Shakespeare

Script, Stage, Screen

David Bevington
The University of Chicago

Anne Marie Welsh
University of California, San Diego

Michael L. Greenwald
Texas A&M University

PEARSON

Longman

New York San Francisco Boston
London Toronto Sydney Tokyo Singapore Madrid
Mexico City Munich Paris Cape Town Hong Kong Montreal

Managing Editor: Erika Berg
Development Editor: Gianna Marsella
Executive Marketing Manager: Ann Stypuloski
Senior Supplements Editor: Donna Campion
Project Coordination, Text Design, and Electronic Page Make-up: Electronic Publishing Services Inc., New York City
Cover Designer/Manager: Wendy Ann Fredericks
Cover Photos (clockwise from top left): *Romeo and Juliet* by Ford Madox Brown 1868–1871/Christie's Images/Corbis;
John Gielgud, British actor of stage and film, with Adele Dixon in the final scene of *Romeo and Juliet,* Mary Evans Picture Library Ltd.;
Leonardo DiCaprio and Claire Danes in Baz Luhrmann's 1996 film production of *Romeo+Juliet,* 20th Century Fox/The Kobal
Collection/Morton, Merrick; and Frontispiece for book of Shakespeare's *Romeo & Juliet,* dated 1599, Mary Evans Picture Library Ltd.
Photo Researcher: Linda Sykes
Manufacturing Buyer: Lucy Hebard
Printer and Binder: Hamilton Printing Co.
Cover Printer: Coral Graphic Services, Inc.

We gratefully acknowledge the following for permission to use copyrighted material: From *Much Ado About Nothing* by William Shakespeare, screenplay, intro, and notes by Kenneth Branagh. Synopsis and character notes copyright © 1993 by Russel Jackson. Used by permission of W. W. Norton & Company, Inc.

Library of Congress Cataloging-in-Publication Data

Bevington, David M.
  Shakespeare : script, stage, screen / David Bevington, Anne Marie Welsh, Michael L. Greenwald.
    p. cm.
  Videography: p.
  Includes bibliographical references (p.   ) and index.
  ISBN 0-321-19813-1
  1. Shakespeare, William, 1564-1616—Criticism and interpretation. 2. Shakespeare, William, 1564-1616—Film and video adaptations. 3. Shakespeare, William, 1564-1616—Stage history. I. Welsh, Anne Marie. II. Greenwald, Michael L. III. Title.
  PR2976.B4427 2005
  822.3′3—dc22
                        2005014340

Please visit our website at http://www.ablongman.com

ISBN 0-321-19813-1

  2 3 4 5 6 7 8 9 10—HT—08 07 06 05

Contents

Preface

Shakespeare: Script, Stage, Screen is the first anthology to combine scrupulously edited, annotated texts of Shakespeare's most-filmed plays with detailed histories of their stage productions and analyses of the films. This abundantly illustrated book is grounded in fourteen essential plays, descriptions of key stage, film, and video interpretations, and film theory with an emphasis upon the differing directorial strategies required of stage, film, and television. We have presented each staging—whether in a theater, in a warehouse, or on film or television—as an interpretation of the play, its point of view conditioned by the times, the medium, and the artist's vision.

This collection of fourteen plays includes five comedies, three history plays, five tragedies, and one of the late romances; it surveys the development of Shakespeare's drama with a particular emphasis upon those works that are available in film or video formats and in multiple versions. Decades of teaching experience have taught us that film and video can provide an honorable "way in" to Shakespeare's plays for students; seeing and hearing actors speak his words offer a ready cure for their frequently encountered fear of his language. While we believe in a careful reading of the plays as great works of literature, we recognize that today's students often are more visually literate than their literature professors. Many students readily apprehend Shakespeare's language through performance, film, and other visual media. Professional actors help students become more sensitive to poetic rhythms, pauses, and shifts between verse and prose. Directors, designers, and performers also offer holistic interpretations of the plays as they must consider every word in a text even as they cut or rearrange it. We approach the plays from these artists' perspective, emphasizing that Shakespeare's plays often were "translations" or "interpretations" of other narratives. Later interpretations, with their varying degrees of fidelity, rivalry, and anxiety, are part of a tradition that now extends to the student as reader, viewer, and interpreter. This approach empowers students to emulate the imaginative daring of contemporary directors in their own critical analyses and imagined stagings of Shakespeare's plays.

We also draw from our differing academic and practical perspectives to offer students as full an account as possible of these plays as literary texts, performance scripts, and cultural documents. The texts have been edited and glossed by University of Chicago scholar David Bevington. The commentary flows from Bevington's decades of study of the playwright's life and creative output; from Michael L. Greenwald's experience directing or acting in sixteen of Shakespeare's plays, researching his book on the Royal Shakespeare Company director John Barton, and teaching a popular Texas A&M course, Shakespeare on Film; and from Anne Marie Welsh's nearly thirty years teaching the plays and reviewing Shakespeare productions as a theater critic for newspapers.

Each play is preceded by a thorough commentary covering scholarly and literary matters such as dating, context, characters, action, language, and theme while emphasizing:

- The dynamic nature of interpretation. Each commentary samples early critical responses to both text and productions, as well as notable historic stagings and the most recent films and adaptations. By emphasizing changing approaches to certain scenes and characters (Falstaff, for instance, as dishonorable and seductive descendant of the Vice, and/or as life-loving speaker of universal truth; Katharina as stereotypical shrew and/or winking lover) and by highlighting often antithetical interpretations (the Laurence Olivier view of patriotism in his *Henry V* contrasted with Kenneth Branagh's; the metaphysics of Peter Brook's cosmically cruel *Lear* compared to Grigori Kozintsev's redemptive reading), these introductory sketches suggest the continuum of responses that make each play a cultural touchstone and Shakespeare our continually reinvented contemporary.

- Those factors that may have inspired Shakespeare to write the play. This section includes not only commentary on the source material for a play such as *Macbeth* (e.g., Raphael Holinshed's *Chronicles*), but also discussion of the social and political contexts that made the play relevant to Shakespeare's audiences (James I's essay on witchcraft and the Gunpowder Plot). Because real events have inspired subsequent theater or film artists to stage or film the play (e.g., Welles's anti-fascist film after World War II), students may thus appreciate the "drama surrounding the drama" that accompanies many of Shakespeare's plays in his lifetime and ours.

■ An analysis of principal themes and concerns of the play with reference to patterns of imagery and specific lines that address these themes. These literary analyses do not pretend to be definitive; rather they are intended to serve as springboards for discussion of the play. Where possible, specific films or stage productions that explore a notable theme are cited.

■ Particular stylistic problems (plots and subplots, genre, language) that will alert students to potential challenges that may affect their understanding of the play. Brief explanations of particularly complex issues, especially of language and wordplay, should allay student qualms.

■ The staging challenges a particular play presents to theater artists (for example, visualizing the fairies in *A Midsummer Night's Dream* or the banquet scene in *The Tempest*) are highlighted so that students come to appreciate acting, directing, and design choices as they watch a play or video. Post-play discussions survey a variety of stage and film solutions to these challenges.

Special Features

Five introductory chapters examine:

■ Shakespeare's life and times, with a particular emphasis upon Shakespeare as a man of the theater;

■ The history of interpretation beginning with actors, and charting the reciprocal relationship of literary theory and performance practice;

■ The interpretive possibilities currently facing readers and artists, a spectrum that ranges from traditional interpretation, to updating and recontextualization, to outright adaptation and spin-off, to purely filmic responses;

■ The process of staging Shakespeare's scripts on stage, film, and television, including the particular conventions of each medium and the responsibilities of artists (directors, actors, cinematographers, and designers) in each medium and the tension between the essentially aural nature of Shakespeare's stage and the visual media of film and television.

Additional Features

■ **Close-ups** focus upon major stage and film directors, actors, and producers who have been especially significant interpreters of Shakespeare on stage and in the cinema. These include Laurence Olivier, Orson Welles, Akira Kurosawa, Franco Zeffirelli, Peter Brook, and Kenneth Branagh. Additional "Close-ups" are devoted to "Silent Shakespeare" (an examination of silent-film adaptations of his work), a pictorial "Hamlet from Burbage to Branagh," and the producer and actress Madame Vestris.

■ **Frame-by-Frame** essays analyze specific film scenes and model close readings of comparative scenes in various films, stage productions, and adaptations.

■ Sixteen pages of **color images** and dozens of **black-and-white illustrations** help students visualize the design and performance styles of various historical periods, as well as contemporary stage works and rare films and videos they may never see.

■ A **screenplay excerpt** allows students to see exactly how a screenwriter and film director have cut, rearranged, or altered scenes from Shakespeare for film treatment. By comparing Shakespeare's text, the screenplay, and the filmed scene, students are able to discern the ways in which film imagery can supplant verbal images; they can also begin to discern the director's style, thematic emphases, and ultimately, interpretation of the play.

■ **Appendices:** a bibliography for each subdivision of the text; an extensive videography; a timeline encapsulating production history; family trees for the Lancaster and York dynasties in the War of the Roses; and a glossary of film terms.

Because *Shakespeare: Script, Stage, Screen* illuminates the historical, cultural, and stylistic aspects of each play as both a literary and a performance text, students are encouraged to appreciate that a play grows out of "the age and body of its time" and can reflect the "age and body" of subsequent ages. Discussions of the many adaptations and spin-offs that Shakespeare's plays have inspired suggest the myriad possibilities of adapting Shakespeare for audiences. Our approach enables students to see that a movie version of one of his plays essentially replicates what Shakespeare typically did with his own sources as he transformed the "original," as one reviewer of this project noted quoting Ben Jonson, to make it "easy and modern for the times." In other words, this anthology demonstrates just how much Shakespeare has in common with the Kenneth Branaghs and Baz Luhrmanns of our day.

A Brief Guide to Editorial Practices and Style

The running title at the top of each page of play text gives the Through Line Numbers (TLN) of each play based on the Norton First Folio of Shakespeare. That facsimile provides line numberings throughout, one number for each line of type. The advantage of this system is that it is universal, applying to all editions whether new or old. Such editions vary in line numbering depending upon how the text is divided into scenes and how prose is numbered in columns of varying width. Because the TLN system is truly universal it is often used by textual scholars.

Line numbers in the text indicate that a gloss is to be found at the foot of the column for a word or phrase in that line.

Stage directions in square brackets are editorially added. Those without brackets, or in parentheses, are from the original Folio or Quarto text. The same is true of the numberings of acts and scenes.

Acknowledgments

We are grateful to the reviewers who made many valuable suggestions for improving this text. For their thoughtful suggestions we would like to thank:

Russell A. Peck, University of Rochester

Mark Aune, North Dakota State University

Joe Black, University of Tennessee, Knoxville

Bill Dynes, University of Indianapolis

Gloria Eastman, SUNY Buffalo State College

Vivianne Foss, University of Wisconsin, Oshkosh

Marc Geisler, Western Washington University

Peter Greenfield, University of Puget Sound

Ervene Gulley, Bloomsburg University

Don Hedrick, Kansas State University

Michael Hennessey, Southwest Texas State University

W. Scott Howard, University of Denver

Kathy Howlett, Northeastern University

Lori Humphrey Newcomb, University of Illinois

Nicholas Jones, Oberlin College

Jeffrey Kahan, University of La Verne

Ivo Kamps, University of Mississippi

Sergei Lobanov-Rostovsky, Kenyon College

Kelli Marshal, University of Texas, Dallas

Steve Marx, California Polytechnic University

Donald McDonough, Central Connecticut State University

David Mikics, University of Houston

Clifford Ronan, Texas State University

Charles Ross, Purdue University

George Rowe, University of Oregon

Diana Major Spencer, Snow College

David Sterritt, Long Island University and Columbia University

Joseph Tate, University of Washington

Toby Widdicombe, University of Alaska, Anchorage

Our project was first conceived by our editor at Pearson-Longman, Erika Berg; she brought us together for this collaboration and shepherded the book through every stage from conception to printing with wisdom, insight, and good-humored support. We thank her for her vision, her flexibility, and her patience. We also wish to thank our developmental editor, Gianna Marsella, whose organizational skills and gentle prodding kept the project on track, despite multiple commitments and a good deal of international travel by all three authors. Many of the scholars, critics, and artists who came before us as interpreters of Shakespeare are mentioned in the references for each section of the text and in the bibliography. We are grateful to them.

Our greatest debt is to our families. They have inspired and supported us even when our engagement with *Shakespeare: Script, Stage, Screen* has drawn our attention away from them. We dedicate this book to our children and grandchildren with thanks and love.

David Bevington
Anne Marie Welsh
Michael Greenwald

Supplements

The following supplements are available free when ordered with this text. Please consult your local Longman representative if you would like to set up a value pack.

Evaluating a Performance informs students about stage and theatrical performance and helps them to become more critical viewers of dramatic productions (ISBN 0-321-09541-3).

Evaluating Plays on Film and Video is designed to prepare students to assess film versions of plays, including Shakespeare's, in reviews or longer critical essays (ISBN 0-321-18794-6).

Screening Shakespeare: Using Film to Understand the Plays is a brief, practical guide to select feature films of the most commonly taught plays (ISBN 0-321-19479-9).

PART ONE

*Introduction
to Shakespeare
and His Interpreters*

Prologue: Discovering Shakespeare, the World's Playwright

Admit me Chorus to this history,
Who, Prologue-like, your humble patience pray
Gently to hear, kindly to judge, our play.

From the opening of The Life of King Henry V

John Barton, a director for the Royal Shakespeare Company, says that each time he begins work on a new production of a Shakespeare play it is "a journey of discovery." Reading or watching one of Shakespeare's works, especially as a student, also means embarking upon that kind of journey. Because Shakespeare is often described in superlatives—as the world's most often-produced playwright, the greatest writer who ever lived, a literary genius, a brilliant poet, a great storyteller, an unsurpassed psychologist of character, and so on—the prospect of getting to know his work can seem daunting.

This book offers a starting place for any reader seeking to discover reasons such extraordinary praise may seem justified. It gathers relevant material about Shakespeare as a man of his time, as a practical theater artist who was an actor and part-owner of his acting company, and as a writer whose output included thirty-eight plays (depending on what one counts as wholly or partly his), one hundred fifty-four sonnets, and two long poems. This volume provides the texts of fourteen of Shakespeare's most popular plays, along with background information to illuminate the contexts in which those plays were written, to trace Shakespeare's artistic development, and to suggest some of the reasons why these plays are still produced and filmed throughout the world.

Shakespeare's popularity is truly worldwide. Consider the following statistics:

- During an eighteen-day festival in 1988, in Beijing and Shanghai, the People's Republic of China, twenty-two of Shakespeare's plays were performed by professional, amateur, and student companies in a variety of styles from quasi-Elizabethan to Chinese operatic. Coal miners from a remote province staged *A Midsummer Night's Dream*. Workers in gray Mao jackets joined students in T-shirts and businessmen in Western suits to see plays of a man who had written in English some four hundred years earlier with hardly a mention of China or the Chinese.

- The Japanese produce almost as much written material today about Shakespeare and his plays as does the English-speaking world. In addition, Japanese film adaptations of *Macbeth* (Akira Kurosawa's *The Throne of Blood*) and *King Lear* (Kurosawa's *Ran*), for instance, translate the original stories to the world of the samurai and are among the finest in the history of the cinema.

- Actors in Italy commonly refer to Shakespeare as "our playwright." Verona is a tourist mecca for lovers of *Romeo and Juliet* and *The Two Gentlemen of Verona*; Venice proudly serves as the setting for *The Merchant of Venice* and *Othello*. Italian towns like Orvieto or Arezzo commonly feature one or more Shakespeare plays on their theater season's bill. The great Italian opera composer Giuseppe Verdi is justly famous for his brilliant operatic adaptation of *Macbeth*, and then, at the climax of his career, of *Othello* (as *Otello*), and portions of *The Merry Wives of Windsor* (as *Falstaff*).

- Russians have produced some of the most vital stage productions and films of Shakespeare's plays in the twentieth century, notably Grigori Kozintsev's

3

Hamlet and *King Lear*. In the eighteenth century the empress Catherine the Great translated *The Merry Wives of Windsor* into Russian, while in the twentieth century the seminal acting teacher and stage director Konstantin Stanislavski directed as many Shakespeare plays at the Moscow Art Theater as those by Anton Chekhov, Russia's foremost playwright. To be sure, Shakespeare wrote more plays than did Chekhov, but the statistic is still compelling.

■ Only the Judeo-Christian Bible has been translated into more languages than Shakespeare's plays—more than eighty languages, and counting.

■ Since 1950 more than one hundred versions of Shakespeare's plays have been filmed, and at least that many have been televised, most notably the BBC's productions of thirty-seven of Shakespeare's plays over a fifteen-year span during the 1970s and 1980s. Numerous "spin-offs" have included musicals (*West Side Story*), rock musicals, movies (*10 Things I Hate About You*, a teen version of *The Taming of the Shrew*), plays (*Rosencrantz and Guildenstern Are Dead*), and television shows.

■ In 1999 the Academy Award for Best Picture went to *Shakespeare in Love*, a fictional biography of the playwright that incorporated a compact rendition of *Romeo and Juliet* into its Oscar-winning screenplay by playwright Tom Stoppard and Marc Norman.

■ Each year more than a million people visit Shakespeare's birthplace in Stratford-upon-Avon in the English Midlands. Many are international visitors from such diverse lands as Burma, Haiti, Iran, and Borneo.

Shakespeare has earned this enduring and international popularity for reasons that can only be briefly suggested here. Among his many achievements, he offers us the following:

■ Fascinating stories, usually derived and adapted from other sources, that further adapt themselves to the particulars of multiple places and moments in history.

■ Vital characters drawn from the full spectrum of humanity, each rendered in a psychological depth not previously seen on the world's stages.

■ A rich variety of ideas and issues.

■ A vigorous, varied, and expressive language.

Despite the enormous contribution Shakespeare made to English language, theater, and literature, only about half of his plays appeared in print during his lifetime, and he did not supervise their publication. (Those that were published while he was alive appeared in quarto format, in which the large two-sided printing sheet is folded twice to yield eight pages to a sheet. The individual pages are smaller than those of the luxurious folio format, whose one fold yields four pages to a sheet.) When his acting company sold plays to a publisher, usually some time after the play had finished its initial run in the theater, the play became the property of that publisher (and Shakespeare seems not to have read proofs).

This lack of oversight on Shakespeare's part is commonly perceived as suggesting that he did not care about his fame as a writer. This assumption, however, is not really justified. His own writings attest to the idea that immortality matters greatly to one who creates through words. Surely he knew that he was a great writer and that his major output was in his plays. During his latter years, from about 1608 until he died in 1616, no new play appeared in print, as though the plan was to publish his works in collected form after he died. Indeed, two colleagues of his acting company, John Heminges and Henry Condell, assembled an impressive collection of his plays for publication in 1623. We can well imagine that Shakespeare encouraged the enterprise. The two editors had full access to his manuscripts and printed editions of the nineteen plays already in print.

Shakespeare may not have been much involved with the publication of his plays, but he was fully engaged with his acting company, the Lord Chamberlain's Men (renamed the King's Men in 1603), and with his writing. He was evidently loyal to his company and actively concerned with its success: he agreed to publishing schedules that were to everyone's advantage. He was a company man, and he clearly regarded his plays as scripts for the actors' performance. He tested the plays in the theater with his colleagues and may well have rewritten to accommodate their talents and wishes.

Several of his greatest plays, including *Hamlet* and *King Lear*, are too long to have been performed in their entirety during the short afternoon performance times that were available at the Globe Theatre, which was situated across the Thames River from London. His plays were published in the 1623 Folio in their entirety by his acting colleagues because they represented the wonderful things that Shakespeare had written for the theater. He was, in the fullest sense, both a poet and a practical man of the theater.

The Lord Chamberlain's Men was a repertory ensemble in which Shakespeare was a shareholder and to which he belonged and in which he performed, at least to 1603. The acting company gave Shakespeare his first and most vital means of communicating his plays to the public and thereby ensured his immortality as a writer. He knew that his actors could take his words and characters and breathe life into them, making his stories, arguments, and intricate plots understandable even to the many unschooled members of Elizabethan audiences. By suiting "the action to the word, the word to the action" (as Hamlet advises the troupe of actors who visit Elsinore Castle), the actors were able to communicate complex ideas and feelings in the lively and understandable language of performance. Ever since, across four centuries, actors from Shakespeare's time (Richard Burbage) to those of the eighteenth and nineteenth centuries (David Garrick, Edmund Kean, Sarah Siddons, and Ellen Terry) to such modern stars as Kenneth Branagh, Kevin Kline, Mel Gibson, Emma Thompson, Judi Dench, and Leonardo DiCaprio have continued that tradition of making Shakespeare accessible to a broad audience.

Shakespeare: Script, Stage, Screen has a similar purpose. Without downplaying Shakespeare's accomplishments as a storyteller, philosopher, and ever-evolving poet and playwright, we focus on him primarily as he must have been known to the actors and audiences of his first performances: a practical man of the theater. Furthermore, we believe that generations of actors, directors, designers, and cinematographers need to be understood as critics and interpreters in their own right, fully as capable as literary critics of offering themselves as compelling guides to Shakespeare's work. We view each production—whether it occurs on the stage, in a warehouse, or outdoors; is translated to film or video; is given traditional or subversive treatment—as an interpretation. Every student's considered response to these performances is a critical step in the larger journey of discovering Shakespeare.

CHAPTER 1

Shakespeare's Life

The word "Shakespeare" refers to several distinct entities:

- William Shakespeare (1564–1616), a man from the English Midlands who traveled to London sometime in the mid-to-late 1580s and became a professional theater artist and writer.
- Thirty-eight plays, one hundred fifty-four sonnets, two long narrative poems, and several short poems; i.e., his literary output.
- The production of his dramatic works on stage, and for film, television, and radio.
- The so-called "Shakespeare Industry," which includes everything from critical analyses of his works and histories of their productions to T-shirts, drinking mugs, this textbook, and college courses devoted to the study of Shakespeare's plays.

We begin with the first Shakespeare—the person. In one of those strange ironies of fate, we know relatively little about this man who created so many characters with whom we are so well acquainted.

The Early Years

Although Shakespeare's actual birth date is uncertain, the parish register of Holy Trinity Church in Stratford-upon-Avon, in Warwickshire, records in Latin the baptism of "Gulielmus filius Johannes Shakspeare," that is, William, son of John Shakespeare, on April 26, 1564. Mary Arden was the mother. This was the year in which the extraordinary Italian artist Michelangelo died, and in which Christopher Marlowe, Shakespeare's fellow playwright, was born. Because babies were customarily baptized very soon after birth, we celebrate the birth of William Shakespeare on April 23, which also is the Feast of St. George, the patron of the English people. Shakespeare's King Henry V invokes the saint in his famous battle prayer: "God for Harry [i.e., King Henry]! England and St. George!" (*Henry V*, 3.1.34).

John Shakespeare was a tanner and glover; that is, he cured skins, made gloves and other leather goods, and sold them from his shop. He also dealt in wood, grain, malt, and other farm produce. He became an important community leader and holder of city offices. His position as high bailiff, which was akin to being a mayor, meant that William and his brothers, Gilbert, Richard, and Edmund, could attend the town's grammar school. William's sister, Joan, could not, for women in Elizabethan England enjoyed fewer privileges and freedoms than did men. (Shakespeare had three other sisters, but all died young.) At this quaint, timber-roofed school, which still exists, the future playwright learned his Latin by translating the works of the Roman writers, such as Ovid, Seneca, and Plautus. Ovid's tales of ancient gods and humans provided Shakespeare with source material for many of his plays. From Seneca Shakespeare would have learned about tragedy and the theatrical appeal of sensational, violent endings. Plautus would have introduced him to the stock characters of classical comedy. *The Comedy of Errors*, among Shakespeare's earliest plays, is adapted from Plautus's *Menaechmi* (*The Twins*).

Some admirers of Shakespeare's work argue that he could not have written the plays for which he is credited because a grammar school education would not have adequately prepared him to write knowledgeably about such diverse subjects as law, medicine, horticulture, seafaring, the military life, and so on. Therefore, this argument goes, the plays must have been written by someone more educated, such as Marlowe or philosopher Francis Bacon, or by some nobleman such as the Earl of Oxford. Yet some of these candidates died too early to have written many of the plays (Marlowe in 1593, Oxford in 1604). Moreover, we should not judge Shakespeare's education by comparing it with today's schooling. A grammar school education in the 1570s was far more demanding than in our modern-day system. Students were in class from dawn until dusk, receiving rigorous training in classical literature and languages, especially Latin, along with extensive study of rhetoric (the art of argumentation) and discourse, both written and spoken. The rigors of a grammar school education are amusingly dramatized in a scene (4.1) in *The Merry Wives of Windsor*, Shakespeare's only comedy set in a Stratford-like English town. In this scene a lad named William is put through his paces by a pedantic schoolteacher who threatens the boy with a whipping if he falters in his recitation of Latin paradigms. Universities such as Cambridge were primarily training grounds for the clergy and lawyers, so that young men could serve the church and the state. A late sixteenth-century grammar school education would have provided a curious and intelligent young man with a solid foundation for the profession that eventually chose him. And London in the last decades of the sixteenth century was another training ground for an inquisitive mind that absorbed travel tales from mariners and soldiers, business acumen from merchants and traders, and philosophical ideas from clergy and intellectuals who were reshaping English thought. No one who knew Shakespeare doubted that he was in fact the author of the plays and poems attributed to him.

Why did Shakespeare not attend a university, as did many of his contemporaries, such as Marlowe, who came from a shoemaking family? One possible reason is that in about 1579 his father seems to have suffered a series of financial setbacks. Another explanation may be that Shakespeare's early marriage made higher education impossible. At age eighteen, he married Anne Hathaway, a woman almost nine years his senior and pregnant with the first of their three children, Susanna. The marriage had to be hastily arranged because of Anne's pregnancy. She later bore twins, daughter Judith and son Hamnet, who died as a boy in 1596. Perhaps the demands of marriage and fatherhood did not permit the luxury of university schooling.

Life as a young person in Stratford must have afforded Shakespeare rich experiences of the sort that are reflected in his plays and poems. He knew firsthand the rhythms of life in an English country town. These included a perhaps surprising number of opportunities to see theatrical performances by small troupes of itinerant actors who brought their entertainments to country towns like Stratford. Records indicate that seven different acting companies performed in Stratford between 1579 and 1584. In 1575 a lavish aquatic show, attended by Queen Elizabeth, was held at nearby Kenilworth Castle.

Shakespeare and his contemporaries probably enjoyed such merriments, but they also lived in a time that inherited medieval traditions in which virtues and vices battled for the souls of humankind. Folklore and tales of fairies, witches, and hobgoblins (see the introduction to *A Midsummer Night's Dream*) were omnipresent. The local Guild Chapel in Stratford featured a vivid painting of the Last Judgment, with Christ as judge of the dead and cavorting devils dragging hapless sinners off into a monstrous hell mouth with jaws open to receive them into a fiery abyss. This painting was covered with whitewash at some point by the Protestant reformers who objected to its Catholic iconography, but Shakespeare may well have known it during his youth. In any event, such vivid scenes of damnation were common in medieval biblical and morality plays, the remnants of which were performed throughout much of England, particularly during the Feast of Corpus Christi in early summer. Among the most famous Corpus Christi pageants was that held at Coventry, only eighteen miles from Stratford. We hear echoes of the morality plays when Falstaff is referred to as a "reverend Vice" and an "old white-bearded Satan" (*Henry IV, Part One*, 2.4) or when an allegorical character named Rumor introduces *Henry IV, Part Two*. Shakespeare's mature tragedies—*Hamlet*, *Othello*, *Macbeth*, *King Lear*—are extraordinary for their ability to make concrete, complex, and psychologically penetrating characters out of figures who in an earlier time might have been called Everyman or Humanitas.

The "Lost" Years

For a period of about seven years, from 1585 to 1592, known as "the lost years," we know virtually nothing of Shakespeare's life. Traditional stories about him speculate that he served as a schoolmaster or a teacher's assistant in the Midlands, or served an apprenticeship in Stratford to his father's trade. Even more gossipy stories about him suggest that he had to leave Stratford after having been apprehended and punished for poaching deer and rabbits. Conceivably he joined an acting company on tour. One early biographer, Edmund Malone, offers the unsupported assertion that Shakespeare's "first office in the theater was that of prompter's assistant." Certainly his later work reveals an intimate and practical acquaintance with technical matters of stagecraft, so that it is not unreasonable to suppose that he worked his way up from basic assignments in a theatrical company. At some point, at any rate, he seems to have left his family behind and made his way to the great metropolis of London.

London

By 1592 Shakespeare was in London. In an outburst of envious rancor, a rival playwright named Robert Greene denounced Shakespeare in that year as "an upstart crow, beautified by our feathers"—that is, a plagiarizer of the work of other dramatists like Greene himself, Marlowe, and Thomas Nashe.

Shakespeare and His Times

PLATE 1

Queen Elizabeth I. *Queen Elizabeth's long reign (1558-1603) extended through the first fourteen years of Shakespeare's playwriting career. She was celebrated during her lifetime with such mythological renderings as this one, which commemorates the English defeat of the Spanish Armada in 1588; she stands with her right hand on the globe, as if she were empress of the world.* (Private Collection/Bridgeman Art Library)

PLATE 2

London. *When Shakespeare arrived in the city, London Bridge afforded the only means of land transport across the River Thames; boats and barges ferried passengers, including the Queen and her court, between venues on opposite sides of the river. Clearly visible in the lower left of this anonymous seventeenth-century painting are the theaters of Southwark, flags flying.* (Museum of London)

PLATE 3
Stratford-upon-Avon. *This house belonged to the family of Shakespeare's mother, Mary Arden, a gentlewoman whom the glove-maker John Shakespeare married around 1557. Like many houses and other buildings in the picturesque town, including Shakespeare's birthplace, the home has been preserved by the Shakespeare Trust.* (Robert Harding Picture Library, Ltd./Alamy)

PLATE 4

The Globe Theatre. *Performances began in 1996 at the new Globe on the south bank of the River Thames in London near the site of Shakespeare's original Globe. The open theater includes such features of the Elizabethan public playhouse as a thrust stage, tiered galleries, and standing room for hundreds of patrons on three sides of the action.* (Getty Images)

PLATE 5

William Shakespeare. *This portrait, possibly by a painter named John Taylor, is the only one that has a real claim to have been painted from life. Called the Chandos portrait after the name of a previous owner, it is dated around 1610 and is owned by the National Gallery of Great Britain.* (National Portrait Gallery, London)

PLATE 6

Shakespeare in Love. *Actor Joseph Fiennes plays Will Shakespeare in the Academy Award-winning film scripted by Tom Stoppard and Marc Norman. Here the character struggles against writer's block to complete a play about Romeo and a girl he imagines to be named "Ethel, the Pirate's Daughter."* (The Kobal Collection/Miramax Films/Universal Pictures/Photo by Laurie Sparham)

Exactly when, where, and how Shakespeare entered the professional theater cannot be determined. One romantic and apocryphal story has him holding horses for patrons attending the Theater in Shoreditch, an occupation that would have allowed him to hear first-hand the opinions of audiences entering and especially exiting the theater structure built by James Burbage in 1576. Perhaps Shakespeare gradually worked his way into the theater as an attendant to the actors who were performing plays by Marlowe and Greene, and eventually onto the stage itself, first playing small roles, later graduating to more demanding parts. As an attendant he would have been paid a flat wage for his services; as a bit-part actor he would have been paid as a "hired man." Only the nine or so leading actors in the acting company would have owned a part of the company, sharing both its profits and its risks.

By 1594 Shakespeare did belong to a newly formed and highly successful company known as the Lord Chamberlain's Men, meaning that they were sponsored by the Lord Chamberlain. James Burbage's son Richard, as leading man, owned half the shares with other members of his family; the remaining half were divided among the other chief actors. Shortly thereafter Shakespeare became a shareholder. The company flourished, and it shareholders quickly became prosperous. Shakespeare's new fortune enabled him to purchase one of the largest homes ("New Place") in Stratford in 1597 and then to acquire other substantial real estate in the vicinity. He himself resided in London. He rented a room in a house owned by the Mountjoy family and located in the north of London, and he also is said to have lived in an area near the Globe Theatre (built in 1599), on the south bank of the River Thames. Though he could have purchased property in London he did not do so, choosing instead to acquire land in and near Stratford over a ten-year period. Shakespeare considered Stratford his home and seems to have planned carefully for his retirement years in that Midlands village.

Shakespeare evidently began writing plays around the time of his arrival in London. *Titus Andronicus*, inspired by the bloody tragedies of the Roman Seneca whom Shakespeare had studied as a schoolboy, was his first printed play (1594), along with *The First Part of the Contention Betwixt The Two Famous Houses of York and Lancaster*, a version of *Henry VI, Part Two* published the same year. He must have been writing plays well before this time. Scholars have determined the order in which they were probably written, although some of the dates are still disputed. Shakespeare averaged two to three scripts a year during the years of his professional career. His was a prodigious accomplishment by any standard. When Theseus defines the poet's task as creating reality for all things "from heaven to earth, from earth to heaven" (*A Midsummer Night's Dream*, 5.1.13), he could be describing the scope of Shakespeare's works.

Periodically during Shakespeare's career, London theaters were closed during episodes of plague. When those outbreaks were especially severe, in 1592 and 1593, giving Shakespeare periods of enforced leisure, he seems to have turned his artistic energies to writing two narrative poems, *Venus and Adonis* and *The Rape of Lucrece*. He probably composed some of his sonnets during this time as well, though they were not published until considerably later. We will consider the poems briefly in Chapter 3. The sonnets, in particular, offer tantalizing hints about Shakespeare's private life. Many are addressed to a well-born young man, often identified with Shakespeare's benefactor, the Earl of Southampton. Although these sonnets deny a consummated sexual relationship between the poet and the young man, they richly portray an emotional relationship that is dependent and deeply loving. Absence from his friend is torture to the poet; he feels jealously threatened by the friend's relationships with other young men and women. Does this remarkable series of sonnets tell us anything biographical about Shakespeare the man? The evidence is ambiguous, and any conclusion is speculative. Later sonnets, which address a "dark lady," exhibit a profound disillusionment with erotic love. Collectively, the sonnets—like the plays—offer ample evidence that Shakespeare possessed extraordinary feeling and remarkable rhetorical skill.

The order in which Shakespeare wrote his plays reveals an author who continually takes up, explores, and then moves beyond established dramatic forms, themes, and literary fashions. The shape of Shakespeare's career also responds to the historical and cultural pressures of the times in which he lived. After some early plays (*The Comedy of Errors* and *Titus Andronicus*) based on Roman models he had read at Stratford, and an erudite comedy (*Love's Labor's Lost*) in the mannered style of John Lyly, Shakespeare seems to have concentrated primarily on English history plays and romantic comedies. The year 1588 marked the failure of Catholic Spain to invade England with its Spanish Armada, a triumph for this small Protestant nation and a celebration of her growing naval power. The London theater, emerging at that time as a cultural force in English life, was a natural venue for the celebration of English pride. Shakespeare's earliest plays often reflect an abiding interest in English history and culture, as for example in the *Henry VI* cycle, which ends with the defeat of Richard III and the triumph of the Tudor royal dynasty. The early comedies, such as *The Taming of the Shrew* and *The Two Gentlemen of Verona*, are no less responsive to the age for which they were written. In the middle and late 1590s, Shakespeare experimented with a tragedy of young love in *Romeo and Juliet*, wrote his best romantic comedies in *The Merchant of Venice*, *Much Ado About Nothing*, and *As You Like It*, and perfected the chronicle play with *Henry V*, a commemoration of England's stirring victory over the French at Agincourt.

Around the turn of the century we see Shakespeare's drama grow increasingly dark as he takes on complex metaphysical themes and explores the genre of tragedy. These were troubled times in England. Because the aging Elizabeth had no heirs, her Protestant subjects feared a return to Catholic rule as in the reign of her older sister Mary (1553–1558). Plots against Elizabeth were rife, most famously in 1601 when the Earl of Essex mounted an abortive rebellion against the Queen's ministers. *Julius Caesar*, a play about the assassination of a charismatic emperor, was written about 1599, followed by a comedy, *Twelfth Night*, in which the strain of melancholy is pronounced. *Hamlet*, in part a meditation upon death, was written in the last years of Elizabeth's life. By this time Shakespeare was clearly the most prominent playwright in London. He seems to have given up acting some time after 1603.

When the Queen died that year, she was succeeded by James VI of Scotland (the son of her first cousin once removed, Mary Queen of Scots), now also James I of England. The English, though generally grateful to have a Protestant monarch and admiring of James's learned dedication to peace, found him personally eccentric. Conflicts between James and the reforming wing of the English church grew in intensity.

These were the years in which Shakespeare experimented with new genres: with the so-called "problem plays" like *All's Well That Ends Well* and *Measure for Measure* that complicated the happy resolutions of romantic comedy, and *Troilus and Cressida* in which satiric comedy, tragedy, and ancient history come together in a disillusioning view of war and human destiny. Ahead lay Shakespeare's greatest tragedies, including *Othello*, *King Lear*, *Macbeth*, and *Antony and Cleopatra*. Although it is a vast oversimplification to speak of "Jacobean pessimism" (i.e., worries about political conflict, the increasingly strident demands of Puritan reformers, uncertainties about foreign policy, and the like) in these early years of James's reign, we can see that Shakespeare's work moved decisively beyond the romantic comedies and patriotic history plays of his first decade of productive work to a drama of increasing complexity and darkness of vision.

Near the end of that first decade of the new century, Shakespeare turned to a new dramatic genre, variously called tragicomedy or romance (as distinguished from romantic comedy). The playwrights Francis Beaumont and John Fletcher contributed to this new genre as well; Fletcher was to be Shakespeare's successor as chief playwright for his acting company, renamed the King's Men in 1603 on the accession of James I. Shakespeare wrote four plays usually identified as belonging to this new genre: *Pericles*, *Cymbeline*, *The Winter's Tale*, and *The Tempest*. His late history play, *Henry VIII*, written in 1613 in collaboration with Fletcher after Shakespeare had retired, shares many romance characteristics as well. The four "romances" are set in exotic locales and feature sea journeys, storms, shipwrecks, separations, the presumed loss of children or loved members of the family, and eventual reunions. They were performed by the King's Men at the Globe Theatre for large public audiences and also (at least in some instances) in the company's winter playhouse, the Blackfriars Theater, located within the City walls and frequented by well-to-do audiences accustomed to the comforts of indoor performance. (Blackfriars could be equipped with new scenic devices, and the Globe too became increasingly capable of special effects, such as the descent of gods and goddesses from the "heavens"—the roof over the stage.) *Pericles* takes its noble, long-suffering hero on a journey through the world of the eastern Mediterranean before reuniting him with his virtuous daughter and then his dear wife, whom he supposes to have died at sea. In *Cymbeline*, Jupiter appears from the "heavens" above the stage in a burst of thunder to offer divine comfort to the beleaguered hero. *The Winter's Tale* concludes with the coming to life of a seeming statue. "You must awake your faith," says the lady-in-waiting, Paulina, as she prepares King Leontes for the apparent miracle of his wife's transformation into a living being. Forgiveness and faith in the power of dramatic art are key themes in these last plays. The romances represent both a synthesis of Shakespeare's dramatic efforts and a transcending of tragedy. They fuse the potential of tragedy with the joyous resolution of comedy in expansive and joyous dramas of reconciliation.

The last of these plays, *The Tempest*, contains a speech by the magician Prospero hinting that Shakespeare was perhaps ready to retire from his "potent art":

> Our revels now are ended. These our actors,
> As I foretold you, were all spirits and
> Are melted into air, into thin air;
> And, like the baseless fabric of this vision,
> The cloud-capped towers, the gorgeous palaces,
> The solemn temples, the great globe itself,
> Yea, all which it inherit, shall dissolve,
> And, like this insubstantial pageant faded,
> Leave not a rack behind.
>
> (4.1.148–156)

The degree to which Shakespeare's evolving art was shaped by the external events outlined here or by the internal compulsions of his own creativity is a subject to which we shall often return in our discussions of individual plays.

Return to Stratford

Shakespeare seems to have chosen to retire from the London stage some time around 1612 and 1613. The reasons are unknown. He was still in his late forties, but may have felt that he was growing old; he died in 1616, seemingly after a bout of ill health. Shakespeare may have felt that he had said what he had to say. He was quite prosperous and had been canny with his real estate investments. His mother had died in 1608, seven years after her husband; Shakespeare's brother Edmund had died in 1607; Gilbert died in 1612, Richard in 1613. William's wife, nearly nine years his senior, outlived him by seven years. The Globe Theatre, where he had lived out much of his career, burned in 1613 during a performance of *Henry VIII*. Hot sparks from a cannon fired as part of the play's special effects ignited the thatching of the theater's roof and burned the building to the ground. Stratford itself was visited by a devastating fire in 1614. The playwright, who had written so profoundly about human mortality during his career, may have been acutely aware of his own mortality. Whatever the reasons, he returned to Stratford, which presumably he had visited frequently during the London years. He seems to have visited London for intervals of writing (he collaborated with Fletcher also in writing *The Two Noble Kinsmen*), but Stratford was now his home.

Shakespeare was buried on April 25, 1616, two days after St. George's Day, which is conventionally regarded as the date of both Shakespeare's birth and death. It would have been his fifty-second birthday. The cause of his death is unknown. A provision of his will, leaving to Anne, his wife of more than 30 years, his "second best bed," has caused a great deal of speculation about the success or lack of success of his marriage, especially in view of his having lived apart from his family for most of that time and his having sired no more children with Anne after 1585. One scholar, Ernst Honigmann, has studied other wills of the period and has concluded that Shakespeare's will is indeed churlish in regard to his wife, though she was comfortably provided for by law. Another controversial document is the epitaph placed in Holy Trinity Church, where Shakespeare had been baptized some fifty-two years earlier; it is written in a doggerel that strikes some observers as not in keeping with Shakespeare's poetic genius:

> Good friend, for Jesus' sake forbear
> To dig the dust enclosèd here.
> Blest be the man that spares these stones,
> And curst be he that moves my bones.

Shakespeare left no heirs. His daughter Judith was married shortly before his death to Thomas Quiney, a man with whom Shakespeare seems not to have been on good terms. Susanna had earlier (1607) married a local and highly reputable physician, John Hall. Their handsome house, known today as Hall's Croft, is one of the finest properties belonging to the Shakespeare Trust in Stratford, and is well worth a visit. Neither daughter produced heirs to continue Shakespeare's lineage. Fortunately, he had better success with his writings as a way to ensure that he would not be forgotten. Two of his

The cover of the First Folio (1623) edition of Shakespeare's plays included this mask-like portrait of the poet and playwright.

theater colleagues, John Heminges and Henry Condell, gathered his scripts that were owned by the acting company, along with printed editions of those plays (approximately half of the total) that had already appeared in quarto format. From these documents they produced the great Folio edition of Shakespeare's plays in 1623. Literary critic and playwright Ben Jonson had published his own collected works of plays, poems, and masques in 1616. The actors with whom Shakespeare worked so closely for more than two decades no doubt wanted to insure that his works, like Jonson's, would be preserved for posterity, and Shakespeare may well have given his blessing to the undertaking. The so-called First Folio became Shakespeare's true heir. Jonson's commendatory verse in the front matter of the First Folio remains a succinct testament to the universality of William Shakespeare, a gentleman, theater owner, actor, poet, and playwright from Stratford:

> Thou art a monument without a tomb,
> And art alive still while thy book doth live,
> And we have wits to read, and praise to give.

CHAPTER 2

Shakespeare: Man of the Theater

Shakespeare: Actor, Poet, and Playwright

The order in which Shakespeare's professions are listed in the subheading above is quite deliberate. Although today we think of Shakespeare first as a poet and playwright, as well we should, in his lifetime his primary career—that is, the "job" in which he made his fortune—was that of an actor who owned a commercial share in his acting company. Certainly he made a reputation in his own day as a poet, but poetry was not a reliable source of income; most professional poets of the time, like Edmund Spenser, were supported by patrons or took positions as secretaries to important men, or both.

Shortly after teaming up with Richard Burbage and others to form the new acting company in 1594 known as the Lord Chamberlain's Men, Shakespeare became an actor-sharer in that company. By paying a substantial stake (which traditionally is supposed to have come to him from the Earl of Southampton in recognition of Shakespeare's having dedicated *Venus and Adonis* and *The Rape of Lucrece* to him), Shakespeare took on a substantial share of the financial risks and potential rewards of a capitalist venture. His fellow shareholders were Burbage, who with his father and brothers owned half the company, and four other actors, John Heminges, Thomas Pope, Augustine Phillips, and Will Kemp. They all took major roles in whatever plays they staged, with Burbage the lead actor and Kemp as the clown. They performed at first in a playhouse called The Theater, built by Burbage's father James in 1576 outside London's walls to the northeast, and then in the nearby Curtain Theater. When the company moved across the Thames River in 1599 they took their theater building with them and rebuilt it as the Globe. Beginning in 1608, they also played indoors at Blackfriars to smaller and more select audiences.

Shakespeare acted in plays through at least 1603. His name appears in a cast list for Ben Jonson's *Every Man In His Humor* (1599) and in some other Jonson plays through *Sejanus* (1603). He must have acted in his own plays as well, though cast lists do not survive. Theater tradition credits him with playing the old servant Adam in *As You Like It* (1598) and the Ghost in *Hamlet;* a contemporary poem lauds him for his skill in "Kingly parts." If these assignments are to be believed, Shakespeare did not take very dominant roles, even in his own plays. This may have been because he was recognized from the start as an important dramatist, and though he acted for the Lord Chamberlain's Men, his chief contribution to them was as a writer of highly successful scripts. His company's commercial success owed a great deal to his genius. As a result, he held a special place: other dramatists might be actors too, but no other writer became an actor-sharer in a major company primarily on the basis of his playwriting. Other writers had to peddle their wares and sell plays to acting companies; Shakespeare enjoyed an institutional advantage.

Competition was keen among acting companies active in London during the 1590s and 1600s. The Lord Chamberlain's Men's chief rivals were the Admiral's Men, with Edward Alleyn as their leading player. Like other groups of actors, the Lord Chamberlain's Men were hungry for plays—as many as forty each year—that would appeal to the tastes of a broad spectrum of London's citizenry. Social heterogeneity was a genuine factor in theater life of the period, and it helped foster a drama that was broadly national and patriotic in its appeal. The proliferation of London theaters in the late sixteenth century coincided with the defeat of the Spanish Armada in 1588, an event that signaled the beginnings of English explorations overseas. Sir Francis Drake's daring raids against the Spanish signaled that England was an international power to be reckoned with. And London, with a population in 1600 of nearly 200,000 and growing, was its bustling center.

The city's so-called public theaters—The Theater, the Globe, the Rose, the Curtain, the Swan, the Fortune, built at various times from 1576 through the early 1600s—held performances in the afternoons in amphitheaters open to the sky. General admission to these theaters was a penny for standing room; seats cost somewhat more, depending on where one sat. A prosperous merchant class in London gave active patronage to the public theaters, along with apprentices and others further down the social scale. The many references to what Hamlet calls the "groundlings," standing around the stage and expecting to be entertained for their pennyworth of admission, attest to a significant social mix in the public theaters. Nonetheless, ordinary day laborers, street sweepers, farmhands, house servants, and the like could not usually afford the theater.

The social diversity of the audiences must not be overstated. If those on the lowest rungs of society could not afford to attend public performances, those on the highest rungs chose not to. Queen Elizabeth I never attended public performances (Judi Dench's queen in *Shakespeare in Love* notwithstanding); neither did her successor, James I. They could and did issue much-coveted invitations for private performances at court. Other aristocrats and wealthy gentlemen may have preferred court entertainments and the private theaters.

Shakespeare and Elizabethan Thought

When we attend a play or movie today, we bring a wealth of perspectives that shape our viewing experience. Education, social background, political leanings, religious preferences (if any), ethnic background, past cultural experiences, and other variables all define the attitudes and beliefs that ultimately affect our reaction. A playwright or screenwriter needs to be aware of such influences in order to enhance our response to the play or film. Some writers do so by challenging our beliefs and social norms, which are themselves in a state of ceaseless flux.

Shakespeare's society was more homogeneous in certain respects than ours. Ethnically it was predominantly Anglo-Saxon. Persons of color were essentially unknown except for an occasional stranger brought to England as a freak exhibit. Jews had been officially expelled from England in the time of Edward I (in 1290), though some still lived unobtrusively in London, outwardly conforming to the English church as a matter of prudence. Other nationalities could be observed in London, especially refugee cloth workers from the Low Countries, but many English citizens were apprenticed to traditional trades and seldom or never left the town in which they had been born. Patriarchal authority was strong, in the family as in the state. Nominally the English worshipped in one church of the Protestant faith. Yet social, economic, and religious conflicts were observable at every turn. Food riots troubled the authorities and were ruthlessly put down. Religious strife divided Anglican Protestants from loyal Catholics on the one hand and reforming Protestants on the other. Inequalities of wealth and social importance were great in an economy based on a huge workforce (mostly agricultural) subordinated to a small elite. London was more socially diverse than other parts of the nation, and was proudly ruled by a merchant class in which nonaristocrats could become very wealthy, but even so the social distance between rich and poor was vast.

Given these social and cultural disparities, along with an awakening sense of national identity, what were the preferences of Shakespeare's audience? To what tastes and opinions did Shakespeare and his fellow playwrights need to appeal to attract audiences? In some ways the answers must have seemed timeless. Then as now, audiences would expect to be diverted by fetching love stories; battles between good and evil; heroic deeds; wicked villains; sprites, ghosts, and witches; exotic locales; miraculous endings; moments of crisis; tear-jerking predicaments; absurdly comic situations; and so on. At the same time, England's particular concerns in the 1590s and 1600s were of vital importance to a theater that was asking its audience to take stock of its cultural heritage and potential.

Shakespeare's plays succeeded in part because they were able to represent a world of changing religious beliefs, of new excitement and hope in individual human achievement, of shifting political allegiances, and of a desire for expanding economic opportunity. England was reinventing itself just as Shakespeare began his writing career in the 1590s. Certainly the victory over the Armada in 1588 encouraged a wave of national pride that Shakespeare was able to explore in his history plays, even as the subject also provided him ample opportunity to dramatize the horrors of political and social conflict. From 1399 (with the deposition of Richard II) until 1485 (when Richard III was slain by Henry Tudor, Earl of Richmond, Queen Elizabeth's grandfather), England had been involved in a series of bloody civil wars. Memories of these wars were fresh in the minds of the Elizabethan English.

Shakespeare wrote eight plays that deal with this century of violence: *Richard II*; *Henry IV, Parts One* and *Two*; *Henry V*; *Henry VI, Parts One, Two,* and *Three*; and *Richard III*. He wrote the latter part of the story first, from Henry VI to Richard III, in the early 1590s, and then took up the earlier story of the rise of Henry IV's son, Prince Hal, to become Henry V. Each four-play sequence ends on a positive note, with Henry V's great victory over the French at Agincourt and with Henry Tudor's victory over Richard III at Bosworth Field. This latter victory signaled the accession to the throne of Henry VII, the first of the Tudor kings. In both four-play series, Shakespeare's audiences were invited to congratulate themselves that their country had survived the perils of civil conflict, much as they had triumphed more recently over the Catholic forces of Spain. Shakespeare's history plays thus appealed to a surge of patriotic feeling even as they also sounded warnings to the British people to be ever vigilant against tyranny and the chaos of regicide and civil war.

Shakespeare extensively reshaped the history of England's civil wars to his own artistic and theatrical purposes, compressing historical time, rearranging dates and events, altering the ages of his characters, and highlighting the achievements that worked best for him as playwright. The account of Prince Hal's wild youth in the company of Falstaff, so essential to the plays of Shakespeare's second four-play cycle, is far more mythical than historically accurate. Similarly, his account of the defeat of Richard III at the hands of the Earl of Richmond, who then became King Henry VII and the Tudor grandfather of Queen Elizabeth, is highly prejudicial toward Richard and flattering toward the new Tudor dynasty. Was Shakespeare indulging in propagandist rewriting of history to please the subjects of England's popular queen in the 1590s? His account owes many of its most piquant details to Sir Thomas More's life of Richard III; More was a man of great integrity, who nevertheless had his own reasons for remaining on good terms with Henry VII and his son Henry VIII. The matter is the subject of much debate. No doubt the Tudor regime was gratified to see history rewritten from its own point of view, all the more so since Henry VII had succeeded Richard III by military rather than constitutional means. Elizabeth's government was sensitive to any attempts to glorify regicide. Shakespeare thus needed to be discreet in dramatizing such a potentially explosive issue. His solution was to blacken the character of Richard III and to depict Henry Tudor as a man of God-fearing probity. The closing prayer in *Richard III* seems intended to glorify the Tudor dynasty:

> Oh, now let Richmond and Elizabeth,
> The true succeeders of each royal house,
> By God's fair ordinance conjoin together!
> And let their heirs, God, if thy will be so,
> Enrich the time to come with smooth-faced peace,
> With smiling plenty, and fair prosperous days!
>
> (5.5.29–34)

At the same time, the ending of *Richard III* seems well designed from an artistic and theatrical point of view. It provides a suitable closure to a prolonged dramatization of civil conflict, much as Henry V's victory over the French at Agincourt in *Henry V* also brings to a close the saga of a young man educating himself in the canny arts of statesmanship.

Henry VII provided some much-needed political and economic stability to war-torn England. His son, Henry VIII, coming to the throne in 1508, was popular and vigorous in his younger years, giving humanist intellectuals some hope that England might become an important center of culture. Yet Henry VIII was also financially extravagant and personally ambitious to cut a major figure in European affairs. When his first wife, Catherine of Aragon, bore him a daughter (Mary) but then proved unable to bear him a male heir, he began divorce proceedings against her so that he might marry Anne Boleyn, who would be Elizabeth's mother. Henry took the view that his marriage to Catherine was invalid because she had been married previously at a young age to Henry's now-dead older brother, Arthur. The Roman Catholic Church, strong in its support for Catherine's powerful royal family in Spain, held that Henry's marriage to Catherine was valid and inviolable. Over this contentious issue, Henry broke with Rome and introduced into England a Protestant Reformation of the church that had begun in 1517 in Wittenberg, Germany, with Martin Luther's challenge to Roman ecclesiastical authority. Under Henry's minister, Thomas Cromwell, the monasteries were suppressed and William Tyndale's English Bible was authorized. Catholics and Protestants alike were martyred as the struggle continued and intensified.

Henry grew more conservative on church matters in his latter years, but when his young son Edward came to the throne in 1547 as Edward VI, reforming Protestantism advanced its cause with vigor. When the sickly Edward died in 1553, his older sister Mary came to the throne because there was no surviving male heir of Henry VIII. Determined as she was to restore the Catholic faith as the exclusive denomination of England, Mary nevertheless found that the monastic properties sold and pillaged by her father were unrecoverable. Her death in 1558 led to a crisis: would her younger sister Elizabeth succeed to the throne, or would some other expedient be found? Conspiracies abounded, and young Elizabeth's life was in danger. Finally she did succeed to the throne, and with her the Protestant Reformation was once again assured of royal support. To a new generation of reformers, eager to proceed after their years of exile on the Continent, fell the task of building a new Protestant culture. With this movement came a sense of a reinvented national identity and a vital economy. Elizabeth's skill for several decades in keeping England out of war with Catholic powers on the Continent was essential to the prosperity of the nation, and helped provide the material basis for the extraordinary flourishing of the arts that England was to experience in the 1580s and in subsequent decades.

Religious and social conflict continued on into the Stuart reigns of the seventeenth century, and indeed led to the execution of King Charles II (1649) and open civil war in mid-century. The discovery in 1605 of the infamous Gunpowder Plot by Guy Fawkes and his fellow Catholic conspirators to blow up the houses of Parliament raised hysteria to new levels of intensity (see discussion under *Macbeth*). The battles were also intellectual and philosophical. Specific issues will be addressed later in conjunction with individual plays, but we should consider here in large terms the intellectual implications of religious reform and new social and economic forces at work in early modern England. Although we must avoid easy generalizations about the new spirit of the Renaissance (a term that came into play only centuries later) and acknowledge that other periods of intellectual reawakening had taken place during the Middle Ages (in the so-called twelfth-century Renaissance, for example), we can still discern ways in which individual choice and a spirit of inquiry were on the rise. Protestant religion tended to decenter the role of the institutional church and its clergy in the quest for salvation. Individual Christians were increasingly being urged to read the Bible for themselves, in vernacular translations newly provided all over Europe. Simultaneously, geographical exploration of new overseas worlds and scientific exploration of the cosmography and the physical world encouraged experimental investigation and inductive reasoning in ways that had seemed foreign to many of the great thinkers of the medieval period like Saint Thomas Aquinas. Shakespeare was able to dramatize an increased sense of personal choice in human life, and with it the increased potential for tragic failure. The individual was more on his own than before, both for better and for worse.

Conceptions of the universe, and of the place of our world in that universe, experienced a major upheaval during Shakespeare's lifetime. Medieval cosmology generally saw the world as flat and as encircled by heavenly bodies moving in symmetrical concentric circles around it, with the moon as the nearest heavenly body, then Mercury, Venus, the sun, Mars, Jupiter, Saturn, the fixed stars on a single plane, and lastly the *primum mobile*, imparting motion to the whole system. Some variations in the pattern were proposed, but the overall design remained constant and essentially unchallenged for centuries. The system is known as the Ptolemaic universe, after the Egyptian astronomer who had formulated its essential design in the second century C.E. All beneath the moon was thought to be subject to mutability and decay; all beyond the moon was eternal. Heaven was to be found at the highest point of the cosmology, with angels and archangels in formal and hierarchical array; hell occupied the center of the earth in a fiery pit under the rule of Satan, whom God had thrown out of heaven. Witches, goblins, and ghosts entered incessantly into life on earth. This cosmology had the authority of the accumulated centuries, and it had an aesthetic beauty all its own. It put the world at the center of the universe in such a way as to suggest the supreme importance of life on earth as the focus of a great spiritual battle between heaven above and hell beneath.

For these reasons, the challenge posed by Copernicus in 1543 was a profound one. In his *De revolutionibus orbium coelestium*, he proposed a mathematical model that put the sun at the center of a solar universe with the earth as one of its satellite bodies. He offered no physical proof; what he demonstrated was that the motions of the heavenly bodies could be much more simply explained by the sun-centered model. Ptolemy had had to rely on epicycles in planetary movements to explain the fact that the planets do not move in a steady progression around the earth; at times, they seem to reverse course. Copernicus saw that these movements could be interpreted as the phenomena of relative motion caused by the fact that the earth also was a planet in motion around the sun. His ideas, reaching England in the late sixteenth century, were highly controversial. They decentered medieval life, and seemed to be in sharp disagreement with the Bible and human learning. The discovery of a new star (a nova or exploding star) in Cassiopeia in 1572 provided a new challenge, with seeming evidence that even the "fixed" stars were not immutable. When Galileo published in 1610 his results of telescopic exploration of the moon and of the moons around Jupiter that could be seen to circle that planet, the physical evidence appeared to confirm Copernicus's theories. Traditionalists fought these new ideas. Galileo's discoveries came a little late in Shakespeare's career to have had a direct impact on his writing, but uncertainties about the cosmos were very much a part of the intellectual world he knew.

Advances in medicine and chemistry, though by no means steady, added to the sense of intellectual excitement during this period. The name of Galen (c. 130 C.E.) was associated with traditional medicine and its dependence on the theory of four humours making up the human body, just as four elements (earth, air, fire, and water) were thought to be the basic constituents of life. A more radical and modern school of thought was that of Paracelsus (c. 1493–1541). In the exploration of human anatomy, which church authorities had long resisted, Vesalius (1514–1564) was a new and very controversial name. William Harvey's investigations of the human blood circulation system were published in 1616. In philosophy and learning, the revered name of Aristotle had to face new challenges from thinkers like Petrus Ramus (1515–1572), who defiantly proclaimed that "everything that Aristotle taught is false." In England, Sir Francis Bacon fought against blind acceptance of ancient authority in his *The Advancement of Learning* (1605). Neoplatonic thinkers like Giovanni Pico della Mirandola (1463–1494) celebrated the seemingly limitless potential of the unfettered human will.

A thinker whom Shakespeare read and admired was Michel de Montaigne (1533–1592). His essays provided a challengingly heterodox, or unconventional, way of thinking about human imperfection. He questioned the generally assumed superiority of the human race to the animal kingdom and the superiority of supposedly "civilized" Europeans to the inhabitants of unknown continents overseas. His emphasis on human arrogance, vanity, and frailty informs Hamlet's meditations on humanity as a "quintessence of dust," and his speculations about the wisdom of supposed "savages" are essential to Shakespeare's portrayal of Caliban in *The Tempest*.

A new and disturbing approach to politics and statecraft presented itself in the writings of Niccolò Machiavelli. His analysis of governing as an art of manipulation seemed to challenge traditional ideas of the divine right of rulers and the fixed hierarchy of social structures. In his *Discourses* and *The Prince*, order was no longer defended as an immutable idea attuned to a higher spiritual law of hierarchical order in the heavens. To Machiavelli, politics was a science best governed by the dictates of social expediency. He was accused of being an atheist, and indeed was so hated and feared by the authorities that his writings were banned in England during Shakespeare's lifetime. Nonetheless, Shakespeare and his contemporaries were plainly acquainted with Machiavelli's ideas. Those ideas turn up in Renaissance plays by Christopher Marlowe (*Tamburlaine*, *The Jew of Malta*, *Edward II*) and in Shakespeare's history plays. This is not to argue that Shakespeare endorsed Machiavellianism, but to suggest that ambitious rulers like King John, Henry IV, and Henry V availed themselves of strategies beyond the dictates of medieval political theology.

For all the excitement of this new spirit of inquiry, we should not expect to find its cause uniformly advanced. In many ways, Elizabethan social attitudes strike us today as not very progressive. We need to remember that Shakespeare wrote some four hundred years ago and that a great deal has changed in the interim. The status of women, who were often treated as property in that essentially patriarchal system, and attitudes toward people of other countries (Spaniards, Turks), races (blacks), and religions (Jews) are particularly disturbing topics that will be explored in conjunction with specific plays. Whether Shakespeare was anti-Semitic is a source of legitimate debate. No doubt the majority of his audience held anti-Semitic beliefs, living as they did in a country that had expelled the Jews from England in 1290 and still enforced stringent laws against them (some of these laws are still technically on the books in

England). The English despised the Spanish, against whom they were fighting even as Shakespeare wrote. To call someone a "Turk" was the vilest of insults. People with dark skin were looked upon suspiciously as being devils. One only has to look at medieval depictions of hellfire to appreciate the history of such prejudices: devils are invariably portrayed as black-skinned beings. Even Shakespeare's most admirable characters exhibit racist sentiments. The heroine of *The Merchant of Venice*, Portia, dismisses an African suitor with an ugly remark ("Let all of his complexion choose me so" [2.7.79], though she does greet him earlier with the far more generous comment that he seems to her "as fair / As any comer I have looked on yet" [2.1.20–21]).

At the same time, we can see that Shakespeare approaches the intellectual battleground of his era with an open and inquiring mind. A good example is to be seen in *Troilus and Cressida* (c. 1601), when Ulysses addresses his fellow officers at the siege of Troy on the importance of order and degree. These were sacrosanct ideas to many Elizabethans, deriving their coherence from intellectual traditions of the Great Chain of Being, with the heavens at the top of a great cosmic hierarchy in which human life must attempt to model itself on the order that the heavens present. Ulysses puts it this way:

> The heavens themselves, the planets, and this center
> Observe degree, priority, and place . . .
>   But when the planets
> In evil mixture to disorder wander,
> What plagues and what portents, what mutiny,
> What raging in the sea, shaking of earth,
> Commotion in the winds, frights, changes, horrors,
> Divert and crack, rend and deracinate
> The unity and married calm of states
> Quite from their fixure! Oh, when degree is shaked,
> Which is the ladder to all high designs,
> The enterprise is sick . . .
> Take but degree away, untune the string,
> And hark what discord follows.
>
>   (1.3.85ff.)

This is an eloquent plea for orderly hierarchy, basing its argument on the essential premise of an order inherent in the universe itself. The speech used to be quoted as an example of Renaissance thinking and its supposed embracing of the concept of the Great Chain of Being. Yet in this play, Ulysses is himself a canny and even Machiavellian manipulator, working behind the scenes with half-truths or even lies as a means of achieving his ends. The Trojan War itself, in this play, is a vastly disillusioning experience in which most of the participants are their own worst enemies. Ulysses's great speech on order and degree needs to be read in this dramatic context. It certainly attests to the pervasiveness of an ideology defending order and degree as essential to civilized life. At the same time, the play shows how such speeches can be empty or cynical attempts at image-making. Many traditional ideas were being contested in Shakespeare's day, and he was genius enough to realize that in such disputes lay the materials for a vital drama of the clash of ideas.

Shakespeare and other playwrights responded to ideas of hierarchy in very practical ways. A quick scan of the cast of characters before each play in this collection, especially the histories and tragedies, will reveal that the characters are not listed in order of their dramatic importance, nor in the order of their appearance on the stage. Renaissance playwrights customarily listed characters in a strict hierarchical order that reflected the society in which they lived. Although he has a relatively small role in *The Taming of the Shrew*, Signor Baptista is listed first because he is gentleman of Padua. The women in this play are generally listed separately from—and only after—the male roles, as appropriate to the relative power and authority of men and women. Most Elizabethan cast lists observe this separation. Traditionally, women were regarded as subservient to men, and biblical authority sanctioned this view. Hence, women could be treated as property to be bartered by their fathers, as in *The Taming of the Shrew* and *Romeo and Juliet*. (This despite the fact that England was ruled by a queen during the first thirty-six years of Shakespeare's life, and she proved herself to be an unusually capable monarch.) Women in England, unlike many continental nations, actually attended plays, though usually with a male escort or while wearing a mask.

Another hierarchical reflection in the drama is to be found in the final speeches of most plays. Usually the last speaker is the person of highest social rank. Prince Escalus speaks last in *Romeo and Juliet*, Fortinbras in *Hamlet*, Malcolm in *Macbeth*, Edgar in *King Lear*, Octavius Caesar in *Antony and Cleopatra*. Such formality often prevails in comedy as well. Duke Theseus brings the festivities of his court to a close in *A Midsummer Night's Dream*, even if Oberon and Puck are then allowed their final say and epilogue. Prospero is the speaker of the epilogue in *The Tempest*, in a Renaissance version of what in the ancient Roman theater was called a *plaudite*, or a request for applause. More unconventionally, Shakespeare gives the epilogue in *As You Like It* to his young heroine, Rosalind (played by a preadolescent male). Such moments raise questions about the degree to which Shakespeare challenged old norms. Was Shakespeare a reformer who championed change in England? Was he a conservative who spoke for the status quo? Or was he a moderate who stood midway between these divergent viewpoints? The answer to each question is "yes" and "we don't know." This paradox is best understood by perceiving the richness of his plays, which encompass so wide a spectrum of

human thought that each reader, viewer, director, actor, critic, and student can respond to the plays in accordance with his or her own experience. Shakespeare is a dramatist, not a writer of lectures or political essays with a "message." He exploits social difference for dramatic effect, allowing speakers of varied persuasions to speak from character rather than as mouthpieces for the playwright. We shall continue to explore this phenomenon in conjunction with specific plays.

Although England was undergoing a major transformation in its thought and social structures in the late sixteenth century, older and more traditional aspects of English society persisted, affording Shakespeare a blend of new thought and old customs and thereby investing his plays with extraordinary richness of possibility. Festive rites were a vital part of Elizabethan life, even if they were also under pressure of attack from newer ideas of reform. Festivity was much needed, because life in Shakespeare's England was difficult. Working hours were long and hard, sanitary conditions were dreadful, the threat of plague was omnipresent. Political intrigues and religious conflicts threatened civil war. Carnival days, folk customs, and other entertainment were therefore welcome respites. Many such customs had originated in pagan rites that were then absorbed by Christian culture and made an integral part of the liturgical calendar. Not surprisingly, Shakespeare draws upon folk custom in many of his plays:

- *A Midsummer Night's Dream* (although set in May) conjures up visions of summer solstice celebrations as the English celebrated the coming of summer.

- *Twelfth Night* (i.e., twelve days after Christmas) is set against the backdrop of the Christmas season and its attendant merrymaking; to be sure, the play is equal parts merrymaking and melancholy, as Twelfth Night marked the formal end of the midwinter holidays.

- *The Merry Wives of Windsor* features the fat, comical knight Sir John Falstaff as a Lord of Misrule whose chicanery upsets the placid social order of a provincial English town. The play ends with mock heroic pageant about Herne the Hunter, a mythic being that wears enormous deer antlers. His exploits are celebrated by village folk—on stage and off—who knew the importance of the hunt in their lives.

Frequently in Shakespeare's plays we encounter characters wearing masks and disguises, or performing in theatrical entertainments. Romeo slips into the Capulet's ball while dressed as a masker. In *Love's Labor's Lost* we are treated to "The Pageant of the Nine Worthies," in which the well-born and rustics join forces to put on an elaborate spectacle, not unlike those one might find in conjunction with a holiday celebration.

Some public spectacles and ceremonies were a good deal more violent and even gruesome. These included executions, torture, and animal baiting.

Prisoners were usually executed in public places, such as Tower Hill and Tyburn. Executions and bloody displays were intended to be a stern warning against horrible crimes and treason, but they also were a source of entertainment. People even brought or bought food and drink, thereby turning an execution into a macabre picnic. Hanging was a common form of execution. Heretics were burned. Traitors were brutally tortured before their deaths: they were hanged for a short time, then revived so that they might suffer the drawing out of their entrails, and then were "quartered" or pulled apart, limb from limb. The heads of traitors were often publicly displayed, sometimes atop London Bridge. More private slayings might take extraordinary forms. In *Richard III* the Duke of Clarence is stabbed and then thrown into "a butt of malmsey" (a barrel full of liquor).

Vagrants and other scofflaws were placed in public stocks where they were humiliated by passersby, or, for more serious offenses, were often flogged or branded on the face or ear. We find reference to such punishments in various plays, most notably *Measure for Measure* (1604), with its vivid portrayal of a seamy demimonde and of prison life.

Baiting animals was another popular public pastime. Not every "wooden O" built south of the River Thames was a theater. Other large buildings, whose silhouettes resembled playhouses, contained "baiting rings" where bears, bulls, and other large animals were tied to posts and set upon by ravenous dogs, much to the amusement of human audiences. Game birds battled one another to death in arenas called cockpits. The Chorus in *Henry V* refers to such places of sport when he asks if "this cockpit" can "hold / The vasty fields of France." Sometimes a single building could accommodate both animal baitings and the performances of plays. The famous stage direction in *The Winter's Tale* (c. 1610), "*Exit pursued by a bear*," may point to the availability to the King's Men of live animals from the nearby baiting rings.

Shakespeare's Theaters

Public vs. Private Playhouses

The Globe Theater is certainly the best-known theater from its day, but it was by no means the only building used to accommodate plays in Shakespeare's London. The theaters were classified into two broad categories: "private" (indoor) or public (outdoor, i.e., with at least a portion of its roof open to the elements). "Private" means that the audiences for the indoor theaters tended

(UNIVERSITATBIBLIOTHEK, UTRECHT)

This diagram of the Swan Theater by Van Buchell (c. 1596), based upon the observations of Johannes De Witt, shows the general features of the public playhouse shared by James Burbage's Theater and the Globe.

to be wealthy and especially interested in satirical drama; they were willing to pay the relatively high price of admission at sixpence for the privilege of belonging to a select and courtly clientele. The "public" theaters charged a penny for general admission standing room, although with higher prices for seats; hence these theaters were "public" in the sense of being patronized by a large cross-section of the London theater-going populace. Among the various indoor theaters were the following four types, all of them "private" to the significant degree of attracting a select and wealthy clientele:

- Academic playing spaces, as for example at the Middle Temple and the other Inns of Court, which were affixed to institutions of higher learning and were used for performances by the academic residents or by visiting adult companies giving special performances (see *Twelfth Night*). Cambridge and Oxford universities provided similar playing spaces in great halls.

- Nonscenic court playhouses, such as the great banqueting hall at Hampton Court, where plays were held on an ad hoc basis and a playing space was adapted for the occasion.

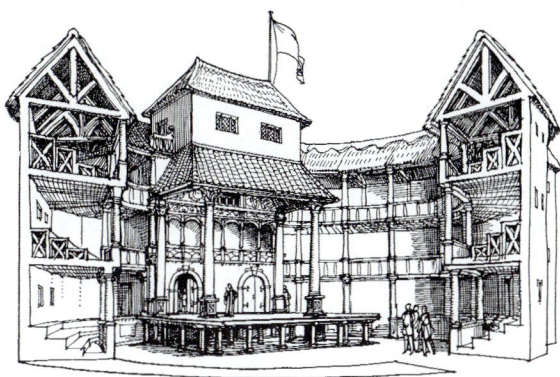

This modern sketch of the Swan Theater shows the open, encircling roof, and a full view of the tiring house. Like the other open theaters, the Swan seems to resemble an Elizabethan innyard, with and added stage. (Courtesy Walter Hodges)

- Scenic court playhouses, such as the Great Hall at Whitehall, where plays and masques were regularly performed in a space created to house scenery and other accouterments of performance.

- Private playhouses with fully functional theater spaces, usually within the city limits or closely nearby, where children's and professional acting companies performed for an exclusive clientele. Among the major private theaters at various times were the playhouse for Paul's Boys (1580s), the first Blackfriars (also 1580s), the second Blackfriars (from 1599 onwards), and the Whitefriars (seventeenth century). During most of the 1590s the children's companies were forbidden to perform because many of their satirical plays were viewed by the authorities as a danger to the state and to public decency.

Two types of public outdoor theaters were used by professional adult acting companies:

- Makeshift playhouses adapted from preexisting spaces such as inn yards (hotels) or animal baiting rings. (The Boar's Head was such a theater.)

- Permanent public playhouses that were specifically constructed for dramatic performances, usually beyond London's city limits. The Globe Theater is the best known of these, but there were others: The Theater (see below), the Curtain, the Rose, the Swan, the Fortune, the Hope, and the Red Bull. Of these, the Swan is noteworthy because a Dutch traveler, Johannes de Witt, sketched its interior in his diary in about 1596. Although De Witt's drawing is now lost, a copy by Arend van Buchell survives to give us the only extant contemporary illustration of the whole interior of an Elizabethan public theater (see the De Witt drawing on p. 18 and a modern rendition by C. Walter Hodges here on p. 19).

The distinctive features of the public and "private" playhouses can perhaps be seen most clearly in the following comparison:

Public Theaters: *The Globe, the Swan, etc.*	**Private Theaters:** *The Globe, Blackfriars*
Bankside or Shoreditch; outside the City to the west, in "liberties" with restrictions	Within the city limits or nearby city's borders
Open air; sunlit and exposed to the elements	Enclosed; roofed; artificial lighting
Daytime performances	Evening performances
Round or polygonal amphitheater	Rectangular hall
"Tiring house" backstage	Attiring area behind the stage
Two entrance doors flanking a "discovery" space	Two entrance doors flanking a "discovery" space
Gallery over the stage, rear	Gallery over the stage, rear
A large rectangular stage, c. 27' x 43', raised c. 5'	A smaller rectangular stage, c. 29' x 18.5', only slightly raised
Capacity: c. 2000 spectators	c. 600–700 spectators
Some spectators stood in the yard on three sides of the stage, others sat either in front of the stage or in galleries on three sides	All audience members were seated, in what we would call the orchestra
Audiences were drawn from a broad spectrum of English society	Audiences were well-educated, homogeneously belonging to the gentlemanly or aristocratic class

Although Shakespeare and his colleagues performed in several of these venues—at the court for both Queen Elizabeth and later King James I, at the Middle Temple where young men studied law, in banqueting halls at manor houses, and at other public theaters such as the Curtain—three theaters may rightly be called Shakespeare's "home" theater at one time or another. The Globe, located across the river from London, is of course best known, but The Theater and the second Blackfriars also merit attention.

The Globe Theater

No playhouse in the history of Western theater has been the subject of such intense scrutiny by scholars as the Globe. Decades of research were rewarded in June 1997 when the new Globe Theater opened in London, not far from the original site of the original building. It is as accurate a reconstruction of the original as possible, given the limitations of knowledge about the first Globe. (We have a drawing of the Swan, but not of the Globe.) Today, patrons can pay a moderate admission price to stand in the pit close to the stage like the "groundlings" of Shakespeare's day, or to sit on wooden benches in the stands. The theater is both a highly popular performance space and a laboratory where the plays can be acted under the conditions for which they were written.

The Globe, like most of its Elizabethan counterparts, had four distinct areas:

The *main stage* was a wooden rectangular platform measuring about twenty-seven feet in depth by forty-three feet in width (see table on p. 19). It stood some five to six feet above the floor of the yard in which spectators could watch performances. Two columns passing from ground level through the stage held up a small roof over the main playing area on the under side of which were painted astrological signs to signify the "heavens." In the facade of the tiring house backstage were at least two doors (the Swan drawing shows two large hinged doors), one to each side of a center line.

The Globe appears also to have had a "discovery space," probably midway between the two doors, where characters could be "discovered" by the thrusting onstage of a bed (as in the final act of *Othello*, when Desdemona enters thus on the bed in which she is to be murdered by her husband), or by the drawing aside of a curtain, as when Prospero *"discovers Ferdinand and Miranda, playing at chess"* (*The Tempest*, 5.1.172.1–2). Scenes were not extensively acted in this discovery space; sight lines were not adequate for that. Instead, discoveries or concealments could be used to introduce actors onto the stage (as in *The Tempest*) or to hide actors from view (as when Polonius hides behind the *arras* or curtain in Queen Gertrude's private rooms to overhear her conversation with Hamlet and is stabbed through the curtain by Hamlet under the plausible assumption that the hidden person is King Claudius). Falstaff is able to exit from the great tavern scene in *1 Henry IV* by hiding behind an arras (presumably in the "discovery space") where he falls asleep, snoring so loudly as to give away his presence there; Prince Henry thereupon bids Peto to pick Falstaff's pockets and see what evidence they may give as to Falstaff's eating and drinking habits.

The main stage also probably featured at least one trap door, from which spirits, ghosts, and other ethereal beings could emerge, or into which the gravediggers in Hamlet could mime their digging of Ophelia's grave and in which Hamlet and Laertes subsequently grapple over her dead body.

Above the stage doors and "discovery space" was a *gallery* with perhaps six bays (such as is shown in the Swan drawing). Here actors could occasionally appear in scenes *"above,"* as when the defenders of a city in a tragedy or history play are addressed by the besiegers on the main stage, or when in *Romeo and Juliet* the heroine appears at her window and is courted by Romeo on the main stage below. Note that Juliet's space is never called a balcony; the term "balcony scene" is an anachronism derived from eighteenth-century staging practice, when her window was indeed made to look like a balcony. This upper acting area is seldom used for complex or lengthy dramatic scenes involving several characters; as with the "discovery space," sight lines did not favor such a use of theatrical facilities. Instead, appearances *"above"* are almost always devoted to scenes in which one or two figures in some elevated location speak to characters below. Juliet is at her window, and so we understand that Romeo is in the garden or orchard behind her house. In scenes of siege warfare, the main stage represents the ground lying before a besieged castle or walled city, in which the gallery doors then come to represent for the duration of the military action the walls of the castle or city. In *Richard II*, King Richard is besieged at Berkeley Castle by Bolingbroke and his forces and is obliged to come down to accede to the demands of his attackers.

Many important plays, like *Hamlet* and *King Lear*, seem to make no use of the upper acting area, which might then be used for spectators; audience members appear to be occupying the bays of the gallery in the Swan drawing, and a similar arrangement is seemingly on display in seventeenth-century illustrations for William Alabaster's *Roxana* (1632) and Francis Kirkman's *The Wits* (c. 1662).

The *tiring house* was essentially the space in back of the stage. Here the actors could "attire" themselves (hence the name) and could store the relatively few properties they needed, such as thrones, chairs, beds, and a variety of hand props. Cannonballs could be rolled across the space's wooden floors to suggest thunder. A musicians' room somewhere in the theater provided space for the instrumentalists who sometimes accompanied the action. (Musicians occasionally appeared onstage as well.) High atop the building above the tiring house was a small hut from which a pennant could be flown to alert the citizens across the river that a play was being performed that day.

The *auditorium*, or what we today might call the "house," provided a yard in which audience members paying a single penny for admission could stand on the ground (hence, the term "groundlings"), and three tiers of galleries surrounding the stage on three sides. To close the distance between spectators and stage as much as possible, the Globe was roughly circular or octagonal in shape. Shakespeare refers to this configuration in the first Chorus speech in *Henry V* when he talks about "this wooden O." The building seems to have had a special room, called "the Lord's room," for distinguished patrons. The auditorium thus was able to house an audience that was at once socially heterogeneous and hierarchically differentiated.

Peter Brook, among the most influential stage and film directors of the twentieth and twenty-first centuries, has called the Elizabethan public theater "the perfect actors' machine." Burbage's ingenious design was indeed a versatile space that allowed for a variety of impressive theatrical effects. Brook also calls such a theater the "perfect philosopher's machine" because its design acknowledged the heavens and all that they portend, the array of human activity that traversed the stage proper, and the nether world beneath the stage. The versatility of the Globe as both an actors' machine and as a place for cosmic musings will be addressed frequently throughout this book, particularly in conjunction with *A Midsummer Night's Dream.*

The Theater

Erected by James Burbage in 1576, The Theater was located northeast of the City in an area known as Shoreditch. In this first successful permanent public playhouse in London, Shakespeare joined with Burbage's sons, Richard and Cuthbert, and other actors to form the Lord Chamberlain's Men in 1594. There they prospered for several years until, in 1598–1599, they ran into leasing difficulties with the owner of the land on which the building stood. At that point the actors literally dismantled The Theater, timber by timber, and hauled it across the Thames (perhaps skidding the timbers over the frozen river in an extraordinarily cold winter) to a Southwark neighborhood noted for its scruffy taverns, houses of prostitution, and baiting rings. Because its timbers were reused in erecting their new playhouse, the Globe must have identical in many respects to The Theater, though the actors could also have introduced modifications based on practical experience.

The Second Blackfriars

Some time after the Reformation of the English church and the abolition of the monasteries in the sixteenth century, the large dining hall of a monastery in the Blackfriars district close to Saint Paul's Cathedral had been converted into a playing space for a company of boy actors. It was closed down in about 1590 for satirical excesses, and the space was put to other use. James Burbage acquired the property in 1597 and fitted out a new, second Blackfriars. He died shortly thereafter. The second Blackfriars passed to his son, Richard, who leased it to a boy's company known as the Children of the Royal Chapel and then, on the death of Queen Elizabeth in 1603, as the Children of the Queen's Revels. (Boys' companies were allowed to reopen in 1599, as we shall see in *Hamlet.*) In 1608, the King's Men reclaimed this indoor theater for their own dramatic activities during the winter, though continuing to perform at the Globe in the summer months. The company liked their new indoor acting space for financial, artistic, and climatic reasons. They increased their revenues by catering to a wealthier, better educated audience.

New technological devices were introduced at the second Blackfriars, as at the Globe. *The Tempest* is filled with wondrous theatrical effects, including a banquet table that is made to disappear *"with a quaint device"* (3.3.52) and the descent of the goddess Juno from the "heavens" above the stage (4.1). Some features of the second Blackfriars were not unlike those at the Globe: suspension gear for flying effects; a gallery rear-stage for action above the stage level; and a "discovery space" located in the center of the rear wall of the stage with two large doors on either side.

Despite the similarities between the two theaters, there also were significant differences. All of the second Blackfriars audience was comfortably seated, including those directly in front of the stage. Indoor lighting, in the form of handsome chandeliers, though not easily dimmed or brightened, illuminated the house. A more elegant clientele inevitably encouraged the company to produce plays to patrician tastes, with fewer military battles and with more satirical comedy making fun of the London bourgeoisie.

Shakespeare's Actors

A number of professional adult acting companies working in London and its environs, as well as the boys' companies in the private theaters, competed for the favor of London's audiences. The best known of these were the Lord Chamberlain's Men, renamed the King's Men in 1603, and the Lord Admiral's Men, whose leading actor was Edward Alleyn and who had some Marlowe plays in their repertory. Other companies, including the Queen's Men, the Earl of Leicester's Men, Lord Strange's Men, the Earl of Pembroke's Men, the Earl of Sussex's Men, and the Earl of Worcester's Men, were also at least briefly a part of the theatrical scene, though the competition among the companies was fierce and the casualty rate high. The title page of Shakespeare's *Titus Andronicus* (1594) announces that it was played by the Right Honorable the Earl of Derby, Earl of Pembroke, and Sussex their Servants. Ferdinando Stanley, Lord Strange, had become the Earl of Derby in 1593. A version of Shakespeare's *Henry VI, Part Three* was published in 1595 as having been "sundry times acted by the Right Honorable the Earl of Pembroke His Servants." Shakespeare might have acted with any of these troupes when he first came to London, before joining the new Lord Chamberlain's Men in 1594. Wealthy and powerful men and women (such as Elizabeth herself) advanced the popular acting companies' prestige by sponsoring them; the company members wore their respective noble's livery.

The boys' companies, including the Children of Paul's, the Children of the Chapel, and the Children of Blackfriars, often drew their young actors from choirs attached to the royal or other aristocratic households. They performed for select paying audience under the pretext of rehearsing for performances at court, where they were much in demand. A number of these juvenile actors graduated to the adult companies, who employed boy actors of their own. As we have seen, Shakespeare's company moved into Blackfriars for winter performances starting in 1608, so that the theatrical fortunes of adult and boys' companies were intertwined in many ways, especially in later years. Nevertheless, the competition for audiences between adult and juvenile companies was at times very sharp, and was exacerbated by contrasts in style: writers for the boys' companies often put their young actors' talent for mimicry to satirical use. Shakespeare devotes a passage in *Hamlet* to the "little eyases" (young hawks), who became a threat to the livelihood of the adult troupes when the boy companies were allowed to reopen in 1599 after nearly a decade of being closed.

Theatrical activity in London was regulated by the Revels Office, founded by Henry VIII to supervise the court spectacles he enjoyed. The office was administered by the Master of the Revels acting on behalf of the crown. (In *Shakespeare in Love*, the Master of the Revels repeatedly attempts to shut down the acting companies for various violations.) Because the Tudor and Stuart monarchs alike were generally fond of theater, however, the London acting companies were given license to perform, though the Master of the Revels was responsible for collecting licensing fees and censoring new play scripts to guard against sacrilegious or seditious material. (For instance, an act of 1606 forbidding the profane use of God's name in stage plays led to many euphemisms and word substitutions that we can see in Shakespeare's texts.)

The London mayor and aldermen were inclined to be suspicious of the theater. Part of their concern was a matter of public health, as plague was such a serious problem. The authorities worried too about unruly crowds, where pickpockets and prostitutes might flourish. Mostly, though, the authorities reflected the moral concerns of a London populace that was becoming increasingly Puritan. Whereas in the earlier years of the sixteenth century the stage had been seen as a potent vehicle for furthering the cause of the Protestant Reformation, Puritan preachers in the late years of the century and on into the seventeenth century were distressed by the increasing freedom of the theater to hold London values up to ridicule. Puritan preachers thundered that the playhouses were "the workhouses of the devil," frequented by prostitutes and thieves. Shakespeare stayed out of the fray for the most part, but Maria's identifying Malvolio in *Twelfth Night* as "a kind of Puritan" who deserves to be made the butt of a satirical plot suggests that Shakespeare did see in the killjoy attitudes of some Puritans a threat to the very idea of holiday that theater can so vividly celebrate. *Measure for Measure* hints at a similar anxiety about the repressive mentality of those who would deny to others the pleasures of this world. Despite such obstacles, however, the theater remained relatively free during Shakespeare's lifetime because the monarchy and ruling class saw the benefits of providing suitable patronage and protection, as long as the players did not overstep certain bounds.

The Lord Chamberlain's-King's Men

Largely because of Shakespeare's remarkable ability to draw enthusiastic audiences, and also because the company contained some unusually talented actors, the Lord Chamberlain's Men grew to become the best known of the Elizabethan acting companies. They were given the title of the King's Men when King James I assumed the throne in 1603, in recognition of their being the premier troupe of the realm. The 1623 Folio lists the names of twenty-seven men who belonged at one time to the Chamberlain's or King's ensemble, performing with either or both of these companies. The list begins with William Shakespeare's name, followed by the names of his colleagues who had belonged to the Lord Chamberlain's Men in 1597, most of them since the time they had had first formed in 1594: Richard Burbage, John Heminges, Thomas Pope, Augustine Phillips, Will Kempe, and Henry Condell. The leading actor, Richard Burbage, and the two company members who would subsequently edit the 1623 Folio, Heminges and Condell, were thus Shakespeare's colleagues for most of his working career. Indeed, the company employed a stable roster and was in the truest sense a repertory company.

A typical Elizabethan acting company was comprised of about ten or twelve men, a handful of hired men, and perhaps three or more boys for the women's roles. Because Shakespeare's plays and those of his contemporaries often have thirty or more speaking roles, the actors frequently had to double in multiple roles. Burbage, as leading actor, was ordinarily not asked to take on more than a single demanding central part, like that of Richard III, Hamlet, Othello, or King Lear, and the company's clown (Will Kempe, and then Robert Armin after Kempe left in 1597) specialized in important clowning roles, but the other actors needed to be versatile. Certain familiar "types" of characters, like the clever servant, the dashing lover, the suspicious father, the gregarious old man, and the braggart soldier, lent themselves to a speedy rehearsal process, and the actors must have learned a number of conventional blocking patterns to make their work easier, as they did not have much time for rehearsal. With a playing season of upwards of forty plays, as well as the occasional revival, everyone had to move fast. They had no time for "concept" directing. Indeed, no one acted officially as director, though Shakespeare's company presumably enjoyed the advantage of having him at hand to answer any questions about his script. The actors were not given complete scripts, because paper was expensive; their roles were copied out individually.

Ever the practical man of the theater, Shakespeare adapted his plots and characters to fit the talents of the actors with whom he worked and whom he knew well. Richard Burbage, a large, imposing man, played the great heroic roles in Shakespeare's plays (and others, such as Hieronimo in Kyd's *The Spanish Tragedy*). Shakespeare, as we have seen, is credited on somewhat shaky authority with several relatively minor roles, including old Adam in *As You Like It* and the Ghost in *Hamlet*. Clownish roles, then as now, demanded a special comic talent. Will Kempe, who once danced a Morris jig from London to Norwich on a bet, was noted for broad comedy. For him Shakespeare wrote such roles as Dogberry in *Much Ado About Nothing* and (probably) Nick Bottom the Weaver in *A Midsummer Night's Dream*. After Kempe left the company in the 1597, Robert

Armin replaced him as the company's leading clown. Armin had a different line as a comic actor, one that was more attuned to the witty antithetical nonsense of the professional fool. Accordingly, Shakespeare wrote for him the parts of Touchstone in *As You Like It* (though this assignment has recently been challenged), Feste in *Twelfth Night*, the Fool Lavatch in *All's Well That Ends Well*, and Lear's Fool in *King Lear*. As we read *Much Ado About Nothing* and *Twelfth Night*, we can compare the speeches by Dogberry and Feste as representing a change in acting style. In a similar way, we can discern ways in which Shakespeare wrote to the capacities of his leading boy actors at any given moment; as they matured their voices would change and they would have to be replaced by others who had been trained in less demanding roles. In *A Midsummer Night's Dream* and *As You Like It*, the script makes comic capital out of the fact that one boy actor is taller than the other. Yet for the important remainder of his casting, Shakespeare could rely on the deep acting experience of the supporting members of his acting company to double roles as needed. They were a remarkably versatile group, and they gave him the material he needed to cast his plays in the best way possible.

CHAPTER 3

Shakespeare the Writer

When and Why Playwriting?

The profession of playwriting was less valued as a cultural achievement in Shakespeare's day than that of poet. The name of the playwright was often not even mentioned on the title page of a published play; Shakespeare's name did not appear on a title page until 1598, after he'd been writing for more than a decade, when finally *Love's Labor's Lost* was attributed to him, presumably in recognition of his growing importance and visibility. Play scripts were essentially anonymous in many cases. How often, even today, do we go to see a film not knowing the name of the screenwriter? We are much more apt to know the names of the director and the leading actors. Yet to be a poet—T. S. Eliot, Sylvia Plath, Robert Frost, Emily Dickinson—is to be known by one's name.

For roughly comparable reasons, perhaps, Shakespeare seems to have entertained the ambition of being a professional poet. When bouts of plague in London closed the theaters and gave him some enforced leisure from acting in the years 1593–1594, he wrote and published two lengthy narrative poems, *Venus and Adonis* and *The Rape of Lucrece*, dedicating them to the Earl of Southampton in hopes of continuing patronage. They added substantially to his reputation as an artist, as did his sonnets, which probably he wrote over a number of years and which, we are told, were circulated "among his private friends." Many sonneteers took this course of private circulation; it was considered gentlemanly to write sonnets as an amateur, whereas to do so for money was "professional" and by that very token not gentlemanly. A young man in need of supporting himself thus had difficult choices to make. Money was to be had in playwriting. London acting companies, newly expanding their repertories, were hungry for new plays, and paid as much as £5 for a script. *Shakespeare in Love* gives a lively and funny impression of what the competition must have been like as theater companies and entrepreneurs looked for new talent while young men in search of careers struggled to make themselves known. Many such would-be writers had been at Oxford or Cambridge, over-educating themselves for anything but the clergy or, if they had connections, a career at court. Those who for personal reasons chose not to become ministers in the church and lacked the social credentials for becoming a courtier found themselves in need of employment. They were called the "University Wits," and to a degree they anticipated the "angry young men" of England after World War II, like John Osborne; they found themselves too well educated to do anything but offer their talents to the competitive world of professional writing.

Shakespeare had not had the good fortune to attend one of the universities, but he was well educated in Stratford's King Edward VI grammar school; he'd had perhaps seven years of Latin, and he obviously read a lot. In London he saw plays and acted in them, and learned about playwriting in that way. Success came early, with (among others) *The First Part of King Henry VI*, whose hero, Lord Talbot, stirred audiences to the extent that the achievement was noted in 1592 by writer Thomas Nashe. In that same year, rival playwright Robert Greene, as we have seen, jeered at Shakespeare in 1592 as an "upstart crow." Greene's mischievous misquotation of a line about "a tiger's heart" from *Henry VI, Part Three* demonstrates that Shakespeare was by then a writer as well as an actor in London's theatrical world. Two years later, in 1594, his reputation as a poet and dramatist was already secure.

Shakespeare evidently cared a good deal about his two narrative poems, *Venus and Adonis* and *The Rape of Lucrece*, for he worked closely with the publisher by whom they were issued in 1593 and 1594. He took care to make sure they were accurately published in a way that he did not when his plays began to appear in print. He prefaced these two poems to Southampton with dedications that are warm, even fulsome, in their expressions of gratitude. He chose to write these poems in the fashionable literary forms expected of a gentleman: *Venus and Adonis* is in the tradition of the Roman poet Ovid's amatory narratives, whereas *The Rape of Lucrece* follows the tradition of the Complaint. They were much noticed and handsomely praised. Henry Willobie's *Willobie His Avisa* (1594) lauded Shakespeare for his poetic skill in depicting "poor Lucrece's rape." Richard Barnfield, in his *Poems in Divers Humors* (1598), commended the "honey-flowing vein" of both poems. Francis Meres, in the same year, rhapsodized that the "sweet, witty soul of Ovid" lives in "mellifluous and honey-tongued Shakespeare: witness his *Venus and Adonis*, his *Lucrece*, and his sugared sonnets among his private friends, etc." (*Palladis Tamia*, 1598). The next year, John Weever offered his praise for "Honey-tongued Shakespeare" as the creator of "Rose-cheeked Adonis, with his amber tresses, / Fair fire-hot Venus, charming him to love her, / Chaste Lucretia virgin-like her dresses, / Proud lust-stung Tarquin seeking still to prove her" (*Epigrams in the Oldest Cut and Newest Fashion*, 1599). The esteemed classical scholar Gabriel Harvey noted some time around 1598–1601 that "The younger sort takes much delight in Shakespeare's *Venus and Adonis*, but his *Lucrece* and his tragedy of *Hamlet, Prince of Denmark* have it in them to please the wiser sort." Few of us today would lump together *The Rape of Lucrece* and *Hamlet* in assessing the greatness of Shakespeare as a writer, but his contemporaries did. Shakespeare was taken seriously as both a nondramatic poet and a playwright.

The Sonnets

The sonnet was a premier genre for a writer ambitious to achieve literary fame, and it was all the rage in the late 1580s and the 1590s. Francesco Petrarcha, or Petrarch (1304–1374), did much to establish the fashion with his sonnet sequence that was widely imitated in England, beginning with Sir Thomas Wyatt and the Earl of Surrey during Henry VIII's reign. Sir Philip Sidney and Edmund Spenser, leading poets of the 1580s and 1590s, wrote sonnet sequences as well. Shakespeare's sonnets were not published until 1609, after the rage for sonneteering had passed. He seems to have composed them over a number of years, and then did not see them through the press. We cannot be sure that they are printed in the order that Shakespeare would have intended, though increasingly today most scholars and readers accept that order as the only arrangement we have. The sonnets are linked thematically by ideas about the ravages of time, the hope for eternity through the power of the written word, and the parallel hope that eternity may be achieved through the begetting of children. They are eloquent in their evocation of deep love, admi-

ration, jealousy, fear of separation, and despair over lost love. Many seem written to a young man, perhaps a wealthy benefactor. Later sonnets in the sequence are obsessed with shame and jealousy over a "dark lady" whom the poet loses as mistress to his friend.

The Printed Sequence

Few literary mysteries have provoked so much speculation and produced so little agreement as do the apparently unanswerable questions of these sonnets. To whom are the sonnets addressed? Do they tell a story? Do they tell us anything important about Shakespeare's life? Who is the "Mr. W. H." to whom the sonnets are dedicated? Is "the Only Begetter of These Ensuing Sonnets" Shakespeare or the publisher, Thomas Thorpe? Although the sonnets seem highly personal and indeed confessional in nature, with their fears of rejection, their self-hatred and humiliation, as well as their gratitude for love returned, are these cries from the heart based on experiences that Shakespeare himself suffered or are they brilliant demonstrations of his ability as poet and dramatist to create character through voice?

Shakespeare was keenly aware of the Petrarchan tradition of sonneteering. Mercutio, in *Romeo and Juliet*, mocks Romeo's state of infatuation by comparing it with that of Petrarch: "Now is he [Romeo] for the numbers that Petrarch flowed in. Laura to his lady was but a kitchen wench" (2.4.38–40). Laura is the lady whom Petrarch worshiped and perhaps invented in his sonnets, the unattainable beauty symbolically placed on a pedestal beyond the poet's reach. The "numbers" that Petrarch "flowed in" are the formal features of the sonnet as a literary form.

Shakespeare did not choose to follow Petrarch's characteristic sonnet structure, however, which divided its fourteen lines into eight and six, consisting of two four-line units (quatrains) followed by a sestet. (Sir Philip Sidney chose this Italianate form as well.) Instead, the "English" or "Shakespearean" sonnet (so known because Shakespeare is its greatest practitioner) patterns itself in three four-line units followed by a final couplet. The four-line units, or quatrains, are rhymed alternatively, a b a b / c d c d / e f e f; the couplet then achieves closure by its more compact and insistent rhyme scheme of gg. The Shakespearean sonnet was thus a highly demanding, highly organized form, requiring from the sonneteer considerable wit and literary acumen. How is the poet to write a unified poem in exactly fourteen lines with a specific rhyme scheme and at the same time incorporate into it serious ideas and passionate feelings that can appear spontaneous and genuine? That so many people (men and women alike) wrote so many fine sonnets is quite remarkable given the rigorous parameters of the form.

Popular music of our own day deals similarly in strong rhythms and rhyming patterns, of course, so that the playful word games and rhythmic effects practiced by Elizabethan writers need not seem unfamiliar to us. The names and the patterns are distinctive, but the poetic intent is similar. Shakespeare's sonnets are composed in *iambic pentameter*, the rhythmic pattern that also underlies the unrhymed verse in so many of his plays. "Iambic pentameter" means simply that each verse line ideally is composed of ten syllables, arranged in five "feet." Penta means five, as it does in "Pentagon," that five-sided structure housing the Defense Department. The phrase "iambic pentameter" is Latin, since the terminology had been devised for describing the metrics of Latin poetry. Various "feet" are described in this system, including "trochaic," consisting of a stressed and unstressed syllable, "anapestic," or unstressed-unstressed-stressed in three syllables, and "dactylic," or stressed-unstressed-unstressed, also in three syllables. "Iambic" in this scheme is the reverse of trochaic; that is, it contains an unstressed syllable followed by a stressed syllable. An iambic pentameter line will ideally have five of these feet in a line, adding up to a total of ten syllables in an alternating rhythm of unstressed and stressed. If we use "u" to signify unstressed and a slash (/) for each stressed syllable, the pattern looks like this:

u / u / u / u / u

Or to illustrate with a line from Sonnet 29:

That THEN I SCORN to CHANGE my STATE with KINGS.

Like his contemporaries, Shakespeare used this metrical form to approximate the natural speaking rhythms of the English language. He and other writers of the day also learned to vary the iambic pattern with graceful variation so that it would not be too predictably regular. Much poetry and drama of the mid sixteenth century sounds singsong to our ears; the poets of that era learned their craft at first by erring on the side of too strict a regularity. John Barton, a director for the Royal Shakespeare Company and one who was intent upon developing its distinctive and revolutionary verse speaking style, argues that it was Shakespeare who invented naturalistic speech on the English stage. Shakespeare and his contemporaries learned to vary the iambic pattern by sometimes placing stresses on words that would not ordinarily be emphasized and by introducing added unstressed syllables.

In Romeo and Juliet

A section of dialogue from *Romeo and Juliet* illustrates how Shakespeare, at a relatively early point in his career, uses poetic structure and rhythm expressively. The passage in question is a sonnet embedded in the discourse, containing the first words that Romeo and Juliet speak to each other. The lovers devise a sonnet between them, and in fact launch into a second sonnet when they are interrupted by Juliet's Nurse after the first four lines. The exchange begins with Romeo as he speaks to Juliet, having touched her hand in the dance. Romeo is in a dangerous situation: his family (the Montagues) are enemies of Juliet's family (the Capulets), and he is now dancing in a masque amidst men who have sworn hatred toward him, especially Juliet's cousin Tybalt. Romeo's conversation with Juliet commences in the context of this threatening situation:

ROMEO: If I profane with my unworthiest hand a
 This holy shrine, the gentle sin is this: b
My lips, two blushing pilgrims, ready stand a
 To smooth that rough touch with a tender kiss. b
     [End of first quatrain]

JULIET: Good pilgrim, you do wrong your hand too much, c
 Which mannerly devotion shows in this; d
For saints have hands that pilgrims' hands do touch, c
 And palm to palm is holy palmers' kiss. d
     [End of second quatrain]

ROMEO: Have not saints lips, and holy palmers, too? e
JULIET: Ay, pilgrim, lips that they must use in prayer. f
ROMEO: Oh, then, dear saint, let lips do what hands do. e
 They pray; grant thou, lest faith turn to despair. f
     [End of third quatrain]
JULIET: Saints do not move, though grant for prayers' sake. g
ROMEO: Then move not, while my prayer's effect I take. g
    [*They kiss.*] [Couplet]
    [Beginning of second sonnet:]
ROMEO: Thus from my lips, by thine, my sin is purged. a
JULIET: Then have my lips the sin that they have took. b
ROMEO: Sin from my lips? Oh, trespass sweetly urged! a
 Give me my sin again. [*They kiss again.*]
JULIET: You kiss by th'book. b
    [End of first quatrain]
NURSE: Madam, your mother craves a word with you.
    [New sonnet aborted]

This sonnet created by the two lovers is typical of the structure of many, though not all, sonnets. It also reflects Shakespeare's formal training in the arts of language. Shakespeare lived in an age when rhetoric, the art of using persuasive language well, was at the heart of the educational system, whether one was a schoolboy in Stratford or a lawyer at the Inns of Court in London. A persuasive argument was supposed to be divided into three parts: the proposition or statement of an idea, the exploration or development of it, and its resolution or conclusive proof. In the first quatrain Romeo puts forth an idea: he is a poor (and lusty) sinner come to a holy shrine (Juliet's body). Note that virtually all of the images he uses—and upon which she builds—have to do with pilgrimage, an integral element in religious practice of medieval life. (Chaucer wrote *The Canterbury Tales* about a group of pilgrims journeying to Canterbury Cathedral to pay homage to St. Thomas Beckett, who had been martyred by King Henry II; Shakespeare's *Two Noble Kinsmen,* which he co-authored with John Fletcher c. 1613, is based on the Knight's tale from Chaucer's work.) Words and phrases such as "profane," "holy shrine," "sin," "pilgrims," "mannerly devotion," "palm to palm," "palmers," "saints," "lips . . . in prayer," "faith," "despair," "move" (with multiple meanings here), "grant," "purged," "trespass," and "th'book" all have strong religious connotations in this context. Collectively they form a *conceit,* an extended and elaborate metaphor or comparison. Rhetoricians (and of course poets) use conceits to make abstract ideas and hypothetical constructs concrete and accessible. Shakespeare uses such devices plentifully throughout his plays, and generally we can find a cluster of over-arching conceits that dominate a play: blood and things foul in *Macbeth,* cancerous agents in *Hamlet,* beasts in *Othello,* and so on.

Because *Romeo and Juliet* is set in the fiercely Catholic world of Italy, where vendettas thrive among Christians who should know better how to practice charity and forgiveness, Shakespeare uses religious imagery ironically throughout the play, most famously in this passage. The individual words within this elaborate conceit are *tropes,* or figures of speech. Conceits and tropes are still with us in film, where visual images and sounds, many of them musical, act as recurring motifs. Consider, for example, the recurring use of close-ups of eyes in *Chicago,* a film in which everyone is scrutinized in the public eye. Similarly, Baz Luhrmann's modern-idiom film, *Shakespeare's Romeo+Juliet* (1996), creates visual motifs by means of overhead shots of religious statues looming over Verona Beach. These are precisely the kinds of audience-engaging effects that Shakespeare achieves when he uses verbal images. Romeo initiates the conceit of the pilgrim and its religious connotations into the dialogue while at the same time injecting humor, or wit, into his speech through the cleverness of his analogies. Having "violated" the shrine with his impetuous touch of her hand, he asks Juliet if he might make amends by kissing the statue to which he has made his pilgrimage; pilgrims traditionally kiss statues and holy relics as a sign of humility. Through his artful appeal to self-abasing worship of a deity, Romeo thus begins what is essentially an ingenious come-on to an attractive young woman.

Juliet's response is certainly no less witty than Romeo's initiating of their dialogue. She must respond in kind, both by using the four-line structure of the sonnet's second quatrain and by adapting his extended metaphor of pilgrimage to the point she wishes to make in reply. Her answer is both modest and decorously encouraging: she points out to him that it is entirely natural for pilgrims to touch and even kiss the sacred images to which they have journeyed, but she also parries his implied request for a mouth-to-mouth kiss by suggesting that palmers "kiss" by touching hands rather than lips. When Romeo replies in turn by asking if saints do not have lips, hinting that she might offer her lips to him rather than the hands with which they are already touching each other in the dance, she retorts by pointing out that saints' and palmers' lips alike are surely to be used in prayer rather than in kissing; if she is a "saint," as he insists, then should she not restrict herself to prayer rather than kissing lip to lip? Throughout, Juliet cleverly puns on the word "palm," in reference to the hand that he has touched as the dance, but also to the palm branches that pilgrims traditionally carried on their journey in remembrance of the Palm Sunday events described in the New Testament.

The wit combat of these two young people is thus simultaneously laden with religious and erotic meaning. Romeo and Juliet are trying to impress each other with their wit, while at the same time expressing deeply felt desires. The scene becomes a spirited competition to see who can outdo the other in clever wordplay. Its cleverness is accentuated by our awareness that the dramatist is writing in the formal style of the sonnet, with its demanding pattern of rhymes. When Romeo makes his move to kiss Juliet—"Have not saints lips, and holy palmers too?"—her response is teasing in the sense of reminding him that both saints and palmers should use their lips in prayer, and yet she also encourages him indirectly by suggesting that he use his lips to pray that his "saint" will grant what his desires. When Romeo takes up this hint by proposing that their lips might also join in prayer—that is, in a kiss—Juliet finds her decorous way to accede to his request by pointing out that saints do not "move" when they are petitioned thus: i.e., (1) saints do not initiate the petition, but respond to it; (2) saints, being statues, remain motionless. A saint, says Juliet, must not be so immodest as to request a kiss, but neither will a saint step away (i.e., move) if the petitioner offers to kiss. This is her way of "granting" his petition without casting aside the modesty that befits a virgin meeting a young man for the first time. Romeo immediately takes up her use of the word "move" in her second sense by asking that she remain perfectly still and unresisting while he kisses her. Shakespeare has meantime exploited and varied his sonnet structure in the third quatrain by abandoning the longer four-line exchanges of the poem's first eight lines in favor of more rapid interchange of question and reply, sally and riposte. The speakers' words and ideas are increasingly intertwined and dependent on each other.

The lovers' first kiss then takes place at the end of the fourteenth line of their dialogue, that is to say, at the end of the sonnet. The insistent rhyme of the concluding couplet, "sake" and "take," brings closure to their brief and exquisite courtship. The proposition initiated in the first quatrain has been resolved.

Varieties of Verse and Prose

As he matures as a writer, Shakespeare's style evolves toward greater freedom of metrical effects and verbal complexity. Compare the above exchange between Romeo and Juliet with the more naturalistic prose exchanges between Beatrice and Benedick in *Much Ado About Nothing*. The passages at 2.1.119ff. and especially 2.3.242ff. are useful samples, particularly the latter, in which Shakespeare explores the wordplay in double meanings. And when he returns to creating such innocent young lovers as Romeo and Juliet at the end of his career in *The Tempest* (c. 1610–1611), Shakespeare's language reveals how much he has moved in the direction of flexibility. Here is what Ferdinand says of his beloved Miranda:

> Full many a lady
> I have eyed with best regard, and many a time
> The harmony of their tongues hath into bondage
> Brought my too diligent ear. For several virtues
> Have I liked several women, never any
> With so full soul but some defect in her
> Did quarrel with the noblest grace she owed
> And put it to the foil. But you, oh, you,
> So perfect and so peerless, are created
> Of every creature's best!
>
> (3.1.39–48)

Although these lines are still in blank verse like those of *Romeo and Juliet*, the thought and grammar virtually never halt at the end of the verse line. Instead, the transitions from one sentence or phrase to another occur in mid line. Then, too, several lines end with what are called "feminine" endings, that is, with an extra unstressed syllable rather than with the emphasized final stress of the iambic pattern: "lady," "bondage," "virtues," and "created" are all patterned in this way, with the stress falling on the next-to-last syllable. The result is a spontaneous flow of thought and feeling as Ferdinand's lines spill from one into the next without hesitation. The more highly structured sonnet form of Shakespeare's early career, with its rhetorical argument, has been left behind.

At least one rhetorical device remains central to Shakespeare's art of language as he develops and challenges literary forms from *Romeo and Juliet* to *The Tempest*: the device of *antithesis*. Sometimes, especially in the early plays, it takes the exuberant form of *oxymoron*, or inherent contradiction, as when Romeo meditates on the antithesis of love and hate that is so vividly displayed in the feuding of the Capulets and Montagues:

> Why, then, O brawling love, O loving hate,
> O anything of nothing first create,
> O heavy lightness, serious vanity,
> Misshapen chaos of well-seeming forms,
> Feather of lead, bright smoke, cold fire, sick health
> Still-waking sleep, that is not what it is!
> This love feel I, that feel no love in this.
>
> (1.1.176–182)

Juliet is no less adept at the figure of oxymoron, as it can so deeply express her conflicting emotions when she first learns that the young man with whom she has fallen in love belongs to the rival clan of Montagues:

> My only love sprung from my only hate!
> Too early seen unknown, and known too late.
> Prodigious birth of love it is to me to
> That I must love a loathèd enemy.
>
> (1.5.139–142)

Oxymoron later offers her a means of expressing her conflicting emotions about Romeo as her dear new husband and the slayer of her dear cousin Tybalt:

> Just opposite to what thou justly seem'st,
> A damnèd saint, an honorable villain!
>
> (3.2.78–79)

This is all poetically appropriate to a play that is about the inexorable battle between love and hatred as contenders for human loyalties. As Friar Lawrence puts it, "Two such opposèd kings encamp them still / In man as well as herbs—grace and rude will; / And where the worser is predominant, / Full soon the canker death eats up that plant" (2.3.27–30). Drama is all about conflict, and in such rhetorical use of antithesis Shakespeare discovers a way to reflect the conflicts of his story in the figural language of his characters. Antitheses create conflict in and of themselves, and they also help actors project aural variety in the delivery of their speeches. When actors consciously play the antithetical words off one another, they must invariably do so by coloring the words so that the audience hears the verbal clash. John Barton, who has directed virtually every play in the canon for the Royal Shakespeare Company, repeatedly tells his actors: "Look for the antitheses and play them." That is useful advice for readers of Shakespeare as well.

Shakespeare uses rhetorical devices to cue his actors as to when they should pick up the pace of their language or slow it down, almost as if he were writing stage directions. He achieves dramatic effects by setting up iambic pentameter as the norm for dramatic speech and then breaking the pattern to highlight key moments. The metrical variation encourages actors to stress certain words within the line. As students of Shakespeare's theatrical language we can discover his devices of rhetoric best if we memorize and speak his words aloud, putting the speech, as actors like to say, "on its feet." Take for example the famous chorus speech that opens *King Henry V* (1599).

This speech is not only a good actor's exercise; it is also an invitation to audiences, viewers, and readers to use their imaginations. Shakespeare repeatedly refers to the theater for which he wrote and in which he acted: it is his "wooden O," his "cockpit." He points to it with pride, yet at the same time he acknowledges the limitations that he and his acting associates necessarily encounter as they perform in it—a space that can only approximate the scene that the words of his play invoke.

The actors must play many roles, asking the audience to "divide one man" into "a thousand parts," so that the acting company of perhaps ten adult actors and a few hired hands can represent an army of thousands in one of the greatest battles in English history. By means of a mathematical conceit, whereby a "crooked figure" or cipher can "Attest in little place a million," the performers will substitute the part for the whole and invite the audience to imagine the rest. The Chorus is saying, in modern parlance, "I cannot tell the story of Agincourt, the greatest victory in English history until the Armada, fought by two large armies over vast amounts of territory unless you—my audience—use your imaginations. If you do, you will see hundreds, even thousands, of men in the figure of a single actor on this bare platform of about 600 square feet." Because the Chorus is imploring the audience to do something, to imagine, he relies on action verbs that appeal to the senses; imperative verbs of command dominate his speech. Shakespeare's control of his verse line directs the actor as to the way in which the active verbs are to be stressed:

> Oh, for a Muse of fire, that would ascend
> The brightest heaven of invention!
> A kingdom for a stage, princes to act,
> And monarchs to behold the swelling scene!
> Then should the warlike Harry, like himself,   5
> Assume the port of Mars; and at his heels,
> Leashed in like hounds, should famine, sword, and fire
> Crouch for employment. But pardon, gentles all,
> The flat unraisèd spirits that hath dared
> On this unworthy scaffold to bring forth
> So great an object. Can this cockpit hold   10
> The vasty fields of France? Or may we cram
> Within this wooden O the very casques
> That did affright the air at Agincourt?
> Oh, pardon! Since a crooked figure may
> Attest in little place a million;   15
> And let us, ciphers to this great account,

> On your imaginary forces work.
> Suppose within the girdle of these walls
> Are now confined two mighty monarchies,
> Whose high uprearèd and abutting fronts   20
> The perilous narrow ocean parts asunder.
> Piece out our imperfections with your thoughts:
> Into a thousand parts divide one man,
> And make imaginary puissance.
> Think, when we talk of horses, that you see them   25
> Printing their proud hoofs i' th' receiving earth.
> For 'tis your thoughts that now must deck our kings,
> Carry them here and there, jumping o'er times,
> Turning th'accomplishment of many years
> Into an hourglass—for the which supply,   30
> Admit me Chorus to this history,
> Who, Prologue-like, your humble patience pray
> Gently to hear, kindly to judge, our play.

Though written in iambic pentameter, this passage contains few if any lines that are perfectly regular, that is, with exactly ten syllables in perfect alternation of unstressed and stressed. The Chorus's excitement expresses itself as much through subtle irregularities of meter as through the powerful imagery of war. Even a seemingly regular line like "For 'tis your thoughts that now must deck our kings" is not what it appears at first: an actor will surely want to stress YOUR and OUR to stress the antithesis of the thought, and both of these words occupy spaces that in the iambic pattern are nominally unstressed. To read the line as unimaginatively regular,

> u / u   /   u / u / u   /
> For 'tis your thoughts that now must deck our kings,

would be to miss the drama and conflict of the essential idea.

Many lines in this passage start with a stressed word in the contrapuntal position, that is, placed where the iambic pattern normally calls for a stress: "Then," "Crouch," "Hold," "Piece," "Think," "Printing," "Carry," "Turning," "Gently." Among these instances, the polysyllabic words are the easiest to identify as contrapuntal: "Printing," "Carry," "Turning," and "Gently" are all stressed on the first syllable in English speech. The others are contrapuntal in context: "THEN should the WARlike HARry" fits the sense of what the Chorus is saying better than "Then SHOULD the WARlike HARry," since "THEN" is vital to the argument: *If* we had a kingdom for a stage, *then* King Harry could appear in his own person. Similarly, in line 8, "Crouch FOR employment" would make little sense; "for" is only a function word, a preposition, whereas "CROUCH" is the active verb of the sentence. In general, prepositions, articles ("the," "a"), and conjunctions ("and," "but," "yet") are not as likely to receive a needed stress as are nouns and verbs, though one must be watchful for exceptions.

Sometimes an inversion will set in motion a sequence of inversions following in rhythmic pattern. The entire speech ends, indeed, with such a rhythmic effect:

Gently to hear, kindly to judge, our play.

If we measure what the iambic pattern would normally specify—

GentLY to HEAR, kindLY to JUDGE, our PLAY.

against what the sense demands—

GENTly to HEAR, KINDly to JUDGE, OUR PLAY.

we can sense the distance between what would be a nearly unintelligible sequence of words and an utterance in which symmetrical balance is exquisitely at work. GENTLY is balanced against KINDLY, pairing two bi-syllabic adverbs ending in "LY." HEAR and JUDGE stand in symmetrical relation to each other as monosyllabic verbs; and the unstressed preposition "to" is repeated to underscore the iteration of sound and sense. Because the word OUR is no less important than PLAY, the line ends with what the rhetoricians would call a *spondee*, or foot of two stresses. (The phrase "So great" in line 11 is another instance; one cannot stress "So" at the expense of "great," or vice versa.) Spondee, a metrical foot consisting of two long or stressed syllables, is an effective way of ending the speech. The very fact that OUR is stressed out of the expected position for a stress adds to it a marked emphasis. The Chorus finishes by introducing to the audience OUR play.

Shakespeare's use of vocatives, rhetorical questions, and imperatives helps to provide this stirring speech with its clarity of structure. The Chorus opens by invoking a muse, if there were such a muse, to inspire the heroic subject of Henry V's great victory at Agincourt. The vocative "O" in line one is the conventional way of invoking a muse, as at the start of a heroic poem like the *Iliad*, the *Odyssey*, or the *Aeneid*. From such an invocation the Chorus soon shifts into a series of questions that are not really questions, but rhetorical statements: Can this cockpit hold the vasty fields of France? Can we cram within this wooden O the very casques that did affright the air at Agincourt? These questions need no answer, because they are rhetorical: the answer is a resounding No. That thought leads in turn to the matter of what the acting company is then to do, given the impossibility of replicating the field of Agincourt inside a theater building, and this proposition resolves itself into a series of imperative commands addressed to the audience: Suppose, Piece, Think. As we saw above, these imperative verbs all occupy initial positions in the iambic line that would normally be unstressed. Because they are stressed, the inversion adds rhetorical empha-

sis to the inherently emphatic nature of verbs of command. We as audience are bidden to participate in the magic of theatrical illusion by thinking and supposing that we see horses when the actors talk of them. We are to piece out the actors' thoughts. We are conspirators in the process of staging a great play.

The decisions as to which word to stress and when to take a pause are choices an actor makes in rehearsal; the hints are there in Shakespeare's text. Actors may choose to play against the text, but they should know the principles upon which the metrics are structured and think of them as invaluable guides. As Ben Kingsley insists, on the basis of his performing many roles for the Royal Shakespeare Company and other ensembles, "In Shakespeare, the language *is* the character." The excitement of the Chorus at the outset of *Henry V*, his frequent exclamations and entreaties, his calls to our imaginations, and his use of impassioned military imagery all create excitement and anticipation in the audience, making this character a kind of advance man for the king and for the play that tells his story. Scanning a text for such clues as an actor finds to speak the lines can make reading them a more active and meaningful experience.

In addition to blank verse, Shakespeare and his contemporaries used a variety of writing styles in their plays, including rhymed verse and song, couplets, and prose.

Shakespeare used rhyme and stanzaic structure when he wanted to call particular attention to the formality of language. Songs invariably stand apart from the dialogue. They must be sung, often with instrumental accompaniment, by singers of vocal ability; not infrequently, a special performer or performers must be brought onstage. Songs can comment thematically on the surrounding action, as when, in *Twelfth Night*, Feste the clown sings,

What is love? 'Tis not hereafter;
Present mirth hath present laughter;
　　What's to come is still unsure.
In delay there lies no plenty.
Then come and kiss me, sweet and twenty;
　　Youth's a stuff will not endure.

(2.3.47–52)

At other times, rhymed verse can sound consciously archaic, as when the Player King in *Hamlet* recites an old set piece on the death of King Priam and the grief of Queen Hecuba; the traditional cadences and archaic diction stand in meaningful contrast to the more supple blank verse and colloquial prose of the larger play of *Hamlet*. Singsong verse can be used to characterize otherworldly beings like the witches in *Macbeth* or the fairies in *A Midsummer Night's Dream*. Doggerel serves admirably as a way to parody inept verse-writing in the play written and performed by handicraftsmen in *A Midsummer Night's Dream*.

Couplets provide closure to Shakespeare's sonnets, as we have seen. Especially in his earlier plays, Shakespeare relies also on couplets to give weight to the formality of state utterances (as when, in *Richard II*, the King attempts to reconcile two angry opponents by saying, "Forget, forgive; conclude and be agreed; / Our doctors say this is no month to bleed," 1.1.156–157) or when characters are speaking sententiously (as when Helena offers her opinion, in *A Midsummer Night's Dream*, that "Love looks not with the eyes, but with the mind, / And therefore is winged Cupid painted blind," 1.1.234–235). Such couplets provided an aural cue to the audience that the scene has rounded to a close, while also giving a clue to the actors that it is time to leave the stage. In the Elizabethan public theaters, lights could not "fade to black," nor could a curtain be lowered to conclude a scene. Besides, the couplet makes for an energetic exit line.

As the language of everyday speech, prose serves Shakespeare well in passages that strive more for witty banter or straightforward narrative than for the high emotional registers of tragedy. The famous interview (1.5.164ff.) between Lady Olivia and Viola (disguised as a young man named Cesario) in *Twelfth Night* illustrates the way in which prose and verse can intersect contrastingly in a single scene. The interview begins in prose, with the Countess and the seeming young man speaking conversationally. Viola, as ambassador from Duke Orsino, then praises Olivia's beauty in the contrived verse of courtly flattery. Speaking more in her own voice, Viola shows that she can utter blank verse of piercing eloquence on the subject of love. For her part, Olivia, smitten by the direct and refreshing candor of her young guest, conveys the intensity of her feeling in graceful and eloquent metrical language. Shakespeare also uses prose when he needs to convey specific, detailed information (as in letters), or to suggest a relaxed informality, as when Hamlet, Rosencrantz, and Guildenstern recall their boyhood friendship (*Hamlet*, 2.2). Prose is generally the vehicle for the speeches of commoners, like the gravediggers in *Hamlet* or the denizens of the tavern in *Henry IV, Part One*. In *Henry IV, Part One*, Prince Henry converses with Falstaff in prose until the final act of the play, when in the battle of Shrewsbury the Prince's choice of blank verse signals his coming of age as a noble warrior and his necessary distancing of himself from Falstaff. Earlier in that same play, the Prince anticipates the greatness to come by addressing the audience in a verse soliloquy (1.2) promising a reformation of his debased behavior with Falstaff. Shakespeare turned to prose often in his mature comedies, such as *Much Ado About Nothing* (c. 1598), where commoners and gentlemen alike speak in prose. The supple use of prose in a play like *Much Ado* was to prove a potent model for plays acted at the end of the seventeenth century on the Restoration stage.

Shakespeare's rhythmic language, along with his powerful imagery and vivid characterization, is integral to the dramatic action of his plays. It not only defines character and situation; its very structure helps us, as well as actors, to read and understand what it is that he wrote.

Shakespeare and Modern English

One myth that interferes with our proper understanding and appreciation of Shakespeare as a writer is that he wrote in "Old English" or "medieval English." He did not do so, nor is his English archaic, even though it contains words and phrases no longer in use or given different meanings. His language, and that of his actors and audience, was Modern English, or as some scholars refer to it, Early Modern English. Shakespeare contributed importantly to what we mean by Early Modern English, for his vast vocabulary (larger by far than that of any other writer in English of any era) contains many words that he coined. He has had such a huge influence as a writer that a number of his expressions have passed into the English language. We often quote him without realizing that we are doing so. When we say "that's Greek to me," for example, meaning that something is unintelligible to us, we are quoting Casca in *Julius Caesar*. The phrase "more honored in the breach than the observance," meaning that some customs are better left unobserved, comes from Hamlet's caustic observation on the heavy ceremonial drinking of his stepfather. To say that "the apparel oft proclaims the man" is to quote Polonius to his son Laertes in *Hamlet*.

The history of the English language can be divided roughly into three phases, the last of which began shortly before Shakespeare was born.

Old English came into England in about the fifth century C.E. with invading tribes from northwestern Germany, especially the Angles and the Saxons; hence the language is known as Anglo-Saxon. It replaced the native Celtic tongue predominantly in the south of England, though Celtic persisted, and persists still, in the mountainous regions of Wales, Scotland, and Ireland. The epic poem *Beowulf* is the best known literary work composed in Old English. Essentially a Germanic language, Old English requires intensive study for today's English student, even though it provides modern English with its underlying linguistic structure. Many of its expressions and grammatical structures persist in English today, in common words like "this" and "wolf" and "can." Some more specialized words are intriguingly relevant to the study of Shakespeare, like "wyrd." In the ancient Anglo-Saxon world it meant "fate," especially as applied to supernatural phenomena that were thought to control human lives. In the Middle Ages the word became "wird" or "werd," and eventually "weird." The three witches who foretell and help to determine Macbeth's fate are called "the Weird Sisters."

The progression to Middle English is somewhat circuitous. After William the Conqueror and his French legions defeated the Saxons to gain control of Britain at the Battle of Hastings in 1066, French became the official language of the English court. As a Romance language, French contained many elements of Latin in a vernacular form. When the Chorus in *Henry V* speaks of "puissance," he is using a French term. French blended and intermingled with Old English to produce Middle English, the dominant form of English speech until the end of the fifteenth century. Chaucer's *Canterbury Tales* gives us Middle English at its very best, and can be read and understood with a little background and a good Middle English dictionary. We encounter in Middle English the occasional infusion of other languages as well, including some Arabic terms that came back with Crusaders to the Holy Lands. The word "assassin" derives from an Arabic word referring to "hashish"; assassins (hashshashin) were Muslim warriors whose fearlessness in attacking the Crusaders was thought to have been whetted by their ingesting of hashish. Shakespeare, who frequently invented words by making verbs from nouns (and vice versa), gave the word its verb form, "assassinate."

A number of factors hastened the development of an Early Modern English that is essentially the language we speak today (Modern English). The fifteenth century was a time of severe economic and social dislocation, owing to nearly continuous warfare and the breakdown of feudalism that led eventually to the establishment of the Tudor line under King Henry VII (1485). In the later part of the century, however, the development of printing facilitated the importation into England of classical and European texts, many of which were translated into English. Meanwhile, the reformation of the Church and repeated confrontations with the Catholic powers of the Continent gave England a growing sense of national identity with a language capable of eloquent expression. Educational reforms under the reforming ministers provided England with a substantial increase in literacy. London prospered as a cultural center. Tudor monarchs and aristocrats prided themselves as patrons of literary and artistic culture. Overseas exploration to the New World and the Far East were rapidly expanding, in a spirit of discovery and adventure that became part of England's new language. The date at which medieval English evolved into Early Modern English is impossible to fix with absolute precision, and indeed the language continued to expand and evolve throughout Shakespeare's lifetime. Because English was not codified into rules governing spelling, grammar, and pronunciation until the eighteenth century, practices varied widely in Shakespeare's day. Even

so, the English of Shakespeare and his contemporaries is recognizably our own.

Shakespeare's English, therefore, is not radically different from the way we speak today. Because language is continually changing and taking on new words, the four centuries separating the Elizabethans from ourselves create a language gulf that can pose difficulties for readers, especially beginning readers, of Shakespeare. Even so, many of these difficulties can diminish when his language is spoken by a good actor. The famous British actress, Dame Maggie Smith, proved the point when she was rehearsing her role of Rosalind in *As You Like It*. She and the director were perplexed by a particularly difficult sentence; even with glosses (the explanation of a word or passage, such as those found at the bottom of the page in the plays section of this anthology), they were unsure that they understood what the line meant. The director suggested cutting the knotty phrase, but Dame Maggie was adamant about retaining it. "I'll find a way to make it work," she declared. She did—and nightly the line got one of the biggest laughs in the production. Two lessons are to be learned from this story. First, even experienced modern actors and directors are challenged by words and phrases that were presumably comprehensible to audiences at the Globe; and second, we can make sense of Shakespeare's language if we approach it in a creatively theatrical context. And after all, might we not expect a well-educated Elizabethan, perhaps a graduate of Cambridge, to be perplexed by words we readily use in our daily lives, such as "interface," "multitask," "cell phone," "Kleenex," "rayon," "high-five," or "ka-ching"?

Often the challenge presented by Shakespeare's language rests not in the actual words, which are usually explained by the glosses, but in the unusual (to our ears) syntax or word order. Conventions of word order and grammatical structure were in flux in Shakespeare's day, and were based in some instances on Latin or German word order in ways that seems unfamiliar to us. Verbs sometimes appear after their objects at the end of a line, as when the Chorus in *Henry V* urges: "let us . . . On your imaginary forces work." Adjectives can follow nouns, as in "adders fanged." Actually, any student who has studied Spanish, French, or Italian knows this is a common practice in such languages. Shakespeare also regularly uses double negatives ("not never") and double superlatives ("most best") in ways that are frowned upon by grammarians today. Other discrepancies between Shakespeare's use of language and ours are best addressed as we explore specific plays. For now we need remember only that Shakespeare's theater offered an exciting feeling of playfulness to audiences who reveled in a newly discovered sense of language and its extraordinary potential. Classical rhetoric valued qualities of invention and copiousness in language; Shakespeare added to this by exploring, extending, and challenging traditional values. To witness or read Shakespeare's plays must have been a liberating experience. Today we can share in that excitement by entering the plays with the same spirit of discovery that created them on both the page and stage.

One final myth about pronunciation can also be dispelled here at the outset. Certainly Elizabethan pronunciation of English differed from our own today, whether we are British, American, Canadian, or Australian; pronunciation evolves no less than do vocabulary and idiom. The Elizabethans seem to have pronounced "now" as "noo," "time" as "toime," and "blood" as "blude." They gave full voice to sounds we sometimes shorten, pronouncing "preparation" in five syllables: "pre-par-a-tsi-oon." They rolled their "r's" in such a way that "war" sounded like "wharre." They sounded "k" in a word like "knight." In many ways English seems to have been a more energetic language than we are accustomed to hear from well-spoken British actors such as Emma Thompson or the late Sir John Gielgud. And that is precisely the point: contemporary British speech is more elegant than that spoken and heard during Shakespeare's time. Arguably, American and Australian actors are more naturally fitted to speak Shakespeare's lines than are the British, for all the skill with which British actors are trained. Speech experts claim that some of the most likely places to find the English spoken in Shakespeare's time may be in the pockets of the Appalachian Mountains and on islands off the coast of Maryland where English sailors settled in the early seventeenth century. On many levels, we are much closer to Shakespeare's language than we might at first suspect.

CHAPTER 4

Shakespeare and His Interpreters

The Spectrum of Interpretive Possibilities

From Shakespeare's generation down to our own, actors have consistently ranked among the most astute interpreters of his work. Each production of a play in the four-hundred-year-long history of Shakespeare on stage, in film, and on television is necessarily an interpretation, one in which Shakespeare's script is filtered through the minds of the acting company and its audience. The same is true of Shakespeare criticism, whether in a theater review or a critical essay. Reviewers, critics, directors, and actors all bring to the plays their own backgrounds, prejudices, and personal experiences, and do so in ways that must take into account the tastes and predilections of their audiences in the theater or in the reading public. For these reasons, any single interpretation of Shakespeare, in production or in a critical essay, cannot make claim to knowing the absolute truth about the text. The histories of performance and of criticism are richly varied and intertwined. The critical and theatrical preoccupations of one cultural period differ, often vastly, from those of other periods. As various nations turn to Shakespeare, translating him into many languages and presenting him in theaters with their own theatrical traditions, the wealth of interpretive possibilities continues to expand. "Shakespeare" becomes a shorthand way of naming something that is much larger than the individual who was born in Stratford-upon-Avon in 1564, and much larger even than the plays he wrote for London audiences. "Shakespeare" signifies a multiform tradition in performance history and criticism that can never stay still.

Theater people and literary critics do not always see eye to eye on matters of interpretation. This statement may be putting the matter mildly. Consider, for example, the conflicting points of view of Jonathan Miller and Richard David. Miller, who (besides being a practicing neurosurgeon) directed many of the BBC Television presentations of the complete canon of Shakespeare's plays, offers the following observation about the power of the plays and the importance of critical interpretation: "With the passage of time Shakespeare's plays have quite properly assumed the status of myths, and it is the honorable fate of all great myths to suffer imaginative distortions at the hands of those to whom they give consolation and nourishment." Miller speaks from the point of view of a director, arguing that reinterpretation of myth by way of performance must be fresh and challenging, even at the cost of "imaginative distortion." By implication, the director must be given a degree of license to update the play in its setting, alter the text, and find analogies to contemporary life. Richard David, speaking as a critic, is more wary of what can happen in performance. To him, Miller's "imaginative distortions" are a form of "translation," a process that "always implies a diminution, and for that reason the aim should always be to make very minimum use of this resource." The director, in this view, must try to make his own personality subservient to the text rather than bend it to his will. Miller and David are talking about "concept" directing, in which the director shapes his production to a dominant interpretive idea, as for example staging the Battle of Agincourt in *Henry V* in such a way as to remind audiences of the nightmare of modern totalitarian warfare.

Fruitful arguments like these are integral to the interpretation of Shakespeare's texts, both in production and in critical writing. What follows is a brief history of that process.

Elizabethan and Jacobean Interpretations

The Elizabethans had no professional theater critics, or talk-show hosts to interview theater personalities, or marketing experts with their advertising campaigns. Nor did the acting companies employ directors. The few accounts of performances that survive from the

Elizabethan period often do little more than summarize the plot and offer a few appreciative (or adverse) comments. Simon Forman is a case in point. An astrologer and doctor of sorts, he was an avid theatergoer who jotted down in a notebook his impressions of what he saw. His remarks tend to summarize his experience of each play with a platitude. He does not bother to name the actors or the playwright, though usually we can tell what play he has seen from the plot description. What interests him are the characters' emotional responses to the action. Macbeth, he wrote in 1611, "fell into a great passion of fear and fury" upon seeing Banquo's ghost. Similarly, a don at Oxford named Henry Jackson noted the effects of the action upon the audience. Witnessing a performance in 1610 of *Othello* by the visiting King's Men, he reported that the audience was deeply moved by Desdemona's death: "by her very countenance she invoked the tearful pity of those who saw her." As Professor Stanley Wells observes in his *Shakespeare and Theatre Critics*, Jackson refers to Desdemona as though she were a real person; he does not mention the boy-actor who performed the role.

Actors spoke their lines rapidly on the Elizabethan stage, and made their entrances and exits with scarcely a pause between scenes. They were able to move quickly because no change of scenery was required. The reference of the Chorus in *Romeo and Juliet* to "the two hours' traffic of our stage" is no doubt a figure rounded off to the nearest whole number, but in any case, the Chorus does not talk about a "three-hour" performance. Some of Shakespeare's plays, like *Hamlet* and *King Lear*, were evidently too long to be performed in their entirety. Even so, the actors were able to deliver more lines in the limited amount of time available to them than are actors generally today; Elizabethan actors employed a rhetorical style of delivery that audiences were able to follow with ease and understanding. Gestures were conventional and designed for actors who were performing in a large amphitheater before sizable audiences. As Andrew Gurr puts it, the audience consisted of "practiced listeners," and the plays "galloped along."

Although today we probably would find the Elizabethan acting style formal, audiences then were struck with the naturalism of what they admired in the best actors of the day. Here, for example, is praise for Richard Burbage portraying a wholly convincing impression of dying:

> I would have sworn he meant to die;
> So lively that spectators and the rest
> Of his sad crew, whilst he but seemed to bleed,
> Amazèd thought even then he died indeed.

This is the kind of praise that any generation bestows on its leading actors; we all want *mimesis*, or mimicry,

in the theater to be persuasively real. Yet any theatrical presentation is put together from gestures and blocking that are shaped to the necessity of addressing audiences in ways that the actors would not do if they were simply communicating with another person. Theater needs to be a heightened reality in this sense.

Shakespeare's company probably employed an acting style that, in Renaissance scholar Arthur Kinney's words, achieved its artistic "counterfeiting" by acting that was "somewhere between stock convention and what we know as realism" (*Shakespeare By Stages*, 56). They surely believed that they had reformed what they perceived as a more bombastic style of an early generation. As Hamlet advises the players who visit Elsinore Castle, actors must aim at "discretion," learning not to "tear a passion to tatters, to very rags, to split the ears of the groundlings." "Suit the action to the word, the word to the action," he admonishes the actors, "with this special observance, that you o'erstep not the modesty of nature." The purpose of playing is "to hold as 'twere the mirror up to nature, to show virtue her feature, scorn her own image, and the very age and body of the time his form and pressure" (*Hamlet*, 3.2.9–24). This sage and essentially timeless advice aims at a "natural" acting style. At the same time, the variety of verbal styles in the best of Renaissance plays, including Shakespeare's, suggests that the actors must also have used a variety of styles in the delivery of the language, ranging from the most sublimely poetic to the lyric, the prosaic, and the doggerel. The theater of that time, outdoors and large-scale, must have reflected the robustness of the age. Elaborate gowns and wigs turned young boys into Shakespeare's female characters. What the scene may have been like can perhaps be glimpsed today from the opening of Laurence Oliver's film of *Henry V* set in a mock-up of an Elizabethan theater in period costume, or from Tom Stoppard and Marc Norman's *Shakespeare in Love*, or from Mark Rylance's 2003 all-male staging of *Twelfth Night*. The effect is anything but stuffy or static.

Shakespeare's tremendous success as a playwright is surprising given the generally low esteem bestowed on actors and playwrights of his generation. That success can be measured in part by the many tributes that poured forth in his honor. Contemporary author Francis Meres compared him to Ovid, Plautus, and Seneca, proclaiming Shakespeare to be England's finest writer for both comedy and tragedy. Writer and poet John Weever rhapsodized about "honey-tongued Shakespeare." Ben Jonson, in his poem of praise prefaced to the great Folio collection of Shakespeare's plays in 1623, wrote, "to the memory of my beloved, the author, Mr. William Shakespeare, and what he hath left us," and compared Shakespeare favorably to the Greek tragic writers Aeschylus, Sophocles, and Euripides before going on to say that in the writing of comedy Shakespeare simply has no equal in any age. This is praise indeed from a rival dramatist who was keenly and even jealously concerned with his own fame:

> Soul of the age!
> The applause, delight, the wonder of our stage!
> My Shakespeare, rise. I will not lodge thee by
> Chaucer, or Spenser, or bid Beaumont lie
> A little further to make thee a room.
> Thou art a monument without a tomb,
> And art alive still, while thy book doth live
> And we have wits to read, and praise to give.

Shakespeare is thus, for Jonson, not only the premier dramatist of England and the greatest comedian of all times, he is peerless among the finest nondramatic poets that England has ever known. Even discounting the conventional nature of extravagant compliments that were expected to adorn and advertise the Folio publication, this is strong praise, and a critical judgment borne out over four centuries and throughout the world.

Jonson did not hesitate, however, to criticize some aspects of Shakespeare's work. Even in the Folio poem he inserted the caveat that Shakespeare had "small Latin and less Greek." Jonson was himself an admirable linguist, and as a neoclassicist felt that Shakespeare could have improved himself as a writer by a better classical training. Jonson complained too on one occasion that Shakespeare "never blotted out [a] line," as he should have done: "Would he had blotted a thousand!" Jonson was sensitive of the charge that he himself wrote too carefully and laboriously, and he complained to Scottish poet William Drummond of Hawthornden that Shakespeare "wanted art." What bothered Jonson particularly was that Shakespeare (in *The Winter's Tale*) "brought in a number of men saying they had suffered a shipwreck in Bohemia, where there is no sea near by some hundred miles." In his 1616 preface to his own *Every Man in His Humour*, Jonson loudly deplored English history plays in which the actors, "with three rusty swords, / And help of some few foot-and-half-foot words, / Fight over York and Lancaster's long jars, / And in the tiring-house bring wounds to scars." This reference to the wars of York and Lancaster can only mean the Wars of the Roses as depicted in Shakespeare's *Henry VI* plays and *Richard III*. To Jonson, any attempt to stage the great battles of that conflict with a mere handful of actors was to invite incredulity and laughter. Jonson was similarly unhappy with plays that covered extended periods of time and that wafted the audience "o'er the seas," as in *Henry V*, with its moving back and forth between England and France. As a neoclassicist, Jonson believed that plays should follow the classical "unities" of time, place, and action, limiting the fictional duration of a play to twenty-four or at most forty-eight hours and to a single

location, so that the dramatic action would seem familiar and plausible to its spectators. Jonson also espoused a kind of decorum that excluded fairies and monsters such as could be found in *A Midsummer Night's Dream* and *The Tempest*. Jonson's criticism was thus consistently neoclassical in point of view: He saw Shakespeare as an untutored genius writing undisciplined if brilliant plays for an unrefined age. This is a perspective that was to persist into the latter seventeenth and eighteenth centuries, both in the staging of Shakespeare revivals and in critical evaluations of his work.

Restoration Interpretations: Shakespeare "Made Fit"; the Rise of the Actor-Manager

During the period following the Restoration of the monarchy in 1660, when King Charles II ascended the throne, Jonson's neoclassical perspective had a profound effect on the interpretation of Shakespeare on the English stage. Many courtiers had been abroad in France during the mid-century Interregnum (the time when the English throne was vacant, 1642–1660), soaking up French neoclassicism in the plays of Molière, Racine, and Corneille. Back in England in the 1660s, they were regaled by new comedies of manners written by Wycherley, Congreve, Farquhar, Vanbrugh, and others celebrating the new moral freedom of Restoration court. Actresses appeared for the first time on the English stage, some of them (like Nell Gwynn) notorious as mistresses of Charles.

Samuel Pepys, indefatigable diarist and playgoer, kept a record of his impressions of the new plays and of numerous Shakespeare revivals. What Pepys saw, however, often bore only a slender resemblance to the plays that Shakespeare had written. *A Midsummer Night's Dream* at the King's Theater in 1662 was for Pepys a play "which I have never seen before, nor shall ever again, for it is the most insipid ridiculous play that ever I saw in my life," even if the evening gave him the opportunity to see "some good dancing and some handsome women, which was all my pleasure." In the same year he dismissed *Romeo and Juliet* at the Opera (later the Duke's playhouse) as "of itself the worst that ever I heard in my life, and the worst acted that ever I saw these people do." Before indicting Pepys for a lapse in critical taste, we might well suspect that the productions were heavily cut and rearranged in a way that might disappoint us too. He was better pleased with *Macbeth* in 1667 at the Duke's playhouse: "a most excellent play in all respects, but especially in divertissement, though it be a deep tragedy; which is a strange perfection in a tragedy, it being most proper here and suitable." Later in the same year *The Tempest* struck him as "the most innocent play that ever I saw," with "no great wit, but yet good, above ordinary plays." He saw other plays as well, among them *Hamlet* and *Othello*, often more than once; he saw an adapted version of *Henry IV, Part One* four times in the 1660s.

Adaptation was the key to the revival productions of Shakespeare's plays. Because, in the view of the theater managers of this Restoration period, Shakespeare was a natural genius in need of refinement, the new theater managers pruned, reshaped, and added to his scripts with a view to gratifying the sophisticated tastes of their courtly clientele. John Dryden, the greatest poet, dramatist, and essayist of the age, made it his task to reshape *Antony and Cleopatra* to Restoration standards in an adaptation entitled *All for Love* (1678). Taking a play that had been written in some forty-seven scenes, covering decades of Roman history and traversing the known world of ancient times from Rome to the Adriatic coast and Egypt and still further east, Dryden disciplined the plot narrative into the last forty-eight hours of the lives of Antony and Cleopatra as they faced their deaths in Egypt. All the rest of the story, from the meeting of the two lovers in Asia Minor to their defeat at Actium, was recollected in the dialogue. The number of scenes was severely reduced so that the sets need be changed as little as possible. The cast was made more compact. Much was lost in terms of Shakespeare's sweep of history and imagination, needless to say, but for Restoration audiences the gain in terms of focus and tragic impact must have seemed worth it. The play was successful in this transformed version and replaced the Shakespearean original onstage.

In his *Essay of Dramatic Poesy* (1668) and his *Essay on the Dramatic Poetry of the Last Age* (1672), Dryden spelled out his critical justification for such adaptation. Like Jonson before him, Dryden was compelled to admire Shakespeare's gift and imagination, but disapproved especially of the late romances like *Pericles* and *The Winter's Tale* for "the lameness of their plots" and their "ridiculous incoherent story" grounded on nothing but "impossibilities." In Dryden's view, Shakespeare and his contemporaries "neither understood correct plotting nor that which they call the decorum of the stage." If only Shakespeare had had the good fortune to live in the age of the Restoration, Dryden held, he would certainly have written "more correctly" in a language at once more "courtly" and "refined." Shakespeare, in short, was a poet of remarkable "fancy" but lacking in poetically correct "judgment." The times for which he wrote having been so "ignorant," his spectators having "known no better," Shakespeare was condemned to artistic imperfection. Yet Dryden saw, as did Jonson, that Shakespeare was a towering genius, "the man who of all modern and perhaps all ancient poets had the largest and most comprehensive soul." Hence, the duty of a Restoration writer like Dryden was to rescue Shakespeare from the barbarism of his age and thus to add the refinement that had escaped him.

Two and only two acting companies were licensed for performance in London during these Restoration years. At first these were the Duke of York's Company under William Davenant at Lincoln's Inn Fields and then Dorset Garden, and the King's Company under Thomas Killigrew at Gibbon's Tennis Court and then the Theatre Royal in Drury Lane. After Davenant died in 1668, Thomas Betterton (1635–1710) took his place, going on to become the dominant Shakespearean actor-manager of his day. Like the so-called "private" theaters of Shakespeare's day, the theaters were indoors and relatively small compared with the great public amphitheaters of the early seventeenth century such as the Globe and the Swan. Charles II and his court had no interest in sponsoring a lively commercial theater for all classes of Londoners. Clientele was now distinctly courtly and gentlemanly; the days of heterogeneous public audiences had disappeared. The two licensed theater companies coalesced into one group under Betterton at Drury Lane in 1682, until a secession led to a new theater at Lincoln's Inn Fields in 1695. Hamlet was a favorite role for Betterton, along with Othello, Brutus, and Macbeth. At different times he had great success with both Hotspur and Falstaff in *Henry IV, Part One*. Colley Cibber, a theater entrepreneur of the early eighteenth century, recalled in his autobiography how Betterton found the happy medium between tearing a passion to tatters and underplaying it, "between mouthing and meaning too little." He was able to "keep the attention more pleasingly awake by a tempered spirit than by mere vehemence of voice [which] is of all the master strokes of an actor the most difficult to reach. In this none yet have equalled Betterton."

Betterton's acting style, and that of his contemporaries, tended to be formal, yielding a carefully cadenced delivery of Shakespeare's lines. He stood in the middle and downstage, illuminated by candlelight, and he expected the lesser actors to group themselves around him. Betterton was one of the first of the great actor-managers of the theaters, in a business arrangement that would dominate the theater world of London right on down to the early twentieth century. That is to say, he essentially owned the company, hired other actors as he saw fit, and staged plays like *Hamlet*, *Othello*, *King Lear*, and *Macbeth* that put him in a commanding central position. The 1983 film called *The Dresser*, with Albert Finney as "Sir" and Tom Courtenay as the servant who helps him dress for performance, is based loosely on the life of Donald Wolfit up to the time of the disappearance of the actor-manager system during World War II; allowing of course for some artistic license, it provides a brilliant and moving insight into the life of acting companies under the sometimes tyrannical domination of the actor-manager.

Some Restoration adaptations, of *Hamlet* and *Othello*, for example, were relatively restrained in their cutting and rearranging. *King Lear*, on the other hand, was radically altered by Nahum Tate in a version that held the English stage from its first performance in 1681 until late in the eighteenth century. In Tate's recasting of the story, Cordelia did not die. She was restored to her father and then married Edgar, while her father went off with the Earls of Kent and Gloucester to pass the remainder of their lives in "calm reflection of our fortunes past." *King Lear* was given a happy ending, in other words, so that the destructive eroticism of the bastard Edmund and Lear's two evil daughters, Goneril and Regan, could be balanced by the redemptive love offered by Cordelia and Edgar. Such a sweeping change was needed to meet the demands of "poetic justice." To the refined age of the Restoration and eighteenth century, Cordelia's death violated all ideas of moral proportion; it seemed excessively wanton, a cruel denial of the hope that heavenly mercy will eventually spare and reward those who are virtuous. Even the great writer Samuel Johnson, in the second half of the eighteenth century, could not bear the death of Cordelia; he confessed that he read the play only when obliged to do so by his editorial responsibilities, but that otherwise the play was overwhelmingly and incomprehensively pessimistic to him. Oscar Wilde, a century or so later, makes fun of this moralism in critical interpretation when Miss Prism, in *The Importance of Being Earnest*, intones solemnly of the three-volume novel she has written, "The good end happily and the bad end unhappily. That is what fiction means." We can share Wilde's laughter at too simple a view of fiction, and yet can understand why Tate's *King Lear* replaced the Shakespearean original for more than a century. London audiences, like Dr. Johnson, found the death of Cordelia simply unbearable and inexplicable in a universe where divine justice is supposed ultimately to prevail. And in fact Shakespeare's sources for *King Lear* had also ended the story with Cordelia still alive. Shakespeare provided a daring innovation that was too much for most readers or viewers of a later age.

Many other Shakespeare plays were adapted to Restoration tastes and political inclinations. The *Henry VI* plays were interpreted by playwright John Crowne as warnings against the follies and disasters of civil war, with pointed reference to England's civil wars of the mid-seventeenth-century. Colley Cibber's *Richard III* (1699–1700) provided that energetic actor-manager with an unforgettable line, "Off with his head, so much for Buckingham," which one can search for in vain in the Shakespearean original. A musical adaptation of *The Tempest* by Dryden and Davenant (1670), not content with the story of a young woman on a deserted island who meets and falls in love with a shipwrecked young man, doubled the plot by introducing onto the island a young man (Hippolito) who has never seen a young woman (other than Miranda) until the shipwreck oblig-

ingly enables him to meet Miranda's sister Dorinda. Caliban is also provided with a sister, named Sycorax, while Ariel is teamed up with a fellow spirit named Milcha. In other musical adaptations, songs were freely transferred from one Shakespearean comedy to another in order to provide as much vocal and instrumental entertainment as possible. Movable scenery enabled Restoration acting companies to present a series of scenes in alternating locations with the visual decor of a drawing room or a garden or castle battlements. The audience no longer stood or sat on three sides of a large thrust platform; instead, it watched a verisimilar action as though through an invisible "fourth wall." The use of scenery, actresses in the female parts, and the classical "unities" of time, place, and action all came together in an aesthetic of theatrical verisimilitude that increasingly displaced the presentational and nonscenic theater of imagination for which Shakespeare had written.

Eighteenth Century: Neoclassical Rules and Tastes

The eighteenth-century stage carried on the neoclassical traditions of the Restoration. To the Augustan Age, as it was known, or the Age of Reason, Shakespeare was preeminently the "native" English writer whose "natural" genius needed the polish of refinement. In his edition of Shakespeare (1725), poet, essayist, and critic Alexander Pope "improved" Shakespeare's language by smoothing out what Pope took to be its ragged rhythms and infelicitous diction. Literary critic Thomas Rymer took Shakespeare to task in 1692 for making too much of Desdemona's handkerchief in *Othello*. Voltaire, the great intellectual of French neoclassicism, was sharply critical of Shakespeare's neglect of the critical unities. Dr. Johnson's great edition was more generous in its view of Shakespeare as the poet of nature who "holds up to his readers a faithful mirror of manners and of life. His characters are not modified by the customs of particular places, unpracticed by the rest of the world. In the writings of other poets a character is too often an individual; in those of Shakespeare it is commonly a species" (Preface to the edition, 1765). Johnson's emphasis on universal truth was classical in its point of view. At the same time, he saw the strengths in Shakespeare's transcending the classical rules and thus did much to free Shakespeare from an overly restrictive classical approach.

David Garrick (1717–1779), actor-manager at Drury Lane for many years and the leading Shakespearean actor of the age, performed a similar service for Shakespeare in the theater. Among his best roles were Romeo, Benedick, Richard III, Hamlet, King Lear (in Tate's version still), and Macbeth. His admirers were often rhapsodic in their praise of Garrick's ability to move audiences with the powerful emotions of fear, jealousy, incredulity, guilt, horror, romantic desire, and more. "The dark coloring given by the actor to these abrupt speeches makes the scene awful and tremendous to the auditors!" marveled Thomas Davies of Garrick's Macbeth after the murder of Duncan. "The wonderful expression of heartfelt horror which Garrick felt when he showed his bloody hands can only be conceived and described by those who saw him!" (quoted by Wells in *Shakespeare in the Theatre: An Anthology of Criticism*, 21). Garrick gained a reputation for restoring a number of plays to something approaching their original Shakespearean form, though at times (in his musical versions of *A Midsummer Night's Dream* and *The Tempest*, for instance) he could be as free in his adaptations as Betterton and Cibber had been.

Because the theater buildings of this era grew in size and capacity, without electric means of amplifying the human voice, the actors and actresses of the time practiced a broad acting style with large gestures and opulent costuming. Visually, the scene was framed by a proscenium arch stage, with painted scenery behind the actors that could be quickly moved on and off by means of grooves in the floor. *Romeo and Juliet* acquired a balcony for the meetings of the two lovers. Gardens for *Twelfth Night* or a forest for *A Midsummer Night's Dream* could easily be provided by means of the painted sets. Curtains made possible transitions from scene to scene. Along with David Garrick, the most famous actors of their day included Charles Macklin, Spranger Barry, James Quin, Hannah Pritchard, Peg Woffington, and Susanna Cibber. Charismatic interpreters all, they became celebrities and drew audiences by the force of their personalities and splendid costuming as much as by their acting skills.

Garrick also championed Shakespeare by organizing in 1769 (just five years late to be a bicentennial of Shakespeare's birth) a Shakespeare Jubilee at Stratford-upon-Avon. This event raised money for preservation of monuments in Shakespeare's hometown; it also did much to perpetuate the bardolatry, or deification of the playwright, that is still with us today. Still, the "mending" of Shakespeare proceeded apace; most of Garrick's productions were "altered" Shakespeare. Among them were a simplified *Shrew* that included only the wife-taming plot and a *Macbeth* that omitted the scene of the drunken Porter. Several plays were considered too indecorous to stage at all. Among these were *Measure for Measure*, *All's Well That Ends Well*, and *Troilus and Cressida*.

Nineteenth Century: Character Criticism and Spectacle

In the early nineteenth century, the English theater generally went into decline. The great poets of the Romantic Age (the late eighteenth and nineteenth centuries) did not write for the stage. Wordsworth, Keats, and Byron,

among others, did write "closet" plays in verse to be read, but they were not designed to be acted. Instead, poets and critics alike recreated Shakespeare as a spiritual precursor of Romanticism. In England and on the Continent, literary criticism turned away from the "classical" Shakespeare of Pope and Dr. Johnson to one whose supreme gifts were those of enthusiasm, native genius, and spiritual insight into the human condition. Goethe, in *Wilhelm Meister* (1796), pictured Hamlet as the archetypal "romantic" figure: melancholic, sensitive, philosophical, and more given to deep thought than to action. In England, Samuel Taylor Coleridge was quick to follow suit. He wrote of Hamlet as one who "vacillates from sensibility, and procrastinates from thought, and loses the power of action in the energy of resolve." More recent generations have perceived that Coleridge was writing about himself as much as about Hamlet, but that observation only underscores the point: Romantic readers of Shakespeare conceived him in their own image. At the same time, Coleridge realized that Shakespeare was a deliberate artist, acutely aware of what he was doing: "The judgment of Shakespeare is commensurate with his genius," he wrote. August Wilhelm Schlegel, a German critic of the same era, emphatically agreed. In Shakespeare's writings, he insisted, "The fancy lays claim to be considered as an independent mental power governed according to its own laws." To the English poet John Keats, Shakespeare was remarkable above all for his "negative capability," that is to say, his extraordinary ability to see into the lives of his characters with a self-effacing sympathy and multiplicity of points of view. Thus, the Romantic Shakespeare was to that generation a genius of "sublimity" and "imagination" rather than the student of human universality that the neoclassical age had fostered.

The Romantic age was importantly a time of political revolution and its aftermath, in France and in America. A political liberal like William Hazlitt was troubled by what he took to be Shakespeare's chauvinism and mistrust of mob-inspired political movements. Hazlitt yearned for a Shakespeare as liberal as himself. What did Shakespeare have to say about the Rights of Man? The continuing popularity of Shakespeare as an inspired writer bespoke a longing to find in him a free spirit whose writings could add dignity and weight to the preoccupations of the Romantic Age.

Still, the Romantics consistently showed their unwillingness to think of Shakespeare as a man of the theater. "It may seem a paradox," wrote Charles Lamb, a friend and fellow writer of Coleridge, "but I cannot help being of opinion that the plays of Shakespeare are less calculated for performance on a stage than those of almost any other dramatic observer." Hazlitt similarly expressed his view that "We do not like to see our author's plays acted, and least of all, *Hamlet*. There is no play that suffers so much in being transferred to the stage." Probably we should view these extraordinary statements as comments about the state of English theater at that time. Yet an anti-theatrical bias was also partly inherent in Romanticism. The age's chief preoccupation was with character, with what Lamb called the desire "to know the internal workings and movements of a great mind, of an Othello or a Hamlet for instance, the when and the why and the how far they should be moved." "Character" critics like Maurice Morgann and Thomas Whatley in the late eighteenth century imagined Falstaff and Hamlet as if they were living in the real world; one could ask questions about their childhoods and family histories, as though they had an existence quite independent of the theater. The intensity of this fascination did not lend itself to questions about staging and performance.

Condescended to or ignored by Romantic critics, the London stage went on its own way. The theaters at Covent Garden and Drury Lane were rebuilt to accommodate ever larger audiences in a new industrial age that greatly increased the size of an English middle class able to afford such luxuries as theater entertainment. John Philip Kemble (1757–1833), manager of Covent Garden from 1788 to 1802, performed before audiences of more than three thousand on a large stage with movable scenes and opulent sets capable of spectacular effects of the sort we now associate with Disney musicals. Drury Lane accommodated thirty-six hundred spectators. Kemble's sister, Sarah Siddons (1755–1831), famed for such roles as Rosalind in *As You Like It*, Hermione in *The Winter's Tale*, and Lady Macbeth, was a favorite leading lady at Covent Garden. Hazlitt said of her in the role of Lady Macbeth that she was "tragedy personified." Charles Kemble (1775–1854), though always under the shadow of his more famous siblings Sarah Siddons and John Philip Kemble, rose to become manager of Covent Garden from 1822 to 1832. Edmund Kean's (1787–1833) debut as Shylock in *The Merchant of Venice* in 1814 at Drury Lane brought him instant celebrity. He was the antithesis of John Philip Kemble, free-flowing in his acting style, notorious for his drunkenness and scandalous private life. Kean restored some of the material cut from *King Lear*, bringing it closer to its original version. He excelled as Othello and Richard III. During a tour of the United States, he played opposite Edwin Booth, the first American actor to win fame abroad. Two decades later, in 1840, Madame Elizabeth Vestris and her husband, Charles Matthews, at Covent Garden restored some traditional cuts to *A Midsummer Night's Dream*. They also costumed it in "authentic" Greek clothing.

Indeed, historical authenticity became the rage in the mid and later nineteenth century. Charles Kean, Edmund's son, astonished audiences by introducing a real ship into the storm scene of his *The Tempest* in 1842. William Charles Macready (1793–1873), manager at Covent Garden (1837–1839) and then Drury Lane (1841–1843), undisputed champion of the London stage between his triumphant debut as Richard III in 1819 and his retirement in 1851, created sets for *King John* (1842) that gave an awe-inspiring impression of Gothic interiors with intricate tracery and soaring columns. He and other actor-managers like Henry Irving (1838–1905) did extensive archival research to recreate costumes in the style of the historical event being dramatized. In doing so they exceeded the theatrical practices of Shakespeare and his contemporaries, who had settled for Elizabethan costuming that was very handsome but not in such a way as to recreate the thirteenth or fourteenth centuries. Spectators in Victorian London seemed pleased with historical recreations of Runnymede, for example, where historically King John had signed Magna Carta, even if Shakespeare's play about King John never mentions Magna Carta and does not stage a scene at Runnymede.

These same historical plays gave big roles for the leading actors and actresses of the day like Henry Irving and Ellen Terry (1847–1928) at the Lyceum; *Henry VIII*, for example, became a quasi-operatic vehicle for star performers interpreting the characters of the Duke of Buckingham, Queen Catherine, Cardinal Wolsey, and Henry VIII. Henry Irving was especially impressive as Hamlet in 1874 at the Lyceum.

Beginning in 1843, changes in English law meant that the few patent companies hitherto allowed to produce theater in London could be challenged by new companies in newly built theaters of ever-increasing capacity; Drury Lane and Covent Garden had collapsed almost immediately after 1843, to be replaced by the Haymarket, Sadler's Wells (managed by Samuel Phelps), the Princess's Theatre (managed by Charles Kean), and the Lyceum. At the same time, the opulently realistic sets were expensive, and the competition for paying audiences was fierce. Henry Irving, manager of the Lyceum from 1878 to 1902, was heard to complain that Shakespeare meant financial ruin. Scripts for these productions sometimes replaced the materials that had been excised in eighteenth-century adaptations; notably, Macready restored the death of Cordelia in *King Lear*. At the same time, massive and expensive sets required rearranging of the text to minimize the necessity for scene change. Shakespearean theater was not unlike the performance of the operatic repertory today in the major houses: expensively produced, for large audiences, with long intermissions needed to change extraordinarily elaborate sets, and a "high" and declamatory style of acting designed for a large house.

The Early Twentieth Century: "Presentational" Staging; the Emergence of the Director

Theatrical performances of Shakespeare around the turn of the twentieth century were at first lavishly spectacular, carrying even further the expensive effects of Macready and Irving. Herbert Beerbohm Tree (1853–1917), at His Majesty's Theatre, was the genius of this late Victorian and then Edwardian age. Beerbohm Tree staged the meeting of Antony and Cleopatra on the river of Cydnus in his *Antony and Cleopatra*, complete with ornate barge and smiling Cupids with fans, even though the event in Shakespeare's play is described rather than shown to the audience. (Hollywood's film about this famous couple, starring Richard Burton and Elizabeth Taylor, was to make the same Cecil B. DeMille choice in favor of opulent spectacle.) Tree provided live rabbits for his production of *A Midsummer Night's Dream*. His set for *Twelfth Night* featured a garden at the house of Olivia with real grass and a running fountain, all so elaborately constructed that Tree was obliged to rearrange the scenes of the play in such a way as to minimize scene shifts.

Yet a movement was afoot, spearheaded by William Poel and his London-based Elizabethan Stage Society, to combat the elaborate Victorian theatrical conventions which these reformers saw as stifling. Poel favored swifter speech rhythms, fluid transitions between scenes for continuity, and a greater intimacy between actors and audience. His actors appeared in Elizabethan costume, on a nearly bare stage modeled after the original Globe. A visionary and idealist, Poel influenced such significant early directors as Harley Granville-Barker at the Savoy and Tyrone Guthrie and Lilian Baylis at the Old Vic. Granville-Barker proved an influential critic as well. His *Prefaces to Shakespeare* provide insights into the plays that could be gleaned only from staging them; he has been consulted almost religiously by some theater directors, especially at the RSC. Guthrie radically reinvented the plays on a much-simplified stage and later helped to launch the American regional theater movement at the Guthrie Theater in Minneapolis. He also founded the Stratford (Ontario) Shakespeare Festival, still the most distinguished such gathering in North America. The Old Vic assembled a blue-chip roster of actors, many of whom will be familiar to you from films and video: John Gielgud, Ralph Richardson, Laurence Olivier, Dame Edith Evans, Maurice Evans, Vivien Leigh, Claire Bloom, and Richard Burton, to name a few. (In 1964 the Old Vic became the Royal National Theatre, which still produces Shakespeare and many contemporary playwrights in its theater complex on the south bank of the Thames, not far from the restored Globe.)

The prominence of the director as the artist responsible for the leading ideas of a play, realized through design, costume, and acting style, on a stage that permits the free flow of scenes, became central to twentieth-century stage productions. And film, of course, which emerged at the same time, was even more dom-

inated by the director and thus reinforced this new approach to interpretation and performance.

Studies of Shakespeare, meanwhile, were still deeply involved in the "character" criticism that had emerged with such energy and insight in the late eighteenth and early nineteenth centuries in the writings of Morgann, Goethe, Coleridge, Lamb, and others. Edward Dowden's *Shakespeare: A Critical Study of His Mind and Art* (1875) traced a progression from Shakespeare's early exuberance and delight in romantic comedy through the brooding pessimism of his great tragedies to the final philosophical calm of the late romances, seeing it as the biographical journey of a great mind passing through the stages of human existence from youth to old age. A. C. Bradley's *Shakespearean Tragedy* (1904) summed up the best of "character" criticism by arguing that Shakespeare's tragic world is ultimately explicable and profoundly moral. "Good, in the widest sense, seems thus to be the principle of life and death in world; evil, at least in these worst forms, to be a poison," he wrote. "The world reacts against it violently, and, in the struggle to expel it, is driven to devastate itself." Even if Cordelia in *King Lear* must pay the supreme sacrifice, her transcendent goodness survives eternally.

A further refinement of "character" criticism in the early twentieth century is to be found in Ernest Jones's *Hamlet and Oedipus* (1910), a study directly indebted to the teachings of Sigmund Freud. Jones's central argument, taken from Freud, is that Hamlet is suffering an unresolvable oedipal crisis. He must kill his uncle Claudius to avenge the death of Hamlet's father, and yet in such an undertaking must proceed against a man who is doing what Hamlet himself has unconsciously desired: possessing his own mother. This psychological interpretation serves as an interpretive point of departure for Laurence Olivier's 1948 *Hamlet*, in which a voice-over at the start of the film announces, while the camera pans past the Queen's bedchamber, that "this is the story of a man who could not make up his mind" (see Chapter 15). For all its psychoanalytic theorizing, the emphasis on indecision aligns itself with the moody and melancholic Hamlet of Coleridge.

The study of character is rife with suggestions of ways in which directors can play up nuances of characters' relationships to one another, betraying hidden feelings. The film *Shakespeare in Love* by Tom Stoppard and Marc Norman is being playful when it shows Shakespeare on the analyst's couch, but the idea is a serious one for psychoanalytic critics like Norman O. Brown and Norman Holland for whom the plays are laden with veiled insights into Shakespeare's own psyche. Family relationships in the plays, Shakespeare's attitudes toward women, and images of sexual pleasure and disgust become particularly important in such interpretations and in the many productions based upon such insights. Olivier's Hamlet, for instance, had a peculiarly close relationship to his mother Gertrude, a neurosis even more intense in the Mel Gibson–Glenn Close *Hamlet* film directed by Franco Zeffirelli.

Mid Twentieth Century: Historicism, New Criticism, and Mythological Criticism

"Character" criticism generated a number of critical reactions, the first of which was a new emphasis on historical research. Scholarly journals began to emerge, starting with the *Shakespeare Jahrbuch* in Germany and then *Shakespeare Survey* in England (1948) and *Shakespeare Quarterly* (1950) and *Shakespeare Studies* (1965) in the United States, with still more to follow. Literary and theatrical historians were eager to study the ways in which Shakespeare was responding to the political conflict and intellectual ferment of his own day. Shakespeare's characters could be analyzed as the descendants of certain theatrical types in ancient and neoclassical drama, such as the braggart soldier, the jealous husband, the prying old father, the unwelcome rival wooer, the virtuous young heroine, the nurse or duenna (governess), and still more. Information about his schooling and his reading could provide insight into Shakespeare's use of sources. Improved knowledge of the theatrical buildings of his day, and of the actors for whom he wrote, could provide a valuable context for understanding him as a man of the theater.

Historical criticism became such a prevailing orthodoxy at universities in the 1930s and 1940s that it generated in turn another counter-reaction, a critical movement away from history to what was called the New Criticism. Its proponents included F. R. Leavis, L. C. Knights, and Derek Traversi in Great Britain, and, in the United States, Cleanth Brooks and Robert Heilman, among many others. The rallying cry of this movement was close reading of the text, unencumbered by biographical or historical information. As a protest against dry footnoting it had an enormous appeal. It has led to incisive studies of Shakespeare's artistry with language, as in Caroline Spurgeon's *Shakespeare's Imagery and What It Tells Us* (1935), Sister Miriam Joseph's *Shakespeare's Use of the Arts of Language* (1947), Wolfgang Clemen's *The Development of Shakespeare's Imagery* (1951), and Brian Vickers's *The Artistry of Shakespeare's Prose* (1968).

These studies had important implications for dramatic production of that era. Although Leavis himself showed little interest in theatrical production, his approach to the texts heavily influenced directors Peter Hall and Trevor Nunn at the Royal Shakespeare Company. G. Wilson Knight was another influential practitioner of this form of criticism: his *The Wheel of Fire* and *The Crown of Life* offered models of close reading of par-

ticular passages embracing many possible meanings and ambiguities, including the religious. Such readings came partially in reaction to the excesses of a form of historical criticism that sometimes placed more emphasis on Shakespeare's cultural milieu than on his work, claiming a scientific accuracy for its conclusions about Shakespeare as a product of his environment. A later offshoot of the New Criticism again bridged literary criticism and theatrical performance, when close readings of Knight's imagery found clues in the text as to how Shakespeare might actually have staged his plays and arranged his actors and stage pictures. The span of these works ranges from Francis Fergusson's *The Idea of a Theater* (1949) to Muriel Bradbrook's influential studies of the Shakespearean stage to David Bevington's *Action is Eloquence: Shakespeare's Language of Gesture* (1984). Such approaches as these have inspired the gestural rhetoric of some stage productions, including several by the American opera and theater director Stephen Wadsworth.

Mythological criticism has brought still another perspective to bear on theater production of Shakespeare in the mid twentieth century and after. In his *Anatomy of Criticism* (1957), Northrop Frye argues that Shakespeare's plays (and indeed all significant literary works) well up from our primal associations with nature and the seasons. Comedy is thus associated with spring, romance with summer, tragedy with autumn, irony and satire with winter. C. L. Barber's influential *Shakespeare's Festive Comedy* (1959) is no less fascinated with the links between literary genres on the one hand and seasonal myths and cycles on the other. Both critics view the best of Shakespeare's characters as literary archetypes, evolving from the same area of the collective unconscious that engenders villains, heroes, clowns, and ingenues in cultures around the world. The zany and wildly farcical productions of Shakespeare's comedies that emerged in the 1960s and 1970s (The Flying Karamazov Brothers' production of *The Comedy of Errors*, for instance) can be traced, at least in part, to Barber's and Frye's discussions of Shakespeare's early comedies as variants of Saturnalian revels, May games, and fertility rites.

Most of the critics surveyed thus far, from Shakespeare's own day into the twentieth century, were public figures. They were poets, playwrights, and influential essayists; George Bernard Shaw, for example, was a music and drama critic before he turned to playwriting. Their interpretive criticism expressed the tastes and values of a wide, literate public. Much literary criticism in the twentieth century, on the other hand, has tended to become the province of academic specialists. As multitudinous approaches to literature in general and Shakespeare in particular have taken shape, critical writing has too often cut itself off from the practicalities of Shakespearean production on stage and screen. For that reason, the remainder of our discussion here will focus on critical and interpretive movements that have affected the production of Shakespeare's plays, rather than attempting a survey of all modern and postmodern criticism.

Post-World War II: Marxism and Existentialism—Jan Kott, Bertolt Brecht, and Orson Welles

A critical study that succeeded brilliantly in capturing a mood of disillusionment and horror in the aftermath of World War II was Polish critic Jan Kott's *Shakespeare Our Contemporary* (1964). Kott was well positioned to characterize the terrors of twentieth-century history because he had come of age in war-ravaged Poland during the fighting and then had had to live through the subjugation of his country to Soviet domination under Stalin. His stark analysis of meaningless political violence in Shakespeare has had an enormous influence upon theater directors such as Peter Hall, who became the director of the Royal Shakespeare Company in 1960 at the age of twenty-nine, and upon Peter Brook, the radically innovative director who did several landmark productions for that same company.

Kott himself was shaped by the revolutionary idea of a theater already promulgated by seminal playwright and poet Bertolt Brecht. Brecht felt that "To think, or write, or produce a play also means to transform society, to transform the state, to subject ideologies to close scrutiny." His epic theater was an attempt to break free from the whole Aristotelian notion of catharsis, of theater as a place to purge emotions by our identification with the plight of tragic heroes. This genius of the Berliner Ensemble in the 1930s, whose *Mother Courage and Her Children* attacked both capitalism and the warmongering impulse, and whose cabaret-style *Threepenny Opera* (with Kurt Weill) was a huge popular success, saw many playwrights and directors as "sellers of drugs," peddlers of comforting illusions. To combat that aesthetic, Brecht invented theatrical techniques to estrange or distance the audience from the characters. He theorized that such an audience would be better able to think about the ideas and issues that the play debates and contests.

Kott depicted Henry V as an imperialist warmonger whose tyrannical oppressions of ordinary citizens and foreigners were characteristic of rulers generally, including Stalin. In his analysis of Shakespeare's comedies, similarly, Kott offered ironic and even sardonic readings of heroes and heroines alike. Portia and Bassanio, in *The Merchant of Venice*, along with the other Christians in the play, were seen by Kott as selfish and materialistic young people, flourishing at the expense of the victimized Shylock. Such a reading was bound to resonate in the aftermath of Hitler's attempt to exterminate the Jews during World War II. Kott's vision of *A Midsummer Night's Dream* was no less dark in its inversions of traditional values: the fairies were no longer gossamer creatures of fairy imaginings but the menacing spirits of a nightmare forest, while Bottom the Weaver and his artisan friends triumphed as embodiments of a vital erotic energy and workingmen's class loyalty.

Such skeptical readings appealed especially to the young during the counter-culture movement of the 1960s with its protests against the Vietnam War and widespread fears of nuclear annihilation. Kott's views undercut the notion, fostered by E. M. W. Tillyard, that the plays embodied the cosmic harmonies of the Elizabethan world picture. Shakespeare in performance has not been the same since. Brook's *King Lear* with Paul Scofield (1962 on stage; 1972 on film) presented a mad scene on the heath that was highly modern and expressionistic, filtered as it was through Kott's idea of Shakespeare's darkly cosmic vision as akin to the nihilistic absurdism of Samuel Beckett's *Endgame*. Hall's *Hamlet* (1965) also bore Kott's fingerprints in its suggestion that a Hamlet for our time (David Warner) would look like the American movie star of *Rebel Without a Cause*, James Dean. He should wear jeans, carry a volume of Camus, and behave as an existential hero trapped in the uncongenial role of the bloody revenger.

To be sure, Kott's *Shakespeare Our Contemporary* was not the first work to pursue radical revisionary interpretations of Shakespeare in a modern world. An important predecessor was Orson Welles (see the "Close-up" on Welles) at his Mercury Theatre in the 1930s, as world war seemed more and more unavoidable. By drawing analogies between the title figure of *Julius Caesar* and the Italian fascist dictator Benito Mussolini, Welles transformed that play into a savage satire of dictatorial rule and the suppression of civil liberties. Later, in the same vein, a Royal Shakespeare Company production of *Macbeth* starring Alec Guinness and Simone Signoret depicted the Scottish kingdom as a kind of Auschwitz. As late as 1982, director Adrian Noble again invoked the spirit of Kott by interpreting his new and powerful *King Lear* as a commentary on the war hysteria produced in England by the Falklands War. Noble's images extended the notion of a society in a state of dissolution to a vision of the universe in apocalypse.

Contemporary Criticism and Interpretation: Deconstruction, New Historicism, and Feminism

Since the late 1960s, postmodernism in the arts has fostered many new approaches to literary theory and thus to Shakespeare criticism and performance. The New Criticism of the mid twentieth century had focused on literary and dramatic texts as self-contained units to be scrutinized closely and analyzed formally for technique, structure, imagery, and style as keys to meaning. "Form is content" was the motto of such analyses. In the 1960s, this formalism transformed itself into a more radical and destabilized vision of language that was interdisciplinary and contextual in its method, much of it originating in France. Ever since then, the revolutionary semiotics and deconstructive methods of Michel Foucault, Jacques Derrida, and Jacques Lacan have claimed a new dominance in the field of literary criticism. Yale University scholars J. Hillis Miller and Paul de Man have championed the new deconstructionist ideology in the United States. Lacan argues that in order to achieve mastery of language, the child subject relinquishes a sensuous, experiential access to the world and moves into a more abstract understanding mediated by language, the symbolic. Language arbitrarily "privileges" some people and experiences over others. The deconstructionist project insists that words, or as they are more often called, "signifiers," are arbitrary; their meanings and the authorial intent are impossible to fix. These thinkers focus upon the primacy of the text and avoid attaching words (signifiers) to intended meanings or messages or authorial intentions, preferring instead the open play of language. Each individual can read the text differently, making for a potentially infinite subjectivity. This philosophical approach, based in new linguistic theories, dismantles or at least unsettles traditional ways of constructing meaning through language. Detractors of deconstructionism view it less as a critical tool than as an ideological movement, which, intentionally or not, undermines Western orthodoxy and subverts other schools of critical interpretation. At an extreme, its opponents charge, it has led to cultural relativism, political correctness, and the culture wars of American universities in the 1980s and 1990s.

These poststructuralist ideas undoubtedly represent a radical departure from traditional Euro-American humanism. They are widely published and have transformed many academic disciplines, including film studies. Less visibly, perhaps, but no less decisively, they have invigorated many theatrical productions. Because postmodern theory, along with other late-twentieth-century developments, has reoriented literary and theatrical history, and has opened up and complicated the meanings of that history, Shakespeare studies are no longer viewed as separate from the histories of politics, economics, race relations, and the role of women and minorities in society. These new contextual approaches have become both subject and strategy for theater artists. A provocative recent anthology of essays, *Shakespeare the Movie: Popularizing the Plays on Film, TV, and Video* (eds. Lynda E. Boose and Richard Burt), exemplifies postmodern critical studies by including important discussions of "Shakesqueer Cinema" and gender roles and inversions in *The Taming of the Shrew*.

Although Derrida's ideas no longer evoke as many anguished cries of alarm from traditionalists as in the heady first days of the postmodern revolution, they have coalesced with other forms of social upheaval in the 1960s and 1970s, including the civil rights movement, rapid changes in sexual mores, and protest against the Vietnam War. These rapid social and cultural shifts have had a crucial impact on contemporary theater practice. Postmodernism has made possible, and even respectable, an ironic or multivalent (having many values or meanings) reading of Shakespeare's texts that is more extensive than in the early days of Jan Kott and Peter Brook. Theater directors frequently play against the traditional historical and cultural meaning of the Shakespearean text. By framing that text with distancing irony, directors encourage a debate between contemporary society and the Elizabethan one that originally generated the work. In the 1980s, for instance, Peter Zadek, an Austrian director known for his provocative stagings of classical texts, applied deconstructionist theory and practice to his treatment of *Othello*. He gave the part of *Othello* to a Caucasian actor in blackface to underscore the ethnic disparity between actor and role, and perhaps subliminally to remind audiences of the American tradition of blackface minstrelsy; by design, the actor's makeup rubbed off on all with whom he came into contact. Desdemona, dressed in a bikini, visibly became a sex object over whom men fought. A gaudy vaudevillian style of acting undercut any idealized romantic notion of Othello and Desdemona as tragic hero and heroine. By directorial choices such as these, at variance with traditional perceptions of Shakespeare, the production audaciously obliged its audiences to reconsider the racism and sexism inherent in Shakespeare's culture and in our own.

These movements have encouraged an openness to the other, an acceptance of a multiplicity of perspectives that has enlarged the arena for criticism, thereby expanding both the number of Shakespeare plays in repertory (the history plays and the sprawling early romances are very popular at this time) and the means of staging them. Along with deconstruction—and in part because of it—have come other modes of postmodern inquiry: women's studies, gender studies, queer theory, and multivalent approaches to Chicano, African American, and Asian American cultures. All share the common impulse to free the literary and theatrical canon and critical practice from a once-dominant white male Eurocentric viewpoint. Differences of sex, race, class, ethnicity, and sexual preference are essential to the postmodern sensibility because they give us a sense of personal identity that has too often been marginalized, distorted, or suppressed in academic culture and in idolatrous stagings of Shakespeare.

In the late 1960s, as the women's movement gained momentum in the United States, a number of seminal studies spelled out important implications for literary and theatrical criticism. Kate Millett's groundbreaking study *Sexual Politics* (1969), among others, dramatized the extent to which the classical canon of literature and the plays produced by most theaters were not written for women, or by them. Roles for male stage actors continued to outnumber those for females by three to one, and still do so. Similarly, as the various civil rights movements of the 1960s gathered force, scholars began to analyze the ways in which African Americans, Latinos, Jews, and other ethnic groups, as well as other minorities, such as gay men and lesbian women, were historically depicted in distorted images and underrepresented on stage, even as they were also misrepresented and underrepresented in the academy. Until the late 1960s, drama anthologies such as this one would have listed very few, if any, books, articles, and productions by women, by people of color, or by openly gay men and lesbians.

By theorizing the social, political, and cultural reasons for the old distortions, and by thus framing and critiquing the inherited body of dramatic literature (including Shakespeare), the new criticism began to clear a space for the voices and truths of the heretofore invisible others to be heard. Arguing that gender and race are chiefly constructed by representational forms in theater and film, feminist scholars such as Jill Dolan, Sandra Gilbert, and Susan Gubar have shown that the inherited conventions of academic curriculums, commercial theater, and Hollywood film have too often led to the subtle oppression of "difference." These scholars' studies have encouraged theater directors to explore new modes of staging that can foreground fundamental issues in the portrayal of women. Innovative directors have found new ways to subvert canonical texts, as in Lee Breuer's production of *King Lear* at Mabou Mines, with the actress Ruth Maleczich in the role of Shakespeare's aging monarch and Karen Kandel as Edgar/Edna. Increasingly, directors today choose to cast their productions so as to be cross-generational, cross-gender, and colorblind. Many American regional theaters have recently staged all-black or all-Latino productions of Shakespeare, including a jazz-flavored, African American *A Midsummer Night's Dream* at La Jolla Playhouse in 1992, and a Mexican American *Dream* employing Day of the Dead motifs and mariachi music in San Antonio that same year.

As the feminist movement evolved and diversified during the theoretical ferment of the 1980s, critics began to study gender and sexual difference not only in literature, but also in science and in history. Once the field of gender studies was well established on campus, queer theory took up the cause of rescuing the representation of homoeroticism from the nearly invisible terrain that it had previously occupied. Representations of homosexuality and homophobia could become means for under-standing the gender system as a whole. Antonio's sadness at the opening of *The Merchant of Venice*, for instance, could now be read and played as homoerotic feeling denied—though whether the representation is identifiably homosexual or closer to the male networking that poet and queer-theory scholar Eve Sedgwick calls "homosocial" remains a matter of debate. So too with Antonio's feelings for Sebastian in *Twelfth Night*, and with Shakespeare's portrayal of intense friendship in the Sonnets and in *The Two Noble Kinsmen*.

The results of feminist criticism for Shakespeare studies have been lively, controversial, and again influential on stage and film productions. Specialized studies of female representation and women's roles in Shakespeare's world are generally agreed to have begun with Juliet Dusinberre's *Shakespeare and the Nature of Women* (1975; second edition, 1999), and include Marjorie Garber's *Coming of Age in Shakespeare* (1981) and Lisa Jardine's *Still Harping on Daughters: Women and Drama in the Age of Shakespeare* (1983), as well as studies of "unruly women" in individual plays including *The Merchant of Venice* and *The Taming of the Shrew*. Other feminist criticism has analyzed male anxieties about women in Shakespeare by close analysis of misogynist passages in *Shrew*, *Hamlet*, and *Lear*. Still other writers, all listed in the bibliography, focus on the construction of gender identity during Elizabethan times, emphasizing the social and material conditions during that period historically and as they are represented in the plays. Feminist scholarship has asked new questions about Shakespearean texts and has uncovered previously unknown texts by women of the Renaissance period along with studies of women as writers, readers, patrons, and audiences.

Some ethnic, feminist, and gay critics argue that when whites attempt to speak for nonwhites (or men for women, or straights for gays), they are engaging in ventriloquism and in a form of cultural imperialism. One effect of this cultural consciousness-raising has been that white actors now are seldom cast as Othello the Moor in blackface makeup when so many black or African American actors are available. Shylock, the Jewish moneylender in *The Merchant of Venice*, is now usually made a sympathetic figure—if this play, which many find distasteful in its exploration of materialism and anti-Semitism, gets produced at all. So, too, with *The Taming of the Shrew*, one of the most frequently filmed of Shakespeare's plays, yet nonetheless a comedy that seems painfully sexist to many viewers.

The current pluralism of twenty-first–century Shakespeare criticism and performance should not surprise us. The universally admired Shakespeare remains essential to postmodern inquiry about history and the ways in which literature, theater, and film construct culture and contribute to the creation of personal identity.

As this brief survey has attempted to show, Shakespeare's plays are elastic—exceptionally responsive to new questions and new approaches. Before we look at the strategies actors and directors employ to bring the plays to stage or screen, let us conclude our study of Shakespeare and his interpreters with a brief examination of the slippery boundaries between interpretations, adaptations, spin-offs, and parodies.

Adaptations, Spin-offs, and Parodies

Except for some seventeenth- and eighteenth-century alterations to the plays, our survey thus far has been of interpretations of Shakespeare, that is, ideas derived from his texts that become the primary focus of the actor's or director's stage production or film. The dialogue remains essentially Shakespearean, although it may be cut and slightly rewritten (usually substituting a more accessible term or phrase for an archaic one). His plot and characters remain intact, even though the sequence of events may be reordered, or scenes may be split to accommodate film's demand for quick cutting. Orson Welles's films show a particular adeptness at restructuring the plays, and many subsequent filmmakers have used his work as a guide for this daunting task. Ultimately, however, what audiences see in such an interpretation is Shakespeare's play, even when the director gives it an entirely new setting; the director and the actors are interpreting the play as they understand it.

Adaptations

In an adaptation, on the other hand, the Shakespeare play serves as a source for a new story and its characters. At times Shakespeare's scripts provide some language and situation, to which the adapters add their material, as Dryden did with his 1678 *All for Love*. Cole Porter's Broadway musical *Kiss Me Kate* (1947) is a useful example. It uses large chunks of *The Taming of the Shrew* to tell the story of a vain Broadway actor (Fredrick) forced to reunite with his former wife (Lilli) for a production of Shakespeare's play. To this Porter adds a dozen pop songs, including "Brush Up Your Shakespeare," sung by two gangsters. (See *The Taming of the Shrew* in Chapter 6 for more details.) The 1957 Broadway musical *West Side Story* (and its 1961 film version) does not use Shakespeare's text of *Romeo and Juliet*, although it follows the original plotline so closely that it may be considered an adaptation rather than a spin-off.

Classical composers, in particular, have shown great skill in adapting Shakespeare to other artistic forms. Among the many operatic version that remain in the repertory today, Giuseppe Verdi's *Otello* (1887) and *Falstaff* (1893) rival in passionate intensity the Shakespearean originals on which they are based. Felix Mendelssohn's incidental music for *A Midsummer Night's Dream* (1843) brilliantly captures the play's varying textures as it employs hunting horns to characterize the court of Duke Theseus, violins to capture the soaring romantic idealism of the four young lovers, pizzicato effects to suggest fairy magic, and bumptious bassoon passages to emphasize the clownishness of Bottom and his fellow tradesmen. Some productions of *A Midsummer* with Mendelssohn's music have made excellent use of ballet as well, thereby extending the artistic range into still another art form.

Even though the adaptations that we will study in this book might strike some readers as overly ingenious and apt to stray from their Shakespearean originals, they are arguably in the spirit of the way Shakespeare himself worked as an artist. He generally adapted stories he found in short stories, poems, histories, and plays, following the plotline and characters of the original to a remarkable degree. Among his plays, only *Love's Labor's Lost*, *A Midsummer Night's Dream*, and *The Tempest* lack a primary original source. Sometimes Shakespeare cleverly combines two or more sources, as in *King Lear* and *Much Ado About Nothing*, and even his most "original" plays make use of familiar plot elements. In any case, Shakespeare was a past master at adaptation.

Spin-offs

The spin-off (or derivative) takes adaptation a step further and creates something that is entirely new and may bear only the slightest relationship to Shakespeare's original. Key plot moments and the general sense of character may be discernible, but for all practical purposes audiences experience an essentially new work. Among numerous examples of film spin-offs are the following:

- *My Own Private Idaho* (1991), inspired by the Henry IV plays, depicts young street hustlers (Keanu Reeves and River Phoenix) tempted by an older man who guzzles bottles of Falstaff beer.

- *Tempest* (1981), which is not Shakespeare's *The Tempest*, but writer-director Paul Mazursky's inventive story of a New York architect who abandons his career to sail the Mediterranean with his daughter and a group of wealthy jet-setters. A shipwreck on a Greek island forces them to evaluate their deepest assumptions about themselves.

- *Broken Lance* (1954), *A Thousand Acres* (1997), and *The King of Texas* (2002), all variants on the *King Lear* story, are set in the American west. All depict tyrannical fathers whose children battle with one another for the family farm or ranch. All end with death and the dissolution of families, obliging us to reconsider the original and its meaning.

Satires and Parodies

Because they are so well known, Shakespeare's plays haven been subjected to numerous satires and parodies. While these exist primarily to entertain, they can also provoke consideration of the original and they attest to the popularity of Shakespeare; a parody is worthless unless the audience knows something of the original. Shakespearean parodies were especially popular in the American west, where gold miners in California could see such oddities as *Romeo and Suet: or, A Cup o' Pizen* (poison) and *Odd Fellow, the Boor of Venice*. During the Vietnam era, the ambition and military policies of President Lyndon Johnson, whose wife was nicknamed Ladybird, were mocked in a popular Macbeth spinoff, *Macbird!* Contemporary playwright Tom Stoppard turns often to Shakespeare as a springboard for his playfully absurdist sensibility. *Dogg's Hamlet, Cahoots Macbeth* sends up linguistic philosophy by applying its concepts to those two plays. Stoppard's *Rosencrantz and Guildenstern Are Dead* pursues the conversations of those minor characters, the boyhood friends of Hamlet, while they are offstage; the pair of bit players who are sent to their deaths in the Shakespearean tragedy get their own bleak comedy.

Television comedy moved into the Shakespeare industry from its beginning in skits written by Mel Brooks for himself and for Sid Cesar's *Your Show of Shows* (1950–1954). The more recent television show *Moonlighting* provided one of the most amusing and popular parodies of *The Taming of the Shrew* ("Atomic Shakespeare," 1987), in which Bruce Willis and Cybill Shepherd played Petruchio and Kate. Here the famous capitulation speech is delivered by Petruchio, not Kate, a role reversal to please (or perhaps provoke) audiences accustomed to late–twentieth-century feminism. Even here, in TV's vast and varied land of situation comedy, Shakespeare helps negotiate the relationship of our present culture to the past.

CHAPTER 5

Shakespeare: From Page to Stage; Screenplay to Screen

When theater and film artists talk to each other, they often use phrases such as "I like your choices there." Directors exhort actors to "make bold choices," while a costume designer researches fashion history to make the right choices for the silhouette for a show and a scout seeks locations to choose an appropriate one for each outdoor scene in a film. Thus, *choice* is a crucial term for theater and film artists, just as Shakespeare's plays are about the characters' crucial human choices and their consequences.

Clear, innovative choices can heighten the theater and film experience, while predictable or ill-conceived ones can produce a long evening for everyone. These comments apply to a performed play or film, but what of the play on the page? Reading can be a richer experience if you think along with the artists who are charged with the responsibility of bringing Shakespeare's plays to life. A Shakespearean script or screenplay is only a blueprint for a production, the equivalent of a musical score for an orchestra. Dramatists, including Shakespeare, write for artists who can transform a script into something richer than even the playwright envisioned. Many commentators feel that Shakespeare anticipated certain cinematic techniques in the way he cuts from scene to scene, mixes tones, and intuitively creates a rhythm between soloist and crowd scenes, internal monologue (the soliloquy) and external bustle. This chapter provides tools for understanding the similarities and differences between presentations of the plays on stage and film, while asking for an imaginative leap into the step-by-step collaborative process—and the artistic and interpretive choices—behind every production.

The Verbal and the Visual

There's an old saying among writers that plays reveal character through speech and films reveal character through action. Although the contrast is not always that extreme, it does convey a basic truth. The stage, especially during Shakespeare's age, has been basically a verbal medium, with a strong visual component; movies are basically visual, with a less elaborated verbal text. From that major difference flow many others that confront directors in the two media. As you study Shakespeare's scripts and come to appreciate their various representations on stage and screen, keep in mind at least some of the following distinctions, remembering that elements on opposite sides of this comparative chart are not always mutually exclusive. These contrasting elements have been outlined and analyzed many times, notably in *As You Like It: Audio-Visual Shakespeare*, edited by C. Grant; in *Shakespeare on the Screen: Kenneth Branagh's Adaptations*, by critic Tanja Weiss; and in *What Is Cinema?* by film theorist Andre Bazin, who points out that drama can exist on screen without actors, but not on stage.

Verbal Medium/ Live Performance	Visual Medium/ Fixed Film or Video
Play script	*Screenplay*
Happens now; made fresh each time the play is performed	Fixed in its time of making; a finished product
Performers present; limited in number	Performers absent; unlimited number

Play script	Screenplay
Audience integral and acknowledged as a group or community	Audience separate, individuals
Audience's physical relationship to stage and actors is fixed	Audience viewpoint shifted by director
Audience chooses where to look and focus	Director determines audience focus
Action confined to stage space; language and imagination conjure other places in the mind	Action occurs in many locales: set decoration physically realized rather than imagined
Actors often enter and leave	Actors can be "discovered" in space and seen traveling to other spaces
Characters consistent in size and visible from head to toe	Characters change size; often only portions of the body seen: close-up
Character movement limited	Movement virtually unlimited
Script allows players to externalize emotion	Screenplay often internalizes feeling
Special effects limited and costly	Special effects relatively easy, frequent
Complete scene is basic structural unit	Each shot is the unit of construction
Illusion of reality based on evocative use of language; stage visible	Illusion of reality created by visual images, action; no visible stage
Viewer feels tension between self and the actors	Viewer more easily identifies with actors; gives self over to the illusion

Clearly, film directors and theater directors work in very different media, and directors of Shakespeare films, however much they may respect their source, must take these differences into account.

Viewers, therefore, may also have to reconsider their criteria rather than judge the success or failure of a film by its fidelity to every word of the play. Photographed images can replace whole speeches of description, a single close-up of a reaction can take the place of many words, and a camera panning over a landscape while music swells in the background can establish tone and atmosphere as effectively in its own way as a long passage of detailed and affecting poetry. The opening shots of the countryside in Tuscany in Branagh's film of *Much Ado* are a good example of this substitution of photographic images for verbal ones. We see a villa set upon rolling hills, architecturally ornate gardens, beautiful green vistas, and relaxed people clothed in natural colors picnicking beneath a bright, hot sun. The camera, by con-

trolling and selecting the images we see, seldom shows us many things at once, however, and thus may deprive the viewer of the thoughtful engagement required to change mental focus from the isolated figure to the group, or from one portion of the total stage space to another. But because the camera can record natural scenes so realistically, it can make some of Shakespeare's evocations in words—Ophelia's drowning in a flowing river (*Hamlet*, 4.7.167–184), for instance—inappropriate for film. Verbal poetry is "an essential part of cinematic expression; the lack of poetry in film impoverishes and depletes the art" (Lawson, *Film: The Creative Process*, 196). In the theater, too, as the previous chapter has demonstrated, certain words, speeches, or scenes are cut or rearranged depending upon the taste of the times and the choice of themes the director wishes to emphasize and explore.

Stage Artists at Work

The Actors

Even if Shakespeare is best known as a playwright, any discussion of theater artists must begin with actors, not only because they are the most visible, but because they are the first artists of the theater. Actors were performing before there were playwrights, directors, and designers. More importantly, the actor is the least dispensable artist in the theater: a solo performer improvising on a bare floor or street corner can create memorable theater.

Put simply, an actor is one who performs or impersonates. (The "-or" suffix is gender neutral and is used at times throughout this text to denote both male and female performers.) Yet "performs" and "impersonates" do not begin to define the reality of what the actor does. As Charles Marowitz, a Shakespearean director and critic, writes, an actor is one who remembers all of the emotions, sensory experiences, triumphs, and defeats known to humanity. Such comments remind us that the first actors evolved from priests or shamans whose duty was to heal people. Magic was integral to their work, and perhaps we have retained some of that sense of the magical and mysterious as we watch actors transform themselves into other beings. As we have seen, the earliest Shakespearean performances led audiences to identify with characters such as Burbage's Macbeth.

Humans are the most imitative of living creatures, according to Aristotle's *Poetics*, which is to say that each of us brings a wealth of intuitive experience to the theater and to our study of Shakespeare. Film star Marlon Brando once told an interviewer: "Acting is something

CLOSE-UP

SILENT SHAKESPEARE

No single writer in the history of the English language has coined more new words or has been quoted more often. A Shakespeare play or poem is indeed "a thing of words."

Ironically, Shakespeare's splendid words and theatrical images provided inspiration for numerous films in the earliest days of the cinema. The first "talkie" film of a Shakespeare play did not appear until 1929—the still-fascinating *The Taming of the Shrew*, with the swashbuckling Douglas Fairbanks as Petruchio and Mary Pickford, "America's sweetheart," as Kate. (See Part One, Chapter 5 and Part Two, Chapter 6 for further discussion of this classic film.) By the time Fairbanks and Pickford allowed audiences to hear Shakespeare on film for the first time (in other than lip-synched to phonograph versions), thirty-four silent-film versions of a dozen Shakespeare plays had already appeared; even more impressively, the *Cambridge Companion to Shakespeare on Film* (2000) estimates that there were over four hundred films "on Shakespearean subjects" in the silent era.

In 1889 Thomas Alva Edison invented the Kinetoscope, a predecessor to the cinema, and in 1895 the projector was invented to allow audiences to view a film on a large screen. Soon thereafter the first film of a Shakespeare play—or, more accurately, a portion of a play—appeared: Sir Herbert Beerbohm Tree's eighty-second scene from *King John*. Tree was then in the midst of an ambitious project to stage thirteen Shakespeare plays at London's newest theater, Her Majesty's, which he opened in 1897. In 1899 he staged *King John,* adding a spectacular tableau of the signing of the Magna Carta in 1215 even though Shakespeare does not include this historical milestone in his play. While the event is the one for which King John (*r.* 1199–1216) is most remembered by posterity, Tree's short film portrays the monarch in his death throes. Today we would likely laugh at Tree's histrionics—which were better suited for a cavernous theater like Her Majesty's than for the camera—much the way we laugh at Nick Bottom's tortuous death scene as Pyramus in *A Midsummer Night's Dream.* Yet audiences in 1899 were no doubt moved by Tree's acting (and, of course, the magic of film), a useful reminder to us that acting styles and audience's perceptions of "reality" reflect "the age and body of the time."

Tree filmed two additional "shorts" based on Shakespeare's plays, and he even made money on the enterprise. His cinematic Shakespeare was especially remarkable because the new medium was considered more of a curiosity intended for the working class than a respectable outlet for the talents of a major classical actor of the era. Appropriately, it was Tree, ever the bold experimenter in his stage work, who saw the potential for film as a medium through which millions could encounter Shakespeare. (Tree made his own film debut in a 1907 French film, *Shakespeare Writing Julius Caesar.*)

Soon after Tree's film enthralled London audiences, others followed to contribute to that most curious of oxymorons: "silent Shakespeare." Actually, one noteworthy attempt to introduce sound into a Shakespeare film was made long before Fairbanks and Pickford traded their verbal darts in the 1929 *Shrew.* In 1900 the renowned French actress Sarah Bernhardt was filmed playing Hamlet, a role she played frequently on the stage. This three-minute film features the climactic duel between the prince and Laertes. The sound of the fencing foils was recorded on Edison's cylinders (remember, he also invented the phonograph) and then synchronized with the moving pictures to convince audiences they were actually hearing the sword fight.

Coincidentally, two of the most notable silent-screen *Hamlets* (eight were filmed) featured women in the title role: the Bernhardt version, and an important German film *Hamlet: The Drama of Vengeance*, made in 1920 by the Danish director, Svend Gade and starring Asta Nielsen. Its adaptation of Shakespeare's tragedy is extraordinarily free. The film presents Gertrude giving birth to a girl, whom the queen fears will not be accepted as a ruler. The queen announces that the child is actually a prince and thereby sets in motion a lifetime of confused identity, sexual anxieties, and a host of other Freudian issues (e.g., Hamlet berates Ophelia because s/he fears the girl is attracted to Horatio, to whom Hamlet is attracted). Gade's film anticipates themes that dominate much late-twentieth-century criticism of the play.

Both the Tree *King John* and the Bernhardt *Hamlet* used a single camera mounted in a fixed position to film a stage production. Thus the picture audiences viewed was essentially static: the setting remained the same, camera angles did not change, there was no editing, and there were no alternating close-ups, medium, and long shots—techniques we now accept as integral parts of the vocabulary of film. As filmmakers learned to tell stories using the camera as a narrative eye, the quality of filmed Shakespeare improved. The New York-based Vitagraph Company, headed by the visionary Stuart Blackton, was largely responsible for creating truly cinematic Shakespeare.

From 1908 to 1912 Vitagraph produced a series of fifteen-minute, one-reel film versions of a dozen Shakespearean plays, including *Romeo and Juliet, Julius Caesar*, and *King Lear*. We might think of these as "highlight reels" because they focused on a play's best-known scenes, thus minimizing the need for dialogue. *Romeo and Juliet* (1908) was especially significant because for the first time the camera was used not merely to record the play (as Tree had done in 1899), but as a conspicuously artistic entity to enhance the storytelling. The Vitagraph *Romeo* used almost twenty different camera positions (shots), thirteen title cards (e.g., "Love at First Sight"), and artistic editing to compress the play's "two hours' traffic" into a fifteen-minute spectacle of the Capulet ball, the wooing scene (filmed at a Long Island mansion), the marriage in Friar Laurence's cell, the duel between Romeo and Tybalt (shot in Central Park), and, of course, the tomb scene. Thus the film allowed each member of the audience to do something heretofore impossible in the theater: view the action from a variety of perspectives and depths of field. Though crude by current standards, the Vitagraph *Romeo and Juliet* may be considered the first Shakespearean "art film." *Romeo and Juliet*, by the way, was among the most filmed of the plays during the silent era, including a 1916 American version with Theda Bara—the notorious "vamp" (seductive woman) of the silent screen—as Juliet.

The Vitagraph films were among the first to go "on location," although most settings were generally recognizable New York landmarks. This limitation was not necessarily a negative aspect of the films, as audiences (at least those in New York) appreciated these films. When the image of Puck was superimposed over a long shot of Central Park, *A Midsummer Night's Dream* acquired an immediacy to 1909 audiences it might not have otherwise enjoyed.

Important cinematic advancements were made in Europe as well as in the United States. The Italians, steeped in a rich tradition of operatic spectacle, produced a number of silent Shakespeare films noted for their visual splendor. The best of these include *Romeo and Juliet* (1911) and *Brutus* (1910), an eight-minute gloss of *Julius Caesar* that set a standard for large crowd scenes. In 1913 a French adaptation of *The Merchant of Venice*, simply called *Shylock*, used cardboard cutouts to recreate the Rialto; they represent an honest—if generally unsuccessful—attempt to create authentic worlds for the plays. Unfortunately, history itself would provide the most "authentic" reality for that play. Henry Baur, the Jewish actor who played Shylock, became a victim of the Holocaust in the 1930s.

The films mentioned to this point were "shorts," none lasting more than a half hour. The first feature-length Shakespeare film in England was *Hamlet* in 1913; it ran fifty-nine minutes and featured the esteemed British Shakespearean, Sir Johnston Forbes-Robertson, noted for his noble profile. It was he who established the norm for the strikingly handsome prince, a tradition that would last into the 1960s when a generation of "boorish" Hamlets was born (see Chapter 15). Americans also produced feature-length Shakespeare films, i.e., those with a running time of forty minutes or more. A five-reel *Richard III* was made in 1912, and starred Frederick B. Warde, a middling British actor who made several Shakespeare films. Warde often made personal appearances at showings of his films to lecture audiences on the plays and to recite significant passages as the projectionist changed the reels. In 1916 Warde played King Lear in an inventive film that opened with a prolonged shot of the actor smoking in his study while reading Shakespeare's script. Enveloped at first in a thick cloud of cigar smoke, Warde was then magically transformed into the aged monarch.

Such visual gimmicks were not uncommon in the silent era (nor are they now), because filmmakers realized that film's strength was its ability to tell the story through pictures, often at the expense of character and Shakespeare's poetry. Consider a couple of examples that illustrate the power of the picture, as well as the gross liberties artists took with the scripts. A 1912 version of *Richard III* (*The Life and Death of King Richard the Third*) reduced the play to the cheapest kind of melodrama. After the hunchbacked king killed Henry VI, he ran his fingers along the sword blade, then licked the dead king's blood from his fingers. A 1922 *Othello*, filmed in Germany by Dimitri Buchowetzki, featured such vivid shots as Iago trying to eat the incriminating strawberry handkerchief. Although Laurence Olivier's *Henry V* (1944, see Chapter 13) is considered the first color version of a Shakespeare play on film, there were early attempts to "colorize" film, even as early as 1905. Charles Urban directed a two-minute film version of Tree's staging of *The Tempest* at Her Majesty's Theater. Urban had his technicians hand-tint individual frames to suggest the color of Prospero's magic island.

people think they are incapable of, but they do it from morning to night." Or as Shakespeare's philosophical Jaques puts it:

> All the world's a stage,
> And all the men and women merely players.
> They have their exits and their entrances,
> And one man in his time plays many parts.
> (*As You Like It*, 2.7.138–141)

Actor training—and therefore acting style—has changed considerably over the roughly twenty-six centuries since the Greek Thespis established the profession for Western culture. Traditionally, most approaches to acting fall into one of two broad categories: *external* (vocal and physical) technique and *internal* (psychological) technique. Shakespeare's tradition was decidedly in the external mode, though the psychological reality of his characters can be just as at home with the internal mode. Best of all for our purposes are *integrated* actors who fuse the external and internal approaches. Whatever their technique, the goal remains constant for actors: to create memorable characters that engage audiences.

External actors work largely from the outside in. They begin with rigorous physical and vocal training because they use the body and especially the voice as their primary tools. Some actors are famous for their obsession with external details. Sir Laurence Olivier felt he must find the right nose for his character before he could come to grips with his inner reality; the crooked nose he devised for Richard III is perhaps his most famous example. Virtually all of pre–twentieth-century drama, including Shakespeare's, necessitated an external approach. The size of the theaters, many of which were outdoor; scripts whose poetry and song demanded an exceptional vocal range; conventions such as boys playing women's roles; few rehearsals; an oratorical acting tradition; and many other factors demanded an external—or "technical"—style. Voice, breathing, and elocution exercises were compulsory, as was training in dance, mime, acrobatics, juggling, swordplay, posture, and balance. At the same time, external acting does not preclude strongly felt inner emotion or truth. Aristotle believed that those who feel emotion are most convincing through natural sympathy with the characters they represent. Hamlet counsels his actors to "use all gently . . . let your own discretion be your tutor. Suit the action to the word, the word to the action, with this special observance, that you o'erstep not the modesty of nature" (3.2.5–29).

Such advice by Aristotle and Shakespeare point the way toward *internal* acting that is largely a modern and Western approach to performance. The late–nineteenth-century plays of Ibsen, Chekhov, and other social realists demanded intimacy in playing style, as well as playing spaces. Thus a subtler, internally based style emerged, largely under the teaching of Konstantin Stanislavski, co-founder of the Moscow Art Theatre in 1897. Stanislavski had become convinced that certain laws govern the art of acting just as certain natural laws govern others areas of life. He defined the actor's goal as creating a truthful representation of life within the limitations imposed by the nature of theater. He encouraged actors to tap their inner resources by using *emotion memory*, among other things, to project themselves into the characters they play. For instance, an actor who plays Hamlet might recall the pain he experienced when a close relative or friend died. Theoretically, this triggers the appropriate response when the actor must grieve for the death of Old Hamlet. Internal actors can place too much emphasis on inner feeling, which can lead to self-indulgence and a breakdown of the vocal and physical demands of performance. In truth, Stanislavski stressed that actors must first develop the voice and body before advancing to the internal aspects of performance: "You must have a strong, well-trained voice of pleasant, expressive timbre, perfect diction, plasticity of movement—without being a poseur." Ultimately he joined his solutions to the problems of speech and diction he encountered as an actor and of movement he experienced as a director into a psycho-technical method enshrined in his book, *Building a Character*. His advice is also applicable to the Shakespearean actor since he staged many of Shakespeare's plays with his Russian actors and excelled as Benedick in *Much Ado About Nothing* himself.

The American equivalent of Stanislavski's training system developed at the Actors Studio in New York where Lee Strasberg evolved his famous Method. Marlon Brando was one of the earliest Method actors, one who turned his talents to Shakespeare for the 1953 *Julius Caesar* movie, in which he played Mark Antony. The Method became the predominant acting style in Hollywood, with such Actors Studio veterans as Ellen Burstyn and Al Pacino (who were co-presidents of the Actors Studio in 2003) performing in both media. Pacino makes his Method training a thematic element in his updated film about Richard III, *Looking for Richard* (see Part Two, Chapter 5).

Though a reader need not have formal actor training to peruse Shakespeare, a familiarity with fundamental technique can enliven both the reading and viewing experiences. Actors must confront four texts:

- The *scripted text*, i.e., the words on the page.
- The *context* in which the characters find themselves.
- The *subtext* or what the text actually implies.
- The *intentional text*, or the reason a character must say those lines at that moment.

For an instant acting lesson, say this simple line from *A Midsummer Night's Dream:* "Here come the lovers." Now repeat the line as if:

1. You are a messenger announcing the arrival of the lovers at court.
2. You are the prank-playing Puck and can't wait to create more mischief for them.
3. You are the Duke who is delighted to see that the quarrelsome lovers have made up and that he and his beloved queen can be married with them.

Without much thought or training you probably came up with a good subtext for each situation. Your subtext ("the text beneath the text") for the first was probably, "My lord, you need to know that the lovers are about to enter the room." Perhaps your subtext for the second was, "I can't wait to make them miserable and get a good laugh," while the third was, "Thank God all this nonsense is over and we can now live happily ever after!" In each case there was a very specific reason for saying the line: i.e., to get the Duke's attention, to get energized for the fun to follow, to put everyone at ease after a night of chaos and confusion.

The Director

Although stage directors were historically among the last artists to enter the theater, they have become a potent force in the shaping of a production. In theory, directors are meant to be the intermediaries between the script and the audience. However, they often rival writers, to the point where we glibly speak of "Brook's *Dream,*" when we actually mean Peter Brook's 1970 production of Shakespeare's *A Midsummer Night's Dream* by the Royal Shakespeare Company. Thoughtful directorial interpretation—which may border on invention—can be so illuminating that audiences feel as if they are seeing a new play and therefore append the director's name to the title. At another extreme, directors may impose their vision on a script to the point where it is something other than what the playwright wrote. This runs the gamut from putting an orange-spiked-haired Hamlet on roller skates to restructuring or rewriting the play, as Charles Marowitz did with *Othello* in 1972. He incorporated material from the writings of the radical Black Panthers, cast a black man as Iago, and used a script comprised of only one-third of Shakespeare's writing. He billed his production as *An Othello* to emphasize that it was an experiment. In this case, Marowitz functioned as an *auteur,* that is, an author-director who creates a new work and has complete control over its realization in production.

Despite their considerable influence on the stage, theater directors do not necessarily enjoy the absolute power of film directors who can choose, frame-by-frame, every picture and sound they wish the audience to see and hear. Once the play begins in the theater, stage directors relinquish their power to the actors and the audience, some of whom may choose to look at the spear-carrier in the back row despite the director's best intentions.

Directors wear many hats, but they have four primary tasks as they guide a play to opening night.

Devising the Directorial Approach. The director's first task is to devise the directorial approach, a process that begins with a great deal of research. Long before a play is cast, the director studies the play. In some ways the director must know the play better than Shakespeare did. This necessitates research on the period in which it was written; the period in which it is set; the philosophical, historical, social, political, and perhaps religious attitudes that shaped it; its production history; and commentaries by critics and scholars. Some plays demand a particular expertise. When directors work on a Shakespearean play such as *King Henry V* and decide to set it in its period, they will immerse themselves in the culture of the early fifteenth century. They should know how a soldier used a longbow or broadsword, how a French princess may have reacted to the overtures of an English monarch, the particulars of arcane Salic laws concerning legitimate successions of title and property, how to pronounce obscure French words and names, the historical realities of the battles of Harfleur and Agincourt, and so on and so on. Again, we are talking about "context" and "given circumstances," terms that are as important to the director as to the actor.

Once directors have considered the myriad possibilities a play offers, they develop a vision or *concept* for the production, that is, an interpretation of the play and the means to express it. The concept usually works on two levels, internal and external. Internally, the director—like the actor—looks for the central idea that holds the play together. One director might say that the superobjective for *A Midsummer Night's Dream* is "humans act foolishly in their pursuit of love and power." Another might believe that it exists "to celebrate the human imagination," while a third might conclude that it is "an enchanted fairy tale that must only amuse." The directorial concept narrows the field of choices for the performers and designers, thereby allowing them to work more efficiently. In an ideal world, all of the artists involved in a production contribute to the discovery of the concept, but the exigencies of getting the show open often preclude this practice, especially in the commercial theater where time is indeed money. Some companies—London's Young Vic, for instance—are noted for the democratic way in which they let a production of a Shakespeare play evolve.

After grappling with the intellectual and emotional center of the play, directors consider the visual and aural elements that may best realize the concept. Much of this may be done in conferences with the designers, though often a director will have a strong image from the outset. Like designers, directors think in terms of graphic metaphors. When the RSC produced *The War of the Roses* in 1963, director Peter Hall and designer John Bury underscored the decay of England by having set pieces and costumes covered in corrosion and rust.

When dealing with plays written before social realism came to prominence, the choice of a period in which to "dress" the play can be an important step toward realizing the directorial concept. There are times when the setting actually *is* the concept, as when John Houseman directed *Much Ado About Nothing* at Stratford, Connecticut, in 1955. To make the play instantly accessible to American audiences, Houseman set the play in the American Wild West. By contrast, John Barton's 1977 production of the same play for the Royal Shakespeare Company placed the play's action in colonial India in the late nineteenth century. Benedick and his fellow soldiers wore the bright red coats of the British Raj, while Dogberry and the Watch were native Sikhs.

The "translation" of Shakespeare into modern or contemporary settings, earlier or timeless periods, or into other theatrical styles (Kabuki *Macbeth*, for instance, or circus *Comedy of Errors*) has been a distinguishing feature of many modern and postmodern productions and adaptations. Shakespeare, of course, wrote at a particular time in history, for particular theater conditions, and for an audience that was conditioned by the culture in which it lived. But because Shakespeare is the most universal of playwrights, his plays now invite a variety of approaches to accommodate "the age and body" of subsequent times and countries. A production of any Shakespeare play—including those most specific to time and place (e.g., the English and Roman histories)—can generally be located in one of four settings:

In Period. First, a play can be set in either the Elizabethan or Jacobean era, as it was done in Shakespeare's lifetime, or in the specific time and locale of the play's action. *King John,* for instance, could be played in Elizabethan doublet and hose or set in the early thirteenth century when John ruled England. (It was a London production of *King John* in 1823 that initiated the practice of historically "accurate" costuming—a full two hundred years after Shakespeare's death.) "In period" settings and costumes offer several advantages:

- There is no disjunction between the language of the play and the décor and costumes. Franco Zeffirelli's meticulous Renaissance settings for *The Taming of the Shrew* (1966) and *Romeo and Juliet* (1968) benefits from the authentic worlds created by the director (a former scene designer for Italian opera). The *Othello* film directed by Oliver Parker in 1996 enjoys a particular authenticity in its Venetian settings and in the exotic locales of Cyprus.

- One need not apologize for changes in weaponry. The various duels and street fights in Zeffirelli's *Romeo and Juliet* provided audiences with some of the best swordplay ever filmed, an important point for a play that borrows much of its language and metaphor from fencing.

- The production avoids the label of "gimmick."

But there are also disadvantages:

- The play can easily take on the appearance of a "museum piece." Audiences, particularly the uninitiated, may assume the play is only about another time, another place.

- Productions can look much the same and take on an aura of predictability.

Modern Dress. Among the easiest—and most obvious—ways of making a play instantly accessible to an audience is to dress it in contemporary clothing and set it in instantly recognizable surroundings. This was essentially the practice during Shakespeare's lifetime and for two hundred years after his death. What are the advantages of "recontextualizing" a Shakespeare play?

- As soon as the lights come up on the stage, or the film begins to roll, the audience knows that this play is about itself, about its particular world.

- Generally, modern-dress productions are less expensive to mount.

- Actors are often more comfortable in modern dress and move more easily, less self-consciously; this is particularly true of younger actors in academic productions.

- There is a freshness of approach.

Modern-dress Shakespeare has its liabilities, of course.

- Shakespeare's elevated and sometimes archaic language is often at odds with what the audience sees; in the early twenty-first century people do not speak with such eloquence.

- In an age of guns and grenades, Shakespeare's weaponry is clearly out-of-date. The swordplay in such plays as *Romeo and Juliet*, *Hamlet*, and *Macbeth* is particularly problematic. In his film *Romeo+Juliet*, Australian director Baz Luhrmann solved this problem by stamping the brand name "Sword" on the barrel of the handguns carried by Verona's gangs.

- There are many specific references to clothing throughout the plays, and often plot and character turn on the fashion of another day (e.g., Malvolio's "cross-gartering" in *Twelfth Night*). Of course, Shakespeare himself encountered such problems; in *Antony and Cleopatra* the queen asks a handmaiden to help her undo undergarments unknown in ancient Egypt.

■ Modern dress can seem a mere gimmick, and especially in film can date quickly. Luhrmann's *Romeo+Juliet*, much admired by young audiences in the late 1990s, may well prove laughable to a subsequent generation of young people, much as the musical adaptation *West Side Story* (1957) seems "corny" to some today.

The most recent film version of *Hamlet* (2000, directed by Michael Almereyda, with Ethan Hawke as the Prince) relocates the play's action to contemporary New York: Denmark is a multinational corporation and its Elsinore a glass-encased office tower. Inventive uses of computers and other electronic gadgetry illustrate the plot for today's technologically savvy audiences; soliloquies are spoken to a camcorder as Hamlet, now a techno-wizard, makes a video diary of his dilemmas. The famous "To be or not to be" soliloquy is spoken as Hamlet wanders through racks of action films in a Blockbuster video store. While it is among the more inventive modern-dress versions of the play, the film's digital gimmickry sometimes overwhelms the text, which has been heavily cut (see Chapter 15 for further discussion of Almereyda's film).

An Alternate Historical Period. The most often used and perhaps most satisfying alternative to traditional "in period" settings and costumes for a Shakespeare play involves placing the play in the third of our four possible settings—a historical period other than the Elizabethan or authentic historical era—because:

■ The milieu is sufficiently removed from the modern age that the incongruity between language and the visual elements is not as disconcerting. The late-nineteenth-century period has proven an especially satisfactory alternative because the clothing suggests antiquity, yet it is just modern enough (especially men's trousers and coats) that the action does not seem antiquated. The Victorian look is also romantic and accommodates the emotional elements of Shakespeare's plays well. Michael Hoffman's film of *A Midsummer Night's Dream* (1999) plays well on the Tuscan landscapes of late–nineteenth-century Italy.

■ The problems with weaponry can be minimized: swords were regularly used well into the nineteenth century, so there is a roughly three-hundred-year window of opportunity for directors and designers to create worlds that are readily compatible with Shakespeare's language and weaponry. Kenneth Brangah's *Hamlet* (1996) is set in the mid nineteenth century; the swordplay and Victorian toy theater seem entirely natural, and the more modern commando-like raid by Fortinbras' army does not seem out of place, even as it appeals to contemporary audience's tastes for action films.

■ With so many visually interesting historical periods to choose from, directors and designers can bring a fresh, innovative look to the production of Shakespeare's plays, without resorting to only modern dress. Consider the ambiance of a variety of recent films of Shakespeare's plays:

■ Branagh's *Much Ado About Nothing* (1991), set in early–nineteenth-century Tuscany, clarifies the military elements of that play more than a traditional Elizabethan setting might do. The crisp military uniforms of the returning soldiers contrast sharply with the rustic look of the women and older men who remain behind, helping to define the clash between the "macho" world of Benedick and his companions with the kinder, gentler nature of the women.

■ Jonathan Miller's *The Merchant of Venice* (1969, with Laurence Olivier as Shylock) is located in early–twentieth-century Europe to highlight the commercial (i.e., capitalistic) themes of the play, as well as the anti-Semitism. Nazi Germany was but a few short years away from the Edwardian era that Miller chose for his production.

■ Trevor Nunn's *Othello* (1987, with Ian McKellen as Iago) underscores the importance of military rank, which is crucial to the play's plot as Michael Cassio is stripped of his rank. By relocating the action to mid–nineteenth-century Europe, Nunn's production defines the military ambience quickly and efficiently. A soldier's rank in the Elizabethan era is perhaps less readily discerned.

At times, well-known speeches enjoy a fresh reading in a nontraditional setting. Richard Loncraine's *Richard III* (1996, with McKellen as Richard) gives the famous "A horse, a horse, my kingdom for a horse" a witty twist in its 1930s setting (devised to draw parallels between Richard and Fascism, and to indict the British aristocracy for their appeasement of Hitler). As he tries to escape Richmond's army, Richard's jeep becomes hopelessly immobilized amid the rubble of the battlefield. In his frustration, Richard bellows out the famous line, which has seldom been funnier, or more pathetic.

An inventive relocation of a text can produce an entirely new experience for the audience, as in Branagh's *Love's Labor's Lost* film (2000). The director-actor, who plays Berowne, has refashioned the play as a 1930s-style Hollywood musical and has spliced songs by Cole Porter, Irving Berlin, and George Gershwin into Shakespeare's text so nimbly that many seem written for Shakespeare's play.

Branagh's film, which has met with mixed to negative reviews, is closer to adaptation than interpretation, yet it captures some of the giddy romanticism of this early comedy; Mercade's ominous entrance in Act 5 to announce the death of the King of France is all the more solemn for it. The Pageant of the Nine Worthies is sung and danced to the Broadway anthem, "There's No Business Like Show Business"; audiences immediately understand the big production number Shakespeare created for his finale.

There are, of course, liabilities to even the most inventive recontextualizations, most notably the dreaded "g" word: gimmick. Some ingenious productions and films convey fresh insight, while others come closer to being bright ideas either unrealized in production or existing only for the moment.

"Universal Timeless." The fourth possible setting for a play or film is referred to as "universal timeless," "time neutral," "no period," or some variation thereon. Of late, there is a growing movement among theater and film directors to underscore the universality of Shakespeare's plays by setting them in such a milieu. John Gielgud's admired Broadway production of *Hamlet* in 1964 (with Richard Burton) came to be known as "the rehearsal clothes *Hamlet*" because the director wanted the audience to focus on Shakespeare's word and emotions, undistracted by spectacular scenery and beautiful costumes. Hence, the actors wore baggy sweaters and workaday clothing as they performed on an essentially bare set defined mostly by unpainted stage scenery. Perhaps the most famous "universal timeless" stage production of a Shakespeare play was that directed by Peter Brook for the RSC in 1970: *A Midsummer Night's Dream* featured actors in formless costumes who were distinguished from one another by a single bright color (purple, gold, green) that defined a character's essence (king, clown, queen of the forest). This timeless, circus-themed production is discussed more fully in Part Two.

In postmodern theater and film, directors often attempt to define a play's universality by freely mixing costumes and settings culled from a spectrum of history. Julie Taymor's *Titus* (2000, adapted from *Titus Andronicus*, with Anthony Hopkins in the title role) is among the most visually inventive films to accomplish this. Taymor has combined costumes from Imperial Rome with contemporary dress, chariots with motorcycles, Roman ruins with modern architecture, and ritual music with pop songs to draw parallels between the savagery of decadent Rome and the modern West. Taymor's notes for the film emphasize her desire "to blend and collide time, to create a singular period that juxtaposed elements of ancient barbaric ritual with familiar, contemporary attitude and style." The effect is to disorient the audience so that it cannot tell where the ancient civilization ends and its own begins.

In his provocative assessment of the modern theater, *The Empty Space*, Brook questions directors who claim to let a play speak for itself because, in his estimation, a play may not make a sound. If the play is to be heard, Brook insists, the director must often "conjure its sound." At its best, "conjuring the sound" can provide us with perceptive insights into a script, much the way a good essay by a literary critic can. At its worst, such "conjuring" can become indulgent, anarchic, confusing, and unfair to the playwright, not to mention audiences.

Coordinating the Artists' Contributions. If the first task a director must accomplish is to develop the directorial vision of a play, the second, and often related, task is to coordinate the other artists' contributions. Ideally, the collaboration between the director and the designers and technicians, as well as the performers, is somewhat democratic. In practice, however, many directors are autocratic; they know exactly what they want and will accept nothing less. Yet in the rehearsal hall or around the conference table, the director's task is rife with paradox, as Brook notes in *The Empty Space*:

> It is a strange role, that of the director: he does not ask to be God and yet his role implies it. He wants to be fallible, and yet an instinctive conspiracy of the actors [and designers] is to make him the arbiter, because an arbiter is so desperately wanted all the time. In a sense the director is always an imposter, a guide at night who does not know the territory, and yet has no choice—he must guide, learning the route as he goes.

Creating an Aesthetic Experience. The director's third task is to create an aesthetic experience for the audience, because audiences perceive a play aesthetically as well as intellectually and emotionally. Visually and aurally, directors attempt to make the theater experience artistically pleasing by composing stage pictures and establishing the rhythm of the play. Some directors meticulously choreograph the movement of the actors in the privacy of their studies, while others allow the blocking to evolve organically from the actors' instincts. Directors need the eye of a master painter to group actors on stage, especially when staging those scenes that require pageantry such as processions and coronations. A popular exercise for students of directing is to look at the paintings of the Renaissance masters to learn about groupings and body attitudes. Directors provide visual variety by using different areas of the stage, height levels, linear and curved patterns, and other techniques to create a pleasing picture. If a play seems dull or static, it may not be entirely the actors' fault; perhaps the director has not provided a variety of visual stimuli.

Helping the Actors. Finally, the director must help the actors. Tyrone Guthrie, cofounder of the Stratford,

Ontario (Canada), Shakespeare Festival in 1953, once labeled the director "an audience of one"; that is, the director functions as an impartial observer who audits, evaluates, and adjusts the actors' work to develop truth and clarity. Early in the production process the director often meets with actors for some "table talk," at which the individual characters and Shakespeare's language are dissected. In rehearsal the director helps the actors make choices, always with an eye toward the whole. As the play takes shape and the individual actors bring their characters to life, the director helps them coalesce into an ensemble. As the actors advance beyond the exploratory stages, some directors merely sit back and react to scenes. Many of the reactions are strictly technical: "I can't hear you there," or "You're speaking too quickly." Others get to the psychological and emotional life of the character: "Why is he always so angry—aren't there other ways to react to a situation?" The director raises many of the same questions and criticisms that an audience member might—and this is not always an easy task, particularly as the director gets to know the play better and better. Paradoxically, often the director is least prepared to help the actors when they need it most: just before opening. In many theater companies, other directors attend late rehearsals to bring fresh eyes and ears to the production.

The Designers

The very term *theater* or "the seeing place" implies that the visual dimension is an important part of the audience's experience. Often our memories of a Shakespeare play in the theater are most colored by what we have seen, rather than heard, for instance:

- The ferocious storm and shipwreck that opens *The Tempest*.

- The spectacular appearance of the three goddesses and the dancing shepherds and nymphs in Act 4; this *masque* derives from the entertainments popular in the royal courts of Italy, France, and England in which royalty dressed in extraordinary costumes and were often hoisted into the heavens on cloud-machines.

- The costume and especially the makeup that helps define Caliban as a half-man, half-monster.

Scenery, costumes, makeup, masks, props, sound, and even lighting effects have been central to theater events since some ancient hunter donned an animal skin for a tribal dance. Although Renaissance designers, such as Inigo Jones, produced spectacular costumes, usually meant to be worn by royalty and their entourages at court entertainments, costuming in the non-court theaters developed more slowly. Shakespeare and his actors customarily wore Elizabethan and Jacobean clothing, sometimes bequeathed to them by nobles. A sketch of actors performing *Titus Andronicus* suggests that the Lord Chamberlain's Men wore a combination of contemporary and archaic clothing especially for a play set in Roman or ancient times. Pictures of seventeenth- and eighteenth-century actors indicate that actors wore contemporary dress, even when doing revivals of period plays such as Shakespeare's. In fact, actors customarily provided clothing from their own wardrobes. Not until the nineteenth century did historically accurate costuming come into vogue. The English actor-manager Charles Kemble produced Shakespeare's *King John* in 1823 with an authentic thirteenth-century setting. The production was enormously popular with audiences who filled the Kemble's theater to see the "precise habits of the period"—that is, faithful reproductions of the dress and armor of King John's reign. As designers do today, Kemble's costumer, James Robinson Planché, methodically researched the period and produced apparel that was "never equaled on the English stage." Kemble's financial success inspired imitation, and soon authentic costuming became the norm. As with scenery, costuming became more of a reproductive art than a creative one as the realists demanded that their actors be clothed in authentic garb.

Today, lighting often replaces scenery as the primary visual element in a production, partly because it is relatively inexpensive, primarily because it is versatile and strikingly dramatic. Shafts of colored light, highlighted by smoke or fog effects, cutting through a black space may elicit as much response from an audience as mammoth sets. An open space can instantly be transformed into a forest, a prison, or a moonlit beach by the use of *gobos*, the metal disks inserted into a lighting instrument to create patterns on stage. Because stage lighting is a technology as well as an art, designers must be knowledgeable electricians and computer literate as well, for most lighting systems are now computer programmed. Although Shakespeare's company, especially at The Theater and the Globe, performed in daylight and relied on the poet's words to create atmospheric effects ("the morn in russet mantle clad / Walks o'er the dew of yon high eastward hill"; *Hamlet*, 1.1.172–173), today lighting designers can create a visual poetry that enhances the text. The danger, of course, is that such effects can overwhelm the actors, even render the script superfluous.

Like the lighting designer, the sound designer is mostly a twentieth-century phenomenon in the theater, although records do attest to the existence of sound effects throughout the history of the stage. Elizabethan actors, for instance, rolled cannonballs across wooden troughs backstage to suggest thunder, while nineteenth-century melodramas were punctuated by effects from wind machines, thunder sheets, and "crash boxes." Such effects—as well as recorded sound effects—are usually further attempts at realism. The work of the sound designer has been improved by sophisticated digital stereo systems to suggest a variety of sound locations. Tony Richardson's 1968 production of *Hamlet* (with Nicol Williamson as the Prince), available in video, uses a stunning combination of light and sound to suggest the ghost of Old Hamlet: a pin spot of light illuminates only Williamson's face while the "voice" of Old Hamlet eerily moves about the theater, thanks to a multiple-speaker sound system.

How Designers Work. Although each designer has objectives particular to a specific area of expertise, certain requirements hold for all for scenic, costume, and lighting designs:

■ They should be consistent with the directorial concept and they should complement each other as they reinforce the production's visual metaphor.

■ They should support the work of the actors functionally and aesthetically by providing focus upon their performances.

■ They should help establish the degree of reality or theatricality for the production.

■ They should reinforce the emotional atmosphere of the production.

■ They should provide the audience with relevant information about the historical period, the locale, and the characters and their relationships with one another and their environment.

To put it succinctly, good designs work together to create exactly the right ambience for *this* production of *this* play. Theoni V. Aldredge once suggested that "good design is design you are not aware of." She meant, of course, that a good design does not compete with a production, but enhances it.

Once a concept has been agreed upon, the designers begin informally sketching potential sets and costumes. They also busy themselves by thoroughly researching the play and the period in which it is set. Many resources are available: history books, museums, paintings, etchings, woodcuts, photographs, even vintage Sears Roebuck catalogs (among the best sources for discovering the appearance of authentic 1920s clothing). Such research informs the sketches, which get increasingly specific. The director and designers evaluate the sketches, choosing things that work and rejecting those that don't. As the several artistic minds become one in this process, the designers produce more formal drawings and models of the set and costumes. The scene designer drafts a floor plan of the set to help the actors and director as they rehearse. Perhaps a scale model of the set is constructed to suggest its dimensionality and spatial relationships; miniature stage lights may illuminate it to approximate the finished product. The costume designer often affixes swatches of cloth to the renderings to suggest texture, color, and sheen. The

lighting designer watches, listens, and examines the evolving designs, thinking ahead to lighting areas, color medium, and the emotional pitch of the play. When true collaboration takes place among these artists, the process by which a play's design evolves is one of the most invigorating aspects of making theater.

While actors talk about subtext and motivations to describe their craft, designers refer to line, mass, form, color, palette, silhouette, balance, symmetry, asymmetry, intensity, texture, and other qualities that define their concerns. Each play dictates the manner in which they are used. For instance, line—e.g., straight, curved, geometrically shaped, irregular—might suggest conflict if predominantly curved lines converge on sharply angled ones. Mass—the comparative size and weight of objects—can suggest oppression. Adrian Noble's 1984 production of *Henry V* featured enormous doors that dwarfed the pawns of history; a variant of this design is in Branagh's film of *Henry V*. Silhouettes for comedy are often oversized, rounded, horizontal, and out-of-balance, while those for more dramatic plays are often proportioned, straight-lined, and vertical. Color and intensity affect mood and perceptions. Texture can subtly—even subliminally—affect an audience's perception of the play. Rough textures, such as a coarse cloth, pocked stones, or decaying metalwork, can add weight to a serious play. Lighting designers sometimes prefer heavily textured sets and costumes because they produce interesting effects by creating sharper contrasts between light and shadow.

Set designers know that scenery must be more than a mere backdrop for the action. Because the audience often sees the scenery before the play begins, the scene design is often the first element to affect an audience's response. And just as the playwright must create intrigue for the audience, so, too, must the scene designer arouse the audience's expectancy when it first views the setting. An aptly chosen visual metaphor may suggest the thematic concerns of the play. The Guthrie Theater's 1985 production of *A Midsummer Night's Dream,* directed by Liviu Cuili, featured an enormous moon as its primary set piece; it seemed to say that moonstruck people do bizarre things.

The scene designer's first task is to transform a bare space into an environment for the actors to do their work. Though the design should have an aesthetic appeal, it needs to be practical by providing entrances and exits, playing levels that encourage a variety of stage pictures, and places to sit, stand, or recline. A good set design provides focal points for key moments of action; down stage center may be a traditional "hot spot" on stage, but designers seek alternatives. While the scenery must support the actors, it cannot dominate them—even in plays where the environment controls the characters. If audiences are distracted by an overly massive or too-cluttered scenic environment, they tend to stop listening and merely look at the setting. As visually splendid as it was, the late Maria Bjornson's enormous set of Prospero's island, complete with a half-submerged ship, for the RSC's production of *The Tempest* (1984), often competed with the stage action for the audience's attention.

Costume designers also have their particular concerns. "Dressing" the actors, the first task, is complicated by the fact that stage clothing—even in realistic plays—is not the same thing as everyday apparel. Polonius's observation in *Hamlet* that "the apparel oft proclaims the man" is particularly true of stage costumes. A thoughtfully conceived and executed costume design is a particularly expedient way to define a character, almost instantaneously. This was the premise of the colorful *commedia dell'arte* costumes in the Renaissance. The brightly colored, diamond-shaped patches of Arlecchino and the vivid red cape of Pantalone immediately told audiences that they were looking at the trickster and the lecherous old man. While costumes quickly tell us about one's social status, profession, and other details, they can also hint at the character's personality. That Shakespeare knew this well is evidenced by his description of Petruchio's comical wedding garb in *The Taming of the Shrew*:

> . . . a new hat and an old jerkin, a pair of old breeches thrice turned; a pair of boots that have been candle-cases, one buckled, another laced; an old rusty sword ta'en out of the town armory, with a broken hilt, and chapeless.
>
> (3.2.43–47)

And the ensuing description of Petruchio's horse is just as humorous and indicative of character.

Well-designed costumes greatly enhance the work of actors by easing the transformation from self to other. Theoni Aldredge, one of the commercial theater's busiest designers, cautions, "a performance will suffer if an actor doesn't love his costume, and it's your job to make him love it." Shakespearean actors often wear bits and pieces of period costuming during rehearsals to help them prepare for their roles.

Not only do costumes tell us much about the individual characters, they show relationships among the characters. Major characters are distinguished from minor ones, and groups are contrasted with one another through a costume plot—a term which suggests that the designer must carefully calculate the effects costumes will have on an audience. The feuding families in *Romeo and Juliet* are quickly distinguished from one another by costumes. Romeo and Benvolio are kinsmen, but the costumer would usually give Romeo more flair in his costume to accent his importance.

Lighting designers traditionally begin their work after the scenery and costume designers have submitted their renderings for final approval by the director. Usually designers observe a few rehearsals to learn where key actions are played, the mood of a scene, and where to focus particular lighting instruments designated for a particular effect. The lighting designer also wants a strong feel for the colors and silhouette of the costumes. Much of the lighting designer's work is mechanical and is undertaken solely to make sure the actors are visible. The artistic dimension involves planning intensities, back and side lighting, and fade times, work that can be done only in final rehearsals when the other components are brought together. The lighting design is the glue that binds all of the visual embellishments of the production.

Prior to technical rehearsals many artisans contribute to the execution of the designs; a typical Shakespeare festival company often employs two or three times as many technicians as it does actors. The scenery is built under the supervision of a technical director, who oversees carpenters, electricians, scene painters, and other specialty workers. A costumer (or *costumier*) supervises cutters, stitchers, and tailors to construct the designer's renderings. Actors are fit for costumes, footwear, and even wigs when necessary. Shortly before "tech week" a costume parade may be organized to give the director and design team an opportunity to see how the garments look on stage under light. During technical rehearsals designers take notes concerning corrections, additions, deletions, and touch-ups. On opening night—if the design team has done its job well months in advance of the opening—the audience sees a fully integrated production that appears to have arrived effortlessly on the stage. To be sure, the popular Reduced Shakespeare Company—the "other" RSC—manages to perform "all" of Shakespeare's plays in thirty-six hilarious minutes on a bare stage with three actors and with a small trunk full of props. Shakespeare and his actors, and the few men employed to assist them in the tiring house, may have successfully produced a play with as few as four or five rehearsals, but the demands of today's theater require an extraordinary effort by many people, each working hundreds of hours, to realize Shakespeare in production.

Film Artists at Work

Many of the artistic personnel required to stage a play are the same as those required when a director or production company decides to turn a play into a film. But the filmmaking process is generally more complex, with a pre-production period during which a screenwriter works with the director to transform the play script into a screenplay, often with a lavishly illustrated outline called a storyboard; a period of shooting requiring a cinematographer, cameramen, lighting technicians, designers, and many other technical workers; and a post-production period when the director works with film and sound editors to meld the many individual shots and mix the sound into a continuous film. The credits of any feature film usually list scores of contributors to this expensive enterprise. Because our discussion moves chronologically through the film-making process, some of these contributors will be familiar from our survey of stage artists, while others will be new.

A word of clarification at the outset, however. As noted in the previous chapter, "Shakespeare and His Interpreters," the director is ultimately responsible for the emphases, final quality, and impact of a film, and so he or she makes the initial choices regarding thematic interpretation, setting (Elizabethan or earlier, modern, indeterminate, universal timeless), and casting. Some of these choices may be modified during shooting, particularly when actors make useful discoveries along the way. Still, in the end the director takes most of the credit for success or the blame for failure. In the first, and still one of the most important full-length studies of our subject, *Shakespeare on Film*, Jack Jorgens outlines three basic approaches (choices, again) a director may envision for the film early on, each of which creates a ripple effect of consequences.

The first of these is a theatrical mode in which the film looks and feels like a performance worked out in a small, stage-like space before an audience. The acting style here can be more assertive and continuous, more theatrical, for it determines the rhythms of the film. Clearly the early, live television presentations of Shakespeare, such as Peter Brook's 1953 *Lear* (with Orson Welles) on the CBS *Omnibus* series, partially employed this mode, as did the Elizabethan sections of Olivier's *Henry V* film. John Gielgud's "rehearsal" *Hamlet* on a bare stage explored this style of presentation, and many of the BBC productions summarized in later chapters of Part Two were designed for educational purposes and were basically documentary recordings of stage performances. (Six of these were broadcast on American television in 1979 and all are widely available.) The strengths of such films derive from the same source as their potential weakness: external fidelity to Shakespeare's range of verbal and dramatic styles within a stage frame does not guarantee a lively and engaging film.

Next is a realistic mode that takes advantage of the camera's ability to show us things and people photographically—a great sweeping landscape filled with flowers or soldiers, an intimate bedroom, a raucous dinner party, a forest by moonlight. Most Shakespeare films are realistic at least in part—Zeffirelli's lush *Romeo and Juliet*, Brooks's stark *Lear*, Branagh's war-torn *Henry V*— because the plays themselves depict (or sometimes imply) such a sweep of action and conversation. The specific style of realism may vary with the genre and mood of the play, although one danger always lurks; an over-emphasis upon realistic detail can overwhelm both the actors and Shakespeare's poetic language. Formal groupings of characters, emblematic scenes, stylized contrasts, duels of wit, and florid speeches are sometimes cut, thus leveling the many-layered illusions Shakespeare usually created through language. Visual literalism can kill the imaginative flights of verbal poetry.

Last is a filmic mode that employs the elements of cinema as a language parallel to Shakespeare's poetic use of words. Instead of simply finding visual contexts (an interior close-up, an exterior long shot) in which actors speak Shakespeare's lines, an imaginative film director transforms the verbal language into visual poetry and creates a visual rhythm sympathetic to Shakespeare's own. Each scene in Orson Welles's Shakespeare-based films is meticulously composed and lit, then shot from emotionally suggestive, often oblique, almost "questioning" angles. Both Akira Kurosawa in his *Macbeth* adaptation *Throne of Blood* and Olivier in his *Henry V* brilliantly mix styles, the realistic and the frankly artificial, avoiding simple theatricality and literal realism, setting up what film theorist Andre Bazin and critic John Fuegi have both called an oscillation between things and art, the real and the imagined—in fact, the kind of rhythm that invests the plays themselves with their extraordinary life.

The three modes outlined above are not mutually exclusive, of course; rather, they suggest a continuum across which directors might choose to work. As always, such critical categories are meant to be an aid to clear thinking and understanding, not a rigidly codified system in which we "murder to dissect."

The Screenwriter

In the case of filmed Shakespeare, the lead actor, the director, and the screenwriter are sometimes the same person. Orson Welles, Laurence Olivier, and Kenneth Branagh, creators of some of the most artistically significant and successful Shakespeare movies, all worked in this way, and their strategies for turning the raw material of a play into screenplays have been as various as their motives for making the films. One such motive was admiration for and competition with one another, the "anxiety of influence" pattern outlined by critic Harold Bloom and precisely and insightfully related to these three Shakespearean filmmakers in several essays noted in the bibliography. In film terms, the most conservative, and sometimes the dullest, Shakespeare movies are those which, as Shakespeare scholar Russell Jackson points out in his essay "From Play-script to Screenplay," adopt as many features of a given play's structure and language as possible while "adapting them to the accepted rules of mainstream cinema in continuity editing, clarity of character and story, and intelligibility of speech." The more radical films, such as Peter Greenaway's fantastically imagistic *Tempest* adaptation, *Prospero's Books*, attempt to embody the play's themes and motifs by exploring the medium of film, with its ability to cut, fade, or dissolve between images; to shift the point of view; and generally to employ what Jackson calls "montage editing," meaning the juxtaposition of successive shots rather than the continuous linear succession of scenes that we associate with the stage.

But whether the director chooses a conservative approach, faithful to the specifics of language and structure in the play, or a more radical one, the screenwriter will first create a screenplay that will no doubt contain many fewer words than Shakespeare's original text. A few exceptions are to be found, to be sure, such as Branagh's almost uncut *Hamlet*. The best directors view their modifications to Shakespeare's play script as expressive possibilities, a way of sharpening emphasis and collaborating with the source. Reading the screenplays for Branagh's other films, for instance, and comparing them to the original texts of Shakespeare can provide important insights into the themes the director wishes to highlight. The cleverly seamless internal cuts he made in speeches (Benedick and Beatrice's wordplay in *Much Ado*) to shorten the film open it to greater physical realism and retain the attention of a contemporary audience. In Act 4 of his *Henry V*, the screenplay eliminates one-third of the lines from Scene 1, more than half from Scene 2, cuts half the lines and reassigns others in Scene 3, dispenses with Scene 4 entirely, uses only two lines from Scene 6, and cuts much more than half the lines from Scenes 7 and 8. No one has complained that the muddy, violent battle of Agincourt is too short in the film, and yet the one scene completely excised from this section of the film is the only actual battle scene in the original play script: a confrontation that parodies Henry's military heroism by showing us the braggart liar Pistol redeeming a French captive, not for honor, but for money. Significantly, also, Branagh erases the angry Henry's command to slash the throats of the French prisoners of war.

In Olivier's superb *Henry V,* created during World War II to arouse British patriotism, the director significantly cuts the young monarch's speech threatening rape, murder, and torture of the enemy citizens of the French city of Harfleur. Olivier's influential film thus simplifies the King's character, depicting him as a model Christian solider-hero whose violent impulses and expansionist mentality, both suggested in the play script, are minimized in the film. Few critics have quarreled with the abridgments in Russian novelist Boris Pasternak's screenplay for Grigori Kozintsev's much-admired *Hamlet* or with the poetic richness of this profound and affecting film in which many speeches are excised while the camera lingers on five central images of stone, fire, iron, sea, and earth.

The Actors

Perhaps the most obvious elements of the film treatment of a play are the actors who assume the characters' roles. Because film and video can use the close-ups made possible by the camera, these media tend to create popular stars and celebrities out of actors even more than theater performance does. If the film has just one or two major roles, as in *Hamlet*, for instance, or *Romeo and Juliet*, these may be cast with the familiar faces of stars. The precedent for this kind of casting goes back at least to 1929, when United Artists produced *The Taming of the Shrew* with those romantic favorites Douglas Fairbanks and Mary Pickford as Petruchio and Kate. The 1935 *A Midsummer Night's Dream,* directed by the Austrian stage genius Max Reinhardt and the Hollywood veteran William Dieterle, featured such Metro-Goldwyn-Mayer contract players as Mickey Rooney as Puck, James Cagney as Bottom, and Olivia de Havilland as Hermia. A more recent film that would probably never have been made without its stars is Michael Hoffman's *A Midsummer Night's Dream* with Michelle Pfeiffer as Titania and Kevin Kline as Bottom. These films, as English professor Stephen M. Buhler states in his book *Shakespeare in the Cinema: Ocular Proof*, are "primarily defined by their commercial aspects, especially by audience appeal" (2002, 3). Surely Welles, Olivier, and Branagh would never have found the money to create their Shakespeare films if they had not established their reputations and box office appeal on stage first. This tradition extends back as far as the first silent film recording a performance by the spectacle-loving actor-impresario Herbert Beerbohm Tree. Yet one danger of such star power is that the film can be warped out of thematic shape to accommodate the actor's demands and strengths. Many critics have complained that Hoffman's film distorts *Dream* by giving Kline's appealing and sympathetic Bottom too substantial a place in the complex interweaving of plots and realities, even if other critics have found his interpretation of a dandified and henpecked man illuminating.

The emotional quality, credibility, and integrity of the acting are key elements of any film's effect. The possibilities are seemingly endless as the range of acting styles in cinematic Shakespeare has widened over time. Even the verbally limited performances of Leonardo DiCaprio and Claire Danes in Baz Luhrmann's *Romeo+Juliet* have proved highly effective, despite their unfamiliarity with Shakespeare's language, because the lovers' performances are of a piece with the punk-inflected, MTV style of the film's setting and rhythm. As noted, Al Pacino explores his Method training in

Looking for Richard, while the thrilling vocal timbres and rhythms of John Gielgud have brought a classical style of performance to his many appearances on screen, from his gaunt King Henry IV in Welles's *Falstaff: Chimes at Midnight* to his omnipresent Prospero in Greenaway's *Tempest* adaptation. Other actorly elements crucial to the film's effect include the casting of subordinate roles. The gifted comic Billy Crystal plays the gravedigger in Branagh's *Hamlet* film; his presence and the audience's knowledge of him as a pop star bring another dimension to this scene of darkly humorous comic relief. By noting specific aspects of the actors' interpretations, viewers begin to form an overall assessment of the performances and of the film. It is especially important that scenes in which the main players are not the focus have their own vividness. In other words, a strong argument can be made for creating an ensemble atmosphere and effect, even in a film dominated by a star performance.

This kind of balance is especially pertinent to a film version of *Hamlet*. Most video stores will yield film versions with Laurence Olivier, Kenneth Branagh, Mel Gibson, and Ethan Hawke in this coveted leading role. (These films are all discussed further in Part Two, Chapter 15). When watching such a film dominated by a single character, soliloquies become increasingly important as examples of the actor's skill in conveying private thoughts and emotions. These scenes help to characterize the ways in which various directors have chosen to record these crucial solo moments, thus revealing both their command of film technique and their insights into the hero at various points in the action. By noting the actor's and the director's approaches to these scenes, one can try to discern whether the public hero, say Hamlet—the man who secretly orders the murders of Rosencrantz and Guildenstern, gives instructions to the players, and frightens Ophelia with his madness—is the same man who reveals his near-despair in the soliloquies. Exploring the depiction of his other relationships—to his mother, Polonius, his friend Horatio, and his mood in the graveyard scene—will yield more facets of the interpretation. If one is called upon to write a review or essay, one may need at first to identify only two or three of the actors playing the leading roles. Even so, responding to even the minor figures will help any viewer form an estimate of the quality of the director's casting overall. Does he or she have an "eye" for matching actor to role? Sometimes smaller supporting roles, especially if they are stock or archetypal characters, are better cast and even more memorable than the principal actors. Noting this can aid in analyzing and assessing the film.

Finally, we make a distinction again between two very different approaches to acting:

- a presentational approach in which the actor speaks directly to the audience and both he and the viewer are aware that this is a fiction, not the shared illusion of everyday reality.

- a representational approach in which the actor creates the illusion that the "fourth wall" has been cut away and we are overhearing and seeing real life.

Although most films require a form of representational acting, those that are inspired by a Brechtian desire to cut through the comforting illusions of the stage and meditate upon the elements of filmmaking itself take a more presentational approach, as in sections of Reinhardt's *A Midsummer Night's Dream*, for instance, and all of Peter Greenaway's *Prospero's Books*. Others, such as Branagh's *Love's Labor's Lost* (2000) with its Cole Porter tunes, unfold like a movie musical, veering back and forth between the two styles. Two of Shakespeare's villains, Richard III in the history play that bears his name and Iago in *Othello*, attempt to seduce others, including the audience; very often actors in these roles adopt a presentational style as they try to pull the viewer into their spells.

Animated Shakespeare, those reconstructions of Shakespeare narratives into truncated cartoon stories, and animal Shakespeare are the only forms of Shakespearean performance no longer tied to the actor and his or her body. Yet even here, any imaginary representations of play scenes by the Simpsons and the Shakespeare-talking dog on the *Wishbone* series on PBS television still require the actor's voice.

The Film Director

The film director has all the responsibilities of a stage director, and more. In addition to making the initial interpretive choices, deciding upon the setting, casting the piece, supervising the screenwriter(s), and working with the lighting, costume, and set designers, he or she must work with a crew to scout exterior locations, decide upon the camera angles and lenses with a cinematographer, and spend a very long period in post-production editing both sound and images. Very often the director must also answer to the producer, the representative of the financial backers of a film. In some cases, because the financial stakes are so high, conflicts over directorial choices can create further pressure to cut, alter, or highlight certain elements thought to make the movie more marketable. Orson Welles spent four years making his *Othello* in various locations throughout Europe because of these kinds of financial pressures; now, decades later, this fascinating work has been remastered and reissued with an introduction by his daughter. More recently, Richard Loncraine described the vagaries of shooting his 1930s-set *Richard III* with Ian McKellen on almost no budget: "It was chaos," he told a BBC interviewer. "We'd run out of money halfway through the film. In fact we were shooting the film knowing we could never finish it. We went bankrupt, and we all put our own money in. The actors all put their own money in. Fifty thousand dollars is what they got paid, and they would get three million normally. So that helped. There was a camaraderie of everyone pulling together" (www.bbc.co.uk/education/lzone/master/richard.shtml).

Even Franco Zeffirelli, despite his long-established reputation as a popularly successful director of Shakespeare's plays on film, ran into such constraints with his 1991 *Hamlet*. When he sought funding for the film, he had to sign a contract with the producers promising to use a "name" star (Mel Gibson), and to keep the film at two hours in length (it actually ran two hours and fifteen minutes).

Directors of Shakespeare on film often emerge, as Welles, Olivier, and Branagh did, from the theater world, and as noted previously, they may sometimes take an essentially theatrical approach to filming. Just as often, however, they have become adept at playing with the new tool kit afforded them by film. Since the late 1960s, when critics and scholars began theorizing about film as a separate art form and film studies became an academic field of intellectual inquiry, the French have celebrated the kind of author-director who creates an original work and has complete control over its realization as an *auteur* (Jean-Luc Godard is a famous example, as is thrill master Alfred Hitchcock). The production of *An Othello* by Charles Marowitz mentioned earlier in this chapter is a good example of an *auteur* approach to staging Shakespeare. Orson Welles's *Falstaff: Chimes at Midnight* is an *auteur* treatment of Shakespeare's *Henry IV* plays on the screen. Welles, who also plays the fat knight, makes Falstaff the center of his own film, basing his heavily adapted text on Shakespeare's own *Henry IV* plays and envisioning the bustling, close-in, down-and-dirty Eastcheap tavern where Falstaff and Prince Hal (the handsome young Keith Baxter) pick pockets, filch purses, womanize, drink, and carouse together. Brooks's 1953 television production of *King Lear* comes close to being an *auteur* version, for it cuts the text to the bone, and has a starkness and intensity that colored his later, fuller production for the Royal Shakespeare Company. Greenaway's *Prospero's Books* definitely falls under the *auteur* category of realizing Shakespeare; the film, with its water-filled design, its repeated images and gestures, its dance-like movement, and its language, nearly all spoken by Gielgud in voice-over, resembles Greenaway's other works more than it resembles any other Shakespeare movie. The director is in charge, not Shakespeare—an approach very different from that of Akira Kurosawa, the great Japanese director. Although his two Shakespeare films are more like his own *Seven Samurai* than like anything by Shakespeare, Kurosawa meets the Elizabethan on Shakespeare's own emotional and poetic

terms in *Throne of Blood* (based on *Macbeth*) and *Ran* (based on *Lear*). Both movies have a stunning visual beauty and a harrowing intensity, and convey a truly tragic view of their protagonists' worlds.

More frequently, however, directors of Shakespeare films are content to cede control of some aspects of the filmmaking to other artists, most notably the cinematographer. Each of Kenneth Branagh's films is quite individual in style and presentation. Rather than imposing a single original artistic vision on each, he attempts to let the genre and style of the play suggest an appropriate cinematic style. Olivier's Shakespeare films have a similar range, their look determined by the play itself, and very definitely by the period in which it is set and the social and cultural influences of that period.

The Cinematographer

The chart contrasting film and theater (on pp. 48–49) notes that in a theater space the audience is free to look at whatever part of the stage appeals to the eye, whereas in film, the director (i.e., the person holding the camera lens) can manipulate the viewer's attention by drawing the eye to whatever the camera is focused upon. The person holding the camera or supervising those who hold the cameras is not the director himself but the cinematographer or director of photography.

This artist is the chief of both the camera and lighting crews working on a film, the person responsible for achieving the artistic and technical decisions relating to how each shot looks. (To be sure, the director will often look through the camera lens to see if the scene fulfills his expectations.) The cinematographer typically selects the film stock, lens, and filters to realize each scene in accordance with the intentions of the director. The relationship between the cinematographer and director can vary widely. In some cases the cinematographer has a great deal of autonomy and independence, earned because of a trusting, almost symbiotic relationship developed with a director. Kurosawa and his director of photography, Asakazu Nakai, worked in this closely collaborative way, as did Ingmar Bergman and his famed cinematographer Sven Nykvist. Both directors, in fact, worked repeatedly with the same artistic team; in Kurosawa's case, this included the heroic actor Toshiro Mifune and the art director Yoshihiro Muraki. That collaborative approach helps to account for the depth, intensity, and integrity of his films.

In other cases, such as Welles's, the director determines even such details as aperture, shutter speed, film stock, angles, and so on, with the cinematographer fulfilling those marching orders. On some shoots, the director assumes the duties of a cinematographer, especially when shooting physically intimate scenes where the director wishes to have as few people as possible present on the set, or when, as in the case of Greenaway and Julie Taymor, the director is an accomplished visual artist for whom recording the image exactly as imagined takes on even greater significance.

As noted earlier, the camera's focus directs and controls what the audience sees. This is most obviously true of the close-up, when the camera records the reactions of a face that may belong to the character speaking or acting, but sometimes focuses upon the face of a person listening or reacting, or being acted upon. Whereas in live theater subtleties of facial expression can project to audiences only if the theater is small, on film, the viewer's close identification with the characters is created by these intimate close-ups.

Think about how the use of the close-up affects the cinematic presentation of a particular play:

- Language may have been deleted in favor of facial expressions or gesture.

- Characters we know only from afar in the play can become more significant in close-up.

- Attention can be shifted away from the main character or the active ones toward minor figures, or even the community responding to a speech or an event.

- The close-up allows directors to zero in on an actor's thoughtful face and turn a soliloquy (Hamlet's "To be or not to be . . .") into a voice-over. Olivier and Branagh both do this in their *Henry V* films when the king worries about his father's crime in deposing Richard II, and prays quietly not to be punished for it.

Long shots (sometimes called deep focus) allow the camera to take in a large swath of action or landscape, crowd scenes, or good-bye scenes from a distance. Along with the medium shot, these different angles and distances between camera and actor (or other subject) are among the film director's most basic tools of storytelling. Many films end with a long shot as the camera recedes from the final action or confrontation, pulling viewers away with it and back into the real world.

Experienced feature film directors, working with their cinematographers, set up a variety of shots, creating a rhythm and interest just in the movement from one kind of shot and distance to another. Other theatrical presentations of Shakespeare, and many television productions, use a very still camera and very few changes of location. As you watch various Shakespeare films, note where each film fits in to this spectrum of cinematographic possibilities and what emotional effect the camera's distance, angle, lens, and filter (clear, dark, hazy?) have upon each scene.

The Designers

Feature films are seldom shot on a stage set within a theater. There are, of course, interesting and important exceptions to this rule; live 1950s television broadcasts, for instance, were shot continuously in real time on the equivalent of a stage in a television studio. The early and closing scenes of Laurence Olivier's *Henry V* were shot on a mock-up of London's Globe Theater, and later this brilliant and unusual film "opens up" to the battlefield and castle shots at the center of the action, before shifting styles again to return to the Elizabethan Globe (and a boy actor playing Katharine of France) for the ending. Similarly, Orson Welles paid close attention to details of setting and design. *Falstaff: Chimes at Midnight*, for instance, has few exterior scenes, since Welles thought such scenes did not mesh well with Shakespeare's stylized language. Instead, the designs often seem dark and cramped, much of the action occurring in low-ceilinged taverns where the thieves meet. The camera angles are odd, even distorted, and even the most beautiful of long shots create shadows and silhouettes as if the action is filtered through memory. The setting helps to create the elegiac tone of the production for this film exploring loss; it presents action "in reflection," and as Jorgens says, it is "saturated in pastness." Similarly in his *Macbeth* (1948), Welles creates a sense of the hero's isolation and confinement by using studio settings in a manner that calls to mind German Expressionist painters of the 1920s such as Emile Nolde. Even the outdoor locations in Kurosawa's *Throne of Blood* are more symbolic than realist, shrouded as they are in fog, and, in the case of the Forest of the Spider Web, suggesting the psychological and moral inversions of nature brought about by Macbeth and Lady Macbeth. As noted before, Kurosawa worked for decades with art director Yoshiro Muraki, developing a sympathetic understanding and shared vocabulary that contributed to the emotional and visual coherence of his films.

Other, more "hip" uses of design, even in exteriors, characterize Baz Luhrmann's *Romeo+Juliet* and Julie Taymor's *Titus*. Luhrmann's designer, Catherine Martin, creates a unified apocalyptic look for the exteriors, including the Romeo flight scene suggesting the sterile, loveless landscape of the Arizona desert. Taymor, having moved into filmmaking from stage direction and design, brilliantly mixes periods, locales, and motifs to give her film its sense of timelessness and relevance.

More frequently, filmed Shakespeare moves the action into realistic environments, taking advantage of the camera's ability to move about capturing people and action from many angles, and substituting images captured by the camera for stage sets built in imitation of real places. Kenneth Branagh's *Much Ado About Nothing* moves joyously about the Italian countryside, lingering on sunny outdoor scenes and festive nighttime parties. As will be noted in the longer discussion of Part Two, Chapter 8, both time and place are changed from Shakespeare's script, and this "opening up" includes vigorous outdoor scenes with the men returning home from war on thundering horses and characters of both sexes happily bathing (separately) before they meet again.

By noting the setting of the play on film, you can determine whether it is different from, an enhancement of, or the same as the setting in the play script. Sensitivity to what effect the new setting has upon your response to characters and theme will become part of your assessment of the play. Remember that sometimes a new setting may seem jarring at first, but could be intentionally dissonant, rather than simply a bad choice on the part of the director.

Other Designers: Lighting, Music, and Mood. Even more than in play production, lighting is a key visual component of film, and, like music, can greatly enhance—or diminish—its emotional effect. Lighting can be both more natural and more sophisticated in film than onstage, and therefore can take on an artistic dimension that involves such elements as contrasts between light and shadow, many variations in intensity, the subtle use of black and white or sepia tones, the bold use of color, and emotionally satisfying or exciting use of cuts, fades, cross-cuts, and dissolves. (See the Glossary of Film Terms for the meaning of such film terms.) Orson Welles was a master at creating atmosphere through lighting, shadows, and silhouettes. He often achieved painterly effects like Rembrandt's by shining light on his actors from below, deforming their faces. Kurosawa's lighting designs have similar originality and power. Not surprisingly, the lighting designer for a film is supervised by the cinematographer or director of photography, for the camera can record a scene only if, and in the way that, it is illuminated.

If lighting is often the element that makes a film feel coherent visually, music can be the element that makes it cohere aurally. This is why so many film producers commission original scores from composers. Many of these take on a life of their own, carrying within the musical metaphors the conflicts and resolutions of the play, in the same way that opera and ballet scores encapsulate theme and action. Felix Mendelssohn's incidental music to *A Midsummer Night's Dream* enriches the atmosphere of the 1935 Reinhardt film, especially in the fairy scenes, with its glittering delicacy and speed. Masaro Sato's highly dramatic and suspenseful score for Kurosawa's *Throne of Blood* underlines the intense emotions of the protagonist and his wife, with a sound design by Fumio Yanoguchi growing especially stirring during the battle scenes and in the death-by-arrows demise of Macbeth. Eliot Goldenthal's eclectic score for Taymor's *Titus* parallels the director's visual approach by creating a sound matrix in which old and new musical materials from around the world are mixed.

Some Shakespeare-on-film directors, including Richard Loncraine, are leery of music, feeling that it can be a distraction from language, character development, and imagery (although he uses pop songs and big band music to brilliant effect in several scenes of his 1930s-set *Richard III*). But again, the effectiveness of musical underscoring and song depends upon how judiciously it is used. Branagh employed the same composer, Patrick Doyle, to create the highly varied musical scores for his *Henry V, Much Ado*, and *Hamlet*. For *Love's Labor's Lost*, on the other hand, he used "found music," tunes already being hummed in the popular imagination as a way of bringing contemporary familiarity to this seldom-performed Shakespearean comedy.

The Film Editor

Various theories of film have insisted upon the primacy of different artists in the filmmaking process. For a time, recounts Robin Wood in "Ideology, Genre, Auteur" (reprinted in *Film Theory and Criticism*, eds. Leo Braudy and Marshall Cohen, 1974/1999), the film editor was ascendant, because "montage theory enthroned editing as the essential creative act at the expense of other aspects of film." The reason such theorists emphasized the film editor is that the ultimate rhythm of a film is determined by its editing and its juxtaposition or linear flow of shots, taking into account their length, mood, look, camera placement, and the kinds of transitions between them. At the two extremes, portions of Baz Luhrmann's *Romeo+Juliet* have a jumpy, agitated quality created by its editor to mimic the quick cuts of MTV; Grigori Kozintsev's *King Lear*, on the other hand, opens with a slowly unfolding wide-screen panorama. An entire kingdom seems to be harmoniously proceeding, with the Fool's melancholy music under their feet, on a timeless journey toward Lear's castle. Something of great and of solemn import is clearly about to happen.

Both kinds of editing are valid, each reflecting the overall spirit of the play, the director's choice of setting, and his overall interpretation. Editing is a painstaking and time-consuming process that involves choosing exactly the right frames to be spliced together as the images make a transition from shot to shot, creating the desired effect. Film editors work closely with the director to achieve his or her vision, although some directors, such as Kurosawa, also serve as their own editors. In big-budget feature films, producers often become involved toward the end of the editing process, making suggestions about length, mood, music, and other matters in an effort to make the film congenial to the widest possible audience—in other words, to make it a "hit." For this reason, several different versions of the same film sometimes exist, such as the studio's final cut and the so-called "director's cut," which more fully realizes the artistic vision of the director. Many of the Shakespeare films in our survey were protected from such outside pressures

CLOSE-UP

PETER BROOK

The Director as Conjurer

When I hear a director speaking glibly of serving the author, of letting a play speak for itself, my suspicions are aroused, because this is the hardest job of all. If you just let a play speak, it may not make a sound. If what you want is for the play to be heard, then you must conjure its sound from it.

Peter Brook, *The Empty Space* (1968)

Peter Brook (b. 1925) is arguably the most significant stage director in the second half of the twentieth century. While he has staged numerous acclaimed and often controversial productions of Shakespeare's plays, his work has extended into other realms, most notably in his nine-hour staging of *The Mahabharata*, India's sacred epic poem. His productions have been performed in the world's most prestigious theaters, in commercial houses in the West End and on Broadway, in experimental spaces (a converted railway station in Paris), and, as importantly, in "found" spaces such as the sands of Africa and before ancient stone carvings in Iran. Whatever and wherever Brook directs, he is bound by one philosophy: "I want to know what theater is—and to know what it is, is to know what it could be" (Croyden, 285).

The son of a former Russian *Menshevik* (a member of the Russian Social-Democratic Workers' Party) turned prosperous pharmaceutical manufacturer in England, Brook first turned to staging Shakespeare with a three-hour *Hamlet*, which he presented in a toy theater rigged with lights—at the age of five. A life-threatening illness confined Brook to a hospital bed in Switzerland when he was twelve; vociferously reading the world's finest literature provided his recreation. He claims this period as the only truly educative one of his youth. Brook entered Oxford University in 1942 with the intention of becoming a film director. He quickly established himself as a visionary when—at age seventeen—he rented a small theater in London to stage Christopher Marlowe's *Doctor Faustus*. A year later he directed his first film with the Oxford Film Society, using a lawnmower as a camera dolly. While searching for film locations, Brook met John Gielgud, who allowed the precocious artist to use Gielgud's Haymarket Theatre for rehearsals; the renowned actor remained instrumental in advancing Brook's career.

In 1945 Sir Barry Jackson, the artistic director of the Birmingham Repertory Company, asked Brook to direct Shaw's notoriously difficult *Man and Superman*. The twenty-year-old cast the then unknown Paul Scofield in the leading role of Jack Tanner. The Brook-Scofield relationship proved to be a boon to English theater; the actor played central roles in Brook's productions of Shakespeare's *King John*, Ibsen's *The Lady from the Sea*, and most famously in the controversial *King Lear* (1962) for the Royal Shakespeare Company, which Brook filmed in 1965.

By the 1950s Brook had established himself as an important director of Shakespeare's plays. In 1951 he directed *Measure for Measure* at the Shakespeare Memorial Theatre in Stratford and sparked controversy when he asked the actor playing Isabella to pause until she felt the audience could no longer stand the silence before sparing Angelo's life; the pause lasted for almost two minutes. In 1955 Brook directed Laurence Olivier in the rarely performed *Titus Andronicus* at the SMT, a production for which he also designed the scenery and wrote the eerie musical score. The production transformed the work from "a grotesque neo-Senecan melodrama of primitive bloodlust . . . into a rite of authentic passions and suffering by *suggesting* a horrendous reality with simple stylized eloquence" (Williams, 4). For instance, when Lavinia appeared, her arms and tongue severed by Tamara's wicked sons, the stumps of her arms were represented by long blood-red ribbons, her mouth stuffed with crimson silks. The effect caused some spectators to faint and have to be carried from the theater.

When Peter Hall assumed the leadership of the SMT in 1960—and changed its name to the Royal Shakespeare Theatre—Brook was named an associate director of the Royal Shakespeare Company. At the RSC Brook's most notable achievements were the innovative "white box" *A Midsummer Night's Dream* (1970, see the stage history of the play, p. 160-ff) and the Theater of Cruelty seasons (1962–1964), which produced the aforementioned *King Lear* and the RSC's most celebrated non-Shakespeare work, *The Persecution and Assassination of Jean Paul Marat as Performed by the Inmates of the Asylum of Charenton under the Direction of the Marquis de Sade* (or simply, *Marat/Sade*).

Brook's experimentation with the Theater of Cruelty, founded upon principles espoused by the French visionary Antonin Artaud, produced other stunning and controversial Shakespearean works, most notably *The Tempest* (1968) as performed at London's Round House. This location was transformed into an open space (much like a gymnasium), permitting the audience to sit among the actors. Brook had previously directed the play twice at Stratford: in 1957 with John Gielgud as Prospero, and in 1963 for the fledgling RSC. Both were relatively conventional productions, but in 1968 Brook used the text of Shakespeare's play as a springboard for an alternative work suggesting that Caliban commits sexual violence against Miranda and Prospero (see the stage history of *The Tempest*). Brook's intention was not to merely shock audiences (although the production did precisely that) but to experiment with sound, movement, and text in ways that realized the Boatswain's description of Prospero's magic isle, reverberating

> with strange and several noises
> Of roaring, shrieking, howling, jingling chains,
> And more diversity of sounds, all horrible . . .
> (5.1.234–236)

Bold experimentation, particularly with primitive communicative and theatrical techniques, characterized Brook's work throughout the late 1960s and the 1970s. He put together an itinerant company of actors (including Helen Mirren) that functioned under the banner of *Le Centre International de Recherche Theatrale* (*CIRT*), the Center for International Theater Research, and trekked to remote locales to "increase the general understanding of the mysterious nature of [theatre] by trying out things that have not been tried before" (Brook, in Williams, 169). In 1971 CIRT created a modern twelve-hour ritual, *Orghast at Persopolis*, based on Middle Eastern ancient myths. It was performed on carpets in the village of Shiraz, Persia (now Iran), backed by enormous cliffs containing the tombs of Persia's warrior-kings. In 1973 CIRT created *The Ik*, a drama about displaced Africans based on anthropological studies of native Ugandans. For Brook, *The Ik* became a symbol of moderns displaced by technology and commercialism. The work was performed in Africa to indigenous audiences who had not seen Western theater, as well as in Paris and many other cities. Brook's experimentation with primitive theatrical forms and spaces influenced his direction of more conventional Western works, most notably Bizet's opera, *La tragedie du Carmen*, which was staged partly in a sandpit and reduced to its most essential elements.

Perhaps Brook's most ambitious work was his 1985 anti-war epic, *The Mahabharata*, first staged in a rock quarry near Avignon, France. The production featured an international cast from all continents (save Antarctica) and freely mixed theatrical styles (e.g., Japanese Kabuki, Indian Kath Kali, Western realism), thereby creating a unique synthesis of communication modes to produce an "everyday story of superfolk [through] a combination of spectacular theatrical magic and simplicity of playing" (Hunt, 257). Despite its length, *The Mahabharata* was performed before huge audiences in a variety of venues (other quarries, railroad depots, a boathouse in Switzerland) as well as in conventional theaters; it was also filmed and is now available in video and DVD formats.

Brook's directorial work, Shakespearean and otherwise, is motivated by a lifelong quest to find an "immediate theater" that is a "spike in the side of an audience," or, in other words, a theater that is "out of tune with society—not seeking to celebrate the accepted values but to challenge them." Brook's theater, as defined in his manifesto, *The Empty Space*, is the antithesis of the Deadly Theater that he defines as "depressingly active" in its use of old formulae and old methods. "Nowhere does the Deadly Theater install itself so securely . . . as in the works of William Shakespeare" when he is approached "from the viewpoint that somewhere, someone has found and defined how the play should be done." Yet Brook is Shakespeare's staunchest defender in that his "aim continually is holy, metaphysical, yet he never makes the mistake of staying too long on the highest plane." For Brook, Shakespeare's plays are an ideal synthesis of:

- a *Holy Theater* (or "the Theatre of the Invisible-Made-Visible") that celebrates ritual and ceremony as did our ancestors who created theater; it contains "all the hidden impulses known to man"; and

(continued)

■ a *Rough Theater* that is close to the people in that it deals with "men's actions . . . it is down to earth and direct because it admits wickedness and laughter."

Brook's Shakespearean work has been sporadic, partly because the director is drawn to a vast variety of the world's myths and literature, mostly because he passionately believes that a production, Shakespearean or otherwise, is "only right at a given moment and anything it asserts dogmatically today may well be wrong fifty years from now." Because he has been faithful to that tenet, Brook "has found the means of making actual Shakespeare's ongoing theatrical potential in relevant and immediate pro-

ductions which speak to and of our time without falsifying the plays' universality" (Jones, 123).

References and Related Reading
Brook, Peter. *The Empty Space*. New York, 1968.
Croyden, Margaret. *Lunatics, Lovers, and Poets: The Contemporary Experimental Theater*. New York, 1974.
Hunt, Alfred, and Geoffrey Reeves. *Peter Brook*. Cambridge, Eng., 1995.
Jones, Edward Trostle. *Following Directions: A Study of Peter Brook*. New York, 1985.
Todd, Andrew, and Jean-Guy Lecat. *The Open Circle: Peter Brook's Theatrical Environments*. New York, 2003.
Williams, David. *Peter Brook: A Theatrical Casebook*. London, 1988.

because the director himself (Welles, especially) served as the film's producer and chief fundraiser. When any film involves more than one cut, the fact will be duly noted in the stage and screen histories following each play.

Now that we have examined the basic processes required to bring a Shakespeare script to stage or screen, we will begin our in-depth look at fourteen of his most frequently staged (and filmed) plays, describing each with a survey of its creative inspirations, sources, language, and themes. We also present a history of its most significant realizations on stage and screen. Our hope is that visiting these stage and screen productions will lead to deeper understanding of Shakespeare's plays, and from there to sharper critical insights and more refined interpretive skills. We have organized the plays by genre and include a brief description of each genre (comedy, history, tragedy, and romance) in the corresponding group of plays.

A Word About Genres

Genre is a literary term that describes the classification of a work into a distinctive type according to the treatment of its subject matter, its tone and structure, and the perspective of the writer. In his *The Poetics*, the Greek philosopher Aristotle was the first to describe tragedy, basing his discussion upon his experience of plays by the ancient writers Aeschylus, Sophocles, and Euripides. Aristotle's codification of the elements and requirements of tragedy affected Roman ideas of drama that in turn came down to such Elizabethan writers as Marlowe and Shakespeare. *The Poetics* also contains an outline of a theory of comedy, although not a fully elaborated discussion. Shakespeare's art, as scholar David

Galbraith notes, "assumed a system of genres" (in Leggatt, 13). But Shakespeare's practice, in both comedy and tragedy, did not adhere to theoretical formulations. In *Hamlet*, Shakespeare mocks the fine distinctions among genres when he has the old royal counselor Polonius catalog the genres popular during the playwright's day, taking them to ludicrous extremes when he names "tragedy, comedy, history, pastoral, pastoral-comical, historical-pastoral, tragical-historical, tragical-comical-historical-pastoral" (2.2.397–399) as the kinds of works that traveling players might perform when they visit Elsinore. When Heminges and Condell printed the First Folio in 1623, they were more economical than Polonius, naming only Comedies, Histories, and Tragedies as the principal genres in Shakespeare's canon. To those, scholars and editors add a fourth genre: the Romance, which evolved from the pastoral dramas of which Polonius speaks. Romances combine the impulse of tragedy (usually a monarch makes a disastrous error in judgment), the epic sweep of the histories, and the resolution of comedy (i.e., the happy ending). There are, of course, subgenres of these primary genres; farce is a subset of comedy, for instance. Several of Shakespeare's history plays were actually treated—and even titled—as tragic plays.

In their purest, "unmixed" forms, tragedy and comedy, the oldest and most elemental dramatic genres, reflect a playwright's opposite approaches to an examination of human behavior. The eighteenth-century British writer Horace Walpole observed that tragedy is for "those who feel," while comedy is "for those who think," a distinction that suggests the degree to which the playwright involves the audience in the theater experience. Tragedy, or at least serious drama, asks the audience to engage more fully in the emotions of the protagonists, while comedy asks audiences to step back and judge the folly of a play's characters.

Both those genres and history plays share two common premises: our actions often do go wrong and even so, we are accountable for them. Causality—the recognition that actions lead to other actions—is central to the telling of a story, be it serious, comic, or historical. In tragedies and history plays actions have serious consequences that lead to suffering and death, and perhaps the peril of a nation; in comedy, though there may be momentary threats of dire consequences, transgressions are ultimately forgiven and misfortune gives way to celebration. In those plays that we know as the problem plays (e.g., *Measure for Measure*, *All's Well That Ends Well*, and *Troilus and Cressida*), Shakespeare challenged traditional notions of comedy; their resolutions are less satisfying (one might say more realistic) and the plays are closer in spirit to what we now recognize as tragicomedy.

This anthology is divided into the four principal genres, with representative samples of each. We address the specifics of each genre in a brief introduction to each section. We have not included any of the so-called "problem plays," which are slipperier to categorize by genre; we omit them from this collection mostly, however, because they have not inspired important films or videos. Perhaps because they are so unconventional and are in some cases lesser known to much of the public, filmmakers have tended to ignore them. They are included in the BBC Shakespeare series, however, though none of these productions is particularly distinguished.

PART TWO

The Plays

PLATE 7
The Taming of the Shrew. *Playing a lusty Petruchio in Franco Zeffirelli's 1967 film, Richard Burton publicly plants a kiss upon the lips of a surprised Katharine played by his real-life wife, Elizabeth Taylor.* (Ronald Grant Archive)

PLATE 8

A Midsummer Night's Dream. *In director Peter Brook's landmark, circus-styled production (1970), Titania wakes upon her bed of red feathers and, under the influence of a love potion, falls in love with Bottom the Weaver. His clown nose is one of many Brook inventions; the script (and most productions) call for an ass's head.* (©Photo by Max Waldman Archives. All rights reserved.)

PLATE 10
Much Ado About Nothing. *Beatrice and Benedick share a quiet moment in which their true feelings for one another are unmasked. In the
distance are the rolling hills of Tuscany which lends its sunny, sensuous atmosphere to the 1993 film starring its director Kenneth Branagh
and Emma Thompson.* (Bureau L. A. Collection/Corbis)

PLATE 11

Much Ado About Nothing. *During the dazzling opening scenes of Kenneth Branagh's 1993 film, picnickers on a verdant Italian hillside run toward the nearby villa so they can prepare to greet a cadre of soldiers now thundering on horseback toward home.* (Photofest)

PLATE 12

Twelfth Night. *In director Trevor Nunn's 1996 film, actor Ben Kingsley brings a melancholy edge to the role of the music-loving jester, Feste. After three couples join hands in the final scenes, Kingsley's Feste wanders off from his mistress Olivia to seek other employment.* (Ronald Grant Archive)

SHAKESPEARE AND COMEDY

Defining Comedy

Dr. Samuel Johnson, who devised one of the first English dictionaries, wrote that "Comedy has been unpropitious to definers." While there is general agreement about what constitutes a tragedy, scholars and theorists have reached little accord on comedy. Even more than tragedy, comedy is usually dependent on the particulars of a given culture. Because it is customarily about the here and now, comedy may not always translate well for subsequent generations; therefore, directors often feel the need to relocate a Shakespearean comedy into a more familiar setting. Although all of Shakespeare's comedies are set in foreign locales—save *The Merry Wives of Windsor*, his sole comedy located in England—each retains a distinctly Elizabethan quality, especially among the common characters. Although they may be billed as working men of Athens, the rustics in *A Midsummer Night's Dream* are as thoroughly English as shepherd's pie and a tankard of ale.

The Types of Shakespearean Comedy

To further complicate the issue, comedy has numerous subsets, most of which can be found in Shakespeare's canon: romantic comedy, the romance, the comedy of manners, farce and slapstick, bawdy comedy, grotesque comedy, gallows humor, benign comedy, sentimental comedy, and others discussed in conjunction with specific plays. Additionally, such genres and subsets themselves are in a constant state of transformation. Attempting to define precisely what constitutes a "Shakespearean comedy," much less defining the genre, is a daunting task. In 1973 Bertrand Evans noted that "to date no one has been quite successful in composing a definition of Shakespearean comedy that is at the same time broad enough . . . and precise enough to be of much use." Notable attempts have been made, yet Evans's comment remains valid.

Fourteen of the thirty-five plays in the First Folio are placed under the heading of "Comedies." Two of these,

The Tempest and *The Winter's Tale*, are now regarded as romances, a subset of comedy inclining toward the tragicomic, albeit with joyful endings reflecting the spirit of comedy. Two others, *Measure for Measure* and *All's Well That Ends Well*, are often classified as "problem comedies." They deal with intractable social problems and end in problematic marriages, although they do provide some very funny scenes and characters. Some of the history plays, notably those in which Sir John Falstaff appears, contain important elements of comedy and were classified as such by Francis Meres in 1599, though their main concern is the often-vexed topic of English history. *Richard III* and *Henry V* provide triumphant—and in that sense comic—resolutions to the tetralogies they conclude.

Comedy extends beyond our normal assumption that it makes people laugh and ends happily. We offer here a survey of relevant general notions about the purpose and spirit of comedy, applied to the specifics of Shakespeare's comic endeavors. As a starting point, consider the paradox that lies at the heart of comedy and tragedy (see "A Word About Genres," pp. 68–69). Tragedy, though serious and about death, begins with the ennobling premise that human beings possess nearly unlimited potential—a central tenet of humanist thought in the Renaissance. Comedy grows from a more sardonic notion that we mortals are, in Puck's estimation, "fools" (*MND*, 3.2.115). Whereas only a select few have the nobility of spirit to achieve tragic heroism, comedy is fundamentally democratic in that virtually all people, by nature of their folly, are candidates for comedy. As Thornton Wilder wrote in *Our Town*, "Whenever you come near the human race, you find layers and layers of nonsense."

What is the difference between comedy and tragedy if both spring from human weakness? On one level, tragic heroes seek absolute knowledge about the limits of their humanity and play for much higher stakes to obtain it. The stakes are rarely as high in comedy. An angry father may threaten his daughter with death, as in *A Midsummer Night's Dream*, and Beatrice may command Benedick to "Kill Claudio" in *Much Ado About*

Nothing, but we understand through the tone and conventions of comedy that death is unlikely. Because we, as audience, enjoy a superior perspective as we sit comfortably outside the play's action, we know intuitively, with Puck, that by the final act "Naught shall go ill . . . and all shall be well" (3.2.462–465).

If tragedy deals with an individual, a Hamlet or a King Lear, at odds with the cosmos, comedy is immersed in the social world. In many comedies, especially those of Shakespeare's rival, Ben Jonson, and the later-seventeenth-century French comedian, Molière, the comic protagonist is at odds with the norms of society and must be reformed. Shakespeare's comedies are sometime referred to as "benevolent" because he is rarely as harshly critical of his comic creations as were Jonson and Molière. These writers are generally more cynical in their treatment of human folly than is Shakespeare, whose audiences are most often asked to laugh with the characters rather than at them.

Comedy often serves as a social corrective insofar as it challenges those societal norms that may be outmoded or stultifying. In this sense comedy is subversive, even anarchic. Shakespeare's comedies are frequently initiated by an "irrational law" (Frye, 127) that the action of the comedy eventually overturns. In *The Taming of the Shrew* a young woman, Bianca, may not marry until her older sister, Kate, marries; Kate resents being property to be bartered to the highest bidder in the male-dominated world of Padua. Hermia in *A Midsummer Night's Dream* is threatened with death by her father and Duke Theseus if she refuses to marry the man her father has selected as her husband. She and her lover, Lysander, are thus forced escape from the cruel world of Athens into the woods. In the first act of *As You Like It*, Rosalind is banished from "the envious court" of Duke Frederick, a place of political gamesmanship and strife between brothers. She is an outcast simply because she is her father's daughter and thereby an assumed enemy of the duke. After discovering that the laws of nature found in the forest are superior to those of the court, Rosalind and other banished figures return in Act 5 to revitalize the man-made world. Shakespearean comedies often contrast the natural laws of "the green world" with the artificial laws of the court (Frye, 147).

The spirit of carnival is among the primary impulses underlying comedy. Throughout history and across many cultural borders, we find examples of people celebrating anarchy in a sanctioned manner by subverting societal norms, if only for a day or two. As they take to the streets to celebrate freedom from restraint, the participants in a carnival often wear masks and festive costumes to liberate them from their customary inhibitions. During the Middle Ages, a holiday known as the Feast of Fools gave license to such behavior; that day was set aside for role-reversals as underlings mocked royalty, while those in power played commoners. Men often dressed as women to indulge in food, drink, and perhaps sexual activity during the merrymaking. Presiding over the Feast of Fools was the Lord of Misrule, a mock-king embodying the anarchic spirit. Sir John Falstaff (the *Henry IV* plays) and Sir Toby Belch (*Twelfth Night*) are among Shakespeare's best-known Lords of Misrule.

Masks and costumes, particularly women in male clothing, are central to many of Shakespeare's comedies. We learn an important idea from this playful convention of Shakespearean comedy: in his mature comedies, those written from about 1595 on, invariably a woman subverts the status quo to forge a better society. (Conversely, almost never in Shakespeare's tragedies is a woman of importance to the plot alive at the end of the play.) Consider some examples of Shakespeare's women who dress as men to survive in male-dominated worlds. Portia, the refined lady of Belmont in *The Merchant of Venice*, assumes the identity of a law clerk to rescue Antonio from Shylock's cruel plot to extract a pound of flesh; while dressed as a man she also teaches her betrothed, Bassanio, and his friend, Gratiano, an important lesson about keeping promises. Rosalind in *As You Like It*, like Sylvia in the early comedy *Two Gentlemen of Verona*, dresses as a man as she escapes into the Forest of Arden, where her wisdom and forbearance restore harmony to the chaos around her. Viola in *Twelfth Night* wears "concealing" garb to serve Duke Orsino; her unstinting loyalty and good sense are antidotes to the madness that rules in Illyria. Even those women who do not dress as men (Kate in *The Taming of the Shrew* and Beatrice in *Much Ado About Nothing*) rail against the boorish behavior of the men and ultimately force them to be more tolerant of women. Although it is not a comedy written by Shakespeare, the film *Shakespeare in Love* plays with the Elizabethan convention of cross-dressing when a woman, Viola de Lesseps, dresses as a man to gain entry into Shakespeare's theater. One of the film's best lines provides us with an insight into the issues raised by Shakespeare's strong-willed women; Queen Elizabeth sympathizes with Viola when she says, "I know what it is to be a woman in a man's world."

Shakespeare's depiction of women in the comedies has provoked competing viewpoints among contemporary critics. Those aligned with one school of criticism, the New Historicism, such as Leonard Tennenhouse, argue that such poses by women are merely requirements of a patriarchal society. The women only revolt symbolically against male domination, but in the final analysis—or in the last act—they succumb to the old norm in which women best serve society by being dutiful wives to their husbands and loyal subjects to their monarchs. Other social critics, such as Jonathan Dollimore and Graham Holderness, offer alternative readings of the same texts: The women truly are subversives who alter society by refusing to play the conventional roles assigned them. The marriages into which they enter figure to be shared experiences because power is equitably distributed between husband and wife.

The marriages are remnants of ancient rites. Most classical comedies, including Shakespeare's, end with a marriage (or two or three), a dance, or a banquet—joyful ceremonies that distinguish Shakespeare's "festive comedies," as C. L. Barber termed them. The Greeks referred to such rites as a *komos* ("joyful union"), marking a new beginning for those who have endured the chaos of the play's action. The *komos* suggests fertility (symbolized by marriages), long life (banquets that nourish life), and the harmonious restoration of the community's social order (dances). Such comedic resolutions derive from ancient planting and/or harvest festivals found in virtually all cultures. Few moments in modern cinema capture the unabashed joy of the ancient *komos* as does the final sequence of Kenneth Branagh's *Much Ado About Nothing*; cascades of flower petals descend on the revelers as they dance in circles symbolic of unity and harmony.

Thus far we have discussed Shakespeare's comedy in philosophical and social terms; some practical elements of Shakespeare's comedies also merit attention, particularly his comic diction. Much Shakespearean comedy is dependent on ingenious wordplay, especially puns, malaprops, and elaborate turns of phrase. Puns are especially common in Shakespeare's plays, much to the dismay of Dr. Samuel Johnson, who attributed such wordplay to "some malignant power over [Shakespeare's] mind." Most comedies contain about eighty puns, while *Love's Labor's Lost*—a comedy of manners satirizing the newly educated—features almost two hundred. Some scenes are built almost entirely on puns and wordplay, some of it intentionally silly (e.g., the twin Dromios in *The Comedy of Errors*), much of it genuinely witty. For Shakespeare, puns were not always the lowest form of humor. In the first encounter between Petruchio and Kate in *The Taming of the Shrew* (2.1.182–277), the humor is predicated on the numerous puns and word games that enhance the relationship between the wooer and the wooed. Petruchio becomes attracted to Kate, and she to him (as she is not to Padua's other dullards), because their witticisms indicate the quality and nimbleness of mind, attractive qualities to Elizabethan lovers.

Malaprops, the misuse of one word when another is intended (Bottom tells Quince that he and his fellow actors will "rehearse most obscenely"), are quite the opposite of puns. Generally, they indicate a lack of education and sophistication, a way in which Shakespeare created likably foolish characters such as Nick Bottom, Dogberry, and the Dromios. Although Shakespeare excelled in using the malaprop in his plays, the actual term comes from a character, Mrs. Malaprop, created by Richard Brinsley Sheridan in his still popular English comedy, *The Rivals* (1775).

English men and women were exploring—even reveling in—their language as Shakespeare wrote. On occasion Shakespeare pokes fun at those who would extend the boundaries of the language too far. Much of his humor is the product of a character using language not wisely but certainly too much. In *Love's Labor's Lost* Don Armado's linguistic embellishments provide many of that play's biggest laughs. Consider a portion of a twenty-line speech in which the foolish Spaniard expounds upon his affection for the wench, Jaquenetta:

> I do affect the very ground, which is base, where
> her shoe, which is baser, guided by her foot, which
> is basest, doth tread. I shall be foresworn, which
> is a great argument of falsehood, if I love. And how
> can that be true love which is falsely attempted?
> Love is familiar; Love is a devil. There is no evil
> angel but Love.
>
> (1.2.161–167)

On the page, such verbosity may seem less comical, although from the mouth of a skilled actor such speeches are as amusing today as they were in the Globe in c. 1600. The conflation of inventive plots, memorable characters, and well-crafted speeches encourages actors to use their comedic talents to make many scenes in Shakespeare's comic plays laugh-out-loud funny.

References and Related Reading

Barber, C. L. *Shakespeare's Festive Comedy*. Princeton, 1959.

Barton, Anne. *The Names of Comedy*. Toronto, 1990.

Brown, John Russell. *Shakespeare and His Comedies*. London, 1968.

Dollimore, Jonathan, and Alan Sinfield, eds. *Political Shakespeare*. Manchester, Eng., 1985.

Evans, Bertrand. *Shakespeare's Comedies*. Oxford, 1960.

Friedman, Michael D. *"The World Must Be Peopled:" Shakespeare's Comedies of Forgiveness.* Madison, N.J., and London; 2002.

Frye, Northrop. *Anatomy of Criticism.* Princeton, 1957.

———. *A Natural Perspective: The Development of Shakespearean Comedy and Romance.* New York, 1965.

Holderness, Graham. "Radical Potentiality and Institutional Closure: Shakespeare in Film and Television." In Dollimore and Sinfield (see above).

Jensen, Ejner J. *Shakespeare and the Ends of Comedy.* Manchester, Eng., 1999.

Nevo, Ruth. *Comic Transformations in Shakespeare.* London, 1980.

Salinger, Leo. *Shakespeare and the Traditions of Comedy.* Cambridge, Eng., 1974.

Tennenhouse, Leonard. *Power on Display: The Politics of Shakespeare's Genres.* New York and London, 1986.

Traversi, Derek. *Shakespeare: The Early Comedies.* London, 1960.

Williamson, Marilyn. *The Patriarchy of Shakespeare's Comedies.* Detroit, 1986.

CHAPTER 6

The Taming of the Shrew

(1590–1594)

Context and Dating: Misogynist Tradition in Elizabethan England

Although Shakespeare's ingenious *The Taming of the Shrew* has long been an audience favorite, contemporary critics and directors often find it difficult to reconcile the play's depiction of relationships between the sexes with today's standards for courtship and marriage. *Shrew* is an early example of Shakespeare's robust comic genius, written before his comedies achieved the warmth and depth of characterization and the romantic intensity that flowered in such lyrical later works as *A Midsummer Night's Dream* and *Twelfth Night*. Borrowing in *Shrew* from many sources while inventing most details of the shrew taming, Shakespeare smoothly weaves together two plots with a framing plot, a third plot, called the Induction. Farce, realism, and the idealized romance associated with the Italian poet Petrarch coexist in this comic world. Its scenes are located in the English countryside in the Induction and in the Italian locales of Padua, Petruchio's country estate, and the road between them during the play proper. Together the three plots offer sharply contrasting views of sexual love and multiple perspectives upon contested Elizabethan views of women and marriage in a patriarchal society.

What offends some modern sensibilities—and entertains others—is the plot that gives the play its title, the taming of Katharina, who is also known as Katharine and Kate. At one extreme is the assessment of George Bernard Shaw, playwright and defender of the "modern" woman, who wrote in 1888 that *Shrew* presents "one vile insult to womanhood and manhood from first to last." Petruchio tames his wife exactly as brutal people tame animals or children, Shaw felt, "by breaking their spirit by domineering cruelty." Other commenta-

tors (Marianne Novy, John Bean) view the Katharina-Petruchio plot as one in which two spirited, mutually attracted people struggle through self-discovery toward a genuine accommodation, though on masculine terms, in marriage. Still others view the play as a raucous farce (Jack Jorgens, Robert Heilman, many stage directors) and little more. Jorgens memorably describes *Shrew* as "a play not for a sober Monday morning but for a drunken Saturday night, a vacation from morality, psychology, and seriousness in which we can sit back and laugh at a caricature of the battle of the sexes" (67–68).

As the stage history below indicates, actor-managers and directors have cut, adapted, or shaped their stagings of the play to suppress the supposed cruelty of the taming plot. Actresses playing Kate have often been encouraged to employ nods, winks, and erotic physical action to give an ironic twist to their delivery of her final speech praising obedience to husbands. The unvarnished text does explore the role of women in patriarchy during the early modern period, and some of the most shrewd and revealing contemporary critics of Shakespeare (see "References and Related Reading") have studied the play within its historical, material, and social context.

Scholars do not agree upon the date of its composition. Nor do we know the date of its first performance. The play was not printed until the First Folio of 1623, and a different play called the *The Taming of A Shrew* (1594) has complicated debate over the early history of Shakespeare's *Shrew* (see "Sources and Inspirations"). In general, Shakespeare's *The Taming of the Shrew* is thought to have been composed between 1590 and no later than 1594, which makes it an early comedy composed around the same period as three others: *The Comedy of Errors*, with which *Shrew* shares a delight in neoclassical plotting and many farcical elements; the very different *Love's Labor's Lost*, with which it shares some conventions of Petrarchan lyric poetry; and *The Two Gentlemen of Verona*, also dated 1590–1594, which may be Shakespeare's first romantic comedy—that is, a story in which lovers overcome blocking forces, conflict, and dangers before finally achieving their goal of marriage.

The Taming of the Shrew is set within another dramatic action that nearly disappears after two opening scenes that form what is called the Induction. A nobleman and his party discover a drunken tinker, Christopher Sly, and trick him into believing that he is a lord who has been dreaming for fifteen years. Outfitting him luxuriously, they sit him down to watch a group of strolling players entertain with a "pleasant comedy." He would rather be in bed with the "wife" (a cross-dressed page) whom the nobles have duped him into believing is his. Still, he watches the play at least until he declares himself bored with it. In many productions he falls asleep at this point. (The ending to Sly's "play" has been either omitted by Shakespeare or is lost; see "Sources and Inspirations.")

The play these noblemen present to him has an Italian setting. It is about the wealthy Paduan, Baptista, and the two daughters he wants to see married—the shrewish older sister Katharina (Kate) and the seemingly docile younger one, Bianca. Several men are competing to win Bianca, and she cannot be wed until Kate has been married off first. Petruchio and Kate commit to a wedding day, although Petruchio arrives at the ceremony in colorfully mismatched rags, ignores the wedding feast, and takes his unwilling bride to his country house where he begins a taming ritual by keeping her hungry (saying the food is not good enough for her), ill dressed (saying simple garments suit her better), sleepless, and frustrated until she will agree to anything. In a final public test of the sisters' docility, the passive Bianca proves less pliable and more proudly defiant, once married, than her formerly aggressive sister. Katharina responds obediently to her new husband's request that she come when he summons her and then bring the other ladies, then lectures the other two brides on the joy that derives from being an obedient wife:

> Such duty as the subject owes the prince,
> Even such a woman oweth to her husband;
> And when she is froward, peevish, sullen, sour,
> And not obedient to his honest will,
> What is she but a foul contending rebel
> And graceless traitor to her loving lord?
>
> (5.2.159–164)

Characters

When first we meet them, Kate may seem a standard virago (a loud, overbearing woman) from farce and Petruchio may appear a variant of the braggart from Roman comedy. She hurls invective and, in most productions, throws flowerpots at her father, sister, and suitors; he swaggers, bullies, and demands attention with provocative remarks. He mocks the wedding with his mismatched clothes and refuses the wedding feast and dance, preferring instead to take his bride to a country estate. Kate's strong-willed, feisty behavior can be funny, yet the characterization is not particularly deep, and her motives go mostly unexplored. As Kate is subjected to Petruchio's taming, she changes dramatically, though initially for physical reasons: he leaves her tired, hungry, and overwhelmed. Kate's capitulation on the journey back to Padua and her lecture on obedience at the end are sometimes prepared for by actors who imply that these two are consciously playacting all along. Petruchio's speeches reflect a tug-of-war between brutal, near-violent behavior and the kind, gentle words that even Kate adopts at the end of the play, words that may mark the beginning of a happily married relationship now that peace has succeeded the couple's initial war.

Baptista, father to the girls, is looking to marry off his daughters to the highest bidder. He can be played quite sternly as a cold man looking to enlarge his landholdings and get the best bargain possible through pairing off his marriageable girls. He has also been interpreted as a warm and avuncular traditional father, as bound by social codes surrounding the marriage contract as are his daughters. He can also be played as an exasperated father who is simply at his wits' end. Bianca's three suitors are comic archetypes: Gremio is listed as a pantaloon or capering fool, Hortensio is an amorous fop, and Lucentio is a stock young lover. Many productions draw from these roots in Roman comedy and stage the play as a kind of topsy-turvy carnival. The largest of the secondary roles goes to Tranio, the clever servant who disguises himself as his master Lucentio, while the latter woos Bianca.

Sources and Inspirations

The "Other" Shrew

Shakespeare's comedy, as it was first printed in 1623 in the First Folio, stands in a still-contested relationship to an earlier play printed in 1594 called *The Taming of A Shrew*. That comedy, with different names for some characters, has a framing plot that does satisfactorily complete itself with the Sly character setting off for home, having learned from the play how to tame his own wife. This work may have been an earlier version of Shakespeare's play *The Taming of the Shrew*, a different play altogether derived from similar sources, or, most likely, a script reconstructed from memory from

Shakespeare's comedy, reported by actors, and changed by the person who wrote down the dialogue. Scholars do not agree on this issue. They do agree upon the various sources from which Shakespeare took each of his three plots and then closely wove into the fabric of the play that has come down to us.

Roman Comedy

The plot involving Lucentio and Bianca comes from George Gascoigne's comedy *Supposes*, itself a translation of Ludovico Ariosto's *I Suppositi*. Ariosto's work is based upon two Roman classical sources, Terence's *Eunuchus* and Plautus's *Captivi;* these ancient plays account for the farcical elements of trickery and disguise (hence the "supposes" of the title), and the stock nature of characters such as Hortensio and Gremio. Many directors cast actors adept at classical clowning in the roles, as they do in Shakespeare's earlier *The Comedy of Errors*, also based upon comedies by Plautus. Shakespeare's tone, at least in the Bianca plot, is less ribald, however, than in the earlier *Errors* and the Roman source comedies.

The Induction, with its story of a beggar tricked into believing himself a wealthy lord, is a recurring tale found in the *Arabian Nights* and in several later tellings in French and English.

Popular Ballads

The Kate-Petruchio plot draws upon an ancient comic tradition of misogyny that reaches back at least to Chaucer's depiction of the Wife of Bath and the representation of Noah's wife in medieval Corpus Christi plays. The tradition was continued in folktales and ballads popular during Shakespeare's day. Since 1964, when scholar Richard Hosley proposed that Shakespeare likely borrowed from the ballad *A Merry Jest of a Shrewd and Curst Wife Lapped in Morel's Skin, for her Good Behavior*, others have explored this populist tradition of misogyny, most notably Frances E. Dolan in the Bedford edition, *Texts and Contexts*. In the ballad, printed around 1550, the husband beats his wife until she bleeds, then wraps her in the salted skin of an old work horse named Morel. The shrewish wife has a gentle younger sister whom their father favors. The shrew's suitor ignores her father's warnings of the girl's fiery nature and goes about taming her. At a dinner celebration afterward, he is congratulated for his success. As Dolan's chapter on shrew-taming literature shows (244–326), *A Merry Jest* may not have been the only source for the taming plot, for the play comes during a period of English history when society was preoccupied with women who posed a threat to the patriarchal system in which men controlled property and exercised authority in both domestic and political settings. The

marriageable women in *Shrew* (like the daughters later in *A Midsummer Night's Dream*, *Twelfth Night*, *Othello*, *Hamlet*, and *Lear*) have no living mothers. When Katharina is at Petruchio's home, his servants and even an ill-used tailor who supplies a rejected dress for Katharina become part of the play-acting in this disciplinary domestic drama. "Katherine is without allies or even sympathetic bystanders" (Orgel, Introduction, xxxix). And though women, then as now, were much more likely to be victims of male violence, new legislation in the 1590s, increased rates of prosecution of women, and ballads, folktales, jokes, and plays about assertive women suggest that society found such disorderly women as Kate both threatening and fascinating.

Language and Silence

Each of the three plots has its characteristic forms of speech. The Induction begins with Sly arguing with the Hostess in earthy prose over the damage he's caused: "I'll not budge an inch, boy," he says before passing out. The Lord, who arrives, discussing with his huntsman the merits of various sporting dogs, adopts a courtly style of blank verse as he orders the deception of Sly who now lies "like a swine" and soon will be persuaded he's a lord:

> Carry him gently to my fairest chamber,
> And hang it round with all my wanton pictures.
> Balm his foul head in warm distillèd waters,
> And burn sweet wood to make the lodging sweet.
> Procure me music ready when he wakes,
> To make a dulcet and a heavenly sound.
>
> (Induction 1.45–50)

Surrounded by such seductive sights and sounds, Sly awakes from his stupor and continues to speak in his blunt prose: "I have not more doublets than backs, no more stockings than legs, no more shoes than feet—nay sometime more feet than shoes, or such shoes as my toes look through the overleather" (Ind.2.8–12). But once he has been persuaded that he is "a lord and nothing but a lord" with a "lady far more beautiful / than any in this waning age," Sly adopts verse speaking as well:

> Am I a lord? And have I such a lady?
> Or do I dream? Or have I dreamed till now?
> I do not sleep: I see, I hear, I speak,
> I smell sweet savors, and I feel soft things.
> Upon my life, I am a lord indeed,
> And not a tinker nor Christopher Sly.
>
> (Ind.2.68–73)

Clothes, scents, and sense impressions not only promote the man to lord, but also transform his language.

In the Bianca-Lucentio plot, the romantic wooer speaks the language and imagery of Petrarchan love poetry. The servant Tranio, for instance, asks Lucentio whether it be possible that "love should of a sudden take such hold." His master replies:

> Oh, Tranio, till I found it to be true,
> I never thought it possible or likely.
> But see, while idly I stood looking on,
> I found the effect of love in idleness,
> And now in plainness do confess to thee,
> That art to me as secret and as dear
> As Anna to the Queen of Carthage was,
> Tranio, I burn, I pine, I perish, Tranio,
> If I achieve not this young modest girl . . .
> Tranio, I saw her coral lips to move,
> And with her breath she did perfume the air.
> Sacred and sweet was all I saw in her.
>
> (1.1.149–156, 175–177)

Lucentio has fallen in love at first sight, for he has seen Bianca side by side with the fiery Kate ("in the other's silence do I see / Maid's mild behavior and sobriety") and has heard her speak just these four lines to her sister and father:

> Sister, content you in my discontent.—
> Sir, to your pleasure humbly I subscribe.
> My books and instruments shall be my company,
> On them to look and practice by myself.
>
> (1.1.80–83)

Bianca's public voice barely rises above a whisper, although perhaps we are to understand that it is she who is actually willful, getting the man she wants by pretending to be pliable.

Kate and Petruchio speak a far more earthy, if often comically embellished, rhetoric. Petruchio's servant Grumio describes his master's manner of speaking when he tells Hortensio that if Kate knew his master she would know that scolding him would have no effect at all. The servant reports that once Petruchio begins, he proceeds with his verbal "rope tricks," throwing "a figure" (meaning a figure of speech) in her face enough to disfigure her with it "that she shall have no more eyes to see withal than a cat" (1.2.112–114). In their first exchanges Kate and Petruchio both employ such figures and elaborate deftly upon them—a sign, perhaps, of their compatibility. She immediately meets and matches his challenges, even to his puns filled with sexual innuendo. Shakespeare's writing here is not as crude as that in the Roman comedies, but nonetheless a series of jokes about intercourse, childbearing, the male organ, and cuckoldry make their way into the dialogue. The couple's farcical competition already involves punning and simile making; it is not very dif-

ferent from, though it is less intellectually witty than, the competitive banter that will appear in later plays—the verbal gamesmanship of Beatrice and Benedick in *Much Ado About Nothing*, and the battle of similes between Falstaff and Prince Hal in the tavern scenes of the *Henry IV* plays. The sexual directness of the Kate-Petruchio plot stands in high contrast to the romanticism of the Bianca-Lucentio plot as these courtships first present themselves in language.

As the comedy develops, and as Kate comes to realize that she is being wooed and then tamed by a man she takes to be mad, her verbal shrewishness ultimately declines. Once wedded, and subjected to the physical taming rituals, she intermittently responds with silence or a kind of empathetic sincerity, as when she intervenes on behalf of Petruchio's cruelly treated servants. These moments when she is silent have proven puzzling to critics, actors, and directors. When Petruchio insists that they are going to marry, she says she would rather see him hanged than marry him (2.1.292). Yet she remains silent while Petruchio explains her reticence as part of their a compact: " 'Tis bargained twixt us twain, being alone, / That she shall still be curst in company." After expressing the humiliation she feels when Petruchio does not come to the wedding, she retreats again into silence, just as she does after he arrives and refuses to attend the wedding feast. She hears his "She is my goods, my chattels" speech and quietly leaves with him. Actresses sometimes use gestures, winks, and nods to suggest she is of another mind; Shakespeare does not directly signal such irony in the words. Katharina is never seen alone explaining the motives for her silence or her seeming transformation from shrew to docile wife. Petruchio, on the other hand, often soliloquizes and speaks twice as many lines overall as Katharina. When Kate gives her final speech admonishing wives to obey, this very public declaration comes so unprepared for that actresses and readers often interpret it as just that, a public speech which likely contrasts with the more egalitarian private behavior of this newly loving couple.

Themes and Issues

Women's Roles and Rights: Then and Now

Despite the powerful political roles played by Queen Mary and Queen Elizabeth, women during Shakespeare's time (as historians have shown) had few alternatives besides marriage. Katharina twice indicates that she understands what is expected of her and acknowledges that she does want to get married. She complains bitterly to her father, for instance, that his favoritism towards Bianca is destroying her own chances of finding a husband:

> Nay, now I see
> She is your treasure, she must have a husband;
> I must dance barefoot on her wedding day,
> And for your love to her lead apes in hell.
> Talk not to me. I will go sit and weep
> Till I can find occasion of revenge.
>
> (2.1.31–36)

Knowing that marriage is her fate, Katharina falls several times into silences, which can be interpreted as moments of reflection as she learns to control her assertiveness.

In demanding that Kate forego the wedding feast and come with him immediately, Petruchio says that others may do as Kate asks and carouse at the feast, but he has different plans for her. "But for my bonny Kate, she must with me. / Nay, look not big, nor stamp, nor stare, nor fret," he says, the implied stage direction suggesting Kate *has* glared and stamped her feet at his command. Then in an infamous speech, he describes the Elizabethan concept of marriage as allied to property rights:

> I will be master of what is mine own.
> She is my goods, my chattels; she is my house,
> My household stuff, my field, my barn,
> My horse, my ox, my ass, my anything;
> And here she stands, touch her whoever dare.
>
> (3.2.230–234)

The reaction of the others onstage is not shock, but laughter. Gremio says, "Went they not quickly I should die with laughing." Tranio, still disguised as Lucentio, says, "Of all mad matches never was the like." And Bianca thinks jocularly that they are well matched: "That being mad herself, she's madly mated" (3.2.243ff.). Clearly Petruchio's unreasonable demands and Kate's silent acquiescence are accepted, if not expected, in this historical context.

Fathers and Daughters; Men and Marriage

According to Elizabethan custom, Baptista's daughters are his property. Kate is such a bad bargain that he quickly consents to her marrying Petruchio, the only man who has asked, remarking, "Faith, gentlemen, now I play a merchant's part, / And venture madly on a desperate mart" (2.1.324–325). Tranio counters by comparing Kate to stale meat or bread: " 'Twas a commodity that lay" rotting on his hands, and now will bring him gain. Baptista says his only gain is "quiet in the match," for he will be relieved of his noxious

daughter. When Baptista turns to the more "valuable" daughter, Bianca, he opens business negotiations:

> Content you, gentlemen, I will compound this strife.
> 'Tis deeds must win the prize, and he of both
> That can assure my daughter greatest dower
> Shall have my Bianca's love.
> Say, Signor Gremio, what can you assure her?
>
> (2.1.339–343)

No one in the play balks at such bargaining; it is the way of their world. Similarly, Petruchio has come to Padua to "wive and thrive." When Hortensio jokingly recommends the local shrew as a match, Petruchio says he'll take any "rich enough to be [my] wife" no matter how ugly, cursed, shrewish, and turbulent she may be, for

> I come to wive it wealthily in Padua;
> If wealthily, then happily in Padua.
>
> (1.2.74–75)

Katharina brings property with her, but she will no longer own nor control that property—or her husband's—once she is married.

In addition to representing these notions of women as property and conveyors of property and of marriage as a financial contract between fathers and husbands, the play also outlines the taming strategies Petruchio will use to gain mastery over Katharina. Falconry provides the dominant imagery for this process (see Dolan, 304–311). Part of his strategy is to insist (in words) that she is not a shrew, thus offering an ideal image of who she might be: the woman he desires, rather than the one everyone reports she is. A second image he presents to her is of his own terrible treatment of her and his servants during the wedding (3.2) and at his house (4.1). Many critics have remarked that Petruchio is here taming a shrew by behaving like one. Petruchio can get away with this kind of behavior and be considered merry and mad for it; Katharina, on the other hand, cannot (see Hodgdon).

Role-Playing: Supposes

In all three plots, a supposition or impersonation induces others to act a certain way. Language and disguise are used to deceive others into changing behavior, with the theme unfolding at three different levels of complexity. In the Induction, Christopher Sly is tricked into believing (and acting) as if he were someone else, a long-slumbering lord, married to a woman who is actually a young male page in disguise. The impersonation is easily forced upon him from outside, simply for the sport of the noblemen and hunters who have found him. Once the "pleasant comedy" begins, the impersonations are multiple in the wooing of Bianca. Her young suitor Lucentio exchanges clothing with his servant Tranio and, thus disguised, pretends to be the Latin teacher Cambio. Hortensio impersonates a music teacher, and Lucentio's servant Tranio most effectively impersonates his master. These disguises both serve the plotting and raise questions about the nature of artifice in the social hierarchy. If, with a good wash and change of clothes, a drunken tinker can seem a lord, then what is nobility? And if a servant can seem a proper suitor, then what is the moral basis for the social hierarchy?

In the more psychologically complex impersonations, Kate has adopted the personality of a classic shrew. We know very little of her motives, for during many moments when she might be expected to speak, she is actually silent. Yet there are some hints, which actors and directors have elaborated. Kate's persona may have come in response to her father's rejection of her spirit and his obvious preference for the passive younger sister Bianca. Or perhaps the limited roles afforded women then have driven Kate into the assertive pose as a defense. Petruchio, seen as affable and merry in his first scenes, takes on the part of both an antic ruffian and a verbal gentleman in relationship to Katharina. In his first scene with her, he reflects back to Kate the image of the docile gentlewoman he wishes her to become, yet problematically; it's only when he's starved her and deprived her of sleep that she willingly adopts that new persona of an obedient and loyal wife.

Staging Challenges

The Induction Scenes

Because the Sly plot virtually disappears after two scenes, directors and filmmakers often cut the framing story, and thus deprive the play of one of its metatheatrical layers. Others have borrowed ideas and dialogue from *A Shrew* to end Shakespeare's play. Thus amended, the Sly plot completes itself with the character merrily leaving for home to practice upon his own wife the taming he's seen in the "pleasant comedy." One of many clever (and also economical) solutions to staging the Induction originated in England and has made its way to America. In the summer of 2002, director John Rando (a Tony Award winner for *Urinetown*) fooled audiences at San Diego's Old Globe Theater. As his *Shrew* was about to open on the theater's outdoor stage, there was a commotion in the aisles. An usher was unable to prevent a drunken man, in punk leather clothing, from barging into the theater with a female companion who appeared to be his girlfriend. Actors milling about on stage took notice, and patrons, unaware of the ruse, nervously looked away as the usher

and then the actors spoke to the drunk and eventually forced him on stage, dressed him in Renaissance costume, and sat him down to watch their play. They gave him a script as well. When this man, named Christopher Sly, sobered up, he joined the onstage action by playing Petruchio; his "girlfriend" played Kate.

Boys Playing Kate and Bianca

Before the Restoration, when Sly asked "Am I a lord? / And have I such a lady?" his words would have called attention to the fact that this "lady" was actually a beardless boy playing the role of a page playing a woman. Thus Bartholomew the Page was equivalent in at least the reality of his gender to Kate and Bianca, who would also have been played by boys. Rather than disguising this knowledge, Shakespeare several times highlights it—in the Induction, in Katharina's accusations of feminine playacting to Bianca, and most elaborately in Katharina's final lecture on the proper nature and role of women.

> Why are our bodies soft, and weak, and smooth,
> Unapt to toil and trouble in the world,
> But that our soft conditions and our hearts
> Should well agree with our external parts?
>
> (5.2.169–172)

Whether interpreted ironically or whimsically or "straight," this speech, as delivered by a boy actor, would have conveyed at least some awareness that the obedient wife Kate may be as much an adopted role as her earlier shrew persona—and perhaps as far from her real nature as the boy actor's is from a real woman's. As critic Karen Newman notes in her essay appended to the Folger edition of the play, at the moment when the ideology of women's silence and submission is most powerfully articulated, "we find a woman, or at any rate a boy playing a woman's part, speaking forcefully and in public the longest speech in the play, at the most dramatic moment in the action. In short, Kate's speaking as she does contradicts the very sentiments she affirms" (234).

Locales, Interiors, Exteriors, and Roadways

Shrew moves. The action occurs in three different places in two different countries, and much of Act Four is set on the road leading from Petruchio's country house back to Padua from Verona. The Induction requires a second story or gallery space above from which Sly can watch the play. Few productions (excepting those well-budgeted enough to employ an indoor/outdoor revolving turntable) actually take the action indoors, except to show a long table in Petruchio's house upon which food is set before Katharina—and then taken away from her. The return to Padua very often involves a horse or mule, which is sometimes comically embodied by a two-man vaudevillian animal. The scene can be played in front of a curtain, with the couple crossing over from one side of the stage to the other. Shakespeare's theater, of course, had no such curtain. Lighting can also serve to isolate the moving figures as they make their way, arguing all the while, from the house of Katharina's husband back to the house of her father. If a fabricated horse is part of the procession, Katharina usually walks beside the beast while Petruchio rides. Only when she says the sun is the moon and the moon the sun is he pleased enough with her submission to allow her to ride.

The Taming of the Shrew

[*Dramatis Personae*

CHRISTOPHER SLY, *a tinker and beggar,*
HOSTESS *of an alehouse,*
A LORD,
A PAGE, SERVANTS, HUNTSMEN,
PLAYERS,
}
Persons in the Induction

BAPTISTA, *a rich gentleman of Padua*
KATHARINA, *the shrew, also called Katharine and Kate, Baptista's elder daughter*
BIANCA, *Baptista's younger daughter*

PETRUCHIO, *a gentleman of Verona, suitor to Katharina*
GRUMIO, *Petruchio's servant*
CURTIS, NATHANIEL, PHILIP, JOSEPH, NICHOLAS, PETER, *and other servants of Petruchio*

GREMIO, *elderly suitor to Bianca*
HORTENSIO, *suitor to Bianca*
LUCENTIO, *son of Vincentio, in love with Bianca*
TRANIO, *Lucentio's servant*
BIONDELLO, *Lucentio's servant*
VINCENTIO, *a gentleman of Pisa*
A PEDANT *(or Merchant) of Mantua*
A WIDOW, *courted by Hortensio*

A TAILOR
A HABERDASHER
AN OFFICER
Other Servants of Baptista and Lucentio

SCENE: *Padua, and Petruchio's country house in Italy; the Induction is located in the countryside and at a Lord's house in England*]

[Induction.1]

Enter Beggar (Christopher Sly) and Hostess.

SLY   I'll feeze you, in faith.   1
HOSTESS   A pair of stocks, you rogue!   2
SLY   You're a baggage. The Slys are no rogues. Look in   3
the chronicles; we came in with Richard Conqueror.   4
Therefore *paucas pallabris*, let the world slide. Sessa!   5
HOSTESS   You will not pay for the glasses you have
burst?

SLY   No, not a denier. Go by, Saint Jeronimy, go to thy   8
cold bed and warm thee.   9
HOSTESS   I know my remedy; I must go fetch the third-   10
borough.   [*Exit.*]   11
SLY   Third, or fourth, or fifth borough, I'll answer him   12
by law. I'll not budge an inch, boy. Let him come, and   13
kindly.   *Falls asleep.*   14

Wind horns [*within*]. *Enter a Lord from hunting, with his train.*

Induction.1. Location: Before an alehouse and, subsequently, before the Lord's house nearby. (See lines 75, 135.)
1 feeze you i.e., fix you, get even with you   2 A . . . stocks i.e., I'll have you put in the stocks   3 baggage contemptible woman or prostitute.   4 Richard (Sly's mistake for "William.")   5 paucas pallabris i.e., *pocas palabras,* "few words." (Spanish.)   Sessa (Of doubtful meaning; perhaps "be quiet," "cease," or "let it go.")

8 denier French copper coin of little value.   Go . . . Jeronimy (Sly's variation of an often quoted line from Kyd's *The Spanish Tragedy,* urging caution.)   8–9 go . . . thee (Perhaps a proverb; see *King Lear,* 3.4.46–7.)   10–11 thirdborough constable.   12 Third (Sly shows his ignorance; the *third* in "thirdborough" derives from the Old English word *frith,* "peace.")   13 by law in the law courts.   14 kindly welcome. (Said ironically.)   14.1 *Wind* Blow   14.2 *train* retinue.

LORD
Huntsman, I charge thee, tender well my hounds.   15
Breathe Merriman—the poor cur is embossed—   16
And couple Clowder with the deep-mouthed brach.   17
Saw'st thou not, boy, how Silver made it good   18
At the hedge corner, in the coldest fault?   19
I would not lose the dog for twenty pound.

FIRST HUNTSMAN
Why, Bellman is as good as he, my lord.
He cried upon it at the merest loss,   22
And twice today picked out the dullest scent.
Trust me, I take him for the better dog.

LORD
Thou art a fool. If Echo were as fleet,
I would esteem him worth a dozen such.
But sup them well and look unto them all.   27
Tomorrow I intend to hunt again.

FIRST HUNTSMAN   I will, my lord.

LORD [seeing Sly]
What's here? One dead, or drunk? See, doth he breathe?

SECOND HUNTSMAN [examining Sly]
He breathes, my lord. Were he not warmed with ale,
This were a bed but cold to sleep so soundly.

LORD
Oh, monstrous beast, how like a swine he lies!
Grim death, how foul and loathsome is thine image!   34
Sirs, I will practice on this drunken man.   35
What think you, if he were conveyed to bed,
Wrapped in sweet clothes, rings put upon his fingers,   37
A most delicious banquet by his bed,   38
And brave attendants near him when he wakes,   39
Would not the beggar then forget himself?

FIRST HUNTSMAN
Believe me, lord, I think he cannot choose.   41

SECOND HUNTSMAN
It would seem strange unto him when he waked.

LORD
Even as a flatt'ring dream or worthless fancy.   43
Then take him up, and manage well the jest.
Carry him gently to my fairest chamber,
And hang it round with all my wanton pictures.
Balm his foul head in warm distillèd waters,   47
And burn sweet wood to make the lodging sweet.
Procure me music ready when he wakes,
To make a dulcet and a heavenly sound.   50
And if he chance to speak, be ready straight,   51
And with a low submissive reverence   52
Say, "What is it Your Honor will command?"

Let one attend him with a silver basin
Full of rosewater and bestrewed with flowers;
Another bear the ewer, the third a diaper,   56
And say, "Will 't please Your Lordship cool your hands?"
Someone be ready with a costly suit,
And ask him what apparel he will wear;
Another tell him of his hounds and horse,   60
And that his lady mourns at his disease.   61
Persuade him that he hath been lunatic,
And when he says he is, say that he dreams,   63
For he is nothing but a mighty lord.
This do, and do it kindly, gentle sirs.   65
It will be pastime passing excellent,   66
If it be husbanded with modesty.   67

FIRST HUNTSMAN
My lord, I warrant you we will play our part
As he shall think by our true diligence   69
He is no less than what we say he is.

LORD
Take him up gently, and to bed with him,
And each one to his office when he wakes.   72
        [Some bear out Sly.] Sound trumpets [within].
Sirrah, go see what trumpet 'tis that sounds.   73
                [Exit a Servingman.]
Belike some noble gentleman that means,   74
Traveling some journey, to repose him here.

        Enter [a] Servingman.

How now? Who is it?

SERVINGMAN   An't please Your Honor, players   76
That offer service to Your Lordship.

        Enter Players.

LORD
Bid them come near.—Now, fellows, you are welcome.

PLAYERS   We thank Your Honor.

LORD
Do you intend to stay with me tonight?

FIRST PLAYER
So please Your Lordship to accept our duty.   81

LORD
With all my heart. This fellow I remember
Since once he played a farmer's eldest son.—
'Twas where you wooed the gentlewoman so well.
I have forgot your name, but sure that part
Was aptly fitted and naturally performed.

SECOND PLAYER
I think 'twas Soto that Your Honor means.

LORD
'Tis very true. Thou didst it excellent.
Well, you are come to me in happy time,   89

---

15 **tender** care for   16 **Breathe Merriman** Give the dog Merriman time to recover its breath. **embossed** foaming at the mouth from exhaustion   17 **couple** leash together. **deep-mouthed brach** bitch hound with the deep baying voice.   18 **made it good** i.e., picked up the lost scent   19 **in the coldest fault** when the scent was lost by a *fault* or break in the scent.   22 **cried . . . loss** bayed to signal his recovery of the scent after it had been completely lost   27 **sup them well** feed them a good supper   34 **image** likeness (since sleep was regarded as a likeness of death).   35 **practice on** play a joke on   37 **sweet** perfumed   38 **banquet** light repast   39 **brave** finely arrayed   41 **cannot choose** is bound to.   43 **fancy** flight of imagination.   47 **Balm** Bathe, anoint   50 **dulcet** melodious   51 **straight** at once   52 **reverence** bow

56 **ewer** jug, pitcher. **diaper** towel   60 **horse** horses   61 **disease** i.e., mental derangement.   63 **when . . . is** i.e., when he says he must be mad indeed. (The *is* is stressed.)   65 **kindly** naturally (and thus persuasively). **gentle** kind   66 **passing** surpassingly   67 **husbanded with modesty** managed with decorum.   69 **As** so that. **by** as a result of   72 **office** duty   73 **Sirrah** (Usual form of address to inferiors.)   74 **Belike** Perhaps   76 **An't** If it   81 **So please** If it please. **duty** expression of respect and dutiful service.   89 **happy** opportune

The rather for I have some sport in hand   90
Wherein your cunning can assist me much.   91
There is a lord will hear you play tonight.
But I am doubtful of your modesties,   93
Lest, overeeying of his odd behavior—   94
For yet His Honor never heard a play—
You break into some merry passion   96
And so offend him; for I tell you, sirs,
If you should smile, he grows impatient.

FIRST PLAYER
Fear not, my lord, we can contain ourselves,
Were he the veriest antic in the world.   100

LORD [*to a Servingman*]
Go, sirrah, take them to the buttery,   101
And give them friendly welcome every one.
Let them want nothing that my house affords.   103
                              Exit one with the Players.
Sirrah, go you to Barthol'mew my page,
And see him dressed in all suits like a lady.   105
That done, conduct him to the drunkard's chamber,
And call him "madam," do him obeisance.   107
Tell him from me, as he will win my love,   108
He bear himself with honorable action
Such as he hath observed in noble ladies
Unto their lords by them accomplishèd.   111
Such duty to the drunkard let him do
With soft low tongue and lowly courtesy,
And say, "What is't Your Honor will command,
Wherein your lady and your humble wife
May show her duty and make known her love?"
And then with kind embracements, tempting kisses,
And with declining head into his bosom,
Bid him shed tears, as being overjoyed
To see her noble lord restored to health,
Who for this seven years hath esteemèd him   121
No better than a poor and loathsome beggar.
And if the boy have not a woman's gift
To rain a shower of commanded tears,
An onion will do well for such a shift,   125
Which in a napkin being close conveyed   126
Shall in despite enforce a watery eye.   127
See this dispatched with all the haste thou canst.
Anon I'll give thee more instructions.   129
                              Exit a Servingman.
I know the boy will well usurp the grace,   130
Voice, gait, and action of a gentlewoman.
I long to hear him call the drunkard husband,
And how my men will stay themselves from laughter 133

When they do homage to this simple peasant.
I'll in to counsel them. Haply my presence   135
May well abate the overmerry spleen   136
Which otherwise would grow into extremes.
                              [*Exeunt.*]

[Induction.2]

*Enter aloft the drunkard [Sly], with attendants;
some with apparel, basin, and ewer and other
appurtenances; and Lord.*

SLY   For God's sake, a pot of small ale.   1
FIRST SERVINGMAN
Will't please Your Lordship drink a cup of sack?   2
SECOND SERVINGMAN
Will't please Your Honor taste of these conserves?   3
THIRD SERVINGMAN
What raiment will Your Honor wear today?
SLY   I am Christophero Sly. Call not me "Honor" nor
"Lordship." I ne'er drank sack in my life; and if you
give me any conserves, give me conserves of beef.   7
Ne'er ask me what raiment I'll wear, for I have no
more doublets than backs, no more stockings than   9
legs, nor no more shoes than feet—nay, sometimes
more feet than shoes, or such shoes as my toes look   11
through the overleather.   12
LORD
Heaven cease this idle humor in Your Honor!   13
Oh, that a mighty man of such descent,
Of such possessions and so high esteem,
Should be infusèd with so foul a spirit!
SLY   What, would you make me mad? Am not I Christopher Sly, old Sly's son of Burton-heath, by birth a   18
peddler, by education a cardmaker, by transmutation   19
a bearherd, and now by present profession a tinker?   20
Ask Marian Hacket, the fat alewife of Wincot, if she   21
know me not. If she say I am not fourteen pence on   22
the score for sheer ale, score me up for the lyingest   23
knave in Christendom. What, I am not bestraught: 24
here's—
THIRD SERVINGMAN
Oh, this it is that makes your lady mourn!
SECOND SERVINGMAN
Oh, this is it that makes your servants droop!

135 I'll in I'll go in   **136 spleen** mood. (The spleen was the supposed
seat of laughter and anger.)
Induction.2. Location: A bedchamber in the Lord's house.
0.1 *aloft* i.e., in the gallery over the rear facade of the stage   **1 small**
weak (and therefore cheap)   **2 sack** sweet Spanish wine (suited for a
gentleman to drink).   **3 conserves** candied fruit.   **7 conserves of
beef** preserved (salted) beef.   **9 doublets** men's jackets   **11 as** that
12 overleather upper leather of the shoe.   **13 idle humor** foolish
whim   **18 Burton-heath** (Perhaps Barton on the Heath, about sixteen
miles from Stratford, the home of Shakespeare's aunt.)   **19 cardmaker** maker of cards or combs used to prepare wool for spinning
20 bearherd keeper of a performing bear.   **tinker** pot mender.
21 alewife woman who keeps an alehouse.   **Wincot** small village about
four miles from Stratford. (The parish register shows that there were
Hackets living there in 1591.)   **22–3 on the score** in debt (since such
reckonings were originally notched or scored on a stick)   **23 sheer** nothing but.   **score me up for** reckon me to be   **24 bestraught** distracted

90 The rather for the more so since   **91 cunning** professional skill
93 doubtful apprehensive.   **modesties** discretion, self-control   **94
overeeying** of witnessing   **96 merry passion** outburst of laughter
100 veriest antic oddest buffoon or eccentric   **101 buttery** pantry, or
a room for storing liquor (in butts) and other provisions   **103 want**
lack   **105 in all suits** in every detail. (With a pun on *suits* of clothes.)
107 do him obeisance show him dutiful respect.   **108 him** i.e., the
page Bartholomew.   **as he will** if he wishes to   **111 by them accomplishèd** performed by the ladies.   **121 him** himself   **125 shift** purpose   **126 napkin** handkerchief.   **close** secretly   **127 in despite** i.e.,
notwithstanding a natural inclination to laugh rather than cry   **129
Anon** Soon   **130 usurp** assume   **133 And how** i.e., and to see how

LORD
    Hence comes it that your kindred shuns your house,
    As beaten hence by your strange lunacy.   29
    Oh, noble lord, bethink thee of thy birth.
    Call home thy ancient thoughts from banishment,   31
    And banish hence these abject lowly dreams.
    Look how thy servants do attend on thee,
    Each in his office ready at thy beck.   34
    Wilt thou have music? Hark, Apollo plays,   *Music.*   35
    And twenty cagèd nightingales do sing.
    Or wilt thou sleep? We'll have thee to a couch,
    Softer and sweeter than the lustful bed
    On purpose trimmed up for Semiramis.   39
    Say thou wilt walk; we will bestrew the ground.   40
    Or wilt thou ride? Thy horses shall be trapped,   41
    Their harness studded all with gold and pearl.
    Dost thou love hawking? Thou hast hawks will soar
    Above the morning lark. Or wilt thou hunt?
    Thy hounds shall make the welkin answer them   45
    And fetch shrill echoes from the hollow earth.
FIRST SERVINGMAN
    Say thou wilt course, thy greyhounds are as swift   47
    As breathèd stags, ay, fleeter than the roe.   48
SECOND SERVINGMAN
    Dost thou love pictures? We will fetch thee straight
    Adonis painted by a running brook,   50
    And Cytherea all in sedges hid,   51
    Which seem to move and wanton with her breath,   52
    Even as the waving sedges play wi'th'wind.
LORD
    We'll show thee Io as she was a maid,   54
    And how she was beguilèd and surprised,
    As lively painted as the deed was done.   56
THIRD SERVINGMAN
    Or Daphne roaming through a thorny wood,   57
    Scratching her legs that one shall swear she bleeds,
    And at that sight shall sad Apollo weep,
    So workmanly the blood and tears are drawn.   60
LORD
    Thou art a lord, and nothing but a lord.
    Thou hast a lady far more beautiful
    Than any woman in this waning age.   63
FIRST SERVINGMAN
    And till the tears that she hath shed for thee
    Like envious floods o'errun her lovely face,   65
    She was the fairest creature in the world;
    And yet she is inferior to none.   67

SLY
    Am I a lord? And have I such a lady?
    Or do I dream? Or have I dreamed till now?
    I do not sleep: I see, I hear, I speak,
    I smell sweet savors, and I feel soft things.
    Upon my life, I am a lord indeed,
    And not a tinker nor Christopher Sly.
    Well, bring our lady hither to our sight,
    And once again a pot o'th' smallest ale.
SECOND SERVINGMAN
    Will 't please Your Mightiness to wash your hands?
    Oh, how we joy to see your wit restored!   77
    Oh, that once more you knew but what you are!   78
    These fifteen years you have been in a dream,
    Or when you waked, so waked as if you slept.
SLY
    These fifteen years! By my fay, a goodly nap.   81
    But did I never speak of all that time?   82
FIRST SERVINGMAN
    Oh, yes, my lord, but very idle words;
    For though you lay here in this goodly chamber,
    Yet would you say ye were beaten out of door,
    And rail upon the hostess of the house,   86
    And say you would present her at the leet   87
    Because she brought stone jugs and no sealed quarts.   88
    Sometimes you would call out for Cicely Hacket.
SLY
    Ay, the woman's maid of the house.
THIRD SERVINGMAN
    Why, sir, you know no house, nor no such maid,
    Nor no such men as you have reckoned up,
    As Stephen Sly, and old John Naps of Greet,   93
    And Peter Turf, and Henry Pimpernel,
    And twenty more such names and men as these,
    Which never were, nor no man ever saw.
SLY
    Now Lord be thankèd for my good amends!   97
ALL
    Amen.

        Enter [the Page as a] lady, with Attendants.

SLY   I thank thee. Thou shalt not lose by it.   98
PAGE
    How fares my noble lord?
SLY   Marry, I fare well,   99
    For here is cheer enough. Where is my wife?
PAGE
    Here, noble lord. What is thy will with her?
SLY
    Are you my wife, and will not call me husband?

---

29 As as if **31 ancient** former **34 beck** nod. **35 Apollo** i.e., as god of
music **39 Semiramis** legendary queen of Assyria, famous for her
voluptuousness. **40 bestrew** i.e., scatter rushes on **41 trapped**
adorned **45 welkin** sky, heavens **47 course** hunt the hare
48 breathèd in good physical condition, with good wind. **roe** small,
swift deer. **50 Adonis** a young huntsman with whom Venus is vainly
in love. (See Ovid's *Metamorphoses*, Book 10, and Shakespeare's poem,
Venus and Adonis.) **51 Cytherea** one of the names for Venus (because
of her association with the island of Cythera). **sedges** grassy marsh
plants **52 wanton** play seductively **54 Io** a woman who, according
to Ovid, was seduced by Jove concealed in a mist and afterwards transformed into a heifer **56 as** as if **57 Daphne** a wood nymph beloved
by Apollo, changed by Diana into a laurel tree to preserve her from
Apollo's assault (*Metamorphoses*, Book 1) **60 workmanly** skillfully
63 waning degenerate **65 envious** spiteful **67 yet** even today

77 wit mental faculties **78 knew but** only knew **81 fay** faith **82 of**
during **86 house** tavern **87 present** bring accusation against. **leet**
manorial court **88 sealed quarts** quart containers officially stamped
as a guarantee of that capacity. (The irregular stoneware quarts might
be used to cheat customers.) **93 Stephen . . . Greet** (A Stephen Sly
lived in Stratford during Shakespeare's day. *Greet* is a Gloucestershire
hamlet not far from Stratford. The Folio reading, "Greece," is an easy
misreading if Shakespeare wrote "Greete.") **97 amends** recovery
98 Thou . . . it i.e., I will reward your solicitude toward me.
99 Marry (A mild oath, derived from "by Mary.") **fare well** (1) am
fine (2) have plenty of good *cheer* (line 100), refreshment

My men should call me "lord"; I am your goodman. 103

PAGE

My husband and my lord, my lord and husband;
I am your wife in all obedience.

SLY

I know it well.—What must I call her?

LORD   Madam.

SLY   Al'ce madam, or Joan madam?

LORD

Madam, and nothing else. So lords call ladies.

SLY

Madam wife, they say that I have dreamed
And slept above some fifteen year or more.

PAGE

Ay, and the time seems thirty unto me,
Being all this time abandoned from your bed. 112

SLY

'Tis much.—Servants, leave me and her alone.—
Madam, undress you and come now to bed.

PAGE

Thrice-noble lord, let me entreat of you
To pardon me yet for a night or two,
Or, if not so, until the sun be set.
For your physicians have expressly charged,
In peril to incur your former malady,
That I should yet absent me from your bed.
I hope this reason stands for my excuse.

SLY   Ay, it stands so that I may hardly tarry so long. But 122
I would be loath to fall into my dreams again. I will
therefore tarry in despite of the flesh and the blood.

Enter a [Servingman as] messenger.

SERVINGMAN

Your Honor's players, hearing your amendment,
Are come to play a pleasant comedy,
For so your doctors hold it very meet, 127
Seeing too much sadness hath congealed your blood,
And melancholy is the nurse of frenzy.
Therefore they thought it good you hear a play
And frame your mind to mirth and merriment,
Which bars a thousand harms and lengthens life.

SLY   Marry, I will let them play it. Is not a comonty a 133
Christmas gambold or a tumbling-trick? 134

PAGE

No, my good lord, it is more pleasing stuff.

SLY   What, household stuff? 136

PAGE   It is a kind of history. 137

SLY   Well, we'll see 't. Come, madam wife, sit by my side
and let the world slip; we shall ne'er be younger. 139
                    [They sit over the stage.] Flourish.

1.1

Enter Lucentio and his man, Tranio.

LUCENTIO

Tranio, since for the great desire I had
To see fair Padua, nursery of arts, 2
I am arrived fore fruitful Lombardy, 3
The pleasant garden of great Italy,
And by my father's love and leave am armed
With his good will and thy good company,
My trusty servant, well approved in all, 7
Here let us breathe and haply institute 8
A course of learning and ingenious studies. 9
Pisa, renownèd for grave citizens,
Gave me my being, and my father first— 11
A merchant of great traffic through the world, 12
Vincentio, come of the Bentivolii. 13
Vincentio's son, brought up in Florence, 14
It shall become to serve all hopes conceived 15
To deck his fortune with his virtuous deeds. 16
And therefore, Tranio, for the time I study, 17
Virtue and that part of philosophy
Will I apply that treats of happiness 19
By virtue specially to be achieved.
Tell me thy mind, for I have Pisa left
And am to Padua come as he that leaves
A shallow plash to plunge him in the deep, 23
And with satiety seeks to quench his thirst.

TRANIO

Mi perdonate, gentle master mine. 25
I am in all affected as yourself, 26
Glad that you thus continue your resolve
To suck the sweets of sweet philosophy.
Only, good master, while we do admire
This virtue and this moral discipline,
Let's be no stoics nor no stocks, I pray, 31
Or so devote to Aristotle's checks 32
As Ovid be an outcast quite abjured. 33
Balk logic with acquaintance that you have, 34
And practice rhetoric in your common talk. 35
Music and poesy use to quicken you; 36

1.1 Location: Padua. A street before Baptista's house.
2 Padua . . . arts (Padua's was one of the most renowned of universities during Shakespeare's time.) **3 am arrived fore** have arrived at, or at the gates of, before. (Padua is not in Lombardy, but imprecise maps may have allowed Shakespeare to think of Lombardy as comprising all of northern Italy.) **7 approved** tested and proved trustworthy **8 breathe** pause, settle down. **haply institute** begin, as circumstances permit **9 ingenious** i.e., "ingenuous," liberal, befitting a wellborn person **11 first** i.e., before me **12 of great traffic** involved in extensive trade **13 come of** descended from **14–16 Vincentio's . . . deeds** It will befit Vincentio's son, brought up in Florence, to fulfill all the hopes of his family by adding virtuous deeds to what fortune has bestowed on him. **17 for . . . study** for my term of study **19 apply** study. **treats of** discusses, concerns **23 plash** pool **25 Mi perdonate** Pardon me **26 affected** disposed **31 stocks** persons devoid of feeling, like wooden posts. (With a play on *stoics.*) **32 devote** devoted. **checks** restraints **33 As** so that. **Ovid** Latin love poet. (Used here to typify amorous light entertainment, as contrasted with the constraining philosophic study of Aristotle.) **34 Balk logic** Argue, bandy words. **acquaintance** acquaintances **35 common talk** ordinary conversation. **36 Music . . . you** Use music and poetry to refresh yourself

---

103 goodman (A homely term for "husband.") **112 abandoned** banished **122 stands** (1) is the case (2) punningly, "is giving me an erection." The joke picks up on *stands,* meaning "serves," in line 121. **127 meet** suitable **133 Marry . . . play it** (Perhaps the Folio punctuation should be emended to "Marry, I will. Let them play it.") **comonty** (Sly's approximation of "comedy.") **134 gambold** (Sly's version of "gambol," frolicsome merrymaking and leaping about.) **136 household stuff** i.e., domestic doings. **137 history** story. **139.1 They sit over the stage** (Possibly the Lord and some servingmen exeunt here or at line 113. At 1.1.249 ff., a servingman, the Page, and Sly speak, while the Lord is no longer heard from.)

The mathematics and the metaphysics,
Fall to them as you find your stomach serves you.   38
No profit grows where is no pleasure ta'en.
In brief, sir, study what you most affect.   40

LUCENTIO
Gramercies, Tranio, well dost thou advise.   41
If, Biondello, thou wert come ashore,   42
We could at once put us in readiness
And take a lodging fit to entertain
Such friends as time in Padua shall beget.
But stay awhile, what company is this?

TRANIO
Master, some show to welcome us to town.   47

Enter Baptista with his two daughters, Katharina and Bianca; Gremio, a pantaloon; [and] Hortensio, suitor to Bianca. Lucentio [and] Tranio stand by.

BAPTISTA
Gentlemen, importune me no farther,
For how I firmly am resolved you know:
That is, not to bestow my youngest daughter
Before I have a husband for the elder.
If either of you both love Katharina,
Because I know you well and love you well,
Leave shall you have to court her at your pleasure.

GREMIO
To cart her rather. She's too rough for me.   55
There, there, Hortensio, will you any wife?

KATHARINA [*to Baptista*]
I pray you, sir, is it your will
To make a stale of me amongst these mates?   58

HORTENSIO
"Mates," maid? How mean you that? No mates for you,
Unless you were of gentler, milder mold.

KATHARINA
I'faith, sir, you shall never need to fear;
Iwis it is not halfway to her heart.   62
But if it were, doubt not her care should be
To comb your noddle with a three-legged stool,   64
And paint your face, and use you like a fool.   65

HORTENSIO
From all such devils, good Lord deliver us!

GREMIO   And me too, good Lord!

TRANIO [*aside to Lucentio*]
Husht, master, here's some good pastime toward.   68

That wench is stark mad or wonderful froward.   69

LUCENTIO [*aside to Tranio*]
But in the other's silence do I see
Maid's mild behavior and sobriety.
Peace, Tranio!

TRANIO [*aside to Lucentio*]
Well said, master. Mum, and gaze your fill.

BAPTISTA
Gentlemen, that I may soon make good
What I have said—Bianca, get you in.
And let it not displease thee, good Bianca,
For I will love thee ne'er the less, my girl.

KATHARINA   A pretty peat! It is best   78
Put finger in the eye, an she knew why.   79

BIANCA
Sister, content you in my discontent.—
Sir, to your pleasure humbly I subscribe.   81
My books and instruments shall be my company,
On them to look and practice by myself.

LUCENTIO [*aside to Tranio*]
Hark, Tranio, thou mayst hear Minerva speak.   84

HORTENSIO
Signor Baptista, will you be so strange?   85
Sorry am I that our good will effects   86
Bianca's grief.

GREMIO   Why will you mew her up,   87
Signor Baptista, for this fiend of hell,
And make her bear the penance of her tongue?   89

BAPTISTA
Gentlemen, content ye. I am resolved.
Go in, Bianca.   [*Exit Bianca.*]
And for I know she taketh most delight   92
In music, instruments, and poetry,
Schoolmasters will I keep within my house
Fit to instruct her youth. If you, Hortensio,
Or, Signor Gremio, you know any such,
Prefer them hither; for to cunning men   97
I will be very kind, and liberal
To mine own children in good bringing up.
And so farewell.—Katharina, you may stay,
For I have more to commune with Bianca.   *Exit.* 101

KATHARINA
Why, and I trust I may go too, may I not?
What, shall I be appointed hours,   103
As though, belike, I knew not what to take,   104
And what to leave? Ha!   *Exit.* 105

GREMIO   You may go to the devil's dam. Your gifts are 106
so good, here's none will hold you.—Their love is not 107

38 stomach inclination, appetite   **40 affect** find pleasant.   **41 Gramercies** Many thanks   **42 Biondello** (Lucentio apostrophizes his absent servant.)   **come ashore** (Padua, though inland, is given a harbor by Shakespeare, unless he is thinking of the canals that crossed northern Italy in the sixteenth century.)   **47.2 pantaloon** foolish old man, a stock character in Italian comedy   **55 cart** carry in a cart through the streets by way of punishment or public exposure. (With a play on *court*.)   **58 stale** laughingstock. (With a play on the meaning "harlot," since a harlot might well be carted.)   **mates** rude fellows. (But Hortensio takes the word in the sense of "husband.")   **62 Iwis . . . heart** indeed, marriage is not even halfway suited to my inclination. (Katharina speaks of herself in the third person here and in line 63.)   **64 comb your noddle** rake your head   **65 paint** i.e., make red with scratches   **68 toward** in prospect.

69 wonderful froward incredibly perverse.   **78–9 A . . . why** i.e., A fine spoiled darling she is! She does well to put on a show of weeping, knowing what's good for her. (Said sardonically.)   **81 pleasure** will.   **subscribe** submit.   **84 Minerva** goddess of wisdom   **85 strange** distant, unfeeling.   **86 effects** causes   **87 mew** coop (as one would a falcon)   **89 her . . . her** i.e., Bianca . . . Katharina's   **92 for** because   **97 Prefer** recommend.   **cunning** skillful, learned   **101 commune** discuss   **103 appointed hours** given a timetable   **104–5 As . . . leave?** as though, forsooth, I didn't know how to choose for myself?   **106 dam** mother.   **gifts** endowments. (Said ironically.)   **107 hold** detain.   **Their love** i.e., The love of women

so great, Hortensio, but we may blow our nails togeth- 108
er and fast it fairly out. Our cake's dough on both 109
sides. Farewell. Yet, for the love I bear my sweet 110
Bianca, if I can by any means light on a fit man to teach
her that wherein she delights, I will wish him to 112
her father.

HORTENSIO   So will I, Signor Gremio. But a word, I pray.
Though the nature of our quarrel yet never brooked 115
parle, know now, upon advice, it toucheth us both, 116
that we may yet again have access to our fair mistress
and be happy rivals in Bianca's love, to labor and effect
one thing specially.

GREMIO   What's that, I pray?

HORTENSIO   Marry, sir, to get a husband for her sister.

GREMIO   A husband? A devil.

HORTENSIO   I say a husband.

GREMIO   I say a devil. Think'st thou, Hortensio, though
her father be very rich, any man is so very a fool to be 125
married to hell?

HORTENSIO   Tush, Gremio, though it pass your patience 127
and mine to endure her loud alarums, why, man, there 128
be good fellows in the world, an a man could light on 129
them, would take her with all faults, and money 130
enough.

GREMIO   I cannot tell. But I had as lief take her dowry 132
with this condition: to be whipped at the high cross 133
every morning.

HORTENSIO   Faith, as you say, there's small choice in
rotten apples. But come, since this bar in law makes us 136
friends, it shall be so far forth friendly maintained till
by helping Baptista's eldest daughter to a husband we
set his youngest free for a husband, and then have to't 139
afresh. Sweet Bianca! Happy man be his dole! He that 140
runs fastest gets the ring. How say you, Signor 141
Gremio?

gremio   I am agreed, and would I had given him the best
horse in Padua to begin his wooing that would thoroughly woo her, wed her, and bed her and rid the
house of her! Come on.   Exeunt ambo. Manent 146
                                Tranio and Lucentio.

TRANIO
I pray, sir, tell me, is it possible
That love should of a sudden take such hold?

LUCENTIO
Oh, Tranio, till I found it to be true,
I never thought it possible or likely.
But see, while idly I stood looking on,

I found the effect of love in idleness,   152
And now in plainness do confess to thee,
That art to me as secret and as dear   154
As Anna to the Queen of Carthage was,   155
Tranio, I burn, I pine, I perish, Tranio,
If I achieve not this young modest girl.
Counsel me, Tranio, for I know thou canst;
Assist me, Tranio, for I know thou wilt.

TRANIO
Master, it is no time to chide you now.
Affection is not rated from the heart.   161
If love have touched you, naught remains but so,
"Redime te captum quam queas minimo."   163

LUCENTIO
Gramercies, lad. Go forward. This contents;   164
The rest will comfort, for thy counsel's sound.   165

TRANIO
Master, you looked so longly on the maid,   166
Perhaps you marked not what's the pith of all.   167

LUCENTIO
Oh, yes, I saw sweet beauty in her face,
Such as the daughter of Agenor had,   169
That made great Jove to humble him to her hand,   170
When with his knees he kissed the Cretan strand.   171

TRANIO
Saw you no more? Marked you not how her sister
Began to scold and raise up such a storm
That mortal ears might hardly endure the din?

LUCENTIO
Tranio, I saw her coral lips to move,
And with her breath she did perfume the air.
Sacred and sweet was all I saw in her.

TRANIO [aside]
Nay, then, 'tis time to stir him from his trance.—
I pray, awake, sir. If you love the maid,
Bend thoughts and wits to achieve her. Thus it stands:
Her elder sister is so curst and shrewd   181
That till the father rid his hands of her,
Master, your love must live a maid at home,   183
And therefore has he closely mewed her up,
Because she will not be annoyed with suitors.   185

LUCENTIO
Ah, Tranio, what a cruel father's he!
But art thou not advised he took some care   187
To get her cunning schoolmasters to instruct her?   188

TRANIO
Ay, marry, am I, sir; and now 'tis plotted.

108–9 blow . . . together i.e., twiddle our thumbs, wait patiently
109 fast . . . out abstain as best we can.   109–10 Our cake's . . . sides
i.e., We're both out of luck, getting nowhere.   112 wish commend
115-16 brooked conference   116 advice reflection.
toucheth concerns   125 very a utterly a   127 pass exceed
128 alarums i.e., loud, startling noises. (In military terms, a call to
arms.)   129 an if   130 would who would   132 I cannot tell i.e., I
don't know about that, don't know what to say.   had as lief would
as willingly   133 high cross cross set on a pedestal in a marketplace
or center of a town   136 bar in law legal impediment, i.e., Baptista's
refusal to receive suitors for Bianca   139 have to't renew combat
140 Happy . . . dole! i.e., May happiness be the reward of him who
wins! (Proverbial.)   141 the ring (An allusion to the sport of riding at
the ring, with quibble on "wedding ring" and also sexual sense, "vul-
var ring.")   146 s.d. ambo both.   Manent They remain onstage

152 love in idleness i.e., (1) desire bred by idleness (2) a popular name
for the pansy, thought to induce love   154 secret trusted, intimate
155 Anna confidante of her sister Dido, Queen of Carthage, beloved of
Aeneas   161 rated driven away by chiding   163 Redime . . . minimo
Buy yourself out of bondage for as little as you can. (From Terence's
Eunuchus as quoted in William Lilly's Latin Grammar.)   164 Gramercies Thanks   165 The rest rest of what you have to say   166 so
longly (1) for such a long time (2) so longingly   167 marked noted.
pith core, essence   169 daughter of Agenor Europa, beloved of Jove;
Jove took the form of a bull in order to abduct her   170 him himself
171 kissed i.e., knelt on   181 curst and shrewd shrewish and ill-
natured   183 must . . . home must remain unattached, unmated
185 Because so that   187 advised aware (that)   188 cunning expert

LUCENTIO
I have it, Tranio.

TRANIO   Master, for my hand,   190
Both our inventions meet and jump in one.   191

LUCENTIO
Tell me thine first.

TRANIO   You will be schoolmaster
And undertake the teaching of the maid:
That's your device.

LUCENTIO   It is. May it be done?

TRANIO
Not possible; for who shall bear your part
And be in Padua here Vincentio's son,
Keep house and ply his book, welcome his friends,   197
Visit his countrymen, and banquet them?

LUCENTIO
Basta, content thee, for I have it full.   199
We have not yet been seen in any house,
Nor can we be distinguished by our faces
For man or master. Then it follows thus:
Thou shalt be master, Tranio, in my stead,
Keep house, and port, and servants, as I should.   204
I will some other be, some Florentine,
Some Neapolitan, or meaner man of Pisa.   206
'Tis hatched and shall be so. Tranio, at once
Uncase thee. Take my colored hat and cloak.   208
When Biondello comes, he waits on thee,
But I will charm him first to keep his tongue.   210

TRANIO   So had you need.
In brief, sir, sith it your pleasure is,   212
And I am tied to be obedient—
For so your father charged me at our parting,
"Be serviceable to my son," quoth he,
Although I think 'twas in another sense—
I am content to be Lucentio,
Because so well I love Lucentio.
                            [*They exchange clothes.*]

LUCENTIO
Tranio, be so, because Lucentio loves.
And let me be a slave t'achieve that maid
Whose sudden sight hath thralled my wounded eye.   221

        Enter Biondello.

Here comes the rogue.—Sirrah, where have you been?

BIONDELLO
Where have I been? Nay, how now, where are you?
Master, has my fellow Tranio stol'n your clothes?
Or you stol'n his? Or both? Pray, what's the news?

LUCENTIO
Sirrah, come hither. 'Tis no time to jest,
And therefore frame your manners to the time.   227
Your fellow Tranio here, to save my life,
Puts my apparel and my countenance on,   229

And I for my escape have put on his;
For in a quarrel since I came ashore,
I killed a man, and fear I was descried.   232
Wait you on him, I charge you, as becomes,   233
While I make way from hence to save my life.
You understand me?

BIONDELLO   I, sir?—Ne'er a whit.   235

LUCENTIO
And not a jot of Tranio in your mouth.
Tranio is changed into Lucentio.

BIONDELLO
The better for him. Would I were so, too!

TRANIO
So could I, faith, boy, to have the next wish after,
That Lucentio indeed had Baptista's youngest
    daughter.
But, sirrah, not for my sake, but your master's, I
    advise
You use your manners discreetly in all kind of com-
    panies.
When I am alone, why, then I am Tranio,
But in all places else your master Lucentio.

LUCENTIO   Tranio, let's go.
One thing more rests, that thyself execute: 246
To make one among these wooers. If thou ask me
    why,
Sufficeth my reasons are both good and weighty.   248
                                    Exeunt.

        The presenters above speak.

FIRST SERVINGMAN
My lord, you nod. You do not mind the play.   249

SLY   Yes, by Saint Anne, do I. A good matter, surely.
Comes there any more of it?

PAGE [*as lady*]   My lord, 'tis but begun.

SLY   'Tis a very excellent piece of work, madam lady.
Would 'twere done!   *They sit and mark.* 254

                        ❧

[1.2]

        Enter Petruchio and his man, Grumio.

PETRUCHIO
Verona, for a while I take my leave
To see my friends in Padua, but of all   2
My best belovèd and approvèd friend,
Hortensio; and I trow this is his house.   4
Here, sirrah Grumio, knock, I say.

GRUMIO   Knock, sir? Whom should I knock? Is there any
man has rebused Your Worship?   7

PETRUCHIO   Villain, I say, knock me here soundly.   8

---

190 **for my hand** (A mild oath.)   191 **inventions** plans.   **jump** tally,
agree   197 **Keep . . . book** entertain guests and pursue his studies
199 ***Basta*** Enough.   **full** i.e., fully thought out.   204 **port** state, style
of living   206 **meaner** of a lower social class   208 **Uncase thee**
Remove your outer garments.   210 **charm** i.e., command, persuade
212 **sith** since   221 **Whose . . . thralled** the sudden sight of whom has
captured   227 **frame** adapt, suit   229 **countenance** bearing, manner

232 **descried** observed.   233 **as becomes** as is suitable   235 **I, sir**
(Lucentio may hear this as "Ay, sir.")   **Ne'er a whit** Not in the least.
246 **rests** remains to be done   248 **Sufficeth** it suffices that
248.2 *presenters* characters of the Induction, whose role it is to "present" the play proper   249 **mind** attend to   254 s.d. *mark* observe.
1.2. **Location: Padua. Before Hortensio's house.**
2 **of all** above all   4 **trow** believe   7 **rebused** (A blunder for
"abused.")   8 **Villain** i.e., Wretch. (A term of abuse.)   **me** i.e., for me.
(But Grumio, perhaps intentionally, misunderstands.)

GRUMIO   Knock you here, sir? Why, sir, what am I, sir,
that I should knock you here, sir?

PETRUCHIO
Villain, I say, knock me at this gate,   11
And rap me well, or I'll knock your knave's pate.

GRUMIO
My master is grown quarrelsome. I should knock
     you first,   13
And then I know after who comes by the worst.   14

PETRUCHIO   Will it not be?   15
Faith, sirrah, an you'll not knock, I'll ring it.   16
I'll try how you can *sol fa* and sing it.   17

He wrings him by the ears.

GRUMIO
Help, masters, help! My master is mad.   18

PETRUCHIO
Now knock when I bid you, sirrah villain.

Enter Hortensio.

HORTENSIO   How now, what's the matter? My old
friend Grumio and my good friend Petruchio? How
do you all at Verona?

PETRUCHIO
Signor Hortensio, come you to part the fray?
Con tutto il cuore ben trovato, may I say.   24

HORTENSIO
Alla nostra casa ben venuto,   25
Molto onorato signor mio Petruchio.—   26
Rise, Grumio, rise. We will compound this quarrel.   27

GRUMIO   Nay, 'tis no matter, sir, what he 'leges in Latin.   28
If this be not a lawful cause for me to leave his service!
Look you, sir: he bid me knock him and rap him
soundly, sir. Well, was it fit for a servant to use his
master so, being perhaps, for aught I see, two-and-   32
thirty, a pip out?   33
Whom would to God I had well knocked at first!
Then had not Grumio come by the worst.

PETRUCHIO
A senseless villain! Good Hortensio,
I bade the rascal knock upon your gate,
And could not get him for my heart to do it.   38

GRUMIO   Knock at the gate? Oh, heavens! Spake you not
these words plain, "Sirrah, knock me here, rap me
here, knock me well, and knock me soundly"? And
come you now with "knocking at the gate"?   42

PETRUCHIO
Sirrah, begone, or talk not, I advise you.

HORTENSIO
Petruchio, patience. I am Grumio's pledge.   44
Why, this's a heavy chance twixt him and you,   45
Your ancient, trusty, pleasant servant Grumio.   46
And tell me now, sweet friend, what happy gale
Blows you to Padua here from old Verona?

PETRUCHIO
Such wind as scatters young men through the world
To seek their fortunes farther than at home,
Where small experience grows. But in a few,   51
Signor Hortensio, thus it stands with me:
Antonio, my father, is deceased,
And I have thrust myself into this maze,
Happily to wive and thrive as best I may.   55
Crowns in my purse I have, and goods at home,   56
And so am come abroad to see the world.

HORTENSIO
Petruchio, shall I then come roundly to thee   58
And wish thee to a shrewd, ill-favored wife?   59
Thou'dst thank me but a little for my counsel.
And yet I'll promise thee she shall be rich,
And very rich. But thou'rt too much my friend,
And I'll not wish thee to her.

PETRUCHIO
Signor Hortensio, twixt such friends as we
Few words suffice. And therefore, if thou know
One rich enough to be Petruchio's wife—
As wealth is burden of my wooing dance—   67
Be she as foul as was Florentius' love,   68
As old as Sibyl, and as curst and shrewd   69
As Socrates' Xanthippe, or a worse,   70
She moves me not, or not removes, at least,   71
Affection's edge in me, were she as rough   72
As are the swelling Adriatic seas.
I come to wive it wealthily in Padua;
If wealthily, then happily in Padua.

GRUMIO   Nay, look you, sir, he tells you flatly what his
mind is. Why, give him gold enough and marry him
to a puppet or an aglet-baby, or an old trot with ne'er   78
a tooth in her head, though she have as many diseases
as two-and-fifty horses. Why, nothing comes amiss, so   80
money comes withal.   81

---

44 pledge surety.   **45 this's . . . chance** this is a sad occurrence
46 ancient long-standing.   **pleasant** merry   **51 in a few** in short
55 Happily with good luck. (*Happily* and *haply* were not always distinguished.)   **56 Crowns** Gold coins   **58 come roundly** speak
plainly   **59 shrewd** shrewish.   **ill-favored** ill-natured (? Kate is not
"ugly," the usual meaning of this term; see line 85.)   **67 burden**
undersong, i.e., basis   **68 foul** ugly   **Florentius' love** (An allusion
to John Gower's version in *Confessio Amantis* of the fairy tale of the
knight who promises to marry an ugly old woman if she solves the
riddle he must answer. After the fulfillment of all promises, she
becomes young and beautiful. Another version of this story is
Chaucer's "Tale of the Wife of Bath," from *The Canterbury Tales*.)
69 Sibyl prophetess of Cumae, to whom Apollo gave as many
years of life as she held grains of sand in her hand   **70 Xanthippe**
the philosopher's notoriously shrewish wife   **71 moves** affects,
disturbs. (Setting up wordplay on *removes*.)   **72 Affection's edge**
the keen edge of desire   **78 aglet-baby** small figure carved on the
metal tip of a lace, i.e., a tiny baby.   **trot** hag   **80 so** provided
81 withal with it.

---

11 gate door   **13–14 I should . . . worst** i.e., You're asking me to hit
you—and I know who then will get the worst of it.   **15 Will it not
be?** i.e., Aren't you going to do what I said?   **16 an** if   **ring it** sound
loudly, using a circular knocker or a bell. (With a pun on *wring*.)
17 I'll . . . sing it i.e., I'll make you cry out. (To *sol fa* is to sing a scale.)
18 masters i.e., sirs. (Addressed to the audience.)   **24 Con . . . trovato**
With all my heart, well met   **25–6 Alla . . . Petruchio** Welcome to our
house, my much-honored Signor Petruchio. (Italian.)   **27 compound**
settle   **28 'leges** alleges   **32–3 two . . . out** i.e., drunk, or not quite
right in the head. (Derived from the card game called *one-and-thirty*.)
33 a pip a spot on a playing card. (Hence, *a pip out* means "off by
one," or "one in excess of thirty one.")   **38 for my heart** i.e., for my
life   **42 come you now with** do you now change your tune to

HORTENSIO
Petruchio, since we are stepped thus far in,
I will continue that I broached in jest.   83
I can, Petruchio, help thee to a wife
With wealth enough, and young and beauteous,
Brought up as best becomes a gentlewoman.
Her only fault, and that is faults enough,
Is that she is intolerable curst   88
And shrewd, and froward, so beyond all measure   89
That, were my state far worser than it is,   90
I would not wed her for a mine of gold.

PETRUCHIO
Hortensio, peace! Thou know'st not gold's effect.
Tell me her father's name and 'tis enough;
For I will board her, though she chide as loud   94
As thunder when the clouds in autumn crack.   95

HORTENSIO
Her father is Baptista Minola,
An affable and courteous gentleman.
Her name is Katharina Minola,
Renowned in Padua for her scolding tongue.

PETRUCHIO
I know her father, though I know not her,
And he knew my deceasèd father well.
I will not sleep, Hortensio, till I see her;
And therefore let me be thus bold with you
To give you over at this first encounter,   104
Unless you will accompany me thither.

GRUMIO [to Hortensio]   I pray you, sir, let him go while
the humor lasts. O' my word, an she knew him as well 107
as I do, she would think scolding would do little good
upon him. She may perhaps call him half a score
knaves or so. Why, that's nothing; an he begin once,
he'll rail in his rope tricks. I'll tell you what, sir: an she 111
stand him but a little, he will throw a figure in her face 112
and so disfigure her with it that she shall have no more 113
eyes to see withal than a cat. You know him not, sir.   114

HORTENSIO
Tarry, Petruchio, I must go with thee,
For in Baptista's keep my treasure is.   116
He hath the jewel of my life in hold,   117
His youngest daughter, beautiful Bianca,
And her withholds from me and other more,   119
Suitors to her and rivals in my love,
Supposing it a thing impossible,
For those defects I have before rehearsed,   120
That ever Katharina will be wooed.
Therefore this order hath Baptista ta'en,   124
That none shall have access unto Bianca

Till Katharine the curst have got a husband.
GRUMIO   Katharine the curst!
A title for a maid of all titles the worst.
HORTENSIO
Now shall my friend Petruchio do me grace,   129
And offer me disguised in sober robes
To old Baptista as a schoolmaster
Well seen in music, to instruct Bianca,   132
That so I may by this device at least
Have leave and leisure to make love to her,   134
And unsuspected court her by herself.

        Enter Gremio [with a paper], and Lucentio dis-
        guised [as a schoolmaster].

GRUMIO   Here's no knavery! See, to beguile the old 136
folks, how the young folks lay their heads together!
Master, master, look about you. Who goes there, ha?
HORTENSIO
Peace, Grumio, it is the rival of my love.
Petruchio, stand by awhile.   [*They stand aside.*]
GRUMIO [*aside*]
A proper stripling and an amorous!   141
GREMIO [*to Lucentio*]
Oh, very well, I have perused the note.   142
Hark you, sir, I'll have them very fairly bound—
All books of love, see that at any hand—   144
And see you read no other lectures to her.   145
You understand me. Over and beside
Signor Baptista's liberality,
I'll mend it with a largess. Take your paper too,   148
                    [*giving Lucentio the note*]
And let me have them very well perfumed,   149
For she is sweeter than perfume itself
To whom they go to. What will you read to her?
LUCENTIO
Whate'er I read to her, I'll plead for you
As for my patron, stand you so assured,
As firmly as yourself were still in place—   154
Yea, and perhaps with more successful words
Than you, unless you were a scholar, sir.
GREMIO
Oh, this learning, what a thing it is!
GRUMIO [*aside*]
Oh, this woodcock, what an ass it is!   158
PETRUCHIO   Peace, sirrah!
HORTENSIO [*coming forward*]
Grumio, mum!—God save you, Signor Gremio.
GREMIO
And you are well met, Signor Hortensio.   161
Trow you whither I am going? To Baptista Minola.   162

---

83 **that I broached** what I began   88–9 **intolerable . . . froward** intolerably ill-natured and willful   90 **state** estate   94 **board** woo aggressively, accost, have intercourse with, rape   95 **crack** make an explosive noise.   104 **give you over** leave you   107 **humor** whim.   **O' my
word, an** On my word, if   111 **he'll . . . tricks** i.e., he has tricks up his
sleeve to answer her scolding.   112–14 **he will . . . cat** i.e., he will
utterly dazzle and disable her with his rhetorical tricks. (A *figure* is a
figure of speech.)   116 **keep** (1) place to store treasure (2) keeping
117 **in hold** (1) in his custody (2) in his stronghold   118 **And . . . more**
and witholds her from me and others besides   122 **rehearsed** related,
described   124 **this order** these measures

129 **grace** a favor   132 **seen** skilled   134 **make love to** woo
136 **Here's no knavery!** (Said sarcastically.)   141 **proper stripling**
handsome young fellow. (Said ironically, in reference to Gremio.)
142 **note** (Evidently, a list of books for Bianca's tutoring.)
144 **see** see to.   **at any hand** in any case   145 **read . . . lectures** teach
no other lessons   148 **mend** improve, increase.   **largess** gift of
money.   149 **them** i.e., the books   154 **as** as if.   **still in place** present
all the time   158 **woodcock** (A bird easily caught; proverbially stupid.)   161 **you are well met** i.e., how opportune to meet you just
now   162 **Trow** Know

I promised to inquire carefully
About a schoolmaster for the fair Bianca,
And by good fortune I have lighted well   165
On this young man, for learning and behavior
Fit for her turn, well read in poetry   167
And other books—good ones, I warrant ye.

HORTENSIO
'Tis well. And I have met a gentleman
Hath promised me to help me to another,   170
A fine musician to instruct our mistress.
So shall I no whit be behind in duty
To fair Bianca, so beloved of me.

GREMIO
Beloved of me, and that my deeds shall prove.

GRUMIO [aside]   And that his bags shall prove.   175

HORTENSIO
Gremio, 'tis now no time to vent our love.   176
Listen to me, and if you speak me fair,   177
I'll tell you news indifferent good for either.   178
Here is a gentleman whom by chance I met,
Upon agreement from us to his liking,   180
Will undertake to woo curst Katharine,
Yea, and to marry her, if her dowry please.

GREMIO   So said, so done, is well.   183
Hortensio, have you told him all her faults?

PETRUCHIO
I know she is an irksome brawling scold.
If that be all, masters, I hear no harm.   186

GREMIO
No? Say'st me so, friend? What countryman?

PETRUCHIO
Born in Verona, old Antonio's son.
My father dead, his fortune lives for me,
And I do hope good days and long to see.   190

GREMIO
Oh, sir, such a life with such a wife were strange.   191
But if you have a stomach, to't, i' God's name.   192
You shall have me assisting you in all.
But will you woo this wildcat?

PETRUCHIO   Will I live?

GRUMIO
Will he woo her? Ay, or I'll hang her.

PETRUCHIO
Why came I hither but to that intent?
Think you a little din can daunt mine ears?
Have I not in my time heard lions roar?
Have I not heard the sea, puffed up with winds,
Rage like an angry boar chafèd with sweat?
Have I not heard great ordnance in the field,   201
And heaven's artillery thunder in the skies?

Have I not in a pitchèd battle heard   203
Loud 'larums, neighing steeds, and trumpets' clang?   204
And do you tell me of a woman's tongue,
That gives not half so great a blow to hear
As will a chestnut in a farmer's fire?   207
Tush, tush! Fear boys with bugs.

GRUMIO   For he fears none. 208

GREMIO   Hortensio, hark.
This gentleman is happily arrived,   210
My mind presumes, for his own good and ours.

HORTENSIO
I promised we would be contributors
And bear his charge of wooing, whatsoe'er.   213

GREMIO
And so we will, provided that he win her.

GRUMIO
I would I were as sure of a good dinner.   215

    Enter Tranio, brave [as Lucentio], and
    Biondello.

TRANIO
Gentlemen, God save you. If I may be bold,
Tell me, I beseech you, which is the readiest way
To the house of Signor Baptista Minola?

BIONDELLO   He that has the two fair daughters, is't he
you mean?

TRANIO   Even he, Biondello.   221

GREMIO
Hark you, sir, you mean not her to—

TRANIO
Perhaps him and her, sir. What have you to do?   223

PETRUCHIO
Not her that chides, sir, at any hand, I pray.   224

TRANIO
I love no chiders, sir.—Biondello, let's away.

LUCENTIO [aside]
Well begun, Tranio.

HORTENSIO   Sir, a word ere you go.
Are you a suitor to the maid you talk of, yea or no?

TRANIO
An if I be, sir, is it any offense?

GREMIO
No, if without more words you will get you hence.

TRANIO
Why, sir, I pray, are not the streets as free
For me as for you?

GREMIO   But so is not she.

TRANIO
For what reason, I beseech you?

GREMIO   For this reason, if you'll know,
That she's the choice love of Signor Gremio.

---

165 **lighted** alighted   167 **Fit for her turn** suited to her needs. (Something that is true in more ways than Gremio realizes.)   170 **Hath . . .
another** who has promised to help me to obtain another   175 **bags**
moneybags   176 **vent** express   177 **speak me fair** deal with me
courteously   178 **indifferent** equally   180 **Upon . . . liking** who, if
we agree to terms satisfactory to him   183 **So . . . is well** i.e., That's
all very well, when his deeds match his words (which may not be
soon).   186 **masters** good sirs   190 **And . . . see** and I hope to see
many happy days.   191 **were** would be   192 **a stomach** an appetite,
inclination   201 **ordnance** artillery.   **field** battlefield

203 **a pitchèd battle** a planned battle set in orderly array (unlike a
skirmish)   204 **'larums** calls to arms   207 **chestnut** (Chestnuts roasted will pop open or explode with a loud report.)   208 **Fear . . . bugs**
Frighten children with bugbears, bogeymen.   210 **happily** fortunately, just when needed   213 **charge** expense   215.1 **brave** elegantly
dressed   221 **Even he** Yes, precisely, he   223 **Perhaps . . . do?** i.e.,
Perhaps I mean to woo both Baptista Minola and Katharina, sir.
What's that to you?   224 **at any hand** on any account

HORTENSIO
  That she's the chosen of Signor Hortensio.
TRANIO
  Softly, my masters! If you be gentlemen,
  Do me this right: hear me with patience.
  Baptista is a noble gentleman,
  To whom my father is not all unknown;   238
  And were his daughter fairer than she is,
  She may more suitors have, and me for one.
  Fair Leda's daughter had a thousand wooers;   241
  Then well one more may fair Bianca have,
  And so she shall. Lucentio shall make one,
  Though Paris came in hope to speed alone.   244
GREMIO
  What, this gentleman will out-talk us all!
LUCENTIO
  Sir, give him head. I know he'll prove a jade.   246
PETRUCHIO
  Hortensio, to what end are all these words?
HORTENSIO [to Tranio]
  Sir, let me be so bold as ask you,   248
  Did you yet ever see Baptista's daughter?
TRANIO
  No, sir, but hear I do that he hath two,
  The one as famous for a scolding tongue
  As is the other for beauteous modesty.
PETRUCHIO
  Sir, sir, the first's for me. Let her go by.   253
GREMIO
  Yea, leave that labor to great Hercules,
  And let it be more than Alcides' twelve.   255
PETRUCHIO
  Sir, understand you this of me, in sooth: 256
  The youngest daughter, whom you hearken for,   257
  Her father keeps from all access of suitors,
  And will not promise her to any man
  Until the elder sister first be wed.
  The younger then is free, and not before.
TRANIO
  If it be so, sir, that you are the man
  Must stead us all, and me amongst the rest;   263
  And if you break the ice and do this feat,
  Achieve the elder, set the younger free
  For our access, whose hap shall be to have her   266
  Will not so graceless be to be ingrate.   267
HORTENSIO
  Sir, you say well, and well you do conceive.   268
  And since you do profess to be a suitor,
  You must, as we do, gratify this gentleman,   270

  To whom we all rest generally beholding.   271
TRANIO
  Sir, I shall not be slack. In sign whereof,
  Please ye we may contrive this afternoon,   273
  And quaff carouses to our mistress' health,   274
  And do as adversaries do in law—   275
  Strive mightily, but eat and drink as friends.
GRUMIO, BIONDELLO
  Oh, excellent motion! Fellows, let's be gone.   277
HORTENSIO
  The motion's good indeed, and be it so.
  Petruchio, I shall be your ben venuto.   Exeunt. 279

❖

[2.1]

Enter Katharina and Bianca [with her hands tied].

BIANCA
  Good sister, wrong me not, nor wrong yourself,
  To make a bondmaid and a slave of me.
  That I disdain. But for these other goods,   3
  Unbind my hands, I'll pull them off myself,   4
  Yea, all my raiment, to my petticoat,
  Or what you will command me will I do,
  So well I know my duty to my elders.
KATHARINA
  Of all thy suitors here I charge thee tell
  Whom thou lov'st best. See thou dissemble not.
BIANCA
  Believe me, sister, of all the men alive
  I never yet beheld that special face
  Which I could fancy more than any other.
KATHARINA
  Minion, thou liest. Is't not Hortensio?   13
BIANCA
  If you affect him, sister, here I swear   14
  I'll plead for you myself but you shall have him.   15
KATHARINA
  Oh, then belike you fancy riches more.   16
  You will have Gremio to keep you fair.   17
BIANCA
  Is it for him you do envy me so?
  Nay, then, you jest, and now I well perceive
  You have but jested with me all this while.
  I prithee, sister Kate, untie my hands.
KATHARINA (strikes her)
  If that be jest, then all the rest was so.

  Enter Baptista.

238 all entirely   241 Leda's daughter Helen of Troy   244 Though . . .
alone even if Paris (who abducted Helen from her husband,
Menelaus) were to come in hopes of succeeding above all others.
246 Sir . . . jade Sir, give him a loose bridle; i.e., let him talk freely. I
know he'll prove to be a worthless horse, soon tired.   248 as ask as
to ask   253 Let her go by Pass over her.   255 And . . . twelve (Hercules, called *Alcides* because he was the reputed grandson of Alcaeus,
had to perform twelve huge labors.)   256 of me from me.   sooth
truth   257 hearken for seek to win   263 Must stead who must help
266 whose hap he whose good fortune   267 to be ingrate as to be
ungrateful.   268 conceive understand.   270 gratify this gentleman
reward Petruchio

271 beholding beholden, indebted.   273 contrive manage our affairs,
pass the time (?)   274 quaff carouses drink toasts   275 adversaries
opposing lawyers   277 motion suggestion.   279 ben venuto welcome, i.e., host.
2.1. Location: Padua. Baptista's house.
3 for as for.   goods i.e., clothes, jewels, love tokens   4 Unbind if you
will unbind   13 Minion Hussy   14 affect love   15 but . . . him if
necessary for you to win him.   16 belike perhaps   17 fair resplendent with finery.

BAPTISTA
Why, how now, dame, whence grows this
    insolence?—
Bianca, stand aside. Poor girl, she weeps.
Go ply thy needle, meddle not with her.—   25
For shame, thou hilding of a devilish spirit,   26
Why dost thou wrong her that did ne'er wrong thee?
When did she cross thee with a bitter word?   28

KATHARINA
Her silence flouts me, and I'll be revenged.   29
                               [*She*] *flies after Bianca.*

BAPTISTA
What, in my sight? Bianca, get thee in.   *Exit* [*Bianca*].

KATHARINA
What, will you not suffer me? Nay, now I see   31
She is your treasure, she must have a husband;
I must dance barefoot on her wedding day,   33
And for your love to her lead apes in hell.   34
Talk not to me. I will go sit and weep
Till I can find occasion of revenge.   [*Exit.*]

BAPTISTA
Was ever gentleman thus grieved as I?
But who comes here?   38

    Enter Gremio, Lucentio [*as a schoolmaster*] *in the*
    habit of a mean man, Petruchio, with [*Hortensio as*
    a musician, and] *Tranio* [*as Lucentio*] *with his boy*
    [*Biondello*] *bearing a lute and books.*

GREMIO   Good morrow, neighbor Baptista.
BAPTISTA   Good morrow, neighbor Gremio. God save
you, gentlemen.
PETRUCHIO
And you, good sir. Pray, have you not a daughter
Called Katharina, fair and virtuous?

BAPTISTA
I have a daughter, sir, called Katharina.

GREMIO
You are too blunt. Go to it orderly.   45

PETRUCHIO
You wrong me, Signor Gremio; give me leave.—   46
I am a gentleman of Verona, sir,
That, hearing of her beauty and her wit,
Her affability and bashful modesty,
Her wondrous qualities and mild behavior,
Am bold to show myself a forward guest
Within your house, to make mine eye the witness
Of that report which I so oft have heard.
And, for an entrance to my entertainment,   54
I do present you with a man of mine,
              [*presenting Hortensio*]
Cunning in music and the mathematics,   56

To instruct her fully in those sciences,   57
Whereof I know she is not ignorant.
Accept of him, or else you do me wrong.   59
His name is Litio, born in Mantua.

BAPTISTA
You're welcome, sir, and he, for your good sake.
But for my daughter Katharine, this I know,   62
She is not for your turn, the more my grief.

PETRUCHIO
I see you do not mean to part with her,
Or else you like not of my company.   65

BAPTISTA
Mistake me not, I speak but as I find.
Whence are you, sir? What may I call your name?

PETRUCHIO
Petruchio is my name, Antonio's son,
A man well known throughout all Italy.

BAPTISTA
I know him well. You are welcome for his sake.   70

GREMIO
Saving your tale, Petruchio, I pray,   71
Let us that are poor petitioners speak too.
Bacare! You are marvelous forward.   73

PETRUCHIO
Oh, pardon me, Signor Gremio, I would fain be doing. 74

GREMIO
I doubt it not, sir, but you will curse your wooing.—
Neighbors, this is a gift very grateful, I am sure of 76
it. [*To Baptista*] To express the like kindness, myself, that have been more kindly beholding to you
than any, freely give unto you this young scholar
[*presenting Lucentio*], that hath been long studying at
Rheims, as cunning in Greek, Latin, and other
languages as the other in music and mathematics. His 82
name is Cambio. Pray, accept his service.   83

BAPTISTA   A thousand thanks, Signor Gremio.—Welcome, good Cambio. [*To Tranio*] But, gentle sir,
methinks you walk like a stranger. May I be so bold to
know the cause of your coming?

TRANIO
Pardon me, sir, the boldness is mine own,
That, being a stranger in this city here,
Do make myself a suitor to your daughter,
Unto Bianca, fair and virtuous.
Nor is your firm resolve unknown to me
In the preferment of the eldest sister.   93
This liberty is all that I request,
That, upon knowledge of my parentage,   95
I may have welcome 'mongst the rest that woo,
And free access and favor as the rest.   97

25 **meddle not with** have nothing to do with   26 **hilding** vicious
(hence worthless) beast   28 **cross** contradict, thwart   29 **flouts**
mocks, insults   31 **suffer me** let me have my own way.   33, 34 **dance
. . . day, lead . . . hell** (Popularly supposed to be the fate of old maids.)
38.2 *habit* dress.   *mean* of low social station. (Said here of a schoolmaster.)   45 **orderly** in a properly orderly manner.   46 **give me
leave** excuse me, let me do this my way.   54 **entrance** entrance fee.
entertainment reception   56 **Cunning** skillful

57 **sciences** subjects, branches of knowledge   59 **Accept of** Accept
62 **for** as for   65 **like not of** do not like   70 **know** know of. (See also
lines 104–5.)   71 **Saving** With all due respect for   73 *Bacare!* Stand
back!   74 **fain** gladly.   **doing** getting on with the business. (With
sexual suggestion.)   76 **grateful** pleasing   82 **the other** i.e., Hortensio   83 **Cambio** (In Italian, appropriately, the word means "change"
or "exchange.")   93 **In the preferment of** in the precedence you give
to   95 **upon knowledge of** when you know about   97 **favor** leave,
permission

And toward the education of your daughters
I here bestow a simple instrument,
And this small packet of Greek and Latin books.
If you accept them, then their worth is great.
    [Biondello brings forward the lute and books.]

BAPTISTA
Lucentio is your name? Of whence, I pray? 102

TRANIO
Of Pisa, sir, son to Vincentio.

BAPTISTA
A mighty man of Pisa. By report
I know him well. You are very welcome, sir.
[To Hortensio] Take you the lute, *[to Lucentio]* and
  you the set of books;
You shall go see your pupils presently.—
Holla, within!

    Enter a Servant.

     Sirrah, lead these gentlemen
To my daughters, and tell them both
These are their tutors. Bid them use them well.
    [Exit Servant, with Lucentio and Hortensio.]
We will go walk a little in the orchard,
And then to dinner. You are passing welcome, 112
And so I pray you all to think yourselves.

PETRUCHIO
Signor Baptista, my business asketh haste,
And every day I cannot come to woo.
You knew my father well, and in him me,
Left solely heir to all his lands and goods,
Which I have bettered rather than decreased.
Then tell me, if I get your daughter's love,
What dowry shall I have with her to wife?

BAPTISTA
After my death the one half of my lands,
And in possession twenty thousand crowns. 122

PETRUCHIO
And for that dowry I'll assure her of 123
Her widowhood, be it that she survive me, 124
In all my lands and leases whatsoever.
Let specialties be therefore drawn between us, 126
That covenants may be kept on either hand.

BAPTISTA
Ay, when the special thing is well obtained,
That is, her love; for that is all in all.

PETRUCHIO
Why, that is nothing, for I tell you, father, 130
I am as peremptory as she proud-minded;
And where two raging fires meet together,
They do consume the thing that feeds their fury.
Though little fire grows great with little wind,
Yet extreme gusts will blow out fire and all.
So I to her, and so she yields to me, 136

For I am rough and woo not like a babe.

BAPTISTA
Well mayst thou woo, and happy be thy speed! 138
But be thou armed for some unhappy words.

PETRUCHIO
Ay, to the proof, as mountains are for winds, 140
That shakes not, though they blow perpetually. 141

  Enter Hortensio [as Litio], with his head broke.

BAPTISTA
How now, my friend, why dost thou look so pale?

HORTENSIO
For fear, I promise you, if I look pale. 143

BAPTISTA
What, will my daughter prove a good musician?

HORTENSIO
I think she'll sooner prove a soldier. 145
Iron may hold with her, but never lutes. 146

BAPTISTA
Why then, thou canst not break her to the lute? 147

HORTENSIO
Why, no, for she hath broke the lute to me.
I did but tell her she mistook her frets, 149
And bowed her hand to teach her fingering,
When, with a most impatient devilish spirit,
"Frets, call you these?" quoth she, "I'll fume with
  them."
And with that word she struck me on the head,
And through the instrument my pate made way;
And there I stood amazèd for a while, 155
As on a pillory, looking through the lute, 156
While she did call me rascal fiddler
And twangling Jack, with twenty such vile terms, 158
As had she studied to misuse me so. 159

PETRUCHIO
Now, by the world, it is a lusty wench! 160
I love her ten times more than e'er I did.
Oh, how I long to have some chat with her!

BAPTISTA *[to Hortensio]*
Well, go with me, and be not so discomfited.
Proceed in practice with my younger daughter; 164
She's apt to learn and thankful for good turns.—
Signor Petruchio, will you go with us,
Or shall I send my daughter Kate to you?

PETRUCHIO
I pray you, do.   *Exeunt. Manet Petruchio.*
   I'll attend her here, 168
And woo her with some spirit when she comes.

---

102 Lucentio . . . name? (Baptista may have learned this information from a note accompanying the books and lute.) **112 passing** exceedingly **122 in possession** in immediate possession **123 for** in exchange for **124 widowhood** i.e., widow's share of the estate. **be it that she** if she should **126 specialties** terms of contract **130 father** father-in-law **136 So I** i.e., So I behave, like an extreme gust of wind

138 happy . . . speed! may fortune give you success! **140 to the proof** i.e., in armor, proof against her shrewishness **141 shakes** shake. **141.1 broke** with a bleeding cut. (Hortensio usually appears on stage with his head emerging through a broken lute.) **143 promise** assure **145 I think . . . soldier** i.e., She's better suited for the manly career of soldiering. **146 hold with** hold out against **147 break** train. (With pun in the next line.) **149 frets** ridges or bars on the fingerboard of the lute. (But Kate puns on the sense of "fume," "be indignant.") **155 amazèd** bewildered **156 As on a pillory** as if with my head in a wooden collar used as punishment **158 Jack** knave **159 As . . . so** as if she had planned how to abuse me so. **160 lusty** lively **164 practice** instruction **168 s.d. Manet** He remains onstage

Say that she rail, why then I'll tell her plain
She sings as sweetly as a nightingale.
Say that she frown, I'll say she looks as clear   172
As morning roses newly washed with dew.
Say she be mute and will not speak a word,
Then I'll commend her volubility
And say she uttereth piercing eloquence.   176
If she do bid me pack, I'll give her thanks,   177
As though she bid me stay by her a week.
If she deny to wed, I'll crave the day   179
When I shall ask the banns and when be married.   180
But here she comes; and now, Petruchio, speak.

    Enter Katharina.

Good morrow, Kate, for that's your name, I hear.
KATHARINA
Well have you heard, but something hard of hearing.   183
They call me Katharine that do talk of me.
PETRUCHIO
You lie, in faith, for you are called plain Kate,
And bonny Kate, and sometimes Kate the curst;
But Kate, the prettiest Kate in Christendom,
Kate of Kate Hall, my superdainty Kate,
For dainties are all Kates, and therefore, Kate,   189
Take this of me, Kate of my consolation: 190
Hearing thy mildness praised in every town,
Thy virtues spoke of, and thy beauty sounded,   192
Yet not so deeply as to thee belongs,
Myself am moved to woo thee for my wife.   194
KATHARINA
Moved? In good time! Let him that moved you hither 195
Remove you hence. I knew you at the first
You were a movable.
PETRUCHIO   Why, what's a movable?   197
KATHARINA
A joint stool.
PETRUCHIO   Thou hast hit it. Come, sit on me.   198
KATHARINA
Asses are made to bear, and so are you.   199
PETRUCHIO
Women are made to bear, and so are you.
KATHARINA
No such jade as you, if me you mean.   201
PETRUCHIO
Alas, good Kate, I will not burden thee,   202

For knowing thee to be but young and light.   203
KATHARINA
Too light for such a swain as you to catch,   204
And yet as heavy as my weight should be.
PETRUCHIO
Should be? Should—buzz!
KATHARINA   Well ta'en, and like a buzzard. 206
PETRUCHIO
Oh, slow-winged turtle, shall a buzzard take thee?
KATHARINA
Ay, for a turtle, as he takes a buzzard.
PETRUCHIO
Come, come, you wasp, i'faith you are too angry.   209
KATHARINA
If I be waspish, best beware my sting.
PETRUCHIO
My remedy is then to pluck it out.
KATHARINA
Ay, if the fool could find it where it lies.
PETRUCHIO
Who knows not where a wasp does wear his sting?
In his tail.
KATHARINA   In his tongue.
PETRUCHIO   Whose tongue?
KATHARINA
Yours, if you talk of tales, and so farewell.   217
PETRUCHIO
What, with my tongue in your tail? Nay, come again.
Good Kate, I am a gentleman—
KATHARINA   That I'll try.
                    She strikes him.
PETRUCHIO
I swear I'll cuff you if you strike again.
KATHARINA   So may you lose your arms.
If you strike me, you are no gentleman,
And if no gentleman, why then no arms.   223
PETRUCHIO
A herald, Kate? Oh, put me in thy books!   224
KATHARINA   What is your crest, a coxcomb?   225
PETRUCHIO
A combless cock, so Kate will be my hen.   226
KATHARINA
No cock of mine. You crow too like a craven.   227

---

172 **clear** serene 176 **piercing** moving 177 **pack** begone 179 **deny** refuse. **crave the day** ask her to name the day 180 **ask the banns** have a reading of the required announcement in church of a forthcoming marriage 183 **heard, hard** (Pronounced nearly alike.) 189 **all Kates** (With a quibble on "cates," confections, delicacies.) 190 **of me** from me. **consolation** comfort 192 **sounded** proclaimed. (With a quibble on "plumbed," as indicated by *deeply* in the next line.) 194 **moved** impelled. (Followed by wordplay on the more literal meaning of *move* and *remove*.) 195 **In good time!** Forsooth! Indeed! 197 **movable** (1) one easily changed or dissuaded (2) an article of furniture. 198 **A joint stool** a well-fitted stool made by an expert craftsman. 199 **bear** carry. (With puns in the following lines suggesting "bear children" and "support a man during sexual intercourse.") 201 **jade** an ill-conditioned horse 202 **burden** (1) oppress with a heavy load—a term appropriate to *asses* and *bear* in line 199, since asses are beasts of *burden* (2) lie on during sexual intercourse, impregnate. (See notes on lines 199 and 203.)

203 **For knowing** because I know. **light** (1) of delicate stature (2) lascivious (3) lacking a *burden* (see previous line) in the musical sense of lacking a bass undersong or accompaniment (4) elusive (in the following line). 204 **swain** young rustic in love 206 **Should . . . buzz!** (Petruchio puns on *be* and "bee," and uses *buzz* in perhaps three senses: [1] an interjection of impatience or contempt [2] a bee's sound [3] a rumor being buzzed about, to which, he implies, Kate had better listen.) **buzzard** (1) figuratively, a fool (2) in the next line, an inferior kind of hawk, fit only to overtake a slow-winged *turtle* or turtledove, as Petruchio might overtake Kate (3) a buzzing insect, caught by a turtledove. 209 **wasp** i.e., waspish, scolding woman. (But suggested by *buzzard*, buzzing insect.) 217 **talk of tales** i.e., idly tell stories. (With pun on "tail.") 223 **no arms** no coat of arms. (With pun on *arms* as limbs of the body.) 224 **books** (1) books of heraldry, heraldic registers (2) grace, favor. 225 **crest** (1) armorial device (2) a rooster's comb, setting up the joke on *coxcomb*, the cap of the court fool 226 **A combless cock** i.e., A gentle rooster. (With suggestion of the male sexual organ.) **so** provided that 227 **a craven** a cock that is not "game" or willing to fight.

PETRUCHIO
Nay, come, Kate, come. You must not look so sour.
KATHARINA
It is my fashion when I see a crab.   229
PETRUCHIO
Why, here's no crab, and therefore look not sour.
KATHARINA   There is, there is.
PETRUCHIO
Then show it me.
KATHARINA   Had I a glass, I would.
PETRUCHIO   What, you mean my face?
KATHARINA   Well aimed of such a young one.   234
PETRUCHIO
Now, by Saint George, I am too young for you.
KATHARINA
Yet you are withered.
PETRUCHIO   'Tis with cares.
KATHARINA   I care not.
PETRUCHIO
Nay, hear you, Kate. In sooth, you scape not so.   237
KATHARINA
I chafe you if I tarry. Let me go.   238
PETRUCHIO
No, not a whit. I find you passing gentle.   239
'Twas told me you were rough, and coy, and sullen,   240
And now I find report a very liar,   241
For thou art pleasant, gamesome, passing courteous, 242
But slow in speech, yet sweet as springtime flowers. 243
Thou canst not frown, thou canst not look askance,   244
Nor bite the lip, as angry wenches will,
Nor hast thou pleasure to be cross in talk;   246
But thou with mildness entertain'st thy wooers,   247
With gentle conference, soft and affable.   248
Why does the world report that Kate doth limp?
Oh, sland'rous world! Kate like the hazel twig
Is straight and slender, and as brown in hue
As hazelnuts, and sweeter than the kernels.
Oh, let me see thee walk. Thou dost not halt.   253
KATHARINA
Go, fool, and whom thou keep'st command.   254
PETRUCHIO
Did ever Dian so become a grove   255
As Kate this chamber with her princely gait?
Oh, be thou Dian, and let her be Kate,
And then let Kate be chaste and Dian sportful!   258
KATHARINA
Where did you study all this goodly speech?   259
PETRUCHIO
It is extempore, from my mother wit.   260

KATHARINA
A witty mother! Witless else her son.   261
PETRUCHIO   Am I not wise?   262
KATHARINA   Yes, keep you warm.   263
PETRUCHIO
Marry, so I mean, sweet Katharine, in thy bed.
And therefore, setting all this chat aside,
Thus in plain terms: your father hath consented
That you shall be my wife; your dowry 'greed on;
And will you, nill you, I will marry you.   268
Now, Kate, I am a husband for your turn,   269
For by this light, whereby I see thy beauty—
Thy beauty that doth make me like thee well—
Thou must be married to no man but me.

*Enter Baptista, Gremio, [and] Tranio [as
Lucentio].*

For I am he am born to tame you, Kate,
And bring you from a wild Kate to a Kate   274
Conformable as other household Kates.   275
Here comes your father. Never make denial;
I must and will have Katharine to my wife.
BAPTISTA
Now, Signor Petruchio, how speed you with my
    daughter?   278
PETRUCHIO
How but well, sir, how but well?
It were impossible I should speed amiss.
BAPTISTA
Why, how now, daughter Katharine, in your dumps? 281
KATHARINA
Call you me daughter? Now, I promise you,   282
You have showed a tender fatherly regard,
To wish me wed to one half-lunatic,
A madcap ruffian and a swearing Jack,   285
That thinks with oaths to face the matter out.   286
PETRUCHIO
Father, 'tis thus: yourself and all the world
That talked of her have talked amiss of her.
If she be curst, it is for policy,   289
For she's not froward, but modest as the dove.   290
She is not hot, but temperate as the morn.
For patience she will prove a second Grissel,   292
And Roman Lucrece for her chastity.   293
And to conclude, we have 'greed so well together
That upon Sunday is the wedding day.

229 crab crab apple.   234 aimed of guessed for.   young i.e., inexperienced. (But Petruchio picks up the word in the sense of "strong," "virile.")   237 scape escape   238 chafe irritate, arouse   239 passing very. (Also in line 242.)   240 coy disdainful   241 a very an utter   242 pleasant, gamesome merry, spirited   243 But slow never anything but slow   244 askance scornfully   246 cross in talk always contradicting   247 entertain'st receive   248 conference conversation   253 halt limp.   254 whom thou keep'st command i.e., order about those whom you employ, your servants, not me.   255 Dian Diana, goddess of the hunt and of chastity.   become adorn   258 sportful amorous.   259 study memorize   260 mother wit native intelligence.

261 Witless . . . son i.e., Without the intelligence inherited from her, he would have none at all.   262–3 wise . . . warm (An allusion to the proverbial phrase "enough wit to keep oneself warm.")   268 will you, nill you whether you're willing or not   269 for your turn to suit you   274 wild Kate (With a quibble on "wildcat.")   275 Conformable compliant   278 speed fare, get on   281 in your dumps in low spirits.   282 promise assure   285 Jack ill-mannered fellow   286 face brazen   289 policy cunning, ulterior motive   290 froward willful, perverse   292 Grissel patient Griselda, the epitome of wifely patience and devotion (whose story was told by Chaucer in "The Clerk's Tale" of The Canterbury Tales and earlier by Boccaccio and Petrarch)   293 Roman Lucrece Lucretia, a Roman lady who took her own life after her chastity had been violated by the Tarquin prince, Sextus. (Shakespeare tells the story in The Rape of Lucrece.)

KATHARINA
    I'll see thee hanged on Sunday first.

GREMIO   Hark, Petruchio, she says she'll see thee
    hanged first.

TRANIO
    Is this your speeding? Nay then, good night our part! 299

PETRUCHIO
    Be patient, gentlemen. I choose her for myself.
    If she and I be pleased, what's that to you?
    'Tis bargained twixt us twain, being alone,
    That she shall still be curst in company.
    I tell you, 'tis incredible to believe
    How much she loves me. Oh, the kindest Kate!
    She hung about my neck, and kiss on kiss
    She vied so fast, protesting oath on oath,   307
    That in a twink she won me to her love.
    Oh, you are novices! 'Tis a world to see   309
    How tame, when men and women are alone,
    A meacock wretch can make the curstest shrew.—   311
    Give me thy hand, Kate. I will unto Venice
    To buy apparel gainst the wedding day.—   313
    Provide the feast, father, and bid the guests.
    I will be sure my Katharine shall be fine.   315

BAPTISTA
    I know not what to say. But give me your hands.
    God send you joy, Petruchio! 'Tis a match.

GREMIO, TRANIO
    Amen, say we. We will be witnesses.

PETRUCHIO
    Father, and wife, and gentlemen, adieu.
    I will to Venice. Sunday comes apace.
    We will have rings, and things, and fine array;
    And kiss me, Kate. We will be married o'Sunday.   322
        Exeunt Petruchio and Katharine [separately].

GREMIO
    Was ever match clapped up so suddenly?   323

BAPTISTA
    Faith, gentlemen, now I play a merchant's part,   324
    And venture madly on a desperate mart.   325

TRANIO
    'Twas a commodity lay fretting by you;   326
    'Twill bring you gain, or perish on the seas.

BAPTISTA
    The gain I seek is quiet in the match.

GREMIO
    No doubt but he hath got a quiet catch.   329
    But now, Baptista, to your younger daughter.
    Now is the day we long have lookèd for.
    I am your neighbor, and was suitor first.

TRANIO
    And I am one that love Bianca more
    Than words can witness, or your thoughts can guess.

GREMIO
    Youngling, thou canst not love so dear as I.

TRANIO
    Graybeard, thy love doth freeze.

GREMIO   But thine doth fry.
    Skipper, stand back. 'Tis age that nourisheth.   337

TRANIO
    But youth in ladies' eyes that flourisheth.

BAPTISTA
    Content you, gentlemen, I will compound this strife.   339
    'Tis deeds must win the prize, and he of both   340
    That can assure my daughter greatest dower   341
    Shall have my Bianca's love.
    Say, Signor Gremio, what can you assure her?

GREMIO
    First, as you know, my house within the city
    Is richly furnishèd with plate and gold,   345
    Basins and ewers to lave her dainty hands;   346
    My hangings all of Tyrian tapestry;   347
    In ivory coffers I have stuffed my crowns;   348
    In cypress chests my arras counterpoints,   349
    Costly apparel, tents, and canopies,   350
    Fine linen, Turkey cushions bossed with pearl,   351
    Valance of Venice gold in needlework,   352
    Pewter and brass, and all things that belongs
    To house or housekeeping. Then at my farm
    I have a hundred milch kine to the pail,   355
    Sixscore fat oxen standing in my stalls,
    And all things answerable to this portion.   357
    Myself am struck in years, I must confess,   358
    And if I die tomorrow, this is hers,
    If whilst I live she will be only mine.

TRANIO
    That "only" came well in.—Sir, list to me:
    I am my father's heir and only son.
    If I may have your daughter to my wife,
    I'll leave her houses three or four as good,
    Within rich Pisa walls, as any one
    Old Signor Gremio has in Padua,
    Besides two thousand ducats by the year   367
    Of fruitful land, all which shall be her jointure.—   368
    What, have I pinched you, Signor Gremio?

GREMIO
    Two thousand ducats by the year of land!
    [*Aside*] My land amounts not to so much in all.—
    That she shall have, besides an argosy   372

---

299 **speeding** success. **good night our part** good-bye to what we hoped to get. **307 vied** went me one better, kiss for kiss **309 a world** worth a whole world **311 meacock** cowardly **313 gainst** in anticipation of **315 fine** elegantly dressed. **322 kiss me** (Petruchio probably kisses her.) **323 clapped up** settled (by a shaking of hands) **324 Faith** In faith **325 desperate mart** risky venture. **326 lay fretting** i.e., which lay in storage being destroyed by moths, weevils, or spoilage. (With a pun on "chafing.") **329 quiet catch** (Said ironically; Gremio is sure that Kate will be anything but quiet.)

337 Skipper Flighty fellow **339 compound** settle **340 deeds** (1) actions (2) legal deeds. **he of both** the one of you two **341 dower** portion of a husband's estate settled on his wife in his will. (Also at line 387 and 4.4.45.) **345 plate** silver utensils **346 ewers to lave** pitchers to wash **347 hangings** draperies hung on beds and walls. **Tyrian** dark red or purple **348 crowns** five-shilling coins **349 arras counterpoints** counterpanes of tapestry **350 tents** bed curtains **351 Turkey** Turkish. **bossed** embossed **352 Valance** fringes of drapery around the canopy or bed frame **355 milch kine to the pail** dairy cattle **357 answerable to** on the same scale as **358 struck** advanced **367 ducats** gold coins **368 Of** from. **jointure** marriage settlement. **372 argosy** merchant vessel of the largest size

That now is lying in Marseilles road.   373
[*To Tranio*] What, have I choked you with an argosy?

TRANIO
Gremio, 'tis known my father hath no less
Than three great argosies, besides two galliases   376
And twelve tight galleys. These I will assure her,   377
And twice as much, whate'er thou off'rest next.

GREMIO
Nay, I have offered all. I have no more,
And she can have no more than all I have.
[*To Baptista*] If you like me, she shall have me and
    mine.

TRANIO
Why then, the maid is mine from all the world,
By your firm promise. Gremio is outvied.   383

BAPTISTA
I must confess your offer is the best;
And, let your father make her the assurance,   385
She is your own; else, you must pardon me.
If you should die before him, where's her dower?

TRANIO
That's but a cavil. He is old, I young.   388

GREMIO
And may not young men die, as well as old?

BAPTISTA
Well, gentlemen, I am thus resolved:
On Sunday next, you know
My daughter Katharine is to be married.
Now, on the Sunday following shall Bianca
Be bride [*to Tranio*] to you, if you make this assurance;
If not, to Signor Gremio.
And so I take my leave, and thank you both.   *Exit.*

GREMIO
Adieu, good neighbor.—Now I fear thee not.
Sirrah, young gamester, your father were a fool
To give thee all, and in his waning age
Set foot under thy table. Tut, a toy!   400
An old Italian fox is not so kind, my boy.   *Exit.*

TRANIO
A vengeance on your crafty withered hide!
Yet I have faced it with a card of ten.   403
'Tis in my head to do my master good.
I see no reason but supposed Lucentio
Must get a father, called supposed Vincentio—
And that's a wonder. Fathers commonly
Do get their children; but in this case of wooing,   408
A child shall get a sire, if I fail not of my cunning.
                                              Exit.

❖

3.1

Enter Lucentio [*as Cambio*], *Hortensio* [*as
Litio*], *and Bianca.*

LUCENTIO
Fiddler, forbear. You grow too forward, sir.
Have you so soon forgot the entertainment
Her sister Katharine welcomed you withal?

HORTENSIO
But, wrangling pedant, this is   4
The patroness of heavenly harmony.
Then give me leave to have prerogative,   6
And when in music we have spent an hour,
Your lecture shall have leisure for as much.   8

LUCENTIO
Preposterous ass, that never read so far
To know the cause why music was ordained!   10
Was it not to refresh the mind of man
After his studies or his usual pain?   12
Then give me leave to read philosophy,   13
And, while I pause, serve in your harmony.   14

HORTENSIO
Sirrah, I will not bear these braves of thine.   15

BIANCA
Why, gentlemen, you do me double wrong
To strive for that which resteth in my choice.
I am no breeching scholar in the schools;   18
I'll not be tied to hours nor 'pointed times,
But learn my lessons as I please myself.
And, to cut off all strife, here sit we down.
[*To Hortensio*] Take you your instrument, play you the
    whiles;   22
His lecture will be done ere you have tuned.

HORTENSIO
You'll leave his lecture when I am in tune?

LUCENTIO
That will be never. Tune your instrument.
              [*Hortensio moves aside and tunes.*]

BIANCA   Where left we last?

LUCENTIO   Here, madam. [*He reads.*]
    "*Hic ibat Simois; hic est Sigeia tellus;*   28
    Hic steterat Priami regia celsa senis."   29

BIANCA   Conster them.   30

LUCENTIO   "*Hic ibat,*" as I told you before, "*Simois,*" I
am Lucentio, "*hic est,*" son unto Vincentio of Pisa, "*Sigeia
tellus,*" disguised thus to get your love; "*Hic
steterat,*" and that Lucentio that comes a-wooing,
"*Priami,*" is my man Tranio, "*regia,*" bearing my port,   35
"*celsa senis,*" that we might beguile the old panta-   36
loon.   37

---

373 **road** roadstead, harbor.   376 **galliases** heavy, low-built vessels
377 **tight** watertight   383 **outvied** outbidden.   385 **let** provided
388 **but a cavil** merely a frivolous objection.   400 **Set . . . toy!** i.e.,
become a dependent in your household. Tut, nonsense!   403 **faced . . .
ten** brazened it out with only a ten-spot of cards.   408 **get** beget.
(With a play on *get*, "obtain," in line 406.)

3.1. Location: The same.
4 **this** i.e., Bianca   6 **prerogative** precedence   8 **lecture** lesson
10 **To know** as to know   12 **usual pain** regular labors.   13 **read** teach
14 **serve in** present, serve up   15 **braves** insults   18 **breeching scholar** i.e., schoolboy liable to be whipped   22 **the whiles** meantime
28–9 *Hic . . . senis* Here flowed the river Simois; here is the Sigeian
land; here stood the lofty palace of old Priam. (Ovid, *Heroides*, 1.33–4.)
30 **Conster** Construe   35 **bearing my port** i.e., pretending to be me
36–7 **pantaloon** foolish old man, i.e., Gremio.

HORTENSIO   Madam, my instrument's in tune.
BIANCA   Let's hear. [*He plays.*] Oh, fie! The treble jars.
LUCENTIO   Spit in the hole, man, and tune again.   40
                                            [*Hortensio moves aside.*]
BIANCA   Now let me see if I can conster it: *"Hic ibat
Simois,"* I know you not, *"hic est Sigeia tellus,"* I trust
you not; *"Hic steterat Priami,"* take heed he hear us not,
"regia," presume not, *"celsa senis,"* despair not.
HORTENSIO
Madam, 'tis now in tune.   [*He plays again.*]
LUCENTIO   All but the bass.
HORTENSIO
The bass is right, 'tis the base knave that jars.
[*Aside*] How fiery and forward our pedant is!
Now, for my life, the knave doth court my love.
Pedascule, I'll watch you better yet.   49
BIANCA [*to Lucentio*]
In time I may believe, yet I mistrust.
LUCENTIO
Mistrust it not, for, sure, Aeacides   51
Was Ajax, called so from his grandfather.
BIANCA
I must believe my master; else, I promise you,
I should be arguing still upon that doubt.
But let it rest.—Now, Litio, to you:
Good master, take it not unkindly, pray,
That I have been thus pleasant with you both.   57
HORTENSIO [*to Lucentio*]
You may go walk, and give me leave awhile.
My lessons make no music in three parts.
LUCENTIO
Are you so formal, sir? Well, I must wait.   60
[*Aside*] And watch withal; for, but I be deceived,   61
Our fine musician groweth amorous.
                                            [*He moves aside.*]
HORTENSIO
Madam, before you touch the instrument,
To learn the order of my fingering,   64
I must begin with rudiments of art,
To teach you gamut in a briefer sort,   66
More pleasant, pithy, and effectual
Than hath been taught by any of my trade.
And there it is in writing, fairly drawn.   69
                                            [*He gives her a paper.*]
BIANCA
Why, I am past my gamut long ago.

HORTENSIO
Yet read the gamut of Hortensio.
BIANCA [*reads*]
"Gamut I am, the ground of all accord,   72
A re, to plead Hortensio's passion;
B mi, Bianca, take him for thy lord,   74
C fa ut, that loves with all affection.   75
D sol re, one clef, two notes have I;   76
E la mi, show pity, or I die."   77
Call you this gamut? Tut, I like it not.
Old fashions please me best; I am not so nice   79
To change true rules for odd inventions.

        Enter a [Servant as] messenger.

SERVANT
Mistress, your father prays you leave your books
And help to dress your sister's chamber up.
You know tomorrow is the wedding day.
BIANCA
Farewell, sweet masters both. I must be gone.
LUCENTIO
Faith, mistress, then I have no cause to stay.
                    [*Exeunt Bianca, Servant, and Lucentio.*]
HORTENSIO
But I have cause to pry into this pedant.
Methinks he looks as though he were in love.
Yet if thy thoughts, Bianca, be so humble
To cast thy wandering eyes on every stale,   89
Seize thee that list. If once I find thee ranging,   90
Hortensio will be quit with thee by changing.   *Exit.* 91

                        ❖

[3.2]

        Enter Baptista, Gremio, Tranio [as Lucentio],
        Katharine, Bianca, [Lucentio as Cambio], and
        others, attendants.

BAPTISTA [*to Tranio*]
Signor Lucentio, this is the 'pointed day
That Katharine and Petruchio should be married,
And yet we hear not of our son-in-law.
What will be said? What mockery will it be,   4
To want the bridegroom when the priest attends   5
To speak the ceremonial rites of marriage?
What says Lucentio to this shame of ours?

---

40 Spit in the hole i.e., to make the peg stick   **49** *Pedascule* (A word
contemptuously coined by Hortensio, presumably the vocative of an
invented Latinism, *pedasculus*, "little pedant.")   **51 Mistrust** (Lucentio plays upon Bianca's *mistrust* in line 50, in which she expresses
skepticism about his secret wooing; his answer seeks to reassure her,
while at the same time in "Litio's" hearing he seems to emphasize the
truth of his instruction as he goes on with his lesson from the
Heroides. Her reply is ambiguous in the same way.)   **Aeacides**
descendant of Aeacus, King of Aegina, father of Telamon and grandfather of Ajax   **57 pleasant** merry   **60 formal** precise   **61 but** unless
64 order method   **66 gamut** the scale, from the alphabet name
(*gamma*) of the first note plus *ut*, its syllable name, now commonly
called *do*. (The *gamut* of Hortensio begins on G instead of on C.)
69 drawn set out, copied.

72 ground bass note, foundation.   **accord** harmony   **74** *B mi* (With a
suggestion of "be my.")   **75** *fa ut* (The note C is the fourth note, or *fa*,
of a scale based on G but is the first note, *ut*, or *do*, of the more universal major scale based on C. Similarly, D is the fifth note, or *sol*, in the
G scale but is the second, or *re*, in the C scale; similarly, with E as
sixth and third.)   **76 two notes** (Hinting at Hortensio's disguise.)
77 *E la mi* (Suggesting "Ill am I.")   **79 nice** capricious   **89 stale**
ridiculous rival   **90 Seize . . . list** let him who wants you have you.
ranging inconstant. (The metaphor is that of a straying hawk.)
91 be quit get even.   **changing** loving another.
3.2. Location: Padua. Before Baptista's house.
4 What . . . said? What will people say?   **5 want** lack

KATHARINA
No shame but mine. I must, forsooth, be forced
To give my hand opposed against my heart
Unto a mad-brain rudesby full of spleen,   10
Who wooed in haste and means to wed at leisure.
I told you, I, he was a frantic fool,
Hiding his bitter jests in blunt behavior.
And, to be noted for a merry man,   14
He'll woo a thousand, 'point the day of marriage,
Make friends, invite, and proclaim the banns,   16
Yet never means to wed where he hath wooed.
Now must the world point at poor Katharine
And say, "Lo, there is mad Petruchio's wife,
If it would please him come and marry her!"

TRANIO
Patience, good Katharine, and Baptista, too.
Upon my life, Petruchio means but well,
Whatever fortune stays him from his word.   23
Though he be blunt, I know him passing wise;   24
Though he be merry, yet withal he's honest.   25

KATHARINA
Would Katharine had never seen him, though!
                                    Exit weeping.

BAPTISTA
Go, girl, I cannot blame thee now to weep,
For such an injury would vex a very saint,
Much more a shrew of thy impatient humor.

        Enter Biondello.

BIONDELLO   Master, master! News, and such old news   30
as you never heard of!
BAPTISTA   Is it new and old too? How may that be?
BIONDELLO   Why, is it not news to hear of Petruchio's
coming?
BAPTISTA   Is he come?
BIONDELLO   Why, no, sir.
BAPTISTA   What, then?
BIONDELLO   He is coming.
BAPTISTA   When will he be here?
BIONDELLO   When he stands where I am and sees you
there.
TRANIO   But say, what to thine old news?   42
BIONDELLO   Why, Petruchio is coming in a new hat and
an old jerkin; a pair of old breeches thrice turned; a   44
pair of boots that have been candle-cases, one buckled,   45
another laced; an old rusty sword ta'en out of the town
armory, with a broken hilt, and chapeless; with two   47
broken points; his horse hipped, with an old mothy   48

saddle and stirrups of no kindred; besides, possessed   49
with the glanders and like to mose in the chine, trou-   50
bled with the lampass, infected with the fashions, full   51
of windgalls, sped with spavins, rayed with the yel-   52
lows, past cure of the fives, stark spoiled with the stag- 53
gers, begnawn with the bots, swayed in the back and   54
shoulder-shotten; near-legged before, and with a half-   55
cheeked bit and a headstall of sheep's leather which,   56
being restrained to keep him from stumbling, hath   57
been often burst and now repaired with knots; one
girth six times pieced, and a woman's crupper of   59
velour, which hath two letters for her name fairly   60
set down in studs, and here and there pieced
with packthread.   62
BAPTISTA   Who comes with him?
BIONDELLO   Oh, sir, his lackey, for all the world capari- 64
soned like the horse; with a linen stock on one leg and   65
a kersey boot-hose on the other, gartered with a red   66
and blue list; an old hat, and the humor of forty fan-   67
cies pricked in 't for a feather—a monster, a very mon-   68
ster in apparel, and not like a Christian footboy or a
gentleman's lackey.

TRANIO
'Tis some odd humor pricks him to this fashion;   71
Yet oftentimes he goes but mean-appareled.   72
BAPTISTA   I am glad he's come, howsoe'er he comes.
BIONDELLO   Why, sir, he comes not.
BAPTISTA   Didst thou not say he comes?
BIONDELLO   Who? That Petruchio came?
BAPTISTA   Ay, that Petruchio came.
BIONDELLO   No, sir, I say his horse comes, with him on
his back.
BAPTISTA   Why, that's all one.   80
BIONDELLO
Nay, by Saint Jamy,

---

10 rudesby unmannerly fellow.   **spleen** i.e., changeable temper
14 to be noted for in order to get a reputation as   **16 banns** wedding
announcement   **23 Whatever . . . word** whatever accident keeps him
from fulfilling his promise.   **24 passing** exceedingly   **25 merry**
given to joking   **30 old** rare; and referring to Petruchio's old clothes
42 to about   **44 jerkin** man's jacket.   **turned** i.e., with the material
reversed to get more wear   **45 candle-cases** i.e., discarded boots,
used only as a receptacle for candle ends   **47 chapeless** without the
chape, the metal plate or mounting of a scabbard, especially that
which covers the point   **48 points** tagged laces for attaching hose to
doublet.   **hipped** lamed in the hip. (Almost all the diseases here
named are described in Gervase Markham's *How to Choose, Ride,
Train, and Diet both Hunting Horses and Running Horses . . . Also a Discourse of Horsemanship*, probably first published in 1593.)

49 of no kindred that don't match   **50 glanders** contagious disease in
horses causing swelling beneath the jaw and mucous discharge from
the nostrils.   **50 mose in the chine** suffer from glanders   **51 lampass** a
thick, spongy flesh growing over a horse's upper teeth and hindering
his eating.   **fashions** i.e., or farcins, or farcy, a disease like glanders.
52 windgalls soft tumors or swellings generally found on the fetlock
joint, so called from having been supposed to contain air.   **sped** far
gone.   **spavins** a disease of the hock, marked by a small bony enlargement inside the leg.   **rayed** bespattered, defiled   **52–3 yellows** jaundice   **53 fives** avives, a glandular disease causing swelling behind the
ear   **53–4 stark . . . staggers** completely destroyed by a disease causing
palsylike staggering   **54 bots** parasitic worms   **55 shoulder-shotten**
with sprained or dislocated shoulder.   **near-legged before** with knock-
kneed forelegs   **55–6 half-cheeked bit** one to which the bridle is
attached halfway up the cheek or sidepiece and thus not giving sufficient control over the horse   **56 headstall** part of the bridle over the
head.   **sheep's leather** (i.e., of inferior quality; pigskin was used for
strongest harness)   **57 restrained** drawn back   **59 girth** saddle-strap
passing under the horse's belly.   **pieced** mended.   **crupper** leather
loop passing under the horse's tail and fastened to the saddle
60 velour velvet.   **two . . . name** her initials   **62 packthread** twine for
securing parcels.   **64–5 for . . . caparisoned** in all respects outfitted
65 stock stocking   **66 kersey boot-hose** overstocking of coarse material
for wearing under boots   **67 list** strip of cloth   **67–8 the humor . . .
feather** a trite motto incised in it instead of a feather   **68 pricked**
pinned.   **for** in place of   **71 humor pricks** whim that spurs   **72 mean-
appareled** poorly dressed.   **80 all one** the same thing.

I hold you a penny,   82
A horse and a man
Is more than one,
And yet not many.

Enter Petruchio and Grumio.

PETRUCHIO
Come, where be these gallants? Who's at home?
BAPTISTA   You are welcome, sir.
PETRUCHIO   And yet I come not well.   88
BAPTISTA   And yet you halt not.   89
TRANIO
Not so well apparelled as I wish you were.
PETRUCHIO
Were it better, I should rush in thus.   91
But where is Kate? Where is my lovely bride?
How does my father? Gentles, methinks you frown.
And wherefore gaze this goodly company,
As if they saw some wondrous monument,   95
Some comet, or unusual prodigy?   96
BAPTISTA
Why, sir, you know this is your wedding day.
First were we sad, fearing you would not come,
Now sadder that you come so unprovided.   99
Fie, doff this habit, shame to your estate,   100
An eyesore to our solemn festival!
TRANIO
And tell us, what occasion of import
Hath all so long detained you from your wife
And sent you hither so unlike yourself?
PETRUCHIO
Tedious it were to tell, and harsh to hear.
Sufficeth I am come to keep my word,   106
Though in some part enforcèd to digress,   107
Which at more leisure I will so excuse
As you shall well be satisfied withal.
But where is Kate? I stay too long from her.
The morning wears; 'tis time we were at church.
TRANIO
See not your bride in these unreverent robes.
Go to my chamber. Put on clothes of mine.
PETRUCHIO
Not I, believe me. Thus I'll visit her.
BAPTISTA
But thus, I trust, you will not marry her.
PETRUCHIO
Good sooth, even thus. Therefore ha' done with
    words.   116
To me she's married, not unto my clothes.
Could I repair what she will wear in me   118
As I can change these poor accoutrements,
'Twere well for Kate and better for myself.

But what a fool am I to chat with you,
When I should bid good morrow to my bride
And seal the title with a lovely kiss!   *Exit.* 123
TRANIO
He hath some meaning in his mad attire.
We will persuade him, be it possible,
To put on better ere he go to church.
BAPTISTA
I'll after him, and see the event of this.   127
        Exit [with all but Tranio and Lucentio].
TRANIO
But, sir, to love concerneth us to add   128
Her father's liking, which to bring to pass,
As I before imparted to Your Worship,   130
I am to get a man—whate'er he be
It skills not much, we'll fit him to our turn—   132
And he shall be Vincentio of Pisa
And make assurance here in Padua
Of greater sums than I have promisèd.
So shall you quietly enjoy your hope
And marry sweet Bianca with consent.
LUCENTIO
Were it not that my fellow schoolmaster
Doth watch Bianca's steps so narrowly,
'Twere good, methinks, to steal our marriage,   140
Which once performed, let all the world say no,
I'll keep mine own, despite of all the world.
TRANIO
That by degrees we mean to look into,
And watch our vantage in this business.   144
We'll overreach the graybeard, Gremio,
The narrow-prying father, Minola,   146
The quaint musician, amorous Litio,   147
All for my master's sake, Lucentio.

Enter Gremio.

Signor Gremio, came you from the church?
GREMIO
As willingly as e'er I came from school.
TRANIO
And is the bride and bridegroom coming home?
GREMIO
A bridegroom, say you? 'Tis a groom indeed,   152
A grumbling groom, and that the girl shall find.
TRANIO
Curster than she? Why, 'tis impossible.
GREMIO
Why, he 's a devil, a devil, a very fiend.
TRANIO
Why, she's a devil, a devil, the devil's dam.   156

82 hold wager   **88 I come not well** i.e., I am not made to feel welcome; or, I come admittedly not well apparelled.   **89 halt** limp, move
slowly   **91 Were it** Even if it (my apparel) were.   **rush** come quickly.
(Referring to *halt not* in line 89.)   **95 monument** portent   **96 prodigy**
omen.   **99 unprovided** ill equipped.   **100 habit** outfit.   **estate** position, station   **106 Sufficeth** It is enough that   **107 digress** i.e., devi-
ate   **116 Good sooth** i.e., Yes, indeed   **118 Could . . . me** If I could
amend in my character what she'll have to put up with

123 lovely loving   **127 event** outcome   **128 to love . . . add** besides
obtaining the love of the lady, it behooves us to add   **130 to Your
Worship** (Tranio privately drops the fiction that he is Lucentio's master.)   **132 skills** matters   **140 steal our marriage** elope   **144 watch
our vantage** look out for our best opportunity, advantage   **146 narrow-prying** suspicious, watchful   **147 quaint** skillful   **152 'Tis a
groom indeed** A fine bridegroom he is. (Said ironically, with pun on
the sense of "servant," "rough fellow.")   **156 dam** mother.

GREMIO
Tut, she's a lamb, a dove, a fool to him.   157
I'll tell you, Sir Lucentio. When the priest
Should ask if Katharine should be his wife,   159
"Ay, by Gog's wouns," quoth he, and swore so loud   160
That all amazed the priest let fall the book,
And as he stooped again to take it up,
This mad-brained bridegroom took him such a cuff   163
That down fell priest and book, and book and priest.
"Now take them up," quoth he, "if any list."   165

TRANIO
What said the wench when he rose again?

GREMIO
Trembled and shook, forwhy he stamped and swore   167
As if the vicar meant to cozen him.   168
But after many ceremonies done
He calls for wine. "A health!" quoth he, as if
He had been aboard, carousing to his mates   171
After a storm; quaffed off the muscatel
And threw the sops all in the sexton's face,   173
Having no other reason
But that his beard grew thin and hungerly   175
And seemed to ask him sops as he was drinking.   176
This done, he took the bride about the neck
And kissed her lips with such a clamorous smack
That at the parting all the church did echo.
And I seeing this came thence for very shame,
And after me, I know, the rout is coming.   181
Such a mad marriage never was before.   *Music plays.*
Hark, hark! I hear the minstrels play.

Enter Petruchio, Kate, Bianca, Hortensio [as Litio],
Baptista, [with Grumio, and train].

PETRUCHIO
Gentlemen and friends, I thank you for your pains.
I know you think to dine with me today,
And have prepared great store of wedding cheer;
But so it is my haste doth call me hence,
And therefore here I mean to take my leave.

BAPTISTA
Is't possible you will away tonight?

PETRUCHIO
I must away today, before night come.
Make it no wonder. If you knew my business,   191
You would entreat me rather go than stay.
And, honest company, I thank you all   193
That have beheld me give away myself
To this most patient, sweet, and virtuous wife.
Dine with my father, drink a health to me,
For I must hence; and farewell to you all.

TRANIO
Let us entreat you stay till after dinner.

PETRUCHIO
It may not be.

GREMIO   Let me entreat you.

PETRUCHIO
It cannot be.

KATHARINA   Let me entreat you.

PETRUCHIO
I am content.

KATHARINA   Are you content to stay?

PETRUCHIO
I am content you shall entreat me stay;
But yet not stay, entreat me how you can.

KATHARINA
Now, if you love me, stay.

PETRUCHIO   Grumio, my horse.   204

GRUMIO   Ay, sir, they be ready. The oats have eaten the 205
horses.   206

KATHARINA   Nay, then,
Do what thou canst, I will not go today,
No, nor tomorrow—not till I please myself.
The door is open, sir; there lies your way.
You may be jogging whiles your boots are green.   211
For me, I'll not be gone till I please myself.   212
'Tis like you'll prove a jolly, surly groom,   213
That take it on you at the first so roundly.   214

PETRUCHIO
Oh, Kate, content thee. Prithee, be not angry.

KATHARINA
I will be angry. What hast thou to do?—   216
Father, be quiet. He shall stay my leisure.   217

GREMIO
Ay, marry, sir, now it begins to work.   218

KATHARINA
Gentlemen, forward to the bridal dinner.
I see a woman may be made a fool
If she had not a spirit to resist.

PETRUCHIO
They shall go forward, Kate, at thy command.—
Obey the bride, you that attend on her.
Go to the feast, revel and domineer.   224
Carouse full measure to her maidenhead,   225
Be mad and merry, or go hang yourselves.
But for my bonny Kate, she must with me.   227
Nay, look not big, nor stamp, nor stare, nor fret;   228
I will be master of what is mine own.
She is my goods, my chattels; she is my house,
My household stuff, my field, my barn,
My horse, my ox, my ass, my anything;   232
And here she stands, touch her whoever dare.

---

157 **a fool to** i.e., a pitiable weak creature compared with
159 **Should ask** came to the point (in the service) where he is directed
to ask   160 **Gog's wouns** God's (Christ's) wounds   163 **took** gave,
struck   165 **list** choose.   167 **forwhy** for   168 **cozen** cheat
171 **aboard** aboard ship   173 **sops** cakes or bread soaked in the wine
175 **hungerly** hungry looking, having a starved or famished look
176 **And . . . drinking** and seemed to invite the throwing in his face of
what Petruchio was drinking.   181 **rout** crowd, wedding party
191 **Make it no wonder** Don't be surprised.   193 **honest** worthy, kind

204 **horse** horses.   205–6 **oats . . . horses** (A comic inversion.)
211 **be . . . green** (Proverbial for "getting an early start," with a sarcastic allusion to his unseemly attire.)   **green** fresh, new.   212 **For** As
for   213 **like** likely.   **jolly** (Said sarcastically.)   214 **take it on you**
i.e., throw your weight around.   **roundly** unceremoniously.
216 **What . . . do?** What business is it of yours?   217 **stay my leisure**
wait until I am ready.   218 **now . . . work** now it starts.   224 **domineer** feast riotously   225 **to her maidenhead** to her loss of virginity
227 **for** as for   228 **big** threatening   232 **ox . . . anything** (This catalogue of a man's possessions is from the Tenth Commandment.)

I'll bring mine action on the proudest he 234
That stops my way in Padua.—Grumio,
Draw forth thy weapon. We are beset with thieves. 236
Rescue thy mistress, if thou be a man.—
Fear not, sweet wench, they shall not touch thee, Kate!
I'll buckler thee against a million. 239

Exeunt Petruchio, Katharina, [and Grumio].

BAPTISTA
Nay, let them go—a couple of quiet ones!
GREMIO
Went they not quickly, I should die with laughing.
TRANIO
Of all mad matches never was the like.
LUCENTIO
Mistress, what's your opinion of your sister?
BIANCA
That, being mad herself, she's madly mated.
GREMIO
I warrant him, Petruchio is Kated. 245
BAPTISTA
Neighbors and friends, though bride and bridegroom
    wants 246
For to supply the places at the table, 247
You know there wants no junkets at the feast. 248
Lucentio, you shall supply the bridegroom's place,
And let Bianca take her sister's room.
TRANIO
Shall sweet Bianca practice how to bride it? 251
BAPTISTA
She shall, Lucentio.—Come, gentlemen, let's go.

Exeunt.

❧

[4.1]

Enter Grumio.

GRUMIO   Fie, fie on all tired jades, on all mad masters, 1
and all foul ways! Was ever man so beaten? Was ever 2
man so rayed? Was ever man so weary? I am sent be- 3
fore to make a fire, and they are coming after to warm
them. Now, were not I a little pot and soon hot, my 5
very lips might freeze to my teeth, my tongue to the
roof of my mouth, my heart in my belly, ere I should
come by a fire to thaw me. But I with blowing the fire 8
shall warm myself; for, considering the weather, a
taller man than I will take cold.—Holla, ho! Curtis! 10

Enter Curtis.

CURTIS   Who is that calls so coldly?

GRUMIO   A piece of ice. If thou doubt it, thou mayst
slide from my shoulder to my heel with no greater a
run but my head and my neck. A fire, good Curtis! 14
CURTIS   Is my master and his wife coming, Grumio?
GRUMIO   Oh, ay, Curtis, ay, and therefore fire, fire! Cast 16
on no water. 17
CURTIS   Is she so hot a shrew as she's reported?
GRUMIO   She was, good Curtis, before this frost. But,
thou know'st, winter tames man, woman, and beast;
for it hath tamed my old master and my new mistress
and myself, fellow Curtis.
CURTIS   Away, you three-inch fool! I am no beast. 23
GRUMIO   Am I but three inches? Why, thy horn is a foot, 24
and so long am I, at the least. But wilt thou make a fire, 25
or shall I complain on thee to our mistress, whose
hand—she being now at hand—thou shalt soon feel,
to thy cold comfort, for being slow in thy hot office? 28
CURTIS   I prithee, good Grumio, tell me, how goes the
world?
GRUMIO   A cold world, Curtis, in every office but thine,
and therefore fire. Do thy duty, and have thy duty, for 32
my master and mistress are almost frozen to death.
CURTIS   There's fire ready, and therefore, good Grumio,
the news.
GRUMIO   Why, "Jack boy, ho, boy!" and as much news 36
as wilt thou.
CURTIS   Come, you are so full of coney-catching. 38
GRUMIO   Why, therefore fire, for I have caught extreme
cold. Where's the cook? Is supper ready, the house
trimmed, rushes strewed, cobwebs swept, the serv- 41
ingmen in their new fustian, the white stockings, and 42
every officer his wedding garment on? Be the Jacks 43
fair within, the Jills fair without, the carpets laid, and 44
everything in order?
CURTIS   All ready; and therefore, I pray thee, news.
GRUMIO   First, know my horse is tired, my master and
mistress fallen out. 48
CURTIS   How?
GRUMIO   Out of their saddles into the dirt—and there- 50
by hangs a tale. 51

---

234 **action** (1) lawsuit (2) attack   236 **Draw** (Perhaps Petruchio and
Grumio actually draw their swords.)   239 **buckler** shield, defend
245 **Kated** (Gremio's invention for "mated and matched with Kate.")
246–7 **wants For to supply** are not present to fill   248 **there wants no
junkets** there is no lack of sweetmeats   251 **bride it** play the bride.
**4.1. Location: Petruchio's country house. A table is set out,
with seats.**
1 **jades** ill-conditioned horses   2 **ways** roads.   3 **rayed** bespattered.
5 **a little . . . hot** (Proverbial expression for a person of small stature
soon angered.)   8 **come by** find   10 **taller** (With play on the meaning
"better," "finer.")

14 **run** running start   16–17 **Cast . . . water** (Alludes to the round
"Scotland's burning," in which the phrase "Fire, fire!" is followed by
"Pour on water, pour on water.")   23 **three-inch fool** (Another reference to Grumio's size.)   **I am no beast** (Curtis protests being called
fellow by Grumio, since Grumio in line 20 has paralleled himself with
beast.)   24–5 **Why . . . least** (Grumio hints that Curtis is a beast with a
prominent *horn*, and hence a cuckold; suggesting too that Grumio's
horn, i.e., *penis*, is as long as Curtis's or longer.)   28 **hot office** i.e.,
duty of providing a fire.   32 **have thy duty** have what's coming to
you, your due   36 **Jack . . . boy** (The first line of another round or
catch.)   38 **coney-catching** cheating, trickery. (With wordplay on
catch, or round, like "Jack boy, ho, boy" in line 36.)
41 **rushes** (Used to cover the floor.)   42 **fustian** coarse cloth of cotton
and flax   43 **officer** household servant.   **Jacks** (1) servingmen (2)
drinking vessels, usually of leather and hence needing to be clean
within   44 **Jills** (1) maidservants (2) "gills," drinking vessels holding
a quarter pint, often of metal and hence in need of polishing *without*.
(Grumio may joke that the maidservants cannot be expected to be
clean *within*.)   48 **fallen out** quarreling. (But with a pun on the literal
sense in line 50.)   50–1 **thereby hangs a tale** there's quite a story to
tell about that. (But with a risible suggestion of hanging by one's tail.)

CURTIS Let's ha 't, good Grumio.   52
GRUMIO Lend thine ear.
CURTIS Here.
GRUMIO There.   [*He cuffs Curtis.*]
CURTIS This 'tis to feel a tale, not to hear a tale.
GRUMIO And therefore 'tis called a sensible tale, and   57
this cuff was but to knock at your ear and beseech
listening. Now I begin: Imprimis, we came down a   59
foul hill, my master riding behind my mistress—   60
CURTIS Both of one horse?   61
GRUMIO What's that to thee?
CURTIS Why, a horse.
GRUMIO Tell thou the tale. But hadst thou not crossed   64
me, thou shouldst have heard how her horse fell and
she under her horse; thou shouldst have heard in how
miry a place, how she was bemoiled, how he left her   67
with the horse upon her, how he beat me because her
horse stumbled, how she waded through the dirt to
pluck him off me, how he swore, how she prayed that
never prayed before, how I cried, how the horses ran
away, how her bridle was burst, how I lost my
crupper, with many things of worthy memory, which   73
now shall die in oblivion and thou return unexperi-
enced to thy grave.
CURTIS By this reckoning he is more shrew than she.
GRUMIO Ay, and that thou and the proudest of you all
shall find when he comes home. But what talk I of   78
this? Call forth Nathaniel, Joseph, Nicholas, Philip,
Walter, Sugarsop, and the rest. Let their heads be
sleekly combed, their blue coats brushed, and their   81
garters of an indifferent knit; let them curtsy with their   82
left legs, and not presume to touch a hair of my
master's horsetail till they kiss their hands. Are they
all ready?
CURTIS They are.
GRUMIO Call them forth.
CURTIS [*calling*] Do you hear, ho? You must meet my
master to countenance my mistress.   89
GRUMIO Why, she hath a face of her own.
CURTIS Who knows not that?
GRUMIO Thou, it seems, that calls for company to
countenance her.
CURTIS I call them forth to credit her.   94

Enter four or five Servingmen.

GRUMIO Why, she comes to borrow nothing of them.
NATHANIEL Welcome home, Grumio!
PHILIP How now, Grumio?
JOSEPH What, Grumio!
NICHOLAS Fellow Grumio!
NATHANIEL How now, old lad?

GRUMIO Welcome, you; how now, you; what, you; fellow, you—and thus much for greeting. Now, my
spruce companions, is all ready, and all things neat?   103
NATHANIEL All things is ready. How near is our
master?
GRUMIO E'en at hand, alighted by this; and therefore
be not—Cock's passion, silence! I hear my master.   107

Enter Petruchio and Kate.

PETRUCHIO
Where be these knaves? What, no man at door
To hold my stirrup nor to take my horse?   109
Where is Nathaniel, Gregory, Philip?
ALL SERVANTS Here, here, sir, here, sir.
PETRUCHIO
Here, sir! Here, sir! Here, sir! Here, sir!
You loggerheaded and unpolished grooms!
What, no attendance? No regard? No duty?
Where is the foolish knave I sent before?   115
GRUMIO
Here, sir, as foolish as I was before.
PETRUCHIO
You peasant swain, you whoreson, malt-horse
drudge!   117
Did I not bid thee meet me in the park
And bring along these rascal knaves with thee?
GRUMIO
Nathaniel's coat, sir, was not fully made,
And Gabriel's pumps were all unpinked i'the heel.   121
There was no link to color Peter's hat,   122
And Walter's dagger was not come from sheathing.   123
There were none fine but Adam, Ralph, and Gregory;   124
The rest were ragged, old, and beggarly.
Yet, as they are, here are they come to meet you.
PETRUCHIO
Go, rascals, go and fetch my supper in.
                                    Exeunt Servants.
[*He sings.*] "Where is the life that late I led?   128
Where are those—" Sit down, Kate, and welcome.—   129
                                    [*They sit at table.*]
Soud, soud, soud, soud!   130

Enter Servants with supper.

Why, when, I say?—Nay, good sweet Kate, be
merry.—   131
Off with my boots, you rogues! You villains, when?
                [*A Servant takes off Petruchio's boots.*]
[*He sings.*] "It was the friar of orders gray,   133
As he forth walkèd on his way—"   134

---

103 spruce lively, trim in appearance   **107 Cock's passion** By God's
(Christ's) suffering   **109 hold my stirrup** i.e., help me dismount
115 before ahead. (With pun in next line on "previously.")
117 swain rustic.   **whoreson . . . drudge** worthless plodding work
animal, such as would be used on a treadmill to grind malt.
121 pumps low-cut shoes.   **unpinked** lacking in eyelets or in ornamental tracing in the leather   **122 link** blacking made from burnt
"links" or torches   **123 sheathing** being fitted with a sheath.
124 fine well clothed   **128–9 Where . . . those** (A fragment of a lost
ballad, probably lamenting the man's loss of freedom in marriage.)
130 Soud (A nonsense song, or expression of impatience, or perhaps
"food!")   **131 when** (An exclamation of impatience.)   **133–4 "It . . .
way"** (A fragment of a lost ballad, probably bawdy.)

---

52 ha 't have it   **57 sensible** (1) capable of being felt (2) showing
good sense   **59 Imprimis** In the first place   **60 foul** muddy   **61 of**
on   **64 crossed** thwarted, interrupted   **67 bemoiled** befouled with
mire   **73 crupper** (See 3.2.59.)   **of worthy** worthy of   **78 what** why
81 blue coats (Usual dress for servingmen.)   **82 indifferent** well-
matched, identical   **89 countenance** pay respects to. (With a following pun on the meaning "face.")   **94 credit** pay respects to. (With
another pun following, on "extend financial credit.")

Out, you rogue! You pluck my foot awry.   135
                              [*He kicks the Servant.*]
Take that, and mend the plucking of the other.—   136
Be merry, Kate.—Some water, here. What, ho!

        Enter one with water.

Where's my spaniel Troilus? Sirrah, get you hence,
And bid my cousin Ferdinand come hither—
                              [*Exit Servant.*]
One, Kate, that you must kiss and be acquainted with.
Where are my slippers? Shall I have some water?
Come, Kate, and wash, and welcome heartily.
              [*A Servant offers water, but spills some.*]
You whoreson villain, will you let it fall?
                              [*He strikes the Servant.*]

KATHARINA
Patience, I pray you, 'twas a fault unwilling.   144
PETRUCHIO
A whoreson, beetleheaded, flap-eared knave!—   145
Come, Kate, sit down. I know you have a stomach.   146
Will you give thanks, sweet Kate, or else shall I?—   147
What's this? Mutton?
FIRST SERVANT   Ay.
PETRUCHIO   Who brought it?
PETER   I.
PETRUCHIO
'Tis burnt, and so is all the meat.
What dogs are these? Where is the rascal cook?
How durst you, villains, bring it from the dresser   151
And serve it thus to me that love it not?
There, take it to you, trenchers, cups, and all.   153
                  [*He throws the meat, etc., at them.*]
You heedless jolt-heads and unmannered slaves!   154
What, do you grumble? I'll be with you straight.   155
                              [*They run out.*]

KATHARINA
I pray you, husband, be not so disquiet.
The meat was well, if you were so contented.   157
PETRUCHIO
I tell thee, Kate, 'twas burnt and dried away,
And I expressly am forbid to touch it;
For it engenders choler, planteth anger,   160
And better 'twere that both of us did fast,
Since, of ourselves, ourselves are choleric,   162
Than feed it with such overroasted flesh.
Be patient. Tomorrow 't shall be mended,
And for this night we'll fast for company.   165
Come, I will bring thee to thy bridal chamber.   166
                              Exeunt.

        Enter Servants severally.

NATHANIEL   Peter, didst ever see the like?
PETER   He kills her in her own humor.   168

        Enter Curtis.

GRUMIO   Where is he?
CURTIS   In her chamber,
Making a sermon of continency to her,   171
And rails, and swears, and rates, that she, poor soul,   172
Knows not which way to stand, to look, to speak,
And sits as one new risen from a dream.
Away, away! For he is coming hither.   [*Exeunt.*]

        Enter Petruchio.

PETRUCHIO
Thus have I politicly begun my reign,   176
And 'tis my hope to end successfully.
My falcon now is sharp and passing empty,   178
And till she stoop she must not be full-gorged,   179
For then she never looks upon her lure.
Another way I have to man my haggard,   181
To make her come and know her keeper's call:
That is, to watch her, as we watch these kites   183
That bate and beat and will not be obedient.   184
She ate no meat today, nor none shall eat.
Last night she slept not, nor tonight she shall not.
As with the meat, some undeservèd fault
I'll find about the making of the bed,
And here I'll fling the pillow, there the bolster,
This way the coverlet, another way the sheets.
Ay, and amid this hurly I intend   191
That all is done in reverent care of her.
And in conclusion she shall watch all night,   193
And if she chance to nod I'll rail and brawl,
And with the clamor keep her still awake.
This is a way to kill a wife with kindness;
And thus I'll curb her mad and headstrong humor.   197
He that knows better how to tame a shrew,
Now let him speak. 'Tis charity to show.   *Exit.* 199

                        ❖

[4.2]

        *Enter Tranio [as Lucentio] and Hortensio
        [as Litio].*

TRANIO
Is't possible, friend Litio, that Mistress Bianca
Doth fancy any other but Lucentio?
I tell you, sir, she bears me fair in hand.   3

135 **Out** (Exclamation of anger or reproach.)   136 **mend the plucking of** do a better job of pulling off   144 **unwilling** not intentional.
145 **beetleheaded** i.e., blockheaded (since a *beetle* is a pounding tool)   146 **stomach** appetite. (With a suggestion also of "temper.")
147 **give thanks** say grace   151 **dresser** one who "dresses" or prepares the food; or, sideboard   153 **trenchers** wooden dishes or plates   154 **jolt-heads** blockheads   155 **with you straight** after you at once (to get even for this).   157 **if . . . contented** if you had chosen to be pleased with it.   160 **choler** the humor or bodily fluid, hot and dry in character, that supposedly produced ill temper and was thought to be aggravated by the eating of roast meat   162 **of ourselves** by our natures   165 **for company** together.   166.2 *severally* separately.

168 **He . . . humor** He subdues her shrewishness with his own greater shrewishness.   171 **sermon of continency** lecture on self-restraint   172 **rates** scolds.   **that** so that   176 **politicly** with skillful calculation   178 **sharp** hungry.   **passing** very   179 **stoop** fly down to the lure   181 **man** tame, assert masculine authority over.   **haggard** wild female hawk; hence, an intractable woman   183 **watch her** keep her watching, i.e., awake.   **kites** a kind of hawk. (With a pun on *Kate*.)   184 **bate and beat** beat the wings impatiently and flutter away from the hand or perch   191 **hurly** commotion.   **intend** pretend   193 **watch** stay awake   197 **humor** disposition.   199 **'Tis charity to show** This is to perform an act of Christian benevolence. (On the rhyme with *shrew*, see also the play's final lines.)
4.2. Location: Padua. Before Baptista's house.
3 **bears . . . hand** gives me encouragement, leads me on.

HORTENSIO
Sir, to satisfy you in what I have said,   4
Stand by and mark the manner of his teaching.
                                    [*They stand aside.*]

                    Enter Bianca [and Lucentio as Cambio].

LUCENTIO
Now, mistress, profit you in what you read?   6
BIANCA
What, master, read you? First resolve me that.   7
LUCENTIO
I read that I profess, *The Art to Love.*   8
BIANCA
And may you prove, sir, master of your art!
LUCENTIO
While you, sweet dear, prove mistress of my heart!
                    [*They move aside and court each other.*]
HORTENSIO [*to Tranio, coming forward*]
Quick proceeders, marry! Now, tell me, I pray,   11
You that durst swear that your mistress Bianca
Loved none in the world so well as Lucentio.
TRANIO
Oh, despiteful love! Unconstant womankind!   14
I tell thee, Litio, this is wonderful.   15
HORTENSIO
Mistake no more. I am not Litio,
Nor a musician, as I seem to be,
But one that scorn to live in this disguise   18
For such a one as leaves a gentleman   19
And makes a god of such a cullion.   20
Know, sir, that I am called Hortensio.
TRANIO
Signor Hortensio, I have often heard
Of your entire affection to Bianca;   23
And since mine eyes are witness of her lightness,   24
I will with you, if you be so contented,
Forswear Bianca and her love forever.
HORTENSIO
See how they kiss and court! Signor Lucentio,
Here is my hand, and here I firmly vow
                                    [*giving his hand*]
Never to woo her more, but do forswear her,
As one unworthy all the former favors
That I have fondly flattered her withal.   31
TRANIO
And here I take the like unfeignèd oath,
Never to marry with her though she would entreat.
Fie on her, see how beastly she doth court him!
HORTENSIO
Would all the world but he had quite forsworn!   35

For me, that I may surely keep mine oath,   36
I will be married to a wealthy widow,
Ere three days pass, which hath as long loved me
As I have loved this proud disdainful haggard.   39
And so farewell, Signor Lucentio.
Kindness in women, not their beauteous looks,
Shall win my love. And so I take my leave,
In resolution as I swore before.   [*Exit.*]   43
TRANIO [*as Lucentio and Bianca come forward again*]
Mistress Bianca, bless you with such grace
As 'longeth to a lover's blessèd case!   45
Nay, I have ta'en you napping, gentle love,   46
And have forsworn you with Hortensio.
BIANCA
Tranio, you jest. But have you both forsworn me?
TRANIO
Mistress, we have.
LUCENTIO   Then we are rid of Litio.
TRANIO
I' faith, he'll have a lusty widow now,   50
That shall be wooed and wedded in a day.
BIANCA   God give him joy!
TRANIO   Ay, and he'll tame her.
BIANCA   He says so, Tranio?
TRANIO
Faith, he is gone unto the taming-school.
BIANCA
The taming-school! What, is there such a place?
TRANIO
Ay, mistress, and Petruchio is the master,
That teacheth tricks eleven-and-twenty long   58
To tame a shrew and charm her chattering tongue.

                    Enter Biondello.

BIONDELLO
Oh, master, master, I have watched so long
That I am dog-weary, but at last I spied
An ancient angel coming down the hill   62
Will serve the turn.
TRANIO   What is he, Biondello?   63
BIONDELLO
Master, a marcantant, or a pedant,   64
I know not what, but formal in apparel,
In gait and countenance surely like a father.
LUCENTIO   And what of him, Tranio?
TRANIO
If he be credulous and trust my tale,
I'll make him glad to seem Vincentio,
And give assurance to Baptista Minola

---

4 **satisfy** convince   6 **read** (Evidently, both Bianca and "Cambio" carry books.)   7 **resolve** answer   8 **I read . . . Love** I read what I practice, Ovid's *Ars Amatoria.*   11 **proceeders** (1) workers, doers (2) candidates for academic degrees (as suggested by the phrase *master of your art* in line 9)   14 **despiteful** cruel   15 **wonderful** cause for wonder.   18 **scorn** scorns   19 **such a one** i.e., Bianca   20 **cullion** base fellow. (Referring to "Cambio"; literally, *cullion* means "testicle.")   23 **entire** sincere   24 **lightness** wantonness   31 **fondly** foolishly   35 **Would . . . forsworn!** i.e., May everyone in the world forsake her except the penniless "Cambio," and may she thus get what she deserves!

36 **For** As for   39 **haggard** wild hawk.   43 **In resolution** determined   45 **'longeth** belongs   46 **ta'en you napping** taken you by surprise   50 **lusty** merry, lively   58 **eleven . . . long** i.e., right on the money. (Alluding to the card game called "one-and-thirty" referred to at 1.2.32–3.)   62 **ancient angel** i.e., fellow of the good old stamp. (Literally, an "angel" or gold coin bearing the stamp of the archangel Michael and thus distinguishable from more recent debased coinage.)   63 **Will . . . turn** who will serve our purposes.   64 **marcantant** merchant.   **pedant** schoolmaster. (Though at lines 90–1 he speaks more like a merchant.)

As if he were the right Vincentio.
Take in your love, and then let me alone.   72
                                    [*Exeunt Lucentio and Bianca.*]

    Enter a Pedant.

PEDANT
  God save you, sir!
TRANIO   And you sir! You are welcome.
  Travel you farre on, or are you at the farthest?   74
PEDANT
  Sir, at the farthest for a week or two,
  But then up farther, and as far as Rome,
  And so to Tripoli, if God lend me life.
TRANIO
  What countryman, I pray?
PEDANT   Of Mantua.
TRANIO
  Of Mantua, sir? Marry, God forbid!
  And come to Padua, careless of your life?
PEDANT
  My life, sir? How, I pray? For that goes hard.   81
TRANIO
  'Tis death for anyone in Mantua
  To come to Padua. Know you not the cause?
  Your ships are stayed at Venice, and the Duke,   84
  For private quarrel twixt your Duke and him,
  Hath published and proclaimed it openly.
  'Tis marvel, but that you are but newly come,
  You might have heard it else proclaimed about.
PEDANT
  Alas, sir, it is worse for me than so,   89
  For I have bills for money by exchange   90
  From Florence, and must here deliver them.
TRANIO
  Well, sir, to do you courtesy,
  This will I do, and this I will advise you—
  First, tell me, have you ever been at Pisa?
PEDANT
  Ay, sir, in Pisa have I often been,
  Pisa renownèd for grave citizens.
TRANIO
  Among them know you one Vincentio?
PEDANT
  I know him not, but I have heard of him;
  A merchant of incomparable wealth.
TRANIO
  He is my father, sir, and, sooth to say,
  In count'nance somewhat doth resemble you.
BIONDELLO [*aside*] As much as an apple doth an oy-
  ster, and all one.   103
TRANIO
  To save your life in this extremity,
  This favor will I do you for his sake;
  And think it not the worst of all your fortunes
  That you are like to Sir Vincentio.

His name and credit shall you undertake,   108
And in my house you shall be friendly lodged.
Look that you take upon you as you should.   110
You understand me, sir. So shall you stay
Till you have done your business in the city.
If this be courtesy, sir, accept of it.
PEDANT
  Oh, sir, I do, and will repute you ever   114
  The patron of my life and liberty.
TRANIO
  Then go with me to make the matter good.   116
  This, by the way, I let you understand:
  My father is here looked for every day
  To pass assurance of a dower in marriage   119
  Twixt me and one Baptista's daughter here.
  In all these circumstances I'll instruct you.
  Go with me to clothe you as becomes you.
                                    Exeunt.

                        ❖

4.[3]

    Enter Katharina and Grumio.

GRUMIO
  No, no, forsooth, I dare not for my life.
KATHARINA
  The more my wrong, the more his spite appears.   2
  What, did he marry me to famish me?
  Beggars that come unto my father's door
  Upon entreaty have a present alms;   5
  If not, elsewhere they meet with charity.
  But I, who never knew how to entreat,
  Nor never needed that I should entreat,
  Am starved for meat, giddy for lack of sleep,
  With oaths kept waking, and with brawling fed.
  And that which spites me more than all these wants,
  He does it under name of perfect love,
  As who should say, if I should sleep or eat   13
  'Twere deadly sickness or else present death.
  I prithee, go and get me some repast,
  I care not what, so it be wholesome food.   16
GRUMIO   What say you to a neat's foot?   17
KATHARINA
  'Tis passing good. I prithee, let me have it.   18
GRUMIO
  I fear it is too choleric a meat.
  How say you to a fat tripe finely broiled?
KATHARINA
  I like it well. Good Grumio, fetch it me.
GRUMIO
  I cannot tell. I fear 'tis choleric.   22
  What say you to a piece of beef and mustard?

---

72 **let me alone** leave things to me.   74 **farre** farther   81 **goes hard**
is serious indeed.   84 **stayed** detained   89 **than so** than that
90 **bills . . . exchange** promissory notes   103 **all one** no matter.

108 **credit** reputation   110 **take upon you** play your part   114 **repute
you** regard you as   116 **make . . . good** carry out the plan.   119 **pass
assurance** convey a legal guarantee
4.3. Location: Petruchio's house. A table is set out, with seats.
2 **my wrong** the wrong done to me   5 **present** immediate. (As in line
14.)   13 **As who** as if one   16 **so** so long as   17 **neat's** ox's   18 **passing** extremely   22 **I cannot tell** I don't know what to say.

KATHARINA
A dish that I do love to feed upon.
GRUMIO
Ay, but the mustard is too hot a little.
KATHARINA
Why then, the beef, and let the mustard rest.   26
GRUMIO
Nay then, I will not. You shall have the mustard,
Or else you get no beef of Grumio.
KATHARINA
Then both, or one, or anything thou wilt.
GRUMIO
Why then, the mustard without the beef.
KATHARINA
Go, get thee gone, thou false, deluding slave,
                                [*She*] *beats him.*
That feed'st me with the very name of meat!   32
Sorrow on thee and all the pack of you,
That triumph thus upon my misery!
Go, get thee gone, I say.

                Enter Petruchio and Hortensio with meat.

PETRUCHIO
How fares my Kate? What, sweeting, all amort?   36
HORTENSIO
Mistress, what cheer?
KATHARINA   Faith, as cold as can be.
PETRUCHIO
Pluck up thy spirits; look cheerfully upon me.
Here, love, thou see'st how diligent I am
To dress thy meat myself and bring it thee.   40
I am sure, sweet Kate, this kindness merits thanks.
What, not a word? Nay, then thou lov'st it not,
And all my pains is sorted to no proof.—   43
Here, take away this dish.
KATHARINA   I pray you, let it stand.
PETRUCHIO
The poorest service is repaid with thanks,
And so shall mine before you touch the meat.
KATHARINA   I thank you, sir.
HORTENSIO
Signor Petruchio, fie, you are to blame.
Come, Mistress Kate, I'll bear you company.
PETRUCHIO [*aside to Hortensio*]
Eat it up all, Hortensio, if thou lovest me.—
Much good do it unto thy gentle heart!
Kate, eat apace. And now, my honey love,
Will we return unto thy father's house
And revel it as bravely as the best,   54
With silken coats and caps and golden rings,
With ruffs, and cuffs, and farthingales, and things,   56
With scarves, and fans, and double change of brav'ry,   57
With amber bracelets, beads, and all this knav'ry.

What, hast thou dined? The tailor stays thy leisure,   59
To deck thy body with his ruffling treasure.   60

                Enter Tailor [with a gown].

Come, tailor, let us see these ornaments.
Lay forth the gown.

                Enter Haberdasher [with a cap].

                    What news with you, sir?
HABERDASHER
Here is the cap Your Worship did bespeak.   63
PETRUCHIO
Why, this was molded on a porringer—   64
A velvet dish. Fie, fie, 'tis lewd and filthy.   65
Why, 'tis a cockle or a walnut shell,   66
A knack, a toy, a trick, a baby's cap.   67
Away with it! Come, let me have a bigger.
KATHARINA
I'll have no bigger. This doth fit the time,   69
And gentlewomen wear such caps as these.
PETRUCHIO
When you are gentle, you shall have one too,   71
And not till then.
HORTENSIO [*aside*]   That will not be in haste.
KATHARINA
Why, sir, I trust I may have leave to speak,
And speak I will. I am no child, no babe.
Your betters have endured me say my mind,   75
And if you cannot, best you stop your ears.
My tongue will tell the anger of my heart,
Or else my heart, concealing it, will break.
And rather than it shall, I will be free
Even to the uttermost, as I please, in words.
PETRUCHIO
Why, thou say'st true. It is a paltry cap,
A custard-coffin, a bauble, a silken pie.   82
I love thee well in that thou lik'st it not.
KATHARINA
Love me or love me not, I like the cap,
And it I will have, or I will have none.
                            [*Exit Haberdasher.*]
PETRUCHIO
Thy gown? Why, ay. Come, tailor, let us see't.
Oh, mercy, God, what masquing stuff is here?   87
What's this, a sleeve? 'Tis like a demicannon.   88
What, up and down carved like an apple tart?   89
Here's snip, and nip, and cut, and slish and slash,
Like to a censer in a barber's shop.   91
Why, what i' devil's name, tailor, call'st thou this?

---

59 stays awaits   **60 ruffling treasure** finery trimmed with ruffles.
63 bespeak order.   **64 porringer** porridge bowl   **65 lewd** vile
66 cockle cockleshell   **67 trick** trifle   **69 fit the time** suit the current
fashion   **71 gentle** mild. (Petruchio plays on Kate's *gentlewomen,*
line 70, i.e., women of high social station.)   **75 endured me say**
suffered me to say   **82 custard-coffin** pastry crust for a custard
87 masquing i.e., suited only for a masque   **88 demicannon** large
cannon.   **89 What . . . tart?** What, carved from one end to the other
with slits like those in the crust of an apple tart? (Such slits in gowns
were designed to reveal the fabric underneath.)   **91 censer** perfum-
ing pan having an ornamental lid

26 let . . . rest i.e., forget about the mustard.   **32 very** mere   **36 all
amort** dejected, dispirited.   **40 dress** prepare   **43 is . . . proof** have
proved to be to no purpose.   **54 bravely** splendidly   **56 farthingales**
hooped petticoats   **57 brav'ry** finery

HORTENSIO [*aside*]
    I see she's like to have neither cap nor gown.   93
TAILOR
    You bid me make it orderly and well,
    According to the fashion and the time.
PETRUCHIO
    Marry, and did. But if you be remembered,   96
    I did not bid you mar it to the time.
    Go hop me over every kennel home,   98
    For you shall hop without my custom, sir.
    I'll none of it. Hence, make your best of it.
KATHARINA
    I never saw a better fashioned gown,
    More quaint, more pleasing, nor more
        commendable.   102
    Belike you mean to make a puppet of me.   103
PETRUCHIO
    Why, true, he means to make a puppet of thee.
TAILOR
    She says Your Worship means to make a puppet of her.
PETRUCHIO
    Oh, monstrous arrogance! Thou liest, thou thread,
        thou thimble,   106
    Thou yard, three-quarters, half-yard, quarter, nail!   107
    Thou flea, thou nit, thou winter cricket, thou!   108
    Braved in mine own house with a skein of thread?   109
    Away, thou rag, thou quantity, thou remnant,   110
    Or I shall so be-mete thee with thy yard   111
    As thou shalt think on prating whilst thou liv'st!   112
    I tell thee, I, that thou hast marred her gown.
TAILOR
    Your Worship is deceived. The gown is made
    Just as my master had direction.
    Grumio gave order how it should be done.
GRUMIO   I gave him no order. I gave him the stuff.   117
TAILOR
    But how did you desire it should be made?
GRUMIO   Marry, sir, with needle and thread.
TAILOR
    But did you not request to have it cut?
GRUMIO   Thou hast faced many things.   121
TAILOR   I have.
GRUMIO   Face not me. Thou hast braved many men;   123
    brave not me. I will neither be faced nor braved. I say   124
    unto thee, I bid thy master cut out the gown, but I did
    not bid him cut it to pieces. Ergo, thou liest.   126
TAILOR   Why, here is the note of the fashion to testify.
                                        [*He displays his bill.*]
PETRUCHIO   Read it.

GRUMIO   The note lies in 's throat if he say I said so.   129
TAILOR [*reads*]   "Imprimis, a loose-bodied gown—"   130
GRUMIO   Master, if ever I said loose-bodied gown,   131
    sew me in the skirts of it and beat me to death with a
    bottom of brown thread. I said a gown.   133
PETRUCHIO   Proceed.
TAILOR [*reads*]   "With a small compassed cape—"   135
GRUMIO   I confess the cape.
TAILOR [*reads*]   "With a trunk sleeve—"   137
GRUMIO   I confess two sleeves.
TAILOR [*reads*]   "The sleeves curiously cut."   139
PETRUCHIO   Ay, there's the villainy.
GRUMIO   Error i'the bill, sir, error i'the bill. I command-
    ed
    the sleeves should be cut out and sewed up again, and   143
    that I'll prove upon thee, though thy little finger be
    armed in a thimble.   145
TAILOR   This is true that I say. An I had thee in place   146
    where, thou shouldst know it.   147
GRUMIO   I am for thee straight. Take thou the bill, give   148
    me thy mete-yard, and spare not me.   149
HORTENSIO   God-a-mercy, Grumio, then he shall have   150
    no odds.
PETRUCHIO   Well, sir, in brief, the gown is not for me.
GRUMIO   You are i'the right, sir, 'tis for my mistress.   153
PETRUCHIO   Go, take it up unto thy master's use.
GRUMIO [*to the Tailor*]   Villain, not for thy life! Take up
    my mistress' gown for thy master's use!   156
PETRUCHIO   Why sir, what's your conceit in that?
GRUMIO   157
    Oh, sir, the conceit is deeper than you think for:
    Take up my mistress' gown to his master's use!
    Oh, fie, fie, fie!
PETRUCHIO [*aside to Hortensio*]
    Hortensio, say thou wilt see the tailor paid.
    [*To Tailor*] Go, take it hence. Begone, and say no more.
HORTENSIO [*aside to the Tailor*]
    Tailor, I'll pay thee for thy gown tomorrow.
    Take no unkindness of his hasty words.
    Away, I say. Commend me to thy master.
                                            Exit Tailor.
PETRUCHIO
    Well, come, my Kate. We will unto your father's   166
    Even in these honest, mean habiliments.
    Our purses shall be proud, our garments poor,
    For 'tis the mind that makes the body rich;
    And as the sun breaks through the darkest clouds,

93 **like** likely   96 **Marry . . remembered** I did indeed. But if you rec-
ollect   98 **hop . . . home** hop on home over every street gutter
102 **quaint** elegant   103 **Belike** Perhaps   106–10 **thou thread . . .
remnant** Petruchio attacks the tailor's proverbial thinness and effeminacy using metaphors from tailoring.   107 **nail** a measure of length
for cloth: 2 ¼ inches.   108 **nit** louse egg   109 **Braved** Defied.   **with**
by   110 **quantity** fragment   111 **be-mete** measure, i.e., thrash.   **yard**
yardstick   112 **think on prating** i.e., remember this thrashing and
think twice before talking so again   117 **stuff** material.
121 **faced** trimmed, decked   123 **Face** Bully.   **braved** dressed finely
124 **brave** defy   126 **Ergo** Therefore

129 **lies in 's throat** i.e., lies utterly   130 **Imprimis** First   131 **loose-
bodied gown** (Grumio plays on *loose*, "wanton"; a gown fit for a
prostitute.)   133 **bottom** i.e., ball or skein. (A weaver's term for the
bobbin.)   135 **compassed** flared, cut on the bias so as to fall in a circle
137 **trunk** full, wide   139 **curiously** elaborately   143 **prove upon
thee** prove by fighting you   145–6 **in place where** in a suitable place
147 **bill** (1) the note ordering the gown (2) a weapon, a halberd
148 **mete-yard** measuring stick   149 **God-a-mercy** Thanks   150 **no
odds** no advantage. (The contest between Grumio and the Tailor will
be evenly matched.)   153 **take it up** take it away.   **use** i.e., whatever
use he can make of it. (But Grumio deliberately misinterprets both
expressions in a bawdy sense.)   156 **conceit** idea   157 **deeper** more
serious. (But continuing the sexual idea of lifting up the dress and
entering for sexual "use," as in lines 155 and 158.)   166 **honest, mean
habiliments** respectable, plain clothes.

So honor peereth in the meanest habit.   170
What, is the jay more precious than the lark
Because his feathers are more beautiful?
Or is the adder better than the eel
Because his painted skin contents the eye?   174
Oh, no, good Kate; neither art thou the worse
For this poor furniture and mean array.   176
If thou account'st it shame, lay it on me.
And therefore frolic; we will hence forthwith,
To feast and sport us at thy father's house.
[*To Grumio*] Go call my men, and let us straight
    to him;
And bring our horses unto Long Lane end.
There will we mount, and thither walk on foot.
Let's see, I think 'tis now some seven o'clock,
And well we may come there by dinnertime.   184

KATHARINA
I dare assure you, sir, 'tis almost two,
And 'twill be suppertime ere you come there.

PETRUCHIO
It shall be seven ere I go to horse.
Look what I speak, or do, or think to do,   188
You are still crossing it.—Sirs, let 't alone.   189
I will not go today, and ere I do,
It shall be what o'clock I say it is.

HORTENSIO [*aside*]
Why, so this gallant will command the sun.   192

                                                    [*Exeunt.*]

                              ❖

[4.4]

*Enter Tranio [as Lucentio], and the Pedant
dressed like Vincentio [booted].*

TRANIO
Sir, this is the house. Please it you that I call?

PEDANT
Ay, what else? And but I be deceived,   2
Signor Baptista may remember me,   3
Near twenty years ago, in Genoa—   4

TRANIO
Where we were lodgers at the Pegasus.—   5
'Tis well; and hold your own in any case   6
With such austerity as 'longeth to a father.

                Enter Biondello.

PEDANT
I warrant you. But, sir, here comes your boy.
'Twere good he were schooled.   9

TRANIO
Fear you not him.—Sirrah Biondello,
Now do your duty throughly, I advise you.   11
Imagine 'twere the right Vincentio.   12

BIONDELLO   Tut, fear not me.   13

TRANIO
But hast thou done thy errand to Baptista?

BIONDELLO
I told him that your father was at Venice
And that you looked for him this day in Padua.

TRANIO [*giving money*]
Thou'rt a tall fellow. Hold thee that to drink.   17
Here comes Baptista. Set your countenance, sir.   18

            *Enter Baptista, and Lucentio [as Cambio].
            [The] Pedant [stands] bareheaded.*

Signor Baptista, you are happily met.   19
[*To the Pedant*] Sir, this is the gentleman I told you of.
I pray you, stand good father to me now;
Give me Bianca for my patrimony.

PEDANT   Soft, son!—   23
Sir, by your leave, having come to Padua
To gather in some debts, my son Lucentio
Made me acquainted with a weighty cause
Of love between your daughter and himself;
And, for the good report I hear of you   28
And for the love he beareth to your daughter
And she to him, to stay him not too long,   30
I am content, in a good father's care,
To have him matched. And if you please to like   32
No worse than I, upon some agreement
Me shall you find ready and willing
With one consent to have her so bestowed;   35
For curious I cannot be with you,   36
Signor Baptista, of whom I hear so well.

BAPTISTA
Sir, pardon me in what I have to say.
Your plainness and your shortness please me well.
Right true it is your son Lucentio here
Doth love my daughter, and she loveth him,
Or both dissemble deeply their affections.
And therefore, if you say no more than this,
That like a father you will deal with him
And pass my daughter a sufficient dower,   45
The match is made, and all is done.
Your son shall have my daughter with consent.

TRANIO
I thank you, sir. Where then do you know best   48
We be affied and such assurance ta'en   49
As shall with either part's agreement stand?   50

---

170 peereth . . . habit peeps through the humblest attire.
174 painted colorfully patterned   **176 furniture** furnishings of attire
184 dinnertime i.e., about noon.   **188 Look what** Whatever
189 still crossing always contradicting or defying   **192 so** at this rate
4.4. Location: Padua. Before Baptista's house.
0.2 booted (signifying travel)   **2 but** unless   **3–4 Signor . . . Genoa**
(The Pedant rehearses what he is to say.)   **5 Where . . . Pegasus**
(Tranio is coaching the Pedant in further details of his story.)   **the
Pegasus** i.e., an inn, so named after the famous winged horse of classical myth.   **6 hold your own** play your part   **9 schooled** i.e.,
rehearsed in his part.

11 throughly thoroughly   **12 right** real   **13 fear not me** don't worry
about my doing my part.   **17 tall** fine.   **Hold . . . drink** Take that
and buy a drink.   **18 Set your countenance** i.e., Put on the expression of an austere father (line 7).   **19 happily** fortunately   **23 Soft**
i.e., Steady, take it easy   **28 for** because of   **30 to stay him not** not to
keep him waiting   **32 like** i.e., approve of the match   **35 one** i.e.,
firm   **36 curious** overly particular   **45 pass** settle on, give
48–50 Where . . . stand? Where in your view is the best place for
us to be betrothed and for legal assurances to be made that will
confirm an agreement satisfactory to both parties?

BAPTISTA

Not in my house, Lucentio, for you know
Pitchers have ears, and I have many servants.
Besides, old Gremio is heark'ning still,   53
And happily we might be interrupted.   54

TRANIO

Then at my lodging, an it like you.   55
There doth my father lie, and there this night   56
We'll pass the business privately and well.   57
Send for your daughter by your servant here.
          [*He indicates Lucentio, and winks at him.*]
My boy shall fetch the scrivener presently.   59
The worst is this, that at so slender warning
You are like to have a thin and slender pittance.   61

BAPTISTA

It likes me well. Cambio, hie you home,
And bid Bianca make her ready straight.
And if you will, tell what hath happened:
Lucentio's father is arrived in Padua,
And how she's like to be Lucentio's wife.
                              [*Exit Lucentio.*]

BIONDELLO

I pray the gods she may with all my heart!

TRANIO

Dally not with the gods, but get thee gone.
                                   Exit [*Biondello*].
Signor Baptista, shall I lead the way?
Welcome! One mess is like to be your cheer.   70
Come, sir, we will better it in Pisa.

BAPTISTA   I follow you.   72
                    Exeunt [*Tranio, Pedant, and Baptista*].

          Enter Lucentio [*as Cambio*] *and Biondello.*

BIONDELLO   Cambio!
LUCENTIO   What say'st thou, Biondello?
BIONDELLO   You saw my master wink and laugh upon
you?
LUCENTIO   Biondello, what of that?
BIONDELLO   Faith, nothing; but he's left me here behind
to expound the meaning or moral of his signs and to-   79
kens.
LUCENTIO   I pray thee, moralize them.   81
BIONDELLO   Then thus. Baptista is safe, talking with   82
the deceiving father of a deceitful son.
LUCENTIO   And what of him?
BIONDELLO   His daughter is to be brought by you to
the supper.
LUCENTIO   And then?
BIONDELLO   The old priest at Saint Luke's church is at
your command at all hours.
LUCENTIO   And what of all this?

BIONDELLO   I cannot tell, except they are busied about a   91
counterfeit assurance. Take you assurance of her   92
cum privilegio ad imprimendum solum. To th'   93
church take the priest, clerk, and some sufficient hon-   94
est witnesses.
If this be not that you look for, I have no more to say,   96
But bid Bianca farewell forever and a day.
                         [*Biondello starts to leave.*]
LUCENTIO   Hear'st thou, Biondello?
BIONDELLO   I cannot tarry. I knew a wench married in
an afternoon as she went to the garden for parsley to
stuff a rabbit, and so may you, sir. And so, adieu, sir.
My master hath appointed me to go to Saint Luke's, to
bid the priest be ready to come against you come with   103
your appendix.   *Exit.* 104

LUCENTIO

I may, and will, if she be so contented.
She will be pleased; then wherefore should I doubt?
Hap what hap may, I'll roundly go about her.   107
It shall go hard if Cambio go without her.   *Exit.* 108

[4.5]

          Enter Petruchio, Kate, [*and*] *Hortensio.*

PETRUCHIO

Come on, i'God's name, once more toward our father's.   1
Good Lord, how bright and goodly shines the moon!

KATHARINA

The moon? The sun. It is not moonlight now.

PETRUCHIO

I say it is the moon that shines so bright.

KATHARINA

I know it is the sun that shines so bright.

PETRUCHIO

Now, by my mother's son, and that's myself,
It shall be moon, or star, or what I list   7
Or ere I journey to your father's house.—   8
Go on, and fetch our horses back again—
Evermore crossed and crossed, nothing but crossed!

HORTENSIO [*to Katharina*]

Say as he says, or we shall never go.

KATHARINA

Forward, I pray, since we have come so far,
And be it moon, or sun, or what you please;
An if you please to call it a rush candle,   14

53 heark'ning still continually listening   **54 happily** haply   **55 an it like** if it please   **56 lie** lodge   **57 pass** transact   **59 scrivener** notary, one to draw up contracts.   **presently** at once.   **61 like** likely.   **slender pittance** i.e., scanty banquet.   **70 mess** dish.   **cheer** entertainment.   **72.1 *Exeunt*** (Technically, the cleared stage may mark a new scene, but the conversation of Lucentio and Biondello suggests that they come creeping back on stage as the others leave rather than doing the errands Baptista and Tranio bid them.)   **79 moral** hidden meaning   **81 moralize** elucidate   **82 safe** i.e., safely out of the way

91 except unless   **92 counterfeit assurance** pretended betrothal agreement.   **Take . . . of her** Legalize your claim to her (by marriage)   **93 *cum . . . solum*** with exclusive printing rights. (A copyright formula often appearing on the title pages of books, here jokingly applied to the marriage and to procreation as an act of imprinting.)   **94 sufficient** meeting the legal requirement in number and social standing   **96 that you look for** what you are looking for   **103 against you come** in anticipation of your arrival   **104 appendix** something appended, i.e., the bride. (Continuing the metaphor of printing.)   **107 roundly . . . her** set about marrying her in no uncertain terms.   **108 It . . . her** i.e., I'm determined to have her. (With pun about erection.)   **4.5. Location: A road on the way to Padua.**
1 our father's our father's house.   **7 list** please   **8 Or ere** before   **14 a rush candle** a rush dipped into tallow; hence a very feeble light

Henceforth I vow it shall be so for me.

PETRUCHIO
I say it is the moon.

KATHARINA   I know it is the moon.

PETRUCHIO
Nay, then you lie. It is the blessèd sun.

KATHARINA
Then, God be blessed, it is the blessèd sun.
But sun it is not, when you say it is not,
And the moon changes even as your mind.
What you will have it named, even that it is,
And so it shall be so for Katharine.

HORTENSIO
Petruchio, go thy ways. The field is won.   23

PETRUCHIO
Well, forward, forward. Thus the bowl should run,
And not unluckily against the bias.   25
But soft! Company is coming here.

          Enter Vincentio.

[To Vincentio] Good morrow, gentle mistress. Where
          away?—   27
Tell me, sweet Kate, and tell me truly too,
Hast thou beheld a fresher gentlewoman?
Such war of white and red within her cheeks!
What stars do spangle heaven with such beauty
As those two eyes become that heavenly face?—
Fair lovely maid, once more good day to thee.—
Sweet Kate, embrace her for her beauty's sake.

HORTENSIO [aside]
'A will make the man mad, to make a woman of him.   35

KATHARINA [embracing Vincentio]
Young budding virgin, fair, and fresh, and sweet,
Whither away, or where is thy abode?
Happy the parents of so fair a child!
Happier the man whom favorable stars
Allots thee for his lovely bedfellow!   40

PETRUCHIO
Why, how now, Kate? I hope thou art not mad.
This is a man, old, wrinkled, faded, withered,
And not a maiden, as thou say'st he is.

KATHARINA
Pardon, old father, my mistaking eyes,
That have been so bedazzled with the sun
That everything I look on seemeth green.   46
Now I perceive thou art a reverend father.
Pardon, I pray thee, for my mad mistaking.

PETRUCHIO
Do, good old grandsire, and withal make known
Which way thou travelest—if along with us,
We shall be joyful of thy company.

VINCENTIO
Fair sir, and you, my merry mistress,
That with your strange encounter much amazed me,

My name is called Vincentio, my dwelling Pisa,
And bound I am to Padua, there to visit
A son of mine, which long I have not seen.

PETRUCHIO
What is his name?

VINCENTIO   Lucentio, gentle sir.

PETRUCHIO
Happily met, the happier for thy son.
And now by law as well as reverend age
I may entitle thee my loving father.
The sister to my wife, this gentlewoman,
Thy son by this hath married. Wonder not,   62
Nor be not grieved. She is of good esteem,   63
Her dowry wealthy, and of worthy birth;
Besides, so qualified as may beseem   65
The spouse of any noble gentleman.
Let me embrace with old Vincentio,
And wander we to see thy honest son,   68
Who will of thy arrival be full joyous.
          [He embraces Vincentio.]

VINCENTIO
But is this true? Or is it else your pleasure,
Like pleasant travelers, to break a jest   71
Upon the company you overtake?

HORTENSIO
I do assure thee, father, so it is.

PETRUCHIO
Come, go along, and see the truth hereof,
For our first merriment hath made thee jealous.   75
          Exeunt [all but Hortensio].

HORTENSIO
Well, Petruchio, this has put me in heart.   76
Have to my widow! And if she be froward,   77
Then hast thou taught Hortensio to be untoward.   78
                                        Exit.

          ❦

[5.1]

Enter Biondello, Lucentio [no longer disguised],
and Bianca. Gremio is out before [and stands
aside].

BIONDELLO   Softly and swiftly, sir, for the priest is
ready.

LUCENTIO   I fly, Biondello. But they may chance to need
thee at home; therefore leave us.

BIONDELLO   Nay, faith, I'll see the church a' your back,   5
and then come back to my master's as soon as I can.
          [Exeunt Lucentio, Bianca, and Biondello.]

---

62 **by this** by this time   63 **esteem** reputation   65 **so qualified** having
such qualities.   **beseem** befit   68 **wander** go (having changed plans)
71 **pleasant** humorous, jocular.   **break a jest** play a practical joke
75 **jealous** suspicious.   76 **put me in heart** encouraged me.   77 **Have
to** i.e., Now for.   **froward** perverse   78 **untoward** unmannerly.
5.1. Location: Padua. Before Lucentio's house.
0.2 out before i.e., onstage first. (Gremio does not see Biondello,
Lucentio, and Bianca as they steal to church, or else he does not
recognize Lucentio in his own person.)   5 **a' your back** at your
back, behind you. (Biondello first wants to see them in church
and safely married.)

---

23 **go thy ways** i.e., well done, carry on.   25 **against the bias** off its
proper course. (The *bias* is an off-center weight in a bowling ball
enabling the bowler to roll the ball in an oblique or curving path.)
27 **Where away?** Where are you going?   35 **'A** He   40 **Allots** allot
46 **green** young and fresh.

GREMIO
I marvel Cambio comes not all this while.

Enter Petruchio, Kate, Vincentio, Grumio, with
attendants.

PETRUCHIO
Sir, here's the door. This is Lucentio's house.
My father's bears more toward the marketplace;   9
Thither must I, and here I leave you, sir.

VINCENTIO
You shall not choose but drink before you go.   11
I think I shall command your welcome here,
And by all likelihood some cheer is toward.   *Knock.*   13

GREMIO [*advancing*]   They're busy within. You were
best knock louder.   15

Pedant looks out of the window.

PEDANT   What's he that knocks as he would beat down
the gate?

VINCENTIO   Is Signor Lucentio within, sir?

PEDANT   He's within, sir, but not to be spoken withal.   19

VINCENTIO   What if a man bring him a hundred pound
or two to make merry withal?

PEDANT   Keep your hundred pounds to yourself. He
shall need none, so long as I live.

PETRUCHIO [*to Vincentio*]   Nay, I told you your son was
well beloved in Padua.—Do you hear, sir? To leave
frivolous circumstances, I pray you, tell Signor Lucen-   26
tio that his father is come from Pisa and is here at the
door to speak with him.

PEDANT   Thou liest. His father is come from Padua and   29
here looking out at the window.

VINCENTIO   Art thou his father?

PEDANT   Ay, sir, so his mother says, if I may believe
her.

PETRUCHIO [*to Vincentio*]   Why, how now, gentleman!
Why, this is flat knavery, to take upon you another   35
man's name.

PEDANT   Lay hands on the villain. I believe 'a means to
cozen somebody in this city under my countenance.   38

Enter Biondello.

BIONDELLO [*aside*]   I have seen them in the church
together, God send 'em good shipping! But who is   40
here? Mine old master Vincentio! Now we are undone
and brought to nothing.

VINCENTIO [*seeing Biondello*]   Come hither, crackhemp.   43

BIONDELLO   I hope I may choose, sir.   44

VINCENTIO   Come hither, you rogue. What, have you
forgot me?

BIONDELLO   Forgot you? No, sir. I could not forget you,
for I never saw you before in all my life.

VINCENTIO   What, you notorious villain, didst thou
never see thy master's father, Vincentio?

BIONDELLO   What, my old worshipful old master? Yes,
marry, sir, see where he looks out of the window.

VINCENTIO   Is't so, indeed?   *He beats Biondello.*

BIONDELLO   Help, help, help! Here's a madman will
murder me.   [*Exit.*]

PEDANT   Help, son! Help, Signor Baptista!
[*Exit from the window.*]

PETRUCHIO   Prithee, Kate, let's stand aside and see the
end of this controversy.   [*They stand aside.*]

Enter [*below*] *Pedant with servants, Baptista,*
[*and*] *Tranio* [*as Lucentio*].

TRANIO   Sir, what are you that offer to beat my servant?   59

VINCENTIO   What am I, sir? Nay, what are you, sir? O
immortal gods! Oh, fine villain! A silken doublet, a velvet hose, a scarlet cloak, and a copintank hat! Oh, I am   62
undone, I am undone! While I play the good husband   63
at home, my son and my servant spend all at the university.

TRANIO   How now, what's the matter?

BAPTISTA   What, is the man lunatic?

TRANIO   Sir, you seem a sober ancient gentleman by
your habit, but your words show you a madman.   69
Why, sir, what 'cerns it you if I wear pearl and gold?   70
I thank my good father, I am able to maintain it.   71

VINCENTIO   Thy father! Oh, villain, he is a sailmaker in
Bergamo.

BAPTISTA   You mistake, sir, you mistake, sir. Pray, what
do you think is his name?

VINCENTIO   His name! As if I knew not his name! I have
brought him up ever since he was three years old, and
his name is Tranio.

PEDANT   Away, away, mad ass! His name is Lucentio,
and he is mine only son, and heir to the lands of me,
Signor Vincentio.

VINCENTIO   Lucentio! Oh, he hath murdered his master!
Lay hold on him, I charge you, in the Duke's name.
Oh, my son, my son! Tell me, thou villain, where is my
son Lucentio?

TRANIO   Call forth an officer.

[*Enter an Officer.*]

Carry this mad knave to the jail. Father Baptista, I
charge you see that he be forthcoming.   88

VINCENTIO   Carry me to the jail?

GREMIO   Stay, officer, he shall not go to prison.

BAPTISTA   Talk not, Signor Gremio. I say he shall go to
prison.

GREMIO   Take heed, Signor Baptista, lest you be coney-   93
catched in this business. I dare swear this is the right   94
Vincentio.

PEDANT   Swear, if thou dar'st.

GREMIO   Nay, I dare not swear it.

TRANIO   Then thou wert best say that I am not Lucentio.   98

GREMIO   Yes, I know thee to be Signor Lucentio.

BAPTISTA   Away with the dotard! To the jail with him!

Enter Biondello, Lucentio, and Bianca.

VINCENTIO   Thus strangers may be haled and abused.   101
—Oh, monstrous villain!

BIONDELLO   Oh! We are spoiled and—yonder he is.   103
Deny him, forswear him, or else we are all undone.
*Exeunt Biondello, Tranio, and Pedant as fast as
may be. [Lucentio and Bianca] kneel.*

LUCENTIO
Pardon, sweet father.

VINCENTIO   Lives my sweet son?

BIANCA
Pardon, dear father.

BAPTISTA   How hast thou offended?
Where is Lucentio?

LUCENTIO   Here's Lucentio,
Right son to the right Vincentio,
That have by marriage made thy daughter mine,
While counterfeit supposes bleared thine eyne.   110

GREMIO
Here's packing, with a witness, to deceive us all!   111

VINCENTIO
Where is that damnèd villain Tranio,
That faced and braved me in this matter so?   113

BAPTISTA
Why, tell me, is not this my Cambio?

BIANCA
Cambio is changed into Lucentio.   115

LUCENTIO
Love wrought these miracles. Bianca's love
Made me exchange my state with Tranio,   117
While he did bear my countenance in the town,   118
And happily I have arrivèd at the last
Unto the wishèd haven of my bliss.
What Tranio did, myself enforced him to;
Then pardon him, sweet father, for my sake.

VINCENTIO   I'll slit the villain's nose, that would have
sent me to the jail.

BAPTISTA   [*to Lucentio*]   But do you hear, sir? Have you
married my daughter without asking my good will?

VINCENTIO   Fear not, Baptista, we will content you. Go   127
to. But I will in, to be revenged for this villainy.   128
Exit.

BAPTISTA   And I, to sound the depth of this knavery.
Exit.

LUCENTIO   Look not pale, Bianca. Thy father will not
frown.   *Exeunt [Lucentio and Bianca].*

GREMIO
My cake is dough, but I'll in among the rest,   132
Out of hope of all but my share of the feast.   [*Exit.*]   133

KATHARINA   Husband, let's follow, to see the end of
this ado.

PETRUCHIO   First kiss me, Kate, and we will.

KATHARINA   What, in the midst of the street?

PETRUCHIO   What, art thou ashamed of me?

KATHARINA   No, sir, God forbid, but ashamed to kiss.

PETRUCHIO
Why, then let's home again. [*To Grumio*] Come, sirrah,
let's away.

KATHARINA
Nay, I will give thee a kiss. [*She kisses him.*] Now pray
thee, love, stay.

PETRUCHIO
Is not this well? Come, my sweet Kate.
Better once than never, for never too late.   *Exeunt.*   143

5.[2]

*Enter Baptista, Vincentio, Gremio, the Pedant,
Lucentio, and Bianca; [Petruchio, Kate, Hortensio,] Tranio, Biondello, Grumio, and [the]
Widow; the servingmen with Tranio bringing
in a banquet.*

LUCENTIO
At last, though long, our jarring notes agree,   1
And time it is, when raging war is done,
To smile at scapes and perils overblown.   3
My fair Bianca, bid my father welcome,
While I with selfsame kindness welcome thine.
Brother Petruchio, sister Katharina,
And thou, Hortensio, with thy loving widow,
Feast with the best, and welcome to my house.
My banquet is to close our stomachs up   9
After our great good cheer. Pray you, sit down,   10
For now we sit to chat as well as eat.   [*They sit.*]

PETRUCHIO
Nothing but sit and sit, and eat and eat!

BAPTISTA
Padua affords this kindness, son Petruchio.

PETRUCHIO
Padua affords nothing but what is kind.

93–4 coney-catched tricked   **98 wert best** might as well
101 haled hauled about, maltreated   **103 spoiled** ruined   **110 supposes** suppositions, false appearances. (With an allusion to Gascoigne's *Supposes*, an adaptation of *I Suppositi* by Ariosto, from
which Shakespeare took the Lucentio-Bianca plot of intrigue.)
eyne eyes.   **111 Here's . . . all!** Here's evidence of a conspiracy, no
mistake about it!   **113 faced and braved** stood up to and defied
115 Cambio is changed (A pun. *Cambio* in Italian means "change"
or "exchange.")   **117 state** social station   **118 countenance** appearance, identity

127–8 Go to i.e., Don't worry. (An expression of impatience or annoyance.)   **132 My . . . dough** i.e., I'm out of luck, I failed
133 Out . . . but having hope for nothing other than   **143 once** at
some time. (Compare with "better late than never.")
5.2. Location: Padua. Lucentio's house.
1 long after long time   **3 scapes** close calls   **9 stomachs** (1) appetites
(2) quarrels   **10 cheer** i.e., wedding feast.

HORTENSIO
For both our sakes, I would that word were true.
PETRUCHIO
Now, for my life, Hortensio fears his widow.   16
WIDOW
Then never trust me if I be afeard.   17
PETRUCHIO
You are very sensible, and yet you miss my sense:
I mean Hortensio is afeard of you.
WIDOW
He that is giddy thinks the world turns round.
PETRUCHIO
Roundly replied.
KATHARINA   Mistress, how mean you that?   21
WIDOW   Thus I conceive by him.   22
PETRUCHIO
Conceives by me! How likes Hortensio that?
HORTENSIO
My widow says, thus she conceives her tale.   24
PETRUCHIO
Very well mended. Kiss him for that, good widow.
KATHARINA
"He that is giddy thinks the world turns round":
I pray you, tell me what you meant by that.
WIDOW
Your husband, being troubled with a shrew,
Measures my husband's sorrow by his woe.
And now you know my meaning.   29
KATHARINA
A very mean meaning.
WIDOW   Right, I mean you.   31
KATHARINA
And I am mean indeed, respecting you.   32
PETRUCHIO   To her, Kate!   33
HORTENSIO   To her, widow!
PETRUCHIO
A hundred marks, my Kate does put her down.   35
HORTENSIO   That's my office.
PETRUCHIO
Spoke like an officer. Ha' to thee, lad!   37
                           [He] drinks to Hortensio.
BAPTISTA
How likes Gremio these quick-witted folks?
GREMIO
Believe me, sir, they butt together well.   39
BIANCA
Head, and butt! An hasty-witted body   40
Would say your head and butt were head and horn.   41

VINCENTIO
Ay, mistress bride, hath that awakened you?
BIANCA
Ay, but not frighted me. Therefore I'll sleep again.
PETRUCHIO
Nay, that you shall not. Since you have begun,
Have at you for a bitter jest or two!   45
BIANCA
Am I your bird? I mean to shift my bush;   46
And then pursue me as you draw your bow.
You are welcome all.
                   Exit Bianca [with Katharina and the Widow].
PETRUCHIO
She hath prevented me. Here, Signor Tranio,   49
This bird you aimed at, though you hit her not.   50
Therefore a health to all that shot and missed.   51
                                          [He offers a toast.]
TRANIO
Oh, sir, Lucentio slipped me like his greyhound,   52
Which runs himself and catches for his master.
PETRUCHIO
A good swift simile, but something currish.   54
TRANIO
'Tis well, sir, that you hunted for yourself.
'Tis thought your deer does hold you at a bay.   56
BAPTISTA
Oho, Petruchio! Tranio hits you now.
LUCENTIO
I thank thee for that gird, good Tranio.   58
HORTENSIO
Confess, confess, hath he not hit you here?
PETRUCHIO
'A has a little galled me, I confess;   60
And as the jest did glance away from me,
'Tis ten to one it maimed you two outright.
BAPTISTA
Now, in good sadness, son Petruchio,   63
I think thou hast the veriest shrew of all.
PETRUCHIO
Well, I say no. And therefore for assurance   65
Let's each one send unto his wife;
And he whose wife is most obedient
To come at first when he doth send for her
Shall win the wager which we will propose.
HORTENSIO
Content. What's the wager?
LUCENTIO   Twenty crowns.
PETRUCHIO   Twenty crowns!
I'll venture so much of my hawk or hound,   72
But twenty times so much upon my wife.

16 for my life upon my life. fears is afraid of   17 afeard frightened
(by Hortensio).   21 Roundly Boldly, bluntly   22 Thus . . . him i.e.,
That's what I think of him, Petruchio. (But Petruchio takes up
conceives in the sense of "is made pregnant.")   24 conceives intends,
interprets. (With a possible pun on *tale* and "tail.")   35 marks coins
worth thirteen shillings
31 very mean contemptible. (But the Widow takes up *mean* in the
sense of "have in mind," and Kate replies in the sense of "moderate
in shrewishness.")   32 respecting compared to   33 To her (A cry used
to egg on fighting roosters.)   35 marks coins worth thirteen shillings
four pence.   put her down overcome her. (But Hortensio takes up the
phrase in a bawdy sense.)   37 officer (playing on Hortensio's speaking of his *office* or function).   Ha' Have, i.e., Here's   39 butt butt heads
40 An hasty-witted body A quick-witted person   41 head and horn
(Alluding to the familiar joke about cuckolds' horns.)

45 Have at you for Here comes   46 Am . . . bush i.e., If you mean to
shoot your barbs at me, I intend to move out of the way, as a bird
would fly to another bush. (With a possible bawdy double meaning;
bush can suggest pubic hair.)   49 prevented forestalled   50 This bird
i.e., Bianca, whom Tranio courted (*aimed at*) in his disguise as Lucentio   51 a health a toast   52 slipped unleashed   54 swift (1) quick-
witted (2) concerning swiftness.   currish (1) ignoble (2) concerning
dogs.   56 deer (Punning on "dear.")   does . . . bay turns on you like
a cornered animal and holds you at a distance.   58 gird sharp, biting
jest   60 galled scratched, chafed   63 sadness seriousness   65 assurance proof   72 of on

LUCENTIO   A hundred then.
HORTENSIO   Content.
PETRUCHIO   A match. 'Tis done.
HORTENSIO   Who shall begin?
LUCENTIO   That will I.
    Go, Biondello, bid your mistress come to me.
BIONDELLO   I go.   *Exit.*
BAPTISTA
    Son, I'll be your half Bianca comes.   81
LUCENTIO
    I'll have no halves; I'll bear it all myself.

        Enter Biondello.

    How now, what news?
BIONDELLO
    Sir, my mistress sends you word
    That she is busy and she cannot come.
PETRUCHIO
    How? She's busy and she cannot come?
    Is that an answer?
GREMIO   Ay, and a kind one too.
    Pray God, sir, your wife send you not a worse.
PETRUCHIO   I hope better.
HORTENSIO
    Sirrah Biondello, go and entreat my wife
    To come to me forthwith.   *Exit Biondello.*
PETRUCHIO   Oho, entreat her!
    Nay, then she must needs come.
HORTENSIO   I am afraid, sir,
    Do what you can, yours will not be entreated.

        Enter Biondello.

    Now, where's my wife?
BIONDELLO
    She says you have some goodly jest in hand.
    She will not come. She bids you come to her.
PETRUCHIO
    Worse and worse. She will not come!
    Oh, vile, intolerable, not to be endured!—
    Sirrah Grumio, go to your mistress.
    Say I command her come to me.   *Exit [Grumio].*
HORTENSIO
    I know her answer.
PETRUCHIO   What?
HORTENSIO   She will not.
PETRUCHIO
    The fouler fortune mine, and there an end.   102

        Enter Katharina.

BAPTISTA
    Now, by my halidom, here comes Katharina!   103
KATHARINA
    What is your will, sir, that you send for me?
PETRUCHIO
    Where is your sister, and Hortensio's wife?

KATHARINA
    They sit conferring by the parlor fire.
PETRUCHIO
    Go fetch them hither. If they deny to come,
    Swinge me them soundly forth unto their husbands.   108
    Away, I say, and bring them hither straight.
                                    [Exit Katharina.]
LUCENTIO
    Here is a wonder, if you talk of a wonder.
HORTENSIO
    And so it is. I wonder what it bodes.
PETRUCHIO
    Marry, peace it bodes, and love, and quiet life,
    An awful rule, and right supremacy,   113
    And, to be short, what not that's sweet and happy.
BAPTISTA
    Now, fair befall thee, good Petruchio!   115
    The wager thou hast won, and I will add
    Unto their losses twenty thousand crowns,
    Another dowry to another daughter,
    For she is changed, as she had never been.   119
PETRUCHIO
    Nay, I will win my wager better yet,
    And show more sign of her obedience,
    Her new-built virtue and obedience.

        Enter Kate, Bianca, and [the] Widow.

    See where she comes and brings your froward wives
    As prisoners to her womanly persuasion.—
    Katharine, that cap of yours becomes you not.
    Off with that bauble. Throw it underfoot.
                                    [She obeys.]
WIDOW
    Lord, let me never have a cause to sigh
    Till I be brought to such a silly pass!   128
BIANCA
    Fie, what a foolish duty call you this?
LUCENTIO
    I would your duty were as foolish, too.
    The wisdom of your duty, fair Bianca,
    Hath cost me a hundred crowns since suppertime.
BIANCA
    The more fool you, for laying on my duty.   133
PETRUCHIO
    Katharine, I charge thee tell these headstrong women
    What duty they do owe their lords and husbands.
WIDOW
    Come, come, you're mocking. We will have no telling.
PETRUCHIO
    Come on, I say, and first begin with her.
WIDOW   She shall not.
PETRUCHIO
    I say she shall—and first begin with her.

---

81 **be your half** take half your bet   102 **there an end** that's that.
103 **by my halidom** (Originally an oath by the holy relics, but confused with an oath to the Virgin Mary.)

108 **Swinge** thrash.   **me** i.e., at my behest. (*Me* is used colloquially.)
113 **awful rule** authority commanding awe or respect   115 **fair befall
thee** good luck to you, and congratulations   119 **as . . . been** as if she
had never existed, i.e., she is totally changed.   128 **pass** state of
affairs.   133 **laying** wagering

KATHARINA
Fie, fie! Unknit that threatening, unkind brow,
And dart not scornful glances from those eyes
To wound thy lord, thy king, thy governor.
It blots thy beauty as frosts do bite the meads,   143
Confounds thy fame as whirlwinds shake fair buds,   144
And in no sense is meet or amiable.
A woman moved is like a fountain troubled,   146
Muddy, ill-seeming, thick, bereft of beauty;
And while it is so, none so dry or thirsty   148
Will deign to sip or touch one drop of it.
Thy husband is thy lord, thy life, thy keeper,
Thy head, thy sovereign; one that cares for thee,
And for thy maintenance commits his body
To painful labor both by sea and land,   153
To watch the night in storms, the day in cold,   154
Whilst thou liest warm at home, secure and safe;
And craves no other tribute at thy hands
But love, fair looks, and true obedience—
Too little payment for so great a debt.
Such duty as the subject owes the prince,
Even such a woman oweth to her husband;
And when she is froward, peevish, sullen, sour,   161
And not obedient to his honest will,   162
What is she but a foul contending rebel
And graceless traitor to her loving lord?
I am ashamed that women are so simple   165
To offer war where they should kneel for peace,
Or seek for rule, supremacy, and sway,
When they are bound to serve, love, and obey.
Why are our bodies soft, and weak, and smooth,
Unapt to toil and trouble in the world,   170
But that our soft conditions and our hearts   171
Should well agree with our external parts?

Come, come, you froward and unable worms!   173
My mind hath been as big as one of yours,   174
My heart as great, my reason haply more,
To bandy word for word and frown for frown;
But now I see our lances are but straws,
Our strength as weak, our weakness past compare,   178
That seeming to be most which we indeed least are. 179
Then vail your stomachs, for it is no boot,   180
And place your hands below your husband's foot,
In token of which duty, if he please,
My hand is ready; may it do him ease.   183
PETRUCHIO
Why, there's a wench! Come on, and kiss me, Kate.
                                              [They kiss.]
LUCENTIO
Well, go thy ways, old lad, for thou shalt ha 't.   185
VINCENTIO
'Tis a good hearing when children are toward.   186
LUCENTIO
But a harsh hearing when women are froward.
PETRUCHIO   Come, Kate, we'll to bed.
We three are married, but you two are sped.   189
[To Lucentio] 'Twas I won the wager, though you hit
    the white,   190
And, being a winner, God give you good night!   191
                         Exit Petruchio [with Katharina].
HORTENSIO
Now go thy ways. Thou hast tamed a curst shrew.   192
LUCENTIO
'Tis a wonder, by your leave, she will be tamed so.
                                              [Exeunt.]

143 meads meadows   144 Confounds thy fame ruins your reputation   146 moved angry   148 none . . . thirsty there is no one so
thirsty that he   153 painful onerous   154 watch stay awake
throughout   161 peevish obstinate   162 to his honest will (Kate
may suggest that she will be obedient when his will is decent and virtuous, not that his will is always so.)   165 simple foolish   170 Unapt
to unfit for   171 conditions qualities

173 unable worms i.e., poor feeble creatures.   174 big haughty
178 as weak i.e., as weak as straws   179 That seeming to be seeming
to be that   180 Then . . . boot Then lower your pride, for it is no use
striving   183 do him ease give him pleasure.   185 go thy ways well
done.   ha 't have it, the prize.   186 'Tis . . . toward i.e., One likes to
hear when children are obedient.   189 We . . . sped i.e., All we three
men have taken wives, but you two are done for (sped) through disobedient wives.   190 the white the center of the target. (With quibble
on the name of Bianca, which in Italian means "white.")   191 being
since I am   192 shrew pronounced "shrow" (and thus spelled in the
Folio). See also 4.1.198 and 5.2.28.

The Taming of the Shrew on Stage

As in the case of *The Merchant of Venice* (see below), the
stage and film histories of *The Taming of the Shrew*
reflect radical changes in social attitudes and theatrical
tastes. The four-hundred-year performance history of
the play includes areas of human discourse that the
Shrew's first audiences could not have imagined; the
play has become a cultural touchstone.

The Elizabethan Era: Popular Fare

An entry in Philip Henslowe's diary states that on June
13, 1594, the Lord Chamberlain's Men presented "*the*

Tamynge of a Shrowe" as an evening performance at Newington Butts, a lesser London theater about which little
is known. Although this is the first known performance
of a very similar play, there is reason to believe that the
Earl of Pembroke's Men performed *A Shrew* in the English provinces (Chambers, IV, 48). As Shakespeare was a
member of the Chamberlain's Men in 1594, the play produced at Newington Butts may have been an early version of Shakespeare's play. *A Shrew* or the later comedy
printed in the First Folio was performed often in the late
sixteenth century and well into the seventeenth. Shakespeare's play may have been staged in Elizabeth's court
in 1594 (Sharpe, 46) and was certainly performed at St.
James Palace before King Charles I in November 1633.

(1922).(Hulton Archive/Getty Images)

(Photofest/Metro-Goldwyn-Mayer film)

(Photofest/Elton Productions/Pickford Production – England)

At age fifteen, Laurence Olivier played Katharina.

Howard Keel spanks Kathryn Grayson in the movie musical Kiss Me Kate *(1953).*

Patricia Morrison's Katharina bites the hand of Alfred Drake's Petruchio.

(TopFoto.co.uk)

(United Artists/The Kobal Collection)

(Columbia Pictures/The Kobal Collection)

Janet McTeer as Petruchio ignores the pleas of Janet Hunter's Katharina in this all-female staging at London's New Globe Theatre (2003).

Douglas Fairbanks, Sr. holds the tamer's whip in the 1929 Shrew *film with Mary Pickford.*

Playing Petruchio and Katharina in Franco Zeffirelli's 1967 film, Elizabeth Taylor and Richard Burton fall into feathers.

At Newington Butts or the Globe, an open platform served as a neutral playing space for the play's numerous locales. Most Elizabethan public theaters had at least two doors, so that the many entrances and exits in this fast-paced comedy could be easily accommodated. Sly seems to have watched "the play" from the gallery to the rear of the main stage over the tiring house, as suggested by the Folio stage direction, "*Enter aloft the drunkard with attendants.*" The playing style was farcical and, as the text implies, relied on slapstick to win its laughs: Petruchio twists Grumio's ear; Kate slaps Bianca, Petruchio, and Grumio; and the hapless Hortensio enters with a broken lute about his shoulders.

The Restoration: A Different Tamer

When the English theaters reopened after the Interregnum (1642–1660), the King's Company, under Thomas Killigrew at the Theatre Royal, held the rights to the play. Shakespeare's script, as printed in the Folio editions, was not performed after his lifetime until 1844; instead, before that date it was regularly rewritten to conform to current tastes. (Shakespeare's *Shrew* may have been performed at Court in 1663–1664, as recorded by the Master of the Revels.) Restoration comedy, typified by the works of William Congreve and Mrs. Aphra Behn, relied upon wit and double-entendres, and playwrights in the late seventeenth century frequently replaced Shakespeare's humor with their own. In 1667 John Lacy, a comic actor, adapted the *Shrew* to enlarge the role of Grumio, which he played. Retitled *Sauny, the Scot, or The Taming of the Shrew*, Lacy's script follows Shakespeare's plot but adds even more tribulations for poor Margaret (i.e., Kate), who willingly marries Petruchio in order to tame his coarse manners. To avenge her audacity, Petruchio forces Margaret to smoke tobacco and drink strong liquor; he threatens to extract her teeth or bury her alive. Performed until 1736, *Sauny* was an enormously popular piece precisely reflecting its society's view of the battle of the sexes. Another Restoration-era adaptation, Charles Johnson's *The Cobbler of Preston* (1716), expanded the Sly Induction into a two-act farce.

The Eighteenth Century: Garrick's Catherine and Petruchio

The century's greatest actor-manager, David Garrick, revised Shakespeare's comedy in 1754. His *Catherine and Petruchio* remains the most important adaptation of the *Shrew* in the play's rich history; it dominated English and American stages until well into the nineteenth century, was still performed in the twentieth, and rivaled *Romeo and Juliet* and *Richard III* as the most popular Shakespeare play on both sides of the Atlantic. Garrick reduced the play's three plots (Sly, Kate-Petruchio, and Bianca-Lucentio) to one, focusing solely on the eventual submission of Catherine (Garrick Anglicized the name) to Petruchio. In this three-act version, Catherine is actually a stronger, more sympathetic (and certainly less bawdy) character than Shakespeare's; her final submission is honest and heartfelt as she becomes the ideal wife prescribed by cultural codes and church teachings. Like Lacy's Margaret and John Fletcher's Maria in *The Tamer Tamed* (1611, see "A Sequel and Spin-offs" below), Garrick's Catherine actually wishes to marry Petruchio to tame him: "A Plague upon his Impudence! I'll marry my Revenge, but I will tame him." Garrick's approach to the taming plot may say as much about the neoclassical taste for symmetry as it does about any proto-feminist leanings in the actor. Unlike Shakespeare's Kate, who is never seen alone, Garrick's Catherine has a soliloquy in which she lets the audience in on her secret—that she will be the tamer too. She even uses the same hawk metaphor employed by Petruchio in Shakespeare's plot, saying she'll make her husband "stoop onto her lure." If she fails, she promises to "tie her tongue up, and pare down her nails." Garrick's Petruchio was a gentlemanly adversary. Still, Garrick introduced a bullwhip as part of the tamer's weaponry, a piece of business which can be found into the twenty-first century. Not everyone in that age approved of Garrick's revision, not so much because of its theme, but because it violated Shakespeare's original: Dr. Samuel Johnson argued that the twin love plots in *The Taming of the Shrew* were "so well united, that they can hardly be called the two plots without injury to the art with which they are interwoven."

Nonetheless the Garrick version was the principal acting edition of the original until 1844. The first performances in America were at Philadelphia's Southwark Theater in 1766 by the American (formerly Hallam) Company. The Continental Congress outlawed the public performance of plays at the outset of the Revolutionary War, and, when the theaters reopened, *Catherine and Petruchio* was one of the first plays to return to the professional stage. The acting was broad, farcical, and declamatory—and Petruchio still carried that bullwhip.

In England, John Philip Kemble challenged the popularity of Garrick's adaptation. Kemble's *Katharine and Petruchio* used Garrick's edition as a basis but made further alterations. Kemble, who first played the role at the Drury Lane in 1786, built on the tradition of a more genteel Petruchio, largely by deleting much of his rude behavior (including Biondello's description of Petruchio's outlandish costume and actions during the wedding) and his quest for Baptista's fortune. Kemble's cutting also "tamed" Katharine, played often by Kemble's sister, Sarah Siddons, who was best known for her performances in tragedies. Kemble's cuts, which included minimizing the farcical/slapstick elements of the play, may have been motivated as much by his own strengths and weaknesses as an actor as by any sentimental impulses to bring dignity and morality to the stage. Charles Kemble restored some of the broader comedy in 1828 when he incorporated new business at Petruchio's house: Katharine had to scramble under the dining table as the servants threw food about the stage.

The Nineteenth Century: Shakespeare's Shrew Restored

In 1844 Shakespeare's Induction and the original text (minus two dozen bawdy lines) reappeared at London's Haymarket Theatre. There Robert Strickland made history as the first Christopher Sly on British stages for more than two hundred years. J. R. Planché, a noted antiquarian who inaugurated the fashion for historically accurate settings, recreated a Tudor banqueting hall as the play's setting; strolling players in Italianate costumes erected a makeshift stage for the action; and signboards were used to identify locales. Sly remained on stage throughout, falling asleep during the banquet in Act 5, only to be carried off by the company after their curtain call. This popular restoration inspired others to return to Shakespeare's text, most notably Samuel Phelps, who played Sly to considerable acclaim at the Sadler's Wells Theatre in 1856.

The most admired and scenically impressive of the "restored" *Shrews* could be found in America, where, in 1887, Augustin Daly mounted the first American production of the play, "a pictorial delight," according to theater historian George C. D. Odell (v. 2, 438). Odell describes the interior of Baptista's house as a "very handsome room, with a superb old rug covering most of the floor, and with a set of massive, heavily carved gold furniture, said to have been brought from an old Italian Palace" (v. 2, 439). At a great banquet in Act Five, at which all the warring elements were appeased, Daly used a set that suggested "a great picture by Paul Veronese. The costumes and the groupings were beautiful." A soloist and choir boys sang.

Daly deleted passages that he judged to be of poor literary quality. Still, he shaped the production to showcase the talents of his leading lady, the imposing and much admired Ada Rehan who appeared in a gorgeous mahogany-red brocade gown and a fiery wig for her first tiger-like entry. The Daly-Rehan interpretation restored Katharina's importance, and she, for the first time in the nineteenth century, became a true match to Petruchio. John Drew's Petruchio was dashing and charming, not a rough-and-tumble hellion, although the bullwhip was still a prominent prop. Daly's version of the play was more polite than most previous productions and it proved so popular that it played in London (where Shaw disapproved), Edinburgh, and Paris.

The Twentieth Century: Rethinking The Shrew

The suffragette movement advanced the cause of women in the years before and after World War I. As women became a more potent political force, productions of *The Taming of the Shrew* reflected these changes. Twentieth-century productions of the play have fallen into four major categories that sometimes overlap:

1. Slapstick farce, which reduces characters to comic automatons and thereby distances the audience from the human issues in the play. Such productions often set the play in a *commedia dell'arte*, circus, or similar milieu or recontextualize it (e.g., a Wild West setting) to estrange the audience.

2. Love stories, in which Kate and Petruchio fall in love early and their seemingly aberrant behaviors are masquerades and/or mating rituals; a number of these productions reflect the metatheatrical nature of the play to argue that Kate and Petruchio are merely playing roles.

3. Metatheatrical interpretations emphasizing the play-within-the-play that the traveling actors perform for Sly; these often suggest that the mistreatment of women is Sly's male fantasy.

4. Renderings that attempt to expose abusive behaviors; such productions have been especially noticeable since the late 1970s.

Fin de siècle productions of the play (e.g., Frank Benson's at Manchester and Stratford in 1899, and Oscar Asche's in London, 1900) generally featured caterwauling, cantankerous Kates. From 1905 to 1914, the famed American acting team of Richard Southern and Julia Marlowe advanced a kinder interpretation of the Petruchio-Kate romance, for Southern's Petruchio sincerely loved Kate who was childish in her shrewishness. Southern directed Bianca to be the provocateur in the battle between sisters, thus making Kate more victim than aggressor. Although considerable slapstick comedy dominated the production, the play seemed a sentimental comedy in which love conquers all. Margaret Anglin, who played Kate and doubled as director, continued the Southern-Marlowe tradition of a dignified Petruchio-Kate relationship in productions in San Francisco (1913) and New York (1914).

An admired "slapstick between a loving couple" production starred Alfred Lunt and Lynn Fontaine, America's preeminent stage duo of the 1930s. In 1935 the Lunts first performed the play in a circus milieu that opened with a parade of clowns, acrobats, and tumbling midgets. All was done to amuse Christopher Sly, who—like the larger audience beyond the footlights—watched the comedic spectacle with childlike amusement. Lunt's Petruchio entered on a horse (two men in costume) wearing a serape and sombrero, as the production freely mixed cultural contexts for the play. Fontaine's Katharina matched Lunt's audaciousness as she stole fruit, stuffed sausages down her bodice, and concluded the lecture to wives by stepping into a golden chariot with Petruchio to ascend into the clouds as heavenly music played. Given the Lunts' reputation as serious actors, their over-the-top clown show gave succeeding productions permission to combine popular entertainment with Shakespeare.

Although they were not necessarily inspired by the Lunts' *Shrew*, other productions of note followed: the Russian Theodore Komisarjevsky staged a deliriously slapstick version at Stratford-upon-Avon in 1939 (even as the Lunts were touring their hugely successful version in the U.S.); Katharine Hepburn and Alfred Drake performed a Wild West version at Stratford, Connecticut, in 1955; and William Ball directed a buoyant and exuberant *commedia dell'arte* production in San Francisco in 1976 (see films below). These, like so many other slapstick *Shrews*, reduced the play's misogynist elements to a giddy puppet show to mitigate the troubling aspects of the play for modern audiences.

In 1960 the Royal Shakespeare Company included *The Taming of the Shrew* in its first season, enlisting John Barton, whom RSC director Peter Hall knew from his university days at Cambridge, to direct the play. Barton bolstered Shakespeare's text, especially the Induction, by adding passages from the earlier *Taming of A Shrew* to complete the Sly subplot. The performance, which was played on a revolving stage that showed the interior and exterior of a Tudor inn, included Sly as a boisterous character commenting on the plot. A young Peter O'Toole (then age twenty-seven) played Petruchio to Dame Peggy Ashcroft's decidedly older (fifty-three) Kate. The emphasis was on the games played between the romantic antagonists; they clearly knew they were merely playing at "fighting" and undertook their mission with twinkles in the eye and smirks on their faces—and considerably less slapstick than had become popular in the post-Lunts era. Sly vowed to race home to apply what he'd learned to *his* wife. Barton's popular production was kept in the RSC repertory for three years, and inspired others to follow a similar format at such venues as the Shakespeare Festivals in Stratford,

Ontario, Canada (Michael Langham, 1962), and Stratford-upon-Avon (Trevor Nunn, 1967). The latter further undercut the play's rougher elements by introducing a Chekhovian pathos and melancholy, both Nunn trademarks, into its unabashedly theatrical concept. Petruchio's final speech ("Why there's a wench. Come and kiss me Kate") was less a conqueror's victory cry than a lover's awe-struck realization that his taming had wrought an extraordinary woman and that this special moment would be all too fleeting.

By contrast, a number of productions in the last quarter of the twentieth century have deconstructed the play to expose Petruchio's brutality. Charles Marowitz noted that virtually all of Petruchio's tactics used to tame his shrew (starvation, sleep deprivation, withholding promised favors) are precisely those used in brainwashing. Accordingly Marowitz, who codirected the RSC's "Season of Cruelty" (1962–1964) with Peter Brook, devised his own version of the play, a collage simply called *The Shrew* (1973). It emphasized violence (Petruchio raped Kate) to transform the comedy into "a Gothic Tragedy" (Marowitz, 117). In the concluding scene, Kate, dressed in an institutional gown, was brought before a tribunal in shackles. Petruchio was the presiding officer. There she delivered her speech mechanically, devoid of human feeling. Like the lobotomized hero of Ken Kesey's popular novel of that era, *One Flew Over the Cuckoo's Nest* (1973), Kate too had been reduced to a mindless ghost of herself.

In 1976 Michael Bogdanov directed a similarly controversial *Shrew* for the RSC. Stratford audiences entered the theater to discover a conventional-looking "Shakespearean setting," all prim and steeped in tradition. At this point, however, a drunken soccer hooligan in the audience insulted a shocked usherette and then climbed on stage to dismantle the setting. Beneath these disguise identities, the hooligan turned out to be Sly/Petruchio (Jonathan Pryce) and the usherette (Paola Dionisotti) to be Kate. Sly/Petruchio continued his boorish assault; a motorcycle established this anti-hero as a "wild one." He was, however, no rebellious teen à la Marlon Brando in the famous 1950s film. This Petruchio was a greedy mercenary whose shrew-taming was strictly a business enterprise. Those who saw the production—which was both controversial and popular—saw that the use of women as chattel by men in power was being exposed to bitter satire by the production.

Two 1985 productions of the play explored such notions in remarkably innovative ways. Di Trevis, directing the play for the RSC, opened the action with a lengthy procession of the actors, headed by the actress playing Kithara (Siam Thomas) carrying a baby and dragging a huge basket on which a banner told audiences they were about to witness "The Taming of the Shrew—A Kind of History." The image immediately conjured memories of Brecht's *Mother Courage*, and indeed the ensuing production treated the play as a political tract. That same year, the Medieval Players offered a provocative variant on the "exploited and abused" women theme by having men play Katharina and Bianca as extensions of male fantasies about women. None of these productions, however, could match the extraordinary ending of a 1989 production in Turkey. After she concluded her sermon on the duties of a wife, Kate slit her wrists rather than succumb to Petruchio's domination (Elsom, 74–75).

The Taming of the Shrew on Film and Video

Shrew has been filmed at least eighteen times in England and North America, placing it, as Diana E. Henderson points out in her article "A Shrew for the Times," in a select league with the "big four" tragedies. On film it outpaces the more poetic later comedies (149). Most of the film versions, to be sure, are adaptations as free with the script as Garrick's *Catherine and Petruchio*. A nickelodeon-era short film about a boxer tamed by a lady who loves Shakespeare's plays was called *The Taming of the Shrew*. The first film of Shakespeare's play was a one-reeler made in 1908 by the pioneer director D. W. Griffith. Mack Sennett, best known for his slapstick comedies in the silent era, assisted Griffith; the film was largely an excuse for knockabout farce. Other silent *Shrews* could be found in Italy (1913), France (1911), and England (1911). *Shrew* later inaugurated the modern era of film as the first "Shakespeare talkie."

- 1929—Director Sam Taylor, with Douglas Fairbanks (Petruchio) and Mary Pickford (Katharina). (68 min.)
  In 1927 Al Jolson starred in *The Jazz Singer*, generally considered the first "sound film." Within two years of that historic event, Shakespeare's characters first "talked" in a film version of *The Taming of the Shrew* that featured the most popular actor of the 1920s, Douglas Fairbanks Senior, and his equally popular wife, Mary Pickford. Known as "America's sweetheart" and loved for her golden curls and coy manner, Pickford lent considerable charm to Katharina, whom she played as a strong-willed woman asserting her independence in a male-dominated world. In the wooing scene Kate first appears atop a lengthy staircase (the unattainable woman on a pedestal), and, in a twist upon tradition, it is she who cracks the bullwhip. Fairbanks, noted for his swashbuckling roles, plays Petruchio as a charming rogue who is genuinely captivated by Kate. The film, produced by Charlie Chaplin's United Artists, takes advantage of the camera's

FRANCO ZEFFIRELLI
Verismo *Shakespeare*

Although he has directed only three Shakespeare plays for film—*The Taming of the Shrew* (1967), *Romeo and Juliet* (1968), and *Hamlet* (1991)—Franco Zeffirelli has secured an important place among interpreters of Shakespeare in the cinema. Just as Kenneth Branagh popularized Shakespeare-on-film for a young generation in the 1990s, Zeffirelli introduced the Elizabethan playwright to movie-going youth of the 1960s. Critic Deborah Cartmell recently noted that Zeffirelli's "films implicitly and daringly argue that pictures can speak as loudly and as eloquently as Shakespeare's words" (220).

Zeffirelli's films of the Italian plays are known for their sumptuous visuals, the cinematic equivalent of Renaissance painting. Given that he was born and educated in Florence, the Tuscan city that spawned Renaissance art, this is hardly surprising. Zeffirelli's father was a wealthy Florentine merchant whose ancestry can be traced to Leonardo da Vinci. He kept a mistress, a prominent fashion designer, who gave birth to Gianfranco Corsi in 1923 and then rechristened the baby "Franco Zeffirelli" according to a Florentine tradition that illegitimate babies should receive a fictitious name beginning with "Z." After his mother's death, young Franco was raised by an English nanny who integrated him into a circle of British expatriates living in Florence. Known as *"I Scorpioni"* because of their stinging wit, these remarkable women introduced the boy to the arts, literature, and culture. Zeffirelli's 1998 film, *Tea with Mussolini* (featuring a cast of England's finest actresses), is based upon his relationship with the *Scorpioni* and provides a revealing look at the artist-director's formative years.

Aspiring to be an architect, Zeffirelli entered the University of Florence's renowned architecture program in 1941; there he began his theatrical career by staging plays and operas. (Zeffirelli, whose aunt was a respected soprano, remains one of Italy's most distinguished opera directors.) In 1943 he joined the Italian resistance to fight the Nazi occupation of his homeland (a subplot in *Tea with Mussolini* is based on his experiences in the underground). Zeffirelli's encounter with British troops increased his passion for dramatic literature and inspired him to devote his artistic training to scenic and costume design, talents that can be seen in his Shakespeare films. Laurence Olivier, who supplies voice-overs for Zeffirelli's *Romeo and Juliet*, also had a profound influence on the Italian director's decision to pursue a career in theater and film. After seeing Olivier's *Henry V* (1944), Zeffirelli asserted, "Architecture was not for me; it had to be the stage. I wanted to do something like [*Henry V*] . . . When the lights went up my head was clearer than it had been for months" (Zeffirelli, 216).

In 1949 Zeffirelli began his film career as an assistant to the noted Italian filmmaker, Luchino Visconti, famous for his *verismo* (ultra-realistic) depictions of post-war Italy. From Visconti—whose bleak films contrast with Zeffirelli's bathed-in-gold Shakespearean works—the young director learned the importance of meticulously creating an authentic world in which to place the action of Shakespeare's plays and Verdi's operas. The opening moments of the famed Old Vic production of *Romeo and Juliet* in 1960 illustrates Zeffirelli's preoccupation with meticulous realism in classical works. Some critics have disparaged this significant element of the director's style, claiming that such attention to detail is detrimental to the words. Pauline Kael, film critic for *The New Yorker*, articulated such reservations in her review of *Romeo and Juliet*:

> [Zeffirelli] brings to the screen the filler of opera—all that coarse, earthy stuff that comes on when the main singers are off. And Zeffirelli's "robust" realistic detail is ludicrous; when he throws a close-up of the marketplace . . . and we see peppers and onions, it's like the obligatory setting of the scene in the first act of an opera when the peasant girl walks on with the basket in her arms.
>
> (Kael, 156)

ability to create farce visually. To force Kate to sit at his command, Petruchio glides a chair fifty feet across a polished floor; it stops magically at her derriere. The film's "induction" sets the farcical tone of the play: instead of a drunken Sly, the audience sees Punch-and-Judy puppets beating one another while proclaiming their love. The movie offers glimpses of the couple during its bridal

Audiences and most other critics did not agree. Zeffirelli counters Kael by arguing that Shakespeare was "a frustrated traveler who wanted to take his audiences on a trip to Italy. The director has to fill in the details of the scene Shakespeare never really saw" (Cole and Chinoy, 439). Whether he is interpreting opera, Shakespeare, the lives of the saints (*Brother Sun, Sister Moon,* a biopic about Francis of Assisi, 1972), or the Bible (his televised miniseries on the life of Christ was seen by more than nine hundred million viewers), Zeffirelli consistently fights "a crusade against boredom." Much of his arsenal consists of imaginative shots (e.g., close ups of Elizabeth Taylor's eyes peering at Petruchio through a grate) and sequences (the dizzying Morosco dance in *Romeo and Juliet* and the numerous chase sequences in *Shrew*) that he imagines as the visual equivalent of Shakespeare's verbal imagery.

The director often crusades against boredom by heavily cutting Shakespeare's texts. Zeffirelli retained only about thirty percent of *The Taming of the Shrew*, thirty-five percent of *Romeo and Juliet*, and thirty-seven percent of *Hamlet* in his screenplays (Pilkington, 165). Some critics wonder whether such drastic cutting of Shakespeare renders a product that is truly "Shakespeare," or, as a writer for the *Financial Times* (London) suggests, "Zeffirelli's aim seems to elicit from his audience an active contempt for the words" (Cartmell, 212). To be fair, it should be noted that Zeffirelli was contractually obligated by his producers to render a two-hour version of *Hamlet* (the film runs 2:15). Still, Zeffirelli perhaps too readily substitutes visual splendor for the complex poetry of the text.

The director freely borrows techniques from Italian artists whose masterpieces abound in Florence. Both *The Taming of the Shrew* and *Romeo and Juliet* often seem like masterfully composed paintings brought to life. While filming *Shrew*, Zeffirelli and his cinematographer, Ossie Morris, studied the works of Antonio Allegri da Corregio (c. 1490–1534) as they created their storyboards. Zeffirelli often employs framing devices popularized by painters to introduce key characters, as in *Romeo and Juliet:* Juliet is first glimpsed through a window, perfectly framed by the villa's woodwork, while Romeo walks up a country lane, framed by trees and an ancient archway.

Like his countryman and fellow film director, Federico Fellini, Zeffirelli often invokes Italy's rich folklore to add authenticity to his films. *Shrew* opens with an elaborate parade through the alleyways of medieval Padua, a lively reenactment of the Feast of Fools that the director substitutes for Shakespeare's Induction and the Christopher Sly subplot. In *Romeo and Juliet,* Mercutio, Romeo, and other of the Montagues cavort through Verona's streets wearing carnival masks and singing bawdy songs from ancient fertility rites. Such revelries reinforce a favorite theme explored by the director: the battle between the staid world of oldsters and the free-spirited younger generation. Such themes resonated with the Counter-Culture Revolution of the 1960s.

Though popular with young audiences (thanks to Mel Gibson's presence more than the director's artistry), Zeffirelli's *Hamlet* remains less successful than the two Italian films, perhaps because the director was on less familiar terrain. Still, it is the Shakespeare work that has obsessed Zeffirelli throughout his artistic life. In 1960 he told the *Times* (London) that he saw Hamlet living "in a hard world—with no elasticity about it—a closed world, with high walls, no windows, lots of storms. Like a prisoner in a tower" (Cole and Chinoy, 440). Elements of this vision (which he admits have been influenced by Olivier's film) were partially realized in his film, especially in the famous "To be or not to be . . ." soliloquy. Despite its deficiencies—most notably in the extensive cutting and odd restructuring that defies Shakespeare's text—the 1991 *Hamlet* is a worthy culmination of the director's filmed Shakespeare, if only for its many memorable visual images.

References and Related Reading

Cartmell, Deborah. "Franco Zeffirelli and Shakespeare." *The Cambridge Companion to Shakespeare on Film.* Ed. Russell Jackson. Cambridge, Eng., 2000. 212–223.

Cole, Toby, and Helen Krich Chinoy. *Directors on Directing: A Source Book of the Modern Theater.* Indianapolis, 1963.

Kael, Pauline. *Going Steady.* London, 1970.

Pilkington, Ace G. "Zeffirelli's Shakespeare." *Shakespeare and the Moving Image.* Eds. Anthony Davis and Stanley Wells. Cambridge, Eng., 1994. 163–169.

Zeffirelli, Franco. *Zeffirelli: The Autobiography of Franco Zeffirelli.* New York, 1986.

night, with Pickford consoling Petruchio after she's bashed his head with a stool. She then throws her whip into the fireplace, signaling their egalitarian sexual union. Pickford concludes the capitulation speech, which Kate delivers solely to Bianca in this heavily cut text, with a sly wink to the audience as the film fades to black; Kate is only pretending to accede to Petruchio's demands.

■ 1967—Director Franco Zeffirelli, with Elizabeth Taylor (Katharina), Richard Burton (Petruchio), and Michael Horden (Baptista). (122 min.)

The success of Zeffirelli's *Shrew* film can be attributed in good part to his casting of a legendary screen couple in the leading roles. Audiences were familiar with the tempestuous love affair between Elizabeth Taylor and Richard Burton, who met as they filmed the then-most expensive film of all time, *Cleopatra*. After divorcing their respective spouses, they married, whereupon their off-screen battles filled gossip columns and magazines. Burton played Petruchio as a drunkard, a choice that reinforced the notion that the film provided a peek at the real-life dilemmas of Hollywood's most talked-about lovers. They wanted so much to work together on the Shakespeare project that they underwrote the film by working for minimal compensation.

Private lives aside, the film succeeds on its own terms, largely because Zeffirelli, an opera director-designer who made his screen debut with the *Shrew*, meticulously recreates a Renaissance world in both its beauty and its seamy reality. The director has devised his own induction to initiate the film: as the credits roll, the audience sees a celebration of the Feast of Fools to mark the beginning of a term at Padua's famed university (the second founded in Italy). As revelers cavort through crowded streets with effigies of church figures and town fathers (there is a shot of a drunk—Sly?—aloft in a cage), it is evident that Zeffirelli intends that Petruchio and Katharina are the Lord and Lady of Misrule who combine energies to expose Padua's outmoded customs, especially those concerning women.

The film was made in the early days of the Women's Liberation Movement. Zeffirelli adheres to the tradition of staging the play as knockabout farce: the wooing scene is a dizzying chase through Baptista's villa and ends with Kate falling through the roof into a pile of goose feathers. While it may offer visual delight, the approach minimizes the scene's witty banter, the very thing that makes these adversaries attractive to one another in Shakespeare's text. To avoid the comedic violence, Zeffirelli inserts a number of brief shots in which Petruchio and Kate silently observe one another—lovingly and longingly. In one of his most inspired choices, the director illustrates Gremio's lengthy description of the off-stage wedding (3.2.149ff.), a textbook case of how the camera can often visualize images described in the text.

The film's most significant nod to changing values occurs in the Act Five material. As Petruchio and Kate prepare to enter Baptista's house for Bianca's wedding, Petruchio demands a kiss from his "tamed" bride. She obliges with a perfunctory peck on his cheek and races off as he stands embarrassed, his bravado punctured. The scene anticipates Zeffirelli's handling of the capitulation speech. After Kate delivers her sermon to the wives in apparent sincerity before the shocked Paduans, she quickly disappears into a crowd of women, and Petruchio is last seen desperately chasing after her amidst the laughter of his male companions.

While Kate may have bested Petruchio in the play's finale, Burton's performance is far better spoken than Taylor's (he was an experienced Shakespearean, she a novice). Taylor's nasal and tart delivery makes her as much nag as shrew. Still, as Barbara Hodgdon notes, for many viewers "Taylor's body language over-matches Burton's facility with Shakespeare. The film not only eroticizes her spectacular body but also capitalizes upon her attraction for Burton" (166). Zeffirelli's film remains a landmark in the history of cinematic bardolatry; it launched a renaissance of Shakespeare films, much the way Kenneth Branagh's *Much Ado About Nothing* did a quarter century later.

■ 1976—Director William Ball, with Marc Singer (Petruchio) and Fredi Olster (Katharina). (120 min.)

Preserved on videotape as part of the Broadway Archives series, Ball's *commedia dell'arte* production of *The Taming of the Shrew* for San Francisco's American Conservatory Theater (ACT) is a masterpiece of comedic playing, with Shakespeare's words still audible beneath the physical antics and the extraordinarily rapid pacing. The actors are costumed in predominantly white and red *commedia* gear (albeit with few masks) as they play on a trestle stage. Actors standing on the perimeter of the action provide sound effects, while those who play roles punctuate virtually every line with broad physical gestures. Ball's production thus skirts any social and political issues by reducing the play to a traditional Punch-and-Judy show played by live actors. The video is useful mostly as a casebook on comic shtick, yet a worthy reminder that the *Shrew* is indebted to the stock characters of Roman and Italian comedy.

■ 1980—Director Jonathan Miller, with John Cleese (Petruchio) and Sarah Badel (Katharina). (163 min.)

Like Zeffirelli's film, this BBC Shakespeare production of the *Shrew* creates a distinctly (English) Renaissance world. Yet instead of offering a colorful, energetic ambience, Miller's Padua is stifling and drab, befitting the ultra-realistic approach to the play. Many scenes are filmed from a distance and framed by sterile corridors; the audience is never asked to warm to Katharina or Petruchio. The superb British comedian John Cleese (of Monty Python fame) as Petruchio should have made this a memorably comic production, but Cleese is miscast and proves dull and dour instead of delightful. He and Sarah Badel play the wooing scene listlessly with little affect. Miller's interpretation is grounded in late-sixteenth-century texts and sermons about men enjoying supremacy over their wives, the antithesis of post-sixties feminism. Miller argued that he had to give the play "an explicitly religious format so people could see it not just as the highjinks of an intolerably selfish man . . . but a sacramental view of the nature of marriage" (Miller, 200). Accordingly, Badel's heartfelt reading of the speech on wifely obedience is punctuated by a high-Anglican hymn glorifying wives as gifts to their husbands. The BBC *Shrew* mutes the comedy.

- 1981—Director Peter Dews, with Len Cariou (Petruchio) and Sherry Flett (Katharina). (163 min.)

   Like the recording of Ball's *commedia* version, this video is an archival record of a production, premiered at the Stratford (Canada) Shakespeare Festival. Dews's Stratford *Shrew* attests that the play can work without excessive or abusive slapstick. Filmed on a thrust stage before a live audience, the production records the reactions of the viewers, thereby adding another joyous element to the experience. As Petruchio, Len Cariou (a Broadway musical star) "tames" Katharina strictly through charm and a playful wit. The uncut wooing scene is among the funniest ever filmed, yet there is scarcely any physical contact. The actors (Cariou and Sherry Flett) turn the battle of the sexes into a witty battle of words, and it is apparent that the lovers thoroughly enjoy their verbal tussles. Because she is so attracted to him, Katharina is completely deflated when Petruchio tells her "by St. George, I am too young for you" (2.1.235). No other film makes it so abundantly clear that these romantic antagonists are drawn to each other by the sexiness of their wit, and thus the Stratford production remains an antidote to the choreographed wrestling matches that dominate other films. Furthermore, this is the only film in which the Induction is included; after his initial encounter with the actors, Sly sits on a platform above the stage enjoying their performance.

Adaptations

- 1948/1953—*Kiss Me Kate* (theater and film productions), director George Sidney, with Howard Keel (Fred Graham/Petruchio), Kathryn Grayson (Kate/Lili Vanessi), Ann Miller (Lois Lane/Bianca), and Tommy Rall (Bill Calhoun/Lucentio).

   The Taming of the Shrew has inspired what theater critics consider the best Broadway musical adapted from Shakespeare. Cole Porter composed the 1948 "backstage musical" *Kiss Me Kate,* in which divorced Broadway stars Fred Graham and Lili Vanessi are reunited to play Petruchio and Kate in a New York revival of Shakespeare's play. Their offstage battles mirror those of the shrew and her tamer, and Porter provides witty musical soliloquies that define characters and their dilemmas. Kate sings "I Hate Men" as she tosses tankards about the stage, while Fred's Petruchio brags that "I Have Come to Wive It Wealthily in Padua." Later, as Fred destroys his little black book of phone numbers, he sings the melancholic "Where Is the Life That Late I Led?" Two gangsters attempting to collect a gambling debt sing "Brush Up Your Shakespeare" when they are trapped on stage in the play within the play; the song abounds with bawdy puns ("Kick him in the Coriolanus") and captures the spirit of Shakespeare's rustics. The capitulation speech becomes a sentimental afterthought in which Fred and Lili kiss and make up before an enthusiastic audience. Filmed in 1953 with the strong cast named above, *Kate* is a staple of the American musical theater and is regularly revived on Broadway, most recently in a multiple Tony Award–winning production directed by Michael Blakemore and telecast in 2003.

A Sequel and Spin-offs

By the early seventeenth century, *The Taming of the Shrew* had already inspired a sequel, John Fletcher's *The Woman's Prize: or the Tamer Tamed* (c. 1611), in which Petruchio, now a widower, marries once more. After his tempestuous life with his first wife Kate, Petruchio looks forward to a peaceful existence with young Maria. In the interim between wedding and bedding, Maria, inspired by Bianca, stalls the consummation. Although one of their female allies remarks "'Tis as easy with a sieve to scoop the ocean, as to tame Petruchio," ultimately Maria succeeds in turning the tables and taming her new husband. The play has been a recent popular hit at the Royal Shakespeare Company and is sometimes paired with *Shrew,* as it was during the 2004 summer season at Shakespeare Santa Cruz in California. Fletcher eventually succeeded Shakespeare as the chief playwright for the King's Men, and they co-wrote *Henry VIII* (c. 1613) and *The Two Noble Kinsmen* (c. 1613–1614) after Shakespeare ostensibly retired from the stage.

   Nearly four centuries later, *Shrew* inspired a popular episode of an American sitcom, *Moonlighting,* among the top-rated television shows in the 1980s. The episode, aired on November 2, 1987, offered a charming and thoughtful spoof of Shakespeare's play and was the most talked-about show among the series' sixty-five episodes. Like the Induction of *The Taming of the Shrew,* "Atomic Shakespeare" (as the episode is known) provides its own framing device as a mother and her young son watch a television show that becomes a parody of Shakespeare's play. Using Shakespeare's plot as a template, *Moonlighting* gently mocks the *Shrew*, especially in its witty variations on the Petruchio-Kate banter about day and night, the sun and the moon. True to the show's premise (women outthink men), the parody ends with Petruchio (Bruce Willis) capitulating to Kate (Cybill Shepherd), much to the delight of Padua's citizenry. Kate and Petruchio vow to live happily ever after, bound by their mutual hatred of iambic pentameter. With sitcom humor, "Atomic Shakespeare" critiques *Shrew*'s sexism and provides a satisfying resolution its audience.

10 Things I Hate About You (1999), a teenflick set in a Seattle's Padua High School, depicts Patrick Verona (Heath Ledger) as a rebellious outsider/rock guitarist attracted to the school's beautiful contrarian, Kat (Julia Stiles). The film is both a comedy about nineties youth and a thoughtful, entertaining adaptation of Shakespeare's play for moderns. Bianca, a beautiful if vacuous sophomore, cannot date unless her older sister, Kat, does too. When Joey Donner decides to date Bianca, he and his conniving friends pay wild Australian Pat one hundred dollars to spend time with Kat. Eventually Pat wins her over with his (initially) bogus caring and a spectacular rendition of Frankie Valli's "Can't Take My Eyes Off of You" accompanied by the school's marching band. Director Gil Junger and cast provide many new emotional twists and turns, sealing the tempestuous romance and the couple's real feelings with Kat's recitation of her own Shakespearean sonnet. She lists all of Pat's flaws, most significant of which, she acknowledges, is that "I hate the way I don't hate you."

Choreographer John Cranko, the Englishman who brought Germany's Stuttgart Ballet to international prominence, created a vivacious 1969 balletic comedy closely based upon the play and starring his lead dancers Richard Cragun and Marcia Haydee. Stuffed with incident, caricature, slapstick, and even romantic dancing, the two-act ballet is set to music inspired by Domenico Scarlatti and is now performed by classical dance companies, including Chicago's Joffrey Ballet, worldwide.

References and Related Reading

Bate, Jonathan, and Russell Jackson. *The Oxford Illustrated History of Shakespeare on Stage*. Oxford, 2001.

Bean, John. "Comic Structure and the Humanizing of Kate in *The Taming of the Shrew*." *The Woman's Part: Feminist Criticism of Shakespeare*. Eds. Carolyn Ruth Swift Lenz, Gayle Green, and Carol Thomas Neely. Urbana, 1980. 65–78.

Bevington, David. *Shakespeare: The Complete Works*. 5th ed. New York, 2003.

Brown, Pamela Allen. " 'Fie, What a foolish duty call you this?' *The Taming of the Shrew*, Women's Jest and the Divided Audience." *A Companion to Shakespeare's Works: The Comedies*. Eds. Richard Dutton and Jean E. Howard. London, 2003. 289–306.

Buhler, Stephen M. *Shakespeare in the Cinema: Ocular Proof*. Albany, 2002.

Chambers, E. K. *The Elizabethan Stage*. Oxford, 1923.

DiGangi, Mario. "The Social Relations of Shakespeare's Comic Households." *A Companion to Shakespeare's Works: The Comedies*. Eds. Richard Dutton and Jean E. Howard. London, 2003. 90–113.

Dolan, Frances E., ed. *The Taming of the Shrew: Texts and Contexts*. New York, 1996.

Elsom, John. *Is Shakespeare Still Our Contemporary?* London, 1989.

Freedman, Barbara. *Staging the Gaze: Post-modernism, Psychoanalysis and Shakespearean Comedy*. Ithaca and London, 1991.

Hall, Jonathan. *Anxious Pleasures: Shakespearean Comedy and the Nation-State*. London, 1995.

Haring-Smith, Tori. *From Farce to Metadrama: A Stage History of "The Taming of the Shrew," 1594–1983*. Westport, Conn., 1985.

Henderson, Diana E. "A Shrew for the Times." *Shakespeare: The Movie*. Eds. Lynda E. Boose and Richard Burt. London and New York, 1997/99. 148–168.

Hodgdon, Barbara. "Katherina Bound; or, Play(K)ating the Strictures of Everyday Life." *Shakespeare on Film*. Ed. Robert Shaughnessy. New York, 1998. 156–172.

Holderness, Graham. *Shakespeare in Performance: The Taming of the Shrew*. Manchester and New York, 1989.

Leggatt, Alexander, ed. *The Cambridge Companion to Shakespearean Comedy*. Cambridge, Eng., 2002.

Leiter, Samuel L. *Shakespeare Around the Globe: A Guide to Notable Postwar Revivals*. Westport, Conn., 1986.

Marowitz, Charles. *The Marowitz Shakespeare*. New York, 1978.

Newman, Karen. "A Modern Perspective." *The Taming of the Shrew*. New York, 1992. 229–238.

Novy, Marianne. *Love's Argument: Gender Relations in Shakespeare*. Chapel Hill, 1984.

Odell, George C. D. *Shakespeare From Betterton to Irving*. 2 vols. New York, 1920/63.

Orgel, Stephen. "Introduction." *The Pelican Shakespeare: "The Taming of the Shrew."* London and New York, 2000. ix–xl.

Parsons, Keith, and Pamela Mason. *Shakespeare in Performance*. London, 1995.

Paster, Gail Kerns. "The Humour of It: Bodies, Fluids, and Social Discipline in Shakespearean Comedy." *A Companion to Shakespeare's Works: The Comedies*. Eds. Richard Dutton and Jean E. Howard. London, 2003. 47–66.

CHAPTER 7

A Midsummer Night's Dream

c. 1595

Context and Dating

By the winter of 1594–1595, the approximate date for *A Midsummer Night's Dream* and *Romeo and Juliet*, Shakespeare was at full stride as a playwright. We cannot say with certainty which of these plays was written first, but we are reasonably sure that they were penned one right after the other, in late 1594 or early 1595. Taken together, the scripts suggest that Shakespeare was interested in "oer-hasty marriages" and the consequences of falling in love too quickly. Whereas *Romeo and Juliet* treats the subject matter tragically in a domestic setting, the comedic *A Midsummer Night's Dream* frames the theme with mystery and the supernatural. This profound and sophisticated comedy encourages audiences to "glance from heaven to earth, from earth to heaven" (5.1.13).

Known in theatrical shorthand simply as *The Dream*, the play is a catalog of the elements that all people seek in theatrical entertainment. Typical of Shakespeare's comedies, it is a romantic tale, with four love stories unfolding simultaneously—five if you count the ill-fated Greek lovers, Pyramus and Thisbe, whose myth inspired elements in both this play and *Romeo and Juliet*. Not only does Shakespeare give us the obligatory fare of lovely ladies and handsome men, lovers' quarrels, powerful passions, a meddling father, battles between both the generations and the sexes, mistaken identities, and comic chases, he also presents a magical forest, a beautiful fairy queen, apparitions and disappearances by spirits and sprites, men in drag, and even kinky sex. Predictably, there is a happy ending that celebrates weddings galore. Consequently, *The Dream* has been played on virtually every continent by professional and amateur actors for hundreds of years as it is nearly fail-proof theater.

The Dream posed a then-radical departure for Shakespeare: in no previous play had he experimented with such disparate elements. He devised multiple plots borrowed from legend, literature, and folktales from various cultures; the characters represent royalty, commoners, and the spirit world. The mixture of these differences allows for a play that explores the reconciliation of opposites.

Plots

Four plots run concurrently in *The Dream*, each with contrasting tones and textures. These involve:

- the courtship and marriage of **the noble lovers**, Duke Theseus and Hippolyta;
- the tribulations of **the young lovers**, Hermia and Lysander, and Helena and Demetrius;
- the custody battle of **the fairy regents**, Oberon and Titania, over a child from India;
- the hilarious attempts of **the workingmen** to present a play about Pyramus and Thisbe for Duke Theseus's wedding to the Queen of the Amazons.

The philosophical implications of these multiple plots resonate in the finale as the fairies watch the courtly lovers watch the actors perform a play about lovers, while we, the audience, watch them all. Who then, Shakespeare seems to ask, is watching us?

The play moves from the apparently civilized world of the court—a world tarnished by petty jealousies and the oppression of women—to the natural world of Athens Wood. Even nature itself is at strife, as evidenced by the clash between Oberon and Titania. After four acts of "discord," much of it orchestrated by the hobgoblin Puck, the action on all levels reaches "concord." Made wiser by their trek into the woods—to use the title of Steven Sondheim's fairy-tale musical that counsels us to go *Into the Woods* to discover ourselves—the lovers return to build a "sweet peace" and produce offspring that "ever shall be fortunate" (5.1.401).

Characters

Shakespeare borrows popular characters from Roman and Renaissance comedy, though they are not as fully etched as in his later comedies. They exist instead to move the intricate plots forward at a brisk pace. The four lovers are the stock *amorati* of Italian comedy; they are likable yet flawed. Hermia and Lysander are too full of grand sentiments, while Demetrius is callow and self-serving. Among the young lovers only Helena, an emblem of fidelity, emerges as thoughtful and individualized. In the first scene, Egeus, the grumpy old man of Roman comedy (i.e., the *Senex*), threatens Hermia with death or life in a convent; his ultimatum invests the play with the potential for a tragic resolution. The Theseus-Hippolyta relationship is also disconcerting: the Amazon Queen is the Duke's prisoner of war, so that their marriage takes place under duress. (In contemporary productions Hippolyta is sometimes first seen in chains.) Oberon is a majestic and poetic fairy king, but he also succumbs to his darker side by having his royal paramour do "some vile thing." Titania, though radiant and queenly, can be as petty and possessive as Oberon. Puck (a.k.a. "Robin Goodfellow," a folk euphemism for the devil himself) is the ubiquitous trickster, a lord of misrule whom humans throughout the world blame for mishap and chaos. Bottom, a weaver and would-be actor, is an amalgam of stock characters drawn from world comedy: the bragging impostor (or *alazon*), both in his egotistical pronouncements about his acting prowess and in his hammy overacting, and the ancient fool (or *bomolochos*), whose misuse of words and self-important posturing elicit laughter. However flawed these characters may be, they are not figures to be scorned. This is one of Shakespeare's most benevolent and festive comedies, despite the threats of death and danger.

Sources and Inspirations

The Elizabethans and the Spirit World

Growing up in the richly wooded countryside of his native Warwickshire, the young Shakespeare may have heard many a tale of creatures of the night who could fright

> . . . the maidens of the villagery,
> Skim milk, and sometimes labor in the quern,
> And bootless make the breathless huswife churn,
> And sometimes make the drink to bear no barn,
> Mislead night wanderers, laughing at their harm.
> (2.1.35–39)

Shakespeare and his audiences shared a fascination with the spirit world that still delights in our time. Today's moviegoers flock to such films as *The Lord of the Rings* and *Star Wars* for many of the same reasons that London audiences were attracted to *A Midsummer Night's Dream*. Tales about supernatural beings are not only inherently fascinating, but from a theatrical standpoint they allow artists to indulge their imaginations to create enthralling images for audiences.

Today the fairies and hobgoblins seem whimsical creatures of folklore and myth, but to many Elizabethans, especially the uneducated, fairies—as well as ghosts and witches—were actual beings. Elizabethan housewives often paid obeisance to fairies who watched over their firesides and bedrooms. A contemporary of Shakespeare wrote that women in his village "were wont to set a bowl of milk before [the fairies] and Robin Good-fellow [a.k.a. Puck], for grinding of malt or mustard, and sweeping the house at midnight." Should such tasks be neglected, fairies were feared as being capable of wreaking havoc on an Elizabethan housewife. In *The Merry Wives of Windsor*, Shakespeare's lone comedy set entirely in his native country, Pistol warns that

> Where fires thou find'st unraked and hearths unswept,
> There pinch the maids as blue as bilberry.
> Our radiant Queen [i.e., Titania] hates sluts and sluttery.
> (5.5.43–45)

To the Elizabethans, fairies were the source of practical jokes (e.g., tipping milk pails), and leading travelers astray was a favorite trick—a device that Shakespeare incorporates into Puck's antics in Act 4 of *The Dream*.

A Courtly Wedding

Although there is no record of the play being performed until 1598 (and no publication until 1600), evidence suggests that *The Dream* was written during the winter of 1594–1595. Some scholars believe that it may have been a commissioned work intended to honor a prestigious wedding (no less than six weddings have been suggested as sources), possibly that of the earl of Darby, brother to a patron of Shakespeare's acting company, and Lady Elizabeth Vere, granddaughter of the Queen's counselor, Lord Burghley. The couple was married at Whitehall in January 1595. Given the play's emphasis on wedding preparations, and particularly the blessing on the multiple newlyweds that concludes the play (5.1.396–415), the hypothesis that Shakespeare wrote the play for a specific wedding continues to invite speculation. Yet no one has ever proved that the play was written for any specific occasion beyond the public performances noted in 1600 in the First Quarto: "as it hath been sundry times publickely acted, by the Right honourable, the Lord Chamberlaine his seruants."

Literary Sources

Although no specific source can be cited as the source of the plots for *A Midsummer Night's Dream*, Shakespeare seems to have drawn from a variety of well-known works. Chaucer's *The Knight's Tale* provides elements of the Theseus-Hippolyta story, with reliance, too, on Thomas North's translation of Plutarch's *Lives of the Noble Grecians and Romans* (1579) for material about Theseus. Oberon, a figure from Teutonic (German) myth, can be traced to a medieval romance called *Huon of Boreaux* (translated into English c. 1540), which describes Oberon as the offspring of Julius Ceasar and Morgan le Fay, the temptress of Arthurian legend. Titania is the Faerie Queen immortalized in a lengthy poem by Edmund Spenser (1552–1599). Shakespeare, however, specifically calls her "Titania," a name he perhaps borrowed from the Latin poet, Ovid, who refers to the moon by that title. Shakespeare also composes an amusing parody of St. Paul's letter to the Corinthians for Bottom's attempt to articulate the extraordinary "dream" celebrating his night in Titania's bower. St. Paul wrote, "What no eye has seen, nor ear heard, nor the heart of man conceived" (1 Cor., 2:9), which in Bottom's convoluted logic becomes, "The eye of man hath not heard, the ear of man hath not seen, man's hand is not able to taste, his tongue to conceive, nor his heart to report, what my dream was" (4.1.209–212).

The story of the ill-fated lovers Pyramus and Thisbe provided Shakespeare with the both a primary plot (a young man and a young woman whose fathers attempt to keep them apart) and the metatheatrical device of a play-within-the-play. The Greek myth, as recounted by Ovid in his *Metamorphoses*, also provided material for *Romeo and Juliet*. Shakespeare may have written *The Dream* as a comic antidote to *Romeo and Juliet*, or, depending on the chronology, perhaps he wished to explore the theme of star-crossed lovers tragically after composing a comedy on the subject.

Language, Music, and Dance

Stylistically, there are four sorts of language in *The Dream*, as well as music and dance, each defining character and establishing tone:

1. *Singsong rhyme:* There are two instances, quite distinct from one another, when Shakespeare uses stylized language to abet his purpose. The fairies—and Puck in particular—speak in exaggerated verse to denote that they are not humans but "unearthly" creatures. In addition, the play-within-the-play is written in rhymed verse that borders on doggerel, partly because Shakespeare is satirizing a style that was popular in much medieval drama. He also may have been mocking the bombastic verse of his contemporaries.

2. *Rhymed couplets:* The four young lovers often speak in couplets because they are uttering sentiments and oaths expected of the Renaissance lover. Hermia's speech at 1.2.171–179 is an especially useful example. At times the playwright is parodying the overblown sentiments of the lovesick by underscoring the artificiality of their speech—and their emotions. After their awakening in Act 4, the lovers rarely speak in such mannered couplets.

3. *Prose:* As is typical of most of Shakespeare's plays, the common folk—those "rough, rude mechanicals"—employ the language of everyday speech in prose. Even here Shakespeare invests the talk, notably Bottom's speeches, with a richness that approaches poetry. The speech in which Bottom tries to articulate his feelings upon waking in Titania's bower in 4.1 sounds as poetic as anything uttered by the mellifluous Oberon. Elsewhere, some of the play's humor derives from the mechanicals' misuse of the language, as malapropisms, puns, and wordplay abound.

4. *Blank verse:* The courtiers and royalty among the fairies most often speak in blank verse (i.e., unrhymed verse in iambic pentameter), although their actions often undercut the dignity of their language.

On a stage that employed little scenery to create its effects, Shakespeare necessarily had to rely on costuming and the evocative power of words, particularly the language of poetry. Oberon's description of "the bank where the wild thyme grows" (2.1.249) is an often-cited example of the playwright's talent for creating ambience through words.

Music, song, and dance also permeate the play, which itself has inspired several operas and ballets. Felix Mendelssohn's popular incidental music, composed between 1826 and 1843, has accompanied many productions of the play (see below). The fairies sing Titania to sleep and dance a lovely roundel in Act 2, in contrast with the earthy stomping dance, or Bergomask, with which the working men conclude their play. *A Midsummer Night's Dream* concludes with yet another dance; Oberon and Titania sing together as they had done to signal their reconciliation in Act 4. Their songs are in marked contrast to their tempestuous meeting in Act 2 and underscore the play's theme of finding harmony out of discord.

Themes and Issues

Shakespeare's multiple plots create a prism through which an idea can be examined from different perspectives. Among *The Dream*'s primary themes are:

Lunatics, Lovers, and Poets

Although Shakespeare explores the nature of love in all of his romantic comedies, in *The Dream* he seems especially interested in the irrational behaviors that often accompany love. There are frequent references to the moon throughout the text—three times in the first ten lines alone. The Latin word for moon (*luna*) provides a term applied to irrational people: *lunatic*, i.e., one who is *moonstruck*. Lunatics, as well as lovers and poets, according to Duke Theseus (see 5.1.2–22), see things existing only in their fantastic imaginations. In *The Dream*, moonstruck courtiers, commoners, and fairies experience the hilarious and horrifying consequences of their sexual desires during the long night in Athens Wood. Ironically, they are ultimately redeemed by Diana, goddess of the hunt and of virgins, who is personified by the moon. By the end of Act 4, false love, lust, and indulgence—satirized by the misplaced drops from Oberon's magic flower—give way to honest and unselfish love. Moonlight itself gives way to a universal symbol of hope, the dawn, the beacon of the champion of reason, Apollo. Thus passion and rationality temper one another to create the whole person—or fairy king and queen.

Imagination and Mind Games

As in so many of his plays, Shakespeare is also concerned with discovering the difference between what "seems" and what "is." In Act 1 Theseus and Hippolyta prepare for marriage, normally a celebratory event; in reality Hippolyta is a prisoner of war who sees in Hermia another young woman dominated by male laws and egos. Acts 2 and 3 mock the notion of love at first sight—which can be as false as it is fleeting—through the running joke about the misplaced love drops that cause both Lysander and Demetrius to dote on Helena. Despite their supernatural status, Oberon and Titania—who ought to epitomize love at its most refined—often behave more irresponsibly (and comically) than the earthly lovers. Despite their comic ineptitude, the mechanicals portray the truest love—that between Pyramus and Thisbe, who are not self-serving—in the artificial world of the theater. This "mirthful tragedy," ill-suited for a wedding, reminds us that even the most unselfish love is subject to discord and to the fatal misunderstandings that bring about the tragedy in *Romeo and Juliet*.

A play—whether by the world's best known dramatist or by Peter Quince, who scripts *Pyramis and Thisbe* for the mechanicals—is the product of the human imagination, and *The Dream* is nothing if not a celebration of the imagination. A dream takes us into the innermost recesses of the mind to create "the forms of things unknown" (5.1.15); accordingly, it need not be bound by an absolute logic, for a dream weaves its disparate elements together to create its own logic. So is it with *A Midsummer Night's Dream*: into a single cohesive tale Shakespeare weaves three distinct worlds peopled by diverse characters drawn from "antique fables." He illustrates, often hilariously, that reason can be overwhelmed by unbridled passion and ego-driven delusions. Shakespeare stretches his imagination—and ours—in this tale of "musical confusion" (4.1.109). Just as Bottom realizes that the ballad he plans to write (4.1.213) cannot hope to capture all the ineffable mystery of that which "the eye hath not heard, the ear of man hath not seen," so, too, does the playwright use his theater to make concrete the most abstract of human creations—a dream.

Staging Challenges

Like his last plays—collectively known as the Romances—*The Dream* is filled with fantasy. It presents exceptional challenges to those who perform the play. And to those who read it. Among them:

The Fairies

What do fairies look like? Are they gossamer-winged little creatures, such as those depicted in Victorian storybooks? Are they hobbit-like gnomes out of Tolkien's *The Lord of the Rings*? Wee folk from Celtic lore? Our culture has many received impressions of fairies, none absolute, all possible for a production of *A Midsummer Night's Dream*. We do possess a drawing of Puck from the frontispiece of a 1639 edition of a play called "Robin Goodfellow, His Mad Pranks and Merry Jests" that offers one early–seventeenth-century view of that "merry wanderer of the night." He appears half-man, half-goat, a satyr and keeper of the Greek god Dionysus, whose spring rites, Aristotle wrote, provided the birth of Western drama in the sixth century B.C.E. Fittingly for Shakespeare's play, Dionysus and his satyrs embodied the creative and irrational drives in humans; they were associated with lust and carnal desires (often displaying a naked phallus). Robin Goodfellow is also surrounded by icons of necromancy (the circle, the dark bird, the black-clad figures), which align him with the darker forces that underpin the comedy. Robin, like Shakespeare's Puck, carries a broom "to sweep the dust behind the door" (5.1.385). Yet Puck represents only one faction within the fairy kingdom. Titania's keepers—Mustardseed, Peaseblossom, *et al.*—are more benign. In contrast to Puck's darker incantations and mischief-making, they sing a beautiful lullaby and dance a graceful roundel.

The Settings

The play begins amid the splendor of Theseus's court before moving quickly to a more primal setting in Athens's Wood. In Act 5 we return to the court, where the inhabitants have been changed by their night in the forest. The appearance of the court itself in the theater often reflects that change. Although on Shakespeare's stage the words and situations themselves were sufficient to convey shifts in locale and demeanor, modern audiences, conditioned by such visual media as film and television, generally expect some sort of optical effect. The court in Act 1 is not necessarily a happy place, and lighting designers can use their imaginations to effect the transformation from the court of Act 1 to that of Act 5. How literal ought the forest to look? If Shakespeare asks us to use our imaginations, should the scenery do that work for us? If the setting is too graphic, Shakespeare's text is rendered superfluous. Worse yet, an audience is more inclined to watch than listen, especially in early scenes filled with exposition about characters and plot.

Bottom's Transformation

When Bottom enters wearing an ass's head (3.1.97), the custom for centuries has been to use a full donkey's head mask to mark the transformation, and the device is unquestionably funny. Of late, however, directors and actors (who feel they communicate with their facial expressions as much as words) have tended to favor partial masks or mere suggestions of one, such as a pair of ears. In his celebrated (and controversial) staging of the play in 1970 (see below), Peter Brook simply used the time-honored "clown nose" to transform Bottom into an ass. The pros and cons of such solutions are described in the "Frame-by-Frame" analysis below (pp. 166–168).

The Play-Within-the-Play

The performance of "The most lamentable comedy and cruel death of Pyramus and Thisbe" is among the most famous finales in Shakespeare. Certainly it is crowd-pleasing and rarely fails to delight, even in the hands of amateur actors—which is precisely the point. The working men of Athens are amateurs, unschooled in the ways of the theater (as their often-hilarious discussions of how best to stage the play suggest). Today the play is frequently performed by trained actors who enjoy a rich history of stage and film productions of the play to inspire them. As a consequence, the play-within-the-play can too quickly become a catalog of actors' tricks calculated to induce laughter, rather than, as Shakespeare must have intended, a too-honest performance by actors whose bumbling performance happens to be funny. Lysander's observation that "it is not enough to speak, but to speak true" (5.1.120–121) may well apply to over-calculating actors who layer on already amusing situation with excessive business. Conversely, recent productions of *The Dream* have an almost obsessive aversion to playing the play-within-the-play too comically, thereby blunting the joy of the play's finale.

A Midsummer Night's Dream

[*Dramatis Personae*

THESEUS, *Duke of Athens*

HIPPOLYTA, *Queen of the Amazons, betrothed to Theseus*
PHILOSTRATE, *Master of the Revels*
EGEUS, *father of Hermia*

HERMIA, *daughter of Egeus, in love with Lysander*
LYSANDER, *in love with Hermia*
DEMETRIUS, *in love with Hermia and favored by Egeus*
HELENA, *in love with Demetrius*

OBERON, *King of the Fairies*
TITANIA, *Queen of the Fairies*
PUCK, *or* ROBIN GOODFELLOW

PEASEBLOSSOM,
COBWEB,
MOTE,   } *fairies attending Titania*
MUSTARDSEED,
Other FAIRIES *attending*

PETER QUINCE, *a carpenter,*   }   PROLOGUE
NICK BOTTOM, *a weaver,*   PYRAMUS
FRANCIS FLUTE, *a bellows*
    mender,   *repre-*   THISBE
TOM SNOUT, *a tinker,*   *senting*   WALL
SNUG, *a joiner,*   LION
ROBIN STARVELING, *a tailor,* }   MOONSHINE

Lords and Attendants on Theseus and Hippolyta

SCENE: *Athens, and a wood near it*]

[1.1]

*Enter Theseus, Hippolyta, [and Philostrate,]
with others.*

THESEUS
Now, fair Hippolyta, our nuptial hour
Draws on apace. Four happy days bring in
Another moon; but, oh, methinks, how slow
This old moon wanes! She lingers my desires,   4
Like to a stepdame or a dowager   5
Long withering out a young man's revenue.   6

HIPPOLYTA
Four days will quickly steep themselves in night; 7
Four nights will quickly dream away the time;
And then the moon, like to a silver bow
New bent in heaven, shall behold the night
Of our solemnities.

THESEUS   Go, Philostrate,   11
Stir up the Athenian youth to merriments.
Awake the pert and nimble spirit of mirth.
Turn melancholy forth to funerals;
The pale companion is not for our pomp.   15
                        [*Exit Philostrate.*]
Hippolyta, I wooed thee with my sword   16
And won thy love doing thee injuries;
But I will wed thee in another key,
With pomp, with triumph, and with reveling.   19

*Enter Egeus and his daughter Hermia, and
Lysander, and Demetrius.*

EGEUS
Happy be Theseus, our renownèd duke!

THESEUS
Thanks, good Egeus. What's the news with thee?

EGEUS
Full of vexation come I, with complaint
Against my child, my daughter Hermia.—
Stand forth, Demetrius.—My noble lord,
This man hath my consent to marry her.—
Stand forth, Lysander.—And, my gracious Duke,
This man hath bewitched the bosom of my child.—
Thou, thou Lysander, thou hast given her rhymes
And interchanged love tokens with my child.
Thou hast by moonlight at her window sung
With feigning voice verses of feigning love,   31
And stol'n the impression of her fantasy   32
With bracelets of thy hair, rings, gauds, conceits, 33

Knacks, trifles, nosegays, sweetmeats—messengers 34
Of strong prevailment in unhardened youth.   35
With cunning hast thou filched my daughter's heart,
Turned her obedience, which is due to me,
To stubborn harshness. And, my gracious Duke,
Be it so she will not here before Your Grace   39
Consent to marry with Demetrius,
I beg the ancient privilege of Athens:
As she is mine, I may dispose of her,
Which shall be either to this gentleman
Or to her death, according to our law
Immediately provided in that case.   45

THESEUS
What say you, Hermia? Be advised, fair maid.
To you your father should be as a god—
One that composed your beauties, yea, and one
To whom you are but as a form in wax
By him imprinted, and within his power
To leave the figure or disfigure it.   51
Demetrius is a worthy gentleman.

HERMIA
So is Lysander.

THESEUS   In himself he is;
But in this kind, wanting your father's voice,   54
The other must be held the worthier.

HERMIA
I would my father looked but with my eyes.

THESEUS
Rather your eyes must with his judgment look.

HERMIA
I do entreat Your Grace to pardon me.
I know not by what power I am made bold,
Nor how it may concern my modesty
In such a presence here to plead my thoughts;
But I beseech Your Grace that I may know
The worst that may befall me in this case
If I refuse to wed Demetrius.

THESEUS
Either to die the death or to abjure   65
Forever the society of men.
Therefore, fair Hermia, question your desires,
Know of your youth, examine well your blood,   68
Whether, if you yield not to your father's choice,
You can endure the livery of a nun,   70
For aye to be in shady cloister mewed,   71
To live a barren sister all your life,
Chanting faint hymns to the cold fruitless moon.
Thrice blessèd they that master so their blood
To undergo such maiden pilgrimage;
But earthlier happy is the rose distilled   76
Than that which, withering on the virgin thorn,
Grows, lives, and dies in single blessedness.

1.1. Location: Athens. Theseus's court.
4 lingers frustrates   **5 stepdame** stepmother.   **a dowager** i.e., a
widow (whose right of inheritance from her dead husband is eating
into her son's estate)   **6 withering out** causing to dwindle
7 Four . . . night (The image is of the day sinking into the ocean as
night comes on.)   **11 solemnities** festive ceremonies of marriage.
15 companion fellow. (A pale complexion is linked to melancholy.)
pomp ceremonial magnificence.   **16 with my sword** i.e., in a military
engagement against the Amazons, when Hippolyta was taken captive   **19 triumph** public festivity   **31 feigning** (1) counterfeiting
(2) faining, desirous   **32 And . . . fantasy** and made her fall in love
with you (imprinting your image on her imagination) by stealthy and
dishonest means   **33 gauds, conceits** playthings, fanciful trifles

34 Knacks . . . sweetmeats knicknacks, trinkets, bouquets, candies
35 prevailment in influence on   **39 Be it so** if   **45 Immediately**
directly, with nothing intervening   **51 leave** i.e., leave unaltered
54 kind respect.   **wanting** lacking.   **voice** approval   **65 die the**
death be executed by legal process   **68 blood** passions   **70 livery**
habit, costume   **71 aye** ever.   **mewed** shut in. (Said of a hawk, poultry, etc.)   **76 earthlier happy** happier as respects this world.
distilled i.e., to make perfume

HERMIA
So will I grow, so live, so die, my lord,
Ere I will yield my virgin patent up   80
Unto His Lordship, whose unwishèd yoke
My soul consents not to give sovereignty.

THESEUS
Take time to pause, and by the next new moon—
The sealing day betwixt my love and me
For everlasting bond of fellowship—
Upon that day either prepare to die
For disobedience to your father's will,
Or else to wed Demetrius, as he would,
Or on Diana's altar to protest   89
For aye austerity and single life.

DEMETRIUS
Relent, sweet Hermia, and, Lysander, yield
Thy crazèd title to my certain right.   92

LYSANDER
You have her father's love, Demetrius;
Let me have Hermia's. Do you marry him.

EGEUS
Scornful Lysander! True, he hath my love,
And what is mine my love shall render him.
And she is mine, and all my right of her
I do estate unto Demetrius.   98

LYSANDER
I am, my lord, as well derived as he,   99
As well possessed; my love is more than his;   100
My fortunes every way as fairly ranked,   101
If not with vantage, as Demetrius';   102
And, which is more than all these boasts can be,
I am beloved of beauteous Hermia.
Why should not I then prosecute my right?
Demetrius, I'll avouch it to his head,   106
Made love to Nedar's daughter, Helena,
And won her soul; and she, sweet lady, dotes,
Devoutly dotes, dotes in idolatry
Upon this spotted and inconstant man.   110

THESEUS
I must confess that I have heard so much,
And with Demetrius thought to have spoke thereof;
But, being overfull of self-affairs,   113
My mind did lose it. But, Demetrius, come,
And come, Egeus, you shall go with me;
I have some private schooling for you both.   116
For you, fair Hermia, look you arm yourself   117
To fit your fancies to your father's will,   118
Or else the law of Athens yields you up—
Which by no means we may extenuate—   120
To death or to a vow of single life.
Come, my Hippolyta. What cheer, my love?
Demetrius and Egeus, go along.   123

I must employ you in some business
Against our nuptial, and confer with you   125
Of something nearly that concerns yourselves.   126

EGEUS
With duty and desire we follow you.
   Exeunt [all but Lysander and Hermia].

LYSANDER
How now, my love, why is your cheek so pale?
How chance the roses there do fade so fast?

HERMIA
Belike for want of rain, which I could well   130
Beteem them from the tempest of my eyes.   131

LYSANDER
Ay me! For aught that I could ever read,
Could ever hear by tale or history,
The course of true love never did run smooth;
But either it was different in blood—   135

HERMIA
Oh, cross! Too high to be enthralled to low.   136

LYSANDER
Or else misgrafted in respect of years—   137

HERMIA
Oh, spite! Too old to be engaged to young.

LYSANDER
Or else it stood upon the choice of friends—   139

HERMIA
Oh, hell, to choose love by another's eyes!

LYSANDER
Or if there were a sympathy in choice,   141
War, death, or sickness did lay siege to it,
Making it momentany as a sound,   143
Swift as a shadow, short as any dream,
Brief as the lightning in the collied night   145
That in a spleen unfolds both heaven and earth,   146
And ere a man hath power to say "Behold!"
The jaws of darkness do devour it up.
So quick bright things come to confusion.   149

HERMIA
If then true lovers have been ever crossed,   150
It stands as an edict in destiny.
Then let us teach our trial patience,   152
Because it is a customary cross,
As due to love as thoughts, and dreams, and sighs,
Wishes, and tears, poor fancy's followers.   155

LYSANDER
A good persuasion. Therefore, hear me, Hermia: 156
I have a widow aunt, a dowager
Of great revenue, and she hath no child.
From Athens is her house remote seven leagues;   159
And she respects me as her only son.   160

---

80 patent privilege **89 protest** vow **92 crazèd** cracked, unsound
98 estate unto settle or bestow upon **99 as well derived** as well born
and descended **100 possessed** endowed with wealth **101 fairly**
handsomely **102 vantage** superiority **106 head** i.e., face **110 spotted** i.e., morally stained **113 self-affairs** my own concerns
116 schooling admonition **117 look you arm** take care you prepare
118 fancies likings, thoughts of love **120 extenuate** mitigate, relax
123 go i.e., come

125 Against in preparation for **126 nearly that** that closely
130 Belike Very likely **131 Beteem** grant, afford **135 blood** hereditary rank **136 cross** vexation. **137 misgrafted** ill grafted, badly
matched **139 friends** relatives **141 sympathy** agreement
143 momentany lasting but a moment **145 collied** blackened (as
with coal dust), darkened **146 in a spleen** in a swift impulse, in a
violent flash. **unfolds** reveals **149 confusion** ruin. **150 ever
crossed** always thwarted **152 teach . . . patience** i.e., teach ourselves
patience in this trial **155 fancy's** amorous passion's **156 persuasion** doctrine. **159 seven leagues** about 21 miles **160 respects**
regards

There, gentle Hermia, may I marry thee,
And to that place the sharp Athenian law
Cannot pursue us. If thou lovest me, then,
Steal forth thy father's house tomorrow night;
And in the wood, a league without the town,   165
Where I did meet thee once with Helena
To do observance to a morn of May,   167
There will I stay for thee.

HERMIA   My good Lysander!
I swear to thee, by Cupid's strongest bow,
By his best arrow with the golden head,   170
By the simplicity of Venus' doves,   171
By that which knitteth souls and prospers loves,
And by that fire which burned the Carthage queen   173
When the false Trojan under sail was seen,   174
By all the vows that ever men have broke,
In number more than ever women spoke,
In that same place thou hast appointed me
Tomorrow truly will I meet with thee.

LYSANDER
Keep promise, love. Look, here comes Helena.

Enter Helena.

HERMIA
God speed, fair Helena! Whither away?   180

HELENA
Call you me fair? That "fair" again unsay.
Demetrius loves your fair. Oh, happy fair!   182
Your eyes are lodestars, and your tongue's sweet air 183
More tunable than lark to shepherd's ear   184
When wheat is green, when hawthorn buds appear.
Sickness is catching. Oh, were favor so,   186
Yours would I catch, fair Hermia, ere I go;
My ear should catch your voice, my eye your eye,
My tongue should catch your tongue's sweet melody.
Were the world mine, Demetrius being bated,   190
The rest I'd give to be to you translated.   191
Oh, teach me how you look and with what art
You sway the motion of Demetrius' heart.   193

HERMIA
I frown upon him, yet he loves me still.

HELENA
Oh, that your frowns would teach my smiles such
   skill!

HERMIA
I give him curses, yet he gives me love.

HELENA
Oh, that my prayers could such affection move!   197

HERMIA
The more I hate, the more he follows me.

HELENA
The more I love, the more he hateth me.

HERMIA
His folly, Helena, is no fault of mine.

HELENA
None, but your beauty. Would that fault were mine!

HERMIA
Take comfort. He no more shall see my face.
Lysander and myself will fly this place.
Before the time I did Lysander see   204
Seemed Athens as a paradise to me.   205
Oh, then, what graces in my love do dwell,
That he hath turned a heaven unto a hell?

LYSANDER
Helen, to you our minds we will unfold.
Tomorrow night, when Phoebe doth behold   209
Her silver visage in the watery glass,   210
Decking with liquid pearl the bladed grass,   211
A time that lovers' flights doth still conceal,   212
Through Athens' gates have we devised to steal.

HERMIA
And in the wood, where often you and I
Upon faint primrose beds were wont to lie,   215
Emptying our bosoms of their counsel sweet,   216
There my Lysander and myself shall meet,
And thence from Athens turn away our eyes
To seek new friends and stranger companies.   219
Farewell, sweet playfellow. Pray thou for us,
And good luck grant thee thy Demetrius!
Keep word, Lysander. We must starve our sight
From lovers' food till morrow deep midnight.

LYSANDER
I will, my Hermia.   *Exit Hermia.*
                 Helena, adieu!
As you on him, Demetrius dote on you!
                                   Exit Lysander.

HELENA
How happy some o'er other some can be!   226
Through Athens I am thought as fair as she.
But what of that? Demetrius thinks not so;
He will not know what all but he do know.
And as he errs, doting on Hermia's eyes,
So I, admiring of his qualities.
Things base and vile, holding no quantity,   232
Love can transpose to form and dignity.
Love looks not with the eyes, but with the mind,
And therefore is winged Cupid painted blind.

---

165 **without** outside   167 **To do . . . May** to perform the ceremonies
of May Day   170 **best arrow** (Cupid's best gold-pointed arrows were
supposed to induce love; his blunt leaden arrows, aversion.)
171 **simplicity** innocence.   **doves** i.e., those that drew Venus's chariot
173, 174 **Carthage queen, false Trojan** (Dido, Queen of Carthage,
immolated herself on a funeral pyre after having been deserted by
the Trojan hero Aeneas.)   180 **fair** fair-complexioned. (Generally
regarded by the Elizabethans as more beautiful than a dark complexion.)   182 **your fair** your beauty (even though Hermia is dark com-
plexioned).   **happy fair** lucky fair one.   183 **lodestars** guiding stars.
air music   184 **tunable** tuneful, melodious   186 **favor** appearance,
looks   190 **bated** excepted   191 **translated** transformed.   193 **sway
the motion** control the impulses

197 **Oh, that . . . move!** Would that my prayers could arouse such
desire!   204–5 **Before . . . to me** (Love has led to complications and
jealousies, making Athens hell for Hermia.)   209 **Phoebe** Diana, the
moon   210 **glass** reflecting surface (of a lake, etc.)   211 **liquid pearl**
i.e., dew   212 **still** always   215 **faint** pale   216 **counsel** secret
thought   219 **stranger companies** the company of strangers.
226 **o'er . . . can be** can be in comparison to some others.   232 **holding no quantity** i.e., unsubstantial, unshapely

Nor hath Love's mind of any judgment taste;   236
Wings and no eyes figure unheedy haste.   237
And therefore is Love said to be a child,
Because in choice he is so oft beguiled.   239
As waggish boys in game themselves forswear,   240
So the boy Love is perjured everywhere.
For ere Demetrius looked on Hermia's eyne,   242
He hailed down oaths that he was only mine;
And when this hail some heat from Hermia felt,
So he dissolved, and showers of oaths did melt.
I will go tell him of fair Hermia's flight.
Then to the wood will he tomorrow night
Pursue her; and for this intelligence   248
If I have thanks, it is a dear expense.   249
But herein mean I to enrich my pain,
To have his sight thither and back again.   *Exit.*

❧

[1.2]

Enter Quince the carpenter, and Snug the join-
er, and Bottom the weaver, and Flute the bel-
lows mender, and Snout the tinker, and
Starveling the tailor.

QUINCE   Is all our company here?

BOTTOM   You were best to call them generally, man by   2
man, according to the scrip.   3

QUINCE   Here is the scroll of every man's name which
is thought fit, through all Athens, to play in our inter-   5
lude before the Duke and the Duchess on his wedding   6
day at night.

BOTTOM   First, good Peter Quince, say what the play
treats on, then read the names of the actors, and so
grow to a point.   10

QUINCE   Marry, our play is "The most lamentable com-   11
edy and most cruel death of Pyramus and Thisbe."

BOTTOM   A very good piece of work, I assure you, and
a merry. Now, good Peter Quince, call forth your
actors by the scroll. Masters, spread yourselves.

QUINCE   Answer as I call you. Nick Bottom, the weaver.   16

BOTTOM   Ready. Name what part I am for, and proceed.

QUINCE   You, Nick Bottom, are set down for Pyramus.

BOTTOM   What is Pyramus? A lover or a tyrant?

QUINCE   A lover, that kills himself most gallant for love.

BOTTOM   That will ask some tears in the true performing
of it. If I do it, let the audience look to their eyes. I will
move storms; I will condole in some measure. To the   23
rest—yet my chief humor is for a tyrant. I could play   24

Ercles rarely, or a part to tear a cat in, to make all split.   25
    "The raging rocks
    And shivering shocks
    Shall break the locks
        Of prison gates;
    And Phibbus' car   30
    Shall shine from far
    And make and mar
        The foolish Fates."
This was lofty! Now name the rest of the players. This is
Ercles' vein, a tyrant's vein. A lover is more condoling.

QUINCE   Francis Flute, the bellows mender.

FLUTE   Here, Peter Quince.

QUINCE   Flute, you must take Thisbe on you.

FLUTE   What is Thisbe? A wandering knight?

QUINCE   It is the lady that Pyramus must love.

FLUTE   Nay, faith, let not me play a woman. I have a
beard coming.

QUINCE   That's all one. You shall play it in a mask, and   43
you may speak as small as you will.   44

BOTTOM   An I may hide my face, let me play Thisbe too.   45
I'll speak in a monstrous little voice: "Thisne, Thisne!"
"Ah, Pyramus, my lover dear! Thy Thisbe dear, and
lady dear!"

QUINCE   No, no, you must play Pyramus, and Flute, you
Thisbe.

BOTTOM   Well, proceed.

QUINCE   Robin Starveling, the tailor.

STARVELING   Here, Peter Quince.

QUINCE   Robin Starveling, you must play Thisbe's
mother. Tom Snout, the tinker.

SNOUT   Here, Peter Quince.

QUINCE   You, Pyramus' father; myself, Thisbe's father;
Snug, the joiner, you, the lion's part; and I hope here is
a play fitted.

SNUG   Have you the lion's part written? Pray you, if it
be, give it me, for I am slow of study.

QUINCE   You may do it extempore, for it is nothing but
roaring.

BOTTOM   Let me play the lion too. I will roar that I will
do any man's heart good to hear me. I will roar that I
will make the Duke say, "Let him roar again, let him
roar again."

QUINCE   An you should do it too terribly, you would
fright the Duchess and the ladies, that they would
shriek; and that were enough to hang us all.

ALL   That would hang us, every mother's son.

BOTTOM   I grant you, friends, if you should fright the
ladies out of their wits, they would have no more discretion but to hang us; but I will aggravate my voice   74
so that I will roar you as gently as any sucking dove; I   75
will roar you an 'twere any nightingale.   76

---

236 Nor . . . taste i.e., Nor has Love, which dwells in the fancy or imagination, any least bit of judgment or reason   **237 figure** signify   **239 in choice** in choosing.   **beguiled** self-deluded, making unaccountable choices.   **240 waggish** playful, mischievous.   **game** sport, jest   **242 eyne** eyes. (Old form of plural.)   **248 intelligence** information   **249 a dear expense** i.e., a trouble worth taking on my part.   **1.2. Location: Athens.**
2 generally (Bottom's blunder for "individually.")   **3 scrip** script.   **5–6 interlude** play   **10 grow to** come to   **11 Marry** (A mild oath; originally the name of the Virgin Mary.)   **16 Bottom** (As a weaver's term, a *bottom* was an object around which thread was wound.)   **23 condole** lament, arouse pity   **24 humor** inclination

25 Ercles Hercules. (The tradition of ranting came from Seneca's *Hercules Furens.*)   **tear a cat** i.e., rant.   **make all split** i.e., cause a stir, bring the house down.   **30 Phibbus' car** Phoebus's, the sun god's, chariot   **43 That's all one** It makes no difference.   **44 small** high-pitched   **45 An** If. (Also at line 68.)   **74 aggravate** (Bottom's blunder for "moderate.")   **75 roar you** i.e., roar for you. **sucking dove** (Bottom conflates *sitting dove* and *sucking lamb*, two proverbial images of innocence.)   **76 an 'twere** as if it were

QUINCE   You can play no part but Pyramus; for Pyramus is a sweet-faced man, a proper man as one shall   78
see in a summer's day, a most lovely gentlemanlike
man. Therefore you must needs play Pyramus.

BOTTOM   Well, I will undertake it. What beard were I
best to play it in?

QUINCE   Why, what you will.

BOTTOM   I will discharge it in either your straw-color   84
beard, your orange-tawny beard, your purple-in-grain   85
beard, or your French-crown-color beard, your perfect   86
yellow.

QUINCE   Some of your French crowns have no hair at all,   88
and then you will play barefaced. But, masters, here
are your parts. [*He distributes parts.*] And I am to
entreat you, request you, and desire you to con them   91
by tomorrow night, and meet me in the palace wood,
a mile without the town, by moonlight. There will we
rehearse; for if we meet in the city, we shall be dogged
with company, and our devices known. In the mean-   95
time I will draw a bill of properties, such as our play   96
wants. I pray you, fail me not.

BOTTOM   We will meet, and there we may rehearse most
obscenely and courageously. Take pains, be perfect.   99
Adieu.

QUINCE   At the Duke's oak we meet.

BOTTOM   Enough. Hold, or cut bowstrings.   *Exeunt.*   102

❖

[2.1]

Enter a Fairy at one door, and Robin Goodfellow
[*Puck*] *at another.*

PUCK
How now, spirit, whither wander you?

FAIRY
Over hill, over dale,
    Thorough bush, thorough brier,   3
Over park, over pale,   4
    Thorough flood, thorough fire,
I do wander everywhere,
Swifter than the moon's sphere;   7
And I serve the Fairy Queen,
To dew her orbs upon the green.   9
The cowslips tall her pensioners be.   10
In their gold coats spots you see;

Those be rubies, fairy favors;   12
    In those freckles live their savors.   13
I must go seek some dewdrops here
And hang a pearl in every cowslip's ear.
Farewell, thou lob of spirits; I'll be gone.   16
Our Queen and all her elves come here anon.   17

PUCK
The King doth keep his revels here tonight.
Take heed the Queen come not within his sight.
For Oberon is passing fell and wrath,   20
Because that she as her attendant hath
A lovely boy, stolen from an Indian king;
She never had so sweet a changeling.   23
And jealous Oberon would have the child
Knight of his train, to trace the forests wild.   25
But she perforce withholds the lovèd boy,   26
Crowns him with flowers, and makes him all her joy.
And now they never meet in grove or green,
By fountain clear, or spangled starlight sheen,   29
But they do square, that all their elves for fear   30
Creep into acorn cups and hide them there.

FAIRY
Either I mistake your shape and making quite,
Or else you are that shrewd and knavish sprite   33
Called Robin Goodfellow. Are not you he
That frights the maidens of the villagery,   35
Skim milk, and sometimes labor in the quern,   36
And bootless make the breathless huswife churn,   37
And sometimes make the drink to bear no barm,   38
Mislead night wanderers, laughing at their harm?   39
Those that "Hobgoblin" call you, and "Sweet Puck,"   40
You do their work, and they shall have good luck.
Are you not he?

PUCK   Thou speakest aright;
I am that merry wanderer of the night.
I jest to Oberon and make him smile
When I a fat and bean-fed horse beguile,   45
Neighing in likeness of a filly foal;   46
And sometimes lurk I in a gossip's bowl   47
In very likeness of a roasted crab,   48
And when she drinks, against her lips I bob
And on her withered dewlap pour the ale.   50
The wisest aunt, telling the saddest tale,   51

Sometime for three-foot stool mistaketh me;
Then slip I from her bum, down topples she,
And "Tailor" cries, and falls into a cough;   54
And then the whole choir hold their hips and laugh,   55
And waxen in their mirth, and neeze, and swear   56
A merrier hour was never wasted there.   57
But, room, fairy! Here comes Oberon.   58

FAIRY
And here my mistress. Would that he were gone!

Enter [Oberon] the King of Fairies at one door,
with his train, and [Titania] the Queen at
another, with hers.

OBERON
Ill met by moonlight, proud Titania.

TITANIA
What, jealous Oberon? Fairies, skip hence.
I have forsworn his bed and company.

OBERON
Tarry, rash wanton. Am not I thy lord?   63

TITANIA
Then I must be thy lady; but I know
When thou hast stolen away from Fairyland
And in the shape of Corin sat all day,   66
Playing on pipes of corn and versing love   67
To amorous Phillida. Why art thou here   68
Come from the farthest step of India,   69
But that, forsooth, the bouncing Amazon,
Your buskined mistress and your warrior love,   71
To Theseus must be wedded, and you come
To give their bed joy and prosperity.

OBERON
How canst thou thus for shame, Titania,
Glance at my credit with Hippolyta,   75
Knowing I know thy love to Theseus?
Didst not thou lead him through the glimmering night
From Perigenia, whom he ravishèd?   78
And make him with fair Aegles break his faith,   79
With Ariadne and Antiopa?   80

TITANIA
These are the forgeries of jealousy;
And never, since the middle summer's spring,   82
Met we on hill, in dale, forest, or mead,   83

By pavèd fountain or by rushy brook,   84
Or in the beachèd margent of the sea,   85
To dance our ringlets to the whistling wind,   86
But with thy brawls thou hast disturbed our sport.
Therefore the winds, piping to us in vain,
As in revenge, have sucked up from the sea
Contagious fogs which, falling in the land,   90
Hath every pelting river made so proud   91
That they have overborne their continents.   92
The ox hath therefore stretched his yoke in vain,   93
The plowman lost his sweat, and the green corn   94
Hath rotted ere his youth attained a beard;
The fold stands empty in the drownèd field,   96
And crows are fatted with the murrain flock;   97
The nine-men's morris is filled up with mud,   98
And the quaint mazes in the wanton green   99
For lack of tread are undistinguishable.
The human mortals want their winter here;   101
No night is now with hymn or carol blessed.
Therefore the moon, the governess of floods,   103
Pale in her anger, washes all the air,   104
That rheumatic diseases do abound.   105
And thorough this distemperature we see   106
The seasons alter: hoary-headed frosts
Fall in the fresh lap of the crimson rose,
And on old Hiems' thin and icy crown   109
An odorous chaplet of sweet summer buds
Is, as in mockery, set. The spring, the summer,
The childing autumn, angry winter, change   112
Their wonted liveries, and the mazèd world   113
By their increase now knows not which is which.   114
And this same progeny of evils comes
From our debate, from our dissension.   116
We are their parents and original.   117

OBERON
Do you amend it, then. It lies in you.
Why should Titania cross her Oberon?
I do but beg a little changeling boy
To be my henchman.

TITANIA   Set your heart at rest.   121
The fairy land buys not the child of me.
His mother was a vot'ress of my order,   123

---

54 **"Tailor"** (Seemingly a cry of distress or embarrassment.) 55 **choir** company 56 **waxen** increase. **neeze** sneeze 57 **wasted** spent 58 **room** stand aside, make room 63 **wanton** headstrong creature. 66, 68 **Corin, Phillida** (Conventional names of pastoral lovers.) 67 **corn** (Here, oat stalks.) **versing love** writing love verses 69 **step** farthest limit of travel, or, perhaps, *steep,* "mountain range" 71 **buskined** wearing half-boots called buskins 75 **Glance . . . Hippolyta** make insinuations about my favored relationship with Hippolyta 78 **Perigenia** i.e., Perigouna, one of Theseus's conquests. (This and the following women are named in Thomas North's translation of Plutarch's "Life of Theseus.") 79 **Aegles** i.e., Aegle, for whom Theseus deserted Ariadne according to some accounts 80 **Ariadne** the daughter of Minos, King of Crete, who helped Theseus to escape the labyrinth after killing the Minotaur; later she was abandoned by Theseus. **Antiopa** Queen of the Amazons and wife of Theseus; elsewhere identified with Hippolyta, but here thought of as a separate woman. 82 **middle summer's spring** beginning of midsummer 83 **mead** meadow

84 **pavèd** with pebbled bottom. **rushy** bordered with rushes 85 **in** on. **margent** edge, border 86 **ringlets** dances in a ring. (See *orbs* in line 9.) **to** to the sound of 90 **Contagious** noxious 91 **pelting** paltry 92 **continents** banks that contain them. 93 **stretched his yoke** i.e., pulled at his yoke in plowing 94 **corn** grain of any kind 96 **fold** pen for sheep or cattle 97 **murrain** having died of the plague 98 **nine-men's morris** i.e., portion of the village green marked out in a square for a game played with nine pebbles or pegs 99 **quaint mazes** i.e., intricate paths marked out on the village green to be followed rapidly on foot as a kind of contest. **wanton** luxuriant 101 **want** lack. **winter** i.e., regular winter season; or, proper observances of winter, such as the *hymn* or *carol* in the next line (?) 103 **Therefore** i.e., As a result of our quarrel 104 **washes** saturates with moisture 105 **rheumatic diseases** colds, flu, and other respiratory infections 106 **distemperature** disturbance in nature 109 **Hiems'** the winter god's 112 **childing** fruitful, pregnant 113 **wonted liveries** usual apparel. **mazèd** bewildered 114 **their increase** the increasing pace of change; or, their produce 116 **debate** quarrel 117 **original** origin. 121 **henchman** attendant, page. 123 **was . . . order** had taken a vow to serve me

And in the spicèd Indian air by night
Full often hath she gossiped by my side
And sat with me on Neptune's yellow sands,
Marking th'embarkèd traders on the flood,   127
When we have laughed to see the sails conceive
And grow big-bellied with the wanton wind;   129
Which she, with pretty and with swimming gait,   130
Following—her womb then rich with my young
      squire—
Would imitate, and sail upon the land
To fetch me trifles, and return again
As from a voyage, rich with merchandise.
But she, being mortal, of that boy did die;
And for her sake do I rear up her boy,
And for her sake I will not part with him.

OBERON
Give me that boy, and I will go with thee.

OBERON
How long within this wood intend you stay?

TITANIA
Perchance till after Theseus' wedding day.
If you will patiently dance in our round   140
And see our moonlight revels, go with us;
If not, shun me, and I will spare your haunts.   142

OBERON
Give me that boy, and I will go with thee.

TITANIA
Not for thy fairy kingdom. Fairies, away!
We shall chide downright, if I longer stay.
                    Exeunt [Titania with her train].

OBERON
Well, go thy way. Thou shalt not from this grove   146
Till I torment thee for this injury.
My gentle Puck, come hither. Thou rememb'rest
Since once I sat upon a promontory,   149
And heard a mermaid on a dolphin's back
Uttering such dulcet and harmonious breath   151
That the rude sea grew civil at her song,   152
And certain stars shot madly from their spheres
To hear the sea-maid's music?

PUCK   I remember.

OBERON
That very time I saw, but thou couldst not,
Flying between the cold moon and the earth
Cupid, all armed. A certain aim he took   157
At a fair vestal thronèd by the west,   158
And loosed his love shaft smartly from his bow   159
As it should pierce a hundred thousand hearts;   160
But I might see young Cupid's fiery shaft   161
Quenched in the chaste beams of the wat'ry moon,
And the imperial vot'ress passèd on,
In maiden meditation, fancy-free.   164
Yet marked I where the bolt of Cupid fell: 165

It fell upon a little western flower,
Before milk-white, now purple with love's wound,
And maidens call it love-in-idleness.   168
Fetch me that flower; the herb I showed thee once.
The juice of it on sleeping eyelids laid
Will make or man or woman madly dote   171
Upon the next live creature that it sees.
Fetch me this herb, and be thou here again
Ere the leviathan can swim a league.   174

PUCK
I'll put a girdle round about the earth
In forty minutes.   [Exit.]

OBERON   Having once this juice,
I'll watch Titania when she is asleep
And drop the liquor of it in her eyes.
The next thing then she waking looks upon,
Be it on lion, bear, or wolf, or bull,
On meddling monkey, or on busy ape,
She shall pursue it with the soul of love.
And ere I take this charm from off her sight,
As I can take it with another herb,
I'll make her render up her page to me.
But who comes here? I am invisible,
And I will overhear their conference.

                    [He stands aside.]

      Enter Demetrius, Helena following him.

DEMETRIUS
I love thee not; therefore pursue me not.
Where is Lysander and fair Hermia?
The one I'll slay; the other slayeth me.
Thou told'st me they were stol'n unto this wood;
And here am I, and wood within this wood   192
Because I cannot meet my Hermia.
Hence, get thee gone, and follow me no more.

HELENA
You draw me, you hardhearted adamant!   195
But yet you draw not iron, for my heart
Is true as steel. Leave you your power to draw,   197
And I shall have no power to follow you.

DEMETRIUS
Do I entice you? Do I speak you fair?   199
Or rather do I not in plainest truth
Tell you I do not nor I cannot love you?

HELENA
And even for that do I love you the more.
I am your spaniel; and, Demetrius,
The more you beat me I will fawn on you.
Use me but as your spaniel, spurn me, strike me,
Neglect me, lose me; only give me leave,
Unworthy as I am, to follow you.
What worser place can I beg in your love—
And yet a place of high respect with me—
Than to be usèd as you use your dog?

---

127 **traders** trading vessels.   **129 wanton** (1) playful (2) amorous   **130 swimming** smooth, gliding   **140 round** circular
dance   **142 spare** shun   **146 from** go from   **149 Since** when
151 dulcet sweet.   **breath** voice, song   **152 rude** rough   **157 all**
fully.   **certain** sure   **158 vestal** vestal virgin. (Contains a complimentary allusion to Queen Elizabeth as a votaress of Diana and probably
refers to an actual entertainment in her honor at Elvetham in 1591.)
by in the region of   **159 loosed** released   **160 As** as if   **161 might**
could   **164 fancy-free** free of love's spell.   **165 bolt** arrow

168 **love-in-idleness** pansy, heartsease.   **171 or man** either man
174 **leviathan** sea monster, whale   **192 wood** mad, frantic. (With an
obvious wordplay on *wood*, meaning "woods.")   **195 adamant** lode-
stone, magnet. (With pun on *hardhearted*, since adamant was also
thought to be the hardest of all stones and was confused with the diamond.)   **197 Leave you** Give up   **199 speak you fair** speak courteously to you.

DEMETRIUS
Tempt not too much the hatred of my spirit,
For I am sick when I do look on thee.
HELENA
And I am sick when I look not on you.
DEMETRIUS
You do impeach your modesty too much   214
To leave the city and commit yourself   215
Into the hands of one that loves you not,
To trust the opportunity of night
And the ill counsel of a desert place   218
With the rich worth of your virginity.
HELENA
Your virtue is my privilege. For that   220
It is not night when I do see your face,
Therefore I think I am not in the night;
Nor doth this wood lack worlds of company,
For you, in my respect, are all the world.   224
Then how can it be said I am alone
When all the world is here to look on me?
DEMETRIUS
I'll run from thee and hide me in the brakes,   227
And leave thee to the mercy of wild beasts.
HELENA
The wildest hath not such a heart as you.
Run when you will. The story shall be changed:
Apollo flies and Daphne holds the chase,   231
The dove pursues the griffin, the mild hind   232
Makes speed to catch the tiger—bootless speed,   233
When cowardice pursues and valor flies!
DEMETRIUS
I will not stay thy questions. Let me go!   235
Or if thou follow me, do not believe
But I shall do thee mischief in the wood.
HELENA
Ay, in the temple, in the town, the field,
You do me mischief. Fie, Demetrius!
Your wrongs do set a scandal on my sex.   240
We cannot fight for love, as men may do;
We should be wooed and were not made to woo.
                              [Exit Demetrius.]
I'll follow thee and make a heaven of hell,
To die upon the hand I love so well.   [Exit.] 244
OBERON
Fare thee well, nymph. Ere he do leave this grove
Thou shalt fly him, and he shall seek thy love.

        Enter Puck.

Hast thou the flower there? Welcome, wanderer.

PUCK
Ay, there it is.   [He offers the flower.]
OBERON   I pray thee, give it me.
I know a bank where the wild thyme blows,   249
Where oxlips and the nodding violet grows,   250
Quite overcanopied with luscious woodbine,   251
With sweet muskroses and with eglantine.   252
There sleeps Titania sometime of the night,   253
Lulled in these flowers with dances and delight;
And there the snake throws her enameled skin,   255
Weed wide enough to wrap a fairy in.   256
And with the juice of this I'll streak her eyes   257
And make her full of hateful fantasies.
Take thou some of it, and seek through this grove.
                          [He gives some love juice.]
A sweet Athenian lady is in love
With a disdainful youth. Anoint his eyes,
But do it when the next thing he espies
May be the lady. Thou shalt know the man
By the Athenian garments he hath on.
Effect it with some care, that he may prove
More fond on her than she upon her love;   266
And look thou meet me ere the first cock crow.
PUCK
Fear not, my lord, your servant shall do so.
                          Exeunt [separately].

                              ❖

[2.2]

        Enter Titania, Queen of Fairies, with her train.

TITANIA
Come, now a roundel and a fairy song;   1
Then, for the third part of a minute, hence—
Some to kill cankers in the muskrose buds,   3
Some war with reremice for their leathern wings   4
To make my small elves coats, and some keep back
The clamorous owl, that nightly hoots and wonders
At our quaint spirits. Sing me now asleep.   7
Then to your offices, and let me rest.

        Fairies sing.

FIRST FAIRY
        You spotted snakes with double tongue,   9
            Thorny hedgehogs, be not seen;
        Newts and blindworms, do no wrong;   11
            Come not near our Fairy Queen.

---

214 **impeach** call into question   215 **To leave** by leaving   218 **desert** deserted   220 **privilege** safeguard, warrant.   **For that** Because 224 **in my respect** as far as I am concerned, in my esteem 227 **brakes** thickets   231 **Apollo . . . chase** (In the ancient myth, Daphne fled from Apollo and was saved from rape by being transformed into a laurel tree; here it is the female who *holds the chase,* or pursues, instead of the male.)   232 **griffin** a fabulous monster with the head and wings of an eagle and the body of a lion.   **hind** female deer   233 **bootless** fruitless   235 **stay** wait for, put up with. **questions** talk or argument.   240 **Your . . . sex** i.e., The wrongs that you do me cause me to act in a manner that disgraces my sex. 244 **upon** by

249 **blows** blooms   250 **oxlips** flowers resembling cowslip and primrose   251 **woodbine** honeysuckle   252 **muskroses** a kind of large, sweet-scented rose.   **eglantine** sweetbrier, another kind of rose. 253 **sometime of** for part of   255 **throws** sloughs off, sheds 256 **Weed** garment   257 **streak** anoint, touch gently   266 **fond on** doting on 2.2. **Location: The wood.** 1 **roundel** dance in a ring   3 **cankers** cankerworms (i.e., caterpillars or grubs)   4 **reremice** bats   7 **quaint** dainty   9 **double** forked 11 **Newts** water lizards. (Considered poisonous, as were *blindworms*— small snakes with tiny eyes—and spiders.)

CHORUS [*dancing*]
> Philomel, with melody   13
> Sing in our sweet lullaby;
> Lulla, lulla, lullaby, lulla, lulla, lullaby.
> Never harm
> Nor spell nor charm
> Come our lovely lady nigh.
> So good night, with lullaby.

FIRST FAIRY
> Weaving spiders, come not here;
> Hence, you long-legged spinners, hence!
> Beetles black, approach not near;
> Worm nor snail, do no offense.   23

CHORUS [*dancing*]
> Philomel, with melody
> Sing in our sweet lullaby;
> Lulla, lulla, lullaby, lulla, lulla, lullaby.
> Never harm
> Nor spell nor charm
> Come our lovely lady nigh.
> So good night, with lullaby.   [*Titania sleeps.*]

SECOND FAIRY
> Hence, away! Now all is well.
> One aloof stand sentinel.   32
>   [*Exeunt Fairies, leaving one sentinel.*]

*Enter Oberon [and squeezes the flower on
Titania's eyelids].*

OBERON
> What thou see'st when thou dost wake,
> Do it for thy true love take;
> Love and languish for his sake.
> Be it ounce, or cat, or bear,   36
> Pard, or boar with bristled hair,   37
> In thy eye that shall appear
> When thou wak'st, it is thy dear.
> Wake when some vile thing is near.   [*Exit.*]

Enter Lysander and Hermia.

LYSANDER
> Fair love, you faint with wand'ring in the wood;
> And to speak truth, I have forgot our way.
> We'll rest us, Hermia, if you think it good,
> And tarry for the comfort of the day.

HERMIA
> Be it so, Lysander. Find you out a bed,
> For I upon this bank will rest my head.

LYSANDER
> One turf shall serve as pillow for us both;
> One heart, one bed, two bosoms, and one troth.   48

HERMIA
> Nay, good Lysander, for my sake, my dear,
> Lie further off yet. Do not lie so near.

LYSANDER
> Oh, take the sense, sweet, of my innocence!   51
> Love takes the meaning in love's conference.   52
> I mean that my heart unto yours is knit,
> So that but one heart we can make of it;
> Two bosoms interchainèd with an oath—
> So then two bosoms and a single troth.
> Then by your side no bed-room me deny,
> For lying so, Hermia, I do not lie.   58

HERMIA
> Lysander riddles very prettily.
> Now much beshrew my manners and my pride   60
> If Hermia meant to say Lysander lied.
> But, gentle friend, for love and courtesy
> Lie further off, in human modesty.
> Such separation as may well be said
> Becomes a virtuous bachelor and a maid,
> So far be distant; and, good night, sweet friend.
> Thy love ne'er alter till thy sweet life end!

LYSANDER
> Amen, amen, to that fair prayer, say I,
> And then end life when I end loyalty!
> Here is my bed. Sleep give thee all his rest!

HERMIA
> With half that wish the wisher's eyes be pressed!   71
>   [*They sleep, separated by a short distance.*]

Enter Puck.

PUCK
> Through the forest have I gone,
> But Athenian found I none
> On whose eyes I might approve   74
> This flower's force in stirring love.
> Night and silence.—Who is here?
> Weeds of Athens he doth wear.
> This is he, my master said,
> Despisèd the Athenian maid;
> And here the maiden, sleeping sound,
> On the dank and dirty ground.
> Pretty soul, she durst not lie
> Near this lack-love, this kill-courtesy.
> Churl, upon thy eyes I throw
> All the power this charm doth owe.   85
>   [*He applies the love juice.*]
> When thou wak'st, let love forbid   86
> Sleep his seat on thy eyelid.   87
> So awake when I am gone,
> For I must now to Oberon.   *Exit.*

Enter Demetrius and Helena, running.

HELENA
> Stay, though thou kill me, sweet Demetrius!

---

13 Philomel the nightingale. (Philomela, daughter of King Pandion, was transformed into a nightingale, according to Ovid's *Metamorphoses* 6, after she had been raped by her sister Procne's husband, Tereus.) **23 offense** harm. **32 sentinel** (Presumably Oberon is able to outwit or intimidate this guard.) **36 ounce** lynx **37 Pard** leopard **48 troth** faith, trothplight.

51–2 take . . . conference take my meaning in an innocent sense, with generosity and sympathy! True lovers do so when they converse. **58 lie** tell a falsehood. (With a riddling pun on *lie*, "recline.") **60 beshrew** (A mild oath.) **71 With . . . pressed!** i.e., I return half that wish, so that you, the wisher, may sleep well too (instead of Sleep giving all his rest to me)! **74 approve** test **85 owe** own. **86–7 let . . . eyelid** may love, heretofore denied, be enthroned in your eyes.

DEMETRIUS
I charge thee, hence, and do not haunt me thus.
HELENA
Oh, wilt thou darkling leave me? Do not so.   92
DEMETRIUS
Stay, on thy peril! I alone will go.   [*Exit.*] 93
HELENA
Oh, I am out of breath in this fond chase!   94
The more my prayer, the lesser is my grace.   95
Happy is Hermia, wheresoe'er she lies,   96
For she hath blessèd and attractive eyes.
How came her eyes so bright? Not with salt tears;
If so, my eyes are oft'ner washed than hers.
No, no, I am as ugly as a bear,
For beasts that meet me run away for fear.
Therefore no marvel though Demetrius   102
Do, as a monster, fly my presence thus.   103
What wicked and dissembling glass of mine   104
Made me compare with Hermia's sphery eyne?   105
But who is here? Lysander, on the ground?
Dead, or asleep? I see no blood, no wound.
Lysander, if you live, good sir, awake.
LYSANDER [*awaking*]
And run through fire I will for thy sweet sake.
Transparent Helena! Nature shows art,   110
That through thy bosom makes me see thy heart.
Where is Demetrius? Oh, how fit a word
Is that vile name to perish on my sword!
HELENA
Do not say so, Lysander; say not so.
What though he love your Hermia? Lord, what
    though?
Yet Hermia still loves you. Then be content.
LYSANDER
Content with Hermia? No! I do repent
The tedious minutes I with her have spent.
Not Hermia but Helena I love.
Who will not change a raven for a dove?
The will of man is by his reason swayed,   121
And reason says you are the worthier maid.
Things growing are not ripe until their season;
So I, being young, till now ripe not to reason.   124
And, touching now the point of human skill,   125
Reason becomes the marshal to my will
And leads me to your eyes, where I o'erlook   127
Love's stories written in love's richest book.
HELENA
Wherefore was I to this keen mockery born?   129
When at your hands did I deserve this scorn?
Is't not enough, is't not enough, young man,
That I did never—no, nor never can—
Deserve a sweet look from Demetrius' eye,

But you must flout my insufficiency?
Good troth, you do me wrong, good sooth, you do,   135
In such disdainful manner me to woo.
But fare you well. Perforce I must confess
I thought you lord of more true gentleness.   138
Oh, that a lady, of one man refused,   139
Should of another therefore be abused!   *Exit.* 140
LYSANDER
She sees not Hermia. Hermia, sleep thou there,
And never mayst thou come Lysander near!
For as a surfeit of the sweetest things
The deepest loathing to the stomach brings,
Or as the heresies that men do leave   145
Are hated most of those they did deceive,   146
So thou, my surfeit and my heresy,
Of all be hated, but the most of me!   148
And, all my powers, address your love and might   149
To honor Helen and to be her knight!   *Exit.*
HERMIA [*awaking*]
Help me, Lysander, help me! Do thy best
To pluck this crawling serpent from my breast!
Ay me, for pity! What a dream was here!
Lysander, look how I do quake with fear.
Methought a serpent ate my heart away,
And you sat smiling at his cruel prey.   156
Lysander! What, removed? Lysander! Lord!
What, out of hearing? Gone? No sound, no word?
Alack, where are you? Speak, an if you hear;   159
Speak, of all loves! I swoon almost with fear.   160
No? Then I well perceive you are not nigh.
Either death, or you, I'll find immediately.
                Exit. [*The sleeping Titania remains.*]

❧

3.1

*Enter the clowns [Quince, Snug, Bottom, Flute,
Snout, and Starveling].*

BOTTOM   Are we all met?
QUINCE   Pat, pat; and here's a marvelous convenient   2
place for our rehearsal. This green plot shall be our
stage, this hawthorn brake our tiring-house, and we   4
will do it in action as we will do it before the Duke.
BOTTOM   Peter Quince?
QUINCE   What sayest thou, bully Bottom?   7
BOTTOM   There are things in this comedy of Pyramus
and Thisbe that will never please. First, Pyramus must
draw a sword to kill himself, which the ladies cannot
abide. How answer you that?
SNOUT   By'r lakin, a parlous fear.   12

92 darkling in the dark   **93 on thy peril** i.e., on pain of reprisal if you don't obey me and stay.   **94 fond** doting   **95 my grace** the favor I obtain.   **96 lies** dwells   **102–3 no marvel . . . thus** i.e., no wonder that Demetrius flies from me as from a monster.   **104 glass** mirror   **105 compare** compare myself.   **sphery eyne** eyes as bright as stars in their spheres.   **110 Transparent** Radiant, pure.   **art** skill, magic power   **121 will** desire   **124 ripe not** have not ripened   **125 touching . . . skill** reaching now the age of mature judgment   **127 o'erlook** read over   **129 Wherefore** Why
135 Good troth, good sooth i.e., Indeed, truly   **138 lord of** i.e., possessor of.   **gentleness** courtesy.   **139 of** by   **140 abused** ill treated.   **145–6 as . . . deceive** as renounced heresies are hated most by those persons who formerly were deceived by them   **148 Of . . . of** by . . . by   **149 address** direct, apply   **156 prey** act of preying.   **159 an if** if   **160 of all loves** for love's sake.
3.1. Location: The action is continuous.
0.1 *clowns* rustics   **2 Pat** On the dot, punctually   **4 brake** thicket.   **tiring-house** attiring area, hence backstage   **7 bully** i.e., worthy, jolly, fine fellow   **12 By'r lakin** By our ladykin, i.e., the Virgin Mary.   **parlous** perilous, alarming

STARVELING   I believe we must leave the killing out, when all is done.   14

BOTTOM   Not a whit. I have a device to make all well. Write me a prologue, and let the prologue seem to say,   16 we will do no harm with our swords, and that Pyramus is not killed indeed; and for the more better assurance, tell them that I, Pyramus, am not Pyramus but Bottom the weaver. This will put them out of fear.

QUINCE   Well, we will have such a prologue, and it shall be written in eight and six.   22

BOTTOM   No, make it two more: let it be written in eight and eight.

SNOUT   Will not the ladies be afeard of the lion?

STARVELING   I fear it, I promise you.

BOTTOM   Masters, you ought to consider with yourself, to bring in—God shield us!—a lion among ladies is a   28 most dreadful thing. For there is not a more fearful   29 wildfowl than your lion living, and we ought to look to 't.

SNOUT   Therefore another prologue must tell he is not a lion.

BOTTOM   Nay, you must name his name, and half his face must be seen through the lion's neck, and he himself must speak through, saying thus or to the same defect: "Ladies," or "Fair ladies, I would wish you," or   37 "I would request you," or "I would entreat you, not to fear, not to tremble; my life for yours. If you think I   39 come hither as a lion, it were pity of my life. No, I am   40 no such thing; I am a man as other men are." And there indeed let him name his name, and tell them plainly he is Snug the joiner.

QUINCE   Well, it shall be so. But there is two hard things: that is, to bring the moonlight into a chamber; for, you know, Pyramus and Thisbe meet by moonlight.

SNOUT   Doth the moon shine that night we play our play?

BOTTOM   A calendar, a calendar! Look in the almanac. Find out moonshine, find out moonshine.

[They consult an almanac.]

QUINCE   Yes, it doth shine that night.

BOTTOM   Why then may you leave a casement of the great chamber window where we play open, and the moon may shine in at the casement.

QUINCE   Ay; or else one must come in with a bush of   55 thorns and a lantern and say he comes to disfigure, or   56 to present, the person of Moonshine. Then there is another thing: we must have a wall in the great cham-

ber; for Pyramus and Thisbe, says the story, did talk through the chink of a wall.

SNOUT   You can never bring in a wall. What say you, Bottom?

BOTTOM   Some man or other must present Wall. And let him have some plaster, or some loam, or some rough-   64 cast about him, to signify wall; or let him hold his   65 fingers thus, and through that cranny shall Pyramus and Thisbe whisper.

QUINCE   If that may be, then all is well. Come, sit down, every mother's son, and rehearse your parts. Pyramus, you begin. When you have spoken your speech, enter into that brake, and so everyone according to his cue.

Enter Robin [Puck].

PUCK *[aside]*
What hempen homespuns have we swagg'ring here   72
So near the cradle of the Fairy Queen?   73
What, a play toward? I'll be an auditor;   74
   An actor, too, perhaps, if I see cause.

QUINCE   Speak, Pyramus. Thisbe, stand forth.

BOTTOM *[as Pyramus]*
"Thisbe, the flowers of odious savors sweet—"

QUINCE   Odors, odors.

BOTTOM   "—Odors savors sweet;
   So hath thy breath, my dearest Thisbe dear.
But hark, a voice! Stay thou but here awhile,
   And by and by I will to thee appear."   *Exit.*

PUCK   A stranger Pyramus than e'er played here. *[Exit.]*   83

FLUTE   Must I speak now?

QUINCE   Ay, marry, must you; for you must understand he goes but to see a noise that he heard, and is to come again.

FLUTE *[as Thisbe]*
"Most radiant Pyramus, most lily-white of hue,
   Of color like the red rose on triumphant brier,   89
Most brisky juvenal and eke most lovely Jew,   90
   As true as truest horse that yet would never tire.
I'll meet thee, Pyramus, at Ninny's tomb."

QUINCE   "Ninus' tomb," man. Why, you must not speak   93 that yet. That you answer to Pyramus. You speak all your part at once, cues and all. Pyramus, enter. Your   95 cue is past; it is "never tire."

FLUTE
Oh—"As true as truest horse that yet would never tire."   97

[Enter Puck, and Bottom as Pyramus with the ass head.]

---

14 **when all is done** i.e., when all is said and done.   16 **Write me** i.e., Write at my suggestion. (*Me* is used colloquially.)   22 **eight and six** alternate lines of eight and six syllables, a common ballad measure.   28 **lion among ladies** (A contemporary pamphlet tells how, at the christening in 1594 of Prince Henry, eldest son of King James VI of Scotland, later James I of England, a "blackamoor" instead of a lion drew the triumphal chariot, since the lion's presence might have "brought some fear to the nearest.")   29 **fearful** fear-inspiring   37 **defect** (Bottom's blunder for "effect.")   39 **my life for yours** i.e., I pledge my life to make your lives safe.   40 **it were . . . life** i.e., I should be sorry, by my life; or, my life would be endangered.   55–6 **bush of thorns** bundle of thornbush fagots. (Part of the accoutrements of the man in the moon, according to the popular notions of the time, along with his lantern and his dog.)   56 **disfigure** (Quince's blunder for "figure," "represent.")

64–5 **roughcast** a mixture of lime and gravel used to plaster the outside of buildings   72 **hempen homespuns** i.e., rustics dressed in homespun fabric made from hemp   73 **cradle** i.e., Titania's bower   74 **toward** about to take place.   83 **A stranger . . . here** The strangest Pyramus you ever saw.   89 **triumphant** magnificent   90 **brisky juvenal** lively youth.   **eke** also.   **Jew** (A desperate attempt to rhyme with *hue*, inspired perhaps by the first syllable of *juvenal*.)   93 **Ninus** mythical founder of Nineveh (whose wife, Semiramis, was supposed to have built the walls of Babylon where the story of Pyramus and Thisbe takes place)   95 **part** (An actor's *part* was a script consisting only of his speeches and their cues.)   97.1–2 **with the ass head** (This stage direction, taken from the Folio, presumably refers to a standard stage property.)

BOTTOM
  "If I were fair, Thisbe, I were only thine."   98
QUINCE   Oh, monstrous! Oh, strange! We are haunted.
  Pray, masters! Fly, masters! Help!
> [*Exeunt Quince, Snug, Flute,*
> *Snout, and Starveling.*]

PUCK
  I'll follow you: I'll lead you about a round,   101
    Through bog, through bush, through brake,
      through brier.
  Sometimes a horse I'll be, sometimes a hound,
    A hog, a headless bear, sometimes a fire;   104
  And neigh, and bark, and grunt, and roar, and burn,
  Like horse, hound, hog, bear, fire, at every turn.   *Exit.*
BOTTOM   Why do they run away? This is a knavery of
  them to make me afeard.

    Enter Snout.

SNOUT   Oh, Bottom, thou art changed! What do I see on
  thee?
BOTTOM   What do you see? You see an ass head of your
  own, do you?   [*Exit Snout.*]

    Enter Quince.

QUINCE   Bless thee, Bottom, bless thee! Thou art trans-   113
  lated.   *Exit.*   114
BOTTOM   I see their knavery. This is to make an ass of
  me, to fright me, if they could. But I will not stir from
  this place, do what they can. I will walk up and down
  here, and I will sing, that they shall hear I am not
  afraid.   [*He sings.*]
    The ouzel cock so black of hue,   120
      With orange-tawny bill,
    The throstle with his note so true,   122
      The wren with little quill—   123
TITANIA [*awaking*]
  What angel wakes me from my flow'ry bed?
BOTTOM [*sings*]
    The finch, the sparrow, and the lark,
    The plainsong cuckoo gray,   126
    Whose note full many a man doth mark,
      And dares not answer nay—   128
  For indeed, who would set his wit to so foolish a bird?   129
  Who would give a bird the lie, though he cry "cuckoo"   130
  never so?   131
TITANIA
  I pray thee, gentle mortal, sing again.
  Mine ear is much enamored of thy note;
  So is mine eye enthrallèd to thy shape;
  And thy fair virtue's force perforce doth move me   135
  On the first view to say, to swear, I love thee.

BOTTOM   Methinks, mistress, you should have little rea-
  son for that. And yet, to say the truth, reason and love
  keep little company together nowadays—the more the
  pity that some honest neighbors will not make them
  friends. Nay, I can gleek upon occasion.   141
TITANIA
  Thou art as wise as thou art beautiful.
BOTTOM   Not so, neither. But if I had wit enough to get
  out of this wood, I have enough to serve mine own   144
  turn.   145
TITANIA
  Out of this wood do not desire to go.
  Thou shalt remain here, whether thou wilt or no.
  I am a spirit of no common rate.   148
  The summer still doth tend upon my state,   149
  And I do love thee. Therefore, go with me.
  I'll give thee fairies to attend on thee,
  And they shall fetch thee jewels from the deep,
  And sing while thou on pressèd flowers dost sleep.
  And I will purge thy mortal grossness so
  That thou shalt like an airy spirit go.—
  Peaseblossom, Cobweb, Mote, and Mustardseed!   156

    Enter four Fairies [*Peaseblossom, Cobweb,*
    Mote, and Mustardseed].

PEASEBLOSSOM   Ready.
COBWEB
  And I.
MOTE   And I.
MUSTARDSEED And I.
ALL   Where shall we go?
TITANIA
  Be kind and courteous to this gentleman.
  Hop in his walks and gambol in his eyes;   160
  Feed him with apricots and dewberries,   161
  With purple grapes, green figs, and mulberries;
  The honey bags steal from the humble-bees,
  And for night tapers crop their waxen thighs,   164
  And light them at the fiery glowworms' eyes,   165
  To have my love to bed and to arise;
  And pluck the wings from painted butterflies
  To fan the moonbeams from his sleeping eyes.
  Nod to him, elves, and do him courtesies.
PEASEBLOSSOM   Hail, mortal!
COBWEB   Hail!
MOTE   Hail!
MUSTARDSEED   Hail!
BOTTOM   I cry Your Worships mercy, heartily. I beseech   174
  Your Worship's name.
COBWEB   Cobweb.

---

98 If Even if. **fair** handsome. **were** would be   **101 about a round**
roundabout   **104 fire** will-o'-the-wisp   **113–14 translated** transformed.   **120 ouzel cock** male blackbird   **122 throstle** song thrush
123 with little quill with small pipe, i.e., high-pitched note; or else
with small feathers   **126 plainsong** singing a melody without variations   **128 dares . . . nay** i.e., cannot deny that he is a cuckold
129 set his wit to employ his intelligence to answer   **130 give . . . lie**
call the bird a liar   **131 never so** ever so much.   **135 thy . . . force** the
power of your unblemished excellence

141 gleek jest   **144–5 serve . . . turn** answer my purpose.   **148 rate**
rank, value.   **149 still . . . state** always waits upon me as a part of my
royal retinue   **156 Mote** i.e., speck. (The two words *moth* and *mote*
were pronounced alike, and both meanings may be present.)   **160 in
his eyes** in his sight (i.e., before him)   **161 dewberries** blackberries
164 night . . . thighs (The waxen thighs of the bumble-bee are to be
fashioned into wax candles to light Bottom's way in the dark.)   **165
eyes** (In fact, the light is emitted by the abdomen. *Eyes* may be
metaphorical.)   **174 I cry . . . mercy** I beg pardon of Your Worships
(for presuming to ask a question)

BOTTOM I shall desire you of more acquaintance, good 177
Master Cobweb. If I cut my finger, I shall make bold 178
with you.—Your name, honest gentleman? 179

PEASEBLOSSOM Peaseblossom.

BOTTOM I pray you, commend me to Mistress Squash, 181
your mother, and to Master Peascod, your father. 182
Good Master Peaseblossom, I shall desire you of more
acquaintance too.—Your name, I beseech you, sir?

MUSTARDSEED Mustardseed.

BOTTOM Good Master Mustardseed, I know your 186
patience well. That same cowardly, giantlike ox-beef 187
hath devoured many a gentleman of your house. I
promise you, your kindred hath made my eyes water 189
ere now. I desire you of more acquaintance, good
Master Mustardseed.

TITANIA
Come wait upon him; lead him to my bower.
The moon methinks looks with a wat'ry eye;
And when she weeps, weeps every little flower, 194
Lamenting some enforcèd chastity. 195
Tie up my lover's tongue; bring him silently. 196
Exeunt.

❖

[3.2]

Enter [Oberon,] King of Fairies.

OBERON
I wonder if Titania be awaked;
Then, what it was that next came in her eye,
Which she must dote on in extremity.

[Enter] Robin Goodfellow [Puck].

Here comes my messenger. How now, mad spirit?
What night-rule now about this haunted grove? 5

PUCK
My mistress with a monster is in love.
Near to her close and consecrated bower, 7
While she was in her dull and sleeping hour, 8
A crew of patches, rude mechanicals, 9
That work for bread upon Athenian stalls, 10
Were met together to rehearse a play
Intended for great Theseus' nuptial day.
The shallowest thickskin of that barren sort, 13
Who Pyramus presented, in their sport 14
Forsook his scene and entered in a brake. 15
When I did him at this advantage take,

An ass's noll I fixèd on his head. 17
Anon his Thisbe must be answerèd,
And forth my mimic comes. When they him spy, 19
As wild geese that the creeping fowler eye, 20
Or russet-pated choughs, many in sort, 21
Rising and cawing at the gun's report,
Sever themselves and madly sweep the sky, 23
So, at his sight, away his fellows fly;
And, at our stamp, here o'er and o'er one falls;
He "Murder!" cries and help from Athens calls.
Their sense thus weak, lost with their fears thus
strong, 27
Made senseless things begin to do them wrong, 28
For briers and thorns at their apparel snatch;
Some, sleeves—some, hats; from yielders all things
catch. 30
I led them on in this distracted fear
And left sweet Pyramus translated there,
When in that moment, so it came to pass,
Titania waked and straightway loved an ass.

OBERON
This falls out better than I could devise.
But hast thou yet latched the Athenian's eyes 36
With the love juice, as I did bid thee do?

PUCK
I took him sleeping—that is finished too—
And the Athenian woman by his side,
That, when he waked, of force she must be eyed. 40

Enter Demetrius and Hermia.

OBERON
Stand close. This is the same Athenian.

PUCK
This is the woman, but not this the man.
[They stand aside.]

DEMETRIUS
Oh, why rebuke you him that loves you so?
Lay breath so bitter on your bitter foe.

HERMIA
Now I but chide; but I should use thee worse,
For thou, I fear, hast given me cause to curse.
If thou hast slain Lysander in his sleep,
Being o'er shoes in blood, plunge in the deep, 48
And kill me too.
The sun was not so true unto the day
As he to me. Would he have stolen away
From sleeping Hermia? I'll believe as soon
This whole earth may be bored, and that the moon 53
May through the center creep, and so displease
Her brother's noontide with th'Antipodes. 55

---

177 I . . . acquaintance I crave to be better acquainted with you
178–9 If . . . you (Cobwebs were used to stanch bleeding.)
181 Squash unripe pea pod 182 Peascod ripe pea pod 186–7 your
patience what you have endured. (Mustard is eaten with beef.)
189 water (1) weep for sympathy (2) smart, sting 194 And . . .
flower (Dew was thought to fall from the heavens in greater proportion as the moon shown fully.) 195 enforcèd violated. (The moon is
associated throughout the play with the goddess Diana and chastity.)
196 Tie . . . tongue (Presumably Bottom is braying like an ass.)
3.2. Location: The wood.
5 night-rule diversion or misrule for the night 7 close secret 8 dull
drowsy 9 patches clowns, fools. rude mechanicals ignorant artisans 10 stalls market booths 13 barren sort stupid company or
crew 14 presented acted 15 scene playing area

17 noll noddle, head 19 mimic actor 20 fowler hunter of game
birds 21 russet-pated choughs reddish brown or gray-headed jackdaws. in sort in a flock 23 Sever themselves i.e., scatter
27–8 Their . . . wrong Their weakened physical senses, disabled by
their strong fears, made it seem to them as though inanimate things
in the forest were attacking them 30 from . . . catch the forest
snatches away everything from those who yield to it. 36 latched
snared, taken prisoner 40 of force perforce 48 Being o'er shoes
having waded in so far 53 whole solid 55 Her . . . Antipodes i.e.,
the sun's noontime on the opposite side of the earth, among the people who live there, the Antipodes.

It cannot be but thou hast murdered him;
So should a murderer look, so dead, so grim. 57
DEMETRIUS
So should the murdered look, and so should I,
Pierced through the heart with your stern cruelty.
Yet you, the murderer, look as bright, as clear
As yonder Venus in her glimmering sphere.
HERMIA
What's this to my Lysander? Where is he? 62
Ah, good Demetrius, wilt thou give him me?
DEMETRIUS
I had rather give his carcass to my hounds.
HERMIA
Out, dog! Out, cur! Thou driv'st me past the bounds
Of maiden's patience. Hast thou slain him, then?
Henceforth be never numbered among men.
Oh, once tell true, tell true, even for my sake: 68
Durst thou have looked upon him being awake? 69
And hast thou killed him sleeping? Oh, brave touch! 70
Could not a worm, an adder, do so much? 71
An adder did it; for with doubler tongue 72
Than thine, thou serpent, never adder stung.
DEMETRIUS
You spend your passion on a misprised mood. 74
I am not guilty of Lysander's blood,
Nor is he dead, for aught that I can tell.
HERMIA
I pray thee, tell me then that he is well.
DEMETRIUS
And if I could, what should I get therefor? 78
HERMIA
A privilege never to see me more.
And from thy hated presence part I so.
See me no more, whether he be dead or no.   *Exit.*
DEMETRIUS
There is no following her in this fierce vein.
Here therefore for a while I will remain.
So sorrow's heaviness doth heavier grow 84
For debt that bankrupt sleep doth sorrow owe, 85
Which now in some slight measure it will pay, 86
If for his tender here I make some stay. 87
                   [He] lie[s] down [and sleeps].
OBERON
What hast thou done? Thou hast mistaken quite
And laid the love juice on some true love's sight.
Of thy misprision must perforce ensue 90
Some true love turned, and not a false turned true.
PUCK
Then fate o'errules, that, one man holding troth, 92
A million fail, confounding oath on oath. 93

OBERON
About the wood go swifter than the wind,
And Helena of Athens look thou find.
All fancy-sick she is and pale of cheer 96
With sighs of love, that cost the fresh blood dear. 97
By some illusion see thou bring her here.
I'll charm his eyes against she do appear. 99
PUCK
I go, I go, look how I go,
Swifter than arrow from the Tartar's bow.   *[Exit.]* 101
OBERON *[applying love juice to Demetrius's eyes]*
    Flower of this purple dye,
    Hit with Cupid's archery,
    Sink in apple of his eye. 104
    When his love he doth espy,
    Let her shine as gloriously
    As the Venus of the sky.
    When thou wak'st, if she be by,
    Beg of her for remedy.

    Enter Puck.

PUCK
    Captain of our fairy band,
    Helena is here at hand,
    And the youth, mistook by me,
    Pleading for a lover's fee. 113
    Shall we their fond pageant see? 114
    Lord, what fools these mortals be!
OBERON
    Stand aside. The noise they make
    Will cause Demetrius to awake.
PUCK
    Then will two at once woo one;
    That must needs be sport alone. 119
    And those things do best please me
    That befall preposterously. 121
                    [They stand aside.]

    Enter Lysander and Helena.

LYSANDER
Why should you think that I should woo in scorn?
    Scorn and derision never come in tears.
Look when I vow, I weep; and vows so born, 124
    In their nativity all truth appears. 125
How can these things in me seem scorn to you,
Bearing the badge of faith to prove them true?
HELENA
You do advance your cunning more and more. 128
    When truth kills truth, oh, devilish-holy fray! 129
These vows are Hermia's. Will you give her o'er?
    Weigh oath with oath, and you will nothing weigh;

57 dead deadly, or deathly pale   **62 to** to do with   **68 once** once and for all   **69 being awake** when he was awake.   **70 brave touch!** fine stroke! (Said ironically.)   **71 worm** serpent   **72 doubler** (1) more forked (2) more deceitful   **74 You . . . mood** Your anger is misdirected.   **78 therefor** in return for that.   **84–7 So . . . stay** The heaviness of sorrow grows still heavier when sleepiness adds to the weariness caused by sorrow, which debt to sleepiness I will now repay in part if I can stop here and accept what sleep has to offer.
90 misprision mistake   **92–3 Then . . . oath** If so, then fate prevails; for each male who is able to keep true faith in love, a million will fail, breaking oath on oath.

96 fancy-sick lovesick. **cheer** face   **97 sighs . . . dear** (Each sigh was supposed to cost the heart a drop of blood.)   **99 against . . . appear** in anticipation of her coming.   **101 Tartar's bow** (Tartars were famed for their skill with the bow.)   **104 apple** pupil   **113 fee** privilege, reward.   **114 fond pageant** foolish spectacle   **119 alone** unequaled.   **121 preposterously** out of the natural order.   **124 Look when** Whenever   **124–5 vows . . . appears** i.e., vows made by one who is weeping give evidence thereby of their sincerity.
128 advance carry forward, display   **129 When . . . truth** i.e., When one of your vows cancels the other

Your vows to her and me, put in two scales,
Will even weigh, and both as light as tales. 133

LYSANDER
I had no judgment when to her I swore.

HELENA
Nor none, in my mind, now you give her o'er.

LYSANDER
Demetrius loves her, and he loves not you.

DEMETRIUS [*awaking*]
O Helen, goddess, nymph, perfect, divine!
To what, my love, shall I compare thine eyne?
Crystal is muddy. Oh, how ripe in show 139
Thy lips, those kissing cherries, tempting grow!
That pure congealèd white, high Taurus' snow, 141
Fanned with the eastern wind, turns to a crow 142
When thou hold'st up thy hand. Oh, let me kiss
This princess of pure white, this seal of bliss! 144

HELENA
Oh, spite! Oh, hell! I see you all are bent
To set against me for your merriment. 146
If you were civil and knew courtesy,
You would not do me thus much injury.
Can you not hate me, as I know you do,
But you must join in souls to mock me too? 150
If you were men, as men you are in show,
You would not use a gentle lady so—
To vow, and swear, and superpraise my parts, 153
When I am sure you hate me with your hearts.
You both are rivals, and love Hermia,
And now both rivals to mock Helena.
A trim exploit, a manly enterprise, 157
To conjure tears up in a poor maid's eyes
With your derision! None of noble sort 159
Would so offend a virgin and extort 160
A poor soul's patience, all to make you sport.

LYSANDER
You are unkind, Demetrius. Be not so.
For you love Hermia; this you know I know.
And here, with all good will, with all my heart,
In Hermia's love I yield you up my part;
And yours of Helena to me bequeath,
Whom I do love, and will do till my death.

HELENA
Never did mockers waste more idle breath.

DEMETRIUS
Lysander, keep thy Hermia; I will none. 169
If e'er I loved her, all that love is gone.
My heart to her but as guestwise sojourned, 171
And now to Helen is it home returned,
There to remain.

LYSANDER　　　　Helen, it is not so.

DEMETRIUS
Disparage not the faith thou dost not know,
Lest, to thy peril, thou aby it dear. 175
Look where thy love comes; yonder is thy dear.

Enter Hermia.

HERMIA
Dark night, that from the eye his function takes, 177
The ear more quick of apprehension makes;
Wherein it doth impair the seeing sense,
It pays the hearing double recompense.
Thou art not by mine eye, Lysander, found;
Mine ear, I thank it, brought me to thy sound.
But why unkindly didst thou leave me so?

LYSANDER
Why should he stay, whom love doth press to go?

HERMIA
What love could press Lysander from my side?

LYSANDER
Lysander's love, that would not let him bide—
Fair Helena, who more engilds the night
Than all yon fiery oes and eyes of light. 188
Why seek'st thou me? Could not this make thee
　　know
The hate I bear thee made me leave thee so?

HERMIA
You speak not as you think. It cannot be.

HELENA
Lo, she is one of this confederacy!
Now I perceive they have conjoined all three
To fashion this false sport, in spite of me. 194
Injurious Hermia, most ungrateful maid!
Have you conspired, have you with these contrived
To bait me with this foul derision? 197
Is all the counsel that we two have shared— 198
The sisters' vows, the hours that we have spent
When we have chid the hasty-footed time
For parting us—oh, is all forgot?
All schooldays' friendship, childhood innocence?
We, Hermia, like two artificial gods 203
Have with our needles created both one flower,
Both on one sampler, sitting on one cushion,
Both warbling of one song, both in one key,
As if our hands, our sides, voices, and minds
Had been incorporate. So we grew together, 208
Like to a double cherry, seeming parted,
But yet an union in partition,
Two lovely berries molded on one stem;
So, with two seeming bodies but one heart,
Two of the first, like coats in heraldry, 213
Due but to one and crownèd with one crest. 214
And will you rend our ancient love asunder,
To join with men in scorning your poor friend?
It is not friendly, 'tis not maidenly.

---

133 **tales** lies.　**139 show** appearance　**141 Taurus** a lofty mountain range in Asia Minor　**142 turns to a crow** i.e., seems black by contrast　**144 seal** pledge　**146 set against** attack　**150 in souls** i.e., heart and soul　**153 superpraise** overpraise. **parts** qualities　**157 trim** pretty, fine. (Said ironically.)　**159 sort** character, quality　**160 extort** twist, torture　**169 will none** i.e., want no part of her　**171 to . . . sojourned** only visited with her.

175 **aby** pay for　**177 his** its　**188 oes** spangles (here, stars)　**194 in spite of me** to vex me.　**197 bait** torment, as one sets on dogs to bait a bear　**198 counsel** confidential talk　**203 artificial** skilled in art or creation　**208 incorporate** of one body.　**213–14 Two . . . crest** i.e., we have two separate bodies, just as a coat of arms in heraldry can be represented twice on a shield but surmounted by a single crest.

Our sex, as well as I, may chide you for it,
Though I alone do feel the injury.

HERMIA
I am amazèd at your passionate words.
I scorn you not. It seems that you scorn me.

HELENA
Have you not set Lysander, as in scorn,
To follow me and praise my eyes and face?
And made your other love, Demetrius,
Who even but now did spurn me with his foot,
To call me goddess, nymph, divine, and rare,
Precious, celestial? Wherefore speaks he this
To her he hates? And wherefore doth Lysander
Deny your love, so rich within his soul,
And tender me, forsooth, affection,   230
But by your setting on, by your consent?
What though I be not so in grace as you,   232
So hung upon with love, so fortunate,
But miserable most, to love unloved?
This you should pity rather than despise.

HERMIA
I understand not what you mean by this.

HELENA
Ay, do! Persever, counterfeit sad looks,   237
Make mouths upon me when I turn my back,   238
Wink each at other, hold the sweet jest up.   239
This sport, well carried, shall be chronicled.   240
If you have any pity, grace, or manners,
You would not make me such an argument.   242
But fare ye well. 'Tis partly my own fault,
Which death, or absence, soon shall remedy.

LYSANDER
Stay, gentle Helena; hear my excuse,
My love, my life, my soul, fair Helena!

HELENA
Oh, excellent!

HERMIA [to Lysander]   Sweet, do not scorn her so.

DEMETRIUS [to Lysander]
If she cannot entreat, I can compel.   248

LYSANDER
Thou canst compel no more than she entreat.
Thy threats have no more strength than her weak
    prayers.—
Helen, I love thee, by my life, I do!
I swear by that which I will lose for thee,
To prove him false that says I love thee not.

DEMETRIUS [to Helena]
I say I love thee more than he can do.

LYSANDER
If thou say so, withdraw, and prove it too.   255

DEMETRIUS
Quick, come!

HERMIA   Lysander, whereto tends all this?

LYSANDER
Away, you Ethiope!

[He tries to break away from Hermia.]

DEMETRIUS   No, no; he'll   257
Seem to break loose; take on as you would follow,   258
But yet come not. You are a tame man. Go!

LYSANDER [to Hermia]
Hang off, thou cat, thou burr! Vile thing, let loose,   260
Or I will shake thee from me like a serpent!

HERMIA
Why are you grown so rude? What change is this,
Sweet love?

LYSANDER   Thy love? Out, tawny Tartar, out!
Out, loathèd med'cine! O hated potion, hence!   264

HERMIA
Do you not jest?

HELENA   Yes, sooth, and so do you.   265

LYSANDER
Demetrius, I will keep my word with thee.

DEMETRIUS
I would I had your bond, for I perceive
A weak bond holds you. I'll not trust your word.   268

LYSANDER
What, should I hurt her, strike her, kill her dead?
Although I hate her, I'll not harm her so.

HERMIA
What, can you do me greater harm than hate?
Hate me? Wherefore? Oh, me, what news, my love?   272
Am not I Hermia? Are not you Lysander?
I am as fair now as I was erewhile.   274
Since night you loved me; yet since night you left me.
Why, then you left me—oh, the gods forbid!—
In earnest, shall I say?

LYSANDER   Ay, by my life!
And never did desire to see thee more.
Therefore be out of hope, of question, of doubt;
Be certain, nothing truer. 'Tis no jest
That I do hate thee and love Helena.

HERMIA [to Helena]
Oh, me! You juggler! You cankerblossom!   282
You thief of love! What, have you come by night
And stol'n my love's heart from him?

HELENA   Fine, i'faith!
Have you no modesty, no maiden shame,
No touch of bashfulness? What, will you tear
Impatient answers from my gentle tongue?
Fie, fie! You counterfeit, you puppet, you!   288

HERMIA
"Puppet"? Why, so! Ay, that way goes the game.
Now I perceive that she hath made compare
Between our statures; she hath urged her height,
And with her personage, her tall personage,

230 tender offer   232 grace favor   237 sad grave, serious
238 mouths i.e., mows, faces, grimaces. upon at   239 hold . . . up
keep up the joke.   240 carried carried out, brought off   242 argument subject for a jest.   248 entreat i.e., succeed by entreaty
255 withdraw . . . too i.e., withdraw with me and prove your claim
in a duel. (The two gentlemen are armed.)

257 Ethiope (Referring to Hermia's relatively dark hair and complexion; see also tawny Tartar six lines later.)   258 take on as act as if,
make a fuss as if   260 Hang off Let go   264 med'cine i.e., poison
265 sooth truly   268 weak bond i.e., Hermia's arm. (With a pun on
bond, "oath," in the previous line.)   272 what news what is the matter   274 erewhile just now.   282 cankerblossom worm that destroys
the flower bud, or wild rose.   288 puppet (1) counterfeit (2) dwarfish
woman (in reference to Hermia's smaller stature)

Her height, forsooth, she hath prevailed with him.
And are you grown so high in his esteem
Because I am so dwarfish and so low?
How low am I, thou painted maypole? Speak!
How low am I? I am not yet so low
But that my nails can reach unto thine eyes.

[*She flails at Helena but is restrained.*]

HELENA
I pray you, though you mock me, gentlemen,
Let her not hurt me. I was never curst;   300
I have no gift at all in shrewishness;
I am a right maid for my cowardice.   302
Let her not strike me. You perhaps may think,
Because she is something lower than myself,   304
That I can match her.

HERMIA   Lower? Hark, again!

HELENA
Good Hermia, do not be so bitter with me.
I evermore did love you, Hermia,
Did ever keep your counsels, never wronged you,
Save that, in love unto Demetrius,
I told him of your stealth unto this wood.   310
He followed you; for love I followed him.
But he hath chid me hence and threatened me   312
To strike me, spurn me, nay, to kill me too.   313
And now, so you will let me quiet go,   314
To Athens will I bear my folly back
And follow you no further. Let me go.
You see how simple and how fond I am.   317

HERMIA
Why, get you gone. Who is't that hinders you?

HELENA
A foolish heart, that I leave here behind.

HERMIA
What, with Lysander?

HELENA   With Demetrius.

LYSANDER
Be not afraid; she shall not harm thee, Helena.

DEMETRIUS
No, sir, she shall not, though you take her part.

HELENA
Oh, when she is angry, she is keen and shrewd.   323
She was a vixen when she went to school;
And though she be but little, she is fierce.

HERMIA
"Little" again? Nothing but "low" and "little"?—
Why will you suffer her to flout me thus?
Let me come to her.

LYSANDER   Get you gone, you dwarf!
You minimus, of hind'ring knotgrass made!   329
You bead, you acorn!

DEMETRIUS   You are too officious
In her behalf that scorns your services.
Let her alone. Speak not of Helena;

Take not her part. For, if thou dost intend   333
Never so little show of love to her,
Thou shalt aby it.

LYSANDER   Now she holds me not.   335
Now follow, if thou dar'st, to try whose right,
Of thine or mine, is most in Helena.   [*Exit.*]

DEMETRIUS
Follow? Nay, I'll go with thee, cheek by jowl.   338

[*Exit, following Lysander.*]

HERMIA
You, mistress, all this coil is 'long of you.   339
Nay, go not back.

HELENA   I will not trust you, I,   340
Nor longer stay in your curst company.
Your hands than mine are quicker for a fray;
My legs are longer, though, to run away.   [*Exit.*]

HERMIA
I am amazed and know not what to say.   *Exit.*

[*Oberon and Puck come forward.*]

OBERON
This is thy negligence. Still thou mistak'st,
Or else commit'st thy knaveries willfully.

PUCK
Believe me, king of shadows, I mistook.
Did not you tell me I should know the man
By the Athenian garments he had on?
And so far blameless proves my enterprise
That I have 'nointed an Athenian's eyes;
And so far am I glad it so did sort,   352
As this their jangling I esteem a sport.   353

OBERON
Thou see'st these lovers seek a place to fight.
Hie therefore, Robin, overcast the night;   355
The starry welkin cover thou anon   356
With drooping fog as black as Acheron,   357
And lead these testy rivals so astray
As one come not within another's way.   359
Like to Lysander sometimes frame thy tongue,   360
Then stir Demetrius up with bitter wrong;   361
And sometimes rail thou like Demetrius.
And from each other look thou lead them thus,
Till o'er their brows death-counterfeiting sleep
With leaden legs and batty wings doth creep.   365
Then crush this herb into Lysander's eye,   366

[*giving herb*]

Whose liquor hath this virtuous property,   367
To take from thence all error with his might   368
And make his eyeballs roll with wonted sight.   369
When they next wake, all this derision   370
Shall seem a dream and fruitless vision,

---

300 **curst** shrewish 302 **right** true 304 **something** somewhat
310 **stealth** stealing away 312 **chid me hence** driven me away with
his scolding 313 **spurn** kick 314 **so** if only 317 **fond** foolish
323 **keen and shrewd** fierce and shrewish. 329 **minimus** diminutive
creature. **knotgrass** a weed, an infusion of which was thought to
stunt the growth

333 **intend** give sign of 335 **aby** pay for 338 **cheek by jowl** i.e.,
side by side. 339 **coil** turmoil, dissension. **'long of** on account of
340 **go not back** i.e., don't retreat. (Hermia is again proposing a fight.)
352 **so far** at least to this extent. **sort** turn out 353 **As** in that
355 **Hie** Hasten 356 **welkin** sky 357 **Acheron** river of Hades (here
representing Hades itself) 359 **As** that 360 **frame thy tongue** fashion your speech 361 **wrong** insults 365 **batty** batlike 366 **this
herb** i.e., the antidote (mentioned in 2.1.184) to love-in-idleness
367 **virtuous** efficacious 368 **his** its 369 **wonted** accustomed
370 **derision** laughable business

And back to Athens shall the lovers wend
With league whose date till death shall never end.　373
Whiles I in this affair do thee employ,
I'll to my queen and beg her Indian boy;
And then I will her charmèd eye release
From monster's view, and all things shall be peace.

PUCK
My fairy lord, this must be done with haste,
For night's swift dragons cut the clouds full fast,　379
And yonder shines Aurora's harbinger,　380
At whose approach ghosts, wand'ring here and there,
Troop home to churchyards. Damnèd spirits all,
That in crossways and floods have burial,　383
Already to their wormy beds are gone.
For fear lest day should look their shames upon,
They willfully themselves exile from light
And must for aye consort with black-browed night.　387

OBERON
But we are spirits of another sort.
I with the Morning's love have oft made sport,　389
And, like a forester, the groves may tread　390
Even till the eastern gate, all fiery red,
Opening on Neptune with fair blessèd beams,
Turns into yellow gold his salt green streams.
But notwithstanding, haste, make no delay.
We may effect this business yet ere day.　[Exit.]

PUCK
　　　Up and down, up and down,
　　　I will lead them up and down.
　　　I am feared in field and town.
　　　Goblin, lead them up and down.　399
Here comes one.

　　　Enter Lysander.

LYSANDER
Where art thou, proud Demetrius? Speak thou now.

PUCK [mimicking Demetrius]
Here, villain, drawn and ready. Where art thou?　402

LYSANDER
I will be with thee straight.

PUCK　　　　　　　　　　　Follow me, then,　403
To plainer ground.
　　　[Lysander wanders about, following the voice.]

　　　Enter Demetrius.

DEMETRIUS　　　　　Lysander! Speak again!　404
Thou runaway, thou coward, art thou fled?
Speak! In some bush? Where dost thou hide thy head?

PUCK [mimicking Lysander]
Thou coward, art thou bragging to the stars,
Telling the bushes that thou look'st for wars,
And wilt not come? Come, recreant; come, thou child,　409
I'll whip thee with a rod. He is defiled
That draws a sword on thee.

DEMETRIUS　　　　　　　　Yea, art thou there?

PUCK
Follow my voice. We'll try no manhood here.　412
　　　　　　　　　　　　　　　　　Exeunt.

　　　[Lysander returns.]

LYSANDER
He goes before me and still dares me on.
When I come where he calls, then he is gone.
The villain is much lighter-heeled than I.
I followed fast, but faster he did fly,
That fallen am I in dark uneven way,
And here will rest me. [He lies down.] Come, thou
　　　gentle day!
For if but once thou show me thy gray light,
I'll find Demetrius and revenge this spite. [He sleeps.]

　　　[Enter] Robin [Puck] and Demetrius.

PUCK
Ho, ho, ho! Coward, why com'st thou not?

DEMETRIUS
Abide me, if thou dar'st; for well I wot　422
Thou runn'st before me, shifting every place,
And dar'st not stand nor look me in the face.
Where art thou now?

PUCK　　　　　　　Come hither. I am here.

DEMETRIUS
Nay, then, thou mock'st me. Thou shalt buy this dear,　426
If ever I thy face by daylight see.
Now go thy way. Faintness constraineth me
To measure out my length on this cold bed.
By day's approach look to be visited.
　　　　　　　　　[He lies down and sleeps.]

　　　Enter Helena.

HELENA
O weary night, O long and tedious night,
　Abate thy hours! Shine comforts from the east,　432
That I may back to Athens by daylight
　From these that my poor company detest;
And sleep, that sometimes shuts up sorrow's eye,
Steal me awhile from mine own company!
　　　　　　　　[She lies down and] sleep[s].

PUCK
　　　Yet but three? Come one more;
　　　Two of both kinds makes up four.
　　　Here she comes, curst and sad.　439
　　　Cupid is a knavish lad,
　　　Thus to make poor females mad.

　　　[Enter Hermia.]

373 date term of existence　379 dragons (Supposed here to be yoked
to the car of the goddess of night or the moon.)　380 Aurora's harbinger the morning star, precursor of dawn　383 crossways . . . burial (Those who had committed suicide were buried at crossways,
with a stake driven through them; those who intentionally or accidentally drowned [in floods or deep water] would be condemned to
wander disconsolately for lack of burial rites.)　387 for aye forever
389 the Morning's love Cephalus, a beautiful youth beloved by
Aurora; or perhaps the goddess of the dawn herself　390 forester
keeper of a royal forest　399 Goblin Hobgoblin. (Puck refers to himself.)　402 drawn with drawn sword　403 straight immediately.
404 plainer more open.　s.d. Lysander wanders about (Lysander may
exit here, but perhaps not; neither exit nor reentrance is indicated in
the early texts.)

409 recreant cowardly wretch　412 try test　422 Abide Confront,
face.　wot know　426 buy this dear pay for this dearly　432 Abate
lessen, shorten　439 curst ill-tempered

HERMIA
    Never so weary, never so in woe,
        Bedabbled with the dew and torn with briers,
    I can no further crawl, no further go;
        My legs can keep no pace with my desires.
    Here will I rest me till the break of day.
    Heavens shield Lysander, if they mean a fray!
                      [She lies down and sleeps.]

PUCK
      On the ground
      Sleep sound.
      I'll apply
      To your eye,
    Gentle lover, remedy.
           [He squeezes the juice on Lysander's eyes.]
      When thou wak'st,
      Thou tak'st
      True delight
      In the sight
    Of thy former lady's eye;
    And the country proverb known,
    That every man should take his own,
    In your waking shall be shown:
      Jack shall have Jill;   461
      Naught shall go ill;
    The man shall have his mare again, and all shall
      be well.   *[Exit. The four sleeping lovers remain.]*

[4.1]

    Enter [Titania,] Queen of Fairies, and [Bottom
    the] clown, and Fairies; and [Oberon,] the King,
    behind them.

TITANIA
    Come, sit thee down upon this flow'ry bed,
        While I thy amiable cheeks do coy,   2
    And stick muskroses in thy sleek smooth head,
        And kiss thy fair large ears, my gentle joy.
                        [They recline.]
BOTTOM   Where's Peaseblossom?
PEASEBLOSSOM   Ready.
BOTTOM   Scratch my head, Peaseblossom. Where's
Monsieur Cobweb?
COBWEB   Ready.
BOTTOM   Monsieur Cobweb, good monsieur, get you
your weapons in your hand, and kill me a red-hipped
humble-bee on the top of a thistle; and, good monsieur, bring me the honey bag. Do not fret yourself too
much in the action, monsieur; and, good monsieur,
have a care the honey bag break not. I would be loath
to have you overflown with a honey bag, signor.
                            [Exit Cobweb.]

    Where's Monsieur Mustardseed?
MUSTARDSEED   Ready.

BOTTOM   Give me your neaf, Monsieur Mustardseed. 19
    Pray you, leave your courtesy, good monsieur. 20
MUSTARDSEED   What's your will?
BOTTOM   Nothing, good monsieur, but to help Cavalery 22
Cobweb to scratch. I must to the barber's, monsieur, 23
for methinks I am marvelous hairy about the face; and
I am such a tender ass, if my hair do but tickle me I
must scratch.
TITANIA
    What, wilt thou hear some music, my sweet love?
BOTTOM   I have a reasonable good ear in music. Let's
have the tongs and the bones. 29
                      [Music: tongs, rural music.]
TITANIA
    Or say, sweet love, what thou desirest to eat.
BOTTOM   Truly, a peck of provender. I could munch 31
your good dry oats. Methinks I have a great desire to
a bottle of hay. Good hay, sweet hay, hath no fellow. 33
TITANIA
    I have a venturous fairy that shall seek
    The squirrel's hoard, and fetch thee new nuts.
BOTTOM   I had rather have a handful or two of dried
peas. But, I pray you, let none of your people stir me. 37
I have an exposition of sleep come upon me. 38
TITANIA
    Sleep thou, and I will wind thee in my arms.—
    Fairies, begone, and be all ways away. 40
                           [Exeunt Fairies.]
    So doth the woodbine the sweet honeysuckle 41
    Gently entwist; the female ivy so
    Enrings the barky fingers of the elm.
    Oh, how I love thee! How I dote on thee!
                           [They sleep.]

    Enter Robin Goodfellow [Puck].

OBERON *[coming forward]*
    Welcome, good Robin. See'st thou this sweet sight?
    Her dotage now I do begin to pity.
    For, meeting her of late behind the wood
    Seeking sweet favors for this hateful fool, 48
    I did upbraid her and fall out with her.
    For she his hairy temples then had rounded
    With coronet of fresh and fragrant flowers;
    And that same dew, which sometime on the buds 52
    Was wont to swell like round and orient pearls, 53
    Stood now within the pretty flowerets' eyes
    Like tears that did their own disgrace bewail.
    When I had at my pleasure taunted her,

---

461 Jack shall have Jill (Proverbial for "boy gets girl.")
4.1. Location: The action is continuous. The four lovers are still
asleep onstage. (Compare with the Folio stage direction: *"They sleep
all the act."*)
2 amiable lovely. **coy** caress

19 neaf fist **20 leave your courtesy** i.e., stop bowing, or put on your
hat **22 Cavalery** Cavalier. (Form of address for a gentleman.)
23 Cobweb (Seemingly an error, since Cobweb has been sent to bring
honey, while Peaseblossom has been asked to scratch.) **29 tongs . . .
bones** instruments for rustic music. (The tongs were played like a triangle, whereas the bones were held between the fingers and used as
clappers.) **29.1** *Music . . . music* (This stage direction is added from
the Folio.) **31 peck of provender** one-quarter bushel of grain.
33 bottle bundle. **fellow** equal. **37 stir** disturb **38 exposition of**
(Bottom's phrase for "disposition to.") **40 all ways** in all directions
41 woodbine bindweed, a climbing plant **48 favors** i.e., gifts of
flowers **52 sometime** formerly **53 orient** lustrous

And she in mild terms begged my patience,
I then did ask of her her changeling child,
Which straight she gave me, and her fairy sent
To bear him to my bower in Fairyland.
And, now I have the boy, I will undo
This hateful imperfection of her eyes.
And, gentle Puck, take this transformèd scalp
From off the head of this Athenian swain,
That he, awaking when the other do,   65
May all to Athens back again repair,   66
And think no more of this night's accidents
But as the fierce vexation of a dream.
But first I will release the Fairy Queen.
                    [*He squeezes an herb on her eyes.*]
    Be as thou wast wont to be;
    See as thou wast wont to see.
    Dian's bud o'er Cupid's flower   72
    Hath such force and blessèd power.
Now, my Titania, wake you, my sweet queen.

TITANIA [*awaking*]
My Oberon! What visions have I seen!
Methought I was enamored of an ass.

OBERON
There lies your love.

TITANIA   How came these things to pass?
Oh, how mine eyes do loathe his visage now!

OBERON
Silence awhile. Robin, take off this head.
Titania, music call, and strike more dead
Than common sleep of all these five the sense.   81

TITANIA
Music, ho! Music, such as charmeth sleep!   [*Music.*]   82

PUCK [*removing the ass head*]
Now, when thou wak'st, with thine own fool's eyes
    peep.

OBERON
Sound, music! Come, my queen, take hands with me,
And rock the ground whereon these sleepers be.
                    [*They dance.*]
Now thou and I are new in amity,
And will tomorrow midnight solemnly   87
Dance in Duke Theseus' house triumphantly,
And bless it to all fair prosperity.
There shall the pairs of faithful lovers be
Wedded, with Theseus, all in jollity.

PUCK
    Fairy King, attend, and mark:
    I do hear the morning lark.

OBERON
    Then, my queen, in silence sad,   94
    Trip we after night's shade.
    We the globe can compass soon,
    Swifter than the wand'ring moon.

TITANIA
Come, my lord, and in our flight
Tell me how it came this night
That I sleeping here was found
With these mortals on the ground.
          Exeunt [*Oberon, Titania, and Puck*].
          Wind horn [*within*].

    Enter Theseus and all his train; [*Hippolyta,*
Egeus].

THESEUS
Go, one of you, find out the forester,
For now our observation is performed;   103
And since we have the vaward of the day,   104
My love shall hear the music of my hounds.
Uncouple in the western valley; let them go.   106
Dispatch, I say, and find the forester.
               [*Exit an Attendant.*]
We will, fair queen, up to the mountain's top
And mark the musical confusion
Of hounds and echo in conjunction.

HIPPOLYTA
I was with Hercules and Cadmus once   111
When in a wood of Crete they bayed the bear   112
With hounds of Sparta. Never did I hear   113
Such gallant chiding; for, besides the groves,   114
The skies, the fountains, every region near
Seemed all one mutual cry. I never heard
So musical a discord, such sweet thunder.

THESEUS
My hounds are bred out of the Spartan kind,   118
So flewed, so sanded; and their heads are hung   119
With ears that sweep away the morning dew;
Crook-kneed, and dewlapped like Thessalian bulls;   121
Slow in pursuit, but matched in mouth like bells,   122
Each under each. A cry more tunable   123
Was never holloed to nor cheered with horn   124
In Crete, in Sparta, nor in Thessaly.
Judge when you hear. [*He sees the sleepers.*] But soft!
    What nymphs are these?   126

EGEUS
My lord, this is my daughter here asleep,
And this Lysander; this Demetrius is;
This Helena, old Nedar's Helena.
I wonder of their being here together.   130

THESEUS
No doubt they rose up early to observe
The rite of May, and hearing our intent,

---

65 **other** others 66 **repair** return 72 **Dian's bud** (Perhaps the flower of the *agnus castus* or chaste-tree, supposed to preserve chastity; or perhaps referring simply to Oberon's herb by which he can undo the effects of "Cupid's flower," the love-in-idleness of 2.1.166–8.)
81 **these five** i.e., the four lovers and Bottom 82 **charmeth** brings about, as though by a charm 87 **solemnly** ceremoniously
94 **sad** solemn

103 **observation** i.e., observance to a morn of May (1.1.167)
104 **vaward** vanguard, i.e., earliest part 106 **Uncouple** Set free for the hunt 111 **Cadmus** mythical founder of Thebes. (This story about him is unknown.) 112 **bayed** brought to bay 113 **hounds of Sparta** (A breed famous in antiquity for their hunting skill.) 114 **chiding** i.e., yelping 118 **kind** strain, breed 119 **So flewed** similarly having large hanging chaps or fleshy covering of the jaw. **sanded** of sandy color 121 **dewlapped** having pendulous folds of skin under the neck. **Thessalian** from Thessaly, in Greece 122–3 **matched . . . each** i.e., harmoniously matched in their various cries like a set of bells, from treble down to bass. 123 **cry** pack of hounds. **tunable** well tuned, melodious 124 **cheered** encouraged 126 **soft** i.e., gently, wait a minute. 130 **of** at

Came here in grace of our solemnity.   133
But speak, Egeus. Is not this the day
That Hermia should give answer of her choice?

EGEUS   It is, my lord.

THESEUS
Go bid the huntsmen wake them with their horns.

                                        [*Exit an Attendant.*]

            Shout within. Wind horns. They all start up.

Good morrow, friends. Saint Valentine is past.   138
Begin these woodbirds but to couple now?

LYSANDER
Pardon, my lord.   [*They kneel.*]

THESEUS   I pray you all, stand up.

                                              [*They stand.*]

I know you two are rival enemies;
How comes this gentle concord in the world,
That hatred is so far from jealousy
To sleep by hate and fear no enmity?

LYSANDER
My lord, I shall reply amazedly,
Half sleep, half waking; but as yet, I swear,
I cannot truly say how I came here.
But, as I think—for truly would I speak,
And now I do bethink me, so it is—
I came with Hermia hither. Our intent
Was to be gone from Athens, where we might,
Without the peril of the Athenian law—

EGEUS
Enough, enough, my lord; you have enough.
I beg the law, the law, upon his head.
They would have stol'n away; they would, Demetrius,
Thereby to have defeated you and me,
You of your wife and me of my consent,
Of my consent that she should be your wife.

DEMETRIUS
My lord, fair Helen told me of their stealth,
Of this their purpose hither to this wood,
And I in fury hither followed them,
Fair Helena in fancy following me.   162
But, my good lord, I wot not by what power—
But by some power it is—my love to Hermia,
Melted as the snow, seems to me now
As the remembrance of an idle gaud   166
Which in my childhood I did dote upon;
And all the faith, the virtue of my heart,
The object and the pleasure of mine eye,
Is only Helena. To her, my lord,
Was I betrothed ere I saw Hermia,
But like a sickness did I loathe this food;
But, as in health, come to my natural taste,
Now I do wish it, love it, long for it,
And will forevermore be true to it.

THESEUS
Fair lovers, you are fortunately met.
Of this discourse we more will hear anon.

Egeus, I will overbear your will;
For in the temple, by and by, with us
These couples shall eternally be knit.
And, for the morning now is something worn,   181
Our purposed hunting shall be set aside.
Away with us to Athens. Three and three,
We'll hold a feast in great solemnity.   184
Come, Hippolyta.
            [*Exeunt Theseus, Hippolyta, Egeus, and train.*]

DEMETRIUS
These things seem small and undistinguishable,
Like far-off mountains turnèd into clouds.

HERMIA
Methinks I see these things with parted eye,   188
When everything seems double.

HELENA   So methinks;
And I have found Demetrius like a jewel,   190
Mine own, and not mine own.

DEMETRIUS   Are you sure   191
That we are awake? It seems to me
That yet we sleep, we dream. Do not you think
The Duke was here, and bid us follow him?

HERMIA
Yea, and my father.

HELENA   And Hippolyta.

LYSANDER
And he did bid us follow to the temple.

DEMETRIUS
Why, then, we are awake. Let's follow him,
And by the way let us recount our dreams.

                                        [*Exeunt the lovers.*]

BOTTOM [*awaking*]   When my cue comes, call me, and I
will answer. My next is "Most fair Pyramus." Heigh-
ho! Peter Quince! Flute, the bellows mender! Snout,
the tinker! Starveling! God's my life, stolen hence and   202
left me asleep! I have had a most rare vision. I have
had a dream, past the wit of man to say what dream
it was. Man is but an ass if he go about to expound this   205
dream. Methought I was—there is no man can tell
what. Methought I was—and methought I had—but
man is but a patched fool if he will offer to say what   208
methought I had. The eye of man hath not heard, the   209
ear of man hath not seen, man's hand is not able to   210
taste, his tongue to conceive, nor his heart to report,   211
what my dream was. I will get Peter Quince to write
a ballad of this dream. It shall be called "Bottom's   213
Dream," because it hath no bottom; and I will sing it   214
in the latter end of a play, before the Duke. Peradventure, to make it the more gracious, I shall sing it at her 216
death.   [*Exit.*]

---

133 **in . . . solemnity** in honor of our wedding ceremony. 138 **Saint Valentine** (Birds were supposed to choose their mates on Saint Valentine's Day.) 162 **in fancy** driven by love 166 **idle gaud** worthless trinket

181 **for** since. **something** somewhat 184 **in great solemnity** with great ceremony. 188 **parted** i.e., improperly focused 190–1 **like . . . own** i.e., something precious that seems mine and yet so mysteriously found that I can hardly believe it is mine. 202 **God's** May God save 205 **go about** attempt 208 **patched** wearing motley, i.e., a dress of various colors. **offer** venture 209–11 **The eye . . . report** (Bottom garbles 1 Corinthians 2:9.) 213 **ballad** (The proper medium for relating sensational stories and preposterous events.) 214 **hath no bottom** is unfathomable 216 **her** Thisbe's (?)

[4.2]

Enter Quince, Flute, [Snout, and Starveling].

QUINCE   Have you sent to Bottom's house? Is he come home yet?

STARVELING   He cannot be heard of. Out of doubt he is transported.   4

FLUTE   If he come not, then the play is marred. It goes not forward. Doth it?

QUINCE   It is not possible. You have not a man in all Athens able to discharge Pyramus but he.   8

FLUTE   No, he hath simply the best wit of any handicraft   9
man in Athens.

QUINCE   Yea, and the best person too, and he is a very   11
paramour for a sweet voice.

FLUTE   You must say "paragon." A paramour is, God bless us, a thing of naught.   14

Enter Snug the joiner.

SNUG   Masters, the Duke is coming from the temple, and there is two or three lords and ladies more married. If our sport had gone forward, we had all   17
been made men.   18

FLUTE   Oh, sweet bully Bottom! Thus hath he lost sixpence a day during his life; he could not have   20
scaped sixpence a day. An the Duke had not given him sixpence a day for playing Pyramus, I'll be hanged. He would have deserved it. Sixpence a day in Pyramus, or nothing.

Enter Bottom.

BOTTOM   Where are these lads? Where are these hearts?   25

QUINCE   Bottom! Oh, most courageous day! Oh, most happy hour!

BOTTOM   Masters, I am to discourse wonders. But ask   28
me not what; for if I tell you, I am no true Athenian. I will tell you everything, right as it fell out.

QUINCE   Let us hear, sweet Bottom.

BOTTOM   Not a word of me. All that I will tell you is that   32
the Duke hath dined. Get your apparel together, good strings to your beards, new ribbons to your   34
pumps; meet presently at the palace; every man look   35
o'er his part; for the short and the long is, our play is preferred. In any case, let Thisbe have clean linen; and   37
let not him that plays the lion pare his nails, for they shall hang out for the lion's claws. And, most dear actors, eat no onions nor garlic, for we are to utter sweet breath; and I do not doubt but to hear them say it is a sweet comedy. No more words. Away! Go, away!
    [Exeunt.]

❧

4.2. Location: Athens.
4 **transported** carried off by fairies; or, transformed.   **8 discharge** perform   **9 wit** intellect   **11 person** appearance   **14 a . . . naught** a shameful thing   **17–18 we . . . men** i.e., we would have had our fortunes made.   **20 sixpence a day** i.e., as a royal pension   **25 hearts** good fellows.   **28 am . . . wonders** have wonders to relate.   **32 of** out of   **34 strings** (to attach the beards)   **35 pumps** light shoes or slippers   **37 preferred** selected for consideration.

[5.1]

Enter Theseus, Hippolyta, and Philostrate,
[lords, and attendants].

HIPPOLYTA
'Tis strange, my Theseus, that these lovers speak of.   1

THESEUS
More strange than true. I never may believe   2
These antique fables nor these fairy toys.   3
Lovers and madmen have such seething brains,
Such shaping fantasies, that apprehend   5
More than cool reason ever comprehends.   6
The lunatic, the lover, and the poet
Are of imagination all compact.   8
One sees more devils than vast hell can hold;
That is the madman. The lover, all as frantic,
Sees Helen's beauty in a brow of Egypt.   11
The poet's eye, in a fine frenzy rolling,
Doth glance from heaven to earth, from earth to
    heaven;
And as imagination bodies forth
The forms of things unknown, the poet's pen
Turns them to shapes and gives to airy nothing
A local habitation and a name.
Such tricks hath strong imagination
That, if it would but apprehend some joy,
It comprehends some bringer of that joy;   20
Or in the night, imagining some fear,   21
How easy is a bush supposed a bear!

HIPPOLYTA
But all the story of the night told over,
And all their minds transfigured so together,
More witnesseth than fancy's images   25
And grows to something of great constancy;   26
But, howsoever, strange and admirable.   27

Enter lovers: Lysander, Demetrius, Hermia,
and Helena.

THESEUS
Here come the lovers, full of joy and mirth.
Joy, gentle friends! Joy and fresh days of love
Accompany your hearts!

LYSANDER   More than to us
Wait in your royal walks, your board, your bed!

THESEUS
Come now, what masques, what dances shall we
    have,   32
To wear away this long age of three hours
Between our after-supper and bedtime?
Where is our usual manager of mirth?

5.1. Location: Athens. The palace of Theseus.
1 that that which   **2 may** can   **3 antique** old-fashioned. (Punning, too, on *antic*, "strange," "grotesque.")   **fairy toys** trifling stories about fairies.   **5 fantasies** imaginations.   **apprehend** conceive, imagine   **6 comprehends** understands.   **8 compact** formed, composed.   **11 Helen's** i.e., of Helen of Troy, pattern of beauty.   **brow of Egypt** i.e., face of a gypsy.   **20 bringer** i.e., source   **21 fear** object of fear   **25 More . . . images** testifies to something more substantial than mere imaginings   **26 constancy** certainty   **27 howsoever** in any case.   **admirable** a source of wonder.   **32 masques** courtly entertainments

What revels are in hand? Is there no play
To ease the anguish of a torturing hour?
Call Philostrate.
PHILOSTRATE   Here, mighty Theseus.
THESEUS
Say, what abridgment have you for this evening?   39
What masque? What music? How shall we beguile
The lazy time, if not with some delight?
PHILOSTRATE [*giving him a paper*]
There is a brief how many sports are ripe.   42
Make choice of which Your Highness will see first.
THESEUS [*reads*]
"The battle with the Centaurs, to be sung   44
By an Athenian eunuch to the harp"?
We'll none of that. That have I told my love,
In glory of my kinsman Hercules.   47
[*He reads.*] "The riot of the tipsy Bacchanals,   48
Tearing the Thracian singer in their rage"?   49
That is an old device; and it was played   50
When I from Thebes came last a conqueror.
[*He reads.*] "The thrice three Muses mourning for the
death   52
Of Learning, late deceased in beggary"?   53
That is some satire, keen and critical,
Not sorting with a nuptial ceremony.   55
[*He reads.*] "A tedious brief scene of young Pyramus
And his love Thisbe; very tragical mirth"?
Merry and tragical? Tedious and brief?
That is, hot ice and wondrous strange snow.   59
How shall we find the concord of this discord?
PHILOSTRATE
A play there is, my lord, some ten words long,
Which is as brief as I have known a play;
But by ten words, my lord, it is too long,
Which makes it tedious. For in all the play
There is not one word apt, one player fitted.
And tragical, my noble lord, it is,
For Pyramus therein doth kill himself.
Which, when I saw rehearsed, I must confess,
Made mine eyes water; but more merry tears
The passion of loud laughter never shed.
THESEUS   What are they that do play it?
PHILOSTRATE
Hardhanded men that work in Athens here,
Which never labored in their minds till now,
And now have toiled their unbreathed memories   74

With this same play, against your nuptial.   75
THESEUS
And we will hear it.
PHILOSTRATE   No, my noble lord,
It is not for you. I have heard it over,
And it is nothing, nothing in the world;
Unless you can find sport in their intents,
Extremely stretched and conned with cruel pain   80
To do you service.
THESEUS   I will hear that play;
For never anything can be amiss
When simpleness and duty tender it.
Go, bring them in; and take your places, ladies.
          [*Philostrate goes to summon the players.*]
HIPPOLYTA
I love not to see wretchedness o'ercharged,   85
And duty in his service perishing.   86
THESEUS
Why, gentle sweet, you shall see no such thing.
HIPPOLYTA
He says they can do nothing in this kind.   88
THESEUS
The kinder we, to give them thanks for nothing.
Our sport shall be to take what they mistake;
And what poor duty cannot do, noble respect   91
Takes it in might, not merit.   92
Where I have come, great clerks have purposèd   93
To greet me with premeditated welcomes;
Where I have seen them shiver and look pale,
Make periods in the midst of sentences,
Throttle their practiced accent in their fears,   97
And in conclusion dumbly have broke off,
Not paying me a welcome. Trust me, sweet,
Out of this silence yet I picked a welcome;
And in the modesty of fearful duty
I read as much as from the rattling tongue
Of saucy and audacious eloquence.
Love, therefore, and tongue-tied simplicity
In least speak most, to my capacity.   105

          [*Philostrate returns.*]

PHILOSTRATE
So please Your Grace, the Prologue is addressed.   106
THESEUS   Let him approach.   [*A flourish of trumpets.*]

          Enter the Prologue [*Quince*].

PROLOGUE
If we offend, it is with our good will.
     That you should think, we come not to offend,
But with good will. To show our simple skill,
     That is the true beginning of our end.

39 abridgment pastime (to abridge or shorten the evening)
42 brief summary   **44 battle . . . Centaurs** (Probably refers to the battle of the Centaurs and the Lapithae, when the Centaurs attempted to
carry off Hippodamia, bride of Theseus's friend Pirothous. The story
is told in Ovid's *Metamorphoses* 12.)   **47 kinsman** (Plutarch's "Life of
Theseus" states that Hercules and Theseus were near kinsmen. Theseus is referring to a version of the battle of the Centaurs in which
Hercules was said to be present.)   **48–9 The riot . . . rage** (This was
the story of the death of Orpheus, as told in *Metamorphoses* 11.)
50 device show, performance   **52–3 The thrice . . . beggary** (Possibly
an allusion to Spenser's *Teares of the Muses*, 1591, though "satires"
deploring the neglect of learning and the creative arts were commonplace.)   **55 sorting with** befitting   **59 strange** (Sometimes emended
to an adjective that would contrast with *snow*, just as *hot* contrasts
with *ice*.)   **74 toiled** taxed.   **unbreathed** unexercised

75 against in preparation for   **80 conned** memorized   **85 wretchedness o'ercharged** social or intellectual inferiority overburdened
86 his service its attempt to serve   **88 kind** kind of thing.
91–2 noble . . . merit noble consideration values it for the effort made
rather than for the actual worth.   **93 clerks** learned men   **97 practiced accent** i.e., rehearsed speech; or, usual way of speaking
105 least i.e., saying least.   **to my capacity** in my judgment and
understanding.   **106 Prologue** speaker of the prologue.   **addressed**
ready.

Consider, then, we come but in despite.
    We do not come, as minding to content you,   113
Our true intent is. All for your delight
    We are not here. That you should here repent you,
The actors are at hand; and, by their show,
You shall know all that you are like to know.

THESEUS   This fellow doth not stand upon points.   118

LYSANDER   He hath rid his prologue like a rough colt; he   119
knows not the stop. A good moral, my lord: it is not   120
enough to speak, but to speak true.

HIPPOLYTA   Indeed, he hath played on his prologue like
a child on a recorder: a sound, but not in government.   123

THESEUS   His speech was like a tangled chain: nothing   124
impaired, but all disordered. Who is next?

    Enter Pyramus [Bottom], and Thisbe [Flute],
    and Wall [Snout], and Moonshine [Starveling],
    and Lion [Snug].

PROLOGUE
Gentles, perchance you wonder at this show;
    But wonder on, till truth make all things plain.
This man is Pyramus, if you would know;
    This beauteous lady Thisbe is, certain.
This man with lime and roughcast doth present
    Wall, that vile wall which did these lovers sunder;
And through Wall's chink, poor souls, they are content
    To whisper. At the which let no man wonder.
This man with lantern, dog, and bush of thorn
    Presenteth Moonshine; for, if you will know,
By moonshine did these lovers think no scorn   136
    To meet at Ninus' tomb, there, there to woo.
This grisly beast, which Lion hight by name,   138
The trusty Thisbe coming first by night
Did scare away, or rather did affright;
And as she fled, her mantle she did fall,   141
    Which Lion vile with bloody mouth did stain.
Anon comes Pyramus, sweet youth and tall,   143
    And finds his trusty Thisbe's mantle slain;
Whereat, with blade, with bloody, blameful blade,
    He bravely broached his boiling bloody breast.   146
And Thisbe, tarrying in mulberry shade,
    His dagger drew, and died. For all the rest,
Let Lion, Moonshine, Wall, and lovers twain
At large discourse, while here they do remain.   150
    Exeunt Lion, Thisbe, and Moonshine.

THESEUS   I wonder if the lion be to speak.

DEMETRIUS   No wonder, my lord. One lion may, when
many asses do.

WALL
In this same interlude it doth befall   154
That I, one Snout by name, present a wall;
And such a wall as I would have you think

That had in it a crannied hole or chink,
Through which the lovers, Pyramus and Thisbe,
Did whisper often, very secretly.
This loam, this roughcast, and this stone doth show
That I am that same wall; the truth is so.
And this the cranny is, right and sinister,   162
Through which the fearful lovers are to whisper.

THESEUS   Would you desire lime and hair to speak
better?

DEMETRIUS   It is the wittiest partition that ever I heard   166
discourse, my lord.

    [Pyramus comes forward.]

THESEUS   Pyramus draws near the wall. Silence!

PYRAMUS
O grim-looked night! O night with hue so black!   169
    O night, which ever art when day is not!
O night, O night! Alack, alack, alack,
    I fear my Thisbe's promise is forgot.
And thou, O wall, O sweet, O lovely wall,
    That stand'st between her father's ground and
    mine,
Thou wall, O wall, O sweet and lovely wall,
    Show me thy chink, to blink through with mine
    eyne.   *[Wall makes a chink with his fingers.]*
Thanks, courteous wall. Jove shield thee well for
    this.
    But what see I? No Thisbe do I see.
O wicked wall, through whom I see no bliss!
    Cursed be thy stones for thus deceiving me!

THESEUS   The wall, methinks, being sensible, should   181
curse again.   182

PYRAMUS   No, in truth, sir, he should not. "Deceiving
me" is Thisbe's cue: she is to enter now, and I am to
spy her through the wall. You shall see, it will fall pat   185
as I told you. Yonder she comes.

    Enter Thisbe.

THISBE
O wall, full often hast thou heard my moans
    For parting my fair Pyramus and me.
My cherry lips have often kissed thy stones,
    Thy stones with lime and hair knit up in thee.

PYRAMUS
I see a voice. Now will I to the chink,
    To spy an I can hear my Thisbe's face.   192
Thisbe!

THISBE   My love! Thou art my love, I think.

PYRAMUS
    Think what thou wilt, I am thy lover's grace,   194
And like Limander am I trusty still.   195

THISBE
And I like Helen, till the Fates me kill.   196

---

113 minding intending   **118 stand upon points** (1) heed niceties or small points (2) pay attention to punctuation in his reading. (The humor of Quince's speech is in the blunders of its punctuation.) **119 rid** ridden.   **rough** unbroken   **120 stop** (1) stopping of a colt by reining it in (2) punctuation mark.   **123 recorder** wind instrument like a flute.   **government** control.   **124 nothing** not at all   **136 think no scorn** think it no disgraceful matter   **138 hight** is called   **141 fall** let fall   **143 tall** courageous   **146 broached** stabbed   **150 At large** in full, at length   **154 interlude** play

162 right and sinister from right to left   **166 partition** (1) wall (2) section of a learned treatise or oration   **169 grim-looked** grim-looking   **181 sensible** capable of feeling   **182 again** in return.   **185 pat** exactly   **192 an** if   **194 lover's grace** i.e., gracious lover   **195, 196 Limander, Helen** (Blunders for "Leander" and "Hero.")

PYRAMUS
Not Shafalus to Procrus was so true.   197
THISBE
As Shafalus to Procrus, I to you.
PYRAMUS
Oh, kiss me through the hole of this vile wall!
THISBE
I kiss the wall's hole, not your lips at all.
PYRAMUS
Wilt thou at Ninny's tomb meet me straightway?
THISBE
'Tide life, 'tide death, I come without delay.   202
                        [*Exeunt Pyramus and Thisbe.*]
WALL
Thus have I, Wall, my part dischargèd so;
And, being done, thus Wall away doth go.   [*Exit.*]
THESEUS   Now is the mural down between the two
    neighbors.
DEMETRIUS   No remedy, my lord, when walls are so
    willful to hear without warning.   208
HIPPOLYTA   This is the silliest stuff that ever I heard.
THESEUS   The best in this kind are but shadows; and the   210
    worst are no worse, if imagination amend them.
HIPPOLYTA   It must be your imagination then, and not
    theirs.
THESEUS   If we imagine no worse of them than they of
    themselves, they may pass for excellent men. Here
    come two noble beasts in, a man and a lion.

                    Enter Lion and Moonshine.

LION
You, ladies, you, whose gentle hearts do fear
    The smallest monstrous mouse that creeps on
        floor,
May now perchance both quake and tremble here,
    When lion rough in wildest rage doth roar.
Then know that I, as Snug the joiner, am   221
A lion fell, nor else no lion's dam;   222
For, if I should as lion come in strife
Into this place, 'twere pity on my life.
THESEUS   A very gentle beast, and of a good conscience.
DEMETRIUS   The very best at a beast, my lord, that e'er I
    saw.
LYSANDER   This lion is a very fox for his valor.   228
THESEUS   True; and a goose for his discretion.   229
DEMETRIUS   Not so, my lord, for his valor cannot carry
    his discretion, and the fox carries the goose.
THESEUS   His discretion, I am sure, cannot carry his
    valor; for the goose carries not the fox. It is well. Leave
    it to his discretion, and let us listen to the moon.

MOON
This lanthorn doth the hornèd moon present—   235
DEMETRIUS   He should have worn the horns on his   236
    head.   237
THESEUS   He is no crescent, and his horns are invisible   238
    within the circumference.
MOON
This lanthorn doth the hornèd moon present;
Myself the man i'th' moon do seem to be.
THESEUS   This is the greatest error of all the rest. The
    man should be put into the lanthorn. How is it else the
    man i'th' moon?
DEMETRIUS   He dares not come there for the candle, for   245
    you see it is already in snuff.   246
HIPPOLYTA   I am aweary of this moon. Would he would
    change!
THESEUS   It appears, by his small light of discretion, that
    he is in the wane; but yet, in courtesy, in all reason, we
    must stay the time.
LYSANDER   Proceed, Moon.
MOON   All that I have to say is to tell you that the lan-
    thorn is the moon, I, the man i'th' moon, this thorn-
    bush my thornbush, and this dog my dog.
DEMETRIUS   Why, all these should be in the lanthorn,
    for all these are in the moon. But silence! Here comes
    Thisbe.

                    Enter Thisbe.

THISBE
This is old Ninny's tomb. Where is my love?
LION [*roaring*]   Oh!
DEMETRIUS   Well roared, Lion.
                    [*Thisbe runs off, dropping her mantle.*]
THESEUS   Well run, Thisbe.
HIPPOLYTA   Well shone, Moon. Truly, the moon shines
    with a good grace.
                    [*The Lion worries Thisbe's mantle.*]
THESEUS   Well moused, Lion.   265

        Enter Pyramus.   [*Exit Lion.*]

DEMETRIUS   And then came Pyramus.
LYSANDER   And so the lion vanished.
PYRAMUS
Sweet Moon, I thank thee for thy sunny beams;
    I thank thee, Moon, for shining now so bright;
For, by thy gracious, golden, glittering gleams,
    I trust to take of truest Thisbe sight.
        But stay, oh, spite!
        But mark, poor knight,
    What dreadful dole is here?   274
        Eyes, do you see?
        How can it be?

---

197 **Shafalus, Procrus** (Blunders for "Cephalus" and "Procris," also famous lovers.)   202 **'Tide** Betide, come   208 **willful** willing.   **without warning** i.e., without warning the parents. (Demetrius makes a joke on the proverb "Walls have ears.")   210 **in this kind** of this sort. **shadows** likenesses, representations   221–2 **am . . . dam** enact the part of a fierce lion, but otherwise am not really a lion. (*Dam* means "mother"; in Shakespeare's source the beast is a lioness.)
228 **is . . . valor** i.e., his valor consists of craftiness and discretion.
229 **a goose . . . discretion** i.e., as discreet as a goose, that is, more foolish than discreet.

---

235 **lanthorn** (This original spelling, "lanthorne," may suggest a play on the *horn* of which lanterns were made and also on a cuckold's horns; however, the spelling "lanthorne" is not used consistently for comic effect in this play or elsewhere. At 5.1.134, for example, the word is "lanterne" in the original.)   236–7 **on his head** (As a sign of cuckoldry.)   238 **crescent** a waxing moon   245 **for** because of, for fear of   246 **in snuff** (1) offended (2) in need of snuffing or trimming.
265 **moused** shaken, torn, bitten   274 **dole** grievous event

   Oh, dainty duck! Oh, dear!
    Thy mantle good,
    What, stained with blood?
   Approach, ye Furies fell!   280
    O Fates, come, come,   281
    Cut thread and thrum;   282
   Quail, crush, conclude, and quell!   283

THESEUS This passion, and the death of a dear friend, 284
  would go near to make a man look sad. 285

HIPPOLYTA Beshrew my heart, but I pity the man. 286

PYRAMUS
  Oh, wherefore, Nature, didst thou lions frame? 287
  Since lion vile hath here deflowered my dear,
  Which is—no, no, which was—the fairest dame
  That lived, that loved, that liked, that looked with
    cheer.   290
    Come, tears, confound,
    Out, sword, and wound
  The pap of Pyramus;   293
    Ay, that left pap,
    Where heart doth hop. [*He stabs himself.*]
  Thus die I, thus, thus, thus.
    Now am I dead,
    Now am I fled;
  My soul is in the sky.
    Tongue, lose thy light;
    Moon, take thy flight. [*Exit Moonshine.*]
  Now die, die, die, die, die. [*Pyramus dies.*]

DEMETRIUS No die, but an ace, for him; for he is 303
  but one.   304

LYSANDER Less than an ace, man; for he is dead, he is
  nothing.

THESEUS With the help of a surgeon he might yet
  recover, and yet prove an ass.   308

HIPPOLYTA How chance Moonshine is gone before
  Thisbe comes back and finds her lover?

THESEUS She will find him by starlight.

   [*Enter Thisbe.*]

  Here she comes; and her passion ends the play.

HIPPOLYTA Methinks she should not use a long one for
  such a Pyramus. I hope she will be brief.

DEMETRIUS A mote will turn the balance, which Pyra- 315
  mus which Thisbe, is the better: he for a man, God 316
  warrant us; she for a woman, God bless us.

LYSANDER She hath spied him already with those sweet
  eyes.

DEMETRIUS And thus she means, videlicet: 320
THISBE
   Asleep, my love?
    What, dead, my dove?
  O Pyramus, arise!
   Speak, speak. Quite dumb?
   Dead, dead? A tomb
  Must cover thy sweet eyes.
    These lily lips,
    This cherry nose,
  These yellow cowslip cheeks,
    Are gone, are gone!
    Lovers, make moan.
  His eyes were green as leeks.
    O Sisters Three,   333
    Come, come to me,
  With hands as pale as milk;
    Lay them in gore,
    Since you have shore   337
  With shears his thread of silk.
    Tongue, not a word.
    Come, trusty sword,
  Come, blade, my breast imbrue! 341
        [*She stabs herself.*]
    And farewell, friends.
    Thus Thisbe ends.
   Adieu, adieu, adieu.   [*She dies.*]

THESEUS Moonshine and Lion are left to bury the dead.
DEMETRIUS Ay, and Wall too.
BOTTOM [*starting up, as Flute does also*] No, I assure you,
  the wall is down that parted their fathers. Will it please
  you to see the epilogue, or to hear a Bergomask dance 349
  between two of our company?

   [*The other players enter.*]

THESEUS No epilogue, I pray you; for your play needs
  no excuse. Never excuse; for when the players are all
  dead, there need none to be blamed. Marry, if he that
  writ it had played Pyramus and hanged himself in
  Thisbe's garter, it would have been a fine tragedy; and
  so it is, truly, and very notably discharged. But, come,
  your Bergomask. Let your epilogue alone. [*A dance.*]
  The iron tongue of midnight hath told twelve. 358
  Lovers, to bed, 'tis almost fairy time.
  I fear we shall outsleep the coming morn
  As much as we this night have overwatched. 361
  This palpable-gross play hath well beguiled 362
  The heavy gait of night. Sweet friends, to bed. 363
  A fortnight hold we this solemnity,
  In nightly revels and new jollity. [*Exeunt.*]

   Enter Puck [*carrying a broom*].

---

280 **Furies fell** fierce avenging goddesses of Greek myth. 281 **Fates** the three goddesses (Clotho, Lachesis, Atropos) of Greek myth who spun, drew, and cut the thread of human life 282 **thread and thrum** i.e., everything—the good and bad alike; literally, the warp in weaving and the loose end of the warp 283 **Quail** overpower. **quell** kill, destroy. 284–5 **This . . . sad** i.e., If one had other reason to grieve, one might be sad, but not from this absurd portrayal of passion. 286 **Beshrew** Curse. (A mild curse.) 287 **frame** create. 290 **cheer** countenance. 293 **pap** breast 303 **ace** the side of the die featuring the single pip, or spot. (The pun is on *die* as a singular of *dice*; Bottom's performance is not worth a whole *die* but rather one single face of it, one small portion.) 304 **one** (1) an individual person (2) unique. 308 **ass** (With a pun on *ace*.) 315 **mote** small particle 315–16 **which . . . which** whether . . . or

320 **means** moans, laments. (With a pun on the meaning, "lodge a formal complaint.") **videlicet** to wit 333 **Sisters Three** the Fates 337 **shore** shorn 341 **imbrue** stain with blood. 349 **Bergomask dance** a rustic dance named from Bergamo, a province in the state of Venice 358 **iron tongue** i.e., of a bell. **told** counted, struck ("tolled") 361 **overwatched** stayed up too late. 362 **palpable-gross** palpably gross, obviously crude 363 **heavy** drowsy, dull

PUCK

Now the hungry lion roars,
   And the wolf behowls the moon,
Whilst the heavy plowman snores,   368
   All with weary task fordone.   369
Now the wasted brands do glow,   370
   Whilst the screech owl, screeching loud,
Puts the wretch that lies in woe
   In remembrance of a shroud.
Now it is the time of night
   That the graves, all gaping wide,
Every one lets forth his sprite,   376
   In the churchway paths to glide.
And we fairies, that do run
   By the triple Hecate's team.   379
From the presence of the sun,
   Following darkness like a dream,
Now are frolic. Not a mouse   382
   Shall disturb this hallowed house.
I am sent with broom before,
To sweep the dust behind the door.   385

Enter [Oberon and Titania,] King and Queen of
Fairies, with all their train.

OBERON

Through the house give glimmering light,
   By the dead and drowsy fire;
Every elf and fairy sprite
   Hop as light as bird from brier;
And this ditty, after me,
Sing, and dance it trippingly.

TITANIA

First, rehearse your song by rote,   392
To each word a warbling note.
Hand in hand, with fairy grace,
Will we sing, and bless this place.

[Song and dance.]

OBERON

Now, until the break of day,
Through this house each fairy stray.
To the best bride-bed will we,
Which by us shall blessèd be;
And the issue there create   400
Ever shall be fortunate.
So shall all the couples three
Ever true in loving be;
And the blots of Nature's hand
Shall not in their issue stand;
Never mole, harelip, nor scar,
Nor mark prodigious, such as are   407
Despisèd in nativity,
Shall upon their children be.
With this field dew consecrate,   410
Every fairy take his gait,   411
And each several chamber bless,   412
Through this palace, with sweet peace;
And the owner of it blest
Ever shall in safety rest.
Trip away; make no stay;
Meet me all by break of day.

Exeunt [Oberon, Titania, and train].

PUCK [*to the audience*]

If we shadows have offended,
Think but this, and all is mended,
That you have but slumbered here   420
While these visions did appear.
And this weak and idle theme,
No more yielding but a dream,   423
Gentles, do not reprehend.
If you pardon, we will mend.   425
And, as I am an honest Puck,
If we have unearnèd luck
Now to scape the serpent's tongue,   428
We will make amends ere long;
Else the Puck a liar call.
So, good night unto you all.
Give me your hands, if we be friends,   432
And Robin shall restore amends.   *[Exit.]* 433

368 **heavy** tired   369 **fordone** exhausted.   370 **wasted brands** burned-out logs   376 **Every . . . sprite** every grave lets forth its ghost 379 **triple Hecate's** (Hecate ruled in three capacities: as Luna or Cynthia in heaven, as Diana on earth, and as Proserpina in hell.) 382 **frolic** merry.   385 **behind** from behind, or else like sweeping the dirt under the carpet. (Robin Goodfellow was a household spirit who helped good housemaids and punished lazy ones, but he could, of course, be mischievous.)   392 **rehearse** recite

400 **issue** offspring. **create** created   407 **prodigious** monstrous, unnatural 410 **consecrate** consecrated 411 **take his gait** go his way 412 **several** separate 420 **That . . . here** i.e., that it is a "midsummer night's dream" 423 **No . . . but** yielding no more than 425 **mend** improve. 428 **serpent's tongue** i.e., hissing 432 **Give . . . hands** Applaud 433 **restore amends** give satisfaction in return.

The Dream on Stage

The Elizabethan Era: In a Public Theater

At their theater in Shoreditch, or in a revival at the Globe, the Lord Chamberlain's Men performed *A Midsummer Night's Dream* with little scenery. Yet the very structure and the performance conventions of an Elizabethan public theater accommodated the needs of this imaginative play. The great posts that supported the roof (with the "heavens" representing the moon and stars painted on its underside) could suggest tree trunks and provide hiding places for Oberon and Puck to observe the action. Titania's bower could have been enclosed near or in the "discovery space," shrouded by the colorful curtain that may have separated it from the stage proper. Quince's actors probably rehearsed their play on the down stage platform, near the yard where less wealthy spectators stood to watch the play. Musicians, sitting perhaps offstage or in their gallery high above the stage, accompanied the fairy dances and roundel. Special effects were possible: flashes of gunpowder may have punctuated entrances by the fairy king and queen, and a cannonball rolled across the floor of the tiring house may have suggested thunder.

The fairies were probably played by boy apprentices. The actor who played Puck was likely an acrobat, his face perhaps covered in wheat-paste for an otherworldly effect. Burbage, the company's leading actor, may have played Oberon, while Will Kempe, a popular comedian whose specialty was coarse word play, portrayed Nick Bottom. If Shakespeare played Peter Quince, as some surmise, the dialogue between the frustrated carpenter-turned-playwright and the pompous Bottom would have produced an especially rich irony among the Lord Chamberlain's Men.

The play's nine scenes flowed seamlessly from one to another; audiences were alerted to shifts in locale—from Theseus's court to Athens Wood—by dialogue and gestures by the actors. The effect is comparable to that of modern film as one scene "cuts" to another as a soundtrack plays.

The Seventeenth, Eighteenth, and Early Nineteenth Centuries: Adaptations, Truncated and Musicalized

Throughout this book you will find many accounts of theater and film artists "reinventing" Shakespeare, a practice that goes back to the later seventeenth century, when his plays were heavily cut, revised, and rewritten to accommodate then contemporary tastes. Because of its fantasy elements, *A Midsummer Night's Dream* has been a particularly popular target for artistic license. The diarist Samuel Pepys, writing less than fifty years after Shakespeare's death, called the adapted, truncated version of the play he saw "insipid" and "ridiculous." In 1692 Henry Purcell wrote music for an operatic version of the play, renamed *The Fairie Queen*, that included such exotic features as a Chinese chorus and dancing monkeys. During the late seventeenth and the eighteenth centuries the play was rarely performed in its entirety, and it was common practice to delete the fifth act with its play-within-the-play. David Garrick, the premier English actor in the eighteenth century, and George Colman, a respected theater manager, both produced truncated versions of *The Dream*, each with the mock tragedy deleted. In 1777, a short piece entitled *A Fairy Tale* was produced in London containing "a few scenes" from *The Dream*; it was remembered by an 1853 reviewer for the *Times* of London as

too insignificant to be styled a reproduction of [*A Midsummer Night's Dream*]. We have seen *A Fairy Tale* and cannot conceive what it was about. The only *dramatis personae* seem to have been the clowns and the fairies, and yet not only the burlesque tragedy, but also the incident of the ass's head was left out.

Frederick Reynolds (1764–1841) adapted many of Shakespeare's comedies, most famously *A Midsummer Night's Dream*, for extravagant spectacles at London's popular Covent Garden Theatre from 1816 to 1828. With music composed by Sir Henry Bishop, Reynolds's adaptations may be best described as "loosely based on a play by Shakespeare," for they were strange amalgams of popular songs, poetry, operatic flights, and pageantry. For almost two hundred years after his death in 1616, Shakespeare's heavily cut *Dream* bore little resemblance to the play he wrote.

The Germans and The Dream

In 1826 Felix Mendelssohn, then only seventeen years old, composed an overture for a Berlin production of *A Midsummer Night's Dream*. Mendelssohn's score, completed in 1843, was among the first to employ themes from the overture as motifs in the incidental music that accompanies the play's action. It beautifully evokes the fairy world as well as that of the mechanicals. Mendelssohn's ingenious *Dream* music provided an orchestral score and ballet music for most European and American productions of the play until Harley Granville-Barker broke with tradition in 1914 (see below). The Max Reinhardt film (1935) retains the famous score and offers contemporary audiences an opportunity to appreciate the music in conjunction with the play.

Ludwig Tieck, a scholar turned theater artist, employed Mendelssohn's score in his admired production of *The Dream* in 1843. Tieck, who had reconstructed (as best he could at the time) London's Fortune Theatre in 1836, adapted many Elizabethan staging conditions—a thrust stage, an elevated playing area behind the forestage—for his innovative production of Shakespeare's comedy. The combination of Mendelssohn's music and Tieck's artistry so pleased German audiences that the production was repeated forty times in the 1843–1844 season and numerous times for the next half-century.

The Dream *from 1840 to World War II*

Madame Elizabeth Vestris and her husband Charles Matthews assumed the artistic leadership of London's Covent Garden Theatre in 1839; among their most admirable projects was the restoration of Shakespeare's texts in performance. (See "Close-up: Madame Lucia

Elizabetta Bartolozzi Vestris," pp. 169–171.) Their staging of *A Midsummer Night's Dream* in 1840 was the first production to restore much of the script since Shakespeare's time. The vogue for historically accurate costuming and scenery had begun two decades earlier with John Philip Kemble's production of *King John*, featuring early medieval costumes and weaponry. In a similar spirit, the Covent Garden production of *A Midsummer Night's Dream* exhibited "authentic" ancient Greek clothing. Madame Vestris played not Hippolyta or Titania, as one might expect, but Oberon; it was considered the best role for a serious (as opposed to comic) actor, and as the company's actor-manager she could assign herself the choice role. Madame Vestris's shapely legs in men's breeches may have sold more than a few extra tickets in this early Victorian age when the mere sight of a woman's ankle was considered risqué. Throughout the Victorian era, actresses not infrequently played both Oberon and Puck.

Mid– and late–nineteenth-century *Dream*s were spectacular affairs, as theater owners and actor-managers competed fiercely to give audiences extraordinary scenic effects. When Charles Kean produced the play at London's Princess's Theatre in October 1855, he plastered the city with playbills promising to recreate ancient Athens in vivid detail, so that audiences might see "the Acropolis on its rocky eminence, surrounded by marble Temples . . . together with the Theater of Bacchus [i.e., Dionysus], wherein multitudes once thronged to listen to the majestic poetry of Aeschylus, Sophocles, and Euripides." Kean was responding to a similarly spectacular production of *The Dream* by Samuel Phelps at Sadler's Wells Theatre two years earlier. News of Phelps's sumptuous production soon reached New York, a city that was then establishing itself as the theater capital of the United States, and by February 1854 two simultaneous productions of the play were enthralling New York audiences. An excerpt from an enthusiastic review suggests the kind of spectacle that accompanied most nineteenth-century productions. Here we can visualize the

> magic change from Theseus' palace to the fairy land. A cloud opens [to reveal] a working sun, within it the first fairy. After it opens, Titania, Oberon, and four fairy children get onto a platform, which is masked by clouds, attached to the sun. Then the sun goes down . . . [as] eight fairies are discovered with garlands in tableau. As the sun goes down, they move with it. The fairies that are on in front . . . pirouette with the principal dancers in center and continue so until the grand tableau is formed.
>
> (*Some Accounts of the Grand Performance at Burton's Theater,* 1854)

Spectacles of this sort culminated in Herbert Beerbohm Tree's production of the play at London's Haymarket Theatre in 1900, featuring scores of children dressed as fairies, a stage strewn with hundreds of pounds of leaves, and live rabbits competing with Shakespeare's words for the audience's attention.

A reaction to such elaborate stagings of *The Dream* came from William Poel's productions for London's Elizabethan Society in the 1890s. Poel dressed the actors in Elizabethan clothing to perform the plays on an approximation of the Globe's stage. In a much-admired 1914 production, Harley Granville-Barker went further as he boldly attempted to restore the play to the realm of the audience's imagination, rather than that of the designers. Instead of creating the illusion of an actual forest onstage, Granville-Barker placed his actors in front of a simple curtain on which was painted fantasy woodlands inspired by the Impressionistic paintings of Renoir and Van Gogh. The fairies, painted gold from head to toe, moved in a ritual fashion quite unlike that of the balletic *Dream*s of the nineteenth century. As with Poel's productions, Granville-Barker attempted to simplify Shakespeare by allowing his actors (who were rigorously rehearsed) to create the magic of the play. He also abandoned the Victorian tendency to cast women in the roles of Oberon and Puck. This production traveled to the United States in 1915 and altered American audience's perceptions of how Shakespeare should be staged.

The Twentieth Century: Post–World War II to the Present

While the mid twentieth century saw some interesting alternatives to the spectacular *Dream*s of theatrical tradition—notably a futuristic, "sci-fi" version conceived by George Devine at Stratford-upon-Avon in 1954—most were decidedly conventional until 1960 when Peter Hall, just five years out of Cambridge University, founded the Royal Shakespeare Company in Stratford and immediately sought to revitalize the manner in which Shakespeare was performed. In 1961 Hall set *The Dream* in a Tudor garden as it might have been staged for a wedding in 1595 and then recreated this production for film in 1968 (see "Frame-by-Frame," below, pp. 166–168). Hall's most radical departure from tradition was to play the spirits as nearly nude beings, covered in green paint; a very youthful Judi Dench played Titania with strategically placed leaves about her body. This was among the first productions to abandon the full ass's head for Nick Bottom, who wore only the animal ears.

A still more revolutionary *A Midsummer Night's Dream* was Peter Brook's production of the play for the RSC in 1970. "Brook's *Dream*," as it now known, may be the most influential production of a Shakespeare play in the twentieth century. The production was so successful that it was kept in the RSC repertory for an unprecedented five years and toured every continent (save

Antarctica). Using Hippolyta's Act 5 line "It must be in [the audience's] imagination" as their credo, along with Jan Kott's cynical interpretation of the darker aspects of the play in *Shakespeare Our Contemporary*, Brook and his actors created a minimalist *Dream*. Sally Jacobs designed a white box set on which the actors, clad in satin gowns of vivid colors, flew on trapezes, created the magic flower out of a juggler's plate and wand, and fought through a forest suggested by metal coils. Fairies "disappeared" through invisible doors in the white walls, then appeared above to watch the action below; they accompanied the action with various musical instruments, including electric guitars. The Bottom-Titania affair was lusty and far more sensual than had been seen on an English stage; the giddy Bottom was led to Titania's bower astride the shoulders of a burly fairy whose bare arm protruded bawdily between Bottom's legs. Brook's influential *Dream* was equal parts street carnival, Dionysian rite, and *avant-garde* theater. (Although there is no film or video of the complete production available, a 2002 video [33 min.] issued by Films for the Humanities under the title *A Midsummer Night's Dream: What to Make of Magic* contains several minutes of Brook's innovative approach to the play.)

Brook's darker reading of the play spawned other such productions. In 1985 the Romanian director Liviu Ciulei staged the play at Minneapolis's Guthrie Theater in such a way as to emphasize the brutal treatment of the women: Hippolyta was savagely stripped of her clothing by Oberon's troops, while Lysander and Demetrius threatened to kill Helena with switchblade knives. The Oberon-Titania scenes were played as a ferocious marital battle. After she made love to the ass, Titania was horrified to discover Oberon under the ass's head, not Bottom. Ciulei's production—and many like it—represent a postmodern approach to Shakespeare in its ironic reading of the text, its bold combination of many performance and cultural styles, and its irreverence for older theater traditions. Even more revisionary was a German production at the Gorky Theater in East Berlin in 1980: Theseus, Oberon, and Puck manipulated the other characters as puppets suspended from enormous chains. Director Thomas Hoff thus took aim at an oppressive Communist regime.

In addition to its exploration of the play's ominous elements, Brook's 1970 production influenced casting decisions for a number of subsequent productions of *The Dream*. Brook double-cast the roles of Theseus-Oberon, Hippolyta-Titania, and Philistrate-Puck "so that the two very different worlds of daylight and moonlight, practical life and dream, were visibly intertwined" (Dawson, 19). Double casting the courtly roles with those of the fairy kingdom can lead to some intriguing Freudian implications for the play. The casting device, now rather standard in professional productions (its economic advantages are attractive), was carried to a fascinating

extreme at the Stratford Ontario Shakespeare Festival in 1976. Director Robin Phillips conceived a production in which the comedy was actually a dream in the mind of Queen Elizabeth I. In a Chinese-box effect, Hippolyta, costumed in a replica of the gown in the famous portrait of Shakespeare's monarch, conjured the image of Titania-as-Elizabeth in her onstage dream. Hermia and Helena appeared as younger images of Elizabeth and her cousin, Mary Stuart.

The most discussed production of *The Dream* at the end of the twentieth century was that staged in 1992 at the National Theatre of Great Britain. Quebec-based Robert Lepage (the first North American to direct for the NT) set out to "reinvent" the play, much as Brook had done more than twenty years earlier. He featured artists from Canada's renowned *Cirque du Soleil* to create the play's magic. Puck (Angela Laurier) was a contortionist who could walk, crab-like, with her head between her legs, especially in the production's closing moment; Titania (Sally Dexter) slept, not in a bower, but dangling upside down from a rope high above the stage. The most memorable aspect of the production may have been its thoroughly unconventional setting. Whereas Brook and the RSC performed within a white box, the NT actors performed on a stage dominated by a huge, eight-feet-deep pool of water. Much of the action took place in the water (patrons in the first three rows were given plastic rain gear) to create a dream-like effect as the figures of the living actors, their reflections, and their shadows merged eerily. The fairies, dressed in black and wearing blue facial makeup, rearranged simple chairs into various tree-like configurations, both within and beyond the water. An antique bed frame defined Theseus's palace and later served as a door, an observation deck for Puck and Oberon as they spied on the lovers, and finally the stage for the mechanicals performance. The mattress was rigged to allow actors, especially Puck, to appear and disappear mysteriously. Although the production's many surreal visual elements perhaps competed too much with Shakespeare's text (virtually uncut by Lepage), its overall effect was to create "the forms of things unknown," such as might be experienced in a dream.

The Dream on Film and Video

A Midsummer Night's Dream is especially "film friendly." Various photographic tricks (dissolves, super-impositions, montage) can be used to create the illusion of fairies appearing and disappearing, of dream states, and other visual magic. Thus the play is among the most filmed of Shakespeare's works. There have been several animated films (see videography) and a puppet version, superbly conceived and directed in 1959 by Jiri Trnka, Czechoslovakia. The first "live action" film of *The Dream* appeared in 1908 when Vitagraph, one of the first film companies, released an eight-minute version of Puck and several fairies cavorting in New York's Central Park. This was the age of German Expressionism, with its distortions of "reality" calculated to explore the unconscious on the stage and in the cinema; the play's dream sequences provided German artists with an ideal subject for their bold experiments with dream-states. In 1925 the German director Hans Neumann produced a fifty-minute version of *The Dream* so replete with nudity and overtly sexual entanglements that it was officially censored.

Among the most significant and accessible films versions of *A Midsummer Night's Dream* are:

■ 1935—Directors Max Reinhardt and William Deterle, Warner Brothers, with Mickey Rooney (Puck), James Cagney (Bottom), Olivia de Havilland (Hermia), Victor Jory (Oberon), Dick Powell (Demetrius), and Joe E. Brown (Flute). (132 min.)

Reinhardt's was the first full-length, commercially successful production of a Shakespeare play on film. Jack Warner, the famed Hollywood producer, persuaded the Austrian director to make the film after seeing his stage production at the Hollywood Bowl. To Reinhardt's chagrin, Warner insisted that the director employ actors under contract to his studio instead of unknown stage actors. Few in the American cast had experience acting Shakespeare, and thus the acting runs from the excellent (Jimmy Cagney, whose Brooklyn accent made him indeed a rough, rude mechanical) to the silly (Dick Powell's laughable-for-all-the-wrong-reasons Demetrius). The film uses Mendelssohn's famous score and suggests how a nineteenth-century stage production may have looked and sounded.

Still, Reinhardt's expressionistic film remains a significant example of Shakespeare in the cinema, largely for the "movie magic" that still enchants. Shot in black-and-white with effective contrasts between light and shadow, the film is a visual delight, as with the cascade of stars from the heavens on which Titania's fairies enter and Oberon's seemingly miles-long black cloak. Reinhardt built what was at the time Hollywood's largest sound stage (350' x 175') to create an enormous, mysterious forest full of dancing fairies, choreographed by the Russian ballerina, Bronislava Nijinska, sister to the famed Vaslav Nijinsky. The film's strength is its recognition of the play's darker elements (see "Frame-by-Frame" below). Victor Jory's Oberon is a mostly frightful being and Mickey Rooney's child-like Puck suggests the Dionysian side of this merry wanderer. Despite some undeniably campy elements, the film creates a darker *Dream* than most audiences had seen. As importantly, the film has shown mass audiences that some

American actors could do Shakespeare credibly in their native accents.

■ 1968—Director Peter Hall, with the Royal Shakespeare Company, including Judi Dench (Titania), Ian Holm (Puck), Ian Richardson (Oberon), and Paul Rogers (Bottom). (124 min.)

As he had been when he staged *The Wars of the Roses* for the RSC in 1963, Hall was influenced by Jan Kott's abrasive, ironic readings of Shakespeare's plays in *Shakespeare Our Contemporary*. Drawing upon his staging of *The Dream* for the RSC in its second season (see above), Hall filmed the play—using hand-held cameras to effect a documentary style—on the grounds of a stately English manor. Hall was determined to counter several centuries' worth of "pretty" *Dream*s. To de-glamorize the play, Hall and his actors waited until October and its treacherous weather for filming. Courtiers and the nearly-nude fairies alike are drenched in rain and are covered with mud on a dimly lit landscape. There is little magic in these woods, save for some flickering lights meant to suggest fairies flying. Though perhaps the best-spoken *Dream* on film (the director actually recorded the actors after the film had been shot, synching their lines to the visuals), Hall's version remains heavy-handed, and even he considered it a failure. Its primary value is that it preserved an early performance by the then-young RSC and many of its finest actors.

■ 1981—Director Elijah Moshinsky, BBC Television, with Helen Mirren (Titania) and Nigel Davenport (Bottom). (120 min.)

When Jonathan Miller assumed the role of artistic director for the BBC's ambitious project to film the entire canon, he took a generally conservative approach to the interpretation of Shakespeare's plays. Television director Elijah Moshinsky's *A Midsummer Night's Dream*, with its richly detailed Renaissance-era costuming, is memorable mostly for its mannered reconstruction of famous paintings by European masters. For instance, Bottom and the mechanicals are discovered in an artificial pose that suggests Hans Bol's painting, "Members of the Wine Merchants' Guild." There is little humor in the mechanicals' scenes; the production offers a largely naturalistic reading of the play in which understatement is the norm. The quartet of lovers slogs through a muddy swamp in their pursuit of one another, a directorial choice that can also be seen in Michael Hoffman's 1999 film (see below).

■ 1988—Director James Lapine, with William Hurt (Oberon), Jeffrey DeMunn (Bottom), and Marcell Rosenblatt (Puck). (165 min.)

A 1982 production of the play at Joseph Papp's Delacorte Theatre in New York's Central Park has been preserved on video. In keeping with Papp's mission to bring free and multicultural Shakespeare to large audiences, the production prompted considerable laughter by using campy humor, though on film it retains a charm of its own in its honest quest to be a crowd-pleasing entertainment. The fairies represent an odd-ball assortment of types and cultures, including Pacific islanders. Bottom wears a Yankee baseball hat, carries a bat, and speaks in a thick "Noo Yawk" accent, thereby giving some fresh readings to that character's many humorous lines. As an alternative to the unusually serious renderings of the mechanicals' play about Pyramus and Thisbe in the Hall and BBC versions discussed above, Papp's actors play the scene for as many laughs as they can conjure from their audience.

- 1996—Director Adrian Noble, Guild Films, with the Royal Shakespeare Company, including Alex Jennings (Theseus/Oberon), Lindsay Duncan (Hippolyta/Titania), and Desmond Barrit (Bottom). (103 min.)

In 1994 Noble directed the play at Stratford, proclaimedly under the influence of Brook's staging of *The Dream*, which he saw in 1970 as a university student while standing in the back of the Royal Shakespeare Theater auditorium. Like Brook's version, Noble's placed a premium on the audience's imagination. His stage featured an array of freestanding doorways and dangling light bulbs to suggest stars. Titania's bower was rendered as an enormous hot-pink parasol that was lowered onto the stage and ceremoniously raised into the "heavens" as the Fairy Queen passionately embraced Bottom. Parasols were, in fact, the recurrent image on the RSC's stage: Quince carried a bulky bumbershoot, and fairies wore funny hats made from parasols. The text was played more lightly than Brook's famous version, befitting Noble's notion that the audience ought to view the play through the wonderment of a child's eyes. The film reproduces the stage version and is thus self-consciously theatrical and confined to a limited space. For the film Noble adds a short prologue and epilogue featuring a young boy conjuring up *The Dream* by peeping through a keyhole (à la *Alice in Wonderland*). The film does suggest that an imaginative theatricality can be as appealing as the Hollywood razzle-dazzle of Reinhardt and later, Hoffman.

- 1999—Director Michael Hoffman, Fox Searchlight, with Kevin Kline (Bottom), Michelle Pfeiffer (Titania), Rupert Everett (Oberon), Calista Flockhart (Helena), and Stanley Tucci (Puck). (120 min.)

In a written prologue to the film, Hoffman notes that he has set the action in the late nineteenth century when the bicycle and phonograph had recently been invented. Hoffman's *Dream* thus relies on a new technology that is as magical to the fairies as Shakespeare's play to generations of theater audiences. We are shown inventive and amusing scenes in which the fairies are mystified by a gramophone. Puck (played as "the anti-Rooney" by a middle-aged, balding Stanley Tucci) is confounded by riding a bike for the first time. For Hoffman, magic is a relative term: fairies can be as "wowed" by humans as humans are by fairies, portrayed herein as an intriguing blend of types. Some are clearly in the Victorian mode, while others seem more aligned with George Lucas's space epics.

Filmed in Italy against beautiful Tuscan landscapes (cf. Kenneth Branagh's *Much Ado About Nothing*), the film is fittingly underscored by operatic music to enhance the Italian setting and the play's grand passions. Hoffman melds the traditional with the daring (see the "Frame-by-Frame" for a discussion of the fairy kingdom). The director's most inventive touches involve the mechanicals and Nick Bottom. Played by a dapper Kevin Kline in a white suit and rakish straw hat, Bottom emerges as a sophisticated, charming, henpecked Italian husband. During his bombastic audition for the roles in Quince's play, he becomes the butt of a cruel practical joke played by some village youngsters; the humiliated Bottom returns home to confront his wife (an invention by Hoffman). Thus, when he becomes Titania's lover the audience feels life has finally rewarded him for the slings and arrows he has endured in marriage. Hoffman brings a similar inventiveness and sympathy to the Pyramus and Thisbe play, beautifully staged in Theseus's baroque theater. The scene swerves from the truly comic (the mechanicals open the casement to allow for moonshine only to discover that the window has been bricked over) to the genuinely moving. The young man who plays Thisbe in Act 5, stung by the laughter his "monstrous little voice" elicits from the courtly audience, removes his wig and speaks Thisbe's farewell from the heart and in a natural voice. The court is reduced to tears, both by the lad's honest performance and by the recognition that there is indeed such a thing as honest love, something they had collectively failed to acknowledge for the play's first four acts.

Spin-offs

Given its frequent use of music and its tonal variety, *A Midsummer Night's Dream* lends itself to musical adaptations. Mendelssohn's incidental music to the play, discussed with the stage history of the play, has become well-known on concert stages and as the springboard for *Dream* ballets, including a significant one (filmed in 1966) by the New York City Ballet's late choreographer,

"BOTTOM, THOU ART TRANSLATED!"

Act 3, Scene 1 on Film

A visual and comedic high point of *A Midsummer Night's Dream* occurs in Act 3, Scene 1 when Bottom re-enters the stage wearing an ass's head thrust upon him by Puck during the rehearsal of the Pyramus-Thisbe play. This grotesquely comic moment is followed by a sublime one: the appearance of Titania and her retinue of fairies. The scene is Shakespeare's variant of that ancient legend of the Beauty and the Beast, and it remains among the most painted and photographed in all of Shakespearean lore. Staging/filming this scene presents a series of challenges to the director, if only because it is familiar. The spirit of a theater production or movie can be measured by isolating this scene for analysis. Three films introduced earlier provide a test of how directors have met the challenges of 3.1:

- Max Reinhardt's 1935 black-and-white film;
- Peter Hall's 1968 version, based loosely on an earlier stage production for the Royal Shakespeare Company; and
- Michael Hoffman's 1999 movie featuring a cast of international film stars.

Although it is the oldest of the three films, Reinhardt employs the technology of cinema to good effect in the transformation scene. On one of Warner's largest sound stages Reinhardt uses a variety of long and close-up shots to suggest the expanse of the forest, generously employing dissolves and other photographic tricks to create magical effects. For instance, Puck's line—"Sometimes a horse I'll be; sometimes a hound, / A hog, a headless bear, sometimes a fire" (3.1.103–104)—takes visible shape on screen as the hobgoblin dissolves into superimposed shots of a dog, a pig, and a flame. Because Reinhardt's version is an enchanted fairy tale à la the 1930s Warner Brothers musical, the line and image of the "headless bear" are omitted. After Puck blows dandelion petals on him, Bottom is transformed into an ass through a clever series of superimposed shots that gradually turn man into beast. A traditional madcap chase takes place among the working men after Bottom has been "translated," with Puck riding repeatedly upon the backs of an unsuspecting worker. Flute/Thisbe falls into a pond as the others scramble into a donkey cart to escape.

In one of his boldest choices, Reinhardt allows Bottom (played by movie tough-guy Jimmy Cagney) to become aware of his ass-like predicament as he kneels before a pool to see his face reflected in the water. To be sure, the moment plays against the text because Bottom's line to Snout ("You see an ass head of your own, do you?" [111–112]) is more amusing if Bottom is ignorant of his situation. Shakespeare's point is that Bottom's behavior is frequently "asinine" whether he sports an actual donkey's head or not.

Everything in Reinhardt's depiction of the transformation and its aftermath is intended to reinforce the notion of fairy magic: Titania appears in a shimmering gown, back lit to make her radiant against the darker background; the fairies in general, and the four named fairies (Peaseblossom *et al.*) in particular, glisten with a surreal beauty. As Bottom is led to Titania's bower, to the strains of Mendelssohn's famous wedding march, a spider weaves an enormous veil that is then placed on Titania's head by her attendants. As Bottom and Titania fall into each other's arms in the bower—a spot beneath a tree onto which the fairies scatters shimmering flower petals—the fairies envelop the lovers in the fragile web in an especially beautiful shot that suggests an innocence not manifested in the other films discussed here. Titania's luminescent veil contrasts strikingly with the gigantic black cape worn by Oberon. In Reinhardt's reading of the play, Oberon represents a sinister force in Athens Wood, the Jungian "shadow" of our darker side. Titania, pale and blond, is an almost sexless innocent who, in the best Warner Brothers musical fashion, sings a lullaby to Bottom.

Reinhardt's most provocative interpretive choice in the scene makes clear that Bottom's transformation into an ass, and Titania's infatuation with the beast, is a diversion enabling Oberon to steal the Child of India from the Fairy Queen. When she is awakened by Bottom's song (ll. 123–124), we see in close-up Titania sleeping with the child snuggled next to her in her bower. The Indian boy repeatedly becomes agitated at Titania's doting on Bottom. A close-up of Oberon peering at the scene from behind some foliage is followed by a shot of the boy crying in alarm. After Bottom and Titania settle into their slumber, Oberon bursts upon the scene, snatches the boy, and says, "This falls out better than I could devise"—a line Reinhardt has moved from 3.2.35. In Shakespeare's text Oberon is unaware of the transformation until Puck informs him in a detailed account of the scene (3.2.6–34). Throughout Reinhardt's version Oberon omnisciently controls the comings and goings in Athens Wood.

For all its technical wizardry Reinhardt's film allows us to experience a nineteenth-century approach to Shakespeare in its sumptuous costumes, elaborate scenic effects, and cast of hundreds. Quince amusingly attempts to place Flute/Thisbe into various histrionic positions, the kind which actors prior to the twentieth century were rigorously taught to indicate through emotions. Visually splendid though it may be, Reinhardt's film leaves very little to the audience's imagination.

Hall's film is, in effect, a rebuttal to Reinhardt's ostentatious *Dream*. Virtually every choice he makes seems the antithesis of the 1935 film—as well as almost two hundred years of spectacular *Dream* productions on European and American stages. As an antidote to visually resplendent *Dream*s, the director was determined to "de-prettify" the play. It was intentionally filmed in late autumn during wretched weather on a sprawling estate in the north of England.

In Hall's version the rehearsal for the Pyramus and Thisbe play by the mechanicals is understated, almost solemn. There are no cheap laughs, as in the Reinhardt version. Bottom seems peevish in his relationship with Quince, the apparent result of a long-standing feud between the two. Bottom's attempts to direct the play are more a case of one-upsmanship than the over-eagerness of a hammy actor. Consequently, Bottom emerges as unsympathetic, boorish—an interpretive choice that affects the audience's response to his dalliance with Tita-

nia. He truly becomes the "vile thing" that Oberon wishes upon Titania (2.2.40).

The actual transformation of Bottom into the ass is scrupulously attendant to Shakespeare's stage direction: *"Enter . . . Bottom as Pyramus with the ass head."* In both the Reinhardt and Hoffman versions, the audience sees Puck work his magic on Bottom to effect the transformation. Hall, however, uses no cinematic gimmickry to alter Bottom's appearance. A quick cut simply reveals Bottom fully transformed. Curiously, Hall places a complete donkey's head on Bottom in the film, although in his 1961 stage version, only the ears and some facial hair suggested the full head. Hall again disdains tradition to show the most restrained reaction by the mechanicals imaginable. The brief exchange with Snout (3.1.109–112) is played almost matter-of-factly, save a subdued double take by the bewildered Joiner.

In another break with tradition Hall's film uses no incidental music to underscore the meeting of Titania and the Ass—no strains of Mendelssohn as in Reinhardt's film or arias from the Italian opera as in Hoffman's. Hall's version is stark, anti-romantic, and conforms precisely to Titania's admonition that her fairy retinue should bring Bottom to her bower "silently" (3.1.196). Although nude and covered in green body-paint, Titania is disheveled and sexually less appealing than is customary. She is the antithesis of Reinhardt's vision or Michelle Pfeiffer's Titania in Hoffman's movie. Peaseblossom *et al.* are played by scruffy children who are dirty, unkempt, and shabbily dressed like refugees from a Dickens novel. The bower itself is nondescript, merely a patch of earth under a tree.

Though less comical than the majority of *Dream*s on stage and film, Hall's version of 3.1 allows audiences to focus solely on Shakespeare's language in the scene, which is virtually uncut and unaltered. Hall filmed the scene in a series of intimate tight shots—more typical of television than film—to place maximum emphasis on the actors and their words. Whenever the actors can motivate a line to the audience, they turn to face the camera in what was in the 1960s an innovative manner of filming Shakespeare.

Hoffman's film may be placed somewhere between the visual splendor of Reinhardt's and the intimate, more naturalistic approach employed by Hall. It, too, is visually sumptuous. Whereas

(continued)

Reinhardt uses black-and-white photography to underscore the differences between the innocence of Titania's court and the sinister forces of Oberon, Hoffman uses color to distinguish between the workaday world of the mechanicals (bland earth tones) and the enchanted kingdom of the fairies (rich hues). To alert the audience that the mechanicals are near the Fairy Queen, Hoffman inserts between 3.1 and the previous scene (2.2) a brief shot of Titania sleeping alone in her bower, ending the sequence with Hermia terrified and abandoned by Lysander. The mechanicals, as they enter singing a boisterous song, encounter their "hawthorne brake" adjacent to the ruins of a Greek temple in an apt reminder of the mythological source of the Pyramus and Thisbe legend. As the workers rehearse the play, the self-centered Bottom has difficulty remembering Thisbe's name. Roger Rees, an experienced Royal Shakespeare Company actor, plays Quince, a fitting choice because Rees, whose specialty was romantic roles in his youth, makes Quince seem a weary old actor who has seen it all in his career.

Hoffman makes other choices that distinguish his film from the earlier two. His Peaseblossom *et al.* are played, not by children as in the earlier films, but by attractive young women dressed in pseudo-Grecian gowns. Other spirits—grotesque in their appearance, more *Star Trek* than Shakespeare—stand in the background. (Earlier Hoffman has inserted a cocktail party for the spirits, clearly a spoof of the famous alien bar scene created for R2D2 and friends in *Star Wars*.)

Bottom's transformation into the ass and his ensuing encounter with Titania are notably unconventional in Hoffman's film. Usually, Bottom is played by an older, portly man, even though the script does not specify his age or physique. Hoffman chooses instead to assign the part to Kevin Kline, as a younger, more dashing, even romantic figure whose encounter with Titania is suffused with eroticism not often seen in the role. Bottom is thus contrasted with Puck (Stanley Tucci), conspicuously older, balding, and weary of the forest world and put off by the antics of both the humans and his fellow spirits. To initiate Bottom's transformation, Puck blows golden fairy dust upon the actor as he rehearses his Pyramus speeches alone in the forest. Some dust alights on a tree stump, which is thereby transformed into liquid gold. As Bottom gazes into the miraculous substance, both he and the audience witness the eerie change. Kline's disguise as an ass is subtle and minimal: nothing more than a bit of facial hair, pronounced teeth, and a pair of ears that are suddenly visible to Bottom's fellow-artisans when he removes his top hat. Hoffman has prepared audiences for the transformation early in the film by showing us a merchant leading a donkey, while Bottom, resplendent in white suit and straw hat, sits in an outdoor café in the bustling piazza of a nineteenth-century Italian village.

As Bottom sings his song about "The ouzel cock so black of hue," Hoffman's camera pulls back to reveal Titania's bower: an enormous basket covered in foliage suspended high above the forest floor. The initial exchange between Bottom the Ass and Titania the Queen maintains a separation between the two so that Bottom must gaze heavenward to see the image of the lovely queen. This, however, is a queen to be reckoned with. As Bottom turns to leave ("if I had wit enough to get out of this wood"), Titania commands him to stay: "Out of this wood do not desire to go" (l. 146). Customarily her line is said as a desperate entreaty by a woman afraid she may lose her lover; Michele Pfeiffer instead reads the line almost violently. The forest comes alive to enforce her command; a vine from a tree snakes outward and coils itself about the hapless Bottom. Pfeiffer takes a hint of the dominatrix from Shakespeare's text:

> Thou shalt remain here, whether thou wilt or no.
> I am a spirit of no common rate.
> The summer still doth tend upon my state.
> (ll. 147–149)

Her lover firmly in tow, Titania summons her retinue to serve Bottom.

Pfeiffer's Titania is the most aggressively sexual of the three Titanias discussed here. Her reading of "the moon methinks weeps with a wat'ry eye" speech is sensuous and passionate, befitting the lovely operatic aria that underscores Titania's tryst with Bottom. Whereas Reinhardt's film provokes amusement and innocence in his rendering of the scene, and Hall's promotes a detached coolness that counters more than three centuries of romanticized *Dream*s, Hoffman is unabashed in his pursuit of a passionate and genuinely erotic—though not salacious—representation of the scene. The eroticism makes Oberon's opening line in 3.2—"I wonder if Titania be awaked"—all the funnier, especially as read by Rupert Everett's lethargic Fairy King. As he reclines listlessly in the grass, his ladylove has truly been "awakened" in her bower.

CLOSE-UP

MADAME LUCIA ELIZABETTA BARTOLOZZI VESTRIS
Shakespeare's "Leading Lady"

Women were not allowed to perform on Eng-lish stages during Shakespeare's lifetime. Not until 1660—when the public theaters reopened after eighteen years of Puritan rule—did women participate in theatrical productions. Margaret Hughes is acknowledged to have been England's first Shakespearean tragedienne. She probably played Desdemona to Thomas Betterton's Othello in December 1660. (Playwright Jeffrey Hatcher has recently dramatized this transition from men to women in female parts on the Restoration stage in his rambunctious 2001 historical drama *Compleat Female Stage Beauty,* later filmed as *Stage Beauty.*) Although a few plays had been written by women in the Elizabethan era, such as Elizabeth Carey's *The Tragedy of Miriam,* these plays were not publicly performed; women were not supposed to write for the commercial stage. After the Restoration, Mrs. Aphra Behn (c. 1640–1689) was the first to script commercially successful plays.

Despite these advances by women in the late seventeenth century, and although women actors became box-office draws in the eighteenth (e.g., Sarah Siddons was acclaimed for her Shakespearean roles), not until the nineteenth century did women achieve some real power and prominence in the male-dominated world of the theater. The visionary actor-manager, Madame Vestris (born Lucia Elizabetta Bartolozzi), pioneered Shakespearean stage production by women in the English-speaking world. Even so, women would not become consistently and permanently involved in production management until the twentieth century. Lillian Bayless at London's Old Vic Theatre, Margaret Webster in America, Ariane Mnouchkine in France, and most recently Tina Packer, Julie Taymor, and Libby Appel are beholden to Madame Vestris's groundbreaking work at London's Covent Garden Theatre in the 1840s, as well as to her earlier, non-Shakespearean work at the Olympic. Vestris was, in the estimation of one of her biographers, "the first woman in England to show a genuine capacity for effective and imaginative direction" (Gilder, 259).

Born in London on March 2, 1797, Elizabetta Vestris inherited her artistic sensibilities from her family. Her grandfather, Francesco Bartolozzi, was an Italian immigrant who served as engraver to King George III; her father, Gaetano, was an accomplished violinist who introduced her to London's artistic circles. Elizabeth began her career in music, both as a pianist (the renowned composer Josef Haydn considered her among the city's finest players) and as a singer. Although her extraordinary contralto voice might have led her to a career in opera, the self-confident young woman preferred the theater. At sixteen, she married Armand Vestris, the premier French dancing-master and mime at the King's Theatre, where he once danced in a ballet version of *Macbeth.* Armand, whose father Auguste and grandfather had been chief ballet masters at the Paris Opera, taught his young wife movement skills that served her well during her theatrical career. (The Vestris family made significant contributions to the technique, repertory, and performance of classical ballet in England, France, Denmark, and Russia; as a young virtuoso in Leningrad, star dancer Mikhail Baryshnikov often performed a gestural solo called "Vestris," created in tribute to Auguste Vestris and based upon Jaques's "Seven Ages of Man" speech in Shakespeare's *As You Like It.*)

After her marriage failed in 1820, Elizabetta embarked on a solo stage career. She played a man's (or breeches) role in a burlesque of Mozart's opera *Don Giovanni* and became a sensation on both London and Paris stages. In France she acted at the prestigious *Comédie Français* with Talma, the country's foremost tragedian. This actor passionately discussed authentically realistic costuming with her, a topic that would form an important basis for managerial work back in England. In 1830 she returned permanently to London where—in an audacious move for a woman—she rented London's Olympic Theatre, thus becoming the first female lessee in theater history; her competitors actually referred to her as "the Great Lessee." Although the fare she produced at the Olympic consisted mostly of burlesques and light comedies, she quickly gained a

(continued)

reputation as London's most innovative manager. She insisted on real, as opposed to fake, props, and authentic costuming specifically designed for a given show. She also introduced the so-called "box set" to the English stage; it consisted of three realistic walls and a ceiling for interior scenes. Indeed, this innovation is often considered Madame Vestris's major gift to the theater. Furthermore, she raised performance standards by carefully selecting casts for a particular play at a time when most theater companies were comprised of "stock" actors, and, to create an ensemble effect, she carefully rehearsed her company, usually with herself in a leading role. Nine successful seasons at the Olympic established Madame Vestris as a leading actor-manager in London to the extent that she rivaled William Charles Macready, England's most accomplished Shakespearean in the 1830s and 1840s.

In 1838 she defied polite custom by taking a second husband, this time a middling actor named Charles Matthews. The two toured the United States to considerable acclaim and returned to London in 1839 to assume the leadership of the Covent Garden Theatre. As one of the city's two patent theaters (Drury Lane was the other), Covent Garden provided Madame Vestris with the opportunity to stage Shakespeare's plays. Ever daring, she chose *Love's Labor's Lost* as her novel first Shakespearean production, in what may be been the English theater's first performance of this early comedy (c. 1592) since the closing of the theaters in 1642. Because this erudite comedy is so different from the Shakespearean comedies London audiences were accustomed to seeing, such as Garrick's *Catherine and Petruchio* (a revision of *The Taming of the Shrew*), the actors were unable to cope with the play's verbal gymnastics, and the result was a theatrical failure. Earlier, William Hazlitt, a leading literary and theater critic of the day, dismissed the play, suggesting that "if we were to part with any of [Shakespeare's] comedies, it should be this." Vestris also miscalculated her audience by trying to suppress noisy patrons in the gallery seats, thereby inciting a riot that damaged business.

Despite the failure of *Love's Labor's Lost*, Vestris continued to produce Shakespeare. *The Merry Wives of Windsor,* with Vestris as Mistress Page, pleased audiences so much that they clamored for more of her "authentic" Shakespeare. In her second season (1840) at Covent Garden, Vestris produced *A Midsummer Night's Dream,* her finest and historically most important Shakespearean production. For the first time since the text had been notoriously revised and turned into an opera in 1692, Shakespeare's original script received its due. Some cuts were necessary to allow for Mendelssohn's music (and other pieces by Beethoven and Weber), but not a word was added, and the play was rightly advertised as being "wrote by Mr. Shakespeare." Supported by the famed designer James Planché's sumptuous settings, Vestris's obsession with accuracy and detail was manifest so much so the spectacle influenced subsequent productions by Charles Kean and Samuel Phelps (see "*The Dream* on Stage," pp. 160–161). As Covent Garden's most popular actress, Vestris assigned herself the plum role of Oberon, and she appeared in a Grecian tunic, a variant on the many breeches roles for which she became well known. London audiences and theater critics delighted in the Planché-Vestris rendering of *The Dream*. One observer announced that

> A just, generous, and graceful homage has been paid to Shakespeare, and the management is entitled to our high approval of almost to invent a fairyland for the stage—to invest it with a dreamy spirit—to produce beautiful contrasts of scenery—to people it with an elfin world costumed with fantastic splendor which tells a tale of power, riches, and romance.
>
> (Pearce, 258–259)

Vestris followed her success with *A Midsummer Night's Dream* by staging *Romeo and Juliet*, also restored to something like its original condition. No longer did Juliet awaken for a sentimental reunion with the dying Romeo, as she had done since Garrick (see "*Romeo and Juliet* on Stage," p. 555). This production was less successful than *The Dream* because audiences craved the sentimental ending devised by Garrick and others. Although Vestris did not produce other of Shakespeare's plays, she and a few others inspired actor-managers to return to Shakespeare's original texts to discover the playwright's intentions. Such is her legacy to Shakespearean stage production. Remarkably, her theatrical vision as a woman enabled her to restore Shakespeare's texts to something like their original, as some other actor-managers had done also.

Vestris completed her stewardship of Covent Garden by producing *London Assurance*, a comedy of manners by Dion Boucicault, which she staged with realistic detail, the first such effort on the modern London stage. The play ran for fifty-two performances, a phenomenal record for that time.

After some financial setbacks, which landed her husband in prison for a short time, Vestris took over the Lyceum Theatre with Matthews in 1847. There she took on many non-Shakespearean tragic roles to acclaim. George Henry Lewes, among London's leading theater critics at mid-century, called Vestris "the pet of the public," praising her tragic acting and claiming that "no actress on our stage could do it . . . [she] will startle even her greatest admirers, for assuredly no one believed her powers lay at all in that direction." Given Vestris's history of accepting the extraordinary challenges that the theater could offer, Lewes should perhaps not have been surprised at her skills. A nearly forty-year career in the theater proved she could undertake almost any assignment. She died in August 1856, even as European theater was about to undergo a radical transformation. The realistic works of T. W. Robertson and Eugene Scribe were, in some ways, by-products of the work begun by Madame Vestris. And as importantly, her Shakespearean productions, though few, helped to change the way Shakespeare's scripts were approached by actor-managers and directors who, like Vestris, returned to the originals.

References and Related Reading

Appleton, William W. *Madame Vestris and the London Stage.* New York and London, 1974.

Gilder, Rosamond. *Enter the Actress.* New York, 1931. (See Chapter Twelve: "Madame Vestris: The First Lady of the English Stage.")

Pearce, Charles. *Madame Vestris and Her Time.* New York, 1969.

George Balanchine. Mendelssohn's "Wedding March," with its ceremonial horns, is a favorite choice for real-life weddings, and his orchestral colors (a jaunty bassoon for the "rude mechanicals," pizzicato strings for the fairies) poetically conjure up the play's various interweaving worlds. In 1960 Benjamin Britten composed a notable opera that retains much of Shakespeare's text in the libretto as well as the play's air of mystery. At least one Broadway musical, *Babes in the Woods* (1950), is based on the play; various rock and pop music versions have been less successful.

In *A Midsummer Night's Sex Comedy* (1982), writer-director Woody Allen abandons his beloved Manhattan to fuse Shakespeare and Ingmar Bergman (*Smiles of a Summer Night*) in an intentionally anachronistic retelling of *The Dream* set in c. 1905. Here the lovers are—typically in Allen's worldview—neurotic and sex-obsessed. The spirit world is conjured by a magical globe that allows the fantasy world to coexist with the real world. Though it is decidedly not Shakespeare's play, the film illuminates some of the sexual frustrations felt among the various sets of lovers in the original.

The Dream makes cameo appearances in several popular films, notably *Dead Poets Society* (1989) and even in a recently issued Beatles DVD, *Fun with the Fab Four* (2002), containing footage of the rockers enacting the play-within-the-play in 1964 as part of London's celebration of the four-hundredth anniversary of Shakespeare's birth.

More recently, a dance version of the play, directed by Celestino Coronado, has been preserved on film by the Lindsey Kemp Company. Coronado takes extraordinary liberties with Shakespeare's text (more than seventy percent of the original has been cut). Among his most memorable "inventions" include Lysander awaking to fall in love with Demetrius, Quince's company performing *Romeo and Juliet*, and Titania enacted by a drag queen. Lest we too quickly dismiss such liberties as postmodernism run amok, we might recall that similar liberties have been taken with *A Midsummer Night's Dream* during its four-hundred-year history.

References and Related Reading

Barber, C. L. *Shakespeare's Festive Comedy.* Princeton, 1959.

Greenwald, Michael L. "Broadway's Theatre War of 1854: The Burton and Broadway Productions of *A Midsummer Night's Dream.*" *Journal of American Drama and Theatre* 3:3 (Fall 1992): 5–17.

Halio, Jay. *A Midsummer Night's Dream (Shakespeare in Performance series).* Manchester, Eng., 1994.

Kott, Jan. "Shakespeare's Bitter Arcadia." *Shakespeare Our Contemporary.* New York, 1964.

Loney, Glen. *Peter Brook's Production of William Shakespeare's "A Midsummer Night's Dream" for the Royal Shakespeare Company: The Complete and Authorized Acting Edition.* Stratford-upon-Avon, 1974.

Selbourne, David. *The Making of "A Midsummer Night's Dream."* London, 1982.

Warren, Roger. *A Midsummer Night's Dream: Text and Performance.* London, 1983.

Watkins, Ronald, and Jeremy Lemmon. *In Shakespeare's Playhouse: "A Midsummer Night's Dream."* Totowa, N.J., 1974.

Williams, Gary Jay. *Our Moonlight Revels: "A Midsummer Night's Dream" in the Theatre.* Ames, Iowa, 1997.

Williamson, Marilyn. *The Patriarchy of Shakespeare's Comedies.* Detroit, 1986.

Young, David P. *Something of Great Constancy: The Art of "A Midsummer Night's Dream."* New Haven, Conn., 1966.

CHAPTER 8

The Merchant of Venice

(c. 1596–1597)

Context and Dating: Problem Comedy

The Merchant of Venice is a multifaceted comedy, episodic in structure, and complex in tone. Although the role of Shylock is the most famous part (and has drawn nearly every actor of note), the merchant of the title is a less prominent character, the melancholy Antonio whose trading ships sail from his home port of Venice. To finance his friend Bassanio's courtship of the wealthy heiress Portia, Antonio borrows money from Shylock, the Jewish moneylender who is the villain of this love comedy. Shylock is treated with disdain by the Christian inhabitants of the imagined place, Belmont, where the romantic episodes unfold, and Venice, where Antonio and the other commercially oriented characters drive their bargains. The merchant, whose ships are at sea, pledges "a pound of flesh" as his bond for the loan. In performance, Shylock's vengeful struggle to extract his pound of flesh becomes the emotional and dramatic center of the play. The three contrasting love affairs (Bassanio and Portia, Gratiano and Nerissa, and Lorenzo and Jessica) tend toward fairy tale and parable; on stage, these romantic encounters often pale by comparison to the near-tragedy of Shylock and the pound of flesh.

Because Shylock's bitter eloquence is so impressive, this story has become an uncomfortable one for today's audiences. Shakespeare now strikes us as equivocal in his depiction of Shylock as a resentful and unwelcome outsider cruelly forced to convert to Christianity as punishment for seeking Antonio's flesh—"to bait fish withal."

The play's other major character, Portia, is at the center of the most conspicuous of the interwoven romantic love stories. When she dons a lawyer's disguise to argue against Shylock in court, she grows from an ingénue heroine into a deep, witty, and philosophical woman. She extols the Christian virtues of charity, mercy, and forgiveness, then shrewdly tricks Shylock, oversees his punishment, and ultimately earns married happiness with the appropriate suitor, Bassanio. Although the play has been popular throughout its history, interpretation of Shylock has changed radically over the centuries, as actors and directors emphasize different facets of the character and the play in which he has such a key role. Shakespeare's sympathies here seem divided; the play's point of view is Christian, yet its author exposes the hedonistic, cruel, and racist behavior of some of these culturally privileged Christians, while also humanizing Shylock's authentic and well-justified desire for revenge.

The play was entered in the Stationers' Register, the official record of the London company of printers, on July 22, 1598. Although the play was recorded then, it was not printed until 1600 in a quarto text accurate enough to become the basis of modern editions. Establishing the earliest date for a first performance has not been so easy. Some scholars have seen a connection between the possible first performance dates and the indictment of Queen Elizabeth I's physician, the Portuguese Jew Roderigo Lopez, in a 1594 plot upon her life. The unfortunate Lopez was hanged, drawn, and quartered, having been implicated by the Earl of Essex and (perhaps) falsely accused. Christopher Marlowe's audience-pleasing, melodramatic caricature, *The Jew of Malta* (1589), was revived in 1594 to capitalize upon anti-Lopez feeling; its popularity may have inspired Shakespeare to stake his claim in similar territory (see stage history below, pp. 212ff.). Yet other allusions in the play to the capture of a Spanish ship at Cadiz in 1596 and to a 1595 publication on usury, suggest a later date of composition, perhaps 1596–1597.

An unattributed fifteenth-century woodcut depicts a supplicant farmer before a Jewish moneylender.

Henry Irving created a sympathetic Shylock in this 1879 Merchant of Venice.

Laurence Olivier's Shylock argues with the disguised Portia (Joan Plowright) in the National Theatre's 1973, Edwardian-set production.

Henry Goodman's Shylock has a tender moment with Jessica (Gabrielle Jourdan) in director Trevor Nunn's 1999 staging.

In any case, during the period when Shakespeare wrote the play, Jews had been expelled from England for more than three hundred years. According to some estimates, fewer than two hundred persons of the Jewish faith—and those mostly conforming outwardly to the practice of Protestantism—lived in England of the Elizabethan era, though James Shapiro (*Shakespeare and the Jews*) has argued cogently for a larger figure. The anti-Semitic traditions on which Shakespeare drew to create his portrait of Shylock and the Christians were only partly based upon actual observation. Continental traditions judged Jews and usurers as sinister and anti-Christian; English Renaissance thinking viewed the Old Testament God of Moses as a wrathful, demanding deity and its judicial ethic as one that insists, as Shylock does, upon an eye for an eye and the strict letter of the law.

Characters

The title character is the Venetian merchant Antonio, yet his role is subordinate and ambiguous. He has been variously depicted as shy and sad, or cold and stiff. He serves largely as a foil to Shylock, the Jewish money-lender, and to his more conventionally depicted friend, Bassanio. Contemporary productions have made much of Antonio's melancholy amidst wealth and of his devoted love, perhaps tinged with homoerotic desire, for his friend Bassanio.

Bassanio is an amiable character who has traditionally been seen as open-hearted and honest. When asked by Portia to choose among three caskets—one of gold, one of silver, and one of lead—so that she might assess his character and thus determine his worthiness as a potential husband, he chooses lead because he values truth and reality in a world easily deceived by ornament and appearance.

Bassanio and Portia are well matched. When she is confronted with situations of increasing seriousness during the play, Portia achieves a degree of maturity and integrity matching that of her new husband. In the wooing scenes and in her decision to appear in court, Portia is, as one critic put it, "rich, bright, and bored." She busies herself playing games—with the suitors, in the lawyer's disguise, and with the keepsake rings. In the trial scene, on the other hand, Portia discovers and reveals her depth of character. Her "quality of mercy" speech is not merely about legal rhetoric but about human truth, as is her equally heartfelt love test for Bassanio. As her character becomes more mature, so does the poetry of her speeches, and from her comes a radiant warmth that contrasts with the mercenary Shylock-Antonio plot. Hers is the role that has attracted actresses from Sarah Siddons to Ellen Terry and Katharine Hepburn. Like Shakespeare's most complex comic heroines, Beatrice in *Much Ado About Nothing* and Rosalind in *As You Like It*, Portia—more worldly than those later characters—is brighter than her intended.

So is Nerissa, who is paired with Gratiano (a man who Bassanio says, "speaks an infinite deal of nothing"). Gratiano also offers the most offensive anti-Semitic exclamations against Shylock—"O Jew! An upright judge, a learnèd judge!"—during the trial scene and proves slow-witted in the final act when Nerissa reveals she had been the clerk. We sense a mild and sophisticated irony in those pairings, while Lorenzo and especially Jessica prove double-edged. Jessica's spirited rebellion against her father has lent itself to varied interpretations by actresses. She is both an innocent girl who feels oppressed by Shylock's possessiveness and at the same time one who betrays her father, steals his money, runs away from his "house of hell," and renounces her Jewishness to marry a Christian.

Shylock remains the most fascinating character in the play. Other characters, including his own daughter, view him as a creature of darkness. His servant calls him "the fiend at mine elbow." Antonio and Bassanio treat him with mistrust and aversion, which he reciprocates, even as they borrow money from him. In the trial scene he is seen as a villain sharpening his knife to take the pound of flesh, his eye-for-an-eye vengeance the opposite of "Christian" charity as it is expressed in Portia's "quality of mercy" speech. When Portia succeeds in tricking him, we may feel joy and relief, until the cruelty of Gratiano's anti-Semitic words sinks in. Shylock's world—built upon his religion, his wealth, his daughter, and his antipathy to such jeering Christians as Antonio—has collapsed around him. But because his forced conversion to Christianity serves as punishment, not as salvation, he can gain a near tragic stature at the end.

Katharine Hepburn played Portia, seen here in the courtroom scene with Morris Carnovsky as Shylock at the Stratford (Connecticut) Shakespeare Festival in 1957.

Certainly the revolution in interpretation of the play and of his part—from darkly comical villain to nearly tragic victim (see stage history, p. 212)—recapitulates the evolution of English and European views of Jews in history. Although Shakespeare's play is a product of its times and enshrines both the ignorance about real Jewish people and the anti-Semitic feelings then current, it also explores the personal side of a character (see, for example, the famous "Hath not a Jew eyes . . . ?" speech) who has become larger than his play, and thus exposes the limitations of those who hold such prejudices.

Also depicted as less-than-desirable "others" are two of Portia's suitors, the Spaniard (Prince of Aragon) and the Moor (Prince of Morocco), both dismissed and condemned to lives of celibacy. Serving a structural function as well as comic relief is the clown figure of Shylock's servant, Lancelot Gobbo. His predicaments involving changing masters and reuniting with his father offer ironic commentaries upon the play's themes of indentured service and familial fidelity.

Sources and Inspirations

An ancient traditional story circulated in Persia, India, and Italy involves a bond given for human flesh. When the story first appeared in England in the thirteenth century, the creditor was identified as a Jew. Shakespeare's most likely source for that aspect of *The Merchant of*

THE MERCHANT OF VENICE 175

Venice was the version in *Il Pecorone* (*The Simpleton*) by Ser Giovanni Fiorentino. Published in the mid sixteenth century in Milan, it may have come to Shakespeare in a now-lost translation, or in some other accounts. In this source, an heiress tests her would-be suitors by ordeal, confiscating their goods and sending them off when they fail to remain awake long enough to sleep with her. What they do not know is that she has drugged them with a sleeping potion. One suitor, Giannetto, who is befriended by a wealthy merchant of Venice, fails the test twice, but obtains more money from his friend, who in turn borrows it from a Jew, to make a successful third attempt. (He does not drink the sleeping potion.) When the debt is called in, Giannetto's ladylove disguises herself as a lawyer, pleads his case in court, and wins. The Jew is reviled and receives no money. The "doctor of laws" asks payment from Giannetto in the form of the ring given him by his lady. Reluctantly he gives it and returns to Belmont. Despite her torturing him about the ring, they live happily ever after. The moneylender is a lesser figure. The story is a kind of fairy tale. Although it contains the narrative elements of *The Merchant*—the wooing, the borrowing from a Jewish usurer, the story of the pound of flesh, the young woman's disguise at the trial, and the conflict over the keepsake ring—it has only one set of lovers, no daughter for the moneylender, and no clown.

Several of those elements appear to be Shakespeare's inventions, while others—such as the story of an heiress who must be won by choosing among three caskets—are more certainly located in known sources. The casket story is a popular legend found in Boccaccio's *Decameron,* in John Gower's *Confessio Amantis,* and in the *Gesta Romanorum,* which was translated into English in 1577 and 1595. Christopher Marlowe's play *The Jew of Malta* (1589) contains a despicable Jewish villain whose daughter, Abigail, loves a Christian and, like Jessica in *The Merchant*, renounces her religion.

Language and Structure

The triple love plot and the Shylock-Antonio story are linked by the appearance throughout of Bassanio, Portia, and Jessica. As the two plots interweave, the characters create a series of interlocked obligations to one another based upon money. Bassanio requires money to repay his debts and hopes to marry a wealthy woman, the heiress Portia, in order to achieve that. But to make that money he must ask help from Antonio who borrows from Shylock who claims to borrow it from his associate Tubal. When Portia accepts Bassanio, she becomes involved in these male debts, and tells Bassanio that she will not consummate their love until he is freed from his debt to Antonio, which means Antonio must be freed from his bond to Shylock. Because the men are incapable of right-

ing the situation they have created, Portia travels to Venice, disguises herself as a lawyer, and resolves the dilemma of Shylock's "pound of flesh." Now the freed Antonio is bound to the young lawyer (Portia), who demands that he/she receive the keepsake ring from Bassanio. Jessica's obligations move in the opposite direction. Although she acknowledges her duties to her father, she abjures them, creating heartache and humiliation for him. Shylock is mocked even further because of the betrayal by his daughter—the opposite of Antonio's fidelity to Bassanio and, eventually, of Portia's to her husband. Shylock, who has sought to possess all, loses all, including his daughter, his religion, and his wealth.

As the play moves between two contrasting locales—the fairy-tale Belmont and mercantile Venice—and through several allegorical levels, its language creates and mirrors the complexity of the characters' multiple and simultaneous bonds and bindings. Among its most obvious linguistic contrasts are those between Shylock's bitterly intense eloquence and Portia's poetic explication of the Christian doctrine of mercy in the courtroom scene. Lancelot Gobbo's anarchic prose parodies at times the biblical story of the Prodigal Son (and also forecasts elements of the Edgar/Gloucester plot in *King Lear*). The language of parable in the casket scenes is a smooth blend of courtly Petrarchan imagery and down-to-earth psychological realism, and seems aptly suited to the scenes in which the princes of Morocco and Aragon make their wrong choices.

Perhaps the most versatile uses of language come in Act 5, serving for directors, critics, and audiences alike as a kind of coda to the action. Lorenzo's praise of music at the beginning of the act leads him to remember the stories of tragic heroines with whom Jessica teasingly aligns herself. Lorenzo then explains to his wife the doctrine of the music of the spheres, the perfect harmony that human beings have not been able to hear since they were expelled from the Garden of Eden. Music here represents order, harmony, and concord in human relationships. Yet, as if to prove the truth that such concord will always be imperfect this side of paradise, Shakespeare reintroduces a comic quarrel that the ever-loyal Antonio redeems, as well as the bawdy talk of Gratiano. This blend of seriously stated themes and earthy comedy creates a characteristically full Shakespearean close.

Themes and Issues

Unabashed Racism

The Merchant of Venice draws from, explores, and exploits the anti-Semitism of its time. Several racist elements exist in the play (e.g., Portia's foreign suitors, all of whom are teased for their foreignness), but to contemporary audiences, Shakespeare's depiction of Shylock is the most disturbing of these. Shylock is ostracized not only because he is an outsider, but also because he is a usurer—he lends money with interest, a practice still frowned upon among Christians in the 1590s because the New Testament, and for many centuries the Catholic Church, had condemned it. Usurers were seen as getting something for nothing, so the practice was viewed as corrupt and its practitioners as greedy misers. In some European countries only Jews were allowed to practice usury—and then were despised, as Antonio hates Shylock, for doing precisely that. Antonio does not dispute Shylock's report of having been abused; this merchant has indeed kicked and spat upon "the Jew" for charging interest. Many times, Shylock says, he has been berated for his wealth and usury and "Still have I borne it with a patient shrug, / For sufferance is the badge of all our tribe." Shylock reminds Antonio of his ill-treatment, then continues:

> You call me a misbeliever, cutthroat dog,
> And spit on my Jewish gaberdine
> And all for use of that which is mine own.
> Well then, it now appears you need my help . . .
> You, that did void your rheum upon my beard,
> And foot me as you would spurn a stranger cur
> Over your threshold.
>
> (1.3.109–112, 115–117)

Such ill-treatment by Antonio, and worse by Gratiano, complicates our response to these intolerant Christians.

Beyond the question of usury, Shylock, who is referred to by name only three times in the play, is often demonized by imagery that associates him with animals such as dogs, wolves, and ravens or, most explicitly, with the devil. Lancelot Gobbo identifies Shylock as "the very devil incarnation." Salanio calls him "the devil . . . in the likeness of a Jew," and Bassanio calls him a "cruel devil." In one of the play's most quoted lines, Antonio notes how Shylock's arguments in favor of usury remind him that "the devil can cite Scripture for his purpose" (1.3.96). Several of Shylock's speeches suggest that he really would rather murder Antonio— "have the heart of him if he forfeit"—than be repaid, because Antonio is a competitor in business; without him in Venice, Shylock could become wealthier. This notion of the devilish, murderous, greedy Jew descends from Marlowe's *The Jew of Malta*, in which Barabas, that play's moneylender, is portrayed as a villain who poisons wells, thus underscoring a prominent myth that Jews ritually murdered Christians, especially children, and drank their blood. Shakespeare's depiction of Shylock, on the other hand, is more nuanced and less flamboyant than Marlowe's caricature of Barabas.

As literary scholar James Shapiro points out in his *Shakespeare and the Jews*, certain questions about *The*

Merchant cannot be easily resolved. Nonetheless—or perhaps because of this—he defends keeping *The Merchant* in the contemporary repertory. The dark impulses of irrational bigotry are elusive and may never disappear, but plays that illuminate them at least give us a "glimpse of these cultural fault lines". Thus, censoring the play is always more dangerous than staging it, he contends. It must also be noted that when American regional theaters produce the play, they almost always acknowledge its difficulties, reach out for community dialogue about anti-Semitism, and direct the play in ways that control or contextualize the prejudice that in the real world has had such catastrophic effects, especially in the twentieth century.

The Status of Women

Portia can choose a suitor only under the terms of her late father's will. Thus, the culture's patriarchal system requires her obedience to her father, even though he is dead and even though she finds the suitors from Morocco and Aragon distasteful. When she accepts Bassanio as her choice, she knows (like Kate in *The Taming of the Shrew*) that she is giving up control of her inheritance to him. (The fairy-tale quality of the Belmont plot comes in part from the sense that the risk of the wrong man choosing the casket of lead somehow has been minimized, as if Portia's benevolent father or divine providence were shaping the choices.) Although Portia's strength and intelligence, which are so evident when she resolves the legal dilemmas the men cannot untangle, suggest that she may be more spirited than her husband, she remains nonetheless submissive and ready to call Bassanio her lord. Yet her teasing of Bassanio in the comic business of the keepsake ring shows that she is neither silenced nor oppressed by the relationship.

Because Jessica has a far less benign father, she can find happiness in marriage only by leaving her faith and her father behind. Like Portia, she experiences and illustrates the central paradox of the lead casket: "Who chooseth me must give and hazard all he hath." In other words, only if one is willing to lose all can one find happiness. Still, Jessica's spirits are low at the end of the play, and though she is accepted into her new world, the joking of Lancelot Gobbo and her discomfort about taking on a male disguise seem to suggest anxiety about whether she—and the Christian society she has entered—will be able to make the deep changes needed for her to achieve happiness as a convert. Other complications emerge in and after the trial scene. That the husbands are so readily fooled by their shrewd wives suggests that women, for all their external submissiveness, hold on to their own intellectual and emotional powers behind the facade of traditional marriage, in which women forfeited all of their rights. As critic Lisa Jardine suggests, however, in "Cultural Confusion and Shakespeare's Learned Heroine: 'These are old paradoxes,'" Portia's knowledge of the law provokes a divided response: she shows herself both chastely loyal as a woman of manly spirit and mind and also authoritative enough to be feared by men.

False Appearances

Many characters in *The Merchant* must learn to distinguish appearance from reality. This is the riddle of the caskets: that what appears most valuable may have little real substance, while what seems least appealing may contain the thing of true value. Thus, Portia's picture resides in the lead casket. Accordingly, her suitors reveal their true quality when confronted with her puzzle. The Prince of Morocco chooses the gold, thinking that the casket's inscription, "Who chooseth me shall gain what many men desire," refers to Portia herself, whom he sees as the most desirable merchandise in the marriage mart. And so he loses. The Prince of Aragon comes closer to recognizing the difference between false and true when he assesses the golden chest with its inscription. He notes:

> That "many" may be meant
> By the fool multitude, that choose by show,
> Not learning more than the fond eye doth teach,
> Which pries not to th'interior, but like the martlet
> Builds in the weather on the outward wall,
> Even in the force and road of casualty.
>
> (2.9.25–30)

Yet Aragon's real and far less lofty reason for not choosing gold involves arrogance: He will not rank himself with the "barbarous multitudes." Instead, with clear self-regard, he chooses the silver casket, inscribed "Who chooseth me shall get as much as he deserves." He also loses. Bassanio can never succeed in his quest for Portia until he learns that the financial motives that have brought him to Belmont must be supplanted by the desire to choose a woman of substance. Bassanio's eloquent and lengthy speech, when his turn to choose arrives, encapsulates this theme. He proceeds through a series of images drawn from law, religion, warfare, and aesthetics to illustrate his opening premise "So may the outward shows be least themselves; / The world is still deceived with ornament" (3.2.73–74).

Legalism

The Merchant of Venice is governed by legalisms, by (as critic Anthony Miller notes): "contracts, wills, marriage oaths, fidelity to bonds and release from bonds." Shylock, as an alien Jew in Christendom, must depend upon a system of laws for his rights. Yet his collision with Antonio and then Portia shows that Shakespeare's Venice can use its laws not only to achieve a just socie-

ty but to privilege Christians and enrich itself at the expense of those it perceives as being outsiders. The confrontation between Portia and Shylock during the trial scene has often been viewed as a conflict of the New Testament rule of mercy against (and superceding) the Old Testament law of revenge. Yet the play, as Miller points out in his "Matters of State" (Leggatt, 112–214), "conforms only with difficulty to this dichotomy." Portia, despite the beauty of her "quality of mercy" speech, insists upon enforcing the law against Shylock, until the duke intervenes. Her "mercy" does not drop "as the gentle rain" but rather pelts Shylock. And, excepting death, the final judgment upon him could hardly be harsher punishment: Shylock is forgiven at the expense of his wealth and his cherished religion, and he is forced to become a kind of ward of his enemy Antonio. The revenge feels so cruel that even the lighthearted final scenes, with their mock trial at Belmont, cannot make audiences forget it. Shylock's forced conversion transforms the traditional gestures of inclusiveness at the conclusion of the entertainment into a grotesque, exclusionary parody.

Staging Challenges

The Antonio-Bassanio Relationship

Antonio lacks energy at the beginning of the play; in contemporary terms, he is depressed. "In sooth, I know not why I am so sad. / It wearies me, You say it wearies you," he tells Solanio in the opening lines. And, although this melancholy merchant becomes the focus of his friends' love and concern throughout the action, he is excluded from the happiness of the wedded couples at the end of the play. Because he cannot fathom, and also resists revealing to others, the possible reasons for his sadness, at least one character suggests to him, "Why then, you are in love." His reply "Fie, fie!" is evasive.

We are left with the possibility that Antonio's passionate loyalty to Bassanio has a depth that separates it from conventional friendship. Referring to Antonio's emotional dependence upon Bassanio, Solanio says (at 2.8.50), "I think he only loves the world for him." Still later, in the trial scene, Antonio is willing to accept death as the cost of this friendship. Thus, although Antonio encourages and supports Bassanio's marriage, the character is often played as homoerotically bound to his friend. Especially in modern-dress versions of the play, Antonio has been interpreted as a repressed homosexual, tongue-tied about the true nature of his love, and willing to sustain his sadness, even until death, rather than reveal his feelings directly. Alexander Leggatt notes in an essay appended to the 1992 Folger edition of the play that the term "homosexual" did not exist until the early twentieth century and "Our own language of desire and love does not necessarily apply in other cultures" (218). Accordingly, whether the homoerotic undertones are made explicit or not, actors must convey the intensity of Antonio's feelings and the irony that, because he is excluded from the wedded society represented by the couples, he shares with Shylock a kind of outsider status as the play closes. In this, he resembles two very different characters excluded from marriage in the next two comedies in this anthology—Malvolio in *Twelfth Night* and Don Pedro in *Much Ado About Nothing*.

"Jewish Gaberdine": Shylock's Appearance

Because Shylock is one of the half dozen best-known roles in Shakespeare (though also one of the shortest), interpretive choices, including what he should look like and wear, take on highly charged significance. Actors initially made him appear as a malignant fiend, and may even have played him with the traditional red wig of the stereotypical Jew, a choice that would have associated him in the audience's mind with the betrayer of Christ, Judas Iscariot. Yet by 1814 when Edmund Kean assumed the role at London's Drury Lane Theatre, Shylock became a man of religious pride who was plausibly resentful, even noble. Still later, the great Victorian actor Henry Irving played him as a dignified victim embodying the qualities of a persecuted and long-suffering race. In 1970, in Jonathan Miller's production for the Royal Shakespeare Company, Sir Laurence Olivier visualized him as a prosperous private banker in Edwardian top hat and yarmulke (i.e., Jewish skullcap). This interpretation influenced many subsequent actors, including Hal Holbrook, who took on the role in a chic, Italian modern-dress staging directed by Jack O'Brien at San Diego's Old Globe Theater in 1991. He played a shrewd and elegant businessman in mercantile Venice, a man persecuted, vengeful, but justly punished.

In a fascinating Royal Shakespeare Company video (and the accompanying text), "Exploring a Character," actors Patrick Stewart and David Suchet describe their very different interpretations of the role in a way that illuminates its expansive history. Stewart, who says that his first inclination was to refuse the controversial part, visualizes Shylock as shabby and down-at-the-heels, yet with a refined accent. Suchet, who is Jewish, never wants anyone to forget that Shylock is an outsider—even in his language and accent. But, Suchet notes, "Shylock and *The Merchant of Venice* in comparison to the literature of the time were pretty mild, and Shylock himself is perhaps the first Jew in (Western) literature to have the chance of his soul being saved." The two actors agree that the key to an effective stage interpretation of the character is to "play the inconsistencies." This video is discussed in greater detail in the stage history below.

The Suitors

The play's inherent racism can prove difficult for directors and actors in performance, as noted earlier. Offending lines such as Portia's dismissal of the Prince of Morocco ("A gentle riddance. Draw the curtains, go. / Let all of his complexion choose me so") are sometimes excised. More often, contemporary directors highlight these words to show that even Portia participates in the prejudices of her era. In a rare stage direction referring to costumes, Shakespeare's text dramatically underscores Morocco's color: "*Enter [the Prince] of Morocco, a tawny Moor all in white*" (2.1). Given these prejudices, directors sometimes choose a comic approach that encourages the kind of exclusionary laughter that may have greeted the Prince of Morocco, the Prince of Aragon, and Shylock during the Elizabethan era, and that today elicits nervous or sardonic laughter.

A second challenge is to be found in the length, rhetorical intricacy, and mixed tone of the speeches in 2.7, 2.9, and 3.2. Portia arrives with Nerissa and a suitor for each of the three scenes. Staging can adopt a stylized manner that suggests the realm of fairy tale, parable, or romance. Yet at the end of the first two scenes, Portia is undeniably cruel in her dismissal of the foreign princes; she calls them "fools." Nerissa quotes the old saying "Hanging and wiving go by destiny" to mock the losers. Directors can underscore either the romance in a kind of balletic repetition of the choosing motif, or the commercial bargaining involved, or (most effectively) blend the two into a full expression of the contradictory position into which Portia has been placed once she accedes to the terms of her father's will.

"Hath Not a Jew Eyes?"—Sympathy or Menace?

Shylock's presumed villainy is a key element of the play's story. Brilliantly, Shakespeare both exploits the prejudice of his age while also creating a character toward whom it is possible to feel sympathy. Thus, actors and directors are faced with a central decision—how to play Shylock's famously compelling self-defense (3.1.57ff.), which begins "Hath not a Jew eyes?" Such nineteenth-century actors as Kean, and especially the Victorian Henry Irving, explored these speeches as those of a wronged victim, a dignified representative of his religion. In such a reading, the speech becomes a plea for the recognition of commonalities. Empathy for Shylock erases his outsider status, at least emotionally, for he becomes a member of the same human race as Antonio, Portia, and Bassanio. Other actors, however, have emphasized that this speech, at least in its dramatic context, is not so much a plea for tolerance as a defense of Shylock's cruelty. Shylock's tone can shift to the ominous when he completes his catalog of shared human traits: "If you prick us do we not bleed? If you tickle us do we not laugh?" he says, but follows up with the threat, "And if you wrong us, shall we not revenge?" (3.1.60–63). The implacable emotional logic of Shylock's conclusion increases the sense of menace: "The villainy you teach me I will execute and it shall go hard but I will better the instruction" (3.1.67–69). Shylock does exactly that in the trial scene, until the moment that Portia "betters the instruction" by insisting that the letter of the law be followed at his expense.

The Ring Trick and a Bawdy Ending

With the episode of the keepsake rings comes a final, light-hearted variation upon the paradox of winning by losing. Still disguised as a doctor of law and his clerk, Portia and Nerissa force their new husbands to make a difficult choice. Because they have just saved Antonio from Shylock's knife, the two disguised wives ask for the rings on the fingers of Bassanio and Gratiano as payment. The men are forced to choose between their love for the women and their friendship with Antonio. They give away the rings, and, as the play circles to a close, the women tease the men mercilessly about their "betrayal." Portia claims that she will be "as liberal" with her favors to the lawyer as Bassanio was with the ring:

> I'll not deny him anything I have,
> No, not my body nor my husband's bed . . .
> > Watch me like Argus;
> If you do not, if I be left alone,
> Now, by mine honor, which is yet mine own,
> I'll have that doctor for my bedfellow.
> > (5.1.227–228; 230–233)

The last scene now descends from the idealized realm of the earlier romantic speeches to a far more physical and human ending filled with sexual suggestion, as the couples stand on the threshold of consummating their marriages. In fact, the play ends with a bawdy double-entendre as Gratiano jokes of wishing for dark so he can couch with the "doctor's clerk," claiming he now fears nothing as much as "keeping safe Nerissa's ring." The scene's adultery jokes restate the notion of a claim or bond of the speaker upon another's body, thus mixing the final images of harmony with remembrances of pain, even Shylock's, and with anxiety, however mild, about the future. Lorenzo and Jessica recall stories of tragic love to which they laughingly compare their own. Thus, while the lovers' concord may be tuned to the music that plays throughout the scene, their final joy has risen out of a discord that remains imperfectly resolved. The subtlest productions suggest both the harmony and the unresolved issues (gender and money conflicts, the fates of Shylock and Antonio) that complicate the play's slightly melancholy and contemplative ending.

The Merchant of Venice

[*Dramatis Personae*

THE DUKE OF VENICE
ANTONIO, *a merchant of Venice*
BASSANIO, *his friend, suitor to Portia*
GRATIANO, *a follower of Bassanio, in love with Nerissa*
SOLANIO, } *friends to Antonio*
SALERIO, } *and Bassanio*
LORENZO, *in love with Jessica*
LEONARDO, *servant to Bassanio*

PORTIA, *a rich heiress of Belmont*
NERISSA, *her waiting-gentlewoman*
BALTHASAR, *servant to Portia*
STEPHANO, *servant to Portia*

THE PRINCE OF MOROCCO, *suitor to Portia*
THE PRINCE OF ARAGON, *suitor to Portia*
A MESSENGER *to Portia*

SHYLOCK, *a rich Jew*
JESSICA, *his daughter*
TUBAL, *a Jew, Shylock's friend*
LANCELOT GOBBO, *a clown, servant to Shylock and then to Bassanio*
OLD GOBBO, *Lancelot's father*

Magnificoes of Venice, Officers of the Court of Justice, Jailor, Servants to Portia, and other Attendants

SCENE: *Partly at Venice and partly at Belmont, the seat of Portia*]

[1.1]

Enter Antonio, Salerio, and Solanio.

ANTONIO
In sooth, I know not why I am so sad.   1
It wearies me, you say it wearies you;
But how I caught it, found it, or came by it,
What stuff 'tis made of, whereof it is born,
I am to learn;   5
And such a want-wit sadness makes of me   6
That I have much ado to know myself.

SALERIO
Your mind is tossing on the ocean,
There where your argosies with portly sail,   9
Like signors and rich burghers on the flood,   10
Or as it were the pageants of the sea,   11
Do overpeer the petty traffickers   12
That curtsy to them, do them reverence,   13
As they fly by them with their woven wings.   14

SOLANIO
Believe me, sir, had I such venture forth,   15
The better part of my affections would
Be with my hopes abroad. I should be still   17
Plucking the grass to know where sits the wind,
Peering in maps for ports and piers and roads;   19
And every object that might make me fear
Misfortune to my ventures, out of doubt
Would make me sad.

SALERIO   My wind cooling my broth
Would blow me to an ague when I thought   23
What harm a wind too great might do at sea.
I should not see the sandy hourglass run
But I should think of shallows and of flats,   26
And see my wealthy *Andrew* docked in sand,   27
Vailing her high-top lower than her ribs   28
To kiss her burial. Should I go to church   29
And see the holy edifice of stone
And not bethink me straight of dangerous rocks   31
Which, touching but my gentle vessel's side,
Would scatter all her spices on the stream,
Enrobe the roaring waters with my silks,
And, in a word, but even now worth this,   35
And now worth nothing? Shall I have the thought
To think on this, and shall I lack the thought
That such a thing bechanced would make me sad?   38
But tell not me. I know Antonio
Is sad to think upon his merchandise.

ANTONIO
Believe me, no. I thank my fortune for it,
My ventures are not in one bottom trusted,   42
Nor to one place; nor is my whole estate
Upon the fortune of this present year.   44
Therefore my merchandise makes me not sad.
SOLANIO
Why then, you are in love.
ANTONIO   Fie, fie!
SOLANIO
Not in love neither? Then let us say you are sad
Because you are not merry; and 'twere as easy
For you to laugh and leap, and say you are merry
Because you are not sad. Now, by two-headed
          Janus,   50
Nature hath framed strange fellows in her time: 51
Some that will evermore peep through their eyes   52
And laugh like parrots at a bagpiper,   53
And other of such vinegar aspect   54
That they'll not show their teeth in way of smile
Though Nestor swear the jest be laughable.   56

Enter Bassanio, Lorenzo, and Gratiano.

Here comes Bassanio, your most noble kinsman,
Gratiano, and Lorenzo. Fare ye well.
We leave you now with better company.
SALERIO
I would have stayed till I had made you merry,
If worthier friends had not prevented me.   61
ANTONIO
Your worth is very dear in my regard.
I take it your own business calls on you,
And you embrace th'occasion to depart.   64
SALERIO   Good morrow, my good lords.
BASSANIO
Good signors both, when shall we laugh? Say,
          when?   66
You grow exceeding strange. Must it be so?   67
SALERIO
We'll make our leisures to attend on yours.   68
          Exeunt Salerio and Solanio.
LORENZO
My lord Bassanio, since you have found Antonio,
We two will leave you, but at dinnertime,
I pray you, have in mind where we must meet.
BASSANIO   I will not fail you.
GRATIANO
You look not well, Signor Antonio.
You have too much respect upon the world.   74
They lose it that do buy it with much care.
Believe me, you are marvelously changed.

1.1. Location: A street in Venice.
1 In sooth Truly. sad morose, dismal-looking. 5 am to learn have
yet to learn 6 such . . . of me such sadness makes me so distracted,
lacking in good sense 9 argosies large merchant ships. (So named
from *Ragusa*, the modern city of Dubrovnik.) portly majestic 10 signors gentlemen. flood sea 11 pageants mobile stages used in plays
or processions 12 overpeer look down upon 13 curtsy i.e., bob up
and down, or lower topsails in token of respect (*reverence*) 14 woven
wings canvas sails. 15 venture forth investment at risk 17 still
continually 19 roads anchorages, open harbors 23 blow . . . ague
i.e., start me shivering 26 flats shoals 27 *Andrew* name of a ship.
(Perhaps after the *St. Andrew*, a Spanish galleon captured at Cadiz in
1596.) 28 Vailing lowering. (Usually as a sign of submission.)
high-top topmast 29 burial burial place. 31 bethink me straight
be put in mind immediately 35 even now a short while ago. this
i.e., the cargo of spices and silks 38 bechanced having happened

42 bottom ship's hold 44 Upon . . . year i.e., risked upon the chance
of the present year. 50 two-headed Janus a Roman god of all beginnings, represented by a figure with two faces 51 framed fashioned
52 peep . . . eyes i.e., look with eyes narrowed by laughter 53 at a
bagpiper i.e., even at a bagpiper, whose music was regarded as
melancholic 54 other others. vinegar aspect sour, sullen looks
56 Nestor venerable senior officer in the *Iliad*, noted for gravity
61 prevented forestalled 64 th'occasion the opportunity 66 laugh
i.e., be merry together. 67 strange distant. Must it be so? Must
you go? or, Must you show reserve? 68 We'll . . . yours We'll adjust
our spare time to accommodate your schedule. 74 respect . . . world
concern for worldly affairs of business.

ANTONIO

I hold the world but as the world, Gratiano—
A stage where every man must play a part,
And mine a sad one.

GRATIANO   Let me play the fool.

With mirth and laughter let old wrinkles come,
And let my liver rather heat with wine   81
Than my heart cool with mortifying groans.   82
Why should a man whose blood is warm within
Sit like his grandsire cut in alabaster?   84
Sleep when he wakes, and creep into the jaundice   85
By being peevish? I tell thee what, Antonio—
I love thee, and 'tis my love that speaks—
There are a sort of men whose visages
Do cream and mantle like a standing pond,   89
And do a willful stillness entertain   90
With purpose to be dressed in an opinion   91
Of wisdom, gravity, profound conceit,   92
As who should say, "I am Sir Oracle,   93
And when I ope my lips let no dog bark!"   94
Oh, my Antonio, I do know of these
That therefore only are reputed wise
For saying nothing, when, I am very sure,
If they should speak, would almost damn those ears   98
Which, hearing them, would call their brothers
       fools.   99
I'll tell thee more of this another time.
But fish not with this melancholy bait   101
For this fool gudgeon, this opinion.—   102
Come, good Lorenzo.—Fare ye well awhile.
I'll end my exhortation after dinner.

LORENZO [to Antonio and Bassanio]

Well, we will leave you then till dinnertime.
I must be one of these same dumb wise men,   106
For Gratiano never lets me speak.

GRATIANO

Well, keep me company but two years more,   108
Thou shalt not know the sound of thine own
       tongue.

ANTONIO

Fare you well. I'll grow a talker for this gear.   110

GRATIANO

Thanks, i'faith, for silence is only commendable
In a neat's tongue dried and a maid not vendible.   112
              Exeunt [*Gratiano and Lorenzo*].

ANTONIO   Is that anything now?   113

BASSANIO   Gratiano speaks an infinite deal of nothing,
more than any man in all Venice. His reasons are as   115
two grains of wheat hid in two bushels of chaff; you
shall seek all day ere you find them, and when you
have them they are not worth the search.

ANTONIO

Well, tell me now what lady is the same   119
To whom you swore a secret pilgrimage,
That you today promised to tell me of.

BASSANIO

'Tis not unknown to you, Antonio,
How much I have disabled mine estate
By something showing a more swelling port   124
Than my faint means would grant continuance.   125
Nor do I now make moan to be abridged   126
From such a noble rate; but my chief care   127
Is to come fairly off from the great debts   128
Wherein my time, something too prodigal,   129
Hath left me gaged. To you, Antonio,   130
I owe the most, in money and in love,
And from your love I have a warranty   132
To unburden all my plots and purposes   133
How to get clear of all the debts I owe.

ANTONIO

I pray you, good Bassanio, let me know it;
And if it stand, as you yourself still do,   136
Within the eye of honor, be assured   137
My purse, my person, my extremest means
Lie all unlocked to your occasions.

BASSANIO

In my schooldays, when I had lost one shaft,   140
I shot his fellow of the selfsame flight   141
The selfsame way with more advisèd watch   142
To find the other forth, and by adventuring both   143
I oft found both. I urge this childhood proof
Because what follows is pure innocence.   145
I owe you much, and, like a willful youth,
That which I owe is lost; but if you please
To shoot another arrow that self way   148
Which you did shoot the first, I do not doubt,
As I will watch the aim, or to find both   150
Or bring your latter hazard back again   151
And thankfully rest debtor for the first.   152

ANTONIO

You know me well, and herein spend but time   153
To wind about my love with circumstance;   154
And out of doubt you do me now more wrong

---

81 heat with wine (The liver was regarded as the seat of the passions and wine as an agency for inflaming them.) **82 mortifying** penitential and deadly. (Sighs were thought to cost the heart a drop of blood.) **84 in alabaster** i.e., in a stone effigy upon a tomb. **85 jaundice** (Regarded as arising from the effects of too much choler or yellow bile, one of the four humors, in the blood.) **89 cream and mantle** become covered with scum, i.e., acquire a lifeless, stiff expression. **standing** stagnant **90–2 And . . . conceit** and who maintain a willful silence in order to acquire a reputation for gravity and deep thought **93 As . . . say** as if to say **94 let . . . bark** i.e., let no creature dare to interrupt me. **98–9 would . . . fools** i.e., would virtually condemn their hearers into calling them fools. (Compare Matthew 5:22, in which anyone calling another a fool is threatened with damnation.) **101–2 fish . . . opinion** i.e., don't go fishing for a reputation of being wise, using your melancholy silence as the bait to fool people. (*Gudgeon,* a small fish, was thought of as a type of gullibility.) **106 dumb** mute, speechless **108 keep** if you keep **110 for this gear** in view of what you say. **112 neat's** ox's. **not vendible** i.e., not yet salable in the marriage market.

113 Is . . . now? i.e., Was all that talk about anything? **115 reasons** reasonable ideas **119 the same** i.e., the one **124 By . . . port** by showing a somewhat more lavish style of living **125 grant continuance** allow to continue. **126–7 make . . . rate** complain at being cut back from such a high style of living **128 to . . . off** honorably to extricate myself **129 time** youthful lifetime **130 gaged** pledged, in pawn. **132 warranty** authorization **133 unburden** disclose **136–7 if . . . honor** if it looks honorable, as your conduct has always done **140 shaft** arrow **141 his** its. **selfsame flight** same kind and range **142 advisèd** careful **143 forth** out. **adventuring** risking **145 innocence** ingenuousness, sincerity. **148 self** same **150 or** either **151 hazard** that which was risked **152 rest** remain **153 spend but time** only waste time **154 To . . . circumstance** i.e., in not asking plainly what you want. (*Circumstance* here means "circumlocution.")

In making question of my uttermost   156
Than if you had made waste of all I have.
Then do but say to me what I should do
That in your knowledge may by me be done,
And I am prest unto it. Therefore speak.   160

BASSANIO
In Belmont is a lady richly left;   161
And she is fair and, fairer than that word,
Of wondrous virtues. Sometimes from her eyes   163
I did receive fair speechless messages.
Her name is Portia, nothing undervalued   165
To Cato's daughter, Brutus' Portia.   166
Nor is the wide world ignorant of her worth,
For the four winds blow in from every coast
Renownèd suitors, and her sunny locks
Hang on her temples like a golden fleece,
Which makes her seat of Belmont Colchis' strand, 171
And many Jasons come in quest of her.
Oh, my Antonio, had I but the means
To hold a rival place with one of them,
I have a mind presages me such thrift   175
That I should questionless be fortunate.

ANTONIO
Thou know'st that all my fortunes are at sea;
Neither have I money nor commodity   178
To raise a present sum. Therefore go forth.   179
Try what my credit can in Venice do;
That shall be racked even to the uttermost   181
To furnish thee to Belmont, to fair Portia.
Go presently inquire, and so will I,   183
Where money is, and I no question make   184
To have it of my trust or for my sake.   *Exeunt.* 185

❖

[1.2]

Enter Portia with her waiting woman, Nerissa.

PORTIA   By my troth, Nerissa, my little body is aweary   1
of this great world.

NERISSA   You would be, sweet madam, if your miseries   3
were in the same abundance as your good fortunes
are; and yet, for aught I see, they are as sick that surfeit   5
with too much as they that starve with nothing. It is
no mean happiness, therefore, to be seated in the   7
mean. Superfluity comes sooner by white hairs, but   8
competency lives longer.   9

PORTIA   Good sentences, and well pronounced.   10

NERISSA   They would be better if well followed.

PORTIA   If to do were as easy as to know what were
good to do, chapels had been churches and poor
men's cottages princes' palaces. It is a good divine that   14
follows his own instructions. I can easier teach twenty what were good to be done than to be one of the
twenty to follow mine own teaching. The brain may
devise laws for the blood, but a hot temper leaps o'er   18
a cold decree; such a hare is madness, the youth, to
skip o'er the meshes of good counsel, the cripple. But   20
this reasoning is not in the fashion to choose me a   21
husband. Oh, me, the word "choose"! I may neither   22
choose who I would nor refuse who I dislike; so is the
will of a living daughter curbed by the will of a dead   24
father. Is it not hard, Nerissa, that I cannot choose one
nor refuse none?

NERISSA   Your father was ever virtuous, and holy men
at their death have good inspirations; therefore the
lottery that he hath devised in these three chests of
gold, silver, and lead, whereof who chooses his mean-   30
ing chooses you, will no doubt never be chosen by
any rightly but one who you shall rightly love. But   32
what warmth is there in your affection towards any of
these princely suitors that are already come?

PORTIA   I pray thee, overname them, and as thou nam-   35
est them I will describe them; and according to my
description level at my affection.   37

NERISSA   First, there is the Neapolitan prince.

PORTIA   Ay, that's a colt indeed, for he doth nothing but   39
talk of his horse, and he makes it a great appropriation   40
to his own good parts that he can shoe him him-   41
self. I am much afeard my lady his mother played false
with a smith.

NERISSA   Then is there the County Palatine.   44

PORTIA   He doth nothing but frown, as who should say,   45
"An you will not have me, choose." He hears merry   46
tales and smiles not. I fear he will prove the weeping   47
philosopher when he grows old, being so full of un-   48
mannerly sadness in his youth. I had rather be mar-   49
ried to a death's-head with a bone in his mouth than
to either of these. God defend me from these two!

NERISSA   How say you by the French lord, Monsieur   52
Le Bon?

PORTIA   God made him, and therefore let him pass for a
man. In truth, I know it is a sin to be a mocker, but
he! Why, he hath a horse better than the Neapolitan's,

<hr />

156 **In . . . uttermost** in showing any doubt of my intention to do all I can
160 **prest** ready   161 **richly left** left a large fortune (by her father's will)
163 **Sometimes** Once   165–6 **nothing undervalued To** of no less worth
than   166 **Portia** (The same Portia as in Shakespeare's *Julius Caesar*.)
171 **Colchis'** (Jason adventured for the golden fleece in the land of
Colchis, on the Black Sea.)   **strand** shore   175 **presages** i.e., that presages.
thrift profit and good fortune   178 **commodity** merchandise   179 **a
present sum** ready money.   181 **racked** stretched   183 **presently**
immediately   184 **no question make** have no doubt   185 **of my trust**
on the basis of my credit as a merchant.   **sake** i.e., personal sake.
1.2. Location: Belmont. Portia's house.
1 **troth** faith   3 **would be** would have reason to be (weary)   5 **surfeit**
overindulge   7 **mean** small. (With a pun; see next note.)   7–8 **in the
mean** having neither too much nor too little.   8 **comes sooner by**
acquires sooner   9 **competency** modest means   10 **sentences** maxims.
pronounced delivered.

14 **divine** clergyman   18 **blood** (Thought of as a chief agent of the
passions, which in turn were regarded as the enemies of reason.)
20 **meshes** nets. (Used here for hunting hares.)   **good counsel, the
cripple** (Wisdom is portrayed as old and no longer agile.)   20–2 **But
. . . husband** But this talk is not the way to help me choose a husband.
24 **will . . . will** volition . . . testament   30 **who** whoever.   **his** i.e., the
father's   32 **rightly . . . rightly** correctly . . . truly   35 **overname
them** name them over   37 **level** aim, guess   39 **colt** i.e., wanton and
foolish young man. (With a punning appropriateness to his interest in
horses.)   40 **appropriation** addition   41 **good parts** accomplishments   44 **County Palatine** a count entitled to supreme jurisdiction
in his province.   45 **as who should say** as one might say   46 **An** If.
choose i.e., do as you please.   47–8 **the weeping philosopher** i.e.,
Heraclitus of Ephesus, a melancholic and retiring philosopher of
about 500 B.C., often contrasted with Democritus, the "laughing
philosopher"   49 **sadness** melancholy   52 **How . . . by** What do you
have to say about

a better bad habit of frowning than the Count Palatine; he is every man in no man. If a throstle sing, he falls straight a-capering. He will fence with his own shadow. If I should marry him, I should marry twenty husbands. If he would despise me, I would forgive him, for if he love me to madness, I shall never requite him. 58 59 62

NERISSA   What say you, then, to Falconbridge, the young baron of England? 64

PORTIA   You know I say nothing to him, for he understands not me, nor I him. He hath neither Latin, French, nor Italian, and you will come into the court and swear that I have a poor pennyworth in the English. He is a proper man's picture, but alas, who can converse with a dumb show? How oddly he is suited! I think he bought his doublet in Italy, his round hose in France, his bonnet in Germany, and his behavior everywhere. 68 69 70 71 72 73

NERISSA   What think you of the Scottish lord, his neighbor?

PORTIA   That he hath a neighborly charity in him, for he borrowed a box of the ear of the Englishman and swore he would pay him again when he was able. I think the Frenchman became his surety and sealed under for another. 78 80 81

NERISSA   How like you the young German, the Duke of Saxony's nephew?

PORTIA   Very vilely in the morning, when he is sober, and most vilely in the afternoon, when he is drunk. When he is best he is a little worse than a man, and when he is worst he is little better than a beast. An the worst fall that ever fell, I hope I shall make shift to go without him. 87 88

NERISSA   If he should offer to choose, and choose the right casket, you should refuse to perform your father's will if you should refuse to accept him. 90

PORTIA   Therefore, for fear of the worst, I pray thee, set a deep glass of Rhenish wine on the contrary casket, for if the devil be within and that temptation without, I know he will choose it. I will do anything, Nerissa, ere I will be married to a sponge. 94 95 96

NERISSA   You need not fear, lady, the having any of these lords. They have acquainted me with their determinations, which is indeed to return to their home and to trouble you with no more suit, unless you may

be won by some other sort than your father's imposition depending on the caskets. 102 103

PORTIA   If I live to be as old as Sibylla, I will die as chaste as Diana, unless I be obtained by the manner of my father's will. I am glad this parcel of wooers are so reasonable, for there is not one among them but I dote on his very absence, and I pray God grant them a fair departure. 104 105 106

NERISSA   Do you not remember, lady, in your father's time, a Venetian, a scholar and a soldier, that came hither in company of the Marquess of Montferrat?

PORTIA   Yes, yes, it was Bassanio—as I think, so was he called.

NERISSA   True, madam. He, of all the men that ever my foolish eyes looked upon was the best deserving a fair lady.

PORTIA   I remember him well, and I remember him worthy of thy praise.

Enter a Servingman.

How now, what news?

SERVINGMAN   The four strangers seek for you, madam, to take their leave; and there is a forerunner come from a fifth, the Prince of Morocco, who brings word the Prince his master will be here tonight. 121 122

PORTIA   If I could bid the fifth welcome with so good heart as I can bid the other four farewell, I should be glad of his approach. If he have the condition of a saint and the complexion of a devil, I had rather he should shrive me than wive me. 127 128 129

Come, Nerissa. [*To Servingman*] Sirrah, go before. Whiles we shut the gate upon one wooer, another knocks at the door.   *Exeunt.* 130

❧

[1.3]

Enter Bassanio with Shylock the Jew.

SHYLOCK   Three thousand ducats, well. 1

BASSANIO   Ay, sir, for three months.

SHYLOCK   For three months, well.

BASSANIO   For the which, as I told you, Antonio shall be bound.

SHYLOCK   Antonio shall become bound, well.

BASSANIO   May you stead me? Will you pleasure me? Shall I know your answer? 7

SHYLOCK   Three thousand ducats for three months and Antonio bound.

BASSANIO   Your answer to that.

---

58 **he is . . . no man** i.e., he borrows aspects from everyone but has no character of his own.   **throstle** thrush   59 **straight** at once   62 **if** even if   64 **say you . . . to** do you say about. (But Portia wittily puns, in her reply, on the literal sense of "speak to.")   68–70 **come . . . English** i.e., bear witness that I can speak very little English.   70 **He . . . picture** i.e., He looks handsome   71 **dumb show** pantomime. **suited** dressed.   72 **doublet** upper garment corresponding to a jacket.   **round hose** short, puffed-out breeches   73 **bonnet** hat   78 **borrowed** received. (But with a play on the idea of something that must be repaid.)   80–1 **became . . . another** offered to back up the Scottish lord and promised (with as solemn a vow as if he were signing and sealing a document) to add a blow of his own. (An allusion to the age-old alliance of the French and the Scots against the English.)   87 **An** If   88 **fall** befall.   **make shift** manage   90 **offer** undertake   94 **Rhenish wine** a German white wine from the Rhine Valley.   **contrary** i.e., wrong   95 **if** even if   96 **it** i.e., the tempting red wine.

102 **sort** means. (With perhaps a suggestion too of "casting or drawing of lots.")   102–3 **imposition** command, charge   104 **Sibylla** the Cumaean Sibyl, to whom Apollo gave as many years as there were grains in her handful of sand   105 **Diana** goddess of chastity and of the hunt   106 **parcel** assembly, group   121 **four** (Nerissa actually names six suitors; possibly a sign of revision or the author's early draft.)   122 **forerunner** herald   127 **condition** disposition, character   128 **complexion of a devil** (Devils were thought to be black; but *complexion* can also mean "temperament," "disposition.")   129 **shrive me** pardon me, excuse me from having to be wooed. (Literally, act as my confessor and give absolution.)   130 **Sirrah** (Form of address to social inferior.)   **1.3. Location: Venice. A public place.**   1 **ducats** gold coins   7 **stead** supply, assist.   **pleasure** oblige

SHYLOCK   Antonio is a good man.   12

BASSANIO   Have you heard any imputation to the
contrary?

SHYLOCK   Ho, no, no, no, no! My meaning in saying he
is a good man is to have you understand me that he is
sufficient. Yet his means are in supposition. He hath an   17
argosy bound to Tripolis, another to the Indies. I understand, moreover, upon the Rialto, he hath a third   19
at Mexico, a fourth for England, and other ventures he
hath squandered abroad. But ships are but boards,   21
sailors but men. There be land rats and water rats,
water thieves and land thieves—I mean pirates—and
then there is the peril of waters, winds, and rocks. The
man is, notwithstanding, sufficient. Three thousand
ducats. I think I may take his bond.

BASSANIO   Be assured you may.   27

SHYLOCK   I will be assured I may; and that I may be   28
assured, I will bethink me. May I speak with Antonio?

BASSANIO   If it please you to dine with us.

SHYLOCK   Yes, to smell pork, to eat of the habitation
which your prophet the Nazarite conjured the devil   32
into. I will buy with you, sell with you, talk with you,
walk with you, and so following, but I will not eat   34
with you, drink with you, nor pray with you. What
news on the Rialto? Who is he comes here?

Enter Antonio.

BASSANIO   This is Signor Antonio.

SHYLOCK [*aside*]
How like a fawning publican he looks!   38
I hate him for he is a Christian,   39
But more for that in low simplicity   40
He lends out money gratis and brings down   41
The rate of usance here with us in Venice.   42
If I can catch him once upon the hip,   43
I will feed fat the ancient grudge I bear him.   44
He hates our sacred nation, and he rails,   45
Even there where merchants most do congregate,
On me, my bargains, and my well-won thrift,
Which he calls interest. Cursèd be my tribe
If I forgive him!

BASSANIO   Shylock, do you hear?

SHYLOCK   I am debating of my present store,   50
And, by the near guess of my memory,
I cannot instantly raise up the gross   52
Of full three thousand ducats. What of that?
Tubal, a wealthy Hebrew of my tribe,

Will furnish me. But soft, how many months   55
Do you desire? [*To Antonio*] Rest you fair, good
signor!
Your Worship was the last man in our mouths.   57

ANTONIO
Shylock, albeit I neither lend nor borrow
By taking nor by giving of excess,   59
Yet, to supply the ripe wants of my friend,   60
I'll break a custom. [*To Bassanio*] Is he yet possessed   61
How much ye would?   62

SHYLOCK   Ay, ay, three thousand ducats.

ANTONIO   And for three months.

SHYLOCK
I had forgot—three months, you told me so.
Well then, your bond. And let me see—but hear
you,
Methought you said you neither lend nor borrow
Upon advantage.

ANTONIO   I do never use it.   68

SHYLOCK
When Jacob grazed his uncle Laban's sheep—   69
This Jacob from our holy Abram was,   70
As his wise mother wrought in his behalf,
The third possessor; ay, he was the third—   72

ANTONIO
And what of him? Did he take interest?

SHYLOCK
No, not take interest, not as you would say
Directly interest. Mark what Jacob did.
When Laban and himself were compromised   76
That all the eanlings which were streaked and pied   77
Should fall as Jacob's hire, the ewes, being rank,   78
In end of autumn turnèd to the rams,
And when the work of generation was   80
Between these woolly breeders in the act,
The skillful shepherd peeled me certain wands,   82
And in the doing of the deed of kind   83
He stuck them up before the fulsome ewes,   84
Who then conceiving did in eaning time   85
Fall parti-colored lambs, and those were Jacob's.   86
This was a way to thrive, and he was blest;
And thrift is blessing, if men steal it not.   88

ANTONIO
This was a venture, sir, that Jacob served for,   89
A thing not in his power to bring to pass,
But swayed and fashioned by the hand of heaven.
Was this inserted to make interest good?   92
Or is your gold and silver ewes and rams?

---

12 good (Shylock means "solvent," a good credit risk; Bassanio interprets it in the moral sense.)   **17 sufficient** i.e., a good security.
in supposition doubtful, uncertain.   **19 the Rialto** the merchants'
exchange in Venice and the center of commercial activity   **21 squandered** scattered   **27, 28 assured** (Bassanio means that Shylock may
trust Antonio, whereas Shylock means that he will obtain legal assurances.)   **32 Nazarite** Nazarene. (For the reference to Christ's casting
evil spirits into a herd of swine, see Matthew 8:30–2, Mark 5:1–13,
and Luke 8:32–3.)   **34 so following** so forth   **38 publican** Roman tax
gatherer (a term of opprobrium; see Luke 18:9–14); or, innkeeper
39 for because   **40 low simplicity** humble foolishness   **41 gratis**
without charging interest   **42 usance** usury, interest   **43 upon the
hip** i.e., at my mercy. (A figure of speech from wrestling; see Genesis
32:24–9.)   **44 fat** until fatted for the kill   **45 our sacred nation** i.e., the
Hebrew people   **50 I am . . . store** I am considering my current supply of money   **52 gross** total

55 soft i.e., wait a minute   **57 Your . . . mouths** i.e., We were just
speaking of you. (But with ominous connotation of devouring; compare line 44.)   **59 excess** interest   **60 ripe wants** pressing needs
61 possessed informed   **62 ye would** you want.   **68 advantage**
interest.   **69 Jacob** (See Genesis 27, 30:25–43.)   **70 Abram** Abraham
72 third i.e., after Abraham and Isaac.   **possessor** i.e., of the birthright
of which, with the help of Rebecca, he was able to cheat Esau, his
elder brother   **76 compromised** agreed   **77 eanlings** young lambs or
kids. **pied** spotted   **78 hire** wages, share.   **rank** in heat   **80 work of
generation** mating   **82 peeled . . . wands** i.e., partly stripped the bark
of some sticks. (*Me* is used colloquially.)   **83 deed of kind** i.e., copulation   **84 fulsome** lustful, well-fed   **85 eaning** lambing   **86 Fall**
give birth to   **88 thrift** thriving, profit   **89 venture . . . for** uncertain
commercial venture on which Jacob risked his wages   **92 inserted . . .
good** brought in to justify the practice of usury.

SHYLOCK
I cannot tell. I make it breed as fast.   94
But note me, signor—
ANTONIO   Mark you this, Bassanio,
The devil can cite Scripture for his purpose.   96
An evil soul producing holy witness
Is like a villain with a smiling cheek,
A goodly apple rotten at the heart.
Oh, what a goodly outside falsehood hath!
SHYLOCK
Three thousand ducats. 'Tis a good round sum.
Three months from twelve, then let me see, the rate—
ANTONIO
Well, Shylock, shall we be beholding to you?   103
SHYLOCK
Signor Antonio, many a time and oft
In the Rialto you have rated me   105
About my moneys and my usances.
Still have I borne it with a patient shrug,
For sufferance is the badge of all our tribe.   108
You call me misbeliever, cutthroat dog,
And spit upon my Jewish gaberdine,   110
And all for use of that which is mine own.
Well then, it now appears you need my help.
Go to, then. You come to me and you say,   113
"Shylock, we would have moneys"—you say so,
You, that did void your rheum upon my beard   115
And foot me as you spurn a stranger cur   116
Over your threshold. Moneys is your suit.   117
What should I say to you? Should I not say,
"Hath a dog money? Is it possible
A cur can lend three thousand ducats?" Or
Shall I bend low, and in a bondman's key,   121
With bated breath and whispering humbleness,   122
Say this:
"Fair sir, you spit on me on Wednesday last,
You spurned me such a day, another time
You called me dog, and for these courtesies
I'll lend you thus much moneys"?
ANTONIO
I am as like to call thee so again,   128
To spit on thee again, to spurn thee too.
If thou wilt lend this money, lend it not
As to thy friends, for when did friendship take
A breed for barren metal of his friend?   132
But lend it rather to thine enemy,   133
Who, if he break, thou mayst with better face   134
Exact the penalty.
SHYLOCK   Why, look you how you storm!
I would be friends with you and have your love,
Forget the shames that you have stained me with,

Supply your present wants, and take no doit   138
Of usance for my moneys, and you'll not hear me.
This is kind I offer.   140
BASSANIO   This were kindness.   141
SHYLOCK   This kindness will I show.
Go with me to a notary, seal me there
Your single bond; and, in a merry sport,   144
If you repay me not on such a day,
In such a place, such sum or sums as are
Expressed in the condition, let the forfeit
Be nominated for an equal pound   148
Of your fair flesh, to be cut off and taken
In what part of your body pleaseth me.
ANTONIO
Content, in faith. I'll seal to such a bond
And say there is much kindness in the Jew.
BASSANIO
You shall not seal to such a bond for me!
I'll rather dwell in my necessity.   154
ANTONIO
Why, fear not, man, I will not forfeit it.
Within these two months—that's a month before
This bond expires—I do expect return
Of thrice three times the value of this bond.
SHYLOCK
O father Abram, what these Christians are,
Whose own hard dealings teaches them suspect
The thoughts of others! Pray you, tell me this:
If he should break his day, what should I gain
By the exaction of the forfeiture?
A pound of man's flesh taken from a man
Is not so estimable, profitable neither,   165
As flesh of muttons, beefs, or goats. I say
To buy his favor I extend this friendship.
If he will take it, so; if not, adieu.   168
And for my love, I pray you, wrong me not.   169
ANTONIO
Yes, Shylock, I will seal unto this bond.
SHYLOCK
Then meet me forthwith at the notary's.
Give him direction for this merry bond,
And I will go and purse the ducats straight,
See to my house, left in the fearful guard   174
Of an unthrifty knave, and presently
I'll be with you.   Exit.
ANTONIO   Hie thee, gentle Jew.—   176
The Hebrew will turn Christian; he grows kind.
BASSANIO
I like not fair terms and a villain's mind.
ANTONIO
Come on. In this there can be no dismay;
My ships come home a month before the day.
                                                          [Exeunt.]

♣

94 I cannot tell i.e., I don't know about that.   **96 devil . . . Scripture**
(See Matthew 4:6.)   **103 beholding** beholden, indebted   **105 rated**
berated, rebuked   **108 sufferance** endurance   **110 gaberdine** loose
outer garment like a cape or mantle   **113 Go to** (An exclamation of
impatience or annoyance.)   **115 rheum** spittle   **116 spurn** kick
117 suit request.   **121 bondman's key** serf's tone of voice   **122 bated**
subdued   **128 like** likely   **132 A breed . . . metal** offspring from
money, which cannot naturally breed. (One of the oldest arguments
against usury was that it was thereby "unnatural.")   **of** from
133 to as if to   **134 Who** from whom.   **break** fail to pay on time

138 doit a Dutch coin of very small value   **140 kind** kindly   **141 were**
would be (if seriously offered)   **144 single bond** bond signed alone
without other security; unconditional. (Shylock pretends the *condition*,
line 147, is only a joke.)   **148 nominated for** named, specified as.
equal exact   **154 dwell** remain   **165 estimable** valuable   **168 so** well
and good   **169 wrong me not** do not think evil of me.   **174 fearful** to be
mistrusted   **176 gentle** gracious, courteous. (With a play on "gentile.")

[2.1]

[Flourish of cornets.] Enter [the Prince of]
Morocco, a tawny Moor all in white, and three
or four followers accordingly, with Portia, Ner-
issa, and their train.

MOROCCO

Mislike me not for my complexion,
The shadowed livery of the burnished sun,   2
To whom I am a neighbor and near bred.   3
Bring me the fairest creature northward born,
Where Phoebus' fire scarce thaws the icicles,   5
And let us make incision for your love
To prove whose blood is reddest, his or mine.   7
I tell thee, lady, this aspect of mine   8
Hath feared the valiant. By my love I swear,   9
The best-regarded virgins of our clime
Have loved it too. I would not change this hue,
Except to steal your thoughts, my gentle queen.

PORTIA

In terms of choice I am not solely led
By nice direction of a maiden's eyes;   14
Besides, the lott'ry of my destiny
Bars me the right of voluntary choosing.
But if my father had not scanted me,   17
And hedged me by his wit to yield myself   18
His wife who wins me by that means I told you,   19
Yourself, renownèd prince, then stood as fair   20
As any comer I have looked on yet
For my affection.

MOROCCO   Even for that I thank you.   22
Therefore, I pray you, lead me to the caskets
To try my fortune. By this scimitar
That slew the Sophy and a Persian prince,   25
That won three fields of Sultan Solyman,   26
I would o'erstare the sternest eyes that look,   27
Outbrave the heart most daring on the earth,
Pluck the young sucking cubs from the she-bear,
Yea, mock the lion when 'a roars for prey,   30
To win thee, lady. But alas the while!
If Hercules and Lichas play at dice   32
Which is the better man, the greater throw
May turn by fortune from the weaker hand.
So is Alcides beaten by his page,
And so may I, blind Fortune leading me,
Miss that which one unworthier may attain,
And die with grieving.

PORTIA   You must take your chance,
And either not attempt to choose at all

Or swear before you choose, if you choose wrong
Never to speak to lady afterward
In way of marriage. Therefore be advised.   42

MOROCCO

Nor will not. Come, bring me unto my chance.   43

PORTIA

First, forward to the temple. After dinner   44
Your hazard shall be made.

MOROCCO   Good fortune then!
To make me blest or cursed'st among men.
                    [Cornets, and] exeunt.

[2.2]

Enter [Lancelot] the clown, alone.

LANCELOT   Certainly my conscience will serve me to   1
run from this Jew my master. The fiend is at mine
elbow and tempts me, saying to me, "Gobbo, Lancelot
Gobbo, good Lancelot," or "Good Gobbo," or "Good
Lancelot Gobbo, use your legs, take the start, run
away." My conscience says, "No, take heed, honest
Lancelot, take heed, honest Gobbo," or, as aforesaid,
"Honest Lancelot Gobbo, do not run; scorn running
with thy heels." Well, the most courageous fiend bids   9
me pack. "Fia!" says the fiend. "Away!" says the fiend. 10
"For the heavens, rouse up a brave mind," says the   11
fiend, "and run." Well, my conscience, hanging about   12
the neck of my heart, says very wisely to me, "My hon- 13
est friend Lancelot, being an honest man's son," or
rather an honest woman's son—for indeed my father
did something smack, something grow to, he had a   16
kind of taste—well, my conscience says, "Lancelot,   17
budge not." "Budge," says the fiend "Budge not," says
my conscience. "Conscience," say I, "you counsel
well." "Fiend," say I, "you counsel well." To be ruled by
my conscience, I should stay with the Jew my master,
who, God bless the mark, is a kind of devil; and to run 22
away from the Jew, I should be ruled by the fiend, who,
saving your reverence, is the devil himself. Certainly
the Jew is the very devil incarnation; and, in my con- 25
science, my conscience is but a kind of hard conscience
to offer to counsel me to stay with the Jew. The fiend
gives the more friendly counsel. I will run, fiend. My
heels are at your commandment. I will run.

Enter Old Gobbo, with a basket.

GOBBO   Master young man, you, I pray you, which is   30
the way to master Jew's?

2.1. Location: Belmont. Portia's house.
0.3 *accordingly* similarly (i.e., dressed in white and dark-skinned like
Morocco)   **2 shadowed livery** i.e., dark complexion, worn as though
it were a costume of the sun's servants   **3 near bred** closely related.
5 Phoebus' i.e., the sun's   **7 reddest** (Red blood was regarded as a
sign of courage.)   **8 aspect** visage   **9 feared** frightened   **14 nice
direction** careful guidance   **17 scanted** limited   **18 wit** wisdom
18–19 yield . . . who give myself to be the wife of him who   **20 then
. . . fair** would then have looked as attractive and stood as fair a
chance. (With a play on "fair-skinned.")   **22 For my** of gaining my
25 Sophy Shah of Persia   **26 fields** battles.   **Solyman** a Turkish sultan ruling from 1520 to 1566   **27 o'erstare** outstare   **30 'a** he
32 Lichas a page of Hercules (Alcides). See the note for 3.2.55.

42 be advised take warning, consider.   **43 Nor will not** i.e., Nor indeed
will I violate the oath.   **44 to the temple** i.e., in order to take the oaths.
2.2. Location: Venice. A street.
0.1 *clown* (1) country bumpkin (2) comic type in an Elizabethan acting company   **1 serve** permit   **9 with thy heels** i.e., emphatically.
(With a pun on the literal sense.)   **10 pack** begone.   **Fia!** i.e., Via,
away!   **11 For the heavens** i.e., In heaven's name   **12–13 hanging . . .
heart** i.e., timidly   **16–17 did something . . . taste** i.e., had a tendency
to lechery   **22 God . . . mark** (An expression by way of apology for
introducing something potentially offensive, as also in *saving your
reverence* in line 24.)   **25 incarnation** (Lancelot means "incarnate.")
30 you (Gobbo uses the formal *you* but switches to the familiar *thou*,
line 88, when he accepts Lancelot as his son.)

LANCELOT　[*aside*]　Oh, heavens, this is my true-
begotten father, who, being more than sand-blind, 33
high-gravel-blind, knows me not. I will try confusions 34
with him.

GOBBO　Master young gentleman, I pray you, which is
the way to master Jew's?

LANCELOT　Turn up on your right hand at the next
turning, but at the next turning of all on your left;
marry, at the very next turning, turn of no hand, but 40
turn down indirectly to the Jew's house.

GOBBO　By God's sonties, 'twill be a hard way to hit. 42
Can you tell me whether one Lancelot, that dwells
with him, dwell with him or no?

LANCELOT　Talk you of young Master Lancelot? [*Aside*]
Mark me now; now will I raise the waters.—Talk you 46
of young Master Lancelot?

GOBBO　No master, sir, but a poor man's son. His father, 48
though I say't, is an honest exceeding poor man and,
God be thanked, well to live. 50

LANCELOT　Well, let his father be what 'a will, we talk 51
of young Master Lancelot.

GOBBO　Your Worship's friend, and Lancelot, sir. 53

LANCELOT　But I pray you, ergo, old man, ergo, I be- 54
seech you, talk you of young Master Lancelot?

GOBBO　Of Lancelot, an't please Your Mastership?

LANCELOT　Ergo, Master Lancelot. Talk not of Master
Lancelot, father, for the young gentleman, according 58
to Fates and Destinies and such odd sayings, the Sis- 59
ters Three and such branches of learning, is indeed 60
deceased, or, as you would say in plain terms, gone to
heaven.

GOBBO　Marry, God forbid! The boy was the very staff
of my age, my very prop.

LANCELOT　Do I look like a cudgel or a hovel post, a 65
staff, or a prop? Do you know me, father?

GOBBO　Alack the day, I know you not, young gentleman. But I pray you, tell me, is my boy, God rest his
soul, alive or dead?

LANCELOT　Do you not know me, father?

GOBBO　Alack, sir, I am sand-blind. I know you not.

LANCELOT　Nay, indeed, if you had your eyes you
might fail of the knowing me; it is a wise father that 73
knows his own child. Well, old man, I will tell you 74
news of your son. [*He kneels.*] Give me your blessing.
Truth will come to light; murder cannot be hid long; a
man's son may, but in the end truth will out.

GOBBO　Pray you, sir, stand up. I am sure you are not
Lancelot, my boy.

LANCELOT　Pray you, let's have no more fooling about
it, but give me your blessing. I am Lancelot, your 81
boy that was, your son that is, your child that shall be. 82

GOBBO　I cannot think you are my son.

LANCELOT　I know not what I shall think of that; but I
am Lancelot, the Jew's man, and I am sure Margery
your wife is my mother.

GOBBO　Her name is Margery indeed. I'll be sworn, if
thou be Lancelot, thou art mine own flesh and blood.
Lord worshiped might he be, what a beard hast thou 89
got! Thou hast got more hair on thy chin than Dobbin
my fill horse has on his tail. 91

LANCELOT　[*rising*]　It should seem then that Dobbin's
tail grows backward. I am sure he had more hair of 93
his tail than I have of my face when I last saw him. 94

GOBBO　Lord, how art thou changed! How dost thou and
thy master agree? I have brought him a present. How
'gree you now?

LANCELOT　Well, well; but for mine own part, as I have
set up my rest to run away, so I will not rest till 99
I have run some ground. My master's a very Jew. Give 100
him a present? Give him a halter! I am famished in his 101
service; you may tell every finger I have with my ribs. 102
Father, I am glad you are come. Give me your present 103
to one Master Bassanio, who indeed gives rare new 104
liveries. If I serve not him, I will run as far as God has 105
any ground. Oh, rare fortune! Here comes the man. To
him, father, for I am a Jew if I serve the Jew any longer. 107

*Enter Bassanio, with [Leonardo and] a follower
or two.*

BASSANIO　You may do so, but let it be so hasted that 108
supper be ready at the farthest by five of the clock. See 109
these letters delivered, put the liveries to making, and
desire Gratiano to come anon to my lodging.
[*Exit a Servant.*]

LANCELOT　To him, father.

GOBBO　[*advancing*]　God bless Your Worship!

BASSANIO　Gramercy. Wouldst thou aught with me? 114

GOBBO　Here's my son, sir, a poor boy— 115

LANCELOT　Not a poor boy, sir, but the rich Jew's man,
that would, sir, as my father shall specify—

GOBBO　He hath a great infection, sir, as one would say, 118
to serve—

LANCELOT　Indeed, the short and the long is, I serve the
Jew, and have a desire, as my father shall specify—

81–2 your . . . shall be (Echoes the *Gloria* from the Book of Common
Prayer: "As it was in the beginning, is now, and ever shall be.")
89 beard (Stage tradition has Old Gobbo mistaking Lancelot's long hair
for a beard.)　**91 fill horse** cart horse　**93 grows backward** grows at
the wrong end.　**94 of** on　**99 set up my rest** determined, risked all.
(A metaphor from the card game *primero*, in which a final wager is
made, with a pun also on *rest* as "place of residence.")　**not rest** i.e., not
stop running. (More punning on *rest*.)　**100 very** veritable.　**Jew** (1)
Hebrew (2) grasping old usurer.　**101 halter** hangman's noose.　**102 tell**
count.　**tell . . . ribs** (Comically reverses the usual saying of counting
one's ribs with one's fingers.)　**103 Give me** Give. (*Me* suggests "on my
behalf.")　**104 rare** splendid　**105 liveries** uniforms or costumes for
servants.　**107 a Jew** i.e., a villain. (Punning on the literal sense in *the
Jew*. Compare with line 100.)　**108 hasted** hastened, hurried　**109 farthest** latest　**114 Gramercy** Many thanks.　**aught** anything　**115 poor**
(1) unfortunate (2) penniless (contrasted with *rich* in the next line)
118 infection (Blunder for "affection" or "inclination.")

---

33 sand-blind dim-sighted　**34 high-gravel-blind** blinder than sand-
blind. (A term seemingly invented by Lancelot.)　**try confusions**
(Lancelot's blunder for "try conclusions," i.e., experiment, though his
error is comically apt.)　**40 marry** i.e., by the Virgin Mary, indeed. (A
mild interjection.)　**of no hand** neither right nor left　**42 sonties** little
saints　**46 raise the waters** i.e., start tears.　**48 master** (The title was
applied to gentlefolk only.)　**50 well to live** prospering, in good
health.　**51 'a** he　**53 Your . . . Lancelot** (Again, Old Gobbo denies
that Lancelot is entitled to be called "Master.")　**54 ergo** therefore.
(But Lancelot may use this Latin word with no particular meaning in
mind.)　**58 father** (1) old man (2) father　**59–60 the Sisters Three** the
three Fates　**65 hovel post** post holding up a hovel or open shed
73–4 it is . . . child (Reverses the proverb "It is a wise child that
knows his own father.")

GOBBO   His master and he, saving Your Worship's
reverence, are scarce cater-cousins—   123
LANCELOT   To be brief, the very truth is that the Jew,
having done me wrong, doth cause me, as my father,
being, I hope, an old man, shall frutify unto you—   126
GOBBO   I have here a dish of doves that I would bestow
upon Your Worship, and my suit is—
LANCELOT   In very brief, the suit is impertinent to   129
myself, as Your Worship shall know by this honest old
man, and, though I say it, though old man, yet poor
man, my father.
BASSANIO   One speak for both. What would you?
LANCELOT   Serve you, sir.
GOBBO   That is the very defect of the matter, sir.   135
BASSANIO
I know thee well; thou hast obtained thy suit.
Shylock thy master spoke with me this day,
And hath preferred thee, if it be preferment   138
To leave a rich Jew's service to become
The follower of so poor a gentleman.
LANCELOT   The old proverb is very well parted be- 141
tween my master Shylock and you, sir: you have the
grace of God, sir, and he hath enough.
BASSANIO
Thou speak'st it well. Go, father, with thy son.
Take leave of thy old master, and inquire
My lodging out. [*To a Servant*] Give him a livery
More guarded than his fellows'. See it done.   147
LANCELOT   Father, in. I cannot get a service, no! I have
ne'er a tongue in my head, well! [*He looks at his palm.*]
If any man in Italy have a fairer table which doth offer 150
to swear upon a book, I shall have good fortune. Go 151
to, here's a simple line of life. Here's a small trifle of 152
wives! Alas, fifteen wives is nothing. Eleven widows
and nine maids is a simple coming-in for one man. 154
And then to scape drowning thrice, and to be in peril
of my life with the edge of a feather bed! Here are 156
simple scapes. Well, if Fortune be a woman, she's a 157
good wench for this gear. Father, come. I'll take my 158
leave of the Jew in the twinkling.
                          Exit clown [*Lancelot, with Old Gobbo*].
BASSANIO [*giving Leonardo a list*]
I pray thee, good Leonardo, think on this:
These things being bought and orderly bestowed,   161
Return in haste, for I do feast tonight   162
My best-esteemed acquaintance. Hie thee, go.

LEONARDO
My best endeavors shall be done herein.
                                              [*He starts to leave.*]

          Enter Gratiano.

GRATIANO [*to Leonardo*]
Where's your master?
LEONARDO   Yonder, sir, he walks.
                                              Exit Leonardo.
GRATIANO   Signor Bassanio!
BASSANIO   Gratiano!
GRATIANO
I have a suit to you.
BASSANIO   You have obtained it.
GRATIANO   You must not deny me. I must go with you
to Belmont.
BASSANIO
Why, then you must. But hear thee, Gratiano;
Thou art too wild, too rude and bold of voice—
Parts that become thee happily enough,   173
And in such eyes as ours appear not faults,
But where thou art not known, why, there they show
Something too liberal. Pray thee, take pain   176
To allay with some cold drops of modesty   177
Thy skipping spirit, lest through thy wild behavior
I be misconstered in the place I go to   179
And lose my hopes.
GRATIANO   Signor Bassanio, hear me:
If I do not put on a sober habit,   181
Talk with respect and swear but now and then,
Wear prayer books in my pocket, look demurely,
Nay more, while grace is saying, hood mine eyes   184
Thus with my hat, and sigh and say "amen,"
Use all the observance of civility,
Like one well studied in a sad ostent   187
To please his grandam, never trust me more.   188
BASSANIO   Well, we shall see your bearing.
GRATIANO
Nay, but I bar tonight. You shall not gauge me
By what we do tonight.
BASSANIO   No, that were pity.
I would entreat you rather to put on
Your boldest suit of mirth, for we have friends
That purpose merriment. But fare you well;
I have some business.
GRATIANO
And I must to Lorenzo and the rest,
But we will visit you at suppertime.   *Exeunt.*

[2.3]

          Enter Jessica and [*Lancelot*] *the clown.*

JESSICA
I am sorry thou wilt leave my father so.

---

123 **cater-cousins** good friends   126 **frutify** (Lancelot may be trying
to say "fructify," but he means "certify" or "notify.")   129 **impertinent**
(Blunder for "pertinent.")   135 **defect** (Blunder for "effect," i.e., "purport.")   138 **preferred** recommended   141 **proverb** i.e., "He who has
the grace of God has enough."   **parted** divided   147 **guarded** trimmed
with braided ornament   150 **table** palm of the hand. (Lancelot now
reads the lines of his palm.)   151 **book** i.e., Bible. (The image is of a
hand being laid on the Bible to take an oath.)   151–2 **Go to** (An
expression of impatience.)   152 **simple** unremarkable. (Said ironically.)   **line of life** curved line at the base of the thumb.   154 **simple
coming-in** modest beginning or income. (With sexual suggestion.)
156 **feather bed** (Suggesting marriage bed or love bed; Lancelot sees
sexual adventure and the dangers of marriage in his palm reading.)
157 **scapes** (1) adventures (2) transgressions.   **Fortune . . . woman**
(Fortune was personified as a goddess.)   158 **gear** matter.
161 **bestowed** i.e., stowed on board ship   162 **feast** give a feast for

173 **Parts** qualities   176 **liberal** free of manner. (Often with sexual
connotation.)   177 **allay** temper, moderate.   **modesty** decorum
179 **misconstered** misconstrued   181 **habit** demeanor. (With a suggestion of "clothes.")   184 **saying** being said   187 **sad ostent** grave
appearance   188 **grandam** grandmother
2.3. **Location:** Venice. Shylock's house.

Our house is hell, and thou, a merry devil,
Didst rob it of some taste of tediousness.
But fare thee well. There is a ducat for thee.
                                    [*Giving money.*]
And, Lancelot, soon at supper shalt thou see
Lorenzo, who is thy new master's guest.
Give him this letter; do it secretly.   [*Giving a letter.*]
And so farewell. I would not have my father
See me in talk with thee.

LANCELOT   Adieu! Tears exhibit my tongue. Most   10
beautiful pagan, most sweet Jew! If a Christian did not
play the knave and get thee, I am much deceived. But,   12
adieu! These foolish drops do something drown my
manly spirit. Adieu!

JESSICA   Farewell, good Lancelot.   [*Exit Lancelot.*]
Alack, what heinous sin is it in me
To be ashamed to be my father's child!
But though I am a daughter to his blood,
I am not to his manners. O Lorenzo,
If thou keep promise, I shall end this strife,
Become a Christian and thy loving wife.   *Exit.*

❖

[2.4]

Enter Gratiano, Lorenzo, Salerio, and Solanio.

LORENZO
Nay, we will slink away in suppertime,   1
Disguise us at my lodging, and return
All in an hour.

GRATIANO
We have not made good preparation.

SALERIO
We have not spoke us yet of torchbearers.   5

SOLANIO
'Tis vile, unless it may be quaintly ordered,   6
And better in my mind not undertook.

LORENZO
'Tis now but four o'clock. We have two hours
To furnish us.

Enter Lancelot [with a letter].

    Friend Lancelot, what's the news?

LANCELOT   An it shall please you to break up this, it   10
shall seem to signify.   [*Giving the letter.*]

LORENZO
I know the hand. In faith, 'tis a fair hand,
And whiter than the paper it writ on
Is the fair hand that writ.

GRATIANO   Love news, in faith.

LANCELOT   By your leave, sir.   [*He starts to leave.*]

LORENZO   Whither goest thou?

LANCELOT   Marry, sir, to bid my old master the Jew to
sup tonight with my new master the Christian.

LORENZO
Hold here, take this. [*He gives money.*] Tell gentle
    Jessica
I will not fail her. Speak it privately.
                                    Exit clown [Lancelot].
Go, gentlemen,
Will you prepare you for this masque tonight?
I am provided of a torchbearer.

SALERIO
Ay, marry, I'll be gone about it straight.   24

SOLANIO
And so will I.

LORENZO   Meet me and Gratiano.
At Gratiano's lodging some hour hence.   26

SALERIO   'Tis good we do so.   *Exit [with Solanio].*

GRATIANO
Was not that letter from fair Jessica?

LORENZO
I must needs tell thee all. She hath directed   29
How I shall take her from her father's house,
What gold and jewels she is furnished with,
What page's suit she hath in readiness.
If e'er the Jew her father come to heaven,
It will be for his gentle daughter's sake;   34
And never dare misfortune cross her foot,   35
Unless she do it under this excuse,   36
That she is issue to a faithless Jew.   37
Come, go with me. Peruse this as thou goest.
                            [*He gives Gratiano the letter.*]
Fair Jessica shall be my torchbearer.   *Exeunt.*

❖

[2.5]

*Enter [Shylock the] Jew and [Lancelot,] his man
that was, the clown.*

SHYLOCK
Well, thou shalt see, thy eyes shall be thy judge,
The difference of old Shylock and Bassanio.—   2
What, Jessica!—Thou shalt not gormandize,   3
As thou hast done with me—What, Jessica!—
And sleep and snore, and rend apparel out—   5
Why, Jessica, I say!

LANCELOT   Why, Jessica!

SHYLOCK
Who bids thee call? I do not bid thee call.

LANCELOT   Your Worship was wont to tell me I could
do nothing without bidding.

Enter Jessica.

JESSICA   Call you? What is your will?

SHYLOCK
I am bid forth to supper, Jessica.
There are my keys. But wherefore should I go?   13
I am not bid for love—they flatter me—

---

10 exhibit (Blunder for "inhibit," "restrain.")   **12 get** beget
2.4. Location: Venice. A street.
1 in during   **5 spoke . . . of** yet bespoken, ordered   **6 quaintly
ordered** skillfully and tastefully managed   **10 An** If.   **break up this**
unseal the letter

24 straight at once.   **26 some hour** about an hour   **29 must needs** must
34 gentle (With pun on "gentile"?)   **35 foot** footpath   **36 she** i.e.,
Misfortune   **37 she is issue** i.e., Jessica is daughter.   **faithless** pagan
2.5. Location: Venice. Before Shylock's house.
2 of between   **3 gormandize** eat gluttonously   **5 rend apparel out**
i.e., wear out your clothes   **13 wherefore** why

But yet I'll go in hate, to feed upon
The prodigal Christian. Jessica, my girl,
Look to my house. I am right loath to go.   17
There is some ill a-brewing towards my rest,
For I did dream of moneybags tonight.   19

LANCELOT   I beseech you, sir, go. My young master
doth expect your reproach.   21

SHYLOCK   So do I his.

LANCELOT   And they have conspired together. I will
not say you shall see a masque, but if you do, then it
was not for nothing that my nose fell a-bleeding on
Black Monday last at six o'clock i'th' morning, falling   26
out that year on Ash Wednesday was four year in
th'afternoon.

SHYLOCK
What, are there masques? Hear you me, Jessica:
Lock up my doors, and when you hear the drum
And the vile squealing of the wry-necked fife,   31
Clamber not you up to the casements then,
Nor thrust your head into the public street
To gaze on Christian fools with varnished faces,   34
But stop my house's ears—I mean my casements.
Let not the sound of shallow fopp'ry enter
My sober house. By Jacob's staff I swear   37
I have no mind of feasting forth tonight.
But I will go.—Go you before me, sirrah.
Say I will come.

LANCELOT   I will go before, sir. [Aside to Jessica] Mistress, look out at window, for all this;
          There will come a Christian by,
          Will be worth a Jewess' eye.   [Exit.]

SHYLOCK
What says that fool of Hagar's offspring, ha?   45

JESSICA
His words were "Farewell, mistress," nothing else.

SHYLOCK
The patch is kind enough, but a huge feeder,   47
Snail-slow in profit, and he sleeps by day   48
More than the wildcat. Drones hive not with me;
Therefore I part with him, and part with him
To one that I would have him help to waste
His borrowed purse. Well, Jessica, go in.
Perhaps I will return immediately.
Do as I bid you. Shut doors after you.
Fast bind, fast find—   55
A proverb never stale in thrifty mind.   Exit.

JESSICA
Farewell, and if my fortune be not crossed,
I have a father, you a daughter, lost.   Exit.

❧

[2.6]

Enter the masquers, Gratiano and Salerio.

GRATIANO
This is the penthouse under which Lorenzo   1
Desired us to make stand.

SALERIO   His hour is almost past.

GRATIANO
And it is marvel he outdwells his hour,   4
For lovers ever run before the clock.

SALERIO
Oh, ten times faster Venus' pigeons fly   6
To seal love's bonds new-made than they are wont   7
To keep obligèd faith unforfeited.   8

GRATIANO
That ever holds. Who riseth from a feast   9
With that keen appetite that he sits down?
Where is the horse that doth untread again   11
His tedious measures with the unbated fire   12
That he did pace them first? All things that are
Are with more spirit chasèd than enjoyed.
How like a younger or a prodigal   15
The scarfèd bark puts from her native bay,   16
Hugged and embracèd by the strumpet wind!   17
How like the prodigal doth she return,
With overweathered ribs and ragged sails,   19
Lean, rent, and beggared by the strumpet wind!   20

Enter Lorenzo.

SALERIO
Here comes Lorenzo. More of this hereafter.

LORENZO
Sweet friends, your patience for my long abode;   22
Not I, but my affairs, have made you wait.
When you shall please to play the thieves for wives,
I'll watch as long for you then. Approach;   25
Here dwells my father Jew.—Ho! Who's within?   26

[Enter] Jessica, above [in boy's clothes].

JESSICA
Who are you? Tell me for more certainty,
Albeit I'll swear that I do know your tongue.

LORENZO   Lorenzo, and thy love.

JESSICA
Lorenzo, certain, and my love indeed,
For who love I so much? And now who knows

---

17 right loath reluctant   **19 tonight** last night.   **21 reproach**
(Lancelot's blunder for "approach." Shylock takes it in grim humor.)
26 Black Monday Easter Monday. (Lancelot's talk of omens is perhaps intentional gibberish, a parody of Shylock's fears.)   **31 wry-
necked** i.e., played with the musician's head awry; or possibly comparing the fife's *vile squealing* to the call of the wryneck, a bird with a
high-pitched call and a writhing movement of head and neck
34 varnished faces i.e., painted masks   **37 Jacob's staff** (See Genesis
32:10 and Hebrews 11:21.)   **45 Hagar's offspring** (Hagar, a gentile
and Abraham's servant, gave birth to Ishmael; both mother and son
were cast out after the birth of Isaac.)   **47 patch** fool   **48 profit** profitable labor   **55 Fast . . . find** i.e., Keep your property secure and you
will always know where it is. (Proverbial.)

2.6. Location: Before Shylock's house, as in 2.5.
1 penthouse projecting roof or upper story of a house   **4 it . . . hour**
i.e., it is surprising that he is late   **6–8 Oh, ten . . . unforfeited** i.e.,
Oh, lovers are ten times more alacritous in their first pledge of love
than in keeping faith in a long-term commitment. (*Venus' pigeons* are
the doves that draw her chariot.)   **9 ever holds** always holds true.
11 untread retrace   **12 measures** paces   **15 younger** i.e., younger
son, as in the parable of the Prodigal Son (Luke 15). (Often emended
to *younker*, youth.)   **16 scarfèd bark** sailing vessel festooned with
flags or streamers   **17 strumpet** i.e., inconsistent, variable. (Likened
metaphorically to the harlots with whom the Prodigal Son wasted his
fortune.)   **19 overweathered ribs** i.e., weather-beaten and leaking
timbers   **20 rent** torn   **22 your patience** i.e., I beg your patience.
abode delay   **25 watch** keep watch   **26 father** i.e., father-in-law

But you, Lorenzo, whether I am yours?   32

LORENZO
Heaven and thy thoughts are witness that thou art.

JESSICA [*throwing down a casket*]
Here, catch this casket. It is worth the pains.
I am glad 'tis night, you do not look on me,
For I am much ashamed of my exchange.   36
But love is blind, and lovers cannot see
The pretty follies that themselves commit,   38
For if they could, Cupid himself would blush
To see me thus transformèd to a boy.

LORENZO
Descend, for you must be my torchbearer.

JESSICA
What, must I hold a candle to my shames?   42
They in themselves, good sooth, are too too light.   43
Why, 'tis an office of discovery, love,   44
And I should be obscured.

LORENZO   So are you, sweet,
Even in the lovely garnish of a boy.   46
But come at once,
For the close night doth play the runaway,   48
And we are stayed for at Bassanio's feast.   49

JESSICA
I will make fast the doors, and gild myself   50
With some more ducats, and be with you straight.
                                    [*Exit above.*]

GRATIANO
Now, by my hood, a gentle and no Jew.   52

LORENZO
Beshrew me but I love her heartily,   53
For she is wise, if I can judge of her,
And fair she is, if that mine eyes be true,
And true she is, as she hath proved herself;
And therefore, like herself, wise, fair, and true,
Shall she be placèd in my constant soul.

              Enter Jessica [below].

What, art thou come? On, gentlemen, away!
Our masquing mates by this time for us stay.   60
                  Exit [with Jessica and Salerio;
                  Gratiano is about to follow them].

              Enter Antonio.

ANTONIO   Who's there?
GRATIANO   Signor Antonio?
ANTONIO
Fie, fie, Gratiano! Where are all the rest?
'Tis nine o'clock; our friends all stay for you.
No masque tonight. The wind is come about;
Bassanio presently will go aboard.

I have sent twenty out to seek for you.

GRATIANO
I am glad on 't. I desire no more delight
Than to be under sail and gone tonight.   *Exeunt.*

                        ❧

[2.7]

              [Flourish of cornets.] Enter Portia, with [the
              Prince of] Morocco, and both their trains.

PORTIA
Go, draw aside the curtains and discover   1
The several caskets to this noble prince.   2
Now make your choice.   [*The curtains are drawn.*]

MOROCCO
The first, of gold, who this inscription bears,   4
"Who chooseth me shall gain what many men desire";
The second, silver, which this promise carries,
"Who chooseth me shall get as much as he deserves";
This third, dull lead, with warning all as blunt,   8
"Who chooseth me must give and hazard all he hath."
How shall I know if I do choose the right?

PORTIA
The one of them contains my picture, Prince.
If you choose that, then I am yours withal.   12

MOROCCO
Some god direct my judgment! Let me see,
I will survey th'inscriptions back again.
What says this leaden casket?
"Who chooseth me must give and hazard all he hath."
Must give—for what? For lead? Hazard for lead?
This casket threatens. Men that hazard all
Do it in hope of fair advantages.
A golden mind stoops not to shows of dross.   20
I'll then nor give nor hazard aught for lead.   21
What says the silver with her virgin hue?
"Who chooseth me shall get as much as he deserves."
As much as he deserves! Pause there, Morocco,
And weigh thy value with an even hand.   25
If thou be'st rated by thy estimation,   26
Thou dost deserve enough; and yet enough
May not extend so far as to the lady;
And yet to be afeard of my deserving
Were but a weak disabling of myself.   30
As much as I deserve? Why, that's the lady.
I do in birth deserve her, and in fortunes,
In graces, and in qualities of breeding;
But more than these, in love I do deserve.
What if I strayed no farther, but chose here?
Let's see once more this saying graved in gold: 36
"Who chooseth me shall gain what many men desire."
Why, that's the lady; all the world desires her.
From the four corners of the earth they come
To kiss this shrine, this mortal breathing saint.   40

---

32 **But you** better than you   36 **exchange** change of clothes.   38 **pretty** ingenious, artful   42 **hold a candle** i.e., stand by and witness. (With a play on the idea of acting as torchbearer.)   43 **light** (1) immodest (2) illuminated.   44 **'tis . . . discovery** i.e., torchbearing is intended to shed light on matters   46 **garnish** outfit, trimmings   48 **close** dark, secretive.   **doth . . . runaway** i.e., is quickly passing   49 **stayed** waited   50 **gild** adorn. (Literally, cover with gold.)   52 **by my hood** (An asseveration.)   **gentle** gracious person. (With pun on "gentile," as at 2.4.34.)   53 **Beshrew** i.e., A mischief on. (A mild oath.)   60 **stay** wait. (Also in line 64.)

2.7. Location: Belmont. Portia's house.
0.2 *trains* followers   1 **discover** reveal   2 **several** different, various   4 **who** which   8 **dull** (1) dull-colored (2) blunt.   **all as blunt** as blunt as lead   12 **withal** with it.   20 **dross** worthless matter. (Literally, the impurities cast off in the melting down of metals.)   21 **nor give** neither give   25 **even** impartial   26 **estimation** worth   30 **disabling** underrating   36 **graved** engraved   40 **mortal breathing** living

The Hyrcanian deserts and the vasty wilds   41
Of wide Arabia are as throughfares now
For princes to come view fair Portia.
The watery kingdom, whose ambitious head
Spits in the face of heaven, is no bar   45
To stop the foreign spirits, but they come,   46
As o'er a brook, to see fair Portia.
One of these three contains her heavenly picture.
Is't like that lead contains her? 'Twere damnation   49
To think so base a thought; it were too gross   50
To rib her cerecloth in the obscure grave.   51
Or shall I think in silver she's immured,   52
Being ten times undervalued to tried gold?   53
Oh, sinful thought! Never so rich a gem
Was set in worse than gold. They have in England   55
A coin that bears the figure of an angel   56
Stamped in gold, but that's insculped upon;   57
But here an angel in a golden bed
Lies all within. Deliver me the key.
Here do I choose, and thrive I as I may!

PORTIA
There, take it, Prince; and if my form lie there,   61
Then I am yours.
                           [*He unlocks the golden casket.*]
MOROCCO   Oh, hell! What have we here?
A carrion Death, within whose empty eye   63
There is a written scroll! I'll read the writing.
[*He reads.*]
      "All that glisters is not gold;
      Often have you heard that told.
      Many a man his life hath sold
      But my outside to behold.   68
      Gilded tombs do worms infold.
      Had you been as wise as bold,
      Young in limbs, in judgment old,
      Your answer had not been inscrolled.   72
      Fare you well; your suit is cold."
   Cold, indeed, and labor lost.
   Then, farewell, heat, and welcome, frost!
Portia, adieu. I have too grieved a heart
To take a tedious leave. Thus losers part.   77
                    Exit [*with his train. Flourish of cornets.*]
PORTIA
A gentle riddance. Draw the curtains, go.
Let all of his complexion choose me so.   79
                    [*The curtains are closed, and*] *exeunt.*

❖

41 **Hyrcanian** (Hyrcania was the country south of the Caspian Sea
celebrated for its wildness.) **vasty** vast   45 **Spits** (The image is of
huge waves breaking at sea.)   46 **spirits** i.e., men of courage   49 **like**
likely   50 **base** (1) ignoble (2) low in the natural scale, as with lead, a
base metal   50–1 **it were . . . grave** i.e., it would be too gross an insult
to inter her, as it were, wrapped in a waxed cloth, in a lead casket.
52 **immured** enclosed, confined   53 **Being . . . gold** which has only
one-tenth the value of assayed and purified gold.   55 **set** fixed, as a
precious stone, in a border of metal   56 **coin** i.e., the gold coin known
as the *angel*, which bore the device of the archangel Michael treading
on the dragon   57 **insculped upon** merely engraved upon the surface
61 **form** image   63 **carrion Death** death's-head   68 **But** only
72 **inscrolled** i.e., written on this scroll.   77 **part** depart.
79 **complexion** temperament (not merely skin color)

[2.8]

Enter Salerio and Solanio.

SALERIO
Why, man, I saw Bassanio under sail.
With him is Gratiano gone along,
And in their ship I am sure Lorenzo is not.
SOLANIO
The villain Jew with outcries raised the Duke,   4
Who went with him to search Bassanio's ship.
SALERIO
He came too late. The ship was under sail.
But there the Duke was given to understand
That in a gondola were seen together
Lorenzo and his amorous Jessica.
Besides, Antonio certified the Duke
They were not with Bassanio in his ship.
SOLANIO
I never heard a passion so confused,   12
So strange, outrageous, and so variable
As the dog Jew did utter in the streets:
"My daughter! Oh, my ducats! Oh, my daughter!
Fled with a Christian! Oh, my Christian ducats!
Justice! The law! My ducats, and my daughter!
A sealèd bag, two sealèd bags of ducats,
Of double ducats, stol'n from me by my daughter!
And jewels, two stones, two rich and precious
   stones,
Stol'n by my daughter! Justice! Find the girl!
She hath the stones upon her, and the ducats."
SALERIO
Why, all the boys in Venice follow him,
Crying his stones, his daughter, and his ducats.   24
SOLANIO
Let good Antonio look he keep his day,   25
Or he shall pay for this.
SALERIO   Marry, well remembered.
I reasoned with a Frenchman yesterday,   27
Who told me, in the narrow seas that part   28
The French and English, there miscarrièd
A vessel of our country richly fraught.   30
I thought upon Antonio when he told me,
And wished in silence that it were not his.
SOLANIO
You were best to tell Antonio what you hear.
Yet do not suddenly, for it may grieve him.
SALERIO
A kinder gentleman treads not the earth.
I saw Bassanio and Antonio part.
Bassanio told him he would make some speed
Of his return; he answered, "Do not so.
Slubber not business for my sake, Bassanio,   39
But stay the very riping of the time;   40

2.8. **Location: Venice. A street.**
4 **raised** roused   12 **passion** passionate outburst   24 **stones** (In the
boys' jeering cry, the *two stones* suggest testicles; see line 20.)   25 **look . . .
day** see to it that he repays his loan on time   27 **reasoned** talked
28 **narrow seas** English Channel   30 **fraught** freighted.   39 **Slubber
not business** Don't do the business hastily and badly   40 **But . . . time**
i.e., pursue your business at Belmont until it is brought to completion

And for the Jew's bond which he hath of me,   41
Let it not enter in your mind of love.   42
Be merry, and employ your chiefest thoughts
To courtship and such fair ostents of love   44
As shall conveniently become you there."
And even there, his eye being big with tears,   46
Turning his face, he put his hand behind him,   47
And with affection wondrous sensible   48
He wrung Bassanio's hand; and so they parted.

SOLANIO
I think he only loves the world for him.   50
I pray thee, let us go and find him out
And quicken his embracèd heaviness   52
With some delight or other.

SALERIO   Do we so.   *Exeunt.*

❖

[2.9]

Enter Nerissa and a Servitor.

NERISSA
Quick, quick, I pray thee, draw the curtain straight.   1
The Prince of Aragon hath ta'en his oath,
And comes to his election presently.   3
                             [*The curtains are drawn back.*]

[*Flourish of cornets.*] *Enter* [*the Prince of*]
Aragon, his train, and Portia.

PORTIA
Behold, there stand the caskets, noble Prince.
If you choose that wherein I am contained,
Straight shall our nuptial rites be solemnized;
But if you fail, without more speech, my lord,
You must be gone from hence immediately.

ARAGON
I am enjoined by oath to observe three things:
First, never to unfold to anyone   10
Which casket 'twas I chose; next, if I fail
Of the right casket, never in my life
To woo a maid in way of marriage;
Lastly,
If I do fail in fortune of my choice,
Immediately to leave you and be gone.

PORTIA
To these injunctions everyone doth swear
That comes to hazard for my worthless self.

ARAGON
And so have I addressed me. Fortune now   19
To my heart's hope! Gold, silver, and base lead.
"Who chooseth me must give and hazard all he hath."

You shall look fairer ere I give or hazard.
What says the golden chest? Ha, let me see:
"Who chooseth me shall gain what many men desire."
What many men desire! That "many" may be meant
By the fool multitude, that choose by show,   26
Not learning more than the fond eye doth teach,   27
Which pries not to th'interior, but like the martlet   28
Builds in the weather on the outward wall,   29
Even in the force and road of casualty.   30
I will not choose what many men desire,
Because I will not jump with common spirits   32
And rank me with the barbarous multitudes.
Why then, to thee, thou silver treasure-house!
Tell me once more what title thou dost bear:
"Who chooseth me shall get as much as he deserves."
And well said too; for who shall go about
To cozen fortune, and be honorable   38
Without the stamp of merit? Let none presume   39
To wear an undeservèd dignity.
Oh, that estates, degrees, and offices   41
Were not derived corruptly, and that clear honor
Were purchased by the merit of the wearer!
How many then should cover that stand bare?   44
How many be commanded that command?   45
How much low peasantry would then be gleaned   46
From the true seed of honor, and how much honor   47
Picked from the chaff and ruin of the times
To be new-varnished? Well, but to my choice: 49
"Who chooseth me shall get as much as he deserves."
I will assume desert. Give me a key for this,
And instantly unlock my fortunes here.
                             [*He opens the silver casket.*]

PORTIA
Too long a pause for that which you find there.

ARAGON
What's here? The portrait of a blinking idiot,
Presenting me a schedule! I will read it.   55
How much unlike art thou to Portia!
How much unlike my hopes and my deservings!
"Who chooseth me shall have as much as he
   deserves."
Did I deserve no more than a fool's head?
Is that my prize? Are my deserts no better?

PORTIA
To offend and judge are distinct offices   61
And of opposèd natures.

ARAGON   What is here?   62

---

41 for as for   **42 of** preoccupied with   **44 ostents** expressions, shows
46 there thereupon, then   **47 behind him** (Antonio turns away in
tears while extending his hand back to Bassanio.)   **48 affection wondrous sensible** wondrously sensitive and keen emotion   **50 he . . .
him** i.e., Bassanio is all he lives for.   **52 quicken . . . heaviness** light-
en the sorrow he has embraced
2.9. Location: Belmont. Portia's house.
0.1 *Servitor* servant   **1 straight** at once.   **3 election presently** choice
immediately.   **10 unfold** disclose   **19 addressed me** prepared myself
(by this swearing).

26 By for, to signify   **27 fond** foolish   **28 martlet** swift   **29 in**
exposed to   **30 force . . . casualty** power and path of mischance.
32 jump agree   **38 cozen** cheat   **39 stamp** seal of approval
41 estates, degrees status, social rank   **44 cover . . . bare** i.e., wear
hats (of authority) who now stand bareheaded.   **45 How . . . command?** How many then should be servants that are now masters?
46 gleaned culled out and discarded   **47 the true seed of honor** i.e.,
persons of noble descent   **49 new-varnished** i.e., having the luster of
their true nobility restored to them.   **55 schedule** written paper.
61–2 To offend . . . natures i.e., You have no right, having submitted
your case to judgment, to attempt to judge your own case; or, it is not
for me to say, since I've been the indirect cause of your discomfiture.

[*He reads.*]"The fire seven times tried this;   63
        Seven times tried that judgment is
        That did never choose amiss.
        Some there be that shadows kiss;   66
        Such have but a shadow's bliss.
        There be fools alive, iwis,   68
        Silvered o'er, and so was this.   69
        Take what wife you will to bed;
        I will ever be your head.   71
        So begone; you are sped."   72

Still more fool I shall appear   73
By the time I linger here.   74
With one fool's head I came to woo,
But I go away with two.
Sweet, adieu. I'll keep my oath,
Patiently to bear my wroth.   78
                            [*Exeunt Aragon and train.*]
PORTIA
    Thus hath the candle singed the moth.
    Oh, these deliberate fools! When they do choose,   80
    They have the wisdom by their wit to lose.
NERISSA
    The ancient saying is no heresy:
    Hanging and wiving goes by destiny.
PORTIA   Come, draw the curtain, Nerissa.
                            [*The curtains are closed.*]

                    Enter Messenger.

MESSENGER
    Where is my lady?
PORTIA   Here. What would my lord?   85
MESSENGER
    Madam, there is alighted at your gate
    A young Venetian, one that comes before
    To signify th'approaching of his lord,
    From whom he bringeth sensible regreets,   89
    To wit, besides commends and courteous breath,   90
    Gifts of rich value. Yet I have not seen   91
    So likely an ambassador of love.
    A day in April never came so sweet,
    To show how costly summer was at hand,   94
    As this fore-spurrer comes before his lord.   95
PORTIA
    No more, I pray thee. I am half afeard
    Thou wilt say anon he is some kin to thee,
    Thou spend'st such high-day wit in praising him.   98
    Come, come, Nerissa, for I long to see
    Quick Cupid's post that comes so mannerly.   100

NERISSA
    Bassanio, Lord Love, if thy will it be!   *Exeunt.*

[3.1]

        [*Enter*] *Solanio and Salerio.*

SOLANIO   Now, what news on the Rialto?
SALERIO   Why, yet it lives there unchecked that Anto-   2
    nio hath a ship of rich lading wrecked on the narrow   3
    seas—the Goodwins, I think they call the place, a   4
    very dangerous flat, and fatal, where the carcasses of 5
    many a tall ship lie buried, as they say, if my gossip 6
    Report be an honest woman of her word.   7
SOLANIO   I would she were as lying a gossip in that as
    ever knapped ginger or made her neighbors believe   9
    she wept for the death of a third husband. But it is
    true, without any slips of prolixity or crossing the   11
    plain highway of talk, that the good Antonio, the   12
    honest Antonio—oh, that I had a title good enough to
    keep his name company!—
SALERIO   Come, the full stop.   15
SOLANIO   Ha, what sayest thou? Why, the end is, he
    hath lost a ship.
SALERIO   I would it might prove the end of his losses.
SOLANIO   Let me say "amen" betimes, lest the devil   19
    cross my prayer, for here he comes in the likeness of   20
    a Jew.

                    Enter Shylock.

    How now, Shylock, what news among the merchants?
SHYLOCK   You knew, none so well, none so well as
    you, of my daughter's flight.
SALERIO   That's certain. I for my part knew the tailor
    that made the wings she flew withal.   26
SOLANIO   And Shylock for his own part knew the bird
    was fledge, and then it is the complexion of them all   28
    to leave the dam.   29
SHYLOCK   She is damned for it.
SALERIO   That's certain, if the devil may be her judge.
SHYLOCK   My own flesh and blood to rebel!
SOLANIO   Out upon it, old carrion! Rebels it at these   33
    years?   34
SHYLOCK   I say my daughter is my flesh and my blood.

---

63 The fire . . . this This silver has been seven times tested and purified   **66 shadows** illusions   **68 iwis** certainly   **69 Silvered o'er** i.e.,
with silver hair and so apparently wise   **71 I . . . head** i.e., you will
always have a fool's head, be a fool.   **72 sped** done for.   **73–4 Still . . .
here** i.e., I shall seem all the greater fool for wasting any more time
here.   **78 wroth** sorrow, unhappy lot (a variant of *ruth*); or, anger.
80 deliberate reasoning, calculating   **85 my lord** (A jesting response
to "my lady.")   **89 sensible regreets** tangible gifts, greetings
90 commends greetings.   **breath** speech   **91 Yet** Heretofore
94 costly lavish, rich   **95 fore-spurrer** herald, harbinger
98 high-day holiday (i.e., extravagant)   **100 post** messenger

3.1. Location: Venice. A street.
2 yet . . . unchecked i.e., a rumor is spreading undenied   **3–4 the narrow seas** the English Channel, as at 2.8.28   **4 Goodwins** Goodwin
Sands, off the Kentish coast near the Thames estuary   **5 flat** shoal,
sandbank   **6 tall** gallant   **6–7 gossip Report** i.e., Dame Rumor
9 knapped nibbled   **11 slips of prolixity** lapses into long-winded-
ness; or, long-winded lies. *Slips* may be the cuttings or offshoots of
tediousness.   **11–12 crossing . . . talk** deviating from honest, plain
speech   **15 Come . . . stop** Finish your sentence; rein in your tongue
as a horse is checked in its manage.   **19 betimes** while there is yet
time   **20 cross** thwart; make the sign of the cross following
26 the wings . . . withal i.e., the disguise she escaped in. (With a play
on *wings* or ornamented shoulder flaps sewn on garments.)
28 fledge ready to fly.   **complexion** natural disposition, as at 2.7.79
29 dam mother.   **33–4 Rebels . . . years?** (Solanio pretends to interpret Shylock's cry about the rebellion of his own flesh and blood as
referring to his own carnal desires, his own erection.)

SALERIO   There is more difference between thy flesh and
hers than between jet and ivory, more between your   37
bloods than there is between red wine and Rhenish.   38
But tell us, do you hear whether Antonio have had
any loss at sea or no?

SHYLOCK   There I have another bad match! A bankrupt,   41
a prodigal, who dare scarce show his head on the
Rialto; a beggar, that was used to come so smug upon
the mart! Let him look to his bond. He was wont to   44
call me usurer. Let him look to his bond. He was wont
to lend money for a Christian courtesy. Let him look to
his bond.

SALERIO   Why, I am sure, if he forfeit, thou wilt not take
his flesh. What's that good for?

SHYLOCK   To bait fish withal. If it will feed nothing else,
it will feed my revenge. He hath disgraced me, and
hindered me half a million, laughed at my losses,
mocked at my gains, scorned my nation, thwarted my
bargains, cooled my friends, heated mine enemies;
and what's his reason? I am a Jew. Hath not a Jew
eyes? Hath not a Jew hands, organs, dimensions, senses, affections, passions? Fed with the same food, hurt
with the same weapons, subject to the same diseases,
healed by the same means, warmed and cooled by the
same winter and summer, as a Christian is? If you
prick us, do we not bleed? If you tickle us, do we not
laugh? If you poison us, do we not die? And if you
wrong us, shall we not revenge? If we are like you in
the rest, we will resemble you in that. If a Jew wrong
a Christian, what is his humility? Revenge. If a   65
Christian wrong a Jew, what should his sufferance be   66
by Christian example? Why, revenge. The villainy you
teach me I will execute, and it shall go hard but I will   68
better the instruction.

Enter a Man from Antonio.

MAN   Gentlemen, my master Antonio is at his house
and desires to speak with you both.

SALERIO   We have been up and down to seek him.   72

Enter Tubal.

SOLANIO   Here comes another of the tribe. A third
cannot be matched, unless the devil himself turn Jew.   74
          Exeunt gentlemen [Solanio, Salerio, with Man].

SHYLOCK   How now, Tubal, what news from Genoa?
Hast thou found my daughter?

TUBAL   I often came where I did hear of her, but cannot
find her.

SHYLOCK   Why, there, there, there, there! A diamond
gone, cost me two thousand ducats in Frankfort! The   80
curse never fell upon our nation till now; I never felt it   81

till now. Two thousand ducats in that, and other
precious, precious jewels. I would my daughter were
dead at my foot, and the jewels in her ear! Would she
were hearsed at my foot, and the ducats in her coffin!   85
No news of them? Why, so—and I know not what's
spent in the search. Why, thou loss upon loss! The
thief gone with so much, and so much to find the
thief, and no satisfaction, no revenge! Nor no ill luck
stirring but what lights o' my shoulders, no sighs but
o' my breathing, no tears but o' my shedding.

TUBAL   Yes, other men have ill luck too. Antonio, as I
heard in Genoa—

SHYLOCK   What, what, what? Ill luck, ill luck?

TUBAL   hath an argosy cast away, coming from Tripolis.   95

SHYLOCK   I thank God, I thank God. Is it true, is it true?

TUBAL   I spoke with some of the sailors that escaped the
wreck.

SHYLOCK   I thank thee, good Tubal. Good news, good
news! Ha, ha! Heard in Genoa?

TUBAL   Your daughter spent in Genoa, as I heard, one
night fourscore ducats.

SHYLOCK   Thou stick'st a dagger in me. I shall never see
my gold again. Fourscore ducats at a sitting? Fourscore ducats?

TUBAL   There came divers of Antonio's creditors in my
company to Venice that swear he cannot choose but
break.   108

SHYLOCK   I am very glad of it. I'll plague him, I'll torture
him. I am glad of it.

TUBAL   One of them showed me a ring that he had of
your daughter for a monkey.

SHYLOCK   Out upon her! Thou torturest me, Tubal. It
was my turquoise; I had it of Leah when I was a   114
bachelor. I would not have given it for a wilderness of
monkeys.

TUBAL   But Antonio is certainly undone.

SHYLOCK   Nay, that's true, that's very true. Go, Tubal,
fee me an officer; bespeak him a fortnight before. I will   119
have the heart of him if he forfeit, for were he out of
Venice I can make what merchandise I will. Go, Tubal,   121
and meet me at our synagogue. Go, good Tubal; at our
synagogue, Tubal.   *Exeunt [separately].*

❦

[3.2]

*Enter Bassanio, Portia, Gratiano, [Nerissa,]
and all their trains.*

PORTIA
I pray you, tarry. Pause a day or two
Before you hazard, for in choosing wrong   2
I lose your company. Therefore forbear awhile.
There's something tells me—but it is not love—
I would not lose you; and you know yourself
Hate counsels not in such a quality.   6

---

37 jet a black, hard mineral, here contrasted with the whiteness of
ivory and Jessica's fair complexion   **38 Rhenish** i.e., a German white
wine from the Rhine valley. (Salerio seems to prefer the white wine as
more refined than the red.)   **41 match** bargain.   **44 mart** marketplace, Rialto.   **65 what . . . Revenge** i.e., in what spirit does the Christian receive the injury, that of Christian humility? No, he seeks
revenge.   **66 his sufferance** the Jew's patient endurance   **68 it shall
. . . but** i.e., assuredly; unless difficulties intervene   **72 up and down**
i.e., everywhere   **74 matched** i.e., found to match them   **80–1 The
curse** God's curse (such as the plagues visited upon Egypt in Exodus
7–12)

85 hearsed coffined   **95 cast away** shipwrecked   **108 break** go bankrupt.   **114 Leah** Shylock's wife   **119 fee** hire.   **officer** bailiff.
bespeak engage   **121 make . . . I will** drive whatever bargains I
please.
3.2. Location: Belmont. Portia's house.
2 in choosing if you choose   **6 quality** way, manner.

But lest you should not understand me well—
And yet a maiden hath no tongue but thought—
I would detain you here some month or two
Before you venture for me. I could teach you
How to choose right, but then I am forsworn.
So will I never be. So may you miss me.   12
But if you do, you'll make me wish a sin,
That I had been forsworn. Beshrew your eyes,
They have o'erlooked me and divided me!   15
One half of me is yours, the other half yours—
Mine own, I would say; but if mine, then yours,
And so all yours. Oh, these naughty times   18
Puts bars between the owners and their rights!   19
And so, though yours, not yours. Prove it so,   20
Let Fortune go to hell for it, not I.   21
I speak too long, but 'tis to peise the time,   22
To eke it and to draw it out in length,   23
To stay you from election.
BASSANIO   Let me choose,   24
For as I am, I live upon the rack.
PORTIA
Upon the rack, Bassanio? Then confess   26
What treason there is mingled with your love.   27
BASSANIO
None but that ugly treason of mistrust,   28
Which makes me fear th'enjoying of my love.   29
There may as well be amity and life
'Tween snow and fire, as treason and my love.   31
PORTIA
Ay, but I fear you speak upon the rack,
Where men enforcèd do speak anything.
BASSANIO
Promise me life, and I'll confess the truth.
PORTIA
Well then, confess and live.
BASSANIO   "Confess and love"
Had been the very sum of my confession.
Oh, happy torment, when my torturer
Doth teach me answers for deliverance!
But let me to my fortune and the caskets.   39
PORTIA
Away, then! I am locked in one of them.
If you do love me, you will find me out.
Nerissa and the rest, stand all aloof.
Let music sound while he doth make his choice;   42
Then, if he lose, he makes a swanlike end,   44
Fading in music. That the comparison
May stand more proper, my eye shall be the stream

And wat'ry deathbed for him. He may win;
And what is music then? Then music is
Even as the flourish when true subjects bow   49
To a new-crownèd monarch. Such it is
As are those dulcet sounds in break of day
That creep into the dreaming bridegroom's ear
And summon him to marriage. Now he goes,
With no less presence, but with much more love,   54
Than young Alcides when he did redeem   55
The virgin tribute paid by howling Troy   56
To the sea monster. I stand for sacrifice;   57
The rest aloof are the Dardanian wives,   58
With blearèd visages, come forth to view   59
The issue of th'exploit. Go, Hercules!   60
Live thou, I live. With much, much more dismay   61
I view the fight than thou that mak'st the fray.

*A song, the whilst Bassanio comments on the
caskets to himself.*

Tell me where is fancy bred,   63
Or in the heart or in the head?   64
How begot, how nourishèd?
    Reply, reply.
It is engendered in the eyes,   67
With gazing fed, and fancy dies
In the cradle where it lies.   69
    Let us all ring fancy's knell.
    I'll begin it—Ding, dong, bell.
ALL   Ding, dong, bell.
BASSANIO
So may the outward shows be least themselves;   73
The world is still deceived with ornament.   74
In law, what plea so tainted and corrupt
But, being seasoned with a gracious voice,
Obscures the show of evil? In religion,
What damnèd error but some sober brow   78
Will bless it and approve it with a text,   79
Hiding the grossness with fair ornament?
There is no vice so simple but assumes   81
Some mark of virtue on his outward parts.   82
How many cowards, whose hearts are all as false
As stairs of sand, wear yet upon their chins   84
The beards of Hercules and frowning Mars,
Who, inward searched, have livers white as milk?   86
And these assume but valor's excrement   87

---

12 **So** i.e., Forsworn.   **So may . . . me** That being the case, you may
fail to win me.   15 **o'erlooked** bewitched   18 **naughty** wicked
19 **bars** barriers   20 **though yours, not yours** (I am) yours by right but
not by actual possession.   20–1 **Prove . . . not I** i.e., If it turn out thus
(that you are cheated of what is justly yours, i.e., of me), let Fortune be
blamed for it, not I, for I will not be forsworn.   22 **peise** retard (by
hanging on of weights)   23 **eke it** stretch it out, make it last   24 **election** choice.   26–7 **confess What treason** (The rack was used to force
traitors to confess.)   28 **mistrust** misapprehension   29 **fear** fearful
about   31 **as** as between   39 **fortune . . . caskets** (Presumably the curtains are drawn at about this point, as in the previous "casket" scenes,
revealing the three caskets.)   42 **aloof** apart, at a distance.   44 **swanlike** (Swans were believed to sing when they came to die.)

49 **flourish** sounding of trumpets   54 **presence** noble bearing
55 **Alcides** Hercules (called *Alcides*, as at 2.1.32–5, because he was the
grandson of Alcaeus) rescued Hesione, daughter of the Trojan king
Laomedon, from a monster to which, by command of Neptune, she
was about to be sacrificed. Hercules was rewarded, however, not
with the lady's love, but with a famous pair of horses.   56 **howling**
lamenting   57 **stand for sacrifice** represent the sacrificial victim
58 **Dardanian** Trojan   59 **blearèd** tear-stained   60 **issue** outcome
61 **Live thou** If you live   63 **fancy** love   64 **Or** either   67 **eyes** (Love
entered the heart especially through the eyes.)   69 **In the cradle** i.e.,
in its infancy, in the eyes   73 **be least themselves** least represent the
inner reality   74 **still** ever   78 **sober brow** i.e., solemn-faced clergyman   79 **approve** confirm   81 **simple** unadulterated   82 **his** its
84 **stairs** steps   86 **searched** surgically probed.   **livers** (The liver was
thought to be the seat of courage; for it to be deserted by the blood
would be the condition of cowardice.)   87 **excrement** outgrowth,
here a beard

To render them redoubted. Look on beauty,   88
And you shall see 'tis purchased by the weight,   89
Which therein works a miracle in nature,
Making them lightest that wear most of it.   91
So are those crispèd, snaky, golden locks,   92
Which maketh such wanton gambols with the wind
Upon supposèd fairness, often known   94
To be the dowry of a second head,   95
The skull that bred them in the sepulcher.   96
Thus ornament is but the guilèd shore   97
To a most dangerous sea, the beauteous scarf
Veiling an Indian beauty; in a word,   99
The seeming truth which cunning times put on
To entrap the wisest. Therefore, thou gaudy gold,
Hard food for Midas, I will none of thee;   102
Nor none of thee, thou pale and common drudge   103
'Tween man and man. But thou, thou meager lead,   104
Which rather threaten'st than dost promise aught,
Thy paleness moves me more than eloquence;
And here choose I. Joy be the consequence!

PORTIA [*aside*]
How all the other passions fleet to air,
As doubtful thoughts, and rash-embraced despair,   109
And shuddering fear, and green-eyed jealousy!
O love, be moderate, allay thy ecstasy,
In measure rain thy joy, scant this excess!   112
I feel too much thy blessing. Make it less,
For fear I surfeit.

BASSANIO [*opening the leaden casket*]
            What find I here?
Fair Portia's counterfeit! What demigod   115
Hath come so near creation? Move these eyes?
Or whether, riding on the balls of mine,
Seem they in motion? Here are severed lips,
Parted with sugar breath; so sweet a bar   119
Should sunder such sweet friends. Here in her hairs   120
The painter plays the spider, and hath woven
A golden mesh t'entrap the hearts of men
Faster than gnats in cobwebs. But her eyes—   123
How could he see to do them? Having made one,
Methinks it should have power to steal both his
And leave itself unfurnished. Yet look how far   126
The substance of my praise doth wrong this shadow   127
In underprizing it, so far this shadow   128
Doth limp behind the substance. Here's the scroll,   129

The continent and summary of my fortune.   130
[*He reads.*] "You that choose not by the view
    Chance as fair, and choose as true.   132
    Since this fortune falls to you,
    Be content and seek no new.
    If you be well pleased with this,
    And hold your fortune for your bliss,
    Turn you where your lady is
    And claim her with a loving kiss."
A gentle scroll. Fair lady, by your leave,
I come by note, to give and to receive.   140
Like one of two contending in a prize,   141
That thinks he hath done well in people's eyes,
Hearing applause and universal shout,
Giddy in spirit, still gazing in a doubt
Whether those peals of praise be his or no,   145
So, thrice-fair lady, stand I, even so,
As doubtful whether what I see be true,
Until confirmed, signed, ratified by you.

PORTIA
You see me, Lord Bassanio, where I stand,
Such as I am. Though for myself alone
I would not be ambitious in my wish
To wish myself much better, yet for you
I would be trebled twenty times myself,
A thousand times more fair, ten thousand times
    more rich,
That only to stand high in your account   155
I might in virtues, beauties, livings, friends,   156
Exceed account. But the full sum of me   157
Is sum of something, which, to term in gross,   158
Is an unlessoned girl, unschooled, unpracticèd;
Happy in this, she is not yet so old
But she may learn; happier than this,
She is not bred so dull but she can learn;
Happiest of all is that her gentle spirit
Commits itself to yours to be directed
As from her lord, her governor, her king.
Myself and what is mine to you and yours
Is now converted. But now I was the lord   167
Of this fair mansion, master of my servants,
Queen o'er myself; and even now, but now,
This house, these servants, and this same myself
Are yours, my lord's. I give them with this ring,
Which when you part from, lose, or give away,
Let it presage the ruin of your love
And be my vantage to exclaim on you.   174
            [*She puts a ring on his finger.*]

BASSANIO
Madam, you have bereft me of all words.
Only my blood speaks to you in my veins,

---

88 redoubted feared.   **89 purchased by the weight** bought (as cosmetics) at so much per ounce   **91 lightest** most frivolous or lascivious. (With pun on the sense of "least heavy.")   **92 crispèd** curly   **94 Upon supposèd fairness** i.e., on a woman supposed beautiful and fair-haired   **95–6 To . . . sepulcher** i.e., to be a wig of hair taken from a woman now dead.   **97 guilèd** treacherous   **99 Indian** i.e., swarthy, not fair   **102 Midas** the Phrygian king whose touch turned everything to gold, including his food   **103–4 pale . . . man** i.e., silver, used in commerce.   **104 meager** wanting in richness   **109 As** such as   **112 rain** rain down, or perhaps "rein."   **scant** lessen   **115 counterfeit** portrait.   **demigod** i.e., the painter as creator   **119–20 so . . . friends** i.e., only so sweet a barrier as her mouth and breath should be allowed to part such sweet friends as her two lips.   **123 Faster** (1) more tightly (2) quicker   **126 unfurnished** i.e., without a companion.   **look how far** however far   **127 shadow** painting, semblance   **128 underprizing it** failing to do it justice.   **so far** to a similar extent   **129 the substance** the subject, i.e., Portia.

130 continent container   **132 Chance as fair** take your chances fortunately   **140 by note** by a bill of dues (i.e., the scroll). The commercial metaphor continues in *confirmed, signed, ratified* (line 148), *account* (155), *sum* (157), *term in gross* (158), etc.   **141 prize** competition   **145 his** for him   **155 account** estimation   **156 livings** possessions   **157 account** calculation. (Playing on *account*, estimation, in line 155.)   **157–8 But . . . something** i.e., But the full sum of my worth can only be the sum of whatever I am   **158 term in gross** denote in full   **167 But now** A moment ago   **174 vantage to exclaim on** opportunity to reproach

And there is such confusion in my powers   177
As, after some oration fairly spoke
By a belovèd prince, there doth appear
Among the buzzing pleasèd multitude,
Where every something being blent together   181
Turns to a wild of nothing save of joy   182
Expressed and not expressed. But when this ring   183
Parts from this finger, then parts life from hence.
Oh, then be bold to say Bassanio's dead!

NERISSA
My lord and lady, it is now our time,
That have stood by and seen our wishes prosper,   187
To cry, "good joy." Good joy, my lord and lady!

GRATIANO
My lord Bassanio and my gentle lady,
I wish you all the joy that you can wish—
For I am sure you can wish none from me.   191
And when Your Honors mean to solemnize
The bargain of your faith, I do beseech you
Even at that time I may be married too.

BASSANIO
With all my heart, so thou canst get a wife.   195

GRATIANO
I thank Your Lordship, you have got me one.
My eyes, my lord, can look as swift as yours.
You saw the mistress, I beheld the maid;   198
You loved, I loved; for intermission   199
No more pertains to me, my lord, than you.
Your fortune stood upon the caskets there,
And so did mine too, as the matter falls;   202
For wooing here until I sweat again,   203
And swearing till my very roof was dry   204
With oaths of love, at last, if promise last,   205
I got a promise of this fair one here
To have her love, provided that your fortune
Achieved her mistress.

PORTIA   Is this true, Nerissa?

NERISSA
Madam, it is, so you stand pleased withal.   209

BASSANIO
And do you, Gratiano, mean good faith?

GRATIANO   Yes, faith, my lord.

BASSANIO
Our feast shall be much honored in your marriage.

GRATIANO   We'll play with them the first boy for a thou- 213
sand ducats.

NERISSA   What, and stake down?   215

GRATIANO   No, we shall ne'er win at that sport, and   177
stake down.

*Enter Lorenzo, Jessica, and Salerio, a messenger
from Venice.*

But who comes here? Lorenzo and his infidel?
What, and my old Venetian friend Salerio?

BASSANIO
Lorenzo and Salerio, welcome hither,
If that the youth of my new interest here   221
Have power to bid you welcome.—By your leave,
I bid my very friends and countrymen,   223
Sweet Portia, welcome.

PORTIA   So do I, my lord.
They are entirely welcome.

LORENZO
I thank Your Honor. For my part, my lord,
My purpose was not to have seen you here,
But, meeting with Salerio by the way,
He did entreat me, past all saying nay,
To come with him along.

SALERIO   I did, my lord,
And I have reason for it. Signor Antonio
Commends him to you.   [*He gives Bassanio a letter.*]

BASSANIO   Ere I ope his letter,   232
I pray you tell me how my good friend doth.

SALERIO
Not sick, my lord, unless it be in mind,
Nor well, unless in mind. His letter there
Will show you his estate.   [*Bassanio*] open[*s*] *the letter.* 236

GRATIANO [*indicating Jessica*]
Nerissa, cheer yond stranger, bid her welcome.   237
Your hand, Salerio. What's the news from Venice?
How doth that royal merchant, good Antonio?   239
I know he will be glad of our success.
We are the Jasons; we have won the fleece.   241

SALERIO
I would you had won the fleece that he hath lost.

PORTIA
There are some shrewd contents in yond same paper 243
That steals the color from Bassanio's cheek—
Some dear friend dead, else nothing in the world
Could turn so much the constitution
Of any constant man. What, worse and worse?   247
With leave, Bassanio; I am half yourself,   248
And I must freely have the half of anything
That this same paper brings you.

BASSANIO   O sweet Portia,
Here are a few of the unpleasant'st words
That ever blotted paper! Gentle lady,
When I did first impart my love to you,
I freely told you all the wealth I had
Ran in my veins, I was a gentleman;
And then I told you true. And yet, dear lady,

---

177 **powers** faculties   181–3 **Where . . . expressed** i.e., in which every individual utterance, being blended and confused, turns into a hubbub of joy.   187 **That** we who   191 **For . . . me** i.e., I'm sure I can't wish you any more joy than you could wish for yourselves, or, I'm sure your wishes for happiness cannot take away from my happiness. 195 **so** provided   198 **maid** (Nerissa is a lady-in-waiting, not a house servant.)   199 **intermission** delay (in loving)   202 **falls** falls out, happens   203 **sweat again** sweated repeatedly   204 **roof** roof of my mouth   205 **if promise last** i.e., if Nerissa's promise should last, hold out. (With a play on *last* and *at last*, "finally.")   209 **so** provided 213 **We'll . . . boy** We'll wager with them to see who has the first male heir   215 **stake down** cash placed in advance. (But Gratiano, in his reply, turns the phrase into a bawdy joke; *stake down* to him suggests a non-erect phallus.)

221 **youth . . . interest** i.e., newness of my household authority 223 **very** true   232 **Commends him** desires to be remembered 236 **estate** situation.   237 **stranger** alien   239 **royal merchant** i.e., chief among merchants   241 **Jasons . . . fleece** (Compare with 1.1.170–2.)   243 **shrewd** cursed, grievous   247 **constant** settled, not swayed by passion   248 **With leave** With your permission

Rating myself at nothing, you shall see
How much I was a braggart. When I told you
My state was nothing, I should then have told you   259
That I was worse than nothing; for indeed
I have engaged myself to a dear friend,
Engaged my friend to his mere enemy,   262
To feed my means. Here is a letter, lady,
The paper as the body of my friend,
And every word in it a gaping wound
Issuing lifeblood. But is it true, Salerio?
Hath all his ventures failed? What, not one hit?   267
From Tripolis, from Mexico, and England,
From Lisbon, Barbary, and India,
And not one vessel scape the dreadful touch
Of merchant-marring rocks?

SALERIO   Not one, my lord.   271
Besides, it should appear that if he had
The present money to discharge the Jew   273
He would not take it. Never did I know   274
A creature that did bear the shape of man
So keen and greedy to confound a man.   276
He plies the Duke at morning and at night,
And doth impeach the freedom of the state   278
If they deny him justice. Twenty merchants,
The Duke himself, and the magnificoes   280
Of greatest port have all persuaded with him,   281
But none can drive him from the envious plea   282
Of forfeiture, of justice, and his bond.

JESSICA
When I was with him I have heard him swear
To Tubal and to Chus, his countrymen,   285
That he would rather have Antonio's flesh
Than twenty times the value of the sum
That he did owe him; and I know, my lord,
If law, authority, and power deny not,
It will go hard with poor Antonio.

PORTIA [to Bassanio]
Is it your dear friend that is thus in trouble?

BASSANIO
The dearest friend to me, the kindest man,
The best-conditioned and unwearied spirit   293
In doing courtesies, and one in whom
The ancient Roman honor more appears
Than any that draws breath in Italy.

PORTIA   What sum owes he the Jew?

BASSANIO
For me, three thousand ducats.

PORTIA   What, no more?
Pay him six thousand, and deface the bond;   299
Double six thousand, and then treble that,
Before a friend of this description

Shall lose a hair through Bassanio's fault.
First go with me to church and call me wife,
And then away to Venice to your friend;
For never shall you lie by Portia's side
With an unquiet soul. You shall have gold
To pay the petty debt twenty times over.
When it is paid, bring your true friend along.
My maid Nerissa and myself meantime
Will live as maids and widows. Come, away!
For you shall hence upon your wedding day.
Bid your friends welcome, show a merry cheer;   312
Since you are dear bought, I will love you dear.   313
But let me hear the letter of your friend.

BASSANIO [reads]   "Sweet Bassanio, my ships have all
miscarried, my creditors grow cruel, my estate is
very low, my bond to the Jew is forfeit; and since in
paying it, it is impossible I should live, all debts are
cleared between you and I if I might but see you at
my death. Notwithstanding, use your pleasure. If
your love do not persuade you to come, let not my
letter."

PORTIA
O love, dispatch all business, and begone!

BASSANIO
Since I have your good leave to go away,
I will make haste; but till I come again
No bed shall e'er be guilty of my stay,
Nor rest be interposer twixt us twain.   Exeunt.

❖

[3.3]

Enter [Shylock] the Jew and Solanio and Antonio
and the Jailer.

SHYLOCK
Jailer, look to him. Tell not me of mercy.
This is the fool that lent out money gratis.   2
Jailer, look to him.

ANTONIO   Hear me yet, good Shylock.

SHYLOCK
I'll have my bond. Speak not against my bond.
I have sworn an oath that I will have my bond.
Thou called'st me dog before thou hadst a cause,
But since I am a dog, beware my fangs.
The Duke shall grant me justice. I do wonder,
Thou naughty jailer, that thou art so fond   9
To come abroad with him at his request.   10

ANTONIO   I pray thee, hear me speak.

SHYLOCK
I'll have my bond. I will not hear thee speak.
I'll have my bond, and therefore speak no more.
I'll not be made a soft and dull-eyed fool,   14
To shake the head, relent, and sigh, and yield
To Christian intercessors. Follow not.
I'll have no speaking. I will have my bond.   Exit Jew.

---

259 **state** estate   262 **mere** absolute   267 **hit** success.   271 **merchant-marring** capable of damaging a merchant ship   273 **present** available. **discharge** pay off   274 **He** i.e., Shylock   276 **confound** destroy   278 **doth . . . state** i.e., calls in question the ability of Venice to defend legally the freedom of commerce of its citizens   280 **magnificoes** chief men of Venice   281 **port** dignity.   **persuaded** argued   282 **envious** malicious   285 **Chus** the Bishops' Bible spelling of *Cush*, son of Ham and grandson of Noah. *Tubal* was son of Japheth and grandson of Noah (Genesis 10:2, 6).   293 **best-conditioned** best-natured   299 **deface** erase

312 **cheer** countenance   313 **dear . . . dear** at great cost . . . dearly.   **3.3. Location: Venice. A street.**
2 **gratis** free (of interest).   9 **naughty** worthless, wicked.   **fond** foolish   10 **abroad** outside   14 **dull-eyed** easily duped

SOLANIO
It is the most impenetrable cur
That ever kept with men.

ANTONIO   Let him alone.   19
I'll follow him no more with bootless prayers.   20
He seeks my life. His reason well I know:
I oft delivered from his forfeitures
Many that have at times made moan to me;
Therefore he hates me.

SOLANIO   I am sure the Duke
Will never grant this forfeiture to hold.

ANTONIO
The Duke cannot deny the course of law;
For the commodity that strangers have   27
With us in Venice, if it be denied,
Will much impeach the justice of the state,
Since that the trade and profit of the city   30
Consisteth of all nations. Therefore go.
These griefs and losses have so bated me   32
That I shall hardly spare a pound of flesh
Tomorrow to my bloody creditor.—
Well, jailer, on. Pray God Bassanio come
To see me pay his debt, and then I care not.   *Exeunt.*

❖

[3.4]

*Enter Portia, Nerissa, Lorenzo, Jessica, and
[Balthasar,] a man of Portia's.*

LORENZO
Madam, although I speak it in your presence,
You have a noble and a true conceit   2
Of godlike amity, which appears most strongly   3
In bearing thus the absence of your lord.
But if you knew to whom you show this honor,   5
How true a gentleman you send relief,
How dear a lover of my lord your husband,   7
I know you would be prouder of the work
Than customary bounty can enforce you.   9

PORTIA
I never did repent for doing good,
Nor shall not now; for in companions
That do converse and waste the time together,   12
Whose souls do bear an equal yoke of love,
There must be needs a like proportion   14
Of lineaments, of manners, and of spirit;   15
Which makes me think that this Antonio,
Being the bosom lover of my lord,   17
Must needs be like my lord. If it be so,
How little is the cost I have bestowed
In purchasing the semblance of my soul   20

From out the state of hellish cruelty!   21
This comes too near the praising of myself;
Therefore no more of it. Hear other things:
Lorenzo, I commit into your hands
The husbandry and manage of my house   25
Until my lord's return. For mine own part,
I have toward heaven breathed a secret vow
To live in prayer and contemplation,
Only attended by Nerissa here,
Until her husband and my lord's return.
There is a monastery two miles off,
And there we will abide. I do desire you
Not to deny this imposition,   33
The which my love and some necessity
Now lays upon you.

LORENZO   Madam, with all my heart,
I shall obey you in all fair commands.

PORTIA
My people do already know my mind,   37
And will acknowledge you and Jessica
In place of Lord Bassanio and myself.
So fare you well till we shall meet again.

LORENZO
Fair thoughts and happy hours attend on you!

JESSICA
I wish Your Ladyship all heart's content.

PORTIA
I thank you for your wish and am well pleased
To wish it back on you. Fare you well, Jessica.
                Exeunt [Jessica and Lorenzo].
Now, Balthasar,
As I have ever found thee honest-true,
So let me find thee still. Take this same letter,
                [giving a letter]
And use thou all th'endeavor of a man
In speed to Padua. See thou render this
Into my cousin's hands, Doctor Bellario;
And look what notes and garments he doth give thee,   51
Bring them, I pray thee, with imagined speed   52
Unto the traject, to the common ferry   53
Which trades to Venice. Waste no time in words,   54
But get thee gone. I shall be there before thee.

BALTHASAR
Madam, I go with all convenient speed.   *[Exit.]*

PORTIA
Come on, Nerissa, I have work in hand
That you yet know not of. We'll see our husbands
Before they think of us.

NERISSA   Shall they see us?

PORTIA
They shall, Nerissa, but in such a habit   60
That they shall think we are accomplishèd   61
With that we lack. I'll hold thee any wager,   62

---

19 kept associated, dwelt   **20 bootless** unavailing   **27 commodity** facilities or privileges for trading.   **strangers** noncitizens, including Jews   **30 Since that** since   **32 bated** reduced
3.4. Location: Belmont. Portia's house.
2 conceit understanding   **3 amity** friendship and love   **5 to whom . . . honor** i.e., Antonio, who you honor by sending money to relieve him   **7 lover** friend   **9 Than . . . you** than ordinary benevolence can make you.   **12 waste** spend   **14 must be needs** must be   **15 lineaments** physical features   **17 bosom lover** dear friend   **20 the semblance of my soul** i.e., Antonio, so like my Bassanio

21 From . . . cruelty from the cruel state in which he presently stands. **25 husbandry and manage** care and management   **33 deny this imposition** refuse this charge imposed   **37 people** servants   **51 look what** whatever   **52 imagined** all imaginable   **53 traject** ferry. (Italian *traghetto*.)   **common** public   **54 trades** plies back and forth   **60 habit** apparel, garb   **61 accomplishèd** supplied   **62 that** that which. (With a bawdy suggestion.)

When we are both accoutered like young men
I'll prove the prettier fellow of the two,
And wear my dagger with the braver grace,
And speak between the change of man and boy
With a reed voice, and turn two mincing steps
Into a manly stride, and speak of frays
Like a fine bragging youth, and tell quaint lies,   69
How honorable ladies sought my love,
Which I denying, they fell sick and died—
I could not do withal! Then I'll repent,   72
And wish, for all that, that I had not killed them;
And twenty of these puny lies I'll tell,   74
That men shall swear I have discontinued school   75
Above a twelvemonth. I have within my mind   76
A thousand raw tricks of these bragging Jacks,   77
Which I will practice.
NERISSA   Why, shall we turn to men?   78
PORTIA   Fie, what a question's that,
If thou wert near a lewd interpreter!
But come, I'll tell thee all my whole device   81
When I am in my coach, which stays for us
At the park gate; and therefore haste away,
For we must measure twenty miles today.   *Exeunt.*   84

❧

[3.5]

Enter [Lancelot the] clown and Jessica.

LANCELOT   Yes, truly, for look you, the sins of the father are to be laid upon the children; therefore, I prom-   2
ise you, I fear you. I was always plain with you, and   3
so now I speak my agitation of the matter. Therefore   4
be o' good cheer, for truly I think you are damned.
There is but one hope in it that can do you any good,
and that is but a kind of bastard hope, neither.   7
JESSICA   And what hope is that, I pray thee?
LANCELOT   Marry, you may partly hope that your father got you not, that you are not the Jew's daughter.   10
JESSICA   That were a kind of bastard hope, indeed! So
the sins of my mother should be visited upon me.
LANCELOT   Truly, then, I fear you are damned both by
father and mother. Thus when I shun Scylla, your   14
father, I fall into Charybdis, your mother. Well, you   15
are gone both ways.   16
JESSICA   I shall be saved by my husband. He hath made   17
me a Christian.

LANCELOT   Truly, the more to blame he! We were   19
Christians enough before, e'en as many as could well   20
live one by another. This making of Christians will   21
raise the price of hogs. If we grow all to be pork eaters,
we shall not shortly have a rasher on the coals for   23
money.   24

Enter Lorenzo.

JESSICA   I'll tell my husband, Lancelot, what you say.
Here he comes.
LORENZO   I shall grow jealous of you shortly, Lancelot,
if you thus get my wife into corners.
JESSICA   Nay, you need not fear us, Lorenzo. Lancelot
and I are out. He tells me flatly there's no mercy for me   30
in heaven because I am a Jew's daughter; and he says
you are no good member of the commonwealth, for in
converting Jews to Christians you raise the price of
pork.
LORENZO [*to Lancelot*]   I shall answer that better to the
commonwealth than you can the getting up of the
Negro's belly. The Moor is with child by you, Lancelot.   37
LANCELOT   It is much that the Moor should be more   38
than reason; but if she be less than an honest woman,   39
she is indeed more than I took her for.   40
LORENZO   How every fool can play upon the word! I
think the best grace of wit will shortly turn into   42
silence, and discourse grow commendable in none
only but parrots. Go in, sirrah, bid them prepare for
dinner.
LANCELOT   That is done, sir. They have all stomachs.   46
LORENZO   Goodly Lord, what a wit-snapper are you!
Then bid them prepare dinner.
LANCELOT   That is done too, sir, only "cover" is the   49
word.
LORENZO   Will you cover then, sir?   51
LANCELOT   Not so, sir, neither. I know my duty.   52
LORENZO   Yet more quarreling with occasion! Wilt thou   53
show the whole wealth of thy wit in an instant? I pray
thee, understand a plain man in his plain meaning: go
to thy fellows, bid them cover the table, serve in the
meat, and we will come in to dinner.   57
LANCELOT   For the table, sir, it shall be served in; for the 58
meat, sir, it shall be covered; for your coming in to   59

---

69 **quaint** elaborate, clever   72 **do withal** help it.   74 **puny** childish
75–6 **I . . . twelvemonth** i.e., that I am no mere schoolboy.   76 **Above**
more than   77 **Jacks** fellows   78 **turn to** turn into. (But Portia sees
the occasion for a bawdy quibble on the idea of "turning toward,
lying next to.")   81 **device** plan   84 **measure** traverse
3.5. Location: Belmont. Outside Portia's house.
2–3 **promise** assure   3 **fear you** fear for you.   4 **my agitation of** my
sense of agitation about   7 **bastard** i.e., unfounded. (But also anticipating the usual meaning in lines 9–10.)   **neither** i.e., to be sure.
10 **got** begot   14, 15 **Scylla, Charybdis** twin dangers of the *Odyssey*,
12.255, a monster and a whirlpool guarding the straits presumably
between Italy and Sicily. (*Fall into* plays on the idea of entering the
female sexual anatomy.)   16 **gone** done for   17 **I . . . husband**
(Compare 1 Corinthians 7:14: "the unbelieving wife is sanctified by
the husband.")

19–20 **We . . . enough** There were enough of us Christians   21 **one by
another** (1) as neighbors (2) off one another.   23 **rasher** i.e., of bacon
23–4 **for money** even for ready money, at any price.   30 **are out** have
fallen out.   37 **The Moor** (Lancelot has evidently impregnated some
woman of the household, who, being of African heritage, is referred
to as both "Negro" and "Moor.")   38–40 **It is . . . for** i.e., It is a matter
of concern that the Moor is larger (being pregnant) than usual, larger
than she should be; but if it turns out that she is less than perfectly
chaste, she is something more than I originally supposed. (Lancelot
professes to be surprised by what has happened. With wordplay on
less/more and *more/Moor*.)   42 **the best . . . wit** true wittiness   46 **They
. . . stomachs** The guests all have appetites, and are prepared in that
sense. (Lancelot quibbles with Lorenzo's meaning that the cooks and
servants should be told to get dinner ready.)   49, 51 **cover** spread the
table for the meal. (But in line 52 Lancelot uses the word to mean
"put on one's hat.")   52 **my duty** i.e., my duty to remain bareheaded.
53 **Yet . . . occasion!** i.e., Still quibbling at every opportunity!
57 **meat** food   58 **For** As for.   **table** (Here Lancelot quibblingly takes
the word to mean the food itself.)   59 **covered** (Here used in the
sense of providing a cover for each separate dish.)

dinner, sir, why, let it be as humors and conceits shall   60
govern.   *Exit [Lancelot the] clown.*

LORENZO
Oh, dear discretion, how his words are suited!   62
The fool hath planted in his memory
An army of good words; and I do know
A many fools, that stand in better place,   65
Garnished like him, that for a tricksy word   66
Defy the matter. How cheer'st thou, Jessica?   67
And now, good sweet, say thy opinion:
How dost thou like the Lord Bassanio's wife?

JESSICA
Past all expressing. It is very meet   70
The Lord Bassanio live an upright life,
For, having such a blessing in his lady,
He finds the joys of heaven here on earth;
And if on earth he do not merit it,
In reason he should never come to heaven.   75
Why, if two gods should play some heavenly match
And on the wager lay two earthly women,   77
And Portia one, there must be something else   78
Pawned with the other, for the poor rude world   79
Hath not her fellow.

LORENZO   Even such a husband   80
Hast thou of me as she is for a wife.

JESSICA
Nay, but ask my opinion too of that!

LORENZO
I will anon. First let us go to dinner.

JESSICA
Nay, let me praise you while I have a stomach.   84

LORENZO
No, pray thee, let it serve for table talk;
Then, howsome'er thou speak'st, 'mong other things
I shall digest it.

JESSICA   Well, I'll set you forth.   *Exeunt.*   87

♣

[4.1]

Enter the Duke, the Magnificoes, Antonio, Bas-
sanio, [Salerio,] and Gratiano [with others. The
judges take their places.]

DUKE   What, is Antonio here?
ANTONIO   Ready, so please Your Grace.

DUKE
I am sorry for thee. Thou art come to answer   3
A stony adversary, an inhuman wretch
Uncapable of pity, void and empty
From any dram of mercy.

ANTONIO   I have heard   6
Your Grace hath ta'en great pains to qualify   7
His rigorous course; but since he stands obdurate
And that no lawful means can carry me
Out of his envy's reach, I do oppose   10
My patience to his fury and am armed
To suffer with a quietness of spirit
The very tyranny and rage of his.   13

DUKE
Go one, and call the Jew into the court.

SALERIO
He is ready at the door. He comes, my lord.

Enter Shylock.

DUKE
Make room, and let him stand before our face.—   16
Shylock, the world thinks, and I think so too,
That thou but leadest this fashion of thy malice   18
To the last hour of act, and then 'tis thought   19
Thou'lt show thy mercy and remorse more strange   20
Than is thy strange apparent cruelty;   21
And where thou now exacts the penalty,
Which is a pound of this poor merchant's flesh,
Thou wilt not only loose the forfeiture,   24
But, touched with human gentleness and love,
Forgive a moiety of the principal,   26
Glancing an eye of pity on his losses
That have of late so huddled on his back—
Enough to press a royal merchant down
And pluck commiseration of his state   30
From brassy bosoms and rough hearts of flint,   31
From stubborn Turks and Tartars never trained
To offices of tender courtesy.
We all expect a gentle answer, Jew.

SHYLOCK
I have possessed Your Grace of what I purpose,   35
And by our holy Sabbath have I sworn
To have the due and forfeit of my bond.
If you deny it, let the danger light   38
Upon your charter and your city's freedom!   39
You'll ask me why I rather choose to have
A weight of carrion flesh than to receive
Three thousand ducats. I'll not answer that,
But say it is my humor. Is it answered?   43
What if my house be troubled with a rat
And I be pleased to give ten thousand ducats

---

60 humors and conceits whims and fancies   **62 Oh, dear discretion**
Oh, what precious discrimination.)   **suited** suited to the occasion
65 A many many.   **better place** higher social station   **66 Garnished**
i.e., furnished with words, or with garments   **66–7 that . . . matter**
who for the sake of ingenious wordplay torture the plain meaning.
67 How cheer'st thou i.e., What cheer, how are you doing   **70 meet**
fitting   **75 In reason** it stands to reason. (Jessica jokes that for Bassanio to receive unmerited bliss on earth—unmerited because no person can earn bliss through his or her own deserving—is to run the
risk of eternal damnation.)   **77 lay** stake   **78 else** more   **79 Pawned**
staked, wagered   **80 fellow** equal.   **84 stomach** (1) appetite (2) inclination.   **87 digest** (1) ponder, analyze (2) "swallow," put up with.
(With a play also on the gastronomic sense.)   **set you forth** (1) serve
you up, as at a feast (2) set forth your praises.
4.1. Location: Venice. A court of justice. Benches, etc., are provided
for the justices.

3 answer defend yourself against. (A legal term.)   **6 dram** sixty
grains apothecaries' weight, a tiny quantity   **7 qualify** moderate
10 envy's malice's   **13 tyranny** cruelty   **16 our** (The royal plural.)
18 That . . . fashion that you only maintain this pretense or form
19 the last . . . act the brink of action   **20 remorse** pity.   **strange**
remarkable   **21 strange** unnatural, foreign.   **apparent** (1) manifest,
overt (2) seeming   **24 loose** release, waive   **26 moiety** part, portion
30 of for   **31 brassy** unfeeling, hard like brass   **35 possessed**
informed   **38 danger** injury   **39 Upon . . . freedom** (See 3.2.278.)
43 humor whim.

To have it baned? What, are you answered yet?   46
Some men there are love not a gaping pig,   47
Some that are mad if they behold a cat,
And others, when the bagpipe sings i'th' nose,
Cannot contain their urine; for affection,   50
Mistress of passion, sways it to the mood
Of what it likes or loathes. Now, for your answer:
As there is no firm reason to be rendered
Why he cannot abide a gaping pig,   54
Why he a harmless necessary cat,   55
Why he a woolen bagpipe, but of force   56
Must yield to such inevitable shame
As to offend, himself being offended,
So can I give no reason, nor I will not,
More than a lodged hate and a certain loathing   60
I bear Antonio, that I follow thus
A losing suit against him. Are you answered?   62

BASSANIO
This is no answer, thou unfeeling man,
To excuse the current of thy cruelty.   64

SHYLOCK
I am not bound to please thee with my answers.

BASSANIO
Do all men kill the things they do not love?

SHYLOCK
Hates any man the thing he would not kill?

BASSANIO
Every offense is not a hate at first.

SHYLOCK
What, wouldst thou have a serpent sting thee twice?

ANTONIO
I pray you, think you question with the Jew.   70
You may as well go stand upon the beach
And bid the main flood bate his usual height;   72
You may as well use question with the wolf   73
Why he hath made the ewe bleat for the lamb;
You may as well forbid the mountain pines
To wag their high tops and to make no noise
When they are fretten with the gusts of heaven;   77
You may as well do anything most hard
As seek to soften that—than which what's harder?—
His Jewish heart. Therefore, I do beseech you,
Make no more offers, use no farther means,
But with all brief and plain conveniency
Let me have judgment, and the Jew his will.

BASSANIO [to Shylock]
For thy three thousand ducats here is six.

SHYLOCK
If every ducat in six thousand ducats
Were in six parts, and every part a ducat,
I would not draw them. I would have my bond.   87

DUKE
How shalt thou hope for mercy, rendering none?

SHYLOCK
What judgment shall I dread, doing no wrong?   89
You have among you many a purchased slave,
Which, like your asses and your dogs and mules,
You use in abject and in slavish parts,   92
Because you bought them. Shall I say to you,
"Let them be free, marry them to your heirs!
Why sweat they under burdens? Let their beds
Be made as soft as yours, and let their palates
Be seasoned with such viands"? You will answer   97
"The slaves are ours." So do I answer you:
The pound of flesh which I demand of him
Is dearly bought, is mine, and I will have it.
If you deny me, fie upon your law!
There is no force in the decrees of Venice.
I stand for judgment. Answer: shall I have it?

DUKE
Upon my power I may dismiss this court,   104
Unless Bellario, a learnèd doctor,   105
Whom I have sent for to determine this,   106
Come here today.

SALERIO   My lord, here stays without   107
A messenger with letters from the doctor,
New come from Padua.

DUKE
Bring us the letters. Call the messenger.   [Exit one.]

BASSANIO
Good cheer, Antonio. What, man, courage yet!
The Jew shall have my flesh, blood, bones, and all,
Ere thou shalt lose for me one drop of blood.

ANTONIO
I am a tainted wether of the flock,   114
Meetest for death. The weakest kind of fruit   115
Drops earliest to the ground, and so let me.
You cannot better be employed, Bassanio,
Than to live still and write mine epitaph.

                    Enter Nerissa [dressed like a lawyer's clerk].

DUKE
Came you from Padua, from Bellario?

NERISSA
From both, my lord. Bellario greets Your Grace.
     [She presents a letter. Shylock whets his knife on his shoe.]

BASSANIO
Why dost thou whet thy knife so earnestly?

SHYLOCK
To cut the forfeiture from that bankrupt there.

GRATIANO
Not on thy sole, but on thy soul, harsh Jew,
Thou mak'st thy knife keen; but no metal can,
No, not the hangman's ax, bear half the keenness   125
Of thy sharp envy. Can no prayers pierce thee?   126

---

46 **baned** poisoned.   **47 love** who love.   **gaping pig** pig roasted whole with its mouth open   **50 affection** feeling, desire   **54, 55, 56 he, he, he** one person, another, yet another   **55 necessary** i.e., useful for catching rats and mice   **56 woolen** i.e., with flannel-covered bag   **60 lodged** settled, steadfast.   **certain** unwavering, fixed   **62 losing** unprofitable   **64 current** flow, tendency   **70 think** bear in mind. **question** argue   **72 And . . . height** and bid the ocean put an end to its usual high tide   **73 use question with** interrogate   **77 fretten** fretted, i.e., disturbed, ruffled   **87 draw** receive

89 wrong legal wrong.   **92 parts** duties, capacities   **97 such viands** food such as you eat.   **104 Upon** In accordance with   **105 doctor** person of learning. (Here, of law.)   **106 determine this** resolve this legal dispute   **107 stays without** waits outside   **114 wether** ram, especially a castrated ram   **115 Meetest** fittest   **125 hangman's** executioner's.   **keenness** (1) sharpness (2) savagery   **126 envy** malice.

SHYLOCK
No, none that thou hast wit enough to make.

GRATIANO
Oh, be thou damned, inexecrable dog,   128
And for thy life let Justice be accused!   129
Thou almost mak'st me waver in my faith
To hold opinion with Pythagoras   131
That souls of animals infuse themselves
Into the trunks of men. Thy currish spirit
Governed a wolf who, hanged for human slaughter,   134
Even from the gallows did his fell soul fleet,   135
And, whilst thou layest in thy unhallowed dam,   136
Infused itself in thee; for thy desires
Are wolvish, bloody, starved, and ravenous.

SHYLOCK
Till thou canst rail the seal from off my bond,   139
Thou but offend'st thy lungs to speak so loud.   140
Repair thy wit, good youth, or it will fall
To cureless ruin. I stand here for law.   142

DUKE
This letter from Bellario doth commend
A young and learnèd doctor to our court.
Where is he?

NERISSA   He attendeth here hard by
To know your answer, whether you'll admit him.

DUKE
With all my heart. Some three or four of you
Go give him courteous conduct to this place.
                         [Exeunt some.]
Meantime the court shall hear Bellario's letter.
[He reads.] "Your Grace shall understand that at the   150
receipt of your letter I am very sick; but in the instant
that your messenger came, in loving visitation was
with me a young doctor of Rome. His name is Balthasar. I acquainted him with the cause in controversy between the Jew and Antonio the merchant. We
turned o'er many books together. He is furnished with
my opinion, which, bettered with his own learning,
the greatness whereof I cannot enough commend,
comes with him, at my importunity, to fill up Your   159
Grace's request in my stead. I beseech you, let his lack
of years be no impediment to let him lack a reverend   161
estimation, for I never knew so young a body with so
old a head. I leave him to your gracious acceptance,
whose trial shall better publish his commendation."   164

          Enter Portia for Balthasar [dressed like a doctor
          of laws, escorted].

128 inexecrable thoroughly execrable   129 And . . . accused! and may
Justice herself be accused for allowing you to live!   131 Pythagoras
ancient Greek philosopher who argued for the transmigration of souls
134 hanged for human slaughter (A possible allusion to the Elizabethan practice of trying and punishing animals for various crimes.)
135 fell fierce, cruel.   fleet flit, i.e., pass from the body   136 dam
mother. (Usually used of animals.)   139 rail remove by your abusive
language   140 Thou but offend'st you merely injure   142 cureless
incurable   150 [He reads.] (In many modern editions, the reading of
the letter is assigned to a clerk, but the original text gives no such indication.)   159 comes with him accompanies him in the form of my
learned opinion.   importunity insistence   161 to let him lack such as
would deprive him of   164 whose . . . commendation the demonstration of whose excellence will proclaim what is commendable in him
better than my letter can.   164.1 for i.e., disguised as

You hear the learn'd Bellario, what he writes;
And here, I take it, is the doctor come.—
Give me your hand. Come you from old Bellario?

PORTIA
I did, my lord.

DUKE   You are welcome. Take your place.
                         [Portia takes her place.]
Are you acquainted with the difference   169
That holds this present question in the court?

PORTIA
I am informèd throughly of the cause.   171
Which is the merchant here, and which the Jew?

DUKE
Antonio and old Shylock, both stand forth.
                    [Antonio and Shylock stand forth.]

PORTIA
Is your name Shylock?

SHYLOCK   Shylock is my name.

PORTIA
Of a strange nature is the suit you follow,
Yet in such rule that the Venetian law   176
Cannot impugn you as you do proceed.—   177
You stand within his danger, do you not?

ANTONIO
Ay, so he says.

PORTIA   Do you confess the bond?

ANTONIO
I do.

PORTIA   Then must the Jew be merciful.

SHYLOCK
On what compulsion must I? Tell me that.

PORTIA
The quality of mercy is not strained.   182
It droppeth as the gentle rain from heaven
Upon the place beneath. It is twice blest: 184
It blesseth him that gives and him that takes.
'Tis mightiest in the mightiest; it becomes
The thronèd monarch better than his crown.
His scepter shows the force of temporal power,   188
The attribute to awe and majesty,   189
Wherein doth sit the dread and fear of kings.
But mercy is above this sceptered sway;
It is enthronèd in the hearts of kings;
It is an attribute to God himself;
And earthly power doth then show likest God's
When mercy seasons justice. Therefore, Jew,
Though justice be thy plea, consider this,
That in the course of justice none of us   197
Should see salvation. We do pray for mercy,
And that same prayer doth teach us all to render
The deeds of mercy. I have spoke thus much
To mitigate the justice of thy plea,   201
Which if thou follow, this strict court of Venice
Must needs give sentence 'gainst the merchant there.

169 difference argument   171 throughly thoroughly.   cause case.
176 rule order   177 impugn find fault with   182 strained forced,
constrained.   184 is twice blest grants a double blessing   188 His
i.e., The monarch's   189 attribute to symbol of   197 justice divine
justice   201 To . . . plea i.e., to show the way in which your call for
justice needs to be mitigated or reduced in severity

SHYLOCK

My deeds upon my head! I crave the law,   204
The penalty and forfeit of my bond.

PORTIA

Is he not able to discharge the money?

BASSANIO

Yes, here I tender it for him in the court,
Yea, twice the sum. If that will not suffice,
I will be bound to pay it ten times o'er,
On forfeit of my hands, my head, my heart.
If this will not suffice, it must appear
That malice bears down truth. And I beseech you,   212
Wrest once the law to your authority.   213
To do a great right, do a little wrong,
And curb this cruel devil of his will.

PORTIA

It must not be. There is no power in Venice
Can alter a decree establishèd.
'Twill be recorded for a precedent,
And many an error by the same example
Will rush into the state. It cannot be.

SHYLOCK

A Daniel come to judgment! Yea, a Daniel!   221
O wise young judge, how I do honor thee!

PORTIA

I pray you, let me look upon the bond.

SHYLOCK [giving the bond]

Here 'tis, most reverend doctor, here it is.

PORTIA

Shylock, there's thrice thy money offered thee.

SHYLOCK

An oath, an oath! I have an oath in heaven.
Shall I lay perjury upon my soul?
No, not for Venice.

PORTIA   Why, this bond is forfeit,
And lawfully by this the Jew may claim
A pound of flesh, to be by him cut off
Nearest the merchant's heart.—Be merciful.
Take thrice thy money; bid me tear the bond.

SHYLOCK

When it is paid according to the tenor.   233
It doth appear you are a worthy judge.
You know the law. Your exposition
Hath been most sound. I charge you by the law,
Whereof you are a well-deserving pillar,
Proceed to judgment. By my soul I swear
There is no power in the tongue of man
To alter me. I stay here on my bond.   240

ANTONIO

Most heartily I do beseech the court
To give the judgment.

PORTIA   Why then, thus it is:
You must prepare your bosom for his knife.

SHYLOCK

O noble judge! O excellent young man!

PORTIA

For the intent and purpose of the law
Hath full relation to the penalty   246
Which here appeareth due upon the bond.

SHYLOCK

'Tis very true. O wise and upright judge!
How much more elder art thou than thy looks!

PORTIA

Therefore lay bare your bosom.

SHYLOCK   Ay, his breast.
So says the bond, doth it not, noble judge?
"Nearest his heart," those are the very words.

PORTIA

It is so. Are there balance here   253
To weigh the flesh?

SHYLOCK   I have them ready.

PORTIA

Have by some surgeon, Shylock, on your charge,   255
To stop his wounds, lest he do bleed to death.

SHYLOCK

Is it so nominated in the bond?

PORTIA

It is not so expressed, but what of that?
'Twere good you do so much for charity.

SHYLOCK

I cannot find it. 'Tis not in the bond.

PORTIA

You, merchant, have you anything to say?

ANTONIO

But little. I am armed and well prepared.—   262
Give me your hand, Bassanio; fare you well!
Grieve not that I am fall'n to this for you,
For herein Fortune shows herself more kind
Than is her custom. It is still her use   266
To let the wretched man outlive his wealth
To view with hollow eye and wrinkled brow
An age of poverty; from which ling'ring penance
Of such misery doth she cut me off.
Commend me to your honorable wife.
Tell her the process of Antonio's end,   272
Say how I loved you, speak me fair in death;   273
And, when the tale is told, bid her be judge
Whether Bassanio had not once a love.   275
Repent but you that you shall lose your friend,   276
And he repents not that he pays your debt.
For if the Jew do cut but deep enough,
I'll pay it instantly with all my heart.   279

BASSANIO

Antonio, I am married to a wife,
Which is as dear to me as life itself;
But life itself, my wife, and all the world

---

204 My . . . head! (Compare the cry of the crowd at Jesus' crucifixion: "His blood be on us, and on our children," Matthew 27:25.)
212 bears down truth overwhelms righteousness.   **213 Wrest once** for once, forcibly subject   **221 Daniel** (In the Apocrypha's story of Susannah and the Elders, Daniel is the young man who rescues Susannah from her false accusers.)   **233 tenor** conditions.   **240 stay** stand, insist

246 Hath . . . to is fully in accord with   **253 balance** scales   **255 Have by** Have ready at hand.   **on your charge** at your personal expense   **262 armed** i.e., fortified in spirit   **266 still her use** i.e., commonly Fortune's practice   **272 process** story, manner   **273 speak me fair** speak well of me   **275 a love** a friend's love.   **276 Repent but you** Grieve only   **279 with . . . heart** (1) wholeheartedly (2) literally, with my heart's blood.

Are not with me esteemed above thy life.
I would lose all, ay, sacrifice them all
Here to this devil, to deliver you.

PORTIA
Your wife would give you little thanks for that,
If she were by to hear you make the offer.   287

GRATIANO
I have a wife who, I protest, I love;
I would she were in heaven, so she could
Entreat some power to change this currish Jew.

NERISSA
'Tis well you offer it behind her back;
The wish would make else an unquiet house.

SHYLOCK
These be the Christian husbands. I have a daughter;
Would any of the stock of Barabbas   294
Had been her husband rather than a Christian!—
We trifle time. I pray thee, pursue sentence.   296

PORTIA
A pound of that same merchant's flesh is thine.
The court awards it, and the law doth give it.

SHYLOCK   Most rightful judge!

PORTIA
And you must cut this flesh from off his breast.
The law allows it, and the court awards it.

SHYLOCK
Most learnèd judge! A sentence!—Come, prepare.

PORTIA
Tarry a little; there is something else.
This bond doth give thee here no jot of blood;
The words expressly are "a pound of flesh."
Take then thy bond, take thou thy pound of flesh,
But in the cutting it if thou dost shed
One drop of Christian blood, thy lands and goods
Are by the laws of Venice confiscate
Unto the state of Venice.

GRATIANO
O upright judge! Mark, Jew. O learnèd judge!

SHYLOCK
Is that the law?

PORTIA   Thyself shalt see the act;
For, as thou urgest justice, be assured
Thou shalt have justice, more than thou desir'st.

GRATIANO
O learnèd judge! Mark, Jew, a learnèd judge!

SHYLOCK
I take this offer, then. Pay the bond thrice
And let the Christian go.

BASSANIO   Here is the money.

PORTIA   Soft!   318
The Jew shall have all justice. Soft, no haste.   319
He shall have nothing but the penalty.

GRATIANO
O Jew! An upright judge, a learnèd judge!

PORTIA
Therefore prepare thee to cut off the flesh.
Shed thou no blood, nor cut thou less nor more
But just a pound of flesh. If thou tak'st more
Or less than a just pound, be it but so much
As makes it light or heavy in the substance   326
Or the division of the twentieth part   327
Of one poor scruple, nay, if the scale do turn   328
But in the estimation of a hair,
Thou diest, and all thy goods are confiscate.

GRATIANO
A second Daniel, a Daniel, Jew!   331
Now, infidel, I have you on the hip.   332

PORTIA
Why doth the Jew pause? Take thy forfeiture.

SHYLOCK
Give me my principal, and let me go.

BASSANIO
I have it ready for thee. Here it is.

PORTIA
He hath refused it in the open court.
He shall have merely justice and his bond.

GRATIANO
A Daniel, still say I, a second Daniel!
I thank thee, Jew, for teaching me that word.

SHYLOCK
Shall I not have barely my principal?

PORTIA
Thou shalt have nothing but the forfeiture,
To be so taken at thy peril, Jew.

SHYLOCK
Why, then the devil give him good of it!
I'll stay no longer question.   [*He starts to go.*]

PORTIA   Tarry, Jew!   344
The law hath yet another hold on you.
It is enacted in the laws of Venice,
If it be proved against an alien
That by direct or indirect attempts
He seek the life of any citizen,
The party 'gainst the which he doth contrive
Shall seize one half his goods; the other half
Comes to the privy coffer of the state,   352
And the offender's life lies in the mercy   353
Of the Duke only, 'gainst all other voice.   354
In which predicament, I say, thou stand'st;
For it appears, by manifest proceeding,
That indirectly and directly too
Thou hast contrived against the very life
Of the defendant; and thou hast incurred
The danger formerly by me rehearsed.   360
Down therefore, and beg mercy of the Duke.   361

---

287 **by** nearby   294 **Barabbas** a thief whom Pontius Pilate set free instead of Christ in response to the people's demand (see Mark 15); also, the villainous protagonist of Marlowe's *The Jew of Malta*   296 **trifle** waste.   **pursue** proceed with   318 **Soft!** i.e., Not so fast!   319 **all justice** precisely what the law provides.

326 **substance** mass or gross weight   327 **division** fraction   328 **scruple** twenty grains apothecaries' weight, a small quantity   331 **Daniel** (See line 221 above and note.)   332 **on the hip** i.e., at a disadvantage. (A phrase from wrestling.)   344 **I'll . . . question** I'll stay no further pursuing of the case.   352 **privy coffer** private treasury   353 **lies in** lies at   354 **'gainst . . . voice** without appeal   360 **The danger . . . rehearsed** the penalty already cited by me.   361 **Down** Down on your knees

GRATIANO
Beg that thou mayst have leave to hang thyself!
And yet, thy wealth being forfeit to the state,
Thou hast not left the value of a cord;
Therefore thou must be hanged at the state's charge.   365
DUKE
That thou shalt see the difference of our spirit,
I pardon thee thy life before thou ask it.
For half thy wealth, it is Antonio's;   368
The other half comes to the general state,
Which humbleness may drive unto a fine.   370
PORTIA
Ay, for the state, not for Antonio.   371
SHYLOCK
Nay, take my life and all! Pardon not that!
You take my house when you do take the prop
That doth sustain my house. You take my life
When you do take the means whereby I live.
PORTIA
What mercy can you render him, Antonio?
GRATIANO
A halter gratis! Nothing else, for God's sake.   377
ANTONIO
So please my lord the Duke and all the court
To quit the fine for one half of his goods,   379
I am content, so he will let me have   380
The other half in use, to render it,   381
Upon his death, unto the gentleman
That lately stole his daughter.
Two things provided more: that for this favor
He presently become a Christian;   385
The other, that he do record a gift
Here in the court of all he dies possessed   387
Unto his son Lorenzo and his daughter.
DUKE
He shall do this, or else I do recant
The pardon that I late pronouncèd here.   389
PORTIA
Art thou contented, Jew? What dost thou say?
SHYLOCK
I am content.
PORTIA   Clerk, draw a deed of gift.
SHYLOCK
I pray you, give me leave to go from hence;
I am not well. Send the deed after me,
And I will sign it.
DUKE   Get thee gone, but do it.
GRATIANO
In christening shalt thou have two godfathers.
Had I been judge, thou shouldst have had ten more,   397

To bring thee to the gallows, not the font.
                                        Exit [Shylock].
DUKE [to Portia]
Sir, I entreat you home with me to dinner.
PORTIA
I humbly do desire Your Grace of pardon.
I must away this night toward Padua,
And it is meet I presently set forth.   402
DUKE
I am sorry that your leisure serves you not.
Antonio, gratify this gentleman,   404
For in my mind you are much bound to him.
                          Exeunt Duke and his train.
BASSANIO [to Portia]
Most worthy gentleman, I and my friend
Have by your wisdom been this day acquitted
Of grievous penalties, in lieu whereof,   408
Three thousand ducats due unto the Jew
We freely cope your courteous pains withal.   410
                                  [He offers money.]
ANTONIO
And stand indebted over and above
In love and service to you evermore.
PORTIA
He is well paid that is well satisfied,
And I, delivering you, am satisfied,
And therein do account myself well paid.
My mind was never yet more mercenary.
I pray you, know me when we meet again.   417
I wish you well, and so I take my leave.
                                  [She starts to leave.]
BASSANIO
Dear sir, of force I must attempt you further.   419
Take some remembrance of us as a tribute,
Not as fee. Grant me two things, I pray you:
Not to deny me, and to pardon me.   422
PORTIA
You press me far, and therefore I will yield.
Give me your gloves, I'll wear them for your sake.   424
And, for your love, I'll take this ring from you.   425
Do not draw back your hand; I'll take no more,
And you in love shall not deny me this.
BASSANIO
This ring, good sir? Alas, it is a trifle!
I will not shame myself to give you this.
PORTIA
I will have nothing else but only this;
And now, methinks, I have a mind to it.
BASSANIO
There's more depends on this than on the value.

The dearest ring in Venice will I give you,   433
And find it out by proclamation.
Only for this, I pray you, pardon me.

PORTIA
I see, sir, you are liberal in offers.   436
You taught me first to beg, and now, methinks,
You teach me how a beggar should be answered.

BASSANIO
Good sir, this ring was given me by my wife,
And when she put it on she made me vow
That I should neither sell nor give nor lose it.

PORTIA
That 'scuse serves many men to save their gifts.
An if your wife be not a madwoman,   443
And know how well I have deserved this ring,
She would not hold out enemy forever
For giving it to me. Well, peace be with you!
                    Exeunt [*Portia and Nerissa*].

ANTONIO
My lord Bassanio, let him have the ring.
Let his deservings and my love withal
Be valued 'gainst your wife's commandement.   449

BASSANIO
Go, Gratiano, run and overtake him;
Give him the ring, and bring him, if thou canst,
Unto Antonio's house. Away, make haste!
                    Exit Gratiano [*with the ring*].
Come, you and I will thither presently,
And in the morning early will we both
Fly toward Belmont. Come, Antonio.   *Exeunt.*

❧

[4.2]

Enter [*Portia and*] *Nerissa* [*still disguised*].

PORTIA [*giving a deed to Nerissa*]
Inquire the Jew's house out; give him this deed   1
And let him sign it. We'll away tonight
And be a day before our husbands home.
This deed will be well welcome to Lorenzo.

Enter Gratiano.

GRATIANO   Fair sir, you are well o'erta'en.   5
My lord Bassanio upon more advice   6
Hath sent you here this ring and doth entreat
Your company at dinner.   [*He gives a ring.*]

PORTIA   That cannot be.
His ring I do accept most thankfully,
And so, I pray you, tell him. Furthermore,
I pray you, show my youth old Shylock's house.

GRATIANO
That will I do.

NERISSA   Sir, I would speak with you.
[*Aside to Portia*] I'll see if I can get my husband's
    ring,
Which I did make him swear to keep forever.

PORTIA [*aside to Nerissa*]
Thou mayst, I warrant. We shall have old swearing   15
That they did give the rings away to men;
But we'll outface them, and outswear them too.—   17
Away, make haste! Thou know'st where I will tarry.

NERISSA [*to Gratiano*]
Come, good sir, will you show me to this house?
        [*Exeunt, Portia separately from the others.*]

[5.1]

Enter Lorenzo and Jessica.

LORENZO
The moon shines bright. In such a night as this,
When the sweet wind did gently kiss the trees
And they did make no noise, in such a night
Troilus methinks mounted the Trojan walls   4
And sighed his soul toward the Grecian tents
Where Cressid lay that night.

JESSICA   In such a night
Did Thisbe fearfully o'ertrip the dew,   7
And saw the lion's shadow ere himself,
And ran dismayed away.

LORENZO   In such a night
Stood Dido with a willow in her hand   10
Upon the wild sea banks, and waft her love   11
To come again to Carthage.

JESSICA   In such a night
Medea gathered the enchanted herbs   13
That did renew old Aeson.

LORENZO   In such a night
Did Jessica steal from the wealthy Jew   15
And with an unthrift love did run from Venice   16
As far as Belmont.

JESSICA   In such a night
Did young Lorenzo swear he loved her well,
Stealing her soul with many vows of faith,
And ne'er a true one.

LORENZO   In such a night
Did pretty Jessica, like a little shrew,
Slander her love, and he forgave it her.

JESSICA
I would out-night you, did nobody come.   23
But hark, I hear the footing of a man.   24

Enter [*Stephano,*] *a messenger.*

LORENZO
Who comes so fast in silence of the night?

15 **old** plenty of   17 **outface** boldly contradict
5.1. Location: Belmont. Outside Portia's house.
4 **Troilus** Trojan prince deserted by his beloved, Cressida, after she had
been transferred to the Greek camp   7 **Thisbe** beloved of Pyramus
who, arranging to meet him by night, was frightened by a lion and fled;
the tragic misunderstanding of her absence led to the suicides of both
lovers. (See *A Midsummer Night's Dream*, Act 5.)   10 **Dido** Queen of
Carthage, deserted by Aeneas.   **willow** (A symbol of forsaken love.)
11 **waft** wafted, beckoned   13 **Medea** famous sorceress of Colchis who,
after falling in love with Jason and helping him to gain the Golden
Fleece, used her magic to restore youth to Aeson, Jason's father
15 **steal** (1) escape (2) rob   16 **unthrift** prodigal   23 **out-night** i.e.,
outdo in the verbal games we've been playing   24 **footing** footsteps

433 **dearest** most expensive   436 **liberal** generous   443 **An if** If
449 **commandement** (Pronounced in four syllables.)
4.2. Location: Venice. A street.
1 **this deed** i.e., the deed of gift   5 **you . . . o'erta'en** I'm happy to
have caught up with you.   6 **advice** consideration

STEPHANO   A friend.

LORENZO

A friend? What friend? Your name, I pray you,
    friend?

STEPHANO

Stephano is my name, and I bring word
My mistress will before the break of day
Be here at Belmont. She doth stray about
By holy crosses, where she kneels and prays   31
For happy wedlock hours.

LORENZO   Who comes with her?

STEPHANO

None but a holy hermit and her maid.
I pray you, is my master yet returned?

LORENZO

He is not, nor we have not heard from him.
But go we in, I pray thee, Jessica,
And ceremoniously let us prepare
Some welcome for the mistress of the house.

        Enter [Lancelot, the] clown.

LANCELOT   Sola, sola! Wo ha, ho! Sola, sola!   39

LORENZO   Who calls?

LANCELOT   Sola! Did you see Master Lorenzo? Master
Lorenzo, sola, sola!

LORENZO   Leave holloing, man! Here.

LANCELOT   Sola! Where, where?

LORENZO   Here.

LANCELOT   Tell him there's a post come from my mas-   46
ter, with his horn full of good news: my master will be 47
here ere morning.   [Exit.]

LORENZO

Sweet soul, let's in, and there expect their coming.   49
And yet no matter. Why should we go in?
My friend Stephano, signify, I pray you,   51
Within the house, your mistress is at hand,
And bring your music forth into the air.

                            [Exit Stephano.]

How sweet the moonlight sleeps upon this bank!
Here will we sit and let the sounds of music
Creep in our ears. Soft stillness and the night
Become the touches of sweet harmony.   57
Sit, Jessica. [They sit.] Look how the floor of heaven
Is thick inlaid with patens of bright gold.   59
There's not the smallest orb which thou behold'st
But in his motion like an angel sings,
Still choiring to the young-eyed cherubins.   62
Such harmony is in immortal souls,
But whilst this muddy vesture of decay   64
Doth grossly close it in, we cannot hear it.   65

        [Enter musicians.]

Come, ho, and wake Diana with a hymn!   66
With sweetest touches pierce your mistress' ear
And draw her home with music.   *Play music.*

JESSICA

I am never merry when I hear sweet music.

LORENZO

The reason is, your spirits are attentive.   70
For do but note a wild and wanton herd,
Or race of youthful and unhandled colts,   72
Fetching mad bounds, bellowing and neighing loud,
Which is the hot condition of their blood;
If they but hear perchance a trumpet sound,
Or any air of music touch their ears,
You shall perceive them make a mutual stand,   77
Their savage eyes turned to a modest gaze
By the sweet power of music. Therefore the poet   79
Did feign that Orpheus drew trees, stones, and
    floods,   80
Since naught so stockish, hard, and full of rage   81
But music for the time doth change his nature.   82
The man that hath no music in himself,
Nor is not moved with concord of sweet sounds,
Is fit for treasons, stratagems, and spoils;   85
The motions of his spirit are dull as night
And his affections dark as Erebus.   87
Let no such man be trusted. Mark the music.

        Enter Portia and Nerissa.

PORTIA

That light we see is burning in my hall.
How far that little candle throws his beams!
So shines a good deed in a naughty world.   91

NERISSA

When the moon shone, we did not see the candle.

PORTIA

So doth the greater glory dim the less.
A substitute shines brightly as a king
Until a king be by, and then his state   95
Empties itself, as doth an inland brook
Into the main of waters. Music! Hark!   97

NERISSA

It is your music, madam, of the house.

PORTIA

Nothing is good, I see, without respect.   99
Methinks it sounds much sweeter than by day.

NERISSA

Silence bestows that virtue on it, madam.

PORTIA

The crow doth sing as sweetly as the lark
When neither is attended; and I think   103
The nightingale, if she should sing by day,

---

31 holy crosses wayside shrines **39 Sola** (Imitation of a post horn.)
46 post courier **47 horn** (Lancelot jestingly compares the courier's
post horn to a cornucopia; perhaps too with a glance at the frayed jest
about cuckolds' horns.) **49 expect** await **51 signify** make known
57 Become suit. **touches** strains, notes (produced by the fingering of
an instrument) **59 patens** thin, circular plates of metal **62 Still
choiring** continually singing. **young-eyed** eternally clear-sighted.
(In Ezekiel 10:12, the bodies and wings of cherubim are "full of eyes
round about.") **64 muddy . . . decay** i.e., mortal flesh **65 close it in**
i.e., enclose the soul. **hear it** i.e., hear the music of the spheres.

66 Diana (Here, goddess of the moon; compare with 1.2.105.)
70 spirits are attentive (The spirits would be in motion within the
body in merriment, whereas in sadness they would be drawn to the
heart and, as it were, busy listening.) **72 race** herd **77 mutual** common or simultaneous **79 poet** perhaps Ovid, with whom the story of
Orpheus was a favorite theme **80 Orpheus** legendary musician.
drew attracted, charmed. **floods** rivers **81 stockish** unfeeling
82 his its (a tree, a stone, etc.) **85 spoils** acts of pillage **87 Erebus** a
place of primeval darkness on the way to Hades. **91 naughty**
wicked **95 his** i.e., the substitute's **97 main of waters** sea.
99 respect comparison, context. **103 attended** listened to

When every goose is cackling, would be thought
No better a musician than the wren.
How many things by season seasoned are   107
To their right praise and true perfection!
Peace, ho! The moon sleeps with Endymion   109
And would not be awaked.   *[The music ceases.]*

LORENZO   That is the voice,
Or I am much deceived, of Portia.

PORTIA
He knows me as the blind man knows the cuckoo,
By the bad voice.

LORENZO   Dear lady, welcome home.

PORTIA
We have been praying for our husbands' welfare,
Which speed, we hope, the better for our words.   115
Are they returned?

LORENZO   Madam, they are not yet;
But there is come a messenger before,
To signify their coming.

PORTIA   Go in, Nerissa.
Give order to my servants that they take
No note at all of our being absent hence;
Nor you, Lorenzo; Jessica, nor you. *[A tucket sounds.]* 121

LORENZO
Your husband is at hand. I hear his trumpet.
We are no telltales, madam, fear you not.

PORTIA
This night, methinks, is but the daylight sick;   124
It looks a little paler. 'Tis a day
Such as the day is when the sun is hid.

*Enter Bassanio, Antonio, Gratiano, and their
followers.*

BASSANIO
We should hold day with the Antipodes,   127
If you would walk in absence of the sun.   128

PORTIA
Let me give light, but let me not be light;   129
For a light wife doth make a heavy husband,   130
And never be Bassanio so for me.
But God sort all! You are welcome home, my lord.   132

BASSANIO
I thank you, madam. Give welcome to my friend.
This is the man, this is Antonio,
To whom I am so infinitely bound.

PORTIA
You should in all sense be much bound to him,   136
For, as I hear, he was much bound for you.   137

ANTONIO
No more than I am well acquitted of.   138

PORTIA
Sir, you are very welcome to our house.
It must appear in other ways than words;
Therefore I scant this breathing courtesy.   141

GRATIANO *[to Nerissa]*
By yonder moon I swear you do me wrong!
In faith, I gave it to the judge's clerk.
Would he were gelt that had it, for my part,   144
Since you do take it, love, so much at heart.

PORTIA
A quarrel, ho, already? What's the matter?

GRATIANO
About a hoop of gold, a paltry ring
That she did give me, whose posy was   148
For all the world like cutler's poetry
Upon a knife, "Love me, and leave me not."

NERISSA
What talk you of the posy or the value?
You swore to me, when I did give it you,
That you would wear it till your hour of death
And that it should lie with you in your grave.
Though not for me, yet for your vehement oaths
You should have been respective and have kept it.   156
Gave it a judge's clerk! No, God's my judge,
The clerk will ne'er wear hair on 's face that had it.

GRATIANO
He will, an if he live to be a man.   159

NERISSA
Ay, if a woman live to be a man.

GRATIANO
Now, by this hand, I gave it to a youth,
A kind of boy, a little scrubbèd boy   162
No higher than thyself, the judge's clerk,
A prating boy, that begged it as a fee.   164
I could not for my heart deny it him.

PORTIA
You were to blame—I must be plain with you—
To part so slightly with your wife's first gift,
A thing stuck on with oaths upon your finger,
And so riveted with faith unto your flesh.
I gave my love a ring and made him swear
Never to part with it; and here he stands.
I dare be sworn for him he would not leave it,
Nor pluck it from his finger, for the wealth
That the world masters. Now, in faith, Gratiano,   174
You give your wife too unkind a cause of grief.
An 'twere to me, I should be mad at it.   176

BASSANIO *[aside]*
Why, I were best to cut my left hand off
And swear I lost the ring defending it.

GRATIANO
My lord Bassanio gave his ring away

---

107 season fit occasion. (But playing on the idea of seasoning, spices.)
109 Endymion a shepherd loved by the moon goddess, who caused him to sleep a perennial sleep in a cave on Mount Latmos where she could visit him   **115 Which . . . words** who prosper and return speedily, we hope, because we prayed for them.   **121 s.d. tucket** flourish on a trumpet   **124 sick** i.e., made pale by the approach of dawn   **127–8 We . . . sun** i.e., If you, Portia, like a second sun, would always walk about during the sun's absence, we should never have night but would enjoy daylight even when the Antipodes, those who dwell on the opposite side of the globe, enjoy daylight.   **129 be light** be wanton, unchaste   **130 heavy** sad. (With wordplay on the antithesis of *light* and *heavy*.)   **132 sort** decide, dispose   **136 in all sense** in every way, with every reason   **136–7 bound . . . bound** Portia plays on (1) obligated (2) indebted and imprisoned.

138 acquitted of freed from and amply repaid (by thanks and love).
141 scant . . . courtesy make brief these empty (i.e., merely verbal) compliments.   **144 gelt** gelded, castrated. **for my part** as far as I'm concerned   **148 posy** a motto on a ring   **156 respective** mindful, careful   **159 an if** if   **162 scrubbèd** diminutive   **164 prating** chattering   **174 masters** owns.   **176 An** If. **mad** beside myself

Unto the judge that begged it and indeed
Deserved it too; and then the boy, his clerk,
That took some pains in writing, he begged mine;
And neither man nor master would take aught   183
But the two rings.

PORTIA [*to Bassanio*]   What ring gave you, my lord?
Not that, I hope, which you received of me.

BASSANIO
If I could add a lie unto a fault,
I would deny it; but you see my finger
Hath not the ring upon it. It is gone.

PORTIA
Even so void is your false heart of truth.
By heaven, I will ne'er come in your bed
Until I see the ring!

NERISSA [*to Gratiano*]   Nor I in yours
Till I again see mine.

BASSANIO   Sweet Portia,
If you did know to whom I gave the ring,
If you did know for whom I gave the ring,
And would conceive for what I gave the ring,
And how unwillingly I left the ring,
When naught would be accepted but the ring,
You would abate the strength of your displeasure.

PORTIA
If you had known the virtue of the ring,   199
Or half her worthiness that gave the ring,
Or your own honor to contain the ring,   201
You would not then have parted with the ring.
What man is there so much unreasonable,
If you had pleased to have defended it
With any terms of zeal, wanted the modesty   205
To urge the thing held as a ceremony?   206
Nerissa teaches me what to believe:
I'll die for't but some woman had the ring.

BASSANIO
No, by my honor, madam! By my soul,
No woman had it, but a civil doctor,   210
Which did refuse three thousand ducats of me
And begged the ring, the which I did deny him
And suffered him to go displeased away—   213
Even he that had held up the very life
Of my dear friend. What should I say, sweet lady?
I was enforced to send it after him.
I was beset with shame and courtesy.
My honor would not let ingratitude
So much besmear it. Pardon me, good lady!   219
For by these blessèd candles of the night,   220
Had you been there, I think you would have begged
The ring of me to give the worthy doctor.

PORTIA
Let not that doctor e'er come near my house.
Since he hath got the jewel that I loved,
And that which you did swear to keep for me,

I will become as liberal as you: 226
I'll not deny him anything I have,
No, not my body nor my husband's bed.
Know him I shall, I am well sure of it.   229
Lie not a night from home. Watch me like Argus;   230
If you do not, if I be left alone,
Now, by mine honor, which is yet mine own,   232
I'll have that doctor for my bedfellow.

NERISSA
And I his clerk; therefore be well advised   234
How you do leave me to mine own protection.

GRATIANO
Well, do you so. Let not me take him, then!   236
For if I do, I'll mar the young clerk's pen.   237

ANTONIO
I am th'unhappy subject of these quarrels.

PORTIA
Sir, grieve not you; you are welcome notwithstanding.

BASSANIO
Portia, forgive me this enforcèd wrong,
And in the hearing of these many friends
I swear to thee, even by thine own fair eyes
Wherein I see myself—

PORTIA   Mark you but that!
In both my eyes he doubly sees himself;
In each eye, one. Swear by your double self,   245
And there's an oath of credit.

BASSANIO   Nay, but hear me.   246
Pardon this fault, and by my soul I swear
I never more will break an oath with thee.

ANTONIO
I once did lend my body for his wealth,   249
Which, but for him that had your husband's ring,
Had quite miscarried. I dare be bound again,
My soul upon the forfeit, that your lord   252
Will nevermore break faith advisedly.   253

PORTIA
Then you shall be his surety. Give him this,   254
And bid him keep it better than the other.
   [*She gives the ring to Antonio, who gives it to Bassanio.*]

ANTONIO
Here, Lord Bassanio. Swear to keep this ring.

BASSANIO
By heaven, it is the same I gave the doctor!

PORTIA
I had it of him. Pardon me, Bassanio,
For by this ring the doctor lay with me.

NERISSA
And pardon me, my gentle Gratiano,
For that same scrubbèd boy, the doctor's clerk,
In lieu of this last night did lie with me.   262
   [*Presenting her ring.*]

---

226 liberal generous (sexually as well as otherwise) **229 Know** (With the suggestion of carnal knowledge.) **230 from** away from. **Argus** mythological monster with a hundred eyes **232 honor** (1) honorable name (2) chastity **234 be well advised** take care **236 take** apprehend **237 pen** (With sexual double meaning.) **245 double** i.e., deceitful **246 of credit** worthy to be believed. (Said ironically.) **249 wealth** welfare **252 My . . . forfeit** at the risk of eternal damnation **253 advisedly** intentionally. **254 surety** guarantor. **262 In lieu of** in return for

---

183 aught anything **199 virtue** moral efficacy **201 contain** keep safe **205 wanted the modesty** who would have been so lacking in consideration as **206 urge** insist upon receiving. **ceremony** something sacred. **210 civil doctor** i.e., doctor of civil law **213 suffered** allowed **219 it** i.e., my honor. **220 blessèd . . . night** i.e., stars

GRATIANO
Why, this is like the mending of highways
In summer, where the ways are fair enough.   264
What, are we cuckolds ere we have deserved it?   265
PORTIA
Speak not so grossly. You are all amazed.
Here is a letter; read it at your leisure.
                                    [*She gives a letter.*]
It comes from Padua, from Bellario.
There you shall find that Portia was the doctor,
Nerissa there her clerk. Lorenzo here
Shall witness I set forth as soon as you,
And even but now returned; I have not yet
Entered my house. Antonio, you are welcome,
And I have better news in store for you
Than you expect. Unseal this letter soon.
                                [*She gives him a letter.*]
There you shall find three of your argosies
Are richly come to harbor suddenly.
You shall not know by what strange accident
I chancèd on this letter.
ANTONIO   I am dumb.   279
BASSANIO [*to Portia*]
Were you the doctor and I knew you not?
GRATIANO [*to Nerissa*]
Were you the clerk that is to make me cuckold?
NERISSA
Ay, but the clerk that never means to do it,
Unless he live until he be a man.
BASSANIO
Sweet doctor, you shall be my bedfellow.

When I am absent, then lie with my wife.
ANTONIO
Sweet lady, you have given me life and living;
For here I read for certain that my ships
Are safely come to road.
PORTIA   How now, Lorenzo?   288
My clerk hath some good comforts too for you.
NERISSA
Ay, and I'll give them him without a fee.
                                    [*She gives a deed.*]
There do I give to you and Jessica,
From the rich Jew, a special deed of gift,
After his death, of all he dies possessed of.
LORENZO
Fair ladies, you drop manna in the way   294
Of starved people.
PORTIA   It is almost morning,
And yet I am sure you are not satisfied
Of these events at full. Let us go in;
And charge us there upon inter'gatories,   298
And we will answer all things faithfully.
GRATIANO
Let it be so. The first inter'gatory
That my Nerissa shall be sworn on is
Whether till the next night she had rather stay   302
Or go to bed now, being two hours to day.
But were the day come, I should wish it dark
Till I were couching with the doctor's clerk.   305
Well, while I live I'll fear no other thing
So sore as keeping safe Nerissa's ring.   *Exeunt.* 307

---

264 are fair enough i.e., are not in need of repair.   **265 cuckolds** husbands whose wives are unfaithful   **279 dumb** at a loss for words.

288 road anchorage.   **294 manna** the food from heaven that was miraculously supplied to the Israelites in the wilderness (Exodus 16)   **298 And . . . inter'gatories** and put questions to us (as in a court of law)   **302 stay** wait   **305 couching** going to bed   **307 ring** (With sexual suggestion.)

The Merchant of Venice on Stage

The Merchant of Venice has been popular throughout its four-hundred-year history; despite its prejudices and controversy, audiences have consistently filled theaters to see Shakespeare's most celebrated Jewish character. Prior to the Holocaust, the play was often comically staged, although, as previously discussed, notable actors such as Kean and Irving played Shylock with sympathy and even tragic stature. Since World War II, few have attempted to play Shylock as a figure of ridicule, while a number of directors (e.g., Charles Marowitz and Peter Sellars) have deconstructed the play to attack its anti-Semitic elements. Virtually all stage histories of the play focus on Shylock and the actors who play him. John O'Connor's "Shylock in Performance" (Mahon and Mahon, 2002) and Charles

Edelman's "Introduction" (Edelman, 2002) provide vivid accounts of the play in performance, including video, from its debut through the twentieth century.

The Elizabethan Era: Speculating About Shylock

Considerable debate embroils modern examination of Elizabethan perceptions of Shylock. Did the people of Shakespeare's time see him as a grotesquely comic character played by an actor in a red "Jew's wig" (a tradition that goes back to medieval biblical plays)? As a laughably heinous villain like Marlowe's Barabas in *The Jew of Malta*? Or as a loathsome figure who fueled passions in wake of a recent attempt on Queen Elizabeth's life by, among others, her Jewish physician? As there are no records of audience reactions to the play in Shakespeare's lifetime, these questions cannot be answered with authority. If Thomas Pope, a member of the Lord Chamberlain's Men, played Shylock, as some surmise, then the character was likely viewed as a ridiculous figure, for that actor may have specialized in broadly comic roles (e.g., Sir Toby Belch). If Richard Burbage, who was emerging as company's principal actor by the late sixteenth century, first brought Shylock to life, then Elizabethan audiences likely encountered a more serious personage, for Burbage was on the verge of playing Shakespeare's great tragic roles. However Shylock was received in Bankside, the play was immediately popular: the quarto text (1600) states that the play had been presented "divers times" (diverse, or many, times) since its c. 1596 debut, and the King's Men twice took the play to James I's court in February 1605. No matter how the play's religious and social issues may have been received, the trial scene was a favorite among playgoers: Shakespeare's audiences delighted in legal battles and debates.

The Restoration and the Eighteenth Century: Shylock, from Caricature to Man

While London's public theaters were closed during the Civil War, 1642–1660, Jews were slowly being readmitted to English society. In 1656 Oliver Cromwell granted Jews permission to remain in England and to build a synagogue. Yet The Merchant of Venice was not among the first Shakespearean plays to be revived when theaters reopened in 1660 with the restoration to the throne of King Charles II. After the Restoration, the play was not presented until 1701, and then only in poet and playwright George Granville's drastically cut and altered version, The Jew of Venice. Audiences at Lincoln's Inn Fields did not see Morocco or Aragon, Gobbo, or even Solanio and Salerio. Granville's revision emphasized commercial trade because recent (1697) legislation permitted a dozen Jews and other "aliens" to compete in stock ventures with English businessmen. Granville wrote a prologue, spoken by an actor called Shakespeare, attacking the "stock-jobbing Jews" whom the playwright-businessman believed a threat to English commerce. The popular comic actor Thomas Doggett played Shylock, probably as a broadly humorous "stage Jew." Granville's adaptation was virtually the only acting version of Shakespeare's play for the next forty years.

By 1741 Drury Lane became one of London's two premier theaters, thanks to licensing laws (1737) that granted it and Covent Garden a monopoly on spoken plays. Something approximating Shakespeare's original play, not Granville's pastiche, was performed as part of the Drury Lane's 1741–1742 season. It soon became that theater's most popular production, thanks to actor-manager Charles Macklin's Shylock, a role the actor would play for fifty years (he attempted the role at age 90 but could only get through Shylock's first scene). Macklin

was anything but comedic in his approach: he was fiery and fierce in his hatred of Antonio and the Christians who spat upon him and called him "dog." Macklin secretly prepared for the role by visiting the London Exchange, where both gentiles and Jews traded; then he imitated the manners and gestures of the Jewish merchants he had observed. Macklin kept his revolutionary interpretation to himself: during rehearsals he played the role quietly if rather conventionally, and only on opening night did he unleash the fury that would make him the first great Shylock in recorded theater history. Of Macklin's performance the famous essayist and poet Alexander Pope allegedly wrote this couplet: "This is the Jew / That Shakespeare drew."

John Philip Kemble, the subsequent actor-manager at Drury Lane, attempted Shylock in 1789 opposite his sister, actor Sarah Siddons's, Portia, but he was too aristocratic to play Shylock adequately and relegated the role to Tom King, a popular comedian. Kemble's contributions to the play's stage history have more to do with his alterations. To account for the excision of Morocco and Aragon, he rewrote lines in Bassanio's speech about choosing the caskets in 3.2, and in Act 5 he inserted some romantic ballads for Lorenzo and Jessica; this musical tradition would continue into the twentieth century.

Macklin's legacy and the popularity of The Merchant of Venice enabled the play to be among the first performed in the American colonies. America's first permanent acting troupe, the Hallam Company, rehearsed the play on the deck of The Charming Sally as they sailed to the Virginia Colony in 1752. A subsequent English actor, George Frederick Cooke, struck gold in America in 1810 by playing Richard III and Shylock to considerable acclaim. His Shylock was, like Macklin's, fierce and frightening, and is considered the first tour de force performance of a Shakespearean role in North America.

In the late eighteenth century the German theater blossomed as a viable entity in Europe, largely because of the establishment of a state theater in Hamburg. In 1777 The Merchant of Venice was added to the Hamburg repertory and became an instant sensation throughout Germany. August Wilhelm Iffland played a stereotypically comic Jew with a foreign accent in a sumptuously mounted production in Mannheim. Such anti-Semitic performances were, unfortunately, the norm in Germany until 1866 when Bogumil Dawison, a Polish actor, played Shylock in Germany, Austria, and eventually in New York. Dawison was the first European Jew to enact Shylock. His performance continued the Macklin tradition of the angry alien tormented by his Christian oppressors.

The Nineteenth Century: Sympathy and Spectacle

With some notable exceptions, Romantic and Victorian critics largely perceived Shylock as a sympathetic victim, and actors reflected these sentiments in their interpretations. Edmund Kean acted Shylock in 1834, shocking audiences and his fellow actors by appearing in a *black* wig (Edelman, 12). This innovation lends some credence to the belief that actors to that point wore the traditional and stereotypical red wig—pictorial evidence suggests that Macklin had dark brown hair while playing the role. Kean's illegitimate birth and impoverished childhood provided him with material to play a downtrodden "outsider," and his Shylock, while passionate and vengeful, was by all accounts the most sympathetic to date on the English stage. William Charles Macready succeeded Kean as Shylock, whom he played on both sides of the Atlantic. An 1839 reviewer for a London journal observed that Macready gave "personal dignity to the Jew" to make audiences "wonder that a man of his appearance should belong to a despised race." The comment reflects both the changing sentiments toward Shylock specifically and lingering prejudices toward Jews in general. Edmund Booth, nineteenth-century America's premier actor, also played Shylock, but his performance did not earn him the adulation of his Iago or Hamlet. Booth, who had seen Macready's "dignified" performance, wrote that he had "searched in vain for the slightest hint of anything resembling dignity or worthiness in [Shylock]" (Watermeir, 256). This statement may explain why Booth's reading of the role reduced Shylock to yet another portrait of a mere stage villain.

As with so many other classical works, especially Shakespeare's, *The Merchant of Venice* became a vehicle for stage spectacle in the mid nineteenth century. Given England's fascination with all things Italian, it was natural that the play would invite lavish recreations of Italy. Charles Kean's elegant 1858 production at the Princess's Theatre unfolded on an "authentic" recreation of St. Mark's Square filled with throngs of Venetian nobles congregating to watch a procession by the powerful Doge and his magnificoes. Gondoliers, exotic foreigners, and flower girls adorned the stage, as Kean, the son of Edmund, sought to bring the many period paintings of the mystical city to life. Kean played Shylock, but was dwarfed by the sheer size of scenic elements that were to became the staple of most productions thereafter.

The finest of the late–nineteenth-century Shylocks was that of Sir Henry Irving, the esteemed actor-manager of London's cavernous Lyceum Theatre, where scenic splendor was a specialty. Irving modeled his Shylock on a Jewish gentleman he observed while sailing the Mediterranean; thus his 1879 performance depicted a dignified and well-heeled, if controversial, character. A reviewer for *The Spectator* (November 8, 1879) delighted in this "novel and unexpected" interpretation, noting that Irving's Shylock was "a man whom none can despise, who can raise emotions of both pity and fear, and make us Christians thrill with a retrospective sense of shame."

Irving also invented material to evoke more sympathy for the Jew, most notably the moment when Shylock discovers that his daughter has fled his house forever. As the Lyceum's enormous curtain slowly descended, the actor stood motionless in the Venetian moonlight after knocking on his door to summon Jessica; no parent who had lost a child could fail to empathize with this broken man. Irving's performance became the benchmark for actors playing Shylock until well into the twentieth century, and it had a profound impact on subsequent actors of his generation. In 1893 the American actor Richard Mansfield actually went so far as to slash his wrists after saying "I am not well" in the trial scene (Lelyveld, 102–104), reasoning that Shylock would have chosen death as a Jew over life among such vicious Christians.

Irving's production was also notable for making leading lady Ellen Terry the first actor in the play's then nearly three-hundred-year history to enhance her reputation by playing Portia. Terry was equal parts "New Woman" in her amorousness, "while still fulfilling the Victorian role of the ideal woman" (Gay in Mahan, 436), and she was more admired for the coy frankness with which she pursued Bassanio than for her witty and powerful treatment of the trial scene.

The Twentieth Century: Politics and Playing

Even as Irving's thoughtful approach to Shylock was taking hold in the minds of Victorian audiences and other actors, some theater artists attempted to preserve many of the outmoded traditions associated with the role. William Poel, the founder of the Elizabethan Stage Society, did much to retrieve Shakespeare from the scenic excesses of the nineteenth century and to restore Shakespeare's texts as written, but his 1898 production of *The Merchant* proved to be unattractive in its insistence on an "Elizabethan" and hence repellent Shylock. Convinced that Shakespeare intended Shylock to be played as a comic figure, Poel dressed in a red wig and shabby clothes. He spoke his lines in a shrill accent, evoking the ugliest stereotypes associated with the stage Jew. Poel was not alone in this approach; variants on this costume and demeanor continued into the twentieth century.

Sir Herbert Beerbohm Tree, noted for his opulent settings and casts of hundreds, played Shylock in 1908 wearing much the same makeup (a grotesque nose and tangled beard) he had used when he played Fagin in an adaptation of Dickens's *Oliver Twist*; Tree also added a number of Yiddish expressions to his performance. Though Tree's intent may not have been to demean

Shylock, the effect of his costume and accent inevitably contributed to the stereotyping of Jews. As late as 1953 Michael Redgrave played Shylock at Stratford-upon-Avon as visibly Jewish; the respected actor prepared for the role by visiting Jewish ghettos in Europe. By contrast, a 1971 production in Tel Aviv (directed by Yossi Yzraely) intentionally dressed Shylock in blatantly stereotypical costuming to underscore the prejudices some Christians and Muslims held toward Jews, while the Christians were presented through "Jewish eyes," that is: very white, very blonde, and costumed in gowns that evoked the Ku Klux Klan. The play ended with Shylock, a martyr to Christian bigotry, being carried away as he laughed uncontrollably at the absurdity of his forced conversion.

Jewish actors have a long history of trying to assert their proud heritage in what is perceived to be an anti-Semitic play. In 1901 Jacob Adler, patriarch of one of America's most influential theatrical families, played Shylock in Yiddish at the People's Theater in New York. The production was so popular that Adler revived it in English, although Adler as Shylock continued to speak Yiddish. Adler, whose son Luther played the role a half-century later, argued that Shylock was inherently a good man representing a persecuted race. The actor had seen Irving's performance and attempted to invest the character with even greater dignity than his English colleague had done. Jewish director Leopold Jessner, an influential *avant-garde* theater artist in Germany in the 1920s, staged *The Merchant* in Hebrew at Tel Aviv's Habimah Theater in 1936; he had fled Nazi Germany a year earlier. Jessner directed the actors playing Shylock (Ahron Meskin alternated with Shim'on Finkel) to avoid the image of the patient, long-suffering Jew; rather, audiences saw the character as a heroic rebel who proudly wore a yellow Star of David on his cloak. Unfortunately, audiences felt Jessner's concept was anti-Semitic, and a mock trial was held in which Shakespeare and the Habimah were accused of maligning the race, even though both were acquitted and Jessner was actually thanked for raising such difficult issues in those troubled times.

As news of anti-Jewish hatred in Germany grew more disturbing, *The Merchant of Venice* vanished from some stages. It was apparently not performed professionally in America from the late 1920s until after World War II, and—despite the myth that it was the Nazi's favorite Shakespeare play—*The Merchant* also was absent from German stages (Hortmann, 134–135). Max Reinhardt's 1924 production was the last in Berlin until the 1950s. The English continued to produce it, although with reservations. John Gielgud, who had directed the play in the early 1930s, staged it in 1938, playing Shylock for the first time. To soften the play's anti-Jewish elements (the likes of which could be seen in newsreels from central Europe), Gielgud chose a fairy-tale setting for the Venetian comedy. Perhaps he was responding to director Harley Granville-Barker's pronouncement that the play is indeed a children's fable: "There is no more reality in Shylock's bond or the Lord of Belmont's will than in Jack and the Beanstalk" (Granville-Barker, 30). Ten years earlier Russian director Theodore Komisarjevsky devised a spectacular Venetian carnival for the play at Stratford. Gielgud's production continued in that decidedly escapist vein, with one exception: Shylock was played as a repulsive ogre (in a russet wig!) out of the Brothers Grimm. Despite Gielgud's grotesquerie, some journals (e.g., *The New Statesman*, May 1938) lamented that the play's anti-Jewish harangues became "unbearable . . . at a time when Jews are being driven to mass-suicide by unsurpassed brutalities."

As western European and American understanding of the horrors of the Holocaust increased after the war, productions of *The Merchant* provided even more sympathetic renderings of Shylock. In the Royal Shakespeare Company's inaugural season (1960), Michael Langham directed the play and cast a young (twenty-seven) Peter O'Toole as Shylock. Wearing ringlets and a beard, O'Toole's Jewish moneylender was handsome, well-dressed, and dignified. Given Europe's recent history, audiences understood, perhaps more than ever before, the reasons why Shylock sought revenge against the Christians. Three years later, in 1963, Erwin Piscator mounted *The Merchant* in Berlin at the Frei Volksbuhne, using virtually every device of the Epic Theater (signboards, projections, harangues) to expose both Nazi brutality toward Jews and the economic inequalities that divided the peoples of Europe. Though it was a blatantly political tract, the production is also remembered for the embittered performance of the Austrian actor Ernst Deutsch who had escaped from a ghetto to avoid the Nazis.

Several directors, each Jewish, with reputations for iconoclastic Shakespeare have deconstructed the play to expose its anti-Semitism. Austrian Peter Zadek directed the play in Germany in 1972, turning it into a grotesque (and mostly incoherent) fairy tale played amidst a maze of winding canals extending into the auditorium. Shylock was so violently angry that he became a nightmarish depiction of the wronged Jew. In 1976 Charles Marowitz's *Variations on The Merchant of Venice* placed the action in British Palestine in 1946 as Israel was being created as an independent country. Shylock, a covert supporter of the independence movement, provided money for guerilla activities against the British (Venetian) colonists. Marowitz defended his revision: "To give his villainy some kind of moral justification, I turned [Shylock] into a man with a passionate commitment to a political cause." To underscore his point, Marowitz inserted numerous speeches from

Marlowe's *The Jew of Malta* into *Merchant*, turning the play into a deliberate pastiche of vastly different styles.

The truly seminal post-War *Merchant* was that directed by Jonathan Miller for Britain's National Theatre in 1970, featuring the greatest Shakespearean actor of the century, Laurence Olivier, as Shylock. At Olivier's suggestion, Miller relocated the action to the Edwardian era of the early twentieth century, a moment when Europe was headed toward the war (World War I) that would lead to the war (World War II) that murdered millions of Jews. The production—which has been preserved on videotape (see below)—began and ended with a *kaddish*, the traditional Hebrew song of the dead. Olivier—dressed in a black top hat, under which he wore a yarmulke—dominated the stage. Initially, Olivier's Shylock, ever the pragmatic survivor, tried to ingratiate himself to his Christian tormentors by aping their language and mannerisms. His apparent good will dissolved with Jessica's elopement. Shylock became a demented revenger whose "Hath not a Jew eyes?" speech, long considered to be a plea for equality, became a cold, calculated justification for the murder of Antonio. After his humiliation in the trial (Portia was played by Olivier's wife, Joan Plowright), Olivier provided one of the storied moments of his acting career: having accepted his punishment with apparent dignity ("I am content"), he left the stage and only then could be heard to utter an anguished wail that shook the theater. Because of its daring originality, the production had both detractors and admirers.

As if to countermand Miller's interpretation of the play, the RSC then offered a version of *The Merchant* set in the early twentieth century, although it seemed more Chekhovian than Edwardian. John Barton directed the play at the Other Place, in Stratford-upon-Avon, in 1980 with Patrick Stewart as Shylock. The actor's first inclination was to refuse the offer because he didn't want to be "trapped" by the accumulated traditions associated with Shylock (ringlets, exotic clothing, a "hooked nose," an accent, etc.). Yet Barton gave Stewart enough rein to create a portrait of the Jew that would demonstrate "for the first time that it was perfectly possible to engender a healthy disgust for anti-Semitism without having to play Shylock as a tragic hero and martyr" (O'Connor, 408). Stewart wore shabby clothing and constantly smoked the butts of cigarettes that he hoarded in a tin box. He ingratiated himself to the Christians by joking and kowtowing to them; he slapped Jessica in their domestic scene. Stewart's analysis of the text led him to the conclusion that Shylock is obsessed "with the retention and acquisition of wealth . . . it transcends race and religion and is felt to be as important as life itself" (Stewart, 16). To emphasize that Shylock was an unlikable human being who happened to be Jewish, Barton presented a Tubal who was every inch a gentle-man and who shook his head in disapproval of Shylock's actions. At the conclusion of the trial scene, Stewart's Shylock left the stage amidst convulsive laughter, in response to Gratiano's vile joke about the Jew's christening; the moment was the antithesis to Olivier's famous howl earlier in the decade.

When the production transferred to London, David Suchet replaced Stewart (who had a film commitment). Suchet, a Jew, played a far more sympathetic Shylock. These are the markedly different approaches to the role by Stewart and Suchet, in what is virtually the same production, mentioned before in "Exploring a Character," a fifty-minute video in the RSC's *Playing Shakespeare* series. Barton moderates a discussion between the actors who recreate Shylock's major scenes and speeches. The video gives one of the best explications of the play and its issues in any medium. Stewart also developed a one-man show, "Shylock: Shakespeare's Alien," based on his experiences in playing the role.

Two other London productions merit note. In 1989 Peter Hall directed *The Merchant of Venice* with well-known film actor Dustin Hoffman as Shylock. Hoffman had recently played Willy Loman on Broadway (and in a CBS video of that production); several critics noted the link between the two roles. The diminutive Hoffman rendered Shylock, like "Low-man," as the "little man" trapped by forces he cannot control. The actor used his sardonic wit and wry smile to good effect, although his verse-speaking was noticeably weaker than that of his British colleagues. Hoffman, who trained at the Actors Studio in New York, was more successful in the naturalistic prose passages.

Although Hoffman brought undeniable "star power" to the role, it was the Shylock of a relatively unknown actor—Henry Goodman, a Jew—that brought twentieth-century productions of *The Merchant* to a stunning conclusion. Under Trevor Nunn's thoughtful direction for the National Theatre (1999), Goodman garnered the most impressive reviews in the role since Olivier's. Played in modern dress (Goodman wore a prayer shawl beneath his business suit) yet without overt references to modern anti-Semitism (graffiti, swastikas, abusive behaviors, etc.), the production explored the great cultural divide between Jews and Christians. Shylock, a conservative Jew tired of animosities between the religions, sealed the bond with Antonio as a genuine peace offering. Not until Jessica's elopement, coupled with the (mentioned) death of Shylock's wife Leah (whom Goodman mourned from the outset), was Shylock impelled into vengeance. Goodman's richly nuanced performance, which must be seen to be appreciated, has been preserved on television as part of the *Masterpiece Theater* series (see below).

This overview of the play's stage history has concentrated on the actors' approach to Shakespeare's most controversial character. Other aspects of the play's production deserve mention, however, as additional types of prejudice have come to the fore in the last half of the twentieth century, including homosexuality and violence against blacks.

Canadian audiences were presented with a then-revolutionary treatment of the relationship between Antonio and Bassanio when Sir Tyrone Guthrie directed *The Merchant of Venice* at the Stratford Festival in Ontario in 1955. For the first time in a major production on a professional stage, Guthrie suggested that Antonio's "sadness" was the product of a frustrated love—for Bassanio. Writing for the *Saturday Review* (July 23), Henry Hewes argued that Guthrie's acknowledgment of Antonio's homosexual attraction for Bassanio "lends the play a logical base. Antonio is established as a man ready to make any sacrifice for the boy he loves." Freud had written about Antonio's sexual frustration, yet apparently no twentieth-century production had pursued this theme until Guthrie's. It is now commonplace to at least suggest the possibility of a homosexual attraction between the older, wealthier Antonio and the younger, desperate Bassanio.

Director Bill Alexander's production at the RSC in 1989 (with Antony Sher as a wildly disheveled Shylock) advanced the play's homoerotic possibilities by presenting an older Solanio and a younger Salerio as lovers whose mutual fondness mirrored the Antonio-Bassanio relationship. Bassanio was played as a bisexual exploiter who teased Antonio into agreeing to the bond; the latter kissed Bassanio passionately on the lips after agreeing to lend him three thousand ducats (Bulman, 126–127). Alexander's production intended to explore all prejudices in contemporary society, including homophobia and racism: in the trial scene, Shylock pointed to a black attendant in the court as he said, "You have among you many a purchased slave . . ." (4.1.90).

In 1994 the American theater's *enfant terrible*, Peter Sellars, created a four-hour version of the play in which actors held cameras to televise the onstage action, while the audience watched on banks of monitors about the theater. The "live action" video feeds were interrupted by footage from the "evening news"—the beating of African American Rodney King by Los Angeles police and the riots that followed the acquittal of the cops. The Jewish roles were played by African American actors. Venice was relocated to Venice Beach in Los Angeles., a contemporary bastion of multiculturalism. Sellars's inventions, judged as indulgent by much of the press, raises an interesting question about such overt modernizations: if Shakespeare's plays in general, and *The Merchant of Venice* specifically, are admired for the universality of their themes, does a director have to "spell out" a play's relevance to contemporary audiences? The production was widely excoriated when it was taken to London.

The Merchant of Venice on Film and Video

The most recent feature film of *The Merchant of Venice,* starring Al Pacino, was distributed in 2005. There were several silent versions made between 1908 and 1923: three American, and one each from Italy, France, England, and Germany (Buhler, 159). In 1910 Gerolamo Lo Savio directed two of Italy's most famous performers, Ermete Novelli and Francesca Bertini, in compressed versions of *King Lear* and *The Merchant of Venice*. The nine-minute (unfinished?) Italian film, *Il Mercante de Venezia*, was shot in Venice and hand-colored. It focuses on Jessica more than on Portia, while Shylock wears a turban and is seen methodically sharpening his knife in anticipation of obtaining his pound of flesh. (This film may be seen in *Silent Shakespeare* [Milestone Films, 2000], an eighty-eight–minute video of seven Shakespeare films made between 1899 and 1911.) Although the title of the 1913 French film, *Shylock, ou le More de Venice*, seems to confuse *The Merchant* and *Othello*, it perpetuates the negative stereotype of the Jew. An opening title card identifies Shylock as "The crafty Money Lender who for centuries has stood forth a living symbol of cunning and greed." Most shots reinforce the notion of Shylock as a hoarder of money: he is first seen giddily tossing coins from a pile of ducats. The film's most innovative moment occurs at the end: after Portia retrieves her ring from Bassanio, Shylock reappears to beg the principal of his loan. He is rebuked and leaves weeping as the Christians laugh mercilessly at him. Audiences today would likely find the scene pathetic, but in 1913 audiences no doubt joined in the laughter.

Orson Welles, who directed his Mercury Theatre Company in a respected 1938 radio broadcast of *The Merchant of Venice*, began shooting a film version of the play in the early 1960s. The director-actor (Shylock) set the play in eighteenth-century Europe and chose locations in Venice and Yugoslavia (a one-time holding of the Venetian Republic). Unfortunately, Welles died before the project was completed and only four minutes of the film have been retrieved.

■ 2005—Director Michael Radford, A Sony Pictures Classic, with Al Pacino (Shylock), Jeremy Irons (Antonio), Joseph Fiennes (Bassanio), Lynn Collins (Portia), Zuleikha Robinson (Jessica). (131 min.)

Actor Al Pacino told the *Los Angeles Times* that he had seen Laurence Olivier and Dustin Hoffman play Shylock on stage, but the part had never resonated with him until he read the screenplay by director Michael Radford and there saw what he could do with the role. "You pick a thing and you go with it," Pacino explained. "My impulse said, 'Go for being lonely.' " That state has been his specialty since his evolving portrayal of mob boss Michael Corleone in

The Godfather movies made him a star; a similar sense of isolation afflicted his interpretation of the scheming, power-brokering attorney Roy Cohn, dying of AIDS, in the 2003 HBO adaptation of Tony Kushner's *Angels in America*.

Radford cut large chunks of Shakespeare's dialogue, instead creating powerful images, many of which seem like teeming Renaissance paintings come to life. Radford, best known for the popular *Il Postino*, goes to great lengths, especially during the opening sequence, to place his *Merchant* in the context of Elizabethan intolerance. An opening crawl explains the prejudice: Jews in this Venice have been forced to live in a ghetto, observe strict curfews, and wear an identifying red hat whenever they stray outside the ghetto. Because they cannot own property, they often secure their fortunes by becoming moneylenders. Among the onlookers in a mob watching books being burned and a Jew being thrown off a bridge are the characters who become the story's central antagonists, Shylock and Antonio. The crowd pushes them together. Shylock speaks a new first word, "Antonio." When they lock eyes, the moment briefly suggests a connection between two sad men from different worlds. Then Radford visualizes the spitting, which Shylock describes in the play at 1.3.109–111; Pacino's Shylock wipes off the spittle with the sleeve of his gabardine coat. His mesmerizing Shylock grows in stature as his anger and bitterness deepen, while Jeremy Irons makes of his Christian foe, Antonio, a complex and sympathetic figure as well.

With two Oscar winners playing these antagonists, Radford still gives Portia her due as central to the dark comedy and its themes of intolerance, mercy, and forgiveness. Reviewers have been surprised, given her few television and movie appearances, by Lynn Collins's radiant authority as Portia. Beautiful and subtle, she brings a combination of shrewd seductiveness and moral intelligence to the part, making the courtroom scene an intense, emotionally volatile confrontation dominated by her charismatic presence and Shakespeare's language.

New York Times film critic A. O. Scott aptly assessed the film as "better-than-average screen Shakespeare: intelligent without being showily clever, and motivated more by genuine fascination with the play's language and ideas than by a desire to cannibalize its author's cultural prestige" (*New York Times* [December 29, 2004], E-1).

Video versions of the play include:

■ 1973—Director Jonathan Miller, with Laurence Olivier (Shylock) and Joan Plowright (Portia). (131 min.)

Based on his 1970 stage production at the National Theatre of Great Britain (see above), Miller redirected the play for video in an understated, naturalistic style that is more compatible with the medium. Still, it preserves Olivier's famous performance, and the many close-ups allow audiences to get closer to Shylock, the person, than they might in a theater. (Olivier, by the way, had a prosthesis manufactured for the role: his upper teeth project behind his lip and it is difficult to recognize the actor.) Because the camera can isolate a moment via close-ups, the video contains some stunning images. When he learns that Jessica has sold his wedding ring for a monkey in Tunis, Shylock, now alone forever, slowly pulls a prayer shawl about his shoulders and weeps. The moment is echoed later at Belmont as the camera focuses on Jessica, who sadly reads a letter describing her father's fate. Such moments are underscored by the haunting sound of the Jewish *shofar*, the ancient ram's horn that calls the faithful to penance. Joan Plowright is superb as Portia.

■ 1980—Director Jack Gold, BBC, with Warren Mitchell (Shylock), and Gemma Jones (Portia). (157 min.)

Although he did not direct the BBC production of the play, Miller's influence is manifest in this production directed by Jack Gold. The action is set in Renaissance Venice where the Christians are every bit as hostile and self-serving as Miller revealed them to be in his 1970 stage production. In a prebroadcast interview, Miller, who produced this televised play, said that the drama's conflict is between Old and New Testament worldviews and that Shakespeare "shows us that those who are exponents of mercy act unmercifully when given the opportunity to use the law against the Jew." Solanio and Salerio physically harass Shylock as he delivers the "Hath not a Jew eyes?" speech, and Gratiano actually knocks Shylock to the ground after his defeat in the trial scene; Jessica is played as a rebellious daughter eager to escape the prejudices against her race by joining the Christians. Warren Mitchell's Shylock speaks in a thick accent and uses the camera to advantage as he takes his case directly to the viewing audience; that intimacy builds as much sympathy for him as any of the physical abuses directed against him by the Christians. The production has a distinctly "low-budget" look about it that minimizes the splendor of its two worlds, the bustling mercantile center of Venice and the sumptuous Belmont. The mostly naturalistic delivery of the lines further reduces the play's passions, and the result, visually and aurally, is a maddeningly dull production that is neither powerful theater nor compelling television.

■ 1996—Director Alex Horrox, Thames Television, with Bob Peck (Shylock) and Haydn Gwynne (Portia). (75 min.)

Although only seventy-five minutes in length and thus a "highlight" film, this Thames Television (an alternative to the BBC) video attests that a made-for-television production need not be visually limited. Director Alex Horrox uses actual locations in Venice—retaining much of its red-and-gold Renaissance glory—to create the economic atmosphere necessary to the play. The late Bob Peck, an actor noted for his "tough guy" roles, plays an impish Shylock, milking genuine humor from the lines; Shylock thus becomes something more of a character out of playwright Harold Pinter's world as menace lurks beneath the congenial humor. The Pinter connection is not without cause: the noted British playwright descends from Portuguese Jews (Da Pinta) and was raised in London's tough East End, where he learned to use ironic humor to deflect the insults and physical attacks on him.

■ 2002—Director Trevor Nunn, PBS, with Henry Goodman (Shylock), and Derbhle Crotty (Portia). (120 min.)

Nunn's much-praised production at the National Theatre of Great Britain (see above)—and more importantly, Goodman's Shylock—is preserved in this PBS *Masterpiece Theater* broadcast. It bears some resemblance to the Miller and Barton productions in that it is set in modern Europe on the cusp of war, specifically the tuxedoed 1920s when, as Nunn noted in an interview, it became fashionable to make anti-Semitic jokes and witticisms. That the Holocaust was less than a decade away makes the production all the more chilling. Many of the NT production's most salutary features have been discussed above. The television version is especially good at capturing Goodman's subtle facial expressions. The show's finest moment is its last: Jessica sings a plaintive song in English after reading the letter about her father's fate, and then sings it a second time—in Hebrew—to affirm his identity to the Christians, who still see her as an alien in her unwillingness to abandon her identity.

Spin-offs

Although *The Merchant of Venice* has not inspired as many derivatives as have other of Shakespeare's most popular plays, there have been at least two Italian operas (the most notable by Mario Castelnuovo-Tedesco in 1958) and several stage plays. Of the plays, Arnold Wesker's *The Merchant* (1977), intended as a modernist's "reply" to the original play, alters the dynamic of Shakespeare's plot by portraying Antonio and Shylock as close friends drawn to one another because of their shared hatred of Venice's anti-Semitism. Shylock offered to lend his friend money without bond or interest, but Antonio insisted that they adhere to Venice's laws and the bond was sealed. That decision led to tragedy as Antonio, distraught by the loss of his fortune, turned viciously on his one-time friend.

In 1979 Hungarian playwright George Tabori (whose family died at Auschwitz) wrote *Improvisations on the Merchant of Venice: or I Wish My Daughter Were Dead at My Feet, a Jewel in Her Ear*, combining Shakespeare's text with material from Nazi documents. Tabori cut Portia from the plot to emphasize the familial relationship between Jessica and Shylock (who was variously played by twelve actors in broad-brimmed hats and hooked noses). Jewish puppets were mutilated on stage, and Shylock was "converted" to Christianity by having his hair dyed blond; he was "baptized" in a puddle of Jewish blood.

A. R. "Pete" Gurney's *Overtime: A Modern Sequel to The Merchant of Venice* (1996), which debuted at San Diego's Old Globe Theater as part of its summer Shakespeare Festival, invented an Act 6 for the play. Gurney, who specializes in distinctly WASPish worlds, alternated between contemporary inventions (e.g., Gratiano, an African American, and Nerissa, a Latina, rebel against their subservient roles) and darker explorations of the play's themes (especially racial and religious intolerance) in this bittersweet return to Belmont. Passions cooled, affections were redirected, and all did not end well over time for the Venetians in this tragicomedy that seemed inspired as much by Chekhov as by Shakespeare.

In *Shylock* (2000), playwright Marc Leiren-Young created a solo play in which the character, actor Jon Davies "cast" as Shylock, conducted a talk-back with audiences after a fictional production of *Merchant* had been canceled due to protests within the Jewish community and by some powerful theater patrons. The play thus explored the prismatic nature of theatrical illusion as Davies demonstrates several of the many ways Shylock has been portrayed over the years (clown, victim, melodramatic villain). Citing the writings of a fictional English professor holding the shrill but frequently stated view that *Merchant* is an "example of hate literature masquerading as theater," Leiren-Young also interrogated issues of anti-Semitism, political correctness, and free speech versus censorship.

References and Related Reading

Barton, John. *Playing Shakespeare*. London, 1984.
Buhler, Stephen M. *Shakespeare in the Cinema: Ocular Proof*. Albany, 2002.

Bulman, James C. *Shakespeare in Performance: "The Merchant of Venice."* Manchester and New York, 1991.

Cusack, Sinead. "Portia in *The Merchant of Venice*." *Players of Shakespeare*, Vol. 1. Ed. Philip Brockbank,. Cambridge, Eng., 1985. 29–40.

Edelman, Charles, ed. *The Merchant of Venice*. Cambridge, Eng., 2002. See especially Edelman's "Introduction," 1–92, for a thorough history of the play on stage and in film/video.

Fiedler, Leslie A. *The Stranger in Shakespeare*. New York, 1972.

Gilbert, Miriam. *Shakespeare at Stratford: "The Merchant of Venice."* London, 2002.

Granville-Barker, Harley. *Prefaces to Shakespeare: "The Merchant of Venice."* London, 1993.

Hortmann, Wilhelm. *Shakespeare on the German Stage: The Twentieth Century*. Cambridge, Eng., 1998.

Jardine, Lisa. "Cultural Confusion and Shakespeare's Learned Heroine: 'These Are Old Paradoxes.'" *Shakespeare Quarterly* 38 (1987): 1–18.

Leggatt, Alexander. "*The Merchant of Venice*: A Modern Perspective." The New Folger Library Shakespeare: *The Merchant of Venice*. New York, 1992.

Lelyveld, Toby. *Shylock on the Stage*. Cleveland, 1960.

Mahon, John W., and Ellen Macleod Mahon, eds. *"The Merchant of Venice": New Critical Essays*. New York and London, 2002. See especially John O'Connor's "Shylock in Performance" (387–430) and Penny Gay's "Portia Performs: Playing the Role in the Twentieth-Century English Theater" (431–454).

Shapiro, James. *Shakespeare and the Jews*. New York, 1996.

Stewart, Patrick. "Shylock in *The Merchant of Venice*." *Players of Shakespeare*, Vol. I. Ed. Philip Brockbank, Cambridge, Eng., 1985. 11–28.

Watermeier, Daniel D. *Between Actor and Critic: Selected Letters of Edmund Booth and William Winter*. Princeton, 1971.

CHAPTER 9

Much Ado About Nothing

(1598–1599)

Context and Dating

Much Ado About Nothing belongs with Shakespeare's mature comedies, *Twelfth Night* and *As You Like*, for like them it is an expansive, philosophical, and mostly festive investigation of romantic love. Shakespeare wrote it during the same period in which he simultaneously brought to fruition his exploration of the history play with the two parts of *Henry IV* and *Henry V*. At the same time, several aspects of *Much Ado* distinguish it from his other comedies of the period 1598–1600. Although the "merry war" of Benedick and Beatrice stands out in high relief in most productions of the play, the darker, nearly tragic love plot involving Hero and Claudio anticipates concerns that will emerge in such "problem" plays as *Measure for Measure* and *All's Well That Ends Well*. The action of *Much Ado* takes place in Messina, a real place in Sicily, not a mythical setting such as the Illyria of *Twelfth Night* or the forest of Arden in *As You Like It*. Nor does it move into a "green world" of sexual confusion as does *A Midsummer Night's Dream* or *As You Like It*. There is no contrast between the worlds of court and country in the play. And perhaps most obviously, the language of three-quarters of *Much Ado About Nothing* is prose of a supple, witty, and often highly figurative variety.

With their barbed dialogue, Beatrice and Benedick have engendered a centuries-long dramatic tradition of fancifully sparring lovers, men and women whose candid verbal darts demonstrate their deep compatibility and the ultimate rightness of their unions. Plays spanning three centuries by William Congreve, William Wycherley, Richard Brinsley Sheridan, Oscar Wilde, George Bernard Shaw, and Noel Coward owe a debt to this dramatic pair, as do many screenplays for 1930s film comedies, including several featuring Fred Astaire and Ginger Rogers and others with Katharine Hepburn and Spencer Tracy. Precedents can be found in Shakespeare's earlier comedies for this kind of combative courtship in the relationship of Berowne and Rosaline in *Love's Labor's Lost* and Petruchio and Katharine in *The Taming of the Shrew*, but Benedick and Beatrice refine and perfect the sparring of intelligent and perceptive lovers. They at first resist each other, but ultimately and quite happily, as Millimant puts it in William Congreve's *The Way of the World* (1700), "decline" into marriage.

Structurally *Much Ado About Nothing* involves two contrasting love plots. In both, we find a journey toward candor and mutual understanding that involves throwing off the defenses and deceptions of outward appearances. Although the young women, Beatrice and Hero, are cousins, their contrasting characters typify the differences in tone of their respective love plots: Beatrice's is a high comedy and Hero's a melodrama with potentially tragic consequences. Shakespeare freely blends these two seemingly irreconcilable genres, giving each its special language: highly figured prose for the comedy, blank verse for the melodrama. He moves freely between the prose and verse, scene by scene, sometimes even within scenes.

Characters

Beatrice and Benedick usually dominate productions of *Much Ado*, particularly in the twentieth and twenty-first centuries when star actors are drawn to the roles. Yet despite the greater popular appeal of their comic entanglements than of the Hero-Claudio plot, Shakespeare balances character traits, arranging the four lovers as foils to one another. Although Benedick and Claudio are both Italian gentlemen and soldiers under the command

221

of Don Pedro, the differences in their characters are immediately apparent when we see the women to whom they are drawn. In the early scenes, Hero is modest, retiring, usually silent, and certainly obedient to her father. Claudio, who is respectful of authority and speaks of Hero in an idealized, almost courtly fashion, seems well-matched to her. Benedick, on the other hand, already has a reputation as a bachelor and as a combatant in his tempestuous relationship with Beatrice. He is self-protective, and much of the comedy in his character emerges from the clash of this trait with the increasing seriousness of his emotional situation—especially as Don John's plot against Claudio unfolds. Both Benedick and Beatrice are independent thinkers, willing to question authorities such as Leonato and Don Pedro. Both are highly skeptical of marriage. In their joking fascination with one another, they also seem a good match, although their satiric barbs against marriage, Benedick's oft-expressed anxiety about cuckoldry, and their shared intolerance of sentimental romance leave them trapped in the mask of unconcern each has adopted. Still, their sometimes cruel jesting, their basic candor, and their willingness to engage in the kind of introspection that can lead to self-knowledge suggest that their charged relationship will ultimately be all the more stable because it has been so often tested. Claudio is more callow, shallow, and pliable than Benedick. Partly for this reason, the play tilts toward the more sophisticated love affair with its ironic unpredictability. In the best, well-balanced stage productions, Claudio moves through pain and self-loathing into insight, and can seem to blossom into greater wisdom in Act 5. Hero's radiant forgiveness of Claudio's slander at the end prefigures the almost symbolic female figures of Shakespeare's last plays.

Other characters in *Much Ado About Nothing* are aligned two-by-two, as well. Don Pedro and Don John are noble Spanish brothers, each of whom engages in elaborate deceptions during the course of the play. Yet Don Pedro's deceptions are viewed as beneficent, while the bastard Don John's are destructive. John is the classic malcontent linked to earlier Elizabethan villain-heroes in plays by Christopher Marlowe. He also exhibits the kind of malignity associated with Shakespeare's Richard III and Iago, although he lacks their energetic and darkly comic enjoyment of his own villainy. The princely Don Pedro enjoys deceptions in the form of tricks and charades. Even when Beatrice rejects his own brief and unexpected proposal of marriage, he quickly suggests tricking her into thinking Benedick is in love with her. Like Claudio, he is readily deceived and believes the slander against Hero immediately, even though he has reason to distrust his bastard brother who delivers the falsehood. Although Don Pedro is the head of the state of Aragon and a fine warrior, he explains that he has decided to play Cupid instead of Mars. In many productions since the 1960s, he has been played ambiguously as melancholy, isolated, and alone at the end, or even as vaguely sinister in his manipulations.

Leonato is a genial middle-aged man who enjoys his role as governor of Messina. He entertains himself, his family, and his guests with masked balls, charades, and all manner of "games and sports." Like the other men—excepting Benedick and the Friar—he is quick to believe even his own innocent daughter guilty of faithlessness, crying out in near despair, "Wherefore? Why doth not every earthly thing / Cry shame upon her?" We hear an edge of darkness in this patriarch's character as the play-acting proceeds into the charade of Hero's death.

As in *A Midsummer Night's Dream* with its "rude mechanicals," Dogberry and his associates—Verges the constable, Francis Seacoal the sexton, and George Seacoal the watchman—serve as contrasting foils to the upper-class authorities. As they interrogate Don John's henchmen, Borachio and Conrade, in 4.2, Dogberry's mouth-mangling malapropisms, their jostling for position, and Dogberry's fixation on being insulted as an "ass" serve to parody elements of the Hero-Claudio plot. And of course, it is these shallow fools—not the prince, the governor, or the true wits—who discover the truth about Hero.

Sources and Inspirations

No source has been found for the "merry war" between Benedick and Beatrice, although precedents are to be found in Shakespeare's earlier plays, especially in the contest of wits between Rosaline and Berowne in *Love's Labor's Lost* and Petruchio and Kate in *The Taming of the Shrew*. Similarly, no source has been identified for the business of Dogberry and the Watch stumbling across the evil machinations of Don John and his henchmen.

The Hero-Claudio plot, on the other hand, has a long literary history. Shakespeare's likely immediate source was a story from the *Novelle* of Matteo Bandello (1554). Yet the narrative of the maiden falsely accused of infidelity is an older one, found as early as the fifth century B.C.E. in Greek literature in a story in which the hero Chaereas is told by envious rivals that his wife has been unfaithful, then watches in the evening as the maid allows a stranger into the house where she lives. The husband strikes the wife he believes unfaithful, but when the maid confesses he is acquitted of murder. Later the wife awakens from her death-like trance. This version made its way into Ariosto's *Orlando Furioso*, which in turn became a source for a section in Edmund Spenser's *The Faerie Queene* and thus would have become familiar to Shakespeare. He then uses the invented plot for the witty lovers to comment and elaborate upon the one he has borrowed.

Language

The language of the comedy is filled with wordplay, double meanings, verbal figures, and malapropisms as several characters speak a kind of playful badinage; Beatrice and Benedick are the most skillful players in the contest. From the messenger's first announcement that Claudio has done "in the figure of a lamb the feats of a lion," and Beatrice's first line borrowing a sexually charged fencing metaphor to call Benedick "Señor Mountanto," others join in the verbal gamesmanship. Several are actually defined by their use of language: Beatrice with her "sharp tongue," Benedick with his ever-more elaborate metaphoric wordplay, and Dogberry with his malapropisms. Critic Frank Kermode, in his *Shakespeare's Language*, calls this range of prose styles "certainly extraordinary," even while he acknowledges that some of the lovers' "flytings" are a little tedious. "Beatrice and Benedick announce themselves as wits, but the habit spreads to minor characters like Margaret (see 3.4), with whom the effect can be tedious" (Kermode, 77).

The play's two basic modes of expression—verse for the melodramatic love plot and vigorous colloquial prose for the high comedy—also suggest linguistic differences appropriate not just to characters but to differing thoughts and actions. When Claudio is conversing with Benedick, he speaks in prose. When, on the other hand, he speaks to the Prince of his feeling for Hero, he adopts the more stately meter of blank verse. Hero, too, speaks in verse. Similar rhythms are adopted by Leonato when he falls into a fury over Hero's supposed infidelity and by the Friar whom he asks to help the family temporize and thus find a resolution. Dogberry's use (actually misuse) of language extends to the other members of the Watch. These speakers parody the higher-class characters, often saying, without realizing it, the exact opposite of what they mean. The entire play, as many have noted, depends very much upon the misunderstanding of words during conversations overheard and upon the mistaking of appearance for reality. Hence comes the glittering irony that the members of the Watch, who are the most frequent abusers and misusers of language, are the ones who stumble upon the truth. Similarly, the truth about the lovers' relationship emerges when they cease talking altogether and stop each other's mouths with a kiss.

Given the intricacies of the wordplay and the confusions it can engender—whether intentional or not—the dialogue should be read with an alertness to the use of metaphor and to possible double meanings, both bawdy and poetic.

Themes and Issues

The Battle of the Sexes

Benedick and Beatrice engage in the kind of "merry war" that was a staple of English medieval humor in Chaucer's depiction of the Wife of Bath and in the Wakefield Master's comic depiction of Noah's Wife as a shrew and termagant in the Wakefield Cycle's pageant about Noah's Flood. Yet Beatrice differs from these shrewish wives, overturning gender expectations not only with her independence and assertiveness, but also with her verbal dexterity, moral clarity, and agile mind. When Benedick first returns from the wars and addresses Beatrice, he immediately calls her Lady Disdain, bringing to mind their previous skirmishes. And although the tone of their courtship is lighthearted, bantering, and so reassuring that we expect it will turn out happily, their story has deeper resonances that many actors and directors have underscored. Some actors imply that these two have previously been close, but have been hurt and disappointed by one another. Actresses often emphasize the pain of that previous relationship, as Judi Dench did in John Barton's 1976 production. The key to her interpretation was taking the lines about that previous encounter, when Benedick won her heart "with false dice" and she gave a double heart to him in return for his one (2.1.265–268). Benedick's vanity now prevents him from professing what he feels, and Beatrice herself is a powerful contender; that he is attracted to her is a sign of the strength of character she knows he possesses.

The play thus challenges conventional gender stereotypes by balancing the insights of these lovers against expressions of traditional patriarchal ideology (see "Cuckolds and Misogynists" below, pp. 224–225), many of these voiced by Benedick. This stage misogynist has clearly met his match in the articulate Beatrice, whose wit sometimes outruns his own. As John D. Cox concludes in his *Plays in Performance* edition of *Much Ado*, "The ideological power play of this contest undoubtedly brought new pungency and suspense to the perennial stage interest of the battle of the sexes" (Cox, 5).

False Fronts

Both Beatrice and Benedick adopt postures that protect them from revealing their true feelings, and thus their "weakness," for the other. From the start Beatrice demonstrates concern for Benedick, albeit under the guise of abusive joking. She wonders whether he has returned safely from the wars. She is curious whether he has shown himself valiant in battle and wishes to know who his current friends are. Independent as she is, lecturing her more docile cousin that she should choose her own mate rather than acquiesce in her father's choice of a husband, Beatrice scoffs at marriage; but, since that is the fate of women of her time, she also takes so seriously the duty of choosing the right husband that she cannot compromise. She fears revealing her love for Benedick because she worries that he will prove unfaithful or will mock her feelings.

Benedick professes to be a "tyrant to their sex." He has established a public reputation as a confirmed bachelor and is amused at Claudio's passion for Hero, and yet he confesses that he finds Beatrice, "were she not possessed with a fury," far more beautiful than Hero. He concedes that he could be won over by a "perfect" woman—one who gathers all the gifts he desires in one unlikely person. He (at 2.3.8–34) realizes that his idealizing perfectionism is a kind of defense. He begins his litany of desirable womanly traits, saying she should be rich, wise, virtuous, mild, of good discourse, an excellent musician. He closes the litany with a throwaway punch line: "and her hair shall be of what color it please God." Clearly he would not be drawn to the sweet submissiveness of a Hero. He needs a woman who is his intellectual equal, one favored with fortune's gifts, in a word, Beatrice. Like her, he fears revealing his feelings lest she make him the object of her jesting scorn; her doing just that at the masked ball confirms his worst fears.

Here the defenses that Beatrice and Benedick adopt toward each other become intensely hurtful. Benedick, hiding himself behind the mask of a stranger, abuses Beatrice at the masked ball in Act 2 by telling her of her reputation as Lady Disdain, while she—intuiting who the "stranger" is—retaliates by telling the man what she really feels about Benedick. Both emerge from the encounter more deeply wounded; ironically, each can be shaken free from his defensive posture only when their friends practice benign deceptions upon them. When Benedick overhears his friends' conversation suggesting that Beatrice really does love him but has hidden her affection behind a false front of scorn, he becomes confident enough to acknowledge his love for her. Similarly, when she learns by an overheard conversation that even her friends view her as disdainful, she is courageous enough to accept the accusation as true, to change, and to acknowledge honestly what she feels toward Benedick.

Many others in the play adopt false fronts for less amiable purposes. Don John, for instance, speaks to the masked Claudio at the ball, as if his listener were Benedick, and thus he creates the false impression that Don Pedro is actually wooing Beatrice for himself. Claudio wrongly concludes that both his noble friend and the woman he loves are false to him. In both plots, then, society's rigid concern with appearance leads to falsehoods and contrivances because class decorum, manners, patterns of behavior, even clothing all lay themselves open to deception. Don John purports to be the opposite of all of this. He presents himself a plain-dealing villain, saying, "I cannot hide what I am" and "I had rather be a canker in a hedge than a rose in his grace." Yet of course he is the greatest dissembler of all, feigning reconciliation to his brother and a concern about Hero's virtue and Claudio's reputation that he does not possess.

Cuckolds and Misogynists

From the very first scene, *Much Ado* insistently explores the twin themes of cuckoldry—that is, a man being made a "fool with horns" by his wife's infidelity—and a male fear of, bordering upon hostility toward, women. When Don Pedro asks if the young woman standing beside Leonato is that man's daughter, Leonato replies, "Her mother hath many times told me so." The remark may be played as casual, witty, even teasing, but Benedick senses an edge in the words and uses the occasion to make a joke: "Were you in doubt, sir, that you asked her?" Gail Paster suggests in her essay "A Modern Perspective" in the Folger edition of the play that Benedick here "calls our attention to the trace of an old suspicion." Yet whether Leonato was teasing or not, Benedick is unusually sensitive to the issue of wifely fidelity as a defense against marrying.

Later in the scene, when Benedick queries Claudio about whether he is contemplating marriage, he exclaims "Shall I never see a bachelor of threescore again? Go to, i'faith; an thou wilt needs thrust thy neck into a yoke, wear the print of it and sigh away Sundays" (1.1.191–193). In his only half-joking opinion, Claudio's marriage would imprison the younger man and deprive Benedick himself of a yet another bachelor friend. The reason for Benedick's disdain of marriage becomes clear: he is afraid of being humiliated by an unfaithful wife who would plant upon his forehead the horns of a cuckold. In one revealing speech, after thanking a woman for conceiving him and bringing him up, he says, referring to a military bugle horn, "But that I will have a recheat winded in my forehead or hang my bugle in an invisible baldrick, all women shall pardon me. Because I will not do them the wrong to mistrust any, I will do myself the right to trust none; and the fine is, for the which I may go the finer, I will live a bachelor" (1.1.230–235). He goes on to insist that if ever he is found sick with love, the men should go ahead and shoot at him. When Don Pedro counters that in time "the savage bull doth bear the yoke," Benedick comically retorts that if ever the "sensible Benedick" bears the marriage yoke, his friends should pluck off the bull's horns and set them in his forehead as cuckold's horns, hanging a sign on him: "Here you may see Benedick the married man."

This anxiety about women pervades Messina, coloring both plots, though in different ways. Beatrice joins occasionally in the horn imagery. In Claudio, as with Othello and later with Leontes of *The Winter's Tale*, we see a fear of the loved one's infidelity that suggests these valiant men are insecure about their sexuality. They are easily persuaded to reject and humiliate innocent women they purport to love, and to believe the worst of any woman. Claudio loves Hero for her beauty, wealth, and family, and for her modesty and purity. In this society, that purity is all too easily sullied by false appearances. In his rejection of Hero, Claudio betrays a deep cynicism about women. Like Othello, Claudio demonstrates what Freud describes as the virgin-whore syndrome, in which men are inclined neurotically to polarize women as either ideal and chaste or worthless and debauched. Such men experience no middle ground. Thus misogyny and idealization are two aspects of the same attitude that generalizes women instead of accepting each as an individual person. Only Hero's generous forgiveness of Claudio's humiliation of her brings about the happy resolution. And though he is older and a prince, Don Pedro is just as ready to believe the young woman guilty. Having been deceived by his brother in the past, he might have been more skeptical of him now. The male bond—one critic calls these characters "The Men's Club of Messina"—renders them unable to pull away from the group and defend Hero's virtue when it is under suspicion. Only the Friar and then Benedick join the clear-headed Beatrice in seeing this deep fear of women's perfidy for what it is: a sign of male insecurity.

Even at the end of the Act 5 wedding scene, Don Pedro makes pejorative references to Benedick's marriage that involve setting the savage bull's horns in his head. He and Claudio perpetuate this male badinage—a kind of locker room joke—that Benedick now rejects. Claudio repeats another joke about the savage bull; even the mention of Benedick's marriage is accompanied by another reference to cuckolding.

> I think he thinks upon the savage bull.
> Tush, fear not, man! We'll tip thy horns with gold,
> And all Europa shall rejoice at thee,
> As once Europa did at lusty Jove
> When he would play the noble beast in love.
>   (5.4.43–47)

Benedick counters with a clever retort about Claudio's parentage, continuing the classical allusion. He suggest that "Bull Jove" had an "amiable low" and some such bull leaped your father's cow and got a calf much like Claudio,"for you have just his bleat" (5.4.51).

After Benedick is united publicly to Beatrice, when peace among the men is re-established, we perceive still some remnant of the male obsession with infidelity. Benedick tells Claudio that now that he is "like to be my kinsman, live unbruised and love my cousin." Claudio replies that if Benedick had married someone besides Beatrice, he surely would have been an adulterer and might still be if "my cousin do not look exceedingly narrowly to thee" (5.4.114–115). Similarly, after Benedick is converted to love and marriage by Beatrice and encourages Don Pedro to join the procession to the altar, Benedick still associates marriage jestingly with the humiliation of cuckoldom: "Get thee a wife," he says, "get thee a wife. There is no staff more reverend than one tipped with horn" (5.4.121–122). Thus the anxiety over female infidelity and the potential for tragedy are undercurrents throughout. The song heard in 2.3.60 challenges the stereotype of women as faithless, calling men "deceivers ever." Peace and happiness do come to both couples, but only after they experience such pain and distrust. Gail Paster concludes that in such a world still touched by a dispersed misogyny, resistance to marriage is not a psychological problem afflicting Beatrice and Benedick alone; such resistance can be viewed as rational in a patriarchal system that gives men and women good reasons to distrust one another.

Staging Challenges

Eavesdropping

A central theme and device of the play involves eavesdropping, or, less overtly, overhearing. This kind of spying is benign when the friends of Benedick and Beatrice trick him and then her into believing the other is in love; it is malevolent in the deception stage-managed by Don John, and comical (yet important to the plot) when the watch overhears Borachio brag to Conrade about the success of their scheme and how well paid he was to carry it out. The eavesdropping can also be simply a way of showing how such overhearing can lead to misperceptions, as when in 1.2, Leonato's brother reports what his man has overheard. He says that Don Pedro loves and will woo Hero when, of course, the man has heard only a portion of the conversation and thus has misunderstood it. The Prince has offered to woo on behalf of Claudio, who is too shy and inexperienced to do so for himself. Scenes in the play (1.2 and 3.1) refer to a "pleachèd alley" and a "bower" where such overhearings occur; engravings of the period suggest that this bower is a kind of tunnel created from a trellis overgrown with flowers. On Leonato's estate, the bower is in his orchard. Today, the eavesdropping scenes are often staged by employing several levels or several playing areas in the set design, so that the audience can see the characters watching and overhearing as well as the actors from whom the eavesdroppers are hidden. Shakespeare's "orchard" and "bower" have sometimes been visualized on stage and on film as "alleys" between rows of trees in an orchard; thus the listener can be in one alley and the speaker in another row between the trees. This was the device chosen by Stuart Burge for his BBC production and by Kenneth Branagh for his film (see p. 265). In the Elizabethan public theaters, on the other hand, Benedick could simply hide behind a pillar. The audience's dual perspective—a physical manifestation of dramatic irony—proves pleasurable in the lighter plot with Beatrice and Benedick and painful in the darker one with Hero and Claudio. We should note, however, that Shakespeare does not actually dramatize one of the key overhearings, that of Don John and Borachio's deception involving Margaret in Hero's clothing. The clandestine meeting is reported in a speech. For the sake of clarity, nonetheless, many stage directors as well as Branagh in his 1993 film invent a scene to show Don Pedro, Don John, and Claudio actually watching by night as Borachio visits and takes his leave (sometimes with a kiss) from a woman who appears to be Hero. Other directors prefer to follow the script and leave the encounter up the audience's imagination.

"Kill Claudio"

This moment has become a test of directorial interpretation and actors' timing and technique. It comes (at 4.1) after Claudio has spurned Hero. Once the wedding ceremony is abruptly ended by Claudio's accusation, the confusion clears and Beatrice and Benedick are left alone. She weeps (and in some productions he, as well) for the slandered Hero's plight. Beatrice and Benedick relinquish their resistance to marriage, and declare their love for one another. Benedick, alone among the men except the Friar, immediately has intuited that Hero must be innocent. "Come," he says to Beatrice, "bid me do anything for thee." She turns to him and sharply demands, "Kill Claudio." His shocked response: "Ha! Not for the wide world." The exchange, with its sudden shift of tone, very often brings jarring, if nervous, laughter. In John Gielgud's famed production in 1952 at the Phoenix, Beatrice reportedly paused in a long, electrically charged silence before "Kill Claudio" was almost forced from her. Gielgud's response, as Benedick, was described as just as serious, the horrified reply of a man who had never realized love could conflict with friendship in such stark terms. In Trevor Nunn's Renaissance-set production at Stratford-upon-

Avon in 1968, reviewers report that the demand from Beatrice (Janet Suzman) provoked uneasy laughter from the audience because it broke what had been a solemn, ritualized moment in church. When the production transferred to London, Suzman's Beatrice modified her performance by speaking with a slight break in her voice that revealed the terrible nature of her request. Benedick (Alan Howard) paused as well before firmly and gently speaking his refusal. Their new timing and pauses sustained the grave tone.

As the scene continues, Beatrice begins to leave in anger, but Benedick persuades her to return. She insists that Claudio is indeed her enemy and works herself into rage because this "villain" has "slandered, scorned, dishonored my kinswoman." Beatrice exclaims "Oh, that I were a man!" a wish she repeats twice more during the scene when she realizes that Claudio's slander may go unpunished.

> Oh, that I were a man for his sake! Or that I had any friend would be a man for my sake! But manhood is melted into curtsies, valor into compliment, and men are only turned into tongue, and trim ones, too. He is now as valiant as Hercules that only tells a lie and swears it. I cannot be a man with wishing, therefore I will die a woman with grieving.
>
> (316–322)

When she turns to leave again, Benedick stops her with a simple profession of his feeling. "Tarry, good Beatrice. By this hand, I love thee." Again setting aside the figures and elaborate images that have marked their conversation, she asks him directly to use his hand for something other than "swearing by it." He now speaks plainly too, asking whether she thinks in her soul that Count Claudio has wronged Hero. "Yea, as sure as I have a thought or a soul," she responds. Benedick accepts her challenge, saying "Enough I am engaged. I will challenge him." The effect of the scene—its strong emotional impact—depends upon two factors: the credibility of the actors and their timing. Benedick is truly taken aback, quite shocked that Beatrice would ask him to murder a friend. As the seriousness of her request settles in, and he feels its justice, the tone of the relationship changes; their courtship loses some of its combative sense of one-upmanship, as both drop their guards to reveal their feelings toward one another and the dire situation directly, passionately. As Kermode has written, "The most impressive moment of the play is the scene when Beatrice commands her lover to kill Claudio; there is a certain relief involved, for they converse for a moment rather more like persons who have momentarily forgotten their reputations" (77).

Much Ado About Nothing

[*Dramatis Personae*

DON PEDRO, *Prince of Aragon*
LEONATO, *Governor of Messina*
ANTONIO, *his brother*

BENEDICK, *a young lord of Padua*
BEATRICE, *Leonato's niece*
CLAUDIO, *a young lord of Florence*
HERO, *Leonato's daughter*
MARGARET,⎫
URSULA,⎭ *gentlewomen attending Hero*

DON JOHN, *Don Pedro's bastard brother*
BORACHIO,⎫
CONRADE,⎭ *followers of Don John*

DOGBERRY, *Constable in charge of the Watch*
VERGES, *the Headborough, or parish constable, Dogberry's partner*
A SEXTON (FRANCIS SEACOAL)
FIRST WATCHMAN
SECOND WATCHMAN (GEORGE SEACOAL)

BALTHASAR, *a singer attending Don Pedro*
FRIAR FRANCIS
A BOY
MESSENGER *to Leonato*
Another MESSENGER

Attendants, Musicians, Members of the Watch, Antonio's Son, and other Kinsmen

SCENE: *Messina*]

[1.1]

Enter Leonato, Governor of Messina, Hero his daughter, and Beatrice his niece, with a Messenger.

LEONATO [*holding a letter*]   I learn in this letter that Don Pedro of Aragon comes this night to Messina.

MESSENGER   He is very near by this. He was not three leagues off when I left him. 4

LEONATO   How many gentlemen have you lost in this action? 6

MESSENGER   But few of any sort and none of name. 7

LEONATO   A victory is twice itself when the achiever brings home full numbers. I find here that Don Pedro hath bestowed much honor on a young Florentine called Claudio.

MESSENGER   Much deserved on his part and equally remembered by Don Pedro. He hath borne himself 13 beyond the promise of his age, doing in the figure of a lamb the feats of a lion. He hath indeed better bettered expectation than you must expect of me to tell 16 you how.

LEONATO   He hath an uncle here in Messina will be 18 very much glad of it.

MESSENGER   I have already delivered him letters, and there appears much joy in him, even so much that joy 21 could not show itself modest enough without a badge 22 of bitterness. 23

LEONATO   Did he break out into tears?

MESSENGER   In great measure.

LEONATO   A kind overflow of kindness. There are no 26 faces truer than those that are so washed. How much better is it to weep at joy than to joy at weeping!

BEATRICE   I pray you, is Signor Mountanto returned 29 from the wars or no?

MESSENGER   I know none of that name, lady. There was none such in the army of any sort.

LEONATO   What is he that you ask for, niece?

1.1. Location: Messina. Before Leonato's house.
4 leagues units of about three miles   **6 action** battle.   **7 sort** rank.
name reputation, or noble name.   **13 remembered** rewarded

16 bettered surpassed   **18 will** who will   **21–3 joy . . . bitterness** joy could show a decorous moderation only by weeping at the same time.   **26 kind** natural   **29 Mountanto** montanto, an upward blow or thrust in fencing

HERO   My cousin means Signor Benedick of Padua.

MESSENGER   Oh, he's returned, and as pleasant as ever 35
he was.

BEATRICE   He set up his bills here in Messina and chal- 37
lenged Cupid at the flight; and my uncle's fool, reading 38
the challenge, subscribed for Cupid and challenged 39
him at the bird-bolt. I pray you, how many hath he 40
killed and eaten in these wars? But how many hath he
killed? For indeed I promised to eat all of his killing.

LEONATO   Faith, niece, you tax Signor Benedick too 43
much, but he'll be meet with you, I doubt it not. 44

MESSENGER   He hath done good service, lady, in these
wars.

BEATRICE   You had musty victual, and he hath holp to 47
eat it. He is a very valiant trencherman; he hath an 48
excellent stomach. 49

MESSENGER   And a good soldier too, lady.

BEATRICE   And a good soldier to a lady, but what is he 51
to a lord? 52

MESSENGER   A lord to a lord, a man to a man, stuffed 53
with all honorable virtues.

BEATRICE   It is so, indeed, he is no less than a stuffed 55
man. But for the stuffing—well, we are all mortal. 56

LEONATO   You must not, sir, mistake my niece. There is
a kind of merry war betwixt Signor Benedick and her.
They never meet but there's a skirmish of wit between
them.

BEATRICE   Alas! He gets nothing by that. In our last
conflict, four of his five wits went halting off, and now 62
is the whole man governed with one; so that if he have
wit enough to keep himself warm, let him bear it for a
difference between himself and his horse, for it is all 65
the wealth that he hath left to be known a reasonable 66
creature. Who is his companion now? He hath every 67
month a new sworn brother. 68

MESSENGER   Is't possible?

BEATRICE   Very easily possible. He wears his faith but as 70
the fashion of his hat; it ever changes with the next
block. 72

MESSENGER   I see, lady, the gentleman is not in your 73
books. 74

BEATRICE   No. An he were, I would burn my study. But 75
I pray you, who is his companion? Is there no young
squarer now that will make a voyage with him to the 77
devil?

MESSENGER   He is most in the company of the right
noble Claudio.

BEATRICE   Oh, Lord, he will hang upon him like a 81
disease! He is sooner caught than the pestilence, and
the taker runs presently mad. God help the noble 83
Claudio! If he have caught the Benedick, it will cost 84
him a thousand pound ere 'a be cured. 85

MESSENGER   I will hold friends with you, lady. 86

BEATRICE   Do, good friend.

LEONATO   You will never run mad, niece. 88

BEATRICE   No, not till a hot January. 89

MESSENGER   Don Pedro is approached.

*Enter Don Pedro, Claudio, Benedick, Balthasar,
and [Don] John the Bastard.*

DON PEDRO   Good Signor Leonato, are you come to
meet your trouble? The fashion of the world is to 92
avoid cost, and you encounter it. 93

LEONATO   Never came trouble to my house in the
likeness of Your Grace. For trouble being gone,
comfort should remain; but when you depart from
me, sorrow abides and happiness takes his leave.

DON PEDRO   You embrace your charge too willingly.—I 98
think this is your daughter.

[*Presenting himself to Hero.*]

LEONATO   Her mother hath many times told me so.

BENEDICK   Were you in doubt, sir, that you asked her?

LEONATO   Signor Benedick, no; for then were you a
child.

DON PEDRO   You have it full, Benedick. We may guess 104
by this what you are, being a man. Truly, the lady
fathers herself. Be happy, lady, for you are like an 106
honorable father.

BENEDICK   If Signor Leonato be her father, she would
not have his head on her shoulders for all Messina, as 109
like him as she is.   [*Don Pedro and Leonato talk aside.*]

BEATRICE   I wonder that you will still be talking, Signor
Benedick. Nobody marks you.

BENEDICK   What, my dear Lady Disdain! Are you yet
living?

BEATRICE   Is it possible disdain should die while she
hath such meet food to feed it as Signor Benedick? 116

---

35 pleasant jocular   **37 bills** placards, advertisements   **38 at the
flight** to a long-distance archery contest. (Beatrice mocks Benedick's
pretentions as a lady killer.)   **my uncle's fool** (Perhaps a professional fool in her uncle's service.)   **39 subscribed for** accepted on
behalf of   **40 bird-bolt** a blunt-headed arrow used for fowling.
(Sometimes used by children because of its relative harmlessness
and thus conventionally appropriate to Cupid.)   **43 tax** disparage
44 meet even, quits   **47 musty victual** stale food.   **holp** helped
48 valiant trencherman great eater   **49 stomach** appetite. (With a
mocking suggestion also of "courage.")   **51 soldier to a lady** lady
killer. (With a play on *to/too*.)   **52 to** compared to   **53 stuffed**
amply supplied   **55–6 a stuffed man** i.e., a figure stuffed to resemble a man.   **56 the stuffing** i.e., what he's truly made of.   **well . . .
mortal** i.e., well, we all have our faults.   **62 five wits** i.e., not the
five senses, but the five faculties: memory, imagination, judgment,
fantasy, common sense.   **halting** limping   **65 difference** heraldic
feature distinguishing a junior member or branch of a family. (With
a play on the usual sense.)   **65–7 it is . . . creature** i.e., his feeble wit
is all he has left to identify him as rationally human.   **68 sworn
brother** brother in arms (*frater juratus*, an allusion to the ancient
practice of swearing brotherhood).   **70 faith** allegiance, or fidelity
72 block mold for shaping hats.

73–4 in your books in favor with you, in your good books. (But Beatrice, in her reply, takes *books* in the literal sense of something to be
found in a library.)   **75 An** If. (Also in line 131.)   **77 squarer** quarreler   **81 he** i.e., Benedick   **83 presently** immediately   **84 the
Benedick** i.e., as if this were a disease   **85 'a** he   **86 hold friends**
keep on friendly terms (so as not to earn your enmity)   **88 run mad**
i.e., "catch the Benedick"   **89 not . . . January** i.e., not any time soon.
92 your trouble i.e., the expense of entertaining me and my retinue.
93 encounter go to meet   **98 charge** social responsibility and expense
104 have it full are well answered   **106 fathers herself** shows by
appearance who her father is.   **109 his head** i.e., with Leonato's
white beard and signs of age   **116 meet** suitable. (With a pun on
"meat.")

Courtesy itself must convert to disdain, if you come in 117
her presence.

BENEDICK   Then is courtesy a turncoat. But it is certain
I am loved of all ladies, only you excepted; and I
would I could find in my heart that I had not a hard
heart, for truly I love none.

BEATRICE   A dear happiness to women! They would 123
else have been troubled with a pernicious suitor. I
thank God and my cold blood I am of your humor for 125
that. I had rather hear my dog bark at a crow than a 126
man swear he loves me.

BENEDICK   God keep Your Ladyship still in that mind!
So some gentleman or other shall scape a predestinate 129
scratched face.

BEATRICE   Scratching could not make it worse, an 'twere
such a face as yours were.   132

BENEDICK   Well, you are a rare parrot-teacher.   133

BEATRICE   A bird of my tongue is better than a beast of 134
yours.   135

BENEDICK   I would my horse had the speed of your
tongue and so good a continuer. But keep your way, 137
i'God's name; I have done.

BEATRICE   You always end with a jade's trick. I know 139
you of old.

DON PEDRO   That is the sum of all, Leonato. Signor 141
Claudio and Signor Benedick, my dear friend Leonato hath invited you all. I tell him we shall stay here at
the least a month, and he heartily prays some occasion
may detain us longer. I dare swear he is no hypocrite,
but prays from his heart.

LEONATO   If you swear, my lord, you shall not be forsworn. [*To Don John*] Let me bid you welcome, my
lord, being reconciled to the Prince your brother. I owe 149
you all duty.

DON JOHN   I thank you. I am not of many words, but I
thank you.

LEONATO   Please it Your Grace lead on?   153

DON PEDRO   Your hand, Leonato. We will go together. 154
      Exeunt. Manent Benedick and Claudio.

CLAUDIO   Benedick, didst thou note the daughter of
Signor Leonato?

BENEDICK   I noted her not, but I looked on her.   157

CLAUDIO   Is she not a modest young lady?

BENEDICK   Do you question me as an honest man
should do, for my simple true judgment? Or would

you have me speak after my custom, as being a
professed tyrant to their sex?   162

CLAUDIO   No, I pray thee, speak in sober judgment.

BENEDICK   Why, i'faith, methinks she's too low for a 164
high praise, too brown for a fair praise, and too little
for a great praise. Only this commendation I can afford
her, that were she other than she is, she were unhandsome, and being no other but as she is, I do not like her.

CLAUDIO   Thou thinkest I am in sport. I pray thee, tell
me truly how thou lik'st her.

BENEDICK   Would you buy her, that you inquire after
her?

CLAUDIO   Can the world buy such a jewel?

BENEDICK   Yea, and a case to put it into. But speak you
this with a sad brow? Or do you play the flouting Jack, 175
to tell us Cupid is a good hare-finder and Vulcan a rare 176
carpenter? Come, in what key shall a man take you, to 177
go in the song?   178

CLAUDIO   In mine eye she is the sweetest lady that ever 179
I looked on.

BENEDICK   I can see yet without spectacles, and I see no
such matter. There's her cousin, an she were not possessed with a fury, exceeds her as much in beauty as the
first of May doth the last of December. But I hope you 184
have no intent to turn husband, have you?

CLAUDIO   I would scarce trust myself, though I had
sworn the contrary, if Hero would be my wife.

BENEDICK   Is't come to this? In faith, hath not the world
one man but he will wear his cap with suspicion? Shall 189
I never see a bachelor of threescore again? Go to, 190
i'faith; an thou wilt needs thrust thy neck into a yoke, 191
wear the print of it and sigh away Sundays. Look, Don
Pedro is returned to seek you.   193

      Enter Don Pedro.

DON PEDRO   What secret hath held you here, that you
followed not to Leonato's?

BENEDICK   I would Your Grace would constrain me to
tell.   197

DON PEDRO   I charge thee on thy allegiance.

BENEDICK   You hear, Count Claudio. I can be secret as a
dumb man—I would have you think so—but on my
allegiance, mark you this, on my allegiance! He is in
love. With who? Now that is Your Grace's part. Mark
how short his answer is: with Hero, Leonato's short 203
daughter.

CLAUDIO   If this were so, so were it uttered.

---

117 convert change   **123 dear happiness** precious piece of luck
125–6 I am . . . that I am of the same disposition in that matter, i.e., of
loving no one.   **129 scape** escape.   **predestinate** inevitable (for any
man who should woo Beatrice)   **132 were** i.e., is.   **133 rare** outstanding.   **parrot-teacher** i.e., one who would teach a parrot well, because
you merely "parrot" my lines.   **134 of my tongue** taught to speak
like me, i.e., incessantly   **134–5 of yours** taught to speak like you.
137 and . . . continuer i.e., and as much staying power in running as
you have in talking.   **139 a jade's trick** i.e., an ill-tempered horse's
habit of slipping its head out of the collar or stopping suddenly (just
as Benedick proposes to abandon this exchange of witticisms when
he thinks he has had the last word).   **141 sum of all** (Don Pedro and
Leonato have been conversing apart on other matters.)   **149 being**
since you are   **153 Please it** May it please   **154 go together** i.e., go
arm in arm (thus avoiding the question of precedence in order of
leaving).   **154.1 *Manent*** They remain onstage   **157 noted her not**
gave her no special attention

162 tyrant one cruel or pitiless in attitude   **164 low** short   **175 case**
(1) jewel case (2) clothing, outer garments. (There is also a bawdy
play on the meaning "female pudenda.")   **176 sad** serious.   **flouting
Jack** i.e., mocking rascal   **177–8 to tell . . . carpenter?** i.e., are you
mocking us with nonsense? (Cupid was blind, not sharp-eyed like a
hunter, and Vulcan was a blacksmith, not a carpenter.)   **178–9 to . . .
song** as the song expresses it. (Alluding perhaps to some popular
song.)   **184 with a fury** by an avenging, infernal spirit   **189–90 hath
. . . suspicion?** i.e., isn't there a man left alive who will regard marriage with a jaundiced eye? (A cap might be used, unsuccessfully perhaps, in an attempt to hide a cuckold's horns.)   **191 Go to** (An
expression of impatience.)   **193 wear . . . Sundays** i.e., display the
marks of your domestic enslavement resignedly.   **197 constrain**
order   **203 part** speaking part. (I.e., to say, "With who?")

BENEDICK   Like the old tale, my lord: "It is not so, nor 206
'twas not so, but indeed, God forbid it should be so." 207

CLAUDIO   If my passion change not shortly, God forbid
it should be otherwise.

DON PEDRO   Amen, if you love her, for the lady is very
well worthy.

CLAUDIO   You speak this to fetch me in, my lord.

DON PEDRO   By my troth, I speak my thought. 213

CLAUDIO   And in faith, my lord, I spoke mine. 214

BENEDICK   And by my two faiths and troths, my lord, I
spoke mine. 216

CLAUDIO   That I love her, I feel.

DON PEDRO   That she is worthy, I know.

BENEDICK   That I neither feel how she should be loved
nor know how she should be worthy is the opinion
that fire cannot melt out of me. I will die in it at the
stake.

DON PEDRO   Thou wast ever an obstinate heretic in the
despite of beauty.

CLAUDIO   And never could maintain his part but in the 225
force of his will. 226

BENEDICK   That a woman conceived me, I thank her; 227
that she brought me up, I likewise give her most humble thanks. But that I will have a recheat winded in my
forehead or hang my bugle in an invisible baldrick, all 230
women shall pardon me. Because I will not do them 231
the wrong to mistrust any, I will do myself the right to 232
trust none; and the fine is, for the which I may go the
finer, I will live a bachelor. 234

DON PEDRO   I shall see thee, ere I die, look pale with 235
love.

BENEDICK   With anger, with sickness, or with hunger,
my lord, not with love. Prove that ever I lose more
blood with love than I will get again with drinking, 239
pick out mine eyes with a ballad-maker's pen and 240
hang me up at the door of a brothel house for the sign 241
of blind Cupid. 242

DON PEDRO   Well, if ever thou dost fall from this faith,
thou wilt prove a notable argument.

245

BENEDICK   If I do, hang me in a bottle like a cat and 246
shoot at me, and he that hits me, let him be clapped on
the shoulder and called Adam. 248

DON PEDRO   Well, as time shall try:
"In time the savage bull doth bear the yoke." 250

BENEDICK   The savage bull may; but if ever the sensible
Benedick bear it, pluck off the bull's horns and set
them in my forehead, and let me be vilely painted, and
in such great letters as they write, "Here is good horse
to hire," let them signify under my sign, "Here you
may see Benedick the married man."

CLAUDIO   If this should ever happen, thou wouldst be
horn-mad. 258

DON PEDRO   Nay, if Cupid have not spent all his quiver
in Venice, thou wilt quake for this shortly. 260

BENEDICK   I look for an earthquake too, then. 261

DON PEDRO   Well, you will temporize with the hours. In 262
the meantime, good Signor Benedick, repair to Leonat-
o's. Commend me to him, and tell him I will not fail
him at supper, for indeed he hath made great preparation.

BENEDICK   I have almost matter enough in me for such 267
an embassage; and so I commit you— 268

CLAUDIO   To the tuition of God. From my house, if I had 269
it—

DON PEDRO   The sixth of July. Your loving friend,
Benedick.

BENEDICK   Nay, mock not, mock not. The body of your
discourse is sometime guarded with fragments, and 274
the guards are but slightly basted on neither. Ere you 275
flout old ends any further, examine your conscience. 276
And so I leave you.   *Exit.*

CLAUDIO
My liege, Your Highness now may do me good. 278

DON PEDRO
My love is thine to teach. Teach it but how,
And thou shalt see how apt it is to learn
Any hard lesson that may do thee good.

CLAUDIO
Hath Leonato any son, my lord?

DON PEDRO
No child but Hero; she's his only heir.
Dost thou affect her, Claudio?

CLAUDIO   O my lord, 284

---

206 **If . . . uttered** If this were true, it might be told in words to this
effect.   207 **old tale** (In the English fairy tale known as "Mr. Fox," a
murderous wooer, discovered in his crimes by the lady he seeks to
marry and victimize, repeatedly disclaims her recital of what she has
seen by the refrain here set in quotations. The story is a variant of the
theme known as "the Robber Bridegroom." Benedick uses it mockingly here to characterize Claudio's reluctance to admit his "crime" of
falling in love.)   213 **fetch me in** get me to confess   214 **By my troth**
By my faith, upon my word. (A mild oath.)   216 **by . . . troths** as it
were, by my loyalty to you both   225 **despite** contempt   226–7 **in . . .
will** by mere obstinacy (which, as defined by the Schoolmen, was the
state of the heretic.)   230–2 **But that . . . me** i.e., Women must pardon
me for refusing to have a horn placed on my head as if I were a cuckold. (A *recheat* is a hunting call sounded [*winded*] on a horn to assemble the hounds; a *baldrick* is a strap that supports the horn, here
invisible because the horn is the metaphorical one of cuckoldry.)
234 **fine** conclusion   234–5 **go the finer** be more finely dressed (since
without a wife I will have more money to spend on clothing)
239 **Prove** If you can prove   239–40 **lose . . . drinking** (According to
Elizabethan theory, each sigh cost the heart a drop of blood, whereas
blood was replenished by wine.)   241 **ballad-maker's pen** i.e., such
as would be used to write love ballads or satires   242 **sign** painted
sign, such as hung over inns and shops   245 **notable argument** notorious subject for conversation, example.

246 **bottle** wicker or leather basket (to hold the cat sometimes used as
an archery target)   248 **Adam** (Probably refers to Adam Bell, archer
outlaw of the ballads.)   250 **In . . . yoke** (Proverbial.)   258 **horn-mad**
stark mad. (From the fury of horned beasts; with allusion to cuckoldry.)   260 **Venice** (A city noted for licentiousness.)   **quake** (With a
pun on *quiver* in the previous line.)   261 **I . . . then** i.e., My falling in
love will be at least as rare as an earthquake.   262 **temporize . . .
hours** come to terms, or become milder, in time. (With perhaps a
bawdy pun on *hours,* "whores," pronounced something like "hoors.")
267 **matter** wit, intelligence   268 **embassage** mission.   **and so . . . you**
(A conventional close, which Claudio and Don Pedro mockingly play
with as though it were the complimentary close of a letter.)
269 **tuition** protection   274 **guarded** ornamented, trimmed
275 **guards . . . neither** trimmings are tenuously stitched on at best,
have only the flimsiest connection.   276 **flout old ends** quote or recite
mockingly proverbial tags of wisdom (as well as fragments of cloth, or
the *ends* of letters that Claudio and Don Pedro have been parodying).
examine your conscience look to your own behavior or speech.
278 **do me good** do me some good, help me.   284 **affect** love

When you went onward on this ended action,   285
I looked upon her with a soldier's eye,
That liked, but had a rougher task in hand
Than to drive liking to the name of love.
But now I am returned and that war thoughts   289
Have left their places vacant, in their rooms
Come thronging soft and delicate desires,
All prompting me how fair young Hero is,
Saying, I liked her ere I went to wars.

DON PEDRO
Thou wilt be like a lover presently
And tire the hearer with a book of words.
If thou dost love fair Hero, cherish it,
And I will break with her and with her father,   297
And thou shalt have her. Was't not to this end
That thou began'st to twist so fine a story?   299

CLAUDIO
How sweetly you do minister to love,
That know love's grief by his complexion!   301
But lest my liking might too sudden seem,
I would have salved it with a longer treatise.   303

DON PEDRO
What need the bridge much broader than the flood?   304
The fairest grant is the necessity.   305
Look what will serve is fit. 'Tis once: thou lovest,   306
And I will fit thee with the remedy.
I know we shall have reveling tonight;
I will assume thy part in some disguise
And tell fair Hero I am Claudio,
And in her bosom I'll unclasp my heart
And take her hearing prisoner with the force
And strong encounter of my amorous tale.
Then after to her father will I break,
And the conclusion is, she shall be thine.
In practice let us put it presently.   *Exeunt.*

❧

[1.2]

Enter Leonato and an old man [Antonio],
brother to Leonato, [meeting].

LEONATO   How now, brother, where is my cousin,   1
your son? Hath he provided this music?
ANTONIO   He is very busy about it. But brother, I can
tell you strange news that you yet dreamt not of.
LEONATO   Are they good?   5
ANTONIO   As the event stamps them, but they have a   6
good cover; they show well outward. The Prince and   7

Count Claudio, walking in a thick-pleached alley in   8
mine orchard, were thus much overheard by a man of   9
mine: the Prince discovered to Claudio that he loved   10
my niece your daughter and meant to acknowledge it
this night in a dance, and if he found her accordant, he   12
meant to take the present time by the top and instant-   13
ly break with you of it.
LEONATO   Hath the fellow any wit that told you this?   15
ANTONIO   A good sharp fellow. I will send for him, and
question him yourself.
LEONATO   No, no; we will hold it as a dream till it
appear itself. But I will acquaint my daughter withal,
that she may be the better prepared for an answer, if
peradventure this be true. Go you and tell her of it.

[Enter Antonio's Son, with a musician and
others.]

Cousins, you know what you have to do.—Oh, I cry   22
you mercy, friend; go you with me, and I will use your   23
skill.—Good cousin, have a care this busy time.

Exeunt.

❧

[1.3]

Enter Sir [Don] John the Bastard and Conrade,
his companion.

CONRADE   What the goodyear, my lord! Why are you   1
thus out of measure sad?   2
DON JOHN   There is no measure in the occasion that
breeds; therefore the sadness is without limit.
CONRADE   You should hear reason.   5
DON JOHN   And when I have heard it, what blessing
brings it?
CONRADE   If not a present remedy, at least a patient
sufferance.   9
DON JOHN   I wonder that thou, being, as thou say'st
thou art, born under Saturn, goest about to apply a   11
moral medicine to a mortifying mischief. I cannot hide   12
what I am: I must be sad when I have cause and smile
at no man's jests, eat when I have stomach and wait   14
for no man's leisure, sleep when I am drowsy and
tend on no man's business, laugh when I am merry   16
and claw no man in his humor.   17
CONRADE   Yea, but you must not make the full show of
this till you may do it without controlment. You have   19
of late stood out against your brother, and he hath   20
ta'en you newly into his grace, where it is impossible   21
you should take true root but by the fair weather that

---

285 ended action military action now ended   **289 now** now that
297 break open the subject. (As also in line 314.)   **299 twist** draw out
the thread of   **301 his complexion** its outward appearance.
303 salved soothed, eased the way for   **304 What need** Why need be.
flood river.   **305 The fairest . . . necessity** The best thing to do is simply what is necessary.   **306 Look what** Whatever.   **'Tis once** In
short, once and for all. (This speech of Don Pedro's is overheard by a
servant of Antonio's, as we learn in the next scene.)
1.2 Location: Leonato's house.
1 cousin kinsman   **5 they** i.e., the news. (Often treated as a plural
noun, as at 2.1.167.)   **6 event** outcome   **6–7 they . . . cover** (The
image is of a printed book, promising well by its cover.)

8 thick-pleached alley walk lined with dense hedges of intertwined
shrubs   **9 orchard** garden.   **man** servant   **10 discovered** disclosed
12 accordant agreeing, consenting   **13 take . . . top** i.e., seize the
opportunity. (Proverbially, Occasion was imagined bald in the back of
the head but with a forelock hair in the front that opportunistically
could be grabbed.)   **15 wit** sense, intelligence   **22–3 cry you mercy**
beg your pardon   **23 friend** (Addressed perhaps to the musician.)
1.3. Location: Leonato's house.
1 What the goodyear i.e., What the deuce   **2 out of measure** immoderately   **5 hear** listen to   **9 suffereance** endurance.   **11 under Saturn**
(Hence, of a morose disposition.)   **11–12 goest . . . mischief** endeavor
to cure with moral commonplaces a deadly disease.   **14 stomach**
appetite   **16 tend on** attend to   **17 claw** flatter.   **humor** whim.
19 controlment restraint.   **20 stood out** rebelled   **21 grace** favor

you make yourself. It is needful that you frame the   23
season for your own harvest.

DON JOHN   I had rather be a canker in a hedge than a   25
rose in his grace, and it better fits my blood to be dis-   26
dained of all than to fashion a carriage to rob love from   27
any. In this, though I cannot be said to be a flattering
honest man, it must not be denied but I am a plain-
dealing villain. I am trusted with a muzzle and   30
enfranchised with a clog; therefore I have decreed not   31
to sing in my cage. If I had my mouth, I would bite; if
I had my liberty, I would do my liking. In the
meantime let me be that I am, and seek not to alter me.

CONRADE   Can you make no use of your discontent?

DON JOHN   I make all use of it, for I use it only. Who   36
comes here?

Enter Borachio.

What news, Borachio?

BORACHIO   I came yonder from a great supper. The
Prince your brother is royally entertained by Leonato,
and I can give you intelligence of an intended mar-   41
riage.

DON JOHN   Will it serve for any model to build mischief
on? What is he for a fool that betroths himself to   44
unquietness?

BORACHIO   Marry, it is your brother's right hand.   46

DON JOHN   Who, the most exquisite Claudio?

BORACHIO   Even he.

DON JOHN   A proper squire! And who, and who? Which   49
way looks he?

BORACHIO   Marry, one Hero, the daughter and heir of
Leonato.

DON JOHN   A very forward March chick! How came   53
you to this?

BORACHIO   Being entertained for a perfumer, as I was   55
smoking a musty room, comes me the Prince and   56
Claudio, hand in hand, in sad conference. I whipped   57
me behind the arras, and there heard it agreed upon   58
that the Prince should woo Hero for himself and,
having obtained her, give her to Count Claudio.

DON JOHN   Come, come, let us thither. This may prove
food to my displeasure. That young start-up hath all   62
the glory of my overthrow. If I can cross him any way,   63
I bless myself every way. You are both sure, and will   64
assist me?

CONRADE   To the death, my lord.

DON JOHN   Let us to the great supper. Their cheer is the
greater that I am subdued. Would the cook were o' my   68
mind! Shall we go prove what's to be done?   69

BORACHIO   We'll wait upon Your Lordship.   *Exeunt.*

[2.1]

*Enter Leonato, his brother [Antonio], Hero his
daughter, and Beatrice his niece [with Margaret
and Ursula].*

LEONATO   Was not Count John here at supper?

ANTONIO   I saw him not.

BEATRICE   How tartly that gentleman looks! I never can   3
see him but I am heartburned an hour after.   4

HERO   He is of a very melancholy disposition.

BEATRICE   He were an excellent man that were made   6
just in the midway between him and Benedick. The
one is too like an image and says nothing, and the   8
other too like my lady's eldest son, evermore tattling.   9

LEONATO   Then half Signor Benedick's tongue in Count
John's mouth, and half Count John's melancholy in
Signor Benedick's face—

BEATRICE   With a good leg and a good foot, uncle, and
money enough in his purse, such a man would win
any woman in the world, if 'a could get her good will.   15

LEONATO   By my troth, niece, thou wilt never get thee a
husband if thou be so shrewd of thy tongue.   17

ANTONIO   In faith, she's too curst.   18

BEATRICE   Too curst is more than curst. I shall lessen
God's sending that way; for it is said, "God sends a   20
curst cow short horns," but to a cow too curst he sends   21
none.

LEONATO   So, by being too curst, God will send you no
horns.

BEATRICE   Just, if he send me no husband, for the which   25
blessing I am at him upon my knees every morning
and evening. Lord, I could not endure a husband with
a beard on his face! I had rather lie in the woolen.   28

LEONATO   You may light on a husband that hath no
beard.

BEATRICE   What should I do with him? Dress him in my
apparel and make him my waiting-gentlewoman? He
that hath a beard is more than a youth, and he that
hath no beard is less than a man; and he that is more
than a youth is not for me, and he that is less than a
man, I am not for him. Therefore I will even take

---

23 frame fashion   **25 canker** dog rose, one that grows wild rather
than being cultivated in formal gardens   **26 blood** mood, disposition
27 fashion . . . love counterfeit a behavior to gain undeserved attention   **30–1 I . . . clog** I am trusted only with my muzzle on and am
allowed freedom only to the extent of being hampered by a heavy
wooden block   **31 decreed** determined   **36 I . . . only** Discontent is
my only resource, and I cultivate it alone.   **41 intelligence** news
44 What . . . fool What kind of fool is he   **46 Marry** By the Virgin
Mary, i.e., indeed   **49 proper squire** fine young man. (Said contemptuously.)   **53 forward March chick** precocious young thing (like a
chick hatched early).   **55 entertained for** hired as   **56 smoking**
sweetening the air of (with aromatic smoke).   **comes me** comes. (*Me*
is used colloquially, as also in line 58.)   **57 sad** serious   **58 arras** tapestry, wall hanging   **62 start-up** upstart   **63 cross** thwart
64 sure trustworthy

68–9 o' my mind i.e., of a mind to poison the food.   **69 prove** try out
2.1. Location: Leonato's house.
3 tartly sour of disposition   **4 heartburned** afflicted with heartburn or
indigestion   **6 He were** A man would be   **8 image** statue   **9 my . . .
son** i.e., a spoiled child.   **tattling** chattering.   **15 'a** he   **17 shrewd**
sharp   **18 curst** shrewish.   **20 that way** in that respect   **21 curst** i.e.,
savage, vicious. (God proverbially takes care that the vicious are limited in their ability to do harm.)   **25 Just** Right, exactly so.   **no husband** If Beatrice has no husband, there can be no prospect of cuckold's horns. (She may also be jesting about a short penis here and in
lines 20–2.)   **28 in the woolen** between blankets, without sheets.

sixpence in earnest of the bearward, and lead his apes 37
into hell. 38

LEONATO   Well, then, go you into hell?

BEATRICE   No, but to the gate; and there will the devil
meet me, like an old cuckold, with horns on his head,
and say, "Get you to heaven, Beatrice, get you to
heaven, here's no place for you maids." So deliver I up
my apes, and away to Saint Peter, for the heavens; he 44
shows me where the bachelors sit, and there live we 45
as merry as the day is long.

ANTONIO [to Hero]   Well, niece, I trust you will be ruled
by your father.

BEATRICE   Yes, faith, it is my cousin's duty to make
curtsy and say, "Father, as it please you." But yet for
all that, cousin, let him be a handsome fellow, or else
make another curtsy and say, "Father, as it please me."

LEONATO   Well, niece, I hope to see you one day fitted
with a husband.

BEATRICE   Not till God make men of some other metal 55
than earth. Would it not grieve a woman to be over-
mastered with a piece of valiant dust? To make an
account of her life to a clod of wayward marl? No, 58
uncle, I'll none. Adam's sons are my brethren, and 59
truly I hold it a sin to match in my kindred. 60

LEONATO [to Hero]   Daughter, remember what I told
you. If the Prince do solicit you in that kind, you know 62
your answer.

BEATRICE   The fault will be in the music, cousin, if you
be not wooed in good time. If the Prince be too 65
important, tell him there is measure in everything, 66
and so dance out the answer. For, hear me, Hero:
wooing, wedding, and repenting is as a Scotch jig, a 68
measure, and a cinquepace. The first suit is hot and 69
hasty, like a Scotch jig, and full as fantastical; the
wedding, mannerly-modest, as a measure, full of state 71
and ancientry; and then comes Repentance, and with 72
his bad legs falls into the cinquepace faster and faster
till he sink into his grave.

LEONATO   Cousin, you apprehend passing shrewdly. 75

BEATRICE   I have a good eye, uncle; I can see a church by 76
daylight. 77

LEONATO   The revelers are entering, brother. Make good
room.   [The men put on their masks.]

Enter [as maskers] Prince [Don] Pedro, Claudio, and Benedick, and Balthasar, [Borachio,]
and Don John.

DON PEDRO   Lady, will you walk a bout with your 80
friend?   [The couples pair off for the dance.] 81

HERO   So you walk softly and look sweetly and say
nothing, I am yours for the walk, and especially when
I walk away.

DON PEDRO   With me in your company?

HERO   I may say so, when I please.

DON PEDRO   And when please you to say so?

HERO   When I like your favor, for God defend the lute 88
should be like the case! 89

DON PEDRO   My visor is Philemon's roof; within the 90
house is Jove.

HERO   Why, then, your visor should be thatched. 92

DON PEDRO   Speak low, if you speak love. 93
[They dance to one side.]

BALTHASAR   Well, I would you did like me. 94

MARGARET   So would not I for your own sake, for I have
many ill qualities.

BALTHASAR   Which is one?

MARGARET   I say my prayers aloud.

BALTHASAR   I love you the better. The hearers may cry
Amen.

MARGARET   God match me with a good dancer!

BALTHASAR   Amen.

MARGARET   And God keep him out of my sight when
the dance is done! Answer, clerk. 104

BALTHASAR   No more words. The clerk is answered. 105
[They dance to one side.]

URSULA   I know you well enough. You are Signor
Antonio.

ANTONIO   At a word, I am not. 108

URSULA   I know you by the waggling of your head.

ANTONIO   To tell you true, I counterfeit him.

URSULA   You could never do him so ill-well unless you 111
were the very man. Here's his dry hand up and down. 112
You are he, you are he.

ANTONIO   At a word, I am not.

URSULA   Come, come, do you think I do not know you
by your excellent wit? Can virtue hide itself? Go to,
mum, you are he. Graces will appear, and there's an 117
end.   [They dance to one side.] 118

---

37 in earnest in token advance payment for.   **bearward** one who
keeps and exhibits a bear (and sometimes apes)   **37–8 lead . . . hell**
(An ancient proverb says, "Such as die maids do all lead apes in
hell.")   **44 for the heavens** (A common interjection, like "Good heavens!" but here also carrying its literal meaning, i.e., bound for heav-
en.)   **45 bachelors** unmarried persons of either sex   **55 metal** substance. (With play on "mettle.")   **58 marl** clay, earth (such as was
used by God to make Adam in Genesis 2).   **59–60 Adam's . . . kindred** (Beatrice jests that since men and women are all descended from
Adam, it would be incestuous for her to marry a man.)   **62 in that
kind** to that effect (i.e., to marriage)   **65 in good time** (1) soon (2) in
time to the music, rhythmically.   **66 important** importunate, urgent.
measure (1) moderation (2) rhythm, dance   **68–9 a measure** a formal
dance   **69 cinquepace** five-step lively dance, galliard. (The pun on
"sink apace," as it was pronounced, is evident in lines 72–4: repentance will *sink faster and faster,* with a suggestion of detumescence.)
71–2 state and ancientry dignity and traditional stateliness
75 apprehend passing shrewdly understand with unusual perspicac-
ity.   **76–7 see . . . daylight** i.e., see something as plain as the nose on
your face.

80 walk a bout take a turn, join in a section of a dance. (Here probably a slow, stately pavane.)   **81 friend** wooer.   **88 favor** face
88–9 God . . . case! i.e., God forbid the face within should be as
unhandsome as its cover, your visor!   **90–3 My . . . love** (A fourteen-
syllable rhymed couplet, the verse form of Arthur Golding's translation of the *Metamorphoses,* 1567.)   **90 Philemon's roof** i.e., the humble
cottage in which the peasants Philemon and Baucis entertained Jove,
or Jupiter, unawares. (See Ovid, *Metamorphoses,* 8.)   **92 visor** mask.
thatched i.e., whiskered, to resemble the thatch of a humble cottage.
94–105 BALTHASAR (The speech prefixes in the Quarto text for
Balthasar's lines read *Bene.* and *Balth.* Some editors speculate that
Borachio is intended.)   **104 clerk** (So addressed because of Balthasar's
repeatedly answering "Amen" like the parish clerk saying the
responses.)   **108 At a word** In short   **111 do . . . ill-well** imitate his
imperfections so perfectly   **112 dry hand** (A sign of age.)   **up and
down** up exactly.   **117 mum** be silent   **117–18 an end** no more to
be said.

BEATRICE	Will you not tell me who told you so?
BENEDICK	No, you shall pardon me.
BEATRICE	Nor will you not tell me who you are?
BENEDICK	Not now.
BEATRICE	That I was disdainful and that I had my good

BEATRICE   Will you not tell me who told you so?
BENEDICK   No, you shall pardon me.
BEATRICE   Nor will you not tell me who you are?
BENEDICK   Not now.
BEATRICE   That I was disdainful and that I had my good
wit out of the *Hundred Merry Tales*—well, this was 124
Signor Benedick that said so.
BENEDICK   What's he?
BEATRICE   I am sure you know him well enough.
BENEDICK   Not I, believe me.
BEATRICE   Did he never make you laugh?
BENEDICK   I pray you, what is he?
BEATRICE   Why, he is the Prince's jester, a very dull fool.
Only his gift is in devising impossible slanders. None 132
but libertines delight in him, and the commendation 133
is not in his wit but in his villainy, for he both pleases 134
men and angers them, and then they laugh at him and 135
beat him. I am sure he is in the fleet. I would he had 136
boarded me.   137
BENEDICK   When I know the gentleman, I'll tell him 138
what you say.
BEATRICE   Do, do. He'll but break a comparison or two 140
on me, which peradventure not marked or not laughed 141
at strikes him into melancholy; and then there's a partridge wing saved, for the fool will eat no supper that
night. [*Music.*] We must follow the leaders.   144
BENEDICK   In every good thing.
BEATRICE   Nay, if they lead to any ill, I will leave them
at the next turning.   147
                Dance. Exeunt [all except Don John, Borachio, and
                Claudio. Don John and Borachio are unmasked.]
DON JOHN   [*to Borachio*]   Sure my brother is amorous on
Hero and hath withdrawn her father to break with
him about it. The ladies follow her, and but one visor
remains.
BORACHIO   And that is Claudio. I know him by his
bearing.
DON JOHN   [*advancing to Claudio*]   Are not you Signor
Benedick?
CLAUDIO   You know me well. I am he.
DON JOHN   Signor, you are very near my brother in his 157
love. He is enamored on Hero. I pray you, dissuade 158
him from her; she is no equal for his birth. You may do 159
the part of an honest man in it.
CLAUDIO   How know you he loves her?
DON JOHN   I heard him swear his affection.
BORACHIO   So did I, too, and he swore he would marry
her tonight.

DON JOHN   Come, let us to the banquet.   165
                        Exeunt. Manet Claudio.
CLAUDIO
Thus answer I in name of Benedick,
But hear these ill news with the ears of Claudio.
'Tis certain so. The Prince woos for himself.
Friendship is constant in all other things
Save in the office and affairs of love;
Therefore all hearts in love use their own tongues.
Let every eye negotiate for itself
And trust no agent; for beauty is a witch
Against whose charms faith melteth into blood.   174
This is an accident of hourly proof,   175
Which I mistrusted not. Farewell therefore Hero!   176

                Enter Benedick [unmasked].

BENEDICK   Count Claudio?
CLAUDIO   Yea, the same.
BENEDICK   Come, will you go with me?
CLAUDIO   Whither?
BENEDICK   Even to the next willow, about your own 181
business, County. What fashion will you wear the gar- 182
land of? About your neck, like an usurer's chain? Or 183
under your arm, like a lieutenant's scarf? You must 184
wear it one way, for the Prince hath got your Hero.   185
CLAUDIO   I wish him joy of her.
BENEDICK   Why, that's spoken like an honest drover; so 187
they sell bullocks. But did you think the Prince would 188
have served you thus?
CLAUDIO   I pray you, leave me.
BENEDICK   Ho, now you strike like the blind man. 'Twas 191
the boy that stole your meat, and you'll beat the post. 192
CLAUDIO   If it will not be, I'll leave you.   *Exit.* 193
BENEDICK   Alas, poor hurt fowl! Now will he creep into 194
sedges. But that my Lady Beatrice should know me, 195
and not know me! The Prince's fool! Ha? It may be I 196
go under that title because I am merry. Yea, but so I am
apt to do myself wrong. I am not so reputed. It is the 198
base, though bitter, disposition of Beatrice that puts the 199
world into her person and so gives me out. Well, I'll be 200
revenged as I may.

                Enter the Prince [Don Pedro], Hero, [and]
                Leonato. [All are unmasked.]

---

124 *Hundred Merry Tales* (A popular collection of anecdotes first published by John Rastell in 1526.)   132 **Only his gift** His only talent.
impossible incredible   133 **libertines** i.e., those who disregard conventional moral laws   134 **villainy** i.e., mocking, raillery; also,
clownishness   134–5 **pleases . . . angers them** i.e., amuses some
with his rudeness and angers others with his slanders   136 **fleet** i.e.,
crowd, company sailing past in the dance.   137 **boarded** i.e., accosted. (Continuing the nautical metaphor begun in *fleet.*)
138 **know** become acquainted with   140 **break a comparison** i.e.,
make a scornful simile (as in a tilting or breaking of lances)   141 **peradventure** if it is   144 **leaders** i.e., of the dance.   147 **turning** turning
figure in the dance.   157–8 **near . . . love** close to my brother.
159 **birth** aristocratic rank.

165 **banquet** light repast of fruit, wine, and dessert.   165.1 *Manet*
He remains onstage   174 **faith . . . blood** loyalty gives way to passion.   175 **accident** occurrence   176 **mistrusted** suspected   181 **willow** (An emblem of disappointed love.)   182 **County** count.
182–3 **garland** i.e., of willow   183 **usurer's chain** heavy gold chain,
worn by rich men as if it were a badge of office.   184 **scarf** sling.
185 **one way** one way or the other   187 **drover** cattle dealer
188 **bullocks** oxen.   191 **strike . . . man** lash out blindly in every
direction.   191–2 **'Twas . . . post** i.e., You're ready to blame anything
but the true cause of your distress. (Benedick seemingly alludes to
some fable about a boy and an innocent postman that demonstrates
this object lesson.)   193 **If . . . be** i.e., If you won't leave me as I asked
194–5 **creep into sedges** i.e., hide himself away, as wounded fowl
creep into rushes along the river.   195–6 **know me, and not know
me** i.e., be of my long acquaintance, and yet misjudge me so cruelly.
198–200 **It is . . . out** It is Beatrice's low and harsh disposition to assume
that she speaks for everyone when she characterizes me this way.

DON PEDRO   Now, signor, where's the Count? Did you see him?

BENEDICK   Troth, my lord, I have played the part of Lady 204 Fame. I found him here as melancholy as a lodge in a 205 warren. I told him, and I think I told him true, that 206 Your Grace had got the good will of this young lady, and I offered him my company to a willow tree, either 208 to make him a garland, as being forsaken, or to bind 209 him up a rod, as being worthy to be whipped. 210

DON PEDRO   To be whipped! What's his fault?

BENEDICK   The flat transgression of a schoolboy, who, 212 being overjoyed with finding a bird's nest, shows it his companion, and he steals it.

DON PEDRO   Wilt thou make a trust a transgression? The 215 transgression is in the stealer.

BENEDICK   Yet it had not been amiss the rod had been made, and the garland too; for the garland he might have worn himself, and the rod he might have bestowed on you, who, as I take it, have stolen his bird's nest.

DON PEDRO   I will but teach them to sing and restore 222 them to the owner.

BENEDICK   If their singing answer your saying, by my 224 faith, you say honestly.

DON PEDRO   The Lady Beatrice hath a quarrel to you. 226 The gentleman that danced with her told her she is much wronged by you.

BENEDICK   Oh, she misused me past the endurance of a block! An oak but with one green leaf on it would have 230 answered her. My very visor began to assume life and scold with her. She told me, not thinking I had been myself, that I was the Prince's jester, that I was duller than a great thaw; huddling jest upon jest with such 234 impossible conveyance upon me that I stood like a 235 man at a mark, with a whole army shooting at me. She 236 speaks poniards, and every word stabs. If her breath 237 were as terrible as her terminations, there were no liv- 238 ing near her; she would infect to the North Star. I 239 would not marry her, though she were endowed with all that Adam had left him before he transgressed. She 241 would have made Hercules have turned spit, yea, and 242 have cleft his club to make the fire, too. Come, talk not 243 of her. You shall find her the infernal Ate in good 244 apparel. I would to God some scholar would conjure 245 her, for certainly, while she is here, a man may live as 246 quiet in hell as in a sanctuary, and people sin upon purpose because they would go thither; so indeed all disquiet, horror, and perturbation follows her.

Enter Claudio and Beatrice.

DON PEDRO   Look, here she comes.

BENEDICK   Will Your Grace command me any service to the world's end? I will go on the slightest errand now to the Antipodes that you can devise to send me on; I 253 will fetch you a toothpicker now from the furthest inch 254 of Asia, bring you the length of Prester John's foot, 255 fetch you a hair off the great Cham's beard, do you any 256 embassage to the Pygmies, rather than hold three 257 words' conference with this harpy. You have no 258 employment for me?

DON PEDRO   None but to desire your good company.

BENEDICK   Oh, God, sir, here's a dish I love not! I cannot endure my Lady Tongue.   *Exit.*

DON PEDRO   Come, lady, come, you have lost the heart of Signor Benedick.

BEATRICE   Indeed, my lord, he lent it me awhile, and I 265 gave him use for it, a double heart for his single one. 266 Marry, once before he won it of me with false dice; 267 therefore Your Grace may well say I have lost it.

DON PEDRO   You have put him down, lady, you have 269 put him down.

BEATRICE   So I would not he should do me, my lord, lest I should prove the mother of fools. I have brought Count Claudio, whom you sent me to seek.

DON PEDRO   Why, how now, Count? Wherefore are you sad?

CLAUDIO   Not sad, my lord.

DON PEDRO   How then? Sick?

CLAUDIO   Neither, my lord.

BEATRICE   The Count is neither sad, nor sick, nor merry, nor well; but civil count, civil as an orange, and some- 280 thing of that jealous complexion. 281

DON PEDRO   I'faith, lady, I think your blazon to be true, 282 though I'll be sworn, if he be so, his conceit is false. 283 Here, Claudio, I have wooed in thy name, and fair

---

204 **Troth** By my faith   204–5 **Lady Fame** Dame Rumor.
205–6 **lodge in a warren** isolated gamekeeper's hut in a large game preserve.   208 **offered . . . to** offered to accompany him to
209–10 **bind . . . rod** tie several willow switches into a scourge for him   212 **flat** plain   215 **a trust** a trusted assignment (here, the Prince's having taken in trust the wooing of Hero for Claudio, not himself)   222 **them** i.e., the young birds in the nest   224 **answer your saying** correspond to what you say   226 **to** with   230 **block** (of wood).   234 **great thaw** i.e., time when roads are muddy and impassable, obliging one to stay dully at home. **huddling** piling, heaping up   235 **impossible conveyance** incredible dexterity
236 **at a mark** at the target, marking where the arrows hit
237 **poniards** daggers   238 **terminations** terms, expressions
239 **North Star** (Popularly supposed to be the most remote of stars.)
241 **all . . . him** i.e., Paradise before the fall of man   242 **Hercules . . . spit** (The Amazon Omphale forced the captive Hercules to wear women's clothing and spin; turning the spit would be an even more menial kitchen duty.)   243 **cleft** split   244 **Ate** goddess of discord

245 **scholar . . . conjure** (Scholars were supposed to be able to conjure evil spirits back into hell by addressing them in Latin.)   246 **here** i.e., on earth. (As long as Beatrice is on earth, hell will seem like a place of refuge.)   253 **Antipodes** people and region on the opposite side of the earth   254 **toothpicker** toothpick   255 **Prester John** a legendary Christian king of the Far East   256 **great Cham** the Khan of Tartary, ruler of the Mongols   257 **Pygmies** legendary small race thought to live in India   258 **harpy** legendary creature with a woman's face and body and a bird's wings and claws.   265–7 **he . . . dice** (Beatrice refers seemingly to a previous courtship in which she feels that Benedick prevailed over her unfairly, in return for which she now has paid him back with *use* or interest, two to one.)   269 **put him down** got the better of him. (But Beatrice plays with the phrase in its literal and sexual sense.)   280 **civil** serious, grave. (Punning on *Seville* for the city in Spain whence came bitter-tasting oranges.)   280–1 **something** somewhat   281 **jealous complexion**, i.e., yellow, associated with melancholy and symbolic of jealousy.   282 **blazon** description. (A heraldic term.)   283 **conceit** (1) notion, idea (2) heraldic device. (Continuing the metaphor of *blazon*.)

Hero is won. I have broke with her father and his good 285
will obtained. Name the day of marriage, and God
give thee joy!

LEONATO   Count, take of me my daughter and with her
my fortunes. His Grace hath made the match, and all 289
grace say Amen to it.   290

BEATRICE   Speak, Count, 'tis your cue.

CLAUDIO   Silence is the perfectest herald of joy. I were
but little happy if I could say how much!—Lady, as
you are mine, I am yours. I give away myself for you
and dote upon the exchange.

BEATRICE   Speak, cousin, or if you cannot, stop his
mouth with a kiss, and let not him speak neither.
                        [*Claudio and Hero kiss.*]

DON PEDRO   In faith, lady, you have a merry heart.

BEATRICE   Yea, my lord; I thank it, poor fool, it keeps on
the windy side of care. My cousin tells him in his ear 300
that he is in her heart.

CLAUDIO   And so she doth, cousin.

BEATRICE   Good Lord, for alliance! Thus goes everyone 303
to the world but I, and I am sunburnt. I may sit in a 304
corner and cry, "Heigh-ho for a husband!"   305

DON PEDRO   Lady Beatrice, I will get you one.

BEATRICE   I would rather have one of your father's
getting. Hath Your Grace ne'er a brother like you? 308
Your father got excellent husbands, if a maid could come
by them.

DON PEDRO   Will you have me, lady?

BEATRICE   No, my lord, unless I might have another for
working days. Your Grace is too costly to wear every
day. But I beseech Your Grace, pardon me. I was born
to speak all mirth and no matter.   315

DON PEDRO   Your silence most offends me, and to be
merry best becomes you, for out o' question you were
born in a merry hour.

BEATRICE   No, sure, my lord, my mother cried; but then
there was a star danced, and under that was I born.
Cousins, God give you joy!

LEONATO   Niece, will you look to those things I told you
of?

BEATRICE   I cry you mercy, uncle. [*To Don Pedro*] By Your 324
Grace's pardon.   *Exit Beatrice.* 325

DON PEDRO   By my troth, a pleasant-spirited lady.

LEONATO   There's little of the melancholy element in 327
her, my lord. She is never sad but when she sleeps, and
not ever sad then; for I have heard my daughter say 329
she hath often dreamt of unhappiness and waked 330
herself with laughing.

DON PEDRO   She cannot endure to hear tell of a husband.

LEONATO   Oh, by no means. She mocks all her wooers 333
out of suit.   334

DON PEDRO   She were an excellent wife for Benedick.

LEONATO   Oh, Lord, my lord, if they were but a week
married they would talk themselves mad.

DON PEDRO   County Claudio, when mean you to go to
church?

CLAUDIO   Tomorrow, my lord. Time goes on crutches till
Love have all his rites.

LEONATO   Not till Monday, my dear son, which is hence
a just sevennight and a time too brief, too, to have all 343
things answer my mind.   344

DON PEDRO   Come, you shake the head at so long a
breathing, but I warrant thee, Claudio, the time shall 346
not go dully by us. I will in the interim undertake one
of Hercules' labors, which is to bring Signor Benedick
and the Lady Beatrice into a mountain of affection
th'one with th'other. I would fain have it a match, and 350
I doubt not but to fashion it, if you three will but
minister such assistance as I shall give you direction. 352

LEONATO   My lord, I am for you, though it cost me ten
nights' watchings.   354

CLAUDIO   And I, my lord.

DON PEDRO   And you too, gentle Hero?

HERO   I will do any modest office, my lord, to help my 357
cousin to a good husband.

DON PEDRO   And Benedick is not the unhopefullest hus- 359
band that I know. Thus far can I praise him: he is of a
noble strain, of approved valor and confirmed honesty. 361
I will teach you how to humor your cousin, that she
shall fall in love with Benedick; and I, with your two
helps, will so practice on Benedick that, in despite of
his quick wit and his queasy stomach, he shall fall in 365
love with Beatrice. If we can do this, Cupid is no longer
an archer; his glory shall be ours, for we are the
only love gods. Go in with me, and I will tell you my
drift.   *Exeunt.* 369

[2.2]

Enter [Don] John and Borachio.

DON JOHN   It is so. The Count Claudio shall marry the 1
daughter of Leonato.

BORACHIO   Yea, my lord, but I can cross it.   3

DON JOHN   Any bar, any cross, any impediment will be 4
medicinable to me. I am sick in displeasure to him,   5

---

285 broke spoken   **289–90 all . . . to it** i.e., we thank God for this
union.   **300 windy** windward, safe. (In sailing, the ship to windward
has the advantage.)   **303 alliance** relationship by marriage. (Claudio
has just called her "cousin.")   **303–4 goes . . . world** i.e., gets
married   **304 sunburnt** (The Renaissance considered dark complexions unattractive.)   **305 Heigh-ho . . . husband!** (The title of a ballad.)
308 getting begetting. (Playing on *get*, "procure," in the previous
speech.)   **315 matter** substance.   **324 cry you mercy** beg your pardon (for not having obeyed earlier)   **324–5 By . . . pardon** i.e., I beg
you to excuse my departure.   **327 melancholy element** i.e., earth,
associated with the humor of melancholy in the old physiology
329 ever always   **330 unhappiness** misfortune

333–4 She . . . suit She discomfits and discourages all her wooers.
343 a just sevennight exactly a week   **344 answer my mind** suit my
wishes.   **346 breathing** pause, interval   **350 fain** gladly   **352 minister** furnish, supply   **354 watchings** staying awake.   **357 do . . . office**
play any seemly role   **359 unhopefullest** most unpromising
361 strain ancestry.   **approved** tested.   **honesty** honor.   **365 queasy**
squeamish, delicate (about marriage)   **369 drift** purpose.
2.2. Location: Leonato's house.
1 shall is going to   **3 cross** thwart. (Also in line 7.)   **4 bar** obstacle
5 medicinable medicinal.   **in displeasure to** with dislike of

and whatsoever comes athwart his affection ranges 6
evenly with mine. How canst thou cross this mar- 7
riage?

BORACHIO   Not honestly, my lord, but so covertly that
no dishonesty shall appear in me.

DON JOHN   Show me briefly how.

BORACHIO   I think I told Your Lordship, a year since, 12
how much I am in the favor of Margaret, the waiting
gentlewoman to Hero.

DON JOHN   I remember.

BORACHIO   I can, at any unseasonable instant of the 16
night, appoint her to look out at her lady's chamber
window.

DON JOHN   What life is in that, to be the death of this
marriage?

BORACHIO   The poison of that lies in you to temper. Go 21
you to the Prince your brother; spare not to tell him
that he hath wronged his honor in marrying the renowned Claudio—whose estimation do you mightily 24
hold up—to a contaminated stale, such a one as Hero. 25

DON JOHN   What proof shall I make of that?

BORACHIO   Proof enough to misuse the Prince, to vex 27
Claudio, to undo Hero, and kill Leonato. Look you for
any other issue? 29

DON JOHN   Only to despite them I will endeavor any- 30
thing.

BORACHIO   Go, then, find me a meet hour to draw Don 32
Pedro and the Count Claudio alone. Tell them that you
know that Hero loves me. Intend a kind of zeal both to 34
the Prince and Claudio, as—in love of your brother's 35
honor, who hath made this match, and his friend's
reputation, who is thus like to be cozened with the 37
semblance of a maid—that you have discovered thus. 38
They will scarcely believe this without trial. Offer
them instances, which shall bear no less likelihood 40
than to see me at her chamber window, hear me call
Margaret Hero, hear Margaret term me Claudio; and 42
bring them to see this the very night before the
intended wedding—for in the meantime I will so
fashion the matter that Hero shall be absent—and
there shall appear such seeming truth of Hero's
disloyalty that jealousy shall be called assurance and 47
all the preparation overthrown. 48

DON JOHN   Grow this to what adverse issue it can, I will 49
put it in practice. Be cunning in the working this, and
thy fee is a thousand ducats. 51

BORACHIO   Be you constant in the accusation, and my
cunning shall not shame me.

DON JOHN   I will presently go learn their day of mar- 54
riage.   *Exit* [*with Borachio*].

❧

[2.3]

Enter Benedick alone.

BENEDICK   Boy!

[*Enter Boy.*]

BOY   Signor?

BENEDICK   In my chamber window lies a book. Bring it
hither to me in the orchard. 4

BOY   I am here already, sir. 5

BENEDICK   I know that, but I would have thee hence and
here again.   *Exit* [*Boy*].
I do much wonder that one man, seeing how much
another man is a fool when he dedicates his behaviors
to love, will, after he hath laughed at such shallow follies in others, become the argument of his own scorn 11
by falling in love; and such a man is Claudio. I have
known when there was no music with him but the 13
drum and the fife, and now had he rather hear the 14
tabor and the pipe. I have known when he would have 15
walked ten mile afoot to see a good armor, and now 16
will he lie ten nights awake carving the fashion of a 17
new doublet. He was wont to speak plain and to the 18
purpose, like an honest man and a soldier, and now is
he turned orthography—his words are a very fantas- 20
tical banquet, just so many strange dishes. May I be so
converted and see with these eyes? I cannot tell; I think
not. I will not be sworn but Love may transform me to
an oyster, but I'll take my oath on it, till he have made
an oyster of me, he shall never make me such a fool.
One woman is fair, yet I am well; another is wise, yet
I am well; another virtuous, yet I am well; but till all
graces be in one woman, one woman shall not come
in my grace. Rich she shall be, that's certain; wise, or
I'll none; virtuous, or I'll never cheapen her; fair, or I'll 30
never look on her; mild, or come not near me; noble, 31
or not I for an angel; of good discourse, an excellent 32
musician, and her hair shall be of what color it please
God. Ha! The Prince and Monsieur Love. I will hide
me in the arbor.   [*He hides.*]

Enter Prince [*Don Pedro*], *Leonato, Claudio.*

DON PEDRO   Come, shall we hear this music?

6–7 whatsoever . . . mine whatever crosses his inclination runs parallel
with mine.   12 since ago   16 unseasonable unsuitable, unseemly
21 lies in rests with.   temper mix, compound.   24–5 whose . . . up and
emphasize how much you admire his reputation   25 stale prostitute
27 misuse abuse, deceive   29 issue outcome. (With a pun on children
as the product of marriage; cf. 4.1.132.)   30 despite torture, injure
32 meet suitable   34 Intend Pretend   35 as i.e., saying as follows. (The
words between the dashes are to be understood as instructions to Don
John as to what he is to say.)   37 like likely.   cozened deceived, cheated   38 semblance semblance only, outward appearance.   discovered
revealed   40 instances proofs   42 hear . . . Claudio (Many editors read
Borachio for *Claudio.* The present reading may be defended if one imagines that, by arrangement with Margaret, Borachio is playing the part of
Claudio, but the reading may also be an inconsistency.)
47 jealousy suspicion.   assurance certainty   48 preparation i.e., for
marriage   49 Grow this Let this ripen   51 ducats gold coins.

54 presently immediately
2.3. Location: Leonato's garden.
4 orchard garden   5 I . . . already i.e., I will be so quick as to use no
time at all. (But Benedick quibbles on the literal sense.)   11 argument
subject   13-14 there was . . . fife i.e., his only commitment was to soldiering   15 tabor . . . pipe (Symbols of peaceful merriment and wooing.)   16 armor suit of armor   17 carving planning   18 doublet jacket.
20 turned orthography become fastidious and fashionable in his choice
of language   30 I'll none I'll have none of her.   cheapen make a bid
for. (The idea of lessening her value by using her may also be suggested,
though historically it is a later meaning.)   31, 32 noble, angel (Each of
these words involves a pun on the meaning "a coin," a noble being
worth six shillings eightpence and an angel, ten shillings.)

CLAUDIO
  Yea, my good lord. How still the evening is,
  As hushed on purpose to grace harmony!   38
DON PEDRO [*apart to them*]
  See you where Benedick hath hid himself?
CLAUDIO [*apart in reply*]
  Oh, very well, my lord. The music ended,   40
  We'll fit the kid-fox with a pennyworth.   41

        Enter Balthasar with music.

DON PEDRO
  Come, Balthasar, we'll hear that song again.
BALTHASAR
  Oh, good my lord, tax not so bad a voice   43
  To slander music any more than once.
DON PEDRO
  It is the witness still of excellency   45
  To put a strange face on his own perfection.   46
  I pray thee, sing, and let me woo no more.   47
BALTHASAR
  Because you talk of wooing, I will sing,   48
  Since many a wooer doth commence his suit   49
  To her he thinks not worthy, yet he woos,   50
  Yet will he swear he loves.
DON PEDRO   Nay, pray thee, come,   51
  Or if thou wilt hold longer argument,
  Do it in notes.
BALTHASAR   Note this before my notes: 53
  There's not a note of mine that's worth the noting.
DON PEDRO
  Why, these are very crotchets that he speaks!   55
  Note, notes, forsooth, and nothing.   [*Music.*]   56
BENEDICK [*aside*] Now, divine air! Now is his soul rav-   57
  ished! Is it not strange that sheeps' guts should hale   58
  souls out of men's bodies? Well, a horn for my money,   59
  when all's done.

        The Song.

BALTHASAR
      Sigh no more, ladies, sigh no more.
        Men were deceivers ever,
      One foot in sea and one on shore,
        To one thing constant never.

      Then sigh not so, but let them go,
        And be you blithe and bonny,   66
      Converting all your sounds of woe
        Into Hey nonny, nonny.   68

      Sing no more ditties, sing no moe,   69
        Of dumps so dull and heavy;   70
      The fraud of men was ever so,
        Since summer first was leavy.   72
      Then sigh not so, but let them go,
        And be you blithe and bonny,
      Converting all your sounds of woe
        Into Hey nonny, nonny.

DON PEDRO By my troth, a good song.
BALTHASAR And an ill singer, my lord.
DON PEDRO Ha, no, no, faith, thou sing'st well enough
  for a shift.   80
BENEDICK [*aside*] An he had been a dog that should   81
  have howled thus, they would have hanged him, and
  I pray God his bad voice bode no mischief. I has as
  lief have heard the night raven, come what plague   84
  could have come after it.
DON PEDRO Yea, marry, dost thou hear, Balthasar? I   86
  pray thee, get us some excellent music, for tomorrow
  night we would have it at the Lady Hero's chamber
  window.
BALTHASAR The best I can, my lord.
DON PEDRO Do so. Farewell.   *Exit Balthasar.*
  Come hither, Leonato. What was it you told me of
  today, that your niece Beatrice was in love with Sign-
  or Benedick?
CLAUDIO Oh, ay! [*Aside to Pedro*] Stalk on, stalk on; the   95
  fowl sits.—I did never think that lady would have   96
  loved any man.
LEONATO No, nor I neither, but most wonderful that she
  should so dote on Signor Benedick, whom she hath in
  all outward behaviors seemed ever to abhor.
BENEDICK [*aside*] Is't possible? Sits the wind in that   101
  corner?   102
LEONATO By my troth, my lord, I cannot tell what to
  think of it but that she loves him with an enraged   104
  affection; it is past the infinite of thought.   105
DON PEDRO Maybe she doth but counterfeit.
CLAUDIO Faith, like enough.   107
LEONATO Oh, God, counterfeit? There was never coun-
  terfeit of passion came so near the life of passion as she
  discovers it.   110
DON PEDRO Why, what effects of passion shows she?
CLAUDIO [*aside to them*] Bait the hook well; this fish will
  bite.

---

38 As as if. **grace harmony** do honor to music. **40 The music ended** When the music is over **41 We'll . . . pennyworth** i.e., we'll give our sly victim more than he bargained for. (A *kid-fox* is presumably a young fox, as in beast fable; *kid*, i.e., young goat, also suggests one whom they are stalking as their quarry. Claudio may be referring to some children's game.) **43 tax** task **45–6 It . . . perfection** It is always characteristic of excellence to pretend not to know its own skill. **47 woo** entreat **48–51 Because . . . he loves** (Balthasar modestly claims to be unworthy of being *wooed*, i.e., entreated, but will comply, since he knows Don Pedro speaks with the hyperbole all wooers use in addressing women they actually consider unworthy.) **53 notes** music. **55 crotchets** (1) whims, fancies (2) musical notes of brief duration **56 nothing** (With a pun on *noting*; the two words were pronounced alike. Compare the same pun in the title of the play, where *Nothing* suggests "noting," or eavesdropping.) **57 air** melody. **58 sheeps' guts** strings on musical instruments. **hale** draw **59 a horn** a hunting horn, a more masculine instrument than a lute. (But with a perhaps unconscious allusion to a cuckold's horns.)

66 blithe and bonny cheerful and carefree **68 Hey nonny, nonny** (A nonsense refrain.) **69 moe** more **70 dumps** mournful songs; also, dances **72 leavy** leafy. **80 for a shift** in a pinch. **81 An** If. (Also in line 161.) **84 lief** willingly. **night raven** a bird of night, portending disaster **86 Yea, marry** (A continuation of Don Pedro's speech preceding Benedick's aside.) **95–6 Stalk . . . sits** i.e., Proceed stealthily; the hunted bird is hiding in the bush. **101–2 Sits . . . corner?** Is that the way the wind is blowing? **104 enraged** maddened with passion **105 infinite** farthest reach. (It's unbelievable but true.) **107 like** likely **110 discovers** betrays

LEONATO   What effects, my lord? She will sit you—you 114
heard my daughter tell you how.

CLAUDIO   She did indeed.

DON PEDRO   How, how, I pray you? You amaze me. I
would have thought her spirit had been invincible
against all assaults of affection.

LEONATO   I would have sworn it had, my lord—especially against Benedick.

BENEDICK   [aside]   I should think this a gull but that the 122
white-bearded fellow speaks it. Knavery cannot, sure,
hide himself in such reverence.

CLAUDIO   [apart to them]   He hath ta'en th'infection.
Hold it up.   126

DON PEDRO   Hath she made her affection known to
Benedick?

LEONATO   No, and swears she never will. That's her
torment.

CLAUDIO   'Tis true, indeed. So your daughter says.
"Shall I," says she, "that have so oft encountered him 132
with scorn, write to him that I love him?"

LEONATO   This says she now when she is beginning to
write to him, for she'll be up twenty times a night, and
there will she sit in her smock till she have writ a sheet 136
of paper. My daughter tells us all.

CLAUDIO   Now you talk of a sheet of paper, I remember
a pretty jest your daughter told us of.

LEONATO   Oh, when she had writ it and was reading it
over, she found "Benedick" and "Beatrice" between
the sheet?

CLAUDIO   That.   143

LEONATO   Oh, she tore the letter into a thousand half- 144
pence; railed at herself, that she should be so immod- 145
est to write to one that she knew would flout her. "I 146
measure him," says she, "by my own spirit, for I
should flout him if he writ to me. Yea, though I love
him, I should."

CLAUDIO   Then down upon her knees she falls, weeps,
sobs, beats her heart, tears her hair, prays, curses: "O
sweet Benedick! God give me patience!"

LEONATO   She doth indeed; my daughter says so. And
the ecstasy hath so much overborne her that my 154
daughter is sometime afeard she will do a desperate
outrage to herself. It is very true.

DON PEDRO   It were good that Benedick knew of it by
some other, if she will not discover it.   158

CLAUDIO   To what end? He would make but a sport of
it and torment the poor lady worse.

DON PEDRO   An he should, it were an alms to hang him. 161
She's an excellent sweet lady, and, out of all suspicion, 162
she is virtuous.

CLAUDIO   And she is exceeding wise.

DON PEDRO   In everything but in loving Benedick.

LEONATO   O my lord, wisdom and blood combating in 166

so tender a body, we have ten proofs to one that blood
hath the victory. I am sorry for her, as I have just
cause, being her uncle and her guardian.

DON PEDRO   I would she had bestowed this dotage on 170
me. I would have doffed all other respects and made 171
her half myself. I pray you, tell Benedick of it, and hear 172
what 'a will say.

LEONATO   Were it good, think you?

CLAUDIO   Hero thinks surely she will die; for she says
she will die if he love her not, and she will die ere she
make her love known, and she will die if he woo her,
rather than she will bate one breath of her accustomed 178
crossness.   179

DON PEDRO   She doth well. If she should make tender 180
of her love, 'tis very possible he'll scorn it; for the man,
as you know all, hath a contemptible spirit.   182

CLAUDIO   He is a very proper man.   183

DON PEDRO   He hath indeed a good outward happiness. 184

CLAUDIO   Before God, and in my mind, very wise.   185

DON PEDRO   He doth indeed show some sparks that are
like wit.

CLAUDIO   And I take him to be valiant.

DON PEDRO   As Hector, I assure you; and in the manag- 189
ing of quarrels you may say he is wise, for either he
avoids them with great discretion or undertakes them
with a most Christian-like fear.

LEONATO   If he do fear God, 'a must necessarily keep
peace. If he break the peace, he ought to enter into a
quarrel with fear and trembling.

DON PEDRO   And so will he do, for the man doth fear
God, howsoever it seems not in him by some large 197
jests he will make. Well, I am sorry for your niece. Shall
we go seek Benedick and tell him of her love?

CLAUDIO   Never tell him, my lord. Let her wear it out 200
with good counsel.   201

LEONATO   Nay, that's impossible. She may wear her
heart out first.

DON PEDRO   Well, we will hear further of it by your
daughter. Let it cool the while. I love Benedick well,
and I could wish he would modestly examine himself,
to see how much he is unworthy so good a lady.

LEONATO   My lord, will you walk? Dinner is ready.
                                          [They walk aside.]

CLAUDIO   If he do not dote on her upon this, I will never 209
trust my expectation.

DON PEDRO   Let there be the same net spread for her;
and that must your daughter and her gentlewomen
carry. The sport will be when they hold one an opinion 213
of another's dotage, and no such matter; that's the 214

---

114 **sit you** i.e., sit. (*You* is used idiomatically.)   122 **gull** trick, deception.   **but** except for the fact   126 **Hold it up** Keep up the jest.
132 **she** i.e., Beatrice   136 **smock** chemise   143 **That** i.e., That's it.
144–5 **halfpence** i.e., small pieces   146 **flout** mock   154 **overborne**
overwhelmed   158 **discover** reveal   161 **alms** good deed. (Hanging
would be too good for him.)   162 **out of** beyond   166 **blood** natural
feeling

170 **dotage** doting affection   171 **doffed** put or turned aside.
respects considerations   172 **half myself** i.e., my wife.   178 **bate**
abate   179 **crossness** perversity, contrariety.   180 **tender** offer
182 **contemptible** contemptuous   183 **proper** handsome   184 **outward happiness** fortune in his good looks.   185 **Before God** i.e., By
God, you're absolutely right   189 **Hector** the mightiest of the Trojans   197 **by** to judge by.   **large** broad, indelicate   200 **wear it out**
eradicate it   201 **counsel** reflection, deliberation.   209 **upon** as a
result of, after   213 **carry** carry out.   213–14 **they . . . dotage** each
believes the other to be in love   214 **no such matter** the reality is
quite otherwise

scene that I would see, which will be merely a dumb 215
show. Let us send her to call him in to dinner. 216
[*Exeunt Don Pedro, Claudio, and Leonato.*]
BENEDICK [*coming forward*]   This can be no trick. The
conference was sadly borne. They have the truth of 218
this from Hero. They seem to pity the lady. It seems
her affections have their full bent. Love me? Why, it 220
must be requited. I hear how I am censured. They say
I will bear myself proudly if I perceive the love come
from her; they say too that she will rather die than give
any sign of affection. I did never think to marry. I must
not seem proud; happy are they that hear their detrac- 225
tions and can put them to mending. They say the lady 226
is fair; 'tis a truth, I can bear them witness; and virtuous; 'tis so, I cannot reprove it; and wise but for loving 228
me; by my troth, it is no addition to her wit, nor no
great argument of her folly, for I will be horribly in
love with her. I may chance have some odd quirks and 231
remnants of wit broken on me, because I have railed
so long against marriage. But doth not the appetite
alter? A man loves the meat in his youth that he cannot endure in his age. Shall quips and sentences and 235
these paper bullets of the brain awe a man from the 236
career of his humor? No, the world must be peopled. 237
When I said I would die a bachelor, I did not think I
should live till I were married. Here comes Beatrice.
By this day, she's a fair lady! I do spy some marks of
love in her.

Enter Beatrice.

BEATRICE   Against my will I am sent to bid you come in
to dinner.
BENEDICK   Fair Beatrice, I thank you for your pains.
BEATRICE   I took no more pains for those thanks than
you take pains to thank me. If it had been painful I
would not have come.
BENEDICK   You take pleasure then in the message?
BEATRICE   Yea, just so much as you may take upon a 249
knife's point and choke a daw withal. You have no 250
stomach, signor. Fare you well.   *Exit.* 251
BENEDICK   Ha! "Against my will I am sent to bid you
come in to dinner." There's a double meaning in that.
"I took no more pains for those thanks than you took
pains to thank me." That's as much as to say, "Any
pains that I take for you is as easy as thanks." If I do
not take pity of her, I am a villain; if I do not love her,
I am a Jew. I will go get her picture.   *Exit.*

215–16 **dumb show** pantomime (lacking their usual banter)
218 **sadly borne** soberly conducted.   220 **have . . . bent** i.e., are fully
engaged. (The image is of a bow pulled taut.)   225–6 **that . . . mending** that can hear themselves criticized and undertake to remedy the
defect.   228 **reprove** refute   231 **quirks** witty conceits or jokes
235 **sentences** saws, maxims   236 **paper bullets** i.e., words
237 **career of his humor** pursuit of his inclination. (In horsemanship,
a *career* is a short gallop.)   249–50 **just . . . withal** i.e., very little. (A
daw or jackdaw is a common blackbird, smaller than a crow.)
251 **stomach** appetite

[3.1]

*Enter Hero and two gentlewomen, Margaret
and Ursula.*

HERO
Good Margaret, run thee to the parlor.
There shalt thou find my cousin Beatrice
Proposing with the Prince and Claudio.   3
Whisper her ear and tell her I and Ursley   4
Walk in the orchard, and our whole discourse
Is all of her. Say that thou overheard'st us,
And bid her steal into the pleachèd bower,   7
Where honeysuckles, ripened by the sun,
Forbid the sun to enter, like favorites,
Made proud by princes, that advance their pride   10
Against that power that bred it. There will she hide
her,   11
To listen our propose. This is thy office.   12
Bear thee well in it and leave us alone.   13
MARGARET
I'll make her come, I warrant you, presently.   [*Exit.*] 14
HERO
Now, Ursula, when Beatrice doth come,
As we do trace this alley up and down,   16
Our talk must only be of Benedick.
When I do name him, let it be thy part
To praise him more than ever man did merit.
My talk to thee must be how Benedick
Is sick in love with Beatrice. Of this matter
Is little Cupid's crafty arrow made,
That only wounds by hearsay.

Enter Beatrice [behind].

                              Now begin,   23
For look where Beatrice, like a lapwing, runs   24
Close by the ground, to hear our conference.
URSULA [*to Hero*]
The pleasant'st angling is to see the fish
Cut with her golden oars the silver stream   27
And greedily devour the treacherous bait.
So angle we for Beatrice, who even now
Is couchèd in the woodbine coverture.   30
Fear you not my part of the dialogue.   31
HERO [*to Ursula*]
Then go we near her, that her ear lose nothing
Of the false sweet bait that we lay for it.
                              [*They approach the bower.*]
No, truly, Ursula, she is too disdainful;
I know her spirits are as coy and wild   35
As haggards of the rock.
URSULA   But are you sure   36

3.1 **Location: Leonato's garden.**
3 **Proposing** conversing   4 **Ursley** (A nickname for *Ursula*).
7 **pleachèd** formed by densely interwoven branches   10–11 **that . . . it**
i.e., who dare set themselves up against the very princes who advanced
them.   12 **listen our propose** listen to our conversation.   **office** responsibility.   13 **leave us alone** leave the rest to us.   14 **presently** immediately.   16 **trace** walk   23 **only . . . hearsay** wounds by mere report.
24 **lapwing** bird of the plover family   27 **oars** i.e., fins   30 **Is . . . coverture** is hid in the honeysuckle bower.   31 **Fear . . . dialogue** Don't worry
about my not holding up my part in the conversation.   35 **coy** disdainful   36 **As . . . rock** as untamed female hawks in mountainous terrain.

That Benedick loves Beatrice so entirely?

HERO
So says the Prince and my new-trothèd lord.

URSULA
And did they bid you tell her of it, madam?

HERO
They did entreat me to acquaint her of it;
But I persuaded them, if they loved Benedick,
To wish him wrestle with affection
And never to let Beatrice know of it.

URSULA
Why did you so? Doth not the gentleman
Deserve as full as fortunate a bed   45
As ever Beatrice shall couch upon?   46

HERO
O god of love! I know he doth deserve
As much as may be yielded to a man;
But Nature never framed a woman's heart
Of prouder stuff than that of Beatrice.
Disdain and scorn ride sparkling in her eyes,
Misprizing what they look on, and her wit   52
Values itself so highly that to her
All matter else seems weak. She cannot love,   54
Nor take no shape nor project of affection,   55
She is so self-endearèd.

URSULA   Sure I think so,   56
And therefore certainly it were not good
She knew his love, lest she'll make sport at it.

HERO
Why, you speak truth. I never yet saw man,
How wise, how noble, young, how rarely featured,   60
But she would spell him backward. If fair-faced,   61
She would swear the gentleman should be her
    sister;
If black, why, Nature, drawing of an antic,   63
Made a foul blot; if tall, a lance ill-headed;
If low, an agate very vilely cut;   65
If speaking, why, a vane blown with all winds;
If silent, why, a block movèd with none.
So turns she every man the wrong side out
And never gives to truth and virtue that
Which simpleness and merit purchaseth.   70

URSULA
Sure, sure, such carping is not commendable.

HERO
No, not to be so odd and from all fashions   72
As Beatrice is cannot be commendable.
But who dare tell her so? If I should speak,
She would mock me into air; oh, she would laugh me   75
Out of myself, press me to death with wit.   76

Therefore let Benedick, like covered fire,
Consume away in sighs, waste inwardly.   78
It were a better death than die with mocks,
Which is as bad as die with tickling.

URSULA
Yet tell her of it. Hear what she will say.

HERO
No, rather I will go to Benedick
And counsel him to fight against his passion.
And truly, I'll devise some honest slanders   84
To stain my cousin with. One doth not know
How much an ill word may empoison liking.

URSULA
Oh, do not do your cousin such a wrong!
She cannot be so much without true judgment—
Having so swift and excellent a wit
As she is prized to have—as to refuse   90
So rare a gentleman as Signor Benedick.

HERO
He is the only man of Italy,
Always excepted my dear Claudio.

URSULA
I pray you, be not angry with me, madam,
Speaking my fancy: Signor Benedick,
For shape, for bearing, argument, and valor,   96
Goes foremost in report through Italy.

HERO
Indeed, he hath an excellent good name.

URSULA
His excellence did earn it ere he had it.
When are you married, madam?

HERO
Why, every day, tomorrow. Come, go in.   101
I'll show thee some attires and have thy counsel
Which is the best to furnish me tomorrow.
                             [*They walk away.*]

URSULA [*to Hero*]
She's limed, I warrant you. We have caught her,
    madam.   104

HERO [*to Ursula*]
If it prove so, then loving goes by haps;   105
Some Cupid kills with arrows, some with traps.   106
                [*Exeunt Hero and Ursula.*]

BEATRICE [*coming forward*]
What fire is in mine ears? Can this be true?   107
    Stand I condemned for pride and scorn so much?
Contempt, farewell, and maiden pride, adieu!
    No glory lives behind the back of such.   110
And Benedick, love on; I will requite thee,
    Taming my wild heart to thy loving hand.   112

45–6 as full . . . upon i.e., as good a wife as Beatrice. **52 Misprizing** undervaluing, despising **54 weak** unimportant. **55 project** conception, idea **56 self-endearèd** full of self-love. **60 How** however. **rarely** excellently **61 spell him backward** i.e., speak contrarily of him by characterizing his virtues as vices. **63 black** dark. **antic** buffoon, grotesque figure **65 agate** i.e., diminutive person. (Alluding to the small figures cut in agate for rings.) **70 simpleness** integrity, plainness. **purchaseth** earn, deserve. **72 from** contrary to **75–6 she . . . myself** she would mockingly put me down **76 press me to death** (Pressing to death with weights was the usual punishment for those accused of crimes who refused to plead either guilty or not guilty.)

78 Consume . . . sighs (An allusion to the belief that each sigh cost the heart a drop of blood.) **84 honest slanders** i.e., slanders that do not involve her virtue **90 prized** esteemed **96 argument** skill in discourse **101 every day, tomorrow** tomorrow and every day thereafter. **104 limed** caught, like a bird in birdlime, a sticky substance spread on branches to trap the birds that perch on them **105 by haps** by chance **106 Some Cupid kills** Cupid kills some **107 What . . . ears?** (An allusion to the old saying that a person's ears burn when one is being discussed in one's absence.) **110 No . . . such** Nothing is gained by hiding behind such defenses. **112 Taming . . . hand** (A figure derived from the taming of the hawk by the hand of the falconer.)

If thou dost love, my kindness shall incite thee
   To bind our loves up in a holy band;   114
For others say thou dost deserve, and I
Believe it better than reportingly.   *Exit.* 116

❦

[3.2]

*Enter Prince [Don Pedro], Claudio, Benedick,
and Leonato.*

DON PEDRO   I do but stay till your marriage be con- 1
summate, and then go I toward Aragon. 2
CLAUDIO   I'll bring you thither, my lord, if you'll 3
vouchsafe me. 4
DON PEDRO   Nay, that would be as great a soil in the 5
new gloss of your marriage as to show a child his new
coat and forbid him to wear it. I will only be bold with 7
Benedick for his company, for from the crown of his
head to the sole of his foot he is all mirth. He hath
twice or thrice cut Cupid's bowstring, and the little
hangman dare not shoot at him. He hath a heart as 11
sound as a bell, and his tongue is the clapper, for what
his heart thinks his tongue speaks.
BENEDICK   Gallants, I am not as I have been.
LEONATO   So say I. Methinks you are sadder. 15
CLAUDIO   I hope he be in love.
DON PEDRO   Hang him, truant! There's no true drop of 17
blood in him, to be truly touched with love. If he be
sad, he wants money. 19
BENEDICK   I have the toothache. 20
DON PEDRO   Draw it. 21
BENEDICK   Hang it! 22
CLAUDIO   You must hang it first and draw it after-
wards.
DON PEDRO   What, sigh for the toothache?
LEONATO   Where is but a humor or a worm. 26
BENEDICK   Well, everyone can master a grief but he that 27
has it.
CLAUDIO   Yet say I, he is in love.
DON PEDRO   There is no appearance of fancy in him, 30
unless it be a fancy that he hath to strange disguises; 31
as, to be a Dutchman today, a Frenchman tomorrow,
or in the shape of two countries at once, as, a German
from the waist downward, all slops, and a Spaniard 34
from the hip upward, no doublet. Unless he have a 35

fancy to this foolery, as it appears he hath, he is no fool 36
for fancy, as you would have it appear he is. 37
CLAUDIO   If he be not in love with some woman, there
is no believing old signs. 'A brushes his hat o'
mornings. What should that bode?
DON PEDRO   Hath any man seen him at the barber's?
CLAUDIO   No, but the barber's man hath been seen with
him, and the old ornament of his cheek hath already 43
stuffed tennis balls. 44
LEONATO   Indeed he looks younger than he did by the
loss of a beard.
DON PEDRO   Nay, 'a rubs himself with civet. Can you 47
smell him out by that? 48
CLAUDIO   That's as much as to say the sweet youth's in
love.
DON PEDRO   The greatest note of it is his melancholy. 51
CLAUDIO   And when was he wont to wash his face? 52
DON PEDRO   Yea, or to paint himself? For the which I 53
hear what they say of him. 54
CLAUDIO   Nay, but his jesting spirit, which is now crept
into a lute string and now governed by stops. 56
DON PEDRO   Indeed, that tells a heavy tale for him.
Conclude, conclude he is in love.
CLAUDIO   Nay, but I know who loves him.
DON PEDRO   That would I know too. I warrant, one that
knows him not.
CLAUDIO   Yes, and his ill conditions; and, in despite of 62
all, dies for him.
DON PEDRO   She shall be buried with her face upwards. 64
BENEDICK   Yet is this no charm for the toothache. Old
signor, walk aside with me. I have studied eight or
nine wise words to speak to you, which these hobby- 67
horses must not hear.   *[Exeunt Benedick and Leonato.]* 68
DON PEDRO   For my life, to break with him about 69
Beatrice.
CLAUDIO   'Tis even so. Hero and Margaret have by this 71
played their parts with Beatrice, and then the two
bears will not bite one another when they meet.

Enter [Don] John the Bastard.

DON JOHN   My lord and brother, God save you!
DON PEDRO   Good e'en, brother. 75
DON JOHN   If your leisure served, I would speak with
you.
DON PEDRO   In private?

---

114 **band** bond   116 **better than reportingly** on better evidence than mere report.
3.2. Location: Leonato's house.
1–2 **consummate** consummated   3 **bring** escort   4 **vouchsafe** allow
5 **soil** stain   7 **be bold with** ask   11 **hangman** executioner; rogue. (Playfully applied to Cupid.)   15 **sadder** more serious.   17 **truant** i.e., from love.   19 **wants** lacks   20 **toothache** (Thought to be a common ailment of lovers.)   21 **Draw** Extract. (But Claudio jokes on the method of executing traitors, who were hanged first and then cut down alive and drawn, i.e., disemboweled, and finally quartered.)   22 **Hang it!** Confound it!   26 **Where** Where there.   **humor or a worm** (A toothache was ascribed to "humors," or unhealthy secretions, and to actual worms in the teeth.)   27 **grief** pain.   **but** except   30 **fancy** love   31 **fancy** whim, liking   34 **slops** loose breeches   35 **no doublet** i.e., with a hip-length cloak in place of, or covering, the close-fitting doublet.

36–7 **fool for fancy** i.e., lover   43–4 **the old . . . tennis balls** i.e., Benedick's beard has gone to stuff tennis balls. (He appears on stage beardless in this scene for the first time.)   47 **civet** perfume derived from the civet cat.   48 **smell him out** (1) discern his secret (2) smell him coming   51 **note** mark   52 **wont** accustomed.   **wash** i.e., with cosmetics; similarly with *paint* in the next line   53–4 **For . . . him** That's what I hear people saying about him.   56 **stops** (1) frets on the fingerboard (2) restraints.   62 **ill conditions** bad qualities   64 **buried . . . upwards** i.e., as the faithful, not as a suicide, who were sometimes buried face downwards (?). (There is also a sexual suggestion of her being smothered under Benedick, continuing the joke on *dies for him,* meaning to have an orgasm.)   67–8 **hobbyhorses** i.e., buffoons. (Originally, figures in a morris dance made to resemble a horse and rider.)   69 **For** Upon.   **break** speak   71 **Margaret** (Ursula joined Hero in playing the trick on Beatrice, but Margaret has been in on it.)   75 **e'en** evening, i.e., afternoon

DON JOHN   If it please you. Yet Count Claudio may hear,
for what I would speak of concerns him.

DON PEDRO   What's the matter?

DON JOHN   [to Claudio]   Means Your Lordship to be married tomorrow?

DON PEDRO   You know he does.

DON JOHN   I know not that, when he knows what I
know.

CLAUDIO   If there be any impediment, I pray you
discover it.   88

DON JOHN   You may think I love you not. Let that
appear hereafter, and aim better at me by that I now   90
will manifest. For my brother, I think he holds you   91
well and in dearness of heart hath holp to effect your   92
ensuing marriage—surely suit ill spent and labor ill
bestowed.

DON PEDRO   Why, what's the matter?

DON JOHN   I came hither to tell you, and, circumstances   96
shortened—for she has been too long a-talking of—   97
the lady is disloyal.   98

CLAUDIO   Who, Hero?

DON JOHN   Even she—Leonato's Hero, your Hero,
every man's Hero.

CLAUDIO   Disloyal?

DON JOHN   The word is too good to paint out her   103
wickedness. I could say she were worse; think you of
a worse title, and I will fit her to it. Wonder not till fur-   105
ther warrant. Go but with me tonight, you shall see her   106
chamber window entered, even the night before her
wedding day. If you love her then, tomorrow wed her;
but it would better fit your honor to change your
mind.

CLAUDIO   May this be so?

DON PEDRO   I will not think it.

DON JOHN   If you dare not trust that you see, confess not   113
that you know. If you will follow me, I will show you   114
enough; and when you have seen more and heard
more, proceed accordingly.

CLAUDIO   If I see anything tonight why I should not
marry her, tomorrow in the congregation, where I
should wed, there will I shame her.

DON PEDRO   And, as I wooed for thee to obtain her, I
will join with thee to disgrace her.

DON JOHN   I will disparage her no farther till you are my
witnesses. Bear it coldly but till midnight, and let the   123
issue show itself.   124

DON PEDRO   O day untowardly turned!   125

CLAUDIO   O mischief strangely thwarting!

DON JOHN   O plague right well prevented! So will you
say when you have seen the sequel.   [Exeunt.]

88 **discover** reveal   90 **aim better at** judge better of.   **that** that which
91–2 **holds you well** thinks well of you   92 **holp** helped   96–7 **circumstances shortened** without unnecessary details   97 **a-talking of**
under discussion (by us)   98 **disloyal** unfaithful.   103 **paint out** portray in full   105–6 **till further warrant** till further proof appears.
113–14 **If . . . know** i.e., If you are unwilling to believe what you see,
then don't claim to know the truth.   123 **coldly** calmly   124 **issue**
outcome   125 **untowardly turned** wretchedly altered.

[3.3]

*Enter Dogberry and his compartner [Verges]
with the Watch.*

DOGBERRY   Are you good men and true?

VERGES   Yea, or else it were pity but they should suffer
salvation, body and soul.   3

DOGBERRY   Nay, that were a punishment too good for
them, if they should have any allegiance in them,   5
being chosen for the Prince's watch.

VERGES   Well, give them their charge, neighbor Dog-   7
berry.

DOGBERRY   First, who think you the most desartless   9
man to be constable?

FIRST WATCH   Hugh Oatcake, sir, or George Seacoal, for
they can write and read.

DOGBERRY   Come hither, neighbor Seacoal. [*Seacoal, or
Second Watch, steps forward.*] God hath blessed you
with a good name. To be a well-favored man is the gift   15
of fortune, but to write and read comes by nature.

SEACOAL   Both which, Master Constable—

DOGBERRY   You have. I knew it would be your answer.
Well, for your favor, sir, why, give God thanks, and
make no boast of it; and for your writing and reading,
let that appear when there is no need of such vanity.
You are thought here to be the most senseless and fit   22
man for the constable of the watch; therefore bear you
the lantern. This is your charge: you shall comprehend   24
all vagrom men; you are to bid any man stand, in the   25
Prince's name.

SEACOAL   How if 'a will not stand?

DOGBERRY   Why, then, take no note of him, but let him
go, and presently call the rest of the watch together
and thank God you are rid of a knave.

VERGES   If he will not stand when he is bidden, he is
none of the Prince's subjects.

DOGBERRY   True, and they are to meddle with none but
the Prince's subjects. You shall also make no noise in
the streets; for, for the watch to babble and to talk is
most tolerable and not to be endured.   36

WATCH   We will rather sleep than talk. We know what
belongs to a watch.   38

DOGBERRY   Why, you speak like an ancient and most   39
quiet watchman, for I cannot see how sleeping should
offend. Only have a care that your bills be not stolen.   41
Well, you are to call at all the alehouses and bid those
that are drunk get them to bed.

WATCH   How if they will not?

3.3. Location: A street.
3 salvation (A blunder for "damnation.")   **5 allegiance** (For "treachery.")   **7 charge** instructions   **9 desartless** (For "deserving.")
15 a good name (Sea coal was high-grade coal shipped from Newcas-
tle, not the charcoal usually sold by London colliers.)   **well-favored**
good-looking   **22 senseless** (For "sensible.")   **24 comprehend** (For
"apprehend.")   **25 vagrom** vagrant.   **stand** stand still, stop   **36 tolerable** (For "intolerable.")   **37 WATCH** (Here and at lines 44, 48, 53,
and 66 Shakespeare's text does not specify which watchman speaks.
These lines are sometimes assigned to the Second Watch, Seacoal, but
could be spoken by others of the watch.)   **38 belongs to** are the
duties of   **39 ancient** venerable, experienced   **41 bills** pikes, with
axes fixed to long poles

DOGBERRY   Why, then, let them alone till they are sober. If they make you not then the better answer, you may say they are not the men you took them for.

WATCH   Well, sir.

DOGBERRY   If you meet a thief, you may suspect him, by virtue of your office, to be no true man; and for such 50 kind of men, the less you meddle or make with them, 51 why, the more is for your honesty. 52

WATCH   If we know him to be a thief, shall we not lay hands on him?

DOGBERRY   Truly, by your office you may, but I think they that touch pitch will be defiled. The most 56 peaceable way for you, if you do take a thief, is to let him show himself what he is and steal out of your company.

VERGES   You have been always called a merciful man, partner.

DOGBERRY   Truly, I would not hang a dog by my will, much more a man who hath any honesty in him.

VERGES   If you hear a child cry in the night, you must call to the nurse and bid her still it.

WATCH   How if the nurse be asleep and will not hear us?

DOGBERRY   Why, then, depart in peace and let the child wake her with crying, for the ewe that will not hear her lamb when it baas will never answer a calf when he bleats.

VERGES   'Tis very true.

DOGBERRY   This is the end of the charge: you, Constable, are to present the Prince's own person. If you meet 74 the Prince in the night, you may stay him.

VERGES   Nay, by'r Lady, that I think 'a cannot. 76

DOGBERRY   Five shillings to one on't, with any man that knows the statutes, he may stay him; marry, not without the Prince be willing, for indeed the watch ought to offend no man, and it is an offense to stay a man against his will.

VERGES   By'r Lady, I think it be so.

DOGBERRY   Ha, ah ha! Well, masters, good night. An there be any matter of weight chances, call up me. Keep your fellows' counsels and your own, and good night. Come, neighbor. [*He starts to leave with Verges.*]

SEACOAL   Well, masters, we hear our charge. Let us go sit here upon the church bench till two, and then all to bed.

DOGBERRY   One word more, honest neighbors. I pray you, watch about Signor Leonato's door, for the wedding being there tomorrow, there is a great coil 92 tonight. Adieu. Be vigitant, I beseech you. 93

Exeunt [Dogberry and Verges].

Enter Borachio and Conrade.

BORACHIO   What, Conrade!

SEACOAL   [*aside*]   Peace! Stir not.

BORACHIO   Conrade, I say!

CONRADE   Here, man. I am at thy elbow.

BORACHIO   Mass, and my elbow itched; I thought there 98 would a scab follow. 99

CONRADE   I will owe thee an answer for that. And now, 100 forward with thy tale.

BORACHIO   Stand thee close, then, under this penthouse, 102 for it drizzles rain, and I will, like a true drunkard, 103 utter all to thee.

SEACOAL   [*aside*]   Some treason, masters. Yet stand 105 close. 106

BORACHIO   Therefore know I have earned of Don John a thousand ducats.

CONRADE   Is it possible that any villainy should be so dear? 110

BORACHIO   Thou shouldst rather ask if it were possible any villainy should be so rich; for when rich villains 112 have need of poor ones, poor ones may make what price they will.

CONRADE   I wonder at it.

BORACHIO   That shows thou art unconfirmed. Thou 116 knowest that the fashion of a doublet, or a hat, or a cloak, is nothing to a man. 118

CONRADE   Yes, it is apparel.

BORACHIO   I mean, the fashion. 120

CONRADE   Yes, the fashion is the fashion.

BORACHIO   Tush, I may as well say the fool's the fool. But see'st thou not what a deformed thief this fashion 123 is?

SEACOAL   [*aside*]   I know that Deformed. 'A has been a vile thief this seven year; 'a goes up and down like a 126 gentleman. I remember his name.

BORACHIO   Didst thou not hear somebody?

CONRADE   No, 'twas the vane on the house.

BORACHIO   See'st thou not, I say, what a deformed thief this fashion is, how giddily 'a turns about all the hot bloods between fourteen and five-and-thirty, sometimes fashioning them like Pharaoh's soldiers in the reechy painting, sometime like god Bel's priests in the 134 old church-window, sometime like the shaven 135 Hercules in the smirched worm-eaten tapestry, where 136 his codpiece seems as massy as his club? 137

---

98 **Mass** i.e., By the Mass.   **my elbow itched** (Proverbially, a warning against questionable companions.)   99 **scab** i.e., scoundrel. (With play on literal meaning.)   100 **owe thee an answer** answer later
102 **penthouse** overhanging structure   103 **true drunkard** (Alludes to the commonplace that the drunkard tells all; Borachio's name in Spanish means "drunkard.")   105–6 **stand close** stay hidden.
110 **dear** expensive.   112 **rich** well-paid   116 **unconfirmed** inexperienced.   118 **is . . . man** does not make the man. (But Conrade plays on the phrase in the sense of "means nothing to a man.")   120 **I . . . fashion** i.e., My emphasis was on the mere fashion, not on the apparel itself. (But Conrade wittily refuses to allow the difference.)
123 **deformed thief** i.e., so called because fashion takes such varied and extreme shapes and because it impoverishes those who follow fashion   126 **up and down** about, here and there   134 **reechy** dirty, grimy. (Perhaps this painting is of the Israelites passing through the Red Sea.)   **god Bel's priests** (Probably alludes to the story of Bel and the Dragon, from the apocryphal Book of Daniel, depicted in a stained-glass window.)   135–6 **shaven Hercules** (A reference either to young Hercules at the crossroads, choosing between virtue and vice, or in the service of Omphale—see 2.1.242, note—or, confusedly, to the story of Samson.)   137 **codpiece** decorative pouch at the front of a man's breeches (indelicately conspicuous in this tapestry)

---

50 **true** honest   51 **meddle or make** have to do   52 **is** it is   56 **they . . . defiled** (A commonplace, derived from Ecclesiasticus 13:1.)
74 **present** represent   76 **by'r Lady** i.e., by Our Lady. (A mild oath.)
92 **coil** to-do   93 **vigitant** (For "vigilant.")

CONRADE   All this I see, and I see that the fashion wears 138
out more apparel than the man. But art not thou 139
thyself giddy with the fashion, too, that thou hast
shifted out of thy tale into telling me of the fashion?
BORACHIO   Not so, neither. But know that I have tonight
wooed Margaret, the Lady Hero's gentlewoman, by
the name of Hero. She leans me out at her mistress' 144
chamber window, bids me a thousand times good
night—I tell this tale vilely; I should first tell thee how
the Prince, Claudio, and my master, planted and
placed and possessed by my master Don John, saw 148
afar off in the orchard this amiable encounter. 149
CONRADE   And thought they Margaret was Hero?
BORACHIO   Two of them did, the Prince and Claudio,
but the devil my master knew she was Margaret; and
partly by his oaths, which first possessed them, partly by the dark night, which did deceive them, but
chiefly by my villainy, which did confirm any slander
that Don John had made, away went Claudio enraged;
swore he would meet her, as he was appointed, next
morning at the temple, and there, before the whole
congregation, shame her with what he saw o'ernight
and send her home again without a husband.
SEACOAL   We charge you, in the Prince's name, stand!
FIRST WATCH   Call up the Right Master Constable. We 162
have here recovered the most dangerous piece of 163
lechery that ever was known in the commonwealth. 164
SEACOAL   And one Deformed is one of them. I know
him; 'a wears a lock. 166
CONRADE   Masters, masters—
FIRST WATCH   You'll be made bring Deformed forth, I
warrant you.
CONRADE   Masters—
SEACOAL   Never speak, we charge you. Let us obey you 171
to go with us.
BORACHIO   We are like to prove a goodly commodity, 173
being taken up of these men's bills. 174
CONRADE   A commodity in question, I warrant you. 175
Come, we'll obey you.   *Exeunt.*

[3.4]

Enter Hero, and Margaret and Ursula.

HERO   Good Ursula, wake my cousin Beatrice, and
desire her to rise.
URSULA   I will, lady.
HERO   And bid her come hither.
URSULA   Well.   [*Exit.*]   5

MARGARET   Troth, I think your other rabato were better.   6
HERO   No, pray thee, good Meg, I'll wear this.
MARGARET   By my troth, 's not so good, and I warrant   8
your cousin will say so.
HERO   My cousin's a fool, and thou art another. I'll wear
none but this.
MARGARET   I like the new tire within excellently, if the   12
hair were a thought browner; and your gown's a most   13
rare fashion, i'faith. I saw the Duchess of Milan's gown
that they praise so.
HERO   Oh, that exceeds, they say.   16
MARGARET   By my troth, 's but a nightgown in respect   17
of yours: cloth o' gold, and cuts, and laced with silver,   18
set with pearls, down sleeves, side sleeves, and skirts,   19
round underborne with a bluish tinsel. But for a fine,   20
quaint, graceful, and excellent fashion, yours is worth   21
ten on't.   22
HERO   God give me joy to wear it! For my heart is
exceeding heavy.
MARGARET   'Twill be heavier soon by the weight of a
man.
HERO   Fie upon thee! Art not ashamed?
MARGARET   Of what, lady? Of speaking honorably? Is
not marriage honorable in a beggar? Is not your lord   29
honorable without marriage? I think you would have
me say, "saving your reverence, a husband." An bad   31
thinking do not wrest true speaking, I'll offend   32
nobody. Is there any harm in "the heavier for a husband"? None, I think, an it be the right husband and
the right wife; otherwise 'tis light, and not heavy. Ask   35
my Lady Beatrice else. Here she comes.

Enter Beatrice.

HERO   Good morrow, coz.
BEATRICE   Good morrow, sweet Hero.
HERO   Why, how now? Do you speak in the sick tune?   39
BEATRICE   I am out of all other tune, methinks.
MARGARET   Clap 's into "Light o 'love." That goes   41
without a burden; do you sing it, and I'll dance it.   42
BEATRICE   Ye light o' love with your heels! Then, if your   43
husband have stables enough, you'll see he shall lack
no barns.   45
MARGARET   Oh, illegitimate construction! I scorn that   46
with my heels.   47

138–9 **fashion . . . man** i.e., fashion prompts the discarding of clothes
faster than honest use.   144 **leans me** leans. (*Me* is an emphatic
marker.)   148 **possessed** (misleadingly) informed; also, perhaps, possessed, as by the devil   149 **amiable** amorous   162 **Right Master
Constable** (A comic title on the pattern of "Right Worshipful," etc.)
163 **recovered** (For "discovered.")   164 **lechery** (For "treachery.")
166 **lock** lock of hair hanging down on the left shoulder; the lovelock.
171 **obey** (For "oblige," "command.")   173 **commodity** goods
acquired   174 **taken up** (1) arrested (2) obtained on credit.   **bills**
(1) pikes (2) bonds given as security.   175 **in question** (1) subject to
judicial examination (2) of doubtful value
3.4. Location: Leonato's house.
5 **Well** Very well, as you wish.

6 **rabato** tall collar supporting a ruff, stiffened with wire or starch
8 **troth, 's** faith, it is   12 **tire within** headdress in the inner room
13 **hair** hairpiece attached to the *tire* (line 12)   16 **exceeds** i.e., exceeds
comparison   17 **nightgown** dressing gown   17–18 **in respect of** compared to   18 **cuts . . . silver** slashes in a garment revealing the underlying fabic, and laced with silver thread   19 **down sleeves** tight-fitting
sleeves to the wrist.   **side sleeves** secondary ornamental sleeves hanging from the shoulder   20 **round underborne** with a lining around the
edge of the skirt.   **tinsel** cloth, usually silk, interwoven with threads of
silver or gold.   21 **quaint** elegant   22 **on't** of it.   29 **in** even in
31 **saving . . . husband** (By this apologetic formula, Margaret suggests
that Hero is too prudish even to hear the word *husband* mentioned.)
An bad If bawdy   32 **wrest** misinterpret   35 **light** harmless. (With a
play on the meaning "wanton."   39 **tune** i.e., mood.   41 **Clap 's** Let's
shift.   **Light o' love** (A popular song.)   42 **burden** bass accompaniment. (With play on the idea of "the weight of a man.")   43 **Ye . . .
heels!** i.e., You're light-heeled, wanton!   45 **barns** (With pun on
"bairns," children.)   46 **illegitimate construction** false inference. (But
with a play on the idea of bastard "bairns.")   47 **with my heels** (A
proverbial expression of scorn.)

BEATRICE   'Tis almost five o'clock, cousin; 'tis time you were ready. By my troth, I am exceeding ill. Heigh-ho!

MARGARET   For a hawk, a horse, or a husband? 50

BEATRICE   For the letter that begins them all, H. 51

MARGARET   Well, an you be not turned Turk, there's no 52
more sailing by the star. 53

BEATRICE   What means the fool, trow? 54

MARGARET   Nothing, I; but God send everyone their heart's desire!

HERO   These gloves the Count sent me, they are an excellent perfume. 58

BEATRICE   I am stuffed, cousin. I cannot smell. 59

MARGARET   A maid, and stuffed! There's goodly catching of cold.

BEATRICE   Oh, God help me, God help me! How long have you professed apprehension? 63

MARGARET   Ever since you left it. Doth not my wit 64
become me rarely?

BEATRICE   It is not seen enough; you should wear it in 66
your cap. By my troth, I am sick. 67

MARGARET   Get you some of this distilled *carduus bene-* 68
dictus, and lay it to your heart. It is the only thing for a 69
qualm. 70

HERO   There thou prick'st her with a thistle.

BEATRICE   *Benedictus!* Why *benedictus?* You have some moral in this *benedictus.* 73

MARGARET   Moral? No, by my troth, I have no moral meaning, I meant plain holy thistle. You may think 75
perchance that I think you are in love. Nay, by'r Lady, I am not such a fool to think what I list, nor I list not to 77
think what I can, nor indeed I cannot think, if I would think my heart out of thinking, that you are in love or 79
that you will be in love or that you can be in love. Yet Benedick was such another, and now is he become a 81
man. He swore he would never marry, and yet now, 82
in despite of his heart, he eats his meat without grudg- 83
ing; and how you may be converted I know not, but 84
methinks you look with your eyes as other women do.

BEATRICE   What pace is this that thy tongue keeps?

MARGARET   Not a false gallop. 87

Enter Ursula.

URSULA   Madam, withdraw. The Prince, the Count, Signor Benedick, Don John, and all the gallants of the town are come to fetch you to church.

HERO   Help to dress me, good coz, good Meg, good Ursula.   [*Exeunt.*]

[3.5]

*Enter Leonato and the Constable [Dogberry]
and the Headborough [Verges].*

LEONATO   What would you with me, honest neighbor?

DOGBERRY   Marry, sir, I would have some confidence 2
with you that decerns you nearly. 3

LEONATO   Brief, I pray you, for you see it is a busy time with me.

DOGBERRY   Marry, this it is, sir.

VERGES   Yes, in truth it is, sir.

LEONATO   What is it, my good friends?

DOGBERRY   Goodman Verges, sir, speaks a little off the 9
matter—an old man, sir, and his wits are not so blunt 10
as, God help, I would desire they were, but, in faith, honest as the skin between his brows. 12

VERGES   Yes, I thank God I am as honest as any man living that is an old man and no honester than I.

DOGBERRY   Comparisons are odorous. *Palabras,* neigh- 15
bor Verges.

LEONATO   Neighbors, you are tedious.

DOGBERRY   It pleases Your Worship to say so, but we are the poor Duke's officers. But truly, for mine own part, 19
if I were as tedious as a king, I could find in my heart 20
to bestow it all of Your Worship. 21

LEONATO   All thy tediousness on me, ah?

DOGBERRY   Yea, an 'twere a thousand pound more than 'tis; for I hear as good exclamation on Your Worship as 24
of any man in the city, and though I be but a poor man, I am glad to hear it.

VERGES   And so am I.

LEONATO   I would fain know what you have to say.

VERGES   Marry, sir, our watch tonight, excepting Your 29
Worship's presence, ha' ta'en a couple of as arrant 30
knaves as any in Messina.

DOGBERRY   A good old man, sir; he will be talking. As they say, when the age is in, the wit is out. God help 33
us, it is a world to see! Well said, i'faith, neighbor 34

---

50 For . . . husband? (*Heigh-ho* might be a cry of encouragement in the hunt or else "Heigh-ho for a husband!" as at 2.1.305.)   51 H (With a pun on "ache," pronounced "aitch." Beatrice complains of aching of a cold.)   52 turned Turk i.e., turned apostate to the true faith (by violating your oath not to become a lover)   52–3 no . . . star no more navigating by the North Star, i.e., no certain truth in which to trust.   54 trow I wonder.   58 perfume (Gloves were often perfumed.)   59 stuffed i.e., stuffed up with a cold. (But Margaret takes it in a bawdy sense.)   63 professed apprehension made claim to be witty.   64 left it gave it up. (Margaret gibes at Beatrice's pretending not to know what the joking is all about.)   66–7 wear . . . cap i.e., wear it prominently visible, as a fool wears his coxcomb. (Beatrice jokes that Margaret's supposed wit is imperceptible.)   68–9 *carduus benedictus* the blessed thistle, noted for medicinal properties. (With a pun on "Benedick.")   70 a qualm an attack of nausea (or misgiving).   73 moral hidden meaning   75 holy thistle the blessed thistle or *carduus benedictus* of 68–9.   77 list please   79 think . . . thinking i.e., rack my brains   81 such another i.e., seemingly proof against love   81–2 a man i.e., like other men.   83–4 eats . . . grudging i.e., is content to be like other men, to be in love   87 Not . . . gallop. i.e., I'm not speaking at a false pace, at a canter; I speak the truth.

3.5. Location: Leonato's house.
0.2 *Headborough* local constable   2 confidence (A blunder for "conference.")   3 decerns (For "concerns.")   9 Goodman (Title of a person under the social rank of gentleman.)   10 blunt (He means "sharp.")   12 honest . . . brows (Proverbial expression of honesty.)   15 odorous (For "odious.")   *Palabras* (For *pocas palabras,* "few words" in Spanish.)   19 poor Duke's officers (For "Duke's poor officers.")   20 tedious (Dogberry evidently thinks *tedious* means "rich.")   21 of on   24 exclamation (Possibly for "acclamation.")   29 tonight last night   29–30 excepting . . . presence (The normal meaning, "with the exception of your honored self," comically implies that Leonato is an even more arrant knave than the men arrested. Verges probably means, "begging Your Worship's pardon.")   30 ha' ta'en have taken   33 when . . . out (An adaptation of the proverb, "When ale is in, wit is out.")   34 a world i.e., wonderful. (Proverbial.)

Verges. Well, God's a good man. An two men ride 35
of a horse, one must ride behind. An honest soul, 36
i'faith, sir, by my troth he is, as ever broke bread. But, God
is to be worshiped, all men are not alike, alas, good
neighbor!

LEONATO   Indeed, neighbor, he comes too short of you.

DOGBERRY   Gifts that God gives.

LEONATO   I must leave you.

DOGBERRY   One word, sir. Our watch, sir, have indeed
comprehended two aspicious persons, and we would 44
have them this morning examined before Your Worship.

LEONATO   Take their examination yourself and bring
it me. I am now in great haste, as it may appear
unto you.

DOGBERRY   It shall be suffigance. 50

LEONATO   Drink some wine ere you go. Fare you well.

[Enter a Messenger.]

MESSENGER   My lord, they stay for you to give your
daughter to her husband.

LEONATO   I'll wait upon them. I am ready. 54

[Exeunt Leonato and Messenger.]

DOGBERRY   Go, good partner, go, get you to Francis Sea- 55
coal. Bid him bring his pen and inkhorn to the jail. We 56
are now to examination these men. 57

VERGES   And we must do it wisely.

DOGBERRY   We will spare for no wit, I warrant you.
Here's that shall drive some of them to a noncome. 60
Only get the learned writer to set down our excom- 61
munication, and meet me at the jail.   [Exeunt.] 62

[4.1]

Enter Prince [Don Pedro], [Don John the]
Bastard, Leonato, Friar [Francis], Claudio,
Benedick, Hero, and Beatrice [with attendants].

LEONATO   Come, Friar Francis, be brief—only to the
plain form of marriage, and you shall recount their
particular duties afterwards.

FRIAR   You come hither, my lord, to marry this lady?

CLAUDIO   No.

LEONATO   To be married to her. Friar, you come to
marry her.

FRIAR   Lady, you come hither to be married to this
Count?

HERO   I do.

FRIAR   If either of you know any inward impediment 11

why you should not be conjoined, I charge you on
your souls to utter it.

CLAUDIO   Know you any, Hero?

HERO   None, my lord.

FRIAR   Know you any, Count?

LEONATO   I dare make his answer: none.

CLAUDIO   Oh, what men dare do! What men may do!
What men daily do, not knowing what they do!

BENEDICK   How now? Interjections? Why, then, some be 20
of laughing, as, ah, ha, he! 21

CLAUDIO
Stand thee by, Friar.—Father, by your leave, 22
Will you with free and unconstrainèd soul
Give me this maid, your daughter?

LEONATO
As freely, son, as God did give her me.

CLAUDIO
And what have I to give you back, whose worth
May counterpoise this rich and precious gift? 27

DON PEDRO
Nothing, unless you render her again.

CLAUDIO
Sweet Prince, you learn me noble thankfulness. 29
[He hands Hero to Leonato.]
There, Leonato, take her back again.
Give not this rotten orange to your friend;
She's but the sign and semblance of her honor. 32
Behold how like a maid she blushes here!
Oh, what authority and show of truth
Can cunning sin cover itself withal!
Comes not that blood as modest evidence 36
To witness simple virtue? Would you not swear, 37
All you that see her, that she were a maid,
By these exterior shows? But she is none:
She knows the heat of a luxurious bed. 40
Her blush is guiltiness, not modesty.

LEONATO
What do you mean, my lord?

CLAUDIO   Not to be married, 42
Not to knit my soul to an approvèd wanton. 43

LEONATO
Dear my lord, if you, in your own proof, 44
Have vanquished the resistance of her youth,
And made defeat of her virginity—

CLAUDIO
I know what you would say: if I have known her, 47
You will say, she did embrace me as a husband,
And so extenuate the forehand sin. 49
No, Leonato,
I never tempted her with word too large, 51

35 God's . . . man i.e., God is good. (A proverbial saying.) **36 of** on
44 comprehended (For "apprehended.") **aspicious** (For "suspicious.") **50 suffigance** (For "sufficient.") **54 wait upon** attend
55–6 Francis Seacoal i.e., the Sexton of 4.2, not George, the member
of the watch in 3.3. **57 examination** (For "examine.") **60 noncome**
(Probably an unintended contraction for *non compos mentis*, "not of
sound mind," but Dogberry may have intended "nonplus.")
61–2 excommunication (For "examination" or "communication.")
4.1. Location: A church.
11 inward secret

20–1 some . . . he (Benedick quotes from Lilly's Latin grammar on the
subject of interjections; according to Lilly, these are to be classified as
laughing interjections.) **22 Stand thee by** Stand aside **27 counterpoise** balance, be equivalent to **29 learn** teach **32 sign and semblance** pretense and outward show **36 blood** i.e., blush. **modest
evidence** evidence of modesty **37 witness** bear witness to **40 luxurious** lascivious, lustful **42 mean** imply, suggest. (But Claudio bitterly replies in the sense of "intend.") **43 approvèd** proved **44 in . . .
proof** in making trial of her yourself **47 known her** i.e., known her
sexually **49 extenuate** excuse, lessen. **forehand sin** sin of anticipating (marriage). **51 large** broad, immodest

But, as a brother to his sister, showed
Bashful sincerity and comely love.

HERO
And seemed I ever otherwise to you?

CLAUDIO
Out on thee, seeming! I will write against it.   55
You seem to me as Dian in her orb,   56
As chaste as is the bud ere it be blown;   57
But you are more intemperate in your blood
Than Venus, or those pampered animals
That rage in savage sensuality.

HERO
Is my lord well, that he doth speak so wide?   61

LEONATO
Sweet Prince, why speak not you?

DON PEDRO   What should I speak?
I stand dishonored, that have gone about   63
To link my dear friend to a common stale.   64

LEONATO
Are these things spoken, or do I but dream?

DON JOHN
Sir, they are spoken, and these things are true.

BENEDICK   This looks not like a nuptial.

HERO   "True"! Oh, God!   68

CLAUDIO   Leonato, stand I here?
Is this the Prince? Is this the Prince's brother?
Is this face Hero's? Are our eyes our own?

LEONATO
All this is so. But what of this, my lord?

CLAUDIO
Let me but move one question to your daughter,   73
And by that fatherly and kindly power   74
That you have in her, bid her answer truly.

LEONATO [to Hero]
I charge thee do so, as thou art my child.

HERO
Oh, God defend me, how am I beset!
What kind of catechizing call you this?   78

CLAUDIO
To make you answer truly to your name.

HERO
Is it not Hero? Who can blot that name
With any just reproach?

CLAUDIO   Marry, that can Hero!
Hero itself can blot out Hero's virtue.   82
What man was he talked with you yesternight
Out at your window betwixt twelve and one?
Now, if you are a maid, answer to this.

HERO
I talked with no man at that hour, my lord.

DON PEDRO
Why, then are you no maiden. Leonato,
I am sorry you must hear. Upon mine honor,
Myself, my brother, and this grievèd Count   89
Did see her, hear her, at that hour last night
Talk with a ruffian at her chamber window,
Who hath indeed, most like a liberal villain,   92
Confessed the vile encounters they have had
A thousand times in secret.

DON JOHN
Fie, fie, they are not to be named, my lord,
Not to be spoke of!
There is not chastity enough in language
Without offense to utter them. Thus, pretty lady,
I am sorry for thy much misgovernment.   99

CLAUDIO
O Hero, what a Hero hadst thou been
If half thy outward graces had been placed
About thy thoughts and counsels of thy heart!
But fare thee well, most foul, most fair! Farewell,
Thou pure impiety and impious purity!
For thee I'll lock up all the gates of love,   105
And on my eyelids shall conjecture hang,   106
To turn all beauty into thoughts of harm,
And never shall it more be gracious.   108

LEONATO
Hath no man's dagger here a point for me?
                                        [Hero swoons.]

BEATRICE
Why, how now, cousin, wherefore sink you down?

DON JOHN
Come, let us go. These things, come thus to light,
Smother her spirits up.
              [Exeunt Don Pedro, Don John, and Claudio.]

BENEDICK
How doth the lady?

BEATRICE   Dead, I think. Help, uncle!
Hero, why, Hero! Uncle! Signor Benedick! Friar!

LEONATO
O Fate, take not away thy heavy hand!
Death is the fairest cover for her shame
That may be wished for.

BEATRICE   How now, cousin Hero?

FRIAR   Have comfort, lady.

LEONATO
Dost thou look up?

FRIAR   Yea, wherefore should she not?   119

LEONATO
Wherefore? Why, doth not every earthly thing
Cry shame upon her? Could she here deny
The story that is printed in her blood?   122
Do not live, Hero, do not ope thine eyes;
For, did I think thou wouldst not quickly die,
Thought I thy spirits were stronger than thy shames,   125

---

55 Out . . . seeming! i.e., Shame on you, a mere semblance of good!
56 Dian . . . orb i.e., Diana, goddess of chastity, enthroned in the
moon   57 be blown open, flowering   61 wide wide of the mark.
63 gone about undertaken   64 stale whore.   68 True (A response
to Don John's use of the term.)   73 move put   74 kindly natural
78 catechizing formal questioning used by the Church to teach the
principles of faith. The first question in the Church of England's
catechism is, "What is your name?"   82 Hero itself The very name
of Hero (who, in the story of Hero and Leander, is the faithful tragic heroine)

89 grievèd (1) aggrieved, wronged (2) struck with grief   92 liberal
licentious   99 much misgovernment gross misconduct.   105 For
thee Because of you   106 conjecture evil suspicion   108 be gracious
seem attractive, graceful.   110, 119 wherefore why   122 blood i.e.,
blushes.   125 spirits life-giving energies, vital powers

Myself would, on the rearward of reproaches,   126
Strike at thy life. Grieved I I had but one?
Chid I for that at frugal nature's frame?   128
Oh, one too much by thee! Why had I one?
Why ever wast thou lovely in my eyes?
Why had I not with charitable hand
Took up a beggar's issue at my gates,   132
Who, smirchèd thus and mired with infamy,
I might have said, "No part of it is mine;
This shame derives itself from unknown loins"?
But mine, and mine I loved, and mine I praised,   136
And mine that I was proud on, mine so much
That I myself was to myself not mine,   138
Valuing of her—why, she, oh, she, is fallen   139
Into a pit of ink, that the wide sea   140
Hath drops too few to wash her clean again
And salt too little which may season give   142
To her foul-tainted flesh!

BENEDICK   Sir, sir, be patient.
For my part, I am so attired in wonder,
I know not what to say.

BEATRICE
Oh, on my soul, my cousin is belied!

BENEDICK
Lady, were you her bedfellow last night?

BEATRICE
No, truly, not; although, until last night,
I have this twelvemonth been her bedfellow.

LEONATO
Confirmed, confirmed! Oh, that is stronger made
Which was before barred up with ribs of iron!   151
Would the two princes lie and Claudio lie,
Who loved her so that, speaking of her foulness,
Washed it with tears? Hence from her! Let her die.

FRIAR   Hear me a little;
For I have only been silent so long
And given way unto this course of fortune   157
By noting of the lady. I have marked
A thousand blushing apparitions
To start into her face, a thousand innocent shames
In angel whiteness beat away those blushes,
And in her eye there hath appeared a fire
To burn the errors that these princes hold
Against her maiden truth. Call me a fool;
Trust not my reading nor my observations,
Which with experimental seal doth warrant   166
The tenor of my book; trust not my age,   167
My reverence, calling, nor divinity,
If this sweet lady lie not guiltless here
Under some biting error.

LEONATO   Friar, it cannot be.
Thou see'st that all the grace that she hath left
Is that she will not add to her damnation

A sin of perjury; she not denies it.
Why seek'st thou then to cover with excuse
That which appears in proper nakedness?   175

FRIAR
Lady, what man is he you are accused of?

HERO
They know that do accuse me; I know none.
If I know more of any man alive
Than that which maiden modesty doth warrant,   179
Let all my sins lack mercy! O my father,
Prove you that any man with me conversed   181
At hours unmeet or that I yesternight   182
Maintained the change of words with any creature,   183
Refuse me, hate me, torture me to death!   184

FRIAR
There is some strange misprision in the princes.   185

BENEDICK
Two of them have the very bent of honor;   186
And if their wisdoms be misled in this,
The practice of it lives in John the Bastard,   188
Whose spirits toil in frame of villainies.   189

LEONATO
I know not. If they speak but truth of her,
These hands shall tear her; if they wrong her honor,
The proudest of them shall well hear of it.
Time hath not yet so dried this blood of mine,
Nor age so eat up my invention,   194
Nor fortune made such havoc of my means,
Nor my bad life reft me so much of friends,   196
But they shall find, awaked in such a kind,   197
Both strength of limb and policy of mind,   198
Ability in means, and choice of friends,
To quit me of them throughly.

FRIAR   Pause awhile,   200
And let my counsel sway you in this case.
Your daughter here the princes left for dead,   202
Let her awhile be secretly kept in,   203
And publish it that she is dead indeed.
Maintain a mourning ostentation,   205
And on your family's old monument   206
Hang mournful epitaphs, and do all rites
That appertain unto a burial.

LEONATO
What shall become of this? What will this do?   209

FRIAR
Marry, this, well carried, shall on her behalf   210
Change slander to remorse. That is some good.
But not for that dream I on this strange course,   212

---

126 on . . . reproaches following this public disgrace   **128 Chid** Chided.   **frame** plan, order.   **132 Took . . . issue** taken up a beggar's child   **136 mine** i.e., my own daughter   **138–9 That . . . her** i.e., that I set no value on myself in caring so much for her   **140 that** such that   **142 season** preservative   **151 before** already   **157 given . . . fortune** yielded to this turn of events   **166–7 Which . . . book** i.e., by means of which observations and experience I have confirmed what I learned from books

175 proper true   **179 warrant** sanction, permit   **181 Prove you** if you prove   **182 unmeet** improper   **183 Maintained the change** held exchange   **184 Refuse** disown   **185 misprision** mistake, misunderstanding   **186 Two . . . honor** i.e., Don Pedro and Claudio are wholly honorable   **188 practice** scheming   **189 frame** contriving   **194 eat** eaten. (Pronounced "et.")   **invention** power to plan (vengeance)   **196 reft** robbed   **197 kind** manner   **198 policy** shrewdness   **200 quit . . . throughly** settle accounts with them thoroughly.   **202 the princes** i.e., (whom) Don Pedro and Claudio   **203 in** in hiding, at home   **205 Maintain . . . ostentation** Perform all the outward signs of mourning   **206 monument** burial vault   **209 become of** result from   **210 carried** managed   **212 not for that** not for that reason alone

But on this travail look for greater birth.   213
She—dying, as it must be so maintained,
Upon the instant that she was accused—
Shall be lamented, pitied, and excused
Of every hearer; for it so falls out
That what we have we prize not to the worth   218
Whiles we enjoy it, but, being lacked and lost,
Why then we rack the value, then we find   220
The virtue that possession would not show us
Whiles it was ours. So will it fare with Claudio.
When he shall hear she died upon his words,   223
Th'idea of her life shall sweetly creep
Into his study of imagination,   225
And every lovely organ of her life   226
Shall come appareled in more precious habit,   227
More moving-delicate, and full of life,
Into the eye and prospect of his soul,   229
Than when she lived indeed. Then shall he mourn,
If ever love had interest in his liver,   231
And wish he had not so accusèd her,
No, though he thought his accusation true.
Let this be so, and doubt not but success   234
Will fashion the event in better shape   235
Than I can lay it down in likelihood.   236
But if all aim but this be leveled false,   237
The supposition of the lady's death
Will quench the wonder of her infamy.
And if it sort not well, you may conceal her,   240
As best befits her wounded reputation,
In some reclusive and religious life,   242
Out of all eyes, tongues, minds, and injuries.   243
BENEDICK
  Signor Leonato, let the Friar advise you.
  And though you know my inwardness and love   245
  Is very much unto the Prince and Claudio,
  Yet, by mine honor, I will deal in this
  As secretly and justly as your soul
  Should with your body.
LEONATO   Being that I flow in grief,   249
  The smallest twine may lead me.
FRIAR
  'Tis well consented. Presently away;   251
      For to strange sores strangely they strain the cure.   252
  Come, lady, die to live. This wedding day
      Perhaps is but prolonged. Have patience, and
      endure.   254
              Exit [with all but Benedick and Beatrice].
BENDICK   Lady Beatrice, have you wept all this while?

BEATRICE   Yea, and I will weep a while longer.
BENEDICK   I will not desire that.
BEATRICE   You have no reason. I do it freely.   258
BENEDICK   Surely I do believe your fair cousin is
  wronged.
BEATRICE   Ah, how much might the man deserve of me
  that would right her!
BENEDICK   Is there any way to show such friendship?
BEATRICE   A very even way, but no such friend.   264
BENEDICK   May a man do it?
BEATRICE   It is a man's office, but not yours.   266
BENEDICK   I do love nothing in the world so well as you.
  Is not that strange?
BEATRICE   As strange as the thing I know not. It were as
  possible for me to say I loved nothing so well as you.
  But believe me not; and yet I lie not. I confess nothing,
  nor I deny nothing. I am sorry for my cousin.
BENEDICK   By my sword, Beatrice, thou lovest me.
BEATRICE   Do not swear and eat it.   274
BENEDICK   I will swear by it that you love me, and I will
  make him eat it that says I love not you.   276
BEATRICE   Will you not eat your word?
BENEDICK   With no sauce that can be devised to it. I
  protest I love thee.   279
BEATRICE   Why, then, God forgive me!
BENEDICK   What offense, sweet Beatrice?
BEATRICE   You have stayed me in a happy hour. I was   282
  about to protest I loved you.
BENEDICK   And do it with all thy heart.
BEATRICE   I love you with so much of my heart that
  none is left to protest.   286
BENEDICK   Come, bid me do anything for thee.
BEATRICE   Kill Claudio.
BENEDICK   Ha! Not for the wide world.
BEATRICE   You kill me to deny it. Farewell.   *[Going.]*
BENEDICK   Tarry, sweet Beatrice.
BEATRICE   I am gone, though I am here. There is no love   292
  in you. Nay, I pray you, let me go.
BENEDICK   Beatrice—
BEATRICE   In faith, I will go.
BENEDICK   We'll be friends first.
BEATRICE   You dare easier be friends with me than fight
  with mine enemy.
BENEDICK   Is Claudio thine enemy?
BEATRICE   Is 'a not approved in the height a villain, that 300
  hath slandered, scorned, dishonored my kinswoman?
  Oh, that I were a man! What, bear her in hand until   302
  they come to take hands, and then, with public accus-
  ation, uncovered slander, unmitigated rancor—Oh,   304
  God, that I were a man! I would eat his heart in the
  marketplace.

213 **on this travail** from this effort (which is metaphorically like the *travail*, or labor, of childbirth)   218 **to the worth** as fully as it deserves   220 **rack** stretch, extend   223 **upon** in consequence of   225 **Into . . . imagination** into his thoughts   226 **organ . . . life** aspect of her when she was alive   227 **habit** apparel   229 **prospect** range of vision   231 **interest in** claim upon.   **liver** (The supposed seat of the passion of love.)   234 **success** i.e., what succeeds or happens in time as my plan might   235 **event** outcome   236 **lay . . . likelihood** anticipate its probable course.   237 **if . . . false** i.e., if every other aim miscarry   240 **sort** turn out   242 **reclusive** cloistered   243 **injuries** insults.   245 **inwardness and love** close friendship   249 **Being . . . grief** Since I overflow in grief   251 **Presently** Immediately   252 **For . . . cure** for strange diseases require strange and desperate cures.   254 **prolonged** deferred.

258 **You . . . reason** (Beatrice twists Benedick's "I wish you weren't so unhappy," line 257, into "There's no need for you to bid me stop weeping.")   264 **even** direct, straightforward   266 **office** duty   274 **eat it** i.e., eat your words.   276 **eat it** i.e., eat my sword, be stabbed by it   279 **protest** affirm. (Also in line 283.)   282 **stayed** stopped.   **in . . . hour** at an appropriate moment.   286 **protest** object. (With a play on the sense of "affirm" in 279 and 283.)   292 **gone** i.e., in spirit   300 **approved in the height** proved in the highest degree   302 **bear her in hand** delude Hero with false hopes   304 **uncovered** open, unconcealed

BENEDICK   Hear me, Beatrice—

BEATRICE   Talk with a man out at a window! A proper 308
saying! 309

BENEDICK   Nay, but Beatrice—

BEATRICE   Sweet Hero! She is wronged, she is slandered,
she is undone.

BENEDICK   Beat—

BEATRICE   Princes and counties! Surely, a princely testi- 314
mony, a goodly count, Count Comfect; a sweet gallant, 315
surely! Oh, that I were a man for his sake! Or that I had
any friend would be a man for my sake! But manhood
is melted into curtsies, valor into compliment, and
men are only turned into tongue, and trim ones too. 319
He is now as valiant as Hercules that only tells a lie 320
and swears it. I cannot be a man with wishing, there- 321
fore I will die a woman with grieving.

BENEDICK   Tarry, good Beatrice. By this hand, I love
thee.

BEATRICE   Use it for my love some other way than
swearing by it.

BENEDICK   Think you in your soul the Count Claudio
hath wronged Hero?

BEATRICE   Yea, as sure as I have a thought or a soul.

BENEDICK   Enough, I am engaged. I will challenge him. 330
I will kiss your hand, and so I leave you. By this hand,
Claudio shall render me a dear account. As you hear 332
of me, so think of me. Go comfort your cousin. I must
say she is dead. And so, farewell. [*Exeunt separately.*]

✿

[4.2]

*Enter the Constables [Dogberry and Verges]
and the Town Clerk [Sexton] in gowns, Borachio, [Conrade, and Watch].*

DOGBERRY   Is our whole dissembly appeared? 1

VERGES   Oh, a stool and a cushion for the sexton.
[*Stool and cushion are brought. The Sexton sits.*]

SEXTON   Which be the malefactors?

DOGBERRY   Marry, that am I and my partner. 4

VERGES   Nay, that's certain; we have the exhibition to 5
examine.

SEXTON   But which are the offenders that are to be
examined? Let them come before Master Constable.

DOGBERRY   Yea, marry, let them come before me. [*The
prisoners are brought forward.*] What is your name,
friend?

BORACHIO   Borachio.

DOGBERRY   Pray, write down Borachio.—Yours, sirrah? 13

CONRADE   I am a gentleman, sir, and my name is
Conrade.

DOGBERRY   Write down Master Gentleman Conrade.
Masters, do you serve God?

CONRADE, BORACHIO   Yea, sir, we hope.

DOGBERRY   Write down that they hope they serve God;
and write God first, for God defend but God should 20
go before such villains! Masters, it is proved already
that you are little better than false knaves, and it will
go near to be thought so shortly. How answer you for
yourselves?

CONRADE   Marry, sir, we say we are none.

DOGBERRY   A marvelous witty fellow, I assure you, but 26
I will go about with him. [*To Borachio*] Come you 27
hither, sirrah. A word in your ear. Sir, I say to you, it is
thought you are false knaves.

BORACHIO   Sir, I say to you we are none.

DOGBERRY   Well, stand aside. 'Fore God, they are both
in a tale. Have you writ down that they are none? 32

SEXTON   Master Constable, you go not the way to
examine. You must call forth the watch that are their
accusers.

DOGBERRY   Yea, marry, that's the eftest way. Let the 36
watch come forth.—Masters, I charge you in the
Prince's name accuse these men.

SEACOAL   This man said, sir, that Don John, the Prince's
brother, was a villain.

DOGBERRY   Write down Prince John a villain. Why, this
is flat perjury, to call a prince's brother villain. 42

BORACHIO   Master Constable—

DOGBERRY   Pray thee, fellow, peace. I do not like thy
look, I promise thee.

SEXTON   What heard you him say else?

FIRST WATCH   Marry, that he had received a thousand
ducats of Don John for accusing the Lady Hero
wrongfully.

DOGBERRY   Flat burglary as ever was committed.

VERGES   Yea, by Mass, that it is. 51

SEXTON   What else, fellow?

SEACOAL   And that Count Claudio did mean, upon his 53
words, to disgrace Hero before the whole assembly, 54
and not marry her.

DOGBERRY   Oh, villain! Thou wilt be condemned into
everlasting redemption for this. 57

SEXTON   What else?

WATCH   This is all. 59

SEXTON   And this is more, masters, than you can deny:
Prince John is this morning secretly stolen away. Hero
was in this manner accused, in this very manner
refused, and upon the grief of this suddenly died.—
Master Constable, let these men be bound and
brought to Leonato's. I will go before and show him
their examination. [*Exit.*]

308–9 **proper saying** likely story.   314 **counties** counts.   315 **count**
(1) the title (2) declaration of complaint in an indictment (3) account.
Comfect candy or sweetmeat   319 **are . . . tongue** have become mere
(flattering) voices.   **trim** nice, elegant, fine. (Used ironically.)
320–1 **He . . . swears it** A man need only tell lies and swear they are
true to gain a reputation for bravery nowadays.   330 **I am engaged** I
pledge myself.   332 **dear** costly
4.2. Location: The jail.
1 **dissembly** (A blunder for "assembly.")   4 **that am I** (Dogberry evidently understands *malefactors* to mean "factors," agents.)   5 **exhibition** (Possibly for "commission.")   13 **sirrah** (Used to address inferiors; Conrade objects.)

20 **defend** forbid   26 **witty** clever, cunning   27 **go about with** get
the better of, deal with   32 **in a tale** in agreement.   36 **eftest** (Some
sort of invention for "easiest" or "deftest.")   42 **perjury** (Dogberry
means "slander.")   51 **by Mass** by the Mass   53–4 **upon his words**
on the basis of Borachio's testimony   57 **redemption** (Dogberry
means "damnation.")   59 **WATCH** (Perhaps both Seacoal and his partner speak.)

DOGBERRY   Come, let them be opinioned.   67
VERGES   Let them be in the hands—
CONRADE   Off, coxcomb!
DOGBERRY   God's my life, where's the sexton? Let him   70
write down the Prince's officer coxcomb. Come, bind
them. Thou naughty varlet!   72
CONRADE   Away! You are an ass, you are an ass.
DOGBERRY   Dost thou not suspect my place? Dost thou   74
not suspect my years? Oh, that he were here to write   75
me down an ass! But masters, remember that I am an
ass; though it be not written down, yet forget not that
I am an ass. No, thou villain, thou art full of piety, as   78
shall be proved upon thee by good witness. I am a
wise fellow, and, which is more, an officer, and, which
is more, a householder, and, which is more, as pretty
a piece of flesh as any is in Messina, and one that
knows the law, go to, and a rich fellow enough, go to,
and a fellow that hath had losses, and one that hath
two gowns and everything handsome about him.—
Bring him away. Oh, that I had been writ down an ass!
Exeunt.

❧

5.1

Enter Leonato and his brother [Antonio].

ANTONIO
If you go on thus, you will kill yourself;
And 'tis not wisdom thus to second grief   2
Against yourself.
LEONATO   I pray thee, cease thy counsel,
Which falls into mine ears as profitless
As water in a sieve. Give not me counsel,
Nor let no comforter delight mine ear
But such a one whose wrongs do suit with mine.   7
Bring me a father that so loved his child,
Whose joy of her is overwhelmed like mine,
And bid him speak of patience;
Measure his woe the length and breadth of mine,   11
And let it answer every strain for strain,   12
As thus for thus, and such a grief for such,
In every lineament, branch, shape, and form;
If such a one will smile and stroke his beard,
Bid sorrow wag, cry "hem!" when he should groan,   16
Patch grief with proverbs, make misfortune drunk   17
With candle wasters, bring him yet to me,   18
And I of him will gather patience.
But there is no such man. For, brother, men
Can counsel and speak comfort to that grief
Which they themselves not feel; but tasting it,

Their counsel turns to passion, which before
Would give preceptial medicine to rage,   24
Fetter strong madness in a silken thread,
Charm ache with air and agony with words.   26
No, no, 'tis all men's office to speak patience   27
To those that wring under the load of sorrow,   28
But no man's virtue nor sufficiency   29
To be so moral when he shall endure   30
The like himself. Therefore give me no counsel.
My griefs cry louder than advertisement.   32
ANTONIO
Therein do men from children nothing differ.   33
LEONATO
I pray thee, peace. I will be flesh and blood;
For there was never yet philosopher
That could endure the toothache patiently,
However they have writ the style of gods   37
And made a push at chance and sufferance.   38
ANTONIO
Yet bend not all the harm upon yourself.
Make those that do offend you suffer, too.
LEONATO
There thou speak'st reason. Nay, I will do so.
My soul doth tell me Hero is belied,
And that shall Claudio know; so shall the Prince
And all of them that thus dishonor her.

Enter Prince [Don Pedro] and Claudio.

ANTONIO
Here comes the Prince and Claudio hastily.
DON PEDRO
Good e'en, good e'en.
CLAUDIO   Good day to both of you.
LEONATO
Hear you, my lords—
DON PEDRO   We have some haste, Leonato.
LEONATO
Some haste, my lord! Well, fare you well, my lord.
Are you so hasty now? Well, all is one.   49
DON PEDRO
Nay, do not quarrel with us, good old man.
ANTONIO
If he could right himself with quarreling,   51
Some of us would lie low.
CLAUDIO   Who wrongs him?   52
LEONATO
Marry, thou dost wrong me, thou dissembler, thou!   53
Nay, never lay thy hand upon thy sword;
I fear thee not.
CLAUDIO   Marry, beshrew my hand   55
If it should give your age such cause of fear.
In faith, my hand meant nothing to my sword.   57

---

67 opinioned (For "pinioned.")   **70 God's** May God save
72 naughty wicked   **74 suspect** (For "respect.")   **75 my years** (With
an unconscious suggestion of "my ears," i.e., ass's ears.)   **78 piety**
(For "impiety.")
5.1. Location: Near Leonato's house.
2 second assist, encourage   **7 suit with** match   **11 Measure his woe**
let his woe equal in scope   **12 answer . . . for strain** correspond, pang
for pang. (With a musical sense also of echoing a refrain.)   **16 wag** be
off.   **cry "hem"** i.e., clear the throat as before some wordy speech
17 drunk i.e., insensible to pain   **18 candle wasters** those who waste
candles by late study, bookworms, moral philosophers

24 preceptial consisting of precepts   **26 air** mere breath, words
27 office duty   **28 wring** writhe   **29 sufficiency** ability, power
30 moral prone to moralizing   **32 advertisement** advice, counsel.
33 Therein . . . differ i.e., It is childish to be so inconsolable.   **37 writ . . .
gods** uttered godlike wisdom   **38 made . . . sufferance** scoffed at misfortune and suffering.   **49 all is one** it makes no difference.   **51 he** i.e.,
Leonato   **52 Some of us** i.e., Don Pedro and Claudio   **53 thou** (Used
contemptuously instead of the more polite *you*.)   **55 beshrew** curse
57 my . . . sword I had no intention of using my sword.

LEONATO

Tush, tush, man, never fleer and jest at me.   58
I speak not like a dotard nor a fool,
As under privilege of age to brag
What I have done being young or what would do
Were I not old. Know, Claudio, to thy head,   62
Thou hast so wronged mine innocent child and me
That I am forced to lay my reverence by,   64
And with gray hairs and bruise of many days
Do challenge thee to trial of a man.   66
I say thou hast belied mine innocent child.
Thy slander hath gone through and through her
    heart,
And she lies buried with her ancestors—
Oh, in a tomb where never scandal slept,
Save this of hers, framed by thy villainy!   71

CLAUDIO

My villainy?

LEONATO   Thine, Claudio, thine, I say.

DON PEDRO

You say not right, old man.

LEONATO   My lord, my lord,
I'll prove it on his body if he dare,
Despite his nice fence and his active practice,   75
His May of youth and bloom of lustihood.   76

CLAUDIO

Away! I will not have to do with you.

LEONATO

Canst thou so daff me? Thou hast killed my child.   78
If thou kill'st me, boy, thou shalt kill a man.

ANTONIO

He shall kill two of us, and men indeed.
But that's no matter; let him kill one first.
Win me and wear me! Let him answer me.   82
Come follow me, boy. Come, sir boy, come follow me,
Sir boy, I'll whip you from your foining fence!   84
Nay, as I am a gentleman, I will.

LEONATO   Brother—

ANTONIO

Content yourself. God knows I loved my niece,   87
And she is dead, slandered to death by villains
That dare as well answer a man indeed
As I dare take a serpent by the tongue.
Boys, apes, braggarts, jacks, milksops!

LEONATO   Brother Antony—

ANTONIO

Hold you content. What, man! I know them, yea,
And what they weigh, even to the utmost scruple—   94
Scambling, outfacing, fashionmonging boys,   95
That lie and cog and flout, deprave and slander,   96

Go anticly, show outward hideousness,   97
And speak off half a dozen dangerous words   98
How they might hurt their enemies, if they durst,
And this is all.

LEONATO

But brother Antony—

ANTONIO   Come, 'tis no matter.
Do not you meddle; let me deal in this.

DON PEDRO

Gentlemen both, we will not wake your patience.   103
My heart is sorry for your daughter's death;
But, on my honor, she was charged with nothing
But what was true and very full of proof.

LEONATO   My lord, my lord—

DON PEDRO   I will not hear you.

LEONATO

No? Come, brother, away! I will be heard.

ANTONIO

And shall, or some of us will smart for it.   110

Exeunt ambo [Leonato and Antonio].

Enter Benedick.

DON PEDRO

See, see, here comes the man we went to seek.

CLAUDIO   Now, signor, what news?

BENEDICK   Good day, my lord.

DON PEDRO   Welcome, signor. You are almost come to
part almost a fray.

CLAUDIO   We had like to have had our two noses   116
snapped off with two old men without teeth.   117

DON PEDRO   Leonato and his brother. What think'st
thou? Had we fought, I doubt we should have been   119
too young for them.

BENEDICK   In a false quarrel there is no true valor. I came
to seek you both.

CLAUDIO   We have been up and down to seek thee, for
we are high-proof melancholy and would fain have it   124
beaten away. Wilt thou use thy wit?

BENEDICK   It is in my scabbard. Shall I draw it?

DON PEDRO   Dost thou wear thy wit by thy side?

CLAUDIO   Never any did so, though very many have
been beside their wit. I will bid thee draw as we do the   129
minstrels, draw to pleasure us.   130

DON PEDRO   As I am an honest man, he looks pale. Art
thou sick, or angry?

CLAUDIO   What, courage, man! What though care killed
a cat, thou hast mettle enough in thee to kill care.

BENEDICK   Sir, I shall meet your wit in the career, an you   135
charge it against me. I pray you, choose another sub-   136
ject.

---

58 **fleer** sneer, jeer   62 **head** i.e., face   64 **my reverence** i.e., the reverence due old age   66 **trial of a man** manly contest, i.e., duel.
71 **framed** devised   75 **nice fence** dexterous swordsmanship. (Said
contemptuously.)   76 **lustihood** bodily vigor.   78 **daff** doff, brush
aside   82 **Win . . . me!** (A proverbial expression, used as a challenge,
meaning he'll have to overcome me before he can claim me as a
prize.)   **answer me** i.e., in a duel.   84 **foining** thrusting   87 **Content
yourself** i.e., Don't try to stop me.   94 **scruple** small measure of
weight   95 **Scambling . . . boys** contentious, swaggering, dandified
boys   96 **cog** cheat.   **deprave** defame, traduce

97 **anticly** fantastically dressed.   **hideousness** frightening appearance   98 **dangerous** threatening, haughty   103 **wake your patience**
put your patience to any further test.   110.1 *ambo* both   116 **We had
. . . had** We almost had   117 **with** by   119 **doubt** fear, suspect. (Said
ironically.)   124 **high-proof** to the highest degree.   **fain** gladly
129 **beside their wit** out of their wits. (Playing on *by thy side* in line
127.)   130 **draw** (1) draw your weapon (2) draw a bow across a musical instrument   135 **career** short gallop at full speed (as in a tourney).
an if   136 **charge** level (as a weapon)

CLAUDIO   Nay, then, give him another staff. This last 138
was broke cross. 139

DON PEDRO   By this light, he changes more and more. I
think he be angry indeed.

CLAUDIO   If he be, he knows how to turn his girdle. 142

BENEDICK   Shall I speak a word in your ear?

CLAUDIO   God bless me from a challenge!

BENEDICK [aside to Claudio]   You are a villain. I jest not. I
will make it good how you dare, with what you dare,
and when you dare. Do me right, or I will protest your 147
cowardice. You have killed a sweet lady, and her death
shall fall heavy on you. Let me hear from you.

CLAUDIO   Well, I will meet you, so I may have good
cheer. 151

DON PEDRO   What, a feast, a feast?

CLAUDIO   I'faith, I thank him, he hath bid me to a calf's 153
head and a capon, the which if I do not carve most 154
curiously, say my knife's naught. Shall I not find a 155
woodcock too? 156

BENEDICK   Sir, your wit ambles well; it goes easily. 157

DON PEDRO   I'll tell thee how Beatrice praised thy wit
the other day. I said thou hadst a fine wit. "True," said
she, "a fine little one." "No," said I, "a great wit."
"Right," says she, "a great gross one." "Nay," said I, "a
good wit." "Just," said she, "it hurts nobody." "Nay," 162
said I, "the gentleman is wise." "Certain," said she,
"a wise gentleman." "Nay," said I, "he hath the 164
tongues." "That I believe," said she, "for he swore a 165
thing to me on Monday night which he forswore on
Tuesday morning. There's a double tongue; there's
two tongues." Thus did she, an hour together, trans- 168
shape thy particular virtues. Yet at last she concluded 169
with a sigh, thou wast the proper'st man in Italy. 170

CLAUDIO   For the which she wept heartily and said she
cared not.

DON PEDRO   Yea, that she did. But yet for all that, an if
she did not hate him deadly, she would love him
dearly. The old man's daughter told us all. 175

CLAUDIO   All, all. And, moreover, God saw him when 176
he was hid in the garden. 177

DON PEDRO   But when shall we set the savage bull's
horns on the sensible Benedick's head?

CLAUDIO   Yea, and text underneath, "Here dwells 180
Benedick, the married man"?

BENEDICK   Fare you well, boy. You know my mind. I
will leave you now to your gossiplike humor. You
break jests as braggarts do their blades, which, God be 184
thanked, hurt not.—My lord, for your many courtesies I thank you. I must discontinue your company.
Your brother the bastard is fled from Messina. You
have among you killed a sweet and innocent lady. For
my Lord Lackbeard there, he and I shall meet, and till
then peace be with him. [Exit.]

DON PEDRO   He is in earnest.

CLAUDIO   In most profound earnest, and, I'll warrant
you, for the love of Beatrice.

DON PEDRO   And hath challenged thee?

CLAUDIO   Most sincerely.

DON PEDRO   What a pretty thing man is when he goes 196
in his doublet and hose and leaves off his wit! 197

CLAUDIO   He is then a giant to an ape; but then is an ape 198
a doctor to such a man. 199

DON PEDRO   But, soft you, let me be. Pluck up, my heart, 200
and be sad. Did he not say my brother was fled? 201

Enter Constables, [Dogberry and Verges, and
the Watch, with] Conrade and Borachio.

DOGBERRY   Come you, sir. If Justice cannot tame you,
she shall ne'er weigh more reasons in her balance. 203
Nay, an you be a cursing hypocrite once, you must be 204
looked to.

DON PEDRO   How now, two of my brother's men
bound? Borachio one!

CLAUDIO   Hearken after their offense, my lord. 208

DON PEDRO   Officers, what offense have these men
done?

DOGBERRY   Marry, sir, they have committed false report;
moreover, they have spoken untruths; secondarily,
they are slanders; sixth and lastly, they have belied a 213
lady; thirdly, they have verified unjust things; and to
conclude, they are lying knaves.

DON PEDRO   First, I ask thee what they have done;
thirdly, I ask thee what's their offense; sixth and lastly,
why they are committed; and to conclude, what you
lay to their charge.

CLAUDIO   Rightly reasoned, and in his own division; 220
and, by my troth, there's one meaning well suited. 221

DON PEDRO   Who have you offended, masters, that you
are thus bound to your answer? This learned consta- 223
ble is too cunning to be understood. What's your
offense?

138 staff spear shaft.   139 broke cross i.e., broken by clumsily allowing the spear to break crosswise against the opponent's shield. (In
other words, Claudio accuses Benedick of having failed in his sally of
wit.)   142 turn his girdle i.e., turn his sword belt around so that he's
ready to fight. (A proverbial expression of uncertain meaning.)
147 Do me right Give me satisfaction.   protest proclaim before witnesses   151 cheer entertainment. (Claudio is ready to fight, he says,
for the pleasant diversion it should offer.)   153–6 calf's head, capon,
woodcock (In the proposed feast of dueling, Claudio plans to carve
various dishes connoting foolishness, effeminate cowardice, and stupidity.)   155 curiously daintily.   naught good for nothing.
157 ambles i.e., minces along   162 good (1) keen (2) harmless.   Just
Exactly   164 a wise gentleman i.e., an old fool.   164–5 hath the
tongues masters several languages.   168–9 trans-shape distort, turn
the wrong side out   170 proper'st handsomest   175 old man's
daughter i.e., Hero   176–7 God . . . garden (Alluding to the trick
played on Benedick to love Beatrice, and also to Genesis 3:8.)
180 text (In 1.1.251–6, Benedick vowed that, if he were ever to fall in
love, his friends might set a bull's horns on his head and label him
"Benedick the married man.")

184 as . . . blades i.e., as braggarts furtively damage their blades to
make it appear they have been fighting fiercely   196–7 goes . . . wit
goes about fully dressed like a rational creature but forgets to equip
himself with good sense.   198–9 He . . . man i.e., Such a man looks
like a hero in a fool's eyes, but actually the fool is a wise man compared to him.   200–1 soft . . . be sad wait a minute, not so fast; let me
think. Rouse yourself, my heart, and be serious.   201.1–2 (The quarto
placement of this stage direction after line 197 suggests that Dogberry
is visible, strutting and fussing with his prisoners, before he speaks.)
203 ne'er . . . balance never again weigh arguments of reason in her
scales. (But the pronunciation of reason as "raisin" invokes the comic
image of a shopkeeper weighing produce.)   204 cursing accursed.
once in a word   208 Hearken after Inquire into   213 slanders (For
"slanderers.")   220 his own division its own partition in a logical
arrangement. (Said ironically.)   221 well suited nicely dressed up in
the trappings of language.   223 bound (Playing on the meanings
"pinioned" and "headed for a destination.")   answer trial, account.

BORACHIO　　Sweet Prince, let me go no farther to mine answer. Do you hear me, and let this count kill me. I have deceived even your very eyes. What your wisdoms could not discover, these shallow fools have brought to light, who in the night overheard me confessing to this man how Don John your brother incensed me to slander the Lady Hero, how you were brought into the orchard and saw me court Margaret 232 in Hero's garments, how you disgraced her when you should marry her. My villainy they have upon record, which I had rather seal with my death than repeat over to my shame. The lady is dead upon mine and 237 my master's false accusation; and, briefly, I desire nothing but the reward of a villain.

DON PEDRO　[*to Claudio*]
Runs not this speech like iron through your blood?

CLAUDIO
I have drunk poison whiles he uttered it.

DON PEDRO　[*to Borachio*]
But did my brother set thee on to this?

BORACHIO　　Yea, and paid me richly for the practice of it. 243

DON PEDRO
He is composed and framed of treachery,
And fled he is upon this villainy. 245

CLAUDIO
Sweet Hero! Now thy image doth appear
In the rare semblance that I loved it first. 247

DOGBERRY　　Come, bring away the plaintiffs. By this time 248
our sexton hath reformed Signor Leonato of the 249
matter. And masters, do not forget to specify, when 250
time and place shall serve, that I am an ass.

VERGES　　Here, here comes Master Signor Leonato, and
the sexton, too.

Enter Leonato, his brother [Antonio], and the Sexton.

LEONATO
Which is the villain? Let me see his eyes,
That when I note another man like him,
I may avoid him. Which of these is he?

BORACHIO
If you would know your wronger, look on me.

LEONATO
Art thou the slave that with thy breath hast killed
Mine innocent child?

BORACHIO　　　　　　　　Yea, even I alone.

LEONATO
No, not so, villain, thou beliest thyself. 261
Here stand a pair of honorable men—
A third is fled—that had a hand in it.
I thank you, princes, for my daughter's death.
Record it with your high and worthy deeds.
'Twas bravely done, if you bethink you of it.

CLAUDIO
I know not how to pray your patience,
Yet I must speak. Choose your revenge yourself;

Impose me to what penance your invention 268
Can lay upon my sin. Yet sinned I not
But in mistaking.

DON PEDRO　　　　　By my soul, nor I.
And yet, to satisfy this good old man,
I would bend under any heavy weight
That he'll enjoin me to.

LEONATO
I cannot bid you bid my daughter live—
That were impossible—but, I pray you both,
Possess the people in Messina here 276
How innocent she died; and if your love
Can labor aught in sad invention, 278
Hang her an epitaph upon her tomb,
And sing it to her bones; sing it tonight.
Tomorrow morning come you to my house,
And since you could not be my son-in-law,
Be yet my nephew. My brother hath a daughter,
Almost the copy of my child that's dead,
And she alone is heir to both of us. 285
Give her the right you should have giv'n her cousin, 286
And so dies my revenge.

CLAUDIO　　　　　　　　O noble sir,
Your overkindness doth wring tears from me!
I do embrace your offer; and dispose 289
For henceforth of poor Claudio. 290

LEONATO
Tomorrow then I will expect your coming;
Tonight I take my leave. This naughty man 292
Shall face to face be brought to Margaret,
Who I believe was packed in all this wrong, 294
Hired to it by your brother.

BORACHIO　　No, by my soul, she was not,
Nor knew not what she did when she spoke to me,
But always hath been just and virtuous
In anything that I do know by her. 299

DOGBERRY　　Moreover, sir, which indeed is not under 300
white and black, this plaintiff here, the offender, did 301
call me ass. I beseech you, let it be remembered in his
punishment. And also the watch heard them talk of
one Deformed. They say he wears a key in his ear and 304
a lock hanging by it and borrows money in God's 305
name, the which he hath used so long and never paid 306
that now men grow hardhearted and will lend nothing for God's sake. Pray you, examine him upon that point.

LEONATO　　I thank thee for thy care and honest pains.

DOGBERRY　　Your Worship speaks like a most thankful
and reverend youth, and I praise God for you.

LEONATO　　There's for thy pains.　　[*He gives money.*]

DOGBERRY　　God save the foundation! 314

268 **Impose me to** Impose on me　276 **Possess** inform　278 **aught** to any extent　285 **heir to both** (Leonato overlooks Antonio's son mentioned in 1.2.2.)　286 **right** equitable treatment. (Quibbling on "rite," "ceremony.")　289 **dispose** you may dispose　290 **For henceforth** for the future　292 **naughty** wicked　294 **packed** involved as an accomplice　299 **by** concerning　300–301 **under . . . black** written down in black and white　304–5 **key . . . by it** (This is what Dogberry has made out of the lovelock mentioned in 3.3.166.)　305–6 **in God's name** (A phrase of the professional beggar.)　314 **God . . . foundation!** (A formula of those who received alms at religious houses or charitable foundations.)

232 **incensed** incited　237 **upon** in consequence of　243 **practice** cunning execution　245 **upon** i.e., having committed　247 **rare semblance** splendid likeness　248 **plaintiffs** (For "defendants.")　249 **reformed** (For "informed.")　250 **specify** (For "testify"?)　261 **honorable men** i.e., Don Pedro and Claudio, men of rank

LEONATO   Go, I discharge thee of thy prisoner, and I
thank thee.
DOGBERRY   I leave an arrant knave with Your Worship,
which I beseech Your Worship to correct yourself, for
the example of others. God keep Your Worship! I wish
Your Worship well. God restore you to health! I
humbly give you leave to depart; and if a merry meet- 321
ing may be wished, God prohibit it! Come, neighbor. 322
                            [*Exeunt Dogberry and Verges.*]
LEONATO
Until tomorrow morning, lords, farewell.
ANTONIO
Farewell, my lords. We look for you tomorrow.
DON PEDRO
We will not fail.
CLAUDIO   Tonight I'll mourn with Hero.
LEONATO [*to the Watch*]
Bring you these fellows on.—We'll talk with Margaret,
How her acquaintance grew with this lewd fellow. 327
                            Exeunt [*separately*].

[5.2]

Enter Benedick and Margaret, [*meeting*].

BENEDICK   Pray thee, sweet Mistress Margaret, deserve
well at my hands by helping me to the speech of 2
Beatrice.
MARGARET   Will you then write me a sonnet in praise of
my beauty?
BENEDICK   In so high a style, Margaret, that no man 6
living shall come over it, for in most comely truth thou 7
deservest it.
MARGARET   To have no man come over me! Why, shall
I always keep below stairs? 10
BENEDICK   Thy wit is as quick as the greyhound's
mouth; it catches.
MARGARET   And yours as blunt as the fencer's foils,
which hit but hurt not.
BENEDICK   A most manly wit, Margaret; it will not hurt
a woman. And so, I pray thee, call Beatrice. I give thee 16
the bucklers. 17
MARGARET   Give us the swords. We have bucklers of
our own.
BENEDICK   If you use them, Margaret, you must put in
the pikes with a vice, and they are dangerous weapons 21
for maids.

MARGARET   Well, I will call Beatrice to you, who I think
hath legs.   *Exit Margaret.*
BENEDICK   And therefore will come.
[*He sings.*] "The god of love, 26
            That sits above,
            And knows me, and knows me,
            How pitiful I deserve—" 29
I mean in singing; but in loving, Leander the good 30
swimmer, Troilus the first employer of panders, and a 31
whole bookful of these quondam carpetmongers, 32
whose names yet run smoothly in the even road of a
blank verse, why, they were never so truly turned over 34
and over as my poor self in love. Marry, I cannot show 35
it in rhyme. I have tried. I can find out no rhyme to
"lady" but "baby," an innocent rhyme; for "scorn," 37
"horn," a hard rhyme; for "school," "fool," a babbling 38
rhyme; very ominous endings. No, I was not born
under a rhyming planet, nor I cannot woo in festival
terms.

Enter Beatrice.

Sweet Beatrice, wouldst thou come when I called thee?
BEATRICE   Yea, signor, and depart when you bid me.
BENEDICK   Oh, stay but till then!   [*She starts to leave.*]
BEATRICE   "Then" is spoken; fare you well now. And
yet, ere I go, let me go with that I came, which is, with 46
knowing what hath passed between you and Claudio.
BENEDICK   Only foul words; and thereupon I will kiss
thee.
BEATRICE   Foul words is but foul wind, and foul wind
is but foul breath, and foul breath is noisome; there- 51
fore I will depart unkissed.
BENEDICK   Thou hast frighted the word out of his right 53
sense, so forcible is thy wit. But I must tell thee plainly,
Claudio undergoes my challenge; and either I must
shortly hear from him, or I will subscribe him a 56
coward. And I pray thee now tell me, for which of my
bad parts didst thou first fall in love with me?
BEATRICE   For them all together, which maintained so
politic a state of evil that they will not admit any good 60
part to intermingle with them. But for which of my
good parts did you first suffer love for me? 62
BENEDICK   Suffer love! A good epithet. I do suffer love 63
indeed, for I love thee against my will.
BEATRICE   In spite of your heart, I think. Alas, poor
heart, if you spite it for my sake I will spite it for yours,
for I will never love that which my friend hates.
BENEDICK   Thou and I are too wise to woo peaceably.

321 give you leave (For "ask your leave.")   **322 prohibit** (For "permit.")   **327 lewd** wicked, worthless
**5.2. Location: Leonato's garden (? At the scene's end, Leonato's
house is some distance away.)**
2 to the speech of to speak with   **6 style** (1) poetic style (2) stile,
stairs over a fence   **7 come over** (1) excel beyond (2) traverse, as one
would cross a stile (3) in Margaret's next speech, the phrase is taken
to mean "mount sexually."   **comely** good. (With an allusion to Margaret's beauty.)   **10 keep below stairs** dwell in the servants' quarters.
16–17 I . . . bucklers i.e., I acknowledge myself beaten (in repartee).
(Bucklers are shields with spikes [pikes] in their centers. Margaret
uses the word in a bawdy sense in her reply.)   **21 pikes** spikes in the
center of a shield.   **vice** screw. (Benedick's bawdy sense continues
Margaret's jest.)

26–9 The god . . . deserve (The beginning of an old song by William
Elderton.)   **29 How . . . deserve** how I deserve pity. (But Benedick
uses the phrase to mean "how little I deserve.")   **30 Leander** lover of
Hero of Sestos; he swam the Hellespont nightly to see her until he
drowned   **31 Troilus** lover of Cressida, whose affair was assisted by
her uncle Pandarus   **32 quondam carpetmongers** ladies' men of old,
such as one might find in the carpeted boudoirs of the women they
woo   **34–5 over and over** i.e., head over heels   **37 innocent** childish
38 hard (1) exact (2) unpleasant, because of the association with cuckold's horns   **46 that I came** what I came for   **51 noisome** noxious
53 his its   **56 subscribe** formally proclaim in writing   **60 politic** prudently governed   **62 suffer** (1) experience (2) feel the pain of
63 epithet expression.

BEATRICE   It appears not in this confession. There's not ⁶⁹
one wise man among twenty that will praise himself.
BENEDICK   An old, an old instance, Beatrice, that lived ⁷¹
in the time of good neighbors. If a man do not erect in ⁷²
this age his own tomb ere he dies, he shall live no ⁷³
longer in monument than the bell rings and the ⁷⁴
widow weeps. ⁷⁵
BEATRICE   And how long is that, think you?
BENEDICK   Question: why, an hour in clamor and a ⁷⁷
quarter in rheum. Therefore is it most expedient for ⁷⁸
the wise, if Don Worm, his conscience, find no imped- ⁷⁹
iment to the contrary, to be the trumpet of his own
virtues, as I am to myself. So much for praising myself,
who, I myself will bear witness, is praiseworthy. And
now tell me, how doth your cousin?
BEATRICE   Very ill.
BENEDICK   And how do you?
BEATRICE   Very ill too.
BENEDICK   Serve God, love me, and mend. There will I
leave you too, for here comes one in haste.

Enter Ursula.

URSULA   Madam, you must come to your uncle. Yonder's old coil at home. It is proved my lady Hero hath ⁹⁰
been falsely accused, the Prince and Claudio mightily
abused, and Don John is the author of all, who is fled ⁹²
and gone. Will you come presently? ⁹³
BEATRICE   Will you go hear this news, signor?
BENEDICK   I will live in thy heart, die in thy lap, and be ⁹⁵
buried in thy eyes; and moreover I will go with thee to
thy uncle's.   *Exeunt.*

❧

[5.3]

*Enter Claudio, Prince [Don Pedro, Balthasar],
and three or four with tapers.*

CLAUDIO   Is this the monument of Leonato?
A LORD   It is, my lord.
CLAUDIO   [*reading from a scroll*]

Epitaph.

"Done to death by slanderous tongues
    Was the Hero that here lies.
Death, in guerdon of her wrongs,   ⁵
    Gives her fame which never dies.
So the life that died with shame
Lives in death with glorious fame."

69 **It . . . confession** i.e., You don't show your wisdom in praising
yourself for being wise.   71 **instance** proverb (i.e., "He has ill neighbors that is fain to praise himself").   72 **time . . . neighbors** good old
times (when one's neighbors spoke well of one).   73–5 **he shall . . .
weeps** i.e., he will be memorialized only during the (brief) time of the
funeral service and the official mourning.   77 **Question** i.e., An easy
question, which I will answer as follows.   **clamor** noise (of the bell)
78 **rheum** tears (of the widow).   79 **Don . . . conscience** (The action
of the conscience was traditionally described as the gnawing of a
worm; compare with Mark 9:44–8.)   90 **old coil** great confusion
92 **abused** deceived   93 **presently** immediately.   95 **die** (With the
common connotation of "experience sexual climax.")
5.3. Location: A churchyard.
5 **guerdon** recompense

Hang thou there upon the tomb,
Praising her when I am dumb.
                          [*He hangs up the scroll.*]
Now, music, sound, and sing your solemn hymn.

Song.

BALTHASAR
    Pardon, goddess of the night,   ¹²
    Those that slew thy virgin knight;   ¹³
    For the which, with songs of woe,
    Round about her tomb they go.
        Midnight, assist our moan;
        Help us to sigh and groan,
            Heavily, heavily.
        Graves, yawn and yield your dead,
        Till death be utterèd,   ²⁰
            Heavily, heavily.

CLAUDIO
    Now, unto thy bones good night!
    Yearly will I do this rite.
DON PEDRO
    Good morrow, masters. Put your torches out.
        The wolves have preyed; and look, the gentle day, ²⁵
    Before the wheels of Phoebus, round about   ²⁶
        Dapples the drowsy east with spots of gray.
    Thanks to you all, and leave us. Fare you well.
CLAUDIO
    Good morrow, masters. Each his several way.   ²⁹
DON PEDRO
    Come, let us hence, and put on other weeds,   ³⁰
        And then to Leonato's we will go.
CLAUDIO
    And Hymen now with luckier issue speed's   ³²
        Than this for whom we rendered up this woe.
                                                Exeunt.

[5.4]

*Enter Leonato, Benedick, [Beatrice], Margaret,
Ursula, old man [Antonio], Friar [Francis, and]
Hero.*

FRIAR
    Did I not tell you she was innocent?
LEONATO
    So are the Prince and Claudio, who accused her
    Upon the error that you heard debated.   ³
    But Margaret was in some fault for this,
    Although against her will, as it appears   ⁵
    In the true course of all the question.   ⁶

12 **goddess of the night** i.e., Diana, moon goddess, patroness of
chastity   13 **knight** i.e., follower   20 **utterèd** fully expressed
25 **have preyed** i.e., have done their preying   26 **wheels of Phoebus**
i.e., chariot of the sun god   29 **several** separate   30 **weeds** garments
32 **And . . . speed's** And may the god of marriage favor us with better
fortune
5.4. Location: Leonato's house.
3 **Upon** on the basis of   5 **against her will** unintentionally   6 **question** investigation.

ANTONIO
Well, I am glad that all things sorts so well.   7

BENEDICK
And so am I, being else by faith enforced   8
To call young Claudio to a reckoning for it.

LEONATO
Well, daughter, and you gentlewomen all,
Withdraw into a chamber by yourselves,
And when I send for you, come hither masked.
The Prince and Claudio promised by this hour
To visit me. You know your office, brother:
You must be father to your brother's daughter,
And give her to young Claudio.   *Exeunt ladies.*

ANTONIO
Which I will do with confirmed countenance.   17

BENEDICK
Friar, I must entreat your pains, I think.   18

FRIAR   To do what, signor?

BENEDICK
To bind me or undo me—one of them.   20
Signor Leonato, truth it is, good signor,
Your niece regards me with an eye of favor.

LEONATO
That eye my daughter lent her. 'Tis most true.   23

BENEDICK
And I do with an eye of love requite her.

LEONATO
The sight whereof I think you had from me,   25
From Claudio, and the Prince. But what's your will?   26

BENEDICK
Your answer, sir, is enigmatical.
But, for my will, my will is your good will   28
May stand with ours, this day to be conjoined
In the state of honorable marriage,
In which, good Friar, I shall desire your help.

LEONATO
My heart is with your liking.

FRIAR   And my help.
Here comes the Prince and Claudio.

        Enter Prince [Don Pedro] and Claudio, and
        two or three other.

DON PEDRO
Good morrow to this fair assembly.

LEONATO
Good morrow, Prince. Good morrow, Claudio.
We here attend you. Are you yet determined   36
Today to marry with my brother's daughter?

CLAUDIO
I'll hold my mind, were she an Ethiope.

LEONATO
Call her forth, brother. Here's the Friar ready.
                                        [*Exit Antonio.*]

DON PEDRO
Good morrow, Benedick. Why, what's the matter,
That you have such a February face,
So full of frost, of storm, and cloudiness?

CLAUDIO
I think he thinks upon the savage bull.   43
Tush, fear not, man! We'll tip thy horns with gold,
And all Europa shall rejoice at thee,   45
As once Europa did at lusty Jove   46
When he would play the noble beast in love.

BENEDICK
Bull Jove, sir, had an amiable low,
And some such strange bull leapt your father's cow
And got a calf in that same noble feat
Much like to you, for you have just his bleat.

        Enter [Leonato's] brother [Antonio], Hero,
        Beatrice, Margaret, [and] Ursula, [the ladies
        masked].

CLAUDIO
For this I owe you. Here comes other reckonings.   52
Which is the lady I must seize upon?

ANTONIO
This same is she, and I do give you her.

CLAUDIO
Why then, she's mine. Sweet, let me see your face.

LEONATO
No, that you shall not, till you take her hand
Before this friar and swear to marry her.

CLAUDIO
Give me your hand before this holy friar.
I am your husband, if you like of me.   59

HERO [*unmasking*]
And when I lived, I was your other wife;
And when you loved, you were my other husband.

CLAUDIO
Another Hero!

HERO   Nothing certainer.
One Hero died defiled, but I do live,
And surely as I live, I am a maid.

DON PEDRO
The former Hero! Hero that is dead!

LEONATO
She died, my lord, but whiles her slander lived.   66

FRIAR
All this amazement can I qualify,   67
When, after that the holy rites are ended,
I'll tell you largely of fair Hero's death.   69
Meantime let wonder seem familiar,   70
And to the chapel let us presently.   71

BENEDICK
Soft and fair, Friar. Which is Beatrice?   72

---

7 sorts turn out   **8 being . . . enforced** since otherwise I would be enforced by my promise to Beatrice   **17 confirmed countenance** straight face.   **18 entreat your pains** beg your help   **20 undo** (1) ruin (2) untie, unbind   **23 That . . . her** (Alludes to Hero's role in tricking Beatrice into confessing her love for Benedick.)   **25–6 The sight . . . Prince** (Alludes to their role in tricking Benedick into confessing his love for Beatrice.)   **28 for** as for.   **is** is that   **36 yet** still

43 I . . . bull (A jocular reminiscence of the conversation in 1.1.250 ff.)   **45 Europa** Europe   **46 Europa** a princess whom Jove approached in the form of a white bull and bore on his back through the sea to Crete   **52 I owe you** i.e., I'll pay you back later (for calling me a calf and a bastard).   **other reckonings** i.e., other matters to be settled first.   **59 like of** care for   **66 but whiles** only while   **67 qualify** moderate   **69 largely** at large, in full   **70 let . . . familiar** treat these marvels as ordinary matters   **71 let us presently** let us go at once.   **72 Soft and fair** i.e., Wait a minute

BEATRICE *[unmasking]*
I answer to that name. What is your will?
BENEDICK
Do not you love me?
BEATRICE　　　　　　　　　Why, no, no more than reason.
BENEDICK
Why, then your uncle and the Prince and Claudio
Have been deceived. They swore you did.
BEATRICE
Do not you love me?
BENEDICK　　　　　　　Troth, no, no more than reason.
BEATRICE
Why, then my cousin, Margaret, and Ursula　　　78
Are much deceived, for they did swear you did.
BENEDICK
They swore that you were almost sick for me.
BEATRICE
They swore that you were well-nigh dead for me.
BENEDICK
'Tis no such matter. Then you do not love me?
BEATRICE
No, truly, but in friendly recompense.
LEONATO
Come, cousin, I am sure you love the gentleman.　84
CLAUDIO
And I'll be sworn upon't that he loves her;
For here's a paper written in his hand,
A halting sonnet of his own pure brain,　　　　87
Fashioned to Beatrice. *[He shows a paper.]*
HERO　　　　　　　　　　And here's another
Writ in my cousin's hand, stol'n from her pocket,
Containing her affection unto Benedick.
　　　　　　　　　　　[She shows another paper.]
BENEDICK　A miracle! Here's our own hands against our　91
hearts. Come, I will have thee, but by this light I take　92
thee for pity.
BEATRICE　I would not deny you, but by this good day,
I yield upon great persuasion, and partly to save your
life, for I was told you were in a consumption.　　96

BENEDICK　Peace! I will stop your mouth. *[Kissing her.]*
DON PEDRO　How dost thou, Benedick, the married
　man?
BENEDICK　I'll tell thee what, Prince: a college of wit-　100
crackers cannot flout me out of my humor. Dost thou
think I care for a satire or an epigram? No. If a man　102
will be beaten with brains, 'a shall wear nothing hand-　103
some about him. In brief, since I do purpose to marry,　104
I will think nothing to any purpose that the world can
say against it; and therefore never flout at me for what　106
I have said against it; for man is a giddy thing, and this
is my conclusion. For thy part, Claudio, I did think to
have beaten thee, but in that thou art like to be my　109
kinsman, live unbruised, and love my cousin.
CLAUDIO　I had well hoped thou wouldst have denied
Beatrice, that I might have cudgeled thee out of thy
single life, to make thee a double-dealer, which out of　113
question thou wilt be, if my cousin do not look　114
exceeding narrowly to thee.　　　　　　　　　　115
BENEDICK　Come, come, we are friends. Let's have a
dance ere we are married, that we may lighten our
own hearts and our wives' heels.
LEONATO　We'll have dancing afterward.
BENEDICK　First, of my word! Therefore play, music.　120
Prince, thou art sad. Get thee a wife, get thee a wife.
There is no staff more reverend than one tipped with　122
horn.　　　　　　　　　　　　　　　　　　　123

　　　　　　Enter Messenger.

MESSENGER
My lord, your brother John is ta'en in flight
And brought with armèd men back to Messina.
BENEDICK　Think not on him till tomorrow. I'll devise
thee brave punishments for him. Strike up, pipers!　127
　　　　　　　　　　　Dance. [Exeunt.]

78 my cousin i.e., Hero　**84 cousin** i.e., niece　**87 halting** limping.
his own pure purely his own　**91–2 against our hearts** i.e., to prove
our hearts guilty as charged.　**96 in a consumption** i.e., wasting
away in sighs.

100 college assembly　**102–4 If . . . him** i.e., If a man allows himself
to be cowed by ridicule, he'll never dare dress handsomely or do anything conspicuous that will draw attention.　**106 flout** mock　**109 in
that** in view of the fact that.　**like** likely　**113 a double-dealer** (1) a
married man (2) a deceiver, adulterer　**114–15 look . . . narrowly to**
keep close watch over　**120 of** on　**122–3 tipped with horn** (Alludes
to the usual joke about cuckolds, as at line 44).　**127 brave** fine

---

Much Ado About Nothing on Stage

The Elizabethan Era: Fluid Movement

Much Ado was a popular play, remaining in the repertory until the theaters were closed by Parliament in
1642. King Charles I wrote "Benedik and Betrice" next
to the title of the play in his copy of the Second Folio of
Shakespeare's plays, while other seventeenth-century
references to the witty lovers suggest that readers

knew the play well and already viewed it as dominated by this comic pair. As Leonard Digges wrote in his
preface to the 1640 edition of Shakespeare's poems: "let
but *Betrice* / And *Benedicke* be seene, loe in a trice / the
Cockpit Galleries, Boxes, all are full."
　　The unlocalized space of the Elizabethan public theater would have allowed the play to move without
scene changes from everyday conversation and gesture
to more stylized language and ritualistic modes of
behavior. In the Quarto edition of 1600, the names of

Will Kempe, the specialist in clown roles, and Richard Cowley appear as speech headings in 4.2, suggesting that these were the members of Shakespeare's company who played Dogberry and Verges. Burbage presumably played Benedick, with boy players as Beatrice and Hero.

The Restoration and the Eighteenth Century: Adaptations and Practice

After the relicensing of theater companies by royal patent, Beatrice and Benedick returned to the stage in an adaptation by William Davenant much altered from Shakespeare's original. Davenant's *The Law Against Lovers*, performed at Lincoln's Inn Fields in 1662, placed the lovers as characters in a new concoction that also borrowed heavily from *Measure for Measure*. Benedick became a Restoration rake, obliged to fight Duke Angelo (from *Measure*) since the Duke's new law against lovers had sent Claudio and Julietta to prison. Davenant understood the appeal of Benedick and Beatrice's witty repartee for his Restoration audiences. Davenant wrote in a more blunt, less highly figured style than Shakespeare, and employed more bawdy dialogue, suiting Restoration taste. His play dispenses with the Hero-Claudio plot altogether, perhaps because Restoration audiences rejected such idealized and melodramatic romance. Davenant added three other women to the plots and thus could display a quartet of actresses who, according to the positive report of a pair of Dutch visitors, frequently sang and danced.

The first revival of the play in something like its Shakespearean form in London came in 1721; other revivals followed in 1737, 1739, and 1746. When David Garrick took over the management of Drury Lane in 1747, he staged *Much Ado* more than any Shakespearean comedy. Benedick and Beatrice were the primary interest in his swift and lively productions, with Garrick himself acting Benedick in a light-hearted and eccentric vein. When he performed the role opposite Hanna Pritchard from 1748 to 1756, the witty combatants vigorously competed for supremacy in wit with a speed which one reviewer compared to that of a game of badminton. Garrick last played the part in the 1775-1776 season opposite Frances Abington as Beatrice, who went on to play the role at Covent Garden for another ten years. She created a high-born Beatrice whose "every word stabbed" (Gilliland, *Dramatic Mirror*, quoted in Cox, 13). Critics liked her assertive intelligence and appreciated her social status, for Mrs. Abington, like other eighteenth-century actresses before her, wore her own fashionable clothing in the part. She was sixty-one when she played her last Beatrice at Covent Garden.

The Nineteenth Century: Sensibility and Comedy

New approaches to the performance of *Much Ado* and its central roles emerged at the end of the eighteenth century as actors (John and Charles Kemble and Robert Elliston) and actresses (Elizabeth Younge, Elizabeth Farren, and Dorothy Jordan) began portraying the witty pair as creatures of sensibility and feeling as well as of wit. The Hero-Claudio plot was restored to a more nearly equal balance, and interpreters of Beatrice especially were praised if they demonstrated heartfelt emotion rather than simply a strong, caustic spirit. John Philip Kemble played Benedick at Drury Lane from 1788 to 1802, and, though he suggested a dignity and seriousness in the part (Hazlitt, 459-460), he was deemed too stiff for comedy and gave over the part to his brother Charles, who became one of the most-praised Benedicks in theater history. Charles Kemble either performed in or staged nearly every London performance of *Much Ado* between 1817 and 1836, as well as performing the play in America and returning to the role of Benedick for a royal command performance in 1840. Kemble's *Much Ado* took a keener interest in the lovers' motivations than Garrick's; Kemble's performances hinted early on that Beatrice and Benedick were long fascinated with one another. Kemble himself is reported to have added the ease and elegance of a distinguished gentleman to the usual buoyancy and wit in the role of Benedick. During the latter half of the play, when Benedick distances himself from the prevailing male slanders of women, Kemble showed the character's capacity for nobility and honor. Similarly, prominent actresses such as Eliza Chester, Maria Foote, and Fanny Kemble softened the part of Beatrice, turning her wit into a less cutting, more playful banter, and portraying her as a woman of sensibility whose strong moral sense emerged especially in the latter half of the play. Don John, on the other hand, became a melodramatic stage villain.

By the time William Charles Macready essayed the role of Benedick in 1843, the play was staged in spectacular fashion, commencing in the Italian grandeur of Leonato's home with its portico overlooking the harbor of Messina and a garden including a grove of orange trees. Victorian scene changes were frequent and the scenery itself ponderously expensive, with the masked ball in a candlelit ballroom, and the gulling scenes staged in an ornamental garden, sometimes with a fountain. The text was usually heavily cut in these spectacular productions to make room for the time-consuming scene changes that were occasionally advertised in their own right as "authentic." Macready's Benedick contrasted with Kemble's: Macready reportedly created a hard, caustic character, his contempt for women not lightly worn but a settled attitude.

Henry Irving and Ellen Terry were Benedick and Beatrice in Irving's much-travelled production that premiered in 1888; pictured here is what Irving called "the cathedral scene." (TopFoto)

In the second half of the century, Charles and Ellen Kean often performed the leading roles in England and America in a sumptuously mounted production that prepared the way for Henry Irving's *Much Ado* of 1882 at London's Lyceum. That almost universally acclaimed production toured North America and was twice revived. Reviewers praised Irving's attention to detail, the strong sense of ensemble, and the quality of the individual performances, especially Ellen Terry's as Beatrice. She and Irving implied that Beatrice and Benedick love each other unawares from the very first, and suggested real seriousness beneath their jesting. Their Lyceum production was so popular it ran for more than two hundred successive performances prior to various tours and revivals. Terry's warm, refined performances, somewhat bowdlerized by Irving so that Beatrice's barbs lost some of their sting, were among the most admired in the history of the play.

The Twentieth Century: Interpreters, Directors, and Updates

As with other Shakespearean dramas, the turn-of-the-century period brought opulent revivals of *Much Ado* by Augustin Daly in the United States and by Herbert Beerbohm Tree and others in England. Tree's production expressed what he called the luxury and extravagance of the Renaissance in sixteenth-century Italy. Filled with color, with nearly a dozen set changes and scores of costumes, and employing an offstage chorus and orchestra, Tree's production met a mixed response

from critics who felt the grand effects in the four-hour-long performance overwhelmed the essential playfulness of the comedy. Tree played Benedick, emphasizing the contrast between the gruff soldier early on and the polished lover in later scenes. The production gave prominence to the Hero-Claudio plot, with Viola Tree's Hero realizing the emotional potential of the innocent young woman's humiliation.

Change was already coming, however, despite opulent Victorian productions. William Poel and Gordon Craig were exploring the simpler, non-naturalistic settings that were to take precedence in *Much Ado* stagings during the first half of the twentieth century. Poel's 1904 production on a replica of an Elizabethan stage revived the use of simple movable props and employed Renaissance instruments for the music. By 1920, the play was staged experimentally by Birmingham Repertory on a simple set using "strong primary colours and bright lighting to suggest a dominant tone of hard brilliance . . . The acting was consistent with the visual effect, with Douglas Clark-Smith giving Benedick 'a hard veneer of brilliance,' and Margaret Chatwin playing Beatrice with a front of shrewishness beneath which the pleasantry was till visible" (Cox, 51).

In the 1930s, contemporary concepts took the form of modern-dress productions, beginning at the Hull Playgoers' Society in 1930 and later at the Old Vic (i.e., London's Royal Victoria Theatre) with an irreverent staging that mixed Elizabethan and Regency costume styles against a cartoon backdrop. A more successful modern-dress production at the Bristol Old Vic in 1947,

John Gielgud and Diana Wynard, shown here at the Masked Ball, made a sparkling Benedick and Beatrice at London's Phoenix Theatre in 1952. (Corbis/Hulton-Deutsch Collection)

directed by Hugh Hunt, envisioned the returning soldiers as coming home at the end of World War II. Don John was a member of a fascist black-shirt militia; Dogberry entered as an air raid warden on a bicycle. During this period Edith Evans was a noted Beatrice, tilting the role back toward wit and artifice after its Victorian softening, while John Gielgud was esteemed for his quick, darting wit as Benedick. Also noteworthy was Sybil Thorndike as a robust Beatrice, emphasizing the bawdy lines cut from Victorian productions.

As the nineteenth-century emphasis upon character criticism diminished, directors and reviewers looked with more interest toward the play's structure, its mixing of genres, and its variety of verbal styles. When Gielgud staged the play in the 1950s, he emphasized the harmonizing of these elements in a festive romantic fantasy. Gielgud's production, set in the High Renaissance in Italy, played at Stratford-upon-Avon with Gielgud and Peggy Ashcroft, then in London in 1952 with Gielgud and Diana Wynyard. Light and buoyant, it was acclaimed for its high stylishness and was considered as the definitive production for its time as Irving's had been for his. Gielgud was praised as the best Benedick since Irving: a poised, urbane courtier whose ironic detachment was offset by touches of self-mockery.

An opposite reading of Gielgud's came from John Houseman and Jack Landau at the American Shakespeare Festival in Stratford, Connecticut, in 1957. Their staging set the play in nineteenth-century Texas where Spanish Mexicans governed. The tone alternated between farce and romantic sentimentality. Dogberry was a Western sheriff. This kind of recontextualizing continues to this day as directors attempt to find times, places, and cultural moments that make the play's interrogations of gender politics accessible to contemporary audiences.

Similarly, many other producers and actors have offered the play in a range of settings. Douglas Seale's 1958 production was set in the mid–nineteenth-century Italy of Verdi and Rossini; Michael Redgrave was Benedick with Googie Withers as a radiantly mocking Beatrice in this Stratford-upon-Avon production. The frothy operetta style of that staging spread to others as, for example, to a Stratford, Ontario, production with Christopher Plummer as Benedick. At New York's Public Theatre, Joseph Papp and A. J. Antoon staged a popular if controversial *Much Ado* in 1972 that transferred to Broadway and subsequently appeared on national television. Set in small-town America in the early years of the twentieth century, the play began with soldiers returning home in Rough Rider uniforms. Dogberry and his men were Keystone Kops, and the messenger was a reporter photographing the ladies. Other American productions have set the play in Latin America, the United States, outposts of the British Empire, the Netherlands, nineteenth-century Italy, post–World War I Sicily, Spain throughout the ages, and even upon a cruise ship called the *S. S. Messina*. The Royal Shakespeare Company at Stratford-upon-Avon opened its 1988 season with a *Much Ado* that was set loosely in the mid twentieth century with the women in stylish post-war dress and the soldiers arriving by helicopter. That production relied upon broad comedy; one moment frequently remarked upon involved shtick with a folding deck chair that upstaged the actors and may have been the source for Branagh's shenanigans with a folding chair in the gulling scene of his film (see pp. 264–265).

More important than these changes in setting and context were several interpretations influenced by the cultural revolutions of the 1960s and the emergence of feminism. Both Katharine Hepburn at Stratford, Connecticut, and Maggie Smith at the National Theatre of Great Britain challenged the "womanliness" that had become an attribute of Beatrice by offering more fiercely aggressive readings in which her biting wit again had sharp teeth. Such readings, culminating in Janet McTeer's Amazonian performance of Beatrice (1993), have viewed the play's tensions and sexual anxieties as more interesting than the harmonizing impulses shaping productions earlier in the twentieth century. Such postmodern performance practice underscores the dissonances of the play. Even traditional productions, including Branagh's Renaissance Theatre staging (and later film), have viewed Don Pedro as a somewhat isolated and ambiguous figure, rejected by Beatrice and sad during the wedding festivities.

Several directors have sought to re-imagine the play in an atmosphere fraught with male privilege. Franco Zeffirelli's Sicilian setting (1965) and John Barton's Indian Raj production (1976) presented patriarchal cultures steeped in the ideology of male power, with its double standard, its misogyny, and its assumption of male superiority. Barton's production was particularly praised for creating an artificial society full of game-playing and disguise in which spoiled men, waited upon by turbaned servants, amused themselves with sports, jokes, and such heartless games as slandering an innocent young woman. Zeffirelli's exuberant turn-of-the-century Sicilian romp for the National Company at the Old Vic proved festive and flamboyant, although controversial in its modernity and in its music, composed by Nino Rota. Maggie Smith and Robert Stephens engaged in a "merry war." Some critics found the production exhausting in its ceaseless, eager-to-please invention, and challenged its textual revisions by poet Robert Graves. The BBC filmed the production and aired it in 1967.

The play has had a lively history on the British commercial stage in the so-called West End, which is equivalent to Broadway in the United States. In 1989, actors Felicity Kendal and Alan Bates made a middle-aged Beatrice and Benedick, sharing a moment of tender comedy when, confronted by their own letters as evidence against them, the two lovers were shown to be short- and long-sighted respectively. In a similarly effective bit of middle-aged casting, actors Richard Easton and Katherine

McGrath at San Diego's Old Globe Theater in 1995 donned spectacles for that scene, as the potential spinster and confirmed bachelor studied their implicating love poems before stopping each other's banter with a kiss.

Much Ado About Nothing on Film and Television

The first film of *Much Ado About Nothing* was a silent released in 1926, followed by an East German film in 1963 and two in Russian movies in 1956 and 1973. Franco Zeffirelli's stage version in 1965 was filmed for television, as was Joseph Papp's for his Public Theatre in 1973. The BBC filmed its production for the series co-produced with Time-Life in 1984. The best-known film is Kenneth Branagh's 1993 adaptation shot in Tuscany, set indeterminately around 1800-1900, and cast with a mix of British stage veterans (Branagh, Emma Thompson, and Richard Briers) and American film stars (Denzel Washington, Keanu Reeves, Michael Keaton, and Robert Sean Leonard).

■ 1984—Director Stuart Burge, BBC Films, with Royal Shakespeare Company members Robert Lindsay (Benedick), Robert Reynolds (Claudio), Cherie Lunghi (Beatrice), Katharine Levy (Hero), Lee Montague (Leonato), Jon Finch (Don Pedro), Michael Elphick (Dogberry), and Graham Crowden (Friar Francis). (120 min.)

This was the BBC's second attempt to film *Much Ado*. The first, filmed and edited with Michael York as Benedick and Penelope Keith as Beatrice, was never released. The reasons for that decision reportedly had more to do with internal studio politics than any single defect in the production. This second production, directed by Stuart Burge in 1984 with a less well-known cast, proved more acceptable and was aired during the last winter of the BBC's six-year-long Shakespeare series. The studio setting conjures an opulent villa, with Moorish, Florentine, and Spanish influences. The costuming is rich and varied—some have called it distracting—and the language is unusually well-spoken, although generally the acting here is not a high point of the series. The production opens with period music and a leisurely rhythm as Leonato welcomes his guests. Benedick seems quite serious when he asks his host whether he actually doubted that Hero was his daughter; that seriousness pervades Jon Finch's interpretation of Don Pedro in these early scenes as well. Robert Reynolds's Claudio has a physical youth and attractiveness that matches Hero's. Robert Lindsay as Benedick and Cherie Lunghi as Beatrice convey some of the complexity of Benedick and Beatrice's feelings for one another.

The ballroom scene is notable for its period music and choreography; all the dance metaphors in Beatrice's speeches come to life, and the dancing patterns break open now and again for close-ups of various encounters between characters who very often are only pretending not to know the identity of the person beneath the disguise. Benedick shows himself a merry soul, leaping with Margaret to the music. His barbs directed at Beatrice hit the mark, although hers prove even sharper and more wounding. The Don John scenes make effective if conventional use of candlelight and shadow to suggest the plotters' dark designs. The camerawork is rudimentary and occasionally distracting as when the focus moves abruptly from a close-up of Benedick to an explanatory close-up of the "white-bearded fellow," Leonato, about whom he is speaking. High-spirited comedy marks the male-bonding scene in which Benedick returns after the gull, now clean-shaven and ridiculous in love. The costuming during the wedding scene is especially opulent, with Claudio dressed in white and gold trimmed with a crimson silk sash, and Hero a silent, more generalized vision in white by comparison. Claudio is physically rough with Hero as he pushes her away, calling her a "rotten orange." The Friar proves a gently compassionate and appealing character, whose wisdom calms the storm in the church and suggests that divine grace will somehow bring about the wished-for redemption with Hero's resurrection. Evenhanded and steady, the production makes few bold interpretive choices and moves on to a plausibly happy ending signaled again by a lively circle dance accompanied by a dozen musicians.

■ 1993—Director Kenneth Branagh, Renaissance Film Productions, with Branagh (Benedick), Emma Thompson (Beatrice), Kate Beckinsale (Hero), Denzel Washington (Don Pedro), Keanu Reeves (Don John), Michael Keaton (Dogberry), and Richard Briers (Leonato). (120 min.)

Branagh first appeared as Benedick in a production directed by Judi Dench for his Renaissance Theatre in 1988. In most ways traditional and focused upon the psychology of the characters rather than upon any political or gender ideology, the production was enormously popular and made the play both accessible and entertaining. Both of those traits mark Branagh's visually lush film; it exploits the gently undulating Tuscan landscape for its brilliant light and sensuous beauty, even as it emphasizes the eroticism at the core of the two-plotted story. Branagh signals the sexually vigorous yet mild and harmonizing tone of the production with his opening. As a painting of the villa comes gradually to life we see a hillside scene in which the members of Leonato's extended household are joyously picnicking. The relaxed women all wear white, open-necked, full-skirted dresses of indeterminate period. Their hair is long and tousled. The men wear similarly casual clothing in white and soft shades of beige, with many of the younger men bare-chested. Emma Thompson's Beatrice, barefooted and sitting in a tree, is swinging her suntanned legs as she wryly reads the words to Balthasar's song transposed here from later in the play. Her "Sigh no more, ladies, sigh no more. / Men were deceivers ever, / One foot in sea and one on shore, / To one thing constant never" is spoken with such playful irony that clearly the faithlessness of male lovers is here taken as a given. The news of the soldiers' return from the wars arrives quickly, and with it Beatrice's first demonstration of her fascination with Benedick.

From their perch on the hillside, the picnickers see the soldiers approaching. Then in a nod to the classic Western, *The Magnificent Seven*, Branagh's seven lead male characters thunder towards the villa on horseback. After slow-motion close-ups of their exciting and virile ride, the entire household leaps to its collective feet as if on cue and races towards the house to bathe. Clothes fly off in every direction, as the women move into bathing houses, lather one another's backs, and just as quickly dress again, while their scenes are intercut with parallel images of naked men jumping into baths, shaving, and preparing to present themselves properly to Leonato and the ladies. Desire and sex are in the air. Before the actual greetings occur, Branagh uses an overhead shot to show the wedge-shaped phalanx of seven men led by Don Pedro moving like an arrow towards the domestic grouping arrayed in its own formation to welcome them. Both the erotic nature of the comedy to ensue and the theme of apparel and social convention as potentially problematic are established without recourse to any of Shakespeare's language (other than the song).

Throughout the film, the simplified action unfolds swiftly, as Branagh cuts and rearranges scenes, shortens certain speeches, and uses visual cues to replace speech (see "Close-up," pp. 266–276, with an excerpt from the published screenplay). Branagh's Benedick is vivacious and charming, his vanity undercut with self-mockery. Although Thompson's Beatrice is a strong, compelling personality, she is also soft and conventionally feminine. Her warmth and joyous wit do not have a bitter edge. The chemistry between these two—at the time of the filming they were offstage husband and wife—is unusually strong. She bows her head with sorrow when she describes to Don Pedro how she previously lent Benedick her heart and he played her false, while his comically exaggerated exasperation with her swiftly stabbing wit suggests a similar disappointment in their earlier love. Branagh makes substantial cuts to the gulling scenes, adding the shtick with a chair for him, and sending Beatrice behind trees and statuary as she overhears herself described as disdainful by Hero and Ursula. Both lovers quickly accept the responsibility of reformation, as the action fluently moves on to Don John's plot (reassigned from earlier in the play). Robert Sean Leonard's naïve young Claudio is indeed a "Lackbeard" as Benedick later calls him. As conventionally handsome as Kate Beckinsale's Hero is beautiful, the American actor Leonard flattens his speeches early on, but grows more convincing in his passionate disappointment when he thinks he has seen his Hero making love to Borachio in her chamber. This added scene, with Borachio slipping off Margaret's dress and roughly pushing her against a balcony railing, has a crudity at the opposite extreme from Claudio's idealizations of Hero. Its explicitness shocks and implicates Margaret in ways Shakespeare doesn't, though it does prepare for Claudio's rough handling of Hero when he spurns her at the wedding. That wedding is staged simply outdoors. Richard Briers's Leonato is as quickly and passionately overwhelmed by the "evidence" of his daughter's infidelity as Claudio.

Branagh sets the ensuing "Kill Claudio" scene in a small chapel inside the villa, lending this turning point, with its first heartfelt declarations of love by Beatrice and Benedick, both seriousness and intimacy. Benedick's parting of the ways with the male club of Claudio and Don Pedro comes as a shock to them, yet the alienation is short lived, for Branagh swiftly presents a shortened deposition scene. He allows Michael Keaton's Dogberry to use facial tics and mannerisms and only a few of the character-defining malapropisms. Branagh reports in the published screenplay (xv) that he subjectively cut Dogberry's "unfunniest lines" because he had had "bitter experience" playing one of Shakespeare's "great unfunny clowns": Touchstone in *As You Like It*.

Once Branagh's Benedick has declared his love, he submits to the conventions of rhyming, singing, and sonneteering with a giddy awareness of his own ridiculousness. He capers idiotically in a fountain, and raises his arms in triumph (as Beatrice does too) when he knows he is loved. In Act 5, standing by a wall overgrown with pink flowers and overlooking the distant hills, he encounters a Beatrice who claims to be ill for the slandered Hero, though clearly she is sick with love for him. Benedick seriously and empathetically delivers the line: "Serve God, love me, and mend." Then risking ridicule from the men, he leaves her to ask Leonato for this niece's hand in marriage. The resolution comes quickly, as a quartet of veiled women

arrives for the second wedding, and Claudio's amazement at Hero's "resurrection" leads on to the engagement of Beatrice and Benedick. Branagh has cut many of the cuckolding references and much of the misogynist banter from the play, thus softening it on both sides of the gender divide. He makes a similar excision of the cuckolding jokes in this final, exuberantly happy scene. Only Washington's empathetic Don Pedro is left out of the general rejoicing as the camera tracks up and away to capture a circle dance that snakes its way through the gardens of the villa, while the insouciant ballad again converts all "sounds of woe" into "Hey nonny, nonny." Branagh uses mood music extensively in the film, and, having sought approval from a young, popular audience, he achieves it in this genuinely amusing and generally well-received film.

Adaptations

- 1862—*Beatrice et Benedict* (opera), book and music by Hector Berlioz.

    This *opera-comique* in two acts was adapted from Shakespeare's play, with both words and music by Hector Berlioz. It was first performed at Baden-Baden and as Berlioz's last major work has remained popular. Its overture, like many of his, is still often played in symphonic concerts. The title suggests the nature of the adaptation. There is no slander of Hero; the young lovers are united after the war, their union contrasting to the double tricking of Beatrice and Benedick. The resolution for the witty lovers depends upon a love sonnet that each has written to the other.

- 1901—*Much Ado About Nothing* (opera), book and music by Charles Villiers Stanford.

    This lesser-known opera by Charles Villiers Stanford premiered at the Royal Opera House, Covent Garden in 1901. This adaptation includes Don John's plot against Hero and Claudio, along with a window scene enacting Borachio's deception. The libretto follows the play quite closely (F. H. Mares, Cambridge edition, 29); but although the first reviews were enthusiastic, the opera has disappeared from the repertory.

References and Related Reading

Cox, John D., ed. *Plays in Performance: "Much Ado About Nothing."* Cambridge, Eng., 1998.

Findlay, Alison. "*Much Ado About Nothing.*" *A Companion to Shakespeare's Works: The Comedies.* Oxford, 2003. 393–410.

Mason, Pamela. *Text and Performance: "Much Ado About Nothing."* London, 1992.

Paster, Gail Kern. "A Modern Perspective." *The New Folger Edition of "Much Ado About Nothing."* New York, 1995.

CLOSE-UP

KENNETH BRANAGH
Ireland's Renaissance Man

In the spring of 1984 a relatively unknown twenty-three-year-old actor played King Henry V in the Royal Shakespeare Company's opening production of the new season at Stratford-upon-Avon. Never in the long history of Shakespeare at Stratford had an actor that young been entrusted with the demanding role of England's fabled monarch. Just five years later the actor not only portrayed the king in the first major film of *Henry V* since Sir Laurence Olivier's acclaimed version in 1944, but he also directed a stellar cast of English actors. That film, coupled with his popular *Much Ado About Nothing* in 1993, helped to launch the Shakespeare-on-Film Renaissance of the 1990s. The actor was Kenneth Branagh (pronounced "BRAN-ah"), whose subsequent Shakespeare films—the "uncut" *Hamlet* (1996), the 1930s-style movie musical *Love's Labor's Lost* (1999), a wintry *Twelfth Night* (1991), and *Othello* (in which he played Iago for director Oliver Parker in 1995)—as well as a *Hamlet* spin-off (*A Midwinter's Tale*, a.k.a. *In the Bleak Midwinter*, for which Branagh also wrote the screenplay; 1996), have made him an heir to Olivier and Orson Welles as an interpreter of cinematic Shakespeare. All this from a man who has been acting and directing Shakespeare for only twenty years.

Born in Belfast, Northern Ireland, in 1960, Branagh credits his Irish/Celtic heritage for much of his success as a Shakespearean actor and filmmaker. He specifically cites the Irish love of language and storytelling, an affinity for and acceptance of melancholy, and especially the rituals of Irish life: "There was quite a healthy attitude to the ways in which people allowed themselves . . . to react to death and to ceremonies with which they marked the passing of people" (Wray and Burnett, 166). (*Much Ado About Nothing*, to cite an important example from Branagh's films, contains a beautiful sequence that marks the burial of Hero.) In the mid-1970s the Branagh family moved to England where, as a teen, young Kenneth acted multiple roles in a school production of Joan Littlewood's anti-war comedy, *O What a Lovely War!* His director, Roger Lewis, encouraged Branagh to consider acting as a profession, a suggestion that the youth accepted with passion. Also as a teenager Branagh was introduced to

Shakespeare via a touring production of *Romeo and Juliet* (which featured as Romeo Peter McEnery, the much-admired Mercutio in Zeffirelli's 1968 film), but it was the Hamlet of renowned actor Derek Jacobi at Oxford (and subsequently at the Old Vic in the late-1970s) that most stirred Branagh's enthusiasm for Shakespeare. Jacobi played the Chorus in Branagh's film of *Henry V* and Claudius in *Hamlet*; during the filming of *Hamlet* Jacobi presented Branagh with the tattered old acting edition of the play that is traditionally passed down from one "great Hamlet" to the next generation's "great Hamlet."

Branagh received his actor-training at the Royal Academy of Dramatic Art (RADA), which specializes in classical training and is generally regarded as England's premier school for stage talent. While a student at RADA, Branagh was cast in a major Chekhov role and, quite audaciously, wrote a letter to Olivier asking his advice. The revered actor, to Branagh's surprise, responded to his query. Branagh met another legendary Shakespearean actor, Sir John Gielgud, at a seventy-fifth anniversary celebration for RADA, at which Branagh recited a soliloquy from *Hamlet* for Gielgud. (Today young RADA actors look to Branagh much as Branagh looked to the admired Olivier and Gielgud during his own apprenticeship.) Upon completion of his RADA training (which included a praised performance as Hamlet), the faculty named Branagh the school's finest performer in his class.

While at RADA Branagh began working professionally, notably in a television drama called *Too Late to Talk to Billy*, the first in a series of *Billy* plays set in his native Belfast. Branagh earned high praise for his portrait of a troubled Irish youth caught in the horrible civil war that has plagued his homeland for four hundred years. His status as a RADA "star" and his television work led to other professional roles and film work in Australia. He auditioned for the Royal Shakespeare Company, but was not cast. However, a successful one-man show based on a long poem by Tennyson (*Maud*) and an engagement as St. Francis of Assisi in a stage drama caught the attention of RSC director Ron Daniels, who wanted Branagh to play Henry V for him. Though the

Daniels production did not materialize, Branagh was again approached by the RSC and was contracted to play several roles in the 1984–1985 season, including Henry V in Adrian Noble's highly regarded, though controversial, post–Falklands War production. Noble's anti-romantic, Brechtian reading of the play influenced Branagh's 1989 film. Branagh's youth and relative inexperience as a Shakespearean actor actually worked in his favor when he played Henry. He seemed every inch the boy-king struggling to assert himself in an acting company/army of veterans. Assert he did and emerged as a significant presence on the British stage. Branagh has meticulously detailed his work on *Henry V* in his autobiography, *Beginning*; his commentary provides some thoughtful analysis of one of Shakespeare's most enigmatic roles, a stepping-stone for Hamlet. (As part of his rehearsal preparation for the role, Branagh asked for, and received, an interview with Prince Charles, who provided the actor with insights about royal responsibilities and thought processes. The Prince and Lady Diana attended a performance of the play at Stratford; Branagh secured seats for his parents directly behind the royals.)

Branagh freely admits that he wrote *Beginning* for a single reason: money (ix). Specifically, he needed financial backing for a major undertaking—the formation of a classical acting company that would rival the RSC. Although he enjoyed his work with the RSC, he was frustrated by "the size of a merciless timetable of productions [which] was working against a consistently high quality in the work, and the burgeoning bureaucracy created tensions and fears among the members of the Company that were far from healthy" (Branagh, 166). While working on several television projects (including Ibsen's *Ghosts* with Judi Dench and Michael Gambon), Branagh envisioned a company of noted actors that would focus its efforts on a single classical work. In 1986 Branagh directed *Romeo and Juliet*, and played Romeo, at the historically important Lyric Hammersmith Theatre (Hammersmith is a western neighborhood of London). Performed in the Lyric's Studio, which seated one hundred and ten, the production received good notices from the press and from theater professionals such as RSC director Terry Hands. The grounds were laid for an enterprise that would eventually become known as the Renaissance Theatre Company. The RTC included actors such as Richard Briers, Francis Barber, and Emma Thompson, who would play Beatrice to Branagh's Benedick in the *Much Ado* film. (Branagh

and Thompson married in 1989, although they are now divorced.) Judi Dench directed *Much Ado* for the RTC, a production that set Branagh imagining the comedy as a Tuscany-set film (see screenplay excerpt on p. 270). Anthony Hopkins directed *Macbeth*. Derek Jacobi also agreed to direct a play and an actor of his choosing—Branagh in *Hamlet*, a production that was the cornerstone of the 1996 film (Branagh also played Hamlet for Noble at the RSC in 1992; this experience also influenced his film). In essence the RTC was a home for fine actors directing other fine actors, free from the constraints of size and bureaucracy that plagued the RSC and the National Theatre.

Both Branagh's stage productions and especially his films are known for the clarity of their verse speaking, their inventiveness (which rarely resorts to mere gimmickry), and especially their ability to provide a specific, concrete world for a classical play—though, ironically, that world is rarely the Renaissance. Branagh relocated *Much Ado* to early–nineteenth-century Tuscany (as opposed to its sixteenth-century Sicilian setting); *Love's Labor's Lost* is set in England during the years leading to World War II; and *Hamlet* takes place in a vaguely Bismarckian world of the nineteenth century. Branagh made this last choice because he believed that "the sense of power was very important to convey and to show that [Hamlet is] not just the life of one man and one family that will change but the life of an entire nation . . . the period in which we impressionistically set [the play] was also the case in a million European wars occurring in the latter part of the nineteenth century" (Wray and Burnett, 171). Only the history play, *Henry V*, retained a true-to-the-period setting and costumes, yet Branagh radically parted company from Olivier's romantic, chivalrous rendering of the text by grounding the play in a grimy reality. All was mud and blood, best seen in the glorious post-Agincourt sequence in which Branagh/Henry carries a dead boy the length of the battlefield to the somber tones of a Latin dirge sung by a boys' choir.

That particular shot, one of the most memorable in a film of superb visual images, is emblematic of what scholar-critic Cary Mazur refers to as Branagh's love of the "BMS"—the Big Memorable Sequence (Skovmund, 9). In the BMS Branagh employs (some might say "indulges in") spectacular cinematic effects that remind audiences that they are watching first a movie, and only second a play by Shakespeare. *Much Ado* opens with a rousing shot of the men returning from war, their horses straining at the bit (Branagh actually recreates a moment

(continued)

from the Western classic, *The Magnificent Seven*); the film ends with a long, uninterrupted shot of the men and women dancing into, out of, and throughout the grounds of a Tuscan villa as (apparently) God smiles down on the revelers. Shakespeare's "Pageant of the Nine Worthies" in *Love's Labor's Lost*, under Branagh's direction, becomes a song and dance number ("There's No Business Like Show Business") in the best MGM movie-musical style; Bertram's ruminations on love segue into a giddy flight of fancy—quite literally as Bertram and his three love-struck colleagues float into the "heavens" of a library while singing "I'm in Heaven." That particular BMS provides one of Branagh's most amusing Shakespearean in-jokes as audiences are reminded that the Globe Theatre was adorned with its own "heavens." In *Hamlet*, the appearance of the Ghost, the Claudius-Gertrude nuptial celebration, Branagh's rendering of Act 4's "How all occasions do inform against me" soliloquy (shot against snow-capped mountains), and especially Fortinbras's SWAT-team attack on Elsinore all qualify as BMSs.

Branagh is not apologetic for such stunning cinematic showmanship, which Pauline Kael claims makes him a "flamboyant realist" (Crowe, 223). Branagh admits to being an avid moviegoer himself and enjoys "quoting" bits from other movies in his Shakespearean work (e.g., the *Casablanca*-like parting of the lovers that concludes *Love's Labor's Lost*) because, for him

> Part of the challenge with Shakespeare films, which remain a sort of backbone to what I do, seems necessarily and healthily influenced by exposure to, as a performer and as a director, story-telling in other kinds of genres (with the idea being that one is constantly trying to challenge the ways in which Shakespeare can be offered up on film). Therefore, to be familiar with the ways popular cinema tells its stories is very important.
>
> (Wray and Burnett, 167)

Branagh also gains such experience by performing in other films, like Welles, largely to raise money for his classical theater and Shakespearean film projects. As an actor he has appeared in a range of motion pictures, from pop-Westerns (*The Wild Wild West*, in which he played a hilarious quadriplegic villain), murder mysteries (*The Gingerbread Man*, based on a John Grisham novel), art films, and in children's adventure films (*Harry Potter and the Chamber of Secrets*). Branagh has also written screenplays, such as his melancholy comedy *A Midwinter's Tale*, which won the 1995 Venice International Film Festival, and he adapted Mary Shelley's *Frankenstein* for the cinema (1994). As Artistic Director of the RTC he wrote two stage plays: *Tell Me Honestly* and *Public Enemy*. As of this writing, Branagh is planning film versions of *Macbeth* and *As You Like It*, providing he can find "the world, a unifying concept. You have gut instincts about images or ways of doing [them], and then you spend years with the play tripping you up saying 'But that scene won't work!' " (Wray and Burnett, 177). He does, however, find the current era an ideal time to film Shakespeare:

> I've been very encouraged by the liveliness with which the academic Shakespeare community has responded to this last seven/eight years of film-making, It's a lively moment. It's an exciting moment. It's reinvented things a little, and even if people have been against some of this work, they have been passionate.
>
> (Wray and Burnett, 178)

References and Related Reading

Branagh, Kenneth. *Beginning*. New York and London, 1990.

Crowe, Samuel. "Flamboyant Realist: Kenneth Branagh." *The Cambridge Companion to Shakespeare on Film*. Ed. Russell Jackson. Cambridge, Eng., 2000. 222–238.

Skovmund, Michael. "Introduction with a Discussion on Branagh and *Much Ado*." *Screen Shakespeare*. Arhaus, Denmark, 1994. 7–12.

Wray, Ramona, and Mark Thornton Burnett. "From the Horse's Mouth: Branagh on the Bard." *Shakespeare, Film, Fin de Siècle*. Eds. Wray and Burnett. Houndmills and London, 2000. 165–178.

Kenneth Branagh's Screenplay for *Much Ado About Nothing*

In the published screenplay for his popular film adaptation of *Much Ado About Nothing*, actor-director Kenneth Branagh describes a visual concept that seized his imagination four years before he had the opportunity to actually make the 1993 film:

> The opening images for this film of *Much Ado About Nothing* came to me during an actual stage performance of the play when I have to confess my attention wandered. I was playing Benedick in a

beautiful production directed by Dame Judi Dench on a U.K. tour. One night during Balthasar's song "Sigh No More, Ladies," the title sequence of his film played over and over in my mind: heat, haze and dust, grapes and horseflesh, and a nod to *The Magnificent Seven.* . . . Opening the story for the cinema, I thought should not mean drowning the words and characters in endless vistas and production value. Yet the play seemed to beg to live outside, in a vivid, lush countryside.

(viii)

Branagh goes on to say that it took several years and three motion pictures before he could make the right stylistic connection between Shakespeare's words and those images in his head.

When Branagh finally did find the means to create the film, he had made that connection, and he realized quite precisely the vision he saw years before. As the following excerpt comprising the first twenty pages of the screenplay demonstrates, the film begins with Balthasar's song, its words seen written on the screen as a woman's voice speaks the lines "Sigh no more, ladies, sigh no more." The screenplay is very specific in describing the quality of her voice as "peaceful and steady." Branagh instructs the actor (and audience) that we should sense a "subtle uplift in the voice, an expectancy and lightness" coloring the lines about transforming "all your sounds of woe / Into Hey nonny, nonny."

Instead of opening the film with Shakespeare's first scene, which shows Leonato announcing the contents of a letter he has just read, Branagh transposes the song from Act 3, using it to establish a wry theme and mild tone while his visual images establish place (rural Tuscany) and period (indeterminate late eighteenth to early nineteenth century). A watercolor painting of Leonato's villa appears in the lingering sun of a late afternoon. Laughter is heard, and the sound of music as the song picks up again and the painting dissolves into the "real" villa where a group of picnickers is being read to by the voice which only gradually is revealed as belonging to Beatrice. Before the camera pans over to show her radiantly healthy and beautiful face, it "introduces" many other characters in the drama, men and women, old and young, who seem to have just finished a picnic during this rural idyll. Branagh is specific about how this leisurely movement of the camera mirrors the relaxed mood of the picnickers and how the sound of laughter must be heard before a cut moves us to the image of a young man galloping toward Leonato and the camera.

As noted in Chapter 5, "From Page to Stage; Screenplay to Screen," the basic unit of construction in a film is the shot, not (as in theater) the scene. Many different shots are called for in the screenplay excerpt before a word is uttered. The words "My lord" spoken by the messenger are interpolated before we hear the first

speech from Shakespeare's script. After reading the letter delivered to him by the messenger, Leonato's jaw drops and he announces, "I learn in this letter that Don Pedro of Aragon comes this night to Messina." Scene, mood, and atmosphere have all been established; now the action begins.

For the speeches in the screenplay taken from 1.1 of *Much Ado,* Branagh dispenses with nearly half of the words that appear in Shakespeare's text; he also provides very specific directions and cues for the actors and for the movement of the camera. Upon hearing the messenger's news, for instance, the company is instructed: "There is the briefest of pauses before everyone [Leonato included] lets out an enormous scream. Petite pandemonium." We swiftly learn that Claudio has shown heroism (as the messenger reports), that Hero is smitten (a direction calling for "wicked ooing . . . laughs, looks and leers" among the women), and that Beatrice is very curious about Benedick ("there is no stopping Beatrice who is now well into her stride").

The next twenty-seven shots are wordless. Branagh calls for the thundering arrival of the horsemen (recall his *The Magnificent Seven* idea), the excited reaction of the picnickers, more riding, the frantic undressing of the women preparing to bathe, and more shots of the men, "their chests heaving," their "taut leather thighs against horseflesh" as they ride toward the villa. Each of these shots calls for a certain camera angle and distance, and in some cases, a particular kind of camera, such as the Steadicam®, which can be moved more readily than a larger, heavier, mounted machine. The cuts back and forth from male-centered scenes to female-dominated ones as the two groups prepare to meet again become a rhythm; this rhythm soon takes on an erotic charge. The freshly bathed men march toward Leonato and the women like a swift human arrow; this musical mating dance culminates in the initial dialogue of Benedick and Beatrice, the reconciliation of the bastard Don John to Leonato, and all the other elements of Shakespeare's 1.1.

Comparing this screenplay excerpt with the text of *Much Ado* can provide important insights into the themes the director wishes to highlight and the mood he hopes to convey. Often Branagh makes cleverly seamless internal cuts in long speeches, especially those involving highly figured and elaborate wordplay for Benedick and Beatrice. The cuts were intended to shorten the film, to open it to greater physical realism than that of the stage, and to keep the attention of a contemporary movie audience. Branagh is essentially collaborating with Shakespeare, respecting his language while attempting to make the comedy easily accessible. Placing Balthasar's song at the beginning, in the director's view, "allows the audience to 'tune in' to the new language they are about to experience and to realize that they will easily understand the simplicity, gravity, and beauty of the song lyrics" (viii). Do you agree? As you compare script, screenplay, and film, you might ask yourself whether Branagh has sacrificed too much of the language to achieve his goal of telling the story "with the utmost clarity and simplicity." Or has he instead, found visual equivalents for his interpretation of Shakespeare's words?

The Opening Scenes
Reading

> BLACK. *A series of lines from a song appear one by one on the screen, in bold white against the darkness. As each* LEGEND *materialises, we hear a woman's voice speak the line simultaneously.*

VOICE [OFFSCREEN]
Sigh no more, ladies [DISSOLVE]**,**
Sigh no more [DISSOLVE]**,**

> *The voice is wise, compassionate, knowing. The reading seems personal, read to herself. As if we were merely overhearing it.*

VOICE [OFFSCREEN]
Men were deceivers ever [DISSOLVE]**,**

> *The rhythm of the dissolves and of the voice is peaceful, steady.*

VOICE [OFFSCREEN]
One foot in sea and one on shore [DISSOLVE]**,**
To one thing constant never [DISSOLVE]**,**

> *As the next lines follow, we sense a subtle uplift in the voice, an expectancy and lightness that is in sympathy with the unstuffy typeface before us.*

VOICE [OFFSCREEN]
Then sigh not so [DISSOLVE]**,**
But let them go [DISSOLVE]**,**
And be you blithe and bonny [DISSOLVE]**,**
Converting all your sounds of woe [DISSOLVE]**,**
Into Hey nonny, nonny!
[DISSOLVE TO]

> *Exterior /* **PICNIC SITE** */ Day*

> *A misty watercolour painting which fills the entire frame. It is a view of* LEONATO'S *villa. Nestling on top of the hillside, it sits alone, away from Messina itself. Looking more like a rather grand, expansive farmhouse, it suns itself in the beauty of the autumnal late afternoon. The painting shows us the villa's rather crumbling grandeur: the orchard behind, the formal garden to the side, the little chapel, and here and there the farm workers occupied in tending to this self-contained rural Italian paradise. We have dwelt on the painting but a moment until the group laughter has subsided. As*

> *it does the* VOICE OFFSCREEN *begins again. The sounds of the country and a light, as yet distant, musical Air fills the soundtrack as we pan left to reveal.*

> *Exterior /* **PICNIC SITE** */ Day*

> *Leonato's villa itself. We are on a grassy knoll looking up at the actual house.*

> *An idyllic picnic is in progress. As our pan from the painting across the group proceeds, the Voice continues, and it becomes clear that the group is being read to.*

VOICE [OFFSCREEN]
Sing no more ditties,
Sing no more,

> *Into frame comes Leonato, waistcoat, sun hat, and pleasantly distracted air.*

VOICE [OFFSCREEN]
Of dumps so dull and heavy,

> *More laughter. We continue our pan to find Hero.*

VOICE [OFFSCREEN]
The fraud of men was ever so,
Since summer first was leafy.

> *As the pan continues, we also pull out to reveal more of the whole scene, which includes everyone we've seen to date plus* FRIAR FRANCIS *sitting on a raised path behind the group, gently strumming his guitar, and* ANTONIO, LEONATO'S *brother. Toiling in the background are the* VILLA/VINEYARD *workers.* FOUR YOUNG GIRLS *(two household servants, the other two peasants) plus* TWO OLDER PEASANT WOMEN *are variously distributed among poppies, olive trees, and vines. This group of workers is completed by three men who do most of the labour on* LEONATO'S *estate and who we discover later on will make up* THE WATCH, *Messina's amateur police force. These men are* GEORGE SEACOLE, FRANCES SEACOLE, *and* HUGH OATCAKE.

VOICE [OFFSCREEN]
Then sigh not so, but let them go,
And be you blithe and bonny,

> *We have now* PULLED BACK *even farther, revealing a tethered donkey and a picnic cloth with the remains of a simple but delicious meal.* URSULA, *older, elegant, still vivacious, sits at the right of our frame peeling and eating a pear. With the* VILLA *still in the background, the whole scene looks like an impressionist painting.*

> *Everyone is now gently chanting the words, but our original voice is drawing closer to us. As our camera finishes its reveal of the sun - drenched rural idyll, strong in* LEFT FOREGROUND, *book in hand, from which she reads the last lines, emerges the glorious red-haired profile of* BEATRICE.

BEATRICE

Converting all your sounds of woe,
Into Hey nonny, nonny!

> *She finishes with a flourish and the most heart-*
> *warming laugh, which turns rather bashful as the*
> *others raucously applaud her. Teasing and laughter*
> *continue as we CUT.*

> *Exterior / PICNIC SITE / Day*

> *LEONATO, laughing away to himself, dabbing at his*
> *watercolour. Down the hillside path towards cam-*
> *era is galloping a young male rider. He covers the*
> *ground like the wind and pulls up sharply beside*
> *LEONATO, who, aware of his approach, has begun to*
> *clean brushes and tidy up.*

> *Exterior / PICNIC SITE / Day*

> *On The Messenger as he dismounts and hands a*
> *letter to LEONATO.*

MESSENGER

My lord.

> *He reads for a moment. His jaw drops. He takes a*
> *moment, then slowly to the group of women,*

LEONATO

I learn in this letter that Don Pedro of
Arragon comes this night to Messina.

> *There is the briefest of pauses before everyone*
> *(LEONATO included) lets out an enormous scream.*
> *Petite pandemonium.*

MESSENGER

He is very near by this. He was not three
leagues off when I left him.

LEONATO

How many gentlemen have you lost in this action?

MESSENGER

But few of any sort, and none of name.

> *LEONATO nods solemnly.*

LEONATO [*REFERRING BACK TO THE NOTE*]

I find here that Don Pedro hath bestowed
much honour on a young Florentine
called Claudio.

> *There is much wicked 'oooing' at this from HERO,*
> *MARGARET, and URSULA. As they exchange*
> *laughs, looks, and leers, The Messenger tries to*
> *maintain his youthful composure.*

MESSENGER

He hath borne himself beyond the promise of his age,
doing in the figure of a lamb, the feats of a lion.

> *Something of a lamb himself, he stands a little*
> *apart and a little uneasy, having now delivered his*
> *news. The others continue to clear away, but he*
> *finds himself fixed by the defiantly provocative*

> *stare of BEATRICE, who has refrained from all of this*
> *hub-bubbling and sits exactly where she was when*
> *he arrived. She begins with ominous politeness.*

BEATRICE

Is Signior Mountanto returned
from the wars or no?

> *The other girls' ears prick up. THE MESSENGER*
> *shifts uneasily.*

MESSENGER

I know none of that name, lady.

> *Stifled giggles begin to be heard as HERO in mid-*
> *tidy almost laughs the following into THE MESSEN-*
> *GER'S ear as she rushes past him.*

HERO

My cousin means Signior Benedick of Padua.

> *THE MESSENGER first startled, then relieved.*

MESSENGER

O, he's returned; and as pleasant as ever he was.

BEATRICE

I pray you, how many hath he killed and eaten
in these wars? But how many hath he killed?
For indeed I promised to eat all of his killing.

> *THE MESSENGER grows bold and rather proud.*

MESSENGER

He hath done good service. And a good
soldier too, lady.

> *THE MESSENGER is delicious honey to BEATRICE'S*
> *smiling Bee.*

BEATRICE

And a good soldier to a lady. But what is he to a lord?

MESSENGER [*UNCOMFORTABLE*]

A lord to a lord, a man to a man;
stuffed with all honourable virtues.

BEATRICE

It is so, indeed: he is no less than a stuffed man.

> *General hilarity, during which LEONATO takes the bat-*
> *tered youth aside. The women's excitement is rising.*

LEONATO

You must not, sir, mistake my niece. There is a
kind of merry war betwixt Signior Benedick
and her: they never meet but there's a skirmish
of wit between them.

> *There is a distant rumble that we begin to be aware*
> *of, but there is no stopping BEATRICE, who is now*
> *well into her stride.*

BEATRICE

Who is his companion now? He hath every
month a new sworn brother.

MESSENGER

He is most in the company of the right noble
Claudio.

BEATRICE
O Lord, he will hang upon him like a disease.
He is sooner caught than the pestilence, and
the taker runs presently mad. God help the
noble Claudio! If he have caught the Benedick,
it will cost him a thousand pound ere a' be cured.

Renewed laughter, during which the mildly con-
fused young MESSENGER offers a sheepish grin to
BEATRICE.

MESSENGER
I will keep friends with you, lady.

BEATRICE rushes to him and plants a smiling, gen-
erous kiss on his cheek.

BEATRICE
Do, good friend.

With all things gathered it's time to make their
return to the villa. AS BEATRICE lifts her bundle,
LEONATO shares an intimate moment with her.

LEONATO [*KNOWINGLY*]
You will never run mad, niece.
BEATRICE [*EYES ATWINKLE*]
No, not till a hot January.

A great cloud of dust heralds the imminent arrival
of Horsemen. As one, LEONATO, HERO, MAR-
GARET, URSULA, BEATRICE, THE MESSENGER, THE
DONKEY, and the OTHER SERVANTS start to make
down the hillside to reach the Villa in time to wel-
come their guests. As we watch their manic retreat,
we hear, screamed.

MESSENGER
Don Pedro is approaching!

The CREDITS begin to roll over the following sequence
of rapid intercutting between the men and the women.
Drums will lead us into the full orchestral accompani-
ment. The mood is glorious, celebratory, fun!

*Exterior / **DIRT ROAD** / Day*

Road and sky and heat haze. All we can hear is the
drumming of hooves. The flutter of two flags
appears, over the crest of the road. CUT.

*Exterior / **HILLSIDE** / Day*

Wide shot looking up at the top of the hill. A
moment of silence before, Geronimo-like, all the
women and other picnickers surge over the top
towards us. We CUT in to see each individual
CLOSE, as they bound down the hill. A mixture of
REAL TIME and SLOW MOTION.

*Exterior / **DIRT ROAD** / Day*

Close on horses' hooves and rippling horseflesh. A
mixture of REAL TIME and SLOW MOTION. CUT.

*Exterior / **DIRT ROAD** / Day*

At last, over the brow of the road, fully revealed, are
DON PEDRO and his men. Riding through a mist of
dust and heat haze, they look like a combination of
Omar Sharif riding into Lawrence of Arabia and
The Magnificent Seven. They ride abreast span-
ning the width of the road and our screen. With
tight leather trousers and boots, a mixture of
sweaty shirts and military jackets, they canter in
uniform rhythm as one beast.

*Exterior / **CYPRESS ALLEY** / Day*

Through a gap in this alley of tall trees we see
HUGH OATCAKE and the other picnickers race up
the hillside. As they reach the gap, we PAN right
and let the Steadicam follow Beatrice, Hero, and
company as they run down the dip in the alley and
up the other side towards the house. The
STEADICAM chases them. Runs in front of them.
Gives us their point of view.

*Exterior / **VINEYARD** / Day*

The horsemen in the distance. We RACK FOCUS to see
FRANCES SEACOLE running breathlessly towards us.
As he flies past camera, we Pan and Track left at
great speed along parallel lines of vines stretching
down the hill away from us. Up each of the alleys
come roaring our increasingly fatigued picnickers. A
panting and wheezing LEONATO brings up the rear.

*Exterior / **DIRT ROAD** / Day*

WIDE SHOT of DON PEDRO's men.

*Exterior / **DON PEDRO'S POINT OF VIEW***
***OF VILLA FROM THE ROAD** / Day*

We see frantic activity in front of the Villa. Farm
workers scurry around, and on the highest roof we
see a flag of welcome raised. CUT. CLOSE on
GEORGE SEACOLE raising flag. CLOSE on the flag.

*Exterior / **DIRT ROAD** / Day*

Wide shot reaction to the flag being raised. All six
lead riders throw their arms in the air, as one. CUT to

*Interior / **WOMEN'S BEDROOM** / Day*

STEADICAM moving frantically in this large,
uncluttered, cool, dormitory-style bedroom.
Catching clothes as they fly through the air. Watch-
ing bodices being undone, female flesh being
released all over.

*Exterior / **DIRT ROAD** / Day*

A collection of shots close on the riders. Some real
time, some slow motion. Chests heaving. Taut

leather thighs against horseflesh. Deeply tanned biceps and pectorals.

Exterior / **ROAD** */ Day*

Introductory CLOSE-UPS *on all the riders. DON PEDRO is in the centre riding in front, a natural commander. All muscle. To his right, CLAUDIO, very young, very beautiful, nervous. To DON PEDRO's left, his brother DON JOHN, THE BASTARD, sexy, dark, reserved. By his side, Conrade, part of their entourage, young and ferociously fit. To the right of CLAUDIO, BORACHIO, the cocky sidekick to DON JOHN. On the far right of the group, bland, smiling, and warmest of all is BENEDICK, who is clearly leading the fun and excitement.*

Interior / **WOMEN'S SHOWER ROOM** */ Day*

The STEADICAM *races down the centre of this primitive shower cubicle. On either side huge leather bags of water are dousing the women, who occasionally streak across in front of camera to steal soap or splash the others. The camera meanwhile continues its progress to the end of the room and the enormous window with a view out to the front of the Villa. The horsemen are rounding a corner of the road, almost at the Villa itself.*

Interior / **WOMEN'S SHOWER ROOM**

CLOSE *on breasts and backs being lathered.*

Exterior / **WASH HOUSE** */ Day*

Whoosh! From behind we see one of the riders leap straight off his horse and into the elaborate Wash House, which serves as the laundry and refreshment centre for the Villa. A series of quick cuts follow, in which we see—leather trousers and boots being hauled off. A mixture of REAL TIME *and* SLOW MOTION—*chests and buttocks being lathered. The men splashing each other with wild abandon, all in the tank bar DON PEDRO and DON JOHN. The former is redressed by an attendant. The latter stands apart, apparently unmoved by the scene.*

Interior / **WOMEN'S BEDROOM** */ Day*

CLOSE *on a pleasing cleavage, which is then dabbed with a huge powder puff and then, by the pull of some strings, is yanked together into an even more fulsome display. We tilt up quickly to see the delighted face of MARGARET observing herself in the mirror. HERO is fixing her hair while URSULA ties her dress at the back. The room is abustle with the other picnicking female servants rushing hither and thither. BEATRICE attempts to maintain a relative indifference to this but continues to make up her toilet and is not averse to the odd shriek.*

Interior / **LEONATO'S ROOM** */ Day*

LEONATO *struggling to get into an old pair of 'good' trousers, which have mysteriously shrunk over the years. The attempt causes him to fall over. He gets up to shout at and hit his servant. ANTONIO is laughing at this and fixing his own jacket at the same time. He sniffs under his armpit.*

Exterior / **WASH HOUSE** */ Day*

We TRACK *along the front of the arched facade with the men pulling shirts on and doing up trousers (leather and equally tight), attended by some menservants who brought up the rear in supply carts. Be-bronzed, be-silken, damp hair glinting in the sun with still enough firm flesh on show to have an effect, the men start to assemble.*

Exterior / **INNER COURTYARD VILLA** */ Day*

LEONATO *and the women rushing across the upper loggia that looks into the Courtyard. They hear a trumpet from outside.*

Exterior / **WASH HOUSE** */ Day*

CLOSE *on DON PEDRO as he motions the others to form up behind him in the pedestrian version of the symmetrical arrowhead of before. We watch them climb the steps from the Wash House up to the formal Garden.*

Exterior / **INNER COURTYARD VILLA** */ Day*

LEONATO *and all the picnickers gather in a formal group as they wait for the men.*

Exterior / **FORMAL GARDEN** */ Day*

The STEADICAM *races towards the formal grouping of soldiers as they march towards camera. They make a sharp, disciplined left turn and continue to the great double doors. We follow and halt sharply as they do.*

Exterior / **INNER COURTYARD VILLA** */ Day*

The huge doors fill our frame. Across them appears the last credit of the title sequence. The whole opening section has proceeded to this point like a funny and brisk musical mating dance. End of opening CREDITS.

Exterior / **INNER COURTYARD VILLA** */ Day*

Formal TOP SHOT *of the two groups approaching each other.*

Exterior / **INNER COURTYARD VILLA** */ Day*

The doors open. DON PEDRO steps forward. So does LEONATO. These two are old friends.

DON PEDRO
Good Signior Leonato, are you come to meet
your trouble? The fashion of the world is to
avoid cost, and you encounter it.

LEONATO [*warmly*]
Never came trouble to my house
in the likeness of your grace.

> *An audible 'Ah' from the household group followed
> by gentle applause as the two men hug. This is a
> cue for the groups to loosen up. Hot looks begin to
> be exchanged between the men and women.*

> Exterior / **INNER COURTYARD VILLA** / *Day /
> DON PEDRO's Group*

DON PEDRO [*TO LEONATO, INDICATING HERO*]
I think this is your daughter.

LEONATO
Her mother hath many times told me so.

> *Laughter all around. BENEDICK sees his opportunity.*

BENEDICK
Were you in doubt, sir, that you asked her?

> *Even more amusement. LEONATO laughs the next
> line as he leads DON PEDRO away for more intro-
> ductions.*

LEONATO
Signior Benedick, no!

> *The groups are beginning to disperse, and
> BENEDICK begins to make his way towards the
> clearly Hero-struck CLAUDIO. His jabber begins
> almost to himself.*

BENEDICK
If Signior Leonato be her father, she would not
have his head on her shoulders for all Messina,
as like him as she is.

> *He has failed to distract CLAUDIO's attention, but
> someone has heard him and forces him into the fol-
> lowing semi-public skirmish, conducted against the
> to-ing and fro-ing of the household and visitor traffic.*

BEATRICE
I wonder that you will still be talking,
Signior Benedick. Nobody marks you.

> *Stopping first to 'act' trying to discover where the
> sound has come from, he turns to face her.*

BENEDICK [*INNOCENT*]
What, my dear Lady Disdain!
Are you yet living?

BEATRICE
Is it possible disdain should die while she
hath such meet food to feed it as Signior
Benedick? Courtesy itself must convert to
disdain if you come in her presence.

BENEDICK
Then is courtesy a turncoat. But it is certain
I am loved of all ladies, only you excepted; and

I would I could find in my heart that I had not
a hard heart; for truly, I love none.

BEATRICE
A dear happiness to women: they would else
have been troubled with a pernicious suitor. I
thank God and my cold blood, I am of your
humour for that, I had rather hear my dog bark
at a crow than a man swear he loves me.

BENEDICK
God keep your ladyship still in that mind, so
some gentlemen or other shall 'scape a
pre-destinate scratched face.

> *Now the gloves are really off. The crowd begins to
> prick up.*

BEATRICE
Scratching could not make it worse, an 'twere
such a face as yours.

BENEDICK [*OUTRAGED*]
Well, you are a rare parrot teacher.

BEATRICE [*NO MERCY*]
A bird of my tongue is better than
a beast of yours.

> *She's laid herself open.*

BENEDICK
I would my horse had the speed of your tongue!

> *She tries to retaliate. Too late. The crowd has
> laughed. He swishes away out of arm's and
> tongue's length to rejoin DON PEDRO.*

BENEDICK
But keep you way, i'God's name. I have done.

> *CLOSE on BEATRICE. Her face sad, knowing. She
> speaks almost to herself.*

BEATRICE
You always end with a jade's trick. I know
you of old.

> Exterior / **INNER COURTYARD VILLA** / *Day /
> The whole group*

> *DON PEDRO in public voice addresses all his men.
> Everyone stands attentive. This is important news.*

DON PEDRO
Signior Claudio and Signior Benedick, my dear
friend Leonato hath invited you all.

> *Much 'oooing' and gasping. The girls and boys are
> in for some fun, but for how long?*

DON PEDRO
I tell him we shall stay here at the least a month.

> *Applause and delight all round. We feature CLOSE-
> ups on CLAUDIO's, HERO's, BEATRICE's, and
> BENEDICK's reactions. LEONATO comes forward to
> Don John, who alone has been standing a little to
> one side, his frosty presence having kept everyone
> at bay. This introduction also becomes a piece of
> theatre for the group.*

LEONATO
**Let me bid you welcome, my lord: being
reconciled to the prince your brother, I owe
you all duty.**

*A breathless pause filled with worried looks. A beat,
then* DON JOHN *goes to* LEONATO.

DON JOHN
I thank you. [*The crowd continues to hold its breath*]
I am not of many words, but I thank you.

*An almost audible sigh of relief passes through the
group.* LEONATO *leads a gentle progress back into
the main house.*

LEONATO [*TO DON PEDRO*]
Please it your grace lead on?

DON PEDRO
Your hand, Leonato; we will go together.

BENEDICK and CLAUDIO *are left beside one of the
courtyard wells.* BENEDICK *immediately sits on it
and pours himself a drink.* CLAUDIO *is deeply smitten and stands rooted to the spot gazing after the
retreating Hero, who throws him back a glance.*

Exterior / **INNER COURTYARD MAIN WELL**
/ Day

CLAUDIO
**Benedick, didst thou note the daughter of
Signior Leonato?**

BENEDICK
I noted her not, but I looked on her.

CLAUDIO
Is she not a modest young lady?

BENEDICK
**Do you question me, as an honest man should
do, for my simple true judgment? Or would you
have me speak after my custom, as being a
professed tyrant to their sex?**

CLAUDIO
No; I pray thee speak in sober judgment.

BENEDICK
**Why, i'faith, methinks she's too low for a
high praise, too brown for a fair praise, and
too little for a great praise. Only this
commendation I can afford her, that were she
other than she is, she were unhandsome; and
being no other than as she is** (*He pauses for effect after
this analysis*). ***I do not like her.***

*CLAUDIO will not be beaten down by Benedictine
wit, and now that the object of his affection has
completely disappeared into the house, he engages
with him face to face.*

CLAUDIO
**Thou thinkest I am in sport. I pray thee
tell me truly how thou likest her.**

*BENEDICK turns to look at him with a deliberate,
scrutinising gaze.*

BENEDICK
Would you buy her that you inquire after her?

CLAUDIO
Can the world buy such a jewel?

This is getting serious.

BENEDICK
**Yea, and a case to put it into. But speak you
this with a sad brow?**

CLAUDIO rises to stare again at the palace that is
LEONATO's *house.*

CLAUDIO
**In mine eye she is the sweetest lady that
ever I looked on.**

*BENEDICK also gets up and looks in the same direc-
tion, more worried now.*

BENEDICK
**I can see yet without spectacles and I see
no such matter.**

At that moment BEATRICE *walks across the upper
loggia, and* BENEDICK *finds himself saying the following almost to himself.*

BENEDICK
**There's her cousin, an she were not possessed
with a fury, exceeds her as much in beauty as
the first of May doth the last of December.**

*He shakes himself out of this reverie to turn on his
companion.*

BENEDICK
**But I hope you have no intent to turn husband,
have you?**

CLAUDIO [*SOLEMNLY*]
**I would scarce trust myself, though I had sworn the
contrary, if Hero would be my wife.**

The final straw. BENEDICK's *comic outrage lets rip.*

BENEDICK [*HITTING HIM*]
**Is't come to this? Shall I never see a bachelor of
threescore again?**

*DON PEDRO has returned from the house, glass in
hand.*

Exterior / **INNER COURTYARD MAIN WELL**
/ Day

DON PEDRO
**Gentlemen, what secret hath held you here, that
you followed not to Leonato's?**

BENEDICK
He [*pauses, gathers himself*] **is 'in love'**
[*still contemptuous*]. ***With who? That is your***
**grace's part. With Hero, Leonato's short
daughter.**

Before CLAUDIO *has a chance to protest, the smiling Don smooths all.*

DON PEDRO
Amen if you love her; for the lady is very
well worthy.

The bashful and battered CLAUDIO *is still uncertain if he is being taken seriously.* BENEDICK *is hovering, ready to pounce with bachelor indignation.*

CLAUDIO
You speak this to fetch me in, my lord.

DON PEDRO [*KINDLY*]
By my troth, I speak my thought.

CLAUDIO
And in faith, my lord, I spoke mine.

BENEDICK [*DESPERATELY*]
And, by my two faiths and
troths, my lord, I spoke mine.

CLAUDIO
That I love her, I feel.

DON PEDRO
That she is worthy, I know.

*BENEDICK, the mad fly, continues to buzz around
them.*

BENEDICK
That I neither feel how she should be loved
nor know how she should be worthy, is the
opinion that fire cannot melt out of me. I
will die in it at the stake.

DON PEDRO
Thou wast ever an obstinate heretic in the
despite of beauty.

*BENEDICK now warming to his theme, sure of him-
self. This man has obviously been hurt.*

BENEDICK
That a women conceived me, I thank her; that
she brought me up, I likewise give her most
humble thanks. But that I will hang my bugle
in an invisible baldrick, all women shall
pardon me. I will live a bachelor.

DON PEDRO [*CERTAIN*]
I shall see thee, ere I die,
look pale with love.

Red rag to a bull.

BENEDICK
With anger, with sickness, or with hunger,
my lord, not with love.

DON PEDRO [*CAT-LIKE, TEASING*]
Well as time shall try:
'In time the savage bull doth bear the yoke.'

CHAPTER 10

Twelfth Night; or, What You Will

(c. 1601)

Context and Dating: The Melancholy Comedy

Twelfth Night was written about 1601 as Shakespeare was completing a series of festive comedies. The term "festive comedy," that so well describes this thoughtful and joyous vein of comic writing, was coined by the influential critic C. L. Barber to describe *A Midsummer Night's Dream, Much Ado About Nothing, As You Like It,* and *Twelfth Night*. The English poet laureate John Masefield (1878–1967) once judged *Twelfth Night* "the most perfect comedy in the English language," and many recent critics have agreed that it is the greatest of Shakespeare's romantic comedies. *Twelfth Night* was performed for an audience of law students in 1602; it may have been written as early as 1599 for public audiences at the Globe. During this period Shakespeare was turning to more somber work such as *Julius Caesar* and *Hamlet. Twelfth Night's* melancholy elements reflect the playwright's concern with darker matters, and his subsequent attempts at comedy (*Measure for Measure, All's Well That Ends Well*) emerge as conspicuously troubling works (as you have read in previous chapters, the term "problem comedies" often is used to describe them). Thus *Twelfth Night* is both a culmination of one phase of Shakespeare's dramatic career and the beginning of a new one.

To appreciate the complexity of *Twelfth Night*, one might begin with the final moments of the play. After nearly five acts of comic confusion in the play's love plot, two sets of lovers leave the stage to celebrate both a recent and a pending marriage. All's well that ends well, or so it seems with this gloriously happy ending, including as it does a miraculous reunion of a long-lost brother and his sister. Yet, Shakespeare chooses to con-

clude the play with one of the most melancholy songs in his repertory, one that he will use again when writing his late tragedy, *King Lear* (3.2.74–77). Alone on stage, Feste, the play's clown and its voice of common sense, sings

> But when I came, alas, to wive,
> With hey, ho, the wind and the rain,
> By swaggering could I never thrive,
> For the rain it raineth every day,
>
> (5.1.397–400)

This is hardly the kind of song one would expect to celebrate reunions and multiple marriages. While it can be argued that the song is simply about Feste's own forlorn experiences, it is typical of the underlying melancholy that permeates this comedy.

The shift between delightful comedy and bittersweet reflections on life's temporalities ("Youth's a stuff will not endure," Feste sings in Act 2) makes *Twelfth Night* a rich and satisfying work. Several scenes (2.3, 2.5, and 3.4) occasion raucous laughter while others (1.5, 2.4, and 5.1) provoke tears of both sadness and joy. Royal Shakespeare Company director John Barton, who in 1969 staged perhaps the twentieth century's most admired production of the play, cites the "violence of contrast" in such plays as *Twelfth Night* as the source of our emotional and intellectual satisfaction with Shakespeare's work.

The Title

These contrasting emotions are found in the play's title: *Twelfth Night*. Twelve days after Christmas (January 6), Christians celebrate the Epiphany, or Feast of the Magi, a time of traditional gift-giving and merrymaking commemorating the visitation by the three kings who offered rich gifts to the Christ Child. A 1979 production of the play in Rome actually costumed Sir Toby, Maria, and Feste as the Three Kings in the Sir Topas scene in Act 4. Amid the joy and celebration of the day is the sober reality that the lengthy holiday season is over for another year and that all must return to more mundane concerns on January 7. Today we talk about the post-Christmas letdown and an upsurge in depression-related illnesses after the winter holiday season.

In Shakespeare's time the period between Christmas and Epiphany included another holiday: the Feast of Fools, a remnant of a medieval practice of allowing lesser clergy in the Catholic Church's hierarchy as well as choir boys and sextons to mock their betters in a carnival of role-reversals and inversions of power. The Feast of Fools is probably a vestige of pagan rites, particularly the Roman Saturnalia, appropriated by the Church in the Middle Ages. The opening sequence of Franco Zeffirelli's 1966 film *The Taming of the Shrew* features a lively recreation of a Feast of Fools as university students celebrate the opening of their new term by parading through Padua's streets.

By the seventeenth century the Feast of Fools had become a partly secular holiday intended to mark the end of the Christmas season. In Shakespeare's England in the winter of 1601, the year *Twelfth Night* may have been composed, life would bring uncompromisingly dreary days for months to come. Houses were poorly heated; roads were muddy and often impassable; many foods, especially fresh produce, were in short supply. There was little prospect for relief until the Easter season. Little wonder the Elizabethans frantically celebrated the end of the Christmas season; and little wonder there was invariably more than a touch of melancholy beneath the merrymaking.

Thus the play and the holiday *Twelfth Night* mark a self-conscious frivolity, and both celebrate role-reversals, disguisings, practical jokes, and other confusions. You will find all of these in excess (to use a key word that marks the opening of the play) in Shakespeare's melancholy comedy—or is it his funniest drama?

Two plots dominate *Twelfth Night*: a love plot (the Viola-Orsino-Olivia triangle) that anticipates Shakespeare's last plays, the Romances, and a satirical subplot sometimes referred to as "the gulling [tricking] of Malvolio." Both make demands on the audience's ability to suspend disbelief; coincidences, mistaken identities, cross-dressing, outlandish dressing, eavesdropping, and a miraculous ending characterize the action. Shakespeare points to his own improbable plotting when Fabian comments upon the comic duel between the hapless Sir Andrew and the disguised Viola: "If this were played upon the stage, now, I could condemn it as an improbable fiction" (3.4.129–130). In this play human folly leads to some oddly improbable behaviors, and yet there is method to the madcap mayhem of *Twelfth Night*.

Characters

The parallel plots, though divergent in mood and style, consistently complement one another, largely through their characters, who manifest two facets of human nature. Duke Orsino's aggrandized statements about love are nearly as comically exaggerated as Malvolio's churlish pronouncements; Toby's love of the bottle is as excessive as the indulgently mourning Olivia; and Sir Andrew Aguecheek is as foolish as the Fool (Feste) is wise. The raucous "caterwauling" of the drinkers contrasts with the melancholic songs of Feste. Typical of Shakespeare's dramaturgy, one scene comments upon its predecessor even as it foreshadows the issues of the ensuing action. The twin plots intersect twice: first, in the comic duel between Aguecheek and Viola (3.1); and predictably in the climax (5.1) when "the madly used Malvolio" brings a somber note—and a disturbing curse—on the joyful reunion and impending marriages.

Viola stands at the center of the play. She and her twin brother, Sebastian, have been separated in a shipwreck. Assuming that her brother is dead, she takes on a masculine identity, adopting the name Cesario. She embodies service to others in a world where self-serving indulgence seems the norm. Viola finds a parallel in Antonio, the sea captain who rescues Sebastian from the sea and from Aguecheek's cowardly swordplay; like Viola, Antonio places the needs of others ahead of his own. He is one of Shakespeare's most enigmatic characters. Just as Viola is a quick-witted woman whose actions propel the romantic plot, her comic counterpart, Maria, Olivia's outspoken lady-in-waiting, provides the impetus for the jocular subplot.

The lovers (Orsino, Olivia, Sebastian, and, to a lesser degree, Viola) are gently satirical comic portraits of Renaissance lovers, the offspring of Petrarch, Dante, and other writers who made unrequited love an art form. Though we sympathize with the characters' plight, we are amused by the overblown declarations and grand sentiments of Orsino and Olivia. The subplot recasts stock characters from Roman comedy into distinctly English molds. We find a braggart (Toby), an imposter (Aguecheek), and a sassy serving wench (Maria), all of whom may be traced to Plautus and Terence, those twin pillars of Roman comedy. Straddling the two plots is Feste, the *eiron* or "wise fool," who stands on the fringe of the action to comment wittily on the folly of those around him.

Sources and Inspirations

English and Italian Precedents

The sources for *Twelfth Night* include several works of Renaissance literature, both Italian and English, that feature mistaken identity among twins or a woman disguised in "breeches" to serve the man she loves. Three of these in English were Philip Sidney's *Arcadia*, Emmanuel Forde's *Parismus*, and most importantly for Shakespeare's comedy, Barnabe Riche's moralistic tale *Apollonius and Silla*. Most of the plot elements of *Twelfth Night* appear in Riche's tale, though these events are represented as warnings against the destructive power of irrational, carnal love. Shakespeare's handling of the material is closer in tone to several Italian comedies of the mid-1500s, which contain some characters that appear in *Twelfth Night*, notably Sir Toby and company. The *Menaechmi* of Plautus had already well-served Shakespeare when he reconceived its mistaken identities among two sets of twins as *The Comedy of Errors*. As in such earlier plays, however, Shakespeare combines his own plots and devices with action and character ideas from both English and Italian sources. In *Twelfth Night*, he gives the new combination a thematic richness by employing the contrasting figures of Feste and Malvolio.

Her Majesty Requests a Twelfth Night Entertainment

During the final moments of the film *Shakespeare in Love*, Queen Elizabeth asks Shakespeare to write another play, ostensibly about Viola de Lesseps, the determined heroine who dresses as a man. The final shot of that award-winning film shows Viola, who has survived a shipwreck en route to the New World, walking alone on a vast stretch of beach, a stranger in a strange land who must survive by her wits. Although *Twelfth Night* is indeed founded on the premise of a shipwrecked young woman named Viola, there is no evidence that Shakespeare ever loved a woman named Viola or that Queen Elizabeth asked England's finest young playwright to create a play about her. Still, the text of *Twelfth Night* did lead to speculation by scholar Leslie Hotson that its first performance may have been at the Queen's bidding, and this guess informed the movie's screenwriters, Tom Stoppard and Marc Norman. Harley Granville-Barker, an influential Shakespearean director of the early twentieth century, maintains in his indispensable *Prefaces to Shakespeare* (1946–1947) that "there is much to show that the play was designed for performance upon a bare platform stage without [curtains] or inner rooms. . . . The scene changes constantly from anywhere suitable to anywhere else that is equally so. . . . Scenery is an inconvenience" (27). These sparse requirements—a bench or two and perhaps something to indicate the "box tree" in 2.5—support the view that the play could have been handily mounted at Whitehall or the Middle Temple, an academy for would-be lawyers. The simple staging requirements would have served just as well for public performances at the Globe, for the court, or for the Inns of Court. When Mark Rylance, artistic director of Shakespeare's Globe Theatre in London, toured his vivid, all-male production of the play to the United States in 2003, he reconfigured theaters at such tour stops as UCLA to resemble the long, narrow great hall of the Middle Temple, seating the audience on either side of the players.

Twelfth Night was certainly performed on February 2, 1602, at the Middle Temple. John Manningham, a law student at the Inns of Court; his fellow students; and their faculty and guests observed "a play called . . . 'Twelve [sic] Night, or What You Will,' much like 'The Comedy of Errors' or 'Menaechmi' in Plautus, but most like and near to that in Italian called *Inganni*." Even though Manningham's brief diary entry mentions only the comedy's subplot, it remains one of the few accounts of a Shakespeare play in performance during his lifetime. Several elements in the play would have appealed to an audience of law students, most notably the parody of legal and theological debates in 4.2, when Feste disguises himself as the gibberish-spouting Sir Topas to torment Malvolio. Yet these features are also suited for popular audiences, and surely the play was also staged commercially at the Globe.

Manningham's reference to *Inganni* identifies one of the primary analogues for the Viola-Olivia-Orsino plot: a popular comedy by Niccolo Secchi, *Gl'Ingannati* (translated as "The Deceived" or "The Frauds"), produced in Siena in 1531. Both Secchi's play and Shakespeare's direct source, Riche's previously cited *Apollonius and Silla*, deal with a young woman disguised as a man, a gender-bending love triangle, and a long-lost brother whose arrival provides a happy conclusion for the confusion.

The Puritan Strain

The source for play's subplot, in which carousing merrymakers inhabiting Olivia's house humiliate her foul-tempered steward through an ingenious trick, is harder to pin down. Shakespeare may have based this subplot on events well known to London's citizens. Some possible models for Malvolio include Sir William Knollys and John Darrell.

Knollys was the Comptroller of the Queen's household, notorious for his puritanical disposition and his tight-fisted fiscal policies that, according to Hotson, did not sit well with the Queen's ladies-in-waiting. Knollys is reported to have broken up a late-night party at the palace while wearing his nightshirt (and, according to legend, carrying a volume of Italian pornography).

Darrell was a controversial Puritan preacher (cf. Makepeace in *Shakespeare in Love*) who initiated a "war of pamphlets" from about 1596 to 1602. He was especially known for his exorcisms of the possessed, particularly young Thomas Darling (a.k.a. the Boy of Burton). Again, Shakespeare may have openly mocked a well-known Puritan by turning the tables on him: Sir Toby, Maria, and Fabian perform a mock exorcism on Malvolio in 3.4, and the aforementioned Sir Topas scene (4.2) actually contains language, "bibble-babble" (97), associated with Darrell's exorcism of young Darling.

Such tales about priggish Puritans reinforce the fact that there was indeed friction between some of the religious righteous and theater artists: Shakespeare's own career was often threatened by Puritans who wanted the theaters closed. Given a chance to tweak some sanctimonious noses, Shakespeare created his most unctuously comical villain, Malvolio.

One other figure who may have influenced Shakespeare while he was writing *Twelfth Night* merits consideration here. Will Kempe, the comedian who specialized in low comedy roles such as Dogberry and Nick Bottom, left the Lord Chamberlain's Men at the end of the sixteenth century and was replaced by Robert Armin, whose specialty was sophisticated comedy and wordplay. Shakespeare probably created the role of Feste to accommodate Armin's admirable comedic and singing abilities. Armin was particularly adept at improvising verses upon demand. He published some of his best poems extempore in c. 1601 under the title *Quips upon Questions*. These include a verse called "He Plays the Fool." Viola's description of Feste's art in 3.1 (ll.60ff.: "This fellow is wise enough to play the fool . . .") is essentially a paraphrase of Armin's poem.

Language and Music

Each plot in *Twelfth Night* is marked by a distinct use of language. The love plot provides some of the most lyrical passages in all of Shakespeare, particularly Viola-Cesario's praise in Act 1 for Olivia's beauty, in which she declares that, were she a suitor to Olivia, she would

> Make me a willow cabin at your gate
> And call upon my soul within the house;
> Write loyal cantons of contemnèd love
> And sing them loud even in the dead of night;
> Hallow your name to the reverberate hills,
> And make the babbling gossip of the air
> Cry out "Olivia!"
>
> (1.5.263–269)

The scene actually begins in prose but shifts to verse as the emotional pitch of the scene rises and Viola's paean to Olivia grows both more beautiful in expression and more intense. The subplot involving the knights, Sir Toby and Sir Andrew, is firmly rooted in earthy prose. Malvolio speaks only in prose.

The play is sprinkled with riddles, syllogisms, and other brain teasers. The most interesting of these is Viola's subtle description of herself to Orsino in Act 2 ("I am all the daughters of my father's house, / And all the brothers, too," 2.4.120–121). This is a play about finding answers, and its riddles and word games reflect this. Linguistically, the most challenging scene (4.2) is Sir Topas's interrogation of Malvolio, who has been locked in a dark room because Olivia thinks him mad. It is filled with cryptic references to law, theology, and the ancient world. Though it may require the glosses for readers to appreciate fully the arcane references, the scene plays beautifully on stage in the hands of inventive actors.

The second word of the play is "music," and fittingly *Twelfth Night* is one of Shakespeare's most musical plays. The play begins with an unnamed piece of music which the Duke interrupts—"That strain again! it had a dying fall"—with his request for an encore. As the action unfolds, songs both precipitate the action (as in the caterwauling of the drunks that rouse Malvolio) and comment upon it (Feste mocks the Duke's melancholy with the mournful "Come away, come away, Death" in 2.4). And, as has been noted, the play ends with a sad ballad that reminds us that the "rain it raineth every day."

Music, as Orsino says in the first line, is both "the food of love" and a direct route to the heart. In a play about emotions and the excesses that result when the heart rules the mind, the songs and snatches heighten the play's emotional impact. Music enhances the emotional resonance of *Twelfth Night,* for the songs invariably introduce moments of intense emotion amid all the improbable fictions. Shakespeare did not compose the music for the songs in the play; Armin, a superb musician as well as comedian, may well have contributed some music. Some of the songs in *Twelfth Night* were in fact popular songs of the period—and new ones at that. The lyrics for "O mistress mine" (2.3) are Shakespeare's, but "Farewell, my heart, since I must needs be gone" was a popular song of about 1600. Shakespeare, ever attentive to "the street," quickly incorporated such fresh material into his plays; fortunately, he was not bound by copyright laws. Borrowing material from other playwrights or inserting popular songs in a play was common practice in Shakespeare's day.

Twelfth Night rewards the special effort required to hear its music. Some directors (and readers) have substituted a relevant contemporary pop song for one in the text. In 1998 Sheldon Epps transformed the play into a successful Broadway musical, *Play On!*, using Duke Ellington's big band music as the source for his lively 1940s-era adaptation (see p. 321). Similarly, the Orlando Shakespeare Festival recently used Jimmy Buffett's music, itself a celebration of the spirit of carnival, for a production in which Viola washed up on the shores of the Caribbean: Illyria as Margaritaville!

Themes and Issues

Love, Infatuation, and Lust

In *Twelfth Night* Shakespeare returns to many of the themes he explored in the earlier comedies and in *Romeo and Juliet*.

The comedy portrays affairs of the heart in its many forms—genuine love, infatuation, even self-love. In the opening scene we meet a duke who is in love with being in love; in Scene 2 a woman, Viola, who epitomizes the credo that "Love sought is good, but given unsought is better" (3.1.156); in Scene 3 another woman, Olivia, whose love for a dead brother prompts irrational behavior; and a pompous steward who is "sick of self-love." We get love-at-first-sight (Olivia for "Cesario," then Sebastian for Olivia), imagined love (Orsino for Olivia), and cultivated and selfless love (Viola for Orsino, Antonio for Sebastian). In the normal course of Shakespearean comedy, the fooleries of love are resolved by play's end, but in *Twelfth Night* there is something unsettling about the resolution. Olivia marries Sebastian, and he her, solely on exterior appearances, and the Duke marries a "woman" he has never seen—i.e., the boy Cesario. Even that melancholic song that ends the play does not speak well for love and marriage; it provides hardly the kind of joyful *komos* we expect in Shakespeare's comedies. Yet there is hope in the person of Viola, the generous heroine who put aside her own feelings to court happiness for the man she loves.

Hypocrisy and Disguises

When Viola discovers the nature of her dilemma at the beginning of Act 2, she laments that her disguises have become a "wickedness / Wherein the pregnant enemy does much" (2.2.27–28). Shakespeare's plays invariably examine the nature of reality versus its mere appearance (where better to do this than in the theater?); this theme is especially pronounced in *Twelfth Night*, given its association with the Feast of Fools and of carnival. In Illyria many characters wear masks, some literal (Feste's "gown and beard" as Sir Topas), some psychological (Duke Orsino's obsession with love). The subplot is predicated on perhaps the most famous—certainly the funniest—costume in Shakespeare's canon: Malvolio's ludicrous "cross-gartering." The tricksters induce Malvolio to don this sportive attire, so against his puritanical nature, to woo Olivia. He is humiliated when she rejects him as a madman. The cross-garters (garish ribbons dandies wrapped about their legs to attract women) are ludicrous on Malvolio, but on a deeper level they manifest his hypocrisy. By succumbing to his own vanity (and the letter Maria concocts is designed to prompt Malvolio to read into it precisely what he wishes), Malvolio proves himself to be the consummate hypocrite; he becomes the very thing he professes to dislike.

Carnival vs. Lent

"Dost thou think, because thou art virtuous," asks Toby of Malvolio, "there shall be no more cakes and ale?" (2.3.114–115). The line, among the most quoted from the play, crystallizes the battle between what we might call the expansive and the repressive forces in *Twelfth Night*. The former represents the spirit of carnival, the latter is associated with Lent and its reminder that "from dust you came and to dust you will return." (A 1980 production of the play in Czechoslovakia renamed Feste as "Carnival.") Malvolio's puritanical disposition attempts to negate the free-spirited impulses of Toby and company. Olivia's vow to abjure "the sight / And company of men" for seven years is also an anti-life choice, which is reversed when she meets the life-giving goodness of Viola-Cesario.

Madness

"My master, are you mad?" Malvolio demands of the midnight revelers in 2.3, an apt question for virtually all of the Illyrians. In Act 4 Sebastian deduces that either he is mad or Olivia is mad, in a speech (see 4.3.15–16) immediately following the scene in which Malvolio is tormented as a madman by Sir Topas/Feste. Here, as in *A Midsummer Night's Dream*, Shakespeare shows how perilously close passion is to madness; the various lovers behave erratically in their pursuit of one another (or oneself in the case of Malvolio), the bottle, the delights of carnival, and merry pranks and jests. *Twelfth Night* does not necessarily condemn a little madness; rather, it—like the novel *Zorba the Greek* (Nikos Kazantzakis 1953)—proclaims that "Man must have a little madness to be free." The play condones some madness as a means of divesting ourselves of the rigidity in our day-to-day lives. In excess, irrationality becomes destructive, but in moderation a fine madness is liberating. Thus, the emphasis on madness in *Twelfth Night* is an extension of its carnival-like spirit.

Staging Challenges

The Many Moods of Twelfth Night

The most daunting task facing interpreters of this comedy is finding the balance among its diverse moods. *Twelfth Night* displays the one of the widest emotional ranges of Shakespeare's comedies (the same may be said of *Hamlet* among the tragedies). While it can be played mostly for boisterous laughter, the play works best when it moves seamlessly between the uproarious and the melancholic. Consider one example: the principal exchange between Viola-Cesario and the Duke (2.4) is bracketed by the late-night carousing of Sir Toby and Company (2.3) and the masterful "letter scene" (2.5) in which Malvolio convolutes Maria's well-crafted note to aggrandize himself. Directors must find the balance between the extremes of hilarity and melancholia.

Where Is Illyria?

Geographically, Illyria comprised the eastern shore of the Adriatic Sea, now the coastal region of modern Croatia. Shakespeare set most of his comic plays in Italy or the lower Mediterranean (Greece, Turkey), balmy places that seems to have had special appeal to his cold-climate audience. Situated between Europe and the East, Illyria perhaps seems a more exotic locale than the usual ones. Given the play's emphasis on "improbable fictions," it creates an instant image of a strange land of even stranger behaviors. While a vaguely Italianate milieu is perhaps the most common setting for *Twelfth Night*, directors have been especially inventive in their choice of location for the play. The BBC televised version moves the play's action forward in time to the Cavalier period (mid seventeenth century), thus heightening the friction between the puritanical Malvolio and the laced-and-plumed cavaliers. Trevor Nunn's 1996 film situates Illyria in the nineteenth century; Viola's smart-looking military apparel enhances her attempts at masculinity. These, however, are fairly conventional approaches, especially when we consider the many ingenious recontextualizations of the play: at New Orleans's Mardi Gras, the Venetian carnival, and the silent movie era (in which Viola was a Charlie Chaplin-like figure, and Laurel and Hardy served as models for the Toby-Andrew pairing). A 1978 Illinois Shakespeare Festival production placed the action on some distant planet onto which Viola's spaceship crashed; ray guns, robots, and electronic music provided additional comedy. While these innovative settings offer visual variety, they run the risk of muting the play's more somber moods.

Identical Twins and the Love Triangle

One physical challenge offered by *Twelfth Night* is the need to find a woman and a man who may pass as identical twins. While costuming and makeup can partly solve this dilemma, it is not often that a woman and a man of the same general build and voice quality are available simultaneously. Film can create effects not often available to theater companies, although close-ups can undercut the twinning. Shakespeare relied on a young man to play Viola, making "her" transition to a man all the more credible. In 2002 at London's new Globe Theatre, Mark Rylance staged *Twelfth Night* featuring an all-male cast. Although the actors were adults, not boys, this staging did replicate many conventions of the Elizabethan theater. Rylance himself played Olivia in an exquisitely balanced production that toured to several American cities. Nunn's film addresses the problem of the twins immediately as the director invents a charming prologue: Viola and Sebastian appear as identically dressed entertainers on a nineteenth-century "cruise ship" to emphasize that Viola and her brother are indeed like "An apple cleft in two" (5.1.223). For four centuries audiences have accepted the twins as a given even if they do not look alike. What is perhaps more interesting is the love triangle that the female-as-male conceit provokes. The sexual indeterminism in *Twelfth Night* can be highlighted if Orsino is unquestionably attracted to Viola's male countenance, while Olivia finds to her chagrin that she has been "betrothed both to a maid and man" (5.3.263).

The Tyranny of the Subplot

"The Gulling of Malvolio," often performed as a piece unto itself, can easily dwarf the love plot if care is not taken to balance the extraordinary pathos and comedy of the Viola-Orsino-Olivia plot. Played too comically, the main love plot cannot hope to hold its own against the raucous subplot; played too heavily, even morosely, the love plot can easily weigh down the entire play. The cruel and serious elements of the Malvolio subplot also present a potential problem, especially the scene (4.2) in which the steward is imprisoned in the "dark room" and tormented by Feste in the guise of Sir Topas. The prank—so funny in the letter scene (2.4) and in the scene in which Malvolio appears cross-gartered (3.4)—suddenly turns cruel, and our sympathies perhaps shift more in favor of the hapless Puritan, perhaps away from the clowns. Even Sir Toby realizes he may have overstepped into cruelty when he dismisses himself from the Sir Topas scene ("I would we were well rid of this knavery," 4.2.67–68), and Olivia judges that Malvolio "hath been most notoriously abused" (5.1.379).

(TopFoto)

At London's Globe Theatre in 2002 and later on tour, Mark Rylance, right, played Olivia in an all-male Twelfth Night *with Michael Brown and Rhys Meredith.*

Poor Antonio

Shakespeare relegates Antonio, Sebastian's savior, to an inconspicuous position in the joyful ending. He stands silently for almost two hundred lines after his final pronouncement (5.1.208–214), and even though the final stage direction [*Exeunt all, except Feste*] does not specifically exclude Antonio from the celebration, he is not included in any of the speeches that mark the occasion. Harley Granville-Barker notes that the final scene is "scandalously ill-arranged . . . the despair of any stage manager" because so many characters must be accounted for in the finale. Antonio can, of course, exit en masse with the rest of the characters, although audiences tend to forget his importance to the play if that happens. He can be left alone on stage to wander off in another direction, a solitary figure who is ill-rewarded for his valiant efforts by those whom he served so well. Or can be "reclaimed" by Sebastian and his new bride who return to lead him to that "solemn celebration."

Contemporary critics have sometimes suggested a homoerotic bond between Antonio and Sebastian. Such matters are all subject to interpretation and staging. In any case, it is clear that Shakespeare makes Antonio, like Viola, an admirable character who forsakes personal gain for the love of another. Is it merely Platonic love of one man for another? Or is there something more sexual? Sexual ambiguities abound in the play. A production at the 1981 Alabama Shakespeare Festival emphasized and exaggerated the ambiguity by featuring an overtly gay Orsino, who directed his egotistical pronouncements about his ability to love—to a rubber duck while seated in an aqua-colored bathtub.

The Miraculous Ending

In *The Comedy of Errors* Shakespeare creates one of his most improbable and amusing finales: two sets of twins are reunited with one another, and one pair meets their long-lost father—and mother! The ending trumps the play's farcical action so fantastically as to be laughable. In *Twelfth Night* Shakespeare provides a resolution, in which Viola is reunited with Sebastian, that has cosmic implications. While it is no doubt amusing to audiences unfamiliar with the play, the Act 5 reunion has the effect of a miracle: Time has indeed untangled the knotty situation in which Viola has found herself. Here Shakespeare's last great comedy for several years foreshadows one of Shakespeare's later themes: there is a divinity that shapes our ends. The key to understanding the scene is the lengthy twenty-eight-line exchange between sister and brother in which they affirm their identities. Were the playwright interested only in hearty laughter, he might have climaxed the reunion with Olivia's line, "Most wonderful" (5.1.210), but he prolongs the moment. The effect creates not only suspense but also a sense of awe, of the miraculous. Unfortunately, the Viola-Sebastian interrogation is often trimmed by some directors who feel it is anti-climactic. However, the reunion can be heightened to intensify the moment and raise it to a spiritual level. In his admired 1969 production for the RSC, Barton underscored the reunion with the faint echoes of the sea, to suggest that a universal hand had guided Sebastian back to his sister.

Twelfth Night; or, What You Will

[*Dramatis Personae*

ORSINO, *Duke (sometimes called Count) of Illyria*
VALENTINE, *gentleman attending on Orsino*
CURIO, *gentleman attending on Orsino*

VIOLA, *a shipwrecked lady, later disguised as Cesario*
SEBASTIAN, *twin brother of Viola*
ANTONIO, *a sea captain, friend to Sebastian*
CAPTAIN *of the shipwrecked vessel*

OLIVIA, *a rich countess of Illyria*
MARIA, *gentlewoman in Olivia's household*

SCENE: *Illyria*]

SIR TOBY BELCH, *Olivia's uncle*
SIR ANDREW AGUECHEEK, *a companion of Sir Toby*
MALVOLIO, *steward of Olivia's household*
FABIAN, *a member of Olivia's household*
FESTE, *a clown, also called* FOOL, *Olivia's jester*

A PRIEST
FIRST OFFICER
SECOND OFFICER

Lords, Sailors, Musicians, and other Attendants

1.1

Enter Orsino Duke of Illyria, Curio, and other lords [*with musicians*].

ORSINO
If music be the food of love, play on;
Give me excess of it, that surfeiting,
The appetite may sicken and so die.
That strain again! It had a dying fall;   4
Oh, it came o'er my ear like the sweet sound
That breathes upon a bank of violets,
Stealing and giving odor. Enough, no more.
'Tis not so sweet now as it was before.
O spirit of love, how quick and fresh art thou,   9
That, notwithstanding thy capacity
Receiveth as the sea, naught enters there,
Of what validity and pitch soe'er,   12
But falls into abatement and low price   13
Even in a minute! So full of shapes is fancy   14
That it alone is high fantastical.   15
CURIO
Will you go hunt, my lord?
ORSINO   What, Curio?
CURIO   The hart.

ORSINO
Why, so I do, the noblest that I have.   17
Oh, when mine eyes did see Olivia first,
Methought she purged the air of pestilence.
That instant was I turned into a hart,
And my desires, like fell and cruel hounds,   21
E'er since pursue me.

Enter Valentine.

                           How now, what news from her? 22
VALENTINE
So please my lord, I might not be admitted,
But from her handmaid do return this answer:
The element itself, till seven years' heat,   25
Shall not behold her face at ample view;
But like a cloistress she will veilèd walk,   27
And water once a day her chamber round
With eye-offending brine—all this to season   29
A brother's dead love, which she would keep fresh   30
And lasting in her sad remembrance.
ORSINO
Oh, she that hath a heart of that fine frame   32
To pay this debt of love but to a brother,

1.1 Location: Orsino's court.
0.1 *Illyria* Nominally on the east coast of the Adriatic Sea, but with a suggestion also of "illusion" and "delirium." **4 fall** cadence **9 quick and fresh** keen and hungry **12 validity** value. **pitch** superiority. (Literally, the highest point of a falcon's flight.) **13 abatement** depreciation. (The lover's brain entertains innumerable fantasies but soon tires of them all.) **14 shapes** imagined forms. **fancy** love **15 it ... fantastical** it surpasses everything else in imaginative power.

17 the noblest . . . have i.e., my noblest part, my heart. (Punning on *hart*.) **21 fell** fierce **22 pursue me** (Alludes to the story in Ovid of Actaeon, who, having seen Diana bathing, was transformed into a stag and killed by his own hounds.) **25 element** sky. **seven years' heat** seven summers **27 cloistress** nun secluded in a religious community **29 season** keep fresh. (Playing on the idea of the salt in her tears.) **30 A brother's dead love** her love for her dead brother and the memory of his love for her **32 frame** construction

How will she love, when the rich golden shaft   34
Hath killed the flock of all affections else   35
That live in her; when liver, brain, and heart,   36
These sovereign thrones, are all supplied, and filled   37
Her sweet perfections, with one self king!   38
Away before me to sweet beds of flowers.
Love-thoughts lie rich when canopied with bowers.

Exeunt.

❧

1.2

Enter Viola, a Captain, and sailors.

VIOLA   What country, friends, is this?
CAPTAIN   This is Illyria, lady.
VIOLA
And what should I do in Illyria?
My brother he is in Elysium.   4
Perchance he is not drowned. What think you, sailors?   5
CAPTAIN
It is perchance that you yourself were saved.   6
VIOLA
Oh, my poor brother! And so perchance may he be.
CAPTAIN
True, madam, and to comfort you with chance,   8
Assure yourself, after our ship did split,
When you and those poor number saved with you
Hung on our driving boat, I saw your brother,   11
Most provident in peril, bind himself,
Courage and hope both teaching him the practice,
To a strong mast that lived upon the sea;   14
Where, like Arion on the dolphin's back,   15
I saw him hold acquaintance with the waves
So long as I could see.
VIOLA   For saying so, there's gold.   [*She gives money.*]
Mine own escape unfoldeth to my hope,   19
Whereto thy speech serves for authority,   20
The like of him. Know'st thou this country?   21
CAPTAIN
Ay, madam, well, for I was bred and born
Not three hours' travel from this very place.

VIOLA   Who governs here?
CAPTAIN   A noble duke, in nature as in name.
VIOLA   What is his name?
CAPTAIN   Orsino.
VIOLA
Orsino! I have heard my father name him.
He was a bachelor then.
CAPTAIN
And so is now, or was so very late;   30
For but a month ago I went from hence,
And then 'twas fresh in murmur—as, you know,   32
What great ones do the less will prattle of—   33
That he did seek the love of fair Olivia.
VIOLA   What's she?
CAPTAIN
A virtuous maid, the daughter of a count
That died some twelvemonth since, then leaving her
In the protection of his son, her brother,
Who shortly also died; for whose dear love,
They say, she hath abjured the sight
And company of men.
VIOLA   Oh, that I served that lady,
And might not be delivered to the world   42
Till I had made mine own occasion mellow,   43
What my estate is!
CAPTAIN   That were hard to compass,   44
Because she will admit no kind of suit,
No, not the Duke's.   46
VIOLA
There is a fair behavior in thee, Captain,
And though that nature with a beauteous wall   48
Doth oft close in pollution, yet of thee
I will believe thou hast a mind that suits
With this thy fair and outward character.   51
I prithee, and I'll pay thee bounteously,
Conceal me what I am, and be my aid
For such disguise as haply shall become   54
The form of my intent. I'll serve this duke.   55
Thou shalt present me as an eunuch to him.   56
It may be worth thy pains, for I can sing
And speak to him in many sorts of music
That will allow me very worth his service.   59
What else may hap, to time I will commit;
Only shape thou thy silence to my wit.   61
CAPTAIN
Be you his eunuch, and your mute I'll be;   62
When my tongue blabs, then let mine eyes not see.
VIOLA   I thank thee. Lead me on.   *Exeunt.*

---

34 golden shaft Cupid's golden-tipped arrow, causing love. (His lead-tipped arrow causes aversion.) **35 affections else** other feelings **36–8 when . . . king** i.e., when passion, thought, and feeling all sit in majesty in their proper thrones (liver, brain, and heart), and her sweet perfections are brought to completion by her union with a single lord and husband.
1.2 Location: The seacoast.
4 Elysium classical abode of the blessed dead. **5-6 Perchance . . . perchance** Perhaps . . . by mere chance **8 chance** i.e., what one may hope that chance will bring about **11 driving** drifting, driven by the seas **14 lived** i.e., kept afloat **15 Arion** a Greek poet who so charmed the dolphins with his lyre that they saved him when he leaped into the sea to escape murderous sailors **19-21 unfoldeth . . . him** offers a hopeful example that he may have escaped similarly, to which hope your speech provides support.

30 late lately **32 murmur** rumor **33 less** social inferiors **42 delivered** revealed, made known. (With suggestion of "born.") **43 Till . . . mellow** until the time is ripe for my purpose **44 estate** social rank. **compass** encompass, bring about **46 not** not even **48 though that** though **51 character** face or features as indicating moral qualities.
54-5 as haply . . . intent as may suit the nature of my purpose.
56 eunuch castrato, high-voiced singer **59 allow** prove **61 wit** plan, invention. **62 mute** silent attendant. (Sometimes used of non-speaking actors.)

1.3

Enter Sir Toby [Belch] and Maria.

SIR TOBY What a plague means my niece to take the death of her brother thus? I am sure care's an enemy to life.

MARIA By my troth, Sir Toby, you must come in earlier o'nights. Your cousin, my lady, takes great exceptions 5 to your ill hours.

SIR TOBY Why, let her except before excepted. 7

MARIA Ay, but you must confine yourself within the modest limits of order. 9

SIR TOBY Confine? I'll confine myself no finer than I am. 10 These clothes are good enough to drink in, and so be these boots too. An they be not, let them hang them- 12 selves in their own straps.

MARIA That quaffing and drinking will undo you. I heard my lady talk of it yesterday, and of a foolish knight that you brought in one night here to be her wooer.

SIR TOBY Who, Sir Andrew Aguecheek?

MARIA Ay, he.

SIR TOBY He's as tall a man as any's in Illyria. 20

MARIA What's that to the purpose?

SIR TOBY Why, he has three thousand ducats a year. 22

MARIA Ay, but he'll have but a year in all these ducats. 23 He's a very fool and a prodigal.

SIR TOBY Fie, that you'll say so! He plays o'th' viol-de- 25 gamboys, and speaks three or four languages word 26 for word without book, and hath all the good gifts of 27 nature.

MARIA He hath indeed, almost natural, for, besides that 29 he's a fool, he's a great quarreler, and but that he hath the gift of a coward to allay the gust he hath in quar- 31 reling, 'tis thought among the prudent he would quickly have the gift of a grave.

SIR TOBY By this hand, they are scoundrels and sub- 34 stractors that say so of him. Who are they? 35

MARIA They that add, moreover, he's drunk nightly in your company.

SIR TOBY With drinking healths to my niece. I'll drink to her as long as there is a passage in my throat and drink in Illyria. He's a coward and a coistrel that will 40 not drink to my niece till his brains turn o'th' toe like

a parish top. What, wench? *Castiliano vulgo!* For here 42 comes Sir Andrew Agueface. 43

Enter Sir Andrew [Aguecheek].

SIR ANDREW Sir Toby Belch! How now, Sir Toby Belch?

SIR TOBY Sweet Sir Andrew!

SIR ANDREW [*to Maria*] Bless you, fair shrew. 46

MARIA And you too, sir.

SIR TOBY Accost, Sir Andrew, accost. 48

SIR ANDREW What's that?

SIR TOBY My niece's chambermaid. 50

SIR ANDREW Good Mistress Accost, I desire better acquaintance.

MARIA My name is Mary, sir.

SIR ANDREW Good Mistress Mary Accost—

SIR TOBY You mistake, knight. "Accost" is front her, 55 board her, woo her, assail her. 56

SIR ANDREW By my troth, I would not undertake her in 57 this company. Is that the meaning of "accost"?

MARIA Fare you well, gentlemen. [*Going.*]

SIR TOBY An thou let part so, Sir Andrew, would thou 60 mightst never draw sword again.

SIR ANDREW An you part so, mistress, I would I might never draw sword again. Fair lady, do you think you have fools in hand? 64

MARIA Sir, I have not you by the hand.

SIR ANDREW Marry, but you shall have, and here's my 66 hand. [*He gives her his hand.*]

MARIA Now, sir, thought is free. I pray you, bring your 68 hand to th' buttery-bar, and let it drink. 69

SIR ANDREW Wherefore, sweetheart? What's your metaphor?

MARIA It's dry, sir. 72

SIR ANDREW Why, I think so. I am not such an ass but I can keep my hand dry. But what's your jest?

MARIA A dry jest, sir. 75

SIR ANDREW Are you full of them?

MARIA Ay, sir, I have them at my fingers' ends. Marry, 77 now I let go your hand, I am barren. 78

[*She lets go his hand.*] *Exit Maria.*

1.3 Location: Olivia's house.

5 cousin kinswoman **7 let . . . excepted** i.e., let her take exception to my conduct all she wants; I don't care. (Plays on the legal phrase *exceptis excipiendis*, "with the exceptions before named.") **9 modest** moderate **10 I'll . . . finer** (1) I'll constrain myself no more rigorously (2) I'll dress myself no more finely **12 An** If **20 tall** brave. (But Maria pretends to take the word in the common sense.)
22 ducats coins worth about four or five shillings **23 he'll . . . ducats** he'll spend all his money within a year. **25–6 viol-de-gamboys** viola da gamba, leg-viol, bass viol **27 without book** by heart
29 natural (With a play on the sense "born idiot.") **31 gift** natural ability. (But shifted to mean "present" in line 33.) **allay the gust** moderate the taste **34–5 substractors** detractors **40 coistrel** horse-groom, base fellow

42 parish top a large top provided by the parish to be spun by whip-ping, apparently for exercise. *Castiliano vulgo!* (Of uncertain mean-ing. Possibly Sir Toby is saying "Speak of the devil!" Castiliano is the name adopted by a devil in Haughton's *Grim the Collier of Croydon.*)
43 Agueface (Like *Aguecheek*, this name betokens the thin, pale coun-tenance of one suffering from an ague or fever.) **46 shrew** i.e., diminutive creature. (But with probably unintended suggestion of shrewishness.) **48 Accost** Go alongside (a nautical term), i.e., greet her, address her **50 chambermaid** lady-in-waiting (a gentlewoman, not one who would do menial tasks). **55 front** confront, come along-side **56 board** greet, approach (as though preparing to board in a naval encounter) **57 undertake** have to do with. (Here with unin-tended sexual suggestion, to which Maria mirthfully replies with her jokes about *dry jests, barren,* and *buttery-bar.*) **60 An . . . part** If you let her leave **64 have . . . hand** i.e., have to deal with fools. (But Maria puns on the literal sense.) **66 Marry** i.e., Indeed. (Originally, "By the Virgin Mary.") **68 thought is free** i.e., I may think what I like. (Proverbial; replying to *do you think . . . in hand,* above.) **69 buttery-bar** ledge on top of the half-door to the buttery or the wine cellar. (Maria's language is sexually suggestive, though Sir Andrew seems oblivious to that.) **72 dry** thirsty; also dried up, a sign of age and sexual debility **75 dry** (1) ironic (2) dull, barren. (Referring to Sir Andrew.) **77 at my fingers' ends** (1) at the ready (2) by the hand.
78 barren i.e., empty of jests and of Sir Andrew's hand.

SIR TOBY   Oh, knight, thou lack'st a cup of canary! When   79
did I see thee so put down?

SIR ANDREW   Never in your life, I think, unless you see
canary put me down. Methinks sometimes I have no   82
more wit than a Christian or an ordinary man has. But
I am a great eater of beef, and I believe that does harm
to my wit.

SIR TOBY   No question.

SIR ANDREW   An I thought that, I'd forswear it. I'll ride
home tomorrow, Sir Toby.

SIR TOBY   *Pourquoi*, my dear knight?   89

SIR ANDREW   What is "*pourquoi*"? Do or not do? I would
I had bestowed that time in the tongues that I   91
have in fencing, dancing, and bearbaiting. Oh, had I   92
but followed the arts!   93

SIR TOBY   Then hadst thou had an excellent head of hair.

SIR ANDREW   Why, would that have mended my hair?   95

SIR TOBY   Past question, for thou see'st it will not curl by
nature.

SIR ANDREW   But it becomes me well enough, does't
not?

SIR TOBY   Excellent. It hangs like flax on a distaff; and I   100
hope to see a huswife take thee between her legs and
spin it off.   102

SIR ANDREW   Faith, I'll home tomorrow, Sir Toby. Your
niece will not be seen, or if she be, it's four to one
she'll none of me. The Count himself here hard by   105
woos her.

SIR TOBY   She'll none o'th' Count. She'll not match
above her degree, neither in estate, years, nor wit; I   108
have heard her swear't. Tut, there's life in't, man.   109

SIR ANDREW   I'll stay a month longer. I am a fellow o'th'
strangest mind i'th' world; I delight in masques and
revels sometimes altogether.

SIR TOBY   Art thou good at these kickshawses, knight?   113

SIR ANDREW   As any man in Illyria, whatsoever he be,
under the degree of my betters, and yet I will not   115
compare with an old man.   116

SIR TOBY   What is thy excellence in a galliard, knight?   117

SIR ANDREW   Faith, I can cut a caper.   118

SIR TOBY   And I can cut the mutton to't.

SIR ANDREW   And I think I have the back-trick simply   120
as strong as any man in Illyria.

SIR TOBY   Wherefore are these things hid? Wherefore
have these gifts a curtain before 'em? Are they like to   123
take dust, like Mistress Mall's picture? Why dost thou   124
not go to church in a galliard and come home in a
coranto? My very walk should be a jig; I would not so   126
much as make water but in a sink-a-pace. What dost   127
thou mean? Is it a world to hide virtues in? I did think,   128
by the excellent constitution of thy leg, it was formed
under the star of a galliard.   130

SIR ANDREW   Ay, 'tis strong, and it does indifferent well   131
in a dun-colored stock. Shall we set about some   132
revels?

SIR TOBY   What shall we do else? Were we not born
under Taurus?   135

SIR ANDREW   Taurus? That's sides and heart.

SIR TOBY   No, sir, it is legs and thighs. Let me see thee
caper. [*Sir Andrew capers.*] Ha, higher! Ha, ha, excellent!   *Exeunt.*

1.4

Enter Valentine, and Viola in man's attire.

VALENTINE   If the Duke continue these favors towards
you, Cesario, you are like to be much advanced. He   2
hath known you but three days, and already you are
no stranger.

VIOLA   You either fear his humor or my negligence,   5
that you call in question the continuance of his love. Is
he inconstant, sir, in his favors?

VALENTINE   No, believe me.

Enter Duke [Orsino], Curio, and attendants.

VIOLA   I thank you. Here comes the Count.

ORSINO   Who saw Cesario, ho?

VIOLA   On your attendance, my lord, here.   11

ORSINO
Stand you awhile aloof. [*The others stand aside.*]
   Cesario,   12
Thou know'st no less but all. I have unclasped
To thee the book even of my secret soul.
Therefore, good youth, address thy gait unto her;   15
Be not denied access, stand at her doors,

---

79 thou . . . canary i.e., you look as if you need a drink. (*Canary* is a
sweet wine from the Canary Islands.)   **82 put me down** (1) baffle my
wits (2) lay me out flat.   **89 *Pourquoi*** Why   **91 tongues** languages.
(Sir Toby then puns on "tongs," curling irons.)   **92 bearbaiting** the
sport of setting dogs on a chained bear.   **93 the arts** the liberal arts,
learning. (But Sir Toby plays on the phrase as meaning "artifice," the
antithesis of *nature*.)   **95 mended** improved   **100 distaff** a staff for
holding the flax, tow, or wool in spinning   **102 spin it off** i.e.,
(1) treat your flaxen hair as though it were flax on a distaff to be spun
(2) cause you to lose hair as a result of venereal disease (3) make you
ejaculate. (*Huswife* suggests "hussy," "whore.")   **105 Count** i.e., Duke
Orsino, sometimes referred to as Count.   **hard** near   **108 degree**
social position.   **estate** fortune, social position   **109 there's life in't**
i.e., while there's life there's hope   **113 kickshawses** delicacies, fancy
trifles. (From the French, *quelque chose*.)   **115 under . . . betters**
excepting those who are above me   **116 old man** i.e., one experienced through age.   **117 galliard** lively dance in triple time   **118 cut
a caper** make a lively leap. (But Sir Toby puns on the *caper* used to
make a sauce served with mutton. *Mutton*, in turn, suggests
"whore.")

120 back-trick backward step in the galliard. (With sexual innuendo;
the back was associated with sexual vigor.)   **123–4 like to take** likely
to collect   **124 Mistress Mall's picture** i.e., perhaps the portrait of
some woman protected from light and dust, as many pictures were,
by curtains. (*Mall* is a diminutive of *Mary*.)   **126 coranto** lively running dance.   **127 sink-a-pace** dance like the galliard. (French
cinquepace. *Sink* also suggests a cesspool into which one might uri-
nate.)   **128 virtues** talents   **130 under . . . galliard** i.e., under a star
favorable to dancing.   **131 indifferent well** well enough. (Said complacently.)   **132 dun-colored stock** mouse-colored stocking.
135 Taurus zodiacal sign. (Sir Andrew is mistaken, since Leo governed sides and hearts in medical astrology. Taurus governed legs
and thighs, or, more commonly, neck and throat.)
1.4 Location: Orsino's court.
2 like likely   **5 humor** changeableness   **11 On your attendance**
Ready to do you service   **12 aloof** aside.   **15 address thy gait** go

And tell them, there thy fixèd foot shall grow   17
Till thou have audience.

VIOLA   Sure, my noble lord,
If she be so abandoned to her sorrow
As it is spoke, she never will admit me.

ORSINO
Be clamorous and leap all civil bounds   21
Rather than make unprofited return.

VIOLA
Say I do speak with her, my lord, what then?

ORSINO
Oh, then unfold the passion of my love;
Surprise her with discourse of my dear faith.   25
It shall become thee well to act my woes;   26
She will attend it better in thy youth
Than in a nuncio's of more grave aspect.   28

VIOLA
I think not so, my lord.

ORSINO   Dear lad, believe it;
For they shall yet belie thy happy years
That say thou art a man. Diana's lip
Is not more smooth and rubious; thy small pipe   32
Is as the maiden's organ, shrill and sound,   33
And all is semblative a woman's part.   34
I know thy constellation is right apt   35
For this affair.—Some four or five attend him.
All, if you will, for I myself am best
When least in company.—Prosper well in this,
And thou shalt live as freely as thy lord,
To call his fortunes thine.

VIOLA   I'll do my best
To woo your lady. [Aside] Yet a barful strife!   41
Whoe'er I woo, myself would be his wife.   Exeunt.

❧

1.5

Enter Maria and Clown [Feste].

MARIA   Nay, either tell me where thou hast been, or I
will not open my lips so wide as a bristle may enter in
way of thy excuse. My lady will hang thee for thy
absence.

FESTE   Let her hang me. He that is well hanged in this
world needs to fear no colors.   6

MARIA   Make that good.   7

FESTE   He shall see none to fear.   8

MARIA   A good Lenten answer. I can tell thee where   9
that saying was born, of "I fear no colors."

FESTE   Where, good Mistress Mary?

MARIA   In the wars, and that may you be bold to say in   12
your foolery.   13

FESTE   Well, God give them wisdom that have it; and
those that are fools, let them use their talents.   15

MARIA   Yet you will be hanged for being so long absent;
or to be turned away, is not that as good as a hanging   17
to you?

FESTE   Many a good hanging prevents a bad marriage;   19
and for turning away, let summer bear it out.   20

MARIA   You are resolute, then?

FESTE   Not so, neither, but I am resolved on two
points.   23

MARIA   That if one break, the other will hold; or if both
break, your gaskins fall.   25

FESTE   Apt, in good faith, very apt. Well, go thy way. If
Sir Toby would leave drinking, thou wert as witty a   27
piece of Eve's flesh as any in Illyria.   28

MARIA   Peace, you rogue, no more o' that. Here comes
my lady. Make your excuse wisely, you were best.   30

[Exit.]

*Enter Lady Olivia with Malvolio, [and
attendants].*

FESTE   [aside]   Wit, an't be thy will, put me into good   31
fooling! Those wits that think they have thee do very
oft prove fools, and I that am sure I lack thee may pass
for a wise man. For what says Quinapalus? "Better a   34
witty fool than a foolish wit."—God bless thee, lady!

OLIVIA   [to attendants]   Take the fool away.

FESTE   Do you not hear, fellows? Take away the lady.

OLIVIA   Go to, you're a dry fool. I'll no more of you.   38
Besides, you grow dishonest.

FESTE   Two faults, madonna, that drink and good   40
counsel will amend. For give the dry fool drink, then
is the fool not dry. Bid the dishonest man mend
himself; if he mend, he is no longer dishonest; if he
cannot, let the botcher mend him. Anything that's   44
mended is but patched; virtue that transgresses is but   45
patched with sin, and sin that amends is but patched
with virtue. If that this simple syllogism will serve, so;   47
if it will not, what remedy? As there is no true cuckold   48
but calamity, so beauty's a flower. The lady bade take   49

17 them i.e., Olivia's servants   **21 civil bounds** bounds of civility
25 Surprise Take by storm. (A military term.)   **dear** heartfelt
26 become suit   **28 nuncio's** messenger's   **32 rubious** ruby red.
pipe voice, throat   **33 shrill and sound** high and clear, uncracked
34 semblative resembling, like   **35 constellation** i.e., nature as determined by your horoscope   **41 barful strife** endeavor full of impediments.
1.5 Location: Olivia's house.
6 fear no colors i.e., fear no foe, fear nothing. (With pun on *colors*,
worldly deceptions, and "collars," halters or nooses.)   **7 Make that
good** Explain that.   **8 He . . . fear** i.e., The hanged man will be dead
and unable to see anything.   **9 Lenten** meager, scanty (like Lenten
fare), and morbid

12 In the wars (Where *colors* would mean "military standards, enemy
flags"—the literal meaning of the proverb.)   **12–13 that . . . foolery**
that's an answer you may be bold to use in your fool's conundrums.
(*Colors* here refer to military banners and insignia used to align rows
of fighting men in battle.)   **15 talents** abilities. (Also alluding to the
parable of the talents, Matthew 25:14–29, and to "talons," claws.)
17 turned away dismissed. (Possibly also meaning "turned off,"
"hanged.")   **19 good hanging** (With possible bawdy pun on "being
well hung.")   **20 for** as for.   **let . . . out** i.e., let mild weather make
dismissal endurable.   **23 points** (Maria plays on the meaning "laces
used to hold up hose or breeches.")   **25 gaskins** wide breeches
27–8 thou . . . Illyria (Feste may be hinting ironically that Maria
would be a suitable mate for Sir Toby.)   **30 you were best** it would be
best for you.   **31 an't** if it   **34 Quinapalus** (Feste's invented authority.)   **38 Go to** (An expression of annoyance or expostulation.)   **dry**
dull   **40 madonna** my lady   **44 botcher** mender of old clothes and
shoes. (Playing on two senses of *mend*: "reform" and "repair.")
44–5 Anything . . . patched i.e., Life is patched or parti-colored like
the Fool's garment, a mix of good and bad   **47 so** well and good
48–9 As . . . flower (Nonsense, yet with a suggestion that Olivia has
wedded calamity but should not be faithful to it, for the natural
course is to seize the moment of youth and beauty before we lose it.)

away the fool; therefore I say again, take her away.

OLIVIA   Sir, I bade them take away you.

FESTE   Misprision in the highest degree! Lady, *cucullus* 52
non facit monachum; that's as much to say as I wear not 53
motley in my brain. Good madonna, give me leave to 54
prove you a fool.

OLIVIA   Can you do it?

FESTE   Dexteriously, good madonna.

OLIVIA   Make your proof.

FESTE   I must catechize you for it, madonna. Good my 59
mouse of virtue, answer me. 60

OLIVIA   Well, sir, for want of other idleness, I'll bide 61
your proof.

FESTE   Good madonna, why mourn'st thou?

OLIVIA   Good fool, for my brother's death.

FESTE   I think his soul is in hell, madonna.

OLIVIA   I know his soul is in heaven, fool.

FESTE   The more fool, madonna, to mourn for your
brother's soul, being in heaven.—Take away the fool,
gentlemen.

OLIVIA   What think you of this fool, Malvolio? Doth he
not mend? 71

MALVOLIO   Yes, and shall do till the pangs of death
shake him. Infirmity, that decays the wise, doth ever
make the better fool.

FESTE   God send you, sir, a speedy infirmity for the
better increasing your folly! Sir Toby will be sworn
that I am no fox, but he will not pass his word for 77
twopence that you are no fool.

OLIVIA   How say you to that, Malvolio?

MALVOLIO   I marvel Your Ladyship takes delight in such
a barren rascal. I saw him put down the other day
with an ordinary fool that has no more brain than a 82
stone. Look you now, he's out of his guard already. 83
Unless you laugh and minister occasion to him, he is 84
gagged. I protest I take these wise men that crow so at 85
these set kind of fools no better than the fools' zanies. 86

OLIVIA   Oh, you are sick of self-love, Malvolio, and taste
with a distempered appetite. To be generous, guiltless, 88
and of free disposition is to take those things for bird- 89
bolts that you deem cannon bullets. There is no slan- 90
der in an allowed fool, though he do nothing but rail; 91
nor no railing in a known discreet man, though he do 92
nothing but reprove. 93

FESTE   Now Mercury endue thee with leasing, for thou 94
speak'st well of fools!

Enter Maria.

MARIA   Madam, there is at the gate a young gentleman
much desires to speak with you.

OLIVIA   From the Count Orsino, is it?

MARIA   I know not, madam. 'Tis a fair young man, and
well attended.

OLIVIA   Who of my people hold him in delay?

MARIA   Sir Toby, madam, your kinsman.

OLIVIA   Fetch him off, I pray you. He speaks nothing
but madman. Fie on him!   [*Exit Maria.*] 104
Go you, Malvolio. If it be a suit from the Count, I am
sick or not at home; what you will, to dismiss it.
                                        Exit Malvolio.
Now you see, sir, how your fooling grows old, and 107
people dislike it.

FESTE   Thou hast spoke for us, madonna, as if thy eldest
son should be a fool; whose skull Jove cram with
brains, for—here he comes—

Enter Sir Toby.

one of thy kin has a most weak *pia mater.* 112

OLIVIA   By mine honor, half drunk.—What is he at the
gate, cousin?

SIR TOBY   A gentleman.

OLIVIA   A gentleman? What gentleman?

SIR TOBY   'Tis a gentleman here—[*He belches.*] A plague
o' these pickle-herring! [*To Feste*] How now, sot? 118

FESTE   Good Sir Toby.

OLIVIA   Cousin, cousin, how have you come so early by 120
this lethargy?

SIR TOBY   Lechery? I defy lechery. There's one at the
gate.

OLIVIA   Ay, marry, what is he?

SIR TOBY   Let him be the devil an he will, I care not.
Give me faith, say I. Well, it's all one.   *Exit.* 126

OLIVIA   What's a drunken man like, Fool?

FESTE   Like a drowned man, a fool, and a madman.
One draft above heat makes him a fool, the second 129
mads him, and a third drowns him.

OLIVIA   Go thou and seek the crowner, and let him sit 131
o' my coz; for he's in the third degree of drink, he's 132
drowned. Go, look after him.

FESTE   He is but mad yet, madonna; and the fool shall
look to the madman.   [*Exit.*]

Enter Malvolio.

MALVOLIO   Madam, yond young fellow swears he will
speak with you. I told him you were sick; he takes on
him to understand so much, and therefore comes to
speak with you. I told him you were asleep; he seems

---

52 Misprision Mistake, misunderstanding. (A legal term meaning a
wrongful action or misdemeanor.)   **52–3 *cucullus . . . monachum*** the
cowl does not make the monk   **54 motley** the many-colored garment
of jesters   **59–60 Good . . . virtue** My good, virtuous mouse. (A term
of endearment.)   **61 idleness** pastime.   **bide** endure   **71 mend** i.e.,
improve, grow more amusing. (But Malvolio uses the word to mean
"grow more like a fool.")   **77 pass** give   **82 with** by   **83 out of his
guard** defenseless, unprovided with a witty answer   **84 minister
occasion** provide opportunity (for his fooling)   **85 protest** avow,
declare.   **crow** laugh stridently   **86 set** artificial, stereotyped.
zanies assistants, aping attendants.   **88 distempered** diseased.
generous noble-minded   **89 free** magnanimous   **89–90 bird-bolts**
blunt arrows for shooting small birds   **90–3 There . . . reprove** Both a
licensed fool and a man known for discretion can criticize freely
without being accused of slander in the first instance or railing in
the second. (In rebuking Malvolio here, Olivia implies that he is not
behaving like a "known discreet man.")   **91 allowed** licensed (to
speak freely)

94 Now . . . leasing i.e., May Mercury, the god of deception, make
you a skillful liar   **104 madman** i.e., the words of madness.   **107 old**
stale   **112 *pia mater*** i.e., brain. (Actually the soft membrane enclosing the brain.)   **118 sot** (1) fool (2) drunkard.   **120 Cousin** Kinsman.
(Here, uncle.)   **126 Give me faith** i.e., to resist the devil.   **it's all one**
it doesn't matter.   **129 draft above heat** helping of drink raising his
temperature above normal bodily warmth   **131 crowner** coroner
131–2 sit o' my coz hold an inquest on my kinsman (Sir Toby)

to have a foreknowledge of that too, and therefore comes to speak with you. What is to be said to him, lady? He's fortified against any denial.

OLIVIA   Tell him he shall not speak with me.

MALVOLIO   He's been told so; and he says he'll stand at your door like a sheriff's post, and be the supporter to 145 a bench, but he'll speak with you.

OLIVIA   What kind o' man is he?

MALVOLIO   Why, of mankind.

OLIVIA   What manner of man?

MALVOLIO   Of very ill manner. He'll speak with you, will you or no.

OLIVIA   Of what personage and years is he?

MALVOLIO   Not yet old enough for a man, nor young enough for a boy; as a squash is before 'tis a peascod, 154 or a codling when 'tis almost an apple. 'Tis with him in 155 standing water between boy and man. He is very 156 well-favored, and he speaks very shrewishly. One 157 would think his mother's milk were scarce out of him.

OLIVIA   Let him approach. Call in my gentlewoman.

MALVOLIO   Gentlewoman, my lady calls.   Exit.

Enter Maria.

OLIVIA
Give me my veil. Come, throw it o'er my face.
We'll once more hear Orsino's embassy. [*Olivia veils.*]

Enter Viola.

VIOLA   The honorable lady of the house, which is she?

OLIVIA   Speak to me; I shall answer for her. Your will?

VIOLA   Most radiant, exquisite, and unmatchable beauty—I pray you, tell me if this be the lady of the house, for I never saw her. I would be loath to cast away my speech; for besides that it is excellently well penned, I have taken great pains to con it. Good 170 beauties, let me sustain no scorn; I am very comptible, 171 even to the least sinister usage. 172

OLIVIA   Whence came you, sir?

VIOLA   I can say little more than I have studied, and that question's out of my part. Good gentle one, give me modest assurance if you be the lady of the house, 176 that I may proceed in my speech.

OLIVIA   Are you a comedian? 178

VIOLA   No, my profound heart; and yet, by the very 179 fangs of malice, I swear I am not that I play. Are you 180 the lady of the house?

OLIVIA   If I do not usurp myself, I am. 182

VIOLA   Most certain, if you are she, you do usurp your- 183 self; for what is yours to bestow is not yours to reserve. 184

But this is from my commission. I will on with my 185 speech in your praise, and then show you the heart of my message.

OLIVIA   Come to what is important in't. I forgive you 188 the praise.

VIOLA   Alas, I took great pains to study it, and 'tis poetical.

OLIVIA   It is the more like to be feigned. I pray you, keep it in. I heard you were saucy at my gates, and allowed your approach rather to wonder at you than to hear you. If you be not mad, begone; if you have 195 reason, be brief. 'Tis not that time of moon with me to 196 make one in so skipping a dialogue. 197

MARIA   Will you hoist sail, sir? Here lies your way.

VIOLA   No, good swabber, I am to hull here a little 199 longer.—Some mollification for your giant, sweet 200 lady. Tell me your mind; I am a messenger.

OLIVIA   Sure you have some hideous matter to deliver, when the courtesy of it is so fearful. Speak your office. 203

VIOLA   It alone concerns your ear. I bring no overture of 204 war, no taxation of homage. I hold the olive in my 205 hand; my words are as full of peace as matter.

OLIVIA   Yet you began rudely. What are you? What 207 would you?

VIOLA   The rudeness that hath appeared in me have I learned from my entertainment. What I am and what 210 I would are as secret as maidenhead—to your ears, 211 divinity; to any other's, profanation. 212

OLIVIA [*to the others*]   Give us the place here alone. We will hear this divinity.   [*Exeunt Maria and attendants.*] Now, sir, what is your text?

VIOLA   Most sweet lady—

OLIVIA   A comfortable doctrine, and much may be said 217 of it. Where lies your text?

VIOLA   In Orsino's bosom.

OLIVIA   In his bosom? In what chapter of his bosom?

VIOLA   To answer by the method, in the first of his 221 heart.

OLIVIA   Oh, I have read it. It is heresy. Have you no more to say?

VIOLA   Good madam, let me see your face.

OLIVIA   Have you any commission from your lord to negotiate with my face? You are now out of your text. 227 But we will draw the curtain and show you the

---

145 sheriff's post post before the sheriff's door to mark a residence of authority, often elaborately carved and decorated.   **supporter** prop **154 squash** unripe pea pod.   **peascod** ripe pea pod. (The image suggests that the boy's testicles have not yet dropped.)   **155 codling** unripe apple   **155–6 in standing water** at the turn of the tide **157 well-favored** good-looking.   **shrewishly** sharply.   **170 con** memorize   **171 comptible** susceptible, sensitive   **172 least sinister** slightest discourteous   **176 modest** reasonable   **178 comedian** actor. **179 my profound heart** my most wise lady; or, in all sincerity **179–80 by . . . I play** (Viola hints at her true identity, which malice itself might not detect.)   **182 do . . . myself** am not an impostor **183–4 usurp yourself** i.e., misappropriate yourself, by withholding yourself from love and marriage

185 from outside of   **188 forgive you** excuse you from repeating **195 not mad** i.e., not altogether mad   **196 reason** sanity.   **moon** (The moon was thought to affect lunatics according to its changing phases.)   **197 make one** take part   **199 swabber** one in charge of washing the decks. (A nautical retort to *hoist sail.*)   **hull** lie with sails furled   **200 Some . . . for** i.e., Please mollify, pacify.   **giant** i.e., the diminutive Maria who, like many giants in medieval romances, is guarding the lady   **203 courtesy** i.e., complimentary, "poetical" introduction. (Or Olivia may refer to Cesario's importunate manner at her gate, as reported by Malvolio.)   **office** commission, business. **204 overture** declaration. (Literally, opening.)   **205 taxation of homage** demand for tribute.   **olive** olive-branch (signifying peace) **207 Yet . . . rudely** i.e., Yet you were saucy at my gates.   **210 entertainment** reception.   **211 maidenhead** virginity   **212 divinity** sacred discourse   **217 comfortable** comforting   **221 To . . . method** i.e., To continue the metaphor of delivering a sermon, begun with *divinity* and *what is your text* and continued in *doctrine, heresy,* etc.   **227 out of** straying from

picture. [*Unveiling.*] Look you, sir, such a one I was   229
this present. Is't not well done?   230

VIOLA   Excellently done, if God did all.

OLIVIA   'Tis in grain, sir; 'twill endure wind and   232
weather.

VIOLA
'Tis beauty truly blent, whose red and white   234
Nature's own sweet and cunning hand laid on.   235
Lady, you are the cruel'st she alive
If you will lead these graces to the grave
And leave the world no copy.   238

OLIVIA   Oh, sir, I will not be so hardhearted. I will give
out divers schedules of my beauty. It shall be invento-   240
ried, and every particle and utensil labeled to my   241
will: as, item, two lips, indifferent red; item, two gray   242
eyes, with lids to them; item, one neck, one chin, and
so forth. Were you sent hither to praise me?   244

VIOLA
I see you what you are: you are too proud.
But, if you were the devil, you are fair.   246
My lord and master loves you. Oh, such love   247
Could be but recompensed, though you were
crowned   248
The nonpareil of beauty!

OLIVIA   How does he love me?   249

VIOLA
With adorations, fertile tears,   250
With groans that thunder love, with sighs of fire.

OLIVIA
Your lord does know my mind; I cannot love him.
Yet I suppose him virtuous, know him noble,
Of great estate, of fresh and stainless youth,
In voices well divulged, free, learned, and valiant,   255
And in dimension and the shape of nature   256
A gracious person. But yet I cannot love him.   257
He might have took his answer long ago.

VIOLA
If I did love you in my master's flame,   259
With such a suff'ring, such a deadly life,   260
In your denial I would find no sense;
I would not understand it.

OLIVIA   Why, what would you?

VIOLA
Make me a willow cabin at your gate   263
And call upon my soul within the house;   264
Write loyal cantons of contemnèd love   265

And sing them loud even in the dead of night;
Hallow your name to the reverberate hills,   267
And make the babbling gossip of the air   268
Cry out "Olivia!" Oh, you should not rest
Between the elements of air and earth   270
But you should pity me!

OLIVIA   You might do much.
What is your parentage?

VIOLA
Above my fortunes, yet my state is well: 273
I am a gentleman.

OLIVIA   Get you to your lord.
I cannot love him. Let him send no more—
Unless, perchance, you come to me again
To tell me how he takes it. Fare you well.
I thank you for your pains. Spend this for me.
[*She offers a purse.*]

VIOLA
I am no fee'd post, lady. Keep your purse.   279
My master, not myself, lacks recompense.
Love make his heart of flint that you shall love,   281
And let your fervor, like my master's, be
Placed in contempt! Farewell, fair cruelty.   *Exit.*

OLIVIA   "What is your parentage?"
"Above my fortunes, yet my state is well:
I am a gentleman." I'll be sworn thou art!
Thy tongue, thy face, thy limbs, actions, and spirit
Do give thee fivefold blazon. Not too fast! Soft, soft!   288
Unless the master were the man. How now?   289
Even so quickly may one catch the plague?
Methinks I feel this youth's perfections
With an invisible and subtle stealth
To creep in at mine eyes. Well, let it be.—
What ho, Malvolio!

Enter Malvolio.

MALVOLIO   Here, madam, at your service.

OLIVIA
Run after that same peevish messenger,
The County's man. He left this ring behind him,   296
[*giving a ring*]
Would I or not. Tell him I'll none of it.   297
Desire him not to flatter with his lord,   298
Nor hold him up with hopes; I am not for him.
If that the youth will come this way tomorrow,
I'll give him reasons for't. Hie thee, Malvolio.   301

MALVOLIO   Madam, I will.   *Exit.*

OLIVIA
I do I know not what, and fear to find
Mine eye too great a flatterer for my mind.   304

229–30 **such . . . present** this is a recent portrait of me. (Since it was customary to hang curtains in front of pictures, Olivia in unveiling speaks as if she were displaying a picture of herself.) 232 **in grain** fast dyed 234 **blent** blended 235 **cunning** skillful 238 **copy** i.e., a child. (But Olivia uses the word to mean "transcript.") 240 **schedules** inventories 241 **utensil** article, item. **labeled** added as a codicil 242 **indifferent** somewhat 244 **praise** (With pun on "appraise.") 246 **if** even if 247–9 **Oh . . . beauty!** i.e., Even if you were the most beautiful woman alive, that beauty could do no more than repay my master's love for you! 250 **fertile** copious 255 **In . . . divulged** well spoken of. **free** generous 256 **in . . . nature** in his physical form 257 **gracious** graceful, attractive 259 **flame** passion 260 **deadly** deathlike 263 **willow cabin** shelter, hut. (Willow was a symbol of unrequited love.) 264 **my soul** i.e., Olivia 265 **cantons** songs. **contemnèd** rejected

267 **Hallow** (1) halloo (2) bless 268 **babbling . . . air** echo 270 **Between . . . air** i.e., anywhere 273 **state** social standing 279 **fee'd post** messenger to be tipped 281 **Love . . . love** May Cupid make the heart of the man you love as hard as flint 288 **blazon** heraldic description. **Soft** Wait a minute 289 **Unless . . . man** i.e., Unless Cesario and Orsino changed places. 296 **County's** Count's, i.e., Duke's 297 **Would I or not** whether I wanted it or not. 298 **flatter with** encourage 301 **Hie thee** Hasten 304 **Mine . . . mind** i.e., that my eyes (through which love enters the soul) have deceived my reason.

Fate, show thy force. Ourselves we do not owe.   305
What is decreed must be; and be this so.   [*Exit.*]

❖

2.1

Enter Antonio and Sebastian.

ANTONIO   Will you stay no longer? Nor will you not   1
that I go with you?

SEBASTIAN   By your patience, no. My stars shine darkly   3
over me. The malignancy of my fate might perhaps   4
distemper yours; therefore I shall crave of you your   5
leave that I may bear my evils alone. It were a bad
recompense for your love to lay any of them on you.

ANTONIO   Let me yet know of you whither you are
bound.

SEBASTIAN   No, sooth, sir; my determinate voyage is   10
mere extravagancy. But I perceive in you so excellent   11
a touch of modesty that you will not extort from me
what I am willing to keep in; therefore it charges me in   13
manners the rather to express myself. You must know   14
of me then, Antonio, my name is Sebastian, which I
called Roderigo. My father was that Sebastian of
Messaline whom I know you have heard of. He left   17
behind him myself and a sister, both born in an hour.   18
If the heavens had been pleased, would we had so
ended! But you, sir, altered that, for some hour before   20
you took me from the breach of the sea was my sister   21
drowned.

ANTONIO   Alas the day!

SEBASTIAN   A lady, sir, though it was said she much resembled me, was yet of many accounted beautiful. But
though I could not with such estimable wonder over-   26
far believe that, yet thus far I will boldly publish her: 27
she bore a mind that envy could not but call fair. She   28
is drowned already, sir, with salt water, though I seem
to drown her remembrance again with more.

ANTONIO   Pardon me, sir, your bad entertainment.   31

SEBASTIAN   O good Antonio, forgive me your trouble.   32

ANTONIO   If you will not murder me for my love, let me   33
be your servant.

SEBASTIAN   If you will not undo what you have done,
that is, kill him whom you have recovered, desire it   36
not. Fare ye well at once. My bosom is full of

kindness, and I am yet so near the manners of my   38
mother that upon the least occasion more mine eyes   39
will tell tales of me. I am bound to the Count Orsino's
court. Farewell.   *Exit.*

ANTONIO
The gentleness of all the gods go with thee!
I have many enemies in Orsino's court,
Else would I very shortly see thee there.
But come what may, I do adore thee so
That danger shall seem sport, and I will go.   *Exit.*

❖

2.2

Enter Viola and Malvolio, at several doors.

MALVOLIO   Were not you even now with the Countess
Olivia?

VIOLA   Even now, sir. On a moderate pace I have since
arrived but hither.

MALVOLIO   She returns this ring to you, sir. You might
have saved me my pains, to have taken it away   6
yourself. She adds, moreover, that you should put
your lord into a desperate assurance she will none of   8
him. And one thing more: that you be never so hardy   9
to come again in his affairs, unless it be to report your   10
lord's taking of this. Receive it so.

VIOLA   She took the ring of me. I'll none of it.   12

MALVOLIO   Come, sir, you peevishly threw it to her,
and her will is it should be so returned. [*He throws
down the ring.*] If it be worth stooping for, there it lies,
in your eye; if not, be it his that finds it.   *Exit.*   16

VIOLA   [*picking up the ring*]
I left no ring with her. What means this lady?
Fortune forbid my outside have not charmed her!   18
She made good view of me, indeed so much
That sure methought her eyes had lost her tongue,   20
For she did speak in starts, distractedly.
She loves me, sure! The cunning of her passion
Invites me in this churlish messenger.   23
None of my lord's ring? Why, he sent her none.
I am the man. If it be so—as 'tis—   25
Poor lady, she were better love a dream.
Disguise, I see, thou art a wickedness
Wherein the pregnant enemy does much.   28
How easy is it for the proper false   29
In women's waxen hearts to set their forms!   30
Alas, our frailty is the cause, not we,   31
For such as we are made of, such we be.   32

---

305 owe own, control.
2.1 Location: Somewhere in Illyria.
1 Nor will you not Do you not wish   **3 patience** leave   **4 malignancy** malevolence (of the stars; also in a medical sense)   **5 distemper**
infect   **10 sooth** truly.   **determinate** intended, determined upon   **11
extravagancy** aimless wandering.   **13 am willing . . . in** wish to keep
secret   **13–14 it . . . manners** it is incumbent upon me in all courtesy
14 express reveal   **17 Messaline** possibly Messina, or, more likely,
Massila (the modern Marseilles). In Plautus's *Menaechmi,* Massilians
and Illyrians are mentioned together.   **18 in an hour** in the same
hour   **20 some hour** about an hour.   **21 breach of the sea** surf   **26
estimable wonder** admiring judgment   **27 publish** proclaim   **28
envy** even malice   **31 Pardon . . . entertainment** i.e., I'm sorry I cannot offer you better hospitality and comfort.   **32 your trouble** the
trouble I put you to.   **33 murder . . . love** i.e., cause me to die from
lacking your love   **36 recovered** rescued, restored

38 kindness emotion, affection   **38–9 manners of my mother** i.e.,
womanly inclination to weep
2.2 Location: Near Olivia's house.
0.1 several different   **6 to have taken** by taking   **8 desperate** without hope   **9–10 so hardy to come** so bold as to come   **12 She . . . it**
(Viola tells a quick and friendly lie to shield Olivia.)   **16 in your eye**
in plain sight   **18 charmed** enchanted   **20 her eyes . . . tongue** i.e.,
the sight of me had deprived her of speech   **23 in** in the person of
25 the man the man of her choice.   **28 the pregnant enemy** the
resourceful enemy (either Satan or Cupid)   **29 the proper false**
deceptively handsome men   **30 waxen** i.e., malleable, impression-
able.   **set their forms** stamp their images (as of a seal).   **31–2 our . . .
be** i.e., the fault lies not in us as individuals, but in the frailty of
female nature.

How will this fadge? My master loves her dearly,   33
And I, poor monster, fond as much on him;   34
And she, mistaken, seems to dote on me.
What will become of this? As I am man,
My state is desperate for my master's love;
As I am woman—now, alas the day!—
What thriftless sighs shall poor Olivia breathe!   39
O Time, thou must untangle this, not I;
It is too hard a knot for me t'untie.   [*Exit.*]

❖

2.3

Enter Sir Toby and Sir Andrew.

SIR TOBY   Approach, Sir Andrew. Not to be abed after
midnight is to be up betimes; and *diluculo surgere,* thou   2
know'st—

SIR ANDREW   Nay, by my troth, I know not, but I know
to be up late is to be up late.

SIR TOBY   A false conclusion. I hate it as an unfilled can.   6
To be up after midnight and to go to bed then, is early;
so that to go to bed after midnight is to go to bed
betimes. Does not our lives consist of the four   9
elements?   10

SIR ANDREW   Faith, so they say, but I think it rather
consists of eating and drinking.

SIR TOBY   Thou'rt a scholar; let us therefore eat and
drink.—Marian, I say, a stoup of wine!   14

Enter Clown [Feste].

SIR ANDREW   Here comes the Fool, i'faith.

FESTE   How now, my hearts! Did you never see the
picture of "we three"?   17

SIR TOBY   Welcome, ass. Now let's have a catch.   18

SIR ANDREW   By my troth, the Fool has an excellent
breast. I had rather than forty shillings I had such a   20
leg, and so sweet a breath to sing, as the Fool has. In   21
sooth, thou wast in very gracious fooling last night,
when thou spok'st of Pigrogromitus, of the Vapians   23
passing the equinoctial of Queubus. 'Twas very good,   24
i'faith. I sent thee sixpence for thy leman. Hadst it?   25

FESTE   I did impeticos thy gratillity; for Malvolio's nose   26
is no whipstock. My lady has a white hand, and the   27
Myrmidons are no bottle-ale houses.   28

SIR ANDREW   Excellent! Why, this is the best fooling,
when all is done. Now, a song.

SIR TOBY   Come on, there is sixpence for you. [*He gives
money.*] Let's have a song.

SIR ANDREW   There's a testril of me too. [*He gives money.*]   33
If one knight give a—

FESTE   Would you have a love song, or a song of good   35
life?   36

SIR TOBY   A love song, a love song.

SIR ANDREW   Ay, ay, I care not for good life.

FESTE (*sings*)
        O mistress mine, where are you roaming?
        Oh, stay and hear, your true love 's coming,
            That can sing both high and low.
        Trip no further, pretty sweeting;
        Journeys end in lovers' meeting,
            Every wise man's son doth know.

SIR ANDREW   Excellent good, i'faith.

SIR TOBY   Good, good.

FESTE [*sings*]
        What is love? 'Tis not hereafter;
        Present mirth hath present laughter;
            What's to come is still unsure.   49
        In delay there lies no plenty.
        Then come kiss me, sweet and twenty;   51
            Youth's a stuff will not endure.

SIR ANDREW   A mellifluous voice, as I am true knight.

SIR TOBY   A contagious breath.   54

SIR ANDREW   Very sweet and contagious, i'faith.

SIR TOBY   To hear by the nose, it is dulcet in contagion.   56
But shall we make the welkin dance indeed? Shall we   57
rouse the night owl in a catch that will draw three   58
souls out of one weaver? Shall we do that?   59

SIR ANDREW   An you love me, let's do't. I am dog at a   60
catch.   61

FESTE   By'r Lady, sir, and some dogs will catch well.   62

SIR ANDREW   Most certain. Let our catch be "Thou   63
knave."   64

FESTE   "Hold thy peace, thou knave," knight? I shall be   65
constrained in't to call thee knave, knight.   66

SIR ANDREW   'Tis not the first time I have constrained
one to call me knave. Begin, Fool. It begins, "Hold thy
peace."

---

33 fadge turn out   **34 monster** i.e., being both man and woman.
fond dote   **39 thriftless** unprofitable
2.3. Location: Olivia's house.
2 betimes early. *diluculo surgere* (*saluberrimum est*) to rise early is
most healthful. (A sentence from Lilly's *Latin Grammar.*)   **6 can**
tankard.   **9-10 four elements** i.e., fire, air, water, and earth, the elements that were thought to make up all matter.   **14 stoup** drinking
vessel   **17 picture of "we three"** picture of two fools or asses
inscribed "we three," the spectator being the third.   **18 catch** round.
20 breast voice.   **21 leg** (for dancing)   **23-4 Pigrogromitus . . .
Queubus** (Feste's mock erudition.)   **25 leman** sweetheart.
26 impeticos thy gratillity (Suggests "impetticoat, or pocket up, thy
gratuity.")   **27 is no whipstock** is no whip-handle. (More nonsense,
but perhaps suggesting that Malvolio's nose for smelling out faults
does not give him the right to punish, so that he need not be feared.)
has a white hand i.e., is lady-like. (But Feste's speech may be mere
nonsense.)   **28 Myrmidons** followers of Achilles.   **bottle-ale houses**
(Used contemptuously of taverns because they sold low-class drink.)

33 testril tester, a coin worth sixpence   **35-6 good life** virtuous living. (Or perhaps Feste means simply "life's pleasures," but is misunderstood by Sir Andrew to mean "virtuous living.")   **49 still** always
51 sweet and twenty i.e., sweet and twenty times sweet, or twenty
years old   **54 contagious** infectiously delightful   **56 To . . . contagion** i.e., If we were to describe hearing in olfactory terms, we could
say it is sweet in stench.   **57 make . . . dance** i.e., drink till the sky
seems to turn around   **58-9 draw three souls** (Refers to the threefold
nature of the soul—vegetal, sensible, and intellectual—or to the three
singers of the three-part catch; or, just a comic exaggeration.)
59 weaver (Weavers were often associated with psalm singing.)
60 dog at very clever at. (But Feste uses the word literally.)   **61 catch**
round. (But Feste uses it to mean "seize.")   **62 By 'r Lady** (An oath,
originally, "by the Virgin Mary.")   **63-4 "Thou knave"** (This popular
round is arranged so that the three singers repeatedly accost one
another with "Thou knave.")   **65-6 "Hold . . . knight** ("Knight and
knave" is a common antithesis, like "rich and poor.")

FESTE   I shall never begin if I hold my peace.
SIR ANDREW   Good, i'faith. Come, begin.   *Catch sung.*

Enter Maria.

MARIA   What a caterwauling do you keep here! If my   72
lady have not called up her steward Malvolio and bid
him turn you out of doors, never trust me.
SIR TOBY   My lady's a Cataian, we are politicians,   75
Malvolio's a Peg-o'-Ramsey, and [*he sings*] "Three   76
merry men be we." Am not I consanguineous? Am I   77
not of her blood? Tillyvally! Lady! [*He sings.*] "There   78
dwelt a man in Babylon, lady, lady."   79
FESTE   Beshrew me, the knight's in admirable fooling.   80
SIR ANDREW   Ay, he does well enough if he be disposed,
and so do I too. He does it with a better grace,
but I do it more natural.   83
SIR TOBY [*sings*]
    "O' the twelfth day of December"—   84
MARIA   For the love o' God, peace!

Enter Malvolio.

MALVOLIO   My masters, are you mad? Or what are you?
Have you no wit, manners, nor honesty but to gabble   87
like tinkers at this time of night? Do ye make an alehouse of my lady's house, that ye squeak out your coz-   89
iers' catches without any mitigation or remorse of   90
voice? Is there no respect of place, persons, nor time in
you?
SIR TOBY   We did keep time, sir, in our catches. Sneck   93
up!   94
MALVOLIO   Sir Toby, I must be round with you. My   95
lady bade me tell you that though she harbors you as
her kinsman, she's nothing allied to your disorders. If
you can separate yourself and your misdemeanors,
you are welcome to the house; if not, an it would
please you to take leave of her, she is very willing to
bid you farewell.
SIR TOBY [*sings*]
    "Farewell, dear heart, since I must needs be gone."   102
MARIA   Nay, good Sir Toby.
FESTE [*sings*]
    "His eyes do show his days are almost done."
MALVOLIO   Is't even so?
SIR TOBY [*sings*]
    "But I will never die."
FESTE
    "Sir Toby, there you lie."

MALVOLIO   This is much credit to you.
SIR TOBY [*sings*]
    "Shall I bid him go?"
FESTE [*sings*]
    "What an if you do?"
SIR TOBY [*sings*]
    "Shall I bid him go, and spare not?"
FESTE [*sings*]
    "Oh, no, no, no, no, you dare not."
SIR TOBY   Out o' tune, sir? Ye lie. Art any more than a   113
steward? Dost thou think, because thou art virtuous,
there shall be no more cakes and ale?
FESTE   Yes, by Saint Anne, and ginger shall be hot i'th'   116
mouth, too.
SIR TOBY   Thou'rt i'the right.—Go, sir, rub your chain   118
with crumbs.—A stoup of wine, Maria!   119
MALVOLIO   Mistress Mary, if you prized my lady's
favor at anything more than contempt, you would not
give means for this uncivil rule. She shall know of it,   122
by this hand.   *Exit.*
MARIA   Go shake your ears.   124
SIR ANDREW   'Twere as good a deed as to drink when a
man's a-hungry to challenge him the field and then to   126
break promise with him and make a fool of him.
SIR TOBY   Do't, knight. I'll write thee a challenge, or I'll
deliver thy indignation to him by word of mouth.
MARIA   Sweet Sir Toby, be patient for tonight. Since the
youth of the Count's was today with my lady, she is
much out of quiet. For Monsieur Malvolio, let me   132
alone with him. If I do not gull him into a nayword   133
and make him a common recreation, do not think I   134
have wit enough to lie straight in my bed. I know I can
do it.
SIR TOBY   Possess us, possess us. Tell us something of   137
him.
MARIA   Marry, sir, sometimes he is a kind of puritan.   139
SIR ANDREW   Oh, if I thought that, I'd beat him like a
dog.
SIR TOBY   What, for being a puritan? Thy exquisite
reason, dear knight?
SIR ANDREW   I have no exquisite reason for't, but I
have reason good enough.

72 keep keep up   **75 Cataian** Cathayan, i.e., Chinese, a trickster or inscrutable; or, just nonsense.   **politicians** schemers, intriguers   **76 Peg-o'-Ramsey** character in a popular song. (Used here contemptuously.)   **76–7 "Three . . . we"** (A snatch of an old song.)   **77 consanguineous** i.e., a blood relative of Olivia.   **78 Tillyvally!** Nonsense, fiddle-faddle!   **78–9 "There . . . lady"** (The first line of a ballad, "The Constancy of Susanna," together with the refrain, "Lady, lady.")   **80 Beshrew** i.e., The devil take. (A mild curse.)   **83 natural** naturally. (But unconsciously suggesting idiocy.)   **84 "O' . . . December"** (Possibly part of a ballad about the Battle of Musselburgh Field, or Toby's error for the "twelfth day of Christmas," i.e., Twelfth Night.)   **87 wit** common sense.   **honesty** decency   **89–90 coziers'** cobblers'   **90 mitigation or remorse** i.e., considerate lowering   **93–4 Sneck up!** Go hang!   **95 round** blunt   **102 "Farewell . . . gone"** (From the ballad "Corydon's Farewell to Phyllis.")

113 Out o' tune (Perhaps a quibbling reply—"We did too keep time in our tune"—to Malvolio's accusation of having no respect for place or time, line 91. Often emended to *Out o' time,* easily misread in secretary hand.)   **116 Saint Anne** mother of the Virgin Mary. (Her cult was derided in the Reformation, much as Puritan reformers also derided the tradition of *cakes and ale* at church feasts.)   **ginger** (Commonly used to spice ale.)   **118–19 rub . . . crumbs** i.e., scour or polish your steward's chain; attend to your own business and remember your station.   **122 give means** i.e., supply drink.   **rule** conduct.   **124 your ears** i.e., your ass's ears.   **126 the field** i.e., to a duel   **132 For** As for   **132–3 let . . . him** leave him to me.   **133 gull** trick.   **nayword** byword. (His name will be synonymous with "dupe.")   **134 recreation** sport   **137 Possess** Inform   **139 puritan** (Maria's point is that Malvolio is sometimes a *kind* of puritan, insofar as he is precise about moral conduct and censorious of others for immoral conduct, but that he is nothing consistently except a time-server. He is not, then, simply a satirical type of the Puritan sect. The extent of the resemblance is left unstated.)

MARIA The devil a puritan that he is, or anything con- 146
stantly, but a time-pleaser; an affectioned ass, that cons 147
state without book and utters it by great swaths; the 148
best persuaded of himself, so crammed, as he thinks, 149
with excellencies, that it is his grounds of faith that all 150
that look on him love him; and on that vice in him
will my revenge find notable cause to work.

SIR TOBY What wilt thou do?

MARIA I will drop in his way some obscure epistles of 154
love, wherein by the color of his beard, the shape of
his leg, the manner of his gait, the expressure of his 156
eye, forehead, and complexion, he shall find himself
most feelingly personated. I can write very like my 158
lady your niece; on a forgotten matter we can hardly 159
make distinction of our hands. 160

SIR TOBY Excellent! I smell a device.

SIR ANDREW I have't in my nose too.

SIR TOBY He shall think, by the letters that thou wilt
drop, that they come from my niece, and that she's in
love with him.

MARIA My purpose is indeed a horse of that color.

SIR ANDREW And your horse now would make him an
ass.

MARIA Ass, I doubt not. 169

SIR ANDREW Oh, 'twill be admirable!

MARIA Sport royal, I warrant you. I know my physic 171
will work with him. I will plant you two, and let the
Fool make a third, where he shall find the letter. Observe his construction of it. For this night, to bed, 174
and dream on the event. Farewell.   *Exit.* 175

SIR TOBY Good night, Penthesilea. 176

SIR ANDREW Before me, she's a good wench. 177

SIR TOBY She's a beagle true-bred and one that adores 178
me. What o'that?

SIR ANDREW I was adored once, too.

SIR TOBY Let's to bed, knight. Thou hadst need send
for more money.

SIR ANDREW If I cannot recover your niece, I am a foul 183
way out. 184

SIR TOBY Send for money, knight. If thou hast her not
i'th' end, call me cut. 186

SIR ANDREW If I do not, never trust me, take it how
you will.

SIR TOBY Come, come, I'll go burn some sack. 'Tis too 189
late to go to bed now. Come, knight; come, knight. 190
                                                   Exeunt.

2.4

Enter Duke [Orsino], Viola, Curio, and others.

ORSINO
Give me some music. Now, good morrow, friends.   1
Now, good Cesario, but that piece of song,   2
That old and antique song we heard last night.   3
Methought it did relieve my passion much,
More than light airs and recollected terms   5
Of these most brisk and giddy-pacèd times.
Come, but one verse.

CURIO He is not here, so please Your Lordship, that
should sing it.

ORSINO Who was it?

CURIO Feste the jester, my lord, a fool that the Lady
Olivia's father took much delight in. He is about the
house.

ORSINO
Seek him out, and play the tune the while.
                   [Exit Curio.] Music plays.
[To Viola] Come hither, boy. If ever thou shalt love,
In the sweet pangs of it remember me;
For such as I am, all true lovers are,
Unstaid and skittish in all motions else   18
Save in the constant image of the creature
That is beloved. How dost thou like this tune?

VIOLA
It gives a very echo to the seat   21
Where Love is throned.

ORSINO   Thou dost speak masterly.
My life upon't, young though thou art, thine eye
Hath stayed upon some favor that it loves.   24
Hath it not, boy?

VIOLA   A little, by your favor.   25

ORSINO
What kind of woman is't?

VIOLA   Of your complexion.

ORSINO
She is not worth thee, then. What years, i'faith?

VIOLA About your years, my lord.

ORSINO
Too old, by heaven. Let still the woman take   29
An elder than herself. So wears she to him;   30
So sways she level in her husband's heart.   31
For, boy, however we do praise ourselves,

146–7 **constantly** consistently   147 **time-pleaser** time-server, syco-
phant.   **affectioned** affected   147–8 **cons . . . book** learns by heart
the phrases and mannerisms of the great   148 **by great swaths** in
great sweeps, like rows of mown grain   148–9 **the best persuaded**
having the best opinion   150 **grounds of faith** creed, belief
154 **some obscure epistles** an ambiguously worded letter
156 **expressure** expression   158 **personated** represented.   159 **on a
forgotten matter** when we've forgotten which of us wrote something
or what it was about   160 **hands** handwriting.   169 **Ass, I** (With a
pun on "as I.")   171 **physic** medicine   174 **construction** interpretation   175 **event** outcome.   176 **Penthesilea** Queen of the Amazons.
(Another ironical allusion to Maria's diminutive stature.)
177 **Before me** i.e., On my soul. (A mild oath.)   178 **beagle** a small,
intelligent hunting dog   183 **recover** win   183–4 **foul way out** i.e.,
miserably out of pocket. (Literally, out of my way and in the mire.)
186 **cut** a proverbial term of abuse: literally, a horse with a docked
tail; also, a gelding, or the female genital organ.

189 **burn some sack** warm some Spanish wine.   190.1 *Exeunt* (Feste
may have left earlier; he says nothing after line 117 and is perhaps
referred to without his being present at 172–3.)
2.4 Location: Orsino's court.
1 **morrow** morning   2 **but** i.e., I ask only   3 **antique** old, quaint, fantastic   5 **recollected terms** studied and artificial expressions   18 **all
motions else** all other thoughts and emotions   21 **the seat** i.e., the
heart   24 **stayed . . . favor** rested upon some face   25 **by your favor**
if you please. (But also hinting at "like you in feature.")   29 **still**
always   30 **wears she** she adapts herself   31 **sways she level** she
keeps a perfect equipoise and steady affection

Our fancies are more giddy and unfirm,
More longing, wavering, sooner lost and worn,   34
Than women's are.
VIOLA   I think it well, my lord.
ORSINO
Then let thy love be younger than thyself,
Or thy affection cannot hold the bent;   37
For women are as roses, whose fair flower
Being once displayed, doth fall that very hour.   39
VIOLA
And so they are. Alas that they are so,
To die even when they to perfection grow!   41

        Enter Curio and Clown [Feste].

ORSINO
Oh, fellow, come, the song we had last night.
Mark it, Cesario, it is old and plain;
The spinsters and the knitters in the sun,   44
And the free maids that weave their thread with
    bones,   45
Do use to chant it. It is silly sooth,   46
And dallies with the innocence of love,   47
Like the old age.   48
FESTE   Are you ready, sir?
ORSINO   Ay, prithee, sing.   Music.

        The Song.

FESTE [sings]
        Come away, come away, death,   51
            And in sad cypress let me be laid.   52
        Fly away, fly away, breath;
            I am slain by a fair cruel maid.
        My shroud of white, stuck all with yew,   55
            Oh, prepare it!
        My part of death, no one so true   57
            Did share it.   58

        Not a flower, not a flower sweet
            On my black coffin let there be strown;   60
        Not a friend, not a friend greet
            My poor corpse, where my bones shall be
                thrown.
        A thousand thousand sighs to save,
            Lay me, oh, where
        Sad true lover never find my grave,
            To weep there!

ORSINO [offering money]   There's for thy pains.
FESTE   No pains, sir. I take pleasure in singing, sir.
ORSINO   I'll pay thy pleasure then.

FESTE   Truly, sir, and pleasure will be paid, one time   70
    or another.   71
ORSINO   Give me now leave to leave thee.   72
FESTE   Now, the melancholy god protect thee, and the   73
    tailor make thy doublet of changeable taffeta, for thy 74
    mind is a very opal. I would have men of such con-   75
    stancy put to sea, that their business might be every- 76
    thing and their intent everywhere, for that's it that   77
    always makes a good voyage of nothing. Farewell.   78
                                                    Exit.
ORSINO
Let all the rest give place.
            [Curio and attendants withdraw.]
                    Once more, Cesario,   79
Get thee to yond same sovereign cruelty.
Tell her, my love, more noble than the world,
Prizes not quantity of dirty lands;
The parts that fortune hath bestowed upon her,   83
Tell her, I hold as giddily as fortune;   84
But 'tis that miracle and queen of gems   85
That nature pranks her in attracts my soul.   86
VIOLA   But if she cannot love you, sir?
ORSINO
I cannot be so answered.
VIOLA   Sooth, but you must.   88
Say that some lady—as perhaps there is—
Hath for your love as great a pang of heart
As you have for Olivia. You cannot love her;
You tell her so. Must she not then be answered?   92
ORSINO   There is no woman's sides
Can bide the beating of so strong a passion   94
As love doth give my heart; no woman's heart
So big, to hold so much. They lack retention.   96
Alas, their love may be called appetite,
No motion of the liver, but the palate,   98
That suffer surfeit, cloyment, and revolt;   99
But mine is all as hungry as the sea,
And can digest as much. Make no compare   101
Between that love a woman can bear me
And that I owe Olivia.
VIOLA   Ay, but I know—   103
ORSINO   What dost thou know?

34 worn exhausted. (Sometimes emended to won.)   37 hold the bent
hold steady, keep the intensity (like the tension of a bow)   39 displayed full blown   41 even when just as   44 spinsters spinners
45 free carefree, innocent.   bones bobbins on which bone-lace was
made   46 Do use are accustomed.   silly sooth simple truth   47 dallies with dwells lovingly on, sports with   48 Like . . . age as in the
good old times.   51 Come away Come hither   52 cypress i.e., a coffin of cypress wood, or bier strewn with sprigs of cypress   55 yew
yew sprigs. (Emblematic of mourning, like cypress.)   57–8 My . . . it
No one died for love so true to love as I.   60 strown strewn

70–1 pleasure . . . another sooner or later one must pay for indulgence.   72 leave to leave permission to take leave of, dismiss   73 the
melancholy god i.e., Saturn, whose planet was thought to control the
melancholy temperament   74 doublet close-fitting jacket.
changeable taffeta a silk so woven of various-colored threads that its
color shifts with changing perspective   75 opal an iridescent precious stone that changes color when seen from various angles or in
different lights.   76–7 that . . . everywhere i.e., so that in the changeableness of the sea their inconstancy could always be exercised
77–8 for . . . nothing because that's the quality that is satisfied with
an aimless voyage.   79 give place withdraw.   83 parts attributes
such as wealth or rank   84 I . . . fortune I esteem as carelessly as I do
fortune, that fickle goddess   85 that miracle . . . gems i.e., her beauty
86 pranks adorns.   attracts that attracts   88 Sooth In truth   92 be
answered be satisfied with your answer.   94 bide withstand   96 to
hold as to contain.   retention constancy, the power of retaining.
98 motion impulse.   liver . . . palate (Real love is a passion of the
liver, whereas fancy, light love, is born in the eye and nourished in
the palate.)   99 cloyment satiety.   revolt revulsion   101 compare
comparison   103 owe have for

VIOLA
  Too well what love women to men may owe.
  In faith, they are as true of heart as we.
  My father had a daughter loved a man
  As it might be, perhaps, were I a woman,
  I should Your Lordship.
ORSINO   And what's her history?
VIOLA
  A blank, my lord. She never told her love,
  But let concealment, like a worm i'th' bud,
  Feed on her damask cheek. She pined in thought,   112
  And with a green and yellow melancholy;   113
  She sat like Patience on a monument,   114
  Smiling at grief. Was not this love indeed?
  We men may say more, swear more, but indeed
  Our shows are more than will; for still we prove   117
  Much in our vows, but little in our love.
ORSINO
  But died thy sister of her love, my boy?
VIOLA
  I am all the daughters of my father's house,
  And all the brothers too—and yet I know not.
  Sir, shall I to this lady?
ORSINO   Ay, that's the theme.
  To her in haste; give her this jewel. [*He gives a jewel.*]
    Say
  My love can give no place, bide no denay.   124
                              Exeunt [*separately*].

2.5

Enter Sir Toby, Sir Andrew, and Fabian.

SIR TOBY   Come thy ways, Signor Fabian.   1
FABIAN   Nay, I'll come. If I lose a scruple of this sport,   2
  let me be boiled to death with melancholy.   3
SIR TOBY   Wouldst thou not be glad to have the niggardly rascally sheep-biter come by some notable   5
  shame?
FABIAN   I would exult, man. You know he brought me
  out o'favor with my lady about a bearbaiting here. 8
SIR TOBY   To anger him we'll have the bear again, and
  we will fool him black and blue. Shall we not, Sir An- 10
  drew?
SIR ANDREW   An we do not, it is pity of our lives. 12

Enter Maria [*with a letter*].

SIR TOBY   Here comes the little villain.—How now, my 13
  metal of India!   14
MARIA   Get ye all three into the boxtree. Malvolio's 15
  coming down this walk. He has been yonder i'the sun
  practicing behavior to his own shadow this half hour.
  Observe him, for the love of mockery, for I know this
  letter will make a contemplative idiot of him. Close, in 19
  the name of jesting! [*The others hide.*] Lie thou there
  [*throwing down a letter*]; for here comes the trout that
  must be caught with tickling.   *Exit.* 22

Enter Malvolio.

MALVOLIO   'Tis but fortune; all is fortune. Maria once
  told me she did affect me; and I have heard herself 24
  come thus near, that should she fancy, it should be 25
  one of my complexion. Besides, she uses me with a
  more exalted respect than anyone else that follows 27
  her. What should I think on't?
SIR TOBY   Here's an overweening rogue!
FABIAN   Oh, peace! Contemplation makes a rare turkey- 30
  cock of him. How he jets under his advanced plumes! 31
SIR ANDREW   'Slight, I could so beat the rogue!   32
SIR TOBY   Peace, I say.
MALVOLIO   To be Count Malvolio.
SIR TOBY   Ah, rogue!
SIR ANDREW   Pistol him, pistol him.
SIR TOBY   Peace, peace!
MALVOLIO   There is example for't. The lady of the Stra- 38
  chy married the yeoman of the wardrobe.   39
SIR ANDREW   Fie on him, Jezebel!   40
FABIAN   Oh, peace! Now he's deeply in. Look how imag-
  ination blows him.   42
MALVOLIO   Having been three months married to her,
  sitting in my state—   44
SIR TOBY   Oh, for a stone-bow, to hit him in the eye! 45
MALVOLIO   Calling my officers about me, in my
  branched velvet gown; having come from a daybed, 47
  where I have left Olivia sleeping—
SIR TOBY   Fire and brimstone!
FABIAN   Oh, peace, peace!
MALVOLIO   And then to have the humor of state; and 51
  after a demure travel of regard, telling them I know 52
  my place as I would they should do theirs, to ask for
  my kinsman Toby.   54
SIR TOBY   Bolts and shackles!
FABIAN   Oh, peace, peace, peace! Now, now.

---

112 damask pink and white like the damask rose   **113 green and yellow** pale and sallow   **114 on a monument** carved in statuary on a
tomb   **117 shows** displays of passion.   **more than will** greater than
our determination.   **still** always   **124 can . . . denay** cannot yield or
endure denial.
2.5 Location: Olivia's garden.
1 Come thy ways Come along   **2 a scruple** the least bit   **3 boiled**
(With a pun on "biled"; black bile was the "humor" of melancholy
and was thought to be a cold humor.)   **5 sheep-biter** a dog that bites
sheep, i.e., a scoundrel   **8 bearbaiting** (A special target of Puritan
disapproval.)   **10 fool . . . blue** mock him until he is figuratively
black and blue.   **12 An** If.   **pity of our lives** a pity we should live.

13 villain (Here, a term of endearment.)   **14 metal** gold, i.e., priceless
one   **15 boxtree** an evergreen shrub.   **19 contemplative** i.e., from
his musings.   **Close** i.e., Keep close, stay hidden   **22 tickling**
(1) stroking gently about the gills—an actual method of fishing
(2) deception.   **24 she** Olivia.   **affect** have fondness for   **25 fancy**
fall in love   **27 follows** serves   **30 rare** extraordinary   **31 jets** struts.
advanced prominent   **32 'Slight** By His (God's) light   **38 example**
precedent   **38–9 lady of the Strachy** (Apparently a lady who had
married below her station; no certain identification.)   **40 Jezebel** the
proud queen of Ahab, King of Israel.   **42 blows** puffs up   **44 state**
chair of state   **45 stone-bow** crossbow that shoots stones
47 branched adorned with a figured pattern suggesting branched
leaves or flowers.   **daybed** sofa, couch   **51 have . . . state** adopt the
imperious manner of authority   **52 demure . . . regard** grave survey
of the company   **54 Toby** (Malvolio omits the title *Sir*.)

MALVOLIO   Seven of my people, with an obedient start, make out for him. I frown the while, and perchance wind up my watch, or play with my—some rich jewel. Toby approaches; curtsies there to me—   59 60

SIR TOBY   Shall this fellow live?

FABIAN   Though our silence be drawn from us with cars, yet peace.   62 63

MALVOLIO   I extend my hand to him thus, quenching my familiar smile with an austere regard of control—   65

SIR TOBY   And does not Toby take you a blow o'the lips then?   66

MALVOLIO   Saying, "Cousin Toby, my fortunes having cast me on your niece give me this prerogative of speech—"

SIR TOBY   What, what?

MALVOLIO   "You must amend your drunkenness."

SIR TOBY   Out, scab!   73

FABIAN   Nay, patience, or we break the sinews of our plot.   74

MALVOLIO   "Besides, you waste the treasure of your time with a foolish knight—"

SIR ANDREW   That's me, I warrant you.

MALVOLIO   "One Sir Andrew."

SIR ANDREW   I knew 'twas I, for many do call me fool.

MALVOLIO   What employment have we here?   81
    [*Taking up the letter.*]

FABIAN   Now is the woodcock near the gin.   82

SIR TOBY   Oh, peace, and the spirit of humors intimate reading aloud to him!   83

MALVOLIO   By my life, this is my lady's hand. These be her very c's, her u's, and her t's; and thus makes she her great P's. It is in contempt of question her hand.   86 87

SIR ANDREW   Her c's, her u's, and her t's. Why that?

MALVOLIO [*reads*]   "To the unknown beloved, this, and my good wishes."—Her very phrases! By your leave, wax. Soft! And the impressure her Lucrece, with which she uses to seal. 'Tis my lady. To whom should this be?   [*He opens the letter.*]   90 91 92

FABIAN   This wins him, liver and all.   94

MALVOLIO [*reads*]
    "Jove knows I love,
        But who?
    Lips, do not move;
        No man must know."
"No man must know." What follows? The numbers altered! "No man must know." If this should be thee, Malvolio?   99 100

SIR TOBY   Marry, hang thee, brock!   102

MALVOLIO [*reads*]
    "I may command where I adore,
        But silence, like a Lucrece knife,
    With bloodless stroke my heart doth gore;
        M.O.A.I. doth sway my life."

FABIAN   A fustian riddle!   107

SIR TOBY   Excellent wench, say I.

MALVOLIO   "M.O.A.I. doth sway my life." Nay, but first, let me see, let me see, let me see.

FABIAN   What dish o'poison has she dressed him!   111

SIR TOBY   And with what wing the staniel checks at it!   112 113

MALVOLIO   "I may command where I adore." Why, she may command me; I serve her, she is my lady. Why, this is evident to any formal capacity. There is no obstruction in this. And the end—what should that alphabetical position portend? If I could make that resemble something in me! Softly! "M.O.A.I."—   116 118

SIR TOBY   Oh, ay, make up that. He is now at a cold scent.   120

FABIAN   Sowter will cry upon't for all this, though it be as rank as a fox.   121 122

MALVOLIO   "M"—Malvolio. "M"! Why, that begins my name!

FABIAN   Did not I say he would work it out? The cur is excellent at faults.   126

MALVOLIO   "M"—But then there is no consonancy in the sequel that suffers under probation: "A" should follow, but "O" does.   127 128

FABIAN   And "O" shall end, I hope.   130

SIR TOBY   Ay, or I'll cudgel him, and make him cry "Oh!"

MALVOLIO   And then "I" comes behind.

FABIAN   Ay, an you had any eye behind you, you might see more detraction at your heels than fortunes before you.   133 134

MALVOLIO   "M.O.A.I." This simulation is not as the former. And yet, to crush this a little, it would bow to me, for every one of these letters are in my name. Soft! Here follows prose.   136

---

59 play with my (Malvolio perhaps means his steward's chain but checks himself in time; as "Count Malvolio," he would not be wearing it. A bawdy meaning of playing with himself is also suggested.) **60 curtsies** bows   **62–3 with cars** with chariots, i.e., pulling apart by force   **65 familiar** (1) customary (2) friendly.   **regard of control** look of authority   **66 take** deliver   **73 scab** scurvy fellow.   **74 break . . . of** hamstring, disable   **81 employment** business   **82 woodcock** (A bird proverbial for its stupidity.)   **gin** snare.   **83 humors** whim, caprice   **86 c's . . . t's** i.e., *cut,* slang for the female pudenda   **87 great** (1) uppercase (2) copious. (*P* suggests "pee.")   **in contempt of** beyond   **90–1 By . . . wax** (Addressed to the seal on the letter.)   **91 Soft** Softly, not so fast.   **impressure** device imprinted on the seal.   **Lucrece** Lucretia, chaste matron who, ravished by Tarquin, committed suicide   **92 uses** is accustomed   **94 liver** i.e., the seat of passion   **99–100 The numbers altered!** More verses, in a different meter!

102 brock badger. (Used contemptuously.)   **107 fustian** bombastic, ridiculously pompous   **111 What** What a.   **dressed** prepared for   **112 wing** speed.   **staniel** kestrel, a sparrow hawk. (The word is used contemptuously because of the uselessness of the staniel for falconry.)   **112–13 checks at it** turns to fly at it.   **116 formal capacity** normal understanding.   **118 position** arrangement   **120 Oh, ay** (Playing on *O.I.* of *M.O.A.I.*)   **make up** work out   **121–2 Sowter . . . fox** The hound Sowter (literally, "Cobbler") will bay triumphantly at picking up this false scent, even though the smell is as rank as a fox. ("M.O.A.I." is a false lead that reeks.)   **126 at faults** i.e., at maneuvering his way past breaks in the line of scent—in this case, on a false trail.   **127–8 no consonancy . . . probation** no pattern in the following letters that stands up under examination. (In fact, the letters "M.O.A.I." represent the first, last, second, and next to last letters of Malvolio's name.)   **130 "O" shall end** (1) "O" ends Malvolio's name (2) *omega* ends the Greek alphabet and is thus a symbol for the ending of the world, *alpha* to *omega* (3) Malvolio's cry of pain will end the matter, as Sir Toby suggests in the next line.   **133 eye** (punning on the "I" of "Oh, ay" and "M.O.A.I.")   **134 detraction . . . heels** defamation pursuing you   **136 simulation** disguise, puzzle

[*He reads.*] "If this fall into thy hand, revolve. In my 140
stars I am above thee, but be not afraid of greatness. 141
Some are born great, some achieve greatness, and
some have greatness thrust upon 'em. Thy Fates open 143
their hands; let thy blood and spirit embrace them; 144
and, to inure thyself to what thou art like to be, cast 145
thy humble slough and appear fresh. Be opposite with 146
a kinsman, surly with servants. Let thy tongue tang 147
arguments of state; put thyself into the trick of 148
singularity. She thus advises thee that sighs for thee. 149
Remember who commended thy yellow stockings,
and wished to see thee ever cross-gartered. I say, 151
remember. Go to, thou art made, if thou desir'st to be 152
so. If not, let me see thee a steward still, the fellow of
servants, and not worthy to touch Fortune's fingers.
Farewell. She that would alter services with thee, 155
                          The Fortunate-Unhappy."
Daylight and champaign discovers not more! This is 157
open. I will be proud, I will read politic authors, I will 158
baffle Sir Toby, I will wash off gross acquaintance, I 159
will be point-devise the very man. I do not now fool 160
myself, to let imagination jade me; for every reason 161
excites to this, that my lady loves me. She did com- 162
mend my yellow stockings of late, she did praise my
leg being cross-gartered; and in this she manifests herself to my love, and with a kind of injunction drives
me to these habits of her liking. I thank my stars, I am 166
happy. I will be strange, stout, in yellow stockings 167
and cross-gartered, even with the swiftness of putting
on. Jove and my stars be praised! Here is yet a postscript. [*He reads.*] "Thou canst not choose but know who
I am. If thou entertain'st my love, let it appear in thy 171
smiling; thy smiles become thee well. Therefore in my
presence still smile, dear my sweet, I prithee." 173
Jove, I thank thee. I will smile; I will do everything that
thou wilt have me.   *Exit.*

[*Sir Toby, Sir Andrew, and Fabian come from hiding.*]

FABIAN   I will not give my part of this sport for a
pension of thousands to be paid from the Sophy. 177
SIR TOBY   I could marry this wench for this device.
SIR ANDREW   So could I too.
SIR TOBY   And ask no other dowry with her but such
another jest.

Enter Maria.

SIR ANDREW   Nor I neither.
FABIAN   Here comes my noble gull-catcher. 183
SIR TOBY   Wilt thou set thy foot o' my neck?
SIR ANDREW   Or o' mine either?
SIR TOBY   Shall I play my freedom at tray-trip, and 186
become thy bondslave?
SIR ANDREW   I'faith, or I either?
SIR TOBY   Why, thou hast put him in such a dream that
when the image of it leaves him he must run mad.
MARIA   Nay, but say true, does it work upon him?
SIR TOBY   Like aqua vitae with a midwife. 192
MARIA   If you will then see the fruits of the sport, mark
his first approach before my lady. He will come to her
in yellow stockings, and 'tis a color she abhors, and
cross-gartered, a fashion she detests; and he will smile
upon her, which will now be so unsuitable to her
disposition, being addicted to a melancholy as she is,
that it cannot but turn him into a notable contempt. If 199
you will see it, follow me.
SIR TOBY   To the gates of Tartar, thou most excellent 201
devil of wit!
SIR ANDREW   I'll make one too.   *Exeunt.* 203

3.1

*Enter Viola, and Clown [Feste, playing his pipe
and tabor].*

VIOLA   Save thee, friend, and thy music. Dost thou live 1
by thy tabor? 2
FESTE   No, sir, I live by the church.
VIOLA   Art thou a churchman?
FESTE   No such matter, sir. I do live by the church, for
I do live at my house, and my house doth stand by the
church.
VIOLA   So thou mayst say the king lies by a beggar if 8
a beggar dwell near him, or the church stands by thy 9
tabor if thy tabor stand by the church. 10
FESTE   You have said, sir. To see this age! A sentence is 11
but a cheveril glove to a good wit. How quickly the 12
wrong side may be turned outward!
VIOLA   Nay, that's certain. They that dally nicely with 14
words may quickly make them wanton. 15
FESTE   I would therefore my sister had had no name,
sir.
VIOLA   Why, man?

140 revolve consider.   **141 stars** fortune   **143–4 open their hands**
offer their bounty   **145 inure** accustom.   **like** likely.   **cast** cast off
146 slough skin of a snake; hence, former demeanor of humbleness.
opposite contradictory   **147 tang** sound loud with   **148 state** politics, statecraft   **148–9 trick of singularity** eccentricity of manner.
151 cross-gartered wearing garters above and below the knee so as to
cross behind it.   **152 Go to** (An expression of remonstrance.)
155 alter services i.e., exchange place of mistress and servant
157 champaign open country.   **discovers** discloses   **158 politic** dealing with state affairs   **159 baffle** deride, degrade. (A technical chivalric term used to describe the disgrace of a perjured knight.)   **gross**
base   **160 point-devise** correct to the letter   **161 to let** by letting.
jade me trick me, make me look ridiculous (as an unruly horse might
do)   **162 excites to this** prompts this conclusion   **164 this** this letter
166 these habits this attire   **167 happy** fortunate.   **strange, stout**
aloof, haughty   **171 thou entertain'st** you accept   **173 still** continually   **177 Sophy** Shah of Persia.

183 gull-catcher tricker of *gulls* or dupes.   **186 play** gamble.   **tray-
trip** a game of dice, success in which depended on throwing a three
(*tray*)   **192 aqua vitae** brandy or other distilled liquor   **199 notable
contempt** notorious object of contempt.   **201 Tartar** Tartarus, the
infernal regions   **203 make one** i.e., tag along
3.1 Location: Olivia's garden.
1 Save God save   **1–2 live by** earn your living with. (But Feste uses
the phrase to mean "dwell near.")   **2 tabor** small drum.   **8 lies by**
(1) lies sexually with (2) dwells near   **9–10 stands by . . . stand by**
(1) is maintained by (2) is placed near   **11 You have said** You've
expressed your opinion.   **sentence** maxim, judgment, opinion
12 cheveril kidskin   **14 dally nicely** (1) play subtly (2) toy amorously
15 wanton (1) equivocal (2) licentious, unchaste. (Feste then "dallies"
with the word in its sexual sense; see line 20.)

FESTE   Why, sir, her name's a word, and to dally with
that word might make my sister wanton. But indeed,
words are very rascals since bonds disgraced them.   21

VIOLA   Thy reason, man?

FESTE   Troth, sir, I can yield you none without words,
and words are grown so false I am loath to prove
reason with them.

VIOLA   I warrant thou art a merry fellow and car'st for   26
nothing.   27

FESTE   Not so, sir, I do care for something; but in my
conscience, sir, I do not care for you. If that be to care
for nothing, sir, I would it would make you invisible.   30

VIOLA   Art not thou the Lady Olivia's fool?

FESTE   No indeed, sir. The Lady Olivia has no folly. She
will keep no fool, sir, till she be married, and fools are
as like husbands as pilchers are to herrings—the   34
husband's the bigger. I am indeed not her fool but   35
her corrupter of words.

VIOLA   I saw thee late at the Count Orsino's.   37

FESTE   Foolery, sir, does walk about the orb like the   38
sun; it shines everywhere. I would be sorry, sir, but   39
the fool should be as oft with your master as with my   40
mistress. I think I saw Your Wisdom there.   41

VIOLA   Nay, an thou pass upon me, I'll no more with   42
thee. Hold, there's expenses for thee.

[*She gives a coin.*]

FESTE   Now Jove, in his next commodity of hair, send   44
thee a beard!

VIOLA   By my troth, I'll tell thee, I am almost sick for   46
one—[*aside*] though I would not have it grow on my   47
chin.—Is thy lady within?

FESTE   Would not a pair of these have bred, sir?

VIOLA   Yes, being kept together and put to use.   50

FESTE   I would play Lord Pandarus of Phrygia, sir, to   51
bring a Cressida to this Troilus.

VIOLA   I understand you, sir. 'Tis well begged.

[*She gives another coin.*]

FESTE   The matter, I hope, is not great, sir, begging   54
but a beggar; Cressida was a beggar. My lady is   55
within, sir. I will conster to them whence you come.   56
Who you are and what you would are out of my
welkin—I might say "element," but the word is   58
overworn.   *Exit.*

VIOLA
This fellow is wise enough to play the fool,
And to do that well craves a kind of wit.
He must observe their mood on whom he jests,
The quality of persons, and the time,   63
Not, like the haggard, check at every feather   64
That comes before his eye. This is a practice   65
As full of labor as a wise man's art;
For folly that he wisely shows is fit,   67
But wise men, folly-fall'n, quite taint their wit.   68

Enter Sir Toby and [Sir] Andrew.

SIR TOBY   Save you, gentleman.

VIOLA   And you, sir.

SIR ANDREW   *Dieu vous garde, monsieur.*   71

VIOLA   *Et vous aussi; votre serviteur.*   72

SIR ANDREW   I hope, sir, you are, and I am yours.

SIR TOBY   Will you encounter the house? My niece is   74
desirous you should enter, if your trade be to her.   75

VIOLA   I am bound to your niece, sir; I mean, she is the   76
list of my voyage.   77

SIR TOBY   Taste your legs, sir. Put them to motion.   78

VIOLA   My legs do better understand me, sir, than I un-   79
derstand what you mean by bidding me taste my legs.

SIR TOBY   I mean, to go, sir, to enter.

VIOLA   I will answer you with gait and entrance.—But   82
we are prevented.   83

Enter Olivia and gentlewoman [Maria].

Most excellent accomplished lady, the heavens rain
odors on you!

SIR ANDREW   [*to Sir Toby*]   That youth's a rare courtier.
"Rain odors"—well.

VIOLA   [*to Olivia*]   My matter hath no voice, lady, but to   88
your own most pregnant and vouchsafed ear.   89

SIR ANDREW   [*to Sir Toby*]   "Odors," "pregnant," and
"vouchsafed." I'll get 'em all three all ready.   91

OLIVIA   Let the garden door be shut, and leave me to
my hearing. [*Exeunt Sir Toby, Sir Andrew, and Maria.*]
Give me your hand, sir.

VIOLA
My duty, madam, and most humble service.

OLIVIA   What is your name?

VIOLA
Cesario is your servant's name, fair princess.

---

21 since . . . them i.e., since bonds have been needed to make sworn statements good. (Words cannot be relied on since not even contractual promises are reliable.)   **26–7 car'st for nothing** are without any worries. (But Feste puns on *care for* in lines 29–30 in the sense of "like.")   **30 invisible** i.e., nothing; absent.   **34 pilchers** pilchards, fish resembling herring but smaller   **35 the bigger** (1) the larger (2) the bigger fool.   **37 late** recently   **38 orb** earth   **39–41 I would . . . mistress** (1) I should be sorry not to visit Orsino's house often (2) It would be a shame if folly were no less common there than in Olivia's household.   **41 Your Wisdom** i.e., you. (A title of mock courtesy.)   **42 an . . . me** if you fence (verbally) with me, pass judgment on me   **44 commodity** supply   **46–7 sick for one** (1) eager to have a beard (2) in love with a bearded man   **50 put to use** put out at interest.   **51 Pandarus** the go-between in the love story of Troilus and Cressida; uncle to Cressida   **54–5 begging . . . was a beggar** (A reference to Henryson's *Testament of Cresseid* in which Cressida became a leper and a beggar. Feste desires another coin to be the mate of the one he has, just as Cressida, the beggar, was mate to Troilus.)   **56 conster** construe, explain   **58 welkin** sky. **element** (The word can be synonymous with *welkin*, but the common phrase *out of my element* means "beyond my scope.")

63 quality character, rank   **64 haggard** untrained adult hawk, hence unmanageable   **64–5 check . . . eye** strike at every bird it sees, i.e., dart from subject to subject.   **65 practice** exercise of skill   **67–8 For . . . wit** for the folly he judiciously displays is appropriate and clever, whereas when wise men fall into folly they utterly infect their own intelligence.   **71 Dieu . . . monsieur** God keep you, sir.   **72 Et . . . serviteur** And you, too; (I am) your servant. (Sir Andrew is not quite up to a reply in French.)   **74 encounter** (High-sounding word to express "approach.")   **75 trade** business. (Suggesting also a commercial venture.)   **76 I am bound** (1) I am on a journey. (Continuing Sir Toby's metaphor in *trade*.) (2) I am confined, obligated   **77 list** limit, destination   **78 Taste** Try   **79 understand** stand under, support   **82 gait and entrance** going and entering. (With a pun on *gate*: [1] stride [2] entryway.)   **83 prevented** anticipated.   **88 hath no voice** cannot be uttered   **89 pregnant and vouchsafed** receptive and attentive   **91 all ready** committed to memory for future use.

OLIVIA

My servant, sir? 'Twas never merry world   98
Since lowly feigning was called compliment.   99
You're servant to the Count Orsino, youth.

VIOLA

And he is yours, and his must needs be yours;   101
Your servant's servant is your servant, madam.

OLIVIA

For him, I think not on him. For his thoughts,   103
Would they were blanks, rather than filled with me!   104

VIOLA

Madam, I come to whet your gentle thoughts
On his behalf.

OLIVIA   Oh, by your leave, I pray you.   106
I bade you never speak again of him.
But, would you undertake another suit,
I had rather hear you to solicit that
Than music from the spheres.

VIOLA   Dear lady—   110

OLIVIA

Give me leave, beseech you. I did send,
After the last enchantment you did here,
A ring in chase of you; so did I abuse   113
Myself, my servant, and, I fear me, you.
Under your hard construction must I sit,   115
To force that on you in a shameful cunning   116
Which you knew none of yours. What might you
    think?
Have you not set mine honor at the stake   118
And baited it with all th'unmuzzled thoughts   119
That tyrannous heart can think? To one of your
    receiving   120
Enough is shown; a cypress, not a bosom,   121
Hides my heart. So, let me hear you speak.   122

VIOLA

I pity you.

OLIVIA   That's a degree to love.

VIOLA

No, not a grece; for 'tis a vulgar proof   124
That very oft we pity enemies.

OLIVIA

Why then, methinks 'tis time to smile again.   126
Oh, world, how apt the poor are to be proud!   127
If one should be a prey, how much the better

To fall before the lion than the wolf!   *Clock strikes.* 129
The clock upbraids me with the waste of time.
Be not afraid, good youth, I will not have you;
And yet, when wit and youth is come to harvest
Your wife is like to reap a proper man.   133
There lies your way, due west.

VIOLA   Then westward ho!   134
Grace and good disposition attend Your Ladyship.   135
You'll nothing, madam, to my lord by me?

OLIVIA   Stay.
I prithee, tell me what thou think'st of me.

VIOLA

That you do think you are not what you are.   139

OLIVIA

If I think so, I think the same of you.   140

VIOLA

Then think you right. I am not what I am.

OLIVIA

I would you were as I would have you be!

VIOLA

Would it be better, madam, than I am?
I wish it might, for now I am your fool.   144

OLIVIA [*aside*]

Oh, what a deal of scorn looks beautiful
In the contempt and anger of his lip!
A murderous guilt shows not itself more soon
Than love that would seem hid; love's night is noon.—   148
Cesario, by the roses of the spring,
By maidhood, honor, truth, and everything,
I love thee so that, maugre all thy pride,   151
Nor wit nor reason can my passion hide.   152
Do not extort thy reasons from this clause,   153
For that I woo, thou therefore hast no cause.   154
But rather reason thus with reason fetter: 155
Love sought is good, but given unsought is better.

VIOLA

By innocence I swear, and by my youth,
I have one heart, one bosom, and one truth,
And that no woman has, nor never none
Shall mistress be of it save I alone.
And so adieu, good madam. Nevermore
Will I my master's tears to you deplore.   162

OLIVIA

Yet come again, for thou perhaps mayst move
That heart, which now abhors, to like his love.
                                        Exeunt [*separately*].

98–9 'Twas . . . compliment Things have never been the same since affected humility (like calling oneself another's servant) began to be mistaken for courtesy.   101 is yours is your servant.   his those belonging to him   103 For As for   104 blanks blank coins ready to be stamped or empty sheets of paper   106 by your leave i.e., allow me to interrupt   110 music from the spheres (The heavenly bodies were thought to be fixed in hollow concentric spheres that revolved one about the other, producing a harmony too exquisite to be heard by human ears.)   113 abuse wrong, mislead   115 hard construction harsh interpretation   116 To force that for forcing the ring   118 at the stake (The figure is from bearbaiting.)   119 baited harassed. (Literally, set the unmuzzled dogs on to bite the bear.)   120 receiving capacity, intelligence   121–2 a cypress . . . heart i.e., I have shown my heart to you, veiled only with thin, gauzelike cypress cloth rather than the opaque flesh of my bosom.   124 grece step. (Synonymous with *degree* in the preceding line.)   vulgar proof common experience   126 smile i.e., cast off love's melancholy   127 how . . . proud! how ready the unfortunate and rejected (like myself) are to find something to be proud of in their distress! Or, how apt are persons of comparatively low social station like yourself to show pride in rejecting love!

129 To fall . . . wolf! i.e., to fall before a noble adversary rather than to a person like you who attacks me thus!   133 like likely.   proper handsome, worthy   134 westward ho (The cry of Thames watermen to attract westward-bound passengers.)   135 Grace . . . Ladyship May you enjoy God's blessing and a happy frame of mind.   139 That . . . are i.e., That you think you are in love with a man, and you are mistaken.   140 If . . . you (Olivia may interpret Viola's cryptic statement as suggesting that Olivia "does not know herself," i.e., is distracted with passion; she may also hint at her suspicion that "Cesario" is higher born than he admits.)   144 fool butt.   148 love's . . . noon i.e., love, despite its attempt to be secret, reveals itself as plain as day.   151 maugre in spite of   152 Nor neither   153–4 Do . . . cause Do not rationalize your indifference along these lines, that because I am the wooer you have no cause to reciprocate.   155 But . . . fetter But instead control your reasoning with the following reason   162 deplore beweep.

3.2

Enter Sir Toby, Sir Andrew, and Fabian.

SIR ANDREW   No, faith, I'll not stay a jot longer.

SIR TOBY   Thy reason, dear venom, give thy reason.   2

FABIAN   You must needs yield your reason, Sir Andrew.

SIR ANDREW   Marry, I saw your niece do more favors to
the Count's servingman than ever she bestowed upon
me. I saw't i'th' orchard.   6

SIR TOBY   Did she see thee the while, old boy? Tell me
that.

SIR ANDREW   As plain as I see you now.

FABIAN   This was a great argument of love in her toward   10
you.

SIR ANDREW   'Slight, will you make an ass o'me?   12

FABIAN   I will prove it legitimate, sir, upon the oaths of   13
judgment and reason.

SIR TOBY   And they have been grand-jurymen since
before Noah was a sailor.

FABIAN   She did show favor to the youth in your sight
only to exasperate you, to awake your dormouse valor,   18
to put fire in your heart and brimstone in your liver.
You should then have accosted her, and with some
excellent jests, fire-new from the mint, you should   21
have banged the youth into dumbness. This was   22
looked for at your hand, and this was balked. The dou-   23
ble gilt of this opportunity you let time wash off, and   24
you are now sailed into the north of my lady's opinion,   25
where you will hang like an icicle on a Dutchman's   26
beard unless you do redeem it by some laudable at-   27
tempt either of valor or policy.   28

SIR ANDREW   An't be any way, it must be with valor,
for policy I hate. I had as lief be a Brownist as a poli-   30
tician.   31

SIR TOBY   Why, then, build me thy fortunes upon the   32
basis of valor. Challenge me the Count's youth to fight   33
with him; hurt him in eleven places. My niece shall
take note of it; and assure thyself, there is no
love-broker in the world can more prevail in man's   36
commendation with woman than report of valor.

FABIAN   There is no way but this, Sir Andrew.

SIR ANDREW   Will either of you bear me a challenge to
him?

SIR TOBY   Go, write it in a martial hand. Be curst and   41
brief; it is no matter how witty, so it be eloquent and
full of invention. Taunt him with the license of ink. If   43

thou "thou"-est him some thrice, it shall not be amiss;   44
and as many lies as will lie in thy sheet of paper,   45
although the sheet were big enough for the bed of   46
Ware in England, set 'em down. Go, about it. Let   47
there be gall enough in thy ink, though thou write   48
with a goose pen, no matter. About it.   49

SIR ANDREW   Where shall I find you?

SIR TOBY   We'll call thee at the cubiculo. Go.   51

Exit Sir Andrew.

FABIAN   This is a dear manikin to you, Sir Toby.   52

SIR TOBY   I have been dear to him, lad, some two   53
thousand strong or so.

FABIAN   We shall have a rare letter from him; but you'll   55
not deliver't?

SIR TOBY   Never trust me, then; and by all means stir on
the youth to an answer. I think oxen and wainropes   58
cannot hale them together. For Andrew, if he were   59
opened and you find so much blood in his liver as will   60
clog the foot of a flea, I'll eat the rest of th'anatomy.   61

FABIAN   And his opposite, the youth, bears in his   62
visage no great presage of cruelty.

Enter Maria.

SIR TOBY   Look where the youngest wren of nine   64
comes.

MARIA   If you desire the spleen, and will laugh your-   66
selves into stitches, follow me. Yond gull Malvolio is
turned heathen, a very renegado; for there is no   68
Christian that means to be saved by believing rightly
can ever believe such impossible passages of gross-   70
ness. He's in yellow stockings.   71

SIR TOBY   And cross-gartered?

MARIA   Most villainously, like a pedant that keeps a   73
school i'th' church. I have dogged him like his
murderer. He does obey every point of the letter that
I dropped to betray him. He does smile his face into
more lines than is in the new map with the augmen-   77
tation of the Indies. You have not seen such a thing as   78
'tis. I can hardly forbear hurling things at him. I know
my lady will strike him. If she do, he'll smile and
take't for a great favor.

SIR TOBY   Come, bring us, bring us where he is.

Exeunt omnes.

3.2. Location: Olivia's house.
2 venom i.e., person filled with venomous anger   **6 orchard** garden.
10 argument proof   **12 'Slight** By his (God's) light   **13 it** my contention.   **oaths** i.e., testimony under oath   **18 dormouse** i.e., sleepy
and timid   **21 fire-new . . . mint** newly coined   **22 banged** struck
23 balked missed, neglected.   **23–4 double gilt** thick layer of gold,
i.e., rare worth   **25 into . . . opinion** i.e., out of the warmth and sunshine of Olivia's favor   **26–7 icicle . . . beard** (Alludes to the arctic
voyage of William Barents in 1596–1597.)   **28 policy** stratagem.
30 Brownist (An early name of the Congregationalists, from the name
of the founder, Robert Browne.)   **30–1 politician** intriguer. (Sir
Andrew misinterprets more neutral use of *policy*, "clever stratagem.")
32–3 build me . . . Challenge me build . . . Challenge. ("Me" is
idiomatic.)   **36 love-broker** agent between lovers   **41 curst** fierce
43 with . . . ink i.e., with all the unfettered eloquence at your diposal
as a writer.

44 "thou"-est ("Thou" was used only between friends or to inferiors.)
45 lies charges of lying   **46–7 bed of Ware** a famous bedstead capable
of holding twelve persons, about eleven feet square, said to have been
at the Stag Inn in Ware, Hertfordshire   **48 gall** (1) bitterness, rancor
(2) a growth found on certain oaks, used as an ingredient of ink
49 goose pen (1) goose quill (2) foolish style   **51 call thee** call for you.
cubiculo little chamber, bedchamber.   **52 manikin** puppet   **53 dear**
expensive. (Playing on *dear,* "fond," in the previous speech.)   **55 rare**
extraordinary   **58 wainropes** wagon ropes   **59 hale** haul.   **For** As
for   **60 liver** (A pale and bloodless liver was a sign of cowardice.)
61 th'anatomy the cadaver.   **62 opposite** adversary   **64 youngest . . .**
nine the last hatched and smallest of a nest of wrens   **66 the spleen** a
laughing fit. (The spleen was thought to be the seat of immoderate
laughter.)   **68 renegado** renegade, deserter of his religion
70–1 impossible . . . grossness gross impossibilities (i.e., in the letter).
73 villainously i.e., abominably.   **pedant** schoolmaster   **77–8 the new**
. . . Indies (Probably a reference to a map made by Emmeric Mollineux
in 1599–1600 to be printed in Hakluyt's *Voyages,* showing more of the
East indies, including Japan, than had ever been mapped before.)

3.3

Enter Sebastian and Antonio.

SEBASTIAN
I would not by my will have troubled you,
But since you make your pleasure of your pains,
I will no further chide you.

ANTONIO
I could not stay behind you. My desire,
More sharp than filèd steel, did spur me forth,
And not all love to see you—though so much   6
As might have drawn one to a longer voyage—
But jealousy what might befall your travel,   8
Being skilless in these parts, which to a stranger,   9
Unguided and unfriended, often prove
Rough and unhospitable. My willing love,
The rather by these arguments of fear,   12
Set forth in your pursuit.

SEBASTIAN   My kind Antonio,
I can no other answer make but thanks,
And thanks; and ever oft good turns   15
Are shuffled off with such uncurrent pay.   16
But were my worth, as is my conscience, firm,   17
You should find better dealing. What's to do?   18
Shall we go see the relics of this town?   19

ANTONIO
Tomorrow, sir. Best first go see your lodging.

SEBASTIAN
I am not weary, and 'tis long to night.
I pray you, let us satisfy our eyes
With the memorials and the things of fame
That do renown this city.

ANTONIO   Would you'd pardon me.   24
I do not without danger walk these streets.
Once in a sea fight 'gainst the Count his galleys   26
I did some service, of such note indeed
That were I ta'en here it would scarce be answered. 28

SEBASTIAN
Belike you slew great number of his people?   29

ANTONIO
Th'offense is not of such a bloody nature,
Albeit the quality of the time and quarrel
Might well have given us bloody argument.   32
It might have since been answered in repaying   33
What we took from them, which for traffic's sake   34
Most of our city did. Only myself stood out,
For which, if I be lapsèd in this place,   36
I shall pay dear.

SEBASTIAN   Do not then walk too open.

ANTONIO
It doth not fit me. Hold, sir, here's my purse.
                                [He gives his purse.]
In the south suburbs, at the Elephant,   39
Is best to lodge. I will bespeak our diet,   40
Whiles you beguile the time and feed your knowl-
    edge
With viewing of the town. There shall you have me.   42

SEBASTIAN   Why I your purse?

ANTONIO
Haply your eye shall light upon some toy   44
You have desire to purchase; and your store   45
I think is not for idle markets, sir.   46

SEBASTIAN
I'll be your purse-bearer and leave you
For an hour.

ANTONIO   To th'Elephant.

SEBASTIAN   I do remember.
                                Exeunt [separately].

3.4

Enter Olivia and Maria.

OLIVIA *[aside]*
I have sent after him; he says he'll come.   1
How shall I feast him? What bestow of him?   2
For youth is bought more oft than begged or
    borrowed.
I speak too loud.—
Where's Malvolio? He is sad and civil,   5
And suits well for a servant with my fortunes.
Where is Malvolio?

MARIA He's coming, madam, but in very strange
manner. He is, sure, possessed, madam.   9

OLIVIA Why, what's the matter? Does he rave?

MARIA No, madam, he does nothing but smile. Your
Ladyship were best to have some guard about you if he
come, for sure the man is tainted in's wits.   13

OLIVIA
Go call him hither. *[Maria summons Malvolio.]* I am as
    mad as he,
If sad and merry madness equal be.   15

    *Enter Malvolio, [cross-gartered and in yellow
    stockings].*

How now, Malvolio?

MALVOLIO Sweet lady, ho, ho!

OLIVIA Smil'st thou? I sent for thee upon a sad   18
occasion.

3.3. Location: A Street.
6 all only, merely. **so much** i.e., that was great enough **8 jealousy**
anxiety **9 skilless in** unacquainted with **12 The rather** made all the
more willing **15 And . . . turns** (This probably corrupt line is usually
made to read, "And thanks and ever thanks; and oft good turns.")
16 shuffled off turned aside. **uncurrent** worthless (such as mere
thanks) **17 worth** wealth. **conscience** i.e., moral inclination to assist
18 dealing treatment, payment. **19 relics** antiquities **24 renown**
make famous **26 Count his** Count's, i.e., Duke's **28 it . . . answered**
I'd be hard put to offer a defense. **29 Belike** Perhaps **32 bloody**
argument cause for bloodshed. **33 answered** compensated **34 traf-**
fic's trade's **36 lapsèd** caught off guard, surprised

39 Elephant the name of an inn **40 bespeak our diet** order our food
42 have find **44 Haply** Perhaps. **toy** trifle **45 store** store of money
46 is not . . . markets cannot afford luxuries
3.4. Location: Olivia's garden.
1 he . . . come i.e., suppose he says he'll come. **2 of** on **5 sad and**
civil sober and decorous **9 possessed** (1) possessed with an evil
spirit (2) mad **13 in's** in his **15 If . . . equal be** i.e., if love melancholy and smiling madness are essentially alike. (Love melancholy
was regarded as a kind of madness.) **18 sad** serious

MALVOLIO   Sad, lady? I could be sad. This does make 20
some obstruction in the blood, this cross-gartering,
but what of that? If it please the eye of one, it is with
me as the very true sonnet is, "Please one and please 23
all." 24

OLIVIA   Why, how dost thou, man? What is the matter
with thee?

MALVOLIO   Not black in my mind, though yellow in my 27
legs. It did come to his hands, and commands shall be 28
executed. I think we do know the sweet roman hand. 29

OLIVIA   Wilt thou go to bed, Malvolio? 30

MALVOLIO   To bed! "Ay, sweetheart, and I'll come to 31
thee." 32

OLIVIA   God comfort thee! Why dost thou smile so and
kiss thy hand so oft?

MARIA   How do you, Malvolio?

MALVOLIO   At your request? Yes, nightingales answer 36
daws. 37

MARIA   Why appear you with this ridiculous boldness
before my lady?

MALVOLIO   "Be not afraid of greatness." 'Twas well writ.

OLIVIA   What mean'st thou by that, Malvolio?

MALVOLIO   "Some are born great—"

OLIVIA   Ha?

MALVOLIO   "Some achieve greatness—"

OLIVIA   What say'st thou?

MALVOLIO   "And some have greatness thrust upon them."

OLIVIA   Heaven restore thee!

MALVOLIO   "Remember who commended thy yellow
stockings—"

OLIVIA   Thy yellow stockings?

MALVOLIO   "And wished to see thee cross-gartered."

OLIVIA   Cross-gartered?

MALVOLIO   "Go to, thou art made, if thou desir'st to
be so—"

OLIVIA   Am I made?

MALVOLIO   "If not, let me see thee a servant still."

OLIVIA   Why, this is very midsummer madness. 57

Enter Servant.

SERVANT   Madam, the young gentleman of the Count
Orsino's is returned. I could hardly entreat him back.
He attends Your Ladyship's pleasure.

OLIVIA   I'll come to him.   [*Exit Servant.*]
Good Maria, let this fellow be looked to. Where's my
cousin Toby? Let some of my people have a special

care of him. I would not have him miscarry for the half 64
of my dowry.

Exeunt [Olivia and Maria, different ways].

MALVOLIO   Oho, do you come near me now? No worse 66
man than Sir Toby to look to me! This concurs directly
with the letter. She sends him on purpose that I may
appear stubborn to him, for she incites me to that in
the letter. "Cast thy humble slough," says she; "be opposite with a kinsman, surly with servants; let thy
tongue tang with arguments of state; put thyself into
the trick of singularity." And consequently sets down 73
the manner how: as, a sad face, a reverend carriage, a 74
slow tongue, in the habit of some sir of note, and so 75
forth. I have limed her, but it is Jove's doing, and Jove 76
make me thankful! And when she went away now,
"Let this fellow be looked to." "Fellow!" Not "Malvo- 78
lio," nor after my degree, but "fellow." Why, every- 79
thing adheres together, that no dram of a scruple, no 80
scruple of a scruple, no obstacle, no incredulous or un- 81
safe circumstance—what can be said?—nothing that 82
can be can come between me and the full prospect of
my hopes. Well, Jove, not I, is the doer of this, and he
is to be thanked.

Enter [Sir] Toby, Fabian, and Maria.

SIR TOBY   Which way is he, in the name of sanctity? If
all the devils of hell be drawn in little, and Legion him- 87
self possessed him, yet I'll speak to him.

FABIAN   Here he is, here he is.—How is't with you,
sir? How is't with you, man?

MALVOLIO   Go off. I discard you. Let me enjoy my
private. Go off. 92

MARIA   Lo, how hollow the fiend speaks within him!
Did not I tell you? Sir Toby, my lady prays you to have
a care of him.

MALVOLIO   Aha, does she so?

SIR TOBY   Go to, go to! Peace, peace, we must deal
gently with him. Let me alone.—How do you, 98
Malvolio? How is't with you? What, man, defy the 99
devil! Consider, he's an enemy to mankind.

MALVOLIO   Do you know what you say?

MARIA   La you, an you speak ill of the devil, how he 102
takes it at heart! Pray God he be not bewitched!

FABIAN   Carry his water to th' wise woman. 104

MARIA   Marry, and it shall be done tomorrow morning,
if I live. My lady would not lose him for more than
I'll say.

MALVOLIO   How now, mistress?

---

20 sad (1) serious (2) melancholy.   **23 sonnet** song, ballad
23–4 "Please . . . all" "To please one special person is as good as to
please everybody." (The refrain of a ballad.)   **27 black** i.e., melancholic
28 It i.e., The letter.   **his** Malvolio's   **29 roman hand** fashionable italic
or Italian style of handwriting rather than English "secretary" handwriting.   **30 go to bed** i.e., try to sleep off your mental distress. (But
Malvolio misinterprets as a sexual invitation.)   **31–2 "Ay . . . thee"**
(Malvolio quotes from a popular song of the day.)   **36–7 nightingales
answer daws** i.e. (to Maria), do you suppose a fine fellow like me
would answer a lowly creature (a *daw*, a "jackdaw") like you?
57 midsummer madness (A proverbial phrase; the midsummer
moon was supposed to cause madness.)

64 miscarry come to harm   **66 come near** understand, appreciate
73 consequently thereafter   **74 sad** serious   **75 habit . . . note** attire
suited to a man of distinction   **76 limed** caught like a bird with
birdlime (a sticky substance spread on branches)   **78 Fellow** (Malvolio takes the basic meaning, "companion.")   **79 after my degree**
according to my position   **80 dram** (Literally, one-eighth of a fluid
ounce.)   **scruple** (Literally, one-third of a dram.)   **81 incredulous**
incredible   **81–2 unsafe** uncertain, unreliable   **87 drawn in little**
(1) portrayed in miniature (2) gathered into a small space.   **Legion**
an unclean spirit. ("My name is Legion, for we are many," Mark 5:9.)
92 private privacy.   **98 Let me alone** Leave him to me.   **99 defy**
renounce   **102 La you** Look you   **104 water** urine (for medical
analysis). **wise woman** sorceress.

MARIA   Oh, Lord!

SIR TOBY   Prithee, hold thy peace; this is not the way. Do you not see you move him? Let me alone with him. 111

FABIAN   No way but gentleness, gently, gently. The fiend is rough, and will not be roughly used.

SIR TOBY   Why, how now, my bawcock! How dost thou, chuck? 115 116

MALVOLIO   Sir!

SIR TOBY   Ay, biddy, come with me. What, man, 'tis not for gravity to play at cherry-pit with Satan. Hang him, foul collier! 118 119 120

MARIA   Get him to say his prayers, good Sir Toby, get him to pray.

MALVOLIO   My prayers, minx?

MARIA   No, I warrant you, he will not hear of godliness.

MALVOLIO   Go hang yourselves all! You are idle, shallow things; I am not of your element. You shall know more hereafter.   *Exit.* 125 126 127

SIR TOBY   Is't possible?

FABIAN   If this were played upon a stage, now, I could condemn it as an improbable fiction.

SIR TOBY   His very genius hath taken the infection of the device, man. 131

MARIA   Nay, pursue him now, lest the device take air and taint. 133 134

FABIAN   Why, we shall make him mad indeed.

MARIA   The house will be the quieter.

SIR TOBY   Come, we'll have him in a dark room and bound. My niece is already in the belief that he's mad. We may carry it thus for our pleasure and his penance till our very pastime, tired out of breath, prompt us to have mercy on him, at which time we will bring the device to the bar and crown thee for a finder of madmen. But see, but see! 137 138 139 142 143

Enter Sir Andrew [with a letter].

FABIAN   More matter for a May morning. 144

SIR ANDREW   Here's the challenge. Read it. I warrant there's vinegar and pepper in't.

FABIAN   Is't so saucy? 147

SIR ANDREW   Ay, is't, I warrant him. Do but read. 148

SIR TOBY   Give me. [*He reads.*] "Youth, whatsoever thou art, thou art but a scurvy fellow."

FABIAN   Good, and valiant.

SIR TOBY [*reads*]   "Wonder not, nor admire not in thy mind, why I do call thee so, for I will show thee no reason for't." 152

FABIAN   A good note, that keeps you from the blow of the law. 155

SIR TOBY [*reads*]   "Thou com'st to the Lady Olivia, and in my sight she uses thee kindly. But thou liest in thy throat; that is not the matter I challenge thee for."

FABIAN   Very brief, and to exceeding good sense—less.

SIR TOBY [*reads*]   "I will waylay thee going home, where if it be thy chance to kill me—"

FABIAN   Good.

SIR TOBY [*reads*]   "Thou kill'st me like a rogue and a villain."

FABIAN   Still you keep o' th' windy side of the law. Good. 166

SIR TOBY [*reads*]   "Fare thee well, and God have mercy upon one of our souls! He may have mercy upon mine, but my hope is better, and so look to thyself. Thy friend, as thou usest him, and thy sworn enemy,   Andrew Aguecheek." 170

If this letter move him not, his legs cannot. I'll give't him. 173

MARIA   You may have very fit occasion for't. He is now in some commerce with my lady, and will by and by depart. 176

SIR TOBY   Go, Sir Andrew. Scout me for him at the corner of the orchard like a bum-baily. So soon as ever thou see'st him, draw, and as thou draw'st, swear horrible; for it comes to pass oft that a terrible oath, with a swaggering accent sharply twanged off, gives manhood more approbation than ever proof itself would have earned him. Away! 178 179 180 181 183

SIR ANDREW   Nay, let me alone for swearing.   *Exit.* 185

SIR TOBY   Now will not I deliver his letter, for the behavior of the young gentleman gives him out to be of good capacity and breeding; his employment between his lord and my niece confirms no less. Therefore this letter, being so excellently ignorant, will breed no terror in the youth. He will find it comes from a clodpoll. But, sir, I will deliver his challenge by word of mouth, set upon Aguecheek a notable report of valor, and drive the gentleman—as I know his youth will aptly receive it—into a most hideous opinion of his rage, skill, fury, and impetuosity. This will so fright them both that they will kill one another by the look, like cockatrices. 191 194 195 198

Enter Olivia and Viola.

FABIAN   Here he comes with your niece. Give them way till he take leave, and presently after him. 199 200

---

111 **move** upset, excite   115 **bawcock** fine fellow. (From the French *beau-coq*.)   116 **chuck** (A form of "chick," term of endearment.) 118 **biddy** chicken   119 **for gravity** suitable for a man of your dignity.   **cherry-pit** a children's game consisting of throwing cherry stones into a little hole   120 **collier** i.e., Satan. (Literally, a coal vendor.)   125 **idle** foolish   126 **element** sphere.   126–7 **know more** i.e., hear about this   131 **genius** i.e., soul, spirit   133–4 **take . . . taint** become exposed to air (i.e., become known) and thus spoil. 137–8 **have . . . bound** (The standard treatment for insanity at this time.)   139 **carry** manage   142 **bar** i.e., bar of judgment 142–3 **finder of madmen** member of a jury changed with "finding" if the accused is insane.   144 **matter . . . morning** sport for Mayday plays or games.   147 **saucy** (1) spicy (2) insolent.   148 **him** it. 152 **admire** marvel

155 **note** observation, remark   166 **windy** windward, i.e., safe, where one is less likely to be driven onto legal rocks and shoals   170 **my hope is better** (Sir Andrew's comically inept way of saying he hopes to be the survivor; instead, he seems to say, "May I be damned.") 173 **move** (1) stir up (2) set in motion   176 **commerce** transaction 178 **Scout me** Keep watch   179 **bum-baily** minor sheriff's officer employed in making arrests.   180–1 **horrible** horribly   183 **approbation** reputation (for courage).   **proof** performance   185 **let . . . swearing** don't worry about my ability in swearing.   191 **clodpoll** blockhead.   194–5 **his . . . it** his inexperience will make him all the more ready to believe it   198 **cockatrices** basilisks, fabulous serpents reputed to be able to kill by a mere look.   199 **Give them way** Stay out of their way   200 **presently** immediately

SIR TOBY   I will meditate the while upon some horrid 201
message for a challenge.

[*Exeunt Sir Toby, Fabian, and Maria.*]

OLIVIA
I have said too much unto a heart of stone
And laid mine honor too unchary on't.   204
There's something in me that reproves my fault,
But such a headstrong potent fault it is
That it but mocks reproof.

VIOLA
With the same havior that your passion bears   208
Goes on my master's griefs.   209

OLIVIA [*giving a locket*]
Here, wear this jewel for me. 'Tis my picture.
Refuse it not; it hath no tongue to vex you.
And I beseech you come again tomorrow.
What shall you ask of me that I'll deny,
That honor, saved, may upon asking give?   214

VIOLA
Nothing but this: your true love for my master.

OLIVIA
How with mine honor may I give him that
Which I have given to you?

VIOLA   I will acquit you.   217

OLIVIA
Well, come again tomorrow. Fare thee well.
A fiend like thee might bear my soul to hell.   [*Exit.*] 219

Enter [Sir] Toby and Fabian.

SIR TOBY   Gentleman, God save thee.

VIOLA   And you, sir.

SIR TOBY   That defense thou hast, betake thee to't. Of 222
what nature the wrongs are thou hast done him, I
know not, but thy intercepter, full of despite, bloody 224
as the hunter, attends thee at the orchard end. 225
Dismount thy tuck, be yare in thy preparation, for thy 226
assailant is quick, skillful, and deadly.

VIOLA   You mistake sir. I am sure no man hath any
quarrel to me. My remembrance is very free and clear 229
from any image of offense done to any man.

SIR TOBY   You'll find it otherwise, I assure you. Therefore, if you hold your life at any price, betake you to
your guard, for your opposite hath in him what youth, 233
strength, skill, and wrath can furnish man withal. 234

VIOLA   I pray you, sir, what is he?

SIR TOBY   He is knight, dubbed with unhatched rapier 236

and on carpet consideration, but he is a devil in 237
private brawl. Souls and bodies hath he divorced
three, and his incensement at this moment is so implacable that satisfaction can be none but by pangs of
death and sepulchre. Hob, nob is his word; give't or 241
take't.

VIOLA   I will return again into the house and desire
some conduct of the lady. I am no fighter. I have 244
heard of some kind of men that put quarrels purposely
on others, to taste their valor. Belike this is a 246
man of that quirk. 247

SIR TOBY   Sir, no. His indignation derives itself out of a
very competent injury; therefore, get you on and give 249
him his desire. Back you shall not to the house unless
you undertake that with me which with as much
safety you might answer him. Therefore, on, or strip 252
your sword stark naked; for meddle you must, that's 253
certain, or forswear to wear iron about you. 254

VIOLA   This is as uncivil as strange. I beseech you, do
me this courteous office as to know of the knight what 256
my offense to him is. It is something of my negligence, 257
nothing of my purpose. 258

SIR TOBY   I will do so.—Signor Fabian, stay you by this
gentleman till my return.   *Exit [Sir] Toby.*

VIOLA   Pray you, sir, do you know of this matter?

FABIAN   I know the knight is incensed against you,
even to a mortal arbitrament, but nothing of the 263
circumstance more.

VIOLA   I beseech you, what manner of man is he?

FABIAN   Nothing of that wonderful promise, to read 266
him by his form, as you are like to find him in 267
proof of his valor. He is, indeed, sir, the most skillful,
bloody, and fatal opposite that you could possibly
have found in any part of Illyria. Will you walk 270
towards him, I will make your peace with him if I can.

VIOLA   I shall be much bound to you for't. I am one
that had rather go with Sir Priest than Sir Knight. I 273
care not who knows so much of my mettle.   *Exeunt.*

Enter [Sir] Toby and [Sir] Andrew.

SIR TOBY   Why, man, he's a very devil; I have not seen
such a firago. I had a pass with him, rapier, scabbard, 276
and all, and he gives me the stuck-in with such a 277
mortal motion that it is inevitable; and on the answer, 278
he pays you as surely as your feet hits the ground they
step on. They say he has been fencer to the Sophy. 280

SIR ANDREW   Pox on't, I'll not meddle with him.

---

201 horrid terrifying. (Literally, "bristling.")   **204 laid** hazarded.
unchary on't recklessly on it.   **208–9 With . . . griefs** i.e., Orsino's sufferings in love are as reckless and uncontrollable as your feelings.
214 That . . . give? that can be granted without compromising my
honor?   **217 acquit you** release you of your promise.   **219 A fiend . . .
hell** i.e., You are my torment. (*Like thee* means "in your likeness.")
222 That . . . to't Get ready to deploy whatever skill you have in fencing.   **224 intercepter** he who lies in wait.   **despite** defiance, ill will
224–5 bloody as the hunter bloodthirsty as a hunting dog   **226 Dismount thy tuck** Draw your rapier.   **yare** ready, nimble   **229 to** with
233 opposite opponent.   **what** whatsoever   **234 withal** with.
236 unhatched unhacked, unused in battle

237 carpet consideration (A carpet knight was one whose title was
obtained, not in battle, but through connections at court.)   **241 Hob,
nob** Have or have not, i.e., give it or take it, kill or be killed.   **word**
motto   **244 conduct** safe-conduct, escort   **246 taste** test, prove
Belike Probably   **247 quirk** peculiar humor.   **249 competent** sufficient   **252–3 strip . . . naked** draw your sword from its sheath
253 meddle engage (in conflict)   **254 forswear . . . iron** give up your
right to wear a sword   **256 know of** inquire from   **257–8 It is . . .
purpose** It is the result of some oversight, not anything I intended.
263 mortal arbitrament trial to the death   **266–7 read . . . form** judge
him by his appearance   **267 like** likely   **270 Will you** If you will
273 go with associate with.   **Sir Priest** (*Sir* was a courtesy title for
priests.)   **276 firago** virago.   **pass** bout   **277 stuck-in** stoccado, a
thrust in fencing   **278 answer** return hit   **280 to** in the service of

SIR TOBY　Ay, but he will not now be pacified. Fabian can scarce hold him yonder.

SIR ANDREW　Plague on't, an I thought he had been valiant and so cunning in fence, I'd have seen him damned ere I'd have challenged him. Let him let the matter slip and I'll give him my horse, gray Capilet. 287

SIR TOBY　I'll make the motion. Stand here, make a 288 good show on't. This shall end without the perdition 289 of souls. [Aside, as he crosses to meet Fabian] Marry, I'll 290 ride your horse as well as I ride you.

Enter Fabian and Viola.

[Aside to Fabian] I have his horse to take up the 292 quarrel. I have persuaded him the youth's a devil.

FABIAN　He is as horribly conceited of him, and pants 294 and looks pale as if a bear were at his heels.

SIR TOBY　[to Viola] There's no remedy, sir, he will fight with you for's oath's sake. Marry, he hath better bethought him of his quarrel, and he finds that now scarce to be worth talking of. Therefore draw, for the supportance of his vow; he protests he 300 will not hurt you.

VIOLA　[aside] Pray God defend me! A little thing 302 would make me tell them how much I lack of a man. 303

FABIAN　Give ground, if you see him furious.

SIR TOBY　[crossing to Sir Andrew] Come, Sir Andrew, there's no remedy. The gentleman will, for his honor's sake, have one bout with you. He cannot by the *duello* avoid it. But he has promised me, as he is 308 a gentleman and a soldier, he will not hurt you. Come on, to't.

SIR ANDREW　Pray God he keep his oath!

Enter Antonio.

VIOLA　[to Fabian] I do assure you, 'tis against my will.
[They draw.]

ANTONIO　[drawing, to Sir Andrew] Put up your sword. If this young gentleman Have done offense, I take the fault on me; If you offend him, I for him defy you.

SIR TOBY　You, sir? Why, what are you?

ANTONIO One, sir, that for his love dares yet do more Than you have heard him brag to you he will.

SIR TOBY　[drawing] Nay, if you be an undertaker, I am for you. 319

Enter Officers.

FABIAN　Oh, good Sir Toby, hold! Here come the officers.

SIR TOBY　[to Antonio] I'll be with you anon.

VIOLA　[to Sir Andrew] Pray, sir, put your sword up, if you please.

SIR ANDREW　Marry, will I, sir; and for that I promised 324 you, I'll be as good as my word. He will bear you 325 easily, and reins well.

FIRST OFFICER　This is the man. Do thy office.

SECOND OFFICER Antonio, I arrest thee at the suit Of Count Orsino.

ANTONIO　　　　　You do mistake me, sir.

FIRST OFFICER No, sir, no jot. I know your favor well, 330 Though now you have no sea-cap on your head.— Take him away. He knows I know him well.

ANTONIO I must obey. [To Viola] This comes with seeking you. But there's no remedy; I shall answer it. 334 What will you do, now my necessity Makes me to ask you for my purse? It grieves me Much more for what I cannot do for you Than what befalls myself. You stand amazed, But be of comfort.

SECOND OFFICER　　　　Come, sir, away.

ANTONIO　[to Viola] I must entreat of you some of that money.

VIOLA　What money, sir? For the fair kindness you have showed me here, And part being prompted by your present trouble, 343 Out of my lean and low ability I'll lend you something. My having is not much; 345 I'll make division of my present with you. 346 Hold, there's half my coffer. [She offers money.] 347

ANTONIO　Will you deny me now? Is't possible that my deserts to you 349 Can lack persuasion? Do not tempt my misery, 350 Lest that it make me so unsound a man 351 As to upbraid you with those kindnesses That I have done for you.

VIOLA　　　　　　　I know of none, Nor know I you by voice or any feature. I hate ingratitude more in a man Than lying, vainness, babbling drunkenness, 356 Or any taint of vice whose strong corruption Inhabits our frail blood.

ANTONIO　Oh, heavens themselves!

SECOND OFFICER　Come, sir, I pray you, go.

ANTONIO Let me speak a little. This youth that you see here I snatched one half out of the jaws of death, Relieved him with such sanctity of love, 363 And to his image, which methought did promise 364 Most venerable worth, did I devotion. 365

---

287 **Capilet** i.e., "little horse." (From "capel," a nag.) **288 motion** offer. **289–90 perdition of souls** i.e., loss of lives. **292 take up** settle, make up **294 He . . . him** i.e., Cesario has as horrible a conception of Sir Andrew **300 supportance** upholding **302–3 A little . . . man** (With bawdy suggestion of the penis.) **308** *duello* dueling code **319 undertaker** one who takes upon himself a task or business; here, a challenger. **for you** ready for you.

324 **for that** as for what **325 He** i.e., The horse **330 favor** face **334 answer it** stand trial and make reparation for it. **343 part** partly **345 having** wealth **346 present** present store **347 coffer** purse. (Literally, strongbox.) **349–50 deserts . . . persuasion** claims on you can fail to persuade you to help me. **350 tempt** try too severely **351 unsound** morally weak, lacking in self-control **356 vainness** vaingloriousness **363 such . . . love** i.e., such veneration as is due to a sacred relic **364 image** what he appeared to be. (Playing on the idea of a religious icon to be venerated.) **365 venerable worth** worthiness of being venerated

FIRST OFFICER
What's that to us? The time goes by. Away!

ANTONIO
But, oh, how vile an idol proves this god!
Thou hast, Sebastian, done good feature shame.   368
In nature there's no blemish but the mind;
None can be called deformed but the unkind.   370
Virtue is beauty, but the beauteous evil   371
Are empty trunks o'erflourished by the devil.   372

FIRST OFFICER
The man grows mad. Away with him! Come, come,
sir.

ANTONIO   Lead me on.   *Exit [with Officers].*

VIOLA *[aside]*
Methinks his words do from such passion fly
That he believes himself. So do not I.   376
Prove true, imagination, oh, prove true,
That I, dear brother, be now ta'en for you!

SIR TOBY   Come hither, knight. Come hither, Fabian.
We'll whisper o'er a couplet or two of most sage saws. 380
                    [They gather apart from Viola.]

VIOLA
He named Sebastian. I my brother know   381
Yet living in my glass; even such and so   382
In favor was my brother, and he went   383
Still in this fashion, color, ornament,   384
For him I imitate. Oh, if it prove,   385
Tempests are kind, and salt waves fresh in love!
                                        [Exit.]

SIR TOBY   A very dishonest paltry boy, and more a   387
coward than a hare. His dishonesty appears in leaving 388
his friend here in necessity and denying him; and for 389
his cowardship, ask Fabian.

FABIAN   A coward, a most devout coward, religious in it. 391

SIR ANDREW   'Slid, I'll after him again and beat him. 392

SIR TOBY   Do, cuff him soundly, but never draw thy
sword.

SIR ANDREW   An I do not—   *[Exit.]*

FABIAN   Come, let's see the event.   396

SIR TOBY   I dare lay any money 'twill be nothing yet. 397
                                        Exeunt.

❧

4.1

Enter Sebastian and Clown [Feste].

FESTE   Will you make me believe that I am not sent for
you?

SEBASTIAN   Go to, go to, thou art a foolish fellow. Let
me be clear of thee.

FESTE   Well held out, i'faith! No, I do not know you,   5
nor I am not sent to you by my lady to bid you come
speak with her, nor your name is not Master Cesario,
nor this is not my nose, neither. Nothing that is so is so.

SEBASTIAN   I prithee, vent thy folly somewhere else.   9
Thou know'st not me.

FESTE   Vent my folly! He has heard that word of some   11
great man, and now applies it to a fool. Vent my folly!
I am afraid this great lubber, the world, will prove a   13
cockney. I prithee now, ungird thy strangeness and   14
tell me what I shall vent to my lady. Shall I vent to her
that thou art coming?

SEBASTIAN   I prithee, foolish Greek, depart from me.   17
There's money for thee. [*He gives money.*] If you tarry
longer, I shall give worse payment.

FESTE   By my troth, thou hast an open hand. These   20
wise men that give fools money get themselves a good
report—after fourteen years' purchase.   22

Enter [Sir] Andrew, [Sir] Toby, and Fabian.

SIR ANDREW   Now, sir, have I met you again? There's
for you!   [*He strikes Sebastian.*]

SEBASTIAN   Why, there's for thee, and there, and there!
          [*He beats Sir Andrew with the hilt of his dagger.*]
Are all the people mad?

SIR TOBY   Hold, sir, or I'll throw your dagger o'er the
house.

FESTE   This will I tell my lady straight. I would not be in 29
some of your coats for twopence.   [*Exit.*]   30

SIR TOBY   Come on, sir, hold!   [*He grips Sebastian.*]

SIR ANDREW   Nay, let him alone. I'll go another way to
work with him. I'll have an action of battery against   33
him, if there be any law in Illyria. Though I struck him
first, yet it's no matter for that.

SEBASTIAN   Let go thy hand!

SIR TOBY   Come, sir, I will not let you go. Come, my
young soldier, put up your iron. You are well fleshed.   38
Come on.

SEBASTIAN
I will be free from thee. [*He breaks free and draws his
          sword.*] What wouldst thou now?
If thou dar'st tempt me further, draw thy sword.   41

SIR TOBY   What, what? Nay, then I must have an ounce
or two of this malapert blood from you.   [*He draws.*] 43

Enter Olivia.

---

368 Thou . . . shame i.e., You have shamed physical beauty by
showing that it does not always reflect inner beauty.   **370 unkind**
ungrateful, unnatural.   **371 beauteous evil** those who are outwardly beautiful but evil within   **372 trunks** (1) chests (2) bodies.
o'erflourished (1) covered with ornamental carvings (2) made outwardly beautiful   **376 So . . . I** i.e., I do not believe myself (in the
hope that has arisen in me).   **380 We'll . . . saws** i.e., Let's converse
privately. (*Saws* are sayings.)   **381–2 I . . . glass** i.e., I know that my
brother's likeness lives in me   **383 favor** appearance   **384 Still**
always   **385 prove** prove true   **387 dishonest** dishonorable
388 dishonesty dishonor   **389 denying** refusing to acknowledge
391 religious in it making a religion of cowardice.   **392 'Slid** By his
(God's) eyelid   **396 event** outcome.   **397 lay** wager.   **yet** nevertheless, after all.
4.1. Location: Before Olivia's house.

5 held out kept up   **9 vent** (1) utter (2) void, excrete, get rid of   **11 of**
from, suited to the diction of; or, with reference to   **13 lubber** lout
14 cockney effeminate or foppish fellow. (Feste comically despairs of
finding common sense anywhere if people start using affected phrases like those Sebastian uses.)   **ungird thy strangeness** put off your
affectation of being a stranger. (Feste apes the kind of high-flown
speech he has just deplored.)   **17 Greek** (1) one who speaks gibberish (as in "It's all Greek to me") (2) buffoon (as in "merry Greek")   **20
open** generous. (With money or with blows.)   **22 report** reputation.
after . . . purchase i.e., at great cost and after long delays. (Land was
ordinarily valued at the price of twelve years' rental; the Fool adds
two years to this figure.)   **29 straight** at once.   **29–30 in . . . coats** i.e.,
in your shoes   **33 action of battery** lawsuit for physical assault   **38
fleshed** initiated into battle.   **41 tempt** make trial of   **43 malapert**
saucy, impudent

OLIVIA
Hold, Toby! On thy life I charge thee, hold!

SIR TOBY   Madam—

OLIVIA
Will it be ever thus? Ungracious wretch,
Fit for the mountains and the barbarous caves,
Where manners ne'er were preached! Out of my
    sight!—
Be not offended, dear Cesario.—
Rudesby, begone!
            [Exeunt Sir Toby, Sir Andrew, and Fabian.]
                    I prithee, gentle friend,   50
Let thy fair wisdom, not thy passion, sway
In this uncivil and unjust extent   52
Against thy peace. Go with me to my house,
And hear thou there how many fruitless pranks
This ruffian hath botched up, that thou thereby   55
Mayst smile at this. Thou shalt not choose but go.   56
Do not deny. Beshrew his soul for me!   57
He started one poor heart of mine, in thee.   58

SEBASTIAN [aside]
What relish is in this? How runs the stream?   59
Or I am mad, or else this is a dream.   60
Let fancy still my sense in Lethe steep;   61
If it be thus to dream, still let me sleep!

OLIVIA
Nay, come, I prithee. Would thou'dst be ruled by me!

SEBASTIAN
Madam, I will.

OLIVIA   Oh, say so, and so be!   Exeunt.

❧

4.2

Enter Maria [carrying a gown and a false
beard], and Clown [Feste].

MARIA   Nay, I prithee, put on this gown and this beard;
make him believe thou art Sir Topas the curate. Do it   2
quickly. I'll call Sir Toby the whilst.   [Exit.]   3

FESTE   Well, I'll put it on, and I will dissemble myself   4
in't, and I would I were the first that ever dissembled
in such a gown. [He disguises himself in gown and
beard.] I am not tall enough to become the function   7
well, nor lean enough to be thought a good student;   8

but to be said an honest man and a good housekeeper   9
goes as fairly as to say a careful man and a great   10
scholar. The competitors enter.   11

Enter [Sir] Toby [and Maria].

SIR TOBY   Jove bless thee, Master Parson.

FESTE   *Bonos dies,* Sir Toby. For, as the old hermit of   13
Prague, that never saw pen and ink, very wittily said   14
to a niece of King Gorboduc, "That that is, is"; so I,   15
being Master Parson, am Master Parson; for what is
"that" but "that," and "is" but "is"?

SIR TOBY   To him, Sir Topas.

FESTE   What, ho, I say! Peace in this prison!
                [He approaches the door
                behind which Malvolio is confined.]

SIR TOBY   The knave counterfeits well; a good knave.

MALVOLIO (within)   Who calls there?

FESTE   Sir Topas the curate, who comes to visit Malvolio
the lunatic.

MALVOLIO   Sir Topas, Sir Topas, good Sir Topas, go to
my lady—

FESTE   Out, hyperbolical fiend! How vexest thou this   26
man! Talkest thou nothing but of ladies?

SIR TOBY   Well said, Master Parson.

MALVOLIO   Sir Topas, never was man thus wronged.
Good Sir Topas, do not think I am mad. They have
laid me here in hideous darkness.

FESTE   Fie, thou dishonest Satan! I call thee by the most
modest terms, for I am one of those gentle ones that   33
will use the devil himself with courtesy. Say'st thou
that house is dark?   35

MALVOLIO   As hell, Sir Topas.

FESTE   Why, it hath bay windows transparent as barri-   37
cadoes, and the clerestories toward the south north   38
are as lustrous as ebony; and yet complainest thou of
obstruction?

MALVOLIO   I am not mad, Sir Topas. I say to you this
house is dark.

FESTE   Madman, thou errest. I say there is no darkness
but ignorance, in which thou art more puzzled than
the Egyptians in their fog.   45

MALVOLIO   I say this house is as dark as ignorance,
though ignorance were as dark as hell; and I say there
was never man thus abused. I am no more mad than
you are. Make the trial of it in any constant question.   49

---

50 Rudesby Ruffian   **52 extent** attack   **55 botched up** clumsily contrived   **56 Thou . . . go** I insist on your going with me.   **57 deny**
refuse.   **Beshrew** Curse. (A mild oath.)   **for me** for my part.
58 He . . . thee i.e., He alarmed that part of my heart which lies in
your bosom. (To *start* is also to drive an animal such as a *hart* [*heart*]
from its cover.)   **59 What . . . this?** i.e., What am I to make of this?
(*Relish* means "taste.")   **60 Or** Either   **61 Let . . . steep** i.e., Let this
fantasy continue to steep my senses in forgetfulness. (*Lethe* is the river
of forgetfulness in the underworld.)
4.2. Location: Olivia's house.
2 Sir (An honorific title for priests.)   **Topas** (A name perhaps derived
from Chaucer's comic knight in the "Rime of Sir Thopas" or from a
similar character in Lyly's *Endymion*. Topaz, a semiprecious stone,
was believed to be a cure for lunacy.)   **3 the whilst** in the meantime.
4 dissemble disguise. (With a play on "feign.")   **7 become the function** adorn the priestly office   **8 lean** (Scholars were proverbially
sparing of diet.)   **student** scholar (in divinity)

9–11 to be . . . scholar to be accounted honest and hospitable is as
good as being known as a painstaking scholar. (Feste suggests that
honesty and charity are found as often in ordinary men as in clerics.)
11 competitors associates, partners (in this plot)   **13 Bonos dies** Good
day   **13–14 hermit of Prague** (Probably another invented authority.)
15 King Gorboduc a legendary king of ancient Britain, protagonist in
the English tragedy *Gorboduc* (1562)   **26 hyperbolical** vehement,
boisterous.   **fiend** i.e., the devil supposedly possessing Malvolio.
33 modest moderate   **35 house** i.e., room   **37–8 barricadoes** barri-
cades. (Which are opaque. Feste speaks comically in impossible paradoxes, but Malvolio seems not to notice.)   **38 clerestories** windows
in an upper wall   **45 Egyptians . . . fog** (Alluding to the darkness
brought upon Egypt by Moses; see Exodus 10:21–3.)   **49 constant
question** problem that requires consecutive reasoning.

FESTE   What is the opinion of Pythagoras concerning 50
wildfowl?   51

MALVOLIO   That the soul of our grandam might haply 52
inhabit a bird.

FESTE   What think'st thou of his opinion?

MALVOLIO   I think nobly of the soul, and no way
approve his opinion.

FESTE   Fare thee well. Remain thou still in darkness.
Thou shalt hold th'opinion of Pythagoras ere I will
allow of thy wits, and fear to kill a woodcock lest thou 59
dispossess the soul of thy grandam. Fare thee well.
                [*He moves away from Malvolio's prison.*]

MALVOLIO   Sir Topas, Sir Topas!

SIR TOBY   My most exquisite Sir Topas!

FESTE   Nay, I am for all waters.   63

MARIA   Thou mightst have done this without thy beard
and gown. He sees thee not.

SIR TOBY   To him in thine own voice, and bring me
word how thou find'st him.—I would we were well rid
of this knavery. If he may be conveniently delivered, I 68
would he were, for I am now so far in offense with
my niece that I cannot pursue with any safety this
sport to the upshot. Come by and by to my chamber. 71
                            Exit [*with Maria*].

FESTE [*singing as he approaches Malvolio's prison*]
        "Hey, Robin, jolly Robin,   72
        Tell me how thy lady does."   73

MALVOLIO   Fool!

FESTE   "My lady is unkind, pardie."   75

MALVOLIO   Fool!

FESTE   "Alas, why is she so?"

MALVOLIO   Fool, I say!

FESTE   "She loves another—" Who calls, ha?

MALVOLIO   Good Fool, as ever thou wilt deserve well at
my hand, help me to a candle, and pen, ink, and
paper. As I am a gentleman, I will live to be thankful
to thee for't.

FESTE   Master Malvolio?

MALVOLIO   Ay, good Fool.

FESTE   Alas, sir, how fell you besides your five wits? 86

MALVOLIO   Fool, there was never man so notoriously 87
abused. I am as well in my wits, Fool, as thou art.   88

FESTE   But as well? Then you are mad indeed, if you be 89
no better in your wits than a fool.

MALVOLIO   They have here propertied me, keep me in 91
darkness, send ministers to me—asses—and do all
they can to face me out of my wits.   93

FESTE   Advise you what you say. The minister is here. 94
[*He speaks as Sir Topas.*] Malvolio, Malvolio, thy wits
the heavens restore! Endeavor thyself to sleep, and
leave thy vain bibble-babble.

MALVOLIO   Sir Topas!

FESTE [*in Sir Topas's voice*]   Maintain no words with
him, good fellow. [*In his own voice*] Who, I, sir? Not
I, sir. God b'wi'you, good Sir Topas. [*In Sir Topas's
voice*] Marry, amen. [*In his own voice*] I will, sir, I will.

MALVOLIO   Fool! Fool! Fool, I say!

FESTE   Alas, sir, be patient. What say you, sir? I am
shent for speaking to you.   105

MALVOLIO   Good Fool, help me to some light and some
paper. I tell thee I am as well in my wits as any man in
Illyria.

FESTE   Welladay that you were, sir!   109

MALVOLIO   By this hand, I am. Good Fool, some ink,
paper, and light; and convey what I will set down to
my lady. It shall advantage thee more than ever the
bearing of letter did.

FESTE   I will help you to't. But tell me true, are you
not mad indeed, or do you but counterfeit?

MALVOLIO   Believe me, I am not. I tell thee true.

FESTE   Nay, I'll ne'er believe a madman till I see his
brains. I will fetch you light and paper and ink.

MALVOLIO   Fool, I'll requite it in the highest degree. I
prithee, begone.

FESTE [*sings*]
        I am gone, sir,
        And anon, sir,
    I'll be with you again,
        In a trice,
        Like to the old Vice,   125
    Your need to sustain;

        Who, with dagger of lath,   127
        In his rage and his wrath,
    Cries, "Aha!" to the devil;
        Like a mad lad,
        "Pare thy nails, dad?   131
    Adieu, goodman devil!"   *Exit.* 132

                        ❖

4.3

Enter Sebastian [*with a pearl*].

SEBASTIAN
This is the air; that is the glorious sun;

50–1 Pythagoras . . . wildfowl (An opening for the discussion of
transmigration of souls, a doctrine held by Pythagoras.)   **52 haply**
perhaps   **59 allow of thy wits** certify your sanity.   **woodcock** (A
proverbially stupid bird, easily caught.)   **63 Nay . . . waters** i.e.,
Indeed, I can turn my hand to anything.   **68 delivered** i.e., delivered
from prison   **71 upshot** conclusion.   **72–3 "Hey, Robin . . . does"**
(Another fragment of an old song, a version of which is attributed to
Sir Thomas Wyatt.)   **75 pardie** i.e., by God, certainly.   **86 besides**
out of.   **five wits** The intellectual faculties, usually listed as common
wit, imagination, fantasy, judgment, and memory.   **87–8 notoriously
abused** egregiously ill treated.   **89 But** Only   **91 propertied me** i.e.,
treated me as property and thrown me into the lumber-room
93 face . . . wits brazenly represent me as having lost my wits.

94 Advise you Take care   **105 shent** scolded, rebuked   **109 Welladay** Alas, would that   **125 Vice** comic tempter of the "old" morality
plays   **127 dagger of lath** comic weapon of the Vice in at least some
morality plays   **131 Pare thy nails** (This may allude to the belief that
evil spirits could use nail parings to get control of their victims; cf.
Dromio of Syracuse in *The Comedy of Errors*, 4.3.69, "Some devils ask
but the parings of one's nail," and the Boy's characterization of Pistol
in *Henry V*, 4.4.72–3, as "this roaring devil i'th' old play, that everyone
may pare his nails with a wooden dagger.")   **132 goodman** title for a
person of substance but not of gentle birth. (This line could be Feste's
farewell to Malvolio and his "devil.")
4.3. Location: Olivia's garden.

This pearl she gave me, I do feel't and see't;
And though 'tis wonder that enwraps me thus,
Yet 'tis not madness. Where's Antonio, then?
I could not find him at the Elephant;
Yet there he was, and there I found this credit,   6
That he did range the town to seek me out.
His counsel now might do me golden service;
For though my soul disputes well with my sense   9
That this may be some error, but no madness,
Yet doth this accident and flood of fortune   11
So far exceed all instance, all discourse,   12
That I am ready to distrust mine eyes
And wrangle with my reason that persuades me
To any other trust but that I am mad,   15
Or else the lady's mad. Yet if 'twere so,
She could not sway her house, command her
    followers,   17
Take and give back affairs and their dispatch   18
With such a smooth, discreet, and stable bearing
As I perceive she does. There's something in't
That is deceivable. But here the lady comes.   21

Enter Olivia and Priest.

OLIVIA
Blame not this haste of mine. If you mean well,
Now go with me and with this holy man
Into the chantry by. There, before him,   24
And underneath that consecrated roof,
Plight me the full assurance of your faith,
That my most jealous and too doubtful soul   27
May live at peace. He shall conceal it
Whiles you are willing it shall come to note,   29
What time we will our celebration keep   30
According to my birth. What do you say?   31

SEBASTIAN
I'll follow this good man, and go with you,
And having sworn truth, ever will be true.

OLIVIA
Then lead the way, good father, and heavens so shine
That they may fairly note this act of mine!   *Exeunt.*   35

5.1

Enter Clown [Feste] and Fabian.

FABIAN   Now, as thou lov'st me, let me see his letter.
FESTE   Good Master Fabian, grant me another request.
FABIAN   Anything.

---

6 was was previously.   **credit** report   **9 my soul . . . sense** i.e., both my rational faculties and my physical senses come to the conclusion   **11 accident** unexpected event   **12 instance** precedent.   **discourse** reason   **15 trust** belief   **17 sway** rule   **18 Take . . . dispatch** receive reports on matters of household business and see to their execution   **21 deceivable** deceptive.   **24 chantry by** private endowed chapel nearby (where mass would be said for the souls of the dead, including Olivia's brother).   **27 jealous** anxious, mistrustful.   **doubtful** full of doubts   **29 Whiles** until.   **come to note** become known   **30 What time** at which time.   **our celebration** i.e., the actual marriage. (What they are about to perform is a binding betrothal.)   **31 birth** social position.   **35 fairly note** look upon with favor   **5.1. Location:** Before Olivia's house.

FESTE   Do not desire to see this letter.
FABIAN   This is to give a dog and in recompense desire   5
    my dog again.   6

Enter Duke [Orsino], Viola, Curio, and lords.

ORSINO   Belong you to the Lady Olivia, friends?
FESTE   Ay, sir, we are some of her trappings.   8
ORSINO   I know thee well. How dost thou, my good fellow?
FESTE   Truly, sir, the better for my foes and the worse   10
    for my friends.
ORSINO   Just the contrary—the better for thy friends.
FESTE   No, sir, the worse.
ORSINO   How can that be?
FESTE   Marry, sir, they praise me, and make an ass of   15
    me. Now my foes tell me plainly I am an ass, so that   16
    by my foes, sir, I profit in the knowledge of myself,
    and by my friends I am abused; so that, conclusions to   18
    be as kisses, if your four negatives make your two   19
    affirmatives, why then the worse for my friends and   20
    the better for my foes.
ORSINO   Why, this is excellent.
FESTE   By my troth, sir, no, though it please you to be   23
    one of my friends.   24
ORSINO   Thou shalt not be the worse for me. There's gold.
    [*He gives a coin.*]
FESTE   But that it would be double-dealing, sir, I would   26
    you could make it another.
ORSINO   Oh, you give me ill counsel.
FESTE   Put your grace in your pocket, sir, for this once,   29
    and let your flesh and blood obey it.   30
ORSINO   Well, I will be so much a sinner to be a   31
    double-dealer. There's another. [*He gives another coin.*]
FESTE   *Primo, secundo, tertio,* is a good play, and the old   33
    saying is, the third pays for all. The triplex, sir, is a   34
    good tripping measure; or the bells of Saint Bennet,   35
    sir, may put you in mind—one, two, three.
ORSINO   You can fool no more money out of me at this
    throw. If you will let your lady know I am here to   38
    speak with her, and bring her along with you, it may
    awake my bounty further.
FESTE   Marry, sir, lullaby to your bounty till I come
    again. I go, sir, but I would not have you to think that

5–6 This . . . again (Apparently a reference to a well-known reply of Dr. Bulleyn when Queen Elizabeth asked for his dog and promised a gift of his choosing in return; he asked to have his dog back.)   **8 trappings** ornaments, decorations.   **10 for** because of   **15–16 make an ass of me** i.e., flatter me into foolishly thinking well of myself.   **18 abused** flatteringly deceived   **18–20 conclusions . . . affirmatives** i.e., as when a young lady, asked for a kiss, says "no, no" really meaning "yes"; or, in grammar, two negatives make an affirmative   **23 though** even though   **24 friends** i.e., those who, according to Feste's syllogism, flatter him.   **26 But** Except for the fact.   **double-dealing** (1) giving twice (2) deceit, duplicity   **29 Put . . . pocket** (1) Pay no attention to your honor, put it away (2) Reach in your pocket or purse and show your customary grace or munificence. (*Your Grace* is also the formal way of addressing a duke.)   **30 it** i.e., my "ill counsel."   **31 to be** as to be   **33 *Primo . . . tertio*** Latin ordinals: first, second, third.   **play** (Perhaps a mathematical game or game of dice.)   **34 the third . . . all** the third time is lucky. (Proverbial.)   **triplex** triple time in music   **35 Saint Bennet** church of St. Benedict   **38 throw** (1) time (2) throw of the dice.

my desire of having is the sin of covetousness. But as
you say, sir, let your bounty take a nap. I will awake
it anon.   *Exit.*

Enter Antonio and Officers.

VIOLA
Here comes the man, sir, that did rescue me.

ORSINO
That face of his I do remember well,
Yet when I saw it last it was besmeared
As black as Vulcan in the smoke of war.   49
A baubling vessel was he captain of,   50
For shallow draft and bulk unprizable,   51
With which such scatheful grapple did he make   52
With the most noble bottom of our fleet   53
That very envy and the tongue of loss   54
Cried fame and honor on him. What's the matter?

FIRST OFFICER
Orsino, this is that Antonio
That took the *Phoenix* and her freight from Candy,   57
And this is he that did the *Tiger* board
When your young nephew Titus lost his leg.
Here in the streets, desperate of shame and state,   60
In private brabble did we apprehend him.   61

VIOLA
He did me kindness, sir, drew on my side,
But in conclusion put strange speech upon me.   63
I know not what 'twas but distraction.   64

ORSINO
Notable pirate, thou saltwater thief,   65
What foolish boldness brought thee to their mercies
Whom thou in terms so bloody and so dear   67
Hast made thine enemies?

ANTONIO   Orsino, noble sir,
Be pleased that I shake off these names you give me.   69
Antonio never yet was thief or pirate,
Though, I confess, on base and ground enough   71
Orsino's enemy. A witchcraft drew me hither.
That most ingrateful boy there by your side
From the rude sea's enragèd and foamy mouth
Did I redeem; a wreck past hope he was.   75
His life I gave him, and did thereto add
My love, without retention or restraint,   77
All his in dedication. For his sake   78
Did I expose myself—pure for his love—   79
Into the danger of this adverse town,   80
Drew to defend him when he was beset;

Where being apprehended, his false cunning,
Not meaning to partake with me in danger,
Taught him to face me out of his acquaintance   84
And grew a twenty years' removèd thing   85
While one would wink; denied me mine own purse,   86
Which I had recommended to his use   87
Not half an hour before.

VIOLA   How can this be?

ORSINO   When came he to this town?

ANTONIO
Today, my lord; and for three months before,
No interim, not a minute's vacancy,
Both day and night did we keep company.

Enter Olivia and attendants.

ORSINO
Here comes the Countess. Now heaven walks on
    earth.
But for thee, fellow—fellow, thy words are madness.   95
Three months this youth hath tended upon me;
But more of that anon.—Take him aside.

OLIVIA [*to Orsino*]
What would my lord—but that he may not have—   98
Wherein Olivia may seem serviceable?—
Cesario, you do not keep promise with me.

VIOLA   Madam?

ORSINO   Gracious Olivia—

OLIVIA
What do you say, Cesario?—Good my lord—   103

VIOLA
My lord would speak. My duty hushes me.

OLIVIA
If it be aught to the old tune, my lord,
It is as fat and fulsome to mine ear   106
As howling after music.

ORSINO   Still so cruel?

OLIVIA   Still so constant, lord.

ORSINO
What, to perverseness? You uncivil lady,
To whose ingrate and unauspicious altars   111
My soul the faithfull'st off'rings have breathed out
That e'er devotion tendered! What shall I do?

OLIVIA
Even what it please my lord that shall become him.   114

ORSINO
Why should I not, had I the heart to do it,
Like to th'Egyptian thief at point of death   116
Kill what I love?—a savage jealousy
That sometime savors nobly. But hear me this: 118

---

49 **Vulcan** Roman god of fire and smith to the other gods; his face
was blackened by the fire   50 **baubling** insignificant, trifling   51 **For**
because of.   **draft** depth of water a ship draws.   **unprizable** of value
too slight to be estimated, not worth taking as a "prize"   52 **scatheful** destructive   53 **bottom** ship   54 **very envy** i.e., even those who
had most reason to hate him, his enemies.   **loss** i.e., the losers
57 **from Candy** on her return from Candia, or Crete   60 **desperate . . .
state** recklessly disregarding the disgrace and danger to himself
61 **brabble** brawl   63 **put . . . me** spoke to me strangely.   64 **but distraction** unless (it was) madness.   65 **Notable** Notorious   67 **in
terms . . . dear** in so bloodthirsty and costly a manner   69 **Be pleased
that I** Allow me to   71 **base and ground** solid grounds   75 **wreck**
shipwrecked person   77 **retention** reservation   78 **All . . . dedication**
devoted wholly to him.   79 **pure** entirely, purely   80 **Into** unto.
adverse hostile

84 **face . . . acquaintance** brazenly deny he knew me   85–6 **grew . . .
wink** in the twinkling of an eye acted as though we had been
estranged for twenty years   87 **recommended** consigned   95 **for** as
for   98 **but . . . have** except that which he may not have—i.e., my
love   103 **Good my lord** (Olivia urges Orsino to listen to Cesario.)
106 **fat and fulsome** gross and offensive   111 **ingrate and unauspicious** thankless and unpropitious   114 **become** suit   116 **th'Egyptian thief** (An allusion to the story of Theagenes and Chariclea in the
Ethiopica, a Greek romance by Heliodorus. The robber chief, Thyamis
of Memphis, having captured Chariclea and fallen in love with her, is
attacked by a larger band of robbers; threatened with death, he
attempts to slay her first.)   118 **savors nobly** is not without nobility.

Since you to nonregardance cast my faith,   119
And that I partly know the instrument   120
That screws me from my true place in your favor,   121
Live you the marble-breasted tyrant still.
But this your minion, whom I know you love,   123
And whom, by heaven I swear, I tender dearly,   124
Him will I tear out of that cruel eye   125
Where he sits crownèd in his master's spite.—   126
Come, boy, with me. My thoughts are ripe in
   mischief.
I'll sacrifice the lamb that I do love,   128
To spite a raven's heart within a dove.   [*Going.*] 129

VIOLA
And I, most jocund, apt, and willingly,   130
To do you rest, a thousand deaths would die.   131
                                                 [*Going.*]

OLIVIA
Where goes Cesario?

VIOLA   After him I love
More than I love these eyes, more than my life,
More by all mores than e'er I shall love wife.   134
If I do feign, you witnesses above
Punish my life for tainting of my love!   136

OLIVIA
Ay me, detested! How am I beguiled!   137

VIOLA
Who does beguile you? Who does do you wrong?

OLIVIA
Hast thou forgot thyself? Is it so long?
Call forth the holy father.   [*Exit an attendant.*]

ORSINO [*to Viola*]   Come, away!

OLIVIA
Whither, my lord?—Cesario, husband, stay.

ORSINO
Husband?

OLIVIA   Ay, husband. Can he that deny?

ORSINO [*to Viola*]
Her husband, sirrah?

VIOLA   No, my lord, not I.   143

OLIVIA
Alas, it is the baseness of thy fear
That makes thee strangle thy propriety.   145
Fear not, Cesario, take thy fortunes up;
Be that thou know'st thou art, and then thou art   147
As great as that thou fear'st.

           Enter Priest.

                         Oh, welcome, father!   148
Father, I charge thee by thy reverence

Here to unfold—though lately we intended
To keep in darkness what occasion now   151
Reveals before 'tis ripe—what thou dost know
Hath newly passed between this youth and me.

PRIEST
A contract of eternal bond of love,
Confirmed by mutual joinder of your hands,   155
Attested by the holy close of lips,   156
Strengthened by interchangement of your rings,
And all the ceremony of this compact
Sealed in my function, by my testimony;   159
Since when, my watch hath told me, toward my
   grave
I have traveled but two hours.

ORSINO [*to Viola*]
Oh, thou dissembling cub! What wilt thou be
When time hath sowed a grizzle on thy case?   163
Or will not else thy craft so quickly grow
That thine own trip shall be thine overthrow?   165
Farewell, and take her, but direct thy feet
Where thou and I henceforth may never meet.

VIOLA
My Lord, I do protest—

OLIVIA   Oh, do not swear!
Hold little faith, though thou hast too much fear.   169

           Enter Sir Andrew.

SIR ANDREW   For the love of God, a surgeon! Send one
   presently to Sir Toby.   171

OLIVIA   What's the matter?

SIR ANDREW   He's broke my head across, and has given   173
   Sir Toby a bloody coxcomb too. For the love of God,   174
   your help! I had rather than forty pound I were at
   home.

OLIVIA   Who has done this, Sir Andrew?

SIR ANDREW   The Count's gentleman, one Cesario. We
   took him for a coward, but he's the very devil
   incardinate.   180

ORSINO   My gentleman, Cesario?

SIR ANDREW   'Od's lifelings, here he is!—You broke my   182
   head for nothing, and that that I did I was set on to
   do't by Sir Toby.

VIOLA
Why do you speak to me? I never hurt you.
You drew your sword upon me without cause,
But I bespake you fair, and hurt you not.   187

SIR ANDREW   If a bloody coxcomb be a hurt, you have
   hurt me. I think you set nothing by a bloody cox-   189
   comb.

           Enter [Sir] Toby and Clown [Feste].

---

119 nonregardance neglect   **120 that** since   **121 screws** pries, forces
123 minion darling, favorite   **124 tender** regard   **125–6 Him . . . spite**
I will tear Cesario away from Olivia, in whose cruel eye sits like a
king to spite me, his true master.   **128–9 I'll . . . dove** i.e., I'll kill
Cesario, whom I love, to revenge myself on this seemingly gracious
but black-hearted lady.   **130 apt** readily   **131 do you rest** give you
ease   **134 by all mores** by all such comparisons   **136 Punish . . . love!**
punish me with death for being disloyal to the love I feel!
137 detested hated and denounced by another.   **143 sirrah** (The normal way of addressing an inferior.)   **145 strangle thy propriety** i.e.,
deny what is properly yours, disavow your marriage to me.   **147 that**
that which   **148 as that thou fear'st** as him you fear, i.e., Orsino.

151 occasion necessity   **155 joinder** joining   **156 close** meeting
159 Sealed . . . function ratified through my carrying out of my
priestly office   **163 grizzle** scattering of gray hair.   **case** skin.
165 trip wrestling trick used to throw an opponent. (You'll get over-
clever and trip yourself up.)   **169 Hold . . . fear** Keep to your oath as
well as you can, even if you are frightened by Orsino's threats.
171 presently immediately   **173 broke** broken the skin, cut   **174 coxcomb** fool's cap resembling the crest of a cock; here, head   **180 incardinate** (For "incarnate.")   **182 'Od's lifelings** By God's little lives
187 bespake you fair addressed you courteously   **189 set nothing by**
regard as insignificant

Here comes Sir Toby, halting. You shall hear more. 191
But if he had not been in drink, he would have tickled
you othergates than he did.   193
ORSINO   How now, gentleman? How is't with you?
SIR TOBY   That's all one. He's hurt me, and there's 195
th'end on't.—Sot, didst see Dick surgeon, sot?   196
FESTE   Oh, he's drunk, Sir Toby, an hour agone; his eyes 197
were set at eight i'th' morning.   198
SIR TOBY   Then he's a rogue, and a passy measures 199
pavane. I hate a drunken rogue.   200
OLIVIA   Away with him! Who hath made this havoc
with them?
SIR ANDREW   I'll help you, Sir Toby, because we'll be 203
dressed together.   204
SIR TOBY   Will you help? An ass-head and a coxcomb
and a knave, a thin-faced knave, a gull!

OLIVIA
Get him to bed, and let his hurt be looked to.
[Exeunt Feste, Fabian, Sir Toby, and Sir Andrew.]

Enter Sebastian.

SEBASTIAN
I am sorry, madam, I have hurt your kinsman;
But, had it been the brother of my blood,   209
I must have done no less with wit and safety.—   210
You throw a strange regard upon me, and by that   211
I do perceive it hath offended you.
Pardon me, sweet one, even for the vows
We made each other but so late ago.
ORSINO
One face, one voice, one habit, and two persons,   215
A natural perspective, that is and is not!   216
SEBASTIAN
Antonio, O my dear Antonio!
How have the hours racked and tortured me   218
Since I have lost thee!
ANTONIO   Sebastian are you?
SEBASTIAN   Fear'st thou that, Antonio?   221
ANTONIO
How have you made division of yourself?
An apple cleft in two is not more twin
Than these two creatures. Which is Sebastian?
OLIVIA   Most wonderful!
SEBASTIAN [seeing Viola]
Do I stand there? I never had a brother;
Nor can there be that deity in my nature
Of here and everywhere. I had a sister,   228
Whom the blind waves and surges have devoured.   229
Of charity, what kin are you to me?   230

What countryman? What name? What parentage?
VIOLA
Of Messaline. Sebastian was my father.
Such a Sebastian was my brother, too.
So went he suited to his watery tomb.   234
If spirits can assume both form and suit,   235
You come to fright us.
SEBASTIAN   A spirit I am indeed,
But am in that dimension grossly clad   237
Which from the womb I did participate.   238
Were you a woman, as the rest goes even,   239
I should my tears let fall upon your cheek
And say, "Thrice welcome, drownèd Viola!"
VIOLA
My father had a mole upon his brow.
SEBASTIAN   And so had mine.
VIOLA
And died that day when Viola from her birth
Had numbered thirteen years.
SEBASTIAN
Oh, that record is lively in my soul!   246
He finishèd indeed his mortal act
That day that made my sister thirteen years.
VIOLA
If nothing lets to make us happy both   249
But this my masculine usurped attire,
Do not embrace me till each circumstance
Of place, time, fortune, do cohere and jump   252
That I am Viola—which to confirm
I'll bring you to a captain in this town
Where lie my maiden weeds, by whose gentle help   255
I was preserved to serve this noble count.
All the occurrence of my fortune since
Hath been between this lady and this lord.
SEBASTIAN [to Olivia]
So comes it, lady, you have been mistook.
But nature to her bias drew in that.   260
You would have been contracted to a maid,
Nor are you therein, by my life, deceived.
You are betrothed both to a maid and man.   263
ORSINO [to Olivia]
Be not amazed; right noble is his blood.
If this be so, as yet the glass seems true,   265
I shall have share in this most happy wreck.   266
[To Viola] Boy, thou hast said to me a thousand times
Thou never shouldst love woman like to me.   268
VIOLA
And all those sayings will I over swear,   269
And all those swearings keep as true in soul

191 halting limping.   193 othergates otherwise   195 That's all one
It doesn't matter; never mind.   195–6 there's . . . on't that's all there
is to it.   196 Sot (1) Fool (2) Drunkard   197 agone ago   198 set fixed
or closed   199–200 passy measures pavane passe-measure pavane, a
slow-moving, stately dance. (Suggesting Sir Toby's impatience to
have his wounds dressed.)   203–4 be dressed have our wounds surgically dressed   209 the brother . . . blood my own brother
210 with wit and safety with intelligent concern for my own safety.
211 You . . . me You look strangely at me   215 habit dress   216 A
natural perspective an optical device or illusion created in this
instance by nature   218 racked tortured   221 Fear'st thou that Do
you doubt that   228 here and everywhere omnipresence.
229 blind heedless, indiscriminate   230 Of charity (Tell me) in kindness

234 suited dressed; clad in human form   235 form and suit physical
appearance and dress   237 in . . . clad clothed in that fleshly shape
238 participate possess in common with all humanity.   239 as . . .
even since everything else agrees   246 record recollection   249 lets
hinders   252 jump coincide, fit exactly   255 weeds clothes
260 nature . . . that nature followed her bent in that. (The metaphor is
from the game of bowls.)   263 a maid i.e., a virgin man   265 the
glass i.e., the natural perspective of line 216   266 wreck shipwreck,
accident.   268 like to me as well as you love me.   269 over swear
swear again

As doth that orbèd continent the fire   271
That severs day from night.

ORSINO   Give me thy hand,
And let me see thee in thy woman's weeds.

VIOLA
The captain that did bring me first on shore
Hath my maid's garments. He upon some action   275
Is now in durance, at Malvolio's suit,   276
A gentleman and follower of my lady's.

OLIVIA
He shall enlarge him. Fetch Malvolio hither.   278
And yet, alas, now I remember me,
They say, poor gentleman, he's much distract.

Enter Clown [Feste] with a letter, and Fabian.

A most extracting frenzy of mine own   281
From my remembrance clearly banished his.   282
How does he, sirrah?

FESTE   Truly, madam, he holds Beelzebub at the stave's 284
end as well as a man in his case may do. He's here   285
writ a letter to you; I should have given't you today
morning. But as a madman's epistles are no gospels,   287
so it skills not much when they are delivered.   288

OLIVIA   Open't and read it.

FESTE   Look then to be well edified when the fool
delivers the madman. [*He reads loudly.*] "By the Lord, 291
madam—"

OLIVIA   How now, art thou mad?

FESTE   No, madam, I do but read madness. An Your
Ladyship will have it as it ought to be, you must allow
vox.   296

OLIVIA   Prithee, read i'thy right wits.

FESTE   So I do, madonna; but to read his right wits is to 298
read thus. Therefore perpend, my princess, and give   299
ear.

OLIVIA [*to Fabian*]   Read it you, sirrah.

FABIAN (*reads*)   "By the Lord, madam, you wrong me,
and the world shall know it. Though you have put me
into darkness and given your drunken cousin rule
over me, yet have I the benefit of my senses as well
as Your Ladyship. I have your own letter that induced
me to the semblance I put on, with the which I   307
doubt not but to do myself much right or you much
shame. Think of me as you please. I leave my duty   309
a little unthought of, and speak out of my injury.   310
                           The madly used Malvolio."

OLIVIA   Did he write this?

FESTE   Ay, madam.

ORSINO   This savors not much of distraction.

OLIVIA
See him delivered, Fabian. Bring him hither.   315
                              [*Exit Fabian.*]
My lord, so please you, these things further thought
on,   316
To think me as well a sister as a wife,   317
One day shall crown th'alliance on't, so please you,   318
Here at my house and at my proper cost.   319

ORSINO
Madam, I am most apt t'embrace your offer.   320
[*To Viola*] Your master quits you; and for your
service done him,   321
So much against the mettle of your sex,   322
So far beneath your soft and tender breeding,
And since you called me master for so long,
Here is my hand. You shall from this time be
Your master's mistress.

OLIVIA   A sister! You are she.

Enter [Fabian, with] Malvolio.

ORSINO
Is this the madman?

OLIVIA   Ay, my lord, this same.
How now, Malvolio?

MALVOLIO   Madam, you have done me wrong,
Notorious wrong.

OLIVIA   Have I, Malvolio? No.

MALVOLIO [*showing a letter*]
Lady, you have. Pray you, peruse that letter.
You must not now deny it is your hand.
Write from it, if you can, in hand or phrase,   332
Or say 'tis not your seal, not your invention.   333
You can say none of this. Well, grant it then,
And tell me, in the modesty of honor,   335
Why you have given me such clear lights of favor,   336
Bade me come smiling and cross-gartered to you,
To put on yellow stockings, and to frown
Upon Sir Toby and the lighter people?   339
And, acting this in an obedient hope,   340
Why have you suffered me to be imprisoned,
Kept in a dark house, visited by the priest,   342
And made the most notorious geck and gull   343
That e'er invention played on? Tell me why?   344

OLIVIA
Alas, Malvolio, this is not my writing,
Though, I confess, much like the character;   346

---

271 **As . . . fire** i.e., as the sphere of the sun keeps the fire   275 **action** legal charge   276 **in durance** imprisoned   278 **enlarge** release
281 **extracting** i.e., that obsessed me and drew all thoughts except of Cesario from my mind   282 **his** i.e., his madness.   284–5 **holds . . . end** i.e., keeps the devil at a safe distance. (The metaphor is of fighting with quarterstaffs or long poles.)   287 **a madman's . . . gospels** i.e., there is no truth in a madman's letters. (An allusion to readings in the church service of selected passages from the epistles and the gospels.)   288 **skills** matters.   **delivered** (1) delivered to their recipient (2) read aloud.   291 **delivers** speaks the words of   296 *vox* voice, i.e., an appropriately loud voice.   298 **to read . . . wits** to express his true state of mind   299 **perpend** consider, attend. (A deliberately lofty word.)   307 **the which** i.e., the letter   309–10 **I leave . . . injury** I leave unsaid the expressions of duty with which I would normally conclude, and convey instead my sense of having been wronged.

315 **delivered** released   316 **so . . . on** if you are pleased on further consideration of all that has happened   317 **To . . . wife** to regard me as favorably as a sister-in-law as you had hoped to regard me as a wife   318 **crown . . . on't** i.e., serve as occasion for two marriages confirming our new relationships   319 **proper** own   320 **apt** ready   321 **quits** releases   322 **mettle** natural disposition   332 **from it** differently   333 **invention** composition.   335 **in . . . honor** in the name of all that is decent and honorable   336 **clear lights** evident signs   339 **lighter** lesser   340 **acting . . . hope** when I acted thus out of obedience to you and in hope of your favor   342 **priest** i.e., Feste   343 **geck** dupe   344 **invention played on** contrivance sported with.   346 **the character** my handwriting

But out of question 'tis Maria's hand.   347
And now I do bethink me, it was she
First told me thou wast mad; then cam'st in smiling,   349
And in such forms which here were presupposed   350
Upon thee in the letter. Prithee, be content.
This practice hath most shrewdly passed upon thee;   352
But when we know the grounds and authors of it,
Thou shalt be both the plaintiff and the judge
Of thine own cause.
FABIAN   Good madam, hear me speak,
And let no quarrel nor no brawl to come   356
Taint the condition of this present hour,   357
Which I have wondered at. In hope it shall not,
Most freely I confess, myself and Toby
Set this device against Malvolio here,
Upon some stubborn and uncourteous parts   361
We had conceived against him. Maria writ   362
The letter at Sir Toby's great importance,   363
In recompense whereof he hath married her.
How with a sportful malice it was followed   365
May rather pluck on laughter than revenge,   366
If that the injuries be justly weighed   367
That have on both sides passed.
OLIVIA [to Malvolio]
Alas, poor fool, how have they baffled thee!   369
FESTE   Why, "Some are born great, some achieve
greatness, and some have greatness thrown upon
them." I was one, sir, in this interlude, one Sir Topas,   372
sir, but that's all one. "By the Lord, fool, I am not   373
mad." But do you remember? "Madam, why laugh
you at such a barren rascal? An you smile not, he's
gagged." And thus the whirligig of time brings in his   376
revenges.
MALVOLIO   I'll be revenged on the whole pack of you!
[Exit.]

347 **out of** beyond   349 **cam'st** you came   350 **presupposed** specified beforehand   352 **practice** plot.   **shrewdly passed** mischievously
been perpetrated   356 **to come** in the future   357 **condition** (happy)
nature   361 **Upon** on account of.   **parts** qualities, deeds   362 **conceived against him** seen and resented in him.   363 **importance**
importunity   365 **followed** carried out   366 **pluck on** induce
367 **If that** if   369 **baffled** disgraced, quelled   372 **interlude** little play
373 **that's all one** no matter for that.   376 **whirligig** spinning top

OLIVIA
He hath been most notoriously abused.
ORSINO
Pursue him, and entreat him to a peace.
He hath not told us of the captain yet.
When that is known, and golden time convents,   382
A solemn combination shall be made
Of our dear souls. Meantime, sweet sister,
We will not part from hence. Cesario, come—
For so you shall be, while you are a man;
But when in other habits you are seen,   387
Orsino's mistress and his fancy's queen.   388
                              Exeunt [all, except Feste].
FESTE (sings)
When that I was and a little tiny boy,   389
    With hey, ho, the wind and the rain,
A foolish thing was but a toy,   391
    For the rain it raineth every day.

But when I came to man's estate,
    With hey, ho, the wind and the rain,
'Gainst knaves and thieves men shut their gate,
    For the rain it raineth every day.

But when I came, alas, to wive,
    With hey, ho, the wind and the rain,
By swaggering could I never thrive,
    For the rain it raineth every day.

But when I came unto my beds,   401
    With hey, ho, the wind and the rain,
With tosspots still had drunken heads,   403
    For the rain it raineth every day.

A great while ago the world begun,
    With hey, ho, the wind and the rain,
But that's all one, our play is done,
    And we'll strive to please you every day.
                                          [Exit.]

382 **convents** (1) summons, calls together (2) suits   387 **habits** attire
388 **fancy's** love's   389 **and a little** a little   391 **toy** trifle   401 **unto
my beds** i.e., (1) drunk to bed, or, perhaps, (2) in the evening of life
403 **tosspots** drunkards

Twelfth Night on Stage

Although it is among the most performed of Shakespeare's plays, *Twelfth Night* has had relatively few
memorable productions on stage or in film. We do not
find pages of scintillating photos of famous *Twelfth
Night*s as we do with Peter Brook's *A Midsummer
Night's Dream* at the RSC or Laurence Olivier's award-
winning films, *Henry V* and *Hamlet*. Much of this has
to do with the uncommon simplicity required to stage
the play. More significantly, this melancholic comedy

is ultimately an actors' vehicle with its many plum
roles for the entire ensemble.

The Elizabethan Era: Twelfth Night
During Shakespeare's Lifetime

Other than the comedian-musician Robert Armin, for
whom Shakespeare seems to have created the role of
Feste (this is undocumented), we have little knowledge
as to who in the Lord Chamberlain's Men played which
roles in *Twelfth Night*. A tall, slender actor named John

Sincklo may have played Aguecheek. Surely an accomplished boy-actor was needed to play Viola, among the most lyrically and intellectually challenging roles in Shakespeare, because the lines ("a voice as is a maiden's organ, / And all is semblative a woman's part," 1.4.32–33) demand a boy who could pass for a woman. Did Burbage play the romantic and stately Orsino, or would he have played the most prized role, Malvolio?

A similar issue is how the theater itself might have been used by the actors during this play. Shakespeare's actors undoubtedly used the building's structural amenities to good effect—although no one is sure of how. Toby, Andrew, and Fabian most likely hid from Malvolio, as he read the letter, behind either of the two posts supporting the small roof that covered a portion of the stage. On the other hand, Donald Sinden, who played Malvolio at the RSC in 1969, believes that at the Globe the three pranksters were hidden in the gallery above the stage, although no evidence supports this conjecture. In 4.2 Malvolio is locked in "a dark room" where he is tormented by Feste in the role of the curate, Sir Topas. At the Globe—or even Whitehall and/or the Middle Temple, which used screens to partition the temporary stage and thus mask entrances—Malvolio may have been sequestered in the discovery space upstage. It is also possible that he was placed below the stage with his head protruding from the trap door. The latter may be more satisfying, as Malvolio does suffer the torments of the damned and the trap was often used to suggest the netherworld. It is also more amusing to see a "talking head" peeking from the stage floor.

The Late Seventeenth and the Eighteenth Centuries: Amended, Musicalized, and Rediscovered

Despite its popularity today, *Twelfth Night* was among the least-performed of Shakespeare's comedies until the mid eighteenth century. Samuel Pepys saw a performance on January 6, 1663, three years after the theaters were reopened in London and women finally were allowed to act roles such as Viola and Olivia; he dismissed the play as "silly" and "weak." Assessing the comedy on the page, Dr. Samuel Johnson professed that he enjoyed it, despite its want of "credibility," complaining that the play fails "to produce the proper instruction required in the drama, as it exhibits no just picture of life." Several heavily modified versions of the play were staged in the early eighteenth century, but none of consequence until 1741 when Shakespeare's text was (chiefly) restored at the Drury Lane Theatre, with Charles Macklin in the role of Malvolio. Macklin was famous for playing Shylock, then clearly a broadly comic villain on the English stage.

The success of this *Twelfth Night* at the Drury Lane reinvigorated the comedy and it became a staple of the English repertory thereafter. Like *A Midsummer Night's Dream*, *Twelfth Night* was transformed into a quasi-opera by Sir Frederick Reynolds and Henry Bishop by the insertion of songs from other of Shakespeare's plays, a practice that continued throughout the nineteenth century. For instance, "Who Is Sylvia?" from *The Two Gentlemen of Verona* (set to music by Franz Schubert in 1826), was converted to "Who Is Olivia? What Is She?" by the American director-producer Augustin Daly in 1894. Feste's sad lamentations ("Come Away Death" and "The Rain It Raineth Everyday") were often cut in favor of lighter fare, an indication that producers and audiences alike were discomfited by the play's darker elements.

The Nineteenth Century: Romanticism

Romantics of the early nineteenth century found in *Twelfth Night* (and especially in *Hamlet*) elements that were entirely compatible with their obsession with the sweet brevity of life. In the 1820s actor-manager John Philip Kemble began what has become a not uncommon practice in contemporary stage and film versions of *Twelfth Night*: Kemble reversed the order of the first two scenes so that the play would begin with a (potentially) visually exciting shipwreck and at the same time impart the sea captain's important exposition about the Duke and Olivia. Other nineteenth-century producers revised the play's chronology, most notably by reversing Scenes 1 and 2 of Act 2, so that Sebastian enters after Viola's plea to "Time" to untangle the Gordian knot in which she finds herself. Some productions actually opened with 2.1—the scene in which Sebastian and Antonio are discovered on Illyria's shores. Most commentaries on nineteenth-century productions of *Twelfth Night* center upon such textual liberties, as though setting and character interpretation were not particularly important.

The Twentieth Century: Spectacle, Melancholy, and Feste Foregrounded

During the late nineteenth and early twentieth centuries, some theater artists embellished the play's simple setting, as when Daly opened his 1894 production with a spectacular shipwreck inspired by *The Tempest*; he even included the "Come Unto These Yellow Sands" song from that play. In 1901 Sir Herbert Beerbohm Tree created a spectacular three-dimensional Victorian garden with multilevel terraces, inspired by a photograph in *Country Life*. Another magazine of the time, *Era*, describes the setting's "real and solid holly hedges at the right entrance, the seat at the left, and two 'rakes' of grass-covered steps. Beyond this the garden walk stretches up and away, seemingly for nearly a half mile" (Mazer, 46). Although Tree's enormous garden could not be moved and therefore confined the play's action to the garden, including the scenes on the seashore, similar elaborate gardens became a standard for many productions in the following years. Tree assigned himself the role of Malvolio and was apparently the first to dress the steward in a nightgown for his entrance in the carousing scene (2.3), a tradition still observed in many productions today. Tree also cast four identically dressed miniature Malvolios who aped his pompous demeanor. The actor-manager's comic performance dominated the play and "left an unforgettable impression of Beerbohm Tree's Malvolio, with incidental verbal music by William Shakespeare" (Pearson, 130).

In 1912 Harley Granville-Barker reacted to the excesses of Tree and his ostensibly realistic, spectacle-oriented approach to the play by staging the work at the Savoy Theatre with simplified settings. Granville-Barker also featured a garden, but its trees were represented by anti-illusionistic conical shapes. He and his costumer clothed the actors in stylish Elizabethan garb, yet the actors actually seemed "to ape the success of Edwardian fashionable drawing-room comedy [for example, that of Bernard Shaw], such as was playing elsewhere in the West End" (Mazur, 145). The director's most influential choice, however, was concerned not with costumes and sets but with Feste; breaking with tradition, Granville-Barker cast an older actor to underscore the plaintive notion proclaimed in Feste's "Youth's a stuff will not endure" (2.3.52). Subsequent twentieth-century productions of *Twelfth Night* continued to focus on the wise fool and his impact on the play.

In 1948 actor Alec Guinness directed the comedy at London's Old Vic Theatre and moved Feste squarely to the play's center. As the curtain was raised, the Fool, a Hamlet-like specter who cast an ominous shadow over Illyria's landscape, sifted through the wreckage of the ship that carried Viola and Sebastian to Orsino's kingdom. (Trevor Nunn's 1996 film pays homage to Guinness's invention.) The London *Times* described Feste as "a lugubrious fellow . . . tormented by his view of life and thoroughly sorry for himself" because of his unrequited love for Olivia. Subsequent productions have shown a dark side to Feste and thereby the play at large.

Feste has sometimes been portrayed as a "director" of Illyria's comic drama. In 1982 the Swedish director Claes Lundberg depicted a Feste who was equal parts Chaplin and punk-rock artist, and who operated as a master-puppeteer that controlled the strings of the other characters. A 1975 production in Bulgaria actually had Feste, a Prospero-like sorcerer, conjure the storm that brought the twins to Illyria. More recently, Nunn's film (see p. 320) endowed Feste with apparent omniscience as he stood atop huge cliffs to watch the action

unfold. Such choices, though perhaps extreme, are not unjustified: in the text Feste moves freely between the Duke's court and Olivia's house, and he seems to appear, almost mystically, whenever necessary.

As the approach to Feste has changed through the years, so has the perception and portrayal of Malvolio. Once played almost exclusively as a pompous figure who deserves a comeuppance, the character has been invested with more dignity in increasing numbers of twentieth-century productions. A noteworthy example was the Malvolio of Laurence Olivier in a 1955 production directed by John Gielgud in Stratford-upon-Avon. J. C. Trewin wrote that Olivier's Malvolio was "not just a part for a comedian barnacled with antique business," but one "who takes his proper place in the Illyrian household" (179). In 1979 Ingmar Bergman, Sweden's premier filmmaker and stage director, went so far as to suggest that Malvolio was a "mock-Hamlet" in his solemn examination of his plight. Even when Malvolio has been played with requisite dignity, he can still elicit laughter, as did Donald Sinden at the RSC in Barton's 1969 production. For instance, in 2.2 the ring that Malvolio delivers to Cesario from Olivia became stuck on his finger; he struggled mightily to maintain his composure as he frantically tried to remove it. Later, his yellow garters were laced so tightly that his legs could scarcely move, yet he plodded on with feigned dignity.

The predilection for increasingly somber productions of the play has led directors to place its action in autumnal and blustery winter settings; such stagings emphasize that like youth, the seasons themselves will not endure. Peter Hall's 1958 production at Stratford was among the first to portray a conspicuously autumnal setting, with Carolingian costumes in shades of russet, purple, and gold. A decade later Barton staged the play in a long, bare gallery of latticework through which sunlight only half penetrated; critic Sheila Bannock described the setting as "a dream tunnel, a journeying place of the mind." In 1979 Terry Hands took the fading sun images even further into winter: the opening scenes were played on a snowy landscape, dotted with leafless trees that sprouted leaves as Illyria's problems dissipated. Kenneth Branagh's production for the Renaissance Theatre Company (preserved on film) featured such a wintry landscape. While sitting in a Victorian garden adorned with monuments to the dead, the Duke delivered the opening monologue somberly as snow fell upon him.

Michael Benthall's 1958 Old Vic production (later moved to Broadway) seemed inspired more by Chekhov than by Shakespeare in its deliberate, melancholic pacing; actors were dressed in costumes from an earlier era, the paintings of Jean-Antoine Watteau and Giovanni Battista Tiepolo. Aguecheek, usually a giddy fop, was played as a pathetic simpleton who dimly suspected his foolishness; Sir Toby shared traits with Chekhov's frustrated Uncle Vanya more than with Falstaff. Barton's 1969 staging was labeled "Chekhovian" by many critics, especially in its handling of the Toby-Maria relationship. Considerably older than is customary, Maria was an aging spinster who saw in Toby her last chance to marry. After humiliating Malvolio in 3.4, Toby pulled Maria aside to deliver "Come by and by to my chamber," a line traditionally directed to Feste, and gave her a ring as she wept happily while Feste softly reprised the line, "Youth's a stuff will not endure."

Regardless of whether the approach to it is light-hearted or dark, *Twelfth Night* has been embraced throughout the world; the first feature film of the play was actually Russian. In 1959 the play was performed before 20,000 people in an ancient Greek amphitheater in Aspendus, Turkey, and in 1957 it was staged in China, where it still enjoys regular productions in both traditional Western and Chinese opera styles. The Japanese have an extraordinary fondness for Shakespeare, and a play such as *Twelfth Night* is especially compatible with the Kabuki theater, which has a long tradition of cross-dressing. In 1981 France's Théâtre du Soleil, under the direction of Ariane Mnouchkine, combined quasi-Elizabethan costuming with India's classical *bharatnatyam* dance to potent aesthetic effect. The two forms complemented one another; as the gestural stylization of the traditional Indian dance melded with the (perhaps) more familiar English clothing and characters, East met West in a provocative and even subliminal global fusion.

The company at London's new Globe Theatre brought its most recent staging of the play to the U.S. in 2003. This all-male production attempted fidelity to what we know of some Elizabethan theatrical practices—musicians played period instruments; the day-like lighting remained unchanged; and actors used only the simplest of props—while exploring contemporary interest in gender roles. The designers reproduced the dimensions of a long, narrow Elizabethan hall—like that of Whitehall or the Middle Temple—in theaters in Los Angeles and Philadelphia, seating the audience on three sides of the playing space. Company director Mark Rylance portrayed a regal, feminine, and self-mocking Olivia, opulently dressed in the manner of Queen Elizabeth I.

Twelfth Night on Film and Television

Although *Twelfth Night* is among the most produced of Shakespeare's plays on the world's stages, it has not been filmed as often as some of Shakespeare's comedies. There exist only two feature films of the play, one in English (Trevor Nunn, 1996), and one in Russian (1955). However, it has enjoyed at least eight television productions, including two sexually explicit versions, one with a rock-star Orsino in 1972 directed by Ron Wertheim, and the other for Hugh Hefner's Playboy Channel in 1988.

The earliest filmed version was a twelve-minute silent film in 1910. It portrayed Viola emerging from the sea with her brother's trunk, and then a snippet of the interview between Orsino and Cesario; Feste and Malvolio are shown, but there is only a fleeting suggestion of the subplot. The first feature-length *Twelfth Night* was *Dvenadtsataia noch*, the Russian film made by Yakov Friedland in 1955. Shot in color and trimmed to 90 minutes, it is noted for its high spirits and *bawdry* (coarse or obscene language), a marked departure from stereotypical notions about Russia's often-ponderous dramatic art. The Friedland film's most inventive touches involve Viola and her twin, both played by the same actress, thanks to some skillful inter-cutting and montage effects. The Russian director created the film as a subtle statement about Russia itself, then recovering from years of repression under Josef Stalin, who died two years prior to the film's release.

Twelfth Night was the first Shakespeare play to be shown in its entirety on television by the BBC (the network had broadcast an eleven-minute sequence from *As You Like It* in 1937). Using a stage production of the comedy at London's Phoenix Theatre as its source, the BBC televised *Twelfth Night* in 1939. In addition to a 1957 Hallmark Hall of Fame production for NBC, in which the action appeared as a dream in the mind of Feste, the principal television and film versions of *Twelfth Night* include:

- 1970—Director John Dexter, BBC, with Joan Plowright (Viola/Sebastion), Alec Guinness (Malvolio), and Ralph Richardson (Sir Toby). (120 min.)

   As did *Dvenadtsataia noch*, Dexter uses electronic magic to enable Joan Plowright, one of England's most admired actresses, to appear as both Viola and Sebastian. Continuing a tradition begun in the nineteenth century, Dexter restructures Shakespeare's text to take advantage of television's ability to superimpose one scene onto another. For instance, the Captain's description of Orsino in 1.2 is interspersed with shots of the Duke's melancholic pronouncements in 1.1 and with Olivia's mourning in 1.3; later, the Sebastian-Antonio scenes (2.1 and 3.3) are conflated into a single sequence.

- 1980—Director Cedric Messina, BBC Shakespeare, with Felicity Kendal (Viola), Sinead Cusack (Olivia), and Alec McCowen (Malvolio). (120 min.)

   Like so many of the BBC Shakespeare plays, *Twelfth Night* is given a reverential treatment, and

Messina's version is acted in a mostly naturalistic style that mitigates the "improbable fictions" upon which the comedy rests. The production always looks lovely: Olivia's stately English manor house is surrounded by lush gardens, while the beautiful Restoration-era lace costumes and high-fashion wigs also serve to underscore the feud between Toby's cavaliers and the puritanical Malvolio. Messina frequently uses the subjective camera to allow TV audiences to view the action from the perspective of a particular character. For instance, the camera slowly pans up Malvolio's body, first revealing his gaudy yellow stockings, ultimately his wicked grin. Like Olivia, the audience may well be repulsed by the view. Later, Feste and the audience peer together at the "notoriously abused" Malvolio as he cowers in the dark room. The camera work also proves effective during the "letter scene" (2.5), in which the audience views Malvolio as he reads Maria's letter from the perspective of the three clowns hiding in the box tree. The comedy aspects of Messina's production, however, are diminished because the film is slowly paced and unduly melancholic. Appropriately, the play was first televised in 1980 on January 6, the Feast of the Epiphany.

- 1988—Directors Kenneth Branagh and Paul Kafno (for television), with Frances Barber (Viola) and Richard Briers (Malvolio). (130 min.)

This video, shot mostly in drab grays, preserves Branagh's Renaissance Theatre Company production and offers a decidedly dark view of the play. The opening sequence creates the violent storm that casts Viola on Illyria's shores, followed by a dissolve to a glum Orsino, covered by snow, reciting the opening monologue. Branagh places the action in the Christmas season; the letter scene (2.5) is played with the clowns hiding behind a discarded Christmas tree in the garden of a Victorian country house. As is often the case with film and television, the camera's penchant for capturing real life undercuts this patently theatrical moment as the three fools talk to one another with Malvolio obviously within earshot. A hollow-eyed Feste, dressed as something of a nineteenth-century hippie, seems oddly disconnected from both Orsino's retinue and Olivia's household. His rendition of the final song, as he slowly leaves Olivia's estate, is truly haunting, yet with so little humor preceding it that the song becomes simply another expression of the melancholy that pervades the production.

- 1996—Director Trevor Nunn, Fine Line Features, with Imogen Stubbs (Viola), Helena Bonham Carter (Olivia), Toby Stephens (Duke Orsino), Ben Kings-

ley (Feste), Nigel Hawthorne (Malvolio), Mel Smith (Sir Toby), and Imelda Staunton (Maria). (133 min.)

Filmed on the rugged coast of Cornwall in southwestern England during the autumn months, Nunn's film is the most attractive *Twelfth Night* available. Nunn has skillfully reconstructed Shakespeare's text into a workable screenplay. He begins by inventing a prologue to introduce both the twins and the theatrical nature of the play. Viola and Sebastian are a pair of English music-hall performers, singing and dancing a lively song on board a ship somewhere at sea. A violent storm erupts, splitting the ship and hurling Viola into the waters in a scene eerily reminiscent of the shipwreck that nearly drowns Viola de Lesseps in *Shakespeare in Love*.

Viola, obviously a skilled performer, is highly credible as she transforms herself into Cesario. Nunn includes a number of transition shots of Viola (superbly acted by Imogen Stubbs) practicing the walk and carriage of a man. The "boy talk" scene in 2.4 is especially amusing, as Cesario attends Orsino, who is immersed in a Victorian bathtub. The funniest moments in the play, however, are not reserved for the clowns; rather, Helena Bonham Carter's Olivia, truly "the nonpareil of beauty," so transforms herself from the dutifully mourning sister to a giddy love-struck maiden that the result is an extraordinary comic delight. The erotic charge between Olivia and Viola-Cesario vibrates throughout the film, as do the scenes between Orsino and Cesario-Viola, so rich in sexual ambiguity. Nunn flirts with the homoerotic as the Duke nearly kisses Cesario in 2.4. Ben Kingsley's Feste has proved to be the most controversial interpretation in the film. Kingsley is curiously asexual, almost androgynous, a suggestion that underscores the fact that he belongs to neither house of Illyria nor to the lovelorn inhabitants of those two houses. Kingsley delivers his lines with uncommon bitterness, complicating his melancholy with the sardonic. The reunion between Viola and Sebastian, however, clears the atmosphere created by Feste; the reunion and finale bring forth the miraculous, spiritual possibilities suggested by Shakespeare.

- 2001—Director Nick Hytner, PBS, with Helen Hunt (Viola) and Kyra Sedgwick (Olivia).

This beautifully filmed documentation of Hytner's 1999 stage production at New York's Lincoln Center was later broadcast as part of PBS's *Great Performances* series; shot before a live audience, it captures the appeal of a stage production while providing the visual variety of film. Hytner sets the action in a vaguely Middle Eastern kingdom. The stage floor is dominated by a large, irregularly shaped pool of water upon which flower petals float. As the lights come up, Orsino languidly dangles his hand in the water as he listens to exotic sitar music. (The exceptional musical score, now available on CD, is by Jeanine Tesori.) Later the Duke swims in the pool while interrogating Cesario in 2.4. Viola emerges mysteriously from a mist of fog—like a lady from the sea who arrives to release Illyria from its madness. Hytner's illusion-filled, unabashedly theatrical production creates an aura of mystery as characters appear from, and later disappear into, the cavernous reaches of the enormous Vivian Beaumont stage. For instance, the mourning Olivia's first entrance is highlighted by a single hand carrying a skull eerily protruding from the water. Such otherworldly inventions by the director helped make the Act 5 reunion of Viola and her brother as sublime as can be imagined. The text is especially well-spoken by actors whose reputations rest upon popular films and television.

Spin-offs

Surprisingly, no one has written a modern opera/operetta version of *Twelfth Night,* although there have been several musical versions of note. In 1947 a Spanish film, *Noche de Reyes* (*Night of the Kings*), converted the play into a *zarzuela,* or Spanish musical. In 1968 a moderately successful rock-musical, *Your Own Thing,* portrayed Toby and company as members of a rock band who spar with a pompous record producer. This musical, rarely produced today, mirrors the 1960's preoccupation with free love and gender bending, and predictably its music smacks of the Beatles. Another rock musical adaptation, *Music Is* (1976), was an instant failure.

The most successful musical adaptation, *Play On!,* was conceived by Sheldon Epps at San Diego's Old Globe Theater in 1999; its success prompted a year-long run on Broadway (and a telecast by PBS's *American*

Masterpieces series). Epps relocates the play to Harlem in the 1940s, where a would-be songwriter (Vi-Man) dresses herself as a man seeking the tutelage of "the Duke," proprietor of Harlem's famed Cotton Club. The Duke is modeled on Duke Ellington, and the show was created to mark the one-hundredth anniversary of the musician's birth. More than a dozen of Ellington's best songs are featured, many sung by Lady Liv (Olivia), a torch-singer at the Cotton Club presided over by The Rev (Malvolio). Several musicians (cf. Toby, Andrew, and Feste) enlist Lady Liv's dresser (Mary) to torment the pompous Rev; in one of the musical's surprises the singing pranksters induce the Rev to "scat" and dance to "It Don't Mean a Thing (If It Ain't Got That Swing)." Later, the Rev appears in a yellow zoot suit to woo Lady Liv, whose hand he eventually wins. *Play On!* embodies the spirit of carnival, while its poetry derives from the jive-talk of the musicians.

References and Further Reading

Barber, C. L. *Shakespeare's Festive Comedy.* Princeton, 1959.

Bloom, Harold. *Shakespeare: The Invention of the Human.* New York, 1998.

_____, ed. *Modern Critical Interpretations of "Twelfth Night."* New York, 1987.

Bryant, J. A., Jr. *Shakespeare and the Uses of Comedy.* Lexington, Ky., 1986.

Hotson, Leslie. *The First Night of "Twelfth Night."* New York, 1954.

Leech, Clifford. *Twelfth Night and Shakespearean Comedy.* Toronto, 1965.

Leggatt, Alexander. *Shakespeare's Comedies of Love.* London and New York, 1974.

Mazur, Cary M. *Shakespeare Refashioned: Elizabethan Plays on Edwardian Stages.* Ann Arbor, Mich., 1981.

Osbourne, Lisa. *The Trick of Singularity: The Performance Editions.* Iowa City, Iowa, 1996.

Pearson, Hesketh. *Beerbohm Tree.* New York, 1956.

Potter, Lois. *"Twelfth Night": Text and Performance.* London, 1985.

Trewin, J. C. *Going to Shakespeare.* London and Boston, 1978.

SHAKESPEARE AND THE ENGLISH HISTORY PLAY

Historical chronicles and history plays based upon them were extremely popular in London after the defeat of the Spanish Armada in 1588. Just thirty years before that victory, when Elizabeth I ascended the throne at the age of twenty-five, England had been a nation deeply torn by religious controversy and violence. Now in the 1590s, England viewed herself as a great country, "one that had defeated in the Spanish Armada, the most formidable armed expedition ever launched against its shores without losing a single vessel in the process. America, discovered less than a century before, had proved a source of riches beyond her subjects' wildest dreams," writes historian John Julius Norwich (6). Although the English still worried about the Catholic powers on the Continent, about the aging Queen who had no successor, and about economic pressures and unrest resulting from immigrant labor populations, the country was filled with a new and unfamiliar pride. That pride extended to its language, which, as we have seen in our introductory chapters, was flowering into a vigorous and varied new idiom. Shakespeare's history plays used and created that language to examine complex issues of kingship, nationhood, and personal and political morality. Similarly, these plays both recreated and intervened in the nation's history. Shakespeare dramatizes a period of transition from a dynastic kingdom to a modern nation, one that was closely bound to shifts in the cultural understanding of gender and of the social roles then available to men and women (see reference to studies by Phyllis Rackin, Jean E. Howard, and Richard Dutton, p. 325). In the histories, Shakespeare views such themes through the lens of the dynastic struggles that began after the death of Edward III (who reigned from 1327 to 1377) and reached their bloody peak in the fifteenth-century civil wars, known collectively as The War of the Roses. The combatants were the families of Lancaster, and their allies, the Tudors and Beauforts, against the house of York and its allies, the Mortimers and Nevills. (See the table in the appendix, "The Houses of Lancaster, Tudor, Mortimer, and York.")

Despite the popularity of chronicle-based drama, the history play as a genre was not well defined during the 1590s. It had not been theorized in the way that comedy and tragedy had been described and analyzed since the time of Aristotle. Shakespeare contributed to the establishment of the genre, stamping it as his own as he explored his thematic and artistic interests through what appears to be an ambitious and adventurous process of trial and error. As his facility with language and structure matured, so did his approach to historical characters, their actions and motives, and the political themes that sound through their lives and the nation's. The history play was uncharted territory when Shakespeare wrote during the first decade of his playwriting career. And so this Stratford writer, still new to London, had "not only to create a suitable dramatic form for the History Play," notes critic Robert Ornstein in *A Kingdom for a Stage*, "but he had also to recreate that form again and again as his vision of politics and history deepened" (2).

Shakespeare wrote ten English history plays in all—eleven, if we count, as many contemporary scholars do, at least portions of *Edward III*, which is now included in several British editions and the Riverside edition of the complete works. Eight of these ten plays were fashioned into two four-play sequences usually referred to as *tetralogies*. Shakespeare did not write these in the order in which the historical events actually occurred. His first four-play sequence (c. 1591–1594) begins with three plays about the reign of Henry VI and culminates in *Richard III*, with its centering on the vitally evil last of the Yorkist kings. Called a tragedy in both early printings and recent editions, *Richard III* charts the monarch's rise to power through a dazzling, if conscienceless, command of rhetoric; it concludes with Richard's fall at Bosworth Field at the hands of the right-minded Earl of Richmond. Shakespeare's second four-play sequence chronicles earlier events. It begins with the deposition and murder of *Richard II* (written c. 1595–1596), continues with the two parts of *Henry IV* (written c. 1596–1598), and concludes with the epic *Henry V* (written in 1599). Three of these eight—*Richard III*; *Henry IV, Part One*; and *Henry V*—are included in this anthology. All three have been filmed several times, and the first two have been produced in the style of differing historical periods. All three have been often performed during the second half of the twentieth century and into the new millennium.

Although Shakespeare borrowed from many sources, he turned to two primary chronicles, and two secondary ones, for the bulk of the record he re-imagined. The Englishman Edward Hall completed *The Union of the Two Noble and Illustre Families of Lancaster and York* in 1530. Published in 1548, his work served as the basic source for Shakespeare's first tetralogy. Raphael Holinshed's *Chronicles* (the abbreviated title of a work titled *The chronicles of England Scotlande and Ireland . . . conteyning the description and chronicles of England from first inhabiting unto the Conquest*) was first published in 1577, then enlarged and slightly censored in the 1587 edition. Shakespeare used this second edition for his major history plays as well as for the tragedies, *King Lear* and *Macbeth*. Other important sources were the English translation by John Bourchier, Lord Berners (1525) of the Frenchman Jean Froissart's four-volume *Chroniques* about the Hundred Years War, and finally, English poet Samuel Daniel's account of the civil wars between Lancastrians and Yorkists, published in 1595.

Holinshed and especially Hall, who was a government official under Queen Elizabeth's father Henry VIII, are considered by many contemporary scholars to be architects of "the Tudor myth," that is to say a providential reading of fifteenth-century English history in which the bloody and murderous events of the so-called War of the Roses were all interpreted as leading forward, through divine guidance, to the foundation of the Tudor dynasty under Elizabeth's grandfather, Henry VII. In that view, the English nation had to be punished for the murder of Richard II, and thus Richard III becomes the scourge of God, an agent who thinks he is furthering his own ambitions when what he actually has done is to execute God's wrath against a wayward people. His murderous reign crystallizes their fall into fratricide and disobedience. The Elizabethan nation, now purged over time of the crime of deposing and murdering Richard II, has settled on a hard-won, divinely blessed stability. Similarly, the Lancastrian Henry V's short-lived victory and harmonious reign were seen as a forecast of the civic virtue and the strength that England was now enjoying under the Tudors. Such a providential reading can illuminate aspects of plays like *Richard II* and *Richard III*, but its hopefully propagandistic view is seriously undercut by the pointless carnage of historical events and Machiavellian political maneuvering that dominates the action of so much of this historical series. Shakespeare apprehended that civil and cosmic order depend not just upon concepts of hierarchy and class, as set forth in the much-touted Great Chain of Being or Elizabethan World Picture, but also upon the kind of personal relationships that a villain such as Richard III is incapable of sustaining.

The many plays and poems written by Elizabethans on English history take varied approaches to the past. The history drama, often patriotic, flourished on the public stage during the years when Shakespeare wrote his two tetralogies. Thomas Heywood contributed to the genre between 1592 and 1599; so did Henry Chettle and Anthony Munday. The Admiral's Men, in competition with Shakespeare's company, staged the two parts of *Sir John Oldcastle* by Michael Drayton and others written in competition with Shakespeare's two parts of *Henry IV*.

The chroniclers draw on common sources, borrow from and plagiarize one another, or simply incorporate their predecessors' accounts in their own. Still, even these sources vary in their opinions of their subjects as well as in their mix of significant and trivial facts. Thus, any playwright—and certainly Shakespeare, whose interest in history ran deep—had to edit, conflate scenes, and create a dramatically coherent narrative from these sometimes rambling accounts. "The miracle is [that Shakespeare] was able to stick as closely to the truth as he did, weaving together all the various strands to create a single epic masterpiece which, for all its minor inaccuracies, is almost always right when it really matters" (Norwich, 7).

We, of course, do not know whether Shakespeare set out to write these eight or ten or eleven plays as a series when he began; indeed, it was not until the nineteenth century when a producer in Weimar, Germany, staged them in sequence that they were even considered as a series. German scholars had prepared the theoretical ground for this production by viewing the two tetralogies as England's "national epic." The three *Henry VI* plays read awkwardly as scripts, but can be highly effective and exciting in performance, as a vigorous 2001 staging at London's Young Vic Theatre attested. The first of the *Henry VI* plays was extremely popular during its initial run; scholars estimate from their reading of producer Philip Henslowe's records of receipts that at least 20,000 people saw the play in 1592. Yet this play and its sequels were unappreciated and unperformed in their original forms from the seventeenth through most of the twentieth century.

More recently, however, interest in these series has increased. California's Pasadena Playhouse and director Gilmore Browne revived interest in these plays with their 1935 season of all of Shakespeare's historical cycle—ten plays presented in the chronological order of the kings' reigns. Then in the early 1950s, England's Birmingham Repertory Company presented the three *Henry VI* plays over several seasons; the same trilogy appeared at the Old Vic in the summer of 1953. An ambitious and important adaptation followed ten years later: John Barton's famed *The Wars of the Roses* premiered at Stratford-upon-Avon in 1963, with a script cut, rearranged, and confidently amplified with hundreds of his own lines. The result was a new trilogy—*Henry VI, Edward IV,* and *Richard III*—and a new interest, worldwide, in the histories. Michael Bogdanov's English Shakespeare Company mounted a different *The War of the Roses* in 1988, based largely on *Henry VI, Parts One, Two, and Three.* The Royal Shakespeare Company produced another history marathon called *The Plantagenets* in 1989. Then, in the spring of 2001, the RSC staged all eight plays, which could be seen over a weekend in historical sequence—though staged by different directors in different styles—at the Barbican and Young Vic theaters in London. Last, and more generally, Jean E. Howard and Phyllis Rackin note in their *Engendering a Nation* that these same often ignored plays have become a favorite subject for feminist scholarship and criticism, owing to the prominence of such fascinating female characters as Queen Margaret and Joan of Arc (21–24).

The introductions and notes to the three history plays in this anthology delve further into their quite differing themes and their forms, which border, respectively, upon melodrama, comedy, and Epic Theater. Interest in the history plays has intensified as English and European colonialism and Soviet Communism have all been overturned. The achievement of these plays has been examined in postcolonial literary theo-

ry, in theater criticism, and in directorial interpretations of Shakespeare on stage. Even as the United States and England ventured into Iraq in 2003, launching what many commentators have viewed as a new age of American imperialism, U.S. fighting troops were offered, along with two classic American novels, specially formatted, battle-friendly copies of *Henry V.* Thus this still-controversial and clearly relevant play about Shakespeare's soldier-king and his successful invasion of France has once again entered into the historical process.

References and Related Reading

Holderness, Graham. *Shakespeare: The Histories.* New York, 2000.

Howard, Jean E., and Rackin, Phyllis. *Engendering a Nation: A Feminist Account of Shakespeare's English Histories.* London and New York, 1997.

Kewes, Paulina. "The Elizabethan History Play: A True Genre?" *A Companion to Shakespeare's Plays, Vol. III: The Histories.* Eds. Richard Dutton and Jean E. Howard. Malden, Mass.; Oxford; and Victoria, 2003.

Norwich, John Julius. *Shakespeare's Kings.* London and New York, 2000.

Ornstein, Robert. *A Kingdom for a Stage.* Cambridge, 1972.

Rackin, Phyllis. *Stages of History: Shakespeare's English Chronicles.* Ithaca, 1990.

Saccio, Peter. *Shakespeare's English Kings: History, Chronicle and Drama.* Oxford, 1977/2000.

CHAPTER 11

The Tragedy of King Richard III

(1592–1594)

Context and Dating: A Theatrical Villain, Fact, and Shakespeare's Fiction

One of Shakespeare's most theatrical villains, Richard III has proven such a plum role for actors that the play bearing his name has seldom been out of the repertory since the first performances by Richard Burbage in about 1593. Although *The Tragedy of Richard III* is long, uneven, and potentially confusing to modern audiences—so much so that it was drastically overhauled for nearly one hundred and fifty years during the eighteenth and nineteenth centuries—it remains one of the most popular of Shakespeare's plays. During the latter half of the historically conscious twentieth century and into this new millennium, it has been often staged (or adapted) as part of a War of the Roses tetralogy with the three parts of *Henry VI*, as the literary and dramatic culmination of that series. A dozen film versions of the play are available, including four silent films, as well as movie adaptations in German and Russian.

The Tragedy of Richard III continues the story of the *Henry VI* plays about the fifteenth-century dynastic rivalry of the houses of Lancaster and York. The tragedy opens in the year 1471, with Edward IV sitting upon the throne while his brother Richard plots to become the next king of England. The play chronicles Richard's breathtaking rise to power as Richard III and ends with his precipitous fall: the Earl of Richmond, who will become Henry VII, kills this last monarch of the Yorkist line at the Battle of Bosworth (1485). Richmond thus becomes the progenitor of the line of Tudor monarchs that culminated with Elizabeth I. History aside, *Richard III* is also the first of Shakespeare's plays to strike an authentic, if only fitfully, tragic note, approaching the dimension and grandeur of myth. Though it is not list-

ed with the tragedies in the First Folio, it shares aspects of tragedy, along with those of several other genres: the morality play with its insinuating Vice; the melodrama of overreaching heroes favored by Christopher Marlowe; and comedy with its trumpet-blaring happy ending announcing the emergence of the Tudor dynasty in the person of Henry, Earl of Richmond. Hence, this tonally mixed play, dominated by the titular villain-hero who literally plots the course of the action, stands in a literary class of its own. It is also a celebration of the power of a virtuoso actor over audiences.

The First Quarto (1597) of *Richard III* titles the play in the sensational language that today we associate with trailers for action movies: "The Tragedy of King Richard the Third, Containing, His treacherous Plots again his brother Clarence: the pitiful murder of his innocent nephews: his tyrannical usurpation: with the whole course of his detested life, and most deserved death." Subsequent editions drop such potboiling rhetoric. Yet the best recent productions and film adaptations of *Richard III* do not quench the blazing melodrama of the play and the perverse gusto with which the central character fulfills his ambition. Artistically, and in terms of audience interest, the evil in this play is more fascinating than good. (One of Richard's more recent analogs is the character Roy Cohn, the Red-baiting McCarthy-era lawyer who dominates the first part of Tony Kushner's quasi-historical epic of the Reagan era, *Angels in America: Part I, Millennium Approaches*.)

Richard, eventually Duke of Gloucester, emerges from the welter of personalities and events in the second and especially the third parts of *Henry VI* (1589–1592), ending the trilogy in which Shakespeare first tried his hand at representing the history of the emerging modern nation. In Part Three, the hunchback with a withered arm disarmingly reveals himself and his plan:

I can add colors to the chameleon,
Change shapes with Proteus for advantages,
And set the murderous Machiavel to school.
Can I do this, and cannot get a crown?
Tut! Were it farther off, I'll pluck it down.
                    (*Henry VI, Part Three*, 3.2.191–195)

His means to that end are presaged by his final actions in *Henry VI, Part Three*: he helps to stab Henry's son Edward on the battlefield, then murders Henry himself in the Tower of London. Finally, comparing himself to Judas, he kisses his brother's son, the infant Prince Edward. Now, in *Richard III*, with few Lancastrians left to murder, this protean avenger takes his aim at his own family.

Shakespeare places his villain-hero within a political and metaphysical framework that suggests several uses of history. For such critics as E. M. W. Tillyard and Lily B. Campbell, Shakespeare's histories in general, and this play in particular, represent Richard III's murderous career as part of a providential plan of retribution for evil and injustice. These critics see in the progression of the action evidence of a divine order with Richard serving as the scourge, sent to cleanse England and heal the nation's divisions by making way for Richmond as the agent of divine justice. This view has been challenged, however, first by the large and lasting appeal of the villain as a stage character, and second, by critics such as Henry A. Kelly who, in *Divine Providence in the England of Shakespeare's Histories*, has shown how the plays of this tetralogy can be viewed as explorations of political topics that concerned Shakespeare's audience, rather than as *teleological* (i.e., exhibiting design or purpose) narratives supporting any simple and celebratory Tudor Myth. With other views of gender, sexual preference, and the making of history also conditioning later responses to the play, *Richard III* has become a more complicated and variously interpreted play script than its early history might have suggested.

Characters: Conspirators

Richard dominates most of the play. At 1164 lines his role is second in length in the Shakespeare canon only to that of Hamlet. We meet Richard of Gloucester in the highly dramatic opening where he leers toward the audience to begin his famous soliloquy, "Now is the winter of our discontent." Like his many subsequent private moments with the audience, the speech ingratiates him with his listeners, and establishes the postwar scene and the plots he has already laid. He justifies his villainy by grounding it in his physical deformity which, he says, prevents him from being a lover, and therefore has made him "determinèd to prove a villain." Richard is the consummate actor, asking his brother Clarence, who passes by

led by the lieutenant of the Tower, "What means this armèd guard / that waits upon Your Grace?" Richard has played upon their older brother Edward's fears, maneuvered him into arresting Clarence, yet here affects concern for the man whose imprisonment he has caused. "I will deliver you," he says, punning outrageously: "deliver" can mean free from prison, or deliver into the hands of death. Richard is both performer and his own best audience; when he succeeds in wooing Lady Anne, despite having killed her husband and his brothers, he gloats, reviewing his own performance:

Was ever woman in this humour wooed?
Was ever woman in this humour won?
I'll have her, but I will not keep her long.

                                            (1.2.230–232)

Many of the forty other characters are well etched. Among the most important are the Duke of Buckingham, "the deep-revolving, witty Buckingham" (4.2) who assists Richard's plots, but is captured and executed when he deserts Richard's cause and Richard's brothers: Edward IV, sick in body and soul, who dies in Act 2, and George, Duke of Clarence, whose death in the Tower overwhelms Edward and contributes to his demise. William, Lord Hastings, supports Edward's "heirs of true descent" and is cut down for his opposition to Richard. Lady Anne, the daughter-in-law of Henry VI, marries Richard after the wooing, but then largely disappears from the play after she has been crowned queen. Queen Margaret, "a prophetess" as Buckingham calls her, acts as vituperative chorus, especially in 1.3 and 4.4, unlike the historical Queen Margaret who was still confined during these years to France. Richard's chief antagonist and his nemesis, Richmond, appears in the later scenes, praying piously before Bosworth Field and calling upon God to make him and his soldiers "thy ministers of chastisement."

Amidst the "alarums and excursions" of the battle, Richard is finally unseated. He famously shouts "A horse! A horse! My kingdom for a horse!" before he is surrounded by Richmond and his troops and killed. "The bloody dog is dead," shouts Henry Tudor as Lord Stanley places the crown upon his head. The new King Henry VII announces that he and his wife, Elizabeth of York, "The true succeeders of each royal house," will be by God's fair ordinance wed, thus ending the bloody civil war and healing the nation's wounds.

Sources and Inspirations

Revisionism and the Tudor Myth

The historical reign of King Richard III has lately been subject to revisionism, with an English organization and a series of high-profile writers challenging Shakespeare's depiction of him as a thoroughgoing villain. Those who would rehabilitate his reputation blame Richard's successor, Henry VII, for defaming his character. They also accuse Sir Thomas More of vilifying him in the Tudor cause, pointing to More's account of his reign in one of Shakespeare's key sources, Edward Hall's *Union of the Two Noble and Illustre Families of Lancaster and York* (1548), as a fount of this Tudor Myth. Richard's most effective latter-day apologist has been Josephine Tey, whose mystery novel *The Daughter of Time* has rescued Richard from the ranks of the damned, seeking to clear him of the charge of murdering the little princes in the Tower. Still, despite these latter-day attempts to repair his reputation, nearly all Elizabethan writers—and certainly those sources upon whom Shakespeare based the play—view Richard in a negative light.

The English Chronicles

Shakespeare's major sources were Hall's *Union* and Raphael Holinshed's 1587 edition of *The Chronicles of England, Scotland, and Ireland*. Both of these historical compilations found their hostile view of Richard III in works by Polydore Vergil and Thomas More. In *Shakespeare's Kings*, John Julian Norwich notes that Vergil, who, though he arrived in England only in 1502, "tells us that he personally interviewed 'every elderly man pointed out to me as having once held an important position in public life.'" Vergil's patron, Henry VII, may have commissioned him to write his *Anglica Historia*; still, his living sources, the chronicles, and much other evidence besides, Norwich concludes, leave no doubt that "Richard's reputation had already reached its nadir during his lifetime; no subsequent blackening of it was possible" (Norwich, 357). Shakespeare may have been familiar since childhood with a chronicle-based excerpt titled "King Richard III, the Cruel Tyrant" in a grammar-school primer called *The Foundation of Rhetoric* (1563). Thus it is the chronology of events, derived from Hall and Holinshed, that has been changed more than the subject's perceived character. Shakespeare elided material and generally restructured the action for greater dramatic effect, compressing the events of fourteen years into a three-hour play. In the first two acts, King Henry VI's funeral, the courting of Lady Anne, Clarence's murder in the Tower, and Edward's death—events that historically spanned twelve years—occur within days as the plot careens toward Richard's coronation.

Shakespeare has embellished the historical image of a deformed Richard, but he has also made him charismatic and persuasive, thus complicating both his character and the response of audiences who are put immediately on intimate terms with him. And though many major episodes early in the play are fictional, and many events after the murder of the young princes are imagined as well, history does supply, at least intermittently, the primary inspiration.

Stage Machiavels and Christopher Marlowe's Villainous Heroes

Several literary works and an English stage tradition were also important inspirations for this play, including *The Mirror for Magistrates*, the bloody tragedies of the Roman playwright Seneca, and the convention of the stage Machiavel. The first of these is a homiletic work that sets the *Chronicles* stories to rhyme; each of its many sections deals with the fall of a historical figure. The Senecan influences include the lamentation of the women who have lost children at Richard's hands, some aspects of the wooing of Lady Anne, and the imagery of drowning and being transported to the underworld in the recital of Clarence's dream—comically so unlike his inglorious end in a vat of wine. Atmospherically as well, the play echoes these Roman sources in its employment of ghosts and prophecies suggesting the tragedy of inevitable fate. From the native traditions of the medieval morality play, from Christopher Marlowe, and from other playwrights of the Elizabethan era, all of which had their version of the stage Machiavel, Shakespeare gained insight into his villain-hero's energy, his self-revealing theatricality, and his sheer pleasure in manipulating people and circumstances.

In the last of the *Henry VI* plays, Richard has declared himself able to "set the murderous Machiavel to school." Now in the tragedy of *Richard III*, he climaxes the literary tradition that extends back to the morality-play Vice and to Marlowe's flamboyantly theatrical heroes. The character of the Vice, of whom Sir John Falstaff in the *Henry IV* plays is also partly a descendant, dominated the morality play as a malign jester, skilled at conspiring gleefully with his audience. In moral terms, the Vice is the allegorical representation of sin, sent by the devil to tempt humanity; but in artistic terms he is the character audiences want to see, for he delivers many of the best lines, the wisecracking equivalent of today's stand-up comic. Richard actually describes himself as a Vice in an aside as he plots against the little princes; he behaves "like the formal Vice, Iniquity" (3.1.82). In *Richard III*, Shakespeare enlarges the two-dimensional figure of the Vice with human plausibility, though with little internal emotional complexity, giving him a moralizing function, along with the brilliant thrust-and-parry of political (and sexual) intrigue, thus blending morality and history in a nascent tradition of English tragedy that contains also moments of grim farce.

Another precedent comes from Marlowe. Like Barabas in Marlowe's *The Jew of Malta* (c. 1590), Richard opens the play by addressing the audience directly in a soliloquy. Yet Marlowe introduced Barabas's soliloquy in his study with a Prologue by Machiavel, the stage version of the historical Machiavelli who was considered a subversive and an atheist because of the cynical political theories he espoused in his manual, *The Prince*. Shakespeare dispenses with the formal device of a Prologue, allowing Richard to move directly towards the audience, which quickly becomes complicit in his schemes; before the action begins, we know—or think we know—more about this eloquent and sarcastic outsider than do the characters in the play.

Language and Structure

Richard's speeches span the stylistic range of the play. Often they are filled with rhetorical devices of repetition and antithesis. Certainly the poetically lurid recitals of dreams and portents, and the invective spat at him by Lady Anne and Queen Margaret, share in this classical tradition. At times these speeches can seem static and artificial, especially when compared with the fluid prose and nimble blank verse of Shakespeare's later work.

From the start of the play Richard also makes exaggerated claims for himself as a villain, determined to revenge himself upon the world—and the family—that have rejected him. His hyperbolic speeches, his rants, and his blustering promises are so tonally ambiguous they are as likely to elicit laughter as fear. And so his wit and irony, his use of puns and hostile imagery, his demonic glee give many of his scenes a sardonic edge. At times, the give-and-take of Richard and his ally Buckingham has the easygoing rhythms and casual camaraderie of a well-rehearsed comedy duo. Not surprisingly, this over-the-top quality has been highlighted in many interpretations of the play. The spirit of camp, defined by critic Jonathan Dollimore in *Political Shakespeare: New Essays in Cultural Materialism* as the "deep truth of the superficial: if it's worth doing, it's worth overdoing" (147), has permeated several notable interpretations of the play, including the whole of the Richard Loncraine film of *Richard III* with Ian McKellen.

The structure of the action in *Richard III* is such that, although the external events are real, they are also part of a pattern subject to prophecies and visitations from a spiritual world over which the characters, and even the willful Richard, have no control. Determined "to prove a villain" and to stage-manage the action, Gloucester consistently does so even if temporarily fazed by Queen Margaret (1.3.112); she represents the remnants of the defeated Lancastrian past and a forecast of the Tudor future. Theatrically, her curses suggest the wild-eyed desperation of the aggrieved, yet she also speaks of the machinery of divine retribution in ways that prefigure the progress, and certainly the ending, of the play.

Other women in the play, speaking largely a declamatory language of curses, express this sense of loss, grief, and grievance, as do some of the noble characters, especially as they approach death. Margaret understands that many of Richard's murders contribute to her cause of revenge; and as Vaughan, Rivers, Grey, Hastings, and Buckingham die, Richard's actions bring her prophecies closer to fulfillment. Thus Richard's fate is represented as part of a larger order with him as the nation's scourge and Richmond as the instrument of divine justice, or as the future Tudor monarch prays, a minister of "chastisement." This structure of foreordained events turns in such a way that the very actions Richard takes to insure his power, once he reaches the pinnacle, assure his downfall and the fulfillment of Margaret's prophecies. Richard's is not the kind of tragedy Shakespeare will later achieve: what catharsis occurs at its end purges not so much the audience, as England.

Themes and Issues

Conscience and Amorality

Conscience and amorality are key themes in *Richard III*, for the hero is radically and exuberantly amoral, while other noble evil-doers experience, sometimes in dreams, nightmares, and ghostly visitations, the pangs of their consciences. Conscience is plentifully in evidence in the play, although not always in pure form. Buckingham, who for much of the play is Richard's "other self," is executed on All Souls' Day; the holy day of remembrance brings to his "fearful soul . . . the determined respite of (his) wrongs" with Margaret's curse fallen upon his head. Queen Margaret, widow to the murdered Henry VI, appears like the ghost of bad conscience spewing her invective and prophecies. The executioners who argue whether they should kill Clarence while their intended victim sleeps do so in a grotesquely comic fashion, yet their discussion contains a kind of human moralizing. Just as in Tyrrel's account of the killing of the princes, these henchmen show some "dregs of conscience."

Most importantly, Shakespeare contrasts Richard and Richmond to make fully clear the extent of the former's evil. Shakespeare constructs much of Act 5 to juxtapose the sweet dreams of the pious future king before battle to the troubled sleep of murderous Richard who wakes (at 5.3.179) afflicted by "coward conscience," and "Cold fearful drops" standing on his "trembling flesh." Richard has been associated all along with the inhuman and the monstrous—a dog, a hell-hound, the bottled spider and foul toad—whereas Richmond has been portrayed as calm, blessed, princely, humane, and pious. In the nightmare scene, Richard's usual extroversion and wit disintegrate as he confronts the ghosts of those he has murdered and questions himself in the conscience-stricken terms of Christian polemics. (Characters in later plays, such as Hamlet and Rosalind, will also indulge in speeches of remembered narrative.) Strikingly, when Richard wakes he seems to move away from any moral self-awareness the nightmare might have imparted. Unlike even his brother Clarence and Buckingham, Richard faces his death unrepentant, aware that he is in communion with neither God nor himself.

Elizabethan audiences would have taken Richard's deformity, to which he attributes his lust for power, as a correlative for his moral corruption, and until the final act he demonstrates a remorseless, sometimes terrifying absence of conscience. Unlike Iago, the agent of evil in *Othello*, whose iniquity Coleridge called "motiveless malignity," Richard rationalizes his evil as the effect of his physical deformation:

> I, that am curtailed of this fair proportion,
> Cheated of feature by dissembling Nature,
> Deformed, unfinished, sent before my time
> Into this breathing world scarce half made up,
> And that so lamely and unfashionable
> That dogs bark at me as I halt by them—
> . . . .
> And therefore, since I cannot prove a lover
> To entertain these fair well-spoken days,
> I am determinèd to prove a villain.
>
> (1.1.18–23; 28–30)

Sex and power are games for him, both played ruthlessly to win, with all the resources of a "subtle, false, and treacherous" genius. Whatever persons stand between him and the throne must die, be they brothers, nephews, a wife, or loyal associates. Richard surges forward vampire-like, seeking more victims, nearly a dozen of them haunting his dream, all dismissed in the next scene when he tells Norfolk:

> Let not our babbling dreams affright our souls;
> Conscience is but a word that cowards use,
> Devised at first to keep the strong in awe.
> Our strong arms be our conscience, swords our law!
>
> (5.3.308–311)

Might, in Richard's diseased mind, is the only right—a theme underscored in several productions set during fascist eras.

Regicide and Its Consequences

Shakespeare frames Richard's individual evil within his role as the scourge of England. According to this theory,

Richard is a devil figure come to cleanse the kingdom for its earlier crime in deposing and murdering the king (Richard II) whose murder set off the wars of which Bosworth is the final battle. Shakespeare will deal with the earlier history later in his career. In the last of those plays, *Henry V*, the young, conscience-stricken king on the verge of the battle of Agincourt, begs his God not to "think upon the fault / My father made in compassing the crown" (4.1.291–292). Henry's miraculous victory at Agincourt becomes proof to him that "God fought for us." Yet despite Henry V's wedding to the French princess Katherine, the peace is short-lived, and when their son is crowned king at nine months, another cycle of power rivalries and violence is unleashed. Innocent and pious, Henry VI is incapable of negotiating, or protecting himself from, the factions that surround him; in fact, he would rather not be wearing the crown at all. And as the body count rises and the list of atrocities lengthens during the second and third installments of *Henry VI*, Richard emerges as the most energetic villain among a cadre of noble murderers who will assemble at the court of the next king, Edward IV. Critic John Danby in *Shakespeare's Doctrine of Nature* (60) notes that, thanks to Richard, "the corruption of his time is made aware of itself. This is the ambiguity of his role: to be the logical outcome of this society, and yet a pariah rejected by that society; a hypocrite, yet more sincere in his self-awareness than those he ruins and deceives." Uniquely deformed in body and soul, Richard in death at last cleanses the emergent nation, not only of the crime of deposing Richard II, but also of the corruption that has turned the previous century into an age of disorder, misrule, and a violence that is both pathological and political.

The Art of the Actor and the Seductive Power of Words

Richard's theatricality has been remarked upon already. This virtuoso actor's power over others through the medium of words is explored to brilliant effect in the scene with Lady Anne. Essayist William Hazlitt suggests that this seduction should be conducted entirely as an actor might, his "progress of wily adulation, of encroaching humility and smiling villainy" suggesting that Richard attracts women not as a lover but as a performer—"to show his mental superiority, and power to make others the playthings of his will." Hazlitt describes Edmund Kean's attitude, in leaning against the side of the stage before he comes forward in this scene, as "one of the most graceful and striking we remember to have seen. It would have done for Titian to paint" (in Wells, *Shakespeare in the Theatre: An Anthology of Theatre Criticism*, 40). Royal Shakespeare Company director John Barton, demonstrating the same scene with actors Sinead Cusack and Alan Howard for his

Playing Shakespeare video and accompanying text (43), calls this "a piece of ding-dong dialogue where two actors will get lost if they don't go with the rhythm and pick up the cues as Shakespeare wrote them. Often in this passage a character comes in half-way through the verse-line." When the RSC actors had completed the first volley (1.295ff.), Barton praised their nimble deliveries, noting, "the verse works there like a rally at tennis. You both served the text up to each other, which is clearly the way it's written" (Barton, 44).

Staging Challenges

Cutting/Adapting the (Long) Script

The tradition of cutting and amending *Richard III* goes back at least to 1700, when the actor/manager Colley Cibber cut the play in half, inserting other lines from Shakespeare and many of his own (see below) to assemble the acting script that was to predominate for one hundred fifty years. Even during the twentieth and twenty-first centuries, few productions have staged the entire script. Part of the reason for this is problems with the play's language. For instance, even Richard's rhetoric in some late scenes of the play becomes as artificial (e.g., 4.4) as that of lesser characters. Before that, his speeches are often the only ones with a sense of personal animation and a variety of tone that distinguishes them from the more generalized bickering of the courtiers. And the classically derived choral and ritual scenes have a sententiousness inimical to Richard's sardonic spirit and to modern tastes.

The passages most often omitted are such rhetorically formal arguments as Richard's with the Queen in 4.4, a scene in which their dialogue is a textbook example of the ancient back-and-forth device of *stichomythia*. Other excisions include cutting the longer speeches in the middle or omitting characters (Stanley and Queen Margaret often go) in order to simplify the plotting, reduce the number of lines, and shorten the evening. Laurence Olivier chose to cut most of Richard's conscience-afflicted speeches before Bosworth, thus depicting the King as unrepentant and largely unself-aware before death.

Visualizing the Crook-backed King

Richard himself descants upon his own deformity, and others in the play speak of him with other forms of bestial imagery. The sorrowful Queen approaches Margaret, assuring her that her predictions were accurate and that the king is a monster:

> Oh, thou didst prophesy the time would come
> That I should wish for thee to help me curse
> That bottled spider, that foul bunch-backed toad!
> (4.4.79–81)

Hence, able-bodied actors have to confront the physical demands of a man "curtailed" of fair proportion. How big a hump, which he himself describes as "an envious mountain" (*3 Henry VI*, 3.2.157)? How noticeably a limp (*Richard III*, 1.1.23)? How grotesquely withered an arm (3.4.68–69)? And beyond that, what are the interpretive and moral implications of these forms of crookedness? Richard is both disabled and energetic, a monster who may have been bred in hell and yet serves as an almost irresistibly attractive and funny guide to his own play. The actor must take care not to immobilize himself with prosthetic devices that would cut against that energy. Olivier managed to both drag his leg and suggest (as Sir Thomas More tells us) that one shoulder was higher than the other, while still maintaining a nimbleness, even on the battlefield, that made his Richard a swaggering boaster. Others, such as Antony Sher during the 1980s, have created such exaggerated disabilities—a large hump and spidery crutches for a figure barely able to walk—that his physical pain has mitigated some of his cruelty.

Richard's Nightmare

One of the challenges faced by directors of *Richard III* is that posed by the nightmare scene. In it, a dozen figures Richard has murdered appear to him and to his nemesis Richmond in their simultaneous dreams. Because the rivals are sleeping, however, we seldom see stage directors create the characters' reactions to the ghosts' curses and benedictions. Richard may start up moaning, or turn in his bed, but generally the ghosts are envisioned as a long procession of figures, moving past the sleeping antagonists. On stage, the special effects are usually limited to stage fog, ominous music, and perhaps an offstage fan to rustle the clothing of the ghosts. Such scenic modesty appears in the famous drawing of the scene by William Hogarth, as a circle of finger-pointing victims encircle the murderer's bed. "Despair and die," they are saying to Richard, as contrasted with their good wishes for Richmond: "Live and flourish." Hogarth's circle foreshadows the scene the next day when Richard is unhorsed and surrounded by enemy soldiers.

Bosworth Field and Other Scenes of Murder

Stage versions of the battle can be thrilling when the fights are well choreographed, the action is swift, and effective musical underscoring and brassy "alarums and excursions" accompany the scene. In his 2003 production, part of the RSC's historic "My England—the Histories" marathon, director Michael Boyd turned the limitations of the in-the-round setting at

London's Young Vic theater (formerly an open industrial space) into an advantage by making the battle highly energetic, chaotic, and acrobatic. The misshapen Richard (Aidan McArdle), nonetheless as nimble as Olivier's was, climbed poles and ropes to the mezzanine level, while various soldiers, nobles, and secret enemies, such as Lord Stanley, raced in and out from great bronze doors and the many exits and entrances surrounding the audience on all sides. The excitement was palpable.

The Tragedy of King Richard III

[Dramatis Personae

KING EDWARD THE FOURTH
QUEEN ELIZABETH, *wife of King Edward*
EDWARD, PRINCE OF WALES, } *sons of Edward and*
RICHARD, DUKE OF YORK, } *Elizabeth*
GEORGE, DUKE OF CLARENCE,
RICHARD, DUKE OF GLOUCESTER, } *brothers of the King*
   later King Richard III,
DUCHESS OF YORK, *mother of Edward IV,*
   Clarence, and Richard, Duke of Gloucester
LADY ANNE, *widow of Edward, Prince of Wales*
   (son of Henry VI); later wife of Richard, Duke of
   Gloucester
MARGARET, *widow of King Henry VI*
BOY, *son of Clarence (Edward Plantagenet, Earl of*
   Warwick)
GIRL, *daughter of Clarence (Margaret Plantagenet,*
   Countess of Salisbury)

ANTHONY WOODVILLE, EARL RIVERS, *brother of*
   Queen Elizabeth
MARQUESS OF DORSET, } *sons of Queen*
LORD GREY, } *Elizabeth*
SIR THOMAS VAUGHAN, *executed with Rivers and*
   Grey

WILLIAM, LORD HASTINGS, *the Lord Chamberlain*
DUKE OF BUCKINGHAM, *Richard's supporter, later*
   in opposition
SIR WILLIAM CATESBY,
SIR RICHARD RATCLIFFE, } *Richard's supporters*
LORD LOVELL, } *and henchmen*
SIR JAMES TYRREL,
DUKE OF NORFOLK, } *Richard's generals*
EARL OF SURREY, }

HENRY, EARL OF RICHMOND, *later King Henry VII*

   SCENE: *England.*]

LORD STANLEY, EARL OF DERBY,
EARL OF OXFORD,
SIR JAMES BLUNT, } *supporters of*
SIR WALTER HERBERT, } *Richmond*
SIR WILLIAM BRANDON,
CHRISTOPHER URSWICK, *a priest,*

CARDINAL BOURCHIER, *Archbishop of Canterbury*
ARCHBISHOP OF YORK (*Thomas Rotherham*)
BISHOP OF ELY (*John Morton*)
GHOSTS *of King Henry VI, Edward Prince of*
   Wales, and others murdered by Richard
   (Clarence, Rivers, Grey, Vaughan, Hastings, the
   two young princes, Anne, and Buckingham)
SIR ROBERT BRACKENBURY, *Lieutenant of the Tower*
TRESSEL,
BERKELEY, } *attending the*
HALBERDIER, } *Lady Anne*
GENTLEMAN,
Two MURDERERS
KEEPER *in the Tower*
Three CITIZENS
MESSENGER *to Queen Elizabeth*
LORD MAYOR OF LONDON
MESSENGER *to Lord Hastings*
PURSUIVANT
PRIEST
SCRIVENER
Two BISHOPS
PAGE *to Richard III*
Four MESSENGERS *to Richard III*
SHERIFF OF WILTSHIRE

Lords, Attendants, Aldermen, Citizens, Councilors,
   Soldiers

1.1

Enter Richard, Duke of Gloucester, solus.

RICHARD
    Now is the winter of our discontent
    Made glorious summer by this son of York,   2
    And all the clouds that loured upon our house   3
    In the deep bosom of the ocean buried.
    Now are our brows bound with victorious wreaths,   5
    Our bruisèd arms hung up for monuments,   6
    Our stern alarums changed to merry meetings,   7
    Our dreadful marches to delightful measures.   8
    Grim-visaged War hath smoothed his wrinkled
        front;   9
    And now, instead of mounting barbèd steeds   10
    To fright the souls of fearful adversaries,   11
    He capers nimbly in a lady's chamber
    To the lascivious pleasing of a lute.
    But I, that am not shaped for sportive tricks,   14
    Nor made to court an amorous looking glass;
    I, that am rudely stamped, and want love's majesty   16
    To strut before a wanton ambling nymph;   17
    I, that am curtailed of this fair proportion,   18
    Cheated of feature by dissembling Nature,   19
    Deformed, unfinished, sent before my time
    Into this breathing world scarce half made up,
    And that so lamely and unfashionable   22
    That dogs bark at me as I halt by them—   23
    Why, I, in this weak piping time of peace,   24
    Have no delight to pass away the time,
    Unless to see my shadow in the sun
    And descant on mine own deformity.   27
    And therefore, since I cannot prove a lover
    To entertain these fair well-spoken days,   29
    I am determinèd to prove a villain
    And hate the idle pleasures of these days.
    Plots have I laid, inductions dangerous,   32
    By drunken prophecies, libels, and dreams,
    To set my brother Clarence and the King
    In deadly hate the one against the other;
    And if King Edward be as true and just

As I am subtle, false, and treacherous,
This day should Clarence closely be mewed up   38
About a prophecy, which says that G   39
Of Edward's heirs the murderer shall be.
Dive, thoughts, down to my soul; here Clarence
    comes.

        Enter Clarence, guarded, and Brackenbury,
        [Lieutenant of the Tower].

Brother, good day. What means this armèd guard
That waits upon Your Grace?
CLARENCE   His Majesty,   43
    Tend'ring my person's safety, hath appointed   44
    This conduct to convey me to the Tower.   45
RICHARD
    Upon what cause?
CLARENCE   Because my name is George.
RICHARD
    Alack, my lord, that fault is none of yours.
    He should, for that, commit your godfathers.
    Oh, belike His Majesty hath some intent   49
    That you should be new christened in the Tower.   50
    But what's the matter, Clarence, may I know?   51
CLARENCE
    Yea, Richard, when I know; for I protest
    As yet I do not. But, as I can learn,
    He hearkens after prophecies and dreams,
    And from the crossrow plucks the letter G,   55
    And says a wizard told him that by G
    His issue disinherited should be;   57
    And, for my name of George begins with G,   58
    It follows in his thought that I am he.
    These, as I learn, and suchlike toys as these   60
    Hath moved His Highness to commit me now.   61
RICHARD
    Why, this it is when men are ruled by women.
    'Tis not the King that sends you to the Tower;
    My Lady Grey his wife, Clarence, 'tis she   64
    That tempers him to this extremity.   65
    Was it not she, and that good man of worship,   66
    Anthony Woodville, her brother there,   67

1.1. Location: London. Near the Tower.
0.1 *solus* alone.   **2 son** Edward IV was the son of Richard, Duke of
York. (With a pun on "sun"; Edward IV used the sun on his badge.)
3 loured looked threateningly   **5 brows** foreheads   **6 arms** armor.
monuments trophies   **7 alarums** calls to arms, or assaults   **8 dreadful**
formidable, awe-inspiring.   **measures** stately dances.   **9 wrinkled**
front furrowed forehead   **10 barbéd** armored   **11 fearful** frightened
14 sportive amorous   **16 rudely stamped** roughly fashioned, coined.
want lack   **17 ambling** walking affectedly, i.e., wantonly   **18 curtailed**
cut short, denied.   **proportion** shape   **19 feature** shapeliness of
body   **22 unfashionable** badly fashioned   **23 halt** limp   **24 piping**
time i.e., a time when the music heard is that of pipes and not fifes
and drums   **27 descant** compose variations, comment on   **29 entertain**
pass away pleasurably.   **well-spoken** refined, elegant   **32 inductions**
preparations

38 mewed up confined (like a hawk)   **39 prophecy . . . G** (The prophecy
is mentioned in the chronicles; the quibble is that *G* stands for
Gloucester and not for *George*, the given name of the Duke of Clarence.)
43 waits attends   **44 Tend'ring** having care for   **45 conduct** escort
49 belike probably   **50 new christened** (Anticipates, ironically,
Clarence's death by drowning in 1.4.)   **51 matter** reason, cause
55 crossrow Christ-crossrow, or alphabet (so called from the cross
printed before the alphabet in the hornbook)   **57 issue** offspring
58 for because   **60 toys** trifles   **61 commit** arrest   **64 My Lady Grey**
(A disrespectful reference to the Queen, whose maiden name was
Elizabeth Woodville and who, when the King married her, was the
widow of Sir John Grey.)   **65 tempers** governs, directs   **66 worship**
honor. (Said ironically.)   **67 Woodville** i.e., Earl Rivers (whom
Richard also disrespectfully refers to by his family name rather than
by his recently acquired title)

That made him send Lord Hastings to the Tower,
From whence this present day he is delivered?
We are not safe, Clarence, we are not safe.

CLARENCE
By heaven, I think there is no man secure
But the Queen's kindred and night-walking heralds   72
That trudge betwixt the King and Mistress Shore.   73
Heard you not what an humble suppliant
Lord Hastings was to her for his delivery?   75

RICHARD
Humbly complaining to Her Deity   76
Got my Lord Chamberlain his liberty.   77
I'll tell you what: I think it is our way,   78
If we will keep in favor with the King,
To be her men and wear her livery.   80
The jealous, o'erworn widow and herself,   81
Since that our brother dubbed them gentlewomen,   82
Are mighty gossips in our monarchy.   83

BRACKENBURY
I beseech Your Graces both to pardon me:
His Majesty hath straitly given in charge   85
That no man shall have private conference,
Of what degree soever, with your brother.   87

RICHARD
Even so? An't please Your Worship, Brackenbury,   88
You may partake of anything we say.
We speak no treason, man. We say the King
Is wise and virtuous, and his noble queen
Well struck in years, fair, and not jealous.   92
We say that Shore's wife hath a pretty foot,
A cherry lip, a bonny eye, a passing pleasing tongue;   94
And that the Queen's kindred are made gentlefolks.
How say you, sir? Can you deny all this?

BRACKENBURY
With this, my lord, myself have naught to do.

RICHARD
Naught to do with Mistress Shore? I tell thee, fellow,   98
He that doth naught with her, excepting one,
Were best to do it secretly, alone.

BRACKENBURY   What one, my lord?

RICHARD
Her husband, knave. Wouldst thou betray me?   102

BRACKENBURY
I beseech Your Grace to pardon me, and withal   103
Forbear your conference with the noble Duke.

CLARENCE
We know thy charge, Brackenbury, and will obey.

RICHARD
We are the Queen's abjects, and must obey.   106
Brother, farewell. I will unto the King;
And whatsoe'er you will employ me in,
Were it to call King Edward's widow sister,   109
I will perform it to enfranchise you.   110
Meantime, this deep disgrace in brotherhood
Touches me deeper than you can imagine.   112

CLARENCE
I know it pleaseth neither of us well.

RICHARD
Well, your imprisonment shall not be long;
I will deliver you, or else lie for you.   115
Meantime, have patience.

CLARENCE   I must perforce. Farewell.   116

Exit Clarence [with Brackenbury and guard].

RICHARD
Go tread the path that thou shalt ne'er return.
Simple, plain Clarence, I do love thee so
That I will shortly send thy soul to heaven,
If heaven will take the present at our hands.
But who comes here? The new-delivered Hastings?   121

Enter Lord Hastings.

HASTINGS
Good time of day unto my gracious lord.

RICHARD
As much unto my good Lord Chamberlain.
Well are you welcome to the open air.
How hath Your Lordship brooked imprisonment?   125

HASTINGS
With patience, noble lord, as prisoners must.
But I shall live, my lord, to give them thanks   127
That were the cause of my imprisonment.

RICHARD
No doubt, no doubt; and so shall Clarence too,
For they that were your enemies are his,
And have prevailed as much on him as you.

HASTINGS
More pity that the eagles should be mewed,
Whiles kites and buzzards prey at liberty.   133

RICHARD   What news abroad?   134

HASTINGS
No news so bad abroad as this at home:

---

72 night-walking heralds i.e., secret messengers for an assignation
73 Mistress Shore Jane Shore, the King's mistress, and wife of a gold-
smith in Lombard Street. (The title *Mistress* is a respectful form of
address for any woman, married or unmarried.)   **75 her** i.e., Jane
Shore   **76 Her Deity** (A mock title for Jane Shore, suggesting she is
even more elevated than "Her Grace" or "Her Majesty.")   **77 Lord
Chamberlain** i.e., Lord Hastings   **78 our way** i.e., our only way (to
succeed)   **80 men** servants   **81 widow** i.e., Queen Elizabeth. (See the
note for line 64.)   **herself** i.e., Jane Shore   **82 Since that** since.   **gentlewomen** (A sneer at the Queen's family, which was gentle but not
noble until after her marriage with the King; Jane Shore was, of
course, neither gentle nor noble.)   **83 mighty gossips** i.e., influential
busybodies   **85 straitly . . . charge** strictly ordered   **87 degree** rank
88 An't If it   **92 Well struck** i.e., well along.   **not jealous** (Implies
there are things she might be jealous about.)   **94 passing** surpassingly   **98 Naught** (Richard quibbles on the meanings "nothing" and
"naughtiness," "the sexual act.")   **102 betray me** i.e., into naming
the King as a person who does "naught" with Mistress Shore.

103 withal furthermore   **106 abjects** abjectly servile subjects
109 King Edward's widow i.e., the widow whom Edward has made
queen   **110 enfranchise** release from imprisonment   **112 Touches . . .
imagine** (1) distresses me more than can be imagined (2) concerns me
(in my personal ambition) more than you could possibly guess.
115 lie for you (1) take your place in prison (2) tell lies about you.
116 perforce necessarily.   **121 new-delivered** recently released
125 brooked endured   **127 give them thanks** i.e., pay them back.
(Said ironically.)   **133 kites** scavengers of the hawk family
134 abroad at large, circulating.

The King is sickly, weak, and melancholy,
And his physicians fear him mightily.   137

RICHARD

Now, by Saint John, that news is bad indeed!
Oh, he hath kept an evil diet long   139
And overmuch consumed his royal person.
'Tis very grievous to be thought upon.
Where is he, in his bed?

HASTINGS   He is.

RICHARD

Go you before, and I will follow you.   *Exit Hastings.*
He cannot live, I hope, and must not die
Till George be packed with post-horse up to heaven.   146
I'll in, to urge his hatred more to Clarence
With lies well steeled with weighty arguments;   148
And, if I fail not in my deep intent,
Clarence hath not another day to live.
Which done, God take King Edward to his mercy
And leave the world for me to bustle in!
For then I'll marry Warwick's youngest daughter.   153
What though I killed her husband and her father?   154
The readiest way to make the wench amends
Is to become her husband and her father,
The which will I; not all so much for love
As for another secret close intent   158
By marrying her which I must reach unto.
But yet I run before my horse to market.
Clarence still breathes, Edward still lives and reigns;
When they are gone, then must I count my gains.
                                                       Exit.

❖

1.2

*Enter the corpse of [King] Henry the Sixth, with
Halberds to guard it; Lady Anne being the
mourner [attended by Tressel and Berkeley].*

ANNE

Set down, set down your honorable load—
If honor may be shrouded in a hearse—   2
Whilst I awhile obsequiously lament   3
Th'untimely fall of virtuous Lancaster.
            [The bearers set down the coffin.]
Poor key-cold figure of a holy king,   5
Pale ashes of the house of Lancaster,
Thou bloodless remnant of that royal blood,
Be it lawful that I invocate thy ghost   8
To hear the lamentations of poor Anne,

Wife to thy Edward, to thy slaughtered son,
Stabbed by the selfsame hand that made these wounds!
Lo, in these windows that let forth thy life   12
I pour the helpless balm of my poor eyes.   13
Oh, cursèd be the hand that made these holes!
Cursèd the heart that had the heart to do it!
Cursèd the blood that let this blood from hence!
More direful hap betide that hated wretch   17
That makes us wretched by the death of thee
Than I can wish to wolves, to spiders, toads,
Or any creeping venomed thing that lives!
If ever he have child, abortive be it,   21
Prodigious, and untimely brought to light,   22
Whose ugly and unnatural aspect   23
May fright the hopeful mother at the view,
And that be heir to his unhappiness!   25
If ever he have wife, let her be made
More miserable by the life of him
Than I am made by my young lord and thee!—   28
Come now towards Chertsey with your holy load,   29
Taken from Paul's to be interrèd there.   30
            [The bearers take up the hearse.]
And still as you are weary of this weight,   31
Rest you, whiles I lament King Henry's corpse.

Enter Richard, Duke of Gloucester.

RICHARD

Stay, you that bear the corpse, and set it down.

ANNE

What black magician conjures up this fiend
To stop devoted charitable deeds?   35

RICHARD

Villains, set down the corpse, or, by Saint Paul,
I'll make a corpse of him that disobeys.

HALBERDIER *[advancing with his halberd lowered]*

My lord, stand back, and let the coffin pass.

RICHARD

Unmannered dog, stand thou when I command!   39
Advance thy halberd higher than my breast,   40
Or, by Saint Paul, I'll strike thee to my foot
And spurn upon thee, beggar, for thy boldness.   42
            [The bearers set down the hearse.]

ANNE

What do you tremble? Are you all afraid?   43
Alas, I blame you not, for you are mortal,
And mortal eyes cannot endure the devil.—
Avaunt, thou dreadful minister of hell!   46
Thou hadst but power over his mortal body;
His soul thou canst not have. Therefore, begone.

---

137 fear fear for **139 diet** course of life, regimen **146 with post-horse** by post-horses, i.e., by swiftest possible means **148 steeled** reinforced **153 Warwick's youngest daughter** the Lady Anne Neville, widow of Edward, Prince of Wales, son of King Henry VI. **154 father** i.e., father-in-law (Henry VI). **158 intent** design (i.e., Richard hopes to ally himself with the house of Lancaster to bolster his claim to the throne)
1.2. Location: London. A street.
0.2 *Halberds* halberdiers, guards with halberds, or long poleaxes
2 hearse (Probably here an open coffin on a bier.) **3 obsequiously** as befits a funeral, mournfully **5 key-cold** extremely cold, cold as a metal key. (Proverbial.) **8 Be it** Let it be. **invocate** invoke

12 windows i.e., wounds **13 helpless** useless, unavailing **17 hap betide** fortune befall **21 abortive** misshapen, premature **22 Prodigious** monstrous, unnatural **23 aspect** appearance **25 unhappiness** evil nature, bad luck. **28 by . . . thee** i.e., by the deaths of Prince Edward and King Henry VI. **29 Chertsey** monastery in Surrey, near London, where King Henry's body is to be buried **30 Paul's** Saint Paul's Cathedral in London **31 still as** as often as **35 devoted** holy **39 stand** halt **40 Advance . . . breast** Raise your halberd upright **42 spurn** trample **43 What** Why **46 Avaunt** Begone

RICHARD

Sweet saint, for charity, be not so curst.   49

ANNE

Foul devil, for God's sake hence and trouble us not,   50
For thou hast made the happy earth thy hell,
Filled it with cursing cries and deep exclaims.   52
If thou delight to view thy heinous deeds,
Behold this pattern of thy butcheries.   54

[*She uncovers the corpse.*]

Oh, gentlemen, see, see dead Henry's wounds
Open their congealed mouths and bleed afresh!   56
Blush, blush, thou lump of foul deformity!
For 'tis thy presence that exhales this blood   58
From cold and empty veins where no blood dwells.
Thy deeds inhuman and unnatural
Provokes this deluge most unnatural.
O God, which this blood mad'st, revenge his death!
O earth, which this blood drink'st, revenge his death!
Either heav'n with lightning strike the murd'rer dead,
Or earth gape open wide and eat him quick,   65
As thou dost swallow up this good king's blood,
Which his hell-governed arm hath butcherèd!

RICHARD

Lady, you know no rules of charity,
Which renders good for bad, blessings for curses.

ANNE

Villain, thou know'st nor law of God nor man.   70
No beast so fierce but knows some touch of pity.   71

RICHARD

But I know none, and therefore am no beast.

ANNE

Oh, wonderful, when devils tell the truth!   73

RICHARD

More wonderful, when angels are so angry.
Vouchsafe, divine perfection of a woman,   75
Of these supposèd crimes to give me leave
By circumstance but to acquit myself.   77

ANNE

Vouchsafe, defused infection of a man,   78
Of these known evils but to give me leave
By circumstance t'accuse thy cursèd self.

RICHARD

Fairer than tongue can name thee, let me have
Some patient leisure to excuse myself.

ANNE

Fouler than heart can think thee, thou canst make
No excuse current but to hang thyself.   84

RICHARD

By such despair I should accuse myself.

ANNE

And by despairing shalt thou stand excused
For doing worthy vengeance on thyself
That didst unworthy slaughter upon others.

RICHARD   Say that I slew them not?

ANNE   Then say they were not slain.
But dead they are, and, devilish slave, by thee.

RICHARD   I did not kill your husband.

ANNE   Why, then he is alive.

RICHARD

Nay, he is dead, and slain by Edward's hand.

ANNE

In thy foul throat thou liest! Queen Margaret saw
Thy murd'rous falchion smoking in his blood,   96
The which thou once didst bend against her breast,   97
But that thy brothers beat aside the point.

RICHARD

I was provokèd by her sland'rous tongue,
That laid their guilt upon my guiltless shoulders.   100

ANNE

Thou wast provokèd by thy bloody mind,
That never dream'st on aught but butcheries.   102
Didst thou not kill this king?

RICHARD   I grant ye.

ANNE

Dost grant me, hedgehog? Then God grant me too   104
Thou mayst be damnèd for that wicked deed!
Oh, he was gentle, mild, and virtuous!

RICHARD

The better for the King of Heaven that hath him.

ANNE

He is in heaven, where thou shalt never come.

RICHARD

Let him thank me that holp to send him thither;   109
For he was fitter for that place than earth.

ANNE

And thou unfit for any place but hell.

RICHARD

Yes, one place else, if you will hear me name it.

ANNE   Some dungeon.

RICHARD   Your bedchamber.

ANNE

Ill rest betide the chamber where thou liest!   115

RICHARD

So will it, madam, till I lie with you.

ANNE

I hope so.

RICHARD   I know so. But, gentle Lady Anne,
To leave this keen encounter of our wits
And fall something into a slower method,   119
Is not the causer of the timeless deaths   120
Of these Plantagenets, Henry and Edward,
As blameful as the executioner?

49 curst spiteful, shrewish.   50 hence go hence, depart   52 exclaims
exclamations.   54 pattern example   56 bleed afresh (A phenomenon popularly supposed to occur in the presence of the murderer.)
58 exhales draws out   65 quick alive   70 nor . . . nor neither . . . nor
71 so fierce but knows is so savage that it has not   73 Oh . . . truth
(Anne bitterly reinterprets Richard's *am no beast,* "am not beastly," to
mean that he is neither man nor beast, but devil.)   75 Vouchsafe
Deign, consent   77 circumstance detailed argument   78 defused
diffused, disordered, shapeless; *defused infection* means "spreading
plague"   84 current genuine, acceptable (as in coinage)

96 falchion curved sword   97 bend direct, aim   100 their my
brothers'   102 aught anything   104 hedgehog (Richard's heraldic
emblem featured a boar or wild hog.)   109 holp helped
115 betide befall   119 something into a into a somewhat   120 timeless untimely

ANNE
  Thou wast the cause and most accurst effect.   123
RICHARD
  Your beauty was the cause of that effect—   124
  Your beauty, that did haunt me in my sleep
  To undertake the death of all the world,
  So I might live one hour in your sweet bosom.
ANNE
  If I thought that, I tell thee, homicide,   128
  These nails should rend that beauty from my cheeks.   129
RICHARD
  These eyes could not endure that beauty's wrack;   130
  You should not blemish it, if I stood by.
  As all the world is cheerèd by the sun,
  So I by that. It is my day, my life.
ANNE
  Black night o'ershade thy day, and death thy life!
RICHARD
  Curse not thyself, fair creature—thou art both.
ANNE
  I would I were, to be revenged on thee.   136
RICHARD
  It is a quarrel most unnatural
  To be revenged on him that loveth thee.
ANNE
  It is a quarrel just and reasonable
  To be revenged on him that killed my husband.
RICHARD
  He that bereft thee, lady, of thy husband
  Did it to help thee to a better husband.
ANNE
  His better doth not breathe upon the earth.
RICHARD
  He lives that loves thee better than he could.   144
ANNE
  Name him.
RICHARD   Plantagenet.
ANNE   Why, that was he. 145
RICHARD
  The selfsame name, but one of better nature.
ANNE
  Where is he?
RICHARD   Here.   [She] spits at him.
  Why dost thou spit at me?
ANNE
  Would it were mortal poison for thy sake!
RICHARD
  Never came poison from so sweet a place.
ANNE
  Never hung poison on a fouler toad.   150

  Out of my sight! Thou dost infect mine eyes.
RICHARD
  Thine eyes, sweet lady, have infected mine.   152
ANNE
  Would they were basilisks, to strike thee dead!   153
RICHARD
  I would they were, that I might die at once;
  For now they kill me with a living death.
  Those eyes of thine from mine have drawn salt tears,
  Shamed their aspects with store of childish drops;   157
  These eyes, which never shed remorseful tear—
  No, when my father York and Edward wept
  To hear the piteous moan that Rutland made   160
  When black-faced Clifford shook his sword at him;   161
  Nor when thy warlike father, like a child,   162
  Told the sad story of my father's death
  And twenty times made pause to sob and weep,
  That all the standers-by had wet their cheeks   165
  Like trees bedashed with rain—in that sad time
  My manly eyes did scorn an humble tear;
  And what these sorrows could not thence exhale,   168
  Thy beauty hath, and made them blind with weeping.
  I never sued to friend nor enemy;   170
  My tongue could never learn sweet smoothing words;   171
  But now thy beauty is proposed my fee,   172
  My proud heart sues and prompts my tongue to speak.
                            She looks scornfully at him.
  Teach not thy lip such scorn, for it was made
  For kissing, lady, not for such contempt.
  If thy revengeful heart cannot forgive,
  Lo, here I lend thee this sharp-pointed sword,
  Which if thou please to hide in this true breast
  And let the soul forth that adoreth thee,
  I lay it naked to the deadly stroke
  And humbly beg the death upon my knee.   181
              He [kneels and] lays his breast open; she offers at [it]
                                      with his sword.
  Nay, do not pause; for I did kill King Henry—
  But 'twas thy beauty that provokèd me.
  Nay, now dispatch; 'twas I that stabbed young Edward—
  But 'twas thy heavenly face that set me on.   185
                                  She falls the sword.
  Take up the sword again, or take up me.
ANNE
  Arise, dissembler. Though I wish thy death,
  I will not be thy executioner.
RICHARD [*rising*]
  Then bid me kill myself, and I will do it.

---

123 effect fulfillment.   **124 effect** result   **128 homicide** murderer
129 rend tear   **130 wrack** destruction   **136 I would I were** (If Anne
were truly both Richard's day and his life, she could terminate both.)
144 He lives i.e., There is a man.   **he** i.e., Prince Edward   **145 Plantagenet** (Richard's father, the Duke of York, adopted this name when
he made his claim to the English throne—see *1 Henry VI*, 2.4.36—but
the name had been in the family of England's Angevin rulers since
the time of Henry II and thus could also be claimed by Henry VI and
his son, Prince Edward.)   **150 poison . . . toad** (Toads were popularly
regarded as poisonous.)

152 infected i.e., with love (since love was thought to enter through
the eyes)   **153 basilisks** mythical reptiles reputed to kill by their
looks   **157 aspects** appearance   **160 Rutland** second son of Richard,
Duke of York. (See *3 Henry VI*, 1.3, for his death scene.)   **161 black-
faced** i.e., foreboding in appearance   **162 thy warlike father** i.e., the
Earl of Warwick   **165 That** so that   **168 exhale** draw out   **170 sued**
supplicated, appealed   **171 smoothing** flattering   **172 now** now
that.   **proposed my fee** proposed as my reward   **181 the death**
death after sentencing.   **181.1 *offers*** aims   **185.1 *falls*** lets fall

ANNE
  I have already.
RICHARD   That was in thy rage.
  Speak it again, and even with the word
  This hand, which for thy love did kill thy love,
  Shall for thy love kill a far truer love.
  To both their deaths shalt thou be accessory.
ANNE   I would I knew thy heart.   195
RICHARD   'Tis figured in my tongue.   196
ANNE   I fear me both are false.
RICHARD   Then never man was true.
ANNE   Well, well, put up your sword.
RICHARD   Say, then, my peace is made.
ANNE   That shalt thou know hereafter.
RICHARD   But shall I live in hope?
ANNE   All men, I hope, live so.
RICHARD   Vouchsafe to wear this ring.   204
ANNE   To take is not to give.   205
              [He slips the ring on her finger.]

RICHARD
  Look how my ring encompasseth thy finger,   206
  Even so thy breast encloseth my poor heart;
  Wear both of them, for both of them are thine.
  And if thy poor devoted servant may   209
  But beg one favor at thy gracious hand,
  Thou dost confirm his happiness forever.
ANNE   What is it?
RICHARD
  That it may please you leave these sad designs
  To him that hath most cause to be a mourner,
  And presently repair to Crosby House,   215
  Where, after I have solemnly interred
  At Chertsey monast'ry this noble king
  And wet his grave with my repentant tears,
  I will with all expedient duty see you.   219
  For divers unknown reasons, I beseech you,   220
  Grant me this boon.
ANNE
  With all my heart, and much it joys me, too,
  To see you are become so penitent.—
  Tressel and Berkeley, go along with me.
RICHARD
  Bid me farewell.
ANNE   'Tis more than you deserve;
  But since you teach me how to flatter you,
  Imagine I have said farewell already.
              Exeunt two [Tressel and Berkeley] with Anne.
RICHARD
  Sirs, take up the corpse.
GENTLEMAN   Towards Chertsey, noble lord?
RICHARD
  No, to Whitefriars. There attend my coming.   229
              Exeunt [bearers with] corpse.

195 would wish   **196 figured** portrayed   **204 Vouchsafe** Consent
205 To take . . . give i.e., I accept the ring but I make no promises.
206 Look how Just as   **209 servant** i.e., male admirer, one whom she
may command   **215 presently repair** go right away.   **Crosby House**
(One of Richard's London dwellings; built originally by Sir John Crosby.)
219 expedient expeditious   **220 unknown** secret   **229 Whitefriars**
the Carmelite priory in London.   **attend** await

Was ever woman in this humor wooed?
Was ever woman in this humor won?
I'll have her, but I will not keep her long.
What? I, that killed her husband and his father,
To take her in her heart's extremest hate,
With curses in her mouth, tears in her eyes,
The bleeding witness of my hatred by,
Having God, her conscience, and these bars against me,   237
And I no friends to back my suit withal
But the plain devil and dissembling looks?
And yet to win her! All the world to nothing!   240
Ha!
Hath she forgot already that brave prince,
Edward, her lord, whom I, some three months since,
Stabbed in my angry mood at Tewkesbury?
A sweeter and a lovelier gentleman,
Framed in the prodigality of nature,   246
Young, valiant, wise, and, no doubt, right royal,
The spacious world cannot again afford.   248
And will she yet abase her eyes on me,   249
That cropped the golden prime of this sweet prince   250
And made her widow to a woeful bed?
On me, whose all not equals Edward's moiety?   252
On me, that halts and am misshapen thus?   253
My dukedom to a beggarly denier,   254
I do mistake my person all this while.
Upon my life, she finds, although I cannot,
Myself to be a marv'lous proper man.   257
I'll be at charges for a looking glass,   258
And entertain a score or two of tailors   259
To study fashions to adorn my body.
Since I am crept in favor with myself,
I will maintain it with some little cost.
But first I'll turn yon fellow in his grave,   263
And then return lamenting to my love.
Shine out, fair sun, till I have bought a glass,   265
That I may see my shadow as I pass.   *Exit.*

❧

1.3

*Enter the Queen Mother [Elizabeth], Lord Rivers,
[Marquess of Dorset,] and Lord Grey.*

RIVERS
  Have patience, madam. There's no doubt His Majesty
  Will soon recover his accustomed health.
GREY
  In that you brook it ill, it makes him worse.   3
  Therefore, for God's sake, entertain good comfort,   4
  And cheer His Grace with quick and merry eyes.

237 bars obstacles   **240 All . . . nothing** i.e., Against infinite odds.
246 Framed . . . nature i.e., formed in nature's most lavish mood
248 afford (because Nature was so lavish).   **249 abase her eyes** degrade
herself by looking favorably   **250 cropped** cut short.   **prime** springtime, early manhood   **252 Edward's moiety** half of Edward's worth.
253 halts limps   **254 denier** small copper coin, the twelfth part of a sou
257 proper handsome   **258 be . . . for** undertake the expense of
259 entertain retain, employ   **263 in** into   **265 glass** mirror
1.3. Location: London. The royal court.
3 brook endure   **4 entertain . . . comfort** cheer up

QUEEN ELIZABETH
If he were dead, what would betide on me?   6

GREY
No other harm but loss of such a lord.

QUEEN ELIZABETH
The loss of such a lord includes all harms.

GREY
The heavens have blessed you with a goodly son
To be your comforter when he is gone.

QUEEN ELIZABETH
Ah, he is young, and his minority
Is put unto the trust of Richard Gloucester,
A man that loves not me, nor none of you.

RIVERS
Is it concluded he shall be Protector?

QUEEN ELIZABETH
It is determined, not concluded yet;   15
But so it must be, if the King miscarry.   16

Enter Buckingham and [Lord Stanley Earl of] Derby.

GREY
Here come the lords of Buckingham and Derby.

BUCKINGHAM
Good time of day unto Your Royal Grace!

STANLEY
God make Your Majesty joyful, as you have been!

QUEEN ELIZABETH
The Countess Richmond, good my lord of Derby,   20
To your good prayer will scarcely say amen.
Yet, Derby, notwithstanding she's your wife
And loves not me, be you, good lord, assured
I hate not you for her proud arrogance.   24

STANLEY
I do beseech you, either not believe
The envious slanders of her false accusers,   26
Or, if she be accused on true report,
Bear with her weakness, which I think proceeds
From wayward sickness and no grounded malice.   29

QUEEN ELIZABETH
Saw you the King today, my lord of Derby?

STANLEY
But now the Duke of Buckingham and I   31
Are come from visiting His Majesty.

QUEEN ELIZABETH
What likelihood of his amendment, lords?   33

BUCKINGHAM
Madam, good hope; His Grace speaks cheerfully.

QUEEN ELIZABETH
God grant him health! Did you confer with him?

BUCKINGHAM
Ay, madam. He desires to make atonement   36
Between the Duke of Gloucester and your brothers,   37
And between them and my Lord Chamberlain,   38
And sent to warn them to his royal presence.   39

QUEEN ELIZABETH
Would all were well! But that will never be.
I fear our happiness is at the height.

Enter Richard [Duke of Gloucester, and Lord Hastings].

RICHARD
They do me wrong, and I will not endure it!
Who is it that complains unto the King
That I, forsooth, am stern and love them not?
By holy Paul, they love His Grace but lightly
That fill his ears with such dissentious rumors.   46
Because I cannot flatter and look fair,   47
Smile in men's faces, smooth, deceive, and cog,   48
Duck with French nods and apish courtesy,   49
I must be held a rancorous enemy.
Cannot a plain man live and think no harm,
But thus his simple truth must be abused
With silken, sly, insinuating Jacks?   53

GREY
To whom in all this presence speaks Your Grace?   54

RICHARD
To thee, that hast nor honesty nor grace.   55
When have I injured thee? When done thee wrong?
Or thee? Or thee? Or any of your faction?
A plague upon you all! His Royal Grace—
Whom God preserve better than you would wish!—
Cannot be quiet scarce a breathing while   60
But you must trouble him with lewd complaints.   61

QUEEN ELIZABETH
Brother of Gloucester, you mistake the matter.
The King, on his own royal disposition,   63
And not provoked by any suitor else,
Aiming, belike, at your interior hatred,   65
That in your outward action shows itself
Against my children, brothers, and myself,
Makes him to send, that he may learn the ground   68
Of your ill will, and thereby to remove it.

RICHARD
I cannot tell. The world is grown so bad   70
That wrens make prey where eagles dare not perch.

---

6 **betide on** become of   15 **determined, not concluded** i.e., decided though not officially passed   16 **miscarry** perish.   20 **The Countess Richmond** i.e., Margaret Beaufort (1443–1509), who married, successively, Edmund Tudor (Earl of Richmond), Lord Henry Stafford, and Thomas Lord Stanley (here called the Earl of Derby), to whom she is currently married. By the Earl of Richmond, she was mother of the future Henry VII.   24 **arrogance** i.e., ambition for her son.   26 **envious** malicious   29 **wayward** not yielding readily to treatment. **grounded** firmly fixed   31 **But now** Just now   33 **amendment** recovery

36 **atonement** reconciliation   37 **brothers** (Only one brother, Earl Rivers, is mentioned in the play, though historically Elizabeth had others; Shakespeare may be thinking of other kinsmen, including her sons, whom she helped to advance.)   38 **Lord Chamberlain** Hastings   39 **warn** summon   46 **dissentious** quarrelsome, discordant   47 **look fair** put on a pleasing appearance   48 **smooth** flatter. **cog** deceive   49 **Duck . . . nods** i.e., bow affectedly   53 **With silken** by smooth. **Jacks** lowbred persons.   54 **presence** company   55 **grace** sense of duty or propriety. (Playing upon *Your Grace* in the preceding line.)   60 **breathing while** i.e., brief time   61 **lewd** vile, base   63 **disposition** inclination   65 **Aiming** guessing. **belike** probably   68 **Makes him** causes him. (The implied subject is "The king's own disposition.") **ground** cause   70 **I cannot tell** i.e., I don't know what to think. (Richard plays the role of the exasperated moralist.)

Since every Jack became a gentleman,
There's many a gentle person made a Jack.

QUEEN ELIZABETH
Come, come, we know your meaning, brother Gloucester;
You envy my advancement and my friends'.   75
God grant we never may have need of you!

RICHARD
Meantime, God grants that I have need of you.
Our brother is imprisoned by your means,   78
Myself disgraced, and the nobility
Held in contempt, while great promotions
Are daily given to ennoble those
That scarce some two days since were worth a noble.   82

QUEEN ELIZABETH
By Him that raised me to this careful height   83
From that contented hap which I enjoyed,   84
I never did incense His Majesty
Against the Duke of Clarence, but have been
An earnest advocate to plead for him.
My lord, you do me shameful injury
Falsely to draw me in these vile suspects.   89

RICHARD
You may deny that you were not the mean   90
Of my Lord Hastings' late imprisonment.

RIVERS   She may, my lord, for—

RICHARD
She may, Lord Rivers! Why, who knows not so?
She may do more, sir, than denying that:
She may help you to many fair preferments,   95
And then deny her aiding hand therein,
And lay those honors on your high desert.   97
What may she not? She may, ay, marry, may she—   98

RIVERS   What, marry, may she?

RICHARD
What, marry, may she? Marry with a king,   100
A bachelor, and a handsome stripling too!   101
Iwis your grandam had a worser match.   102

QUEEN ELIZABETH
My lord of Gloucester, I have too long borne
Your blunt upbraidings and your bitter scoffs.
By heaven, I will acquaint His Majesty
Of those gross taunts that oft I have endured.
I had rather be a country servant maid
Than a great queen with this condition,
To be so baited, scorned, and stormèd at.   109

Enter old Queen Margaret [behind].

Small joy have I in being England's queen.

QUEEN MARGARET [*aside*]
And lessened be that small, God I beseech him!
Thy honor, state, and seat is due to me.   112

RICHARD
What? Threat you me with telling of the King?   113
Tell him, and spare not. Look what I have said   114
I will avouch 't in presence of the King.
I dare adventure to be sent to the Tower.   116
'Tis time to speak; my pains are quite forgot.   117

QUEEN MARGARET [*aside*]
Out, devil! I do remember them too well: 118
Thou killed'st my husband Henry in the Tower,
And Edward, my poor son, at Tewkesbury.

RICHARD
Ere you were queen, ay, or your husband king,
I was a packhorse in his great affairs,   122
A weeder-out of his proud adversaries,
A liberal rewarder of his friends.
To royalize his blood I spent mine own.

QUEEN MARGARET [*aside*]
Ay, and much better blood than his or thine.

RICHARD
In all which time you and your husband Grey
Were factious for the house of Lancaster;   128
And, Rivers, so were you. Was not your husband   129
In Margaret's battle at Saint Albans slain?
Let me put in your minds, if you forget,
What you have been ere this, and what you are;
Withal, what I have been, and what I am.   133

QUEEN MARGARET [*aside*]
A murd'rous villain, and so still thou art.

RICHARD
Poor Clarence did forsake his father, Warwick,   135
Ay, and forswore himself—which Jesu pardon!—

QUEEN MARGARET [*aside*]   Which God revenge!

RICHARD
To fight on Edward's party for the crown;
And for his meed, poor lord, he is mewed up.   139
I would to God my heart were flint, like Edward's,
Or Edward's soft and pitiful, like mine.
I am too childish-foolish for this world.

QUEEN MARGARET [*aside*]
Hie thee to hell for shame, and leave this world,   143
Thou cacodemon! There thy kingdom is.   144

RIVERS
My lord of Gloucester, in those busy days
Which here you urge to prove us enemies,   146

75 friends' i.e., kinsmen's.   **78 Our brother** i.e., Clarence   **82 noble** (1) gold coin worth six shillings eight pence (2) nobleman.   **83 careful** full of cares   **84 hap** fortune   **89 in** into.   **suspects** suspicions.   **90 mean** means   **95 preferments** advantages, promotions   **97 lay . . . desert** attribute these high honors to your rich deservings.   **98 marry** i.e., indeed. (A mild oath, literally, "by the Virgin Mary.")   **100 Marry with** Wed. (Punning on *marry*, indeed, in line 98.)   **101 stripling** young man   **102 Iwis** (1) Certainly (2) *I wis,* I know   **109 baited** harassed, as in bearbaiting   **109.1 Queen Margaret** (Historically, the widow of Henry VI was held prisoner in England for five years following the battle of Tewkesbury in 1471 and then was sent to France; see the note to line 167 below.)

112 state degree, high rank.   **seat** throne   **113 Threat** Threaten   **114 Look what** Whatever   **116 adventure to be** risk being   **117 pains** efforts (in King Edward's behalf)   **118 Out** (An exclamation of anger.)   **122 packhorse** workhorse, beast of burden   **128 Were factious for** fought factiously on the side of   **129 husband** (Queen Elizabeth's first husband, Sir John Grey, fell fighting on the Lancastrian side at Saint Albans.)   **133 Withal** in addition   **135 father** i.e., father-in-law. (See *3 Henry VI,* 4.1, when Clarence deserted his brothers to marry Warwick's daughter Isabella and supported the Lancastrian cause for a time; thereafter, he forswore his oath to Warwick by returning to fight on Edward's *party* [line 138] or side.)   **139 meed** reward.   **mewed** caged (like a hawk)   **143 Hie** Hasten   **144 cacodemon** evil spirit.   **146 urge** cite

We followed then our lord, our sovereign king.
So should we you, if you should be our king.

RICHARD
If I should be? I had rather be a peddler.
Far be it from my heart, the thought thereof!

QUEEN ELIZABETH
As little joy, my lord, as you suppose
You should enjoy were you this country's king,
As little joy you may suppose in me
That I enjoy, being the queen thereof.

QUEEN MARGARET [aside]
Ah, little joy enjoys the queen thereof,
For I am she, and altogether joyless.
I can no longer hold me patient.   [Advancing.]
Hear me, you wrangling pirates, that fall out
In sharing that which you have pilled from me!   159
Which of you trembles not that looks on me?
If not, that I am queen, you bow like subjects,   161
Yet that, by you deposed, you quake like rebels?   162
[To Richard] Ah, gentle villain, do not turn away!   163

RICHARD
Foul wrinkled witch, what mak'st thou in my sight?   164

QUEEN MARGARET
But repetition of what thou hast marred;   165
That will I make before I let thee go.   166

RICHARD
Wert thou not banishèd on pain of death?   167

QUEEN MARGARET
I was; but I do find more pain in banishment
Than death can yield me here by my abode.
A husband and a son thou ow'st to me,   170
And thou a kingdom; all of you allegiance.   171
This sorrow that I have by right is yours,
And all the pleasures you usurp are mine.

RICHARD
The curse my noble father laid on thee   174
When thou didst crown his warlike brows with paper
And with thy scorns drew'st rivers from his eyes,
And then, to dry them, gav'st the Duke a clout   177
Steeped in the faultless blood of pretty Rutland—   178
His curses then, from bitterness of soul
Denounced against thee, are all fall'n upon thee;   180
And God, not we, hath plagued thy bloody deed.

QUEEN ELIZABETH
So just is God, to right the innocent.

HASTINGS
Oh, 'twas the foulest deed to slay that babe,   183
And the most merciless, that e'er was heard of!

RIVERS
Tyrants themselves wept when it was reported.   185

DORSET
No man but prophesied revenge for it.   186

BUCKINGHAM
Northumberland, then present, wept to see it.

QUEEN MARGARET
What? Were you snarling all before I came,
Ready to catch each other by the throat,
And turn you all your hatred now on me?
Did York's dread curse prevail so much with heaven
That Henry's death, my lovely Edward's death,
Their kingdom's loss, my woeful banishment,
Should all but answer for that peevish brat?   194
Can curses pierce the clouds and enter heaven?
Why, then, give way, dull clouds, to my quick curses! 196
Though not by war, by surfeit die your king,   197
As ours by murder, to make him a king!
Edward thy son, that now is Prince of Wales,
For Edward our son, that was Prince of Wales,
Die in his youth by like untimely violence!
Thyself a queen, for me that was a queen,
Outlive thy glory, like my wretched self!
Long mayst thou live to wail thy children's death
And see another, as I see thee now,
Decked in thy rights, as thou art stalled in mine!   206
Long die thy happy days before thy death,
And, after many lengthened hours of grief,
Die neither mother, wife, nor England's queen!
Rivers and Dorset, you were standers-by,   210
And so wast thou, Lord Hastings, when my son   211
Was stabbed with bloody daggers: God, I pray him,
That none of you may live his natural age,   213
But by some unlooked accident cut off!   214

RICHARD
Have done thy charm, thou hateful withered hag!   215

QUEEN MARGARET
And leave out thee? Stay, dog, for thou shalt hear me.
If heaven have any grievous plague in store
Exceeding those that I can wish upon thee,
Oh, let them keep it till thy sins be ripe,   219
And then hurl down their indignation
On thee, the troubler of the poor world's peace!
The worm of conscience still begnaw thy soul!   222
Thy friends suspect for traitors while thou liv'st,
And take deep traitors for thy dearest friends!
No sleep close up that deadly eye of thine,
Unless it be while some tormenting dream
Affrights thee with a hell of ugly devils!
Thou elvish-marked, abortive, rooting hog,   228

---

159 **pilled** pillaged, robbed   161–2 **If . . . rebels** i.e., Even if you do
not bow low to me as your queen, you quake as rebels who have
deposed me.   163 **gentle** nobly born. *Gentle villain* is an oxymoron,
since *villain* can mean "one ignobly born."   164 **mak'st thou** are you
doing   165 **But . . . marred** Only reciting your crimes   166 **That** that
repetition or recital   167 **banishèd** (Margaret was banished in 1464,
returned to England in 1471, and after the Battle of Tewkesbury was
confined in the Tower until 1476, when she returned to France, dying
there in 1482, one year before the historical time of this scene.)
170 **thou** i.e., Richard   171 **thou** i.e., Elizabeth   174 **The curse** (See *3
Henry VI*, 1.4.164–6.)   177 **clout** cloth, handkerchief   178 **faultless**
innocent   180 **Denounced** proclaimed vengefully   183 **that babe**
i.e., Rutland (who historically was an older brother of Richard)

185 **Tyrants** Even pitiless men   186 **No . . . prophesied** There was no
one who did not prophesy   194 **but answer for** merely atone for,
equal.   **peevish** silly, senseless   196 **quick** lively, piercing
197 **surfeit** dissipated living   206 **Decked** dressed.   **stalled** installed
210–11 **Rivers, Dorset, Hastings** (Not present in Shakespeare's
dramatization of the event in *3 Henry VI*, 5.5, but named in the chronicles as having been present.)   213 **natural age** full course of life
214 **unlooked** unexpected   215 **charm** magic curse, pronounced by a
witch   219 **them** i.e., the heavens, heaven   222 **still begnaw** continually gnaw   228 **elvish-marked** marked by elves at birth.   **hog**
(Alludes to Richard's badge, the wild boar.)

Thou that wast sealed in thy nativity   229
The slave of nature and the son of hell!   230
Thou slander of thy heavy mother's womb,   231
Thou loathèd issue of thy father's loins,
Thou rag of honor, thou detested—   233

RICHARD
Margaret.

QUEEN MARGARET   Richard!

RICHARD   Ha?

QUEEN MARGARET   I call thee not.

RICHARD
I cry thee mercy then, for I did think   235
That thou hadst called me all these bitter names.

QUEEN MARGARET
Why, so I did, but looked for no reply.
Oh, let me make the period to my curse!   238

RICHARD
'Tis done by me, and ends in "Margaret."

QUEEN ELIZABETH [to Queen Margaret]
Thus have you breathed your curse against yourself.

QUEEN MARGARET
Poor painted queen, vain flourish of my fortune!   241
Why strew'st thou sugar on that bottled spider,   242
Whose deadly web ensnareth thee about?
Fool, fool, thou whet'st a knife to kill thyself.
The day will come that thou shalt wish for me
To help thee curse this poisonous bunch-backed toad. 246

HASTINGS
False-boding woman, end thy frantic curse,   247
Lest to thy harm thou move our patience.

QUEEN MARGARET
Foul shame upon you! You have all moved mine.

RIVERS
Were you well served, you would be taught your duty. 250

QUEEN MARGARET
To serve me well, you all should do me duty,   251
Teach me to be your queen, and you my subjects.   252
Oh, serve me well, and teach yourselves that duty!

DORSET
Dispute not with her. She is lunatic.

QUEEN MARGARET
Peace, Master Marquess, you are malapert.   255
Your fire-new stamp of honor is scarce current.   256
Oh, that your young nobility could judge
What 'twere to lose it and be miserable!
They that stand high have many blasts to shake them, 259
And if they fall, they dash themselves to pieces.

RICHARD
Good counsel, marry! Learn it, learn it, Marquess.

DORSET
It touches you, my lord, as much as me.

RICHARD
Ay, and much more; but I was born so high.   263
Our aerie buildeth in the cedar's top,   264
And dallies with the wind and scorns the sun.

QUEEN MARGARET
And turns the sun to shade; alas, alas!   266
Witness my son, now in the shade of death,
Whose bright outshining beams thy cloudy wrath
Hath in eternal darkness folded up.
Your aerie buildeth in our aerie's nest.
O God, that see'st it, do not suffer it!
As it is won with blood, lost be it so!

BUCKINGHAM
Peace, peace, for shame, if not for charity!

QUEEN MARGARET
Urge neither charity nor shame to me.
                                        [Turning to the others.]
Uncharitably with me have you dealt,
And shamefully my hopes by you are butchered.
My charity is outrage, life my shame,   277
And in that shame still live my sorrow's rage!

BUCKINGHAM   Have done, have done.

QUEEN MARGARET
O princely Buckingham, I'll kiss thy hand
In sign of league and amity with thee.
Now fair befall thee and thy noble house!   282
Thy garments are not spotted with our blood,
Nor thou within the compass of my curse.   284

BUCKINGHAM
Nor no one here; for curses never pass   285
The lips of those that breathe them in the air.

QUEEN MARGARET
I will not think but they ascend the sky   287
And there awake God's gentle-sleeping peace.
O Buckingham, take heed of yonder dog!
Look when he fawns, he bites; and when he bites, 290
His venom tooth will rankle to the death.   291
Have not to do with him, beware of him;
Sin, death, and hell have set their marks on him,
And all their ministers attend on him.

RICHARD
What doth she say, my lord of Buckingham?

BUCKINGHAM
Nothing that I respect, my gracious lord.   296

QUEEN MARGARET
What, dost thou scorn me for my gentle counsel?

---

229 **sealed** stamped   230 **slave of nature** i.e., wretch made by the malignancy of nature (as seen in his deformity)   231 **heavy** (1) sorrowful (2) weighted down in pregnancy   233 **rag** tattered remnant   235 **cry thee mercy** beg your pardon. (Said sarcastically.)   238 **period** conclusion   241 **painted** counterfeit. **vain ... fortune** i.e., mere ornament of a position that is mine by right.   242 **bottled** bottle-shaped, swollen   246 **bunch-backed** hunch-backed   247 **False-boding** Falsely prophesying   250 **well served** treated as you deserve. (But Margaret turns the phrase around to mean "served as befitting one of royal rank.")   **your duty** your place (i.e., to be obedient).   251 **duty** reverence   252 **Teach me** i.e., show by your obedience what is my role   255 **Master** (A title for a boy of good family, used insultingly here.)   **malapert** impudent.   256 **fire-new** newly coined.   **current** genuine as legal tender.   259 **blasts** strong gusts of wind

263 **born so high** i.e., born noble—unlike you.   264 **aerie** eagle's brood   266 **sun** (With a play on *son* in the next line.)   277 **My ... shame** i.e., Instead of charity I receive outrage, and the only life given me is one of shame; or, outrage is all the charity I feel, and shame is my only life   282 **fair befall** good luck to   284 **compass** scope, boundary   285 **pass** get any further than   287 **I ... but** I must believe that   290 **Look when** (1) Whenever (2) Expect that when   291 **venom** envenomed.   **rankle** cause a festering wound   296 **respect** heed

And soothe the devil that I warn thee from?   298
Oh, but remember this another day,
When he shall split thy very heart with sorrow,
And say poor Margaret was a prophetess!
Live each of you the subjects to his hate,   302
And he to yours, and all of you to God's!   *Exit.*

BUCKINGHAM
My hair doth stand on end to hear her curses.

RIVERS
And so doth mine. I muse why she's at liberty.   305

RICHARD
I cannot blame her. By God's holy mother,
She hath had too much wrong, and I repent
My part thereof that I have done to her.

QUEEN ELIZABETH
I never did her any, to my knowledge.

RICHARD
Yet you have all the vantage of her wrong.   310
I was too hot to do somebody good   311
That is too cold in thinking of it now.   312
Marry, as for Clarence, he is well repaid;
He is franked up to fatting for his pains—   314
God pardon them that are the cause thereof!

RIVERS
A virtuous and a Christian-like conclusion,
To pray for them that have done scathe to us.   317

RICHARD
So do I ever—(*speaks to himself*) being well advised.   318
For had I cursed now, I had cursed myself.

Enter Catesby.

CATESBY
Madam, His Majesty doth call for you,
And for Your Grace, and yours, my gracious lord.

QUEEN ELIZABETH
Catesby, I come.—Lords, will you go with me?

RIVERS
We wait upon Your Grace.   323
            Exeunt all but [Richard Duke of] Gloucester.

RICHARD
I do the wrong, and first begin to brawl.
The secret mischiefs that I set abroach   325
I lay unto the grievous charge of others.   326
Clarence, who I indeed have cast in darkness,
I do beweep to many simple gulls—   328
Namely, to Derby, Hastings, Buckingham—
And tell them 'tis the Queen and her allies
That stir the King against the Duke my brother.
Now they believe it, and withal whet me   332
To be revenged on Rivers, Dorset, Grey.
But then I sigh and, with a piece of Scripture,

Tell them that God bids us do good for evil.   335
And thus I clothe my naked villainy
With odd old ends stol'n forth of Holy Writ,   337
And seem a saint when most I play the devil.

Enter two Murderers.

But soft! Here come my executioners.—   339
How now, my hardy, stout, resolvèd mates,   340
Are you now going to dispatch this thing?

FIRST MURDERER
We are, my lord, and come to have the warrant
That we may be admitted where he is.

RICHARD
Well thought upon. I have it here about me.
                                [He gives the warrant.]
When you have done, repair to Crosby Place.   345
But sirs, be sudden in the execution,
Withal obdurate; do not hear him plead;   347
For Clarence is well-spoken, and perhaps
May move your hearts to pity if you mark him.   349

FIRST MURDERER
Tut, tut, my lord, we will not stand to prate;   350
Talkers are no good doers. Be assured
We go to use our hands and not our tongues.

RICHARD
Your eyes drop millstones when fools' eyes fall tears.   353
I like you, lads. About your business straight.
Go, go, dispatch.

FIRST MURDERER   We will, my noble lord.   *[Exeunt.]*

❖

1.4

Enter Clarence and Keeper.

KEEPER
Why looks Your Grace so heavily today?   1

CLARENCE
Oh, I have passed a miserable night,
So full of fearful dreams, of ugly sights,
That, as I am a Christian faithful man,
I would not spend another such a night
Though 'twere to buy a world of happy days,
So full of dismal terror was the time!

KEEPER
What was your dream, my lord? I pray you, tell me.

CLARENCE
Methoughts that I had broken from the Tower   9
And was embarked to cross to Burgundy,   10
And in my company my brother Gloucester,
Who from my cabin tempted me to walk

---

298 soothe flatter   **302 the subjects to** subjugated to   **305 muse**
wonder   **310 vantage of her wrong** benefits derived from the
wrongs she has suffered.   **311 too hot . . . good** i.e., too eager in
helping Edward to the throne   **312 That . . . cold** who is too ungrateful   **314 franked . . . fatting** shut up in a frank or sty to be fattened
for slaughter   **317 scathe** harm   **318 well advised** cautious.
323 wait upon attend   **325 set abroach** set flowing   **326 lay . . . of**
impute as a serious accusation against   **328 gulls** credulous persons
332 withal furthermore.   **whet** urge, incite

335 for in return for   **337 ends** fragments, tags   **339 soft** gently; wait
a minute.   **340 stout . . . mates** bold, resolute fellows   **345 repair**
betake yourselves   **347 Withal** at the same time   **349 mark** pay
attention to   **350 prate** prattle   **353 millstones** heavy stone disks
used for grinding. (To *drop millstones* was proverbially to show signs
of hardheartedness.)   **fall** let fall
1.4. Location: London. The Tower.
1 heavily sad   **9 Methoughts** It seemed to me   **10 Burgundy**
(Clarence and Richard, according to the chronicles, had been sent to
Burgundy for protection following their father's death.)

Upon the hatches. Thence we looked toward England 13
And cited up a thousand heavy times, 14
During the wars of York and Lancaster,
That had befall'n us. As we paced along
Upon the giddy footing of the hatches, 17
Methought that Gloucester stumbled, and in falling
Struck me, that thought to stay him, overboard 19
Into the tumbling billows of the main. 20
Oh, Lord, methought what pain it was to drown!
What dreadful noise of waters in my ears!
What sights of ugly death within my eyes!
Methought I saw a thousand fearful wracks; 24
Ten thousand men that fishes gnawed upon;
Wedges of gold, great anchors, heaps of pearl, 26
Inestimable stones, unvalued jewels, 27
All scattered in the bottom of the sea.
Some lay in dead men's skulls, and in the holes
Where eyes did once inhabit there were crept,
As 'twere in scorn of eyes, reflecting gems,
That wooed the slimy bottom of the deep 32
And mocked the dead bones that lay scattered by.

KEEPER
Had you such leisure in the time of death
To gaze upon these secrets of the deep?

CLARENCE
Methought I had, and often did I strive
To yield the ghost; but still the envious flood 37
Stopped in my soul and would not let it forth 38
To seek the empty, vast, and wand'ring air,
But smothered it within my panting bulk, 40
Which almost burst to belch it in the sea.

KEEPER
Awaked you not in this sore agony?

CLARENCE
No, no, my dream was lengthened after life.
Oh, then began the tempest to my soul!
I passed, methought, the melancholy flood, 45
With that sour ferryman which poets write of, 46
Unto the kingdom of perpetual night.
The first that there did greet my stranger soul 48
Was my great father-in-law, renownèd Warwick,
Who spake aloud, "What scourge for perjury
Can this dark monarchy afford false Clarence?"
And so he vanished. Then came wand'ring by
A shadow like an angel, with bright hair 53
Dabbled in blood, and he shrieked out aloud,
"Clarence is come—false, fleeting, perjured Clarence, 55
That stabbed me in the field by Tewkesbury.
Seize on him, Furies, take him unto torment!"
With that, methought, a legion of foul fiends

Environed me and howlèd in mine ears
Such hideous cries that with the very noise
I trembling waked, and for a season after 61
Could not believe but that I was in hell,
Such terrible impression made my dream.

KEEPER
No marvel, my lord, though it affrighted you.
I am afraid, methinks, to hear you tell it.

CLARENCE
Ah, keeper, keeper, I have done these things,
That now give evidence against my soul,
For Edward's sake, and see how he requites me! 68
O God! If my deep prayers cannot appease thee,
But thou wilt be avenged on my misdeeds,
Yet execute thy wrath in me alone!
Oh, spare my guiltless wife and my poor children!
Keeper, I prithee, sit by me awhile.
My soul is heavy, and I fain would sleep. 74

KEEPER
I will, my lord. God give Your Grace good rest!

                     [*Clarence sleeps.*]

      Enter Brackenbury, the Lieutenant.

BRACKENBURY
Sorrow breaks seasons and reposing hours, 76
Makes the night morning and the noontide night.
Princes have but their titles for their glories,
An outward honor for an inward toil,
And, for unfelt imaginations, 80
They often feel a world of restless cares;
So that between their titles and low name 82
There's nothing differs but the outward fame. 83

        Enter two Murderers.

FIRST MURDERER Ho! Who's here?

BRACKENBURY
What would'st thou, fellow, and how cam'st thou hither?

SECOND MURDERER I would speak with Clarence, and I
came hither on my legs.

BRACKENBURY What, so brief?

FIRST MURDERER 'Tis better, sir, than to be tedious.—
Let him see our commission, and talk no more.

                [*Brackenbury*] *reads* [*it*].

BRACKENBURY
I am in this commanded to deliver
The noble Duke of Clarence to your hands.
I will not reason what is meant hereby,
Because I will be guiltless from the meaning. 94
There lies the Duke asleep, and there the keys.

                    [*He gives keys.*]

I'll to the King and signify to him
That thus I have resigned to you my charge.

---

13 **hatches** movable planks forming a deck. 14 **cited up** recalled.
heavy difficult 17 **giddy** unsteady 19 **stay** hold, steady 20 **main**
ocean. 24 **wracks** shipwrecked vessels 26 **Wedges** ingots
27 **Inestimable** precious and innumerable. **unvalued** priceless
32 **wooed** (These lifeless eyes have nothing to flirt with but the
murky depths.) 37 **envious flood** malicious water 38 **Stopped**
held 40 **bulk** body 45 **melancholy flood** i.e., River Styx 46 **ferryman** i.e., Charon, who ferried souls to Hades, *the kingdom of perpetual
night* (line 47) 48 **stranger** i.e., newly arrived 53 **shadow** i.e., ghost of
Edward, Prince of Wales, son of Henry VI 55 **fleeting** fickle, deceitful

61 **season** time 68 **requites** repays 74 **fain** willingly 76 **breaks . . .
hours** disrupts the normal rhythms of life and hours properly devoted to sleep 80 **for unfelt imaginations** in return for glories that are
merely illusory 82 **low name** i.e., the lowly position of ordinary
men 83 **fame** reputation. 94 **will be** wish to be

FIRST MURDERER   You may, sir; 'tis a point of wisdom.
Fare you well.   *Exit [Brackenbury with Keeper].*

SECOND MURDERER   What, shall I stab him as he
sleeps?

FIRST MURDERER   No. He'll say 'twas done cowardly,
when he wakes.

SECOND MURDERER   Why, he shall never wake until the
great Judgment Day.

FIRST MURDERER   Why, then he'll say we stabbed him
sleeping.

SECOND MURDERER   The urging of that word "judgment" hath bred a kind of remorse in me.

FIRST MURDERER   What, art thou afraid?

SECOND MURDERER   Not to kill him, having a warrant,
but to be damned for killing him, from the which no
warrant can defend me.

FIRST MURDERER   I thought thou hadst been resolute.

SECOND MURDERER   So I am—to let him live.

FIRST MURDERER   I'll back to the Duke of Gloucester
and tell him so.

SECOND MURDERER   Nay, I prithee, stay a little. I hope
this passionate humor of mine will change. It was 119
wont to hold me but while one tells twenty.   120

FIRST MURDERER   How dost thou feel thyself now?

SECOND MURDERER   Faith, some certain dregs of conscience are yet within me.

FIRST MURDERER   Remember our reward when the
deed 's done.

SECOND MURDERER   Zounds, he dies! I had forgot the 126
reward.

FIRST MURDERER   Where's thy conscience now?

SECOND MURDERER   Oh, in the Duke of Gloucester's
purse.

FIRST MURDERER   When he opens his purse to give us
our reward, thy conscience flies out.

SECOND MURDERER   'Tis no matter; let it go. There's few
or none will entertain it.   134

FIRST MURDERER   What if it come to thee again?

SECOND MURDERER   I'll not meddle with it; it makes a
man a coward. A man cannot steal but it accuseth him;
a man cannot swear but it checks him; a man cannot 138
lie with his neighbor's wife but it detects him. 'Tis a
blushing, shamefaced spirit that mutinies in a man's
bosom. It fills a man full of obstacles. It made me once
restore a purse of gold that by chance I found. It
beggars any man that keeps it. It is turned out of
towns and cities for a dangerous thing, and every man
that means to live well endeavors to trust to himself
and live without it.

FIRST MURDERER   Zounds, 'tis even now at my elbow,
persuading me not to kill the Duke.

SECOND MURDERER   Take the devil in thy mind, and 149
believe him not. He would insinuate with thee but to 150
make thee sigh.   151

FIRST MURDERER   Tut, I am strong-framed; he cannot
prevail with me.

SECOND MURDERER   Spoke like a tall man that respects 154
thy reputation. Come, shall we fall to work?

FIRST MURDERER   Take him on the costard with the hilts 156
of thy sword, and then throw him into the malmsey 157
butt in the next room.   158

SECOND MURDERER   Oh, excellent device! And make a sop 159
of him.

FIRST MURDERER   Soft, he wakes.

SECOND MURDERER   Strike!

FIRST MURDERER   No, we'll reason with him.   163

CLARENCE *[waking]*
Where art thou, keeper? Give me a cup of wine.

SECOND MURDERER
You shall have wine enough, my lord, anon.

CLARENCE   In God's name, what art thou?

FIRST MURDERER   A man, as you are.

CLARENCE   But not, as I am, royal.

FIRST MURDERER   Nor you, as we are, loyal.

CLARENCE
Thy voice is thunder, but thy looks are humble.

FIRST MURDERER
My voice is now the King's, my looks mine own.

CLARENCE
How darkly and how deadly dost thou speak!   172
Your eyes do menace me. Why look you pale?
Who sent you hither? Wherefore do you come?

SECOND MURDERER   To, to, to—

CLARENCE   To murder me?

BOTH   Ay, ay.

CLARENCE
You scarcely have the hearts to tell me so,
And therefore cannot have the hearts to do it.
Wherein, my friends, have I offended you?

FIRST MURDERER
Offended us you have not, but the King.

CLARENCE
I shall be reconciled to him again.

SECOND MURDERER
Never, my lord; therefore prepare to die.

CLARENCE
Are you drawn forth among a world of men   184
To slay the innocent? What is my offense?
Where is the evidence that doth accuse me?
What lawful quest have given their verdict up   187
Unto the frowning judge? Or who pronounced
The bitter sentence of poor Clarence' death
Before I be convict by course of law?   190
To threaten me with death is most unlawful.
I charge you, as you hope to have redemption
By Christ's dear blood shed for our grievous sins,
That you depart and lay no hands on me.
The deed you undertake is damnable.

---

119 **passionate humor** compassionate mood   120 **wont** accustomed.
tells counts   126 **Zounds** i.e., By God's (Christ's) wounds   134 **entertain it** receive it, give it welcome.   138 **checks** reproves, stops
149–50 **Take . . . not** i.e., Listen to the devil and pay no heed to conscience.
150–1 **He . . . sigh** Your conscience would ingratiate itself with you merely
for the purpose of making you unhappy.

154 **tall** brave   156 **Take** Strike.   **costard** head. (Literally, a kind of
apple.)   157–8 **malmsey butt** wine barrel. (Malmsey is a sweet wine.)
159 **sop** bread or cake soaked in wine   163 **reason** talk   172 **darkly**
ominously   184 **drawn . . . men** especially selected from the whole
human race   187 **quest** inquest, i.e., jury   190 **convict** convicted

FIRST MURDERER
What we will do, we do upon command.

SECOND MURDERER
And he that hath commanded is our king.

CLARENCE
Erroneous vassals! The great King of kings   198
Hath in the table of His law commanded   199
That thou shalt do no murder. Will you then
Spurn at His edict and fulfill a man's?
Take heed; for He holds vengeance in His hand
To hurl upon their heads that break His law.

SECOND MURDERER
And that same vengeance doth He hurl on thee
For false forswearing and for murder, too.
Thou didst receive the Sacrament to fight   206
In quarrel of the house of Lancaster.

FIRST MURDERER
And, like a traitor to the name of God,
Didst break that vow, and with thy treacherous blade
Unripped'st the bowels of thy sovereign's son.   210

SECOND MURDERER
Whom thou wast sworn to cherish and defend.

FIRST MURDERER
How canst thou urge God's dreadful law to us
When thou hast broke it in such dear degree?   213

CLARENCE
Alas! For whose sake did I that ill deed?
For Edward, for my brother, for his sake.
He sends you not to murder me for this,
For in that sin he is as deep as I.
If God will be avengèd for the deed,
Oh, know you yet he doth it publicly!
Take not the quarrel from His powerful arm.
He needs no indirect or lawless course
To cut off those that have offended Him.

FIRST MURDERER
Who made thee, then, a bloody minister   223
When gallant-springing brave Plantagenet,   224
That princely novice, was struck dead by thee?   225

CLARENCE
My brother's love, the devil, and my rage.   226

FIRST MURDERER
Thy brother's love, our duty, and thy faults
Provoke us hither now to slaughter thee.

CLARENCE
If you do love my brother, hate not me!
I am his brother, and I love him well.
If you are hired for meed, go back again,   231
And I will send you to my brother Gloucester,
Who shall reward you better for my life
Than Edward will for tidings of my death.

SECOND MURDERER
You are deceived. Your brother Gloucester hates you.

CLARENCE
Oh, no, he loves me, and he holds me dear.
Go you to him from me.

FIRST MURDERER   Ay, so we will.

CLARENCE
Tell him, when that our princely father York
Blessed his three sons with his victorious arm
And charged us from his soul to love each other,
He little thought of this divided friendship.
Bid Gloucester think of this, and he will weep.

FIRST MURDERER
Ay, millstones, as he lessoned us to weep.   243

CLARENCE
Oh, do not slander him, for he is kind.

FIRST MURDERER
Right, as snow in harvest. Come, you deceive
  yourself.   245
'Tis he that sends us to destroy you here.

CLARENCE
It cannot be, for he bewept my fortune,
And hugged me in his arms, and swore with sobs
That he would labor my delivery.   249

FIRST MURDERER
Why, so he doth, when he delivers you
From this earth's thralldom to the joys of heaven.   251

SECOND MURDERER
Make peace with God, for you must die, my lord.

CLARENCE
Have you that holy feeling in your souls
To counsel me to make my peace with God,
And are you yet to your own souls so blind
That you will war with God by murd'ring me?
Oh, sirs, consider, they that set you on
To do this deed will hate you for the deed.

SECOND MURDERER [to First Murderer]
What shall we do?

CLARENCE   Relent, and save your souls.
Which of you, if you were a prince's son,
Being pent from liberty, as I am now,   261
If two such murderers as yourselves came to you,
Would not entreat for life?

FIRST MURDERER
Relent? No. 'Tis cowardly and womanish.

CLARENCE
Not to relent is beastly, savage, devilish.
[To Second Murderer] My friend, I spy some pity in thy looks..
Oh, if thine eye be not a flatterer,
Come thou on my side, and entreat for me,
As you would beg, were you in my distress.
A begging prince what beggar pities not?

SECOND MURDERER   Look behind you, my lord.

---

198 **Erroneous vassals!** Sinful and mistaken wretches! 199 **table**
tablet (the Ten Commandments) 206 **receive the Sacrament** i.e.,
swear upon the Sacrament 210 **sovereign's son** i.e., Prince Edward,
son of Henry VI. 213 **dear** grievous, costly 223 **minister** agent of
God 224 **gallant-springing** i.e., gallant and sprightly, aspiring.
Plantagenet i.e., the Lancastrian Prince Edward, killed in *3 Henry VI*,
5.5. (See the note at 1.2.145 on Edward's claim to this name.)
225 **novice** youth 226 **My brother's love** i.e., My love for my brother
231 **meed** financial reward

243 **lessoned** taught 245 **Right . . . harvest** i.e., He's just as kind and
natural—that is, both affectionate and with the natural feelings of a
brother—as is snow at harvest time. 249 **labor my delivery** work for
my release. 251 **thralldom** bondage, captivity 261 **pent** shut up

FIRST MURDERER
Take that, and that! (*Stabs him.*) If all this will not do,
I'll drown you in the malmsey butt within.
                                      Exit [*with the body*].

SECOND MURDERER
A bloody deed, and desperately dispatched!
How fain, like Pilate, would I wash my hands   275
Of this most grievous murder!

    Enter First Murderer.

FIRST MURDERER
How now? What mean'st thou that thou help'st me not?
By heaven, the Duke shall know how slack you
    have been.

SECOND MURDERER
I would he knew that I had saved his brother!
Take thou the fee, and tell him what I say,
For I repent me that the Duke is slain.   *Exit.*

FIRST MURDERER
So do not I. Go, coward as thou art.—
Well, I'll go hide his body in some hole
Till that the Duke give order for his burial;
And when I have my meed, I will away,
For this will out, and then I must not stay.   *Exit.* 286

    ❖

2.1

    Flourish. Enter the King [*Edward*], *sick, the*
    Queen [*Elizabeth*], *Lord Marquess Dorset,* [*Grey,*]
    Rivers, Hastings, Catesby, Buckingham, [*and*
    others].

KING EDWARD
Why, so. Now have I done a good day's work.
You peers, continue this united league.
I every day expect an embassage
From my Redeemer to redeem me hence;
And more in peace my soul shall part to heaven,
Since I have made my friends at peace on earth.
Rivers and Hastings, take each other's hand;
Dissemble not your hatred, swear your love.   8

RIVERS [*taking Hastings' hand*]
By heaven, my soul is purged from grudging hate,
And with my hand I seal my true heart's love.

HASTINGS
So thrive I, as I truly swear the like!

KING EDWARD
Take heed you dally not before your king,   12
Lest he that is the supreme King of kings
Confound your hidden falsehood, and award   14
Either of you to be the other's end.   15

HASTINGS
So prosper I, as I swear perfect love!

RIVERS
And I, as I love Hastings with my heart!

KING EDWARD
Madam, yourself is not exempt from this,
Nor you, son Dorset, Buckingham, nor you;   19
You have been factious one against the other.   20
Wife, love Lord Hastings; let him kiss your hand;
And what you do, do it unfeignedly.

QUEEN ELIZABETH
There, Hastings, I will never more remember
Our former hatred, so thrive I and mine!   24
    [*Hastings kisses her hand.*]

KING EDWARD
Dorset, embrace him. Hastings, love Lord Marquess.

DORSET
This interchange of love, I here protest,   26
Upon my part shall be inviolable.

HASTINGS   And so swear I.   [*They embrace.*]

KING EDWARD
Now, princely Buckingham, seal thou this league
With thy embracements to my wife's allies,
And make me happy in your unity.

BUCKINGHAM [*to the Queen*]
Whenever Buckingham doth turn his hate
Upon Your Grace, but with all duteous love   33
Doth cherish you and yours, God punish me
With hate in those where I expect most love!
When I have most need to employ a friend,
And most assurèd that he is a friend,
Deep, hollow, treacherous, and full of guile   38
Be he unto me! This do I beg of God,
When I am cold in love to you or yours.
    [*They*] *embrace.*

KING EDWARD
A pleasing cordial, princely Buckingham,   41
Is this thy vow unto my sickly heart.
There wanteth now our brother Gloucester here   43
To make the blessèd period of this peace.   44

BUCKINGHAM   And, in good time,
Here comes Sir Richard Ratcliffe and the Duke.

    Enter Ratcliffe and [*Richard Duke of*] *Gloucester.*

RICHARD
Good morrow to my sovereign king and queen;
And, princely peers, a happy time of day!

KING EDWARD
Happy, indeed, as we have spent the day.
Gloucester, we have done deeds of charity,
Made peace of enmity, fair love of hate,
Between these swelling wrong-incensèd peers.   52

---

275 fain gladly. **Pilate** The Roman governor of Judaea who ordered the crucifixion of Jesus at the behest of the chief priests but symbolically washed his hands of the business (Matthew 27:24). **286 this will out** ("Murder will out" was a proverbial saying.)
2.1. Location: London. The royal court.
0.1 *Flourish* Trumpet call to announce the arrival of a distinguished person. **8 Dissemble** conceal, disguise (under a false appearance of love) **12 dally** trifle **14 Confound** defeat **15 Either . . . end** each of you to be the agent of death of the other.

19 son stepson **20 factious** quarrelsome **24 mine** my family and children. **26 protest** declare **33 but** and does not **38 Deep** subtle, crafty **41 cordial** restorative **43 wanteth** is lacking **44 period** conclusion **52 swelling** i.e., with anger or rivalry

RICHARD
A blessèd labor, my most sovereign lord.
Among this princely heap, if any here,   54
By false intelligence, or wrong surmise,   55
Hold me a foe;
If I unwittingly, or in my rage,
Have aught committed that is hardly borne   58
By any in this presence, I desire
To reconcile me to his friendly peace.
'Tis death to me to be at enmity;
I hate it, and desire all good men's love.
First, madam, I entreat true peace of you,
Which I will purchase with my duteous service;
Of you, my noble cousin Buckingham,
If ever any grudge were lodged between us;
Of you and you, Lord Rivers, and of Dorset,
That all without desert have frowned on me;   68
Dukes, earls, lords, gentlemen—indeed, of all.
I do not know that Englishman alive
With whom my soul is any jot at odds
More than the infant that is born tonight.   72
I thank my God for my humility.

QUEEN ELIZABETH
A holy day shall this be kept hereafter.
I would to God all strifes were well compounded.   75
My sovereign lord, I do beseech Your Highness
To take our brother Clarence to your grace.

RICHARD
Why, madam, have I offered love for this,
To be so flouted in this royal presence?   79
Who knows not that the gentle Duke is dead?   80
                                          They all start.
You do him injury to scorn his corpse.

KING EDWARD
Who knows not he is dead? Who knows he is?

QUEEN ELIZABETH
All-seeing heaven, what a world is this!

BUCKINGHAM
Look I so pale, Lord Dorset, as the rest?

DORSET
Ay, my good lord, and no man in the presence   85
But his red color hath forsook his cheeks.

KING EDWARD
Is Clarence dead? The order was reversed.

RICHARD
But he, poor man, by your first order died,
And that a wingèd Mercury did bear;   89
Some tardy cripple bare the countermand,   90
That came too lag to see him buried.   91

God grant that some, less noble and less loyal,   92
Nearer in bloody thoughts but not in blood,   93
Deserve not worse than wretched Clarence did,   94
And yet go current from suspicion!   95

          Enter [Lord Stanley] Earl of Derby.

STANLEY [*kneeling*]
A boon, my sovereign, for my service done!   96

KING EDWARD
I prithee, peace. My soul is full of sorrow.

STANLEY
I will not rise unless Your Highness hear me.

KING EDWARD
Then say at once what is it thou requests.

STANLEY
The forfeit, sovereign, of my servant's life,   100
Who slew today a riotous gentleman
Lately attendant on the Duke of Norfolk.

KING EDWARD
Have I a tongue to doom my brother's death,   103
And shall that tongue give pardon to a slave?   104
My brother killed no man; his fault was thought,
And yet his punishment was bitter death.
Who sued to me for him? Who, in my wrath,
Kneeled at my feet, and bid me be advised?   108
Who spoke of brotherhood? Who spoke of love?
Who told me how the poor soul did forsake
The mighty Warwick and did fight for me?
Who told me, in the field at Tewkesbury,
When Oxford had me down, he rescued me   113
And said, "Dear brother, live, and be a king"?
Who told me, when we both lay in the field
Frozen almost to death, how he did lap me   116
Even in his garments, and did give himself,
All thin and naked, to the numb-cold night?   118
All this from my remembrance brutish wrath
Sinfully plucked, and not a man of you
Had so much grace to put it in my mind.
But when your carters or your waiting vassals   122
Have done a drunken slaughter and defaced   123
The precious image of our dear Redeemer,   124
You straight are on your knees for pardon, pardon;   125
And I, unjustly too, must grant it you.
                                          [*Stanley rises.*]
But for my brother not a man would speak,
Nor I, ungracious, speak unto myself
For him, poor soul. The proudest of you all
Have been beholding to him in his life;   130

92–5 God . . . suspicion! i.e., (ironically) Pray God there be not persons who deserve worse than Clarence got, persons less noble or related by blood to the King than he, although closely involved in bloody plots, who yet go undetected! (Richard means the Queen and her kindred.) **95 go current** are accepted at face value (like legal currency).   **from** free from   **96 A boon** (I crave) a favor   **100 The forfeit** i.e., The remission of the forfeit   **103 doom** decree   **104 slave** servant, wretch. **108 advised** cautious.   **113 Oxford** (See *3 Henry VI*, 5.5.2; this episode has no historical basis.)   **116 lap** wrap   **118 thin** thinly clad   **122 your carters . . . vassals** your cart drivers or your attendants   **123–4 defaced . . . Redeemer** i.e., killed a man. (God made humanity in his own image; Genesis 1:27.)   **125 straight** at once   **130 beholding** beholden

54 heap assembly   **55 false intelligence** being misinformed **58 hardly borne** taken amiss, deeply resented   **68 all without desert** wholly without my having deserved it   **72 More than the infant** i.e., more than is that infant's soul   **75 compounded** settled.   **79 flouted** mocked   **80 gentle** noble   **85 presence** i.e., royal presence   **89 Mercury** messenger of the classical gods   **90 tardy cripple** (Richard privately shares with the audience a jest on his own role in this.)   **bare** bore   **91 lag** late

Yet none of you would once beg for his life.
O God, I fear thy justice will take hold
On me and you, and mine and yours, for this!
Come, Hastings, help me to my closet. Ah, poor Clarence! 134
                    Exeunt some with King and Queen.

RICHARD
This is the fruits of rashness. Marked you not
How that the guilty kindred of the Queen
Looked pale when they did hear of Clarence' death?
Oh, they did urge it still unto the King.   138
God will revenge it. Come, lords, will you go
To comfort Edward with our company?
BUCKINGHAM   We wait upon Your Grace.   *Exeunt.*

2.2

*Enter the old Duchess of York, with the two
children of Clarence, [Edward and Margaret
Plantagenet].*

BOY
Good grandam, tell us, is our father dead?
DUCHESS   No, boy.
GIRL
Why do you weep so oft, and beat your breast,
And cry, "O Clarence, my unhappy son"?
BOY
Why do you look on us, and shake your head,
And call us orphans, wretches, castaways,
If that our noble father were alive?   7
DUCHESS
My pretty cousins, you mistake me both.   8
I do lament the sickness of the King,
As loath to lose him, not your father's death;
It were lost sorrow to wail one that's lost.
BOY
Then, you conclude, my grandam, he is dead.
The King mine uncle is to blame for it.
God will revenge it, whom I will importune   14
With earnest prayers all to that effect.
GIRL   And so will I.
DUCHESS
Peace, children, peace! The King doth love you well.
Incapable and shallow innocents,   18
You cannot guess who caused your father's death.
BOY
Grandam, we can; for my good uncle Gloucester
Told me the King, provoked to it by the Queen,
Devised impeachments to imprison him;   22
And when my uncle told me so, he wept,
And pitied me, and kindly kissed my cheek;
Bade me rely on him as on my father,
And he would love me dearly as his child.

DUCHESS
Ah, that deceit should steal such gentle shape,
And with a virtuous visor hide deep vice!   28
He is my son—ay, and therein my shame;
Yet from my dugs he drew not this deceit.   30
BOY
Think you my uncle did dissemble, grandam?
DUCHESS   Ay, boy.
BOY
I cannot think it. Hark, what noise is this?   33

*Enter the Queen [Elizabeth], with her hair about
her ears; Rivers and Dorset after her.*

QUEEN ELIZABETH
Ah, who shall hinder me to wail and weep,
To chide my fortune and torment myself?
I'll join with black despair against my soul,
And to myself become an enemy.
DUCHESS
What means this scene of rude impatience?   38
QUEEN ELIZABETH
To make an act of tragic violence.   39
Edward, my lord, thy son, our king, is dead!   40
Why grow the branches when the root is gone?
Why wither not the leaves that want their sap?
If you will live, lament; if die, be brief,   43
That our swift-wingèd souls may catch the King's
Or, like obedient subjects, follow him
To his new kingdom of ne'er-changing night.
DUCHESS
Ah, so much interest have I in thy sorrow
As I had title in thy noble husband!   48
I have bewept a worthy husband's death
And lived with looking on his images;   50
But now two mirrors of his princely semblance   51
Are cracked in pieces by malignant death,
And I for comfort have but one false glass,   53
That grieves me when I see my shame in him.   54
Thou art a widow; yet thou art a mother,
And hast the comfort of thy children left;
But death hath snatched my husband from mine arms
And plucked two crutches from my feeble hands,
Clarence and Edward. Oh, what cause have I,   59
Thine being but a moiety of my moan,   60
To overgo thy woes and drown thy cries!   61
BOY
Ah, aunt! You wept not for our father's death.
How can we aid you with our kindred tears?   63

---

134 closet private chambers.   138 still continually
2.2. Location: London. The royal court.
7 If that if   8 cousins kinfolks   14 importune solicit, beg
18 Incapable Unable to understand   22 impeachments accusations

28 visor mask   30 dugs breasts   33.1–2 *with her . . . ears* (A conventional sign of grief.)   38 rude impatience violent unwillingness to accept misfortune.   39 make perform. (Continues the theatrical metaphor in the previous line.)   40 Edward . . . dead (Clarence's death, February 1478, and Edward IV's death, April 1483, are treated as if they had occurred nearly together.)   43 brief quick   48 title i.e., as mother of the King   50 images likenesses; here, children   51 two mirrors i.e., Edward and Clarence. (The Duchess does not count Rutland.)   53 false glass i.e., Richard   54 my . . . him a son of whom to be ashamed.   59 what . . . I what a cause I have   60 moiety of my moan half (the cause) of my grief   61 overgo exceed   63 kindred tears i.e., tears of kinfolks.

GIRL
  Our fatherless distress was left unmoaned;
  Your widow-dolor likewise be unwept!   65
QUEEN ELIZABETH
  Give me no help in lamentation;
  I am not barren to bring forth complaints.   67
  All springs reduce their currents to mine eyes,   68
  That I, being governed by the watery moon,   69
  May send forth plenteous tears to drown the world!
  Ah for my husband, for my dear lord Edward!
CHILDREN
  Ah for our father, for our dear lord Clarence!
DUCHESS
  Alas for both, both mine, Edward and Clarence!
QUEEN ELIZABETH
  What stay had I but Edward? And he's gone.   74
CHILDREN
  What stay had we but Clarence? And he's gone.
DUCHESS
  What stays had I but they? And they are gone.
QUEEN ELIZABETH
  Was never widow had so dear a loss!   77
CHILDREN
  Were never orphans had so dear a loss!
DUCHESS
  Was never mother had so dear a loss!
  Alas, I am the mother of these griefs;
  Their woes are parceled, mine is general.   81
  She for an Edward weeps, and so do I;
  I for a Clarence weep, so doth not she.
  These babes for Clarence weep, and so do I;
  I for an Edward weep, so do not they.
  Alas, you three, on me, threefold distressed,
  Pour all your tears! I am your sorrow's nurse,   87
  And I will pamper it with lamentation.   88
DORSET [to Queen Elizabeth]
  Comfort, dear mother. God is much displeased
  That you take with unthankfulness his doing.
  In common worldly things 'tis called ungrateful
  With dull unwillingness to repay a debt   92
  Which with a bounteous hand was kindly lent;
  Much more to be thus opposite with heaven   94
  For it requires the royal debt it lent you.   95
RIVERS
  Madam, bethink you like a careful mother
  Of the young Prince your son. Send straight for him;
  Let him be crowned. In him your comfort lives.
  Drown desperate sorrow in dead Edward's grave

And plant your joys in living Edward's throne.

    Enter Richard [Duke of Gloucester], Buckingham,
    [Lord Stanley Earl of] Derby, Hastings, and
    Ratcliffe.

RICHARD [to Queen Elizabeth]
  Sister, have comfort. All of us have cause
  To wail the dimming of our shining star,
  But none can help our harms by wailing them.—
  Madam, my mother, I do cry you mercy;   104
  I did not see Your Grace. Humbly on my knee
  I crave your blessing.   [He kneels.]
DUCHESS
  God bless thee, and put meekness in thy breast,
  Love, charity, obedience, and true duty!
RICHARD
  Amen! [Aside] And make me die a good old man!
  That is the butt end of a mother's blessing;   110
  I marvel that Her Grace did leave it out.
BUCKINGHAM
  You cloudy princes and heart-sorrowing peers,   112
  That bear this heavy mutual load of moan,   113
  Now cheer each other in each other's love.
  Though we have spent our harvest of this king,
  We are to reap the harvest of his son.
  The broken rancor of your high-swoll'n hates,
  But lately splintered, knit, and joined together,   118
  Must gently be preserved, cherished, and kept.   119
  Me seemeth good that with some little train   120
  Forthwith from Ludlow the young Prince be fet   121
  Hither to London, to be crowned our king.
RIVERS
  Why with some little train, my lord of Buckingham?
BUCKINGHAM
  Marry, my lord, lest by a multitude   124
  The new-healed wound of malice should break out,
  Which would be so much the more dangerous
  By how much the estate is green and yet ungoverned. 127
  Where every horse bears his commanding rein   128
  And may direct his course as please himself,   129
  As well the fear of harm, as harm apparent,   130
  In my opinion, ought to be prevented.
RICHARD
  I hope the King made peace with all of us;
  And the compact is firm and true in me.
RIVERS
  And so in me, and so, I think, in all.
  Yet since it is but green, it should be put
  To no apparent likelihood of breach,

---

65 **widow-dolor** widow's grief   67 **barren to** i.e., unable to. (She is pregnant with grief.)   68 **All . . . eyes** Let all springs be concentrated in my eyes   69 **I . . . moon** (Her grief is now a sea, fed by springs and her tides governed by the moon.)   74 **stay** support   77 **dear** costly, grievous   81 **Their . . . general** the woes of Queen Elizabeth and these children are particular to each of them, mine is all-embracing.   87 **nurse** source of sustenance   88 **pamper** feed luxuriously, nourish   92 **dull** sluggish   94 **opposite with** contrary toward   95 **For it requires** because it calls back

104 **cry you mercy** beg your pardon   110 **butt end** concluding portion. (The *butt* is the end of a spear shaft.)   112 **cloudy** clouded with grief   113 **moan** lamentation   118 **But lately splintered** only recently bound together (as with a splint)   119 **Must . . . preserved** i.e., the recent mending of differences must be preserved   120 **Me seemeth** It seems to me.   **train** entourage   121 **Ludlow** royal castle in Shropshire, near the Welsh border.   **fet** fetched   124 **multitude** i.e., large train or entourage   127 **estate** state, government.   **green** unripe, i.e., newly established   128 **bears . . . rein** controls the reins that ought to control him   129 **as please** as it pleases   130 **As . . . apparent** both the fear of trouble and the actual manifestation of it

Which haply by much company might be urged.   137
Therefore I say with noble Buckingham
That it is meet so few should fetch the Prince.   139

HASTINGS   And so say I.

RICHARD
Then be it so; and go we to determine
Who they shall be that straight shall post to Ludlow.   142
Madam, and you, my sister, will you go
To give your censures in this business?   144

QUEEN ELIZABETH, DUCHESS   With all our hearts.   145

Exeunt. Manent Buckingham and Richard.

BUCKINGHAM
My lord, whoever journeys to the Prince,
For God's sake let not us two stay at home;
For by the way I'll sort occasion,   148
As index to the story we late talked of,   149
To part the Queen's proud kindred from the Prince.

RICHARD
My other self, my counsel's consistory,   151
My oracle, my prophet! My dear cousin,
I, as a child, will go by thy direction.
Toward Ludlow then, for we'll not stay behind.

Exeunt.

❖

2.3

Enter one Citizen at one door, and another at the other.

FIRST CITIZEN
Good morrow, neighbor. Whither away so fast?

SECOND CITIZEN
I promise you, I scarcely know myself.   2
Hear you the news abroad?

FIRST CITIZEN   Yes, that the King is dead.

SECOND CITIZEN
Ill news, by'r Lady; seldom comes the better.   5
I fear, I fear 'twill prove a giddy world.   6

Enter another Citizen.

THIRD CITIZEN
Neighbors, God speed!

FIRST CITIZEN   Give you good morrow, sir.

THIRD CITIZEN
Doth the news hold of good King Edward's death?   8

SECOND CITIZEN
Ay, sir, it is too true, God help the while!

THIRD CITIZEN
Then, masters, look to see a troublous world.   10

FIRST CITIZEN
No, no; by God's good grace his son shall reign.

THIRD CITIZEN
Woe to that land that's governed by a child!   12

SECOND CITIZEN
In him there is a hope of government,
Which in his nonage, council under him,   14
And in his full and ripened years, himself,
No doubt shall then, and till then, govern well.

FIRST CITIZEN
So stood the state when Henry the Sixth
Was crowned in Paris but at nine months old.

THIRD CITIZEN
Stood the state so? No, no, good friends, God wot,   19
For then this land was famously enriched
With politic, grave counsel; then the King   21
Had virtuous uncles to protect His Grace.

FIRST CITIZEN
Why, so hath this, both by his father and mother.

THIRD CITIZEN
Better it were they all came by his father,
Or by his father there were none at all;
For emulation who shall now be nearest   26
Will touch us all too near, if God prevent not.
Oh, full of danger is the Duke of Gloucester,
And the Queen's sons and brothers haught and proud!   29
And were they to be ruled, and not to rule,
This sickly land might solace as before.   31

FIRST CITIZEN
Come, come, we fear the worst. All will be well.

THIRD CITIZEN
When clouds are seen, wise men put on their cloaks;
When great leaves fall, then winter is at hand;
When the sun sets, who doth not look for night?
Untimely storms makes men expect a dearth.
All may be well; but if God sort it so,   37
'Tis more than we deserve or I expect.

SECOND CITIZEN
Truly, the hearts of men are full of fear.
You cannot reason almost with a man   40
That looks not heavily and full of dread.   41

THIRD CITIZEN
Before the days of change, still is it so.   42
By a divine instinct men's minds mistrust   43
Ensuing danger; as, by proof, we see   44
The water swell before a boist'rous storm.
But leave it all to God. Whither away?

SECOND CITIZEN
Marry, we were sent for to the justices.

THIRD CITIZEN
And so was I. I'll bear you company.   *Exeunt.*

❖

---

137 haply perhaps.   **urged** encouraged, provoked.   **139 meet** fitting
142 post hasten   **144 censures** judgments   **145.1** *Manent* They
remain onstage   **148 by** on.   **sort** find, contrive   **149 index** prologue.   **late** lately   **151 consistory** council chamber
2.3. Location: London. A street.
2 promise assure   **5 Ill . . . better** Ill news, by Our Lady. Good news
comes seldom; most news is bad news.   **6 giddy** mad   **8 Doth the
news hold** Is the news true   **10 masters** good sirs.   **troublous** troubled, disorderly

12 Woe . . . child! (Compare with Ecclesiastes 10:16: "Woe to thee, O
land, when thy king is a child.")   **14 nonage** minority.   **council
under him** i.e., with the Privy Council governing in his name
19 wot knows   **21 politic** sagacious   **26 emulation** ambitious rivalry
29 haught haughty   **31 solace** be happy, have comfort   **37 sort** dispose   **40 You . . . man** There is scarcely anyone with whom you can
talk   **41 heavily** sad   **42 still** ever   **43 mistrust** suspect, fear
44 proof experience

2.4

*Enter [the] Archbishop [of York], [the] young
[Duke of] York, the Queen [Elizabeth], and the
Duchess [of York].*

ARCHBISHOP
Last night, I hear, they lay at Stony Stratford,   1
And at Northampton they do rest tonight.   2
Tomorrow, or next day, they will be here.

DUCHESS
I long with all my heart to see the Prince.
I hope he is much grown since last I saw him.

QUEEN ELIZABETH
But I hear, no; they say my son of York
Has almost overta'en him in his growth.

YORK
Ay, mother, but I would not have it so.

DUCHESS
Why, my young cousin? It is good to grow.

YORK
Grandam, one night as we did sit at supper,
My uncle Rivers talked how I did grow
More than my brother. "Ay," quoth my uncle Gloucester,
"Small herbs have grace; great weeds do grow apace."   13
And since, methinks, I would not grow so fast,   14
Because sweet flow'rs are slow and weeds make haste.

DUCHESS
Good faith, good faith, the saying did not hold   16
In him that did object the same to thee.   17
He was the wretched'st thing when he was young,
So long a-growing and so leisurely,
That, if his rule were true, he should be gracious.

ARCHBISHOP
And so no doubt he is, my gracious madam.

DUCHESS
I hope he is, but yet let mothers doubt.

YORK
Now, by my troth, if I had been remembered,   23
I could have given my uncle's Grace a flout   24
To touch his growth nearer than he touched mine.   25

DUCHESS
How, my young York? I prithee, let me hear it.

YORK
Marry, they say my uncle grew so fast
That he could gnaw a crust at two hours old;
'Twas full two years ere I could get a tooth.
Grandam, this would have been a biting jest.   30

DUCHESS
I prithee, pretty York, who told thee this?
YORK   Grandam, his nurse.
DUCHESS
His nurse? Why, she was dead ere thou wast born.
YORK
If 'twere not she, I cannot tell who told me.
QUEEN ELIZABETH
A parlous boy! Go to, you are too shrewd.   35
DUCHESS
Good madam, be not angry with the child.
QUEEN ELIZABETH   Pitchers have ears.   37

Enter a Messenger.

ARCHBISHOP
Here comes a messenger.—What news?
MESSENGER
Such news, my lord, as grieves me to report.
QUEEN ELIZABETH
How doth the Prince?
MESSENGER   Well, madam, and in health.
DUCHESS   What is thy news?
MESSENGER
Lord Rivers and Lord Grey are sent to Pomfret,   42
And with them Sir Thomas Vaughan, prisoners.
DUCHESS
Who hath committed them?
MESSENGER   The mighty dukes
Gloucester and Buckingham.
ARCHBISHOP   For what offense?
MESSENGER
The sum of all I can, I have disclosed.
Why or for what the nobles were committed
Is all unknown to me, my gracious lord.
QUEEN ELIZABETH
Ay me, I see the ruin of my house!
The tiger now hath seized the gentle hind;   50
Insulting tyranny begins to jut   51
Upon the innocent and aweless throne.   52
Welcome, destruction, blood, and massacre!
I see, as in a map, the end of all.   54
DUCHESS
Accursèd and unquiet wrangling days,
How many of you have mine eyes beheld!
My husband lost his life to get the crown,
And often up and down my sons were tossed   58
For me to joy and weep their gain and loss;
And being seated, and domestic broils   60
Clean overblown, themselves the conquerors   61
Make war upon themselves, brother to brother,
Blood to blood, self against self. O preposterous   63

2.4. Location: London. The royal court.
1 Stony Stratford village in Buckinghamshire   **2 Northampton** town
in Northamptonshire and hence farther from London than Stony
Stratford. The Prince was taken back to Northampton after the arrest
of Rivers, Grey, and Vaughan. The Archbishop does not yet know of
that arrest, but the Folio version of his speech, followed here, is based
misleadingly on historical information of subsequent events. (The quartos reverse the order in which the two towns are named.)   **13 grace**
virtuous qualities.   **apace** rapidly.   **14 since** ever since   **16–17 the
saying . . . thee** the saying did not at all apply to the person who
applied it to you, i.e., Richard.   **23 troth** truth, faith.   **had been
remembered** had recollected   **24 my . . . flout** His Grace, my uncle, a
mocking gibe   **25 touch . . . nearer** i.e., taunt him about his growth
more tellingly   **30 biting** (With a play on the idea of teething.)

35 parlous cunning, precocious.   **Go to** (An expression of remonstrance.)   **shrewd** sharp-tongued.   **37 Pitchers have ears** Little
pitchers have large ears. (Proverbial.)   **42 Pomfret** the castle at Pontefract in Yorkshire   **50 hind** doe   **51 Insulting** scornfully triumphing.   **jut** encroach   **52 aweless** inspiring no awe (because of the
youth of the King)   **54 map** i.e., of future events   **58 up . . . tossed**
i.e., my sons were raised and then lowered on fortune's wheel
60 seated i.e., on the throne   **61 Clean overblown** entirely finished
63 preposterous monstrous, perverse

And frantic outrage, end thy damnèd spleen,   64
Or let me die, to look on death no more!

QUEEN ELIZABETH
Come, come, my boy, we will to sanctuary.   66
Madam, farewell.

DUCHESS   Stay, I will go with you.

QUEEN ELIZABETH
You have no cause.

ARCHBISHOP [*to the Queen*]   My gracious lady, go,
And thither bear your treasure and your goods.
For my part, I'll resign unto Your Grace
The seal I keep; and so betide to me   71
As well I tender you and all of yours!   72
Go, I'll conduct you to the sanctuary.   *Exeunt.*

3.1

*The trumpets sound. Enter [the] young Prince
[Edward], the Dukes of Gloucester and
Buckingham, [Lord] Cardinal [Bourchier, Catesby],
etc.*

BUCKINGHAM
Welcome, sweet Prince, to London, to your chamber.   1

RICHARD
Welcome, dear cousin, my thoughts' sovereign!
The weary way hath made you melancholy.

PRINCE EDWARD
No, uncle, but our crosses on the way   4
Have made it tedious, wearisome, and heavy.
I want more uncles here to welcome me.   6

RICHARD
Sweet Prince, the untainted virtue of your years
Hath not yet dived into the world's deceit.
Nor more can you distinguish of a man
Than of his outward show—which, God he knows,
Seldom or never jumpeth with the heart.   11
Those uncles which you want were dangerous.
Your Grace attended to their sugared words
But looked not on the poison of their hearts.
God keep you from them, and from such false
    friends!

PRINCE EDWARD
God keep me from false friends! But they were none.

RICHARD
My lord, the Mayor of London comes to greet you.

Enter [the] Lord Mayor [and his train].

MAYOR
God bless Your Grace with health and happy days!

PRINCE EDWARD
I thank you, good my lord, and thank you all.
            [*The Mayor and his train stand aside.*]
I thought my mother and my brother York
Would long ere this have met us on the way.
Fie, what a slug is Hastings, that he comes not   22
To tell us whether they will come or no!

Enter Lord Hastings.

BUCKINGHAM
And, in good time, here comes the sweating lord.

PRINCE EDWARD
Welcome, my lord. What, will our mother come?

HASTINGS
On what occasion God he knows, not I,   26
The Queen your mother and your brother York
Have taken sanctuary. The tender Prince
Would fain have come with me to meet Your Grace,
But by his mother was perforce withheld.   30

BUCKINGHAM
Fie, what an indirect and peevish course   31
Is this of hers!—Lord Cardinal, will Your Grace
Persuade the Queen to send the Duke of York
Unto his princely brother presently?   34
If she deny, Lord Hastings, go with him,
And from her jealous arms pluck him perforce.   36

CARDINAL
My lord of Buckingham, if my weak oratory
Can from his mother win the Duke of York,
Anon expect him here; but if she be obdurate   39
To mild entreaties, God in heaven forbid
We should infringe the holy privilege
Of blessèd sanctuary! Not for all this land
Would I be guilty of so deep a sin.

BUCKINGHAM
You are too senseless-obstinate, my lord,
Too ceremonious and traditional.   45
Weigh it but with the grossness of this age,   46
You break not sanctuary in seizing him.
The benefit thereof is always granted
To those whose dealings have deserved the place
And those who have the wit to claim the place.
This prince hath neither claimed it nor deserved it,
And therefore, in mine opinion, cannot have it.
Then, taking him from thence that is not there,   53
You break no privilege nor charter there.
Oft have I heard of sanctuary men,
But sanctuary children never till now.

CARDINAL
My lord, you shall o'errule my mind for once.
Come on, Lord Hastings, will you go with me?

---

64 **spleen** i.e., malice, hatred   66 **sanctuary** (Queen Elizabeth, with her son, daughters, and kinsmen, lodged in the precincts of Westminster Abbey, which served as a legal refuge for criminals and persons in danger of their lives.)   71 **seal** seal of office i.e., the Great Seal of England. (The Archbishop's giving the Great Seal to Elizabeth is an unusual and extralegal action.)   71–2 **so . . . you** may my fortunes be measured by the care I take of you
3.1. Location: London. A street.
1 **chamber** (London was called the *camera regis*, or King's chamber.)
4 **crosses** vexations (i.e., the arrests of the Queen's kindred)   6 **want** (1) lack (2) wish   11 **jumpeth** agrees

22 **slug** sluggard   26 **On what occasion** For what reason   30 **perforce** by force   31 **peevish** perverse   34 **presently** at once   36 **jealous** suspicious   39 **Anon** shortly   45 **ceremonious** bound by formalities   46 **grossness** lack of moral refinement   53 **taking . . . there** i.e., taking the Prince from a place that cannot properly be called a sanctuary in his case

HASTINGS   I go, my lord.

PRINCE EDWARD
Good lords, make all the speedy haste you may.
                    [*Exeunt Cardinal and Hastings.*]
Say, uncle Gloucester, if our brother come,
Where shall we sojourn till our coronation?   62

RICHARD
Where it seems best unto your royal self.
If I may counsel you, some day or two
Your Highness shall repose you at the Tower;   65
Then where you please, and shall be thought most fit
For your best health and recreation.

PRINCE EDWARD
I do not like the Tower, of any place.   68
Did Julius Caesar build that place, my lord?

BUCKINGHAM
He did, my gracious lord, begin that place,
Which, since, succeeding ages have re-edified.   71

PRINCE EDWARD
Is it upon record, or else reported   72
Successively from age to age, he built it?

BUCKINGHAM   Upon record, my gracious lord.

PRINCE EDWARD
But say, my lord, it were not registered,   75
Methinks the truth should live from age to age,
As 'twere retailed to all posterity,   77
Even to the general all-ending day.   78

RICHARD [*aside*]
So wise so young, they say, do never live long.

PRINCE EDWARD   What say you, uncle?

RICHARD
I say, without characters fame lives long.   81
[*Aside*] Thus, like the formal Vice, Iniquity,   82
I moralize two meanings in one word.   83

PRINCE EDWARD
That Julius Caesar was a famous man;
With what his valor did enrich his wit,   85
His wit set down to make his valor live.   86
Death makes no conquest of this conqueror,
For now he lives in fame, though not in life.
I'll tell you what, my cousin Buckingham—

BUCKINGHAM   What, my gracious lord?

PRINCE EDWARD
An if I live until I be a man,   91
I'll win our ancient right in France again
Or die a soldier, as I lived a king.

RICHARD [*aside*]
Short summers lightly have a forward spring.   94

            Enter young York, Hastings, [and the] Cardinal.

BUCKINGHAM
Now, in good time, here comes the Duke of York.

PRINCE EDWARD
Richard of York, how fares our loving brother?   96

YORK
Well, my dread lord—so must I call you now.   97

PRINCE EDWARD
Ay, brother, to our grief, as it is yours.
Too late he died that might have kept that title,   99
Which by his death hath lost much majesty.

RICHARD
How fares our cousin, noble lord of York?

YORK
I thank you, gentle uncle. Oh, my lord,   102
You said that idle weeds are fast in growth;   103
The Prince my brother hath outgrown me far.

RICHARD
He hath, my lord.

YORK   And therefore is he idle?

RICHARD
Oh, my fair cousin, I must not say so.

YORK
Then he is more beholding to you than I.   107

RICHARD
He may command me as my sovereign,
But you have power in me as in a kinsman.

YORK
I pray you, uncle, give me this dagger.

RICHARD
My dagger, little cousin? With all my heart.   111

PRINCE EDWARD   A beggar, brother?

YORK
Of my kind uncle, that I know will give;   113
And being but a toy, which is no grief to give.   114

RICHARD
A greater gift than that I'll give my cousin.

YORK
A greater gift? Oh, that's the sword to it.

RICHARD
Ay, gentle cousin, were it light enough.

YORK
Oh, then I see you will part but with light gifts.   118
In weightier things you'll say a beggar nay.

RICHARD
It is too heavy for Your Grace to wear.

YORK
I weigh it lightly, were it heavier.   121

---

62 sojourn reside   **65 Tower** (Although in the fifteenth century—the historical time this play represents—the Tower of London was a royal palace, by Shakespeare's day it had acquired a sinister reputation.) **68 of any place** of all places.   **71 re-edified** rebuilt.   **72 upon record** in the written record.   **reported** i.e., by oral tradition   **75 say** suppose.   **registered** written down   **77 retailed** repeated, handed down from one to another   **78 general . . . day** Day of Judgment.   **81 without characters** even lacking written records   **82 formal Vice** i.e., the conventional Vice figure of the morality play, a comic tempter to evil, who would habitually *moralize two meanings in one word*, that is, play on double meanings in a single phrase, as Richard does in the phrase *live long*   **83 moralize** interpret, illustrate   **85–6 With . . . live** having improved his understanding through his military achievements, he used his understanding to set down in writing an account (the *Gallic Wars*) that would make his valor immortal.   **91 An if** If

94 lightly commonly, often.   **forward** early. (Alludes to Edward's precociousness.)   **96 our** i.e., my. (The royal "we.")   **97 dread** inspiring reverential fear (as King)   **99 late** lately   **102 gentle** noble   **103 idle** worthless   **107 beholding** beholden   **111 With . . . heart** Willingly. (Richard combines in one phrase an overt generosity and a hidden threat.)   **113 that** who   **114 toy** trifle   **118 light** trivial   **121 I weigh . . . heavier** I consider it a trifle (playing on the literal meanings of "light" and "heavy") and would do so even if it were heavier.

RICHARD
    What, would you have my weapon, little lord?
YORK
    I would, that I might thank you as you call me.
RICHARD   How?
YORK   Little.   125
PRINCE EDWARD
    My lord of York will still be cross in talk.   126
    Uncle, Your Grace knows how to bear with him.
YORK
    You mean, to bear me, not to bear with me.
    Uncle, my brother mocks both you and me:
    Because that I am little, like an ape,
    He thinks that you should bear me on your shoulders.   131
BUCKINGHAM [*aside to Hastings*]
    With what a sharp-provided wit he reasons!   132
    To mitigate the scorn he gives his uncle,
    He prettily and aptly taunts himself.
    So cunning and so young is wonderful.
RICHARD [*to the Prince*]
    My lord, will't please you pass along?
    Myself and my good cousin Buckingham
    Will to your mother, to entreat of her
    To meet you at the Tower and welcome you.
YORK [*to the Prince*]
    What, will you go unto the Tower, my lord?
PRINCE EDWARD
    My Lord Protector needs will have it so.
YORK
    I shall not sleep in quiet at the Tower.
RICHARD   Why, what should you fear?
YORK
    Marry, my uncle Clarence' angry ghost.
    My grandam told me he was murdered there.
PRINCE EDWARD   I fear no uncles dead.
RICHARD   Nor none that live, I hope.
PRINCE EDWARD
    An if they live, I hope I need not fear.   148
    But come, my lord; with a heavy heart,
    Thinking on them, go I unto the Tower.   150
                                [*A sennet.*] *Exeunt Prince, York,*
                        Hastings, [Cardinal, and others]. Manent
                              Richard, Buckingham, [and Catesby].
BUCKINGHAM
    Think you, my lord, this little prating York   151
    Was not incensèd by his subtle mother   152
    To taunt and scorn you thus opprobriously?

RICHARD
    No doubt, no doubt. Oh, 'tis a parlous boy,   154
    Bold, quick, ingenious, forward, capable.
    He is all the mother's, from the top to toe.
BUCKINGHAM
    Well, let them rest.—Come hither, Catesby.   157
    Thou art sworn as deeply to effect what we intend
    As closely to conceal what we impart.
    Thou know'st our reasons urged upon the way.   160
    What think'st thou? Is it not an easy matter
    To make William Lord Hastings of our mind
    For the installment of this noble Duke
    In the seat royal of this famous isle?
CATESBY
    He for his father's sake so loves the Prince   165
    That he will not be won to aught against him.
BUCKINGHAM
    What think'st thou, then, of Stanley? Will not he?
CATESBY
    He will do all in all as Hastings doth.
BUCKINGHAM
    Well, then, no more but this: go, gentle Catesby,
    And, as it were far off, sound thou Lord Hastings   170
    How he doth stand affected to our purpose,   171
    And summon him tomorrow to the Tower
    To sit about the coronation.   173
    If thou dost find him tractable to us,
    Encourage him, and tell him all our reasons.
    If he be leaden, icy, cold, unwilling,
    Be thou so too; and so break off the talk,
    And give us notice of his inclination.
    For we tomorrow hold divided councils,   179
    Wherein thyself shalt highly be employed.
RICHARD
    Commend me to Lord William. Tell him, Catesby,   181
    His ancient knot of dangerous adversaries   182
    Tomorrow are let blood at Pomfret Castle;   183
    And bid my lord, for joy of this good news,
    Give Mistress Shore one gentle kiss the more.   185
BUCKINGHAM
    Good Catesby, go, effect this business soundly.   186
CATESBY
    My good lords both, with all the heed I can.   187
RICHARD
    Shall we hear from you, Catesby, ere we sleep?
CATESBY   You shall, my lord.
RICHARD
    At Crosby House, there shall you find us both.
                                                                    Exit Catesby.

---

125 Little (York saucily suggests that he would give little thanks for such a "light" gift.)   **126 My . . . talk** i.e., My younger brother is always twisting words in his wittily perverse but annoying way.   **131 bear me . . . shoulders** (At fairs, the bear commonly carried an ape on his back. The speech is doubtless an allusion to Richard's hump and puns triply on *bear with*, "put up with," *bear*, "carry," and *bear*, "an animal.")   **132 sharp-provided** nimble and ready   **148 An if** If.   **they** i.e., Rivers and Grey. (Grey was, in fact, Edward's stepbrother, not his uncle. See the note to 1.3.37.)   **150.1 sennet** trumpet call to announce the approach or departure of processions.   **150.2 Manent** They remain onstage   **151 prating** chattering, prattling   **152 incensèd** incited

154 parlous clever, but also dangerous   **157 let them rest** leave them for the moment.   **160 the way** i.e., the journey to London from Ludlow.   **165 He . . . sake** i.e., Hastings for King Edward IV's sake   **170 sound** sound out   **171 doth stand affected** is disposed   **173 sit** sit in council   **179 divided councils** (While the regular Council meets about the coronation, Richard plans also to have his own private consultation at Crosby House.)   **181 Lord William** i.e., Hastings.   **182 knot** group   **183 are let blood** will be bled, i.e., executed   **185 Mistress Shore** (According to Thomas More, Jane Shore had become the mistress of Hastings after the death of Edward IV.)   **186 soundly** thoroughly.   **187 heed** attention, care

BUCKINGHAM
    Now, my lord, what shall we do if we perceive
    Lord Hastings will not yield to our complots?   192
RICHARD
    Chop off his head. Something we will determine.
    And look when I am king, claim thou of me   194
    The earldom of Hereford and all the movables   195
    Whereof the King my brother was possessed.
BUCKINGHAM
    I'll claim that promise at Your Grace's hand.
RICHARD
    And look to have it yielded with all kindness.
    Come, let us sup betimes, that afterwards   199
    We may digest our complots in some form.   *Exeunt.* 200

❦

3.2

Enter a Messenger to the door of Hastings.

MESSENGER   My lord! My lord!
HASTINGS [*within*]   Who knocks?
MESSENGER   One from the Lord Stanley.
HASTINGS [*within*]   What is't o'clock?   4
MESSENGER   Upon the stroke of four.

Enter Lord Hastings.

HASTINGS
    Cannot my Lord Stanley sleep these tedious nights?
MESSENGER
    So it appears by that I have to say.
    First, he commends him to your noble self.
HASTINGS   What then?
MESSENGER
    Then certifies Your Lordship that this night   10
    He dreamt the boar had razèd off his helm.   11
    Besides, he says there are two councils kept,
    And that may be determined at the one
    Which may make you and him to rue at th'other.   14
    Therefore he sends to know Your Lordship's pleasure,
    If you will presently take horse with him   16
    And with all speed post with him toward the north,
    To shun the danger that his soul divines.
HASTINGS
    Go, fellow, go, return unto thy lord.
    Bid him not fear the separated councils.
    His Honor and myself are at the one,   21
    And at the other is my good friend Catesby,
    Where nothing can proceed that toucheth us
    Whereof I shall not have intelligence.   24
    Tell him his fears are shallow, without instance. 25

    And for his dreams, I wonder he's so simple   26
    To trust the mock'ry of unquiet slumbers.
    To fly the boar before the boar pursues   28
    Were to incense the boar to follow us,
    And make pursuit where he did mean no chase.
    Go, bid thy master rise and come to me,
    And we will both together to the Tower,
    Where he shall see the boar will use us kindly.
MESSENGER
    I'll go, my lord, and tell him what you say.   *Exit.*

Enter Catesby.

CATESBY
    Many good morrows to my noble lord!
HASTINGS
    Good morrow, Catesby. You are early stirring.
    What news, what news, in this our tott'ring state?
CATESBY
    It is a reeling world, indeed, my lord,
    And I believe will never stand upright
    Till Richard wear the garland of the realm.
HASTINGS
    How? Wear the garland? Dost thou mean the crown?
CATESBY   Ay, my good lord.
HASTINGS
    I'll have this crown of mine cut from my shoulders 43
    Before I'll see the crown so foul misplaced.
    But canst thou guess that he doth aim at it?
CATESBY
    Ay, on my life, and hopes to find you forward   46
    Upon his party for the gain thereof;   47
    And thereupon he sends you this good news,
    That this same very day your enemies,
    The kindred of the Queen, must die at Pomfret.
HASTINGS
    Indeed, I am no mourner for that news,
    Because they have been still my adversaries.   52
    But that I'll give my voice on Richard's side
    To bar my master's heirs in true descent,
    God knows I will not do it, to the death.   55
CATESBY
    God keep Your Lordship in that gracious mind!
HASTINGS
    But I shall laugh at this a twelvemonth hence,
    That they which brought me in my master's hate,   58
    I live to look upon their tragedy.   59
    Well, Catesby, ere a fortnight make me older,
    I'll send some packing that yet think not on't.
CATESBY
    'Tis a vile thing to die, my gracious lord,
    When men are unprepared and look not for it.

---

192 complots conspiracies.   **194 look when** as soon as   **195 movables**
personal property, other than real estate   **199 betimes** early, soon
200 digest arrange, perfect.   **form** good order.
3.2. Location: Before Lord Hastings' house.
4 What is't o'clock? What time is it?   **10 certifies** informs   **11 boar**
i.e., Richard.   **razèd** torn, slashed   **14 th'other** i.e., the regular Council meeting in the Tower, in which Hastings and Stanley will participate.   **16 presently** immediately   **21 His Honor** Lord Stanley
24 intelligence information.   **25 instance** grounds.

26 for as for.   **simple** simpleminded (as)   **28 fly** flee   **43 crown** i.e.,
head. (Recalls Stanley's dream in line 11 and anticipates Hastings'
execution by beheading.)   **46 forward** inclined   **47 Upon his party**
on his side   **52 still** always   **55 to the death** i.e., though I lose my
life. (A common asseveration, but here with ironic meaning.)
58–9 That . . . tragedy that I will live to see the fatal end of those who
brought me out of favor with King Edward IV.

HASTINGS
  Oh, monstrous, monstrous! And so falls it out   64
  With Rivers, Vaughan, Grey; and so 'twill do
  With some men else, that think themselves as safe
  As thou and I—who, as thou know'st, are dear
  To princely Richard and to Buckingham.
CATESBY
  The princes both make high account of you—   69
  [*Aside*] For they account his head upon the Bridge.   70
HASTINGS
  I know they do, and I have well deserved it.

      Enter Lord Stanley [Earl of Derby].

  Come on, come on, where is your boar spear, man?
  Fear you the boar, and go so unprovided?
STANLEY
  My lord, good morrow. Good morrow, Catesby.
  You may jest on, but, by the Holy Rood,   75
  I do not like these several councils, I.   76
HASTINGS   My lord,
  I hold my life as dear as you do yours,
  And never in my days, I do protest,
  Was it so precious to me as 'tis now.
  Think you, but that I know our state secure,   81
  I would be so triumphant as I am?
STANLEY
  The lords at Pomfret, when they rode from London,   83
  Were jocund and supposed their states were sure,   84
  And they indeed had no cause to mistrust;
  But yet you see how soon the day o'ercast.   86
  This sudden stab of rancor I misdoubt.   87
  Pray God, I say, I prove a needless coward!
  What, shall we toward the Tower? The day is spent.   89
HASTINGS
  Come, come, have with you. Wot you what, my lord?   90
  Today the lords you talk of are beheaded.
STANLEY
  They, for their truth, might better wear their heads   92
  Than some that have accused them wear their hats.   93
  But come, my lord, let's away.   94

      Enter a Pursuivant.

HASTINGS
  Go on before. I'll talk with this good fellow.
      Exit Lord Stanley [Earl of Derby] and Catesby.

  How now, sirrah? How goes the world with thee?   96
PURSUIVANT
  The better that Your Lordship please to ask.
HASTINGS
  I tell thee, man, 'tis better with me now
  Than when thou met'st me last where now we meet.
  Then was I going prisoner to the Tower,
  By the suggestion of the Queen's allies;   101
  But now, I tell thee—keep it to thyself—
  This day those enemies are put to death,
  And I in better state than e'er I was.
PURSUIVANT
  God hold it, to Your Honor's good content!   105
HASTINGS
  Gramercy, fellow. There, drink that for me.   106
                Throws him his purse.
PURSUIVANT   I thank Your Honor.   *Exit Pursuivant.*

      Enter a Priest.

PRIEST
  Well met, my lord. I am glad to see Your Honor.
HASTINGS
  I thank thee, good Sir John, with all my heart.   109
  I am in your debt for your last exercise;   110
  Come the next Sabbath, and I will content you.   111
                [He whispers in his ear.]
PRIEST   I'll wait upon Your Lordship.

      Enter Buckingham.

BUCKINGHAM
  What, talking with a priest, Lord Chamberlain?
  Your friends at Pomfret, they do need the priest;
  Your Honor hath no shriving work in hand.   115
HASTINGS
  Good faith, and when I met this holy man,
  The men you talk of came into my mind.
  What, go you toward the Tower?
BUCKINGHAM
  I do, my lord, but long I cannot stay there.
  I shall return before Your Lordship thence.
HASTINGS
  Nay, like enough, for I stay dinner there.   121
BUCKINGHAM [*aside*]
  And supper too, although thou know'st it not.—   122
  Come, will you go?
HASTINGS   I'll wait upon Your Lordship.
                                          Exeunt.

                              ❧

---

64 **so . . . out** so it has happened   69 **high account** great estimation. (The quibble on *high* appears in the next line.)   70 **account** expect, reckon. (Punning on *account* in the previous line.)   **the Bridge** London Bridge, on a tower of which the heads of traitors were exposed. 75 **Rood** cross   76 **several** separate   81 **our state** the positions we (Stanley and Hastings) occupy   83 **London** (An error for "Ludlow"?) 84 **jocund** merry   86 **o'ercast** became overcast.   87 **This . . . misdoubt** This sudden rancorous vengeance (against Rivers, Vaughan, and Grey) makes me uneasy.   89 **spent** i.e., well advanced (although the scene began at 4:00 A.M.).   90 **have with you** let's go together.   **Wot** Know 92-3 **They . . . hats** They, for their honest loyalty (to King Edward and now his son), might more justly be allowed to keep their heads than some of their accusers wear their hats of office.   94.1 *Pursuivant* attendant on a herald with authority to serve warrants.

96 **sirrah** (Form of address to inferiors.)   101 **suggestion** instigation 105 **hold it** continue it (i.e., the better state)   106 **Gramercy** Many thanks   109 **Sir** (Common title for addressing any priest.) 110 **exercise** sermon or devotional exercise   111 **content** compensate 115 **shriving work** confession and absolution   121 **stay** stay for 122 **And supper . . . not** i.e., You won't be leaving as soon as you think. (Also suggesting that Hastings will be a feast for worms.)

3.3

*Enter Sir Richard Ratcliffe, with Halberds, carrying
the nobles [Rivers, Grey, and Vaughan] to death
at Pomfret.*

RATCLIFFE   Come, bring forth the prisoners.

RIVERS
Sir Richard Ratcliffe, let me tell thee this:
Today shalt thou behold a subject die
For truth, for duty, and for loyalty.

GREY
God bless the Prince from all the pack of you!   5
A knot you are of damnèd bloodsuckers.   6

VAUGHAN
You live that shall cry woe for this hereafter.

RATCLIFFE
Dispatch. The limit of your lives is out.   8

RIVERS
O Pomfret, Pomfret! O thou bloody prison,
Fatal and ominous to noble peers!
Within the guilty closure of thy walls   11
Richard the Second here was hacked to death;
And, for more slander to thy dismal seat,   13
We give to thee our guiltless blood to drink.

GREY
Now Margaret's curse is fall'n upon our heads,
When she exclaimed on Hastings, you, and I,
For standing by when Richard stabbed her son.

RIVERS
Then cursed she Richard, then cursed she Buckingham,
Then cursed she Hastings. Oh, remember, God,
To hear her prayer for them, as now for us!
And for my sister and her princely sons,
Be satisfied, dear God, with our true blood,
Which, as thou know'st, unjustly must be spilt.

RATCLIFFE
Make haste. The hour of death is expiate.   24

RIVERS
Come, Grey, come, Vaughan, let us here embrace.
                                  [*They embrace.*]
Farewell, until we meet again in heaven.   *Exeunt.*

❖

3.4

*Enter Buckingham, [Lord Stanley Earl of] Derby,
Hastings, Bishop of Ely, Norfolk, Ratcliffe, Lovell,
with others, at a table.*

HASTINGS
Now, noble peers, the cause why we are met
Is to determine of the coronation.   2
In God's name, speak. When is the royal day?

BUCKINGHAM
Is all things ready for the royal time?

STANLEY
It is, and wants but nomination.   5

ELY
Tomorrow, then, I judge a happy day.   6

BUCKINGHAM
Who knows the Lord Protector's mind herein?
Who is most inward with the noble Duke?   8

ELY
Your Grace, methinks, should soonest know his mind.

BUCKINGHAM
We know each other's faces; for our hearts,   10
He knows no more of mine than I of yours,
Or I of his, my lord, than you of mine.
Lord Hastings, you and he are near in love.

HASTINGS
I thank His Grace, I know he loves me well;
But, for his purpose in the coronation,
I have not sounded him, nor he delivered
His gracious pleasure any way therein.
But you, my honorable lords, may name the time,
And in the Duke's behalf I'll give my voice,   19
Which I presume he'll take in gentle part.   20

Enter [Richard Duke of] Gloucester.

ELY
In happy time, here comes the Duke himself.

RICHARD
My noble lords and cousins all, good morrow.   22
I have been long a sleeper; but I trust
My absence doth neglect no great design   24
Which by my presence might have been concluded.

BUCKINGHAM
Had you not come upon your cue, my lord,
William Lord Hastings had pronounced your part,
I mean your voice for crowning of the King.

RICHARD
Than my Lord Hastings no man might be bolder.
His Lordship knows me well, and loves me well.—
My lord of Ely, when I was last in Holborn,   31
I saw good strawberries in your garden there.
I do beseech you send for some of them.

ELY
Marry, and will, my lord, with all my heart.
                                  Exit Bishop.

RICHARD
Cousin of Buckingham, a word with you.
                              [*Drawing him aside.*]
Catesby hath sounded Hastings in our business,
And finds the testy gentleman so hot
That he will lose his head ere give consent
His master's child, as worshipfully he terms it,   39
Shall lose the royalty of England's throne.

3.3. Location: Pomfret (Pontefract) Castle.
5 pack gang   **6 knot** group   **8 Dispatch** Hurry.   **is out** has been
reached.   **11 closure** enclosure   **13 for . . . seat** i.e., to add further to
the evil reputation of this place   **24 expiate** fully come.
3.4. Location: London. The Tower.
2 determine of decide upon

5 wants but nomination lacks only naming of the day.   **6 happy**
favorable   **8 inward** intimate   **10 for** as for   **19 voice** vote
20 in gentle part with gracious acceptance.   **22 cousins** i.e., peers
24 neglect cause the neglect of   **31 Holborn** (location of the Bishop's
London palace)   **39 worshipfully** reverently. (Said contemptuously.)

BUCKINGHAM
  Withdraw yourself awhile. I'll go with you.
                    Exeunt [Richard and Buckingham].

STANLEY
  We have not yet set down this day of triumph.
  Tomorrow, in my judgment, is too sudden,
  For I myself am not so well provided   44
  As else I would be, were the day prolonged.   45

      Enter the Bishop of Ely.

ELY
  Where is my lord the Duke of Gloucester?
  I have sent for these strawberries.

HASTINGS
  His Grace looks cheerfully and smooth this morning;   48
  There's some conceit or other likes him well   49
  When that he bids good morrow with such spirit.
  I think there's never a man in Christendom
  Can lesser hide his love or hate than he,
  For by his face straight shall you know his heart.

STANLEY
  What of his heart perceive you in his face
  By any likelihood he showed today?

HASTINGS
  Marry, that with no man here he is offended;
  For, were he, he had shown it in his looks.

STANLEY   I pray God he be not, I say.

      Enter Richard and Buckingham.

RICHARD
  I pray you all, tell me what they deserve
  That do conspire my death with devilish plots
  Of damnèd witchcraft, and that have prevailed
  Upon my body with their hellish charms?

HASTINGS
  The tender love I bear Your Grace, my lord,   63
  Makes me most forward in this princely presence
  To doom th'offenders, whosoe'er they be:
  I say, my lord, they have deservèd death.

RICHARD
  Then be your eyes the witness of their evil.
                       [He bares his arm.]
  Look how I am bewitched! Behold, mine arm
  Is like a blasted sapling withered up.   69
  And this is Edward's wife, that monstrous witch,
  Consorted with that harlot strumpet Shore,   71
  That by their witchcraft thus have markèd me.

HASTINGS
  If they have done this deed, my noble lord—

RICHARD
  If? Thou protector of this damnèd strumpet,
  Talk'st thou to me of "ifs"? Thou art a traitor.—
  Off with his head! Now, by Saint Paul I swear,
  I will not dine until I see the same.
  Lovell and Ratcliffe, look that it be done.   78

  The rest that love me, rise and follow me.   79
      Exeunt. Manent Lovell and Ratcliffe, with the Lord
                                  Hastings.

HASTINGS
  Woe, woe for England! Not a whit for me,
  For I, too fond, might have prevented this.   81
  Stanley did dream the boar did raze our helms,
  And I did scorn it and disdain to fly.
  Three times today my footcloth horse did stumble,   84
  And started, when he looked upon the Tower,
  As loath to bear me to the slaughterhouse.
  Oh, now I need the priest that spake to me!
  I now repent I told the pursuivant,
  As too triumphing, how mine enemies
  Today at Pomfret bloodily were butchered,
  And I myself secure in grace and favor.
  O Margaret, Margaret, now thy heavy curse
  Is lighted on poor Hastings' wretched head!

RATCLIFFE
  Come, come, dispatch. The Duke would be at
    dinner.
  Make a short shrift. He longs to see your head.   95

HASTINGS
  Oh, momentary grace of mortal men,   96
  Which we more hunt for than the grace of God!
  Who builds his hope in air of your good looks   98
  Lives like a drunken sailor on a mast,
  Ready with every nod to tumble down
  Into the fatal bowels of the deep.

LOVELL
  Come, come, dispatch. 'Tis bootless to exclaim.   102

HASTINGS
  Oh, bloody Richard! Miserable England!
  I prophesy the fearful'st time to thee
  That ever wretched age hath looked upon.
  Come, lead me to the block; bear him my head.
  They smile at me who shortly shall be dead.
                            Exeunt.

❖

[3.5]

      Enter Richard [Duke of Gloucester] and
      Buckingham in rotten armor, marvelous
      ill-favored.

RICHARD
  Come, cousin, canst thou quake and change thy color,
  Murder thy breath in middle of a word,   2
  And then again begin, and stop again,
  As if thou wert distraught and mad with terror?

79.1 Manent They remain onstage **81 fond** foolish **84 footcloth**
large, richly ornamented cloth laid over the back of a horse and hanging to the ground on each side. **stumble** (An omen of misfortune.)
95 shrift confession. **96 grace** favor, fortune **98 Who** Anyone who.
in . . . looks on the insubstantial foundation of your favor **102 boot-**
less useless
3.5. Location: London. The Tower.
0.2 rotten rusty **0.2–3 marvelous ill-favored** remarkably unattractive. **2 Murder** i.e., stop, catch

---

44 provided equipped **45 prolonged** postponed. **48 smooth** pleasant **49 conceit** fancy, idea. **likes** pleases **63 tender** dear
69 blasted shriveled **71 Consorted** associated **78 look** see to it

BUCKINGHAM
Tut, I can counterfeit the deep tragedian,
Speak and look back, and pry on every side,   6
Tremble and start at wagging of a straw;
Intending deep suspicion, ghastly looks   8
Are at my service, like enforcèd smiles;
And both are ready in their offices,   10
At any time, to grace my stratagems.
But what, is Catesby gone?

RICHARD
He is; and, see, he brings the Mayor along.

Enter the Mayor and Catesby.

BUCKINGHAM   Lord Mayor—
RICHARD   Look to the drawbridge there!
BUCKINGHAM   Hark, a drum!
RICHARD   Catesby, o'erlook the walls.   [*Exit Catesby.*]   17

BUCKINGHAM
Lord Mayor, the reason we have sent—

RICHARD
Look back, defend thee, here are enemies!

BUCKINGHAM
God and our innocence defend and guard us!

Enter Lovell and Ratcliffe, with Hastings' head.

RICHARD
Be patient. They are friends, Ratcliffe and Lovell.

LOVELL
Here is the head of that ignoble traitor,
The dangerous and unsuspected Hastings.

RICHARD
So dear I loved the man that I must weep.
I took him for the plainest harmless creature
That breathed upon the earth a Christian,
Made him my book wherein my soul recorded   27
The history of all her secret thoughts.
So smooth he daubed his vice with show of virtue
That, his apparent open guilt omitted—   30
I mean, his conversation with Shore's wife—   31
He lived from all attainder of suspects.   32

BUCKINGHAM
Well, well, he was the covert'st sheltered traitor   33
That ever lived. Look ye, my Lord Mayor,
Would you imagine, or almost believe,   35
Were't not that by great preservation   36
We live to tell it, that the subtle traitor
This day had plotted, in the Council House,
To murder me and my good lord of Gloucester?

MAYOR   Had he done so?   39

RICHARD
What, think you we are Turks or infidels?
Or that we would, against the form of law,

Proceed thus rashly in the villain's death,
But that the extreme peril of the case,
The peace of England, and our persons' safety,
Enforced us to this execution?

MAYOR
Now fair befall you! He deserved his death,   47
And Your good Graces both have well proceeded   48
To warn false traitors from the like attempts.

BUCKINGHAM
I never looked for better at his hands
After he once fell in with Mistress Shore.
Yet had we not determined he should die   52
Until Your Lordship came to see his end,
Which now the loving haste of these our friends,
Something against our meanings, have prevented;   55
Because, my lord, we would have had you hear   56
The traitor speak and timorously confess
The manner and the purpose of his treasons,
That you might well have signified the same
Unto the citizens, who haply may   60
Misconster us in him and wail his death.   61

MAYOR
But, my good lord, Your Grace's words shall serve
As well as I had seen and heard him speak.   63
And do not doubt, right noble princes both,
But I'll acquaint our duteous citizens
With all your just proceedings in this cause.

RICHARD
And to that end we wished Your Lordship here,
T'avoid the censures of the carping world.

BUCKINGHAM
Which, since you come too late of our intent,   69
Yet witness what you hear we did intend.   70
And so, my good Lord Mayor, we bid farewell.
                                                                    Exit Mayor.

RICHARD
Go, after, after, cousin Buckingham.
The Mayor towards Guildhall hies him in all post.   73
There, at your meet'st advantage of the time,   74
Infer the bastardy of Edward's children.   75
Tell them how Edward put to death a citizen
Only for saying he would make his son
Heir to the Crown—meaning indeed his house,   78
Which, by the sign thereof, was termèd so.   79
Moreover, urge his hateful luxury   80

6 **back** over my shoulder.   **pry** peer   8 **Intending** pretending
10 **offices** uses, functions   17 **o'erlook** inspect   27 **book** i.e., table
book or diary   30 **his . . . omitted** apart from his manifest open guilt
31 **conversation** sexual intimacy   32 **from . . . suspects** free from all
stain of suspicion.   33 **covert'st sheltered** most secret, hidden
35 **almost** even   36 **great preservation** providential protection
39 **Had he** Would he have

47 **fair** good fortune   48 **Your . . . proceeded** Your Graces (the Dukes
of Gloucester and Buckingham) have done well   52 **had we . . . die**
we had determined he should not die   55 **Something . . . meanings**
somewhat contrary to our intent   56 **we . . . heard** we would have
wished you to have heard   60 **haply** perhaps   61 **Misconster . . . him**
i.e., misconstrue our intentions regarding him   63 **as** as if   69 **of** to
accord with   70 **witness** bear witness to   73 **Guildhall** central hall
for municipal affairs.   **hies . . . post** hurries with all possible speed.
74 **meet'st advantage** most suitable opportunity   75 **Infer** allege,
adduce   78 **the Crown** i.e., a tavern in Cheapside identified by the
sign of the Crown. (King Edward is portrayed as having been so sensitive to possible rivals that he put to death a man merely for naming
his son heir to "the Crown," even though the poor fellow innocently
meant nothing more than his own tavern. The story is from Sir
Thomas More's *History of King Richard III*.)   79 **sign** tavern or shop
sign displayed over the door   80 **luxury** lechery

PLATE 13

Henry V. *When King Henry V, a fairy tale prince, sets sail for France, actor-director Laurence Olivier's rousing 1944 film opens out and away from the Elizabethan public theater of its early scenes. Colorful and patriotic in its imagery, this harbor scene ends with the King's cry "Cheerly to sea! The signs of war advance! / No king of England, if not king of France!" (2.2.193-194). (Photofest)*

PLATE 14

Henry V. *In contrast to Olivier's patriotic pageant, Kenneth Branagh's 1989 film employs a gritty war-is-hell style of realism. In this scene, Branagh's Henry V has just placed the body of a murdered boy on the cart beside him, and, although the Battle of Agincourt is now won, the imagery seems to ask "What price victory?"* (Terry O'Neil/ Corbis-Sygma)

PLATE 15

Richard III. *Laurence Olivier wore a long, lank wig and witch-like nose in his terrifying stage portrayal of Shakespeare's murderous monarch. Here, in a scene from his widely seen 1955 film based on that production, Olivier's Richard prepares to fight his nemesis, the Earl of Richmond, at Bosworth Field.* (The Kobal Collection)

PLATE 16

Richard III. *Al Pacino tracked Shakespeare's character as an actor's quarry in the documentary sections of his 1996 film* Looking for Richard. *Pictured here is the actor with a prop arrow in his chest and members of the cast and crew as they prepare to shoot the final Battle of Bosworth.* (20th Century Fox/The Kobal Collection/Michael Halsband)

PLATE 17
Richard III. *In his taut 1995 film starring Ian McKellen, director Richard Loncraine parallels Richard's reign of terror with the fascistic violence of Hitler and Mussolini. He relocates the action to the 1930s, clarifying the political rivalries and highlighting the perverted sexuality of Shakespeare's deformed anti-hero.* (Mayfair/Bayly/Pare/ The Kobal Collection)

PLATE 18
Henry IV. *Kevin Kline created a muted Falstaff, witty and empathetic, in director Jack O'Brien's autumnal 2003 staging of* Henry IV *at New York's Lincoln Center. In the tavern scene (from Part One, 2.4.374 ff), Kline's Falstaff wears a cushion for a crown to play at being Prince Hal's disapproving father, Henry IV.* (Photo by Sara Kulwich/the *New York Times*)

And bestial appetite in change of lust,   81
Which stretched unto their servants, daughters, wives,   82
Even where his raging eye or savage heart,
Without control, lusted to make a prey.
Nay, for a need, thus far come near my person: 85
Tell them, when that my mother went with child   86
Of that insatiate Edward, noble York   87
My princely father then had wars in France,
And by true computation of the time
Found that the issue was not his begot—
Which well appearèd in his lineaments,   91
Being nothing like the noble duke my father.
Yet touch this sparingly, as 'twere far off,
Because, my lord, you know my mother lives.

BUCKINGHAM
Doubt not, my lord, I'll play the orator
As if the golden fee for which I plead   96
Were for myself. And so, my lord, adieu.

RICHARD
If you thrive well, bring them to Baynard's Castle,   98
Where you shall find me well accompanied
With reverend fathers and well-learnèd bishops.

BUCKINGHAM
I go; and towards three or four o'clock
Look for the news that the Guildhall affords.
                                                   Exit Buckingham.

RICHARD
Go, Lovell, with all speed to Doctor Shaw.   103
[*To Ratcliffe*] Go thou to Friar Penker. Bid them both   104
Meet me within this hour at Baynard's Castle.
                                           Exeunt [all but Richard].
Now will I go to take some privy order   106
To draw the brats of Clarence out of sight,
And to give order that no manner person   108
Have any time recourse unto the princes.   *Exit.* 109

❧

[3.6]

Enter a Scrivener [with a paper in his hand].

SCRIVENER
Here is the indictment of the good Lord Hastings,
Which in a set hand fairly is engrossed   2
That it may be today read o'er in Paul's.   3
And mark how well the sequel hangs together: 4

Eleven hours I have spent to write it over,
For yesternight by Catesby was it sent me;
The precedent was full as long a-doing.   7
And yet within these five hours Hastings lived,
Untainted, unexamined, free, at liberty.   9
Here's a good world the while! Who is so gross   10
That cannot see this palpable device?
Yet who so bold but says he sees it not?
Bad is the world, and all will come to naught
When such ill dealing must be seen in thought.   14
                                                   Exit.

❧

[3.7]

*Enter Richard [Duke of Gloucester] and
Buckingham, at several doors.*

RICHARD
How now, how now, what say the citizens?

BUCKINGHAM
Now, by the holy mother of our Lord,
The citizens are mum, say not a word.

RICHARD
Touched you the bastardy of Edward's children?   4

BUCKINGHAM
I did; with his contract with Lady Lucy   5
And his contract by deputy in France;   6
Th'insatiate greediness of his desire   7
And his enforcement of the city wives;   8
His tyranny for trifles; his own bastardy,   9
As being got, your father then in France,   10
And his resemblance, being not like the Duke.
Withal I did infer your lineaments,   12
Being the right idea of your father   13
Both in your form and nobleness of mind;
Laid open all your victories in Scotland,   15
Your discipline in war, wisdom in peace,   16
Your bounty, virtue, fair humility;
Indeed, left nothing fitting for your purpose
Untouched or slightly handled in discourse.
And when mine oratory drew toward end,
I bid them that did love their country's good
Cry, "God save Richard, England's royal king!"

RICHARD   And did they so?

---

7 **precedent** prepared indictment serving as a first draft   9 **Untainted,
unexamined** not yet accused or interrogated   10 **Here's . . . while!**
Here's a fine state of affairs! **gross** dull, stupid   14 **seen in thought**
i.e., perceived in silence.
3.7. **Location:** The courtyard of Baynard's Castle.
0.2 *several* separate   4 **Touched you** Did you deal with, touch upon,
discuss   5 **contract** betrothal.   **Lady Lucy** Elizabeth Lucy (by whom
Edward had a child, though there was no formal contract of
betrothal)   6 **deputy** (See *3 Henry VI,* 3.3.49 ff., where Warwick, as
deputy, contracts with Louis XI of France for the marriage of King
Edward to Lady Bona, sister of the French queen.)   7 **Th'insatiate** the
insatiable   8 **enforcement** forcible seduction   9 **tyranny for trifles**
harsh punishment of minor offenses, or cruel behavior over trifles
10 **got** begot   12 **Withal . . . lineaments** Besides that, I pointed to
your features   13 **right idea** true image   15 **Laid . . . Scotland** I elaborated on your successful expedition against Scotland in 1482
16 **discipline** skill, training

---

81 **in . . . lust** i.e., constantly desiring new mistresses   82 **their** i.e.,
the citizens'   85 **for a need** if necessary   86–7 **when . . . Of** when my
mother was pregnant with   91 **his lineaments** Edward's features
96 **golden fee** i.e., crown   98 **Baynard's Castle** Richard's residence
on the north bank of the Thames. It was founded by Baynard, a
nobleman in the time of the Conquest, and had belonged to Richard's
father.   103, 104 **Doctor Shaw, Friar Penker** (Well-known divines
who delivered sermons in Richard's favor.)   106 **take . . . order** give
some secret instruction   108 **no manner person** no one at all
109 **Have . . . recourse** have access at any time
3.6. **Location:** London. A street.
2 **in . . . engrossed** is written out in a style of script used for legal documents   3 **read . . . Paul's** posted and read publicly in St. Paul's
Cathedral.   4 **the sequel** what follows

BUCKINGHAM
No, so God help me, they spake not a word,
But, like dumb statues or breathing stones,
Stared each on other and looked deadly pale.
Which when I saw, I reprehended them,
And asked the Mayor what meant this willful silence.
His answer was, the people were not used
To be spoke to but by the Recorder.   30
Then he was urged to tell my tale again:
"Thus saith the Duke, thus hath the Duke inferred"—   32
But nothing spake in warrant from himself.   33
When he had done, some followers of mine own,
At lower end of the hall, hurled up their caps,
And some ten voices cried, "God save King Richard!"
And thus I took the vantage of those few: 37
"Thanks, gentle citizens and friends," quoth I,
"This general applause and cheerful shout
Argues your wisdoms and your love to Richard"—
And even here brake off and came away.   41
RICHARD
What tongueless blocks were they! Would they not speak?
BUCKINGHAM   No, by my troth, my lord.
RICHARD
Will not the Mayor, then, and his brethren come?   44
BUCKINGHAM
The Mayor is here at hand. Intend some fear;   45
Be not you spoke with but by mighty suit.   46
And look you get a prayer book in your hand,
And stand between two churchmen, good my lord,
For on that ground I'll make a holy descant;   49
And be not easily won to our requests.
Play the maid's part: still answer nay and take it.
RICHARD
I go; and if you plead as well for them
As I can say nay to thee for myself,
No doubt we'll bring it to a happy issue.   54
BUCKINGHAM
Go, go, up to the leads. The Lord Mayor knocks.   55
                                       [Exit Richard.]

        Enter the Mayor, [aldermen,] and citizens.

Welcome, my lord. I dance attendance here;   56
I think the Duke will not be spoke withal.   57

        Enter Catesby.

Now, Catesby, what says your lord to my request?
CATESBY
He doth entreat Your Grace, my noble lord,
To visit him tomorrow or next day.
He is within, with two right reverend fathers,
Divinely bent to meditation,

And in no worldly suits would he be moved
To draw him from his holy exercise.
BUCKINGHAM
Return, good Catesby, to the gracious Duke.
Tell him myself, the Mayor and aldermen,
In deep designs, in matter of great moment,
No less importing than our general good,   68
Are come to have some conference with His Grace.
CATESBY
I'll signify so much unto him straight.   Exit.
BUCKINGHAM
Aha, my lord, this prince is not an Edward!
He is not lolling on a lewd love bed
But on his knees at meditation;
Not dallying with a brace of courtesans   74
But meditating with two deep divines;   75
Not sleeping, to engross his idle body,   76
But praying, to enrich his watchful soul.
Happy were England, would this virtuous prince
Take on His Grace the sovereignty thereof;
But sure I fear we shall not win him to it.
MAYOR
Marry, God defend His Grace should say us nay!   81
BUCKINGHAM
I fear he will.—Here Catesby comes again.

        Enter Catesby.

Now, Catesby, what says His Grace?
CATESBY   My lord,
He wonders to what end you have assembled
Such troops of citizens to come to him,
His Grace not being warned thereof before.
He fears, my lord, you mean no good to him.
BUCKINGHAM
Sorry I am my noble cousin should
Suspect me that I mean no good to him.
By heaven, we come to him in perfect love,
And so once more return and tell His Grace.
                                       Exit [Catesby].
When holy and devout religious men
Are at their beads, 'tis much to draw them thence,   93
So sweet is zealous contemplation.   94

        Enter Richard aloft, between two bishops. [Catesby
        returns to the main stage.]

MAYOR
See where His Grace stands, 'tween two clergymen!
BUCKINGHAM
Two props of virtue for a Christian prince,
To stay him from the fall of vanity.   97
And, see, a book of prayer in his hand,
True ornaments to know a holy man.—   99
Famous Plantagenet, most gracious prince,

---

30 the Recorder London's chief legal officer.   32 inferred alleged,
asserted   33 in . . . himself on his own authority.   37 vantage
advantage   41 brake broke   44 brethren fellow aldermen
45 Intend Pretend   46 mighty suit importunate entreaty.
49 ground the plainsong or melody on which a *descant* or melodious
accompaniment is raised   54 issue outcome.   55 leads flat lead cov-
erings for roof; hence, the roof itself.   56 dance attendance i.e., am
kept waiting   57 withal with.

68 No less importing concerned with nothing less   74 brace pair
75 deep learned   76 engross fatten   81 defend forbid   93 beads i.e.,
prayers beads.   much hard   94.1 *aloft* i.e., on the gallery above the
stage, rear. (The tiring-house facade in this scene is imagined to be the
facade of Baynard's Castle.)   97 stay steady or keep   99 ornaments
i.e., the bishops as well as the prayer book

Lend favorable ear to our requests,
And pardon us the interruption
Of thy devotion and right Christian zeal.

RICHARD
My lord, there needs no such apology.
I do beseech Your Grace to pardon me,
Who, earnest in the service of my God,
Deferred the visitation of my friends.
But, leaving this, what is Your Grace's pleasure?

BUCKINGHAM
Even that, I hope, which pleaseth God above,
And all good men of this ungoverned isle.

RICHARD
I do suspect I have done some offense
That seems disgracious in the city's eye,   112
And that you come to reprehend my ignorance.

BUCKINGHAM
You have, my lord. Would it might please Your Grace,
On our entreaties, to amend your fault!

RICHARD
Else wherefore breathe I in a Christian land?   116

BUCKINGHAM
Know then, it is your fault that you resign
The supreme seat, the throne majestical,
The sceptered office of your ancestors,
Your state of fortune and your due of birth,   120
The lineal glory of your royal house,
To the corruption of a blemished stock;   122
While, in the mildness of your sleepy thoughts,   123
Which here we waken to our country's good,
The noble isle doth want her proper limbs;   125
Her face defaced with scars of infamy,
Her royal stock graft with ignoble plants,   127
And almost shouldered in the swallowing gulf   128
Of dark forgetfulness and deep oblivion.
Which to recure, we heartily solicit   130
Your gracious self to take on you the charge
And kingly government of this your land—
Not as protector, steward, substitute,
Or lowly factor for another's gain,   134
But as successively from blood to blood,   135
Your right of birth, your empery, your own.   136
For this, consorted with the citizens,   137
Your very worshipful and loving friends,   138
And by their vehement instigation,
In this just cause come I to move Your Grace.

RICHARD
I cannot tell if to depart in silence
Or bitterly to speak in your reproof

Best fitteth my degree or your condition.   143
If not to answer, you might haply think   144
Tongue-tied ambition, not replying, yielded   145
To bear the golden yoke of sovereignty,
Which fondly you would here impose on me.   147
If to reprove you for this suit of yours,
So seasoned with your faithful love to me,   149
Then on the other side I checked my friends.   150
Therefore, to speak, and to avoid the first,
And then, in speaking, not to incur the last,
Definitively thus I answer you.   153
Your love deserves my thanks, but my desert   154
Unmeritable shuns your high request.   155
First, if all obstacles were cut away,
And that my path were even to the crown   157
As the ripe revenue and due of birth,   158
Yet so much is my poverty of spirit,
So mighty and so many my defects,
That I would rather hide me from my greatness—   161
Being a bark to brook no mighty sea—   162
Than in my greatness covet to be hid   163
And in the vapor of my glory smothered.
But, God be thanked, there is no need of me,
And much I need to help you, were there need.   166
The royal tree hath left us royal fruit,
Which, mellowed by the stealing hours of time,   168
Will well become the seat of majesty
And make, no doubt, us happy by his reign.
On him I lay that you would lay on me,   171
The right and fortune of his happy stars,
Which God defend that I should wring from him!   173

BUCKINGHAM
My lord, this argues conscience in Your Grace;
But the respects thereof are nice and trivial,   175
All circumstances well considerèd.
You say that Edward is your brother's son.
So say we too, but not by Edward's wife;
For first was he contract to Lady Lucy—   179
Your mother lives a witness to his vow—   180
And afterward by substitute betrothed   181
To Bona, sister to the King of France.   182
These both put off, a poor petitioner,
A care-crazed mother to a many sons,

143 **degree** rank. **condition** social status. 144 **haply** perhaps
145 **Tongue-tied** silent. (Silence gives consent.) **yielded** consented
147 **fondly** foolishly 149 **seasoned** i.e., made agreeable or palatable
150 **checked** rebuked, i.e., would have rebuked 153 **Definitively**
once and for all 154–5 **my desert Unmeritable** my unworthiness
157 **even** smooth 158 **ripe revenue** possession ready to be inherited
161 **my greatness** i.e., my claim to the throne 162 **bark** ship. **brook**
endure 163 **Than . . . hid** than wish to be enveloped in and overwhelmed by my greatness, i.e., the throne. 166 **I need** I lack the requisite ability 168 **stealing** stealthily moving 171 **that** what
173 **defend** forbid 175 **respects thereof** considerations by which
you support your argument. **nice** overscrupulous 179 **contract**
contracted 180 **Your . . . vow** (According to the chronicles, Richard's
mother, in opposing Edward's intention of marrying Lady Grey because
it was interfering with the negotiations for his marriage to Lady Bona
of Savoy, asserted that Lady Elizabeth Lucy was already Edward's
trothplight wife. Compare with 3.5.75 and 3.7.6.) 181 **substitute**
proxy 182 **sister** i.e., sister-in-law, the Queen's sister

112 **disgracious** unbecoming, displeasing 116 **Else . . . land?** i.e.,
How could I call myself a Christian if I am not prepared to amend my
faults? 120 **state of fortune** position to which fortune entitles you
122 **blemished** i.e., through bastardy; see lines 177–91 below
123 **sleepy** passive 125 **want her proper limbs** lack its own limbs, is
crippled 127 **graft** engrafted 128 **shouldered in** jostled into, or
immersed up to the shoulders in 130 **recure** restore, make whole
134 **factor** agent 135 **successively** in order of succession 136 **empery**
empire 137 **consorted** associated, leagued 138 **worshipful** respectful

A beauty-waning and distressèd widow,
Even in the afternoon of her best days,
Made prize and purchase of his wanton eye,   187
Seduced the pitch and height of his degree   188
To base declension and loathed bigamy.   189
By her, in his unlawful bed, he got
This Edward, whom our manners call the Prince.   191
More bitterly could I expostulate,   192
Save that, for reverence to some alive,   193
I give a sparing limit to my tongue.
Then, good my lord, take to your royal self   195
This proffered benefit of dignity,
If not to bless us and the land withal,
Yet to draw forth your noble ancestry   198
From the corruption of abusing times
Unto a lineal true-derivèd course.

MAYOR
  Do, good my lord. Your citizens entreat you.
BUCKINGHAM
  Refuse not, mighty lord, this proffered love.
CATESBY
  Oh, make them joyful. Grant their lawful suit!
RICHARD
  Alas, why would you heap this care on me?
  I am unfit for state and majesty.
  I do beseech you, take it not amiss;
  I cannot nor I will not yield to you.
BUCKINGHAM
  If you refuse it—as, in love and zeal,   208
  Loath to depose the child, your brother's son,
  As well we know your tenderness of heart   210
  And gentle, kind, effeminate remorse,   211
  Which we have noted in you to your kindred
  And equally indeed to all estates—   213
  Yet know, whe'er you accept our suit or no,   214
  Your brother's son shall never reign our king,
  But we will plant some other in the throne
  To the disgrace and downfall of your house.
  And in this resolution here we leave you.—
  Come, citizens. Zounds! I'll entreat no more.   219
RICHARD
  Oh, do not swear, my lord of Buckingham.
                              Exeunt [*Buckingham,*
                          Mayor, aldermen, and the citizens].
CATESBY
  Call him again, sweet prince. Accept their suit.
  If you deny them, all the land will rue it.

RICHARD
  Will you enforce me to a world of cares?
  Call them again. I am not made of stone,
  But penetrable to your kind entreaties,
  Albeit against my conscience and my soul.

              Enter Buckingham and the rest.

  Cousin of Buckingham, and sage, grave men,
  Since you will buckle fortune on my back,
  To bear her burden, whe'er I will or no,
  I must have patience to endure the load.
  But if black scandal or foul-faced reproach
  Attend the sequel of your imposition,   232
  Your mere enforcement shall acquittance me   233
  From all the impure blots and stains thereof;
  For God doth know, and you may partly see,
  How far I am from the desire of this.
MAYOR
  God bless Your Grace! We see it and will say it.
RICHARD
  In saying so, you shall but say the truth.
BUCKINGHAM
  Then I salute you with this royal title:
  Long live Richard, England's worthy king!
MAYOR AND CITIZENS   Amen.
BUCKINGHAM
  Tomorrow may it please you to be crowned?
RICHARD
  Even when you please, for you will have it so.
BUCKINGHAM
  Tomorrow, then, we will attend Your Grace.
  And so most joyfully we take our leave.
RICHARD [*to the Bishops*]
  Come, let us to our holy work again.—
  Farewell, my cousin. Farewell, gentle friends. *Exeunt.*

                              ✤

4.1

              Enter [at one door] the Queen [Elizabeth], the
              Duchess of York, and Marquess [of] Dorset; [at
              another door] Anne, Duchess of Gloucester,
              [leading Lady Margaret Plantagenet, Clarence's
              young daughter].

DUCHESS
  Who meets us here? My niece Plantagenet   1
  Led in the hand of her kind aunt of Gloucester?
  Now, for my life, she's wand'ring to the Tower,   3
  On pure heart's love to greet the tender Prince.   4
  Daughter, well met.
ANNE   God give Your Graces both   5
  A happy and a joyful time of day!
QUEEN ELIZABETH
  As much to you, good sister. Whither away?   7

---

187 **purchase** booty   188–9 **Seduced . . . declension** i.e., seduced him away from his high rank to ignoble decline. (*Pitch* is the highest point in a falcon's flight.)   189 **bigamy** (Edward was not only bound by previous contracts, as indicated in lines 178–82 above, but also, by marrying a widow, entered into a union that was widely regarded as bigamous.)   191 **manners** sense of politeness   192 **expostulate** discuss, dilate   193 **some alive** i.e., the Duchess of York. (See 3.5.93–4.)   195 **good my lord** my good lord   198 **draw forth** rescue, extract   208 **as** from being   210 **As . . . know** since we know well   211 **kind, effeminate remorse** natural, tender pity   213 **estates** ranks. (Buckingham argues that this virtue of pity is found in Richard's treatment of everyone.)   214 **whe'er** whether   219 **Zounds!** By His (God's) wounds!

232 **your imposition** the duty that you lay upon me   233 **Your . . . acquittance me** the mere fact of your insistence will exonerate me   **4.1. Location:** London. Before the Tower.   1 **niece** i.e., granddaughter   3 **for** on   4 **On** out of.   **tender** young   5 **Daughter** i.e., Daughter-in-law   7 **sister** i.e., sister-in-law.

ANNE
No farther than the Tower, and, as I guess,
Upon the like devotion as yourselves,   9
To gratulate the gentle princes there.   10

QUEEN ELIZABETH
Kind sister, thanks. We'll enter all together.

Enter [Brackenbury] the Lieutenant.

And, in good time, here the Lieutenant comes.—
Master Lieutenant, pray you, by your leave,
How doth the Prince and my young son of York?

BRACKENBURY
Right well, dear madam. By your patience,
I may not suffer you to visit them;   16
The King hath strictly charged the contrary.

QUEEN ELIZABETH
The King! Who's that?

BRACKENBURY   I mean the Lord Protector.

QUEEN ELIZABETH
The Lord protect him from that kingly title!
Hath he set bounds between their love and me?   20
I am their mother; who shall bar me from them?

DUCHESS
I am their father's mother; I will see them.

ANNE
Their aunt I am in law, in love their mother;
Then bring me to their sights. I'll bear thy blame
And take thy office from thee, on my peril.   25

BRACKENBURY
No, madam, no; I may not leave it so.
I am bound by oath, and therefore pardon me.

                      Exit Lieutenant.

Enter [Lord] Stanley [Earl of Derby].

STANLEY
Let me but meet you, ladies, one hour hence,
And I'll salute Your Grace of York as mother,   29
And reverend looker-on, of two fair queens.   30
[*To Anne*] Come, madam, you must straight to
    Westminster,
There to be crownèd Richard's royal queen.

QUEEN ELIZABETH   Ah, cut my lace asunder,   33
That my pent heart may have some scope to beat,
Or else I swoon with this dead-killing news!

ANNE
Despiteful tidings! Oh, unpleasing news!

DORSET
Be of good cheer. Mother, how fares Your Grace?

QUEEN ELIZABETH
Oh, Dorset, speak not to me. Get thee gone!
Death and destruction dogs thee at thy heels;
Thy mother's name is ominous to children.
If thou wilt outstrip death, go cross the seas

And live with Richmond, from the reach of hell.   42
Go, hie thee, hie thee from this slaughterhouse,   43
Lest thou increase the number of the dead
And make me die the thrall of Margaret's curse,   45
Nor mother, wife, nor England's counted queen.   46

STANLEY
Full of wise care is this your counsel, madam.
[*To Dorset*] Take all the swift advantage of the hours.
You shall have letters from me to my son   49
In your behalf, to meet you on the way.   50
Be not ta'en tardy by unwise delay.   51

DUCHESS
Oh, ill-dispersing wind of misery!   52
Oh, my accursèd womb, the bed of death!
A cockatrice hast thou hatched to the world,   54
Whose unavoided eye is murderous.

STANLEY [*to Anne*]
Come, madam, come. I in all haste was sent.

ANNE
And I with all unwillingness will go.
Oh, would to God that the inclusive verge   58
Of golden metal that must round my brow
Were red-hot steel, to sear me to the brains!
Anointed let me be with deadly venom   61
And die ere men can say, "God save the Queen!"

QUEEN ELIZABETH
Go, go, poor soul. I envy not thy glory.
To feed my humor, wish thyself no harm.   64

ANNE
No? Why? When he that is my husband now
Came to me, as I followed Henry's corpse,
When scarce the blood was well washed from his hands
Which issued from my other angel husband   68
And that dear saint which then I weeping followed—   69
Oh, when, I say, I looked on Richard's face,
This was my wish: "Be thou," quoth I, "accurst
For making me, so young, so old a widow!   72
And, when thou wed'st, let sorrow haunt thy bed;
And be thy wife—if any be so mad—
More miserable by the life of thee
Than thou hast made me by my dear lord's death!"
Lo, ere I can repeat this curse again,
Within so small a time, my woman's heart
Grossly grew captive to his honey words   79
And proved the subject of mine own soul's curse,

---

9 **like devotion** same devout errand   10 **gratulate** greet, salute
16 **suffer** permit   20 **bounds** barriers   25 **take . . . thee** i.e., relieve
you of the responsibility   29 **mother** i.e., mother-in-law (of Elizabeth
as widow of Edward and of Anne as wife of King Richard)
30 **looker-on** beholder.   **two fair queens** i.e., Elizabeth and Anne,
since Anne's husband, Richard, is about to be crowned.   33 **lace** cord
used to lace the bodice

42 **with Richmond** i.e., with Henry Tudor, Earl of Richmond, at this
time in Brittany   43 **hie** hasten   45 **thrall** subject, victim   46 **Nor**
neither.   **counted** accepted, esteemed   49–50 **You . . . way** i.e., I will
arrange to have a letter catch up with you on your journey, recom-
mending you to my stepson, the Earl of Richmond. (Lord Stanley's
own son, George Stanley, may also be involved in this rapid negotiation; see 4.4.494–6 ff. below.)   51 **ta'en** taken, caught   52 **ill-dispersing**
evil-spreading   54 **cockatrice** basilisk. (See the note for 1.2.153.)
58 **inclusive verge** enclosing circle, i.e., the crown, here likened to an
instrument of torture used to punish regicides or other criminals
61 **Anointed** (Anne desires to be anointed with poison rather than
with holy oil, as in the ceremony of coronation.)   64 **To . . . harm** Do
not curse yourself (or, possibly, I do not wish you harm) just to satisfy
my vengeful mood.   68 **angel husband** Edward, son of Henry VI
69 **saint** Henry VI   72 **so old a widow** i.e., destined to live so long as
a widow.   79 **Grossly** stupidly

Which hitherto hath held mine eyes from rest;   81
For never yet one hour in his bed
Did I enjoy the golden dew of sleep,
But with his timorous dreams was still awaked.   84
Besides, he hates me for my father Warwick,
And will, no doubt, shortly be rid of me.

QUEEN ELIZABETH
Poor heart, adieu! I pity thy complaining.

ANNE
No more than with my soul I mourn for yours.

DORSET
Farewell, thou woeful welcomer of glory!   89

ANNE
Adieu, poor soul, that tak'st thy leave of it!

DUCHESS [to Dorset]
Go thou to Richmond, and good fortune guide thee!
[To Anne] Go thou to Richard, and good angels tend thee!
[To Queen Elizabeth] Go thou to sanctuary, and good
    thoughts possess thee!
I to my grave, where peace and rest lie with me!
Eighty-odd years of sorrow have I seen,
And each hour's joy wracked with a week of teen.   96
                                [They start to go.]

QUEEN ELIZABETH
Stay, yet look back with me unto the Tower.
Pity, you ancient stones, those tender babes
Whom envy hath immured within your walls—   99
Rough cradle for such little pretty ones!
Rude ragged nurse, old sullen playfellow   101
For tender princes, use my babies well!
So foolish sorrows bids your stones farewell.   Exeunt.

❧

4.2

Sound a sennet. Enter Richard, in pomp;
Buckingham, Catesby, Ratcliffe, Lovell, [a Page,
and others].

KING RICHARD
Stand all apart. Cousin of Buckingham!   1
            [The others stand aside, out of earshot.]

BUCKINGHAM   My gracious sovereign?

KING RICHARD
Give me thy hand.
            Sound [trumpets. Here he ascends the throne.]
                        Thus high, by thy advice
And thy assistance, is King Richard seated.
But shall we wear these glories for a day?
Or shall they last, and we rejoice in them?

BUCKINGHAM
Still live they, and forever let them last!

KING RICHARD
Ah, Buckingham, now do I play the touch,   8
To try if thou be current gold indeed: 9
Young Edward lives. Think now what I would speak.

BUCKINGHAM   Say on, my loving lord.

KING RICHARD
Why, Buckingham, I say I would be king.

BUCKINGHAM
Why, so you are, my thrice-renownèd lord.

KING RICHARD
Ha! Am I king? 'Tis so. But Edward lives.

BUCKINGHAM
True, noble prince.

KING RICHARD   Oh, bitter consequence,   15
That Edward still should live "true, noble prince"!   16
Cousin, thou wast not wont to be so dull.   17
Shall I be plain? I wish the bastards dead,
And I would have it suddenly performed.   19
What say'st thou now? Speak suddenly; be brief.

BUCKINGHAM   Your Grace may do your pleasure.

KING RICHARD
Tut, tut, thou art all ice; thy kindness freezes.
Say, have I thy consent that they shall die?

BUCKINGHAM
Give me some little breath, some pause, dear lord,
Before I positively speak in this.
I will resolve you herein presently.   *Exit Buckingham.*   26

CATESBY [to those standing aside]
The King is angry. See, he gnaws his lip.

KING RICHARD [aside]
I will converse with iron-witted fools   28
And unrespective boys. None are for me   29
That look into me with considerate eyes.   30
High-reaching Buckingham grows circumspect.—   31
Boy!

PAGE [approaching]   My lord?

KING RICHARD
Know'st thou not any whom corrupting gold
Will tempt unto a close exploit of death?   35

PAGE
My lord, I know a discontented gentleman
Whose humble means match not his haughty spirit.
Gold were as good as twenty orators,
And will, no doubt, tempt him to anything.

KING RICHARD
What is his name?

PAGE   His name, my lord, is Tyrrel.

KING RICHARD
I partly know the man. Go call him hither, boy.
                                        Exit [Page].

---

81 **hitherto** until now   84 **timorous** full of fears.   **still** continually
89 **glory** i.e., the rank of queen—*woeful* because it involves marriage
to Richard.   96 **wracked** destroyed, or, *racked*, tortured.   **teen** woe.
99 **envy** malice.   **immured** walled up   101 **Rude** Rough
4.2. Location: London. The royal court.
1 **apart** aside.

8 **play the touch** play the part of a touchstone (to test the quality of
gold)   9 **current** sterling, genuine   15 **bitter consequence** i.e., intolerable answer to my words, and an intolerable fact   16 **"true, noble
prince"** (Richard mockingly repeats Buckingham's evasive reply in
line 15 and applies it to the irritating fact that young Edward still
lives and is a noble prince.)   17 **wast not wont** used not   19 **suddenly** swiftly   26 **resolve** answer   28–31 **I will . . . circumspect** i.e.,
Apparently I have no choice but to communicate my intentions to
dim-witted fools and inattentive boys. I will have nothing more to do
with men who look into my thoughts too searchingly. Ambitious
Buckingham grows wary.   35 **close** secret

[*Aside*] The deep-revolving, witty Buckingham   42
No more shall be the neighbor to my counsels.
Hath he so long held out with me untired,
And stops he now for breath? Well, be it so.

Enter [Lord] Stanley [Earl of Derby].

How now, Lord Stanley? What's the news?
STANLEY   Know, my loving lord,
The Marquess Dorset, as I hear, is fled
To Richmond, in the parts where he abides.
                                          [*He stands apart.*]
KING RICHARD
Come hither, Catesby. Rumor it abroad
That Anne my wife is very grievous sick;
I will take order for her keeping close.   52
Inquire me out some mean poor gentleman,   53
Whom I will marry straight to Clarence' daughter.
The boy is foolish, and I fear not him.   55
Look how thou dream'st! I say again, give out
That Anne my queen is sick and like to die.   57
About it, for it stands me much upon   58
To stop all hopes whose growth may damage me.
                                          [*Exit Catesby.*]
I must be married to my brother's daughter,   60
Or else my kingdom stands on brittle glass.
Murder her brothers, and then marry her—
Uncertain way of gain! But I am in
So far in blood that sin will pluck on sin.   64
Tear-falling pity dwells not in this eye.   65

Enter [Page, with] Tyrrel.

Is thy name Tyrrel?
TYRREL
James Tyrrel, and your most obedient subject.
KING RICHARD
Art thou, indeed?
TYRREL   Prove me, my gracious lord.   68
KING RICHARD
Dar'st thou resolve to kill a friend of mine?
TYRREL   Please you;   70
But I had rather kill two enemies.
KING RICHARD
Why, there thou hast it: two deep enemies,
Foes to my rest and my sweet sleep's disturbers
Are they that I would have thee deal upon—   74
Tyrrel, I mean those bastards in the Tower.
TYRREL
Let me have open means to come to them,   76
And soon I'll rid you from the fear of them.

KING RICHARD
Thou sing'st sweet music. Hark, come hither, Tyrrel.
Go, by this token. [*He gives him a token.*] Rise, and lend
    thine ear.   *Whispers.*
There is no more but so. Say it is done,
And I will love thee and prefer thee for it.   81
TYRREL   I will dispatch it straight.   *Exit.*

Enter Buckingham.

BUCKINGHAM
My lord, I have considered in my mind
The late request that you did sound me in.   84
KING RICHARD
Well, let that rest. Dorset is fled to Richmond.
BUCKINGHAM   I hear the news, my lord.
KING RICHARD
Stanley, he is your wife's son. Well, look to it.   87
BUCKINGHAM
My lord, I claim the gift, my due by promise,
For which your honor and your faith is pawned: 89
Th'earldom of Hereford and the movables
Which you have promisèd I shall possess.
KING RICHARD
Stanley, look to your wife. If she convey
Letters to Richmond, you shall answer it.   93
BUCKINGHAM
What says Your Highness to my just request?
KING RICHARD
I do remember me, Henry the Sixth
Did prophesy that Richmond should be king,
When Richmond was a little peevish boy.
A king! Perhaps, perhaps—
BUCKINGHAM   My lord!
KING RICHARD
How chance the prophet could not at that time   100
Have told me, I being by, that I should kill him?   101
BUCKINGHAM
My lord, your promise for the earldom!
KING RICHARD
Richmond! When last I was at Exeter,
The Mayor in courtesy showed me the castle
And called it Rougemont, at which name I started,   105
Because a bard of Ireland told me once
I should not live long after I saw Richmond.
BUCKINGHAM   My lord!
KING RICHARD   Ay, what's o'clock?   109
BUCKINGHAM
I am thus bold to put Your Grace in mind
Of what you promised me.
KING RICHARD   Well, but what's o'clock?
BUCKINGHAM   Upon the stroke of ten.
KING RICHARD   Well, let it strike.
BUCKINGHAM   Why let it strike?

---

42 **deep-revolving** deeply scheming.   **witty** cunning   52 **I will . . .
close** I will give orders for her close confinement.   53 **mean** of humble station   55 **boy** i.e., Clarence's eldest son, Edward Plantagenet,
Earl of Warwick   57 **like** likely   58 **stands . . . upon** is a matter of the
utmost importance to me   60 **brother's daughter** i.e., Elizabeth of
York, daughter to Edward IV, who will, in fact, later become the
queen of Henry VII; see 4.5.7–9 and 5.5.29–31   64 **pluck on** draw on
65 **Tear-falling** Tear-dropping   68 **Prove** Test   70 **Please** If it please
74 **deal upon** proceed against   76 **open** unhampered

81 **prefer** promote, advance   84 **late** recent.   **sound me in** ask me
about.   87 **he** i.e., Richmond   89 **pawned** pledged   93 **it** for it.
100 **the prophet** i.e., Henry VI   101 **by** nearby.   **him** (The word
applies to Richmond and Henry VI.)   105 **Rougemont** i.e., Red Hill.
(With a play on "Richmond.")   109 **what's o'clock?** what time is it?

KING RICHARD
    Because that, like a jack, thou keep'st the stroke   116
    Betwixt thy begging and my meditation.
    I am not in the giving vein today.   118
BUCKINGHAM
    May it please you to resolve me in my suit.   119
KING RICHARD
    Thou troublest me. I am not in the vein.
                          Exit [with all but Buckingham].
BUCKINGHAM
    And is it thus? Repays he my deep service
    With such contempt? Made I him king for this?
    O, let me think on Hastings, and be gone
    To Brecknock, while my fearful head is on!   *Exit.* 124

[4.3]

          Enter Tyrrel.

TYRREL
    The tyrannous and bloody act is done,
    The most arch deed of piteous massacre   2
    That ever yet this land was guilty of.
    Dighton and Forrest, whom I did suborn   4
    To do this piece of ruthless butchery,
    Albeit they were fleshed villains, bloody dogs,   6
    Melted with tenderness and mild compassion,
    Wept like to children in their deaths' sad story.   8
    "Oh, thus," quoth Dighton, "lay the gentle babes."
    "Thus, thus," quoth Forrest, "girdling one another
    Within their alabaster innocent arms.
    Their lips were four red roses on a stalk,
    Which in their summer beauty kissed each other.
    A book of prayers on their pillow lay,
    Which once," quoth Forrest, "almost changed my mind;
    But oh, the devil!"—there the villain stopped;
    When Dighton thus told on: "We smotherèd
    The most replenishèd sweet work of Nature   18
    That from the prime creation e'er she framed."   19
    Hence both are gone; with conscience and remorse   20
    They could not speak; and so I left them both,
    To bear this tidings to the bloody king.

          Enter [King] Richard.

    And here he comes.—All health, my sovereign lord!
KING RICHARD
    Kind Tyrrel, am I happy in thy news?

TYRREL
    If to have done the thing you gave in charge   25
    Beget your happiness, be happy then,
    For it is done.
KING RICHARD   But didst thou see them dead?
TYRREL
    I did, my lord.
KING RICHARD   And buried, gentle Tyrrel?
TYRREL
    The chaplain of the Tower hath buried them;
    But where, to say the truth, I do not know.
KING RICHARD
    Come to me, Tyrrel, soon at after-supper,   31
    When thou shalt tell the process of their death.   32
    Meantime, but think how I may do thee good,
    And be inheritor of thy desire.   34
    Farewell till then.
TYRREL   I humbly take my leave.   *[Exit.]*
KING RICHARD
    The son of Clarence have I pent up close,   36
    His daughter meanly have I matched in marriage,   37
    The sons of Edward sleep in Abraham's bosom,   38
    And Anne my wife hath bid this world good night.
    Now, for I know the Breton Richmond aims   40
    At young Elizabeth, my brother's daughter,   41
    And by that knot looks proudly on the crown,   42
    To her go I, a jolly thriving wooer.

          Enter Ratcliffe.

RATCLIFFE   My lord!
KING RICHARD
    Good or bad news, that thou com'st in so bluntly?
RATCLIFFE
    Bad news, my lord. Morton is fled to Richmond,   46
    And Buckingham, backed with the hardy Welshmen,
    Is in the field, and still his power increaseth.   48
KING RICHARD
    Ely with Richmond troubles me more near   49
    Than Buckingham and his rash-levied strength.   50
    Come, I have learned that fearful commenting   51
    Is leaden servitor to dull delay;   52
    Delay leads impotent and snail-paced beggary.   53
    Then fiery expedition be my wing,   54
    Jove's Mercury, and herald for a king!   55

---

116 **jack** the figure of a man that strikes the bell on the outside of a clock. (With a play on the meaning "lowbred fellow." Richard's complaint is that Buckingham, like the jack of a clock, being on the point of striking the hour—i.e., speaking his request—breaks the continuity of Richard's reflections.)   118 **vein** mood   119 **resolve me** give me a final answer   124 **Brecknock** i.e., Brecon, Buckingham's family seat in Wales.   **fearful** full of fears
4.3. Location: London. The royal court.
2 **arch deed** i.e., chief or notorious act   4 **suborn** bribe   6 **fleshed** experienced in bloodshed   8 **in their . . . story** in telling the story of their deaths.   18 **replenishèd** complete, perfect   19 **prime** first   20 **gone** undone, unnerved

25 **gave in charge** ordered, commanded   31 **after-supper** dessert after supper   32 **process** story   34 **be . . . desire** expect to get what you ask.   36 **pent up close** strictly confined   37 **His . . . marriage** (Margaret Plantagenet was about twelve years old when Richard died. Shakespeare may have confused her with Lady Cicely, a daughter of Edward IV, whom Richard, according to Holinshed, intended to marry to "a man found in a cloud, and of an unknown lineage and family.")   38 **Abraham's bosom** (See Luke 16:22.)   40 **for** because. **Breton** located in Brittany   41 **my brother's** Edward's   42 **by that knot** by virtue of that alliance   46 **Morton** i.e., John Morton, Bishop of Ely, who had been kept prisoner at Brecknock (or Brecon) Castle; he is the Ely of 3.4.   48 **power** army   49 **near** deeply   50 **rash-levied** hastily recruited   51 **fearful commenting** timorous talk   52 **leaden servitor** sluggish attendant   53 **leads** leads to. **beggary** ruin.   54 **expedition** speed   55 **Mercury** messenger of the gods

Go muster men. My counsel is my shield;   56
We must be brief when traitors brave the field.   57

Exeunt.

❖

4.[4]

Enter old Queen Margaret.

QUEEN MARGARET
So now prosperity begins to mellow   1
And drop into the rotten mouth of death.
Here in these confines slyly have I lurked   3
To watch the waning of mine enemies.
A dire induction am I witness to,   5
And will to France, hoping the consequence   6
Will prove as bitter, black, and tragical.
Withdraw thee, wretched Margaret. Who comes here?

[She steps aside.]

Enter Duchess [of York] and Queen [Elizabeth].

QUEEN ELIZABETH
Ah, my poor princes! Ah, my tender babes!
My unblown flowers, new-appearing sweets!   10
If yet your gentle souls fly in the air
And be not fixed in doom perpetual,   12
Hover about me with your airy wings
And hear your mother's lamentation!

QUEEN MARGARET *[aside]*
Hover about her; say that right for right   15
Hath dimmed your infant morn to agèd night.   16

DUCHESS
So many miseries have crazed my voice   17
That my woe-wearied tongue is still and mute.
Edward Plantagenet, why art thou dead?   19

QUEEN MARGARET *[aside]*
Plantagenet doth quit Plantagenet.   20
Edward for Edward pays a dying debt.   21

QUEEN ELIZABETH
Wilt thou, O God, fly from such gentle lambs   22
And throw them in the entrails of the wolf?
When didst thou sleep when such a deed was done?   24

QUEEN MARGARET *[aside]*
When holy Harry died, and my sweet son.   25

DUCHESS
Dead life, blind sight, poor mortal-living ghost,   26

Woe's scene, world's shame, grave's due by life usurped,   27
Brief abstract and record of tedious days,   28
Rest thy unrest on England's lawful earth,

[sitting down]

Unlawfully made drunk with innocent blood!   30

QUEEN ELIZABETH
Ah, that thou wouldst as soon afford a grave   31
As thou canst yield a melancholy seat!
Then would I hide my bones, not rest them here.
Ah, who hath any cause to mourn but we?

[Sitting down by her.]

QUEEN MARGARET *[coming forward]*
If ancient sorrow be most reverend,   35
Give mine the benefit of seniory   36
And let my griefs frown on the upper hand.   37
If sorrow can admit society,   *[sitting down with them]*
Tell o'er your woes again by viewing mine:
I had an Edward, till a Richard killed him;   40
I had a Harry, till a Richard killed him: 41
Thou hadst an Edward, till a Richard killed him;   42
Thou hadst a Richard, till a Richard killed him.   43

DUCHESS
I had a Richard too, and thou didst kill him;   44
I had a Rutland too, thou holp'st to kill him.   45

QUEEN MARGARET
Thou hadst a Clarence too, and Richard killed him.
From forth the kennel of thy womb hath crept
A hellhound that doth hunt us all to death.
That dog, that had his teeth before his eyes   49
To worry lambs and lap their gentle blood,   50
That foul defacer of God's handiwork,
That excellent grand tyrant of the earth   52
That reigns in gallèd eyes of weeping souls,   53
Thy womb let loose, to chase us to our graves.
O upright, just, and true-disposing God,
How do I thank thee that this carnal cur   56
Preys on the issue of his mother's body   57
And makes her pew-fellow with others' moan!   58

DUCHESS
O Harry's wife, triumph not in my woes!
God witness with me, I have wept for thine.

QUEEN MARGARET
Bear with me. I am hungry for revenge,
And now I cloy me with beholding it.   62

---

56 My . . . shield i.e., I will take counsel by arming myself and trust no adviser other than my own weapons   **57 brave** challenge
4.4. Location: London. Near the royal court.
1 mellow mature   **3 confines** regions.   **slyly** stealthily   **5 induction** beginning (as of a play)   **6 will** will go.   **the consequence** what follows, the sequel and conclusion (as in a play)   **10 unblown** unopened.   **sweets** flowers.   **12 doom perpetual** eternal destiny
15 right for right i.e., a just punishment for an offense against justice
16 dimmed . . . night i.e., brought the youthful promise of your children to ruin and death.   **17 crazed** cracked   **19 Edward Plantagenet** the Duchess's son, the dead King Edward IV; or, his son Edward V
20 quit requite   **21 Edward . . . debt** Edward IV (or else Edward V) for Edward, the son of Margaret and Henry VI.   **dying debt** debt paid through death.   **22 fly . . . lambs** i.e., abandon my two sons
24 When i.e., Whenever till now   **25 Harry** i.e., Henry VI   **26 mortal-living ghost** i.e., a dead person still among the living

27 grave's . . . usurped i.e., one who, by living too long, deprives the grave of its due   **28 abstract** epitome   **30 Unlawfully . . . drunk** i.e., England's earth, which is unlawfully made drunk   **31 that thou** would that you, England's earth   **35 reverend** worthy of respect
36 seniory seniority of claim   **37 on . . . hand** i.e., from a place of precedence.   **40 Edward** i.e., my son, the former Prince of Wales
41 Harry i.e., my husband, King Henry VI   **42 Thou** i.e., Queen Elizabeth.   **Edward** i.e., Edward V   **43 Thou . . . Richard** You, Queen Elizabeth, had a son, the young Duke of York   **44 Richard** i.e., Duke of York, the Duchess's husband and father of Richard III, killed by Margaret's army at the Battle of Wakefield in 1460   **45 Rutland** i.e., Edmund, son of the Duke of York, also killed at Wakefield   **49 teeth** (Richard was supposedly born with teeth.)   **50 worry** bite on the throat, tear to pieces   **52 excellent** unparalleled   **53 gallèd** sore with weeping   **56 carnal** flesh-eating   **57 issue** offspring   **58 pew-fellow** i.e., intimate associate   **62 cloy me** gorge myself

Thy Edward he is dead that killed my Edward;   63
Thy other Edward dead, to quit my Edward;   64
Young York he is but boot, because both they   65
Matched not the high perfection of my loss.
Thy Clarence he is dead that stabbed my Edward;   68
And the beholders of this frantic play,   68
Th'adulterate Hastings, Rivers, Vaughan, Grey,   69
Untimely smothered in their dusky graves.   70
Richard yet lives, hell's black intelligencer,   71
Only reserved their factor to buy souls   72
And send them thither; but at hand, at hand
Ensues his piteous and unpitied end.   74
Earth gapes, hell burns, fiends roar, saints pray,
To have him suddenly conveyed from hence.
Cancel his bond of life, dear God, I pray,
That I may live and say, "The dog is dead!"

QUEEN ELIZABETH
  Oh, thou didst prophesy the time would come
  That I should wish for thee to help me curse
  That bottled spider, that foul bunch-backed toad!   81

QUEEN MARGARET
  I called thee then vain flourish of my fortune;   82
  I called thee then poor shadow, painted queen,
  The presentation of but what I was,   84
  The flattering index of a direful pageant,   85
  One heaved a-high to be hurled down below,
  A mother only mocked with two fair babes,
  A dream of what thou wast, a garish flag   88
  To be the aim of every dangerous shot;   89
  A sign of dignity, a breath, a bubble,   90
  A queen in jest, only to fill the scene.
  Where is thy husband now? Where be thy brothers?
  Where be thy two sons? Wherein dost thou joy?
  Who sues and kneels and says, "God save the Queen"
  Where be the bending peers that flattered thee?   95
  Where be the thronging troops that followed thee?   96
  Decline all this, and see what now thou art: 97
  For happy wife, a most distressèd widow;
  For joyful mother, one that wails the name;
  For one being sued to, one that humbly sues;
  For queen, a very caitiff crowned with care;   101
  For she that scorned at me, now scorned of me;   102
  For she being feared of all, now fearing one;
  For she commanding all, obeyed of none.
  Thus hath the course of justice whirled about

And left thee but a very prey to time,
Having no more but thought of what thou wast   107
To torture thee the more, being what thou art.
Thou didst usurp my place, and dost thou not
Usurp the just proportion of my sorrow?
Now thy proud neck bears half my burdened yoke,   111
From which even here I slip my weary head
And leave the burden of it all on thee.
Farewell, York's wife, and queen of sad mischance!
These English woes shall make me smile in France.
                                    [She starts to leave.]
QUEEN ELIZABETH
  O thou well skilled in curses, stay awhile,
  And teach me how to curse mine enemies!
QUEEN MARGARET
  Forbear to sleep the nights, and fast the days;
  Compare dead happiness with living woe;
  Think that thy babes were sweeter than they were
  And he that slew them fouler than he is.
  Bett'ring thy loss makes the bad causer worse;   122
  Revolving this will teach thee how to curse.   123
QUEEN ELIZABETH
  My words are dull. Oh, quicken them with thine!   124
QUEEN MARGARET
  Thy woes will make them sharp, and pierce like mine.
                                          Exit Margaret.
DUCHESS
  Why should calamity be full of words?
QUEEN ELIZABETH
  Windy attorneys to their client's woes,   127
  Airy succeeders of intestate joys,   128
  Poor breathing orators of miseries,   129
  Let them have scope! Though what they will impart
  Help nothing else, yet do they ease the heart.
DUCHESS
  If so, then be not tongue-tied. Go with me,
  And in the breath of bitter words let's smother
  My damnèd son that thy two sweet sons smothered.
                                         [Sound trumpet.]
  The trumpet sounds. Be copious in exclaims.   135

    Enter King Richard and his train [marching, with
    drums and trumpets].

KING RICHARD
  Who intercepts me in my expedition?   136
DUCHESS
  Oh, she that might have intercepted thee,
  By strangling thee in her accursèd womb,
  From all the slaughters, wretch, that thou hast done!
QUEEN ELIZABETH
  Hid'st thou that forehead with a golden crown
  Where should be branded, if that right were right,

63 **Thy Edward** Edward IV.   **my Edward** the son of Henry VI   **64 other Edward** Edward V.   **quit** requite   **65 Young York** Richard, Duke of York, the younger of the princes murdered in the Tower.   **but boot** merely into the bargain   **68 frantic** frenzied, insane   **69 Th'adulterate** the adulterous   **70 smothered** buried   **71 intelligencer** agent, go-between, spy   **72 Only . . . factor** chosen above all others as their (hell's) agent, and sent to earth for no other purpose   **74 piteous** deplorable   **81 bottled** bottle-shaped, swollen (as at 1.3.242).   **bunch-backed** hunchbacked   **82 flourish** mere ornament, embellishment. (See 1.3.241.)   **84 presentation** representation, semblance   **85 index** argument, preface, prologue.   **pageant** spectacular entertainment   **88–9 garish . . . shot** i.e., standard-bearer, conspicuous in appearance, and thus the target of enemy fire   **90 sign** mere token   **95 bending** bowing   **96 troops** supporters, followers   **97 Decline** Go through in order. (A grammatical metaphor.)   **101 caitiff** wretch, slave   **102 of** by. (Also in lines 103 and 104.)

107 **no . . . thought** only the memory   **111 burdened** burdensome   **122 Bett'ring** Magnifying   **123 Revolving** meditating on   **124 quicken** put life into   **127 Windy . . . woes** i.e., Words, which are airy pleaders on behalf of one who is suffering   **128 Airy . . . joys** insubstantial words, all that is left of joys that died unfulfilled. (Literally, having died without anything to bequeath.)   **129 breathing** speaking   **135 exclaims** exclamations.   **136 expedition** (1) haste (2) military undertaking.

The slaughter of the prince that owed that crown   142
And the dire death of my poor sons and brothers?
Tell me, thou villain slave, where are my children?

DUCHESS
Thou toad, thou toad, where is thy brother Clarence?
And little Ned Plantagenet, his son?   146

QUEEN ELIZABETH
Where is the gentle Rivers, Vaughan, Grey?

DUCHESS   Where is kind Hastings?

KING RICHARD
A flourish, trumpets! Strike alarum, drums!   149
Let not the heavens hear these telltale women   150
Rail on the Lord's anointed. Strike, I say!
                                    Flourish. Alarums.
Either be patient and entreat me fair,   152
Or with the clamorous report of war   153
Thus will I drown your exclamations.

DUCHESS   Art thou my son?

KING RICHARD
Ay, I thank God, my father, and yourself.

DUCHESS
Then patiently hear my impatience.

KING RICHARD
Madam, I have a touch of your condition,   158
That cannot brook the accent of reproof.

DUCHESS
Oh, let me speak!

KING RICHARD   Do then, but I'll not hear.

DUCHESS
I will be mild and gentle in my words.

KING RICHARD
And brief, good mother, for I am in haste.

DUCHESS
Art thou so hasty? I have stayed for thee,   163
God knows, in torment and in agony.   164

KING RICHARD
And came I not at last to comfort you?

DUCHESS
No, by the Holy Rood, thou know'st it well,   166
Thou cam'st on earth to make the earth my hell.
A grievous burden was thy birth to me;
Tetchy and wayward was thy infancy;   169
Thy schooldays frightful, desp'rate, wild, and furious;
Thy prime of manhood daring, bold, and venturous;
Thy age confirmed, proud, subtle, sly, and bloody,   172
More mild, but yet more harmful—kind in hatred.   173
What comfortable hour canst thou name
That ever graced me with thy company?

KING RICHARD
Faith, none, but Humphrey Hour, that called Your Grace 176

To breakfast once forth of my company.   177
If I be so disgracious in your eye,   178
Let me march on and not offend you, madam.—
Strike up the drum.

DUCHESS   I prithee, hear me speak.

KING RICHARD
You speak too bitterly.

DUCHESS   Hear me a word,
For I shall never speak to thee again.

KING RICHARD   So.

DUCHESS
Either thou wilt die by God's just ordinance
Ere from this war thou turn a conqueror,   185
Or I with grief and extreme age shall perish
And nevermore behold thy face again.
Therefore take with thee my most grievous curse,
Which in the day of battle tire thee more
Than all the complete armor that thou wear'st!
My prayers on the adverse party fight,   191
And there the little souls of Edward's children
Whisper the spirits of thine enemies   193
And promise them success and victory!
Bloody thou art, bloody will be thy end;
Shame serves thy life and doth thy death attend.   196
                                            Exit.

QUEEN ELIZABETH
Though far more cause, yet much less spirit to curse
Abides in me; I say amen to her.

KING RICHARD
Stay, madam. I must talk a word with you.

QUEEN ELIZABETH
I have no more sons of the royal blood
For thee to slaughter. For my daughters, Richard,   201
They shall be praying nuns, not weeping queens,
And therefore level not to hit their lives.   203

KING RICHARD
You have a daughter called Elizabeth,
Virtuous and fair, royal and gracious.

QUEEN ELIZABETH
And must she die for this? Oh, let her live,
And I'll corrupt her manners, stain her beauty,   207
Slander myself as false to Edward's bed,
Throw over her the veil of infamy;
So she may live unscarred of bleeding slaughter,   210
I will confess she was not Edward's daughter.

KING RICHARD
Wrong not her birth. She is a royal princess.

QUEEN ELIZABETH
To save her life, I'll say she is not so.

KING RICHARD
Her life is safest only in her birth.   214

QUEEN ELIZABETH
And only in that safety died her brothers.

142 owed owned   **146 Ned Plantagenet** (See 4.3.36.)   **149 flourish** fanfare.   **alarum** call to arms   **150 telltale** tattling, gabbling   **152 entreat me fair** treat me with courtesy   **153 report** noise   **158 condition** disposition   **163 stayed** waited   **164 in agony** i.e., in childbirth.
166 Holy Rood Christ's cross   **169 Tetchy** fretful, peevish   **172 age confirmed** riper manhood   **173 kind in hatred** concealing hatred under pretense of kindness.   **176 Humphrey Hour** (To "dine with Duke Humphrey" was to go hungry; hence, Richard flippantly suggests, he was saved from a spare breakfast. The passage is obscure.)

177 forth of away from   **178 disgracious** unpleasing, disliked   **185 turn** return   **191 party** side   **193 Whisper** whisper to   **196 serves** accompanies   **201 For my** As for my   **203 level** aim   **207 manners** morals   **210 So** provided.   **of** by   **214 Her . . . birth** Her best guarantee of personal safety is her high birth.

KING RICHARD
   Lo, at their birth good stars were opposite.   216
QUEEN ELIZABETH
   No, to their lives ill friends were contrary.   217
KING RICHARD
   All unavoided is the doom of destiny.   218
QUEEN ELIZABETH
   True, when avoided grace makes destiny.   219
   My babes were destined to a fairer death,
   If grace had blessed thee with a fairer life.
KING RICHARD
   You speak as if that I had slain my cousins.   222
QUEEN ELIZABETH
   Cousins, indeed, and by their uncle cozened   223
   Of comfort, kingdom, kindred, freedom, life.
   Whose hand soever lanced their tender hearts,   225
   Thy head, all indirectly, gave direction.   226
   No doubt the murd'rous knife was dull and blunt
   Till it was whetted on thy stone-hard heart,
   To revel in the entrails of my lambs.
   But that still use of grief makes wild grief tame,   230
   My tongue should to thy ears not name my boys
   Till that my nails were anchored in thine eyes;
   And I, in such a desp'rate bay of death,   233
   Like a poor bark of sails and tackling reft,   234
   Rush all to pieces on thy rocky bosom.
KING RICHARD
   Madam, so thrive I in my enterprise   236
   And dangerous success of bloody wars   237
   As I intend more good to you and yours
   Than ever you or yours by me were harmed!
QUEEN ELIZABETH
   What good is covered with the face of heaven,   240
   To be discovered, that can do me good?
KING RICHARD
   Th'advancement of your children, gentle lady.
QUEEN ELIZABETH
   Up to some scaffold, there to lose their heads.
KING RICHARD
   Unto the dignity and height of fortune,
   The high imperial type of this earth's glory.   245
QUEEN ELIZABETH
   Flatter my sorrow with report of it;
   Tell me what state, what dignity, what honor,
   Canst thou demise to any child of mine?   248
KING RICHARD
   Even all I have—ay, and myself and all—
   Will I withal endow a child of thine,
   So in the Lethe of thy angry soul   251

   Thou drown the sad remembrance of those wrongs
   Which thou supposest I have done to thee.
QUEEN ELIZABETH
   Be brief, lest that the process of thy kindness   254
   Last longer telling than thy kindness' date.   255
KING RICHARD
   Then know that from my soul I love thy daughter.   256
QUEEN ELIZABETH
   My daughter's mother thinks it with her soul.
KING RICHARD   What do you think?
QUEEN ELIZABETH
   That thou dost love my daughter from thy soul.
   So from thy soul's love didst thou love her brothers,   260
   And from my heart's love I do thank thee for it.
KING RICHARD
   Be not so hasty to confound my meaning.   262
   I mean that with my soul I love thy daughter
   And do intend to make her Queen of England.
QUEEN ELIZABETH
   Well then, who dost thou mean shall be her king?
KING RICHARD
   Even he that makes her queen. Who else should be?
QUEEN ELIZABETH
   What, thou?
KING RICHARD   Even so. How think you of it?
QUEEN ELIZABETH
   How canst thou woo her?
KING RICHARD   That would I learn of you,
   As one being best acquainted with her humor.   269
QUEEN ELIZABETH
   And wilt thou learn of me?
KING RICHARD   Madam, with all my heart.
QUEEN ELIZABETH
   Send to her, by the man that slew her brothers,
   A pair of bleeding hearts; thereon engrave
   "Edward" and "York"; then haply will she weep.   273
   Therefore present to her—as sometime Margaret   274
   Did to thy father, steeped in Rutland's blood—   275
   A handkerchief, which, say to her, did drain
   The purple sap from her sweet brother's body;
   And bid her wipe her weeping eyes withal.
   If this inducement move her not to love,
   Send her a letter of thy noble deeds.
   Tell her thou mad'st away her uncle Clarence,
   Her uncle Rivers, ay, and for her sake
   Mad'st quick conveyance with her good aunt Anne.   283
KING RICHARD
   You mock me, madam. This is not the way
   To win your daughter.
QUEEN ELIZABETH   There is no other way,
   Unless thou couldst put on some other shape
   And not be Richard that hath done all this.

216 opposite hostile. **217 contrary** opposed. **218 unavoided** unavoidable **219 avoided grace** i.e., Richard, in whom grace is void or lacking **222 as if that** as if **223 cozened** cheated **225 Whose hand soever** Whoever it was whose hand **226 all indirectly** by indirect means, and wrongly **230 But . . . grief** Were it not that constant grieving **233 bay** (1) inlet (2) position of a hunted animal turning to face the hounds **234 bark** sailing vessel. **reft** bereft **236 so thrive I** may I so thrive **237 success** sequel, result **240 covered with** hidden by (and therefore not yet revealed to humanity) **245 imperial type** symbol of rule **248 demise** convey, transmit, lease **251 So** provided that. **Lethe** river in the underworld, the waters of which produce forgetfulness

254 process story **255 date** duration. **256 from** with. (But Queen Elizabeth, in lines 259–61, sarcastically uses the word in the sense "apart from," "at variance with.") **260 So** Just so. (Said ironically.) **262 confound** deliberately misconstrue **269 humor** temperament. **273 haply** perhaps **274 sometime** once **275 Rutland's** (See *3 Henry VI*, 1.4.79–83.) **283 conveyance with** disposal of

KING RICHARD
   Say that I did all this for love of her.
QUEEN ELIZABETH
   Nay, then indeed she cannot choose but hate thee,
   Having bought love with such a bloody spoil.   290
KING RICHARD
   Look what is done cannot be now amended.   291
   Men shall deal unadvisedly sometimes,   292
   Which after-hours gives leisure to repent.
   If I did take the kingdom from your sons,
   To make amends I'll give it to your daughter.
   If I have killed the issue of your womb,
   To quicken your increase I will beget   297
   Mine issue of your blood upon your daughter.
   A grandam's name is little less in love
   Than is the doting title of a mother;
   They are as children but one step below,
   Even of your metal, of your very blood,   302
   Of all one pain, save for a night of groans   303
   Endured of her for whom you bid like sorrow.   304
   Your children were vexation to your youth,
   But mine shall be a comfort to your age.
   The loss you have is but a son being king,
   And by that loss your daughter is made queen.
   I cannot make you what amends I would;
   Therefore accept such kindness as I can.   310
   Dorset your son, that with a fearful soul
   Leads discontented steps in foreign soil,
   This fair alliance quickly shall call home
   To high promotions and great dignity.
   The king that calls your beauteous daughter wife
   Familiarly shall call thy Dorset brother;   316
   Again shall you be mother to a king,
   And all the ruins of distressful times
   Repaired with double riches of content.
   What? We have many goodly days to see.
   The liquid drops of tears that you have shed
   Shall come again, transformed to orient pearl,   322
   Advantaging their love with interest   323
   Of ten times double gain of happiness.
   Go then, my mother, to thy daughter go.
   Make bold her bashful years with your experience;
   Prepare her ears to hear a wooer's tale;
   Put in her tender heart th'aspiring flame
   Of golden sovereignty; acquaint the Princess
   With the sweet silent hours of marriage joys.
   And when this arm of mine hath chastisèd
   The petty rebel, dull-brained Buckingham,
   Bound with triumphant garlands will I come
   And lead thy daughter to a conqueror's bed;
   To whom I will retail my conquest won,   335
   And she shall be sole victoress, Caesar's Caesar.

QUEEN ELIZABETH
   What were I best to say? Her father's brother
   Would be her lord? Or shall I say her uncle?
   Or, he that slew her brothers and her uncles?
   Under what title shall I woo for thee
   That God, the law, my honor, and her love
   Can make seem pleasing to her tender years?
KING RICHARD
   Infer fair England's peace by this alliance.   343
QUEEN ELIZABETH
   Which she shall purchase with still-lasting war.   344
KING RICHARD
   Tell her the King, that may command, entreats.
QUEEN ELIZABETH
   That at her hands which the King's King forbids.   346
KING RICHARD
   Say she shall be a high and mighty queen.
QUEEN ELIZABETH
   To vail the title, as her mother doth.   348
KING RICHARD
   Say I will love her everlastingly.
QUEEN ELIZABETH
   But how long shall that title "ever" last?
KING RICHARD
   Sweetly in force unto her fair life's end.
QUEEN ELIZABETH
   But how long fairly shall her sweet life last?   352
KING RICHARD
   As long as heaven and nature lengthens it.
QUEEN ELIZABETH
   As long as hell and Richard likes of it.
KING RICHARD
   Say I, her sovereign, am her subject low.
QUEEN ELIZABETH
   But she, your subject, loathes such sovereignty.
KING RICHARD
   Be eloquent in my behalf to her.
QUEEN ELIZABETH
   An honest tale speeds best being plainly told.   358
KING RICHARD
   Then plainly to her tell my loving tale.
QUEEN ELIZABETH
   Plain and not honest is too harsh a style.
KING RICHARD
   Your reasons are too shallow and too quick.   361
QUEEN ELIZABETH
   Oh, no, my reasons are too deep and dead—
   Too deep and dead, poor infants, in their graves.
KING RICHARD
   Harp not on that string, madam. That is past.
QUEEN ELIZABETH
   Harp on it still shall I till heartstrings break.

---

290 spoil slaughter. (A hunting term.)   **291 Look what** Whatever
292 shall deal cannot but act   **297 quicken your increase** give new
life to your progeny   **302 metal** substance. (With a suggestion also of
mettle, "spirit." The Folio reads "mettall.")   **303 pain** labor, effort   **304
of** by.   **bid** endured, bided   **310 can** am able (to give).   **316 Familiarly** familially   **322 orient** bright, shining   **323 Advantaging their
love** augmenting the love that prompted tears   **335 retail** relate

343 Infer Allege, adduce (as a reason)   **344 still-lasting war** i.e., perpetual domestic strife.   **346 forbids** (*The Book of Common Prayer*,
echoing the injunctions of Leviticus 18, prohibits the marriage of a
man with his brother's daughter.)   **348 vail** yield; lower or abase as a
sign of submission   **352 fairly** without foul play   **358 speeds** succeeds   **361 quick** hasty. (With a pun on the meaning "alive," contrasted with *dead* in the next line, just as *shallow* is punningly contrasted with *deep*.)

KING RICHARD
    Now, by my George, my Garter, and my crown—   366
QUEEN ELIZABETH
    Profaned, dishonored, and the third usurped.
KING RICHARD
    I swear—
QUEEN ELIZABETH   By nothing, for this is no oath.
    Thy George, profaned, hath lost his lordly honor;   369
    Thy Garter, blemished, pawned his knightly virtue;
    Thy crown, usurped, disgraced his kingly glory.
    If something thou wouldst swear to be believed,
    Swear then by something that thou hast not wronged.
KING RICHARD
    Then, by myself—
QUEEN ELIZABETH   Thyself is self-misused.
KING RICHARD
    Now, by the world—
QUEEN ELIZABETH   'Tis full of thy foul wrongs.
KING RICHARD
    My father's death—
QUEEN ELIZABETH   Thy life hath it dishonored.
KING RICHARD
    Why then, by God—
QUEEN ELIZABETH   God's wrong is most of all.
    If thou didst fear to break an oath with Him,
    The unity the King my husband made   379
    Thou hadst not broken, nor my brothers died.
    If thou hadst feared to break an oath by Him,
    Th'imperial metal circling now thy head
    Had graced the tender temples of my child,
    And both the princes had been breathing here,
    Which now, two tender bedfellows for dust,
    Thy broken faith hath made the prey for worms.
    What canst thou swear by now?
KING RICHARD   The time to come.
QUEEN ELIZABETH
    That thou hast wrongèd in the time o'erpast;
    For I myself have many tears to wash
    Hereafter time, for time past wronged by thee.   390
    The children live whose fathers thou hast slaughtered,
    Ungoverned youth, to wail it in their age;   392
    The parents live whose children thou hast butchered,
    Old barren plants, to wail it with their age.
    Swear not by time to come, for that thou hast
    Misused ere used, by times ill-used o'erpast.   396
KING RICHARD
    As I intend to prosper and repent,   397
    So thrive I in my dangerous affairs
    Of hostile arms! Myself myself confound!   399

Heaven and fortune bar me happy hours!
Day, yield me not thy light, nor, night, thy rest!
Be opposite all planets of good luck   402
To my proceeding if, with dear heart's love,
Immaculate devotion, holy thoughts,
I tender not thy beauteous, princely daughter!   405
In her consists my happiness and thine;
Without her follows to myself and thee,
Herself, the land, and many a Christian soul,
Death, desolation, ruin, and decay.
It cannot be avoided but by this;
It will not be avoided but by this.
Therefore, dear mother—I must call you so—
Be the attorney of my love to her.
Plead what I will be, not what I have been,
Not my deserts, but what I will deserve.
Urge the necessity and state of times,   416
And be not peevish-fond in great designs.   417
QUEEN ELIZABETH
    Shall I be tempted of the devil thus?
KING RICHARD
    Ay, if the devil tempt you to do good.
QUEEN ELIZABETH
    Shall I forget myself to be myself?   420
KING RICHARD
    Ay, if yourself's remembrance wrong yourself.   421
QUEEN ELIZABETH
    Yet thou didst kill my children.
KING RICHARD
    But in your daughter's womb I bury them,
    Where in that nest of spicery they will breed   424
    Selves of themselves, to your recomforture.   425
QUEEN ELIZABETH
    Shall I go win my daughter to thy will?
KING RICHARD
    And be a happy mother by the deed.
QUEEN ELIZABETH
    I go. Write to me very shortly,
    And you shall understand from me her mind.
KING RICHARD
    Bear her my true love's kiss; and so, farewell.
                         Exit Queen [*Elizabeth*].
    Relenting fool, and shallow, changing woman!

        Enter Ratcliffe; [*Catesby following*].

    How now, what news?
RATCLIFFE
    Most mighty sovereign, on the western coast
    Rideth a puissant navy; to our shores   434
    Throng many doubtful, hollow-hearted friends,   435

366 George . . . Garter (The George, a badge showing Saint George slaying the dragon, was not added to the insignia of the Order of the Garter until the reign of Henry VII or Henry VIII.)   369 his its (as also in lines 370, 371)   379 The unity i.e., the reconciliation between Queen Elizabeth and her enemies   390 Hereafter time in the future 392 Ungoverned i.e., without a father's guidance or rule 396 Misused . . . o'erpast misused even before it came time to be used, by your ill use of past times.   397 As . . . repent i.e., I swear that as I hope to thrive and intend to repent   399 Myself . . . confound! May I destroy myself!

402 opposite opposed, adverse   405 I tender not I fail to show a tender regard for   416 state of times urgent political need   417 And . . . designs and do not stand by, childishly foolish as great plans are afoot.   420 Shall . . . myself? i.e., Shall I, in order to be queen mother, forget that I am the person you have wronged?   421 wrong yourself i.e., interferes with what is to your advantage.   424 nest of spicery (The fabled phoenix arose anew from the nest of spices, its funeral pyre.)   425 recomforture comfort, consolation.   434 puissant powerful   435 doubtful apprehensive

Unarmed and unresolved to beat them back.
'Tis thought that Richmond is their admiral;   437
And there they hull, expecting but the aid   438
Of Buckingham to welcome them ashore.

KING RICHARD
Some light-foot friend post to the Duke of Norfolk: 440
Ratcliffe, thyself, or Catesby; where is he?

CATESBY
Here, my good lord.

KING RICHARD   Catesby, fly to the Duke.

CATESBY
I will, my lord, with all convenient haste.   443

KING RICHARD
Ratcliffe, come hither. Post to Salisbury.
When thou com'st thither—[*To Catesby*] Dull, unmindful villain,
Why stay'st thou here, and go'st not to the Duke?

CATESBY
First, mighty liege, tell me Your Highness' pleasure,
What from Your Grace I shall deliver to him.

KING RICHARD
Oh, true, good Catesby. Bid him levy straight
The greatest strength and power that he can make,   450
And meet me suddenly at Salisbury.   451

CATESBY   I go.   *Exit.*

RATCLIFFE
What, may it please you, shall I do at Salisbury?

KING RICHARD
Why, what wouldst thou do there before I go?

RATCLIFFE
Your Highness told me I should post before.   455

KING RICHARD
My mind is changed.

      Enter Lord Stanley [Earl of Derby].

               Stanley, what news with you?

STANLEY
None good, my liege, to please you with the hearing,
Nor none so bad but well may be reported.

KING RICHARD
Hoyday, a riddle! Neither good nor bad!   459
What need'st thou run so many miles about,
When thou mayst tell thy tale the nearest way?   461
Once more, what news?

STANLEY   Richmond is on the seas.

KING RICHARD
There let him sink, and be the seas on him!
White-livered runagate, what doth he there?   464

STANLEY
I know not, mighty sovereign, but by guess.

KING RICHARD   Well, as you guess?

STANLEY
Stirred up by Dorset, Buckingham, and Morton,

He makes for England, here to claim the crown.

KING RICHARD
Is the chair empty? Is the sword unswayed?   469
Is the King dead? The empire unpossessed?   470
What heir of York is there alive but we?
And who is England's king but great York's heir?
Then tell me, what makes he upon the seas?   473

STANLEY
Unless for that, my liege, I cannot guess.

KING RICHARD
Unless for that he comes to be your liege,
You cannot guess wherefore the Welshman comes.   476
Thou wilt revolt and fly to him, I fear.

STANLEY
No, my good lord; therefore mistrust me not.

KING RICHARD
Where is thy power, then, to beat him back?   479
Where be thy tenants and thy followers?
Are they not now upon the western shore,
Safe-conducting the rebels from their ships?

STANLEY
No, my good lord, my friends are in the north.

KING RICHARD
Cold friends to me! What do they in the north
When they should serve their sovereign in the west?

STANLEY
They have not been commanded, mighty King.
Pleaseth Your Majesty to give me leave,   487
I'll muster up my friends and meet Your Grace
Where and what time Your Majesty shall please.

KING RICHARD
Ay, thou wouldst be gone to join with Richmond.
But I'll not trust thee.

STANLEY   Most mighty sovereign,
You have no cause to hold my friendship doubtful.
I never was nor never will be false.

KING RICHARD
Go then and muster men, but leave behind
Your son, George Stanley. Look your heart be firm,
Or else his head's assurance is but frail.   496

STANLEY
So deal with him as I prove true to you.

          Exit Stanley [Earl of Derby].

        Enter a Messenger.

FIRST MESSENGER
My gracious sovereign, now in Devonshire,
As I by friends am well advertisèd,   499
Sir Edward Courtney and the haughty prelate,
Bishop of Exeter, his elder brother,   501
With many more confederates, are in arms.

       Enter another Messenger.

---

437 their admiral i.e., of the *puissant navy* named three lines earlier
438 hull drift with the sails furled   **440 light-foot** swift-footed.   **post** hasten   **443 convenient** appropriate, suitable   **450 make** raise
451 suddenly swiftly   **455 post** hasten   **459 Hoyday** Heyday. (Expressing mock wonderment.)   **461 the nearest way** directly, simply.   **464 White-livered runagate** Cowardly renegade, vagabond

469 chair throne   **470 empire** kingdom   **473 makes he** is he doing
476 Welshman (Richmond was the grandson of Owen Tudor, a Welshman of Anglesea, who fathered three sons and a daughter by Katharine of Valois, widow of Henry V.)   **479 power** army
487 Pleaseth May it please   **496 assurance** safety   **499 advertisèd** informed   **501 brother** (Actually, a cousin.)

SECOND MESSENGER
 In Kent, my liege, the Guildfords are in arms,
 And every hour more competitors   504
 Flock to the rebels, and their power grows strong.

   Enter another Messenger.

THIRD MESSENGER
 My lord, the army of great Buckingham—
KING RICHARD
 Out on ye, owls! Nothing but songs of death? 507
           He striketh him.
 There, take thou that, till thou bring better news.
THIRD MESSENGER
 The news I have to tell Your Majesty
 Is that by sudden floods and fall of waters
 Buckingham's army is dispersed and scattered,
 And he himself wandered away alone,
 No man knows whither.
KING RICHARD   I cry thee mercy. 513
 There is my purse to cure that blow of thine.
         [He gives money.]
 Hath any well-advisèd friend proclaimed 515
 Reward to him that brings the traitor in?
THIRD MESSENGER
 Such proclamation hath been made, my lord.

   Enter another Messenger.

FOURTH MESSENGER
 Sir Thomas Lovell and Lord Marquess Dorset, 518
 'Tis said, my liege, in Yorkshire are in arms.
 But this good comfort bring I to Your Highness:
 The Breton navy is dispersed by tempest.
 Richmond, in Dorsetshire, sent out a boat
 Unto the shore, to ask those on the banks
 If they were his assistants, yea or no,
 Who answered him they came from Buckingham
 Upon his party. He, mistrusting them,
 Hoised sail and made his course again for Brittany. 527
KING RICHARD
 March on, march on, since we are up in arms,
 If not to fight with foreign enemies,
 Yet to beat down these rebels here at home.

   Enter Catesby.

CATESBY
 My liege, the Duke of Buckingham is taken!
 That is the best news. That the Earl of Richmond
 Is with a mighty power landed at Milford 533
 Is colder tidings, yet they must be told.
KING RICHARD
 Away towards Salisbury! While we reason here, 535

 A royal battle might be won and lost.
 Someone take order Buckingham be brought
 To Salisbury. The rest march on with me.
        Flourish. Exeunt.

4.[5]

  Enter [Lord Stanley Earl of] Derby and Sir
  Christopher [Urswick, a priest].

STANLEY
 Sir Christopher, tell Richmond this from me:
 That in the sty of the most deadly boar
 My son George Stanley is franked up in hold. 3
 If I revolt, off goes young George's head;
 The fear of that holds off my present aid.
 So get thee gone; commend me to thy lord.
 Withal say that the Queen hath heartily consented 7
 He should espouse Elizabeth her daughter.
 But tell me, where is princely Richmond now?
CHRISTOPHER
 At Pembroke, or at Ha'rfordwest, in Wales. 10
STANLEY What men of name resort to him? 11
CHRISTOPHER
 Sir Walter Herbert, a renownèd soldier,
 Sir Gilbert Talbot, Sir William Stanley,
 Oxford, redoubted Pembroke, Sir James Blunt, 14
 And Rice ap Thomas, with a valiant crew,
 And many other of great name and worth;
 And towards London do they bend their power, 17
 If by the way they be not fought withal.
STANLEY
 Well, hie thee to thy lord; I kiss his hand. 19
 My letter will resolve him of my mind. 20
       [He gives a letter.]
 Farewell.   *Exeunt.*

5.1

  Enter Buckingham, with [Sheriff and] halberds, led
  to execution.

BUCKINGHAM
 Will not King Richard let me speak with him?
SHERIFF
 No, my good lord. Therefore be patient.
BUCKINGHAM
 Hastings, and Edward's children, Grey, and Rivers,
 Holy King Henry, and thy fair son Edward, 4
 Vaughan, and all that have miscarried 5

---

504 **competitors** confederates 507 **owls** (The cry of the owl was thought to portend death.) 513 **I cry thee mercy** I beg your pardon. 515 **well-advisèd** judicious 518 **Sir Thomas Lovell** (Not the Lovell of 3.4 and 3.5, who was historically Sir Francis Lovell, Richard's Lord Chamberlain, but perhaps related to him.) 527 **Hoised** hoisted 533 **Milford** Milford Haven on the coast of Wales in the county of Pembroke. (A gap of two years is bridged here. Richmond's first fruitless expedition was in October 1483; his landing at Milford was in August 1485.) 535 **reason** talk

4.5. Location: London. The house of Lord Stanley, Earl of Derby. **0.1 *Sir*** (Honorific title for a clergyman.) 3 **franked up in hold** shut up in custody, as in a pigpen. 7 **Withal** In addition 10 **Ha'rford-west** Haverfordwest, in Wales 11 **name** rank 14 **redoubted Pembroke** awe-inspiring Jasper Tudor, Earl of Pembroke (uncle to Richmond) 17 **bend their power** direct their forces 19 **hie** hasten 20 **resolve him of** inform him concerning
5.1. Location: Salisbury. An open place.
4 **thy** i.e., Henry VI's 5 **miscarrièd** perished

By underhand corrupted foul injustice:
If that your moody, discontented souls   7
Do through the clouds behold this present hour,
Even for revenge mock my destruction!
This is All Souls' Day, fellow, is it not?   10

SHERIFF   It is, my lord.

BUCKINGHAM
Why, then All Souls' Day is my body's doomsday.
This is the day which, in King Edward's time,
I wished might fall on me when I was found
False to his children and his wife's allies;
This is the day wherein I wished to fall
By the false faith of him whom most I trusted;
This, this All Souls' Day to my fearful soul
Is the determined respite of my wrongs.   19
That high All-Seer which I dallied with
Hath turned my feignèd prayer on my head
And given in earnest what I begged in jest.
Thus doth he force the swords of wicked men
To turn their own points in their masters' bosoms.
Thus Margaret's curse falls heavy on my neck:
"When he," quoth she, "shall split thy heart with sorrow,   26
Remember Margaret was a prophetess."
Come lead me, officers, to the block of shame.
Wrong hath but wrong, and blame the due of blame.

Exeunt Buckingham with officers.

❧

5.2

Enter Richmond, Oxford, [Sir James] Blunt, [Sir Walter] Herbert, and others, with drum and colors.

RICHMOND
Fellows in arms, and my most loving friends
Bruised underneath the yoke of tyranny,
Thus far into the bowels of the land   3
Have we marched on without impediment;
And here receive we from our father Stanley   5
Lines of fair comfort and encouragement.
The wretched, bloody, and usurping boar,
That spoiled your summer fields and fruitful vines,   8
Swills your warm blood like wash, and makes his trough   9
In your emboweled bosoms, this foul swine   10
Is now even in the center of this isle,
Near to the town of Leicester, as we learn.
From Tamworth thither is but one day's march.
In God's name, cheerly on, courageous friends,   14
To reap the harvest of perpetual peace
By this one bloody trial of sharp war.

OXFORD
Every man's conscience is a thousand swords
To fight against this guilty homicide.

HERBERT
I doubt not but his friends will turn to us.

BLUNT
He hath no friends but what are friends for fear,   20
Which in his dearest need will fly from him.   21

RICHMOND
All for our vantage. Then, in God's name, march!
True hope is swift and flies with swallow's wings;
Kings it makes gods and meaner creatures kings.   24

Exeunt omnes.

❧

[5.3]

Enter King Richard in arms, with Norfolk, Ratcliffe, and the Earl of Surrey [and others].

KING RICHARD
Here pitch our tent, even here in Bosworth Field.
My lord of Surrey, why look you so sad?

SURREY
My heart is ten times lighter than my looks.

KING RICHARD
My lord of Norfolk—

NORFOLK   Here, most gracious liege.

KING RICHARD
Norfolk, we must have knocks; ha! Must we not?   5

NORFOLK
We must both give and take, my loving lord.

KING RICHARD
Up with my tent! Here will I lie tonight.
      [*Soldiers begin to set up King Richard's tent.*]
But where tomorrow? Well, all's one for that.   8
Who hath descried the number of the traitors?   9

NORFOLK
Six or seven thousand is their utmost power.

KING RICHARD
Why, our battalia trebles that account.   11
Besides, the King's name is a tower of strength,
Which they upon the adverse faction want.   13
Up with the tent! Come, noble gentlemen,
Let us survey the vantage of the ground.   15
Call for some men of sound direction.   16
Let's lack no discipline, make no delay,
For, lords, tomorrow is a busy day.   *Exeunt.*

Enter [on the other side of the stage] Richmond, Sir William Brandon, Oxford, and Dorset, [Blunt, Herbert, and others. Some of the soldiers pitch Richmond's tent.]

---

7 moody, discontented angry, vengeance-seeking   **10 All Souls' Day** November 2, the day on which the Church intercedes for all Christian souls   **19 the determined . . . wrongs** the ordained date to which the punishment of my evil practices was respited or postponed. **26 he** Richard
5.2. Location: A camp near Tamworth.
3 bowels interior   **5 father** stepfather, Lord Stanley, Earl of Derby   **8 spoiled** despoiled   **9 Swills** gulps.   **wash** hogwash, swill   **10 emboweled** disemboweled   **14 cheerly** cheerily, heartily

20 for fear i.e., out of fearing Richard   **21 dearest** direst   **24 meaner** of lower degree.   **24.1 omnes** all.
5.3. Location: Bosworth Field.
5 knocks blows   **8 all's . . . that** be that as it may.   **9 descried** reconnoitred   **11 battalia** army   **13 want** lack.   **15 vantage of the ground** i.e., way in which the field can best be used for tactical advantage.   **16 direction** judgment, military skill.

RICHMOND
    The weary sun hath made a golden set,
    And, by the bright track of his fiery car,   20
    Gives token of a goodly day tomorrow.
    Sir William Brandon, you shall bear my standard.   22
    Give me some ink and paper in my tent.
    I'll draw the form and model of our battle,
    Limit each leader to his several charge,   25
    And part in just proportion our small power.   26
    My lord of Oxford, you, Sir William Brandon,
    And you, Sir Walter Herbert, stay with me.
    The Earl of Pembroke keeps his regiment;   29
    Good Captain Blunt, bear my good-night to him,
    And by the second hour in the morning
    Desire the Earl to see me in my tent.
    Yet one thing more, good Captain, do for me:
    Where is Lord Stanley quartered, do you know?
BLUNT
    Unless I have mista'en his colors much,
    Which well I am assured I have not done,
    His regiment lies half a mile at least
    South from the mighty power of the King.   38
RICHMOND
    If without peril it be possible,
    Sweet Blunt, make some good means to speak with him,
    And give him from me this most needful note.
                    [He gives a letter.]
BLUNT
    Upon my life, my lord, I'll undertake it.
    And so, God give you quiet rest tonight!
RICHMOND
    Good night, good Captain Blunt.   *[Exit Blunt.]*
                    Come, gentlemen,
    Let us consult upon tomorrow's business.
    Into my tent; the dew is raw and cold.
                   They withdraw into the tent.

        Enter [to his tent, King] Richard, Ratcliffe,
        Norfolk, and Catesby.

KING RICHARD
    What is't o'clock?
CATESBY   It's suppertime, my lord;
    It's nine o'clock.
KING RICHARD   I will not sup tonight.
    Give me some ink and paper.
    What, is my beaver easier than it was,   50
    And all my armor laid into my tent?
CATESBY
    It is, my liege, and all things are in readiness.
KING RICHARD
    Good Norfolk, hie thee to thy charge.
    Use careful watch; choose trusty sentinels.
NORFOLK   I go, my lord.

KING RICHARD
    Stir with the lark tomorrow, gentle Norfolk.
NORFOLK   I warrant you, my lord.   *[Exit.]* 57
KING RICHARD   Catesby!
CATESBY
    My lord?
KING RICHARD   Send out a pursuivant at arms   59
    To Stanley's regiment. Bid him bring his power   60
    Before sunrising, lest his son George fall
    Into the blind cave of eternal night.   *[Exit Catesby.]*
    Fill me a bowl of wine. Give me a watch.   63
    Saddle white Surrey for the field tomorrow.   64
    Look that my staves be sound and not too heavy.   65
    Ratcliffe!
RATCLIFFE   My lord?
KING RICHARD
    Saw'st thou the melancholy Lord Northumberland?
RATCLIFFE
    Thomas the Earl of Surrey and himself,
    Much about cockshut time, from troop to troop   70
    Went through the army, cheering up the soldiers.
KING RICHARD
    So, I am satisfied. Give me a bowl of wine.
    I have not that alacrity of spirit
    Nor cheer of mind that I was wont to have.   74
                   [Wine is brought.]
    Set it down. Is ink and paper ready?
RATCLIFFE
    It is, my lord.
KING RICHARD   Bid my guard watch. Leave me.
    Ratcliffe, about the mid of night come to my tent
    And help to arm me. Leave me, I say.
            Exit Ratcliffe. [Richard sleeps.]

        Enter [Lord Stanley Earl of] Derby, to Richmond
        in his tent, [lords and others attending].

STANLEY
    Fortune and victory sit on thy helm!   79
RICHMOND
    All comfort that the dark night can afford
    Be to thy person, noble father-in-law!   81
    Tell me, how fares our loving mother?
STANLEY
    I, by attorney, bless thee from thy mother,   83
    Who prays continually for Richmond's good.
    So much for that. The silent hours steal on,
    And flaky darkness breaks within the east.   86
    In brief—for so the season bids us be—   87
    Prepare thy battle early in the morning,   88
    And put thy fortune to the arbitrament   89

---

57 warrant guarantee   **59 pursuivant at arms** junior officer acting as messenger   **60 power** forces   **63 watch** watch light, candle marked into equal divisions to show time; or, perhaps, sentinel.   **64 white Surrey** (The name seems to be Shakespeare's invention. The chroniclers say that Richard was mounted on a "great white courser.")   **65 staves** lance shafts   **70 cockshut time** evening twilight; possibly, the time at which the poultry are shut up   **74 was wont** used   **79 helm** helmet.   **81 father-in-law** stepfather.   **83 by attorney** as proxy   **86 flaky** streaked with light   **87 season** time   **88 battle** troops   **89 arbitrament** arbitration

---

20 car chariot (of Phoebus)   **22 standard** flag.   **25 Limit** appoint. **several charge** individual command   **26 And . . . power** and divide proportionately our small army.   **29 keeps** i.e., is with   **38 power** army   **50 beaver** face-guard or visor of helmet.   **easier** looser, better fitting

Of bloody strokes and mortal-staring war.   90
I, as I may—that which I would I cannot—   91
With best advantage will deceive the time   92
And aid thee in this doubtful shock of arms.   93
But on thy side I may not be too forward,   94
Lest, being seen, thy brother, tender George,   95
Be executed in his father's sight.
Farewell. The leisure and the fearful time   97
Cuts off the ceremonious vows of love
And ample interchange of sweet discourse
Which so long sundered friends should dwell upon.
God give us leisure for these rites of love!
Once more, adieu. Be valiant, and speed well!   102

RICHMOND
Good lords, conduct him to his regiment.
I'll strive with troubled thoughts to take a nap,
Lest leaden slumber peise me down tomorrow,   105
When I should mount with wings of victory.
Once more, good night, kind lords and gentlemen.
                          Exeunt. [*Richmond remains.*]
O Thou whose captain I account myself,
Look on my forces with a gracious eye;
Put in their hands thy bruising irons of wrath,
That they may crush down with a heavy fall
The usurping helmets of our adversaries!
Make us thy ministers of chastisement,
That we may praise thee in the victory!
To thee I do commend my watchful soul
Ere I let fall the windows of mine eyes.   116
Sleeping and waking, oh, defend me still!   117
                                        [*He sleeps.*]

Enter the Ghost of young Prince Edward, son [*of*]
Harry the Sixth, to Richard.

GHOST (*to Richard*)
Let me sit heavy on thy soul tomorrow!   118
Think, how thou stabbed'st me in my prime of youth
At Tewkesbury. Despair therefore and die!
(*To Richmond*) Be cheerful, Richmond, for the wrongèd souls
Of butchered princes fight in thy behalf.
King Henry's issue, Richmond, comforts thee. [*Exit.*]

Enter the Ghost of Henry the Sixth.

GHOST (*to Richard*)
When I was mortal, my anointed body   124
By thee was punchèd full of deadly holes.
Think on the Tower and me. Despair and die!   126
Harry the Sixth bids thee despair and die!
(*To Richmond*) Virtuous and holy, be thou conqueror!

Harry, that prophesied thou shouldst be king,   129
Doth comfort thee in thy sleep. Live and flourish!
                                           [*Exit.*]

Enter the Ghost of Clarence.

GHOST [*to Richard*]
Let me sit heavy in thy soul tomorrow,
I, that was washed to death with fulsome wine,   132
Poor Clarence, by thy guile betrayed to death!
Tomorrow in the battle think on me,
And fall thy edgeless sword. Despair and die!   135
(*To Richmond*) Thou offspring of the house of Lancaster,
The wrongèd heirs of York do pray for thee.
Good angels guard thy battle! Live and flourish!   138
                                           [*Exit.*]

Enter the Ghosts of Rivers, Grey, [*and*] *Vaughan.*

GHOST OF RIVERS [*to Richard*]
Let me sit heavy in thy soul tomorrow,
Rivers that died at Pomfret! Despair and die!
GHOST OF GREY [*to Richard*]
Think upon Grey, and let thy soul despair!
GHOST OF VAUGHAN [*to Richard*]
Think upon Vaughan, and, with guilty fear,
Let fall thy lance. Despair and die!
ALL (*to Richmond*)
Awake, and think our wrongs in Richard's bosom
Will conquer him! Awake, and win the day!
                                   [*Exeunt Ghosts.*]

Enter the Ghost of Hastings.

GHOST [*to Richard*]
Bloody and guilty, guiltily awake
And in a bloody battle end thy days!
Think on Lord Hastings. Despair and die!
(*To Richmond*) Quiet untroubled soul, awake, awake!
Arm, fight, and conquer for fair England's sake!
                                           [*Exit.*]

Enter the Ghosts of the two young Princes.

GHOSTS (*to Richard*)
Dream on thy cousins smothered in the Tower.   151
Let us be lead within thy bosom, Richard,
And weigh thee down to ruin, shame, and death!
Thy nephews' souls bid thee despair and die!
(*To Richmond*) Sleep, Richmond, sleep in peace, and
   wake in joy.
Good angels guard thee from the boar's annoy!   156
Live, and beget a happy race of kings!
Edward's unhappy sons do bid thee flourish.
                                   [*Exeunt Ghosts.*]

Enter the Ghost of Lady Anne, his wife.

GHOST [*to Richard*]
Richard, thy wife, that wretched Anne thy wife,
That never slept a quiet hour with thee,

---

90 **mortal-staring** fatal-visaged   91 **that . . . cannot** i.e., I cannot fight openly on your side, though I want to   92 **With . . . time** as best I can I will work for your side without seeming to do so   93 **shock** encounter   94 **forward** zealous   95 **brother** i.e., stepbrother.   **tender** young, of tender years   97 **leisure** i.e., brief time allowed   102 **speed well** may you succeed.   105 **peise** weigh   116 **windows** i.e., eyelids   117 **still** continually.   118 **sit heavy on** be oppressive to   124 **anointed** i.e., with the sacred oil used in the coronation ceremony; compare with 4.4.151   126 **Tower** (Where Henry VI was supposed to have been murdered.)

129 **prophesied** (See *3 Henry VI,* 4.6.68 ff.)   132 **washed to death** i.e., drowned in a butt of malmsey.   **fulsome** cloying   135 **fall** let fall.   **edgeless** blunt, useless   138 **battle** troops.   151 **cousins** i.e., nephews   156 **the boar's annoy** i.e., Richard's attack.

Now fills thy sleep with perturbations.
Tomorrow in the battle think on me,
And fall thy edgeless sword. Despair and die!
(*To Richmond*) Thou quiet soul, sleep thou a quiet sleep;
Dream of success and happy victory!
Thy adversary's wife doth pray for thee.   [*Exit.*]

Enter the Ghost of Buckingham.

GHOST [*to Richard*]
The first was I that helped thee to the crown;
The last was I that felt thy tyranny.
Oh, in the battle think on Buckingham,
And die in terror of thy guiltiness!
Dream on, dream on of bloody deeds and death;
Fainting, despair; despairing, yield thy breath!   172
(*To Richmond*) I died for hope ere I could lend thee aid,   173
But cheer thy heart, and be thou not dismayed.
God and good angels fight on Richmond's side,
And Richard fall in height of all his pride!   [*Exit.*] 176
                Richard starteth up out of a dream.

KING RICHARD
Give me another horse! Bind up my wounds!
Have mercy, Jesu!—Soft, I did but dream.
O coward conscience, how dost thou afflict me!
The lights burn blue. It is now dead midnight.   180
Cold fearful drops stand on my trembling flesh.
What do I fear? Myself? There's none else by.
Richard loves Richard; that is, I am I.   183
Is there a murderer here? No. Yes, I am.
Then fly. What, from myself? Great reason why: 185
Lest I revenge. What, myself upon myself?
Alack, I love myself. Wherefore? For any good   187
That I myself have done unto myself?
Oh, no! Alas, I rather hate myself
For hateful deeds committed by myself!
I am a villain. Yet I lie, I am not.
Fool, of thyself speak well. Fool, do not flatter.
My conscience hath a thousand several tongues,   193
And every tongue brings in a several tale,
And every tale condemns me for a villain.
Perjury, perjury, in the highest degree,
Murder, stern murder, in the direst degree,
All several sins, all used in each degree,   198
Throng to the bar, crying all, "Guilty! Guilty!"   199
I shall despair. There is no creature loves me,   200
And if I die no soul will pity me.
And wherefore should they, since that I myself
Find in myself no pity to myself?
Methought the souls of all that I had murdered

Came to my tent, and every one did threat
Tomorrow's vengeance on the head of Richard.

Enter Ratcliffe.

RATCLIFFE   My lord!
KING RICHARD   Zounds! Who is there?
RATCLIFFE
My lord, 'tis I. The early village cock
Hath twice done salutation to the morn.
Your friends are up and buckle on their armor.
KING RICHARD
Oh, Ratcliffe, I have dreamed a fearful dream!
What think'st thou, will our friends prove all true?
RATCLIFFE
No doubt, my lord.
KING RICHARD   Oh, Ratcliffe, I fear, I fear!
RATCLIFFE
Nay, good my lord, be not afraid of shadows.
KING RICHARD
By the apostle Paul, shadows tonight
Have struck more terror to the soul of Richard
Than can the substance of ten thousand soldiers
Armèd in proof and led by shallow Richmond.   219
'Tis not yet near day. Come, go with me;
Under our tents I'll play the eavesdropper,
To see if any mean to shrink from me.
                Exeunt [*Richard and Ratcliffe*].

Enter the Lords to Richmond, [sitting in his tent].

LORDS   Good morrow, Richmond!
RICHMOND
Cry mercy, lords and watchful gentlemen,   224
That you have ta'en a tardy sluggard here.
A LORD   How have you slept, my lord?
RICHMOND
The sweetest sleep and fairest-boding dreams
That ever entered in a drowsy head
Have I since your departure had, my lords.
Methought their souls whose bodies Richard murdered
Came to my tent and cried on victory.   231
I promise you, my soul is very jocund   232
In the remembrance of so fair a dream.
How far into the morning is it, lords?
A LORD   Upon the stroke of four.
RICHMOND
Why, then 'tis time to arm and give direction.

His oration to his soldiers.

More than I have said, loving countrymen,   237
The leisure and enforcement of the time   238
Forbids to dwell upon. Yet remember this:
God and our good cause fight upon our side.
The prayers of holy saints and wrongèd souls,
Like high-reared bulwarks, stand before our faces.

---

172 Fainting losing heart   **173 for hope** i.e., for hoping to support
you, or for want of hope, hoping in vain to help   **176 Richard fall**
may Richard fall   **180 lights burn blue** (Superstitiously regarded as
evidence of the presence of ghosts.)   **183 I am I** (A blasphemy of
God's "*ego sum*.")   **185 fly** flee.   **187 Wherefore?** Why?   **193 several**
different, separate   **198 used . . . degree** committed in every degree
of infamy, from bad to worst   **199 bar** i.e., bar of justice   **200 despair**
(Considered the only unforgivable sin.)

219 proof armor   **224 Cry mercy** I beg your pardon   **231 cried on
victory** invoked victory, cried out to it.   **232 promise** assure.
jocund cheerful   **237 have said** have already said before
238 leisure i.e., brief time allowed

Richard except, those whom we fight against   243
Had rather have us win than him they follow.
For what is he they follow? Truly, gentlemen,
A bloody tyrant and a homicide;
One raised in blood, and one in blood established;   247
One that made means to come by what he hath,   248
And slaughtered those that were the means to help him;
A base, foul stone, made precious by the foil   250
Of England's chair, where he is falsely set;   251
One that hath ever been God's enemy.
Then if you fight against God's enemy,
God will in justice ward you as his soldiers;   254
If you do sweat to put a tyrant down,
You sleep in peace, the tyrant being slain;
If you do fight against your country's foes,
Your country's fat shall pay your pains the hire;   258
If you do fight in safeguard of your wives,
Your wives shall welcome home the conquerors;
If you do free your children from the sword,
Your children's children quits it in your age.   262
Then, in the name of God and all these rights,
Advance your standards! Draw your willing swords!   264
For me, the ransom of my bold attempt   265
Shall be this cold corpse on the earth's cold face;   266
But if I thrive, the gain of my attempt
The least of you shall share his part thereof.
Sound drums and trumpets boldly and cheerfully;
God and Saint George! Richmond and victory!

[Exeunt.]

*Enter King Richard, Ratcliffe, [attendants and
forces].*

KING RICHARD
What said Northumberland as touching Richmond?
RATCLIFFE
That he was never trainèd up in arms.
KING RICHARD
He said the truth. And what said Surrey then?
RATCLIFFE
He smiled and said, "The better for our purpose."
KING RICHARD
He was in the right, and so indeed it is.
                            The clock striketh.
Tell the clock there. Give me a calendar.   276
Who saw the sun today?   *[He takes an almanac.]*
RATCLIFFE   Not I, my lord.
KING RICHARD
Then he disdains to shine, for by the book   278
He should have braved the east an hour ago.   279
A black day will it be to somebody.

Ratcliffe!
RATCLIFFE
My lord?
KING RICHARD   The sun will not be seen today;
The sky doth frown and lour upon our army.   283
I would these dewy tears were from the ground.
Not shine today? Why, what is that to me
More than to Richmond? For the selfsame heaven
That frowns on me looks sadly upon him.

Enter Norfolk.

NORFOLK
Arm, arm, my lord, the foe vaunts in the field!   288
KING RICHARD
Come, bustle, bustle! Caparison my horse.   289
Call up Lord Stanley; bid him bring his power.
I will lead forth my soldiers to the plain,
And thus my battle shall be orderèd: 292
My foreward shall be drawn out all in length,   293
Consisting equally of horse and foot;
Our archers shall be placèd in the midst.
John Duke of Norfolk, Thomas Earl of Surrey,
Shall have the leading of this foot and horse.
They thus directed, we will follow   298
In the main battle, whose puissance on either side   299
Shall be well wingèd with our chiefest horse.   300
This, and Saint George to boot! What think'st thou,
    Norfolk?   301
NORFOLK
A good direction, warlike sovereign.
This found I on my tent this morning.
                            He showeth him a paper.
KING RICHARD *[reads]*
"Jockey of Norfolk, be not so bold,   304
For Dickon thy master is bought and sold."   305
A thing devised by the enemy.
Go, gentlemen, every man unto his charge.
Let not our babbling dreams affright our souls;
Conscience is but a word that cowards use,
Devised at first to keep the strong in awe.
Our strong arms be our conscience, swords our law!
March on, join bravely! Let us to it pell-mell;   312
If not to heaven, then hand in hand to hell.

His oration to his army.

What shall I say more than I have inferred?   314
Remember whom you are to cope withal:
A sort of vagabonds, rascals, and runaways,   316
A scum of Bretons and base lackey peasants,   317
Whom their o'ercloyèd country vomits forth   318
To desperate adventures and assured destruction.

---

243 except excepted   **247 in blood** by bloodshed   **248 made means**
i.e., has taken advantage, created opportunity   **251 foil** a thin leaf of
metal placed under a gem to set it off to advantage   **251 chair** throne.
set (1) seated (2) set like a jewel   **254 ward** protect   **258 Your . . . hire**
England's prosperity will reward your efforts   **262 Your . . . age** your
grandchildren will requite it when you are old.   **264 Advance** raise
265–6 the ransom . . . face i.e., if I fail, there will be no question of
ransom, but only death   **276 Tell** Count the strokes of.   **calendar**
almanac.   **278 the book** i.e., the almanac   **279 braved** made splendid

283 lour look threateningly   **288 vaunts** boasts his strength
289 Caparison Put on the battle trappings of   **292 battle** troops
293 foreward vanguard   **298 directed** deployed   **299 main battle**
main body of troops.   **puissance** strength   **300 wingèd** flanked.
horse cavalry.   **301 to boot** i.e., to give us aid in addition.   **304 Jockey**
i.e., Jack, John   **305 Dickon** i.e., Dick, Richard.   **bought and sold**
done for, finished.   **312 join** join battle.   **pell-mell** headlong, hand
to hand   **314 inferred** alleged.   **316 sort** gang   **317 lackey** servile
318 o'ercloyèd satiated, glutted

You sleeping safe, they bring to you unrest;
You having lands, and blest with beauteous wives,
They would restrain the one, distain the other.   322
And who doth lead them but a paltry fellow,
Long kept in Brittany at our mother's cost?   324
A milksop, one that never in his life
Felt so much cold as over shoes in snow?   326
Let's whip these stragglers o'er the seas again.
Lash hence these overweening rags of France,   328
These famished beggars, weary of their lives,
Who, but for dreaming on this fond exploit,   330
For want of means, poor rats, had hanged themselves.   331
If we be conquered, let men conquer us,
And not these bastard Bretons, whom our fathers
Have in their own land beaten, bobbed, and thumped,   334
And in record left them the heirs of shame.   335
Shall these enjoy our lands? Lie with our wives?
Ravish our daughters? [*Drum afar off.*] Hark! I hear
   their drum.
Fight, gentlemen of England! Fight, bold yeomen!
Draw, archers, draw your arrows to the head!   339
Spur your proud horses hard, and ride in blood;
Amaze the welkin with your broken staves!   341

              [*Enter a Messenger.*]

What says Lord Stanley? Will he bring his power?
MESSENGER   My lord, he doth deny to come.
KING RICHARD   Off with his son George's head!
NORFOLK
   My lord, the enemy is past the marsh.
   After the battle let George Stanley die.
KING RICHARD
   A thousand hearts are great within my bosom.
   Advance our standards! Set upon our foes!   348
   Our ancient word of courage, fair Saint George,   349
   Inspire us with the spleen of fiery dragons!   350
   Upon them! Victory sits on our helms!   *Exeunt.*

                        ❧

[5.4]

   *Alarum. Excursions. [Norfolk and forces continue
   to make forays, entering and exiting.] Enter [in the
   melee] Catesby.*

CATESBY
   Rescue, my lord of Norfolk, rescue, rescue!
   The King enacts more wonders than a man,   2
   Daring an opposite to every danger.   3
   His horse is slain, and all on foot he fights,
   Seeking for Richmond in the throat of death.
   Rescue, fair lord, or else the day is lost!

       [*Alarums.*] *Enter [King] Richard.*

KING RICHARD
   A horse! A horse! My kingdom for a horse!
CATESBY
   Withdraw, my lord. I'll help you to a horse.
KING RICHARD
   Slave, I have set my life upon a cast,   9
   And I will stand the hazard of the die.   10
   I think there be six Richmonds in the field;   11
   Five have I slain today instead of him.
   A horse! A horse! My kingdom for a horse! [*Exeunt.*]

                        ❧

[5.5]

   *Alarum. Enter Richard and Richmond; they fight.
   Richard is slain. [Exit Richmond.] Then, retreat
   being sounded, [flourish, and] enter Richmond,
   [Lord Stanley Earl of] Derby bearing the crown,
   with other lords, etc.*

RICHMOND
   God and your arms be praised, victorious friends!
   The day is ours; the bloody dog is dead.
STANLEY [*offering him the crown*]
   Courageous Richmond, well hast thou acquit thee.
   Lo, here this long-usurpèd royalty
   From the dead temples of this bloody wretch
   Have I plucked off, to grace thy brows withal.   6
   Wear it, enjoy it, and make much of it.
RICHMOND
   Great God of heaven, say amen to all!
   But, tell me, is young George Stanley living?
STANLEY
   He is, my lord, and safe in Leicester town,
   Whither, if it please you, we may now withdraw us.
RICHMOND
   What men of name are slain on either side?   12
STANLEY
   John Duke of Norfolk, Walter Lord Ferrers,
   Sir Robert Brackenbury, and Sir William Brandon.
RICHMOND
   Inter their bodies as becomes their births.
   Proclaim a pardon to the soldiers fled

322 restrain deprive you of.   **distain** defile, sully   **324 our mother's**
(Richmond's mother was not Richard's. This error occurs in the second
edition of Holinshed's *Chronicles.* The first edition reads "brothers," the
reference being to the fact that Richmond had been supported at the
court of the Duke of Brittany at the cost of Charles, Duke of Burgundy,
Richard's brother-in-law.)   **326 over shoes** i.e., over his shoe-tops
328 rags ragged fellows   **330 fond** foolish   **331 want of means** poverty
334 bobbed thrashed   **335 And . . . shame** and left them with nothing but the promise of a shameful record in history.   **339 to the head**
to the head of the arrow.   **341 Amaze the welkin** Frighten the skies
348 Advance our standards! Raise our flags!   **349 word of courage**
battle cry   **350 dragons** (Richard ironically identifies with the dragon
slain by Saint George.)
5.4. Location: Bosworth Field, as before; the action is continuous.
0.1 *Excursions* Sorties

2 than a man than seems possible for a human being   **3 Daring . . .
danger** boldly facing every danger in battle.   **9 cast** throw of the dice
10 stand the hazard accept the fortune.   **die** (Singular of *dice.*)
11 six Richmonds i.e., Richmond himself and five men dressed like
him as a safety precaution
5.5. Location: Action continues at Bosworth Field.
0.2 *retreat* trumpet signal to withdraw, cease the attack   **6 withal**
with.   **12 of name** of title

That in submission will return to us,
And then, as we have ta'en the Sacrament,   18
We will unite the white rose and the red.
Smile heaven upon this fair conjunction,   20
That long have frowned upon their enmity!
What traitor hears me and says not amen?
England hath long been mad, and scarred herself;
The brother blindly shed the brother's blood,
The father rashly slaughtered his own son,
The son, compelled, been butcher to the sire.
All this divided York and Lancaster,
Divided in their dire division.

18 ta'en the Sacrament sworn a sacred oath on the Sacrament (to marry Princess Elizabeth, daughter of Edward IV, thereby uniting the houses of York and of Lancaster, white rose and red rose)   20 conjunction union. (An astrological metaphor.)

Oh, now let Richmond and Elizabeth,
The true succeeders of each royal house,
By God's fair ordinance conjoin together!   31
And let their heirs, God, if thy will be so,
Enrich the time to come with smooth-faced peace,
With smiling plenty, and fair prosperous days!
Abate the edge of traitors, gracious Lord,   35
That would reduce these bloody days again   36
And make poor England weep in streams of blood!
Let them not live to taste this land's increase
That would with treason wound this fair land's peace!
Now civil wounds are stopped, peace lives again.   40
That she may long live here, God say amen! [*Exeunt.*]

31 ordinance decree   35 Abate Blunt, render ineffective   36 reduce bring back   40 stopped closed up

Richard III on Stage

Because of his wit, wile, and spectacular downfall, Richard has attracted just about every actor of note. Many have emphasized his melodramatic intensity— Edmund Kean, Edwin Booth, and Henry Irving in the nineteenth century, followed by Donald Wolfit, Laurence Olivier, and Antony Sher in the twentieth. Others have taken a more psychologically complex approach, attempting to probe suggested aspects of his mind: his neglect by his mother, his sadomasochism, his sexual frustration or closeted homosexuality, his diabolical appeal to women. Those employing that more psychological approach include David Garrick in the eighteenth century; William Macready in the nineteenth; and John Barrymore, Laurence Olivier (on stage), Alec Guinness, Christopher Plummer, and Ian McKellen in the twentieth. Some have reportedly offered a character that concentrated on external traits while seemingly ignoring the mind behind them, thus creating merely a grotesque and stuttering hunchback, such as might be imagined in a child's fears or medieval fantasies. The variety of approaches to the part also enables, however, of a kind of grandeur, as when Richard assumes what Hazlitt called "a condescending superiority, after he is made king."

The Elizabethan Era: Richard III
During Shakespeare's Day

In stark contrast to the sheer volume and convolutions of *Richard III*'s text, the play can be staged relatively directly and simply, with much of its effect dependent upon the lead actor and the insinuating relationship he establishes with the audience. The first productions probably occurred at The Theater; with its large thrust stage, entries and exits would have been through doors in the rear stage wall. Between these same doors, a throne would have been set for the coronation scene in 4.2. During the final battle, when Richard and Richmond meet, they would have entered separately through those rear doors and those doors would have represented the tents of each general. None of the public playhouses, including, eventually, the Globe, would have used much scenery. Only a few props would have been required, such as the casque (helmet) of Henry VI; the sexually symbolic sword and ring in the wooing scene; and a few banners, drums, and perhaps onstage trumpets for the military expeditions. One stage direction at 3.7 suggests that Richard and his bishops appear above, in the acting space comprising the gallery over the rear stage wall. Probably no use was made of a trap door even for the appearances of the ghosts. The two tents in which Richard and Richmond have their cursed and blessed dreams would have been portable props set up at the two doors, carried on and off by actors representing their soldiers.

The Eighteenth and Nineteenth Centuries:
Spectacle and Melodrama

Between 1700 and 1850, the acting version in use for *Richard III* was a mosaic devised by actor-manager Colley Cibber for production at Drury Lane. His own performance was remembered, as one critic put it, as "the distorted heavings of an unjointed caterpillar," and in the nineteenth century William Hazlitt called this same adaptation a "miserable medley acted for *Richard III.*" Yet it held the stage. Even in our own day, traces of Cibber survive in the Laurence Olivier film in which the actor-director has included such notorious lines as the Cibber-inspired "Off with his head! So much for Buckingham!" Olivier also followed Cibber in deleting some of the more complicating factors from the villain's character, such as Richard's soliloquy on conscience and self-knowledge on the night before the battle at Bosworth Field. Cibber's composite production also borrowed from other histories; added moments of his own making; and dropped the character of Margaret, the wailing women, Clarence (and his dream), and Lord Stanley. The emphasis was almost exclusively, then, upon Richard as an out-and-out villain.

David Garrick took up the part in 1741. It is he who is depicted in William Hogarth's famous drawing of Richard waking after the nightmare phantoms have circled him the night before. "He dwindles neither into the buffoon nor the brute," wrote one admiring contemporary. Garrick's performance was so powerful, according to theatrical legend, that women shrieked when his Richard died. Writer Charles Lamb spoke much less admiringly, on the other hand, of the Covent Garden performances by George Frederick Cooke in 1800, noting in a letter that "the lofty imagery and high sentiments and high passions of poetry come black and prose-smoked from his prose lips."

In one of his most famous pieces of theater criticism (1814), William Hazlitt described Edmund Kean's Richard, favoring him over the dazzling but erratic Cooke or any other interpreter. "He is more refined than Cooke; more bold, varied and original than Kemble in the same character. His courtship scene with Lady Anne was an admirable exhibition of smooth and smiling villainy. The progress of wily adulation, of encroaching humility was finely marked throughout by the action, voice, and eye. He seemed, like the first tempter, to approach his prey, certain of the event, and as if success had smoothed the way before him" (quoted in Wells, *Shakespeare in the Theatre: An Anthology of Criticism*, 39–40). Richard's confident diabolism, Hazlitt implies, is part of his attraction and his terror.

William Charles Macready, who played in the Cibber version at Covent Garden in 1819, was said to have shown a sharp theatrical intelligence and surprising nimbleness in the part. In 1821, he acted in a production more closely based on Shakespeare's text, with about two hundred lines from Cibber. Samuel Phelps partly restored Shakespeare's text in 1845, although another fifty years were to pass before Cibber's medley was fully replaced. In 1877, Henry Irving acted in a badly cut ver-

sion of Shakespeare's text, of which the American novelist Henry James wrote that its effect was "sinister-sardonic" with elements of the "elegant-grotesque."

The Twentieth Century: Psychology and Current Events

Contrasting interpretations of Richard continued into the early years of the twentieth century when the rise of the repertory theater, such as the Old Vic, made possible the enactment of a varied range of plays by a large company. Robert Atkins, who had directed all the plays in the Shakespeare Folio there between 1914 and 1923, performed the crookback as an energetic upstart rather than a princely usurper, while Baliol Holloway, also at the Old Vic, created a grim, if royal, old devil Richard in the Machiavellian tradition. Laurence Olivier chose instead to create a panther-like Richard in Richard Burrell's production at the New Theatre in 1944. Pale, limping, with long, lank black hair and a diabolically debonair manner, Olivier maintained the melodramatic malice while also exploring Richard's strangled rage and the theme of betrayal that permeates the play. Critic Kenneth Tynan wrote of this memorable performance that Olivier "leapt into life, using the circumambient gloom as his springboard. Olivier's Richard eats into memory like acid into metal, but the total impression is one of lightness and deftness" (quoted in Wells, 230). The notion that this youngest of the Duchess of York's children was neglected and even abused creeps into several interpretations after Olivier's, notably Ian McKellen's (see below) on stage and film.

Other notable Richards after mid-century were Alec Guinness, who opened the Stratford Shakespeare Festival in Ontario with a performance that press critics called terrifying and the most exciting night in the history of Canadian theater, and Hume Cronyn, whose performance at the Guthrie Theater in Minneapolis (1965) underscored the black comedy of the role. Antony Sher, in a highly praised 1984 staging directed by Bill Alexander for the RSC, proved a brilliantly grotesque centerpiece to a spectacle that reminded some viewers of grand nineteenth-century interpretations by John Philip Kemble. Hunched over long crutches that suggested his spider-like being, rubbing them together like forelegs, Sher deployed the props and his monstrous hump as weapons. In his review for the *Times Literary Supplement*, Stanley Wells noted that Sher's Richard possessed not only a frightening appearance but also a grim self-knowledge that made this staging an ironic tragedy.

A controversial 1994 production directed in England by Barrie Rutter for Northern Broadsides on tour played up the farcical aspects of the play. A shoulder pad from a rugby league served as Richard's hump, and a used fur

(TopFoto)

In director Barry Kyle's all-female production of Richard III *at London's Globe Theatre, Kathryn Hunter played the gleefully theatrical monarch with Meredith McNeill as his advisor Buckingham.*

coat as the queen's robe passed from one female character to another. Richard died at the hands of the ghosts, who clobbered him with sticks and clogs in what one critic described as a "folk ritual of exorcism of the devil."

The Royal Shakespeare Company's **The War of the Roses**

Peter Hall and John Barton's adapted version of *Richard III* in 1963 followed their two-play adaptation of the *Henry VI* trilogy. The project was acclaimed as a monumental and significant treatment of Shakespeare, for it generated a sense of history as a horrifying process. (Hall acknowledged in his program notes a heavy indebtedness to Ian Kott's vision of the Grand Mechanism of History as described in Kott's *Shakespeare, Our Contemporary*.) In the Hall/Barton production, Richard's deeds were portrayed as being part of the retributive phase of a sequence of events that began with the murder of Richard II. Hall's production, staged on a metallic set, was unabashedly sensational, and Ian Holm created a Richard steeped in the blood of a violent culture—an atmosphere emphasized by staging choices such as displaying around Richard the severed heads of those already executed. Kott had viewed Richard as a kind of faceless mastermind of the Grand Mechanism which he at first operates before being crushed by it. Queen Margaret emerged in this production as a significant antagonist. Played by Peggy Ashcroft and beginning as the beautiful young bride of Henry VI in the first play of that trilogy, Margaret took on a dimension and humanity

absent from most interpretations. *The War of the Roses* was the first in a tradition of Shakespeare stagings influenced by Kott, or more precisely, by the grim post-Holocaust theater of central and Eastern Europe. Others followed, including Terry Hands's 1970 Stratford production emphasizing the atrocities, and a grotesque Brechtian staging by the Rustaveli Company of Tbilisi, Georgia, later made into a feature film.

The RSC's Eight Histories Marathon

Visitors to London could see all eight history plays, more or less uncut, during the RSC's series *This England—The Histories*, which was produced for the 2000–2001 season at the Barbican Centre (which contains two theaters) and the Young Vic (a converted industrial space) and staged by several directors, including Michael Attenborough. During the so-called "Eight Histories Marathon," the *Henry VI* plays and *Richard III* were presented in bloody, close-in stagings by Michael Boyd. The *Henry VI* productions, with their pathetically ineffectual and pious king (played by David Oyelowo), led to the bloodbath that was the *Tragedy of King Richard III* and concluded the marathon. Aidan McArdle starred as an impish and sardonic, but not a very powerful, Richard; his skill with the comedy of dissimulation entertained, even if it did not terrorize. Grand and truly frightening, on the other hand, was Fiona Bell as Queen Margaret, who stalked the scene like a ghost and hauled on stage a large sack carrying the bones of her murdered son.

Richard III on Film and Television

Richard III has been filmed often and to excellent effect for the large and small screens, though with widely varying approaches and interpretations. In contrast to the limits inherent in stage productions, film and television offer an arsenal of special effect and editing tools that can be used by directors to tell the tale.

In the nightmare scene, for instance, film directors have used various means of enhancing the horror. Some use illusions to represent the spirits, such as the strange lights and ghostly transparencies that float across Bosworth Field in Olivier's film; the flashing subliminal faces and voices, and the smoky figures filmed through red filters in Al Pacino's *Looking for Richard*; and floating, disembodied heads. Jane Howell, in her 1982 television production for the BBC, takes the viewer inside the nightmare. The camera moves into a close-up of Richmond settling in to sleep, but when the head turns we see it is Richard's face, his eyes opening as the Duchess of York curses him. Richard is visible within the pupil of his own eye. A flashback shows in procession all the people he has eliminated in his progress to the crown, each bearing either wounds or reminiscences of how he or she was murdered. Wine dribbles down Clarence's face, while those beheaded bear the scars on their necks. A cloth suddenly releases feathers to remind the viewer that the little princes were smothered with a pillow.

Similarly, film is an especially tractable medium for the final scene; its visual realism and flexibility allow for caparisoned horses and formations of soldiers to confront one another on the battlefield. Howell's BBC production overcame many of the limitations of filming in a television studio and "in period" by employing a renowned fight choreographer to arrange the movement and by using the camera and editing techniques to build montages: shots of individual combats and slashing death blows (though not the deaths themselves, except Richard's) are spliced into the larger battle.

Many silent films were made of *Richard III.* After a brief discussion of them we outline four of the dozen films with soundtracks currently in circulation.

Silent Films

A five-reel *Richard III* was made in 1912, starring Frederick B. Warde, a British actor, the producer of several Shakespeare films (see "Close-up: Silent Shakespeare," pp. 50–51). Warde, claiming that he had to "suppress all sense of the ridiculous to complete this project," often made personal appearances at showings of this and others of his films to lecture audiences on the plays and to recite significant passages while the projectionist changed the reels. Visual gimmicks were not uncommon in the silent era (nor are they now), as even the earliest filmmakers realized that films could tell stories through pictures, rather than just with words or even characters. Warde's film, co-directed by James Keane II, used mostly a fixed camera capturing the tableau acting style of the period, although a few tracking shots and other innovations show that this was a quite a creative work for its era.

Warde's film contrasted with a 1911 version of *Richard III* (*The Life and Death of King Richard the Third*), directed by Frank R. Benson, that reduced the play to mere melodrama. Interpolating a scene from the earlier trilogy, Benson's film made the hunchbacked king bloodthirsty: after he killed Henry VI, he ran his fingers along the sword blade and licked the dead king's blood from his fingers.

The first of the silent Richards was a 1908 film directed by J. Stuart Blackton and William V. Ramous. The last was Max Reinhardt's German production in 1919.

More Recent Film Versions

As previously mentioned, a dozen post-silent film versions have been made of *Richard III.* Four of them are discussed below.

- 1955—Director Laurence Olivier, London Film Productions, Ltd., with Olivier (Richard), John Gielgud (Clarence), Ralph Richardson (Buckingham), Cedric Hardwicke (Edward IV), Claire Bloom (Anne), and Helen Hayes (the Duchess of York). (158 min.)

Olivier's film, like his earlier *Henry V*, has been generally praised for the film's casting, its vigor, its attention to the language, and its formal beauty. At the same time it has been viewed as too tidy and one-dimensional in its treatment of Richard, whose lines are significantly cut—most noticeably in the nightmare of conscience scene before Bosworth Field. Also on the cutting room floor are such characters as Queen Margaret and Lord Stanley. Richmond appears as a Prince Valiant antagonist. Among the film's most striking images are the final encirclement of Richard, and his death throes with which the movie ends—with none of the final lines in which Henry Tudor predicts the marriage and peaceful prosperity to follow. Olivier's Richard and the great crown that is the film's central iconic image are the film's focus, although Gielgud's recital of Clarence's poetic dream is one of its highlights. The sheer beauty of Claire Bloom, hypnotized into Richard's baleful spell, is another of the film's many strengths. Richard has to drag Anne toward the throne for his coronation, during which he himself sits as though dazed at having realized his ambition.

Olivier retains the long locks, the huge hump, the limping gait, and the strong, outsized nose that characterized his stage Richard in 1944. At the same time the film domesticates the character he created on stage, partly by cutting so many significant lines, but also by bringing him in close so often that his insinuating charisma casts an intimate spell and makes the audience guiltily complicit. Olivier adds a segment showing Hastings in a scene of domestic intimacy with Jane Shore, thereby clarifying one of Richard's summary actions in beheading Hastings when that gentleman does not immediately agree to have Jane executed as a witch. (Loncraine, in his 1995 film, also shows such mistress figures who never appear in Shakespeare's text: he visualizes them as 1930s flight attendants.) Olivier's Richard quickly shakes off whatever fear his bad dreams have brought to him; he fights, as Jack Jorgens notes, "like a demon" with two horses killed beneath him before he is surrounded by Richmond's men, who pull off his armor and butcher him. Olivier's protracted death throes end the film without the conciliatory final passages about Richmond, now Henry VII, as peacemaker to the kingdom. Instead, the great crown, which has been so central to the production's symbolic design, appears once more as the camera tracks away and the credits roll.

- 1982—Director Jane Howell, BBC, with Ron Cook (Richard), Rowena Cooper (Queen Elizabeth), Annette Crosbie (the Duchess of York), Brian Deacon (Richmond), Julie Foster (Margaret), Paul Jesson (Clarence), and Brian Protheroe (Edward IV). (180 min.)

Jane Howell's film for the BBC Shakespeare productions is one of the more effective of the series. She retains most of the text, as well as the rhetorical set pieces and emblematic groupings of this long play, and manages to exceed the limitations of a unit set and a television studio for the battle scenes in this film and in the *Henry VI* trilogy that preceded it. Though Bosworth Field is the final battle in the War of the Roses, Richard's is the only death shown in Howell's film. Howell's depiction of that scene is brilliant: Richard is pictured on his knees as he is impaled upon Richmond's sword. With the crown now Richmond's, his soldiers kneel around the new king, while Richard appears to be kneeling in eerie allegiance as well.

Howell creates another startling visual irony in the final image, implying her skepticism of the divine order that some other directors have restored to the end of this play. Howell follows the triumphant accession of Henry Tudor with a final scene in which the camera pans over the mangled corpses on Bosworth Field until stopping finally at Queen Margaret. We see her holding the dead body of Richard in her arms, in a reverse-Pieta image. Witch-like and wild-haired, Margaret cackles triumphantly: her prophecies have all come true.

- 1995—Director Richard Loncraine, United Artists, with Ian McKellen (Richard), Maggie Smith (the Duchess of York), Jim Broadbent (Buckingham), Nigel Hawthorne (Clarence), Kristin Scott Thomas (Lady Anne), John Wood (Edward IV), Dominic West (Richmond), and Annette Bening (Elizabeth). (104 min.)

This fast-paced film acknowledges its debt to Richard Eyre's 1990 production for the Royal National Theatre, an interpretation that compared Richard to the fascist leaders of the mid-twentieth century—not only Hitler in Germany and Mussolini in Italy, but the British upper classes who were drawn to their homegrown Union of Fascists. In

adapting that 1930s-set production for the screen, director Richard Loncraine drives the action with hurtling momentum. He establishes that dizzying pace at the start when a huge tank smashes through the walls of an army office. A soldier wearing a gas mask rises out of the tank, shoots a young officer and his father, then peels off the mask: the killer is Richard. When he unloads more rounds from his pistol, the loud gunshots spell out the movie's title in blood-red letters on the screen: *Richard III.*

Appearing pale and sickly, Ian McKellen underscores Richard's malignant sexuality, his outrageous humor, and his status as an alienated outsider. His Richard is unable, for instance, to participate in the elegant dance (to big band music) celebrating the Yorkist victory. He leaves the party for the men's room, turns away from the urinal toward the camera, and facing us, delivers his opening soliloquy. Loncraine and McKellen suggest that Richard's hostility is born of sexual conflict and frustration, and that he was unloved by his steely mother, the Duchess of York (Maggie Smith), who greets his every gesture toward her with contempt and, eventually, curses. Costumed in the blackshirt style of national fascists, with his leather coat, little moustache, cigarette, and ominous riding crop, McKellen's Richard embodies the theory that fascism and denied homosexuality could be interconnected, while also taking some scenes so close to the top that he seems a mordant combination of Adolf Hitler and Dr. Strangelove. His withered arm is usually tucked into a pocket; only once does he pull the ugly appendage out, and then to use it as a weapon to threaten Lord Hastings (Jim Carter). This Gloucester murders with style and relishes the results by repeatedly examining photographs of his victims.

Loncraine's direction assists the audience in several ways. For instance, the director clarifies the opposing sides in this latter-day reign of terror by having the Prime Minister (Hastings) and the air force chief (Edward Hardwicke's Stanley) join the Lancastrian forces of Richmond (Dominic West), here depicted as a handsome young naval commander. In addition, Loncraine creates intimacy between the audience and Richard by giving McKellen many close-ups and asides. Like his predecessor in the role, Olivier, McKellen's Richard delights in speaking directly to the camera, which focuses upon his sinister, smiling face even as he plunges to his death in a fiery furnace. The director makes wonderfully witty use of even the most anachronistic lines. When Richard's jeep becomes stuck during the final battle sequence, he angrily exits the vehicle with his automatic weapon and shouts the famous line, "A horse! A horse! My kingdom for a horse!"

Among the changes in this energetic recontextu-alization is that Margaret is dropped altogether, along with almost all references to the earlier *Henry VI* plays in the cycle, while the roles of the other three women (Lady Anne, Queen Elizabeth, and the usually unseen princess) have been expanded. Lady Anne (Kristin Scott Thomas in gorgeous, fox-trimmed period clothes) meets the villain who will seduce her in a gloomy morgue where the fresh gunshot wounds are clearly visible on her husband's body. Richmond marries the Princess Elizabeth before Bosworth, and his sweet dreams come to him while he is enfolded in her naked arms. Much of the political and historical background has been delet-ed from this film, but it borrows liberally from the tradition of the American gangster film, as James N. Loehlin has pointed out in his essay "Top of the World, Ma" (in *Shakespeare: the Movie*, 67–79). Each victim dies a different sort of death, with the vio-lence, which Shakespeare kept off stage, graphical-ly depicted. The gullible, sympathetic brother Clarence is bathing in the tower when his throat is slit; we see the water in the tub redden as it fills with his blood. Hastings is hanged. Buckingham is beat-en, then garroted like a Mafia don. Little Prince Edward is smothered with a red silk scarf. The most startling death comes to Queen Elizabeth's brother, Rivers. He snuffs out a cigarette and leans back to enjoy his tryst with a flight attendant when a dagger suddenly pierces upward through his back from the hand of an unseen assailant under the bed; we see the knife tip protruding from his belly. This England has indeed become a "slaughterhouse."

Despite these radical re-imaginings, the film is true to the spirit of the play. McKellen retains the pre-battle speech about conscience, though he short-ens it. Tossing painfully and sweating profusely as dawn breaks on the day of battle, he suggests that Richard now truly suffers the pangs of his own long-dormant conscience and gains grimly ironic self-knowledge. This tragic awareness does not exoner-ate him from his crimes, but it does humanize him.

The final confrontation of the two antagonists takes place in a skeletal industrial building (one of many brilliantly employed locations in London) where Richard falls from on high, grinning as he descends in flames while Richmond faces the camera and smiles directly at the audience as Richard did formerly, all to the accompaniment of "Sittin' on Top of the World." This reference to the ending of one of James Cagney's gangster movies, *White Heat*, and other sardonic juxtapositions suggest that Rich-mond's rise to power may be as short-lived and bloody as his predecessor's.

■ 1996—*Looking for Richard*. Conceived, directed, and acted by Al Pacino, Twentieth Century Fox, with Kevin Spacey (Buckingham), Penelope Allen (Queen Margaret), Winona Ryder (Lady Anne), Alec Baldwin (Clarence), and Harris Yulin (Edward IV). (112 min.)

This feature film follows American film star Al Pacino as he takes part in roundtable discussions, conversations with academics, and man-on-the-street interviews in New York City to search for clues about how to interpret the text of the play, how to approach the character, and how to convey the cul-tural relevance of Shakespeare at the end of the twen-tieth century. As much docudrama as performance document, *Looking for Richard* has no real precedent in Shakespearean filmmaking. Like Orson Welles, Laurence Olivier, and Kenneth Branagh before him, Pacino clearly used his own star power to get the film made. Yet instead of presenting an interpretation or even an adaptation of the full play, he shows us frag-mentary scenes, intercutting them with the interview and roundtable material, thereby suggesting differ-ences between filming and staging the play, between American and British approaches to language and character, and between rehearsing (sometimes in para-phrase) and actually performing the script.

The traits long associated with *Richard III*—a sat-urnine menace and hypnotic sexuality—aptly describe the popular image of Pacino himself, known as he is for playing charismatic villains. In *The Godfa-ther* (1972) he personified the don apparent, Michael Corleone; in a more recent production of Oscar Wilde's *Salome* (2003), directed by Estelle Parsons on Broadway, he presented a leering, lascivious Herod; and in the brilliant HBO presentation of Kushner's *Angels in America*, directed by Mike Nichols (2003), he played a theatrical descendant of Richard III, the Republican political operative and Red-baiter, Roy Cohn. Thus, Pacino virtually typecasts himself as Richard III. Yet when he performed the play on Broadway in 1979, critics slammed him for his too slovenly delivery of the language, as if his Method training (at Lee Strasberg's famed Actors Studio in New York) disqualified him from such nonrealistic classical roles. Perhaps that earlier rejection accounts for the film's defensive discussions of various acting styles and possibilities. Traditional British confidence in speaking Shakespeare's verse is here contrasted to the Americans' casual ease in the predominant con-temporary idiom of naturalism. Pacino's self-financed and self-produced *Looking for Richard* breaks open the play, and, as its title implies, hunts the central char-acter as an actor's quarry. Pacino's associates include John Gielgud, in one of his last filmed appearances, explaining that American actors may need to do more research into the context in which Shakespeare wrote. Also on hand is admired theater innovator Peter Brook, discussing how the filmed close-up may have advantages over the stage presentation of certain of Shakespeare's scenes.

In *Looking for Richard*, Pacino and his collaborators move in and out of their characters, asking questions all the while, as they confer with one another, with learned scholars, and with citizens in New York. One notable character in the film is real-life author Frederic Kimball, Pacino's co-writer on the script, who serves as dramaturge, or literary advisor, for the play scenes within the film. In the scenes themselves, Pacino adopts a hump and a lurching gait, but does not pay much attention otherwise to making the characterization consistent: he is bearded in some scenes, and not in others, for instance. The fragmentary, even equivocal nature of the interpretations he discovers is mirrored in the structure of this decidedly postmodern, anti-illusionistic film. (Critic H. R. Coursen dismissed Pacino's effort [in Esche, 23] as "a documentary about making a film of *Richard III* in a city innocent of any knowledge of Shakespeare.") Yet as the film progresses, the Shakespearean scenes become longer, more fully costumed, and "staged," until they culminate in the final scene at Bosworth Field, which gets the full filmic treatment, with horses, weapons, and even the final lines that had been cut from Olivier's film. Pacino reaches some confidence about his interpretation before the nightmare scene when he tells his company: "The pursuit of power has totally corrupted him [Richard]."

Spin-offs

Richard of Gloucester has inspired two horror films, both called *The Tower of London*. The 1939 original starred Basil Rathbone as Richard, Boris Karloff as the executioner Mord, and Vincent Price as Clarence. A low-budget period piece, written by Robert Lee and directed by Rowland Lee, the film charts Richard's progress to the throne as Mord eliminates each person in his way. In the throne room is a large dollhouse from which the accomplices remove a figurine representing each of the murder victims. A silly romantic subplot and several dungeon scenes veer into unintentional comedy. Price, the master of horror, must have enjoyed the filming, for he plays Richard in director Roger Corman's 1962 remake of the movie, in which he is haunted by ghosts and surrounded by bloodcurdling special effects.

References and Related Reading

Burt, Richard. "The Love that Dare Not Speak Shakespeare's Name: New Shakesqueer Cinema." *Shakespeare: The Movie.* Eds. Lynda E. Boose and Richard Burt. London and New York, 1997/99. 240–268.

Cibber, Colley. "*Richard III.*" *Shakespeare Made Fit: Restoration Adaptations of Shakespeare.* Ed. Sandra Clark. London, 1997. 374–459.

Dollimore, Jonathan, and Alan Sinfield, eds. *Political Shakespeare: New Essays in Cultural Materialism.* Manchester, 1985.

Hankey, Julia, ed. *Plays in Performance: Richard III.* Bristol, 1981/88.

Hortmann, William. "Shakespeare on the Political Stage." *Shakespeare on Stage.* Eds. Stanley Wells and Sarah Stanton. Cambridge, 2002. 212–229.

Kelly, Henry A. *Divine Providence in the England of Shakespeare's Histories.* Cambridge, Mass., 1970.

Loehlin, James N. " 'Top of the World, Ma': *Richard III* and Cinematic Convention." *Shakespeare: The Movie.* Eds. Lynda E. Boose and Richard Burt. London and New York, 1997/99, 67–79.

Manheim, Michael. "The English History Play on Screen." *Shakespeare and the Moving Image.* Eds. Anthony Davies and Stanley Wells. Cambridge, Eng., 1994. 121–145.

Norwich, John Julius. *Shakespeare's Kings.* New York and London, 1999/2001.

Siegel, Paul N. *Shakespeare's English and Roman History Plays: A Marxist Approach.* London and Toronto, 1986.

Willis, Susan. *The BBC Shakespeare Plays: Making the Televised Canon.* Chapel Hill and London, 1991.

Wood, Alice Ida. *The Stage History of Shakespeare's "King Richard III."* New York, 1909/65.

CHAPTER 12

Henry IV, Part One

(c. 1596–1597)

Context and Dating: The Appeal of Falstaff

Henry IV, Part One was printed more often during Shakespeare's lifetime than any of his other plays. The prime reason for its popularity during its first two centuries was a single character: Sir John Falstaff, the rotund old knight and "misleader" of the crown prince Hal. The play survived as a skit about the robust, sherry-addicted, subversively witty Falstaff when Puritan forces closed London theaters during the 1640s and 1650s. Yet the seductively comic scenes involving Falstaff comprise only one aspect of this multifaceted history play in which Shakespeare's sympathies flow in many directions. The primary action continues the story of civil conflict begun in *Richard II*. At the close of that play Henry Bolingbroke emerges as King Henry IV; the two-part drama that bears his name is a close successor. Both the personal story of this king, his son Hal, Hal's surrogate father Falstaff, and Hal's rival Hotspur (Henry Percy), and the political story of the civil wars giving birth to modern England continue into the sequels *Henry IV, Part Two* and *Henry V*.

The opening of *Henry IV, Part One* is grave and impassioned, for Shakespeare takes not simply a moral, but a very practical view of the importance of social order and good kingship to the stability of the kingdom. This drama, spanning many locations, emotional tones, and social levels, presents a troubled Henry IV who would prefer to cleanse his guilt over his usurpation of the crown from his cousin Richard II and to unify his nation by engaging in a foreign crusade to the Holy Land. Instead he must face continuing military assaults on his throne at home. The members of the Percy clan, who have helped him to the throne, soon react to what they feel is his ingratitude and hostility.

They organize against him, joining the Scots and the Welsh who are already fighting Henry.

Amid these serious political conflicts are more humorous and personal events at work in the story of Falstaff. "The Falstaff plays," as critic William Empson calls them, "were an enormous hit, appealing to a great variety of people, not all of them very high-minded." And so the complex relationship of the sober history to the raucous comedy, along with the social, poetic, and tonal richness of *Henry IV*, have been cause for lively critical and directorial debate. This argument has pitted those readers who sometimes fail to be taken in by Falstaff's charm on the page against other readers, many of them theater directors and actors, who are more readily seduced by the wide appeal of Falstaff's comic speeches and seemingly spontaneous actions on stage.

Even these divergent camps agree that beginning with *Henry IV, Part One*, Shakespeare redefines history (and by extension the history play) as the record of a much more expansive, humane, and less hierarchical society than that presented by many Renaissance historians, who dealt only with the upper classes, the military, and the state. By stretching the genre of the history play to include Falstaff and other vivid denizens of Eastcheap, a lower-class neighborhood of London, as well as the deftly drawn wives of the rebels, Shakespeare expands traditional notions of who and what are historically important. Artistically, with its fusion of high dramatic verse and robust comic writing, *Henry IV* is almost unmatched in the Shakespeare canon.

Henry IV, Part One was written before early 1598 when it was entered in the Stationers' Register. How long before that publication date the play was performed is uncertain, although early in 1597 seems likely to most theater scholars. This would mean that the Lord Chamberlain's Men performed the play at The Theater in Shoreditch, where they had performed since 1594, or perhaps at the nearby Curtain once their lease had expired at The Theater in March of 1597. In any case, it was first staged before their move across the Thames to the Globe in 1599. The evidence suggests that *Henry IV* was revised before its Register entry, notably to change the name of the character originally called Sir John Old-castle to Sir John Falstaff. Apparently a descendant of the real-life Oldcastle (who was martyred during King Henry V's reign) complained of this secular use of his rel-ative's revered name, and so Shakespeare rechristened the character who was destined to become so famous with a less controversial name from his sources, Falstaff.

Characters

According to the chronicles, Henry IV, the title charac-ter, would have been thirty-seven years old at the time of the play's action, but in the play he seems much older; he is depicted as "wan with care" and is some-times acted as already weak from the illness that even-tually kills him. Now brooding, insecure, and guilt-rid-den, he sees the alliance he formed with other rebels against Richard II begin to dissolve in the first act and lead to further civil conflict in Act 2.

Henry's son, Hal, the Prince of Wales, may seem a kind of slacker early on, a dissolute prankster whose royal blood is something to joke about. Yet interpreters have also seen (and an actor can emphasize, as the stage history shows) a range of different qualities in him, espe-cially during the early scenes with Falstaff. He may appear an attractive young man who does not wish to grow up, who cherishes his youthful irresponsibility, and who wishes to avoid as long as possible the burdens of an unsought kingship. Contrastingly, Hal can also seem, and has been played as, a shrewd actor-manipulator who can persuade us that he is playing a kind of game, edu-cating himself about human nature and the common man when he soliloquizes about his low-life companions:

> I know you all, and will awhile uphold
> The unyoked humor of your idleness.
> Yet herein will I imitate the sun,
> Who doth permit the base contagious clouds
> To smother up his beauty from the world,
> That when he please again to be himself,
> Being wanted he may be more wondered at
> By breaking through the foul and ugly mists
> Of vapors that did seem to strangle him.
>
> (1.2.189–197)

A calculating reading of the soliloquy tests our sym-pathies, for Hal here appears to be using his friends to cre-ate an image of himself as a royal with a common touch. This speech has also been read as a kind of chorus-speech designed to explain to the audience that this irresponsible young man will eventually become the hero known from history as Henry V. The speech explaining his actions can be read another way. A subtle actor can represent Hal as ambivalent, a youth who clearly enjoys romping with the anarchic Falstaff, tricking him in the Gad's Hill scene, and role-playing his future position as a king who will indeed, if sadly and inevitably, put this "loose behavior" behind him. The potentially cold and calculating streak in Prince Hal makes the role notoriously contradictory, and, for many actors, unrewarding. Hal is emotionally veiled, a trait that deepens in the more somber Part Two, and becomes central to his character in the last play in the tetralogy, *Henry V*. Shakespeare seems to have under-stood, as Falstaff does not, that any effective leader, once in a public role, can seldom let down the mask of power.

One of Hal's foils is Hotspur, the role that many young actors, including Laurence Olivier during the 1940s, have preferred to that of Hal. In fact, after Falstaff, Hotspur is the most coveted role in the play. Hotspur, a member of the Percy clan, is charismatic, valiant, and witty. His virtues are old-fashioned ones that include manliness, chivalrous behavior, and a high-toned notion of honor. Fiery by nature and quick to anger (as his name suggests), he is also impatient and proud. When Hotspur explains to Henry IV that he will not deliver his Scottish prisoners because an effete courtier (whom he sardonically imitates and mocks) had come to him in battle to ask, he reveals his narrow conception of chival-ry and manhood. And as soon as Henry IV refuses to ransom Hotspur's brother-in-law Mortimer, Hotspur becomes obsessed with payback: "All studies here I solemnly defy, / Save how to gall and pinch this Bol-ingbroke, / And that same sword-and-buckler Prince of Wales" (1.3.227–229). Hotspur's kinsmen and fellow rebels are clearly accustomed to and affectionately for-give these traits, including his inability to listen: "Why, what a wasp-stung and impatient fool / Art thou to break into this woman's mood, / Tying thine ear to no tongue but thine own!" (1.3.235–237). When these rela-tives—his father, Northumberland, and uncle, Worces-ter—suggest to him that Henry's refusal is politically motivated, Hotspur quickly exaggerates the offense. The hot-blooded young soldier, driven by feudal notions of honor, roused to anger by Henry IV's "for-getful" and "proud" mistreatment, calls the king "this thorn, this canker, Bolingbroke" and joins his uncle and Northumberland in a rebellion against him. He invokes danger from all four corners of the earth, for "Oh, the blood more stirs / To rouse a lion than to start a hare!" (1.3.197–198). The explosive rhythms of his speech, its "poetry as natural as the human voice" (Van Doren) are another part of his appeal to audiences and to actors.

Henry IV admires Hotspur's strong character, and wishes his own son's were more like it. He feels envy that Northumberland

Should be the father to so blest a son—
A son who is the theme of honor's tongue,
Amongst a grove the very straightest plant,
Who is sweet Fortune's minion and her pride,
Whilst I, by looking on the praise of him,
See riot and dishonor stain the brow
Of my young Harry. Oh, that it could be proved
That some night-tripping fairy had exchanged
In cradle clothes our children where they lay,
And called mine Percy, his Plantagenet!
Then would I have his Harry and he mine.

(1.1.79–88)

Hotspur's intemperance, his distracted treatment of his loving, outspoken wife, and his one-dimensional judgments of men and manners are defects of character that Henry IV would correct, however, and which his own son, the more temperate, sophisticated, and nonchalant crown prince, does not share. Still, after Hal kills Hotspur in close combat, his farewell to the corpse of this rival with the "great heart" can be quite moving: it has some of the tender feeling that will later color Horatio's farewell to Hamlet.

Sir John Falstaff is generally considered Shakespeare's fullest comic creation, possessing a robust wit, a keen intelligence, and an exuberant fancy that makes him a prodigious improviser and phrase-maker. Through the ages he has been seen to represent everything from the old corrupt, decadent feudalism whose time has passed, to a disruptive, even subversive, personality threatening the rule of law and order, to the embodiment of all that is most free and joyous in life, to the ultimate realist, a vital truth-teller who exposes the life-denying lies of the powerful (A. C. Bradley). Literary genealogists have viewed him as an archetypal descendant of the medieval Vice (Bernard Spivack, 1958); as the embodiment of the sins of Gluttony and Sloth (Samuel Johnson, 1765); and as a much more complex, ironic, and ambiguous figure as in William Empson's psychic analysis of his corpulence and shame.

Throughout the eighteenth and nineteenth centuries, commentary tended to focus upon Falstaff as a character separate from the historical action; critics and audiences alike were attracted to his irrepressible vitality and were less concerned with his role and functions within the dramatic universe of the play. Such commentators evaluated him as a real person subject to moral judgments and capable of educating or misleading the prince. Even if his failings were noted (as they were by such critics as Dryden and Dr. Johnson), they were sometimes forgiven because of his inventiveness and charm. "For the sake of his wit," wrote Corbin Morris in 1744, "you forgive his cowardice, or rather are fond of his cowardice for the occasions it gives to his wit." This "character" view of Falstaff is most associated with critic Maurice Morgann, whose *Essay on the Dramatic Character of Falstaff* appeared in 1777. Beginning with a defense of the character against the charge of cowardice, Morgann went on to write a wide-ranging

study of his multifaceted personality, "even to the principles of human nature itself." A. C. Bradley summed up the nineteenth-century view of Falstaff as a comic figure of immense enjoyment, a genius of wit devoted and loyal to the young prince; in Bradley's view Hal's rejection of this merry companion is a "catastrophe" for Falstaff.

Later twentieth-century historical critics, including John Dover Wilson, have viewed Falstaff within both the historical and dramatic contexts, noting his function as an intermediary father-figure who must be rejected if Hal is to learn the lessons that will allow him to function effectively as King Henry V. In this view, Falstaff had been sentimentalized earlier. That sentimental glorification of the old rogue has had a resurgence in Harold Bloom's popular recent study, *Shakespeare: The Invention of the Human* and in several productions that, as David Scott Kastan points out in his Arden third edition of the play, do not "subjugate the fat knight to the Prince's desires or designs. Falstaff's exuberance and excess refuse to be comfortably subordinated." Falstaff does prey upon both equals (Justice Shallow) and the lower classes (such as Mistress Quickly and the scores of ill-trained recruits he leads to their deaths in Part Two). But even these negative traits, which Hal eventually rejects, have been taken to give him a kind of perverse moral authority. The play has sometimes been called "The First Part of Sir John Falstaff," and, taken together with the two others in which he appears (*Henry IV, Part Two* and *The Merry Wives of Windsor*), the three have sometimes been grouped as The Falstaff Plays.

If Falstaff's character relates to the archetype of the bluff, amoral braggart from ancient comedy and the Lord of Misrule in medieval entertainments, he is, nonetheless, more self-aware than these types, and invested with a rueful self-consciousness. He exhibits a comprehensiveness of consciousness that puts him beyond us. He has made deliberate choices, preferring pleasure to standard morality, freedom to responsibility, skepticism to conventional notions of honor—and, above all, life to death. He sees that much public discourse is merely empty rhetoric meant to disguise private vice as public good. His "catechism" deriding military honor (5.1.129–140) seems realistic wisdom in its context, and even his cowardice has a rational strain. In the Gad's Hill robbery, he fights only until the poor odds of his winning against two stronger, younger men become clear, just as at the Battle of Shrewsbury he feigns death because he knows he cannot win against the Scottish warrior, Douglas.

Sources and Inspirations

The English Chronicles: Raphael Holinshed and Samuel Daniel

Shakespeare supplemented his chief historical source, Holinshed's 1587 *Chronicles*, with material from Samuel

Daniel's *The First Four Books of the Civil Wars* (1595). The theme of the civil war as punishment for Henry's usurpation of the throne and consent to Richard II's murder is more prominent in Daniel than in Holinshed. Shakespeare changes the age of Hotspur, who was much older than Prince Henry, in order to pair and contrast them. Hal's killing of Hotspur is a fiction; both sources report only that Hal helped rescue his father and that Hotspur was subsequently killed in the battle. From hints in Holinshed, Shakespeare creates Glendower's taste for sorcery and poetry, making him, like so many of the subsidiary characters in the play, a charismatic individual. Hotspur, too, is largely Shakespeare's creation, although Daniel also changed his age, and depicted him, as Shakespeare did, as brave, stubborn, and honorable. Similarly, characters in the rebel camp—including Hotspur's forthright wife, Kate, and Mortimer's lovesick, Welsh-singing bride—are created from the merest hints in Holinshed. Their meetings in the rebel camp of Act 3 are virtually all the work of Shakespeare's imagination.

Most of the historical details of Henry's troubled reign come from Holinshed, but, as mentioned above, many of Shakespeare's plot details were his own and had to do more with propelling the story than with conveying historical accuracy. Here as in the other plays, the record is artfully tightened to reinforce Shakespeare's central symphonic theme: the sources, the justifications for right and wrong use, and the responsibilities, of power. Many crises marked Henry's reign, and these appear in the Richard II and Henry IV plays, though they are tightly compressed, rather than spaced out. Thus, though the plays were not commonly viewed as a series until the twentieth century, their action is indeed continuous and accelerating, possessing a vigorous narrative drive, which translates on stage and film to dramatic momentum. These crises—the Percys' revolt in 1404, Archbishop's Scroop's rebellion in 1405, and Northumberland's in 1408—become part of one smoothly unfolding action.

Shakespeare's conception of Hal as a madcap prince turned wondrous warrior-king is a version of the New Testament's Prodigal Son story; this variant was first launched in Tito Livio's *Vita Henrici Quinti* (c. 1437) and soon translated and expanded. An early treatment of the material in the popular anonymous play, *The Famous Victories of Henry the Fifth* (1587 or 1588), is a charmingly chaotic medley of history and comedy, giving us a version of the underlying plot and many episodes that Shakespeare reconstructed for his new purposes. The wild prince consorts with a pack of low-life companions named Sir John Oldcastle, Tom, and Ned. They commit a robbery, frequent an Eastcheap tavern, and run afoul of the Lord Chief Justice before Hal is reconciled to his father, rejects his friends, and takes the French princess as his wife. The Admiral's Men, who were in competition with Shakespeare's company, also staged the two parts of *Sir John Oldcastle* by Michael Drayton; that play may have been written in response to Shakespeare's play.

Victory over the Armada and English Supremacy

Shakespeare may also have been more generally inspired to complete his series of historical dramas by England's 1588 victory over the Spanish Armada, a force larger and better equipped than the English navy. As suggested in this book's introduction to the history plays, that event was cause for a new burst of national pride in England. Given the freshness of that status, the periods of political instability during Elizabeth's long reign, and the uncertainty about her successor, Shakespeare would naturally have been drawn to explore the horrors of civil strife that led to the Tudor accession and the period of uncertain peace during which he lived. As the (London) *Times* critic Benedict Nightingale noted when assessing the Royal Shakespeare Company's eight-play millennial project *This England—The Histories*, directors and actors have restored "immediacy and urgency to pieces that embody the darkest fears of the aging Elizabeth's England. With no clear heir in sight, and ambitious nobles everywhere, it could all have occurred again: the competing claims, the hatreds and broken vows, the endless battles, the deep divisions" (*The Times*, April 27, 2001).

Themes and Issues

Fathers and Sons

Throughout the play, Shakespeare structures scenes in such a way as to compare the relationships of various fathers and their sons, or would-be sons. Falstaff is a father figure to Prince Hal, an unruly, warm-hearted mentor who teaches lessons in surviving the world that differ from those that Hal's cold, rigid, and guilt-driven father might pass along. Falstaff is a foil both to Henry IV and to Hotspur, whose model of "bright honor" and whose quick-tempered valor contrast so strongly with Falstaff's skeptical realism. In the tavern scene (2.4) when Falstaff and Hal take turns playing the king and crown prince, Falstaff argues that it is better to be guided by an old, fat, merry, and beloved wit than to be cold and denying like "Pharaoh's lean kine," and by implication, like Henry IV. Yet Hal resists the thrust of Falstaff's position, even as he mocks some of the arguments he knows his father will make against him. And when Falstaff questions the prince about whether he will hang thieves when he becomes king, and whether he will banish "plump Jack" or the other rogues, Hal answers " I do, I will"—an ominous phrase that can be played jocularly on stage but also as a threatening promise.

Early on, Henry IV wishes that Hotspur were his son; he admires the valiant Percy so much that he briefly wishes that some fairy has exchanged the two boys in their cradles. Hotspur's outspokenness is part of his manliness, while Hal's personal rebellion seems a dereliction of duty. Viewed this way, the Henry IV plays center upon Hal's coming-of-age, his growth into personal maturity coming simultaneously with his acknowledgment that he is truly the son of Henry IV, however different he may be in character and personality. As that son and heir, he accepts his responsibility, which will involve the unasked-for public role of king. (Yet another father figure emerges very late in this play and into Part Two when the new king calls the Lord Chief Justice "father.") Hotspur has multiple fathers as well. In his admiration for the young man, Henry IV is a putative father. Hotspur himself comes close to criticizing his real father, Northumberland, for falling into the illness that keeps him away from the glories of the battlefield, calling it an "inward sickness" that suggests faintheartedness. Hotspur's uncle, Worcester, cares less about such realities than about appearances. A shrewd and politic aristocrat, Worcester can manipulate his nephew/son. He exploits Hotspur's hair-trigger responses and does not tell him of the King's offer of pardon if the rebels share their grievances and put up their swords. Worcester thus becomes the one cynically dark character in Part One, the father figure whose actions lead his intemperate surrogate boy Hotspur to his death.

Honor—"A Word . . . "

Shakespeare is unusually interested in honor in this play—its meaning, its appearance, and its reality. Hotspur lives (and dies) by a passionate devotion to "bright honor" (1.3.202), a traditional conception of the virtue as a quality that could be plucked from the "pale-faced moon" or dredged up from "the bottom of the deep" (1.3.202–203). Henry IV sees Hotspur as the "theme of honor's tongue," while the Earl of Douglas views him as "the king of honor." The young soldier itches to be off to battle, dreaming always of great exploits that will enhance the glory of his name. Even the absences from the rebel army of his father Northumberland and of Glendower at the Battle of Shrewsbury become opportunities to gain greater fame than they.

At the opposite extreme from Hotspur's adherence to honor is Falstaff's perpetual questioning of it. Alone before the battle begins, Falstaff asks himself, "What is that word 'honor'?" He answers with a skeptical catalog that contrasts utterly with Hotspur's chivalric notions of "bright honor." (Falstaff's speech has since become famous as a realistic counterpoint to military propaganda, for it offers stark commentary on the rousing speeches that stir men in battle to march bravely to their deaths.) "Honor pricks me on," he begins, but

characteristically questions that cliché. "Yea, but how if honor prick me off when I come on? How then? Can honor set to a leg? No. Or an arm? No. Or take away the grief of a wound? No. Honor hath no skill in surgery, then? No. What is honor? A word. What is in that word 'honor'? What is that 'honor'? Air. A trim, reckoning! Who hath it? . . . Detraction will not suffer it. Therefore I'll none of it. Honor is a mere scutcheon. And so ends my catechism" (5.1.130–135, 138–139).

This skeptical countering of the presumed inherent honor of war continues to the end of the act as Falstaff appears three times, comically insisting that surviving with one's life intact is the ultimate wisdom. "There's honor for you" (5.4.32–33), he says, pointing to the corpse of Sir Walter Blunt and adding he likes not such "grinning honor." Then, while Hal and Hotspur engage in mortal combat, Falstaff, confronted by the powerful Scots leader, Douglas, feigns death to save his life. When he rises from the dead, to the amazement of Prince Hal, he asserts: "The better part of valor is discretion, in the which better part I have saved my life" (5.4.119–121).

When Falstaff falsely claims to have killed Hotspur and demands to be made a duke or an earl for his services, Hal allows him the lie, saying he will "gild it with the happiest terms I have." Falstaff, who now has the appearance of honor without the substance, says he will take on the corresponding appearance of a nobleman: "If I do grow great, I'll grow less; for I'll purge, and leave sack, and live cleanly as a nobleman should do" (5.4.161–163).

One interpretation of the theme of honor thus views Hotspur as extreme in his preoccupation with the pursuit of honor as a motivation for courageous acts and Falstaff as the opposite extreme in his pursuit of the appearance of honor when its reality has been replaced by the survival instinct. In this reading, Hal comes to represent the man of moderation between these two extremes. Hal demonstrates his honor only toward the end of the play, at the climactic Battle of Shrewsbury, when he promises to clip Hotspur's honors to make for himself a victory garland for his head. In the real event, Hal's defeat of Hotspur seems honor enough, and he is willing, at least for a time, to let Falstaff claim that honor and whatever titles might accrue to it. Hotspur, meanwhile, dies as he had lived, caring less about the loss "of brittle life" than that his "proud titles have been won" away from him by the rival he underestimated, the slowly reforming Prince Hal.

The Tempters and the Tempted

As C. L. Barber has pointed out in *Shakespeare's Festive Comedy*, his 1959 study of the relationship of social ritual to the plays, Hal and Falstaff can be fruitfully studied as embodying certain patterns of symbolic action: the prodigal son and the temporary king become scapegoat. The material Shakespeare inherited from the popular play *The Famous Victories of Henry V*, Barber argues, casts Hal as the prodigal son and his disreputable companions as tempters in the same fashion as the Vice of the morality plays. But Shakespeare shifts the emphasis from simple moral terms to something more psychologically interesting. When he becomes king, will Hal be noble or degenerate, responsible or forever on holiday? Hal tells the audience that he will change in due course, for "If all the year were playing holidays, / To sport would be as tedious as to work" (1.2.198–199). Through Falstaff, Shakespeare expresses attitudes grounded in a Saturnalian reversal of value, with Sir John a Lord of Misrule. But the structural parallels and contrasts between the Falstaff scenes and the actions at court and with the rebels suggest that the comedy provides an even more radical challenge to traditional order. By acting out disruptive motives in the robbery, drinking, and playacting episodes, Falstaff, Barber argues, takes "away what might have been Hal's bad luck, taking it away, not in a magical way, but by extending the sphere of conscious control. . . . [A] similar mastery of potential aberration is promoted by the experience of seeing through Falstaff's burlesque of the sort of headlong chivalry presented seriously in Hotspur." When Falstaff is helped to his "throne" atop a table in the Boar's Head Tavern, he becomes visually and physically the Lord of Misrule: his "state is taken for a joint stool, [his] golden scepter for a leaden dagger, and [his] precious rich crown for a pitiful bald crown" (2.4.376–378). No matter how much he aggrandizes himself and swells with self-love, Falstaff must submit to the world which he does not control, first by avoiding prosecution by the watch who come beating at the tavern doors and finally by submitting to rejection and banishment as the scapegoat who, in this reading, bears away iniquity and the holiday spirit of misrule.

Staging Challenges

Playing Falstaff

Two of the twentieth century's most admired Falstaffs, Ralph Richardson and Orson Welles, have emphasized divergent qualities in the character; their interpretations begin to suggest the range of interpretations and of choices available to contemporary actors cast in the role. Richardson, in a 1945 production directed by John Burrell, is remembered as a Falstaff whose wise, agile mind and exuberant spirit explored the rich and witty prose with great zest. Welles played Falstaff and directed himself in his film, *Falstaff* (also called *Chimes at Midnight*), in which he emphasized Falstaff's desire to be loved as a father. The film is saturated with wintry foreboding, the melancholy sense of the passing of an age. Specialist comic actors—in and out of padding—have naturally been drawn to the huge role.

Several comic actors in the twentieth century have given more genial if narrower interpretations than either Richardson or Welles. British critics have described such sweetly entertaining performances as belonging to the "sack-and-sugar" school. George Robey, the beloved music hall performer, was one of these. He appeared as Falstaff in the flashback scenes of Olivier's film of *Henry V*, after earning a reputation as a mirth-making delight in the part in 1935. As we shall see in the stage history section following the text of the play, muted interpretations of Falstaff came from others later in the twentieth century when the Henry plays were done in series: Anthony Quayle, who emphasized the character's melancholy streak beginning in 1951 and through the BBC television production (see p. 440) in 1979; Paul Rogers, who was funny, but not carefree, and therefore brought irony and pathos to the role in 1955; and Desmond Barrit who, in the 2001 "histories marathon" staged by Royal Shakespeare Company director Michael Attenborough, was not a universally appealing nor scene-stealing Falstaff, but instead seemed an ignoble man, callous, self-deluding, and opportunistic, despite his wry humor and genuine affection for Hal. In the United States recently, charismatic actors in productions directed by Jack O'Brien created multidimensional Falstaffs. Both John Goodman (swilling sack at San Diego's Old Globe Theater in 1995) and Kevin Kline (imposing, well-padded, and barely able to pull himself up without the help of his sword/cane at Lincoln Center in 2003) showed the exploitive streak that cuts the rogue's immense charm with a dash of the acidic.

Given the tremendous variation of approach to the role of Falstaff, how should he be played? The best Falstaffs possess the warmth and affection to attract Hal, and the wit to seem spontaneous in excuses and rationalizations for bad behavior, but they also reveal a vulnerability, stemming from less savory, even debauched elements in the character. Falstaff's perpetual drunkenness, his easy lies, his exploitation of Mistress Quickly and, in Part Two, his sponging off old Shallow can prepare the way for Hal's rejection. Irony, pathos, and even shame and self-disgust can balance the robust comedy in this multifaceted, shape-shifting role.

The Boar's Head Tavern

The tavern is a pivotal locale in the Henry IV plays, offering the same attractions as well as the dangers of the Elizabethan playhouse (Howard and Rackin, 175). The name of Mistress Quickly's tavern is not specified, but its traditional identification as the Boar's Head is suggested in Part Two (2.2.138–139). The place is both tavern and bawdy house, attracting a disreputable crowd given to fighting, drunkenness, and thievery. The scenes set there must create the illusion of an interior space; this can be achieved as much by intimate, dusky lighting as by scenery. Generally tables and benches, mugs and flagons are required to create the cramped sense of being inside. Assuming the director sets the play in period, a nearby stable can be suggested. The playacting scene in which Falstaff and Hal take turns role-playing as the disappointed King Henry IV requires certain props (a table, a stool, and a pillow) and careful emphasis. Directors usually highlight these moments with lighting, quiet down the peripheral action, and make certain that the witty dialogue, some of it humorously convoluted, is spoken clearly and forcefully. One key interpretive choice here involves the tone of Hal's promise—a joke or a threat?—to hang thieves and banish his old companions. The delivery of the lines and the blocking establish Hal's relationship to the audience and will determine how innocent or shrewd, open-hearted or manipulative Hal may appear to be early on.

The Battle Scenes

Space and the theater's budget as well as directorial vision determine how spectacular or simple these scenes can be. The battle scenes can be effectively (and inexpensively) suggested by offstage noise and smoke, with the spoken dialogue—especially for Falstaff's "catechism" and feigned death, and the hand-to-hand combat of Hal and Hotspur—conceived intimately, like strongly lit cinematic close-ups or the foreground action in a narrative painting. Ordinarily a fight director collaborates with the director in staging these scenes, especially the combat between Hal and Hotspur, which can be protracted and shaped to suggest their equality in skill and valor, or presented swiftly, with Hotspur (and perhaps the audience) badly underestimating his opponent. For the 2000–2001 series of two tetralogies, the RSC designer spread peat moss on the Barbican stage for battle scenes of the Henry IV plays. The effect—even to the aroma—of being outdoors lent a convincing naturalism to the Shrewsbury conflict. At Lincoln Center in 2003, designer Ralph Funicello's four-level, massively timbered set took advantage of the Vivian Beaumont Theater's unusually deep thrust stage. Soldiers moved in deep perspective on all levels, with director Jack O'Brien employing every actor possible in his thirty-three–member cast to lend the scenes their intensity and excitement. Pyrotechnics exploded, smoke filled portions of the stage, and the sounds of clashing broadswords, axes, and lethal pikes made for a thrillingly cinematic Battle of Shrewsbury, culminating quietly in the death of Hotspur and Hal's tender valediction to his corpse. The lighting designer often proves a key collaborator in such scenes, pulling audience focus toward the spoken dialogue even as the fighting continues in dimmer areas of the stage.

The First Part of King Henry the Fourth

[*Dramatis Personae*

KING HENRY THE FOURTH
PRINCE HENRY, *Prince of Wales,*
PRINCE JOHN OF LANCASTER, } *sons of the King*
EARL OF WESTMORLAND
SIR WALTER BLUNT

EARL OF NORTHUMBERLAND, *Henry Percy,*
HARRY PERCY (HOTSPUR), *his son,*
EARL OF WORCESTER, *Northumberland's
    younger brother,*
LORD MORTIMER, *Edmund Mortimer
    also referred to as the Earl of March,*
OWEN GLENDOWER,
EARL OF DOUGLAS, *Archibald Douglas,*
SIR RICHARD VERNON,
ARCHBISHOP OF YORK, *Richard Scroop,*
SIR MICHAEL, *a member of the
    Archbishop's household,*
} *rebels
against
the King*

LADY PERCY, *Hotspur's wife and Mortimer's sister*
LADY MORTIMER, *Mortimer's wife and Glendower's
    daughter*

SCENE: *England and Wales*]

SIR JOHN FALSTAFF
NED POINS
BARDOLPH
PETO
GADSHILL, *arranger of the highway robbery*
HOSTESS OF THE TAVERN, *Mistress Quickly*
FRANCIS, *a drawer, or tapster*
VINTNER, *or tavern keeper*

FIRST CARRIER
SECOND CARRIER
HOSTLER
CHAMBERLAIN
FIRST TRAVELER
SHERIFF
SERVANT *to Hotspur*
MESSENGER
SECOND MESSENGER

Soldiers, Travelers, Lords, Attendants

[1.1]

Enter the King, Lord John of Lancaster, [the] Earl of Westmorland, [Sir Walter Blunt,] with others.

KING
So shaken as we are, so wan with care,
Find we a time for frighted peace to pant,   2
And breathe short-winded accents of new broils   3
To be commenced in strands afar remote.   4
No more the thirsty entrance of this soil   5
Shall daub her lips with her own children's blood;   6
No more shall trenching war channel her fields   7
Nor bruise her flowerets with the armèd hoofs
Of hostile paces. Those opposèd eyes,   9
Which, like the meteors of a troubled heaven,
All of one nature, of one substance bred,
Did lately meet in the intestine shock   12
And furious close of civil butchery,   13
Shall now in mutual well-beseeming ranks
March all one way and be no more opposed
Against acquaintance, kindred, and allies.
The edge of war, like an ill-sheathèd knife,
No more shall cut his master. Therefore, friends,   18
As far as to the sepulcher of Christ—
Whose soldier now, under whose blessèd cross
We are impressèd and engaged to fight—   21
Forthwith a power of English shall we levy,   22
Whose arms were molded in their mothers' womb   23
To chase these pagans in those holy fields
Over whose acres walked those blessèd feet
Which fourteen hundred years ago were nailed
For our advantage on the bitter cross.
But this our purpose now is twelve month old,
And bootless 'tis to tell you we will go.   29
Therefore we meet not now. Then let me hear   30
Of you, my gentle cousin Westmorland,   31
What yesternight our council did decree
In forwarding this dear expedience.   33

WESTMORLAND
My liege, this haste was hot in question,   34
And many limits of the charge set down   35
But yesternight, when all athwart there came   36
A post from Wales loaden with heavy news,   37
Whose worst was that the noble Mortimer,
Leading the men of Herefordshire to fight
Against the irregular and wild Glendower,

Was by the rude hands of that Welshman taken,
A thousand of his people butcherèd—
Upon whose dead corpse there was such misuse,   43
Such beastly shameless transformation,   44
By those Welshwomen done as may not be
Without much shame retold or spoken of.

KING
It seems then that the tidings of this broil
Brake off our business for the Holy Land.

WESTMORLAND
This matched with other did, my gracious lord;   49
For more uneven and unwelcome news   50
Came from the north, and thus it did import:
On Holy Rood Day, the gallant Hotspur there,   52
Young Harry Percy, and brave Archibald,
That ever-valiant and approvèd Scot,   54
At Holmedon met, where they did spend   55
A sad and bloody hour,
As by discharge of their artillery   57
And shape of likelihood the news was told;   58
For he that brought them, in the very heat   59
And pride of their contention did take horse,   60
Uncertain of the issue any way.

KING
Here is a dear, a true industrious friend,   62
Sir Walter Blunt, new lighted from his horse,   63
Stained with the variation of each soil
Betwixt that Holmedon and this seat of ours;
And he hath brought us smooth and welcome news.   66
The Earl of Douglas is discomfited;   67
Ten thousand bold Scots, two-and-twenty knights,
Balked in their own blood, did Sir Walter see   69
On Holmedon's plains. Of prisoners, Hotspur took
Mordake, Earl of Fife and eldest son   71
To beaten Douglas, and the Earl of Atholl,
Of Murray, Angus, and Menteith.
And is not this an honorable spoil?
A gallant prize? Ha, cousin, is it not?

WESTMORLAND
In faith, it is a conquest for a prince to boast of.

KING
Yea, there thou mak'st me sad, and mak'st me sin
In envy that my lord Northumberland
Should be the father to so blest a son—
A son who is the theme of honor's tongue,
Amongst a grove the very straightest plant,   81
Who is sweet Fortune's minion and her pride,   82
Whilst I, by looking on the praise of him,
See riot and dishonor stain the brow   84
Of my young Harry. Oh, that it could be proved

1.1. Location: The royal court.
2 Find we let us find. **frighted** frightened **3 breathe short-winded accents** speak, even though we are out of breath. **accents** words. **broils** battles **4 strands afar remote** far-off shores, i.e., of the Holy Land (to which, at the end of *Richard II*, Henry has pledged himself to a crusade). **5 thirsty entrance** i.e., parched mouth **6 daub** coat, smear **7 trenching** cutting, plowing **9 paces** horses' tread. **12 intestine** internal **13 close** hand-to-hand encounter. **civil** (as in "civil war") **18 his** its **21 impressèd** conscripted **22 power** army **23 their mother's** i.e., England's, but also suggesting *their mothers'* **29 bootless** useless **30 Therefore . . . now** That is not the reason for our present meeting. **31 Of** from. **gentle cousin** noble kinsman **33 dear expedience** urgent expedition. **34 hot in question** being hotly debated **35 limits . . . charge** particulars of military responsibility **36 athwart** at cross purposes, contrarily **37 post** messenger. **loaden** laden

43 corpse corpses **44 transformation** mutilation **49 other** other news **50 uneven** disconcerting, distressing **52 Holy Rood Day** September 14 **54 approvèd** proved by experience **55 Holmedon** Humbleton in Northumberland **57 by** judging from **58 shape of likelihood** likely outcome **59 them** the news **60 pride** height **62–3 Here . . . Blunt** (Whether Blunt enters at the start of the scene, or now, or possibly not at all, is not certain in the original text.) **66 smooth** pleasant **67 discomfited** defeated **69 Balked** heaped up in balks, or ridges **71 Mordake** i.e., Murdoch, son of the Earl of Albany **81 plant** young tree **82 minion** favorite **84 riot** debauchery

That some night-tripping fairy had exchanged   86
In cradle clothes our children where they lay,
And called mine Percy, his Plantagenet!   88
Then would I have his Harry, and he mine.
But let him from my thoughts. What think you, coz,   90
Of this young Percy's pride? The prisoners
Which he in this adventure hath surprised   92
To his own use he keeps, and sends me word   93
I shall have none but Mordake, Earl of Fife.   94

WESTMORLAND
This is his uncle's teaching. This is Worcester,
Malevolent to you in all aspects,   96
Which makes him prune himself and bristle up   97
The crest of youth against your dignity.

KING
But I have sent for him to answer this;
And for this cause awhile we must neglect
Our holy purpose to Jerusalem.
Cousin, on Wednesday next our council we
Will hold at Windsor. So inform the lords.
But come yourself with speed to us again,
For more is to be said and to be done
Than out of anger can be utterèd.

WESTMORLAND   I will, my liege.   *Exeunt.*

[1.2]

Enter Prince of Wales and Sir John Falstaff.

FALSTAFF
Now, Hal, what time of day is it, lad?
PRINCE   Thou art so fat-witted with drinking of old sack,   2
and unbuttoning thee after supper, and sleeping upon
benches after noon, that thou hast forgotten to de-   4
mand that truly which thou wouldst truly know. What
a devil hast thou to do with the time of the day? Unless   6
hours were cups of sack, and minutes capons, and
clocks the tongues of bawds, and dials the signs of   8
leaping houses, and the blessed sun himself a fair hot   9
wench in flame-colored taffeta, I see no reason why   10
thou shouldst be so superfluous to demand the time   11
of the day.
FALSTAFF   Indeed, you come near me now, Hal, for we   13
that take purses go by the moon and the seven stars,   14

and not by Phoebus, "he, that wandering knight so   15
fair." And I prithee, sweet wag, when thou art king,   16
as, God save Thy Grace—Majesty I should say, for   17
grace thou wilt have none—
PRINCE   What, none?
FALSTAFF   No, by my troth, not so much as will serve to   20
be prologue to an egg and butter.   21
PRINCE   Well, how then? Come, roundly, roundly.   22
FALSTAFF   Marry, then, sweet wag, when thou art   23
king, let not us that are squires of the night's body be   24
called thieves of the day's beauty. Let us be Diana's for-   25
esters, gentlemen of the shade, minions of the moon;   26
and let men say we be men of good government,   27
being governed, as the sea is, by our noble and chaste
mistress the moon, under whose countenance we steal.   29
PRINCE   Thou sayest well, and it holds well too, for the   30
fortune of us that are the moon's men doth ebb and
flow like the sea, being governed, as the sea is, by the
moon. As, for proof, now: a purse of gold most
resolutely snatched on Monday night and most disso-
lutely spent on Tuesday morning, got with swearing
"Lay by" and spent with crying "Bring in," now in as   36
low an ebb as the foot of the ladder and by and by in   37
as high a flow as the ridge of the gallows.   38
FALSTAFF   By the Lord, thou say'st true, lad. And is not
my hostess of the tavern a most sweet wench?
PRINCE   As the honey of Hybla, my old lad of the castle.   41
And is not a buff jerkin a most sweet robe of durance?   42
FALSTAFF   How now, how now, mad wag, what, in thy
quips and thy quiddities? What a plague have I to do   44
with a buff jerkin?
PRINCE   Why, what a pox have I to do with my hostess   46
of the tavern?
FALSTAFF   Well, thou hast called her to a reckoning many   48
a time and oft.
PRINCE   Did I ever call for thee to pay thy part?
FALSTAFF   No, I'll give thee thy due, thou hast paid all
there.
PRINCE   Yea, and elsewhere, so far as my coin would
stretch, and where it would not I have used my credit.

---

86 night-tripping i.e., moving nimbly in the night   **88 Plantagenet**
(Family name of English royalty since Henry II.)   **90 let him** let him
go.   **coz** cousin, i.e., kinsman   **92 surprised** ambushed, captured
93 To . . . use i.e., to collect ransom for them   **94 none but Mordake**
(Since Mordake was of royal blood, being grandson to Robert II of
Scotland, Hotspur could not claim him as his prisoner according to
the law of arms.)   **96 Malevolent . . . aspects** (1) implacably hostile to
you (2) in astrological terms, a planet in a disobedient orbit, ominous
as seen from every angle   **97 Which . . . himself** i.e., which teaching
makes Hotspur preen himself (as a falcon preens its feathers)
1.2. Location: London, perhaps in an apartment of the Prince's.
2 sack a Spanish white wine   **4 forgotten** forgotten how   **6 a devil**
in the devil   **8 dials** clocks   **9 leaping houses** houses of prostitution   **10 taffeta** (Commonly worn by prostitutes.)   **11 superfluous**
(1) unnecessarily concerned (2) self-indulgent   **13 you . . . now** i.e.,
you've scored a point on me   **14 go by** (1) travel by the light of
(2) tell time by.   **the seven stars** the Pleiades

15–16 Phoebus . . . fair (Phoebus, god of the sun, is here equated with
the wandering knight of a ballad or popular romance.)   **17 Grace**
royal highness. (With pun on spiritual *grace* and also on the *grace* or
blessing before a meal.)   **20 troth** faith   **21 prologue . . . butter** i.e.,
grace before a brief meal.   **22 roundly** i.e., out with it.   **23 Marry**
Indeed. (Literally, "by the Virgin Mary.")   **wag** joker   **24–5 let . . .
beauty** i.e., let not us who are attendants on the goddess of night,
members of her household, be blamed for stealing daylight by sleeping in the daytime.   **25–6 Diana's foresters** (An elegant name for
thieves by night; Diana is goddess of the moon and the hunt.)
26 minions favorites   **27 government** (1) conduct (2) commonwealth
29 countenance (1) face (2) patronage, approval.   **steal** (1) move
stealthily (2) rob.   **30 it holds well** the comparison is apt   **36 Lay by**
(A cry of highwaymen, like "Hands up!")   **Bring in** (An order given
to a waiter in a tavern.)   **37 ladder** (1) pier ladder (2) gallows ladder
38 ridge crossbar   **41 Hybla** (A town, famed for its honey, in Sicily
near Syracuse.)   **old . . . castle** (1) a roisterer (2) the name, Sir John
Oldcastle, borne by Falstaff in an earlier version of this play.   **42 buff
jerkin** a leather jacket worn by officers of the law.   **durance** (1) imprisonment (2) durability, durable cloth.   **44 quiddities** subtleties of
speech.   **46 pox** syphilis. (Here, *what a pox* is used as an expletive, like
"what the devil.")   **48 reckoning** settlement of the bill. (With bawdy
suggestion that is continued in *pay thy part* and *my coin would stretch*.)

FALSTAFF   Yea, and so used it that, were it not here apparent that thou art heir apparent—But I prithee, sweet wag, shall there be gallows standing in England when thou art king? And resolution thus fubbed as it 58 is with the rusty curb of old father Antic the law? Do 59 not thou, when thou art king, hang a thief.

PRINCE   No, thou shalt.

FALSTAFF   Shall I? Oh, rare! By the Lord, I'll be a brave 62 judge.

PRINCE   Thou judgest false already. I mean, thou shalt have the hanging of the thieves, and so become a rare 65 hangman.

FALSTAFF   Well, Hal, well; and in some sort it jumps 67 with my humor as well as waiting in the court, I can 68 tell you.

PRINCE   For obtaining of suits? 70

FALSTAFF   Yea, for obtaining of suits, whereof the hangman hath no lean wardrobe. 'Sblood, I am as 72 melancholy as a gib cat or a lugged bear. 73

PRINCE   Or an old lion, or a lover's lute.

FALSTAFF   Yea, or the drone of a Lincolnshire bagpipe.

PRINCE   What sayest thou to a hare, or the melancholy 76 of Moorditch? 77

FALSTAFF   Thou hast the most unsavory similes, and art indeed the most comparative, rascalliest, sweet young 79 prince. But Hal, I prithee, trouble me no more with vanity. I would to God thou and I knew where a com- 81 modity of good names were to be bought. An old lord 82 of the council rated me the other day in the street 83 about you, sir, but I marked him not; and yet he talked very wisely, but I regarded him not; and yet he talked wisely, and in the street too.

PRINCE   Thou didst well, for wisdom cries out in the 87 streets and no man regards it. 88

FALSTAFF   Oh, thou hast damnable iteration, and art 89 indeed able to corrupt a saint. Thou hast done much harm upon me, Hal, God forgive thee for it. Before I knew thee, Hal, I knew nothing; and now am I, if a 92 man should speak truly, little better than one of the wicked. I must give over this life, and I will give it over. By the Lord, an I do not I am a villain. I'll be 95 damned for never a king's son in Christendom.

PRINCE   Where shall we take a purse tomorrow, Jack?

FALSTAFF   Zounds, where thou wilt, lad, I'll make one. 98 An I do not, call me villain and baffle me. 99

PRINCE   I see a good amendment of life in thee—from praying to purse taking.

FALSTAFF   Why, Hal, 'tis my vocation, Hal. 'Tis no sin for a man to labor in his vocation. 102

Enter Poins.

Poins! Now shall we know if Gadshill have set a 104 match. Oh, if men were to be saved by merit, what 105 hole in hell were hot enough for him? This is the most omnipotent villain that ever cried "Stand!" to a 107 true man. 108

PRINCE   Good morrow, Ned.

POINS   Good morrow, sweet Hal.—What says Monsieur Remorse? What says Sir John, Sack-and-Sugar Jack? How agrees the devil and thee about thy soul that thou soldest him on Good Friday last for a cup of Madeira and a cold capon's leg?

PRINCE   Sir John stands to his word; the devil shall have 115 his bargain, for he was never yet a breaker of proverbs. He will give the devil his due.

POINS   Then art thou damned for keeping thy word with the devil.

PRINCE   Else he had been damned for cozening the 120 devil.

POINS   But my lads, my lads, tomorrow morning, by four o'clock early, at Gad's Hill, there are pilgrims 123 going to Canterbury with rich offerings and traders riding to London with fat purses. I have vizards for 125 you all; you have horses for yourselves. Gadshill lies 126 tonight in Rochester. I have bespoke supper tomorrow 127 night in Eastcheap. We may do it as secure as sleep. If 128 you will go, I will stuff your purses full of crowns; if 129 you will not, tarry at home and be hanged.

FALSTAFF   Hear ye, Yedward, if I tarry at home and go 131 not, I'll hang you for going. 132

POINS   You will, chops? 133

FALSTAFF   Hal, wilt thou make one?

PRINCE   Who, I rob? I a thief? Not I, by my faith.

FALSTAFF   There's neither honesty, manhood, nor good fellowship in thee, nor thou cam'st not of the blood royal, if thou darest not stand for ten shillings. 138

---

58 **resolution** courage (of a highwayman).   **fubbed** cheated
59 **Antic** buffoon   62 **rare** splendid.   **brave** excellent   65 **have . . . thieves** (1) be in charge of hanging thieves (or protecting them from hanging) (2) hang like other thieves.   **rare** (1) rarely used (2) excellent   67–8 **jumps . . . humor** suits my temperament   68 **waiting in the court** being in attendance at the royal court   70 **suits** petitions. (But Falstaff uses the word to mean suits of clothes; clothes belonging to an executed man were given to the executioner.)   72 **'Sblood** By his (Christ's) blood   73 **gib cat** tomcat.   **lugged bear** bear led by a chain and baited by dogs.   76 **hare** (A proverbially melancholy animal.)   77 **Moorditch** (A foul ditch draining Moorfields, outside London walls.)   79 **comparative** given to abusive comparisons   81 **vanity** worldliness.   81–2 **commodity** supply   82 **names** reputations   83 **rated** chastised   87–8 **wisdom . . . regards it** (Hal paraphrases Proverbs 1:20–4, "Wisdom crieth without, and putteth forth her voice in the streets . . . and no man regarded," in jocose reply to Falstaff's mock sanctimoniousness.)   89 **iteration** repetition (of biblical texts, with a neat twist)   92 **nothing** i.e., no evil   95 **an** if

98 **Zounds** By his (Christ's) wounds.   **make one** be one of the party.   99 **baffle** publicly disgrace   102 **vocation** (A favorite term of the reforming Protestant ministers to describe the function or station to which one is called by God. Falstaff comically misapplies it to justify highway robbery.)   104 **Gadshill** (The name of one of the highwaymen.)   104–5 **set a match** arranged a robbery.   105 **by merit** i.e., according to their deservings rather than by God's grace   107 **omnipotent** unparalleled, utter.   "**Stand!**" "Stand and deliver!" i.e., Hand over your money.   108 **true man** honest citizen.   115 **stands to** keeps   120 **Else** Otherwise.   **cozening** cheating   123 **Gad's Hill** (Location near Rochester on the road from London to Canterbury; one of the highwaymen is called Gadshill.)   125 **vizards** masks   126 **lies** lodges   127 **bespoke** ordered   128 **Eastcheap** market district in London, with many taverns.   129 **crowns** gold coins   131 **Yedward** (Nickname for *Edward*, Poins's first name.)   131–2 **if I . . . going** i.e., there's no chance of my not going; sooner than that, I'd see you hanged instead for going in my place.   133 **chops** i.e., fat jaws or cheeks.   138 **stand . . . shillings** (1) stand up and fight for booty (2) be worth ten shillings, the value of the *royal*, the gold coin alluded to in *blood royal* (line 138).

PRINCE   Well then, once in my days I'll be a madcap.

FALSTAFF   Why, that's well said.

PRINCE   Well, come what will, I'll tarry at home.

FALSTAFF   By the Lord, I'll be a traitor then, when thou art king.

PRINCE   I care not.

POINS   Sir John, I prithee leave the Prince and me alone. I will lay him down such reasons for this adventure that he shall go.

FALSTAFF   Well, God give thee the spirit of persuasion and him the ears of profiting, that what thou speakest may move and what he hears may be believed, that the true prince may, for recreation sake, prove a false thief; for the poor abuses of the time want counte- 152
nance. Farewell. You shall find me in Eastcheap.   153

PRINCE   Farewell, thou latter spring! Farewell, All- 154
hallown summer!   [*Exit Falstaff.*] 155

POINS   Now, my good sweet honey lord, ride with us tomorrow. I have a jest to execute that I cannot manage alone. Falstaff, Peto, Bardolph, and Gadshill shall rob those men that we have already waylaid— 159
yourself and I will not be there—and when they have the booty, if you and I do not rob them, cut this head off from my shoulders.

PRINCE   How shall we part with them in setting forth?

POINS   Why, we will set forth before or after them and appoint them a place of meeting, wherein it is at our pleasure to fail; and then will they adventure upon the 166
exploit themselves, which they shall have no sooner achieved but we'll set upon them.

PRINCE   Yea, but 'tis like that they will know us by our 169
horses, by our habits, and by every other appoint- 170
ment, to be ourselves.   171

POINS   Tut, our horses they shall not see—I'll tie them in the wood; our vizards we will change after we leave them; and, sirrah, I have cases of buckram for the 174
nonce, to immask our noted outward garments.   175

PRINCE   Yea, but I doubt they will be too hard for us.   176

POINS   Well, for two of them, I know them to be as true-bred cowards as ever turned back; and for the 178
third, if he fight longer than he sees reason, I'll for-swear arms. The virtue of this jest will be the incompre- 180
hensible lies that this same fat rogue will tell us when 181
we meet at supper—how thirty at least he fought with, what wards, what blows, what extremities he 183
endured; and in the reproof of this lives the jest.   184

PRINCE   Well, I'll go with thee. Provide us all things nec-essary and meet me tomorrow night in Eastcheap. There I'll sup. Farewell.

POINS   Farewell, my lord.   *Exit Poins.*

PRINCE

I know you all, and will awhile uphold
The unyoked humor of your idleness.   190
Yet herein will I imitate the sun,
Who doth permit the base contagious clouds   192
To smother up his beauty from the world,
That when he please again to be himself,   194
Being wanted he may be more wondered at   195
By breaking through the foul and ugly mists
Of vapors that did seem to strangle him.
If all the year were playing holidays,
To sport would be as tedious as to work;
But when they seldom come, they wished-for come,
And nothing pleaseth but rare accidents.   201
So when this loose behavior I throw off
And pay the debt I never promisèd,
By how much better than my word I am,
By so much shall I falsify men's hopes;   205
And like bright metal on a sullen ground,   206
My reformation, glitt'ring o'er my fault,
Shall show more goodly and attract more eyes
Than that which hath no foil to set it off.   209
I'll so offend to make offense a skill,   210
Redeeming time when men think least I will.   *Exit.* 211

[1.3]

Enter the King, Northumberland, Worcester, Hotspur, Sir Walter Blunt, with others.

KING

My blood hath been too cold and temperate,
Unapt to stir at these indignities,
And you have found me, for accordingly   3
You tread upon my patience. But be sure
I will from henceforth rather be myself,   5
Mighty and to be feared, than my condition,   6
Which hath been smooth as oil, soft as young down,
And therefore lost that title of respect
Which the proud soul ne'er pays but to the proud.

WORCESTER

Our house, my sovereign liege, little deserves   10
The scourge of greatness to be used on it—
And that same greatness too which our own hands
Have holp to make so portly.   13

NORTHUMBERLAND [*to the King*]   My lord—

KING

Worcester, get thee gone, for I do see

152–3 **want countenance** lack sponsorship (from men of rank).
154–5 **All-hallown summer** a season of clement weather around All Saints' Day, November 1; the *latter spring* or "Indian summer" of Fal-staff's old age.   159 **waylaid** set an ambush for   166 **pleasure** choice, discretion   169 **like** likely   170 **habits** garments   170–1 **appoint-ment** accoutrement   174 **sirrah** (Usually addressed to an inferior; here, a sign of intimacy.)   174–5 **cases . . . nonce** suits of buckram, a stiff-finished heavily sized fabric, for the purpose   175 **immask** hide, disguise.   **noted** known   176 **doubt** fear.   **too hard** too formidable   178 **turned back** turned their backs and ran away   180–1 **incompre-hensible** boundless   183 **wards** parries   184 **reproof** disproof

190 **unyoked . . . idleness** unbridled inclination of your frivolity.
192 **contagious** noxious   194 **That** so that   195 **wanted** missed, lacked   201 **accidents** events.   205 **hopes** expectations   206 **sullen ground** dark background, like a *foil*. (See line 209.)   209 **foil** metal sheet laid contrastingly behind a jewel to set off its luster   210 **to** as to.   **skill** i.e., clever tactic, piece of good policy   211 **Redeeming time** i.e., making amends for lost time
1.3. Location: London. The court (historically at Windsor).
3 **found me** found me so   5 **myself** i.e., my royal self   6 **my condi-tion** my natural (mild) disposition   10 **Our house** i.e., The Percy family   13 **holp** helped.   **portly** majestic, prosperous.

Danger and disobedience in thine eye.
Oh, sir, your presence is too bold and peremptory,
And majesty might never yet endure
The moody frontier of a servant brow.   19
You have good leave to leave us. When we need   20
Your use and counsel, we shall send for you.

> *Exit Worcester.*

[*To Northumberland*] You were about to speak.

NORTHUMBERLAND   Yea, my good lord.
Those prisoners in Your Highness' name demanded,
Which Harry Percy here at Holmedon took,
Were, as he says, not with such strength denied
As is delivered to Your Majesty.   26
Either envy, therefore, or misprision   27
Is guilty of this fault, and not my son.

HOTSPUR [*to the King*]
My liege, I did deny no prisoners.
But I remember when the fight was done,
When I was dry with rage and extreme toil,
Breathless and faint, leaning upon my sword,
Came there a certain lord, neat and trimly dressed,
Fresh as a bridegroom, and his chin new reaped   34
Showed like a stubble land at harvest home.   35
He was perfumèd like a milliner,   36
And twixt his finger and his thumb he held
A pouncet box, which ever and anon   38
He gave his nose and took 't away again,
Who therewith angry, who it next came there,   40
Took it in snuff; and still he smiled and talked,   41
And as the soldiers bore dead bodies by
He called them untaught knaves, unmannerly,
To bring a slovenly unhandsome corpse
Betwixt the wind and his nobility.
With many holiday and lady terms   46
He questioned me, amongst the rest demanded
My prisoners in Your Majesty's behalf.
I then, all smarting with my wounds being cold,
To be so pestered with a popinjay,   50
Out of my grief and my impatience   51
Answered neglectingly I know not what,
He should, or he should not; for he made me mad
To see him shine so brisk, and smell so sweet,
And talk so like a waiting-gentlewoman
Of guns and drums and wounds—God save the
   mark!—   56
And telling me the sovereignest thing on earth   57
Was parmacety for an inward bruise,   58

And that it was great pity, so it was,
This villainous saltpeter should be digged   60
Out of the bowels of the harmless earth,
Which many a good tall fellow had destroyed   62
So cowardly, and but for these vile guns
He would himself have been a soldier.
This bald unjointed chat of his, my lord,   65
I answered indirectly, as I said,   66
And I beseech you, let not his report
Come current for an accusation   68
Betwixt my love and your high majesty.

BLUNT [*to the King*]
The circumstance considered, good my lord,
Whate'er Lord Harry Percy then had said
To such a person and in such a place,
At such a time, with all the rest retold,
May reasonably die, and never rise
To do him wrong or any way impeach   75
What then he said, so he unsay it now.   76

KING
Why, yet he doth deny his prisoners,   77
But with proviso and exception   78
That we at our own charge shall ransom straight   79
His brother-in-law, the foolish Mortimer,   80
Who, on my soul, hath willfully betrayed
The lives of those that he did lead to fight
Against that great magician, damned Glendower,
Whose daughter, as we hear, that Earl of March   84
Hath lately married. Shall our coffers then
Be emptied to redeem a traitor home?
Shall we buy treason and indent with fears   87
When they have lost and forfeited themselves?
No, on the barren mountains let him starve!
For I shall never hold that man my friend
Whose tongue shall ask me for one penny cost
To ransom home revolted Mortimer.   92

HOTSPUR   Revolted Mortimer?
He never did fall off, my sovereign liege,   94
But by the chance of war. To prove that true
Needs no more but one tongue for all those wounds,
Those mouthèd wounds, which valiantly he took,   97
When on the gentle Severn's sedgy bank,   98
In single opposition, hand to hand,

---

60 saltpeter potassium nitrate, used to make gunpowder and also used medicinally   **62 tall** brave   **65 bald** trivial   **66 indirectly** inattentively, offhandedly   **68 Come current** (1) be taken at face value (2) come rushing in   **75 impeach** discredit   **76 so** provided that   **77 yet** (emphatic) i.e., even now.   **deny** refuse to surrender   **78 proviso and exception** (synonymous terms)   **79 straight** straightway, at once   **80 Mortimer** (There were two Edmund Mortimers; Shakespeare confuses them and combines their stories. It was the uncle [1376–1409?] who was captured by Glendower and married Glendower's daughter; it was the nephew [1391–1425], fifth Earl of March, who was proclaimed heir presumptive to King Richard II after the death of his father, the fourth earl, whom Richard had named as his heir. The uncle was brother to the fourth earl and to Hotspur's wife, Elizabeth, called Kate in this play.)   **84 Earl of March** (The "Mortimer" of line 80; see note there.)   **87 indent with fears** i.e., make a bargain or come to terms with traitors whom we have reason to fear   **92 revolted** rebellious   **94 fall off** change his allegiance   **97 mouthèd** gaping and eloquent   **98 Severn's** (The Severn River flows from northern Wales and western England into the Bristol Channel.)   **sedgy** bordered with reeds

19 moody frontier i.e., angry brow, frown. (*Frontier* literally means "outwork" or "fortification.")   **20 good leave** full permission   **26 delivered** reported   **27 envy** malice.   **misprision** misunderstanding   **34 chin new reaped** i.e., with beard freshly barbered according to the latest fashion, not like a soldier's beard   **35 Showed** looked.   **harvest home** end of harvest, fields being cut back to stubble.   **36 milliner** dealer in fancy articles, such as gloves and hats   **38 pouncet box** perfume box with perforated lid   **40 Who** i.e., his nose   **41 Took it in snuff** (1) inhaled it (2) took offense.   **still** continually   **46 holiday and lady** dainty and effeminate   **50 popinjay** parrot   **51 grief** pain   **56 God . . . mark** (Probably originally a formula to avert evil omen; here, an expression of impatience.)   **57 sovereignest** most efficacious   **58 parmacety** spermaceti, a fatty substance taken from the head of the sperm whale, used as a medicinal ointment

He did confound the best part of an hour   100
In changing hardiment with great Glendower.   101
Three times they breathed, and three times did they
    drink,   102
Upon agreement, of swift Severn's flood,   103
Who then, affrighted with their bloody looks,   104
Ran fearfully among the trembling reeds
And hid his crisp head in the hollow bank,   106
Bloodstainèd with these valiant combatants.
Never did bare and rotten policy   108
Color her working with such deadly wounds,   109
Nor never could the noble Mortimer
Receive so many, and all willingly.
Then let not him be slandered with revolt.   112

KING
Thou dost belie him, Percy, thou dost belie him.
He never did encounter with Glendower.
I tell thee,
He durst as well have met the devil alone
As Owen Glendower for an enemy.
Art thou not ashamed? But, sirrah, henceforth
Let me not hear you speak of Mortimer.
Send me your prisoners with the speediest means,
Or you shall hear in such a kind from me   121
As will displease you.—My lord Northumberland,
We license your departure with your son.
Send us your prisoners, or you will hear of it.

            Exit King [with Blunt, and train].

HOTSPUR
An if the devil come and roar for them   125
I will not send them. I will after straight   126
And tell him so, for I will ease my heart,
Albeit I make a hazard of my head.   128

NORTHUMBERLAND
What, drunk with choler? Stay and pause awhile.   129
Here comes your uncle.

            Enter Worcester.

HOTSPUR   Speak of Mortimer?
Zounds, I will speak of him, and let my soul
Want mercy if I do not join with him!   132
Yea, on his part I'll empty all these veins,   133
And shed my dear blood drop by drop in the dust,
But I will lift the downtrod Mortimer
As high in the air as this unthankful king,
As this ingrate and cankered Bolingbroke.   137

NORTHUMBERLAND
Brother, the King hath made your nephew mad.

WORCESTER
Who struck this heat up after I was gone?

HOTSPUR
He will forsooth have all my prisoners;
And when I urged the ransom once again
Of my wife's brother, then his cheek looked pale,
And on my face he turned an eye of death,   143
Trembling even at the name of Mortimer.

WORCESTER
I cannot blame him. Was not he proclaimed   145
By Richard, that dead is, the next of blood?   146

NORTHUMBERLAND
He was; I heard the proclamation.
And then it was when the unhappy king—   148
Whose wrongs in us God pardon!—did set forth   149
Upon his Irish expedition;   150
From whence he, intercepted, did return   151
To be deposed and shortly murderèd.

WORCESTER
And for whose death we in the world's wide mouth
Live scandalized and foully spoken of.

HOTSPUR
But, soft, I pray you, did King Richard then   155
Proclaim my brother Edmund Mortimer   156
Heir to the crown?

NORTHUMBERLAND   He did; myself did hear it.

HOTSPUR
Nay, then I cannot blame his cousin king,   158
That wished him on the barren mountains starve.
But shall it be that you that set the crown
Upon the head of this forgetful man,
And for his sake wear the detested blot
Of murderous subornation—shall it be   163
That you a world of curses undergo,
Being the agents, or base second means,   165
The cords, the ladder, or the hangman rather?
Oh, pardon me that I descend so low
To show the line and the predicament   168
Wherein you range under this subtle king!   169
Shall it for shame be spoken in these days,
Or fill up chronicles in time to come,
That men of your nobility and power
Did gage them both in an unjust behalf,   173
As both of you—God pardon it!—have done,
To put down Richard, that sweet lovely rose,
And plant this thorn, this canker, Bolingbroke?   176
And shall it in more shame be further spoken
That you are fooled, discarded, and shook off
By him for whom these shames ye underwent?
No! Yet time serves wherein you may redeem   180
Your banished honors and restore yourselves

---

100 **confound** consume   101 **changing hardiment** exchanging blows, matching valor   102 **breathed** paused for breath   103 **flood** river   104 **Who** i.e., the river   106 **crisp** curly, i.e., rippled   108 **bare** paltry. **policy** cunning   109 **Color** disguise   112 **revolt** i.e., the accusation of rebellion.   121 **kind** manner   125 **An if** If   126 **will after straight** will go after him immediately   128 **Albeit . . . head** even if I risk being beheaded.   129 **choler** anger.   132 **Want mercy** lack mercy, be damned   133 **on his part** i.e., fighting on Mortimer's side   137 **cankered** spoiled, malignant.   **Bolingbroke** i.e., King Henry IV. (Hotspur pointedly refuses to acknowledge his royalty.)

143 **an eye of death** a fearful look   145 **he** i.e., Mortimer   146 **next of blood** heir to the throne.   148 **unhappy** unfortunate   149 **in us** caused by our doings   150 **Irish expedition** (Richard II was putting down a rebellion in Ireland when Bolingbroke returned to England from exile.)   151 **intercepted** interrupted   155 **soft** i.e., wait a minute   156 **brother** brother-in-law   158 **cousin** (With a pun on cozen, "cheat.")   163 **murderous subornation** the suborning of, or inciting to, murder   165 **second means** agents   168 **To . . . predicament** to show the direction things are moving and the danger to you   169 **range** (1) are ranked; (2) stray   173 **gage them** engage, pledge themselves   176 **canker** (1) canker rose or dog rose, wild and unfragrant (2) ulcer   180 **Yet** Still

Into the good thoughts of the world again;
Revenge the jeering and disdained contempt 183
Of this proud king, who studies day and night
To answer all the debt he owes to you 185
Even with the bloody payment of your deaths.
Therefore, I say—
WORCESTER   Peace, cousin, say no more. 187
And now I will unclasp a secret book,
And to your quick-conceiving discontents 189
I'll read you matter deep and dangerous,
As full of peril and adventurous spirit
As to o'erwalk a current roaring loud
On the unsteadfast footing of a spear. 193
HOTSPUR
If he fall in, good night, or sink or swim! 194
Send danger from the east unto the west,
So honor cross it from the north to south, 196
And let them grapple. Oh, the blood more stirs
To rouse a lion than to start a hare!
NORTHUMBERLAND [to Worcester]
Imagination of some great exploit
Drives him beyond the bounds of patience.
HOTSPUR
By heaven, methinks it were an easy leap
To pluck bright honor from the pale-faced moon,
Or dive into the bottom of the deep,
Where fathom line could never touch the ground, 204
And pluck up drownèd honor by the locks,
So he that doth redeem her thence might wear
Without corrival all her dignities; 207
But out upon this half-faced fellowship! 208
WORCESTER [to Northumberland]
He apprehends a world of figures here, 209
But not the form of what he should attend.— 210
Good cousin, give me audience for a while.
HOTSPUR
I cry you mercy.
WORCESTER   Those same noble Scots 212
That are your prisoners—
HOTSPUR   I'll keep them all.
By God, he shall not have a Scot of them, 214
No, if a scot would save his soul, he shall not! 215
I'll keep them, by this hand.
WORCESTER   You start away
And lend no ear unto my purposes.
Those prisoners you shall keep.
HOTSPUR   Nay, I will, that's flat. 218

He said he would not ransom Mortimer,
Forbade my tongue to speak of Mortimer,
But I will find him when he lies asleep,
And in his ear I'll holler "Mortimer!"
Nay, I'll have a starling shall be taught to speak
Nothing but "Mortimer," and give it him
To keep his anger still in motion. 225
WORCESTER   Hear you, cousin, a word.
HOTSPUR
All studies here I solemnly defy, 227
Save how to gall and pinch this Bolingbroke,
And that same sword-and-buckler Prince of Wales. 229
But that I think his father loves him not
And would be glad he met with some mischance,
I would have him poisoned with a pot of ale.
WORCESTER
Farewell, kinsman. I'll talk to you
When you are better tempered to attend.
NORTHUMBERLAND [to Hotspur]
Why, what a wasp-stung and impatient fool
Art thou to break into this woman's mood,
Tying thine ear to no tongue but thine own!
HOTSPUR
Why, look you, I am whipped and scourged with rods,
Nettled and stung with pismires, when I hear 239
Of this vile politician, Bolingbroke. 240
In Richard's time—what do you call the place?—
A plague upon it, it is in Gloucestershire;
'Twas where the madcap duke his uncle kept, 243
His uncle York; where I first bowed my knee
Unto this king of smiles, this Bolingbroke—
'Sblood, when you and he came back from
Ravenspurgh. 246
NORTHUMBERLAND   At Berkeley Castle. 247
HOTSPUR   You say true.
Why, what a candy deal of courtesy 249
This fawning greyhound then did proffer me!
"Look when his infant fortune came to age," 251
And "gentle Harry Percy," and "kind cousin"—
Oh, the devil take such cozeners!—God forgive me! 253
Good uncle, tell your tale; I have done.
WORCESTER
Nay, if you have not, to it again;
We will stay your leisure.
HOTSPUR   I have done, i'faith. 256
WORCESTER
Then once more to your Scottish prisoners.
Deliver them up without their ransom straight, 258
And make the Douglas' son your only mean 259

---

183 **Revenge** and wherein you may revenge yourself against. **disdained** disdainful   185 **answer** satisfy, discharge   187 **cousin** nephew   189 **quick-conceiving** comprehending quickly   193 **spear** i.e., spear laid across a stream as a narrow bridge.   194 **If . . . swim** i.e., Anyone daring such a thing will face a life-or-death challenge. (Hotspur's imagination is fired by the thought of risking everything on such an attempt.)   196 **So** provided that. (Also at line 206.)   204 **fathom line** a weighted line marked at fathom intervals (six feet), used for measuring the depth of water   207 **corrival** rival, competitor   208 **out . . . fellowship!** down with this paltry business of sharing glory with others!   209 **apprehends** snatches at.   **figures** figures of the imagination, or figures of speech   210 **form** essential nature.   **attend** give attention to.   212 **cry you mercy** beg your pardon.   214–15 **Scot . . . scot** Scotsman . . . trifling amount   218 **that's flat** that's for sure.

225 **still** continually   227 **studies** pursuits.   **defy** renounce   229 **sword-and-buckler** swashbuckling. (Gentlemen generally preferred to wear the rapier and the dagger.)   239 **Nettled** stung with nettles.   **pismires** ants. (From the urinous smell of an anthill.)   240 **politician** deceitful schemer   243 **kept** dwelled   246 **Ravenspurgh** on the Yorkshire coast, at the mouth of the Humber River, where Bolingbroke landed on his return from exile (*Richard II*, 2.1.296).   247 **Berkeley Castle** castle near Bristol.   249 **candy** sugared, flattering   251 **Look when** When, as soon as   253 **cozeners** cheats. (With pun on *cousins*.)   256 **stay** await   258 **Deliver them up** Free them   259 **the Douglas' son** i.e., Mordake. (See 1.1.71 and note.)   **mean** i.e., agent

For powers in Scotland, which, for divers reasons   260
Which I shall send you written, be assured
Will easily be granted. [*To Northumberland*] You, my
   lord,
Your son in Scotland being thus employed,
Shall secretly into the bosom creep   264
Of that same noble prelate well beloved,
The Archbishop.
HOTSPUR   Of York, is it not?
WORCESTER   True, who bears hard   268
His brother's death at Bristol, the Lord Scroop.
I speak not this in estimation,   270
As what I think might be, but what I know
Is ruminated, plotted, and set down,
And only stays but to behold the face
Of that occasion that shall bring it on.
HOTSPUR
I smell it. Upon my life, it will do well.
NORTHUMBERLAND
Before the game is afoot thou still let'st slip.   276
HOTSPUR
Why, it cannot choose but be a noble plot.   277
And then the power of Scotland and of York   278
To join with Mortimer, ha?
WORCESTER   And so they shall.
HOTSPUR
In faith, it is exceedingly well aimed.   280
WORCESTER
And 'tis no little reason bids us speed,
To save our heads by raising of a head;   282
For, bear ourselves as even as we can,   283
The King will always think him in our debt,   284
And think we think ourselves unsatisfied
Till he hath found a time to pay us home.   286
And see already how he doth begin
To make us strangers to his looks of love.
HOTSPUR
He does, he does. We'll be revenged on him.
WORCESTER
Cousin, farewell. No further go in this
Than I by letters shall direct your course.
When time is ripe, which will be suddenly,   292
I'll steal to Glendower and Lord Mortimer,
Where you and Douglas and our powers at once,   294
As I will fashion it, shall happily meet   295
To bear our fortunes in our own strong arms,   296
Which now we hold at much uncertainty.
NORTHUMBERLAND
Farewell, good brother. We shall thrive, I trust.
HOTSPUR
Uncle, adieu. Oh, let the hours be short
Till fields and blows and groans applaud our sport!   300
                        Exeunt [*in separate groups*].

260 **For powers** for raising an army   264 **secretly . . . creep** win the confidence   268 **bears hard** resents   270 **estimation** guesswork   276 **still
let'st slip** always let loose the dogs.   277 **cannot choose but be** cannot
help being   278 **power** army   280 **aimed** designed.   282 **head** army
283 **even** carefully   284 **him** himself   286 **home** (1) fully (2) with a
thrust to the heart.   292 **suddenly** soon   294 **at once** all together
295 **happily** fortunately   296 **arms** (1) limbs (2) military might
300 **fields** battlefields

[2.1]

Enter a Carrier with a lantern in his hand.

FIRST CARRIER   Heigh-ho! An it be not four by the day,   1
   I'll be hanged. Charles's Wain is over the new   2
   chimney, and yet our horse not packed. What, hostler!   3
HOSTLER [*within*]   Anon, anon.   4
FIRST CARRIER   I prithee, Tom, beat Cut's saddle, put a   5
   few flocks in the point. Poor jade is wrung in the   6
   withers out of all cess.   7

Enter another Carrier.

SECOND CARRIER   Peas and beans are as dank here as a   8
   dog, and that is the next way to give poor jades the   9
   bots. This house is turned upside down since Robin   10
   Hostler died.
FIRST CARRIER   Poor fellow never joyed since the price
   of oats rose. It was the death of him.
SECOND CARRIER   I think this be the most villainous
   house in all London road for fleas. I am stung like a
   tench.   16
FIRST CARRIER   Like a tench? By the Mass, there is ne'er
   a king Christian could be better bit than I have been   18
   since the first cock.   19
SECOND CARRIER   Why, they will allow us ne'er a jordan,   20
   and then we leak in your chimney, and your chamber-   21
   lye breeds fleas like a loach.   22
FIRST CARRIER [*calling*]   What, Hostler! Come away and   23
   be hanged! Come away.
SECOND CARRIER   I have a gammon of bacon and two   25
   races of ginger, to be delivered as far as Charing Cross.   26
FIRST CARRIER   God's body, the turkeys in my pannier   27
   are quite starved. What, hostler! A plague on thee!
   Hast thou never an eye in thy head? Canst not hear?
   An 'twere not as good deed as drink to break the pate   30
   on thee, I am a very villain. Come, and be hanged!   31
   Hast no faith in thee?   32

Enter Gadshill.

2.1. Location: An innyard on the London-Canterbury road.
0.1 *Carrier* one whose trade was conveying goods, usually by pack-
horses   **1 An** If.   **by the day** in the morning   **2 Charles's Wain**
i.e., Charlemagne's wagon; the constellation Ursa Major (the Big
Dipper)   **3 horse** horses.   **hostler** groom.   **4 Anon** Right away,
coming   **5 beat** soften.   **Cut's saddle** packsaddle of the horse
named *Cut*, meaning "bobtailed"   **6 flocks** tufts of wool.   **point**
pommel of the saddle.   **jade** nag   **6–7 wrung . . . withers** chafed
(by his saddle) on the ridge between his shoulder-blades   **7 cess**
measure, estimate.   **8 Peas and beans** i.e., Horse fodder   **8–9 dank
. . . dog** i.e., damp as can be   **9 next** nearest, quickest   **10 bots**
intestinal maggots.   **house** inn   **16 tench** a spotted fish, whose
spots may have been likened to flea bites.   **18 king Christian**
Christian king, accustomed to have the best of everything   **19 first
cock** i.e., midnight.   **20 jordan** chamberpot   **21 chimney** fireplace
21–2 chamber-lye urine   **22 loach** a small freshwater fish, thought
to harbor parasites.   **23 Come away** Come along   **25 gammon of
bacon** ham   **26 races** roots.   **Charing Cross** a market town lying
between London and Westminster.   **27 pannier** basket   **30 An** If
30–1 An . . . hanged! i.e., I'll be hanged if it wouldn't be a good
idea to smack you on the head. Come along, damn you!   **32 faith**
trustworthiness

GADSHILL   Good morrow, carriers. What's o'clock?
FIRST CARRIER   I think it be two o'clock.   34
GADSHILL   I prithee, lend me thy lantern to see my
gelding in the stable.   36
FIRST CARRIER   Nay, by God, soft, I know a trick worth   37
two of that, i'faith.
GADSHILL [*to the Second Carrier*]   I pray thee, lend me thine.
SECOND CARRIER   Ay, when, canst tell? Lend me thy   40
lantern, quoth he! Marry, I'll see thee hanged first.   41
GADSHILL   Sirrah carrier, what time do you mean to
come to London?
SECOND CARRIER   Time enough to go to bed with a   44
candle, I warrant thee.—Come, neighbor Mugs, we'll   45
call up the gentlemen. They will along with company,   46
for they have great charge.   *Exeunt [Carriers].*   47
GADSHILL   What, ho! Chamberlain!   48

Enter Chamberlain.

CHAMBERLAIN   At hand, quoth pickpurse.   49
GADSHILL   That's even as fair as—at hand, quoth the   50
chamberlain; for thou variest no more from picking of   51
purses than giving direction doth from laboring; thou   52
layest the plot how.   53
CHAMBERLAIN   Good morrow, Master Gadshill. It holds   54
current that I told you yesternight: there's a franklin in   55
the Weald of Kent hath brought three hundred marks   56
with him in gold. I heard him tell it to one of his company last night at supper—a kind of auditor, one that
hath abundance of charge too, God knows what. They
are up already, and call for eggs and butter. They will
away presently.   61
GADSHILL   Sirrah, if they meet not with Saint Nicholas'   62
clerks, I'll give thee this neck.   63
CHAMBERLAIN   No, I'll none of it. I pray thee, keep that   64
for the hangman, for I know thou worshipest Saint
Nicholas as truly as a man of falsehood may.
GADSHILL   What talkest thou to me of the hangman? If   67
I hang, I'll make a fat pair of gallows; for if I hang, old
Sir John hangs with me, and thou knowest he is no
starveling. Tut, there are other Trojans that thou   70
dream'st not of, the which for sport sake are content
to do the profession some grace, that would, if matters   72

should be looked into, for their own credit sake   73
make all whole. I am joined with no foot-landrakers,   74
no long-staff sixpenny strikers, none of these mad   75
mustachio purple-hued malt-worms, but with nobility   76
and tranquillity, burgomasters and great oneyers, such   77
as can hold in, such as will strike sooner than speak,   78
and speak sooner than drink, and drink sooner than
pray. And yet, zounds, I lie, for they pray continually
to their saint, the commonwealth, or rather not pray to
her but prey on her, for they ride up and down on her
and make her their boots.   83
CHAMBERLAIN   What, the commonwealth their boots?
Will she hold out water in foul way?   85
GADSHILL   She will, she will. Justice hath liquored her.   86
We steal as in a castle, cocksure. We have the receipt   87
of fern seed; we walk invisible.   88
CHAMBERLAIN   Nay, by my faith, I think you are more
beholding to the night than to fern seed for your   90
walking invisible.
GADSHILL   Give me thy hand. Thou shalt have a share
in our purchase, as I am a true man.   93
CHAMBERLAIN   Nay, rather let me have it as you are a
false thief.
GADSHILL   Go to; *homo* is a common name to all men.   96
Bid the hostler bring my gelding out of the stable. Farewell, you muddy knave.   *[Exeunt separately.]*   98

❧

[2.2]

Enter Prince, Poins, Peto, and [Bardolph].

POINS   Come, shelter, shelter! I have removed Falstaff's
horse, and he frets like a gummed velvet.   2
PRINCE   Stand close.   *[They step aside.]*   3

Enter Falstaff.

FALSTAFF   Poins! Poins, and be hanged! Poins!
PRINCE [*coming forward*]   Peace, ye fat-kidneyed rascal!
What a brawling dost thou keep!   6
FALSTAFF   Where's Poins, Hal?

---

34 two o'clock (An evasive answer; the First Carrier knows that it is
at least four o'clock; see line 1.)   **36 gelding** castrated male horse
37 soft i.e., wait a minute   **40 Ay . . . tell?** i.e., You must be joking.
41 quoth he forsooth, indeed.   **44–5 Time . . . candle** i.e., Soon
enough. (Another evasive answer.)   **46–7 They . . . charge** i.e., They
wish to travel in company, because they have lots of valuable cargo.
48 Chamberlain (Male equivalent of a chambermaid. His entrance in
the Quarto at line 47 may suggest that he is visible before Gadshill
calls for him, giving point to his remark about being "At hand.")
49 At . . . pickpurse i.e., I am right beside you, as the pickpurse said.
50 fair good, apt   **51–3 thou variest . . . how** i.e., you don't actually
do the stealing, but you give directions, like a master workman to his
apprentices.   **54–5 holds current that** holds true what   **55 a franklin**
a yeoman owning his own land   **56 Weald** wooded region.   **marks**
coins of the value of thirteen shillings four pence   **61 presently**
immediately.   **62–3 Saint Nicholas' clerks** highwaymen. (Saint
Nicholas was popularly supposed the patron of thieves.)   **64 I'll
none** I want none   **67 What** Why   **70 Trojans** i.e., jolly fellows,
roisterers   **72 profession** i.e., robbery.   **grace** credit, favor

73–4 for . . . whole for the sake of their own reputation will make sure
that all goes well. (Gadshill hints that they may be joined by some
persons of social importance, such as the Prince.)   **74 foot-landrakers**
thieves who travel on foot   **75 long-staff six-penny strikers** robbers
with long staves who would knock down their victims for sixpence
76 mustachio . . . malt-worms purple-faced drunkards with huge
mustaches   **77 tranquillity** those who lead easy lives.   **oneyers**
ones, persons (?)   **78 hold in** keep a secret; hold fast   **83 boots** booty.
(With pun on *boots*, "shoes.")   **85 Will . . . way?** Will she let you go
dry in muddy roads? i.e., Will she protect you in tight places?
86 liquored (1) made waterproof by oiling (2) bribed (3) made drunk
87 as in a castle i.e., in complete security.   **receipt** recipe, formula
88 of fern seed i.e., of becoming invisible (since fern seed, almost
invisible itself, was popularly supposed to render its possessor invisible)   **90 beholding** beholden   **93 purchase** booty   **96 Go to** (An
expression of impatience.)   *homo* . . . **men** the Latin name for man
applies to all types; the phrase "true man" applies to me as well as
the next man.   **98 muddy** stupid
2.2. Location: The highway, near Gad's Hill.
2 frets (1) is vexed (2) rubs and frays like *gummed velvet*, velvet made
glossy with a stiffening gum   **3 close** concealed.   **6 keep** keep up.

PRINCE   He is walked up to the top of the hill. I'll go
seek him.   [*He steps aside.*]

FALSTAFF   I am accursed to rob in that thief's company.
The rascal hath removed my horse and tied him I
know not where. If I travel but four foot by the square   12
further afoot, I shall break my wind. Well, I doubt not
but to die a fair death for all this, if I scape hanging for   14
killing that rogue. I have forsworn his company hourly
any time this two-and-twenty years, and yet I am bewitched with the rogue's company. If the rascal have
not given me medicines to make me love him, I'll be   18
hanged; it could not be else—I have drunk medicines.
Poins! Hal! A plague upon you both! Bardolph! Peto!
I'll starve ere I'll rob a foot further. An 'twere not as   21
good a deed as drink to turn true man and to leave   22
these rogues, I am the veriest varlet that ever chewed   23
with a tooth. Eight yards of uneven ground is three-   24
score-and-ten miles afoot with me, and the stony-
hearted villains know it well enough. A plague upon
it when thieves cannot be true one to another! (*They
whistle.*) Whew! A plague upon you all! Give me my   28
horse, you rogues, give me my horse, and be hanged!

PRINCE [*coming forward*]   Peace, ye fat-guts! Lie down.
Lay thine ear close to the ground and list if thou   31
canst hear the tread of travelers.

FALSTAFF   Have you any levers to lift me up again, being
down? 'Sblood, I'll not bear mine own flesh so far
afoot again for all the coin in thy father's Exchequer.
What a plague mean ye to colt me thus?   36

PRINCE   Thou liest. Thou art not colted, thou art
uncolted.

FALSTAFF   I prithee, good Prince Hal, help me to my   39
horse, good king's son.   40

PRINCE   Out, ye rogue! Shall I be your hostler?

FALSTAFF   Go hang thyself in thine own heir-apparent
garters! If I be ta'en, I'll peach for this. An I have not   43
ballads made on you all and sung to filthy tunes, let a
cup of sack be my poison. When a jest is so forward,   45
and afoot too! I hate it.   46

Enter Gadshill.

GADSHILL   Stand!   47

FALSTAFF   So I do, against my will.

POINS [*coming forward with Bardolph and Peto*]   Oh, 'tis our
setter. I know his voice.   50

BARDOLPH   What news?

GADSHILL   Case ye, case ye, on with your vizards!   52

There's money of the King's coming down the hill; 'tis
going to the King's Exchequer.

FALSTAFF   You lie, ye rogue, 'tis going to the King's
Tavern.

GADSHILL   There's enough to make us all.   57

FALSTAFF   To be hanged.

PRINCE   Sirs, you four shall front them in the narrow   59
lane; Ned Poins and I will walk lower. If they scape   60
from your encounter, then they light on us.

PETO   How many be there of them?

GADSHILL   Some eight or ten.

FALSTAFF   Zounds, will they not rob us?

PRINCE   What, a coward, Sir John Paunch?

FALSTAFF   Indeed, I am not John of Gaunt, your   66
grandfather, but yet no coward, Hal.

PRINCE   Well, we leave that to the proof.   68

POINS   Sirrah Jack, thy horse stands behind the hedge.
When thou need'st him, there thou shalt find him.
Farewell, and stand fast.

FALSTAFF   Now cannot I strike him, if I should be   72
hanged.   73

PRINCE [*to Poins*]   Ned, where are our disguises?

POINS [*to Prince*]   Here, hard by. Stand close.
                                      [*Exeunt Prince and Poins.*]

FALSTAFF   Now, my masters, happy man be his dole,   76
say I. Every man to his business.   [*They stand aside.*]

Enter the Travelers.

FIRST TRAVELER   Come, neighbor. The boy shall lead
our horses down the hill; we'll walk afoot awhile, and
ease our legs.

THIEVES [*coming forward*]   Stand!

TRAVELERS   Jesus bless us!

FALSTAFF   Strike! Down with them! Cut the villains'
throats! Ah, whoreson caterpillars, bacon-fed knaves!   84
They hate us youth. Down with them, fleece them!

TRAVELERS   Oh, we are undone, both we and ours forever!

FALSTAFF   Hang ye, gorbellied knaves, are ye undone?   88
No, ye fat chuffs; I would your store were here. On,   89
bacons, on! What, ye knaves, young men must live.   90
You are grandjurors, are ye? We'll jure ye, 'faith.   91
                Here they rob them and bind them. Exeunt.

Enter the Prince and Poins [in buckram].

PRINCE   The thieves have bound the true men. Now
could thou and I rob the thieves and go merrily to
London, it would be argument for a week, laughter   94
for a month, and a good jest forever.

---

12 square a measuring tool   **14 fair** exemplary.   **for all** despite all
18 medicines love potions   **21–4 An . . . tooth** i.e., If I don't think it's a
good idea to reform and turn informer, I'm the damnedest scoundrel
that ever lived. (Cf. 2.1.30–1 and n.)   **28 Whew** (Perhaps Falstaff tries
to answer the whistling he hears or mocks it.)   **31 list** listen   **36 colt**
trick, cheat. (In lines 37–8, Prince Hal puns on the common meaning.)
39–40 help . . . horse help me to find my horse. (But in line 41, the
Prince comically retorts as though having been asked to hold the stirrup while Falstaff mounted, as a hostler would do.)   **43 peach** inform
on you   **45 so forward** so far advanced   **46 afoot** (1) in progress (2)
on foot, i.e., not on horseback   **47 Stand!** Don't move! (But Falstaff
answers in the sense of "stand on one's feet.")   **50 setter** arranger of
the robbery. (See 1.2.104–5 and note.)   **52 Case ye** Put on your masks

57 make us all make our fortunes (or, as Falstaff sees it, make us be
hanged).   **59 front** confront   **60 lower** further downhill.   **66 John of
Gaunt** Henry IV's father, born at Ghent (and hence giving Falstaff a
chance to pun on *gaunt* as the opposite of his fatness)   **68 proof** test.
72–3 Now . . . hanged (Falstaff wishes he could hit Poins, who is too
quick for him.)   **76 happy . . . dole** may happiness be every man's
portion or lot   **84 Ah . . . knaves!** i.e., Ah, you abominable parasites,
you over-fed rascals!   **88 gorbellied** big-bellied   **89 chuffs** churls,
rich but miserly.   **store** total wealth   **90 bacons** fat men   **91 grandjurors** i.e., men of wealth, able to serve on juries   **94 argument** a subject for conversation

POINS   Stand close. I hear them coming.

[They stand aside.]

Enter the thieves again.

FALSTAFF   Come, my masters, let us share, and then to 97
horse before day. An the Prince and Poins be not two
arrant cowards, there's no equity stirring. There's no 99
more valor in that Poins than in a wild duck.

[The thieves begin to share the booty.]

PRINCE   Your money!

POINS   Villains!

*As they are sharing, the Prince and Poins set upon
them. They all run away, and Falstaff, after a blow
or two, runs away too, leaving the booty behind
them.*

PRINCE
Got with much ease. Now merrily to horse.
The thieves are all scattered and possessed with fear
So strongly that they dare not meet each other;
Each takes his fellow for an officer.
Away, good Ned. Falstaff sweats to death
And lards the lean earth as he walks along. 108
Were't not for laughing, I should pity him.

POINS   How the fat rogue roared!   *Exeunt.*

❖

[2.3]

Enter Hotspur, solus, reading a letter.

HOTSPUR   "But, for mine own part, my lord, I could be
well contented to be there, in respect of the love I bear
your house." He could be contented; why is he not, 3
then? In respect of the love he bears our house! He
shows in this he loves his own barn better than he
loves our house. Let me see some more. "The purpose
you undertake is dangerous"—why, that's certain.
'Tis dangerous to take a cold, to sleep, to drink; but I
tell you, my lord fool, out of this nettle, danger, we
pluck this flower, safety. "The purpose you undertake
is dangerous, the friends you have named uncertain,
the time itself unsorted, and your whole plot too light 12
for the counterpoise of so great an opposition." Say 13
you so, say you so? I say unto you again, you are a
shallow, cowardly hind, and you lie. What a lack-brain 15
is this! By the Lord, our plot is a good plot as
ever was laid, our friends true and constant; a good
plot, good friends, and full of expectation; an excellent 18
plot, very good friends. What a frosty-spirited rogue is
this! Why, my lord of York commends the plot and 20

the general course of the action. Zounds, an I were 21
now by this rascal, I could brain him with his lady's 22
fan. Is there not my father, my uncle, and myself? Lord 23
Edmund Mortimer, my lord of York, and Owen Glendower? Is there not besides the Douglas? Have I not all
their letters to meet me in arms by the ninth of the next
month, and are they not some of them set forward
already? What a pagan rascal is this, an infidel! Ha, 28
you shall see now in very sincerity of fear and
cold heart will he to the King and lay open all our
proceedings. Oh, I could divide myself and go to buf- 31
fets for moving such a dish of skim milk with so hon- 32
orable an action! Hang him, let him tell the King, we
are prepared. I will set forward tonight.

Enter his Lady.

How now, Kate? I must leave you within these two
hours.

LADY PERCY
Oh, my good lord, why are you thus alone?
For what offense have I this fortnight been
A banished woman from my Harry's bed?
Tell me, sweet lord, what is't that takes from thee
Thy stomach, pleasure, and thy golden sleep? 41
Why dost thou bend thine eyes upon the earth
And start so often when thou sit'st alone?
Why hast thou lost the fresh blood in thy cheeks
And given my treasures and my rights of thee 45
To thick-eyed musing and curst melancholy? 46
In thy faint slumbers I by thee have watched 47
And heard thee murmur tales of iron wars,
Speak terms of manage to thy bounding steed, 49
Cry, "Courage! To the field!" And thou hast talked
Of sallies and retires, of trenches, tents, 51
Of palisadoes, frontiers, parapets, 52
Of basilisks, of cannon, culverin, 53
Of prisoners' ransom, and of soldiers slain,
And all the currents of a heady fight. 55
Thy spirit within thee hath been so at war,
And thus hath so bestirred thee in thy sleep,
That beads of sweat have stood upon thy brow
Like bubbles in a late-disturbèd stream, 59
And in thy face strange motions have appeared,
Such as we see when men restrain their breath
On some great sudden hest. Oh, what portents are
   these? 62
Some heavy business hath my lord in hand,
And I must know it, else he loves me not.

---

97 **masters** good sirs   99 **arrant** notorious, unmitigated.   **equity**
judgment, discernment   108 **lards** drips fat on, bastes
**2.3. Location: Hotspur's estate (identified historically as Warkworth
Castle in Northumberland).**
0.1 *solus* alone   **3 house** family. (But Hotspur replies derisively in
lines 4–6 as though to the literal sense of a building that one might
compare to a barn.)   **12 unsorted** unsuitable   **13 for . . . of** to counterbalance   **15 hind** menial, peasant   **18 expectation** promise
20 lord of York i.e., Archbishop Scroop. (Also in line 24.)

21–2 an . . . rascal if I were face to face with this rascal, instead of
reading his letter   **22–3 his lady's fan** his wife's fan—a suitable light
weapon with which to chastise such a milktoast.   **28 pagan** unbelieving   **31–2 divide . . . buffets** i.e., fight with myself   **32 moving** urging   **41 stomach** appetite   **45 And . . . thee** and given the precious
right I have as wife to share your thoughts   **46 thick-eyed** dull-sight-
ed, vacant, abstracted.   **curst** ill-tempered   **47 faint** restless.
watched lain awake   **49 manage** horsemanship   **51 retires** retreats
52–3 Of . . . culverin of stakes set in the ground for defense, of ram-
parts, protective walls, of large and smaller cannon   **55 heady** headlong   **59 late-disturbèd** recently stirred up   **62 hest** command;
endeavor.

HOTSPUR [*calling*]
  What, ho!

    [*Enter a Servant.*]

       Is Gilliams with the packet gone?
SERVANT He is, my lord, an hour ago.
HOTSPUR
  Hath Butler brought those horses from the sheriff?   67
SERVANT
  One horse, my lord, he brought even now.   68
HOTSPUR
  What horse? A roan, a crop-ear, is it not?   69
SERVANT
  It is, my lord.
HOTSPUR   That roan shall be my throne.
  Well, I will back him straight. Oh, *Esperance!*   71
  Bid Butler lead him forth into the park.

                  [*Exit Servant.*]
LADY PERCY But hear you, my lord.
HOTSPUR What say'st thou, my lady?
LADY PERCY What is it carries you away?   75
HOTSPUR Why, my horse, my love, my horse.
LADY PERCY Out, you mad-headed ape!   77
  A weasel hath not such a deal of spleen   78
  As you are tossed with. In faith,   79
  I'll know your business, Harry, that I will.
  I fear my brother Mortimer doth stir
  About his title, and hath sent for you   82
  To line his enterprise; but if you go—   83
HOTSPUR
  So far afoot, I shall be weary, love.
LADY PERCY
  Come, come, you paraquito, answer me   85
  Directly unto this question that I ask.
  In faith, I'll break thy little finger, Harry,
  An if thou wilt not tell me all things true.   88
HOTSPUR Away,
  Away, you trifler! Love? I love thee not;
  I care not for thee, Kate. This is no world
  To play with mammets and to tilt with lips.   92
  We must have bloody noses and cracked crowns,   93
  And pass them current too. Gods me, my horse!   94
  What say'st thou, Kate? What wouldst thou have with
    me?
LADY PERCY
  Do you not love me? Do you not, indeed?
  Well, do not, then, for since you love me not

I will not love myself. Do you not love me?
  Nay, tell me if you speak in jest or no.
HOTSPUR Come, wilt thou see me ride?
  And when I am a-horseback I will swear
  I love thee infinitely. But hark you, Kate,
  I must not have you henceforth question me
  Whither I go, nor reason whereabout.   104
  Whither I must, I must; and, to conclude,
  This evening must I leave you, gentle Kate.
  I know you wise, but yet no farther wise
  Than Harry Percy's wife; constant you are,
  But yet a woman; and for secrecy,
  No lady closer, for I well believe   110
  Thou wilt not utter what thou dost not know,
  And so far will I trust thee, gentle Kate.
LADY PERCY How, so far?
HOTSPUR
  Not an inch further. But hark you, Kate:
  Whither I go, thither shall you go too.
  Today will I set forth, tomorrow you.
  Will this content you, Kate?
LADY PERCY   It must, of force.   *Exeunt.* 117

❖

[2.4]

Enter Prince and Poins.

PRINCE Ned, prithee, come out of that fat room, and   1
  lend me thy hand to laugh a little.
POINS Where hast been, Hal?
PRINCE With three or four loggerheads amongst three   4
  or four score hogsheads. I have sounded the very bass   5
  string of humility. Sirrah, I am sworn brother to a
  leash of drawers, and can call them all by their Christian   7
  names, as Tom, Dick, and Francis. They take it already   8
  upon their salvation that, though I be but Prince of   9
  Wales, yet I am the king of courtesy, and tell me flatly
  I am no proud Jack like Falstaff, but a Corinthian, a lad   11
  of mettle, a good boy—by the Lord, so they call me!—
  and when I am King of England I shall command all
  the good lads in Eastcheap. They call drinking deep   14
  "dyeing scarlet"; and when you breathe in your water-   15
  ing they cry "hem!" and bid you "play it off." To con-   16
  clude, I am so good a proficient in one quarter of an
  hour that I can drink with any tinker in his own language during my life. I tell thee, Ned, thou hast lost
  much honor that thou wert not with me in this action.

---

67 sheriff i.e., bailiff. **68 even** just **69 roan** roan-colored, i.e., with white or grey interspersed in the overall color of the coat **71 back** mount. *Esperance* Hope. (The motto of the Percy family.) **75 carries you away** carries you beyond the bounds of reason and judgment. (But Hotspur puns on the literal meaning.) **77 Out** (An expression of impatience.) **78 spleen** (The spleen was thought to be the source of impulsive and irritable behavior.) **79 tossed** tossed about, agitated **82 title** claim to the throne **83 line** strengthen **85 paraquito** little parrot. (A term of endearment.) **88 An if** if **92 mammets** dolls. (With a quibble on the Latin *mamma* meaning "breast.") **93 crowns** (1) heads (2) coins worth five shillings. (Cracked coins would not "pass current," as Hotspur jokes in the next line.) **94 Gods me** God save me

104 reason whereabout ask about what. **110 closer** more close-mouthed **117 of force** perforce, of necessity.
2.4. Location: A tavern in Eastcheap, London, usually identified as the Boar's Head. Some tavern furniture, including stools, is provided onstage.
1 fat stuffy, or, a vat room **4 loggerheads** blockheads **5 hogsheads** wine barrels. **bass** (With a pun on *base.*) **7 leash of drawers** three waiters **8–9 take . . . salvation** already maintain it as they hope to be saved **11 Jack** (1) Jack Falstaff (2) fellow. **Corinthian** i.e., gay blade, good sport. (Corinth was reputed to be licentious.)
14–15 They . . . scarlet (Either because excessive drinking causes a red complexion or because urine, produced by *drinking deep,* was sometimes used for fixing dyes.) **15–16 breathe . . . watering** pause for breath in your drinking **16 play it off** drink it up.

But, sweet Ned—to sweeten which name of Ned, I give thee this pennyworth of sugar, clapped even now 22 into my hand by an underskinker, one that never 23 spake other English in his life than "Eight shillings and sixpence," and "You are welcome," with this shrill addition, "Anon, anon, sir! Score a pint of bas- 26 tard in the Half-Moon," or so. But, Ned, to drive away 27 the time till Falstaff come, I prithee do thou stand in some by-room while I question my puny drawer to 29 what end he gave me the sugar; and do thou never leave calling "Francis," that his tale to me may be nothing but "Anon." Step aside, and I'll show thee a precedent.   [Exit Poins.] 33

POINS [within]   Francis!

PRINCE   Thou art perfect.

POINS [within]   Francis!

Enter [Francis, a] drawer.

FRANCIS   Anon, anon, sir.—Look down into the Pom- 37
garnet, Ralph.   38

PRINCE   Come hither, Francis.

FRANCIS   My lord?

PRINCE   How long hast thou to serve, Francis?   41

FRANCIS   Forsooth, five years, and as much as to—

POINS [within]   Francis!

FRANCIS [calling]   Anon, anon, sir.

PRINCE   Five year! By'r Lady, a long lease for the 45
clinking of pewter. But Francis, darest thou be so
valiant as to play the coward with thy indenture and 47
show it a fair pair of heels and run from it?

FRANCIS   Oh, Lord, sir, I'll be sworn upon all the books in 49
England, I could find in my heart—

POINS [within]   Francis!

FRANCIS [calling]   Anon, sir.

PRINCE   How old art thou, Francis?

FRANCIS   Let me see, about Michaelmas next I shall 54
be—

POINS [within]   Francis!

FRANCIS [calling]   Anon, sir. Pray, stay a little, my lord.

PRINCE   Nay, but hark you, Francis: for the sugar thou
gavest me, 'twas a pennyworth, was 't not?

FRANCIS   Oh, Lord, I would it had been two!

PRINCE   I will give thee for it a thousand pound. Ask
me when thou wilt, and thou shalt have it.

POINS [within]   Francis!

FRANCIS [calling]   Anon, anon.

PRINCE   Anon, Francis? No, Francis; but tomorrow,
Francis, or, Francis, o'Thursday, or indeed, Francis,
when thou wilt. But, Francis—

FRANCIS   My lord?

PRINCE   Wilt thou rob this leathern-jerkin, crystal- 69
button, not-pated, agate-ring, puke-stocking, caddis- 70
garter, smooth-tongue, Spanish-pouch—   71

FRANCIS   Oh, Lord, sir, who do you mean?

PRINCE   Why, then, your brown bastard is your only 73
drink; for look you, Francis, your white canvas 74
doublet will sully. In Barbary, sir, it cannot come to so 75
much.   76

FRANCIS   What, sir?

POINS [within]   Francis!

PRINCE   Away, you rogue! Dost thou not hear them call? 79
*Here they both call him; the drawer stands
amazed, not knowing which way to go.*

Enter Vintner.

VINTNER   What stand'st thou still and hear'st such a 80
calling? Look to the guests within.   [Exit Francis.]
My lord, old Sir John, with half a dozen more, are at the
door. Shall I let them in?

PRINCE   Let them alone awhile, and then open the door.
[Exit Vintner.]

[Calling]   Poins!

Enter Poins.

POINS   Anon, anon, sir.

PRINCE   Sirrah, Falstaff and the rest of the thieves are at
the door. Shall we be merry?

POINS   As merry as crickets, my lad. But hark ye, what
cunning match have you made with this jest of the 90
drawer? Come, what's the issue?   91

PRINCE   I am now of all humors that have showed 92
themselves humors since the old days of Goodman 93
Adam to the pupil age of this present twelve o'clock at 94
midnight.   95

[Enter Francis, hurrying across the stage with
wine.]

What's o'clock, Francis?

FRANCIS   Anon, anon, sir.   [Exit.]

PRINCE   That ever this fellow should have fewer words
than a parrot, and yet the son of a woman! His industry is upstairs and downstairs, his eloquence the parcel 100
of a reckoning. I am not yet of Percy's mind, the Hot- 101
spur of the north, he that kills me some six or seven 102
dozen of Scots at a breakfast, washes his hands, and
says to his wife, "Fie upon this quiet life! I want
work." "Oh, my sweet Harry," says she, "how many

69–71 **Wilt . . . Spanish-pouch** i.e., Will you rob your master of your services by running away, this man with his leather jacket, transparent buttons, cropped hair, a ring with small figures in an agate stone for a seal, dark woolen stockings, worsted garters, an ingratiating flattering manner of speech, wallet of Spanish leather   73–6 **Why . . . much** (The Prince talks seeming nonsense in order to bewilder Francis, but he also implies that Francis should stick to his trade, since he will not cut much of a figure in the world.)   75 **it** i.e., sugar
79.3 **Vintner** i.e., Innkeeper.   80 **What** Why   90 **match** game, contest   91 **issue** outcome, point.   92–5 **I . . . midnight** i.e., I'm now in a mood for anything that has happened in the whole history of the world.   93 **Goodman** (Title for a yeoman.)   94 **pupil** youthful   100–1 **parcel . . . reckoning** items of a bill.   102 **kills me** i.e., kills. (*Me* is used colloquially.)

22 **sugar** (Used to sweeten wine.)   23 **underskinker** assistant to a waiter or bartender   26–7 **Anon . . . Half-Moon** Coming, sir!—Charge a pint of a sweet Spanish wine to the customers in the room of the inn called "the Half-Moon."   29 **by-room** side-room.   **puny drawer** inexperienced tapster or bartender   33 **precedent** example.   37–8 **Pomgarnet** Pomegranate. (Another room in the inn.)   41 **serve** i.e., serve out your apprenticeship   45 **By'r Lady** By Our Lady   47 **indenture** contract of apprenticeship   49 **books** i.e., Bibles   54 **Michaelmas** September 29

hast thou killed today?" "Give my roan horse a
drench," says he, and answers, "Some fourteen," an   107
hour after, "a trifle, a trifle." I prithee, call in Falstaff.
I'll play Percy, and that damned brawn shall play Dame   109
Mortimer his wife. "Rivo!" says the drunkard. Call in   110
ribs, call in tallow.   111

Enter Falstaff, [Gadshill, Bardolph, and Peto;
Francis following with wine].

POINS   Welcome, Jack. Where hast thou been?
FALSTAFF   A plague of all cowards, I say, and a   113
vengeance too! Marry and amen! Give me a cup of
sack, boy. Ere I lead this life long, I'll sew nether-   115
stocks, and mend them and foot them too. A plague   116
of all cowards! Give me a cup of sack, rogue. Is there
no virtue extant?   *He drinketh.*
PRINCE   Didst thou never see Titan kiss a dish of butter,   119
pitiful-hearted Titan, that melted at the sweet tale of   120
the sun's? If thou didst, then behold that compound.   121
FALSTAFF   You rogue, here's lime in this sack too. There   122
is nothing but roguery to be found in villainous man,
yet a coward is worse than a cup of sack with lime in
it. A villainous coward! Go thy ways, old Jack, die
when thou wilt. If manhood, good manhood, be not
forgot upon the face of the earth, then am I a shotten   127
herring. There lives not three good men unhanged in   128
England, and one of them is fat and grows old, God
help the while! A bad world, I say. I would I were a   130
weaver; I could sing psalms or anything. A plague of   131
all cowards, I say still.
PRINCE   How now, woolsack, what mutter you?   133
FALSTAFF   A king's son! If I do not beat thee out of thy
kingdom with a dagger of lath, and drive all thy   135
subjects afore thee like a flock of wild geese, I'll never
wear hair on my face more. You, Prince of Wales!
PRINCE   Why, you whoreson round man, what's the
matter?
FALSTAFF   Are not you a coward? Answer me to that.
And Poins there?
POINS   Zounds, ye fat paunch, an ye call me coward, by
the Lord, I'll stab thee.
FALSTAFF   I call thee coward? I'll see thee damned ere I
call thee coward, but I would give a thousand pound
I could run as fast as thou canst. You are straight
enough in the shoulders; you care not who sees your
back. Call you that backing of your friends? A plague
upon such backing! Give me them that will face me.

Give me a cup of sack. I am a rogue if I drunk today.
PRINCE   Oh, villain, thy lips are scarce wiped since thou
drunk'st last.
FALSTAFF   All is one for that. (*He drinketh.*) A plague of   153
all cowards, still say I.
PRINCE   What's the matter?
FALSTAFF   What's the matter? There be four of us here
have ta'en a thousand pound this day morning.   157
PRINCE   Where is it, Jack, where is it?
FALSTAFF   Where is it? Taken from us it is. A hundred
upon poor four of us.
PRINCE   What, a hundred, man?
FALSTAFF   I am a rogue if I were not at half-sword with   162
a dozen of them two hours together. I have scaped by   163
miracle. I am eight times thrust through the doublet,   164
four through the hose, my buckler cut through and   165
through, my sword hacked like a handsaw—*ecce*   166
signum! I never dealt better since I was a man. All   167
would not do. A plague of all cowards! Let them   168
speak. If they speak more or less than truth, they are
villains and the sons of darkness.
PRINCE   Speak, sirs, how was it?
GADSHILL   We four set upon some dozen—
FALSTAFF   Sixteen at least, my lord.
GADSHILL   And bound them.
PETO   No, no, they were not bound.
FALSTAFF   You rogue, they were bound, every man of
them, or I am a Jew else, an Hebrew Jew.
GADSHILL   As we were sharing, some six or seven fresh
men set upon us—
FALSTAFF   And unbound the rest, and then come in the
other.   181
PRINCE   What, fought you with them all?
FALSTAFF   All? I know not what you call all, but if I
fought not with fifty of them, I am a bunch of radish.
If there were not two- or three-and-fifty upon poor old
Jack, then am I no two-legged creature.
PRINCE   Pray God you have not murdered some of them.
FALSTAFF   Nay, that's past praying for. I have peppered
two of them. Two I am sure I have paid, two rogues
in buckram suits. I tell thee what, Hal, if I tell thee a
lie, spit in my face, call me horse. Thou knowest my
old ward. Here I lay, and thus I bore my point. [*He*   192
demonstrates his stance.] Four rogues in buckram let
drive at me—
PRINCE   What, four? Thou said'st but two even now.   195
FALSTAFF   Four, Hal, I told thee four.
POINS   Ay, ay, he said four.
FALSTAFF   These four came all afront, and mainly thrust   198
at me. I made me no more ado but took all their seven   199
points in my target, thus.   200

---

107 **drench** draft (sometimes of medicine).   **says he** i.e., he tells a servant   109 **brawn** fat boar   110 **Rivo** (An exclamation of uncertain
meaning, but related to drinking.)   111 **ribs** rib roast.   **tallow** fat
drippings.   113 **of** on   115–16 **netherstocks** stockings (the sewing or
mending of which is a menial occupation)   116 **foot** make a new foot
for   119 **Titan** i.e., the sun   120 **that** i.e., the butter   121 **compound**
melting butter, i.e., Falstaff.   122 **lime in this sack** i.e., lime added to
make the wine sparkle   127–8 **a shotten herring** a herring that has
cast its roe and is consequently thin.   130 **the while** i.e., in these bad
times.   131 **weaver** (Many psalm-singing Protestant immigrants
from the Low Countries were weavers.)   133 **woolsack** bale of wool
135 **dagger of lath** (The Vice, a stock comic figure in morality plays,
was so armed.)

153 **All . . . that** No matter.   157 **this day morning** this morning.
162 **at half-sword** fighting at close quarters   163 **scaped** escaped
164 **doublet** Elizabethan upper garment like a jacket   165 **hose** close-
fitting breeches.   **buckler** shield   166–7 **ecce signum** behold the proof.
(Familiar words from the Mass.)   167–8 **All . . . do** All that I did was of
no use.   181 **other** others.   192 **ward** defensive stance, parry.   **lay**
stood   195 **even** just   198 **afront** abreast.   **mainly** powerfully
199 **made me** made. (*Me* is used colloquially.)   200 **target** shield

PRINCE   Seven? Why, there were but four even now.

FALSTAFF   In buckram?

POINS   Ay, four, in buckram suits.

FALSTAFF   Seven, by these hilts, or I am a villain else.   204

PRINCE [*aside to Poins*]   Prithee, let him alone. We shall have more anon.

FALSTAFF   Dost thou hear me, Hal?

PRINCE   Ay, and mark thee too, Jack.   208

FALSTAFF   Do so, for it is worth the listening to. These nine in buckram that I told thee of—

PRINCE   So, two more already.

FALSTAFF   Their points being broken—   212

POINS   Down fell their hose.

FALSTAFF   Began to give me ground; but I followed me   214 close, came in foot and hand; and with a thought   215 seven of the eleven I paid.

PRINCE   Oh, monstrous! Eleven buckram men grown out of two!

FALSTAFF   But, as the devil would have it, three misbegotten knaves in Kendal green came at my back   220 and let drive at me; for it was so dark, Hal, that thou couldst not see thy hand.

PRINCE   These lies are like their father that begets them,   223 gross as a mountain, open, palpable. Why, thou claybrained guts, thou knotty-pated fool, thou whore-   225 son, obscene, greasy tallow-keech—   226

FALSTAFF   What, art thou mad? Art thou mad? Is not the truth the truth?

PRINCE   Why, how couldst thou know these men in Kendal green when it was so dark thou couldst not see thy hand? Come, tell us your reason. What sayest thou to this?

POINS   Come, your reason, Jack, your reason.

FALSTAFF   What, upon compulsion? Zounds, an I were at the strappado, or all the racks in the world, I would   235 not tell you on compulsion. Give you a reason on compulsion? If reasons were as plentiful as blackberries,   237 I would give no man a reason upon compulsion, I.

PRINCE   I'll be no longer guilty of this sin. This sanguine   239 coward, this bed-presser, this horse-backbreaker, this huge hill of flesh—

FALSTAFF   'Sblood, you starveling, you eel-skin, you dried neat's tongue, you bull's pizzle, you stockfish!   243 Oh, for breath to utter what is like thee! You tailor's yard, you sheath, you bowcase, you vile standing   245 tuck—   246

PRINCE   Well, breathe awhile, and then to it again, and when thou hast tired thyself in base comparisons, hear me speak but this.

POINS   Mark, Jack.

PRINCE   We two saw you four set on four and bound them, and were masters of their wealth. Mark now how a plain tale shall put you down. Then did we two set on you four, and, with a word, outfaced you from   254 your prize, and have it, yea, and can show it you here in the house. And, Falstaff, you carried your guts away as nimbly, with as quick dexterity, and roared for mercy, and still run and roared, as ever I heard bull calf. What a slave art thou, to hack thy sword as thou hast done, and then say it was in fight! What trick, what device, what starting-hole canst thou now find   261 out to hide thee from this open and apparent shame?

POINS   Come, let's hear, Jack. What trick hast thou now?

FALSTAFF   By the Lord, I knew ye as well as he that made ye. Why, hear you, my masters, was it for me to kill the heir apparent? Should I turn upon the true prince? Why, thou knowest I am as valiant as Hercules, but beware instinct. The lion will not touch the true prince. Instinct is a great matter; I was now a coward on instinct. I shall think the better of myself and thee during my life—I for a valiant lion, and thou for a true prince. But by the Lord, lads, I am glad you have the money. Hostess, clap to the doors! Watch   273 tonight, pray tomorrow. Gallants, lads, boys, hearts   274 of gold, all the titles of good fellowship come to you! What, shall we be merry? Shall we have a play extempore?

PRINCE   Content; and the argument shall be thy run-   278 ning away.

FALSTAFF   Ah, no more of that, Hal, an thou lovest me!

Enter Hostess.

HOSTESS   Oh, Jesu, my lord the Prince!

PRINCE   How now, my lady the hostess, what say'st thou to me?

HOSTESS   Marry, my lord, there is a nobleman of the court at door would speak with you. He says he comes from your father.

PRINCE   Give him as much as will make him a royal   287 man, and send him back again to my mother.   288

FALSTAFF   What manner of man is he?

HOSTESS   An old man.

FALSTAFF   What doth Gravity out of his bed at mid-   291 night? Shall I give him his answer?

PRINCE   Prithee, do, Jack.

FALSTAFF   Faith, and I'll send him packing.   *Exit.*

PRINCE   Now, sirs. By'r Lady, you fought fair; so did you, Peto; so did you, Bardolph. You are lions too, you ran away upon instinct, you will not touch the true prince; no, fie!

BARDOLPH   Faith, I ran when I saw others run.

PRINCE   Faith, tell me now in earnest, how came Falstaff's sword so hacked?

PETO   Why, he hacked it with his dagger, and said he would swear truth out of England but he would make 303 you believe it was done in fight, and persuaded us to do the like.

BARDOLPH   Yea, and to tickle our noses with spear grass to make them bleed, and then to beslubber our gar- 307 ments with it and swear it was the blood of true men. I did that I did not this seven year before: I blushed to 309 hear his monstrous devices.

PRINCE   Oh, villain, thou stolest a cup of sack eighteen years ago and wert taken with the manner, and ever 312 since thou hast blushed extempore. Thou hadst fire 313 and sword on thy side, and yet thou ran'st away. What instinct hadst thou for it?

BARDOLPH   My lord, do you see these meteors? Do you 316 behold these exhalations?   [Pointing to his own face.] 317

PRINCE   I do.

BARDOLPH   What think you they portend?   319

PRINCE   Hot livers and cold purses.   320

BARDOLPH   Choler, my lord, if rightly taken.   321

PRINCE   No, if rightly taken, halter.   322

Enter Falstaff.

Here comes lean Jack, here comes bare-bone.—How now, my sweet creature of bombast? How long is't 324 ago, Jack, since thou sawest thine own knee?

FALSTAFF   My own knee? When I was about thy years, Hal, I was not an eagle's talon in the waist; I could have crept into any alderman's thumb ring. A plague of sighing and grief! It blows a man up like a bladder. There's villainous news abroad. Here was Sir John Bracy from your father. You must to the court in the morning. That same mad fellow of the north, Percy, and he of Wales that gave Amamon the bastinado and 333 made Lucifer cuckold and swore the devil his true 334 liegeman upon the cross of a Welsh hook—what a 335 plague call you him?

POINS   Owen Glendower.

FALSTAFF   Owen, Owen, the same; and his son-in-law Mortimer, and old Northumberland, and that

sprightly Scot of Scots, Douglas, that runs a-horseback up a hill perpendicular—

PRINCE   He that rides at high speed, and with his pistol kills a sparrow flying.

FALSTAFF   You have hit it.   344

PRINCE   So did he never the sparrow.

FALSTAFF   Well, that rascal hath good mettle in him; he will not run.   347

PRINCE   Why, what a rascal art thou then to praise him so for running!

FALSTAFF   A-horseback, ye cuckoo; but afoot he will not budge a foot.

PRINCE   Yes, Jack, upon instinct.

FALSTAFF   I grant ye, upon instinct. Well, he is there too, and one Mordake, and a thousand blue-caps more. 354 Worcester is stolen away tonight. Thy father's beard is turned white with the news. You may buy land now as cheap as stinking mackerel.

PRINCE   Why, then, it is like, if there come a hot June 358 and this civil buffeting hold, we shall buy maiden- 359 heads as they buy hobnails, by the hundreds.

FALSTAFF   By the mass, lad, thou sayest true; it is like we shall have good trading that way. But tell me, Hal, art not thou horrible afeard? Thou being heir appar- ent, could the world pick thee out three such enemies again as that fiend Douglas, that spirit Percy, and that devil Glendower? Art thou not horribly afraid? Doth not thy blood thrill at it?

PRINCE   Not a whit, i'faith. I lack some of thy instinct.

FALSTAFF   Well, thou wilt be horribly chid tomorrow 369 when thou comest to thy father. If thou love me, practice an answer.

PRINCE   Do thou stand for my father, and examine me upon the particulars of my life.

FALSTAFF   Shall I? Content. This chair shall be my state, 374 this dagger my scepter, and this cushion my crown.
[Falstaff establishes himself on his "throne."]

PRINCE   Thy state is taken for a joint stool, thy golden 376 scepter for a leaden dagger, and thy precious rich 377 crown for a pitiful bald crown.

FALSTAFF   Well, an the fire of grace be not quite out of thee, now shalt thou be moved. Give me a cup of sack to make my eyes look red, that it may be thought I have wept; for I must speak in passion, and I will do it in King Cambyses' vein.   383

PRINCE   Well, here is my leg.   [He bows.]

FALSTAFF   And here is my speech. Stand aside, nobil- ity.

HOSTESS   Oh, Jesu, this is excellent sport, i'faith!

FALSTAFF
Weep not, sweet queen, for trickling tears are vain.

HOSTESS   Oh, the Father, how he holds his countenance! 389

---

303 swear . . . would swear oaths until they go out of fashion if he did not   307 beslubber smear, cover   309 that something   312 taken . . . manner caught with the goods   313 extempore without needing any occasion. (Bardolph is red-faced whether he blushes or not.) fire i.e., a red nose and complexion caused by heavy drinking 316, 317 meteors, exhalations i.e., the red blotches on Bardolph's face. 319 portend signify. (Meteors, comets, and other meteorological phe- nomena were widely regarded as omens of disaster.)   320 Hot . . . purses i.e., Livers inflamed by drink and purses made empty by spending.   321 Choler A choleric or combative temperament.   taken understood. (But the Prince, in his next speech, uses the word to mean "arrested.")   322 halter hangman's noose. (The Prince plays on Bardolph's choler, which he takes as collar.)   322.1 (Falstaff's entry in the Quarto after line 321 suggests he is visible to the audience while the Prince talks of a hangman's halter.)   324 bombast (1) cotton padding (2) fustian speech.   333 Amamon (The name of a demon.) bastinado beating on the soles of the feet   334 made . . . cuckold i.e., gave Lucifer his horns, the sign of cuckoldry   334–5 and swore . . . liegeman and made the devil take an oath of allegiance as a true sub- ject   335 Welsh hook curved-bladed pike lacking the cross shape of the sword on which such oaths were usually sworn

344 hit it described it exactly. (But the Prince takes hit literally in the next line.)   347 run flee. (But the Prince answers punningly in the sense of "ride at high speed.")   354 blue-caps Scottish soldiers 358 like likely   359 hold continues   369 chid chided   374 state chair of state, throne   376 joint stool a stool made by a joiner or furniture maker   377 leaden of soft metal, hence inferior   383 in . . . vein i.e., in the ranting and (by Shakespeare's time) old-fashioned style of Thomas Preston's Cambyses, an early Elizabethan tragedy.   389 the Father i.e., in God's name.   holds his countenance keeps a straight face.

FALSTAFF

For God's sake, lords, convey my tristful queen, 390
For tears do stop the floodgates of her eyes. 391

HOSTESS Oh, Jesu, he doth it as like one of these harlotry 392
players as ever I see! 393

FALSTAFF

Peace, good pint pot; peace, good tickle-brain.— 394
Harry, I do not only marvel where thou spendest thy
time, but also how thou art accompanied; for though 396
the camomile, the more it is trodden on the faster it 397
grows, yet youth, the more it is wasted the sooner it 398
wears. That thou art my son I have partly thy mother's 399
word, partly my own opinion, but chiefly a villainous
trick of thine eye and a foolish hanging of thy nether 401
lip that doth warrant me. If then thou be son to me, 402
here lies the point: why, being son to me, art thou so
pointed at? Shall the blessed sun of heaven prove a
micher and eat blackberries? A question not to be 405
asked. Shall the son of England prove a thief and take
purses? A question to be asked. There is a thing, Harry,
which thou hast often heard of, and it is known
to many in our land by the name of pitch. This pitch, 409
as ancient writers do report, doth defile; so doth the 410
company thou keepest. For, Harry, now I do not speak
to thee in drink but in tears, not in pleasure but in
passion, not in words only but in woes also. And yet 413
there is a virtuous man whom I have often noted in
thy company, but I know not his name.

PRINCE What manner of man, an it like Your Majesty? 416

FALSTAFF A goodly portly man, i'faith, and a corpulent; 417
of a cheerful look, a pleasing eye, and a most noble
carriage; and, as I think, his age some fifty, or, by'r
Lady, inclining to threescore; and now I remember me,
his name is Falstaff. If that man should be lewdly 421
given, he deceiveth me; for, Harry, I see virtue in his
looks. If then the tree may be known by the fruit, as the 423
fruit by the tree, then peremptorily I speak it, there is 424
virtue in that Falstaff. Him keep with, the rest banish.
And tell me now, thou naughty varlet, tell me, where
hast thou been this month?

PRINCE Dost thou speak like a king? Do thou stand for
me, and I'll play my father.

FALSTAFF Depose me? If thou dost it half so gravely, so
majestically, both in word and matter, hang me up by
the heels for a rabbit-sucker or a poulter's hare. 432

[Hal takes Falstaff's place on the "throne."]

PRINCE Well, here I am set. 433

FALSTAFF And here I stand. Judge, my masters.

PRINCE Now, Harry, whence come you?

FALSTAFF My noble lord, from Eastcheap.

PRINCE The complaints I hear of thee are grievous.

FALSTAFF 'Sblood, my lord, they are false.—Nay, I'll 438
tickle ye for a young prince, i'faith. 439

PRINCE Swearest thou, ungracious boy? Henceforth
ne'er look on me. Thou art violently carried away from
grace. There is a devil haunts thee in the likeness of an
old fat man; a tun of man is thy companion. Why dost 443
thou converse with that trunk of humors, that bolting- 444
hutch of beastliness, that swollen parcel of dropsies, 445
that huge bombard of sack, that stuffed cloak-bag of 446
guts, that roasted Manningtree ox with the pudding in 447
his belly, that reverend Vice, that gray Iniquity, that 448
father ruffian, that vanity in years? Wherein is he good 449
but to taste sack and drink it? Wherein neat and
cleanly but to carve a capon and eat it? Wherein 451
cunning but in craft? Wherein crafty but in villainy? 452
Wherein villainous but in all things? Wherein worthy
but in nothing?

FALSTAFF I would Your Grace would take me with 455
you. Whom means Your Grace? 456

PRINCE That villainous abominable misleader of youth,
Falstaff, that old white-bearded Satan.

FALSTAFF My lord, the man I know.

PRINCE I know thee dost.

FALSTAFF But to say I know more harm in him than in
myself were to say more than I know. That he is old,
the more the pity, his white hairs do witness it; but
that he is, saving your reverence, a whoremaster, that 464
I utterly deny. If sack and sugar be a fault, God help
the wicked! If to be old and merry be a sin, then many
an old host that I know is damned. If to be fat be to be 467
hated, then Pharaoh's lean kine are to be loved. No, 468
my good lord, banish Peto, banish Bardolph, banish
Poins; but for sweet Jack Falstaff, kind Jack Falstaff,
true Jack Falstaff, valiant Jack Falstaff, and therefore
more valiant being as he is old Jack Falstaff, banish not
him thy Harry's company, banish not him thy Harry's
company—banish plump Jack, and banish all the
world.

---

390 convey escort away. **tristful** sorrowing **391 stop** fill **392 har-lotry** scurvy, vagabond **393 players** actors **394 tickle-brain** (A slang term for strong liquor, here applied as a nickname for the tavern host-ess.) **396–9 for though . . . wears** (Falstaff parodies the style of John Lyly's *Euphues*, with its elaborate balanced antitheses, alliterative effects, and illustrations drawn from fanciful natural history. *Camomile* is an aromatic creeping herb whose flowers and leaves are used med-icinally.) **401 trick** trait **402 warrant** assure **405 micher** truant **409–10 This . . . defile** (An allusion to the familiar proverb from Ecclesiasticus 13:1 about the defilement of touching pitch.) **pitch** a sticky, black residue from the distillation of tar, used to seal wood from moisture **413 passion** sorrow **416 an it like** if it please **417 portly** (1) stately (2) corpulent **421 lewdly** wickedly **423 If . . . by the fruit** (See Matthew 12:33.) **424 peremptorily** decisively **432 rabbit-sucker** unweaned rabbit. **poulter's** poulterer's

433 set seated. **438 'Sblood** i.e., By Christ's blood **439 tickle ye for** amuse you in the role of **443 tun** (1) large barrel (2) ton **444 con-verse** associate. **humors** body fluids, diseases **444–5 bolting-hutch** large bin **445 dropsies** accumulations of fluids causing swelling **446 bombard** leathern drinking vessel. **cloak-bag** portmanteau **447 Manningtree ox** (Manningtree, a town in Essex, had noted fairs where, no doubt, oxen were roasted whole.) **pudding** sausage-like entrails **448 Vice, Iniquity** (Allegorical names for the chief comic character and tempter in morality plays.) **449 vanity** person given to worldly desires **451 cleanly** (1) pure (2) deft. **a capon** a castrated rooster for the table **452 cunning** (1) skillful (2) crafty **455–6 take me with you** let me catch up with your meaning. **464 saving your reverence** i.e., with my apology for using offensive language **467 host** innkeeper **468 Pharaoh's lean kine** (See Genesis 41, where Pharaoh's dream of seven well-fattened cattle being devoured by seven lean ones is interpreted by Joseph as a prophecy of seven years' famine to come.)

PRINCE   I do, I will.   [*A knocking.*
                            Exeunt Hostess, Francis, and Bardolph.]

        Enter Bardolph, running.

BARDOLPH   Oh, my lord, my lord! The sheriff with a
    most monstrous watch is at the door.   478
FALSTAFF   Out, ye rogue! Play out the play. I have
    much to say in the behalf of that Falstaff.

        Enter the Hostess.

HOSTESS   Oh, Jesu, my lord, my lord!
PRINCE   Heigh, heigh! The devil rides upon a fiddle-   482
    stick. What's the matter?   483
HOSTESS   The sheriff and all the watch are at the door.
    They are come to search the house. Shall I let them in?
FALSTAFF   Dost thou hear, Hal? Never call a true piece   486
    of gold a counterfeit. Thou art essentially made   487
    without seeming so.   488
PRINCE   And thou a natural coward without instinct.
FALSTAFF   I deny your major. If you will deny the   490
    sheriff, so; if not, let him enter. If I become not a cart 491
    as well as another man, a plague on my bringing up!   492
    I hope I shall as soon be strangled with a halter as
    another.
PRINCE   Go hide thee behind the arras. The rest walk   495
    up above. Now, my masters, for a true face and good   496
    conscience.
FALSTAFF   Both which I have had, but their date is out,   498
    and therefore I'll hide me.   [*He hides behind the arras.*]
PRINCE   Call in the sheriff.
                            [*Exeunt all except the Prince and Peto.*]

        Enter Sheriff and the Carrier.

    Now, Master Sheriff, what is your will with me?
SHERIFF
    First, pardon me, my lord. A hue and cry   502
    Hath followed certain men unto this house.
PRINCE   What men?
SHERIFF
    One of them is well known, my gracious lord,
    A gross, fat man.
CARRIER   As fat as butter.
PRINCE
    The man, I do assure you, is not here,
    For I myself at this time have employed him.
    And, Sheriff, I will engage my word to thee   509
    That I will, by tomorrow dinnertime,   510
    Send him to answer thee, or any man,

    For anything he shall be charged withal;
    And so let me entreat you leave the house.
SHERIFF
    I will, my lord. There are two gentlemen
    Have in this robbery lost three hundred marks.
PRINCE
    It may be so. If he have robbed these men,
    He shall be answerable; and so farewell.
SHERIFF   Good night, my noble lord.
PRINCE
    I think it is good morrow, is it not?   519
SHERIFF
    Indeed, my lord, I think it be two o'clock.
                                Exit [*with Carrier*].
PRINCE   This oily rascal is known as well as Paul's. Go   521
    call him forth.
PETO   [*discovering Falstaff*]   Falstaff—Fast asleep behind
    the arras, and snorting like a horse.
PRINCE   Hark, how hard he fetches breath. Search his
    pockets. (*He searcheth his pockets, and findeth certain
    papers.*) What hast thou found?
PETO   Nothing but papers, my lord.
PRINCE   Let's see what they be. Read them.
PETO   [*reads*]
        Item, A capon,.....................................2s. 2d.
        Item, Sauce, ...4d.
        Item, Sack, two gallons, ...5s. 8d.
        Item, Anchovies and sack after
            supper,...2s. 6d.
        Item, Bread, ...ob. 534
PRINCE   Oh, monstrous! But one halfpennyworth of
    bread to this intolerable deal of sack? What there is
    else, keep close; we'll read it at more advantage. There 537
    let him sleep till day. I'll to the court in the morning.
    We must all to the wars, and thy place shall be
    honorable. I'll procure this fat rogue a charge of foot, 540
    and I know his death will be a march of twelve score.   541
    The money shall be paid back again with advantage.   542
    Be with me betimes in the morning; and so, good   543
    morrow, Peto.
PETO   Good morrow, good my lord.   545
                        Exeunt [*separately. Falstaff is concealed
                            once more behind the arras.*]

[3.1]

        *Enter Hotspur, Worcester, Lord Mortimer,
        [and] Owen Glendower.*

478 watch posse of constables   **482–3 The . . . fiddlestick** i.e., Here's
much ado about nothing.   **486–8 Dost . . . seeming so** (In this difficult passage, Falstaff seems to suggest that he is true gold, not counterfeit, and so should not be betrayed to the watch by the Prince,
who, he hopes, is not merely playacting at the tavern but is truly one
of its madcap members.)   **490 deny your major** reject your major
premise.   **deny** refuse entrance to   **491 become** befit, adorn.   **cart**
i.e., hangman's cart   **492 bringing up** (1) upbringing (2) being
brought before the authorities to be hanged.   **495 arras** wall hanging
or tapestry.   **496 up above** upstairs.   **498 date is out** lease has run
out   **502 hue and cry** outcry calling for the pursuit of a felon
509 engage pledge   **510 dinnertime** i.e., about noon

519 morrow morning.   **521 Paul's** Saint Paul's Cathedral.   **534 ob.**
obolus, i.e., halfpenny.   **537 close** hidden.   **advantage** favorable
opportunity.   **540 charge of foot** command of a company of infantry
541 twelve score i.e., two hundred and forty yards.   **542 advantage**
interest.   **543 betimes** early   **545.1–2** *Exeunt . . . arras* (On stage, the
arras is evidently arranged so that Falstaff can exit behind it once the
scene is over.)
3.1 Location: Wales. Glendower's residence. (Holinshed places a
meeting of the rebel deputies at Bangor in the Archdeacon's house,
but in this present "unhistorical" scene, as invented by Shakespeare, Glendower is host throughout.) Seats are provided on stage.

MORTIMER
  These promises are fair, the parties sure,
  And our induction full of prosperous hope.   2
HOTSPUR
  Lord Mortimer, and cousin Glendower,
  Will you sit down? And uncle Worcester—
  A plague upon it, I have forgot the map.
GLENDOWER [*producing a map*]
  No, here it is. Sit, cousin Percy,
  Sit, good cousin Hotspur—for by that name
  As oft as Lancaster doth speak of you   8
  His cheek looks pale, and with a rising sigh
  He wisheth you in heaven.
HOTSPUR   And you in hell,
  As oft as he hears Owen Glendower spoke of.
GLENDOWER
  I cannot blame him. At my nativity
  The front of heaven was full of fiery shapes,   13
  Of burning cressets, and at my birth   14
  The frame and huge foundation of the earth
  Shaked like a coward.
HOTSPUR   Why, so it would have done
  At the same season, if your mother's cat
  Had but kittened, though yourself had never been
      born.
GLENDOWER
  I say the earth did shake when I was born.
HOTSPUR
  And I say the earth was not of my mind,
  If you suppose as fearing you it shook.
GLENDOWER
  The heavens were all on fire; the earth did tremble.
HOTSPUR
  Oh, then the earth shook to see the heavens on fire,
  And not in fear of your nativity.
  Diseasèd nature oftentimes breaks forth
  In strange eruptions; oft the teeming earth
  Is with a kind of colic pinched and vexed
  By the imprisoning of unruly wind
  Within her womb, which, for enlargement striving, 29
  Shakes the old beldam earth and topples down   30
  Steeples and moss-grown towers. At your birth
  Our grandam earth, having this distemp'rature,   32
  In passion shook.
GLENDOWER   Cousin, of many men   33
  I do not bear these crossings. Give me leave   34
  To tell you once again that at my birth
  The front of heaven was full of fiery shapes,
  The goats ran from the mountains, and the herds
  Were strangely clamorous to the frighted fields.
  These signs have marked me extraordinary,
  And all the courses of my life do show
  I am not in the roll of common men.

Where is he living, clipped in with the sea   42
  That chides the banks of England, Scotland, Wales, 43
  Which calls me pupil or hath read to me?   44
  And bring him out that is but woman's son   45
  Can trace me in the tedious ways of art   46
  And hold me pace in deep experiments.   47
HOTSPUR
  I think there's no man speaks better Welsh.   48
  I'll to dinner.
MORTIMER
  Peace, cousin Percy; you will make him mad.
GLENDOWER
  I can call spirits from the vasty deep.   51
HOTSPUR
  Why, so can I, or so can any man;
  But will they come when you do call for them?
GLENDOWER
  Why, I can teach you, cousin, to command the devil.
HOTSPUR
  And I can teach thee, coz, to shame the devil
  By telling truth. Tell truth and shame the devil.
  If thou have power to raise him, bring him hither,
  And I'll be sworn I have power to shame him hence.
  Oh, while you live, tell truth and shame the devil!
MORTIMER
  Come, come, no more of this unprofitable chat.
GLENDOWER
  Three times hath Henry Bolingbroke made head   61
  Against my power; thrice from the banks of Wye   62
  And sandy-bottomed Severn have I sent him
  Bootless home and weather-beaten back.   64
HOTSPUR
  Home without boots, and in foul weather too!
  How scapes he agues, in the devil's name?   66
GLENDOWER
  Come, here is the map. Shall we divide our right
  According to our threefold order ta'en?   68
MORTIMER
  The Archdeacon hath divided it   69
  Into three limits very equally: 70
  England, from Trent and Severn hitherto,   71
  By south and east is to my part assigned;
  All westward, Wales beyond the Severn shore,
  And all the fertile land within that bound,
  To Owen Glendower; and, dear coz, to you   75
  The remnant northward, lying off from Trent.

---

2 induction beginning. **prosperous hope** hope of prospering.
8 Lancaster i.e., King Henry, here demoted to Duke of Lancaster
13 front brow, face. (As also at line 36.) **14 cressets** lights burning in
metal baskets suspended from the ends of long poles or ceilings;
hence, meteors **29 enlargement** release **30 beldam** grandmother
32 distemp'rature disorder **33 passion** suffering. **of** from
34 crossings contradictions.

42–4 Where . . . to me? i.e., Where is there anyone in all of sea-walled
Great Britain who can claim to have been my instructor? **45–7 And . . .
experiments** And I challenge you to produce a single human being
who can follow my tracks in the arcane craft of magic or keep up with
me in occult experiments. **48 speaks better Welsh** (Hotspur hides
an insult behind the literal meaning, since "to speak Welsh" meant
colloquially both "to boast" and "to speak nonsense.") **51 call** summon. (But Hotspur sardonically replies in the sense of "call out to,"
whether or not there is any response.) **vasty deep** lower world.
61 made head raised a force **62 power** army **64 Bootless** without
advantage. (But Hotspur quibbles on the sense of "barefoot.")
66 agues fevers **68 order ta'en** arrangements made. **69 Archdeacon** i.e., the Archdeacon of Bangor, in whose house, according to
Holinshed, a meeting took place between deputies of the rebel leaders **70 limits** regions **71 hitherto** to this point **75 coz** cousin, i.e.,
brother-in-law

And our indentures tripartite are drawn,   77
Which being sealèd interchangeably—
A business that this night may execute—   79
Tomorrow, cousin Percy, you and I
And my good lord of Worcester will set forth
To meet your father and the Scottish power,
As is appointed us, at Shrewsbury.
My father Glendower is not ready yet,   84
Nor shall we need his help these fourteen days.
[*To Glendower*] Within that space you may have drawn
     together   86
Your tenants, friends, and neighboring gentlemen.

GLENDOWER
A shorter time shall send me to you, lords;
And in my conduct shall your ladies come,   89
From whom you now must steal and take no leave,
For there will be a world of water shed
Upon the parting of your wives and you.

HOTSPUR [*consulting the map*]
Methinks my moiety, north from Burton here,   93
In quantity equals not one of yours.
See how this river comes me cranking in   95
And cuts me from the best of all my land
A huge half-moon, a monstrous cantle, out.   97
I'll have the current in this place dammed up,
And here the smug and silver Trent shall run   99
In a new channel, fair and evenly.
It shall not wind with such a deep indent
To rob me of so rich a bottom here.   102

GLENDOWER
Not wind? It shall, it must. You see it doth.

MORTIMER
Yea, but mark how he bears his course and runs me up 104
With like advantage on the other side,
Gelding the opposèd continent as much   106
As on the other side it takes from you.

WORCESTER
Yea, but a little charge will trench him here   108
And on this north side win this cape of land;
And then he runs straight and even.

HOTSPUR
I'll have it so. A little charge will do it.

GLENDOWER   I'll not have it altered.

HOTSPUR   Will not you?

GLENDOWER   No, nor you shall not.

HOTSPUR   Who shall say me nay?

GLENDOWER   Why, that will I.

HOTSPUR
Let me not understand you, then; speak it in Welsh.

GLENDOWER
I can speak English, lord, as well as you;
For I was trained up in the English court,
Where, being but young, I framèd to the harp   120
Many an English ditty lovely well,
And gave the tongue a helpful ornament—   122
A virtue that was never seen in you.

HOTSPUR
Marry, and I am glad of it with all my heart!
I had rather be a kitten and cry "mew"
Than one of these same meter balladmongers.
I had rather hear a brazen can'stick turned   127
Or a dry wheel grate on the axletree,   128
And that would set my teeth nothing on edge,   129
Nothing so much as mincing poetry.
'Tis like the forced gait of a shuffling nag.   131

GLENDOWER   Come, you shall have Trent turned.

HOTSPUR
I do not care. I'll give thrice so much land
To any well-deserving friend;
But in the way of bargain, mark ye me,
I'll cavil on the ninth part of a hair.   136
Are the indentures drawn? Shall we be gone?   137

GLENDOWER
The moon shines fair; you may away by night.
I'll haste the writer and withal   139
Break with your wives of your departure hence.   140
I am afraid my daughter will run mad,
So much she doteth on her Mortimer.   *Exit.*

MORTIMER
Fie, cousin Percy, how you cross my father!

HOTSPUR
I cannot choose. Sometimes he angers me
With telling me of the moldwarp and the ant,   145
Of the dreamer Merlin and his prophecies,   146
And of a dragon and a finless fish,
A clip-winged griffin and a moulten raven,   148
A couching lion and a ramping cat,   149
And such a deal of skimble-skamble stuff   150
As puts me from my faith. I tell you what: 151
He held me last night at least nine hours
In reckoning up the several devils' names   153

---

77 tripartite i.e., drawn up in triplicate, each document *sealèd interchangeably* (line 78) with the seal of all signatories.   **drawn** drawn up   **79 this night may execute** may be carried out tonight   **84 father** father-in-law   **86 may** will be able to   **89 conduct** escort   **93 moiety** share   **95 comes me cranking in** comes bending in on my share. (The Trent, by turning northward to the North Sea instead of continuing eastward into the Wash, cuts Hotspur off from rich land in Lincolnshire and its vicinity.)   **97 cantle** piece   **99 smug** smooth   **102 bottom** valley   **104 runs me** runs. (*Me* is used colloquially.)   **106 Gelding . . . continent** cutting off from the land which it bounds on the opposite side. (The Trent's southerly loop from Stoke to Burton deprives Mortimer of a piece of land, just as its later northerly course deprives Hotspur.)   **108 charge** expenditure.   **trench** provide a new channel

120 framèd to the harp set to harp accompaniment   **122 gave . . . ornament** i.e., added to the words a pleasing ornament of music; also, gave to the English tongue the ornament of music and poetry   **127 can'stick turned** candlestick turned on a lathe   **128 axletree** axle   **129 nothing** not at all   **131 shuffling** hobbled   **136 cavil . . . hair** i.e., argue about the most trivial detail.   **137 drawn** drawn up.   **139 writer** i.e., scrivener who would be drawing the indentures.   **withal** also   **140 Break with** inform   **145 moldwarp** mole. (Holinshed tells us that the division was arranged because of a prophecy that represented King Henry as the mole and the others as the dragon, the lion, and the wolf, who should divide the land among them.)   **146 Merlin** the bard, prophet, and magician of Arthurian story, Welsh in origin   **148 griffin** a fabulous beast, half lion, half eagle.   **moulten** having molted   **149 couching** couchant, crouching. (Heraldic term.)   **ramping** rampant, advancing on its hind legs. (Hotspur is ridiculing the heraldic emblems that Glendower holds so dear.)   **150 skimble-skamble** foolish, nonsensical   **151 puts . . . faith** drives me from my (Christian) faith.   **153 several** various

That were his lackeys. I cried "Hum," and "Well, go to," 154
But marked him not a word. Oh, he is as tedious
As a tirèd horse, a railing wife,
Worse than a smoky house. I had rather live
With cheese and garlic in a windmill, far,
Than feed on cates and have him talk to me   159
In any summer house in Christendom.

MORTIMER
In faith, he is a worthy gentleman,
Exceedingly well read, and profited   162
In strange concealments, valiant as a lion   163
And wondrous affable, and as bountiful
As mines of India. Shall I tell you, cousin?
He holds your temper in a high respect   166
And curbs himself even of his natural scope   167
When you come 'cross his humor. Faith, he does.   168
I warrant you that man is not alive
Might so have tempted him as you have done   170
Without the taste of danger and reproof.
But do not use it oft, let me entreat you.

WORCESTER [to Hotspur]
In faith, my lord, you are too willful-blame,   173
And since your coming hither have done enough
To put him quite besides his patience.   175
You must needs learn, lord, to amend this fault.
Though sometimes it show greatness, courage,
    blood—   177
And that's the dearest grace it renders you—   178
Yet oftentimes it doth present harsh rage,   179
Defect of manners, want of government,   180
Pride, haughtiness, opinion, and disdain,   181
The least of which haunting a nobleman
Loseth men's hearts and leaves behind a stain
Upon the beauty of all parts besides,   184
Beguiling them of commendation.   185

HOTSPUR
Well, I am schooled. Good manners be your speed!   186
Here come our wives, and let us take our leave.

    Enter Glendower with the ladies.

MORTIMER
This is the deadly spite that angers me: 188
My wife can speak no English, I no Welsh.

GLENDOWER
My daughter weeps she'll not part with you;
She'll be a soldier too, she'll to the wars.

MORTIMER
Good father, tell her that she and my aunt Percy   192

Shall follow in your conduct speedily.   193
    *Glendower speaks to her in Welsh, and she answers
                                him in the same.*

GLENDOWER
She is desperate here; a peevish self-willed harlotry, 194
One that no persuasion can do good upon.
                    The lady speaks in Welsh.

MORTIMER [to her]
I understand thy looks. That pretty Welsh   196
Which thou pourest down from these swelling heavens 197
I am too perfect in; and, but for shame,   198
In such a parley should I answer thee.   199
                    The lady again in Welsh.
I understand thy kisses and thou mine,
And that's a feeling disputation.   201
But I will never be a truant, love,
Till I have learned thy language; for thy tongue
Makes Welsh as sweet as ditties highly penned,   204
Sung by a fair queen in a summer's bower,
With ravishing division, to her lute.   206

GLENDOWER
Nay, if you melt, then will she run mad.   207
                The lady speaks again in Welsh.

MORTIMER
Oh, I am ignorance itself in this!

GLENDOWER
She bids you on the wanton rushes lay you down   209
And rest your gentle head upon her lap,
And she will sing the song that pleaseth you
And on your eyelids crown the god of sleep,   212
Charming your blood with pleasing heaviness,   213
Making such difference twixt wake and sleep   214
As is the difference betwixt day and night
The hour before the heavenly-harnessed team   216
Begins his golden progress in the east.

MORTIMER
With all my heart I'll sit and hear her sing.
By that time will our book, I think, be drawn.   219

GLENDOWER   Do so;
And those musicians that shall play to you
Hang in the air a thousand leagues from hence,
And straight they shall be here. Sit, and attend.
                *[Mortimer reclines with his head
                            in his wife's lap.]*

HOTSPUR   Come, Kate, thou art perfect in lying down;
    come, quick, quick, that I may lay my head in thy lap.

LADY PERCY   Go, ye giddy goose.
                    *[Hotspur lies with his head
                    in Kate's lap.] The music plays.*

---

154 **go to** i.e., you don't say   159 **cates** delicacies   162 **profited** proficient   163 **concealments** occult practices   166 **temper** temperament   167 **scope** freedom of speech   168 **come 'cross** contradict   170 **Might** who could   173 **too willful-blame** blameworthy for too much self-will   175 **besides** out of   177 **blood** spirit   178 **dearest grace** best (and costliest) credit   179 **present** represent   180 **want of government** lack of self-control   181 **opinion** vanity, arrogance   184 **all parts besides** all other abilities   185 **Beguiling** depriving   186 **Good . . . speed!** i.e., May these good manners you praise so bring you success! (Said wryly; Hotspur doubts that good manners count for much in a time of war.)   188 **spite** vexation   192 **aunt** (Percy's wife, here called Kate, was aunt of Edmund Mortimer, the fifth Earl of March, but was sister-in-law to the Sir Edward Mortimer who married Glendower's daughter.)

193 **conduct** safe-conduct, escort   194 **desperate here** adamant on this point (i.e., her decision to accompany Mortimer).   **peevish self-willed harlotry** childish, willful, silly wench   196 **That pretty Welsh** i.e., Your eloquent tears   197 **heavens** i.e., eyes   198 **perfect** proficient   199 **such a parley** i.e., the same language (of weeping)   201 **disputation** conversation, debate.   204 **highly penned** eloquently composed, in high style   206 **division** variation, passage in which rapid short notes vary a theme   207 **melt** i.e., weep   209 **wanton rushes** i.e., soft floor covering   212 **crown . . . sleep** make sleep supreme ruler   213 **heaviness** drowsiness   214 **difference** nearly indistinguishable difference   216 **the heavenly-harnessed team** i.e., the team of horses drawing the chariot of the sun   219 **book** document, indentures

HOTSPUR
Now I perceive the devil understands Welsh;
And 'tis no marvel he is so humorous.   228
By'r Lady, he is a good musician.
LADY PERCY   Then should you be nothing but musical,
for you are altogether governed by humors. Lie still,
ye thief, and hear the lady sing in Welsh.   232
HOTSPUR   I had rather hear Lady, my brach, howl in   233
Irish.
LADY PERCY   Wouldst thou have thy head broken?   235
HOTSPUR   No.
LADY PERCY   Then be still.
HOTSPUR   Neither, 'tis a woman's fault.   238
LADY PERCY   Now God help thee!   239
HOTSPUR   To the Welsh lady's bed.
LADY PERCY   What's that?
HOTSPUR   Peace, she sings.
                    Here the lady sings a Welsh song.
HOTSPUR
Come, Kate, I'll have your song too.
LADY PERCY
Not mine, in good sooth.
HOTSPUR   Not yours, in good sooth! Heart, you swear   245
like a comfit maker's wife. "Not you, in good sooth,"   246
and "as true as I live," and "as God shall mend me,"
and "as sure as day,"
And givest such sarcenet surety for thy oaths   249
As if thou never walk'st further than Finsbury.   250
Swear me, Kate, like a lady as thou art,
A good mouth-filling oath, and leave "in sooth,"
And such protest of pepper-gingerbread,   253
To velvet-guards and Sunday citizens.   254
Come, sing.
LADY PERCY   I will not sing.
HOTSPUR   'Tis the next way to turn tailor, or be redbreast 257
teacher. An the indentures be drawn, I'll away within 258
these two hours; and so, come in when ye will.   *Exit.*
GLENDOWER
Come, come, Lord Mortimer. You are as slow
As hot Lord Percy is on fire to go.
By this our book is drawn; we'll but seal,   262
And then to horse immediately.
MORTIMER   With all my heart.   *Exeunt.*

228 **humorous** whimsical, capricious.   232 **thief** i.e., rascal
233 **brach** bitch hound   235 **broken** i.e., struck so as to break the
skin.   238 **Neither . . . fault** i.e., I won't do that either; it's womanish
to be submissive.   239 **help** amend. (But Hotspur answers in the
sense of "assist with an amour.")   245 **Heart** i.e., By Christ's heart
246 **comfit maker's** confectioner's   249 **sarcenet** soft, flimsy. (From
the soft silken material known as *sarcenet*.)   250 **Finsbury** a field just
outside London frequented by the London citizenry. (Hotspur jokes
with Kate as though she were a citizen's wife, using the pious and
modest oaths of such people.)   253 **protest . . . gingerbread** i.e.,
mealy-mouthed protestations   254 **velvet-guards** i.e., wives who
wear velvet trimming   257–8 **'Tis . . . teacher** i.e., The only use one
might put singing to is to become a tailor (since tailors were noted for
effeminacy and singing at their work) or an instructor to caged song-
birds before they are sold. (Hotspur airily dismisses singing, as he
does poetry.)   262 **By this** By this time.   **but** just

[3.2]

Enter the King, Prince of Wales, and others.

KING
Lords, give us leave. The Prince of Wales and I
Must have some private conference; but be near at
    hand,
For we shall presently have need of you.
                                                    Exeunt Lords.
I know not whether God will have it so
For some displeasing service I have done,
That in his secret doom out of my blood   6
He'll breed revengement and a scourge for me;
But thou dost in thy passages of life   8
Make me believe that thou art only marked   9
For the hot vengeance and the rod of heaven   10
To punish my mistreadings. Tell me else,   11
Could such inordinate and low desires,   12
Such poor, such bare, such lewd, such mean attempts, 13
Such barren pleasures, rude society,
As thou art matched withal and grafted to,   15
Accompany the greatness of thy blood
And hold their level with thy princely heart?   17
PRINCE
So please Your Majesty, I would I could
Quit all offenses with as clear excuse   19
As well as I am doubtless I can purge   20
Myself of many I am charged withal.
Yet such extenuation let me beg
As, in reproof of many tales devised,   23
Which oft the ear of greatness needs must hear
By smiling pickthanks and base newsmongers,   25
I may, for some things true, wherein my youth
Hath faulty wandered and irregular,
Find pardon on my true submission.
KING
God pardon thee! Yet let me wonder, Harry,
At thy affections, which do hold a wing   30
Quite from the flight of all thy ancestors.   31
Thy place in Council thou hast rudely lost,   32
Which by thy younger brother is supplied,
And art almost an alien to the hearts
Of all the court and princes of my blood.
The hope and expectation of thy time   36
Is ruined, and the soul of every man
Prophetically do forethink thy fall.

3.2 **Location:** The royal court (historically, Westminster).
6 **doom** judgment.   **blood** offspring   8 **passages** course, conduct
9–11 **thou . . . mistreadings** (1) you are marked as the means of heaven's
vengeance against me, or (2) you are marked to suffer heaven's
vengeance because of my sins.   11 **else** how otherwise   12 **inordinate** (1) immoderate (2) unworthy of your rank   13 **lewd** low, base.
attempts undertakings   15 **withal** with   17 **hold their level** claim
equality   19 **Quit** acquit myself of   20 **doubtless** certain   23 **in
reproof** upon disproof   25 **By . . . newsmongers** from smiling flatterers and ignoble talebearers   30 **affections** inclinations.   **hold a wing**
fly a course   31 **from** at variance with   32 **rudely** by violence.
(According to an apocryphal story, Prince Hal boxed the ears of the
Lord Chief Justice and was sent to prison for it; see *2 Henry IV*,
1.2.54–5, 192, and 5.2.70–1.)   36 **The hope . . . time** The hopes that
people had for you

Had I so lavish of my presence been,
So common-hackneyed in the eyes of men,   40
So stale and cheap to vulgar company,
Opinion, that did help me to the crown,   42
Had still kept loyal to possession   43
And left me in reputeless banishment,
A fellow of no mark nor likelihood.   45
By being seldom seen, I could not stir
But like a comet I was wondered at,
That men would tell their children, "This is he!"
Others would say, "Where, which is Bolingbroke?"
And then I stole all courtesy from heaven,   50
And dressed myself in such humility
That I did pluck allegiance from men's hearts,
Loud shouts and salutations from their mouths,
Even in the presence of the crownèd King.
Thus did I keep my person fresh and new,
My presence, like a robe pontifical,   56
Ne'er seen but wondered at; and so my state,   57
Seldom but sumptuous, showed like a feast   58
And won by rareness such solemnity.   59
The skipping King, he ambled up and down
With shallow jesters and rash bavin wits,   61
Soon kindled and soon burnt; carded his state,   62
Mingled his royalty with cap'ring fools,
Had his great name profanèd with their scorns,   64
And gave his countenance, against his name,   65
To laugh at gibing boys and stand the push   66
Of every beardless vain comparative;   67
Grew a companion to the common streets,
Enfeoffed himself to popularity,   69
That, being daily swallowed by men's eyes,
They surfeited with honey and began
To loathe the taste of sweetness, whereof a little
More than a little is by much too much.
So when he had occasion to be seen,
He was but as the cuckoo is in June,
Heard, not regarded—seen, but with such eyes
As, sick and blunted with community,   77
Afford no extraordinary gaze,
Such as is bent on sunlike majesty
When it shines seldom in admiring eyes;
But rather drowsed and hung their eyelids down,
Slept in his face, and rendered such aspect   82
As cloudy men use to their adversaries,   83

Being with his presence glutted, gorged, and full.
And in that very line, Harry, standest thou;   85
For thou hast lost thy princely privilege
With vile participation. Not an eye   87
But is aweary of thy common sight,
Save mine, which hath desired to see thee more—
Which now doth that I would not have it do,   90
Make blind itself with foolish tenderness.   91

PRINCE
I shall hereafter, my thrice gracious lord,
Be more myself.
KING   For all the world   93
As thou art to this hour was Richard then
When I from France set foot at Ravenspurgh,
And even as I was then is Percy now.
Now, by my scepter, and my soul to boot,   97
He hath more worthy interest to the state   98
Than thou the shadow of succession.   99
For of no right, nor color like to right,   100
He doth fill fields with harness in the realm,   101
Turns head against the lion's armèd jaws,   102
And, being no more in debt to years than thou,   103
Leads ancient lords and reverend bishops on
To bloody battles and to bruising arms.
What never-dying honor hath he got
Against renownèd Douglas! Whose high deeds,   107
Whose hot incursions and great name in arms
Holds from all soldiers chief majority   109
And military title capital   110
Through all the kingdoms that acknowledge Christ.
Thrice hath this Hotspur, Mars in swaddling clothes,
This infant warrior, in his enterprises
Discomfited great Douglas, ta'en him once,   114
Enlargèd him and made a friend of him,   115
To fill the mouth of deep defiance up   116
And shake the peace and safety of our throne.
And what say you to this? Percy, Northumberland,
The Archbishop's Grace of York, Douglas, Mortimer,   119
Capitulate against us and are up.   120
But wherefore do I tell these news to thee?
Why, Harry, do I tell thee of my foes,
Which art my nearest and dearest enemy?   123
Thou that art like enough, through vassal fear,   124
Base inclination, and the start of spleen,   125
To fight against me under Percy's pay,

---

40 common-hackneyed cheapened, vulgarized   **42 Opinion** public opinion   **43 to possession** i.e., to Richard II's sovereignty   **45 mark nor likelihood** importance or likeliness to succeed.   **50 I . . . heaven** i.e., I assumed a bearing of the utmost meekness   **56 pontifical** like that of a pope or archbishop   **57–9 and so . . . solemnity** and so my magnificence on public occasions, infrequent but always sumptuous, looked festive and achieved by this rarity a suitable formal impressiveness.   **61 bavin** brushwood, soon burnt out   **62 carded his state** debased his royal dignity. (To *card* is to stir or mix, hence to adulterate.)   **64 with their scorns** by his favorites' scornful and contemptuous behavior   **65–7 And gave . . . comparative** and lent his authority, to the detriment of his royal dignity and reputation, to find amusement in young scoffers and submit himself to the insolence of every frivolous witcracker   **69 Enfeoffed himself** gave himself up   **77 community** commonness   **82–3 Slept . . . adversaries** dozed off right before his eyes, and looked at the King in the way sullen men look at their adversaries

85 line degree, category   **87 vile participation** base association or companionship.   **90 that** that which   **91 tenderness** i.e., tears.   **93 For all the world** in every way   **97 to boot** in addition   **98–9 He . . . succession** i.e., this rebel Hotspur has a better claim to the throne than your merely hereditary claim unsupported by deeds.   **100 of . . . to right** having no rightful claim or even the pretext of one   **101 harness** armor, i.e., men in armor   **lion's** i.e., King's   **103 being . . . thou** i.e., being no older than you. (Though historically Hotspur was twenty-three years older than the Prince.)   **107 Whose** i.e., Hotspur's   **109 majority** preeminence   **110 capital** chief, principal   **114 Discomfited** defeated   **115 Enlargèd** freed   **116 To . . . up** to swell the roar of deep defiance   **119 The Archbishop's Grace** His Grace the Archbishop   **120 Capitulate** form a league, draw up articles.   **up** up in arms.   **123 dearest** (1) most precious (2) direst   **124 like** likely.   **vassal** slavish   **125 Base . . . spleen** inclination for baseness, and sudden bursts of capricious irascibility

To dog his heels and curtsy at his frowns,
To show how much thou art degenerate.
PRINCE
Do not think so. You shall not find it so.
And God forgive them that so much have swayed
Your Majesty's good thoughts away from me!
I will redeem all this on Percy's head
And in the closing of some glorious day
Be bold to tell you that I am your son,
When I will wear a garment all of blood
And stain my favors in a bloody mask,   136
Which, washed away, shall scour my shame with it.
And that shall be the day, whene'er it lights,   138
That this same child of honor and renown,
This gallant Hotspur, this all-praisèd knight,
And your unthought-of Harry chance to meet.   141
For every honor sitting on his helm,   142
Would they were multitudes, and on my head
My shames redoubled! For the time will come
That I shall make this northern youth exchange
His glorious deeds for my indignities.
Percy is but my factor, good my lord,   147
To engross up glorious deeds on my behalf;   148
And I will call him to so strict account
That he shall render every glory up,
Yea, even the slightest worship of his time,   151
Or I will tear the reckoning from his heart.
This in the name of God I promise here,
The which if He be pleased I shall perform,
I do beseech Your Majesty may salve   155
The long-grown wounds of my intemperance.   156
If not, the end of life cancels all bonds,
And I will die a hundred thousand deaths
Ere break the smallest parcel of this vow.
KING
A hundred thousand rebels die in this!
Thou shalt have charge and sovereign trust herein. 161

Enter Blunt.

How now, good Blunt? Thy looks are full of speed.
BLUNT
So hath the business that I come to speak of.
Lord Mortimer of Scotland hath sent word   164
That Douglas and the English rebels met
The eleventh of this month at Shrewsbury.
A mighty and a fearful head they are,   167
If promises be kept on every hand,
As ever offered foul play in a state.
KING
The Earl of Westmorland set forth today,
With him my son, Lord John of Lancaster;
For this advertisement is five days old.   172
On Wednesday next, Harry, you shall set forward;

On Thursday we ourselves will march. Our meeting 174
Is Bridgnorth. And, Harry, you shall march   175
Through Gloucestershire; by which account,
Our business valuèd, some twelve days hence   177
Our general forces at Bridgnorth shall meet.
Our hands are full of business. Let's away!
Advantage feeds him fat while men delay.   *Exeunt.* 180

[3.3]

Enter Falstaff and Bardolph.

FALSTAFF Bardolph, am I not fallen away vilely since   1
this last action? Do I not bate? Do I not dwindle? Why, 2
my skin hangs about me like an old lady's loose gown;
I am withered like an old applejohn. Well, I'll repent,   4
and that suddenly, while I am in some liking. I shall be 5
out of heart shortly, and then I shall have no strength   6
to repent. An I have not forgotten what the inside of a
church is made of, I am a peppercorn, a brewer's   8
horse. The inside of a church! Company, villainous   9
company, hath been the spoil of me.
BARDOLPH Sir John, you are so fretful you cannot live   11
long.
FALSTAFF Why, there is it. Come sing me a bawdy
song; make me merry. I was as virtuously given as a   14
gentleman need to be, virtuous enough: swore little,
diced not above seven times—a week, went to a
bawdy house not above once in a quarter—of an
hour, paid money that I borrowed—three or four
times, lived well and in good compass; and now I live   19
out of all order, out of all compass.
BARDOLPH Why, you are so fat, Sir John, that you must
needs be out of all compass, out of all reasonable
compass, Sir John.
FALSTAFF Do thou amend thy face, and I'll amend my
life. Thou art our admiral, thou bearest the lantern in   25
the poop, but 'tis in the nose of thee. Thou art the
Knight of the Burning Lamp.   27
BARDOLPH Why, Sir John, my face does you no harm.
FALSTAFF No, I'll be sworn, I make as good use of it as
many a man doth of a death's-head or a *memento mori.*   30
I never see thy face but I think upon hellfire and

---

136 **favors** features   138 **lights** dawns   141 **unthought-of** lightly valued, disregarded   142 **For** As for   147 **factor** agent   148 **engross up** amass, buy up   151 **even . . . time** every smallest honor he has ever won   155 **salve** soothe, heal   156 **intemperance** dissolute living.
161 **charge** command (of troops)   164 **Lord Mortimer of Scotland** (A Scottish nobleman, unrelated to Glendower's son-in-law.)   167 **head** armed force   172 **advertisement** tidings, news

174 **meeting** place of rendezvous   175 **Bridgnorth** a town near Shrewsbury.   177 **Our business valuèd** estimating how long our business will take   180 **Advantage . . . fat** Opportunity (for rebellion) prospers.   **him** himself
3.3. Location: A tavern in Eastcheap, as in 2.4.
1 **fallen away** shrunk   2 **action** i.e., the robbery at Gad's Hill.   **bate** lose weight.   4 **applejohn** a kind of apple still in good eating condition when shriveled.   5 **liking** (1) good bodily condition (2) inclination.   6 **out of heart** (1) disinclined, disheartened (2) out of condition   8 **peppercorn** unground dried pepper berry   8–9 **brewer's horse** i.e., one that is old, withered, and decrepit.   11 **fretful** (1) anxious (2) fretted, frayed   14 **given** inclined   19 **good compass** reasonable limits; also, in Bardolph's speech, girth, circumference   25 **admiral** flagship.   **lantern** i.e., a light for the rest of the fleet to follow; here applied to Bardolph's inflamed nose, red from overdrinking   27 **Knight . . . Lamp** Falstaff parodies the names of heroes in popular chivalric romances.   30 *memento mori* reminder of death, such as a death's head or a skull engraved on a seal ring.

Dives that lived in purple; for there he is in his robes, 32
burning, burning. If thou wert any way given to
virtue, I would swear by thy face; my oath should be
"By this fire, that's God's angel." But thou art 35
altogether given over, and wert indeed, but for the 36
light in thy face, the son of utter darkness. When thou
ran'st up Gad's Hill in the night to catch my horse, if
I did not think thou hadst been an *ignis fatuus* or a ball 39
of wildfire, there's no purchase in money. Oh, thou art 40
a perpetual triumph, an everlasting bonfire light! 41
Thou hast saved me a thousand marks in links and 42
torches, walking with thee in the night betwixt tavern
and tavern; but the sack that thou hast drunk me
would have bought me lights as good cheap at the 45
dearest chandler's in Europe. I have maintained that 46
salamander of yours with fire any time this two-and- 47
thirty years. God reward me for it!

BARDOLPH   'Sblood, I would my face were in your belly! 49

FALSTAFF   God-a-mercy! So should I be sure to be
heartburned.

Enter Hostess.

How now, Dame Partlet the hen? Have you inquired 52
yet who picked my pocket?

HOSTESS   Why, Sir John, what do you think, Sir John?
Do you think I keep thieves in my house? I have
searched, I have inquired, so has my husband, man
by man, boy by boy, servant by servant. The tithe of a 57
hair was never lost in my house before.

FALSTAFF   Ye lie, hostess. Bardolph was shaved and 59
lost many a hair; and I'll be sworn my pocket was 60
picked. Go to, you are a woman, go.

HOSTESS   Who, I? No, I defy thee! God's light, I was 62
never called so in mine own house before.

FALSTAFF   Go to, I know you well enough.

HOSTESS   No, Sir John, you do not know me, Sir John.
I know you, Sir John. You owe me money, Sir John,
and now you pick a quarrel to beguile me of it. I
bought you a dozen of shirts to your back.

FALSTAFF   Dowlas, filthy dowlas. I have given them 69
away to bakers' wives; they have made bolters of 70
them.

HOSTESS   Now, as I am a true woman, holland of eight 72
shillings an ell. You owe money here besides, Sir 73
John, for your diet and by-drinkings, and money lent 74
you, four-and-twenty pound.

FALSTAFF   He had his part of it. Let him pay. 76

HOSTESS   He? Alas, he is poor, he hath nothing.

FALSTAFF   How, poor? Look upon his face. What call
you rich? Let them coin his nose, let them coin his
cheeks. I'll not pay a denier. What, will you make a 80
younker of me? Shall I not take mine ease in mine inn 81
but I shall have my pocket picked? I have lost a seal
ring of my grandfather's worth forty mark.

HOSTESS   Oh, Jesu, I have heard the Prince tell him, I
know not how oft, that that ring was copper.

FALSTAFF   How? The Prince is a Jack, a sneak-up. 86
'Sblood, an he were here, I would cudgel him like a
dog if he would say so. 88

*Enter the Prince [with Peto], marching, and
Falstaff meets him playing upon his truncheon like
a fife.*

How now, lad, is the wind in that door, i'faith? Must 89
we all march?

BARDOLPH   Yea, two and two, Newgate fashion. 91

HOSTESS   My lord, I pray you, hear me.

PRINCE   What say'st thou, Mistress Quickly? How doth
thy husband? I love him well; he is an honest man.

HOSTESS   Good my lord, hear me.

FALSTAFF   Prithee, let her alone and list to me.

PRINCE   What say'st thou, Jack?

FALSTAFF   The other night I fell asleep here behind the
arras and had my pocket picked. This house is turned 99
bawdy house; they pick pockets.

PRINCE   What didst thou lose, Jack?

FALSTAFF   Wilt thou believe me, Hal? Three or four
bonds of forty pound apiece and a seal ring of my
grandfather's.

PRINCE   A trifle, some eightpenny matter.

HOSTESS   So I told him, my lord, and I said I heard Your
Grace say so; and, my lord, he speaks most vilely of
you, like a foulmouthed man as he is, and said he
would cudgel you.

PRINCE   What, he did not!

HOSTESS   There's neither faith, truth, nor womanhood
in me else.

FALSTAFF   There's no more faith in thee than in a stewed 113
prune, nor no more truth in thee than in a drawn fox; 114
and for womanhood, Maid Marian may be the dep- 115
uty's wife of the ward to thee. Go, you thing, go. 116

HOSTESS   Say, what thing, what thing?

FALSTAFF   What thing? Why, a thing to thank God on. 118

HOSTESS   I am no thing to thank God on, I would thou 119
shouldst know it! I am an honest man's wife, and,

32 **Dives** the rich man who went to hell, referred to in Luke 16:19–31
35 **"By . . . angel"** (Psalms 104:4, Hebrews 1:7, and Exodus 3:2
describe angels that appear in flames of fire.)   36 **given over** abandoned to wickedness   39 *ignis fatuus* will-o'-the-wisp   40 **wildfire**
fireworks; lightning; will-o'-the-wisp   41 **triumph** procession led by
torches   42 **links** torches, flares   45 **good cheap** cheap   46 **dearest
chandler's** most expensive candle maker's   47 **salamander** lizard
reputed to be able to live in fire   49 **I . . . belly** (A colloquial way of
objecting to an insult. Falstaff responds in the literal sense: A face like
yours would give me massive indigestion.)   52 **Partlet** (Traditional
name of a hen.)   57 **tithe** tenth part   59 **was shaved** (1) had his
beard cut (2) was cheated and robbed   60 **lost many a hair** (1) was
shaved (2) was made bald by syphilis   62 **God's light** (A mild oath.)
69 **Dowlas** a coarse kind of linen   70 **bolters** cloths for sifting flour
72 **holland** fine linen   73 **an ell** a measure of forty-five inches.
74 **diet** meals.   **by-drinkings** drinks between meals

76 **He** Bardolph   80 **denier** one-twelfth of a French sou; type of very
small coin.   81 **younker** greenhorn   86 **Jack** knave, rascal.   **sneak-
up** sneak.   88.2 **truncheon** officer's staff   89 **is . . . door** i.e., is that the
way the wind is blowing   91 **Newgate** a famous city prison in London.
(Prisoners marched two by two.)   99 **arras** curtain   113–14 **stewed
prune** (Customarily associated with bawdy houses.)   114 **drawn fox**
fox driven from cover and wily in getting back   115–16 **Maid . . .
thee** i.e., Maid Marian, a disreputable woman in Robin Hood ballads,
morris dances, and the like, was a model of respectability compared
with you.   118–19 **What thing . . . no thing** (With sexual quibbles.)

setting thy knighthood aside, thou art a knave to call 121
me so.

FALSTAFF   Setting thy womanhood aside, thou art a
beast to say otherwise.

HOSTESS   Say, what beast, thou knave, thou?

FALSTAFF   What beast? Why, an otter.

PRINCE   An otter, Sir John! Why an otter?

FALSTAFF   Why? She's neither fish nor flesh; a man
knows not where to have her.   129

HOSTESS   Thou art an unjust man in saying so. Thou or
any man knows where to have me, thou knave, thou.

PRINCE   Thou say'st true, hostess, and he slanders thee
most grossly.

HOSTESS   So he doth you, my lord, and said this other
day you owed him a thousand pound.

PRINCE   Sirrah, do I owe you a thousand pound?

FALSTAFF   A thousand pound, Hal? A million. Thy love
is worth a million; thou owest me thy love.

HOSTESS   Nay, my lord, he called you Jack and said he
would cudgel you.

FALSTAFF   Did I, Bardolph?

BARDOLPH   Indeed, Sir John, you said so.

FALSTAFF   Yea, if he said my ring was copper.

PRINCE   I say 'tis copper. Darest thou be as good as thy
word now?

FALSTAFF   Why, Hal, thou knowest, as thou art but
man, I dare; but as thou art prince, I fear thee as I fear
the roaring of the lion's whelp.   148

PRINCE   And why not as the lion?

FALSTAFF   The King himself is to be feared as the lion.
Dost thou think I'll fear thee as I fear thy father? Nay,
an I do, I pray God my girdle break.

PRINCE   Oh, if it should, how would thy guts fall about
thy knees! But, sirrah, there's no room for faith, truth,
nor honesty in this bosom of thine; it is all filled up
with guts and midriff. Charge an honest woman with
picking thy pocket? Why, thou whoreson, impudent,
embossed rascal, if there were anything in thy pocket 158
but tavern reckonings, memorandums of bawdy   159
houses, and one poor pennyworth of sugar candy to
make thee long-winded, if thy pocket were enriched
with any other injuries but these, I am a villain. And 162
yet you will stand to it; you will not pocket up wrong! 163
Art thou not ashamed?

FALSTAFF   Dost thou hear, Hal? Thou knowest in the
state of innocency Adam fell; and what should poor
Jack Falstaff do in the days of villainy? Thou see'st I
have more flesh than another man, and therefore
more frailty. You confess then you picked my pocket.

PRINCE   It appears so by the story.

FALSTAFF   Hostess, I forgive thee. Go make ready breakfast. Love thy husband, look to thy servants, cherish
thy guests. Thou shalt find me tractable to any honest
reason; thou see'st I am pacified still. Nay, prithee, 174
begone.   Exit Hostess.
Now, Hal, to the news at court: for the robbery, lad,
how is that answered?

PRINCE   Oh, my sweet beef, I must still be good angel to
thee. The money is paid back again.

FALSTAFF   Oh, I do not like that paying back. 'Tis a
double labor.   181

PRINCE   I am good friends with my father and may do
anything.

FALSTAFF   Rob me the exchequer the first thing thou
dost, and do it with unwashed hands too.   185

BARDOLPH   Do, my lord.

PRINCE   I have procured thee, Jack, a charge of foot.   187

FALSTAFF   I would it had been of horse. Where shall I
find one that can steal well? Oh, for a fine thief, of the 189
age of two-and-twenty or thereabouts! I am heinously
unprovided. Well, God be thanked for these rebels;   191
they offend none but the virtuous. I laud them, I   192
praise them.

PRINCE   Bardolph!

BARDOLPH   My lord?

PRINCE [giving letters]
Go bear this letter to Lord John of Lancaster,
To my brother John; this to my lord of Westmorland.
                                           [Exit Bardolph.]
Go, Peto, to horse, to horse, for thou and I
Have thirty miles to ride yet ere dinnertime.
                                              [Exit Peto.]
Jack, meet me tomorrow in the Temple Hall   200
At two o'clock in the afternoon.
There shalt thou know thy charge, and there receive
Money and order for their furniture.   203
The land is burning. Percy stands on high,
And either we or they must lower lie.   [Exit.]

FALSTAFF
Rare words! Brave world! Hostess, my breakfast, come! 206
Oh, I could wish this tavern were my drum!   [Exit.] 207

❖

[4.1]

[Enter Hotspur, Worcester, and Douglas.]

HOTSPUR
Well said, my noble Scot. If speaking truth

---

121 setting . . . aside (Mistress Quickly means, "without wishing to
offend your rank of knighthood," but Falstaff replies in line 123 with
the meaning, "setting aside your womanhood as of no value or perti-
nence.")   129 have understand. (With a sly suggestion of sexual possession—a meaning that eludes Mistress Quickly.)   148 whelp cub.
158 embossed (1) swollen with fat (2) foaming at the mouth and
exhausted, like a hunted animal.   rascal (1) scoundrel (2) immature
and inferior deer   159 memorandums souvenirs   162 injuries i.e.,
those things you claim to have lost, thereby suffering harm   163 stand
to it make a stand, insist on your supposed rights.   pocket up
endure silently

174 still always.   181 double labor i.e., the taking and the returning.
185 with unwashed hands without further ado   187 charge of foot
command of a company of infantry.   189 one i.e., a companion in
thievery. (Falstaff sees war as the opportunity for stealing and con-
ning.)   191 unprovided ill-equipped.   192 they . . . virtuous i.e., the
rebels, by providing the occasion of war, give dishonest men a chance
to profiteer and hence offend only those who are honest.   200 Temple Hall i.e., at the Inner Temple, one of the Inns of Court   203 furniture equipment, furnishing.   206 Brave Splendid   207 drum (Possibly Falstaff means that he wishes he could continue to enjoy this
tavern instead of risking his life in battle. He may also be punning on
tavern/taborn, i.e., taborin, a kind of drum.)
4.1. Location: The rebel camp near Shrewsbury.

In this fine age were not thought flattery,
Such attribution should the Douglas have   3
As not a soldier of this season's stamp   4
Should go so general current through the world.   5
By God, I cannot flatter; I do defy   6
The tongues of soothers! But a braver place   7
In my heart's love hath no man than yourself.
Nay, task me to my word; approve me, lord.   9

DOUGLAS   Thou art the king of honor.
No man so potent breathes upon the ground   11
But I will beard him.

Enter one [a Messenger] with letters.

HOTSPUR   Do so, and 'tis well.—   12
What letters hast thou there?—I can but thank you.   13

MESSENGER
These letters come from your father.

HOTSPUR
Letters from him? Why comes he not himself?

MESSENGER
He cannot come, my lord. He is grievous sick.

HOTSPUR
Zounds, how has he the leisure to be sick
In such a jostling time? Who leads his power?   18
Under whose government come they along?   19

MESSENGER
His letters bears his mind, not I, my lord.
                    [*Hotspur reads the letter.*]

WORCESTER
I prithee, tell me, doth he keep his bed?   21

MESSENGER
He did, my lord, four days ere I set forth,
And at the time of my departure thence
He was much feared by his physicians.   24

WORCESTER
I would the state of time had first been whole   25
Ere he by sickness had been visited.
His health was never better worth than now.

HOTSPUR
Sick now? Droop now? This sickness doth infect
The very life-blood of our enterprise;
'Tis catching hither, even to our camp.
He writes me here that inward sickness—
And that his friends by deputation   32
Could not so soon be drawn, nor did he think it meet   33
To lay so dangerous and dear a trust
On any soul removed but on his own.   35
Yet doth he give us bold advertisement   36

That with our small conjunction we should on,   37
To see how fortune is disposed to us;
For, as he writes, there is no quailing now,   39
Because the King is certainly possessed   40
Of all our purposes. What say you to it?

WORCESTER
Your father's sickness is a maim to us.   42

HOTSPUR
A perilous gash, a very limb lopped off.
And yet, in faith, it is not! His present want   44
Seems more than we shall find it. Were it good   45
To set the exact wealth of all our states   46
All at one cast? To set so rich a main   47
On the nice hazard of one doubtful hour?   48
It were not good, for therein should we read   49
The very bottom and the soul of hope,   50
The very list, the very utmost bound   51
Of all our fortunes.

DOUGLAS   Faith, and so we should;
Where now remains a sweet reversion,   53
We may boldly spend upon the hope
Of what is to come in.
A comfort of retirement lives in this.   56

HOTSPUR
A rendezvous, a home to fly unto,
If that the devil and mischance look big   58
Upon the maidenhead of our affairs.   59

WORCESTER
But yet I would your father had been here.
The quality and hair of our attempt   61
Brooks no division. It will be thought   62
By some that know not why he is away
That wisdom, loyalty, and mere dislike   64
Of our proceedings kept the Earl from hence.
And think how such an apprehension   66
May turn the tide of fearful faction   67
And breed a kind of question in our cause.
For well you know we of the off'ring side   69
Must keep aloof from strict arbitrament,   70
And stop all sight-holes, every loop from whence   71
The eye of reason may pry in upon us.
This absence of your father's draws a curtain   73
That shows the ignorant a kind of fear
Before not dreamt of.

HOTSPUR   You strain too far.   75
I rather of his absence make this use:

3 **attribution** praise, tribute   4–5 **As . . . world** that no one coined as
a soldier in this current campaign should enjoy such a current reputation. (To *go . . . current* is to be put into circulation, continuing the
image of coining in line 4.)   6 **defy** proclaim against   7 **soothers** flatterers.   **braver** better, dearer   9 **task . . . word** challenge me to make
good my word.   **approve** test   11–12 **No . . . him** i.e., I am ready to
defy anyone alive.   13 **I can . . . you** (Said to Douglas.)   18 **jostling**
contending, clashing   19 **government** command   21 **keep** keep to
24 **feared** feared for   25 **time** the times   32–3 **And that . . . drawn**
and that his allies could not so soon be assembled by anyone other
than himself, any deputy   33 **meet** appropriate   35 **On . . . own** on
anyone other than himself.   36 **advertisement** counsel, advice

37 **conjunction** joint force.   **on** go on   39 **quailing** losing heart
40 **possessed** informed   42 **maim** injury   44 **want** absence   45 **more**
more serious   46 **To . . . states** to stake the absolute total of our
resources   47 **cast** throw of the dice.   **main** stake in gambling; also, an
army   48 **nice** precarious, delicate.   **hazard** (1) game at dice
(2) venture   49–50 **should . . . hope** we should discover the utmost
foundation and basis of our hopes, the most we could rely on   51 **list**
limit   53 **Where . . . reversion** since as things stand we can expect rein-
forcements. (A *reversion* is literally part of an estate yet to be inherited.)
56 **retirement** something to fall back on   58 **big** threatening   59 **maidenhead** i.e., commencement   61 **hair** kind, nature   62 **Brooks** toler-
ates   64 **loyalty** i.e., to the crown   66 **apprehension** (1) perception
(2) apprehensiveness   67 **fearful faction** timid support   69 **off'ring
side** side that attacks   70 **strict arbitrament** just inquiry or investigation   71 **sight-holes** peep-holes. (*Loop* or *loophole* has the same meaning.)   73 **draws** draws aside, opens   75 **strain too far** exaggerate.

It lends a luster and more great opinion,   77
A larger dare to our great enterprise,   78
Than if the Earl were here; for men must think,
If we without his help can make a head   80
To push against a kingdom, with his help
We shall o'erturn it topsy-turvy down.
Yet all goes well, yet all our joints are whole.   83

DOUGLAS
As heart can think. There is not such a word
Spoke of in Scotland as this term of fear.

Enter Sir Richard Vernon.

HOTSPUR
My cousin Vernon, welcome, by my soul.

VERNON
Pray God my news be worth a welcome, lord.
The Earl of Westmorland, seven thousand strong,
Is marching hitherwards; with him Prince John.

HOTSPUR
No harm. What more?

VERNON   And further I have learned
The King himself in person is set forth,
Or hitherwards intended speedily,   92
With strong and mighty preparation.

HOTSPUR
He shall be welcome too. Where is his son,
The nimble-footed madcap Prince of Wales,
And his comrades, that doffed the world aside   96
And bid it pass?

VERNON   All furnished, all in arms   97
All plumed like estridges, that with the wind   98
Bated like eagles having lately bathed,   99
Glittering in golden coats, like images,   100
As full of spirit as the month of May
And gorgeous as the sun at midsummer,
Wanton as youthful goats, wild as young bulls.   103
I saw young Harry, with his beaver on,   104
His cuisses on his thighs, gallantly armed,   105
Rise from the ground like feathered Mercury,
And vaulted with such ease into his seat   107
As if an angel dropped down from the clouds
To turn and wind a fiery Pegasus   109
And witch the world with noble horsemanship.   110

HOTSPUR
No more, no more! Worse than the sun in March   111
This praise doth nourish agues. Let them come.   112
They come like sacrifices in their trim,   113

And to the fire-eyed maid of smoky war   114
All hot and bleeding will we offer them.
The mailèd Mars shall on his altar sit   116
Up to the ears in blood. I am on fire
To hear this rich reprisal is so nigh,   118
And yet not ours. Come, let me taste my horse,   119
Who is to bear me like a thunderbolt
Against the bosom of the Prince of Wales.
Harry to Harry shall, hot horse to horse,
Meet and ne'er part till one drop down a corse.   123
Oh, that Glendower were come!

VERNON   There is more news:
I learned in Worcester, as I rode along,
He cannot draw his power this fourteen days.   126

DOUGLAS
That's the worst tidings that I hear of yet.

WORCESTER
Ay, by my faith, that bears a frosty sound.

HOTSPUR
What may the King's whole battle reach unto?   129

VERNON
To thirty thousand.

HOTSPUR   Forty let it be!
My father and Glendower being both away,
The powers of us may serve so great a day.   132
Come, let us take a muster speedily.
Doomsday is near; die all, die merrily.

DOUGLAS
Talk not of dying. I am out of fear   135
Of death or death's hand for this one half year.

                                                          Exeunt.

                              ♣

[4.2]

Enter Falstaff, [and] Bardolph.

FALSTAFF   Bardolph, get thee before to Coventry; fill me
a bottle of sack. Our soldiers shall march through; we'll
to Sutton Coldfield tonight.   3

BARDOLPH   Will you give me money, Captain?

FALSTAFF   Lay out, lay out.   5

BARDOLPH   This bottle makes an angel.   6

FALSTAFF   An if it do, take it for thy labor; an if it make
twenty, take them all; I'll answer the coinage. Bid my   8
lieutenant Peto meet me at town's end.

BARDOLPH   I will, Captain. Farewell.   *Exit.*

FALSTAFF   If I be not ashamed of my soldiers, I am a
soused gurnet. I have misused the King's press dam-   12
nably. I have got, in exchange of a hundred and fifty

77 opinion renown   **78 dare** daring   **80 make a head** raise an armed
force   **83 Yet** Still.   **joints** limbs   **92 intended** on the verge of departure   **96–7 that doffed . . . pass?** i.e., that thumbed their noses at
responsibilities, telling the world to mind its own business?   **97 furnished** equipped   **98–9 All . . . bathed** i.e., all plumed with ostrich
feathers, fluttering their wings in the wind like eagles having just
bathed. (The text may be defective.)   **100 coats** (1) coats of mail
(2) heraldic coats of arms.   **images** gilded statues   **103 Wanton**
sportive, frolicsome   **104 beaver** visor; hence, helmet   **105 cuisses**
armor for the thighs   **107 seat** saddle   **109 wind** wheel about.
Pegasus winged horse of Greek mythology   **110 witch** bewitch
111–12 Worse . . . agues (The spring sun was believed to give impetus
to chills and fevers, by drawing up vapors. Vernon's speech, says
Hotspur, gives one the shudders.)   **113 sacrifices** beasts for sacrifice.
trim fine apparel, trappings

114 maid i.e., Bellona, goddess of war   **116 mailèd** dressed in mail,
armor   **118 reprisal** prize   **119 taste** try, feel under me   **123 corse**
corpse.   **126 draw his power** muster his army   **129 battle** army
132 The . . . us our forces   **135 out of** free from
4.2. Location: A public road near Coventry.
3 Sutton Coldfield (In Warwickshire near Coventry.)   **5 Lay out** Pay
for it yourself   **6 makes an angel** i.e., makes ten shillings I've spent
for you. (But Falstaff answers as though *makes* means "produces,"
implying that Bardolph can profit from the transaction.)   **8 I'll . . .
coinage** I'll take responsibility for any proceeds.   **12 soused gurnet** a
kind of pickled fish.   **King's press** royal warrant for the impressment of troops

soldiers, three hundred and odd pounds. I press me 14
none but good householders, yeomen's sons, inquire 15
me out contracted bachelors, such as had been asked 16
twice on the banns—such a commodity of warm 17
slaves as had as lief hear the devil as a drum, such as 18
fear the report of a caliver worse than a struck fowl or 19
a hurt wild duck. I pressed me none but such toasts- 20
and-butter, with hearts in their bellies no bigger than 21
pins' heads, and they have bought out their services; 22
and now my whole charge consists of ancients, cor- 23
porals, lieutenants, gentlemen of companies—slaves 24
as ragged as Lazarus in the painted cloth, where the 25
glutton's dogs licked his sores, and such as indeed
were never soldiers, but discarded unjust servingmen, 27
younger sons to younger brothers, revolted tapsters, 28
and hostlers trade-fallen, the cankers of a calm world 29
and a long peace, ten times more dishonorable-ragged
than an old feazed ancient. And such have I, to fill up 31
the rooms of them as have bought out their services,
that you would think that I had a hundred and fifty tattered prodigals lately come from swine keeping, from 34
eating draff and husks. A mad fellow met me on the way 35
and told me I had unloaded all the gibbets and pressed 36
the dead bodies. No eye hath seen such scarecrows. I'll
not march through Coventry with them, that's flat. 38
Nay, and the villains march wide betwixt the legs as if
they had gyves on, for indeed I had the most of them 40
out of prison. There's not a shirt and a half in all my
company, and the half shirt is two napkins tacked together and thrown over the shoulders like a herald's
coat without sleeves; and the shirt, to say the truth,
stolen from my host at Saint Albans, or the red-nose 45
innkeeper of Daventry. But that's all one; they'll find 46
linen enough on every hedge. 47

Enter the Prince [and the] Lord of Westmorland.

PRINCE How now, blown Jack? How now, quilt? 48
FALSTAFF What, Hal? How now, mad wag? What a
devil dost thou in Warwickshire?—My good lord of

Westmorland, I cry you mercy. I thought Your Honor 51
had already been at Shrewsbury.
WESTMORLAND Faith, Sir John, 'tis more than time that
I were there, and you too; but my powers are there 54
already. The King, I can tell you, looks for us all. We
must away all night. 56
FALSTAFF Tut, never fear me. I am as vigilant as a cat to 57
steal cream.
PRINCE I think, to steal cream indeed, for thy theft hath 59
already made thee butter. But tell me, Jack, whose 60
fellows are these that come after?
FALSTAFF Mine, Hal, mine.
PRINCE I did never see such pitiful rascals.
FALSTAFF Tut, tut, good enough to toss; food for 64
powder, food for powder. They'll fill a pit as well as 65
better. Tush, man, mortal men, mortal men.
WESTMORLAND Ay, but, Sir John, methinks they are
exceeding poor and bare, too beggarly. 68
FALSTAFF Faith, for their poverty, I know not where 69
they had that, and for their bareness, I am sure they
never learned that of me.
PRINCE No, I'll be sworn, unless you call three fingers 72
in the ribs bare. But, sirrah, make haste. Percy is 73
already in the field. *Exit.*
FALSTAFF What, is the King encamped?
WESTMORLAND He is, Sir John. I fear we shall stay too
long. *[Exit.]*
FALSTAFF Well,
To the latter end of a fray and the beginning of a feast 79
Fits a dull fighter and a keen guest. *Exit.* 80

[4.3]

*Enter Hotspur, Worcester, Douglas, [and]
Vernon.*

HOTSPUR
We'll fight with him tonight.
WORCESTER   It may not be.
DOUGLAS
You give him then advantage.
VERNON   Not a whit. 2
HOTSPUR
Why say you so? Looks he not for supply? 3
VERNON
So do we.
HOTSPUR   His is certain; ours is doubtful.

WORCESTER
Good cousin, be advised, stir not tonight.

VERNON
Do not, my lord.

DOUGLAS   You do not counsel well.
You speak it out of fear and cold heart.

VERNON
Do me no slander, Douglas. By my life,
And I dare well maintain it with my life,
If well-respected honor bid me on,   10
I hold as little counsel with weak fear   11
As you, my lord, or any Scot that this day lives.
Let it be seen tomorrow in the battle
Which of us fears.

DOUGLAS   Yea, or tonight.

VERNON   Content.

HOTSPUR   Tonight, say I.

VERNON
Come, come, it may not be. I wonder much,
Being men of such great leading as you are,   19
That you foresee not what impediments
Drag back our expedition. Certain horse   21
Of my cousin Vernon's are not yet come up.
Your uncle Worcester's horse came but today,
And now their pride and mettle is asleep,   24
Their courage with hard labor tame and dull,
That not a horse is half the half of himself.

HOTSPUR
So are the horses of the enemy
In general journey-bated and brought low.   28
The better part of ours are full of rest.

WORCESTER
The number of the King exceedeth our.
For God's sake, cousin, stay till all come in.   31

The trumpet sounds a parley.

Enter Sir Walter Blunt.

BLUNT
I come with gracious offers from the King,
If you vouchsafe me hearing and respect.   33

HOTSPUR
Welcome, Sir Walter Blunt; and would to God
You were of our determination!   35
Some of us love you well; and even those some   36
Envy your great deservings and good name
Because you are not of our quality   38
But stand against us like an enemy.

BLUNT
And God defend but still I should stand so,   40
So long as out of limit and true rule   41
You stand against anointed majesty.
But to my charge. The King hath sent to know   43

The nature of your griefs and whereupon   44
You conjure from the breast of civil peace
Such bold hostility, teaching his duteous land
Audacious cruelty. If that the King   47
Have any way your good deserts forgot,
Which he confesseth to be manifold,
He bids you name your griefs, and with all speed
You shall have your desires with interest
And pardon absolute for yourself and these
Herein misled by your suggestion.   53

HOTSPUR
The King is kind; and well we know the King
Knows at what time to promise, when to pay.
My father and my uncle and myself
Did give him that same royalty he wears,
And when he was not six-and-twenty strong,
Sick in the world's regard, wretched and low,
A poor unminded outlaw sneaking home,   60
My father gave him welcome to the shore;
And when he heard him swear and vow to God
He came but to be Duke of Lancaster,
To sue his livery and beg his peace   64
With tears of innocency and terms of zeal,
My father, in kind heart and pity moved,
Swore him assistance, and performed it too.
Now when the lords and barons of the realm
Perceived Northumberland did lean to him,
The more and less came in with cap and knee,   70
Met him in boroughs, cities, villages,
Attended him on bridges, stood in lanes,   72
Laid gifts before him, proffered him their oaths,
Gave him their heirs as pages, followed him   74
Even at the heels in golden multitudes.   75
He presently, as greatness knows itself,   76
Steps me a little higher than his vow   77
Made to my father while his blood was poor   78
Upon the naked shore at Ravenspurgh,
And now, forsooth, takes on him to reform
Some certain edicts and some strait decrees   81
That lie too heavy on the commonwealth,
Cries out upon abuses, seems to weep
Over his country's wrongs; and by this face,   84
This seeming brow of justice, did he win
The hearts of all that he did angle for;
Proceeded further—cut me off the heads   87
Of all the favorites that the absent King
In deputation left behind him here
When he was personal in the Irish war.   90

---

10 **well-respected** well weighed or considered   11 **I hold . . . counsel**
I have as little to do   19 **leading** leadership   21 **expedition** speedy
progress.   **horse** cavalry. (As also at line 23.)   24 **pride and mettle**
spirit   28 **journey-bated** tired from the journey   31.1 **parley** trumpet
summons to a conference.   33 **respect** attention.   35 **determination**
persuasion (in the fight).   36 **even those some** those same persons
38 **Because** only because.   **quality** party   40 **defend** forbid.   **still**
always   41 **limit** bounds of allegiance   43 **charge** commission.

44 **griefs** grievances   47 **If that** If   53 **suggestion** instigation.
60 **unminded** disregarded   64 **To sue . . . peace** to petition to take
possession of his rightful inheritance and be reconciled with King
Richard II   70 **The more . . . knee** persons of all ranks came to him with
cap in hand and with bended knee   72 **Attended** waited for.   **stood
in lanes** stood row-deep along the roads   74 **Gave . . . pages** i.e.,
brought him their heirs to serve as pages and also as hostages to the
fathers' loyalty   75 **golden** (1) auspicious, celebrating (2) majestically
attired   76 **knows itself** perceives its own strength   77 **Steps me** i.e.,
steps. (*Me* is used colloquially.)   **vow** i.e., Bolingbroke's vow to seek
no more than his inheritance   78 **while . . . poor** i.e., while Bolingbroke's spirits were still humbled and his dynastic claim in question
81 **strait** strict   84 **face** show, pretense   87 **cut me** i.e., cut   90 **personal** in person

BLUNT
Tut, I came not to hear this.

HOTSPUR   Then to the point.
In short time after, he deposed the King,
Soon after that, deprived him of his life,
And in the neck of that tasked the whole state;   94
To make that worse, suffered his kinsman March—
Who is, if every owner were well placed,   96
Indeed his king—to be engaged in Wales,   97
There without ransom to lie forfeited;   98
Disgraced me in my happy victories,   99
Sought to entrap me by intelligence;   100
Rated mine uncle from the Council board;   101
In rage dismissed my father from the court;
Broke oath on oath, committed wrong on wrong,
And in conclusion drove us to seek out
This head of safety, and withal to pry   105
Into his title, the which we find
Too indirect for long continuance.

BLUNT
Shall I return this answer to the King?

HOTSPUR
Not so, Sir Walter. We'll withdraw awhile.
Go to the King; and let there be impawned
Some surety for a safe return again,   110
And in the morning early shall mine uncle
Bring him our purposes. And so farewell.   113

BLUNT
I would you would accept of grace and love.

HOTSPUR
And maybe so we shall.

BLUNT
                              Pray God you do. [*Exeunt.*]

♣

[4.4]

Enter [the] Archbishop of York, [and] Sir Michael.

ARCHBISHOP [*giving letters*]
Hie, good Sir Michael, bear this sealèd brief   1
With wingèd haste to the Lord Marshal,   2
This to my cousin Scroop, and all the rest   3
To whom they are directed. If you knew
How much they do import, you would make haste.

SIR MICHAEL   My good lord, I guess their tenor.

ARCHBISHOP   Like enough you do.   7
Tomorrow, good Sir Michael, is a day

Wherein the fortune of ten thousand men
Must bide the touch; for, sir, at Shrewsbury,   10
As I am truly given to understand,
The King with mighty and quick-raisèd power
Meets with Lord Harry. And I fear, Sir Michael,
What with the sickness of Northumberland,
Whose power was in the first proportion,   15
And what with Owen Glendower's absence thence,
Who with them was a rated sinew too   17
And comes not in, o'erruled by prophecies,
I fear the power of Percy is too weak
To wage an instant trial with the King.   20

SIR MICHAEL
Why, my good lord, you need not fear;
There is Douglas and Lord Mortimer.

ARCHBISHOP   No, Mortimer is not there.

SIR MICHAEL
But there is Mordake, Vernon, Lord Harry Percy,
And there is my lord of Worcester, and a head   25
Of gallant warriors, noble gentlemen.

ARCHBISHOP
And so there is. But yet the King hath drawn
The special head of all the land together: 28
The Prince of Wales, Lord John of Lancaster,
The noble Westmorland, and warlike Blunt,
And many more corrivals and dear men   31
Of estimation and command in arms.   32

SIR MICHAEL
Doubt not, my lord, they shall be well opposed.

ARCHBISHOP
I hope no less, yet needful 'tis to fear;
And, to prevent the worst, Sir Michael, speed.
For if Lord Percy thrive not, ere the King
Dismiss his power he means to visit us,   37
For he hath heard of our confederacy,
And 'tis but wisdom to make strong against him.
Therefore make haste. I must go write again
To other friends; and so farewell, Sir Michael.
                              Exeunt [separately].

♣

[5.1]

*Enter the King, Prince of Wales, Lord John of
Lancaster, Sir Walter Blunt, [and] Falstaff.*

KING
How bloodily the sun begins to peer
Above yon bosky hill! The day looks pale   2
At his distemperature.

PRINCE   The southern wind   3
Doth play the trumpet to his purposes,   4

---

94 in . . . that next, immediately after.   **tasked** laid taxes upon   **96 if
. . . placed** if every claimant were given his proper place   **97 engaged**
held as hostage   **98 lie forfeited** remain prisoner, unreclaimed
99 Disgraced me (by demanding the prisoners; see 1.3.23 ff.)   **happy**
fortunate   **100 intelligence** secret information, i.e., from spies
101 Rated scolded   **105 head of safety** armed force for our protection.
withal also   **110 impawned** pledged   **113 purposes** proposals.
4.4. Location: York. The Archbishop's palace.
1 brief letter, dispatch   **2 Lord Marshal** i.e., Thomas Mowbray, son
of the Duke of Norfolk who is exiled in *Richard II*, and a longtime
enemy of the new King   **3 Scroop** i.e., perhaps Sir Stephen Scroop
of *Richard II*, 3.2.91–218, or Lord Scroop of Masham of *Henry V*, 2.2
7 Like Likely

10 bide the touch be put to the test (like gold)   **15 in . . . proportion**
of the largest size   **17 rated sinew** main strength or support reckoned upon   **20 instant** immediate   **25 head** troop   **28 special head**
notable leaders   **31 corrivals** partners in the enterprise   **32 estimation** reputation, importance   **37 he** i.e., the King
5.1. Location: The King's camp near Shrewsbury.
2 bosky bushy   **3 his distemperature** i.e., the sun's unhealthy
appearance.   **4 trumpet** trumpeter.   **his** its, the sun's

And by his hollow whistling in the leaves
Foretells a tempest and a blust'ring day.

KING
Then with the losers let it sympathize,
For nothing can seem foul to those that win.

The trumpet sounds.

Enter Worcester [and Vernon].

How now, my lord of Worcester? 'Tis not well
That you and I should meet upon such terms
As now we meet. You have deceived our trust
And made us doff our easy robes of peace   12
To crush our old limbs in ungentle steel.
This is not well, my lord, this is not well.
What say you to it? Will you again unknit
This churlish knot of all-abhorrèd war
And move in that obedient orb again   17
Where you did give a fair and natural light,
And be no more an exhaled meteor,   19
A prodigy of fear, and a portent   20
Of broachèd mischief to the unborn times?   21

WORCESTER   Hear me, my liege:
For mine own part, I could be well content
To entertain the lag end of my life   24
With quiet hours, for I protest
I have not sought the day of this dislike.   26

KING
You have not sought it? How comes it, then?

FALSTAFF   Rebellion lay in his way, and he found it.

PRINCE   Peace, chewet, peace!   29

WORCESTER
It pleased Your Majesty to turn your looks
Of favor from myself and all our house;
And yet I must remember you, my lord,   32
We were the first and dearest of your friends.
For you my staff of office did I break
In Richard's time, and posted day and night   35
To meet you on the way, and kiss your hand,
When yet you were in place and in account
Nothing so strong and fortunate as I.   38
It was myself, my brother, and his son
That brought you home and boldly did outdare   40
The dangers of the time. You swore to us,
And you did swear that oath at Doncaster,
That you did nothing purpose 'gainst the state,
Nor claim no further than your new-fall'n right, 44
The seat of Gaunt, dukedom of Lancaster.
To this we swore our aid. But in short space
It rained down fortune show'ring on your head,
And such a flood of greatness fell on you—

What with our help, what with the absent King,
What with the injuries of a wanton time,   50
The seeming sufferances that you had borne,   51
And the contrarious winds that held the King
So long in his unlucky Irish wars
That all in England did repute him dead—
And from this swarm of fair advantages
You took occasion to be quickly wooed   56
To grip the general sway into your hand;
Forgot your oath to us at Doncaster;
And being fed by us, you used us so
As that ungentle gull, the cuckoo's bird,   60
Useth the sparrow; did oppress our nest,
Grew by our feeding to so great a bulk
That even our love durst not come near your sight 63
For fear of swallowing; but with nimble wing
We were enforced, for safety sake, to fly
Out of your sight and raise this present head,   66
Whereby we stand opposèd by such means   67
As you yourself have forged against yourself
By unkind usage, dangerous countenance,   69
And violation of all faith and troth
Sworn to us in your younger enterprise.

KING
These things indeed you have articulate,   72
Proclaimed at market crosses, read in churches,   73
To face the garment of rebellion   74
With some fine color that may please the eye   75
Of fickle changelings and poor discontents,   76
Which gape and rub the elbow at the news   77
Of hurly-burly innovation.   78
And never yet did insurrection want   79
Such water-colors to impaint his cause,   80
Nor moody beggars, starving for a time   81
Of pell-mell havoc and confusion.   82

PRINCE
In both your armies there is many a soul   83
Shall pay full dearly for this encounter,
If once they join in trial. Tell your nephew
The Prince of Wales doth join with all the world
In praise of Henry Percy. By my hopes—   87
This present enterprise set off his head—   88
I do not think a braver gentleman,
More active-valiant or more valiant-young,
More daring or more bold, is now alive
To grace this latter age with noble deeds.

---

12 **easy** comfortable   17 **orb** orbit, sphere of action. (The King's subjects, like planets and stars in the Ptolemaic cosmos, were supposed to revolve around the kingly center, comparable to the earth, in fixed courses.)   19 **exhaled meteor** (Meteors were believed to be vapors drawn up or *exhaled* by the sun and visible as streaks of light; they were regarded as ill omens.)   20 **prodigy of fear** fearful omen   21 **broachèd** set flowing, already begun   24 **entertain** occupy   26 **the . . . dislike** this time of discord.   29 **chewet** chough, jackdaw. (Here, a chatterer.)   32 **remember** remind   35 **posted** rode swiftly   38 **Nothing** not at all   40 **home** back to England from exile   44 **new-fall'n** recently inherited (by the death of John of Gaunt)

50 **injuries** abuses.   **wanton** ill-managed   51 **sufferances** suffering, distress   56 **occasion** the opportunity   60 **ungentle . . . bird** rude nestling, the cuckoo's young offspring. (The cuckoo lays its eggs in other birds' nests.)   63 **our love** we who loved you   66 **head** armed force   67 **opposèd . . . means** goaded into opposition by such factors   69 **dangerous countenance** threatening behavior   72 **articulate** set forth, specified   73 **market crosses** (Christian crosses were often erected in the centers of marketplaces—a good place for public announcements.)   74 **face** trim, adorn   75 **color** (1) hue (2) specious appearance   76 **changelings** turncoats   77 **rub the elbow** i.e., hug themselves with delight   78 **innovation** rebellion.   79 **want** lack   80 **water-colors** i.e., thin excuses. (See *color*, line 75.)   **his** its   81 **moody** sullen, angry   82 **havoc** plundering   83 **both your** i.e., your and our   87 **hopes** i.e., hopes of salvation   88 **This . . . head** i.e., if this present rebellion is taken from his account, not held against him

For my part, I may speak it to my shame,
I have a truant been to chivalry;
And so I hear he doth account me too.
Yet this before my father's majesty:
I am content that he shall take the odds
Of his great name and estimation,   98
And will, to save the blood on either side,
Try fortune with him in a single fight.

KING
And, Prince of Wales, so dare we venture thee,   101
Albeit considerations infinite   102
Do make against it.—No, good Worcester, no.
We love our people well; even those we love
That are misled upon your cousin's part;   105
And, will they take the offer of our grace,   106
Both he and they and you, yea, every man
Shall be my friend again, and I'll be his.
So tell your cousin, and bring me word
What he will do. But if he will not yield,
Rebuke and dread correction wait on us,   111
And they shall do their office. So, begone.
We will not now be troubled with reply.
We offer fair; take it advisedly.

Exit Worcester [with Vernon].

PRINCE
It will not be accepted, on my life.
The Douglas and the Hotspur both together
Are confident against the world in arms.

KING
Hence, therefore, every leader to his charge;
For on their answer will we set on them,
And God befriend us as our cause is just!   120

Exeunt. Manent Prince, Falstaff.

FALSTAFF   Hal, if thou see me down in the battle and
bestride me, so; 'tis a point of friendship.   122
PRINCE   Nothing but a colossus can do thee that friendship. Say thy prayers, and farewell.
FALSTAFF   I would 'twere bedtime, Hal, and all well.
PRINCE   Why, thou owest God a death.   *[Exit.]* 126
FALSTAFF   'Tis not due yet; I would be loath to pay him
before his day. What need I be so forward with him
that calls not on me? Well, 'tis no matter; honor pricks 129
me on. Yea, but how if honor prick me off when I 130
come on? How then? Can honor set to a leg? No. Or 131
an arm? No. Or take away the grief of a wound? No. 132
Honor hath no skill in surgery, then? No. What is
honor? A word. What is in that word "honor"? What is
that "honor"? Air. A trim reckoning! Who hath it? He
that died o' Wednesday. Doth he feel it? No. Doth he
hear it? No. 'Tis insensible, then? Yea, to the dead. But
will it not live with the living? No. Why? Detraction 138

will not suffer it. Therefore I'll none of it. Honor is a 139
mere scutcheon. And so ends my catechism.   140

Exit.

❖

[5.2]

Enter Worcester [and] Sir Richard Vernon.

WORCESTER
Oh, no, my nephew must not know, Sir Richard,
The liberal and kind offer of the King.
VERNON
'Twere best he did.
WORCESTER   Then are we all undone.
It is not possible, it cannot be,
The King should keep his word in loving us;
He will suspect us still and find a time
To punish this offense in other faults.   7
Suspicion all our lives shall be stuck full of eyes;   8
For treason is but trusted like the fox,
Who, never so tame, so cherished, and locked up,   10
Will have a wild trick of his ancestors.   11
Look how we can, or sad or merrily,   12
Interpretation will misquote our looks,
And we shall feed like oxen at a stall,
The better cherished still the nearer death.
My nephew's trespass may be well forgot;
It hath the excuse of youth and heat of blood,
And an adopted name of privilege—   18
A harebrained Hotspur, governed by a spleen.   19
All his offenses live upon my head
And on his father's. We did train him on,   21
And, his corruption being ta'en from us,   22
We as the spring of all shall pay for all.   23
Therefore, good cousin, let not Harry know
In any case the offer of the King.

Enter Hotspur [and Douglas, with soldiers].

VERNON
Deliver what you will; I'll say 'tis so.   26
Here comes your cousin.
HOTSPUR   My uncle is returned.
Deliver up my lord of Westmorland.   28
Uncle, what news?
WORCESTER
The King will bid you battle presently.
DOUGLAS
Defy him by the lord of Westmorland.   31

---

139 suffer allow   **140 scutcheon** heraldic emblem carried in funerals,
displayed on coaches, etc.; it was the lowest form of symbol, having
no pennon or other insignia.   **catechism** the principles of faith given
in the form of question and answer.
5.2. Location: Near the rebel camp.
7 To . . . faults to find other faults in us to punish (as a way of getting
back at us for defying him militarily).   **8 stuck . . . eyes** i.e., provided
with many eyes, suspiciously inquisitive   **10 never so** be he never so
11 trick trait   **12 or sad** either sad   **18 an adopted . . . privilege** i.e., a
nickname, "Hotspur," to justify his rashness   **19 spleen** intemperate
impulse.   **21 train** incite, draw   **22 his . . . us** i.e., since his guilt originated in us   **23 spring** source   **26 Deliver** Report   **28 Deliver up**
Release (as hostage; see 4.3.110–11)   **31 Defy him by** Send back your
defiance with

---

98 estimation reputation   **101 venture** hazard, risk   **102 Albeit**
although it be that. (The subjunctive has the force of "were it not
that.")   **105 cousin's** i.e., nephew's   **106 will they** if they will.
grace pardon   **111 wait on us** are awaiting my royal command
120.1 Manent They remain onstage   **122 bestride** stand over in order
to defend.   **so** well and good   **126 thou . . . death** (Proverbial, with a
pun on *debt*.)   **129 pricks** spurs   **130 prick me off** mark me off (as
one dead)   **131 set to** rejoin or set   **132 grief** pain   **138 Detraction**
Slander

HOTSPUR
Lord Douglas, go you and tell him so.
DOUGLAS
Marry, and shall, and very willingly.   *Exit Douglas.*
WORCESTER
There is no seeming mercy in the King.
HOTSPUR
Did you beg any? God forbid!
WORCESTER
I told him gently of our grievances,
Of his oathbreaking, which he mended thus,
By now forswearing that he is forsworn.
He calls us rebels, traitors, and will scourge
With haughty arms this hateful name in us.

          Enter Douglas.

DOUGLAS
Arm, gentlemen, to arms! For I have thrown
A brave defiance in King Henry's teeth,   42
And Westmorland, that was engaged, did bear it;   43
Which cannot choose but bring him quickly on.
WORCESTER
The Prince of Wales stepped forth before the King,
And, nephew, challenged you to single fight.
HOTSPUR
Oh, would the quarrel lay upon our heads,
And that no man might draw short breath today
But I and Harry Monmouth! Tell me, tell me,   49
How showed his tasking? Seemed it in contempt?   50
VERNON
No, by my soul. I never in my life
Did hear a challenge urged more modestly,   52
Unless a brother should a brother dare
To gentle exercise and proof of arms.   54
He gave you all the duties of a man,   55
Trimmed up your praises with a princely tongue,   56
Spoke your deservings like a chronicle,
Making you ever better than his praise
By still dispraising praise valued with you;   59
And, which became him like a prince indeed,
He made a blushing cital of himself,   61
And chid his truant youth with such a grace
As if he mastered there a double spirit
Of teaching and of learning instantly.   64
There did he pause. But let me tell the world,
If he outlive the envy of this day,   66
England did never owe so sweet a hope,   67
So much misconstrued in his wantonness.   68
HOTSPUR
Cousin, I think thou art enamorèd
On his follies. Never did I hear
Of any prince so wild a liberty.   71

But be he as he will, yet once ere night
I will embrace him with a soldier's arm,
That he shall shrink under my courtesy.   74
Arm, arm with speed! And, fellows, soldiers, friends,
Better consider what you have to do
Than I, that have not well the gift of tongue,
Can lift your blood up with persuasion.

          Enter a Messenger.

FIRST MESSENGER   My lord, here are letters for you.
HOTSPUR   I cannot read them now.
Oh, gentlemen, the time of life is short!
To spend that shortness basely were too long   82
If life did ride upon a dial's point,   83
Still ending at the arrival of an hour.   84
An if we live, we live to tread on kings;
If die, brave death, when princes die with us!   86
Now, for our consciences, the arms are fair   87
When the intent of bearing them is just.

          Enter another [Messenger].

SECOND MESSENGER
My lord, prepare. The King comes on apace.
HOTSPUR
I thank him that he cuts me from my tale,
For I profess not talking. Only this—   91
Let each man do his best. And here draw I
A sword, whose temper I intend to stain
With the best blood that I can meet withal
In the adventure of this perilous day.
Now, *Esperance!* Percy! And set on.   96
Sound all the lofty instruments of war,
And by that music let us all embrace;
For, heaven to earth, some of us never shall   99
A second time do such a courtesy.
          Here they embrace. The trumpets sound. [Exeunt.]

❖

[5.3]

          *The King enters with his power [and passes over
          the stage]. Alarum to the battle. Then enter
          Douglas, and Sir Walter Blunt [dressed like King
          Henry].*

BLUNT
What is thy name, that in the battle thus
Thou crossest me? What honor dost thou seek
Upon my head?
DOUGLAS   Know then my name is Douglas,
And I do haunt thee in the battle thus
Because some tell me that thou art a king.

---

42 **brave** proud   43 **engaged** held as hostage   49 **Monmouth** (A name for the Prince, taken from the Welsh town where he was born.) 50 **showed his tasking** appeared his giving the challenge.   52 **urged** put forward   54 **gentle** befitting noble birth.   **proof of arms** test of martial skill.   55 **duties** due merits   56 **Trimmed . . . praises** adorned his praise of you   59 **By . . . you** by consistently disparaging praise itself as not sufficient to measure your true worth   61 **cital** account, recital   64 **instantly** simultaneously.   66 **envy** hostility   67 **owe** own   68 **wantonness** playful sportiveness.   71 **liberty** licentiousness.

74 **shrink under my courtesy** (1) be daunted by my greater courtesy (2) fall back before my attack.   82–4 **To . . . hour** Life is too short to spend it basely, even if life were to last only the time needed for the dial (or sundial) to advance a single hour, ending when that hour is up.   86 **brave** glorious   87 **for** as for.   **fair** just   91 **I . . . talking** I have no calling as an orator.   96 *Esperance* (The motto of the Percy family.)   99 **heaven to earth** i.e., I'll wager heaven against earth 5.3. **Location: Shrewsbury field. The scene is virtually continuous.** 0.1 *power* army.   0.2 *Alarum* Trumpet signal to advance

BLUNT   They tell thee true.

DOUGLAS
The lord of Stafford dear today hath bought   7
Thy likeness, for instead of thee, King Harry,   8
This sword hath ended him. So shall it thee,
Unless thou yield thee as my prisoner.

BLUNT
I was not born a yielder, thou proud Scot,
And thou shalt find a king that will revenge
Lord Stafford's death.   *They fight. Douglas kills Blunt.*

Then enter Hotspur.

HOTSPUR
Oh, Douglas, hadst thou fought at Holmedon thus,
I never had triumphed upon a Scot.

DOUGLAS
All's done, all's won; here breathless lies the King.   16

HOTSPUR   Where?

DOUGLAS   Here.

HOTSPUR
This, Douglas? No. I know this face full well.
A gallant knight he was; his name was Blunt,
Semblably furnished like the King himself.   21

DOUGLAS
A fool go with thy soul, whither it goes!   22
A borrowed title hast thou bought too dear.
Why didst thou tell me that thou wert a king?

HOTSPUR
The King hath many marching in his coats.   25

DOUGLAS
Now, by my sword, I will kill all his coats!
I'll murder all his wardrobe, piece by piece,
Until I meet the King.

HOTSPUR   Up, and away!
Our soldiers stand full fairly for the day.   [*Exeunt.*]   29

Alarum. Enter Falstaff, solus.

FALSTAFF   Though I could scape shot-free at London, I   30
fear the shot here; here's no scoring but upon the pate.   31
Soft, who are you? Sir Walter Blunt. There's honor for
you. Here's no vanity! I am as hot as molten lead, and   33
as heavy too. God keep lead out of me! I need no more
weight than mine own bowels. I have led my raga-
muffins where they are peppered. There's not three of
my hundred and fifty left alive, and they are for the
town's end, to beg during life. But who comes here?   38

Enter the Prince.

PRINCE
What, stands thou idle here? Lend me thy sword.

Many a nobleman lies stark and stiff
Under the hoofs of vaunting enemies,
Whose deaths are yet unrevenged. I prithee,
Lend me thy sword.

FALSTAFF   Oh, Hal, I prithee, give me leave to breathe
awhile. Turk Gregory never did such deeds in arms as   45
I have done this day. I have paid Percy, I have made   46
him sure.   47

PRINCE
He is, indeed, and living to kill thee.
I prithee, lend me thy sword.

FALSTAFF   Nay, before God, Hal, if Percy be alive, thou
gets not my sword; but take my pistol, if thou wilt.

PRINCE
Give it me. What, is it in the case?

FALSTAFF   Ay, Hal, 'tis hot, 'tis hot. There's that will   53
sack a city.
           *The Prince draws it out and finds it to be a bottle
                                              of sack.*

PRINCE
What, is it a time to jest and dally now?
                        He throws the bottle at him. Exit.

FALSTAFF   Well, if Percy be alive, I'll pierce him. If he do   56
come in my way, so; if he do not, if I come in his   57
willingly, let him make a carbonado of me. I like not   58
such grinning honor as Sir Walter hath. Give me life,
which if I can save, so; if not, honor comes unlooked
for, and there's an end.   [*Exit.*]   61

[5.4]

*Alarum. Excursions. Enter the King, the Prince,
Lord John of Lancaster, [and the] Earl of
Westmorland.*

KING   I prithee,
Harry, withdraw thyself; thou bleedest too much.
Lord John of Lancaster, go you with him.

LANCASTER
Not I, my lord, unless I did bleed too.

PRINCE
I beseech Your Majesty, make up,   5
Lest your retirement do amaze your friends.   6

KING
I will do so. My lord of Westmorland,
Lead him to his tent.

7 dear dearly   7–8 bought Thy likeness paid for his resemblance to
you   16 breathless i.e., dead   21 Semblably furnished similarly
accoutered   22 A . . . soul i.e., May the stigma of "fool" accompany
your soul (for having dressed as a decoy of King Henry)   25 coats
vests worn over armor embroidered with a coat of arms.   29 stand . . .
day i.e., seem in an auspicious position, likely to win the victory.
30 shot-free without paying the tavern bill   31 scoring (1) cutting
(2) marking up of charges, by notches on a stick or on the inn door
33 Here's no vanity! i.e. (ironically), If this doesn't show what I was
saying about honor, then nothing does!   38 town's end i.e., city gate,
frequented by beggars

45 Turk Gregory (*Turk* is an abusive term signifying a tyrant, and
Gregory refers probably to Pope Gregory XIII, who was assumed to
have encouraged the Massacre of Saint Bartholomew [1572], in which
many French Protestants were slain, and to have encouraged plots
against Elizabeth.)   46–7 made him sure made sure of him. (But
Prince Hal takes *sure* in a different sense, meaning "safe.")   53 hot
(Falstaff implies he has been firing at the enemy.)   56 Percy . . .
pierce (Elizabethan pronunciation rendered the pun more obvious
than it is now.)   57 so well and good   58 carbonado meat scored
across for broiling   61 there's an end (1) that concludes the subject of
my catechism (see 5.1.129–40) (2) thus life ends.
5.4 Location: Scene continues at Shrewsbury field.
0.1 Excursions Sorties. (The fallen body of Blunt may be removed at
some point or may be onstage still at 5.4.77 when Hal kills Hotspur.)
5 make up go forward   6 retirement retreat.   amaze alarm

WESTMORLAND
Come, my lord, I'll lead you to your tent.
PRINCE
Lead me, my lord? I do not need your help.
And God forbid a shallow scratch should drive
The Prince of Wales from such a field as this,
Where stained nobility lies trodden on
And rebels' arms triumph in massacres!
LANCASTER
We breathe too long. Come, cousin Westmorland,   15
Our duty this way lies. For God's sake, come.
                    [Exeunt Prince John and Westmorland.]
PRINCE
By God, thou hast deceived me, Lancaster!
I did not think thee lord of such a spirit.
Before, I loved thee as a brother, John,
But now I do respect thee as my soul.
KING
I saw him hold Lord Percy at the point   21
With lustier maintenance than I did look for   22
Of such an ungrown warrior.
PRINCE
Oh, this boy lends mettle to us all!   Exit.

                    [Enter Douglas.]

DOUGLAS
Another king? They grow like Hydra's heads.   25
I am the Douglas, fatal to all those
That wear those colors on them. What art thou   27
That counterfeit'st the person of a king?
KING
The King himself, who, Douglas, grieves at heart
So many of his shadows thou hast met   30
And not the very King. I have two boys
Seek Percy and thyself about the field;   32
But, seeing thou fall'st on me so luckily,
I will assay thee; and defend thyself.   34
DOUGLAS
I fear thou art another counterfeit;
And yet, in faith, thou bearest thee like a king.
But mine I am sure thou art, whoe'er thou be,
And thus I win thee.
                    They fight; the King being in danger,
                    enter Prince of Wales.
PRINCE
Hold up thy head, vile Scot, or thou art like   39
Never to hold it up again! The spirits
Of valiant Shirley, Stafford, Blunt, are in my arms.
It is the Prince of Wales that threatens thee,
Who never promiseth but he means to pay.   43
                    They fight. Douglas flieth.
Cheerly, my lord. How fares Your Grace?

Sir Nicholas Gawsey hath for succor sent,
And so hath Clifton. I'll to Clifton straight.
KING   Stay and breathe awhile.
Thou hast redeemed thy lost opinion,   48
And showed thou mak'st some tender of my life   49
In this fair rescue thou hast brought to me.
PRINCE
Oh, God, they did me too much injury
That ever said I hearkened for your death.   52
If it were so, I might have let alone
The insulting hand of Douglas over you,   54
Which would have been as speedy in your end
As all the poisonous potions in the world,
And saved the treacherous labor of your son.
KING
Make up to Clifton; I'll to Sir Nicholas Gawsey.   58
                    Exit King.

                    Enter Hotspur.

HOTSPUR
If I mistake not, thou art Harry Monmouth.
PRINCE
Thou speak'st as if I would deny my name.
HOTSPUR
My name is Harry Percy.
PRINCE   Why then, I see
A very valiant rebel of the name.
I am the Prince of Wales; and think not, Percy,
To share with me in glory any more.
Two stars keep not their motion in one sphere,
Nor can one England brook a double reign   66
Of Harry Percy and the Prince of Wales.
HOTSPUR
Nor shall it, Harry, for the hour is come
To end the one of us; and would to God
Thy name in arms were now as great as mine!
PRINCE
I'll make it greater ere I part from thee,
And all the budding honors on thy crest
I'll crop to make a garland for my head.   73
HOTSPUR
I can no longer brook thy vanities.   They fight.   74

                    Enter Falstaff.

FALSTAFF   Well said, Hal! To it, Hal! Nay, you shall find   75
no boy's play here, I can tell you.   76

                    Enter Douglas. He fighteth with Falstaff, who falls
                    down as if he were dead.   [Exit Douglas.]
                    The Prince killeth Percy.

HOTSPUR
Oh, Harry, thou hast robbed me of my youth!
I better brook the loss of brittle life
Than those proud titles thou hast won of me;

15 breathe rest, pause for breath (as also at line 47)   21 at the point
at sword's point   22 lustier maintenance more vigorous bearing
25 Hydra's heads (The heads of the Lernaean Hydra grew again as
fast as they were cut off.)   27 colors i.e., the colors of the King's
insignia   30 shadows having form without substance   32 Seek who
seek   34 assay thee put you to the test   39 like likely   43 pay
(1) settle a debt (2) kill.

48 opinion reputation   49 thou . . . of you have some care for
52 hearkened listened (as for welcome news)   54 insulting exulting
58 Make up Advance   66 brook endure   73 crop pluck   74 vanities
empty boasts.   75 Well said Well done   76.3 killeth mortally
wounds

They wound my thoughts worse than thy sword my
   flesh.
But thoughts, the slaves of life, and life, time's fool,   81
And time, that takes survey of all the world,
Must have a stop. Oh, I could prophesy,
But that the earthy and cold hand of death
Lies on my tongue. No, Percy, thou art dust,
And food for—   [He dies.]

PRINCE
For worms, brave Percy. Fare thee well, great heart.
Ill-weaved ambition, how much art thou shrunk!
When that this body did contain a spirit,
A kingdom for it was too small a bound;
But now two paces of the vilest earth
Is room enough. This earth that bears thee dead
Bears not alive so stout a gentleman.   93
If thou wert sensible of courtesy,   94
I should not make so dear a show of zeal;   95
But let my favors hide thy mangled face,   96
And, even in thy behalf, I'll thank myself
For doing these fair rites of tenderness.
            [He covers Hotspur's face with a scarf
                              or other favor.]
Adieu, and take thy praise with thee to heaven!
Thy ignominy sleep with thee in the grave,
But not remembered in thy epitaph!
                 He spieth Falstaff on the ground.
What, old acquaintance, could not all this flesh
Keep in a little life? Poor Jack, farewell!
I could have better spared a better man.
Oh, I should have a heavy miss of thee   105
If I were much in love with vanity.   106
Death hath not struck so fat a deer today,
Though many dearer, in this bloody fray.
Emboweled will I see thee by and by.   109
Till then in blood by noble Percy lie.   Exit.
                      Falstaff riseth up.

FALSTAFF   Emboweled? If thou embowel me today, I'll
give you leave to powder me and eat me too tomor-   112
row. 'Sblood, 'twas time to counterfeit, or that hot ter-   113
magant Scot had paid me, scot and lot too. Counterfeit?   114
I lie, I am no counterfeit. To die is to be a counterfeit,
for he is but the counterfeit of a man who hath not the
life of a man; but to counterfeit dying, when a man
thereby liveth, is to be no counterfeit but the true and
perfect image of life indeed. The better part of valor is   119
discretion, in the which better part I have saved my
life. Zounds, I am afraid of this gunpowder Percy,
though he be dead. How if he should counterfeit too
and rise? By my faith, I am afraid he would prove the

better counterfeit. Therefore I'll make him sure; yea,
and I'll swear I killed him. Why may not he rise as well
as I? Nothing confutes me but eyes, and nobody sees   126
me. Therefore, sirrah [stabbing him], with a new
wound in your thigh, come you along with me.
               He takes up Hotspur on his back.

      Enter Prince [and] John of Lancaster.

PRINCE
Come, brother John; full bravely hast thou fleshed   129
Thy maiden sword.
LANCASTER   But soft, whom have we here?
Did you not tell me this fat man was dead?
PRINCE   I did; I saw him dead,
Breathless and bleeding on the ground.—Art thou
   alive?
Or is it fantasy that plays upon our eyesight?
I prithee, speak. We will not trust our eyes
Without our ears. Thou art not what thou seem'st.
FALSTAFF   No, that's certain, I am not a double man; but   137
if I be not Jack Falstaff, then am I a Jack. There is Percy   138
[throwing the body down]. If your father will do me
any honor, so; if not, let him kill the next Percy himself. I look to be either earl or duke, I can assure you.
PRINCE
Why, Percy I killed myself and saw thee dead.
FALSTAFF   Didst thou? Lord, Lord, how this world is
given to lying! I grant you I was down and out of
breath, and so was he; but we rose both at an instant   145
and fought a long hour by Shrewsbury clock. If I may
be believed, so; if not, let them that should reward
valor bear the sin upon their own heads. I'll take it   148
upon my death I gave him this wound in the thigh.   149
If the man were alive and would deny it, zounds, I
would make him eat a piece of my sword.
LANCASTER
This is the strangest tale that ever I heard.
PRINCE
This is the strangest fellow, brother John.—
Come, bring your luggage nobly on your back.
For my part, if a lie may do thee grace,   155
I'll gild it with the happiest terms I have.   156
                  A retreat is sounded.
The trumpet sounds retreat; the day is our.   157
Come, brother, let us to the highest of the field,   158
To see what friends are living, who are dead.
         Exeunt [Prince of Wales and Lancaster].
FALSTAFF   I'll follow, as they say, for reward. He that re-
wards me, God reward him! If I do grow great, I'll
grow less; for I'll purge, and leave sack, and live   162
cleanly as a nobleman should do.
                 Exit [bearing off the body].

---

81 thoughts . . . fool i.e., our mental consciousness, which is dependent on physical existence, and our life itself, which is subject to time
93 stout valiant   **94 sensible of courtesy** able to hear my praise
95 dear handsome, heartfelt.   **zeal** admiration   **96 favors** plume,
scarf, glove, or similar article   **105 heavy** (1) serious (2) corpulent
106 vanity frivolity.   **109 Emboweled** Disemboweled, i.e., for
embalming and burial   **112 powder** salt   **113–14 termagant** violent
and blustering, like the heathen god of the Saracens in medieval and
Renaissance lore   **114 paid** i.e., killed.   **scot and lot** i.e., in full.
(Originally the phrase was the term for a parish tax.)   **119 part** con-
stituent part, quality, role

126 Nothing . . . eyes i.e., Nothing can contradict me but an eyewit-
ness   **129 fleshed** initiated (in battle)   **137 double man** (1) specter
(2) two men.   **138 a Jack** a knave.   **145 at an instant** simultaneously
148–9 take . . . death i.e., swear with my eternal soul at risk   **155 a lie**
i.e., this lie of yours.   **grace** credit   **156 happiest** most felicitous
157 our ours.   **158 highest** highest vantage point   **162 purge** (1)
reduce in weight, using laxatives (2) repent

[5.5]

The trumpets sound. Enter the King, Prince of Wales, Lord John of Lancaster, Earl of Westmorland, with Worcester and Vernon prisoners.

KING
Thus ever did rebellion find rebuke.
Ill-spirited Worcester! Did not we send grace,
Pardon, and terms of love to all of you?
And wouldst thou turn our offers contrary?
Misuse the tenor of thy kinsman's trust?   5
Three knights upon our party slain today,
A noble earl, and many a creature else
Had been alive this hour,
If like a Christian thou hadst truly borne
Betwixt our armies true intelligence.   10

WORCESTER
What I have done my safety urged me to;
And I embrace this fortune patiently,
Since not to be avoided it falls on me.

KING
Bear Worcester to the death, and Vernon too.
Other offenders we will pause upon.
        [*Exeunt Worcester and Vernon, guarded.*]
How goes the field?

PRINCE
The noble Scot, Lord Douglas, when he saw
The fortune of the day quite turned from him,
The noble Percy slain, and all his men

Upon the foot of fear, fled with the rest;   20
And falling from a hill, he was so bruised
That the pursuers took him. At my tent
The Douglas is; and I beseech Your Grace
I may dispose of him.
KING   With all my heart.
PRINCE
Then, brother John of Lancaster,
To you this honorable bounty shall belong.   26
Go to the Douglas, and deliver him
Up to his pleasure, ransomless and free.
His valors shown upon our crests today   29
Have taught us how to cherish such high deeds
Even in the bosom of our adversaries.
LANCASTER
I thank Your Grace for this high courtesy,
Which I shall give away immediately.   33
KING
Then this remains, that we divide our power.
You, son John, and my cousin Westmorland
Towards York shall bend you with your dearest speed 36
To meet Northumberland and the prelate Scroop,
Who, as we hear, are busily in arms.
Myself and you, son Harry, will towards Wales,
To fight with Glendower and the Earl of March.
Rebellion in this land shall lose his sway,   41
Meeting the check of such another day;   42
And since this business so fair is done,   43
Let us not leave till all our own be won.   *Exeunt.*   44

5.5 Location: The battlefield.
5 Misuse . . . trust? i.e., Would you abuse Hotspur's confidence in you (by concealing the generosity of my offer, in your role as emissary)?   10 intelligence information, report.

20 Upon . . . fear fleeing in panic   26 this honorable bounty the honor of this bounteous act   29 crests i.e., helmets   33 give away pass along, confer on Douglas   36 bend you direct your course. dearest most urgent   41 his its   42 Meeting . . . day i.e., when the rebellion is entirely repulsed at one more battlefield   43 fair successfully   44 leave leave off

---

Henry IV, Part One on Stage

Henry IV, Part One has always been popular on stage. For its first two centuries, as we have seen, Falstaff was the audience favorite. A gradual evolution in interpretation of other characters, as well as a movement toward authenticity in stage settings, combined to make possible different, more integrated readings of the play's action and Falstaff's role in it. In the early nineteenth century, when William Charles Macready proved successful for several decades as Hotspur, the fiery young Percy began sharing the attention that had heretofore been directed to Falstaff. In the twentieth century, the play was increasingly performed as part of a cycle sometimes called *The Henriad*. Viewed as part of a continuous historical narrative, Prince Hal's gradual transformation came to be seen as the play's underlying theme.

The Elizabethan Era: Speculation and Doubling

We cannot say for sure who first played Prince Hal and Falstaff. The scholar Edmund Malone said that he had seen a tract stating that Falstaff was first played by John Heminges (or Hemming), one of the two members of Shakespeare's acting company who later oversaw the publication of the 1623 Folio. Others, including Jean E. Howard, have speculated that the role was originally played either by Will Kempe, the company's favorite clown (see Howard below, and David Wiles, 116–135), or by Thomas Pope, who also played clown roles for the Lord Chamberlain's Men. *Henry IV, Part One* is suited to any of the outdoor London amphitheaters in which it would have been performed during its first few years, for it makes no unusual staging demands. A large stage would serve, allowing the battle scenes to flow in Act 5, and the pillars, such a those at the Globe, to serve as hiding places for Hal and

Poins as they watch the robbery in 2.2. The props required include masks (vizards), daggers, swords, shields, a crown, a throne, tables, chairs, and drinking cups. The play was almost certainly performed in Elizabethan "modern dress" rather than in medieval costumes. With careful doubling, the play's thirty-four speaking roles could be assumed by a company of seventeen actors. Two actors must be able to sound Welsh, and one must sing (3.1.242) in that language.

The Restoration and the Eighteenth Century: Resisting "Improvements"

In 1660, when the public playhouses re-opened, Falstaff already had taken on independent life as the subject of the short, droll play *The Bouncing Knight*. That entertainment was performed during the mid seventeenth century when the theaters were still officially closed. After 1660, the entire *Henry IV, Part One* was performed, though not with the same success as the more sensational *Richard III*. Theater historian Lois Potter suggests that the absence of good roles for women worked against *Henry IV, Part One* and the other plays of the second tetralogy (285). Because beautiful actresses were a novelty and a primary draw to London playhouses during the Restoration era, the fact that there are no women at Henry's court and that women speak only four percent of the lines in *Henry IV, Part One* (see Howard and Rackin, 23ff.) probably affected the play's reception, at least in the first two decades after Charles II assumed the throne. In 1682, actor-manager Thomas Betterton played Hotspur in a performance of "fierce and flashing fire," wrote Colley Cibber (Bevington, 87); in 1700 Betterton played Falstaff to wide acclaim. One commentator wrote that "the critics allow Mr. Betterton has hit the humour of Falstaff better then any that have aimed at it before" (Thorn-Drury, 68 from Kastan edition). Betterton confined his revision of *Henry IV, Part One* to cuts rather than adopting the post-Restoration practice of freely reordering and rewriting scenes. "In essence he did not do much more than any modern director does with a Shakespeare play, seeking cuts that will clarify the conception of the play and speed up its playing" (Kastan, 83). Along with *Julius Caesar, Hamlet,* and *Othello, Henry IV, Part One* was one of few Shakespeare plays to escape Restoration and Neoclassical "improvements."

During the first half of the eighteenth century James Quin was praised as a Falstaff who projected intelligence and refinement. Quin played Falstaff for thirty years until 1751; he cut the playacting scene in the tavern from the second act, an excision that lasted past the midpoint of the nineteenth century. Although a lingering judgment about Shakespeare's blemishes remained—epitomized during the mid eighteenth century by Charlotte Lennox's invidious comparisons of the plays to their sources and by Dr. Johnson's listing of Shakespeare's faults—the indecorous Falstaff remained beloved. Like so many eighteenth-century critics who viewed Falstaff as a real personage living independently from the play, Henry MacKenzie remarked in 1786 that the character's "humor is infinite and his wit admirable," despite his "Epicurean grossness" (in Bevington, *Critical Essays*, 45). Toward the end of Quin's reign in the role, he appeared (in 1746–1747) at Covent Garden with David Garrick as Hotspur. Quin recognized the fundamental change in style that Garrick's acting represented, remarking of the younger man's nimble movement and conversational speaking, "If the young fellow is right, I and the rest of the players have been all wrong."

Garrick dominates the history of Shakespeare in performance from his debut as Richard III in 1741 until his death in 1779. Although Garrick adapted Shakespeare as was the custom, he frequently restored passages to the plays and he consolidated Shakespeare's status as the greatest of English playwrights, acting in and producing most of the tragedies and several of the histories, including *Henry IV, Part One*. Garrick's artistically rigorous and well-attended Theatre Royal, Drury Lane based its repertory on original comedies and the Shakespeare plays just mentioned. Garrick favored well-rehearsed and consistently presented productions opulently costumed in the clothing of his own era. Garrick disciplined his audiences as well as his actors, and one of his most important reforms was the final banishment of spectators from the stage. He approached more closely to the modern concept of a director than anyone before him, putting on plays with exceptional care for overall effect, demonstrating by his own acting what superb roles they contained. To these ends, as we have seen in Chapter 5, he became not only the greatest actor of his age, but also an important technical innovator.

The Nineteenth Century: Historical Accuracy and Unified Approaches

Very early in the nineteenth century, an admired American Falstaff emerged, James Henry Hackett; he performed the role annually for nearly sixty years in the United States and England. He held the opposite view from Quin, performing Falstaff as a character whose intellect and breeding had been corrupted. Stephen Kemble was an entertaining, though apparently one-dimensional, Falstaff during the first two decades of the century; his innovative addition of Falstaff mightily asleep at the beginning of 1.2 has come down to the present day and was part of Kevin Kline's 2003 portrayal at Lincoln Center. The most powerful influences upon later Victorian stagings of *Henry IV, Part One* were another Kemble brother, Charles, and actor-manager William Charles Macready. In 1818, Macready began a long stage reign playing Hotspur in Part One and the King in Part Two. The actor eventually rose to the leadership of his profession, and at Covent Garden and Drury Lane he was known for restoring Shakespeare's texts and enforcing high standards of scenery and costume based upon thorough historical research. His historical reconstructions and his success as Hotspur turned attention away from Falstaff toward the larger historical action and the story of Hal's personal growth toward kingliness.

Charles Kemble also strove for such period accuracy when he produced *Henry IV, Part One* at Covent Garden in 1824. For several decades after Kemble's and Macready's productions, the play was less staged, for producers with a taste for lavish spectacle found it too difficult and expensive to mount with the kind of "authenticity" then in favor. Herbert Beerbohm Tree's production at London's Haymarket Theatre in 1896 was one of the last to espouse this view of Shakespearean stagecraft. Although Tree counseled that such antiquarianism should not be deferred to uncritically, he accepted that the creation of realistic, "accurate" illusions should be the aim of the contemporary stage. He did just that in the psychologically based character acting and lavish production in which he played Falstaff.

The Twentieth Century: From Romanticism to Realism, Cycles and Adaptations

One of the most important influences upon twentieth-century productions of *Henry IV, Part One* was the theory that the eight history plays of the two tetralogies (see the section introduction, "Shakespeare and the English History Play") could be profitably read and staged, and perhaps were written, as a continuous and coherent series. During the first decade of the twentieth century, Frank Benson produced *The Life and Death of King John* and nearly the entire first and second tetralogy at the Memorial Theatre in Stratford-upon-Avon, thus inaugurating the fashion for viewing the plays and their themes in relationship to one another as parts of a single narrative. The plays had been cut, and the scenes, in some cases, had been rearranged. Nonetheless, Benson's "Grand Cycle of Shakespeare's Plays," launched in 1901 and played complete in 1906, was the first attempt that we know of to present the English history plays in English as a sequence. A German production offered precedent for this approach. As Lois Potter notes, mid–nineteenth-century German scholars had already described Shakespeare's English history plays as a national epic. In 1864 Franz Dingelstedt translated and staged all but one of the plays of the two tetralogies in Weimar (Potter, 288). In England, nearly fifty years would pass after Benson's production before the English theater would again stage the histories as a series. Since then, many adapters have compressed the two parts of *Henry IV* into one evening-length work, usually emphasizing the coming-of-age of the crown prince. Orson Welles was such an adapter. He conceived a project for the stage in which the two tetralogies would become a two-part work called *Five Kings*. He showed the first part in 1939 in New York. It failed then and in a revival in Dublin. These stage productions became the basis for his successful and influential rumination upon Falstaff and Prince Hal in his film, *Falstaff: Chimes at Midnight* (1966, see pp. 438–440).

A persuasive critical argument for the narrative unity of the history plays came in 1944 with J. Dover Wilson's *The Fortunes of Falstaff*. Wilson argued that the *Henry IV* plays could be more easily apprehended as a unit. A 1945 production at the Old Vic, directed by John Burrell, with Ralph Richardson as Falstaff and Laurence Olivier as Hotspur in Part One and Justice Shallow in Part Two, proved a landmark. Olivier played Hotspur with what has been called a stabbing, darting fire, and stammered especially in his death throes as he tried to move past the letter "W" to complete the thought "food for w–worms." Richardson is remembered as having reached deeply into Falstaff's agile mind and examined his rich, witty prose with such zest that his delight in his own inventiveness allowed him to transcend even the darkening pathos of the part. His performance elicited universal delight, becoming definitive for most critics who saw it. That Old Vic production took the politics of the play seriously. In the context of World War II, it revealed the political and military tensions in the play; from those tensions and the social institutions that breeds them, Richardson's Falstaff separated himself with child-like gaiety.

Dover Wilson's view that the second tetralogy was conceived as a unit underpinned a Stratford production of the four plays during the 1951 Festival of Britain. Staged on a single set by Tanya Moiseiwitsch, with the same cast playing most roles throughout the series, the tetralogy was well-received even though audiences had to wait one-month intervals between the premieres of each play. Perhaps more importantly, the Stratford production became a kind of template for later stagings by the Royal Shakespeare Company, which emerged from the Stratford organization in 1961.

In 1963 the RSC staged John Barton's bold adaptation of the first tetralogy as *The Wars of the Roses*. Audiences could see that sequence, which now consisted of three plays, in one day or on a weekend. The following season, for the four-hundredth anniversary of Shakespeare's birth, Barton and RSC director Peter Hall staged the second tetralogy along with *The Wars of the Roses*, thus presenting the continuous history from the end of the reign of Richard II to the accession of Henry VII, the Tudor monarch, at the end of *Richard III*. In this historic seven-play series the collaborators emphasized the dark side of the plays; their *Henry IV, Part One* had as its final image the hanging of Worcester and Vernon. Ian Holm was Hal, Hugh Griffith played Falstaff, and Eric Porter was Henry IV. Exploring the histories as specific examples of general historical truths, Hall and Barton viewed the making of the modern nation as a power struggle that corrupted many participants and involved the working out, as in ancient drama, of a kind of curse begun with the deposition of Richard II. The plays announced Hall's taste for relevance and the emergence of an RSC style—spare and muscular.

The last quarter of the century brought many inventive productions of the play. In 1987–1988, English Shakespeare Company director Michael Bogdanov and co-artistic director Michael Pennington toured their own Wars of the Roses, a staging of seven history plays over twenty-five hours (see pp. 440–441) that offered clear parallels to contemporary Great Britain. The directors agreed that Prince Hal was a "dirty rat" and Henry IV a "cold bureaucrat"; they attempted to point up the division between conservative English voters, who had recently re-elected Margaret Thatcher, and the electorate in Scotland, Ireland, and Wales, which had voted against her (Potter, 295–296). The Guthrie Theater in Minneapolis staged a three-hour, fifteen-minute version of the two Henry IV plays in 1990 as part of a three-production repertory with Richard II and Henry V. The Guthrie text owed a large debt to Falstaff: Chimes at Midnight (1966), the Orson Welles amalgam of the Henry IV plays. Welles himself had played Falstaff in his auteur version, which shifted the emotional dynamic from Hal's journey toward kingliness to Falstaff's heartbreaking demise; the film is considered at length below (pp. 438–440). The Shakespeare Theatre of Washington, D.C., produced a three-and-a-half hour version of Part One of the two Henry IV plays in 1994. Add to that the many stagings of Dakin Matthews's compression—at the Goodman Theatre in Chicago (1978), the Baxter Theatre Centre in Denver (1989), the Old Globe Theatre in San Diego (1995), and the Vivian Beaumont Theatre of Lincoln Center in New York (2003, described below)—and it is clear that the play(s) have retained their popularity with producers, actors, and audiences. Henry IV remains artistically exciting and politically relevant into the new millennium. Two twenty-first–century stage productions, one in London and one in New York, are described here.

The Royal Shakespeare Company. Michael Attenborough's 2000 production of Henry IV, Part One for the Royal Shakespeare Company was part of the RSC's millennium celebration, This England—The Histories. The series was resolutely postmodern in that several different directors staged the plays in three theaters at two venues, the Barbican and the Young Vic, with no attempt to unify their approaches. The only conceptual signpost in Attenborough's Henry IV, Part One was a design element—a large high-backed chair sitting in the middle of a bare stage and, depending upon who was sitting in it, serving as a throne at court or a tavern bench in Eastcheap. When David Troughton's Henry IV, pragmatic yet consumed by guilt and remorse, had completed the first scene describing his political and domestic cares, he walked away clearly burdened by the crown he wore. Out crawled his son Prince Hal from under the cloth covering the chair. A large, sleeping Falstaff rose from a trap nearby. William Houston's nervy young prince and Desmond Barrit's Falstaff displayed great physical affection for one another. Falstaff hugged and rocked Hal, and in these early scenes seemed spontaneously to improvise as entertainment for the young man he so clearly loved. In this, he contrasted with Troughton's Henry IV, who was emotionally withheld and physically distant. In Troughton's potent and empathetic interpretation, the King wanted more closeness to Hal and seemed both hurt and angry that Falstaff had replaced him in the boy's affection. He reached out to touch his prodigal heir. But Henry IV won that affection only in the later scenes of Part Two. There, he and Hal sat on the floor at the foot of the king's sickbed, finding mutual trust, respect, and love when the dying monarch gives his last words of paternal advice to his heir.

Barrit revealed many dimensions of Falstaff and proved initially funny. His Falstaff grew increasingly vain, opportunistic, and bitter, despite the moving moments in his "catechism of honor" speech. Adam Levy's Hotspur adopted a counter-cultural punk style, including a leather jacket, out of keeping with the rest of the production, yet his scenes with Lady Percy had affecting emotional chemistry. Because each character was assigned to a given actor throughout the This England series, the historical personages could readily be seen changing and developing over time. Troughton's Henry Bolingbroke, fierce in Richard II, but slowly corroded by feelings of guilt and remorse in the Henry IV plays, proved one of the revelatory highlights of the series; so too with Houston's growth from Prince Hal's real affection toward Falstaff into the coolly politic public role of Henry V.

The Lincoln Center Theater Company. Dakin Matthews revised his compression of the two Henry IV plays for this 2003 production, directed by Jack O'Brien, in which film star Kevin Kline adopted a rumbling baritone for his clear, Welles-influenced, and somewhat muted interpretation of Falstaff. The charismatic Michael Hayden offered a young, ambivalent Hal early on and made plausible the difficult transition from truant prince to true king. In this Hayden was abetted by Ethan Hawke's punk-rocker performance as Hotspur—butch-cut, bare-chested—as well as Richard Easton's crabbed, sympathetically guilt-driven Henry IV; Byron Jennings's sardonic, manipulative Worcester; and adapter Matthews's wild-haired Glendower and later, his imposing, dignified Lord Chief Justice. Jess Goldstein's opulent costuming was derived from fifteenth-century paintings, with enough contemporary touches (leather pants and lace-up jerkins for the men, for instance) to turn up the sexual as well as the political heat. Director O'Brien emphasized the father-son themes, viewing the play largely as a progression of scenes featuring fathers or surrogate fathers in situations of mentoring, play, conflict, or resolution with their respective sons or son figures. The director drew visual parallels to reinforce certain similarities of theme and situation. Hal snuggled into bed with Falstaff and his scurvy mistress Doll Tearsheet; the image was echoed when, after trying on his father's crown, he lay down with the sick king for their final—and in this production—radiant and moving reconciliation. One critic called it a "bedtime story" moment; in any case, this peaceful family snapshot forecast, at least temporarily, an end to civil war and some stability while Hal-as-Henry V was on the throne.

The production's iconic ending was especially effective. After rejecting and banishing Falstaff pending his reformation, Hayden's Henry V, now ermine-caped and surrounded by all of England, moved upstage into the uncertain future of the nation. Yet facing downstage, in a pool of painterly light, stood Kline's Falstaff, first silently weeping, then pulling his monumental body up one last time to desperately assure himself with a last deluded word. "I shall be sent for," he told the boy Francis when every one else, including Justice Shallow, had abandoned him. "I shall be sent for at night." The scene had some of the heartbreak of Welles's filmic treatment. Deluded as he was in the final scene, Falstaff had been such good company that the audience mourned him, understanding that Death was the only powerful personage who could possibly be sending for him at night.

Henry IV, Part One on Film and Television

- 1966—*Falstaff: Chimes at Midnight*, directed by Orson Welles, with Welles (Falstaff), John Gielgud (Henry IV), Keith Baxter (Prince Hal), Norman Rodway (Henry Percy, known as Hotspur), Jeanne Moreau (Doll Tearsheet), and Margaret Rutherford (Mistress Quickly). (119 min.)

    Orson Welles drew from both parts of *Henry IV* and from *Richard II, Henry V,* and *The Merry Wives of Windsor* in this remarkable and highly personal film. (It was released in Europe as *Chimes at Midnight* and in the United States as *Falstaff*.) He played as loosely with Shakespeare's narrative as Shakespeare did with his historical sources, restructuring and rearranging scenes to foreground the story of Falstaff in

In his 1966 Falstaff, *also known as* Chimes at Midnight, *Orson Welles fills the frame as the old knight; here his Falstaff wears armor for the tumultuous battles he avoids. (Internacional Films Espanola/Alpine Films/The Kobal Collection)*

the context of England's dynastic wars. The title reveals Welles's emphasis. This is a film about Shakespeare's old knight in his twilight hours and a nostalgic lament not only for Falstaff—whom Welles played with such memorable dimension, wit, and pathos—but also for "the death of Merrie England" (McMillin, 92). Film students consider it one of the great cinematic adaptations of Shakespeare, despite its technical deficiencies (such as poor synchronization and dubbing) and its psychological simplification of Falstaff. For this reason, and because it is not widely available, we will describe the film at greater than usual length.

Welles minimizes Falstaff's debauchery and other moral failings, making him more humanly attractive than the future Henry V. The extravagant, expansive Welles, once rejected by the Hollywood establishment, creates a Falstaff with whom he can identify, a good man and a genius who now can comment upon Laurence Olivier's concept of this rejected "misleader" and the boy he loved-turned-king. (See discussion of Olivier's 1946 film of *Henry V*, pp. 490–491). Like nineteenth-century character critics (and some scholars today), Welles views Falstaff's story as more important to Shakespeare than the political drama in which it is contained. Falstaff very often fills the frame, his vices virtually disappearing, leaving only the vital, celebratory aspect of the sweetened, sometimes sentimentalized character. In the end, Mistress Quickly's descriptions of his death (taken from *Henry V*) proves heartrending: "The king has killed his heart . . . ," and "all was cold as any stone."

The film opens with just such cold, a wintry scene centered on an ancient oak tree; its expansive limbs might be taken to represent Falstaff himself. Two figures are walking, one huge and with a cane, the other slender and stooped. We overhear Falstaff talking to his old friend, the country justice, Shallow. They recall hearing the "chimes at midnight" that in youth meant late-night carousing but now prefigure death. In a nod to a great interpreter of the Falstaff role, Ralph Richardson is then heard in a voiceover, his narration taken from Shakespeare's primary source, Holinshed's 1587 *Chronicles*. Henry IV is played with icy disdain and painful abstraction by John Gielgud, whose sonorous voice and stately demeanor make him an austere and imposing figure, gaunt, haunted, almost calcified by guilt. When he meditates on "Nature's soft nurse" of sleep in the famous set speech ending "Uneasy lies the head that wears a crown" (*Henry IV, Part Two* [3.1]), Gielgud's performance grows as sympathetic as any interpreter's ever recorded or reviewed in the role. Welles's golden voice is a deeper rumbling baritone by comparison to Gielgud's lighter, more musical tone. The complementary sonorities of these two actors are one of many reasons to hope that the film will eventually be restored, as Welles's *Othello* has been.

Falstaff: Chimes at Midnight, like most of Welles's later projects, had to be made economically (see "Close-up: Orson Welles"). Because Gielgud was such a busy and highly paid actor, Welles had to film all of Gielgud's scenes in Spain in one week. Gielgud recalls, in his book *An Actor and His Time,* that he never "even saw (Welles) made up as Falstaff until I watched the film in the cinema." Body doubles served for the principals in other scenes, with careful editing smoothing the various shots into place. Because the sound was added in two different studios, it suffers both poor synchronization and also a distracting hum in the final scenes.

Nonetheless, the director's intentions are clear. Welles employs diagonal shafts of light, deep shadows, and oblique camera angles to create the somber atmosphere that pervades the court scenes of the film. These were shot on location in a castle that looms above Barcelona, where this Spanish-Swiss co-production was filmed. In the tavern scenes with which the court episodes alternate, Welles places Falstaff,

Hal, and their cohorts Poins, Bardolph, and eventually Pistol in a wood-timbered building with a low-lying roof. Although there is nothing opulent about these surroundings, the wood, the fires, and the presence of others contrast mightily with the stony grandeur of the court. One tavern scene involves a spirited dance that fires the blood of the many participants; in its warmth and energy it evokes the Merrie Olde England that Welles told interviewers he was here eulogizing as its spirit was being replaced by that of a colder imperial modern nation.

Among the strengths of *Falstaff: Chimes at Midnight* is its depiction of the Battle of Shrewsbury in a ten-minute sequence capturing the tumult and savagery of actual warfare. A rude wind blows as the scene begins with a visual allusion to Laurence Olivier's *Henry V* film (see the "Frame-by-Frame" following that play on pp. 493–495): Long arrows and lethal pikes are arrayed in ominous lines, and heavily armored knights are lowered from trees onto their horses. But the differences between the films are immediately apparent. (For one thing, Welles's film was shot in black and white.) Balletic martial choreography lends the opening of Olivier's Battle of Agincourt the stylized beauty of a medieval tapestry, whereas Welles creates a much more naturalistic representation of war's extremes, from the ridiculous sight of Falstaff blustering about to the dehumanizing savagery of soldiers who repeatedly stab their victims with what appears to be passionate relish. In the fog of this war, with horses' breath steaming from exertion, both animals and men are stabbed and pierced indiscriminately, and soon it is impossible to tell which side is which in the civil broil. The common men fight with no armor and the crudest of weapons—axes, maces, and simple bows and arrows. Fear is the only expression on the common soldiers' faces as arrows fly, pikes pierce their backs, and the awful thundering sound of hooves mixes with the screams of men who suffer multiple gashes even as religious music ironically plays in the background. Welles's close-ups and quick cuts heighten the sense of confusion and anxiety; the tension and fury of battle is created as much by the editing as by any complex direction. The virtuoso editing also creates the illusion that many more actors are in the scenes than were actually there.

As the bloody conflict progresses, bodies are seen being tossed into a dirty pile in an image that calls to mind Hotspur's final words: "thou art dust, / And food for—" No glory accrues to anyone in the scene; man is reduced by war to the dust from which he came. Welles also heightens Shakespeare's technique of counterpoint, cutting from the presumably honor-driven battle scenes to their burlesque in bleak Falstaffian comedy. While other knights are hoisted aloft on trapezes and then lowered from the trees onto their horses, the massive Falstaff cannot be raised. He tumbles loudly to the ground, his weight pulling him down. He looks like Humpty-Dumpty encased in bizarre armor as he wanders about brandishing his sword, attempting to avoid engagement. As Stephen Buhler notes in his study of Shakespeare on film, *Ocular Proof*, Welles sees even the Prince's survival as a matter of luck, not Providence, nor even honor (107). The encounter of the two Harrys is swift, with Hal stabbing Hotspur upwards underneath his armor and the Prince's valediction to his rival longer than the hand-to-hand combat itself. Afterward, when Falstaff rises as if from the dead upon the word "Embowelled!" his claim to have killed Hotspur is at least partially believed by Gielgud's surprised Henry IV, who here has overheard the false boast.

Welles conceives Falstaff as a lovable rogue, whose greedy appetite for life, for the rewards of falsified honor, and the pleasures of the flesh eventually turn the Prince against him. In a superb performance, Welles makes the old knight a near-tragic figure, a good man abandoned by an unfeeling new regime, the victim of historical necessity. The film encapsulates many of the accomplishments—and frustrations—of Welles as an actor, writer, and director. Welles called *Falstaff: Chimes at Midnight* a personal favorite among his films, for reasons that most viewers will certainly understand.

- 1979—Director David Giles, producer Cedric Messina, BBC, with Jon Finch (Henry IV), David Gwillim (Prince Hal), Anthony Quayle (Falstaff), Tim Pigott-Smith (Hotspur), Robert Morris (Mortimer), Richard Owens (Glendower), Michele Dotrice (Lady Percy), and Brenda Bruce (Mistress Quickly). (147 min.)

This is a close-in, even-handed, and traditional film version of the play shot in a realistic studio setting that sometimes makes the actors' deliveries appear overly stylized, even stiff. Director David Giles presents the text uncut, with the scenes following the order established in the first complete Quarto and Folio. Anthony Quayle makes a subdued, often anxious Falstaff, not particularly potent or appealing even in the catechism on honor, while David Gwillim is an overtly calculating and detached Prince Hal, weighing his reformation from the start. Giles shows us, for instance, how Hal reacts to others by placing him in the foreground and allowing him to share his first reactions with the audience before he turns to join the scene. The most full-blooded performance comes from Tim Piggott-Smith as an impulsive and appealing Hotspur, nim-

ble of mind and body. Gwillim's performance has been praised, to be sure, by at least one critic (T. F. Wharton in "Henry the Fourth Parts I and II," from *Text and Performance*, 1983) as "very deeply studied playing . . . of a very shallow man."

Henry IV, played by Jon Finch, here seems not much older than his son. In Finch's somewhat monotonously delivered speeches, the King becomes a Lady Macbeth figure, rubbing his hands, washing them, wearing soft gray gloves to soothe them. Giles no doubt is suggesting here the skin disease that eventually led to Henry's death, but the gestures, seen so close up and so early in the action, are often distracting and point more toward Henry's guilt over the usurpation than to his medical condition. Finch strongly emphasizes one thematic possibility—that his badly behaved son, Prince Hal, may have been sent as a scourge to punish Henry for his usurpation.

The secondary roles in the tavern (that of Pistol, for instance) are taken by actors of vigor and individuality, although the aristocrats on both sides are not so well differentiated. The twilight scene in the rebel camp was filmed indoors, and though the relationships of Hotspur to Lady Percy and Mortimer to his Welsh wife lack much erotic charge, the scene, with its Welsh song, becomes an effective domestic interlude before the battle.

The battle scene itself, and especially Henry's tent, have a studied studio air about them. There's a good deal of stage blood, especially unconvincing on Prince Hal's face and as it bubbles up from Hotspur's dying throat. All in all, this is a well-spoken, if rather flat and slowly paced production, lacking charismatic performances and a sense of urgency and excitement in its depiction of the Battle of Shrewsbury. With its companion, Part Two, this *Henry IV* is a middling accomplishment for the BBC television series, now available on digitally remastered DVDs.

- 1989—*The Wars of the Roses.* Director Michael Bogdanov, with Michael Pennington (Prince Hal), Barry Stanton (Falstaff), and Michael Cronin (Henry IV). (160 min.)

Director Michael Bogdanov has said his goal is to create productions of Shakespeare that will appeal especially to young people by using contemporary references, props, and costumes, and by finding associations in the language that will resonate with popular media and culture, current events, and prevailing values. Certainly, the English Shakespeare Company's 1986 staging of *Henry IV, Parts One and Two* was edgy and iconoclastic. The production was the company's first; it opened at the Old Vic Theatre, then toured to England and Canada as an antidote (or at least complement) to the very different RSC style. Within two years of that initial production, Bogdanov had staged seven history plays in a compilation called *The Wars of the Roses* that attempted to fuse past and present ideas about English history. These plays were taped during one intense week of shooting at the Grand Theatre in Swansea; the result is this 1989 television documentary. "There was a live audience and seven cameramen racing about the stage with the actors while I was off in a van watching on four monitors," Bogdanov told the Toronto *Star*. He took the tapes to Hamburg, Germany, where he was then director of the city's main theater, and there "suggested cuts scene by scene."

In this version of *The Wars of the Roses* (vs. the RSC's version), costumes, characters, and other cultural clues mix anachronistically. The costuming, thoroughly eclectic, is not used to place the play in one specific period. (Falstaff, for instance, wears a green velvet smoking jacket that suggests the 1930s, while Prince Hal wears jeans and hiking boots.) Gangland thugs appear instead of medieval villagers. Paratroopers conjure the bloody warfare in urban Belfast. Other scenes evoke the Falklands War, while a half-mad Queen Margaret in the *Henry VI* plays is made up to resemble Prime Minister Margaret Thatcher. The set for the *The Wars of the Roses* consists primarily of two rolling iron scaffolds. As in Brecht's anti-illusionistic theater, lighting instruments, amplifiers, and microphones are fully exposed to view. And within these empty spaces, Bogdanov creates visual images of specific social worlds.

The dramatic universe of *Henry IV* opens with an aggressively Brechtian folk song as a prelude and segues to a political press conference in which King Henry, Westmorland, and Lancaster broadcast their speeches before individual microphones. Michael Cronin's Henry IV is careworn, graying, and gradually sick to death as he pays a heavy psychological price for his usurpation. Certain images recur during the series. The Boar's Head Tavern scene, during which bystanders chant as if at a football game, is echoed during the coronation of Hal as Henry V at the end of Part Two; Hotspur's speech from atop a baggage cart is echoed in *Henry V* when the King speaks from atop a tank at Harfleur. The cold amorality of the court world is revealed in Pennington's complex, tortured, and manipulative Hal, who stabs Hotspur in the back after his rival has chivalrously returned the sword he has just knocked out of his hand in their combat.

In this play, as elsewhere in the series, Bogdanov has been influenced by the artistic and political ideas of Brecht, Peter Brook, and director Peter Stein in Germany. His imaginative, often radical approach is part of what he has called an effort to "cut through the fustian of history and classical tradition." The television version of the history plays, however, hasn't been thoroughly adapted for the small screen, so that the broad canvas of the series, with its intriguingly blended visual inspirations and skeptical views of all political power, sometimes gives way to a series of declaiming heads.

Spin-off

■ 1991—*My Own Private Idaho* (film), director Gus Van Sant, New Line Cinema, with Keanu Reeves (Scott), William Richert (Bob), and River Phoenix (Mike). (102 min.)

Gus Van Sant's idiosyncratic film includes a modern adaptation of *Henry IV, Part One* in scenes portraying as a Falstaffian character the mentor to a couple of young, gay hustlers. One of the two main boys, Scott (Keanu Reeves), is the son of Seattle's sickly, wheelchair–using mayor, and can be viewed as a Prince Hal figure. He turns tricks to make money, while the father seeks out his alienated, marginalized son. The mentor and father figure Bob (William Richert) first appears staggering about when the boys arrive in Portland, Oregon; he is as addicted to cocaine as Falstaff is to sack. Scott chooses Bob as his "real" father; Bob also views Scott as a "ticket out" of the hard life of the streets—just as Falstaff expects to be rewarded, perhaps by being given a dukedom or earlship, when young Hal becomes king. They all conduct business from the seedy Family Tree Motel, equivalent to the Boar's Head Tavern. Other borrowings from and allusions to *Henry IV*, and more specifically to Welles's film *Falstaff: Chimes at Midnight*, include Scott's direct address to the camera, a robbery equivalent to Gad's Hill with the corresponding deception of Bob, and Scott's soliloquy, in which he explains that he will give up this kind of underworld life, analogous to Hal's "loose behavior." Scott seals a contract with his father to reform his behavior and thus come into his inheritance. Eventually Scott leaves the gay life and returns to Seattle with a new wife. Bob is publicly rejected in a restaurant filled with important people from the Portland political establishment. When Bob dies, the boys attend his funeral; when the mayor dies, Scott attends the funeral of his real father.

Van Sant has said that New Line Cinema, the American distributors, was against the Shakespearean scenes, but the foreign distributors wanted as much of the history play—including Shakespeare's language—as they could get. (Interview by Graham Fuller, quoted in Boose and Burt, eds.,

Shakespeare: The Movie, 235.) Although the film's title, taken from a B-52s song, suggests a place of imaginative freedom for the boys, no one in the film finds that place of peace. And as in many productions of *Henry IV, Part One*, the newly reformed young Scott, whose coming-of-age means rejecting a loved "misleader," pays a heavy price for taking on the burden—and here, the hypocrisies—of adulthood.

References and Related Reading

Bevington, David, ed. *"Henry IV, Parts One and Two": Critical Essays*. New York and London, 1986.

Bevington, David, ed. "Introduction: *King Henry IV, Part One*." *The Complete Works of William Shakespeare*. 5th ed. New York, 2003.

Boose, Lynda E., and Richard Burt, eds. *Shakespeare: The Movie: Popularizing the Plays on Film, TV, and Video*. London and New York, 1997.

Bradley, A. C. "The Rejection of Falstaff." *Oxford Lectures in Poetry* (1909). Rpt. in *"Henry IV, Parts I and II": Critical Essays*. Ed. David Bevington. New York and London, 1986. 77–98.

Dutton, Richard, and Jean E. Howard, eds. *A Companion to Shakespeare's Works: The Histories*. Malden, Mass., Oxford, and Victoria, 2003.

Empson, William. "Falstaff." *Essays on Shakespeare*. Cambridge, Eng., 1986.

Hay, John. "Lincoln and the Civil War in the Diaries and Letters of John Hay." Ed. Tyler Dennett. New York, 1938. Cited in *Henry V*. Ed. David Scott Kastan.

Howard, Jean E., and Phyllis Rackin. *Engendering a Nation*. London, 1997.

Jenkins, Harold. *The Structural Problem in Shakespeare's "Henry the Fourth."* London, 1956.

Kastan, David Scott, ed. *King Henry IV, Part One*. London, 2002.

McMillin, Scott. *Shakespeare in Performance: Henry IV, Part One*. Manchester and New York, 1991.

Potter, Lois. "The Second Tetralogy: Performance as Interpretation." *A Companion to Shakespeare's Works: The Histories*. Eds. Richard Dutton and Jean E. Howard. Oxford, 2003. 287–307.

Spivack, Bernard. *Shakespeare and the Allegory of Evil*. New York, 1958.

Weil, Herbert and Judith, eds. *The First Part of "King Henry IV."* Cambridge, Eng., 1997.

Wharton, T. J. *"Henry the Fourth, Parts 1 and 2": Text and Performance*. London, 1983.

Wilson, John Dover. *The Fortunes of Falstaff*. Cambridge, Eng., 1943.

Young, David P., ed. *Twentieth Century Interpretations of "Henry IV, Part Two."* Englewood Cliffs, N.J., 1968.

CHAPTER 13

The Life of King Henry V

(1599)

Context and Dating: Hal as Superhero, Statesman, Manipulator, and Lover

In *The Life of King Henry V*, the slacker Prince Hal, who banished his drinking companion Falstaff in *Henry IV, Part Two*, completes his education as a politician-prince, rules England as Henry V during contentious times, and regains control of France with a miraculous victory at Agincourt. "Oh, for a muse of fire," implores the Chorus in the resounding opening to this still-controversial chronicle in which Henry demonstrates his kingliness, military heroism, and political skill, even as scenes of parody, comedy, and moral questioning challenge the meaning of his honor, his patriotism, and his statesman's rhetoric. Here, too, in this culmination of his eight history plays, Shakespeare slyly demonstrates his confidence in the genre. The Chorus apologizes for being unable to show the actual battles of the French wars on "this wooden O." Instead the speaker and his creator fire the imaginations of his listeners with a series of debate scenes, comic turns, wooings, reported battles, and brilliant set speeches, while also interrogating motives for the military exploits the play seems to celebrate.

Shakespeare's Chorus points often to the artifice of the play. By asking that we, the audience, use our imaginations to embrace the story, he freely moves the action across the sea to France and back again, reporting on taunts, treason, and war, panning across every level of British society and its multinational citizens. He reveals both the public Henry of inspiring speeches and the private man wracked by internal doubt in the kind of epic theater that we now associate with the cinema.

Not surprisingly, because of this breadth of described action, *Henry V* has twice been adapted into popular and now classic films, two of the best examples of the genre: Laurence Olivier's mostly sunny, stylisti-

cally daring 1944 patriotic pageant, and Kenneth Branagh's muddy, close-in, war-is-hell adaptation of 1989. Divergent in impetus, mood, in their portrayals of Henry, and in their explorations of English nationalism and imperialism, these films suggest again that interpretations of Shakespeare reflect "the age and body" of their times. Any production or film can only be provisional, tempered by its historical context.

Henry V can be dated with some certainty, for it contains one of the very few direct and explicit references to contemporary events in all of Shakespeare's plays. At the opening of Act 5, the Chorus compares the pouring forth of London citizens to welcome victorious Henry home from France to the "lower" but still "loving likelihood" that the queen's favorite, Essex, would also return victorious from Ireland:

> Were now the General of our gracious Empress,
> As in good time he may, from Ireland coming,
> Bringing rebellion broachèd on his sword,
> How many would the peaceful city quit
> To welcome him!
>
> (5.0.30–34)

Robert Devereux, Earl of Essex and Governor-General of Ireland, had left London in March of 1599 to put down a rebellion by the Earl of Tyrone. He had been given a vociferous send-off by the people, but returned sooner than anticipated, having made a truce the Queen soon rejected. Shakespeare could not have predicted that Essex's mission would end in his house arrest and, the following year, in a charge of treason and his execution, although *Henry V* does reflect ambivalently upon even the Queen's Irish wars in some scenes with the uncontrollable Irishman Macmorris. Scholars generally accept that the fifth-act Chorus does refer to Essex, and, if this speculation is true, then *Henry V* was first performed between March and September of 1599,

443

and thus written soon after *Henry IV, Part Two*, which was certainly performed in 1598. Also consistent with the 1599 dating is the Chorus's reference to "this wooden O," suggesting that the play may have been staged by the Lord Chamberlain's Men at the new Globe playhouse on the Bankside in Southwark, which we know to have been built that year.

Any reading or production that is true to the entire play must take into account its many and contradictory voices. Henry may be viewed as a patriot prince, the "mirror of a Christian king," or as a complex manipulator, or with unresolved ambivalence, yet always as the center of the play. Critics have described his role in extremes ranging from John Dover Wilson's simple proclamation "The subject is patriotism; Henry is the hero" to a more skeptical view from essayist William Hazlitt in 1817: "He was a hero, that is, he was ready to sacrifice his own life for the pleasure of destroying thousands of other lives . . . [a protagonist] with no idea of any rule of right or wrong, but brute force, glossed over with a little religious hypocrisy." The playwright George Bernard Shaw also deplored Henry V as a prig and imperialist warmonger, a man we might today call a "hawk." The poet William Butler Yeats shared Shaw's assessment: "[Henry] has the gross vices, the coarse nerves of one who is to rule among violent people. He is as remorseless and undistinguished as some natural force." Such modern critics as Michael Neill ("*Henry V*: A Modern Perspective") see both the ironies in Shakespeare's treatment and also the celebratory tone of this flamboyant pageant. In this view, Henry is the "good" Machiavellian prince whose brutality, rhetorical manipulations, and even his hypocritical piety are simply outshone by the youthful, shrewdly employed charisma of England's great soldier king.

Characters: The Manly English and the Arrogant French

As befits a play about the making of a nation and its history, the cast of characters spans many social classes and national origins. Among the English are the clergy of Act 1, the conspirators arrested in Act 2, the trusted nobles Sir Thomas Grey and Thomas Erpingham, and the three regional captains: Fluellen from Wales, Jamy from Scotland, and Macmorris from Ireland, as well as the sturdy Englishman Gower and the soldier commoners, including Williams. On the French side are King Charles VI; his Queen Isabel; their much-ridiculed son, the Dauphin; and the princess Katharine, as well as the Constable (who dies fighting) and the noble envoy Mountjoy. Three scenes involve substantial speeches in French: Shakespeare shows Katharine learning the English names of the parts of her body soon to be colonized by Henry. French words also get mangled in a burlesque of a military ransom during the short scene involving a frightened soldier, Monsieur Le Fer.

Sources and Inspirations

Victories at Agincourt and Over the Armada

One of Shakespeare's many sources for *The Life of King Henry V* was an anonymous play (c. 1588), *The Famous Victories of King Henry V*. Its appearance around the time of the English defeat of the Spanish Armada in 1588 suggests one motivation for turning to the historical Henry: England had been threatened and greatly outnumbered by the continuing broils with Spain, just as the late medieval nation had been threatened by France during the reign of Henry V. Shakespeare's 1599 version of those events celebrates the titular hero's nation-building skills, while acknowledging in the Epilogue how short-lived was the harmony he created out of discord.

Fears of foreign invasion in the late 1590s inflated prices for food, and led to the constant call for soldiers, horses, and supplies for the military in the Low Countries and the continuing campaign to subdue Ireland. All would have made the play topical in 1599. Then, too, Shakespeare had promised in the Epilogue of *Henry IV, Part Two* (1598) to continue that story of King Henry and, despite the banishment of Falstaff, to write a sequel "with Sir John in it, and make you merry with fair Katharine of France. Where, for anything I know, Falstaff shall die of a sweat" (Epilogue, 26–28).

Along with Richard the Lionhearted, Edward III, and his son the Black Prince, Henry V was widely perceived in the 1590s as a genuine hero. Shakespeare's play helped to enhance this reputation. Shakespeare's recreation of history, in other words, intervened in the historical process. The actual Henry V succeeded his father in 1413 and died in 1422 after his triumph at the Battle of Agincourt against the French in 1415. He married Princess Katharine of France in 1420; she joined him during his second French invasion, when their son, whom he never met, was five months old. Soon after, suffering from dysentery, King Henry died. The ensuing struggles after the crowning of the child King Henry VI led into the brutal War of the Roses, depicted by Shakespeare in his earlier tetralogy of the *Henry VI* plays and *Richard III*.

While not yet thirty, then, the historical Henry twice raised large, well-equipped expeditionary forces and transported them to France. In the first instance, he achieved the victory at Agincourt, in one of the most celebrated battles in English history, over an army many times the size of his own. On the other hand, the military adventures in France were justified by a claim that had little legal or moral basis. The Battle of Agincourt climaxed an invasion deemed by some historians to have been foolhardy and irresponsible. Shakespeare both lionizes the charismatic king and creates scenes revealing aspects of his character that qualify our admiration. In viewing both stage and screen productions, we should note how much emphasis is given to these darker elements of plot and character and to the scenes of satiric comedy:

- The lengthy (and often burlesqued) disquisition of the Archbishop of Canterbury on the Salic law justifying Henry's imperial adventure and the Archbishop's promise to guard (1.2) the home front from the "weasel Scot."

- Henry's threats against the French (which significantly Olivier omits from his film) during the siege of Harfleur (3.3) beginning "The gates of mercy shall be all shut up" and ending "Whiles the mad mothers with their howls confused/Do break the clouds, as did the wives of Jewry / At Herod's bloody-hunting slaughtermen."

- The poignant reminiscences of Falstaff "killed" by Prince Hal (2.1; 2.2; 4.7.44–51); the report of the fat knight's death (2.3.5–43), and the hanging of Henry and Falstaff's former comrade Bardolph (3.6.100–113).

- The skepticism of Henry's common soldiers, especially Williams (4.1.134–146); the parodies of honor in scenes with Pistol, Nym, and Bardolph (3.2), and with Pistol and Monsieur Le Fer (4.4).

Such scenes which undercut heroic and rhetorical ideals have alternately been de-emphasized and cut by some directors and emphasized by others in order to stress the horrors of war.

The English Chronicles—and English Myth

Shakespeare's treatment seems to have been derived principally from Raphael Holinshed's *Chronicles* (1587 edition), although Edward Hall's *The Union of the Two Noble and Illustre Families of Lancaster and York* (1542), as well as Samuel Daniel's *The First Four Books of the Civil Wars* (1595) all depict Henry V as a soldier-hero-king. From both Holinshed and Hall came the order of events involving the rivalry with the French Dauphin, who sends tennis balls to mock the young king to remind him of his reputation for profligacy; the machinations of the clergy to support the French escapade so that they could avoid seizure of their lands; a traitorous plot on Henry's life; the siege of Harfleur; and the victory, employing archers, at Agincourt.

Current scholarship suggests many sources including two other contemporary plays about Henry V, several Latin histories translated around the time the play was written, and a popular ballad about the Battle of Agincourt. At the same time, many of Shakespeare's best scenes and characters simply have no precedent: the ramble of "Harry" through his camp on the eve of war, the argumentative scenes between Fluellen and his captains, and of course, Henry's rousing speeches with their "band of brothers" emotional exuberance and effect.

Language and Structure

According to the Archbishop of Canterbury in the opening scene, the young King Henry is a superb rhetorician. "Hear him but reason in divinity," the cleric says, and all admiring listeners would wish him a prelate. Hear him debate policy and you would think politics had "been all in all his study." Listen to him talk of war and "you shall hear / A fearful battle rendered you in music" (1.1.39–50). The play's language is rich in dramatic oratory, public rhetoric, and shorthand characterization. Language is also one of its themes, for Henry V forges in words his public identity as King with God's blessing of an imperial nation:

> Either our history shall with full mouth
> Speak freely of our acts, or else our grave,
> Like Turkish mute, shall have a tongueless mouth,
> Not worshiped with a waxen epitaph.
>
> (1.2.230–233)

When the play ends, Chorus with "full mouth" proclaims him King of both France and England. The prospect of his victory has inspired the French princess to learn his language. He has created, at least theoretically, a multicultural nation from the ethnicities represented by his captains from Ireland, Scotland, Wales and England. In addition to their colorful and often eccentric ways of speaking, there are several other distinct speaking styles in the play: the blank verse of the English aristocrats; the earthy prose humor of Pistol, Nym, and other English commoners; the more florid imagery, as well as bestial humor, in the verse for the French; and two scenes in which Katharine speaks both languages as she haltingly learns both English and the romantic aspect of her soon-to-be-husband, Henry.

Especially characteristic of the play are the stirring public relations speeches by the Chorus and the long set pieces for the King. Shakespeare's rhetorical training underpins, as Wells points out, the high drama of all the histories, as well as the classic expressions of the pastoral ideal revealed in moments of discontent by both Henry IV and Henry V. These great set pieces of *Henry V* are as memorable (and as excerptable as actor exercises) as Hamlet's more psychologically penetrating soliloquies. Even when the sincerity of such speeches is thrown into doubt by ironic counterpointing, the following passages, when well acted, are emotionally effective both inside the play and for audiences:

- King Henry's strong and witty response to the Dauphin's mocking gift of tennis balls (1.2.259–296).

- His inspiring speech at Harfleur beginning "Once more unto the breach" (3.1.1–34).

- His soliloquy on the burden of kingships (4.1.228–282) and his guilt-stricken prayer, before the Battle of Agincourt, that God not think upon his father's sin in "compassing the crown" from Richard II.

- The motivational rhetoric of his St. Crispin's Day speech (4.3.18–67) with its famous promise that valiant fighting will forge a democracy among soldiers from all classes:

> But we in it shall be rememberèd—
> We few, we happy few, we band of brothers.
> For he today that sheds his blood with me
> Shall be my brother; be he ne'er so vile,
> This day shall gentle his condition.
> And gentlemen in England now abed
> Shall think themselves accurst they were not here,
> And hold their manhoods cheap whiles any speaks
> That fought with us upon Saint Crispin's Day.
>
> (4.3.59–67)

- His adoption of the rhetoric of a "blunt soldier" in his wooing scene with Katharine (5.2.98–282).

Themes and Issues

Royal Limits

Although *Henry V* crowns Shakespeare's achievement in the genre of the history play, the celebratory mood surrounding the victorious English monarch is tempered by an exploration of royal limits. Much current-day skepticism about Henry's role as a model Christian king has been answered by other scholars who view that skepticism as anachronistic. Yet Shakespeare does present a complex and balanced portrait of a monarch who behaves according to Renaissance notions (the "good" side of Machiavelli's descriptions of the Prince) of royal leadership. Conflicting explanations or ambiguous ones emerge for some of Henry's less attractive traits. When Henry orders his soldiers to kill their French prisoners, for instance, we are first told (as his sources Holinshed and Hall reported) that Henry does not have enough men to guard the prisoners and still carry on the fight. But later, we learn from Gower that the soldier-king, who has acknowledged his anger over the French killing of the English boys, orders the prisoners murdered in retaliation. Henry's egalitarian language in the St. Crispin's Day speech has been undercut earlier by Williams's reminders of extreme class differences, and will be challenged again when Henry reserves the term "brother" for his aristocratic peers, his blood brother Gloucester, and the conquered "brother France" and "brother Ireland." Yet with the Welsh, the Scots, and the Irish particularly, Shakespeare represents what critic Michael Neill calls an image of nation-building as incorporation that is both dream (the loyal Welshman Fluellen) and nightmare (the wild Macmorris and the "weasel Scot"). The situational ethics of Henry suggest that kings, wearing a mask for their public role, create this public persona out of rhetoric; like a politician who believes his own PR, such a king may actually become the role his words create.

Religious Piety

Henry's religious piety is another topic open to ambiguous readings. Many times he attributes his victories to God, suggesting that not only is the monarchy his by divine blessing, but that France belongs to England too, as the Archbishop of Canterbury has argued in his opening exposition of Salic law. Yet there are elements of satire and anti-clericalism in that scene as well. Henry's request to the Archbishop that he give divine sanction to the war can be played as a shrewd political move rather than a more disinterested request. The request to Henry's bishops can be viewed as a public relations ploy, not a genuine request for understanding and support. Also ambiguous is Henry's questioning of his soldiers, and his debate with Williams during his "little touch of Harry in the night" ramble through the camp. When the plain-spoken Williams says, referring to the sinful or contrite state of the soldiers' souls, "if these men do not die well, it will be a black matter for the King who led them to it" (4.1.144–145), Henry responds with the kind of subtle reasoning in divinity for which the Archbishop of Canterbury had praised him. To modern ears the King's response—"Every subject's duty is the King's, but every subject's soul is his own"—may sound like rationalizing. Henry's piety is shown to be complex in his final moments alone before the Battle of Agincourt, when he prays not to be punished for his father's sin in deposing Richard II and acknowledges that all the prayers he says and pays others to say are worth nothing more than his sincere repentance. Heroically winning the Battle of Agincourt and marrying the French princess will at least lead to a period of peaceful respite from the dynastic crisis that followed that deposition and murder.

Staging Challenges

The Chorus

Sometimes, in American regional theaters, the speeches of the Chorus are divided among several characters. The speakers might adopt the same robe, or stance, or prop, suggesting that they are clearly part of a communal story-telling impulse, and by their variety stressing again the imagination required of the spectators to participate in the action. Richard Olivier's 1997 production during the opening season of the new Globe Theatre in London similarly split the role of Chorus between several actors, with other historical background to Henry's reign narrated in an opening ballad. In more costly and elaborate productions, especially during the nineteenth century, many of the Chorus's speeches were cut, since they referred to limitations in staging that these lavish productions surmounted. When a single actor takes on the role—Leslie Banks in Olivier's film, for instance, or

Derek Jacobi in Branagh's later movie—he may appear in various garbs, as an Elizabethan gentleman or an urbane modern. All are dedicated to prodding the viewers' imaginations, as well as to creating and marketing the magnificent royal personality that is Henry V.

The Brutal and Exhilarating Battles

The play script calls for no actual fighting on stage except for the dishonorable, parodic, and sometimes-cut scene between Pistol and the French soldier Le Fer (4.4). Shakespeare dramatizes this exploit only as the capstone of Henry's French campaign, and yet it is a ridiculous exploit, with Pistol a coward pretending to valor, and the Frenchman ready to be ransomed as Henry was not. We see none of the hand-to-hand combat described and shown as at the end of *Henry IV, Part One* or in the *Henry VI* or *Richard III* plays. Instead, the Chorus tells of armor, armaments, a cannon, and a few ragged foils. Some directors are content to let the reports of these battles create the excitement; others use such stage effects as smoke, blood-red lighting, the recorded sound and shouts of battles, or even glimpses of actors engaged in combat. The Olivier and Branagh films both open up the setting and present stirring, if very different, battle scenes, each sensitive to historical accounts of the muddy field conditions, the ingenious use of archers and arrows, and the Frenchmen's fatally heavy armor overburdening their horses. (See "Frame-by-Frame," pp. 493–495.)

The English vs. the French

Shakespeare describes the French as more effeminate than the plain English "band of brothers." Stage directors can choose to underscore this difference with language delivery and with costuming or to ignore it. Using brighter colors for the French and earth tones for the down-to-earth English is a frequent choice for the distinction, as well as using more iconic means: the fleur de lis symbol, for instance, on the French uniforms and the lion of St. George on the English with the two symbols—and the national colors of blue and red—joined as the English seek victory.

The Life of King Henry V

[*Dramatis Personae*

CHORUS

KING HENRY THE FIFTH
HUMPHREY, DUKE OF GLOUCESTER,
JOHN, DUKE OF BEDFORD,
DUKE OF CLARENCE,   } *the King's brothers*
DUKE OF EXETER, *the King's uncle*
DUKE OF YORK, *the King's cousin*
EARL OF SALISBURY
EARL OF WESTMORLAND
EARL OF WARWICK
EARL OF HUNTINGDON

ARCHBISHOP OF CANTERBURY
BISHOP OF ELY

RICHARD, EARL OF CAMBRIDGE,
HENRY, LORD SCROOP OF MASHAM,   } *conspirators against the King*
SIR THOMAS GREY,

SIR THOMAS ERPINGHAM,
CAPTAIN GOWER,
CAPTAIN FLUELLEN,   } *officers in the King's army*
CAPTAIN MACMORRIS,
CAPTAIN JAMY,
JOHN BATES,
ALEXANDER COURT,   } *soldiers in the King's army*
MICHAEL WILLIAMS,
An English HERALD

SCENE: *England, afterwards France*]

PISTOL,
NYM,   } *Falstaff's former tavern-mates*
BARDOLPH,
BOY, *formerly Falstaff's page*
HOSTESS, *formerly Mistress Quickly, now married to Pistol*

DUKE OF BURGUNDY

FRENCH KING, *Charles the Sixth*
QUEEN ISABEL *of France*
DAUPHIN, *Lewis*
KATHARINE, *Princess of France*
ALICE, *a lady attending Katharine*
DUKE OF ORLEANS
DUKE OF BERRI
DUKE OF BOURBON
DUKE OF BRITTANY
CONSTABLE OF FRANCE
LORD RAMBURES
LORD GRANDPRÉ
GOVERNOR OF HARFLEUR
MONSIEUR LE FER, *a French soldier*
MONTJOY, *the French herald*
French AMBASSADORS *to England*

Lords, Ladies, Officers, Soldiers, Citizens, Messengers, and Attendants

Prologue

Enter [Chorus as] Prologue.

CHORUS

Oh, for a Muse of fire, that would ascend 1
The brightest heaven of invention! 2
A kingdom for a stage, princes to act,
And monarchs to behold the swelling scene! 4
Then should the warlike Harry, like himself, 5
Assume the port of Mars; and at his heels, 6
Leashed in like hounds, should famine, sword, and
  fire
Crouch for employment. But pardon, gentles all, 8
The flat unraisèd spirits that hath dared 9
On this unworthy scaffold to bring forth 10
So great an object. Can this cockpit hold 11
The vasty fields of France? Or may we cram 12
Within this wooden O the very casques 13
That did affright the air at Agincourt?
Oh, pardon! Since a crooked figure may 15
Attest in little place a million; 16
And let us, ciphers to this great account, 17
On your imaginary forces work. 18
Suppose within the girdle of these walls
Are now confined two mighty monarchies,
Whose high uprearèd and abutting fronts 21
The perilous narrow ocean parts asunder. 22
Piece out our imperfections with your thoughts:
Into a thousand parts divide one man,
And make imaginary puissance. 25
Think, when we talk of horses, that you see them
Printing their proud hoofs i'th' receiving earth.
For 'tis your thoughts that now must deck our kings, 28
Carry them here and there, jumping o'er times,
Turning th'accomplishment of many years
Into an hourglass—for the which supply, 31
Admit me Chorus to this history,
Who, Prologue-like, your humble patience pray
Gently to hear, kindly to judge, our play.   *Exit.*

Prologue.
1 Muse of fire (Of the four elements—earth, air, fire, and water—fire
is the most sublime and mounting.)   **2 invention** poetic imagination.
4 swelling splendid, magnificent   **5 like himself** i.e., presented in a
fashion worthy of so great a king.   **6 port** bearing   **8 gentles** gentlemen and gentlewomen   **9 flat unraisèd** uninspired, lifeless.   **spirits**
i.e., actors and playwright.   **hath** (Elizabethan usage often pairs a
plural subject with a singular verb.)   **10 scaffold** stage   **11 cockpit**
(Elizabethan theaters were shaped rather like arenas for animal fighting.)   **12 vasty** vast, spacious   **13 O** (Refers to a round theater such
as the Globe; the play may have been performed at the Curtain Theater.)   **casques** helmets   **15 crooked figure** cipher or zero (which,
added to a number, will multiply its value tenfold)   **16 Attest** stand
for   **17 account** (1) sum total (continuing the metaphor of *crooked figure*) (2) story   **18 imaginary forces** forces of imagination   **21 abutting** touching, bordering.   **fronts** (1) frontiers, i.e., the cliffs of Dover
and Calais (2) foreheads   **22 perilous . . . ocean** i.e., English Channel
25 puissance armed might, army.   **28 deck** dress, adorn   **31 the
which supply** which service

1.1

*Enter the two bishops, [the Archbishop] of
Canterbury and [the Bishop of] Ely.*

CANTERBURY

My lord, I'll tell you. That self bill is urged 1
Which in th'eleventh year of the last king's reign
Was like, and had indeed against us passed, 3
But that the scambling and unquiet time 4
Did push it out of farther question. 5

ELY

But how, my lord, shall we resist it now?

CANTERBURY

It must be thought on. If it pass against us,
We lose the better half of our possession.
For all the temporal lands which men devout 9
By testament have given to the Church
Would they strip from us, being valued thus:
As much as would maintain, to the King's honor,
Full fifteen earls and fifteen hundred knights,
Six thousand and two hundred good esquires, 14
And, to relief of lazars and weak age 15
Of indigent faint souls past corporal toil, 16
A hundred almshouses right well supplied;
And to the coffers of the King beside
A thousand pounds by th' year. Thus runs the bill.

ELY   This would drink deep.

CANTERBURY   'Twould drink the cup and all.

ELY   But what prevention?

CANTERBURY

The King is full of grace and fair regard.

ELY

And a true lover of the holy Church.

CANTERBURY

The courses of his youth promised it not.
The breath no sooner left his father's body
But that his wildness, mortified in him, 27
Seemed to die too; yea, at that very moment
Consideration like an angel came 29
And whipped th'offending Adam out of him, 30
Leaving his body as a paradise
T'envelop and contain celestial spirits.
Never was such a sudden scholar made;
Never came reformation in a flood
With such a heady currance, scouring faults; 35
Nor never Hydra-headed willfulness 36
So soon did lose his seat, and all at once, 37
As in this king.

ELY   We are blessed in the change.

CANTERBURY

Hear him but reason in divinity,

1.1. Location: England. The royal court.
1 self same   **3 like** likely (to have passed)   **4 scambling** unsettled
5 question consideration.   **9 temporal** used for secular purposes
14 esquires members of the gentry, ranking just below knights
15 lazars lepers   **16 corporal** physical   **27 mortified** killed   **29 Consideration** meditation, reflection   **30 offending Adam** original sin
35 heady currance headlong current   **36 Hydra-headed** i.e., many-
headed. (Alludes to the Lernaean Hydra, a monster of many heads
overcome by Hercules.)   **37 his seat** its throne

And, all-admiring, with an inward wish
You would desire the King were made a prelate.
Hear him debate of commonwealth affairs,
You would say it hath been all in all his study.
List his discourse of war, and you shall hear   44
A fearful battle rendered you in music.   45
Turn him to any cause of policy,   46
The Gordian knot of it he will unloose,   47
Familiar as his garter, that, when he speaks,   48
The air, a chartered libertine, is still,   49
And the mute wonder lurketh in men's ears   50
To steal his sweet and honeyed sentences;   51
So that the art and practic part of life   52
Must be the mistress to this theoric.   53
Which is a wonder how His Grace should glean it,
Since his addiction was to courses vain,   55
His companies unlettered, rude, and shallow,   56
His hours filled up with riots, banquets, sports,   57
And never noted in him any study,
Any retirement, any sequestration
From open haunts and popularity.   60

ELY
The strawberry grows underneath the nettle,
And wholesome berries thrive and ripen best
Neighbored by fruit of baser quality;
And so the Prince obscured his contemplation
Under the veil of wildness, which, no doubt,
Grew like the summer grass, fastest by night,
Unseen, yet crescive in his faculty.   67

CANTERBURY
It must be so, for miracles are ceased.   68
And therefore we must needs admit the means   69
How things are perfected.

ELY   But, my good lord,
How now for mitigation of this bill
Urged by the Commons? Doth His Majesty
Incline to it, or no?

CANTERBURY   He seems indifferent,   73
Or rather swaying more upon our part
Than cherishing th'exhibiters against us;   75
For I have made an offer to His Majesty,
Upon our spiritual convocation   77
And in regard of causes now in hand,   78
Which I have opened to His Grace at large,   79

As touching France, to give a greater sum
Than ever at one time the clergy yet
Did to his predecessors part withal.   82

ELY
How did this offer seem received, my lord?

CANTERBURY
With good acceptance of His Majesty,
Save that there was not time enough to hear,
As I perceived His Grace would fain have done,   86
The severals and unhidden passages   87
Of his true titles to some certain dukedoms,
And generally to the crown and seat of France,   89
Derived from Edward, his great-grandfather.   90

ELY
What was th'impediment that broke this off?

CANTERBURY
The French ambassador upon that instant
Craved audience; and the hour I think is come
To give him hearing. Is it four o'clock?

ELY   It is.

CANTERBURY
Then go we in to know his embassy,   96
Which I could with a ready guess declare
Before the Frenchman speak a word of it.

ELY
I'll wait upon you, and I long to hear it.   *Exeunt.*

[1.2]

Enter the King, Humphrey [Duke of Gloucester],
Bedford, Clarence, Warwick, Westmorland, and
Exeter [with attendants].

KING
Where is my gracious lord of Canterbury?

EXETER
Not here in presence.

KING   Send for him, good uncle.

WESTMORLAND
Shall we call in th'ambassador, my liege?

KING
Not yet, my cousin. We would be resolved,   4
Before we hear him, of some things of weight
That task our thoughts, concerning us and France.   6

Enter two bishops, [the Archbishop of Canter-
bury and the Bishop of Ely].

CANTERBURY
God and his angels guard your sacred throne,
And make you long become it!

KING   Sure we thank you.   8
My learnèd lord, we pray you to proceed,

---

44 **List** Listen to   45 **rendered . . . music** i.e., eloquently narrated.
46 **cause of policy** matter of statecraft   47 **Gordian knot** i.e., great
difficulty resolved forcefully. (It was foretold that whoever should
untie the Gordian knot would rule Asia. Alexander solved the problem by cutting the knot.)   48 **Familiar** as offhandedly or routinely.
that so that   49 **chartered libertine** free spirit, licensed to roam at
will   50–1 **the mute . . . sentences** i.e., wonder makes men silent,
eagerly listening to hear more of his sweetly profitable wise sayings
52–3 **So . . . theoric** so that experience in practical life must have been
the teacher by which he acquired his theoretical conception.
55 **addiction** inclination   56 **companies** companions.   **rude** coarse
57 **riots** reveling.   **sports** amusements   60 **open . . . popularity**
places of public resort and low company.   67 **crescive . . . faculty** naturally inclined to grow.   68 **miracles are ceased** (Protestants generally believed that no miracles occurred after the revelation of Christ.)
69 **means** i.e., natural causes   73 **indifferent** impartial   75 **exhibiters** those who introduce bills in Parliament   77 **Upon** on behalf of.
convocation formal assembly of the clergy   78 **in hand** under consideration   79 **opened** expounded.   **at large** in full

82 **withal** with.   86 **fain** gladly   87 **severals** details.   **unhidden passages** clear lines of descent   89 **seat** throne   90 **Edward** Edward III
96 **embassy** message
1.2. Location: England. The royal court.
4 **cousin** (A form of address customarily used by royalty in addressing their nobles. In this case, Westmorland is in fact related to the
King by marriage.)   **be resolved** come to a decision   6 **task** engage,
occupy   8 **become** adorn, grace

And justly and religiously unfold
Why the law Salic that they have in France   11
Or should or should not bar us in our claim.   12
And God forbid, my dear and faithful lord,
That you should fashion, wrest, or bow your reading,
Or nicely charge your understanding soul   15
With opening titles miscreate, whose right   16
Suits not in native colors with the truth;   17
For God doth know how many now in health
Shall drop their blood in approbation   19
Of what your reverence shall incite us to.   20
Therefore take heed how you impawn our person,   21
How you awake our sleeping sword of war.
We charge you in the name of God take heed;
For never two such kingdoms did contend
Without much fall of blood, whose guiltless drops
Are every one a woe, a sore complaint   26
'Gainst him whose wrongs gives edge unto the
    swords   27
That makes such waste in brief mortality.   28
Under this conjuration speak, my lord;   29
For we will hear, note, and believe in heart
That what you speak is in your conscience washed
As pure as sin with baptism.

CANTERBURY
Then hear me, gracious sovereign, and you peers,
That owe yourselves, your lives, and services
To this imperial throne. There is no bar
To make against Your Highness' claim to France
But this, which they produce from Pharamond: 37
"In terram Salicam mulieres ne succedant,"
"No woman shall succeed in Salic land."
Which Salic land the French unjustly gloze   40
To be the realm of France, and Pharamond
The founder of this law and female bar.
Yet their own authors faithfully affirm
That the land Salic is in Germany,
Between the floods of Saale and of Elbe;   45
Where, Charles the Great having subdued the Saxons,   46
There left behind and settled certain French,
Who, holding in disdain the German women
For some dishonest manners of their life,   49
Established then this law: to wit, no female
Should be inheritrix in Salic land—
Which Salic, as I said, twixt Elbe and Saale,
Is at this day in Germany called Meissen.
Then doth it well appear the Salic law
Was not devisèd for the realm of France;
Nor did the French possess the Salic land

Until four hundred one-and-twenty years
After defunction of King Pharamond,   58
Idly supposed the founder of this law,   59
Who died within the year of our redemption
Four hundred twenty-six; and Charles the Great
Subdued the Saxons, and did seat the French
Beyond the River Saale, in the year
Eight hundred five. Besides, their writers say,
King Pepin, which deposèd Childeric,   65
Did, as heir general, being descended   66
Of Blithild, which was daughter to King Clothair,
Make claim and title to the crown of France.
Hugh Capet also, who usurped the crown
Of Charles the Duke of Lorraine, sole heir male
Of the true line and stock of Charles the Great,
To find his title with some shows of truth,   72
Though, in pure truth, it was corrupt and naught,
Conveyed himself as th'heir to th' Lady Lingard,   74
Daughter to Charlemagne, who was the son   75
To Lewis the Emperor, and Lewis the son
Of Charles the Great. Also King Lewis the Tenth,   77
Who was sole heir to the usurper Capet,
Could not keep quiet in his conscience,
Wearing the crown of France, till satisfied
That fair Queen Isabel, his grandmother,
Was lineal of the Lady Ermengard,   82
Daughter to Charles the foresaid Duke of Lorraine;
By the which marriage the line of Charles the Great
Was reunited to the crown of France.
So that, as clear as is the summer's sun,
King Pepin's title and Hugh Capet's claim,
King Lewis his satisfaction, all appear   88
To hold in right and title of the female;
So do the kings of France unto this day,
Howbeit they would hold up this Salic law   91
To bar Your Highness claiming from the female,
And rather choose to hide them in a net   93
Than amply to imbar their crooked titles   94
Usurped from you and your progenitors.

KING
May I with right and conscience make this claim?

CANTERBURY
The sin upon my head, dread sovereign!
For in the Book of Numbers is it writ,
When the man dies, let the inheritance   99
Descend unto the daughter. Gracious lord,   100
Stand for your own; unwind your bloody flag!   101
Look back into your mighty ancestors:

---

58 **defunction** death   59 **Idly** foolishly   65 **which** who. (As also in line 67.)   66 **heir general** heir through male or female line   72 **find** provide   74 **Conveyed himself** passed himself off   75 **Charlemagne** (Holinshed's and Hall's error, followed by Shakespeare, for Charles the Bald or Charles II, emperor of the West; Luitgard [Shakespeare's Lingard] became Charlemagne's wife after the death of Fastrada in 794.)   77 **Lewis the Tenth** (Actually, Louis IX; an error copied from Holinshed.)   82 **lineal of** descended from   88 **Lewis his satisfaction** Lewis's conviction   91 **Howbeit** notwithstanding   93 **hide . . . net** i.e., conceal the weakness of their case in a tangle of contradictions   94 **amply to imbar** frankly to bar claim to   99–100 **When . . . daughter** (This paraphrase leaves out an important phrase. Numbers 27:8 reads, "When a man dies leaving no son, his patrimony shall pass to his daughter.")   101 **unwind** unfurl

---

11 **Salic** (See explanation at lines 39–45.)   12 **Or** either   15 **nicely charge** subtly and foolishly burden   16 **opening titles miscreate** expounding spurious claims   17 **Suits . . . colors** i.e., does not naturally harmonize   19 **approbation** support, proof   20 **your reverence** (1) an honorific title for an archbishop, Your Reverence (2) your sacred authority   21 **impawn** put under an obligation   26 **woe** grievance.   **sore** severe, grievous   27 **wrongs** wrongdoings   28 **in brief mortality** i.e., among mortal, short-lived men.   29 **conjuration** solemn adjuration   37 **Pharamond** legendary Frankish king   40 **gloze** gloss   45 **floods** rivers   46 **Charles the Great** Charlemagne   49 **dishonest** unchaste

Go, my dread lord, to your great-grandsire's tomb, 103
From whom you claim! Invoke his warlike spirit,
And your great-uncle's, Edward the Black Prince,
Who on the French ground played a tragedy, 106
Making defeat on the full power of France, 107
Whiles his most mighty father on a hill
Stood smiling to behold his lion's whelp
Forage in blood of French nobility.
O noble English, that could entertain 111
With half their forces the full pride of France
And let another half stand laughing by,
All out of work and cold for action! 114

ELY
Awake remembrance of these valiant dead,
And with your puissant arm renew their feats!
You are their heir; you sit upon their throne;
The blood and courage that renownèd them 118
Runs in your veins; and my thrice-puissant liege
Is in the very May morn of his youth,
Ripe for exploits and mighty enterprises.

EXETER
Your brother kings and monarchs of the earth
Do all expect that you should rouse yourself
As did the former lions of your blood.

WESTMORLAND
They know Your Grace hath cause, and means, and
    might;
So hath Your Highness. Never king of England 126
Had nobles richer and more loyal subjects,
Whose hearts have left their bodies here in England
And lie pavilioned in the fields of France. 129

CANTERBURY
Oh, let their bodies follow, my dear liege,
With blood, and sword, and fire to win your right!
In aid whereof we of the spiritualty 132
Will raise Your Highness such a mighty sum
As never did the clergy at one time
Bring in to any of your ancestors.

KING
We must not only arm t'invade the French,
But lay down our proportions to defend 137
Against the Scot, who will make road upon us 138
With all advantages. 139

CANTERBURY
They of those marches, gracious sovereign,
Shall be a wall sufficient to defend 140
Our inland from the pilfering borderers.

KING
We do not mean the coursing snatchers only, 143

But fear the main intendment of the Scot, 144
Who hath been still a giddy neighbor to us. 145
For you shall read that my great-grandfather
Never went with his forces into France
But that the Scot on his unfurnished kingdom 148
Came pouring like the tide into a breach
With ample and brim fullness of his force, 150
Galling the gleanèd land with hot assays, 151
Girding with grievous siege castles and towns;
That England, being empty of defense,
Hath shook and trembled at th'ill neighborhood. 154

CANTERBURY
She hath been then more feared than harmed, my
    liege. 155
For hear her but exampled by herself: 156
When all her chivalry hath been in France 157
And she a mourning widow of her nobles, 158
She hath herself not only well defended
But taken and impounded as a stray 160
The King of Scots, whom she did send to France 161
To fill King Edward's fame with prisoner kings
And make her chronicle as rich with praise
As is the ooze and bottom of the sea
With sunken wrack and sumless treasuries. 165

A LORD
But there's a saying very old and true:
    "If that you will France win,
    Then with Scotland first begin."
For once the eagle England being in prey, 169
To her unguarded nest the weasel Scot
Comes sneaking, and so sucks her princely eggs,
Playing the mouse in absence of the cat,
To 'tame and havoc more than she can eat. 173

EXETER
It follows then the cat must stay at home;
Yet that is but a crushed necessity, 175
Since we have locks to safeguard necessaries
And pretty traps to catch the petty thieves. 177
While that the armèd hand doth fight abroad, 178
Th'advisèd head defends itself at home; 179
For government, though high, and low, and lower, 180
Put into parts, doth keep in one consent, 181

103 **great-grandsire's** i.e., Edward III's. His descent through his mother Isabella from the French King Philip IV is the basis of English claims to the French kingdom—a claim through female inheritance. Hence the importance of lines 39–55. 106 **tragedy** i.e., the Battle of Crécy, 1346, a major defeat for the French 107 **power** army 111 **entertain** engage, encounter 114 **for action** for want of action. 118 **renownèd** brought renown to 126 **So** so indeed 129 **pavilioned** tented, encamped 132 **spiritualty** clergy 137 **lay . . . proportions** allocate our forces 138 **road** inroad, raid 139 **With all advantages** whenever a good opportunity presents itself. 140 **They . . . marches** Our English forces in the territories bordering Scotland 143 **coursing snatchers** hit-and-run Scottish raiders on fast-galloping horses

144 **intendment** plan, hostile intent 145 **still** always. **giddy** unstable, fickle 148 **unfurnished** unprovided with defense 150 **brim** absolute, complete 151 **Galling . . . assays** harassing the land stripped of defenders with hot attacks 154 **th'ill neighborhood** the unneighborliness. 155 **feared** frightened 156 **hear . . . herself** i.e., only listen how England can be instructed by an example from her own history 157 **chivalry** knights 158 **And she . . . nobles** and she, England, widowlike in being deprived of her nobility while they fight in France 160–1 **impounded . . . Scots** (King David II of Scotland was captured and imprisoned in 1346 while Edward III was in France.) 161 **to France** (Historically, David II was imprisoned in London, not sent to France.) 165 **wrack** wreckage. **sumless** inestimable 169 **in prey** absent in search of prey 173 **to 'tame and havoc** to attame (i.e., break into) and ravage 175 **crushed necessity** distorted conclusion 177 **pretty** ingenious 178 **While that** While 179 **advisèd** wise, prudent 180 **though . . . lower** i.e., though composed of three broad social ranks (corresponding also to three singing voices from treble to bass) 181 **Put into parts** separated into different functions (and into different parts in part-music). **one consent** mutual harmony

Congreeing in a full and natural close,   182
Like music.
CANTERBURY   Therefore doth heaven divide
The state of man in divers functions,
Setting endeavor in continual motion,
To which is fixèd, as an aim or butt,   186
Obedience; for so work the honeybees,
Creatures that by a rule in nature teach
The act of order to a peopled kingdom.
They have a king, and officers of sorts,   190
Where some, like magistrates, correct at home;   191
Others, like merchants, venture trade abroad;
Others, like soldiers, armèd in their stings,
Make boot upon the summer's velvet buds,   194
Which pillage they with merry march bring home
To the tent royal of their emperor,
Who, busied in his majesty, surveys
The singing masons building roofs of gold,
The civil citizens kneading up the honey,
The poor mechanic porters crowding in   200
Their heavy burdens at his narrow gate,
The sad-eyed justice with his surly hum   202
Delivering o'er to executors pale   203
The lazy yawning drone. I this infer,
That many things, having full reference   205
To one consent, may work contrariously.   206
As many arrows loosèd several ways   207
Come to one mark, as many ways meet in one town,   208
As many fresh streams meet in one salt sea,
As many lines close in the dial's center,   210
So may a thousand actions once afoot
End in one purpose, and be all well borne   212
Without defeat. Therefore to France, my liege!
Divide your happy England into four,
Whereof take you one quarter into France,
And you withal shall make all Gallia shake.   216
If we with thrice such powers left at home
Cannot defend our own doors from the dog,
Let us be worried, and our nation lose   219
The name of hardiness and policy.   220
KING
Call in the messengers sent from the Dauphin.   221
                              [Exeunt some.]
Now are we well resolved, and by God's help
And yours, the noble sinews of our power,
France being ours, we'll bend it to our awe,   224

Or break it all to pieces. Or there we'll sit,   225
Ruling in large and ample empery   226
O'er France and all her almost kingly dukedoms,
Or lay these bones in an unworthy urn,
Tombless, with no remembrance over them.
Either our history shall with full mouth
Speak freely of our acts, or else our grave,
Like Turkish mute, shall have a tongueless mouth,
Not worshiped with a waxen epitaph.   233

          Enter Ambassadors of France.

Now are we well prepared to know the pleasure
Of our fair cousin Dauphin; for we hear   235
Your greeting is from him, not from the King.
FIRST AMBASSADOR
May't please Your Majesty to give us leave
Freely to render what we have in charge,
Or shall we sparingly show you far off
The Dauphin's meaning and our embassy?
KING
We are no tyrant, but a Christian king,
Unto whose grace our passion is as subject
As is our wretches fettered in our prisons.
Therefore with frank and with uncurbèd plainness
Tell us the Dauphin's mind.
FIRST AMBASSADOR   Thus, then, in few:
Your Highness, lately sending into France,
Did claim some certain dukedoms, in the right
Of your great predecessor, King Edward the Third.
In answer of which claim, the Prince our master
Says that you savor too much of your youth,
And bids you be advised there's naught in France
That can be with a nimble galliard won;   252
You cannot revel into dukedoms there.
He therefore sends you, meeter for your spirit,   254
This tun of treasure, and in lieu of this   255
Desires you let the dukedoms that you claim
Hear no more of you. This the Dauphin speaks.
                    [*A casket is presented;*
                    Exeter examines its contents.]
KING
What treasure, uncle?
EXETER   Tennis balls, my liege.
KING
We are glad the Dauphin is so pleasant with us.   259
His present and your pains we thank you for.
When we have matched our rackets to these balls,   261
We will in France, by God's grace, play a set
Shall strike his father's crown into the hazard.   263

---

182 **Congreeing** agreeing together.   **close** musical cadence   186 **aim or butt** target. (All endeavor is to direct itself toward obedience.)   190 **They . . . king** (A common error of early natural history, derived from Aristotle. The simile of the bees appears in Virgil, Sir Thomas Elyot, John Lyly, and others.)   **of sorts** various kinds   191 **correct** administer justice   194 **Make boot** prey   200 **mechanic** engaged in manual labor   202 **sad-eyed** grave-eyed   203 **executors pale** executioners, pale in their terrible sternness   205–6 **having . . . consent** united by a common understanding   207 **As** Just as.   **loosèd several ways** shot from different directions   208 **ways** roads   210 **close** come together.   **dial's** sundial's   212 **borne** carried out, sustained   216 **Gallia** France. (Latin name.)   219 **worried** (1) torn apart or harried, as by dogs (2) made anxious   220 **hardiness and policy** bravery and statesmanship.   221 **Dauphin** heir apparent to the French throne.   224 **ours** i.e., ours by right.   **our awe** submission to us

225 **Or there** Either there   226 **empery** dominion   233 **Not . . . epitaph** i.e., with not even so much as a wax (as opposed to bronze) epitaph; one easily effaced.   235 **cousin** fellow prince (though Henry does also claim a line of descent in the French royal family)   252 **galliard** a lively dance   254 **meeter** more fitting   255 **tun** cask   259 **pleasant** jocular. (Also in line 281.)   261 **rackets** (1) tennis rackets (2) noisy military assaults   263 **crown** (1) royal crown (2) final point scored, or a coin (worth five shillings in English coinage) staked in the game.   **hazard** (1) in "royal" tennis, an opening in one of the high walls enclosing the court; hitting the ball into such a "hazard" scored a winning point (2) jeopardy.

Tell him he hath made a match with such a wrangler 264
That all the courts of France will be disturbed 265
With chases. And we understand him well, 266
How he comes o'er us with our wilder days, 267
Not measuring what use we made of them.
We never valued this poor seat of England, 269
And therefore, living hence, did give ourself 270
To barbarous license—as 'tis ever common
That men are merriest when they are from home. 272
But tell the Dauphin I will keep my state, 273
Be like a king, and show my sail of greatness 274
When I do rouse me in my throne of France.
For that I have laid by my majesty 276
And plodded like a man for working days, 277
But I will rise there with so full a glory
That I will dazzle all the eyes of France,
Yea, strike the Dauphin blind to look on us.
And tell the pleasant Prince this mock of his
Hath turned his balls to gunstones, and his soul 282
Shall stand sore chargèd for the wasteful vengeance 283
That shall fly with them; for many a thousand
   widows
Shall this his mock mock out of their dear husbands,
Mock mothers from their sons, mock castles down,
And some are yet ungotten and unborn 287
That shall have cause to curse the Dauphin's scorn.
But this lies all within the will of God,
To whom I do appeal, and in whose name
Tell you the Dauphin I am coming on
To venge me as I may, and to put forth
My rightful hand in a well-hallowed cause.
So get you hence in peace; and tell the Dauphin
His jest will savor but of shallow wit
When thousands weep more than did laugh at it.—
Convey them with safe conduct.—Fare you well. 297
                          Exeunt Ambassadors.
EXETER This was a merry message.
KING
We hope to make the sender blush at it.
Therefore, my lords, omit no happy hour 300
That may give furth'rance to our expedition; 301
For we have now no thought in us but France,
Save those to God, that run before our business. 303
Therefore let our proportions for these wars 304
Be soon collected, and all things thought upon
That may with reasonable swiftness add
More feathers to our wings; for, God before, 307

We'll chide this Dauphin at his father's door.
Therefore let every man now task his thought, 309
That this fair action may on foot be brought.
                         Flourish. Exeunt.

❖

2.0

Enter Chorus.

CHORUS
Now all the youth of England are on fire,
And silken dalliance in the wardrobe lies. 2
Now thrive the armorers, and honor's thought
Reigns solely in the breast of every man.
They sell the pasture now to buy the horse,
Following the mirror of all Christian kings, 6
With wingèd heels, as English Mercurys. 7
For now sits Expectation in the air
And hides a sword from hilts unto the point 9
With crowns imperial, crowns and coronets, 10
Promised to Harry and his followers.
The French, advised by good intelligence 12
Of this most dreadful preparation,
Shake in their fear, and with pale policy 14
Seek to divert the English purposes.
O England! Model to thy inward greatness, 16
Like little body with a mighty heart,
What mightst thou do, that honor would thee do, 18
Were all thy children kind and natural?
But see, thy fault France hath in thee found out,
A nest of hollow bosoms, which he fills
With treacherous crowns; and three corrupted men, 22
One, Richard Earl of Cambridge, and the second,
Henry Lord Scroop of Masham, and the third,
Sir Thomas Grey, knight, of Northumberland,
Have, for the gilt of France—oh, guilt indeed!— 26
Confirmed conspiracy with fearful France, 27
And by their hands this grace of kings must die,
If hell and treason hold their promises,
Ere he take ship for France, and in Southampton.
Linger your patience on, and we'll digest 31
Th'abuse of distance, force a play. 32
The sum is paid, the traitors are agreed,
The King is set from London, and the scene
Is now transported, gentles, to Southampton.
There is the playhouse now, there must you sit,
And thence to France shall we convey you safe,

---

264 **wrangler** adversary, disputant 265 **courts** (1) tennis courts (2) royal courts 266 **chases** (1) returns of the ball (2) chasing after game (3) chasing the enemy. 267 **comes o'er us** taunts me. (*Us* is the royal plural.) 269 **seat** throne 270 **living hence** not frequenting the royal court 272 **from** away from 273 **keep my state** i.e., fulfill the role of king 274 **sail** full swell. (Henry says he has not yet revealed his full majesty in laying claim to France.) 276 **For that** i.e., In anticipation of that great event 277 **for** suited and ready for 282 **gunstones** cannonballs 283 **sore chargèd** sorely burdened with responsibility. **wasteful** destructive 287 **yet ungotten** not yet conceived 297 **Convey** Escort 300 **omit . . . hour** lose no favorable opportunity 301 **expedition** (1) invasion of France (2) haste 303 **that . . . business** that properly come first. 304 **proportions** levies of men 307 **God before** with God leading, helping

309 **task** tax, exercise
2.0 Chorus.
2 **silken . . . lies** i.e., silken apparel and idle pleasure are packed away. 6 **the mirror . . . kings** i.e., the ideal or model to which all other kings should compare themselves 7 **Mercurys** (Mercury, classical messenger of the gods, always wears winged heels.) 9 **hides a sword** i.e., holds up a sword completely impaled with the prizes of war 10 **With . . . coronets** with the crowns of emperors, kings, and nobles 12 **intelligence** information gathering 14 **pale policy** faint-hearted stratagems 16 **Model to** Outward manifestation of 18 **would** would have 22 **crowns** coins, money (as a bribe) 26 **gilt** gold 27 **fearful** frightened, cowardly 31–2 **digest . . . play** compress long distance (and time) into what can be encompassed in a play, an *abuse* of the unities of time and place.

And bring you back, charming the narrow seas
To give you gentle pass; for, if we may,   39
We'll not offend one stomach with our play.   40
But, when the King come forth, and not till then,   41
Unto Southampton do we shift our scene.   *Exit.*   42

2.1

Enter Corporal Nym and Lieutenant Bardolph.

BARDOLPH   Well met, Corporal Nym.

NYM   Good morrow, Lieutenant Bardolph.

BARDOLPH   What, are Ancient Pistol and you friends   3
yet?

NYM   For my part, I care not. I say little; but when time
shall serve, there shall be smiles—but that shall be as
it may. I dare not fight, but I will wink and hold out   7
mine iron. It is a simple one, but what though? It will   8
toast cheese, and it will endure cold as another man's   9
sword will—and there's an end.   10

BARDOLPH   I will bestow a breakfast to make you
friends, and we'll be all three sworn brothers to
France. Let 't be so, good Corporal Nym.

NYM   Faith, I will live so long as I may, that's the certain
of it; and when I cannot live any longer, I will do as I
may. That is my rest; that is the rendezvous of it.   16

BARDOLPH   It is certain, Corporal, that he is married to
Nell Quickly, and certainly she did you wrong, for
you were trothplight to her.   19

NYM   I cannot tell. Things must be as they may. Men
may sleep, and they may have their throats about
them at that time, and some say knives have edges. It
must be as it may. Though Patience be a tired mare,   23
yet she will plod. There must be conclusions. Well, I   24
cannot tell.

Enter Pistol and [Hostess] Quickly.

BARDOLPH   Here comes Ancient Pistol and his wife.
Good Corporal, be patient here.

NYM   How now, mine host Pistol?

PISTOL
Base tike, call'st thou me host?   29
Now, by this hand, I swear, I scorn the term!
Nor shall my Nell keep lodgers.

HOSTESS   No, by my troth, not long; for we cannot lodge
and board a dozen or fourteen gentlewomen that live

honestly by the prick of their needles, but it will be   34
thought we keep a bawdy house straight. [*Nym and
Pistol draw.*] Oh, welladay, Lady! If he be not hewn   36
now, we shall see willful adultery and murder com-   37
itted.

BARDOLPH   Good Lieutenant! Good Corporal! Offer   39
nothing here.   40

NYM   Pish!

PISTOL
Pish for thee, Iceland dog!   42
Thou prick-eared cur of Iceland!

HOSTESS   Good Corporal Nym, show thy valor, and   44
put up your sword.   [*They sheathe their swords.*]

NYM   Will you shog off? I would have you solus.   46

PISTOL
Solus, egregious dog? O viper vile!
The solus in thy most mervailous face!   48
The solus in thy teeth, and in thy throat,   49
And in thy hateful lungs, yea, in thy maw, pardie,   50
And, which is worse, within thy nasty mouth!
I do retort the solus in thy bowels;
For I can take, and Pistol's cock is up,   53
And flashing fire will follow.

NYM   I am not Barbason; you cannot conjure me. I have   55
an humor to knock you indifferently well. If you grow   56
foul with me, Pistol, I will scour you with my rapier, as 57
I may, in fair terms. If you would walk off, I would   58
prick your guts a little, in good terms, as I may, and
that's the humor of it.   60

PISTOL
O braggart vile and damnèd furious wight!   61
The grave doth gape, and doting death is near.
Therefore exhale!   [*They draw their swords.*]   63

BARDOLPH   [*drawing his sword*]   Hear me, hear me what
I say. He that strikes the first stroke, I'll run him up to
the hilts, as I am a soldier.

PISTOL
An oath of mickle might, and fury shall abate.   67
          [*Pistol and Nym sheathe their swords.*]
[*To Nym*] Give me thy fist, thy forefoot to me give.
Thy spirits are most tall.   69

---

34 prick (With a bawdy double meaning, probably unintended, as also
in *Pistol's cock*, line 53.)   **36 welladay** wellaway, alas.   **Lady** i.e., by
Our Lady. (An oath.)   **hewn** struck down   **37 adultery** (Blunder for
"battery"?)   **39–40 Offer nothing** Attempt no violence   **42 Iceland
dog** a small, shaggy dog often kept as a house pet. (Pistol's humor is
to use extravagant epithets, like this one, tags from current plays, and
scraps of foreign languages.)   **44 valor** (She means "calm," "forbearance.")   **46 shog off** move along.   **solus** alone. (Nym proposes a duel;
see *walk off* in line 58.)   **48 mervailous** marvelous, astonishing
49–50 The solus . . . thy lungs (The most offensive insult possible, as
in *Hamlet*'s "the lie i'th' throat / As deep as to the lungs," 2.2.574–5.)
50 maw belly.   **pardie** *par Dieu*, by God   **53 take** catch fire.   **cock is
up** trigger is cocked. (With bawdy pun.)   **55 Barbason** (The name of
a fiend.)   **conjure** exorcise. (Nym mocks Pistol's hyperbolic rant as
though it were a conjuration.)   **55–6 I have an humor** I'm in the mood.
(*Humor* is a favorite word with Nym, as in lines 60, 71, 97, 116, 121, and
126.)   **57 foul** (1) foulmouthed (2) fouled from firing and in need of
scouring   **58 in fair terms** i.e., make no mistake about it. (*In good terms*
at line 59 means the same.)   **walk off** walk aside (to fight)   **60 that's
. . . it** that's my mood.   **61 wight** person.   **63 exhale** draw (sword, much
as the sun draws forth vapors).   **67 mickle** great   **69 tall** valiant.

---

39 pass passage   **40 offend one stomach** (1) offend anyone's taste by
sudden shifts in scene (2) make anyone seasick   **41–2 But . . . scene**
i.e., The scene will be shifted to Southampton after a scene in London.
(These lines sound as though they were added as an afterthought, to
accommodate the inclusion of the comic scene in 2.1.)
2.1. Location: London. A street.
3 Ancient Ensign, standard-bearer   **7 wink** shut the eyes   **8 iron**
sword.   **though** of that.   **9 endure cold** i.e., doesn't mind being
drawn from its sheath   **10 there's an end** that's all there is to it.
16 rest last stake (in the gambling game of primero).   **rendezvous**
last resort   **19 trothplight** betrothed   **23–4 Though . . . plod** i.e.,
Patient persistence will ultimately achieve its goal. (Nym hints, as
he does elsewhere, at violence toward Pistol.)   **24 conclusions** an
end to matters. (Nym hints darkly that the end must come soon.)
29 tike cur

NYM   I will cut thy throat, one time or other, in fair
terms. That is the humor of it.

PISTOL *Couple a gorge!*   72
That is the word. I thee defy again.
O hound of Crete, think'st thou my spouse to get?   74
No, to the spital go,   75
And from the powdering tub of infamy   76
Fetch forth the lazar kite of Cressid's kind,   77
Doll Tearsheet she by name, and her espouse.
I have, and I will hold, the quondam Quickly   79
For the only she; and—*pauca!* There's enough.   80
Go to.

Enter the Boy.

BOY   Mine host Pistol, you must come to my master,
and you, hostess. He is very sick and would to bed.
Good Bardolph, put thy face between his sheets, and   84
do the office of a warming pan. Faith, he's very ill.

BARDOLPH   Away, you rogue!

HOSTESS   By my troth, he'll yield the crow a pudding   87
one of these days. The King has killed his heart. Good   88
husband, come home presently.   *Exit [with Boy].*   89

BARDOLPH   Come, shall I make you two friends? We
must to France together. Why the devil should we
keep knives to cut one another's throats?

PISTOL
Let floods o'erswell, and fiends for food howl on!

NYM   You'll pay me the eight shillings I won of you at
betting?

PISTOL   Base is the slave that pays.

NYM   That now I will have. That's the humor of it.

PISTOL   As manhood shall compound. Push home.   98
[They] draw.

BARDOLPH *[drawing]*   By this sword, he that makes
the first thrust, I'll kill him! By this sword, I will.

PISTOL
Sword is an oath, and oaths must have their course.   101
[He sheathes his sword.]

BARDOLPH   Corporal Nym, an thou wilt be friends, be   102
friends; an thou wilt not, why, then, be enemies with
me too. Prithee, put up.   104

NYM   I shall have my eight shillings I won of you at
betting?

PISTOL
A noble shalt thou have, and present pay;   107
And liquor likewise will I give to thee,

And friendship shall combine, and brotherhood.
I'll live by Nym, and Nym shall live by me.   110
Is not this just? For I shall sutler be   111
Unto the camp, and profits will accrue.
Give me thy hand.

NYM   I shall have my noble?

PISTOL   In cash most justly paid.

NYM   Well, then, that's the humor of't.
[Nym and Bardolph sheathe their swords.]

Enter Hostess.

HOSTESS   As ever you come of women, come in quickly   117
to Sir John. Ah, poor heart, he is so shaked of a burning quotidian tertian that it is most lamentable to be-   119
hold. Sweet men, come to him.   *[Exit.]*

NYM   The King hath run bad humors on the knight,   121
that's the even of it.   122

PISTOL   Nym, thou hast spoke the right.
His heart is fracted and corroborate.   124

NYM   The King is a good king, but it must be as it may;
he passes some humors and careers.   126

PISTOL
Let us condole the knight, for, lambkins, we will live.   127
[Exeunt.]

[2.2]

Enter Exeter, Bedford, and Westmorland.

BEDFORD
'Fore God, His Grace is bold to trust these traitors.

EXETER
They shall be apprehended by and by.

WESTMORLAND
How smooth and even they do bear themselves!   3
As if allegiance in their bosoms sat,
Crownèd with faith and constant loyalty.

BEDFORD
The King hath note of all that they intend,
By interception which they dream not of.

EXETER
Nay, but the man that was his bedfellow,   8
Whom he hath dulled and cloyed with gracious
favors—   9

---

72 *Couple a gorge! Couper la gorge!*, "Cut the throat!"   74 **hound of
Crete** (Parallel to *Iceland dog,* line 42.)   75 **spital** hospital   76 **powdering tub** (Originally a tub used for salting beef; here, alluding to
a method of curing venereal disease by sweating.)   77 **lazar . . . kind**
i.e., diseased, leprous whore (a *kite* is a bird of prey) like Cressida,
the fallen woman, who, in Robert Henryson's *Testament of Cresseid,* is
shown as being rejected by Diomede and infected with leprosy
79 **quondam** former   80 **only she** i.e., only woman in the world.
pauca i.e., in brief   84 **face** (Bardolph's face is fiery with drinking.)
87 **he'll** (Refers to the Boy or Falstaff.)   **yield . . . pudding** i.e., be
hanged on the gallows and eaten by carrion birds   88 **his** i.e., Falstaff's   89 **presently** immediately.   98 **As . . . compound** As valor
shall settle the matter (in fight).   101 **Sword is an oath** (Quibbling on
sword as *'s word,* i.e., "God's word.")   102 **an** if   104 **put up** i.e., put
up your sword.   107 **A noble . . . pay** i.e., I'll settle for paying you six
shillings eight pence ready money

110 **Nym** (Quibbles on *nim,* meaning "thief.")   111 **sutler** seller of
liquor and provisions to the soldiers   117 **come of** were born of
119 **quotidian tertian** (A *quotidian* fever was one that came daily; a
tertian fever, one that came on alternate days, though some authorities believed that different fevers might mix and intensify their
effects.)   121 **run bad humors** i.e., vented his displeasure   122 **even**
level truth   124 **fracted** broken.   **corroborate** (Blunder for "broken
to pieces" or "corrupted"? The word means "strengthened, confirmed.")   126 **passes . . . careers** lets pass (i.e., indulges in) some
idiosyncrasies and capers. (A *career* is a full gallop.)   127 **condole**
express our commiseration of or sympathy with.   **lambkins** (A term
of endearment.)
2.2. Location: Southampton, a seaport on England's southern coast.
3 smooth and even pleasant and calm   **8 bedfellow** i.e., constant
companion. (Refers to Scroop.)   **9 dulled** dulled the appetite of

That he should, for a foreign purse, so sell
His sovereign's life to death and treachery!

*Sound trumpets. Enter the King, Scroop, Cam-
bridge, and Grey, [and attendants].*

KING
Now sits the wind fair, and we will aboard.   12
My lord of Cambridge, and my kind lord of Masham,
And you, my gentle knight, give me your thoughts.
Think you not that the pow'rs we bear with us   15
Will cut their passage through the force of France,
Doing the execution and the act
For which we have in head assembled them?   18

SCROOP
No doubt, my liege, if each man do his best.

KING
I doubt not that, since we are well persuaded
We carry not a heart with us from hence
That grows not in a fair consent with ours,   22
Nor leave not one behind that doth not wish
Success and conquest to attend on us.

CAMBRIDGE
Never was monarch better feared and loved
Than is Your Majesty. There's not, I think, a subject
That sits in heart-grief and uneasiness
Under the sweet shade of your government.

GREY
True. Those that were your father's enemies
Have steeped their galls in honey, and do serve you   30
With hearts create of duty and of zeal.   31

KING
We therefore have great cause of thankfulness,
And shall forget the office of our hand   33
Sooner than quittance of desert and merit   34
According to the weight and worthiness.

SCROOP
So service shall with steelèd sinews toil,
And labor shall refresh itself with hope,
To do Your Grace incessant services.

KING
We judge no less.—Uncle of Exeter,
Enlarge the man committed yesterday   40
That railed against our person. We consider
It was excess of wine that set him on,
And on his more advice we pardon him.   43

SCROOP
That's mercy, but too much security.   44
Let him be punished, sovereign, lest example
Breed, by his sufferance, more of such a kind.   46

KING   Oh, let us yet be merciful.

CAMBRIDGE
So may Your Highness, and yet punish too.

GREY
Sir, you show great mercy if you give him life   49
After the taste of much correction.   50

KING
Alas, your too much love and care of me
Are heavy orisons 'gainst this poor wretch!   52
If little faults proceeding on distemper   53
Shall not be winked at, how shall we stretch our eye   54
When capital crimes, chewed, swallowed, and
    digested,   55
Appear before us? We'll yet enlarge that man,   56
Though Cambridge, Scroop, and Grey, in their dear
    care
And tender preservation of our person,
Would have him punished. And now to our French
    causes.
Who are the late commissioners?   60

CAMBRIDGE   I one, my lord.
Your Highness bade me ask for it today.   62

SCROOP   So did you me, my liege.

GREY   And I, my royal sovereign.

KING [*giving them papers*]
Then, Richard Earl of Cambridge, there is yours;
There yours, Lord Scroop of Masham; and sir knight,
Grey of Northumberland, this same is yours.
Read them, and know I know your worthiness.—
My lord of Westmorland, and uncle Exeter,
We will aboard tonight.—Why, how now, gentlemen?
What see you in those papers, that you lose
So much complexion?—Look ye how they change!   72
Their cheeks are paper.—Why, what read you there   73
That have so cowarded and chased your blood
Out of appearance?

CAMBRIDGE   I do confess my fault,   75
And do submit me to Your Highness' mercy.

GREY, SCROOP   To which we all appeal.

KING
The mercy that was quick in us but late   78
By your own counsel is suppressed and killed.
You must not dare, for shame, to talk of mercy,
For your own reasons turn into your bosoms,
As dogs upon their masters, worrying you.—   82
See you, my princes and my noble peers,
These English monsters! My lord of Cambridge here,
You know how apt our love was to accord   85
To furnish him with all appurtenants   86
Belonging to his honor; and this man
Hath for a few light crowns lightly conspired   88
And sworn unto the practices of France   89

49 **give him life** allow him to live   50 **correction** punishment.
52 **heavy orisons** weighty prayers, pleas   53 **proceeding on distemper** resulting from unstable condition (caused by excessive drinking)
54 **stretch** open wide, not wink   55 **capital** punishable by death.
chewed ... digested i.e., premeditated   56 **yet** in spite of what you
say   60 **late** recently appointed (to serve while Henry is in France)
62 **it** i.e., my commission   72 **complexion** color.   73 **paper** i.e., white
as a sheet.   75 **appearance** (1) sight (2) your faces. (Presumably
the traitors kneel at this point.)   78 **quick** alive   82 **worrying you**
tearing at your throat.   85 **accord** consent   86 **appurtenants** appurtenances   88 **light** insignificant.   **lightly** readily, casually
89 **practices** plots

12 **sits ... fair** the wind blows from a favorable quarter   15 **pow'rs**
armed forces   18 **in head** as an army   22 **grows ... consent** does not
act in harmony   30 **galls** i.e., resentment   31 **create** composed
33 **office** use, function   34 **quittance** requital   40 **Enlarge** set free
43 **more advice** explaining and apologizing for what happened
44 **security** overconfidence.   46 **sufferance** being pardoned

To kill us here in Hampton. To the which
This knight, no less for bounty bound to us   91
Than Cambridge is, hath likewise sworn. But oh,
What shall I say to thee, Lord Scroop, thou cruel,
Ingrateful, savage, and inhuman creature?
Thou that didst bear the key of all my counsels,
That knew'st the very bottom of my soul,
That almost mightst have coined me into gold,
Wouldst thou have practiced on me for thy use?   98
May it be possible that foreign hire
Could out of thee extract one spark of evil
That might annoy my finger? 'Tis so strange   101
That though the truth of it stands off as gross   102
As black and white, my eye will scarcely see it.
Treason and murder ever kept together,
As two yoke-devils sworn to either's purpose,   105
Working so grossly in a natural cause   106
That admiration did not whoop at them.   107
But thou, 'gainst all proportion, didst bring in   108
Wonder to wait on treason and on murder;   109
And whatsoever cunning fiend it was
That wrought upon thee so preposterously   111
Hath got the voice in hell for excellence.   112
All other devils that suggest by treasons   113
Do botch and bungle up damnation   114
With patches, colors, and with forms being fetched   115
From glist'ring semblances of piety;   116
But he that tempered thee bade thee stand up,   117
Gave thee no instance why thou shouldst do treason,   118
Unless to dub thee with the name of traitor.   119
If that same demon that hath gulled thee thus
Should with his lion gait walk the whole world,   121
He might return to vasty Tartar back   122
And tell the legions, "I can never win
A soul so easy as that Englishman's."
Oh, how hast thou with jealousy infected   125
The sweetness of affiance! Show men dutiful?   126
Why, so didst thou. Seem they grave and learnèd?
Why, so didst thou. Come they of noble family?
Why, so didst thou. Seem they religious?
Why, so didst thou. Or are they spare in diet,
Free from gross passion or of mirth or anger,   131
Constant in spirit, not swerving with the blood,   132

Garnished and decked in modest complement,   133
Not working with the eye without the ear,   134
And but in purgèd judgment trusting neither?   135
Such and so finely bolted didst thou seem.
And thus thy fall hath left a kind of blot   137
To mark the full-fraught man and best endued   138
With some suspicion. I will weep for thee;   139
For this revolt of thine, methinks, is like
Another fall of man.—Their faults are open.   141
Arrest them to the answer of the law;   142
And God acquit them of their practices!
EXETER   I arrest thee of high treason, by the name of
    Richard Earl of Cambridge.
    I arrest thee of high treason, by the name of Henry Lord
    Scroop of Masham.
    I arrest thee of high treason, by the name of Thomas
    Grey, knight, of Northumberland.
SCROOP
    Our purposes God justly hath discovered,   150
    And I repent my fault more than my death,
    Which I beseech Your Highness to forgive,
    Although my body pay the price of it.
CAMBRIDGE
    For me, the gold of France did not seduce,
    Although I did admit it as a motive   155
    The sooner to effect what I intended.   156
    But God be thankèd for prevention,
    Which I in sufferance heartily will rejoice,   158
    Beseeching God and you to pardon me.
GREY
    Never did faithful subject more rejoice
    At the discovery of most dangerous treason
    Than I do at this hour joy o'er myself,
    Prevented from a damnèd enterprise.
    My fault, but not my body, pardon, sovereign.
KING
    God quit you in his mercy! Hear your sentence.   165
    You have conspired against our royal person,
    Joined with an enemy proclaimed, and from his
        coffers
    Received the golden earnest of our death,   168
    Wherein you would have sold your king to slaughter,
    His princes and his peers to servitude,
    His subjects to oppression and contempt,
    And his whole kingdom into desolation.
    Touching our person seek we no revenge,   173

---

91 This knight i.e., Grey   **98 practiced on** plotted against.   **use** profit.
(With play on the meaning "interest derived from usury"; Scroop had
served as Lord Treasurer.)   **101 annoy** injure   **102 stands . . . gross**
appears as obvious   **105 yoke-devils** partners in a diabolical cause
106–7 Working . . . them working together so manifestly toward a
purpose suited to their evil natures that they provoked no outcry of
wonder.   **108 proportion** fitness of things   **109 Wonder** astonishment (that Scroop should be a murderer).   **wait on** attend, accompany   **111 wrought** worked.   **preposterously** unnaturally   **112 voice**
vote   **113–16 All . . . piety** All other devils that tempt make at least
some effort to dress damnation up in a plausible semblance of piety
117–19 But . . . traitor but the devil that tempted you to treason simply ordered you to stand up an unabashed rebel, and gave you no
specious justification to do treason other than for the sheer sake of
having the name of traitor.   **121 lion gait** (The devil, according to 1
Peter 5:8, strides about the world like a roaring lion, "seeking whom
he may devour.")   **122 vasty** vast.   **Tartar** Tartarus, the hell of classical mythology   **125 jealousy** suspicion   **126 affiance** trust.   **Show**
Appear   **131 or of** either of   **132 swerving with the blood** sinning
through passion

133 decked . . . complement wearing the look of modesty   **134–5 Not
. . . neither** trusting neither eye nor ear alone, and not trusting either
one except when refined by wisdom and judgment.   **137–39 And . . .
suspicion** And thus your fall into sin has been such as to cast some
suspicion on even those who seem fully and richly endowed with virtuous qualities.   **141 fall of man** humankind's original disobedience
to God in the Garden of Eden.   **open** apparent, obvious.   **142 to the
answer of** so that they will be answerable to   **150 discovered**
revealed   **155 did . . . motive** i.e., accepted money from France as a
means   **156 The . . . intended** (Cambridge's real motive, barely hinted at here, was to assist his brother-in-law Edmund Mortimer, fifth
Earl of March, to the throne as the standard-bearer of the Yorkist
claim against the Lancastrian Henry.)   **158 sufferance** my suffering
and patient endurance   **165 quit** (1) pardon (2) requite, punish
168 golden earnest advance payment   **173 Touching our person** As
regards my own personal safety

But we our kingdom's safety must so tender,   174
Whose ruin you have sought, that to her laws
We do deliver you. Get you therefore hence,
Poor miserable wretches, to your death,
The taste whereof God of his mercy give
You patience to endure, and true repentance
Of all your dear offenses!—Bear them hence.   180
          Exeunt [Cambridge, Scroop, and Grey, guarded].
Now, lords, for France, the enterprise whereof
Shall be to you, as us, like glorious.   182
We doubt not of a fair and lucky war,
Since God so graciously hath brought to light
This dangerous treason lurking in our way
To hinder our beginnings. We doubt not now
But every rub is smoothèd on our way.   187
Then forth, dear countrymen! Let us deliver
Our puissance into the hand of God,   189
Putting it straight in expedition.   190
Cheerly to sea! The signs of war advance!   191
No king of England, if not king of France!
          Flourish. [Exeunt.]

❖

[2.3]

Enter Pistol, Nym, Bardolph, Boy, and Hostess.

HOSTESS   Prithee, honey-sweet husband, let me bring
thee to Staines.   2
PISTOL   No, for my manly heart doth earn. Bardolph, be   3
blithe; Nym, rouse thy vaunting veins; Boy, bristle thy
courage up; for Falstaff he is dead, and we must earn
therefore.
BARDOLPH   Would I were with him, wheresome'er he is,
either in heaven or in hell!
HOSTESS   Nay, sure he's not in hell. He's in Arthur's   9
bosom, if ever man went to Arthur's bosom. 'A made   10
a finer end, and went away an it had been any   11
christom child. 'A parted ev'n just between twelve   12
and one, ev'n at the turning o'th' tide. For after I saw
him fumble with the sheets, and play with flowers,
and smile upon his finger's end, I knew there was but
one way; for his nose was as sharp as a pen, and 'a   16
babbled of green fields. "How now, Sir John?" quoth I.   17
"What, man? Be o' good cheer." So 'a cried out, "God,
God, God!" three or four times. Now I, to comfort him,
bid him 'a should not think of God; I hoped there was

no need to trouble himself with any such thoughts yet.
So 'a bade me lay more clothes on his feet. I put my
hand into the bed and felt them, and they were as cold
as any stone; then I felt to his knees, and so upward   24
and upward, and all was as cold as any stone.   25
NYM   They say he cried out of sack.   26
HOSTESS   Ay, that 'a did.
BARDOLPH   And of women.
HOSTESS   Nay, that 'a did not.
BOY   Yes, that 'a did, and said they were devils incar-
nate.
HOSTESS   'A could never abide carnation; 'twas a color
he never liked.
BOY   'A said once the devil would have him about
women.
HOSTESS   'A did in some sort, indeed, handle women;   36
but then he was rheumatic, and talked of the Whore of   37
Babylon.
BOY   Do you not remember, 'a saw a flea stick upon
Bardolph's nose, and 'a said it was a black soul
burning in hell?
BARDOLPH   Well, the fuel is gone that maintained that   42
fire. That's all the riches I got in his service.
NYM   Shall we shog? The King will be gone from South-   44
ampton.
PISTOL
  Come, let's away.—My love, give me thy lips.
          [He kisses the Hostess.]
  Look to my chattels and my movables.   47
  Let senses rule. The word is "Pitch and pay."   48
  Trust none,
  For oaths are straws, men's faiths are wafer cakes,   50
  And Holdfast is the only dog, my duck.   51
  Therefore, *caveto* be thy counselor.   52
  Go, clear thy crystals.—Yokefellows in arms,   53
  Let us to France, like horseleeches, my boys,
  To suck, to suck, the very blood to suck!
BOY   And that's but unwholesome food, they say.
PISTOL   Touch her soft mouth, and march.
BARDOLPH   Farewell, hostess.   *[Kissing her.]*
NYM   I cannot kiss, that is the humor of it; but adieu.
PISTOL
  Let huswifery appear. Keep close, I thee command.   60
HOSTESS   Farewell! Adieu!   *Exeunt [separately].*

❖

---

174 tender regard, hold dear   **180 dear** grievous, dire   **182 like**
alike, equally   **187 But** but that.   **rub** obstacle. (A bowling term.)
189 puissance armed might   **190 straight in expedition** immediately
in action.   **191 The signs . . . advance!** Lift high our banners!
2.3. London. A street.
2 Staines town on the road from London to Southampton.   **3 earn**
grieve. (But in line 5 there may also be a play on the sense of "find
other employment," since Pistol and the others are now on their
own.)   **9–10 Arthur's bosom** (Malapropism for "Abraham's bosom";
see Luke 16:22.)   **10 'A** He   **11 an** as if   **12 christom** (Mistress Quickly
means "new christened." A *chrisom* is a white robe put on a child at
baptism to betoken innocence. Christenings were performed soon
after birth because of the high rate of infant mortality.)   **16–17 'a babbled of green fields** (This line contains Theobald's famous emendation. The Folio has "and a Table of greene fields." Mistress Quickly
seems unaware that Falstaff was reciting the Twenty-third Psalm.)

24–5 upward . . . stone (The Hostess seems unaware of the sexual implications of her speech. *Stone* can mean "testicle.")   **26 of sack** against
sack (a Spanish wine).   **36 handle** discuss. (Though an unintended literal sense is also comically present.)   **37 rheumatic** feverish, or perhaps
an error for "lunatic." (Because "Rome" was pronounced "room,"
rheumatic also prepares for the allusion to the Whore of Babylon, i.e., the
Church of Rome. See also Revelation 17:4–5.)   **42 fuel** i.e., liquor, supplied by Falstaff, that has given Bardolph his red face   **44 shog** be off.
47 chattels . . . movables personal property.   **48 Let . . . pay** i.e., Keep
your eyes and ears open, and let your motto as hostess be "cash down."
50 wafer cakes i.e., easily broken   **51 Holdfast . . . dog** i.e., a large
clamp or *holdfast* is best at holding things tight, like a tenacious dog.
(Compare the proverb, "Brag is a good dog, but Holdfast is better.")
Mistress Quickly is bidden to keep a tight hold on things.   **52 caveto**
beware. (The correct imperative plural of the Latin is *cavete*.)   **53 clear
thy crystals** wipe your eyes.   **Yokefellows** Companions   **60 Let . . .
close** i.e., Be a thrifty housekeeper and stay at home

2.4

Flourish. Enter the French King, the Dauphin, the Dukes of Berri and Brittany, [the Constable, and others].

FRENCH KING
Thus comes the English with full power upon us,
And more than carefully it us concerns
To answer royally in our defenses.
Therefore the Dukes of Berri and of Brittany,
Of Brabant and of Orleans, shall make forth,   5
And you, Prince Dauphin, with all swift dispatch,
To line and new-repair our towns of war   7
With men of courage and with means defendant;   8
For England his approaches makes as fierce   9
As waters to the sucking of a gulf.   10
It fits us then to be as provident
As fear may teach us, out of late examples   12
Left by the fatal and neglected English   13
Upon our fields.
DAUPHIN   My most redoubted father,   14
It is most meet we arm us 'gainst the foe;   15
For peace itself should not so dull a kingdom,
Though war nor no known quarrel were in question,
But that defenses, musters, preparations,
Should be maintained, assembled, and collected
As were a war in expectation.   20
Therefore, I say 'tis meet we all go forth
To view the sick and feeble parts of France.
And let us do it with no show of fear—
No, with no more than if we heard that England
Were busied with a Whitsun morris dance.   25
For, my good liege, she is so idly kinged,   26
Her scepter so fantastically borne
By a vain, giddy, shallow, humorous youth,   28
That fear attends her not.
CONSTABLE   Oh, peace, Prince Dauphin!
You are too much mistaken in this king.
Question Your Grace the late ambassadors,
With what great state he heard their embassy,   32
How well supplied with noble counselors,
How modest in exception, and withal   34
How terrible in constant resolution,   35
And you shall find his vanities forespent   36
Were but the outside of the Roman Brutus,   37
Covering discretion with a coat of folly,
As gardeners do with ordure hide those roots   39

That shall first spring and be most delicate.
DAUPHIN
Well, 'tis not so, my Lord High Constable;
But though we think it so, it is no matter.
In cases of defense 'tis best to weigh
The enemy more mighty than he seems.
So the proportions of defense are filled,   45
Which of a weak and niggardly projection   46
Doth, like a miser, spoil his coat with scanting
A little cloth.
FRENCH KING   Think we King Harry strong;
And, princes, look you strongly arm to meet him.   49
The kindred of him hath been fleshed upon us;   50
And he is bred out of that bloody strain
That haunted us in our familiar paths.
Witness our too-much-memorable shame
When Crécy battle fatally was struck,   54
And all our princes captived by the hand
Of that black name, Edward, Black Prince of Wales;
Whiles that his mountain sire, on mountain standing,   57
Up in the air, crowned with the golden sun,
Saw his heroical seed and smiled to see him   59
Mangle the work of nature and deface   60
The patterns that by God and by French fathers   61
Had twenty years been made. This is a stem   62
Of that victorious stock; and let us fear
The native mightiness and fate of him.   64

Enter a Messenger.

MESSENGER
Ambassadors from Harry King of England
Do crave admittance to Your Majesty.
FRENCH KING
We'll give them present audience. Go and bring them.
                                [Exit Messenger.]
You see this chase is hotly followed, friends.
DAUPHIN
Turn head and stop pursuit; for coward dogs   69
Most spend their mouths when what they seem to
   threaten   70
Runs far before them. Good my sovereign,
Take up the English short, and let them know
Of what a monarchy you are the head.
Self-love, my liege, is not so vile a sin
As self-neglecting.

Enter Exeter [and others].

FRENCH KING   From our brother of England?   75

2.4. Location: France. The royal court.
5 make forth set forth   **7 line** reinforce   **8 defendant** defensive
9 England the King of England   **10 gulf** whirlpool.   **12 late** recent
13 fatal and neglected fatally underestimated   **14 redoubted** reverenced   **15 meet** appropriate   **20 As were** as if there were   **25 Whitsun morris dance** folk dance often performed during Whitsuntide, in early summer, by persons in fancy costumes and decked with bells.
26 idly frivolously   **28 humorous** capricious   **32 state** dignity
34 exception making objections.   **withal** in addition   **35 terrible** awesome, terrifying   **36 vanities forespent** follies used up and now a thing of the past   **37 Brutus** i.e., the elder Brutus, Lucius Junius Brutus, who pretended to be stupid (*brutus*) as a ruse to allay the suspicions of the tyrant Tarquin until the time for overthrow was ripe   **39 ordure** manure, mulch

45 So . . . filled In that way an adequate and full defense is provided   **46 Which . . . projection** which defense, if designed on too small and miserly a scale   **49 look** be sure   **50 kindred** i.e., his great-grandfather Edward III and great-uncle Edward the Black Prince.   **fleshed** initiated in the shedding of blood, with foretaste of further success   **54 Crécy** French defeat in 1346.   **struck** waged   **57 mountain sire** i.e., Edward III, born in mountainous Wales, and of sturdy proportions   **59–62 Saw . . . made** beheld his heroical son (the Black Prince) and smiled to see him mangle Nature's handiwork in the shape of young Frenchmen, whom, some twenty or so years earlier, God and their French fathers had created and begotten.   **64 fate** what he is destined to do   **69 Turn . . . pursuit** Turn and face the pursuing hounds. (Hunting terms.)   **70 Most . . . mouths** bay the loudest   **75 brother** fellow monarch

EXETER
   From him, and thus he greets Your Majesty:
   He wills you, in the name of God Almighty,
   That you divest yourself and lay apart   78
   The borrowed glories that by gift of heaven,
   By law of nature and of nations, 'longs   80
   To him and to his heirs, namely, the crown
   And all wide-stretchèd honors that pertain   82
   By custom and the ordinance of times   83
   Unto the crown of France. That you may know
   'Tis no sinister nor no awkward claim,   85
   Picked from the wormholes of long-vanished days,
   Nor from the dust of old oblivion raked,
   He sends you this most memorable line,   88
                          [giving a paper]
   In every branch truly demonstrative,
   Willing you overlook this pedigree.   90
   And when you find him evenly derived   91
   From his most famed of famous ancestors,
   Edward the Third, he bids you then resign
   Your crown and kingdom, indirectly held   94
   From him the native and true challenger.   95
FRENCH KING   Or else what follows?
EXETER
   Bloody constraint; for if you hide the crown   97
   Even in your hearts, there will he rake for it.
   Therefore in fierce tempest is he coming,
   In thunder and in earthquake, like a Jove,
   That if requiring fail, he will compel;   101
   And bids you, in the bowels of the Lord,   102
   Deliver up the crown, and to take mercy
   On the poor souls for whom this hungry war
   Opens his vasty jaws, and on your head   105
   Turning the widows' tears, the orphans' cries,   106
   The dead men's blood, the privèd maidens' groans,   107
   For husbands, fathers, and betrothèd lovers
   That shall be swallowed in this controversy.
   This is his claim, his threat'ning, and my message—
   Unless the Dauphin be in presence here,
   To whom expressly I bring greeting too.
FRENCH KING
   For us, we will consider of this further.
   Tomorrow shall you bear our full intent
   Back to our brother of England.
DAUPHIN   For the Dauphin,
   I stand here for him. What to him from England?
EXETER
   Scorn and defiance, slight regard, contempt,
   And anything that may not misbecome   118
   The mighty sender, doth he prize you at.   119

Thus says my king, and if your father's Highness
Do not, in grant of all demands at large,   121
Sweeten the bitter mock you sent His Majesty,
He'll call you to so hot an answer of it   123
That caves and womby vaultages of France   124
Shall chide your trespass and return your mock
In second accent of his ordinance.   126
DAUPHIN
   Say if my father render fair return   127
   It is against my will, for I desire
   Nothing but odds with England. To that end,   129
   As matching to his youth and vanity,
   I did present him with the Paris balls.   131
EXETER
   He'll make your Paris Louvre shake for it,   132
   Were it the mistress court of mighty Europe.
   And be assured, you'll find a diff'rence,
   As we his subjects have in wonder found,
   Between the promise of his greener days   136
   And these he masters now. Now he weighs time
   Even to the utmost grain. That you shall read   138
   In your own losses, if he stay in France.
FRENCH KING
   Tomorrow shall you know our mind at full.   140
                       Flourish.
EXETER
   Dispatch us with all speed, lest that our king
   Come here himself to question our delay;
   For he is footed in this land already.
FRENCH KING
   You shall be soon dispatched with fair conditions.
   A night is but small breath and little pause
   To answer matters of this consequence.
                   Flourish. Exeunt.

[3.0]

Enter Chorus.

CHORUS
   Thus with imagined wing our swift scene flies   1
   In motion of no less celerity
   Than that of thought. Suppose that you have seen
   The well-appointed King at Dover pier   4
   Embark his royalty, and his brave fleet   5
   With silken streamers the young Phoebus fanning.   6
   Play with your fancies, and in them behold

78 apart aside **80 'longs** belongs **82 wide-stretchèd** stretching far and wide **83 ordinance of times** decrees of tradition **85 sinister** illegitimate. **awkward** oblique **88 line** pedigree **90 Willing you overlook** desiring that you look over **91 evenly** directly **94 indirectly** wrongfully **95 native** natural (by birthright). **challenger** claimant. **97 constraint** coercion, compulsion **101 requiring** requesting **102 in . . . Lord** in the name of God's compassion. (See Philippians 1:8.) **105–6 and on . . . tears** and who, poor souls, are pouring on your head their widows' tears **107 privèd** deprived (by loss of loved ones) **118 misbecome** be inappropriate for **119 prize** value, appraise

121 in grant of in assenting to. **at large** in full **123 of it** for it **124 womby vaultages** hollow recesses **126 In . . . ordinance** in loud echoing of the sound of King Henry's ordnance (cannon). **127 fair return** courteous reply **129 odds** (1) strife (2) betting odds, as in tennis **131 Paris balls** tennis balls. **132 Louvre** the French royal palace **136 greener** younger **138 grain** grain of sand (in an hourglass). **That . . . read** i.e., You will see this new seriousness manifested **140.1 Flourish** (This trumpet call is sounded as the French King arises from his throne, thereby dismissing the embassy, but Exeter boldly insists on speaking further.)
3.0. Chorus.
1 imagined wing wings of imagination **4 well-appointed** well-equipped. **Dover** (Seemingly an error for Hampton, i.e., Southampton.) **5 brave** handsome **6 the . . . fanning** i.e., fluttering in the rising sun.

Upon the hempen tackle shipboys climbing;   8
Hear the shrill whistle, which doth order give
To sounds confused; behold the threaden sails,   10
Borne with th'invisible and creeping wind,
Draw the huge bottoms through the furrowed sea,   12
Breasting the lofty surge. Oh, do but think   13
You stand upon the rivage and behold   14
A city on th'inconstant billows dancing;
For so appears this fleet majestical,
Holding due course to Harfleur. Follow, follow!
Grapple your minds to sternage of this navy,   18
And leave your England as dead midnight still,
Guarded with grandsires, babies, and old women,
Either past or not arrived to pith and puissance;   21
For who is he whose chin is but enriched
With one appearing hair that will not follow
These culled and choice-drawn cavaliers to France?   24
Work, work your thoughts, and therein see a siege;
Behold the ordnance on their carriages,
With fatal mouths gaping on girded Harfleur.   27
Suppose th'ambassador from the French comes back,
Tells Harry that the King doth offer him
Katharine his daughter, and with her, to dowry,
Some petty and unprofitable dukedoms.
The offer likes not; and the nimble gunner   32
With linstock now the devilish cannon touches,   33
                    Alarum, and chambers go off.
And down goes all before them. Still be kind,
And eke out our performance with your mind.
                                              Exit.

❖

[3.1]

Enter the King, Exeter, Bedford, and Gloucester.
Alarum, [with soldiers carrying] scaling ladders at
Harfleur.

KING
Once more unto the breach, dear friends, once more,
Or close the wall up with our English dead!
In peace there's nothing so becomes a man
As modest stillness and humility.
But when the blast of war blows in our ears,
Then imitate the action of the tiger:
Stiffen the sinews, conjure up the blood,
Disguise fair nature with hard-favored rage.   8
Then lend the eye a terrible aspect: 9
Let it pry through the portage of the head   10
Like the brass cannon; let the brow o'erwhelm it   11

As fearfully as doth a gallèd rock   12
O'erhang and jutty his confounded base,   13
Swilled with the wild and wasteful ocean.   14
Now set the teeth and stretch the nostril wide,
Hold hard the breath, and bend up every spirit
To his full height. On, on, you noblest English,
Whose blood is fet from fathers of war-proof,   18
Fathers that, like so many Alexanders,   19
Have in these parts from morn till even fought,   20
And sheathed their swords for lack of argument.   21
Dishonor not your mothers; now attest
That those whom you called fathers did beget you.
Be copy now to men of grosser blood,   24
And teach them how to war. And you, good yeomen,
Whose limbs were made in England, show us here
The mettle of your pasture. Let us swear   27
That you are worth your breeding, which I doubt not,
For there is none of you so mean and base
That hath not noble luster in your eyes.
I see you stand like greyhounds in the slips,   31
Straining upon the start. The game's afoot.   32
Follow your spirit, and upon this charge   33
Cry, "God for Harry! England and Saint George!"   34
          Alarum, and chambers go off. [Exeunt.]

❖

[3.2]

Enter Nym, Bardolph, Pistol, and Boy.

BARDOLPH   On, on, on, on, on! To the breach, to the
breach!
NYM   Pray thee, Corporal, stay. The knocks are too hot,
and for mine own part I have not a case of lives. The   4
humor of it is too hot, that is the very plainsong of it. 5
PISTOL
"The plainsong" is most just; for humors do abound.
Knocks go and come; God's vassals drop and die;   7
[*He sings*] "And sword and shield
        In bloody field
        Doth win immortal fame."
BOY   Would I were in an alehouse in London! I would
give all my fame for a pot of ale and safety.
PISTOL   And I:
     [*He sings*] "If wishes would prevail with me,   14
        My purpose should not fail with me,
           But thither would I hie."   16

---

8 **hempen** rope   10 **threaden** stitched   12 **bottoms** hulls of ships
13 **surge** swell of the sea.   14 **rivage** shore   18 **Grapple** Attach, hook.   **to
sternage** to the sterns   21 **pith** strength   24 **choice-drawn** carefully
selected   27 **fatal** deadly.   **girded** besieged   32 **likes** pleases
33 **linstock** staff holding a gunner's match   33.1 *Alarum* Call to arms.
chambers small cannon (fired off backstage, or "within")
3.1. Location: France. Before Harfleur.
0.2 *scaling ladders* (Presumably these are set up against the facade
of the tiring-house, upstage, which is perceived to be the walls of
Harfleur.)   8 **hard-favored** unsightly, ugly   9 **terrible aspect** terrifying appearance   10 **portage** portholes, eyes   11 **o'erwhelm** project
over

12 **fearfully** frighteningly.   **gallèd** washed away, eroded   13 **O'erhang . . . base** hang and project over its worn-away base   14 **Swilled**
washed.   **wasteful** destructive   18 **fet** fetched, derived.   **of war-
proof** tested in war   19 **Alexanders** (Alexander grieved that there
were no new worlds for him to conquer.)   20 **even** evening
21 **argument** opposition.   24 **copy** models   27 **mettle . . . pasture**
quality of your breeding. (Literally, *pasture* means "feeding.")
31 **slips** leashes   32 **The game's afoot** The quarry is out of its lair and
running.   33 **Follow your spirit** i.e., Obey the impulse of your vital
powers   34 **Saint George** patron saint of England.
**3.2. Location: Before Harfleur, as in the previous scene; the action is
essentially continuous.**
4 **case** set   5 **plainsong** simple melody, simple truth   7 **God's vassals** i.e., mortal men   14 **with me** in my case   16 **hie** hasten.

BOY [*sings*]
     "As duly, but not as truly,
          As bird doth sing on bough."

Enter Fluellen.

FLUELLEN Up to the breach, you dogs! Avaunt, you cul- 19
lions!   [*Driving them forward.*] 20
PISTOL
     Be merciful, great duke, to men of mold. 21
     Abate thy rage, abate thy manly rage,
     Abate thy rage, great duke!
     Good bawcock, bate thy rage! Use lenity, sweet chuck! 24
NYM These be good humors! Your Honor runs bad 25
humors.   *Exit* [*with all but Boy*]. 26
BOY As young as I am, I have observed these three
swashers. I am boy to them all three, but all they three, 28
though they would serve me, could not be man to me; 29
for indeed three such antics do not amount to a man. 30
For Bardolph, he is white-livered and red-faced, by the 31
means whereof 'a faces it out but fights not. For Pistol, 32
he hath a killing tongue and a quiet sword, by the
means whereof 'a breaks words and keeps whole 34
weapons. For Nym, he hath heard that men of few
words are the best men, and therefore he scorns to say
his prayers, lest 'a should be thought a coward; but
his few bad words are matched with as few good
deeds, for 'a never broke any man's head but his own,
and that was against a post when he was drunk. They
will steal anything and call it purchase. Bardolph 41
stole a lute case, bore it twelve leagues, and sold it for 42
three halfpence. Nym and Bardolph are sworn brothers in filching, and in Calais they stole a fire shovel. I
knew by that piece of service the men would carry 45
coals. They would have me as familiar with men's 46
pockets as their gloves or their handkerchiefs, which
makes much against my manhood, if I should take 48
from another's pocket to put into mine, for it is plain
pocketing up of wrongs. I must leave them and seek 50
some better service. Their villainy goes against my 51
weak stomach, and therefore I must cast it up. *Exit.* 52

Enter Gower [*and Fluellen, meeting*].

GOWER Captain Fluellen, you must come presently to
the mines. The Duke of Gloucester would speak with 54
you.
FLUELLEN To the mines? Tell you the Duke it is not so
good to come to the mines; for look you, the mines is
not according to the disciplines of the war. The 58
concavities of it is not sufficient. For look you, th'athver- 59
sary, you may discuss unto the Duke, look you, 60
is digt himself four yard under the countermines. By 61
Cheshu, I think 'a will plow up all, if there is not better 62
directions.
GOWER The Duke of Gloucester, to whom the order of
the siege is given, is altogether directed by an Irishman, a very valiant gentleman, i'faith.
FLUELLEN It is Captain Macmorris, is it not?
GOWER I think it be.
FLUELLEN By Cheshu, he is an ass, as in the world! I
will verify as much in his beard. He has no more di- 70
rections in the true disciplines of the wars, look you,
of the Roman disciplines, than is a puppy dog.

Enter Macmorris and Captain Jamy.

GOWER Here 'a comes, and the Scots captain, Captain
Jamy, with him.
FLUELLEN Captain Jamy is a marvelous falorous gen-
tleman, that is certain, and of great expedition and 76
knowledge in th'aunchient wars, upon my particular
knowledge of his directions. By Cheshu, he will
maintain his argument as well as any military man in
the world, in the disciplines of the pristine wars of the 80
Romans.
JAMY I say gud day, Captain Fluellen.
FLUELLEN Good e'en to Your Worship, good Captain 83
James.
GOWER How now, Captain Macmorris, have you quit
the mines? Have the pioneers given o'er? 86
MACMORRIS By Chrish, la, 'tish ill done! The work ish
give over, the trompet sound the retreat. By my hand
I swear, and my father's soul, the work ish ill done; it
ish give over. I would have blowed up the town, so
Chrish save me, la, in an hour. Oh, 'tish ill done, 'tish
ill done! By my hand, 'tish ill done!
FLUELLEN Captain Macmorris, I beseech you now, will
you voutsafe me, look you, a few disputations with 94
you, as partly touching or concerning the disciplines
of the war, the Roman wars, in the way of argument,

---

19 **Avaunt** Begone   19–20 **cullions** rascals. (The original meaning
was "testicles.")   21 **duke** leader, commander. (Latin *dux*.) A flattering title for a captain.   **men of mold** mere mortals.   24 **bawcock**
fine fellow. (French *beau coq*.)   **chuck** (A term of endearment.)
25–6 **Your . . . humors** i.e., (1) You are behaving very idiosyncratically,
Your Honor (2) Your fury is out of control. (Addressed to Fluellen,
who is doubtless threatening or beating Nym, Bardolph, and Pistol to
make them go forward.)   28 **swashers** swashbucklers.   29 **man**
(1) servant (2) a manly, brave person   30 **antics** buffoons, zanies
31 **For** As for. (Also in lines 32 and 35.)   **white-livered** i.e., cowardly.
(In extreme fear, the blood was thought to sink below the liver, leaving it bloodless.)   32 **'a faces it out** he has the martial-looking face
for it, puts on a brave front   34 **breaks words** (1) misuses language
and fails to keep his word (2) uses words as weapons   41 **purchase**
(1) something paid for (2) thieves' cant for stolen goods.   42 **leagues**
(about three miles each)   45–6 **carry coals** (1) do dirty, hard work,
such as hauling coal (2) put up with insults   48 **makes** goes
50 **pocketing . . . wrongs** (1) putting up with insults (2) receiving
stolen goods.   51–2 **goes . . . stomach** (1) goes against my inclination
(2) makes me sick   52 **cast it up** (1) cast it aside (2) vomit it.   **s.d.**
Exit (A scene break may occur here, though it is not marked as such
in most editions. Possibly Fluellen did not leave the stage at line 26.)

54 **mines** tunnels dug under the walls of the beseiged city to plant
explosives.   58 **disciplines of the war** science of warfare (about
which there were many books from Greek and Roman times down to
the Renaissance; Fluellen's humor involves an obsession with this
study and a preference for traditional methods).   59 **concavities** i.e.,
depth   59–60 **athversary** (Fluellen's pronunciation of *adversary*.)
60 **discuss** explain   61 **is digt . . . countermines** has dug himself
countermines four yards beneath our mines.   62 **Cheshu** Jesu, Jesus.
plow blow. (In Fluellen's Welsh dialect, *p* is regularly substituted for *b*
and *f* for *v*.)   70 **in his beard** i.e., to his face.   76 **expedition** readiness of argument, quickness of wit   80 **pristine** ancient   83 **Good
e'en** Good afternoon or evening   86 **pioneers** sappers, diggers
94 **voutsafe** vouchsafe, permit

look you, and friendly communication—partly to satisfy my opinion, and partly for the satisfaction, look
you, of my mind, as touching the direction of the military discipline, that is the point.

JAMY   It sall be vary gud, gud feith, gud captens bath, 101
and I sall quite you with gud leve, as I may pick 102
occasion. That sall I, marry. 103

MACMORRIS   It is no time to discourse, so Chrish save
me! The day is hot, and the weather, and the wars,
and the King, and the dukes. It is no time to discourse.
The town is beseeched, and the trumpet call us to the 107
breach, and we talk, and, be Chrish, do nothing. 'Tis 108
shame for us all. So God sa' me, 'tis shame to stand
still, it is shame, by my hand! And there is throats to
be cut, and works to be done, and there ish nothing
done, so Chrish sa' me, la! 112

JAMY   By the Mess, ere theise eyes of mine take 113
themselves to slomber, ay'll de gud service, or I'll lig i'th' 114
grund for it, ay, or go to death! And I'll pay't as
valorously as I may, that sall I suerly do, that is the
breff and the long. Marry, I wad full fain heard some 117
question 'tween you twae. 118

FLUELLEN   Captain Macmorris, I think, look you, under
your correction, there is not many of your nation—

MACMORRIS   Of my nation? What ish my nation? Ish a 121
villain, and a bastard, and a knave, and a rascal? What 122
ish my nation? Who talks of my nation?

FLUELLEN   Look you, if you take the matter otherwise
than is meant, Captain Macmorris, peradventure I
shall think you do not use me with that affability as in
discretion you ought to use me, look you, being as
good a man as yourself, both in the disciplines of war
and in the derivation of my birth, and in other partic-
ularities.

MACMORRIS   I do not know you so good a man as myself. So Chrish save me, I will cut off your head!

GOWER   Gentlemen both, you will mistake each other. 133

JAMY   Ah, that's a foul fault!   *A parley [is sounded].* 134

GOWER   The town sounds a parley.

FLUELLEN   Captain Macmorris, when there is more better opportunity to be required, look you, I will be so 137
bold as to tell you I know the disciplines of war; and
there is an end.   *Exit [with others].*

[3.3]

*[Enter the Governor and some citizens on the
walls.] Enter the King [Henry] and all his train
before the gates.*

KING
How yet resolves the Governor of the town?
This is the latest parle we will admit.   2
Therefore to our best mercy give yourselves,
Or, like to men proud of destruction,   4
Defy us to our worst; for as I am a soldier,
A name that in my thoughts becomes me best,
If I begin the batt'ry once again   7
I will not leave the half-achievèd Harfleur
Till in her ashes she lie burièd.
The gates of mercy shall be all shut up,
And the fleshed soldier, rough and hard of heart,   11
In liberty of bloody hand shall range   12
With conscience wide as hell, mowing like grass   13
Your fresh fair virgins and your flow'ring infants.
What is it then to me if impious War,
Arrayed in flames like to the prince of fiends,
Do with his smirched complexion all fell feats   17
Enlinked to waste and desolation?
What is't to me, when you yourselves are cause,
If your pure maidens fall into the hand
Of hot and forcing violation?
What rein can hold licentious Wickedness
When down the hill he holds his fierce career?   23
We may as bootless spend our vain command   24
Upon th'enragèd soldiers in their spoil
As send precepts to the leviathan   26
To come ashore. Therefore, you men of Harfleur,
Take pity of your town and of your people
Whiles yet my soldiers are in my command,
Whiles yet the cool and temperate wind of grace   30
O'erblows the filthy and contagious clouds   31
Of heady murder, spoil, and villainy.   32
If not, why, in a moment look to see   33
The blind and bloody soldier with foul hand   34
Defile the locks of your shrill-shrieking daughters;
Your fathers taken by the silver beards,
And their most reverend heads dashed to the walls;
Your naked infants spitted upon pikes,

101 **bath** both   102 **quite** requite, answer.   **with gud leve** with good
leave, with your kind permission   103 **marry** indeed. (Originally, "by
the Virgin Mary.")   107 **beseeched** besieged   108 **be** by   112 **Chrish
sa' me** Christ save me   113 **Mess** Mass   114 **ay'll de** I'll do.   **lig** lie
117 **breff** brief.   **wad full fain heard** would very willingly have
heard   118 **question** discussion   121 **What ish** i.e., What about
121–2 **Ish a villain** i.e., Is my nation a villain (etc.)?, or Macmorris
may be making a declarative statement, saying that anyone who says
anything against my nation is a villain, etc.   133 **will mistake** (Two
possible meanings: [1] insist on misunderstanding [2] are going to
misunderstand.)   134 s.d. *parley* trumpet summons to a negotiation
137 **required** found

3.3. **Location: Before the gates of Harfleur, as in the previous scene.
The action is essentially continuous, as it is usually in battle
sequences; possibly some of the captains in 3.2 do not need to exit
here. The gates are represented by the tiring-house facade. Those
who appear *on the walls* are seen in the gallery backstage.**
2 **latest parle** last parley   4 **like . . . destruction** i.e., like men elated
at the prospect of slaughter and glorying in destruction   7 **batt'ry**
attack   11 **fleshed** made fierce with the taste of blood   12–13 **In liberty . . . as hell** will range with free license to shed blood and with a
conscience wide and loose enough to sanction anything that hell itself
would justify   17 **smirched** blackened, covered with grime.   **fell**
savage   23 **career** gallop.   24 **bootless** fruitlessly   26 **precepts** written summons.   **leviathan** whale   30 **grace** mercy   31 **O'er blows**
blows away. (Contagion was thought to reside in clouds and mists.)
32 **heady** violent; headstrong   33 **look** expect   34 **blind** i.e., blinded
with lust and rage

Whiles the mad mothers with their howls confused
Do break the clouds, as did the wives of Jewry   40
At Herod's bloody-hunting slaughtermen.   41
What say you? Will you yield, and this avoid,
Or, guilty in defense, be thus destroyed?   43

GOVERNOR
Our expectation hath this day an end.
The Dauphin, whom of succors we entreated,   45
Returns us that his powers are yet not ready   46
To raise so great a siege. Therefore, great King,
We yield our town and lives to thy soft mercy.
Enter our gates, dispose of us and ours,
For we no longer are defensible.

KING
Open your gates.   [Exit Governor.]
           Come, uncle Exeter,
Go you and enter Harfleur; there remain,
And fortify it strongly 'gainst the French.
Use mercy to them all. For us, dear uncle,   54
The winter coming on and sickness growing
Upon our soldiers, we will retire to Calais.
Tonight in Harfleur will we be your guest;
Tomorrow for the march are we addressed.   58

                    Flourish, and enter the town.

[3.4]

Enter Katharine and [Alice,] an old gentlewoman.

KATHARINE   Alice, tu as été en Angleterre, et tu bien   1
parles le langage.
ALICE   Un peu, madame.
KATHARINE   Je te prie, m'enseignez; il faut que
j'apprenne à parler. Comment appelez-vous la main
en anglais?
ALICE   La main? Elle est appelée de hand.
KATHARINE   De hand. Et les doigts?
ALICE   Les doigts? Ma foi, j'oublie les doigts; mais je me
souviendrai. Les doigts? Je pense qu'ils sont appelés   10
de fingres; oui, de fingres.
KATHARINE   La main, de hand; les doigts, de fingres. Je
pense que je suis le bon écolier; j'ai gagné deux
mots d'anglais vîtement. Comment appelez-vous les
ongles?

40 **Jewry** Judaea   41 **Herod's . . . slaughtermen** (For the account of
Herod's slaughter of the innocent children in his attempt to murder the
infant Jesus, see Matthew 2:16–18.)   43 **in defense** i.e., by not surren-
dering   45 **of succors** for help   46 **Returns** replies to   54 **For** As for
58 **addressed** prepared.
3.4. Location: The French court at Rouen.

Translation:
KATHARINE   Alice, you have been in England and speak the language
well.
ALICE   A little, my lady.
KATHARINE   I pray you teach me; I have to learn to speak it. What do
you call *la main* in English?
ALICE   *La main?* It is called de hand.
KATHARINE   De hand. And *les doigts?*
ALICE   *Les doigts?* Dear me, I forget *les doigts;* but I shall remember. I
think that they are called de fingres; yes, de fingres.
KATHARINE   *La main,* de hand; *les doigts,* de fingres. I think that I am a
clever scholar; I have learned two English words in no time. What
do you call *les ongles?*

ALICE   Les ongles? Nous les appelons de nailes.
KATHARINE   De nailes. Écoutez, dites-moi si je parle
bien: de hand, de fingres, et de nailes.
ALICE   C'est bien dit, madame; il est fort bon anglais.
KATHARINE   Dites-moi l'anglais pour le bras.   20
ALICE   De arm, madame.
KATHARINE   Et le coude?
ALICE   D' elbow.
KATHARINE   D' elbow. Je m'en fais la répétition de tous
les mots que vous m'avez appris dès à présent.
ALICE   Il est trop difficile, madame, comme je pense.
KATHARINE   Excusez-moi, Alice; écoutez: d' hand, de
fingre, de nailes, d' arma, de bilbow.
ALICE   D' elbow, madame.
KATHARINE   Oh, Seigneur Dieu, je m'en oublie! D' elbow.   30
Comment appelez-vous le col?
ALICE   De nick, madame.
KATHARINE   De nick. Et le menton?
ALICE   De chin.
KATHARINE   De sin. Le col, de nick; le menton, de sin.
ALICE   Oui. Sauf votre honneur, en vérité, vous pro-
noncez les mots aussi droit que les natifs d'Angleterre.
KATHARINE   Je ne doute point d'apprendre, par la grâce
de Dieu, et en peu de temps.
ALICE   N'avez-vous pas déjà oublié ce que je vous ai   40
enseigné?
KATHARINE   Non, je réciterai à vous promptement: d'
hand, de fingre, de mailes—
ALICE   De nailes, madame.
KATHARINE   De nailes, de arm, de ilbow.
ALICE   Sauf votre honneur, d' elbow.
KATHARINE   Ainsi dis-je; d' elbow, de nick, et de sin.
Comment appelez-vous le pied et la robe?

ALICE   *Les ongles?* We call them de nailes.
KATHARINE   De nailes. Listen; tell me whether or not I speak correctly:
de hand, de fingres, and de nailes.
ALICE   That is correct, my lady; it is very good English.
KATHARINE   Tell me the English for *le bras.*
ALICE   De arm, my lady.
KATHARINE   And *le coude?*
ALICE   D' elbow.
KATHARINE   D' elbow. I am going to repeat all the words you have
taught me so far.
ALICE   It is too hard, my lady, I fear.
KATHARINE   Pardon me, Alice; listen: d' hand, de fingre, de nailes, d'
arma, de bilbow.
ALICE   D' elbow, my lady.
KATHARINE   Oh, Lord, I can't remember! D' elbow. What do you call *le
col?*
ALICE   De nick, my lady.
KATHARINE   De nick. And *le menton?*
ALICE   De chin.
KATHARINE   De sin. *Le col,* de nick; *le menton,* de sin.
ALICE   Yes. If I may say so, really you pronounce the words just as cor-
rectly as native Englishmen.
KATHARINE   I have no doubt that I shall learn, with God's help, in a
very short time.
ALICE   Haven't you already forgotten what I have taught you?
KATHARINE   No. I shall recite to you at once: d' hand, de fingre, de
mailes—
ALICE   De nailes, my lady.
KATHARINE   De nailes, de arm, de ilbow.
ALICE   By your leave, d' elbow.
KATHARINE   That's what I said; d' elbow, de nick, and de sin. What do
you call *le pied* and *la robe?*

ALICE   Le foot, madame, et le count.

KATHARINE   Le foot et le count! Oh, Seigneur Dieu! Ils 50
sont les mots de son mauvais, corruptible, gros, et
impudique, et non pour les dames d'honneur d'user.
Je ne voudrais prononcer ces mots devant les seig-
neurs de France pour tout le monde. Foh! Le foot et le
count! Néanmoins, je réciterai une autre fois ma leçon
ensemble: d' hand, de fingre, de nailes, de arm,
d' elbow, de nick, de sin, de foot, le count.

ALICE   Excellent, madame!

KATHARINE   C'est assez pour une fois. Allons-nous à
dîner.   Exit [with Alice].

❧

[3.5]

*Enter the King of France, the Dauphin, [the Duke
of Brittany,] the Constable of France, and others.*

FRENCH KING
'Tis certain he hath passed the River Somme.

CONSTABLE
And if he be not fought withal, my lord,   2
Let us not live in France; let us quit all
And give our vineyards to a barbarous people.

DAUPHIN
O Dieu vivant! Shall a few sprays of us,   5
The emptying of our fathers' luxury,   6
Our scions, put in wild and savage stock,   7
Spurt up so suddenly into the clouds   8
And overlook their grafters?   9

BRITTANY
Normans, but bastard Normans, Norman bastards!
Mort de ma vie, if they march along   11
Unfought withal, but I will sell my dukedom   12
To buy a slobbery and a dirty farm   13
In that nook-shotten isle of Albion.   14

CONSTABLE
Dieu de batailles, where have they this mettle?   15
Is not their climate foggy, raw, and dull,

On whom as in despite the sun looks pale,   17
Killing their fruit with frowns? Can sodden water,   18
A drench for sur-reined jades, their barley broth,   19
Decoct their cold blood to such valiant heat?   20
And shall our quick blood, spirited with wine,   21
Seem frosty? Oh, for honor of our land,
Let us not hang like roping icicles   23
Upon our houses' thatch, whiles a more frosty people
Sweat drops of gallant youth in our rich fields!
"Poor" may we call them in their native lords.   26

DAUPHIN   By faith and honor,
Our madams mock at us and plainly say   28
Our mettle is bred out, and they will give   29
Their bodies to the lust of English youth
To new-store France with bastard warriors.   31

BRITTANY
They bid us to the English dancing schools   32
And teach lavoltas high and swift corantos,   33
Saying our grace is only in our heels   34
And that we are most lofty runaways.   35

FRENCH KING
Where is Montjoy the herald? Speed him hence.   36
Let him greet England with our sharp defiance.
Up, princes, and with spirit of honor edged   38
More sharper than your swords, hie to the field!   39
Charles Delabreth, High Constable of France,
You Dukes of Orleans, Bourbon, and of Berri,
Alençon, Brabant, Bar, and Burgundy,
Jaques Chatillion, Rambures, Vaudemont,
Beaumont, Grandpré, Roussi, and Faulconbridge,
Foix, Lestrelles, Boucicault, and Charolais,
High dukes, great princes, barons, lords, and knights,
For your great seats now quit you of great shames.   47
Bar Harry England, that sweeps through our land   48
With pennons painted in the blood of Harfleur.   49
Rush on his host, as doth the melted snow   50
Upon the valleys, whose low vassal seat
The Alps doth spit and void his rheum upon.   52
Go down upon him—you have power enough—
And in a captive chariot into Rouen
Bring him our prisoner.

CONSTABLE   This becomes the great.   55
Sorry am I his numbers are so few,
His soldiers sick and famished in their march,
For I am sure, when he shall see our army,

ALICE   Le foot, my lady, and le count. [As she pronounces them, *foot*
sounds to Katharine like *foutre*, fornicate, and *count* (for *gown*) sounds
like French for the female sexual organ, *cunt* in English.]
KATHARINE   Le foot and le count! Oh, Lord! Those are naughty words,
wicked, coarse, and immodest, and are not fit to be used by ladies. I
wouldn't say those words before French gentlemen for the whole
world. Bah! Le foot and le count! Nevertheless, I shall recite my
whole lesson once more: d' hand, de fingre, de nailes, de arm, d'
elbow, de nick, de sin, de foot, le count.
ALICE   Excellent, my lady.
KATHARINE   That's enough for one time. Let's go to dinner.
3.5. Location: The French court at Rouen.
2 withal with. (As also in line 12.)   **5–9** *O . . .* **grafters?** O living God,
shall a few sprigs derived from native French stock, from the pouring
out of our forefathers' lust (during and after the Norman Conquest)
being grafted onto the wild and savage stock (of English Saxons),
sprout up suddenly to lofty heights and domineer over the plants or
trees from which the grafts were taken, i.e., us native French?
11 *Mort de ma vie* Death to my life   **12 but I will** i.e., if I do not
13 slobbery wet and slimy   **14 nook-shotten** full of nooks and
angles. (Refers to the coastline.)   **isle of Albion** island of England,
Scotland, and Wales.   **15** *Dieu de batailles* God of battles.   **where**
from where

17 as in despite as if despising them, the English   **18 sodden water**
boiled water   **19 A drench . . . jades** i.e., stuff no better than what
they give their overridden horses to drink.   **barley broth** ale
20 Decoct warm up   **21 quick** lively   **23 roping** hanging down
like a rope   **26 "Poor" . . . lords** i.e., Our fields, though rich in themselves, may be called poor in that they are owned by a spiritless
aristocracy.   **28 madams** wives, ladies   **29 bred out** exhausted by
breeding   **31 new-store** newly supply   **32 bid us** bid us go
33 lavoltas, corantos fashionable dances   **34 in our heels** (1) in dancing gracefully (2) in running away   **35 lofty** (1) noble (2) leaping.
runaways cowards. (But referring also to the movements of the
dances.)   **36 Montjoy** title of the chief herald of France   **38 edged**
given a sharp edge   **39 hie** hasten   **47 For** in the name of, in defense
of.   **seats** positions.   **quit you** rid, free yourselves   **48 Bar** Stop; bar
the claim of   **49 pennons** banners, streamers   **50 host** army
52 rheum watery discharge, i.e., streams or avalanches   **55 becomes
the great** befits greatness.

He'll drop his heart into the sink of fear   59
And for achievement offer us his ransom.   60

FRENCH KING
Therefore, Lord Constable, haste on Montjoy,
And let him say to England that we send
To know what willing ransom he will give.
Prince Dauphin, you shall stay with us in Rouen.

DAUPHIN
Not so, I do beseech Your Majesty.

FRENCH KING
Be patient, for you shall remain with us.
Now forth, Lord Constable and princes all,
And quickly bring us word of England's fall. *Exeunt.*

[3.6]

*Enter Captains, English and Welsh: Gower and
Fluellen,* [*meeting*].

GOWER   How now, Captain Fluellen? Come you from
the bridge?   2
FLUELLEN   I assure you, there is very excellent services   3
committed at the bridge.
GOWER   Is the Duke of Exeter safe?
FLUELLEN   The Duke of Exeter is as magnanimous as
Agamemnon, and a man that I love and honor with   7
my soul, and my heart, and my duty, and my live,   8
and my living, and my uttermost power. He is not—
God be praised and blessed!—any hurt in the world,
but keeps the bridge most valiantly, with excellent discipline. There is an aunchient lieutenant there at the   12
pridge, I think in my very conscience he is as valiant
a man as Mark Antony, and he is a man of no esti-   14
mation in the world, but I did see him do as gallant   15
service.
GOWER   What do you call him?
FLUELLEN   He is called Aunchient Pistol.
GOWER   I know him not.

Enter Pistol.

FLUELLEN   Here is the man.
PISTOL
Captain, I thee beseech to do me favors.
The Duke of Exeter doth love thee well.
FLUELLEN   Ay, I praise God, and I have merited some
love at his hands.
PISTOL
Bardolph, a soldier, firm and sound of heart,
And of buxom valor, hath, by cruel fate   26
And giddy Fortune's furious fickle wheel,

That goddess blind
That stands upon the rolling restless stone—
FLUELLEN   By your patience, Aunchient Pistol. Fortune
is painted blind, with a muffler afore her eyes, to sig-   31
nify to you that Fortune is blind; and she is painted
also with a wheel, to signify to you, which is the moral
of it, that she is turning, and inconstant, and mutability, and variation; and her foot, look you, is fixed upon
a spherical stone, which rolls, and rolls, and rolls. In
good truth, the poet is make a most excellent descrip-   37
tion of it. Fortune is an excellent moral.   38
PISTOL
Fortune is Bardolph's foe, and frowns on him;   39
For he hath stol'n a pax,   40
And hangèd must 'a be—a damnèd death!
Let gallows gape for dog; let man go free,
And let not hemp his windpipe suffocate.
But Exeter hath given the doom of death   44
For pax of little price.
Therefore, go speak—the Duke will hear thy voice—
And let not Bardolph's vital thread be cut
With edge of penny cord and vile reproach.   48
Speak, Captain, for his life, and I will thee requite.   49
FLUELLEN   Aunchient Pistol, I do partly understand
your meaning.
PISTOL   Why then rejoice therefor.
FLUELLEN   Certainly, Aunchient, it is not a thing to re-
joice at. For if, look you, he were my brother, I would
desire the Duke to use his good pleasure and put him
to execution; for discipline ought to be used.
PISTOL
Die and be damned! And *figo* for thy friendship!   57
FLUELLEN   It is well.
PISTOL   The fig of Spain!   *Exit.*
FLUELLEN   Very good.
GOWER   Why, this is an arrant counterfeit rascal! I
remember him now; a bawd, a cutpurse.
FLUELLEN   I'll assure you, 'a uttered as prave words at
the pridge as you shall see in a summer's day. But it is
very well. What he has spoke to me, that is well, I
warrant you, when time is serve.
GOWER   Why, 'tis a gull, a fool, a rogue, that now and   67
then goes to the wars, to grace himself at his return
into London under the form of a soldier. And such
fellows are perfect in the great commanders' names,   70
and they will learn you by rote where services were   71
done—at such and such a sconce, at such a breach, at   72
such a convoy; who came off bravely, who was shot,
who disgraced, what terms the enemy stood on—and   74
this they con perfectly in the phrase of war, which   75

---

59 **sink** pit   60 **for achievement** instead of achieving victory, as his
sole accomplishment
3.6 Location: The English camp in northern France.
2 **bridge** (According to Holinshed, the French were beaten in their
attempt to break down the bridge over the Ternoise. The audience is
not told this, however, and might assume the river to be the Somme,
mentioned in 3.5.1.)   3 **services** exploits. (As also in line 71.)
7 **Agamemnon** leader of the Greeks against Troy   8 **live** life
12 **aunchient lieutenant** (Pistol is elsewhere given the rank of
ancient, or ensign.)   14–15 **estimation** fame   26 **buxom** (1) vigorous
(2) compliant, meek

31 **muffler** blindfold   37 **is make** has made   38 **moral** emblem.
39 **Fortune . . . foe** (Probably alludes to the ballad "Fortune, my foe!")
40 **pax** metal disk with a crucifix stamped on it, kissed by the priest
and communicants during Mass. (But Holinshed describes an incident in which the object stolen is a *pyx*, the vessel containing the consecrated host.)   44 **doom** judgment, sentence   48 **cord** rope
49 **requite** repay.   57 *figo* gesture of contempt made by thrusting the
thumb between the index and middle fingers   67 **gull** simpleton
70 **are perfect in** i.e., can recite perfectly   71 **learn** teach, recite
72 **sconce** fortification   74 **terms . . . stood on** conditions the enemy
insisted on   75 **con** learn by heart

they trick up with new-tuned oaths. And what a 76
beard of the General's cut and a horrid suit of the 77
camp will do among foaming bottles and ale-washed 78
wits is wonderful to be thought on. But you must
learn to know such slanders of the age, or else you 80
may be marvelously mistook. 81

FLUELLEN I tell you what, Captain Gower, I do perceive
he is not the man that he would gladly make show
to the world he is. If I find a hole in his coat, I will tell 84
him my mind. [*Drum heard.*] Hark you, the King is
coming, and I must speak with him from the pridge. 86

*Drum and colors. Enter the King and his poor
soldiers [and Gloucester].*

God pless Your Majesty!

KING How now, Fluellen, cam'st thou from the bridge?

FLUELLEN Ay, so please Your Majesty. The Duke of
Exeter has very gallantly maintained the pridge. The
French is gone off, look you, and there is gallant and
most prave passages. Marry, th'athversary was have 92
possession of the pridge, but he is enforced to retire,
and the Duke of Exeter is master of the pridge. I can
tell Your Majesty, the Duke is a prave man.

KING What men have you lost, Fluellen?

FLUELLEN The perdition of th'athversary hath been very 97
great, reasonable great. Marry, for my part, I think the
Duke hath lost never a man, but one that is like to be ex- 99
ecuted for robbing a church, one Bardolph, if Your Majesty know the man. His face is all bubukles, and whelks, 101
and knobs, and flames o' fire, and his lips blows at his
nose, and it is like a coal of fire, sometimes plue and
sometimes red; but his nose is executed, and his fire's
out.

KING We would have all such offenders so cut off. And we
give express charge that, in our marches through the 107
country, there be nothing compelled from the villages,
nothing taken but paid for, none of the French up-
braided or abused in disdainful language; for when lenity and cruelty play for a kingdom, the gentler gamester 111
is the soonest winner. 112

Tucket. Enter Montjoy.

MONTJOY You know me by my habit. 113
KING Well then, I know thee. What shall I know of thee?
MONTJOY My master's mind.
KING Unfold it.
MONTJOY Thus says my King: "Say thou to Harry of
England, though we seemed dead, we did but sleep.
Advantage is a better soldier than rashness. Tell him 119
we could have rebuked him at Harfleur, but that we

thought not good to bruise an injury till it were full 121
ripe. Now we speak upon our cue, and our voice is
imperial. England shall repent his folly, see his 123
weakness, and admire our sufferance. Bid him there- 124
fore consider of his ransom, which must proportion 125
the losses we have borne, the subjects we have lost,
the disgrace we have digested; which in weight to re- 127
answer, his pettiness would bow under. For our losses, 128
his exchequer is too poor; for th'effusion of our blood, 129
the muster of his kingdom too faint a number; and for 130
our disgrace, his own person kneeling at our feet but
a weak and worthless satisfaction. To this add defiance; and tell him, for conclusion, he hath betrayed his
followers, whose condemnation is pronounced." So far 134
my King and master; so much my office.

KING
What is thy name? I know thy quality. 136
MONTJOY Montjoy.
KING
Thou dost thy office fairly. Turn thee back
And tell thy King I do not seek him now,
But could be willing to march on to Calais
Without impeachment. For, to say the sooth, 141
Though 'tis no wisdom to confess so much
Unto an enemy of craft and vantage, 143
My people are with sickness much enfeebled,
My numbers lessened, and those few I have
Almost no better than so many French,
Who when they were in health, I tell thee, herald,
I thought upon one pair of English legs 148
Did march three Frenchmen. Yet, forgive me, God, 149
That I do brag thus! This your air of France
Hath blown that vice in me. I must repent. 151
Go, therefore, tell thy master here I am;
My ransom is this frail and worthless trunk, 153
My army but a weak and sickly guard.
Yet, God before, tell him we will come on,
Though France himself and such another neighbor
Stand in our way. There's for thy labor, Montjoy.
[He gives a purse.]
Go bid thy master well advise himself. 158
If we may pass, we will; if we be hindered,
We shall your tawny ground with your red blood
Discolor. And so, Montjoy, fare you well.
The sum of all our answer is but this:
We would not seek a battle as we are,
Nor, as we are, we say we will not shun it. 164
So tell your master.

---

76 **trick** dress. **new-tuned** i.e., of the latest fashion **77–8 horrid . . . camp** fierce battle outfit **80 slanders of the age** persons who are a disgrace to the times **81 mistook** mistaken, deluded. **84 a hole . . . coat** i.e., a weak spot in him. (Proverbial.) **86 from the pridge** with news concerning the bridge. **86.1 poor** bedraggled **92 passages** deeds of arms. **was** did **97 perdition** losses **99 like** likely **101 bubukles** carbuncles. **whelks** boils, pimples **107 express charge** explicit orders **111 gamester** player **112.1 Tucket** Trumpet signal, fanfare. **113 habit** i.e., tabard, herald's coat. **119 Advantage** Knowing how to wait for favorable circumstance and position

121 **bruise an injury** squeeze a boil or pimple **123 England** i.e., King Henry **124 admire our sufferance** wonder at our patience. **125 proportion** be proportional to **127–8 which . . . under** i.e., to compensate for which his means are too slender. **129 exchequer** treasury **130 muster** roll call **134 condemnation** death sentence **136 quality** rank and profession; ability. **141 impeachment** impediment. **sooth** truth **143 vantage** superiority in resources **148–49 upon . . . Frenchman** i.e., an English soldier is worth three Frenchmen. **151 blown** swelled; caused to blossom **153 trunk** body **158 advise himself** consider. **164 as we are** being who we are. (Playing on the meaning "in the condition we are" in the previous line.)

MONTJOY
I shall deliver so. Thanks to Your Highness.   [*Exit.*]
GLOUCESTER
I hope they will not come upon us now.
KING
We are in God's hand, brother, not in theirs.
March to the bridge. It now draws toward night.
Beyond the river we'll encamp ourselves,
And on tomorrow bid them march away.   *Exeunt.* 171

❧

[3.7]

*Enter the Constable of France, the Lord Rambures,
Orleans, Dauphin, with others.*

CONSTABLE   Tut, I have the best armor of the world.
Would it were day!
ORLEANS   You have an excellent armor; but let my
horse have his due.
CONSTABLE   It is the best horse of Europe.
ORLEANS   Will it never be morning?
DAUPHIN   My lord of Orleans and my Lord High
Constable, you talk of horse and armor?
ORLEANS   You are as well provided of both as any
prince in the world.
DAUPHIN   What a long night is this! I will not change
my horse with any that treads but on four pasterns. 12
Ça, ha! He bounds from the earth as if his entrails 13
were hairs; *le cheval volant,* the Pegasus, *qui a les narines* 14
de feu! When I bestride him, I soar, I am a hawk. He 15
trots the air. The earth sings when he touches it. The
basest horn of his hoof is more musical than the pipe 17
of Hermes. 18
ORLEANS   He's of the color of the nutmeg.
DAUPHIN   And of the heat of the ginger. It is a beast for
Perseus. He is pure air and fire; and the dull elements 21
of earth and water never appear in him, but only in 22
patient stillness while his rider mounts him. He is indeed a horse, and all other jades you may call beasts.
CONSTABLE   Indeed, my lord, it is a most absolute and 25
excellent horse.
DAUPHIN   It is the prince of palfreys. His neigh is like 27
the bidding of a monarch, and his countenance
enforces homage.
ORLEANS   No more, cousin.
DAUPHIN   Nay, the man hath no wit that cannot, from
the rising of the lark to the lodging of the lamb, vary 32

deserved praise on my palfrey. It is a theme as fluent
as the sea; turn the sands into eloquent tongues, and
my horse is argument for them all. 'Tis a subject for a 35
sovereign to reason on, and for a sovereign's sovereign 36
to ride on, and for the world, familiar to us and un- 37
known, to lay apart their particular functions and 38
wonder at him. I once writ a sonnet in his praise, and 39
began thus: "Wonder of nature—"
ORLEANS   I have heard a sonnet begin so to one's
mistress.
DAUPHIN   Then did they imitate that which I composed
to my courser, for my horse is my mistress. 44
ORLEANS   Your mistress bears well.
DAUPHIN   Me well, which is the prescript praise and 46
perfection of a good and particular mistress. 47
CONSTABLE   Nay, for methought yesterday your mis-
tress shrewdly shook your back. 49
DAUPHIN   So perhaps did yours.
CONSTABLE   Mine was not bridled. 51
DAUPHIN   Oh, then belike she was old and gentle, and 52
you rode like a kern of Ireland, your French hose off, 53
and in your strait strossers. 54
CONSTABLE   You have good judgment in horsemanship.
DAUPHIN   Be warned by me, then: they that ride so,
and ride not warily, fall into foul bogs. I had rather
have my horse to my mistress. 58
CONSTABLE   I had as lief have my mistress a jade. 59
DAUPHIN   I tell thee, Constable, my mistress wears his 60
own hair. 61
CONSTABLE   I could make as true a boast as that, if I had
a sow to my mistress.
DAUPHIN   *"Le chien est retourné à son propre vomissement,* 64
et la truie lavée au bourbier." Thou mak'st use of 65
anything.
CONSTABLE   Yet do I not use my horse for my mistress,
or any such proverb so little kin to the purpose. 68
RAMBURES   My Lord Constable, the armor that I saw in
your tent tonight, are those stars or suns upon it?
CONSTABLE   Stars, my lord.
DAUPHIN   Some of them will fall tomorrow, I hope.
CONSTABLE   And yet my sky shall not want. 73
DAUPHIN   That may be, for you bear a many superflu- 74
ously, and 'twere more honor some were away. 75

---

171 bid . . . away bid our army march toward Calais.
3.7. Location: The French camp, near Agincourt.
12 pasterns i.e., hooves. (The *pastern* literally is the part of the horse's
leg just above the hoof.)   **13–14 as . . . hairs** i.e., as if he were a tennis
ball. (Tennis balls were stuffed with hair. Or perhaps *hairs* should
read *hares.)*   **14–15 le cheval . . . feu** the flying horse, Pegasus, with
nostrils breathing fire.   **17 basest horn** (1) lowest part (2) hoofbeat
17–18 pipe of Hermes (Hermes, messenger of the gods, charmed
Argus of the hundred eyes asleep with playing on his pipe.)
21 Perseus (According to some Greek legends and to Ovid, Perseus
rode Pegasus when he rescued Andromeda from the dragon.)
21–2 air . . . water (Of the four elements supposed to make up all matter, water and earth are the heavier, while fire and air ascend.)
25 absolute perfect   **27 palfreys** saddle horses.   **32 lodging** lying
down.   **vary** produce variations of

35 argument subject   **36 reason** discourse   **37–9 for . . . him** for both
the known and unknown worlds to put aside their differences and
join in wondering at him.   **44 horse is my mistress** (Here begins a
series of bawdy double entendres involving human and animal sexuality: *bears, shook your back, rode, foul bogs, doing,* etc.)   **46 prescript**
prescribed   **47 particular** acknowledging only one master
49 shrewdly viciously   **51 Mine . . . bridled** i.e., At least my mistress
was not a horse.   **52 belike** probably   **53 kern** Irish foot soldier.
(Here it is used to mean "rustic" or "boor.")   **French hose** wide
breeches   **54 strait strossers** tight trousers, i.e., bare-legged.   **58 to** as
59 lief happily.   **jade** (1) worn-out horse (2) slut.   **60–1 wears . . .
hair** i.e., is not artificially wigged, like an elegant court lady, and perhaps bald from syphilis.   **64–5 "Le chien . . . bourbier"** The dog is
returned to his own vomit, and the washed sow to the mire. (See 2
Peter 2:22.)   **68 kin** related   **73 sky** i.e., sky of honor.   **want** be lacking (in honor).   **74 a many** many. (Parallel to "a few.")   **75 'twere . . .
away** i.e., it would be more honest and proper if some of your stars
were done away with.

CONSTABLE   Even as your horse bears your praises, who would trot as well, were some of your brags dismounted.

DAUPHIN   Would I were able to load him with his desert! Will it never be day? I will trot tomorrow a mile, and my way shall be paved with English faces. 79 80

CONSTABLE   I will not say so, for fear I should be faced out of my way. But I would it were morning, for I would fain be about the ears of the English. 82 83 84

RAMBURES   Who will go to hazard with me for twenty prisoners? 85

CONSTABLE   You must first go yourself to hazard, ere you have them.

DAUPHIN   'Tis midnight. I'll go arm myself.   *Exit.*

ORLEANS   The Dauphin longs for morning.

RAMBURES   He longs to eat the English.

CONSTABLE   I think he will eat all he kills.

ORLEANS   By the white hand of my lady, he's a gallant prince.

CONSTABLE   Swear by her foot, that she may tread out the oath. 95 96

ORLEANS   He is simply the most active gentleman of France.

CONSTABLE   Doing is activity, and he will still be doing. 99

ORLEANS   He never did harm, that I heard of. 100

CONSTABLE   Nor will do none tomorrow. He will keep that good name still.

ORLEANS   I know him to be valiant.

CONSTABLE   I was told that by one that knows him better than you.

ORLEANS   What's he?

CONSTABLE   Marry, he told me so himself, and he said he cared not who knew it.

ORLEANS   He needs not; it is no hidden virtue in him. 109

CONSTABLE   By my faith, sir, but it is. Never anybody saw it but his lackey. 'Tis a hooded valor, and when it appears it will bate. 110 111 112

ORLEANS   Ill will never said well.

CONSTABLE   I will cap that proverb with "There is flattery in friendship."

ORLEANS   And I will take up that with "Give the devil his due." 116 117

CONSTABLE   Well placed. There stands your friend for the devil. Have at the very eye of that proverb with "A pox of the devil." 118 119

ORLEANS   You are the better at proverbs by how much "A fool's bolt is soon shot." 122

CONSTABLE   You have shot over. 123

ORLEANS   'Tis not the first time you were overshot. 124

Enter a Messenger.

MESSENGER   My Lord High Constable, the English lie within fifteen hundred paces of your tents.

CONSTABLE   Who hath measured the ground?

MESSENGER   The Lord Grandpré.

CONSTABLE   A valiant and most expert gentleman.
                    [*Exit Messenger.*]
Would it were day! Alas, poor Harry of England! He longs not for the dawning as we do.

ORLEANS   What a wretched and peevish fellow is this King of England, to mope with his fat-brained followers so far out of his knowledge! 133

CONSTABLE   If the English had any apprehension, they would run away. 135

ORLEANS   That they lack; for if their heads had any intellectual armor, they could never wear such heavy headpieces.

RAMBURES   That island of England breeds very valiant creatures; their mastiffs are of unmatchable courage.

ORLEANS   Foolish curs, that run winking into the mouth of a Russian bear and have their heads crushed like rotten apples. You may as well say "That's a valiant flea that dare eat his breakfast on the lip of a lion." 142

CONSTABLE   Just, just! And the men do sympathize with the mastiffs in robustious and rough coming on, leaving their wits with their wives; and then give them great meals of beef and iron and steel, they will eat like wolves and fight like devils. 146 147

ORLEANS   Ay, but these English are shrewdly out of beef. 151

CONSTABLE   Then shall we find tomorrow they have only stomachs to eat and none to fight. Now is it time to arm. Come, shall we about it? 154

ORLEANS
It is now two o'clock; but let me see, by ten
We shall have each a hundred Englishmen.   *Exeunt.*

[4.0]

[*Enter*] *Chorus.*

CHORUS
Now entertain conjecture of a time 1
When creeping murmur and the poring dark 2
Fills the wide vessel of the universe.
From camp to camp, through the foul womb of night,
The hum of either army stilly sounds, 5

79–80 Would . . . desert! I wish I could find words to equal his deserving! **82–3 faced . . . way** braved out of my way, put to shame. **84 fain** gladly. **about the ears** buffeting the heads **85 go to hazard** bet, play at dice. (But the Constable replies in the sense of "encounter danger.") **95–6 tread . . . oath** (1) fulfill the oath by dancing (2) stamp on, spurn the oath. **99 Doing** (1) Acting, pretending (2) Copulating. **still** continually **100 did harm** i.e., offended. (But the Constable uses it to mean "hurt any enemy.") **109 He needs not** i.e., There is no need for him to proclaim it himself. **it** i.e., valor. **110–11 Never . . . lackey** i.e., He shows "valor" only in beating his servant. **111 hooded valor** (The hawk was kept hooded to prevent it from beating its wings, or "bating.") **112 bate** (1) beat its wings (2) abate, be downcast. **116–17 Give . . . due** Give even the devil his due; everyone deserves some praise. (But the Constable turns this proverb against the Dauphin by likening him to the devil.) **118–19 There . . . devil** i.e., You just called the Dauphin the devil. **119 Have . . . eye** Shoot straight at the mark. (A sporting term appropriate to this verbal contest of "capping proverbs.")

122 bolt short, blunt arrow **123 shot over** i.e., shot over the mark. **124 overshot** i.e., outshot, defeated. **133 mope** (1) wander about (2) be downcast **135 apprehension** (1) sense (2) sense of danger **142 winking** shutting their eyes **146 Just** Exactly. **sympathize with** resemble **147 robustious** violent, boisterous **151 shrewdly out of** devilishly short of **154 stomachs** appetites **4.0. Chorus.** **1 entertain conjecture of** imagine **2 poring** in which one must strain the eyes to see **5 stilly** softly

That the fixed sentinels almost receive
The secret whispers of each other's watch.
Fire answers fire, and through their paly flames   8
Each battle sees the other's umbered face.   9
Steed threatens steed, in high and boastful neighs
Piercing the night's dull ear; and from the tents
The armorers, accomplishing the knights,   12
With busy hammers closing rivets up,
Give dreadful note of preparation.
The country cocks do crow, the clocks do toll,
And the third hour of drowsy morning name.
Proud of their numbers and secure in soul,   17
The confident and overlusty French   18
Do the low-rated English play at dice,   19
And chide the cripple tardy-gaited night,
Who like a foul and ugly witch doth limp
So tediously away. The poor condemnèd English,
Like sacrifices, by their watchful fires
Sit patiently and inly ruminate   24
The morning's danger; and their gesture sad,   25
Investing lank-lean cheeks and war-worn coats,   26
Presenteth them unto the gazing moon
So many horrid ghosts. Oh, now, who will behold
The royal captain of this ruined band
Walking from watch to watch, from tent to tent,
Let him cry, "Praise and glory on his head!"
For forth he goes and visits all his host,   32
Bids them good morrow with a modest smile,
And calls them brothers, friends, and countrymen.
Upon his royal face there is no note
How dread an army hath enrounded him.   36
Nor doth he dedicate one jot of color   37
Unto the weary and all-watchèd night,   38
But freshly looks and overbears attaint   39
With cheerful semblance and sweet majesty;
That every wretch, pining and pale before,
Beholding him, plucks comfort from his looks.
A largess universal like the sun
His liberal eye doth give to everyone,
Thawing cold fear, that mean and gentle all   45
Behold, as may unworthiness define,   46
A little touch of Harry in the night.
And so our scene must to the battle fly;
Where—oh, for pity!—we shall much disgrace
With four or five most vile and ragged foils,   50
Right ill-disposed in brawl ridiculous,
The name of Agincourt. Yet sit and see,
Minding true things by what their mockeries be.   53

Exit.

❖

8 **paly** pale 9 **battle** army. **umbered** shadowed 12 **accomplishing**
equipping 17 **secure** overconfident 18 **overlusty** overly merry
19 **play** gamble for 24 **inly** inwardly 25 **gesture sad** serious bearing
26 **Investing** clothing 32 **host** army 36 **enrounded** surrounded
37 **dedicate** yield up. **color** i.e., bright color of complexion 38 **all-
watchèd** spent entirely in wakefulness and waiting 39 **overbears
attaint** overcomes the effects of weariness and depression 45 **mean
and gentle** those of low and of high birth 46 **unworthiness** I, who am
unworthy of praising so great an object 50 **foils** blunted fencing swords
53 **Minding** bearing in mind. **mockeries** inadequate imitations

[4.1]

Enter the King, Bedford, and Gloucester.

KING
Gloucester, 'tis true that we are in great danger;
The greater therefore should our courage be.
Good morrow, brother Bedford. God Almighty!
There is some soul of goodness in things evil,
Would men observingly distill it out;   5
For our bad neighbor makes us early stirrers,
Which is both healthful and good husbandry.   7
Besides, they are our outward consciences,
And preachers to us all, admonishing
That we should dress us fairly for our end.   10
Thus may we gather honey from the weed
And make a moral of the devil himself.

Enter Erpingham.

Good morrow, old Sir Thomas Erpingham.
A good soft pillow for that good white head
Were better than a churlish turf of France.   15
ERPINGHAM
Not so, my liege. This lodging likes me better,   16
Since I may say, "Now lie I like a king."
KING
'Tis good for men to love their present pains
Upon example; so the spirit is eased.   19
And when the mind is quickened, out of doubt
The organs, though defunct and dead before,
Break up their drowsy grave and newly move   22
With casted slough and fresh legerity.   23
Lend me thy cloak, Sir Thomas. [*The King puts on
    Erpingham's cloak.*] Brothers both,   24
Commend me to the princes in our camp;   25
Do my good morrow to them, and anon
Desire them all to my pavilion.
GLOUCESTER   We shall, my liege.
ERPINGHAM   Shall I attend Your Grace?
KING   No, my good knight,
Go with my brothers to my lords of England.
I and my bosom must debate awhile,
And then I would no other company.
ERPINGHAM
The Lord in heaven bless thee, noble Harry!
                            Exeunt [*all but the King*].
KING
God-a-mercy, old heart! Thou speak'st cheerfully.

Enter Pistol.

PISTOL   *Che vous là?*   36

4.1. Location: The English camp at Agincourt.
5 **Would** men if one could 7 **husbandry** economy, thrift. 10 **dress
us fairly** prepare ourselves well 15 **churlish** rough, hard 16 **likes**
pleases 19 **Upon example** i.e., following or considering the example
of persons such as King Henry and Erpingham 22–3 **Break . . . legerity** break out of their lethargy and move nimbly, like a snake having cast off its old skin. 24 **Brothers both** i.e., Bedford and Gloucester 25 **Commend me** convey my greetings 36 **Che vous là?** i.e., *Qui
va là?* ("Who goes there?") or *Qui vous là?* ("Who are you there?").
(Pistol's imperfect French.)

KING   A friend.

PISTOL

Discuss unto me: art thou officer,   38
Or art thou base, common, and popular?   39

KING   I am a gentleman of a company.   40

PISTOL   Trail'st thou the puissant pike?   41

KING   Even so. What are you?

PISTOL

As good a gentleman as the Emperor.

KING   Then you are a better than the King.

PISTOL

The King's a bawcock and a heart of gold,   45
A lad of life, an imp of fame,   46
Of parents good, of fist most valiant.
I kiss his dirty shoe, and from heartstring
I love the lovely bully. What is thy name?   49

KING   Harry le Roy.

PISTOL

Le Roy? A Cornish name. Art thou of Cornish crew?

KING   No, I am a Welshman.   52

PISTOL   Know'st thou Fluellen?

KING   Yes.

PISTOL

Tell him I'll knock his leek about his pate   55
Upon Saint Davy's Day.   56

KING   Do not you wear your dagger in your cap that
day, lest he knock that about yours.

PISTOL   Art thou his friend?

KING   And his kinsman too.

PISTOL   The *figo* for thee, then!   61

KING   I thank you. God be with you!

PISTOL   My name is Pistol called.   *Exit.*

KING   It sorts well with your fierceness.   64

Manet King [standing apart].

Enter Fluellen and Gower [meeting].

GOWER   Captain Fluellen!

FLUELLEN   So, in the name of Jesu Christ, speak fewer.   66
It is the greatest admiration in the universal world,   67
when the true and aunchient prerogatifes and laws of
the wars is not kept. If you would take the pains but
to examine the wars of Pompey the Great, you shall   70
find, I warrant you, that there is no tiddle-taddle nor   71
pibble-pabble in Pompey's camp. I warrant you, you   72
shall find the ceremonies of the wars, and the cares of
it, and the forms of it, and the sobriety of it, and the   74
modesty of it, to be otherwise.   75

---

38 Discuss Declare   **39 popular** of low birth.   **40 gentleman of a company** gentleman serving as a volunteer.   **41 Trail'st . . . pike?** i.e., Are you in the infantry?   **45 bawcock** fine fellow. (From the French *beau coq.*)   **46 imp of fame** child or scion of renown   **49 bully** (A term of endearment meaning "fine fellow.")   **52 Welshman** (Henry was born at Monmouth, then considered part of Wales.)   **55–6 leek . . . Day** (On Saint David's Day, March 1, the leek was worn in memory of a Welsh victory over the Saxons in 540 A.D., since Saint David, the Welsh leader, had commanded his followers to wear leeks in their caps on that occasion.)   **61 figo** (A provoking gesture of contempt; see the note for 3.6.57.)   **64 sorts** fits, agrees   **64.1 Manet King** The King remains.   **66 fewer** i.e., calmly, more quietly.   **67 admiration** wonder   **70 Pompey the Great** Roman general defeated by Julius Caesar   **71–2 tiddle-taddle nor pibble-pabble** tittle-tattle nor bibble-babble   **74 sobriety** orderliness, decorum   **75 modesty** propriety

---

GOWER   Why, the enemy is loud; you hear him all
night.

FLUELLEN   If the enemy is an ass and a fool and a prating   78
coxcomb, is it meet, think you, that we should also,   79
look you, be an ass and a fool and a prating coxcomb?
In your own conscience, now?

GOWER   I will speak lower.

FLUELLEN   I pray you and beseech you that you will.

Exit [with Gower].

KING

Though it appear a little out of fashion,
There is much care and valor in this Welshman.

*Enter three soldiers, John Bates, Alexander Court,
and Michael Williams.*

COURT   Brother John Bates, is not that the morning
which breaks yonder?

BATES   I think it be. But we have no great cause to
desire the approach of day.

WILLIAMS   We see yonder the beginning of the day, but
I think we shall never see the end of it.—Who goes
there?

KING   A friend.

WILLIAMS   Under what captain serve you?

KING   Under Sir Thomas Erpingham.

WILLIAMS   A good old commander and a most kind
gentleman. I pray you, what thinks he of our estate?   97

KING   Even as men wrecked upon a sand, that look to   98
be washed off the next tide.

BATES   He hath not told his thought to the King?

KING   No, nor it is not meet he should. For, though I   101
speak it to you, I think the King is but a man, as I am.
The violet smells to him as it doth to me; the element   103
shows to him as it doth to me; all his senses have but   104
human conditions. His ceremonies laid by, in his   105
nakedness he appears but a man; and though his
affections are higher mounted than ours, yet when   107
they stoop, they stoop with the like wing. Therefore
when he sees reason of fears, as we do, his fears, out
of doubt, be of the same relish as ours are. Yet, in   110
reason, no man should possess him with any appear-   111
ance of fear, lest he, by showing it, should dishearten
his army.

BATES   He may show what outward courage he will; but
I believe, as cold a night as 'tis, he could wish himself
in Thames up to the neck; and so I would he were,
and I by him, at all adventures, so we were quit here.   117

KING   By my troth, I will speak my conscience of the
King: I think he would not wish himself anywhere but
where he is.

78–9 prating coxcomb chattering fool   **97 estate** situation.
98 wrecked shipwrecked   **101 meet** fitting   **103–4 element shows** sky appears   **105 ceremonies** symbols of royalty   **107 affections . . . mounted** desires soar higher. (A falconry metaphor continued in *stoop,* "descend," "swoop down," and *with the like wing,* "similarly.")
110 relish taste   **111 possess him with** induce in him   **117 at all adventures** at all events (since the Thames would be less risky under any circumstances than the impending battle).   **quit here** out of this situation.

BATES   Then I would he were here alone. So should he be sure to be ransomed, and a many poor men's lives saved.

KING   I dare say you love him not so ill to wish him here alone, howsoever you speak this to feel other men's 125 minds. Methinks I could not die anywhere so contented as in the King's company, his cause being just and his quarrel honorable.

WILLIAMS   That's more than we know.

BATES   Ay, or more than we should seek after; for we know enough if we know we are the King's subjects. If his cause be wrong, our obedience to the King wipes the crime of it out of us.

WILLIAMS   But if the cause be not good, the King himself hath a heavy reckoning to make, when all those legs and arms and heads, chopped off in a battle, shall join together at the Latter Day and cry all, 137 "We died at such a place"—some swearing, some crying for a surgeon, some upon their wives left poor behind them, some upon the debts they owe, some upon their children rawly left. I am afeard there are 141 few die well that die in a battle; for how can they charitably dispose of anything, when blood is their argument? Now, if these men do not die well, it will be a black matter for the King that led them to it; who 145 to disobey were against all proportion of subjection. 146

KING   So, if a son that is by his father sent about merchandise do sinfully miscarry upon the sea, the 148 imputation of his wickedness, by your rule, should be 149 imposed upon his father that sent him; or if a servant, under his master's command transporting a sum of money, be assailed by robbers and die in many 152 irreconciled iniquities, you may call the business of the 153 master the author of the servant's damnation. But this is not so. The King is not bound to answer the particular endings of his soldiers, the father of his son, nor 155 the master of his servant; for they purpose not their 157 deaths when they propose their services. Besides, there is no king, be his cause never so spotless, if it 159 come to the arbitrament of swords, can try it out with 160 all unspotted soldiers. Some, peradventure, have on 161 them the guilt of premeditated and contrived murder; some, of beguiling virgins with the broken seals of 163 perjury; some, making the wars their bulwark, that 164 have before gored the gentle bosom of peace with pillage and robbery. Now, if these men have defeated 166 the law and outrun native punishment, though they 167 can outstrip men, they have no wings to fly from God. War is his beadle, war is his vengeance; so that here 169

men are punished for before-breach of the King's laws 170 in now the King's quarrel. Where they feared the 171 death, they have borne life away; and where they 172 would be safe, they perish. Then if they die unpro- 173 vided, no more is the King guilty of their damnation 174 than he was before guilty of those impieties for the which they are now visited. Every subject's duty is the 176 King's; but every subject's soul is his own. Therefore should every soldier in the wars do as every sick man in his bed, wash every mote out of his conscience; and 179 dying so, death is to him advantage, or not dying, the time was blessedly lost wherein such preparation was gained. And in him that escapes, it were not sin to think that, making God so free an offer, He let him outlive that day to see His greatness and to teach others how they should prepare.

WILLIAMS   'Tis certain, every man that dies ill, the ill 186 upon his own head, the King is not to answer it.

BATES   I do not desire he should answer for me, and yet I determine to fight lustily for him.

KING   I myself heard the King say he would not be ransomed.

WILLIAMS   Ay, he said so, to make us fight cheerfully; but when our throats are cut, he may be ransomed and we ne'er the wiser.

KING   If I live to see it, I will never trust his word after.

WILLIAMS   You pay him then! That's a perilous shot out 196 of an elder-gun, that a poor and a private displeasure 197 can do against a monarch. You may as well go about to turn the sun to ice with fanning in his face with a peacock's feather. You'll never trust his word after! Come, 'tis a foolish saying.

KING   Your reproof is something too round. I should be 202 angry with you, if the time were convenient.

WILLIAMS   Let it be a quarrel between us, if you live.

KING   I embrace it.

WILLIAMS   How shall I know thee again?

KING   Give me any gage of thine, and I will wear it in 207 my bonnet. Then if ever thou dar'st acknowledge it, I will make it my quarrel.

WILLIAMS   Here's my glove. Give me another of thine.

KING   There.   [*They exchange gloves.*]

WILLIAMS   This will I also wear in my cap. If ever thou come to me and say, after tomorrow, "This is my glove," by this hand, I will take thee a box on the ear. 214

KING   If ever I live to see it, I will challenge it.

WILLIAMS   Thou dar'st as well be hanged.

KING   Well, I will do it, though I take thee in the King's company.

WILLIAMS   Keep thy word. Fare thee well.

125 **feel** feel out   137 **Latter Day** last day, Christian Day of Judgment
141 **rawly** without provision   145 **who** whom   146 **proportion of subjection** proper duty of a subject.   148 **sinfully miscarry** die in his sins   149 **imputation . . . wickedness** wickedness imputed to him
152–3 **in . . . iniquities** with his wicked deeds unabsolved   155 **answer** answer for   157 **purpose** intend   159–60 **if . . . swords** if a dispute can be settled only by swords   161 **unspotted** innocent
163 **broken seals** (1) broken promises (2) violated maidenheads
164 **bulwark** refuge from punishment (for offenses committed)
166 **defeated** broken   167 **native** at home   169 **beadle** parish officer responsible for punishing petty offenders

170 **before-breach** prior violation   171–3 **Where . . . perish** i.e., Whereas before they feared execution but escaped punishment, here where they look for safety they die in battle.   173–4 **unprovided** spiritually unprepared   176 **visited** i.e., by punishment.   179 **mote** small impurity   186 **dies ill** dies in sin   196 **You pay him then!** i.e., That will really pay him back for his perfidy, won't it? (Said sarcastically.)   197 **elder-gun** popgun made from a branch of elder with the pith hollowed out   202 **round** direct, brusque.   207 **gage** pledge
214 **take** give, strike

BATES   Be friends, you English fools, be friends. We
   have French quarrels enough, if you could tell how to 221
   reckon.

KING   Indeed, the French may lay twenty French crowns 223
   to one they will beat us, for they bear them on their
   shoulders; but it is no English treason to cut French 225
   crowns, and tomorrow the King himself will be a
   clipper.   *Exeunt soldiers.*
   Upon the King! Let us our lives, our souls,
   Our debts, our careful wives,   229
   Our children, and our sins lay on the King!
   We must bear all. Oh, hard condition,
   Twin-born with greatness, subject to the breath   232
   Of every fool, whose sense no more can feel   233
   But his own wringing! What infinite heartsease   234
   Must kings neglect that private men enjoy!
   And what have kings that privates have not too,   236
   Save ceremony, save general ceremony?
   And what art thou, thou idol ceremony?
   What kind of god art thou, that suffer'st more
   Of mortal griefs than do thy worshipers?
   What are thy rents? What are thy comings-in?   241
   O ceremony, show me but thy worth!
   What is thy soul of adoration?   243
   Art thou aught else but place, degree, and form,   244
   Creating awe and fear in other men?
   Wherein thou art less happy, being feared,
   Than they in fearing.
   What drink'st thou oft, instead of homage sweet,
   But poisoned flattery? Oh, be sick, great greatness, 249
   And bid thy ceremony give thee cure!   250
   Thinks thou the fiery fever will go out   251
   With titles blown from adulation?   252
   Will it give place to flexure and low bending?   253
   Canst thou, when thou command'st the beggar's
      knee,
   Command the health of it? No, thou proud dream,
   That play'st so subtly with a king's repose.
   I am a king that find thee, and I know   257
   'Tis not the balm, the scepter, and the ball,   258
   The sword, the mace, the crown imperial,   259

The intertissued robe of gold and pearl,   260
The farcèd title running 'fore the king,   261
The throne he sits on, nor the tide of pomp
That beats upon the high shore of this world—
No, not all these, thrice-gorgeous ceremony,
Not all these, laid in bed majestical,
Can sleep so soundly as the wretched slave
Who, with a body filled and vacant mind,
Gets him to rest, crammed with distressful bread;   268
Never sees horrid night, the child of hell,
But like a lackey from the rise to set   270
Sweats in the eye of Phoebus, and all night   271
Sleeps in Elysium; next day after dawn   272
Doth rise and help Hyperion to his horse,   273
And follows so the ever-running year
With profitable labor to his grave.
And but for ceremony, such a wretch,
Winding up days with toil and nights with sleep,
Had the forehand and vantage of a king.   278
The slave, a member of the country's peace,   279
Enjoys it, but in gross brain little wots   280
What watch the King keeps to maintain the peace,   281
Whose hours the peasant best advantages.   282

   Enter Erpingham.

ERPINGHAM
   My lord, your nobles, jealous of your absence,   283
   Seek through your camp to find you.
KING   Good old knight,
   Collect them all together at my tent.
   I'll be before thee.
ERPINGHAM   I shall do't, my lord.   *Exit.* 286
KING
   O God of battles, steel my soldiers' hearts;
   Possess them not with fear! Take from them now
   The sense of reck'ning, ere th'opposèd numbers   289
   Pluck their hearts from them. Not today, O Lord,
   Oh, not today, think not upon the fault   291
   My father made in compassing the crown!   292
   I Richard's body have interrèd new,   293
   And on it have bestowed more contrite tears
   Than from it issued forcèd drops of blood.
   Five hundred poor I have in yearly pay
   Who twice a day their withered hands hold up
   Toward heaven, to pardon blood; and I have built
   Two chantries, where the sad and solemn priests   299
   Sing still for Richard's soul. More will I do;   300

221 could tell knew   **223 lay** bet. (But also anticipating the meaning "lay down or lose in battle.")   **crowns** (1) coins (2) heads   **225 English treason** (It was a treasonable offense to clip or "cut" English coins; it obviously is no offense to slash French heads, and even King Henry will be such a "clipper.")   **229 careful** full of cares   **232–4 Twin-born . . . wringing** i.e., inseparable from the condition of being born of royal rank, a condition that makes a king the subject of the idle gossip of every fool, even those whose sensibilities pay attention to nothing other than the rumbling of their own stomachs.   **236 privates** private persons   **241 comings-in** revenues.   **243 thy soul of adoration** the essential quality that makes you so much admired.   **244 place** rank   **249–50 Oh . . . cure!** Learn to cure yourself by being sick, by treating poisoned flattery and ceremoniousness as a medicine that will purge you of being in love with your own great greatness.   **251–2 Thinks . . . adulation?** Do you really think that the fever of vain pride will be extinguished by speeches breathed by flatterers? (*Blown* also suggests "inflated.")   **253 Will . . . bending?** i.e., Will the sickness yield to bowing and scraping?   **257 find thee** i.e., experience greatness and am able to appraise its worth and limitations   **258 balm** consecrating oil used to anoint a king in his coronation.   **ball** orb of sovereignty   **259 mace** ceremonial staff

260 intertissued interwoven   **261 farcèd** stuffed (with pompous phrases)   **268 distressful** earned by hard work   **270 lackey** (1) footman running alongside the chariot of the sun (2) peasant.   **rise to set** sunrise to sunset   **271 Phoebus** the sun god   **272 Elysium** in Greek mythology, the abode of the blessed   **273 Hyperion** the father of the sun, or the sun itself. (The peasant is up before the sun.)   **278 Had** would have.   **forehand** upper hand   **279 member** sharer   **280 it** i.e., peace.   **wots** knows   **281 watch** wakeful guard   **282 the peasant best advantages** most benefit the peasant.   **283 jealous of** apprehensive because of   **286 be** be there   **289 sense of reck'ning** ability to reckon up the odds   **291 the fault** i.e., the deposition and murder of Richard II   **292 compassing** obtaining   **293 new** anew   **299 chantries** chapels in which masses for the dead were celebrated.   **sad** grave   **300 still** continually

Though all that I can do is nothing worth,
Since that my penitence comes after all,   302
Imploring pardon.

Enter Gloucester.

GLOUCESTER   My liege!
KING   My brother Gloucester's voice? Ay;
I know thy errand. I will go with thee.
The day, my friends, and all things stay for me.

Exeunt.

❧

[4.2]

*Enter the Dauphin, Orleans, Rambures, and
Beaumont.*

ORLEANS
The sun doth gild our armor. Up, my lords!
DAUPHIN   *Monte à cheval!* My horse! *Varlet! Lacquais!* Ha!   2
ORLEANS   Oh, brave spirit!
DAUPHIN   *Via, les eaux et terre!*   4
ORLEANS   *Rien puis? L'air et feu?*   5
DAUPHIN   *Cieux,* cousin Orleans.   6

Enter Constable.

Now, my Lord Constable?
CONSTABLE
Hark, how our steeds for present service neigh!   8
DAUPHIN
Mount them, and make incision in their hides,   9
That their hot blood may spin in English eyes   10
And dout them with superfluous courage. Ha!   11
RAMBURES
What, will you have them weep our horses' blood?
How shall we then behold their natural tears?

Enter Messenger.

MESSENGER
The English are embattled, you French peers.   14
CONSTABLE
To horse, you gallant princes, straight to horse!
Do but behold yond poor and starvèd band,
And your fair show shall suck away their souls,   17
Leaving them but the shales and husks of men.   18
There is not work enough for all our hands,
Scarce blood enough in all their sickly veins
To give each naked curtal ax a stain   21

That our French gallants shall today draw out
And sheathe for lack of sport. Let us but blow on
   them,
The vapor of our valor will o'erturn them.
'Tis positive against all exceptions, lords,   25
That our superfluous lackeys and our peasants,
Who in unnecessary action swarm
About our squares of battle, were enough   28
To purge this field of such a hilding foe,   29
Though we upon this mountain's basis by   30
Took stand for idle speculation—   31
But that our honors must not. What's to say?   32
A very little little let us do
And all is done. Then let the trumpets sound
The tucket sonance and the note to mount;   35
For our approach shall so much dare the field   36
That England shall couch down in fear and yield.

Enter Grandpré.

GRANDPRÉ
Why do you stay so long, my lords of France?
Yond island carrions, desperate of their bones,   39
Ill-favoredly become the morning field.   40
Their ragged curtains poorly are let loose,   41
And our air shakes them passing scornfully.   42
Big Mars seems bankrupt in their beggared host   43
And faintly through a rusty beaver peeps.   44
The horsemen sit like fixèd candlesticks,
With torch staves in their hand, and their poor jades 46
Lob down their heads, drooping the hides and hips,   47
The gum down-roping from their pale-dead eyes,   48
And in their pale dull mouths the gimmaled bit   49
Lies foul with chewed grass, still and motionless;
And their executors, the knavish crows,   51
Fly o'er them all impatient for their hour.
Description cannot suit itself in words
To demonstrate the life of such a battle   54
In life so lifeless as it shows itself.
CONSTABLE
They have said their prayers, and they stay for death. 56
DAUPHIN
Shall we go send them dinners and fresh suits,
And give their fasting horses provender,   58
And after fight with them?
CONSTABLE
I stay but for my guard. On to the field!   60
I will the banner from a trumpet take,   61

---

302 **Since that** necessitating that
4.2. Location: The French camp.
0.2 *Beaumont* (The Folio text mentions Lord Beaumont but does not
give him a speaking part.)   2 *Monte à cheval!* To horse!   4 *Via . . .
terre!* Begone, waters and earth! (The Dauphin imagines himself riding through and over rivers and solid ground.)   5 *Rien . . . feu?*
Nothing more? What about air and fire? (i.e., Why not soar above all
four elements, not just water and earth?)   6 *Cieux* The heavens. (The
Dauphin carries the metaphor one step further to its ultimate height.)
8 **present service** immediate action   9 **incision** i.e., with spurs
10 **spin** gush, spatter   11 **And . . . courage** i.e., and put out the English eyes with the horses' superfluous blood, the proof of their excessive courage.   **dout** put out   14 **embattled** arranged in battle order
17 **fair show** impressive appearance   18 **shales** shells   21 **curtal ax**
cutlass, short sword

25 **exceptions** objections   28 **squares of battle** four-sided military
formations   29 **hilding** worthless, base   30 **basis** foot.   **by** nearby
31 **speculation** looking on   32 **But that** except for the fact that
35 **tucket sonance** trumpet call.   **mount** mount our horses   36 **dare**
(1) defy (2) stupify with fear   39 **carrions** cadavers for the scavenger
birds.   **desperate of** without hope of saving   40 **Ill-favoredly
become** i.e., are an eyesore to   41 **curtains** colors, banners   42 **passing** exceedingly   43 **Mars** the god of war   44 **beaver** visor   46 **torch
staves** i.e., tapers in place of lances. (The horsemen themselves look
like carved candleholders.)   47 **Lob down** hang down.   **drooping**
letting droop   48 **gum** watery discharge.   **down-roping** hanging
down ropelike   49 **gimmaled** jointed   51 **their executors** the dis-
posers of their remains   54 **battle** army   56 **stay for** await
58 **provender** fodder   60 **guard** (Including a standard-bearer.)
61 **trumpet** trumpeter

And use it for my haste. Come, come, away!
The sun is high, and we outwear the day.   *Exeunt.*   63

❖

[4.3]

Enter Gloucester, Bedford, Exeter, Erpingham,
with all his host, Salisbury, and Westmorland.

GLOUCESTER   Where is the King?
BEDFORD
The King himself is rode to view their battle.   2
WESTMORLAND
Of fighting men they have full threescore thousand.
EXETER
There's five to one. Besides, they all are fresh.
SALISBURY
God's arm strike with us! 'Tis a fearful odds.
God b'wi' you, princes all; I'll to my charge.   6
If we no more meet till we meet in heaven,
Then, joyfully, my noble lord of Bedford,
My dear lord Gloucester, and my good lord Exeter,
And my kind kinsman, warriors all, adieu!   10
BEDFORD
Farewell, good Salisbury, and good luck go with thee!
EXETER
Farewell, kind lord. Fight valiantly today!
And yet I do thee wrong to mind thee of it,   13
For thou art framed of the firm truth of valor.   14
                    [*Exit Salisbury.*]
BEDFORD
He is as full of valor as of kindness,
Princely in both.

Enter the King.

WESTMORLAND   Oh, that we now had here
But one ten thousand of those men in England
That do no work today!
KING   What's he that wishes so?   18
My cousin Westmorland? No, my fair cousin.
If we are marked to die, we are enough   20
To do our country loss; and if to live,   21
The fewer men, the greater share of honor.
God's will, I pray thee, wish not one man more.
By Jove, I am not covetous for gold,
Nor care I who doth feed upon my cost;   25
It yearns me not if men my garments wear;   26
Such outward things dwell not in my desires.
But if it be a sin to covet honor
I am the most offending soul alive.
No, faith, my coz, wish not a man from England.   30
God's peace, I would not lose so great an honor
As one man more, methinks, would share from me   32
For the best hope I have. Oh, do not wish one more!   33

Rather proclaim it, Westmorland, through my host   34
That he which hath no stomach to this fight,   35
Let him depart; his passport shall be made
And crowns for convoy put into his purse.   37
We would not die in that man's company
That fears his fellowship to die with us.   39
This day is called the Feast of Crispian.   40
He that outlives this day and comes safe home
Will stand a-tiptoe when this day is named
And rouse him at the name of Crispian.
He that shall see this day and live old age   44
Will yearly on the vigil feast his neighbors   45
And say, "Tomorrow is Saint Crispian."
Then will he strip his sleeve and show his scars,
And say, "These wounds I had on Crispin's Day."
Old men forget; yet all shall be forgot,   49
But he'll remember with advantages   50
What feats he did that day. Then shall our names,
Familiar in his mouth as household words—
Harry the King, Bedford and Exeter,
Warwick and Talbot, Salisbury and Gloucester—
Be in their flowing cups freshly remembered.
This story shall the good man teach his son;
And Crispin Crispian shall ne'er go by,
From this day to the ending of the world,
But we in it shall be rememberèd—
We few, we happy few, we band of brothers.
For he today that sheds his blood with me
Shall be my brother; be he ne'er so vile,   62
This day shall gentle his condition.   63
And gentlemen in England now abed
Shall think themselves accurst they were not here,
And hold their manhoods cheap whiles any speaks
That fought with us upon Saint Crispin's Day.

Enter Salisbury.

SALISBURY
My sovereign lord, bestow yourself with speed.   68
The French are bravely in their battles set,   69
And will with all expedience charge on us.   70
KING
All things are ready, if our minds be so.
WESTMORLAND
Perish the man whose mind is backward now!   72
KING
Thou dost not wish more help from England, coz?
WESTMORLAND
God's will, my liege, would you and I alone,
Without more help, could fight this royal battle!

---

63 outwear waste
4.3. Location: The English camp.
2 battle army.   **6 charge** post, command.   **10 kinsman** i.e., Westmorland, whose son had married Salisbury's daughter   **13 mind** remind
14 framed made, built   **18 What's** Who is   **20–1 enough . . . loss**
enough loss for our country to suffer   **25 upon my cost** at my
expense   **26 yearns** grieves   **30 coz** cousin, kinsman   **32 share from
me** take from me as his share   **33 For . . . have** i.e., in exchange for
my hope of eternal life.

34 host army   **35 stomach to** appetite for   **37 crowns for convoy**
travel money   **39 That . . . us** who is afraid to risk his life in my company.   **40 Feast of Crispian** Saint Crispin's Day, October 25. (Crispi-
nus and Crispianus were martyrs who fled from Rome in the third
century; according to legend, they disguised themselves as shoemak-
ers and afterward became the patron saints of that craft.)   **44 live**
live to see   **45 vigil** evening before a feast day   **49 yet** in time
50 advantages additions of his own   **62 vile** lowly   **63 gentle his
condition** i.e., raise his social status to the equivalent of gentleman
in that he is my "brother."   **68 bestow yourself** take up your battle
position   **69 bravely . . . set** finely arrayed in their battalions
70 expedience speed   **72 backward** reluctant

KING
Why, now thou hast unwished five thousand men,
Which likes me better than to wish us one.—   77
You know your places. God be with you all!

Tucket. Enter Montjoy.

MONTJOY
Once more I come to know of thee, King Harry,
If for thy ransom thou wilt now compound   80
Before thy most assurèd overthrow;
For certainly thou art so near the gulf   82
Thou needs must be englutted. Besides, in mercy   83
The Constable desires thee thou wilt mind   84
Thy followers of repentance, that their souls
May make a peaceful and a sweet retire   86
From off these fields where, wretches, their poor
    bodies
Must lie and fester.
KING   Who hath sent thee now?
MONTJOY   The Constable of France.
KING
I pray thee, bear my former answer back:
Bid them achieve me, and then sell my bones.   91
Good God, why should they mock poor fellows thus?
The man that once did sell the lion's skin
While the beast lived was killed with hunting him.
A many of our bodies shall no doubt   95
Find native graves, upon the which, I trust,   96
Shall witness live in brass of this day's work.
And those that leave their valiant bones in France,
Dying like men, though buried in your dunghills,
They shall be famed; for there the sun shall greet them
And draw their honors reeking up to heaven,   101
Leaving their earthly parts to choke your clime,
The smell whereof shall breed a plague in France.
Mark then abounding valor in our English,   104
That, being dead, like to the bullets crazing   105
Break out into a second course of mischief,
Killing in relapse of mortality.   107
Let me speak proudly. Tell the Constable
We are but warriors for the working day.   109
Our gayness and our gilt are all besmirched
With rainy marching in the painful field.
There's not a piece of feather in our host—
Good argument, I hope, we will not fly—
And time hath worn us into slovenry.   114
But, by the Mass, our hearts are in the trim!   115
And my poor soldiers tell me, yet ere night

They'll be in fresher robes, or they will pluck   117
The gay new coats o'er the French soldiers' heads   118
And turn them out of service. If they do this—   119
As, if God please, they shall—my ransom then
Will soon be levied. Herald, save thou thy labor.   121
Come thou no more for ransom, gentle herald.   122
They shall have none, I swear, but these my joints,
Which if they have as I will leave 'em them,
Shall yield them little, tell the Constable.
MONTJOY
I shall, King Harry. And so fare thee well.
Thou never shalt hear herald any more.   *Exit.*
KING
I fear thou wilt once more come again for a ransom.

Enter York [and kneels].

YORK
My lord, most humbly on my knee I beg
The leading of the vaward.   130
KING
Take it, brave York. Now, soldiers, march away.
And how thou pleasest, God, dispose the day!
                                          Exeunt.

❖

[4.4]

*Alarum. Excursions. Enter Pistol, French Soldier,
[and] Boy.*

PISTOL   Yield, cur!
FRENCH SOLDIER   *Je pense que vous êtes le gentilhomme de*   2
bonne qualité.   3
PISTOL
Qualtitie calmie custure me!   4
Art thou a gentleman? What is thy name? Discuss.   5
FRENCH SOLDIER   *O Seigneur Dieu!*   6
PISTOL
Oh, Signieur Dew should be a gentleman.
Perpend my words, O Signieur Dew, and mark: 8
O Signieur Dew, thou diest on point of fox,   9
Except, O signieur, thou do give to me   10
Egregious ransom.   [*He threatens him with his sword.*] 11
FRENCH SOLDIER   *Oh, prenez miséricorde! Ayez pitié de* 12
moi!   13
PISTOL
"Moy" shall not serve. I will have forty moys,   14
Or I will fetch thy rim out at thy throat   15

77 **likes** pleases   80 **compound** make terms   82 **gulf** whirlpool
83 **englutted** swallowed up.   84 **mind** remind   86 **retire** retreat
91 **achieve** capture   95 **A many** Many. (The phrase is an exact parallel to "a few.")   96 **native** in our own land (i.e., England)   101 **reeking** (1) breathing (2) smelling   104 **abounding** overflowing, abundant   105 **crazing** shattering, with a suggestion also of *grazing,*
"ricocheting"   107 **Killing . . . mortality** killing (their foes) as they
(the English) fall back (decompose) into their elements; also, like the
bullet, with a deadly ricochet.   109 **for the working day** to do serious work, not take a holiday.   114 **slovenry** slovenliness, untidiness.
115 **in the trim** fully rigged, ready for action.

117–19 **They'll . . . service** they will be more freshly dressed by nightfall, if no other way than by defrocking the French soldiers like incapable servants being dismissed and stripped of their livery. (Soldiers
got to keep such spoils of war from their victims.)   121 **levied** collected.   122 **gentle** noble   130 **vaward** vanguard
4.4. Location: The field of battle.
0.1 *Excursions* Sorties.   2–3 *Je . . . qualité* I think that you are a gentleman of high rank.   4 *calmie custure me* (These words are perhaps
derived from the refrain of a popular song, supposed to be Irish, "Calen
o custure me.")   5 **Discuss** Speak.   6 *O Seigneur Dieu!* O Lord God!
8 **Perpend** Attend to, consider   9 **fox** sword   10 **Except** unless
11 **Egregious** huge   12–13 *Oh . . . moi!* Oh, have mercy! Take pity on me!
14 **Moy** (Pistol, not understanding, takes *moi* for the name of a coin or
a sum of money, a moiety or half.)   15 **rim** midriff, diaphragm

In drops of crimson blood.

FRENCH SOLDIER   *Est-il impossible d'échapper la force de ton*   17
bras?   18

PISTOL   Brass, cur?
Thou damnèd and luxurious mountain goat,   20
Offer'st me brass?

FRENCH SOLDIER   *Oh, pardonnez-moi!*

PISTOL
Say'st thou me so? Is that a ton of moys?—   23
Come hither, boy. Ask me this slave in French
What is his name.

BOY   *Écoutez: comment êtes-vous appelé?*   26

FRENCH SOLDIER   *Monsieur Le Fer.*

BOY   He says his name is Master Fer.

PISTOL   Master Fer? I'll fer him, and firk him, and ferret   29
him. Discuss the same in French unto him.

BOY   I do not know the French for fer, and ferret, and
firk.

PISTOL
Bid him prepare, for I will cut his throat.

FRENCH SOLDIER   *Que dit-il, monsieur?*   34

BOY   *Il me commande à vous dire que vous faites vous*   35
prêt; car ce soldat ici est disposé tout à cette heure de   36
couper votre gorge.   37

PISTOL
Owy, cuppele gorge, permafoy,   38
Peasant, unless thou give me crowns, brave crowns,
Or mangled shalt thou be by this my sword.

FRENCH SOLDIER   *Oh, je vous supplie, pour l'amour de*   41
Dieu, me pardonner! Je suis le gentilhomme de bonne   42
maison. Gardez ma vie, et je vous donnerai deux cents   43
écus.   44

PISTOL   What are his words?

BOY   He prays you to save his life. He is a gentleman of
a good house, and for his ransom he will give you two   47
hundred crowns.

PISTOL
Tell him my fury shall abate, and I
The crowns will take.

FRENCH SOLDIER   *Petit monsieur, que dit-il?*   51

BOY   *Encore qu'il est contre son jurement de pardonner*   52
aucun prisonnier, néanmoins, pour les écus que vous   53
l'avez promis, il est content à vous donner la liberté,   54
le franchisement.   55

FRENCH SOLDIER   [*kneeling*]   *Sur mes genoux je vous*   56
donne mille remercîments; et je m'estime heureux que   57
j'ai tombé entre les mains d'un chevalier, je pense,   58
le plus brave, vaillant, et très-distingué seigneur   59
d'Angleterre.   60

PISTOL   Expound unto me, boy.

BOY   He gives you, upon his knees, a thousand thanks,
and he esteems himself happy that he hath fallen into
the hands of one, as he thinks, the most brave, valor-
ous, and thrice-worthy signieur of England.

PISTOL
As I suck blood, I will some mercy show.
Follow me!

BOY   *Suivez-vous le grand capitaine.*   68

[*Exeunt Pistol and French Soldier.*]
I did never know so full a voice issue
from so empty a heart! But the saying is true, "The
empty vessel makes the greatest sound." Bardolph and
Nym had ten times more valor than this roaring devil   72
i'th'old play, that everyone may pare his nails with   73
a wooden dagger, and they are both hanged; and so   74
would this be, if he durst steal anything adventur-
ously. I must stay with the lackeys, with the luggage
of our camp. The French might have a good prey of   77
us, if he knew of it, for there is none to guard it but
boys.   *Exit.*

❖

[4.5]

Enter Constable, Orleans, Bourbon, Dauphin, and
Rambures.

CONSTABLE   *Oh, diable!*   1

ORLEANS   *Oh, Seigneur! Le jour est perdu, tout est perdu!*   2

DAUPHIN
Mort de ma vie! All is confounded, all.   3
Reproach and everlasting shame
Sits mocking in our plumes.   *A short alarum.*
Oh, méchante fortune! Do not run away.   6

CONSTABLE   Why, all our ranks are broke.

DAUPHIN
Oh, perdurable shame! Let's stab ourselves.   8
Be these the wretches that we played at dice for?

ORLEANS
Is this the king we sent to for his ransom?

BOURBON
Shame and eternal shame, nothing but shame!
Let us die! In once more! Back again!

17–18 *Est-il . . . bras?* Is it impossible to escape the strength of your
arm? (But Pistol takes *bras*, "arm," for *brass*.)   **20 luxurious** lecherous
23 a ton of moys (This is what Pistol phonetically makes out of
pardonnez-moi.)   **26** *Écoutez . . . appelé*? Listen: what is your name?
29 firk trounce.   **ferret** worry (like a ferret)   **34–7** *Que . . . gorge*
What does he say, sir? BOY He bids me tell you that you must prepare
yourself, because this soldier intends to cut your throat immediately.
38 *Owy Oui*, "yes."   **permafoy** *per ma foi*, by my faith   **41–4** *Oh . . .*
écus Oh, I pray you, for the love of God, to pardon me! I am a gentleman of a good house; preserve my life, and I shall give you two hundred crowns.   **47 house** family   **51–5** *Petit . . . franchisement* What
does he say, little sir? BOY Although it is against his oath to pardon
any prisoner, nevertheless, for the sake of the crowns you have promised, he is willing to give you your liberty, your freedom.

56–60 *Sur . . . d'Angleterre* On my knees, I give you a thousand
thanks, and I consider myself happy that I have fallen into the hands
of a knight, as I think, the bravest, most valiant, and very distinguished gentleman in England.   **68** *Suivez-vous . . . capitaine* Follow
the great captain.   **72–4 this roaring . . . dagger** Shakespeare refers
several times to the devil in the morality play with his dagger of lath;
see *2H6*, 4.2.2 and *Twelfth Night*, 4.2.126. The paring of the devil's nails
was a proverbial act of bravado.   **77 a good prey** i.e., easy pickings
4.5. Location: The field of battle still.
1 *Oh, diable!* Oh, the devil!   **2** *Oh . . . perdu!* Oh, Lord, the day is lost,
all is lost!   **3** *Mort . . . vie!* Death to my life!   **confounded** lost
6 *Oh, méchante fortune!* Oh, malicious fortune!   **8 perdurable** everlasting

And he that will not follow Bourbon now,
Let him go hence, and with his cap in hand,
Like a base pander, hold the chamber door
Whilst by a slave, no gentler than my dog,   16
His fairest daughter is contaminated.

CONSTABLE
Disorder, that hath spoiled us, friend us now!   18
Let us on heaps go offer up our lives.   19

ORLEANS
We are enough yet living in the field
To smother up the English in our throngs,
If any order might be thought upon.

BOURBON
The devil take order now! I'll to the throng.
Let life be short, else shame will be too long.
                                                Exeunt.

❖

[4.6]

*Alarum. Enter the King and his train, [Exeter,
and others,] with prisoners.*

KING
Well have we done, thrice valiant countrymen!
But all's not done; yet keep the French the field.   2

EXETER
The Duke of York commends him to Your Majesty.

KING
Lives he, good uncle? Thrice within this hour
I saw him down, thrice up again and fighting.
From helmet to the spur all blood he was.

EXETER
In which array, brave soldier, doth he lie,
Larding the plain; and by his bloody side,   8
Yokefellow to his honor-owing wounds,   9
The noble Earl of Suffolk also lies.
Suffolk first died; and York, all haggled over,   11
Comes to him, where in gore he lay insteeped,   12
And takes him by the beard, kisses the gashes
That bloodily did yawn upon his face.   14
He cries aloud, "Tarry, my cousin Suffolk!
My soul shall thine keep company to heaven;
Tarry, sweet soul, for mine, then fly abreast,
As in this glorious and well-foughten field
We kept together in our chivalry!"
Upon these words I came and cheered him up.
He smiled me in the face, raught me his hand,   21
And with a feeble grip says, "Dear my lord,
Commend my service to my sovereign."
So did he turn, and over Suffolk's neck
He threw his wounded arm, and kissed his lips,
And so, espoused to death, with blood he sealed

A testament of noble-ending love.
The pretty and sweet manner of it forced
Those waters from me which I would have stopped;   29
But I had not so much of man in me,
And all my mother came into mine eyes   31
And gave me up to tears.

KING   I blame you not;
For, hearing this, I must perforce compound   33
With mistful eyes, or they will issue too.   *Alarum.*   34
But, hark, what new alarum is this same?
The French have reinforced their scattered men.
Then every soldier kill his prisoners!   37
Give the word through.   *Exeunt.*

❖

[4.7]

Enter Fluellen and Gower.

FLUELLEN   Kill the poys and the luggage? 'Tis expressly   1
against the law of arms. 'Tis as arrant a piece of
knavery, mark you now, as can be offert; in your
conscience, now, is it not?

GOWER   'Tis certain there's not a boy left alive; and the
cowardly rascals that ran from the battle ha' done this
slaughter. Besides, they have burned and carried
away all that was in the King's tent, wherefore the
King most worthily hath caused every soldier to cut
his prisoner's throat. Oh, 'tis a gallant king!

FLUELLEN   Ay, he was porn at Monmouth, Captain   11
Gower. What call you the town's name where Alexander the Pig was born?

GOWER   Alexander the Great.

FLUELLEN   Why, I pray you, is not "pig" great? The pig,
or the great, or the mighty, or the huge, or the
magnanimous, are all one reckonings, save the phrase   17
is a little variations.

GOWER   I think Alexander the Great was born in
Macedon. His father was called Philip of Macedon, as
I take it.

FLUELLEN   I think it is e'en Macedon where Alexander is
porn. I tell you, Captain, if you look in the maps of the
'orld, I warrant you sall find, in the comparisons between Macedon and Monmouth, that the situations,
look you, is both alike. There is a river in Macedon,
and there is also moreover a river at Monmouth. It is
called Wye at Monmouth, but it is out of my prains
what is the name of the other river; but 'tis all one, 'tis
alike as my fingers is to my fingers, and there is sal-
mons in both. If you mark Alexander's life well, Harry
of Monmouth's life is come after it indifferent well, for 32
there is figures in all things. Alexander, God knows,   33

---

16 **gentler** (1) more nobly born (2) tenderer   18 **friend** befriend
19 **on** in
4.6. Location: The field of battle still.
2 **yet . . . field** the French are in the field of battle still.   8 **Larding**
fattening, enriching (with his blood)   9 **honor-owing** honor-owning,
honorable   11 **haggled over** mangled, hacked   12 **insteeped**
steeped, soaked   14 **yawn** gape   21 **me in the** in my.   **raught**
reached

29 **waters** i.e., tears   31 **my mother** i.e., the tenderer part of me
33 **perforce** necessarily.   **compound** come to terms   34 **issue** issue
forth tears   37 **kill his prisoners** (This follows Holinshed, who says
that Henry, alarmed by the outcry of the lackeys and boys of the
camp, feared a new attack and ordered the prisoners killed as a precaution. Gower, 4.7.8–10, attributes the King's action to revenge.)
4.7. Location: The field of battle still.
1 **luggage** i.e., lackeys guarding the luggage.   11 **Monmouth** (i.e., in
Wales)   17 **are . . . reckonings** come to the same thing   32 **is . . . well**
resembles it fairly well   33 **figures** comparisons, similes

and you know, in his rages, and his furies, and his
wraths, and his cholers, and his moods, and his dis-
pleasures, and his indignations, and also being a little
intoxicates in his prains, did, in his ales and his angers,   37
look you, kill his best friend, Cleitus.   38

GOWER   Our King is not like him in that. He never killed
any of his friends.

FLUELLEN   It is not well done, mark you now, to take
the tales out of my mouth ere it is made and finished.
I speak but in the figures and comparisons of it. As
Alexander killed his friend Cleitus, being in his ales
and his cups, so also Harry Monmouth, being in his
right wits and his good judgments, turned away the
fat knight with the great-belly doublet. He was full of   47
jests, and gipes, and knaveries, and mocks. I have   48
forgot his name.

GOWER   Sir John Falstaff.

FLUELLEN   That is he. I'll tell you there is good men
porn at Monmouth.

GOWER   Here comes His Majesty.

*Alarum. Enter King Harry, [Warwick, Gloucester,
Exeter, and others,] and Bourbon, with [other]
prisoners. Flourish.*

KING
I was not angry since I came to France
Until this instant. Take a trumpet, herald;   55
Ride thou unto the horsemen on yond hill.
If they will fight with us, bid them come down,
Or void the field. They do offend our sight.   58
If they'll do neither, we will come to them,
And make them skirr away as swift as stones   60
Enforcèd from the old Assyrian slings.   61
Besides, we'll cut the throats of those we have,
And not a man of them that we shall take
Shall taste our mercy. Go and tell them so.

Enter Montjoy.

EXETER
Here comes the herald of the French, my liege.

GLOUCESTER
His eyes are humbler than they used to be.

KING
How now, what means this, herald? Know'st thou
    not
That I have fined these bones of mine for ransom?   68
Com'st thou again for ransom?

MONTJOY   No, great King.
I come to thee for charitable license,
That we may wander o'er this bloody field
To book our dead and then to bury them,   72
To sort our nobles from our common men.

For many of our princes—woe the while!—
Lie drowned and soaked in mercenary blood;   75
So do our vulgar drench their peasant limbs   76
In blood of princes; and the wounded steeds
Fret fetlock-deep in gore and with wild rage   78
Yerk out their armèd heels at their dead masters,   79
Killing them twice. Oh, give us leave, great King,
To view the field in safety, and dispose
Of their dead bodies!

KING   I tell thee truly, herald,
I know not if the day be ours or no,
For yet a many of your horsemen peer   84
And gallop o'er the field.

MONTJOY   The day is yours.

KING
Praisèd be God, and not our strength, for it!
What is this castle called that stands hard by?

MONTJOY   They call it Agincourt.

KING
Then call we this the field of Agincourt,
Fought on the day of Crispin Crispianus.

FLUELLEN   Your grandfather of famous memory, an't   91
please Your Majesty, and your great-uncle Edward the
Plack Prince of Wales, as I have read in the chronicles,
fought a most prave pattle here in France.

KING   They did, Fluellen.

FLUELLEN   Your Majesty says very true. If Your Majesties is remembered of it, the Welshmen did good
service in a garden where leeks did grow, wearing
leeks in their Monmouth caps, which, Your Majesty   99
know, to this hour is an honorable badge of the
service; and I do believe Your Majesty takes no scorn
to wear the leek upon Saint Tavy's Day.   102

KING
I wear it for a memorable honor,
For I am Welsh, you know, good countryman.

FLUELLEN   All the water in Wye cannot wash Your
Majesty's Welsh plood out of your pody, I can tell you
that. God pless it and preserve it, as long as it pleases
His Grace, and His Majesty too!

KING   Thanks, good my countryman.

FLUELLEN   By Jeshu, I am Your Majesty's countryman.
I care not who know it. I will confess it to all the 'orld.
I need not to be ashamed of Your Majesty, praised be
God, so long as Your Majesty is an honest man.

KING
God keep me so!

Enter Williams [with a glove in his cap].

Our heralds go with him.
Bring me just notice of the numbers dead   115

---

37 in his ales i.e., under the influence of ale   **38 Cleitus** a general
and close associate of Alexander, whom Alexander killed in a drinking bout.   **47 great-belly doublet** a man's close-fitting jacket, in
which the lower part was stuffed out with bombast or padding.
48 gipes gibes, jokes   **55 trumpet** trumpeter   **58 void** leave
60 skirr scurry   **61 Enforcèd** discharged   **68 fined . . . ransom** i.e.,
agreed to pay as a fine or ransom only these bones of mine and no
more.   **72 book** record

75 mercenary i.e., of common soldiers, who fought for pay   **76 vulgar** commoners   **78 fetlock-deep** (The *fetlock* is above the hoof, at the
back of the leg.)   **79 Yerk** kick   **84 peer** (1) look about anxiously
(2) appear   **91 grandfather** i.e., great-grandfather, Edward III.   **an't**
if it   **99 Monmouth caps** round and rimless caps with a tapering
crown, commonly worn by the Welsh   **102 Saint Tavy's Day** the festival of Saint David, patron saint of Wales, March 1—an occasion for
the celebration of Welsh traditions, though the wearing of leeks to
commemorate the great victory in 540 against the Saxons did not
begin until well after the setting of this play.   **115 just** exact

On both our parts.
               [*Exeunt Heralds and Gower with Montjoy.*]
               Call yonder fellow hither.

EXETER [*to Williams*]   Soldier, you must come to the King.

KING   Soldier, why wear'st thou that glove in thy cap?

WILLIAMS   An't please Your Majesty, 'tis the gage of
one that I should fight withal, if he be alive.

KING   An Englishman?

WILLIAMS   An't please Your Majesty, a rascal that swaggered with me last night, who, if 'a live and ever dare
to challenge this glove, I have sworn to take him a box
o'th'ear; or if I can see my glove in his cap, which he
swore, as he was a soldier, he would wear if 'a lived, I
will strike it out soundly.

KING   What think you, Captain Fluellen, is it fit this
soldier keep his oath?

FLUELLEN   He is a craven and a villain else, an't please   130
Your Majesty, in my conscience.

KING   It may be his enemy is a gentleman of great sort,   132
quite from the answer of his degree.   133

FLUELLEN   Though he be as good a gentleman as the
devil is, as Lucifer and Beelzebub himself, it is
necessary, look Your Grace, that he keep his vow and
his oath. If he be perjured, see you now, his reputation
is as arrant a villain and a Jack-sauce as ever his   138
black shoe trod upon God's ground and His earth, in
my conscience, la!

KING [*to Williams*]   Then keep thy vow, sirrah, when
thou meet'st the fellow.

WILLIAMS   So I will, my liege, as I live.

KING   Who serv'st thou under?

WILLIAMS   Under Captain Gower, my liege.

FLUELLEN   Gower is a good captain, and is good
knowledge and literatured in the wars.   147

KING   Call him hither to me, soldier.

WILLIAMS   I will, my liege.   *Exit.*

KING   Here, Fluellen, wear thou this favor for me and
stick it in thy cap. [*He gives Fluellen Williams' glove.*]
When Alençon and myself were down together, I
plucked this glove from his helm. If any man challenge   153
this, he is a friend to Alençon and an enemy to our
person. If thou encounter any such, apprehend him,
an thou dost me love.   156

FLUELLEN [*putting the glove in his cap*]   Your Grace doo's 157
me as great honors as can be desired in the hearts of
his subjects. I would fain see the man that   159
has but two legs that shall find himself aggriefed at
this glove, that is all. But I would fain see it once, an't 161
please God of his grace that I might see.

KING   Know'st thou Gower?

FLUELLEN   He is my dear friend, an't please you.

KING   Pray thee, go seek him and bring him to my tent.

FLUELLEN   I will fetch him.   *Exit.*

KING
My lord of Warwick, and my brother Gloucester,
Follow Fluellen closely at the heels.
The glove which I have given him for a favor
May haply purchase him a box o'th'ear.   170
It is the soldier's; I by bargain should
Wear it myself. Follow, good cousin Warwick.
If that the soldier strike him, as I judge
By his blunt bearing he will keep his word,
Some sudden mischief may arise of it;
For I do know Fluellen valiant
And touched with choler, hot as gunpowder,   177
And quickly will return an injury.   178
Follow, and see there be no harm between them.
Go you with me, uncle of Exeter.   *Exeunt [separately].*

[4.8]

Enter Gower and Williams.

WILLIAMS   I warrant it is to knight you, Captain.

Enter Fluellen.

FLUELLEN   God's will and his pleasure, Captain, I
beseech you now, come apace to the King. There is
more good toward you, peradventure, than is in your
knowledge to dream of.

WILLIAMS   Sir, know you this glove?

FLUELLEN   Know the glove? I know the glove is a glove.

WILLIAMS   I know this, and thus I challenge it.
                                              Strikes him.

FLUELLEN   'Sblood, an arrant traitor as any 's in the   9
universal world, or in France, or in England!

GOWER [*to Williams*]   How now, sir? You villain!

WILLIAMS   Do you think I'll be forsworn?

FLUELLEN   Stand away, Captain Gower. I will give
treason his payment into plows, I warrant you.   14

WILLIAMS   I am no traitor.

FLUELLEN   That's a lie in thy throat.—I charge you in His   16
Majesty's name, apprehend him. He's a friend of the
Duke Alençon's.

Enter Warwick and Gloucester.

WARWICK   How now, how now, what's the matter?

FLUELLEN   My lord of Warwick, here is—praised be
God for it!—a most contagious treason come to light,   21
look you, as you shall desire in a summer's day.—
Here is His Majesty.

Enter King [Henry] and Exeter.

KING   How now, what's the matter?

FLUELLEN   My liege, here is a villain and a traitor that,
look Your Grace, has struck the glove which Your
Majesty is take out of the helmet of Alençon.

---

130 craven coward   **132 sort** rank   **133 quite . . . degree** i.e., too high
in rank to answer the challenge of one so low.   **138 Jack-sauce** saucy
knave   **147 literatured** well read   **153 helm** helmet.   **156 an** if
157 doo's does   **159 fain** willingly   **161 an't** if it. (Also in line 164.)

170 haply perhaps   **177 touched with choler** hot-tempered
178 return an injury repay an insult.
4.8. Location: The English camp.
9 'Sblood By His (Christ's) blood   **14 his** its.   **into plows** in blows
16 lie in thy throat i.e., inexcusable lie.   **21 contagious** noxious

WILLIAMS   My liege, this was my glove; here is the fellow of it. [*Showing his other glove.*] And he that I gave it
to in change promised to wear it in his cap. I promised   30
to strike him, if he did. I met this man with my glove
in his cap, and I have been as good as my word.

FLUELLEN   Your Majesty hear now, saving Your Majesty's manhood, what an arrant, rascally, beggarly,
lousy knave it is. I hope Your Majesty is pear me   35
testimony and witness, and will avouchment, that this   36
is the glove of Alençon that Your Majesty is give me,
in your conscience, now.

KING   Give me thy glove, soldier. Look, here is the
fellow of it.   [*He shows his other glove.*]
'Twas I indeed thou promisèd'st to strike,
And thou hast given me most bitter terms.   42

FLUELLEN   An't please Your Majesty, let his neck
answer for it, if there is any martial law in the world.

KING
How canst thou make me satisfaction?

WILLIAMS   All offenses, my lord, come from the heart.
Never came any from mine that might offend Your
Majesty.

KING   It was ourself thou didst abuse.

WILLIAMS   Your Majesty came not like yourself. You
appeared to me but as a common man—witness the
night, your garments, your lowliness. And what Your   52
Highness suffered under that shape, I beseech you take
it for your own fault and not mine; for had you been
as I took you for, I made no offense. Therefore I beseech Your Highness pardon me.

KING
Here, uncle Exeter, fill this glove with crowns,
And give it to this fellow.—Keep it, fellow,
And wear it for an honor in thy cap
Till I do challenge it.—Give him the crowns.
          [*Exeter gives the glove and gold to Williams.*]
And Captain, you must needs be friends with him.

FLUELLEN   By this day and this light, the fellow has
mettle enough in his belly.—Hold, there is twelve-
pence for you. [*He offers Williams a coin.*] And I pray you
to serve God, and keep you out of prawls, and
prabbles, and quarrels, and dissensions, and I warrant   66
you it is the better for you.

WILLIAMS   I will none of your money.

FLUELLEN   It is with a good will. I can tell you, it will
serve you to mend your shoes. Come, wherefore
should you be so pashful? Your shoes is not so good.
'Tis a good silling, I warrant you, or I will change it.

          Enter [an English] Herald.

KING   Now, herald, are the dead numbered?

HERALD [*giving a paper*]
Here is the number of the slaughtered French.

KING
What prisoners of good sort are taken, uncle?   75

EXETER [*reading*]
Charles Duke of Orleans, nephew to the King;   76
John Duke of Bourbon, and Lord Boucicault;
Of other lords and barons, knights and squires,
Full fifteen hundred, besides common men.

KING
This note doth tell me of ten thousand French
That in the field lie slain. Of princes, in this number,
And nobles bearing banners, there lie dead   82
One hundred twenty-six; added to these,
Of knights, esquires, and gallant gentlemen,
Eight thousand and four hundred, of the which
Five hundred were but yesterday dubbed knights.
So that in these ten thousand they have lost
There are but sixteen hundred mercenaries;
The rest are princes, barons, lords, knights, squires,
And gentlemen of blood and quality.
The names of those their nobles that lie dead:
Charles Delabreth, High Constable of France;
Jaques of Chatillion, Admiral of France;
The Master of the Crossbows, Lord Rambures;
Great-Master of France, the brave Sir Guichard
   Dauphin   95
John, Duke of Alençon; Anthony, Duke of Brabant,
The brother to the Duke of Burgundy;
And Edward, Duke of Bar; of lusty earls,   98
Grandpré and Roussi, Faulconbridge and Foix,
Beaumont and Marle, Vaudemont and Lestrelles.
Here was a royal fellowship of death!
Where is the number of our English dead?
                    [*He is given another paper.*]
Edward the Duke of York, the Earl of Suffolk,
Sir Richard Keighley, Davy Gam, esquire;
None else of name, and of all other men   105
But five-and-twenty. O God, thy arm was here!   106
And not to us, but to thy arm alone,
Ascribe we all. When, without stratagem,
But in plain shock and even play of battle,   109
Was ever known so great and little loss
On one part and on th'other? Take it, God,
For it is none but thine.

EXETER   'Tis wonderful.

KING
Come, go we in procession to the village.
And be it death proclaimèd through our host
To boast of this or take that praise from God
Which is his only.

FLUELLEN   Is it not lawful, an't please Your Majesty, to
tell how many is killed?

KING
Yes, Captain, but with this acknowledgment,
That God fought for us.

76–106 Charles . . . here (The catalogue of the captured and slain is
from Holinshed.)   **82 bearing banners** i.e., with coats of arms
95 Great-Master grandmaster, i.e., the chief officer of the royal household   **98 lusty** vigorous   **105 name** rank, social importance
109 even equal

30 change exchange   **35 is pear** will bear   **36 avouchment** avouch
42 terms words.   **52 lowliness** humble mien.
66 prabbles i.e., brabbles, scuffles   **75 good sort** high rank

FLUELLEN   Yes, in my conscience, he did us great good.
KING   Do we all holy rites.
  Let there be sung *Non nobis* and *Te Deum,*   123
  The dead with charity enclosed in clay;
  And then to Calais, and to England then,
  Where ne'er from France arrived more happy men.   126

                                                        Exeunt.

❧

5.0

  Enter Chorus.

CHORUS
  Vouchsafe to those that have not read the story   1
  That I may prompt them; and of such as have,
  I humbly pray them to admit th'excuse   3
  Of time, of numbers, and due course of things,
  Which cannot in their huge and proper life
  Be here presented. Now we bear the King
  Toward Calais. Grant him there. There seen,
  Heave him away upon your wingèd thoughts
  Athwart the sea. Behold, the English beach   9
  Pales in the flood with men, wives, and boys,   10
  Whose shouts and claps outvoice the deep-mouthed
        sea,
  Which like a mighty whiffler 'fore the King   12
  Seems to prepare his way. So let him land,
  And solemnly see him set on to London.
  So swift a pace hath thought that even now
  You may imagine him upon Blackheath,   16
  Where that his lords desire him to have borne   17
  His bruisèd helmet and his bended sword
  Before him through the city. He forbids it,
  Being free from vainness and self-glorious pride,
  Giving full trophy, signal, and ostent   21
  Quite from himself to God. But now behold,
  In the quick forge and working-house of thought,
  How London doth pour out her citizens!
  The Mayor and all his brethren, in best sort,   25
  Like to the senators of th'antique Rome
  With the plebeians swarming at their heels,
  Go forth and fetch their conquering Caesar in;

As by a lower but loving likelihood,   29
Were now the General of our gracious Empress,   30
As in good time he may, from Ireland coming,
Bringing rebellion broachèd on his sword,   32
How many would the peaceful city quit
To welcome him! Much more, and much more cause,   34
Did they this Harry. Now in London place him;
As yet the lamentation of the French   36
Invites the King of England's stay at home;   37
The Emperor's coming in behalf of France,   38
To order peace between them . . . and omit   39
All the occurrences, whatever chanced,
Till Harry's back-return again to France.   41
There must we bring him; and myself have played
The interim by remem'bring you 'tis past.   43
Then brook abridgment, and your eyes advance,   44
After your thoughts, straight back again to France.

                                                         Exit.

❧

[5.1]

  *Enter Fluellen [with a leek in his cap, and a
  cudgel], and Gower.*

GOWER   Nay, that's right. But why wear you your leek
  today? Saint Davy's Day is past.
FLUELLEN   There is occasions and causes why and
  wherefore in all things. I will tell you asse my friend,   4
  Captain Gower. The rascally, scald, beggarly, lousy,   5
  pragging knave, Pistol, which you and yourself and all
  the world know to be no petter than a fellow, look you
  now, of no merits, he is come to me and prings me
  pread and salt yesterday, look you, and bid me eat my
  leek. It was in a place where I could not breed no contention with him; but I will be so bold as to wear it in
  my cap till I see him once again, and then I will tell
  him a little piece of my desires.

  Enter Pistol.

GOWER   Why, here he comes, swelling like a turkey-
  cock.
FLUELLEN   'Tis no matter for his swellings nor his
  turkey-cocks.—God pless you, Aunchient Pistol! You
  scurvy, lousy knave, God pless you!
PISTOL
  Ha, art thou bedlam? Dost thou thirst, base Trojan,   19

123 *Non nobis* i.e., Psalm 115, beginning, "Not unto us, O Lord,
not unto us, but unto thy name give glory."   *Te Deum* a hymn
of thanksgiving, beginning, "We praise thee O God"   **126 happy**
fortunate
**5.0. (Between Acts 4 and 5, there is historically an interval of about
five years during which Henry made a second campaign in France
that brought the French to terms in the Treaty of Troyes, with which
the play ends.)**
1 Vouchsafe Permit it   **3 admit th'excuse** excuse our handling
9 Athwart across   **10 Pales in** hems in, surrounds.   **flood** sea
12 whiffler an usher heading the procession to clear the way
16 Blackheath open area just outside London, to the southeast
17 Where that where   **21 Giving . . . ostent** giving every memorial,
token, and display of victory   **25 sort** array

29–34 As . . . him (Seemingly, an allusion to the Earl of Essex, who left
London on his Irish expedition on March 27, 1599, in an attempt to
put down Tyrone's rebellion; he returned unsuccessful and under a
cloud on September 28 of the same year. These lines, therefore, were
probably written between the dates mentioned.)   **29 a . . . likelihood**
a less exalted comparison but one that shows much love   **30 Empress**
i.e., Elizabeth   **32 broachèd** transfixed, spitted   **36–7 As . . . home**
i.e., the French are so dejected that Henry can stay in England without fear of loss in France   **38 Emperor's coming** (The Holy Roman
Emperor, Sigismund, came to England on behalf of France in May
1416.)   **39 them . . . and omit** (Something appears to be left out here.
Possibly it should read, "them, and the death / O' the Dauphin, leap
we over, and omit . . .")   **41 Harry's back-return** i.e., Henry's second
campaign, commencing in 1417   **43 remem'bring** reminding
44 brook tolerate, excuse
5.1. Location: France. The English camp.
4 asse as   **5 scald** scurvy   **19 bedlam** crazy.   **Trojan** i.e., rascal

To have me fold up Parca's fatal web?   20
Hence, I am qualmish at the smell of leek.   21

FLUELLEN   I peseech you heartily, scurvy, lousy knave,
at my desires, and my requests, and my petitions, to
eat, look you, this leek. [*He offers the leek.*] Because,
look you, you do not love it, nor your affections and
your appetites and your disgestions doo's not agree
with it, I would desire you to eat it.

PISTOL
Not for Cadwallader and all his goats.   28

FLUELLEN   There is one goat for you. (*Strikes him.*) Will
you be so good, scald knave, as eat it?

PISTOL   Base Trojan, thou shalt die.

FLUELLEN   You say very true, scald knave, when God's
will is. I will desire you to live in the meantime and
eat your victuals. Come, there is sauce for it. [*He strikes
him.*] You called me yesterday mountain squire, but I   35
will make you today a squire of low degree. I pray   36
you, fall to. If you can mock a leek, you can eat a leek.

GOWER   Enough, Captain, you have astonished him.   38

FLUELLEN   By Jesu, I will make him eat some part of my
leek, or I will peat his pate four days. Bite, I pray you;   40
it is good for your green wound and your ploody   41
coxcomb.   42

PISTOL   Must I bite?

FLUELLEN   Yes, certainly, and out of doubt and out of
question too, and ambiguities.

PISTOL
By this leek, I will most horribly revenge—
                                    [*Fluellen threatens him.*]
I eat and eat—I swear—

FLUELLEN   Eat, I pray you. Will you have some more
sauce to your leek? There is not enough leek to
swear by.

PISTOL
Quiet thy cudgel; thou dost see I eat.

FLUELLEN   Much good do you, scald knave, heartily.
Nay, pray you, throw none away; the skin is good for
your broken coxcomb. When you take occasions to see   54
leeks hereafter, I pray you, mock at 'em, that is all.

PISTOL   Good.

FLUELLEN   Ay, leeks is good. Hold you, there is a groat   57
to heal your pate.   [*He offers a coin.*]

PISTOL   Me, a groat?

FLUELLEN   Yes, verily, and in truth you shall take it, or
I have another leek in my pocket which you shall eat.

PISTOL
I take thy groat in earnest of revenge.   62

FLUELLEN   If I owe you anything, I will pay you in
cudgels. You shall be a woodmonger and buy nothing
of me but cudgels. God b'wi'you, and keep you, and
heal your pate.   *Exit.*

PISTOL   All hell shall stir for this.

GOWER   Go, go, you are a counterfeit cowardly knave.
Will you mock at an ancient tradition, begun upon an
honorable respect and worn as a memorable trophy of   70
predeceased valor, and dare not avouch in your deeds   71
any of your words? I have seen you gleeking and   72
galling at this gentleman twice or thrice. You thought 73
because he could not speak English in the native garb
he could not therefore handle an English cudgel. You
find it otherwise; and henceforth let a Welsh correction teach you a good English condition. Fare
ye well.   *Exit.*

PISTOL
Doth Fortune play the huswife with me now?   79
News have I that my Doll is dead   80
I'th' spital of a malady of France,   81
And there my rendezvous is quite cut off.
Old I do wax, and from my weary limbs   83
Honor is cudgeled. Well, bawd I'll turn,
And something lean to cutpurse of quick hand.   85
To England will I steal, and there I'll steal;
And patches will I get unto these cudgeled scars,
And swear I got them in the Gallia wars.   *Exit.*   88

[5.2]

Enter, at one door, King Henry, Exeter, Bedford,
[Gloucester, Clarence,] Warwick, [Westmorland,]
and other lords; at another, Queen Isabel, the
[French] King, the Duke of Burgundy, [the
Princess Katharine, Alice,] and other French.

KING HENRY
Peace to this meeting, wherefor we are met!
Unto our brother France and to our sister,
Health and fair time of day; joy and good wishes
To our most fair and princely cousin Katharine;
And, as a branch and member of this royalty,   5
By whom this great assembly is contrived,
We do salute you, Duke of Burgundy;
And princes French, and peers, health to you all!

FRENCH KING
Right joyous are we to behold your face,
Most worthy brother England. Fairly met!
So are you, princes English, every one.

20 Parca's (The Parcae, or Fates, spun, drew out, and cut the thread of
destiny.)   21 qualmish squeamish, nauseated   28 Cadwallader sev-
enth-century Welsh warrior king.   goats (Pistol makes the customary
taunt that the Welsh were goatherds.)   35 mountain squire i.e., a
squire owning mountainous, poor land   36 squire of low degree
(Allusion to a popular medieval romance, *The Squire of Low Degree.*
Fluellen threatens to make Pistol into a lowly, contemptible figure,
towered over by a mountain squire.)   38 astonished dazed, terrified
40 pate head   41 green raw   42 coxcomb fool's cap; here, the scalp.
54 broken bleeding (not "fractured")   57 groat fourpenny coin
62 in earnest of as a down payment for

70 respect consideration   71 predeceased valor valor of those now
dead   72–3 gleeking and galling mocking and scoffing   79 huswife
hussy, fickle jade   80 Doll (At 2.1.17–18 we learn that Pistol was married to Nell Quickly. The similarity of *Doll* and *Nell* could suggest a
textual error here, or authorial forgetfulness, or a change in the characters' fortunes.)   81 spital hospital.   malady of France venereal
disease   83 wax grow   85 something lean to I'll incline somewhat
to   88 Gallia French
5.2. Location: The French court.
5 royalty royal family

QUEEN ISABEL
    So happy be the issue, brother England,   12
    Of this good day and of this gracious meeting,
    As we are now glad to behold your eyes—
    Your eyes, which hitherto have borne in them
    Against the French that met them in their bent   16
    The fatal balls of murdering basilisks.   17
    The venom of such looks, we fairly hope,
    Have lost their quality, and that this day
    Shall change all griefs and quarrels into love.   20
KING HENRY
    To cry amen to that, thus we appear.
QUEEN ISABEL
    You English princes all, I do salute you.
BURGUNDY
    My duty to you both, on equal love,
    Great Kings of France and England! That I have
        labored
    With all my wits, my pains, and strong endeavors
    To bring your most imperial Majesties
    Unto this bar and royal interview,   27
    Your mightiness on both parts best can witness.
    Since, then, my office hath so far prevailed
    That, face to face and royal eye to eye,
    You have congreeted, let it not disgrace me   31
    If I demand, before this royal view,   32
    What rub or what impediment there is   33
    Why that the naked, poor, and mangled Peace,
    Dear nurse of arts, plenties, and joyful births,
    Should not in this best garden of the world,
    Our fertile France, put up her lovely visage?   37
    Alas, she hath from France too long been chased,
    And all her husbandry doth lie on heaps,   39
    Corrupting in it own fertility.   40
    Her vine, the merry cheerer of the heart,
    Unprunèd dies; her hedges even-pleached,   42
    Like prisoners wildly overgrown with hair,
    Put forth disordered twigs; her fallow leas   44
    The darnel, hemlock, and rank fumitory   45
    Doth root upon, while that the coulter rusts   46
    That should deracinate such savagery.   47
    The even mead, that erst brought sweetly forth   48
    The freckled cowslip, burnet, and green clover,   49
    Wanting the scythe, all uncorrected, rank,   50
    Conceives by idleness, and nothing teems   51
    But hateful docks, rough thistles, kecksies, burrs, 52
    Losing both beauty and utility.
    And all our vineyards, fallows, meads, and hedges, 54

    Defective in their natures, grow to wildness;   55
    Even so our houses and ourselves and children   56
    Have lost, or do not learn for want of time,
    The sciences that should become our country,   58
    But grow like savages—as soldiers will
    That nothing do but meditate on blood—
    To swearing and stern looks, diffused attire,   61
    And everything that seems unnatural.
    Which to reduce into our former favor   63
    You are assembled, and my speech entreats
    That I may know the let why gentle Peace   65
    Should not expel these inconveniences
    And bless us with her former qualities.
KING HENRY
    If, Duke of Burgundy, you would the peace,   68
    Whose want gives growth to th'imperfections   69
    Which you have cited, you must buy that peace
    With full accord to all our just demands,
    Whose tenors and particular effects   72
    You have enscheduled briefly in your hands.   73
BURGUNDY
    The King hath heard them, to the which as yet
    There is no answer made.
KING HENRY   Well then, the peace,
    Which you before so urged, lies in his answer.
FRENCH KING
    I have but with a cursitory eye   77
    O'erglanced the articles. Pleaseth Your Grace   78
    To appoint some of your council presently
    To sit with us once more, with better heed
    To re-survey them, we will suddenly   81
    Pass our accept and peremptory answer.   82
KING HENRY
    Brother, we shall.—Go, uncle Exeter,
    And brother Clarence, and you, brother Gloucester,
    Warwick, and Huntingdon, go with the King,
    And take with you free power to ratify,
    Augment, or alter, as your wisdoms best
    Shall see advantageable for our dignity,   88
    Anything in or out of our demands,
    And we'll consign thereto.—Will you, fair sister,   90
    Go with the princes, or stay here with us?
QUEEN ISABEL
    Our gracious brother, I will go with them.
    Haply a woman's voice may do some good   93
    When articles too nicely urged be stood on.   94
KING HENRY
    Yet leave our cousin Katharine here with us.
    She is our capital demand, comprised   96
    Within the fore-rank of our articles.   97

---

12 issue outcome   **16 in their bent** (1) as they were directed (2) in their glance   **17 fatal balls** (1) cannonballs (2) eyeballs.   **basilisks** (1) large cannon (2) monsters supposed to kill with their gaze. **20 griefs** grievances   **27 bar** tribunal   **31 congreeted** greeted each other   **32 demand** ask   **33 rub** obstacle. (A term from bowls.) **37 put up** show, lift up   **39 husbandry** harvest, foison   **40 it** its **42 even-pleached** smoothly intertwined   **44 fallow leas** uncultivated open fields   **45 darnel . . . fumitory** i.e., weeds that grow in cultivated land   **46 coulter** plow blade   **47 deracinate** root out   **48 even mead** level meadow.   **erst** formerly   **49 burnet** a herb   **50 Wanting** lacking   **51 Conceives** gives birth (to weeds).   **teems** flourishes **52 kecksies** dry stalks   **54 fallows** land plowed and left lying

55 Defective . . . natures naturally inclined to wildness   **56 houses** households   **58 sciences** skills   **61 diffused** disordered   **63 reduce . . . favor** return to our former good appearance and good graces **65 let** hindrance   **68 would** wish   **69 want** lack   **72 tenors . . . effects** general purport and specific details   **73 enscheduled** drawn up in writing   **77 cursitory** cursory, hasty   **78 Pleaseth** May it please **81 suddenly** speedily   **82 Pass . . . answer** deliver our agreed-to and final answer.   **88 advantageable** advantageous   **90 consign** agree, subscribe   **93 Haply** Perhaps   **94 nicely** punctiliously, with insistence on detail.   **stood on** insisted on.   **96 capital** chief   **97 fore-rank** first row

QUEEN ISABEL
She hath good leave.

*Exeunt omnes. Manent King [Henry]
and Katharine [with Alice].*

KING HENRY   Fair Katharine, and most fair,   98
Will you vouchsafe to teach a soldier terms
Such as will enter at a lady's ear
And plead his love suit to her gentle heart?

KATHARINE   Your Majesty shall mock at me. I cannot
speak your England.

KING HENRY   O fair Katharine, if you will love me
soundly with your French heart, I will be glad to hear
you confess it brokenly with your English tongue. Do
you like me, Kate?

KATHARINE   *Pardonnez-moi,* I cannot tell wat is "like
me."

KING HENRY   An angel is like you, Kate, and you are
like an angel.

KATHARINE [*to Alice*]   *Que dit-il? Que je suis semblable à*   112
les anges?   113

ALICE   *Oui, vraiment, sauf Votre Grâce, ainsi dit-il.*   114

KING HENRY   I said so, dear Katharine, and I must not
blush to affirm it.

KATHARINE   *Oh, bon Dieu! Les langues des hommes sont
pleines de tromperies.*

KING HENRY   What says she, fair one? That the tongues
of men are full of deceits?

ALICE   *Oui,* dat de tongues of de mans is be full of
deceits. Dat is de Princess.

KING HENRY   The Princess is the better Englishwoman.   123
I'faith, Kate, my wooing is fit for thy understanding.
I am glad thou canst speak no better English, for if
thou couldst, thou wouldst find me such a plain king
that thou wouldst think I had sold my farm to buy my
crown. I know no ways to mince it in love, but directly   128
to say, "I love you." Then if you urge me farther than
to say, "Do you, in faith?" I wear out my suit. Give me   130
your answer, i'faith, do, and so clap hands and a   131
bargain. How say you, lady?

KATHARINE   *Sauf votre honneur,* me understand well.

KING HENRY   Marry, if you would put me to verses or
to dance for your sake, Kate, why, you undid me. For
the one I have neither words nor measure, and for the   136
other I have no strength in measure, yet a reasonable   137
measure in strength. If I could win a lady at leapfrog,   138
or by vaulting into my saddle with my armor on my
back, under the correction of bragging be it spoken, I
should quickly leap into a wife. Or if I might buffet for   141
my love, or bound my horse for her favors, I could lay   142
on like a butcher and sit like a jackanapes, never off.   143
But before God, Kate, I cannot look greenly, nor gasp   144
out my eloquence, nor I have no cunning in protesta-

tion—only downright oaths, which I never use till   146
urged, nor never break for urging. If thou canst love a
fellow of this temper, Kate, whose face is not worth   148
sunburning, that never looks in his glass for love of   149
anything he sees there, let thine eye be thy cook. I   150
speak to thee plain soldier. If thou canst love me for
this, take me. If not, to say to thee that I shall die is
true; but for thy love, by the Lord, no. Yet I love thee
too. And while thou liv'st, dear Kate, take a fellow of
plain and uncoined constancy, for he perforce must   155
do thee right, because he hath not the gift to woo in
other places. For these fellows of infinite tongue that
can rhyme themselves into ladies' favors, they do
always reason themselves out again. What? A speaker
is but a prater, a rhyme is but a ballad. A good leg will
fall, a straight back will stoop, a black beard will turn   161
white, a curled pate will grow bald, a fair face will
wither, a full eye will wax hollow; but a good heart,
Kate, is the sun and the moon—or rather the sun and
not the moon, for it shines bright and never changes,
but keeps his course truly. If thou would have such a
one, take me. And take me, take a soldier; take a
soldier, take a king. And what say'st thou then to my
love? Speak, my fair, and fairly, I pray thee.

KATHARINE   Is it possible dat I sould love de *ennemi* of
France?

KING HENRY   No, it is not possible you should love the
enemy of France, Kate; but in loving me you should
love the friend of France, for I love France so well that
I will not part with a village of it. I will have it all mine.
And, Kate, when France is mine and I am yours, then
yours is France and you are mine.

KATHARINE   I cannot tell wat is dat.

KING HENRY   No, Kate? I will tell thee in French, which
I am sure will hang upon my tongue like a new-
married wife about her husband's neck, hardly to be
shook off. *Je quand sur le possession de France, et quand*   182
vous avez le possession de moi—let me see, what?   183
Saint Denis be my speed!—*donc vôtre est France et vous*   184
êtes mienne. It is as easy for me, Kate, to conquer the   185
kingdom as to speak so much more French. I shall
never move thee in French, unless it be to laugh at
me.

KATHARINE   *Sauf votre honneur, le français que vous parlez,*   189
il est meilleur que l' anglais lequel je parle.   190

KING HENRY   No, faith, is't not, Kate. But thy speaking
of my tongue, and I thine, most truly-falsely, must   192
needs be granted to be much at one. But, Kate, dost   193
thou understand thus much English: Canst thou
love me?

---

98 s.d. *omnes* all. *Manent* They remain onstage   112–14 *Que . . .*
ainsi dit-il? What does he say? That I am like the angels? ALICE Yes,
truly, save Your Grace, he says so.   123 **is . . . Englishwoman** i.e., is
the better for preferring honesty.   128 **mince it** speak coyly
130 **wear out my suit** expend all my resources as a wooer.   131 **clap**
clasp   136 **measure** (skill in) meter   137 **measure** dance
138 **measure** amount, aptitude   141 **buffet** box   142 **bound** make
prance   143 **jackanapes** ape, monkey   144 **greenly** like a lovesick
youth

146 **downright** straightforward   148–9 **not . . . sunburning** i.e.,
already so tanned that more sun could make it worse. (Tanned and
dark complexions were generally considered unhandsome.)
149 **glass** mirror   150 **be thy cook** dress up and garnish my plain
looks.   155 **uncoined** (1) not put into circulation (2) unalloyed, fixed,
steady   161 **fall** shrink, lose its shapeliness   182–5 *Je . . . mienne*
(Henry haltingly translates into French the last sentence of his previous speech.)   184 **Saint Denis** patron saint of France.   **be my speed**
help me.   189–90 *Sauf . . . parle* Saving your honor, the French that
you speak is better than the English that I speak.   192 **truly-falsely**
true-heartedly but incorrectly   193 **at one** alike.

KATHARINE   I cannot tell.

KING HENRY   Can any of your neighbors tell, Kate? I'll ask them. Come, I know thou lovest me. And at night, when you come into your closet, you'll question 199 this gentlewoman about me; and I know, Kate, you will to her dispraise those parts in me that you love with your heart. But, good Kate, mock me mercifully, the rather, gentle Princess, because I love thee cruelly. If ever thou be'st mine, Kate, as I have a saving faith within me tells me thou shalt, I get thee with scambling, and thou must therefore needs prove a 206 good soldier-breeder. Shall not thou and I, between Saint Denis and Saint George, compound a boy, half French, half English, that shall go to Constantinople and take the Turk by the beard? Shall we not? What say'st thou, my fair flower-de-luce? 211

KATHARINE   I do not know dat.

KING HENRY   No; 'tis hereafter to know, but now to promise. Do but now promise, Kate, you will endeavor for your French part of such a boy, and for my English moiety take the word of a king and a bachelor. 216 How answer you, *la plus belle Katharine du monde, mon* 217 *très cher et devin déesse?* 218

KATHARINE   Your Majestee 'ave *fausse* French enough 219 to deceive de most *sage demoiselle* dat is *en France.*

KING HENRY   Now, fie upon my false French! By mine honor, in true English, I love thee, Kate; by which honor I dare not swear thou lovest me, yet my blood begins to flatter me that thou dost, notwithstanding the poor and untempering effect of my visage. Now 225 beshrew my father's ambition! He was thinking of civil 226 wars when he got me; therefore was I created with a stubborn outside, with an aspect of iron, that when I 228 come to woo ladies I fright them. But in faith, Kate, the elder I wax the better I shall appear. My comfort is that old age, that ill layer-up of beauty, can do no more spoil upon my face. Thou hast me, if thou hast me, at the worst; and thou shalt wear me, if thou wear me, better and better. And therefore tell me, most fair Katharine, will you have me? Put off your maiden blushes; avouch the thoughts of your heart with the 236 looks of an empress; take me by the hand, and say, "Harry of England, I am thine." Which word thou shalt no sooner bless mine ear withal, but I will tell thee aloud, "England is thine, Ireland is thine, France is thine, and Henry Plantagenet is thine"—who, though I speak it before his face, if he be not fellow with the best king, thou shalt find the best king 243 of good fellows. Come, your answer in broken music! 244 For thy voice is music, and thy English broken. Therefore, queen of all, Katharine, break thy mind to 246 me in broken English. Wilt thou have me?

KATHARINE   Dat is as it shall please de *roi mon père.* 248

KING HENRY   Nay, it will please him well, Kate. It shall please him, Kate.

KATHARINE   Den it sall also content me.

KING HENRY   Upon that I kiss your hand, and I call you my queen.   [*He attempts to kiss her hand.*]

KATHARINE   *Laissez, mon seigneur, laissez, laissez! Ma* 254 *foi, je ne veux point que vous abaissiez votre grandeur* 255 *en baisant la main d'une—Notre Seigneur!—indigne* 256 *serviteur. Excusez-moi, je vous supplie, mon très-puissant* 257 *seigneur.* 258

KING HENRY   Then I will kiss your lips, Kate.

KATHARINE   *Les dames et demoiselles pour être baisées* 260 *devant leur noces, il n'est pas la coutume de France.* 261

KING HENRY   [*to Alice*]   Madam my interpreter, what says she?

ALICE   Dat it is not be de fashion *pour les* ladies of France—I cannot tell wat is *baiser* en Anglish.

KING HENRY   To kiss.

ALICE   Your Majestee *entend* bettre *que moi.* 267

KING HENRY   It is not a fashion for the maids in France to kiss before they are married, would she say?

ALICE   *Oui, vraiment.* 270

KING HENRY   Oh, Kate, nice customs curtsy to great 271 kings. Dear Kate, you and I cannot be confined within the weak list of a country's fashion. We are the mak- 273 ers of manners, Kate; and the liberty that follows our 274 places stops the mouth of all find-faults, as I will do yours, for upholding the nice fashion of your country in de-nying me a kiss. Therefore, patiently and yielding. [*He kisses her.*] You have witchcraft in your lips, Kate. There is more eloquence in a sugar touch of them than in the tongues of the French council, and they should sooner persuade Harry of England than a general petition of monarchs.—Here comes your father.

Enter the French power and the English lords.

BURGUNDY   God save Your Majesty! My royal cousin, teach you our princess English?

KING HENRY   I would have her learn, my fair cousin, how perfectly I love her, and that is good English.

BURGUNDY   Is she not apt?

KING HENRY   Our tongue is rough, coz, and my condi- 288 tion is not smooth; so that, having neither the voice 289 nor the heart of flattery about me, I cannot so conjure up the spirit of love in her that he will appear in his true likeness.

---

199 **closet** private chamber   206 **scambling** the scuffles of war
211 **flower-de-luce** fleur-de-lis, the emblem of France.   216 **moiety**
half   217–18 *la plus . . . déesse* the most beautiful Katharine in the
world, my very dear and divine goddess.   219 *fausse* i.e., false (both
"incorrect" and "deceptive")   225 **untempering** unsettling, unsoften-
ing   226 **beshrew** curses on   228 **aspect** appearance   236 **avouch**
vouch for, confirm   243 **fellow with** on equal terms with   244 **broken music** (Henry quibbles on the term for music composed in parts
for different instruments.)   246 **break** open

248 *de roi mon père* the King my father.   254–8 *Laissez . . . seigneur*
Don't, my lord, don't, don't! By my faith, I do not wish you to
lower your greatness by kissing the hand of an—our dear Lord!—
unworthy servant; excuse me, I beg you, my most powerful lord.
(*Serviteur* is masculine and not appropriately applied to a lady, but
the error may be Shakespeare's.)   260–1 *Les dames . . . France* It is
not customary in France for ladies and young girls to be kissed before
their marriage.   267 *entend . . . moi* understands better than I.
270 *Oui, vraiment* Yes, truly.   271 **nice** fastidious   273 **list** limit,
barrier   274 **follows our places** attends our (high) rank   288 **Our
tongue** (1) Our English language (2) My soldierly speech   288–9 **condition** soldierly manner

BURGUNDY   Pardon the frankness of my mirth, if I
answer you for that. If you would conjure in her, you 294
must make a circle; if conjure up love in her in his true
likeness, he must appear naked and blind. Can you 296
blame her then, being a maid yet rosed over with the 297
virgin crimson of modesty, if she deny the appearance 298
of a naked blind boy in her naked seeing self? It were, 299
my lord, a hard condition for a maid to consign to. 300
KING HENRY   Yet they do wink and yield, as love is 301
blind and enforces. 302
BURGUNDY   They are then excused, my lord, when they
see not what they do.
KING HENRY   Then, good my lord, teach your cousin to
consent winking.
BURGUNDY   I will wink on her to consent, my lord, if 307
you will teach her to know my meaning; for maids,
well summered and warm kept, are like flies at Bar- 309
tholomew-tide: blind, though they have their eyes, 310
and then they will endure handling, which before 311
would not abide looking on.
KING HENRY   This moral ties me over to time and a hot 313
summer; and so I shall catch the fly, your cousin, in 314
the latter end, and she must be blind too.
BURGUNDY   As love is, my lord, before it loves. 316
KING HENRY   It is so; and you may, some of you, thank
love for my blindness, who cannot see many a fair 318
French city for one fair French maid that stands in 319
my way. 320
FRENCH KING   Yes, my lord, you see them perspectively, 321
the cities turned into a maid; for they are all girdled
with maiden walls that war hath never entered. 323
KING HENRY   Shall Kate be my wife?
FRENCH KING   So please you.
KING HENRY   I am content, so the maiden cities you talk 326
of may wait on her. So the maid that stood in the way 327
for my wish shall show me the way to my will. 328
FRENCH KING
We have consented to all terms of reason.
KING HENRY   Is't so, my lords of England?

WESTMORLAND
The King hath granted every article:
His daughter first, and then in sequel all
According to their firm proposèd natures. 333
EXETER
Only he hath not yet subscribèd this: 334
Where Your Majesty demands that the King of France,
having any occasion to write for matter of grant, shall 336
name Your Highness in this form and with this ad- 337
dition, in French, *Notre très cher fils Henri, Roi* 338
d'Angleterre, Héritier de France; and thus in Latin, 339
Praeclarissimus filius noster Henricus, Rex Angliae et 340
Haeres Franciae.
FRENCH KING
Nor this I have not, brother, so denied 342
But your request shall make me let it pass. 343
KING HENRY
I pray you then, in love and dear alliance,
Let that one article rank with the rest,
And thereupon give me your daughter.
FRENCH KING
Take her, fair son, and from her blood raise up
Issue to me, that the contending kingdoms
Of France and England, whose very shores look pale
With envy of each other's happiness,
May cease their hatred, and this dear conjunction
Plant neighborhood and Christian-like accord
In their sweet bosoms, that never war advance
His bleeding sword twixt England and fair France.
LORDS   Amen!
KING HENRY
Now, welcome, Kate; and bear me witness all,
That here I kiss her as my sovereign queen.
                              [*He kisses her.*] *Flourish.*
QUEEN ISABEL
God, the best maker of all marriages,
Combine your hearts in one, your realms in one!
As man and wife, being two, are one in love,
So be there twixt your kingdoms such a spousal 361
That never may ill office, or fell jealousy, 362
Which troubles oft the bed of blessèd marriage,
Thrust in between the paction of these kingdoms 364
To make divorce of their incorporate league;
That English may as French, French Englishmen,
Receive each other. God speak this "Amen"!
ALL   Amen!
KING HENRY
Prepare we for our marriage, on which day,
My lord of Burgundy, we'll take your oath,
And all the peers', for surety of our leagues.
Then shall I swear to Kate, and you to me;

---

294 conjure in her (with bawdy double meaning of raising up something within her *circle*, line 295) **296 naked and blind** (as Cupid is conventionally portrayed) **297 yet rosed over** still blushing **298–9 if . . . self** if she refuses to admit the entry of a naked boy in her sight, or herself being naked? **300 a hard condition** (Suggesting erection.) **consign** agree **301–2 Yet . . . enforces** Yet young maidens do close their eyes and say yes, prompted to do so by their own bashfulness and male importunity. **307 wink on her** give her an encouraging wink **309 summered** nurtured **309–10 Bartholomew-tide** August 24 (when flies, bees, etc., are sluggish) **311 handling** (1) handling of the beehive (2) sexual handling **313–14 This moral . . . summer** The lesson of your fable would oblige me to wait for the heat of summer **316 As . . . loves** (Love is blind before it loves, because it cannot yet see the beloved and because love has not yet opened the lover's eyes.) **318–20 who . . . my way** i.e., since I am so preoccupied with Katharine that I have forgotten for the moment about all those French towns I want. (He is joking; he gets the French towns, along with her.) **321 perspectively** i.e., as in an optical device that presents different images when viewed from different angles **323 maiden** unbreached. (With a sexual metaphor, continued in *entered*.) **326 so** provided that **327 wait on her** attend her, go along with her (as part of her dowry). **328 will** (1) intention of ruling France (2) sexual desire.

333 According . . . natures exactly as specified in the proposals. **334 subscribèd** agreed to, signed to **336 for . . . grant** in official deeds, granting title to land and the like **337–8 addition** title **338–9 Notre . . . France** i.e., Our very dear son Henry, King of England, Heir of France **340 Praeclarissimus** most famous. (Presumably an error for "*Praecharissimus*" or "*Praecarissimus*," "most dear." Shakespeare is following Holinshed, who took the error from Hall.) **342 so** so firmly **343 But** but that **361 spousal** marriage **362 ill office** unfriendly dealings. **fell** cruel **364 paction** alliance, compact

And may our oaths well kept and prosperous be!

Sennet.   *Exeunt.*

[Epilogue]

Enter Chorus.

CHORUS

Thus far, with rough and all-unable pen,
  Our bending author hath pursued the story,   2
In little room confining mighty men,
  Mangling by starts the full course of their glory.   4

Small time, but in that small most greatly lived   5
  This star of England. Fortune made his sword,
By which the world's best garden he achieved,   7
  And of it left his son imperial lord.
Henry the Sixth, in infant bands crowned King   9
  Of France and England, did this king succeed;
Whose state so many had the managing,
  That they lost France and made his England bleed,
Which oft our stage hath shown; and, for their sake,   13
In your fair minds let this acceptance take.   [*Exit.*]   14

Epilogue.
2 bending i.e., under the weight of his task   **4 by starts** in fits and
starts, in fragments

5 Small time (Henry V ruled for only nine years, dying at the age of
thirty-five.)   **7 best garden** i.e., France   **9 infant bands** swaddling
clothes   **13 Which . . . shown** (Refers to the three parts of *King Henry
VI.*)   **their** i.e., the actors and the author, the presenters on *our stage*
(line 13)   **14 let . . . take** let this play meet with your approval.

Henry V on Stage

The Elizabethan Era: In a Public Theater— A Topical Play

Although scholars generally agree that the play was
first performed in the spring or summer of 1599, the
early historical record is unusually sketchy and conflicting. It was first performed either at the new Globe
in Southwark ("this wooden O") or at the Curtain Theater, from which Shakespeare's company moved to the
Globe. It is also generally accepted that Richard
Burbage, the leading tragedian of the Lord Chamberlain's Men, played Henry V and that many of the smaller roles were doubled as they are today. Boys played the
women's roles. The gallery over the stage doors could
suggest the battlements and gates of Harfleur. Costuming was no doubt contemporary, as the armaments and
weapons would also be, even though the historical setting of the play is circa 1415. The few props required are
a throne, ladders, and small pieces of ordnance off stage
to create sound effects at the end of the Chorus's speech
in Act 3. Compared with the scenic elaboration of later
ages and the thrilling sights and sounds of battle in the
two classic films, the original staging must have been
simplicity itself. When the Chorus asks the audience to
imagine thundering horses "Printing their proud
hooves i'th' receiving earth," who could have predicted the Victorian productions in which Henry rode
proudly into London on a real white steed or the
Branagh movie in which mounted soldiers fight one
another in thick mud?

When the London stages reopened after the
Restoration, we find several mentions of a *Henry V*,
though apparently not exclusively by Shakespeare.
Adapters Colley Cibber, and later Charles Molloy,
seem to have imported certain set pieces from *Henry V*,
including in the first instance several rhetorical flourishes, and in the second, its comic elements featuring
the king's old Boar's Head companions Pistol, Nym,
and Bardolph.

The definitive stage history of *Henry V* does not
begin, ironically enough, until its reclamation in 1738
by the Shakespeare Ladies' Club.

The Eighteenth and Nineteenth Centuries: Spectacle and the Restored Text

That Ladies' Club petitioned Covent Garden's John
Rich to revive more Shakespeare instead of the Restoration comedy then still in vogue. In February 1738, *Henry
V* was performed four times "at the Desire of Several
Ladies of Quality" (Scouten, *The London Stage*, 704) and
soon after was firmly established, with performances
becoming frequent during the wars with France in the
middle and late years of the century. As the productions
became more elaborate owing to the innovation of
changeable scenery, speeches of the Chorus apologizing for the meager means of the theater became problematic for the actor, as they are now for a modern film
director. David Garrick is known to have spoken the
Chorus's lines in 1747 and 1748, but they were omitted
from John Philip Kemble's landmark production that
was popular from 1789 through 1848 as audiences
swelled with anti-French sentiment stoked by the
Napoleonic Wars. Fourteen different sets were
employed for the production's nineteen scenes. A stage
full of extras created such pageantry as military marches
through gates opening onto a bridge. Kemble's production was unabashedly patriotic and spectacular.

Actor-manager William Charles Macready restored
the Chorus to *Henry V* in 1839. He also added a moving
diorama of the fleet sailing to Harfleur, while the Chorus was asking the audience to imagine it. Reviews

remarked upon the lavishness of the costuming and the hero's polished steel armor, even while Macready's performance was disparaged as less heroic than Kemble's.

Charles Kean's 1859 production went several steps farther, reconstructing the gatehouse at the end of the old London Bridge for the King's return. In a watercolor by F. Loyds based on William Telbin's stage designs, the scene depicts a host of girls, dressed in diaphanous gowns, wearing angel wings, and playing tambourines to welcome the King. Others above the gatehouse dropped gold coins on the returning monarch, who was on horseback, surrounded by scores of citizens looking like movie extras. Kean solved what was perceived as another problem—the play's presumed lack of appeal to women—by casting his wife as the Chorus interpreted as the Muse of History. As noted in Part One, Chapter 2, such spectacular productions required long scene changes, and so actor-managers such as Macready and Kean cut the text to make room for the elaborate sets. They and their successor Charles Calvert sought a kind of archeological accuracy in their elaborate, if stylized, stagings. Clearly, these Victorian-era pageant productions viewed Henry as an unalloyed hero.

The Twentieth Century: Stagings Through World War II—Irony and Patriotism

William Poel challenged these elaborate Victorian spectacles with simpler productions by his Elizabethan Stage Society. His 1901 staging of *Henry V*, first in the open air of Stratford and later at Burlington Gardens in London, dispensed with cumbersome sets, although Poel's Henry (Robert Loraine) still entered gallantly on a white horse for his St. Crispin's Day speech. Critical opinion was beginning to turn in Poel's direction; reviewers noted that it is useless to try to make Shakespeare's essentially poetic dramas realistic. *Henry V*, particularly, must "on [our] imaginary forces work." From Poel on, the twentieth century was to begin tilting toward anti-illusionistic, continuous staging instead of the display pieces of the heavily-upholstered Victorians.

Emma Smith, in her *Shakespeare in Production, "King Henry V,"* cites a pair of productions (42) influenced by research into the original staging of Shakespeare's play. John Martin-Harvey's 1916 production was "in the Elizabethan manner," according to the playbill at His Majesty's Theatre in London. William Bridges-Adams also attempted this kind of presumed Elizabethan authenticity again in 1920 with a nearly uncut production that moved quickly and fluently on a relatively uncluttered stage. Bridges-Adams produced and directed, but did not star in, the production, thus forecasting the coming age of the director. And as World War I's devastating lessons about war sank in, *Henry V* began to seem a more thematically complex and emotionally nuanced play.

An influential essay by Gerald Gould in *The English Review* of 1919 radically reinterpreted the play, saying that none of Shakespeare's works had been so "thoroughly misunderstood" as *Henry V*. "Irony is an awkward weapon," he continued, attempting to explain why, hundreds of years after Shakespeare's death, even the educated failed to see that the play was ironic, a satire of the imperialism it seems to promote. The following year, an *Athenaeum* reviewer of Bridges-Adams's production opened another revolutionary new avenue of *Henry V* criticism. He wrote that if Shakespeare had really wanted to write a patriotic pageant, he would never have mentioned that lovable deflater of patriotism and honor, the Sir John Falstaff so cruelly rejected by Henry. These skeptical responses have colored readings of the play ever since—even Olivier's overtly patriotic film.

That famed film is partially based upon the 1937 production directed by Tyrone Guthrie at the Old Vic, featuring Olivier as Henry. Olivier has written in his autobiography (*Confessions of an Actor* 1982) that he was uncomfortable with the traditional declamatory style employed for the part, saying that Guthrie pushed him toward heightening his delivery because "you're taking all the thrill out of the play, and for heaven's sake that's all it's got!" Olivier presented a heroic Henry, but one who was nonetheless filled with self-doubts. The actor later toured the military camps with a one-man show geared to cheering the troops and culminating in Henry's speech before the Battle of Agincourt. "By the time I got to 'God for Harry' I think they would have followed me anywhere," Olivier wrote.

Postmodern Stagings: The Histories in Sequence. When in the 1950s, the history plays were beginning to be viewed as a sequence, *Henry V* seemed in that context to be less of a hero than before. Anthony Quayle's production at Stratford in 1951 was one of the first to stage the play as the culmination of a sequence beginning with *Richard II* and continuing through *Henry IV, Parts One* and *Two*. Richard Burton was Henry, with Michael Redgrave as the Chorus in a production that unfolded on the same utilitarian set as the other three plays. Burton reprised the role effectively in 1955, creating, according to the esteemed critic Kenneth Tynan, "a cunning warrior, stocky and astute, unafraid of harshness or of curling the royal lip."

Peter Hall and John Barton repeated the idea of presenting the play in a historical sequence when they staged the complete cycle of two tetralogies during the Shakespeare Quartercentenary celebrations in 1964. Ian Holm was the young king. The production was strongly influenced by Jan Kott's cynical view of the history plays as a "Grand Mechanism." To most astute reviewers, the production managed to be at once admiring of Henry and yet anti-war, as it conveyed something of the sheer boredom and dogged persistence required in battle. This was the first *Henry V* geared to a rebellious, anti-authoritarian generation. That mood was picked up by an American production, directed by Michael Kahn for the American Shakespeare Festival in Stratford, Connecticut, in 1969. Kahn, who now directs The Shakespeare Theatre in Washington, D.C., employed Brechtian alienation techniques; for example, he prefaced each scene with a wise-cracking announcement of its title, and arranged matters so that the dead of Agincourt remained on stage throughout the later wooing scene. The Englishmen were dressed in jeans, the French in bulky sporting gear. As Henry, Len Cariou perched on a swing in the early and closing scenes in what appeared to be a large playground. Reviewers were as negative as Kahn's view of the protagonist.

Another innovative and strongly ideological staging by the German director Peter Zadek, called *Held Henry,* has been described as a multimedia "pacifist collage." The title is ironic; "Held" means hero in German. Zadek deconstructed the play to show that patriotism is a created emotion and that the hero is a product of cult worship and manipulation. The eclectic production flashed images of Hitler's troops marching into Paris, followed by images of Stalin, Billy Graham, sports stars, and other celebrities. This Henry was telegenic and media-conscious, a demagogic hero for the television age.

Two later productions in the aftermath of the Falklands War presented strikingly postmodern images of the soldier-king. Adrian Noble's 1984 production at Stratford-upon-Avon, starring the young Kenneth Branagh, became the basis for the actor's popular film five years later. Noble (and Branagh) took on the double-edged history of interpretation, presenting a Henry who is complex, neither simply good nor consciously evil. Visually, the production's keynote was the muddy, wet reality of modern warfare. Bardolph was hanged on stage as the troops watched, huddled in the rain. Branagh, who has compared Henry to Hamlet in his haunting by his father and their troubled relationship, consulted Prince Charles of England's royal family to learn something of the conflict between leadership, responsibility, and compassion.

More radical still was Michael Bogdanov's production for the English Shakespeare Company (1986). Determined to work outside the major institutions such as the Royal Shakespeare Company and the National Theatre, and to bring Shakespeare's history plays to people in the provinces far from London, Bogdanov staged the two tetralogies in aggressively modern style, to underscore the basic connection between the political questions raised in the histories and those of late–twentieth-century Britain. Notoriously, Bogdanov visualized Henry's expeditionary army as a crowd of unruly footballers chanting " 'Ere we go" and carrying a banner with the slogan "Fuck the Frogs!" This English Shakespeare Company was untroubled that so many in the audience vociferously cheered and that others protested the subversive production. This challenge to what Bogdanov and actor Michael Pennington viewed as the conservatism of most Shakespeare productions was shared by other touring companies: Cheek by Jowl, who focused on subverting Shakespeare's sexual politics, and Northern Broadsides, whose Northern speech gave a strongly sardonic cast to Henry's attempt to unify a multicultural nation.

Like Poel's experiments in Elizabethan staging at the beginning of the century, Richard Olivier's 1997 production, staged to open London's new Globe Theatre and filmed for television, became part of a countervailing tradition. With the newly built stage created in imitation of the best information historical scholarship could recover, the production used an all-male cast, deemphasized the brutal elements of Henry's character, and played up the comedy scenes. Richard Olivier (son of Sir Laurence and Joan Plowright) said he was exploring the "myth" of the play. The production sought and achieved a lively interchange with audiences, encouraging booing of the French emissaries, approval of the slaughter of the French prisoners, and a winking laughter at the comedy of a cross-dressed man as Katharine. Mark Rylance was Henry V, a pious and conscience-stricken monarch, according to the London reviews.

Henry V on Film and Video

Two great films, different in emphases for their differing times, have been adapted from *The Life of Henry V*. Olivier's, the first of his three Shakespeare films, was released in 1944, at the height of the World War II when Winston Churchill was rousing the British nation with the same rhetorical fervor that marks King Henry's speeches to his soldiers. Kenneth Branagh's darker, more skeptical 1989 film, no doubt undertaken in response to Olivier's as well as to the then-recent Falklands War, engages in a more complex way the ethical issues surrounding war and politics which the play, read as a whole, does certainly raise. Both of these stage actors directed and starred in their films. Two of the seven televised adaptations of *Henry V* are also surveyed below.

■ 1944—Producer and director Laurence Olivier, Rank Films, with Olivier (Henry V), Michael Warre (Gloucester), Brian Nissen (Court/Chorus), Nicholas Hannen (Exeter), Robert Helpmann (Bardolph), and Leo Genn (Constable of France). (137 min.)

Olivier's dazzling film, a popular and artistic success, led on to two decades of international Shakespeare adaptations from such directors as Orson Welles, Franco Zeffirelli, and Akira Kurosawa. Olivier famously opens *Henry V* with an overhead shot of old London and the Globe (a model in reality) on the south side of the Thames, followed by some wonderful backstage comedy of the actors preparing: Olivier himself coughs to ready his voice and a boy player stuffs oranges in his bosom for his female role as Katherine. The Chorus is a gallant (Leslie Banks) in Renaissance dress. And the clergymen who explicate Salic law prove comical figures, bumbling and inept as they disorder their papers and lose them all over the stage. The Globe itself is a boisterous place, filled with life and color. The responsive audience cheers Falstaff's name, mocks the comic actors playing Bardolph, Nym, and Pistol, and applauds Olivier's robust Henry when he rebuffs the French and their insulting gift of tennis balls.

Olivier, creating the picture to rouse the patriotic English against a new enemy, Hitler, succeeded artistically and commercially. The opening scene at the Globe is a kind of archeological charmer, comical and exaggerated. His depiction of the theater suggests (as the Chorus does) the limitations of the stage, but also the intimate, almost democratic relationship among audience members and the actors. Who wouldn't want to be an Englishman in this context? The style shifts closer toward realism when the fleet gathers at Southampton, however, and Olivier's compositional eye delivers scene after scene that—like Shakespeare's language—is both formally precise and beautiful, yet also suggestive of down-to-earth human psychology.

The costume designs reflect the central contrast between the manly English and the more effeminate French here, as the earth-toned aristocrats and soldiers appear plainspoken and human compared to the proud, pastel-dressed French with their mad, vacuous king who sits on the floor amidst bored nobles playing games or painting.

England is the aggressor in this war. Olivier's comical scene with the bishops and several shrewd cuts disguise this fact. The French are depicted as so over-civilized they border on the decadent. The heightened contrasts between the two nations and the cutting of such manipulations as Henry's trap set for the traitors, as well as the threatening speech at the gates of Harfleur, almost guarantee a softened, and positive view of Henry—"no tyrant, but a Christian king."

Still, the film is far more than propaganda. The Falstaff scenes suggest both the cost of kingship when Henry rejects him, and later, a heartfelt melancholy that the old companion has died. The battle sequences (see "Frame-by-Frame") introduce a third visual vocabulary to the film. Shot in the muddy fields of Ireland, the battle scenes are thrilling. Agincourt's pageant-like beginnings devolve into the murder of the boys, the swashbuckling drop of English archers from the trees, the fantastically effective sounds of their whizzing arrows, many glimpses of corpses, and struggling horses without riders, and the *Te Deum* sounding toward the end, all of which is presided over by a charismatic young prince who, in the later French scenes with their return to embroidered romance, seems born from a fairy tale. When the film reverts to its opening conventions in the Elizabethan theater, it is as if we have watched the pages of a storybook turn, its various panels pleasing the eye with three distinct periods and styles, while the whole unites play, filmed play, and film in one highly entertaining, stylistically eclectic, and important work of visual art.

■ 1989—Director Kenneth Branagh, BBC/Renaissance Films; with Derek Jacobi (The Chorus), Paul Scofield (French King), Richard Easton (Constable), Judi Dench (Mistress Quickly), Katherine (Emma Thompson), Alec McCowen (Ely), Ian Holm (Fluellen), and Michael Maloney (Dauphin). (137 min.)

Branagh's interpretation as an actor differs significantly from Olivier's. He portrays Henry as isolated, preoccupied, and betrayed—very much, it turns out, a Hamlet figure. These internalized moments, conveyed in a near-Method acting style, create a hero who is cool, obviously calculating, even ruthless—though serious and genuinely pious, it appears, despite his callowness.

The differences and borrowings from Olivier assert themselves immediately. Branagh's film begins in darkness in a movie studio, site of the twentieth century's predominant art form, not in the sunny outdoors of Olivier's Globe scene. In that darkness, a match is struck, echoing the "Oh, for a Muse of fire" first line. The chorus figure (Derek Jacobi in a scarf and long overcoat) opens great clanking double doors that dwarf the historical figures behind them.

The most distinctive traits of Branagh's film are its almost unrelenting darkness of mood, a muddy, messy, bloody battle, and a careful amassing of interpretive particulars. Unlike Olivier, he does lead the traitors on to trick them into confessing their crime; he does viciously threaten the residents of Harfleur; and he is present (even shedding a tear) when his old pal Bardolph is hanged.

Like Olivier, on the other hand, Branagh interpolates scenes with Falstaff that do not actually appear in the text. One wordless image early on in Branagh's film shows the face of the dying Falstaff with a concerned Mistress Quickly (Judi Dench) leaning over him. We see them in a bedroom at the Boar's Head Tavern, followed by a montage of scenes in flashback: Falstaff is shown in the happy company of Pistol, Nym, and the others, and then distraught as he is rejected by Prince Hal (from *Henry IV, Part Two*, 3.2 and 5.5). Another flashback to the old knight shows Prince Hal in the foreground in an aside repeating what he will do to Falstaff and the "use" he will make of his wild days.

Similarly, when King Henry signals for his former companion Bardolph, who has been raiding French churches, to be hanged, Branagh cuts to the Boar's Head Tavern for a foreshadowing flashback from *Henry IV, Part One*. The camera, returning to Henry, finds him weeping as he justifies the execution on the ground of discipline and the rules of war. In a similar emotional vein, a bloodied Henry carries the body of the murdered Boy through the battleground, thus justifying the retaliatory order to kill French prisoners.

And in that penultimate scene before the negotiations that lead to his marriage, we see the horror and bleakness of victory. The exhausted victors follow Henry to the sounds of a swelling requiem as he places the child in a cart and kisses him. A prolonged tracking shot follows, highlighting his exhausted, bloody, mud-streaked face. Those images are not fully counterbalanced by the harmonies achieved in the final scenes with the defeated French, although Branagh is paired with a witty Katharine (his then wife, Emma Thompson), who projects a kind of sexual autonomy that certainly lightens and complicates her role as the spoils of war.

Branagh's "little touch of Harry in the night" scenes are especially effective when Henry is alone with his doubts and fears. He seems genuinely devout as he prays, worrying that he might inherit the guilt of his father who took the crown from Richard II. (Olivier deletes that particular worry.) Branagh takes a skeptical, cynical approach to the whole idea of war, although his shrewd, cool Harry has many other attractive dimensions—his piety, his easy, seemingly natural rhetorical skill, his courage in battle, and most especially his charm as the unlikely wooer. In a fine historical irony, Branagh was praised for his film by Prince Charles just after the English incursion into the Falklands.

- 1979—Director David Giles, BBC Television, with David Gwillim (Henry), Alec McGowen (Chorus), Jocelyne Boisseau (Katherine), Julian Glover (French Constable), and Thorley Walters (Charles VI). (160 min.)

Not the first televised version of *Henry V*, this production was part of the series co-produced by the BBC and Time-Life, first broadcast in December 1979. Giles treats the studio set anti-illusionistically so that the Chorus's speeches will continue to make sense. He places realistic facades against a white cyclorama; thus his long shots show the limitations of the studio forthrightly before he moves the camera in closer for the "real" scenes. The Chorus moves into the frame from darkness; as he walks forward the lights come up and he steps between various persons from each court as if giving the viewer a guided tour of the political situation before the action begins. Color distinctions between the French and English make the story easier to follow for television viewers, and the small-scale production uses close-ups and medium shots, which lend the production both intimacy and a domestic feeling. Such choices create a static, iconic image of the king by shooting Gwillim so often in ways that turns his profile into iconography.

The production, available on video, has not been well received, partly because it seems an interpretive throwback to a simpler, if not naïve, view of the hero, and also because its studio-bound approach to filmmaking lacked excitement, especially for those accustomed to the Olivier and later, the Branagh film.

- 1990—Director Michael Bogdanov, with Michael Pennington (Henry). Video adaptation of this part of the ESC's second tetralogy.

Bogdanov views the histories as plays for today and sees *Henry V* as particularly modern, with, as he has put it, "its war of expedience, ruthless manipulation, bribery and corruption . . . and, the French superior in numbers but beaten by superior technology." As this statement from *The English Shakespeare Company: The Story of the Wars of the Roses, 1986–1989* suggests, Bogdanov's interpretation is unambiguous: he reads *Henry V* as an anti-war play and its hero (played by Michael Pennington) as a monarch capable of declaring English hegemony.

In one of his more original touches, Pennington repeatedly suggests that Henry V is in the early stages of the dysentery that killed him so soon after his son was born. With that image, underscored by the Epilogue, comes a reminder of the transitoriness of his victories. "Imperialism encourages jingoism. So the Falklands. So Agincourt." Relentless in its cynicism, the staging is a controversial triumph. This profoundly political reading juxtaposes rock and elegiac classical music as the collaborators suggest that not only do kings rise and fall, as this one will, and his father did before him, and his son will after him, but also that nations suffer such unpredictable cycles as well, one of which may have been beginning again as the twentieth century ended with ethnic clashes worldwide.

TWO BATTLES AT AGINCOURT: OLIVIER AND BRANAGH

Although two of the most popular films adapted from Shakespeare contain rousing military scenes depicting the Battle of Agincourt, the playwright did not actually dramatize this famous English victory. The text of *The Life of King Henry V* moves toward this predetermined climax, yet has few of the "alarums and excursions" that signal onstage fighting in other history plays—the *Henry IV, Part One* battles at Shrewsbury, Richard III's at Bosworth Field, or the Roman conspirators' conflicts at Philippi in *Julius Caesar*. The Chorus instead prepares the audience for the scenic minimalism of *Henry V* at the opening of Act 4 when he says:

> And so our scene must to the battle fly;
> Where—oh for pity!—we shall much disgrace
> With four or five most vile and ragged foils,
> Right ill-disposed in brawl ridiculous,
> The name of Agincourt. Yet sit and see,
> Minding true things by what their mockeries be.
>
> (4.0.48–53)

Details of the battle are then reported by soldiers and the Chorus, not enacted. The one scene that might properly be judged a battlefield encounter is something of a joke: the passage at 4.4 introduced by the sole direction *Alarum. Excursions.*" This truly is a "brawl ridiculous," for it involves the cutpurse Pistol, the quaking French soldier Monsieur Le Fer, and the Boy.

In this short comic turn, placed in the Quarto and Folio texts at the beginning of the Agincourt conflict, Pistol, ignorant yet confident and understanding no French, asks the Boy to translate his own speeches and his captive's. When the French soldier learns that Pistol is ready to cut his throat, he offers two hundred crowns to his captor to spare his life, a bargain the greedy Pistol readily accepts. With even the Boy describing Pistol mockingly ("The empty vessel makes the greatest sound" [4.4.70–71]), the scene not only suspends the lofty tone of the St. Crispin's Day rhetoric that comes before it but also burlesques the whole notion of military honor. Both Laurence Olivier in his 1944 film and Kenneth Branagh in 1989 drop the scene altogether, along with the Chorus's disclaimer.

This choice is one of the similarities apparent in the actor-directors' cinematic treatments of the play. More importantly, both visualize the key battle as action-packed in far more detail than Shakespeare's characters describe it. The directors also exhibit core similarities in their approach to cutting, eliding, and omitting scenes from Shakespeare's text.

Some of these excisions can be attributed to the greater photographic realism that allows the camera, as noted earlier, to record images that replace descriptive lines in Shakespeare and in this case, his chief source, Holinshed's *Chronicles*. Yet many other deletions are intended by Branagh and Olivier to present a milder, less bloodthirsty view of the King's character. Each film proved highly effective and popular as cinema, yet each presents a less complex, balanced, and skeptically questioning exploration of such themes as military honor, heroism, expansionism, and moral responsibility than Shakespeare's text does.

Both Olivier and Branagh begin the day-of-battle scene with the news from Westmorland (at 4.3.3) that the French "have full threescore thousand" fighting men. The odds are, therefore, five-to-one in favor of the French, and "Besides, they all are fresh," as Exeter notes. Westmorland wishes that the English had "But one ten thousand of those men in England / That do no work today."

The King responds to this wish with the rousing St. Crispin's Day speech. Olivier—young, charismatic, and handsome, a fairy-tale prince—first answers Westmorland himself, then gathers more soldiers to listen. As the camera moves away, the crowd swells ever larger, and Olivier's King moves into a cart to complete the speech. He delivers it with a graceful carriage and balletic arm movements; at times his posture seems lifted from a dance manual or the "Hours" manuscript (see next page). The ease and grace he showed earlier in grasping a royal seal and flourishing it before stamping it in hot wax as the ships load at Southampton appears here as well. At the end of this "band of brothers" speech, he leaps easily from the wagon to his horse.

(continued)

As the battle proceeds, he further shows his command of graceful equestrian motion when he grasps a sword from the ground while riding. When disarmed, he proves still strong enough to unseat the Constable with a mighty punch from his armored fist. At this point, the camera again pulls back and up, showing how the idealized King can unify and inspire his men. As writer and critic James Agee has noted, "the King seems now to be riding like an unexpectedly mounting wave the astounding size of his sudden proud awareness of the country morning, of his moment in history, of his responsibility and competence, of being full-bloodedly alive, and of being about to die" (211–212). Scholar Jack Jorgens remarks that "Even Henry's horse seems to share his excitement, shaking its head vigorously when the Herald offers ransom before the battle" (129).

Branagh's St. Crispin's Day speech is also beautifully spoken, again from a wagon, and moves to an emotional crescendo. Its dynamism is overtly underscored by Patrick Doyle's swelling music, which the director relies upon throughout the battle scenes for atmospheric effect. Branagh borrows some details in the battle preparations from Olivier's film and their mutual source. Both directors show the English foot soldiers setting stakes to protect the archers, then sharpening them. Both linger on the key historical detail that lightly armed archers took the French by surprise and began routing them.

Despite the similarities of approach discussed above, however, Olivier's and Branagh's interpretations diverge far more often and more dramatically than they coalesce. Clear differences appear when we examine the actors' depictions of Henry and the films' respective visual treatments of the battle scene, their portrayals of the French, and their rhythms.

Olivier's portrayal of the veiled and elusive Henry, the soldier-king at war, is more attractive, outgoing, and idealized than Branagh's introverted, enigmatic, almost neutral monarch (who seems a close kin to Hamlet in some scenes). Indeed, Branagh's portrayal appears to be a response to Olivier's.

Similarly, Olivier's Battle of Agincourt possesses an artful beauty very different from Branagh's violent imagery. The latter's dark, gory scenes and his bloody, close-in view of hand-to-hand combat often seem a direct response to Olivier's choreographed and nearly bloodless skirmishes set amid pristine tents, colorful banners, and medieval pageantry. Olivier borrows some of his imagery from the colorfully illuminated French manuscript, *A Book of Hours* (created as *Les Très Riches Heures du duc de Berry* between 1413–1416), while Branagh borrows much of his scene's imagistic vocabulary from Orson Welles's depiction of the Battle of Shrewsbury in his Falstaff film *Chimes at Midnight* and from such violent Westerns as Sam Peckinpah's *The Wild Bunch* (1969), with its aestheticized, slow-motion violence.

The films diverge most sharply, perhaps, in their treatment of the French. Olivier shows the enemy as comically inept. His own manly English ease contrasts sharply with Frenchmen's arrogance and effeminacy. (And madness, in the case of the King.) Olivier's English soldiers are dressed in earthy colors against the bright-blue, cloud-flecked sky (the kind depicted by the English Romantic painter Turner); the French are dressed too colorfully in pastels. In addition, they drink wine, blithely assume victory, and, in one of the film's most inventive touches, have to be lifted onto their horses by winches because their heavy, ornate, old-fashioned armor makes it impossible for them to mount the animals without help. Branagh's Frenchmen, on the other hand, especially the Constable (played by Richard Easton) and the King (played by Paul Scofield), are not so much arrogant and over-civilized to the point of decadence as they are misinformed. In their eagerness for battle, they show a certain heroism and nobility missing from Olivier's Gallic enemy. Branagh views the French as dignified and worthy opponents, despite the Dauphin's narcissism.

When the scene cuts to the death of the boys, Olivier shows the French nobles actually killing one boy and setting their camp and luggage afire from horseback, though the camera turns away, here as throughout the scene, at the moment of actual contact of French blade and English Boy. The face of the Boy is smeared in blood when Fluellen shows the child's body to Olivier as King. Branagh's treatment here, as throughout, is more graphic than Olivier's, yet the two kings' responses are similarly quiet and restrained despite the bitterness of their words: "I was not angry since I came to France / Until this instant" (4.7.54–55). Olivier deletes the continuation of the scene, in which the king commands (for the second time in the original Shakespeare text) that the English kill their French prisoners (here, by slitting their throats). Branagh's Henry, on the other hand, does speak those lines at 4.7.62–65:

> Besides, we'll cut the throats of those we have,
> And not a man of them that we shall take
> Shall taste our mercy. Go and tell them so.

Last, the two films differ markedly in their rhythms. Olivier's pacing is more leisurely and expansive, in the delivery of the lines, the timing of the transitions, and the use of the camera to show large swaths of action and the landscape of green fields, rolling hills, and blue sky. He shows the military choreography's inherent geometric beauty by means of overhead shots and by frequently cutting to images of Henry's flag, with its red cross, symbolically advancing upon the French fleur de lis. With the nobles on both sides maneuvering on caparisoned horses, the first wave of the assault ends, and a second onslaught, like a wave in an ocean set, begins as if on cue. Like Robin Hood and his merry men, the English archers drop from trees upon their enemies, and more French flags retreat to a nearby hill held by the weak and whining Dauphin.

An abrupt shift of tone follows the killing of the Boy in Olivier's film. In a final battle, the black knight from France proves no match for the white hero of England. After the warriors' horses rear, the French Constable falls to Olivier's monarch. When the Frenchman is down, the Englishmen cheer. The victorious Henry bids the French to come down from their hill because by cowering there, he says, they do "offend our sight." At this point William Walton's supportive though unobtrusive musical score leads into a celebratory victory song.

Unlike Olivier, with his expansive view of the battle, Branagh puts viewers inside his battle, bringing us close to its confusion and its agitated rhythms, and extending the quick-cut technique of the sort Welles employs in *Falstaff: Chimes at Midnight.* The Chorus quickly interrupts the preparations with his speech as spikes are hammered into the ground and arrows are readied. Bowmen warm up, the French are seated in their armor, the Constable pulls down the visor on his helmet. Many close-ups of faces, most looking frightened, are intercut throughout the scene, showing intimate portraits of wet, dirty, and exhausted soldiers. The sounds of thundering hooves, then screams, introduce the moment when a great storm of the English archers' arrows flies directly into the combat, inadvertently killing English soldiers as well as French. Thus, Branagh's depiction of the confusion of battle clearly is more realistic and modern than Olivier's thrilling image of thousands of whistling English arrows neatly taking the French by surprise.

Branagh's nervous, jangly pacing continues as music swells beneath mostly wordless and ignoble action: rain pours down, and horses become stuck in the mud and fall. Close-up scenes of hand-to-hand combat reveal a throat cut here, a purse picked there, a Frenchman drowned. King Henry appears as a kind of medieval Dirty Harry, turning, unhelmeted, from side to side and brandishing his clanking sword. Pistol is stabbed in the back. More horses stumble and land on their riders. War, here, is clearly hell.

At this point in the action, Branagh and his film editor, Michael Bradsell, move into slow motion, showing us the French Constable being thrown from his horse, then dragged off. Two young Englishmen succumb, too. York dies spurting and vomiting blood (as described at 4.6.6: "From helmet to the spur all blood he was"); the Boy runs toward camp, pursued by a Frenchman with a truncheon, and we hear the sound of it making violent contact with flesh.

The action in this slow-motion and invented scene is quite different from Olivier's, which follows Shakespeare's description of the camp being set on fire. Both films, however, drop the early lines in Fluellen and Gower's colloquy about the killing of the boys. Gone, too, are the key lines recalling to mind Falstaff, the friend whom, these soldiers say, Harry Monmouth (King Henry) "killed" metaphorically when he banished him.

Branagh's nobly depicted French herald Montjoy (Christopher Ravenscroft) reveals to Henry that the day belongs to England, and the King, now covered in gore and grime, attributes the victory to God. The image of the Boy's bloodied corpse firmly in his mind's eye (and on the screen), Branagh's Henry drapes the body over his shoulder and trudges through the killing field of the battle. Branagh's exhausted King evades the sharpened pikes, while the camera pans over bodies: some felled by arrows and spikes, some in a sitting position, some stacked, like cordwood, in carts. Injured survivors limp painfully toward camp, while in one of the film's most affecting additions, women—mothers, wives, and daughters—rush onto the field looking for their loved ones. A river of blood runs through a huge puddle. The imagery suggests "What price, victory?"

Despite this gore and waste and grief, the reverential tone of the scene; the religious aura of the *Non nobis* and *Te Deum;* the King's brief triumphant glance at the Dauphin; and most of all the King's sensitivity to the Boy, whose body he places in a cart, balance the violence with a kind of religious and national piety. Branagh's Henry closes the dead child's eyes and kisses his face as the scene slowly dissolves to the French court, where the successful soldier Harry must now win a very different victory over the French princess, Katharine.

References and Related Reading

Berman, Ronald, ed. *Twentieth-Century Interpretations of "Henry V."* Englewood Cliffs, N.J., 1968.

Hedrick, Donald K. "War is Mud: Branagh's Dirty *Harry V* and the Types of Political Ambiguity." *Shakespeare: The Movie.* Eds. Lynda E. Boose and Richard Burt. London and New York, 1997. 45–66.

Howard, Jean E., and Phyllis Rackin. *Engendering a Nation: A Feminist Account of Shakespeare's English History Plays.* London and New York, 1997.

Kermode, Frank. *Shakespeare's Language.* New York, 2000.

Neill, Michael. "'Henry V': A Modern Perspective." The New Folger Shakespeare: *"Henry V."* New York, 1995. 253–278.

Norwich, John Julius. *Shakespeare's Kings.* New York, 2000.

Olivier, Laurence. *Confessions of An Actor.* London, 1982.

Rosenthal, Daniel. *Shakespeare on Screen.* London, 2000.

Saccio, Peter. *Shakespeare's English Kings: History, Chronicle, and Drama.* Oxford and New York, 1977/2000.

Smith, Emma, ed. *Shakespeare in Production: "King Henry V."* Cambridge, Eng., 2002.

Tillyard, E. M. W. *Shakespeare's History Plays.* London, 1944/61.

SHAKESPEARE AND TRAGEDY

Defining Tragedy: Classical and Native Traditions

Shakespeare's dramatic career coincided with the revival of interest in the classics and renewed fascination with tragedy, the dramatic form admired since Aristotle outlined its structural features and analyzed its effect in his *Poetics*. Yet attempts to deduce a formula for Shakespearean tragedy, as Aristotle did for the Greek plays, nearly always falter. Shakespeare wrote in a range of forms and styles about a variety of tragic experiences thereby making each play a unique response to its source and subject.

Aristotle theorized the genre by examining the Greek plays of fifth century (B.C.E.) Athens, most notably Sophocles's *Oedipus the King*. The philosopher postulated that a tragic action must have a beginning, middle, and end, must be of a certain magnitude, and evoke pity and fear in the spectators and, by arousing these emotions, purge them. This reaction Aristotle called catharsis. The tragic hero was an exceptional person, that is, of a certain stature in the community. Because even such a hero could not avoid his fate, neither could the unexceptional common man. Aristotle noted that such heroes possessed a tragic flaw or *hamartia*, the recognition of which accompanied and precipitated the hero's downfall and (in most but not all cases) death. At the conclusion of *Oedipus the King*, the tragic protagonist, learning that he has mistakenly though unavoidably killed his father and married his mother, plucks out his own eyes. He is doomed to spend his remaining days a wandering beggar, guided in his painful progress by his daughter, Antigone.

In clear contrast to comedies, which resolve conflicts happily for most characters, all tragedies involve conflicts that bring about the hero's downfall and often the destruction of others, including his family and sometimes the political order. Without exception, Shakespeare's tragedies do end with the death of the protagonist. After a series of mishaps Romeo and Juliet commit suicide. Hamlet is killed by Laertes's poison-tipped sword. Othello kills himself in self-punishment for his crime of mur-

dering his innocent wife. Macbeth is beheaded in battle. King Lear dies of heartbreak and an overtaxed old age.

Defining Shakespearean Tragedy

Shakespeare and his contemporaries did not model their works upon Greek tragedy, those plays of Aeschylus, Sophocles, and Euripides studied by Aristotle. Rather, they knew these classical dramas through the Roman plays of Seneca, a widely imitated model for such works as Thomas Sackville and Thomas Norton's *Gorboduc* (1565) and Thomas Kyd's revenge play, *The Spanish Tragedy* (1592). Also available as patterns of tragic action and influencing the kinds of experiences represented in Shakespeare's plays were two strains in the native English tradition. The English morality play represented human life as a struggle between good and evil, acknowledging that all human beings sin, suffer, and die. The morality plays frame their stories within a Christian universe in which sin can be redeemed and death releases the immortal soul into salvation in heaven or damnation in hell. In these medieval English plays, human failure and even death are understood as part of a larger providential plan that will eventually lead to the restoration of order, to a kind of cosmic harmony. The second influential strain is the *de causibus* tradition, named for a medieval narrative form that represented the Fall of Princes in such works as the *Mirror for Magistrates*, a frequent source of tragic plots for Shakespeare's contemporaries, including several of Shakespeare's history plays and tragedies.

In comparison to the morality plays and the *de causibus* tradition, Shakespeare's tragedies are secular, although the terms in which several of his heroes (notably Hamlet, Othello, and Macbeth) understand their suffering and death are recognizably Christian. Shakespeare departed from the Greek plays Aristotle described and the Senecan plays he knew in other significant ways. None of Shakespeare's tragedies follows the classical "unities" of time, place, and action. Instead they unfold over long periods of time, usually in many locales, and often with subplots that illuminate or counterpoint the main action.

Three of the tragedies included in this anthology have heroes based upon historical or quasi-historical figures. King Lear and Macbeth are set in early Britain with protagonists modeled on monarchs descended from shadowy realms of myth and legend into Holinshed's *Chronicles*. The Danish prince Amlethus, ultimately based on Saxo Grammaticus's *Historica Danica* (1180–1208), became the subject of *Hamlet*. *Romeo and Juliet* and *Othello*, the first set in Verona, the second in Venice and Cyprus, derive from narrative fictions by Giraldi Cinthio. These five tragedies vary in structure, tone, and style; their range includes the lyricism of the early *Romeo and Juliet*, the psychologically penetrating soliloquies of *Hamlet* (the longest tragedy) and *Macbeth* (the shortest), the domestic pathos of *Othello*, and the cosmic sweep of *King Lear*. Each of the five contains moments of comedy or dark irony; clearly Shakespeare showed no interest in adhering to the Aristotelian or neo-Aristotelian notions that tragic scenes should not be mixed with comedy. A simplified evolutionary view of Shakespeare's career holds that he tends to experiment and perfect one form before embarking upon the next: first comedy simultaneously with the history plays, then tragedy before his last plays, the tragicomic romances. Yet Shakespeare wrote tragedies during both his early and late periods, four during the reign of Queen Elizabeth and six during that of King James I. Some theater historians and scholars have argued that the six tragedies he wrote between 1600 and 1608 (*Hamlet, Othello, King Lear, Macbeth, Antony and Cleopatra,* and *Coriolanus*) reflect a turn to pessimism, as the nation moved uncertainly from the long and largely peaceful reign of Elizabeth I into the less certain era of James I, from optimism into a period when scientific inquiry and philosophical questioning created a brooding sense of unease. Such explanations are speculative at best, and the question of how much Shakespeare's evolving art was influenced by historical events or by the dictates of his own creativity is one that is often broached in the commentaries of this anthology, but may never be satisfactorily answered.

What we do know is that around the turn of the century, after essaying tragedy twice in the previous decade with *Titus Andronicus* and *Romeo and Juliet,* and after perfecting the chronicle play with his stirring depiction of the victory of Henry V at Agincourt, Shakespeare's drama grows increasingly dark as he explores the genre of tragedy and meditates upon complex metaphysical themes, including the nature of evil, the meaning of justice, and the inevitability of death.

While, as we have seen, comedies represent a social order flexible enough to welcome changing values, new perceptions, and aberrant behavior, tragedies represent societies thrown into crisis to which the hero must respond. Shakespeare emphasizes character in his plays and the ways in which individual character—not simply the gods or fate—shapes human destiny. Manifestations of the supernatural are few—the ghost in Hamlet, the weird sisters in Macbeth. Although gods may be invoked, they do not intervene.

Of the five tragedies included in this volume, *Romeo and Juliet* (1594–1596) is the least Aristotelian. Though it ends unhappily, with the lovers' deaths, the play is lyric in impetus, and the action shares many traits with those of comedies of the period, including an emphasis upon romantic love. The young lovers do not possess the tragic stature of later heroes such as Othello, and their tragedy of passion is rooted in the enmity of their warring families. In a fit of passion Romeo chooses to kill Tybalt. Yet this choice is not the sole reason for the tragic outcome. Like several of the history plays (*Richard II* and *Richard III)* that were titled as tragedies, even though not grouped with them in the First Folio, *Romeo and Juliet* stands both inside and outside the generic classification.

Despite their variations in form, style, and moral experience, the four later plays in this section—*Hamlet, Othello, King Lear,* and *Macbeth*—do share certain traits, including a sophisticated psychological realism. Two of these plays, *Othello* and *Macbeth*, represent a catastrophe that flows from a character's tragic flaw or moral failing, a version of the *hamartia* cited by Aristotle. At the outset Macbeth is a man of conscience, a good person infected with a secret ambition to be king. He succumbs to this vice because of the seductive prophecies of the weird sisters whom he meets at the beginning of the action, and through the urgings of his wife, whose desire for the crown is even stronger than his. Together, the foretellings and the lust for power prove fatal. Othello, the most Aristotelian of Shakespeare's heroes in terms of stature, is similarly afflicted with a tragic flaw. Although he is not jealous by nature, once "wrought/Perplexed in the extreme" he allows himself to be seized by an irrational, all-consuming passion, the "green eyed monster" of jealousy. *Othello* becomes a domestic tragedy in which the hero is manipulated by the thoroughgoing villain Iago into murdering his innocent wife. Like Agamemnon in Aeschylus's *Oresteia*, he is seized by an irrational passion; like Oedipus, he comes to recognize his own crime and punishes himself for it.

Hamlet, like the play that bears his name, is *sui generis*, or in a class by himself. Although many critics of the Romantic era, such as Coleridge, and more recent interpreters, such as actor-director Laurence Olivier, have found fault with Hamlet for hesitancy and indecision, the character can hardly be said to have a *hamartia*, or tragic flaw. His own father has demanded that he play the role of avenger; the thoughtful philosophy student home from university for his father's funeral and mother's unexpected wedding naturally wants to find out whether such a command is just. Hamlet's progress is toward acceptance of his fate, even though it may bring about his own death—"the readiness is all." King Lear is rash and impetuous in deciding first to divide his kingdom and then to disinherit his most loving daughter, Cordelia. Like old Gloucester he is blind to the true moral natures of his children. Yet even in those productions, such as Peter Brook's, that emphasize the violence of Lear's knights and the King's arrogant disregard for others, Lear does not possess a fatal flaw or commit a tragic error that explains the cruelty of his two evil daughters or the horrible pain of the ending when he enters carrying the body of his murdered child.

These four later tragedies present their heroes (and sometimes, other characters) in moments of self-reflective soliloquy. These speeches give us insight into the characters' evolving states of mind. Hamlet, Macbeth, Othello, and more obliquely Lear, also reach a point in their progress when they have achieved a state of inward awareness that they call "readiness" or "ripeness." They have experienced new aspects of themselves, gained insight into their failings, and are prepared for death if it should come. All four plays thus take readers and audiences into the deepest and most universal of human desires and fears.

Shakespeare's tragic endings do not always follow the pattern of catharsis defined by Aristotle. King Lear's gradual realization of his fallibility and common humanity does not save his loved daughter Cordelia from being murdered, nor does it leave all audiences with a feeling of tragic enlightenment. As the stage histories following each play will demonstrate, various actors and directors through the ages have shaped or adapted the plays to create varying tones in the final scenes and thus differing responses in the audience. After *Lear* and *Macbeth*, Shakespeare wrote two more tragedies—*Timon of Athens* and *Coriolanus*—in which bitterness and misanthropy run deep; disillusionment over man's ingratitude is pervasive and an ironic skepticism greets even our tragic failures.

The difficulty of defining Shakespearean tragedy may in fact be a symptom of the plays' greatness and their humanity. In his famed Preface to his 1765 edition of the plays, Dr. Samuel Johnson described Shakespeare's lifelong preference for mixed forms:

> Shakespeare's plays are not in the rigorous and critical sense either tragedies or comedies, but compositions of a distinct kind: exhibiting the real state of sublunary nature, which partakes of good and evil, joy and sorrow, mingled with endless variety of proportion and innumerable modes of combination; and expressing the course of the world, in which the loss of one is the gain of another; in which, at the same time, the reveler is hastening to his wine, and the mourner burying his friend; in which the malignity of one is sometimes defeated by the frolick of another; and many mischiefs and many benefits are done and hindered without design.

CHAPTER 14

Romeo and Juliet

(1594–1596)

Context and Dating: Questions of Genre

Some years after his early experiment with *Titus Andronicus*, Shakespeare wrote the first of his great tragedies, *Romeo and Juliet*. The play is one of Shakespeare's most popular. Its story of star-crossed lovers who defy their parents' mutual hatred is one of the most widely told in the world; the names of the hero and heroine are synonymous with impetuous young love. Four hundred years later, Romeo and Juliet are continually invoked as icons of pop culture. Their story has been reframed, parodied, satirized, musicalized, and filmed in scores of adaptations and spin-offs, many of which have effectively brought the play and its issues into the lives of contemporary young people. Because the focus of the play is shared by Romeo and Juliet, lovers who are not figures of tragic greatness in the usual sense and whose only failing is falling passionately in love and hastily marrying, the locus of the tragedy lies elsewhere, especially in the collision of their passionate romantic love with the all-encompassing feud between their families in the city of Verona. The dual focus upon the lovers and the feud makes the city itself an actor in the drama. Like the parents of the dead lovers, Verona suffers from its own penchant for violence and learns from the deaths a certain wisdom.

Although *Romeo and Juliet* ends unhappily and thus differs from *A Midsummer Night's Dream* and other such comedies in which lovers overcome parental opposition, its classification as a tragedy remains problematic. In this play (written about the same time as *Dream*), the sins of the fathers are visited upon their children so that the young lovers themselves can be viewed, at least in part, as victims, rather than as active participants in their fates. Despite its very different outcome, *Romeo and Juliet* contains many parallels with the romantic comedies of the same period and many differences from the mature tragedies (*Hamlet*, *Macbeth*, *Othello*, and *King Lear*) that Shakespeare wrote a half-decade later. *Romeo and Juliet* is lyric in impetus, sharing with the sonnets and portions of *The Merchant of Venice* and *Richard II* an attraction to various rhyme schemes, rhetorical devices, puns, antithesis, and varied verse forms, including the sonnet. Romeo's infatuation with the unseen Rosaline borrows from conventions of the Petrarchan tradition. The play's frequent resort to bawdry (coarse, suggestive language)—as the young men tease Romeo, the nurse teases Juliet, and Juliet expresses her sexual desires and satisfactions—also links it to comedy. One can view the plot as a kind of tragic parody of the *Pyramus and Thisbe* episode enacted by the "rude mechanicals" at the end of *A Midsummer Night's Dream* (unless *Romeo and Juliet* was written earlier).

The play is generally dated 1594–1596, because the first quarto was published in 1597, and because by 1598 Francis Meres had cited it as an example of Shakespeare's mastery of tragedy. As the stage history will reveal, the play's popularity has gone in hand with its dynamism: from the Restoration onward, this cherished love story has been ceaselessly reinvented to reflect the needs and desires of different cultures.

Characters

Romeo and Juliet are *young* lovers: they are teenagers. She would have turned fourteen on Lammas Eve (August) had she lived; he is a bit older. In the opening scene, Romeo's bookish infatuation with Rosaline ("Love is a smoke raised with the fume of sighs; / Being purged, a fire sparkling in lovers' eyes; / Being vexed, a sea nourished with lovers' tears," 1.1.190–192) suggests that he is a typical young lover in the Petrarchan tradition of exaggerated love symptoms. (In one of the better interpretative touches for actor Leonardo DiCaprio's Romeo in Baz Luhrmann's 1996 film, *Romeo+Juliet*, the young hero is a "Shakespeare in bud," as *New Yorker* critic Anthony Lane noted: he keeps a journal of his thoughts and emotions.) In the Shakespeare script, Romeo and his friends, some invited, some not, attend the Capulet's masked ball out of sheer bravado, the fear of being discovered in the enemy camp adding excitement to their adventure. Once there, however, Romeo quickly discovers true passion when he meets Juliet. He now devotes himself not just to his imaginings of a god-like beauty but to an actual young woman, to Juliet. Unlike the unattainable "goddess" Rosaline, Juliet has not the "cunning to be strange" and insists that she and Romeo speak honestly to one another. Loving him and imagining a future as an adult with him, she speaks rapturously, revealing the essential innocence of her nature: "O gentle Romeo, / If thou dost love, pronounce it faithfully. / Or if thou thinkest I am too quickly won, / I'll frown and be perverse and say thee nay, / So thou wilt woo, but else not for the world" (2.2.93–97). She also demonstrates her keen intelligence and fearless sexuality in speeches praying for "love-performing night" so that Romeo may "Leap to these arms, untalked of and unseen." She proves practical in making plans and resilient in the face of misfortune.

Mercutio is the wittiest of the friends, "a gallant spirit," as Benvolio calls him. As his name suggests, he is mercurial. A relative of the Prince, he is something of a prickly and cynical observer who sees situations more clearly than his comrades. His mocking wit lights on Romeo in trying to "conjure" him:

> Romeo! Humors! Madman! Passion! Lover!
> Appear thou in the likeness of a sigh.
> Speak but one rhyme, and I am satisfied;
> Cry but "Ay me!" Pronounce but "love" and "dove."
> Speak to my gossip Venus one fair word,
> One nickname for her purblind son and heir.
>
> (2.1.8–13)

When Mercutio is stabbed by Tybalt "under the arm" of Romeo, who is trying to stop the brawl, he speaks bluntly: "A plague o' both your houses! I am sped" (3.1.90). He spins his most characteristically imaginative speech, and one of the play's most finely wrought, just before the masked ball when he tells his friends of Queen Mab, that bringer of dreams, the "fairies' midwife" who comes in shape "no bigger than an agate stone / On the finger of an alderman" drawn by a team of "little atomi / Over men's noses as they lie asleep," her chariot an empty hazelnut shell, her wagon spokes made of long spiders' legs (1.4.53–104). In its imagery and philosophy the speech recalls *A Midsum-*

mer Night's Dream and forecasts the pastoral magic of the late romances, especially *The Tempest*. Mercutio is doomed, in part by his insistence on fighting Tybalt; he dies in 3.1. His friend Benvolio vanishes from the plot after describing the duel that killed him.

Tybalt, Mercutio's nemesis, is the loving, if rash cousin of Juliet and the nephew of Lady Capulet. He brawls in every scene in which he appears and his death begins the transformation of the play from comedy to tragedy. Friar Laurence and the Nurse, two unusual characters with large roles, serve important functions in the plot and take on thematic significance as well. The Friar proves a somewhat equivocal character, whose well-intentioned advice and ultimate miscalculation contribute to the disaster. Still, he is treated by all in the play with the affection and respect he gives to others. And because he is the character most in touch with the natural world and serves as a kindly surrogate father for Romeo, he shares in the pathos and grief of the ending. The Nurse, derived in part from the garrulous and bawdy figures of Roman comedy, has been played by actresses of many different ages, her character interpreted across a range of possibilities from confused and foolish to maternal, earthy, and wise. As Juliet's wet nurse, she has been with the Capulet family since the girl's birth, providing the warmth and affection of a mother and the nurturing qualities that Juliet's well-to-do parents lack. She provides much of the play's comic relief, her down-to-earth bawdry contrasting with the rhetoric of power that colors the parents' scenes with Juliet. The Nurse appreciates the naturalness of the love between Romeo and Juliet, another of the qualities destroyed by the status-seeking families and their violent feud.

Sources and Inspirations

Shakespeare's chief source for *Romeo and Juliet* was a narrative poem by Arthur Brooke, itself a version of a popular legend by the Italian writer Matteo Bandello: *The Tragical History of Romeus and Juliet, written first in Italian by Bandell and now in English* (1562). The plot device of a sleeping potion to escape an unwanted wedding goes back as far as 500 C.E. to a romance story by Xenophon of Ephesus. By the fifteenth century, the Italian *Il Novellino* by Masuccio of Salerno combined the sleeping draught narrative with a misunderstanding and suicide that derives from the Pyramus and Thisbe story in Ovid's *Metamorphoses*. (See the uses of this story in *A Midsummer Night's Dream*.) Luigi da Porto later shifted the scene of his similar story to Verona. Da Porto in turn inspired Bandello, who is the major source for the Brooke poem that Shakespeare knew. The indebtedness is extensive, especially in the emphasis upon the bold contrasts between love and violent hatred. Shakespeare's changes are many, too. He compresses the time, reduces Juliet's age, and gives imaginative depth to the characters—especially Mercutio, the Nurse, and Juliet—so that they are much fuller and more attractive than they are in the sources. The Nurse especially takes on a larger and warmer role. Most importantly, Shakespeare sympathizes with his young lovers, rather than exposing them to moral judgment.

Language and Structure

The play's structure contrasts violent enmity with passionate love and scenes of public brawling with intimate episodes; the conflicts drive the lovers more fully into themselves and their predicament. Romeo finds himself drawn deeply into the Capulet's environs as he becomes more passionately attached to Juliet. The death of Mercutio and Romeo's slaying of Tybalt change the course of the play, interrupting the progress of the lovers from their secret marriage to the consummation of their love, thereby shifting the tone from comic to tragic. Once these deaths have taken place, Friar Laurence can no longer hope that a Capulet-Montague marriage will be able to heal the ancient feud of the two families, and so he proposes the desperate expedient of the sleeping draught. Juliet's contemplation of her temporary "death," as she prepares to drink the potion, foreshadows her actual death. In many productions the same platform that served as her bed becomes in the final act, her bier.

Famed playwright George Bernard Shaw sensed in *Romeo and Juliet*'s language and structure an "irresistibly impetuous march of music." The play's language, often lyrical and ornate in its imagery, deploys an impressive range of language styles that reflects these structural contrasts and thematic concerns and suits the varied characters and their actions. The opening Chorus in sonnet form introduces a scene between servants in simple prose before the upper-class Benvolio speaks in blank verse when he intervenes in the quarrel. He and Tybalt trade swift verse lines; the Prince delivers the first of his many judicious pronouncements in grave and stentorian language. The tone shifts again when Romeo's name is mentioned. The boy's father, Montague (to whom the son never speaks during the course of the play), describes Romeo's melancholy. Romeo's speeches about his disdainful lady Rosaline are fully in the Petrarchan mode, filled with rhymes and fantastic conceits. He has lost his usual self to love, feels the experience of her disdain, and is hanging back from his friends in a kind of tortured isolation. With the entrance of the young Montague masquers comes Mercutio's dazzling "Queen Mab" speech, a virtuoso set piece so rich in imagery and witty in attitude that young actors often choose it as an audition speech. The "holy palmers" sonnet (see the explication of this wittily poetic scene at 1.5 in Chapter 4) further explores Petrarchan conventions with its paradox-filled rhetoric, until the idealized woman becomes Juliet, a living, embodied girl standing before Romeo. Once together, the lovers employ language (see 3.5 especially) that takes on a rapturous loveliness and natural musicality as they argue over the sound of the nightingale or the lark and Romeo informs her that "jocund day stands tiptoe on the misty mountaintops." Contrastingly, bawdry often colors the vivid speech of Mercutio and the Nurse, the former to debunk Romeo's Petrarchism, the latter simply because she is earthy and direct. Much later, when Romeo is in exile and believes Juliet to be dead, he speaks with a sim-

David Garrick, the leading actor-manager of the eighteenth century, added the dramatic moment pictured on the left to the tomb scene of Romeo and Juliet; *Juliet wakes up for a brief reunion with Romeo before he dies. On the right, the American actress Charlotte Cushman played Romeo to her sister Susan's Juliet, c. 1849.*

Laurence Olivier turned down an offer to star in the first feature film of Romeo and Juliet; *instead, Leslie Howard (left) made a bland Romeo with Norma Shearer as Juliet in director George Cukor's 1936 movie. Set to Sergei Prokofiev's great score, the Bolshoi Ballet's sumptuous 1940 production (right) with Galina Ulanova as a tremulous Juliet dancing with Yuri Zhadanov's impassioned Romeo proved highly effective on stage and screen.*

plicity and directness befitting his real state: "Well, Juliet, I will lie with thee tonight" (5.1.34).

Themes and Issues

O'erhasty Marriages: Passion and Impetuousness

One pattern of imagery in the play suggests a theme of sudden and violent actions—fire, gunpowder, hot blood, lightning, the stormy sea and shipwrecked vessel. These associations with a love that is young and fragile underscore the swiftness and brevity of the lovers' experience, thus intensifying the ecstasy of a joy "too rich for use, for earth too dear" (1.5.48). With its hasty secret marriage, its imagery expressing that haste, and its strong dramatic momentum, *Romeo and Juliet* flies swiftly and lyrically to its tragic conclusion. Although the Chorus's "two hours' traffic of the stage" is a figure of speech rather than a description of the play's running time, the fluency and speed with which one scene blends into the next feels very much like the technique of a "dissolve" in film. Thus, image, structure, and technique reinforce one another, contributing to the sense of time rushing forward and at last running out for the lovers. The first Quarto version of the play even contains a stage direction that suggests the speed and daring of the lovers: Before the wedding at the Friar's cell, the prompt reads, "*Enter Juliet, somewhat fast, and she embraces Romeo*" (Q1, 2.5.8SD from Jill Levenson's 2000 Oxford edition of the play).

Blood Feuds: Self-Perpetuating Revenge

The mindless feuding of the two families is so ancient that we never learn its cause, only its consequences: "My only

love sprung from my only hate," says Juliet (1.5.139). Shakespeare creates three large public scenes during which this theme plays itself out, at the beginning, mid-point, and the close of the play. At the beginning, the brawling has extended even to the bawdy servants, thus prompting the Prince to warn the Capulets and Montagues to cease hostilities, a demand that the vengeful Tybalt simply ignores. Again at 3.1, Prince Escalus dominates the end of the scene, exiling Romeo for Tybalt's death, and again speaking for public order and safety against the irrational forces of violence. At the play's end, it is Escalus who interprets the meaning of events: "See what a scourge is laid upon your hate" (5.3.292), implying that a higher power has intervened to demand the removal of the ancient grudge through the sacrifice of a child from each family. When directors emphasize this aspect of the play in performance, love is pitted against violence and the lovers pay the high cost of their families' hostilities with their lives. The deaths purge hatred from the families, who resolve to learn from the children's sacrifice.

At the same time the feuding can be seen as perpetuating, through rivalry, the male bonds that even the Prince's most dire warnings cannot sever. As scholar Coppélia Kahn suggests in her *Man's Estate: Masculine Identity in Shakespeare*, their feuding reinforces social hierarchy. Servants fight with servants, young men with young men, and old men with old men (83ff.). On stage, the weapons employed in these brawls—from cudgels to rapiers to broadswords—often follow the same socially hierarchical pattern. Some interpretations of the play question whether the deaths of Romeo and Juliet are a sacrifice that actually redeems the ingrained violence and hostility wracking this historically divided city. Even the final scene's reconciliation of the two houses has been staged with an undertow of misapprehension.

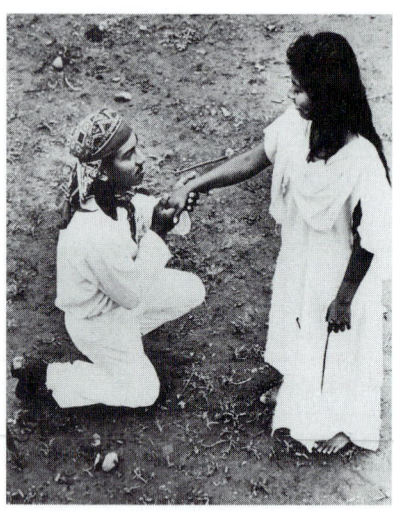

Pictured to the left, Mexico's Laboratorio de Teatro Campesino e Indigena performed its Romeo and Juliet *with Octavio Cervantes and Lesvi Vasquez at the Delacorte Theatre in New York's Central Park. On the right, playing Tybalt as a Latino gang leader, John Leguizamo packs a Sword handgun in Baz Luhrmann's* Romeo+Juliet.

"Fortune's Fools": Tragic Heroes or Victims?

The action of *Romeo and Juliet*, as noted earlier, lacks the "magnitude" Aristotle requires of tragedy. Yet these "star-crossed lovers" are more than mere victims. Their fates derive from a welter of decisions and misapprehensions that, combined with the feud and bad timing, bring about the story's tragic ending. Old Capulet might have forbidden Juliet's marriage to a hated Montague, but he insists upon her marriage to the worthy young aristocrat Paris, not knowing that she is already married to Romeo. Neither does Mercutio know that Romeo is married to Tybalt's kinswoman when he berates his friend for cowardice in the face of the vengeful young Capulet's taunts. Many other events are beyond the control of the lovers: the death of Mercutio "under" Romeo's arm; the outbreak of the plague that prevents the delivery of Friar Laurence's letter; the timing of Romeo's entrance to the tomb before Juliet awakens, and the arrival of the watch just after she stabs herself. Count Paris becomes a victim of his own ignorance of the lovers' true state. The Prince's dignified interpretive speeches at the end of the play—like similar speeches that restore order at the end of the later tragedies—do not account for the terrible experience of waste and loss surrounding these deaths.

Personal Identity and Women's Roles

As scholar Gail Kern Paster notes in an essay appended to the Folger edition of the play, social historians examining changes in private life in Western European culture in Shakespeare's time "offer a complicating perspective on the timelessness of Romeo and Juliet" (253). In England in the late sixteenth century, individual identity, especially a woman's identity, was not, as we define it today, a result of

growth in self-awareness, but a part of an individual's place in her or his family and community. Specifically, a woman's identity derived almost exclusively from her relationship to her father and then her husband. Juliet, however, defies these customs by perceiving herself as an individual independent of her family's authority and prejudices and by actively seeking to fulfill her sexual desires through her secret marriage to Romeo. Shakespeare's depiction of a young woman who has become an autonomous desiring self, disobediently married and invoking the coming of night to "Give me my Romeo," is thus a radical statement of romantic individualism within patriarchal culture. "Instead of an uncomplicated, if lyrically beautiful, contest between young love and 'ancient grudge,' the play becomes a narrative that expresses an historical conflict between old forms of identity and new modes of desire, between authority and freedom, between parental will and romantic individualism" (Paster, 254). Such a reading of the play also requires attentiveness to the differences in the lovers' circumstance that are clearly drawn along the traditional lines of gender. Unlike Romeo, whose emotional ties are to his male friends (seen often in outdoor public spaces), Juliet's ties are to her family, with whom she lives a far more isolated life defined by her status as a daughter and warmed by her relationship with the Nurse.

Staging Challenges

Romeo and Juliet makes substantial demands upon those wishing to produce it on stage. The play has a large cast, requires many props, incorporates a good deal of physical action, and has specific staging requirements such as an upper playing area for the scenes at Juliet's window, a curtained bed in which Juliet takes the sleep-

The Tragedies and a Romance

PLATE 19

Romeo and Juliet. *Franco Zeffirelli's youth-oriented 1968 film, shot on locations in Italy, launched a new era of Shakespeare on the silver screen. Olivia Hussey was just 15 when she played Juliet; here the heroine prepares to stab herself near the corpse of Leonard Whiting's Romeo.* (Photofest)

PLATE 20

Romeo+Juliet. *Australian director Baz Luhrmann relocates the tragic action to a gang-infested coastal city where love offers Romeo and Juliet moments of escape from the violent feuding. After her seeming death, the body of Juliet (Claire Danes) lies in a gloomy cathedral surrounded by flickering candles and guarded by plaster angels.* (20th Century Fox / The Kobal Collection / Merrick Morton)

PLATE 21

King Lear. *In Laurence Olivier's final Shakespearean appearance on screen, he gives a touching performance as a forgetful Lear. Filmed for Granada Television in 1983 when he was 75 years old and weakened by cancer, Olivier emphasizes the character's old age and innate benevolence; here he enters mad, "fantastically dressed with wild flowers" as a stage direction (after 4.6.79) indicates.* (Yorkshire Television)

PLATE 22

Ran. *In Japanese filmmaker Akira Kurosawa's adaptation of* King Lear *as* Ran, *vibrant, color-coded battalions fight against the Lear figure Hidetora and his one loyal son. The presence of the implacable Lady Kaede, whose father and brothers have been killed by Hidetora, turns the epic story into a violent drama of revenge. (Matsumoto Toshi/Corbis Sygma)*

PLATE 23

Othello. *Kenneth Branagh (right) relishes an unaccustomed villain's role as the wily manipulator Iago in Oliver Parker's 1995 film co-starring Laurence Fishburne as the Moor and Irene Jacob as Desdemona. Parker and Fishburne intensify Othello's tragic decline into distrust by underscoring his erotic bond to Desdemona.* (Castle Rock/Dakota Films/The Kobal Collection/Rolf Konow)

PLATE 24

The Tempest. *John Gielgud plays Prospero and voices all the other characters in Peter Greenaway's highly original, resolutely visual adaptation of the last play Shakespeare wrote by himself. In the scene pictured here and in many others, the film's imagery focuses upon water, the favored element of naked sprites and nymphs on the magician's island.* (Photofest)

ing potion, and some representation of a tomb, perhaps with a bier that symbolically parallels the wedding bed.

Duels and Swordplay

Dueling was a "highly topical" issue when the play was first performed. "Despite Tudor edicts against them, street fighting and violent feuds were a constant danger, and dueling was on the rise in the 1590s" (Loehlin, Introduction, 6). Italian and Spanish fencing masters, with their rules of etiquette and elaborate terminology, were teaching their art all over London. Mercutio mocks the fad when he calls Tybalt "The very butcher of a silk button, a duellist, a duellist."

Given the two sword fights at the beginning and middle of the play, that in 1.1 which begins and quickly ends and that in 3.2 which leads to the deaths of Mercutio and Tybalt, the male actors in *Romeo and Juliet* should be trained in fencing. The main characters must be adept at swordplay. In fact, the play itself requires the services of a fight choreographer. Most actors who take on the roles of Romeo, Mercutio, Benvolio, and Tybalt work with the choreographer (under the eye of the stage director) to create and carefully rehearse the fight scenes. These can be as complex as the brawls found in most Shakespeare company productions and in films such as Zeffirelli's that spill over the town square and onto several levels of the set. Or, the action can be as minimal as the few swift strokes described in the script's stage directions. Many details of the fighting are open to significant interpretation. Comical servants begin the swordplay in the first scene, their bravado parodying that of the young men and the well-to-do patriarchs, while also suggesting the divided city's long-standing and widespread culture of violence. Benvolio arrives speaking of peace, and in this scene Romeo does not draw a sword at all; he is too distracted by his infatuation with Rosaline to be involved in violent posturings. In 3.2, Romeo is again a peacemaker who has not told of the secret marriage that now makes Tybalt his kinsman. When Tybalt kills Mercutio, he is thrust "under" the arm of Romeo, who is attempting to stop the fight.

Modern-dress interpretations of the play, of course, must determine how to handle the anachronistic swords mentioned in the dialogue. Director Baz Luhrmann outfits his warring factions with handguns that visibly carry the brand name "Sword."

Two Hours' Traffic: Swift Events

Ironically, the open Elizabethan stage accommodated the play's brisk pace far more handily than the elaborately scene-filled later and modern stages that are the result of the introduction of the proscenium, painted sets, and special effects. Fluid staging upon a playing space thrust into the audience appealed to the viewers' imaginations: the area outside the Capulet villa could become an inte-

rior simply with the introduction of a few props—specifically when servingmen coming forward with napkins for the young men who have just marched past and now are "guests." Romeo and Juliet are together "aloft" in 3.5, whereupon Romeo descends into the Capulet orchard by means of a rope ladder, in full view of the audience. Once he has exited, the main stage becomes Juliet's bedroom into which Capulet's wife enters for a busy scene of confrontation involving her, Juliet, Juliet's father, and the Nurse. This is too busy a scene to stage in the gallery aloft, and for that reason Shakespeare shifts the *mise-en-scène*, or physical setting of the action. Having previously asked us to visualize the main stage as a street (1.1-3), a banquet hall (1.4), and an orchard (2.2), Shakespeare now asks us to suppose that the gallery and then the main stage are Juliet's chambers. Such free and fluent shifts intensify the story's momentum. Later actor-managers and directors have been frustrated in their attempts to move spectacular scenery with similar dispatch. Productions with realistic scenery generally place both parts of the scene at 3.5 in the bedroom and have Romeo climb over a gallery railing at the rear stage.

By the end of the Victorian age of spectacle, Henry Irving conceived the play visually as a series of pictures achieving a *coup de théâtre*, or sudden, dramatic turn of events, by combining scenery, lighting, and music in a painterly succession of scenes. In Act 5, his Romeo killed Paris in a moonlit churchyard, moving the scene into the tomb with cinematic fluency as Romeo dragged the corpse of Paris with him to make the transition. Although Irving cut several passages to accommodate the scenery, his production seems to have reflected an understanding that, like the transformation of Juliet's wedding music to a funeral dirge, physical movement—rather than static pictures—should be a signature of any production of the play. Novelist Henry James (see stage history below, pp. 547–551) felt that Irving's pictorial approach "put the cart before the horse," though it seems to have been the slow pacing, not the visual fluency that so bothered James. John Gielgud's 1935 production inaugurated an opposite trend: using a simple unit set, not very different from an unadorned Elizabethan stage, he created a fast-paced, naturally spoken staging that came very close to realizing the "two hours' traffic of our stage" promised by the Chorus.

The Tomb Scene

The staging of the tomb scene offers directors and actors many possibilities—and poses many difficulties. In productions that use a bed for Juliet's room in 4.3 and 4.5 when she takes potion, the bed can stay on stage or be brought back as a bier. The eighteenth-century tradition of staging a torch-lit funeral procession for Juliet sometimes reappears nowadays. But such a bier and procession can create confusion when Romeo enters, asking

Balthasar to give him "that mattock and the wrenching iron" to open what is presumably a closed tomb or mausoleum on stage. If a large tomb is carried on to the stage, then Romeo must pry it open so the doors can fly open forward, thus revealing Juliet on her bier for the audience to see. Some directors have kept the tomb at the rear of the stage, others closer to the stage apron. Actors following David Garrick's text have then moved

Juliet to the forestage for the lovers' last scene together (see "Frame-by-Frame," pp. 557–559). Also problematic is the fight with Paris, a favored moment during the eighteenth century, but an event often transformed to self-defense in nineteenth-century stagings or excised altogether in the Zeffirelli and Luhrmann films. Neither of those directors wished to shift the focus from Romeo as grieving lover to Romeo as murderer.

Romeo and Juliet

[*Dramatis Personae*

CHORUS

ESCALUS, *Prince of Verona*
MERCUTIO, *the Prince's kinsman and Romeo's friend*
PARIS, *a young count and kinsman of the Prince*
PAGE *to Count Paris*

MONTAGUE
MONTAGUE'S WIFE
ROMEO, *son of the Montagues*
BENVOLIO, *Montague's nephew and Romeo's friend*
ABRAHAM, *a servant of the Montague household*
BALTHASAR, *a servant of the Montague household attending Romeo*

CAPULET
CAPULET'S WIFE
JULIET, *daughter of the Capulets*
NURSE
TYBALT, *nephew of Capulet's Wife*

SCENE: *Verona; Mantua*]

PETRUCHIO, *Capulet's kinsman*
SECOND CAPULET, *an old man, Capulet's kinsman*
PETER, *a servant of the Capulet household attending the Nurse*
SAMSON
GREGORY
ANTHONY   } *servants of the Capulet household*
POTPAN
CLOWN *or* SERVANT
Other SERVANTS

FRIAR LAURENCE } *Franciscan friars*
FRIAR JOHN

APOTHECARY
Three MUSICIANS (*Simon Catling, Hugh Rebeck, and James Soundpost*)
Three WATCHMEN

Citizens, Maskers, Torchbearers, Guards, Servants, and Attendants

The Prologue

[*Enter Chorus.*]

CHORUS
Two households, both alike in dignity,   1
    In fair Verona, where we lay our scene,
From ancient grudge break to new mutiny,   3
    Where civil blood makes civil hands unclean.   4
From forth the fatal loins of these two foes.
    A pair of star-crossed lovers take their life;   6
Whose misadventured piteous overthrows   7

    Doth with their death bury their parents' strife.
The fearful passage of their death-marked love,   9
    And the continuance of their parents' rage,
Which, but their children's end, naught could remove,
    Is now the two hours' traffic of our stage;   12
The which if you with patient ears attend,
What here shall miss, our toil shall strive to mend.   14
                                                    [*Exit.*]

Prologue.
1–14 (The Prologue is in the form of a sonnet.)
1 dignity rank, status   **3 mutiny** strife, discord   **4 Where . . . unclean** where citizens' hands uncivilly are stained in civil strife with their fellow citizens' blood.   **6 star-crossed** thwarted by destiny, by adverse stars   **7 misadventured** unlucky

9 passage progress   **12 two hours' traffic** A conventional way of referring to the length of stage performances in the early modern period, not to be taken too literally, but indicative of a brisk pace   **14 What . . . mend** what is defective or inadequate in the short summary I have given you here, the actors' efforts in the following two hours will amply and fully make clear.

[1.1]

Enter Samson and Gregory, with swords
and bucklers, of the house of Capulet.

SAMSON   Gregory, on my word, we'll not carry coals.   1
GREGORY   No, for then we should be colliers.   2
SAMSON   I mean, an we be in choler, we'll draw.   3
GREGORY   Ay, while you live, draw your neck out of   4
collar.   5
SAMSON   I strike quickly, being moved.   6
GREGORY   But thou art not quickly moved to strike.
SAMSON   A dog of the house of Montague moves me.   8
GREGORY   To move is to stir, and to be valiant is to
stand. Therefore, if thou art moved, thou run'st away.   10
SAMSON   A dog of that house shall move me to stand. I
will take the wall of any man or maid of Montague's.   12
GREGORY   That shows thee a weak slave, for the   13
weakest goes to the wall.   14
SAMSON   'Tis true, and therefore women, being the
weaker vessels, are ever thrust to the wall. Therefore I   16
will push Montague's men from the wall and thrust
his maids to the wall.
GREGORY   The quarrel is between our masters and us   19
their men.   20
SAMSON   'Tis all one. I will show myself a tyrant: when   21
I have fought with the men, I will be civil with the
maids—I will cut off their heads.
GREGORY   The heads of the maids?
SAMSON   Ay, the heads of the maids, or their maidenheads. Take it in what sense thou wilt.   26
GREGORY   They must take it in sense that feel it.   27
SAMSON   Me they shall feel while I am able to stand,   28
and 'tis known I am a pretty piece of flesh.   29
GREGORY   'Tis well thou art not fish; if thou hadst, thou   30
hadst been Poor John. Draw thy tool. Here comes of   31
the house of Montagues.

Enter two other Servingmen
[Abraham and another].

SAMSON   My naked weapon is out. Quarrel, I will back
thee.
GREGORY   How, turn thy back and run?
SAMSON   Fear me not.   36
GREGORY   No, marry. I fear thee!   37
SAMSON   Let us take the law of our side. Let them   38
begin.
GREGORY   I will frown as I pass by, and let them take it
as they list.   41
SAMSON   Nay, as they dare. I will bite my thumb at   42
them, which is disgrace to them if they bear it.
              [*Samson makes taunting gestures.*]
ABRAHAM   Do you bite your thumb at us, sir?
SAMSON   I do bite my thumb, sir.
ABRAHAM   Do you bite your thumb at us, sir?
SAMSON [*aside to Gregory*]   Is the law of our side if I
say ay?
GREGORY [*aside to Samson*]   No.
SAMSON [*to Abraham*]   No, sir, I do not bite my thumb
at you, sir, but I bite my thumb, sir.
GREGORY   Do you quarrel, sir?
ABRAHAM   Quarrel, sir? No, sir.
SAMSON   But if you do, sir, I am for you. I serve as good
a man as you.
ABRAHAM   No better.
SAMSON   Well, sir.

Enter Benvolio.

GREGORY [*to Samson*]   Say "better." Here comes one of   58
my master's kinsmen.   59
SAMSON [*to Abraham*]   Yes, better, sir.
ABRAHAM   You lie.
SAMSON   Draw, if you be men. Gregory, remember thy
washing blow.   *They fight.*   63
BENVOLIO   Part, fools!
Put up your swords. You know not what you do.

Enter Tybalt [with sword drawn].

TYBALT
What, art thou drawn among these heartless hinds?   66
Turn thee, Benvolio. Look upon thy death.
BENVOLIO
I do but keep the peace. Put up thy sword,
Or manage it to part these men with me.   69
TYBALT
What, drawn and talk of peace? I hate the word
As I hate hell, all Montagues, and thee.
Have at thee, coward!   [*They fight.*]   72

Enter three or four Citizens with clubs
or partisans.

1.1. Location: Verona. A public place.
0.2 *bucklers* small shields   **1 carry coals** i.e., endure insults.   **2 colliers**
(Coal carriers were regarded as dirty and of evil repute.)   **3 an** if.
choler anger (produced by one of the four humors).   **draw** draw
swords.   **5 collar** i.e., hangman's noose. (With pun on *colliers* and
choler.)   **6 moved** i.e., to anger. (With pun in next line.)   **8 moves**
incites   **10 stand**, stand one's ground.   **12 take the wall** take the
cleaner side of the walk nearest the wall, thus forcing others out into
the gutter   **13–14 the weakest . . . wall** (A proverb expressing the
idea that the weakest are always forced to give way.)   **16 weaker**
vessels (Saint Paul bids husbands give honor to their wives "as unto
the weaker vessel," 1 Peter 3:7.)   **thrust to the wall** (With suggestion
of amorous assault.)   **19–20 between . . . men** i.e., between the males
of one household and the males of the other household; we have no
quarrel with the women.   **21 one** the same.   **26 what sense** whatever meaning   **27 They . . . feel it** i.e., It is the maids who must receive
by way of physical sensation (*sense*) what I have to offer, because they
are the ones who can feel it.   **28 stand** (With suggestion of "have an
erection," continued in the next few lines in *draw thy tool* and *my
naked weapon is out.*)   **29–30 flesh . . . fish** (Refers to the proverbial
phrase, "neither fish nor flesh.")   **31 Poor John** hake salted and
dried—a poor Lenten kind of food. (Probably with a bawdy suggestion of sexual insufficiency.).   **comes of** i.e., come members of

36 Fear Mistrust. (But Gregory deliberately misunderstands in the
next line, saying, in effect, "No indeed, do you think I'd be afraid of
you?")   **37 marry** i.e., indeed. (Originally an oath, "by the Virgin
Mary.")   **38 take the law of** have the law on   **41 list** please.   **42 bite**
my thumb i.e., make an insulting and probably obscene gesture
58–9 one . . . kinsmen i.e., Tybalt, who is approaching. (Not Benvolio,
who has just entered unobserved by the servingmen.)   **63 washing**
slashing with great force   **66 heartless hinds** cowardly menials.
69 manage use   **72 Have at thee** i.e., On guard, here I come
72.2 *partisans* long-handled spears.

CITIZENS
Clubs, bills, and partisans! Strike! Beat them down!   73
Down with the Capulets! Down with the Montagues!   74

Enter old Capulet in his gown, and his Wife.

CAPULET
What noise is this? Give me my long sword, ho!   75
CAPULET'S WIFE
A crutch, a crutch! Why call you for a sword?
CAPULET
My sword, I say! Old Montague is come
And flourishes his blade in spite of me.   78

Enter old Montague and his Wife.

MONTAGUE
Thou villain Capulet!—Hold me not; let me go.
MONTAGUE'S WIFE
Thou shalt not stir one foot to seek a foe.   80

Enter Prince Escalus, with his train.

PRINCE
Rebellious subjects, enemies to peace,
Profaners of this neighbor-stainèd steel—   82
Will they not hear? What, ho! You men, you beasts,
That quench the fire of your pernicious rage
With purple fountains issuing from your veins,   85
On pain of torture, from those bloody hands
Throw your mistempered weapons to the ground   87
And hear the sentence of your movèd prince.   88
Three civil brawls, bred of an airy word,   89
By thee, old Capulet, and Montague,
Have thrice disturbed the quiet of our streets
And made Verona's ancient citizens
Cast by their grave-beseeming ornaments   93
To wield old partisans in hands as old,
Cankered with peace, to part your cankered hate.   95
If ever you disturb our streets again
Your lives shall pay the forfeit of the peace.   97
For this time all the rest depart away.
You, Capulet, shall go along with me,
And Montague, come you this afternoon,
To know our farther pleasure in this case,
To old Freetown, our common judgment-place.   102
Once more, on pain of death, all men depart.
*Exeunt [all but Montague, Montague's Wife,
and Benvolio].*

MONTAGUE
Who set this ancient quarrel new abroach?   104
Speak, nephew, were you by when it began?   105
BENVOLIO
Here were the servants of your adversary,
And yours, close fighting ere I did approach.
I drew to part them. In the instant came
The fiery Tybalt with his sword prepared,   109
Which, as he breathed defiance to my ears,
He swung about his head and cut the winds
Who, nothing hurt withal, hissed him in scorn.   112
While we were interchanging thrusts and blows,
Came more and more, and fought on part and part   114
Till the Prince came, who parted either part.   115
MONTAGUE'S WIFE
Oh, where is Romeo? Saw you him today?
Right glad I am he was not at this fray.
BENVOLIO
Madam, an hour before the worshiped sun
Peered forth the golden window of the east,   119
A troubled mind drave me to walk abroad,   120
Where, underneath the grove of sycamore
That westward rooteth from this city side,   122
So early walking did I see your son.
Towards him I made, but he was ware of me   124
And stole into the covert of the wood.   125
I, measuring his affections by my own,   126
Which then most sought where most might not be
    found,   127
Being one too many by my weary self,
Pursued my humor, not pursuing his,   129
And gladly shunned who gladly fled from me.   130
MONTAGUE
Many a morning hath he there been seen,
With tears augmenting the fresh morning's dew,
Adding to clouds more clouds with his deep sighs;
But all so soon as the all-cheering sun
Should in the farthest east begin to draw
The shady curtains from Aurora's bed,   136
Away from light steals home my heavy son   137
And private in his chamber pens himself,
Shuts up his windows, locks fair daylight out,
And makes himself an artificial night.
Black and portentous must this humor prove
Unless good counsel may the cause remove.
BENVOLIO
My noble uncle, do you know the cause?
MONTAGUE
I neither know it nor can learn of him.

---

73 **Clubs** rallying cry, summoning apprentices with their clubs.
bills long-handled spears with hooked blades   74.1 *gown* nightgown, dressing gown   75 **long sword** heavy, old-fashioned sword
78 **spite** defiance, despite   80.1 *train* retinue.   82 **Profaners . . . steel**
you who profane your weapons by staining them with neighbors'
blood   85 **purple** bloody, dark red   87 **mistempered** (1) having been
tempered, or hardened, in hot blood rather than cold water (2) malignant, ill-tempered   88 **movèd** angry   89 **airy** flippant, saucy
93 **grave-beseeming ornaments** i.e., staffs and other appurtenances
suited to wise old age   95 **Cankered . . . cankered** corroded (from
disuse) . . . malignant   97 **Your . . . peace** death will be the penalty for
breaking the peace.   102 **Freetown** (Brooke's translation, in his poem
Romeus and Juliet, of *Villa Franca*, as found in the Italian story.)
common public

104 **set . . . abroach** reopened this old quarrel, set it flowing.   105 **by**
near   109 **prepared** drawn, ready   112 **Who . . . withal** which winds,
not at all injured thereby   114 **on part and part** on one side and the
other   115 **either part** both parties.   119 **forth** from forth   120 **drave**
. . . abroad drove me to take a walk   122 **That . . . side** that grows on
the west side of this city   124 **made** moved.   **ware** wary, aware
125 **covert** cover, hiding place   126 **affections** wishes, inclination
127 **Which . . . found** which then chiefly desired a place where I
might be alone   129 **humor** mood   130 **who** him who   136 **Aurora**
goddess of dawn   137 **heavy** (1) sad (2) the opposite of *light*.   **son**
(punning on *sun*, line 134)

BENVOLIO
Have you importuned him by any means? 145
MONTAGUE
Both by myself and many other friends.
But he, his own affections' counselor,
Is to himself—I will not say how true, 148
But to himself so secret and so close, 149
So far from sounding and discovery, 150
As is the bud bit with an envious worm 151
Ere he can spread his sweet leaves to the air
Or dedicate his beauty to the sun.
Could we but learn from whence his sorrows grow,
We would as willingly give cure as know.

Enter Romeo.

BENVOLIO
See where he comes. So please you, step aside. 156
I'll know his grievance or be much denied.
MONTAGUE
I would thou wert so happy by thy stay 158
To hear true shrift.—Come, madam, let's away. 159

Exeunt [Montague and his Wife].

BENVOLIO
Good morrow, cousin.
ROMEO   Is the day so young? 160
BENVOLIO
But new struck nine.
ROMEO   Ay me! Sad hours seem long.
Was that my father that went hence so fast?
BENVOLIO
It was. What sadness lengthens Romeo's hours?
ROMEO
Not having that which, having, makes them short.
BENVOLIO   In love?
ROMEO   Out—
BENVOLIO   Of love?
ROMEO
Out of her favor where I am in love.
BENVOLIO
Alas, that Love, so gentle in his view, 169
Should be so tyrannous and rough in proof! 170
ROMEO
Alas, that Love, whose view is muffled still, 171
Should without eyes see pathways to his will! 172
Where shall we dine?—Oh, me! What fray was here?
Yet tell me not, for I have heard it all.
Here's much to do with hate, but more with love.
Why, then, O brawling love, O loving hate,
O anything of nothing first create, 177
O heavy lightness, serious vanity,
Misshapen chaos of well-seeming forms,
Feather of lead, bright smoke, cold fire, sick health,

Still-waking sleep, that is not what it is! 181
This love feel I, that feel no love in this.
Dost thou not laugh?
BENVOLIO   No, coz, I rather weep. 183
ROMEO
Good heart, at what?
BENVOLIO   At thy good heart's oppression.
ROMEO
Why, such is love's transgression.
Griefs of mine own lie heavy in my breast,
Which thou wilt propagate, to have it pressed 187
With more of thine. This love that thou hast shown 188
Doth add more grief to too much of mine own.
Love is a smoke made with the fume of sighs;
Being purged, a fire sparkling in lovers' eyes; 191
Being vexed, a sea nourished with lovers' tears.
What is it else? A madness most discreet, 193
A choking gall, and a preserving sweet.
Farewell, my coz.
BENVOLIO   Soft! I will go along. 195
An if you leave me so, you do me wrong. 196
ROMEO
Tut, I have lost myself. I am not here.
This is not Romeo; he's some other where.
BENVOLIO
Tell me in sadness, who is that you love? 199
ROMEO   What, shall I groan and tell thee?
BENVOLIO
Groan? Why, no, but sadly tell me who. 201
ROMEO
Bid a sick man in sadness make his will—
A word ill urged to one that is so ill! 203
In sadness, cousin, I do love a woman.
BENVOLIO
I aimed so near when I supposed you loved.
ROMEO
A right good markman! And she's fair I love. 206
BENVOLIO
A right fair mark, fair coz, is soonest hit. 207
ROMEO
Well, in that hit you miss. She'll not be hit
With Cupid's arrow. She hath Dian's wit, 209
And, in strong proof of chastity well armed, 210
From love's weak childish bow she lives unharmed.
She will not stay the siege of loving terms, 212
Nor bide th'encounter of assailing eyes, 213
Nor ope her lap to saint-seducing gold.
Oh, she is rich in beauty, only poor
That when she dies, with beauty dies her store. 216

181 **Still-waking** continually awake   183 **coz** cousin, kinsman
187–8 **propagate . . . thine** increase by having it, i.e., my own grief, oppressed or made still heavier with your grief on my account. (The image of propagating and pressing is appropriately sexual.)
191 **purged** i.e., of smoke   193 **discreet** judicious, prudent   195 **Soft!** i.e., Wait a moment!   196 **An if** If   199 **sadness** seriousness.   **is that** is it that   201 **sadly** seriously. (But Romeo plays on the word, and on *in sadness*, in the sense of "sorrowfully.")   203 **A word** i.e., *sadly* or *in sadness*—too sad a word, says Romeo, for a melancholy lover   206 **fair** beautiful   207 **fair mark** clear, distinct target   209 **Dian** Diana, huntress and goddess of chastity   210 **proof** armor   212 **stay** submit to   213 **bide** abide, endure   216 **store** wealth. (She will die without children, and therefore her beauty will die with her.)

145 **any means** every means possible.   148 **true** i.e., wise in counseling himself   149 **close** secretive   150 **sounding** being fathomed (to discover deep or inner secrets)   151 **envious** malicious   156 **So please you** If you please   158 **happy** fortunate, successful   159 **To** as to.   **shrift** confession.   160 **cousin** kinsman.   169 **Love** Cupid.   **view** appearance   170 **in proof** in reality, in experience.   171 **view . . . still** sight is blindfolded always. (Love is blind.)   172 **to his will** to what he wants.   177 **create** created

BENVOLIO
    Then she hath sworn that she will still live chaste?   217
ROMEO
    She hath, and in that sparing makes huge waste,   218
    For beauty starved with her severity   219
    Cuts beauty off from all posterity.
    She is too fair, too wise, wisely too fair,
    To merit bliss by making me despair.   222
    She hath forsworn to love, and in that vow   223
    Do I live dead, that live to tell it now.
BENVOLIO
    Be ruled by me. Forget to think of her.
ROMEO
    Oh, teach me how I should forget to think!
BENVOLIO
    By giving liberty unto thine eyes:
    Examine other beauties.
ROMEO   'Tis the way
    To call hers, exquisite, in question more.   229
    These happy masks that kiss fair ladies' brows,
    Being black, puts us in mind they hide the fair.
    He that is strucken blind cannot forget
    The precious treasure of his eyesight lost.
    Show me a mistress that is passing fair: 234
    What doth her beauty serve but as a note
    Where I may read who passed that passing fair?   236
    Farewell. Thou canst not teach me to forget.
BENVOLIO
    I'll pay that doctrine, or else die in debt.   *Exeunt.* 238

❦

[1.2]

Enter Capulet, County Paris, and the Clown
[a Servingman].

CAPULET
    But Montague is bound as well as I,   1
    In penalty alike, and 'tis not hard, I think,
    For men so old as we to keep the peace.
PARIS
    Of honorable reckoning are you both,   4
    And pity 'tis you lived at odds so long.
    But now, my lord, what say you to my suit?
CAPULET
    But saying o'er what I have said before: 7
    My child is yet a stranger in the world;
    She hath not seen the change of fourteen years.
    Let two more summers wither in their pride
    Ere we may think her ripe to be a bride.

PARIS
    Younger than she are happy mothers made.
CAPULET
    And too soon marred are those so early made.
    The earth hath swallowed all my hopes but she;
    She is the hopeful lady of my earth.   15
    But woo her, gentle Paris, get her heart;
    My will to her consent is but a part;
    And, she agreed, within her scope of choice   18
    Lies my consent and fair-according voice.   19
    This night I hold an old accustomed feast,   20
    Whereto I have invited many a guest
    Such as I love; and you among the store,   22
    One more, most welcome, makes my number more.
    At my poor house look to behold this night
    Earth-treading stars that make dark heaven light.
    Such comfort as do lusty young men feel   26
    When well-appareled April on the heel   27
    Of limping winter treads, even such delight
    Among fresh fennel buds shall you this night   29
    Inherit at my house. Hear all, all see,   30
    And like her most whose merit most shall be;
    Which on more view of many, mine, being one,   32
    May stand in number, though in reck'ning none.   33
    Come, go with me. [*To the Servingman, giving a paper*]
        Go, sirrah, trudge about   34
    Through fair Verona; find those persons out
    Whose names are written there, and to them say,
    My house and welcome on their pleasure stay.   37
                              Exit [*with Paris*].
SERVINGMAN   Find them out whose names are written
    here! It is written that the shoemaker should meddle   39
    with his yard and the tailor with his last, the fisher   40
    with his pencil, and the painter with his nets; but I am   41
    sent to find those persons whose names are here writ,   42
    and can never find what names the writing person   43
    hath here writ. I must to the learned.—In good time!   44

Enter Benvolio and Romeo.

---

217 **still** always   218 **sparing** miserliness   219 **starved with** killed by
222 **To . . . despair** to achieve her own salvation through chaste living
while driving me to the spiritually dangerous state of despair.
223 **forsworn to** renounced, repudiated   229 **in question more** even
more keenly to mind, into consideration.   234 **mistress** i.e., eligible
young woman.   **passing** surpassingly   236 **passed** surpassed
238 **I'll . . . debt** i.e., I'll fulfill my obligation to do that, or feel I have
failed as a friend.
1.2. Location: Verona.
0.1 *County* Count   1 **bound** legally obligated (to keep the peace)
4 **reckoning** estimation, repute   7 **o'er** again

15 **the hopeful . . . earth** i.e., my heir and hope for posterity. (*Earth*
includes property and lands.)   18 **she** if she be   19 **according** agreeing   20 **old accustomed** traditional   22 **store** group   26 **lusty** lively
27 **well-appareled** newly clothed in green   29 **fennel** flowering herb
thought to have the power of awakening passion   30 **Inherit** possess
32–3 **Which . . . none** i.e., when you have looked over many ladies,
my daughter, being one of them, may be numerically counted among
the lot, but you will not think her worth your notice. (Capulet refers
to the proverbial saying, "one is no number.")   34 **sirrah** (Customary
form of address to servants.)   37 **on . . . stay** wait to serve their pleasure.   39–41 **It is . . . nets** i.e., If a shoemaker cannot be expected to
have any skill with a *yard* (a tailor's yardstick) and conversely a tailor
with a *last* (a shoemaker's form), and similarly with a painter's *pencil*
(a paintbrush) in a fisherman's hands or a net in a painter's hands,
why should I, an illiterate servant, be expected to be able to read a
written note of invitation? (*Meddle, yard*, and *pencil* are often slang
expressions for sexual activity and the male sexual organ, but since
last and *nets* don't seem to convey sexual meaning here, the humor is
more directed at comic inappropriateness.)   42 **find** locate   43 **find**
figure out   44 **In good time** i.e., Here comes help.

BENVOLIO
Tut, man, one fire burns out another's burning,
One pain is lessened by another's anguish;   46
Turn giddy, and be holp by backward turning;   47
One desperate grief cures with another's languish.   48
Take thou some new infection to thy eye,
And the rank poison of the old will die.   50
ROMEO
Your plaintain leaf is excellent for that.   51
BENVOLIO
For what, I pray thee?
ROMEO   For your broken shin.
BENVOLIO   Why, Romeo, art thou mad?
ROMEO
Not mad, but bound more than a madman is;   54
Shut up in prison, kept without my food,
Whipped and tormented and—Good e'en, good
  fellow.   56
SERVINGMAN   God gi' good e'en. I pray, sir, can you read?   57
ROMEO
Ay, mine own fortune in my misery.
SERVINGMAN   Perhaps you have learned it without   59
book. But, I pray, can you read anything you see?   60
ROMEO
Ay, if I know the letters and the language.
SERVINGMAN   Ye say honestly. Rest you merry!   62
                                         [Going.]
ROMEO   Stay, fellow, I can read.   He reads the letter.
  "Signor Martino and his wife and daughters,
  County Anselme and his beauteous sisters,
  The lady widow of Vitruvio,
  Signor Placentio and his lovely nieces,
  Mercutio and his brother Valentine,
  Mine uncle Capulet, his wife, and daughters,
  My fair niece Rosaline, and Livia,
  Signor Valentio and his cousin Tybalt,
  Lucio and the lively Helena."
  A fair assembly. Whither should they come?
SERVINGMAN   Up.
ROMEO   Whither? To supper?
SERVINGMAN   To our house.
ROMEO   Whose house?
SERVINGMAN   My master's.
ROMEO
Indeed, I should have asked thee that before.
SERVINGMAN   Now I'll tell you without asking. My
master is the great rich Capulet; and if you be not of
the house of Montagues, I pray, come and crush a cup   82
of wine. Rest you merry!   [Exit.]

BENVOLIO
At this same ancient feast of Capulet's   84
Sups the fair Rosaline whom thou so loves,
With all the admirèd beauties of Verona.
Go thither, and with unattainted eye   87
Compare her face with some that I shall show,
And I will make thee think thy swan a crow.
ROMEO
When the devout religion of mine eye   90
    Maintains such falsehood, then turn tears to fires;   91
And these who, often drowned, could never die,   92
    Transparent heretics, be burnt for liars!   93
One fairer than my love? The all-seeing sun
Ne'er saw her match since first the world begun.
BENVOLIO
Tut, you saw her fair, none else being by,
Herself poised with herself in either eye;   97
But in that crystal scales let there be weighed   98
Your lady's love against some other maid
That I will show you shining at this feast,
And she shall scant show well that now seems best.   101
ROMEO
I'll go along, no such sight to be shown,
But to rejoice in splendor of mine own.   [Exeunt.] 103

❦

[1.3]

Enter Capulet's Wife and Nurse.

WIFE
Nurse, where's my daughter? Call her forth to me.
NURSE
Now, by my maidenhead at twelve year old,
I bade her come. What, lamb! What, ladybird!   3
God forbid, where's this girl? What, Juliet!   4

        Enter Juliet.

JULIET   How now? Who calls?
NURSE   Your mother.
JULIET
Madam, I am here. What is your will?
WIFE
This is the matter.—Nurse, give leave awhile,   8
We must talk in secret.—Nurse, come back again;
I have remembered me, thou's hear our counsel.   10
Thou knowest my daughter's of a pretty age.

---

46 **another's anguish** the anguish of another pain   47 **holp . . . turning** helped by turning in the reverse direction   48 **cures . . . languish** is cured by the suffering of a second *grief* or pain.   50 **rank** foul   51 **Your . . . that** i.e., (sardonically) Your proverbial nostrums are about as useful in curing my real grief as is a folk remedy for minor abrasions such as a *broken shin* (line 52) or surface wound on the leg— that is, no use at all.   54 **bound** (The usual treatment for madness.)   56 **Good e'en** Good evening. (Used after noon.)   57 **gi'** give you   59–60 **Perhaps . . . book** (1) Perhaps that's some sort of book that you've committed to memory (2) Misery is something one can learn without knowing how to read.   62 **Rest you merry** i.e., Farewell. (The servingman can see he is getting nowhere.)   82 **crush** i.e., drink

84 **ancient** customary   87 **unattainted** unbiased   90–3 **When . . . liars!** (Romeo, recalling that persons suspected of witchcraft were sometimes thrown into water to see if they would drown or float, and that those who did not drown were declared witches and burned at the stake, protests that whenever he is a heretic in love by looking at some woman other than Rosaline he should be similarly burned by having his own tears turn into flames, since he will have shown that his flood of tears could not drown him, i.e., was insufficient. *Transparent* means "manifest," "clear.")   97 **poised** weighed, balanced   98 **crystal scales** i.e., Romeo's eyes   101 **scant** scarcely   103 **mine own** i.e., the sight of my own Rosaline.
1.3. Location: Verona. Capulet's house.
3 **ladybird** (A term of affection.)   4 **God forbid** (A mild oath.)
8 **give leave** leave us   10 **thou's** thou shalt

NURSE
Faith, I can tell her age unto an hour.
WIFE
She's not fourteen.
NURSE   I'll lay fourteen of my teeth—
And yet, to my teen be it spoken, I have but four—   14
She's not fourteen. How long is it now
To Lammastide?
WIFE   A fortnight and odd days.   16
NURSE
Even or odd, of all days in the year,
Come Lammas Eve at night shall she be fourteen.
Susan and she—God rest all Christian souls!—   19
Were of an age. Well, Susan is with God;
She was too good for me. But, as I said,
On Lammas Eve at night shall she be fourteen,
That shall she, marry, I remember it well.   23
'Tis since the earthquake now eleven years,
And she was weaned—I never shall forget it—
Of all the days of the year, upon that day;
For I had then laid wormwood to my dug,   27
Sitting in the sun under the dovehouse wall.
My lord and you were then at Mantua—
Nay, I do bear a brain! But, as I said,   30
When it did taste the wormwood on the nipple
Of my dug and felt it bitter, pretty fool,   32
To see it tetchy and fall out wi'th' dug!   33
"Shake" quoth the dovehouse. 'Twas no need, I trow,   34
To bid me trudge!   35
And since that time it is eleven years,
For then she could stand high-lone; nay, by the rood,   37
She could have run and waddled all about.
For even the day before, she broke her brow,   39
And then my husband—God be with his soul!
'A was a merry man—took up the child.   41
"Yea," quoth he, "dost thou fall upon thy face?
Thou wilt fall backward when thou hast more wit,   43
Wilt thou not, Jule?" and, by my halidom,   44
The pretty wretch left crying and said "Ay."
To see now how a jest shall come about!   46
I warrant, an I should live a thousand years,
I never should forget it. "Wilt thou not, Jule?" quoth
    he,
And, pretty fool, it stinted and said "Ay."   49
WIFE
Enough of this. I pray thee, hold thy peace.

NURSE
Yes, madam. Yet I cannot choose but laugh
To think it should leave crying and say "Ay."
And yet, I warrant, it had upon it brow   53
A bump as big as a young cockerel's stone—   54
A perilous knock—and it cried bitterly.
"Yea," quoth my husband, "fall'st upon thy face?
Thou wilt fall backward when thou comest to age,
Wilt thou not, Jule?" It stinted and said "Ay."
JULIET
And stint thou too, I pray thee, Nurse, say I.   59
NURSE
Peace, I have done. God mark thee to his grace!
Thou wast the prettiest babe that e'er I nursed.
An I might live to see thee married once,   62
I have my wish.
WIFE
Marry, that "marry" is the very theme
I came to talk of. Tell me, daughter Juliet,
How stands your disposition to be married?   66
JULIET
It is an honor that I dream not of.
NURSE
An honor? Were not I thine only nurse,
I would say thou hadst sucked wisdom from thy teat.   69
WIFE
Well, think of marriage now. Younger than you
Here in Verona, ladies of esteem,
Are made already mothers. By my count
I was your mother much upon these years   73
That you are now a maid. Thus then in brief:
The valiant Paris seeks you for his love.
NURSE
A man, young lady! Lady, such a man
As all the world—why, he's a man of wax.   77
WIFE
Verona's summer hath not such a flower.
NURSE
Nay, he's a flower, in faith, a very flower.   79
WIFE
What say you? Can you love the gentleman?
This night you shall behold him at our feast.
Read o'er the volume of young Paris' face,
And find delight writ there with beauty's pen;
Examine every married lineament,   84
And see how one another lends content;   85
And what obscured in this fair volume lies   86
Find written in the margent of his eyes.   87
This precious book of love, this unbound lover,   88

14 teen sorrow. (Playing on *teen* and *four* in *fourteen*.)   16 Lammastide the days near August 1.   19 Susan the Nurse's own child, who has evidently died   23 marry i.e., by the Virgin Mary. (A mild oath.)   27 wormwood (A bitter-tasting plant used to wean the child from the *dug* or "teat.")   30 bear a brain maintain a keen memory.   32 fool (A term of endearment here.)   33 tetchy peevish, irritable   34 "Shake" . . . dovehouse i.e., The dovehouse shook.   trow believe, assure you   35 trudge be off quickly.   37 high-lone on her feet, without help.   rood cross   39 broke her brow bruised her forehead (by falling)   41 'A He   43 wit understanding   44 by my halidom (A mild oath: "by all things holy," but popularly confused with "by my Holy Dame.")   46 come about come true.   49 stinted ceased

53 it its   54 cockerel's stone young rooster's testicle   59 say I (With a pun on *said* "Ay" of previous line.)   62 An If.   once someday   66 disposition inclination   69 thy teat the teat that nourished you.   73 much . . . years at much the same age   77 a man of wax as handsome as a figure modeled in wax.   79 Nay Indeed   84 married lineament harmonized feature   85 And . . . content and see how his handsome features enhance one another   86–7 And what . . . eyes and whatever you don't fully grasp by seeing his handsome features, find explained in his eyes, as though they were a kind of marginal gloss or commentary found in books.   88 unbound i.e., because not bound in marriage. (With a double meaning in the continuing metaphor of an unbound book.)

To beautify him, only lacks a cover.   89
The fish lives in the sea, and 'tis much pride   90
For fair without the fair within to hide.   91
That book in many's eyes doth share the glory,   92
That in gold clasps locks in the golden story;   93
So shall you share all that he doth possess
By having him, making yourself no less.

NURSE
No less? Nay, bigger. Women grow by men.   96

WIFE
Speak briefly, can you like of Paris' love?   97

JULIET
I'll look to like, if looking liking move;   98
But no more deep will I endart mine eye
Than your consent gives strength to make it fly.

Enter Servingman.

SERVINGMAN   Madam, the guests are come, supper
served up, you called, my young lady asked for, the
Nurse cursed in the pantry, and everything in extremity. I must hence to wait. I beseech you, follow straight.   104

WIFE   We follow thee.   [*Exit Servingman.*]
                             Juliet, the County stays.   105

NURSE
Go, girl, seek happy nights to happy days.   *Exeunt.*

❖

[1.4]

*Enter Romeo, Mercutio, Benvolio, with five or
six other masquers; torchbearers.*

ROMEO
What, shall this speech be spoke for our excuse?   1
Or shall we on without apology?   2

BENVOLIO
The date is out of such prolixity.   3
We'll have no Cupid hoodwinked with a scarf,   4
Bearing a Tartar's painted bow of lath,   5
Scaring the ladies like a crowkeeper,   6
Nor no without-book prologue, faintly spoke   7
After the prompter, for our entrance;
But let them measure us by what they will,   9
We'll measure them a measure, and be gone.   10

ROMEO
Give me a torch. I am not for this ambling.   89 *[line 11]*
Being but heavy, I will bear the light.   12

MERCUTIO
Nay, gentle Romeo, we must have you dance.

ROMEO
Not I, believe me. You have dancing shoes
With nimble soles; I have a soul of lead   15
So stakes me to the ground I cannot move.

MERCUTIO
You are a lover; borrow Cupid's wings,
And soar with them above a common bound.   18

ROMEO
I am too sore enpiercèd with his shaft   19
To soar with his light feathers, and so bound
I cannot bound a pitch above dull woe.   21
Under love's heavy burden do I sink.

MERCUTIO
And, to sink in it, should you burden love—   23
Too great oppression for a tender thing.

ROMEO
Is love a tender thing? It is too rough,
Too rude, too boisterous, and it pricks like thorn.

MERCUTIO
If love be rough with you, be rough with love;
Prick love for pricking, and you beat love down.   28
Give me a case to put my visage in.   29
                                [*He puts on a mask.*]
A visor for a visor! What care I   30
What curious eye doth quote deformities?   31
Here are the beetle brows shall blush for me.

BENVOLIO
Come, knock and enter, and no sooner in
But every man betake him to his legs.   34

ROMEO
A torch for me. Let wantons light of heart
Tickle the senseless rushes with their heels,   36
For I am proverbed with a grandsire phrase: 37
I'll be a candle-holder and look on.   38
The game was ne'er so fair, and I am done.   39

---

89 a cover i.e., marriage, an embracing wife.   **90–1 The fish . . . hide**
i.e., The fish has its own suitable environment, and similarly in marriage the fair Juliet (here imagined as a beautiful book cover "binding" Paris) would suitably enhance Paris's worth.   **92–3 That book
. . . story** i.e., In many persons' eyes, a good story is all the more
admirable for being handsomely bound. (*Clasps* means [1] book fas-
tenings [2] embraces.)   **96 bigger** i.e., by pregnancy.   **97 like of** be
pleased with   **98 liking move** may provoke affection   **104 straight**
at once.   **105 County stays** Count (Paris) waits for you.
1.4. Location: Verona. A street.
1 speech (Masquers were customarily preceded by a messenger or
"presenter" with a set speech of compliment.)   **2 on** go on, approach
3 The date . . . prolixity Such windy rhetoric is out of fashion.
4 Cupid i.e., messenger or "presenter," probably a boy, disguised as
Cupid.   **hoodwinked** blindfolded   **5 Tartar's . . . bow** (Tartars'
bows, shorter and more curved than the English longbow, were
thought to have resembled the old Roman bow with which Cupid
was pictured.)   **lath** flimsy wood   **6 crowkeeper** scarecrow
7 without-book memorized   **9 measure** judge   **10 measure . . .
measure** tread a dance for them

12 heavy (1) sad (2) the opposite of *light* (as at 1.1.137)   **15 soul** (Punning on *sole*.)   **18 common bound** (1) ordinary limit (2) normal
dance leap.   **19 sore** sorely. (With pun on *soar*.)   **21 bound** leap.
(With wordplay on *bound*, "confined," in the previous line.)   **pitch**
height. (A term from falconry for the highest point of a hawk's flight.)
23 And . . . love i.e., You wouldn't just sink *under* love's heavy burden, you'd sink *into* it and burden it. (Suggesting sexual penetration.)
28 Prick . . . down i.e., If love gets rough, fight back. (But with bawdy
suggestion of *pricking* as a way to satisfy desire and cause detumescence.)   **29 case** mask   **30 A visor . . . visor** i.e., A mask for an ugly
masklike face.   **31 quote** take notice of   **34 to his legs** to dancing.
36 senseless rushes reeds used as floor covering, or insensate green
rushes   **37 proverbed . . . phrase** furnished with an old proverb
38 candle-holder i.e., bystander. (Referring to the proverbial idea that
one who lacks ability himself can hold the candle and thus provide
light for one who is able to act.)   **39 The game . . . done** (Another
proverbial truism, that it is best to quit when one is ahead.)

MERCUTIO

Tut, dun's the mouse, the constable's own word.   40
If thou art dun, we'll draw thee from the mire   41
Of—save your reverence—love, wherein thou stickest   42
Up to the ears. Come, we burn daylight, ho!   43

ROMEO

Nay, that's not so.

MERCUTIO   I mean, sir, in delay
We waste our lights in vain, like lamps by day.
Take our good meaning, for our judgment sits   46
Five times in that ere once in our five wits.   47

ROMEO

And we mean well in going to this masque,
But 'tis no wit to go.

MERCUTIO   Why, may one ask?   49

ROMEO

I dreamt a dream tonight.

MERCUTIO   And so did I.   50

ROMEO

Well, what was yours?

MERCUTIO   That dreamers often lie. 51

ROMEO

In bed asleep, while they do dream things true.

MERCUTIO

Oh, then, I see Queen Mab hath been with you.   53
She is the fairies' midwife, and she comes
In shape no bigger than an agate stone   55
On the forefinger of an alderman,   56
Drawn with a team of little atomi   57
Over men's noses as they lie asleep.
Her chariot is an empty hazelnut,
Made by the joiner squirrel or old grub,   60
Time out o' mind the fairies' coachmakers.
Her wagon spokes made of long spinners' legs,   62
The cover of the wings of grasshoppers,
Her traces of the smallest spider web,
Her collars of the moonshine's wat'ry beams,
Her whip of cricket's bone, the lash of film,   66
Her wagoner a small gray-coated gnat,   67

Not half so big as a round little worm   68
Pricked from the lazy finger of a maid.   69
And in this state she gallops night by night
Through lovers' brains, and then they dream of love;
O'er courtiers' knees, that dream on curtsies straight; 72
O'er lawyers' fingers, who straight dream on fees;
O'er ladies' lips, who straight on kisses dream,
Which oft the angry Mab with blisters plagues
Because their breaths with sweetmeats tainted are.   76
Sometime she gallops o'er a courtier's nose,
And then dreams he of smelling out a suit.   78
And sometime comes she with a tithe-pig's tail   79
Tickling a parson's nose as 'a lies asleep;
Then dreams he of another benefice.   81
Sometime she driveth o'er a soldier's neck,
And then dreams he of cutting foreign throats,
Of breaches, ambuscadoes, Spanish blades,   84
Of healths five fathom deep, and then anon   85
Drums in his ear, at which he starts and wakes,
And being thus frighted swears a prayer or two
And sleeps again. This is that very Mab
That plats the manes of horses in the night,   89
And bakes the elflocks in foul sluttish hairs,   90
Which once untangled much misfortune bodes.   91
This is the hag, when maids lie on their backs,
That presses them and learns them first to bear,   93
Making them women of good carriage.   94
This is she—

ROMEO   Peace, peace, Mercutio, peace!
Thou talk'st of nothing.

MERCUTIO   True, I talk of dreams,
Which are the children of an idle brain,
Begot of nothing but vain fantasy,   98
Which is as thin of substance as the air,
And more inconstant than the wind, who woos
Even now the frozen bosom of the north,
And being angered, puffs away from thence,
Turning his side to the dew-dropping south.

BENVOLIO

This wind you talk of blows us from ourselves.   104
Supper is done, and we shall come too late.

ROMEO

I fear, too early; for my mind misgives   106
Some consequence yet hanging in the stars

---

40 dun's . . . word i.e., "keep still"—just the sort of thing a constable might say. (Matching proverb with proverb, Mercutio answers Romeo's "I am done" by twitting him for being mousy. Constables were much laughed at for inappropriately pompous speech.)
41–3 If . . . ears (To Mercutio, Romeo's love melancholy recalls the Christmas game called "Dun is in the mire," in which a heavy log, representing a horse named Dun, was hauled out of an imaginary mire by the players. *Save your reverence* is Mercutio's mock apology for speaking of so improper an expression as being mired up to the ears in love.) **43 burn daylight** i.e., waste time. (But Romeo quibbles, protesting that it is not literally daytime.) **46–7 Take . . . wits** Try to understand what I am trying to say (rather than quibbling with phrases like "burn daylight"), for wise judgment is five times more pleased with good meaning than with the ingenious wit of our frail senses. **49 wit** wisdom (playing on *wits* in line 47; *mean* in line 48 plays on *meaning* in line 46) **50 tonight** last night. **51 lie** tell falsehoods. (But Mercutio answers in the sense of "lie down in bed.") **53 Queen Mab** (Possibly a name of Celtic origin for the Fairy Queen.) **55 agate stone** (Precious stone often carved with diminutive figures and set in a ring.) **56 alderman** member of the municipal council **57 atomi** tiny creatures (atoms) **60 joiner** furniture maker. **grub** insect larva (which bores holes in nuts) **62 spinners'** spiders' **66 film** gossamer thread **67 wagoner** chariot driver

68–9 a round . . . maid (Worms proverbially breed in the fingers of the idle.) **72 curtsies** bows, obeisances. **straight** immediately **76 sweetmeats** candies or candied preserves **78 smelling . . . suit** i.e., finding a petitioner who will pay for the use of his influence at court. **79 tithe-pig** pig given to the parson in lieu of money as the parishioner's tithing, or granting of a tenth **81 benefice** ecclesiastical living. **84 Of breaches . . . blades** of opening up gaps in fortifications, of ambushes, of swords from Toledo in Spain, where the best swords were made **85 Of healths . . . deep** of toasts drunk deep **89 That plats . . . night** (According to popular superstition, the tangles that persistently turn up in the manes of horses were "witches' stirrups," i.e., footholds for witches as they rode.) **90–1 And bakes . . . bodes** (*Elflocks* or clumps of matted hair were so named because they were imagined to be the work of elves, who would torment anyone so presumptuous as to untangle the elflocks.) **93 learns** teaches **94 good carriage** (1) commendable deportment (2) skill in bearing the weight of men in sexual intercourse (3) able subsequently to carry a child. **98 vain fantasy** delusive imagination **104 from ourselves** from our plans. **106 misgives** fears

Shall bitterly begin his fearful date   108
With this night's revels, and expire the term   109
Of a despisèd life closed in my breast
By some vile forfeit of untimely death.
But He that hath the steerage of my course
Direct my suit! On, lusty gentlemen.   113
BENVOLIO   Strike, drum.   *They march about the stage,* 114
                                   and [retire to one side].

❖

[1.5]

Servingmen come forth with napkins.

FIRST SERVINGMAN   Where's Potpan, that he helps not
to take away? He shift a trencher? He scrape a trencher?   2

SECOND SERVINGMAN   When good manners shall lie all
in one or two men's hands, and they unwashed too,
'tis a foul thing.

FIRST SERVINGMAN   Away with the joint stools, remove   6
the court cupboard, look to the plate. Good thou, save   7
me a piece of marchpane, and, as thou loves me, let   8
the porter let in Susan Grindstone and Nell.
                                   [Exit Second Servingman.]
Anthony and Potpan!

[Enter two more Servingmen.]

THIRD SERVINGMAN   Ay, boy, ready.

FIRST SERVINGMAN   You are looked for and called for,
asked for and sought for, in the great chamber.

FOURTH SERVINGMAN   We cannot be here and there
too. Cheerly, boys! Be brisk awhile, and the longest   15
liver take all.   *Exeunt.*   16

*Enter [Capulet and family and] all the guests
and gentlewomen to the masquers.*

CAPULET *[to the masquers]*
Welcome, gentlemen! Ladies that have their toes
Unplagued with corns will walk a bout with you.   18
Ah, my mistresses, which of you all
Will now deny to dance? She that makes dainty,   20
She, I'll swear, hath corns. Am I come near ye now?   21
Welcome, gentlemen! I have seen the day
That I have worn a visor and could tell
A whispering tale in a fair lady's ear
Such as would please. 'Tis gone, 'tis gone, 'tis gone.
You are welcome, gentlemen! Come, musicians, play.
                          Music plays, and they dance.

A hall, a hall! Give room! And foot, it, girls.   27
[To Servingmen]   More light, you knaves, and turn the
   tables up,   28
And quench the fire; the room is grown too hot.
[To his cousin]   Ah, sirrah, this unlooked-for sport
   comes well.   30
Nay, sit, nay, sit, good cousin Capulet,   31
For you and I are past our dancing days.
How long is't now since last yourself and I
Were in a mask?
SECOND CAPULET   By'r Lady, thirty years.
CAPULET
What, man? 'Tis not so much, 'tis not so much;
'Tis since the nuptial of Lucentio,
Come Pentecost as quickly as it will,   37
Some five-and-twenty years, and then we masked.
SECOND CAPULET
'Tis more, 'tis more. His son is elder, sir;
His son is thirty.
CAPULET   Will you tell me that?
His son was but a ward two years ago.   41
ROMEO *[to a Servingman]*
What lady's that which doth enrich the hand
Of yonder knight?
SERVINGMAN   I know not, sir.
ROMEO
Oh, she doth teach the torches to burn bright!
It seems she hangs upon the cheek of night
As a rich jewel in an Ethiop's ear—
Beauty too rich for use, for earth too dear!   48
So shows a snowy dove trooping with crows   49
As yonder lady o'er her fellows shows.
The measure done, I'll watch her place of stand,   51
And, touching hers, make blessèd my rude hand.   52
Did my heart love till now? Forswear it, sight!   53
For I ne'er saw true beauty till this night.
TYBALT
This, by his voice, should be a Montague.
Fetch me my rapier, boy. What dares the slave   56
Come hither, covered with an antic face,   57
To fleer and scorn at our solemnity?   58
Now, by the stock and honor of my kin,
To strike him dead I hold it not a sin.
CAPULET
Why, how now, kinsman? Wherefore storm you so?

---

27 A hall i.e., Clear the hall for dancing   **28 turn . . . up** move the tables out of the way for the dancing (by taking up the boards and then removing the supporting trestles)   **30 sirrah** (Normally used in addressing social inferiors. Perhaps Capulet uses a jesting tone toward his kinsman or possibly addresses himself.)   **unlooked-for sport** i.e., arrival of the masquers, providing more men for the dancing   **31 cousin** (*Cousin* often means "kinsman"; at 1.2.69, "Mine uncle Capulet" is named on the invitation list.)   **37 Pentecost** seventh Sunday after Easter (and never as late as mid-July, two weeks before Lammas or August 1, when according to 1.3.16, the play takes place; a seeming inconsistency).   **41 a ward** a minor under guardianship   **48 dear** precious.   **49 shows** appears   **51 The measure done** When this dance is over.   **her place of stand** where she stands   **52 hers** her hand.   **rude** rough   **53 Forswear it** Deny any previous oath   **56 What** How   **57 antic face** grotesque mask   **58 fleer** jeer. **solemnity** time-honored festivity.

---

108 date appointed time   **109 expire** bring to an end   **113 lusty** lively   **114 drum** drummer.
1.5. Location: The action, continuous from the previous scene, is now imaginatively transferred to a hall in Capulet's house.
2 take away clear the table.   **trencher** wooden dish or plate.   **6 joint stools** stools of which the parts are fitted by a joiner or furniture maker   **7 court cupboard** sideboard.   **plate** silverware.   **8 marchpane** cake made from sugar and almonds, marzipan   **15–16 the longest . . . all** (A proverb in defense of merriment.)   **18 walk a bout** dance a turn   **20 makes dainty** seems coyly reluctant (to dance)   **21 Am . . . now?** Have I hit a sensitive point, struck home?

TYBALT
    Uncle, this is a Montague, our foe,
    A villain that is hither come in spite   63
    To scorn at our solemnity this night.
CAPULET
    Young Romeo is it?
TYBALT   'Tis he, that villain Romeo.
CAPULET
    Content thee, gentle coz, let him alone.
    'A bears him like a portly gentleman,   67
    And, to say truth, Verona brags of him
    To be a virtuous and well governed youth.
    I would not for the wealth of all this town
    Here in my house do him disparagement.
    Therefore be patient; take no note of him.
    It is my will, the which if thou respect,
    Show a fair presence and put off these frowns,   74
    An ill-beseeming semblance for a feast.   75
TYBALT
    It fits when such a villain is a guest.
    I'll not endure him.
CAPULET   He shall be endured.
    What, goodman boy? I say he shall. Go to!   78
    Am I the master here, or you? Go to.
    You'll not endure him! God shall mend my soul,
    You'll make a mutiny among my guests!   81
    You will set cock-a-hoop! You'll be the man!   82
TYBALT
    Why, uncle, 'tis a shame.
CAPULET   Go to, go to,
    You are a saucy boy. Is't so, indeed?
    This trick may chance to scathe you. I know what,   85
    You must contrary me. Marry, 'tis time.—   86
    Well said, my hearts!—You are a princox, go.   87
    Be quiet, or—More light, more light!—For shame!
    I'll make you quiet.—What, cheerly, my hearts!
TYBALT
    Patience perforce with willful choler meeting   90
    Makes my flesh tremble in their different greeting.   91
    I will withdraw. But this intrusion shall,
    Now seeming sweet, convert to bitt'rest gall.   Exit.
ROMEO [to Juliet]
    If I profane with my unworthiest hand   94
        This holy shrine, the gentle sin is this: 95
    My lips, two blushing pilgrims, ready stand
        To smooth that rough touch with a tender kiss.
JULIET
    Good pilgrim, you do wrong your hand too much,

    Which mannerly devotion shows in this;
    For saints have hands that pilgrims' hands do touch,   100
    And palm to palm is holy palmers' kiss.   101
ROMEO
    Have not saints lips, and holy palmers too?
JULIET
    Ay, pilgrim, lips that they must use in prayer.
ROMEO
    Oh, then, dear saint, let lips do what hands do.   104
    They pray; grant thou, lest faith turn to despair.
JULIET
    Saints do not move, though grant for prayers' sake. 106
ROMEO
    Then move not, while my prayer's effect I take.   107
                                     [He kisses her.]
    Thus from my lips, by thine, my sin is purged.
JULIET
    Then have my lips the sin that they have took.
ROMEO
    Sin from my lips? Oh, trespass sweetly urged!
    Give me my sin again.   [He kisses her.]
JULIET   You kiss by th' book.   111
NURSE [approaching]
    Madam, your mother craves a word with you.
                                     [Juliet retires.]
ROMEO
    What is her mother?
NURSE   Marry, bachelor,   113
    Her mother is the lady of the house,
    And a good lady, and a wise and virtuous.
    I nursed her daughter that you talked withal.   116
    I tell you, he that can lay hold of her
    Shall have the chinks.
ROMEO [aside]   Is she a Capulet?   118
    Oh, dear account! My life is my foe's debt.   119
BENVOLIO [approaching]
    Away, begone! The sport is at the best.   120
ROMEO
    Ay, so I fear; the more is my unrest.
                         [The masquers prepare to leave.]
CAPULET
    Nay, gentlemen, prepare not to be gone.
    We have a trifling foolish banquet towards.   123
                             [One whispers in his ear.]
    Is it e'en so? Why, then, I thank you all.
    I thank you, honest gentlemen. Good night.   125

---

63 **spite** malice   67 **portly** of good deportment   74 **presence**
demeanor   75 **semblance** facial expression   78 **goodman boy** (A
belittling term for Tybalt; *Goodman* applied to one below the rank of
gentleman but still of some substance, like a wealthy farmer.)   **Go to**
(An expression of irritation.)   81 **mutiny** disturbance   82 **You . . .
man!** i.e., You'll set mischief abroach (literally, turn the tap and let the
liquor flow)! You'll be the big shot!   85 **scathe** harm   86 **contrary**
oppose, thwart.   **'tis time** i.e., it's time you were taught a lesson.
87 **Well said** Well done. (Said to the dancers.)   **princox** saucy boy
90–1 **Patience . . . greeting** The attempt to be patient under duress
when I am so angry causes me to tremble at the contrary meeting of
these two opposite impulses.   94–107 (These lines are in the form of
a Shakespearean sonnet; they are followed by a quatrain.)   95 **shrine**
i.e., Juliet's hand

100 **saints** i.e., images of saints that are venerated by pilgrims
101 **palmers** pilgrims who have been to the Holy Land and have
brought back a palm. (With a pun on the palm of the hand.)   104 **let . . .
do** let lips touch, just as hands touch.   106 **Saints . . . sake** Venerated
images and statues of saints remain motionless but nonetheless inter-
cede on behalf of praying pilgrims.   107 **move** (Romeo quibbles on
Juliet's metaphorical use of the word *move* to urge that she remain
motionless while he kisses her.)   111 **by th' book** by the rules, like
an expert.   113 **What** Who   116 **withal** with.   118 **the chinks** plenty
of coins, money. (A slang expression.)   119 **dear account** heavy reckoning.   **my foe's debt** due to my foe, at his mercy.   120 **The sport . . .
best** i.e., It is time to leave. (Refers to the proverb, "When play is at
the best, it is time to leave"; compare at 1.4.39.)   123 **foolish banquet
towards** insignificant light refreshment just ready.   125 **honest**
honorable

More torches here! Come on then, let's to bed.   126
[*To his cousin*] Ah, sirrah, by my fay, it waxes late.   127
I'll to my rest.
              [*All proceed to leave but Juliet and the Nurse.*]

JULIET
Come hither, Nurse. What is yond gentleman?

NURSE
The son and heir of old Tiberio.

JULIET
What's he that now is going out of door?

NURSE
Marry, that, I think, be young Petruchio.

JULIET
What's he that follows here, that would not dance?

NURSE   I know not.

JULIET
Go ask his name. [*The Nurse goes.*] If he be marrièd,
My grave is like to be my wedding bed.   136

NURSE [*returning*]
His name is Romeo, and a Montague,
The only son of your great enemy.

JULIET
My only love sprung from my only hate!
Too early seen unknown, and known too late!
Prodigious birth of love it is to me   141
That I must love a loathèd enemy.

NURSE
What's tis? What's tis?

JULIET   A rhyme I learned even now   143
Of one I danced withal.   *One calls within* "Juliet."

NURSE   Anon, anon!   144
Come, let's away. The strangers all are gone.   *Exeunt.*

❦

[2.0]

              [*Enter*] Chorus.

CHORUS
Now old desire doth in his deathbed lie,   1
   And young affection gapes to be his heir;   2
That fair for which love groaned for and would die,   3
   With tender Juliet matched, is now not fair.   4
Now Romeo is beloved and loves again,
   Alike bewitchèd by the charm of looks;   6
But to his foe supposed he must complain,   7
   And she steal love's sweet bait from fearful hooks.   8
Being held a foe, he may not have access
   To breathe such vows as lovers use to swear;   10
And she as much in love, her means much less
   To meet her new-belovèd anywhere.

But passion lends them power, time means, to meet,   13
Temp'ring extremities with extreme sweet.   [*Exit.*]   14

❦

[2.1]

              Enter Romeo alone.

ROMEO
Can I go forward when my heart is here?   1
Turn back, dull earth, and find thy center out.   2
                                          [*Romeo retires.*]

              Enter Benvolio with Mercutio.

BENVOLIO
Romeo! My cousin Romeo! Romeo!

MERCUTIO   He is wise
And, on my life, hath stol'n him home to bed.

BENVOLIO
He ran this way and leapt this orchard wall.
Call, good Mercutio.

MERCUTIO   Nay, I'll conjure too.   7
Romeo! Humors! Madman! Passion! Lover!   8
Appear thou in the likeness of a sigh.
Speak but one rhyme, and I am satisfied;
Cry but "Ay me!" Pronounce but "love" and "dove."
Speak to my gossip Venus one fair word,   12
One nickname for her purblind son and heir,   13
Young Abraham Cupid, he that shot so trim   14
When King Cophetua loved the beggar maid.—   15
He heareth not, he stirreth not, he moveth not;
The ape is dead, and I must conjure him.—   17
I conjure thee by Rosaline's bright eyes,
By her high forehead and her scarlet lip,
By her fine foot, straight leg, and quivering thigh,
And the demesnes that there adjacent lie,   21
That in thy likeness thou appear to us.

BENVOLIO
An if he hear thee, thou wilt anger him.   23

MERCUTIO
This cannot anger him. 'Twould anger him
To raise a spirit in his mistress' circle   25
Of some strange nature, letting it there stand   26

---

126 torches i.e., to light the guests as they leave   **127 fay** faith
136 like likely   **141 Prodigious** Ominous   **143 tis** this. (Dialect pronunciation.)   **144 Anon** i.e., We're coming
2.0. Chorus.
1–14 (This chorus is a sonnet.)   **2 gapes** waits open-mouthed   **3 fair**
beauty, i.e., Rosaline   **4 matched** compared   **6 Alike** i.e., equally
with Juliet   **7 foe supposed** i.e., Juliet, a Capulet; also, his opposite
number in the war of love.   **complain** offer his love plaint   **8 And
she . . . hooks** and she must steal moments of happy love from frightening circumstances designed to catch her unawares.   **10 use** are
accustomed

13 time means time lends them means   **14 Temp'ring extremities**
mitigating the hardships.   **sweet** sweetness, pleasure.
2.1. Location: Verona. Outside of Capulet's walled orchard.
1 forward i.e., away   **2 Turn . . . out** (Romeo bids his own earthbound body find out its *center*, its soul or heart (i.e., Juliet), much as
in the Ptolemaic system all earthly things seek out their center, the
earth, standing at the center of the universe. His body is *dull* in that,
like earth, it is the lowest and heaviest of the four elements, associated with melancholy.)   **7 conjure** raise him with magical incantation
8 Humors Moods.   **12 gossip** crony   **13 purblind** dim-sighted
14 Young Abraham i.e., one who is young and yet, like the Biblical
Abraham, old; Cupid was paradoxically the youngest and the oldest
of the gods   **15 King Cophetua** (In an old ballad, the King falls in
love with a beggar maid and makes her his queen.)   **17 ape** (Used as
a term of endearment.)   **21 demesnes** regions. (With bawdy suggestion as to what is adjacent to the thighs; bawdy puns on terms of conjuration continue in *raise*, *spirit*, i.e., "phallus" or "semen," *circle*,
stand, laid it, raise up.)   **23 An if** If   **25 circle** (1) conjuring circle (2)
vagina   **26 strange** belonging to another person. (With suggestion of
a rival possessing Rosaline sexually.)

Till she had laid it and conjured it down;   27
That were some spite. My invocation   28
Is fair and honest; in his mistress' name
I conjure only but to raise up him.

BENVOLIO
Come, he hath hid himself among these trees
To be consorted with the humorous night.   32
Blind is his love, and best befits the dark.

MERCUTIO
If love be blind, love cannot hit the mark.
Now will he sit under a medlar tree   35
And wish his mistress were that kind of fruit
As maids call medlars when they laugh alone.
Oh, Romeo, that she were, oh, that she were
An open-arse, and thou a pop'ring pear!   39
Romeo, good night. I'll to my truckle bed;   40
This field bed is too cold for me to sleep.   41
Come, shall we go?

BENVOLIO   Go, then, for 'tis in vain
To seek him here that means not to be found.
                                   Exit [*with Mercutio*].

[2.2]

ROMEO [*coming forward*]
He jests at scars that never felt a wound.   1
        [*A light appears above, as at Juliet's window.*]
But soft, what light through yonder window breaks?
It is the east, and Juliet is the sun.
Arise, fair sun, and kill the envious moon,
Who is already sick and pale with grief
That thou her maid art far more fair than she.   6
Be not her maid, since she is envious;   7
Her vestal livery is but sick and green   8
And none but fools do wear it. Cast it off.
            [*Juliet appears aloft as at her window.*]
It is my lady, oh, it is my love.
Oh, that she knew she were!
She speaks, yet she says nothing. What of that?

Her eye discourses. I will answer it.
I am too bold. 'Tis not to me she speaks.
Two of the fairest stars in all the heaven,
Having some business, do entreat her eyes
To twinkle in their spheres till they return.   17
What if her eyes were there, they in her head?   18
The brightness of her cheek would shame those stars
As daylight doth a lamp; her eyes in heaven
Would through the airy region stream so bright   21
That birds would sing and think it were not night.
See how she leans her cheek upon her hand!
Oh, that I were a glove upon that hand,
That I might touch that cheek!

JULIET   Ay me!

ROMEO [*aside*]   She speaks.
Oh, speak again, bright angel, for thou art
As glorious to this night, being o'er my head,
As is a wingèd messenger of heaven
Unto the white-upturnèd wond'ring eyes   29
Of mortals that fall back to gaze on him
When he bestrides the lazy puffing clouds
And sails upon the bosom of the air.

JULIET [*to herself*]
Oh, Romeo, Romeo, wherefore art thou Romeo?   33
Deny thy father and refuse thy name!
Or, if thou wilt not, be but sworn my love,
And I'll no longer be a Capulet.

ROMEO [*aside*]
Shall I hear more, or shall I speak at this?

JULIET
'Tis but thy name that is my enemy;
Thou art thyself, though not a Montague.   39
What's Montague? It is nor hand, nor foot,   40
Nor arm, nor face, nor any other part
Belonging to a man. Oh, be some other name!
What's in a name? That which we call a rose
By any other word would smell as sweet;
So Romeo would, were he not Romeo called,
Retain that dear perfection which he owes   46
Without that title. Romeo, doff thy name,   47
And for thy name, which is no part of thee,   48
Take all myself.

ROMEO   I take thee at thy word!
Call me but love, and I'll be new baptized;
Henceforth I never will be Romeo.

JULIET
What man art thou that, thus bescreened in night,   52
So stumblest on my counsel?

ROMEO   By a name   53
I know not how to tell thee who I am.
My name, dear saint, is hateful to myself,
Because it is an enemy to thee;
Had I it written, I would tear the word.

---

27 **laid it** (1) laid the spirit to rest (2) provided sexual satisfaction leading to detumescence   28 **were some spite** would be vexing.   32 **consorted** associated.   **humorous** (1) moist, damp (2) well suited to the *humor* of melancholy   35 **medlar** a fruit that was edible only when partly decayed, used as a slang term for women's sexual organs   39 **open-arse** (Another name for the *medlar*, making explicit the sexual metaphor.)   **pop'ring pear** poppering pear (named after Poperinghe in Flanders). A fruit with phallic associations because of its shape and its suggestive name ("pop 'er in").   40 **truckle bed** a bed on casters to be rolled under a standing bed when not in use   41 **field bed** i.e., the ground
2.2. Location: The action, continuous from the previous scene, is now imaginatively transferred to inside Capulet's orchard. A rhymed couplet links the two scenes. Romeo has been hiding from his friends as though concealed by the orchard wall. He speaks at once and then turns to observe Juliet's window, which is probably in the gallery above, rearstage.
1.1 *A light appears* (Some editors assume that Juliet is visible at line 1.)   6 **maid** i.e., votary of Diana, goddess of the moon and patroness of virgins   7 **her** the moon's, Diana's, as the goddess of chastity. (Addressed to Juliet as the sun; Romeo hopes that she will not be a devotee of chastity.)   8 **Her vestal livery** the uniform of Diana's chaste votaries.   **sick and green** (Suggesting the pallor of moonlight, as well as anemia or *greensickness* [see 3.5.156], to which teenage girls were susceptible.)

---

17 **spheres** transparent concentric shells supposed to carry the heavenly bodies with them in their revolution around the earth   18 **there** i.e., in the spheres   21 **stream** shine   29 **white-upturnèd** looking upward so that the whites of the eyes are visible   33 **wherefore** why   39 **though not** (1) even if you were not (2) though not in anything essential   40 **nor hand** neither hand   46 **owes** owns   47 **doff** cast off   48 **for** in exchange for   52 **bescreened** concealed   53 **counsel** secret thought.

JULIET
My ears have yet not drunk a hundred words
Of thy tongue's uttering, yet I know the sound:
Art thou not Romeo and a Montague?

ROMEO
Neither, fair maid, if either thee dislike.   61

JULIET
How camest thou hither, tell me, and wherefore?
The orchard walls are high and hard to climb,
And the place death, considering who thou art,
If any of my kinsmen find thee here.

ROMEO
With love's light wings did I o'erperch these walls,   66
For stony limits cannot hold love out,
And what love can do, that dares love attempt;
Therefore thy kinsmen are no stop to me.

JULIET
If they do see thee, they will murder thee.

ROMEO
Alack, there lies more peril in thine eye
Than twenty of their swords. Look thou but sweet,
And I am proof against their enmity.   73

JULIET
I would not for the world they saw thee here.

ROMEO
I have night's cloak to hide me from their eyes;
And but thou love me, let them find me here.   76
My life were better ended by their hate
Than death proroguèd, wanting of thy love.   78

JULIET
By whose direction found'st thou out this place?

ROMEO
By love, that first did prompt me to inquire.
He lent me counsel, and I lent him eyes.
I am no pilot; yet, wert thou as far
As that vast shore washed with the farthest sea,
I should adventure for such merchandise.

JULIET
Thou knowest the mask of night is on my face,
Else would a maiden blush bepaint my cheek
For that which thou hast heard me speak tonight.
Fain would I dwell on form—fain, fain deny   88
What I have spoke; but farewell compliment!   89
Dost thou love me? I know thou wilt say "Ay,"
And I will take thy word. Yet if thou swear'st
Thou mayst prove false. At lovers' perjuries,
They say, Jove laughs. O gentle Romeo,
If thou dost love, pronounce it faithfully.
Or if thou thinkest I am too quickly won,
I'll frown and be perverse and say thee nay,
So thou wilt woo, but else not for the world.
In truth, fair Montague, I am too fond,   98
And therefore thou mayst think my havior light.   99
But trust me, gentleman, I'll prove more true
Than those that have more cunning to be strange.   101

I should have been more strange, I must confess,
But that thou overheard'st, ere I was ware,   103
My true-love passion. Therefore pardon me,
And not impute this yielding to light love,
Which the dark night hath so discoverèd.   106

ROMEO
Lady, by yonder blessèd moon I vow,
That tips with silver all these fruit-tree tops—

JULIET
Oh, swear not by the moon, th'inconstant moon,
That monthly changes in her circled orb,   110
Lest that thy love prove likewise variable.

ROMEO
What shall I swear by?

JULIET   Do not swear at all;
Or, if thou wilt, swear by thy gracious self,
Which is the god of my idolatry,
And I'll believe thee.

ROMEO   If my heart's dear love—

JULIET
Well, do not swear. Although I joy in thee,
I have no joy of this contract tonight.   117
It is too rash, too unadvised, too sudden,   118
Too like the lightning, which doth cease to be
Ere one can say it lightens. Sweet, good night!
This bud of love, by summer's ripening breath,
May prove a beauteous flower when next we meet.
Good night, good night! As sweet repose and rest   123
Come to thy heart as that within my breast!

ROMEO
Oh, wilt thou leave me so unsatisfied?

JULIET
What satisfaction canst thou have tonight?

ROMEO
Th'exchange of thy love's faithful vow for mine.

JULIET
I gave thee mine before thou didst request it;
And yet I would it were to give again.

ROMEO
Wouldst thou withdraw it? For what purpose, love?

JULIET
But to be frank and give it thee again.   131
And yet I wish but for the thing I have.
My bounty is as boundless as the sea,
My love as deep; the more I give to thee,
The more I have, for both are infinite.
                                  [The Nurse calls within.]
I hear some noise within. Dear love, adieu!—
Anon, good Nurse!—Sweet Montague, be true.
Stay but a little; I will come again.   [Exit, above.]

ROMEO
Oh, blessèd, blessèd night! I am afeard,
Being in night, all this is but a dream,
Too flattering-sweet to be substantial.

[Enter Juliet, above.]

---

61 **thee dislike** displeases you. 66 **o'erperch** fly over 73 **proof** protected 76 **but** unless 78 **prorogued** postponed. **wanting of** lacking 88 **Fain** Gladly. **dwell on form** preserve the proper formalities 89 **compliment** etiquette, convention. 98 **fond** infatuated 99 **havior light** behavior frivolous. 101 **strange** reserved, aloof, modest.

103 **ware** aware 106 **Which** i.e., which yielding. **discoverèd** revealed. 110 **orb** orbit, sphere 117 **contract** exchanging of vows 118 **unadvised** unconsidered 123 **As** May just as 131 **frank** liberal, bounteous

JULIET
Three words, dear Romeo, and good night indeed.
If that thy bent of love be honorable,   143
Thy purpose marriage, send me word tomorrow,
By one that I'll procure to come to thee,
Where and what time thou wilt perform the rite,
And all my fortunes at thy foot I'll lay
And follow thee my lord throughout the world.
NURSE [within]   Madam!
JULIET
I come, anon.—But if thou meanest not well,
I do beseech thee—
NURSE [within]   Madam!
JULIET   By and by, I come—   151
To cease thy strife and leave me to my grief.   152
Tomorrow will I send.
ROMEO   So thrive my soul—
JULIET   A thousand times good night!   [Exit, above.]
ROMEO
A thousand times the worse, to want thy light.
Love goes toward love as schoolboys from their
    books,
But love from love, toward school with heavy looks.
                                    [He starts to leave.]

        Enter Juliet [above] again.

JULIET
Hist! Romeo, hist! Oh, for a falconer's voice,
To lure this tassel-gentle back again!   160
Bondage is hoarse and may not speak aloud,   161
Else would I tear the cave where Echo lies   162
And make her airy tongue more hoarse than mine
With repetition of "My Romeo!"
ROMEO
It is my soul that calls upon my name.
How silver-sweet sound lovers' tongues by night,
Like softest music to attending ears!
JULIET
Romeo!
ROMEO   My nyas?
JULIET   What o'clock tomorrow   168
Shall I send to thee?
ROMEO   By the hour of nine.
JULIET
I will not fail. 'Tis twenty year till then.—
I have forgot why I did call thee back.
ROMEO
Let me stand here till thou remember it.
JULIET
I shall forget, to have thee still stand there,   173
Remembering how I love thy company.

ROMEO
And I'll still stay, to have thee still forget,
Forgetting any other home but this.
JULIET
'Tis almost morning. I would have thee gone—
And yet no farther than a wanton's bird,   178
That lets it hop a little from his hand,
Like a poor prisoner in his twisted gyves,   180
And with a silken thread plucks it back again,
So loving-jealous of his liberty.   182
ROMEO
I would I were thy bird.
JULIET   Sweet, so would I.
Yet I should kill thee with much cherishing.
Good night, good night! Parting is such sweet sorrow
That I shall say good night till it be morrow.
                                    [Exit, above.]
ROMEO
Sleep dwell upon thine eyes, peace in thy breast!
Would I were sleep and peace, so sweet to rest!
Hence will I to my ghostly friar's close cell,   189
His help to crave, and my dear hap to tell.   Exit. 190

                        ❖

[2.3]

        Enter Friar [Laurence] alone, with a basket.

FRIAR LAURENCE
The gray-eyed morn smiles on the frowning night,
Check'ring the eastern clouds with streaks of light,
And fleckled darkness like a drunkard reels   3
From forth day's path and Titan's fiery wheels.   4
Now, ere the sun advance his burning eye,   5
The day to cheer and night's dank dew to dry,
I must up-fill this osier cage of ours   7
With baleful weeds and precious-juicèd flowers.   8
The earth that's nature's mother is her tomb;
What is her burying grave, that is her womb;
And from her womb children of divers kind
We sucking on her natural bosom find,
Many for many virtues excellent,
None but for some, and yet all different.   14
Oh, mickle is the powerful grace that lies   15
In plants, herbs, stones, and their true qualities.   16
For naught so vile that on the earth doth live   17
But to the earth some special good doth give;
Nor aught so good but, strained from that fair use,   19
Revolts from true birth, stumbling on abuse.
Virtue itself turns vice, being misapplied,
And vice sometime by action dignified.

        Enter Romeo.

143 bent purpose, inclination   151 By and by Immediately
152 strife striving   160 tassel-gentle tercel gentle, the male of the
goshawk   161 Bondage is hoarse i.e., In confinement one can speak
only in a loud whisper   162 tear pierce (with noise).   Echo (In Book
3 of Ovid's *Metamorphoses*, Echo, rejected by Narcissus, pines away in
lonely caves until only her voice is left.)   168 nyas eyas, fledgling
173 still always

178 wanton's spoiled child's   180 gyves fetters   182 his its
189 ghostly spiritual.   close narrow   190 dear hap good fortune
2.3. Location: Verona. Friar Laurence's monastery garden.
3 fleckled dappled   4 From forth out of the way of.   Titan's (Helios,
the sun god, was a descendant of the race of Titans.)   5 advance raise
7 osier cage willow basket   8 baleful harmful   14 None but for some
there are none that are not useful for something   15 mickle great.
grace beneficent virtue   16 true proper, inherent   17 For naught so
vile For there is nothing so vile   19 strained forced, perverted

Within the infant rind of this weak flower
Poison hath residence and medicine power:
For this, being smelt, with that part cheers each part;   25
Being tasted, stays all senses with the heart.   26
Two such opposèd kings encamp them still   27
In man as well as herbs—grace and rude will;
And where the worser is predominant,
Full soon the canker death eats up that plant.   30

ROMEO
Good morrow, Father.

FRIAR LAURENCE   Benedicite!   31
What early tongue so sweet saluteth me?
Young son, it argues a distempered head   33
So soon to bid good morrow to thy bed.
Care keeps his watch in every old man's eye,
And where care lodges sleep will never lie;
But where unbruisèd youth with unstuffed brain   37
Doth couch his limbs, there golden sleep doth reign.
Therefore thy earliness doth me assure
Thou art uproused with some distemp'rature;
Or if not so, then here I hit it right:
Our Romeo hath not been in bed tonight.

ROMEO
That last is true. The sweeter rest was mine.

FRIAR LAURENCE
God pardon sin! Wast thou with Rosaline?

ROMEO
With Rosaline, my ghostly father? No.
I have forgot that name, and that name's woe.

FRIAR LAURENCE
That's my good son. But where hast thou been, then?

ROMEO
I'll tell thee ere thou ask it me again.
I have been feasting with mine enemy,
Where on a sudden one hath wounded me
That's by me wounded. Both our remedies   51
Within thy help and holy physic lies.   52
I bear no hatred, blessèd man, for, lo,
My intercession likewise steads my foe.   54

FRIAR LAURENCE
Be plain, good son, and homely in thy drift.   55
Riddling confession finds but riddling shrift.   56

ROMEO
Then plainly know my heart's dear love is set
On the fair daughter of rich Capulet.
As mine on hers, so hers is set on mine,
And all combined, save what thou must combine
By holy marriage. When and where and how
We met, we wooed, and made exchange of vow
I'll tell thee as we pass; but this I pray,
That thou consent to marry us today.

FRIAR LAURENCE
Holy Saint Francis, what a change is here!
Is Rosaline, that thou didst love so dear,

So soon forsaken? Young men's love then lies
Not truly in their hearts, but in their eyes.
Jesu Maria, what a deal of brine
Hath washed thy sallow cheeks for Rosaline!
How much salt water thrown away in waste
To season love, that of it doth not taste!
The sun not yet thy sighs from heaven clears,
Thy old groans yet ringing in mine ancient ears.
Lo, here upon thy cheek the stain doth sit
Of an old tear that is not washed off yet.
If e'er thou wast thyself and these woes thine,   77
Thou and these woes were all for Rosaline.
And art thou changed? Pronounce this sentence then: 79
Women may fall, when there's no strength in men.

ROMEO
Thou chid'st me oft for loving Rosaline.

FRIAR LAURENCE
For doting, not for loving, pupil mine.

ROMEO
And bad'st me bury love.

FRIAR LAURENCE   Not in a grave
To lay one in, another out to have.

ROMEO
I pray thee, chide not. She whom I love now
Doth grace for grace and love for love allow.   86
The other did not so.

FRIAR LAURENCE   Oh, she knew well
Thy love did read by rote, that could not spell.   88
But come, young waverer, come, go with me,
In one respect I'll thy assistant be;   90
For this alliance may so happy prove
To turn your households' rancor to pure love.   92

ROMEO
Oh, let us hence! I stand on sudden haste.   93

FRIAR LAURENCE
Wisely and slow. They stumble that run fast.

                                                    Exeunt.

❖

[2.4]

Enter Benvolio and Mercutio.

MERCUTIO
Where the devil should this Romeo be?   1
Came he not home tonight?   2

BENVOLIO
Not to his father's. I spoke with his man.

MERCUTIO
Why, that same pale hardhearted wench, that
     Rosaline,
Torments him so that he will sure run mad.

BENVOLIO
Tybalt, the kinsman to old Capulet,
Hath sent a letter to his father's house.

---

25 **that part** i.e., the odor   26 **stays** halts.   **with** together with   27 **them still** themselves always   30 **canker** cankerworm   31 **Benedicite!** A blessing on you!   33 **argues** demonstrates, provides evidence of.   **distempered** disturbed, disordered   37 **unstuffed** not overcharged, carefree   51 **Both our remedies** The remedy for both of us   52 **physic** medicine, healing property   54 **intercession** petition.   **steads** helps   55 **homely** simple   56 **shrift** absolution.

77 **If . . . thine** If ever you had any proper sense of self and understanding of your love sorrows   79 **sentence** maxim   86 **grace** favor, 88 **did read . . . spell** i.e., was like a schoolboy's exercise, repeating words without understanding.   90 **In one respect** for one reason (at least)   92 **To** as to   93 **stand on** am in need of, insist on
2.4. Location: Verona. A street.
1 **should** can   2 **tonight** last night.

MERCUTIO   A challenge, on my life.

BENVOLIO   Romeo will answer it.   9

MERCUTIO   Any man that can write may answer a letter.

BENVOLIO   Nay, he will answer the letter's master, how
he dares, being dared.

MERCUTIO   Alas poor Romeo! He is already dead,
stabbed with a white wench's black eye, run through
the ear with a love song, the very pin of his heart cleft   15
with the blind bow-boy's butt shaft. And is he a man   16
to encounter Tybalt?

BENVOLIO   Why, what is Tybalt?

MERCUTIO   More than prince of cats. Oh, he's the   19
courageous captain of compliments. He fights as you   20
sing prick song, keeps time, distance, and proportion;   21
he rests his minim rests, one, two, and the third in   22
your bosom. The very butcher of a silk button, a   23
duellist, a duellist, a gentleman of the very first house,   24
of the first and second cause. Ah, the immortal   25
passado! The *punto reverso!* The *hay!*   26

BENVOLIO   The what?

MERCUTIO   The pox of such antic, lisping, affecting phan- 28
tasimes, these new tuners of accent! "By Jesu, a very   29
good blade! A very tall man! A very good whore!"   30
Why, is not this a lamentable thing, grandsire, that we   31
should be thus afflicted with these strange flies, these   32
fashionmongers, these pardon-me's, who stand so   33
much on the new form that they cannot sit at ease on   34
the old bench? Oh, their bones, their bones!   35

Enter Romeo.

BENVOLIO   Here comes Romeo, here comes Romeo.

MERCUTIO   Without his roe, like a dried herring. Oh,   37
flesh, flesh, how art thou fishified! Now is he for the
numbers that Petrarch flowed in. Laura to his lady   39
was but a kitchen wench—marry, she had a better

love to berhyme her—Dido a dowdy, Cleopatra a   41
gypsy, Helen and Hero hildings and harlots, Thisbe a   42
gray eye or so, but not to the purpose. Signor Romeo,   43
bonjour! There's a French salutation to your French   44
slop. You gave us the counterfeit fairly last night.   45

ROMEO   Good morrow to you both. What counterfeit
did I give you?

MERCUTIO   The slip, sir, the slip. Can you not conceive?   48

ROMEO   Pardon, good Mercutio. My business was great,
and in such a case as mine a man may strain courtesy.

MERCUTIO   That's as much as to say, such a case as yours   51
constrains a man to bow in the hams.   52

ROMEO   Meaning, to curtsy.   53

MERCUTIO   Thou hast most kindly hit it.   54

ROMEO   A most courteous exposition.

MERCUTIO   Nay, I am the very pink of courtesy.   56

ROMEO   Pink for flower.

MERCUTIO   Right.

ROMEO   Why then is my pump well flowered.   59

MERCUTIO   Sure wit, follow me this jest now till thou
hast worn out thy pump, that when the single sole of
it is worn, the jest may remain, after the wearing,
solely singular.   63

ROMEO   Oh, single-soled jest, solely singular for the   64
singleness!   65

MERCUTIO   Come between us, good Benvolio. My wits
faints.

ROMEO   Switch and spurs, switch and spurs! Or I'll cry   68
a match.   69

MERCUTIO   Nay, if our wits run the wild-goose chase, I   70
am done, for thou hast more of the wild goose in one
of thy wits than, I am sure, I have in my whole five.
Was I with you there for the goose?   73

ROMEO   Thou wast never with me for anything when
thou wast not there for the goose.   75

MERCUTIO   I will bite thee by the ear for that jest.   76

ROMEO   Nay, good goose, bite not.

MERCUTIO   Thy wit is a very bitter sweeting; it is a most   78
sharp sauce.   79

ROMEO   And is it not, then, well served in to a sweet
goose?

---

9 answer it accept the challenge. (But Mercutio replies in the sense of
"write in reply.")   **15 pin** peg in the center of a target   **16 butt shaft**
unbarbed arrow, allotted to children and thus to Cupid.   **19 prince
of cats** (The name of the king of cats in *Reynard the Fox* was Tybalt or
Tybert.)   **20 captain of compliments** master of ceremony and dueling etiquette.   **21 prick song** music written out.   **proportion** rhythm
22 minim rests short rests in musical notation   **23 butcher . . . button**
i.e., one able to strike a specific button on his adversary's person
24 first house best school of fencing   **25 first and second cause** causes according to the code of dueling that would oblige one to seek the
satisfaction of one's honor.   **26 passado** forward thrust.   **punto
reverso** backhanded stroke.   **hay** thrust through. (From the Italian
hai, meaning "you have [it].")   **28 The pox of** Plague take.   **antic**
grotesque   **28–9 phantasimes** coxcombs, fantastically dressed or
mannered   **29 new tuners of accent** those who introduce new foreign words and slang phrases into their speech.   **30 tall** valiant
31 grandsire i.e., one who disapproves of the new fashion and prefers
old custom.   **32 flies** parasites   **33 pardon-me's** i.e., those who affect
overly polite manners.   **stand** (1) insist (2) the opposite of *sit*, line 34
34–5 form . . . bench (*Form* means both "fashion" or "code of manners" and "bench.")   **35 bones** French *bon*, "good" (with play on
English *bone*)   **37 Without his roe** i.e., Looking thin and emaciated,
sexually spent. (With a pun on the first syllable of Romeo's name; the
remaining syllables, *me-oh*, sound like the expression of a melancholy
lover. *Roe* also suggests a female deer or "dear.")   **39 numbers** verses.   **Laura** the lady to whom the Italian Renaissance poet Petrarch
addressed his love poems. (Other romantic heroines are named in the
following passage: Dido, Queen of Carthage; Cleopatra; Helen of
Troy; Hero, beloved of Leander; and Thisbe, beloved of Pyramus.)
to in comparison with

41 dowdy homely woman   **42 gypsy** Egyptian; whore.   **hildings**
good-for-nothings   **43 not** i.e., that is not   **44 to** to match   **44–5 French
slop** loose trousers of French fashion.   **45 fairly** handsomely, effectively
48 slip (Counterfeit coins were called "slips.")   **conceive** i.e., get the
joke.   **51 case** (1) situation (2) physical condition. (Mercutio also bawdily suggests that Romeo has been in a *case*, i.e., the female genitalia.)
52 bow in the hams (1) make a low bow (2) show the effects of venereal
disease.   **53 curtsy** bow, make obeisance.   **54 kindly** graciously. (But
also suggesting natural and physical explanations.)
56 pink embodied perfection. (But suggesting also the flower called
pink, the color, and *pinking* of a shoe; see next note.)   **59 pump well
flowered** shoe expertly pinked or perforated in ornamental figures suggesting flowers.   **63 solely singular** unique.   **64 single-soled** i.e., thin,
contemptible   **65 singleness** feebleness.   **68 Switch and spurs** i.e.,
Keep up the rapid pace of the hunt (in the game of wits)   **68–9 cry a
match** claim the victory.   **70 wild-goose chase** a horse race in which the
leading rider dares his competitors to follow him wherever he goes
73 Was . . . goose? Did I score a point in calling you a goose?   **75 for the
goose** (1) behaving like a goose (2) looking for a prostitute.   **76 bite . . .
ear** i.e., give you an affectionate nibble on the ear. (Said ironically, however, and Romeo parries.)   **78 sweeting** sweet-flavored variety of apple
79 sharp sauce (1) "biting" retort (2) tart sauce, of the sort that should be
served with cooked goose (as Romeo points out).

MERCUTIO   Oh, here's a wit of cheveril, that stretches 82
from an inch narrow to an ell broad! 83
ROMEO   I stretch it out for that word "broad," which,
added to the goose, proves thee far and wide a broad 85
goose.
MERCUTIO   Why, is not this better now than groaning for
love? Now art thou sociable, now art thou Romeo;
now art thou what thou art, by art as well as by nature.
For this driveling love is like a great natural that runs 90
lolling up and down to hide his bauble in a hole. 91
BENVOLIO   Stop there, stop there.
MERCUTIO   Thou desirest me to stop in my tale against 93
the hair. 94
BENVOLIO   Thou wouldst else have made thy tale large.
MERCUTIO   Oh, thou art deceived; I would have made it
short, for I was come to the whole depth of my tale
and meant indeed to occupy the argument no longer.
ROMEO   Here's goodly gear! 99

Enter Nurse and her man [Peter].

A sail, a sail! 100
MERCUTIO   Two, two: a shirt and a smock. 101
NURSE   Peter!
PETER   Anon!
NURSE   My fan, Peter.
MERCUTIO   Good Peter, to hide her face, for her fan's
the fairer face.
NURSE   God gi' good morrow, gentlemen.
MERCUTIO   God gi' good e'en, fair gentlewoman.
NURSE   Is it good e'en? 109
MERCUTIO   'Tis no less, I tell ye, for the bawdy hand of
the dial is now upon the prick of noon. 111
NURSE   Out upon you! What a man are you? 112
ROMEO   One, gentlewoman, that God hath made for
himself to mar. 114
NURSE   By my troth, it is well said. "For himself to mar," 115
quoth 'a? Gentlemen, can any of you tell me where I 116
may find the young Romeo?
ROMEO   I can tell you; but young Romeo will be older
when you have found him than he was when you
sought him. I am the youngest of that name, for fault 120
of a worse.
NURSE   You say well.

MERCUTIO   Yea, is the worst well? Very well took, i'faith, 123
wisely, wisely.
NURSE   If you be he, sir, I desire some confidence with 125
you.
BENVOLIO   She will indite him to some supper. 127
MERCUTIO   A bawd, a bawd, a bawd! So ho! 128
ROMEO   What hast thou found?
MERCUTIO   No hare, sir, unless a hare, sir, in a lenten 130
pie, that is something stale and hoar ere it be spent. 131
                                                    [*He sings.*]
        An old hare hoar,
        And an old hare hoar,
    Is very good meat in Lent.
        But a hare that is hoar
        Is too much for a score, 136
    When it hoars ere it be spent.
Romeo, will you come to your father's? We'll to din-
ner thither.
ROMEO   I will follow you.
MERCUTIO   Farewell, ancient lady. Farewell,   [*singing*]
"Lady, lady, lady."   *Exeunt [Mercutio and Benvolio].* 142
NURSE   I pray you, sir, what saucy merchant was this 143
that was so full of his ropery? 144
ROMEO   A gentleman, Nurse, that loves to hear himself
talk, and will speak more in a minute than he will
stand to in a month. 147
NURSE   An 'a speak anything against me, I'll take him 148
down, an 'a were lustier than he is, and twenty such 149
Jacks; and if I cannot, I'll find those that shall. Scurvy 150
knave! I am none of his flirt-gills. I am none of his 151
skains-mates. [*To Peter*] And thou must stand by, too, 152
and suffer every knave to use me at his pleasure!
PETER   I saw no man use you at his pleasure. If I had,
my weapon should quickly have been out; I warrant 155
you, I dare draw as soon as another man, if I see
occasion in a good quarrel, and the law on my side.
NURSE   Now, afore God, I am so vexed that every part 158
about me quivers. Scurvy knave! Pray you, sir, a 159
word; and as I told you, my young lady bid me
inquire you out. What she bid me say, I will keep to
myself. But first let me tell ye, if ye should lead her
in a fool's paradise, as they say, it were a very gross
kind of behavior, as they say. For the gentlewoman
is young; and therefore if you should deal double

---

82 cheveril kid leather, easily stretched   **83 ell** (forty-five inches)
85 broad large, complete; perhaps also wanton   **90 natural** idiot
91 lolling with his tongue (or bauble) hanging out.   **bauble** (1) jester's
wand (2) phallus   **93 stop in my tale** (1) stop short in my story (2) stuff
in my penis   **93–4 against the hair** against the grain, against my wish.
(With bawdy suggestion of pubic hair. The sexual punning continues
in *large* [erect], *short* [detumescent], *come to the depth of my tale, occupy,*
etc.)   **99 goodly gear** matter for mockery. (With suggestion of "ample
sexual apparatus.")   **100 A sail** (To Romeo, the Nurse is an imposing
galleon in full sail.)   **101 a shirt and a smock** i.e., a man and a woman.
109 Is it good e'en? Is it afternoon already?   **111 prick** point on the
dial of a clock. (With bawdy suggestion.)   **112 Out upon you** (Expression of indignation.)   **What** What kind of   **114 mar** i.e., disfigure
morally through sin. (Humankind, made in God's image, mars that
image sinfully.)   **115 troth** faith   **116 quoth 'a** said he. (A sarcastic
interjection, meaning "forsooth" or "indeed.")   **120 fault** lack

123 took understood   **125 confidence** (The Nurse's mistake for "conference.")   **127 indite** (Benvolio's deliberate malapropism for
"invite.")   **128 So ho** (Cry of hunter sighting game.)   **130 hare**
(Slang word for "prostitute"; similarly, with *stale* and *meat* in the following lines.)   **130–1 a lenten pie** a pie that should contain no meat,
in observance of Lent   **131 hoar** moldy. (With pun on "whore"; *stale*
also can mean "whore.")   **spent** consumed.   **136 for a score** for a
reckoning, to pay good money for   **142 "Lady, lady, lady"** (Refrain
from the ballad *Chaste Susanna*.)   **143 merchant** i.e., fellow   **144 ropery** vulgar humor, knavery.   **147 stand to** carry out, stand in support
of   **148 An 'a** If he   **148–9 take him down** cut him down to size.
(With unintended bawdy suggestion.)   **150 Jacks** knaves   **151 flirt-
gills** loose women.   **152 skains-mates** (Perhaps daggermates, outlaws, or gangster molls.)   **155 weapon** (With bawdy suggestion, perhaps unrecognized by the speaker, as also in *at his pleasure.*)
158–9 every part . . . quivers (More bawdy suggestion, unrecognized
by the Nurse.)

with her, truly it were an ill thing to be offered to any
gentlewoman, and very weak dealing.   167
ROMEO   Nurse, commend me to thy lady and mistress.
I protest unto thee—   169
NURSE   Good heart, and i'faith I will tell her as much.
Lord, Lord, she will be a joyful woman.
ROMEO   What wilt thou tell her, Nurse? Thou dost not
mark me.   173
NURSE   I will tell her, sir, that you do protest, which, as
I take it, is a gentlemanlike offer.
ROMEO   Bid her devise
Some means to come to shrift this afternoon,   177
And there she shall at Friar Laurence' cell
Be shrived and married. Here is for thy pains.   179
                            [*He offers money.*]
NURSE   No, truly, sir, not a penny.
ROMEO   Go to, I say you shall.
NURSE
This afternoon, sir? Well, she shall be there.
ROMEO
And stay, good Nurse, behind the abbey wall.
Within this hour my man shall be with thee
And bring thee cords made like a tackled stair,   185
Which to the high topgallant of my joy   186
Must be my convoy in the secret night.   187
Farewell. Be trusty, and I'll quit thy pains.   188
Farewell. Commend me to thy mistress.
                            [*Romeo starts to leave.*]
NURSE
Now God in heaven bless thee! Hark you, sir.
ROMEO   What say'st thou, my dear Nurse?
NURSE
Is your man secret? Did you ne'er hear say,   192
"Two may keep counsel, putting one away"?   193
ROMEO
'Warrant thee, my man's as true as steel.
NURSE   Well, sir, my mistress is the sweetest lady—
Lord, Lord! When 'twas a little prating thing—Oh,
there is a nobleman in town, one Paris, that would
fain lay knife aboard; but she, good soul, had as lief   198
see a toad, a very toad, as see him. I anger her
sometimes and tell her that Paris is the properer man,   200
but I'll warrant you, when I say so, she looks as pale
as any clout in the versal world. Doth not rosemary   202
and Romeo begin both with a letter?   203
ROMEO   Ay, Nurse, what of that? Both with an R.

NURSE   Ah, mocker! That's the dog's name; R is for   205
the—No; I know it begins with some other letter; and   206
she hath the prettiest sententious of it, of you and   207
rosemary, that it would do you good to hear it.
ROMEO   Commend me to thy lady.
NURSE   Ay, a thousand times.   [*Exit Romeo.*]
Peter!
PETER   Anon!
NURSE   Before, and apace.   *Exeunt.*   212

                            ❖

[2.5]

          Enter Juliet.

JULIET
The clock struck nine when I did send the Nurse;
In half an hour she promised to return.
Perchance she cannot meet him. That's not so.
Oh, she is lame! Love's heralds should be thoughts,
Which ten times faster glides than the sun's beams
Driving back shadows over louring hills.   6
Therefore do nimble-pinioned doves draw Love,   7
And therefore hath the wind-swift Cupid wings.
Now is the sun upon the highmost hill
Of this day's journey, and from nine till twelve
Is three long hours, yet she is not come.
Had she affections and warm youthful blood,   12
She would be as swift in motion as a ball;
My words would bandy her to my sweet love,   14
And his to me.
But old folks, many feign as they were dead—   16
Unwieldy, slow, heavy, and pale as lead.

          Enter Nurse [*and Peter*].

Oh, God, she comes!—O honey Nurse, what news?
Hast thou met with him? Send thy man away.
NURSE   Peter, stay at the gate.   [*Exit Peter.*]
JULIET
Now, good sweet Nurse—Oh, Lord, why lookest thou
     sad?
Though news be sad, yet tell them merrily;
If good, thou shamest the music of sweet news
By playing it to me with so sour a face.
NURSE
I am aweary. Give me leave awhile.   25
Fie, how my bones ache! What a jaunce have I had!   26
JULIET
I would thou hadst my bones and I thy news.
Nay, come, I pray thee, speak. Good, good Nurse,
     speak.

---

167 **weak** contemptible   169 **protest** vow. (Romeo may intend only
to protest his good intentions, but the Nurse seemingly takes the
word to mean "propose," as if Romeo is making a *gentlemanlike offer*
[line 175] of marriage that would ensure against Juliet's being led into
a *fool's paradise* [line 163]—i.e., being seduced.)   173 **mark** attend to
177 **shrift** confession and absolution   179 **shrived** absolved
185 **tackled stair** rope ladder   186 **topgallant** highest mast and sail of
a ship, the summit   187 **convoy** conveyance, means of passage
188 **quit** reward, requite   192 **secret** trustworthy   193 **keep counsel**
keep a secret   198 **fain lay knife aboard** like to assert his claim (just
as a guest at an inn did by bringing his knife to the dinner table; with
sexual suggestion also).   **lief** willingly   200 **properer** handsomer
202 **clout** faded rag.   **versal** universal.   **rosemary** (Associated with
weddings and funerals.)   203 **a letter** one and the same letter.

205 **the dog's name** (The letter *R* was thought to resemble the dog's
growl.)   205–6 **R is for . . . letter** (Perhaps the Nurse is about to say
"arse," but has a notion that it begins with some other letter. In any case,
she decides against saying such an indelicate word.)   207 **sententious**
(The Nurse probably means "sentences," maxims.)   212 **Before, and
apace** Go before me quickly.
2.5. **Location:** Verona. Outside Capulet's house, perhaps in the
orchard or garden.
6 **louring** dark, threatening   7 **Love** i.e., Venus, whose chariot was
drawn by swift-winged doves   12 **affections** desires   14 **bandy** toss
to and fro, as in tennis   16 **feign as** act as though   25 **Give me leave**
Let me alone   26 **jaunce** jouncing, jolting

NURSE
Jesu, what haste! Can you not stay awhile?   29
Do you not see that I am out of breath?

JULIET
How art thou out of breath, when thou hast breath
To say to me that thou art out of breath?
The excuse that thou dost make in this delay
Is longer than the tale thou dost excuse.   34
Is thy news good or bad? Answer to that;
Say either, and I'll stay the circumstance.   36
Let me be satisfied: is't good or bad?

NURSE   Well, you have made a simple choice. You know   38
not how to choose a man. Romeo? No, not he. Though
his face be better than any man's, yet his leg excels all
men's; and for a hand, and a foot, and a body, though
they be not to be talked on, yet they are past compare.   42
He is not the flower of courtesy, but, I'll warrant him,
as gentle as a lamb. Go thy ways, wench. Serve God.
What, have you dined at home?

JULIET
No, no; but all this did I know before.
What says he of our marriage? What of that?

NURSE
Lord, how my head aches! What a head have I!
It beats as it would fall in twenty pieces.
My back o' t'other side—ah, my back, my back!   50
Beshrew your heart for sending me about   51
To catch my death with jauncing up and down!

JULIET
I'faith, I am sorry that thou art not well.
Sweet, sweet, sweet Nurse, tell me, what says my
    love?

NURSE
Your love says, like an honest gentleman,
And a courteous, and a kind, and a handsome,
And, I warrant, a virtuous—Where is your mother?

JULIET
Where is my mother? Why, she is within,
Where should she be? How oddly thou repliest!
"Your love says, like an honest gentleman,   60
'Where is your mother?' "

NURSE   O God's Lady dear!
Are you so hot? Marry, come up, I trow.   62
Is this the poultice for my aching bones?
Henceforward do your messages yourself.

JULIET
Here's such a coil! Come, what says Romeo?   65

NURSE
Have you got leave to go to shrift today?

JULIET   I have.

NURSE
Then hie you hence to Friar Laurence' cell;   68
There stays a husband to make you a wife.

Now comes the wanton blood up in your cheeks;
They'll be in scarlet straight at any news.   71
Hie you to church. I must another way,
To fetch a ladder, by the which your love
Must climb a bird's nest soon when it is dark.   74
I am the drudge, and toil in your delight,
But you shall bear the burden soon at night.
Go. I'll to dinner. Hie you to the cell.

JULIET
Hie to high fortune! Honest Nurse, farewell.
                                    Exeunt [*separately*].

[2.6]

Enter Friar [Laurence] and Romeo.

FRIAR LAURENCE
So smile the heavens upon this holy act   1
That after-hours with sorrow chide us not!

ROMEO
Amen, amen! But come what sorrow can,
It cannot countervail the exchange of joy   4
That one short minute gives me in her sight.
Do thou but close our hands with holy words,   6
Then love-devouring death do what he dare;
It is enough I may but call her mine.

FRIAR LAURENCE
These violent delights have violent ends
And in their triumph die, like fire and powder,   10
Which as they kiss consume. The sweetest honey
Is loathsome in his own deliciousness,   12
And in the taste confounds the appetite.   13
Therefore love moderately. Long love doth so;
Too swift arrives as tardy as too slow.

    Enter Juliet.

Here comes the lady. Oh, so light a foot
Will ne'er wear out the everlasting flint.
A lover may bestride the gossamers   18
That idles in the wanton summer air,   19
And yet not fall, so light is vanity.   20

JULIET
Good even to my ghostly confessor.   21

FRIAR LAURENCE
Romeo shall thank thee, daughter, for us both.   22

JULIET
As much to him, else is his thanks too much.   23

---

29 stay wait   **34 excuse** excuse yourself from telling.   **36 stay the circumstance** wait patiently for the details.   **38 simple** foolish   **42 be
not to be talked on** are beneath mention (especially in refined lady-
like company)   **50 o' t'other** on the other   **51 Beshrew** A curse on.
(Used as a mild oath.)   **60 honest** honorable   **62 hot** impatient.
Marry, come up (An expression of impatient reproof.)   **65 coil** turmoil, fuss.   **68 hie** hasten

71 in scarlet straight i.e., blushing immediately   **74 bird's nest** i.e.,
Juliet's room. (Continues the association of Juliet as a bird, as at 1.3.3,
2.2.168–82, with erotic suggestion. The bawdry is continued in *bear
the burden* two lines later.)
2.6. Location: Verona. Friar Laurence's cell.
1 So . . . heavens May the heavens so smile   **4 countervail** outweigh,
counterbalance   **6 close** join   **10 powder** gunpowder   **12 his** its
13 confounds destroys   **18 gossamers** filmy cobwebs   **19 wanton**
playful   **20 vanity** transitory human joy.   **21 ghostly** spiritual
22 thank thee i.e., give a kiss in thanks for your greeting   **23 As . . .
too much** either (1) Then I must repay him with a kiss, lest I be over-
paid, or (2) My greeting is to Romeo as much as to you; otherwise, his
greeting would exceed mine.

ROMEO
Ah, Juliet, if the measure of thy joy
Be heaped like mine, and that thy skill be more   25
To blazon it, then sweeten with thy breath   26
This neighbor air, and let rich music's tongue
Unfold the imagined happiness that both   28
Receive in either by this dear encounter.   29

JULIET
Conceit, more rich in matter than in words,   30
Brags of his substance, not of ornament.   31
They are but beggars that can count their worth.
But my true love is grown to such excess
I cannot sum up sum of half my wealth.   34

FRIAR LAURENCE
Come, come with me, and we will make short work;
For, by your leaves, you shall not stay alone
Till Holy Church incorporate two in one.   [*Exeunt.*]

[3.1]

Enter Mercutio, Benvolio, and men.

BENVOLIO
I pray thee, good Mercutio, let's retire.
The day is hot, the Capels are abroad,   2
And if we meet we shall not scape a brawl,
For now, these hot days, is the mad blood stirring.

MERCUTIO   Thou art like one of these fellows that when
he enters the confines of a tavern, claps me his sword   6
upon the table and says, "God send me no need of
thee!" and by the operation of the second cup draws   8
him on the drawer, when indeed there is no need.   9

BENVOLIO   Am I like such a fellow?

MERCUTIO   Come, come, thou art as hot a Jack in thy   11
mood as any in Italy, and as soon moved to be moody,   12
and as soon moody to be moved.   13

BENVOLIO   And what to?

MERCUTIO   Nay, an there were two such, we should   15
have none shortly, for one would kill the other. Thou!
Why, thou wilt quarrel with a man that hath a hair
more or a hair less in his beard than thou hast. Thou
wilt quarrel with a man for cracking nuts, having no
other reason but because thou hast hazel eyes. What
eye but such an eye would spy out such a quarrel? Thy
head is as full of quarrels as an egg is full of meat, and 22
yet thy head hath been beaten as addle as an egg for   23
quarreling. Thou hast quarreled with a man for cough-
ing in the street, because he hath wakened thy dog that

hath lain asleep in the sun. Didst thou not fall out
with a tailor for wearing his new doublet before East-   27
er? With another, for tying his new shoes with old
ribbon? And yet thou wilt tutor me from quarreling!

BENVOLIO   An I were so apt to quarrel as thou art, any
man should buy the fee simple of my life for an hour   31
and a quarter.   32

MERCUTIO   The fee simple! Oh, simple!   33

Enter Tybalt, Petruchio, and others.

BENVOLIO   By my head, here comes the Capulets.
MERCUTIO   By my heel, I care not.
TYBALT   [*to his companions*]
Follow me close, for I will speak to them.—
Gentlemen, good e'en. A word with one of you.

MERCUTIO   And but one word with one of us? Couple it
with something: make it a word and a blow.

TYBALT   You shall find me apt enough to that, sir, an
you will give me occasion.

MERCUTIO   Could you not take some occasion without
giving?

TYBALT   Mercutio, thou consortest with Romeo.   44

MERCUTIO   "Consort"? What, dost thou make us minstrels? An thou make minstrels of us, look to hear
nothing but discords. Here's my fiddlestick; here's   47
that shall make you dance. Zounds, "consort"!   48

BENVOLIO
We talk here in the public haunt of men.
Either withdraw unto some private place,
Or reason coldly of your grievances,   51
Or else depart; here all eyes gaze on us.   52

MERCUTIO
Men's eyes were made to look, and let them gaze.
I will not budge for no man's pleasure, I.

Enter Romeo.

TYBALT
Well, peace be with you, sir. Here comes my man.

MERCUTIO
But I'll be hanged, sir, if he wear your livery.   56
Marry, go before to field, he'll be your follower;   57
Your Worship in that sense may call him "man."   58

TYBALT
Romeo, the love I bear thee can afford
No better term than this: thou art a villain.

ROMEO
Tybalt, the reason that I have to love thee
Doth much excuse the appertaining rage   62
To such a greeting. Villain am I none.

---

25 that if   **26 blazon** describe, set forth. (A heraldic term.)
28 Unfold make known.   **imagined** i.e., unexpressed   **29 in either**
from each other   **30–1 Conceit . . . ornament** True understanding,
more enriched by the actual reality (of love) than by mere words, finds
more worth in the substance of that reality than in outward show.
34 sum up sum add up the total
3.1. Location: Verona. A public place.
2 Capels Capulets   **6 claps me** claps. (*Me* is a now-archaic dative of
reference, used colloquially.)   **8–9 draws . . . drawer** draws his sword
against the tapster or waiter   **9 there is no need** i.e., of his sword.
11 as hot a Jack as hot-tempered a fellow   **12 moody** angry   **13 to be
moved** at being provoked.   **15 an** if   **22 meat** i.e., edible matter
23 addle addled, confused

27 doublet man's jacket   **31 fee simple** outright possession   **31–2 an
hour . . . quarter** i.e., my life would last no longer in such circumstances.
33 Oh, simple! Oh, how stupid!   **44 consortest** keep company with.
(But Mercutio quibbles on its musical sense of "accompany" or "play
together.")   **47 fiddlestick** (Mercutio means his sword.)   **48 that** that
which.   **Zounds** By God's (Christ's) wounds   **51 coldly** calmly
52 depart go away separately   **56 livery** servant's uniform. (Mercutio
deliberately mistakes Tybalt's phrase *my man* to mean "my servant.")
57 field field where a duel might occur   **58 Your Worship** (A title of
honor used here with mock politeness.)   **62 the appertaining rage** the
rage that would ordinarily be appropriate to

Therefore, farewell. I see thou knowest me not.

TYBALT
Boy, this shall not excuse the injuries   65
That thou hast done me. Therefore turn and draw.

ROMEO
I do protest I never injured thee,
But love thee better than thou canst devise   68
Till thou shalt know the reason of my love.
And so, good Capulet—which name I tender   70
As dearly as mine own—be satisfied.

MERCUTIO
Oh, calm, dishonorable, vile submission!
Alla stoccata carries it away.   [*He draws.*] 73
Tybalt, you ratcatcher, will you walk?   74

TYBALT   What wouldst thou have with me?

MERCUTIO   Good king of cats, nothing but one of your
nine lives, that I mean to make bold withal, and, as   77
you shall use me hereafter, dry-beat the rest of the   78
eight. Will you pluck your sword out of his pilcher by   79
the ears? Make haste, lest mine be about your ears ere   80
it be out.

TYBALT   I am for you.   [*He draws.*]

ROMEO
Gentle Mercutio, put thy rapier up.

MERCUTIO   Come, sir, your *passado*.   [*They fight.*] 84

ROMEO
Draw, Benvolio, beat down their weapons.
Gentlemen, for shame, forbear this outrage!
Tybalt, Mercutio, the Prince expressly hath
Forbid this bandying in Verona streets.
Hold, Tybalt! Good Mercutio!
          [*Tybalt under Romeo's arm stabs Mercutio.*] *Away*
                    Tybalt [*with his followers*].

MERCUTIO   I am hurt.   89
A plague o' both your houses! I am sped.   90
Is he gone, and hath nothing?

BENVOLIO   What, art thou hurt?

MERCUTIO
Ay, ay, a scratch, a scratch; marry, 'tis enough.
Where is my page? Go, villain, fetch a surgeon.
                              [*Exit Page.*]

ROMEO
Courage, man, the hurt cannot be much.

MERCUTIO   No, 'tis not so deep as a well, nor so wide as
a church door, but 'tis enough, 'twill serve. Ask for me
tomorrow, and you shall find me a grave man. I am   97
peppered, I warrant, for this world. A plague o' both   98
your houses! Zounds, a dog, a rat, a mouse, a cat, to
scratch a man to death! A braggart, a rogue, a villain,
that fights by the book of arithmetic! Why the devil   101
came you between us? I was hurt under your arm.

ROMEO   I thought all for the best.

MERCUTIO
Help me into some house, Benvolio,
Or I shall faint. A plague o' both your houses!
They have made worm's meat of me. I have it,
And soundly too. Your houses!
                    Exit [*supported by Benvolio*].

ROMEO
This gentleman, the Prince's near ally,   108
My very friend, hath got this mortal hurt   109
In my behalf; my reputation stained
With Tybalt's slander—Tybalt, that an hour
Hath been my cousin! O sweet Juliet,   112
Thy beauty hath made me effeminate,   113
And in my temper softened valor's steel.   114

          Enter Benvolio.

BENVOLIO
O Romeo, Romeo, brave Mercutio is dead!
That gallant spirit hath aspired the clouds,   116
Which too untimely here did scorn the earth.

ROMEO
This day's black fate on more days doth depend;   118
This but begins the woe others must end.   119

          [*Enter Tybalt.*]

BENVOLIO
Here comes the furious Tybalt back again.

ROMEO
Alive in triumph, and Mercutio slain!
Away to heaven, respective lenity,   122
And fire-eyed fury be my conduct now!   123
Now, Tybalt, take the "villain" back again
That late thou gavest me, for Mercutio's soul
Is but a little way above our heads,
Staying for thine to keep him company.
Either thou or I, or both, must go with him.

TYBALT
Thou, wretched boy, that didst consort him here,
Shalt with him hence.

ROMEO   This shall determine that.
                    They fight. Tybalt falls.

BENVOLIO   Romeo, away, begone!
The citizens are up, and Tybalt slain.

---

65 Boy (A deliberate and grave insult when addressed to a grown
man. Tybalt's use of *thee* and *thou* in lines 59–60 and following is similarly insulting; Romeo's use of this personal form in lines 61–4 and
67–9, on the other hand, is appropriate to a close family tie that he
privately acknowledges but is of course misunderstood by Tybalt and
the bystanders.)   **68 devise** imagine   **70 tender** value   **73 *Alla stoccata . . . away*** i.e. (scornfully), This elegant Italian way of fencing,
and the fancy terminology to go with it, will win the day, I suppose.
(*Alla stoccata* means "at the thrust.")   **74 ratcatcher** (An allusion to
Tybalt as king of cats; see 2.4.19.)   **77 make bold withal** make free
with   **78 dry-beat** beat soundly (without drawing blood)   **79–80 out
. . . ears** out of its scabbard by the handle or hilt.   **84 *passado*** forward thrust. (Another fancy Italian fencing term of the sort Mercutio
despises.)   **89 s.d. *Away Tybalt*** (Because the phrase is unusual for an
exit stage direction, some editors plausibly assign this as a speech to
Petruchio, who enters at line 33.1 and is otherwise silent.)   **90 sped**
done for.

97 grave (Mercutio thus puns with his last breath.)   **98 peppered** finished, done for   **101 by . . . arithmetic** by the numbers, as in a textbook on fencing (as at 2.4.20–3).   **108 ally** kinsman   **109 very** true
112 cousin kinsman.   **113 effeminate** weak   **114 temper** disposition.
(But with a play on the tempering of a steel sword.)   **116 aspired**
ascended to   **118 This day's . . . depend** This day hangs threateningly over the time to come   **119 others** other days to come
122 respective lenity considerate gentleness   **123 conduct** guide

Stand not amazed. The Prince will doom thee death   133
If thou art taken. Hence, begone, away!

ROMEO
Oh, I am fortune's fool!

BENVOLIO   Why dost thou stay?   135

Exit Romeo.

Enter Citizens.

FIRST CITIZEN
Which way ran he that killed Mercutio?
Tybalt, that murderer, which way ran he?

BENVOLIO
There lies that Tybalt.

FIRST CITIZEN   Up, sir, go with me.
I charge thee in the Prince's name, obey.

Enter Prince [attended], old Montague,
Capulet, their Wives, and all.

PRINCE
Where are the vile beginners of this fray?

BENVOLIO
O noble Prince, I can discover all   141
The unlucky manage of this fatal brawl.   142
There lies the man, slain by young Romeo,
That slew thy kinsman, brave Mercutio.

CAPULET'S WIFE
Tybalt, my cousin! O my brother's child!
O Prince! O cousin! Husband! Oh, the blood is spilled
Of my dear kinsman! Prince, as thou art true,
For blood of ours shed blood of Montague.
O cousin, cousin!

PRINCE
Benvolio, who began this bloody fray?

BENVOLIO
Tybalt, here slain, whom Romeo's hand did slay.
Romeo, that spoke him fair, bid him bethink   152
How nice the quarrel was, and urged withal   153
Your high displeasure. All this—utterèd
With gentle breath, calm look, knees humbly bowed—
Could not take truce with the unruly spleen   156
Of Tybalt deaf to peace, but that he tilts
With piercing steel at bold Mercutio's breast,
Who, all as hot, turns deadly point to point,
And, with a martial scorn, with one hand beats
Cold death aside and with the other sends
It back to Tybalt, whose dexterity
Retorts it. Romeo he cries aloud,   163
"Hold, friends! Friends, part!" and swifter than his
    tongue
His agile arm beats down their fatal points,
And twixt them rushes; underneath whose arm
An envious thrust from Tybalt hit the life   167
Of stout Mercutio, and then Tybalt fled;   168
But by and by comes back to Romeo,
Who had but newly entertained revenge,   170

And to't they go like lightning, for, ere I
Could draw to part them was stout Tybalt slain,
And, as he fell, did Romeo turn and fly.
This is the truth, or let Benvolio die.

CAPULET'S WIFE
He is a kinsman to the Montague.
Affection makes him false; he speaks not true.   176
Some twenty of them fought in this black strife,
And all those twenty could but kill one life.
I beg for justice, which thou, Prince, must give.
Romeo slew Tybalt; Romeo must not live.

PRINCE
Romeo slew him, he slew Mercutio.
Who now the price of his dear blood doth owe?

MONTAGUE
Not Romeo, Prince, he was Mercutio's friend;
His fault concludes but what the law should end,   184
The life of Tybalt.

PRINCE   And for that offense
Immediately we do exile him hence.
I have an interest in your hate's proceeding;
My blood for your rude brawls doth lie a-bleeding;   188
But I'll amerce you with so strong a fine   189
That you shall all repent the loss of mine.
I will be deaf to pleading and excuses.
Nor tears nor prayers shall purchase out abuses.   192
Therefore use none. Let Romeo hence in haste,   193
Else, when he is found, that hour is his last.   194
Bear hence this body and attend our will.   195
Mercy but murders, pardoning those that kill.   196

Exeunt, [some carrying Tybalt's body].

❧

[3.2]

Enter Juliet alone.

JULIET
Gallop apace, you fiery-footed steeds,   1
Towards Phoebus' lodging! Such a wagoner   2
As Phaëthon would whip you to the west   3
And bring in cloudy night immediately.   4
Spread thy close curtain, love-performing night,   5

---

176 **Affection** Partiality   184 **concludes but** only finishes   188 **My
blood** i.e., blood of my kinsman. (Here we learn that Mercutio is kin
to the Prince.)   189 **amerce** penalize   192 **Nor** neither.   **purchase
out abuses** redeem misdeeds.   193 **hence** depart   194 **Else** Otherwise   195 **attend our will** be on hand to hear further judgment.
196 **but murders** merely encourages murder by excessive leniency
3.2. Location: Verona. Capulet's house.
1 **apace** quickly.   **steeds** i.e., the horses of the sun god's chariot
2 **Phoebus** (Often equated with Helios, the sun god.)   **lodging** i.e., in
the west, below the horizon.   2–4 **Such . . . immediately** i.e., One
who is impetuously young, as we are, would understand the need to
make the day as short as possible and would quickly bring it to an
end. (The mythical allusion is sadly ironic, for Phaëthon drove the
chariot of the sun so badly that he had to be destroyed by Zeus.)
5 **close** enclosing

---

133 **amazed** dazed.   **doom thee death** sentence you to death
135 **fool** dupe.   141 **discover** reveal   142 **manage** conduct   152 **fair**
civilly.   **bethink** consider   153 **nice** trivial.   **withal** besides
156 **take truce** make peace   163 **Retorts** returns   167 **envious** malicious   168 **stout** brave   170 **entertained** harbored thoughts of

That runaways' eyes may wink, and Romeo   6
Leap to these arms, untalked of and unseen.   7
Lovers can see to do their amorous rites
By their own beauties; or, if love be blind,
It best agrees with night. Come, civil night,   10
Thou sober-suited matron all in black,
And learn me how to lose a winning match   12
Played for a pair of stainless maidenhoods.
Hood my unmanned blood, bating in my cheeks,   14
With thy black mantle till strange love grown bold   15
Think true love acted simple modesty.
Come, night. Come, Romeo. Come, thou day in night;
For thou wilt lie upon the wings of night
Whiter than new snow upon a raven's back.
Come, gentle night, come, loving, black-browed night,
Give me my Romeo, and when I shall die   21
Take him and cut him out in little stars,
And he will make the face of heaven so fine
That all the world will be in love with night
And pay no worship to the garish sun.   25
Oh, I have bought the mansion of a love
But not possessed it, and though I am sold,
Not yet enjoyed. So tedious is this day
As is the night before some festival
To an impatient child that hath new robes
And may not wear them. Oh, here comes my nurse,   31

          Enter Nurse, with cords.

And she brings news, and every tongue that speaks
But Romeo's name speaks heavenly eloquence.
Now, Nurse, what news? What hast thou there? The
     cords
That Romeo bid thee fetch?
NURSE   Ay, ay, the cords.
                              [*She throws them down.*]
JULIET
Ay me, what news? Why dost thou wring thy hands?
NURSE
Ah, weraday! He's dead, he's dead, he's dead!   37
We are undone, lady, we are undone!
Alack the day, he's gone, he's killed, he's dead!
JULIET
Can heaven be so envious?
NURSE   Romeo can,   40
Though heaven cannot. Oh, Romeo, Romeo!
Who ever would have thought it? Romeo!

JULIET
What devil art thou that dost torment me thus?
This torture should be roared in dismal hell.
Hath Romeo slain himself? Say thou but "Ay,"
And that bare vowel "I" shall poison more   46
Than the death-darting eye of cockatrice.   47
I am not I, if there be such an "Ay,"
Or those eyes shut, that makes thee answer "Ay."   49
If he be slain, say "Ay," or if not, "No."
Brief sounds determine of my weal or woe.   51
NURSE
I saw the wound. I saw it with mine eyes—
God save the mark!—here on his manly breast.   53
A piteous corpse, a bloody piteous corpse;
Pale, pale as ashes, all bedaubed in blood,
All in gore-blood. I swoonèd at the sight.   56
JULIET
Oh, break, my heart! Poor bankrupt, break at once!
To prison, eyes; ne'er look on liberty!
Vile earth, to earth resign; end motion here,   59
And thou and Romeo press one heavy bier!   60
NURSE
O Tybalt, Tybalt, the best friend I had!
O courteous Tybalt! Honest gentleman!   62
That ever I should live to see thee dead!
JULIET
What storm is this that blows so contrary?
Is Romeo slaughtered, and is Tybalt dead?
My dearest cousin, and my dearer lord?
Then, dreadful trumpet, sound the general doom!   67
For who is living, if those two are gone?
NURSE
Tybalt is gone, and Romeo banishèd;
Romeo that killed him, he is banishèd.
JULIET
Oh, God! Did Romeo's hand shed Tybalt's blood?
NURSE
It did, it did. Alas the day it did!
JULIET
O serpent heart, hid with a flow'ring face!   73
Did ever dragon keep so fair a cave?   74
Beautiful tyrant! Fiend angelical!
Dove-feathered raven! Wolvish-ravening lamb!
Despisèd substance of divinest show!   77
Just opposite to what thou justly seem'st,
A damnèd saint, an honorable villain!
O nature, what hadst thou to do in hell
When thou didst bower the spirit of a fiend   81
In mortal paradise of such sweet flesh?
Was ever book containing such vile matter

6–7 That runaways' . . . unseen (Perhaps Juliet is thinking of the
elopement that will surely be necessary once she and Romeo secretly
marry; they will embrace in the dark of *love-performing night*,
untalked of and unseen by others and by each other. A difficult passage that is sometimes interpreted, uncertainly, as referring to the
sun's horses as the *runaways*. *Wink* means "close, be shut.") **10 civil**
circumspect, somberly attired **12 learn** teach **14 Hood** Cover. (A
term in falconry; the hawk's eyes were covered so that it would not
bate or beat its wings.) **unmanned** untamed (in falconry; with a pun
on "not yet sexually possessed") **15 strange** diffident **21 I** (Often
emended to *he*, following the Fourth Quarto, but Juliet may mean
that when she is dead she will share Romeo's beauty with the world.
Dying may also hint at sexual climax.) **25 garish** dazzling
31.1 *cords* ropes (for the ladder). **37 weraday!** welladay, alas!
40 envious malicious.

46 "I" (Pronounced identically with "Ay.") **47 cockatrice** basilisk, a
mythical serpent that could kill by its look. **49 those eyes shut** if
Romeo's eyes are shut (in death) **51 weal** welfare, happiness
53 God . . . mark (An oath registering shock and horror.) **56 gore-
blood** clotted blood. **59 Vile . . . here** May my vile body resign itself
to burial, ending life itself **60 press** weigh down. **bier** litter for carrying corpses. **62 Honest** Honorable **67 trumpet** i.e., the last trumpet. **general doom** Day of Judgment. **73 hid . . . face** concealed
beneath a beautiful face. **74 keep** occupy, guard. **cave** i.e., one with
treasure in it. **77 show** appearance. **81 bower** give lodging to

So fairly bound? Oh, that deceit should dwell
In such a gorgeous palace!

NURSE   There's no trust,
No faith, no honesty in men; all perjured,
All forsworn, all naught, all dissemblers.   87
Ah, where's my man? Give me some aqua vitae.   88
These griefs, these woes, these sorrows make me old.
Shame come to Romeo!

JULIET   Blistered be thy tongue
For such a wish! He was not born to shame.
Upon his brow shame is ashamed to sit,
For 'tis a throne where honor may be crowned
Sole monarch of the universal earth.
Oh, what a beast was I to chide at him!

NURSE
Will you speak well of him that killed your cousin?

JULIET
Shall I speak ill of him that is my husband?
Ah, poor my lord, what tongue shall smooth thy name   98
When I, thy three-hours wife, have mangled it?
But wherefore, villain, didst thou kill my cousin?
That villain cousin would have killed my husband.
Back, foolish tears, back to your native spring!
Your tributary drops belong to woe,   103
Which you, mistaking, offer up to joy.
My husband lives, that Tybalt would have slain,   105
And Tybalt's dead, that would have slain my
    husband.
All this is comfort. Wherefore weep I then?
Some word there was, worser than Tybalt's death,
That murdered me. I would forget it fain,   109
But oh, it presses to my memory
Like damnèd guilty deeds to sinners' minds!
"Tybalt is dead, and Romeo—banishèd."
That "banishèd," that one word "banishèd"
Hath slain ten thousand Tybalts. Tybalt's death
Was woe enough, if it had ended there;
Or, if sour woe delights in fellowship
And needly will be ranked with other griefs,   117
Why followed not, when she said "Tybalt's dead,"
"Thy father," or "thy mother," nay, or both,
Which modern lamentation might have moved?   120
But with a rearward following Tybalt's death,   121
"Romeo is banishèd"—to speak that word
Is father, mother, Tybalt, Romeo, Juliet,
All slain, all dead. "Romeo is banishèd!"
There is no end, no limit, measure, bound,
In that word's death; no words can that woe sound.   126
Where is my father and my mother, Nurse?

NURSE
Weeping and wailing over Tybalt's corpse.
Will you go to them? I will bring you thither.

JULIET
Wash they his wounds with tears? Mine shall be spent,
When theirs are dry, for Romeo's banishment.
Take up those cords.—Poor ropes, you are beguiled,
Both you and I, for Romeo is exiled.
He made you for a highway to my bed,
But I, a maid, die maiden-widowèd.
Come, cords, come, Nurse. I'll to my wedding bed,
And death, not Romeo, take my maidenhead.

NURSE [taking up the cords]
Hie to your chamber. I'll find Romeo
To comfort you. I wot well where he is.   139
Hark ye, your Romeo will be here at night.
I'll to him. He is hid at Laurence' cell.

JULIET [giving a ring]
Oh, find him! Give this ring to my true knight,
And bid him come to take his last farewell.
                                        Exeunt [separately].

[3.3]

        Enter Friar [Laurence].

FRIAR LAURENCE
Romeo, come forth; come forth, thou fearful man.   1
Affliction is enamored of thy parts,   2
And thou art wedded to calamity.

        [Enter] Romeo.

ROMEO
Father, what news? What is the Prince's doom?   4
What sorrow craves acquaintance at my hand
That I yet know not?

FRIAR LAURENCE   Too familiar
Is my dear son with such sour company.
I bring thee tidings of the Prince's doom.

ROMEO
What less than doomsday is the Prince's doom?   9

FRIAR LAURENCE
A gentler judgment vanished from his lips: 10
Not body's death, but body's banishment.

ROMEO
Ha, banishment? Be merciful, say "death";
For exile hath more terror in his look,
Much more than death. Do not say "banishment."

FRIAR LAURENCE
Here from Verona art thou banishèd.
Be patient, for the world is broad and wide.

ROMEO
There is no world without Verona walls   17
But purgatory, torture, hell itself.
Hence "banishèd" is banished from the world,
And world's exile is death. Then "banishèd,"   20
Is death mistermed. Calling death "banishèd,"

87 naught worthless, evil   88 man servant.   aqua vitae alcoholic
spirits.   98 poor my lord my poor lord.   smooth thy name speak
your name kindly   103 Your . . . woe You should be shed, offered as
a tribute, on some occasion of real woe   105 that whom   109 fain
gladly   117 needly of necessity.   ranked with accompanied by
120 Which . . . moved which might have prompted a normal griefstricken response.   121 rearward rearguard, following afterward
126 sound (1) fathom (2) express.

139 wot know
3.3. Location: Verona. Friar Laurence's cell.
1 fearful full of fear   2 parts qualities   4 doom judgment.
9 doomsday the Day of judgment, i.e., end of the world
10 vanished issued (into air)   17 without outside of   20 world's
exile exile from the world

Thou cut'st my head off with a golden ax
And smilest upon the stroke that murders me.

FRIAR LAURENCE
Oh, deadly sin! Oh, rude unthankfulness!
Thy fault our law calls death, but the kind Prince,   25
Taking thy part, hath rushed aside the law   26
And turned that black word "death" to "banishment."
This is dear mercy, and thou see'st it not.

ROMEO
'Tis torture, and not mercy. Heaven is here
Where Juliet lives, and every cat and dog
And little mouse, every unworthy thing,
Live here in heaven and may look on her,
But Romeo may not. More validity,   33
More honorable state, more courtship lives   34
In carrion flies than Romeo. They may seize
On the white wonder of dear Juliet's hand
And steal immortal blessing from her lips,
Who even in pure and vestal modesty   38
Still blush, as thinking their own kisses sin;   39
But Romeo may not, he is banishèd.
Flies may do this, but I from this must fly.
They are free men, but I am banishèd.
And sayest thou yet that exile is not death?
Hadst thou no poison mixed, no sharp-ground knife,
No sudden mean of death, though ne'er so mean,   45
But "banishèd" to kill me? "Banishèd"?
Oh, Friar, the damnèd use that word in hell;
Howling attends it. How hast thou the heart,
Being a divine, a ghostly confessor,
A sin absolver, and my friend professed,
To mangle me with that word "banishèd"?

FRIAR LAURENCE
Thou fond mad man, hear me a little speak.   52

ROMEO
Oh, thou wilt speak again of banishment.

FRIAR LAURENCE
I'll give thee armor to keep off that word,
Adversity's sweet milk, philosophy,
To comfort thee, though thou art banishèd.

ROMEO
Yet "banishèd"? Hang up philosophy!   57
Unless philosophy can make a Juliet,
Displant a town, reverse a prince's doom,   59
It helps not, it prevails not. Talk no more.

FRIAR LAURENCE
Oh, then I see that madmen have no ears.

ROMEO
How should they, when that wise men have no eyes?

FRIAR LAURENCE
Let me dispute with thee of thy estate.   63

ROMEO
Thou canst not speak of that thou dost not feel.   64
Wert thou as young as I, Juliet thy love,
An hour but married, Tybalt murderèd,
Doting like me, and like me banishèd,
Then mightst thou speak, then mightst thou tear thy
   hair,
And fall upon the ground, as I do now,
Taking the measure of an unmade grave.
                    [*He falls upon the ground.*] Knock [*within*].

FRIAR LAURENCE
Arise. One knocks. Good Romeo, hide thyself.

ROMEO
Not I, unless the breath of heartsick groans,
Mistlike, infold me from the search of eyes.   *Knock.*

FRIAR LAURENCE
Hark, how they knock!—Who's there?—Romeo, arise.
Thou wilt be taken.—Stay awhile!—Stand up.
                                                  Knock.
Run to my study.—By and by!—God's will,
What simpleness is this?—I come, I come!   *Knock.* 77
Who knocks so hard? Whence come you? What's your
   will?   [*Going to the door.*]

NURSE [*within*]
Let me come in, and you shall know my errand.
I come from Lady Juliet.

FRIAR LAURENCE   Welcome, then.
                              [*He opens the door.*]

        Enter Nurse.

NURSE
O holy Friar, oh, tell me, holy Friar,
Where's my lady's lord, where's Romeo?

FRIAR LAURENCE
There on the ground, with his own tears made drunk.

NURSE
Oh, he is even in my mistress' case,   84
Just in her case! Oh, woeful sympathy!   85
Piteous predicament! Even so lies she,
Blubb'ring and weeping, weeping and blubb'ring.—
Stand up, stand up! Stand, an you be a man.
For Juliet's sake, for her sake, rise and stand!
Why should you fall into so deep an O?   90

ROMEO   Nurse!   [*He rises.*]

NURSE
Ah sir, ah sir! Death's the end of all.

ROMEO
Spakest thou of Juliet? How is it with her?
Doth not she think me an old murderer,   94
Now I have stained the childhood of our joy
With blood removed but little from her own?
Where is she? And how doth she? And what says
My concealed lady to our canceled love?   98

---

25 **Thy fault . . . death** For your crime, the law demands a death sentence 26 **rushed** thrust 33 **validity** true worth 34 **courtship** (1) courtliness (2) occasion for wooing 38 **vestal** maidenly 39 **Still . . . sin** continually look red, as though blushing to think that their touching each other is sin 45 **mean . . . mean** means . . . base 52 **fond** foolish, frantic 57 **Yet** Still 59 **Displant** uproot 63 **dispute** reason. **estate** situation.

64 **that** that which 77 **simpleness** foolishness 84 **even** exactly. **case** situation 85 **woeful sympathy** mutuality of grief. 90 **an O** a fit of groaning. (A sexual meaning, unrecognized by the speaker, is suggested by *rise and stand* in the previous line.) 94 **old** hardened 98 **concealed** secret. **canceled** nullified (by the impending exile)

NURSE
    Oh, she says nothing, sir, but weeps and weeps,
    And now falls on her bed, and then starts up,
    And "Tybalt" calls, and then on Romeo cries,
    And then down falls again.
ROMEO   As if that name,
    Shot from the deadly level of a gun,   103
    Did murder her, as that name's cursèd hand
    Murdered her kinsman. Oh, tell me, Friar, tell me,
    In what vile part of this anatomy
    Doth my name lodge? Tell me, that I may sack   107
    The hateful mansion.
                      [*He draws a weapon, but is restrained.*]
FRIAR LAURENCE   Hold thy desperate hand!
    Art thou a man? Thy form cries out thou art;
    Thy tears are womanish, thy wild acts denote
    The unreasonable fury of a beast.
    Unseemly woman in a seeming man,
    And ill-beseeming beast in seeming both!
    Thou hast amazed me. By my holy order,
    I thought thy disposition better tempered.   115
    Hast thou slain Tybalt? Wilt thou slay thyself,
    And slay thy lady, that in thy life lives,
    By doing damnèd hate upon thyself?
    Why railest thou on thy birth, the heaven, and earth,
    Since birth, and heaven, and earth, all three do meet   120
    In thee at once, which thou at once wouldst lose?
    Fie, fie, thou shamest thy shape, thy love, thy wit,   122
    Which, like a usurer, abound'st in all,   123
    And usest none in that true use indeed   124
    Which should bedeck thy shape, thy love, thy wit.   125
    Thy noble shape is but a form of wax,   126
    Digressing from the valor of a man;
    Thy dear love sworn but hollow perjury,
    Killing that love which thou hast vowed to cherish;
    Thy wit, that ornament to shape and love,
    Misshapen in the conduct of them both,   131
    Like powder in a skilless soldier's flask   132
    Is set afire by thine own ignorance,
    And thou dismembered with thine own defense.   134
    What, rouse thee, man! Thy Juliet is alive,
    For whose dear sake thou wast but lately dead;   136
    There art thou happy. Tybalt would kill thee,   137
    But thou slewest Tybalt; there art thou happy.
    The law that threatened death becomes thy friend
    And turns it to exile; there art thou happy.
    A pack of blessings light upon thy back,
    Happiness courts thee in her best array,
    But like a mishavèd and sullen wench   143
    Thou pout'st upon thy fortune and thy love.

    Take heed, take heed, for such die miserable.
    Go, get thee to thy love, as was decreed.   146
    Ascend her chamber; hence and comfort her.
    But look thou stay not till the watch be set,   148
    For then thou canst not pass to Mantua,
    Where thou shalt live till we can find a time
    To blaze your marriage, reconcile your friends,   151
    Beg pardon of the Prince, and call thee back
    With twenty hundred thousand times more joy
    Than thou went'st forth in lamentation.
    Go before, Nurse. Commend me to thy lady,
    And bid her hasten all the house to bed,
    Which heavy sorrow makes them apt unto.
    Romeo is coming.
NURSE
    Oh, Lord, I could have stayed here all the night
    To hear good counsel. Oh, what learning is!—
    My lord, I'll tell my lady you will come.
ROMEO
    Do so, and bid my sweet prepare to chide.
NURSE [*giving a ring*]
    Here, sir, a ring she bid me give you, sir.
    Hie you, make haste, for it grows very late.   [*Exit.*]
ROMEO
    How well my comfort is revived by this!
FRIAR LAURENCE
    Go hence. Good night. And here stands all your state: 166
    Either be gone before the watch be set,
    Or by the break of day disguised from hence.
    Sojourn in Mantua. I'll find out your man,
    And he shall signify from time to time
    Every good hap to you that chances here.   171
    Give me thy hand. 'Tis late. Farewell, good night.
ROMEO
    But that a joy past joy calls out on me,
    It were a grief so brief to part with thee.   174
    Farewell.   *Exeunt* [*separately*].

❖

[3.4]

Enter old Capulet, his Wife, and Paris.

CAPULET
    Things have fall'n out, sir, so unluckily,   1
    That we have had no time to move our daughter.   2
    Look you, she loved her kinsman Tybalt dearly,
    And so did I. Well, we were born to die.
    'Tis very late. She'll not come down tonight.
    I promise you, but for your company   6
    I would have been abed an hour ago.
PARIS
    These times of woe afford no times to woo.
    Madam, good night. Commend me to your daughter.

103 **level** aim   107 **sack** destroy   115 **tempered** harmonized, balanced.   120 **birth . . . earth** life, soul, and body   122–5 **thou shamest
. . . wit** you shame your physical form, love, and mind (corresponding to life, soul, and body), all of which you have in abundance but
which you misuse as a usurer misuses wealth, using improperly the
treasure that you should put to proper use.   126 **form of wax** wax-
work, mere outer form   131 **conduct** guidance   132 **powder** gunpowder.   **flask** powder horn   134 **dismembered . . . defense** blown
to pieces by that which should defend you, i.e., your *wit*, or intellect.
136 **wast . . . dead** i.e., only recently were wishing yourself dead. (See
line 70.)   137 **happy** fortunate.   143 **mishavèd** misbehaved

146 **decreed** (1) arranged earlier (2) decreed by heaven for those who
have married.   148 **the watch be set** guards are posted (at the city
gates)   151 **blaze** publish, divulge.   **friends** relations   166 **here . . .
state** your fortune depends on what follows   171 **good hap** fortunate
event   174 **brief** quickly
3.4. Location: Verona. Capulet's house.
1 **fall'n out** happened   2 **move** persuade   6 **promise** assure

WIFE
> I will, and know her mind early tomorrow.
> Tonight she's mewed up to her heaviness.   11
CAPULET
> Sir Paris, I will make a desperate tender   12
> Of my child's love. I think she will be ruled
> In all respects by me; nay, more, I doubt it not.
> Wife, go you to her ere you go to bed.
> Acquaint her here of my son Paris' love,
> And bid her, mark you me, on Wednesday next—   17
> But soft, what day is this?
PARIS   Monday, my lord.   18
CAPULET
> Monday! Ha, ha! Well, Wednesday is too soon;
> O' Thursday let it be. O'Thursday, tell her,
> She shall be married to this noble earl.
> Will you be ready? Do you like this haste?
> We'll keep no great ado—a friend or two;
> For hark you, Tybalt being slain so late,   24
> It may be thought we held him carelessly,   25
> Being our kinsman, if we revel much.
> Therefore we'll have some half a dozen friends,
> And there an end. But what say you to Thursday?
PARIS
> My lord, I would that Thursday were tomorrow.
CAPULET
> Well, get you gone. O' Thursday be it, then.
> [*To his Wife*] Go you to Juliet ere you go to bed;
> Prepare her, wife, against this wedding day.—   32
> Farewell, my lord.—Light to my chamber, ho!—
> Afore me, it is so very late   34
> That we may call it early by and by.
> Good night.   *Exeunt.*

❦

[3.5]

Enter Romeo and Juliet aloft [at the window].

JULIET
> Wilt thou be gone? It is not yet near day.
> It was the nightingale, and not the lark,
> That pierced the fearful hollow of thine ear;   3
> Nightly she sings on yond pomegranate tree.
> Believe me, love, it was the nightingale.
ROMEO
> It was the lark, the herald of the morn,
> No nightingale. Look, love, what envious streaks
> Do lace the severing clouds in yonder east.   8
> Night's candles are burnt out, and jocund day   9
> Stands tiptoe on the misty mountain tops.
> I must be gone and live, or stay and die.

JULIET
> Yond light is not daylight, I know it, I.
> It is some meteor that the sun exhaled   13
> To be to thee this night a torchbearer
> And light thee on thy way to Mantua.
> Therefore stay yet. Thou need'st not to be gone.
ROMEO
> Let me be ta'en; let me be put to death.
> I am content, so thou wilt have it so.   18
> I'll say yon gray is not the morning's eye;
> 'Tis but the pale reflex of Cynthia's brow.   20
> Nor that is not the lark whose notes do beat
> The vaulty heaven so high above our heads.
> I have more care to stay than will to go.   23
> Come, death, and welcome! Juliet wills it so.
> How is't, my soul? Let's talk. It is not day.
JULIET
> It is, it is. Hie hence, begone, away!   26
> It is the lark that sings so out of tune,
> Straining harsh discords and unpleasing sharps.   28
> Some say the lark makes sweet division;   29
> This doth not so, for she divideth us.
> Some say the lark and loathèd toad changed eyes;   31
> Oh, now I would they had changed voices too,
> Since arm from arm that voice doth us affray,   33
> Hunting thee hence with hunt's-up to the day.   34
> Oh, now begone! More light and light it grows.
ROMEO
> More light and light, more dark and dark our woes!

Enter Nurse [hastily].

NURSE   Madam!
JULIET   Nurse?
NURSE
> Your lady mother is coming to your chamber.
> The day is broke; be wary, look about.   [*Exit.*]
JULIET
> Then window, let day in, and let life out.
ROMEO
> Farewell, farewell! One kiss, and I'll descend.
>   [*They kiss. He climbs down from the window.*]
JULIET
> Art thou gone so? Love, lord, ay, husband, friend!   43
> I must hear from thee every day in the hour,
> For in a minute there are many days.
> Oh, by this count I shall be much in years   46
> Ere I again behold my Romeo!
ROMEO [*from below her window*]   Farewell!

---

11 mewed up to cooped up with. (A term from falconry, reminiscent of 2.2.159–68.)   **heaviness** sorrow.   **12 desperate tender** bold offer   **17 mark you me** listen to this   **18 soft** wait a minute   **24 late** recently   **25 held him carelessly** did not regard him highly   **32 against** in anticipation of   **34 Afore me** i.e., By my life. (A mild oath.)
3.5. Location: Verona. Capulet's orchard with Juliet's chamber window above, and, at lines 68 ff., the interior of Juliet's chamber.
3 fearful apprehensive, anxious   **8 severing** separating   **9 jocund** cheerful

13 exhaled i.e., has drawn out of the ground. (Meteors were thought to be vapors of luminous gas drawn up by the sun.)   **18 so** as long as, since   **20 reflex** reflection.   **Cynthia's** the moon's   **23 care** desire, concern   **26 Hie hence** Hasten away   **28 sharps** notes relatively high in pitch and hence discordant.   **29 division** variations on a melody, made by dividing each note into notes of briefer duration   **31 changed** exchanged. (A popular saying, to account for the observation that the lark has very ordinary eyes and the toad remarkable ones.)   **33 arm from arm** from one another's arms.   **affray** frighten   **34 hunt's-up** a song or tune originally designed to awaken huntsmen; later, used also to serenade a newly married couple   **43 friend** lover.   **46 much in years** much older

I will omit no opportunity
That may convey my greetings, love, to thee.

JULIET
Oh, think'st thou we shall ever meet again?

ROMEO
I doubt it not, and all these woes shall serve
For sweet discourses in our times to come.

JULIET
Oh, God, I have an ill-divining soul!   54
Methinks I see thee, now thou art so low,
As one dead in the bottom of a tomb.
Either my eyesight fails or thou lookest pale.

ROMEO
And trust me, love, in my eye so do you.
Dry sorrow drinks our blood. Adieu, adieu!   *Exit.* 59

JULIET
O Fortune, Fortune! All men call thee fickle.
If thou art fickle, what dost thou with him
That is renowned for faith? Be fickle, Fortune.
For then, I hope, thou wilt not keep him long,
But send him back.

         Enter Mother [Capulet's Wife].

WIFE   Ho, daughter, are you up?

JULIET
Who is't that calls? It is my lady mother.
Is she not down so late, or up so early?   66
What unaccustomed cause procures her hither?   67
         [She goeth down from the window.]

WIFE
Why, how now, Juliet?

JULIET   Madam, I am not well.

WIFE
Evermore weeping for your cousin's death?
What, wilt thou wash him from his grave with tears?
An if thou couldst, thou couldst not make him live;
Therefore, have done. Some grief shows much of love, 72
But much of grief shows still some want of wit. 73

JULIET
Yet let me weep for such a feeling loss.   74

WIFE
So shall you feel the loss, but not the friend
Which you weep for.

JULIET   Feeling so the loss,
I cannot choose but ever weep the friend.   77

WIFE
Well, girl, thou weep'st not so much for his death
As that the villain lives which slaughtered him.

JULIET
What villain, madam?

WIFE   That same villain, Romeo.

JULIET *[aside]*
Villain and he be many miles asunder.—
God pardon him! I do, with all my heart;
And yet no man like he doth grieve my heart. 83

WIFE
That is because the traitor murderer lives.

JULIET
Ay, madam, from the reach of these my hands.
Would none but I might venge my cousin's death!

WIFE
We will have vengeance for it, fear thou not.
Then weep no more. I'll send to one in Mantua,
Where that same banished runagate doth live, 89
Shall give him such an unaccustomed dram 90
That he shall soon keep Tybalt company.
And then, I hope, thou wilt be satisfied.

JULIET
Indeed, I never shall be satisfied
With Romeo till I behold him—dead—
Is my poor heart so for a kinsman vexed.
Madam, if you could find out but a man
To bear a poison, I would temper it, 97
That Romeo should, upon receipt thereof,
Soon sleep in quiet. Oh, how my heart abhors
To hear him named, and cannot come to him
To wreak the love I bore my cousin 101
Upon his body that hath slaughtered him! 102

WIFE
Find thou the means, and I'll find such a man.
But now I'll tell thee joyful tidings, girl.

JULIET
And joy comes well in such a needy time.
What are they, beseech Your Ladyship?

WIFE
Well, well, thou hast a careful father, child, 107
One who, to put thee from thy heaviness, 108
Hath sorted out a sudden day of joy 109
That thou expects not, nor I looked not for.

JULIET
Madam, in happy time, what day is that?

WIFE
Marry, my child, early next Thursday morn, 112
The gallant, young, and noble gentleman,
The County Paris, at Saint Peter's Church
Shall happily make thee there a joyful bride.

JULIET
Now, by Saint Peter's Church, and Peter too,
He shall not make me there a joyful bride!

---

54 ill-divining prophesying of evil **59 Dry sorrow** (The heat of the body in sorrow and despair was thought to descend into the bowels and dry up the blood.) **66 down** in bed **67 procures** induces to come. **67.1** (As indicated by the bracketed stage direction, which is from the First Quarto, Juliet, who has appeared until now at her "window" above the stage, evidently descends quickly to the main stage and joins her mother for the remainder of the scene. The stage, which before was to have been imagined as Capulet's orchard, is now Juliet's chamber. Juliet's mother has entered onto the main stage four lines earlier.) **72 have done** cease. **73 want of wit** lack of intelligence. **74 feeling** deeply felt **77 the friend** (Juliet secretly means "my lover," as at line 43, but, of course, her mother hears it as "Tybalt.")

83 no man like he no man so much as he. **grieve** (1) anger (2) grieve with longing. (Juliet speaks to her mother throughout in intentional ambiguities, at lines 85, 86, 99, 100–2, etc.) **89 runagate** renegade, fugitive **90 Shall** who will. **dram** dose. (Literally, one-eighth of a fluid ounce.) **97 temper** (1) mix, concoct (2) alloy, dilute. (In her intended double meanings about Romeo dead, poisoned, and sleeping in quiet, Juliet is, of course, unaware of an ironic anticipation of how these things will be fulfilled.) **101 wreak** (1) avenge (2) bestow **102 his body that** the body of him who **107 careful** full of care (for you) **108 heaviness** sorrow **109 sorted** chosen **112 Marry** i.e., By the Virgin Mary

I wonder at this haste, that I must wed
Ere he that should be husband comes to woo.
I pray you, tell my lord and father, madam,
I will not marry yet, and when I do I swear
It shall be Romeo, whom you know I hate,
Rather than Paris. These are news indeed!

WIFE
Here comes your father. Tell him so yourself,
And see how he will take it at your hands.

Enter Capulet and Nurse.

CAPULET
When the sun sets, the earth doth drizzle dew,
But for the sunset of my brother's son
It rains downright.—
How now, a conduit, girl? What, still in tears?   129
Evermore show'ring? In one little body
Thou counterfeits a bark, a sea, a wind;   131
For still thy eyes, which I may call the sea,
Do ebb and flow with tears; the bark thy body is,
Sailing in this salt flood; the winds, thy sighs,
Who, raging with thy tears, and they with them,
Without a sudden calm, will overset   136
Thy tempest-tossèd body.—How now, wife?
Have you delivered to her our decree?

WIFE
Ay, sir, but she will none, she gives you thanks.   139
I would the fool were married to her grave!

CAPULET
Soft, take me with you, take me with you, wife.   141
How? Will she none? Doth she not give us thanks?
Is she not proud? Doth she not count her blest,   143
Unworthy as she is, that we have wrought   144
So worthy a gentleman to be her bride?   145

JULIET
Not proud you have, but thankful that you have.
Proud can I never be of what I hate,
But thankful even for hate that is meant love.   148

CAPULET
How, how, how, how, chopped logic? What is this?
"Proud," and "I thank you," and "I thank you not,"
And yet "not proud"? Mistress minion, you,   151
Thank me no thankings, nor proud me no prouds,
But fettle your fine joints 'gainst Thursday next   153
To go with Paris to Saint Peter's Church,
Or I will drag thee on a hurdle thither.   155
Out, you greensickness carrion! Out, you baggage!   156
You tallow-face!

WIFE [*to Capulet*] Fie, fie! What, are you mad?   157

JULIET [*kneeling*]
Good father, I beseech you on my knees,
Hear me with patience but to speak a word.

CAPULET
Hang thee, young baggage, disobedient wretch!
I tell thee what: get thee to church o' Thursday
Or never after look me in the face.
Speak not, reply not, do not answer me!
My fingers itch. Wife, we scarce thought us blest
That God had lent us but this only child;
But now I see this one is one too much,
And that we have a curse in having her.
Out on her, hilding!

NURSE   God in heaven bless her!   168
You are to blame, my lord, to rate her so.   169

CAPULET
And why, my Lady Wisdom? Hold your tongue,
Good Prudence. Smatter with your gossips, go.   171

NURSE
I speak no treason.

CAPULET   Oh, God-i'-good-e'en!   172

NURSE
May not one speak?

CAPULET   Peace, you mumbling fool!
Utter your gravity o'er a gossip's bowl,   174
For here we need it not.

WIFE   You are too hot.

CAPULET God's bread, it makes me mad!   176
Day, night, hour, tide, time, work, play,   177
Alone, in company, still my care hath been
To have her matched. And having now provided
A gentleman of noble parentage,
Of fair demesnes, youthful, and nobly liened,   181
Stuffed, as they say, with honorable parts,   182
Proportioned as one's thought would wish a man—
And then to have a wretched puling fool,   184
A whining mammet, in her fortune's tender,   185
To answer, "I'll not wed, I cannot love,
I am too young; I pray you, pardon me."
But, an you will not wed, I'll pardon you.   188
Graze where you will, you shall not house with me.
Look to 't, think on 't. I do not use to jest.   190
Thursday is near. Lay hand on heart; advise.   191
An you be mine, I'll give you to my friend;
An you be not, hang, beg, starve, die in the streets,
For, by my soul, I'll ne'er acknowledge thee,
Nor what is mine shall never do thee good.
Trust to 't, bethink you. I'll not be forsworn.   *Exit.* 196

JULIET
Is there no pity sitting in the clouds
That sees into the bottom of my grief?

---

129 **conduit** water pipe, fountain 131 **bark** sailing vessel 136 **With-out** unless there is 139 **will . . . thanks** says "no thank you," she'll have no part of it. 141 **take . . . you** let me understand you 143 **count her** consider herself 144 **wrought** arranged for 145 **bride** bridegroom. 148 **hate . . . love** that which is hateful but which was meant lovingly. 151 **minion** spoiled darling, minx 153 **fettle** make ready. **'gainst** in anticipation of 155 **a hurdle** a conveyance on which criminals were dragged to execution 156 **greensickness** (An anemic ailment of young unmarried women; it suggests Juliet's paleness.) **baggage** hussy. 157 **tallow-face** paleface.

168 **hilding** jade, baggage. 169 **rate** berate, scold 171 **Smatter** Chatter. **gossips** gossiping women friends 172 **God-i'-good-e'en** i.e., For God's sake. (Literally, God give you good evening.) 174 **gravity** wisdom. (Said contemptuously.) 176 **God's bread** i.e., By God's (Christ's) Sacrament 177 **tide** season 181 **demesnes** estates. **liened** descended 182 **parts** qualities 184 **puling** whining 185 **mammet** doll. **in . . . tender** when an offer of good fortune is made to her 188 **pardon you** i.e., allow you to depart. (Said caustically.) 190 **do not use** am not accustomed 191 **advise** consider carefully. 196 **be forsworn** i.e., go back on my word.

O sweet my mother, cast me not away!
Delay this marriage for a month, a week;
Or if you do not, make the bridal bed
In that dim monument where Tybalt lies.
WIFE
    Talk not to me, for I'll not speak a word.
    Do as thou wilt, for I have done with thee.   *Exit.*
JULIET   [*rising*]
    Oh, God!—O Nurse, how shall this be prevented?
    My husband is on earth, my faith in heaven.   206
    How shall that faith return again to earth,   207
    Unless that husband send it me from heaven   208
    By leaving earth? Comfort me, counsel me.   209
    Alack, alack, that heaven should practice stratagems
    Upon so soft a subject as myself!
    What say'st thou? Hast thou not a word of joy?
    Some comfort, Nurse.
NURSE   Faith, here it is.
    Romeo is banished, and all the world to nothing   214
    That he dares ne'er come back to challenge you,   215
    Or if he do, it needs must be by stealth.
    Then, since the case so stands as now it doth,
    I think it best you married with the County.
    Oh, he's a lovely gentleman!
    Romeo's a dishclout to him. An eagle, madam,   220
    Hath not so green, so quick, so fair an eye
    As Paris hath. Beshrew my very heart,   222
    I think you are happy in this second match,
    For it excels your first; or if it did not,
    Your first is dead—or 'twere as good he were,
    As living here and you no use of him.
JULIET   Speak'st thou from thy heart?
NURSE
    And from my soul too. Else beshrew them both.
JULIET   Amen!   229
NURSE   What?
JULIET
    Well, thou hast comforted me marvelous much.
    Go in, and tell my lady I am gone,
    Having displeased my father, to Laurence' cell
    To make confession and to be absolved.
NURSE
    Marry, I will; and this is wisely done.   [*Exit.*]
JULIET
    Ancient damnation! Oh, most wicked fiend!   236
    Is it more sin to wish me thus forsworn,   237
    Or to dispraise my lord with that same tongue
    Which she hath praised him with above compare
    So many thousand times? Go, counselor,
    Thou and my bosom henceforth shall be twain.   241

I'll to the Friar to know his remedy.
If all else fail, myself have power to die.   *Exit.*

[4.1]

Enter Friar [Laurence] and County Paris.

FRIAR LAURENCE
    On Thursday, sir? The time is very short.
PARIS
    My father Capulet will have it so,
    And I am nothing slow to slack his haste.   3
FRIAR LAURENCE
    You say you do not know the lady's mind?
    Uneven is the course. I like it not.
PARIS
    Immoderately she weeps for Tybalt's death,
    And therefore have I little talked of love,
    For Venus smiles not in a house of tears.   8
    Now, sir, her father counts it dangerous
    That she do give her sorrow so much sway,
    And in his wisdom hastes our marriage
    To stop the inundation of her tears,
    Which, too much minded by herself alone,   13
    May be put from her by society.   14
    Now do you know the reason of this haste.
FRIAR LAURENCE   [*aside*]
    I would I knew not why it should be slowed.—
    Look, sir, here comes the lady toward my cell.

        Enter Juliet.

PARIS
    Happily met, my lady and my wife!
JULIET
    That may be, sir, when I may be a wife.
PARIS
    That "may be" must be, love, on Thursday next.
JULIET
    What must be shall be.
FRIAR LAURENCE   That's a certain text.
PARIS
    Come you to make confession to this father?
JULIET
    To answer that, I should confess to you.
PARIS
    Do not deny to him that you love me.
JULIET
    I will confess to you that I love him.
PARIS
    So will ye, I am sure, that you love me.
JULIET
    If I do so, it will be of more price,   27
    Being spoke behind your back, than to your face.

---

206 my faith in heaven i.e., I am married to Romeo in the sight of
heaven.   **207–9 How . . . leaving earth?** i.e., How can I remarry while
Romeo is still alive?   **214 all . . . nothing** the odds are overwhelming
215 challenge lay claim to   **220 dishclout** dishrag   **222 Beshrew** (A
mild oath. Also in line 228.)   **229 Amen** (Juliet says "Amen" as
though to answer the Nurse's prayer that her heart and soul be
cursed. The Nurse does not get the point.)   **236 Ancient damnation!**
Damnable old woman!   **237 forsworn** i.e., false to my marriage vows
241 bosom secret thoughts.   **twain** separated.

4.1. Location: Verona. Friar Laurence's cell.
3 nothing . . . haste not at all reluctant to lessen his haste, i.e., willing to
speed matters along.   **8 Venus . . . tears** (1) amorousness is not appropriate in a house of mourning (2) the planet Venus does not exert a
favorable influence when it is in an inauspicious *house* or constellation
of the zodiac.   **13 too . . . alone** too mind-consuming when she is alone
14 society companionship.   **27 more price** greater worth

PARIS

    Poor soul, thy face is much abused with tears.

JULIET

    The tears have got small victory by that,

    For it was bad enough before their spite.   31

PARIS

    Thou wrong'st it more than tears with that report.   32

JULIET

    That is no slander, sir, which is a truth;

    And what I spake, I spake it to my face.   34

PARIS

    Thy face is mine, and thou hast slandered it.

JULIET

    It may be so, for it is not mine own.—   36

    Are you at leisure, holy Father, now,

    Or shall I come to you at evening Mass?

FRIAR LAURENCE

    My leisure serves me, pensive daughter, now.—   39

    My lord, we must entreat the time alone.   40

PARIS

    God shield I should disturb devotion!   41

    Juliet, on Thursday early will I rouse ye.

    Till then, adieu, and keep this holy kiss.   *Exit.*

JULIET

    Oh, shut the door! And when thou hast done so,

    Come weep with me—past hope, past cure, past help!

FRIAR LAURENCE

    Ah, Juliet, I already know thy grief;

    It strains me past the compass of my wits.   47

    I hear thou must, and nothing may prorogue it,   48

    On Thursday next be married to this county.

JULIET

    Tell me not, Friar, that thou hearest of this,

    Unless thou tell me how I may prevent it.

    If in thy wisdom thou canst give no help,

    Do thou but call my resolution wise

    And with this knife I'll help it presently.   54

                           [She shows a knife.]

    God joined my heart and Romeo's, thou our hands;

    And ere this hand, by thee to Romeo sealed,

    Shall be the label to another deed,   57

    Or my true heart with treacherous revolt

    Turn to another, this shall slay them both.   59

    Therefore, out of thy long-experienced time,   60

    Give me some present counsel, or, behold,

    Twixt my extremes and me this bloody knife   62

    Shall play the umpire, arbitrating that

    Which the commission of thy years and art   64

    Could to no issue of true honor bring.

    Be not so long to speak; I long to die   66

    If what thou speak'st speak not of remedy.

FRIAR LAURENCE

    Hold, daughter. I do spy a kind of hope,

    Which craves as desperate an execution

    As that is desperate which we would prevent.

    If, rather than to marry County Paris,

    Thou hast the strength of will to slay thyself,

    Then is it likely thou wilt undertake

    A thing like death to chide away this shame,

    That cop'st with Death himself to scape from it;   75

    And if thou darest, I'll give thee remedy.

JULIET

    Oh, bid me leap, rather than marry Paris,

    From off the battlements of any tower,

    Or walk in thievish ways, or bid me lurk   79

    Where serpents are; chain me with roaring bears,

    Or hide me nightly in a charnel house,   81

    O'ercovered quite with dead men's rattling bones,

    With reeky shanks and yellow chopless skulls;   83

    Or bid me go into a new-made grave

    And hide me with a dead man in his tomb—

    Things that, to hear them told, have made me

        tremble—

    And I will do it without fear or doubt,

    To live an unstained wife to my sweet love.

FRIAR LAURENCE

    Hold, then. Go home, be merry, give consent

    To marry Paris. Wednesday is tomorrow.

    Tomorrow night look that thou lie alone;

    Let not the Nurse lie with thee in thy chamber.

    Take thou this vial, being then in bed,

                         [showing her a vial]

    And this distilling liquor drink thou off,   94

    When presently through all thy veins shall run

    A cold and drowsy humor; for no pulse   96

    Shall keep his native progress, but surcease;   97

    No warmth, no breath shall testify thou livest;

    The roses in thy lips and cheeks shall fade

    To wanny ashes, thy eyes' windows fall   100

    Like death when he shuts up the day of life;

    Each part, deprived of supple government,   102

    Shall, stiff and stark and cold, appear like death.

    And in this borrowed likeness of shrunk death

    Thou shalt continue two-and-forty hours,

    And then awake as from a pleasant sleep.

    Now, when the bridegroom in the morning comes

    To rouse thee from thy bed, there art thou dead.

    Then, as the manner of our country is,

    In thy best robes uncovered on the bier

    Thou shalt be borne to that same ancient vault

    Where all the kindred of the Capulets lie.

    In the meantime, against thou shalt awake,   113

    Shall Romeo by my letters know our drift,   114

---

31 spite malice. **32 Thou . . . report** Your apology for your face slanders it more than your tears do. **34 to my face** (1) openly (2) about my face. **36 is not mine own** (1) is beyond my control, does not reveal me truly (2) belongs to Romeo. **39 pensive** sorrowful **40 entreat . . . alone** ask you to leave us alone. **41 God shield** God forbid **47 compass** bounds **48 prorogue** delay **54 presently** at once. **57 label** strip attached to a deed to carry the seal; hence, confirmation, seal **59 both** i.e., hand and heart. **60 time** age **62 extremes** extreme difficulties. **64 commission** authority. **art** skill **66 so long** so slow. (With wordplay on *long*, "yearn," later in this same line.)

75 That . . . himself either (1) you who are willing to encounter Death by killing yourself, or (2) that simulates Death itself. **it** this shame **79 thievish ways** roads frequented by thieves **81 charnel house** vault for human bones **83 reeky** reeking, malodorous. **chopless** without the lower jaw **94 distilling** infusing the body, or distilled **96 humor** fluid **97 his native** its natural. **surcease** cease **100 wanny** wan, pale **102 supple government** control of motion **113 against** anticipating when **114 drift** plan

And hither shall he come; and he and I
Will watch thy waking, and that very night   116
Shall Romeo bear thee hence to Mantua.
And this shall free thee from this present shame,
If no inconstant toy nor womanish fear   119
Abate thy valor in the acting it.

JULIET [*taking the vial*]
Give me, give me! Oh, tell not me of fear!

FRIAR LAURENCE
Hold, get you gone. Be strong and prosperous   122
In this resolve. I'll send a friar with speed
To Mantua, with my letters to thy lord.

JULIET
Love give me strength, and strength shall help afford. 125
Farewell, dear Father!   *Exeunt* [*separately*].

❖

[4.2]

Enter Father Capulet, Mother [*Capulet's Wife*],
Nurse, and Servingmen, two or three.

CAPULET
So many guests invite as here are writ.
              [*Exit one or two servingmen.*]
Sirrah, go hire me twenty cunning cooks.   2

SERVINGMAN   You shall have none ill, sir, for I'll try if   3
they can lick their fingers.

CAPULET   How canst thou try them so?

SERVINGMAN   Marry, sir, 'tis an ill cook that cannot lick
his own fingers; therefore he that cannot lick his
fingers goes not with me.

CAPULET   Go, begone.   [*Exit Servingman.*]
We shall be much unfurnished for this time.   10
What, is my daughter gone to Friar Laurence?

NURSE   Ay, forsooth.

CAPULET
Well, he may chance to do some good on her.
A peevish self-willed harlotry it is.   14

Enter Juliet.

NURSE
See where she comes from shrift with merry look.

CAPULET
How now, my headstrong, where have you been
              gadding?

JULIET
Where I have learned me to repent the sin
Of disobedient opposition
To you and your behests, and am enjoined   19
By holy Laurence to fall prostrate here,   [*kneeling*]
To beg your pardon. Pardon, I beseech you!
Henceforward I am ever ruled by you.

CAPULET
Send for the County! Go tell him of this.
I'll have this knot knit up tomorrow morning.

JULIET
I met the youthful lord at Laurence' cell
And gave him what becomèd love I might,   26
Not stepping o'er the bounds of modesty.

CAPULET
Why, I am glad on't. This is well. Stand up.
                        [*Juliet rises.*]
This is as 't should be. Let me see the County;
Ay, marry, go, I say, and fetch him hither.
Now, afore God, this reverend holy friar,
All our whole city is much bound to him.   32

JULIET
Nurse, will you go with me into my closet   33
To help me sort such needful ornaments   34
As you think fit to furnish me tomorrow?

WIFE
No, not till Thursday. There is time enough.

CAPULET
Go, Nurse, go with her. We'll to church tomorrow.
              Exeunt [*Juliet and Nurse*].

WIFE
We shall be short in our provision.
'Tis now near night.

CAPULET   Tush, I will stir about,
And all things shall be well, I warrant thee, wife.
Go thou to Juliet, help to deck up her.
I'll not to bed tonight. Let me alone.   42
I'll play the huswife for this once.—What, ho!—   43
They are all forth. Well, I will walk myself
To County Paris, to prepare up him
Against tomorrow. My heart is wondrous light,
Since this same wayward girl is so reclaimed.
                        Exeunt.

❖

[4.3]

Enter Juliet and Nurse.

JULIET
Ay, those attires are best. But, gentle Nurse,
I pray thee, leave me to myself tonight;
For I have need of many orisons   3
To move the heavens to smile upon my state,
Which, well thou knowest, is cross and full of sin. 5

Enter Mother [*Capulet's Wife*].

WIFE
What, are you busy, ho? Need you my help?

JULIET
No, madam, we have culled such necessaries   7
As are behooveful for our state tomorrow.   8
So please you, let me now be left alone,
And let the Nurse this night sit up with you,

116 **watch** keep a watch over, be on hand for   119 **toy** idle fancy
122 **prosperous** successful   125 **help afford** provide help.
4.2. Location: Verona. Capulet's house.
2 **cunning** skilled   3 **none ill** no bad ones.   **try** test   10 **unfurnished** unprovided   14 **A peevish . . . is** i.e., She's a silly good-for-
nothing.   19 **behests** commands

26 **becomèd** befitting   32 **bound** indebted   33 **closet** chamber
34 **sort** choose   42 **Let me alone** Leave things to me.   43 **huswife**
housewife
**4.3. Location: Verona. Capulet's house; Juliet's bed, enclosed by
bedcurtains, is set up in the discovery space.**
3 **orisons** prayers   5 **cross** perverse   7 **culled** picked out
8 **behooveful** needful.   **state** ceremony

For I am sure you have your hands full all
In this so sudden business.
WIFE   Good night.
Get thee to bed and rest, for thou hast need.
                    Exeunt [Capulet's Wife and Nurse].
JULIET
Farewell! God knows when we shall meet again.
I have a faint cold fear thrills through my veins   15
That almost freezes up the heat of life.
I'll call them back again to comfort me.—
Nurse!—What should she do here?
My dismal scene I needs must act alone.
Come, vial.   *[She takes out the vial.]*
What if this mixture do not work at all?
Shall I be married then tomorrow morning?
No, no, this shall forbid it. Lie thou there.
                        [She lays down a dagger.]
What if it be a poison, which the Friar
Subtly hath ministered to have me dead,
Lest in this marriage he should be dishonored
Because he married me before to Romeo?
I fear it is; and yet methinks it should not,
For he hath still been tried a holy man.   29
How if, when I am laid into the tomb,
I wake before the time that Romeo
Come to redeem me? There's a fearful point!
Shall I not then be stifled in the vault,
To whose foul mouth no healthsome air breathes in,
And there die strangled ere my Romeo comes?
Or, if I live, is it not very like   36
The horrible conceit of death and night,   37
Together with the terror of the place—
As in a vault, an ancient receptacle,   39
Where for this many hundred years the bones
Of all my buried ancestors are packed;
Where bloody Tybalt, yet but green in earth,   42
Lies fest'ring in his shroud; where, as they say,
At some hours in the night spirits resort—
Alack, alack, is it not like that I,
So early waking, what with loathsome smells,
And shrieks like mandrakes torn out of the earth,   47
That living mortals, hearing them, run mad—   48
Oh, if I wake, shall I not be distraught,
Environèd with all these hideous fears,   50
And madly play with my forefathers' joints,
And pluck the mangled Tybalt from his shroud,
And in this rage, with some great kinsman's bone   53
As with a club dash out my desp'rate brains?
Oh, look! Methinks I see my cousin's ghost
Seeking out Romeo, that did spit his body   56

Upon a rapier's point. Stay, Tybalt, stay!   57
Romeo, Romeo, Romeo! Here's drink—I drink to thee.
                    [She drinks and falls upon her bed,
                                within the curtains.]

[4.4]

Enter Lady of the House [Capulet's Wife]
and Nurse.

WIFE
Hold, take these keys, and fetch more spices, Nurse.
NURSE
They call for dates and quinces in the pastry.   2

                Enter old Capulet.

CAPULET
Come, stir, stir, stir! The second cock hath crowed.
The curfew bell hath rung; 'tis three o'clock.
Look to the baked meats, good Angelica.   5
Spare not for cost.
NURSE   Go, you cotquean, go,   6
Get you to bed. Faith, you'll be sick tomorrow
For this night's watching.   8
CAPULET
No, not a whit. What, I have watched ere now
All night for lesser cause, and ne'er been sick.
WIFE
Ay, you have been a mouse-hunt in your time,   11
But I will watch you from such watching now.   12
                        Exeunt Lady and Nurse.
CAPULET   A jealous hood, a jealous hood!   13

        Enter three or four [Servingmen] with spits and
        logs, and baskets.

Now, fellow, what is there?
FIRST SERVINGMAN
Things for the cook, sir, but I know not what.
CAPULET   Make haste, make haste. *[Exit First Servingman.]*
[To Second Servingman]   Sirrah, fetch drier logs.
Call Peter. He will show thee where they are.
SECOND SERVINGMAN
I have a head, sir, that will find out logs   18
And never trouble Peter for the matter.
CAPULET
Mass, and well said. A merry whoreson, ha!   20

57 Stay Stop, wait
4.4. Location: Scene continues. Juliet's bed remains visible.
2 pastry room in which pastry was made.   **5 baked meats** pies, pastry   **6 cotquean** i.e., a man who acts the housewife. (Literally, a cottage housewife.)   **8 watching** being awake.   **11 mouse-hunt** i.e., hunter of women. (Literally, a weasel.)   **12 watch . . . watching** i.e., keep an eye on you to prevent such nighttime activity. (Playing on *watching* in line 8.)   **13 A jealous hood** i.e., You wear the cap of jealousy   **18 I . . . logs** i.e., (1) I have a good head for finding things (2) My wooden head knows all about logs   **20 Mass** By the Mass. **whoreson** i.e., fellow. (An abusive term used familiarly.)

15 faint producing faintness.   **thrills** that pierces, shivers   **29 still been tried** always been tried and proven to be   **36 like** likely. (Also at line 45.)   **37 conceit** idea   **39 As** namely   **42 green** new, freshly   **47 mandrakes** (The root of the mandragora or mandrake resembled the human form; the plant was fabled to utter a shriek when torn from the ground.)   **48 That** so that   **50 fears** objects of fear   **53 rage** madness.   **great** i.e., of an earlier generation, as in *great*-grandfather   **56 spit** impale

Thou shalt be loggerhead.   [*Exit Servingman.*]
                        Good faith, 'tis day.   21
The County will be here with music straight,   22
For so he said he would.   *Play music* [*within*].
                        I hear him near.
Nurse! Wife! What, ho! What, Nurse, I say!

        Enter Nurse.

Go waken Juliet, go and trim her up.
I'll go and chat with Paris. Hie, make haste,
Make haste. The bridegroom he is come already.
Make haste, I say.   [*Exit Capulet.*]

[4.5]

        [*The Nurse goes to the bed.*]

NURSE
    Mistress! What, mistress! Juliet!—Fast, I warrant her,
        she.   1
    Why, lamb, why, lady! Fie, you slugabed!
    Why, love, I say! Madam! Sweetheart! Why, bride!
    What, not a word? You take your pennyworths now.   4
    Sleep for a week; for the next night, I warrant,
    The County Paris hath set up his rest   6
    That you shall rest but little. God forgive me,   7
    Marry, and amen! How sound is she asleep!   8
    I needs must wake her.—Madam, madam, madam!
    Ay, let the County take you in your bed;   10
    He'll fright you up, i'faith.—Will it not be?
                        [*She opens the bedcurtains.*]
    What, dressed, and in your clothes, and down again?
    I must needs wake you. Lady, lady, lady!
    Alas, alas! Help, help! My lady's dead!
    Oh, weraday, that ever I was born!   15
    Some aqua vitae, ho! My lord! My lady!   16

        [*Enter Capulet's Wife.*]

WIFE
    What noise is here?
NURSE   Oh, lamentable day!
WIFE
    What is the matter?
NURSE   Look, look! Oh, heavy day!   18
WIFE
    Oh, me, oh, me! My child, my only life!
    Revive, look up, or I will die with thee!
    Help, help! Call help.

        Enter Father [*Capulet*].

CAPULET
    For shame, bring Juliet forth. Her lord is come.

---

21 loggerhead (1) put in charge of getting logs (2) a blockhead.
22 straight straightway, immediately
4.5. Location: Scene continues. Juliet's bed remains visible.
1 Fast Fast asleep   **4 pennyworths** small portions (of sleep)   **6 set . . .
rest** staked his all, resolved to play all out. (From the card game of
primero, here with obviously bawdy meaning.)   **7–8 God . . . amen!**
(The Nurse apologizes amiably for her bawdy talk.)   **10 take . . . bed**
(1) find you still abed (2) possess you sexually   **15 weraday** wellaway,
alas   **16 aqua vitae** strong alcoholic spirits   **18 heavy** sorrowful

---

NURSE
    She's dead, deceased. She's dead, alack the day!
WIFE
    Alack the day, she's dead, she's dead, she's dead!
CAPULET
    Ha! Let me see her. Out, alas! She's cold.
    Her blood is settled, and her joints are stiff;   26
    Life and these lips have long been separated.
    Death lies on her like an untimely frost
    Upon the sweetest flower of all the field.
NURSE
    Oh, lamentable day!
WIFE   Oh, woeful time!
CAPULET
    Death, that hath ta'en her hence to make me wail,
    Ties up my tongue and will not let me speak.

        Enter Friar [*Laurence*] *and the County* [*Paris,
        with Musicians*].

FRIAR LAURENCE
    Come, is the bride ready to go to church?
CAPULET
    Ready to go, but never to return.
    Oh, son, the night before thy wedding day
    Hath Death lain with thy wife. There she lies,
    Flower as she was, deflowered by him.
    Death is my son-in-law, Death is my heir;
    My daughter he hath wedded. I will die,
    And leave him all; life, living, all is Death's.   40
PARIS
    Have I thought long to see this morning's face,   41
    And doth it give me such a sight as this?
WIFE
    Accurst, unhappy, wretched, hateful day!
    Most miserable hour that e'er time saw
    In lasting labor of his pilgrimage!   45
    But one, poor one, one poor and loving child,
    But one thing to rejoice and solace in,
    And cruel Death hath catched it from my sight!
NURSE
    O woe! O woeful, woeful, woeful day!
    Most lamentable day, most woeful day
    That ever, ever I did yet behold!
    O day, O day, O day! O hateful day!
    Never was seen so black a day as this.
    O woeful day, O woeful day!
PARIS
    Beguiled, divorcèd, wrongèd, spited, slain!
    Most detestable Death, by thee beguiled,
    By cruel, cruel thee quite overthrown!
    O love! O life! Not life, but love in death!
CAPULET
    Despised, distressèd, hated, martyred, killed!
    Uncomfortable time, why cam'st thou now   60

---

26 settled congealed   **40 living** means of living, property
41–64 Have . . . burièd (A stage direction in the First Quarto, "*All at
once cry out and wring their hands,*" may suggest that the four mourners are to speak simultaneously, a possibility since all have six lines of
text.)   **45 lasting** unceasing   **60 Uncomfortable** Comfortless

To murder, murder our solemnity?
O child! O child! My soul, and not my child!
Dead art thou! Alack, my child is dead,
And with my child my joys are burièd.

FRIAR LAURENCE
Peace, ho, for shame! Confusion's cure lives not
In these confusions. Heaven and yourself
Had part in this fair maid; now heaven hath all,
And all the better is it for the maid.
Your part in her you could not keep from death,
But heaven keeps his part in eternal life.
The most you sought was her promotion,
For 'twas your heaven she should be advanced;
And weep ye now, seeing she is advanced
Above the clouds, as high as heaven itself?
Oh, in this love you love your child so ill
That you run mad, seeing that she is well.
She's not well married that lives married long,
But she's best married that dies married young.
Dry up your tears, and stick your rosemary
On this fair corpse, and, as the custom is,
And in her best array, bear her to church;
For though fond nature bids us all lament,
Yet nature's tears are reason's merriment.

CAPULET
All things that we ordainèd festival
Turn from their office to black funeral:
Our instruments to melancholy bells,
Our wedding cheer to a sad burial feast,
Our solemn hymns to sullen dirges change,
Our bridal flowers serve for a buried corpse,
And all things change them to the contrary.

FRIAR LAURENCE
Sir, go you in, and, madam, go with him,
And go, Sir Paris. Everyone prepare
To follow this fair corpse unto her grave.
The heavens do lour upon you for some ill;
Move them no more by crossing their high will.

             Exeunt. Manet [*Nurse with Musicians*].

FIRST MUSICIAN
Faith, we may put up our pipes and be gone.

NURSE
Honest good fellows, ah, put up, put up!
For well you know this is a pitiful case.   [*Exit.*]

FIRST MUSICIAN
Ay, by my troth, the case may be amended.

    Enter Peter.

61
64

65

69

71
72

79

82
83

84
85

88

90

94
95

99

PETER Musicians, oh, musicians, "Heart's ease," | 100
"Heart's ease." Oh, an you will have me live, play
"Heart's ease."

FIRST MUSICIAN Why "Heart's ease"?

PETER Oh, musicians, because my heart itself plays "My
heart is full." Oh, play me some merry dump to | 105
comfort me.

FIRST MUSICIAN Not a dump we! 'Tis no time to play
now.

PETER You will not, then?

FIRST MUSICIAN No.

PETER I will then give it you soundly.

FIRST MUSICIAN What will you give us?

PETER No money, on my faith, but the gleek; I will give | 113
you the minstrel. | 114

FIRST MUSICIAN Then will I give you the serving- | 115
creature. | 116

PETER Then will I lay the serving-creature's dagger on | 117
your pate. I will carry no crotchets. I'll re you, I'll fa | 118
you. Do you note me? | 119

FIRST MUSICIAN An you re us and fa us, you note us.

SECOND MUSICIAN Pray you, put up your dagger and | 121
put out your wit. | 122

PETER Then have at you with my wit! I will dry-beat | 123
you with an iron wit, and put up my iron dagger.
Answer me like men:
    "When griping griefs the heart doth wound, | 126
      And doleful dumps the mind oppress,
    Then music with her silver sound—" | 128
Why "silver sound"? Why "music with her silver
sound"? What say you, Simon Catling? | 130

FIRST MUSICIAN Marry, sir, because silver hath a sweet
sound.

PETER Pretty! What say you, Hugh Rebeck? | 133

SECOND MUSICIAN I say "silver sound" because musi-
cians sound for silver. | 135

PETER Pretty too! What say you, James Soundpost? | 136

THIRD MUSICIAN Faith, I know not what to say.

---

61 **solemnity** ceremony, festivity.   65 **Confusion's** Calamity's   69 **Your part** i.e., The mortal part you begot   71 **promotion** social advancement   72 **your heaven** i.e., your idea of the greatest good   79 **rosemary** symbol of immortality and enduring love; therefore used at both funerals and weddings   82 **fond nature** foolish human nature   83 **nature's ... merriment** that which causes human nature to weep is an occasion of joy to reason.   84 **ordainèd festival** intended to be festive   85 **office** function   88 **sullen** mournful   90 **them** themselves   94 **lour ... ill** frown upon you because of some sinfulness   95 **Move** anger.
95.1 *Manet* She remains onstage   99 **the case ... amended** things generally could be much better. (With a punning suggestion of an instrument case that is in need of repair.)   99.1 *Peter* (The Second Quarto has *Enter Will Kemp*, the actor for whom Shakespeare or perhaps the bookkeeper intended this role.)

100 **"Heart's ease"** (A popular ballad; so too with "My heart is full" in lines 104–5.)   105 **dump** mournful tune or dance   113 **gleek** scornful rebuke   113–14 **I will ... minstrel** I will insult you by calling you what you are, a minstrel. (Minstrels were widely regarded as vagabonds.)   115–16 **Then ... serving-creature** Then I'll insult you right back by calling you what you are, a servant.   117–18 **Then ... crotchets** Then I'll knock you about the head with my dagger. I'll not put up with your whims. (*Crotchets* are also quarter notes, appropriate to the musicians' trade.)   118–19 **I'll re ... me?** i.e., I'll give you a thrashing, do you hear? (Again using musical terms: *re* and *fa* are the names of notes, and *note* can mean "set to music.")   121–2 **put up ... wit** sheathe your dagger and stop being a smart aleck. (But *put up* and *put out* can also mean "display." Peter chooses to answer to this meaning.)   123 **have at you** i.e., here I come.   **dry-beat** thrash (without drawing blood)   126–8 **"When ... sound"** (From Richard Edwards's song, "In Commendation of Music," published in *The Paradise of Dainty Devices*, 1576.)   130 **Catling** (A catling was a small lute-string made of catgut.)   133 **Rebeck** (A rebeck was a fiddle with three strings.)   135 **sound** make music   136 **Soundpost** (A soundpost is the pillar or peg that supports the sounding board of a stringed instrument.)

PETER   Oh, I cry you mercy, you are the singer. I will say   138
for you. It is "music with her silver sound" because
musicians have no gold for sounding: 140
      "Then music with her silver sound
          With speedy help doth lend redress."   *Exit.*
FIRST MUSICIAN   What a pestilent knave is this same!
SECOND MUSICIAN   Hang him, Jack! Come, we'll in here,
tarry for the mourners, and stay dinner.   *Exeunt.*   145

[5.1]

Enter Romeo.

ROMEO
If I may trust the flattering truth of sleep,   1
My dreams presage some joyful news at hand.
My bosom's lord sits lightly in his throne,   3
And all this day an unaccustomed spirit
Lifts me above the ground with cheerful thoughts.
I dreamt my lady came and found me dead—
Strange dream, that gives a dead man leave to
    think!—
And breathed such life with kisses in my lips
That I revived and was an emperor.
Ah me, how sweet is love itself possessed   10
When but love's shadows are so rich in joy!   11

Enter Romeo's man [Balthasar, booted].

News from Verona! How now, Balthasar,
Dost thou not bring me letters from the Friar?
How doth my lady? Is my father well?
How fares my Juliet? That I ask again,
For nothing can be ill if she be well.
BALTHASAR
Then she is well, and nothing can be ill.
Her body sleeps in Capels' monument,
And her immortal part with angels lives.
I saw her laid low in her kindred's vault,
And presently took post to tell it you.   21
Oh, pardon me for bringing these ill news,
Since you did leave it for my office, sir.   23
ROMEO
Is it e'en so? Then I defy you, stars!—
Thou knowest my lodging. Get me ink and paper,
And hire post-horses. I will hence tonight.
BALTHASAR
I do beseech you, sir, have patience.
Your looks are pale and wild, and do import   28
Some misadventure.
ROMEO   Tush, thou art deceived.
Leave me, and do the thing I bid thee do.
Hast thou no letters to me from the Friar?

BALTHASAR
No, my good lord.
ROMEO   No matter. Get thee gone,
And hire those horses. I'll be with thee straight.
                              Exit [Balthasar].
Well, Juliet, I will lie with thee tonight.
Let's see for means. O mischief, thou art swift   35
To enter in the thoughts of desperate men!
I do remember an apothecary—   37
And hereabouts 'a dwells—which late I noted   38
In tattered weeds, with overwhelming brows,   39
Culling of simples. Meager were his looks;   40
Sharp misery had worn him to the bones;
And in his needy shop a tortoise hung,
An alligator stuffed, and other skins
Of ill-shaped fishes; and about his shelves
A beggarly account of empty boxes,   45
Green earthen pots, bladders, and musty seeds,
Remnants of packthread, and old cakes of roses   47
Were thinly scattered to make up a show.
Noting this penury, to myself I said,
"An if a man did need a poison now,   50
Whose sale is present death in Mantua,   51
Here lives a caitiff wretch would sell it him."   52
Oh, this same thought did but forerun my need,
And this same needy man must sell it me.
As I remember, this should be the house.
Being holiday, the beggar's shop is shut.—
What, ho! Apothecary!

[Enter Apothecary.]

APOTHECARY   Who calls so loud?
ROMEO
Come hither, man. I see that thou art poor.
Hold, there is forty ducats. [*He shows gold.*] Let me
    have   59
A dram of poison, such soon-speeding gear   60
As will disperse itself through all the veins
That the life-weary taker may fall dead,
And that the trunk may be discharged of breath   63
As violently as hasty powder fired
Doth hurry from the fatal cannon's womb.
APOTHECARY
Such mortal drugs I have, but Mantua's law   66
Is death to any he that utters them.   67
ROMEO
Art thou so bare and full of wretchedness,
And fearest to die? Famine is in thy cheeks,

---

138 cry you mercy beg your pardon   **140 have . . . sounding** i.e., (1) are paid only silver for playing (2) have no gold to jingle in their pockets   **145 stay** await
5.1. Location: Mantua. A street.
1 flattering i.e., telling me what I want to believe   **3 bosom's lord** i.e., heart   **10 itself possessed** actually enjoyed   **11 love's shadows** dreams of love   **11.1 booted** wearing riding boots—a conventional stage sign of traveling   **21 presently took post** at once started off with post-horses   **23 for my office** as my duty   **28 import** denote

35 for means by what means.   **37 apothecary** druggist   **38 which . . . noted** whom lately I noticed   **39 weeds** garments.   **overwhelming brows** forehead and eyebrows jutting out over his eyes   **40 simples** medicinal herbs.   **Meager** Impoverished   **45 beggarly account** poor array   **47 cakes of roses** petals pressed into cakes to be used as perfume   **50 An if** If   **51 present** immediate   **52 caitiff** miserable. **would** who would   **59 ducats** gold coins.   **60 soon-speeding gear** quickly effective stuff   **63 trunk** body   **66 mortal** deadly   **67 any he** anyone.   **utters** issues, sells

Need and oppression starveth in thy eyes,   70
Contempt and beggary hangs upon thy back.
The world is not thy friend, nor the world's law;
The world affords no law to make thee rich.
Then be not poor, but break it, and take this.

APOTHECARY
My poverty but not my will consents.

ROMEO
I pay thy poverty and not thy will.

APOTHECARY [*giving poison*]
Put this in any liquid thing you will
And drink it off, and if you had the strength
Of twenty men it would dispatch you straight.

ROMEO [*giving gold*]
There is thy gold—worse poison to men's souls,
Doing more murder in this loathsome world
Than these poor compounds that thou mayst not sell.
I sell thee poison; thou hast sold me none.
Farewell. Buy food, and get thyself in flesh.
                                             [*Exit Apothecary.*]
Come, cordial and not poison, go with me   85
To Juliet's grave, for there must I use thee.   *Exit.*

❧

[5.2]

Enter Friar John to Friar Laurence.

FRIAR JOHN
Holy Franciscan friar! Brother, ho!

Enter [Friar] Laurence.

FRIAR LAURENCE
This same should be the voice of Friar John.
Welcome from Mantua! What says Romeo?
Or if his mind be writ, give me his letter.

FRIAR JOHN
Going to find a barefoot brother out—
One of our order—to associate me   6
Here in this city visiting the sick,
And finding him, the searchers of the town,   8
Suspecting that we both were in a house
Where the infectious pestilence did reign,
Sealed up the doors and would not let us forth,
So that my speed to Mantua there was stayed.   12

FRIAR LAURENCE
Who bare my letter, then, to Romeo?

FRIAR JOHN
I could not send it—here it is again—
Nor get a messenger to bring it thee,
So fearful were they of infection.   [*He gives a letter.*]

FRIAR LAURENCE
Unhappy fortune! By my brotherhood,
The letter was not nice but full of charge,   18
Of dear import, and the neglecting it   19
May do much danger. Friar John, go hence.
Get me an iron crow and bring it straight   21
Unto my cell.

FRIAR JOHN   Brother, I'll go and bring it thee.   *Exit.*

FRIAR LAURENCE
Now must I to the monument alone.
Within this three hours will fair Juliet wake.
She will beshrew me much that Romeo   26
Hath had no notice of these accidents;   27
But I will write again to Mantua,
And keep her at my cell till Romeo come—
Poor living corpse, closed in a dead man's tomb!
                                                       Exit.

❧

[5.3]

Enter Paris, and his Page [bearing flowers, perfumed water, and a torch. Juliet, lying in seeming death atop her bier and perhaps concealed at first from the audience's view, is understood to be in the Capulets' burial vault, with Tybalt's body also there.]

PARIS
Give me thy torch, boy. Hence, and stand aloof.   1
Yet put it out, for I would not be seen.
Under yond yew trees lay thee all along,   3
Holding thy ear close to the hollow ground.
So shall no foot upon the churchyard tread,
Being loose, unfirm, with digging up of graves,   6
But thou shalt hear it. Whistle then to me
As signal that thou hearest something approach.
Give me those flowers. Do as I bid thee. Go.

PAGE [*aside*]
I am almost afraid to stand alone   10
Here in the churchyard, yet I will adventure.
                                              [*He retires.*]

PARIS [*strewing flowers and perfumed water*]
Sweet flower, with flowers thy bridal bed I strew—   12
   Oh, woe! Thy canopy is dust and stones—   13
Which with sweet water nightly I will dew,   14
   Or wanting that, with tears distilled by moans.   15
The obsequies that I for thee will keep   16
Nightly shall be to strew thy grave and weep.
                                             Whistle Boy.
The boy gives warning something doth approach.
What cursèd foot wanders this way tonight

18 **nice** trivial. **charge** importance **19 dear** precious, urgent **21 crow** crowbar **26 beshrew** i.e., reprove **27 accidents** events
5.3. Location: Verona. A churchyard and the vault or tomb belonging to the Capulets. Juliet's bier may be thrust on stage from the "discovery" space or may be concealed until the tomb is "opened" by Romeo at 83.1, perhaps by the drawing back of curtains.
1 aloof to one side, at a distance. **3 all along** at full length **6 Being** i.e., the soil being **10 stand** stay **12 Sweet flower** i.e., Juliet **13 canopy** covering **14 sweet** perfumed. **dew** moisten **15 wanting** lacking **16 obsequies** ceremonies in memory of the dead

70 starveth are revealed by the starving look **85 cordial** restorative for the heart
5.2. Location: Verona. Friar Laurence's cell.
6 associate accompany **8 searchers of the town** town officials charged with public health (and especially concerned about the *pestilence* or plague) **12 speed** successful journey, progress. **stayed** stopped.

To cross my obsequies and true love's rite?   20
What, with a torch? Muffle me, night, awhile.   21
                                        [*He retires.*]

      Enter Romeo and Balthasar, [with a torch, a
      mattock, and a crowbar].

ROMEO
Give me that mattock and the wrenching iron.   22
                                        [*He takes the tools.*]
Hold, take this letter. Early in the morning
See thou deliver it to my lord and father.
                        [*He gives a letter and takes a torch.*]
Give me the light. Upon thy life I charge thee,
Whate'er thou hearest or see'st, stand all aloof
And do not interrupt me in my course.   27
Why I descend into this bed of death
Is partly to behold my lady's face,
But chiefly to take thence from her dead finger
A precious ring—a ring that I must use
In dear employment. Therefore hence, begone.   32
But if thou, jealous, dost return to pry   33
In what I farther shall intend to do,
By heaven, I will tear thee joint by joint
And strew this hungry churchyard with thy limbs.   36
The time and my intents are savage-wild,
More fierce and more inexorable far
Than empty tigers or the roaring sea.   39
BALTHASAR
I will be gone, sir, and not trouble ye.
ROMEO
So shalt thou show me friendship. Take thou that.
                                        [*He gives him money.*]
Live, and be prosperous; and farewell, good fellow.
BALTHASAR [*aside*]
For all this same, I'll hide me hereabout.   43
His looks I fear, and his intents I doubt.   [*He retires.*]   44
ROMEO
Thou detestable maw, thou womb of death,   45
Gorged with the dearest morsel of the earth,
Thus I enforce thy rotten jaws to open,
And in despite I'll cram thee with more food.   48
                        [*He begins to open the tomb.*]
PARIS
This is that banished haughty Montague
That murdered my love's cousin, with which grief
It is supposèd the fair creature died,
And here is come to do some villainous shame
To the dead bodies. I will apprehend him.
                                        [*He comes forward.*]
Stop thy unhallowed toil, vile Montague!
Can vengeance be pursued further than death?

Condemnèd villain, I do apprehend thee.
Obey and go with me, for thou must die.
ROMEO
I must indeed, and therefore came I hither.
Good gentle youth, tempt not a desperate man.
Fly hence and leave me. Think upon these gone;   60
Let them affright thee. I beseech thee, youth,
Put not another sin upon my head
By urging me to fury. Oh, begone!
By heaven, I love thee better than myself,
For I come hither armed against myself.
Stay not, begone. Live, and hereafter say
A madman's mercy bid thee run away.
PARIS
I do defy thy conjuration,   68
And apprehend thee for a felon here.
ROMEO
Wilt thou provoke me? Then have at thee, boy!
                                        [*They fight.*]
PAGE
Oh, Lord, they fight! I will go call the watch.   [*Exit.*]
PARIS
Oh, I am slain! [*He falls.*] If thou be merciful,
Open the tomb, lay me with Juliet.   [*He dies.*]
ROMEO
In faith, I will. Let me peruse this face.
Mercutio's kinsman, noble County Paris!
What said my man when my betossèd soul
Did not attend him as we rode? I think
He told me Paris should have married Juliet.   78
Said he not so? Or did I dream it so?
Or am I mad, hearing him talk of Juliet,
To think it was so? Oh, give me thy hand,
One writ with me in sour misfortune's book.
I'll bury thee in a triumphant grave.
                                        [*He opens the tomb.*]
A grave? Oh, no! A lantern, slaughtered youth,   84
For here lies Juliet, and her beauty makes
This vault a feasting presence full of light.   86
Death, lie thou there, by a dead man interred.
                                [*He lays Paris in the tomb.*]
How oft when men are at the point of death
Have they been merry, which their keepers call   89
A lightening before death! Oh, how may I   90
Call this a lightening? O my love, my wife!
Death, that hath sucked the honey of thy breath,
Hath had no power yet upon thy beauty.
Thou art not conquered; beauty's ensign yet   94
Is crimson in thy lips and in thy cheeks,
And death's pale flag is not advancèd there.   96
Tybalt, liest thou there in thy bloody sheet?   97
Oh, what more favor can I do to thee
Than with that hand that cut thy youth in twain
To sunder his that was thine enemy?   100

---

20 cross interrupt   **21 Muffle** Conceal.   **22 wrenching iron** crowbar.
27 course intended action.   **32 dear employment** important business.
33 jealous suspicious   **36 hungry** hungry for corpses   **39 empty**
hungry   **43 For all this same** All the same   **44 fear** distrust.   **doubt**
suspect.   **45 womb** belly   **48 in despite** defiantly   **48.1 He . . . tomb**
Whether the tomb is represented by a bier thrust onstage or by a curtained recess (see indication of scene location above at the start of
5.3), Romeo may mime the action here and at line 83.1 of using tools
to open it.

60 gone dead   **68 conjuration** solemn entreaty   **78 should have** was
to have   **84 lantern** turret room full of windows   **86 feasting presence** reception chamber for feasting   **89 keepers** attendants, jailers
90 lightening exhilaration (supposed to occur just before death)
94 ensign banner   **96 advancèd** raised   **97 sheet** shroud.   **100 his**
i.e., my (Romeo's) own

Forgive me, cousin!—Ah, dear Juliet,
Why art thou yet so fair? Shall I believe
That unsubstantial Death is amorous,   103
And that the lean abhorrèd monster keeps
Thee here in dark to be his paramour?
For fear of that I still will stay with thee   106
And never from this palace of dim night
Depart again. Here, here will I remain
With worms that are thy chambermaids. Oh, here
Will I set up my everlasting rest   110
And shake the yoke of inauspicious stars
From this world-wearied flesh. Eyes, look your last!
Arms, take your last embrace! And lips, O you
The doors of breath, seal with a righteous kiss
A dateless bargain to engrossing death!   115
                                   [*He kisses Juliet.*]
Come, bitter conduct, come, unsavory guide,   116
Thou desperate pilot, now at once run on   117
The dashing rocks thy seasick weary bark!
Here's to my love. [*He drinks.*] O true apothecary!
Thy drugs are quick. Thus with a kiss I die. [*He dies.*]

            Enter Friar [Laurence] with lantern, crow,
            and spade.

FRIAR LAURENCE
Saint Francis be my speed! How oft tonight   121
Have my old feet stumbled at graves! Who's there?
BALTHASAR
Here's one, a friend, and one that knows you well.
FRIAR LAURENCE
Bliss be upon you. Tell me, good my friend,
What torch is yond that vainly lends his light   125
To grubs and eyeless skulls? As I discern,   126
It burneth in the Capels' monument.
BALTHASAR
It doth so, holy sir, and there's my master,
One that you love.
FRIAR LAURENCE   Who is it?
BALTHASAR   Romeo.
FRIAR LAURENCE
How long hath he been there?
BALTHASAR   Full half an hour.
FRIAR LAURENCE
Go with me to the vault.
BALTHASAR   I dare not, sir.
My master knows not but I am gone hence,
And fearfully did menace me with death
If I did stay to look on his intents.
FRIAR LAURENCE
Stay, then, I'll go alone. Fear comes upon me.
Oh, much I fear some ill unthrifty thing.   136

BALTHASAR
As I did sleep under this yew tree here
I dreamt my master and another fought,
And that my master slew him.
FRIAR LAURENCE [*advancing to the tomb*]   Romeo!
Alack, alack, what blood is this which stains
The stony entrance of this sepulcher?
What mean these masterless and gory swords
To lie discolored by this place of peace?   143
                                   [*He looks in the tomb.*]
Romeo! Oh, pale! Who else? What, Paris too?
And steeped in blood? Ah, what an unkind hour   145
Is guilty of this lamentable chance!
The lady stirs.   [*Juliet wakes.*]
JULIET
O comfortable Friar, where is my lord?   148
I do remember well where I should be,
And there I am. Where is my Romeo?
                                   [*A noise within.*]
FRIAR LAURENCE
I hear some noise. Lady, come from that nest
Of death, contagion, and unnatural sleep.
A greater power than we can contradict
Hath thwarted our intents. Come, come away.
Thy husband in thy bosom there lies dead,
And Paris, too. Come, I'll dispose of thee
Among a sisterhood of holy nuns.
Stay not to question, for the watch is coming.
Come, go, good Juliet. [*A noise again.*] I dare no longer
     stay.   *Exit [Friar Laurence].*
JULIET
Go, get thee hence, for I will not away.
What's here? A cup, closed in my true love's hand?
Poison, I see, hath been his timeless end.   162
O churl, drunk all, and left no friendly drop   163
To help me after? I will kiss thy lips;
Haply some poison yet doth hang on them,   165
To make me die with a restorative.   [*She kisses him.*]
Thy lips are warm.

            Enter [Paris's] Boy and Watch.

FIRST WATCH   Lead, boy. Which way?
JULIET
Yea, noise? Then I'll be brief. O happy dagger!   169
                                   [*She takes Romeo's dagger.*]
This is thy sheath. There rust, and let me die.
                                   [*She stabs herself and dies.*]
PAGE
This is the place, there where the torch doth burn.
FIRST WATCH
The ground is bloody. Search about the churchyard.
Go, some of you, whoe'er you find attach.   173
                                   [*Exeunt some.*]
Pitiful sight! Here lies the County slain,

---

103 **unsubstantial** lacking material existence   106 **still** always
110 **set . . . rest** (See 4.5.6. The meaning is, "make my final determination," with allusion to the idea of repose.)   115 **dateless bargain**
everlasting contract.   **engrossing** monopolizing, taking all; also,
drawing up the contract   116 **conduct** guide (i.e., the poison)
117 **desperate** reckless, despairing   121 **be my speed** prosper me and
let me arrive in time.   125 **vainly** uselessly   126 **grubs** insect larvae
136 **unthrifty** unfortunate.

143.1 **He looks . . . tomb** Whether the Friar is to enter the tomb
depends on staging arrangements.   145 **unkind** unnatural
148 **comfortable** comforting   162 **timeless** (1) untimely (2) everlasting   163 **churl** miser   165 **Haply** perhaps   169 **happy** opportune
173 **attach** arrest, detain.

And Juliet bleeding, warm, and newly dead,
Who here hath lain these two days burièd.
Go tell the Prince. Run to the Capulets.
Raise up the Montagues. Some others search.
                                    [*Exeunt others.*]
We see the ground whereon these woes do lie,
But the true ground of all these piteous woes   180
We cannot without circumstance descry.   181

          Enter [*some of the Watch, with*] *Romeo's*
          man [*Balthasar*].

SECOND WATCH
   Here's Romeo's man. We found him in the
   churchyard.
FIRST WATCH
   Hold him in safety till the Prince come hither.   183

          Enter Friar [*Laurence*], *and another Watchman*
          [*with tools*].

THIRD WATCH
   Here is a friar, that trembles, sighs, and weeps.
   We took this mattock and this spade from him
   As he was coming from this churchyard's side.
FIRST WATCH
   A great suspicion. Stay the Friar, too.   187

          Enter the Prince [*and attendants*].

PRINCE
   What misadventure is so early up
   That calls our person from our morning rest?   189

          Enter Capels [*Capulet and his Wife*].

CAPULET
   What should it be that is so shrieked abroad?
CAPULET'S WIFE
   Oh, the people in the street cry "Romeo,"
   Some "Juliet," and some "Paris," and all run
   With open outcry toward our monument.
PRINCE
   What fear is this which startles in our ears?   194
FIRST WATCH
   Sovereign, here lies the County Paris slain,
   And Romeo dead, and Juliet, dead before,
   Warm and new killed.
PRINCE
   Search, seek, and know how this foul murder comes. 198
FIRST WATCH
   Here is a friar, and slaughtered Romeo's man,
   With instruments upon them fit to open   200
   These dead men's tombs.
CAPULET
   O heavens! O wife, look how our daughter bleeds!
   This dagger hath mista'en, for lo, his house   203
   Is empty on the back of Montague,
   And it mis-sheathèd in my daughter's bosom!

CAPULET'S WIFE
   Oh, me! This sight of death is as a bell
   That warns my old age to a sepulcher.

          Enter Montague.

PRINCE
   Come, Montague, for thou art early up
   To see thy son and heir more early down.
MONTAGUE
   Alas, my liege, my wife is dead tonight;
   Grief of my son's exile hath stopped her breath.
   What further woe conspires against mine age?
PRINCE   Look, and thou shalt see.
MONTAGUE   [*seeing Romeo's body*]
   O thou untaught! What manners is in this,   214
   To press before thy father to a grave?   215
PRINCE
   Seal up the mouth of outrage for a while,   216
   Till we can clear these ambiguities
   And know their spring, their head, their true descent; 218
   And then will I be general of your woes   219
   And lead you even to death. Meantime, forbear,   220
   And let mischance be slave to patience.   221
   Bring forth the parties of suspicion.   222
FRIAR LAURENCE
   I am the greatest, able to do least,
   Yet most suspected, as the time and place
   Doth make against me, of this direful murder;   225
   And here I stand, both to impeach and purge   226
   Myself condemnèd and myself excused.   227
PRINCE
   Then say at once what thou dost know in this.
FRIAR LAURENCE
   I will be brief, for my short date of breath   229
   Is not so long as is a tedious tale.
   Romeo, there dead, was husband to that Juliet,
   And she, there dead, that Romeo's faithful wife.
   I married them, and their stol'n marriage day
   Was Tybalt's doomsday, whose untimely death
   Banished the new-made bridegroom from this city,
   For whom, and not for Tybalt, Juliet pined.
   You, to remove that siege of grief from her,
   Betrothed and would have married her perforce   238
   To County Paris. Then comes she to me,
   And with wild looks bid me devise some means
   To rid her from this second marriage,
   Or in my cell there would she kill herself.
   Then gave I her—so tutored by my art—
   A sleeping potion, which so took effect
   As I intended, for it wrought on her   245
   The form of death. Meantime I writ to Romeo   246

214 **untaught** ill-mannered youth. (Said with affectionate irony.)
215 **press** hasten, go   216 **mouth of outrage** (1) popular outcry (2)
entrance to the tomb   218 **spring, head** (Both words mean "source.")
219 **be . . . woes** be leader in lamentation   220 **even to death** in
lamentation for the dead.   221 **let . . . patience** i.e., let us bear our
misfortune patiently.   222 **of** under   225 **make** conspire, tell
226–7 **to . . . excused** to accuse myself of what is to be condemned in
me and to exonerate myself where I ought to be excused.   229 **date
of breath** time left to live   238 **perforce** by compulsion   245 **wrought**
fashioned   246 **form** appearance

180 **ground** basis. (Playing on the meaning "earth" in line 179.)   181
circumstance details   183 **in safety** under guard   187 **Stay** Detain
189 **our person** (The royal "we.")   194 **startles** cries alarmingly
198 **know** learn   200 **instruments** tools   203 **his house** its scabbard

That he should hither come as this dire night   247
To help to take her from her borrowed grave,
Being the time the potion's force should cease.
But he which bore my letter, Friar John,
Was stayed by accident, and yesternight   251
Returned my letter back. Then all alone
At the prefixèd hour of her waking
Came I to take her from her kindred's vault,
Meaning to keep her closely at my cell   255
Till I conveniently could send to Romeo.
But when I came, some minute ere the time
Of her awakening, here untimely lay
The noble Paris and true Romeo dead.
She wakes, and I entreated her come forth
And bear this work of heaven with patience.
But then a noise did scare me from the tomb,
And she, too desperate, would not go with me,
But, as it seems, did violence on herself.
All this I know, and to the marriage
Her nurse is privy; and if aught in this   266
Miscarried by my fault, let my old life
Be sacrificed some hour before his time   268
Unto the rigor of severest law.

PRINCE
We still have known thee for a holy man.   270
Where's Romeo's man? What can he say to this?

BALTHASAR
I brought my master news of Juliet's death,
And then in post he came from Mantua   273
To this same place, to this same monument.
This letter he early bid me give his father,   275
                              [showing a letter]
And threatened me with death, going in the vault,
If I departed not and left him there.

PRINCE [taking the letter]
Give me the letter. I will look on it.
Where is the County's page, that raised the watch?
Sirrah, what made your master in this place?   280

PAGE
He came with flowers to strew his lady's grave,
And bid me stand aloof, and so I did.
Anon comes one with light to ope the tomb,
And by and by my master drew on him,
And then I ran away to call the watch.

PRINCE
This letter doth make good the Friar's words,
Their course of love, the tidings of her death;
And here he writes that he did buy a poison
Of a poor 'pothecary, and therewithal   289
Came to this vault to die, and lie with Juliet.
Where be these enemies? Capulet, Montague,
See what a scourge is laid upon your hate,
That heaven finds means to kill your joys with love.   293
And I, for winking at your discords, too   294
Have lost a brace of kinsmen. All are punished.   295

CAPULET
O brother Montague, give me thy hand.
This is my daughter's jointure, for no more   297
Can I demand.

MONTAGUE   But I can give thee more,
For I will raise her statue in pure gold,   299
That whiles Verona by that name is known
There shall no figure at such rate be set   301
As that of true and faithful Juliet.

CAPULET
As rich shall Romeo's by his lady's lie;
Poor sacrifices of our enmity!

PRINCE
A glooming peace this morning with it brings;
    The sun, for sorrow, will not show his head.
Go hence to have more talk of these sad things.
    Some shall be pardoned, and some punishèd;
For never was a story of more woe
Than this of Juliet and her Romeo.   [Exeunt.]

---

247 as this this very **251 stayed** stopped **255 closely** secretly **266 privy** in on the secret **268 his** its **270 still** always **273 post haste** **275 This . . . father** He bade me give this letter to his father early in the morning (5.3.23–4) **280 made** did

289 therewithal with the poison **293 kill your joys** (1) destroy your happiness (2) kill your children. **with** by means of **294 winking at** shutting my eyes to **295 a brace** of two **297 jointure** marriage settlement **299 raise** (The Second Quarto reading, "raie," is defended by some editors in the sense of "array," make ready.) **301 rate** value

---

Romeo and Juliet on Stage

To appreciate the stage and film popularity of *Romeo and Juliet*, consider a 1981 performance at the Shanghai Drama Institute in the People's Republic of China. That the play was performed in Mandarin before an enthusiastic audience is not especially noteworthy, for Shakespeare is regularly produced on Chinese stages, especially after the Cultural Revolution (1966–1976). Rather, the Shanghai production was remarkable because its young actors from remote Tibet learned Mandarin to portray the world's most famous lovers. Such is—and has always been—the universal appeal of *Romeo and*

Juliet since its first performances in the mid-1590s at The Theater and later at the Curtain in the north of London. A fanciful recreation of that first performance may be seen in John Madden's Academy Award-winning film *Shakespeare in Love* (1998), discussed below (p. 556).

The Elizabethan Era: Swift Transitions

Whether played at either The Theater, the Curtain, or in revivals at the Globe, the Elizabethan *Romeo and Juliet* was performed on an open platform without scenery—an important point, as we have discussed, for a play in which speed and haste are central issues. The unadorned stage allowed for quick transitions between scenes as the play hurtled toward its tragic resolution. The vast Elizabethan forestage, so close to the "groundlings" who enjoyed bawdry and sword fights, could accommodate the first violent encounter between the Capulets and Montagues, as well as the later brawl in which Mercutio and Tybalt die (3.2). These public encounters contrast with the story's intimate domestic and monastic scenes (e.g., 1.2, 1.3, 2.6). *Romeo and Juliet* requires several specific locales, most famously Juliet's window and the tomb. In the wooing scene (2.2), Juliet is visible at her "window" (2.2.2). Later in the scene, the script requires Juliet to enter and exit above (at 138, 141, 155, and 186). Juliet being above is also symbolic: elevated some ten or twelve feet above Romeo, Juliet epitomizes the idealized woman popularized in Petrarch's love poetry for Laura (see 2.4.38–40 for a specific reference to these Renaissance lovers).

The scenes in Juliet's bedchamber (4.3–5) and the tomb (5.3) conceivably require the discovery space. The bedchamber scene would have involved a bed thrust forward; significantly, Juliet describes the terrors of the tomb in which she must awaken in Act 5, actually preparing the audience's imagination for that event, thereby negating the need for scenic embellishment. While the bed scene may possibly have been staged within the discovery space, Leslie Thompson suggests that it is more likely that a bed—hidden behind a curtain separating the discovery space from the stage proper—could have been thrust onto the stage, or else that a special structure may have been built specifically for the play (150–151). The same bed probably doubled as the bier on which Juliet rests in the tomb. The very simplicity of the Elizabethan stage and its conventions frequently contributes to a play's impact; what an audience sees in an earlier scene (a young girl, alone in her bed, deliberating whether to take a potion that will reunite her with her lover) resonates in a later one (the dead girl is locked in an eternal embrace with her deceased lover).

With about forty speaking roles (and extras), *Romeo and Juliet* required doubling among the acting company's ten or so adult shareholders (i.e., each actor had to play more than one part), plus a few extras. Doubling was a standard practice for these professionals, as a matter of economic practicability. The finale requires thirteen speaking roles in its final scene, as the warring families come together before the Prince amidst the "glooming peace" of the tomb.

The Restoration and Eighteenth Century: Radical Revisions

Romeo and Juliet was among the first of Shakespeare's plays to be revived when the public theaters in England reopened after the Civil War (1642–1660). In March 1662 the tragedy was performed at Lincoln's Inn Fields, where the diarist Samuel Pepys judged it to be "the worst ever I heard in my life." What Pepys saw was substantially altered from Shakespeare's play. Pepys's objections notwithstanding, this radically altered version of the play found new life in the Restoration—and affected performances into the nineteenth century. In 1679–1680 Thomas Otway, a notable tragedian, adapted the play to a setting in ancient Rome. Known as *The History and Fall of Caius Marcus*, Otway's play had the heroine (Lavinia) awaken before the hero died to allow for a reunion, thus heightening the play's pathos. This trend continued throughout the eighteenth century. In 1744 writer-actor Theophilus Cibber, son of actor-manager Colley Cibber, returned the tale to Verona and retained Otway's ending.

David Garrick's important revision of 1748 became a staple of London's two major theaters, Drury Lane and Covent Garden, for thirty years. Garrick restored much of Shakespeare's text; he detested Otway's "vile and scandalous" revision, although he, like his Restoration predecessor, devised a reunion for the lovers as Juliet awoke before Romeo expired. Garrick wrote some seventy-five lines guaranteed to magnify the tragic effect, as evidenced by Romeo's final speech:

> My powers are blasted,
> Twixt death and love I'm torn, I am distracted!
> But death's strongest—and must I leave thee, Juliet?
> O cruel, cursèd fate!

Garrick further enhanced the scene by devising a spectacular setting for the tomb, an enormous vault bathed in moonlight and guarded by girls spreading flowers about the stage of Drury Lane Theatre (see illustration on p. 502); Juliet was carried to this magnificent mausoleum in a torch-lit procession while a choir sang music composed by William Boyce. All was calculated to maximize the pathos of the finale. It worked, at least in the opinion of MacNamara Morgan, a 1753 observer, who judged Garrick's finale as "the finest picture of Grief and Despair . . . that ever was exhibited in any Scene." Garrick did not confine his emendations to the fifth act. He cut all references to Rosaline so that Romeo would not appear callous in jilting his first love; he also deleted many of the script's alternating rhymes and couplets (mere "jingle," thought Garrick), including much of the justly famous "holy palmers" sonnet in 1.5. And true to the age and body of his time, Garrick excised most of the puns and virtually all of the play's bawdry as being indecorous for tragedy. Though we may find Garrick's revision audacious, London audiences embraced the altered play enthusiastically; it was performed more than three hundred times in a twenty-year span.

While Otway and Garrick devised a brief reunion for the lovers before their deaths, some revisions actually provided a joyful ending to the play. James Howard turned the play into a "Tragi-comedy" by allowing the lovers to live, in a variation on Garrick's revision; according to an eighteenth-century commentator, the Garrick and Howard scripts were "Played Alternately, Tragical one day, and Tragicomical another for several days together." Such alterations of tragic endings were not uncommon in the eighteenth century (see *King Lear*). Middle-class values, informed by the doctrine of "Benevolence" positing that bad things should not happen to good people, dictated such anti-tragic impulses. The Royal Shakespeare Company's 1982 nine-hour production of Dickens's *Nicholas Nickleby* (available on videotape) features a sequence in which a nineteenth-century acting troupe performs an altered *Romeo and Juliet* where all of the dead characters (save Tybalt) are revived; to provide a love match for Paris, Benvolio announces that he is really *Benvolia*, a woman disguised as a man. Although a burlesque, the sequence illustrates the lengths to which theater artists in the eighteenth and nineteenth centuries went to "improve" Shakespeare. Even in our time, the spirit of the Garrick-Otway reunions remains alive: Baz Luhrmann's 1996 film (see below) teases its audience by inserting a close-up of Juliet's eyes opening even as Romeo draws the poison to his lips.

The Nineteenth Century: Breeches Romeos and Admired Juliets

Few actors in the eighteenth and early nineteenth centuries enhanced their reputations by playing Romeo, perhaps because most were considerably older than the callow youth of Shakespeare's script. Several actresses, on the other hand, emerged as memorable Juliets, most notably Maria Isabella Nossiter (at Drury Lane in 1753), whose rendering of the potion speech in 4.1 was admired for its naturalness. In the Romantic Age, Eliza O'Neill, for whom Percy Shelley wrote roles, was an acclaimed Juliet noted for a "re-active" style that, in critic William Hazlitt's estimation, led to "conformity of mind and disposition to [Juliet] as if she had unconsciously become the very person." The American Charlotte Cushman earned her renown in *Romeo and Juliet*, however, by playing Romeo to the Juliet of her sister, Susan, from 1837 to 1860, including a sensationally popular run at London's Haymarket Theatre during the 1845–1846 season. Cushman was not the only actress to play Romeo during the nineteenth century; at least sixteen women attempted the role in America and Europe. Cushman's was the most admired of these "breeches Romeos" (so-named for the pants women wore) because she brought a vigor and passion to Romeo hitherto unseen; "a living, breathing, burning Italian on the boards," proclaimed the London *Times* in 1846. Cush-

man also restored Shakespeare's text by deleting the sentimental reunion popularized by Otway and especially Garrick, although as a woman in the Victorian age she excised even more of the sexual content from Shakespeare's text (e.g., the Nurse's discussion of breast-feeding Juliet).

Although *Romeo and Juliet* remained among the most popular of Shakespeare's plays on stage throughout the nineteenth century, few productions stand out. Producers were, in the main, content to stage the audience-pleasing tragedy with little invention other than spectacular scenery. Henry James, in the *Atlantic Monthly* (August 1882), crystallized such approaches to the play while assessing Sir Henry Irving's production at London's Lyceum Theatre:

> It is the last word in stage-carpentering, and is full of beautiful effect of colour and costume. The stage is crowded with figures; there are at moments too many; the play moves slowly through a succession of glowing and deceptive pictures. The fault of all this splendour of detail is that . . . it puts the cart before the horse. The play is not acted, it is costumed; the immortal lovers of Verona become subordinate and ineffectual figures.

The Twentieth Century: Romeo and Mercutio Return

The first truly significant production of *Romeo and Juliet* in the twentieth century was directed by John Gielgud at London's New Theatre in 1935. Gielgud and Laurence Olivier alternated the roles of Romeo and Mercutio, while Peggy Ashcroft (Juliet) and Edith Evans (the Nurse) were also featured. Gielgud, then England's foremost Shakespearean actor, had directed the play at Oxford University three years earlier (using Ashcroft and Evans as professional artists within a predominantly student cast) and learned that the play was especially powerful when played nearly uncut and in the order Shakespeare proscribed. To avoid cumbersome scenic changes, Gielgud's London production employed a simple unit set that, like Elizabethan public theaters, enabled one scene to flow directly—and dramatically—into the next. Gielgud also encouraged his actors to avoid rhetorical flourishes in their verse-speaking; they also found more comedy and bawdry in the lines than in any production in memory. The result was a fast-paced, naturalistically spoken show that came very near to realizing the "two hours' traffic of our stage" promised by the Chorus. It was also a spectacularly beautiful show in its simplicity. Gielgud placed the action in Renaissance Italy, using the paintings of Botticelli and Carpaccio as sources for the costumes that were designed by a trio of women collectively known as Motley. Gielgud's innovative approach to what had become an over-solemn, spectacle-bound play met with audience approval; the production ran for one hundred–eighty-five performances, thirty more than the previous record for *Romeo and Juliet*. More importantly, it influenced numerous subsequent productions throughout the century.

Olivier, who was building his reputation as an actor of the first order, played Romeo more naturally than did the eloquent Gielgud. Olivier's Romeo was an awkward, often tongue-tied youth; his robust Mercutio was more favored by critics than his Romeo. Gielgud's reading of Romeo was lyrical, though somewhat more restrained than Olivier's impassioned lover. James Agate, among the finest theater critics of that generation, compared the Romeos of the two actors:

> Mr. Olivier's Romeo showed himself very much in love but rather butchered the poetry, whereas Mr. Gielgud carves the verse so exquisitely . . .Yet is this Romeo ever really in love with anyone but himself? I have a feeling that [Gielgud's] Romeo never warms up to Juliet until she is cold (Agate, 214).

Olivier's Mercutio (and to a lesser degree, Gielgud's) almost single-handedly restored this pivotal role to its schematic importance after three centuries of neglect. As Mercutio said "A sail, a sail" in Act 3, Olivier lifted the Nurse's skirts with the tip of his sword, a piece of business that can be seen, slightly altered, in Franco Zeffirelli's 1968 film (see below, pp. 552–553).

A dozen years later, in 1947, Peter Brook, a young director who would become an important interpreter of Shakespeare in the theater, cast young, unknown actors as the lovers—as well as a young and then-unknown Paul Scofield as Mercutio—in a production that continued the Gielgud legacy of uncluttered staging. Brook used simple, impressionistic sets to underscore what he considered to be the play's signature line: "For now, these hot days, is the mad blood stirring" (3.1.4). The production's most memorable moment occurred when Scofield's Mercutio was "lying on the stage in torch-light, arm raised and eyes rapt as he let the words [of the Queen Mab speech] flower into the silence of the grotesquely-visaged masquers" (Trewin, 154).

Despite the innovations by Gielgud and Brook, most productions during the 1950s could be categorized as picturesque. Robert Helpmann's staging at the Old Vic in 1955 typified such approaches with its extensive pageantry and processions contributing to the production's three-plus hour running time. Renato Castellani's grittily realistic 1954 film (see below, p. 552) did much to alter perceptions about ways in which the love tragedy could be approached, and in 1960 Franco Zeffirelli staged a hallmark production at the Old Vic that showed Castellani's influence. No director in the twentieth century is more associated with *Romeo and Juliet*

than Zeffirelli, an Italian who began his career as a scenic artist. Because of its fame, we usually think first of his 1968 film, even though much of the film is an enlargement upon the ideas tried in London.

Zeffirelli's production was influenced not only by Castellani's film but also by two major theater events. First, dramatist John Osborne's *Look Back in Anger* (1956) invested the British theater with a new and exciting sense of anger and social relevance. Then, the Broadway musical *West Side Story* (1957), which relocated the play's action to New York's mean streets (see below, p. 555), underscored the relevance of Shakespeare's play to a new generation of disenfranchised youth. Consequently, Zeffirelli injected into his film version the angry energy of growing discontent among young people that would explode in the 1960s. Mercutio's Queen Mab speech (1.4.53–95), for instance, became the utterance of "a wittily aggressive 'angry man,'" with Benvolio a kind of sympathetic interlocutor to the central figure as if they were characters in Osborne's play (Jackson, 227). Actor Peter McHenry's controversial interpretation of Mercutio was thus, in part at least, a product of Zeffirelli's fascination with *Look Back in Anger*.

In contrast to the romantic renderings of Verona usually associated with the play, Zeffirelli designed a setting—narrow alleys dividing decaying buildings—that was the Renaissance Italian equivalent of New York's Upper West Side; thus the production reflected the *verismo* (pictorial realism) of Italian post-war film. Judi Dench, who played Juliet at the age of twenty, recalls the reaction of the audience at the Old Vic: "[They] gasped when the curtain went up because it was all misty in the very real looking Italian street and people were throwing sheets out to the air: nothing as realistic had been seen for a very long time in Shakespeare" (Dench, 201). Perhaps because English was not his first language, Zeffirelli did little to help the actors with the verse-speaking, which was universally criticized by the press. The production, however, was not without invention: Mercutio was accidentally stabbed during some comic by-play with Tybalt, a moment that is recreated in the 1968 film. The production (and the ensuing film) is best remembered for its visual realism and its youthful energy. In 1964 the director restaged the play in Verona's beautifully preserved Roman amphitheater; the scenery was designed to blend with the fabled city's skyline.

The social and political relevance of Shakespeare's love tragedy became commonplace on the world's stages in the wake of *West Side Story* and Zeffirelli's stage version. Name almost any internecine, or mutually destructive, conflict, and one could find a production of *Romeo and Juliet* to illustrate it: Israeli-Arab (several versions, including a 1990 film, *Torn Apart*), Muslim girl-Hindu boy (India, 1992), Northern Irish Free State (Boston

Shakespeare Company, 1982), or anti-Fascist (Stratford, Canada, 1985; preserved on video). Interracial *Romeos* are not uncommon. In 1968 the Washington, D.C., Shakespeare Festival relocated the play to "New Verona, Louisiana" where the African American Capulets confronted the Anglo Montagues. A 1971 production in Budapest, Hungary, served as a commentary on that country's ill-fated uprising against the Russians in 1956; similarly, a Madrid production in 1971, using a translation by Nobel Laureate Pablo Neruda, called up memories of Spain's Civil War of the 1930s. As South Africa struggled to overthrow apartheid, the tragedy was used to parallel contemporary problems. A 1984 production in Durban (on South Africa's Cape), performed by a mixed-race cast speaking Afrikaans, portrayed Juliet as an orthodox Muslim girl in love with a Christian boy. Director Celliers Delport describes how he invented an apt meeting place for the lovers, since Muslims do not attend dances, much less fancy dress balls:

> In the Cape, the Muslims have a tradition of big weddings—the most colorful thing. Right there is my setting: a Muslim wedding at home. We had a real Malay band at the wedding with guests singing these old traditional songs. Now a Muslim . . . will never turn you away if you come there. And Romeo living in the same street—naturally he can go there easily. So who is Juliet? One of the bridesmaids. When Romeo comes in, the custom is that you must go and congratulate the bride and groom and also the bridesmaids. She was the last bridesmaid, wearing beautiful Malay clothes, and he touches her hand.
>
> (Quince, 123)

The play ended with the reconciliation of the families as the Muslim father helped the grieving Christian father to his feet while a tape recorder played the final speech against the sounds of Christian bells and a Muslim chanter calling the faithful to prayer.

In the spirit of *West Side Story*, other productions have contemporized the play by dressing it in current fashions and employing modern cultural artifacts. To indict contemporary Western decadence, Michael Bogdanov's 1986 Royal Shakespeare Company treatment put on stage Italian motorbikes and an Alfa-Romeo, the radio antenna of which became the sword that Tybalt used to kill Mercutio. The families lolled in outdoor cafes, dressed in trendy leather suits, sipping Campari. Romeo killed himself with a hypodermic needle. Bogdanov ended the action immediately after Juliet's death, and, as the dead lovers quickly reappeared in golden cloaks as statues in "pure gold" (5.3.299), paparazzi and TV crews rushed through the aisles of the Royal Shakespeare Theatre to get their headlines about the love-suicide. Capulet read a prepared statement (the opening prologue spoken in past tense) to end the production that seemed to say, "In the capitalist, competitive world of this Verona, the priorities remained wealth, status, and power. . .The story of the star-crossed lovers was being exploited by the families and the media for its commercial possibilities" (Parsons and Mason, 194). Luhrmann's 1996 film seems indebted to Bogdanov's audacious reading of the play.

Romeo and Juliet on Film and Television

Romeo and Juliet is the most filmed play throughout the world. Thomas Edison, who helped invent the motion picture, attempted the first American film of the play in 1902; actually it was a short satire (*Burlesque of Romeo and Juliet*) of an earlier French film by Georges Méliès. Regrettably, both of these early *Romeos* have been lost. In 1908 Vitagraph released a ten-minute film of the balcony scene. The first "on location" version (1915), filmed in Verona by Girolamo Lo Savio, included the Mercutio-Tybalt-Romeo street brawl. The most successful of the silent-era films was released by Metro in 1916 and featured the Leonardo DiCaprio of that time, Francis X. Bushman. A rival company (Fox) rushed its version into production; in an unlikely casting, Theda ("the Vamp") Bara, the famed silent-screen temptress, starred as Juliet. The first "talkie" *Romeo and Juliet* made its debut in 1929 when John Gilbert recited the window scene (2.2) as part of *The Hollywood Review of 1929*; Norma Shearer played Juliet, a role she reprised seven years later in the first full-length film version of the play.

Several of the most significant film and video versions of the play are discussed below.

- 1936—Director George Cukor, MGM, with Leslie Howard (Romeo), Norma Shearer (Juliet), Basil Rathbone (Tybalt), John Barrymore (Mercutio) and Andy Devine (Peter). (126 min.)

  Once Max Reinhardt's 1935 film of *A Midsummer Night's Dream* for Warner Brothers had launched big studio productions of Shakespeare, MGM chose *Romeo and Juliet* in 1936 for its inaugural attempt at screen Shakespeare. Despite an all-star cast, this 1930s film was actually a critical and box office failure, perhaps because the leads were too old (Howard was forty-two, Shearer thirty-seven) to play the young lovers convincingly. Though aware of the enormous expense of filming on location (the movie cost more than two million dollars), producer Irving Thalberg dispatched a design team to Verona in order to mount a meticulous recreation on a mammoth sound stage. To insure fidelity to the text, Thalberg also hired academics and a verse-speaking teacher for Shearer. The finished product included fragments from other Shakespeare plays and a song from *Twelfth Night*. Such efforts, however well intended, produced stilted, self-conscious performances from an otherwise accomplished group of actors. Only John Barrymore's Mercutio, played as a dashing ladies' man (befitting the actor's off-screen persona), and Basil Rathbone's unusually sympathetic Tybalt emerge as credible performances.

The film works best in its atmospheric shots:

- the bustling, donkey-and-merchant filled streets of Renaissance Verona where, in the opening sequence, the feuding families—not their servants—initiate hostilities;

- the fight between Tybalt and Romeo, which anticipates Zeffirelli's thrilling chase through the narrow streets;

- the lavish dances at the Capulet ball, staged by Agnes DeMille, who would emerge in the 1940s as America's foremost theater choreographer.

Director George Cukor invented some interesting touches that would be difficult to replicate on stage. His film begins with a shot of a Renaissance painting of Verona that dissolves into the real thing, a device that moves the play from the artificial world of the stage to the actual world of Italy. At the film's end, the crowd recites the Prince's final words ("Some shall be pardoned, some punishèd") in unison as they dissolve into the artificial painting that opened the film. Earlier, to emphasize a sense of pastoral beginning, Juliet is discovered petting a baby deer, Romeo in a field of sheep. Juliet creates a rope ladder to allow Romeo to climb into her chamber on their wedding night. To make room for such creations, Cukor has excised portions of the script, most notably many of Friar Laurence's lines, thereby diminishing his role as an unintentional contributor to the tragic consequences. The Thalberg-Cukor experiment in filming "true Shakespeare" failed with audiences, as it was deemed too intellectual and too "artsy" for the masses. The films of Orson Welles aside (and even these had notorious problems getting financing), American movie studios would not return to Shakespeare until after the success of Zeffirelli's *Romeo and Juliet* in the late sixties. In the meantime, Shakespeare-on-film would be largely in the hands of the British (notably Olivier) and Europeans.

- 1954—Director Renato Castellani, with Laurence Harvey (Romeo), Susan Shentall (Juliet), and John Gielgud (Chorus). (141 min.)

Although it is far from a definitive interpretation of the play, Castellani's film is significant because it was the first film—and among the first professional stage plays—to use actors close to the ages of Shakespeare's lovers. Harvey, twenty-five, was already an experienced and admired stage actor, while Shentall, nineteen, was a not a trained performer. The director cast for her innocent looks after seeing her in a British pub. Unfortunately, her inexperience mars the film, as does Harvey's understated, passionless, and too naturalistic delivery of Shakespeare's fervent love poetry. More successfully, Castellani filmed the play "authentically," that is, on location. He selected ten Italian towns, replete with crumbling walls and dark passageways, to represent Verona; the result was the most intensely realistic, claustrophobic, and dangerous set of locales for the play to date. Such visuals undercut the sentimentally romantic view of the play that had held the stage for three hundred years to create an authentic vitality that makes the ill-fated love affair more genuinely tragic in Romeo's need to overcome many obstacles in his pursuit of Juliet. If it had had stronger performances by the lovers, and had not Castellani reduced Mercutio to a bit part, the film might be a masterpiece; it remains more an ingenious travelogue that presages Zeffirelli's film fourteen years later.

- 1968—Director Franco Zeffirelli, with Leonard Whiting (Romeo), Olivia Hussey (Juliet), Milo O'Shea (Friar Laurence), and Laurence Olivier (Chorus, voice-over only). (138 min.)

This may be the most viewed Shakespeare film of all time, if only because it has been shown in high schools and universities for well over thirty years. Having successfully staged the play at the Old Vic and in Verona (see above), Zeffirelli retained the best features of those productions while making "a movie," rather than a filmed stage play. Like his countryman Castellani, Zeffirelli also used young, unknown actors (though formally trained) in the title roles. He, too, scoured Tuscany and Umbria to find authentic early-Renaissance locations for his film. (Verona is a distinctly northern Italian town, mostly flat and less rustic than the picturesque hill towns of central Italy. Only the opening sequence shows the actual Verona.) The thrilling fight between Romeo and Tybalt, a chase through winding, hillside alleyways, particularly benefited from the locales chosen by the director, who excelled at creating precisely the right atmosphere for this play set in "these hot days" when the blood of youth stirs. Peace in the dusty, sweltering piazza gives way to the initial fight between the Montagues and Capulets. The fatal Mercutio-Tybalt-Romeo duels of Act 3 also take place in choking heat. As Mercutio—played by Peter McEnery, "the cinema's finest Mercutio" (Rosenthal, 128)—bathes himself in the town water font, he engages Tybalt in witty, macho banter that escalates into a playful fencing match and thence to a furious fight in which Tybalt gives

Mercutio the fatal wound. The high-spirited laughter of the rival gangs underscores the scene; the laughter continues even as Mercutio, ironist to the end, notes that he will meet a "grave" ending. Laughter gives way to horror in Zeffirelli's most thoughtful interpretive statement: *Romeo and Juliet* is the tragedy of accidents. The director invents scenes on the road to Mantua to reinforce this reading. Balthazar races past Friar John en route to Mantua with the news that Juliet is "dead." Romeo fails to see Friar John, who is watering his donkey, as he gallops back to Verona. Romeo truly becomes "Fortune's fool."

In contrast to the sweltering street scenes, the sequences with the lovers are in cooler, more hospitable locales. Juliet's room overlooks a woodland that provides Romeo with a natural ladder to climb to his love. In one of the film's most comic moments, he dangles giddily from a branch. Friar Laurence's cell, the church in which the lovers are married, and especially Juliet's bedchamber become oases in Verona's steaming cauldron of hate and vengeance. When the dead lovers are displayed in the closing shot, Verona is shrouded in a cold fog; all is grey and lifeless.

The torch-lit Capulet ball is a thing of beauty. Zeffirelli inserts a lively dance from North Africa, the Morosco, to symbolize another theme of the play: haste and impetuosity lead to catastrophe. "They stumble that run fast," says the Friar to Romeo at 2.3.94. As the dancers whirl madly in a circle, Juliet is foregrounded in the frame as the only identifiable character. The action abruptly stops as a young man sings a melancholic song by composer Nino Rota ("What Is a Youth"); its message—"so dies the rose, so dies the youth, so dies the fair young maid"—is actually drawn from *Twelfth Night* ("women are as roses . . . To die even when they to perfection grow," 2.4.38–41). Though a sentimental moment in Shakespeare's most sentimental tragedy, this Zeffirelli-invented sequence became the play in microcosm illustrating as it does that beauty is too easily and quickly lost in a hostile, vengeful world. In 1968 audiences readily understood Zeffirelli's intentions as they, too, used the music of youth to protest against war and social injustice.

- 1978—Director Alvin Rakoff, BBC Shakespeare Series, with Patrick Ryecart (Romeo), Rebecca Saire (Juliet), Michael Hordern (Capulet), and John Gielgud (Chorus). (120 min.)

After Zeffirelli's spectacular rendering of the play in authentic Italian locales, virtually any made-for-television version (with all its budgetary and space limitations) would seem confined. Perhaps then it is unfair to judge the BBC's *Romeo and Juliet* against studio film versions. Still, this production is as stodgy and unappealing as any of the BBC's rever-

ential approaches to Shakespeare. It contains, however, one redeeming feature that neither Zeffirelli nor Luhrmann's films did: director Alvin Rakoff wisely retains Juliet's potion speech (4.3.14–58). Rebecca Saire's delivery of it is viewed through a gauzy curtain to enhance Juliet's eerie atmospheric talk of waking in a tomb full of decaying corpses. The speech is crucial to the development of Juliet's character (played by Saire as a very young and rather plain-looking girl), and it underscores a major point in this play about impetuous actions: Juliet is virtually the only character in the play to consider the consequences of one's choices. That she takes the potion after weighing the possible outcomes, all horrific, speaks volumes about this wise girl, only thirteen.

- 1997—*William Shakespeare's Romeo+Juliet*. Director Baz Luhrmann, with Leonardo DiCaprio (Romeo), Claire Danes (Juliet), Paul Sorvino (Capulet), Brian Dennehy (Montague), and Peter Postlethwaite (Friar Laurence). (120 min.)

If Zeffirelli attempted to please sixties' "flower children" and their Beatles-inspired "all you need is love" credo, Luhrmann courted the MTV generation with equal fervor. A pulsing soundtrack of contemporary pop music (including disco, soul, and electronica, as well as songs by Radiohead), rapidly edited montages of three-to-four-second shots, and surrealistic visuals combine to create an action-film aimed at an audience immersed in popular culture. The opening shot of a TV anchor intoning the Chorus's speech decrees that the ensuing film is not a stage play but a new creation for a new generation (note the altered title). Luhrmann's suggests that today's newscasts are "the abstract and brief chronicles" of our time (*Hamlet*, 2.2.524). The director returns to the image at the film's end: after the news anchor reads the Prince's final speech from a teleprompter, the TV goes blank—the visual equivalent of Hamlet's "the rest is silence."

Whereas the Italian Zeffirelli meticulously recreated a Renaissance world for the play and cast young unknowns in the title roles, the Australian Luhrmann invents a modern setting—Verona Beach (prompting some to refer to the film as "the Miami" or "L.A." *Romeo and Juliet*, although it was filmed in Mexico City and Vera Cruz)—in which well-heeled Anglos clash with Latinos led by John Leguizamo's sneering, *vato*-dressed Tybalt. The families drive fast cars, and the young men carry lethal weapons (their guns have the brand name "Sword" emblazoned on their barrels). In the opening gunfight a gas station is immolated in the best action-flick style.

Other divergences of style from previous films mark Luhrmann's production. Whereas Zeffirelli's lovers rebelled against rigidly strict parents, Luhrmann's—teen-favorite Leonardo DiCaprio as Romeo and Claire Danes, a dewy, intelligent actress who was sixteen when the movie was filmed, as Juliet—are the products of grotesquely dysfunctional families. The fathers are more interested in financial empire-building (with hints of Mafia backgrounds) than in their children. Lady Capulet (Diane Venora) is a shrill, chain-smoking, pill-popping cartoon mother, as funny as she is frightening; little wonder that Juliet wants out of the house. In addition, Luhrmann's inspired casting involves two African Americans, as the Prince ("Joe Prince," chief detective of Verona Beach's PD) and Mercutio, which makes plausible Shakespeare's notation that the two are "kinsmen." Their ethnicity sets them apart from the feuding families, and Mercutio's dying line ("A plague o' both your houses") resonates with uncommon irony. Whereas Shakespeare may have intended Mercutio to be an ironist who comments wryly on the folly of the Veronese, Luhrmann transforms him into an analog to a Jacobean-era "fantastic" (cf. Lucio in *Measure for Measure*). He arrives for the Capulet's ball, where most of the revelers are costumed as Shakespearean characters, dressed in a glittery spandex mini-skirt and a platinum wig; he's a drag queen, making a magnificently campy entrance disco-dancing with an all-male chorus. Mercutio's Queen Mab speech becomes an ode to the hallucinatory drug he gives to Romeo before the Capulet party and his meeting with Juliet.

Luhrmann clearly knows and respects his Shakespeare; his film abounds with visual details that pick up on images in the speeches and with clever references to various plays, including a glimpse of the Shylock Bank. Two audacious breaks from tradition are especially memorable. The wooing scene (2.2), perhaps predictable through its familiarity, gets a fresh update by taking place in the Montague swimming pool. As Romeo declares, "Call me but love, and I'll be new baptized" (2.2.50), he pulls Juliet into the pool. Yet the sinister world in which they live intrudes upon their revels as the lovers are monitored by Capulet's guards via security cameras. Another scene that breaks from tradition also happens to be the most cinematically beautiful sequence in the film: the tomb scene, which Luhrmann situates in an empty cathedral. He has prepared the audience for this moment throughout the film by filling the screen with religious icons (e.g., Friar Laurence's Hawaiian shirt bears an image of Christ). After dodging police helicopters to find his Juliet, Romeo enters the cathedral and sees her on a bier surrounded by neon crosses and thousands of candles. In a tradition dating to the late seventeenth century, Juliet awakens just as Romeo takes the poison, although there is no sentimental reunion as in the altered versions of Otway, Garrick, and others. Luhrmann's mystical rendering of the tomb scene employs a visual style associated with the magic realism (*realismo majico*) found in such films as Alfonso Arau's *Like Water for Chocolate*, providing a fitting climax for a film with a distinctly Latino ambience. Juliet's suicide is as disturbing as it is pitiable: after Romeo dies she lifts his sword (a handgun) to her head and cocks the hammer; as the camera pulls back she pulls the trigger. Earlier, Luhrmann photographed Romeo pumping numerous bullets into Tybalt to conclude a car chase through wet streets. The violence is another inheritance from the feuding families in this imaginative if sometimes excessive film, with its many positive values, not the least of which is the ability to engage its target audience.

Adaptations

An extraordinary number of artists in a variety of artistic forms have adapted the Romeo and Juliet story. Many will never be seen again, but collectively these works—only a few of which can be mentioned here—further attest to the appeal of the source story that inspired them.

Ballets, Operas, and Musicals

Romeo and Juliet's combination of romantic emotion and physical speed are among the qualities that have made the story so attractive not only to filmmakers, but also to dancers and choreographers. Because the Veronese lovers meet at a dance, ballet provides a natural medium for the tragedy. Ever since Eusebio Luzzi's five-act ballet opened in Venice in 1785, more than a dozen distinct ballet versions of *Romeo and Juliet* have been created. Some used music written specifically for the ballet; others adapted music by such masters as Vivaldi and Chopin; still others have used music written for operas based on the play (e.g., Gounod). The most famous ballet scores are those written by Tchaikovsky (1869, revised in 1880) and Sergei Prokofiev (1938); the latter is the most often performed and is generally regarded as the greatest ballet score of the twentieth century.

Prokofiev's score was written for the Bolshoi Ballet's production, which featured original choreography by Leonid Lavrovsky and which starred the great Bolshoi ballerina Galina Ulanova as Juliet. Lavrovsky's choreography was heavy on pantomime and theatrical gesture, but Ulanova's dancing proved to be rapturous and ultimately tragic. Her interpretation has been preserved in a readily available 1955 film shown widely in the United States. The Bolshoi *Romeo and Juliet* has toured frequently under the management of the legendary impresario Sol Hurok and his successors.

In 1965, London's Royal Ballet produced its own version, which was choreographed by Sir Kenneth MacMillan and featured two of the twentieth century's finest dancers, Rudolf Nureyev and Margot Fonteyn, as the lovers. The performance has been preserved on video and is worth seeing if only for the extraordinary *pas de deux* in the final act. In MacMillan's interpretation, Romeo enters the tomb disguised as a hooded monk and finds the sleeping Juliet. After killing Paris, he attempts to revive her, yet her body remains rigid and lifeless. The moment, so exquisitely captured in ballet, provides audiences with a glimpse of the lovers united in a passionate dance of death; Fonteyn's superb body control and Nureyev's impetuous passion and abandonment to grief create an emotionally satisfying alternative to Shakespeare's tomb scene.

Romeo and Juliet has been rendered as an opera in at least thirty-three versions, the first in 1776 by a German composer, Georg Anton Brenda, the most recent (2002) by the French composer Gerard Presgurvic. Charles Gounod's 1867 *tragedie lyrique* is the best-known of the operatic *Romeo*s. Though not as popular as his *Faust*, Gounod's opera captures the play's passion in an overtly sentimental vein; the opera has been called "a love song with occasional interruptions." It begins at the Capulet ball where Romeo discovers Juliet, alone, dancing a waltz as she implores "sprites from fairyland" to help her find love. Gounod sets the famous "holy palmers" sonnet to music ("Angel Adorable"). The wooing scene comprises Act 2 and contains the opera's most lyrical music (e.g., "Linger But a Moment"). The tomb scene concludes with a famous duet in which the lovers greet death as a "happy moment." In 1901 Frederick Delius wrote a less upper-class opera, *A Village Romeo and Juliet*, that uses folk airs; it is second only to Gounod's opera in number of performances in the twentieth century.

Although it was written for the Broadway stage, *West Side Story* (1957) is now recognized as a legitimate opera. The Metropolitan Opera in New York and Rome's Civic Opera, among other companies, have included the Leonard Bernstein musical (with lyrics by Stephen Sondheim and book by Arthur Laurents) in their opera seasons. A recent CD features the Met's finest artists singing Bernstein's admired score, which fuses European classical music, American popular music, jazz, Latin, and rock-and-roll. *West Side Story*—which inaugurated the vogue for the serious musical—follows Shakespeare's plot and characterizations, but shifts the action to Manhattan's shabby Upper West Side, where Anglo ("the Jets") and Puerto Rican ("the Sharks") gangs fight over cement turf. A Polish immigrant (Tony) falls in love with a newly arrived *Puertoriquena* (Maria) when they meet at a gymnasium dance. Maria's brother Nardo (Tybalt) objects and the gangs "rumble" under a highway overpass. Nardo kills Tony's best friend, Riff (Mercutio), and Tony retaliates, which prompts Chino, a Shark, to kill Tony on the cement playground over which the gangs have fought. Maria lives to plea for an end to the mindless violence that perpetuates the bloodshed.

West Side Story remains a much-performed staple of the contemporary musical theater. Bernstein and Sondheim (who was only twenty-one when he wrote the show's lyrics) find viable parallels to Shakespeare's most famous scenes in their songs: the wooing scene ("Tonight, Tonight") takes place on a tenement fire escape; the wedding scene ("Make of Our Hands One Hand") is located in a bridal shop (actually, a sweat shop where Puerto Rican women are exploited for low wages); and the tomb scene ("There's a Place for Us") on New York's meanest streets. The musical was made into an Academy Award-winning film in 1961 (dir. Robert Wise), and it may be argued that the play and subsequent film did much to advance the Civil Rights movement of the 1960s, because it was embraced by a generation of young people who mostly had not been confronted by issues of race and inequality. Two songs—"Gee, Sgt. Krupke" and "America"—anticipate the antiestablishment resentment by young people that marked the 1960s. For all the play's good intentions, Maria was played by an Anglo both on stage and in the film (Carol Lawrence and Natalie Wood, respectively) because a Latina could not have been cast in a leading role.

Spin-offs

Stage Plays

Two of the most prominent stage plays to have been inspired by *Romeo and Juliet* are Maxwell Anderson's *Winterset* (1935) and Peter Ustinov's *Romanoff and Juliet* (1956; filmed in 1961). Anderson's verse drama is based on the infamous Sacco-Vanzetti murder trial in which two Italian immigrants were charged with homicide, partly because of their ethnicity, mostly because they were Communists. *Winterset* portrays a love affair between Mio (Romeo), the son of an Italian unjustly accused of murder, and Miramne, whose brother (cf. Tybalt) has evidence that might clear Mio's father, but he fears for his life in a corrupt justice system. Ustinov's comedy places the play's action in the 1950s Cold War era where Russian and American diplomats feud openly, whereas their children (the Juliet counterpart is aptly named Concordia) fall in love and help resolve international tensions. Although Peter Parnell's *Romance Language* (1985) is not based directly on *Romeo and Juliet*, it does contain an imaginative scene in which actress

Charlotte Cushman (see above, p. 549) plays Romeo to the Juliet of stellar English actress Ellen Terry.

Films

Like *Hamlet*, *Romeo and Juliet* has inspired numerous film variants on the classic story, most updated to contemporary settings, as shown by some of the movies already mentioned. The play's universal appeal has induced international filmmakers to craft versions of the famous story for their cultures: Eygpt's *Shulhadda el gharam* (1942) and India's *Anjuman* (1948) are representative of such works.

Two Academy Award-winning films of the 1990s are indebted to *Romeo and Juliet*. James Cameron's *Titanic* (1998) borrows elements of Shakespeare's love story to provide the recreation of the catastrophic sinking of the *S.S. Titanic* in 1912 with a centuries-old emotional appeal that transcends its historical interest. Jack, a poor Irish immigrant, falls in love with a wealthy socialite (Rose) aboard the ship. He first glimpses his "Juliet" as she stands atop a ship's deck, the nautical equivalent of Shakespeare's "above;" later he takes her to a rousing Irish dance below decks in a scene that pays homage to Zeffirelli's famed Morosco sequence. Though Rose survives the sinking, the farewell scene between the lovers while adrift at sea enjoys the sentimental impact of Shakespeare's tomb scene.

Shakespeare in Love (directed by John Madden, 1998) does not parallel the Romeo and Juliet story as do the other entrants in this section on *Romeo*-inspired works. Rather it attempts to recreate the first production of the play at the Curtain in c. 1595—with varying degrees of fidelity (Queen Elizabeth did not attend public theaters, the actors came to her). The film introduces a number of authentic personages such as Richard Burbage, Philip Henslowe, Christopher Marlowe, and a very young John Webster whose fascination with things ghoulish anticipates his Jacobean tragedies (e.g., *The White Devil*). Though often whimsical, the Marc Norman-Tom Stoppard screenplay represents the cutthroat competition among the public theaters and the constant need to produce new works. The film engages issues of gender-bending ("I know what it is to be a woman in a man's world" the Queen tells the heroine, Viola de Lesseps), of Puritan opposition to the theaters, and, perhaps most importantly, of acting and staging conventions in the Elizabethan theaters. The film outrageously suggests that the passions and philosophical musings displayed in *Romeo and Juliet* grew out of Shakespeare's new-found love for Viola (like his Romeo, he, too, was originally smitten by a woman named Rosaline). The film's most glorious sequence—the first audience sits mouths agape at the deaths of the lovers—is a monument to the lasting popularity of *Romeo and Juliet*.

Since the 1980s several films have emerged that seem as much inspired by *West Side Story*—gang warfare substitutes for family feuds—as Shakespeare's play. While the concepts for each may be inventive, these films are ultimately melodramas that substitute violence for dramatic action. In their unrelenting nihilism, the films are more in akin to the most decadent of the Jacobean revenge tragedies (e.g., *The Revenger's Tragedy*) than to Shakespeare's vision. Several of these films are briefly discussed below.

- *China Girl* (Director Abel Ferrara, 1987): The battle here is between newly arrived Chinese immigrants and established Italian street gangs in New York. Tragedy occurs when Tony Monte (Romeo) falls in love with a beautiful immigrant named Tyan Hue. The film contains considerable violence, and the lovers are accidentally killed during an Italian street festival that erupts into all-out war between the gangs.

- *Zebrahead* (Director Anthony Drazan, 1992): Set in Detroit, this variant portrays a Jewish young man named Zach who falls for Nikki, an African American girl. Although most of the Shakespeare-inspired secondary characters die, Zach and Nikki actually live. The love poetry is supplied by old Johnny Mathis songs, and the "heat" associated with Shakespeare's original derives from a character who tosses matches about his lawn, which explodes in flames, to prove that pollution is turning the country into a volatile wasteland.

- *Romeo Must Die* (Director Andrzej Bartkowiak, 2000): Like *China Girl*, this film also features a Chinese street gang, but here they fight African Americans in Oakland. Han Singh (Romeo) is a martial arts expert who falls for Trish, the daughter of an African American gang member. The lovers finally escape together, but only after most of the other characters die in this violent exploitation film.

- *Tromeo* [sic] *and Juliet* (Director Lloyd Kaufman, 1996): This production is an intentional travesty by Troma Films, which specializes in tongue-in-cheek exploitation films. Here the families of porn kings Cap Capulet and Monty Que feud as Tromeo and Juliet, who is also involved in a lesbian relationship with the Nurse, more or less love each other ("She: "Parting is such sweet sorrow." He: "Yeah, totally sucks.""). Romeo and Juliet are actually (half) brother and sister, thanks to an adulterous affair between his father and her mother. Friar Laurence is a pedophile. Numerous severed limbs, decapitations, graphic sex, and other salacious episodes suggest that Kaufman's film deliberately "o'ersteps the modesty of nature."

Other *Romeo and Juliet* derivatives conspicuously appeal to teen audiences. Actor Joseph Bologna wrote and directed *Love Is All There Is* (1996), a contemporary New York comedy of manners about a poor girl (Angelina

FRAME-BY-FRAME

THE CRYPT SCENE IN *ROMEO AND JULIET*

Shakespeare's tragedy of love and mischance ends with the deaths of the lovers (5.3) in the Capulet burial vault, or crypt, where Juliet, seeming dead, has been laid to rest. This scene's combination of atmospheric gloom and intense emotion has challenged filmmakers and choreographers to visualize the young lovers' deaths as a pitiable, yet transcendent release from this world. As Shakespeare wrote the scene, it includes Romeo's killing of Paris; the Friar's greeting to the waking Juliet; and the arrival of the watch, the Prince, and the feuding families who must puzzle out the deaths, which the Friar explains in a long summary of his miscarried scheme. We examine here how two directors and one choreographer have met this challenge; outlined below are the crypt scenes from Franco Zeffirelli's and Baz Luhrmann's films and Kenneth MacMillan's ballet.

These three versions of the scene differ from the original in various ways. Each film excises significant actions and many speeches from Shakespeare's text in order to focus upon the couple. None of the scenes retains the Friar's explanation for the deaths. Only the ballet includes the detail of Romeo killing Paris, while only the Zeffirelli film places the frightened, distraught Friar in the crypt when Juliet awakens. Luhrmann transposes the entire scene to the altar of a cathedral where Juliet lies in her wedding dress upon a bier, surrounded by Catholic iconography and thousands of glimmering candles and neon crosses. All three directors make much of Juliet's awakening back into life, a moment Shakespeare signals only with the Friar's line, "The lady stirs." All three also emphasize motion and music, using musical cues, dynamic changes, shifts of key and instrumentation, as well as charged silences, to strongly underscore the emotion, both religious and romantic, of the scene.

Franco Zeffirelli's Film

Zeffirelli's 1968 film stars Leonard Whiting as Romeo, Olivia Hussey as Juliet, and Milo O'Shea as Friar Laurence. Its tomb in the Italian countryside really is an underground crypt, which is entered through imposing metal doors. O'Shea's Friar Laurence wears a knowing smile as the funeral procession moves prayerfully toward this place where Juliet is interred by the grieving family. His look signals that he thinks his scheme is unfolding according to plan. All too soon, however, we see Romeo racing back to Verona on horseback with Balthazar, who has taken Juliet's seeming death and burial at face value and has brought the sad news to Romeo. They pass the dawdling Friar John and his mule along the way; this is a moment of painful dramatic irony as we understand that the message about Friar Laurence's ruse will go undelivered. When Romeo arrives at the crypt, he finds the metal doors locked and smashes them open with a rock. His radiant face, the light of a torch, and swelling violin music establish a mood of expectancy as he looks for Juliet among a long row of shrouded corpses. A harp picks up composer Nino Rota's love theme when Romeo finds and holds Juliet, calling her "my love, my wife," as he smiles down upon her in her pearl-trimmed cap and gown. When he recognizes the corpse of Tybalt in his "bloody sheet" he moves toward him and asks forgiveness for killing him.

Whiting's Romeo seems at peace in these first passages of the scene; he tells the lifeless Tybalt that he will do him the favor of self-slaughter. Positioning himself near the feet of Juliet, his Romeo asks why "art thou yet so fair" and promises to remain with her forever. Only now does he cry, sobbing as the music swells again. Zeffirelli's experience as an opera director surfaces here as Whiting quaffs the deadly poison at the exact climax of a musical phrase. Placing his hand on Juliet's, he speaks his last words— "Thus with a kiss I die"—and falls to the ground.

The next shot moves outside the tomb where the Friar sees Balthazar and fears some "ill, unthrifty thing." Entering the tomb, he sees Romeo dead and cries out "Ah, what an unkind hour / Is guilty of this lamentable chance!" He himself has, of course, helped bring about the boy's death; this agonizing knowledge is apparent on O'Shea's face here and later, when he hurriedly leaves the scene. Zeffirelli's camera, inside the crypt again, focuses upon Juliet's hand, which begins to move. She fingers the diaphanous cloth that had been her shroud and, to a melody for flute and oboe, she touches her own face, realizing she is awake. She directs her first words (as in the Shakespeare script) to the Friar:

(continued)

"Where is my lord?" Friar Laurence hopes to move her away from this "nest of death, contagion, and unnatural sleep" before she sees Romeo's body. Hearing the horns and horses of the watch, he fears for his life, however, and flees. As the musical love theme returns, Juliet sees Romeo, takes the phial of poison, and tries to drink at least "a friendly drop to help me after" him into death. She sobs as she kisses him, and cries out as the sounds of the watch and the Friar's page come nearer to her. "Then I'll be brief," she says, fearlessly taking Romeo's dagger and plunging it into her chest. Her body falls forward in such a way that the two young faces are still looking toward one another in death.

Zeffirelli takes us back outside for the final speeches by the Prince. He composes this scene atop stone stairs where the two bodies are laid out. The two fathers, Capulet and Montague, must rise from the crowd to stand at the foot of the biers and hear the Prince say, "See what a scourge is laid upon your hate." The lingering image underscores the theme of the sins of the fathers truly being visited upon the children. The Prince repeats his final words, "All are punished," first as a kind of quiet moral, and then in a loud, angry scream. Shakespeare's concluding couplet ("For never was a story of more woe / Than this of Juliet and her Romeo," [308–309]) is spoken in voice-over by Laurence Olivier, becoming a kind of epilogue to the drama and to this groundbreaking and deservedly popular film.

Kenneth MacMillan's Ballet

Kenneth MacMillan's work for England's Royal Ballet was filmed by director Paul Czinner as a feature-length film in 1966. Set to Sergei Prokofiev's score, it stars legendary dancers Rudolf Nureyev and Margot Fonteyn as Romeo and Juliet, respectively, with Derek Rencher as Paris and Ronald Hynd as Friar Laurence. In this movie, the crypt scene is called Act 3, Scene 4. Like the entire Royal Ballet production, a monumental one with opulent costumes and massive sets by Nicholas Georgiadis, the scene was filmed in such a way as to duplicate the feeling of live performance in a theater.

Initially the scene appears as Juliet's bedroom, but then it is transformed, becoming a stony underground space with two angel sculptures—now, it is her tomb. The set change accomplishes this in a literal way that may mirror the original Elizabethan staging solution: Juliet's marriage bed becomes her funeral bier. As in Zeffirelli's film, shrouded bodies lie on nearby tombs; one of them belongs to Tybalt. A procession of monks enters the crypt with Juliet's parents, her nurse, and Paris; they lament her death and pay their final respects. Off to one side is a caped monk, who reveals himself—in dramatic Nureyev fashion—to be Romeo. Paris also has lingered in the crypt. When he and Romeo recognize one another, Romeo soon attacks, stabs, and kills him.

Romeo now leaps onto Juliet's bier. As he tries to hold her in his arms, she slips from his embrace. He raises her off the tomb, carrying her away, as if acting out the lines: "Death, that hath sucked the honey of thy breath, / Hath had no power yet upon thy beauty" (5.3.92–93). Throughout the ballet, but especially in the duets and solos, MacMillan's choreography conveys this sense of words just below the surface, propelling the music and motion. Juliet's body is straight as an arrow, though her arms and legs flop almost ludicrously as the music swells. Twice Romeo attempts to hang on to her, thinking that he can revive her, but she eludes his grasp. Desperate to hold her, Nureyev's passionate Romeo drags her body by one arm, as Fonteyn's limp Juliet trails behind him like a rag doll. He clings to her, imparting passionate kisses on her lips and face, and then raises her aloft in a series of lifts that express his adoration, before her body falls again to the ground and then into his arms.

He places her tenderly upon her bier. First facing her, then turning away, he takes the phial of poison he has brought with him and swallows the liquid. With crabbed, painful movements as the poison does its work, he maneuvers himself back to Juliet's side. As his shudders subside and he approaches death, the light music of strings accompanies his final embrace and kiss. Then he falls backward next to the bier. Fonteyn's Juliet awakens from the heart first: her diaphragm rises, then her arms feel the air before she sits up, startled, to the sound of strings and flute. She dashes, swiftly and lyrically, from one side of the vault to the other, encountering the frightening shrouded bodies, and then discovers the body of her Romeo. She stops, staring (as she had stared straight ahead, still and scared, in the protracted dance-soliloquy before taking the sleeping draught). She runs to him, expecting to find him alive, perhaps asleep. But her joy becomes terror when she touches him. She kisses his hand, and knows for certain he is dead. She walks straight toward the dagger that dropped from the lifeless hand of Paris. With both hands, she plunges it into her heart. Then she crawls back atop her stone bier as the music lightens yet again, and she reaches toward Romeo's body, bringing his dead hand to her lips for a kiss. As Fonteyn's Juliet releases his hand it falls, a dead weight, back down, and she dies, her body draped over the side of the bier as if reaching in death for her love.

Baz Luhrmann's *Romeo+Juliet*

Baz Luhrmann's *William Shakespeare's Romeo+Juliet* is a lush, violent, and thoroughly contemporary take on Shakespeare's story, and stars Claire Danes as Juliet and Leonardo DiCaprio as Romeo. Luhrmann's treatment of the scene replaces the crypt with a soaring cathedral; the scene is the most visually stunning of the many settings he and designer Catherine Martin envisioned for this 1996 film. When the scene opens, a police dragnet encircles the church; in order to enter this house of God, where he knows he will find Juliet, DiCaprio's Romeo must get past this human barrier. In an exciting sequence of shots, he shoots his way up the steps, takes a night watchman hostage by holding a gun to his head, and muscles past the cathedral's huge doors into the darkened vestibule. There, the sounds of wailing sirens, explosive gunshots, and whirring police helicopters suddenly fall silent. In that long silence, time seems to stop. The camera gradually focuses upon a sheaf of light emanating from a crack between the inner doors; as Romeo opens the doors, religious music surges forth. The unearthly glow of thousands of flickering candles and scores of kitschy blue neon crosses lining the aisle beckon him towards the sacristy where Juliet lies in her wedding dress, as if in state. A lily has been placed upon her torso, and two plaster angels stand guard over her. Romeo, his eyes misting, slowly makes his way down the candlelit aisle toward her. He carefully sets his gun down, intones "my love, my wife," and continues speaking to her tenderly as if she were alive and death were "amorous."

Luhrmann adds several significant details that heighten the pathos of the scene. Romeo places upon Juliet's finger the ring and chain necklace she had given him as a love token. She soon begins to move her fingers against his hand, but he is so griefstricken that he does not feel the life

returning to her. As he is about to take the dram of poison (purchased from a drug dealer whose seedy upstairs place resembles the "needy shop" Shakespeare describes for his apothecary), Danes's Juliet suddenly opens her wide eyes, a look of recognition spreading across her face. Her expression turns quizzical as she sees Romeo raise the yellow liquid to his lips; clearly she is still too sedated to raise her arm or speak to stop him. When he turns toward her, Romeo acknowledges her coming back to life with a startled, then pained look. It is too late; he has swallowed the fatal draught. She kisses his lips, hoping to find a drop there for herself, and her eyes well with tears as he dies next to her. There will be no sentimental reunion as there was in David Garrick's eighteenth-century adaptation.

Luhrmann now has Juliet spy Romeo's abandoned gun, which has fallen near a mute, kneeling angel. She raises the weapon, feeling its unfamiliar shape in her hand. Then she cocks it and, looking terrified, raises the barrel to her temple. We hear the shot ring out as the camera tracks away and the music dissolves into the Liebestod, or love-death theme, from Richard Wagner's *Tristan and Isolde*. As the camera moves upward, the candles below, centered by the youthful bodies, begin to look like a burst of fireworks from the celebrations during an earlier scene. For the second time in the film, Luhrmann now presents an anthology of remembered images; as if flipping though a family album, he shows bits of hearts-on-fire Roman Catholic imagery and the dreamy vision of DiCaprio and Danes floating underwater as they did in her parents' pool after their first furtive meeting in the ballroom. The rich, deep voice of opera legend Leontyne Price sings wave after wave of repeated melody mingling erotic desire and the wish for death.

After this scene, Luhrmann completes the film swiftly, moving from the Latin-inflected magical-realist world of the cathedral back out into the cold light of reality. The sheet-draped bodies are placed in ambulances for the trip to the morgue. To the uncomprehending parents, Captain Prince repeats, as Zeffirelli's Prince did, first quietly and then in a rage, "All are punished." The film ends as it began with a television newscaster on a snowy screen concluding "For never was a story of more woe / Than this of Juliet and her Romeo." When the TV set turns off, the movie screen goes dark, and stays that way for a time before the credits roll.

BAZ LUHRMANN ON FILM AND THEATER

"I have an international passport and it's called the vernacular of story."

Ed. note: Anne Marie Welsh interviewed director Baz Luhrmann in New York City on December 10, 2002, the night before his updated staging of Puccini's *La Bohème* opened on Broadway. Portions of this interview appeared in the *San Diego Union-Tribune* and are reprinted with the newspaper's permission.

No Shakespeare film has gripped the imagination of a global teenage audience with such startling power as Baz Luhrmann's gangland *Romeo+Juliet*. Although critics were at first divided about the 1996 film, set in a Miami-like Verona Beach, stars Leonardo DiCaprio and Claire Danes became the archetypal young lovers for their generation. Even those who have felt that Luhrmann buried the lyrical tragedy in a cascade of visual effects, choppy MTV-style editing, and pop songs have also acknowledged that the film confirms Luhrmann, the protean Australian director, as an original visual stylist. He envisioned his *Romeo and Juliet* project as part of a trilogy of movies that would draw inspiration as much from the worlds of theater, dance, and opera as from the conventions of cinema. Frankly artificial, highly stylized, and telling simple mythological stories, his *Strictly Ballroom, Romeo+Juliet,* and *Moulin Rouge* all testify to what Luhrmann describes as "my goal of accessing a direct emotional response through a kind of twisting of simple melodrama."

Luhrmann began his artistic life as a dancer, competing in the kind of ballroom dance competitions that are depicted, with only mild exaggeration, in the kitschy contests of his surprise box office hit, *Strictly Ballroom.* He lived in rural New South Wales where, he explains, "My Dad was sort of crazy in that he wanted us to have some culture even though we lived in such an isolated place." Thus came the long drives for dance lessons far from the combination pig farm and gas station where young Bazmark Anthony Luhrmann worked and met a startling array of real-life characters. He became a champion dancer himself, though he felt thwarted by the restrictions placed upon his fertile imagination by the competition format's strict rules. Luhrmann landed at the National Institute of Dramatic Arts and at the age of nineteen began developing his experience of ballroom dance culture into a play about the struggle of a gifted young artist for love and against artistic repression. It is his recurring story.

"That was the beginning of this cinematic language," he says, "the whole idea of placing those near-mythic stories in worlds. I was beginning to go down that road already. Even that film has one foot in the work of Shakespeare, because it's not about psychological naturalism—it's about a stylized theatrical world. You enter a created world and it draws you in." Luhrmann says that as a young stage director helming plays and operas, he was impacted by film in part because no one in the culture can be isolated from the movies. He contends that once an artist has "the primary story and knows the plot, the work is not about revealing that. In psychological naturalism, the story may be about hiding the plot. You're trying to use all your machinery for making invisible the inevitable in, say, *Oedipus Rex.*"

That is definitely not his method, he says. For Luhrmann and, he contends, for Shakespeare, "Theater is more like football. People gather as a group and they commune over a love story, and a child has a completely different experience of it than does an adult intellectual. And yet they commune together in the event. I think that's why [the stylized approach] is so effective as storytelling, as if the story becomes elastic. We worked with very serious Shakespeare scholars to find our way in."

American distributors of *William Shakespeare's Romeo+Juliet* sold the film, he says, "as an MTV thing, but in Great Britain, where it won the prizes that year, people knew it came out of years of academic study by me and my team about the Elizabethan notion of Shakespeare, instead of what is really a kind of generalized quasi-Victorian notion that so many people take to be the *real* Shakespeare. I thought, let's all learn from Shakespeare. So we spent a year stripping away that nineteenth century—all that notion of language. Peter Hall demonstrated that the sound of Shakespeare would have been completely different. It was an extraordinary revelation, but above everything else, Shakespeare had to deal with a city of nearly three hundred thousand people and a theater that held four thousand and everyone from the street sweeper upwards. He used everything to arrest and stop that audience—bawdy comedy and then, wham! something really beautiful and poetic. We decided we would be fearless about the lowness of the comedy."

Luhrmann confesses to being amused that his mostly American cast was sometimes criticized by people who said, " 'They're not speaking like Shakespeare sounds, not correctly.' Well, yes they are; there's a lot of drivel written about Shakespeare. There's really very little that we really know. We know a few primary things and we certainly know that linguistically Americans on the East coast toward the South may sound more like Shakespeare's actors did than Gielgud and Olivier. Not to denigrate them; of course, they were great. But they are old-fashioned and people start making these hugely crazy generalizations about what should and shouldn't be. The thing about the film we made was that, sure MTV is referenced, but that's another place where stylistic cinema is used in this kind of vernacular. The bottom line is that from the standup comedy in the beginning, cutting to low comedy, cutting to high tragedy—that has very little to do with MTV, it has to do with the Elizabethan stage. Putting a pop song into Shakespeare is doing exactly what Shakespeare did."

Shakespeare's drama had to play to the queen (Elizabeth I) and to the streets, Luhrmann continues, attributing the plays' bawdry to that attempted reach. "Shakespeare's audience would make the roughest multiplex look positively tame. If, to get their attention, he had to use the bawdiest comment or make a double-entendre, he did it—to shock and engage, with crass humor. Then the crassness would lead to an odd beauty."

Describing the elasticity of Shakespeare's love tragedy, he characteristically skips across the centuries speaking of the tale of Pyramus and Thisbe and the contemporary Middle East almost in the same breath. "It really is two households both alike in dignity; in Palestine today, both have their children coming home in body bags. It's a primary human story. It happens in life in all cultures, so therefore we have many derivations of the story that project it."

And summing up his Shakespearean lessons, he says he wondered whether "one person could have nailed the human condition so well and written poems on the side. I'd like to go back to him every now and again as a gymnasium for the mind."

Luhrmann is part of a generation of post-French New Wave film directors who emerged in the 1990s and move easily back and forth from stage to film as Laurence Olivier and Orson Welles and Elia Kazan once did. Among them are Rob Marshall, Sam Mendes, Neil La Bute, Richard Eyre, and, in the Shakespeare field, Kenneth Branagh. Midway through Luhrmann's ravishing stage production of *La Bohème,* a kind of fool-the-eye illusion might stand as an emblem of their accomplishment. As the distraught seamstress Mimi stands before the tavern Au Port de Marseille, shivering, ill, wrapped in a white trench coat, she seeks solace from her friends, Marcello and Musetta. The tavern vanishes into the distance, fading into a photo-realist landscape as Mimi is reunited with her beloved, Rodolfo. All eyes and the spotlight now focus on the lovers. That smooth rhythmic shift of perspective felt so much like a dissolve into a close-up that for a moment, audiences at the Broadway theater were not sure whether they were watching a film or a stage play. The vivid presence of the actors and then their passionate voices rising in Puccini's tender *Addio, dolce svegliare* revealed that the production was both and neither.

That brief moment of confusion—the blurring of boundaries between media and genres—suggests the ease with which Luhrmann and some others now bring techniques learned in theater into the movies and from moviemaking back into the theater.

Such border crossing comes naturally to Luhrmann who, at the age of twenty-three, was directing a state opera company and a national theater troupe in Australia. "I was making films when I ran an opera and a theater because for me there is no border. I have an international passport and it's called the vernacular of story," he says. "I work with the currency of the time. And whether we're editing for *Vogue* magazine, or making a record, or doing a film or doing an election campaign, all of which we've done, it's all part of the same creative activity."

The same eclectic range of reference that makes his *Romeo+Juliet* so rich in detail peppers his darting conversation. He says there is not that much difference between a writer and an actor and a politician: the question for all three involves how to best express content. "I acted too when I was a kid. I'd have an idea, and then I'd write, direct, act, whatever I felt like doing or needed to do to get my meaning across. I've done documentaries. I am not driven by what makes for a successful career or how you get rich. I'm driven and my collaborators are driven by what will make our lives, and what will make our life journey rich and fulfilling. . . . We want to make New York our second home; that's why *La Bohème* is

(continued)

on Broadway. Lord knows there are easier ways to make money than to open an Italian opera on Broadway, but we wanted to be in New York."

Thinking creatively about what to do next has led him to projects like *Moulin Rouge*, which he says came out of his desire to "reinvent the postmodern movie musical while still making my life interesting and rich."

Casting, he says, is key to his work. "You can't get past script and cast—if you get one of those wrong you might as well forget it," he says, while acknowledging that the precision and fullness of each project's visual world is something he works out in tandem with the woman he calls "CM," his set designer and wife, Catherine Martin.

When he cast DiCaprio as Romeo, Luhrmann recalls, "There was a whole lot of 'Oh my god he'll never be able to do it' from people. But he did. I knew he could be the romantic hero. He was tremendous as an actor, which he is, and a movie star, which he is, but then we tried to capture the essence of the tragic romantic hero of his particular generation." So, too, with the deeply intelligent Claire Danes, who was sixteen years old when *Romeo+Juliet* was filmed and who shows an intuitive command of the role and an easy grace in speaking the verse.

Luhrmann credits his casting director, Ronna Kress, for steering him toward such surprising actors as Harold Perrineau (who makes Shakespeare's complex Mercutio a flamboyant disco-hopping drag queen half in love with Romeo) and comic monologist John Leguizamo (who makes a sneering flamenco-style Latin lover of Tybalt) in *Romeo+Juliet*. Leguizamo, whom Kress championed until Luhrmann saw what she saw in him, went on to play the sexually ambiguous dwarf of *Moulin Rouge*.

"My goal is to help actors reveal that which is within themselves. I always knew that Nicole could be warm and funny," Luhrmann says, referring to fellow Australian Nicole Kidman, who sings and stars as Satine, the Eurydice figure in *Moulin Rouge*. Like *Romeo+Juliet*, that final film in the "Red Curtain" trilogy has a soundtrack as diverse as its visual attack, referencing a wild variety of pop tunes and styles in an approach that Luhrmann calls "free-basing." The sounds of Elton John waft through mid–nineteenth-century Paris in *Moulin Rouge*, and the signature theme is the Eden Ahbez's tune "Nature Boy," popularized by Nat "King" Cole. Luhrmann's mantra comes from its simple lyric: "The greatest thing / You'll ever learn / Is just to love / And be loved in return."

Because he bases his moviemaking upon a theater company model, close in concept to the multi-disciplinary approach of Serge Diaghilev and his Ballets Russes company, actors working on one of his films have to commit to Luhrmann for a period of months. "I don't do auditions; I kind of do workshops for actors in which we create text. If you want to be in one of my films you can't just turn up and act. You have to be involved in several workshops, several months of rehearsals."

Luhrmann's sensibility persistently flirts with gay and camp attitudes; his movies include sexually ambivalent and sometimes what he calls "omnisexual" characters. His casts also have an international look, global in reach. In his Broadway-scaled production of *La Bohème*, the three rotating casts came from every corner of the world—"an English boy like James Dean with a Chinese girl, Weng Wang, who's from Shanghai," he says ticking off names of the handsome boy from Colorado, the soprano from Russia, and all the other young singers with him in New York for the opening. "To be sure, it's not a generic version of Rodolfo and Mimi. I've been working on the production for two years because it took me that long to find them all," he says.

"My work is never about the leather jacket," he contends, referring to the Brandoesque costuming for Rodolfo in his 1957-set *Bohème*. It's never "about being Hamlet in Hawaii, nor about being groovy for the sake of it. Every choice I made in every production was made to reveal text."

In *Romeo+Juliet* that can mean a quite literal translation of verbal to visual. The run-down Sycamore Grove amusement park and theater of the opening scenes is rooted in Shakespeare's description of young Romeo as isolating himself in a "sycamore grove." There he pines over his idealized, loved-from-afar Rosaline. When DiCaprio's Romeo, who, like his fellow Montagues, does wear a Hawaiian shirt in the film, jots down his Petrarchan musings and his clever oxymorons in a little journal, he's being true to a strong implication of the play. This Romeo is, as Anthony Lane of the *New Yorker* put it, "a Shakespeare in bud."

Luhrmann earned the artistic backing of Twentieth-Century-Fox for *Romeo+Juliet* because his life was, as he says, "irreversibly changed in that euphoric moment when *Strictly Ballroom* sold more tickets in twenty-four hours at the Cannes Film Festival than any movie in the festival's history. I mean I was offered huge amounts of money by the studios, but I made a deal with Fox that if they would allow us to work from Australia I would go with them. So since then I've had a deal with Fox so that I can make what I want, when I want, where I want. So basically artistic freedom is worth more to me than money."

The costs, by today's movie budget standards, have been small, but escalating—eighteen million dollars for *Strictly Ballroom*, twenty million dollars for *Romeo+Juliet*, and fifty million dollars for *Moulin Rouge.*

Asked how free he really is, Luhrmann answers, "It's pretty hard for them to sack me and put someone in to do iambic pentameter in modern dress. We can make what we want, how we want. The only constraint is: not for any budget. *Moulin Rouge* was

$45 million originally, and then it went to $50. That was a big ask. $50 million was a bit of a worry. Over $50 million would have been a very big worry. Thankfully, we've paid the bill and we can continue to fly the flag of creative freedom. I don't just consider that to be important, I consider it to be everything. Whether you work for a king, a government body, or a producer in Hollywood, it's still the same relationship. You've got to have your artistic vision and they've got to want to finance that. But if they start saying, 'Well, it's O.K., I'll do it if you wear less clothes,' then no, that's not for me. We are not for hire. I don't want to be. I would never take a directing job if I didn't think it would be fulfilling, if it didn't make my life more rich and interesting."

Jolie in her film debut) who falls for her Romeo as they perform in a high school production of Shakespeare's play. *Fire with Fire* (1986) takes place in a Catholic boarding school where a prim young woman falls for an escapee from a nearby prison; the lovers attempt suicide by jumping off a cliff, but miraculously they are swept downstream where they are saved and live happily ever after. *Under the Boardwalk* (1989) is a surfer film in which Romeo (Nick, a member of a San Fernando Valley surf gang) goes head to head against his enemy in a "surf to the death duel," all of which proves, dudes, that Shakespeare's tragedies and their derivatives continue to be "acted over / In states unborn and accents yet unknown!" (*Julius Caesar*, 3.1.113–114).

References and Related Reading

Agate, James. *Brief Chronicles*. London, 1943.

Bode, Douglas. *Shakespeare in the Movies*. New York, 2001.

Dench, Judi. "A Career in Shakespeare." *The Oxford Illustrated History of Shakespeare on Stage*. Eds. Jonathan Bate and Russell Jackson. Oxford, 2001. 199–210.

Evans, G. Blakemore, ed. *"Romeo and Juliet."* The New Cambridge Shakespeare. Cambridge, Eng., 1984.

Jackson, Russell. "Shakespeare in Opposition." *The Oxford Illustrated History of Shakespeare on Stage*. Eds. Jonathan Bate and Russell Jackson. Oxford, 2001.

Melchiori, Giorgio. "Peter, Balthasar, and Shakespeare's Art of Doubling." *Modern Language Review* 55: 4 (October 1983): 777–792.

Parsons, Keith, and Pamela Mason. *Shakespeare in Performance*. London, 1995.

Quince, Rohan. *Shakespeare in South Africa: Stage Productions in the Apartheid Era*. New York, 2000.

Rosenthal, Daniel. *Shakespeare on Screen*. London, 2000.

Thompson, Leslie. "How the Lovers' Scenes Were Staged in Elizabethan Times." *Readings on Romeo and Juliet*. Ed. Don Nardo., 1998. 125–134.

Trewin, J. C. *Going to Shakespeare*. London and Boston, 1978.

CHAPTER 15

Hamlet

c. 1601

Context and Dating

Having written the Roman tragedy *Julius Caesar* in 1599 and *Twelfth Night* in c. 1601, Shakespeare turned his attention to the first of his four "great tragedies": *Hamlet*. No play in Shakespeare's canon has been performed more often than this tragedy of the Danish Prince. Western actors from Richard Burbage, who created the role, to Kenneth Branagh, whose four-hour film presents the text in its entirety, have been judged upon their interpretations of Hamlet. More than forty films of the play and its derivatives exist, including one starring Mel Gibson who portrays the Prince as a "lethal weapon." Actors throughout Asia, Africa, and Latin America now perform the role regularly. Many women have played Hamlet, including the great French actor Sarah Bernhardt at the end of the nineteenth century. Dame Judith Anderson was seventy-two when she enacted the Prince on a world tour in the 1970s. In Denver an enterprising gambler actually won a hundred-dollar bet in 1861 when he memorized Hamlet's lines in three days to play the role in "a highly creditable" manner (Davidson, 39). All this for a man who is—as the Prince says in another context—"a fiction," a "dream of passion" (2.2.552).

Hamlet intrigues all who meet him because he does not seem the creation of a playwright—yet he assuredly is. Shakespeare creates a human portrait of such complexity and contradictions that audiences cannot help but think of him as a real person, or, as Samuel Taylor Coleridge said, "I have a smack of Hamlet." Each person who encounters him on the page, the stage, or film also has "a smack of Hamlet," for he is the archetype of the decent person confronted by an onerous task.

While scholars and actors focus upon Hamlet's multifaceted character as a source of the play's enduring appeal, the drama itself is memorable as superb storytelling and spectacular theater. In the opening seconds a ghost stalks a medieval castle seeking revenge for his death—a chilling prologue to a tale of an adulterous love affair, court intrigues, a pathetic suicide, and several ruthless murders. The play concludes with a suspense-filled sword fight, bizarre poisonings, and the arrival of another young prince who, like Hamlet, seeks a crown lost by his slain father. As Horatio tells the Danish court in a remarkably concise plot summary, the story is one

> Of carnal, bloody, and unnatural acts,
> Of accidental judgments, casual slaughters,
> Of deaths put on by cunning and forced cause.
> (5.2.383–385)

Plots and Counterplots

From a structural standpoint *Hamlet* is as complex as any of Shakespeare's great tragedies. *Othello* and *Macbeth* have single plots; *King Lear* has two. *Hamlet* relies on three interlinked stories to advance its principal concern of avenging patricide. Three sons from different families—the Danish Prince Hamlet, Laertes, and young Prince Fortinbras of Norway—are each called upon to avenge a father's murder, and each follows his own path to accomplish his mission. Laertes, whose father, Polonius, is killed by Hamlet near the end of Act 3, returns from France "in a riotous head" (4. 5.104); his unchecked passion causes him to be "justly killed with [his] own treachery" (5.2.310). By contrast, Hamlet admits that he thinks "too precisely on th'event" (4.4.42), and thereby delays the revenge commanded by his father's death. Fortinbras, on the other hand, successfully achieves his end as he carefully and methodically avenges his father's murder at the hands of Old

564

Hamlet. Fortinbras's success poses a critical problem for us, as for Hamlet, since being simply "strong in arms" is not seen in the play as clearly a better answer than Hamlet's submitting himself to the will of Providence. Yet Fortinbras does become the new king of Denmark. Because of the play's length, the Fortinbras subplot is often cut, although the deletion diminishes the multiple perspectives on the consequences of human actions—or inaction—inherent in Shakespeare's design.

Shakespeare, in the estimation of Harvard scholar Stephen Greenblatt, seems to have discovered a new means of advancing plot as he crafted *Hamlet*. Rather than presenting lengthy exposition in the early portions of the play and then following that with a rapid move to denouement, Shakespeare consciously made "a play about what it is like to live inwardly in the queasy interval between a murderous design and its fulfillment" (Greenblatt, 304). The playwright had hinted at this technique in his previous tragedy, *Julius Caesar*, particularly in Brutus's anguished deliberations about assassinating Caesar. That play, however, resolves itself midway through the third act. With *Hamlet*, Shakespeare seems to have "conceived the possibility of writing about a character suspended, for virtually the whole length of a play, in this strange interim" between impulse and action (302). Thus, *Hamlet* emerges as the drama of character, rather than one of mere action—although it offers its audiences thrilling action throughout its five acts.

Both in the theater and in the study, Hamlet observers invariably ask the question: given the Ghost's command at the end of Act 1 that Hamlet "Revenge his foul and most unnatural murder" (1.5.26) at the hands of Claudius, why does it take the Prince four acts to comply with his father's charge? Hamlet himself apparently suspects that Claudius killed his father: "Oh, my prophetic soul!" he says in response to the Ghost's indictment (1.5.42). Nonetheless, Hamlet does not immediately avenge his father's death. The text offers some hints concerning Hamlet's delay. Hamlet fears that the Ghost may be the devil in disguise, tempting him to a heinous act (2.2.599ff.). He has a moral aversion to murder—and suicide—and fears the consequences of his actions: "conscience does make cowards of us all" (3.1.84). Questions of morality aside, Hamlet suspects that he is simply a coward who is "pigeon-livered and lack[s] gall / To make oppression bitter" (see 2.2.571–578). Furthermore, the Prince, the new Renaissance Man, is trapped in a medieval world and its blood-for-blood system of justice; thus he intellectualizes the situation as he might have done on an ethics examination at Wittenberg. In the final analysis, Shakespeare does not tell us why Hamlet delays; he only shows Hamlet's lack of action in the matter of retribution. The great trick of *Hamlet* is that it remains a compelling story even as its hero follows what critics variously refer to as its "action of inaction." Peter Alexander offers insight into the unusual structure of Shakespeare's tragedy:

> The play is not a series of random scenes but an ordered and highly controlled pattern . . . Within this pattern of action and language the theme of violent death followed by equally violent revenge and retaliation is repeated in different circumstances by different players. As death answers to death in the play, the audience [is] required to examine the nature of this act of violence. The play is more than a murder story: it is an examination of the kind of response provoked by murder.
>
> (Alexander, 3)

Characters: Theater's Most Famous Enigmatic Hero

If *Hamlet* were merely a cautionary tale about the conflict between reason and passion, or thought and action, it would not be the world's most scrutinized play. Rather, the play's fascination emanates from the many contradictions in the makeup of its central character. Commentators frequently suppose that Hamlet's problem, his "flaw," is that he procrastinates. Olivier begins his film with a voice-over proclaiming that *Hamlet* "is the tragedy of a man who cannot make up his mind." Such characterizations, however, provoke more questions than they answer. Does a procrastinator follow the "most horrible" spirit of his father despite the warnings of his friends whom he threatens to kill if they stop him? Can a man of inaction instantaneously devise a scheme to have traveling actors play "something like the murder of [his] father" (2.2.596)? He then quickly composes "some dozen or sixteen lines" to insert in their play. Does a man paralyzed by indecision leap into the grave of his betrothed to fight her brother as proof that "Forty thousand brothers / Could not with all their quantity of love / Make up the sum" of his love (5.1.272–273)?

Other erroneous perceptions cloud our view of this man fraught with inconsistencies:

- Hamlet has been called the consummate rationalist, yet throughout much of the play audiences can never be sure whether he is feigning madness or has indeed slipped into madness.
- We often refer to Hamlet as "a delicate and tender prince" (4.4.49, a phrase the Prince coins to describe Fortinbras) because he is repulsed at the thought of having to murder. Nonetheless he coolly dispatches his schoolmates, Rosencrantz and Guildenstern, to their deaths, saying they are "not near my conscience" (5.2.58).

- Although he is consumed by melancholy and frequently meditates on death, Hamlet is Shakespeare's only tragic hero with an enviable sense of humor. He speaks some of Shakespeare's wittiest lines as he mocks those about him—and himself.

- Ophelia tells us he is "the scholar's eye . . . the expectancy and rose of the fair state" (3.1.154–155; i.e., the ideal gentleman), yet he attacks her and his mother with crude language and insinuations.

- He will not kill himself because he fears that the Almighty has "fixed / His canon 'gainst self-slaughter" (1.2.131–132). Yet in 3.3, he deliberately refuses to kill his uncle, whom he knows to be his father's murderer, choosing to wait until he is certain that death will dispatch Claudius to eternal damnation, an act reserved for the Almighty Himself.

Hamlet is not unaware of the many contradictions in his nature. No Shakespearean character is alone on stage more than he, attempting in soliloquy to resolve his ambiguities. The soliloquies mark the Prince's movement from paralysis ("I must hold my tongue," see 1.2.129–159) to action ("from this time forth / My thoughts be bloody or be nothing worth," 4.4.66–67). That Hamlet entrusts us, his audience, with the privilege of sharing his innermost doubts further endears him to us.

The potentially oedipal aspect of Hamlet's character has emerged as a major consideration of theater directors during the past century. Because of Hamlet's apparent obsession with his mother's sex life, Sigmund Freud argues in *The Interpretations of Dreams* (1901) that the Prince "is able to do anything—except take vengeance on the man [Claudius] who did away with his father and took that father's place with his mother, the man who shows him the repressed wishes of his own childhood realized." Among others, psychologist Ernest Jones advances Freud's analysis in an influential study, *Hamlet and Oedipus* (1949). While few scholars endorse such readings, the oedipal implications of the Hamlet-Gertrude relationship are prominent in the films of Olivier (1948) and Zeffirelli (1990), as well as a number of stage productions.

The play's other characters are overshadowed by Shakespeare's extraordinary portrait of the Prince, but, as he does in so many of his plays, the playwright invests well-known stage characters from popular genres such as the revenge tragedy with complex human traits: a wicked uncle-king (Claudius); a garrulous and meddling counselor (Polonius); an innocent ingénue who becomes a pawn in the struggle among Elsinore's men (Ophelia); a fiery brother (Laertes); a faithful friend and confidant (Horatio, without whom Hamlet would require more soliloquies); manipulative and manipulated schoolmates (Rosencrantz and Guildenstern, who serve as foils to faithful Horatio). Ultimately all are destroyed in Denmark's courtly intrigues. Of the prin-

cipal roles, Gertrude emerges as epecially complex, torn as she is between her roles as queen-lover and mother-protector. For centuries scholars and actors have asked a central question about her: to what extent does she know about—or is involved in—the murder of Hamlet's father? The Ghost commands his son "to leave her [the Queen] to heaven" (1.5.87), an intriguingly ambiguous line that suggests guilt but that does not verify it.

For actors, the most intriguing secondary character is Polonius, who has been portrayed between the extremes of a comically meddlesome father and a ruthless Machiavel who plays the games at court well. Shakespeare's rich text supports a variety of readings for this "wretched, rash, intruding fool" (3.4.32). To illustrate, consider the testimony of Tony Church, who played the role twice for the Royal Shakespeare Company. In Peter Hall's 1964 production, Church characterized the old counselor as "an absolute bastard." Later (1980), under John Barton's direction, Church emphasized the benevolence in Polonius: "I played him as the good old man described by the Queen (4.1.12)." The audience's perception of Polonius affects its response to Hamlet's "rash and bloody deed" in 3.4. If the Prince kills a villainous counselor the tragic import is diminished; if he kills an essentially good man, then Hamlet—and his audience—experiences a moral shock as he senses that this murder will not go unpunished by the "divinity that shapes our ends" (5.2.10).

Even seemingly minor characters abet Hamlet as he acquires the knowledge to confront his dilemma. From Fortinbras, the future king of Denmark, Hamlet learns that

> Rightly to be great
> Is not to stir without great argument,
> But greatly to find quarrel in a straw
> When honor's at the stake.
>
> (4.4.56–57)

The Gravediggers, or Clowns, provoke Hamlet to an appreciation of the inevitability of death. Turning the practical need for gravediggers to thematic advantage, Shakespeare gives these homely men a significant role in contributing to Hamlet's awareness of life's transitory nature. Hamlet also learns much from long-dead Yorick, his father's jester who carried the child-prince "on [his] back a thousand times" (5.2.185). As he stands staring at Yorick's grinning skull, the Prince comprehends a truth that allows him to meet death with courage and peace of spirit. The rich result of Hamlet's thoughtfully acquired wisdom becomes evident in his explanation to Horatio as to why he will not attempt to evade destiny in the duel with Laertes: "The readiness is all. Since no man of aught he leaves knows, what is't to leave betimes? Let be" (5.2.220–222). Thus the man of infinite words accepts his fate—willingly? sardonically?—with the simplest of lines: "Let be." Ben Kingsley, who played Hamlet at

Stratford in 1978, says of this speech: "Very delicate, small words but they are mobilized by somebody who is almost at the end of his massive journey who now has the capacity, grace, and maturity to use 'a sparrow,' 'let be,' and 'not now.' They are tiny, tiny words that are immediately contagious to an audience."

Sources and Inspirations

The Spanish Tragedy

London's public theaters frequently offered patrons plays about "bloody and unnatural acts." *The Spanish Tragedy*, among the most popular dramas in England at the end of the sixteenth century, was written in approximately 1588 by Thomas Kyd. The success of *The Spanish Tragedy* initiated the vogue for the revenge tragedy in England. Though the British did not invent the genre —the Roman Seneca is usually credited with this feat— they made it a mainstay of their tradition. (Shakespeare's first tragedy, *Titus Andronicus* [c. 1593], is Senecan in its structure and themes.) Kyd's sensational, passionate drama, which includes a vengeful ghost that provokes the action, portrays a crazed father, Hieronimo, who attempts to avenge the death of his son, Horatio, by performing in a play re-enacting the son's death before the court. During the play-within-the-play, Hieronimo stabs one of his son's murderers, another actor in the tragedy. Rather than divulge his secrets to the court, Hieronimo stabs himself—but only after he "bites out his tongue." The play, with its gory sights that delighted London audiences, was often revived at the Rose and other theaters. An especially popular revival in 1598 may have prompted Shakespeare to write a play to compete with Kyd's work, which provides some incidents, character names, and even language for *Hamlet*. (For a thorough discussion of the similarities between Kyd's play and *Hamlet*, see Harold Jenkins's "Introduction" to The Arden Shakespeare *Hamlet*.)

Another play that some scholars believe influenced Shakespeare is the so-called *Ur-Hamlet*, perhaps written by Kyd. A 1589 pamphlet by Thomas Nashe suggests, via a pun on the playwright's name, that Kyd wrote an early version of the Hamlet story. Peter Alexander has suggested that the *Ur-Hamlet* was actually an early play written by the young Shakespeare; when he joined the Lord Chamberlain's Men in 1594 three news plays were added to the company's repertory, including one called *Hamlet*. Whether Kyd, Shakespeare, or an unknown author wrote the *Ur-Hamlet* is still debated, but it is clear that the early play includes many elements—the Ghost, the Laertes subplot, the play-within-the-play, and the climactic duel between the prince and his young rival—that are integral to the *Hamlet* of c. 1601.

Saxo Grammaticus and Belleforest

Kyd and the *Ur-Hamlet* notwithstanding, an ancient Viking saga remains the primary source of the Danish Prince's tragedy. The Norse myth of Amlothi (also: Amlethus, Amlodi) worked its way into the Elizabethan world through Saxo Grammaticus's *Historia Danica* ("History of the Danish People," c. 1180–1208). A French version by François de Belleforest (*Histories Tragiques*, 1576) significantly altered the Amlothi myth. In the ancient myth Amlothi is hardly the introspective character Shakespeare presents. Rather, he is a stern warrior who kills without qualms, setting fire to the King's courtiers whom he has ensnared in a tapestry, and dispatching his wicked Uncle Fen in a bloody sword fight. Amlothi convinces his people, the Jutlanders, that his cause is just, becomes king, and eventually dies during a battle in Britain. Belleforest's version builds upon the Norse myth by investing the Prince with a melancholy disposition and suggesting that the Prince's mother is an adulteress. Shakespeare's ability to meld a variety of popular works into a single play that has become the touchstone of Western literature further attests to his creative powers.

1601 is generally accepted as the date of the play's composition because the discussion of the "little eyases"—i.e., the children's acting companies—between Hamlet and Rosencrantz at 2.2.328–362 refers to specific events in London's theaters in 1601. It is possible, however, that this brief passage may have been inserted into a revision of an earlier text. That year, 1601, is an especially significant date in Shakespeare's private life: his father, John, died in September. Whether Shakespeare had written or was currently writing *Hamlet* when his father died cannot be known. In any event, *Hamlet* evinces a particular fascination with death, "The undiscovered country from whose bourn / No traveler returns" (3.1.80–81). The death of his father must have affected Shakespeare, the human being (Wells, 20–21). *Hamlet* offers an especially rich experience if we understand that the speeches by sons about their dead fathers were written by a man coming to terms with his own father's death. Stephen Greenblatt's new biography of Shakespeare (2004) provides a thoughtful reading of *Hamlet* as it reflects the playwright's grief for John Shakespeare's death (307–322).

Language and Music

Several images dominate the language of *Hamlet*, notably those describing corruption and decay. Marcellus declares that "Something is rotten in the state of Denmark" (1.4.90). The play contains many comparable images: "sterile promontory," "unweeded garden," "black and grainèd spots," "mildewed ear," "rank sweat of an enseamèd bed," "limèd soul," and "ulcerous place." While the recurring motif of decay creates a psychological ambience for the play, it also reinforces a principal idea: an evil act (fratricide, the primal sin) soils everyone, even as the corrupt maintain a pretense of virtue. Even Hamlet himself becomes affected by Elsinore's corruption as he denigrates Ophelia and his mother, slays an old man, and dispassionately arranges the death of his school friends. Only late in the play does the corruption destroy Claudius, "the enginer" who is ultimately "Hoist with his own petard" (3.4.213–214).

In this play of contradictions, base images are continually set against those of beauty and nobility. Horatio's description of the rising sun (1.1.172ff.) contrasts with the horror of the ghost's appearance. Throughout, the play moves from the beautiful to the harrowing, nowhere more so than in Hamlet's famous paean to humankind that begins with "What a piece of work is a man" only to conclude by negating all that he has said before: "And yet, to me, what is this quintessence of dust? Man delights not me" (2.2.304ff.). As much as any play in the canon, *Hamlet* explores the gap between our human ideals and the reality of our condition.

Hamlet represents Shakespeare's most ambitious attempt to that point in his career to create a psychological complexity in his characters through language. The Prince's diction, syntax, self-interruptions, contradictions, and other irregularities mirror his violent internal struggle to come to terms with a time that is "out of joint" (1.5.197). We find this particularly in the soliloquies, the first of which—"Oh, that this too too sullied flesh" (1.2.129–159)—provides an especially rich example of Hamlet's tortured thought. Though his language is as disjointed as the circumstances in which Hamlet finds himself, the very words he utters are the product of the skillful, deliberate artistry of the playwright. Shakespeare uses some six hundred words in *Hamlet* that he had not used in the previous twenty-plus plays and two long poems; indeed, many of these words cannot be found in the English language prior to this play (Greenblatt, 308). Shakespeare seems to have so completely entered the mind of his tragic hero that he was forced to create a language known only in Hamlet's world.

Anne Barton, whose criticism assesses the metatheatrical elements in Shakespeare's plays, notes that *Hamlet* is "unique in the density and pervasiveness of its theatrical self-reference" (Barton, 28). Obviously Hamlet's encounter with the traveling actors (2.2.42), his advice to the players (3.2.1–44), and the play-within-the-play lend themselves to the discourse of the theater. Yet theatrical language permeates the entire play. Hamlet talks about "actions that a man might play" (1.2.84), a phrase modern actors frequently use as they work. He assumes a role—a madman—when he puts on the "antic disposition" (1.5.181), and, after his encounter with the players in 2.2, he chastises himself for playing the villain poorly in the melodrama that is his life (see 2.2.550–606). He casts other characters in roles—Ophelia becomes a cheap whore who paints her face (3.1.144ff.), Claudius "a king of shreds and patches" out of the *commedia dell'arte* (3.4.106), and most especially his mother, whom he paints as an incestuous adulteress (1.2.157). For Hamlet the theater is a place where "guilty creatures sitting at a play" might be reformed (2.2.589–593). The preponderance of theater language in the play reinforces an essential Shakespearean concept: drama holds art's mirror up to itself "to remind the audience that elements of illusions are present in ordinary life, and that between the world and the stage there exists a complicated interplay of resemblance that is part of the perfection and nobility of the drama itself as a form" (Righter, 86).

Hamlet contains three songs of note. The hero sings a jaunty tune (3.2.269–282) to celebrate the triumph of the "mousetrap" he set for Claudius; while its message is obvious, the song sets up Hamlet's confrontation with Rosencrantz and Guildenstern (289–371) in which he makes bold threats to them and to the King. Musical references abound throughout this testy exchange. Ophelia's song before the dismayed court (4.5.23–67) is among the bawdiest songs found in Shakespeare. It reinforces—even parodies—Hamlet's preoccupation with his mother's sexuality. Whereas Hamlet apparently feigns madness, Ophelia has clearly become mad, and to the Elizabethans sexual obsessions were a sign of insanity. The Gravedigger's nonsensical ditty at 5.1.61–121 is an absurd rejoinder to Ophelia's raunchy tune even as he digs her grave.

Themes and Issues

No play in the history of the theater has generated more commentary than *Hamlet*. In 1964 the Polish critic Jan Kott observed that a bibliography of books and essays written about the play would be twice the size of the Warsaw telephone directory—and the volume of *Hamlet* analyses has increased exponentially since then as further complexities of meaning and alternative approaches to critical methodologies have emerged. A brief sampling of a half-dozen twentieth-century commentators on a *possible* (not *the*) meaning of *Hamlet* suggests only a few of the many concerns the play raises:

- *Hamlet* as a religious treatise:

   "While Hamlet certainly cannot be called in the specific sense a "religious drama," there is in it nevertheless both a freer use of popular religious ideas, and a more decided, though always imaginative, intimation of a supreme power concerned in human evil and good, than can be found in any other of Shakespeare's tragedies."

   (A. C. Bradley, Shakespearean Tragedy, 1904)

- *Hamlet* as a cry of despair:

"Hamlet's soul is sick. The symptoms are horror at the fact of death and an equal detestation of life, a sense of uncleanliness and evil in things of nature; a disgust at the physical body of man; bitterness, cynicism, hate . . . He can describe the glories of heaven and earth—but for him those glories are gone."
(G. Wilson Knight, *The Wheel of Fire*, 1930)

- *Hamlet* as an interrogation into the human condition:

"Hamlet opens with a question: "Who's there?" and seems to lie closer to the illogical logic of life than Shakespeare's other tragedies . . . Hamlet's world is pre-eminently in the interrogative mood. It reverberates with questions, anguished, meditative, alarmed. There are questions that in this play, to an extent I think unparalleled in any other, mark the phases and even nuances of the action, helping to establish its peculiar baffled tone."
(Maynard Mack, "The World of *Hamlet*," 1952)

- *Hamlet* as an existentialist tract:

"Every Hamlet has a book in his hand. What book would the modern Hamlet read? Hamlet in the Krakow [Poland] production in the late autumn of 1956 read only newspapers. He shouted "Denmark's a prison," and wanted to improve the world. He was a rebellious ideologist and lived only for action. Hamlet in the Warsaw production of 1959 was full of doubts again; and again was "the sad boy with a book in his hand." We can easily visualize him in black sweater and jeans. The book he is holding is not by Montaigne, but by Sartre, Camus, or Kafka . . . he is tormented by thought of the fundamental absurdity of existence."
(Jan Kott, *Shakespeare Our Contemporary*, 1964)

- *Hamlet* as a political document:

"The question whether it is nobler to suffer in Christian patience or to take arms against a secular injustice is not resolved in [revenge] plays. It is ultimately a question about authority—God's, the sovereign's or the subjects. To the extent that the plays condemn revenge, they stay within orthodoxy which permits only passive disobedience and prescribes no remedy for the subject when the sovereign breaks the law. But in order to be revenge plays at all, they are compelled to throw into relief the social and political weaknesses of this ethical and political position. To the extent that they consequently endorse revenge, they participate in the installation of the sovereign subject, entitled to take action in accordance with conscience and on behalf of law."
(Catherine Belsey, *The Subject of Tragedy: Identity and Difference in Renaissance Drama*, 1985)

- *Hamlet* as feminist discourse:

"In their brief appearances, Ophelia and the Queen illustrate the destructiveness for women of adopting

an alien set of values . . . .In [Hamlet] Shakespeare explores some of the ways in which male dominance and patriarchal expectations can warp women's lives.
(Irene Dash, *Women's Worlds in Shakespeare's Plays*, 1997)

Staging Challenges

Which Text?—And How Do We Cut It?

The textual problems of *Hamlet* are as complicated as the interpretive ones. Three texts survive from the seventeenth century.

1. The first is the so-called "Unauthorized Quarto" (Q1): This edition, sometimes erroneously referred to as "the Bad Quarto," seems to have been a memorial reconstruction by actors who toured the play and had no authoritative script. Perhaps the actor playing Marcellus jotted down the play as he heard it backstage and sold it to a printer in c. 1603. Marcellus's lines, as well as those of minor characters (Lucianus, Voltimand), are remarkably accurate to the other scripts, while much of Q1 is a mishmash of only 2154 lines. Some scholars argue that Q1 is either a fragment of the *Ur-Hamlet* or the remnant of a scaled-down touring version of the play performed in the provinces. (The 1603 text claims the play was performed at Cambridge and Oxford.)

2. The second is the "Authorized Quarto" (Q2): In c. 1604 the King's Men, aggrieved by the publication of Q1, apparently took pains to publish "the true and perfect Coppie" of the playing text (3723 lines) Shakespeare wrote. It is the most complete and most accepted version of the play.

3. The third is the 1623 Folio (F): Published seven years after Shakespeare's death by the actors who worked with the playwright, this edition is compatible with Q2, with some notable exceptions. It is about two hundred lines shorter than Q2.

There are notable differences among the three versions, such as the location of the "To be or not to be" soliloquy. As located in Q2 and in the Folio, immediately before the Nunnery Scene with Ophelia, the soliloquy seems decidedly contrary to Hamlet's previous speech—the "Oh, what a rogue and peasant slave" soliloquy that concludes Act 2 with the hope that Hamlet will catch the conscience of the King. Contrastingly, in Q1 the speech is placed *after* the Nunnery Scene, which itself appears in Act 2 after Polonius tells Claudius that he will "loose his daughter on the Prince." Q1's placement of the soliloquy is thus at variance with that of Q2 and the Folio. A number of stage productions such as Edwin Booth's, as well as the

Olivier and Zeffirelli films, have relocated the soliloquy to another scene in the play.

The version of *Hamlet* printed in the present edition is probably longer than any version acted during Shakespeare's day. At almost four thousand lines the play wants cutting for the stage, although this anthology includes Q2 and lines found only in the First Folio to create the fullest coherent text for *reading*. The play must have been trimmed in Shakespeare's time, especially as daylight grew short in London. *Hamlet*, like so many of Shakespeare's texts, was altered and abridged by succeeding generations of theater artists whose audiences could not tolerate a four-hour–plus production, or, during certain centuries, the so-called "mixing" of comic scenes with tragic. Branagh's 1996 film boldly attempts to present the "complete text" because "with the full text, the gravitational weight of the play seemed to increase" (Branagh, xiv). True, but the practical exigencies of theater production do not usually allow the luxury afforded Branagh. Directors usually approach a production of *Hamlet* asking, "Where does one begin to cut the world's most famous play?"

Old Hamlet's Ghost

Like *Macbeth*, *Hamlet* opens with an eerie scene in which the supernatural hovers over the landscape. Soldiers standing watch in the chilly Denmark air jump at shadows because they have seen a ghost stalking Elsinore Castle. Shakespeare is quite specific that the Ghost is dressed in "fair and warlike form" (1.1.51)—that is, as a soldier. The watchmen, Horatio, and even Hamlet are terrified at the sight of the Ghost, and the audience ought to experience this fear to enter the tormented Prince's mind. Grigori Kozintsev's 1964 film presents a towering ghost with an enormous billowing cloak. At the other end of the spectrum, Tony Richardson's 1968 production at London's Roundhouse (and later on film) did not show the Ghost: a multitrack stereo system suggested that the spirit floated about the darkened theater while only a tiny beam of light played upon Hamlet's face, which seemed suspended in space. Both approaches—the spectacular and the minimalist—can effectively set a tone for the Ghost's horrific revelations.

In what may have been a theatrical first, John Barton's RSC production (1980) allowed Gertrude to see the Ghost during the Closet Scene (3.4). As Hamlet knelt facing his mother, the Ghost entered from behind her. At first the Queen is baffled by Hamlet's stare ("you do bend your eye on vacancy"), prompting Hamlet to take her gently by the head and turn it toward the Ghost at "Why, look you there" (l.140). Gertrude fainted as the Ghost reached out to touch her. Barton intensified the scene by splicing 3.4 onto 4.1 (deleting the King's first speech). The Queen knelt humbly and greeted Claudius with "Ah, mine own lord, what I have

seen tonight!" Tony Church (Polonius) defended Barton's innovation: "It doesn't interfere with the text. It's extraordinary that she doesn't see him [as do the soldiers and Horatio] . . . surely every Gertrude has asked this question in rehearsal." Of Barton's audacious invention Irving Wardle, theater critic of the London *Times*, said: "You can hear the ice cracking all round, but thanks to the preparation that has gone into it, the surface just holds" (July 3, 1980).

The Players and the Dumb Show

The traveling players, who arrive at Elsinore at precisely the time Hamlet needs them most, embody the play-life theme that permeates this and to a lesser extent every other Shakespearean play. The contemporary British playwright Tom Stoppard elevates them to principal-role status in his wittily absurdist retelling of the Hamlet story from the bit players' point of view, *Rosencrantz and Guildenstern Are Dead* (1966, see below, p. 633). The Player King and his colleagues provide a colorful interlude in the midst of Elsinore's gloom, while also validating Hamlet's belief that "The play's the thing" to expose malefactions (2.2.605). Their performance of "The Murder of Gonzago" exposes Claudius's wicked deeds; just as importantly, the Player King's recital (2.2.450–518) about the Greek warrior Pyrrhus, who must avenge *his* father's death, motivates Hamlet. Thus the Players transcend their performance and emerge as a mystical force that, much like the pirates who intervene to return Hamlet to England, teach the Prince that there is indeed "special providence in the fall of a sparrow" (5.2.217–218)—or the apparition of traveling players. In the Barton production, the Players emerged eerily from—and later disappeared into—the black void of the upstage recesses of the theater. In contrast to the "Players Have Arrived" tumble of gaudy costumes and tambourines found in most productions, this group of drably costumed actors merely appeared and disappeared much like the Ghost in Act 1.

Hamlet's Treatment of Women

In his first soliloquy Hamlet, frustrated by his mother's o'erhasty marriage to his uncle, cries, "frailty, thy name is woman!" (1.2.146) Later, Ophelia's apparent duplicity in the Claudius-Polonius scheme to spy on Hamlet compounds the Prince's disillusionment with women. To what extent do Hamlet's perceptions of women, particularly the two women dearest to him, translate into verbal and/or physical violence? The question must be asked by actors because their answers affect the degree to which audiences sympathize with Hamlet. In 3.1 (the Nunnery Scene) and 3.4 (the Closet Scene, i.e., Gertrude's bedchamber) Hamlet angrily rebukes Ophelia and then his mother. The text allows for the potential of physical violence, and bits of stage business toward that end have become increasingly prominent on stage and in film. After Ophelia assures Hamlet that her father is "At home, my lord" (3.1.132), the Prince flies into a rage because he seems to know that Polonius is eavesdropping on them, probably with Claudius. Convinced that his love has betrayed him, Hamlet verbally assaults her and then—in many productions—grasps her chin in his hand at "God hath given you one face," etc. In the BBC television production (1980) Derek Jacobi enacts this traditional business as he forces her to the floor; he stops suddenly to say "It *hath* made me mad" (l.149) as a stunning realization that he has indeed lost his reason, as predicted by Horatio (1.5.73–74). Hamlet similarly berates his mother in 3.4: actors often physically force Gertrude to look at the pictures of her first and second husbands (3.4.54ff.), justifying such aggressive behavior because, they argue, the audience must witness the extent to which Hamlet feels the necessity of turning his mother's life around. If, however, physical violence is "overdone or come tardy off" (3.2.25), the actor risks alienating the audience's sympathy for Hamlet. Perhaps inspired by John Osborne's seminal play, *Look Back in Anger* (1956), in the 1960s and 1970s actors such as Nicol Williamson and Steven Berkoff played Hamlet as an "angry young man," even as a boorish lout, often to the detriment of the play's tragic impact.

The Graveyard

Hamlet and Horatio pass through the graveyard adjacent to the castle as the Prince returns to Elsinore. After Hamlet's encounter with the gravediggers and Yorick's skull, he discovers the funeral cortège carrying Ophelia to her burial site. The scene represents a curious mixture of emotions: it runs from broad comedy (the banter between Hamlet and the First Clown), to philosophic introspection (Hamlet's meditation on death), to heroic bravado ("This is I, / Hamlet the Dane!" 5.1.257–258), and finally to violent action as Laertes and Hamlet grapple with each other in Ophelia's grave. Michael Pennington, who played Hamlet at Stratford-upon-Avon in 1980, says of the moment: "The fight is ridiculous and ugly: there is no room, and there is a dead body . . . and the exercise of pulling men out [of the grave] is ungainly and difficult . . . everybody is at their worst" (Pennington, 139). Shakespeare apparently scripts the scene to provide a visual metaphor emphasizing the rot that has infected Denmark. Nonetheless, as Pennington suggests, the fight in the grave must be staged with care or this crucial moment can lapse into an absurd farce.

Hamlet, Prince of Denmark

[*Dramatis Personae*

GHOST *of Hamlet, the former King of Denmark*
CLAUDIUS, *King of Denmark, the former King's brother*
GERTRUDE, *Queen of Denmark, widow of the former King and now wife of Claudius*
HAMLET, *Prince of Denmark, son of the late King and of Gertrude*

POLONIUS, *councillor to the King*
LAERTES, *his son*
OPHELIA, *his daughter*
REYNALDO, *his servant*

HORATIO, *Hamlet's friend and fellow student*

VOLTIMAND,
CORNELIUS,
ROSENCRANTZ,
GUILDENSTERN, } *members of the Danish court*
OSRIC,
A GENTLEMAN,
A LORD,

BERNARDO,
FRANCISCO, } *officers and soldiers on watch*
MARCELLUS,

FORTINBRAS, *Prince of Norway*
CAPTAIN *in his army*

Three or Four PLAYERS, *taking the roles of* PROLOGUE, PLAYER KING, PLAYER QUEEN, *and* LUCIANUS
Two MESSENGERS
FIRST SAILOR
Two CLOWNS, *a gravedigger and his companion*
PRIEST
FIRST AMBASSADOR *from England*

Lords, Soldiers, Attendants, Guards, other Players, Followers of Laertes, other Sailors, another Ambassador or Ambassadors from England

SCENE: *Denmark*]

[1.1]

Enter Bernardo and Francisco, two sentinels,
[meeting].

BERNARDO   Who's there?

FRANCISCO

Nay, answer me. Stand and unfold yourself.   2

BERNARDO   Long live the King!

FRANCISCO   Bernardo?

BERNARDO   He.

FRANCISCO

You come most carefully upon your hour.

BERNARDO

'Tis now struck twelve. Get thee to bed, Francisco.

FRANCISCO

For this relief much thanks. 'Tis bitter cold,
And I am sick at heart.

BERNARDO   Have you had quiet guard?

FRANCISCO   Not a mouse stirring.

BERNARDO   Well, good night.

If you do meet Horatio and Marcellus,
The rivals of my watch, bid them make haste.   14

Enter Horatio and Marcellus.

FRANCISCO

I think I hear them.—Stand, ho! Who is there?

HORATIO   Friends to this ground.   16

MARCELLUS   And liegemen to the Dane.   17

FRANCISCO   Give you good night.   18

MARCELLUS

Oh, farewell, honest soldier. Who hath relieved you?

FRANCISCO

Bernardo hath my place. Give you good night.

Exit Francisco.

MARCELLUS   Holla! Bernardo!

BERNARDO   Say, what, is Horatio there?

HORATIO   A piece of him.

BERNARDO

Welcome, Horatio. Welcome, good Marcellus.

HORATIO

What, has this thing appeared again tonight?

BERNARDO   I have seen nothing.

MARCELLUS

Horatio says 'tis but our fantasy,   27
And will not let belief take hold of him
Touching this dreaded sight twice seen of us.
Therefore I have entreated him along   30
With us to watch the minutes of this night,   31
That if again this apparition come
He may approve our eyes and speak to it.   33

HORATIO

Tush, tush, 'twill not appear.

BERNARDO   Sit down awhile

And let us once again assail your ears,
That are so fortified against our story,
What we have two nights seen.

HORATIO   Well, sit we down,
And let us hear Bernardo speak of this.

BERNARDO   Last night of all,   39
When yond same star that's westward from the pole   40
Had made his course t'illume that part of heaven   41
Where now it burns, Marcellus and myself,
The bell then beating one—

Enter Ghost.

MARCELLUS

Peace, break thee off! Look where it comes again!

BERNARDO

In the same figure like the King that's dead.

MARCELLUS

Thou art a scholar. Speak to it, Horatio.   46

BERNARDO

Looks 'a not like the King? Mark it, Horatio.   47

HORATIO

Most like. It harrows me with fear and wonder.

BERNARDO

It would be spoke to.

MARCELLUS   Speak to it, Horatio.   49

HORATIO

What art thou that usurp'st this time of night,   50
Together with that fair and warlike form
In which the majesty of buried Denmark   52
Did sometimes march? By heaven, I charge thee, speak! 53

MARCELLUS

It is offended.

BERNARDO   See, it stalks away.

HORATIO

Stay! Speak, speak! I charge thee, speak!   *Exit Ghost.*

MARCELLUS   'Tis gone and will not answer.

BERNARDO

How now, Horatio? You tremble and look pale.
Is not this something more than fantasy?
What think you on't?   59

HORATIO

Before my God, I might not this believe
Without the sensible and true avouch   61
Of mine own eyes.

MARCELLUS   Is it not like the King?

HORATIO   As thou art to thyself.

Such was the very armor he had on
When he the ambitious Norway combated.   65
So frowned he once when, in an angry parle,   66
He smote the sledded Polacks on the ice.   67
'Tis strange.

1.1 **Location: Elsinore castle. A guard platform.**
2 **me** (Francisco emphasizes that *he* is the sentry currently on watch.)
unfold yourself reveal your identity.   14 **rivals** partners   16 **ground**
country, land.   17 **liegemen to the Dane** men sworn to serve the
Danish king.   18 **Give** May God give   27 **fantasy** imagination
30 **along** to come along   31 **watch** keep watch during   33 **approve**
corroborate

39 **Last . . . all** i.e., This *very* last night. (Emphatic.)   40 **pole** polestar,
north star   41 **his** its.   **t'illume** to illuminate   46 **scholar** one
learned enough to know how to question a ghost properly.   47 **'a** he
49 **It . . . to** (It was commonly believed that a ghost could not speak
until spoken to.)   50 **usurp'st** wrongfully takes over   52 **buried
Denmark** the buried King of Denmark   53 **sometimes** formerly
59 **on't** of it.   61 **sensible** confirmed by the senses.   **avouch** warrant,
evidence   65 **Norway** King of Norway   66 **parle** parley   67 **sledded**
traveling on sleds.   **Polacks** Poles

MARCELLUS
Thus twice before, and jump at this dead hour,   69
With martial stalk hath he gone by our watch.   70

HORATIO
In what particular thought to work I know not,   71
But in the gross and scope of mine opinion   72
This bodes some strange eruption to our state.

MARCELLUS
Good now, sit down, and tell me, he that knows,   74
Why this same strict and most observant watch
So nightly toils the subject of the land,   76
And why such daily cast of brazen cannon   77
And foreign mart for implements of war,   78
Why such impress of shipwrights, whose sore task   79
Does not divide the Sunday from the week.
What might be toward, that this sweaty haste   81
Doth make the night joint-laborer with the day?
Who is't that can inform me?

HORATIO   That can I;
At least, the whisper goes so. Our last king,
Whose image even but now appeared to us,
Was, as you know, by Fortinbras of Norway,
Thereto pricked on by a most emulate pride,   87
Dared to the combat; in which our valiant Hamlet—
For so this side of our known world esteemed him—   89
Did slay this Fortinbras; who by a sealed compact   90
Well ratified by law and heraldry   91
Did forfeit, with his life, all those his lands
Which he stood seized of, to the conqueror;   93
Against the which a moiety competent   94
Was gagèd by our king, which had returned   95
To the inheritance of Fortinbras   96
Had he been vanquisher, as, by the same cov'nant   97
And carriage of the article designed,   98
His fell to Hamlet. Now, sir, young Fortinbras,
Of unimprovèd mettle hot and full,   100
Hath in the skirts of Norway here and there   101
Sharked up a list of lawless resolutes   102
For food and diet to some enterprise   103
That hath a stomach in't, which is no other—   104
As it doth well appear unto our state—
But to recover of us, by strong hand
And terms compulsatory, those foresaid lands
So by his father lost. And this, I take it,
Is the main motive of our preparations,

The source of this our watch, and the chief head   110
Of this posthaste and rummage in the land.   111

BERNARDO
I think it be no other but e'en so.
Well may it sort that this portentous figure   113
Comes armèd through our watch so like the King
That was and is the question of these wars.   115

HORATIO
A mote it is to trouble the mind's eye.   116
In the most high and palmy state of Rome,   117
A little ere the mightiest Julius fell,   118
The graves stood tenantless, and the sheeted dead   119
Did squeak and gibber in the Roman streets;
As stars with trains of fire and dews of blood,   121
Disasters in the sun; and the moist star   122
Upon whose influence Neptune's empire stands   123
Was sick almost to doomsday with eclipse.   124
And even the like precurse of feared events,   125
As harbingers preceding still the fates   126
And prologue to the omen coming on,   127
Have heaven and earth together demonstrated
Unto our climatures and countrymen.   129

        Enter Ghost.

But soft, behold! Lo, where it comes again!   130
I'll cross it, though it blast me. (*It spreads his arms.*) Stay,
        illusion!   131
If thou hast any sound or use of voice,
Speak to me!
If there be any good thing to be done
That may to thee do ease and grace to me,
Speak to me!
If thou art privy to thy country's fate,   137
Which, happily, foreknowing may avoid,   138
Oh, speak!
Or if thou hast uphoarded in thy life
Extorted treasure in the womb of earth,
For which, they say, you spirits oft walk in death,
Speak of it! (*The cock crows.*) Stay and speak!—Stop it,
        Marcellus.

MARCELLUS
Shall I strike at it with my partisan?   144
HORATIO   Do, if it will not stand.   [*They strike at it.*]
BERNARDO   'Tis here!   146
HORATIO   'Tis here!   [*Exit Ghost.*] 147

---

69 jump exactly **70 stalk** stride **71 to work** i.e., to collect my thoughts and try to understand this **72 gross and scope** general drift **74 Good now** (An expression denoting entreaty or expostulation.) **76 toils** causes to toil. **subject** subjects **77 cast** casting **78 mart** shopping **79 impress** impressment, conscription **81 toward** in preparation **87 Thereto . . . pride** (Refers to old Fortinbras, not the Danish King.) **pricked on** incited. **emulate** emulous, ambitious **89 this . . . world** i.e., all Europe, the Western world **90 sealed** certified, confirmed **91 heraldry** chivalry **93 seized** possessed **94 Against the** in return for. **moiety competent** corresponding portion **95 gagèd** engaged, pledged. **had returned** would have passed **96 inheritance** possession **97 cov'nant** i.e., the *sealed compact* of line 90 **98 carriage . . . designed** purport of the article referred to **100 unimprovèd mettle** untried, undisciplined spirits **101 skirts** outlying regions, outskirts **102–4 Sharked . . . in't** rounded up (as a shark scoops up fish) a troop of lawless desperadoes to feed and supply an enterprise of considerable daring

110 head source **111 posthaste and rummage** frenetic activity and bustle **113 Well . . . sort** That would explain why **115 question** focus of contention **116 mote** speck of dust **117 palmy** flourishing **118 Julius** Julius Caesar **119 sheeted** shrouded **121 As** (This abrupt transition suggests that matter is possibly omitted between lines 120 and 121.) **trains** trails **122 Disasters** unfavorable signs or aspects. **moist star** i.e., moon, governing tides **123 Neptune's . . . stands** the sea depends **124 Was . . . eclipse** was eclipsed nearly to the cosmic darkness predicted for the second coming of Christ and the ending of the world. (See Matthew 24:29 and Revelation 6:12.) **125 precurse** heralding, foreshadowing **126 harbingers** forerunners. **still** always **127 omen** calamitous event **129 climatures** climes, regions **130 soft** i.e., enough, break off **131 cross** stand in its path, confront. **blast** wither, strike with a curse. **131 s.d. his** its **137 privy to** in on the secret of **138 happily** haply, perchance **144 partisan** long-handled spear. **146–7 'Tis Here! / 'Tis here!** (Perhaps they attempt to strike at the Ghost, but are baffled by its seeming ability to be here and there and nowhere.)

MARCELLUS 'Tis gone.
We do it wrong, being so majestical,
To offer it the show of violence,
For it is as the air invulnerable,
And our vain blows malicious mockery.

BERNARDO
It was about to speak when the cock crew.

HORATIO
And then it started like a guilty thing
Upon a fearful summons. I have heard
The cock, that is the trumpet to the morn,   156
Doth with his lofty and shrill-sounding throat
Awake the god of day, and at his warning,
Whether in sea or fire, in earth or air,
Th'extravagant and erring spirit hies   160
To his confine; and of the truth herein
This present object made probation.   162

MARCELLUS
It faded on the crowing of the cock.
Some say that ever 'gainst that season comes   164
Wherein our Savior's birth is celebrated,
This bird of dawning singeth all night long,
And then, they say, no spirit dare stir abroad;
The nights are wholesome, then no planets strike,   168
No fairy takes, nor witch hath power to charm,   169
So hallowed and so gracious is that time.   170

HORATIO
So have I heard and do in part believe it.
But, look, the morn in russet mantle clad   172
Walks o'er the dew of yon high eastward hill.
Break we our watch up, and by my advice
Let us impart what we have seen tonight
Unto young Hamlet; for upon my life,
This spirit, dumb to us, will speak to him.
Do you consent we shall acquaint him with it,
As needful in our loves, fitting our duty?

MARCELLUS
Let's do't, I pray, and I this morning know
Where we shall find him most conveniently.
                                                    Exeunt.

❖

[1.2]

*Flourish. Enter Claudius, King of Denmark,
Gertrude the Queen, [the] Council, as Polonius
and his son Laertes, Hamlet, cum aliis [including
Voltimand and Cornelius].*

KING
Though yet of Hamlet our dear brother's death   1
The memory be green, and that it us befitted
To bear our hearts in grief and our whole kingdom

To be contracted in one brow of woe,
Yet so far hath discretion fought with nature
That we with wisest sorrow think on him
Together with remembrance of ourselves.
Therefore our sometime sister, now our queen,   8
Th'imperial jointress to this warlike state,   9
Have we, as 'twere with a defeated joy—
With an auspicious and a dropping eye,   11
With mirth in funeral and with dirge in marriage,
In equal scale weighing delight and dole—   13
Taken to wife. Nor have we herein barred
Your better wisdoms, which have freely gone
With this affair along. For all, our thanks.
Now follows that you know young Fortinbras,   17
Holding a weak supposal of our worth,   18
Or thinking by our late dear brother's death
Our state to be disjoint and out of frame,   20
Co-leaguèd with this dream of his advantage,   21
He hath not failed to pester us with message
Importing the surrender of those lands   23
Lost by his father, with all bonds of law,   24
To our most valiant brother. So much for him.
Now for ourself and for this time of meeting.
Thus much the business is: we have here writ
To Norway, uncle of young Fortinbras—
Who, impotent and bed-rid, scarcely hears   29
Of this his nephew's purpose—to suppress
His further gait herein, in that the levies,   31
The lists, and full proportions are all made   32
Out of his subject; and we here dispatch   33
You, good Cornelius, and you, Voltimand,
For bearers of this greeting to old Norway,
Giving to you no further personal power
To business with the King more than the scope
Of these dilated articles allow.   [*He gives a paper.*]   38
Farewell, and let your haste commend your duty.   39

CORNELIUS, VOLTIMAND
In that, and all things, will we show our duty.

KING
We doubt it nothing. Heartily farewell.   41
                [*Exeunt Voltimand and Cornelius.*]
And now, Laertes, what's the news with you?
You told us of some suit; what is't, Laertes?
You cannot speak of reason to the Dane   44
And lose your voice. What wouldst thou beg, Laertes,   45
That shall not be my offer, not thy asking?
The head is not more native to the heart,   47

---

156 **trumpet** trumpeter   160 **extravagant and erring** wandering
beyond bounds. (The words have similar meaning.)   **hies** hastens
162 **probation** proof.   164 **'gainst** just before   168 **strike** destroy by
evil influence   169 **takes** bewitches.   **charm** cast a spell, control by
enchantment   170 **gracious** full of grace   172 **russet** reddish brown
1.2 Location: The castle.
0.2 *as* i.e., such as, including.   0.3 *cum aliis* with others   1 **our** my.
(The royal "we"; also in the following lines.)

8 **sometime** former   9 **jointress** woman possessing property with
her husband   11 **With . . . eye** with one eye smiling and the other
weeping   13 **dole** grief   17 **Now . . . know** Next, you need to be
informed that   18 **weak supposal** low estimate   20 **disjoint . . .
frame** in a state of total disorder   21 **Co-leaguèd . . . advantage**
joined to his illusory sense of having the advantage over us and to
his vision of future success   23 **Importing** having for its substance
24 **with . . . law** (See 1.1.91, "Well ratified by law and heraldry.")
29 **impotent** helpless   31 **His** i.e., Fortinbras'.   **gait** proceeding
31–3 **in that . . . subject** since the levying of troops and supplies is
drawn entirely from the King of Norway's own subjects   38 **dilated**
set out at length   39 **let . . . duty** let your swift obeying of orders,
rather than mere words, express your dutifulness.   41 **nothing** not
at all.   44 **the Dane** the Danish king   45 **lose your voice** waste your
speech.   47 **native** closely connected, related

The hand more instrumental to the mouth,   48
Than is the throne of Denmark to thy father.
What wouldst thou have, Laertes?

LAERTES   My dread lord,
Your leave and favor to return to France,   51
From whence though willingly I came to Denmark
To show my duty in your coronation,
Yet now I must confess, that duty done,
My thoughts and wishes bend again toward France
And bow them to your gracious leave and pardon.   56

KING
Have you your father's leave? What says Polonius?

POLONIUS
H'ath, my lord, wrung from me my slow leave   58
By laborsome petition, and at last
Upon his will I sealed my hard consent.   60
I do beseech you, give him leave to go.

KING
Take thy fair hour, Laertes. Time be thine,   62
And thy best graces spend it at thy will.   63
But now, my cousin Hamlet, and my son—   64

HAMLET
A little more than kin, and less than kind.   65

KING
How is it that the clouds still hang on you?

HAMLET
Not so, my lord. I am too much in the sun.   67

QUEEN
Good Hamlet, cast thy nighted color off,   68
And let thine eye look like a friend on Denmark.   69
Do not forever with thy vailèd lids   70
Seek for thy noble father in the dust.
Thou know'st 'tis common, all that lives must die,   72
Passing through nature to eternity.

HAMLET
Ay, madam, it is common.

QUEEN   If it be,
Why seems it so particular with thee?   75

HAMLET
Seems, madam? Nay, it is. I know not "seems."
'Tis not alone my inky cloak, good mother,
Nor customary suits of solemn black,   78
Nor windy suspiration of forced breath,   79

No, nor the fruitful river in the eye,   80
Nor the dejected havior of the visage,   81
Together with all forms, moods, shapes of grief,   82
That can denote me truly. These indeed seem,
For they are actions that a man might play.
But I have that within which passes show;
These but the trappings and the suits of woe.

KING
'Tis sweet and commendable in your nature, Hamlet,
To give these mourning duties to your father.
But you must know your father lost a father,
That father lost, lost his, and the survivor bound
In filial obligation for some term
To do obsequious sorrow. But to persever   92
In obstinate condolement is a course   93
Of impious stubbornness. 'Tis unmanly grief.
It shows a will most incorrect to heaven,
A heart unfortified, a mind impatient,   96
An understanding simple and unschooled.   97
For what we know must be and is as common
As any the most vulgar thing to sense,   99
Why should we in our peevish opposition
Take it to heart? Fie, 'tis a fault to heaven,
A fault against the dead, a fault to nature,
To reason most absurd, whose common theme
Is death of fathers, and who still hath cried,   104
From the first corpse till he that died today,   105
"This must be so." We pray you, throw to earth
This unprevailing woe and think of us   107
As of a father; for let the world take note,
You are the most immediate to our throne,   109
And with no less nobility of love
Than that which dearest father bears his son
Do I impart toward you. For your intent   112
In going back to school in Wittenberg,   113
It is most retrograde to our desire,   114
And we beseech you bend you to remain   115
Here in the cheer and comfort of our eye,
Our chiefest courtier, cousin, and our son.

QUEEN
Let not thy mother lose her prayers, Hamlet.
I pray thee, stay with us, go not to Wittenberg.

HAMLET
I shall in all my best obey you, madam.   120

KING
Why, 'tis a loving and a fair reply.
Be as ourself in Denmark. Madam, come.
This gentle and unforced accord of Hamlet
Sits smiling to my heart, in grace whereof   124
No jocund health that Denmark drinks today   125

---

48 instrumental serviceable   **51 leave and favor** kind permission **56 bow . . . pardon** entreatingly make a deep bow, asking your permission to depart.   **58 H'ath** He has   **60 sealed** (as if sealing a legal document).   **hard** reluctant   **62 Take thy fair hour** Enjoy your time of youth   **63 And . . . will** and may your time be spent in exercising your best qualities.   **64 cousin** any kin not of the immediate family **65 A little . . . kind** Too close a blood relation, and yet we are less than kinsmen in that our relationship lacks affection and is indeed unnatural. (Hamlet plays on *kind* as [1] kindly [2] belonging to nature, suggesting that Claudius is not the same kind of being as the rest of humanity. The line is often delivered as an aside, though it need not be.)   **67 the sun** i.e., the sunshine of the King's royal favor. (With pun on *son*.)   **68 nighted color** (1) mourning garments of black (2) dark melancholy   **69 Denmark** the King of Denmark.   **70 vailèd lids** lowered eyes   **72 common** of universal occurrence. (But Hamlet plays on the sense of "vulgar" in line 74.)   **75 particular** personal **78 customary** customary to mourning   **79 suspiration** sighing

80 fruitful abundant   **81 havior** expression   **82 moods** outward expression of feeling   **92 obsequious** suited to obsequies or funerals **93 condolement** sorrowing   **96 unfortified** i.e., against adversity **97 simple** ignorant   **99 As . . . sense** as the most ordinary experience **104 still** always   **105 the first corpse** (Abel's)   **107 unprevailing** unavailing, useless   **109 most immediate** next in succession **112 impart toward** liberally bestow on.   **For** As for   **113 to school** i.e., to your studies.   **Wittenberg** famous German university founded in 1502   **114 retrograde** contrary   **115 bend you** incline yourself **120 in all my best** to the best of my ability   **124 to** i.e., at.   **grace** thanksgiving   **125 jocund** merry

But the great cannon to the clouds shall tell,
And the King's rouse the heaven shall bruit again, 127
Respeaking earthly thunder. Come away. 128

Flourish. Exeunt all but Hamlet.

HAMLET
Oh, that this too too sullied flesh would melt, 129
Thaw, and resolve itself into a dew!
Or that the Everlasting had not fixed
His canon 'gainst self-slaughter! Oh, God, God, 132
How weary, stale, flat, and unprofitable
Seem to me all the uses of this world!
Fie on't, ah fie! 'Tis an unweeded garden
That grows to seed. Things rank and gross in nature
Possess it merely. That it should come to this! 137
But two months dead—nay, not so much, not two.
So excellent a king, that was to this 139
Hyperion to a satyr, so loving to my mother 140
That he might not beteem the winds of heaven 141
Visit her face too roughly. Heaven and earth,
Must I remember? Why, she would hang on him
As if increase of appetite had grown
By what it fed on, and yet within a month—
Let me not think on't; frailty, thy name is woman!—
A little month, or ere those shoes were old 147
With which she followed my poor father's body,
Like Niobe, all tears, why she, even she— 149
Oh, God, a beast, that wants discourse of reason, 150
Would have mourned longer—married with my
    uncle,
My father's brother, but no more like my father
Than I to Hercules. Within a month,
Ere yet the salt of most unrighteous tears
Had left the flushing in her gallèd eyes, 155
She married. Oh, most wicked speed, to post 156
With such dexterity to incestuous sheets! 157
It is not, nor it cannot come to good.
But break, my heart, for I must hold my tongue.

Enter Horatio, Marcellus, and Bernardo.

HORATIO
Hail to Your Lordship!
HAMLET   I am glad to see you well.
Horatio!—or I do forget myself.
HORATIO
The same, my lord, and your poor servant ever.

HAMLET
Sir, my good friend; I'll change that name with you. 163
And what make you from Wittenberg, Horatio?— 164
Marcellus.
MARCELLUS   My good lord.
HAMLET
I am very glad to see you. [*To Bernardo*] Good even,
    sir.—
But what in faith make you from Wittenberg?
HORATIO
A truant disposition, good my lord.
HAMLET
I would not hear your enemy say so,
Nor shall you do my ear that violence
To make it truster of your own report 172
Against yourself. I know you are no truant.
But what is your affair in Elsinore?
We'll teach you to drink deep ere you depart.
HORATIO
My lord, I came to see your father's funeral.
HAMLET
I prithee, do not mock me, fellow student;
I think it was to see my mother's wedding.
HORATIO
Indeed, my lord, it followed hard upon. 179
HAMLET
Thrift, thrift, Horatio! The funeral baked meats 180
Did coldly furnish forth the marriage tables. 181
Would I had met my dearest foe in heaven 182
Or ever I had seen that day, Horatio! 183
My father!—Methinks I see my father.
HORATIO
Where, my lord?
HAMLET   In my mind's eye, Horatio.
HORATIO
I saw him once. 'A was a goodly king. 186
HAMLET
'A was a man. Take him for all in all,
I shall not look upon his like again.
HORATIO
My lord, I think I saw him yesternight.
HAMLET   Saw? Who?
HORATIO   My lord, the King your father.
HAMLET   The King my father?
HORATIO
Season your admiration for a while 193
With an attent ear till I may deliver, 194
Upon the witness of these gentlemen,
This marvel to you.
HAMLET   For God's love, let me hear!
HORATIO
Two nights together had these gentlemen,

---

127 rouse drinking of a draft of liquor. **bruit again** loudly echo
128 thunder i.e., of trumpet and kettledrum, sounded when the King
drinks; see 1.4.8–12. **129 sullied** defiled. (The early quartos read
"sallied"; the Folio, "solid.") **132 canon** law **137 merely** completely. **139 to** in comparison to **140 Hyperion** Titan sun-god, father of
Helios. **satyr** a lecherous creature of classical mythology, half-
human but with a goat's legs, tail, ears, and horns **141 beteem** allow
147 or ere even before **149 Niobe** Tantalus's daughter, Queen of
Thebes, who boasted that she had more sons and daughters than
Leto; for this, Apollo and Artemis, children of Leto, slew her fourteen
children. She was turned by Zeus into a stone that continually
dropped tears. **150 wants . . . reason** lacks the faculty of reason **155
gallèd** irritated, inflamed **156 post** hasten **157 incestuous** (In
Shakespeare's day, the marriage of a man like Claudius to his
deceased brother's wife was considered incestuous.)

163 change that name i.e., give and receive reciprocally the name of
"friend" rather than talk of "servant." Or Hamlet may be saying,
"No, I am *your* servant." **164 make you from** are you doing away
from **172 To . . . of** to make it trust **179 hard** close **180 baked
meats** meat pies **181 coldly** i.e., as cold leftovers **182 dearest** clos-
est (and therefore deadliest) **183 Or ever** ere, before **186 'A** He
193 Season your admiration Moderate your astonishment
194 attent attentive

Marcellus and Bernardo, on their watch,
In the dead waste and middle of the night,   199
Been thus encountered. A figure like your father,
Armèd at point exactly, cap-à-pie,   201
Appears before them, and with solemn march
Goes slow and stately by them. Thrice he walked
By their oppressed and fear-surprisèd eyes
Within his truncheon's length, whilst they, distilled   205
Almost to jelly with the act of fear,   206
Stand dumb and speak not to him. This to me
In dreadful secrecy impart they did,   208
And I with them the third night kept the watch,
Where, as they had delivered, both in time,
Form of the thing, each word made true and good,
The apparition comes. I knew your father;
These hands are not more like.

HAMLET   But where was this?

MARCELLUS
My lord, upon the platform where we watch.

HAMLET
Did you not speak to it?

HORATIO   My lord, I did,
But answer made it none. Yet once methought
It lifted up it head and did address   217
Itself to motion, like as it would speak;   218
But even then the morning cock crew loud,   219
And at the sound it shrunk in haste away
And vanished from our sight.

HAMLET   'Tis very strange.

HORATIO
As I do live, my honored lord, 'tis true,
And we did think it writ down in our duty
To let you know of it.

HAMLET
Indeed, indeed, sirs. But this troubles me.
Hold you the watch tonight?

ALL   We do, my lord.

HAMLET Armed, say you?

ALL Armed, my lord.

HAMLET From top to toe?

ALL My lord, from head to foot.

HAMLET Then saw you not his face?

HORATIO
Oh, yes, my lord, he wore his beaver up.   232

HAMLET What looked he, frowningly?   233

HORATIO
A countenance more in sorrow than in anger.

HAMLET Pale or red?

HORATIO Nay, very pale.

HAMLET And fixed his eyes upon you?

HORATIO Most constantly.

HAMLET I would I had been there.

HORATIO It would have much amazed you.

HAMLET Very like, very like. Stayed it long?

HORATIO
While one with moderate haste might tell a hundred.   242

MARCELLUS, BERNARDO   Longer, longer.

HORATIO   Not when I saw't.

HAMLET   His beard was grizzled—no?

HORATIO
It was, as I have seen it in his life,
A sable silvered.

HAMLET   I will watch tonight.
Perchance 'twill walk again.

HORATIO   I warr'nt it will.

HAMLET
If it assume my noble father's person,
I'll speak to it though hell itself should gape
And bid me hold my peace. I pray you all,
If you have hitherto concealed this sight,
Let it be tenable in your silence still,   253
And whatsomever else shall hap tonight,
Give it an understanding but no tongue.
I will requite your loves. So, fare you well.
Upon the platform twixt eleven and twelve
I'll visit you.

ALL   Our duty to Your Honor.

HAMLET
Your loves, as mine to you. Farewell.   259
                            Exeunt [all but Hamlet].
My father's spirit in arms! All is not well.
I doubt some foul play. Would the night were come!   261
Till then sit still, my soul. Foul deeds will rise,
Though all the earth o'erwhelm them, to men's eyes.
                                                                Exit.

❧

[1.3]

Enter Laertes and Ophelia, his sister.

LAERTES
My necessaries are embarked. Farewell.
And, sister, as the winds give benefit
And convoy is assistant, do not sleep   3
But let me hear from you.

OPHELIA   Do you doubt that?

LAERTES
For Hamlet, and the trifling of his favor,   5
Hold it a fashion and a toy in blood,   6
A violet in the youth of primy nature,   7
Forward, not permanent, sweet, not lasting,   8
The perfume and suppliance of a minute—   9
No more.

OPHELIA   No more but so?

LAERTES   Think it no more.

---

199 dead waste desolate stillness   **201 at point** correctly in every detail.   **cap-à-pie** from head to foot   **205 truncheon** officer's staff. **distilled** dissolved   **206 act** action, operation   **208 dreadful** full of dread   **217 it** its   **217–18 did . . . speak** prepared to move as though it was about to speak   **219 even then** at that very instant **232 beaver** visor on the helmet   **233 What** How

242 tell count   **253 tenable** held   **259 Your loves** i.e., Say "Your loves" to me, not just your "duty."   **261 doubt** suspect
1.3. Location: Polonius's chambers.
3 convoy is assistant means of conveyance are available   **5 For** As for   **6 toy in blood** passing amorous fancy   **7 primy** in its prime, springtime   **8 Forward** precocious   **9 suppliance** pastime, something to fill the time

For nature crescent does not grow alone   11
In thews and bulk, but as this temple waxes   12
The inward service of the mind and soul
Grows wide withal. Perhaps he loves you now,   14
And now no soil nor cautel doth besmirch   15
The virtue of his will; but you must fear,   16
His greatness weighed, his will is not his own.   17
For he himself is subject to his birth.
He may not, as unvalued persons do,
Carve for himself, for on his choice depends   20
The safety and health of this whole state,
And therefore must his choice be circumscribed
Unto the voice and yielding of that body   23
Whereof he is the head. Then if he says he loves you,
It fits your wisdom so far to believe it
As he in his particular act and place   26
May give his saying deed, which is no further
Than the main voice of Denmark goes withal.   28
Then weigh what loss your honor may sustain
If with too credent ear you list his songs,   30
Or lose your heart, or your chaste treasure open
To his unmastered importunity.   32
Fear it, Ophelia, fear it, my dear sister,
And keep you in the rear of your affection,   34
Out of the shot and danger of desire.
The chariest maid is prodigal enough   36
If she unmask her beauty to the moon.   37
Virtue itself scapes not calumnious strokes.
The canker galls the infants of the spring   39
Too oft before their buttons be disclosed,   40
And in the morn and liquid dew of youth   41
Contagious blastments are most imminent.   42
Be wary then; best safety lies in fear.
Youth to itself rebels, though none else near.   44

OPHELIA
I shall the effect of this good lesson keep
As watchman to my heart. But, good my brother,
Do not, as some ungracious pastors do,   47
Show me the steep and thorny way to heaven,
Whiles like a puffed and reckless libertine   49
Himself the primrose path of dalliance treads,
And recks not his own rede.

      Enter Polonius.

LAERTES   Oh, fear me not.   51

11–14 For nature . . . withal For nature, as it ripens, does not grow only
in physical strength, but as the body matures the inner qualities of mind
and soul grow along with it. (Laertes warns Ophelia that the mature
Hamlet may not cling to his youthful interests.)   **15 soil nor cautel**
blemish nor deceit   **16 The . . . will** the purity of his desire   **17 His
greatness weighed** taking into account his high fortune   **20 Carve** i.e.,
choose   **23 voice and yielding** assent, approval   **26 in . . . place** in his
particular restricted circumstances   **28 main voice** general assent.
withal along with.   **30 credent** credulous.   **list** listen to   **32 unmastered** uncontrolled   **34 keep . . . affection** don't advance as far as your
affection might lead you. (A military metaphor.)   **36 chariest** most
scrupulously modest   **37 If she unmask** if she does no more than show
her beauty.   **moon** (Symbol of chastity.)   **39 canker galls** cankerworm
destroys   **40 buttons be disclosed** buds be opened   **41 liquid dew** i.e.,
time when dew is fresh and bright   **42 blastments** blights   **44 Youth
. . . rebels** Youth yields to the rebellion of the flesh   **47 ungracious**
ungodly   **49 puffed** bloated, or swollen with pride   **51 recks** heeds.
rede counsel.   **fear me not** don't worry on my account.

I stay too long. But here my father comes.
A double blessing is a double grace;   53
Occasion smiles upon a second leave.   54

POLONIUS
Yet here, Laertes? Aboard, aboard, for shame!
The wind sits in the shoulder of your sail,
And you are stayed for. There—my blessing with thee!
And these few precepts in thy memory
Look thou character. Give thy thoughts no tongue,   59
Nor any unproportioned thought his act.   60
Be thou familiar, but by no means vulgar.   61
Those friends thou hast, and their adoption tried,   62
Grapple them unto thy soul with hoops of steel,
But do not dull thy palm with entertainment   64
Of each new-hatched, unfledged courage. Beware   65
Of entrance to a quarrel, but being in,
Bear't that th'opposèd may beware of thee.   67
Give every man thy ear, but few thy voice;
Take each man's censure, but reserve thy judgment.   69
Costly thy habit as thy purse can buy,   70
But not expressed in fancy; rich, not gaudy,   71
For the apparel oft proclaims the man,
And they in France of the best rank and station
Are of a most select and generous chief in that.   74
Neither a borrower nor a lender be,
For loan oft loses both itself and friend,
And borrowing dulleth edge of husbandry.   77
This above all: to thine own self be true,
And it must follow, as the night the day,
Thou canst not then be false to any man.
Farewell. My blessing season this in thee!   81

LAERTES
Most humbly do I take my leave, my lord.

POLONIUS
The time invests you. Go, your servants tend.   83

LAERTES
Farewell, Ophelia, and remember well
What I have said to you.

OPHELIA   'Tis in my memory locked,
And you yourself shall keep the key of it.

LAERTES   Farewell.   *Exit Laertes.*

POLONIUS
What is't, Ophelia, he hath said to you?

OPHELIA
So please you, something touching the Lord Hamlet.

POLONIUS   Marry, well bethought.   91
'Tis told me he hath very oft of late
Given private time to you, and you yourself

53–4 A double . . . leave The goddess Occasion or Opportunity smiles
on the happy circumstance of being able to say good-bye twice and
thus receive a second blessing.   **59 Look thou character** see to it that
you inscribe.   **60 unproportioned** badly calculated, intemperate.   **his**
its   **61 familiar** sociable.   **vulgar** common.   **62 and . . . tried** and
their suitability to be your friends having been put to the test   **64 dull
thy palm** i.e., shake hands so often as to make the gesture meaningless   **65 courage** swashbuckler.   **67 Bear't that** manage it so that
69 censure opinion, judgment   **70 habit** clothing   **71 fancy** excessive
ornament, decadent fashion   **74 Are . . . that** are of a most refined
and well-bred preeminence in choosing what to wear.   **77 husbandry** thrift.   **81 season** mature   **83 invests** besieges, presses upon.
tend attend, wait.   **91 Marry** i.e., By the Virgin Mary. (A mild oath.)

Have of your audience been most free and bounteous.
If it be so—as so 'tis put on me, 95
And that in way of caution—I must tell you
You do not understand yourself so clearly
As it behooves my daughter and your honor. 98
What is between you? Give me up the truth.

OPHELIA
He hath, my lord, of late made many tenders 100
Of his affection to me.

POLONIUS
Affection? Pooh! You speak like a green girl,
Unsifted in such perilous circumstance. 103
Do you believe his tenders, as you call them?

OPHELIA
I do not know, my lord, what I should think.

POLONIUS
Marry, I will teach you. Think yourself a baby
That you have ta'en these tenders for true pay
Which are not sterling. Tender yourself more dearly, 108
Or—not to crack the wind of the poor phrase, 109
Running it thus—you'll tender me a fool. 110

OPHELIA
My lord, he hath importuned me with love
In honorable fashion.

POLONIUS
Ay, fashion you may call it. Go to, go to. 113

OPHELIA
And hath given countenance to his speech, my lord, 114
With almost all the holy vows of heaven.

POLONIUS
Ay, springes to catch woodcocks. I do know, 116
When the blood burns, how prodigal the soul 117
Lends the tongue vows. These blazes, daughter,
Giving more light than heat, extinct in both
Even in their promise as it is a-making, 120
You must not take for fire. From this time
Be something scanter of your maiden presence. 122
Set your entreatments at a higher rate 123
Than a command to parle. For Lord Hamlet, 124
Believe so much in him that he is young, 125
And with a larger tether may he walk
Than may be given you. In few, Ophelia, 127
Do not believe his vows, for they are brokers, 128
Not of that dye which their investments show, 129
But mere implorators of unholy suits, 130

Breathing like sanctified and pious bawds, 131
The better to beguile. This is for all: 132
I would not, in plain terms, from this time forth
Have you so slander any moment leisure 134
As to give words or talk with the Lord Hamlet.
Look to't, I charge you. Come your ways. 136

OPHELIA　　I shall obey, my lord.　　　　　　　　*Exeunt.*

❦

[1.4]

Enter Hamlet, Horatio, and Marcellus.

HAMLET
The air bites shrewdly; it is very cold. 1

HORATIO
It is a nipping and an eager air. 2

HAMLET
What hour now?

HORATIO　　　　　　　I think it lacks of twelve. 3

MARCELLUS
No, it is struck.

HORATIO　　　　　　Indeed? I heard it not.
It then draws near the season 5
Wherein the spirit held his wont to walk. 6
A flourish of trumpets, and two pieces go off
[within].
What does this mean, my lord?

HAMLET
The King doth wake tonight and takes his rouse, 8
Keeps wassail, and the swagg'ring upspring reels; 9
And as he drains his drafts of Rhenish down, 10
The kettledrum and trumpet thus bray out
The triumph of his pledge.

HORATIO　　　　　　　　　　Is it a custom? 12

HAMLET　　Ay, marry, is't,
But to my mind, though I am native here
And to the manner born, it is a custom 15
More honored in the breach than the observance. 16
This heavy-headed revel east and west 17
Makes us traduced and taxed of other nations. 18
They clepe us drunkards, and with swinish phrase 19
Soil our addition; and indeed it takes 20
From our achievements, though performed at height, 21
The pith and marrow of our attribute. 22

So, oft it chances in particular men,
That for some vicious mole of nature in them,   24
As in their birth—wherein they are not guilty,
Since nature cannot choose his origin—   26
By their o'ergrowth of some complexion,   27
Oft breaking down the pales and forts of reason,   28
Or by some habit that too much o'erleavens   29
The form of plausive manners, that these men,   30
Carrying, I say, the stamp of one defect,
Being nature's livery or fortune's star,   32
His virtues else, be they as pure as grace,   33
As infinite as man may undergo,   34
Shall in the general censure take corruption   35
From that particular fault. The dram of evil   36
Doth all the noble substance often dout   37
To his own scandal.

Enter Ghost.

HORATIO   Look, my lord, it comes!   38
HAMLET
Angels and ministers of grace defend us!   39
Be thou a spirit of health or goblin damned,   40
Bring with thee airs from heaven or blasts from hell,   41
Be thy intents wicked or charitable,   42
Thou com'st in such a questionable shape   43
That I will speak to thee. I'll call thee Hamlet,
King, father, royal Dane. Oh, answer me!
Let me not burst in ignorance, but tell
Why thy canonized bones, hearsèd in death,   47
Have burst their cerements; why the sepulcher   48
Wherein we saw thee quietly inurned   49
Hath oped his ponderous and marble jaws
To cast thee up again. What may this mean,
That thou, dead corpse, again in complete steel,   52
Revisits thus the glimpses of the moon,   53
Making night hideous, and we fools of nature   54
So horridly to shake our disposition   55
With thoughts beyond the reaches of our souls?
Say, why is this? Wherefore? What should we do?
                       [The Ghost] beckons [Hamlet].

HORATIO
It beckons you to go away with it,
As if it some impartment did desire   59
To you alone.
MARCELLUS   Look with what courteous action
It wafts you to a more removèd ground.
But do not go with it.
HORATIO   No, by no means.
HAMLET
It will not speak. Then I will follow it.
HORATIO
Do not, my lord!
HAMLET   Why, what should be the fear?
I do not set my life at a pin's fee,   65
And for my soul, what can it do to that,   66
Being a thing immortal as itself?
It waves me forth again. I'll follow it.
HORATIO
What if it tempt you toward the flood, my lord,   69
Or to the dreadful summit of the cliff
That beetles o'er his base into the sea,   71
And there assume some other horrible form
Which might deprive your sovereignty of reason   73
And draw you into madness? Think of it.
The very place puts toys of desperation,   75
Without more motive, into every brain
That looks so many fathoms to the sea
And hears it roar beneath.
HAMLET
It wafts me still.—Go on, I'll follow thee.
MARCELLUS
You shall not go, my lord.   *[They try to stop him.]*
HAMLET   Hold off your hands!
HORATIO
Be ruled. You shall not go.
HAMLET   My fate cries out,   81
And makes each petty artery in this body   82
As hardy as the Nemean lion's nerve.   83
Still am I called. Unhand me, gentlemen.
By heaven, I'll make a ghost of him that lets me!   85
I say, away!—Go on, I'll follow thee.
                       Exeunt Ghost and Hamlet.
HORATIO
He waxes desperate with imagination.
MARCELLUS
Let's follow. 'Tis not fit thus to obey him.
HORATIO
Have after. To what issue will this come?   89
MARCELLUS
Something is rotten in the state of Denmark.

---

24 **for . . . mole** on account of some natural defect in their constitutions   26 **his** its   27 **their o'ergrowth . . . complexion** the excessive growth in individuals of some natural trait   28 **pales** palings, fences (as of a fortification)   29–30 **o'erleavens . . . manners** i.e., infects the way we should behave (much as bad yeast spoils the dough). *Plausive* means "pleasing."   32 **Being . . . star** (that stamp of defect) being a sign identifying one as wearing the livery of, and hence being the servant to, nature (unfortunate inherited qualities) or fortune (mischance)   33 **His virtues else** i.e., the other qualities of *these men* (line 30)   34 **may undergo** can sustain   35 **in . . . censure** in overall appraisal, in people's opinion generally   36-8 **The dram . . . scandal** i.e., The small drop of evil blots out or works against the noble substance of the whole and brings it into disrepute. (To *dout* is to blot out. A famous crux.)   39 **ministers of grace** messengers of God   40 **Be . . . health** Whether you are a good angel   41 **Bring** whether you bring   42 **Be thy intents** whether your intentions are   43 **questionable** inviting question   47 **canonized** buried according to the canons of the church.   **hearsèd** coffined   48 **cerements** grave clothes   49 **inurned** entombed   52 **complete steel** full armor   53 **the glimpses . . . moon** i.e., the sublunary world, all that is beneath the moon   54 **fools of nature** mere mortals, limited to natural knowledge and subject to nature   55 **So . . . disposition** to distress our mental composure so violently

59 **impartment** communication   65 **fee** value   66 **for** as for   69 **flood** sea   71 **beetles o'er** overhangs threateningly (like bushy eyebrows).   **his** its   73 **deprive . . . reason** take away the rule of reason over your mind   75 **toys of desperation** fancies of desperate acts, i.e., suicide   81 **My fate cries out** My destiny summons me   82 **petty** weak.   **artery** blood vessel system through which the vital spirits were thought to have been conveyed   83 **as the . . . nerve** as a sinew of the huge lion slain by Hercules as the first of his twelve labors.   85 **lets** hinders   89 **Have after** Let's go after him.   **issue** outcome

HORATIO
Heaven will direct it.
MARCELLUS   Nay, let's follow him.   *Exeunt.* 91

❧

[1.5]

Enter Ghost and Hamlet.

HAMLET
Whither wilt thou lead me? Speak. I'll go no further.
GHOST
Mark me.
HAMLET   I will.
GHOST   My hour is almost come,
When I to sulf'rous and tormenting flames
Must render up myself.
HAMLET   Alas, poor ghost!
GHOST
Pity me not, but lend thy serious hearing
To what I shall unfold.
HAMLET   Speak. I am bound to hear.   7
GHOST
So art thou to revenge, when thou shalt hear.
HAMLET   What?
GHOST   I am thy father's spirit,
Doomed for a certain term to walk the night,
And for the day confined to fast in fires,   12
Till the foul crimes done in my days of nature   13
Are burnt and purged away. But that I am forbid   14
To tell the secrets of my prison house,
I could a tale unfold whose lightest word
Would harrow up thy soul, freeze thy young blood,   17
Make thy two eyes like stars start from their spheres, 18
Thy knotted and combinèd locks to part,   19
And each particular hair to stand on end
Like quills upon the fretful porcupine.
But this eternal blazon must not be   22
To ears of flesh and blood. List, list, oh, list!
If thou didst ever thy dear father love—
HAMLET   Oh, God!
GHOST
Revenge his foul and most unnatural murder.
HAMLET   Murder?
GHOST
Murder most foul, as in the best it is,   28
But this most foul, strange, and unnatural.
HAMLET
Haste me to know't, that I, with wings as swift
As meditation or the thoughts of love,
May sweep to my revenge.
GHOST   I find thee apt;

And duller shouldst thou be than the fat weed   33
That roots itself in ease on Lethe wharf,   34
Wouldst thou not stir in this. Now, Hamlet, hear.
'Tis given out that, sleeping in my orchard,   36
A serpent stung me. So the whole ear of Denmark
Is by a forgèd process of my death   38
Rankly abused. But know, thou noble youth,   39
The serpent that did sting thy father's life
Now wears his crown.
HAMLET   Oh, my prophetic soul! My uncle!
GHOST
Ay, that incestuous, that adulterate beast,   43
With witchcraft of his wit, with traitorous gifts—   44
Oh, wicked wit and gifts, that have the power
So to seduce!—won to his shameful lust
The will of my most seeming-virtuous queen.
Oh, Hamlet, what a falling off was there!
From me, whose love was of that dignity
That it went hand in hand even with the vow   50
I made to her in marriage, and to decline
Upon a wretch whose natural gifts were poor
To those of mine!   53
But virtue, as it never will be moved,   54
Though lewdness court it in a shape of heaven,   55
So lust, though to a radiant angel linked,
Will sate itself in a celestial bed   57
And prey on garbage.
But soft, methinks I scent the morning air.
Brief let me be. Sleeping within my orchard,
My custom always of the afternoon,
Upon my secure hour thy uncle stole,   62
With juice of cursèd hebona in a vial,   63
And in the porches of my ears did pour   64
The leprous distillment, whose effect   65
Holds such an enmity with blood of man
That swift as quicksilver it courses through
The natural gates and alleys of the body,   68
And with a sudden vigor it doth posset   69
And curd, like eager droppings into milk,   70
The thin and wholesome blood. So did it mine,
And a most instant tetter barked about,   72
Most lazar-like, with vile and loathsome crust,   73
All my smooth body.
Thus was I, sleeping, by a brother's hand
Of life, of crown, of queen at once dispatched,   76

---

91 it i.e., the outcome.
1.5 Location: The battlements of the castle.
7 bound (1) ready (2) obligated by duty and fate. (The Ghost, in line 8, answers in the second sense.)   **12 fast** do penance by fasting
13 crimes sins.   **of nature** as a mortal   **14 But that** Were it not that
17 harrow up lacerate, tear   **18 spheres** i.e., eye-sockets, here compared to the orbits or transparent revolving spheres in which, according to Ptolemaic astronomy, the heavenly bodies were fixed
19 knotted . . . locks hair neatly arranged and confined   **22 eternal blazon** revelation of the secrets of eternity   **28 in the best** even at best

33 shouldst thou be you would have to be.   **fat** torpid, lethargic
34 Lethe the river of forgetfulness in Hades   **36 orchard** garden
38 forgèd process falsified account   **39 abused** deceived.   **43 adulterate** adulterous   **44 gifts** (1) talents (2) presents   **50 even with the vow** with the very vow   **53 To** compared with   **54 virtue, as it** just as virtue   **55 shape of heaven** heavenly form   **57 sate . . . bed** gratify its lustful appetite to the point of revulsion or ennui, even in a virtuously lawful marriage   **62 secure hour** time of being free from worries   **63 hebona** a poison. (The word seems to be a form of *ebony*, though it is thought perhaps to be related to *henbane*, a poison, or to *ebenus*, "yew.")   **64 porches** gateways   **65 leprous distillment** distillation causing leprosylike disfigurement   **68 gates** entry ways
69–70 posset . . . curd coagulate and curdle   **70 eager** sour, acid
72 tetter eruption of scabs.   **barked** covered with a rough covering, like bark on a tree   **73 lazar-like** leperlike   **76 dispatched** suddenly deprived

Cut off even in the blossoms of my sin,
Unhouseled, disappointed, unaneled,   78
No reck'ning made, but sent to my account   79
With all my imperfections on my head.
Oh, horrible! Oh, horrible, most horrible!
If thou hast nature in thee, bear it not.   82
Let not the royal bed of Denmark be
A couch for luxury and damnèd incest.   84
But, howsomever thou pursues this act,
Taint not thy mind nor let thy soul contrive
Against thy mother aught. Leave her to heaven
And to those thorns that in her bosom lodge,
To prick and sting her. Fare thee well at once.
The glowworm shows the matin to be near,   90
And 'gins to pale his uneffectual fire.   91
Adieu, adieu, adieu! Remember me.   [*Exit.*]

HAMLET
O all you host of heaven! O earth! What else?
And shall I couple hell? Oh, fie! Hold, hold, my heart,   94
And you, my sinews, grow not instant old,   95
But bear me stiffly up. Remember thee?
Ay, thou poor ghost, whiles memory holds a seat
In this distracted globe. Remember thee?   98
Yea, from the table of my memory   99
I'll wipe away all trivial fond records,   100
All saws of books, all forms, all pressures past   101
That youth and observation copied there,
And thy commandment all alone shall live
Within the book and volume of my brain,
Unmixed with baser matter. Yes, by heaven!
Oh, most pernicious woman!
Oh, villain, villain, smiling, damnèd villain!
My tables—meet it is I set it down   108
That one may smile, and smile, and be a villain.
At least I am sure it may be so in Denmark.
So, uncle, there you are. Now to my word: 111
It is "Adieu, adieu! Remember me."
I have sworn't.

Enter Horatio and Marcellus.

HORATIO   My lord, my lord!
MARCELLUS   Lord Hamlet!
HORATIO   Heavens secure him!   116
HAMLET   So be it.
MARCELLUS   Hillo, ho, ho, my lord!
HAMLET   Hillo, ho, ho, boy! Come, bird, come.   119
MARCELLUS   How is't, my noble lord?

HORATIO   What news, my lord?
HAMLET   Oh, wonderful!
HORATIO   Good my lord, tell it.
HAMLET   No, you will reveal it.
HORATIO   Not I, my lord, by heaven.
MARCELLUS   Nor I, my lord
HAMLET
How say you, then, would heart of man once think it?   127
But you'll be secret?
HORATIO, MARCELLUS   Ay, by heaven, my lord.
HAMLET
There's never a villain dwelling in all Denmark
But he's an arrant knave.   130
HORATIO
There needs no ghost, my lord, come from the grave
To tell us this.
HAMLET   Why, right, you are in the right.
And so, without more circumstance at all,   133
I hold it fit that we shake hands and part,
You as your business and desire shall point you—
For every man hath business and desire,
Such as it is—and for my own poor part,
Look you, I'll go pray.
HORATIO
These are but wild and whirling words, my lord.
HAMLET
I am sorry they offend you, heartily;
Yes, faith, heartily.
HORATIO   There's no offense, my lord.
HAMLET
Yes, by Saint Patrick, but there is, Horatio,   142
And much offense too. Touching this vision here,   143
It is an honest ghost, that let me tell you.   144
For your desire to know what is between us,
O'ermaster't as you may. And now, good friends,
As you are friends, scholars, and soldiers,
Give me one poor request.
HORATIO   What is't, my lord? We will.
HAMLET
Never make known what you have seen tonight.
HORATIO, MARCELLUS   My lord, we will not.
HAMLET   Nay, but swear't.
HORATIO   In faith, my lord, not I.   153
MARCELLUS   Nor I, my lord, in faith.
HAMLET   Upon my sword.   [*He holds out his sword.*]   155
MARCELLUS   We have sworn, my lord, already.   156
HAMLET   Indeed, upon my sword, indeed.
GHOST (*cries under the stage*)   Swear.
HAMLET
Ha, ha, boy, say'st thou so? Art thou there, truepenny?   159

78 Unhouseled . . . unaneled without having received the Sacrament or other last rites including confession, absolution, and the holy oil of extreme unction   **79 reck'ning** settling of accounts   **82 nature** i.e., the promptings of a son   **84 luxury** lechery   **90 matin** morning   **91 his** its   **94 couple** add.   **Hold** Hold together   **95 instant** instantly   **98 globe** (1) head (2) world (3) Globe Theater.   **99 table** tablet, slate   **100 fond** foolish   **101 All . . . past** all wise sayings, all shapes or images imprinted on the tablets of my memory, all past impressions   **108 My tables . . . down** (Editors often specify that Hamlet makes a note in his writing tablet, but he may simply mean that he is making a mental observation of lasting impression.)   **111 there you are** i.e., there, I've noted that against you.   **116 secure him** keep him safe.   **119 Hillo . . . come** (A falconer's call to a hawk in air. Hamlet mocks the hallooing as though it were a part of hawking.)

127 once ever   **130 But . . . knave** (Hamlet jokingly gives a self-evident answer: every villain is a thoroughgoing knave.)   **133 circumstance** ceremony, elaboration   **142 Saint Patrick** the keeper of Purgatory   **143 offense** (Hamlet deliberately changes Horatio's "no offense taken" to "an offense against all decency.")   **144 honest** genuine   **153 In faith . . . I** i.e., I swear not to tell what I have seen. (Horatio is not refusing to swear.)   **155 sword** i.e., the hilt in the form of a cross.   **156 We . . . already** i.e., We swore *in faith*.   **159 truepenny** honest old fellow.

Come on, you hear this fellow in the cellarage.
Consent to swear.

HORATIO   Propose the oath, my lord.

HAMLET
Never to speak of this that you have seen,
Swear by my sword.

GHOST [*beneath*]   Swear.   [*They swear.*] 164

HAMLET
Hic et ubique? Then we'll shift our ground.   165
                        [*He moves to another spot.*]
Come hither, gentlemen,
And lay your hands again upon my sword.
Swear by my sword
Never to speak of this that you have heard.

GHOST [*beneath*]   Swear by his sword.   [*They swear.*]

HAMLET
Well said, old mole. Canst work i'th'earth so fast?
A worthy pioneer!—Once more remove, good friends. 172
                        [*He moves again.*]

HORATIO
Oh, day and night, but this is wondrous strange!

HAMLET
And therefore as a stranger give it welcome.   174
There are more things in heaven and earth, Horatio,
Than are dreamt of in your philosophy.   176
But come;
Here, as before, never, so help you mercy,   178
How strange or odd some'er I bear myself—
As I perchance hereafter shall think meet
To put an antic disposition on—   181
That you, at such times seeing me, never shall,
With arms encumbered thus, or this headshake,   183
Or by pronouncing of some doubtful phrase
As "Well, we know," or "We could, an if we would,"   185
Or "If we list to speak," or "There be, an if they
    might,"   186
Or such ambiguous giving out, to note   187
That you know aught of me—this do swear,   188
So grace and mercy at your most need help you.

GHOST [*beneath*]   Swear.   [*They swear.*]

HAMLET
Rest, rest, perturbèd spirit!—So, gentlemen,
With all my love I do commend me to you;   192
And what so poor a man as Hamlet is
May do t'express his love and friending to you,   194
God willing, shall not lack. Let us go in together,   195
And still your fingers on your lips, I pray.   196

The time is out of joint. Oh, cursèd spite   197
That ever I was born to set it right!
                [*They wait for him to leave first.*]
Nay, come, let's go together.   *Exeunt.* 199

[2.1]

Enter old Polonius with his man [Reynaldo].

POLONIUS
Give him this money and these notes, Reynaldo.
                [*He gives money and papers.*]

REYNALDO   I will, my lord.

POLONIUS
You shall do marvelous wisely, good Reynaldo,   3
Before you visit him, to make inquire   4
Of his behavior.

REYNALDO   My lord, I did intend it.

POLONIUS
Marry, well said, very well said. Look you, sir,
Inquire me first what Danskers are in Paris,   7
And how, and who, what means, and where they
    keep,   8
What company, at what expense; and finding
By this encompassment and drift of question   10
That they do know my son, come you more nearer   11
Than your particular demands will touch it.   12
Take you, as 'twere, some distant knowledge of him,   13
As thus, "I know his father and his friends,
And in part him." Do you mark this, Reynaldo?

REYNALDO   Ay, very well, my lord.

POLONIUS
"And in part him, but," you may say, "not well.
But if't be he I mean, he's very wild,
Addicted so and so," and there put on him   19
What forgeries you please—marry, none so rank   20
As may dishonor him, take heed of that,
But, sir, such wanton, wild, and usual slips   22
As are companions noted and most known
To youth and liberty.

REYNALDO   As gaming, my lord.

POLONIUS   Ay, or drinking, fencing, swearing,
Quarreling, drabbing—you may go so far.   27

REYNALDO   My lord, that would dishonor him.

POLONIUS
Faith, no, as you may season it in the charge.   29
You must not put another scandal on him
That he is open to incontinency;   31

---

164 s.d. *They swear* (Seemingly they swear here, and at lines 170 and
190, as they lay their hands on Hamlet's sword. Triple oaths would
have particular force; these three oaths deal with what they have
seen, what they have heard, and what they promise about Hamlet's
antic disposition.)   165 *Hic et ubique?* Here and everywhere? (Latin.)
172 **pioneer** foot soldier assigned to dig tunnels and excavations.
174 **as a stranger** i.e., needing your hospitality   176 **your philosophy**
this subject that is called "natural philosophy" or "science." (*Your* is
not personal.)   178 **so help you mercy** as you hope for God's mercy
when you are judged   181 **antic** grotesque, strange   183 **encumbered** folded   185 **an if** if   186 **list** wished.   **There . . . might** There
are those who could talk if they were at liberty to do so   187 **note**
indicate   188 **aught** anything   192 **commend . . . you** give you my
best wishes   194 **friending** friendliness   195 **lack** be lacking.
196 **still** always

---

197 **out of joint** in utter disorder.   199 **let's go together** (Probably
they wait for him to leave first, but he refuses this ceremoniousness.)
2.1 Location: Polonius's chambers.
3 **marvelous** marvelously   4 **inquire** inquiry   7 **Danskers** Danes
8 **what means** what wealth (they have).   **keep** dwell   10 **encompassment . . . question** roundabout way of questioning   11-12 **come . . .
it** you will find out more this way than by asking pointed questions
(*particular demands*).   13 **Take you** Assume, pretend   19 **put on**
impute to   20 **forgeries** invented tales.   **rank** gross   22 **wanton**
sportive, unrestrained   27 **drabbing** whoring   29 **season** temper,
soften   31 **incontinency** habitual sexual excess

That's not my meaning. But breathe his faults so
    quaintly   32
That they may seem the taints of liberty,   33
The flash and outbreak of a fiery mind,
A savageness in unreclaimèd blood,   35
Of general assault.   36
REYNALDO   But, my good lord—
POLONIUS   Wherefore should you do this?
REYNALDO   Ay, my lord, I would know that.
POLONIUS   Marry, sir, here's my drift,
    And I believe it is a fetch of warrant.   41
    You laying these slight sullies on my son,
    As 'twere a thing a little soiled wi'th' working,   43
    Mark you,
    Your party in converse, him you would sound,   45
    Having ever seen in the prenominate crimes   46
    The youth you breathe of guilty, be assured   47
    He closes with you in this consequence: 48
    "Good sir," or so, or "friend," or "gentleman,"
    According to the phrase or the addition   50
    Of man and country.
REYNALDO   Very good, my lord.
POLONIUS   And then, sir, does 'a this—'a does—what
    was I about to say? By the Mass, I was about to say
    something. Where did I leave?
REYNALDO   At "closes in the consequence."
POLONIUS
    At "closes in the consequence," ay, marry.
    He closes thus: "I know the gentleman,
    I saw him yesterday," or "th'other day,"
    Or then, or then, with such or such, "and as you say,
    There was 'a gaming," "there o'ertook in 's rouse,"   60
    "There falling out at tennis," or perchance   61
    "I saw him enter such a house of sale,"
    Videlicet a brothel, or so forth. See you now,   63
    Your bait of falsehood takes this carp of truth;   64
    And thus do we of wisdom and of reach,   65
    With windlasses and with assays of bias,   66
    By indirections find directions out.   67
    So by my former lecture and advice   68
    Shall you my son. You have me, have you not?   69
REYNALDO
    My lord, I have.
POLONIUS   God b'wi'ye; fare ye well.
REYNALDO   Good my lord.

POLONIUS
    Observe his inclination in yourself.   72
REYNALDO   I shall, my lord.
POLONIUS   And let him ply his music.
REYNALDO   Well, my lord.
POLONIUS
    Farewell.   *Exit Reynaldo.*

        Enter Ophelia.

            How now, Ophelia, what's the matter?
OPHELIA
    Oh, my lord, my lord, I have been so affrighted!
POLONIUS   With what, i'th' name of God?
OPHELIA
    My lord, as I was sewing in my closet,   79
    Lord Hamlet, with his doublet all unbraced,   80
    No hat upon his head, his stockings fouled,
    Ungartered, and down-gyvèd to his ankle,   82
    Pale as his shirt, his knees knocking each other,
    And with a look so piteous in purport   84
    As if he had been loosèd out of hell
    To speak of horrors—he comes before me.
POLONIUS
    Mad for thy love?
OPHELIA   My lord, I do not know,
    But truly I do fear it.
POLONIUS   What said he?
OPHELIA
    He took me by the wrist and held me hard.
    Then goes he to the length of all his arm,
    And, with his other hand thus o'er his brow
    He falls to such perusal of my face
    As 'a would draw it. Long stayed he so.   93
    At last, a little shaking of mine arm
    And thrice his head thus waving up and down,
    He raised a sigh so piteous and profound
    As it did seem to shatter all his bulk   97
    And end his being. That done, he lets me go,
    And with his head over his shoulder turned
    He seemed to find his way without his eyes,
    For out o' doors he went without their helps,
    And to the last bended their light on me.
POLONIUS
    Come, go with me. I will go seek the King.
    This is the very ecstasy of love,   104
    Whose violent property fordoes itself   105
    And leads the will to desperate undertakings
    As oft as any passion under heaven
    That does afflict our natures. I am sorry.
    What, have you given him any hard words of late?
OPHELIA
    No, my good lord, but as you did command
    I did repel his letters and denied

---

32 **quaintly** artfully, subtly   33 **taints of liberty** faults resulting from free living   35-6 **A savageness . . . assault** a wildness in untamed youth that assails all indiscriminately.   41 **fetch of warrant** legitimate trick.   43 **wi'th' working** in the process of being made, i.e., in everyday experience   45 **Your . . . converse** the person you are conversing with.   **sound** sound out   46 **Having ever** if he has ever.   **prenominate crimes** aforenamed offenses   47 **breathe** speak   48 **closes . . . consequence** takes you into his confidence as follows   50 **addition** title   60 **o'ertook in 's rouse** overcome by drink   61 **falling out** quarreling   63 **Videlicet** namely   64 **carp** a fish   65 **reach** capacity, ability   66 **windlasses** i.e., circuitous paths. (Literally, circuits made to head off the game in hunting.)   **assays of bias** attempts through indirection (like the curving path of the bowling ball, which is biased or weighted to one side)   67 **directions** i.e., the way things really are   68 **former lecture** just-ended set of instructions   69 **have** understand

72 **in yourself** in your own person (as well as by asking questions of others).   79 **closet** private chamber   80 **doublet** close-fitting jacket.   **unbraced** unfastened   82 **down-gyvèd** fallen to the ankles (like gyves or fetters)   84 **in purport** in what it expressed   93 **As** as if   97 **As** that.   **bulk** body   104 **ecstasy** madness   105 **property fordoes** nature destroys

His access to me.
POLONIUS   That hath made him mad.
I am sorry that with better heed and judgment
I had not quoted him. I feared he did but trifle   114
And meant to wrack thee. But beshrew my jealousy!   115
By heaven, it is as proper to our age   116
To cast beyond ourselves in our opinions   117
As it is common for the younger sort
To lack discretion. Come, go we to the King.
This must be known, which, being kept close, might
   move   120
More grief to hide than hate to utter love.   121
Come.   *Exeunt.*

❖

[2.2]

Flourish. Enter King and Queen, Rosencrantz,
and Guildenstern [with others].

KING
Welcome, dear Rosencrantz and Guildenstern.
Moreover that we much did long to see you,   2
The need we have to use you did provoke
Our hasty sending. Something have you heard
Of Hamlet's transformation—so call it,
Sith nor th'exterior nor the inward man   6
Resembles that it was. What it should be,   7
More than his father's death, that thus hath put him
So much from th'understanding of himself,
I cannot dream of. I entreat you both
That, being of so young days brought up with him,   11
And sith so neighbored to his youth and havior,   12
That you vouchsafe your rest here in our court   13
Some little time, so by your companies
To draw him on to pleasures, and to gather
So much as from occasion you may glean,   16
Whether aught to us unknown afflicts him thus
That, opened, lies within our remedy.   18
QUEEN
Good gentlemen, he hath much talked of you,
And sure I am two men there is not living
To whom he more adheres. If it will please you
To show us so much gentry and good will
As to expend your time with us awhile   22
For the supply and profit of our hope,   24

Your visitation shall receive such thanks
As fits a kings's remembrance.
ROSENCRANTZ   Both Your Majesties   26
Might, by the sovereign power you have of us,   27
Put your dread pleasures more into command   28
Than to entreaty.
GUILDENSTERN   But we both obey,
And here give up ourselves in the full bent   30
To lay our service freely at your feet,
To be commanded.
KING
Thanks, Rosencrantz and gentle Guildenstern.
QUEEN
Thanks, Guildenstern and gentle Rosencrantz.
And I beseech you instantly to visit
My too much changèd son.—Go, some of you,
And bring these gentlemen where Hamlet is.
GUILDENSTERN
Heavens make our presence and our practices   38
Pleasant and helpful to him!
QUEEN   Ay, amen!
        Exeunt Rosencrantz and Guildenstern [with some
                                        attendants].

        Enter Polonius.

POLONIUS
Th'ambassadors from Norway, my good lord,
Are joyfully returned.
KING
Thou still hast been the father of good news.   42
POLONIUS
Have I, my lord? I assure my good liege
I hold my duty, as I hold my soul,
Both to my God and to my gracious king;
And I do think, or else this brain of mine
Hunts not the trail of policy so sure   47
As it hath used to do, that I have found
The very cause of Hamlet's lunacy.
KING
Oh, speak of that! That do I long to hear.
POLONIUS
Give first admittance to th'ambassadors.
My news shall be the fruit to that great feast.   52
KING
Thyself do grace to them and bring them in.   53
                                    [Exit Polonius.]
He tells me, my dear Gertrude, he hath found
The head and source of all your son's distemper.
QUEEN
I doubt it is no other but the main,   56
His father's death and our o'erhasty marriage.

        Enter Ambassadors [Voltimand and Cornelius,
        with Polonius].

114 quoted observed   **115 wrack** ruin, seduce.   **beshrew my jealousy!** a plague upon my suspicious nature!   **116 proper . . . age** characteristic of us (old) men   **117 cast beyond** overshoot, miscalculate. (A metaphor from hunting.)   **120 known** made known (to the King). **close** secret   **120-1 might . . . love** i.e., might cause more grief (because of what Hamlet might do) by hiding the knowledge of Hamlet's strange behavior to Ophelia than unpleasantness by telling it.
2.2 Location: The castle.
2 Moreover that Besides the fact that   **6 Sith nor** since neither   **7 that** what   **11–12 That . . . havior** that, seeing as you were brought up with him from early youth (see 3.4.209, where Hamlet refers to Rosencrantz and Guildenstern as "my two schoolfellows"), and since you have been intimately acquainted with his youthful ways **13 vouchsafe your rest** consent to stay   **16 occasion** opportunity **18 opened** being revealed   **22 gentry** courtesy   **24 supply . . . hope** aid and furtherance of what we hope for

26 As fits . . . remembrance as would be a fitting gift of a king who rewards true service.   **27 of** over   **28 dread** inspiring awe   **30 in . . . bent** to the utmost degree of our capacity. (An archery metaphor.) **38 practices** doings   **42 still** always   **47 policy** statecraft   **52 fruit** dessert   **53 grace** honor. (Punning on *grace* said before a *feast*, line 52.)   **56 doubt** fear, suspect

KING
    Well, we shall sift him.—Welcome, my good friends!   58
    Say, Voltimand, what from our brother Norway?   59
VOLTIMAND
    Most fair return of greetings and desires.   60
    Upon our first, he sent out to suppress   61
    His nephew's levies, which to him appeared
    To be a preparation 'gainst the Polack,
    But, better looked into, he truly found
    It was against Your Highness. Whereat grieved
    That so his sickness, age, and impotence   66
    Was falsely borne in hand, sends out arrests   67
    On Fortinbras, which he, in brief, obeys,
    Receives rebuke from Norway, and in fine   69
    Makes vow before his uncle never more
    To give th'assay of arms against Your Majesty.   71
    Whereon old Norway, overcome with joy,
    Gives him three thousand crowns in annual fee
    And his commission to employ those soldiers,
    So levied as before, against the Polack,
    With an entreaty, herein further shown,
                               [giving a paper]
    That it might please you to give quiet pass
    Through your dominions for this enterprise
    On such regards of safety and allowance   79
    As therein are set down.
KING   It likes us well,   80
    And at our more considered time we'll read,   81
    Answer, and think upon this business.
    Meantime we thank you for your well-took labor.
    Go to your rest; at night we'll feast together.
    Most welcome home!   *Exeunt Ambassadors.*
POLONIUS   This business is well ended.
    My liege, and madam, to expostulate   86
    What majesty should be, what duty is,
    Why day is day, night night, and time is time,
    Were nothing but to waste night, day, and time.
    Therefore, since brevity is the soul of wit,   90
    And tediousness the limbs and outward flourishes,
    I will be brief. Your noble son is mad.
    Mad call I it, for, to define true madness,
    What is't but to be nothing else but mad?
    But let that go.
QUEEN   More matter, with less art.
POLONIUS
    Madam, I swear I use no art at all.
    That he's mad, 'tis true; 'tis true 'tis pity,
    And pity 'tis 'tis true—a foolish figure,   98
    But farewell it, for I will use no art.
    Mad let us grant him, then, and now remains
    That we find out the cause of this effect,

    Or rather say, the cause of this defect,
    For this effect defective comes by cause.   103
    Thus it remains, and the remainder thus.
    Perpend.   105
    I have a daughter—have while she is mine—
    Who, in her duty and obedience, mark,
    Hath given me this. Now gather and surmise.   108
    [He reads the letter.] "To the celestial and my soul's
    idol, the most beautified Ophelia"—
    That's an ill phrase, a vile phrase; "beautified" is a
    vile phrase. But you shall hear. Thus: *[He reads.]*
    "In her excellent white bosom, these, etc."   113
QUEEN   Came this from Hamlet to her?
POLONIUS
    Good madam, stay awhile, I will be faithful.   115
                                [He reads.]
    "Doubt thou the stars are fire,
      Doubt that the sun doth move,
      Doubt truth to be a liar,   118
      But never doubt I love.
    O dear Ophelia, I am ill at these numbers. I have not   120
    art to reckon my groans. But that I love thee best, O   121
    most best, believe it. Adieu.
                  Thine evermore, most dear lady, whilst this
                        machine is to him, Hamlet."   124
    This in obedience hath my daughter shown me,
    And, more above, hath his solicitings,   126
    As they fell out by time, by means, and place,   127
    All given to mine ear.
KING   But how hath she   128
    Received his love?
POLONIUS   What do you think of me?
KING
    As of a man faithful and honorable.
POLONIUS
    I would fain prove so. But what might you think,   131
    When I had seen this hot love on the wing—
    As I perceived it, I must tell you that,
    Before my daughter told me—what might you,
    Or my dear Majesty your queen here, think,
    If I had played the desk or table book,   136
    Or given my heart a winking, mute and dumb,   137
    Or looked upon this love with idle sight?   138
    What might you think? No, I went round to work,   139
    And my young mistress thus I did bespeak: 140
    "Lord Hamlet is a prince out of thy star;   141
    This must not be." And then I prescripts gave her,   142

---

58 **sift him** question Polonius (or Hamlet) closely.   59 **brother** fellow king   60 **desires** good wishes.   61 **Upon our first** At our first words on the business   66 **impotence** weakness   67 **borne in hand** deluded, taken advantage of.   **arrests** orders to desist   69 **in fine** in conclusion   71 **give th'assay** make trial of strength, challenge   79 **On . . . allowance** i.e., with such considerations for the safety of Denmark and permission for Fortinbras   80 **likes** pleases   81 **considered** suitable for deliberation   86 **expostulate** expound, inquire into   90 **wit** sense or judgment   98 **figure** figure of speech

103 **For . . . cause** i.e., for this defective behavior, this madness, must have a cause.   105 **Perpend** Consider.   108 **gather and surmise** draw your own conclusions.   113 **"In . . . etc."** (The letter is poetically addressed to her heart, where a letter would be kept by a young lady.)   115 **stay . . . faithful** i.e., hold on, I will do as you wish.   118 **Doubt** suspect   120 **ill . . . numbers** unskilled at writing verses.   121 **reckon** (1) count (2) number metrically, scan   124 **machine** i.e., body   126–8 **And . . . ear** and moreover she has told me when, how, and where his solicitings of her occurred.   131 **fain** gladly   136–7 **If . . . dumb** if I had acted as go-between, passing love notes, or if I had refused to let my heart acknowledge what my eyes could see   138 **with idle sight** complacently or incomprehendingly.   139 **round** roundly, plainly   140 **bespeak** address   141 **out of thy star** above your sphere, position   142 **prescripts** orders

That she should lock herself from his resort,
Admit no messengers, receive no tokens.
Which done, she took the fruits of my advice;
And he, repellèd—a short tale to make—
Fell into a sadness, then into a fast,
Thence to a watch, thence into a weakness,   148
Thence to a lightness, and by this declension   149
Into the madness wherein now he raves,
And all we mourn for.
KING [to the Queen]   Do you think 'tis this?
QUEEN   It may be, very like.
POLONIUS
Hath there been such a time—I would fain know
    that—
That I have positively said "'Tis so,"
When it proved otherwise?
KING   Not that I know.
POLONIUS
Take this from this, if this be otherwise.   156
If circumstances lead me, I will find
Where truth is hid, though it were hid indeed
Within the center.
KING   How may we try it further?   159
POLONIUS
You know sometimes he walks four hours together
Here in the lobby.
QUEEN   So he does indeed.
POLONIUS
At such a time I'll loose my daughter to him.   162
Be you and I behind an arras then.   163
Mark the encounter. If he love her not
And be not from his reason fall'n thereon,   165
Let me be no assistant for a state,
But keep a farm and carters.
KING   We will try it.   167

Enter Hamlet [reading on a book].

QUEEN
But look where sadly the poor wretch comes reading.
POLONIUS
Away, I do beseech you both, away.
I'll board him presently. Oh, give me leave.   170
            Exeunt King and Queen [with attendants].
How does my good Lord Hamlet?
HAMLET   Well, God-a-mercy.   172
POLONIUS   Do you know me, my lord?
HAMLET   Excellent well. You are a fishmonger.   174
POLONIUS   Not I, my lord.
HAMLET   Then I would you were so honest a man.

POLONIUS   Honest, my lord?
HAMLET   Ay, sir. To be honest, as this world goes, is to
be one man picked out of ten thousand.
POLONIUS   That's very true, my lord.
HAMLET   For if the sun breed maggots in a dead dog,
being a good kissing carrion—Have you a daughter?   182
POLONIUS   I have, my lord.
HAMLET   Let her not walk i'th' sun. Conception is a   184
blessing, but as your daughter may conceive, friend,
look to't.
POLONIUS [aside]   How say you by that? Still harping
on my daughter. Yet he knew me not at first; 'a said
I was a fishmonger. 'A is far gone. And truly in my
youth I suffered much extremity for love, very near
this. I'll speak to him again.—What do you read,
my lord?
HAMLET   Words, words, words.
POLONIUS   What is the matter, my lord?   194
HAMLET   Between who?
POLONIUS   I mean, the matter that you read, my lord.
HAMLET   Slanders, sir; for the satirical rogue says here
that old men have gray beards, that their faces are wrinkled, their eyes purging thick amber and plum-tree   199
gum, and that they have a plentiful lack of wit, to- 200
gether with most weak hams. All which, sir, though I
most powerfully and potently believe, yet I hold it not
honesty to have it thus set down, for yourself, sir, shall 203
grow old as I am, if like a crab you could go backward. 204
POLONIUS [aside]   Though this be madness, yet there is
method in't.—Will you walk out of the air, my lord?   206
HAMLET   Into my grave.
POLONIUS   Indeed, that's out of the air. [Aside] How
pregnant sometimes his replies are! A happiness that   209
often madness hits on, which reason and sanity could
not so prosperously be delivered of. I will leave him   211
and suddenly contrive the means of meeting between   212
him and my daughter.—My honorable lord, I will
most humbly take my leave of you.
HAMLET   You cannot, sir, take from me anything that I
will more willingly part withal—except my life, except   216
my life, except my life.

Enter Guildenstern and Rosencrantz.

POLONIUS   Fare you well, my lord.
HAMLET   These tedious old fools!
POLONIUS   You go to seek the Lord Hamlet. There he is.
ROSENCRANTZ [to Polonius]   God save you, sir!
                                    [Exit Polonius.]
GUILDENSTERN   My honored lord!

---

148 **watch** state of sleeplessness   149 **lightness** lightheadedness.
declension decline, deterioration. (With a pun on the grammatical
sense.)   156 **Take this from this** (The actor probably gestures, indicating that he means his head from his shoulders, or his staff of office
or chain from his hands or neck, or something similar.)   159 **center**
center of the earth, traditionally an extraordinarily inaccessible place.
try test   162 **loose** (As one might release an animal that is being
mated.)   163 **arras** hanging, tapestry   165 **thereon** on that account
167 **carters** wagon drivers.   170 **I'll . . . leave** I'll accost him at once.
Please leave us alone; leave him to me.   172 **God-a-mercy** God have
mercy, i.e., thank you.   174 **fishmonger** fish merchant.

182 **a good kissing carrion** i.e., a good piece of flesh for kissing, or for
the sun to kiss   184 **i'th' sun** in public. (With additional implication
of the sunshine of princely favors.)   **Conception** (1) Understanding
(2) Pregnancy   194 **matter** substance. (But Hamlet plays on the sense
of "basis for a dispute.")   199 **purging** discharging.   **amber** i.e.,
resin, like the resinous *plum-tree gum*   200 **wit** understanding
203 **honesty** decency, decorum   204 **old** as old   206 **out of the air**
(The open air was considered dangerous for sick people.)   209 **pregnant** quick-witted, full of meaning.   **happiness** felicity of expression
211 **prosperously** successfully   212 **suddenly** immediately
216 **withal** with

ROSENCRANTZ   My most dear lord!

HAMLET   My excellent good friends! How dost thou, Guildenstern? Ah, Rosencrantz! Good lads, how do you both?

ROSENCRANTZ
As the indifferent children of the earth.   227

GUILDENSTERN
Happy in that we are not overhappy.
On Fortune's cap we are not the very button.

HAMLET   Nor the soles of her shoe?

ROSENCRANTZ   Neither, my lord.

HAMLET   Then you live about her waist, or in the mid-   232
dle of her favors?   233

GUILDENSTERN   Faith, her privates we.   234

HAMLET   In the secret parts of Fortune? Oh, most true,
she is a strumpet. What news?   236

ROSENCRANTZ   None, my lord, but the world's grown honest.

HAMLET   Then is doomsday near. But your news is not true. Let me question more in particular. What have you, my good friends, deserved at the hands of Fortune that she sends you to prison hither?

GUILDENSTERN   Prison, my lord?

HAMLET   Denmark's a prison.

ROSENCRANTZ   Then is the world one.

HAMLET   A goodly one, in which there are many confines, wards, and dungeons, Denmark being one   247
o'th' worst.

ROSENCRANTZ   We think not so, my lord.

HAMLET   Why then 'tis none to you, for there is nothing either good or bad but thinking makes it so. To me it is a prison.

ROSENCRANTZ   Why then, your ambition makes it one. 'Tis too narrow for your mind.

HAMLET   Oh, God, I could be bounded in a nutshell and count myself a king of infinite space, were it not that I have bad dreams.

GUILDENSTERN   Which dreams indeed are ambition, for the very substance of the ambitious is merely the   259
shadow of a dream.

HAMLET   A dream itself is but a shadow.

ROSENCRANTZ   Truly, and I hold ambition of so airy and light a quality that it is but a shadow's shadow.

HAMLET   Then are our beggars bodies, and our mon-   264
archs and outstretched heroes the beggars' shadows.   265
Shall we to th' court? For, by my fay, I cannot reason.   266

ROSENCRANTZ, GUILDENSTERN   We'll wait upon you.   267

HAMLET   No such matter. I will not sort you with the   268
rest of my servants, for, to speak to you like an honest
man, I am most dreadfully attended. But, in the   270
beaten way of friendship, what make you at Elsinore?   271

ROSENCRANTZ   To visit you, my lord, no other occasion.

HAMLET   Beggar that I am, I am even poor in thanks;
but I thank you, and sure, dear friends, my thanks are
too dear a halfpenny. Were you not sent for? Is it your   275
own inclining? Is it a free visitation? Come, come, deal   276
justly with me. Come, come. Nay, speak.

GUILDENSTERN   What should we say, my lord?

HAMLET   Anything but to th' purpose. You were sent   279
for, and there is a kind of confession in your looks
which your modesties have not craft enough to color.   281
I know the good King and Queen have sent for you.

ROSENCRANTZ   To what end, my lord?

HAMLET   That you must teach me. But let me conjure   284
you, by the rights of our fellowship, by the consonancy   285
of our youth, by the obligation of our ever-preserved   286
love, and by what more dear a better proposer   287
could charge you withal, be even and direct with me   288
whether you were sent for or no.

ROSENCRANTZ [aside to Guildenstern]   What say you?

HAMLET [aside]   Nay, then, I have an eye of you.—If   291
you love me, hold not off.   292

GUILDENSTERN   My lord, we were sent for.

HAMLET   I will tell you why; so shall my anticipation   294
prevent your discovery, and your secrecy to the King   295
and Queen molt no feather. I have of late—but   296
wherefore I know not—lost all my mirth, forgone all
custom of exercises; and indeed it goes so heavily with
my disposition that this goodly frame, the earth,
seems to me a sterile promontory; this most excellent
canopy, the air, look you, this brave o'erhanging   301
firmament, this majestical roof fretted with golden   302
fire, why, it appeareth nothing to me but a foul and
pestilent congregation of vapors. What a piece of work   304
is a man! How noble in reason, how infinite in faculties,
in form and moving how express and admirable, in   306
action how like an angel, in apprehension how like a   307
god! The beauty of the world, the paragon of animals!
And yet, to me, what is this quintessence of dust?   309
Man delights not me—no, nor woman neither,
though by your smiling you seem to say so.

---

227 **indifferent** ordinary, at neither extreme of fortune or misfortune   232–3 **the middle . . . favors** i.e., her genitals.   234 **her privates we** (1) we dwell in her privates, her genitals, in the middle of her favors (2) we are her ordinary footsoldiers.   236 **strumpet** (Fortune was proverbially thought of as fickle.)   247 **confines** places of confinement   259 **the very . . . ambitious** that seemingly very substantial thing that the ambitious pursue   264–5 **Then . . . shadows** (Hamlet pursues their argument about ambition to its absurd extreme: if ambition is only a shadow of a shadow, then beggars (who are presumably without ambition) must be real, whereas monarchs and heroes are only their shadows—*outstretched* like elongated shadows, made to look bigger than they are.)   266 **fay** faith   267 **wait upon** accompany, attend. (But Hamlet uses the phrase in the sense of providing menial service.)

268 **sort** class, categorize   270 **dreadfully attended** waited upon in slovenly fashion.   271 **beaten way** familiar path, tried-and-true course.   **make** do   275 **too dear a halfpenny** (1) too expensive at even a halfpenny, i.e., of little worth (2) too expensive by a halfpenny in return for worthless kindness.   276 **free** voluntary   279 **Anything but to th' purpose** Anything except a straightforward answer. (Said ironically.)   281 **color** disguise.   284 **conjure** adjure, entreat   285–6 **the consonancy of our youth** our closeness in our younger days   287 **better** more skillful   288 **charge** urge.   **even** straight, honest   291 **of** on   292 **hold not off** don't hold back.   294–5 **so . . . discovery** in that way my saying it first will spare you from having to reveal the truth   296 **molt no feather** i.e., not diminish in the least.   301 **brave** splendid   302 **fretted** adorned (with fretwork, as in a vaulted ceiling)   304 **congregation** mass.   **piece of work** masterpiece   306 **express** well-framed, exact, expressive   307 **apprehension** power of comprehending   309 **quintessence** very essence. (Literally, the fifth essence beyond earth, water, air, and fire, supposed to be extractable from them.)

ROSENCRANTZ   My lord, there was no such stuff in my
    thoughts.
HAMLET   Why did you laugh, then, when I said man
    delights not me?
ROSENCRANTZ   To think, my lord, if you delight not in
    man, what Lenten entertainment the players shall   317
    receive from you. We coted them on the way, and   318
    hither are they coming to offer you service.
HAMLET   He that plays the king shall be welcome; His
    Majesty shall have tribute of me. The adventurous   321
    knight shall use his foil and target, the lover shall not   322
    sigh gratis, the humorous man shall end his part in   323
    peace, the clown shall make those laugh whose lungs   324
    are tickle o'th' sear, and the lady shall say her mind   325
    freely, or the blank verse shall halt for't. What players   326
    are they?
ROSENCRANTZ   Even those you were wont to take such
    delight in, the tragedians of the city.   329
HAMLET   How chances it they travel? Their residence,   330
    both in reputation and profit, was better both ways.
ROSENCRANTZ   I think their inhibition comes by the   332
    means of the late innovation.   333
HAMLET   Do they hold the same estimation they did
    when I was in the city? Are they so followed?
ROSENCRANTZ   No, indeed are they not.
HAMLET   How comes it? Do they grow rusty?   337
ROSENCRANTZ   Nay, their endeavor keeps in the wonted   338
    pace. But there is, sir, an aerie of children, little eyases,   339
    that cry out on the top of question and are most tyran-   340
    nically clapped for't. These are now the fashion, and   341
    so berattle the common stages—so they call them—   342
    that many wearing rapiers are afraid of goose quills   343
    and dare scarce come thither.
HAMLET   What, are they children? Who maintains 'em?
    How are they escotted? Will they pursue the quality no   346
    longer than they can sing? Will they not say after-   347

wards, if they should grow themselves to common   348
    players—as it is most like, if their means are no   349
    better—their writers do them wrong to make them   350
    exclaim against their own succession?   351
ROSENCRANTZ   Faith, there has been much to-do on   352
    both sides, and the nation holds it no sin to tar them to   353
    controversy. There was for a while no money bid for   354
    argument unless the poet and the player went to cuffs   355
    in the question.   356
HAMLET   Is't possible?
GUILDENSTERN   Oh, there has been much throwing
    about of brains.
HAMLET   Do the boys carry it away?   360
ROSENCRANTZ   Ay, that they do, my lord—Hercules   361
    and his load too.   362
HAMLET   It is not very strange; for my uncle is King of
    Denmark, and those that would make mouths at him   364
    while my father lived give twenty, forty, fifty, a
    hundred ducats apiece for his picture in little. 'Sblood,   366
    there is something in this more than natural, if philos-
    ophy could find it out.

                    A flourish [of trumpets within].

GUILDENSTERN   There are the players.
HAMLET   Gentlemen, you are welcome to Elsinore. Your
    hands, come then. Th'appurtenance of welcome is   371
    fashion and ceremony. Let me comply with you in this   372
    garb, lest my extent to the players, which, I tell you,   373
    must show fairly outwards, should more appear like   374
    entertainment than yours. You are welcome. But my   375
    uncle-father and aunt-mother are deceived.
GUILDENSTERN   In what, my dear lord?
HAMLET   I am but mad north-north-west. When the   378
    wind is southerly I know a hawk from a handsaw.   379

                    Enter Polonius.

POLONIUS   Well be with you, gentlemen!
HAMLET   Hark you, Guildenstern, and you too; at each
    ear a hearer. That great baby you see there is not yet
    out of his swaddling clouts.   383
ROSENCRANTZ   Haply he is the second time come to   384
    them, for they say an old man is twice a child.

---

317 Lenten entertainment meager reception (appropriate to Lent)
318 coted overtook and passed by   **321 tribute** (1) applause (2) homage paid in money.   **of** from   **322 foil and target** sword and shield
323 gratis for nothing.   **humorous man** eccentric character, dominated by one trait or "humor"   **323–4 in peace** i.e., with full license
325 tickle o'th' sear hair trigger, ready to laugh easily. (A *sear* is part
of a gun-lock.)   **326 halt** limp   **329 tragedians** actors
330 residence remaining in their usual place, i.e., in the city
332 inhibition formal prohibition (from acting plays in the city)
333 late innovation i.e., recent new fashion in satirical plays performed by boy actors in the "private" theaters; or the Earl of Essex's
abortive rebellion in 1601 against Elizabeth's government. (A much
debated passage of seemingly topical reference.)   **337 How . . . rusty?**
Have they lost their polish, gone out of fashion? (This passage,
through line 362, alludes to the rivalry between the children's companies and the adult actors, given strong impetus by the reopening of
the Children of the Chapel at the Blackfriars Theater in late 1600.)
338 keeps . . . wonted continues in the usual   **339 aerie** nest.   **eyases**
young hawks   **340 cry . . . question** speak shrilly, dominating the
controversy (in decrying the public theaters)   **340–1 tyrannically**
vehemently   **342 berattle . . . stages** clamor against the public theaters   **343 many wearing rapiers** i.e., many men of fashion, afraid to
patronize the common players for fear of being satirized by the poets
writing for the boy actors.   **goose quills** i.e., pens of satirists
346 escotted maintained.   **quality** (acting) profession   **346–7 no
longer . . . sing** i.e., only until their voices change.

348 common regular, adult   **349 like** likely   **349–50 if . . . better** if
they find no better way to support themselves   **351 succession** i.e.,
future careers.   **352 to-do** ado   **353 tar** incite (as in inciting dogs to
attack a chained bear)   **354–6 There . . . question** i.e., For a while, no
money was offered by the acting companies to playwrights for the
plot to a play unless the satirical poets who wrote for the boys and
the adult actors came to blows in the play itself.   **360 carry it away**
i.e., win the day.   **361–2 Hercules . . . load** (Thought to be an allusion
to the sign of the Globe Theatre, which allegedly was Hercules bearing the world on his shoulders.)   **364 mouths** faces   **366 ducats** gold
coins.   **in little** in miniature.   **'Sblood** By God's (Christ's) blood
371 Th'appurtenance The proper accompaniment   **372 comply**
observe the formalities of courtesy   **373 garb** i.e., manner.   **my
extent** that which I extend, i.e., my polite behavior   **374 show fairly
outwards** show every evidence of cordiality   **375 entertainment** a
(warm) reception   **378 north-north-west** just off true north, only
partly.   **379 I . . . handsaw** (Speaking in his mad guise, Hamlet perhaps suggests that he can tell true from false. A *handsaw* may be a
hernshaw or heron. Still, a supposedly mad disposition might compare hawks and handsaws.)   **383 swaddling clouts** cloths in which
to wrap a newborn baby.   **384 Haply** Perhaps

HAMLET   I will prophesy he comes to tell me of the
players. Mark it.—You say right, sir, o' Monday 387
morning, 'twas then indeed.   388

POLONIUS   My lord, I have news to tell you.

HAMLET   My lord, I have news to tell you. When Roscius 390
was an actor in Rome—

POLONIUS   The actors are come hither, my lord.

HAMLET   Buzz, buzz!   393

POLONIUS   Upon my honor—

HAMLET   Then came each actor on his ass.

POLONIUS   The best actors in the world, either for
tragedy, comedy, history, pastoral, pastoral-comical,
historical-pastoral, tragical-historical, tragical-comical-
historical-pastoral, scene individable, or poem unlim- 399
ited. Seneca cannot be too heavy, nor Plautus too   400
light. For the law of writ and the liberty, these are the 401
only men.

HAMLET   O Jephthah, judge of Israel, what a treasure 403
hadst thou!

POLONIUS   What a treasure had he, my lord?

HAMLET   Why,
   "One fair daughter, and no more,
   The which he lovèd passing well."   408

POLONIUS   [aside] Still on my daughter.

HAMLET   Am I not i'th' right, old Jephthah?

POLONIUS   If you call me Jephthah, my lord, I have a
daughter that I love passing well.

HAMLET   Nay, that follows not.   413

POLONIUS   What follows then, my lord?   414

HAMLET   Why,
   "As by lot, God wot,"   416
and then, you know,
   "It came to pass, as most like it was"—   418
the first row of the pious chanson will show you more, 419
for look where my abridgment comes.   420

               Enter the Players.

You are welcome, masters; welcome, all. I am glad to 421
see thee well. Welcome, good friends. Oh, old friend!
Why, thy face is valanced since I saw thee last. Com'st 423
thou to beard me in Denmark? What, my young lady 424

and mistress! By'r Lady, Your Ladyship is nearer to 425
heaven than when I saw you last, by the altitude of a 426
chopine. Pray God your voice, like a piece of uncur- 427
rent gold, be not cracked within the ring. Masters, you 428
are all welcome. We'll e'en to't like French falconers, 429
fly at anything we see. We'll have a speech straight. 430
Come, give us a taste of your quality. Come, a 431
passionate speech.

FIRST PLAYER   What speech, my good lord?

HAMLET   I heard thee speak me a speech once, but it
was never acted, or if it was, not above once, for the
play, I remember, pleased not the million; 'twas cav- 436
iar to the general. But it was—as I received it, and 437
others, whose judgments in such matters cried in the 438
top of mine—an excellent play, well digested in the 439
scenes, set down with as much modesty as cunning. I 440
remember one said there were no sallets in the lines to 441
make the matter savory, nor no matter in the phrase
that might indict the author of affectation, but called it 443
an honest method, as wholesome as sweet, and by very
much more handsome than fine. One speech in't I 445
chiefly loved: 'twas Aeneas' tale to Dido, and there-
about of it especially when he speaks of Priam's 447
slaughter. If it live in your memory, begin at this line: 448
let me see, let me see—
   "The rugged Pyrrhus, like th' Hyrcanian beast"— 450
'Tis not so. It begins with Pyrrhus:
   "The rugged Pyrrhus, he whose sable arms,   452
   Black as his purpose, did the night resemble
   When he lay couchèd in th' ominous horse,   454
   Hath now this dread and black complexion
      smeared
   With heraldry more dismal. Head to foot   456
   Now is he total gules, horridly tricked   457
   With blood of fathers, mothers, daughters, sons,
   Baked and impasted with the parching streets,   459
   That lend a tyrannous and a damnèd light   460

387–8 You say . . . then indeed (Said to impress upon Polonius the idea
that Hamlet is in serious conversation with his friends.) 390 Roscius a
famous Roman actor who died in 62 B.C. 393 Buzz (An interjection
used to denote stale news.) 399–400 scene . . . unlimited plays that
are unclassifiable and all-inclusive. (An absurdly catchall conclusion to
Polonius's pompous list of categories.) 400 Seneca writer of Latin
tragedies. Plautus writer of Latin comedies 401 law . . . liberty dramatic composition both according to the rules and disregarding the
rules. these i.e., the actors 403 Jephthah . . . Israel (Jephthah had to
sacrifice his daughter; see Judges 11. Hamlet goes on to quote from a
ballad on the theme.) 408 passing surpassingly 413 that follows not
i.e., just because you resemble Jephthah in having a daughter does not
logically prove that you love her. 414 What . . . lord? What does follow logically? (But Hamlet, pretending madness, answers with a fragment of a ballad, as if Polonius had asked, "What comes next?" See
419n.) 416 lot chance. wot knows 418 like likely, probable
419 the first . . . more the first stanza of this biblically based ballad will
satisfy your stated desire to know *what follows* (line 414) 420 my
abridgment something that cuts short my conversation; also, a diversion 421 masters good sirs 423 valanced fringed (with a beard)
424 beard confront, challenge. (With obvious pun.) young lady i.e.,
boy playing women's parts

425 By'r Lady By Our Lady 425–6 nearer to heaven i.e., taller
427 chopine thick-soled shoe of Italian fashion. 427–8 uncurrent not
passable as lawful coinage 428 cracked . . . ring i.e., changed from
adolescent to male voice, no longer suitable for women's roles. (Coins
featured rings enclosing the sovereign's head; if the coin was sufficiently clipped to invade within this ring, it was unfit for currency.)
429 e'en to't go at it 430 straight at once. 431 quality professional
skill. 436–7 caviar to the general i.e., an expensive delicacy not generally palatable to uneducated tastes. 438–9 cried in the top of i.e.,
spoke with greater authority than 439 digested arranged, ordered
440 modesty moderation, restraint. cunning skill. 441 sallets i.e.,
something savory, spicy improprieties 443 indict convict
445 handsome well-proportioned. fine elaborately ornamented,
showy. 447–8 Priam's slaughter the slaying of the ruler of Troy,
when the Greeks finally took the city. 450 Pyrrhus a Greek hero in
the Trojan War, also known as Neoptolemus, son of Achilles—another
avenging son. th' Hyrcanian beast i.e., the tiger. (On the death of
Priam, see Virgil, *Aeneid*, 2.506 ff.; compare the whole speech with
Marlowe's *Dido Queen of Carthage*, 2.1.214 ff. On the *Hyrcanian* tiger,
see *Aeneid*, 4.366–7. Hyrcania is on the Caspian Sea.) 452 rugged
shaggy, savage. sable black (for reasons of camouflage during the
episode of the Trojan horse) 454 couchèd concealed. ominous
horse fateful Trojan horse, by which the Greeks gained access to Troy
456 dismal calamitous. 457 total gules entirely red. (A heraldic
term.) tricked spotted and smeared. (Heraldic.) 459 Baked . . .
streets roasted and encrusted, like a thick paste, by the parching heat
of the streets (because of the fires everywhere) 460 tyrannous cruel

To their lord's murder. Roasted in wrath and fire, 461
And thus o'ersizèd with coagulate gore, 462
With eyes like carbuncles, the hellish Pyrrhus 463
Old grandsire Priam seeks."
So proceed you.

POLONIUS 'Fore God, my lord, well spoken, with good accent and good discretion.

FIRST PLAYER   "Anon he finds him
Striking too short at Greeks. His antique sword, 469
Rebellious to his arm, lies where it falls,
Repugnant to command. Unequal matched, 471
Pyrrhus at Priam drives, in rage strikes wide,
But with the whiff and wind of his fell sword 473
Th'unnervèd father falls. Then senseless Ilium, 474
Seeming to feel this blow, with flaming top
Stoops to his base, and with a hideous crash 476
Takes prisoner Pyrrhus' ear. For, lo! His sword,
Which was declining on the milky head 478
Of reverend Priam, seemed i'th'air to stick.
So as a painted tyrant Pyrrhus stood, 480
And, like a neutral to his will and matter, 481
Did nothing.
But as we often see against some storm 483
A silence in the heavens, the rack stand still, 484
The bold winds speechless, and the orb below 485
As hush as death, anon the dreadful thunder
Doth rend the region, so, after Pyrrhus' pause, 487
A rousèd vengeance sets him new a-work,
And never did the Cyclops' hammers fall 489
On Mars's armor forged for proof eterne 490
With less remorse than Pyrrhus' bleeding sword 491
Now falls on Priam.
Out, out, thou strumpet Fortune! All you gods
In general synod take away her power! 494
Break all the spokes and fellies from her wheel, 495
And bowl the round nave down the hill of heaven 496
As low as to the fiends!"

POLONIUS This is too long.

HAMLET It shall to the barber's with your beard.—Prithee, say on. He's for a jig or a tale of bawdry, or he 500
sleeps. Say on; come to Hecuba. 501

FIRST PLAYER
"But who, ah woe! had seen the moblèd queen"— 502

HAMLET "The moblèd queen"?

POLONIUS That's good. "Moblèd queen" is good.

FIRST PLAYER
"Run barefoot up and down, threat'ning the flames 505
With bisson rheum, a clout upon that head 506
Where late the diadem stood, and, for a robe, 507
About her lank and all o'erteemèd loins 508
A blanket, in the alarm of fear caught up—
Who this had seen, with tongue in venom steeped,
'Gainst Fortune's state would treason have
    pronounced. 511
But if the gods themselves did see her then
When she saw Pyrrhus make malicious sport
In mincing with his sword her husband's limbs,
The instant burst of clamor that she made,
Unless things mortal move them not at all,
Would have made milch the burning eyes of heaven, 517
And passion in the gods." 518

POLONIUS Look whe'er he has not turned his color and 519
has tears in 's eyes. Prithee, no more.

HAMLET 'Tis well; I'll have thee speak out the rest of
this soon.—Good my lord, will you see the players well
bestowed? Do you hear, let them be well used, for they 523
are the abstract and brief chronicles of the time. After 524
your death you were better have a bad epitaph than
their ill report while you live.

POLONIUS My lord, I will use them according to their
desert.

HAMLET God's bodikin, man, much better. Use every 529
man after his desert, and who shall scape whipping?
Use them after your own honor and dignity. The less 531
they deserve, the more merit is in your bounty. Take
them in.

POLONIUS Come, sirs.   [Exit.]

HAMLET Follow him, friends. We'll hear a play tomorrow. [As they start to leave, Hamlet detains the First
Player.] Dost thou hear me, old friend? Can you play
The Murder of Gonzago?

FIRST PLAYER Ay, my lord.

HAMLET We'll ha 't tomorrow night. You could, for a 540
need, study a speech of some dozen or sixteen lines 541
which I would set down and insert in't, could you not?

FIRST PLAYER Ay, my lord.

HAMLET Very well. Follow that lord, and look you mock
him not.   Exeunt players.
My good friends, I'll leave you till night. You are welcome to Elsinore.

ROSENCRANTZ Good my lord!
            Exeunt [Rosencrantz and Guildenstern].

HAMLET
Ay, so, goodbye to you.—Now I am alone.
Oh, what a rogue and peasant slave am I!

---

461 their lord's i.e., Priam's **462 o'ersizèd** covered as with size or glue **463 carbuncles** large fiery-red precious stones thought to emit their own light **469 antique** ancient, long-used **471 Repugnant** disobedient, resistant **473 fell** cruel **474 Th'unnervèd** the strengthless. **senseless Ilium** inanimate citadel of Troy **476 his** its **478 declining** descending. **milky** white-haired **480 painted** motionless, as in a painting **481 like . . . matter** i.e., as though suspended between his intention and its fulfillment **483 against** just before **484 rack** mass of clouds **485 orb** globe, earth **487 region** sky **489 Cyclops** giant armor makers in the smithy of Vulcan **490 proof** proven or tested resistance to assault **491 remorse** pity **494 synod** assembly **495 fellies** pieces of wood forming the rim of a wheel **496 nave** hub. **hill of heaven** Mount Olympus **500 jig** comic song and dance often given at the end of a play **501 Hecuba** wife of Priam. **502 who . . . had** anyone who had. (Also in line 510.) **moblèd** muffled

505 threat'ning the flames i.e., weeping hard enough to dampen the flames **506 bisson rheum** blinding tears. **clout** cloth **507 late** lately **508 all o'erteemèd** utterly worn out with bearing children **511 state** rule, managing. **pronounced** proclaimed. **517 milch** milky, moist with tears. **burning eyes of heaven** i.e., stars, heavenly bodies **518 passion** overpowering emotion **519 whe'er** whether **523 bestowed** lodged. **524 abstract** summary account **529 God's bodikin** By God's (Christ's) little body, *bodykin*. (Not to be confused with *bodkin*, "dagger.") **531 after** according to **540 ha 't** have it **541 study** memorize

Is it not monstrous that this player here,
But in a fiction, in a dream of passion,   552
Could force his soul so to his own conceit   553
That from her working all his visage wanned,   554
Tears in his eyes, distraction in his aspect,   555
A broken voice, and his whole function suiting   556
With forms to his conceit? And all for nothing!   557
For Hecuba!
What's Hecuba to him, or he to Hecuba,
That he should weep for her? What would he do
Had he the motive and the cue for passion
That I have? He would drown the stage with tears
And cleave the general ear with horrid speech,   563
Make mad the guilty and appall the free,   564
Confound the ignorant, and amaze indeed   565
The very faculties of eyes and ears. Yet I,
A dull and muddy-mettled rascal, peak   567
Like John-a-dreams, unpregnant of my cause,   568
And can say nothing—no, not for a king
Upon whose property and most dear life   570
A damned defeat was made. Am I a coward?   571
Who calls me villain? Breaks my pate across?   572
Plucks off my beard and blows it in my face?
Tweaks me by the nose? Gives me the lie i'th' throat   574
As deep as to the lungs? Who does me this?
Ha, 'swounds, I should take it; for it cannot be   576
But I am pigeon-livered and lack gall   577
To make oppression bitter, or ere this   578
I should ha' fatted all the region kites   579
With this slave's offal. Bloody, bawdy villain!   580
Remorseless, treacherous, lecherous, kindless villain!   581
Oh, vengeance!
Why, what an ass am I! This is most brave,   583
That I, the son of a dear father murdered,
Prompted to my revenge by heaven and hell,
Must like a whore unpack my heart with words
And fall a-cursing, like a very drab,   587
A scullion! Fie upon't, foh! About, my brains!   588
Hum, I have heard
That guilty creatures sitting at a play
Have by the very cunning of the scene   591
Been struck so to the soul that presently   592

552 **But** merely   553 **force . . . conceit** bring his innermost being so
entirely into accord with his conception (of the role)   554 **from her
working** as a result of, or in response to, his soul's activity.   **wanned**
grew pale   555 **aspect** look, glance   556–7 **his whole . . . conceit** all
his bodily powers responding with actions to suit his thought.
563 **the general ear** everyone's ear.   **horrid** horrible   564 **appall** (Literally, make pale.)   **free** innocent   565 **Confound the ignorant** i.e.,
dumbfound those who know nothing of the crime that has been
committed.   **amaze** stun   567 **muddy-mettled** dull-spirited
567–8 **peak . . . cause** mope, like a dreaming idler, not quickened by
my cause   570 **property** person and function   571 **damned defeat**
damnable act of destruction   572 **pate** head   574 **Gives . . . throat**
Calls me an out-and-out liar   576 **'swounds** by his (Christ's) wounds
577 **pigeon-livered** (The pigeon or dove was popularly supposed to
be mild because it secreted no gall.)   578 **To . . . bitter** to make things
bitter for oppressors   579 **region kites** kites (birds of prey) of the air
580 **offal** entrails.   581 **Remorseless** Pitiless.   **kindless** unnatural
583 **brave** fine, admirable. (Said ironically.)   587 **drab** whore
588 **scullion** menial kitchen servant. (Apt to be foul-mouthed.)
About About it, to work   591 **cunning** art, skill.   **scene** dramatic
presentation   592 **presently** at once

They have proclaimed their malefactions;
For murder, though it have no tongue, will speak
With most miraculous organ. I'll have these players
Play something like the murder of my father
Before mine uncle. I'll observe his looks;
I'll tent him to the quick. If 'a do blench,   598
I know my course. The spirit that I have seen
May be the devil, and the devil hath power
T'assume a pleasing shape; yea, and perhaps,
Out of my weakness and my melancholy,
As he is very potent with such spirits,   603
Abuses me to damn me. I'll have grounds   604
More relative than this. The play's the thing   605
Wherein I'll catch the conscience of the King.   *Exit.*

[3.1]

*Enter King, Queen, Polonius, Ophelia,
Rosencrantz, Guildenstern, lords.*

KING
And can you by no drift of conference   1
Get from him why he puts on this confusion,
Grating so harshly all his days of quiet
With turbulent and dangerous lunacy?
ROSENCRANTZ
He does confess he feels himself distracted,
But from what cause 'a will by no means speak.
GUILDENSTERN
Nor do we find him forward to be sounded,   7
But with a crafty madness keeps aloof
When we would bring him on to some confession
Of his true state.
QUEEN   Did he receive you well?
ROSENCRANTZ   Most like a gentleman.
GUILDENSTERN
But with much forcing of his disposition.   12
ROSENCRANTZ
Niggard of question, but of our demands   13
Most free in his reply.
QUEEN   Did you assay him   14
To any pastime?
ROSENCRANTZ
Madam, it so fell out that certain players
We o'erraught on the way. Of these we told him,   17
And there did seem in him a kind of joy
To hear of it. They are here about the court,
And, as I think, they have already order
This night to play before him.
POLONIUS   'Tis most true,
And he beseeched me to entreat Your Majesties
To hear and see the matter.

598 **tent** probe.   **the quick** the tender part of a wound, the core.
blench quail, flinch   603 **spirits** humors (of melancholy)
604 **Abuses** deludes   605 **relative** cogent, pertinent
3.1 Location: The castle.
1 **drift of conference** course of talk   7 **forward** willing.   **sounded**
questioned   12 **disposition** inclination.   13 **Niggard of question**
Laconic.   **demands** questions   14 **assay** try to win   17 **o'erraught**
overtook

KING
　　With all my heart, and it doth much content me
　　To hear him so inclined.
　　Good gentlemen, give him a further edge　　　　　　　26
　　And drive his purpose into these delights.

ROSENCRANTZ
　　We shall, my lord.
　　　　　　　　　Exeunt Rosencrantz and Guildenstern.

KING　　　　　　　　　Sweet Gertrude, leave us too,
　　For we have closely sent for Hamlet hither,　　　　29
　　That he, as 'twere by accident, may here
　　Affront Ophelia.　　　　　　　　　　　　　　　　31
　　Her father and myself, lawful espials,　　　　　　32
　　Will so bestow ourselves that seeing, unseen,
　　We may of their encounter frankly judge,
　　And gather by him, as he is behaved,
　　If 't be th'affliction of his love or no
　　That thus he suffers for.

QUEEN　　　　　　　　　I shall obey you.
　　And for your part, Ophelia, I do wish
　　That your good beauties be the happy cause
　　Of Hamlet's wildness. So shall I hope your virtues
　　Will bring him to his wonted way again,
　　To both your honors.

OPHELIA　　　　　　　　Madam, I wish it may.
　　　　　　　　　　　　　　　　　[*Exit Queen.*]

POLONIUS
　　Ophelia, walk you here.—Gracious, so please you,　43
　　We will bestow ourselves. [*To Ophelia*] Read on this
　　　　book,　　　　　　　　　　　[*giving her a book*]　44
　　That show of such an exercise may color　　　　　45
　　Your loneliness. We are oft to blame in this—　　46
　　'Tis too much proved—that with devotion's visage　47
　　And pious action we do sugar o'er
　　The devil himself.

KING [*aside*]　Oh, 'tis too true!
　　How smart a lash that speech doth give my
　　　　conscience!
　　The harlot's cheek, beautied with plast'ring art,
　　Is not more ugly to the thing that helps it　　　　53
　　Than is my deed to my most painted word.　　　　54
　　Oh, heavy burden!

POLONIUS
　　I hear him coming. Let's withdraw, my lord.　　　56
　　　　　　　　　　[*The King and Polonius withdraw.*]

　　　　Enter Hamlet. [*Ophelia pretends to read a book.*]

HAMLET
　　To be, or not to be, that is the question:
　　Whether 'tis nobler in the mind to suffer
　　The slings and arrows of outrageous fortune,

Or to take arms against a sea of troubles
And by opposing end them. To die, to sleep—
No more—and by a sleep to say we end
The heartache and the thousand natural shocks
That flesh is heir to. 'Tis a consummation
Devoutly to be wished. To die, to sleep;
To sleep, perchance to dream. Ay, there's the rub,　66
For in that sleep of death what dreams may come,
When we have shuffled off this mortal coil,　　　68
Must give us pause. There's the respect　　　　　69
That makes calamity of so long life.　　　　　　70
For who would bear the whips and scorns of time,
Th'oppressor's wrong, the proud man's contumely,　72
The pangs of disprized love, the law's delay,　　73
The insolence of office, and the spurns　　　　　74
That patient merit of th'unworthy takes,　　　　75
When he himself might his quietus make　　　　76
With a bare bodkin? Who would fardels bear,　　77
To grunt and sweat under a weary life,
But that the dread of something after death,
The undiscovered country from whose bourn　　　80
No traveler returns, puzzles the will,
And makes us rather bear those ills we have
Than fly to others that we know not of?
Thus conscience does make cowards of us all;
And thus the native hue of resolution　　　　　85
Is sicklied o'er with the pale cast of thought,　86
And enterprises of great pitch and moment　　　87
With this regard their currents turn awry　　　88
And lose the name of action.—Soft you now,　　89
The fair Ophelia.—Nymph, in thy orisons　　　90
Be all my sins remembered.

OPHELIA　　　　　　　　Good my lord,　　　　91
　　How does Your Honor for this many a day?

HAMLET
　　I humbly thank you; well, well, well.

OPHELIA
　　My lord, I have remembrances of yours,
　　That I have longèd long to redeliver.
　　I pray you, now receive them.　　　[*She offers tokens.*]

HAMLET
　　No, not I, I never gave you aught.

OPHELIA
　　My honored lord, you know right well you did,
　　And with them words of so sweet breath composed
　　As made the things more rich. Their perfume lost,
　　Take these again, for to the noble mind

---

26 **edge** incitement　29 **closely** privately　31 **Affront** confront, meet
32 **espials** spies　43 **Gracious** Your Grace (i.e., the King)
44 **bestow** conceal　45 **exercise** religious exercise. (The book she
reads is one of devotion.)　**color** give a plausible appearance to
46 **loneliness** being alone.　47 **too much proved** too often shown to
be true, too often practiced　53 **to . . . helps it** in comparison with the
cosmetic that fashions the cheek's false beauty　54 **painted word**
deceptive utterances.　56.1 *withdraw* (The King and Polonius may
retire behind an arras. The stage directions specify that they "enter"
again near the end of the scene.)

66 **rub** (Literally, an obstacle in the game of bowls.)　68 **shuffled**
sloughed, cast.　**coil** turmoil　69 **respect** consideration　70 **of . . .
life** so long-lived, something we willingly endure for so long. (Also
suggesting that long life is itself a calamity.)　72 **contumely** insolent
abuse　73 **disprized** unvalued　74 **office** officialdom.　**spurns**
insults　75 **of . . . takes** receives from unworthy persons　76 **quietus**
acquittance; here, death　77 **a bare bodkin** a mere dagger,
unsheathed.　**fardels** burdens　80 **bourn** frontier, boundary
85 **native hue** natural color, complexion　86 **cast** tinge, shade of color
87 **pitch** height (as of a falcon's flight).　**moment** importance
88 **regard** respect, consideration.　**currents** courses　89 **Soft you** i.e.,
Wait a minute, gently　90–1 **in . . . remembered** i.e., pray for me, sinner that I am.

Rich gifts wax poor when givers prove unkind.
There, my lord.   [*She gives tokens.*]
HAMLET   Ha, ha! Are you honest?   104
OPHELIA   My lord?
HAMLET   Are you fair?   106
OPHELIA   What means Your Lordship?
HAMLET   That if you be honest and fair, your honesty   108
should admit no discourse to your beauty.   109
OPHELIA   Could beauty, my lord, have better commerce 110
than with honesty?
HAMLET   Ay, truly, for the power of beauty will sooner
transform honesty from what it is to a bawd than the
force of honesty can translate beauty into his likeness. 114
This was sometime a paradox, but now the time gives 115
it proof. I did love you once.   116
OPHELIA   Indeed, my lord, you made me believe so.
HAMLET   You should not have believed me, for virtue   118
cannot so inoculate our old stock but we shall relish of 119
it. I loved you not.   120
OPHELIA   I was the more deceived.
HAMLET   Get thee to a nunnery. Why wouldst thou be a 122
breeder of sinners? I am myself indifferent honest, but 123
yet I could accuse me of such things that it were better
my mother had not borne me: I am very proud,
revengeful, ambitious, with more offenses at my beck 126
than I have thoughts to put them in, imagination to
give them shape, or time to act them in. What should
such fellows as I do crawling between earth and
heaven? We are arrant knaves all; believe none of us.
Go thy ways to a nunnery. Where's your father?
OPHELIA   At home, my lord.
HAMLET   Let the doors be shut upon him, that he may
play the fool nowhere but in 's own house. Farewell.
OPHELIA   Oh, help him, you sweet heavens!
HAMLET   If thou dost marry, I'll give thee this plague for
thy dowry: be thou as chaste as ice, as pure as snow,
thou shalt not escape calumny. Get thee to a nunnery,
farewell. Or, if thou wilt needs marry, marry a fool, for
wise men know well enough what monsters you   140
make of them. To a nunnery, go, and quickly too.
Farewell.
OPHELIA   Heavenly powers, restore him!
HAMLET   I have heard of your paintings too, well   144
enough. God hath given you one face, and you make
yourselves another. You jig, you amble, and you   146
lisp, you nickname God's creatures, and make your   147
wantonness your ignorance. Go to, I'll no more on't;   148

it hath made me mad. I say we will have no more
marriage. Those that are married already—all but
one—shall live. The rest shall keep as they are. To a
nunnery, go.   *Exit.*
OPHELIA
Oh, what a noble mind is here o'erthrown!
The courtier's, soldier's, scholar's, eye, tongue, sword,
Th'expectancy and rose of the fair state,   155
The glass of fashion and the mold of form,   156
Th'observed of all observers, quite, quite down!   157
And I, of ladies most deject and wretched,
That sucked the honey of his music vows,   159
Now see that noble and most sovereign reason
Like sweet bells jangled out of tune and harsh,
That unmatched form and feature of blown youth   162
Blasted with ecstasy. Oh, woe is me,   163
T'have seen what I have seen, see what I see!

Enter King and Polonius.

KING
Love? His affections do not that way tend;   165
Nor what he spake, though it lacked form a little,
Was not like madness. There's something in his soul
O'er which his melancholy sits on brood,   168
And I do doubt the hatch and the disclose   169
Will be some danger; which for to prevent,
I have in quick determination
Thus set it down: he shall with speed to England   172
For the demand of our neglected tribute.
Haply the seas and countries different
With variable objects shall expel   175
This something-settled matter in his heart,   176
Whereon his brains still beating puts him thus   177
From fashion of himself. What think you on't?   178
POLONIUS
It shall do well. But yet do I believe
The origin and commencement of his grief
Sprung from neglected love.—How now, Ophelia?
You need not tell us what Lord Hamlet said;
We heard it all.—My lord, do as you please,
But, if you hold it fit, after the play
Let his queen-mother all alone entreat him
To show his grief. Let her be round with him;   186
And I'll be placed, so please you, in the ear
Of all their conference. If she find him not,   188
To England send him, or confine him where

104 **honest** (1) truthful (2) chaste.   106 **fair** (1) beautiful (2) just, honorable.   108 **your honesty** your chastity   109 **discourse to** familiar dealings with   110 **commerce** dealings, intercourse   114 **his** its   115–16 **This . . . proof** This was formerly an unfashionable view, but now the present age confirms how true it is.   118–20 **virtue . . . of it** virtue cannot be grafted onto our sinful condition without our retaining some taste of the old stock.   122 **nunnery** convent. (With an awareness that the word was also used derisively to denote a brothel.)   123 **indifferent honest** reasonably virtuous   126 **beck** command   140 **monsters** (An illusion to the horns of a cuckold.)   **you** i.e., you women   144 **paintings** use of cosmetics   146–8 **You jig . . . ignorance** i.e., You prance about frivolously and speak with affected coyness, you put new labels on God's creatures (by your use of cosmetics), and you excuse your affectations on the grounds of pretended ignorance.   148 **on't** of it

155 **Th'expectancy and rose** the hope and ornament   156 **The glass . . . form** the mirror of true self-fashioning and the pattern of courtly behavior   157 **Th'observed . . . observers** i.e., the center of attention and honor in the court   159 **music** musical, sweetly uttered   162 **blown** blossoming   163 **Blasted with ecstasy** blighted with madness.   165 **affections** emotions, feelings   168 **sits on brood** sits like a bird on a nest, about to *hatch* mischief (line 169)   169 **doubt** suspect, fear.   **disclose** disclosure, hatching   172 **set it down** resolved   175 **variable objects** various sights and surroundings to divert him   176 **This something . . . heart** the strange matter settled in his heart   177 **still** continually   178 **From . . . himself** out of his natural manner.   186 **round** blunt   188 **find him not** fails to discover what is troubling him

Your wisdom best shall think.

KING   It shall be so.
Madness in great ones must not unwatched go.
                                        Exeunt.

[3.2]

Enter Hamlet and three of the Players.

HAMLET   Speak the speech, I pray you, as I pronounced
it to you, trippingly on the tongue. But if you mouth
it, as many of our players do, I had as lief the town crier   3
spoke my lines. Nor do not saw the air too much with
your hand, thus, but use all gently; for in the very
torrent, tempest, and, as I may say, whirlwind of your
passion, you must acquire and beget a temperance
that may give it smoothness. Oh, it offends me to the
soul to hear a robustious periwig-pated fellow tear a   9
passion to tatters, to very rags, to split the ears of the
groundlings, who for the most part are capable of   11
nothing but inexplicable dumb shows and noise. I   12
would have such a fellow whipped for o'erdoing Ter-   13
magant. It out-Herods Herod. Pray you, avoid it.   14
FIRST PLAYER   I warrant Your Honor.
HAMLET   Be not too tame neither, but let your own
discretion be your tutor. Suit the action to the word,
the word to the action, with this special observance,
that you o'erstep not the modesty of nature. For   19
anything so o'erdone is from the purpose of playing,   20
whose end, both at the first and now, was and is to
hold as 'twere the mirror up to nature, to show virtue
her feature, scorn her own image, and the very age   23
and body of the time his form and pressure. Now this   24
overdone or come tardy off, though it makes the   25
unskillful laugh, cannot but make the judicious grieve,   26
the censure of the which one must in your allowance   27
o'erweigh a whole theater of others. Oh, there be players that I have seen play, and heard others praise, and
that highly, not to speak it profanely, that, neither   30
having th'accent of Christians nor the gait of Chris-   31
tian, pagan, nor man, have so strutted and bellowed   32
that I have thought some of nature's journeymen had   33

made men and not made them well, they imitated
humanity so abominably.   35
FIRST PLAYER   I hope we have reformed that indifferently   36
with us, sir.
HAMLET   Oh, reform it altogether. And let those that play
your clowns speak no more than is set down for them;
for there be of them that will themselves laugh, to set   40
on some quantity of barren spectators to laugh too,   41
though in the meantime some necessary question of
the play be then to be considered. That's villainous,
and shows a most pitiful ambition in the fool that uses
it. Go make you ready.   [*Exeunt Players.*]

Enter Polonius, Guildenstern, and Rosencrantz.

How now, my lord, will the King hear this piece of
work?
POLONIUS   And the Queen too, and that presently.   48
HAMLET   Bid the players make haste.   [*Exit Polonius.*]
Will you two help to hasten them?
ROSENCRANTZ
Ay, my lord.   *Exeunt they two.*
HAMLET   What ho, Horatio!

Enter Horatio.

HORATIO   Here, sweet lord, at your service.
HAMLET
Horatio, thou art e'en as just a man
As e'er my conversation coped withal.   54
HORATIO
Oh, my dear lord—
HAMLET   Nay, do not think I flatter,
For what advancement may I hope from thee
That no revenue hast but thy good spirits
To feed and clothe thee? Why should the poor be
    flattered?
No, let the candied tongue lick absurd pomp,   59
And crook the pregnant hinges of the knee   60
Where thrift may follow fawning. Dost thou hear?   61
Since my dear soul was mistress of her choice
And could of men distinguish her election,   63
Sh' hath sealed thee for herself, for thou hast been   64
As one, in suffering all, that suffers nothing,
A man that Fortune's buffets and rewards
Hast ta'en with equal thanks; and blest are those
Whose blood and judgment are so well commeddled   68
That they are not a pipe for Fortune's finger
To sound what stop she please. Give me that man   70
That is not passion's slave, and I will wear him
In my heart's core, ay, in my heart of heart,
As I do thee.—Something too much of this.—
There is a play tonight before the King.
One scene of it comes near the circumstance
Which I have told thee of my father's death.

3.2 Location: The castle.
3 our players players nowadays.   **I had as lief** I would just as soon
9 robustious violent, boisterous.   **periwig-pated** wearing a wig
11 groundlings spectators who paid least and stood in the yard of the
theater.   **capable of** able to understand   **12 dumb shows and noise**
noisy spectacle (rather than thoughtful drama).   **13–14 Termagant** a
supposed deity of the Mohammedans, not found in any English
medieval play but elsewhere portrayed as violent and blustering.
14 Herod Herod of Jewry. (A character in *The Slaughter of the Innocents*
and other cycle plays. The part was played with great noise and fury.)
19 modesty restraint, moderation   **20 from** contrary to   **23 scorn** i.e.,
something foolish and deserving of scorn   **23–4 and the . . . pressure**
and the present state of affairs its likeness as seen in an impression,
such as wax.   **25 come tardy off** falling short   **25–6 the unskillful**
those lacking in judgment   **27 the censure . . . one** the judgment of
even one of whom.   **your allowance** your scale of values   **30 not . . .
profanely** (Hamlet anticipates his idea in lines 33–4 that some men
were not made by God at all.)   **31-2 Christians** i.e., ordinary decent
folk   **32 nor man** i.e., nor any human being at all   **33 journeymen**
common workmen

35 abominably (Shakespeare's usual spelling, "abhominably," suggests a literal though etymologically incorrect meaning, "removed
from human nature.")   **36 indifferently** tolerably   **40 of them** some
among them   **41 barren** i.e., of wit   **48 presently** at once   **54 my . . .
withal** my dealings encountered.   **59 candied** sugared, flattering
60 pregnant compliant   **61 thrift** profit   **63 could . . . election** could
make distinguishing choices among persons   **64 sealed thee** (Literally, as one would seal a legal document to mark possession.)
68 blood passion.   **commeddled** commingled   **70 stop** hole in a
wind instrument for controlling the sound

I prithee, when thou see'st that act afoot,
Even with the very comment of thy soul   78
Observe my uncle. If his occulted guilt   79
Do not itself unkennel in one speech,   80
It is a damnèd ghost that we have seen,
And my imaginations are as foul
As Vulcan's stithy. Give him heedful note,   83
For I mine eyes will rivet to his face,
And after we will both our judgments join
In censure of his seeming.
HORATIO   Well, my lord.   86
If 'a steal aught the whilst this play is playing   87
And scape detecting, I will pay the theft.

> [*Flourish.*] *Enter trumpets and kettledrums, King,*
> *Queen, Polonius, Ophelia, [Rosencrantz,*
> *Guildenstern, and other lords, with guards*
> *carrying torches].*

HAMLET   They are coming to the play. I must be idle.   89
Get you a place.   [*The King, Queen, and courtiers sit.*]
KING   How fares our cousin Hamlet?   91
HAMLET   Excellent, i'faith, of the chameleon's dish: I eat   92
the air, promise-crammed. You cannot feed capons so.   93
KING   I have nothing with this answer, Hamlet. These   94
words are not mine.   95
HAMLET   No, nor mine now. [*To Polonius*] My lord, you   96
played once i'th'university, you say?
POLONIUS   That did I, my lord, and was accounted a
good actor.
HAMLET   What did you enact?
POLONIUS   I did enact Julius Caesar. I was killed i'th'   101
Capitol; Brutus killed me.   102
HAMLET   It was a brute part of him to kill so capital a   103
calf there.—Be the players ready?   104
ROSENCRANTZ   Ay, my lord. They stay upon your   105
patience.
QUEEN   Come hither, my dear Hamlet, sit by me.
HAMLET   No, good mother, here's metal more attractive.   108
POLONIUS [*to the King*]   Oho, do you mark that?
HAMLET   Lady, shall I lie in your lap?   110
[*Lying down at Ophelia's feet.*]

OPHELIA   No, my lord.
HAMLET   I mean, my head upon your lap?
OPHELIA   Ay, my lord.
HAMLET   Do you think I meant country matters?   114
OPHELIA   I think nothing, my lord.
HAMLET   That's a fair thought to lie between maids'
legs.
OPHELIA   What is, my lord?
HAMLET   Nothing.   119
OPHELIA   You are merry, my lord.
HAMLET   Who, I?
OPHELIA   Ay, my lord.
HAMLET   Oh, God, your only jig maker. What should a   123
man do but be merry? For look you how cheerfully my
mother looks, and my father died within 's two hours.   125
OPHELIA   Nay, 'tis twice two months, my lord.
HAMLET   So long? Nay then, let the devil wear black, for
I'll have a suit of sables. O heavens! Die two months   128
ago, and not forgotten yet? Then there's hope a great
man's memory may outlive his life half a year. But, by'r
Lady, 'a must build churches, then, or else shall 'a
suffer not thinking on, with the hobbyhorse, whose   132
epitaph is "For oh, for oh, the hobbyhorse is forgot."   133

> *The trumpets sound. Dumb show follows.*

> *Enter a King and a Queen [very lovingly]; the*
> *Queen embracing him, and he her. [She kneels,*
> *and makes show of protestation unto him.] He*
> *takes her up, and declines his head upon her neck.*
> *He lies him down upon a bank of flowers. She,*
> *seeing him asleep, leaves him. Anon comes in*
> *another man, takes off his crown, kisses it, pours*
> *poison in the sleeper's ears, and leaves him. The*
> *Queen returns, finds the King dead, makes*
> *passionate action. The Poisoner with some three or*
> *four come in again, seem to condole with her. The*
> *dead body is carried away. The Poisoner woos the*
> *Queen with gifts; she seems harsh awhile, but in*
> *the end accepts love.*

> [*Exeunt players.*]

OPHELIA   What means this, my lord?
HAMLET   Marry, this' miching mallico; it means mis-   135
chief.

---

78 very . . . soul your most penetrating observation and consideration
79 occulted hidden   **80 unkennel** (As one would say of a fox driven
from its lair.)   **83 Vulcan's stithy** the smithy, the place of stiths (anvils)
of the Roman god of fire and metalworking.   **86 censure of his seeming** judgment of his appearance or behavior.   **87 If 'a steal aught** If he
gets away with anything   **89 idle** (1) unoccupied (2) mad.   **91 cousin**
i.e., close relative   **92 chameleon's dish** (Chameleons were supposed
to feed on air. Hamlet deliberately misinterprets the King's *fares* as
"feeds." By his phrase *eat the air* he also plays on the idea of feeding
himself with the promise of succession, of being the *heir*.)   **93 capons**
roosters castrated and *crammed* with feed to make them succulent
94 have . . . with make nothing of, or gain nothing from   **95 are not
mine** do not respond to what I asked.   **96 nor mine now** (Once spoken, words are proverbially no longer the speaker's own—and hence
should be uttered warily.)   **101–2 i'th' Capitol** (where Caesar was
assassinated, according to *Julius Caesar*, 3.1, but see 1.3.126n in that
play)   **103 brute** (The Latin meaning of *brutus*, "stupid," was often
used punningly with the name Brutus.)   **part** (1) deed (2) role
104 calf fool   **105 stay upon** await   **108 metal** substance that is
attractive, i.e., magnetic, but with suggestion also of *mettle*, "disposition"   **110 Lady . . . lap?** Onstage, Hamlet often lies at Ophelia's feet,
but he could instead offer to do this and continue to stand.

114 country matters sexual intercourse. (With a bawdy pun on the
first syllable of *country*.)   **119 Nothing** The figure zero or naught,
suggesting the female sexual anatomy. (*Thing* not infrequently has a
bawdy connotation of male or female anatomy, and the reference here
could be male.)   **123 only jig maker** very best composer of jigs, i.e.,
pointless merriment. (Hamlet replies sardonically to Ophelia's observation that he is merry by saying, "If you're looking for someone who
is really merry, you've come to the right person.")   **125 within 's**
within this (i.e., these)   **128 suit of sables** garments trimmed with
the dark fur of the sable and hence suited for a person in mourning.
132 suffer . . . on undergo oblivion   **133 "For . . . forgot"** (Verse of a
song occurring also in *Love's Labor's Lost*, 3.1.27–8. The hobbyhorse
was a character made up to resemble a horse and rider, appearing in
the morris dance and such May-game sports. This song laments the
disappearance of such customs under pressure from the Puritans.)
133.12 condole with offer sympathy to   **135 this' miching mallico**
this is sneaking mischief

OPHELIA   Belike this show imports the argument of the 137
play.

Enter Prologue.

HAMLET   We shall know by this fellow. The players cannot keep counsel; they'll tell all.   140

OPHELIA   Will 'a tell us what this show meant?

HAMLET   Ay, or any show that you will show him. Be 142
not you ashamed to show, he'll not shame to tell you 143
what it means.

OPHELIA   You are naught, you are naught. I'll mark the 145
play.

PROLOGUE
For us, and for our tragedy,
Here stooping to your clemency,
We beg your hearing patiently.   148
                                  [*Exit.*]

HAMLET   Is this a prologue, or the posy of a ring?   150

OPHELIA   'Tis brief, my lord.

HAMLET   As woman's love.

Enter [two Players as] King and Queen.

PLAYER KING
Full thirty times hath Phoebus' cart gone round   153
Neptune's salt wash and Tellus' orbèd ground,   154
And thirty dozen moons with borrowed sheen   155
About the world have times twelve thirties been,
Since love our hearts and Hymen did our hands   157
Unite commutual in most sacred bands.   158

PLAYER QUEEN
So many journeys may the sun and moon
Make us again count o'er ere love be done!
But, woe is me, you are so sick of late,
So far from cheer and from your former state,
That I distrust you. Yet, though I distrust,   163
Discomfort you, my lord, it nothing must.   164
For women's fear and love hold quantity;   165
In neither aught, or in extremity.   166
Now, what my love is, proof hath made you know,   167
And as my love is sized, my fear is so.
Where love is great, the littlest doubts are fear;   169
Where little fears grow great, great love grows there.

PLAYER KING
Faith, I must leave thee, love, and shortly too;
My operant powers their functions leave to do.   172
And thou shalt live in this fair world behind,   173
Honored, beloved; and haply one as kind
For husband shalt thou—

PLAYER QUEEN   Oh, confound the rest!

Such love must needs be treason in my breast.
In second husband let me be accurst!
None wed the second but who killed the first.   178

HAMLET   Wormwood, wormwood.   179

PLAYER QUEEN
The instances that second marriage move   180
Are base respects of thrift, but none of love.   181
A second time I kill my husband dead
When second husband kisses me in bed.

PLAYER KING
I do believe you think what now you speak,
But what we do determine oft we break.
Purpose is but the slave to memory,   186
Of violent birth, but poor validity,   187
Which now, like fruit unripe, sticks on the tree,   188
But fall unshaken when they mellow be.
Most necessary 'tis that we forget   190
To pay ourselves what to ourselves is debt.   191
What to ourselves in passion we propose,
The passion ending, doth the purpose lose.
The violence of either grief or joy
Their own enactures with themselves destroy.   195
Where joy most revels, grief doth most lament;   196
Grief joys, joy grieves, on slender accident.   197
This world is not for aye, nor 'tis not strange   198
That even our loves should with our fortunes change;
For 'tis a question left us yet to prove,
Whether love lead fortune, or else fortune love.
The great man down, you mark his favorite flies;   202
The poor advanced makes friends of enemies.   203
And hitherto doth love on fortune tend;   204
For who not needs shall never lack a friend,   205
And who in want a hollow friend doth try   206
Directly seasons him his enemy.   207
But, orderly to end where I begun,
Our wills and fates do so contrary run   209
That our devices still are overthrown;   210
Our thoughts are ours, their ends none of our own.   211
So think thou wilt no second husband wed,
But die thy thoughts when thy first lord is dead.

PLAYER QUEEN
Nor earth to me give food, nor heaven light,   214
Sport and repose lock from me day and night,   215

---

137 **Belike** Probably.   **argument** plot   140 **counsel** secret   142–3 **Be
not you** Provided you are not   145 **naught** indecent. (Ophelia is
reacting to Hamlet's pointed remarks about not being ashamed to
show all.)   148 **stooping** bowing   150 **posy . . . ring** brief motto in
verse inscribed in a ring.   153 **Phoebus' cart** the sun-god's chariot,
making its yearly cycle   154 **salt wash** the sea.   **Tellus** goddess of
the earth, of the *orbèd ground*   155 **borrowed** i.e., reflected
157 **Hymen** god of matrimony   158 **commutual** mutually.   **bands**
bonds.   163 **distrust** am anxious about   164 **Discomfort . . . must** it
must not distress you at all.   165 **hold quantity** keep proportion
with one another   166 **In . . . extremity** (women feel) either no anxiety if they do not love or extreme anxiety if they do love.   167 **proof**
experience   169 **the littlest** even the littlest   172 **My . . . to do** my
vital functions are shutting down.   173 **behind** after I have gone

178 **None** (1) Let no woman; or (2) No woman does.   **but who** except
the one who   179 **Wormwood** i.e., How bitter. (Literally, a bitter-tasting plant.)   180 **instances** motives.   **move** motivate   181 **base . . .
thrift** ignoble considerations of material prosperity   186 **Purpose . . .
memory** Our good intentions are subject to forgetfulness   187 **validity** strength, durability   188 **Which** i.e., purpose   190–1 **Most . . .
debt** It's inevitable that in time we forget the obligations we have
imposed on ourselves.   195 **enactures** fulfillments   196–7 **Where . . .
accident** The capacity for extreme joy and grief go together, and often
one extreme is instantly changed into its opposite at the slightest
provocation.   198 **aye** ever   202 **down** fallen in fortune   203 **The
poor . . . enemies** when one of humble station is promoted, you see
his enemies suddenly becoming his friends.   204 **hitherto** up to this
point in the argument, or, to this extent.   **tend** attend   205 **who not
needs** he who is not in need (of wealth)   206 **who in want** he who,
being in need.   **try** test (his generosity)   207 **seasons him** ripens him
into   209 **Our . . . run** what we want and what we get go so contrarily   210 **devices** intentions.   **still** continually   211 **ends** results
214 **Nor** Let neither   215 **Sport . . . night** may day deny me its pastimes and night its repose

To desperation turn my trust and hope,
An anchor's cheer in prison be my scope!   217
Each opposite that blanks the face of joy   218
Meet what I would have well and it destroy!   219
Both here and hence pursue me lasting strife   220
If, once a widow, ever I be wife!

HAMLET   If she should break it now!

PLAYER KING
'Tis deeply sworn. Sweet, leave me here awhile;
My spirits grow dull, and fain I would beguile   224
The tedious day with sleep.

PLAYER QUEEN   Sleep rock thy brain,
And never come mischance between us twain!
                    [He sleeps.] Exit [Player Queen].

HAMLET   Madam, how like you this play?

QUEEN   The lady doth protest too much, methinks.   228

HAMLET   Oh, but she'll keep her word.

KING   Have you heard the argument? Is there no   230
offense in't?

HAMLET   No, no, they do but jest, poison in jest. No of- 232
fense i'th' world.   233

KING   What do you call the play?

HAMLET   The Mousetrap. Marry, how? Tropically.   235
This play is the image of a murder done in Vienna.
Gonzago is the Duke's name, his wife, Baptista. You   237
shall see anon. 'Tis a knavish piece of work, but what
of that? Your Majesty, and we that have free souls, it   239
touches us not. Let the galled jade wince, our withers   240
are unwrung.   241

        Enter Lucianus.

This is one Lucianus, nephew to the King.

OPHELIA   You are as good as a chorus, my lord.   243

HAMLET   I could interpret between you and your love,   244
if I could see the puppets dallying.   245

OPHELIA   You are keen, my lord, you are keen.   246

HAMLET   It would cost you a groaning to take off mine
edge.

OPHELIA   Still better, and worse.   249

HAMLET   So you mis-take your husbands.—Begin, mur-   250
derer; leave thy damnable faces and begin. Come, the
croaking raven doth bellow for revenge.

LUCIANUS
Thoughts black, hands apt, drugs fit, and time
    agreeing,
Confederate season, else no creature seeing,   254
Thou mixture rank, of midnight weeds collected,
With Hecate's ban thrice blasted, thrice infected,   256
Thy natural magic and dire property   257
On wholesome life usurp immediately.
        [He pours the poison into the sleeper's ear.]

HAMLET   'A poisons him i'th' garden for his estate. His 259
name's Gonzago. The story is extant, and written in
very choice Italian. You shall see anon how the
murderer gets the love of Gonzago's wife.
                            [Claudius rises.]

OPHELIA   The King rises.

HAMLET   What, frighted with false fire?   264

QUEEN   How fares my lord?

POLONIUS   Give o'er the play.

KING   Give me some light. Away!

POLONIUS   Lights, lights, lights!
            Exeunt all but Hamlet and Horatio.

HAMLET
"Why, let the strucken deer go weep,   269
    The hart ungallèd play.   270
For some must watch, while some must sleep;   271
    Thus runs the world away."   272
Would not this, sir, and a forest of feathers—if the   273
rest of my fortunes turn Turk with me—with two   274
Provincial roses on my razed shoes, get me a fellow-   275
ship in a cry of players?   276

HORATIO   Half a share.

HAMLET   A whole one, I.
"For thou dost know, O Damon dear,   279
    This realm dismantled was   280
Of Jove himself, and now reigns here   281
    A very, very—pajock."   282

---

217 anchor's cheer anchorite's or hermit's fare.   my scope the extent
of my happiness.   218–19 Each . . . destroy! May every adverse thing
that causes the face of joy to turn pale meet and destroy everything
that I desire to see prosper!   220 hence in the life hereafter   224 spirits vital spirits   228 doth . . . much makes too many promises and
protestations   230 argument plot.   232 jest make believe.
232–3 offense crime, injury. (Hamlet playfully alters the King's use of
the word in line 231 to mean "cause for objection.")   235 Tropically
Figuratively. (The First Quarto reading, "trapically," suggests a pun
on trap in Mousetrap.)   237 Duke's i.e., King's. (An inconsistency that
may be due to Shakespeare's possible acquaintance with a historical
incident, the alleged murder of the Duke of Urbino by Luigi Gonzaga
in 1538.)   239 free guiltless   240 galled jade horse whose hide is
rubbed by saddle or harness.   withers the part between the horse's
shoulder blades   241 unwrung not rubbed sore.   243 chorus (In
many Elizabethan plays, the forthcoming action was explained by an
actor known as the "chorus"; at a puppet show, the actor who spoke
the dialogue was known as an "interpreter," as indicated by the lines
following.)   244 interpret (1) ventriloquize the dialogue, as in a puppet show (2) act as pander   245 puppets dallying (With suggestion
of sexual play, continued in keen, "sexually aroused," groaning,
"moaning in pregnancy," and edge, "sexual desire" or "impetuosity.")
246 keen sharp, bitter   249 Still . . . worse More keen, always
bettering what other people say with witty wordplay, but at the same
time more offensive.

250 So Even thus (in marriage).   mis-take take falseheartedly and
cheat on. (The marriage vows say "for better, for worse.")   254 Confederate . . . seeing the time and occasion conspiring (to assist me),
and also no one seeing me   256 Hecate's ban the curse of Hecate, the
goddess of witchcraft   257 dire property baleful quality   259 estate
i.e., the kingship.   His i.e., the King's   264 false fire the blank discharge of a gun loaded with powder but no shot.   269–72 Why . . .
away (Perhaps from an old ballad, with allusion to the popular belief
that a wounded deer retires to weep and die; compare with As You
Like It, 2.1.33–66.)   270 ungallèd unafflicted   271 watch remain
awake   272 Thus . . . away Thus the world goes.   273 this i.e., this
success with the play I have just presented.   feathers (Allusion to the
plumes that Elizabethan actors were fond of wearing.)   274 turn
Turk with turn renegade against, go back on   275 Provincial roses
rosettes of ribbon, named for roses grown in a part of France.   razed
with ornamental slashing   275–6 fellowship . . . players partnership
in a theatrical company.   276 cry pack (of hounds, etc.)   279 Damon
the friend of Pythias, as Horatio is friend of Hamlet; or, a traditional
pastoral name   280–2 This realm . . . pajock i.e., Jove, representing
divine authority and justice, has abandoned this realm to its own
devices, leaving in his stead only a peacock or vain pretender to
virtue (though the rhyme-word expected in place of pajock or "peacock" suggests that the realm is now ruled over by an "ass").
280 dismantled stripped, divested

HORATIO   You might have rhymed.

HAMLET   Oh, good Horatio, I'll take the ghost's word for a thousand pound. Didst perceive?

HORATIO   Very well, my lord.

HAMLET   Upon the talk of the poisoning?

HORATIO   I did very well note him.

Enter Rosencrantz and Guildenstern.

HAMLET   Aha! Come, some music! Come, the recorders.
   "For if the King like not the comedy,
      Why then, belike, he likes it not, perdy."   292
   Come, some music.

GUILDENSTERN   Good my lord, vouchsafe me a word with you.

HAMLET   Sir, a whole history.

GUILDENSTERN   The King, sir—

HAMLET   Ay, sir, what of him?

GUILDENSTERN   Is in his retirement marvelous dis-   299
tempered.   300

HAMLET   With drink, sir?

GUILDENSTERN   No, my lord, with choler.   302

HAMLET   Your wisdom should show itself more richer to signify this to the doctor, for for me to put him to his purgation would perhaps plunge him into more   305
choler.

GUILDENSTERN   Good my lord, put your discourse into some frame and start not so wildly from my affair.   308

HAMLET   I am tame, sir. Pronounce.

GUILDENSTERN   The Queen, your mother, in most great affliction of spirit, hath sent me to you.

HAMLET   You are welcome.

GUILDENSTERN   Nay, good my lord, this courtesy is not of the right breed. If it shall please you to make me a   314
wholesome answer, I will do your mother's command-
ment; if not, your pardon and my return shall be the   316
end of my business.

HAMLET   Sir, I cannot.

ROSENCRANTZ   What, my lord?

HAMLET   Make you a wholesome answer; my wit's dis-
eased. But, sir, such answer as I can make, you shall command, or rather, as you say, my mother. Therefore no more, but to the matter. My mother, you say—

ROSENCRANTZ   Then thus she says: your behavior hath struck her into amazement and admiration.   325

HAMLET   Oh, wonderful son, that can so 'stonish a mother! But is there no sequel at the heels of this mother's admiration. Impart.

ROSENCRANTZ   She desires to speak with you in her closet ere you go to bed.   330

HAMLET   We shall obey, were she ten times our mother. Have you any further trade with us?

ROSENCRANTZ   My lord, you once did love me.

HAMLET   And do still, by these pickers and stealers.   334

ROSENCRANTZ   Good my lord, what is your cause of distemper? You do surely bar the door upon your own liberty if you deny your griefs to your friend.   337

HAMLET   Sir, I lack advancement.

ROSENCRANTZ   How can that be, when you have the voice of the King himself for your succession in Denmark?

HAMLET   Ay, sir, but "While the grass grows"—the   342
proverb is something musty.   343

Enter the Players with recorders.

Oh, the recorders. Let me see one. [*He takes a recorder.*]
To withdraw with you: why do you go about to recover   345
the wind of me, as if you would drive me into a toil?   346

GUILDENSTERN   Oh, my lord, if my duty be too bold, my   347
love is too unmannerly.   348

HAMLET   I do not well understand that. Will you play   349
upon this pipe?

GUILDENSTERN   My lord, I cannot.

HAMLET   I pray you.

GUILDENSTERN   Believe me, I cannot.

HAMLET   I do beseech you.

GUILDENSTERN   I know no touch of it, my lord.

HAMLET   It is as easy as lying. Govern these ventages   356
with your fingers and thumb, give it breath with your mouth, and it will discourse most eloquent music. Look you, these are the stops.

GUILDENSTERN   But these cannot I command to any utterance of harmony. I have not the skill.

HAMLET   Why, look you now, how unworthy a thing you make of me! You would play upon me, you would seem to know my stops, you would pluck out the heart of my mystery, you would sound me from my lowest   365
note to the top of my compass, and there is much   366
music, excellent voice, in this little organ, yet cannot   367
you make it speak. 'Sblood, do you think I am easier to be played on than a pipe? Call me what instrument you will, though you can fret me, you cannot play   370
upon me.

Enter Polonius.

God bless you, sir!

292 **perdy** (A corruption of the French *par dieu*, "by God.")
299 **retirement** withdrawal to his chambers   299–300 **distempered** out of humor. (But Hamlet deliberately plays on the wider applica-
tion to any illness of mind or body, as in lines 335–6, especially to drunkenness.)   302 **choler** anger. (But Hamlet takes the word in its more basic humoral sense of "bilious disorder.")   305 **purgation** (Hamlet hints at something going beyond medical treatment to bloodletting and the extraction of confession.)   308 **frame** order.
start shy or jump away (like a horse; the opposite of *tame* in line 309)
314 **breed** (1) kind (2) breeding, manners.   316 **pardon** permission to depart   325 **admiration** bewilderment.   330 **closet** private chamber

334 **pickers and stealers** i.e., hands. (So called from the catechism, "to keep my hands from picking and stealing.")   337 **liberty** i.e., being freed from *distemper*, line 336; but perhaps with a veiled threat as well.
deny refuse to share   342 **"While . . . grows"** (The rest of the proverb is "the silly horse starves"; Hamlet implies that his hopes of succession are distant in time at best.)   343 **something** somewhat   343.1 *Players* actors   345 **withdraw** speak privately   345–6 **recover the wind** get to the windward side (thus allowing the game to scent the hunter and thereby be driven in the opposite direction into the *toil* or net)   346 **toil** snare.   347–8 **if . . . unmannerly** if I am using an unmannerly boldness, it is my love that occasions it.   349 **I . . . that** i.e., I don't understand how genuine love can be unmannerly.   356 **ventages** finger-holes or *stops* (line 359) of the recorder   365 **sound** (1) fathom (2) produce sound in   366 **compass** range (of voice)   367 **organ** musical instrument
370 **fret** irritate. (With a quibble on the *frets* or ridges on the fingerboard of some stringed instruments to regulate the fingering.)

POLONIUS   My lord, the Queen would speak with you,
and presently.   374
HAMLET   Do you see yonder cloud that's almost in
shape of a camel?
POLONIUS   By th' Mass and 'tis, like a camel indeed.
HAMLET   Methinks it is like a weasel.
POLONIUS   It is backed like a weasel.
HAMLET   Or like a whale.
POLONIUS   Very like a whale.
HAMLET   Then I will come to my mother by and by.
[Aside] They fool me to the top of my bent.—I will   383
come by and by.
POLONIUS   I will say so.   [Exit.]
HAMLET   "By and by" is easily said. Leave me, friends.
                                    [Exeunt all but Hamlet.]
'Tis now the very witching time of night,   387
When churchyards yawn and hell itself breathes out
Contagion to this world. Now could I drink hot
blood
And do such bitter business as the day
Would quake to look on. Soft, now to my mother.
O heart, lose not thy nature! Let not ever   392
The soul of Nero enter this firm bosom.   393
Let me be cruel, not unnatural;
I will speak daggers to her, but use none.
My tongue and soul in this be hypocrites:
How in my words somever she be shent,   397
To give them seals never my soul consent!   Exit.   398

❖

[3.3]

Enter King, Rosencrantz, and Guildenstern.

KING
I like him not, nor stands it safe with us   1
To let his madness range. Therefore prepare you.
I your commission will forthwith dispatch,   3
And he to England shall along with you.
The terms of our estate may not endure   5
Hazard so near 's as doth hourly grow
Out of his brows.
GUILDENSTERN   We will ourselves provide.   7
Most holy and religious fear it is   8
To keep those many many bodies safe
That live and feed upon Your Majesty.
ROSENCRANTZ
The single and peculiar life is bound   11

With all the strength and armor of the mind
To keep itself from noyance, but much more   13
That spirit upon whose weal depends and rests   14
The lives of many. The cess of majesty   15
Dies not alone, but like a gulf doth draw   16
What's near it with it; or it is a massy wheel   17
Fixed on the summit of the highest mount,
To whose huge spokes ten thousand lesser things
Are mortised and adjoined, which, when it falls,   20
Each small annexment, petty consequence,   21
Attends the boist'rous ruin. Never alone   22
Did the King sigh, but with a general groan.
KING
Arm you, I pray you, to this speedy voyage,   24
For we will fetters put about this fear,
Which now goes too free-footed.
ROSENCRANTZ   We will haste us.
    Exeunt gentlemen [Rosencrantz and Guildenstern].

    Enter Polonius.

POLONIUS
My lord, he's going to his mother's closet.
Behind the arras I'll convey myself   28
To hear the process. I'll warrant she'll tax him home,   29
And, as you said—and wisely was it said—
'Tis meet that some more audience than a mother,   31
Since nature makes them partial, should o'erhear
The speech of vantage. Fare you well, my liege.   33
I'll call upon you ere you go to bed
And tell you what I know.
KING   Thanks, dear my lord.
                                    Exit [Polonius].
Oh, my offense is rank! It smells to heaven.
It hath the primal eldest curse upon't,   37
A brother's murder. Pray can I not,
Though inclination be as sharp as will;   39
My stronger guilt defeats my strong intent,
And like a man to double business bound   41
I stand in pause where I shall first begin,
And both neglect. What if this cursèd hand
Were thicker than itself with brother's blood,
Is there not rain enough in the sweet heavens
To wash it white as snow? Whereto serves mercy   46
But to confront the visage of offense?   47
And what's in prayer but this twofold force,

374 presently at once.   **383 They fool . . . bent** They humor my odd
behavior to the limit of my ability or endurance. (Literally, the extent
to which a bow may be bent.)   **387 witching time** time when spells
are cast and evil is abroad   **392 nature** natural feeling.   **393 Nero**
(This infamous Roman emperor put to death his mother, Agrippina,
who had murdered her husband, Claudius.)   **397–8 How . . . consent!** however much she is to be rebuked by my words, may my soul
never consent to ratify those words with deeds of violence!
3.3. Location: The castle.
1 him i.e., his behavior   **3 dispatch** prepare, cause to be drawn up
5 terms of our estate circumstances of my royal position   **7 Out . . .
brows** i.e., from his brain, in the form of plots and threats.   **We . . .
provide** We'll put ourselves in readiness.   **8 religious fear** sacred
concern   **11 single and peculiar** individual and private

13 noyance harm   **14 weal** well-being   **15 cess** decease, cessation
16 gulf whirlpool   **17 massy** massive   **20 mortised** fastened (as with
a fitted joint).   **when it falls** i.e., when it descends, like the wheel of
Fortune, bringing a king down with it   **21 Each . . . consequence** i.e.,
every hanger-on and unimportant person or thing connected with the
King   **22 Attends** participates in   **24 Arm** Provide, prepare
28 arras screen of tapestry placed around the walls of household
apartments. (On the Elizabethan stage, the arras was presumably
over a door or aperture in the tiring-house facade.)   **29 process** proceedings.   **tax him home** reprove him severely   **31 meet** fitting
33 of vantage from an advantageous place, or, in addition.   **37 the
primal eldest curse** the curse of Cain, the first murderer; he killed his
brother Abel   **39 Though . . . will** though my desire is as strong as
my determination   **41 bound** (1) destined (2) obliged. (The King
wants to repent and still enjoy what he has gained.)   **46–7 Whereto . . .
offense?** What function does mercy serve other than to meet sin face
to face?

To be forestallèd ere we come to fall,   49
Or pardoned being down? Then I'll look up.
My fault is past. But oh, what form of prayer
Can serve my turn? "Forgive me my foul murder"?
That cannot be, since I am still possessed
Of those effects for which I did the murder:
My crown, mine own ambition, and my queen.
May one be pardoned and retain th'offense?   56
In the corrupted currents of this world   57
Offense's gilded hand may shove by justice,   58
And oft 'tis seen the wicked prize itself   59
Buys out the law. But 'tis not so above.
There is no shuffling, there the action lies   61
In his true nature, and we ourselves compelled,   62
Even to the teeth and forehead of our faults,   63
To give in evidence. What then? What rests?   64
Try what repentance can. What can it not?
Yet what can it, when one cannot repent?
O wretched state, O bosom black as death,
O limèd soul that, struggling to be free,   68
Art more engaged! Help, angels! Make assay.   69
Bow, stubborn knees, and heart with strings of steel,
Be soft as sinews of the newborn babe!
All may be well.   [*He kneels.*]

    Enter Hamlet.

HAMLET
Now might I do it pat, now 'a is a-praying;   73
And now I'll do't. [*He draws his sword.*] And so 'a goes
    to heaven,
And so am I revenged. That would be scanned: 75
A villain kills my father, and for that,
I, his sole son, do this same villain send
To heaven.
Why, this is hire and salary, not revenge.
'A took my father grossly, full of bread,   80
With all his crimes broad blown, as flush as May;   81
And how his audit stands who knows save heaven?   82
But in our circumstance and course of thought   83
'Tis heavy with him. And am I then revenged,
To take him in the purging of his soul,
When he is fit and seasoned for his passage?   86
No!
Up, sword, and know thou a more horrid hent.   88
                   [*He puts up his sword.*]

When he is drunk asleep, or in his rage,   89
Or in th'incestuous pleasure of his bed,
At game, a-swearing, or about some act   91
That has no relish of salvation in't—   92
Then trip him, that his heels may kick at heaven,
And that his soul may be as damned and black
As hell, whereto it goes. My mother stays.   95
This physic but prolongs thy sickly days.   *Exit.*   96
KING
My words fly up, my thoughts remain below.
Words without thoughts never to heaven go.   *Exit.*

                     ❧

[3.4]

    Enter [Queen] Gertrude and Polonius.

POLONIUS
'A will come straight. Look you lay home to him.   1
Tell him his pranks have been too broad to bear with,   2
And that Your Grace hath screened and stood
    between
Much heat and him. I'll silence me even here.   4
Pray you, be round with him.   5
HAMLET (*within*)   Mother, mother, mother!
QUEEN   I'll warrant you, fear me not.
Withdraw, I hear him coming.
           [*Polonius hides behind the arras.*]

    Enter Hamlet.

HAMLET   Now, mother, what's the matter?
QUEEN
Hamlet, thou hast thy father much offended.   10
HAMLET
Mother, you have my father much offended.
QUEEN
Come, come, you answer with an idle tongue.   12
HAMLET
Go, go, you question with a wicked tongue.
QUEEN
Why, how now, Hamlet?
HAMLET   What's the matter now?
QUEEN
Have you forgot me?
HAMLET   No, by the rood, not so: 15
You are the Queen, your husband's brother's wife,
And—would it were not so!—you are my mother.
QUEEN
Nay, then, I'll set those to you that can speak.   18

---

49 forestallèd prevented (from sinning)   **56 th'offense** the thing for which one offended.   **57 currents** courses of events   **58 gilded hand** hand offering gold as a bribe.   **shove by** thrust aside   **59 wicked prize** prize won by wickedness   **61 There . . . lies** There in heaven can be no evasion, there the deed lies exposed to view   **62 his** its   **63 to the teeth and forehead** face to face, concealing nothing   **64 give in** provide.   **rests** remains.   **68 limèd** caught as with birdlime, a sticky substance used to ensnare birds   **69 engaged** entangled.   **assay** trial. (Said to himself, or to the angels to try him.)   **73 pat** opportunely   **75 would be scanned** needs to be looked into, or, would be interpreted as follows   **80 grossly, full of bread** i.e., enjoying his worldly pleasures rather than fasting. (See Ezekiel 16:49.)   **81 crimes broad blown** sins in full bloom.   **flush** vigorous   **82 audit** account.   **save** except for   **83 in . . . thought** as we see it from our mortal perspective   **86 seasoned** matured, readied   **88 know . . . hent** await to be grasped by me on a more horrid occasion. (*Hent* means "act of seizing.")

89 drunk . . . rage dead drunk, or in a fit of sexual passion   **91 game** gambling   **92 relish** trace, savor   **95 stays** awaits (me).   **96 physic** purging (by prayer), or, Hamlet's postponement of the killing   **3.4. Location: The Queen's private chamber.**
1 lay . . . him reprove him soundly   **2 broad** unrestrained   **4 Much heat** i.e., the King's anger.   **I'll silence me** I'll quietly conceal myself. (Ironic, since it is his crying out at line 24 that leads to his death. Some editors emend *silence* to "sconce." The First Quarto's reading, "shroud," is attractive.)   **5 round** blunt   **10 thy father** i.e., your stepfather, Claudius   **12 idle** foolish   **15 forgot me** i.e., forgotten that I am your mother.   **rood** cross of Christ   **18 speak** i.e., speak to someone so rude.

HAMLET
   Come, come, and sit you down; you shall not budge.
   You go not till I set you up a glass
   Where you may see the inmost part of you.
QUEEN
   What wilt thou do? Thou wilt not murder me?
   Help, ho!
POLONIUS [*behind the arras*]   What ho! Help!
HAMLET [*drawing*]
   How now? A rat? Dead for a ducat, dead!   25
          [*He thrusts his rapier through the arras.*]
POLONIUS [*behind the arras*]
   Oh, I am slain!   [*He falls and dies.*]
QUEEN   Oh, me, what hast thou done?
HAMLET   Nay, I know not. Is it the King?
QUEEN
   Oh, what a rash and bloody deed is this!
HAMLET
   A bloody deed—almost as bad, good mother,
   As kill a king, and marry with his brother.
QUEEN
   As kill a king!
HAMLET   Ay, lady, it was my word.
      [*He parts the arras and discovers Polonius.*]
   Thou wretched, rash, intruding fool, farewell!
   I took thee for thy better. Take thy fortune.
   Thou find'st to be too busy is some danger.—   34
   Leave wringing of your hands. Peace, sit you down,
   And let me wring your heart, for so I shall,
   If it be made of penetrable stuff,
   If damnèd custom have not brazed it so   38
   That it be proof and bulwark against sense.   39
QUEEN
   What have I done, that thou dar'st wag thy tongue
   In noise so rude against me?
HAMLET   Such an act
   That blurs the grace and blush of modesty,
   Calls virtue hypocrite, takes off the rose
   From the fair forehead of an innocent love
   And sets a blister there, makes marriage vows   45
   As false as dicers' oaths. Oh, such a deed
   As from the body of contraction plucks   47
   The very soul, and sweet religion makes   48
   A rhapsody of words. Heaven's face does glow   49
   O'er this solidity and compound mass   50
   With tristful visage, as against the doom,   51
   Is thought-sick at the act.
QUEEN   Ay me, what act,   52
   That roars so loud and thunders in the index?   53
HAMLET [*showing her two likenesses*]
   Look here upon this picture, and on this,

The counterfeit presentment of two brothers.   55
See what a grace was seated on this brow:
Hyperion's curls, the front of Jove himself,   57
An eye like Mars to threaten and command,   58
A station like the herald Mercury   59
New-lighted on a heaven-kissing hill—   60
A combination and a form indeed
Where every god did seem to set his seal   62
To give the world assurance of a man.
This was your husband. Look you now what follows:
Here is your husband, like a mildewed ear,   65
Blasting his wholesome brother. Have you eyes?   66
Could you on this fair mountain leave to feed   67
And batten on this moor? Ha, have you eyes?   68
You cannot call it love, for at your age
The heyday in the blood is tame, it's humble,   70
And waits upon the judgment, and what judgment
Would step from this to this? Sense, sure, you have,   72
Else could you not have motion, but sure that sense
Is apoplexed, for madness would not err,   74
Nor sense to ecstasy was ne'er so thralled,   75
But it reserved some quantity of choice   76
To serve in such a difference. What devil was't   77
That thus hath cozened you at hoodman-blind?   78
Eyes without feeling, feeling without sight,
Ears without hands or eyes, smelling sans all,   80
Or but a sickly part of one true sense
Could not so mope. O shame, where is thy blush?   82
Rebellious hell,
If thou canst mutine in a matron's bones,   84
To flaming youth let virtue be as wax   85
And melt in her own fire. Proclaim no shame   86
When the compulsive ardor gives the charge,   87
Since frost itself as actively doth burn,   88
And reason panders will.   89
QUEEN   Oh, Hamlet, speak no more!
   Thou turn'st mine eyes into my very soul,
   And there I see such black and grainèd spots   92

---

25 Dead for a ducat i.e., I bet a ducat he's dead; or, a ducat is his life's fee.   **34 busy** nosey   **38 damnèd custom** habitual wickedness. **brazed** brazened, hardened   **39 proof** impenetrable, like *proof* or tested armor.   **sense** feeling.   **45 sets a blister** i.e., brands as a harlot **47 contraction** the marriage contract   **48 sweet religion makes** i.e., makes marriage vows   **49 rhapsody** senseless string   **49–52 Heaven's . . . act** Heaven's face blushes at this solid world compounded of the various elements, with sorrowful face as though the day of doom were near, and is sick with horror at the deed (i.e., Gertrude's marriage).   **53 index** table of contents, prelude or preface.

55 counterfeit presentment representation in portraiture   **57 Hyperion's** the sun-god's.   **front** brow   **58 Mars** god of war   **59 station** manner of standing.   **Mercury** winged messenger of the gods **60 New-lighted** newly alighted.   **heaven-kissing** reaching to the sky **62 set his seal** i.e., affix his approval   **65 ear** i.e., of grain   **66 Blasting** blighting   **67 leave** cease   **68 batten** gorge.   **moor** barren or marshy ground. (Suggesting also "dark-skinned.")   **70 The heyday . . . blood** (The blood was thought to be the source of sexual desire.) **72 Sense** Perception through the five senses (the functions of the middle or sensible soul)   **74 apoplexed** paralyzed.   **err** so err   **75–7 Nor . . . difference** nor could your physical senses ever have been so enthralled to *ecstasy* or lunacy that they could not distinguish to some degree between Hamlet Senior and Claudius.   **78 cozened** cheated. **hoodman-blind** blindman's buff. (In this game, says Hamlet, the devil must have pushed Claudius toward Gertrude while she was blindfolded.)   **80 sans** without   **82 mope** be dazed, act aimlessly. **84 mutine** mutiny   **85–6 To . . . fire** when it comes to sexually passionate youth, let virtue melt like a candle or stick of sealing wax held over a candle flame. (There's no point in hoping for self-restraint among young people when matronly women set such a bad example.)   **86–9 Proclaim . . . will** Call it no shameful business when the compelling ardor of youth delivers the attack, i.e., commits lechery, since the *frost* of advanced age burns with as active a fire of lust and reason perverts itself by fomenting lust rather than restraining it. **92 grainèd** ingrained, indelible

As will not leave their tinct.

HAMLET   Nay, but to live   93
In the rank sweat of an enseamèd bed,   94
Stewed in corruption, honeying and making love   95
Over the nasty sty!   96

QUEEN   Oh, speak to me no more!
These words like daggers enter in my ears.
No more, sweet Hamlet!

HAMLET   A murderer and a villain,
A slave that is not twentieth part the tithe   100
Of your precedent lord, a vice of kings,   101
A cutpurse of the empire and the rule,
That from a shelf the precious diadem stole
And put it in his pocket!

QUEEN   No more!   105

Enter Ghost [in his nightgown].

HAMLET   A king of shreds and patches—   106
Save me, and hover o'er me with your wings,
You heavenly guards! What would your gracious
     figure?

QUEEN   Alas, he's mad!

HAMLET
Do you not come your tardy son to chide,
That, lapsed in time and passion, lets go by   111
Th'important acting of your dread command?   112
Oh, say!

GHOST
Do not forget. This visitation
Is but to whet thy almost blunted purpose.   115
But look, amazement on thy mother sits.   116
Oh, step between her and her fighting soul!
Conceit in weakest bodies strongest works.   118
Speak to her, Hamlet.

HAMLET   How is it with you, lady?

QUEEN   Alas, how is't with you,
That you do bend your eye on vacancy,
And with th'incorporal air do hold discourse?   122
Forth at your eyes your spirits wildly peep,
And, as the sleeping soldiers in th'alarm,   124
Your bedded hair, like life in excrements,   125
Start up and stand on end. O gentle son,
Upon the heat and flame of thy distemper   127
Sprinkle cool patience. Whereon do you look?

HAMLET
On him, on him! Look you how pale he glares!
His form and cause conjoined, preaching to stones,   130
Would make them capable.—Do not look upon me,   131
Lest with this piteous action you convert   132
My stern effects. Then what I have to do   133
Will want true color—tears perchance for blood.   134

QUEEN   To whom do you speak this?

HAMLET   Do you see nothing there?

QUEEN
Nothing at all, yet all that is I see.

HAMLET   Nor did you nothing hear?

QUEEN   No, nothing but ourselves.

HAMLET
Why, look you there, look how it steals away!
My father, in his habit as he lived!   141
Look where he goes even now out at the portal!

Exit Ghost.

QUEEN
This is the very coinage of your brain.   143
This bodiless creation ecstasy   144
Is very cunning in.   145

HAMLET   Ecstasy?
My pulse as yours doth temperately keep time,
And makes as healthful music. It is not madness
That I have uttered. Bring me to the test,
And I the matter will reword, which madness   150
Would gambol from. Mother, for love of grace,   151
Lay not that flattering unction to your soul   152
That not your trespass but my madness speaks.
It will but skin and film the ulcerous place,   154
Whiles rank corruption, mining all within,   155
Infects unseen. Confess yourself to heaven,
Repent what's past, avoid what is to come,
And do not spread the compost on the weeds   158
To make them ranker. Forgive me this my virtue;   159
For in the fatness of these pursy times   160
Virtue itself of vice must pardon beg,
Yea, curb and woo for leave to do him good.   162

QUEEN
Oh, Hamlet, thou hast cleft my heart in twain.

HAMLET
Oh, throw away the worser part of it,
And live the purer with the other half.
Good night. But go not to my uncle's bed;
Assume a virtue, if you have it not.
That monster, custom, who all sense doth eat,   168
Of habits devil, is angel yet in this,   169

---

93 **leave their tinct** surrender their dark stain.   94 **enseamèd** saturated in the grease and filth of passionate lovemaking   95 **Stewed** soaked, bathed. (With a suggestion of "stew," brothel.)   96 **Over . . . sty** (Like barnyard animals.)   100 **tithe** tenth part   101 **precedent lord** former husband.   **vice** (From the morality plays, a model of iniquity and a buffoon.)   105.1 *nightgown* a robe for indoor wear.   106 **A king . . . patches** i.e., a king whose splendor is all sham; a clown or fool dressed in motley   111 **lapsed . . . passion** having let time and passion slip away   112 **Th'important** the importunate, urgent   115 **whet** sharpen   116 **amazement** distraction   118 **Conceit** Imagination   122 **th'incorporal** the immaterial   124 **as . . . th'alarm** like soldiers called out of sleep by an alarum   125 **bedded** laid flat. **like life in excrements** i.e., as though hair, an outgrowth of the body, had a life of its own. (Hair was thought to be lifeless because it lacks sensation, and so its standing on end would be unnatural and ominous.)   127 **distemper** disorder

130 **His . . . conjoined** His appearance joined to his cause for speaking   131 **capable** capable of feeling, receptive.   132–3 **convert . . . effects** divert me from my stern duty.   134 **want . . . blood** lack plausibility so that (with a play on the normal sense of *color*) I shall shed colorless tears instead of blood.   141 **habit** clothes.   **as** as when   143 **very** mere   144–5 **This . . . in** Madness is skillful in creating this kind of hallucination.   150 **reword** repeat word for word   151 **gambol** skip away   152 **unction** ointment   154 **skin** grow a skin over   155 **mining** working under the surface   158 **compost** manure   159 **this my virtue** my virtuous talk in reproving you   160 **fatness** grossness. **pursy** flabby, out of shape   162 **curb** bow, bend the knee.   **leave** permission   168 **who . . . eat** which consumes and overwhelms the physical senses   169 **Of habits devil** devil-like in prompting evil habits

That to the use of actions fair and good
He likewise gives a frock or livery   171
That aptly is put on. Refrain tonight,   172
And that shall lend a kind of easiness
To the next abstinence; the next more easy;
For use almost can change the stamp of nature,   175
And either . . . the devil, or throw him out   176
With wondrous potency. Once more, good night;
And when you are desirous to be blest,   178
I'll blessing beg of you. For this same lord,   179
                    [*pointing to Polonius*]
I do repent; but heaven hath pleased it so
To punish me with this, and this with me,   181
That I must be their scourge and minister.   182
I will bestow him, and will answer well   183
The death I gave him. So, again, good night.
I must be cruel only to be kind.
This bad begins, and worse remains behind.   186
One word more, good lady.
QUEEN   What shall I do?
HAMLET
Not this by no means that I bid you do:
Let the bloat king tempt you again to bed,   189
Pinch wanton on your cheek, call you his mouse,   190
And let him, for a pair of reechy kisses,   191
Or paddling in your neck with his damned fingers,   192
Make you to ravel all this matter out   193
That I essentially am not in madness,
But mad in craft. 'Twere good you let him know,   195
For who that's but a queen, fair, sober, wise,
Would from a paddock, from a bat, a gib,   197
Such dear concernings hide? Who would do so?   198
No, in despite of sense and secrecy,   199
Unpeg the basket on the house's top,   200
Let the birds fly, and like the famous ape,   201
To try conclusions, in the basket creep   202
And break your own neck down.   203
QUEEN
Be thou assured, if words be made of breath,
And breath of life, I have no life to breathe
What thou hast said to me.

HAMLET
I must to England. You know that?
QUEEN   Alack,
I had forgot. 'Tis so concluded on.
HAMLET
There's letters sealed, and my two schoolfellows,
Whom I will trust as I will adders fanged,
They bear the mandate; they must sweep my way   211
And marshal me to knavery. Let it work.   212
For 'tis the sport to have the engineer   213
Hoist with his own petard, and 't shall go hard   214
But I will delve one yard below their mines   215
And blow them at the moon. Oh, 'tis most sweet
When in one line two crafts directly meet.   217
This man shall set me packing.   218
I'll lug the guts into the neighbor room.
Mother, good night indeed. This counselor
Is now most still, most secret, and most grave,
Who was in life a foolish prating knave.—
Come, sir, to draw toward an end with you.—   223
Good night, mother.
        Exeunt [*separately, Hamlet dragging in Polonius*].

[4.1]

*Enter King and Queen, with Rosencrantz and
Guildenstern.*

KING
There's matter in these sighs, these profound heaves.   1
You must translate; 'tis fit we understand them.
Where is your son?
QUEEN
Bestow this place on us a little while.
            [*Exeunt Rosencrantz and Guildenstern.*]
Ah, mine own lord, what have I seen tonight!

---

171 livery an outer appearance, a customary garb (and hence a predisposition easily assumed in time of stress)   **172 aptly** readily   **175 use** habit.   **the stamp of nature** our inborn traits   **176 And either** (A defective line, often emended by inserting the word "master" after *either*, following the Third Quarto and early editors, or some other word such as "shame," "lodge," "curb," or "house.")   **178–9 when . . . you** i.e., when you are ready to be penitent and seek God's blessing, I will ask your blessing as a dutiful son should.   **181 To punish . . . with me** to seek retribution from me for killing Polonius, and from him through my means   **182 their scourge and minister** i.e., agent of heavenly retribution.   **183 bestow** stow, dispose of.   **answer** account or pay for   **186 This** i.e., The killing of Polonius.   **behind** to come.   **189 bloat** bloated   **190 Pinch wanton** i.e., leave his love pinches on your cheeks, branding you as wanton   **191 reechy** dirty, filthy   **192 paddling** fingering amorously   **193 ravel . . . out** unravel, disclose   **195 in craft** by cunning.   **good** (Said sarcastically; also the following eight lines.)   **197 paddock** toad.   **gib** tomcat   **198 dear concernings** important affairs   **199 sense and secrecy** secrecy that common sense requires   **200 Unpeg the basket** open the cage, i.e., let out the secret   **201 famous ape** (In a story now lost.)   **202 try conclusions** test the outcome (in which the ape apparently enters a cage from which birds have been released and then tries to fly out of the cage as they have done, falling to its death)   **203 down** in the fall.

211–12 sweep . . . knavery sweep a path before me and conduct me to some *knavery* or treachery prepared for me.   **212 work** proceed.   **213 engineer** maker of *engines* of war   **214 Hoist with** blown up by.   **petard** an explosive used to blow in a door or make a breach   **214–15 't shall . . . will** unless luck is against me, I will   **215 mines** tunnels used in warfare to undermine the enemy's emplacements; Hamlet will countermine by going under their mines   **217 in one line** i.e., mines and countermines on a collision course, or the countermines directly below the mines.   **crafts** acts of guile, plots   **218 set me packing** set me to making schemes, and set me to lugging (him), and, also, send me off in a hurry.   **223 draw . . . end** finish up. (With a pun on *draw*, "pull.")
4.1 Location: The castle.
0.1 Enter . . . Queen (Some editors argue that Gertrude does not in fact exit at the end of 3.4 and that the scene is continuous here. It is true that the Folio ends 3.4 with "*Exit Hamlet tugging in Polonius*," not naming Gertrude, and opens 4.1 with "*Enter King*." Yet the Second Quarto concludes 3.4 with a simple "*Exit*," which often stands ambiguously for a single exit or an exeunt in early modern texts, and then starts 4.1 with "*Enter King, and Queene, with Rosencraus and Guyldensterne*." The King's opening lines in 4.1 suggest that he has had time, during a brief intervening pause, to become aware of Gertrude's highly wrought emotional state. In line 35, the King refers to Gertrude's *closet* as though it were elsewhere. The differences between the Second Quarto and the Folio offer an alternative staging. In either case, 4.1 follows swiftly upon 3.4.)   **1 matter** significance.   **heaves** heavy sighs.

KING
  What, Gertrude? How does Hamlet?
QUEEN
  Mad as the sea and wind when both contend
  Which is the mightier. In his lawless fit,
  Behind the arras hearing something stir,
  Whips out his rapier, cries, "A rat, a rat!"
  And in this brainish apprehension kills   11
  The unseen good old man.
KING   Oh, heavy deed!   12
  It had been so with us, had we been there.   13
  His liberty is full of threats to all—
  To you yourself, to us, to everyone.
  Alas, how shall this bloody deed be answered?   16
  It will be laid to us, whose providence   17
  Should have kept short, restrained, and out of haunt   18
  This mad young man. But so much was our love,
  We would not understand what was most fit,
  But, like the owner of a foul disease,
  To keep it from divulging, let it feed   22
  Even on the pith of life. Where is he gone?
QUEEN
  To draw apart the body he hath killed,
  O'er whom his very madness, like some ore   25
  Among a mineral of metals base,   26
  Shows itself pure: 'a weeps for what is done.
KING   Oh, Gertrude, come away!
  The sun no sooner shall the mountains touch
  But we will ship him hence, and this vile deed
  We must with all our majesty and skill
  Both countenance and excuse.—Ho, Guildenstern!   32

    Enter Rosencrantz and Guildenstern.

  Friends both, go join you with some further aid.
  Hamlet in madness hath Polonius slain,
  And from his mother's closet hath he dragged him.
  Go seek him out, speak fair, and bring the body   36
  Into the chapel. I pray you, haste in this.
          [*Exeunt Rosencrantz and Guildenstern.*]
  Come, Gertrude, we'll call up our wisest friends
  And let them know both what we mean to do
  And what's untimely done   40
  Whose whisper o'er the world's diameter,   41
  As level as the cannon to his blank,   42
  Transports his poisoned shot, may miss our name
  And hit the woundless air. Oh, come away!   44
  My soul is full of discord and dismay.   *Exeunt.*

11 **brainish apprehension** frenzied misapprehension   12 **heavy** grievous   13 **us** i.e., me. (The royal "we"; also in line 15.)   16 **answered** explained.   17 **providence** foresight   18 **short** i.e., on a short tether.   **out of haunt** secluded   22 **from divulging** from becoming publicly known   25 **ore** vein of gold   26 **mineral** mine   32 **countenance** put the best face on   36 **fair** gently, courteously   40 **And . . . done** (A defective line; conjectures as to the missing words include "So, haply, slander" [Capell and others]; "For, haply, slander" [Theobald and others]; and "So envious slander" [Jenkins].)   41 **diameter** extent from side to side   42 **As level** with as direct aim.   **his blank** its target at point-blank range   44 **woundless** invulnerable

[4.2]

    Enter Hamlet.

HAMLET   Safely stowed.
ROSENCRANTZ, GUILDENSTERN (*within*)   Hamlet! Lord
  Hamlet!
HAMLET   But soft, what noise? Who calls on Hamlet? Oh,
  here they come.

    Enter Rosencrantz and Guildenstern.

ROSENCRANTZ
  What have you done, my lord, with the dead body?
HAMLET
  Compounded it with dust, whereto 'tis kin.
ROSENCRANTZ
  Tell us where 'tis, that we may take it thence
  And bear it to the chapel.
HAMLET   Do not believe it.
ROSENCRANTZ   Believe what?
HAMLET   That I can keep your counsel and not mine   12
  own. Besides, to be demanded of a sponge, what rep-   13
  lication should be made by the son of a king?   14
ROSENCRANTZ   Take you me for a sponge, my lord?
HAMLET   Ay, sir, that soaks up the King's countenance, 16
  his rewards, his authorities. But such officers do the 17
  King best service in the end. He keeps them, like an
  ape, an apple, in the corner of his jaw, first mouthed
  to be last swallowed. When he needs what you have
  gleaned, it is but squeezing you, and, sponge, you
  shall be dry again.
ROSENCRANTZ   I understand you not, my lord.
HAMLET   I am glad of it. A knavish speech sleeps in a   24
  foolish ear.
ROSENCRANTZ   My lord, you must tell us where the
  body is and go with us to the King.
HAMLET   The body is with the King, but the King is not 28
  with the body. The King is a thing—   29
GUILDENSTERN   A thing, my lord?
HAMLET   Of nothing. Bring me to him. Hide fox, and all 31
  after!   *Exeunt* [*running*].   32

    ❖

[4.3]

    Enter King, and two or three.

4.2 Location: The castle.
12–13 That . . . own i.e., Don't expect me to do as you bid me and not follow my own counsel.   **13 demanded of** questioned by **13–14 replication** reply   **16 countenance** favor   **17 authorities** delegated power, influence.   **24 sleeps in** has no meaning to   **28–9 The . . . body** (Perhaps alludes to the legal commonplace of "the king's two bodies," which drew a distinction between the sacred office of kingship and the particular mortal who possessed it at any given time. Hence, although Claudius's body is necessarily a part of him, true kingship is not contained in it. Similarly, Claudius will have Polonius's body when it is found, but there is no kingship in this business either.)   **31 Of nothing** (1) Of no account (2) Lacking the essence of kingship, as in lines 28–9 and note.   **31–2 Hide . . . after** (An old signal cry in the game of hide-and-seek, suggesting that Hamlet now runs away from them.)
4.3. Location: The castle.

KING
> I have sent to seek him, and to find the body.
> How dangerous is it that this man goes loose!
> Yet must not we put the strong law on him.
> He's loved of the distracted multitude,   4
> Who like not in their judgment, but their eyes,   5
> And where 'tis so, th'offender's scourge is weighed,   6
> But never the offense. To bear all smooth and even,   7
> This sudden sending him away must seem
> Deliberate pause. Diseases desperate grown   9
> By desperate appliance are relieved,   10
> Or not at all.

> *Enter Rosencrantz, [Guildenstern,]*
> *and all the rest.*

> How now, what hath befall'n?

ROSENCRANTZ
> Where the dead body is bestowed, my lord,
> We cannot get from him.

KING   But where is he?

ROSENCRANTZ
> Without, my lord; guarded, to know your pleasure.   14

KING
> Bring him before us.

ROSENCRANTZ *[calling]*   Ho! Bring in the lord.

> *They enter [with Hamlet].*

KING   Now, Hamlet, where's Polonius?

HAMLET   At supper.

KING   At supper? Where?

HAMLET   Not where he eats, but where 'a is eaten. A
certain convocation of politic worms are e'en at him.   20
Your worm is your only emperor for diet. We fat all   21
creatures else to fat us, and we fat ourselves for mag-
gots. Your fat king and your lean beggar is but
variable service—two dishes, but to one table. That's   24
the end.

KING   Alas, alas!

HAMLET   A man may fish with the worm that hath eat   27
of a king, and eat of the fish that hath fed of that
worm.

KING   What dost thou mean by this?

HAMLET   Nothing but to show you how a king may go
a progress through the guts of a beggar.   32

KING   Where is Polonius?

HAMLET   In heaven. Send thither to see. If your messenger find him not there, seek him i'th'other place yourself. But if indeed you find him not within this month,

you shall nose him as you go up the stairs into the   37
lobby.

KING *[to some attendants]*   Go seek him there.

HAMLET   'A will stay till you come. *[Exeunt attendants.]*

KING
> Hamlet, this deed, for thine especial safety—
> Which we do tender, as we dearly grieve   42
> For that which thou hast done—must send thee hence
> With fiery quickness. Therefore prepare thyself.
> The bark is ready, and the wind at help,   45
> Th'associates tend, and everything is bent   46
> For England.

HAMLET   For England!

KING   Ay, Hamlet.

HAMLET   Good.

KING
> So is it, if thou knew'st our purposes.

HAMLET   I see a cherub that sees them. But come, for   52
England! Farewell, dear mother.

KING   Thy loving father, Hamlet.

HAMLET   My mother. Father and mother is man and
wife, man and wife is one flesh, and so, my mother.
Come, for England!   *Exit.*

KING
> Follow him at foot; tempt him with speed aboard.   58
> Delay it not. I'll have him hence tonight.
> Away! For everything is sealed and done
> That else leans on th'affair. Pray you, make haste.   61
>   *[Exeunt all but the King.]*
> And, England, if my love thou hold'st at aught—   62
> As my great power thereof may give thee sense,   63
> Since yet thy cicatrice looks raw and red   64
> After the Danish sword, and thy free awe   65
> Pays homage to us—thou mayst not coldly set   66
> Our sovereign process, which imports at full,   67
> By letters congruing to that effect,   68
> The present death of Hamlet. Do it, England,   69
> For like the hectic in my blood he rages,   70
> And thou must cure me. Till I know 'tis done,
> Howe'er my haps, my joys were ne'er begun.   *Exit.*   72

❖

[4.4]

Enter Fortinbras with his army over the stage.

FORTINBRAS
> Go, Captain, from me greet the Danish king.

---

4 of by. **distracted** fickle, unstable   **5 Who . . . eyes** who choose not by judgment but by appearance   **6–7 th'offender's . . . offense** i.e., the populace often takes umbrage at the severity of a punishment without taking into account the gravity of the crime.   **7 To . . . even** To manage the business in an unprovocative way   **9 Deliberate pause** carefully considered action.   **10 appliance** remedies   **14 Without** Outside   **20 politic worms** crafty worms (suited to a master spy like Polonius).   **e'en** even now   **21 Your worm** Your average worm. (Compare *your fat king and your lean beggar* in line 23.)   **diet** food, eating. (With a punning reference to the Diet of Worms, a famous *convocation* held in 1521.)   **24 service** food served at table. (Worms feed on kings and beggars alike.)   **27 eat** eaten. (Pronounced *et.*)   **32 progress** royal journey of state

37 nose smell   **42 tender** regard, hold dear.   **dearly** intensely   **45 bark** sailing vessel   **46 tend** wait.   **bent** in readiness   **52 cherub** (Cherubim are angels of knowledge. Hamlet hints that both he and heaven are onto Claudius's tricks.)   **58 at foot** close behind, at heel   **61 leans on** bears upon, is related to   **62 England** i.e., King of England.   **at aught** at any value   **63 As . . . sense** for so my great power may give you a just appreciation of the importance of valuing my love   **64 cicatrice** scar   **65 free awe** unconstrained show of respect   **66 coldly set** regard with indifference   **67 process** command.   **imports at full** conveys specific directions for   **68 congruing** agreeing   **69 present** immediate   **70 hectic** persistent fever   **72 Howe'er . . . begun** whatever else happens, I cannot begin to be happy.
4.4 Location: The coast of Denmark.

Tell him that by his license Fortinbras   2
Craves the conveyance of a promised march   3
Over his kingdom. You know the rendezvous.
If that His Majesty would aught with us,
We shall express our duty in his eye;   6
And let him know so.
CAPTAIN   I will do't, my lord.
FORTINBRAS   Go softly on.   [*Exeunt all but the Captain.*]   9

Enter Hamlet, Rosencrantz, [Guildenstern,] etc.

HAMLET   Good sir, whose powers are these?   10
CAPTAIN   They are of Norway, sir.
HAMLET   How purposed, sir, I pray you?
CAPTAIN   Against some part of Poland.
HAMLET   Who commands them, sir?
CAPTAIN
The nephew to old Norway, Fortinbras.
HAMLET
Goes it against the main of Poland, sir,   16
Or for some frontier?
CAPTAIN
Truly to speak, and with no addition,   18
We go to gain a little patch of ground
That hath in it no profit but the name.
To pay five ducats, five, I would not farm it;   21
Nor will it yield to Norway or the Pole
A ranker rate, should it be sold in fee.   23
HAMLET
Why, then the Polack never will defend it.
CAPTAIN
Yes, it is already garrisoned.
HAMLET
Two thousand souls and twenty thousand ducats
Will not debate the question of this straw.   27
This is th'impostume of much wealth and peace,   28
That inward breaks, and shows no cause without   29
Why the man dies. I humbly thank you, sir.
CAPTAIN
God b'wi'you, sir.   [*Exit.*]
ROSENCRANTZ   Will't please you go, my lord?
HAMLET
I'll be with you straight. Go a little before.
                                        [*Exeunt all except Hamlet.*]
How all occasions do inform against me   33
And spur my dull revenge! What is a man,
If his chief good and market of his time   35
Be but to sleep and feed? A beast, no more.
Sure he that made us with such large discourse,   37
Looking before and after, gave us not   38
That capability and godlike reason

To fust in us unused. Now, whether it be   40
Bestial oblivion, or some craven scruple   41
Of thinking too precisely on th'event—   42
A thought which, quartered, hath but one part
    wisdom
And ever three parts coward—I do not know
Why yet I live to say "This thing's to do,"
Sith I have cause, and will, and strength, and means   46
To do't. Examples gross as earth exhort me: 47
Witness this army of such mass and charge,   48
Led by a delicate and tender prince,   49
Whose spirit with divine ambition puffed
Makes mouths at the invisible event,   51
Exposing what is mortal and unsure
To all that fortune, death, and danger dare,   53
Even for an eggshell. Rightly to be great   54
Is not to stir without great argument,   55
But greatly to find quarrel in a straw   56
When honor's at the stake. How stand I, then,   57
That have a father killed, a mother stained,
Excitements of my reason and my blood,   59
And let all sleep, while to my shame I see
The imminent death of twenty thousand men
That for a fantasy and trick of fame   62
Go to their graves like beds, fight for a plot   63
Whereon the numbers cannot try the cause,   64
Which is not tomb enough and continent   65
To hide the slain? Oh, from this time forth
My thoughts be bloody or be nothing worth!   *Exit.*

❖

[4.5]

*Enter Horatio, [Queen] Gertrude, and a Gentle-
man.*

QUEEN
I will not speak with her.
GENTLEMAN   She is importunate,
Indeed distract. Her mood will needs be pitied.   2
QUEEN   What would she have?
GENTLEMAN
She speaks much of her father, says she hears
There's tricks i'th' world, and hems, and beats her
    heart,   5
Spurns enviously at straws, speaks things in doubt   6

40 **fust** grow moldy   41 **oblivion** forgetfulness.   **craven** cowardly
42 **precisely** scrupulously.   **th'event** the outcome   46 **Sith** since
47 **gross** obvious   48 **charge** expense   49 **delicate and tender** of fine
and youthful qualities   51 **Makes mouths** makes scornful faces.
invisible event unforeseeable outcome   53 **dare** could do (to him)
54–7 **Rightly . . . stake** True greatness is not a matter of being moved
to action solely by a great cause; rather, it is to respond greatly to an
apparently trivial cause when honor is at the stake.   62 **fantasy** fanciful caprice, illusion.
trick trifle, deceit   63 **plot** plot of ground   64 **Whereon . . . cause** on
which there is insufficient room for the soldiers needed to fight for it
65 **continent** receptacle, container
4.5 Location: The castle.
2 **distract** out of her mind.   5 **tricks** deceptions.   **hems** clears her
throat, makes "hmm" sounds.   **heart** i.e., breast   6 **Spurns . . .**
straws kicks spitefully, takes offense at trifles.   **in doubt** of obscure
meaning

2 **license** permission   3 **conveyance** unhindered passage   6 **We . . .**
eye I will come pay my respects in person   9 **softly** slowly, circum-
spectly   10 **powers** forces   16 **main** main part   18 **addition** exaggeration   21 **To pay** i.e., For a yearly rental of.   **farm it** take a lease
of it   23 **ranker** higher.   **in fee** fee simple, outright.   27 **debate . . .**
straw argue about this trifling matter.   28 **th'impostume** the abscess
29 **inward breaks** festers within.   **without** externally   33 **inform**
against denounce; take shape against   35 **market of** profit of
37 **discourse** power of reasoning   38 **Looking before and after** able
to review past events and anticipate the future

That carry but half sense. Her speech is nothing,
Yet the unshapèd use of it doth move   8
The hearers to collection; they yawn at it,   9
And botch the words up fit to their own thoughts,   10
Which, as her winks and nods and gestures yield
    them,   11
Indeed would make one think there might be thought,   12
Though nothing sure, yet much unhappily.   13

HORATIO
'Twere good she were spoken with, for she may strew
Dangerous conjectures in ill-breeding minds.   15
QUEEN   Let her come in.   [Exit Gentleman.]
[Aside] To my sick soul, as sin's true nature is,
Each toy seems prologue to some great amiss.   18
So full of artless jealousy is guilt,   19
It spills itself in fearing to be spilt.   20

                 Enter Ophelia [distracted].

OPHELIA
Where is the beauteous majesty of Denmark?
QUEEN   How now, Ophelia?
OPHELIA (she sings)
    "How should I your true love know
        From another one?
    By his cockle hat and staff,   25
        And his sandal shoon."   26
QUEEN   Alas, sweet lady, what imports this song?
OPHELIA Say you? Nay, pray you, mark.
    "He is dead and gone, lady,   (Song.)
        He is dead and gone;
    At his head a grass-green turf,
        At his heels a stone."
    Oho!   33
QUEEN   Nay, but Ophelia—
OPHELIA Pray you, mark.
    [Sings] "White his shroud as the mountain snow"—

                 Enter King.

QUEEN   Alas, look here, my lord.
OPHELIA
    "Larded with sweet flowers;   (Song.)   38
    Which bewept to the ground did not go
        With true-love showers."   40
KING   How do you, pretty lady?
OPHELIA Well, God 'ild you! They say the owl was a   42

baker's daughter. Lord, we know what we are, but
know not what we may be. God be at your table!
KING   Conceit upon her father.   45
OPHELIA Pray let's have no words of this; but when
    they ask you what it means, say you this:
    "Tomorrow is Saint Valentine's day,   (Song.)
        All in the morning betime,   49
    And I a maid at your window,
        To be your Valentine.
    Then up he rose, and donned his clothes,
        And dupped the chamber door,   53
    Let in the maid, that out a maid
        Never departed more."
KING   Pretty Ophelia—
OPHELIA Indeed, la, without an oath, I'll make an end
    on't:
    [Sings] "By Gis and by Saint Charity,   59
        Alack, and fie for shame!
    Young men will do't, if they come to't;
        By Cock, they are to blame.   62
    Quoth she, 'Before you tumbled me,
        You promised me to wed.'"
He answers:
    "'So would I ha' done, by yonder sun,
        An thou hadst not come to my bed.'"   67
KING   How long hath she been thus?
OPHELIA I hope all will be well. We must be patient,
    but I cannot choose but weep to think they would lay
    him i'th' cold ground. My brother shall know of it.
    And so I thank you for your good counsel. Come, my
    coach! Good night, ladies, good night, sweet ladies,
    good night, good night.   [Exit.]
KING   [to Horatio]
Follow her close. Give her good watch, I pray you.
                                          [Exit Horatio.]
Oh, this is the poison of deep grief; it springs
All from her father's death—and now behold!
Oh, Gertrude, Gertrude,
When sorrows come, they come not single spies,   79
But in battalions. First, her father slain;
Next, your son gone, and he most violent author
Of his own just remove; the people muddied,   82
Thick and unwholesome in their thoughts and
    whispers
For good Polonius' death—and we have done but
    greenly,   84
In hugger-mugger to inter him; poor Ophelia   85
Divided from herself and her fair judgment,
Without the which we are pictures or mere beasts;
Last, and as much containing as all these,   88
Her brother is in secret come from France,

---

8 **unshapèd use** incoherent manner   9 **collection** inference, a guess
at some sort of meaning.   **yawn** gape, wonder; grasp. (The Folio
reading, "aim," is possible.)   10 **botch** patch   11 **Which** which
words.   **yield** deliver, represent   12–13 **there might . . . unhappily**
that a great deal could be guessed at of a most unfortunate nature,
even if one couldn't be at all sure.   15 **ill-breeding** prone to suspect
the worst and to make mischief   18 **toy** trifle.   **amiss** calamity.
19–20 **So . . . spilt** Guilt is so burdened with conscience and guileless
fear of detection that it reveals itself through apprehension of disaster.   20.1 *Enter Ophelia* (In the First Quarto, Ophelia enters *"playing
on a lute, and her hair down, singing."*)   25 **cockle hat** hat with cockleshell stuck in it as a sign that the wearer had been a pilgrim to the
shrine of Saint James of Compostella in Spain   26 **shoon** shoes.
33 **Oho!** (Perhaps a sigh.)   38 **Larded** strewn, bedecked   40 **showers**
i.e., tears.   42 **God 'ild** God yield or reward.   **owl** (Refers to a legend about a baker's daughter who was turned into an owl for being
ungenerous when Jesus begged a loaf of bread.)

45 **Conceit** Fancy, brooding   49 **betime** early   53 **dupped** did up,
opened   59 **Gis** Jesus   62 **Cock** (A perversion of "God" in oaths;
here also with a quibble on the slang word for penis.)   67 **An** if
79 **spies** scouts sent in advance of the main force   82 **remove**
removal.   **muddied** stirred up, confused   84 **greenly** foolishly
85 **hugger-mugger** secret haste   88 **as much containing** as full of
serious matter

Feeds on this wonder, keeps himself in clouds,   90
And wants not buzzers to infect his ear   91
With pestilent speeches of his father's death,
Wherein necessity, of matter beggared,   93
Will nothing stick our person to arraign   94
In ear and ear. Oh, my dear Gertrude, this,   95
Like to a murd'ring piece, in many places   96
Gives me superfluous death.   *A noise within.*   97

QUEEN   Alack, what noise is this?
KING   Attend!   99
Where is my Switzers? Let them guard the door.   100

Enter a Messenger.

What is the matter?
MESSENGER   Save yourself, my lord!
The ocean, overpeering of his list,   102
Eats not the flats with more impetuous haste   103
Than young Laertes, in a riotous head,   104
O'erbears your officers. The rabble call him lord,
And, as the world were now but to begin,   106
Antiquity forgot, custom not known,   107
The ratifiers and props of every word,   108
They cry, "Choose we! Laertes shall be king!"
Caps, hands, and tongues applaud it to the clouds,   110
"Laertes shall be king, Laertes king!"

QUEEN
How cheerfully on the false trail they cry!
                                     A noise within.
Oh, this is counter, you false Danish dogs!   113

Enter Laertes with others.

KING   The doors are broke.
LAERTES
Where is this King?—Sirs, stand you all without.
ALL   No, let's come in.
LAERTES   I pray you, give me leave.
ALL   We will, we will.
LAERTES   I thank you. Keep the door. [*Exeunt followers.*]
                                    Oh, thou vile king,
Give me my father!
QUEEN [*restraining him*]   Calmly, good Laertes.
LAERTES
That drop of blood that's calm proclaims me bastard,

Cries cuckold to my father, brands the harlot
Even here between the chaste unsmirchèd brow   123
Of my true mother.
KING   What is the cause, Laertes,
That thy rebellion looks so giantlike?   125
Let him go, Gertrude. Do not fear our person.   126
There's such divinity doth hedge a king   127
That treason can but peep to what it would,   128
Acts little of his will. Tell me, Laertes,   129
Why thou art thus incensed. Let him go, Gertrude.
Speak, man.
LAERTES   Where is my father?
KING   Dead.
QUEEN
But not by him.
KING   Let him demand his fill.
LAERTES
How came he dead? I'll not be juggled with.   133
To hell, allegiance! Vows, to the blackest devil!
Conscience and grace, to the profoundest pit!
I dare damnation. To this point I stand,   136
That both the worlds I give to negligence,   137
Let come what comes, only I'll be revenged
Most throughly for my father.   139
KING   Who shall stay you?
LAERTES   My will, not all the world's.   141
And for my means, I'll husband them so well   142
They shall go far with little.
KING   Good Laertes,
If you desire to know the certainty
Of your dear father, is't writ in your revenge
That, swoopstake, you will draw both friend and foe, 146
Winner and loser?
LAERTES   None but his enemies.
KING   Will you know them, then?
LAERTES
To his good friends thus wide I'll ope my arms,
And like the kind life-rendering pelican   151
Repast them with my blood.
KING   Why, now you speak   152
Like a good child and a true gentleman.
That I am guiltless of your father's death,
And am most sensibly in grief for it,   155
It shall as level to your judgment 'pear   156
As day does to your eye.   *A noise within.*

---

90 **Feeds . . . clouds** feeds his resentment on this whole shocking turn
of events, keeps himself aloof and mysterious   91 **wants** lacks.
buzzers gossipers, informers   93 **necessity** i.e., the need to invent
some plausible explanation.   **of matter beggared** unprovided with
facts   94–5 **Will . . . ear** will not hesitate to accuse my (royal) person
in everybody's ears.   96 **murd'ring piece** cannon loaded so as to
scatter its shot   97 **Gives . . . death** kills me over and over.
99 **Attend!** Guard me!   100 **Switzers** Swiss guards, mercenaries.
102 **overpeering of his list** overflowing its shore, boundary   103 **flats**
i.e., flatlands near shore.   **impetuous** violent (perhaps also with the
meaning of *impiteous* ["impitious," Q2], "pitiless")   104 **riotous head**
insurrectionary advance   106–8 **And . . . word** and, as if the world
were to be started all over afresh, utterly setting aside all ancient traditional customs that should confirm and underprop our every word
and promise   110 **Caps** (The caps are thrown in the air.)
113 **counter** (A hunting term, meaning to follow the trail in a direction opposite to that which the game has taken.)

123 **between** amidst   125 **giantlike** (Recalling the rising of the giants
of Greek mythology against Olympus.)   126 **fear our** fear for my
127 **hedge** protect, as with a surrounding barrier   128 **can . . . would**
can only peep furtively, as through a barrier, at what it would intend
129 **Acts . . . will** (but) performs little of what it intends.   133 **juggled
with** cheated, deceived.   136 **To . . . stand** I am resolved in this
137 **both . . . negligence** i.e., both this world and the next are of no
consequence to me   139 **throughly** thoroughly   141 **My will . . .
world's** I'll stop (*stay*) when my will is accomplished, not for anyone
else's.   142 **for** as for   146 **swoopstake** i.e., indiscriminately. (Literally, taking all stakes on the gambling table at once. *Draw* is also a gambling term, meaning "take from.")   151 **pelican** (Refers to the belief
that the female pelican fed its young with its own blood.)
152 **Repast** feed   155 **sensibly** feelingly   156 **level** plain

LAERTES
　How now, what noise is that?

　　　　Enter Ophelia.

KING　　　　　　　　　　　　Let her come in.
LAERTES
　O heat, dry up my brains! Tears seven times salt
　Burn out the sense and virtue of mine eye!　　　160
　By heaven, thy madness shall be paid with weight　161
　Till our scale turn the beam. O rose of May!　　162
　Dear maid, kind sister, sweet Ophelia!
　O heavens, is't possible a young maid's wits
　Should be as mortal as an old man's life?
　Nature is fine in love, and where 'tis fine　　166
　It sends some precious instance of itself　　　167
　After the thing it loves.　　　　　　　　　168

OPHELIA
　　"They bore him barefaced on the bier,　　(*Song.*)
　　　Hey non nonny, nonny, hey nonny,
　　And in his grave rained many a tear—"
　Fare you well, my dove!

LAERTES
　Hadst thou thy wits and didst persuade revenge,
　It could not move thus.
OPHELIA　　You must sing "A-down a-down," and you　175
　"call him a-down-a." Oh, how the wheel becomes it! It　176
　is the false steward that stole his master's daughter.　177
LAERTES　　This nothing's more than matter.　　178
OPHELIA　　There's rosemary, that's for remembrance;　179
　pray you, love, remember. And there is pansies; that's　180
　for thoughts.
LAERTES　　A document in madness, thoughts and re-　182
　membrance fitted.
OPHELIA　　There's fennel for you, and columbines.　184
　There's rue for you, and here's some for me; we may　185
　call it herb of grace o' Sundays. You must wear your
　rue with a difference. There's a daisy. I would give　187
　you some violets, but they withered all when my　188
　father died. They say 'a made a good end—

[*Sings*] "For bonny sweet Robin is all my joy."
LAERTES
　Thought and affliction, passion, hell itself,　　191
　She turns to favor and to prettiness.　　　　192
OPHELIA
　　"And will 'a not come again?　　　　　(*Song.*)
　　And will 'a not come again?
　　　No, no, he is dead.
　　　Go to thy deathbed,
　　He never will come again.

　　"His beard was as white as snow,
　　All flaxen was his poll.　　　　　　　　199
　　　He is gone, he is gone,
　　　And we cast away moan.
　　God ha' mercy on his soul!"
　And of all Christian souls, I pray God. God b'wi'you.
　　　　　　　　　[*Exit, followed by Gertrude.*]
LAERTES　　Do you see this, O God?
KING
　Laertes, I must commune with your grief,
　Or you deny me right. Go but apart,
　Make choice of whom your wisest friends you will,　207
　And they shall hear and judge twixt you and me.
　If by direct or by collateral hand　　　　　209
　They find us touched, we will our kingdom give,　210
　Our crown, our life, and all that we call ours
　To you in satisfaction; but if not,
　Be you content to lend your patience to us,
　And we shall jointly labor with your soul
　To give it due content.
LAERTES　　　　　　　　Let this be so.
　His means of death, his obscure funeral—
　No trophy, sword, nor hatchment o'er his bones,　217
　No noble rite, nor formal ostentation—　　　218
　Cry to be heard, as 'twere from heaven to earth,
　That I must call't in question.
KING　　　　　　　　　　So you shall,　　220
　And where th'offense is, let the great ax fall.
　I pray you, go with me.　　　　　　　*Exeunt.*

❖

[4.6]

　　　　Enter Horatio and others.

HORATIO
　What are they that would speak with me?
GENTLEMAN　　Seafaring men, sir. They say they have
　letters for you.　　　　　　　　　　　　3
HORATIO　　Let them come in.　　[*Exit Gentleman.*]
　I do not know from what part of the world

160 **virtue** faculty, power　161 **paid with weight** repaid, avenged equally or more　162 **beam** crossbar of a balance.　166–8 **Nature . . . loves** Human nature is exquisitely sensitive in matters of love, and in cases of sudden loss it sends some precious part of itself after the lost object of that love. (In this case, Ophelia's sanity deserts her out of sorrow for her lost father and perhaps too out of her love for Hamlet.) 175–6 **You . . . a-down-a** (Ophelia assigns the singing of refrains, like her own "Hey non nonny," to others present.)　176 **wheel** spinning wheel as accompaniment to the song, or refrain　177 **false steward** (The story is unknown.)　178 **This . . . matter** This seeming nonsense is more eloquent than sane utterance.　179 **rosemary** (Used as a symbol of remembrance both at weddings and at funerals.)　180 **pansies** (Emblems of love and courtship; perhaps from French *pensées,* "thoughts.")　182 **document** instruction, lesson　184 **There's fennel . . . columbines** (*Fennel* betokens flattery; *columbines,* unchastity or ingratitude. Throughout, Ophelia addresses her various listeners, giving one flower to one and another to another, perhaps with particular symbolic significance in each case.)　185 **rue** (Emblem of repentance—a signification that is evident in its popular name, *herb of grace.*)　187 **with a difference** (A device used in heraldry to distinguish one family from another on the coat of arms, here suggesting that Ophelia and the others have different causes of sorrow and repentance; perhaps with a play on *rue* in the sense of "ruth," "pity.")　**daisy** (Emblem of love's victims and of faithlessness.)　188 **violets** (Emblems of faithfulness.)

191 **Thought** Melancholy.　**passion** suffering　192 **favor** grace, beauty　199 **poll** head.　207 **whom** whichever of　209 **collateral hand** indirect agency　210 **us touched** me implicated　217 **trophy** memorial.　**hatchment** tablet displaying the armorial bearings of a deceased person　218 **ostentation** ceremony　220 **That** so that.　**call't in question** demand an explanation.
4.6. Location: The castle.
3 **letters** a letter

I should be greeted, if not from Lord Hamlet.

Enter Sailors.

FIRST SAILOR   God bless you, sir.

HORATIO   Let him bless thee too.

FIRST SAILOR   'A shall, sir, an't please him. There's a 9
letter for you, sir—it came from th'ambassador that 10
was bound for England—if your name be Horatio, as
I am let to know it is.   [*He gives a letter.*]

HORATIO [*reads*]   "Horatio, when thou shalt have over- 13
looked this, give these fellows some means to the King; 14
they have letters for him. Ere we were two days old at
sea, a pirate of very warlike appointment gave us 16
chase. Finding ourselves too slow of sail, we put on a
compelled valor, and in the grapple I boarded them.
On the instant they got clear of our ship, so I alone
became their prisoner. They have dealt with me like
thieves of mercy, but they knew what they did: I am to 21
do a good turn for them. Let the King have the letters
I have sent, and repair thou to me with as much speed 23
as thou wouldest fly death. I have words to speak in
thine ear will make thee dumb, yet are they much too
light for the bore of the matter. These good fellows will 26
bring thee where I am. Rosencrantz and Guildenstern
hold their course for England. Of them I have much to
tell thee. Farewell.

          He that thou knowest thine, Hamlet."

Come, I will give you way for these your letters, 31
And do't the speedier that you may direct me
To him from whom you brought them.   *Exeunt.*

[4.7]

Enter King and Laertes.

KING
Now must your conscience my acquittance seal, 1
And you must put me in your heart for friend,
Sith you have heard, and with a knowing ear, 3
That he which hath your noble father slain
Pursued my life.

LAERTES   It well appears. But tell me
Why you proceeded not against these feats 6
So crimeful and so capital in nature, 7
As by your safety, greatness, wisdom, all things else,
You mainly were stirred up. 9

KING   Oh, for two special reasons,
Which may to you perhaps seem much unsinewed, 11
But yet to me they're strong. The Queen his mother
Lives almost by his looks, and for myself—
My virtue or my plague, be it either which—

She is so conjunctive to my life and soul 15
That, as the star moves not but in his sphere, 16
I could not but by her. The other motive
Why to a public count I might not go 18
Is the great love the general gender bear him, 19
Who, dipping all his faults in their affection,
Work like the spring that turneth wood to stone, 21
Convert his gyves to graces, so that my arrows, 22
Too slightly timbered for so loud a wind, 23
Would have reverted to my bow again
But not where I had aimed them.

LAERTES
And so have I a noble father lost,
A sister driven into desp'rate terms, 27
Whose worth, if praises may go back again, 28
Stood challenger on mount of all the age 29
For her perfections. But my revenge will come.

KING
Break not your sleeps for that. You must not think
That we are made of stuff so flat and dull
That we can let our beard be shook with danger
And think it pastime. You shortly shall hear more.
I loved your father, and we love ourself;
And that, I hope, will teach you to imagine—

Enter a Messenger with letters.

How now? What news?

MESSENGER   Letters, my lord, from Hamlet:
This to Your Majesty, this to the Queen.
                    [*He gives letters.*]

KING   From Hamlet? Who brought them?

MESSENGER
Sailors, my lord, they say. I saw them not.
They were given me by Claudio. He received them
Of him that brought them.

KING   Laertes, you shall hear them.—
Leave us.   [*Exit Messenger.*]
[*He reads.*] "High and mighty, you shall know I am set
naked on your kingdom. Tomorrow shall I beg leave 45
to see your kingly eyes, when I shall, first asking your
pardon, thereunto recount the occasion of my sudden 47
and more strange return.   Hamlet."
What should this mean? Are all the rest come back?
Or is it some abuse, and no such thing? 50

LAERTES
Know you the hand?

KING   'Tis Hamlet's character. "Naked!" 51
And in a postscript here he says "alone."

---

9 **an't** if it   10 **th'ambassador** (Hamlet's ostensible role; see 3.1.172-3.)
13–14 **overlooked** looked over   14 **means** means of access
16 **appointment** equipage   21 **thieves of mercy** merciful thieves
23 **repair** come   26 **bore** caliber, i.e., importance   31 **way** means of access

4.7. Location: The castle.
1 **my acquittance seal** confirm or acknowledge my innocence   3 **Sith**
since   6 **feats** acts   7 **capital** punishable by death   9 **mainly** greatly
11 **unsinewed** weak

15 **conjunctive** closely united. (An astronomical metaphor.)   16 **his**
its.   **sphere** one of the hollow spheres in which, according to Ptolemaic astronomy, the planets were supposed to move   18 **count**
account, reckoning, indictment   19 **general gender** common people
21 **Work** operate, act.   **spring** i.e., a spring with such a concentration
of lime that it coats a piece of wood with limestone, in effect gilding
and petrifying it   22 **gyves** fetters (which, gilded by the people's
praise, would look like badges of honor)   23 **Too . . . wind** with too
light a shaft for so powerful a gust (of popular sentiment)   27 **terms**
state, condition   28 **go back** recall what she was   29 **on mount** set
up on high   45 **naked** destitute, unarmed, without following
47 **pardon** (for returning without authorization)   50 **abuse** deceit.
no such thing not what the letter says.   51 **character** handwriting.

Can you devise me?   53

LAERTES
I am lost in it, my lord. But let him come.
It warms the very sickness in my heart
That I shall live and tell him to his teeth,
"Thus didst thou."

KING   If it be so, Laertes—   57
As how should it be so? How otherwise?—   58
Will you be ruled by me?

LAERTES   Ay, my lord,
So you will not o'errule me to a peace.   60

KING
To thine own peace. If he be now returned,
As checking at his voyage, and that he means   62
No more to undertake it, I will work him
To an exploit, now ripe in my device,   64
Under the which he shall not choose but fall;
And for his death no wind of blame shall breathe,
But even his mother shall uncharge the practice   67
And call it accident.

LAERTES   My lord, I will be ruled,
The rather if you could devise it so
That I might be the organ.

KING   It falls right.   70
You have been talked of since your travel much,
And that in Hamlet's hearing, for a quality
Wherein they say you shine. Your sum of parts   73
Did not together pluck such envy from him
As did that one, and that, in my regard,
Of the unworthiest siege.   76

LAERTES   What part is that, my lord?

KING
A very ribbon in the cap of youth,
Yet needful too, for youth no less becomes   79
The light and careless livery that it wears
Than settled age his sables and his weeds   81
Importing health and graveness. Two months since   82
Here was a gentleman of Normandy.
I have seen myself, and served against, the French,
And they can well on horseback, but this gallant   85
Had witchcraft in't; he grew unto his seat,
And to such wondrous doing brought his horse
As had he been incorpsed and demi-natured   88
With the brave beast. So far he topped my thought   89
That I in forgery of shapes and tricks   90
Come short of what he did.

LAERTES   A Norman was't?

KING   A Norman.

LAERTES
Upon my life, Lamord.

KING   The very same.

LAERTES
I know him well. He is the brooch indeed   94
And gem of all the nation.

KING   He made confession of you,   96
And gave you such a masterly report
For art and exercise in your defense,   98
And for your rapier most especial,
That he cried out 'twould be a sight indeed
If one could match you. Th'escrimers of their nation,   101
He swore, had neither motion, guard, nor eye
If you opposed them. Sir, this report of his
Did Hamlet so envenom with his envy
That he could nothing do but wish and beg
Your sudden coming o'er, to play with you.   106
Now, out of this—

LAERTES   What out of this, my lord?

KING
Laertes, was your father dear to you?
Or are you like the painting of a sorrow,
A face without a heart?

LAERTES   Why ask you this?

KING
Not that I think you did not love your father,
But that I know love is begun by time,   112
And that I see, in passages of proof,   113
Time qualifies the spark and fire of it.   114
There lives within the very flame of love
A kind of wick or snuff that will abate it,   116
And nothing is at a like goodness still,   117
For goodness, growing to a pleurisy,   118
Dies in his own too much. That we would do,   119
We should do when we would; for this "would" changes
And hath abatements and delays as many   121
As there are tongues, are hands, are accidents,   122
And then this "should" is like a spendthrift sigh,   123
That hurts by easing. But, to the quick o'th'ulcer: 124
Hamlet comes back. What would you undertake
To show yourself in deed your father's son
More than in words?

LAERTES   To cut his throat i'th' church.

---

53 **devise** explain to   57 **Thus didst thou** i.e., Here's for what you did to my father.   58 **As . . . otherwise?** how can this (Hamlet's return) be true? Yet how otherwise than true (since we have the evidence of his letter)?   60 **So** provided that   62 **checking at** i.e., turning aside from (like a falcon leaving the quarry to fly at a chance bird).   **that** if   64 **device** devising, invention   67 **uncharge the practice** acquit the stratagem of being a plot   70 **organ** agent, instrument.   73 **Your . . . parts** All your other virtues   76 **unworthiest siege** least important rank.   79 **no less becomes** is no less adorned by   81–2 **his sables . . . graveness** its rich robes furred with sable and its garments denoting dignified well-being and seriousness.   85 **can well** are skilled   88–9 **As . . . beast** as if, centaurlike, he had been made into one body with the horse, possessing half its nature.   89 **topped** surpassed   90 **forgery** fabrication

94 **brooch** ornament   96 **confession** testimonial, admission of superiority   98 **For . . . defense** with respect to your skill and practice with your weapon   101 **Th'escrimers** The fencers   106 **sudden** immediate.   **play** fence   112 **begun by time** i.e., created by the right circumstance and hence subject to change   113 **passages of proof** actual well-attested instances   114 **qualifies** weakens, moderates   116 **snuff** the charred part of a candlewick   117 **nothing . . . still** nothing remains at a constant level of perfection   118 **pleurisy** excess, plethora. (Literally, a chest inflammation.)   119 **in . . . much** of its own excess.   **That** That which   121 **abatements** diminutions   122 **As . . . accidents** as there are tongues to dissuade, hands to prevent, and chance events to intervene   123 **spendthrift sigh** (An allusion to the belief that sighs draw blood from the heart.)   124 **hurts by easing** i.e., costs the heart blood and wastes precious opportunity even while it affords emotional relief.   **quick o'th'ulcer** i.e., heart of the matter

KING
 No place, indeed, should murder sanctuarize;   128
 Revenge should have no bounds. But good Laertes,
 Will you do this, keep close within your chamber. 130
 Hamlet returned shall know you are come home.
 We'll put on those shall praise your excellence 132
 And set a double varnish on the fame
 The Frenchman gave you, bring you in fine together, 134
 And wager on your heads. He, being remiss, 135
 Most generous, and free from all contriving, 136
 Will not peruse the foils, so that with ease,
 Or with a little shuffling, you may choose
 A sword unbated, and in a pass of practice 139
 Requite him for your father.
LAERTES   I will do't,
 And for that purpose I'll anoint my sword.
 I bought an unction of a mountebank 142
 So mortal that, but dip a knife in it,
 Where it draws blood no cataplasm so rare, 144
 Collected from all simples that have virtue 145
 Under the moon, can save the thing from death 146
 That is but scratched withal. I'll touch my point
 With this contagion, that if I gall him slightly, 148
 It may be death.
KING   Let's further think of this,
 Weigh what convenience both of time and means
 May fit us to our shape. If this should fail, 151
 And that our drift look through our bad performance, 152
 'Twere better not assayed. Therefore this project
 Should have a back or second, that might hold
 If this did blast in proof. Soft, let me see. 155
 We'll make a solemn wager on your cunnings— 156
 I ha 't!
 When in your motion you are hot and dry—
 As make your bouts more violent to that end— 159
 And that he calls for drink, I'll have prepared him
 A chalice for the nonce, whereon but sipping, 161
 If he by chance escape your venomed stuck, 162
 Our purpose may hold there. [*A cry within.*] But stay,
  what noise?

    Enter Queen.

QUEEN
 One woe doth tread upon another's heel,
 So fast they follow. Your sister's drowned, Laertes.
LAERTES Drowned! Oh, where?

QUEEN
 There is a willow grows askant the brook, 167
 That shows his hoar leaves in the glassy stream; 168
 Therewith fantastic garlands did she make
 Of crowflowers, nettles, daisies, and long purples, 170
 That liberal shepherds give a grosser name, 171
 But our cold maids do dead men's fingers call them. 172
 There on the pendent boughs her crownet weeds 173
 Clamb'ring to hang, an envious sliver broke, 174
 When down her weedy trophies and herself 175
 Fell in the weeping brook. Her clothes spread wide,
 And mermaidlike awhile they bore her up,
 Which time she chanted snatches of old lauds, 178
 As one incapable of her own distress, 179
 Or like a creature native and endued 180
 Unto that element. But long it could not be
 Till that her garments, heavy with their drink,
 Pulled the poor wretch from her melodious lay 183
 To muddy death.
LAERTES   Alas, then she is drowned?
QUEEN Drowned, drowned.
LAERTES
 Too much of water hast thou, poor Ophelia,
 And therefore I forbid my tears. But yet
 It is our trick; nature her custom holds, 188
 Let shame say what it will. [*He weeps.*] When these
  are gone, 189
 The woman will be out. Adieu, my lord. 190
 I have a speech of fire that fain would blaze,
 But that this folly douts it.   *Exit.*
KING   Let's follow, Gertrude. 192
 How much I had to do to calm his rage!
 Now fear I this will give it start again;
 Therefore let's follow.   *Exeunt.*

[5.1]

Enter two Clowns [with spades and mattocks].

FIRST CLOWN Is she to be buried in Christian burial,
 when she willfully seeks her own salvation? 2

---

128 **sanctuarize** protect from punishment. (Alludes to the right of sanctuary with which certain religious places were invested.) 130 **Will you do this** if you wish to do this 132 **put on those shall** arrange for some to 134 **in fine** finally 135 **remiss** negligently unsuspicious 136 **generous** noble-minded 139 **unbated** not blunted, having no button. **pass of practice** treacherous thrust in an arranged bout 142 **unction** ointment. **mountebank** quack doctor 144 **cataplasm** plaster or poultice 145 **simples** herbs. **virtue** potency 146 **Under the moon** i.e., anywhere (with reference perhaps to the belief that herbs gathered at night had a special power) 148 **gall** graze, wound 151 **shape** part we propose to act. 152 **drift . . . performance** intention should be made visible by our bungling 155 **blast in proof** come to grief when put to the test. 156 **cunnings** respective skills 159 **As** i.e., and you should 161 **nonce** occasion 162 **stuck** thrust. (From *stoccado,* a fencing term.)

167 **askant** aslant 168 **hoar leaves** white or gray undersides of the leaves 170 **long purples** early purple orchids 171 **liberal** free-spoken. **a grosser name** (The testicle-resembling tubers of the orchid, which also in some cases resemble *dead men's fingers,* have earned various slang names like "dogstones" and "cullions.") 172 **cold** chaste 173 **pendent** overhanging. **crownet** made into a chaplet or coronet 174 **envious sliver** malicious branch 175 **weedy** i.e., of plants 178 **lauds** hymns 179 **incapable of** lacking capacity to apprehend 180 **endued** adapted by nature 183 **lay** ballad, song 188 **It is our trick** i.e., weeping is our natural way (when sad) 189–90 **When . . . out** When my tears are all shed, the woman in me will be expended, satisfied. 192 **douts** extinguishes. (The Second Quarto reads "drownes.")
5.1 Location: A churchyard.
0.1 *Clowns* rustics 2 **salvation** (A blunder for "damnation," or perhaps a suggestion that Ophelia was taking her own shortcut to heaven.)

SECOND CLOWN   I tell thee she is; therefore make her grave straight. The crowner hath sat on her, and finds it Christian burial.   4 5

FIRST CLOWN   How can that be, unless she drowned herself in her own defense?

SECOND CLOWN   Why, 'tis found so.   8

FIRST CLOWN   It must be *se offendendo*, it cannot be else. For here lies the point: if I drown myself wittingly, it argues an act, and an act hath three branches—it is to act, to do, and to perform. Argal, she drowned herself wittingly.   9 12

SECOND CLOWN   Nay, but hear you, goodman delve—   14

FIRST CLOWN   Give me leave. Here lies the water; good. Here stands the man; good. If the man go to this water and drown himself, it is, will he, nill he, he goes, mark you that. But if the water come to him and drown him, he drowns not himself. Argal, he that is not guilty of his own death shortens not his own life.   17

SECOND CLOWN   But is this law?

FIRST CLOWN   Ay, marry, is't—crowner's quest law.   22

SECOND CLOWN   Will you ha' the truth on't? If this had not been a gentlewoman, she should have been buried out o' Christian burial.

FIRST CLOWN   Why, there thou say'st. And the more pity that great folk should have countenance in this world to drown or hang themselves, more than their even-Christian. Come, my spade. There is no ancient gentlemen but gardeners, ditchers, and grave makers. They hold up Adam's profession.   26 27 29 31

SECOND CLOWN   Was he a gentleman?

FIRST CLOWN   'A was the first that ever bore arms.   33

SECOND CLOWN   Why, he had none.

FIRST CLOWN   What, art a heathen? How dost thou understand the Scripture? The Scripture says Adam digged. Could he dig without arms? I'll put another question to thee. If thou answerest me not to the purpose, confess thyself—   37 39

SECOND CLOWN   Go to.

FIRST CLOWN   What is he that builds stronger than either the mason, the shipwright, or the carpenter?

SECOND CLOWN   The gallows maker, for that frame outlives a thousand tenants.   43

FIRST CLOWN   I like thy wit well, in good faith. The gallows does well. But how does it well? It does well to those that do ill. Now thou dost ill to say the gallows   46

is built stronger than the church. Argal, the gallows may do well to thee. To't again, come.

SECOND CLOWN   "Who builds stronger than a mason, a shipwright, or a carpenter?"

FIRST CLOWN   Ay, tell me that, and unyoke.   52

SECOND CLOWN   Marry, now I can tell.

FIRST CLOWN   To't.

SECOND CLOWN   Mass, I cannot tell.   55

Enter Hamlet and Horatio [at a distance].

FIRST CLOWN   Cudgel thy brains no more about it, for your dull ass will not mend his pace with beating; and when you are asked this question next, say "a grave maker." The houses he makes lasts till doomsday. Go get thee in and fetch me a stoup of liquor.   60

[Exit Second Clown. First Clown digs.]
Song.

"In youth, when I did love, did love,   61
    Methought it was very sweet,
To contract—oh—the time for—a—my behove,   63
    Oh, methought there—a—was nothing—a—
        meet."   64

HAMLET   Has this fellow no feeling of his business, 'a sings in grave-making?   65

HORATIO   Custom hath made it in him a property of easiness.   67 68

HAMLET   'Tis e'en so. The hand of little employment hath the daintier sense.   70

FIRST CLOWN   *Song.*

"But age with his stealing steps
    Hath clawed me in his clutch,
And hath shipped me into the land,   73
    As if I had never been such."

[He throws up a skull.]

HAMLET   That skull had a tongue in it and could sing once. How the knave jowls it to the ground, as if 'twere Cain's jawbone, that did the first murder! This might be the pate of a politician, which this ass now o'erreaches, one that would circumvent God, might it not?   76 78 79

HORATIO   It might, my lord.

HAMLET   Or of a courtier, which could say, "Good morrow, sweet lord! How dost thou, sweet lord?" This might be my Lord Such-a-one, that praised my Lord Such-a-one's horse when 'a meant to beg it, might it not?

HORATIO   Ay, my lord.

HAMLET   Why, e'en so, and now my Lady Worm's, chapless, and knocked about the mazard with a sexton's spade. Here's fine revolution, an we had the trick to see't. Did these bones cost no more the breeding but to play at loggets with them? Mine ache to think on't. 89 90 91 92

FIRST CLOWN   *Song.*
    "A pickax and a spade, a spade,
        For and a shrouding sheet;
    Oh, a pit of clay for to be made
        For such a guest is meet." 95
                    [*He throws up another skull.*]

HAMLET   There's another. Why may not that be the skull of a lawyer? Where be his quiddities now, his quillities, his cases, his tenures, and his tricks? Why does he suffer this mad knave now to knock him about the sconce with a dirty shovel, and will not tell him of his action of battery? Hum, this fellow might be in 's time a great buyer of land, with his statutes, his recognizances, his fines, his double vouchers, his recoveries. Is this the fine of his fines and the recovery of his recoveries, to have his fine pate full of fine dirt? Will his vouchers vouch him no more of his purchases, and double ones too, than the length and breadth of a pair of indentures? The very conveyances of his lands will scarcely lie in this box, and must th'inheritor himself have no more, ha? 99 100 102 103 104 105 106 107 108 109 110 111

HORATIO   Not a jot more, my lord.

HAMLET   Is not parchment made of sheepskins?

HORATIO   Ay, my lord, and of calves' skins too.

HAMLET   They are sheep and calves which seek out assurance in that. I will speak to this fellow.—Whose grave's this, sirrah? 116 117 118

FIRST CLOWN   Mine, sir.
    [*Sings*] "Oh, pit of clay for to be made
        For such a guest is meet."

HAMLET   I think it be thine, indeed, for thou liest in't.

FIRST CLOWN   You lie out on't, sir, and therefore 'tis not yours. For my part, I do not lie in't, yet it is mine.

HAMLET   Thou dost lie in't, to be in't and say it is thine. 'Tis for the dead, not for the quick; therefore thou liest. 126

FIRST CLOWN   'Tis a quick lie, sir; 'twill away again from me to you.

HAMLET   What man dost thou dig it for?

FIRST CLOWN   For no man, sir.

HAMLET   What woman, then?

FIRST CLOWN   For none, neither.

HAMLET   Who is to be buried in't?

FIRST CLOWN   One that was a woman, sir, but, rest her soul, she's dead.

HAMLET   How absolute the knave is! We must speak by the card, or equivocation will undo us. By the Lord, Horatio, this three years I have took note of it: the age is grown so picked that the toe of the peasant comes so near the heel of the courtier he galls his kibe.—How long hast thou been grave maker? 137 138 139 140 141

FIRST CLOWN   Of all the days i'th' year, I came to't that day that our last king Hamlet overcame Fortinbras.

HAMLET   How long is that since?

FIRST CLOWN   Cannot you tell that? Every fool can tell that. It was that very day that young Hamlet was born—he that is mad and sent into England.

HAMLET   Ay, marry, why was he sent into England?

FIRST CLOWN   Why, because 'a was mad. 'A shall recover his wits there, or if 'a do not, 'tis no great matter there.

HAMLET   Why?

FIRST CLOWN   'Twill not be seen in him there. There the men are as mad as he.

HAMLET   How came he mad?

FIRST CLOWN   Very strangely, they say.

HAMLET   How strangely?

FIRST CLOWN   Faith, e'en with losing his wits.

HAMLET   Upon what ground? 160

FIRST CLOWN   Why, here in Denmark. I have been sexton here, man and boy, thirty years.

HAMLET   How long will a man lie i'th'earth ere he rot?

FIRST CLOWN   Faith, if 'a be not rotten before 'a die—as we have many pocky corpses nowadays, that will scarce hold the laying in—'a will last you some eight year or nine year. A tanner will last you nine year. 165 166

HAMLET   Why he more than another?

FIRST CLOWN   Why, sir, his hide is so tanned with his trade that 'a will keep out water a great while, and

---

89 chapless having no lower jaw. **mazard** i.e., head. (Literally, a drinking vessel.) **90 revolution** turn of Fortune's wheel, change. **trick** knack **91–2 cost . . . but** involve so little expense and care in upbringing that we may **92 loggets** a game in which pieces of hard wood shaped like Indian clubs or bowling pins are thrown to lie as near as possible to a stake **95 For and** and moreover **99–100 his quiddities . . . quillities** his subtleties, his legal niceties **100 tenures** the holding of a piece of property or office, or the conditions or period of such holding **102 sconce** head **103 action of battery** lawsuit about physical assault. **104 his statutes** his legal documents acknowledging obligation of a debt **104–5 recognizances** bonds undertaking to repay debts **105 fines** procedures for converting entailed estates into "fee simple" or freehold. **double vouchers** vouchers signed by two signatories guaranteeing the legality of real estate titles. **recoveries** suits to obtain the authority of a court judgment for the holding of land. **106–7 Is this . . . dirt?** Is this the end of his legal maneuvers and profitable land deals, to have the skull of his elegant head filled full of minutely sifted dirt? (With multiple wordplay on *fine* and *fines*.) **107–10 Will . . . indentures?** Will his vouchers, even double ones, guarantee him no more land than is needed to bury him in, being no bigger than the deed of conveyance? (An *indenture* is literally a legal document drawn up in duplicate on a single sheet and then cut apart on a zigzag line so that each pair was uniquely matched.) **111 box** (1) deed box (2) coffin. **th'inheritor** the acquirer, owner **116–17 assurance in that** safety in legal parchments. **118 sirrah** (A term of address to inferiors.)

126 quick living **137 absolute** strict, precise **137–8 by the card** i.e., with precision. (Literally, by the mariner's compass-card, on which the points of the compass were marked.) **138 equivocation** ambiguity in the use of terms **139 took** taken **139–41 the age . . . kibe** i.e., the age has grown so finical and mannered that the lower classes ape their social betters, chafing at their heels. (*Kibes* are chilblains on the heels.) **160 ground** cause. (But, in the next line, the gravedigger takes the word in the sense of "land," "country.") **165 pocky** rotten, diseased. (Literally, with the pox, or syphilis.) **166 hold the laying in** hold together long enough to be interred. **last you** last. (*You* is used colloquially here and in the following lines.)

your water is a sore decayer of your whoreson dead 171
body. [*He picks up a skull.*] Here's a skull now hath
lien you i'th'earth three-and-twenty years.   173

HAMLET   Whose was it?

FIRST CLOWN   A whoreson mad fellow's it was. Whose
do you think it was?

HAMLET   Nay, I know not.

FIRST CLOWN   A pestilence on him for a mad rogue! 'A
poured a flagon of Rhenish on my head once. This 179
same skull, sir, was, sir, Yorick's skull, the King's jester.

HAMLET   This?

FIRST CLOWN   E'en that.

HAMLET   Let me see. [*He takes the skull.*] Alas, poor
Yorick! I knew him, Horatio, a fellow of infinite jest, of
most excellent fancy. He hath bore me on his back a 185
thousand times, and now how abhorred in my
imagination it is! My gorge rises at it. Here hung those 187
lips that I have kissed I know not how oft. Where be
your gibes now? Your gambols, your songs, your 189
flashes of merriment that were wont to set the table on
a roar? Not one now, to mock your own grinning?
Quite chopfallen? Now get you to my lady's chamber 192
and tell her, let her paint an inch thick, to this favor 193
she must come. Make her laugh at that. Prithee,
Horatio, tell me one thing.

HORATIO   What's that, my lord?

HAMLET   Dost thou think Alexander looked o' this
fashion i'th'earth?

HORATIO   E'en so.

HAMLET   And smelt so? Pah! [*He throws down the skull.*]

HORATIO   E'en so, my lord.

HAMLET   To what base uses we may return, Horatio!
Why may not imagination trace the noble dust of
Alexander till 'a find it stopping a bunghole?   204

HORATIO   'Twere to consider too curiously to consider 205
so.

HAMLET   No, faith, not a jot, but to follow him thither
with modesty enough, and likelihood to lead it. As 208
thus: Alexander died, Alexander was buried, Alexander returneth to dust, the dust is earth, of earth we
make loam, and why of that loam whereto he was 211
converted might they not stop a beer barrel?
Imperious Caesar, dead and turned to clay,   213
Might stop a hole to keep the wind away.
Oh, that that earth which kept the world in awe
Should patch a wall t'expel the winter's flaw!   216

    Enter King, Queen, Laertes, and the corpse [*of
Ophelia, in procession, with Priest, lords, etc.*].

But soft, but soft awhile! Here comes the King, 217

The Queen, the courtiers. Who is this they follow?
And with such maimèd rites? This doth betoken   219
The corpse they follow did with desperate hand
Fordo it own life. 'Twas of some estate.   221
Couch we awhile and mark.   222
    [*He and Horatio conceal themselves.
    Ophelia's body is taken to the grave.*]

LAERTES   What ceremony else?

HAMLET [*to Horatio*]
That is Laertes, a very noble youth. Mark.

LAERTES   What ceremony else?

PRIEST
Her obsequies have been as far enlarged
As we have warranty. Her death was doubtful,   227
And but that great command o'ersways the order 228
She should in ground unsanctified been lodged   229
Till the last trumpet. For charitable prayers,   230
Shards, flints, and pebbles should be thrown on her. 231
Yet here she is allowed her virgin crants,   232
Her maiden strewments, and the bringing home   233
Of bell and burial.   234

LAERTES
Must there no more be done?

PRIEST   No more be done.
We should profane the service of the dead
To sing a requiem and such rest to her   237
As to peace-parted souls.

LAERTES   Lay her i'th'earth, 238
And from her fair and unpolluted flesh
May violets spring! I tell thee, churlish priest, 240
A ministering angel shall my sister be
When thou liest howling.

HAMLET [*to Horatio*]   What, the fair Ophelia! 242

QUEEN [*scattering flowers*]   Sweets to the sweet! Farewell.
I hoped thou shouldst have been my Hamlet's wife.
I thought thy bride-bed to have decked, sweet maid,
And not t' have strewed thy grave.

LAERTES   Oh, treble woe
Fall ten times treble on that cursèd head
Whose wicked deed thy most ingenious sense   248
Deprived thee of! Hold off the earth awhile,
Till I have caught her once more in mine arms.
    [*He leaps into the grave and embraces Ophelia.*]
Now pile your dust upon the quick and dead,
Till of this flat a mountain you have made
T' o'ertop old Pelion or the skyish head   253
Of blue Olympus.

---

171 **sore** keen, veritable.   **whoreson** (An expression of contemptuous familiarity.)   173 **lien you** lain. (See the note at line 166.)   179 **Rhenish** Rhine wine   185 **bore** borne   187 **My gorge rises** i.e., I feel nauseated   189 **gibes** taunts   192 **chopfallen** (1) lacking the lower jaw (2) dejected.   193 **favor** aspect, appearance   204 **bunghole** hole for filling or emptying a cask.   205 **curiously** minutely   208 **with . . . lead it** with moderation and plausibility.   211 **loam** a mixture of clay, straw, sand, etc. used to mold bricks, or, in this case, bungs for a beer barrel   213 **Imperious** Imperial   216 **flaw** gust of wind.   217 **soft** i.e., wait, be careful

219 **maimèd** mutilated, incomplete   221 **Fordo it** destroy its.   **estate** rank.   222 **Couch we** Let's hide, lie low   227 **warranty** i.e., ecclesiastical authority.   228 **order** (1) prescribed practice (2) religious order of clerics   229 **She should . . . lodged** she should have been buried in unsanctified ground   230 **For** In place of   231 **Shards** broken bits of pottery   232 **crants** garlands betokening maidenhood   233 **strewments** flowers strewn on a coffin   233–4 **bringing . . . burial** laying the body to rest, to the sound of the bell.   237 **such rest** i.e., to pray for such rest   238 **peace-parted souls** those who have died at peace with God.   240 **violets** (See 4.5.188 and note.)   242 **howling** i.e., in hell.   248 **ingenious sense** a mind that is quick, alert, of fine qualities   253 **Pelion** a mountain in northern Thessaly; compare *Olympus* and *Ossa* in lines 254 and 286. (In their rebellion against the Olympian gods, the giants attempted to heap Ossa on Pelion in order to scale Olympus.)

HAMLET [*coming forward*]   What is he whose grief
  Bears such an emphasis, whose phrase of sorrow   255
  Conjures the wandering stars and makes them stand   256
  Like wonder-wounded hearers? This is I,   257
  Hamlet the Dane.   258
LAERTES [*grappling with him*]   The devil take thy soul!   259
HAMLET   Thou pray'st not well.
  I prithee, take thy fingers from my throat,
  For though I am not splenitive and rash,   262
  Yet have I in me something dangerous,
  Which let thy wisdom fear. Hold off thy hand.
KING   Pluck them asunder.
QUEEN   Hamlet, Hamlet!
ALL   Gentlemen!
HORATIO   Good my lord, be quiet.
                    [*Hamlet and Laertes are parted.*]
HAMLET
  Why, I will fight with him upon this theme
  Until my eyelids will no longer wag.   270
QUEEN   Oh, my son, what theme?
HAMLET
  I loved Ophelia. Forty thousand brothers
  Could not with all their quantity of love
  Make up my sum. What wilt thou do for her?
KING   Oh, he is mad, Laertes.
QUEEN   For love of God, forbear him.   276
HAMLET
  'Swounds, show me what thou'lt do.   277
  Woo't weep? Woo't fight? Woo't fast? Woo't tear
    thyself?   278
  Woo't drink up eisel? Eat a crocodile?   279
  I'll do't. Dost come here to whine?
  To outface me with leaping in her grave?
  Be buried quick with her, and so will I.   282
  And if thou prate of mountains, let them throw
  Millions of acres on us, till our ground,
  Singeing his pate against the burning zone,   285
  Make Ossa like a wart! Nay, an thou'lt mouth,   286
  I'll rant as well as thou.
QUEEN   This is mere madness,   287
  And thus awhile the fit will work on him;
  Anon, as patient as the female dove

When that her golden couplets are disclosed,   290
  His silence will sit drooping.
HAMLET   Hear you, sir.
  What is the reason that you use me thus?
  I loved you ever. But it is no matter.
  Let Hercules himself do what he may,   294
  The cat will mew, and dog will have his day.   295
                    Exit Hamlet.
KING
  I pray thee, good Horatio, wait upon him.
                    [*Exit*] *Horatio.*
  [*To Laertes*] Strengthen your patience in our last
    night's speech;   297
  We'll put the matter to the present push.—   298
  Good Gertrude, set some watch over your son.—
  This grave shall have a living monument.   300
  An hour of quiet shortly shall we see;   301
  Till then, in patience our proceeding be.   *Exeunt.*

[5.2]

Enter Hamlet and Horatio.

HAMLET
  So much for this, sir; now shall you see the other.   1
  You do remember all the circumstance?
HORATIO   Remember it, my lord!
HAMLET
  Sir, in my heart there was a kind of fighting
  That would not let me sleep. Methought I lay
  Worse than the mutines in the bilboes. Rashly,   6
  And praised be rashness for it—let us know   7
  Our indiscretion sometime serves us well   8
  When our deep plots do pall, and that should learn us   9
  There's a divinity that shapes our ends,
  Rough-hew them how we will—
HORATIO   That is most certain.   11
HAMLET   Up from my cabin,
  My sea-gown scarfed about me, in the dark   13
  Groped I to find out them, had my desire,   14
  Fingered their packet, and in fine withdrew   15
  To mine own room again, making so bold,
  My fears forgetting manners, to unseal
  Their grand commission; where I found, Horatio—
  Ah, royal knavery!—an exact command,

255 **emphasis** i.e., rhetorical and florid emphasis. (*Phrase* has a similar rhetorical connotation.)   256 **wandering stars** planets   257 **wonder-wounded** struck with amazement   258 **the Dane** (This title normally signifies the King; see 1.1.17 and note.)   259 **s.d. grappling with him** The testimony of the First Quarto that *"Hamlet leaps in after Laertes"* and of the ballad "Elegy on Burbage," published in *Gentleman's Magazine* in 1825 ("Oft have I seen him leap into a grave") seem to indicate one way in which this fight was staged; however, the difficulty of fitting two contenders and Ophelia's body into a confined space (probably the trapdoor) suggests to many editors the alternative, that Laertes jumps out of the grave to attack Hamlet.)   262 **splenitive** quick-tempered   270 **wag** move. (A fluttering eyelid is a conventional sign that life has not yet gone.)   276 **forbear him** leave him alone.   277 **'Swounds** By His (Christ's) wounds   278 **Woo't** Wilt thou   279 **Woo't . . . eisel?** Will you drink up a whole draft of vinegar? (An extremely self-punishing task as a way of expressing grief.)   **crocodile** (Crocodiles were tough and dangerous, and were supposed to shed crocodile tears.)   282 **quick** alive   285 **his pate** its head, i.e., top.   **burning zone** zone in the celestial sphere containing the sun's orbit, between the tropics of Cancer and Capricorn   286 **Ossa** (See 253n.)   **an thou'lt mouth** if you want to rant   287 **mere** utter

290 **golden couplets** two baby pigeons, covered with yellow down. **disclosed** hatched   294–5 **Let . . . day** i.e., (1) Even Hercules couldn't stop Laertes's theatrical rant (2) I, too, will have my turn; i.e., despite any blustering attempts at interference, every person will sooner or later do what he or she must do.   297 **in** i.e., by recalling   298 **present push** immediate test.   300 **living** lasting. (For Laertes' private understanding, Claudius also hints that Hamlet's death will serve as such a monument.)   301 **hour of quiet** time free of conflict
5.2 Location: The castle.
1 **see the other** hear the other news. (See 4.6.24–6.)   6 **mutines** mutineers.   **bilboes** shackles.   **Rashly** On impulse. (This adverb goes with lines 12 ff.)   7 **know** acknowledge   8 **indiscretion** lack of foresight and judgment (not an indiscreet act)   9 **pall** fail, falter, go stale. **learn** teach   11 **Rough-hew** shape roughly   13 **sea-gown** seaman's coat.   **scarfed** loosely wrapped   14 **them** i.e., Rosencrantz and Guildenstern   15 **Fingered** pilfered, pinched.   **in fine** finally, in conclusion

Larded with many several sorts of reasons   20
Importing Denmark's health and England's too,   21
With, ho! such bugs and goblins in my life,   22
That on the supervise, no leisure bated,   23
No, not to stay the grinding of the ax,   24
My head should be struck off.
HORATIO   Is't possible?
HAMLET [*giving a document*]
Here's the commission. Read it at more leisure.
But wilt thou hear now how I did proceed?
HORATIO   I beseech you.
HAMLET
Being thus benetted round with villainies—
Ere I could make a prologue to my brains,   30
They had begun the play—I sat me down,   31
Devised a new commission, wrote it fair.   32
I once did hold it, as our statists do,   33
A baseness to write fair, and labored much   34
How to forget that learning, but, sir, now
It did me yeoman's service. Wilt thou know
Th'effect of what I wrote?
HORATIO   Ay, good my lord.
HAMLET
An earnest conjuration from the King,   38
As England was his faithful tributary,
As love between them like the palm might flourish,   40
As peace should still her wheaten garland wear   41
And stand a comma 'tween their amities,   42
And many suchlike "as"es of great charge,   43
That on the view and knowing of these contents,
Without debatement further more or less,
He should those bearers put to sudden death,
Not shriving time allowed.
HORATIO   How was this sealed?   47
HAMLET
Why, even in that was heaven ordinant.   48
I had my father's signet in my purse,   49
Which was the model of that Danish seal;   50
Folded the writ up in the form of th'other,   51
Subscribed it, gave't th'impression, placed it safely,   52
The changeling never known. Now, the next day   53
Was our sea fight, and what to this was sequent   54
Thou knowest already.

HORATIO
So Guildenstern and Rosencrantz go to't.
HAMLET
Why, man, they did make love to this employment.
They are not near my conscience. Their defeat   58
Does by their own insinuation grow.   59
'Tis dangerous when the baser nature comes   60
Between the pass and fell incensèd points   61
Of mighty opposites.
HORATIO   Why, what a king is this!   62
HAMLET
Does it not, think thee, stand me now upon—   63
He that hath killed my king and whored my mother,
Popped in between th'election and my hopes,   65
Thrown out his angle for my proper life,   66
And with such coz'nage—is't not perfect conscience   67
To quit him with this arm? And is't not to be damned   68
To let this canker of our nature come   69
In further evil?   70
HORATIO
It must be shortly known to him from England
What is the issue of the business there.
HAMLET
It will be short. The interim is mine,
And a man's life's no more than to say "one."   74
But I am very sorry, good Horatio,
That to Laertes I forgot myself,
For by the image of my cause I see
The portraiture of his. I'll court his favors.
But, sure, the bravery of his grief did put me   79
Into a tow'ring passion.
HORATIO   Peace, who comes here?

Enter a Courtier [Osric].

OSRIC   Your Lordship is right welcome back to Denmark.
HAMLET   I humbly thank you, sir. [*To Horatio*] Dost
know this water fly?
HORATIO   No, my good lord.
HAMLET   Thy state is the more gracious, for 'tis a vice to
know him. He hath much land, and fertile. Let a beast   86
be lord of beasts, and his crib shall stand at the King's   87
mess. 'Tis a chuff, but, as I say, spacious in the   88
possession of dirt.
OSRIC   Sweet lord, if Your Lordship were at leisure, I
should impart a thing to you from His Majesty.
HAMLET   I will receive it, sir, with all diligence of spirit.
Put your bonnet to his right use; 'tis for the head.   93

---

20 Larded garnished.   **several** different   **21 Importing** relating to
22 With . . . life i.e., with all sorts of warnings of imaginary dangers if
I were allowed to continue living. (*Bugs* are bugbears, hobgoblins.)
23 That . . . bated that on the reading of this commission, no delay
being allowed   **24 stay** await   **30–1 Ere . . . play** before I could consciously turn my brain to the matter, it had started working on a plan
32 fair in a clear hand.   **33 statists** politicians, men of public affairs
34 A baseness beneath my dignity   **38 conjuration** entreaty
40 palm (An image of health; see Psalm 92:12.)   **41 still** always.
wheaten garland (Symbolic of fruitful agriculture, of peace and plenty.)   **42 comma** (Indicating continuity, link.)   **43 "as"es** (1) the
"whereases" of a formal document (2) asses.   **charge** (1) import (2)
burden (appropriate to asses)   **47 shriving time** time for confession
and absolution   **48 ordinant** directing.   **49 signet** small seal
50 model replica   **51 writ** writing   **52 Subscribed** signed (with
forged signature).   **impression** i.e., with a wax seal   **53 changeling**
i.e., substituted letter. (Literally, a fairy child substituted for a human
one.)   **54 was sequent** followed

58 defeat destruction   **59 insinuation** intrusive intervention, sticking
their noses in my business   **60 baser** of lower social station   **61 pass**
thrust.   **fell** fierce   **62 opposites** antagonists.   **63 stand me now**
upon become incumbent on me now   **65 th'election** (The Danish
monarch was "elected" by a small number of high-ranking electors.)
66 angle fishhook.   **proper** very   **67 coz'nage** trickery   **68 quit**
requite, pay back   **69 canker** ulcer   **69–70 come In** grow into
74 a man's . . . "one" one's whole life occupies such a short time, only
as long as it takes to count to 1.   **79 bravery** bravado   **86–8 Let . . .**
mess i.e., If a man, no matter how beastlike, is as rich in livestock and
possessions as Osric, he may eat at the King's table.   **87 crib** manger
88 chuff boor, churl. (The Second Quarto spelling, "chough," is a
variant spelling that also suggests the meaning here of "chattering
jackdaw.")   **93 bonnet** any kind of cap or hat.   **his** its

OSRIC   I thank Your Lordship, it is very hot.

HAMLET   No, believe me, 'tis very cold. The wind is northerly.

OSRIC   It is indifferent cold, my lord, indeed.   97

HAMLET   But yet methinks it is very sultry and hot for my complexion.   99

OSRIC   Exceedingly, my lord. It is very sultry, as 'twere—I cannot tell how. My lord, His Majesty bade me signify to you that 'a has laid a great wager on your head. Sir, this is the matter—

HAMLET   I beseech you, remember.

[Hamlet moves him to put on his hat.]

OSRIC   Nay, good my lord; for my ease, in good faith.   105
Sir, here is newly come to court Laertes—believe me, an absolute gentleman, full of most excellent differ-   107
ences, of very soft society and great showing. Indeed,   108
to speak feelingly of him, he is the card or calendar of   109
gentry, for you shall find in him the continent of what   110
part a gentleman would see.   111

HAMLET   Sir, his definement suffers no perdition in   112
you, though I know to divide him inventorially would   113
dozy th'arithmetic of memory, and yet but yaw   114
neither in respect of his quick sail. But, in the verity of   115
extolment, I take him to be a soul of great article, and   116
his infusion of such dearth and rareness as, to make   117
true diction of him, his semblable is his mirror and   118
who else would trace him his umbrage, nothing   119
more.   120

OSRIC   Your Lordship speaks most infallibly of him.

HAMLET   The concernancy, sir? Why do we wrap the   122
gentleman in our more rawer breath?   123

OSRIC   Sir?

HORATIO   Is't not possible to understand in another   125
tongue? You will do't, sir, really.   126

HAMLET   What imports the nomination of this gentle-   127
man?

OSRIC   Of Laertes?

HORATIO   *[to Hamlet]*   His purse is empty already; all 's golden words are spent.

HAMLET   Of him, sir.

OSRIC   I know you are not ignorant—

HAMLET   I would you did, sir. Yet in faith if you did,   134
it would not much approve me. Well, sir?   135

OSRIC   You are not ignorant of what excellence Laertes is—

HAMLET   I dare not confess that, lest I should compare   138
with him in excellence. But to know a man well were   139
to know himself.   140

OSRIC   I mean, sir, for his weapon; but in the imputation   141
laid on him by them, in his meed he's unfellowed.   142

HAMLET   What's his weapon?

OSRIC   Rapier and dagger.

HAMLET   That's two of his weapons—but well.   145

OSRIC   The King, sir, hath wagered with him six Barbary
horses, against the which he has impawned, as I take   147
it, six French rapiers and poniards, with their assigns,   148
as girdle, hangers, and so. Three of the carriages, in   149
faith, are very dear to fancy, very responsive to the   150
hilts, most delicate carriages, and of very liberal con-   151
ceit.   152

HAMLET   What call you the carriages?   153

HORATIO   *[to Hamlet]*   I knew you must be edified by
the margent ere you had done.   155

OSRIC   The carriages, sir, are the hangers.

HAMLET   The phrase would be more germane to the
matter if we could carry a cannon by our sides; I would
it might be hangers till then. But, on: six Barbary horses
against six French swords, their assigns, and three lib-
eral-conceited carriages; that's the French bet against
the Danish. Why is this impawned, as you call it?

OSRIC   The King, sir, hath laid, sir, that in a dozen   163
passes between yourself and him, he shall not exceed   164
you three hits. He hath laid on twelve for nine, and it
would come to immediate trial, if Your Lordship would
vouchsafe the answer.   167

HAMLET   How if I answer no?

---

97 indifferent somewhat   **99 complexion** constitution.   **105 for my ease** (A conventional reply declining the invitation to put the hat back on.)   **107 absolute** perfect   **107–8 differences** special qualities **108 soft society** agreeable manners.   **great showing** distinguished appearance.   **109 feelingly** with just perception   **109–10 the card . . . gentry** the model or paradigm (literally, a chart or directory) of good breeding   **110–11 the continent . . . see** one who contains in himself all the qualities a gentleman would like to see. (A *continent* is that which contains.)   **112–15 his definement . . . sail** the task of defining Laertes's excellences suffers no diminution in your description of him, though I know that to enumerate all his graces would stupify one's powers of memory, and even so could do no more than veer unsteadily off course in a vain attempt to keep up with his rapid forward motion. (Hamlet mocks Osric by parodying his jargon-filled speeches.)   **115–20 But . . . more** But, in true praise of him, I take him to be a person of remarkable value, and his essence of such rarity and excellence as, to speak truly of him, none can compare with him other than his own mirror; anyone following in his footsteps can only hope to be the shadow to his substance, nothing more.   **122 concernancy** import, relevance   **123 rawer breath** unrefined speech that can only come short in praising him.   **125–6 Is't . . . tongue?** i.e., Is it not possible for you, Osric, to understand and communicate in any other tongue than the overblown rhetoric you have used? (Alternatively, Horatio could be asking Hamlet to speak more plainly.)   **126 You will do't** i.e., You can if you try, or, you may well have to try (to speak plainly).   **127 nomination** naming

134–5 I would . . . approve me (Responding to Osric's incompleted sentence as though it were a complete statement, Hamlet says, with mock politeness, "I wish you did know me to be not ignorant [i.e., to be knowledgeable] about matters," and then turns this into an insult: "But if you did, your recommendation of me would be of little value in any case.")   **138–40 I dare . . . himself** I dare not boast of knowing Laertes's excellence lest I seem to imply a comparable excellence in myself. Certainly, to know another person well, one must know oneself.   **141–2 I mean . . . unfellowed** I mean his excellence with his rapier, not his general excellence; in the reputation he enjoys for use of his weapons, his merit is unequaled.   **145 but well** but never mind.   **147 he** i.e., Laertes.   **impawned** staked, wagered **148 poniards** daggers.   **assigns** appurtenances   **149 hangers** straps on the sword belt (*girdle*), from which the sword hung.   **and so** and so on.   **149–52 Three . . . conceit** Three of the hangers, truly, are very pleasing to the fancy, decoratively matched with the hilts, delicate in workmanship, and made with elaborate ingenuity.   **153 What call you** What do you refer to when you say   **155 margent** margin of a book, place for explanatory notes   **163 laid** wagered   **164 passes** bouts. (The odds of the betting are hard to explain. Possibly the King bets that Hamlet will win at least five out of twelve, at which point Laertes raises the odds against himself by betting he will win nine.) **167 vouchsafe the answer** be so good as to accept the challenge. (Hamlet deliberately takes the phrase in its literal sense of replying.)

OSRIC   I mean, my lord, the opposition of your person
in trial.
HAMLET   Sir, I will walk here in the hall. If it please His
Majesty, it is the breathing time of day with me. Let 172
the foils be brought, the gentleman willing, and the
King hold his purpose, I will win for him an I can; if
not, I will gain nothing but my shame and the odd
hits.
OSRIC   Shall I deliver you so?   177
HAMLET   To this effect, sir—after what flourish your
nature will.
OSRIC   I commend my duty to Your Lordship.   180
HAMLET   Yours, yours.   [*Exit Osric.*]
'A does well to commend it himself; there are no tongues
else for 's turn.   183
HORATIO   This lapwing runs away with the shell on his 184
head.
HAMLET   'A did comply with his dug before 'a sucked 186
it. Thus has he—and many more of the same breed 187
that I know the drossy age dotes on—only got the 188
tune of the time, and, out of an habit of encounter, a 189
kind of yeasty collection, which carries them through 190
and through the most fanned and winnowed opin- 191
ions; and do but blow them to their trial, the bubbles 192
are out.   193

Enter a Lord.

LORD   My lord, His Majesty commended him to you by
young Osric, who brings back to him that you attend
him in the hall. He sends to know if your pleasure
hold to play with Laertes, or that you will take longer 197
time.
HAMLET   I am constant to my purposes; they follow the
King's pleasure. If his fitness speaks, mine is ready; 200
now or whensoever, provided I be so able as now.
LORD   The King and Queen and all are coming down.
HAMLET   In happy time.   203
LORD   The Queen desires you to use some gentle enter- 204
tainment to Laertes before you fall to play.   205
HAMLET   She well instructs me.   [*Exit Lord.*]
HORATIO   You will lose, my lord.
HAMLET   I do not think so. Since he went into France, I
have been in continual practice; I shall win at the odds.

But thou wouldst not think how ill all's here about my
heart; but it is no matter.
HORATIO   Nay, good my lord—
HAMLET   It is but foolery, but it is such a kind of gain- 213
giving as would perhaps trouble a woman.   214
HORATIO   If your mind dislike anything, obey it. I will
forestall their repair hither and say you are not fit.   216
HAMLET   Not a whit, we defy augury. There is special 217
providence in the fall of a sparrow. If it be now, 'tis
not to come; if it be not to come, it will be now; if it
be not now, yet it will come. The readiness is all. Since 220
no man of aught he leaves knows, what is't to leave 221
betimes? Let be.   222

*A table prepared. [Enter] trumpets, drums, and
officers with cushions; King, Queen, [Osric,] and
all the state; foils, daggers, [and wine borne in;]
and Laertes.*

KING
Come, Hamlet, come and take this hand from me.
          [*The King puts Laertes's hand into Hamlet's.*]
HAMLET [*to Laertes*]
Give me your pardon, sir. I have done you wrong,
But pardon't as you are a gentleman.
This presence knows,   226
And you must needs have heard, how I am punished 227
With a sore distraction. What I have done
That might your nature, honor, and exception   229
Roughly awake, I here proclaim was madness.
Was't Hamlet wronged Laertes? Never Hamlet.
If Hamlet from himself be ta'en away,
And when he's not himself does wrong Laertes,
Then Hamlet does it not, Hamlet denies it.
Who does it, then? His madness. If't be so,
Hamlet is of the faction that is wronged;   236
His madness is poor Hamlet's enemy.
Sir, in this audience
Let my disclaiming from a purposed evil
Free me so far in your most generous thoughts
That I have shot my arrow o'er the house
And hurt my brother.
LAERTES   I am satisfied in nature,   242
Whose motive in this case should stir me most   243
To my revenge. But in my terms of honor
I stand aloof, and will no reconcilement
Till by some elder masters of known honor
I have a voice and precedent of peace   247
To keep my name ungored. But till that time   248
I do receive your offered love like love,

---

172 **breathing time** exercise period.   **Let** i.e., If   **177 deliver you**
report what you say   **180 commend** commit to your favor. (A conventional salutation, but Hamlet wryly uses a more literal meaning,
"recommend," "praise," in line 182.)   **183 for 's turn** for his purposes, i.e., to do it for him.   **184 lapwing** (A proverbial type of youthful
forwardness. Also, a bird that draws intruders away from its nest and
was thought to run about with its head in the shell when newly
hatched; a seeming reference to Osric's hat.)   **186 comply . . . dug**
observe ceremonious formality toward his nurse's or mother's teat
187–93 Thus . . . are out Thus has he—and many like him of the sort
our frivolous age dotes on—acquired the trendy manner of speech of
the time, and, out of habitual conversation with courtiers of their own
kind, have collected together a kind of frothy medley of current
phrases, which enables such gallants to hold their own among persons of the most select and well-sifted views; and yet do but test them
by merely blowing on them, and their bubbles burst.   **197 play** fence.
that if   **200 If . . . ready** If he declares his readiness, my convenience
waits on his   **203 In happy time** (A phrase of courtesy indicating
that the time is convenient.)   **204–5 entertainment** greeting

213–14 **gaingiving** misgiving   216 **repair** coming   217 **augury** the
attempt to read signs of future events in order to avoid predicted
trouble.   220–2 **Since . . . Let be** Since no one has knowledge of what
he is leaving behind, what does an early death matter after all?
Enough; forbear.   222.1 **trumpets, drums** trumpeters, drummers
222.3 **all the state** the entire court   226 **presence** royal assembly
227 **punished** afflicted   229 **exception** disapproval   236 **faction**
party   242 **in nature** i.e., as to my personal feelings   243 **motive**
prompting   247 **voice** authoritative pronouncement.   **of peace** for
reconcilement   248 **name ungored** reputation unwounded.

And will not wrong it.

HAMLET   I embrace it freely,
And will this brothers' wager frankly play.—   251
Give us the foils. Come on.

LAERTES   Come, one for me.

HAMLET
I'll be your foil, Laertes. In mine ignorance   253
Your skill shall, like a star i'th' darkest night,
Stick fiery off indeed.

LAERTES   You mock me, sir.   255

HAMLET   No, by this hand.

KING
Give them the foils, young Osric. Cousin Hamlet,
You know the wager?

HAMLET   Very well, my lord.
Your Grace has laid the odds o'th' weaker side.   259

KING
I do not fear it; I have seen you both.
But since he is bettered, we have therefore odds.   261

LAERTES
This is too heavy. Let me see another.
                    [He exchanges his foil for another.]

HAMLET
This likes me well. These foils have all a length?   263
                    [They prepare to fence.]

OSRIC   Ay, my good lord.

KING
Set me the stoups of wine upon that table.
If Hamlet give the first or second hit,
Or quit in answer of the third exchange,   267
Let all the battlements their ordnance fire.
The King shall drink to Hamlet's better breath,   269
And in the cup an union shall he throw   270
Richer than that which four successive kings
In Denmark's crown have worn. Give me the cups,
And let the kettle to the trumpet speak,   273
The trumpet to the cannoneer without,
The cannons to the heavens, the heaven to earth,
"Now the King drinks to Hamlet." Come, begin.
                    Trumpets the while.
And you, the judges, bear a wary eye.

HAMLET   Come on, sir.

LAERTES   Come, my lord. [They fence. Hamlet scores a hit.]

HAMLET   One.

LAERTES   No.

HAMLET   Judgment.

OSRIC   A hit, a very palpable hit.   282
                    Drum, trumpets, and shot. Flourish.
                                    A piece goes off.

LAERTES   Well, again.

KING
Stay, give me drink. Hamlet, this pearl is thine.
        [He drinks, and throws a pearl in Hamlet's cup.]
Here's to thy health. Give him the cup.

HAMLET
I'll play this bout first. Set it by awhile.
Come. [They fence.] Another hit; what say you?

LAERTES   A touch, a touch, I do confess't.

KING
Our son shall win.

QUEEN   He's fat and scant of breath.   289
Here, Hamlet, take my napkin, rub thy brows.   290
The Queen carouses to thy fortune, Hamlet.   291

HAMLET   Good madam!

KING   Gertrude, do not drink.

QUEEN
I will, my lord, I pray you pardon me.   [She drinks.]

KING [aside]
It is the poisoned cup. It is too late.

HAMLET
I dare not drink yet, madam; by and by.

QUEEN   Come, let me wipe thy face.

LAERTES [aside to the King]
My lord, I'll hit him now.

KING   I do not think't.

LAERTES [aside]
And yet it is almost against my conscience.

HAMLET
Come, for the third, Laertes. You do but dally.
I pray you, pass with your best violence;   301
I am afeard you make a wanton of me.   302

LAERTES   Say you so? Come on.   [They fence.]

OSRIC   Nothing neither way.

LAERTES
Have at you now!   305
            [Laertes wounds Hamlet; then, in scuffling,
            they change rapiers, and Hamlet wounds Laertes.]

KING   Part them! They are incensed.

HAMLET
Nay, come, again.   [The Queen falls.]

OSRIC   Look to the Queen there, ho!

HORATIO
They bleed on both sides. How is it, my lord?

OSRIC   How is't, Laertes?

LAERTES
Why, as a woodcock to mine own springe, Osric;   309
I am justly killed with mine own treachery.

HAMLET
How does the Queen?

KING   She swoons to see them bleed.

---

251 **frankly** without ill feeling or the burden of rancor   253 **foil** thin metal background which sets a jewel off. (With pun on the blunted rapier for fencing.)   255 **Stick fiery off** stand out brilliantly   259 **laid . . . side** backed the weaker side.   261 **is bettered** is the odds-on favorite. (Laertes's handicap is the "three hits" specified in line 165.)   263 **likes** pleases   267 **Or . . . exchange** or draws even with Laertes by winning the third exchange   269 **better breath** improved vigor   270 **union** pearl. (So called, according to Pliny's *Natural History*, 9, because pearls are *unique*, never identical.)   273 **kettle** kettledrum   282.2 *A piece* A cannon

289 **fat** not physically fit, out of training   290 **napkin** handkerchief   291 **carouses** drinks a toast   301 **pass** thrust   302 **make . . . me** i.e., treat me like a spoiled child, trifle with me.   305.1–2 *in scuffling, they change rapiers* (This stage direction occurs in the Folio. According to a widespread stage tradition, Hamlet receives a scratch, realizes that Laertes's sword is unbated, and accordingly forces an exchange.)   309 **woodcock** a bird, a type of stupidity or as a decoy.   **springe** trap, snare

QUEEN
No, no, the drink, the drink—Oh, my dear Hamlet—
The drink, the drink! I am poisoned.   [*She dies.*]

HAMLET
Oh, villainy! Ho, let the door be locked!
Treachery! Seek it out.   [*Laertes falls. Exit Osric.*]

LAERTES
It is here, Hamlet. Hamlet, thou art slain.
No med'cine in the world can do thee good;
In thee there is not half an hour's life.
The treacherous instrument is in thy hand,
Unbated and envenomed. The foul practice   320
Hath turned itself on me. Lo, here I lie,
Never to rise again. Thy mother's poisoned.
I can no more. The King, the King's to blame.

HAMLET
The point envenomed too? Then, venom, to thy work.
        [*He stabs the King.*]

ALL   Treason! Treason!

KING
Oh, yet defend me, friends! I am but hurt.

HAMLET [*forcing the King to drink*]
Here, thou incestuous, murderous, damnèd Dane,
Drink off this potion. Is thy union here?   328
Follow my mother.   [*The King dies.*]

LAERTES   He is justly served.
It is a poison tempered by himself.   330
Exchange forgiveness with me, noble Hamlet.
Mine and my father's death come not upon thee,
Nor thine on me!   [*He dies.*]

HAMLET
Heaven make thee free of it! I follow thee.
I am dead, Horatio. Wretched Queen, adieu!
You that look pale and tremble at this chance,   336
That are but mutes or audience to this act,   337
Had I but time—as this fell sergeant, Death,   338
Is strict in his arrest—oh, I could tell you—   339
But let it be. Horatio, I am dead;
Thou livest. Report me and my cause aright
To the unsatisfied.

HORATIO   Never believe it.
I am more an antique Roman than a Dane.   343
Here's yet some liquor left.
        [*He attempts to drink from the poisoned cup.
                Hamlet prevents him.*]

HAMLET   As thou'rt a man,
Give me the cup! Let go! By heaven, I'll ha 't.
Oh, God, Horatio, what a wounded name,
Things standing thus unknown, shall I leave behind
    me!
If thou didst ever hold me in thy heart,
Absent thee from felicity awhile,

And in this harsh world draw thy breath in pain
To tell my story. *A march afar off* [*and a volley within*].
    What warlike noise is this?

        Enter Osric.

OSRIC
Young Fortinbras, with conquest come from Poland,
To th'ambassadors of England gives
This warlike volley.

HAMLET   Oh, I die, Horatio!
The potent poison quite o'ercrows my spirit.   355
I cannot live to hear the news from England,
But I do prophesy th'election lights
On Fortinbras. He has my dying voice.   358
So tell him, with th'occurrents more and less   359
Which have solicited. The rest is silence.   [*He dies.*] 360

HORATIO
Now cracks a noble heart. Good night, sweet prince,
And flights of angels sing thee to thy rest!
        [*March within.*]

    Why does the drum come hither?

        Enter Fortinbras, with the [*English*] *Ambassadors*
        [*with drum, colors, and attendants*].

FORTINBRAS
Where is this sight?

HORATIO   What is it you would see?
If aught of woe or wonder, cease your search.

FORTINBRAS
This quarry cries on havoc. O proud Death,   366
What feast is toward in thine eternal cell,   367
That thou so many princes at a shot
So bloodily hast struck?

FIRST AMBASSADOR   The sight is dismal,
And our affairs from England come too late.
The ears are senseless that should give us hearing,
To tell him his commandment is fulfilled,
That Rosencrantz and Guildenstern are dead.
Where should we have our thanks?

HORATIO   Not from his mouth, 374
Had it th'ability of life to thank you.
He never gave commandment for their death.
But since, so jump upon this bloody question,   377
You from the Polack wars and you from England
Are here arrived, give order that these bodies
High on a stage be placèd to the view,   380
And let me speak to th' yet unknowing world
How these things came about. So shall you hear
Of carnal, bloody, and unnatural acts,
Of accidental judgments, casual slaughters,   384

---

320 **Unbated** not blunted with a button.   **practice** plot   328 **union**
pearl. (See line 270; with grim puns on the word's other meanings:
marriage, shared death.)   330 **tempered** mixed   336 **chance** mischance   337 **mutes** silent observers. (Literally, actors with nonspeak-
ing parts.)   338 **fell sergeant** remorseless arresting officer   339 **strict**
(1) severely just (2) unavoidable.   **arrest** (1) taking into custody (2)
stopping my speech   343 **Roman** (Suicide was an honorable choice
for many Romans as an alternative to a dishonorable life.)

355 **o'ercrows** triumphs over (like the winner in a cockfight)
358 **voice** vote.   359 **th'occurrents** the events, incidents
360 **solicited** moved, urged. (Hamlet doesn't finish saying what the
events have prompted—presumably, his acts of vengeance, or his
reporting of those events to Fortinbras.)   366 **This . . . havoc** This
heap of dead bodies loudly proclaims a general slaughter.   367 **feast**
i.e., Death feasting on those who have fallen.   **toward** in preparation
374 **his** Claudius's   377 **so jump . . . question** so hard on the heels of
this bloody business   380 **stage** platform   384 **judgments** retribu-
tions.   **casual** occurring by chance

Of deaths put on by cunning and forced cause,   385
And, in this upshot, purposes mistook
Fall'n on th'inventors' heads. All this can I
Truly deliver.
FORTINBRAS   Let us haste to hear it,
And call the noblest to the audience.
For me, with sorrow I embrace my fortune.
I have some rights of memory in this kingdom,   391
Which now to claim my vantage doth invite me.   392
HORATIO
Of that I shall have also cause to speak,
And from his mouth whose voice will draw on more.   394
But let this same be presently performed,   395

Even while men's minds are wild, lest more
   mischance
On plots and errors happen.
FORTINBRAS   Let four captains   397
Bear Hamlet, like a soldier, to the stage,
For he was likely, had he been put on,   399
To have proved most royal; and for his passage,   400
The soldiers' music and the rite of war
Speak loudly for him.   402
Take up the bodies. Such a sight as this
Becomes the field, but here shows much amiss.   404
Go bid the soldiers shoot.
                Exeunt [*marching, bearing off the dead bodies;
                          a peal of ordnance is shot off*].

385 **put on** instigated.   **forced cause** contrivance   391 **of memory**
traditional, remembered, unforgotten   392 **vantage** favorable opportunity   394 **voice . . . more** vote will influence still others.
395 **presently** immediately

397 **On** on top of   399 **put on** i.e., invested in royal office and so put
to the test   400 **for his passage** to mark his passing   402 **Speak** (let
them) speak   404 **Becomes the field** suits the field of battle

---

Hamlet on Stage

Richard Burbage played Hamlet at the Globe, and it
may be assumed that he adhered to Hamlet's advice to
the players in 3.2 by acting in a "natural" style; regrettably, there is no extant description of Burbage's performance. Fortunately, performances by those who followed Burbage—beginning with Thomas Betterton in
1661—have been memorialized in such meticulous
accounts as *Hamlet on Stage: The Great Tradition* (John A.
Mills, 1985), *Five and Eighty Hamlets* (J. C. Trewin, 1987),
and *Modern Hamlets and Their Soliloquies* (Mary Z.
Maher, 1992). Many of the most admired modern performances (Olivier, Gielgud, Burton, Jacobi, Branagh)
have been preserved on film and video.

The Elizabethan Era: On the Public Stage

Other than Burbage (succeeded by Joseph Taylor in
1619), we have only conjecture about the actors who
assumed the other roles in the play. Tradition says that
Shakespeare himself played the Ghost of Old Hamlet.
Nicholas Rowe, an eighteenth-century editor of Shakespeare's works, wrote that "the top of [Shakespeare's]
performance was the Ghost in his own *Hamlet*."
Bernard Shaw surmises that Shakespeare "would not
trust any one else with [the Ghost] because it is "one of
the wonders of the play" (Wells, 200). No proof exists
to confirm that Shakespeare actually played the role.
The comedian Robert Armin may have played the First
Gravedigger/Clown. Boys played the women's roles,
a fact to which the text itself attests: as Hamlet greets
the Players he notes the young man assigned women's

roles (2.2.424–428). Although specific evidence does
not exist to validate her claim, Cambridge scholar
Muriel Bradbrook suggests an intriguing possibility:
the First Player may have been made up to look like
Burbage himself, so that Hamlet's line about the Player's beard (2.2.423–424) could have been taken as a theatrical "in-joke" (Bradbrook, 120).

With its trap door for ghosts and graves, its pillars
for hiding places, the architecture of the Globe itself
proved ideal for the play's staging demands, as seen in
the Graveyard Scene (5.1). Hamlet and Horatio probably
entered from one of the two portals built into the
façade of the upstage wall. They encountered the gravediggers, one of whom stood in the trap door. The First
Clown extracted Yorick's skull from beneath the stage
to hand it to Hamlet, who recited his meditation on
death close to the audience standing in the pit. At the
entrance of the funeral cortège through an upstage
door, Hamlet and Horatio may have hidden behind the
pillar opposite that door. Conceivably they could not
be seen, nor their lines heard, by the mourners. The
wide expanse of the Globe's thrust stage accommodated this crowd scene. The open trap served as the battleground for the Hamlet-Laertes brawl on Ophelia's
grave. Once the trap has been re-covered, that same
spot on the stage floor could, appropriately, serve as
the site of the climactic fencing match between the
same antagonists in 5.2. Claudius and Gertrude sat on
thrones (common props of Elizabethan acting companies) beneath the "heavens" on the canopy partially
covering the Globe's stage. Fortinbras's entry through
one of two upstage doors initiated the final sequence.
Dressed as a soldier ready for battle—much like the
Ghost of Act 1—Fortinbras became the new king; an

The 1842 painting (left) by Daniel Maclise depicts the play-within-a-play of Hamlet *(3.2.134 ff.) in an elaborate nineteenth-century style; note Ophelia in white, Hamlet at her feet, and the guilty Claudius averting his eyes. By most accounts Sarah Bernhardt (right) made a convincing Hamlet; she often donned tights and a page boy wig for the role.*

Elizabethan audience no doubt appreciated the symbolism of his costume. The new king's first command—"Let four captains / Bear Hamlet, like a soldier, to the stage" (5.2.397–398)—reasserted the play-life theme recurring throughout this tragedy. Elizabethan performances, even of tragedies, often concluded with a song and/or a dance. A recent production of *Hamlet* at the new Globe Theatre (2000) employed this convention to thematic advantage as actors, "drained of their roles, [entered] each carrying a skull on a stick" which they beat on the floor to accompany their dance (Margolies, 21).

The Seventeenth and Eighteenth Centuries: Betterton and Garrick

The foremost Hamlets of the late seventeenth century and the eighteenth century were Thomas Betterton (c. 1635–1710) and David Garrick (1717–1779), each of whom played the role for decades, a common practice in their eras. Drawings indicate that both wore contemporary clothing and wigs (Restoration for Betterton, mid-eighteenth century for Garrick); thus theirs were "modern dress Hamlets," as was that of Burbage. Each employed gestures that today might be considered mannered. Betterton, who acted the part until he was seventy, was especially famous for his passionate reaction to the Ghost, as described here by Colley Cibber, the Restoration-era actor and playwright: "He opened with a pause of mute amazement, then rising slowly to a solemn, trembling voice, he made the Ghost equally terrible to the spectator as himself." Barton Booth, the actor who played the Ghost opposite Betterton's Hamlet, has offered an even better account: "instead of awing him, he terrified me." Despite his

reputation for restoring Shakespeare, Garrick altered the text to enable him to play the Prince more aggressively than in Shakespeare's day; such speeches as "How all occasions do inform against me" (4.4.33ff.) and other lines that reflect Hamlet's self-doubts were cut. His 1763 acting edition retained only about twenty-seven hundred lines of the Folio. He decried "the rubbish of the fifth act" and, responding to French Neoclassical criticism about the mixing of comic and tragic scenes, he deleted the gravediggers and the Laertes-Hamlet fight in the grave. Garrick's Hamlet killed Claudius and then nobly exonerated Laertes. Garrick's contrived ending suited neoclassical tastes that valued poetic justice and moral rectitude.

Elsewhere in eighteenth-century Europe, *Hamlet* was read as an indictment of tyranny. In Russia *Gamlet* opened in 1748 at St. Petersburg's Imperial Theatre; it featured only ten characters (no Ghost, no Players, no Gravediggers) to tell the story of the Prince, who overthrew Tsar Claudius with the help of the common people. Polonius became a scheming mercenary who plotted the death of both Hamlet and Ophelia, although neither died in this version. The triumphant Hamlet forgave the old counselor, who nonetheless cursed the Prince and his daughter before killing himself. In 1790 the play made its way to Hungary via a German translation. As with the Russian version, Hamlet lived to become the new monarch and the symbol of Hungary's new nationalistic pride.

The Nineteenth Century: Hamlet as Romantic Hero

Because of its melancholy preoccupation with death and its depiction of an unscrupulous monarch, *Hamlet*

Laurence Olivier embraces the skull of Yorick to contemplate mortality in his Freud-influenced film of Hamlet *(left, 1948). Like Olivier, Kenneth Branagh directed and starred in his own* Hamlet *feature in 1996, a four-hour film that left the script basically uncut and proved engrossing, if uneven in its inspiration.*

was especially attractive to the Romantics of the early nineteenth century. Samuel Taylor Coleridge, a romantic poet, was also an astute commentator on *Hamlet*; his lectures remain among the most astute analyses of the play. The first truly "melancholic" prince was John Philip Kemble, who acted the role in 1783, around the time that Goethe's *Sorrows of Young Werther* showed the earliest strain of Romanticism, though a full decade before Coleridge and Percy Shelley launched Romanti-

cism as a literary movement in England. Ludwig Tieck, who did much to popularize Shakespeare in Germany, believed that Kemble was especially effective at bringing out "the sad, the melancholy, the nobly suffering aspect of the character." Kemble's Hamlet was also noted for using wit and levity that contrasted with, and thereby heightened, the role's melancholic elements. Kemble set the tone for most nineteenth-century Hamlets on both sides of the Atlantic. Charles Kemble,

Hollywood action hero Mel Gibson played the melancholy Dane in Franco Zeffirelli's otherwise traditional 1990 film of Hamlet. *With Ethan Hawke in the coveted role, director Michael Almereyda set his fast-paced 1999 film in New York, made Denmark a multinational corporation, and Hamlet a filmmaker suffering information overload.*

John's younger brother, was not as successful in the role; he remained noteworthy for interpreting Hamlet as actually mad rather than feigning madness.

Among the foremost Hamlets of the nineteenth century was Edmund Kean (1787–1833). Kean epitomized the Romantic era's brooding interpretation, a style that actually became known as "Hamletism." When he first played the role in 1814, he invented an extraordinary piece of business at the conclusion of the Nunnery Scene: after berating Ophelia for her duplicity, Kean returned to the stage to kiss gently the hand of the weeping girl. William Hazlitt, whose accounts of early nineteenth-century Hamlets in England provide valuable records of major performances, praised Kean's invention as "the finest commentary that was ever made on Shakespeare. It explained the character . . . as one of disappointed hope, of bitter regret, of affection suspended, not obliterated by the distractions of the scene around him." The American actor Edwin Booth (1833–1893) built on the tradition begun by Kemble and Kean, whose Hamlets were decidedly men of action despite their pronounced melancholy. Charles Clarke, who saw Booth's Hamlet eight times, summarized that actor's Prince as "a man of first-class intellect and second class will." Booth's Hamlet was ever the gentleman, even to Gertrude, Rosencrantz, Guildenstern, and the pompous courtier, Osric. He showed remorse after killing Claudius, perhaps because Booth wore about his neck a miniature of his own father (the eccentric actor, Junius Brutus Booth, whose voice Edwin claims to have heard in the Ghost scene). Booth built a new theater in New York to house his Shakespeare productions, which were noted for their lavish, romantic scenery. Booth's *Hamlet* displayed fourteen distinct scenes and "authentic" tenth-century costumes; the production ran for one hundred consecutive performances, the first Shakespeare production to earn that honor.

Henry Irving, whose performances at London's Lyceum Theatre were the finest in England of the late nineteenth century, first played the Dane in 1864, launching the vogue for "psychological Hamlets" in anticipation of Freud's commentaries on the play. Irving played Hamlet as obsessed with his love for Ophelia, who in his estimation betrays him just as his mother had betrayed her husband. At the end of the Nunnery Scene, in which Irving vacillated between genuine tenderness and despair, the actor incorporated Kean's famous business of returning to kiss Ophelia's hand, by refraining at the last second to emphasize his sad realization that he must part from her forever. When Ellen Terry played Ophelia in Irving's Lyceum production, she prepared for the role by visiting an asylum where she observed a pathetic young girl gazing at a wall. Despite the psychological complexities in the acting, Irving's *Hamlet* was as lavish as any nineteenth-century spectacle. He chose a sixth-cen-

tury setting with massive rocks glittering in the moonlight. Hamlet met the Ghost in 1.5 not in the cellarage but on a beach strewn with enormous boulders. The funeral procession used every available actor in the company for a lengthy procession accompanied by tolling bells and a dirge played on an organ. Because such spectacles necessitated heavy cutting to allow time for scene changes, Irving excised the first four scenes of Act 4.

In 1881 William Poel's Elizabethan Stage Society produced the play, using the unauthorized quarto (Q1) of 1603 as they attempted to reconstruct the much simpler conditions of an early seventeenth-century performance. Though it was not successful, the production, like most of Poel's, was an antidote to the grand spectacles of Booth, Irving, and others. In 1897 John Forbes-Robertson combined Booth's "gentlemanly" Prince with elements of Irving's introspective complexity. Significantly, Forbes-Robertson restored the Fortinbras subplot, ending the long-standing custom of lowering the curtain at the Prince's death line, "The rest is silence." Forbes-Robinson also appeared in a twenty-two–minute silent film in 1913, although he was much too old for the part.

The Early Twentieth Century: Barrymore, Olivier, and Gielgud

The American actor John Barrymore was the dominant Hamlet of the early twentieth century, playing the role in New York and in London in 1925. Barrymore eschewed much of the psychological portraiture that had accumulated in the role, arguing in his autobiography that the play is "simple . . . I was no little bewildered that anything of such infinite beauty and simplicity should have acquired centuries of comment." Barrymore's most remarkable invention was to die standing while looking plaintively out over the audience; Horatio slowly lowered him to the floor after "the rest is silence." His simple, manly approach, coupled with his well-known offstage adventures, brought people who might not otherwise have seen *Hamlet* into the theater, much as Mel Gibson did in the Zeffirelli film of 1990. A 1933 screen test of Barrymore reciting the "Now might I do it pat" soliloquy (3.3) exists; unfortunately, the film was never made.

In 1925 Barry Jackson staged a revolutionary production of *Hamlet*, shocking London audiences with a modern dress *Hamlet*. It is sometimes called "the plus-fours *Hamlet*" because men wore the trendy knee breeches of the 1920s. Jackson wanted to free the play from its preconceptions and to emphasize its modernity after World War I, when Europeans were, like Hamlet, experiencing disillusionment and cynicism. Jackson's then bold experiment has been followed by numerous "modern dress" productions of the play. When the Guthrie Theater made its debut in Minneapolis with *Hamlet* in 1964, Tyrone Guthrie costumed his actors in tuxedos and evening gowns. Buzz Goodbody's "Village Hall *Hamlet*" inaugurated the RSC's intimate Other Place in 1975 with actors in second-hand shop clothing. Perhaps the most famous of the post–World War II contemporary-dress *Hamlet*s was that of John Gielgud on Broadway in 1964; known as "the rehearsal clothes Hamlet" (baggy sweaters, unpressed pants), the production placed its emphasis on the spoken word (see the account of the Gielgud-Burton film below).

In the 1930s and 1940s John Gielgud and Laurence Olivier rivaled one another as the premier Hamlets on the English stage. Gielgud played the role five times (once at Elsinore Castle in 1939), invariably as an aristocratic and delicate prince who spoke Shakespeare's language beautifully. Gielgud invented new business for Hamlet in 3.3: the Prince stole Claudius's sword as the King knelt in prayer. The theft was an obvious threat to the King, prompting him to send the Prince to England and his death. In contrast to Gielgud's pale, introspective Prince, Olivier's Hamlet was athletic, masculine, less genteel, more passionate. Olivier's performance, with its overtones of an incestuous obsession with his mother, is discussed below in conjunction with his award-winning film (1948).

The Late Twentieth Century: The Anti-Delicate and Tender Prince

As might be expected, the 1960s offered a number of anti-heroic Hamlets as well as political interpretations that focused upon Claudius as a latter-day Machiavel. In 1965 Peter Hall staged the RSC's first *Hamlet*, casting an unknown, gangly, less-than-handsome actor (David Warner) as the Prince. Dressed in ill-fitted clothing and wearing a floor-length, red wool scarf about his neck, Warner presented a nonconformist Hamlet who "made his own rules and did not mind appearing ridiculous or eccentric. He was making his own discoveries about life and, often enough, he found it ridiculous" (Wells, *Royal Shakespeare*, 34). Students, who were themselves launching the so-called Counter-Cultural Revolution in this age of the Beatles, responded with enthusiasm to the Hall-Warner anti-Establishment interpretation. Although Warner's performance has not been preserved on film, Nicol Williamson also played the role as an anti-heroic outsider on stage and in film (see below under "*Hamlet* on Film"). In 1975 the RSC's experimental production featured Ben Kingsley, a thin, short actor of East Indian descent. Casting a non-Anglo actor established the iconoclastic tone that distinguished this production. Kingsley was cited by reviewers for the uncommon intelligence and ironic humor he brought to the role; in the midst of the "rogue and peasant slave" soliloquy (2.2. 549ff.), Kingsley left the stage (indeed the tiny theater itself) after "a scullion! Fie upon't! Foh!" (l.588), justifying his bold choice as the action of a man, both the character and the actor playing him, who declares, "Goodbye, ladies and gentlemen. I can't do it, you don't think I can do it, you probably don't think I'm a very good Hamlet anyway. So f*** it" (Maher, 80). The ensuing line—"I have heard that guilty creatures sitting at a play, etc."—was delivered sheepishly as he reentered the stage, having reconsidered his rash decision to leave. Director Buzz Goodbody used little scenery and few props in a sparse production notable largely for the speed at which the actors delivered their lines; truly they spoke "trippingly on the tongue" (3.2.2) to give the play a more colloquial quality in the intimate space. The actors also wore modern clothing, much of it evocative of a Mafia-like underworld.

Derek Jacobi (the Old Vic, 1977) and Michael Pennington (RSC, 1980), rebelling against the angry, angst-ridden Hamlets of the 1960s and 1970s, returned to a Prince who was "the glass of fashion and the mold of form" (3.2.156). Jacobi's performance has been preserved by the BBC Shakespeare project in 1980 and is discussed below. Under Barton's direction—in a Pirandellian production that explored the play's numerous theatrical metaphors—Pennington approached the Prince as "graceful and sensitive, a balance to the recent mass of caustic anti-heroes" (Pennington, 13). After two decades of volatile Hamlets, Pennington's Hamlet seemed perhaps too tame; nonetheless his performance, like Jacobi's, marked a significant shift in post-1960s productions of *Hamlet*.

Postmodern Hamlets

For the past forty years *avant-garde* theater artists have rendered *Hamlet* in distinctly postmodern styles—deconstructing the plot, recontextualizing the setting, or reversing its genders to expose its political relevance, its sexism, its absurdist underpinnings, and other contemporary concerns. In 1965 Charles Marowitz, who had recently co-directed the RSC's Theater of Cruelty Seasons, developed *Collage Hamlet* to deconstruct the play. He cut and randomly rearranged the text while inserting new material from other sources. To criticize Hamlet's ineffectuality, Marowitz's actors treated the Prince, who wore clown makeup, as a weakling and buffoon. In New York Joseph Papp's "Naked *Hamlet*" (1967) used modern dress, rock-music, and tacky theatrical jokes—Hamlet gave Claudius an exploding cigar and sold popcorn to the audience—in a ninety-minute romp that rendered the play as Hamlet's hallucinogenic nightmare. The controversial German director Peter Zadek staged the play in 1977 in an empty factory in

Bochum, rendering the play as a curious mixture of operetta, vaudeville, circus, and slapstick. Hamlet was fat and much older than his mother, while Ophelia—played as a mere sex object among the men of Elsinore—was topless. A young woman played Polonius; Guildenstern was a transvestite. Zadek justified his indulgences as an accurate reflection of the preoccupations of contemporary society and its shifting values. Another German production directed by Hansgunther Heyme offered an "electronic *Hamlet*" in 1979. Eighteen television monitors placed about the theater enabled audiences to view live news programs during the play. Hamlet was played by two actors, one on stage (the "public Hamlet") and one in the audience (the "private") who intoned the soliloquies *sotto voce* through the theater's sound system. Ophelia doubled as Fortinbras, and in the production's bizarre finale s/he took possession of the throne situated on a bloody, carcass-littered stage dominated by one hundred TV sets. Robert Wilson's *Hamlet Monologue* (1995) was a striking one-man performance by one of the most original theater artists of the late twentieth century. Wilson, an originator of the so-called "theater of images," offered a deeply personal interpretation of the role while exploring new means of theatrical expression that defy verbal description. Other characters in the play were represented by an eclectic mix of costumes on mannequins, while Hamlet often perched languidly on Wilson-designed set pieces. Wilson's performance may be seen on a sixty-minute video: "The Making of a Monologue: Robert Wilson's *Hamlet*."

Non-Western Hamlets

The German political poet Ferdinand Freiligrath (1810–1876) proclaimed that "Germany is Hamlet!" Based on the extraordinary number of international actors who have played the Prince, it would appear that Freiligrath's sentiments are applicable to many nations, notably Japan and South Africa, each of which has used *Hamlet* as a means to comment upon the modernization of these countries. Although *Hamlet* has been performed in Japan since the 1880s (and there were Kabuki versions a decade prior to that), a notable production of the play at Tokyo's Imperial Theatre in May 1911 ushered in the modern era in Japanese art and literature. Shoyo Tsubouchi directed the play, using professional and amateur actors; school girls played the women's roles, as there were no professional actresses at this time. The production's naturalistic acting style contrasted with the thoroughly theatrical Kabuki and Noh styles familiar to Japanese audiences. In 1964 director Koreya Senda addressed Japan's political problems in the wake of the World War II in a production that employed Bertolt Brecht's alienation tech-

niques to provoke the audience. More recently (1994) a cross-cultural comedy, *Kanadehon Hamlet*, devised by a woman (Harue Tsutsumi), portrayed a Kabuki troupe rehearsing the play in 1887 while coming to terms with its Western issues as distinguished from those of their own culture. In South Africa the play was performed in Afrikaans in 1947 as an affirmation of white superiority; a young Orange Free Stater returned from university to reclaim his land from British, black, and coloured usurpers. Robert Mohr's 1973 production in Johannesburg hinted that the Afrikaans people themselves were to blame for South Africa's brutal politics. The country's evolution from strict apartheid to a degree of tolerance can be measured by these contrasting productions of *Hamlet*. The play is now a staple of white, black, and mixed-race theaters in South Africa.

Hamlet on Film and Television

The extensive archive of film and television adaptations of *Hamlet* offers multiple opportunities to compare the interpretation of the role by many of the most respected actors of the twentieth and the twenty-first centuries.

Hamlet *on Film*

Silent *Hamlet*s. Among nearly a dozen versions of Hamlet filmed during the silent era, the most notable are those featuring women in the title role. In 1900 the renowned French actor Sarah Bernhardt starred in a five-minute rendition of the final duel, enhanced by a crude sound track played on a phonograph. Several Italian, French, and English versions followed, but not until 1920 did a truly memorable film Hamlet appear. Inspired by Edward Vining's controversial book, *The Mystery of Hamlet* (1881), Danish film star Asta Nielsen produced and starred in a seventy-eight–minute film, titled *Hamlet, the Drama of Vengeance* (directed by Svend Gade). The film depicts Hamlet as a woman born of Gertrude, but protected and disguised by the Queen to preserve her succession to the crown. (During the Victorian era it apparently was not uncommon to suppose that Hamlet was actually a woman [Beasley, 135].) Hamlet's reticence to kill Claudius is the result of a sexual identity crisis rather than any oedipal complex or moral scruples. Nielsen, androgynous and charismatic, plays a woman playing a man believed by many to be a woman; she dies in Horatio's arms professing her love for him. Politically, *Hamlet, the Drama of Vengeance* has been also interpreted as a portrait of Germany trying to come to terms with its identity after World War I. The film was the first created and released by Nielsen's own production company; the actress's haunting performance shows why Greta Garbo and Marlene Dietrich considered themselves artistic heirs to the mysterious Nielsen.

- 1948—Director Laurence Olivier, Arthur Rank Productions, with Olivier (Hamlet), Jean Simmons (Ophelia), and Eileen Herlie (Gertrude). (155 min.)

  Enhanced by Olivier's Oscar-winning performance as actor and director, this heavily cut version (c. 1900 lines), filmed mostly in Denmark, fuses an amalgam of styles, each contributing to the mood and meaning of Shakespeare's play. On one level, the film is modeled after a 1930s horror film (e.g., *Dracula*) as the camera tracks movements through an eerie castle; on another, it resembles the *film noir's* preoccupation with alienated, cynical characters (often detectives pursuing a murderer) struggling to survive in dank, dark worlds dominated by corrupt power figures. Olivier uses black-and-white photography partly to achieve "a more majestic, more poetic image, in keeping with the stature of the verse" (Rosenthal, 22); besides, he was angry at Technicolor Corporation for numerous problems it created as he filmed *Henry V* in 1944. Olivier's *Hamlet* freely employs nonrealistic techniques to render the dilemma of a man whose mind seems to waver in and out of madness. We are invited to view Elsinore through Hamlet's troubled mind as the camera leads us through twisting corridors and down bizarrely canted staircases. The "To be or not to be" soliloquy, situated after the Nunnery Scene, is delivered on a precipice above a churning sea. As Olivier intones the speech in a voice-over, shots of violently tumbling waves are inter-cut with cloud formations to create images not unlike those in an ink-blot (Rorschach) test used by psychologists. At the end of the speech, Hamlet drops his "bare bodkin" into the surf below. Olivier was influenced by Freud's and Ernest Jones's explication of the play's oedipal elements; he argued that his film ought to be considered "an essay on Hamlet" rather than a film of a classical play. Accordingly, Olivier illustrates the play's Freudian elements by highlighting Hamlet's attraction to Gertrude, played by an actress (Eileen Herlie) a dozen years younger than himself. The royal bed is covered sensually with conspicuously arranged sheets, upon which Gertrude passionately kisses her son during the closet scene, even as Polonius's corpse lies at the foot of the bed. Despite the psychological probing, Olivier sounds Hamlet's lighter notes, particularly in his banter with Polonius. Olivier uses his fabled athleticism to effect in the finale: Hamlet kills Claudius by plunging a sword into him after leaping headlong from a gallery fifteen feet above the throne. Olivier filmed the famous shot last, without rehears-

al, because he was concerned that he might be injured during the stunt if he landed awkwardly. Branagh pays homage to—but does not match—Olivier's bravado in his 1996 film. Though Olivier's treatment of the play is unmistakably cinematic, his performance is theatrical, a marked contrast to the naturalistic approach found in the Richardson-Williamson Hamlet only twenty years later. The most genuinely affecting moments in the film involve Ophelia and Hamlet, thanks largely to inventive camera-work emphasizing the great divide that circumstances have thrust between them. Olivier faithfully reproduces Sir John Everett Millais's 1851 painting of the drowned Ophelia, inspired by Gertrude's vivid description (4.7.167–184).

- 1964—*Gamlet.* Director Grigori Kozintsev, Lenfilm, with Mikhail Smoktunovsky (Hamlet) and Anastasia Vertinskaia (Ophelia). (149 min.)

  Using the Russian poet-novelist Boris Pasternak's translation and Dmitri Shostakovich's musical score, Kozintsev created one of the most visually satisfying *Hamlet*s on film, although some critics object to the extensive cutting (e.g., there is no dumb show, and most of Hamlet's references to suicide are deleted). Powerful images dominate Kozintsev's screen to make the film a masterpiece of cinematography: the war-torn village beyond Elsinore's walls; the enormous Ghost with its majestic black cape; Fortinbras's massive army advancing upon Elsinore (reminiscent of Sergei Eisenstein's great film epics); and finally Hamlet's death in the presence of hundreds of weeping peasants. Kozintsev emphasizes the social and political realities surrounding the hero. Filmed on a barren Baltic seacoast in gloomy weather, the film creates an oppressive and claustrophobic atmosphere by shooting scenes through iron grates and prison bars. Ophelia is shown encased in an iron skirt that inhibits freedom of movement. Like Olivier, Kozintsev uses shots of the churning sea to suggest Hamlet's tormented mind. The soliloquies are also rendered as voice-overs—at least those that survive the ruthless cutting ("To be or not to be" is deleted). If Olivier's *Hamlet* is sometimes interpreted as the tragedy of a man who could not make up his mind, Kozintsev's is about a man determined to kill his oppressor although every occasion seems to inform against him. Given this interpretation, Kozintsev deleted the scene in which Hamlet fails to kill the praying King. Though the film is not exactly Shakespeare, it is nonetheless outstanding cinema. The director purportedly made the film to expose Stalin's repression of the Soviet people; his lead actor, Mikhail Smoktunovsky, had been imprisoned by the dictator.

■ 1964—Director John Gielgud, Lenfilm, with Richard Burton (Hamlet), Linda Marsh (Ophelia), Alfred Drake (Claudius), and Eileen Herlie (Gertrude). (191 min.)

Although the quality of this film is poor because it was filmed with seven cameras in New York's Lunt-Fontanne Theatre using extant lighting and before a live audience, it provides a valuable record of one of the most important stage productions of *Hamlet* in the post–World War II era. Gielgud applied the knowledge he acquired while playing Hamlet over a twenty-year span to direct the play in a New York engagement that ran for one hundred thirty-eight performances. Like Olivier, Richard Burton also suggests Hamlet's oedipal tendencies, especially as he gives his mother an unusually long, passionate kiss. The Queen is Eileen Herlie, the Gertrude of Olivier's film. Burton renders Hamlet as a passionate prince with an extraordinary sense of humor, especially in the scenes with Polonius, who is played with unusual comic flair by the outstanding actor Hume Cronyn. Gielgud's minimalist staging remains the most memorable aspect of the production. The actors wear sneakers, jeans, and baggy sweaters as they perform on a sparse set consisting of a few stock theatrical flats and platforms. The stark *mise en scène* actually emphasizes the tragedy's metatheatric elements as Hamlet rehearses and improvises his way through Elsinore's drama. Because he wanted to maintain the integrity of his stage performance, Burton allowed the film to be shown for only a two-day period in 1964. All prints of the film were destroyed after that brief engagement. Fortunately, a print was discovered among the actor's possessions after his death and restored, thus preserving one of the most admired performances in the twentieth century.

■ 1967—Director Tony Richardson. Woodfall Films, with Nicol Williamson (Hamlet), Anthony Hopkins (Claudius), and Marianne Faithfull (Ophelia). (114 min.)

While the Gielgud film is clearly a photographic record of a stage play, Richardson attempted to make "a movie" of his production at London's Roundhouse Theatre. Because he was forced to work on a small budget, however, relying on close-ups against black backgrounds, the effect is more like a video version. Despite its financial restrictions, the finished product admirably captures the claustrophobic nature of the play: Hamlet is trapped in a void from which there seems no viable escape. Richardson cuts the script heavily (almost fifty percent), including much of the play's humor. Nicol Williamson's performance, admired by many, derided by others, is the epitome of 1960s–1970s Hamlets: angry, brash, even boorish. Williamson, a Scotsman, speaks in a nasal brogue, yet his readings are often fresh and innovative, grounded in a rapidly spoken, naturalistic style that plays against the heightened language and musicality of Shakespeare's text. The "rogue and peasant slave" soliloquy at the end of 2.2 is used by Williamson's Hamlet to mock himself more humorously than is customary. The Hamlet in this film is very much the common man, not the polished, eloquent gentleman forced into violent acts. The film's most controversial choice involves Ophelia, acted (poorly) by rock singer Marianne Faithfull, who looks like a 1960s flower child. Her affection for her brother Laertes seems incestuous—an intriguing adjunct to the oedipal interpretations of Hamlet's relationship to his mother.

■ 1990—Director Franco Zeffirelli, Warner Brothers/Nelson Entertainment, with Mel Gibson (Hamlet), Glenn Close (Gertrude), Alan Bates (Claudius), and Helena Bonham-Carter (Ophelia). (135 min.)

Despite the commercial success of his late-1960s Shakespeare films (*Romeo and Juliet*, *The Taming of the Shrew*), Zeffirelli could get funding for *Hamlet* only upon two conditions: that he keep the running time to two hours and that he secure an "A-list" star for the title role. Zeffirelli cut and radically restructured the script, using Olivier's screenplay as a model. The film opens in the depths of the castle, where Hamlet, his mother, and stepfather are gathered at the tomb of Old Hamlet. Individual soliloquies are chopped and spread throughout the film to enable the director to tell the story to young audience unfamiliar with the play. Newcomers to *Hamlet* may not notice the alterations, but those who know the play may find the revised text distracting ("What is *that* doing *there*?"). Because Zeffirelli interprets *Hamlet* as an intimate domestic drama, the Fortinbras plot is deleted, as well as any sense of the play's politics, either internal or external. Hamlet seems more outraged at Claudius for stealing his mother than for killing his father; consequently the Hamlet-Gertrude relationship is the most graphic of the Oedipus-inspired interpretations on film. Hamlet seems intent on raping his mother in the Closet Scene (3.4), and seems about to do so before Polonius cries out. As played by action-film superstar Mel Gibson (who received classical training at Australia's Academy of Dramatic Art), Hamlet is an extension of the actor's screen persona, a "lethal weapon" whose madness is reckless and dangerous to all about him. Gibson moves freely (and frantically, inasmuch as he rarely stands still) from the philosophical to the comical, especially in the final duel with Laertes. Helena Bonham Carter emerges as one of the most compelling and pitiable Ophelia's on film, especially in the mad scene; her haunting, pathetic eyes suggest a soul tormented by forces she cannot comprehend, while at the same time "resituating the role squarely in the context of contemporary feminist militancy . . . [she] remains feisty even when driven mad by her men" (Rothwell, 142). Glenn Close, by contrast, creates a Gertrude whose appetites, as one Los Angeles *Times* critic put it, "have been awakened by Alan Bates's simpering roué of a Claudius"; her scenes are often electrifying.

For the most part, Zeffirelli breaks from the tradition of screen Hamlets to create a brighter Elsinore than previously seen on film. Much of the action is washed in bright sunlight, especially Hamlet's "what a piece of work is a man" speech to Rosencrantz and Guildenstern; the scene occurs at a country inn. This Denmark is a prison without bars. When things do darken—within the castle, where the characters lurk everywhere to spy on one another—the effect is all the more striking. Befitting the film's "action flick" status, Zeffirelli's camera is in constant motion; most shots last only seconds. The result is an energetic film that, like its star, appeals to young audiences.

■ 1996—Director Kenneth Branagh, Castle Rock Entertainment, with Kenneth Branagh (Hamlet), Julie Christie (Gertrude), Derek Jacobi (Claudius), and Kate Winslet (Ophelia). (242 min.)

Because he offers the script (a compilation of Q2 and the Folio) in its entirety, Branagh's *Hamlet* is the longest Shakespeare film ever attempted. The fifteen million dollar film features an international cast of established stars, many in small roles (Gérard Depardieu, Jack Lemmon, Robin Williams). The actor-director has created a film that melds a classical tone with a contemporary style. For instance, Fortinbras's army attacks Elsinore much like a SWAT team. England's Blenheim Palace creates the stately milieu for the nineteenth-century setting where the past freely mixes with the present. Branagh's choice of setting visually parallels his desire to convey Shakespeare's language in "a speaking style that is as realistic as a proper adherence to the structure of language will allow" (Branagh, xv). Branagh literally illustrates many key points in the text, often eliminating any ambiguity: the ground erupts with fire at the appearance of the ghost ("blasts from hell"); in a flashback Hamlet and Ophelia are seen in bed making love ("I did love you once"); and much of the Player's narration about the fall of Troy is depicted as the old actor (Charlton Heston) recites the words in a grandiloquent style. Branagh invents other scenes to embellish the text: the crazed Ophelia (Kate Winslet) is doused with torrents of water in a padded cell as she stands wrapped in a straightjacket. At other times, the actors themselves bring clarity to potentially difficult or obscure lines: Billy Crystal's First Gravedigger reminds contemporary audiences just how much this is a masterful comic's role, as does Robin Williams's Osric. Because he had the benefit of studying many notable performances before him, Branagh's soliloquies, particularly the famed set piece "To be or not to be," are consistently well spoken. At times the actor's readings may be too theatrical for the realistic style that dominates the film, perhaps because Branagh had previously played the role on stage in an uncut version for the RSC (1992). Furthermore, Derek Jacobi, who played Hamlet in the BBC production (see below), directed Branagh in another London production (1988). Jacobi's Claudius is among the most sympathetic on film: his affection for Gertrude seems genuine and passionate, and the guilt he suffers for his crime of passion is evident. Julie Christie's Gertrude is properly matronly and clearly in love with Claudius. Branagh minimizes any Freudian overtones between Hamlet and the Queen in his rendering of the play.

Photographed in vivid colors and using the 70 mm format, this *Hamlet* is a larger-than-life epic, best seen in Hamlet's soliloquy in 4.4, "How all occasions do inform against me." After watching Fortinbras's army of thousands march across a snow-covered landscape, Hamlet affirms his resolve to complete the task commanded by his father's ghost as the camera pulls back to reveal a majestic mountain range. Branagh places his intermission after this stirring shot, a fitting choice because the speech marks the climax of the Prince's maturation. Another thoughtful directorial choice enhances the Nunnery Scene. Staged in a long, mirrored hallway, the "To be or not to be" soliloquy is delivered toward the mirrors as an internal self-examination—an inventive way of solving the problem that soliloquies present to filmmakers. As the scene with Ophelia progresses, Hamlet suspects that the King and Polonius are hiding behind these mirrors, which are actually one-way windows. He races to the mirrors to deliver the threat "Those that are married already—all but one—shall live" (3.1.150–151). Branagh's concept here deftly reinforces the play's emphasis on the Prince as actor: he performs for himself in the soliloquy and then explodes madly at his captive audience hidden behind the mirrors. Branagh, the stage actor turned film director, consistently invests his movie with liberal doses of theatricality: Hamlet's plot to have the players "play something like the murder of my father" (2.2.596) materializes as the Prince toys with pasteboard cutouts in a Victorian toy theater. Despite occasional cinematic indulgences, Branagh's film captures "the extraordinary depth of Hamlet and the supporting characters" (Rosenthal, 32).

■ 2000—Director Michael Almereyda, Miramax Films, with Ethan Hawke (Hamlet), Julia Stiles (Ophelia), Bill Murray (Polonius), and Diane Venora (Gertrude). (113 min.)

To the uninitiated Almereyda's film may seem a bold foray into modernity: Denmark is a New York–based mega-corporation, controlled by scheming executives in tailored suits in contrast to Hamlet, a disillusioned, disenfranchised young filmmaker, who wears a woolen ski hat. Yet Almereyda is certainly not the first: Akira Kurosawa, for instance, has recast *Hamlet* as the story of an angry young man fighting corporate malfeasance in modern-day Japan (see *The Bad Sleep Well*, p. 637 below). Almereyda was inspired in turn by a satirical Finnish film (*Hamlet Goes Business*, 1987). Almereyda's film is consistently inventive as it creates an ultra–high-tech world wherein the Ghost appears on a security camera, Ophelia wears a "wire" to entrap her boyfriend, letters are faxed, and the Prince composes soliloquies on a laptop or as voicemails. In perhaps the film's most inspired touch, the "To be or not to be" soliloquy is staged in a Blockbuster video store where Hamlet wanders aimlessly among the section marked "Action." Hamlet seeks to catch the conscience of Denmark's CEO using "The Mousetrap"—not a play, but a genuinely hilarious homemade movie that Hamlet has pieced together from snippets of 1950s sitcoms, old 8-mm home movies, horror and "indie" films. Ethan Hawke's Prince is more surly and self-absorbed than philosophical; his lines are delivered in a monotonous drone that is often overpowered by pulsing music. Bill Murray brings his screen persona—the cynical funnyman whose "shtick" grows progressively less funny—to Polonius and thereby offers a fresh rendering of the character. The actors, save Diane Venora (Gertrude), are not classically trained and rely mostly on a naturalistic acting that is often at odds with Shakespeare's heightened language. To accommodate this "method acting" style so familiar to American actors, Almereyda's heavily cut script emerges as the shortest (113 minutes) *Hamlet* among its modern film versions.

Hamlet *on Television*

Hamlet has been produced specifically for television more than any other Shakespeare play; it is among the most "TV-friendly" plays in the canon because its many soliloquies invite close-ups in the interior of Elsinore. Among the most significant television versions of the play are:

- 1960—Director Franz Peter Wirth, West German TV, with Maximilian Schell (Hamlet). (152 min.)

   Schell, who translated the play into a modern German idiom, played Hamlet to enthusiastic audiences in Munich in August 1960. Fortunately that performance is preserved in this black-and-white film shot for Eurovision. Many judge it to be the best of the TV *Hamlet*s because it treats the play as an intimate chamber play, allowing the camera to indulge in close-ups. During the "To be or not to be soliloquy" the camera focuses tightly on Hamlet's eyes; the scene combines the introspective voice-over technique of Olivier's film with an essentially realistic approach. The minimalist setting invests the two great thrones that fill the tiny screen with political importance. Some notorious dubbing problems mar an otherwise excellent film, dominated by Schell's brooding, yet unusually active, performance. *The Great Hamlets* (see next page) incorporates several scenes from this version, as well as some perceptive insights by Schell into Hamlet's character and his controversial translation.

- 1970—Director Peter Wood, BBC, with Richard Chamberlain (Hamlet), Richard Johnson (Claudius), Margaret Leighton (Gertrude), Michael Redgrave (Polonius), and John Gielgud (Ghost). (180 min.)

   Chamberlain, a popular American television actor, plays Hamlet with a stellar British cast, thus investing the role with an "outsider's status" that contributes to the play's tension. Dressed in early–nineteenth-century clothing to reinforce a Hamlet-as-Byronic-hero interpretation, Chamberlain speaks the verse surprisingly well, especially when judged against his co-actors. The Act 5 sword fight, shot from above, is among the best on film. The play's religious and moral issues are underscored by numerous shots of each of the main characters deep in prayer.

- 1980—Director Rodney Bennett, BBC, with Derek Jacobi (Hamlet), Patrick Stewart (Claudius), Claire Bloom (Gertrude), and Eric Porter (Polonius). (217 min.)

   Among the most successful of the BBC Shakespeare series—if only because it preserves Jacobi's performance, which he had honed during a lengthy run at the Old Vic Theatre—this *Hamlet* counters the then-current vogue for boorish Princes. Jacobi is elegant and introspective, yet he can rise to anger when necessary. His reading of the "To be or not to be" soliloquy and the ensuing Nunnery Scene embrace an uncommonly rich emotional range, at times self-abasing, at others cruelly ironic, yet always thoughtful. Jacobi's inspired handling of the Nunnery Scene has been described above (pp. 570–571) in the discussion of Hamlet's treatment of women. In the Mousetrap Scene, filmed in a faithful recreation of a Renaissance court theater, Jacobi wears a ghoulish skull mask, an ironic foreshadowing of his later encounter with Yorick. As Claudius, Patrick Stewart presents an uncommonly sympathetic King: his reading of the "Bend stubborn knees" soliloquy in 3.3 is genuine and moving, the plea of a man who is trying vainly to repent his "foul deeds." In this film, only Hamlet's soliloquies are audience-centered, while those of other characters (Claudius, Ophelia) are interiorized. Hamlet's speeches are shot in lingering close-ups as Jacobi plays directly to the camera to engage viewers in Hamlet's soul-searching. The BBC *Hamlet* is worth seeing in conjunction with Branagh's 1996 film: audiences can appreciate the influences Jacobi exerted on Branagh's performance.

- 1996—*The Great Hamlets*. Director Derek Bailey, with Trevor Nunn and Mandy Patinkin. (120 min.)

    Although this excellent video does not offer the entire play, it preserves key scenes from ten of the most important stage and film *Hamlets* in the mid-to-late twentieth century. Former RSC Artistic Director Trevor Nunn discusses the play's title role with New York actor Mandy Patinkin; their analyses of the soliloquies are punctuated by excerpts from other productions and interviews with ten actors who have played the role, including Olivier, Gielgud, Burton, Smoktunovsky, Schell, Williamson, and Kingsley. The film allows viewers to see several interpretations of a speech approximate to one another. Smoktunovsky's recitation of the "To be or not to be" soliloquy—in Russian, thirty years after he made the film with Kozintsev (who deleted the speech in the finished product)—encapsulates the universal appeal of Shakespeare's most famous passage.

Adaptations and Spin-offs

Musicals and Ballets

In 1868 Ambroise Thomas revised Shakespeare's plot to accommodate the needs of opera (e.g., Gertrude and Ophelia beg Hamlet to forgo his mad rants in a lyrical duet). The opera's ending is radically altered: Hamlet kills Claudius in the graveyard while his father's ghost looks on and the Danes rally in support of their new King. Though not a great opera—especially compared to Verdi's *Otello*—Thomas's work offers two stirring arias, Hamlet's "To be or not to be" soliloquy ("*Monologo*") and Ophelia's "Mad Scene." In 1976 a pop opera, *Rockabye Hamlet* (libretto and music by Cliff Jones), failed to captivate audiences and closed in a week because it was bad rock and worse theater. Such songs as "He Got It in The Ear" and a scene in which Ophelia strangles herself with a microphone cord contributed to the show's demise.

At least a dozen ballet versions of *Hamlet* have been performed, including those with music by Berlioz,

Liszt, and Copland. The most famous *Hamlet* ballet was a one-act version staged in London (1942) by Robert Helpmann, a superb choreographer-dancer as well as an accomplished stage and film actor. Helpmann used extant music by Tchaikovsky for his nightmarish ballet. Most recently (2000) choreographer Stephen Mills used music by postmodern composer Philip Glass to create an intriguing ballet of the play in which the action was seen as a flashback envisioned by Hamlet as he died from the poison on the bated sword.

Stage Plays

Because *Hamlet* is among the "sacred myths" in Western literature, many playwrights over the past forty years have deconstructed the play in order to critique contemporary society.

- *Rosencrantz and Guildenstern Are Dead* (1966) by Tom Stoppard: This prototype of "mod-*Hamlets*" has initiated an explosion of variations on the *Hamlet* legend, all of which serve as provocative critiques of the original. Stoppard's inventive script makes two of the least consequential supporting roles in Shakespeare's canon the heroes of a quasi-Elizabethan tragicomedy as it might have been written by absurdist playwright Samuel Beckett. Like Beckett's two tramps in *Waiting for Godot* (1953), Rosencrantz and Guildenstern have been thrust into a game that they must play, although they do not know the object of the game. Early in the play Rosencrantz cries out: "What's the game?" His mate responds forlornly, "What are the rules?" In 1988 Stoppard directed a film version of his play, using a screenplay that builds upon the best aspects of the stage play. *Rosencrantz and Guildenstern Are Dead* is often performed in repertory with *Hamlet* at summer Shakespeare festivals, with actors playing their same roles in the two versions.

- "Dogg's Hamlet" (1977) is also by Stoppard. This amusing one-act play satirizes a society in which people speak to each other without a common vocabulary to signify the same object. Inspired by the nonsensical cross-talk between Hamlet and Polonius in Act 2, it is a play about "Words, words, words" (2.2.193).

Other intriguing post–*Rosencrantz and Guildenstern Are Dead* plays are:

- *Poor Murderer* (1977) by Czech playwright Pavel Kohout: A young Russian actor goes mad while playing Hamlet and kills the actor cast as Polonius; he is put in a mental hospital where doctors encourager him to act out a psychodrama explaining the events leading to the murder.

LAURENCE OLIVIER (1907–1989)

The career of Laurence Olivier spanned almost the entire twentieth century and a wider range of parts, both classical and contemporary, than any British actor had essayed before him. As the greatest heroic actor of his day, he was in a line that included David Garrick, Edmund Kean, Henry Irving, and John Gielgud, but he also possessed a lithe physicality and smoldering sexuality that made him a glamorous, popular film star. His cinematic breakthrough occurred when he played a romantic Heathcliff in *Wuthering Heights* (1939). His filmic range went on to include his brilliant portrayal of a high-class restaurateur gripped by obsessive passion in *Carrie* (1950); his barnstorming role as the Muslim fanatic, The Mahdi, in *Khartoum* (1966); and his final cameo as an old soldier in *War Requiem* (1989). As a director and producer he brought Shakespeare perceptively to the screen in three important films—*Henry V, Hamlet,* and *Richard III.* In his last years he also turned television producer, helping to bring several stage works to Britain's Granada Television, including his final filmed Shakespeare performance—and arguably his most touching—in *King Lear.* As *Guardian* critic Michael Billington noted upon Olivier's death, one of the most extraordinary qualities of this protean actor "was his ability to combine the male and female principles in a single performance: one moment as dangerous as a lion, the next as skittish as a gazelle. The qualities that most men hide and suppress, Olivier harbored and displayed; and that is one important source of his greatness."

Olivier was born in Dorking, Surrey, on May 22, 1907, the son of an impoverished Anglican clergyman and a humor-loving mother who died when he was thirteen. He attended All Saints Choir School in London where he made his acting debut as a ten-year-old Brutus in *Julius Caesar.* Legendary British actress Ellen Terry saw that performance and spoke to the surprised boy afterwards, telling him, "Oh don't you love the words?" and later noting in her diary that the child was already a fine actor. At the age of fifteen, Olivier played Katharina in *The Taming of the Shrew;* photographs of him in the role show his beautiful face and compelling eyes flashing a fierce pride. He trained at the Central School of Drama and served his apprenticeship with the Birmingham Repertory Theatre in 1927 and 1928. His

London career began as a leading man in commercial comedies on the West End. In 1930 he married his leading lady, actress Jill Esmond; their appearances together in a Broadway production of Noel Coward's *Private Lives* led to a contract with RKO Studios and a stint in Hollywood.

Olivier filmed and starred in *Henry V* in 1944; the movie made him a national hero and inspired others to attempt his stylistic and interpretive daring in adapting Shakespeare to the screen. Given this reputation, his earlier movie debut, in 1930, was surprisingly unpromising. His first pictures were melodramas that served neither his talents nor the producers' commercial interests. Olivier left Hollywood thinking he would never have a career in the movies. So frustrated was he that he turned down the role of Romeo in MGM's *Romeo and Juliet,* which starred the much older Leslie Howard instead, and proved emotionally pale and cinematically unsatisfactory. Olivier's later vivid performance as Orlando in a relentlessly cheery 1936 *As You Like It* did nothing to change his mind about the viability of Shakespeare on screen.

Instead he rededicated himself to Shakespeare on stage. In 1935, he and John Gielgud alternated as Romeo and Mercutio in a New Theatre staging that proved controversial and very popular. Olivier's natural-seeming speaking of the verse was excoriated as too realistic for the poetry, yet the production secured both actors' reputations. In that famous Gielgud staging, Peggy Ashcroft played Juliet, and Edith Evans the Nurse. Within three years, Olivier had fully launched his classical career at the Old Vic, with star turns as Hamlet, Henry V, Macbeth, and Iago (to Ralph Richardson's Othello), bringing vigor, virility, and a nimble athleticism to each role. Critics were divided at first in their opinions of the actor-director, some finding his approach too external, even flashy. But audiences lined up to see him. *Henry V* set box office records and led to a government request that he film Shakespeare's account of the historic English triumph against a large French army. The film project was meant to stir British patriotism and boost the morale of troops fighting the Germans during World War II. Olivier wished to be a fighter pilot himself, but was given training duties in the Fleet Air Arm, an assignment from which he was released when he was named a co-director of the Old Vic with Ralph

Richardson and John Burrell. There Olivier famously played the tragic Theban king in the poet W. B. Yeats's translation of Sophocles's *Oedipus*. His anguished howl in that seminal tragedy's discovery scene was delivered for maximum impact and was considered unforgettable. He was, as one reviewer put it, "a panther among doves." His supple voice and command of rhetoric now testified to his early vocal training with Elsie Fogerty, whom he acknowledged as his most important mentor. During this highly creative period, Olivier established his personal tradition of building his characters from the outside in by working with elaborately constructed noses and other prostheses to form the physical details first; only then, he often said, could he begin to explore the emotional core of the role.

In the midst of his stage triumphs, the actor returned to Hollywood, where he scored his first major film success with William Wyler's splendid *Wuthering Heights*. Olivier was Heathcliff opposite Merle Oberon's soulful Cathy. Wyler helped Olivier adapt his acting technique to the close-up and the small screen. His Heathcliff brought him his first Oscar nomination and another role, this time as Maxim de Winter in Alfred Hitchcock's *Rebecca*. Olivier and Jill Esmond divorced, and soon after he married his lover, Vivien Leigh, the famous Scarlett O'Hara of *Gone with the Wind*. The celebrated couple sometimes appeared together on stage and screen. Olivier planned a joint appearance in a film of *Macbeth*, a project that never came to fruition.

His epic, style-shifting *Henry V* had proven an even more effective patriotic pageant than the government had hoped for, rousing the nation during the darkest days of the war and winning the Academy Award for Best Picture. In 1947, the beautifully shot film and his own witty and powerful performance as a fairy-tale prince and pious soldier gained him another historic first: he became the youngest actor ever to be knighted. Olivier won two more Oscars (Best Actor and Best Film) for his moody, oedipal interpretation of *Hamlet* (1948), and wide praise for his terrifying portrayal of the hunchbacked smiling villain of *Richard III*, on stage and screen. (Detailed descriptions of all three films are in the chapters on each of these plays.) These notable successes in filmed Shakespeare—each so interpretively and stylistically different from the other—led him to believe that he would find the financing he needed for the proposed *Macbeth* in which he and his fragile wife, Leigh, intended to star as Macbeth and Lady Macbeth. But the financing fell through when the lone producer and patron, Sir Alexander Korda, died, and, after the Oliviers divorced, it became clear to Laurence that the film would never be made. His disappointment was immense, for his Macbeth on stage was considered definitive. Seen during the 1955 Stratford-upon-Avon season, along with his Titus of *Titus Andronicus* and his Malvolio in *Twelfth Night*, Olivier's Macbeth was appreciated for several innovations. Unexpected vocal climaxes in the farewell to sleep speech emphasized Macbeth's horror of the insomnia his crime has generated. Olivier also gave a subtly indirect, almost ironic inflection to his colloquy with the murderers of the good King Duncan. His Titus in Peter Brook's ritualistic production that same season transformed a nearly forgotten play to a bone-chilling tragedy.

Olivier's most acclaimed contemporary role was that of Archie Rice, the cynical musical hall performer in John Osborne's *The Entertainer* (1957); the actor's interpretation was greeted as unparalleled in its virtuosity. Olivier allied himself early on to a new generation of innovators at the Royal Court Theatre where Osborne was becoming the leader of a group of writers dubbed the Angry Young Men. In his portrayal of Osborne's Rice, Olivier evoked the seedy music hall culture of a vanishing past, limned the failed aspirations of a lascivious entertainer, and made the character himself a trenchant symbol of a nation in decline. The Osborne play was filmed in 1960. Olivier devoted his energies for the remainder of that decade to the founding, launching, and financing of the National Theatre of Great Britain. The institution opened in 1962 with Olivier as its first artistic director and the passionate, controversial *Observer* critic, Kenneth Tynan, as its literary manager. The young Tynan, who chronicled so astutely Olivier's 1940s performances, keenly understood Olivier's distinctive gifts: physical relaxation, animal magnetism, commanding eyes and voice, superb timing, and the ability to communicate a sense of danger on stage, as well as enjoyment of vulgar, mischievous comedy. Olivier's acting could be dainty and feminine, but never effeminate, even when he played fops in Restoration comedy.

Newly married in the early 1960s to the charming and gifted actress Joan Plowright, Olivier directed many productions for the National, took on roles in early modern classics by Strindberg, Chekhov, and Ibsen, and continued to explore Shakespearean roles. One highlight was his Astrov, the disillusioned doctor

(continued)

in Chekhov's *Uncle Vanya*, whom Olivier took to be a portrait of the playwright himself. He reached another pinnacle of popularity with his production of *Othello*, in which he played the Moor with little of the pounding rhetoric customarily heard in the role, instead emphasizing the credulous general's descent into animalism. Despite some critical objections to his studied negritude, the staging was a commercial hit for the National, ran off and on for four years, and was filmed in 1965 with Frank Finlay as Iago (see Chapter 16 on *Othello*). His influential portrayal of Shylock came in Jonathan Miller's 1970 production for the Royal Shakespeare Company, the same year Olivier was made a life peer. He was the first actor ever to achieve this honor. His Shylock was harsh, yet elegant, a prosperous private banker in Edwardian top hat and yarmulke. At first ingratiating himself to the Christians and later devolving into a mad revenger, Olivier as Shylock brought his interpretation to a shattering climax as he left his trial scene a broken man uttering an anguished offstage scream.

In 1973, Olivier resigned as director of the National Theatre and quit the stage. By that point, he had been praised as the touring actor and heartbroken husband, James Tyrone, in Eugene O'Neill's harrowing *Long Day's Journey Into Night.* He also had fought serious illness, stage fright, and many battles to keep the theater financially viable, and he was exhausted. He said that he would henceforth limit his appearances to the less demanding electronic media. Tynan assessed the National's first ten years in a caustic journal entry in which he said that the theater had discovered only "one new playwright (Tom Stoppard) and no new directors." Regretting his time there and perhaps smarting from the board's appointment of Peter Hall as Olivier's successor, Tynan concluded that Olivier had little sense of contemporary theater and was "insensitive to current definitions of talent." Still, Olivier, like Orson Welles before him, now happily took on well-paid character parts and cameos in movies and television shows. The father of two sons and two daughters, he said he needed the money and therefore accepted lucrative assignments in advertisements for Polaroid cameras and other American products.

Although weakened by the cancer that had complicated his last years at the National and that now recurred, Olivier nonetheless gave one of his most moving and seemingly heartfelt performances in the Granada Television's production of *King Lear,* filmed in 1983 (described in Chapter 17). The actor was seventy-five when he created this touching portrayal of the old king as a benevolent and forgetful father, his mind wandering, his body broken by the cruelty of his two pitiless elder daughters, no longer able to sustain life in the aftermath of the seemingly wanton death of Cordelia.

Olivier lived six more years, appearing almost to the end in small parts in films and on television. He died in his sleep July 11, 1989, at his home in Sussex, his family by his side. Because as the child of a poor vicar he often felt the sting of want, Olivier always feared poverty and failure—this, despite a catalog of accomplishments that seems impossibly long for one man to have achieved in one life. In death he was extolled as "a Titan" (by director Richard Eyre) and as a man whose "genius shaped the last fifty years" (by Hall, his successor at the National).

At Olivier's memorial service, much of the programmed music was by his friend and collaborator on the great Shakespeare films, composer William Walton. A procession of actors carried mementos from his illustrious career. On a blue-velvet pillow, borne by Douglas Fairbanks, Jr., was Olivier's Order of Merit. Michael Caine carried one of Olivier's Oscars; Peter O'Toole bore his *Hamlet* film script, and Paul Scofield a model of the National Theatre of Great Britain. Frank Finlay came last, carrying Edmund Kean's sword, a gift to Olivier from Gielgud, his old sparring partner. Before they all adjourned for night-long toasts to "Larry" at the National Theatre, the Dean of Westminster Abbey declared that Olivier's ashes would be laid to rest alongside the remains of David Garrick and Henry Irving, the great Shakespearean actor-managers of the eighteenth and nineteenth centuries. Invoking two of Olivier's finest stage and film roles, the Dean continued that the place of internment was "within a stone's throw of the graves of Henry V and the Lady Anne, Queen to Richard III."

References and Related Reading

Billington, Michael. "First Lord of the Stage—A Tribute to the Greatest Actor of the Century." *Guardian* (London) 12 July 1989.

Coveney, Michael. "Olivier Exits in a Blaze of Glory." *Financial Times* (London) 21 Oct. 1989. I:1.

———. "Olivier Dies at 82." *Financial Times* (London) 12 July 1989. I:19.

Holden, Anthony. *Olivier*. London, 1988.

O'Connor, Garry. *Olivier: In Celebration*. London, 1987.

Olivier, Laurence. *Confessions of An Actor.* London, 1982.

Rosenthal, Daniel. *Shakespeare on Screen.* London, 2000.

Tynan, Kenneth. *The Diaries of Kenneth Tynan.* Ed. John Lahr. New York and London, 2001.

- *Hamletmachine* (1977) by Heiner Müller, postwar Germany's most important playwright: Although only eight pages in length (it can run hours in performance), this *avant-garde* work exposes the violence that humans do to themselves and to each other in the name of conflicting social and political ideologies. Müller's play relies on images more than words to portray Hamlet as a misfit trapped in a cycle of violence, while Ophelia is victimized by the patriarchal society that uses and then destroys her.

- *I Hate Hamlet* (1993) by Paul Rudnick: Forced to play Hamlet, a soap-opera actor conjures up the ghost of John Barrymore to coach him through the role in this energetic, mildly subversive farce.

- *Fortinbras* (2002) by Lee Blessing begins where Hamlet ends: Fortinbras enters the royal chamber littered with corpses. To protect his own monarchy, Fortinbras concocts a story blaming the deaths on a Polish spy; the ghosts of the dead return to haunt Fortinbras for tampering with their "truth" in this postmodern satire that examines the rift between truth and myth.

- *Gertrude—The Cry* (2003). Howard Barker, one of England's "shock" playwrights, calls his dramatic style "The Theater of Catastrophe" because it avoids catharsis and moral enlightenment. *Gertrude* concentrates on the sexual life of Hamlet's mother, who gives birth to Claudius's child; Claudius is harassed by a domineering mother (Isola), while Hamlet marries a girl (Ragusa) whom he despises. Barker's play indicts the moral bankruptcy of contemporary society by exposing the most salacious elements of the most revered plays of Western civilization.

Films

Among the most noteworthy of the *Hamlet*-inspired films include:

- *To Be or Not to Be* (1942). Director Ernst Labitsch and writer E. J. Mayer use a performance of *Hamlet* by a Polish acting troupe in World War II to create an ingenious comedy in which the Nazis are duped. The legendary comedian Jack Benny plays the actor-prince. In the film's funniest scene, Benny's mangled delivery of "To be or not to be" becomes (unbeknownst to Benny himself) a signal to his wife's lover, sitting in the audience, that she is available in the dressing room while "the Prince" fumbles through Shakespeare's most famous speech. Mel Brooks remade the film in 1983, substituting crude jokes and parody for the inventive, sophisticated satire of the Labitsch-Mayer film.

- *The Bad Sleep Well* (1960). Akira Kurosawa's Samurai adaptations of *Macbeth* (*Throne of Blood*) and *King Lear* (*Ran*) are considered masterpieces of recontextualization. His 1960s film is set in contemporary Japan to expose corrupt business practices in the post-war era. Instead of samurai, Kurosawa portrays the Yakuza, Mafia-like gangsters, who clash with a young executive (Toshiro Mifune) seeking revenge for his father's death at the hands of an ambitious corporate executive.

- *Johnny Hamlet* (1972). This film relocates the Hamlet story to the American West, where a young cowboy returns from the Civil War to find that his father has been killed by his uncle. The cowboy is aided by a Horatio-like ranch foreman in his quest for revenge. The film was shot in Italy and retains the feel of a spaghetti-Western.

- *A Midwinter's Tale* (1998): After making his four-hour *Hamlet*, Kenneth Branagh wrote and directed (but did not act in) this low-budget, black-and-white film in which a group of eccentric English amateurs perform *Hamlet* in a provincial church. The discussions among the put-upon director (who plays Hamlet) and his cast of misfits provide both thoughtful and comic insights into Shakespeare's play.

In addition to the films just discussed, *Hamlet* has inspired several "troubled and/or angry teen" movies and a few comedies. In 1945 Edgar Ulmer issued *Strange Illusion*, an expressionistic work in which a young man, troubled by his widowed mother's marriage to a drunk, has nightmares that provoke an "antic disposition." Based on a Ross Macdonald crime novel, *Blue City* (1986) uses elements of Shakespeare's plot to create a *film noir* in which a young man (Judd Nelson) attempts to right society's wrongs; it anticipates Michael Almereyda's modern-dress film. *Let the Devil Wear Black* (1999) is a sex-and-violence exploitation film that is generally faithful to Shakespeare's storyline: a young man returns to Los Angeles from a mental hospital and hears a voice telling him that his father was murdered by his gangster uncle.

Three late–twentieth-century comedies use *Hamlet* as stepping-off place for their mayhem. *Strange Brew* (1983) follows the misadventures of two beer-drinking Canadians (Rick Moranis and Dave Thomas) who end up at Elsinore Castle. Those who know Shakespeare's text will find the inventive in-jokes amusing. The only Shakespearean language in *Outrageous Fortune* (1987) is its title (3.1.59), but the film does offer a feminist perspective on the play. A wealthy socialite who wants to play Hamlet is thwarted in her ambition when she becomes involved in espionage with a B-movie actress (Bette Midler). The film shares Hamlet's preoccupation with the "play-life" metaphor; at the end, the woman does in fact get to play the Prince. The plot of *The Renaissance Man* (1994) is not based on Shakespeare's play; rather it offers a useful, though comical, explication of the play's issues in layman's terms as a downtrodden advertising salesman (Danny DeVito) is enlisted to teach thinking skills at an Army boot camp.

References and Related Reading

Alexander, Peter. *Poison, Play, and Duel*. Lincoln, Neb., 1971.

Barton, Anne. "Introduction." *Hamlet*. Ed. T. J. B. Spencer. Hammondsworth, Eng., 1980. 28.

Beasley, Catherine. "Was Hamlet a Man or a Woman? The Prince in the Graveyard, 1800–1920." *"Hamlet": New Critical Essays*. Ed. Arthur F. Kinney. New York and London, 2002. 135–158.

Bloom, Harold. *Shakespeare: The Invention of the Human*. London, 1998.

Bradbrook, Muriel C. *Shakespeare the Craftsman*. London, 1969.

Branagh, Kenneth. *"Hamlet": Screenplay, Introduction and Film Diary*. New York, 1996.

Davidson, Levette J. "Shakespeare in the Rockies." *Shakespeare Quarterly* 4 (1953).

Greenblatt, Stephen. *Will in the World: How Shakespeare Became Shakespeare*. New York, 2004.

Jenkins, Harold. "Introduction." The Arden Shakespeare: *Hamlet*. London and New York, 1982. 97–101.

Jones, Ernest. *Hamlet and Oedipus*. New York, 1949.

Maher, Mary Z. *Modern Hamlets and Their Soliloquies*. Iowa City, Iowa, 2003.

Margolies, Eleanor. "Hamlet." *The Times Literary Supplement* (July 7, 2000): 21.

Pennington, Michael. *Hamlet: A User's Guide*. New York, 1996.

Righter, Anne. *Shakespeare and the Idea of the Play*. Oxford, 1962.

Rosenthal, Daniel. *Shakespeare on Screen*. London, 2000.

Rothwell, Kenneth S. *A History of Shakespeare on Screen: A Century of Film and Television*. Cambridge, Eng., 1999.

Wells, Stanley. *Royal Shakespeare: Four Major Productions at Stratford-upon-Avon*. Manchester, Eng., 1977.

——————. *Shakespeare: For All Time*. Oxford, 2002.

CHAPTER 16

Othello

c. 1604

Context and Dating: Comic Archetypes as Tragic Figures

Othello is unique among Shakespeare's mature tragedies in that it is essentially a domestic play. Written midway into his tragic period, it presents the tale of a once-proud man who concludes sadly that he has "loved not wisely but too well" (5.2.354). The fate of nations is not at stake, for no princes or kings fall, threatening to take their countries with them. The primary action occurs in the hinterlands: a military outpost on the remote island of Cyprus, a thousand miles removed from Venice, the Mediterranean's commercial capital. Although it shares with Shakespeare's other major tragedies a fascination with virulent evil, on its surface *Othello* does not have the cosmic implications of *Hamlet*, *Macbeth*, or *King Lear*. No ghosts come from the grave to seek redress for wrongdoings, no witches to prick the conscience of a would-be king, no storms reflecting a hero's disordered mind. Instead, *Othello* concerns the sexual jealousies and innuendoes that destroy the hero's marriage.

For more than three centuries critics have debated about Shakespeare's plotting and the motives of the play's characters. Most famously, Bernard Shaw dismisses the play as "pure melodrama," although he allows that the dialogue is splendid for its poetry: "Tested by the brain, [*Othello*] is ridiculous; tested by the ear it is sublime." For all its seeming imperfections, *Othello* remains among the most theatrically satisfying plays in the canon. Audiences are still moved by its grand passions and shocking finale. Current interpreters, both theatrical and critical, acknowledge "the play's uncanny ability to evoke thoughts, feelings, and images of a disturbingly intimate nature" (Pechter, 19). Generations of actors have been tested by its central roles—the noble Moor and Iago, one of Western theater's most intriguing villains. *Othello* has also inspired artists in many other media, notably Giuseppe Verdi whose opera *Otello* (1887) is arguably the finest adaptation of a Shakespearean work into another medium (see pp. 696–697).

The first recorded performance of *Othello* was on November 1, 1604. Why Shakespeare chose this domestic story at this point in his career we shall never know. One historical footnote offers an intriguing clue concerning Shakespeare's choice of subject matter in the early seventeenth century. King James, crowned in 1603, wrote a poem about the famous victory of the European armada over the Turks at the Battle of Lepanto in 1571. Perhaps it is not a coincidence that the play emphasizes Othello's heroic leadership of the Venetian forces against the Turkish fleet. Theater historian Lois Potter, however, suggests that Shakespeare may have completed the play well before its first recorded performance, perhaps during the last days of Elizabeth I's reign and before James became king (Potter, 6).

Plot and Structure

Othello's plot is not complicated: a foreign general falls in love with the daughter of a powerful Venetian Senator and she secretly marries him. Despite the Senator's protests, the Duke of Venice condones the marriage and immediately asks Othello to lead an army to Cyprus. On that island a jealous malcontent under the general's command spews the poison that destroys Othello's trust in his bride, leading to a tragic finale. Commentators for at least two centuries have criticized the plot, not for its content, but for its seeming contradictions in the handling of time, such as "double time" structure: Shakespeare employs simultaneously a short time and a long time scheme to advance the plot. Othello's bride, Desdemona, and a young lieutenant, Michael Cassio, simply have no time to indulge in "stolen hours of lust" (3.3.354), as Othello sadly suspects. Cassio, Desdemona, and Othello all travel on separate ships to Cyprus. Yet, as Frank Kermode shows, the play manages through dramaturgical sleight of hand to suggest that sufficient time has elapsed for trouble to have occurred. Unlike the neoclassic plays of France and Italy that rigorously adhered to the unities of time, place, and action, most English plays were episodic and sprawled over time and place. Accordingly, Shakespeare takes advantage of the dual time system by not reminding us of this short time lapse, and "in the immediate absence of such reminders, [we] assume that the action has picked out only certain spots of time" (Kermode, 1199). Director Harley Granville-Barker, whose *Prefaces to Shakespeare* remain among the most useful guides to Shakespeare's plays, dismisses the double time dilemma from a practitioner's viewpoint: "[Shakespeare] is not essentially concerned with time and the calendar . . . The play's essential action lies in the processes of thought and feeling by which the characters are moved and the story forwarded. His imagination is now concerned with fundamental passions, and its swift working demands unencumbered expression" (Vol. 2, 30). Shakespeare may play loosely with the time scheme for his dramatic convenience, but there is no trickery in his depiction of the battle for Othello's soul.

Characters: Heroes, Innocents, and Manipulators

As an intimate domestic drama, *Othello* requires only a half-dozen principal players:

- *Othello*, the Moorish general, who has served Venice well in its wars;
- *Desdemona*, a young Venetian woman who marries him;
- *Iago*, the malevolent ensign whose machinations propel the plot;
- *Emilia*, Iago's wife, confidante and lady-in-waiting to Desdemona, and a voice of reason amidst the tragic confusion;
- *Michael Cassio*, a handsome young lieutenant whom Iago uses to sow suspicion in Othello's mind; and

- *Roderigo*, a hapless and somewhat ridiculous suitor to Desdemona.

Three other characters are important in the action:

- *Brabantio*, Desdemona's aggrieved father and a wealthy Venetian Senator;
- *Bianca*, a Cypriot woman who has bedded with Cassio and whom Iago also uses to feed Othello's jealousy; and
- *Lodovico*, the emissary from Venice who speaks for society when he commands the audience, on stage and off, to "Look upon the tragic loading of [Othello's] bed . . . The object poisons sight" (5.2. 374–375). Lesser characters include the Duke or Doge of Venice; Montano, the Governor of Cyprus, and Gratiano, a Venetian nobleman.

Othello is unique among Shakespeare's tragedies in that its principal roles—Othello and Iago—are nearly equal. Nearly—for it is actually Iago who dominates the play in terms of lines. Fully a third of the lines (1094) are Iago's; only Hamlet and Henry V have more lines than he. Like most villains, Iago precipitates and drives the action; and when played by the right actor, he covers such an extraordinary emotional range that he can overwhelm Othello, the play's protagonist. Achieving the right balance between the two principal roles is a primary concern for directors. In 1956 Richard Burton and John Neville alternated the roles in an admired production of the play in London. Late–twentieth-century productions have tended to make Iago the center of the play or film (as in Oliver Parker's 1996 film: see p. 696).

Iago appeals to actors and audiences because his machinations, often inducing laughter in the early scenes, ingratiate him to both other characters and the audience. He defines himself by creating mischief and revels in his wickedness. The rationales for his destructive actions are difficult to fathom. Although he offers a variety of motives, including the injustice of being overlooked for promotion, none is quite satisfactory; some are contradictory. Commentators have yet to agree upon the source of Iago's evil. Psychologists have written case studies on Iago, suggesting his malevolence is prompted by sexual frustrations—such as a latent homosexuality in his jealousy of Cassio. The most famous analysis of Iago's behavior comes from the English poet and literary commentator Samuel Taylor Coleridge. During a series of lectures delivered between 1809 and 1819, Coleridge assessed Iago's "passionless" character, concluding that a "motiveless malignity" prompted Iago's malevolence. If the villain's actions could be easily or satisfactorily explained, Iago would be a less intriguing character. Although Shakespeare provides hints about Iago's psyche, it is the actor who must flesh these out on stage. *Othello* is perhaps an extraordinary experiment on Shakespeare's part: the villain has nearly become the protagonist of a tragedy, a device to which we will return with *Macbeth*.

Sources and Inspirations

Cinthio's Hecatommithi

Shakespeare's play—and his dramaturgical skills—can be appreciated by comparing *Othello* to its source, a popular Italian novella written by Giraldi Cinthio in 1565. This story, with which Shakespeare was familiar, may have been inspired by an actual murder in Venice about 1508 concerning one Christopher Moro, not a man of color, who killed his wife. Cinthio's lengthy collection of tales, collectively called *Hecatommithi*, includes the sensational story of a nameless Moorish general who marries a beautiful Venetian noblewoman named Disdemona ("unhappy fate"). Shakespeare has improved Cinthio's tale to create the "nobly pitiful tragedy of *Othello*" (Trewin 203). He borrows key events from Cinthio: the marriage of the Moor to the Venetian lady, the assignment of the Moor to the Cypriot garrison, and the ensign's desire to destroy the Moor's happiness with his wife. In the Italian version, the villain is motivated solely by his unrequited love for Disdemona. Shakespeare makes some notable changes. Although Cinthio's tale is narrated by the ensign's wife (cf. Emilia), Shakespeare actively involves the wife in the action and dramatizes her death at the hands of the ensign. The ensign is not punished in the original; he is promoted, then he dies alone and miserable years later. Shakespeare's most profound changes relate to the title character. Shakespeare gives the Moor a name (from *Oteull* or *Otheull*, possibly derived from French romances dating back to Charlemagne) and creates a fascinating past for him. Othello has traveled to the corners of the globe, seeing the Anthropophagi (cannibals) and "men whose heads / Do grow beneath their shoulders" (1.3.146–147). He is a man of boundless imagination and poetic sensibilities, a more sympathetic and engaging figure than Cinthio's violent Moor. In the source story the general, abetted by his ensign, kills the virtuous wife by bludgeoning her with a sock filled with sand; the murderers pull down the ceiling upon the dead bride to suggest an accident. Although the general is brought to trial by the Signiory, he escapes punishment; ultimately he is killed by Disdemona's vengeful relatives. Whereas Cinthio's novella is a lurid, amoral melodrama, Shakespeare's play raises issues of guilt and damnation and, more importantly, creates an ensemble of superbly drawn characters.

Theatrical Traditions

Although Shakespeare inherited the play's principal characters from Cinthio, he also borrows conventional stage figures from two significant genres in Western religious and secular theater: the medieval morality play, and classical Roman comedy with its stock characters.

The Morality Play. Once Othello has fully comprehended Iago's treachery, he comments as follows:

> I look down towards his feet; but that's a fable.
> If thou be'st a devil, I cannot kill thee.
>
> (5.2.294–295)

Othello looks at Iago's feet for a cloven (split) hoof, the legendary sign of a devil. Iago in fact has no cloven hoof, but to the distraught Moor he is still a "demi-devil" (5.2.309), at once human and diabolical. Conversely, the "divine Desdemona" (2.1.75) is described in terms associated with angels and heavenly beings (Gilfoyle, 83–96). Emilia tells Iago that he is "the blacker devil" while Desdemona is "the more angel" (5.2.134–135). The heavens themselves will not touch her ship during the frightful storm (2.1.70–75). As Bernard Spivack argues in *Shakespeare and the Allegory of Evil* (1958), *Othello* can be viewed as a secularized and domesticated version of medieval homiletic drama in which the Vice, a cunning and comically resourceful tempter, employs "his dexterity in effecting, through artful dissimulation and intrigue, the spiritual and physical ruin of frail humanity" (57). In *Othello* and plays like *Richard III*, "Shakespeare conjures up a particular kind of thrill he must have first had as a child watching the Vice in plays like . . . *The Interlude of Youth*: the thrill of fear braided together with transgressive pleasure. The Vice, wickedness personified, is appropriately punished at the end of the play, but for much of the performance he manages to captivate the audience and imagination takes a perverse holiday" (Greenblatt, 34).

Unfortunately Othello succumbs to Iago's captivating temptations. Medieval moralities often portrayed scenes in which the central character is simultaneously courted by a Good and a Bad Angel, a Virtue and a Vice, or other contraries serving as metaphors for one's conscience. This battle for the soul, or *psychomachia*, evokes the medieval theatrical tradition that Shakespeare uses and often acknowledges in his dramas. Falstaff, for instance, is referred to as "that reverend Vice" (*Henry IV, Part One*, 2.4.448) who lures Prince Hal into the irresponsible pleasures of Eastcheap. Shakespeare consistently renders the two-dimensional symbolic figures of the morality play as thoroughly human portraits transcending their homiletic purpose; Iago and Falstaff are his masterpieces of this craft.

Whereas Shakespeare appropriated elements of the morality play to write the tragedy of an everyman named Othello, his intentions have sometimes been distorted by shortsighted critics. In 1693 Thomas Rymer perverted the allegorical elements in *Othello* to suggest that the drama cautions "all Maidens of Quality" about the dangers of running away "with Blackamoors," and warns husbands to ensure "that before their Jealousie be Tragical, the proofs may be mathematical" (Rymer, 132).

The Stock Characters of Roman Comedy. Although their story is tragic, the central characters in *Othello* can also be traced to specific stock types in the Roman comedies of Plautus (c. 254–184 B.C.E.) and Terence (c. 185–159 B.C.E.), whose works Shakespeare must have read as he learned his Latin in the grammar school in Stratford-upon-Avon. Such characters also may be readily found in any number of Renaissance erudite comedies, such as those by Ariosto, from whom Shakespeare borrowed plots for his comic works. They also dominate the popular improvisational street comedy by the *commedia dell'arte*.

- *Othello* is akin to the Braggart Warrior (or Miles Gloriosis)—a boastful soldier who talks a good fight but whose actions fail to match his boasts. Othello's speech in 1.3 about his conquests and adventures to the Senate is a classic braggart warrior speech—only he is, of course, not bragging.

- *Iago*, the trickster or comic servant, uses chicanery to obtain his self-serving goals. Shakespeare transforms the comic trickster into his most pernicious villain.

- *Desdemona* descends from the classic *inamorata* (lover), the virtuous young woman who wins her lover's hand despite her father's protestations. Desdemona is more than the uncorrupted heroine. She is a determined young woman who charts her own destiny by eloping with the Moor, and she asserts herself before the powerful Venetian Senate in a scene (1.3) that may have shocked English audiences in 1604.

- *Brabantio*, her father, is derived from the *Sennex Iratus* of the Roman theater, whose opposition to his daughter's love characteristically provides a blocking mechanism that propels the plot. He is akin to the father in a popular Italian comedy, *Supposes*, that inspired *The Taming of the Shrew*. In *Othello*, Shakespeare transforms "the Grouch" of ancient and neoclassical comedy into a sad, tragic figure.

- *Cassio* is fashioned by Iago into the unwitting *inamorato*, typically a dashing young man who wins the maiden's heart. The inversion of this norm is among Shakespeare's boldest strokes, as Iago subverts, rather than abets, the young man to further his own devious plot.

- *Emilia*, akin to ancient comedy's "sassy serving maid" (or *soubrette*), comments knowingly on the folly of her betters. Like Desdemona, she transcends her roots in classical comedy to emerge as a strong-minded woman who denounces male arrogance.

Language and Music

Two issues concerning Shakespeare's language in *Othello* merit particular attention. First, we hear a strong initial contrast between Othello's speeches, mainly in verse, and Iago's, mainly in prose. The two characters thus occupy "different places in the linguistic hierarchy" (Potter, 4), with Othello representing the high style of the tragic hero and Iago the register of the common man. Othello's language, however, erodes as the play progresses and his confidence in Desdemona's virtue disintegrates. Dominant patterns of imagery contrast light with darkness and the human with the bestial. The play begins in darkness; then, in Act 5, in a superb theatrical moment, Othello must "put out the light" as he prepares to murder Desdemona. The animal imagery depicts the regression of the Moor from one who is almost superhuman to one who becomes nearly bestial. To Othello, in his agony of jealousy, "a hornèd man" (a man whose wife has been unfaithful to him) is "a monster and a beast" (4.1.62). Ironically, Iago says he is determined to destroy Othello because, among other things, he suspects the Moor has slept with Emilia—which would make Iago "a hornèd man" and a "monster and a beast." As the ensign's mischief manipulates Othello's emotions, the Moor, the epitome of eloquence in Act 1, loses control of his language. This linguistic deterioration reaches its nadir in 4.1 when Othello violently strikes Desdemona and exits with the exclamation, "Goats and monkeys!" (271), naming animals that are traditionally associated with uncontrolled sexuality. Lodovico, the emissary from Venice who has witnessed this shocking spectacle, speaks for all as he asks, "Is this the noble Moor whom our full Senate / Call all in all sufficient?" (272–273). We can trace the deterioration of Othello's mind as it yields to raw passion by focusing upon the disturbing changes in his language. Early in the play, Othello's poetic speech contributes to his attractiveness. Desdemona loves him not only for the tales he tells but for the manner in which he tells them: "[She] bade me, if I had a friend that loved her / I should but teach him how to tell my story" (1.3.166–167). In Acts 1 and 2 he is supreme among the characters for his eloquence, even though he modestly claims to be "rude" in speech (1.3.83). Yet by Act 4 he can barely speak coherently, as in this broken and confused prose passage:

Lie with her? Lie on her? We say "lie on her" when they belie her. Lie with her? Zounds, that's fulsome.—Handkerchief—confessions—handkerchief!—To confess and be hanged for his labor—first to be hanged and then to confess.—I tremble at it . . . Pish! Noses, ears, and lips.——Is't possible?—Confess—handkerchief!—O devil!

(4.1.35–43)

The dashes signal that Othello's noble mind, overcome by his jealous rage, is now incapable of a sustained thought. Othello's loss of eloquence is a symptom of his disordered mind and spirit.

By contrast, Iago is a chameleon, adapting his language to all circumstances. In Scene 1 he vents his anger, moving easily between poetic and crude, even scurrilous, diction as he describes Desdemona's purported sexual activity with Othello. He can play the plainspoken soldier when needed. In 2.1 he amuses those awaiting Othello's arrival with some sexually suggestive wordplay. In 3.3—the play's climactic scene in which Iago convinces Othello of Desdemona's infidelity—Iago becomes nearly as eloquent as Othello himself. At times he makes his arguments in the heightened language of poetry, and at others he reverts to a cold, calculated prose that betrays no feeling, as in the crucial "put money in thy purse" speech to Roderigo at the end of 1.3.

Shakespeare also employs song and music to evoke atmosphere and to define themes. The soldiers' bawdy drinking songs, initiated by Iago in 2.3, contrast with Desdemona's "willow" song in 4.3 addressing the plight of women victimized by male cunning and deceit. As with so many songs in his repertory, Shakespeare incorporates popular songs of the day into *Othello* with such precision that they seem as necessary as the dialogue itself.

Themes and Issues

Passion, Reason, and the "Green-eyed Monster"

Audiences customarily think of *Othello* as the play about the "green-eyed monster" because it depicts the destructive power of jealousy. We think first of Othello as a jealous man who destroys the one he loves, yet it is Iago who epitomizes envy. Emilia's description of jealousy applies with equal cogency to all men:

> But jealous souls will not be answered so;
> They are not ever jealous for the cause,
> But jealous for they're jealous. It is a monster
> Begot upon itself, born on itself.

(3.4.160–163)

Shakespeare's plays, and those of his contemporaries, often illustrate the chaos, both comically and tragically, that arises from the excesses of passion. Othello extols his new bride, "when I love thee not, / Chaos is come again" (3.3.99–100), and chaos does indeed come when Othello succumbs to Iago's insinuations. Iago's every move is dictated by an uncontrolled jealousy—that Cassio has been promoted over him, that Othello may have slept with Emilia, that Iago's lust for Desdemona or perhaps even for Othello remains unrequited. To paraphrase Emilia, he is "jealous for he is jealous." Among the most remarkable aspects of Iago's character is his ability to appear so rational and dispassionate—to Roderigo, to Cassio, and especially to Othello—while he is consumed by a malignant passion spawned in part by envy and self-loathing. He hates most in others those things he hates most about himself, and virtually every attack that Iago initiates against Othello, Cassio, or Roderigo is rationalized by a description of his own shortcomings.

The Machiavellian Mind

As has been noted, Iago's character descends from two older stage types: the Vice of the medieval morality plays and the trickster of classical Roman comedy. Shakespeare's audiences would have also recognized in him a variant on the newly popular "stage Machiavel," among the more intriguing characters in Renaissance drama. The term alludes to Niccolò Machiavelli (1469–1527), the historian and political theorist for the powerful Florentine Medici family, who wrote one of the most influential political tracts to emerge from the Renaissance. *The Prince* (1513) argues that those in power are inherently "right" and therefore may use any means to maintain their status. Some unscrupulous royalty and nobles—erroneously dubbed "Machiavels"—corrupted Machiavelli's theories to justify their nefarious deeds in the politically volatile atmosphere of Renaissance Europe. "Machiavel" became synonymous with villainy, and "the stage Machiavel" evolved into a popular character on European stages. While Richard III and Edmund in *King Lear* are among the foremost Machiavels to emerge in the English theater, Iago remains perhaps the consummate example of the type. Although he is neither royal nor nobly born, he exhibits ruthlessness worthy of a tyrant as he manipulates people to secure his ends. If he were seizing political power, as Richard III does, perhaps his malevolence might make sense. Although *Othello* is not an overtly political play in the manner of *Macbeth* or *King Lear*, it depicts the destructive power of an unscrupulous villain who "glories in the serpentine convolutions through which he pursues power, wealth or revenge" (Spivack, 374). England offered no short-age of real-life Machiavels in the turbulent political world of Shakespeare's London. Noting that Machi-avelli did not invent Machiavellianism as much as he affirms its presence in human nature, Spivack asserts that Shakespeare's "age was aware of Machiavellian-ism before it was aware of Machiavelli" (376). Indeed political allegories, such as *The World Tossed at Tennis* (attributed to Thomas Middleton and William Rowley, Shakespeare's contemporaries), featured characters such as Deceit and the Devil that seem kin to Iago, although they do not possess the multidimensionality of Shakespeare's superbly crafted villain.

"The Other": Race, Foreigners, and Women

Anthropologists use the term "the Other" to denote those who are different from, or are not included in, the majority culture. At one level, *Othello* is an intriguing study of Elizabethan-Jacobean prejudices against "the Other." In the play's opening scene, Iago and Roderigo refer to Othello in racist terms: he is thick-lipped, an "old black ram" that is "tupping" (copulating with) Bra-bantio's "white ewe," and a "devil." Medieval paintings often depict devils as black-faced and often with "thick lips," implying that dark-skinned people were also dev-ils. Such prejudices against people of color were com-monplace in Shakespeare's England, and *Othello* is astonishingly bold in its sympathetic depiction of such a person. Kiernan Ryan suggests a motive for Shake-speare's subversive departure from the norms of his time: "*Othello* involves . . . the more complex exposure of a white barbarian, who tries to turn a more truly civ-ilized black man into his degrading image of the kind of creature a Moor ought to be" (54).

Others victims of prejudice are found in the play. To be called "a Turk" was the cruelest of insults in Shake-speare's era, a feeling that dated back to the Crusades and to the more recent Battle of Lepanto (1571) in which the combined forces of Europe defeated the Turkish navy. As he prepares to commit suicide, Othello reminds his audience that he once slew "a malignant and a turbaned Turk . . . [a] circumcisèd dog" who had traduced the Venetian state (5.2.362–366). Significantly, Othello equates himself with that same Turk for having killed innocent Desdemona, suggesting that his heinous crime has made him so despicable that death is the only just remedy. The line must have reverberat-ed powerfully with audiences in 1604, some of whom might have fought against the Turks at Lepanto only a quarter century before.

Ultimately, it is the women who are most victimized in the play. As Desdemona prepares for bed in Act 4,

(Victoria and Albert Museum, London, UK / Art Resource, NY)

Ira Aldridge (c. 1807–1867) was the first African-American to take on the role of Othello; he toured the United States and Europe in this and other roles. In 1833, Aldridge succeeded Edmund Kean as Shakespeare's tragic Moor at Covent Garden.

Emilia delivers a wisely defiant speech (4.3.87–106) in which she catalogs both the injuries women suffer at the hands of men and the ways in which women are equal to men:

> Let husbands know
> Their wives have sense like them. They see, and smell,
> And have their palates both for sweet and sour,
> As husbands have.
>
> (96–99)

Emilia's eloquent argument for the dignity of women echoes Shylock's famous "Hath not a Jew eyes?" speech in *The Merchant of Venice*. If *Othello* is Shakespeare's play dealing most candidly with prejudices against people of color, it does so courageously and rightmindedly, exposing prejudice in its many forms.

Staging Challenges

Depicting Moors? African? Arabic? Or?

Audiences are conditioned to expect a "black" Othello because race-specific lines underscore Othello's blackness. Until the late twentieth century he was customarily depicted as distinctly Negroid. White actors layered their skins with coats of dark makeup, though in the early nineteenth century Edmund Kean introduced a lighter-toned Othello in deference to the poor lighting that made it difficult for audiences to see an actor's face when blackened. Since the mid-1960s, the social consciousness fostered by the American Civil Rights Movement has made whites-in-blackface performances unacceptable; the convention too readily invokes the twin specters of racism and the degradation so ingrained in the nineteenth-century minstrel show and its caricature of blacks. As late as the 1980s, some white British actors still performed Othello, but in American regional theaters and on Broadway the role is now interpreted almost exclusively by actors of color. Historically, however, Moors are Arabic and defined in most dictionaries as "members of a race related to the Arabs, living in Northwest Africa." A number of contemporary productions—most notably that televised by the BBC in 1981—have portrayed Othello in this manner, although there is no evidence Shakespeare and his contemporaries observed such verbal distinctions as are found in modern dictionaries.

Although Othello was played almost exclusively by white actors for four centuries, notable exceptions can be cited. Ira Aldridge (1807–1867), descended from Africans, played the role in America and Europe to considerable acclaim; in 1833 he succeeded Edmund Kean as Othello at Covent Garden. In the twentieth century, well-known actors of color such as Paul Robeson and James Earl Jones have famously interpreted the role (see below, p. 692). In the last quarter of the twentieth century and the early years of the twenty-first, a number of nonwhite, nonblack actors have been cast as Othello, most notably Ben Kingsley (of east Indian descent) and Raul Julia (from Puerto Rico). In perhaps the boldest casting in recent years, Patrick Stewart played a white Othello in a predominantly black cast in Washington, D.C., in 1977; Brabantio's servants were also played by whites in an especially intriguing inversion of the audience's normal expectations. The production was dubbed "the photo-negative *Othello*" because of the reversals of race.

5.2: The Death Scene

Act 5 presents the play's most formidable staging challenge: after Othello violently smothers Desdemona in his fit of passion, nearly three dozen lines are spoken before she revives, almost miraculously, to absolve Othello of his crime. While this may make for splendid romance (and the stuff of opera), it is difficult to play in spoken drama on stage. The more realistic the stage production or film, the more challenging the moment is to portray. To avoid this perilous moment, Oliver Parker simply deleted Desdemona's final speeches in his 1996 movie.

The problem is compounded when Iago slays Emilia after she reveals the truth to Othello. Traditionally she falls onto the bed or at its side; her death is followed by another lengthy exchange among Othello, Lodovico, Montano, and Cassio. During the play's denouement the audience's eyes are transfixed upon the bodies of the dead women. Finally, Othello kills himself with a hidden weapon (an interesting staging challenge in itself) and he, too, falls upon the bed to give Desdemona a final kiss. Whereas Lodovico's reference to "the tragic loading of this bed" emphasizes the tragedy, the moment can, if staged without care, provoke unwanted laughter because of the mechanistic repetition of the murders. To thwart nervous laughter, Shakespeare does break the tension during the final sequence. Othello plays a grimly comic joke on Desdemona's uncle, old Gratiano, by threatening to use "the sword of Spain." The audience is relieved when Othello wounds Iago—though significantly Othello does not kill the villain. The playwright seems to suggest that such evil in the world cannot be eradicated. (In the James Earl Jones production in 1983, Othello castrated Iago by running a sword blade between the ensign's legs, an appropriate wound for a man consumed with sexual jealousy.) Although the final scene is the most difficult to stage among the tragedies, it remains a powerful finale when performed convincingly.

Othello, the Moor of Venice

The Names of the Actors

OTHELLO, *the Moor*
BRABANTIO, *[a senator,] father to Desdemona*
CASSIO, *an honorable lieutenant [to Othello]*
IAGO, *[Othello's ancient,] a villain*
RODERIGO, *a gulled gentleman*
DUKE OF VENICE
SENATORS *[of Venice]*
MONTANO, *Governor of Cyprus*
GENTLEMEN *of Cyprus*
LODOVICO *and* GRATIANO, *[kinsmen to Brabantio,] two noble Venetians*
SAILORS
CLOWN

DESDEMONA, *[daughter to Brabantio and] wife to Othello*
EMILIA, *wife to Iago*
BIANCA, *a courtesan [and mistress to Cassio]*

[A MESSENGER
A HERALD
A MUSICIAN

Servants, Attendants, Officers, Senators, Musicians, Gentlemen

SCENE: *Venice; a seaport in Cyprus]*

1.1

Enter Roderigo and Iago.

RODERIGO
Tush, never tell me! I take it much unkindly   1
That thou, Iago, who hast had my purse
As if the strings were thine, shouldst know of this.   3
IAGO 'Sblood, but you'll not hear me.   4
If ever I did dream of such a matter,
Abhor me.
RODERIGO
Thou told'st me thou didst hold him in thy hate.   7
IAGO Despise me
If I do not. Three great ones of the city,
In personal suit to make me his lieutenant,
Off-capped to him; and by the faith of man,
I know my price, I am worth no worse a place.
But he, as loving his own pride and purposes,
Evades them with a bombast circumstance   14
Horribly stuffed with epithets of war,   15
And, in conclusion,
Nonsuits my mediators. For, "Certes," says he,   17
"I have already chose my officer."

And what was he?
Forsooth, a great arithmetician,   20
One Michael Cassio, a Florentine,
A fellow almost damned in a fair wife,   22
That never set a squadron in the field
Nor the division of a battle knows   24
More than a spinster—unless the bookish theoric,   25
Wherein the togaed consuls can propose   26
As masterly as he. Mere prattle without practice
Is all his soldiership. But he, sir, had th'election;
And I, of whom his eyes had seen the proof   29
At Rhodes, at Cyprus, and on other grounds
Christened and heathen, must be beleed and calmed   31
By debitor and creditor. This countercaster,   32
He, in good time, must his lieutenant be,   33
And I—God bless the mark!—His Moorship's ancient.   34

---

20 arithmetician i.e., a man whose military knowledge is merely theoretical, based on books of tactics **22 A . . . wife** (Cassio does not seem to be married, but his counter-part in Shakespeare's source does have a woman in his house. See also 4.1.131.) **24 division of a battle** disposition of a military unit **25 a spinster** i.e., a housewife, one whose regular occupation is spinning. **theoric** theory **26 togaed consuls** toga-wearing counselors or senators. **propose** discuss **29 his** Othello's **31 beleed and calmed** left to leeward without wind, becalmed. (A sailing metaphor.) **32 debitor and creditor** (A name for a system of bookkeeping, here used as a contemptuous nickname for Cassio.) **countercaster** i.e., bookkeeper, one who tallies with *counters*, or "metal disks." (Said contemptuously.) **33 in good time** opportunely, i.e., forsooth **34 God bless the mark** (Perhaps originally a formula to ward off evil; here an expression of impatience.) **ancient** standard-bearer, ensign.

1.1 Location: Venice. A street.
1 never tell me (An expression of incredulity, like "tell me another one.") **3 this** i.e., Desdemona's elopement. **4 'Sblood** By His (Christ's) blood **7 him** Othello **14 bombast circumstance** wordy evasion. (*Bombast* is cotton padding.) **15 epithets of war** military expressions **17 Nonsuits** rejects the petition of. **Certes** Certainly

RODERIGO
By heaven, I rather would have been his hangman.   35

IAGO
Why, there's no remedy. 'Tis the curse of service;
Preferment goes by letter and affection,   37
And not by old gradation, where each second   38
Stood heir to th' first. Now, sir, be judge yourself
Whether I in any just term am affined   40
To love the Moor.

RODERIGO   I would not follow him then.

IAGO   Oh, sir, content you.   43
I follow him to serve my turn upon him.
We cannot all be masters, nor all masters
Cannot be truly followed. You shall mark   46
Many a duteous and knee-crooking knave
That, doting on his own obsequious bondage,
Wears out his time, much like his master's ass,
For naught but provender, and when he's old,
    cashiered.   50
Whip me such honest knaves. Others there are   51
Who, trimmed in forms and visages of duty,   52
Keep yet their hearts attending on themselves,
And, throwing but shows of service on their lords,
Do well thrive by them, and when they have lined
    their coats,   55
Do themselves homage. These fellows have some
    soul,   56
And such a one do I profess myself. For, sir,
It is as sure as you are Roderigo,
Were I the Moor I would not be Iago.   59
In following him, I follow but myself—
Heaven is my judge, not I for love and duty,
But seeming so for my peculiar end.   62
For when my outward action doth demonstrate
The native act and figure of my heart   64
In compliment extern, 'tis not long after   65
But I will wear my heart upon my sleeve
For daws to peck at. I am not what I am.   67

RODERIGO
What a full fortune does the thick-lips owe   68
If he can carry't thus!

IAGO   Call up her father.   69
Rouse him, make after him, poison his delight,

Proclaim him in the streets; incense her kinsmen,
And, though he in a fertile climate dwell,   72
Plague him with flies. Though that his joy be joy,   73
Yet throw such changes of vexation on't   74
As it may lose some color.   75

RODERIGO
Here is her father's house. I'll call aloud.

IAGO
Do, with like timorous accent and dire yell   77
As when, by night and negligence, the fire   78
Is spied in populous cities.

RODERIGO
What ho, Brabantio! Signor Brabantio, ho!

IAGO
Awake! What ho, Brabantio! Thieves, thieves, thieves!
Look to your house, your daughter, and your bags!
Thieves, thieves!   83

            Brabantio [enters] above [at a window].

BRABANTIO
What is the reason of this terrible summons?
What is the matter there?

RODERIGO
Signor, is all your family within?

IAGO
Are your doors locked?

BRABANTIO   Why, wherefore ask you this?

IAGO
Zounds, sir, you're robbed. For shame, put on your
    gown!   88
Your heart is burst; you have lost half your soul.
Even now, now, very now, an old black ram
Is tupping your white ewe. Arise, arise!   91
Awake the snorting citizens with the bell,   92
Or else the devil will make a grandsire of you.   93
Arise, I say!

BRABANTIO   What, have you lost your wits?

RODERIGO
Most reverend signor, do you know my voice?

BRABANTIO   Not I. What are you?

RODERIGO   My name is Roderigo.

BRABANTIO   The worser welcome.
I have charged thee not to haunt about my doors.
In honest plainness thou hast heard me say
My daughter is not for thee; and now, in madness,
Being full of supper and distemp'ring drafts,   102
Upon malicious bravery dost thou come   103
To start my quiet.   104

---

35 his hangman the executioner of him. 37 Preferment promotion.
letter and affection personal influence and favoritism 38 old gradation step-by-step seniority, the traditional way 40 term respect.
affined bound 43 content you don't you worry about that. 46 truly
faithfully 50 cashiered dismissed from service. 51 Whip me Whip,
as far as I'm concerned 52 trimmed . . . duty dressed up in the mere
form and show of dutifulness 55 lined their coats i.e., stuffed their
purses 56 Do themselves homage i.e., attend to self-interest solely.
59 Were . . . Iago i.e., if I were able to assume command, I certainly
would not choose to remain a subordinate, or, I would keep a suspicious eye on a flattering subordinate. 62 peculiar particular, personal 64 native innate. figure shape, intent 65 compliment extern
outward show (conforming in this case to the inner workings and
intention of the heart) 67 daws small crowlike birds, proverbially
stupid and avaricious. I am not what I am i.e., I am not one who
wears his heart on his sleeve. 68 full swelling. thick-lips (Elizabethans often applied the term "Moor" to Negroes.) owe own
69 carry't thus carry this off.

72–3 though . . . flies though he seems prosperous and happy now,
vex him with misery. 73 Though . . . be joy Although he seems fortunate and happy. (Repeats the idea of line 72.) 74 changes of vexation vexing changes 75 As . . . color that may cause it to lose some
of its first gloss. 77 timorous frightening 78 As . . . fire as when a
fire, having gained hold by negligence at night 83.1 at a window
(This stage direction, from the Quarto, probably calls for an appearance
on the gallery above and rearstage.) 88 Zounds By His (Christ's)
wounds 91 tupping covering, copulating with. (Said of sheep.)
92 snorting snoring 93 the devil (The devil was conventionally pictured as black.) 102 distemp'ring intoxicating 103 Upon malicious
bravery with hostile intent to defy me 104 start startle, disrupt

RODERIGO
  Sir, sir, sir—
BRABANTIO   But thou must needs be sure
  My spirits and my place have in their power   106
  To make this bitter to thee.
RODERIGO   Patience, good sir.
BRABANTIO
  What tell'st thou me of robbing? This is Venice;
  My house is not a grange.
RODERIGO   Most grave Brabantio,   109
  In simple and pure soul I come to you.   110
IAGO   Zounds, sir, you are one of those that will not
  serve God if the devil bid you. Because we come to do
  you service and you think we are ruffians, you'll have
  your daughter covered with a Barbary horse; you'll   114
  have your nephews neigh to you; you'll have coursers   115
  for cousins and jennets for germans.   116
BRABANTIO   What profane wretch art thou?
IAGO   I am one, sir, that comes to tell you your daughter
  and the Moor are now making the beast with two
  backs.
BRABANTIO
  Thou art a villain.
IAGO   You are—a senator.   121
BRABANTIO
  This thou shalt answer. I know thee, Roderigo.   122
RODERIGO
  Sir, I will answer anything. But I beseech you,
  If't be your pleasure and most wise consent—
  As partly I find it is—that your fair daughter,   124
  At this odd-even and dull watch o'th' night,   126
  Transported with no worse nor better guard   127
  But with a knave of common hire, a gondolier,   128
  To the gross clasps of a lascivious Moor—
  If this be known to you and your allowance   130
  We then have done you bold and saucy wrongs.   131
  But if you know not this, my manners tell me
  We have your wrong rebuke. Do not believe
  That, from the sense of all civility,   134
  I thus would play and trifle with your reverence.   135
  Your daughter, if you have not given her leave,
  I say again, hath made a gross revolt,
  Tying her duty, beauty, wit, and fortunes   138
  In an extravagant and wheeling stranger   139
  Of here and everywhere. Straight satisfy yourself.   140

  If she be in her chamber or your house,
  Let loose on me the justice of the state
  For thus deluding you.
BRABANTIO [calling]   Strike on the tinder, ho!   144
  Give me a taper! Call up all my people!
  This accident is not unlike my dream.   146
  Belief of it oppresses me already.
  Light, I say, light!   Exit [above].
IAGO   Farewell, for I must leave you.
  It seems not meet nor wholesome to my place   149
  To be produced—as, if I stay, I shall—   150
  Against the Moor. For I do know the state,
  However this may gall him with some check,   152
  Cannot with safety cast him, for he's embarked   153
  With such loud reason to the Cyprus wars,   154
  Which even now stands in act, that, for their souls,   155
  Another of his fathom they have none   156
  To lead their business; in which regard,   157
  Though I do hate him as I do hell pains,
  Yet for necessity of present life   159
  I must show out a flag and sign of love,
  Which is indeed but sign. That you shall surely find
    him,
  Lead to the Sagittary the raisèd search,   162
  And there will I be with him. So farewell.   Exit. 163

  Enter [below] Brabantio [in his nightgown] with
    servants and torches.

BRABANTIO
  It is too true an evil. Gone she is;
  And what's to come of my despisèd time   165
  Is naught but bitterness. Now, Roderigo,
  Where didst thou see her?—Oh, unhappy girl!—
  With the Moor, say'st thou?—Who would be a father!—
  How didst thou know 'twas she?—Oh, she deceives
    me
  Past thought!—What said she to you?—Get more
    tapers.
  Raise all my kindred.—Are they married, think you?
RODERIGO   Truly, I think they are.
BRABANTIO
  Oh, heaven! How got she out? Oh, treason of the
    blood!
  Fathers, from hence trust not your daughters' minds
  By what you see them act. Is there not charms   175
  By which the property of youth and maidhood   176

---

106 My . . . power my temperament and my authority of office have
it in their power   109 grange isolated country house.   110 simple
sincere   114 Barbary from northern Africa (and hence associated
with Othello)   115 nephews i.e., grandsons   115–16 you'll . . . germans you'll consent to have powerful horses for kinfolks and small
Spanish horses for near relatives.   121 a senator (Said with mock
politeness, as though the word itself were an insult.)   122 answer be
held accountable for.   124 wise well-informed   126 At . . . night at
this hour that is between day and night, neither the one nor the other
127 with by   128 But with a knave than by a low fellow, a servant
130 and your allowance and has your permission   131 saucy
insolent   134 from contrary to.   civility good manners, decency
135 your reverence (1) the respect due to you (2) Your Reverence.
138 wit intelligence   139–40 In . . . everywhere to a wandering and
vagabond foreigner of uncertain origins.   140 Straight Straightaway

144 tinder charred linen ignited by a spark from flint and steel, used
to light torches or tapers (lines 145, 170)   146 accident occurrence,
event   149 meet fitting.   place position (as ensign)   150 produced
produced (as a witness)   152 gall rub; oppress.   check rebuke
153 cast dismiss.   embarked engaged   154 loud urgent   155 stands
in act have started.   for their souls to save their souls   156 fathom
i.e., ability, depth of experience   157 in which regard out of regard
for which   159 life livelihood   162 Sagittary (An inn or house
where Othello and Desdemona are staying, named for its sign of
Sagittarius, or Centaur.)   raisèd search search party roused out of
sleep   163.1 nightgown dressing gown. (This costuming is specified
in the Quarto text.)   165 time i.e., remainder of life   175 charms
spells   176 property special quality, nature

May be abused? Have you not read, Roderigo,   177
Of some such thing?

RODERIGO   Yes, sir, I have indeed.

BRABANTIO
Call up my brother.—Oh, would you had had her!—
Some one way, some another.—Do you know
Where we may apprehend her and the Moor?

RODERIGO
I think I can discover him, if you please   182
To get good guard and go along with me.

BRABANTIO
Pray you, lead on. At every house I'll call;
I may command at most.—Get weapons, ho!   185
And raise some special officers of night.—
On, good Roderigo. I will deserve your pains.   187

                                          Exeunt.

❖

1.2

Enter Othello, Iago, attendants with torches.

IAGO
Though in the trade of war I have slain men,
Yet do I hold it very stuff o'th' conscience   2
To do no contrived murder. I lack iniquity   3
Sometimes to do me service. Nine or ten times
I had thought t'have yerked him here under the ribs.   5

OTHELLO
'Tis better as it is.

IAGO   Nay, but he prated,
And spoke such scurvy and provoking terms
Against your honor
That, with the little godliness I have,
I did full hard forbear him. But, I pray you, sir,   10
Are you fast married? Be assured of this,
That the magnifico is much beloved,   12
And hath in his effect a voice potential   13
As double as the Duke's. He will divorce you,
Or put upon you what restraint or grievance
The law, with all his might to enforce it on,
Will give him cable.

OTHELLO   Let him do his spite.   17
My services which I have done the seigniory   18
Shall out-tongue his complaints. 'Tis yet to know—   19
Which, when I know that boasting is an honor,
I shall promulgate—I fetch my life and being
From men of royal siege, and my demerits   22

May speak unbonneted to as proud a fortune   23
As this that I have reached. For know, Iago,
But that I love the gentle Desdemona,
I would not my unhousèd free condition   26
Put into circumscription and confine   27
For the seas' worth. But look, what lights come yond?   28

Enter Cassio [and officers] with torches.

IAGO
Those are the raisèd father and his friends.
You were best go in.

OTHELLO   Not I. I must be found.
My parts, my title, and my perfect soul   31
Shall manifest me rightly. Is it they?

IAGO   By Janus, I think no.   33

OTHELLO
The servants of the Duke? And my lieutenant?
The goodness of the night upon you, friends!
What is the news?

CASSIO   The Duke does greet you, General,
And he requires your haste-post-haste appearance
Even on the instant.

OTHELLO   What is the matter, think you?

CASSIO
Something from Cyprus, as I may divine.   39
It is a business of some heat. The galleys   40
Have sent a dozen sequent messengers   41
This very night at one another's heels,
And many of the consuls, raised and met,   43
Are at the Duke's already. You have been hotly called
   for;
When, being not at your lodging to be found,
The Senate hath sent about three several quests   46
To search you out.

OTHELLO   'Tis well I am found by you.
I will but spend a word here in the house
And go with you.   *[Exit.]*

CASSIO   Ancient, what makes he here?   49

IAGO
Faith, he tonight hath boarded a land carrack.   50
If it prove lawful prize, he's made forever.   51

CASSIO
I do not understand.

IAGO   He's married.

CASSIO   To who?

[Enter Othello.]

---

177 **abused** deceived.   182 **discover** reveal, uncover   185 **command** demand assistance   187 **deserve** show gratitude for
1.2. Location: Venice. Another street, before Othello's lodgings.
2 **very stuff** essence, basic material. (Continuing the metaphor of *trade* from line 1.)   3 **contrived** premeditated   5 **yerked** stabbed. **him** i.e., Roderigo   10 **I . . . him** I restrained myself with great difficulty from assaulting him.   12 **magnifico** Venetian grandee, i.e., Brabantio   13 **in his effect** at his command.   **potential** powerful   17 **cable** i.e., scope.   18 **seigniory** Venetian government   19 **yet to know** not yet widely known   22 **siege** i.e., rank. (Literally, a seat used by a person of distinction.)   **demerits** deserts

23 **unbonneted** without removing the hat, i.e., on equal terms (? Or "with hat off," "in all due modesty.")   26 **unhoused** unconfined, undomesticated   27 **circumscription and confine** restriction and confinement   28 **the seas' worth** all the riches at the bottom of the sea.   28.1 **officers** (The Quarto text specifies, "*Enter Cassio with lights, Officers, and torches.*")   31 **My . . . soul** My natural gifts, my position or reputation, and my unflawed conscience   33 **Janus** Roman two-faced god of beginnings   39 **divine** guess.   40 **heat** urgency.   41 **sequent** successive   43 **consuls** senators   46 **about** all over the city. **several** separate   49 **makes** does   50 **boarded** gone aboard and seized as an act of piracy. (With sexual suggestion.)   **carrack** large merchant ship.   51 **prize** booty

IAGO
    Marry, to—Come, Captain, will you go?   53

OTHELLO   Have with you.   54

CASSIO
    Here comes another troop to seek for you.   55

        Enter Brabantio, Roderigo, with officers and
        torches.

IAGO
    It is Brabantio. General, be advised.   56
    He comes to bad intent.

OTHELLO   Holla! Stand there!

RODERIGO
    Signor, it is the Moor.

BRABANTIO   Down with him, thief!
        [*They draw on both sides.*]

IAGO
    You, Roderigo! Come, sir, I am for you.

OTHELLO
    Keep up your bright swords, for the dew will rust
        them.   60
    Good signor, you shall more command with years
    Than with your weapons.

BRABANTIO
    O thou foul thief, where hast thou stowed my
        daughter?
    Damned as thou art, thou hast enchanted her!
    For I'll refer me to all things of sense,   65
    If she in chains of magic were not bound
    Whether a maid so tender, fair, and happy,
    So opposite to marriage that she shunned
    The wealthy curlèd darlings of our nation,
    Would ever have, t'incur a general mock,
    Run from her guardage to the sooty bosom   71
    Of such a thing as thou—to fear, not to delight.
    Judge me the world if 'tis not gross in sense   73
    That thou hast practiced on her with foul charms,
    Abused her delicate youth with drugs or minerals   75
    That weakens motion. I'll have't disputed on;   76
    'Tis probable and palpable to thinking.
    I therefore apprehend and do attach thee   78
    For an abuser of the world, a practicer   79
    Of arts inhibited and out of warrant.—   80
    Lay hold upon him! If he do resist,
    Subdue him at his peril.

OTHELLO   Hold your hands,
    Both you of my inclining and the rest.   83
    Were it my cue to fight, I should have known it
    Without a prompter.—Whither will you that I go
    To answer this your charge?

BRABANTIO   To prison, till fit time
    Of law and course of direct session   88
    Call thee to answer.

OTHELLO   What if I do obey?
    How may the Duke be therewith satisfied,
    Whose messengers are here about my side
    Upon some present business of the state
    To bring me to him?

OFFICER   'Tis true, most worthy signor.
    The Duke's in council, and your noble self,
    I am sure, is sent for.

BRABANTIO   How? The Duke in council?
    In this time of the night? Bring him away.   96
    Mine's not an idle cause. The Duke himself,   97
    Or any of my brothers of the state,
    Cannot but feel this wrong as 'twere their own;
    For if such actions may have passage free,   100
    Bondslaves and pagans shall our statesmen be.
        Exeunt.

❖

1.3

    Enter Duke [and] Senators [and sit at a table, with
    lights], and Officers. [The Duke and Senators
    are reading dispatches.]

DUKE
    There is no composition in these news   1
    That gives them credit.

FIRST SENATOR   Indeed, they are disproportioned.   3
    My letters say a hundred and seven galleys.

DUKE
    And mine, a hundred forty.

SECOND SENATOR   And mine, two hundred.
    But though they jump not on a just account—   6
    As in these cases, where the aim reports   7
    'Tis oft with difference—yet do they all confirm
    A Turkish fleet, and bearing up to Cyprus.

DUKE
    Nay, it is possible enough to judgment.
    I do not so secure me in the error   11
    But the main article I do approve   12
    In fearful sense.

SAILOR (*within*)   What ho, what ho, what ho!

        Enter Sailor.

OFFICER   A messenger from the galleys.

DUKE   Now, what's the business?

---

53 Marry (An oath, originally "by the Virgin Mary"; here used with wordplay on *married.*) **54 Have with you** i.e., Let's go. **55.1–2** *officers and torches* (The Quarto text calls for *"others with lights and weapons."*) **56 be advised** be on your guard. **60 Keep up** Keep in the sheath **65 I'll . . . sense** I'll submit my case to one and all **71 guardage** guardianship **73 gross in sense** obvious **75 minerals** i.e., poisons **76 weakens motion** impair the vital faculties. **disputed on** argued in court by professional counsel, debated by experts **78 attach** arrest **79 abuser** deceiver **80 arts inhibited** prohibited arts, black magic. **out of warrant** illegal. **83 inclining** following, party

88 course of direct session regular or specially convened legal proceedings **96 away** right along. **97 idle** trifling **100 may . . . free** are allowed to go unchecked
1.3. Location: Venice. A council chamber.
0.1–2 *Enter . . . Officers* (The Quarto text calls for the Duke and senators to *"set at a Table with lights and Attendants."*) **1 composition** consistency **3 disproportioned** inconsistent. **6 jump** agree. **just** exact **7 the aim** conjecture **11–12 I do not . . . approve** I do not take such (false) comfort in the discrepancies that I fail to perceive the main point, i.e., that the Turkish fleet is threatening

SAILOR

The Turkish preparation makes for Rhodes.   16
So was I bid report here to the state
By Signor Angelo.

DUKE

How say you by this change?

FIRST SENATOR   This cannot be   19
By no assay of reason. 'Tis a pageant   20
To keep us in false gaze. When we consider   21
Th'importancy of Cyprus to the Turk,
And let ourselves again but understand
That, as it more concerns the Turk than Rhodes,
So may he with more facile question bear it,   25
For that it stands not in such warlike brace,   26
But altogether lacks th'abilities   27
That Rhodes is dressed in—if we make thought of this,   28
We must not think the Turk is so unskillful   29
To leave that latest which concerns him first,   30
Neglecting an attempt of ease and gain
To wake and wage a danger profitless.   32

DUKE

Nay, in all confidence, he's not for Rhodes.

OFFICER   Here is more news.

Enter a Messenger.

MESSENGER

The Ottomites, reverend and gracious,
Steering with due course toward the isle of Rhodes,
Have there injointed them with an after fleet.   37

FIRST SENATOR

Ay, so I thought. How many, as you guess?

MESSENGER

Of thirty sail; and now they do restem   39
Their backward course, bearing with frank
appearance   40
Their purposes toward Cyprus. Signor Montano,
Your trusty and most valiant servitor,   42
With his free duty recommends you thus,   43
And prays you to believe him.

DUKE   'Tis certain then for Cyprus.
Marcus Luccicos, is not he in town?

FIRST SENATOR   He's now in Florence.

DUKE

Write from us to him, post-post-haste. Dispatch.

FIRST SENATOR

Here comes Brabantio and the valiant Moor.

Enter Brabantio, Othello, Cassio, Iago, Roderigo, and officers.

DUKE

Valiant Othello, we must straight employ you   50
Against the general enemy Ottoman.   51
[*To Brabantio*] I did not see you; welcome, gentle
signor.   52
We lacked your counsel and your help tonight.

BRABANTIO

So did I yours. Good Your Grace, pardon me;
Neither my place nor aught I heard of business   55
Hath raised me from my bed, nor doth the general
care
Take hold on me, for my particular grief   57
Is of so floodgate and o'erbearing nature   58
That it engluts and swallows other sorrows   59
And it is still itself.

DUKE   Why, what's the matter?   60

BRABANTIO

My daughter! Oh, my daughter!

DUKE AND SENATORS   Dead?

BRABANTIO   Ay, to me.
She is abused, stol'n from me, and corrupted   62
By spells and medicines bought of mountebanks;
For nature so preposterously to err,
Being not deficient, blind, or lame of sense,   65
Sans witchcraft could not.   66

DUKE

Whoe'er he be that in this foul proceeding
Hath thus beguiled your daughter of herself,
And you of her, the bloody book of law
You shall yourself read in the bitter letter
After your own sense—yea, though our proper son   71
Stood in your action.

BRABANTIO   Humbly I thank Your Grace.   72
Here is the man, this Moor, whom now it seems
Your special mandate for the state affairs
Hath hither brought.

ALL   We are very sorry for't.

DUKE [*to Othello*]

What, in your own part, can you say to this?

BRABANTIO   Nothing, but this is so.

OTHELLO

Most potent, grave, and reverend signors,
My very noble and approved good masters: 79
That I have ta'en away this old man's daughter,
It is most true; true, I have married her.
The very head and front of my offending   82
Hath this extent, no more. Rude am I in my speech,   83
And little blessed with the soft phrase of peace;
For since these arms of mine had seven years' pith,   85

16 **preparation** fleet prepared for battle   19 **by** about   20 **assay** test.
pageant mere show   21 **in false gaze** looking the wrong way.   25 **So
may . . . it** so also he (the Turk) can more easily capture it (Cyprus)
26 **For that** since.   **brace** state of defense   27 **th'abilities** the means
of self-defense   28 **dressed in** equipped with   29 **unskillful** deficient in judgment   30 **latest** last   32 **wake and wage** stir up and risk
37 **injointed them** joined themselves.   **after** second, following
39–40 **restem . . . course** retrace their original course   40 **frank
appearance** undisguised intent   42 **servitor** officer under your command   43 **free duty** freely given and loyal service.   **recommends**
commends himself and reports to

50 **straight** straightaway   51 **general enemy** universal enemy to all
Christendom   52 **gentle** noble   55 **place** official position   57 **particular** personal   58 **floodgate** i.e., overwhelming (as when floodgates
are opened)   59 **engluts** engulfs   60 **is still itself** remains undimin-
ished.   62 **abused** deceived   65 **deficient** defective.   **lame of sense**
deficient in sensory perception   66 **Sans** without   71 **After . . .
sense** according to your own interpretation.   **our proper** my own
72 **Stood . . . action** were under your accusation.   79 **approved**
proved, esteemed   82 **head and front** height and breadth, entire
extent   83 **Rude** Unpolished   85 **since . . . pith** i.e., since I was
seven. (*Pith* means "strength, vigor.")

Till now some nine moons wasted, they have used   86
Their dearest action in the tented field;   87
And little of this great world can I speak
More than pertains to feats of broils and battle,
And therefore little shall I grace my cause
In speaking for myself. Yet, by your gracious patience,
I will a round unvarnished tale deliver   92
Of my whole course of love—what drugs, what
     charms,
What conjuration, and what mighty magic,
For such proceeding I am charged withal,   95
I won his daughter.
BRABANTIO   A maiden never bold;
Of spirit so still and quiet that her motion   97
Blushed at herself; and she, in spite of nature,   98
Of years, of country, credit, everything,   99
To fall in love with what she feared to look on!
It is a judgment maimed and most imperfect
That will confess perfection so could err   102
Against all rules of nature, and must be driven
To find out practices of cunning hell   104
Why this should be. I therefore vouch again   105
That with some mixtures powerful o'er the blood,   106
Or with some dram conjured to this effect,   107
He wrought upon her.
DUKE   To vouch this is no proof,
Without more wider and more overt test   109
Than these thin habits and poor likelihoods   110
Of modern seeming do prefer against him.   111
FIRST SENATOR   But Othello, speak.
Did you by indirect and forcèd courses   113
Subdue and poison this young maid's affections?
Or came it by request and such fair question   115
As soul to soul affordeth?
OTHELLO   I do beseech you,
Send for the lady to the Sagittary
And let her speak of me before her father.
If you do find me foul in her report,
The trust, the office I do hold of you
Not only take away, but let your sentence
Even fall upon my life.
DUKE   Fetch Desdemona hither.
OTHELLO   [to Iago]
Ancient, conduct them. You best know the place.
          [Exeunt Iago and attendants.]
And, till she come, as truly as to heaven
I do confess the vices of my blood,   125

So justly to your grave ears I'll present   126
How I did thrive in this fair lady's love,
And she in mine.
DUKE   Say it, Othello.
OTHELLO
Her father loved me, oft invited me,
Still questioned me the story of my life   131
From year to year—the battles, sieges, fortunes
That I have passed.
I ran it through, even from my boyish days
To th' very moment that he bade me tell it,
Wherein I spoke of most disastrous chances,
Of moving accidents by flood and field,   137
Of hairbreadth scapes i'th'imminent deadly breach,   138
Of being taken by the insolent foe
And sold to slavery, of my redemption thence,
And portance in my travels' history,   141
Wherein of antres vast and deserts idle,   142
Rough quarries, rocks, and hills whose heads touch
     heaven,   143
It was my hint to speak—such was my process—   144
And of the Cannibals that each other eat,
The Anthropophagi, and men whose heads   146
Do grow beneath their shoulders. These things to hear
Would Desdemona seriously incline;
But still the house affairs would draw her thence,
Which ever as she could with haste dispatch
She'd come again, and with a greedy ear
Devour up my discourse. Which I, observing,
Took once a pliant hour, and found good means   153
To draw from her a prayer of earnest heart
That I would all my pilgrimage dilate,   155
Whereof by parcels she had something heard,   156
But not intentively. I did consent,   157
And often did beguile her of her tears,
When I did speak of some distressful stroke
That my youth suffered. My story being done,
She gave me for my pains a world of sighs.
She swore, in faith, 'twas strange, 'twas passing
     strange,   162
'Twas pitiful, 'twas wondrous pitiful.
She wished she had not heard it, yet she wished
That heaven had made her such a man. She thanked
     me,   165
And bade me, if I had a friend that loved her,
I should but teach him how to tell my story,
And that would woo her. Upon this hint I spake.   168
She loved me for the dangers I had passed,
And I loved her that she did pity them.

---

86 Till . . . wasted until some nine months ago (since when Othello has evidently not been on active duty, but in Venice)   87 dearest most valuable   92 round plain   95 withal with   97–8 her . . . herself i.e., she blushed easily at herself. (*Motion* can suggest the impulse of the soul or of the emotions, or physical movement.)   99 years i.e., difference in age.   credit virtuous reputation   102 confess concede (that)   104 practices plots   105 vouch assert   106 blood passions   107 dram . . . effect dose made by magical spells to have this effect   109 more wider fuller.   test testimony   110 habits garments, i.e., appearances.   poor likelihoods weak inferences   111 modern seeming commonplace assumption.   prefer bring forth   113 forcèd courses means used against her will   115 question conversation   125 blood passions, human nature

126 justly truthfully, accurately   131 Still continually   137 moving accidents stirring happenings   138 i'th'imminent . . . breach in death-threatening gaps made in a fortification   141 portance conduct   142 antres caverns.   idle barren, desolate   143 Rough quarries rugged rock formations   144 hint occasion, opportunity   146 Anthropophagi man-eaters. (A term from Pliny's *Natural History*.)   153 pliant well-suiting   155 dilate relate in detail   156 by parcels piecemeal   157 intentively with full attention, continuously.   162 passing exceedingly   165 made her (1) created her to be (2) made for her   168 hint opportunity. (Othello does not necessarily mean that she was dropping hints.)

This only is the witchcraft I have used.
Here comes the lady. Let her witness it.

Enter Desdemona, Iago, [and] attendants.

DUKE
I think this tale would win my daughter too.
Good Brabantio,
Take up this mangled matter at the best.   175
Men do their broken weapons rather use
Than their bare hands.

BRABANTIO   I pray you, hear her speak.
If she confess that she was half the wooer,
Destruction on my head if my bad blame
Light on the man!—Come hither, gentle mistress.
Do you perceive in all this noble company
Where most you owe obedience?

DESDEMONA   My noble father,
I do perceive here a divided duty.
To you I am bound for life and education;   184
My life and education both do learn me   185
How to respect you. You are the lord of duty;   186
I am hitherto your daughter. But here's my husband,
And so much duty as my mother showed
To you, preferring you before her father,
So much I challenge that I may profess   190
Due to the Moor my lord.

BRABANTIO   God be with you! I have done.
Please it Your Grace, on to the state affairs.
I had rather to adopt a child than get it.   194
Come hither, Moor.   [*He joins the hands of Othello*
                                  and Desdemona.]
I here do give thee that with all my heart   196
Which, but thou hast already, with all my heart   197
I would keep from thee.—For your sake, jewel,   198
I am glad at soul I have no other child,
For thy escape would teach me tyranny,   200
To hang clogs on them.—I have done, my lord.   201

DUKE
Let me speak like yourself, and lay a sentence   202
Which, as a grece or step, may help these lovers   203
Into your favor.
When remedies are past, the griefs are ended   205
By seeing the worst, which late on hopes depended.   206
To mourn a mischief that is past and gone   207
Is the next way to draw new mischief on.   208
What cannot be preserved when fortune takes,   209
Patience her injury a mock'ry makes.   210

The robbed that smiles steals something from the thief;
He robs himself that spends a bootless grief.   212

BRABANTIO
So let the Turk of Cyprus us beguile,
We lose it not, so long as we can smile.
He bears the sentence well that nothing bears   215
But the free comfort which from thence he hears,   216
But he bears both the sentence and the sorrow   217
That, to pay grief, must of poor patience borrow.   218
These sentences, to sugar or to gall,   219
Being strong on both sides, are equivocal.   220
But words are words. I never yet did hear
That the bruisèd heart was piercèd through the ear.   222
I humbly beseech you, proceed to th'affairs of state.

DUKE   The Turk with a most mighty preparation makes
for Cyprus. Othello, the fortitude of the place is best   225
known to you; and though we have there a substitute   226
of most allowed sufficiency, yet opinion, a sovereign   227
mistress of effects, throws a more safer voice on you.   228
You must therefore be content to slubber the gloss of   229
your new fortunes with this more stubborn and   230
boisterous expedition.   231

OTHELLO
The tyrant custom, most grave senators,
Hath made the flinty and steel couch of war
My thrice-driven bed of down. I do agnize   234
A natural and prompt alacrity
I find in hardness, and do undertake   236
These present wars against the Ottomites.
Most humbly therefore bending to your state,   238
I crave fit disposition for my wife,
Due reference of place and exhibition,   240
With such accommodation and besort   241
As levels with her breeding.   242

DUKE
Why, at her father's.

BRABANTIO   I will not have it so.

OTHELLO
Nor I.

DESDEMONA   Nor I. I would not there reside,
To put my father in impatient thoughts
By being in his eye. Most gracious Duke,
To my unfolding lend your prosperous ear,   247

---

175 **Take . . . best** make the best of a bad bargain.   184 **education** upbringing   185 **learn** teach   186 **of duty** to whom duty is due
190 **challenge** claim   194 **get** beget   196 **with all my heart** wherein my whole affection has been engaged   197 **with all my heart** willingly, gladly   198 **For your sake** Because of you   200 **escape** elopement   201 **clogs** (Literally, blocks of wood fastened to the legs of criminals or animals to inhibit escape.)   202 **like yourself** i.e., as you would, in your proper temper.   **lay a sentence** apply a maxim
203 **grece** step   205–6 **When . . . depended** When all hope of remedy is past, our sorrows are ended by realizing that the worst has already happened which lately we hoped would not happen.   207 **mischief** misfortune, injury   208 **next** nearest   209–10 **What . . . makes** When fortune takes away what cannot be saved, patience makes a mockery of fortune's wrongdoing.

212 **spends a bootless grief** indulges in unavailing grief.   215–18 **He bears . . . borrow** A person can easily be comforted by your maxim that enjoys its platitudinous comfort without having to experience the misfortune that occasions sorrow, but anyone whose grief bankrupts his poor patience is left with your saying and his sorrow, too. (*Bears the sentence* also plays on the meaning, "receives judicial sentence.")
219–20 **These . . . equivocal** These fine maxims are equivocal, being equally appropriate to happiness or bitterness.   222 **piercèd . . . ear** relieved by mere words reaching it through the ear.   225 **fortitude** strength   226 **substitute** deputy   227 **allowed** acknowledged
227–8 **opinion . . . on you** general opinion, an important determiner of affairs, chooses you as the best man.   229 **slubber** soil, sully
230–1 **stubborn . . . expedition** rough and violent expedition, for which haste is needed.   234 **thrice-driven** thrice sifted, winnowed.   **agnize** know in myself, acknowledge   236 **hardness** hardship   238 **bending . . . state** bowing or kneeling to your authority   240–2 **Due . . . breeding** proper respect for her place (as my wife) and maintenance, with such suitable provision and attendance as befits her upbringing.
247 **my unfolding** what I shall unfold or say.   **prosperous** favorable

And let me find a charter in your voice,   248
T'assist my simpleness.
DUKE   What would you, Desdemona?
DESDEMONA
That I did love the Moor to live with him,
My downright violence and storm of fortunes   252
May trumpet to the world. My heart's subdued
Even to the very quality of my lord.   254
I saw Othello's visage in his mind,
And to his honors and his valiant parts   256
Did I my soul and fortunes consecrate.
So that, dear lords, if I be left behind
A moth of peace, and he go to the war,   259
The rites for why I love him are bereft me,   260
And I a heavy interim shall support   261
By his dear absence. Let me go with him.   262
OTHELLO   Let her have your voice.   263
Vouch with me, heaven, I therefor beg it not
To please the palate of my appetite,
Nor to comply with heat—the young affects   266
In me defunct—and proper satisfaction,   267
But to be free and bounteous to her mind.   268
And heaven defend your good souls that you think   269
I will your serious and great business scant
When she is with me. No, when light-winged toys
Of feathered Cupid seel with wanton dullness   272
My speculative and officed instruments,   273
That my disports corrupt and taint my business,   274
Let huswives make a skillet of my helm,
And all indign and base adversities   276
Make head against my estimation!   277
DUKE
Be it as you shall privately determine,
Either for her stay or going. Th'affair cries haste,
And speed must answer it.
A SENATOR   You must away tonight.
DESDEMONA
Tonight, my lord?
DUKE   This night.
OTHELLO   With all my heart.
DUKE
At nine i'th' morning here we'll meet again.
Othello, leave some officer behind,
And he shall our commission bring to you,
With such things else of quality and respect   285
As doth import you.
OTHELLO   So please Your Grace, my ancient; 286

A man he is of honesty and trust.
To his conveyance I assign my wife,
With what else needful Your Good Grace shall think
To be sent after me.
DUKE   Let it be so.
Good night to everyone. [*To Brabantio*] And, noble
    signor,
If virtue no delighted beauty lack,   292
Your son-in-law is far more fair than black.
FIRST SENATOR
Adieu, brave Moor. Use Desdemona well.
BRABANTIO
Look to her, Moor, if thou hast eyes to see.
She has deceived her father, and may thee.
            Exeunt [Duke, Brabantio, Cassio, Senators, and
                                                    officers].
OTHELLO
My life upon her faith!—Honest Iago,
My Desdemona must I leave to thee.
I prithee, let thy wife attend on her,
And bring them after in the best advantage.   300
Come, Desdemona. I have but an hour
Of love, of worldly matters and direction,   302
To spend with thee. We must obey the time.   303
                        Exit [with Desdemona].
RODERIGO   Iago—
IAGO   What say'st thou, noble heart?
RODERIGO   What will I do, think'st thou?
IAGO   Why, go to bed and sleep.
RODERIGO   I will incontinently drown myself.   308
IAGO   If thou dost, I shall never love thee after. Why,
    thou silly gentleman!
RODERIGO   It is silliness to live when to live is torment;
    and then have we a prescription to die when death is   312
    our physician.
IAGO   Oh, villainous! I have looked upon the world for   314
    four times seven years, and, since I could distinguish
    betwixt a benefit and an injury, I never found man
    that knew how to love himself. Ere I would say I
    would drown myself for the love of a guinea hen, I   318
    would change my humanity with a baboon.   319
RODERIGO   What should I do? I confess it is my shame
    to be so fond, but it is not in my virtue to amend it.   321
IAGO   Virtue? A fig! 'Tis in ourselves that we are thus or 322
    thus. Our bodies are our gardens, to the which our
    wills are gardeners; so that if we will plant nettles or
    sow lettuce, set hyssop and weed up thyme, supply it   325
    with one gender of herbs or distract it with many,   326
    either to have it sterile with idleness or manured with 327

industry—why, the power and corrigible authority of 328
this lies in our wills. If the beam of our lives had not 329
one scale of reason to poise another of sensuality, the 330
blood and baseness of our natures would conduct us 331
to most preposterous conclusions. But we have reason
to cool our raging motions, our carnal stings, our 333
unbitted lusts, whereof I take this that you call love to 334
be a sect or scion. 335

RODERIGO   It cannot be.

IAGO   It is merely a lust of the blood and a permission
of the will. Come, be a man. Drown thyself? Drown
cats and blind puppies. I have professed me thy friend, 339
and I confess me knit to thy deserving with cables of
perdurable toughness. I could never better stead thee 341
than now. Put money in thy purse. Follow thou the
wars; defeat thy favor with an usurped beard. I say, 343
put money in thy purse. It cannot be long that Desdemona should continue her love to the Moor—put
money in thy purse—nor he his to her. It was a violent commencement in her, and thou shalt see an an- 347
swerable sequestration—put but money in thy purse. 348
These Moors are changeable in their wills—fill thy 349
purse with money. The food that to him now is as
luscious as locusts shall be to him shortly as bitter as 351
coloquintida. She must change for youth; when she is 352
sated with his body, she will find the error of her
choice. She must have change, she must. Therefore
put money in thy purse. If thou wilt needs damn thyself, do it a more delicate way than drowning. Make 356
all the money thou canst. If sanctimony and a frail vow 357
betwixt an erring barbarian and a supersubtle Vene- 358
tian be not too hard for my wits and all the tribe of
hell, thou shalt enjoy her. Therefore make money. A
pox of drowning thyself! It is clean out of the way. 361
Seek thou rather to be hanged in compassing thy joy 362
than to be drowned and go without her.

RODERIGO   Wilt thou be fast to my hopes if I depend on 364
the issue? 365

IAGO   Thou art sure of me. Go, make money. I have
told thee often, and I retell thee again and again, I hate
the Moor. My cause is hearted; thine hath no less rea- 368
son. Let us be conjunctive in our revenge against him. 369
If thou canst cuckold him, thou dost thyself a pleasure,
me a sport. There are many events in the womb of
time which will be delivered. Traverse, go, provide thy 372
money. We will have more of this tomorrow. Adieu.

RODERIGO   Where shall we meet i'th' morning?

IAGO   At my lodging.

RODERIGO   I'll be with thee betimes. [*He starts to leave.*] 376

IAGO   Go to, farewell.—Do you hear, Roderigo? 377

RODERIGO   What say you?

IAGO   No more of drowning, do you hear?

RODERIGO   I am changed.

IAGO   Go to, farewell. Put money enough in your
purse.

RODERIGO   I'll sell all my land.   *Exit.*

IAGO
Thus do I ever make my fool my purse;
For I mine own gained knowledge should profane
If I would time expend with such a snipe 386
But for my sport and profit. I hate the Moor;
And it is thought abroad that twixt my sheets 388
He's done my office. I know not if't be true; 389
But I, for mere suspicion in that kind,
Will do as if for surety. He holds me well; 391
The better shall my purpose work on him.
Cassio's a proper man. Let me see now: 393
To get his place and to plume up my will 394
In double knavery—How, how?—Let's see:
After some time, to abuse Othello's ear 396
That he is too familiar with his wife. 397
He hath a person and a smooth dispose 398
To be suspected, framed to make women false. 399
The Moor is of a free and open nature, 400
That thinks men honest that but seem to be so,
And will as tenderly be led by the nose 402
As asses are.
I have't. It is engendered. Hell and night
Must bring this monstrous birth to the world's light.
                                              [*Exit.*]

❖

2.1

Enter Montano and two Gentlemen.

MONTANO
What from the cape can you discern at sea?

FIRST GENTLEMAN
Nothing at all. It is a high-wrought flood. 2
I cannot, twixt the heaven and the main, 3
Descry a sail.

MONTANO
Methinks the wind hath spoke aloud at land;
A fuller blast ne'er shook our battlements.
If it hath ruffianed so upon the sea, 7

---

328 **corrigible authority** power to correct   329 **beam** balance
330 **poise** counterbalance   331 **blood** natural passions   333 **motions**
appetites   334 **unbitted** unbridled, uncontrolled   335 **sect or scion**
cutting or offshoot.   339 **blind** i.e., newborn and helpless   341 **perdurable** very durable.   **stead** assist   343 **defeat thy favor** disguise
your face.   **usurped** (The suggestion is that Roderigo is not man
enough to have a beard of his own.)   347–8 **an answerable sequestration** a corresponding cutting off or estrangement   349 **wills** carnal
appetites   351 **locusts** fruit of the carob tree (see Matthew 3:4), or
perhaps honeysuckle   352 **coloquintida** colocynth or bitter apple, a
purgative.   356 **Make** Raise, collect   357 **sanctimony** (1) an aura of
goodness (2) love-worship   358 **erring** wandering, vagabond,
unsteady   361 **clean . . . way** entirely unsuitable as a course of action.
362 **compassing** encompassing, embracing   364 **fast** true   365 **issue**
(successful) outcome.   368 **hearted** fixed in the heart, heartfelt
369 **conjunctive** united   372 **Traverse** (A military marching term.)

376 **betimes** early.   377 **Go to** (An expression of impatience or jolly-
ing along others.)   386 **snipe** woodcock, i.e., fool   388 **it is thought
abroad** it is rumored   389 **my office** i.e., my sexual function as husband.   391 **do . . . surety** act as if on certain knowledge.   **holds me
well** regards me favorably   393 **proper** handsome   394 **plume up**
put a feather in the cap of, i.e., glorify, gratify   396 **abuse** deceive
397 **he** Cassio.   **his** Othello's   398 **dispose** disposition   399 **framed**
formed, made   400 **free and open** frank and unsuspecting   402 **tenderly** readily
2.1. **Location:** A seaport in Cyprus. An open place near the quay.
2 **high-wrought flood** very agitated sea.   3 **main** ocean. (Also at line
41.)   7 **ruffianed** raged

What ribs of oak, when mountains melt on them, 8
Can hold the mortise? What shall we hear of this? 9

SECOND GENTLEMAN
A segregation of the Turkish fleet. 10
For do but stand upon the foaming shore,
The chidden billow seems to pelt the clouds; 12
The wind-shaked surge, with high and monstrous
mane, 13
Seems to cast water on the burning Bear 14
And quench the guards of th'ever-fixèd pole.
I never did like molestation view 16
On the enchafèd flood. 17

MONTANO   If that the Turkish fleet 18
Be not ensheltered and embayed, they are drowned; 19
It is impossible to bear it out. 20

Enter a [Third] Gentleman.

THIRD GENTLEMAN   News, lads! Our wars are done.
The desperate tempest hath so banged the Turks
That their designment halts. A noble ship of Venice 23
Hath seen a grievous wreck and sufferance 24
On most part of their fleet.

MONTANO   How? Is this true?

THIRD GENTLEMAN   The ship is here put in,
A Veronesa; Michael Cassio, 28
Lieutenant to the warlike Moor Othello,
Is come on shore; the Moor himself at sea,
And is in full commission here for Cyprus.

MONTANO
I am glad on't. 'Tis a worthy governor.

THIRD GENTLEMAN
But this same Cassio, though he speak of comfort
Touching the Turkish loss, yet he looks sadly 34
And prays the Moor be safe, for they were parted
With foul and violent tempest.

MONTANO   Pray heaven he be,
For I have served him, and the man commands
Like a full soldier. Let's to the seaside, ho! 38
As well to see the vessel that's come in
As to throw out our eyes for brave Othello,
Even till we make the main and th'aerial blue 41
An indistinct regard.

THIRD GENTLEMAN   Come, let's do so, 42
For every minute is expectancy 43

Of more arrivance. 44

Enter Cassio.

CASSIO
Thanks, you the valiant of this warlike isle,
That so approve the Moor! Oh, let the heavens 46
Give him defense against the elements,
For I have lost him on a dangerous sea.

MONTANO   Is he well shipped?

CASSIO
His bark is stoutly timbered, and his pilot
Of very expert and approved allowance; 51
Therefore my hopes, not surfeited to death, 52
Stand in bold cure.

                    [A cry] within: "A sail, a sail, a sail!" 53

CASSIO   What noise?

A GENTLEMAN
The town is empty. On the brow o'th' sea 55
Stand ranks of people, and they cry "A sail!"

CASSIO
My hopes do shape him for the governor. 57

                                [A shot within.]

SECOND GENTLEMAN
They do discharge their shot of courtesy; 58
Our friends at least.

CASSIO   I pray you, sir, go forth,
And give us truth who 'tis that is arrived.

SECOND GENTLEMAN   I shall.   *Exit.*

MONTANO
But, good Lieutenant, is your general wived?

CASSIO
Most fortunately. He hath achieved a maid
That paragons description and wild fame, 64
One that excels the quirks of blazoning pens, 65
And in th'essential vesture of creation 66
Does tire the engineer.

Enter [Second] Gentleman.

                        How now? Who has put in? 67

SECOND GENTLEMAN
'Tis one Iago, ancient to the General.

CASSIO
He's had most favorable and happy speed.
Tempests themselves, high seas, and howling winds,
The guttered rocks and congregated sands— 71
Traitors ensteeped to clog the guiltless keel— 72
As having sense of beauty, do omit 73
Their mortal natures, letting go safely by 74

---

8 **mountains** i.e., of water   9 **hold the mortise** hold their joints together. (A *mortise* is the socket hollowed out in fitting timbers.) 10 **segregation** dispersal   12 **chidden** i.e., rebuked, repelled (by the shore), and thus shot into the air   13 **monstrous mane** (The surf is like the mane of a wild beast.)   14 **the burning Bear** i.e., the constellation Ursa Minor or the Little Bear, which includes the polestar (and hence regarded as the *guards of th'ever-fixèd pole* in the next line; sometimes the term *guards* is applied to the two "pointers" of the Big Bear or Dipper, which may be intended here.)   16 **like molestation** comparable disturbance   17 **enchafèd** angry   18 **If that** If   19 **embayed** sheltered by a bay   20 **bear it out** survive, weather the storm. 23 **designment halts** enterprise is crippled. (Literally, "is lame.") 24 **wreck** shipwreck.   **sufferance** damage, disaster   28 **Veronesa** from Verona (and perhaps in service with Venice)   34 **sadly** gravely 38 **full** perfect   41 **the main ... blue** the sea and the sky   42 **An indistinct regard** indistinguishable in our view.   43 **is expectancy** gives expectation

---

44 **arrivance** arrival.   46 **approve** admire, honor   51 **approved allowance** tested reputation   52–3 **not ... cure** not worn thin through repeated application or delayed fulfillment, strongly persist. 55 **brow o'th' sea** cliff-edge   57 **My ... governor** I hope and imagine this ship to be Othello's.   58 **discharge ... courtesy** fire a salute in token of respect and courtesy   64 **paragons** surpasses.   **wild fame** extravagant report   65 **quirks** witty conceits.   **blazoning** setting forth as though in heraldic language   66–7 **And in ... engineer** and in her real, God-given, beauty, (she) defeats any attempt to praise her. (An *engineer* is one who devises, here a poet.)   67 **put in** i.e., to harbor.   71 **guttered** jagged, trenched   72 **ensteeped** lying under water 73 **As** as if.   **omit** forbear to exercise   74 **mortal** deadly

The divine Desdemona.

MONTANO   What is she?

CASSIO

She that I spake of, our great captain's captain,
Left in the conduct of the bold Iago,
Whose footing here anticipates our thoughts   78
A sennight's speed. Great Jove, Othello guard,   79
And swell his sail with thine own powerful breath,
That he may bless this bay with his tall ship,   81
Make love's quick pants in Desdemona's arms,
Give renewed fire to our extinct spirits,
And bring all Cyprus comfort!

Enter Desdemona, Iago, Roderigo, and Emilia.

                                Oh, behold,
The riches of the ship is come on shore!
You men of Cyprus, let her have your knees.
          [The gentlemen make curtsy to Desdemona.]
Hail to thee, lady! And the grace of heaven
Before, behind thee, and on every hand
Enwheel thee round!

DESDEMONA   I thank you, valiant Cassio.
What tidings can you tell me of my lord?

CASSIO

He is not yet arrived, nor know I aught
But that he's well and will be shortly here.

DESDEMONA

Oh, but I fear—How lost you company?

CASSIO

The great contention of the sea and skies
Parted our fellowship.
                    (Within) "A sail, a sail!" *[A shot.]*
                    But hark. A sail!

SECOND GENTLEMAN

They give their greeting to the citadel.
This likewise is a friend.

CASSIO   See for the news.
                    [Exit Second Gentleman.]
Good Ancient, you are welcome. *[Kissing Emilia.]*
   Welcome, mistress.
Let it not gall your patience, good Iago,
That I extend my manners; 'tis my breeding   100
That gives me this bold show of courtesy.

IAGO

Sir, would she give you so much of her lips
As of her tongue she oft bestows on me,
You would have enough.

DESDEMONA   Alas, she has no speech!   105

IAGO   In faith, too much.

I find it still, when I have list to sleep.   107
Marry, before Your Ladyship, I grant,
She puts her tongue a little in her heart
And chides with thinking.

EMILIA   You have little cause to say so. 110

IAGO

Come on, come on. You are pictures out of doors,   111
Bells in your parlors, wildcats in your kitchens,   112
Saints in your injuries, devils being offended,   113
Players in your huswifery, and huswives in your beds. 114

DESDEMONA   Oh, fie upon thee, slanderer!

IAGO

Nay, it is true, or else I am a Turk.   116
You rise to play, and go to bed to work.

EMILIA

You shall not write my praise.

IAGO   No, let me not.

DESDEMONA

What wouldst write of me, if thou shouldst praise me?

IAGO

Oh, gentle lady, do not put me to't,
For I am nothing if not critical.   121

DESDEMONA

Come on, essay.—There's one gone to the harbor?   122

IAGO   Ay, madam.

DESDEMONA

I am not merry, but I do beguile
The thing I am by seeming otherwise.   125
Come, how wouldst thou praise me?

IAGO

I am about it, but indeed my invention
Comes from my pate as birdlime does from frieze—   128
It plucks out brains and all. But my Muse labors,   129
And thus she is delivered:
If she be fair and wise, fairness and wit,
The one's for use, the other useth it.   132

DESDEMONA

Well praised! How if she be black and witty?   133

IAGO

If she be black, and thereto have a wit,
She'll find a white that shall her blackness fit.   135

DESDEMONA

Worse and worse.

EMILIA   How if fair and foolish?

IAGO

She never yet was foolish that was fair,
For even her folly helped her to an heir.   138

DESDEMONA   These are old fond paradoxes to make fools 139

78–9 **Whose . . . speed** whose arrival here has happened a week sooner than we expected.   **81 tall** tall-masted   **100 extend** give scope to.
breeding training in the niceties of etiquette   **105 she has no speech**
i.e., she's not a chatterbox, as you allege.   **107 still** always.   **list**
desire   **110 with thinking** i.e., in her thoughts only.

111 **pictures out of doors** i.e., as pretty as pictures, and silently well-
behaved in public   **112 Bells** i.e., jangling, noisy, and brazen.   **in
your kitchens** i.e., in domestic affairs. (Ladies would not do the cooking.)   **113 Saints . . . injuries** i.e., putting on airs of sanctity and innocence when wronged by others   **114 Players . . . beds** play-actors at
domesticity and truly energetic only as lovers in bed.   **116 a Turk** an
infidel, not to be believed.   **121 critical** censorious.   **122 essay** try.
125 The thing I am i.e., my anxious self   **128 birdlime** sticky substance used to catch small birds.   **frieze** coarse woolen cloth
129 labors (1) exerts herself (2) prepares to deliver a child. (With a following pun on *delivered* in line 130.)   **132 The one's . . . it** i.e.,
her cleverness will make use of her beauty.   **133 black** dark-complex-
ioned, brunette   **135 She'll . . . fit** she will find a fair-complexioned
mate suited to her dark complexion. (Punning on *wight*, person, and
contrasting *white* and *black*, with suggestion of sexual coupling.)
138 folly (With added meaning of "lechery, wantonness.")   **to an
heir** i.e., to bear a child.   **139 fond** foolish

laugh i'th'alehouse. What miserable praise hast thou
for her that's foul and foolish?   141

IAGO
There's none so foul and foolish thereunto,   142
But does foul pranks which fair and wise ones do.   143

DESDEMONA   Oh, heavy ignorance! Thou praisest the worst
best. But what praise couldst thou bestow on a deserving woman indeed, one that, in the authority of her merit, did justly put on the vouch of very malice itself?   147

IAGO
She that was ever fair, and never proud,
Had tongue at will, and yet was never loud,   149
Never lacked gold and yet went never gay,   150
Fled from her wish, and yet said, "Now I may,"   151
She that being angered, her revenge being nigh,
Bade her wrong stay and her displeasure fly,   153
She that in wisdom never was so frail
To change the cod's head for the salmon's tail,   155
She that could think and ne'er disclose her mind,
See suitors following and not look behind,
She was a wight, if ever such wight were—

DESDEMONA   To do what?

IAGO
To suckle fools and chronicle small beer.   160

DESDEMONA   Oh, most lame and impotent conclusion! Do
not learn of him, Emilia, though he be thy husband.
How say you, Cassio? Is he not a most profane and   163
liberal counselor?   164

CASSIO   He speaks home, madam. You may relish him   165
more in the soldier than in the scholar.   166

[Cassio and Desdemona stand together,
conversing intimately.]

IAGO *[aside]*   He takes her by the palm. Ay, well said,   167
whisper. With as little a web as this will I ensnare as
great a fly as Cassio. Ay, smile upon her, do; I will
gyve thee in thine own courtship. You say true; 'tis so,   170
indeed. If such tricks as these strip you out of your
lieutenantry, it had been better you had not kissed
your three fingers so oft, which now again you are
most apt to play the sir in. Very good; well kissed! An   174
excellent courtesy! 'Tis so, indeed. Yet again your fingers to your lips? Would they were clyster pipes for   176
your sake! *[Trumpet within.]* The Moor! I know his
trumpet.

CASSIO   'Tis truly so.

DESDEMONA   Let's meet him and receive him.

CASSIO   Lo, where he comes!

Enter Othello and attendants.

OTHELLO
Oh, my fair warrior!

DESDEMONA   My dear Othello!

OTHELLO
It gives me wonder great as my content
To see you here before me. O my soul's joy,
If after every tempest come such calms,
May the winds blow till they have wakened death,
And let the laboring bark climb hills of seas
Olympus-high, and duck again as low
As hell's from heaven! If it were now to die,
'Twere now to be most happy, for I fear
My soul hath her content so absolute
That not another comfort like to this
Succeeds in unknown fate.

DESDEMONA   The heavens forbid   193
But that our loves and comforts should increase
Even as our days do grow!

OTHELLO   Amen to that, sweet powers!
I cannot speak enough of this content.
It stops me here; it is too much of joy.
And this, and this, the greatest discords be   199
                                        [They kiss.]
That e'er our hearts shall make!

IAGO *[aside]*   Oh, you are well tuned now!
But I'll set down the pegs that make this music,   202
As honest as I am.   203

OTHELLO   Come, let us to the castle.
News, friends! Our wars are done, the Turks are
drowned.
How does my old acquaintance of this isle?—
Honey, you shall be well desired in Cyprus;   207
I have found great love amongst them. Oh, my sweet,
I prattle out of fashion, and I dote   209
In mine own comforts.—I prithee, good Iago,
Go to the bay and disembark my coffers.   211
Bring thou the master to the citadel;   212
He is a good one, and his worthiness
Does challenge much respect.—Come, Desdemona.—   214
Once more, well met at Cyprus!
                  Exeunt Othello and Desdemona [and all
                                but Iago and Roderigo].

IAGO *[to a departing attendant]*   Do thou meet me presently at
the harbor. *[To Roderigo]* Come hither. If thou be'st
valiant—as, they say, base men being in love have   218
then a nobility in their natures more than is native to
them—list me. The Lieutenant tonight watches on   220
the court of guard. First, I must tell thee this: 221
Desdemona is directly in love with him.

---

141 foul ugly   **142 thereunto** in addition   **143 foul** sluttish   **147 put
. . . vouch** compel the approval   **149 Had . . . will** was never at a loss
for words   **150 gay** extravagantly clothed   **151 Fled . . . may** avoided
temptation where the choice was hers   **153 Bade . . . stay** i.e.,
resolved to put up with her injury and bade her anger to cease
155 To . . . tail i.e., to be selfishly demanding and ambitious. (The
fish's lower body, below the rib cage, has fewest bones and is generally the succulent portion. With sexual implication as well: *cod's head*
can be slang for "penis," and *tail* for "pudendum.")   **160 To . . . beer**
i.e., To breastfeed babies and keep petty household accounts.
163–4 profane and liberal irreverent and licentious   **165 home** right
to the target. (A term from fencing.)   **relish** appreciate   **166 in** in the
character of   **167 well said** well done   **170 gyve** fetter, shackle.
courtship courtesy, show of courtly manners.   **You say true** i.e.,
That's right, go ahead   **174 the sir** i.e., the fine gentleman
176 clyster pipes tubes used for enemas and douches

193 Succeeds . . . fate i.e., can follow in the unknown future.
199.1 *They kiss* (The direction is from the Quarto.)   **202 set down**
loosen (and hence untune the instrument)   **203 As . . . I am** for all my
supposed honesty.   **207 desired** sought after   **209 out of fashion**
indecorously, incoherently   **211 coffers** chests, baggage.   **212 master**
ship's captain   **214 challenge** lay claim to, deserve   **218 base men**
even ignoble men   **220 list** listen to   **221 court of guard** guardhouse.
(Cassio is in charge of the watch.)

RODERIGO   With him? Why, 'tis not possible.

IAGO   Lay thy finger thus, and let thy soul be instructed. 224
Mark me with what violence she first loved the Moor,
but for bragging and telling her fantastical lies. To love 226
him still for prating? Let not thy discreet heart think it.
Her eye must be fed; and what delight shall she have
to look on the devil? When the blood is made dull with
the act of sport, there should be, again to inflame it 230
and to give satiety a fresh appetite, loveliness in favor, 231
sympathy in years, manners, and beauties—all which 232
the Moor is defective in. Now, for want of these
required conveniences, her delicate tenderness will 234
find itself abused, begin to heave the gorge, disrelish 235
and abhor the Moor. Very nature will instruct her in it 236
and compel her to some second choice. Now, sir, this
granted—as it is a most pregnant and unforced 238
position—who stands so eminent in the degree of this 239
fortune as Cassio does? A knave very voluble, no 240
further conscionable than in putting on the mere form 241
of civil and humane seeming for the better compass- 242
ing of his salt and most hidden loose affection. Why, 243
none, why, none. A slipper and subtle knave, a finder 244
out of occasions, that has an eye can stamp and 245
counterfeit advantages, though true advantage never 246
present itself; a devilish knave. Besides, the knave is
handsome, young, and hath all those requisites in him
that folly and green minds look after. A pestilent 249
complete knave, and the woman hath found him 250
already.

RODERIGO   I cannot believe that in her. She's full of
most blessed condition.   253

IAGO   Blessed fig's end! The wine she drinks is made of 254
grapes. If she had been blessed, she would never have
loved the Moor. Blessed pudding! Didst thou not see 256
her paddle with the palm of his hand? Didst not mark
that?

RODERIGO   Yes, that I did; but that was but courtesy.

IAGO   Lechery, by this hand. An index and obscure pro- 260
logue to the history of lust and foul thoughts. They
met so near with their lips that their breaths embraced
together. Villainous thoughts, Roderigo! When these
mutualities so marshal the way, hard at hand comes 264
the master and main exercise, th'incorporate conclu- 265
sion. Pish! But, sir, be you ruled by me. I have brought

you from Venice. Watch you tonight; for the com- 267
mand, I'll lay't upon you. Cassio knows you not. I'll 268
not be far from you. Do you find some occasion to
anger Cassio, either by speaking too loud, or tainting 270
his discipline, or from what other course you please,
which the time shall more favorably minister.   272

RODERIGO   Well.

IAGO   Sir, he's rash and very sudden in choler, and haply 274
may strike at you. Provoke him that he may, for
even out of that will I cause these of Cyprus to mutiny, 276
whose qualification shall come into no true taste again 277
but by the displanting of Cassio. So shall you have a
shorter journey to your desires by the means I shall
then have to prefer them, and the impediment most 280
profitably removed, without the which there were no
expectation of our prosperity.

RODERIGO   I will do this, if you can bring it to any
opportunity.

IAGO   I warrant thee. Meet me by and by at the citadel. 285
I must fetch his necessaries ashore. Farewell.

RODERIGO   Adieu.   *Exit.*

IAGO
That Cassio loves her, I do well believe't;
That she loves him, 'tis apt and of great credit.   289
The Moor, howbeit that I endure him not,
Is of a constant, loving, noble nature,
And I dare think he'll prove to Desdemona
A most dear husband. Now, I do love her too,
Not out of absolute lust—though peradventure
I stand accountant for as great a sin—   295
But partly led to diet my revenge   296
For that I do suspect the lusty Moor
Hath leaped into my seat, the thought whereof
Doth, like a poisonous mineral, gnaw my innards;
And nothing can or shall content my soul
Till I am evened with him, wife for wife,
Or failing so, yet that I put the Moor
At least into a jealousy so strong
That judgment cannot cure. Which thing to do,
If this poor trash of Venice, whom I trace   305
For his quick hunting, stand the putting on,   306
I'll have our Michael Cassio on the hip,   307
Abuse him to the Moor in the rank garb—   308
For I fear Cassio with my nightcap too—   309
Make the Moor thank me, love me, and reward me
For making him egregiously an ass
And practicing upon his peace and quiet   312

---

224 thus i.e., on your lips   **226 but** only   **230 the act of sport** sex
231 favor appearance   **232 sympathy** correspondence, similarity
233 required conveniences things conducive to sexual compatibility
235 abused cheated, revolted.   **heave the gorge** experience nausea
236 Very nature Her very instincts   **238 pregnant** evident, cogent
239 in . . . of as next in line for   **240 voluble** facile, glib   **241 conscionable** conscientious, conscience-bound   **242 humane** polite,
courteous   **243 salt** licentious.   **affection** passion.   **244 slipper** slippery   **245 an eye can stamp** an eye that can coin, create   **246 advantages** favorable opportunities   **249 folly** wantonness.   **green** immature   **250 found him** sized him up, perceived his intent
253 condition disposition.   **254 fig's end** (See 1.3.322 for the vulgar
gesture of the fig.)   **256 pudding** sausage.   **260 index** table of contents.   **obscure** veiled, hidden   **264 mutualities** exchanges, intima-
cies.   **hard at hand** closely following   **265 th'incorporate** the carnal

267 Watch you Stand watch   **267–8 for . . . you** I'll arrange for you to
be appointed, given orders; or, I'll put you in charge.   **270 tainting**
disparaging   **272 minister** provide.   **274 choler** wrath.   **haply** perhaps   **276 mutiny** riot   **277 qualification** pacification.   **true taste**
i.e., acceptable state   **280 prefer** advance   **285 warrant** assure.
by and by immediately   **289 apt** probable.   **credit** credibility.
295 accountant accountable   **296 diet** feed   **305 trace** i.e., pursue,
dog; or, keep hungry (?) or perhaps *trash*, a hunting term, meaning to
put weights on a hunting dog in order to slow him down   **306 For** to
make more eager for.   **stand . . . on** responds properly when I incite
him to quarrel   **307 on the hip** at my mercy, where I can throw him.
(A wrestling term.)   **308 Abuse** slander.   **rank garb** coarse manner,
gross fashion   **309 with my nightcap** i.e., as a rival in my bed, as one
who gives me cuckold's horns   **312 practicing upon** plotting against

Even to madness. 'Tis here, but yet confused.
Knavery's plain face is never seen till used.   *Exit.*

❖

2.2

Enter Othello's Herald with a proclamation.

HERALD   It is Othello's pleasure, our noble and valiant
general, that, upon certain tidings now arrived, importing the mere perdition of the Turkish fleet, every   3
man put himself into triumph: some to dance, some to   4
make bonfires, each man to what sport and revels his
addiction leads him. For, besides these beneficial   6
news, it is the celebration of his nuptial. So much was
his pleasure should be proclaimed. All offices are open,   8
and there is full liberty of feasting from this present
hour of five till the bell have told eleven. Heaven bless
the isle of Cyprus and our noble general Othello!
                                                                Exit.

❖

[2.3]

*Enter Othello, Desdemona, Cassio, and
attendants.*

OTHELLO
Good Michael, look you to the guard tonight.
Let's teach ourselves that honorable stop   2
Not to outsport discretion.   3
CASSIO
Iago hath direction what to do,
But notwithstanding, with my personal eye
Will I look to't.
OTHELLO   Iago is most honest.
Michael, good night. Tomorrow with your earliest   7
Let me have speech with you. [*To Desdemona*] Come,
    my dear love,
The purchase made, the fruits are to ensue;   9
That profit's yet to come 'tween me and you.—   10
Good night.
            Exit [Othello, with Desdemona and attendants].

            Enter Iago.

CASSIO   Welcome, Iago. We must to the watch.
IAGO   Not this hour, Lieutenant; 'tis not yet ten o'th'   13
clock. Our general cast us thus early for the love of his   14
Desdemona; who let us not therefore blame. He hath   15
not yet made wanton the night with her, and she is
sport for Jove.
CASSIO   She's a most exquisite lady.
IAGO   And, I'll warrant her, full of game.

CASSIO   Indeed, she's a most fresh and delicate creature.
IAGO   What an eye she has! Methinks it sounds a parley   21
to provocation.
CASSIO   An inviting eye, and yet methinks right modest.
IAGO   And when she speaks, is it not an alarum to love?   24
CASSIO   She is indeed perfection.
IAGO   Well, happiness to their sheets! Come, Lieutenant,
I have a stoup of wine, and here without are a brace of   27
Cyprus gallants that would fain have a measure to the   28
health of black Othello.
CASSIO   Not tonight, good Iago. I have very poor and
unhappy brains for drinking. I could well wish cour-
tesy would invent some other custom of entertain-
ment.
IAGO   Oh, they are our friends. But one cup! I'll drink for   34
you.   35
CASSIO   I have drunk but one cup tonight, and that was
craftily qualified too, and behold what innovation it   37
makes here. I am unfortunate in the infirmity and   38
dare not task my weakness with any more.
IAGO   What, man? 'Tis a night of revels. The gallants
desire it.
CASSIO   Where are they?
IAGO   Here at the door. I pray you, call them in.
CASSIO   I'll do't, but it dislikes me.   *Exit.*   44
IAGO
If I can fasten but one cup upon him,
With that which he hath drunk tonight already,
He'll be as full of quarrel and offense   47
As my young mistress' dog. Now, my sick fool
    Roderigo,
Whom love hath turned almost the wrong side out,
To Desdemona hath tonight caroused   50
Potations pottle-deep; and he's to watch.   51
Three lads of Cyprus—noble swelling spirits,   52
That hold their honors in a wary distance,   53
The very elements of this warlike isle—   54
Have I tonight flustered with flowing cups,
And they watch too. Now, 'mongst this flock of
    drunkards   56
Am I to put our Cassio in some action
That may offend the isle.—But here they come.

            *Enter Cassio, Montano, and gentlemen; [servants
            following with wine].*

If consequence do but approve my dream,   59
My boat sails freely both with wind and stream.   60
CASSIO   'Fore God, they have given me a rouse already.   61

2.2. **Location:** Cyprus.
3 **mere perdition** complete destruction   4 **triumph** public celebration
6 **addiction** inclination   8 **offices** rooms where food and drink are kept
2.3. **Location:** Cyprus. The citadel.
2 **stop** restraint   3 **outsport** celebrate beyond the bounds of   7 **with
your earliest** at your earliest convenience   9–10 **The purchase . . .
you** i.e., though married, we haven't yet consummated our love.
(Possibly, too, Othello is referring to pregnancy. At all events, his
desire for sexual union is manifest.)   13 **Not this hour** Not for an
hour yet   14 **cast** dismissed   15 **who** i.e., Othello

21 **sounds a parley** calls for a conference, issues an invitation
24 **alarum** signal calling men to arms. (Continuing the military
metaphor of *parley,* line 21.)   27 **stoup** measure of liquor, two quarts.
without outside.   **brace** pair   28 **fain have a measure** gladly drink a
toast   34–5 **for you** in your place. (Iago will do the steady drinking
to keep the gallants company while Cassio has only one cup.)
37 **qualified** diluted.   **innovation** disturbance, insurrection   38 **here**
i.e., in my head.   44 **it dislikes me** i.e., I'm reluctant.   47 **offense**
readiness to give or take offense   50 **caroused** drunk off   51 **pottle-
deep** to the bottom of the tankard.   **watch** stand watch.
52 **swelling** proud   53 **hold . . . distance** i.e., are extremely sensitive
of their honor   54 **elements** lifeblood   56 **watch** are members of the
guard   59 **If . . . dream** If subsequent events will only confirm my
dreams and hopes   60 **stream** current.   61 **rouse** full draft of liquor

MONTANO   Good faith, a little one; not past a pint, as I
am a soldier.
IAGO   Some wine, ho!
   [*He sings.*]   "And let me the cannikin clink, clink,   65
            And let me the cannikin clink.
               A soldier's a man,
               Oh, man's life's but a span;   68
            Why, then, let a soldier drink."
   Some wine, boys!
CASSIO   'Fore God, an excellent song.
IAGO   I learned it in England, where indeed they are
most potent in potting. Your Dane, your German, and   73
your swag-bellied Hollander—drink, ho!—are noth-
ing to your English.
CASSIO   Is your Englishman so exquisite in his drinking?
IAGO   Why, he drinks you, with facility, your Dane   77
dead drunk; he sweats not to overthrow your Almain;   78
he gives your Hollander a vomit ere the next pottle can
be filled.
CASSIO   To the health of our general!
MONTANO   I am for it, Lieutenant, and I'll do you justice.   82
IAGO   O sweet England! [*He sings.*]

      "King Stephen was and-a worthy peer,
            His breeches cost him but a crown;
      He held them sixpence all too dear,
            With that he called the tailor lown.   87

      He was a wight of high renown,
            And thou art but of low degree.
      'Tis pride that pulls the country down;   90
            Then take thy auld cloak about thee."   91

   Some wine, ho!
CASSIO   'Fore God, this is a more exquisite song than
the other.
IAGO   Will you hear't again?
CASSIO   No, for I hold him to be unworthy of his place
that does those things. Well, God's above all; and
there be souls must be saved, and there be souls must
not be saved.
IAGO   It's true, good Lieutenant.
CASSIO   For mine own part—no offense to the General,
nor any man of quality—I hope to be saved.   102
IAGO   And so do I too, Lieutenant.
CASSIO   Ay, but, by your leave, not before me; the lieutenant is to be saved before the ancient. Let's have no
more of this; let's to our affairs.—God forgive us our
sins!—Gentlemen, let's look to our business. Do not
think, gentlemen, I am drunk. This is my ancient; this
is my right hand, and this is my left. I am not drunk
now. I can stand well enough, and speak well enough.

GENTLEMEN   Excellent well.
CASSIO   Why, very well then; you must not think then
that I am drunk.   *Exit.*
MONTANO
To th' platform, masters. Come, let's set the watch.   114
                                 [*Exeunt Gentlemen.*]
IAGO
You see this fellow that is gone before.
He's a soldier fit to stand by Caesar
And give direction; and do but see his vice.
'Tis to his virtue a just equinox,   118
The one as long as th'other. 'Tis pity of him.
I fear the trust Othello puts him in,
On some odd time of his infirmity,
Will shake this island.
MONTANO   But is he often thus?
IAGO
'Tis evermore the prologue to his sleep.
He'll watch the horologe a double set,   124
If drink rock not his cradle.
MONTANO   It were well
The General were put in mind of it.
Perhaps he sees it not, or his good nature
Prizes the virtue that appears in Cassio
And looks not on his evils. Is not this true?

         Enter Roderigo.

IAGO [*aside to him*]   How now, Roderigo?
   I pray you, after the Lieutenant; go.   [*Exit Roderigo.*]
MONTANO
And 'tis great pity that the noble Moor
Should hazard such a place as his own second   133
With one of an engraffed infirmity.   134
It were an honest action to say so
To the Moor.
IAGO   Not I, for this fair island.
I do love Cassio well and would do much
To cure him of this evil.   [*Cry within:* "Help! Help!"]
                       But, hark! What noise?   138

         Enter Cassio, pursuing Roderigo.

CASSIO   Zounds, you rogue! You rascal!
MONTANO   What's the matter, Lieutenant?
CASSIO   A knave teach me my duty? I'll beat the knave
into a twiggen bottle.   142
RODERIGO   Beat me?
CASSIO   Dost thou prate, rogue?   [*He strikes Roderigo.*]
MONTANO   Nay, good Lieutenant. [*Restraining him.*] I
pray you, sir, hold your hand.
CASSIO   Let me go, sir, or I'll knock you o'er the
mazard.   148

65 cannikin small drinking vessel   **68 span** brief span of time. (Compare Psalm 39:5 as rendered in the Book of Common Prayer: "Thou hast made my days as it were a span long.")   **73 potting** drinking.
77 drinks you drinks.   **your Dane** your typical Dane   **78 sweats not** i.e., need not exert himself.   **Almain** German   **82 I'll . . . justice** i.e., I'll drink as much as you.   **87 lown** lout, rascal.   **90 pride** i.e., extravagance in dress   **91 auld** old   **102 quality** rank

114 set the watch mount the guard.   **118 just equinox** exact counterpart. (*Equinox* is an equal length of days and nights.)   **124 watch . . . set** stay awake twice around the clock or *horologe*   **133–4 hazard . . . With** risk giving such an important position as his second in command to   **134 engraffed** engrafted, inveterate   **138.1 *pursuing*** (The Quarto text reads, "*driuing in.*")   **142 twiggen** wicker-covered. (Cassio vows to assail Roderigo until his skin resembles wickerwork or until he has driven Roderigo through the holes in a wickerwork.)   **148 mazard** i.e., head. (Literally, a drinking vessel.)

MONTANO   Come, come, you're drunk.
CASSIO   Drunk?   [*They fight.*]
IAGO [*aside to Roderigo*]
      Away, I say. Go out and cry a mutiny.   151
                                    [*Exit Roderigo.*]
      Nay, good Lieutenant—God's will, gentlemen—
      Help, ho!—Lieutenant—sir—Montano—sir—
      Help, masters!—Here's a goodly watch indeed!   154
                                    [*A bell rings.*]
      Who's that which rings the bell?—Diablo, ho!   155
      The town will rise. God's will, Lieutenant, hold!   156
      You'll be ashamed forever.

            Enter Othello and attendants [with weapons].

OTHELLO
      What is the matter here?
MONTANO   Zounds, I bleed still.
      I am hurt to th' death. He dies! [*He thrusts at Cassio.*]
OTHELLO   Hold, for your lives!
IAGO
      Hold, ho! Lieutenant—sir—Montano—gentlemen—
      Have you forgot all sense of place and duty?
      Hold! The General speaks to you. Hold, for shame!
OTHELLO
      Why, how now, ho! From whence ariseth this?
      Are we turned Turks, and to ourselves do that   164
      Which heaven hath forbid the Ottomites?   165
      For Christian shame, put by this barbarous brawl!
      He that stirs next to carve for his own rage   167
      Holds his soul light; he dies upon his motion.   168
      Silence that dreadful bell. It frights the isle
      From her propriety. What is the matter, masters?   170
      Honest Iago, that looks dead with grieving,
      Speak. Who began this? On thy love, I charge thee.
IAGO
      I do not know. Friends all but now, even now,
      In quarter and in terms like bride and groom   174
      Devesting them for bed; and then, but now—   175
      As if some planet had unwitted men—
      Swords out, and tilting one at others' breasts
      In opposition bloody. I cannot speak   178
      Any beginning to this peevish odds;   179
      And would in action glorious I had lost
      Those legs that brought me to a part of it!
OTHELLO
      How comes it, Michael, you are thus forgot?   182
CASSIO
      I pray you, pardon me. I cannot speak.

OTHELLO
      Worthy Montano, you were wont be civil;   184
      The gravity and stillness of your youth   185
      The world hath noted, and your name is great
      In mouths of wisest censure. What's the matter   187
      That you unlace your reputation thus   188
      And spend your rich opinion for the name   189
      Of a night-brawler? Give me answer to it.
MONTANO
      Worthy Othello, I am hurt to danger.
      Your officer, Iago, can inform you—
      While I spare speech, which something now offends
        me—   193
      Of all that I do know; nor know I aught
      By me that's said or done amiss this night,
      Unless self-charity be sometimes a vice,
      And to defend ourselves it be a sin
      When violence assails us.
OTHELLO   Now, by heaven,
      My blood begins my safer guides to rule,   199
      And passion, having my best judgment collied,   200
      Essays to lead the way. Zounds, if I stir,   201
      Or do but lift this arm, the best of you
      Shall sink in my rebuke. Give me to know
      How this foul rout began, who set it on;   204
      And he that is approved in this offense,   205
      Though he had twinned with me, both at a birth,
      Shall lose me. What? In a town of war   207
      Yet wild, the people's hearts brim full of fear,
      To manage private and domestic quarrel?   209
      In night, and on the court and guard of safety?   210
      'Tis monstrous. Iago, who began't?
MONTANO [*to Iago*]
      If partially affined, or leagued in office,   212
      Thou dost deliver more or less than truth,
      Thou art no soldier.
IAGO   Touch me not so near.
      I had rather have this tongue cut from my mouth
      Than it should do offense to Michael Cassio;
      Yet, I persuade myself, to speak the truth
      Shall nothing wrong him. Thus it is, General:
      Montano and myself being in speech,
      There comes a fellow crying out for help,
      And Cassio following him with determined sword
      To execute upon him. Sir, this gentleman   222
                                    [*indicating Montano*]
      Steps in to Cassio and entreats his pause.   223
      Myself the crying fellow did pursue,
      Lest by his clamor—as it so fell out—
      The town might fall in fright. He, swift of foot,

---

151 **mutiny** riot.   154 **masters** sirs.   154.1 *A bell rings* (This direction
is from the Quarto, as are *Exit Roderigo* at line 131, *They fight* at line
150, and *with weapons* at line 157.1.)   155 **Diablo** The devil   156 **rise**
grow riotous.   164–5 **to ourselves . . . Ottomites** inflict on ourselves
the harm that heaven has prevented the Turks from doing (by
destroying their fleet).   167 **carve for** i.e., indulge, satisfy with his
sword   168 **Holds . . . light** i.e., places little value on his life.   **upon
his motion** if he moves.   170 **propriety** proper state or condition.
174 **In quarter . . . terms** in conduct and speech   175 **Devesting them**
undressing themselves   178 **speak** explain   179 **peevish odds** childish quarrel   182 **are thus forgot** have forgotten yourself thus.

184 **wont be** accustomed to be   185 **stillness** sobriety   187 **censure**
judgment.   188 **unlace** undo, lay open (as one might loose the strings
of a purse containing reputation)   189 **opinion** reputation
193 **something** somewhat.   **offends** pains   199 **blood** passion (of
anger).   **guides** i.e., reason   200 **collied** darkened   201 **Essays**
undertakes   204 **rout** riot   205 **approved in** found guilty of
207 **town of** town garrisoned for   209 **manage** undertake   210 **on . . .
safety** at the main guardhouse or headquarters and on watch.
212 **If . . . office** If made partial by personal relationship or by your
being fellow officers   222 **execute upon him** (1) proceed violently
against him (2) execute him.   223 **his pause** him to stop.

Outran my purpose, and I returned, the rather   227
For that I heard the clink and fall of swords
And Cassio high in oath, which till tonight
I ne'er might say before. When I came back—
For this was brief—I found them close together
At blow and thrust, even as again they were
When you yourself did part them.
More of this matter cannot I report.
But men are men; the best sometimes forget.   235
Though Cassio did some little wrong to him,
As men in rage strike those that wish them best,   237
Yet surely Cassio, I believe, received
From him that fled some strange indignity,
Which patience could not pass.

OTHELLO   I know, Iago,   240
Thy honesty and love doth mince this matter,
Making it light to Cassio. Cassio, I love thee,
But nevermore be officer of mine.

Enter Desdemona, attended.

Look if my gentle love be not raised up.
I'll make thee an example.

DESDEMONA
What is the matter, dear?

OTHELLO   All's well now, sweeting;
Come away to bed. [*To Montano*] Sir, for your hurts,
Myself will be your surgeon.—Lead him off.   248
                     [*Montano is led off.*]
Iago, look with care about the town
And silence those whom this vile brawl distracted.
Come, Desdemona. 'Tis the soldiers' life
To have their balmy slumbers waked with strife.
                     Exit [with all but Iago and Cassio].

IAGO   What, are you hurt, Lieutenant?

CASSIO   Ay, past all surgery.

IAGO   Marry, God forbid!

CASSIO   Reputation, reputation, reputation! Oh, I have
lost my reputation! I have lost the immortal part of
myself, and what remains is bestial. My reputation,
Iago, my reputation!

IAGO   As I am an honest man, I thought you had
received some bodily wound; there is more sense in
that than in reputation. Reputation is an idle and most
false imposition, oft got without merit and lost with-   263
out deserving. You have lost no reputation at all,
unless you repute yourself such a loser. What, man,
there are more ways to recover the General again. You   266
are but now cast in his mood—a punishment more in   267
policy than in malice, even so as one would beat his   268
offenseless dog to affright an imperious lion. Sue to   269
him again and he's yours.

CASSIO   I will rather sue to be despised than to deceive
so good a commander with so slight, so drunken, and   272
so indiscreet an officer. Drunk? And speak parrot?   273
And squabble? Swagger? Swear? And discourse fustian with one's own shadow? O thou invisible spirit
of wine, if thou hast no name to be known by, let us
call thee devil!

IAGO   What was he that you followed with your sword?
What had he done to you?

CASSIO   I know not.

IAGO   Is't possible?

CASSIO   I remember a mass of things, but nothing
distinctly; a quarrel, but nothing wherefore. Oh, God,   283
that men should put an enemy in their mouths to steal
away their brains! That we should, with joy, pleas-
ance, revel, and applause transform ourselves into   286
beasts!

IAGO   Why, but you are now well enough. How came
you thus recovered?

CASSIO   It hath pleased the devil drunkenness to give
place to the devil wrath. One unperfectness shows me
another, to make me frankly despise myself.

IAGO   Come, you are too severe a moraler. As the time,   293
the place, and the condition of this country stands, I
could heartily wish this had not befallen; but since it is
as it is, mend it for your own good.

CASSIO   I will ask him for my place again; he shall tell
me I am a drunkard. Had I as many mouths as Hydra,   298
such an answer would stop them all. To be now a
sensible man, by and by a fool, and presently a beast!
Oh, strange! Every inordinate cup is unblessed, and the   301
ingredient is a devil.

IAGO   Come, come, good wine is a good familiar
creature, if it be well used. Exclaim no more against it.
And, good Lieutenant, I think you think I love you.

CASSIO   I have well approved it, sir. I drunk!   306

IAGO   You or any man living may be drunk at a time,   307
man. I'll tell you what you shall do. Our general's wife
is now the general—I may say so in this respect, for   309
that he hath devoted and given up himself to the   310
contemplation, mark, and denotement of her parts   311
and graces. Confess yourself freely to her; importune
her help to put you in your place again. She is of so
free, so kind, so apt, so blessed a disposition, she   314
holds it a vice in her goodness not to do more than she
is requested. This broken joint between you and her
husband entreat her to splinter; and, my fortunes   317
against any lay worth naming, this crack of your love   318
shall grow stronger than it was before.

CASSIO   You advise me well.

---

227 **rather** sooner   235 **forget** forget themselves.   237 **those . . . best**
i.e., even those who are well disposed toward them   240 **pass** pass
over, overlook.   248 **be your surgeon** i.e., make sure you receive
medical attention.   263 **false imposition** thing artificially imposed
and of no real value   266 **recover** regain favor with   267 **cast in his
mood** dismissed in a moment of anger   267–8 **in policy** done for
expediency's sake and as a public gesture   268–9 **would . . . lion** i.e.,
would make an example of a minor offender in order to deter more
important and dangerous offenders.   269 **Sue** Petition

272 **slight** worthless   273 **speak parrot** talk nonsense, rant. (*Discourse
fustian*, lines 274–5, has much the same meaning.)   283 **wherefore**
why.   286 **applause** desire for applause   293 **moraler** moralizer.
298 **Hydra** the Lernaean Hydra, a monster with many heads and the
ability to grow two heads when one was cut off, slain by Hercules
as the second of his twelve labors   301 **inordinate** immoderate
306 **approved** proved by experience   307 **at a time** at one time or
another   309–10 **for that** that   311 **mark, and denotement** (Both
words mean "observation.")   **parts** qualities   314 **free** generous
317 **splinter** bind with splints   318 **lay** stake, wager

IAGO   I protest, in the sincerity of love and honest 321
kindness.

CASSIO   I think it freely; and betimes in the morning I 323
will beseech the virtuous Desdemona to undertake for
me. I am desperate of my fortunes if they check me 325
here.

IAGO   You are in the right. Good night, Lieutenant. I
must to the watch.

CASSIO   Good night, honest Iago.   *Exit Cassio.*

IAGO
And what's he then that says I play the villain,
When this advice is free I give, and honest,   331
Probal to thinking, and indeed the course   332
To win the Moor again? For 'tis most easy
Th'inclining Desdemona to subdue   334
In any honest suit; she's framed as fruitful   335
As the free elements. And then for her   336
To win the Moor—were't to renounce his baptism,
All seals and symbols of redeemèd sin—   338
His soul is so enfettered to her love
That she may make, unmake, do what she list,
Even as her appetite shall play the god   341
With his weak function. How am I then a villain,   342
To counsel Cassio to this parallel course   343
Directly to his good? Divinity of hell!   344
When devils will the blackest sins put on,   345
They do suggest at first with heavenly shows,   346
As I do now. For whiles this honest fool
Plies Desdemona to repair his fortune,
And she for him pleads strongly to the Moor,
I'll pour this pestilence into his ear,
That she repeals him for her body's lust;   351
And by how much she strives to do him good,
She shall undo her credit with the Moor.
So will I turn her virtue into pitch,   354
And out of her own goodness make the net
That shall enmesh them all.

                    Enter Roderigo.

                                How now, Roderigo?

RODERIGO   I do follow here in the chase, not like a
hound that hunts, but one that fills up the cry. My 358
money is almost spent; I have been tonight exceedingly well cudgeled; and I think the issue will be I shall 360
have so much experience for my pains, and so, 361
with no money at all and a little more wit, return again
to Venice.

IAGO
How poor are they that have not patience!
What wound did ever heal but by degrees?
Thou know'st we work by wit, and not by witchcraft,
And wit depends on dilatory time.
Does't not go well? Cassio hath beaten thee,
And thou, by that small hurt, hast cashiered Cassio.   369
Though other things grow fair against the sun,   370
Yet fruits that blossom first will first be ripe.   371
Content thyself awhile. By the Mass, 'tis morning!
Pleasure and action make the hours seem short.
Retire thee; go where thou art billeted.
Away, I say! Thou shalt know more hereafter.
Nay, get thee gone.   *Exit Roderigo.*
                Two things are to be done.
My wife must move for Cassio to her mistress;   377
I'll set her on;
Myself the while to draw the Moor apart
And bring him jump when he may Cassio find   380
Soliciting his wife. Ay, that's the way.
Dull not device by coldness and delay.   *Exit.* 382

                        ❧

3.1

                    Enter Cassio [and] Musicians.

CASSIO
Masters, play here—I will content your pains—   1
Something that's brief, and bid "Good morrow,
General."   [*They play.*]

                    [*Enter*] *Clown.*

CLOWN   Why, masters, have your instruments been in
Naples, that they speak i'th' nose thus?   4

A MUSICIAN   How, sir, how?

CLOWN   Are these, I pray you, wind instruments?

A MUSICIAN   Ay, marry, are they, sir.

CLOWN   Oh, thereby hangs a tail.

A MUSICIAN   Whereby hangs a tale, sir?

CLOWN   Marry, sir, by many a wind instrument that I 10
know. But, masters, here's money for you. [*He gives
money.*] And the General so likes your music that he
desires you, for love's sake, to make no more noise
with it.

A MUSICIAN   Well, sir, we will not.

CLOWN   If you have any music that may not be heard, 16
to't again; but, as they say, to hear music the General
does not greatly care.

A MUSICIAN   We have none such, sir.

---

321 protest insist, declare   **323 freely** unreservedly   **325 check**
repulse   **331 free** (1) free from guile (2) freely given   **332 Probal**
probable, reasonable   **334 Th'inclining** the favorably disposed.
subdue persuade   **335 framed as fruitful** created as generous
336 free elements i.e., earth, air, fire, and water, unrestrained and
spontaneous.   **338 seals** tokens   **341 her appetite** her desire, or, perhaps, his desire for her   **342 function** exercise of faculties (weakened
by his fondness for her).   **343 parallel** i.e., seemingly in his best interests but at the same time threatening   **344 Divinity of hell!** Inverted
theology of hell (which seduces the soul to its damnation)!   **345 put
on** further, instigate   **346 suggest** tempt   **351 repeals him** attempts
to get him restored   **354 pitch** i.e., (1) foul blackness (2) a snaring
substance   **358 fills up the cry** merely takes part as one of the pack.
360 issue outcome   **361 so much** just so much and no more

369 cashiered dismissed from service   **370–1 Though . . . ripe** i.e.,
Plans that are well prepared and set expeditiously in motion will
soonest ripen into success.   **377 move** plead   **380 jump** precisely
382 device plot.   **coldness** lack of zeal
3.1. Location: Before the chamber of Othello and Desdemona.
1 Masters Good sirs.   **content your pains** reward your efforts
4 speak i'th' nose (1) sound nasal (2) sound like one whose nose has
been attacked by syphilis. (Naples was popularly supposed to have a
high incidence of venereal disease.)   **10 wind instrument** (With a
joke on flatulence. The *tail*, line 8, that hangs nearby the *wind instrument* suggests the penis.)   **16 may not** cannot

CLOWN   Then put up your pipes in your bag, for I'll
away. Go, vanish into air, away!   *Exeunt Musicians.*
CASSIO   Dost thou hear, mine honest friend?
CLOWN   No, I hear not your honest friend; I hear you.
CASSIO   Prithee, keep up thy quillets. There's a poor   24
piece of gold for thee. [*He gives money.*] If the gentlewoman that attends the General's wife be stirring, tell
her there's one Cassio entreats her a little favor of   27
speech. Wilt thou do this?   28
CLOWN   She is stirring, sir. If she will stir hither, I shall   29
seem to notify unto her.   30
CASSIO
Do, good my friend.   *Exit Clown.*

      Enter Iago.

                         In happy time, Iago.   31
IAGO   You have not been abed, then?
CASSIO   Why, no. The day had broke
Before we parted. I have made bold, Iago,
To send in to your wife. My suit to her
Is that she will to virtuous Desdemona
Procure me some access.
IAGO   I'll send her to you presently;
And I'll devise a mean to draw the Moor
Out of the way, that your converse and business
May be more free.
CASSIO
I humbly thank you for't.   *Exit [Iago].*
                         I never knew
A Florentine more kind and honest.   43

      Enter Emilia.

EMILIA
Good morrow, good Lieutenant. I am sorry
For your displeasure; but all will sure be well.   45
The General and his wife are talking of it,
And she speaks for you stoutly. The Moor replies   47
That he you hurt is of great fame in Cyprus   48
And great affinity, and that in wholesome wisdom   49
He might not but refuse you; but he protests he loves
you   50
And needs no other suitor but his likings
To take the safest occasion by the front   52
To bring you in again.
CASSIO   Yet I beseech you,
If you think fit, or that it may be done,
Give me advantage of some brief discourse
With Desdemon alone.
EMILIA   Pray you, come in.
I will bestow you where you shall have time
To speak your bosom freely.   58

CASSIO   I am much bound to you.   [*Exeunt.*]

❖

3.2

      Enter Othello, Iago, and Gentlemen.

OTHELLO [*giving letters*]
These letters give, Iago, to the pilot,
And by him do my duties to the Senate.   2
That done, I will be walking on the works;   3
Repair there to me.
IAGO   Well, my good lord, I'll do't.   4
OTHELLO
This fortification, gentlemen, shall we see't?
GENTLEMEN   We'll wait upon Your Lordship.   *Exeunt.*   6

❖

3.3

      Enter Desdemona, Cassio, and Emilia.

DESDEMONA
Be thou assured, good Cassio, I will do
All my abilities in thy behalf.
EMILIA
Good madam, do. I warrant it grieves my husband
As if the cause were his.
DESDEMONA
Oh, that's an honest fellow. Do not doubt, Cassio,
But I will have my lord and you again
As friendly as you were.
CASSIO   Bounteous madam,
Whatever shall become of Michael Cassio,
He's never anything but your true servant.
DESDEMONA
I know't. I thank you. You do love my lord;
You have known him long, and be you well assured
He shall in strangeness stand no farther off   12
Than in a politic distance.
CASSIO   Ay, but, lady,   13
That policy may either last so long,
Or feed upon such nice and waterish diet,   15
Or breed itself so out of circumstance,   16
That, I being absent and my place supplied,   17
My general will forget my love and service.
DESDEMONA
Do not doubt that. Before Emilia here   19
I give thee warrant of thy place. Assure thee,   20
If I do vow a friendship I'll perform it
To the last article. My lord shall never rest.
I'll watch him tame and talk him out of patience;   23

24 **keep . . . quillets** refrain from quibbling.   **27–8 a little . . . speech**
the favor of a brief talk.   **29 stir** bestir herself. (With a play on
stirring, "rousing herself from rest.")   **30 seem** deem it good, think fit
31 In happy time i.e., Well met   **43 Florentine** i.e., even a fellow Florentine. (Iago is a Venetian; Cassio is a Florentine.)   **45 displeasure**
fall from favor   **47 stoutly** spiritedly.   **48 fame** reputation, importance   **49 affinity** kindred, family connection   **50 protests** insists
52 occasion . . . front opportunity by the forelock   **58 bosom** inmost
thoughts

3.2. Location: The citadel.
2 do my duties convey my respects   **3 works** breastworks, fortifications   **4 Repair** return, come   **6 wait upon** attend
3.3. Location: The garden of the citadel.
12 strangeness aloofness   **13 politic** required by wise policy
15 Or . . . diet or sustain itself at length upon such trivial and meager
technicalities   **16 breed . . . circumstance** continually renew itself so
out of chance events, or yield so few chances for my being pardoned
17 supplied filled by another person   **19 doubt** fear   **20 warrant**
guarantee   **23 watch him tame** tame him by keeping him from sleeping. (A term from falconry.)   **out of patience** past his endurance

His bed shall seem a school, his board a shrift;   24
I'll intermingle everything he does
With Cassio's suit. Therefore be merry, Cassio,
For thy solicitor shall rather die   27
Than give thy cause away.   28

       Enter Othello and Iago [at a distance].

EMILIA   Madam, here comes my lord.
CASSIO   Madam, I'll take my leave.
DESDEMONA   Why, stay, and hear me speak.
CASSIO
  Madam, not now. I am very ill at ease,
  Unfit for mine own purposes.
DESDEMONA   Well, do your discretion.   *Exit Cassio.*   34
IAGO   Ha? I like not that.
OTHELLO   What dost thou say?
IAGO
  Nothing, my lord; or if—I know not what.
OTHELLO
  Was not that Cassio parted from my wife?
IAGO
  Cassio, my lord? No, sure, I cannot think it,
  That he would steal away so guiltylike,
  Seeing you coming.
OTHELLO   I do believe 'twas he.
DESDEMONA [*joining them*]   How now, my lord?
  I have been talking with a suitor here,
  A man that languishes in your displeasure.
OTHELLO   Who is't you mean?
DESDEMONA
  Why, your lieutenant, Cassio. Good my lord,
  If I have any grace or power to move you,
  His present reconciliation take;   49
  For if he be not one that truly loves you,
  That errs in ignorance and not in cunning,   51
  I have no judgment in an honest face.
  I prithee, call him back.
OTHELLO   Went he hence now?
DESDEMONA   Yes, faith, so humbled
  That he hath left part of his grief with me
  To suffer with him. Good love, call him back.
OTHELLO
  Not now, sweet Desdemon. Some other time.
DESDEMONA   But shall't be shortly?
OTHELLO   The sooner, sweet, for you.
DESDEMONA   Shall't be tonight at supper?
OTHELLO   No, not tonight.
DESDEMONA   Tomorrow dinner, then?   63
OTHELLO   I shall not dine at home.
  I meet the captains at the citadel.
DESDEMONA
  Why, then, tomorrow night, or Tuesday morn,
  On Tuesday noon, or night, on Wednesday morn.
  I prithee, name the time, but let it not
  Exceed three days. In faith, he's penitent;

And yet his trespass, in our common reason—   70
Save that, they say, the wars must make example   71
Out of her best—is not almost a fault   72
T'incur a private check. When shall he come?   73
Tell me, Othello. I wonder in my soul
What you would ask me that I should deny,
Or stand so mamm'ring on. What? Michael Cassio,   76
That came a-wooing with you, and so many a time,
When I have spoke of you dispraisingly,
Hath ta'en your part—to have so much to do
To bring him in! By'r Lady, I could do much—   80
OTHELLO
  Prithee, no more. Let him come when he will;
  I will deny thee nothing.
DESDEMONA   Why, this is not a boon.
  'Tis as I should entreat you wear your gloves,
  Or feed on nourishing dishes, or keep you warm,
  Or sue to you to do a peculiar profit   86
  To your own person. Nay, when I have a suit
  Wherein I mean to touch your love indeed,   88
  It shall be full of poise and difficult weight,   89
  And fearful to be granted.
OTHELLO   I will deny thee nothing.
  Whereon, I do beseech thee, grant me this,   92
  To leave me but a little to myself.
DESDEMONA
  Shall I deny you? No. Farewell, my lord.
OTHELLO
  Farewell, my Desdemona. I'll come to thee straight.   95
DESDEMONA
  Emilia, come.—Be as your fancies teach you;   96
  Whate'er you be, I am obedient.   *Exit [with Emilia].*
OTHELLO
  Excellent wretch! Perdition catch my soul   98
  But I do love thee! And when I love thee not,   99
  Chaos is come again.   100
IAGO   My noble lord—
OTHELLO   What dost thou say, Iago?
IAGO
  Did Michael Cassio, when you wooed my lady,
  Know of your love?
OTHELLO
  He did, from first to last. Why dost thou ask?
IAGO
  But for a satisfaction of my thought;
  No further harm.
OTHELLO   Why of thy thought, Iago?

---

70 common reason everyday judgments   **71–2 Save . . . best** were it not that, as the saying goes, military discipline requires making an example of the very best men. (*Her* refers to wars as a singular concept.)   **72 not almost** scarcely   **73 a private check** even a private reprimand.   **76 mamm'ring on** wavering or muttering about.
80 bring him in restore him to favor.   **86 peculiar** particular, personal   **88 touch** test   **89 poise . . . weight** delicacy and weightiness   **92 Whereon** In return for which   **95 straight** straightaway.   **96 fancies** inclinations   **98 wretch** (A term of affectionate endearment.)   **99–100 And . . . again** i.e., My love for you will last forever, until the end of time when chaos will return. (But with an unconscious, ironic suggestion that, if anything should induce Othello to cease loving Desdemona, the result would be chaos.)

---

24 board dining table.   **shrift** confessional   **27 solicitor** advocate   **28 away** up.   **34 do your discretion** do as you think fit.   **49 His . . . take** let him be reconciled to you right away   **51 in cunning** wittingly   **63 dinner** (The noontime meal.)

IAGO
I did not think he had been acquainted with her.
OTHELLO
Oh, yes, and went between us very oft.
IAGO   Indeed?
OTHELLO
Indeed? Ay, indeed. Discern'st thou aught in that?
Is he not honest?
IAGO   Honest, my lord?
OTHELLO   Honest. Ay, honest.
IAGO   My lord, for aught I know.
OTHELLO   What dost thou think?
IAGO   Think, my lord?
OTHELLO
"Think, my lord?" By heaven, thou echo'st me,
As if there were some monster in thy thought
Too hideous to be shown. Thou dost mean something.
I heard thee say even now, thou lik'st not that,
When Cassio left my wife. What didst not like?
And when I told thee he was of my counsel   123
In my whole course of wooing, thou cried'st "Indeed?"
And didst contract and purse thy brow together   125
As if thou then hadst shut up in thy brain
Some horrible conceit. If thou dost love me,   127
Show me thy thought.
IAGO   My lord, you know I love you.
OTHELLO   I think thou dost;
And, for I know thou'rt full of love and honesty, 131
And weigh'st thy words before thou giv'st them
    breath,
Therefore these stops of thine fright me the more; 133
For such things in a false disloyal knave
Are tricks of custom, but in a man that's just   135
They're close dilations, working from the heart   136
That passion cannot rule.
IAGO   For Michael Cassio,   137
I dare be sworn I think that he is honest.
OTHELLO
I think so too.
IAGO   Men should be what they seem;
Or those that be not, would they might seem none!   140
OTHELLO
Certain, men should be what they seem.
IAGO
Why, then, I think Cassio's an honest man.
OTHELLO   Nay, yet there's more in this.
I prithee, speak to me as to thy thinkings,
As thou dost ruminate, and give thy worst of thoughts
The worst of words.
IAGO   Good my lord, pardon me.
Though I am bound to every act of duty,
I am not bound to that all slaves are free to.   148
Utter my thoughts? Why, say they are vile and false,
As where's that palace whereinto foul things

Sometimes intrude not? Who has that breast so pure
But some uncleanly apprehensions
Keep leets and law days, and in sessions sit   153
With meditations lawful?   154
OTHELLO
Thou dost conspire against thy friend, Iago,   155
If thou but think'st him wronged and mak'st his ear
A stranger to thy thoughts.
IAGO   I do beseech you,
Though I perchance am vicious in my guess—   158
As I confess it is my nature's plague
To spy into abuses, and oft my jealousy   160
Shapes faults that are not—that your wisdom then,
From one that so imperfectly conceits,   162
Would take no notice, nor build yourself a trouble
Out of his scattering and unsure observance.   164
It were not for your quiet nor your good,
Nor for my manhood, honesty, and wisdom,
To let you know my thoughts.
OTHELLO   What dost thou mean?
IAGO
Good name in man and woman, dear my lord,
Is the immediate jewel of their souls.   169
Who steals my purse steals trash; 'tis something,
    nothing;
'Twas mine, 'tis his, and has been slave to thousands;
But he that filches from me my good name
Robs me of that which not enriches him
And makes me poor indeed.
OTHELLO   By heaven, I'll know thy thoughts.
IAGO
You cannot, if my heart were in your hand,   176
Nor shall not, whilst 'tis in my custody.
OTHELLO   Ha?
IAGO   Oh, beware, my lord, of jealousy.
It is the green-eyed monster, which doth mock   179
The meat it feeds on. That cuckold lives in bliss   180
Who, certain of his fate, loves not his wronger;   181
But oh, what damnèd minutes tells he o'er   182
Who dotes, yet doubts, suspects, yet fondly loves!
OTHELLO   Oh, misery!
IAGO
Poor and content is rich, and rich enough,   185
But riches fineless is as poor as winter   186
To him that ever fears he shall be poor.

---

123 **of my counsel** in my confidence   125 **purse** knit   127 **conceit**
fancy.   131 **for** because   133 **stops** pauses   135 **of custom** customary   136–7 **They're . . . rule** they are secret or involuntary expressions of feeling that are too strong to be kept back.   137 **For** As for
140 **seem none** not seem at all, not seem to be honest.   148 **that** that
which.   **free to** free with respect to.

153 **Keep leets and law days** i.e., hold court, set up their authority in
one's heart. (*Leets* are a kind of manor court; *law days* are the days
courts sit in session, or those sessions.)   153–4 **and . . . lawful** i.e.,
and coexist in a kind of spiritual conflict with virtuous thoughts.
155 **thy friend** i.e., Othello   158 **vicious** wrong   160 **jealousy** suspicious nature   162 **one** i.e., myself, Iago.   **conceits** judges, conjectures
164 **scattering** random   169 **immediate** essential, most precious
176 **if** even if   179–80 **which . . . feeds on** (Jealousy mocks both itself
and the sufferer of jealousy; it is self-devouring and is its own punishment.)   180–1 **That . . . wronger** A cuckolded husband who
knows his wife to be unfaithful can at least take comfort in knowing
the truth, so that he will not continue to love her or to befriend her
lover. (Othello echoes this sentiment in lines 204–6, when he vows
that he would end uncertainty and cease to love an unfaithful wife.)
182 **tells** counts   185 **Poor . . . enough** To be content with what little
one has is the greatest wealth of all. (Proverbial.)   186 **fineless**
boundless

Good God, the souls of all my tribe defend
From jealousy!
OTHELLO   Why, why is this?
Think'st thou I'd make a life of jealousy,
To follow still the changes of the moon   192
With fresh suspicions? No! To be once in doubt   193
Is once to be resolved. Exchange me for a goat   194
When I shall turn the business of my soul
To such exsufflicate and blown surmises   196
Matching thy inference. 'Tis not to make me jealous   197
To say my wife is fair, feeds well, loves company,
Is free of speech, sings, plays, and dances well;
Where virtue is, these are more virtuous.
Nor from mine own weak merits will I draw
The smallest fear or doubt of her revolt,   202
For she had eyes, and chose me. No, Iago,
I'll see before I doubt; when I doubt, prove;
And on the proof, there is no more but this—
Away at once with love or jealousy.

IAGO
I am glad of this, for now I shall have reason
To show the love and duty that I bear you
With franker spirit. Therefore, as I am bound,
Receive it from me. I speak not yet of proof.
Look to your wife; observe her well with Cassio.
Wear your eyes thus, not jealous nor secure.   212
I would not have your free and noble nature,
Out of self-bounty, be abused. Look to't.   214
I know our country disposition well;
In Venice they do let God see the pranks
They dare not show their husbands; their best
    conscience
Is not to leave't undone, but keep't unknown.
OTHELLO   Dost thou say so?
IAGO
She did deceive her father, marrying you;
And when she seemed to shake and fear your looks,
She loved them most.
OTHELLO   And so she did.
IAGO   Why, go to, then!   222
She that, so young, could give out such a seeming,   223
To seel her father's eyes up close as oak,   224
He thought 'twas witchcraft! But I am much to blame.
I humbly do beseech you of your pardon
For too much loving you.
OTHELLO   I am bound to thee forever.   228
IAGO
I see this hath a little dashed your spirits.

OTHELLO
Not a jot, not a jot.
IAGO   I'faith, I fear it has.
I hope you will consider what is spoke
Comes from my love. But I do see you're moved.
I am to pray you not to strain my speech
To grosser issues nor to larger reach   234
Than to suspicion.
OTHELLO   I will not.
IAGO   Should you do so, my lord,
My speech should fall into such vile success   238
Which my thoughts aimed not. Cassio's my worthy
    friend.
My lord, I see you're moved.
OTHELLO   No, not much moved.
I do not think but Desdemona's honest.   241
IAGO
Long live she so! And long live you to think so!
OTHELLO
And yet, how nature erring from itself—
IAGO
Ay, there's the point! As—to be bold with you—
Not to affect many proposèd matches   245
Of her own clime, complexion, and degree,   246
Whereto we see in all things nature tends—
Foh! One may smell in such a will most rank,   248
Foul disproportion, thoughts unnatural.   249
But pardon me. I do not in position   250
Distinctly speak of her, though I may fear
Her will, recoiling to her better judgment,   252
May fall to match you with her country forms   253
And happily repent.
OTHELLO   Farewell, farewell!   254
If more thou dost perceive, let me know more.
Set on thy wife to observe. Leave me, Iago.
IAGO [going]   My lord, I take my leave.
OTHELLO
Why did I marry? This honest creature doubtless
Sees and knows more, much more, than he unfolds.
IAGO [returning]
My lord, I would I might entreat Your Honor
To scan this thing no farther. Leave it to time.   261
Although 'tis fit that Cassio have his place—
For, sure, he fills it up with great ability—
Yet, if you please to hold him off awhile,
You shall by that perceive him and his means.   265
Note if your lady strain his entertainment   266
With any strong or vehement importunity;
Much will be seen in that. In the meantime,
Let me be thought too busy in my fears—   269

192–3 To follow . . . suspicions? to be constantly imagining new causes for suspicion, changing incessantly like the moon?   194 once once
and for all.   resolved free of doubt, having settled the matter.   196
exsufflicate and blown inflated and blown up or flyblown, hence,
loathsome, disgusting   197 inference description or allegation.   202
doubt . . . revolt fear of her unfaithfulness   212 not neither.   secure
free from uncertainty.   214 self-bounty inherent or natural goodness
and generosity.   abused deceived.   222 go to (An expression of
impatience.)   223 seeming false appearance   224 seel blind. (A term
from falconry.)   oak (A close-grained wood.)
228 bound indebted. (But perhaps with ironic sense of "tied.")

234 issues significances.   reach meaning, scope   238 success effect,
result   241 honest chaste.   245 affect prefer, desire   246 clime . . .
degree country, temperament or skin color, and social position
248 will sensuality, appetite   249 disproportion abnormality   250 in
position in making this argument or proposition   252 recoiling
reverting.   better i.e., more natural and reconsidered   253 fall . . .
forms undertake to compare you with Venetian norms of handsome-
ness   254 happily repent haply repent her marriage.   261 scan
scrutinize   265 his means the method he uses (to regain his post).
266 strain his entertainment urge his reinstatement   269 busy
officious

As worthy cause I have to fear I am—
And hold her free, I do beseech Your Honor.   271
OTHELLO   Fear not my government.   272
IAGO   I once more take my leave.   *Exit.*
OTHELLO
This fellow's of exceeding honesty,
And knows all qualities, with a learnèd spirit,   275
Of human dealings. If I do prove her haggard,   276
Though that her jesses were my dear heartstrings,   277
I'd whistle her off and let her down the wind   278
To prey at fortune. Haply, for I am black   279
And have not those soft parts of conversation   280
That chamberers have, or for I am declined   281
Into the vale of years—yet that's not much—
She's gone. I am abused, and my relief   283
Must be to loathe her. Oh, curse of marriage,
That we can call these delicate creatures ours
And not their appetites! I had rather be a toad
And live upon the vapor of a dungeon
Than keep a corner in the thing I love
For others' uses. Yet, 'tis the plague of great ones;
Prerogatived are they less than the base.   290
'Tis destiny unshunnable, like death.
Even then this forkèd plague is fated to us   292
When we do quicken. Look where she comes.   293

     Enter Desdemona and Emilia.

If she be false, oh, then heaven mocks itself!
I'll not believe't.
DESDEMONA   How now, my dear Othello?
Your dinner, and the generous islanders   296
By you invited do attend your presence.   297
OTHELLO
I am to blame.
DESDEMONA   Why do you speak so faintly?
Are you not well?
OTHELLO
I have a pain upon my forehead here.
DESDEMONA
Faith, that's with watching. 'Twill away again.   301
         [*She offers her handkerchief.*]
Let me but bind it hard, within this hour
It will be well.
OTHELLO   Your napkin is too little.   303
Let it alone. Come, I'll go in with you.   304
     [*He puts the handkerchief from him, and it drops.*]

DESDEMONA
I am very sorry that you are not well.
           Exit [*with Othello*].
EMILIA [*picking up the handkerchief*]
I am glad I have found this napkin.
This was her first remembrance from the Moor.
My wayward husband hath a hundred times   308
Wooed me to steal it, but she so loves the token—
For he conjured her she should ever keep it—
That she reserves it evermore about her
To kiss and talk to. I'll have the work ta'en out,   312
And give't Iago. What he will do with it
Heaven knows, not I;
I nothing but to please his fantasy.   315

     Enter Iago.

IAGO
How now? What do you here alone?
EMILIA
Do not you chide. I have a thing for you.
IAGO
You have a thing for me? It is a common thing—   318
EMILIA   Ha?
IAGO   To have a foolish wife.
EMILIA
Oh, is that all? What will you give me now
For that same handkerchief?
IAGO   What handkerchief?
EMILIA   What handkerchief?
Why, that the Moor first gave to Desdemona;
That which so often you did bid me steal.
IAGO   Hast stolen it from her?
EMILIA
No, faith. She let it drop by negligence,
And to th'advantage I, being here, took't up.   329
Look, here 'tis.
IAGO   A good wench! Give it me.
EMILIA
What will you do with't, that you have been so earnest
To have me filch it?
IAGO [*snatching it*]   Why, what is that to you?
EMILIA
If it be not for some purpose of import,
Give't me again. Poor lady, she'll run mad
When she shall lack it.
IAGO   Be not acknown on't.   335
I have use for it. Go, leave me.   *Exit Emilia.*
I will in Cassio's lodging lose this napkin   337
And let him find it. Trifles light as air
Are to the jealous confirmations strong
As proofs of Holy Writ. This may do something.
The Moor already changes with my poison.

---

271 **hold her free** regard her as innocent   272 **government** self-control, conduct.   275 **qualities** natures, types   276 **haggard** wild (like a wild female hawk)   277 **jesses** straps fastened around the legs of a trained hawk   278 **I'd . . . wind** i.e., I'd let her go forever. (To release a hawk downwind was to turn it loose.)   279 **prey at fortune** fend for herself in the wild. **Haply, for** Perhaps because   280 **soft . . . conversation** pleasing social graces   281 **chamberers** drawing-room gallants   283 **abused** deceived   290 **Prerogatived** privileged (to have honest wives). **the base** ordinary citizens. (Socially prominent men are especially prone to the common destiny of being cuckolded and to the public shame that goes with it.)   292 **forkèd** (An allusion to the horns of the cuckold.)   293 **quicken** receive life. (*Quicken* may also mean to swarm with maggots as the body festers, as in 4.2.69, in which case lines 292–3 suggest that *even then*, in death, we are cuckolded by *forkèd* worms.)   296 **generous** noble   297 **attend** await   301 **watching** too little sleep.   303 **napkin** handkerchief   304 **Let it alone** i.e., Never mind.

308 **wayward** capricious   312 **work ta'en out** design of the embroidery copied   315 **fantasy** whim.   318 **common thing** (With bawdy suggestion; *common* suggests coarseness and availability to all comers, and *thing* is a slang term for the pudendum.)   329 **to th'advantage** taking the opportunity   335 **lack** miss. **Be . . . on't** Do not confess knowledge of it; keep out of this.   337 **lose** (The Folio spelling, "loose," is a normal spelling for "lose," but it may also contain the idea of "let go," "release.")

Dangerous conceits are in their natures poisons,   342
Which at the first are scarce found to distaste,   343
But with a little act upon the blood   344
Burn like the mines of sulfur.

         Enter Othello.

                          I did say so.
Look where he comes! Not poppy nor mandragora   346
Nor all the drowsy syrups of the world
Shall ever medicine thee to that sweet sleep
Which thou owed'st yesterday.

OTHELLO   Ha, ha, false to me?   349

IAGO
Why, how now, General? No more of that.

OTHELLO
Avaunt! Begone! Thou hast set me on the rack.
I swear 'tis better to be much abused
Than but to know't a little.

IAGO   How now, my lord?

OTHELLO
What sense had I of her stolen hours of lust?
I saw't not, thought it not, it harmed not me.
I slept the next night well, fed well, was free and
    merry;   356
I found not Cassio's kisses on her lips.
He that is robbed, not wanting what is stolen,   358
Let him not know't and he's not robbed at all.

IAGO   I am sorry to hear this.

OTHELLO
I had been happy if the general camp,
Pioneers and all, had tasted her sweet body,   362
So I had nothing known. Oh, now, forever   363
Farewell the tranquil mind! Farewell content!
Farewell the plumèd troops and the big wars   365
That makes ambition virtue! Oh, farewell!
Farewell the neighing steed and the shrill trump,
The spirit-stirring drum, th'ear-piercing fife,
The royal banner, and all quality,   369
Pride, pomp, and circumstance of glorious war!   370
And O you mortal engines, whose rude throats   371
Th'immortal Jove's dread clamors counterfeit,   372
Farewell! Othello's occupation's gone.

IAGO   Is't possible, my lord?

OTHELLO
Villain, be sure thou prove my love a whore!
Be sure of it. Give me the ocular proof,
Or, by the worth of mine eternal soul,
Thou hadst been better have been born a dog
Than answer my waked wrath!

IAGO   Is't come to this?

OTHELLO
Make me to see't, or at the least so prove it

That the probation bear no hinge nor loop   381
To hang a doubt on, or woe upon thy life!

IAGO   My noble lord—

OTHELLO
If thou dost slander her and torture me,
Never pray more; abandon all remorse;   385
On horror's head horrors accumulate;   386
Do deeds to make heaven weep, all earth amazed;   387
For nothing canst thou to damnation add
Greater than that.

IAGO   O grace! O heaven forgive me!
Are you a man? Have you a soul or sense?
God b'wi'you; take mine office. O wretched fool,   391
That lov'st to make thine honesty a vice!   392
O monstrous world! Take note, take note, O world,
To be direct and honest is not safe.
I thank you for this profit, and from hence   395
I'll love no friend, sith love breeds such offense.   396

OTHELLO   Nay, stay. Thou shouldst be honest.   397

IAGO
I should be wise, for honesty's a fool
And loses that it works for.

OTHELLO   By the world,   399
I think my wife be honest and think she is not;
I think that thou art just and think thou art not.
I'll have some proof. My name, that was as fresh
As Dian's visage, is now begrimed and black   403
As mine own face. If there be cords, or knives,
Poison, or fire, or suffocating streams,
I'll not endure it. Would I were satisfied!

IAGO
I see, sir, you are eaten up with passion.
I do repent me that I put it to you.
You would be satisfied?

OTHELLO   Would? Nay, and I will.

IAGO
And may; but how? How satisfied, my lord?
Would you, the supervisor, grossly gape on?   411
Behold her topped?

OTHELLO   Death and damnation! Oh!

IAGO
It were a tedious difficulty, I think,
To bring them to that prospect. Damn them then,   414
If ever mortal eyes do see them bolster   415
More than their own. What then? How then?   416
What shall I say? Where's satisfaction?
It is impossible you should see this,
Were they as prime as goats, as hot as monkeys,   419

---

342 **conceits** fancies, ideas   343 **distaste** be distasteful   344 **act** action, working   346 **mandragora** an opiate made of the mandrake root   349 **thou owed'st** you did own   356 **free** carefree   358 **wanting** missing   362 **Pioneers** diggers of mines, the lowest grade of soldiers   363 **So** provided   365 **big** mighty   369 **quality** character, essential nature   370 **Pride** rich display.   **circumstance** pageantry   371 **mortal engines** i.e., cannon. (*Mortal* means "deadly.")   372 **Jove's dread clamors** i.e., thunder

381 **probation** proof   385 **remorse** pity, penitent hope for salvation   386 **horrors accumulate** add still more horrors   387 **amazed** confounded with horror   391 **O wretched fool** (Iago addresses himself as a fool for having carried honesty too far.)   392 **vice** failing, something overdone.   395 **profit** profitable instruction.   **hence** henceforth   396 **sith** since.   **offense** i.e., harm to the one who offers help and friendship.   397 **Thou shouldst be** It appears that you are. (But Iago replies in the sense of "ought to be.")   399 **that** what   403 **Dian** Diana, goddess of the moon and of chastity   411 **supervisor** onlooker   414 **Damn them then** i.e., They would have to be really incorrigible   415 **bolster** go to bed together, share a bolster   416 **More** other.   **own** own eyes.   419 **prime** lustful

As salt as wolves in pride, and fools as gross   420
As ignorance made drunk. But yet I say,
If imputation and strong circumstances   422
Which lead directly to the door of truth
Will give you satisfaction, you might have't.

OTHELLO
Give me a living reason she's disloyal.

IAGO   I do not like the office.
But sith I am entered in this cause so far,   427
Pricked to't by foolish honesty and love,   428
I will go on. I lay with Cassio lately,
And being troubled with a raging tooth
I could not sleep. There are a kind of men
So loose of soul that in their sleeps will mutter
Their affairs. One of this kind is Cassio.
In sleep I heard him say, "Sweet Desdemona,
Let us be wary, let us hide our loves!"
And then, sir, would he grip and wring my hand,
Cry "O sweet creature!", then kiss me hard,
As if he plucked up kisses by the roots
That grew upon my lips; then laid his leg
Over my thigh, and sighed, and kissed, and then
Cried, "Cursèd fate that gave thee to the Moor!"

OTHELLO
Oh, monstrous! Monstrous!

IAGO   Nay, this was but his dream.

OTHELLO
But this denoted a foregone conclusion.   443
'Tis a shrewd doubt, though it be but a dream.   444

IAGO
And this may help to thicken other proofs
That do demonstrate thinly.

OTHELLO   I'll tear her all to pieces.

IAGO
Nay, but be wise. Yet we see nothing done;
She may be honest yet. Tell me but this:
Have you not sometimes seen a handkerchief
Spotted with strawberries in your wife's hand?   450

OTHELLO
I gave her such a one. 'Twas my first gift.

IAGO
I know not that; but such a handkerchief—
I am sure it was your wife's—did I today
See Cassio wipe his beard with.

OTHELLO   If it be that—

IAGO
If it be that, or any that was hers,
It speaks against her with the other proofs.

OTHELLO
Oh, that the slave had forty thousand lives!   457
One is too poor, too weak for my revenge.
Now do I see 'tis true. Look here, Iago,
All my fond love thus do I blow to heaven.   460

'Tis gone.
Arise, black vengeance, from the hollow hell!
Yield up, O love, thy crown and hearted throne   463
To tyrannous hate! Swell, bosom, with thy freight,   464
For 'tis of aspics' tongues!   465

IAGO   Yet be content.   466

OTHELLO   Oh, blood, blood, blood!

IAGO
Patience, I say. Your mind perhaps may change.

OTHELLO
Never, Iago. Like to the Pontic Sea,   469
Whose icy current and compulsive course
Ne'er feels retiring ebb, but keeps due on
To the Propontic and the Hellespont,   472
Even so my bloody thoughts with violent pace
Shall ne'er look back, ne'er ebb to humble love,
Till that a capable and wide revenge   475
Swallow them up. Now, by yond marble heaven,   476
[Kneeling] In the due reverence of a sacred vow
I here engage my words.

IAGO   Do not rise yet.
[He kneels.] Witness, you ever-burning lights above,   479
You elements that clip us round about,   480
Witness that here Iago doth give up
The execution of his wit, hands, heart,   482
To wronged Othello's service. Let him command,
And to obey shall be in me remorse,   484
What bloody business ever.   [They rise.]

OTHELLO   I greet thy love,   485
Not with vain thanks, but with acceptance bounteous,
And will upon the instant put thee to't.   487
Within these three days let me hear thee say
That Cassio's not alive.

IAGO   My friend is dead;
'Tis done at your request. But let her live.

OTHELLO
Damn her, lewd minx! Oh, damn her, damn her!   491
Come, go with me apart. I will withdraw
To furnish me with some swift means of death
For the fair devil. Now art thou my lieutenant.

IAGO   I am your own forever.   *Exeunt.*

❖

3.4

Enter Desdemona, Emilia, and Clown.

DESDEMONA   Do you know, sirrah, where Lieutenant   1
Cassio lies?   2

---

420 **salt** wanton, sensual.   **pride** heat   422 **imputation . . . circumstances** strong circumstantial evidence   427 **sith** since   428 **Pricked**
spurred   443 **foregone conclusion** previous experience or action.
444 **shrewd doubt** suspicious circumstance   450 **Spotted with strawberries** embroidered with a strawberry pattern   457 **the slave** i.e.,
Cassio   460 **fond** foolish. (But also suggesting "affectionate.")

463 **hearted** fixed in the heart   464 **freight** burden   465 **aspics'**
venomous serpents'   466 **content** calm.   469 **Pontic Sea** Black Sea
472 **Propontic** Sea of Marmora, between the Black Sea and the
Aegean.   **Hellespont** Dardanelles, straits where the Sea of Marmora
joins with the Aegean   475 **capable** ample, comprehensive
476 **marble** i.e., gleaming, polished, and indifferent to human suffering   479 **s.d.** *He kneels* (In the Quarto text, Iago kneels here after
Othello has knelt at line 477.)   480 **clip** encompass   482 **execution**
exercise, action.   **wit** mind   484 **remorse** pity (for Othello's wrongs)
485 **ever** soever.   487 **to't** to the proof.   491 **minx** wanton.
3.4. Location: Before the citadel.
1 **sirrah** (A form of address to an inferior.)   2 **lies** lodges. (But the
Clown makes the obvious pun.)

CLOWN   I dare not say he lies anywhere.

DESDEMONA   Why, man?

CLOWN   He's a soldier, and for me to say a soldier lies, 'tis stabbing.

DESDEMONA   Go to. Where lodges he?

CLOWN   To tell you where he lodges is to tell you where I lie.

DESDEMONA   Can anything be made of this?

CLOWN   I know not where he lodges, and for me to devise a lodging and say he lies here, or he lies there, were to lie in mine own throat.   13

DESDEMONA   Can you inquire him out, and be edified by report?

CLOWN   I will catechize the world for him; that is, make questions, and by them answer.

DESDEMONA   Seek him, bid him come hither. Tell him I have moved my lord on his behalf and hope all will be well.   19

CLOWN   To do this is within the compass of man's wit, and therefore I will attempt the doing it.   *Exit Clown.*

DESDEMONA   Where should I lose that handkerchief, Emilia?

EMILIA   I know not, madam.

DESDEMONA
Believe me, I had rather have lost my purse
Full of crusadoes; and but my noble Moor   26
Is true of mind and made of no such baseness
As jealous creatures are, it were enough
To put him to ill thinking.

EMILIA   Is he not jealous?

DESDEMONA
Who, he? I think the sun where he was born
Drew all such humors from him.

EMILIA   Look where he comes.   31

Enter Othello.

DESDEMONA
I will not leave him now till Cassio
Be called to him.—How is 't with you, my lord?

OTHELLO
Well, my good lady. [*Aside*] Oh, hardness to
dissemble!—
How do you, Desdemona?

DESDEMONA   Well, my good lord.

OTHELLO
Give me your hand. [*She gives her hand.*] This hand is
moist, my lady.

DESDEMONA
It yet hath felt no age nor known no sorrow.

OTHELLO
This argues fruitfulness and liberal heart.   38
Hot, hot, and moist. This hand of yours requires
A sequester from liberty, fasting and prayer,   40

Much castigation, exercise devout;   41
For here's a young and sweating devil here
That commonly rebels. 'Tis a good hand,
A frank one.

DESDEMONA   You may indeed say so,   44
For 'twas that hand that gave away my heart.

OTHELLO
A liberal hand. The hearts of old gave hands,   46
But our new heraldry is hands, not hearts.   47

DESDEMONA
I cannot speak of this. Come now, your promise.

OTHELLO   What promise, chuck?   49

DESDEMONA
I have sent to bid Cassio come speak with you.

OTHELLO
I have a salt and sorry rheum offends me;   51
Lend me thy handkerchief.

DESDEMONA   Here, my lord.   [*She offers a handkerchief.*]

OTHELLO
That which I gave you.

DESDEMONA   I have it not about me.

OTHELLO   Not?

DESDEMONA   No, faith, my lord.

OTHELLO
That's a fault. That handkerchief
Did an Egyptian to my mother give.
She was a charmer, and could almost read   59
The thoughts of people. She told her, while she kept it
'Twould make her amiable and subdue my father   61
Entirely to her love, but if she lost it
Or made a gift of it, my father's eye
Should hold her loathèd and his spirits should hunt
After new fancies. She, dying, gave it me,   65
And bid me, when my fate would have me wived,
To give it her. I did so; and take heed on 't;   67
Make it a darling like your precious eye.
To lose 't or give 't away were such perdition   69
As nothing else could match.

DESDEMONA   Is 't possible?

OTHELLO
'Tis true. There's magic in the web of it.   71
A sibyl, that had numbered in the world
The sun to course two hundred compasses,   73
In her prophetic fury sewed the work;   74
The worms were hallowed that did breed the silk,
And it was dyed in mummy which the skillful   76
Conserved of maidens' hearts.

DESDEMONA   I' faith! Is 't true?   77

---

13 **lie . . . throat** lie egregiously and deliberately.   **19 moved my lord** petitioned Othello   **26 crusadoes** Portuguese gold coins   **31 humors** (Refers to the four bodily fluids thought to determine temperament.)   **38 argues** gives evidence of.   **fruitfulness** generosity, amorousness, and fecundity.   **liberal** generous and sexually free   **40 sequester** sequestration

41 **castigation** corrective discipline.   **exercise devout** i.e., prayer, religious meditation, etc.   **44 frank** generous, open. (With sexual suggestion.)   **46–7 The hearts . . . hearts** i.e., In former times, people would give their hearts when they gave their hands to something, but in our decadent present age the joining of hands no longer has that spiritual sense.   **49 chuck** (A term of endearment.)   **51 salt . . . rheum** distressful head cold or watering of the eyes   **59 charmer** sorceress   **61 amiable** desirable   **65 fancies** loves.   **67 her** i.e., to my wife.   **69 perdition** loss   **71 web** fabric, weaving   **73 compasses** annual circlings. (The *sibyl*, or prophetess, was two hundred years old.)   **74 prophetic fury** frenzy of prophetic inspiration.   **work** embroidered pattern   **76 mummy** medicinal or magical preparation drained from mummified bodies   **77 Conserved of** prepared or preserved out of

OTHELLO
Most veritable. Therefore look to't well.

DESDEMONA
Then would to God that I had never seen't!

OTHELLO   Ha? Wherefore?

DESDEMONA
Why do you speak so startingly and rash?   81

OTHELLO
Is't lost? Is't gone? Speak, is't out o'th' way?   82

DESDEMONA   Heaven bless us!

OTHELLO   Say you?

DESDEMONA
It is not lost; but what an if it were?   85

OTHELLO   How?

DESDEMONA
I say it is not lost.

OTHELLO   Fetch't, let me see't.

DESDEMONA
Why, so I can, sir, but I will not now.
This is a trick to put me from my suit.
Pray you, let Cassio be received again.

OTHELLO
Fetch me the handkerchief! My mind misgives.

DESDEMONA   Come, come,
You'll never meet a more sufficient man.   93

OTHELLO
The handkerchief!

DESDEMONA   I pray, talk me of Cassio.   94

OTHELLO
The handkerchief!

DESDEMONA   A man that all his time   95
Hath founded his good fortunes on your love,   96
Shared dangers with you—

OTHELLO   The handkerchief!

DESDEMONA   I'faith, you are to blame.

OTHELLO   Zounds!   Exit Othello.

EMILIA   Is not this man jealous?

DESDEMONA   I ne'er saw this before.
Sure, there's some wonder in this handkerchief.
I am most unhappy in the loss of it.   104

EMILIA
'Tis not a year or two shows us a man.   105
They are all but stomachs, and we all but food;   106
They eat us hungerly, and when they are full   107
They belch us.

        Enter Iago and Cassio.

                    Look you, Cassio and my husband.

IAGO [to Cassio]
There is no other way; 'tis she must do't.
And, lo, the happiness! Go and importune her.   110

DESDEMONA
How now, good Cassio? What's the news with you?

CASSIO
Madam, my former suit. I do beseech you
That by your virtuous means I may again   113
Exist and be a member of his love
Whom I, with all the office of my heart,   115
Entirely honor. I would not be delayed.
If my offense be of such mortal kind   117
That nor my service past, nor present sorrows,   118
Nor purposed merit in futurity
Can ransom me into his love again,
But to know so must be my benefit;   121
So shall I clothe me in a forced content,
And shut myself up in some other course,   123
To fortune's alms.

DESDEMONA   Alas, thrice-gentle Cassio,   124
My advocation is not now in tune.   125
My lord is not my lord; nor should I know him,
Were he in favor as in humor altered.   127
So help me every spirit sanctified   128
As I have spoken for you all my best
And stood within the blank of his displeasure   130
For my free speech! You must awhile be patient.   131
What I can do I will, and more I will
Than for myself I dare. Let that suffice you.

IAGO
Is my lord angry?

EMILIA   He went hence but now,
And certainly in strange unquietness.

IAGO
Can he be angry? I have seen the cannon
When it hath blown his ranks into the air,
And like the devil from his very arm
Puffed his own brother—and is he angry?
Something of moment then. I will go meet him.   140
There's matter in't indeed, if he be angry.

DESDEMONA
I prithee, do so.   Exit [Iago].
                    Something, sure, of state,   142
Either from Venice, or some unhatched practice   143
Made demonstrable here in Cyprus to him,
Hath puddled his clear spirit; and in such cases   145
Men's natures wrangle with inferior things,
Though great ones are their object. 'Tis even so;
For let our finger ache, and it indues   148
Our other, healthful members even to a sense
Of pain. Nay, we must think men are not gods,

---

81 **startingly and rash** disjointedly and impetuously, excitedly.
82 **out o'th' way** lost, misplaced.   85 **an if** if   93 **sufficient** able,
complete   94 **talk** talk to   95–6 **A man . . . love** A man who throughout his career has relied on your favor for his advancement
104 **unhappy** (1) unfortunate (2) sad   105 **'Tis . . . man** A year or two
is not enough time for us women to know what men really are.
106 **but** nothing but   107 **hungerly** hungrily   110 **the happiness** in
happy time, fortunately met.

113 **virtuous** (1) efficacious (2) morally good   115 **office** loyal service
117 **mortal** fatal   118 **nor . . . nor** neither . . . nor   121 **But . . . benefit**
merely to know that my case is hopeless will have to content me (and
will be better than uncertainty)   123 **shut . . . in** commit myself to
124 **To fortune's alms** throwing myself on the mercy of fortune.
125 **advocation** advocacy   127 **favor** appearance.   **humor** mood
128 **So . . . sanctified** So help me all the heavenly host   130 **within
the blank** within point-blank range. (The *blank* is the center of the target.)   131 **free** frank   140 **of moment** of immediate importance,
momentous   142 **of state** concerning state affairs   143 **unhatched
practice** as yet unexecuted or undiscovered plot   145 **puddled** muddied   148 **indues** endows, brings to the same condition

Nor of them look for such observancy   151
As fits the bridal. Beshrew me much, Emilia,   152
I was, unhandsome warrior as I am,   153
Arraigning his unkindness with my soul;   154
But now I find I had suborned the witness,   155
And he's indicted falsely.

EMILIA   Pray heaven it be
State matters, as you think, and no conception
Nor no jealous toy concerning you.   158

DESDEMONA
Alas the day! I never gave him cause.

EMILIA
But jealous souls will not be answered so;
They are not ever jealous for the cause,
But jealous for they're jealous. It is a monster   162
Begot upon itself, born on itself.   163

DESDEMONA
Heaven keep that monster from Othello's mind!

EMILIA   Lady, amen.

DESDEMONA
I will go seek him. Cassio, walk hereabout.
If I do find him fit, I'll move your suit
And seek to effect it to my uttermost.

CASSIO
I humbly thank Your Ladyship.
                            Exit [*Desdemona with Emilia*].

                    Enter Bianca.

BIANCA
Save you, friend Cassio!

CASSIO   What make you from home?   170
How is't with you, my most fair Bianca?
I' faith, sweet love, I was coming to your house.

BIANCA
And I was going to your lodging, Cassio.
What, keep a week away? Seven days and nights?
Eightscore-eight hours? And lovers' absent hours   175
More tedious than the dial eightscore times?   176
Oh, weary reck'ning!

CASSIO   Pardon me, Bianca.
I have this while with leaden thoughts been pressed;
But I shall, in a more continuate time,   179
Strike off this score of absence. Sweet Bianca,   180
              [*giving her Desdemona's handkerchief*]
Take me this work out.

BIANCA   Oh, Cassio, whence came this?   181
This is some token from a newer friend.   182
To the felt absence now I feel a cause.
Is't come to this? Well, well.

CASSIO   Go to, woman!
Throw your vile guesses in the devil's teeth,

From whence you have them. You are jealous now
That this is from some mistress, some remembrance.
No, by my faith, Bianca.

BIANCA   Why, whose is it?

CASSIO
I know not, neither. I found it in my chamber.
I like the work well. Ere it be demanded—   190
As like enough it will—I would have it copied   191
Take it and do't, and leave me for this time.

BIANCA   Leave you? Wherefore?

CASSIO
I do attend here on the General,
And think it no addition, nor my wish,   195
To have him see me womaned.

BIANCA   Why, I pray you?

CASSIO   Not that I love you not.

BIANCA   But that you do not love me.
I pray you, bring me on the way a little,   200
And say if I shall see you soon at night.

CASSIO
'Tis but a little way that I can bring you,
For I attend here; but I'll see you soon.

BIANCA
'Tis very good. I must be circumstanced.   204
                            Exeunt omnes.

                        ❧

4.1

                Enter Othello and Iago.

IAGO
Will you think so?

OTHELLO   Think so, Iago?

IAGO   What,
To kiss in private?

OTHELLO   An unauthorized kiss!

IAGO
Or to be naked with her friend in bed
An hour or more, not meaning any harm?

OTHELLO
Naked in bed, Iago, and not mean harm?
It is hypocrisy against the devil.
They that mean virtuously and yet do so,
The devil their virtue tempts, and they tempt heaven.

IAGO
If they do nothing, 'tis a venial slip.   9
But if I give my wife a handkerchief—

OTHELLO   What then?

IAGO
Why then, 'tis hers, my lord, and being hers,
She may, I think, bestow't on any man.

OTHELLO
She is protectress of her honor too.
May she give that?

---

151 **observancy** attentiveness   152 **bridal** wedding (when a bride-groom is newly attentive to his bride).   **Beshrew me** (A mild oath.)
153 **unhandsome** insufficient, unskillful   154 **with** before the bar of
155 **suborned the witness** induced the witness to give false testimony
158 **toy** fancy   162 **for** because   163 **Begot upon itself** generated solely from itself   170 **Save** God save.   **make** do   175 **Eightscore-eight** one hundred sixty-eight, the number of hours in a week
176 **the dial** a complete revolution of the clock   179 **continuate** uninterrupted   180 **Strike . . . score** settle this account   181 **Take . . . out** copy this embroidery for me.   182 **friend** mistress.

190 **demanded** inquired for   191 **like** likely   195 **addition** i.e., addition to my reputation   200 **bring** accompany   204 **be circumstanced** be governed by circumstance, yield to your conditions.
4.1. Location: Before the citadel.
9 **venial** pardonable

IAGO

Her honor is an essence that's not seen;
They have it very oft that have it not.   17
But, for the handkerchief—

OTHELLO

By heaven, I would most gladly have forgot it.
Thou said'st—Oh, it comes o'er my memory
As doth the raven o'er the infectious house,   21
Boding to all—he had my handkerchief.

IAGO

Ay, what of that?

OTHELLO   That's not so good now.

IAGO   What

If I had said I had seen him do you wrong?
Or heard him say—as knaves be such abroad,   25
Who having, by their own importunate suit,   26
Or voluntary dotage of some mistress,   27
Convincèd or supplied them, cannot choose   28
But they must blab—

OTHELLO   Hath he said anything?   29

IAGO

He hath, my lord; but, be you well assured,
No more than he'll unswear.

OTHELLO   What hath he said?

IAGO

Faith, that he did—I know not what he did.

OTHELLO   What? What?

IAGO

Lie—

OTHELLO   With her?

IAGO   With her, on her; what you will.

OTHELLO   Lie with her? Lie on her? We say "lie on her"
when they belie her. Lie with her? Zounds, that's ful-   36
some.—Handkerchief—confessions—handkerchief!   37
—To confess and be hanged for his labor—first to be   38
hanged and then to confess.—I tremble at it. Nature   39
would not invest herself in such shadowing passion   40
without some instruction. It is not words that shakes   41
me thus. Pish! Noses, ears, and lips.—Is't possible?
—Confess—handkerchief!—O devil!

                                          Falls in a trance.

IAGO   Work on,
My medicine, work! Thus credulous fools are caught,
And many worthy and chaste dames even thus,
All guiltless, meet reproach.—What, ho! My lord!
My lord, I say! Othello!

                    Enter Cassio.

                    How now, Cassio?

CASSIO   What's the matter?

IAGO

My lord is fall'n into an epilepsy.
This is his second fit. He had one yesterday.

CASSIO

Rub him about the temples.

IAGO   No, forbear.
The lethargy must have his quiet course.   53
If not, he foams at mouth, and by and by
Breaks out to savage madness. Look, he stirs.
Do you withdraw yourself a little while.
He will recover straight. When he is gone,
I would on great occasion speak with you.   58

                                          [*Exit Cassio.*]

How is it, General? Have you not hurt your head?

OTHELLO

Dost thou mock me?

IAGO   I mock you not, by heaven.   60
Would you would bear your fortune like a man!

OTHELLO

A hornèd man's a monster and a beast.

IAGO

There's many a beast then in a populous city,
And many a civil monster.   64

OTHELLO   Did he confess it?

IAGO   Good sir, be a man.
Think every bearded fellow that's but yoked   67
May draw with you. There's millions now alive   68
That nightly lie in those unproper beds   69
Which they dare swear peculiar. Your case is better.   70
Oh, 'tis the spite of hell, the fiend's arch-mock,
To lip a wanton in a secure couch   72
And to suppose her chaste! No, let me know,
And knowing what I am, I know what she shall be.   74

OTHELLO   Oh, thou art wise. 'Tis certain.

IAGO   Stand you awhile apart;
Confine yourself but in a patient list.   77
Whilst you were here o'erwhelmèd with your grief—
A passion most unsuiting such a man—
Cassio came hither. I shifted him away,   80
And laid good 'scuse upon your ecstasy,   81
Bade him anon return and here speak with me,
The which he promised. Do but encave yourself   83
And mark the fleers, the gibes, and notable scorns   84
That dwell in every region of his face;
For I will make him tell the tale anew,
Where, how, how oft, how long ago, and when
He hath and is again to cope your wife.   88

---

17 They have it i.e., They enjoy a reputation for it   **21 raven . . . house** (Allusion to the belief that the raven hovered over a house of sickness or infection, such as one visited by the plague.)   **25–9 as . . . blab—** since there are rascals enough who, having seduced a woman either through their own importunity or through the woman's willing infatuation, cannot keep quiet about it—   **36 belie** slander   **36–7 fulsome** foul.   **38–9 first . . . to confess** (Othello reverses the proverbial *confess and be hanged*; Cassio is to be given no time to confess before he dies.)   **39–41 Nature . . . instruction** i.e., Without some foundation in fact, nature would not have dressed herself in such an overwhelming passion that comes over me now and fills my mind with images, or in such a lifelike fantasy as Cassio had in his dream of lying with Desdemona.   **41 words** mere words

53 lethargy coma.   **his** its   **58 on great occasion** on a matter of great importance   **60 mock me** (Othello takes Iago's question about hurting his head to be a mocking reference to the cuckold's horns.)   **64 civil** i.e., dwelling in a city   **67 yoked** (1) married (2) put into the yoke of infamy and cuckoldry   **68 draw with you** pull as you do, like oxen who are yoked, i.e., share your fate as cuckold.   **69 unproper** not exclusively their own   **70 peculiar** private, their own.   **better** i.e., because you know the truth.   **72 lip** kiss.   **secure** free from suspicion   **74 And . . . shall be** and, knowing myself to be a cuckold, I'll know for certain that she's a whore.   **77 in . . . list** within the bounds of patience.   **80–1 I shifted . . . ecstasy** I got him out of the way, using your fit as my excuse for doing so   **83 encave** conceal   **84 fleers** sneers   **88 cope** encounter with, have sex with

I say, but mark his gesture. Marry, patience!
Or I shall say you're all-in-all in spleen,   90
And nothing of a man.

OTHELLO   Dost thou hear, Iago?
I will be found most cunning in my patience;
But—dost thou hear?—most bloody.

IAGO   That's not amiss;
But yet keep time in all. Will you withdraw?   94
                    [*Othello stands apart.*]
Now will I question Cassio of Bianca,
A huswife that by selling her desires   96
Buys herself bread and clothes. It is a creature
That dotes on Cassio—as 'tis the strumpet's plague
To beguile many and be beguiled by one.
He, when he hears of her, cannot restrain   100
From the excess of laughter. Here he comes.

Enter Cassio.

As he shall smile, Othello shall go mad;
And his unbookish jealousy must conster   103
Poor Cassio's smiles, gestures, and light behaviors
Quite in the wrong.—How do you now, Lieutenant?

CASSIO
The worser that you give me the addition   106
Whose want even kills me.   107

IAGO
Ply Desdemona well and you are sure on't.
[*Speaking lower*] Now, if this suit lay in Bianca's power,
How quickly should you speed!

CASSIO [*laughing*]   Alas, poor caitiff!   111

OTHELLO [*aside*]   Look how he laughs already!

IAGO
I never knew a woman love man so.

CASSIO
Alas, poor rogue! I think, i'faith, she loves me.

OTHELLO [*aside*]
Now he denies it faintly, and laughs it out.

IAGO
Do you hear, Cassio?

OTHELLO [*aside*]   Now he importunes him
To tell it o'er. Go to! Well said, well said.   117

IAGO
She gives it out that you shall marry her.
Do you intend it?

CASSIO   Ha, ha, ha!

OTHELLO [*aside*]
Do you triumph, Roman? Do you triumph?   121

CASSIO   I marry her? What? A customer? Prithee, bear   122
some charity to my wit; do not think it so unwhole-   123
some. Ha, ha, ha!

OTHELLO [*aside*]   So, so, so, so! They laugh that win.   125

IAGO   Faith, the cry goes that you shall marry her.   126

CASSIO   Prithee, say true.

IAGO   I am a very villain else.   128

OTHELLO [*aside*]   Have you scored me? Well.   129

CASSIO   This is the monkey's own giving out. She is
persuaded I will marry her out of her own love and
flattery, not out of my promise.   132

OTHELLO [*aside*]   Iago beckons me. Now he begins the   133
story.

CASSIO   She was here even now; she haunts me in every
place. I was the other day talking on the seabank with   136
certain Venetians, and thither comes the bauble, and,   137
by this hand, she falls me thus about my neck—   138
                    [*He embraces Iago.*]

OTHELLO [*aside*]   Crying, "Oh, dear Cassio!" as it were; his
gesture imports it.

CASSIO   So hangs and lolls and weeps upon me, so
shakes and pulls me. Ha, ha, ha!

OTHELLO [*aside*]   Now he tells how she plucked him to my
chamber. Oh, I see that nose of yours, but not that dog   144
I shall throw it to.   145

CASSIO   Well, I must leave her company.

IAGO   Before me, look where she comes.   147

Enter Bianca [with Othello's handkerchief].

CASSIO   'Tis such another fitchew! Marry, a perfumed   148
one.—What do you mean by this haunting of me?

BIANCA   Let the devil and his dam haunt you! What did   150
you mean by that same handkerchief you gave me
even now? I was a fine fool to take it. I must take out
the work? A likely piece of work, that you should find   153
it in your chamber and know not who left it there!
This is some minx's token, and I must take out the
work? There; give it your hobbyhorse. [*She gives him*   156
the handkerchief.] Wheresoever you had it, I'll take out
no work on't.

CASSIO   How now, my sweet Bianca? How now? How
now?

OTHELLO [*aside*]   By heaven, that should be my hand-   161
kerchief!

BIANCA   If you'll come to supper tonight, you may; if
you will not, come when you are next prepared for.   164
                                        Exit.

IAGO   After her, after her.

CASSIO   Faith, I must. She'll rail in the streets else.

IAGO   Will you sup there?

CASSIO   Faith, I intend so.

IAGO   Well, I may chance to see you, for I would very
fain speak with you.

---

90 all-in-all in spleen utterly governed by passionate impulses
94 keep time keep yourself steady (as in music)   **96 huswife** hussy
100 restrain refrain   **103 his unbookish** Othello's uninstructed.
conster construe   **106 addition** title   **107 Whose want** the lack of
which   **111 caitiff** wretch.   **117 Go to** (An expression of remonstrance.)   **Well said** Well done. (Sarcastic.)   **121 Roman** (The
Romans were noted for their *triumphs* or triumphal processions.)
122 A customer? Who, I, the whore's customer? (Or, *customer* could
mean "prostitute.")   **122–3 bear . . . wit** be more charitable to my
judgment

125 They . . . win i.e., They that laugh last laugh best.   **126 cry** rumor
128 I . . . else Call me a complete rogue if I'm not telling the truth.
129 scored me scored off me, beaten me, made up my reckoning,
branded me.   **132 flattery** self-flattery, self-deception   **133 beckons**
signals to   **136 seabank** seashore   **137 bauble** plaything   **138 by
this hand** I make my vow   **144–5 not . . . to** (Othello imagines himself cutting off Cassio's nose and throwing it to a dog.)   **147 Before
me** i.e., On my soul   **148 'Tis . . . fitchew!** What a whore she is! Just
like all the others. (*Fitchew* or "polecat" was a common term of contempt for a courtesan or prostitute.)   **150 dam** mother   **153 A likely
. . . work** A fine story   **156 hobbyhorse** harlot   **161 should be** must
be   **164 when . . . for** when I'm ready for you (i.e., never).

CASSIO Prithee, come. Will you?
IAGO Go to. Say no more.   [*Exit Cassio.*] 172
OTHELLO [*advancing*] How shall I murder him, Iago?
IAGO Did you perceive how he laughed at his vice?
OTHELLO Oh, Iago!
IAGO And did you see the handkerchief?
OTHELLO Was that mine?
IAGO Yours, by this hand. And to see how he prizes the foolish woman your wife! She gave it him, and he hath given it his whore.
OTHELLO I would have him nine years a-killing. A fine woman! A fair woman! A sweet woman!
IAGO Nay, you must forget that.
OTHELLO Ay, let her rot and perish, and be damned tonight, for she shall not live. No, my heart is turned to stone; I strike it, and it hurts my hand. Oh, the world hath not a sweeter creature! She might lie by an emperor's side and command him tasks.
IAGO Nay, that's not your way.   189
OTHELLO Hang her! I do but say what she is. So delicate with her needle! An admirable musician! Oh, she will sing the savageness out of a bear. Of so high and plenteous wit and invention!   193
IAGO She's the worse for all this.
OTHELLO Oh, a thousand, a thousand times! And then, of so gentle a condition!   196
IAGO Ay, too gentle.   197
OTHELLO Nay, that's certain. But yet the pity of it, Iago! Oh, Iago, the pity of it, Iago!
IAGO If you are so fond over her iniquity, give her patent 200 to offend, for if it touch not you it comes near nobody.
OTHELLO I will chop her into messes. Cuckold me?   202
IAGO Oh, 'tis foul in her.
OTHELLO With mine officer?
IAGO That's fouler.
OTHELLO Get me some poison, Iago, this night. I'll not expostulate with her, lest her body and beauty unpro- 207 vide my mind again. This night, Iago.   208
IAGO Do it not with poison. Strangle her in her bed, even the bed she hath contaminated.
OTHELLO Good, good! The justice of it pleases. Very good.
IAGO And for Cassio, let me be his undertaker. You 212 shall hear more by midnight.
OTHELLO
  Excellent good. [*A trumpet within.*] What trumpet is that same?
IAGO I warrant, something from Venice.

  Enter Lodovico, Desdemona, and attendants.

'Tis Lodovico. This comes from the Duke.
See, your wife's with him.

LODOVICO
  God save you, worthy General!
OTHELLO   With all my heart, sir. 218
LODOVICO [*giving him a letter*]
  The Duke and the senators of Venice greet you.
OTHELLO
  I kiss the instrument of their pleasures.
                          [*He opens the letter, and reads.*]
DESDEMONA
  And what's the news, good cousin Lodovico?
IAGO
  I am very glad to see you, signor.
  Welcome to Cyprus.
LODOVICO
  I thank you. How does Lieutenant Cassio?
IAGO Lives, sir.
DESDEMONA
  Cousin, there's fall'n between him and my lord
  An unkind breach; but you shall make all well.   227
OTHELLO Are you sure of that?
DESDEMONA My lord?
OTHELLO [*reads*] "This fail you not to do, as you will—"
LODOVICO
  He did not call; he's busy in the paper.
  Is there division twixt my lord and Cassio?
DESDEMONA
  A most unhappy one. I would do much
  T'atone them, for the love I bear to Cassio.   234
OTHELLO Fire and brimstone!
DESDEMONA My lord?
OTHELLO Are you wise?
DESDEMONA
  What, is he angry?
LODOVICO   Maybe the letter moved him;
  For, as I think, they do command him home,
  Deputing Cassio in his government.   240
DESDEMONA By my troth, I am glad on't.   241
OTHELLO Indeed?
DESDEMONA My lord?
OTHELLO I am glad to see you mad.   244
DESDEMONA Why, sweet Othello—
OTHELLO [*striking her*] Devil!
DESDEMONA I have not deserved this.
LODOVICO
  My lord, this would not be believed in Venice,
  Though I should swear I saw't. 'Tis very much.   249
  Make her amends; she weeps.
OTHELLO   Oh, devil, devil!
  If that the earth could teem with woman's tears,   251
  Each drop she falls would prove a crocodile.   252
  Out of my sight!
DESDEMONA   I will not stay to offend you. [*Going.*]

172 Go to (An expression of remonstrance.) 189 your way i.e., the way you should think of her. 193 invention imagination. 196 gentle a condition wellborn and well-bred. 197 gentle generous, yielding (to other men). 200 fond foolish. patent license 202 messes portions of meat, i.e., bits. 207–8 unprovide weaken, disarm 212 be his undertaker undertake to dispatch him.

218 With all my heart i.e., I thank you most heartily 227 unkind unnatural, contrary to their natures; hurtful 234 T'atone to reconcile 240 government office. 241 on't of it. 244 I am ... mad i.e., I am glad to see that you are insane enough to rejoice in Cassio's promotion. (? Othello bitterly plays on Desdemona's I am glad.) 249 very much too much, outrageous. 251 teem breed, be impregnated 252 falls lets fall. crocodile (Crocodiles were supposed to weep hypocritical tears for their victims.)

LODOVICO   Truly, an obedient lady.
　　I do beseech Your Lordship, call her back.
OTHELLO [*calling*]   Mistress!
DESDEMONA [*returning*]   My lord?
OTHELLO   What would you with her, sir?   258
LODOVICO   Who, I, my lord?
OTHELLO
　　Ay, you did wish that I would make her turn.
　　Sir, she can turn, and turn, and yet go on
　　And turn again; and she can weep, sir, weep;
　　And she's obedient, as you say, obedient,   263
　　Very obedient.—Proceed you in your tears.—
　　Concerning this, sir—Oh, well-painted passion!—   265
　　I am commanded home.—Get you away;
　　I'll send for you anon.—Sir, I obey the mandate
　　And will return to Venice.—Hence, avaunt!
　　　　　　　　　　　　　　　　　[*Exit Desdemona.*]
　　Cassio shall have my place. And, sir, tonight
　　I do entreat that we may sup together.
　　You are welcome, sir, to Cyprus.—Goats and
　　　　monkeys!   *Exit.* 271
LODOVICO
　　Is this the noble Moor whom our full Senate
　　Call all in all sufficient? Is this the nature
　　Whom passion could not shake? Whose solid virtue
　　The shot of accident nor dart of chance
　　Could neither graze nor pierce?
IAGO   He is much changed.
LODOVICO
　　Are his wits safe? Is he not light of brain?
IAGO
　　He's that he is. I may not breathe my censure   278
　　What he might be. If what he might he is not,   279
　　I would to heaven he were!
LODOVICO   What, strike his wife?   280
IAGO
　　Faith, that was not so well; yet would I knew
　　That stroke would prove the worst!
LODOVICO   Is it his use?   282
　　Or did the letters work upon his blood   283
　　And new-create his fault?
IAGO   Alas, alas!
　　It is not honesty in me to speak
　　What I have seen and known. You shall observe him,
　　And his own courses will denote him so   287
　　That I may save my speech. Do but go after,
　　And mark how he continues.
LODOVICO
　　I am sorry that I am deceived in him.   *Exeunt.*

❖

258 What . . . sir? (Othello implies that Desdemona is pliant and will do a *turn*, lines 257–9, for any man.)   **263 obedient** (With much the same sexual connotation as *turn* in lines 257–9.)   **265 passion** i.e., grief.   **271 Goats and monkeys** (See 3.3.419.)   **278–90 I may . . . were!** I dare not venture an opinion as to whether he's of unsound mind, as you suggest, but, if he isn't, then it might be better to wish he were in fact insane, since only that could excuse his wild behavior!   **282 use** custom.   **283 blood** passions   **287 courses will denote** actions will reveal

4.2

Enter Othello and Emilia.

OTHELLO   You have seen nothing, then?
EMILIA
　　Nor ever heard, nor ever did suspect.
OTHELLO
　　Yes, you have seen Cassio and she together.
EMILIA
　　But then I saw no harm, and then I heard
　　Each syllable that breath made up between them.
OTHELLO   What, did they never whisper?
EMILIA   Never, my lord.
OTHELLO   Nor send you out o'th' way?
EMILIA   Never.
OTHELLO
　　To fetch her fan, her gloves, her mask, nor nothing?
EMILIA   Never, my lord.
OTHELLO   That's strange.
EMILIA
　　I durst, my lord, to wager she is honest,
　　Lay down my soul at stake. If you think other,   14
　　Remove your thought; it doth abuse your bosom.   15
　　If any wretch have put this in your head,
　　Let heaven requite it with the serpent's curse!   17
　　For if she be not honest, chaste, and true,
　　There's no man happy; the purest of their wives
　　Is foul as slander.
OTHELLO   Bid her come hither. Go.
　　　　　　　　　　　　　　　　　Exit Emilia.
　　She says enough; yet she's a simple bawd   21
　　That cannot say as much. This is a subtle whore,   22
　　A closet lock and key of villainous secrets.   23
　　And yet she'll kneel and pray; I have seen her do't.

Enter Desdemona and Emilia.

DESDEMONA   My lord, what is your will?
OTHELLO   Pray you, chuck, come hither.
DESDEMONA
　　What is your pleasure?
OTHELLO   Let me see your eyes.
　　Look in my face.
DESDEMONA   What horrible fancy's this?
OTHELLO [*to Emilia*]   Some of your function, mistress.   29
　　Leave procreants alone and shut the door;   30
　　Cough or cry "hem" if anybody come.
　　Your mystery, your mystery! Nay, dispatch.   32
　　　　　　　　　　　　　　　　　Exit Emilia.
DESDEMONA [*kneeling*]
　　Upon my knees, what doth your speech import?

4.2. Location: The citadel.
14 at stake as the wager.   **15 abuse your bosom** deceive your breast, your heart.   **17 the serpent's curse** the curse pronounced by God on the serpent for deceiving Eve, just as some man has done to Othello and Desdemona. (See Genesis 3:14.)   **21–2 she's . . . much** i.e., any procuress or go-between who couldn't make up as plausible a story as Emilia's would have to be pretty stupid.   **22 This** i.e., Desdemona   **23 closet lock and key** i.e., concealer   **29 Some . . . function** i.e., Practice your chosen profession, that of bawd (by guarding the door)   **30 procreants** mating couples   **32 mystery** trade, occupation

I understand a fury in your words,
But not the words.

OTHELLO
Why, what art thou?

DESDEMONA   Your wife, my lord, your true
And loyal wife.

OTHELLO   Come, swear it, damn thyself,
Lest, being like one of heaven, the devils themselves   38
Should fear to seize thee. Therefore be double
    damned:
Swear thou art honest.

DESDEMONA   Heaven doth truly know it.

OTHELLO
Heaven truly knows that thou art false as hell.

DESDEMONA
To whom, my lord? With whom? How am I false?

OTHELLO [*weeping*]
Ah, Desdemon! Away, away, away!

DESDEMONA
Alas the heavy day! Why do you weep?
Am I the motive of these tears, my lord?   45
If haply you my father do suspect
An instrument of this your calling back,
Lay not your blame on me. If you have lost him,
I have lost him too.

OTHELLO   Had it pleased heaven
To try me with affliction, had they rained   50
All kinds of sores and shames on my bare head,
Steeped me in poverty to the very lips,
Given to captivity me and my utmost hopes,
I should have found in some place of my soul
A drop of patience. But, alas, to make me
A fixèd figure for the time of scorn   56
To point his slow and moving finger at!   57
Yet could I bear that too, well, very well.
But there where I have garnered up my heart,   59
Where either I must live or bear no life,
The fountain from the which my current runs   61
Or else dries up—to be discarded thence!
Or keep it as a cistern for foul toads   63
To knot and gender in! Turn thy complexion there,   64
Patience, thou young and rose-lipped cherubin—   65
Ay, there look grim as hell!   66

DESDEMONA
I hope my noble lord esteems me honest.   67

OTHELLO
Oh, ay, as summer flies are in the shambles,   68
That quicken even with blowing. O thou weed,   69
Who art so lovely fair and smell'st so sweet
That the sense aches at thee, would thou hadst ne'er
    been born!

DESDEMONA
Alas, what ignorant sin have I committed?   72

OTHELLO
Was this fair paper, this most goodly book,
Made to write "whore" upon? What committed?
Committed? Oh, thou public commoner!   75
I should make very forges of my cheeks,
That would to cinders burn up modesty,
Did I but speak thy deeds. What committed?
Heaven stops the nose at it and the moon winks;   79
The bawdy wind, that kisses all it meets,   80
Is hushed within the hollow mine of earth   81
And will not hear't. What committed?
Impudent strumpet!

DESDEMONA   By heaven, you do me wrong.

OTHELLO
Are not you a strumpet?

DESDEMONA   No, as I am a Christian.
If to preserve this vessel for my lord   86
From any other foul unlawful touch
Be not to be a strumpet, I am none.

OTHELLO   What, not a whore?

DESDEMONA   No, as I shall be saved.

OTHELLO   Is't possible?

DESDEMONA
Oh, heaven forgive us!

OTHELLO   I cry you mercy, then.   92
I took you for that cunning whore of Venice
That married with Othello. [*Calling out*] You, mistress,
That have the office opposite to Saint Peter
And keep the gate of hell!

          Enter Emilia.

               You, you, ay, you!
We have done our course. There's money for your
    pains.   [*He gives money.*]   97
I pray you, turn the key and keep our counsel.   *Exit.*

EMILIA
Alas, what does this gentleman conceive?   99
How do you, madam? How do you, my good lady?

DESDEMONA   Faith, half asleep.   101

EMILIA
Good madam, what's the matter with my lord?

DESDEMONA   With who?

EMILIA   Why, with my lord, madam.

DESDEMONA
Who is thy lord?

EMILIA   He that is yours, sweet lady.

DESDEMONA
I have none. Do not talk to me, Emilia.
I cannot weep, nor answers have I none
But what should go by water. Prithee, tonight   108

38 being . . . heaven looking like an angel   **45 motive** cause   **50 they** the heavenly powers   **56–7 A fixèd . . . finger at** a figure of ridicule to be pointed at scornfully for all of eternity by the slowly moving finger of Time.   **59 garnered** stored   **61 fountain** spring   **63 cistern** cesspool   **64 To . . . gender in** to couple sexually and conceive in. **64–6 Turn . . . hell!** Direct your gaze there, Patience, and your youthful and rosy cherubic countenance will turn grim and pale at this hellish spectacle!   **67 honest** chaste.   **68 shambles** slaughterhouse **69 That . . . blowing** that come to life with the puffing up of the rotten meat on which the flies and their maggots are breeding.

72 ignorant sin sin in ignorance   **75 commoner** prostitute. **79 winks** closes her eyes. (The moon symbolizes chastity.) **80 bawdy** kissing one and all   **81 mine** cave (where the winds were thought to dwell)   **86 vessel** body   **92 cry you mercy** beg your pardon. (Sarcastic.)   **97 course** business. (With an indecent suggestion of "trick," turn at sex.)   **99 conceive** suppose, think.   **101 half asleep** i.e., dazed.   **108 go by water** be conveyed by tears.

Lay on my bed my wedding sheets, remember;
And call thy husband hither.
EMILIA   Here's a change indeed!   *Exit.*
DESDEMONA
'Tis meet I should be used so, very meet.   112
How have I been behaved, that he might stick   113
The small'st opinion on my least misuse?   114

Enter Iago and Emilia.

IAGO
What is your pleasure, madam? How is't with you?
DESDEMONA
I cannot tell. Those that do teach young babes
Do it with gentle means and easy tasks.
He might have chid me so, for, in good faith,
I am a child to chiding.
IAGO   What is the matter, lady?
EMILIA
Alas, Iago, my lord hath so bewhored her,
Thrown such despite and heavy terms upon her,
That true hearts cannot bear it.
DESDEMONA   Am I that name, Iago?
IAGO   What name, fair lady?
DESDEMONA
Such as she said my lord did say I was.
EMILIA
He called her whore. A beggar in his drink
Could not have laid such terms upon his callet.   128
IAGO   Why did he so?
DESDEMONA [*weeping*]
I do not know. I am sure I am none such.
IAGO   Do not weep, do not weep. Alas the day!
EMILIA
Hath she forsook so many noble matches,
Her father and her country and her friends,
To be called whore? Would it not make one weep?
DESDEMONA
It is my wretched fortune.
IAGO   Beshrew him for't!   135
How comes this trick upon him?
DESDEMONA   Nay, heaven doth know. 136
EMILIA
I will be hanged if some eternal villain,   137
Some busy and insinuating rogue,   138
Some cogging, cozening slave, to get some office,   139
Have not devised this slander. I will be hanged else.
IAGO
Fie, there is no such man. It is impossible.
DESDEMONA
If any such there be, heaven pardon him!
EMILIA
A halter pardon him! And hell gnaw his bones!   143

Why should he call her whore? Who keeps her
    company?
What place? What time? What form? What
    likelihood?   145
The Moor's abused by some most villainous knave,
Some base notorious knave, some scurvy fellow.
Oh, heavens, that such companions thou'dst unfold, 148
And put in every honest hand a whip
To lash the rascals naked through the world
Even from the east to th' west!
IAGO   Speak within door.   151
EMILIA
Oh, fie upon them! Some such squire he was   152
That turned your wit the seamy side without   153
And made you to suspect me with the Moor.
IAGO
You are a fool. Go to.
DESDEMONA   Oh, God, Iago,   155
What shall I do to win my lord again?
Good friend, go to him; for, by this light of heaven,
I know not how I lost him. Here I kneel. [*She kneels.*]
If e'er my will did trespass 'gainst his love,
Either in discourse of thought or actual deed,   160
Or that mine eyes, mine ears, or any sense   161
Delighted them in any other form;   162
Or that I do not yet, and ever did,   163
And ever will—though he do shake me off
To beggarly divorcement—love him dearly,
Comfort forswear me! Unkindness may do much,   166
And his unkindness may defeat my life,   167
But never taint my love. I cannot say "whore."
It does abhor me now I speak the word;   169
To do the act that might the addition earn   170
Not the world's mass of vanity could make me.   171
                          [*She rises.*]
IAGO
I pray you, be content. 'Tis but his humor.   172
The business of the state does him offense,
And he does chide with you.
DESDEMONA   If 'twere no other—
IAGO   It is but so, I warrant.   [*Trumpets within.*]
Hark, how these instruments summon you to supper!
The messengers of Venice stays the meat.   178
Go in, and weep not. All things shall be well.
              Exeunt Desdemona and Emilia.

Enter Roderigo.

How now, Roderigo?
RODERIGO   I do not find that thou deal'st justly with me.
IAGO   What in the contrary?

---

112 **'Tis . . . very meet** i.e., It must be I somehow have deserved this.
113–14 **How . . . misuse?** What have I done that prompts Othello to
attach even the slightest censure to whatever little fault I may have
committed?   128 **callet** whore.   135 **Beshrew** May evil befall. (An
oath.)   136 **trick** strange behavior, delusion   137 **eternal** inveterate
138 **insinuating** ingratiating, fawning, wheedling   139 **cogging, cozening** cheating, defrauding   143 **halter** hangman's noose

145 **form** manner, circumstance.   148 **that . . . unfold** would that you
would expose such fellows   151 **within door** i.e., not so loud.
152 **squire** fellow   153 **seamy side without** wrong side out   155 **Go
to** i.e., That's enough.   160 **discourse of thought** process of thinking
161 **that** if. (Also in line 163.)   162 **Delighted them** took delight
163 **yet** still   166 **Comfort forswear** may heavenly comfort forsake
167 **defeat** destroy   169 **abhor** (1) fill me with abhorrence (2) make
me whorelike   170 **addition** title   171 **vanity** showy splendor
172 **humor** mood.   178 **stays the meat** are waiting to dine.

RODERIGO   Every day thou daff'st me with some device,   183
Iago, and rather, as it seems to me now, keep'st
from me all conveniency than suppliest me with the   185
least advantage of hope. I will indeed no longer   186
endure it, nor am I yet persuaded to put up in peace   187
what already I have foolishly suffered.

IAGO   Will you hear me, Roderigo?

RODERIGO   Faith, I have heard too much, for your words
and performances are no kin together.

IAGO   You charge me most unjustly.

RODERIGO   With naught but truth. I have wasted myself
out of my means. The jewels you have had from me to
deliver Desdemona would half have corrupted a vo-   195
tarist. You have told me she hath received them and   196
returned me expectations and comforts of sudden re-   197
spect and acquaintance, but I find none.   198

IAGO   Well, go to, very well.

RODERIGO   "Very well"! "Go to"! I cannot go to, man,   200
nor 'tis not very well. By this hand, I think it is scurvy,
and begin to find myself fopped in it.   202

IAGO   Very well.

RODERIGO   I tell you 'tis not very well. I will make myself   204
known to Desdemona. If she will return me my jewels,
I will give over my suit and repent my unlawful solic-
itation; if not, assure yourself I will seek satisfaction   207
of you.

IAGO   You have said now?   209

RODERIGO   Ay, and said nothing but what I protest   210
intendment of doing.   211

IAGO   Why, now I see there's mettle in thee, and even
from this instant do build on thee a better opinion
than ever before. Give me thy hand, Roderigo. Thou
hast taken against me a most just exception; but yet I
protest I have dealt most directly in thy affair.

RODERIGO   It hath not appeared.

IAGO   I grant indeed it hath not appeared, and your
suspicion is not without wit and judgment. But,
Roderigo, if thou hast that in thee indeed which I have
greater reason to believe now than ever—I mean
purpose, courage, and valor—this night show it. If
thou the next night following enjoy not Desdemona,
take me from this world with treachery and devise
engines for my life.   225

RODERIGO   Well, what is it? Is it within reason and
compass?

IAGO   Sir, there is especial commission come from
Venice to depute Cassio in Othello's place.

RODERIGO   Is that true? Why, then Othello and Desdemona return again to Venice.

IAGO   Oh, no; he goes into Mauritania and takes away
with him the fair Desdemona, unless his abode be
lingered here by some accident; wherein none can be
so determinate as the removing of Cassio.   235

RODERIGO   How do you mean, removing of him?

IAGO   Why, by making him uncapable of Othello's
place—knocking out his brains.

RODERIGO   And that you would have me to do?

IAGO   Ay, if you dare do yourself a profit and a right.
He sups tonight with a harlotry, and thither will I go to   241
him. He knows not yet of his honorable fortune. If
you will watch his going thence, which I will fashion
to fall out between twelve and one, you may take him   244
at your pleasure. I will be near to second your attempt,
and he shall fall between us. Come, stand not amazed
at it, but go along with me. I will show you such a
necessity in his death that you shall think yourself
bound to put it on him. It is now high suppertime,   249
and the night grows to waste. About it.   250

RODERIGO   I will hear further reason for this.

IAGO   And you shall be satisfied.   *Exeunt.*

❖

4.3

*Enter Othello, Lodovico, Desdemona, Emilia, and
attendants.*

LODOVICO
I do beseech you, sir, trouble yourself no further.

OTHELLO
Oh, pardon me; 'twill do me good to walk.

LODOVICO
Madam, good night. I humbly thank Your Ladyship.

DESDEMONA
Your Honor is most welcome.

OTHELLO   Will you walk, sir?
Oh, Desdemona!

DESDEMONA   My lord?

OTHELLO   Get you to bed on th'instant. I will be returned forthwith. Dismiss your attendant there. Look't
be done.

DESDEMONA   I will, my lord.
            Exit [Othello, with Lodovico and attendants].

EMILIA   How goes it now? He looks gentler than he did.

DESDEMONA
He says he will return incontinent,   12
And hath commanded me to go to bed,
And bid me to dismiss you.

EMILIA   Dismiss me?

DESDEMONA
It was his bidding. Therefore, good Emilia,
Give me my nightly wearing, and adieu.
We must not now displease him.

EMILIA   I would you had never seen him!

---

183 thou daff'st me you put me off.   **183–4 device** excuse, trick
185 conveniency advantage, opportunity   **186 advantage** increase
187 put up submit to, tolerate   **195 deliver** deliver to   **195–6 votarist**
nun.   **197-8 sudden respect** immediate consideration   **200 I cannot
go to** (Roderigo changes Iago's *go to*, an expression urging patience,
to *I cannot go to*, "I have no opportunity for success in wooing.")
202 fopped fooled, duped   **204 not very well** (Roderigo changes
Iago's *Very well*, "All right, then," to *not very well*, "not at all good.")
207 satisfaction repayment. (The term normally means settling of
accounts in a duel.)   **209 You . . . now?** Have you finished?
210–11 protest intendment avow my intention   **225 engines** plots,
snares

235 determinate conclusive, instrumental   **241 harlotry** slut
244 fall out occur   **249 high** fully   **250 grows to waste** wastes away.
4.3 Location: The citadel.
12 incontinent immediately

DESDEMONA
So would not I. My love doth so approve him
That even his stubbornness, his checks, his frowns—   21
Prithee, unpin me—have grace and favor in them.
                    [*Emilia prepares Desdemona for bed.*]
EMILIA   I have laid those sheets you bade me on the
bed.
DESDEMONA
All's one. Good faith, how foolish are our minds!   25
If I do die before thee, prithee shroud me
In one of these same sheets.
EMILIA   Come, come, you talk.   27
DESDEMONA
My mother had a maid called Barbary.
She was in love, and he she loved proved mad   29
And did forsake her. She had a song of "Willow."
An old thing 'twas, but it expressed her fortune,
And she died singing it. That song tonight
Will not go from my mind; I have much to do   33
But to go hang my head all at one side   34
And sing it like poor Barbary. Prithee, dispatch.
EMILIA   Shall I go fetch your nightgown?   36
DESDEMONA   No, unpin me here.
This Lodovico is a proper man.   38
EMILIA   A very handsome man.
DESDEMONA   He speaks well.
EMILIA   I know a lady in Venice would have walked
barefoot to Palestine for a touch of his nether lip.
DESDEMONA [*singing*]
        "The poor soul sat sighing by a sycamore tree,
            Sing all a green willow;   44
        Her hand on her bosom, her head on her knee,
            Sing willow, willow, willow.
        The fresh streams ran by her and murmured her
                moans;
            Sing willow, willow, willow;
        Her salt tears fell from her, and softened the
                stones—"
Lay by these.
[*Singing*] "Sing willow, willow, willow—"
Prithee, hie thee. He'll come anon.   52
[*Singing*] "Sing all a green willow must be my garland.
        Let nobody blame him; his scorn I approve—"
Nay, that's not next.—Hark! Who is't that knocks?
EMILIA   It's the wind.
DESDEMONA [*singing*]
        "I called my love false love; but what said he
                then?
            Sing willow, willow, willow;
        If I court more women, you'll couch with more
                men."
So, get thee gone. Good night. Mine eyes do itch;
Doth that bode weeping?
EMILIA   'Tis neither here nor there.

DESDEMONA
I have heard it said so. Oh, these men, these men!
Dost thou in conscience think—tell me, Emilia—
That there be women do abuse their husbands   64
In such gross kind?
EMILIA   There be some such, no question.
DESDEMONA
Wouldst thou do such a deed for all the world?
EMILIA
Why, would not you?
DESDEMONA   No, by this heavenly light!
EMILIA
Nor I neither by this heavenly light;
I might do't as well i'th' dark.
DESDEMONA
Wouldst thou do such a deed for all the world?
EMILIA
The world's a huge thing. It is a great price
For a small vice.
DESDEMONA
Good troth, I think thou wouldst not.
EMILIA   By my troth, I think I should, and undo't when
I had done. Marry, I would not do such a thing for a
joint ring, nor for measures of lawn, nor for gowns,   76
petticoats, nor caps, nor any petty exhibition. But for   77
all the whole world! Uds pity, who would not make   78
her husband a cuckold to make him a monarch? I
should venture purgatory for't.
DESDEMONA
Beshrew me if I would do such a wrong
For the whole world.
EMILIA   Why, the wrong is but a wrong i'th' world, and
having the world for your labor, 'tis a wrong in your
own world, and you might quickly make it right.
DESDEMONA
I do not think there is any such woman.
EMILIA   Yes, a dozen, and as many   87
To th' vantage as would store the world they played
        for.   88
But I do think it is their husbands' faults
If wives do fall. Say that they slack their duties   90
And pour our treasures into foreign laps,   91
Or else break out in peevish jealousies,
Throwing restraint upon us? Or say they strike us,   93
Or scant our former having in despite?   94
Why, we have galls, and though we have some grace,   95
Yet have we some revenge. Let husbands know
Their wives have sense like them. They see, and smell,   97
And have their palates both for sweet and sour,
As husbands have. What is it that they do   99

---

21 **stubbornness** roughness. **checks** rebukes   25 **All's one** All
right. It doesn't really matter.   27 **talk** i.e., prattle.   29 **mad** wild,
lunatic   33-4 **I . . . hang** I can scarcely keep myself from hanging
36 **nightgown** dressing gown.   38 **proper** handsome   44 **willow**
(A conventional emblem of disappointed love.)   52 **hie thee** hurry.
anon right away.

64 **abuse** deceive   76 **joint ring** a ring made in separate halves.
lawn fine linen   77 **exhibition** gift.   78 **Uds** God's   87–8 **and . . .
played for** and enough additionally to stock the world men have
gambled and sported sexually for.   90 **they** our husbands.   **duties**
marital duties   91 **pour . . . laps** i.e., are unfaithful, give what is
rightfully ours (semen) to other women   93 **Throwing . . . us** jealously restricting our freedom.   94 **Or . . . despite** or spitefully take away
from us whatever we enjoyed before.   95 **have galls** i.e., are capable
of resenting injury and insult.   **grace** inclination to be merciful   97
sense sensory perception and appetite   99 **they** husbands

When they change us for others? Is it sport?   100
I think it is. And doth affection breed it?   101
I think it doth. Is't frailty that thus errs?
It is so, too. And have not we affections,
Desires for sport, and frailty, as men have?
Then let them use us well; else let them know,
The ills we do, their ills instruct us so.

DESDEMONA
Good night, good night. God me such uses send   107
Not to pick bad from bad, but by bad mend!   108

                                            Exeunt.

❧

5.1

Enter Iago and Roderigo.

IAGO
Here stand behind this bulk. Straight will he come.   1
Wear thy good rapier bare, and put it home.   2
Quick, quick! Fear nothing. I'll be at thy elbow.
It makes us or it mars us. Think on that,
And fix most firm thy resolution.

RODERIGO
Be near at hand. I may miscarry in't.

IAGO
Here, at thy hand. Be bold, and take thy stand.
          [*Iago stands aside, Roderigo conceals himself.*]

RODERIGO
I have no great devotion to the deed;
And yet he hath given me satisfying reasons.
'Tis but a man gone. Forth, my sword! He dies.
                                         [*He draws.*]

IAGO
I have rubbed this young quat almost to the sense,   11
And he grows angry. Now, whether he kill Cassio
Or Cassio him, or each do kill the other,
Every way makes my gain. Live Roderigo,   14
He calls me to a restitution large
Of gold and jewels that I bobbed from him   16
As gifts to Desdemona.
It must not be. If Cassio do remain,
He hath a daily beauty in his life
That makes me ugly; and besides, the Moor
May unfold me to him; there stand I in much peril.   21
No, he must die. Be't so. I hear him coming.

Enter Cassio.

RODERIGO [*coming forth*]
I know his gait, 'tis he.—Villain, thou diest!
                                    [*He attacks Cassio.*]

CASSIO
That thrust had been mine enemy indeed,
But that my coat is better than thou know'st.   25
I will make proof of thine.
                    [*He draws, and wounds Roderigo.*]
RODERIGO   Oh, I am slain! [*He falls.* 26
              *Iago, from behind, wounds Cassio
                        in the leg, and exit.*]

CASSIO
I am maimed forever. Help, ho! Murder! Murder!

Enter Othello.

OTHELLO   The voice of Cassio! Iago keeps his word.
RODERIGO   Oh, villain that I am!
OTHELLO   It is even so.
CASSIO   Oh, help, ho! Light! A surgeon!
OTHELLO
'Tis he. O brave Iago, honest and just,
That hast such noble sense of thy friend's wrong!
Thou teachest me.—Minion, your dear lies dead,   34
And your unblest fate hies. Strumpet, I come.   35
Forth of my heart those charms, thine eyes, are blotted; 36
Thy bed, lust-stained, shall with lust's blood be
      spotted.   *Exit Othello.*

Enter Lodovico and Gratiano.

CASSIO
What ho! No watch? No passage? Murder! Murder!   38
GRATIANO
'Tis some mischance. The voice is very direful.
CASSIO   Oh, help!
LODOVICO   Hark!
RODERIGO   Oh, wretched villain!
LODOVICO
Two or three groan. 'Tis heavy night;   43
These may be counterfeits. Let's think't unsafe
To come in to the cry without more help.   45
                    [*They remain near the entrance.*]
RODERIGO
Nobody come? Then shall I bleed to death.

Enter Iago [in his shirtsleeves, with a light].

LODOVICO   Hark!
GRATIANO
Here's one comes in his shirt, with light and weapons.
IAGO
Who's there? Whose noise is this that cries on murder? 49
LODOVICO
We do not know.
IAGO   Did not you hear a cry?
CASSIO
Here, here! For heaven's sake, help me!
IAGO   What's the matter?
                        [*He moves toward Cassio.*]

---

100 change exchange. **sport** sexual pastime. **101 affection** passion
107 uses habit, practice **108 Not . . . mend** i.e., not to learn bad conduct from others' badness (as Emilia has suggested women learn
from men), but to mend my ways by perceiving what badness is,
making spiritual benefit out of evil and adversity.
5.1 Location: A street in Cyprus.
1 bulk framework projecting from the front of a shop. **2 bare**
unsheathed. **home** all the way into the target. **11 quat** pimple,
pustule. **to the sense** to the quick **14 Live Roderigo** If Roderigo
lives **16 bobbed** swindled **21 unfold** expose

25 coat (Possibly a garment of mail under the outer clothing, or simply a tougher coat than Roderigo expected.) **26 proof** a test
34 Minion Hussy (i.e., Desdemona) **35 hies** hastens on. **36 Forth
of** From out **38 passage** people passing by. **43 heavy** thick, dark
45 come in to approach **49 cries** cries out

GRATIANO [*to Lodovico*]
  This is Othello's ancient, as I take it.
LODOVICO [*to Gratiano*]
  The same indeed, a very valiant fellow.
IAGO [*to Cassio*]
  What are you here that cry so grievously?   54
CASSIO
  Iago? Oh, I am spoiled, undone by villains!   55
  Give me some help.
IAGO
  Oh, me, Lieutenant! What villains have done this?
CASSIO
  I think that one of them is hereabout,
  And cannot make away.
IAGO   Oh, treacherous villains!   59
  [*To Lodovico and Gratiano*] What are you there? Come
    in, and give some help.   [*They advance.*]
RODERIGO   Oh, help me there!
CASSIO
  That's one of them.
IAGO   Oh, murderous slave! Oh, villain!
                       [*He stabs Roderigo.*]
RODERIGO
  Oh, damned Iago! Oh, inhuman dog!
IAGO
  Kill men i'th' dark?—Where be these bloody thieves?—
  How silent is this town!—Ho! Murder, murder!—
  [*To Lodovico and Gratiano*] What may you be? Are you
    of good or evil?
LODOVICO   As you shall prove us, praise us.   67
IAGO   Signor Lodovico?
LODOVICO   He, sir.
IAGO
  I cry you mercy. Here's Cassio hurt by villains.   70
GRATIANO   Cassio?
IAGO   How is't, brother?
CASSIO   My leg is cut in two.
IAGO   Marry, heaven forbid!
  Light, gentlemen! I'll bind it with my shirt.
         [*He hands them the light, and tends to Cassio's
                                          wound.*]

         Enter Bianca.

BIANCA
  What is the matter, ho? Who is't that cried?
IAGO   Who is't that cried?
BIANCA   Oh, my dear Cassio!
  My sweet Cassio! Oh, Cassio, Cassio, Cassio!
IAGO
  Oh, notable strumpet! Cassio, may you suspect
  Who they should be that have thus mangled you?
CASSIO   No.
GRATIANO
  I am sorry to find you thus. I have been to seek you.

IAGO
  Lend me a garter. [*He applies a tourniquet.*] So.—Oh, for
    a chair,   83
  To bear him easily hence!
BIANCA
  Alas, he faints! Oh, Cassio, Cassio, Cassio!
IAGO
  Gentlemen all, I do suspect this trash
  To be a party in this injury.—
  Patience awhile, good Cassio.—Come, come;
  Lend me a light. [*He shines the light on Roderigo.*] Know
    we this face or no?
  Alas, my friend and my dear countryman
  Roderigo! No.—Yes, sure.—Oh, heaven! Roderigo!
GRATIANO   What, of Venice?
IAGO   Even he, sir. Did you know him?
GRATIANO   Know him? Ay.
IAGO
  Signor Gratiano? I cry your gentle pardon.   95
  These bloody accidents must excuse my manners   96
  That so neglected you.
GRATIANO   I am glad to see you.
IAGO
  How do you, Cassio?—Oh, a chair, a chair!
GRATIANO   Roderigo!
IAGO
  He, he, 'tis he. [*A litter is brought in.*] Oh, that's well
    said; the chair.   100
  Some good man bear him carefully from hence;
  I'll fetch the General's surgeon. [*To Bianca*] For you,
    mistress,   102
  Save you your labor.—He that lies slain here, Cassio, 103
  Was my dear friend. What malice was between you?   104
CASSIO
  None in the world, nor do I know the man.
IAGO [*to Bianca*]
  What, look you pale?—Oh, bear him out o'th'air.   106
              [*Cassio and Roderigo are borne off.*]
  Stay you, good gentlemen.—Look you pale,
    mistress?—   107
  Do you perceive the gastness of her eye?—   108
  Nay, if you stare, we shall hear more anon.—   109
  Behold her well; I pray you, look upon her.
  Do you see, gentlemen? Nay, guiltiness
  Will speak, though tongues were out of use.

         [*Enter Emilia.*]

EMILIA
  'Las, what's the matter? What's the matter, husand?
IAGO
  Cassio hath here been set on in the dark
  By Roderigo and fellows that are scaped.
  He's almost slain, and Roderigo dead.

---

83 chair litter   **95 gentle** noble   **96 accidents** sudden events
100 well said well done   **102 For** As for   **103 Save . . . labor** i.e.,
never you mind tending Cassio.   **104 malice** enmity   **106 bear . . .
air** (Fresh air was thought to be dangerous for a wound.)   **107 Stay
you** (Lodovico and Gratiano are evidently about to leave.)   **108 gastness** terror   **109 stare** (Iago pretends to interpret Bianca's wild looks
as an involuntary confession of guilt.)

---

54 What Who. (Also at lines 60 and 66.)   **55 spoiled** ruined, done for
59 make get   **67 prove us** prove us to be.   **praise** appraise   **70 I cry
you mercy** I beg your pardon.

EMILIA
　　Alas, good gentleman! Alas, good Cassio!
IAGO
　　This is the fruits of whoring. Prithee, Emilia,
　　Go know of Cassio where he supped tonight.   119
　　[*To Bianca*] What, do you shake at that?
BIANCA
　　He supped at my house, but I therefore shake not.
IAGO
　　Oh, did he so? I charge you go with me.
EMILIA　　Oh, fie upon thee, strumpet!
BIANCA
　　I am no strumpet, but of life as honest   124
　　As you that thus abuse me.
EMILIA　　As I? Faugh! Fie upon thee!
IAGO
　　Kind gentlemen, let's go see poor Cassio dressed.— 127
　　Come, mistress, you must tell 's another tale.—
　　Emilia, run you to the citadel
　　And tell my lord and lady what hath happed.—
　　Will you go on afore? [*Aside*] This is the night
　　That either makes me or fordoes me quite.   *Exeunt.* 132

5.2

*Enter Othello [with a light], and Desdemona in
her bed.*

OTHELLO
　　It is the cause, it is the cause, my soul.   1
　　Let me not name it to you, you chaste stars!
　　It is the cause. Yet I'll not shed her blood,
　　Nor scar that whiter skin of hers than snow,
　　And smooth as monumental alabaster.   5
　　Yet she must die, else she'll betray more men.
　　Put out the light, and then put out the light.   7
　　If I quench thee, thou flaming minister,   8
　　I can again thy former light restore,
　　Should I repent me; but once put out thy light,   10
　　Thou cunning'st pattern of excelling nature,   11
　　I know not where is that Promethean heat   12
　　That can thy light relume. When I have plucked thy
　　　　rose,   13
　　I cannot give it vital growth again;
　　It needs must wither. I'll smell thee on the tree.
　　　　　　　　　　　　　　　　　　　[*He kisses her.*]
　　Oh, balmy breath, that dost almost persuade
　　Justice to break her sword! One more, one more.

　　Be thus when thou art dead, and I will kill thee,
　　And love thee after. One more, and that's the last.
　　　　　　　　　　　　　　　　　　　[*He kisses her.*]
　　So sweet was ne'er so fatal. I must weep,
　　But they are cruel tears. This sorrow's heavenly;   21
　　It strikes where it doth love. She wakes.   22
DESDEMONA　　Who's there? Othello?
OTHELLO　　Ay, Desdemona.
DESDEMONA　　Will you come to bed, my lord?
OTHELLO　　Have you prayed tonight, Desdemon?
DESDEMONA　　Ay, my lord.
OTHELLO
　　If you bethink yourself of any crime   28
　　Unreconciled as yet to heaven and grace,
　　Solicit for it straight.   30
DESDEMONA
　　Alack, my lord, what may you mean by that?
OTHELLO
　　Well, do it, and be brief. I will walk by.
　　I would not kill thy unprepared spirit.
　　No, heaven forfend! I would not kill thy soul.   34
DESDEMONA
　　Talk you of killing?
OTHELLO　　　　　　　　　Ay, I do.
DESDEMONA　　　　　　　　　　　　Then heaven
　　Have mercy on me!
OTHELLO　　　　　　　　　Amen, with all my heart!
DESDEMONA
　　If you say so, I hope you will not kill me.
OTHELLO　　Humh!
DESDEMONA
　　And yet I fear you; for you're fatal then
　　When your eyes roll so. Why I should fear I know not,
　　Since guiltiness I know not; but yet I feel I fear.
OTHELLO
　　Think on thy sins.
DESDEMONA　　　　　　　　They are loves I bear to you.   42
OTHELLO　　Ay, and for that thou diest.
DESDEMONA
　　That death's unnatural that kills for loving.
　　Alas, why gnaw you so your nether lip?
　　Some bloody passion shakes your very frame.
　　These are portents; but yet I hope, I hope,
　　They do not point on me.
OTHELLO　　Peace, and be still!
DESDEMONA　　I will so. What's the matter?
OTHELLO
　　That handkerchief which I so loved and gave thee
　　Thou gav'st to Cassio.
DESDEMONA　　　　　　　　No, by my life and soul!
　　Send for the man and ask him.
OTHELLO
　　Sweet soul, take heed, take heed of perjury.
　　Thou art on thy deathbed.

---

119 **know** learn   124 **honest** chaste   127 **Cassio dressed** Cassio's
wounds dressed.   132 **fordoes** undoes, ruins
5.2. Location: A bedchamber in the citadel.
0.1–2 *in her bed* (Either the curtains are drawn back to reveal the bed
in a recessed area backstage, or the bed is "thrust out" onstage as the
scene begins.)   1 **cause** i.e., cause of justice, the offense itself, which
must be corrected in the name of justice   5 **monumental** i.e., used in
making tombs and funeral monuments   7 **the light . . . light** the
torch or lamp . . . Desdemona's life.   8 **minister** servant   10 **repent
me** change my mind   11 **Thou . . . pattern** you skillfully wrought
perfect example   12 **Promethean heat** (Alludes to two myths: that of
Prometheus stealing fire from heaven for humanity, and that of his
creating humankind.)   13 **relume** rekindle.

21 **they are cruel tears** these tears betoken a sorrowful cruelty, regret-
table but just.   22 **It . . . love** (Compare Hebrews 12:6: "For whom the
Lord loveth he chasteneth.")   28 **crime** sin   30 **Solicit** petition, pray.
straight immediately.   34 **forfend** forbid.   42 **They . . . you** i.e., My
only sins are my idolatry of loving you too much.

DESDEMONA
 Ay, but not yet to die.
OTHELLO   Yes, presently.   56
 Therefore confess thee freely of thy sin;
 For to deny each article with oath
 Cannot remove nor choke the strong conception   59
 That I do groan withal. Thou art to die.   60
DESDEMONA
 Then Lord have mercy on me!
OTHELLO   I say, amen.
DESDEMONA
 And have you mercy too! I never did
 Offend you in my life; never loved Cassio
 But with such general warranty of heaven   64
 As I might love. I never gave him token.
OTHELLO
 By heaven, I saw my handkerchief in 's hand.
 Oh, perjured woman! Thou dost stone my heart,   67
 And makes me call what I intend to do
 A murder, which I thought a sacrifice.
 I saw the handkerchief.
DESDEMONA   He found it, then.
 I never gave it him. Send for him hither;
 Let him confess a truth.
OTHELLO   He hath confessed.
DESDEMONA   What, my lord?
OTHELLO
 That he hath used thee.
DESDEMONA   How? Unlawfully?
OTHELLO   Ay.
DESDEMONA
 He will not say so.
OTHELLO   No, his mouth is stopped;
 Honest Iago hath ta'en order for't.   76
DESDEMONA
 Oh, my fear interprets. What, is he dead?
OTHELLO
 Had all his hairs been lives, my great revenge
 Had stomach for them all.
DESDEMONA
 Alas, he is betrayed and I undone!   [She weeps.]
OTHELLO
 Out, strumpet! Weep'st thou for him to my face?
DESDEMONA
 Oh, banish me, my lord, but kill me not!
OTHELLO   Down, strumpet!
DESDEMONA
 Kill me tomorrow; let me live tonight!
OTHELLO   Nay, if you strive—
DESDEMONA
 But half an hour!
OTHELLO   Being done, there is no pause.   86

DESDEMONA
 But while I say one prayer!
OTHELLO   It is too late.
                                       Smothers her.
EMILIA (at the door)
 My lord, my lord! What, ho! My lord, my lord!
OTHELLO
 What noise is this? Not dead? Not yet quite dead?
 I that am cruel am yet merciful;
 I would not have thee linger in thy pain.
                                  [He dispatches her.]
 So, so.
EMILIA (within)   What, ho! My lord, my lord!
OTHELLO   Who's there?
EMILIA [within]
 Oh, good my lord, I would speak a word with you!
OTHELLO
 Yes, 'tis Emilia.—By and by.—She's dead.
 'Tis like she comes to speak of Cassio's death.—   95
 The noise was here. Ha! No more moving?   96
 Still as the grave. Shall she come in? Were't good?—
 I think she stirs again. No. What's best to do?
 If she come in, she'll sure speak to my wife.
 My wife! My wife! What wife? I have no wife.
 Oh, insupportable! Oh, heavy hour!
 Methinks it should be now a huge eclipse
 Of sun and moon, and that th'affrighted globe
 Should yawn at alteration.
EMILIA [within]   I do beseech you   104
 That I may speak with you, oh, good my lord!
OTHELLO
 I had forgot thee. Oh, come in, Emilia.—
 Soft, by and by. Let me the curtains draw.—   107
           [He closes the bedcurtains and opens the door.]
 Where art thou?

             Enter Emilia.

                         What's the matter with thee now?
EMILIA
 Oh, my good lord, yonder's foul murders done!
OTHELLO   What, now?
EMILIA   But now, my lord.
OTHELLO
 It is the very error of the moon;   112
 She comes more nearer earth than she was wont,   113
 And makes men mad.   114
EMILIA
 Cassio, my lord, hath killed a young Venetian
 Called Roderigo.
OTHELLO   Roderigo killed?

95 like likely that   96 here (The Folio's "high" is possible, suggesting
that the commotion of the attack on Cassio was loud.)   104 Should . . .
alteration should gape wide in an earthquake, as if expressing
amazement at an eclipse. (According to Pliny, earthquakes often happen during eclipses. The cataclismic event here is especially terrifying
in that it imagines the impossible concurrence of a solar and lunar
eclipse—an apocalyptic scenario befitting the horror of Desdemona's
death.)   107 Soft Wait a minute   112 error aberration, irregularity
113 She Luna, the moon goddess   114 mad i.e., "lunatic."

56 presently immediately.   59 conception (1) belief in your guilt
(2) plan in my mind   60 groan withal (1) groan at in sorrow (2) as in
giving birth.   64 warranty sanction   67 stone turn to stone, harden
76 ta'en order taken measures   86 Being done i.e., Since justice has
begun its relentless course

And Cassio killed?

EMILIA   No, Cassio is not killed.

OTHELLO
Not Cassio killed? Then murder's out of tune,
And sweet revenge grows harsh.

DESDEMONA   Oh, falsely, falsely murdered!

EMILIA   Oh, Lord, what cry is that?

OTHELLO   That? What?

EMILIA
Out and alas, that was my lady's voice.   123
                         [*She opens the bedcurtains.*]
Help, help, ho, help! O lady, speak again!
Sweet Desdemona! O sweet mistress, speak!

DESDEMONA   A guiltless death I die.

EMILIA   Oh, who hath done this deed?

DESDEMONA   Nobody; I myself. Farewell.
Commend me to my kind lord. Oh, farewell! [*She dies.*]

OTHELLO
Why, how should she be murdered?

EMILIA   Alas, who knows?

OTHELLO
You heard her say herself it was not I.

EMILIA
She said so. I must needs report the truth.

OTHELLO
She's like a liar gone to burning hell!
'Twas I that killed her.

EMILIA   Oh, the more angel she,
And you the blacker devil!

OTHELLO
She turned to folly, and she was a whore.   136

EMILIA
Thou dost belie her, and thou art a devil.   137

OTHELLO   She was false as water.

EMILIA   Thou art rash as fire to say
That she was false. Oh, she was heavenly true!

OTHELLO
Cassio did top her. Ask thy husband else.   141
Oh, I were damned beneath all depth in hell
But that I did proceed upon just grounds
To this extremity. Thy husband knew it all.

EMILIA   My husband?

OTHELLO   Thy husband.

EMILIA   That she was false to wedlock?

OTHELLO
Ay, with Cassio. Nay, had she been true,
If heaven would make me such another world
Of one entire and perfect chrysolite,   150
I'd not have sold her for it.

EMILIA   My husband?

OTHELLO
Ay, 'twas he that told me on her first.
An honest man he is, and hates the slime
That sticks on filthy deeds.

EMILIA   My husband?

OTHELLO
What needs this iterance, woman? I say thy husband.   157

EMILIA
Oh, mistress, villainy hath made mocks with love!   158
My husband say she was false?

OTHELLO   He, woman;
I say thy husband. Dost understand the word?
My friend, thy husband, honest, honest Iago.

EMILIA
If he say so, may his pernicious soul
Rot half a grain a day! He lies to th' heart.
She was too fond of her most filthy bargain.

OTHELLO   Ha?   [*He draws.*]

EMILIA   Do thy worst!
This deed of thine is no more worthy heaven
Than thou wast worthy her.

OTHELLO   Peace, you were best.   168

EMILIA
Thou hast not half that power to do me harm
As I have to be hurt. O gull! O dolt!   170
As ignorant as dirt! Thou hast done a deed—
I care not for thy sword; I'll make thee known,
Though I lost twenty lives.—Help! Help, ho, help!
The Moor hath killed my mistress! Murder, murder!

Enter Montano, Gratiano, and Iago.

MONTANO
What is the matter? How now, General?

EMILIA
Oh, are you come, Iago? You have done well,
That men must lay their murders on your neck.   177

GRATIANO   What is the matter?

EMILIA [*to Iago*]
Disprove this villain, if thou be'st a man.
He says thou told'st him that his wife was false.
I know thou didst not; thou'rt not such a villain.   181
Speak, for my heart is full.

IAGO
I told him what I thought, and told no more
Than what he found himself was apt and true.   184

EMILIA
But did you ever tell him she was false?

IAGO   I did.

EMILIA
You told a lie, an odious, damnèd lie!
Upon my soul, a lie, a wicked lie.
She false with Cassio? Did you say with Cassio?

IAGO
With Cassio, mistress. Go to, charm your tongue.   190

EMILIA
I will not charm my tongue; I am bound to speak.
My mistress here lies murdered in her bed—

ALL   Oh, heavens forfend!

EMILIA
And your reports have set the murder on.

---

123 **Out** (A cry of dismay, intensifying *alas.*)   136 **folly** i.e., wantonness, fleshly sin   137 **belie** slander   141 **else** i.e., if you don't believe
me.   150 **chrysolite** precious topaz

157 **iterance** iteration, repetition   158 **made mocks with** made a
mockery of   168 **Peace . . . best** You'd better be quiet.   170 **to be hurt**
i.e., to endure hurt.   **gull** dupe.   177 **on your neck** to your charge.
181 **such a villain** such a villain as all that.   184 **apt** plausible
190 **charm** control

OTHELLO
Nay, stare not, masters. It is true indeed.

GRATIANO   'Tis a strange truth.

MONTANO
Oh, monstrous act!

EMILIA   Villainy, villainy, villainy!
I think upon't—I think I smell't! Oh, villainy!
I thought so then—I'll kill myself for grief—   199
Oh, villainy, villainy!

IAGO
What, are you mad? I charge you, get you home.

EMILIA
Good gentlemen, let me have leave to speak.
'Tis proper I obey him, but not now.
Perchance, Iago, I will ne'er go home.

OTHELLO
Oh! Oh! Oh!   [*Othello falls on the bed.*]

EMILIA   Nay, lay thee down and roar,   205
For thou hast killed the sweetest innocent
That e'er did lift up eye.

OTHELLO [*rising*]   Oh, she was foul!   207
I scarce did know you, uncle. There lies your niece,
Whose breath indeed these hands have newly
     stopped.
I know this act shows horrible and grim.   210

GRATIANO
Poor Desdemon! I am glad thy father's dead.
Thy match was mortal to him, and pure grief
Shore his old thread in twain. Did he live now,   213
This sight would make him do a desperate turn,   214
Yea, curse his better angel from his side,
And fall to reprobance.   216

OTHELLO
'Tis pitiful. But yet Iago knows
That she with Cassio hath the act of shame
A thousand times committed. Cassio confessed it;
And she did gratify his amorous works   220
With that recognizance and pledge of love   221
Which I first gave her. I saw it in his hand;
It was a handkerchief, an antique token
My father gave my mother.

EMILIA   Oh, God! Oh, heavenly God!

IAGO
Zounds, hold your peace.

EMILIA   'Twill out, 'twill out! I peace?
No, I will speak as liberal as the north.   227
Let heaven and men and devils, let them all,
All, all, cry shame against me, yet I'll speak.

IAGO
Be wise, and get you home.

EMILIA   I will not.
         [*Iago threatens Emilia.*]

GRATIANO   Fie,

Your sword upon a woman?

EMILIA
Oh, thou dull Moor! That handkerchief thou speak'st of
I found by fortune and did give my husband;
For often, with a solemn earnestness,
More than indeed belonged to such a trifle,   235
He begged of me to steal't.

IAGO   Villainous whore!

EMILIA
She give it Cassio? No, alas! I found it,
And I did give't my husband.

IAGO   Filth, thou liest!

EMILIA
By heaven, I do not, I do not, gentlemen.
Oh, murderous coxcomb! What should such a fool   240
Do with so good a wife?

OTHELLO   Are there no stones in heaven   242
But what serves for the thunder?—Precious villain!   243
     [*He runs at Iago; Montano disarms Othello. Iago,*
            from behind, stabs Emilia.]

GRATIANO
The woman falls! Sure he hath killed his wife.

EMILIA
Ay, ay. Oh, lay me by my mistress' side.
         [*Exit Iago.*]

GRATIANO   He's gone, but his wife's killed.

MONTANO
'Tis a notorious villain. Take you this weapon,
Which I have here recovered from the Moor.
Come, guard the door without. Let him not pass,
But kill him rather. I'll after that same villain,
For 'tis a damnèd slave.
         Exit [*with all but Othello and Emilia,*
           who has been laid by Desdemona's side].

OTHELLO   I am not valiant neither,
But every puny whipster gets my sword.   253
But why should honor outlive honesty?   254
Let it go all.

EMILIA   What did thy song bode, lady?
Hark, canst thou hear me? I will play the swan,
And die in music. [*She sings*] "Willow, willow, willow."
Moor, she was chaste. She loved thee, cruel Moor.
So come my soul to bliss as I speak true.
So speaking as I think, alas, I die.   [*She dies.*]

OTHELLO
I have another weapon in this chamber;
It was a sword of Spain, the ice-brook's temper—   262
Oh, here it is. [*He finds a sword.*] Uncle, I must come
     forth.

GRATIANO [*within*]
If thou attempt it, it will cost thee dear.

---

199 **then** (Perhaps at 3.3.331–2 and 4.2.137–54.)   205 **s.d. *Othello . . . bed*** (This direction is from the Quarto, as also *He kisses her* at line 19 and *She dies* at line 129.)   207 **lift up eye** i.e., lift her eyes to heaven.   210 **shows** looks   213 **Shore . . . thread** sheared the thread of his old age (as Atropos, one of the three Fates, was thought to do)   214 **turn** deed   216 **reprobance** damnation, i.e., suicide.   220 **gratify** reward   221 **recognizance** token   227 **liberal as the north** freely as the north wind (blows).

235 **belonged** was appropriate   240 **coxcomb** fool. (Addressed to Othello.)   242 **stones** bolts, such as those used for thunderbolts   243 **Precious** i.e., Arrant, utter   243.1–2 *He . . . Emilia* (The Quarto text reads, "*The Moore runnes at* Iago. Iago *kils his wife*." The Quarto also specifies the exit of Iago at line 245 and the death of Emilia at line 260.)   253 **every . . . sword** every whipper-snapper can get the better of me and my sword.   254 **why . . . honesty?** why should a soldier's reputation for bravery outlive true integrity?   262 **the icebrook's temper** tempered in ice-cold water

Thou hast no weapon, and perforce must suffer.

OTHELLO
Look in upon me then and speak with me,
Or, naked as I am, I will assault thee.   267

[Enter Gratiano.]

GRATIANO
What is the matter?

OTHELLO   Behold, I have a weapon;
A better never did itself sustain
Upon a soldier's thigh. I have seen the day
That, with this little arm and this good sword,
I have made my way through more impediments
Than twenty times your stop. But oh, vain boast!   273
Who can control his fate? 'Tis not so now.
Be not afraid, though you do see me weaponed;
Here is my journey's end, here is my butt   276
And very seamark of my utmost sail.   277
                                [Gratiano steps back.]
Do you go back dismayed? 'Tis a lost fear;   278
Man but a rush against Othello's breast   279
And he retires. Where should Othello go?
                                [He turns to Desdemona.]
Now, how dost thou look now? Oh, ill-starred wench!
Pale as thy smock! When we shall meet at compt,   282
This look of thine will hurl my soul from heaven,
And fiends will snatch at it. Cold, cold, my girl?
Even like thy chastity. Oh, cursèd, cursèd slave!   285
Whip me, ye devils,
From the possession of this heavenly sight!
Blow me about in winds! Roast me in sulfur!
Wash me in steep-down gulfs of liquid fire!
Oh, Desdemon! Dead, Desdemon! Dead! Oh! Oh!   290

Enter Lodovico, Cassio [carried in a litter],
Montano, and Iago [prisoner], with officers.

LODOVICO
Where is this rash and most unfortunate man?

OTHELLO
That's he that was Othello. Here I am.

LODOVICO
Where is that viper? Bring the villain forth.
                                [Iago is led forward.]

OTHELLO
I look down towards his feet; but that's a fable.   294
If that thou be'st a devil, I cannot kill thee.
                                [He wounds Iago.]

LODOVICO
Wrench his sword from him.   [Othello is disarmed.]

IAGO   I bleed, sir, but not killed.

OTHELLO
I am not sorry neither. I'd have thee live,

For in my sense 'tis happiness to die.   298

LODOVICO
O thou Othello, that was once so good,
Fall'n in the practice of a cursèd slave,   300
What shall be said to thee?

OTHELLO   Why, anything.
An honorable murderer, if you will,
For naught I did in hate, but all in honor.

LODOVICO
This wretch hath part confessed his villainy.
Did you and he consent in Cassio's death?   305

OTHELLO   Ay.

CASSIO
Dear General, I never gave you cause.

OTHELLO
I do believe it, and I ask your pardon.
Will you, I pray, demand that demi-devil
Why he hath thus ensnared my soul and body?

IAGO
Demand me nothing. What you know, you know.
From this time forth I never will speak word.

LODOVICO   What, not to pray?

GRATIANO   Torments will ope your lips.   314

OTHELLO   Well, thou dost best.   315

LODOVICO
Sir, you shall understand what hath befall'n,
Which, as I think, you know not. Here is a letter
Found in the pocket of the slain Roderigo;
And here another. [He produces letters.] The one of them
    imports
The death of Cassio, to be undertook
By Roderigo.

OTHELLO
Oh, villain!

CASSIO   Most heathenish and most gross!   322

LODOVICO [showing another paper]
Now here's another discontented paper   323
Found in his pocket too. And this, it seems,
Roderigo meant t'have sent this damnèd villain;
But that belike Iago in the interim   326
Came in and satisfied him.   327

OTHELLO [to Iago] Oh, thou pernicious caitiff!—
How came you, Cassio, by that handkerchief
That was my wife's?

CASSIO   I found it in my chamber;
And he himself confessed but even now
That there he dropped it for a special purpose
Which wrought to his desire.

OTHELLO   Oh, fool, fool, fool!   333

CASSIO
There is besides in Roderigo's letter
How he upbraids Iago, that he made him

---

267 **naked** unarmed   273 **your stop** the obstruction you present.
276 **butt** goal, limit. (An archery term.)   277 **seamark** beacon (marking his destination or limit)   278 **lost** groundless   279 **Man . . . rush**
wield no more than a reed   282 **compt** account, judgment day
285 **slave** i.e., Othello himself.   290.1 **in a litter** (The Quarto specifies
that Cassio is "in a Chaire.")   294 **towards his feet** i.e., to see if they
are cloven, as the devil's are fabled to be

298 **in my sense** to one who feels as I do   300 **in the practice** through
the plotting, into the snare.   **slave** villain   305 **consent** agree
314 **Torments** Torture   315 **thou dost best** you (Iago) do best not to
talk.   322 **gross** monstrous.   323 **discontented** full of discontent
326 **belike** most likely   327 **Came . . . him** interposed and gave him
satisfactory explanation.   333 **wrought . . . desire** worked out as he
wished, fitted in with his plan.

Brave me upon the watch, whereon it came   336
That I was cast; and even but now he spake,   337
After long seeming dead, Iago hurt him,
Iago set him on.

LODOVICO [*to Othello*]
You must forsake this room and go with us.
Your power and your command is taken off,   341
And Cassio rules in Cyprus. For this slave,
If there be any cunning cruelty
That can torment him much and hold him long,   344
It shall be his. You shall close prisoner rest   345
Till that the nature of your fault be known
To the Venetian state.—Come, bring away.

OTHELLO
Soft you; a word or two before you go.   348
I have done the state some service, and they know't.
No more of that. I pray you, in your letters,
When you shall these unlucky deeds relate,   351
Speak of me as I am; nothing extenuate,
Nor set down aught in malice. Then must you speak
Of one that loved not wisely but too well;
Of one not easily jealous but, being wrought,   355
Perplexed in the extreme; of one whose hand,   356
Like the base Indian, threw a pearl away   357
Richer than all his tribe; of one whose subdued eyes,   358
Albeit unusèd to the melting mood,
Drops tears as fast as the Arabian trees

Their medicinable gum. Set you down this;   361
And say besides that in Aleppo once,
Where a malignant and a turbaned Turk
Beat a Venetian and traduced the state,
I took by th' throat the circumcisèd dog
And smote him, thus.   [*He stabs himself.*] 366

LODOVICO   Oh, bloody period!   367
GRATIANO   All that is spoke is marred.
OTHELLO
I kissed thee ere I killed thee. No way but this,
Killing myself, to die upon a kiss.
                        [*He kisses Desdemona and*] *dies.*

CASSIO
This did I fear, but thought he had no weapon;
For he was great of heart.
LODOVICO [*to Iago*]   O Spartan dog,   372
More fell than anguish, hunger, or the sea!   373
Look on the tragic loading of this bed.
This is thy work. The object poisons sight;
Let it be hid. Gratiano, keep the house,   376
                        [*The bedcurtains are drawn.*]
And seize upon the fortunes of the Moor,   377
For they succeed on you. [*To Cassio*] To you, Lord
    Governor,   378
Remains the censure of this hellish villain,   379
The time, the place, the torture. Oh, enforce it!
Myself will straight aboard, and to the state
This heavy act with heavy heart relate.   *Exeunt.*

---

336 Brave defy.   **whereon it came** whereof it came about   **337 cast** dismissed   **341 taken off** taken away   **344 hold him long** keep him alive a long time (during his torture)   **345 rest** remain   **348 Soft you** One moment   **351 unlucky** unfortunate   **355 wrought** worked upon, worked into a frenzy   **356 Perplexed** distraught   **357 Indian** (This reading from the Quarto pictures an ignorant savage who cannot recognize the value of a precious jewel. The Folio reading, "Iudean," i.e., infidel or disbeliever, may refer to Herod, who slew Miriamne in a fit of jealousy, or to Judas Iscariot, the betrayer of Christ.)   **358 subdued** i.e., overcome by grief

361 gum i.e., myrrh.   **366 s.d.** *He stabs himself* (This direction is in the Quarto text.)   **367 period** termination, conclusion.   **372 Spartan dog** (Spartan dogs were noted for their savagery and silence.)   **373 fell** cruel   **376 Let it be hid** i.e., draw the bedcurtains. (No stage direction specifies that the dead are to be carried offstage at the end of the play.)   **keep** guard   **377 seize upon** take legal possession of   **378 succeed on** pass as though by inheritance to   **379 censure** sentencing

---

Othello on Stage

The Elizabethan Era: Burbage and What Kind of Iago?

Richard Burbage played Othello; certain verses written to commemorate his death in 1619 note that his performances as the Moor were among his finest. No descriptions of Burbage's performance in the role have survived, however. Textual evidence and historical precedent suggests that the actor blackened his face with coal dust and soot; Brabantio chides Othello for his "sooty bosom" at 1.2.71, a line that may be taken literally as well as metaphorically.

Iago was probably played by an actor noted for his soldier roles, John Lowin, who was 28 in 1604. (Iago similarly says he has lived "four times seven years" at 1.3.315.) Most accounts suggest that Lowin played Iago

demonically, which raises an interesting question that any production must address: if Iago is played overtly as a villain—or even demonically—how does that affect the audience's sympathy for Othello if one grants credibility to a character who is so wicked? Early in the play Iago seems one of Shakespeare's most comic, even admirable, villains. Shakespeare presents him as personable in public settings, though we as the audience are never really fooled by him since he is so candid about his hatred and envy in his private conversations with Roderigo in 1.1. Because the Jacobean thrust stage was ideal for soliloquies, Iago can play to and off the audience effortlessly. For instance, when Cassio begs Iago's aid after the drinking episode in 2.3, he exits saying "Good night, honest Iago." The line invariably gets a laugh from the audience, who knows Iago is anything but "good." Imagine Iago spinning toward the spectators near him to deliver the line "And what's he then that says I play the villain . . . ?" (2.3.330). (Some actors today speak directly to the spectator who laughs loudest at the line.) Such was the dynamic of Shakespeare's theaters.

Both the Globe and the Blackfriars theaters contained the requisite spaces for this tragedy. The great pillars that supported the half-roof at the Globe would have provided hiding places for eavesdropping and spying. The discovery space, common to both theaters, provided an area from which Desdemona's bed in Act 5 could have been thrust onto the main stage. The indoor Blackfriars must have offered an especially effective venue for the murder scene: as Othello ritually "put[s] out the light" of a candle before smothering Desdemona, the theater itself might have been darkened to heighten the mood, an effect not possible in the outdoor Globe. (It may have been difficult too at the Blackfriars.)

The Late Seventeenth and the Eighteenth Centuries: A Female Desdemona

Based on available records, *Othello* seems to have been the first Shakespearean play revived when the theaters reopened after the Interregnum (1642–1660), a good indicator of the play's popularity. Because women were allowed on the English stage starting in 1660, not having been permitted to act publicly before that date, *Othello* may have also been the first play in which a woman played a Shakespearean heroine. (This transitional moment was dramatized by playwright Jeffrey Hatcher in his rambunctious 2002 comedy, *Compleat Female Stage Beauty*, and the subsequent film, *Stage Beauty* [2004], directed by Richard Eyre.) The first Restoration-era Othello-Iago combination was probably Nicholas Burt and Walter Clun; the latter was a popular comedian, suggesting that demonic Iagos were giving way to more multifaceted interpretations. Thomas Betterton, the Restoration's most celebrated actor, did not play the role until 1682. *Othello*'s immediate popularity inspired imitations, notably Thomas Southerne's *Oroonoko* (1695) and *The Revenge* (1721) by Edward Young. The latter play actually reverses the Shakespearean situation as Zanga, the Moor, dupes his lieutenant into killing the Moor's wife and his best friend. William Hazlitt found this alteration more satisfying than Shakespeare's original because it appealed to English prejudices about non-whites "as well as to historical truth." Such racism, not uncommon, reflected Rymer's view that the play was an "improbable lie" because it allowed the Venetians to "set a Negro to be their general."

Othello was among the first of Shakespeare's plays to be performed in the American colonies. In 1752 the governor of Virginia invited the chief of the Iroquois nation to see the play; the performance ended abruptly when the chief ordered his men to stop Othello from killing Desdemona. To escape censorship and anti-theater laws in the Puritan north, acting companies advertised *Othello* not as a play, but as a series of five moral dialogues (i.e., five acts). Handbills promised patrons that such dialogues would depict "the evil effects of Jealousy and other Bad Passions and proving that Happiness can only Spring from the Pursuit of Virtue."

Curiously, David Garrick, the premier eighteenth-century English actor, failed in the role of the Moor, perhaps because of his average stature. His Iago was more favorably received, although it was not among his most praised roles. Traditionally, the noble and dignified Othello has been played by a tall actor (as in Burbage's portrayal); a 1777 acting edition of the play counseled actors cast as the Moor to be "amiably elegant and above middle stature." John Philip Kemble was such an actor, even though Othello was not considered his best role. Edmund Kean proved that shorter actors could succeed as the Moor when he emerged as the early nineteenth century's most admired Othello. He also alternated in the role of Iago. He was one of the first English actors to use light makeup to play the Moor, a decision that seems to have proved salutary in the larger theaters constructed in that era. In America, Edwin Forrest—the country's first native-born superstar—enjoyed his first triumph as the Moor in 1826; Forrest was an imposing figure who specialized in heroic roles such as Spartacus.

The most admired Othello of the mid nineteenth century was an Italian, Tommaso Salvini (1829–1915), whose name became synonymous with the role. He first played Othello in Italy in 1856, and, as word of his passionate interpretation of the role spread westward, he undertook an American and English tour in 1874. Even though he performed in Italian opposite English-speaking actors, audiences were struck by the majesty of his gestures and the musicality of his voice—not to mention the enormous scimitar he wielded. Actresses playing Desdemona were said to be terrified because of his passion and his immersion in the role. Salvini chose to smother Desdemona behind closed bed curtains, thus leaving the death to the audience's imagination. This Italian Othello epitomized the romantic era's interpretation of the Moor as passionate, heroic, and poetic. Salvini's major rival was Edwin Booth, the finest American actor of the late nineteenth century, who played both Othello and Iago throughout his career. Yet Booth's Othello suffered in comparison with that of Salvini's. A San Francisco journalist wrote in 1888 that "Salvini alone is the Othello of Shakespeare. Booth is the Othello of poetry and romance." Booth was, however, the supreme Iago of his generation, thanks largely to his dark, brooding eyes and the subtlety of his interpretation. He eschewed flagrant villainy, and played Iago lightly, even though comedy was not his forte. His most famous moment came near the end of the play: bleeding by Othello, Booth struggled not to allow others to see him bleeding as he clenched his jaws and spat out the line "From this time forth I never will speak word" (5.2.312). Booth then collapsed on a stool, his back to the audience (so as not to steal the scene from Othello), and only later turned to gloat as Othello fell dead next to Desdemona's lifeless body.

The Twentieth Century: Black Actors and Directorial Visions

Historically, the most significant production of Othello in the early twentieth century was that directed by Konstantin Stanislavski, who also played the title role. Stanislavski, co-founder of the Moscow Art Theatre (MAT) and the modern era's premier acting teacher, saw the aging Salvini's performance in 1901 and immediately determined that the MAT should stage the play. In 1904 Stanislavski performed it to only moderate success; he intended another performance in 1930 but it did not materialize. Fortunately, the actor-director left copious notes about the tragedy and its central character; his commentary (*Stanislavski Produces Othello*, 1948) remains required reading for would-be directors of the play. Stanislavski invented the business of having the Moor first appear with an armful of flowers, which became something of a tradition for years afterward. Olivier reduced the bouquet to a single brilliant red rose at the National Theatre in 1964 and in his film (see p. 694). Stanislavski broke from the romantic tradition, even as he built upon it, by emphasizing Desdemona's sexuality.

In the first half of the twentieth century, notable actors on both sides of the Atlantic played Othello, mostly in the romantic tradition so firmly established by Salvini. In 1930, however, perceptions of *Othello* forever changed after Paul Robeson—an actor, a singer, and an Olympic-class athlete—first played the role in London, where he had triumphed in Eugene O'Neill's *The Hairy Ape*. Robeson played Othello again in 1943 (New York) and 1959 (Stratford-upon-Avon). The 1943 production still holds the record for the longest run of a Shakespeare play on Broadway, and it is generally regarded as the best Robeson production because of its cast, including Uta Hagen as Desdemona and José Ferrer as an engaging, witty Iago. Robeson brought to the role not only an imposing presence but an extraordinary, opera-trained voice. Though occasionally too mannered in his delivery— Robeson's musical background led him to "sing" the role at times—he was admired for his unusually intelligent and charming interpretation of the general. The Robeson productions, especially that in London in 1930, are most remembered for their sensuality and for the shock they often produced; for the first time in the modern era a black man passionately kissed a white woman on stage. Audible gasps were heard in the audience when Robeson kissed Peggy Ashcroft in London, and the 1943 Broadway production prompted similar responses. African American actor Earl Hyman, who played Othello in the 1960s and 1970s, argues that Robeson's performance of the Moor was seminal because, for the first time, an actor did not have to "act" the black man.

William Marshall and James Earl Jones became the most admired black actors of Othello after Robeson. Like Robeson, Marshall was a physically imposing figure, an opera singer, and an athlete; unfortunately, these similarities caused audiences and critics to compare him to Robeson, with the result that Marshall never fully escaped that long shadow. His finest performances of the role came late in his career; as an over-sixty Othello, Marshall was able to convey the self-doubts the Moor had about marrying a younger woman, making his eagerness to believe Iago's insinuations more credible. Jones, blessed with a deep, rich speaking voice, is generally regarded as the finest American Othello in the latter twentieth century. Jones's involvement with the role coincides with the Civil Rights Movement: as he spoke the famous "It is the cause" speech to begin the final scene, the line reverberated with contemporary immediacy.

Jones played his final Othello in 1981, to Christopher Plummer's Iago, in a Stratford (Canada) Festival production. Jones was admired for the melancholy interpretation of the Moor, as opposed to the anger he brought to the role in the 1960s. When the Jones-Plummer production opened the following year on Broadway, New York *Times* critic Frank Rich emphasized Plummer's sensational performance: "It is Mr. Plummer's special gift that he gives us peeks into a nihilistic void of a soul—a mysterious, inexplicable blackness that is horrifying precisely because it cannot be explained away" (February 4, 1982).

In England, several non-Anglo actors have played Othello to acclaim. In 1985 Joseph Marcel became the first non-American black to play the role on a major London stage. Ben Kingsley (born Krishna Bhanji) acted Othello at the RSC in 1985–1986; David Harewood performed the role at the National Theatre in 1997–1998. All tapped their personal experiences as men of color in a predominantly white world. By way of contrast, actor Hugh Quarshie co-directed a production in Greenwich, England, in 1989, playing Othello as a distinctly black general, while his Iago (Paul Barber) was a light-skinned black who could not accept a black general who had sold out to the white establishment.

The Kingsley *Othello*, directed by Terry Hands, was especially controversial, not for its racial undertones, but because of the unusual relationship between Othello and Iago (David Suchet). The antagonists looked strikingly similar in their beards. Suchet explored the homoerotic attraction first suggested in Orson Welles's 1952 film (see below, p. 700), and he added a Freudian dimension to suggest that Iago hated Othello because the Moor was so much like himself.

Many nontraditional productions of *Othello* have been staged in the postmodern era. In 1972 Charles Marowitz deconstructed the play in a production he billed as *An Othello* to distinguish it from Shakespeare's text. Marowitz radically reconstructed the script as a collage by inserting the speeches of various Black Power leaders, and by staging the death of Othello at the hands of white men before his body was dragged off stage by a gloating Iago. At a theater in Hamburg, Germany in 1976, Austrian director Peter Zadek turned the play into a political vaudeville to expose racial and gender stereotyping by highlighting their most offensive possibilities. Othello was played by a white actor wearing minstrel show blackface that rubbed off on all with whom he came in contact; the actor also wore a King Kong costume. Desdemona wore a bikini to emphasize that she was a sexual object among the men.

Several non-Western productions have also illuminated the play through inventive interpretations reflecting non-Eurocentric cultures. In the 1960s and 1970s, in Addis Ababa, Ethiopian playwright Tsegaye Gebre-Medhin examined ethnic and religious schisms plaguing his multiracial, multifaith country. Othello was a Black Muslim in conflict with an upper-class Amhara sect of Christians. Typical of Ethiopian theater and culture, the adaptation incorporated slapstick comedy. In India, also a country of mixed ethnicities and faiths, Roysten Abel presented *Othello: A Play in Black and White* (1996), using India's ancient classical dance form, *Kathakali*, to create a play-within-the-play. While rehearsing Shakespeare's *Othello*, a dance company experienced the same frictions portrayed in Shakespeare's tragedy: an older dancer is replaced by a younger one and sought revenge. The Iago-like character was a guru-like mentor to Othello, a transient from one of India's northeast provinces considered inferior by the company. In Singapore Rio Kashida staged *Desdemona* in 2000 utilizing a half-dozen performance styles from the theaters of Asia, including Japanese Noh, Chinese opera, and Indonesian shadow puppetry. Kashida's eclectic style allowed no single person or ethnic group to claim a privileged perspective on the play's themes.

Othello on Film and in Video

Silent Othellos

Its melodramatic elements, exotic locales, and larger-than-life passions have made *Othello* especially attractive to filmmakers. Portions of the play appeared on film as early as 1906, in both an Italian version (since lost) and a German film in which an actor lip-synched Othello's final speech to a gramophone recording. Several short silent versions followed in America (1908), Italy (1911), and Germany (1914), and most importantly again in Germany in 1922. In this last film Werner Krauss, who had played the title role in the seminal expressionistic film *The Cabinet of Dr. Caligari* (1919), infused Iago with the same oversized reactions that served Krauss well in *The Cabinet;* in *Othello* they served only to turn the play into hammy melodrama. In one

bizarre scene, a distraught and irrational Othello (Emil Jannings) tries to eat the contested handkerchief. The film is, as far as can be known, the first silent Shakespeare movie to be sold to the general public.

■ 1952—Director Orson Welles, Mogador/Mercury Productions, with Welles (Othello), Lea Padovani (Desdemona), and Michael MacLiammoir (Iago). (92 min.)

After the box-office failure of his 1948 *Macbeth*, Welles had difficulty raising funds for this ambitious film, correctly titled *The Tragedy of Othello, the Moor of Venice*. The actor-director labored more than four years to complete the project, filmed in Venice, Tuscany, and Morocco, as production frequently stopped while he raised more money. Even when he had financing, Welles often was forced to make do with available costumes and props. Iago slays Roderigo, for instance, in a Turkish bathhouse because costumes were unavailable; paradoxically, the scene benefits from the confined space as the steam hovers eerily about the villain and his dupe. As a result of Welles's financial predicament, the film as released in 1952 ran only ninety-two minutes, roughly half the length of the play's normal duration. The actor-director reduced the play to its essentials, using non-Shakespearean voice-overs to account for the abridgments. Again, financial realities are turned to an advantage; the film speeds to its conclusion and thereby makes Othello's fall from greatness to ignominy all the more disturbing. In 1992 a restored print with added material was issued; Welles's daughter provides an introduction that thoroughly documents her father's vision for the film.

Ever the experimenter with cinematic effects, Welles uses odd camera angles, vertiginous shifts in perspective, strong contrasts between light and shadow, and distorted mirrors to underscore the Moor's transition from a rational, poetic leader to a violently impassioned murderer. As he did with his masterpiece, *Citizen Kane*, Welles invents a prologue to foreshadow the catastrophic fall of a once powerful man. The film opens with the funeral cortège of the dead lovers, and then cuts to a shot of Iago hanging precariously aloft in a cage while he is taunted by an enraged crowd of Cypriots and soldiers. Images of entrapment dominate the film's visual metaphors: cages, grates, and iron bars. In the film's boldest interpretive stroke, Welles characterizes Iago as a repressed homosexual who resents Othello's love for Desdemona. At the same time, Irish actor Michael MacLiammoir's Iago is so venomous that audiences may question why Othello succumbs so readily to such obvious malevolence. Othello's killing of Desdemona provides a fresh twist on the famous scene: instead of smothering her as in the text, the Moor strangles her with the handkerchief that Iago used to convince the Moor of her infidelity. The young woman's body strains against the bed sheets "like a tormented ghost" that creates "an image of horror to rank with any in cinema" (Rosenthal, 100).

Like his *Macbeth*, Welles's *Othello* was not well received by most critics and the public when it was released (it played in only three theaters in the United States); however, recent commentary by film critics and scholars has elevated both its artistic reputation and its cultural significance.

■ 1955—Director Sergei Yutkevitch, MosFilm, with Sergei Bondarchuk (Othello), Irina Skobtseva (Desdemona), and Andrei Popov (Iago). (103 min.)

Using Boris Pasternak's admired translation and Aram Khachaturian's stirring score, this Russian film is an operatic costume drama. Although Shakespeare's script is intimate, the film opens the play to vast vistas as it illustrates sea fights and swashbuckling brawls. Even the famous deathbed scene is given a larger-than-life treatment: after killing Desdemona, Othello carries her lifeless body in his arms—as Lear does with Cordelia—up a stairway leading to the castle battlements where he explains his actions to Lodovico. From its beginning, Yutkevitch's film heightens Desdemona's role: the first shot reveals the young woman gracefully fingering a globe as she traces the adventures Othello describes to her. She later arrives in Cyprus wearing male clothing, a sign of her free-spirited nature. This *Othello*, spectacular to look at (especially in the great naval battle that Othello leads against the Turks), lacks the intimacy of Shakespeare's design. Rooted in nineteenth-century Romanticism, the film only heightens the play's melodramatic elements rather than exploring the honest human emotions in the text. In perhaps the most prominent example of such excess, Othello—played histrionically by Sergei Bondarchuk—is bathed in a blood red light as he smothers Desdemona.

■ 1965—Director Stuart Burge, Eagle Films, with Laurence Olivier (Othello), Maggie Smith (Desdemona), and Frank Finlay (Iago). (166 min.)

In 1964 one of England's most accomplished directors, John Dexter, staged *Othello* at the Old Vic for the National Theatre of Great Britain. Laurence Olivier, ever the master of disguise and makeup, chose to play the Moor as a black man, with facial features and hair reconstructed to look distinctly Negroid. He also worked for months to lower his vocal register into a rich baritone of Jamaican or Caribbean accent, enhanced by mannered poses aimed at portraying what the *National Review* called "a Black Narcissus." The film, directed by Stuart Burge, is essentially an archival preservation of that controversial theatrical performance, undertaken even as the Black Power movement was gaining strength in America and elsewhere. Historically speaking, Olivier's performance was the last truly "blackface" performance of Othello by a white actor of such prominence.

Olivier, performing in his last "big screen" Shakespeare film (both his Shylock and Lear were television productions), brings uncommon stature and dignity to the role. Many observers have felt that these qualities bordered on vanity—a plausible choice for a man who suffers such an ignominious fall. Dressed in a regal whiter-than-white gown—and entering with a red rose clasped to his bosom—Olivier's Othello is every inch the romantic and poetic warrior so loved by Desdemona. She is played with incomparable nobility by Maggie Smith, adorned by a porcelain complexion that is utterly opposite to Olivier's darkened skin. In contrast to Othello's and Desdemona's regal presences, Frank Finlay plays Iago with the distinctly working-class accent of a lowly ensign who resents the Moor's rise to prominence. Othello, in Iago's estimation, has forgotten his African heritage in marrying this aristocratic Venetian woman. Class warfare is pronounced throughout the stage production and film, with perhaps a nod to the counter-culture movement that grew out of the turbulent 1960s.

Ultimately the film is more a record of the stage production than a cinematic entity. It relies on close-ups that occasionally distract because they call attention to Olivier's makeup; the actor no doubt looked more authentic on the stage of the Old Vic. Still, Burge creates some excellent effects, most notably in a stunning overhead shot of Othello as he writhes during the epileptic fit in 4.3. Othello's suicide also provides a memorable moment: the Moor kills himself by slashing his throat with the blade of a knife hidden in an ornate amulet worn on his wrist. The sequence, captured so well on film, is both shocking and tragic.

■ 1980—Director Liz White, a Howard University production, with Yaphet Kotto (Othello), Richard Dixon (Iago), and Audrey Dixon (Desdemona). (115 min.)

Yaphet Kotto, a popular character actor, plays the Moor in this film directed by Canadian Liz White. The film was actually shot in the mid-1960s as an indictment of spousal abuse within the black community. White would not permit a commercial release of the film because she felt blacks had been exploited by the industry. Almost the entire cast in White's feminist film is black; most roles are played by students from Howard University, which retains the rights to the film. Although a largely amateur undertaking, the film can claim a historical significance as the first truly black *Othello* in the cinema.

■ 1981—Director Elijah Moshinsky, BBC Television, with Anthony Hopkins (Othello), Bob Hoskins (Iago), and Penelope Wilton (Desdemona). (205 min.)

The BBC *Othello* has proved to be the most controversial in that ambitious series. James Earl Jones was originally invited to play the Moor, but British Equity (the actors' union) and the British press objected because he was an American. Producer Jonathan Miller created further controversy when he suggested that race is not an issue in the play and that Moors were Arabic, citing several notable Renaissance paintings as evidence. Anthony Hopkins finally was contracted to play Othello as a light-skinned, bearded Arab. The more radical departure from tradition was Hopkins's choice to read Othello as soft-spoken and calmly rational, rather than as a man consumed by passion. Bob Hoskins, noted for a series of "tough-guy" roles in British films, acts Iago with a working-class accent. His giggling and affable Iago is genuinely humorous and likeable, at least initially, making him more credible than the overtly villainous Iagos discussed previously. In one of many original touches, Hoskins's Iago performs magic tricks during the drinking scene, thus symbolizing his ability to conjure mischief as the opportunity presents itself.

Othello is among the most visually compelling productions in the BBC's series, not because it is especially cinematic, but because Moshinsky uses the medium of television and its predilection for close-ups and two-character shots to heighten the domestic nature of the play; the production manages "to work with rather than (as is so often the case) against the medium for which its was made" (Boose, 106). Virtually the entire video was shot indoors on a black-and white set. Moshinsky makes striking use of long hallways and windows from and through which the audience peers as voyeurs into this private world. Like other BBC productions directed by Miller, this one displays a penchant for recreating Renaissance-era paintings: in 4.3, for instance, Desdemona, dramatically backlit, is discovered sitting at a dressing table contemplating a skull, in a scene inspired less by Shakespeare than by Georges de La Tour's *Magdalen with the Smoking Flame* (c. 1638). The video's final shot is disturbing because of its cynicism: the audience views an empty, sterile hallway throughout which Iago's malicious laughter echoes as the scene fades to black.

- 1988—Director Janet Suzman, a Market Theater production, with John Kani (Othello), Richard Haddon Haines (Iago), and Joanna Weinberg (Desdemona). (187 min.)

Suzman, a longtime actress with the RSC, made her directorial debut in her native South Africa with *Othello* at Johannesburg's Market Theater; the film documents this culturally important production. The Market was created in 1976 to promote interracial theater in a society torn by apartheid, and the casting of a black South African with a white woman was a powerful political statement in the late 1980s. Suzman modeled Iago after some of the most racist demagogues in her country, and directed the actor to play the villain as menacingly as possible. As Othello exits muttering line about "Goats and monkeys" in Act 4, Iago repeats the line while striking a gorilla pose and scratching himself. Kani, noted for his work in the plays of Athol Fugard, is a small-framed man who plays the role with remarkable restraint. His Moor, among the most melancholy on record, seems to know that his marriage to Desdemona (played by Joanna Weinberg as a brave woman who challenges her country's outmoded conventions) is doomed in a racist world. The contrast between Kani and the large, hulking Haddon Haines in the role of Iago reinforces the idea that black South Africans, although a majority, are dwarfed by the white minority. Even Emilia is played initially as a product of the racist society, as she eagerly pounces on the lost handkerchief to create mischief; like her husband, this Emilia spits at mention of the black general. In perhaps the play's most telling moment, the dying Emilia stretches her arm toward Othello as if to beg his forgiveness; the wronged Moor gently closes her eyes in a sign of reconciliation among the races.

- 1990—Director Trevor Nunn, with Willard White (Othello), Ian McKellen (Iago), and Imogen Stubbs (Desdemona). (210 min.)

In 1989 Nunn staged the play for the Royal Shakespeare Company in Stratford-upon-Avon's intimate the Other Place; the production was preserved in video format the following year ("as near to perfect a piece of television as you could get," judged *The Observer*). As RSC director John Barton had done almost twenty years earlier, Nunn recreated a late–nineteenth-century military garrison to underscore the importance of rank and uniform in this military world. Opera singer Willard White, a Jamaican black man, brings undeniable passion to the title role in marked contrast to Ian McKellen's purposefully cool, naturalistic Iago. McKellen plays the villain as a dedicated soldier fed up with the inequities of rank. "He is not evil incarnate," McKellen said in an interview. Lois Potter assesses McKellen's costume as an extension of Iago's personality: " . . . everything that can be buttoned is buttoned, in contrast with the relaxed look of the other characters' uniforms. The iconography of repressed sexuality is as obvious as the red cloak that associated Booth and Irving with Mephistopheles" (191–192). Almost unwittingly, Iago creates chaos out of the ordered world of the garrison—part of McKellen's obsession with meticulously putting an inordinate number of props in place on almost every line. Cassio arrives on Cyprus imperiously, much to the annoyance of the common soldiers, even as Iago dutifully tends to his seasick wife, Emilia. As he often does with Shakespeare's plays, Nunn injects a hint of Chekhovian melancholy into *Othello*. Desdemona and Emilia seem more like characters in the Russian playwright's *Three Sisters* than Shakespearean creations; an uncommonly strong bond is established between Desdemona and her confidante. Nunn's decidedly naturalistic approach to the play actually increases its shock value as the Act 5 murders and suicide intrude on an otherwise well-ordered world.

- 1995—Director Oliver Parker, Columbia-Castle Rock, with Laurence Fishburne (Othello), Kenneth Branagh (Iago), and Irene Jacobs (Desdemona). (124 min.)

It is shocking to realize that Parker's *fin de siècle* film was the first to cast a black Othello in a major commercial release. Parker's film features Laurence Fishburne as perhaps the most impressive looking Moor in film history. With his head shaved and adorned with tattoos, the actor makes a sensational entry into Cyprus atop a white steed. Perhaps to compensate for Fishburne's inexperience as a classical actor, Parker has cut the script heavily and restructured the text into a series of short scenes. Kenneth Branagh, who trained at the Royal Academy of Dramatic Art (RADA) and emerged as the most popular Shakespeare-on-film actor of the decade, enacts Iago coolly and dispassionately (shades of McKellen?). His soliloquies are especially effective as he confronts the camera lens directly to create an intimacy with the audience. Occasionally Branagh and Parker lapse into melodrama; Iago concludes a soliloquy by plucking a red-hot log from a fire without feeling any pain. Yes, Iago is a devil; yes, he is a man without feeling; but no, we do not need to be told this in such unsubtle cinematic terms.

Despite Fishburne's occasionally uneven vocal delivery ("Shakespeare's pentameters are alien to an actor who is more at home in the expletive-ridden worlds of 1990s thrillers," asserts Daniel Rosenthal), his performance has both physical amplitude and emotional depth; the film also succeeds visually and remains among the most eye-pleasing and uncompromisingly realistic versions of *Othello*. An opening shot establishes the sumptuous Venetian milieu: Desdemona, wearing a carnival masque, silently skims to her rendezvous with Othello on a gondola (see 1.1.128). The Doge's Palace in Scene 3, a convincing mockup of the original building on the Piazza San Marco in Venice, contrasts markedly with the weathered stone fortress on Cyprus. Parker's *mise en scène* distinguishes the two worlds of the play as well as any film of the play. The island is a place of street brawls and bawdy couplings, all of which define the violent and lustful world that spawns the action. Parker invents several scenes to illustrate that Othello and his new bride are as much given to erotic desire as to spiritual communion: e.g., a passionate kiss upon the Moor's arrival in Cyprus and a graphic suggestion that the marriage is consummated during the drinking scene (2.3). By showing a sexually active Desdemona, Parker dramatizes an erotic fantasy in which Othello's imaginings of her tryst with Cassio become plausible in his jealous mind.

The climactic scene (3.3) in which Othello promotes Iago as his lieutenant is set on a promontory overlooking the restless sea, suggesting a cosmic backdrop for this domestic tragedy. Branagh's look at the camera as he is embraced by Othello while saying "I am your own forever" suggests both the villain's duplicity and his vulnerability. This moment of calm is preceded by a violent confrontation in which Othello attempts to drown Iago in the pounding surf.

To frame the story, Parker inserts key business to illustrate that Iago virtually stage-manages the action. Throughout the film Branagh's Iago is shown as a consummate chess player, as though deftly moving a black king (Othello) and a white Queen (Desdemona) about a chess board. In the final sequence, the bodies of the lovers, Othello shrouded in black, Desdemona in white, are ceremoniously dumped into the ocean. While purists may quibble with Parker's extensive cuts and the graphic emphasis on sexual matters only hinted at in the text, general audiences have found the film as gripping as then-current headlines in 1995, many of which involved the notorious O. J. Simpson murder trial.

Adaptations

Many critics and scholars consider Giuseppe Verdi's four-act opera, *Otello* (1887), the most justly famous and admired adaptation of a Shakespeare into another medium. Arrigo Boito's libretto overcomes the problems encountered by Shakespeare's "double time" scheme by opening the story not in Venice, as does Shakespeare, but on Cyprus as a fierce storm rages. A chorus anxiously anticipates the arrival of Otello (note the Italian spelling) in one of the most stirring opening sequences in all opera. Boito's initial scene immediately initiates the chaotic events that follow. The courtship of Desdemona by Otello is described in a tender duet by the lovers at the close of Act 1, in a thoughtful touch that illustrates how the story moves between moments of tumultuous activity and placidity. The second act ends with one of grand opera's finest male duets, as Iago joins Otello in a mutual vow of vengeance intended for Cassio and Desdemona. Here the opera seems to favor Cinthio's source story over Shakespeare's version. Boito makes another change that is quite contrary to Shakespeare's design: Iago—a nihilist who believes that God created man to be wicked—actually escapes after Emilia reveals his treachery in the final act. The opera concludes with Otello's self-inflicted death-blow with a hidden dagger, followed by his gently kissing the lifeless Desdemona. While the opera libretto foregrounds the play's melodramatic qualities, its music heightens the emotion of Shakespeare's passionate drama. There are several excellent film versions of the opera, most notably Franco Zeffirelli's 1968 film with Placido Domingo as the Moor. (Ironically, Zeffirelli's stage 1961 production of Shakespeare's play, with John Gielgud, is generally regarded as a failure, partially because it was deemed "too operatic" by its critics.)

A rock opera, *Catch My Soul* (1970), had a moderately successful London run as it rode the popularity of the Webber-Rice rock opera, *Jesus Christ Superstar*. Rock guitarist Richie Havens played Othello, the leader of a hippie commune, while Iago seemed a neurotic sociopath à la Charles Manson who got Cassio high on LSD rather than alcohol. This stage opera was filmed for the art-house circuit, where it failed; it was retitled *Santa Fe Satan* and released as an exploitation film.

Spin-offs

The silent screen provided one of the first cinematic spin-offs of *Othello*. *Carnival* (1921), based on a London stage play and filmed by British and Italian filmmakers, tells the story of a modern Venetian actress whose liberal behavior causes her actor-husband to strangle her on stage. It was remade in 1931, with sound, and retitled *Venetian Nights*. Another film, *Men Are Not Gods* (1936), is less an adaptation of the *Othello* story than an intriguing film that portrays a distraught actor (Rex Harrison) who, after receiving scathing reviews as Othello, becomes so obsessed with redeeming himself that he loses himself in the role and nearly strangles Desdemona (Gertrude Lawrence). The expressionistic *A Double Life* (1947) is the most admired of the film spin-offs of *Othello*, largely because it portrays its protagonist with psychological complexity in an otherwise sensational story. Ronald Colman won an Academy Award for his portrait of a second-rate actor attempting to revive his career—and his failed marriage to the actress who plays Desdemona—by playing the Moor. He becomes involved with a young waitress (Shelley Winters) and accidentally strangles her while rehearsing the part. He later commits suicide, as the police close in on him, by using a real knife on stage.

Two recent films reset the Othello story in distinctly modern, nontheatrical contexts, and without Shakespeare's language. *O* (2000), written and directed by Tim Blake Smith, is set in an American high school in the South. Star basketball player Odin (Mekhi Phifer) is victimized by the coach's son, Hugo (Josh Hartnett), who resents losing his spot in the starting lineup. Hugo spreads rumors that Odin's girlfriend Desi (Julia Stiles) is sleeping with another star player, Michael Cassio. Although the film is a clever makeover, especially in its depiction of Southern racism, the teenage settings reduce the play's passions to petty high school jealousies that get out of hand. A British television drama, *Othello*, updates the action to Scotland Yard, where a black police inspector, John Othello, provokes the anger of white detective, Ben Jago, whose career has been sidetracked. Jago also desires Othello's wife, Dessie Brabant. In a twist on Shakespeare's ending, Jago's malevolence is never discovered (except by Othello, who shoots himself without revealing the truth), and he replaces Othello as chief police inspector.

A Brazilian film, *Otelo De Oliveira* (1984), is set in a *favela* (shanty-town) in Rio de Janeiro where Otelo, a light-skinned black man, is the leader of a samba-band who becomes jealous of his lover's flirtations with other members of the band, including Cassio, a white guitarist. Iago is a black man who practices voodoo. The film is equal parts folktale and social tract, underscored by mesmerizing music.

References and Related Reading

Boose, Lynda E. "Grossly Gaping Viewers and Jonathan Miller's *Othello*." *Shakespeare: The Movie*. Eds. Boose and Richard Burt. London and New York, 1997. 186–197.

Bradley, A. C. *Shakespearean Tragedy*. Vol 2. Greenwich, Conn., 1965.

Greenblatt, Stephen. *Will in the World: How Shakespeare Became Shakespeare*. New York and London, 2004.

Guilfoyle, Cheryl. "*Mactacio Desdemonae*: Medieval Scenic Form in the Last Scene of *Othello*." *Shakespeare's Play within Play*. Kalamazoo, Mich., 1990. 83-96.

Hodgdon, Barbara. "Race-ing Othello, Re-engendering White-Out." *Shakespeare: The Movie*. Eds. Lynda E. Boose and Richard Burt. London and New York, 1997. 186–197.

Kermode, Frank. "Othello, the Moor of Venice." *The Riverside Shakespeare*. Ed. G. Blakemore Evans. Dallas, 1974.

Lea, Katherine M. *Italian Popular Comedy; A Study in the Commedia dell'arte, 1560-1620, with Special Reference to the English Stage*. New York, 1962.

Pechter, Edward. *"Othello" and Interpretive Traditions*. Iowa City, Iowa, 1999.

Potter, Lois. *Shakespeare in Performance: "Othello."* Manchester, Eng., 2002.

Rich, Frank. "Jones and Plummer's *Othello*." *New York Times*, 4 Feb. 1982: C15.

Rosenberg, Marvin. *The Masks of Othello: The Search for the Identity of Othello, Iago, and Desdemona by Three Centuries of Actors and Critics*. Berkeley and Los Angeles, 1964.

Rosenthal, Daniel. *Shakespeare on Screen*. London, 2000.

Ryan, Kiernan. *New Readings: Shakespeare*. Atlantic Highlands, N.J., 1989.

Rymer, Thomas "*Othello*: A Bloody Farce." *The Critical Works of Thomas Rymer*. Ed. Curt Zimansky. New Haven, Conn., 1956.

Spivack, Bernard. *Shakespeare and the Allegory of Evil: The History of a Metaphor in Relation to His Major Villains*. New York, 1958.

Trewin, J. C. *Going to Shakespeare*. Boston, 1978.

ORSON WELLES

(1915–1985)

Orson Welles achieved a rare artistry in the fields of theater, film, and broadcasting. His first feature film, *Citizen Kane* (1941), is regarded by many as the best American movie ever made, a breakthrough that changed and elevated the moviemaker's art. Yet over the course of a stormy career Welles was spurned in Hollywood, his taste being considered too artistically subtle for the box office, his perfectionism and ambition too grand for the studio system. He filmed many of his later works in Europe, never having found a steady source of financing for the Shakespeare films that have been described in this anthology—*Falstaff: Chimes at Midnight, Othello,* and *Macbeth.* Yet during the final year of his life, Welles was still at work on a screenplay for *King Lear.* He told potential producers that the tragedy was Shakespeare's masterpiece, "As simple and timeless as any story ever told." He promised them an interpretation stark and down-to-earth, a "new kind of Shakespeare" and a "new kind of film." He died before he could realize that vision.

Welles was already a celebrated stage actor and director when he went to Hollywood in the late 1930s, having directed controversial *avant-garde* theatrical productions in New York, including an all-black *Macbeth* (1936). Two years later, when he was still in his twenties, he stunned the nation with a radio broadcast of H. G. Wells's science fiction fantasy, *The War of the Worlds,* in which he employed a newscast style to create a spoken drama so authentic that frightened listeners believed Martians had landed on earth. Welles's sonorous voice, huge physical presence, and unflagging energy were soon legendary. Appreciation of his genius, however, was often colored by sadness that he never quite fulfilled his promise. Shakespeare on film might have been a richer field of study sooner had he completed the *Julius Caesar* he so often contemplated, or the *Lear* he envisioned in his last year. Yet even that observation stirs controversy. On the day of Welles's death, American director John Houseman, an early and admiring collaborator, commented of his friend: "I knew for a certainty I was working with a genius—we can look back upon his life as extraordinary. He created a number of masterpieces—in

the theater, in film. The world was not very charitable to him. Maybe if people had been kinder to him, he would have done more" (*Los Angeles Times,* October 11, 1985, A-1).

Welles was born George Orson Welles in Kenosha, Wisconsin, the son of a wealthy heir to a manufacturing fortune, Richard Welles, and his arts-loving wife, Beatrice Ives. While his father slipped into alcoholism, his mother groomed Orson for success by teaching him to read with Shakespeare as his primer and to play music on the piano. A friend of the family, a pediatrician called Dr. Bernstein, also took an interest in Welles, publicizing the boy as a "prodigy" from his earliest endeavors. Richard and Beatrice Welles divorced when Orson was six; his mother moved with him to Chicago. There he accompanied her to the theater and to classical music concerts. Beatrice died a few years later. When Orson Welles was eleven years old, his father died too. Acting as his guardian, Dr. Bernstein sent him to the private Todd School in Woodstock, Illinois, where young Welles made his debuts as an actor (in *Hamlet*) and as a filmmaker. Those five years at the Todd School were his only formal education.

When Welles graduated, Bernstein sent him on to Ireland, hoping he would there forget his passion for theater. Instead, Welles made his professional acting debut at Dublin's Gate Theatre, where he had talked his way into a production by lying about his age and fabricating stage experience he did not possess. He was now sixteen years old.

At the Gate, he met Michael MacLiammoir, who would become an actor in several of Welles's Shakespeare projects. When Welles returned to the United States, he met Thornton Wilder, who soon would write the American classic *Our Town.* Welles landed a job with a road company formed by famed actress Katharine Cornell. Employing his deep, resonant voice and handsome stage presence to good effect, he made his Broadway debut with Cornell in 1934, playing the Chorus and Tybalt in *Romeo and Juliet.* During this year he met the producer/director Houseman, who became closely involved with him in several progressive theater projects. Houseman memorably described Welles's contradictions, calling him a "monstrous boy, flat-footed and graceless, yet swift and agile; soft as Jell-O one moment and uncoiled the next, in a spring of such furious energy that, once released, it could be checked by no human intervention." Many others have described Welles in similar terms as an elemental force. His creative output during his next decade was astonishing, a product of chronic insomnia, tremendous talent, and irresistible charisma. His charm enabled him to persuade actors to work tirelessly for very little money; his eloquence seduced rich backers to entrust him with the money he needed to finance his artistic projects. His voice, which Houseman praised for a "clarity and power that tore like the wind through the genteel modulated voices of the well-trained professionals around him," was unforgettable.

Welles was eighteen when he toured with Cornell's company, playing Mercutio in *Romeo and Juliet* as well as Eugene Marchbanks in *Candida* by Bernard Shaw. With Houseman he worked with the New York Federal Theater, a project of the Works Progress Administration (WPA) during the Depression era. In 1934 he wed the Chicago socialite and actress Virginia Nicholson. (His other marriages were to the Hollywood star Rita Hayworth in 1943—they divorced in 1949—and to Paola Mori in 1955.) His most prolific period as a stage actor and director came during the thirties when the federal government provided support to such groundbreaking artists. He teamed with Houseman to direct perhaps his most famous Shakespeare production on stage, the 1936 all-black version of *Macbeth*, set in Haiti, performed in Harlem, and eventually dubbed the "Voodoo *Macbeth*." This breakthrough production established him as a major theatrical figure just as he turned twenty-one.

Controversy soon followed when, the next year, he and Houseman staged Mark Blitzstein's agitprop drama *The Cradle Will Rock*. Conservative politicians, viewing the play as overtly leftist, had federal agents close it down on opening night. Welles and Houseman then moved it down the street to the Venice Theatre, where they stage-managed an improvised performance in the aisles. Welles departed from the Federal Theater Project and Houseman was fired. Together they went on to form the prolific Mercury Theatre Project, which soon produced an updated *Julius Caesar*, one of the earliest examples of recontextualizing a Shakespeare play to underscore thematic points: Shakespeare's tragedy of assassination and retribution became an indictment of totalitarianism. Exchanging Roman togas for Italian black-shirts and turning Caesar into a Fascist leader, Welles directed and played Brutus. During this year, 1937, he also played Shotover in Shaw's *Heartbreak House* and the title role in Christopher Marlowe's Elizabethan drama, *Doctor Faustus*.

Welles's troupe of stage actors evolved into the Mercury Theatre of the Air, a group that became involved in radio and film as well as the stage. In 1938, Welles achieved national notoriety when his October 30 broadcast, *The War of the Worlds*, stirred panic among listeners who thought the intense drama was a true report of an invasion by creatures from outer space. The company also staged Welles's first of several adaptations from Shakespeare's history plays, *Five Kings*, in which the producer/director played Falstaff.

Between 1936 and 1941, Welles extended his popular reach, participating in more than one hundred radio dramas as a writer, an actor, and a director. Many actors from his stage productions participated in the Mercury Theatre of the Air and later appeared in Welles's films. Their radio repertory included Shakespeare, American and European classics, and thrillers such as *The Bride of Death*, *The League of Terror*, and *Dracula*. Welles himself was the voice behind the popular radio series, *The Shadow*.

Welles moved with members of his company to Hollywood to film *Citizen Kane*, which was released in 1941 and universally hailed by critics. The movie, about a newspaper baron modeled upon William Randolph Hearst, indicted an unbridled and immoral form of American capitalism. Welles played the corrupt media tycoon Charles Foster Kane. The motion picture's rich layering of details and effects, its evocative lighting and sound, and its fascination with the dark side of human nature and especially the materialistic side of the American character changed the nation's cinema and the way that movies were made. Still, *Citizen Kane* was a commercial failure, and Welles would henceforth be involved in a lifelong struggle to find financial backing. He followed his artistic and critical success in *Citizen Kane* with a more personal family saga, *The Magnificent Ambersons*; nervous RKO studio executives ordered sixty minutes cut from the film, a fate which also met his *Macbeth* in 1948. Welles continued his stage work as well, directing and designing *Native Son* at the St. James Theatre in New York before *Ambersons* was released.

(continued)

Welles staged and/or filmed multiple productions of the Shakespeare plays that most appealed to him, often adapting their stories of men corrupted by power to contemporary situations. Two more stage productions of *Macbeth* came in 1947 and 1948; the former was filmed in just three weeks on a low budget as an amalgam of cinematic and theatrical techniques. Welles himself plays Macbeth as a man abstracted from himself, an impression intensified when the great soliloquies are presented as voice-overs. Despite an incoherent grab bag of costumes, simple artificial-looking sets, and some unconvincing sound effects, the film often finds striking visual parallels to Shakespeare's language. Although Welles shot the film with actors (notably Jeanette Nolan as a lusty, power-mad Lady Macbeth) who spoke in Scots accents, Republic Studios re-dubbed their voices for the American and British release. Not until 1980, when the film's original dialogue was restored, could its strengths be properly seen and appreciated.

In 1951 Welles directed *Othello* in London, casting himself as the noble Moor. The film version was delayed, again by financial pressures (see pp. 693–694 above). Welles moved the filming from Venice and Tuscany to Morocco, stopping production when he ran out of cash. Making an artistic virtue of financial necessity, he often improvised, staging Iago's murder of Roderigo, for instance, in a Turkish bathhouse because he had no costumes for the actors. When the film was released in 1952, it ran but ninety-two minutes, as Welles distilled the play to its essence and employed voice-overs to fill in the narrative gaps. Experimenting further with the cinematic effects he employed in *Citizen Kane*, Welles uses upward camera angles, shifts in perspective, strong contrasts between light and shadow, distorted mirrors, and images of entrapment as a visual language to convey Shakespeare's themes. In one of his most original interpretative choices, Welles views Iago as a repressed homosexual who resents Othello's love for Desdemona. In 1992, when a restored print with additional scenes was issued, Welles's daughter, Rebecca, provided an introduction that explains her father's vision for the film. That re-issue launched a reassessment of the film and its place in Welles's oeuvre that continues to this day.

Welles's next Shakespeare project—and first foray into television—came in 1953, when he starred in Peter Brook's live television production of a truncated (and controversial) *King Lear* on CBS.

Historian Tony Howard describes both the broadcast and the process of creating that revered and reviled work in "When Peter Met Orson: The 1953 CBS *King Lear*" (Boose and Burt, 121–134; and Chapter 17 stage history following *King Lear*, pp. 760ff.). Welles revisited the play in 1956 and thirty years later was still hoping to film it. By now he was residing in self-imposed exile in Europe and spending more time as an actor in other people's films than as a director on his own.

Welles did not complete another Shakespeare film until his 1966 masterwork in the genre, *Falstaff: Chimes at Midnight*. The film culminated a twenty-five–year process that had begun as an ambitious project of the Mercury Theatre with extracts from the history plays called *Five Kings*. (By 1940 the project had left Welles with a large debt that, as much as any single factor, sent him and his company to Hollywood to make money.) In 1960, he staged a shorter version of the play sequence called *Chimes at Midnight*. The new adaptation opened in Dublin and closed at a loss before reaching London or New York; this script served as the template for the *Chimes* screenplay four years later. Financed from both his own pocket and one million dollars in backing from Spanish financier Emiliano Piedra, the film was shot in inexpensive black-and-white in Spain, though with a star-studded cast that included John Gielgud in the key role of Henry IV, father to the young Prince Hal. The gifted and handsome actor Keith Baxter reprised his Dublin role as Prince Hal, the son who must be king, and Welles again played the prince's surrogate father, Sir John Falstaff. This extraordinary film is discussed at length in the film history section of Chapter Twelve on *Henry IV, Part One* (pp. 439–440). The laborious process by which the film was shot, using body doubles for most scenes because Welles could not afford to pay his leading actors for long, "may have seemed impossible to onlookers and crew alike," writes James Howard in his chronicle of Welles's films. "But Orson the director knew precisely what was needed from each of his performers" (166). In focusing his adaptation upon three men—Prince Hal and his contrasting royal and roguish father figures—and in conceiving his Falstaff as an essentially good man caught in the implacable forward movement of history, Welles achieved a balance of character, emotion, mood, and cinematic effects that rivals that of *Citizen Kane*. Smoothly and masterfully edited, especially in its agitated and violent battle scenes cut and spliced so that they seem to include far more actors than Welles actually used, *Chimes at Midnight* disguises the difficulties Welles encountered while creating the film. Two technical problems mar the final print—poor synchronization in the first reel and a pesky hum during Margaret Rutherford's moving speech as Mistress Quickly recounting Falstaff's death. As James Howard concludes, within the career and life of its director *"Chimes at Midnight* can be seen almost as Orson Welles's lifework—a piece which he had taken some twenty-five years to finally bring to a mass audience" (168).

Welles's television career began with the CBS Omnibus *King Lear* (1953) directed by Brook (see "Close-up: Peter Brook," pp. 66–69) and soon developed into scores of appearances, including *I Love Lucy* (in which he appeared as himself in 1956), a starring role in a Hallmark Hall of Fame production of Kaufman and Hart's *The Man Who Came to Dinner* in 1979, and a guest gig on *Moonlighting* in 1985. During his last decade Welles made a television pilot for *The Orson Welles Show* that was never picked up by the networks, and he earned what he jokingly called "grocery money" by appearing in television commercials, including, famously, advertisements for Paul Masson wines (in which he uttered the phrase "We will sell no wine before its time"). If such commercial and guest appearances seemed a falling-off to many of his admirers, even these were undertaken, as so much of his work had been, to finance projects that never came to be. In August of 1984, Welles was reported to be at work on a film about his famed staging of *The Cradle Will Rock* to be produced by New York's Circle Theater and based upon his collaboration with Houseman on the Blitzstein drama. When that project ran into trouble, Welles returned to his dream of playing and filming *King Lear*. Like so many of his aborted projects, this one, which film historians speculate might have been his greatest, was left unfinished. Welles suffered from a heart condition and diabetes; he died alone, at the age of seventy, of apparent cardiac failure in the upstairs bedroom of his Hollywood house on October 10, 1985.

References and Related Reading

Bogdanovich, Peter, and Jonathan Rosenbaum. *This Is Orson Welles.* New York, 1992.

Howard, James. *The Complete Films of Orson Welles.* New York, 1991.

Howard, Tony. "When Orson Met Peter: The 1953 CBS *King Lear.*" *Shakespeare: The Movie, Popularizing the Plays on Film, TV and Video.* Eds. Lynda E. Boose and Richard Burt. London and New York, 1997. 121–134.

Kael, Pauline. *The* Citizen Kane *Book.* London, 1971.

Rosenthal, Daniel. *Shakespeare on Screen.* London, 2000.

CHAPTER 17

The Tragedy of King Lear

(1605–1606)

Context and Dating: Redemption, Nihilism, and Cosmic Catastrophe

In *King Lear,* Shakespeare has created a drama of old age and family disintegration in which human life often appears meaningless and brutal, no better than an animal's. The tragedy also possesses a political dimension and a philosophical one, cosmic in its resonance and universal in its themes. Only *Hamlet* and *Macbeth* approach it in depicting such thorough devastation—in the mind, the body, and the body politic. *King Lear* ruthlessly reveals the power drives and violent resentment that can corrupt blood relationships and intimate sexual unions. Shakespeare here also gazes clear-eyed at the tenuousness of the patriarchal political order thought in his day to be sustained by strong family and social bonds.

These devastating challenges have proved so harrowing over the past four hundred years that many readers, audiences, and directors have searched anxiously for more hopeful answers, ones that will not seem utterly nihilistic. Many of the stage productions outlined below, especially during the late eighteenth, nineteenth, and early twentieth centuries, have taken as their cue a set of ideas perhaps best summed up in Cordelia's lines when she is reunited with the father who disinherited her. She counsels him, as Edgar has already counseled his father, Gloucester, on the virtues of patient suffering: "We are not the first / Who with best meaning have incurred the worst" (5.3.3–4). With these lines, and Lear's promise to "kneel down / And ask of thee forgiveness," comes the possibility that the compassion Lear has learned from being reduced to the state of a "poor, bare, forked animal" may lead to personal redemption. In some readings this redemptive

process takes on a Christian coloring; other interpreters view it in secular terms as an emotional and psychological reintegration after Lear's madness. Still others have viewed the awful suffering and carnage in the play as necessary to cleanse the realm and restore a moral order that Lear himself violated by relinquishing his throne. In any case, the play has often been read, staged, and filmed as if such patient hope will purge audiences of the strong emotions evoked by the horrifying and unjust deaths with which the play ends. We shall never be certain whether Shakespeare expected audiences to feel redemptive uplift by sharing the perceptions borne of Lear's suffering and the self-knowledge that comes at such cost to him and to Gloucester. Yet generations have viewed the play in this way, and some scholars, directors, and actors still look for textual evidence to support such readings.

In a countervailing trend, especially during the latter part of the twentieth century, these redemptive readings of the tragedy have more often been replaced by nihilistic interpretations that have found little evidence in the play to support the idea of spiritual regeneration and tragic enlightenment. A school of existentialist critics and distinguished directors—Herbert Blau, Peter Brook, and Richard Eyre among them—has emerged in the wake of the twin horrors of the Holocaust and Hiroshima, arguing that nowhere in Shakespeare do evil and injustice triumph for as long, and with the capability of inflicting so much suffering upon the innocent, as in *King Lear*. Gloucester's blinding—first one eye gouged out and then, after the murder of a servant who comes to his aid, the other plucked out as "vile jelly"—may be the most shocking act in the canon. Given the storms on the heath and in the mind of Lear, the brutalities visited upon the aged in both the Lear and the Gloucester family plots, and finally the murder of Cordelia (which English consciences found so morally and aesthetically repugnant that for at least one-hundred and fifty years that brutal act was transformed into a happy ending), these catastrophes have suggested to such interpreters a metaphysic of despair. Associating the play with anxieties about the Cold War and the notion of mutual assured destruction, such directors have seen an image of the apocalypse in the play's ending. "Is this the promised end?" asks Kent as Lear enters bearing the corpse of Cordelia. "Or image of that horror?" replies Edgar (5.3.268–269). Such pessimism, even nihilism—the word "nothing" sounds like the tolling of a death knell throughout the play—has made *King Lear* seem to many during the nuclear age the most existentially modern of the tragedies. A penetrating if one-dimensional essay by Polish critic Jan Kott in his *Shakespeare Our Contemporary*, written after World War II, compares *Lear* with the moral neutrality and black comedy of the Theater of the Absurd. In his apocalyptic staging of the play for San Francisco's Actors' Workshop in 1961, Herbert Blau bleakly asked audiences to consider of Cordelia's tragic fate "not why should she die, but why should she want to live?" (Blau, 282). When filmmaker Akira Kurosawa adapted the tragedy for the screen in 1985, he called it *Ran*, which in Japanese means *Chaos*. He closed the film with a stark image of a blind man staring into the void.

These contradictory readings—redemptive and regenerative; despairing and nihilistic—may also be suspended, as the famed director Brook has suggested in another context, in a "paradox that cannot be argued or resolved, but must be lived." Shakespeare's poetry, he continues, is a "rough magic that fuses opposites" (preface to Kott, x). Such a bifocal reading acknowledges both the aptness of Gloucester's suicidal conclusion that "As flies to wanton boys are we to th' gods; / They kill us for their sport" and the more compassionate and resigned view that Gloucester subsequently learns from the loyal son who has gently guided him out of despair. Stanley Cavell's reading of *King Lear* is similarly paradoxical: suffering is indeed our best teacher, suggests Cavell, and yet we perceive that it teaches us painfully little.

Not surprisingly, then, the play's stage history is fraught with controversy. Nineteenth-century critic Charles Lamb found the play so complex and so violent that, in his view, "the *Lear* of Shakespeare cannot be acted." Yet such esteemed twentieth-century theater artists as Harley Granville-Barker and Peter Brook have insisted that *King Lear* is the greatest *stage* work ever written in English: "a mountain," Brook contends, "whose summit has never been reached." The text of *King Lear*, with its wide divergences of readings between the Quarto and the First Folio, has proved no less controversial. *King Lear* has thus become a tragedy subjected to endless editorial, interpretive, and philosophical debate. As the most intellectually challenging of Shakespeare's tragedies, it asks readers, viewers, and directors for an expansive response, attuned both to an overwhelming sense of loss at the end of the play and to a sense of relief that at least some readers and audiences experience when death removes Lear from the "rack of this tough world."

The first known performance of the play was at Whitehall Palace on December 26, 1606, with King James in attendance. Probably the play had been written the previous year, though severe bouts of plague may well have limited the times when it could have been performed. To be sure, scholars have yet to agree on the exact date of the first performance and of the play's composition. Some argue that the publication of an old play, *The Chronicle History of King Leir*, in May 1605, offers evidence that a publisher may have been trying to capitalize on the popularity of Shakespeare's play by printing the older source. Other indications in the play suggest that Shakespeare did not write the play until late 1605. Gloucester's mention of "These late eclipses in the sun and moon" (1.2.106; see the opening of Jonathan Miller's BBC *Lear* film) may refer to an eclipse of the moon in September and of the sun in October of 1605.

Characters: Friendship, Families, Misjudgments, the Fool

Lear is King of Britain during pagan times. He has three daughters: Goneril, his eldest and the subject of his curse in 1.4; Regan, who is no less heartlessly cruel; and Cordelia, the loving daughter who will not, during the love test, "heave (her) heart" into her mouth and thus is disowned. The eighty-year-old Lear is viewed by the vicious characters in the play, not without some justification, as being irascible, intemperate, and inordinately demanding. Other characters—the Earls of Kent and Gloucester, Gloucester's son Edgar, Lear's knights and servants—treat him with the respect due his age, with loyalty, even love. In the cases of Kent and Cordelia, their love includes a candor that leads to banishment. Lear's decisions to divide his kingdom, disinherit Cordelia, and banish Kent lead on to his own banishment into the cruel night storms that both trigger and reflect the storms in his mind. Kent remains the most loyal of Lear's followers, disguising himself to protect the king he knows has erred, and surviving to see the end.

Goneril is married to the compassionate Albany, whom she upbraids for his mildness. Their incompatibility motivates her lust for the bastard Edmund. The cruelty of the sisters escalates when Regan prods her sadistic husband Cornwall and commands that the blinded Gloucester be "thrust . . . out at gates [to] . . . smell/His way to Dover." Cordelia is their opposite, the loving daughter who returns full of concern for her father and whose reunion with him brings about his cure from madness. Cordelia returns to England with the French army to restore sanity to the kingdom and her father to a place of authority. Her innocent, forgiving nature makes her murder all the more unjust. Victory for Goneril and Regan, however, does not bring them happiness. Their lust-fueled jealous competition for Edmund contributes to their demise, and Edmund too must pay for his crimes with death. The corpses of these wicked sisters, as well as the bodies of Lear and Cordelia, appear together in the last scene. The family has disintegrated, reunited only in death.

In the parallel plot, the Earl of Gloucester has two sons: Edgar, the elder and legitimate, and Edmund, the younger and illegitimate. Gloucester is easily seduced by Edmund's smooth trickery. He credulously believes, on the basis of a forged letter and a play-acted sword fight staged by Edmund, that Edgar wishes his father dead. Thus Edgar, like Cordelia, must live apart from his family. Edmund, who declares Nature to be his goddess, is smooth and full of impudent charm. As Gloucester's illegitimate child, he would have been known as both a bastard and a "natural" child. As the second child, he would not inherit his father's lands and wealth. Thus, in some modern interpretations, Edmund has been played in the early scenes as plausibly victimized by his father's attitudes—why has Edmund been away nine years, for instance?—and by the legalities that rob him of legitimacy and his inheritance. Yet he so scoffs at religion and the metaphysical speculations of others that he becomes a kind of Vice figure and deceiver who boasts of his own villainy.

Edgar may seem a kind of pawn during the early scenes, a son who does not reveal his true self until after he appears as a mysterious knight from a romance to defeat his brother and speak the last wise words of the play. Edgar is not a character in the psychological sense understood by Victorian actors and critics; he is a chameleon figure who assumes various roles depending upon the scene. When he is exiled from his father's good graces by Edmund's scheme, he tells the audience "Edgar I nothing am." From here onwards he becomes a point of reference as he takes on a variety of roles: as the beggar Poor Tom whose assumed madness counterpoints Lear's insanity, as the stoical companion and compassionate guide to his blinded father, and as the avenging knight bringing retribution to Edmund before resuming his own person as a sorrowful and morally insightful survivor. He may bring some continuity to the kingdom at the tragedy's end. To be sure, Edgar's protracted playacting as Poor Tom can raise questions about his motives. Even after his reunion with his desperate father, he continues the deception, perhaps, as Stanley

Cavell has suggested, because of his shame and guilt that he has been so easily gulled (like his father) by Edmund, or perhaps because he cannot bear seeing his father in such distress and wants to imagine him powerful so that Edgar himself "can remain a child" (Cavell, 231). Thus Edgar, though overflowing with filial piety, is a more complex personality than he may at first appear.

Like Edgar, the Fool serves many functions. He is often portrayed as Lear's personified conscience. In some Eastern European and Russian productions in which the tradition of the Wise Fool is strong, he seems Lear's other, better self. He is loyal, but also bitter that his master has sent Cordelia away and in so doing has become foolish himself. Historically the Fool had certain privileges as a kind of professional entertainer and jokester whose childish innocence enabled him to say things that more presumably wise and sane counselors would not be allowed to say. In *King Lear*, the Fool's role is to jest in a way that can clarify the King's understanding of sometimes harsh realities. The comfort he offers the audience is similar to that he affords Lear: not to hide painful reality, but to point it out in images, puns, and jokes, thereby provoking Lear to face up to the horror he has brought upon himself. The Fool's jokes help steer the audience's changing relationship to Lear. The Fool is at first quizzical in his response to Lear's foolish choices and his rage at those whom he should cherish; as he pointedly tells the King, "Thou shouldst not have been old till thou hadst been wise" (1.5.43–44). In the storm the Fool keeps us in touch with Lear's suffering by introducing into these scenes an element of humor that is carefully controlled in its point of view. In some mid– and late–twentieth-century interpretations, Lear, Edgar, and Gloucester have become as clown-like as the Fool because, in the view of some Beckett-influenced directors, foolishness is the common lot of man. After delivering himself of a series of strange predictions, the Fool settles down and mysteriously disappears from the action.

Sources and Inspirations

Celtic Mythology; Tudor Myth

The story of two wicked daughters and their one dutiful, loving sister is well-known in folklore, especially in the tale of Cinderella. The opening scene of *King Lear* belongs, despite its tragic grandeur, to this kind of fairy-tale world, where great decisions are made in an instant and determined by trifles. The specific story of Lear and his daughters is an ancient legend, with the King himself a character type going back to Celtic mythology. The first written mention of Lear's name and story occurs in the *Historia Regum Britanniae* (c. 1136) of Geoffrey of Monmouth, a Welshman. This work, in which much of the purported history is legendary and fictional, places Lear in a line of descent from Brut, the great-grandson of Aeneas of Troy, and then eventually through Cymbeline and King Arthur to the historical kings of England and thus on to the Tudor monarchs in power during Shakespeare's day. This fanciful mixture of legend, myth, and history was taken seriously then, and thus was repeated in various chronicles and literary works during Shakespeare's time. In all of these—including *The Mirror for Magistrates* (1574) and Raphael Holinshed's *Chronicles* (1587)—the story begins as does Shakespeare's play with the dividing of the kingdom, with Cordelia's refusal to flatter and deceive her father as her sisters do, and with her dowerless marriage to the King of the Franks. Once her hypocritical sisters have reduced their father to a single retainer, this Cordelia is finally reunited with her father and is successful in helping Lear to regain his kingdom. The key difference from Shakespeare's version, then, is that in Geoffrey of Monmouth's account and in other early tellings of the story Cordelia lives and Lear reassumes his throne. After his death, Cordelia rules well until she is overthrown by her brothers-in-law, imprisoned, and commits suicide.

An Earlier *Leir*

Shakespeare's immediate source was a play that may have been written as early as 1588 and that was printed in 1605, *The True Chronicle History of King Leir*. An obsequious courtier, the basis for Shakespeare's Oswald, tells the wicked sisters of the King's plan to divide his kingdom and recommends the rhetorical test of their love as a device for apportioning the land. The older play also contains many romance elements such as disguises, an intrigue plot, and a providential thunderstorm that frightens the assassin whom Regan has hired to kill her father. Shakespeare turns the storm to very different psychological and metaphysical purposes in his rewriting of the story. The older play contains models for the loyal Kent, the mild Albany, and the King of France, the latter being the Gallian King who wears a Palmer's disguise to woo Cordella in a scene revealing the virtue of both characters. The old play has a happy ending in which Lear and Cordella are reunited, the Gallian King invades England, and Lear is restored to the throne. Aside from changing the ending, Shakespeare discards the assassination scheme and many of the disguises, and adds the parallel plot of Gloucester, Edgar, and Edmund. Much of the material in this parallel plot is derived from Sir Philip Sidney's *Arcadia* (1590). In Book Two of that great prose romance, two young men meet a son leading his blind father who then tells them his piteous tale. This deposed King of

Paphlagonia now realizes that his bastard son has turned him against his loving son Leonatus, the man who is now his protector and guide. Having escaped his father's wrath and an order of execution, Leonatus has lived poorly and has recently prevented his father's suicide. The bastard son has usurped the throne and at the end of the tale attacks the forgiving true son. Eventually the villain is driven off, the King returns to his court, and the true son Leonatus is crowned his heir. The old King dies; his suffering, betrayal, and newfound joy have proved more than his heart can bear.

Other sources for elements of Shakespeare's tragedy include the allegorical Vice from late-medieval morality plays as a basis for Edmund's self-advertising villainy; parts of *Arcadia* for the disguises adopted by Kent and Edgar; and Samuel Harsnett's *Declaration of Egregious Popish Impostures* (1603) for some of Tom o' Bedlam's mad ravings. (The latter source is discussed at length in Kenneth Muir's 1953 Arden edition of *King Lear* and in R. A. Foakes's more recent Arden edition of 1997.)

Structure and Language

Parallel Families

The formal structure of Shakespeare's double plot is without precedent in Shakespearean tragedy, for *King Lear* involves the parallel tragedies of two families whose fates are closely linked. Gloucester's tragedy provides a commentary and counterpoint to Lear's, while also having its own coherence and sustaining its own interest. The parallels are established early. Though he loves her best, Lear misjudges Cordelia, and hands over his kingdom to the wicked daughters willing to play his rhetorical game. Similarly, old Gloucester mistakes Edmund's villainy for true concern and misjudges his legitimate son, Edgar. Like Cordelia, Edgar is forced into banishment. Both old men are blind to the essential qualities of their children and hence are prey to the hypocrisies of those who would take advantage of them. Both go through a kind of spiritual death—Lear in his madness, Gloucester in his mutilation—that leads them to acknowledge their blindness. Identifying with "unaccommodated man" on the heath, Lear realizes that he has been deceived into believing he was everything and knows now he is not. Gloucester says even more simply as he heads to what he hopes will be death at Dover, "I stumbled when I saw" (4.1.19). Both wronged children return to help the aged fathers recover from the cruelties visited upon them by the wicked. And both old men have the joy—however fleeting—of acknowledging their wronged child. Gloucester's recognition of Edgar as his true son occurs offstage; Edgar reports that the old man's heart was so overwhelmed with joy and sorrow upon learning the true identity of his son that the shock killed him ("'Twixt two extremes of passion, joy and grief, / [his heart] Burst smilingly" [5.3.202–203]).

Lear lives on after his joyous reconciliation with his daughter only to experience further tragedy. Still suffering the aftereffects of his madness, he comes fully to his senses when the doctor and Cordelia confirm for him that the voice he hears is indeed hers. After her murder, he carries her in, lamenting that animals can have life, but not his child. And in a moment of what can be played as illusory hope (see discussion of the excellent Granada Television film with Laurence Olivier, p. 762), Lear thinks he sees her breath after all, and dies. Edmund and Edgar both link the two families—Edmund by erotic bonds that feed the wicked sisters' jealousies, Edgar by analogy to Cordelia. Yet even Edgar and Cordelia, the "good" characters in redemptive readings of the play, possess enigmatic character traits not easy to reconcile with simple, moralistic interpretations of their roles.

Verbal Paradox

The language of the play is wide-ranging and complex. It draws at times from Old Testament sources, especially themes from the Book of Job, and from Christian verbal paradoxes as in the King of France's description of Cordelia as "most rich being poor / Most choice, forsaken, and most loved, despised" (1.1.254–255). Its language also moves into wild, even violent excesses in the apparent unreason of Poor Tom and the ravings of King Lear. By contrast, the scene (1.1) in which Lear divides his kingdom begins in ceremonial formality, as Lear requires from his daughters the pledges of filial love that Goneril and Regan know how to satisfy in empty rhetorical flourishes. When Cordelia can speak only "nothing" in this competition, the King loses his temper, confirming through his rage, as Frank Kermode has pointed out, "that he cannot be temperate in the absence of ceremony; the love he seeks is the sort that can be offered in formal and subservient expressions, and he therefore rejects the love of Cordelia and of Kent" (186).

The Fool often speaks in gnomic paradoxes. Much of the play's invective, initially from Lear, derives from folklore and ancient myth. The sense-in-madness ravings of both Poor Tom and Lear in his fury are yet another idiom in which this expansive plays finds emotional expression, as the poetry develops a dialectic in which madness and folly are heard in counterpoint to "the language of an evil that remains horribly sane" (Kermode, 189). Notable also is the shift in Lear from noisy ranting and shouting during the storm (in 3.2) to a calm, near-prayerful cadence when he identifies with the "Poor naked wretches . . . That bide the pelting of this pitiless

storm" (3.4.28–29) and allows the Fool to first enter the hovel where they find Poor Tom.

Themes and Issues

Natural and Unnatural

One of the most important themes in the play involves divergent meanings of "natural" and "unnatural" as these terms apply to human relationships and behavior. In the second scene of the play, Edmund invokes Nature as his goddess, defying conventional morality and defining the word "natural" to mean an ethic of pure self-interest. He overturns the idea of nature as a benign, humane, civilizing force involving hierarchy and divine order. He replaces such Elizabethan notions of human nature with the idea that survival goes to those who obey the law of the jungle, who, by their wits, learn to kill rather than be killed. Whereas Cordelia, Lear, Kent, and Gloucester see the wicked Goneril and Regan as unnatural, Edmund views them as adhering to nature's law.

Lear's view of nature is revealed in the first scene when he urges France to bestow his love upon a worthier object than the now disinherited Cordelia, a "wretch whom Nature is ashamed / Almost t'acknowledge hers." Because she has not been willing to give him courtly professions of love, Lear considers her unnatural. Thereafter, as Lear suffers the rebuffs and cruelties of the two false daughters who would deprive him of his retinue and other marks of his power, he continually redefines human nature, first viewing it within its moral, emotional, and spiritual dimensions as requiring far more than what animals need. "Allow not nature more than nature needs, / Man's life is cheap as beast's" (2.4.268–269), he tells the cruel daughters in his great speech beginning "Oh, reason not the need!" that marks the beginning of his breakdown into madness. Yet only when Lear has been reduced like Poor Tom to the level of a "poor, bare, forked animal" does he demonstrate the compassion and generosity that should distinguish human from animal nature. Once he has spent time unprotected in the storm and has suffered a broken mind and spirit, he acknowledges the need to share his "additions" with nature's less fortunate. He here achieves a utopian vision of social equality: "Oh, I have tak'n / Too little care of this! Take physic, pomp; / Expose thyself to feel what wretches feel, / That thou mayst shake the superflux to them / And show the heavens more just" (3.4.32–36). He becomes capable of empathizing with the needs and the sufferings of other human beings. He exhibits charity. Paradoxically, Lear achieves this kind of self-knowledge only when he is mad.

J. F. Danby, in his *Shakespeare's Doctrine of Nature*, discusses how Lear and Cordelia are associated with a beneficent natural order, while their enemies represent the self-interest that divorces ethics from politics and society. Edmund embodies certain Jacobean challenges to the older world order in politics, religion, and science. A rationalist and an Epicurean, Edmund describes a "nature" at odds with Elizabethan ideals. Contrastingly, Cordelia, the newly compassionate Lear, Kent, Edgar, and several servants who minister to the savagely treated Gloucester, all exhibit an inborn propensity to be charitable. They follow the best instincts of their own consciences even at the risk of their own safety. Yet Lear's growing awareness does not save him from suffering further injustice and death. Downfall and death come alike to those who view nature as a civilizing force in a divinely ordained hierarchical order and to those, like Edmund, who see the state of nature as one of constant flux, ruthless ambition, and total absence of social restraint and human community. To be sure, in his belated attempt to save the life of Cordelia, even this perceptive villain seems to understand at last that his amoral creed may have been wrong, and that, like Goneril and Regan, he has been destroyed by his own lust for sex and power.

Blindness, Sight, and Insight

The interrelated themes of seeing and self-knowing are omnipresent in the play. Goneril professes that her father is "Dearer than eyesight" (1.1.56). When Lear orders the loyal Kent, who sees clearly the duplicity of Goneril and Regan, "Out of my sight!" Kent replies, "See better, Lear" (1.1.158–159). Regan responds to her father's irrational banishments of those who love him most with the unfeeling statement that "he hath ever but slenderly known himself." By the fourth scene, when Lear begins to realize how badly he has been treated by Goneril, he upbraids himself for self-pity and cries out, "Old fond eyes, / Beweep this cause again, I'll pluck ye out" (1.4.300–301). Yet it is psychological suffering and degradation, not physical blindness, that brings insight and moral vision to Lear. In the parallel plot, Gloucester sees how mistaken he has been in his judgments of his sons only after he is tried for treason and blinded by Cornwall. "I stumbled when I saw," he acknowledges. And as he struggles through his darkened world, he prays, "O dear son Edgar, / The food of thy abusèd father's wrath, / Might I but live to see thee in my touch, / I'd say I had eyes again!" (4.1.19–24). Love requires insight. Although self-awareness and fortitude emerge from Lear's staggering losses and from Gloucester's suffering and blindness, those virtues are all the rewards they are given. For a director such as Brook, when such "characters acquire sight it enables

them to see only into the void" (Marowitz, quoted in Foakes, 33). Still, Lear and Gloucester both eventually perceive that, paradoxically, adversity has brought them precious insight. When they were prosperous, they now understand, they had been spiritually blind. Like Lear, who sees a vision of utopian social justice when he has been shattered by suffering, the blind, humiliated Gloucester prays that arrogant men will be humbled and the poor succored by redistributed wealth. The wealthy "lust-dieted man," Gloucester says, "will not see / because he does not feel" (4.1.66–68). In a socially just world, he now understands, "distribution should undue excess / And each man have enough" (69–70).

Disguise, Illusion, and Reality

Two characters adopt literal disguises in order to survive the wrath of Lear and Gloucester. Transformed, they can protect these impetuous, easily deceived old men. Kent returns to Lear as a servant named Caius, traveling with him and the Fool through Lear's journey into madness and ultimately into compassion once he has stripped away the accommodations and illusions of power. Edgar dons at least three different disguises, first to hide as Poor Tom from his father's wrath and guide the old man toward Dover, later to spin a moral fiction teaching resignation to his father, and finally to become chivalry's agent of retribution. The paradox here is that loyal, loving truth-tellers must seek refuge in disguise, while hypocrites like Edmund, Goneril, and Regan successfully present themselves until late in the play as persons of honest straightforwardness. When the reality of their viciousness is exposed in the last act, their demises swiftly follow. They are consumed by the very lusts have they have attempted to hide. Yet the exposure of their villainy brings only brief consolation, for it is soon followed by the deaths of Lear and Cordelia. The unalleviated harshness of reality is something that Edgar ultimately realizes he must acknowledge with no sentimental illusions.

A Word on This Text of King Lear

King Lear exits in two early texts, the Quarto of 1608 and the considerably changed Folio version of 1623. Similar disparities appear in *Hamlet*, *Othello*, and other plays, but the problem is especially acute in *King Lear*. Shakespeare must have had a hand in the revisions that led to the Folio text. It contains new material. At the same time, the Quarto text contains passages not found in the Folio. The revisions may have resulted from a number of circumstances: cutting for performance (the play as it stands in either version is too long to have been produced in its entirety on the Jacobean stage), censorship, errors in transcription, and still more. The Folio version does alter some matters especially having to do with the French invasion; characters like Albany appear in a different light. The very ending is changed as to which characters speak the concluding lines.

Given these factors, many editions today present two or even three (Quarto, Folio, and composite) texts for the reader, or mark the text with brackets and other indicators of textual variation. This edition does not do so. The reasons for choosing to present here the more traditional composite or eclectic text are these: *King Lear*'s textual variations between Quarto and Folio are more extensive than in some other plays, but are not always different in kind from other plays, so that it is a distortion to treat this play alone as a multiple-text play. To choose either Quarto or Folio is to lose important material that is unquestionably Shakespeare's. To print two or even three versions is to add pages to an already weighty collection. And the presentation of multiple texts, or of a single text that is flagged with bracketed markers, also imposes on the reader a large and confusing task. Sorting out a complex and uncertain textual history that, however important ultimately in studying Shakespeare as a writer and as a reviser, is perhaps best left to subsequent investigation in a full-scale critical edition after one has absorbed the greatness of this play as a piece of writing for the theater. The present composite *King Lear*, based on the Folio text but including the three hundred or so lines found only in the First Quarto along with some Quarto readings where the Folio version seems less textually reliable, is in a sense a compromise, but it is one that seems well suited to the purposes of this anthology.

Staging Challenges

Acting the Old Patriarch

Actors frequently comment upon the paradox that to play Lear, a man must be strong enough to master a role of nearly eight hundred lines, to rage on the heath, and to carry the actress playing Cordelia (among other physical demands), and yet must also appear "Fourscore and upwards" years and frail enough to provoke the tender compassion felt by such sensitive characters as Kent and Albany. One of the many actors who have met these contradictory demands is Ian Holm, whose National Theatre of Great Britain performance can be seen in the 1997 video of *King Lear*, directed by Richard Eyre. So spry that he jumps onto chairs and tables, Holm nonetheless seems believably old and forgetful. Russian director Grigori Kozintsev's *Korol Lir (King Lear)* features actor Yuri Yarvet as the enigmatic, ultimately pitiable old king, with a some-

what similar mix of physical strengths and frailties. The black-and-white photography, the music of Dimitri Shostakovich, and the ritualistic opening procession of the King's subjects all create a near-mythical atmosphere in this reading, one that is more compassionate and clearly Christian than Eyre's. A man, as Lear claims, "more sinned against than sinning," Yarvet's Lear is ultimately redeemed, for Kozintsev endows him and Cordelia with nobility and heroic stature even as they are imprisoned. By contrast, the Lear of Paul Scofield in Brook's film has few of the softened qualities and almost none of the pathos viewers feel in Eyre's and Kozintsev's films and in Michael Elliott's Granada Television film starring a seventy-five-year-old Laurence Olivier. These four interpretations, all discussed at greater length in the stage histories below (pp. 760ff.), suggest the range of possible (and effective) approaches to the role.

Embodying Violence

Once King Lear has initiated the violence that permeates the social atmosphere of *King Lear*, that violence soon escalates to distressing proportions. Lear threatens Kent and strikes Goneril's servant Oswald. These acts, hasty and imperious as they indeed seem, are mild in comparison with the troubling violence that rapidly ensues. Edmund wounds himself in a staged fight with Edgar. The Duke of Cornwall puts Kent in the stocks for beating Oswald. The ungrateful daughters cruelly send out Lear into the night storm. The violence changes in kind, becoming increasingly gratuitous and brutal until it culminates in Cornwall's blinding of Gloucester, first one eye and then the other after a servant has come to Gloucester's defense and has given Cornwall a death blow. Moral values are grotesquely inverted as Edmund is praised for betraying his father to Regan and Cornwall. Still to come are the killing of Oswald, the single combat between Edgar and Edmund, the poisoning of Goneril, the suicide of Regan, and the (off-stage) hanging of Cordelia.

The battle between the French and English is not dramatized in the play, although film and stage directors often suggest scenes of combat (Cordelia is seen in armor in the Eyre film, for instance). Given this degree of violent action, directors can choose to visualize, exaggerate (as in Kurosawa's blood-soaked film adaptation), or minimize the brutality. That decision may depend upon whether the director emphasizes the rehabilitation and redemption of Lear or the familial and political chaos which his intemperance has set in motion.

Perhaps the most difficult scene of all to stage is that of Gloucester's savage blinding. Victorian productions often cut it or reported the action as taking place off stage. Even when the business was enacted on stage,

Gloucester was often seen with his back to the audience as Cornwall bore down upon him. In the latter part of the twentieth century and on film, on the other hand, the scene has been made gruesome and explicit to emphasize the sadistic pleasure Cornwall derives from the act. The Earl is either tied to or held in a chair. Regan goads Cornwall on. When Gloucester defiantly declares that "I shall see / The wingèd vengeance overtake such children," Cornwall responds, "See't shalt thou never.—Fellows, hold the chair. / Upon these eyes of thine I'll set my foot" (3.7.68–71). Departing from Shakespeare's text, Cornwall often attacks with his hands. Blood may spurt from a "blood bag" hidden in the attacker's fist or the victim's hair. The eye itself may appear in Cornwall's hand, with Gloucester's anguished screams adding to the horror. Liquid representing the eyeball's aqueous humor may spurt into the air. The eyeball itself, on some occasions, has rolled across the stage.

In director Peter Brook's 1962 production for the Shakespeare Memorial Theatre in Stratford-upon-Avon and in the film that followed, Cornwall brutally removes one of his spurs, and, in full view of the audience, uses it to gouge out Gloucester's second eye. This gruesome moment comes as the logical consequence of the unceasing violence with which Brook has filmed the story up to this point. Brook locates the violence initially in the behavior of Lear and his knights (as Kurosawa does much later with his opening hunting scene and long backstory). When they are housed at Goneril's castle in the Brook film, Lear's riotous knights drink into the night and then upend tables as they come back to the castle after hunting, nearly wrecking everything in sight. Their behavior offers some small justification for Goneril's (and later Regan's) demand that Lear decrease the number of knights at his service—an act calculated to diminish the destructiveness of Lear and his followers, but also his power and authority. Then, as our sympathies turn increasingly against the daughters in Act 3, Brook shows us in garish detail the gouging out of Gloucester's eyes.

Storm on the Heath, in the Mind

Film has proved an ideal medium for depicting the storm that rages on the heath and in Lear's mind. Even without big-budget special effects, inventive stage directors have created the thunder, lightning, wind, and rain indicated in the text and have given fully realistic rendition to the pelting rain that chillingly pours down upon Lear, Edgar, the Fool, and Gloucester. At the original Globe Theater, Lear's lines invoking the elements may have been accompanied by the kind of early stage effects that Ben Jonson contemptuously described as the "rolled bullet heard / To say, it thunders" or "the tempestuous drum [that] / Rumbles, to tell you when the storm doth come." During the later seventeenth and the eighteenth centuries, theatrical effects became more realistic. Small explosions of saltpeter as well as that sound of cannonballs rolling down wooden troughs were used to create the effect of the storm. By the end of his acting and directing career in the late eighteenth century, David Garrick staged *King Lear* with the authenticity that became a hallmark of Victorian productions, using a backcloth of a stormy sky, wind, and lightning. These lively effects became even more complex in Edmund Kean's use of the so-called "eidophysikon" tricks fashioned by the stage designer de Loutherbourg (Bratton, 27). Kean's use of stage machinery and illusions gave substance to Coleridge's observation that watching Kean as Lear in the storm was like reading Shakespeare by flashes of lightning. An overhead lantern with revolving colored transparencies (roughly comparable to today's gels) bathed Lear in a series of otherworldly colors, while trees creaked on strings and the sea seemed to heave in the background. Victorian productions by Samuel Phelps and Charles Kean heightened these effects of rolling thunder and scudding clouds, with a lurid gloom hovering over the scene. These devices were further enhanced by Henry Irving, whose storms at the Lyceum were admired by audiences expecting elaborate verisimilitude. By 1936, the new sophisticated lighting grids at the Shakespeare Memorial Theatre in Stratford-upon-Avon enabled directors to create storms complete with wind, thunder, and a green sky flecked with clouds turning to a frightening blackness as Lear and his forlorn companions wandered about in the downpour. Since that time, the storm has often been represented simply, as it would have been in Shakespeare's day. In Peter Brook's 1962 production, the actors used mime to suggest the ferocity of the storm. In his 1976 production, Trevor Nunn combined acting stylization with realistic rain, wind, and thunder. Adrian Noble's 1982 production turned back toward pictorial realism by placing Lear and the Fool high above the action, swaying on a tiny platform buffeted by the wind. And for the Olivier/Granada TV *Lear* film, stagehands doused the actors with nine hundred gallons of water during the storm.

Dover Cliff

Act 4 of *King Lear* presents a remarkable staging challenge in the attempted suicide of the Earl of Gloucester. He is accompanied by his son Edgar, still disguised as a peasant, whom the Earl has asked to guide him to a spot where he may throw himself off the cliffs of Dover and thereby end a life he considers no longer tolerable. In 4.6 we thus behold these two figures on what Gloucester believes to be the top of Dover Cliff. A fascinating question arises: do not we, as audience, also assume that they are at the edge of a cliff? In Jonathan Miller's BBC production Edgar carries his father on his back, making Gloucester even more dependent upon the man he takes to be a poor beggar. Edgar assures the old man that he is doing as Gloucester has asked, assisting him to commit suicide, and yet at the same time Edgar turns to us in an aside to reassure us that he has no such intention: "Why I do trifle thus with his despair. / Is done to cure it." Because the scene is deliberately short on specific indications of place, we cannot be sure what to make of Gloucester's repeated puzzlement that he and Poor Tom do not seem to be climbing upwards, and that Gloucester cannot hear any sea sounds nearby. Edgar assures his father that his perceptions are flawed, owing to the fact that he his blind. Thus directors may choose to use an incline to suggest the climb to a cliff top, or may simply keep the pair on flat ground. Some directors pipe in recorded sea sounds, although those make superfluous Edgar's further justifying speech that the "murmuring surge, / That on th'unnumb'red idle pebbles chafes / Cannot be heard so high." Usually, Gloucester kneels on the imagined precipice speaking his farewell to life and his blessing upon his wronged son before falling forward presumably in a swoon or faint. In Miller's production, Gloucester stands, stretches out his arms, and throws himself forward out of the picture frame, thus leaving the audience in suspense.

Olivier's Granada Television production, directed by Michael Elliott, also trades in suspense here, as Gloucester (Leo McKern) kneels, raises his arms, and falls forward, moaning. Very quickly, the camera shows him lying flat in a patch of sand, clearly alive. The camera has thus played meaningful tricks with us: it has led us to wonder if Gloucester is indeed at the edge of a cliff, and then reveals to us the fact that Edgar has brought his father to a place where he is in no such peril.

When Gloucester rouses himself again, realizing he is alive, Edgar adopts another verbal disguise and feigns astonishment that Gloucester has survived so long a fall, telling the blind man, "Thy life's a miracle." Edgar devises a mythology for his dear, superstitious father. He describes for Gloucester a devilish creature upon the crown of the cliff, "some fiend" perhaps who tempted him to suicide. Edgar's fiction is accepted by Gloucester, who resolves henceforth to bear affliction more patiently; Edgar's cure has worked. At the same time, the audience clearly sees that Gloucester's comfort is an illusion, based upon the playacting of his son, not upon miraculous intervention by the gods. The best stagings of the play retain this complex thematic probing, as the lesson of Edgar's little morality play is interrogated by the audience's knowledge that its moral is a fabrication. A saving fiction has been created by a loving son for the despairing old man.

King Lear

[*Dramatis Personae*

KING LEAR
GONERIL,
REGAN,
CORDELIA,
DUKE OF ALBANY, *Goneril's husband*
DUKE OF CORNWALL, *Regan's husband*
KING OF FRANCE, *Cordelia's suitor and husband*
DUKE OF BURGUNDY, *suitor to Cordelia*

EARL OF KENT, *later disguised as Caius*
EARL OF GLOUCESTER
EDGAR, *Gloucester's son and heir, later disguised as poor Tom*
EDMUND, *Gloucester's bastard son*

OSWALD, *Goneril's steward*
A KNIGHT *serving King Lear*
Lear's FOOL
CURAN, *in Gloucester's household*
GENTLEMEN
Three SERVANTS
OLD MAN, *a tenant of Gloucester*
Three MESSENGERS
A GENTLEMAN *attending Cordelia as a Doctor*
Two CAPTAINS
HERALD

Knights, Gentlemen, Attendants, Servants, Officers, Soldiers, Trumpeters

SCENE: *Britain*]

1.1

Enter Kent, Gloucester, and Edmund.

KENT   I thought the King had more affected the Duke of   1
Albany than Cornwall.   2

GLOUCESTER   It did always seem so to us; but now in
the division of the kingdom it appears not which of
the dukes he values most, for equalities are so weighed   5
that curiosity in neither can make choice of either's   6
moiety.   7

KENT   Is not this your son, my lord?

GLOUCESTER   His breeding, sir, hath been at my charge.   9
I have so often blushed to acknowledge him that now
I am brazed to't.   11

KENT   I cannot conceive you.   12

GLOUCESTER   Sir, this young fellow's mother could;
whereupon she grew round-wombed and had indeed,
sir, a son for her cradle ere she had a husband
for her bed. Do you smell a fault?   16

KENT   I cannot wish the fault undone, the issue of it   17
being so proper.   18

GLOUCESTER   But I have a son, sir, by order of law, some   19
year elder than this, who yet is no dearer in my ac-   20
count. Though this knave came something saucily to   21
the world before he was sent for, yet was his mother
fair, there was good sport at his making, and the
whoreson must be acknowledged.—Do you know this   24
noble gentleman, Edmund?

EDMUND   No, my lord.

GLOUCESTER   My lord of Kent. Remember him hereafter
as my honorable friend.

EDMUND   My services to Your Lordship.   29

KENT   I must love you, and sue to know you better.   30

EDMUND   Sir, I shall study deserving.   31

GLOUCESTER   He hath been out nine years, and away   32
he shall again. The King is coming.   33

*Sennet. Enter [one bearing a coronet, then] King
Lear, Cornwall, Albany, Goneril, Regan, Cordelia,
and attendants.*

LEAR
Attend the lords of France and Burgundy, Gloucester.   34

GLOUCESTER   I shall, my liege.   *Exit.*

1.1. Location: King Lear's palace.
1 affected favored   **2 Albany** i.e., Scotland   **5–7 equalities . . .
moiety** the shares balance so equally that close scrutiny cannot find
advantage in either's portion.   **9 breeding** raising, care.   **charge**
expense.   **11 brazed** hardened   **12 conceive** understand. (But
Gloucester puns in the sense of "become pregnant.")   **16 fault** (1) sin
(2) loss of scent by the hounds.   **17 issue** (1) result (2) offspring
18 proper (1) excellent (2) handsome.   **19 by order of law** legitimate
19–20 some year about a year   **20–1 account** estimation.   **21 knave**
young fellow. (Not said disapprovingly, though the word is ironic.)
something somewhat   **24 whoreson** low fellow; suggesting bastardy, but (like *knave* above) used with affectionate condescension
29 services duty   **30 sue** petition, beg   **31 study deserving** strive to
be worthy (of your esteem).   **32 out** i.e., abroad, absent   **33.1 Sennet**
trumpet signal heralding a procession.   *one . . . then* (This direction
is from the Quarto. The *coronet* is perhaps intended for Cordelia or
her betrothed. A coronet signifies nobility below the rank of king.)
34 Attend Wait upon, usher ceremoniously

LEAR
Meantime we shall express our darker purpose.   36
Give me the map there. [*He takes a map.*] Know that we
have divided
In three our kingdom; and 'tis our fast intent   38
To shake all cares and business from our age,
Conferring them on younger strengths while we
Unburdened crawl toward death. Our son of
Cornwall,
And you, our no less loving son of Albany,
We have this hour a constant will to publish   43
Our daughters' several dowers, that future strife   44
May be prevented now. The princes, France and
Burgundy,
Great rivals in our youngest daughter's love,
Long in our court have made their amorous sojourn
And here are to be answered. Tell me, my
daughters—
Since now we will divest us both of rule,
Interest of territory, cares of state—   50
Which of you shall we say doth love us most,
That we our largest bounty may extend
Where nature doth with merit challenge? Goneril,   53
Our eldest born, speak first.

GONERIL
Sir, I love you more than words can wield the matter,
Dearer than eyesight, space, and liberty,   56
Beyond what can be valued, rich or rare,
No less than life, with grace, health, beauty, honor;
As much as child e'er loved, or father found;   59
A love that makes breath poor and speech unable.   60
Beyond all manner of so much I love you.

CORDELIA [*aside*]
What shall Cordelia speak? Love and be silent.

LEAR [*indicating on map*]
Of all these bounds, even from this line to this,
With shadowy forests and with champains riched,   64
With plenteous rivers and wide-skirted meads,   65
We make thee lady. To thine and Albany's issue
Be this perpetual.—What says our second daughter,
Our dearest Regan, wife of Cornwall? Speak.

REGAN
I am made of that self mettle as my sister,   69
And prize me at her worth. In my true heart   70
I find she names my very deed of love;   71
Only she comes too short, that I profess   72
Myself an enemy to all other joys
Which the most precious square of sense possesses,   74

---

36 we, our (The royal plural; also in lines 37–44, etc.)   **darker purpose** undeclared intention.   **38 fast** firm   **43 constant . . . publish**
firm resolve to proclaim   **44 several** individual   **50 Interest of** right
or title to, possession of   **53 Where . . . challenge** where both natural
affection and merit claim our bounty as its due.   **56 space, and liberty** possession of land, and freedom of action   **59 found** i.e., found
himself to be loved   **60 breath . . . unable** utterance impoverished
and speech inadequate.   **64 shadowy** shady.   **champains riched** fertile plains   **65 plenteous . . . meads** abundant rivers bordered with
wide meadows   **69 that self mettle** that same spirited temperament
70 prize . . . worth value myself as her equal (in love for you). (*Prize*
suggests "price.")   **71 names . . . love** describes my love in action
72 that in that   **74 Which . . . possesses** which the most delicately
sensitive part of my nature can enjoy

And find I am alone felicitate   75
In your dear Highness' love.
CORDELIA [*aside*]   Then poor Cordelia!
And yet not so, since I am sure my love's
More ponderous than my tongue.   78
LEAR
To thee and thine hereditary ever
Remain this ample third of our fair kingdom,
No less in space, validity, and pleasure   81
Than that conferred on Goneril.—Now, our joy,
Although our last and least, to whose young love   83
The vines of France and milk of Burgundy   84
Strive to be interested, what can you say to draw   85
A third more opulent than your sisters'? Speak.
CORDELIA   Nothing, my lord.
LEAR   Nothing?
CORDELIA   Nothing.
LEAR
Nothing will come of nothing. Speak again.
CORDELIA
Unhappy that I am, I cannot heave
My heart into my mouth. I love Your Majesty
According to my bond, no more nor less.   93
LEAR
How, how, Cordelia? Mend your speech a little,
Lest you may mar your fortunes.
CORDELIA   Good my lord,
You have begot me, bred me, loved me. I
Return those duties back as are right fit,   97
Obey you, love you, and most honor you.
Why have my sisters husbands if they say
They love you all? Haply, when I shall wed,   100
That lord whose hand must take my plight shall carry   101
Half my love with him, half my care and duty.
Sure I shall never marry like my sisters,
To love my father all.
LEAR
But goes thy heart with this?
CORDELIA   Ay, my good lord.
LEAR   So young, and so untender?
CORDELIA   So young, my lord, and true.
LEAR
Let it be so! Thy truth then be thy dower!
For, by the sacred radiance of the sun,
The mysteries of Hecate and the night,   110
By all the operation of the orbs   111
From whom we do exist and cease to be,   112
Here I disclaim all my paternal care,
Propinquity, and property of blood,   114
And as a stranger to my heart and me

Hold thee from this forever. The barbarous Scythian,   116
Or he that makes his generation messes   117
To gorge his appetite, shall to my bosom
Be as well neighbored, pitied, and relieved   119
As thou my sometime daughter.
KENT   Good my liege—   120
LEAR   Peace, Kent!
Come not between the dragon and his wrath.
I loved her most, and thought to set my rest   123
On her kind nursery. [*To Cordelia*] Hence, and avoid
my sight!—   124
So be my grave my peace, as here I give   125
Her father's heart from her. Call France. Who stirs?   126
Call Burgundy.   [*Exit one.*]
                    Cornwall and Albany,
With my two daughters' dowers digest the third.   128
Let pride, which she calls plainness, marry her.   129
I do invest you jointly with my power,
Preeminence, and all the large effects   131
That troop with majesty. Ourself by monthly course,   132
With reservation of an hundred knights   133
By you to be sustained, shall our abode
Make with you by due turns. Only we shall retain
The name and all th'addition to a king.   136
The sway, revenue, execution of the rest,   137
Belovèd sons, be yours, which to confirm,
This coronet part between you.
KENT   Royal Lear,   139
Whom I have ever honored as my king,
Loved as my father, as my master followed,
As my great patron thought on in my prayers—
LEAR
The bow is bent and drawn. Make from the shaft.   143
KENT
Let it fall rather, though the fork invade   144
The region of my heart. Be Kent unmannerly
When Lear is mad. What wouldst thou do, old man?
Think'st thou that duty shall have dread to speak
When power to flattery bows?
To plainness honor's bound   149
When majesty falls to folly. Reserve thy state,   150
And in thy best consideration check   151
This hideous rashness. Answer my life my judgment,   152

75 **felicitate** made happy   78 **ponderous** weighty   81 **validity** value.
pleasure pleasing features   83 **least** youngest   84 **vines** vineyards.
milk pastures (?)   85 **be interested** be affiliated, establish a claim, be
admitted as to a privilege.   **draw** win   93 **bond** filial obligation
97 **right fit** proper and fitting   100 **all** exclusively, and with all of
themselves.   **Haply** Perhaps, with luck   101 **plight** pledge in marriage   110 **mysteries** secret rites.   **Hecate** goddess of witchcraft and
the moon   111 **operation** influence.   **orbs** planets and stars
112 **From whom** under whose influence   114 **Propinquity . . . blood**
close kinship, and rights and duties entailed in blood ties

116 **this** this time forth.   **Scythian** (Scythians were famous in antiquity for savagery.)   117 **makes . . . messes** makes meals of his children
or parents   119 **neighbored** helped in a neighborly way
120 **sometime** former   123 **set my rest** rely wholly. (A phrase from a
game of cards, meaning "to stake all.")   124 **nursery** nursing, care.
avoid get out of   125 **So . . . peace, as** As I hope to rest peacefully in
my grave   126 **Who stirs?** i.e., Jump to it; don't just stand there.
128 **digest** assimilate, incorporate   129 **Let . . . her** Let pride, which
she calls plain speaking, be her dowry and get her a husband.
131 **effects** outward shows   132 **troop with** accompany, serve.
Ourself (The royal "we.")   133 **With reservation of** reserving to
myself the right to be attended by   136 **th'addition** the honors and
prerogatives   137 **sway** sovereign authority   139 **coronet** (Perhaps
Lear gestures toward this coronet that was to have symbolized
Cordelia's dowry and marriage, hands it to his sons-in-law, or actually attempts to divide it.)   143 **Make from** Get out of the way of
144 **fall** strike.   **fork** barbed head of an arrow   149 **To . . . bound**
Loyalty demands frankness   150 **Reserve thy state** Retain your royal
authority   151 **And . . . check** and with wise deliberation restrain
152 **Answer . . . judgment** I wager my life on my judgment that

Thy youngest daughter does not love thee least,
Nor are those emptyhearted whose low sounds
Reverb no hollowness.

LEAR   Kent, on thy life, no more.   155

KENT

My life I never held but as a pawn   156
To wage against thine enemies, nor fear to lose it,   157
Thy safety being motive.

LEAR   Out of my sight!   158

KENT

See better, Lear, and let me still remain
The true blank of thine eye.   160

LEAR   Now, by Apollo—

KENT   Now, by Apollo, King,
Thou swear'st thy gods in vain.

LEAR   Oh, vassal! Miscreant!   164

[*Laying his hand on his sword.*]

ALBANY, CORNWALL   Dear sir, forbear.

KENT

Kill thy physician, and the fee bestow
Upon the foul disease. Revoke thy gift,
Or whilst I can vent clamor from my throat
I'll tell thee thou dost evil.

LEAR

Hear me, recreant, on thine allegiance hear me!   170
That thou hast sought to make us break our vows,   171
Which we durst never yet, and with strained pride   172
To come betwixt our sentence and our power,   173
Which nor our nature nor our place can bear,   174
Our potency made good, take thy reward.   175
Five days we do allot thee for provision
To shield thee from disasters of the world,
And on the sixth to turn thy hated back
Upon our kingdom. If on the tenth day following
Thy banished trunk be found in our dominions,   180
The moment is thy death. Away! By Jupiter,
This shall not be revoked.

KENT

Fare thee well, King. Sith thus thou wilt appear,   183
Freedom lives hence and banishment is here.
[*To Cordelia*] The gods to their dear shelter take thee,
     maid,
That justly think'st and hast most rightly said!
[*To Regan and Goneril*] And your large speeches may
     your deeds approve,   187
That good effects may spring from words of love.
Thus Kent, O princes, bids you all adieu.

He'll shape his old course in a country new.   *Exit.* 190

*Flourish. Enter Gloucester, with France and
Burgundy; attendants.*

GLOUCESTER

Here's France and Burgundy, my noble lord.

LEAR   My lord of Burgundy,
We first address toward you, who with this king   193
Hath rivaled for our daughter. What in the least   194
Will you require in present dower with her
Or cease your quest of love?

BURGUNDY   Most royal Majesty,
I crave no more than hath Your Highness offered,
Nor will you tender less.

LEAR   Right noble Burgundy,   198
When she was dear to us we did hold her so,   199
But now her price is fallen. Sir, there she stands.
If aught within that little-seeming substance,   201
Or all of it, with our displeasure pieced,   202
And nothing more, may fitly like Your Grace,   203
She's there, and she is yours.

BURGUNDY   I know no answer.

LEAR

Will you, with those infirmities she owes,   205
Unfriended, new-adopted to our hate,
Dowered with our curse and strangered with our
     oath,   207
Take her, or leave her?

BURGUNDY   Pardon me, royal sir.
Election makes not up in such conditions.   209

LEAR

Then leave her, sir, for by the power that made me,
I tell you all her wealth. [*To France*] For you, great King, 211
I would not from your love make such a stray   212
To match you where I hate; therefore beseech you   213
T'avert your liking a more worthier way   214
Than on a wretch whom Nature is ashamed
Almost t'acknowledge hers.

FRANCE   This is most strange,
That she whom even but now was your best object,
The argument of your praise, balm of your age,   218
The best, the dearest, should in this trice of time   219
Commit a thing so monstrous to dismantle   220
So many folds of favor. Sure her offense
Must be of such unnatural degree
That monsters it, or your forevouched affection   223
Fall into taint, which to believe of her

---

155 Reverb no hollowness do not reverberate like a hollow drum,
insincerely.   **156–7 My . . . wage** I never regarded my life other than
as a pledge to hazard in warfare   **158 motive** that which prompts me
to act.   **160 The true . . . eye** i.e., the means to enable you to see better. (*Blank* means "the white center of the target," or, "the true direct
aim," as in "point-blank," traveling in a straight line.)   **164 vassal**
i.e., wretch.   **Miscreant** (Literally, infidel, heretic; hence, villain, rascal.)   **170 recreant** traitor   **171 That** In that, since   **172 strained**
excessive   **173 To . . . power** i.e., to block my power to command and
judge   **174 Which . . . place** which neither my temperament nor my
office as king   **175 Our . . . good** my power enacted, demonstrated
180 trunk body   **183 Sith** Since   **187 your . . . approve** may your
deeds confirm your speeches with their vast claims

190 shape . . . course follow his traditional plainspoken ways
190.1 *Flourish* trumpet fanfare used for the entrance or exit of important persons   **193 address** address myself   **194 rivaled** competed.
in the least at the lowest   **198 tender** offer   **199 so** i.e., *dear*, beloved
and valued at a high price   **201 little-seeming substance** one who
seems substantial but whose substance is, in fact, little, or, one who
refuses to flatter   **202 pieced** added, joined   **203 like** please
205 owes owns   **207 strangered** disowned   **209 Election . . . conditions** No choice is possible under such conditions.   **211 tell you**
(1) inform you of (2) enumerate for you.   **For** As for   **212 make such
a stray** stray so far   **213 To** as to.   **beseech** I beseech   **214 T'avert
your liking** to turn your affections   **218 argument** theme   **219 trice**
moment   **220 to** as to   **223 monsters it** makes it monstrous
223–4 or . . . taint or else the affection for her you have hitherto
affirmed must fall into suspicion

Must be a faith that reason without miracle
Should never plant in me.
CORDELIA   I yet beseech Your Majesty—
    If for I want that glib and oily art   228
    To speak and purpose not, since what I well intend   229
    I'll do't before I speak—that you make known
    It is no vicious blot, murder, or foulness,   231
    No unchaste action or dishonored step
    That hath deprived me of your grace and favor,
    But even for want of that for which I am richer: 234
    A still-soliciting eye and such a tongue   235
    That I am glad I have not, though not to have it
    Hath lost me in your liking.
LEAR   Better thou
    Hadst not been born than not t'have pleased me better.
FRANCE
    Is it but this? A tardiness in nature
    Which often leaves the history unspoke   240
    That it intends to do?—My lord of Burgundy,
    What say you to the lady? Love's not love
    When it is mingled with regards that stands   243
    Aloof from th'entire point. Will you have her?   244
    She is herself a dowry.
BURGUNDY [to Lear]   Royal King,
    Give but that portion which yourself proposed,
    And here I take Cordelia by the hand,
    Duchess of Burgundy.
LEAR
    Nothing. I have sworn. I am firm.
BURGUNDY [to Cordelia]
    I am sorry, then, you have so lost a father
    That you must lose a husband.
CORDELIA   Peace be with Burgundy!
    Since that respects of fortune are his love,   252
    I shall not be his wife.
FRANCE
    Fairest Cordelia, that art most rich being poor,
    Most choice, forsaken, and most loved, despised,
    Thee and thy virtues here I seize upon,
    Be it lawful I take up what's cast away.   257
                    [He takes her hand.]
    Gods, gods! 'Tis strange that from their cold'st neglect   258
    My love should kindle to inflamed respect.—   259
    Thy dowerless daughter, King, thrown to my chance,   260
    Is queen of us, of ours, and our fair France.
    Not all the dukes of wat'rish Burgundy   262
    Can buy this unprized precious maid of me.—   263
    Bid them farewell, Cordelia, though unkind.   264
    Thou losest here, a better where to find.   265

LEAR
    Thou hast her, France. Let her be thine, for we
    Have no such daughter, nor shall ever see
    That face of hers again. Therefore begone
    Without our grace, our love, our benison.   269
    Come, noble Burgundy.
            Flourish. Exeunt [all but France, Goneril, Regan,
                                         and Cordelia].
FRANCE   Bid farewell to your sisters.
CORDELIA
    Ye jewels of our father, with washed eyes   272
    Cordelia leaves you. I know you what you are,
    And like a sister am most loath to call   274
    Your faults as they are named. Love well our father.   275
    To your professèd bosoms I commit him.   276
    But yet, alas, stood I within his grace,
    I would prefer him to a better place.   278
    So, farewell to you both.
REGAN
    Prescribe not us our duty.
GONERIL   Let your study
    Be to content your lord, who hath received you
    At Fortune's alms. You have obedience scanted,   282
    And well are worth the want that you have wanted.   283
CORDELIA
    Time shall unfold what plighted cunning hides;   284
    Who covers faults, at last shame them derides.   285
    Well may you prosper!
FRANCE   Come, my fair Cordelia.
                    Exeunt France and Cordelia.
GONERIL   Sister, it is not little I have to say of what most
    nearly appertains to us both. I think our father will
    hence tonight.
REGAN   That's most certain, and with you; next month
    with us.
GONERIL   You see how full of changes his age is; the
    observation we have made of it hath not been little.
    He always loved our sister most, and with what poor
    judgment he hath now cast her off appears too gross-   295
    ly.
REGAN   'Tis the infirmity of his age. Yet he hath ever
    but slenderly known himself.   298
GONERIL   The best and soundest of his time hath been   299
    but rash. Then must we look from his age to receive   300
    not alone the imperfections of long-ingraffed condi-   301
    tion, but therewithal the unruly waywardness that in-
    firm and choleric years bring with them.   303
REGAN   Such unconstant starts are we like to have from
    him as this of Kent's banishment.

228 for I want because I lack   229 purpose not not intend to do what
I say   231 foulness immorality   234 for which for lack of which
235 still-soliciting ever begging   240 history tale, narrative
243–4 regards . . . point irrelevant considerations.   252 Since . . . fortune Since concern for wealth and position   257 Be it lawful if it be
lawful that   258 from . . . neglect out of the cold neglect of the gods
259 inflamed respect ardent regard.   260 chance lot   262 wat'rish
(1) well-watered with rivers (2) feeble, watery   263 unprized not
appreciated. (With perhaps a sense also of "priceless.")   264 though
unkind though they have behaved unnaturally.   265 here this place.
where place elsewhere

269 benison blessing.   272 washed tear-washed   274 like a sister i.e.,
because I am your sister   275 as . . . named by their true names.
276 professèd bosoms publicly avowed love   278 prefer advance,
recommend   282 At . . . alms as a pittance or dole from Fortune.
283 And well . . . wanted i.e., and well deserve to be without the
dowry and the parental affection that you have both lacked and flouted.   284–5 Time . . . derides Time will bring to light what cunning
attempts to conceal as if in the folds of a cloak; those who hide their
faults may do so for a while, but in time they will be shamed and
derided.   295 grossly obviously.   298–9 The best . . . rash Even in the
prime of his life, he was stormy and unpredictable.   300–1 long-
ingraffed condition long-implanted habit   301 therewithal added
thereto   303 unconstant starts impulsive outbursts.   like likely

GONERIL   There is further compliment of leave-taking 305
  between France and him. Pray you, let us hit together. 306
  If our father carry authority with such disposition as 307
  he bears, this last surrender of his will but offend us. 308
REGAN   We shall further think of it.
GONERIL   We must do something, and i'th' heat. 310

Exeunt.

❧

1.2

Enter Bastard [Edmund, with a letter].

EDMUND
  Thou, Nature, art my goddess; to thy law   1
  My services are bound. Wherefore should I
  Stand in the plague of custom and permit   3
  The curiosity of nations to deprive me,   4
  For that I am some twelve or fourteen moonshines 5
  Lag of a brother? Why bastard? Wherefore base?   6
  When my dimensions are as well compact,   7
  My mind as generous, and my shape as true,   8
  As honest madam's issue? Why brand they us   9
  With base? With baseness? Bastardy? Base, base?
  Who in the lusty stealth of nature take   11
  More composition and fierce quality   12
  Than doth within a dull, stale, tirèd bed
  Go to th' creating a whole tribe of fops   14
  Got 'tween asleep and wake? Well, then,   15
  Legitimate Edgar, I must have your land.
  Our father's love is to the bastard Edmund
  As to th' legitimate. Fine word, "legitimate"!
  Well, my legitimate, if this letter speed   19
  And my invention thrive, Edmund the base   20
  Shall top th' legitimate. I grow, I prosper.
  Now, gods, stand up for bastards!

Enter Gloucester.

GLOUCESTER
  Kent banished thus? And France in choler parted?
  And the King gone tonight? Prescribed his power, 24
  Confined to exhibition? All this done   25
  Upon the gad? Edmund, how now? What news?   26
EDMUND   So please Your Lordship, none.
                                [Putting up the letter.]

GLOUCESTER   Why so earnestly seek you to put up that
  letter?
EDMUND   I know no news, my lord.
GLOUCESTER   What paper were you reading?
EDMUND   Nothing, my lord.
GLOUCESTER   No? What needed then that terrible dis- 33
  patch of it into your pocket? The quality of nothing 34
  hath not such need to hide itself. Let's see. Come, if it
  be nothing I shall not need spectacles.
EDMUND   I beseech you, sir, pardon me. It is a letter
  from my brother, that I have not all o'erread; and for 38
  so much as I have perused, I find it not fit for your
  o'erlooking.   40
GLOUCESTER   Give me the letter, sir.
EDMUND   I shall offend either to detain or give it. The
  contents, as in part I understand them, are to blame. 43
GLOUCESTER   Let's see, let's see.
                                [Edmund gives the letter.]
EDMUND   I hope for my brother's justification he wrote
  this but as an essay or taste of my virtue.   46
GLOUCESTER *(reads)* "This policy and reverence of age 47
  makes the world bitter to the best of our times, keeps 48
  our fortunes from us till our oldness cannot relish
  them. I begin to find an idle and fond bondage in the 50
  oppression of aged tyranny, who sways not as it hath 51
  power but as it is suffered. Come to me, that of this I 52
  may speak more. If our father would sleep till I waked
  him, you should enjoy half his revenue forever and live
  the beloved of your brother,   Edgar."
  Hum! Conspiracy! "Sleep till I waked him, you should
  enjoy half his revenue." My son Edgar! Had he
  a hand to write this? A heart and brain to breed it
  in? When came you to this? Who brought it?   59
EDMUND   It was not brought me, my lord; there's the
  cunning of it. I found it thrown in at the casement of 61
  my closet.   62
GLOUCESTER   You know the character to be your   63
  brother's?
EDMUND   If the matter were good, my lord, I durst   65
  swear it were his; but in respect of that I would fain   66
  think it were not.
GLOUCESTER   It is his.
EDMUND   It is his hand, my lord, but I hope his heart is
  not in the contents.
GLOUCESTER   Has he never before sounded you in this
  business?
EDMUND   Never, my lord. But I have heard him oft
  maintain it to be fit that, sons at perfect age and fathers 74
  declined, the father should be as ward to the son, and   75
  the son manage his revenue.

---

305 compliment ceremony   **306 hit** agree   **307–8 If . . . offend us** If our father continues to boss us around with his accustomed imperiousness, this most recent display of willfulness will do us nothing but harm.   **310 i'th' heat** i.e., while the iron is hot.
1.2. Location: The Earl of Gloucester's house.
1 Nature i.e., the sanction that governs the material world through mechanical amoral forces   **3 Stand . . . custom** submit to the vexatious injustice of convention   **4 The curiosity of nations** arbitrary social gradations   **5 For that** because.   **moonshines** months
6 Lag of lagging behind   **7 dimensions** proportions.   **compact** knit together, fitted   **8 generous** noble, refined   **9 honest** chaste
11–12 Who . . . quality Whose begetting in the sexual act both requires and engenders a fuller mixture and more energetic force
14 fops fools   **15 Got** begotten   **19 speed** succeed, prosper
20 invention thrive scheme prosper   **24 tonight** last night.
Prescribed Limited   **25 exhibition** an allowance, pension.
26 Upon the gad suddenly, as if pricked by a gad or spur.

33–4 terrible dispatch fearful quick disposal   **38 for** as for   **40 o'erlooking** perusal.   **43 to blame** (The Folio reading, "too blame," "too blameworthy to be shown," may be correct.)   **46 essay or taste** assay, test   **47 policy and reverence of** policy of reverencing   **48 the best . . . times** the best years of our lives, i.e., our youth   **50 idle and fond** useless and foolish   **51 who sways** which rules   **52 suffered** permitted.   **59 to this** upon this (letter).   **61 casement** window   **62 closet** private room.   **63 character** handwriting   **65 matter** contents   **66 in . . . that** considering what the contents are.   **fain** gladly   **74 fit** fitting, appropriate.   **perfect age** full maturity   **75 declined** having become feeble

GLOUCESTER   Oh, villain, villain! His very opinion in the 77
letter! Abhorred villain! Unnatural, detested, brutish 78
villain! Worse than brutish! Go, sirrah, seek him. I'll
apprehend him. Abominable villain! Where is he? 79

EDMUND   I do not well know, my lord. If it shall please
you to suspend your indignation against my brother
till you can derive from him better testimony of his
intent, you should run a certain course; where, if you 84
violently proceed against him, mistaking his purpose,
it would make a great gap in your own honor and
shake in pieces the heart of his obedience. I dare pawn 87
down my life for him that he hath writ this to feel my 88
affection to Your Honor, and to no other pretense of 89
danger. 90

GLOUCESTER   Think you so?

EDMUND   If Your Honor judge it meet, I will place you 92
where you shall hear us confer of this, and by an 93
auricular assurance have your satisfaction, and that 94
without any further delay than this very evening.

GLOUCESTER   He cannot be such a monster—

EDMUND   Nor is not, sure.

GLOUCESTER   To his father, that so tenderly and entirely loves him. Heaven and earth! Edmund, seek
him out; wind me into him, I pray you. Frame the 100
business after your own wisdom. I would unstate 101
myself to be in a due resolution. 102

EDMUND   I will seek him, sir, presently, convey the 103
business as I shall find means, and acquaint you
withal. 105

GLOUCESTER   These late eclipses in the sun and moon 106
portend no good to us. Though the wisdom of nature 107
can reason it thus and thus, yet nature finds itself
scourged by the sequent effects. Love cools, friend- 109
ship falls off, brothers divide; in cities, mutinies; in
countries, discord; in palaces, treason; and the bond
cracked twixt son and father. This villain of mine
comes under the prediction; there's son against father.
The King falls from bias of nature; there's father 114
against child. We have seen the best of our time.
Machinations, hollowness, treachery, and all ruinous
disorders follow us disquietly to our graves. Find out
this villain, Edmund; it shall lose thee nothing. Do it 118
carefully. And the noble and truehearted Kent banished! His offense, honesty! 'Tis strange.   *Exit.*

EDMUND   This is the excellent foppery of the world, that 121
when we are sick in fortune—often the surfeits of our 122
own behavior—we make guilty of our disasters the 123
sun, the moon, and stars, as if we were villains on 124
necessity, fools by heavenly compulsion, knaves,
thieves, and treachers by spherical predominance, 126
drunkards, liars, and adulterers by an enforced obedience of planetary influence, and all that we are evil
in, by a divine thrusting on. An admirable evasion of 129
whoremaster man, to lay his goatish disposition on 130
the charge of a star! My father compounded with my 131
mother under the Dragon's tail and my nativity was 132
under Ursa Major, so that it follows I am rough and 133
lecherous. Fut, I should have been that I am, had the 134
maidenliest star in the firmament twinkled on my
bastardizing. Edgar—

Enter Edgar.

and pat he comes like the catastrophe of the old 137
comedy. My cue is villainous melancholy, with a sigh
like Tom o' Bedlam.—Oh, these eclipses do portend 139
these divisions! Fa, sol, la, mi. 140

EDGAR   How now, brother Edmund, what serious
contemplation are you in?

EDMUND   I am thinking, brother, of a prediction I read
this other day, what should follow these eclipses. 144

EDGAR   Do you busy yourself with that?

EDMUND   I promise you, the effects he writes of succeed 146
unhappily, as of unnaturalness between the child and 147
the parent, death, dearth, dissolutions of ancient amities, divisions in state, menaces and maledictions
against king and nobles, needless diffidences, banish- 150
ment of friends, dissipation of cohorts, nuptial 151
breaches, and I know not what.

EDGAR   How long have you been a sectary astronom- 153
ical? 154

EDMUND   Come, come, when saw you my father last?

EDGAR   The night gone by.

EDMUND   Spake you with him?

EDGAR   Ay, two hours together.

EDMUND   Parted you in good terms? Found you no
displeasure in him by word nor countenance? 160

EDGAR   None at all.

122–3 surfeits . . . behavior consequences of our own overindulgence
124 on by   **126 treachers** traitors.   **spherical predominance** astrological determinism, because a certain planet was ascendant at the
hour of our birth   **129 divine** supernatural   **130 goatish** lecherous
130–1 on the charge to the responsibility   **131–2 compounded . . .
Dragon's tail** had sex with my mother under the constellation Draco
(not one of the regular signs of the zodiac), or under the descending
point at which the moon's orbit intersects with the ecliptic or apparent orbit of the sun (when an eclipse might occur)   **133 Ursa Major**
the big bear or dipper—not one of the regular signs of the zodiac
134 Fut i.e., 'Sfoot, by Christ's foot.   **that** what   **137 pat** on cue.
catastrophe conclusion, resolution (of a play)   **139 Tom o' Bedlam** a
lunatic patient of Bethlehem Hospital in London turned out to beg for
his bread.   **140 divisions** social and family conflicts. (But with a
musical sense also of florid variations on a theme, thus prompting
Edmund's singing.)   **144 this other day** the other day   **146 promise**
assure   **146–7 succeed unhappily** follow unluckily   **150 needless
diffidences** groundless distrust of others   **151 dissipation of cohorts**
breaking up of military companies, large-scale desertions   **153–4 sectary astronomical** believer in astrology.   **160 countenance** demeanor.

---

77 villain vile wretch, diabolical schemer   **78 Abhorred** Abhorrent.
detested hated and hateful   **79 sirrah** (Form of address used to inferiors or children.)   **84 run a certain course** proceed with safety and
certainty.   **where** whereas   **87–8 pawn down** stake   **88 feel** feel out
89–90 pretense of danger dangerous purpose.   **92 meet** fitting, proper   **93–4 by an . . . satisfaction** satisfy yourself as to the truth by what
you hear   **100 wind me into him** insinuate yourself into his confidence. (*Me* is used colloquially.)   **Frame** Arrange   **101 after your
own wisdom** as you think best.   **101–2 I would . . . resolution** I
would give up my wealth and rank to know the truth, have my
doubts resolved.   **103 presently** immediately.   **convey** manage
105 withal therewith.   **106 late** recent   **107 the wisdom of nature**
natural science   **109 sequent effects** i.e., devastating consequences.
114 bias of nature natural inclination   **118 lose thee nothing** i.e.,
earn you a reward.   **121 foppery** foolishness

EDMUND Bethink yourself wherein you may have offended him, and at my entreaty forbear his presence 163
until some little time hath qualified the heat of his 164
displeasure, which at this instant so rageth in him that
with the mischief of your person it would scarcely 166
allay. 167

EDGAR Some villain hath done me wrong.

EDMUND That's my fear. I pray you, have a continent 169
forbearance till the speed of his rage goes slower; and, 170
as I say, retire with me to my lodging, from whence I
will fitly bring you to hear my lord speak. Pray ye, go! 172
There's my key. [*He gives a key.*] If you do stir abroad,
go armed.

EDGAR Armed, brother?

EDMUND Brother, I advise you to the best. I am no honest man if there be any good meaning toward you. I 177
have told you what I have seen and heard, but faintly, 178
nothing like the image and horror of it. Pray you, 179
away.

EDGAR Shall I hear from you anon?

EDMUND

I do serve you in this business.   *Exit [Edgar].*
A credulous father and a brother noble,
Whose nature is so far from doing harms
That he suspects none; on whose foolish honesty
My practices ride easy. I see the business.   186
Let me, if not by birth, have lands by wit.   187
All with me's meet that I can fashion fit.   *Exit.* 188

❖

1.3

Enter Goneril, and [Oswald, her] steward.

GONERIL Did my father strike my gentleman for chiding of his fool?

OSWALD Ay, madam.

GONERIL By day and night he wrongs me! Every hour
He flashes into one gross crime or other   5
That sets us all at odds. I'll not endure it.
His knights grow riotous, and himself upbraids us
On every trifle. When he returns from hunting
I will not speak with him. Say I am sick.
If you come slack of former services   10
You shall do well; the fault of it I'll answer.   11
                              [*Horns within.*]

OSWALD He's coming, madam. I hear him.

GONERIL

Put on what weary negligence you please,
You and your fellows. I'd have it come to question.   14
If he distaste it, let him to my sister,   15

Whose mind and mine, I know, in that are one,
Not to be overruled. Idle old man,   17
That still would manage those authorities   18
That he hath given away! Now, by my life,
Old fools are babes again, and must be used
With checks as flatteries, when they are seen abused.   21
Remember what I have said.

OSWALD Well, madam.

GONERIL

And let his knights have colder looks among you.
What grows of it, no matter. Advise your fellows so.
I would breed from hence occasions, and I shall,   26
That I may speak. I'll write straight to my sister   27
To hold my very course. Prepare for dinner.   *Exeunt.*

❖

1.4

Enter Kent [disguised].

KENT

If but as well I other accents borrow   1
That can my speech diffuse, my good intent   2
May carry through itself to that full issue   3
For which I razed my likeness. Now, banished Kent,   4
If thou canst serve where thou dost stand condemned,
So may it come thy master, whom thou lov'st,   6
Shall find thee full of labors.

*Horns within. Enter Lear, [Knights,] and
attendants.*

LEAR Let me not stay a jot for dinner. Go get it ready.   8
                    [*Exit an Attendant.*]
[*To Kent*] How now, what art thou?

KENT A man, sir.

LEAR What dost thou profess? What wouldst thou with 11
us?

KENT I do profess to be no less than I seem: to serve
him truly that will put me in trust, to love him that is
honest, to converse with him that is wise and says 15
little, to fear judgment, to fight when I cannot choose, 16
and to eat no fish. 17

LEAR What art thou?

KENT A very honest-hearted fellow, and as poor as the
King.

---

163 **forbear his presence** avoid meeting him 164 **qualified** moder-
ated 166 **with . . . person** with the harmful effect of your presence;
or, even if there were injury done to you 167 **allay** be allayed.
169–70 **have . . . forbearance** keep a wary distance 172 **fitly** at a fit
time. **my lord** our father 177 **meaning** intention 178 **but faintly**
only with a faint impression 179 **image and horror** horrid reality
186 **practices** plots. **the business** i.e., how my plots should proceed.
187 **wit** cleverness. 188 **meet** justifiable. **fit** to my purpose.
1.3. Location: The Duke of Albany's palace.
5 **crime** offense 10 **come slack** fall short 11 **answer** be answerable
for. 14 **come to question** be made an issue. 15 **distaste** dislike

17 **Idle** Foolish 18 **manage those authorities** exercise those prerogatives 21 **With . . . abused** with rebukes in place of flattering attentiveness, when such flattery is seen to be taken advantage of.
26 **occasions** opportunities for taking offense 27 **speak** speak bluntly. **straight** immediately
1.4. Location: The Duke of Albany's palace still. The sense of time
is virtually continuous.
1 **as well** i.e., as well as I have disguised myself by means of costume
2 **diffuse** render confused or indistinct 3–4 **May . . . likeness** may
achieve the desired result for which I scraped off my beard and
erased my outward appearance. 6 **come** come to pass that 8 **stay**
wait 8.1 *Attendant* (This attendant may be a knight; certainly the
one who speaks at line 50 is a knight.) 11 **What . . . profess?** What is
your special calling? (But Kent puns in his answer on *profess* meaning
to "claim.") 15 **honest** honorable. **converse** associate 16 **judgment** i.e., God's judgment. **choose** i.e., choose but to fight 17 **eat
no fish** i.e., eat a manly diet (?), be a good Protestant (?).

LEAR   If thou be'st as poor for a subject as he's for a king, thou'rt poor enough. What wouldst thou?

KENT   Service.

LEAR   Who wouldst thou serve?

KENT   You.

LEAR   Dost thou know me, fellow?

KENT   No, sir, but you have that in your countenance 27 which I would fain call master.

LEAR   What's that?

KENT   Authority.

LEAR   What services canst do?

KENT   I can keep honest counsel, ride, run, mar a curi- 32 ous tale in telling it, and deliver a plain message 33 bluntly. That which ordinary men are fit for I am qualified in, and the best of me is diligence.

LEAR   How old art thou?

KENT   Not so young, sir, to love a woman for singing, 37 nor so old to dote on her for anything. I have years on my back forty-eight.

LEAR   Follow me; thou shalt serve me. If I like thee no worse after dinner, I will not part from thee yet.— Dinner, ho, dinner! Where's my knave, my fool? Go you and call my fool hither.   [*Exit one.*]

Enter steward [Oswald].

You! You, sirrah, where's my daughter?

OSWALD   So please you—   *Exit.*

LEAR   What says the fellow there? Call the clodpoll back. 46   [*Exit a knight.*]

Where's my fool, ho? I think the world's asleep.

[*Enter Knight.*]

How now? Where's that mongrel?

KNIGHT   He says, my lord, your daughter is not well.

LEAR   Why came not the slave back to me when I called him?

KNIGHT   Sir, he answered me in the roundest manner, 53 he would not.

LEAR   He would not?

KNIGHT   My lord, I know not what the matter is, but to my judgment Your Highness is not entertained with 57 that ceremonious affection as you were wont. There's a great abatement of kindness appears as well in the general dependents as in the Duke himself also and 60 your daughter.

LEAR   Ha? Say'st thou so?

KNIGHT   I beseech you, pardon me, my lord, if I be mistaken, for my duty cannot be silent when I think Your Highness wronged.

LEAR   Thou but rememberest me of mine own concep- 66 tion. I have perceived a most faint neglect of late, 67 which I have rather blamed as mine own jealous 68

curiosity than as a very pretense and purpose of 69 unkindness. I will look further into't. But where's my fool? I have not seen him this two days. 71

KNIGHT   Since my young lady's going into France, sir, the Fool hath much pined away.

LEAR   No more of that. I have noted it well. Go you and tell my daughter I would speak with her. [*Exit one.*] Go you call hither my fool.   [*Exit one.*]

Enter steward [Oswald].

Oh, you, sir, you, come you hither, sir. Who am I, sir?

OSWALD   My lady's father.

LEAR   "My lady's father"? My lord's knave! You whore-son dog, you slave, you cur!

OSWALD   I am none of these, my lord, I beseech your pardon.

LEAR   Do you bandy looks with me, you rascal? 83   [*He strikes Oswald.*]

OSWALD   I'll not be strucken, my lord. 84

KENT   Nor tripped neither, you base football player. 85   [*He trips up Oswald's heels.*]

LEAR   I thank thee, fellow. Thou serv'st me, and I'll love thee.

KENT   Come, sir, arise, away! I'll teach you differences. 88 Away, away! If you will measure your lubber's length 89 again, tarry; but away! Go to. Have you wisdom? So. 90   [*He pushes Oswald out.*]

LEAR   Now, my friendly knave, I thank thee. There's earnest of thy service.   [*He gives Kent money.*] 92

Enter Fool.

FOOL   Let me hire him too. Here's my coxcomb. 93   [*Offering Kent his cap.*]

LEAR   How now, my pretty knave, how dost thou?

FOOL   [*to Kent*]   Sirrah, you were best take my coxcomb. 95

KENT   Why, Fool?

FOOL   Why? For taking one's part that's out of favor. Nay, an thou canst not smile as the wind sits, thou'lt 98 catch cold shortly. There, take my coxcomb. Why, this 99 fellow has banished two on 's daughters and did the 100 third a blessing against his will. If thou follow him, thou 101 must needs wear my coxcomb.—How now, nuncle? 102 Would I had two coxcombs and two daughters.

LEAR   Why, my boy?

27 countenance face and bearing   **32 keep honest counsel** respect confidences   **32–3 curious** ornate, elaborate   **37 to love** as to love **46 clodpoll** blockhead   **53 roundest** bluntest   **57 entertained** treated **60 general dependents** servants generally   **66 rememberest** remind **66–7 conception** idea, thought.   **67 faint** halfhearted   **68–9 jealous curiosity** overscrupulous regard for matters of etiquette

69 very pretense true intention   **71 this** these   **83 bandy looks** exchange glances (in such a way as to imply that Oswald and Lear are social equals)   **84 strucken** struck   **85 football** (A raucous street game played by the lower classes.)   **88 differences** distinctions in rank.   **89–90 If . . . again** i.e., If you want to be laid out flat again, you clumsy ox   **90 Go to** (An expression of impatience or anger.)   **Have you wisdom?** i.e., Wise up.   **92 earnest of** a first payment for **93 coxcomb** fool's cap, crested with a red comb.   **95 you were best** you had better   **98–9 an . . . shortly** i.e., if you can't play along with those in power, you'll find yourself out in the cold.   **100 banished** (Paradoxically, by giving Goneril and Regan his kingdom, Lear has lost them, given them power over him.)   **on 's** of his   **101 blessing** i.e., bestowing Cordelia on France and saving her from the curse of insolent prosperity   **102 nuncle** (Contraction of "mine uncle," the Fool's way of addressing Lear.)

FOOL   If I gave them all my living, I'd keep my 105
coxcombs myself. There's mine; beg another of thy 106
daughters. 107

LEAR   Take heed, sirrah—the whip.

FOOL   Truth's a dog must to kennel. He must be
whipped out, when the Lady Brach may stand by th' 110
fire and stink.

LEAR   A pestilent gall to me! 112

FOOL   Sirrah, I'll teach thee a speech.

LEAR   Do.

FOOL   Mark it, nuncle:
Have more than thou showest, 116
Speak less than thou knowest,
Lend less than thou owest, 118
Ride more than thou goest, 119
Learn more than thou trowest, 120
Set less than thou throwest; 121
Leave thy drink and thy whore,
And keep in-a-door, 123
And thou shalt have more 124
Than two tens to a score. 125

KENT   This is nothing, Fool.

FOOL   Then 'tis like the breath of an unfee'd lawyer; you 127
gave me nothing for't. Can you make no use of nothing, nuncle?

LEAR   Why, no, boy. Nothing can be made out of
nothing.

FOOL   [to Kent]   Prithee, tell him; so much the rent of his 132
land comes to. He will not believe a fool. 133

LEAR   A bitter fool! 134

FOOL   Dost know the difference, my boy, between a
bitter fool and a sweet one?

LEAR   No, lad. Teach me.

FOOL
That lord that counseled thee
To give away thy land,
Come place him here by me;
Do thou for him stand. 141
The sweet and bitter fool
Will presently appear: 143
The one in motley here, 144
The other found out there. 145

LEAR   Dost thou call me fool, boy?

FOOL   All thy other titles thou hast given away; that
thou wast born with.

KENT   This is not altogether fool, my lord.

FOOL   No, faith, lords and great men will not let me; if 150
I had a monopoly out, they would have part on't. And 151
ladies too, they will not let me have all the fool to myself; they'll be snatching. Nuncle, give me an egg and 153
I'll give thee two crowns.

LEAR   What two crowns shall they be?

FOOL   Why, after I have cut the egg i'th' middle and eat 156
up the meat, the two crowns of the egg. When thou 157
clovest thy crown i'th' middle and gav'st away both
parts, thou bor'st thine ass on thy back o'er the dirt. 159
Thou hadst little wit in thy bald crown when thou
gav'st thy golden one away. If I speak like myself in 161
this, let him be whipped that first finds it so. 162
[Sings.]   "Fools had ne'er less grace in a year, 163
For wise men are grown foppish 164
And know not how their wits to wear, 165
Their manners are so apish." 166

LEAR   When were you wont to be so full of songs,
sirrah?

FOOL   I have used it, nuncle, e'er since thou mad'st thy 169
daughters thy mothers; for when thou gav'st them the
rod and putt'st down thine own breeches,
[Sings]   "Then they for sudden joy did weep,
And I for sorrow sung,
That such a king should play bo-peep 174
And go the fools among."
Prithee, nuncle, keep a schoolmaster that can teach
thy fool to lie. I would fain learn to lie.

LEAR   An you lie, sirrah, we'll have you whipped. 178

FOOL   I marvel what kin thou and thy daughters are.
They'll have me whipped for speaking true, thou'lt
have me whipped for lying, and sometimes I am
whipped for holding my peace. I had rather be any
kind o' thing than a fool. And yet I would not be thee,
nuncle. Thou hast pared thy wit o' both sides and left
nothing i'th' middle. Here comes one o' th' parings.

Enter Goneril.

LEAR
How now, daughter? What makes that frontlet on? 186
You are too much of late i'th' frown.

---

105 living property   105–6 keep my coxcombs (as proof of my folly)
106–7 beg . . . daughters i.e., beg for the coxcomb that you deserve for
dealing with your daughters as you did.   110 Brach bitch hound
(here likened to Goneril and Regan, who have been given favored
places despite their reeking of dishonest flattery)   112 gall irritation,
bitterness—literally, a painful swelling, or bile. (Lear is stung by the
Fool's gibe because it is so true.)   116 Have . . . showest don't display your wealth ostentatiously   118 owest own   119 goest i.e., on
foot. (Travel unostentatiously on horseback, not afoot.)   120 Learn
i.e., listen to.   trowest believe   121 Set . . . throwest don't stake
everything on a single throw   123 in-a-door indoors, at home
124–5 And . . . score and you will do better than break even (since a
score equals two tens, or twenty).   127 'tis . . . lawyer i.e., it is free—
and useless—advice. (Lawyers, being proverbially mercenary, would
not give good advice unless paid well.)   132–3 so . . . to (Because
Lear has given away his land, he can collect no rent.)   134 bitter
satirical   141 Do . . . stand take his place.   143 presently immediately   144 motley the parti-colored dress of the professional fool. (The
Fool identifies himself as the sweet fool, Lear as the bitter fool who
counseled himself to give away his kingdom.)   145 found out there
discovered there. (The Fool points at Lear.)

150 No . . . let me i.e., Great persons at court will not let me monopo-
lize folly; I am not *altogether fool* in the sense of being "all the fool
there is"   151 a monopoly out a corner on the market. (The granting
of monopolies was a common abuse under King James and Queen
Elizabeth.)   on't of it.   153 snatching seizing their share (including
sexual pleasure).   156–7 and eat . . . meat and have eaten the edible
part   159 bor'st . . . dirt i.e., bore the ass instead of letting the ass
bear you.   161–2 If . . . so If I speak like a fool in saying this, let the
first person to discover the truth of this be whipped (since in this corrupt world those who speak truth are punished for doing so).
163–6 "Fools . . . apish" "Fools have never been so out of favor, for
wise men foppishly trade places with the fools and no longer know
how to show off their wit to advantage, they have grown so foolish
in their manners."   169 used practiced   174 bo-peep (A child's
game.)   178 An If   186 What . . . on? What is that frown doing on
your forehead?

FOOL   Thou wast a pretty fellow when thou hadst no
need to care for her frowning; now thou art an O with- 189
out a figure. I am better than thou art now; I am a fool, 190
thou art nothing. [*To Goneril*] Yes, forsooth, I will
hold my tongue; so your face bids me, though you say
nothing.
      Mum, mum,
      He that keeps nor crust nor crumb, 195
      Weary of all, shall want some. 196
[*Pointing to Lear*] That's a shelled peascod. 197

GONERIL
Not only, sir, this your all-licensed fool, 198
But other of your insolent retinue
Do hourly carp and quarrel, breaking forth 200
In rank and not-to-be-endurèd riots. Sir, 201
I had thought by making this well known unto you
To have found a safe redress, but now grow fearful, 203
By what yourself too late have spoke and done, 204
That you protect this course and put it on 205
By your allowance; which if you should, the fault 206
Would not scape censure, nor the redresses sleep 207
Which in the tender of a wholesome weal 208
Might in their working do you that offense, 209
Which else were shame, that then necessity 210
Will call discreet proceeding. 211

FOOL   For you know, nuncle,
      "The hedge sparrow fed the cuckoo so long 213
      That it had it head bit off by it young." 214
So, out went the candle, and we were left darkling. 215

LEAR [*to Goneril*]   Are you our daughter?

GONERIL
I would you would make use of your good wisdom,
Whereof I know you are fraught, and put away 218
These dispositions which of late transport you 219
From what you rightly are.

FOOL   May not an ass know when the cart draws the 221
horse? Whoop, Jug! I love thee. 222

LEAR
Does any here know me? This is not Lear.
Does Lear walk thus, speak thus? Where are his eyes?
Either his notion weakens, or his discernings 225
Are lethargied—Ha! Waking? 'Tis not so. 226
Who is it that can tell me who I am?

FOOL   Lear's shadow.

LEAR
I would learn that; for, by the marks of sovereignty, 229
Knowledge, and reason, I should be false persuaded 230
I had daughters. 231

FOOL   Which they will make an obedient father. 232

LEAR   Your name, fair gentlewoman?

GONERIL
This admiration, sir, is much o'th' savor 234
Of other your new pranks. I do beseech you 235
To understand my purposes aright.
As you are old and reverend, should be wise. 237
Here do you keep a hundred knights and squires,
Men so disordered, so debauched and bold 239
That this our court, infected with their manners,
Shows like a riotous inn. Epicurism and lust 241
Makes it more like a tavern or a brothel
Than a graced palace. The shame itself doth speak 243
For instant remedy. Be then desired, 244
By her that else will take the thing she begs,
A little to disquantity your train, 246
And the remainders that shall still depend 247
To be such men as may besort your age, 248
Which know themselves and you.

LEAR   Darkness and devils! 249
Saddle my horses! Call my train together! [*Exit one.*] 250
Degenerate bastard, I'll not trouble thee.
Yet have I left a daughter.

GONERIL
You strike my people, and your disordered rabble
Make servants of their betters.

     Enter Albany.

LEAR
Woe, that too late repents!—Oh, sir, are you come? 255
Is it your will? Speak, sir.—Prepare my horses.
                         [*Exit one.*]
Ingratitude, thou marble-hearted fiend,
More hideous when thou show'st thee in a child
Than the sea monster!

ALBANY   Pray, sir, be patient.

LEAR [*to Goneril*]   Detested kite, thou liest! 261
My train are men of choice and rarest parts, 262
That all particulars of duty know
And in the most exact regard support 264
The worships of their name. Oh, most small fault, 265

189–90 O without a figure zero, cipher of no value unless preceded by a digit.   **195–6 He . . . some** i.e., That person who, having grown weary of his possessions, gives all away, will find himself in need of part of what is gone.   **196 want** lack   **197 shelled peascod** shelled pea pod, empty of its contents.   **198 all-licensed** allowed to speak or act as he pleases   **200 carp** find fault   **201 rank** gross, excessive   **203 safe** certain   **204 too late** all too recently   **205 put it on** encourage it   **206 allowance** approval   **207–11 nor . . . proceeding** nor would the punishments lie dormant which, out of care for the common welfare, might prove unpleasant to you—proceedings that the stern necessity of the times will regard as prudent even if under normal circumstances they might seem shameful.   **213 cuckoo** a bird that lays its eggs in other birds' nests   **214 it** its.   **it young** i.e., the young cuckoo. (A cautionary fable about ungrateful children.)   **215 darkling** in the dark.   **218 fraught** freighted, provided   **219 dispositions** inclinations, moods   **221–2 May . . . horse?** i.e., May not even a fool see that matters are backwards when a daughter lectures her father?   **222 Jug** i.e., Joan. (The origin of this phrase is uncertain.)   **225 notion** intellectual power   **225–6 or his . . . lethargied** or his faculties are asleep   **226 Waking?** i.e., Am I really awake?

229 that i.e., who I am.   **marks of sovereignty** outward and visible evidence of being king   **230–1 I should . . . daughters** i.e., all these outward signs of sanity and status would seem to suggest (falsely) that I am the king who had obedient daughters.   **232 Which** Whom   **234 admiration** (guise of) wonderment   **235 other** other of   **237 should** i.e., you should   **239 Men . . . bold** men so disorderly, so depraved and impudent   **241 Shows** appears.   **Epicurism** Excess, hedonism   **243 graced** dignified   **244 desired** requested   **246 disquantity your train** diminish the number of your attendants   **247 the remainders . . . depend** those who remain to attend you   **248 besort** befit   **249 Which . . . you** servants who have proper self-knowledge and an awareness of how they should serve you.   **250 train** retinue   **255 Woe, that** Woe to the person who   **261 kite** bird of prey   **262 parts** qualities   **264–5 And . . . name** and with utter scrupulousness may uphold the honor of their reputation.

How ugly didst thou in Cordelia show!
Which, like an engine, wrenched my frame of nature 267
From the fixed place, drew from my heart all love, 268
And added to the gall. Oh, Lear, Lear, Lear! 269
Beat at this gate [*striking his head*] that let thy folly in
And thy dear judgment out!—Go, go, my people. 271

          [*Exeunt some.*]

ALBANY
My lord, I am guiltless as I am ignorant
Of what hath moved you.
LEAR   It may be so, my lord.—
Hear, Nature, hear! Dear goddess, hear!
Suspend thy purpose if thou didst intend
To make this creature fruitful!
Into her womb convey sterility;
Dry up in her the organs of increase,
And from her derogate body never spring 279
A babe to honor her! If she must teem, 280
Create her child of spleen, that it may live 281
And be a thwart disnatured torment to her! 282
Let it stamp wrinkles in her brow of youth,
With cadent tears fret channels in her cheeks, 284
Turn all her mother's pains and benefits 285
To laughter and contempt, that she may feel
How sharper than a serpent's tooth it is
To have a thankless child! Away, away!

    Exit [*with Kent and the rest of Lear's followers*].

ALBANY
Now, gods that we adore, whereof comes this?
GONERIL
Never afflict yourself to know more of it, 290
But let his disposition have that scope 291
As dotage gives it. 292

     Enter Lear.

LEAR
What, fifty of my followers at a clap?
Within a fortnight?
ALBANY   What's the matter, sir?
LEAR
I'll tell thee. [*To Goneril*] Life and death! I am ashamed
That thou hast power to shake my manhood thus,
That these hot tears, which break from me perforce,
Should make thee worth them. Blasts and fogs upon
  thee! 298
Th'untented woundings of a father's curse 299
Pierce every sense about thee! Old fond eyes, 300
Beweep this cause again, I'll pluck ye out 301
And cast you, with the waters that you loose, 302

To temper clay. Yea, is't come to this? 303
Ha! Let it be so. I have another daughter,
Who, I am sure, is kind and comfortable. 305
When she shall hear this of thee, with her nails
She'll flay thy wolvish visage. Thou shalt find
That I'll resume the shape which thou dost think 308
I have cast off forever.   *Exit.*
GONERIL [*to Albany*] Do you mark that? 309
ALBANY
I cannot be so partial, Goneril,
To the great love I bear you— 311
GONERIL
Pray you, content.—What, Oswald, ho!
[*To the Fool*] You, sir, more knave than fool, after your
  master.
FOOL   Nuncle Lear, nuncle Lear! Tarry, take the Fool 314
  with thee. 315
     A fox, when one has caught her,
     And such a daughter
     Should sure to the slaughter, 318
     If my cap would buy a halter. 319
     So the Fool follows after.   *Exit.*
GONERIL
This man hath had good counsel. A hundred knights? 321
'Tis politic and safe to let him keep 322
At point a hundred knights—yes, that on every
  dream, 323
Each buzz, each fancy, each complaint, dislike, 324
He may enguard his dotage with their powers 325
And hold our lives in mercy.—Oswald, I say! 326
ALBANY   Well, you may fear too far. 327
GONERIL   Safer than trust too far.
Let me still take away the harms I fear, 329
Not fear still to be taken. I know his heart. 330
What he hath uttered I have writ my sister.
If she sustain him and his hundred knights
When I have showed th'unfitness—

    Enter steward [*Oswald*].

          How now, Oswald?
What, have you writ that letter to my sister?
OSWALD   Ay, madam.
GONERIL
Take you some company and away to horse.
Inform her full of my particular fear,
And thereto add such reasons of your own
As may compact it more. Get you gone, 339

267–8 Which . . . place which, like a powerful mechanical contrivance, wrenched my natural affection away from where it belonged **269 gall** bitterness. **271 dear** precious **279 derogate** debased **280 teem** produce offspring **281 spleen** violent ill nature **282 thwart disnatured** obstinate, perverse, and unnatural, unfilial **284 cadent** cascading. fret wear away **285 benefits** pleasures of motherhood **290 Never . . . know** Don't distress yourself by seeking to know **291 disposition** humor, mood **292 As** that **298 Should . . . them** should seem to suggest that you are worth a king's tears. **Blasts and fogs** Infectious blights and disease-bearing fogs **299 untented** too deep to be probed and cleansed **300 fond** foolish **301 Beweep** if you weep for **302 loose** let loose (in tears)

303 To temper clay to mix with earth. (Lear threatens to cast both his eyes and their tears to the ground.) **305 comfortable** comforting. **308 the shape** i.e., the kingship **309 Do . . . that?** i.e., Did you hear his threat to resume royal power? **311 To** because of **314–15 take . . . thee** (1) take me with you (2) take the name "fool" with you. (A stock phrase of taunting farewell.) **318 Should sure** should certainly be sent **319 halter** (1) rope for leading an animal (2) hangman's noose. **321 This . . . counsel** (Said sarcastically.) **322 politic** prudent. (Said ironically.) **323 At point** armed and ready. dream i.e., imagined wrong **324 buzz** idle rumor **325 enguard** protect **326 in mercy** at his mercy. **327 fear too far** overestimate the danger. **329 still take away** always remove **330 Not . . . taken** rather than dwell continually in the fear of being taken prisoner by such harms. **339 compact** confirm

And hasten your return.   [*Exit Oswald.*]
                         No, no, my lord,
This milky gentleness and course of yours   341
Though I condemn not, yet, under pardon,   342
You're much more attasked for want of wisdom   343
Than praised for harmful mildness.   344

ALBANY
How far your eyes may pierce I cannot tell.   345
Striving to better, oft we mar what's well.

GONERIL   Nay, then—
ALBANY   Well, well, th'event.   *Exeunt.* 348

❦

1.5

Enter Lear, Kent [disguised as Caius], and Fool.

LEAR   [*giving a letter to Kent*]   Go you before to Gloucester   1
with these letters. Acquaint my daughter no further   2
with anything you know than comes from her demand   3
out of the letter. If your diligence be not speedy, I shall 4
be there afore you.

KENT   I will not sleep, my lord, till I have delivered your
letter.   *Exit.*

FOOL   If a man's brains were in 's heels, were't not in   8
danger of kibes?   9

LEAR   Ay, boy.

FOOL   Then, I prithee, be merry. Thy wit shall not go   11
slipshod.   12

LEAR   Ha, ha, ha!

FOOL   Shalt see thy other daughter will use thee kindly, 14
for though she's as like this as a crab's like an apple,   15
yet I can tell what I can tell.

LEAR   What canst tell, boy?

FOOL   She will taste as like this as a crab does to a crab.
Thou canst tell why one's nose stands i'th' middle
on 's face?   20

LEAR   No.

FOOL   Why, to keep one's eyes of either side 's nose,   22
that what a man cannot smell out he may spy into.

LEAR   I did her wrong.   24

FOOL   Canst tell how an oyster makes his shell?

LEAR   No.

FOOL   Nor I neither. But I can tell why a snail has a
house.

LEAR   Why?

FOOL   Why, to put 's head in, not to give it away to his   30
daughters and leave his horns without a case.   31

LEAR   I will forget my nature. So kind a father!—Be my   32
horses ready?

FOOL   Thy asses are gone about 'em. The reason why   34
the seven stars are no more than seven is a pretty   35
reason.

LEAR   Because they are not eight.

FOOL   Yes, indeed. Thou wouldst make a good fool.

LEAR   To take't again perforce! Monster ingratitude!   39

FOOL   If thou wert my fool, nuncle, I'd have thee beaten
for being old before thy time.

LEAR   How's that?

FOOL   Thou shouldst not have been old till thou hadst
been wise.

LEAR
Oh, let me not be mad, not mad, sweet heaven!
Keep me in temper; I would not be mad!   46

[*Enter Gentleman.*]

How now, are the horses ready?
GENTLEMAN   Ready, my lord.
LEAR   Come, boy.   [*Exeunt Lear and Gentleman.*]
FOOL
She that's a maid now, and laughs at my departure,
Shall not be a maid long, unless things be cut
shorter.   *Exit.* 51

❦

2.1

Enter Bastard [Edmund] and Curan, severally.

EDMUND   Save thee, Curan.   1
CURAN   And you, sir. I have been with your father and
given him notice that the Duke of Cornwall and Regan
his duchess will be here with him this night.
EDMUND   How comes that?
CURAN   Nay, I know not. You have heard of the news
abroad—I mean the whispered ones, for they are yet   7
but ear-kissing arguments?   8
EDMUND   Not I. Pray you, what are they?
CURAN   Have you heard of no likely wars toward twixt   10
the Dukes of Cornwall and Albany?
EDMUND   Not a word.
CURAN   You may do, then, in time. Fare you well, sir.
                                        Exit.

---

341 milky . . . course effeminate and gentle way   **342 under pardon**
if you'll excuse my saying so   **343 attasked** taken to task for, blamed
344 harmful mildness mildness that causes harm.   **345 pierce** i.e.,
see into matters   **348 th'event** i.e., time will tell.
1.5. Location: Before Albany's palace.
1 Gloucester i.e., the place in Gloucestershire   **2 these letters** this letter.   **3 demand** inquiry   **4 out of** prompted by   **8–9 were't . . .
kibes?** wouldn't his brains be in danger of that common affliction of
the heel called chilblains?   **11–12 Thy wit . . . slipshod** i.e., Your
brains would have no need for slippers to avoid chafing the
chilblains, since you have no brains. (Anyone who journeys to Regan
in hopes of kind treatment is utterly brainless.)   **14 Shalt** Thou shalt.
kindly (1) with filial kindness (2) according to her own nature
15 crab crab apple   **20 on 's** of his   **22 of either side 's** on either side
of his   **24 her** i.e., Cordelia

30–1 Why, to . . . case i.e., The snail's head and horns are unendan-
gered with its *case* or shell; Lear, conversely, has given away his
crown to his daughters, leaving his brows unadorned and vulnerable.
(With a suggestion too of the cuckold's horned head, as though
Lear's victimization had a sexual dimension.)   **32 nature** natural
affection. (Compare line 14 and note.)   **34 Thy . . . 'em** i.e., Your servants (who labor like asses in your service) have gone about readying
the horses.   **35 seven stars** Pleiades   **39 To take't . . . perforce!** i.e.,
To think that Goneril would forcibly take back again the privileges
guaranteed to me! (Or perhaps Lear is meditating an armed restoration of his monarchy.)   **46 temper** mental equilibrium
51 things i.e., penises.   **cut shorter** (A bawdy joke addressed to the
audience.)
2.1 Location: The Earl of Gloucester's house.
0.1 *severally* separately.   **1 Save** God save   **7 abroad** going the
rounds.   **ones** i.e., the news, regarded as plural   **8 ear-kissing arguments** lightly whispered topics.   **10 toward** impending

EDMUND
The Duke be here tonight? The better! Best!   14
This weaves itself perforce into my business.
My father hath set guard to take my brother,
And I have one thing, of a queasy question,   17
Which I must act. Briefness and fortune, work!—   18
Brother, a word. Descend. Brother, I say!

        Enter Edgar.

My father watches. Oh, sir, fly this place!
Intelligence is given where you are hid.
You have now the good advantage of the night.
Have you not spoken 'gainst the Duke of Cornwall?
He's coming hither, now, i'th' night, i'th' haste,   24
And Regan with him. Have you nothing said
Upon his party 'gainst the Duke of Albany?   26
Advise yourself.
EDGAR   I am sure on't, not a word.   27
EDMUND
I hear my father coming. Pardon me;
In cunning I must draw my sword upon you.
Draw. Seem to defend yourself. Now, quit you well.—
                                    [*They draw.*]   30
Yield! Come before my father!—Light, ho, here!—   31
Fly, brother.—Torches, torches!—So, farewell.   32
                                    Exit Edgar.
Some blood drawn on me would beget opinion   33
Of my more fierce endeavor. I have seen drunkards   34
Do more than this in sport. [*He wounds himself in the
    arm.*] Father, father!
Stop, stop! No help?

        Enter Gloucester, and servants with torches.

GLOUCESTER   Now, Edmund, where's the villain?
EDMUND
Here stood he in the dark, his sharp sword out,
Mumbling of wicked charms, conjuring the moon
To stand 's auspicious mistress.
GLOUCESTER   But where is he?   39
EDMUND
Look, sir, I bleed.
GLOUCESTER   Where is the villain, Edmund?
EDMUND
Fled this way, sir. When by no means he could—
GLOUCESTER   Pursue him, ho! Go after.
                            [*Exeunt some servants.*]
                            By no means what?
EDMUND
Persuade me to the murder of Your Lordship,
But that I told him the revenging gods   44

'Gainst parricides did all the thunder bend,   45
Spoke with how manifold and strong a bond
The child was bound to th' father; sir, in fine,   47
Seeing how loathly opposite I stood   48
To his unnatural purpose, in fell motion   49
With his preparèd sword he charges home   50
My unprovided body, latched mine arm;   51
And when he saw my best alarumed spirits,   52
Bold in the quarrel's right, roused to th'encounter,   53
Or whether ghasted by the noise I made,   54
Full suddenly he fled.
GLOUCESTER   Let him fly far.   55
Not in this land shall he remain uncaught;
And found—dispatch. The noble Duke my master,   57
My worthy arch and patron, comes tonight.   58
By his authority I will proclaim it
That he which finds him shall deserve our thanks,
Bringing the murderous coward to the stake;   61
He that conceals him, death.
EDMUND
When I dissuaded him from his intent
And found him pight to do it, with curst speech   64
I threatened to discover him. He replied,   65
"Thou unpossessing bastard, dost thou think,   66
If I would stand against thee, would the reposal   67
Of any trust, virtue, or worth in thee
Make thy words faithed? No. What I should deny—   69
As this I would, ay, though thou didst produce
My very character—I'd turn it all   71
To thy suggestion, plot, and damnèd practice;   72
And thou must make a dullard of the world   73
If they not thought the profits of my death   74
Were very pregnant and potential spirits   75
To make thee seek it."
GLOUCESTER   Oh, strange and fastened villain!   76
Would he deny his letter, said he?
I never got him.   *Tucket within.*   78
Hark, the Duke's trumpets! I know not why he comes.
All ports I'll bar; the villain shall not scape.   80
The Duke must grant me that. Besides, his picture   81
I will send far and near, that all the kingdom
May have due note of him; and of my land,

14 **The better! Best!** So much the better; in fact, the best that could happen!   17 **queasy question** matter not for queasy stomachs   18 **Briefness and fortune** Expeditious dispatch and good luck   24 **i'th' haste** in great haste   26 **Upon his party** i.e., recklessly on Cornwall's behalf (? It would be dangerous to speak on either side.)   27 **Advise yourself** Consider your situation.   **on't** of it   30 **quit you** defend, acquit yourself   31–2 **Yield . . . farewell** (Edmund speaks loudly as though trying to arrest Edgar, calls for others to help, and privately bids Edgar to flee.)   33–4 **beget . . . endeavor** create an impression of my having fought fiercely.   39 **stand 's** stand his, act as his   44 **that** when

45 **bend** aim   47 **in fine** in conclusion   48 **loathly opposite** loathingly opposed   49 **fell motion** deadly thrust   50 **preparèd** unsheathed and ready.   **home** to the very heart   51 **unprovided** unprotected.   **latched** nicked, lanced   52 **best alarumed** thoroughly aroused to action, as by a trumpet   53 **quarrel's right** justice of the cause   54 **ghasted** frightened   55 **Let him fly far** i.e., Any fleeing, no matter how far, will be in vain.   57 **dispatch** i.e., that will be the end for him.   58 **arch and patron** chief patron   61 **to the stake** i.e., to reckoning   64 **pight** determined.   **curst** angry   65 **discover** expose   66 **unpossessing** unable to inherit, beggarly   67 **reposal** placing   69 **faithed** believed.   **What** That which, whatever   71 **character** written testimony, handwriting.   **turn** attribute   72 **suggestion** instigation.   **practice** scheming   73–6 **And . . . seek it** and you must think everyone slow-witted indeed not to suppose that they would see how the profits to be gained by my death would be fertile and potent tempters to make you seek my death.   76 **strange and fastened** unnatural and hardened   78 **got** begot.   **s.d.** *Tucket* series of notes on the trumpet, here indicating Cornwall's arrival   80 **ports** seaports, or gateways   81 **picture** description

Loyal and natural boy, I'll work the means   84
To make thee capable.   85

Enter Cornwall, Regan, and attendants.

CORNWALL
How now, my noble friend? Since I came hither,
Which I can call but now, I have heard strange news.

REGAN
If it be true, all vengeance comes too short
Which can pursue th'offender. How dost, my lord?

GLOUCESTER
Oh madam, my old heart is cracked, it's cracked!

REGAN
What, did my father's godson seek your life?
He whom my father named? Your Edgar?

GLOUCESTER
Oh, lady, lady, shame would have it hid!

REGAN
Was he not companion with the riotous knights
That tended upon my father?

GLOUCESTER
I know not, madam. 'Tis too bad, too bad.

EDMUND
Yes, madam, he was of that consort.   97

REGAN
No marvel, then, though he were ill affected.   98
'Tis they have put him on the old man's death,   99
To have th'expense and spoil of his revenues.   100
I have this present evening from my sister
Been well informed of them, and with such cautions
That if they come to sojourn at my house
I'll not be there.

CORNWALL   Nor I, assure thee, Regan.
Edmund, I hear that you have shown your father
A childlike office.

EDMUND   It was my duty, sir.   106

GLOUCESTER [*to Cornwall*]
He did bewray his practice, and received   107
This hurt you see striving to apprehend him.   108

CORNWALL   Is he pursued?

GLOUCESTER   Ay, my good lord.

CORNWALL
If he be taken, he shall never more
Be feared of doing harm. Make your own purpose,   112
How in my strength you please. For you, Edmund,   113
Whose virtue and obedience doth this instant
So much commend itself, you shall be ours.
Natures of such deep trust we shall much need;
You we first seize on.

EDMUND   I shall serve you, sir,
Truly, however else.   118

GLOUCESTER   For him I thank Your Grace.

CORNWALL
You know not why we came to visit you—

REGAN
—Thus out of season, threading dark-eyed night:
Occasions, noble Gloucester, of some poise,   122
Wherein we must have use of your advice.
Our father he hath writ, so hath our sister,
Of differences, which I least thought it fit   125
To answer from our home. The several messengers   126
From hence attend dispatch. Our good old friend,   127
Lay comforts to your bosom, and bestow
Your needful counsel to our businesses,
Which craves the instant use.   130

GLOUCESTER   I serve you, madam.
Your Graces are right welcome.   *Flourish. Exeunt.*

❖

2.2

*Enter Kent [disguised as Caius] and steward
[Oswald], severally.*

OSWALD   Good dawning to thee, friend. Art of this   1
house?

KENT   Ay.

OSWALD   Where may we set our horses?

KENT   I'th' mire.

OSWALD   Prithee, if thou lov'st me, tell me.   6

KENT   I love thee not.

OSWALD   Why then, I care not for thee.

KENT   If I had thee in Lipsbury pinfold, I would make 9
thee care for me.   10

OSWALD   Why dost thou use me thus? I know thee not.

KENT   Fellow, I know thee.   12

OSWALD   What dost thou know me for?

KENT   A knave, a rascal, an eater of broken meats;   14
a base, proud, shallow, beggarly, three-suited,   15
hundred-pound, filthy worsted-stocking knave; a   16
lily-livered, action-taking, whoreson, glass-gazing,   17
superserviceable, finical rogue; one-trunk-inheriting 18
slave; one that wouldst be a bawd in way of good ser- 19
vice, and art nothing but the composition of a knave, 20
beggar, coward, pander, and the son and heir of a

---

84 **natural** (1) prompted by natural feelings of loyalty and affection
(2) bastard   85 **capable** legally able to become the inheritor.   97 **consort** crew.   98 **though** if.   **ill affected** ill-disposed, disloyal.   99 **put
him on** incited him to   100 **th'expense and spoil** the squandering
106 **childlike** filial   107 **bewray his practice** expose his (Edgar's)
plot   108 **apprehend** arrest   112–13 **Make . . . please** Go about
achieving your purpose, making free use of my authority and
resources.   113 **For** As for   118 **however else** above all else.

122 **poise** weight   125 **differences** quarrels.   **which** which letters
126 **from our home** while still at our palace in Cornwall.   127 **attend
dispatch** wait to be dispatched.   130 **the instant use** immediate
attention.
2.2 **Location: Before Gloucester's house.**
0.1 *severally* at separate doors.   1 **dawning** (It is not yet day.)   6 **if
thou lov'st me** i.e., if you bear good will toward me. (But Kent deliberately takes the phrase in its literal, not courtly, sense.)   9 **in Lipsbury pinfold** i.e., within the pinfold of the lips, between my teeth. (A
pinfold is a pound for stray animals.)   10 **care for** i.e., be wary of.
(Playing on *care not for*, "do not like," in line 8.)   12 **I know thee** i.e., I
know you for what you are. (Playing on *know thee not*, "am unacquainted with you," in line 11.)   14 **broken meats** scraps of food
(such as were passed out to the most lowly)   15–16 **three-suited . . .
knave** i.e., a steward of a household, with an allowance of three suits
a year and a comfortable income of one hundred pounds, dressed in
dirty wool stockings appropriate to the servant class   16–19 **a lily-
livered . . . slave** a cowardly, litigious, insufferable, self-infatuated,
officious, foppish rogue, whose personal property all fits into one
trunk   19–20 **bawd . . . service** i.e., pimp or pander as a way of providing whatever is wanted   20 **composition** compound

mongrel bitch; one whom I will beat into clamorous
whining if thou deny'st the least syllable of thy addi- 23
tion. 24

OSWALD   Why, what a monstrous fellow art thou thus
to rail on one that is neither known of thee nor knows
thee!

KENT   What a brazen-faced varlet art thou to deny thou
knowest me! Is it two days since I tripped up thy heels
and beat thee before the King? Draw, you rogue, for
though it be night, yet the moon shines. I'll make a
sop o'th' moonshine of you, you whoreson, cullionly 32
barbermonger. Draw!   [*He brandishes his sword.*] 33

OSWALD   Away! I have nothing to do with thee.

KENT   Draw, you rascal! You come with letters against
the King, and take Vanity the puppet's part against 36
the royalty of her father. Draw, you rogue, or I'll so
carbonado your shanks—draw, you rascal! Come 38
your ways. 39

OSWALD   Help, ho! Murder! Help!

KENT   Strike, you slave! Stand, rogue, stand, you neat 41
slave, strike!   [*He beats him.*]

OSWALD   Help, ho! Murder! Murder!

Enter Bastard [Edmund, with his rapier
drawn], Cornwall, Regan, Gloucester, servants.

EDMUND   How now, what's the matter? Part! 44

KENT   With you, goodman boy, an you please! Come, 45
I'll flesh ye. Come on, young master. 46

GLOUCESTER   Weapons? Arms? What's the matter here?

CORNWALL   Keep peace, upon your lives! [*Kent and*
Oswald are parted.] He dies that strikes again. What is
the matter?

REGAN   The messengers from our sister and the King.

CORNWALL   What's your difference? Speak. 52

OSWALD   I am scarce in breath, my lord.

KENT   No marvel, you have so bestirred your valor.
You cowardly rascal, nature disclaims in thee. A tailor 55
made thee.

CORNWALL   Thou art a strange fellow. A tailor make a
man?

KENT   A tailor, sir. A stonecutter or a painter could not
have made him so ill, though they had been but two
years o'th' trade.

CORNWALL   Speak yet, how grew your quarrel?

OSWALD   This ancient ruffian, sir, whose life I have
spared at suit of his gray beard—

KENT   Thou whoreson zed! Thou unnecessary letter!— 65
My lord, if you'll give me leave, I will tread this un- 66
bolted villain into mortar and daub the wall of a jakes 67
with him.—Spare my gray beard, you wagtail? 68

CORNWALL   Peace, sirrah!
You beastly knave, know you no reverence?

KENT
Yes, sir, but anger hath a privilege.

CORNWALL   Why art thou angry?

KENT
That such a slave as this should wear a sword,
Who wears no honesty. Such smiling rogues as these,
Like rats, oft bite the holy cords atwain 75
Which are too intrinse t'unloose; smooth every
    passion 76
That in the natures of their lords rebel, 77
Bring oil to fire, snow to their colder moods, 78
Renege, affirm, and turn their halcyon beaks 79
With every gale and vary of their masters, 80
Knowing naught, like dogs, but following.— 81
A plague upon your epileptic visage! 82
Smile you my speeches, as I were a fool? 83
Goose, an I had you upon Sarum plain, 84
I'd drive ye cackling home to Camelot. 85

CORNWALL   What, art thou mad, old fellow?

GLOUCESTER   How fell you out? Say that.

KENT
No contraries hold more antipathy
Than I and such a knave.

CORNWALL
Why dost thou call him knave? What is his fault?

KENT   His countenance likes me not. 91

CORNWALL
No more, perchance, does mine, nor his, nor hers.

KENT
Sir, 'tis my occupation to be plain:
I have seen better faces in my time
Than stands on any shoulder that I see
Before me at this instant.

CORNWALL   This is some fellow
Who, having been praised for bluntness, doth affect 97

23–4 thy addition the titles I've given you.   **32 sop o'th' moonshine**
something so perforated that it will soak up moonshine as a sop
(floating piece of toast) soaks up liquor   **32–3 cullionly barbermonger** base frequenter of barber shops, fop. (*Cullion* originally meant
"testicle.")   **36 Vanity . . . part** i.e., the part of Goneril (here personified as a character in a morality play)   **38 carbonado** cut crosswise,
like meat for broiling   **38–9 Come your ways** Come on.   **41 neat**
(1) foppish (2) calflike. (*Neat* means "horned cattle.")   **44 matter** i.e.,
trouble. (But Kent takes the meaning "cause for quarrel.")   **45 With
you** I'll fight with you; my quarrel is with you.   **goodman boy** (A
contemptuous epithet, a title of mock respect, addressed seemingly to
Edmund.)   **an if   46 flesh** initiate into combat   **52 difference** quarrel.   **55 disclaims in** disowns

65 zed the letter z (regarded as unnecessary and often not included in
dictionaries of the time).   **66–7 unbolted** unsifted; hence, coarse
67 daub plaster.   **jakes** privy   **68 wagtail** i.e., bird wagging its tail
feathers in pert obsequiousness.   **75 holy cords** sacred bonds of loyalty and order   **76 intrinse** intricate, tightly knotted.   **smooth** flatter,
humor   **77 rebel** rebel against reason   **78 Bring . . . moods** flatteringly fuel the flame of their masters' angry passions, while similarly
exacerbating their downward mood swings   **79 Renege, affirm** nay-
say one moment (when their lords are in a denying mood) and serve
as yes-men the next.   **halcyon beaks** (The halcyon or kingfisher, if
hung up, would supposedly turn its beak into the wind.)   **80 gale
and vary** shifting wind   **81 following** fawning and flattery.
82 epileptic i.e., trembling and pale with fright and distorted with
a grin   **83 Smile you** Do you smile at.   **as** as if   **84–5 Goose . . .
Camelot** (The reference is obscure, but the general sense is that Kent,
if given space and opportunity, would send Oswald packing like a
cackling goose. Camelot, the legendary seat of King Arthur and his
Knights of the Round Table, was thought to have been in the general
vicinity of Salisbury, Sarum, and Gloucester.)   **91 likes** pleases
97 affect adopt the style of

A saucy roughness, and constrains the garb 98
Quite from his nature. He cannot flatter, he; 99
An honest mind and plain, he must speak truth!
An they will take't, so; if not, he's plain. 101
These kind of knaves I know, which in this plainness
Harbor more craft and more corrupter ends
Than twenty silly-ducking observants 104
That stretch their duties nicely. 105

KENT
Sir, in good faith, in sincere verity, 106
Under th'allowance of your great aspect, 107
Whose influence, like the wreath of radiant fire 108
On flickering Phoebus' front—

CORNWALL   What mean'st by this? 109

KENT   To go out of my dialect, which you discommend
so much. I know, sir, I am no flatterer. He that be- 111
guiled you in a plain accent was a plain knave, which 112
for my part I will not be, though I should win your 113
displeasure to entreat me to't. 114

CORNWALL [to Oswald] What was th'offense you gave him?

OSWALD   I never gave him any.
It pleased the King his master very late 117
To strike at me, upon his misconstruction; 118
When he, compact, and flattering his displeasure, 119
Tripped me behind; being down, insulted, railed, 120
And put upon him such a deal of man 121
That worthied him, got praises of the King 122
For him attempting who was self-subdued; 123
And, in the fleshment of this dread exploit, 124
Drew on me here again.

KENT   None of these rogues and cowards 126
But Ajax is their fool.

CORNWALL   Fetch forth the stocks! 127

98–9 constrains . . . nature i.e., distorts plainness quite from its true purpose so that it becomes instead a way of deceiving the listener. 99 He . . . he He professes to be one who abhors the use of flattering speech. (Said sardonically.) 101 An . . . plain If people will take his rudeness, fine; if not, his excuse is that he speaks plain truth. 104–5 Than . . . nicely than twenty foolishly bowing, obsequious courtiers who outdo themselves in the punctilious performance of their courtly duties. 106 Sir, in good faith (Kent assumes the wordy mannerisms of courtly flattery.) 107 th'allowance the approval. aspect (1) countenance (2) astrological position 108 influence astrological power 109 Phoebus' front i.e., the sun's forehead 111–14 He . . . to't The man who used plain speech to you craftily (see lines 102–5) and thereby taught you to suspect plain speakers of being deceitful was in fact a plain rascal, which part I will not play, much as it would please me to incur your displeasure if speaking thus would have that effect. (Kent would prefer to displease Cornwall, since Cornwell is pleased only by flatterers, and Kent has assumed until now that plain speech was the best way to offend, but he now argues mockingly that he can no longer speak plainly, since his honest utterance would be interpreted as duplicity.) 117 late recently 118 upon his misconstruction as a result of the King's misunderstanding (me) 119 When . . . displeasure whereupon Kent, in cahoots with the King and his party, and wishing to gratify the King's anger at me 120 being down, insulted when I was down, he exulted over me 121–2 And put . . . him and acted with a bravado that earned him an accolade 123 For . . . self-subdued for assailing one (i.e., myself) who chose not to resist 124 And . . . exploit and, in the excitement of his first success in this fearless deed. (Said ironically.) 126–7 None . . . fool i.e., You never find any rogues and cowards of this sort who do not outdo the blustering Ajax in their boasting.

You stubborn, ancient knave, you reverend braggart, 128
We'll teach you.

KENT   Sir, I am too old to learn.
Call not your stocks for me. I serve the King,
On whose employment I was sent to you.
You shall do small respect, show too bold malice
Against the grace and person of my master, 133
Stocking his messenger.

CORNWALL
Fetch forth the stocks! As I have life and honor,
There shall he sit till noon.

REGAN
Till noon? Till night, my lord, and all night too.

KENT
Why, madam, if I were your father's dog
You should not use me so. 139

REGAN   Sir, being his knave, I will. 140

CORNWALL
This is a fellow of the selfsame color 141
Our sister speaks of.—Come, bring away the stocks! 142
                              Stocks brought out.

GLOUCESTER
Let me beseech Your Grace not to do so.
His fault is much, and the good King his master
Will check him for't. Your purposed low correction 145
Is such as basest and contemned'st wretches 146
For pilferings and most common trespasses
Are punished with. The King must take it ill
That he, so slightly valued in his messenger,
Should have him thus restrained.

CORNWALL   I'll answer that. 150

REGAN
My sister may receive it much more worse
To have her gentleman abused, assaulted,
For following her affairs. Put in his legs.
                    [Kent is put in the stocks.]
Come, my good lord, away.
                    Exeunt [all but Gloucester and Kent].

GLOUCESTER
I am sorry for thee, friend. 'Tis the Duke's pleasure,
Whose disposition, all the world well knows,
Will not be rubbed nor stopped. I'll entreat for thee. 157

KENT
Pray, do not, sir. I have watched and traveled hard. 158
Some time I shall sleep out; the rest I'll whistle.
A good man's fortune may grow out at heels. 160
Give you good morrow! 161

GLOUCESTER
The Duke's to blame in this. 'Twill be ill taken.   Exit.

128 reverend (because old) 133 grace sovereignty, royal grace 139 should would 140 being since you are 141 color complexion, character 142 away along 145 check rebuke, correct 146 contemned'st most despised 150 answer be answerable for 157 rubbed hindered, obstructed. (A term from bowls.) 158 watched gone sleepless 160 A . . . heels i.e., Even good men suffer decline in fortune at times. (To be out at heels is literally to be threadbare, coming through one's stockings.) 161 Give you i.e., God give you

KENT
    Good King, that must approve the common saw,   163
    Thou out of heaven's benediction com'st
    To the warm sun!   [*He takes out a letter.*]
    Approach, thou beacon to this under globe,   166
    That by thy comfortable beams I may   167
    Peruse this letter. Nothing almost sees miracles   168
    But misery. I know 'tis from Cordelia,   169
    Who hath most fortunately been informed
    Of my obscurèd course, "and shall find time   171
    From this enormous state, seeking to give   172
    Losses their remedies." All weary and o'erwatched,   173
    Take vantage, heavy eyes, not to behold   174
    This shameful lodging.   175
    Fortune, good night. Smile once more; turn thy wheel!   176
                             [*He sleeps.*]

[2.3]

Enter Edgar.

EDGAR   I heard myself proclaimed,
    And by the happy hollow of a tree   2
    Escaped the hunt. No port is free, no place   3
    That guard and most unusual vigilance   4
    Does not attend my taking. Whiles I may scape   5
    I will preserve myself, and am bethought   6
    To take the basest and most poorest shape
    That ever penury, in contempt of man,   8
    Brought near to beast. My face I'll grime with filth,
    Blanket my loins, elf all my hairs in knots,   10
    And with presented nakedness outface   11
    The winds and persecutions of the sky.
    The country gives me proof and precedent   13
    Of Bedlam beggars who with roaring voices   14
    Strike in their numbed and mortifièd arms   15
    Pins, wooden pricks, nails, sprigs of rosemary;   16
    And with this horrible object, from low farms,   17

Poor pelting villages, sheepcotes, and mills,   18
Sometimes with lunatic bans, sometimes with prayers,   19
Enforce their charity. Poor Turlygod! Poor Tom!   20
That's something yet. Edgar I nothing am.   *Exit.*   21

[2.4]

Enter Lear, Fool, and Gentleman.

LEAR
    'Tis strange that they should so depart from home   1
    And not send back my messenger.
GENTLEMAN   As I learned,
    The night before there was no purpose in them
    Of this remove.
KENT   Hail to thee, noble master!   4
LEAR   Ha?
    Mak'st thou this shame thy pastime?
KENT   No, my lord.
FOOL   Ha, ha, he wears cruel garters. Horses are tied by   7
    the heads, dogs and bears by th' neck, monkeys by
    th' loins, and men by th' legs. When a man's over-   9
    lusty at legs, then he wears wooden netherstocks.   10
LEAR
    What's he that hath so much thy place mistook
    To set thee here?
KENT   It is both he and she: 12
    Your son and daughter.
LEAR   No.
KENT   Yes.
LEAR   No, I say.
KENT   I say yea.
LEAR   No, no, they would not.
KENT   Yes, they have.
LEAR   By Jupiter, I swear no.
KENT
    By Juno, I swear ay.
LEAR   They durst not do't!
    They could not, would not do't. 'Tis worse than
        murder
    To do upon respect such violent outrage.   23
    Resolve me with all modest haste which way   24
    Thou mightst deserve, or they impose, this usage,
    Coming from us.

KENT   My lord, when at their home   26
    I did commend Your Highness' letters to them,   27
    Ere I was risen from the place that showed   28
    My duty kneeling, came there a reeking post,   29
    Stewed in his haste, half breathless, panting forth 30
    From Goneril his mistress salutations;
    Delivered letters, spite of intermission,   32
    Which presently they read; on whose contents   33
    They summoned up their meiny, straight took horse,   34
    Commanded me to follow and attend
    The leisure of their answer, gave me cold looks;
    And meeting here the other messenger,
    Whose welcome, I perceived, had poisoned mine—
    Being the very fellow which of late
    Displayed so saucily against Your Highness—   40
    Having more man than wit about me, drew.   41
    He raised the house with loud and coward cries.
    Your son and daughter found this trespass worth
    The shame which here it suffers.
FOOL   Winter's not gone yet if the wild geese fly that 45
way.   46
            Fathers that wear rags
                Do make their children blind,   48
            But fathers that bear bags   49
                Shall see their children kind.
            Fortune, that arrant whore,
                Ne'er turns the key to th' poor.   52
    But, for all this, thou shalt have as many dolors for thy 53
    daughters as thou canst tell in a year.   54
LEAR
    Oh, how this mother swells up toward my heart!   55
    Hysterica passio, down, thou climbing sorrow!   56
    Thy element's below.—Where is this daughter?   57
KENT   With the Earl, sir, here within.
LEAR   Follow me not. Stay here.   *Exit.*
GENTLEMAN
    Made you no more offense but what you speak of?
KENT   None.
    How chance the King comes with so small a number?   62
FOOL   An thou hadst been set i'th' stocks for that ques- 63
    tion, thou'dst well deserved it.
KENT   Why, Fool?

FOOL   We'll set thee to school to an ant to teach thee 66
there's no laboring i'th' winter. All that follow their 67
noses are led by their eyes but blind men, and there's   68
not a nose among twenty but can smell him that's   69
stinking. Let go thy hold when a great wheel runs   70
down a hill lest it break thy neck with following; but
the great one that goes upward, let him draw thee after. When a wise man gives thee better counsel, give
me mine again. I would have none but knaves follow
it, since a fool gives it.
            That sir which serves and seeks for gain,
                And follows but for form,
            Will pack when it begins to rain   78
                And leave thee in the storm.
            But I will tarry; the fool will stay,
                And let the wise man fly.
            The knave turns fool that runs away;   82
                The fool no knave, pardie.   83

            Enter Lear and Gloucester.

KENT   Where learned you this, Fool?
FOOL   Not i'th' stocks, fool.
LEAR
    Deny to speak with me? They are sick? They are
        weary?
    They have traveled all the night? Mere fetches,   87
    The images of revolt and flying off.   88
    Fetch me a better answer.
GLOUCESTER   My dear lord,
    You know the fiery quality of the Duke,
    How unremovable and fixed he is
    In his own course.
LEAR
    Vengeance! Plague! Death! Confusion!   93
    Fiery? What quality? Why, Gloucester, Gloucester,
    I'd speak with the Duke of Cornwall and his wife.
GLOUCESTER
    Well, my good lord, I have informed them so.
LEAR
    Informed them? Dost thou understand me, man?
GLOUCESTER   Ay, my good lord.
LEAR
    The King would speak with Cornwall. The dear father
    Would with his daughter speak, commands, tends
        service.   100
    Are they informed of this? My breath and blood!   101
    Fiery? The fiery Duke? Tell the hot Duke that—
    No, but not yet. Maybe he is not well.
    Infirmity doth still neglect all office   104
    Whereto our health is bound; we are not ourselves   105

26 their home (Kent and Oswald went first to Cornwall's palace after
leaving Albany's palace.)   27 commend deliver   28–9 from . . .
kneeling from the kneeling posture that showed my duty   29 reeking steaming (with heat of travel)   30 Stewed i.e., thoroughly heated, soaked   32 spite of intermission in disregard of interrupting me,
or, in spite of the interruptions caused by his being out of breath   33
presently instantly.   on on the basis of   34 meiny retinue of servants, household   40 Displayed so saucily behaved so insolently
41 more man than wit more courage than good sense   45–6 Winter's
. . . way i.e., The signs still point to continued and worsening fortune;
the wild geese are still flying south.   48 blind i.e., indifferent to their
father's needs   49 bags i.e., of gold   52 turns the key opens the door
53 dolors griefs. (With pun on "dollars," English word for an Austrian or Spanish coin.)   for (1) on account of (2) in exchange for
54 tell (1) relate (2) count   55, 56 mother, *Hysterica passio* i.e., hysteria, giving the sensation of choking or suffocating   57 element's
proper place is. (Hysteria, from the Greek *hystera,* womb, was
thought to be produced by vapors ascending from the uterus or
abdomen.)   62 chance chances it   63 An If

66–7 We'll . . . winter i.e., Just as the ant knows not to labor in the
winter, the wise man knows not to labor for one whose fortunes are
fallen.   67–70 All . . . stinking i.e., One who is out of favor can be
easily detected (he smells of misfortune) and so is easily avoided by
timeservers.   78 pack be off   82 The knave . . . away i.e., Deserting
one's master is the greatest folly   83 pardie *par Dieu* (French), "by
God."   87 fetches pretexts, dodges   88 images signs.   flying off
desertion.   93 Confusion! Destruction!   100 tends attends, waits for
101 My . . . blood! i.e., By my very life. (An oath.)   104–5 Infirmity
. . . bound Sickness always prompts us to neglect all duties which in
good health we are bound to perform

When nature, being oppressed, commands the mind
To suffer with the body. I'll forbear,
And am fallen out with my more headier will,   108
To take the indisposed and sickly fit   109
For the sound man. [*Looking at Kent*] Death on my
    state! Wherefore   110
Should he sit here? This act persuades me
That this remotion of the Duke and her   112
Is practice only. Give me my servant forth.   113
Go tell the Duke and 's wife I'd speak with them,
Now, presently. Bid them come forth and hear me,   115
Or at their chamber door I'll beat the drum
Till it cry sleep to death.   117

GLOUCESTER   I would have all well betwixt you.   *Exit.*

LEAR
Oh, me, my heart, my rising heart! But down!

FOOL   Cry to it, nuncle, as the cockney did to the eels   120
when she put 'em i'th' paste alive. She knapped 'em   121
o'th' coxcombs with a stick and cried, "Down, wan-   122
tons, down!" 'Twas her brother that, in pure kindness 123
to his horse, buttered his hay.   124

    *Enter Cornwall, Regan, Gloucester, [and]
    servants.*

LEAR   Good morrow to you both.
CORNWALL   Hail to Your Grace!
                              Kent here set at liberty.
REGAN   I am glad to see Your Highness.
LEAR
Regan, I think you are. I know what reason
I have to think so. If thou shouldst not be glad,
I would divorce me from thy mother's tomb,   130
Sepulch'ring an adultress. [*To Kent*] Oh, are you free?   131
Some other time for that.—Belovèd Regan,
Thy sister's naught. Oh, Regan, she hath tied   133
Sharp-toothed unkindness, like a vulture, here.
                      [*He lays his hand on his heart.*]
I can scarce speak to thee. Thou'lt not believe
With how depraved a quality—Oh, Regan!   136

REGAN
I pray you, sir, take patience. I have hope   137
You less know how to value her desert   138
Than she to scant her duty.
LEAR   Say? How is that?   139
REGAN
I cannot think my sister in the least
Would fail her obligation. If, sir, perchance
She have restrained the riots of your followers,
'Tis on such ground and to such wholesome end
As clears her from all blame.
LEAR   My curses on her!
REGAN   Oh, sir, you are old;
Nature in you stands on the very verge   147
Of his confine. You should be ruled and led   148
By some discretion that discerns your state   149
Better than you yourself. Therefore, I pray you,
That to our sister you do make return.
Say you have wronged her.
LEAR   Ask her forgiveness?
Do you but mark how this becomes the house: 153
[*Kneeling*] "Dear daughter, I confess that I am old;
Age is unnecessary. On my knees I beg
That you'll vouchsafe me raiment, bed, and food."
REGAN
Good sir, no more. These are unsightly tricks.
Return you to my sister.
LEAR [*rising*]   Never, Regan.
She hath abated me of half my train,   159
Looked black upon me, struck me with her tongue
Most serpentlike upon the very heart.
All the stored vengeances of heaven fall
On her ingrateful top! Strike her young bones,   163
You taking airs, with lameness!
CORNWALL   Fie, sir, fie!   164
LEAR
You nimble lightnings, dart your blinding flames
Into her scornful eyes! Infect her beauty,
You fen-sucked fogs drawn by the powerful sun   167
To fall and blister!   168
REGAN
O the blest gods! So will you wish on me
When the rash mood is on.
LEAR
No, Regan, thou shalt never have my curse.
Thy tender-hafted nature shall not give   172
Thee o'er to harshness. Her eyes are fierce, but thine
Do comfort and not burn. 'Tis not in thee
To grudge my pleasures, to cut off my train,

108–10 And . . . man and now disapprove of my more impetuous will
in having rashly supposed that those who are indisposed and sickly
were in sound health.   **110 Death . . . state!** (A common oath, here
ironically appropriate to a king whose royal authority is dying.)
112 remotion removal, inaccessibility   **113 practice** deception.
forth out of the stocks.   **115 presently** at once.   **117 cry sleep to
death** i.e., puts an end to sleep by the noise.   **120 cockney** i.e., a
Londoner, ignorant of ways of cooking eels   **121 paste** pastry pie.
knapped rapped   **122 coxcombs** heads   **122–3 wantons** playful
creatures, sexy rogues. (A term of affectionate abuse. The cockney
wife is trying to coax and wheedle the eels into laying down their lives
for the making of the pastry pie—a plea that is about as ineffectual as
Lear's imploring his rising heart to subside.)   **123–4 'Twas
. . . hay** (Another city ignorance; the act is well intended, but
horses do not like greasy hay. As with Lear, good intentions are
not enough. The *brother* is related to the cockney wife in that
they are both misguidedly tenderhearted.)   **130–1 I would . . . adultress** i.e., I would cease to honor your dead mother's tomb, since it
would surely contain the dead body of an adultress. (Only such
a fantasy of illegitimacy could explain to Lear filial ingratitude of
the monstrous sort that now confronts him.)   **133 naught** wicked.
136 quality disposition

137–9 I have . . . duty I trust this is more a matter of your undervaluing her merit than of her falling slack in her duty to you.   **139 Say?**
Come again?   **147–8 Nature . . . confine** i.e., Your life has almost
completed its allotted scope.   **149 By . . . state** by some discreet person who understands your situation and condition   **153 becomes the
house** suits domestic decorum and the royal family line. (Said with
bitter irony.)   **159 abated** deprived   **163 ingrateful top** ungrateful
head.   **164 taking** infectious   **167 fen-sucked** (It was supposed that
the sun sucked up poisons from fens or marshes.)   **168 To fall and
blister** to fall upon her and blister her beauty.   **172 tender-hafted**
gentle. (Literally, set in a tender *haft*, i.e., handle or frame.)

To bandy hasty words, to scant my sizes,   176
And, in conclusion, to oppose the bolt   177
Against my coming in. Thou better know'st
The offices of nature, bond of childhood,   179
Effects of courtesy, dues of gratitude.   180
Thy half o'th' kingdom hast thou not forgot,
Wherein I thee endowed.

REGAN   Good sir, to th' purpose.   182

LEAR
Who put my man i'th' stocks?   *Tucket within.*

CORNWALL   What trumpet's that?

REGAN
I know't—my sister's. This approves her letter,   184
That she would soon be here.

          Enter steward [Oswald].

                    Is your lady come?

LEAR
This is a slave, whose easy-borrowed pride   186
Dwells in the fickle grace of her he follows.—   187
Out, varlet, from my sight!

CORNWALL   What means Your Grace?   188

LEAR
Who stocked my servant? Regan, I have good hope
Thou didst not know on't.

          Enter Goneril.

                    Who comes here? O heavens,
If you do love old men, if your sweet sway
Allow obedience, if you yourselves are old,   192
Make it your cause; send down, and take my part!
[*To Goneril*] Art not ashamed to look upon this beard?
          [*Goneril and Regan join hands.*] 194
Oh, Regan, will you take her by the hand?

GONERIL
Why not by th' hand, sir? How have I offended?
All's not offense that indiscretion finds   197
And dotage terms so.

LEAR   O sides, you are too tough!   198
Will you yet hold?—How came my man i'th' stocks?

CORNWALL
I set him there, sir; but his own disorders
Deserved much less advancement.

LEAR   You? Did you?   201

REGAN
I pray you, father, being weak, seem so.   202
If till the expiration of your month
You will return and sojourn with my sister,
Dismissing half your train, come then to me.

I am now from home, and out of that provision   206
Which shall be needful for your entertainment.   207

LEAR
Return to her? And fifty men dismissed?
No! Rather I abjure all roofs, and choose
To wage against the enmity o'th'air,   210
To be a comrade with the wolf and owl—
Necessity's sharp pinch. Return with her?
Why, the hot-blooded France, that dowerless took   213
Our youngest born—I could as well be brought
To knee his throne and, squirelike, pension beg   215
To keep base life afoot. Return with her?
Persuade me rather to be slave and sumpter   217
To this detested groom.   [*He points to Oswald.*]

GONERIL   At your choice, sir.

LEAR
I prithee, daughter, do not make me mad.
I will not trouble thee, my child. Farewell.
We'll no more meet, no more see one another.
But yet thou art my flesh, my blood, my daughter—
Or rather a disease that's in my flesh,
Which I must needs call mine. Thou art a boil,
A plague-sore, or embossèd carbuncle   225
In my corrupted blood. But I'll not chide thee;
Let shame come when it will, I do not call it.   227
I do not bid the thunder-bearer shoot,   228
Nor tell tales of thee to high-judging Jove.   229
Mend when thou canst; be better at thy leisure.
I can be patient. I can stay with Regan,
I and my hundred knights.

REGAN   Not altogether so.
I looked not for you yet, nor am provided   234
For your fit welcome. Give ear, sir, to my sister;
For those that mingle reason with your passion   236
Must be content to think you old, and so—   237
But she knows what she does.

LEAR   Is this well spoken?

REGAN
I dare avouch it, sir. What, fifty followers?   239
Is it not well? What should you need of more?
Yea, or so many, sith that both charge and danger   241
Speak 'gainst so great a number? How in one house
Should many people under two commands
Hold amity? 'Tis hard, almost impossible.

GONERIL
Why might not you, my lord, receive attendance
From those that she calls servants, or from mine?

REGAN
Why not, my lord? If then they chanced to slack ye,   247
We could control them. If you will come to me—   248
For now I spy a danger—I entreat you

---

176 **bandy** volley, exchange.   **scant my sizes** diminish my
allowances   177 **oppose the bolt** lock the door   179 **The offices . . .
childhood** the natural duties and filial obligations due to parents
180 **Effects** outward manifestations   182 **to th' purpose** get to the
point.   184 **approves** confirms   186 **easy-borrowed** easily put on
187 **grace** favor   188 **varlet** worthless fellow   192 **Allow** approve,
sanction   194 **beard** (A sign of age and presumed entitlement to
respect.)   197–8 **All's . . . so** Not everything that the poor judgment
and dotage of old age deem offensive is actually so.   198 **sides** i.e.,
sides of the chest (stretched by the swelling heart)   201 **much less
advancement** far less honor, i.e., far worse treatment.   202 **seem so**
i.e., don't act as if you were strong.

206 **from** away from   207 **entertainment** proper reception.
210 **wage** wage war   213 **hot-blooded** spirited, youthful; choleric
215 **knee** fall on my knees before   217 **sumpter** packhorse; hence,
drudge   225 **embossèd** swollen, tumid   227 **call** summon   228 **the
thunder-bearer** i.e., Jove   229 **high-judging** judging from on high
234 **looked not for** did not expect   236–7 **For . . . old** for those who
dispassionately consider your intemperate outbursts must conclude
that you are old   239 **avouch** vouch for   241 **sith that** since.   **charge**
expense   247 **slack** neglect   248 **control** correct

To bring but five-and-twenty. To no more
Will I give place or notice.   251

LEAR
I gave you all—

REGAN   And in good time you gave it.

LEAR
Made you my guardians, my depositaries,   253
But kept a reservation to be followed   254
With such a number. What, must I come to you
With five-and-twenty? Regan, said you so?

REGAN
And speak't again, my lord. No more with me.

LEAR
Those wicked creatures yet do look well-favored   258
When others are more wicked; not being the worst
Stands in some rank of praise. [*To Goneril*] I'll go with
    thee.   260
Thy fifty yet doth double five-and-twenty,
And thou art twice her love.

GONERIL   Hear me, my lord:
What need you five-and-twenty, ten, or five,
To follow in a house where twice so many   264
Have a command to tend you?

REGAN   What need one?

LEAR
Oh, reason not the need! Our basest beggars   266
Are in the poorest thing superfluous.   267
Allow not nature more than nature needs,   268
Man's life is cheap as beast's. Thou art a lady;
If only to go warm were gorgeous,   270
Why, nature needs not what thou gorgeous wear'st,   271
Which scarcely keeps thee warm. But, for true need—   272
You heavens, give me that patience, patience I need!
You see me here, you gods, a poor old man,
As full of grief as age, wretched in both.
If it be you that stirs these daughters' hearts
Against their father, fool me not so much   277
To bear it tamely; touch me with noble anger,   278
And let not women's weapons, water drops,
Stain my man's cheeks. No, you unnatural hags,
I will have such revenges on you both
That all the world shall—I will do such things—
What they are yet I know not, but they shall be
The terrors of the earth. You think I'll weep;
No, I'll not weep.   *Storm and tempest.*
I have full cause of weeping; but this heart
Shall break into a hundred thousand flaws   287

Or ere I'll weep. Oh, Fool, I shall go mad!   288
    Exeunt [Lear, Gloucester, Kent, Gentleman,
                                        and Fool].

CORNWALL
Let us withdraw. 'Twill be a storm.

REGAN
This house is little. The old man and 's people
Cannot be well bestowed.   291

GONERIL
'Tis his own blame hath put himself from rest,   292
And must needs taste his folly.   293

REGAN
For his particular, I'll receive him gladly,   294
But not one follower.

GONERIL
So am I purposed. Where is my lord of Gloucester?

CORNWALL
Followed the old man forth.

        Enter Gloucester.

                                    He is returned.

GLOUCESTER
The King is in high rage.

CORNWALL   Whither is he going?

GLOUCESTER
He calls to horse, but will I know not whither.

CORNWALL
'Tis best to give him way. He leads himself.   300

GONERIL [*to Gloucester*]
My lord, entreat him by no means to stay.   301

GLOUCESTER
Alack, the night comes on, and the bleak winds
Do sorely ruffle. For many miles about   303
There's scarce a bush.

REGAN   Oh, sir, to willful men
The injuries that they themselves procure
Must be their schoolmasters. Shut up your doors.
He is attended with a desperate train,
And what they may incense him to, being apt   308
To have his ear abused, wisdom bids fear.   309

CORNWALL
Shut up your doors, my lord; 'tis a wild night.
My Regan counsels well. Come out o'th' storm.
                                                    Exeunt.

                        ❦

3.1

Storm still. Enter Kent [disguised as Caius]
and a Gentleman, severally.

KENT   Who's there, besides foul weather?

---

251 place or notice houseroom or recognition.   **253 depositaries** trustees   **254 kept a reservation** reserved a right   **258 well-favored** attractive, fair of feature   **260 Stands . . . praise** achieves, by necessity, some relative deserving of praise.   **264 follow** be your attendants   **266 reason not** do not dispassionately analyze   **266–7 Our . . . superfluous** Even our most destitute beggars have some wretched possessions beyond what they absolutely need.   **268 Allow not** If you do not allow.   **needs** i.e., to survive   **270–2 If . . . warm** If fashions in clothes were determined only by the need for warmth, this natural standard wouldn't justify the rich robes you wear to be gorgeous—which don't serve well for warmth in any case.   **277–8 fool . . . To** do not make me so foolish as to   **287 flaws** fragments

288 Or ere before   **291 bestowed** lodged.   **292 blame** fault.   **hath** that he has, or, that has.   **from rest** i.e., out of the house; also, lacking peace of mind   **293 taste** experience   **294 For his particular** As for him individually   **300 give . . . himself** give him his own way. He is guided only by his own willfulness.   **301 entreat . . . means** by no means entreat him to stay   **303 ruffle** bluster.   **308–9 being . . . abused** (he) being inclined to hearken to wild counsel
3.1. Location: An open place in Gloucestershire.
0.2 *severally* at separate doors.

GENTLEMAN
One minded like the weather, most unquietly.
KENT   I know you. Where's the King?
GENTLEMAN
Contending with the fretful elements;
Bids the wind blow the earth into the sea
Or swell the curlèd waters 'bove the main,   6
That things might change or cease; tears his white hair,   7
Which the impetuous blasts with eyeless rage
Catch in their fury and make nothing of;   9
Strives in his little world of man to outstorm   10
The to-and-fro-conflicting wind and rain.
This night, wherein the cub-drawn bear would couch,   12
The lion and the belly-pinchèd wolf
Keep their fur dry, unbonneted he runs
And bids what will take all.
KENT   But who is with him?   15
GENTLEMAN
None but the Fool, who labors to outjest   16
His heart-struck injuries.
KENT   Sir, I do know you,   17
And dare upon the warrant of my note   18
Commend a dear thing to you. There is division,   19
Although as yet the face of it is covered
With mutual cunning, twixt Albany and Cornwall;
Who have—as who have not, that their great stars   22
Throned and set high?—servants, who seem no less,   23
Which are to France the spies and speculations   24
Intelligent of our state. What hath been seen,   25
Either in snuffs and packings of the dukes,   26
Or the hard rein which both of them hath borne   27
Against the old kind King, or something deeper,   28
Whereof perchance these are but furnishings—   29
But true it is, from France there comes a power   30
Into this scattered kingdom, who already,   31
Wise in our negligence, have secret feet   32
In some of our best ports and are at point   33
To show their open banner. Now to you:
If on my credit you dare build so far   35
To make your speed to Dover, you shall find
Some that will thank you, making just report   37
Of how unnatural and bemadding sorrow
The King hath cause to plain.   39
I am a gentleman of blood and breeding,   40

And from some knowledge and assurance offer   41
This office to you.   42
GENTLEMAN
I will talk further with you.
KENT   No, do not.
For confirmation that I am much more
Than my outwall, open this purse and take   45
What it contains. [*He gives a purse and a ring.*] If you
    shall see Cordelia—
As fear not but you shall—show her this ring,   47
And she will tell you who that fellow is   48
That yet you do not know. Fie on this storm!
I will go seek the King.
GENTLEMAN
Give me your hand. Have you no more to say?
KENT
Few words, but, to effect, more than all yet: 52
That when we have found the King—in which your
    pain   53
That way, I'll this—he that first lights on him   54
Holla the other.   *Exeunt* [*separately*].

3.2

Storm still. Enter Lear and Fool.

LEAR
Blow, winds, and crack your cheeks! Rage, blow!
You cataracts and hurricanoes, spout   2
Till you have drenched our steeples, drowned the
    cocks!   3
You sulfurous and thought-executing fires,   4
Vaunt-couriers of oak-cleaving thunderbolts,   5
Singe my white head! And thou, all-shaking thunder,
Strike flat the thick rotundity o'th' world!
Crack nature's molds, all germens spill at once   8
That makes ingrateful man!
FOOL   Oh, nuncle, court holy water in a dry house is bet- 10
ter than this rainwater out o'door. Good nuncle, in,
ask thy daughters blessing. Here's a night pities   12
neither wise men nor fools.
LEAR
Rumble thy bellyful! Spit, fire! Spout, rain!
Nor rain, wind, thunder, fire are my daughters.   15
I tax not you, you elements, with unkindness;   16
I never gave you kingdom, called you children.
You owe me no subscription. Then let fall   18

6 **main** mainland   7 **things** all things   9 **make nothing of** blow about contemptuously   10 **little world of man** i.e., microcosm, which is an epitome of the macrocosm or universe   12 **cub-drawn** famished, with udders sucked dry (and hence ravenous).   **couch** lie close in its den   15 **bids . . . all** (A cry of desperate defiance: "take all" is the cry of a gambler in staking his last.)   16 **outjest** exorcise or relieve by jesting   17 **heart-struck injuries** injuries that strike to the very heart.   18–19 **And . . . to you** and dare, on the strength of what I know about you, entrust a precious undertaking to you.   22–3 **as . . . high** as who does not, among those whom a mighty destiny has enthroned on high   23 **no less** i.e., no other than servants   24 **speculations** scouts, spies   25 **Intelligent of** supplying intelligence pertinent to   26 **snuffs and packings** resentments and intrigues   27–8 **Or . . . King** or the harsh reining in they both have inflicted on King Lear   29 **furnishings** outward shows   30 **power** army   31 **scattered** divided   32 **Wise in** taking advantage of.   **feet** footholds   33 **at point** ready   35 **credit** trustworthiness.   **so far** so far as   37 **making just report** for making an accurate report   39 **plain** complain.
40 **blood and breeding** good family and education

41 **assurance** confidence, certainty   42 **office** assignment   45 **outwall** exterior appearance   47 **fear not but** be assured that   48 **fellow** i.e., Kent   52 **to effect** in their consequences   53–4 **in which . . . this** in which task, you search in that direction while I go this way
3.2. Location: An open place, as before.
2 **hurricanoes** waterspouts   3 **drenched** drowned.   **cocks** weathercocks.   4 **thought-executing fires** lightning that acts with the quickness of thought   5 **Vaunt-couriers** forerunners   8 **Crack . . . at once** Crack the molds in which nature makes all life; destroy all seeds at once   10 **court holy water** flattery   12 **ask . . . blessing** (For Lear to do so would be to acknowledge their authority.)   15 **Nor** Neither
16 **tax** accuse.   **with** of   18 **subscription** allegiance.

Your horrible pleasure. Here I stand your slave,
A poor, infirm, weak, and despised old man.
But yet I call you servile ministers,   21
That will with two pernicious daughters join
Your high-engendered battles 'gainst a head   23
So old and white as this. Oho! 'Tis foul.

FOOL   He that has a house to put 's head in has a good
headpiece.   26
        The codpiece that will house   27
           Before the head has any,   28
        The head and he shall louse;   29
           So beggars marry many.   30
        The man that makes his toe   31
           What he his heart should make   32
        Shall of a corn cry woe,   33
           And turn his sleep to wake.   34
For there was never yet fair woman but she made   35
mouths in a glass.   36

LEAR
No, I will be the pattern of all patience;
I will say nothing.

    Enter Kent, [disguised as Caius].

KENT   Who's there?
FOOL   Marry, here's grace and a codpiece; that's a wise   40
man and a fool.

KENT
Alas, sir, are you here? Things that love night
Love not such nights as these. The wrathful skies
Gallow the very wanderers of the dark   44
And make them keep their caves. Since I was man,   45
Such sheets of fire, such bursts of horrid thunder,
Such groans of roaring wind and rain I never
Remember to have heard. Man's nature cannot carry 48
Th'affliction nor the fear.

LEAR   Let the great gods,   49
That keep this dreadful pother o'er our heads,   50
Find out their enemies now. Tremble, thou wretch,
That hast within thee undivulgèd crimes
Unwhipped of justice! Hide thee, thou bloody hand,
Thou perjured, and thou simular of virtue   54
That art incestuous! Caitiff, to pieces shake,   55
That under covert and convenient seeming   56

Has practiced on man's life! Close pent-up guilts,   57
Rive your concealing continents and cry   58
These dreadful summoners grace! I am a man   59
More sinned against than sinning.

KENT   Alack, bareheaded?
Gracious my lord, hard by here is a hovel;
Some friendship will it lend you 'gainst the tempest.
Repose you there while I to this hard house—
More harder than the stones whereof 'tis raised,
Which even but now, demanding after you,   65
Denied me to come in—return and force
Their scanted courtesy.

LEAR   My wits begin to turn.   67
Come on, my boy. How dost, my boy? Art cold?
I am cold myself.—Where is this straw, my fellow?
The art of our necessities is strange,
And can make vile things precious. Come, your
hovel.—
Poor fool and knave, I have one part in my heart
That's sorry yet for thee.

FOOL [*sings*]
    "He that has and a little tiny wit,   74
        With heigh-ho, the wind and the rain,
    Must make content with his fortunes fit,
        Though the rain it raineth every day."   77

LEAR
True, boy.—Come, bring us to this hovel.

    Exit [with Kent].

FOOL   This is a brave night to cool a courtesan. I'll speak   79
a prophecy ere I go:

    When priests are more in word than matter;   81
    When brewers mar their malt with water;   82
    When nobles are their tailors' tutors,   83
    No heretics burned but wenches' suitors,   84
    Then shall the realm of Albion   85
    Come to great confusion.

    When every case in law is right,   87
    No squire in debt, nor no poor knight;
    When slanders do not live in tongues,   89
    Nor cutpurses come not to throngs;

---

21 **ministers** agents   23 **high-engendered battles** battalions engendered in the heavens   26 **headpiece** (1) helmetlike covering for the head (2) head for common sense.   27–34 **The codpiece . . . wake** i.e., A man who houses his genitals in a sexual embrace before he has a roof over his head can expect the lice-infested penury of a penniless marriage; and anyone who unwisely places his affection on base things will be afflicted with sorrow and sleeplessness. (The *codpiece* is a covering for the genitals worn by men with their close-fitting hose; here representing the genitals themselves. The *corn* is a bunion on the toe.)   35–6 **made . . . glass** practiced making attractive faces in a mirror.   40 **Marry** (An oath, originally "by the Virgin Mary.")   **grace** royal grace.   **codpiece** (Often prominent in the Fool's costume.)   44 **Gallow . . . dark** frighten the very wild beasts of the night   45 **keep** occupy, remain inside   48 **carry** endure   49 **Th'affliction** the physical affliction   50 **pother** hubbub, turmoil   54 **simular** pretender   55 **Caitiff** Wretch   56 **convenient seeming** deception fitted to the purpose

57 **practiced on** plotted against   57–9 **Close . . . grace!** O you secret and buried consciousnesses of guilt, burst open the hiding places that conceal you, and pray for mercy! (*Summoners* are the officers who cited offenders to appear before ecclesiastical courts.)   65 **Which** i.e., the occupants of which.   **demanding** I inquiring   67 **scanted** stinted   74–7 **"He . . . day"** (Derived from the popular song that Feste sings in *Twelfth Night*, 5.1.389 ff.)   79 **This . . . courtesan** i.e., This night is stormy enough to cool even the lust of a courtesan. (*Brave* means "fine, excellent.")   81 **When priests . . . matter** i.e., When priests do not practice what they preach. (This and the next three lines satirize the present state of affairs.)   82 **mar** adulterate   83 **are . . . tutors** can instruct their own tailors about fashion   84 **No heretics . . . suitors** i.e., when the prevailing heresy is lechery (a heresy, in other words, against love rather than against true religion), punished by burning not at the stake but by means of venereal infection   85 **realm of Albion** kingdom of England. (The Fool is parodying a pseudo-Chaucerian prophetic verse.)   87 **right** just. (This and the next five lines offer a utopian vision of justice and charity that will never be realized in this corrupted world.)   89 **When slanders . . . tongues** when no tongues speak slanders

When usurers tell their gold i'th' field,   91
And bawds and whores do churches build,
Then comes the time, who lives to see't,   93
That going shall be used with feet.   94

This prophecy Merlin shall make, for I live before his   95
time.   *Exit.*

❧

3.3

Enter Gloucester and Edmund [with lights].

GLOUCESTER   Alack, alack, Edmund, I like not this unnatural dealing. When I desired their leave that I might
pity him, they took from me the use of mine own   3
house, charged me on pain of perpetual displeasure
neither to speak of him, entreat for him, or any way
sustain him.

EDMUND   Most savage and unnatural!

GLOUCESTER   Go to; say you nothing. There is division   8
between the dukes, and a worse matter than that. I
have received a letter this night; 'tis dangerous to be
spoken; I have locked the letter in my closet. These in- 11
juries the King now bears will be revenged home;   12
there is part of a power already footed. We must in-   13
cline to the King. I will look him and privily relieve   14
him. Go you and maintain talk with the Duke, that
my charity be not of him perceived. If he ask for me,   16
I am ill and gone to bed. If I die for't, as no less is
threatened me, the King my old master must be relieved. There is strange things toward, Edmund. Pray   19
you, be careful.   *Exit.*

EDMUND
This courtesy forbid thee shall the Duke   21
Instantly know, and of that letter too.
This seems a fair deserving, and must draw me   23
That which my father loses—no less than all.   24
The younger rises when the old doth fall.   *Exit.*

❧

3.4

Enter Lear, Kent [disguised as Caius], and Fool.

KENT
Here is the place, my lord. Good my lord, enter.

The tyranny of the open night's too rough
For nature to endure.   *Storm still.*
LEAR   Let me alone.   3
KENT
Good my lord, enter here.
LEAR   Wilt break my heart?   4
KENT
I had rather break mine own. Good my lord, enter.
LEAR
Thou think'st 'tis much that this contentious storm
Invades us to the skin. So 'tis to thee,
But where the greater malady is fixed   8
The lesser is scarce felt. Thou'dst shun a bear,
But if thy flight lay toward the roaring sea
Thou'dst meet the bear i'th' mouth. When the mind's
    free,   11
The body's delicate. This tempest in my mind   12
Doth from my senses take all feeling else
Save what beats there. Filial ingratitude!
Is it not as this mouth should tear this hand   15
For lifting food to't? But I will punish home.   16
No, I will weep no more. In such a night
To shut me out? Pour on; I will endure.
In such a night as this? Oh, Regan, Goneril,
Your old kind father, whose frank heart gave all—   20
Oh, that way madness lies; let me shun that!
No more of that.
KENT   Good my lord, enter here.
LEAR
Prithee, go in thyself; seek thine own ease.
This tempest will not give me leave to ponder   24
On things would hurt me more. But I'll go in.   25
[*To the Fool*] In, boy; go first. You houseless poverty—
Nay, get thee in. I'll pray, and then I'll sleep.
                    Exit [*Fool into the hovel*].
Poor naked wretches, wheresoe'er you are,
That bide the pelting of this pitiless storm,   29
How shall your houseless heads and unfed sides,   30
Your looped and windowed raggedness, defend you   31
From seasons such as these? Oh, I have ta'en
Too little care of this! Take physic, pomp;   33
Expose thyself to feel what wretches feel,
That thou mayst shake the superflux to them   35
And show the heavens more just.
EDGAR [*within*]   Fathom and half, fathom and half!   37
Poor Tom!

Enter Fool [from the hovel].

---

91 tell count.   **i'th' field** i.e., openly, without fear   **93 who** whoever
94 That . . . feet that walking will be done on foot. (A comical anticli-
max: Nothing will have been changed; don't expect these utopian
dreams to have materialized.)   **95 Merlin** (A great wizard of the
court of King Arthur, who came after Lear. The fool's comical inversion ends his song on a note of paradox and impossibility.)
3.3. Location: Gloucester's house.
3 pity be merciful to, relieve   **8 Go to** i.e., No more of that   **11 closet**
private chamber.   **12 home** thoroughly   **13 power** armed force.
footed landed.   **13–14 incline to** side with   **14 look** look for
16 of by   **19 toward** impending   **21 courtesy forbid thee** kindess
(to Lear) which you were forbidden to show   **23–4 This . . . all** i.e.,
This betraying by me of my father is something he has brought on
himself, and will surely confer upon me the earldom of Gloucester
and all his wealth.
3.4. Location: An open place. Before a hovel.

3 nature human nature   **4 Wilt . . . heart?** i.e., Do you want to relieve
my physical wants and thereby force me to remember my daughters'
ingratitude?   **8 fixed** lodged, implanted   **11 i'th' mouth** i.e., head-
on.   **free** free of anxiety   **12 The body's delicate** i.e., the body's
importunate needs can assert themselves.   **15 as** as if   **16 home**
fully.   **20 frank** liberal   **24 will . . . leave** i.e., keeps me too preoccupied   **25 things would** things (such as filial ingratitude) that would
29 bide endure   **30 unfed sides** i.e., lean ribs   **31 looped and windowed** full of openings like windows and loopholes   **33 Take
physic, pomp** Cure yourself, O distempered great ones   **35 superflux** superfluity. (With suggestion of *flux,* "bodily discharge," introduced by *physic,* "purgative," in line 33.)   **37 Fathom and half** (A
sailor's cry while taking soundings, hence appropriate to a deluge.)

FOOL   Come not in here, nuncle; here's a spirit. Help
me, help me!

KENT   Give me thy hand. Who's there?

FOOL   A spirit, a spirit! He says his name's poor Tom.

KENT
What art thou that dost grumble there i'th' straw?   43
Come forth.

Enter Edgar [disguised as a madman].

EDGAR   Away! The foul fiend follows me! Through the   45
sharp hawthorn blows the cold wind. Hum! Go to thy   46
bed and warm thee.

LEAR   Didst thou give all to thy daughters? And art
thou come to this?

EDGAR   Who gives anything to poor Tom? Whom the
foul fiend hath led through fire and through flame,
through ford and whirlpool, o'er bog and quagmire;
that hath laid knives under his pillow and halters in   53
his pew, set ratsbane by his porridge, made him   54
proud of heart to ride on a bay trotting horse over   55
four-inched bridges to course his own shadow for a   56
traitor. Bless thy five wits! Tom's a-cold. Oh, do de,   57
do de, do de. Bless thee from whirlwinds, star-blast-   58
ing, and taking! Do poor Tom some charity, whom the   59
foul fiend vexes. There could I have him now—and   60
there—and there again—and there.   *Storm still.*

LEAR
Has his daughters brought him to this pass?—   62
Couldst thou save nothing? Wouldst thou give 'em
all?

FOOL   Nay, he reserved a blanket, else we had been all   64
shamed.

LEAR
Now, all the plagues that in the pendulous air   66
Hang fated o'er men's faults light on thy daughters!   67

KENT   He hath no daughters, sir.

LEAR
Death, traitor! Nothing could have subdued nature
To such a lowness but his unkind daughters.
Is it the fashion that discarded fathers
Should have thus little mercy on their flesh?   72
Judicious punishment! 'Twas this flesh begot   73
Those pelican daughters.   74

EDGAR   Pillicock sat on Pillicock Hill. Alow, alow, loo,   75
loo!

FOOL   This cold night will turn us all to fools and madmen.

EDGAR   Take heed o'th' foul fiend. Obey thy parents;
keep thy word's justice; swear not; commit not with   80
man's sworn spouse; set not thy sweet heart on proud
array. Tom's a-cold.

LEAR   What hast thou been?

EDGAR   A servingman, proud in heart and mind, that   84
curled my hair, wore gloves in my cap, served the lust   85
of my mistress' heart, and did the act of darkness with
her; swore as many oaths as I spake words, and broke
them in the sweet face of heaven. One that slept in the
contriving of lust and waked to do it. Wine loved I
deeply, dice dearly, and in woman out-paramoured   90
the Turk. False of heart, light of ear, bloody of hand;   91
hog in sloth, fox in stealth, wolf in greediness, dog in
madness, lion in prey. Let not the creaking of shoes   93
nor the rustling of silks betray thy poor heart to   94
woman. Keep thy foot out of brothels, thy hand out of
plackets, thy pen from lenders' books, and defy the   96
foul fiend. Still through the hawthorn blows the cold
wind; says suum, mun, nonny. Dolphin my boy, boy,   98
sessa! Let him trot by.   *Storm still.*   99

LEAR   Thou wert better in a grave than to answer with
thy uncovered body this extremity of the skies. Is man
no more than this? Consider him well. Thou ow'st the   102
worm no silk, the beast no hide, the sheep no wool,   103
the cat no perfume. Ha! Here's three on 's are sophis-   104
ticated; thou art the thing itself. Unaccommodated   105
man is no more but such a poor, bare, forked animal
as thou art. Off, off, you lendings! Come, unbutton
here.   *[Tearing off his clothes.]*

FOOL   Prithee, nuncle, be contented; 'tis a naughty night   109
to swim in. Now a little fire in a wild field were like   110
an old lecher's heart—a small spark, all the rest on 's   111
body cold.

Enter Gloucester, with a torch.

Look, here comes a walking fire.

---

43 grumble mutter, mumble   **45 Away!** Keep away!   **45–6 Through . . .
wind** (Possibly a line from a ballad.)   **53–4 that hath . . . porridge** (The
fiend has laid in poor Tom's way tempting means to despairing suicide,
the most damnable of sins: knives under his pillow when he is asleep,
nooses in his church pew when he should be at prayer, and rat poison
set beside his soup when he should eat.)   **54–7 made him . . . traitor**
(The next temptation is a prideful act of great bravado that would be
impossible without the devil's aid: riding a horse over bridges only four
inches wide in pursuit of one's own shadow.)   **57 five wits** (Either the
five physical senses—sight, hearing, etc.—or the five faculties of the
mind: common wit, imagination, fantasy, estimation, and memory.)
58–9 star-blasting being blighted by influence of the stars   **59 taking**
infection, evil influence, enchantment.   **60 There** (Perhaps he slaps at
lice and other vermin as if they were devils.)   **62 pass** miserable plight.
64 reserved a blanket kept a wrap (for his nakedness)   **66 pendulous**
suspended, overhanging   **67 fated** having the power of fate   **72 have . . .
flesh** i.e., punish themselves, as Edgar has done (probably with pins
and thorns stuck in his flesh).   **73 Judicious** Appropriate to the crime
74 pelican greedy. (Young pelicans supposedly smote their parents and
fed on the blood of their mothers' breasts.)

75 Pillicock (From an old rhyme, suggested by the sound of *pelican.
Pillicock* in nursery rhyme seems to have been a euphemism for penis;
Pillicock Hill, for the Mount of Venus.)   **80 justice** integrity.   **commit
not** i.e., do not commit adultery. (Edgar's mad homily contains fragments of the Ten Commandments.)   **84 servingman** either a "servant" in the language of courtly love or an ambitious servant in a
household   **85 gloves** i.e., my mistress's favors   **90–1 out-
paramoured the Turk** outdid the Sultan in keeping mistresses.
91 light of ear i.e., listening intently for information that can be used
criminally   **93 prey** preying.   **93–4 creaking . . . silks** (Telltale noises
of lovers in a secret assignation.)   **96 plackets** slits in skirts or petticoats.   **thy pen . . . books** i.e., do not sign a contract for a loan
98 suum . . . nonny (Imitative of the wind?)   **Dolphin my boy** (A
slang phrase or bit of song?)   **99 sessa** i.e., away, cease (?).
102–4 Thou . . . perfume Stripped of your finery, you are not indebted
to the silkworm for silk, cattle for hide, the sheep for wool, or the civet
cat for the perfume derived from its anal pouch.   **104–5 Here . . .
itself** The three of us here (Kent, the Fool, and Lear) are decked out in
the sophistication of supposedly civilized society; you (Edgar) are the
unadorned, natural essence, the natural man.   **105 Unaccommodated**
Unfurnished with the trappings of civilization, such as clothing
109 naughty bad, nasty   **110 wild** barren, uncultivated   **111 on 's**
of his

EDGAR   This is the foul fiend Flibbertigibbet! He begins 114
at curfew and walks till the first cock; he gives the web 115
and the pin, squinnies the eye and makes the harelip, 116
mildews the white wheat, and hurts the poor creature 117
of earth.
      Swithold footed thrice the 'old; 119
      He met the nightmare and her ninefold; 120
        Bid her alight,
        And her troth plight,
      And aroint thee, witch, aroint thee! 123

KENT   How fares Your Grace?

LEAR   What's he?

KENT   Who's there? What is't you seek?

GLOUCESTER   What are you there? Your names?

EDGAR   Poor Tom, that eats the swimming frog, the
toad, the tadpole, the wall newt and the water; that in 129
the fury of his heart, when the foul fiend rages, eats
cow dung for salads, swallows the old rat and the
ditch-dog, drinks the green mantle of the standing 132
pool; who is whipped from tithing to tithing and 133
stock-punished and imprisoned; who hath had three 134
suits to his back, six shirts to his body, 135
      Horse to ride, and weapon to wear;
      But mice and rats and such small deer 137
      Have been Tom's food for seven long year.
Beware my follower. Peace, Smulkin! Peace, thou fiend! 139

GLOUCESTER
What, hath Your Grace no better company?

EDGAR   The Prince of Darkness is a gentleman. Modo 141
he's called, and Mahu.

GLOUCESTER [to Lear]
Our flesh and blood, my lord, is grown so vile 143
That it doth hate what gets it. 144

EDGAR   Poor Tom's a-cold.

GLOUCESTER
Go in with me. My duty cannot suffer 146
T'obey in all your daughters' hard commands. 147
Though their injunction be to bar my doors
And let this tyrannous night take hold upon you,

Yet have I ventured to come seek you out
And bring you where both fire and food is ready.

LEAR
First let me talk with this philosopher.
[To Edgar] What is the cause of thunder?

KENT   Good my lord,
Take his offer. Go into th' house.

LEAR
I'll talk a word with this same learnèd Theban. 155
[To Edgar] What is your study? 156

EDGAR   How to prevent the fiend, and to kill vermin. 157

LEAR   Let me ask you one word in private.
      [Lear and Edgar talk apart.]

KENT [to Gloucester]
Importune him once more to go, my lord.
His wits begin t'unsettle.

GLOUCESTER   Canst thou blame him?
                   Storm still.
His daughters seek his death. Ah, that good Kent!
He said it would be thus, poor banished man.
Thou sayest the King grows mad; I'll tell thee, friend,
I am almost mad myself. I had a son,
Now outlawed from my blood; he sought my life 165
But lately, very late. I loved him, friend,
No father his son dearer. True to tell thee,
The grief hath crazed my wits. What a night's this!—
I do beseech Your Grace—

LEAR   Oh, cry you mercy, sir. 170
[To Edgar] Noble philosopher, your company.

EDGAR   Tom's a-cold.

GLOUCESTER [to Edgar]
In, fellow, there, in th' hovel. Keep thee warm.

LEAR [starting toward the hovel]
Come, let's in all.

KENT   This way, my lord.

LEAR   With him!
I will keep still with my philosopher.

KENT [to Gloucester]
Good my lord, soothe him. Let him take the fellow. 176

GLOUCESTER [to Kent]   Take you him on. 177

KENT [to Edgar]
Sirrah, come on. Go along with us.

LEAR   Come, good Athenian. 179

GLOUCESTER   No words, no words! Hush.

EDGAR
Child Rowland to the dark tower came; 181
His word was still, "Fie, foh, and fum, 182
I smell the blood of a British man."   Exeunt. 183

---

114 Flibbertigibbet (A devil from Elizabethan folklore whose name
appears in Samuel Harsnett's *Declaration of Egregious Popish Impostures*, 1603, and elsewhere.)   **114–15 He . . . cock** He walks from
nightfall till dawn   **115–16 web and the pin** cataract of the eye
116 squinnies squints   **117 white** ripening, ready for harvest
119 Swithold Saint Withold, an Anglo-Saxon exorcist, who here provides defense against the *nightmare*, or demon thought to afflict sleepers, by commanding the nightmare to *alight*, i.e., stop riding over the
sleeper, and *plight* her *troth*, i.e., vow true faith, promise to do no
harm. (Or, an error for *Swithin*.)   **footed . . . 'old** thrice traversed the
wold (tract of hilly upland)   **120 ninefold** nine offspring. (With possible pun on *fold, foal*.)   **123 aroint thee** begone   **129 water** water
newt   **132 ditch-dog** dead dog in a ditch.   **mantle** scum.   **standing**
stagnant   **133 from . . . to tithing** from one ward or parish to another
134 stock-punished placed in the stocks   **134–5 three suits** (Like the
menial servant at 2.2.15.)   **137 deer** animals   **139 follower** familiar,
attendant devil.   **Smulkin** a devil's name (in Samuel Harsnet's *Declaration*, as are *Modo* and *Mahu* in lines 141–2).   **141 The Prince of
Darkness** The devil   **143–4 Our . . . gets it** (1) Children have become
so hardened in sin that they hate their parents (2) Life is so intolerable
that humans cry out at having been born.   **146 suffer** permit me
147 in all in all matters

155 Theban i.e., one deeply versed in "philosophy" or natural science.   **156 study** special competence.   **157 prevent** thwart   **165 outlawed . . . blood** disowned, disinherited, and legally outlawed
170 cry you mercy I beg your pardon   **176 soothe** humor   **177 Take
. . . on** i.e., Go on ahead with Edgar.   **179 Athenian** i.e., philosopher.
181 Child Rowland, etc. (Probably a fragment of a ballad about the
hero of the Charlemagne legends. A *child* is a candidate for knighthood.)   **182 word** watchword   **182–3 "Fie . . . man"** (This is essentially what the Giant says in "Jack, the Giant Killer.")

3.5

Enter Cornwall and Edmund [with a letter].

CORNWALL   I will have my revenge ere I depart his house.

EDMUND   How, my lord, I may be censured, that nature 3
thus gives way to loyalty, something fears me to 4
think of.

CORNWALL   I now perceive it was not altogether your
brother's evil disposition made him seek his death, 7
but a provoking merit set awork by a reprovable 8
badness in himself. 9

EDMUND   How malicious is my fortune, that I must 10
repent to be just! This is the letter he spoke of, which 11
approves him an intelligent party to the advantages 12
of France. Oh, heavens! That this treason were not, or 13
not I the detector!

CORNWALL   Go with me to the Duchess.

EDMUND   If the matter of this paper be certain, you have
mighty business in hand.

CORNWALL   True or false, it hath made thee Earl of
Gloucester. Seek out where thy father is, that he may
be ready for our apprehension. 20

EDMUND   [*aside*]   If I find him comforting the King, it 21
will stuff his suspicion more fully.—I will persevere 22
in my course of loyalty, though the conflict be sore
between that and my blood. 24

CORNWALL   I will lay trust upon thee, and thou shalt
find a dearer father in my love.   *Exeunt.*

3.6

*Enter Kent [disguised as Caius] and
Gloucester.*

GLOUCESTER   Here is better than the open air; take it
thankfully. I will piece out the comfort with what 2
addition I can. I will not be long from you.

KENT   All the power of his wits have given way to his
impatience. The gods reward your kindness! 5

Exit [Gloucester].

Enter Lear, Edgar [as poor Tom], and Fool.

EDGAR   Fraterretto calls me, and tells me Nero is an 6
angler in the lake of darkness. Pray, innocent, and 7
beware the foul fiend.

FOOL   Prithee, nuncle, tell me whether a madman be a
gentleman or a yeoman? 10

LEAR   A king, a king!

FOOL   No, he's a yeoman that has a gentleman to his
son; for he's a mad yeoman that sees his son a
gentleman before him.

LEAR
To have a thousand with red burning spits
Come hizzing in upon 'em— 16

EDGAR   The foul fiend bites my back. 17

FOOL   He's mad that trusts in the tameness of a wolf, a 18
horse's health, a boy's love, or a whore's oath. 19

LEAR
It shall be done; I will arraign them straight. 20
[*To Edgar*] Come, sit thou here, most learnèd justicer. 21
[*To the Fool*] Thou, sapient sir, sit here. Now, you she-
foxes! 22

EDGAR   Look where he stands and glares! Want'st thou 23
eyes at trial, madam? 24
[*Sings.*] "Come o'er the burn, Bessy, to me—" 25

FOOL   [*sings*]
        Her boat hath a leak,
        And she must not speak
    Why she dares not come over to thee.

EDGAR   The foul fiend haunts poor Tom in the voice of a
nightingale. Hoppedance cries in Tom's belly for two 30
white herring. Croak not, black angel; I have no food 31
for thee.

KENT   [*to Lear*]
How do you, sir? Stand you not so amazed. 33
Will you lie down and rest upon the cushions?

LEAR
I'll see their trial first. Bring in their evidence. 35
[*To Edgar*] Thou robèd man of justice, take thy place; 36
[*To the Fool*] And thou, his yokefellow of equity, 37

---

6 Fraterretto (Another of the fiends from Harsnett.)   **6–7 Nero is an
angler** (Chaucer's "Monk's Tale," lines 2474–5, tells how Nero fished
in the Tiber with nets of gold thread; in Rabelais, 2.30, Nero is
described as a hurdy-gurdy player and Trajan an angler for frogs in
the underworld.)   **7 innocent** simpleton, fool (i.e., the Fool)   **10 yeoman** property owner below the rank of gentleman. (The Fool's bitter
jest in lines 12–14 is that such a man might go mad to see his son
advanced over him.)   **16 hizzing** hissing. (Lear imagines his wicked
daughters suffering torments in hell or being attacked by enemies.)
17 bites (i.e., in the shape of a louse)   **18–19 tameness . . . health**
(Wolves are untamable, and horses are prone to disease.)   **20 arraign
them** (Lear now imagines the trial of his cruel daughters.)   **21 justicer** judge, justice.   **22 sapient** wise   **23 he** (Probably one of Edgar's
devils, or, Lear.)   **23–4 Want'st . . . trial** Do you lack spectators at
your trial? or, Can't you see who's looking at you?   **25 Come . . . me**
(First line of a ballad by William Birche, 1558. A *burn* is a brook. The
Fool makes a ribald reply, in which the *leaky boat* suggests the
woman's easy virtue or perhaps her menstrual period.)   **30 nightingale** (Edgar pretends to take the Fool's singing for that of a fiend disguised as a nightingale.)   **Hoppedance** (Harsnett mentions "Hober-
didance.")   **31 white** unsmoked (contrasted with *black angel*, a
demon).   **Croak** (Refers to the rumbling in Edgar's stomach, denoting hunger.)   **33 amazed** bewildered.   **35 their evidence** the witnesses against them.   **36 robèd man** i.e., Edgar, with his blanket
37 yokefellow of equity partner in the law

3.5 Location: Gloucester's house.
3 censured judged.   **nature** attachment to family   **4 something
fears** somewhat frightens   **7 his** his father's   **8–9 but . . . himself**
but the promptings of self-worth stimulated by the reprehensible
badness of the Earl of Gloucester.   **10–11 How . . . just!** i.e., How
cruel of fate to oblige me to be upright and loyal by betraying my
own father!   **11–13 which . . . France** which proves him to be a spy
on behalf of the French.   **20 for our apprehension** for our arresting
of him.   **21 If . . . comforting** If I find Gloucester giving aid and comfort to   **22 his suspicion** suspicion of him   **24 blood** family loyalty,
filial instincts.
**3.6. Location: Within a building on Gloucester's estate, near or
adjoining his house, or part of the house itself. See 3.4.146–54.
Cushions are provided, and stools.**
2 piece eke   **5 impatience** rage, inability to endure more.

Bench by his side. [*To Kent*] You are o'th' commission;   38
Sit you, too.   [*They sit.*]
EDGAR   Let us deal justly.   [*He sings.*]
    Sleepest or wakest thou, jolly shepherd?
        Thy sheep be in the corn;   42
    And for one blast of thy minikin mouth,   43
        Thy sheep shall take no harm.   44
Purr the cat is gray.   45
LEAR   Arraign her first; 'tis Goneril; I here take my oath
before this honorable assembly, kicked the poor King   47
her father.
FOOL   Come hither, mistress. Is your name Goneril?
LEAR   She cannot deny it.
FOOL   Cry you mercy, I took you for a joint stool.   51
LEAR
And here's another, whose warped looks proclaim   52
What store her heart is made on. Stop her there!   53
Arms, arms, sword, fire! Corruption in the place!   54
False justicer, why hast thou let her scape?
EDGAR   Bless thy five wits!
KENT
Oh, pity! Sir, where is the patience now
That you so oft have boasted to retain?
EDGAR [*aside*]
My tears begin to take his part so much
They mar my counterfeiting.
LEAR   The little dogs and all,
Tray, Blanch, and Sweetheart, see, they bark at me.
EDGAR   Tom will throw his head at them.—Avaunt, you   63
curs!
    Be thy mouth or black or white,   65
    Tooth that poisons if it bite,
    Mastiff, greyhound, mongrel grim,
    Hound or spaniel, brach or lym,   68
    Bobtail tike or trundle-tail,   69
    Tom will make him weep and wail;
    For, with throwing thus my head,
    Dogs leap the hatch, and all are fled.   72
Do de, de, de. Sessa! Come, march to wakes and fairs   73
and market towns. Poor Tom, thy horn is dry.   74
LEAR   Then let them anatomize Regan; see what breeds   75
about her heart. Is there any cause in nature that makes
these hard hearts? [*To Edgar*] You, sir, I entertain   77

for one of my hundred; only I do not like the fashion of
your garments. You will say they are Persian; but let   79
them be changed.
KENT
Now, good my lord, lie here and rest awhile.
LEAR [*lying on cushions*]   Make no noise, make no
noise. Draw the curtains. So, so. We'll go to supper   83
i'th' morning.   [*He sleeps.*]
FOOL   And I'll go to bed at noon.

    Enter Gloucester.

GLOUCESTER [*to Kent*]
Come hither, friend. Where is the King my master?
KENT
Here, sir, but trouble him not; his wits are gone.
GLOUCESTER
Good friend, I prithee, take him in thy arms.
I have o'erheard a plot of death upon him.   89
There is a litter ready; lay him in't
And drive toward Dover, friend, where thou shalt
    meet
Both welcome and protection. Take up thy master.
If thou shouldst dally half an hour, his life,
With thine and all that offer to defend him,
Stand in assurèd loss. Take up, take up,   95
And follow me, that will to some provision   96
Give thee quick conduct.
KENT   Oppressèd nature sleeps.   97
This rest might yet have balmed thy broken sinews,   98
Which, if convenience will not allow,   99
Stand in hard cure. [*To the Fool*] Come, help to bear thy
    master.   100
Thou must not stay behind.   [*They pick up Lear.*]
GLOUCESTER   Come, come, away!
               Exeunt [all but Edgar].
EDGAR
When we our betters see bearing our woes,   102
We scarcely think our miseries our foes.   103
Who alone suffers suffers most i'th' mind,   104
Leaving free things and happy shows behind;   105
But then the mind much sufferance doth o'erskip   106
When grief hath mates, and bearing fellowship.   107
How light and portable my pain seems now,   108
When that which makes me bend makes the King
    bow—
He childed as I fathered. Tom, away!   110

---

38 Bench take your place on the bench.   **o'th' commission** one commissioned to be a justice   **42 corn** grainfield   **43–4 And . . . harm** i.e.,
one shout from your dainty (*minikin*) mouth can recall the sheep from
the grainfield and thus save them from dangerous overeating.
45 Purr the cat (A devil or familiar from Harsnett; see the note for
3.4.114. *Purr* may be the sound the familiar makes.)   **47 kicked** who
kicked   **51 joint stool** low stool made by a joiner, or maker of furniture with joined parts. (Proverbially, the phrase "I took . . . stool"
meant "I beg your pardon for failing to notice you." The reference is
also presumably to a real stool onstage.)   **52 another** i.e., Regan
53 store abundance, material.   **on** of.   **54 Corruption in the place!**
i.e., There is iniquity or bribery in this court!   **63 throw his head at**
i.e., threaten   **65 or black** either black   **68 brach or lym** bitch-hound
or bloodhound   **69 Bobtail . . . trundle-tail** mongrel dog with a
docked or bobbed tail, or one that is curly-tailed   **72 hatch** lower half
of a divided door   **73 Sessa** i.e., Away, cease.   **wakes** parish festivals
74 horn horn-bottle, used by beggars to drink from and to beg for
alms   **75 anatomize** dissect   **77 entertain** take into my service

79 Persian (Lear madly asks if Edgar's wretched blanket is a rich Persian fabric.)   **83 curtains** bedcurtains. (They presumably exist only in
Lear's mad imagination.)   **89 upon** against   **95 Stand . . . loss** will
assuredly be lost.   **96 provision** supplies, or, means of providing for
safety   **97 conduct** guidance.   **98 balmed** soothed, healed.   **sinews**
nerves   **99 convenience** circumstances   **100 Stand . . . cure** will be
hard to cure.   **102 our woes** woes like ours   **103 We . . . foes** we
almost forget our own miseries (since we see how human suffering
afflicts even the great).   **104–7 Who . . . fellowship** Anyone who has
no companionship in suffering undergoes the mental anguish of forgetting entirely the carefree ways and happy scenes that were once
enjoyed, whereas fellowship in grief enables the mind to rise above
such suffering. (I.e., Misery loves company.)   **108 portable** bearable,
endurable   **110 He . . . fathered** he suffering cruelty from his children
as I from my father.

Mark the high noises, and thyself bewray   111
When false opinion, whose wrong thoughts defile
    thee,   112
In thy just proof repeals and reconciles thee.   113
What will hap more tonight, safe scape the King!   114
Lurk, lurk.   [*Exit.*]   115

❖

3.7

Enter Cornwall, Regan, Goneril, Bastard
[Edmund], and Servants.

CORNWALL [*to Goneril*] Post speedily to my lord your hus- 1
band; show him this letter. [*He gives a letter.*] The army
of France is landed.—Seek out the traitor Gloucester.
                   [*Exeunt some Servants.*]

REGAN Hang him instantly.
GONERIL Pluck out his eyes.
CORNWALL Leave him to my displeasure. Edmund,
keep you our sister company. The revenges we are   7
bound to take upon your traitorous father are not fit   8
for your beholding. Advise the Duke, where you are   9
going, to a most festinate preparation; we are bound   10
to the like. Our posts shall be swift and intelligent   11
betwixt us. Farewell, dear sister; farewell, my lord of   12
Gloucester.   13

      Enter steward [Oswald].

How now? Where's the King?
OSWALD
My lord of Gloucester hath conveyed him hence.
Some five- or six-and-thirty of his knights,   16
Hot questrists after him, met him at gate,   17
Who, with some other of the lord's dependents,   18
Are gone with him toward Dover, where they boast
To have well-armèd friends.
CORNWALL Get horses for your mistress. [*Exit Oswald.*]
GONERIL Farewell, sweet lord, and sister.
CORNWALL
Edmund, farewell.   *Exeunt [Goneril and Edmund].*
          Go seek the traitor Gloucester.
Pinion him like a thief; bring him before us.
                 [*Exeunt Servants.*]
Though well we may not pass upon his life   25
Without the form of justice, yet our power

Shall do a court'sy to our wrath, which men   27
May blame but not control.

    Enter Gloucester, and Servants [leading him].

               Who's there? The traitor?
REGAN Ingrateful fox! 'Tis he.
CORNWALL Bind fast his corky arms.   30
GLOUCESTER
What means Your Graces? Good my friends, consider
You are my guests. Do me no foul play, friends.
CORNWALL
Bind him, I say.   [*Servants bind him.*]
REGAN   Hard, hard. Oh, filthy traitor!
GLOUCESTER
Unmerciful lady as you are, I'm none.
CORNWALL
To this chair bind him.—Villain, thou shalt find—
          [*Regan plucks Gloucester's beard.*]
GLOUCESTER
By the kind gods, 'tis most ignobly done
To pluck me by the beard.
REGAN
So white, and such a traitor?
GLOUCESTER   Naughty lady,   38
These hairs which thou dost ravish from my chin
Will quicken and accuse thee. I am your host.   40
With robbers' hands my hospitable favors   41
You should not ruffle thus. What will you do?   42
CORNWALL
Come, sir, what letters had you late from France?   43
REGAN
Be simple-answered, for we know the truth.   44
CORNWALL
And what confederacy have you with the traitors
Late footed in the kingdom?
REGAN   To whose hands   46
You have sent the lunatic King. Speak.
GLOUCESTER
I have a letter guessingly set down,   48
Which came from one that's of a neutral heart,
And not from one opposed.
CORNWALL Cunning.
REGAN And false.
CORNWALL Where hast thou sent the King?
GLOUCESTER To Dover.
REGAN
Wherefore to Dover? Wast thou not charged at peril—   55
CORNWALL
Wherefore to Dover? Let him answer that.
GLOUCESTER
I am tied to th' stake, and I must stand the course.   57

111–13 Mark . . . thee Observe what is being said about those in high
places or about great events, and reveal your identity only when the
general opinion that now slanders you, at length establishing your
innocence, recalls you from banishment and restores you to favor.
114 What . . . King! Whatever else happens tonight, may the King
escape safely! **115 Lurk** Keep out of sight
3.7. Location: Gloucester's house.
1 Post speedily Hurry **7 sister** sister-in-law, Goneril **8 bound**
intending; obliged **9 the Duke** Albany **10 festinate** hasty. **are**
bound intend, are committed **11 posts** messengers. **intelligent**
serviceable in bearing information, knowledgeable **12–13 my . . .**
Gloucester i.e., Edmund, the recipient now of his father's forfeited
estate and title. (Two lines later, Oswald uses the same title to refer to
Edmund's father.) **16 his** Lear's **17 questrists after him** searchers
for Lear **18 the lord's** i.e., Gloucester's **25 pass upon his life** pass
the death sentence upon him

27 do a court'sy i.e., bow before, yield precedence **30 corky** withered with age **38 white** white-haired, venerable. **Naughty** Wicked
40 quicken come to life **41–2 With . . . thus** You should not roughly
handle my welcoming face with your hands as though you were robbers. **43 late** lately **44 simple-answered** straightforward in your
answers **46 Late footed** recently landed **48 guessingly set down**
conjecturally written **55 charged at peril** commanded on peril of
your life **57 tied to th' stake** i.e., like a bear to be baited with dogs.
the course the dogs' attack.

REGAN   Wherefore to Dover?

GLOUCESTER
Because I would not see thy cruel nails
Pluck out his poor old eyes, nor thy fierce sister
In his anointed flesh rash boarish fangs.   61
The sea, with such a storm as his bare head
In hell-black night endured, would have buoyed up   63
And quenched the stellèd fires;   64
Yet, poor old heart, he holp the heavens to rain.   65
If wolves had at thy gate howled that dern time,   66
Thou shouldst have said, "Good porter, turn the key."   67
All cruels else subscribe. But I shall see   68
The wingèd Vengeance overtake such children.   69

CORNWALL
See't shalt thou never.—Fellows, hold the chair.
Upon these eyes of thine I'll set my foot.

GLOUCESTER
He that will think to live till he be old,   72
Give me some help!
    [Servants hold the chair as Cornwall grinds
    out one of Gloucester's eyes with his boot.]
                    Oh, cruel! O you gods!

REGAN
One side will mock another. Th'other too.

CORNWALL [to Gloucester]
If you see Vengeance—

FIRST SERVANT   Hold your hand, my lord!
I have served you ever since I was a child;
But better service have I never done you
Than now to bid you hold.

REGAN   How now, you dog?

FIRST SERVANT [to Regan]
If you did wear a beard upon your chin,
I'd shake it on this quarrel.—What do you mean?   80

CORNWALL   My villain?   [He draws his sword.]   81

FIRST SERVANT [drawing]
Nay, then, come on, and take the chance of anger.   82
                [They fight. Cornwall is wounded.]

REGAN [to another Servant]
Give me thy sword. A peasant stand up thus?   83
                [She takes a sword and runs at him behind.]

FIRST SERVANT
Oh, I am slain! My lord, you have one eye left
To see some mischief on him. Oh!   [He dies.]   85

CORNWALL
Lest it see more, prevent it. Out, vile jelly!
                [He puts out Gloucester's other eye.]

Where is thy luster now?

GLOUCESTER
All dark and comfortless. Where's my son Edmund?
Edmund, enkindle all the sparks of nature   89
To quit this horrid act.

REGAN   Out, treacherous villain!   90
Thou call'st on him that hates thee. It was he
That made the overture of thy treasons to us,   92
Who is too good to pity thee.

GLOUCESTER
Oh, my follies! Then Edgar was abused.   94
Kind gods, forgive me that, and prosper him!

REGAN [to a Servant]
Go thrust him out at gates and let him smell
His way to Dover.   Exit [a Servant] with Gloucester.
            How is't, my lord? How look you?   97

CORNWALL
I have received a hurt. Follow me, lady.—
Turn out that eyeless villain. Throw this slave
Upon the dunghill.—Regan, I bleed apace.
Untimely comes this hurt. Give me your arm.
            Exeunt [Cornwall, supported by Regan].

SECOND SERVANT
I'll never care what wickedness I do,
If this man come to good.

THIRD SERVANT   If she live long,
And in the end meet the old course of death,   104
Women will all turn monsters.

SECOND SERVANT
Let's follow the old Earl, and get the Bedlam   106
To lead him where he would. His roguish madness   107
Allows itself to anything.   108

THIRD SERVANT
Go thou. I'll fetch some flax and whites of eggs
To apply to his bleeding face. Now, heaven help him! 110
            Exeunt [with the body].

❖

4.1

Enter Edgar [as poor Tom].

EDGAR
Yet better thus, and known to be contemned,   1
Than still contemned and flattered. To be worst,   2
The lowest and most dejected thing of fortune,   3
Stands still in esperance, lives not in fear.   4

---

61 anointed consecrated with holy oil.   **rash** slash, stick
63–4 would . . . fires would have swelled high enough, like a wave-lifted buoy, to quench the stars. (*Stellèd* means "starry" or "fixed.")
65 holp helped   **66 dern** dire, dread   **67 turn the key** i.e., let them in.   **68 All . . . subscribe** All other cruel creatures would show forgiveness except you; this cruelty is unparalleled.   **69 The wingèd Vengeance** the swift vengeance of the avenging angel of divine wrath
72 will think hopes   **80 I'd . . . quarrel** i.e., I'd pull your beard in vehement defiance in this cause.   **What do you mean?** i.e., What are you thinking of, what do you think you're doing? (Said perhaps to Cornwall.)   **81 villain** servant, bondman. (Cornwall's question implies, "How dare you do such a thing?")   **82 the chance of anger** the risks of an angry encounter.   **83.1 She . . . behind** (This stage direction appears in the Quarto.)   **85 mischief** injury

89 nature i.e., filial love   **90 quit** requite.   **Out** (An exclamation of anger or impatience.)   **92 overture** disclosure   **94 abused** wronged.
97 How look you? How is it with you?   **104 old** customary, natural
106 Bedlam i.e., lunatic discharged from the insane asylum and licensed to beg   **107–8 His . . . anything** His being a madman and derelict allows him to do anything we ask.   **110.1 Exeunt** (At some point after lines 99–100, the body of the slain First Servant must be removed.)
4.1. Location: An open place.
1–2 Yet . . . flattered It is better to be openly despised as a beggar than continually despised behind one's back and flattered to one's face.
3 dejected cast down   **4 Stands . . . fear** gives one some cause for hope, having nothing to fear (since everything is already lost).

The lamentable change is from the best;   5
The worst returns to laughter. Welcome, then,   6
Thou unsubstantial air that I embrace!
The wretch that thou hast blown unto the worst
Owes nothing to thy blasts.

Enter Gloucester, and an Old Man [leading him].

                       But who comes here?   9
My father, poorly led? World, world, O world!
But that thy strange mutations make us hate thee,   11
Life would not yield to age.   12

OLD MAN
Oh, my good lord, I have been your tenant
And your father's tenant these fourscore years.

GLOUCESTER
Away, get thee away! Good friend, begone.
Thy comforts can do me no good at all;
Thee they may hurt.

OLD MAN   You cannot see your way.

GLOUCESTER
I have no way and therefore want no eyes;
I stumbled when I saw. Full oft 'tis seen
Our means secure us, and our mere defects   20
Prove our commodities. O dear son Edgar,   21
The food of thy abusèd father's wrath!   22
Might I but live to see thee in my touch,   23
I'd say I had eyes again!

OLD MAN   How now? Who's there?

EDGAR [*aside*]
O gods! Who is't can say, "I am at the worst"?
I am worse than e'er I was.

OLD MAN   'Tis poor mad Tom.

EDGAR [*aside*]
And worse I may be yet. The worst is not   27
So long as we can say, "This is the worst."   28

OLD MAN [*to Edgar*]
Fellow, where goest?

GLOUCESTER   Is it a beggar-man?

OLD MAN   Madman and beggar too.

GLOUCESTER
He has some reason, else he could not beg.   31
I'th' last night's storm I such a fellow saw,
Which made me think a man a worm. My son
Came then into my mind, and yet my mind
Was then scarce friends with him. I have heard more
  since.
As flies to wanton boys are we to th' gods;   36

They kill us for their sport.

EDGAR [*aside*]   How should this be?   37
Bad is the trade that must play fool to sorrow,   38
Ang'ring itself and others.—Bless thee, master!   39

GLOUCESTER
Is that the naked fellow?

OLD MAN   Ay, my lord.

GLOUCESTER
Then, prithee, get thee gone. If for my sake
Thou wilt o'ertake us hence a mile or twain   42
I'th' way toward Dover, do it for ancient love,   43
And bring some covering for this naked soul,
Which I'll entreat to lead me.

OLD MAN   Alack, sir, he is mad.

GLOUCESTER
'Tis the time's plague, when madmen lead the blind.   46
Do as I bid thee, or rather do thy pleasure;
Above the rest, begone.   48

OLD MAN
I'll bring him the best 'parel that I have,
Come on't what will.   *Exit.*

GLOUCESTER   Sirrah, naked fellow—   50

EDGAR
Poor Tom's a-cold. [*Aside*] I cannot daub it further.   51

GLOUCESTER   Come hither, fellow.

EDGAR [*aside*]
And yet I must.—Bless thy sweet eyes, they bleed.

GLOUCESTER   Know'st thou the way to Dover?

EDGAR   Both stile and gate, horseway and footpath.
Poor Tom hath been scared out of his good wits. Bless
thee, good man's son, from the foul fiend! Five fiends
have been in poor Tom at once: of lust, as Obidicut;   58
Hobbididance, prince of dumbness; Mahu, of stealing;   59
Modo, of murder; Flibbertigibbet, of mopping   60
and mowing, who since possesses chambermaids and   61
waiting women. So, bless thee, master!

GLOUCESTER [*giving a purse*]
Here, take this purse, thou whom the heavens'
  plagues
Have humbled to all strokes. That I am wretched   64
Makes thee the happier. Heavens, deal so still!
Let the superfluous and lust-dieted man,   66

5–6 The lamentable . . . laughter Any change from the best is grievous, just as any change from the worst is bound to be for the better. **9 Owes nothing** can pay no more, is free of obligation **11–12 But . . . age** If it were not for your hateful inconstancy, we would never be reconciled to old age and death. **20–1 Our . . . commodities** Our prosperity makes us proudly overconfident, whereas the sheer afflictions we suffer prove beneficial (by teaching us humility). **22 The . . . wrath** on whom thy deceived father's wrath fed, the object of his anger. **23 in** by means of **27–8 The worst . . . worst** So long as we can speak and act and delude ourselves with false hopes, our fortunes can, in fact, grow worse. **31 reason** sanity **36 wanton** childishly cruel

37 How . . . be? i.e., How can he have suffered so much, changed so much? **38–9 Bad . . . others** It's a bad business to have to play the fool to my sorrowing father, vexing myself and others (with this delay in revealing my true identity). **42 o'ertake us** catch up to us (after you have found clothing for Tom o' Bedlam) **43 ancient love** i.e., the mutually trusting relationship of master and tenant that you and I have long enjoyed **46 'Tis the time's plague** It well expresses the spreading sickness of our present state **48 the rest** all **50 Come . . . will** whatever comes of this as regards myself. **51 I . . . further** i.e., I cannot keep up this pretense any longer. (Literally, "I cannot plaster up the wall.") **58–60 Obidicut . . . Flibbertigibbet** (Fiends borrowed, as before in 3.4.114 and 139–42, from Harsnett.) **60–1 mopping and mowing** making grimaces and mouths **61 since** ever since then **64 Have . . . strokes** have brought so low as to bear every blow of Fortune. **66 superfluous and lust-dieted** immoderately gluttonous and luxuriously fed

That slaves your ordinance, that will not see   67
Because he does not feel, feel your pow'r quickly!   68
So distribution should undo excess
And each man have enough. Dost thou know Dover?

EDGAR   Ay, master.

GLOUCESTER
There is a cliff, whose high and bending head   72
Looks fearfully in the confinèd deep.   73
Bring me but to the very brim of it
And I'll repair the misery thou dost bear
With something rich about me. From that place   76
I shall no leading need.

EDGAR   Give me thy arm.
Poor Tom shall lead thee.   *Exeunt.*

❖

4.2

Enter Goneril [and] Bastard [Edmund].

GONERIL
Welcome, my lord. I marvel our mild husband   1
Not met us on the way.

[Enter] steward [Oswald].

                              Now, where's your master?   2

OSWALD
Madam, within, but never man so changed.
I told him of the army that was landed;
He smiled at it. I told him you were coming;
His answer was "The worse." Of Gloucester's
    treachery
And of the loyal service of his son
When I informed him, then he called me sot   8
And told me I had turned the wrong side out.
What most he should dislike seems pleasant to him;
What like, offensive.

GONERIL [*to Edmund*]   Then shall you go no further.
It is the cowish terror of his spirit,   12
That dares not undertake. He'll not feel wrongs   13
Which tie him to an answer. Our wishes on the way   14
May prove effects. Back, Edmund, to my brother;   15
Hasten his musters and conduct his powers.   16
I must change names at home and give the distaff   17

Into my husband's hands. This trusty servant
Shall pass between us. Ere long you are like to hear,   19
If you dare venture in your own behalf,
A mistress's command. Wear this; spare speech.   21
                                    [She gives him a favor.]
Decline your head. [*She kisses him.*] This kiss, if it durst
    speak,
Would stretch thy spirits up into the air.
Conceive, and fare thee well.   24

EDMUND
Yours in the ranks of death.   *Exit.*

GONERIL   My most dear Gloucester!
Oh, the difference of man and man!
To thee a woman's services are due;
My fool usurps my body.   28

OSWALD   Madam, here comes my lord.   [*Exit.*]   29

Enter Albany.

GONERIL
I have been worth the whistling.

ALBANY   Oh, Goneril,   30
You are not worth the dust which the rude wind
Blows in your face. I fear your disposition;   32
That nature which contemns its origin   33
Cannot be bordered certain in itself.   34
She that herself will sliver and disbranch   35
From her material sap perforce must wither   36
And come to deadly use.   37

GONERIL   No more. The text is foolish.   38

ALBANY
Wisdom and goodness to the vile seem vile;
Filths savor but themselves. What have you done?   40
Tigers, not daughters, what have you performed?
A father, and a gracious agèd man,
Whose reverence even the head-lugged bear would
    lick,   43
Most barbarous, most degenerate, have you madded. 44
Could my good brother suffer you to do it?   45
A man, a prince, by him so benefited?
If that the heavens do not their visible spirits   47
Send quickly down to tame these vile offenses,
It will come,
Humanity must perforce prey on itself,
Like monsters of the deep.

GONERIL   Milk-livered man,   51

---

67 **That . . . ordinance** who enslaves your divine ordinances to his own corrupt will   **67–8 that . . . feel** who is resistant to spiritual insight because, not having suffered himself, he lacks the sympathy of fellow feeling   **72 bending** overhanging   **73 in . . . deep** i.e., into the sea below, which is confined by its shores.   **76 about me** on my person.
4.2. Location: Before the Duke of Albany's palace.
1 Welcome (Goneril, who has just arrived home from Gloucestershire escorted by Edmund, bids him brief welcome before he must return.)
2 Not met has not met   **8 sot** fool   **12 cowish** cowardly   **13 undertake** venture.   **13–14 He'll . . . answer** He will ignore insults that, if he took notice, would oblige him to respond, to fight.   **14–15 Our . . . effects** The hopes we discussed on our journey here (presumably concerning the supplanting of Albany by Edmund) may come to pass.   **15 brother** brother-in-law, Cornwall   **16 musters** assembling of troops.   **powers** armed forces.   **17 change names** i.e., exchange the roles of master and mistress of the household, and exchange the insignia of man and woman: the sword and the *distaff*.   **distaff** spinning staff, symbolizing the wife's role

19 **like** likely   **21 mistress's** (With sexual double meaning.)   **24 Conceive** Understand, take my meaning. (With sexual double entendre, continuing from *stretch thy spirits* in the previous line and continued in *death*, line 25, and *a woman's services*, line 27.)   **28 My fool . . . body** i.e., my husband claims possession of me but is unfitted to do so.   **29 s.d. Exit** (Oswald could exit later with Goneril, at line 88.)   **30 worth the whistling** (Alludes to the proverb, "it is a poor dog that is not worth the whistling.")   **32 fear your disposition** mistrust your nature   **33 contemns** spurns   **34 bordered certain** safely restrained, kept within bounds   **35 sliver** tear off   **36 material sap** nourishing substance, the stock from which she grew   **37 to deadly use** to a bad end, to a destructive purpose.   **38 The text** i.e., on which you have been preaching   **40 savor but themselves** hunger only for that which is filthy.   **43 head-lugged** dragged by the head (or by the ring in its nose) and infuriated   **44 madded** driven mad.   **45 brother** brother-in-law (Cornwall)   **47 If that** If.   **visible** manifested   **51 Milk-livered** White-livered, cowardly

That bear'st a cheek for blows, a head for wrongs,
Who hast not in thy brows an eye discerning   53
Thine honor from thy suffering, that not know'st   54
Fools do those villains pity who are punished   55
Ere they have done their mischief. Where's thy drum?   56
France spreads his banners in our noiseless land,   57
With plumèd helm thy state begins to threat,   58
Whilst thou, a moral fool, sits still and cries,   59
"Alack, why does he so?"
ALBANY   See thyself, devil!   60
Proper deformity shows not in the fiend   61
So horrid as in woman.
GONERIL   Oh, vain fool!   62
ALBANY
Thou changèd and self-covered thing, for shame,   63
Bemonster not thy feature. Were't my fitness   64
To let these hands obey my blood,   65
They are apt enough to dislocate and tear   66
Thy flesh and bones. Howe'er thou art a fiend,   67
A woman's shape doth shield thee.   68
GONERIL   Marry, your manhood! Mew!   69

Enter a Messenger.

ALBANY   What news?
MESSENGER
Oh, my good lord, the Duke of Cornwall's dead,
Slain by his servant, going to put out
The other eye of Gloucester.
ALBANY   Gloucester's eyes!
MESSENGER
A servant that he bred, thrilled with remorse,   74
Opposed against the act, bending his sword   75
To his great master, who, thereat enraged,   76
Flew on him and amongst them felled him dead,   77
But not without that harmful stroke which since
Hath plucked him after.
ALBANY   This shows you are above,   79

You justicers, that these our nether crimes   80
So speedily can venge! But, oh, poor Gloucester!
Lost he his other eye?
MESSENGER   Both, both, my lord.—
This letter, madam, craves a speedy answer;
'Tis from your sister.   [*He gives her a letter.*]
GONERIL [*aside*]   One way I like this well;   84
But being widow, and my Gloucester with her,   85
May all the building in my fancy pluck   86
Upon my hateful life. Another way   87
The news is not so tart.—I'll read, and answer.   88
                                   [*Exit.*]
ALBANY
Where was his son when they did take his eyes?   89
MESSENGER
Come with my lady hither.
ALBANY   He is not here.
MESSENGER
No, my good lord. I met him back again.   91
ALBANY   Knows he the wickedness?
MESSENGER
Ay, my good lord. 'Twas he informed against him,
And quit the house on purpose that their punishment
Might have the freer course.
ALBANY   Gloucester, I live   95
To thank thee for the love thou show'dst the King
And to revenge thine eyes.—Come hither, friend.
Tell me what more thou know'st.   *Exeunt.*

❖

4.[3]

Enter Kent [disguised] and a Gentleman.

KENT   Why the King of France is so suddenly gone back
    know you no reason?
GENTLEMAN   Something he left imperfect in the state,   3
    which since his coming forth is thought of, which im- 4
    ports to the kingdom so much fear and danger that his 5
    personal return was most required and necessary.
KENT
    Who hath he left behind him general?
GENTLEMAN
    The Marshal of France, Monsieur la Far.
KENT   Did your letters pierce the Queen to any demon-
    stration of grief?
GENTLEMAN
    Ay, sir. She took them, read them in my presence,
    And now and then an ample tear trilled down   12
    Her delicate cheek. It seemed she was a queen

53–4 discerning . . . suffering able to tell the difference between an insult to your honor and something you should tolerate   **54–6 that not . . . mischief** you who fail to understand that only fools like yourself are so tenderhearted as to pity villains (like Gloucester, Lear, and Cordelia) who are apprehended and punished before they have committed a crime.   **56 Where's thy drum?** Where is your military preparedness?   **57 noiseless** peaceful, unprepared for war   **58 thy state . . . threat** (France) begins to threaten your kingdom   **59 moral** moralizing   **60 "Alack . . . so?"** (An utterly ineffectual response to invasion.)   **61–2 Proper . . . woman** The deformity that is appropriate in a fiend's features is even uglier in a woman's (since it is so at variance with her nominally feminine appearance).   **63–4 Thou . . . feature** i.e., You creature whose transformation into a fiend now overwhelms your womanliness, do not, however evil you are, take on the outward form of a monster or fiend.   **64 Were't my fitness** If it were suitable for me   **65 blood** passion   **66 apt** ready   **67 Howe'er . . . fiend** However much you may be a fiend in reality   **68 shield** (Since I, as a gentleman, cannot lay violent hands on a lady.)   **69 Mew** (An exclamation of disgust, a derisive catcall: You speak of manhood in shielding me as a woman. Some manhood!)   **74 bred** kept in his household.   **thrilled with remorse** deeply moved with pity   **75 Opposed** opposed himself   **75–6 bending . . . To** directing his sword against   **77 amongst them** together with the others (?) in their midst (?) out of their number (?)   **79 after** along (to death).

80 justicers (heavenly) judges.   **nether** i.e., committed here below, on earth   **84 One way** (i.e., because Edmund is now Duke of Gloucester, and Cornwall, a dangerous rival for the throne, is dead)   **85–7 But . . . life** but she being now a widow, and Edmund in her company, may pull down my imagined happiness (of having the entire kingdom with Edmund), leaving my hopes in ruins.   **88 tart** bitter, sour. (See line 84 and note.)   **89 his son** Edmund.   **his** Gloucester's.   **91 back again** on the way back (from Albany's palace).   **95 Gloucester** The old Earl of Gloucester
4.3. Location: The French camp near Dover.
3 imperfect in the state unsettled in state affairs   **4–5 imports** portends   **12 trilled** trickled

Over her passion, who, most rebel-like,   14
Sought to be king o'er her.
KENT   Oh, then it moved her?
GENTLEMAN
Not to a rage. Patience and sorrow strove
Who should express her goodliest. You have seen   17
Sunshine and rain at once. Her smiles and tears
Were like a better way; those happy smilets   19
That played on her ripe lip seemed not to know   20
What guests were in her eyes, which parted thence   21
As pearls from diamonds dropped. In brief,
Sorrow would be a rarity most beloved   23
If all could so become it.   24
KENT   Made she no verbal question?   25
GENTLEMAN
Faith, once or twice she heaved the name of "father"   26
Pantingly forth, as if it pressed her heart;
Cried, "Sisters, sisters! Shame of ladies, sisters!
Kent! Father! Sisters! What, i'th' storm, i'th' night?
Let pity not be believed!" There she shook   30
The holy water from her heavenly eyes,
And, clamor-moistened, then away she started   32
To deal with grief alone.
KENT   It is the stars,
The stars above us, govern our conditions,   34
Else one self mate and make could not beget   35
Such different issues. You spoke not with her since?   36
GENTLEMAN   No.
KENT
Was this before the King returned?
GENTLEMAN   No, since.   38
KENT
Well, sir, the poor distressèd Lear's i'th' town,
Who sometime in his better tune remembers   40
What we are come about, and by no means
Will yield to see his daughter.
GENTLEMAN   Why, good sir?   42
KENT
A sovereign shame so elbows him—his own
unkindness   43
That stripped her from his benediction, turned her   44
To foreign casualties, gave her dear rights   45
To his dog-hearted daughters—these things sting
His mind so venomously that burning shame
Detains him from Cordelia.   48

GENTLEMAN   Alack, poor gentleman!
KENT
Of Albany's and Cornwall's powers you heard not?   50
GENTLEMAN   'Tis so. They are afoot.   51
KENT
Well, sir, I'll bring you to our master Lear
And leave you to attend him. Some dear cause   53
Will in concealment wrap me up awhile.
When I am known aright, you shall not grieve   55
Lending me this acquaintance. I pray you, go   56
Along with me.   Exeunt.

4.[4]

Enter, with drum and colors, Cordelia,
Gentleman, and soldiers.

CORDELIA
Alack, 'tis he! Why, he was met even now
As mad as the vexed sea, singing aloud,
Crowned with rank fumiter and furrow weeds,   3
With hardocks, hemlock, nettles, cuckooflowers,   4
Darnel, and all the idle weeds that grow   5
In our sustaining corn. A century send forth!   6
Search every acre in the high-grown field
And bring him to our eye.   [*Exit a soldier or soldiers.*]
                                    What can man's wisdom   8
In the restoring his bereavèd sense,
He that helps him take all my outward worth.   10
GENTLEMAN   There is means, madam.
Our foster nurse of nature is repose,
The which he lacks. That to provoke in him   13
Are many simples operative, whose power   14
Will close the eye of anguish.
CORDELIA   All blest secrets,
All you unpublished virtues of the earth,   16
Spring with my tears! Be aidant and remediate   17
In the good man's distress! Seek, seek for him,
Lest his ungoverned rage dissolve the life   19
That wants the means to lead it.

Enter Messenger.

MESSENGER   News, madam.   20
The British powers are marching hitherward.   21

---

14 **who** which   17 **Who . . . goodliest** which of the two could portray her best.   19 **like a better way** better than that, though similar 20–1 **seemed . . . eyes** seemed oblivious of her tears   23 **a rarity** i.e., a precious thing, like a jewel   24 **If . . . it** i.e., if all persons were as attractive in sorrow as she.   25 **verbal** i.e., as distinguished from her tears and looks   26 **heaved** breathed out with difficulty   30 **Let . . . believed**! i.e., Let no show of pity be trusted (since they are proved to be so false)!   32 **clamor-moistened** i.e., her outcry of grief assuaged by tears.   **started** i.e., went   34 **conditions** characters   35 **Else . . . make** otherwise, one couple (husband and wife)   36 **issues** off-spring.   38 **before . . . returned** before the King of France returned to his kingdom.   40 **better tune** more composed state of mind 42 **yield** consent   43 **sovereign** overruling.   **elbows him** i.e., prods his memory, jostles him, thrusts him back   44 **turned her** turned her out   45 **foreign casualties** chances of fortune abroad   48 **Detains him from** holds him back from seeing

50 **powers** troops, armies   51 **afoot** on the march.   53 **dear cause** important purpose   55–6 **grieve . . . acquaintance** regret having made my acquaintance.
4.4. Location: The French camp.
0.2 Gentleman (The Quarto specifies "Doctor" here and at line 11.)
3 **fumiter** fumitory, a weed or herb.   **furrow weeds** weeds growing in plowed furrows   4 **hardocks** probably burdock, a coarse weedy plant.   **cuckooflowers** flowers of late spring, when the cuckoo is heard   5 **Darnel** weed of the grass kind.   **idle** worthless   6 **sustaining corn** sustenance-giving grain.   **A century** (Literally, a troop of one hundred men.)   8 **What . . . wisdom** i.e., What medical knowledge can accomplish   10 **outward** material   13 **That to provoke** To induce that   14 **Are . . . operative** many herbal remedies are efficacious; or, there are many effective remedies. (*Simples* are prepared from a single herb.)   16 **unpublished virtues** little-known benign herbs   17 **Spring** grow.   **aidant and remediate** helpful and remedial 19 **rage** frenzy   20 **That . . . lead it** that lacks the means to live sanely. 21 **powers** armies

CORDELIA
'Tis known before. Our preparation stands
In expectation of them. O dear father,
It is thy business that I go about;
Therefore great France
My mourning and importuned tears hath pitied. 26
No blown ambition doth our arms incite, 27
But love, dear love, and our aged father's right.
Soon may I hear and see him! *Exeunt.*

❧

4.[5]

Enter Regan and steward [Oswald].

REGAN But are my brother's powers set forth? 1
OSWALD Ay, madam.
REGAN Himself in person there?
OSWALD Madam, with much ado. 4
Your sister is the better soldier.
REGAN
Lord Edmund spake not with your lord at home?
OSWALD No, madam.
REGAN
What might import my sister's letters to him? 8
OSWALD I know not, lady.
REGAN
Faith, he is posted hence on serious matter. 10
It was great ignorance, Gloucester's eyes being out, 11
To let him live. Where he arrives he moves
All hearts against us. Edmund, I think, is gone,
In pity of his misery, to dispatch 14
His nighted life; moreover to descry 15
The strength o'th'enemy.
OSWALD
I must needs after him, madam, with my letter.
REGAN
Our troops set forth tomorrow. Stay with us;
The ways are dangerous.
OSWALD I may not, madam.
My lady charged my duty in this business. 20
REGAN
Why should she write to Edmund? Might not you
Transport her purposes by word? Belike 22
Something—I know not what. I'll love thee much;
Let me unseal the letter.
OSWALD Madam, I had rather—
REGAN
I know your lady does not love her husband,
I am sure of that; and at her late being here 26
She gave strange oeillades and most speaking looks 27
To noble Edmund. I know you are of her bosom. 28
OSWALD I, madam?

REGAN
I speak in understanding; y'are, I know't. 30
Therefore I do advise you, take this note: 31
My lord is dead; Edmund and I have talked, 32
And more convenient is he for my hand 33
Than for your lady's. You may gather more. 34
If you do find him, pray you, give him this; 35
And when your mistress hears thus much from you, 36
I pray, desire her call her wisdom to her. 37
So, fare you well.
If you do chance to hear of that blind traitor,
Preferment falls on him that cuts him off. 40
OSWALD
Would I could meet him, madam! I should show
What party I do follow.
REGAN Fare thee well.
Exeunt [separately].

❧

4.[6]

*Enter Gloucester, and Edgar [in peasant's clothes,
leading his father].*

GLOUCESTER
When shall I come to th' top of that same hill? 1
EDGAR
You do climb up it now. Look how we labor.
GLOUCESTER
Methinks the ground is even.
EDGAR Horrible steep.
Hark, do you hear the sea?
GLOUCESTER No, truly.
EDGAR
Why, then, your other senses grow imperfect
By your eyes' anguish.
GLOUCESTER So may it be, indeed.
Methinks thy voice is altered, and thou speak'st
In better phrase and matter than thou didst.
EDGAR
You're much deceived. In nothing am I changed
But in my garments.
GLOUCESTER Methinks you're better spoken.
EDGAR
Come on, sir, here's the place. Stand still. How fearful
And dizzy 'tis to cast one's eyes so low!
The crows and choughs that wing the midway air 13
Show scarce so gross as beetles. Halfway down 14
Hangs one that gathers samphire—dreadful trade! 15
Methinks he seems no bigger than his head.
The fishermen that walk upon the beach

26 **importuned** importunate 27 **blown** swollen
4.5. Location; Gloucester's house.
1 my brother's powers Albany's forces **4 with much ado** after much
fuss and persuasion. **8 import** bear as their purport, express **10 is
posted** has hurried **11 ignorance** error, folly **14 his** Gloucester's
15 nighted benighted, blinded. **descry** spy out **20 charged my
duty** laid great stress on my obedience **22 Belike** It may be **26 late**
recently **27 oeillades** amorous glances **28 of her bosom** in her confidence.

30 **y'are** you are 31 **take this note** take note of this 32 **have talked**
have come to an understanding 33 **convenient** fitting 34 **gather
more** infer what I am trying to suggest. 35 **this** i.e., this information,
or a love token, or possibly a letter (though only one letter, Goneril's,
is found on his dead body at 4.6.262) 36 **thus much** what I have told
you 37 **call . . . to her** recall herself to her senses. 40 **Preferment**
advancement
4.6. Location: Open place near Dover.
1 that same hill i.e., the cliff we talked about (4.1.72–4). **13 choughs**
jackdaws. **midway** halfway down 14 **gross** large 15 **samphire** (A
herb used in pickling.)

Appear like mice, and yond tall anchoring bark   18
Diminished to her cock; her cock, a buoy   19
Almost too small for sight. The murmuring surge,
That on th'unnumbered idle pebble chafes,   21
Cannot be heard so high. I'll look no more,
Lest my brain turn, and the deficient sight   23
Topple down headlong.
GLOUCESTER   Set me where you stand.   24
EDGAR
Give me your hand. You are now within a foot
Of th'extreme verge. For all beneath the moon   26
Would I not leap upright.
GLOUCESTER   Let go my hand.   27
Here, friend, 's another purse; in it a jewel
Well worth a poor man's taking.   [*He gives a purse.*]
    Fairies and gods   29
Prosper it with thee! Go thou further off.   30
Bid me farewell, and let me hear thee going.
EDGAR [*moving away*]
Now fare ye well, good sir.
GLOUCESTER   With all my heart.
EDGAR [*aside*]
Why I do trifle thus with his despair
Is done to cure it.
GLOUCESTER [*kneeling*]   O you mighty gods!
This world I do renounce, and in your sights
Shake patiently my great affliction off.
If I could bear it longer and not fall
To quarrel with your great opposeless wills,   38
My snuff and loathèd part of nature should   39
Burn itself out. If Edgar live, oh, bless him!
Now, fellow, fare thee well.   [*He falls forward.*]
EDGAR   Gone, sir. Farewell.—
And yet I know not how conceit may rob   42
The treasury of life, when life itself
Yields to the theft. Had he been where he thought,   44
By this had thought been past. Alive or dead?—   45
Ho, you, sir! Friend! Hear you, sir! Speak!—
Thus might he pass indeed; yet he revives.—   47
What are you, sir?
GLOUCESTER   Away, and let me die.   48
EDGAR
Hadst thou been aught but gossamer, feathers, air,
So many fathom down precipitating,
Thou'dst shivered like an egg; but thou dost breathe,
Hast heavy substance, bleed'st not, speak'st, art
    sound.   52

Ten masts at each make not the altitude   53
Which thou hast perpendicularly fell.
Thy life's a miracle. Speak yet again.
GLOUCESTER   But have I fall'n or no?
EDGAR
From the dread summit of this chalky bourn.   57
Look up aheight; the shrill-gorged lark so far   58
Cannot be seen or heard. Do but look up.
GLOUCESTER   Alack, I have no eyes.
Is wretchedness deprived that benefit
To end itself by death? 'Twas yet some comfort
When misery could beguile the tyrant's rage   63
And frustrate his proud will.
EDGAR   Give me your arm.
                          [*He lifts him up.*]
Up—so. How is't? Feel you your legs? You stand.
GLOUCESTER
Too well, too well.
EDGAR   This is above all strangeness.
Upon the crown o'th' cliff what thing was that
Which parted from you?
GLOUCESTER   A poor unfortunate beggar.
EDGAR
As I stood here below, methought his eyes
Were two full moons; he had a thousand noses,
Horns whelked and waved like the enridgèd sea.   71
It was some fiend. Therefore, thou happy father,   72
Think that the clearest gods, who make them honors   73
Of men's impossibilities, have preserved thee.   74
GLOUCESTER
I do remember now. Henceforth I'll bear
Affliction till it do cry out itself   76
"Enough, enough," and die. That thing you speak of,   77
I took it for a man; often 'twould say
"The fiend, the fiend." He led me to that place.
EDGAR
Bear free and patient thoughts.

        Enter Lear [*mad, fantastically dressed with wild
        flowers*].

                          But who comes here?   80
The safer sense will ne'er accommodate   81
His master thus.   82
LEAR   No, they cannot touch me for coining. I am the   83
King himself.   84
EDGAR   Oh, thou side-piercing sight!   85

---

18 bark small sailing vessel   **19 Diminished . . . cock** reduced to the size of her cockboat, small ship's boat   **21 th'unnumbered idle pebble** innumerable, randomly shifting, pebbles   **23–4 Lest . . . headlong** lest I become dizzy, and my failing sight topple me headlong. **26 For . . . moon** i.e., For the whole world   **27 upright** i.e., up and down, much less forward.   **29–30 Fairies . . . thee!** May the fairies and gods cause this to multiply in your possession!   **38 To quarrel with** into rebellion against.   **opposeless** irresistible   **39 snuff** i.e., useless residue. (Literally, the smoking wick of a candle.)   **of nature** i.e., of my life   **42 conceit** imagination   **44 Yields** consents   **45 By this** by this time   **47 pass** die   **48 What** Who. (Edgar now speaks in a new voice, differing from that of "poor Tom" and also from the "altered" voice he used at the start of this scene; see lines 7–10.) **52 heavy substance** the substance of the flesh

53 at each end to end   **57 bourn** limit, boundary (i.e., the edge of the sea).   **58 aheight** on high.   **shrill-gorged** shrill-throated   **63 beguile** outwit   **71 whelked** twisted, convoluted.   **enridgèd** furrowed (by the wind)   **72 happy father** lucky old man   **73 clearest** purest, most righteous   **73–4 who . . . impossibilities** who win our awe and reverence by doing things impossible to men   **76–7 till . . . die** i.e., until affliction itself has had enough, or until I die.   **80 free** i.e., free from despair   **81–2 The safer . . . thus** i.e., A person in his right senses would never dress himself in such a fashion. (*His master* is the owner of the *safer sense* or sane mind. *His* means "its.")   **83–4 they . . . himself** they cannot prosecute me for minting coins. As king, I enjoy the exclusive royal prerogative for doing so. (Lear goes on to discuss his need for money to pay his imaginary soldiers.)   **85 side-piercing** heartrending. (With a suggestion of Christ's suffering on the cross.)

LEAR   Nature's above art in that respect. There's your 86
press money. That fellow handles his bow like a crow- 87
keeper. Draw me a clothier's yard. Look, look, a 88
mouse! Peace, peace; this piece of toasted cheese will
do't. There's my gauntlet; I'll prove it on a giant. Bring 90
up the brown bills. Oh, well flown, bird! I'th' clout, 91
i'th' clout—hewgh! Give the word. 92

EDGAR   Sweet marjoram. 93

LEAR   Pass.

GLOUCESTER   I know that voice.

LEAR   Ha! Goneril with a white beard? They flattered
me like a dog and told me I had white hairs in my 97
beard ere the black ones were there. To say ay and 98
no to everything that I said ay and no to was 99
no good divinity. When the rain came to wet me 100
once and the wind to make me chatter, when the 101
thunder would not peace at my bidding, there I found 102
'em, there I smelt 'em out. Go to, they are not men o' 103
their words. They told me I was everything. 'Tis a
lie. I am not ague-proof. 105

GLOUCESTER
The trick of that voice I do well remember. 106
Is't not the King?

LEAR   Ay, every inch a king.
When I do stare, see how the subject quakes.
I pardon that man's life. What was thy cause? 109
Adultery?
Thou shalt not die. Die for adultery? No.
The wren goes to't, and the small gilded fly
Does lecher in my sight.
Let copulation thrive; for Gloucester's bastard son
Was kinder to his father than my daughters
Got 'tween the lawful sheets.
To't, luxury, pell-mell, for I lack soldiers. 117
Behold yond simpering dame,
Whose face between her forks presages snow, 119
That minces virtue and does shake the head 120
To hear of pleasure's name; 121
The fitchew nor the soilèd horse goes to't 122

With a more riotous appetite.
Down from the waist they're centaurs, 124
Though women all above.
But to the girdle do the gods inherit; 126
Beneath is all the fiends'.
There's hell, there's darkness, there is the sulfurous pit,
burning, scalding, stench, consumption. Fie, fie, fie!
Pah, pah! Give me an ounce of civet, good apothecary, 130
sweeten my imagination. There's money for thee.

GLOUCESTER   Oh, let me kiss that hand!

LEAR   Let me wipe it first; it smells of mortality.

GLOUCESTER
Oh, ruined piece of nature! This great world 134
Shall so wear out to naught. Dost thou know me? 135

LEAR   I remember thine eyes well enough. Dost thou
squinny at me? No, do thy worst, blind Cupid; I'll not 137
love. Read thou this challenge. Mark but the penning
of it.

GLOUCESTER
Were all thy letters suns, I could not see.

EDGAR [aside]
I would not take this from report. It is, 141
And my heart breaks at it.

LEAR   Read.

GLOUCESTER   What, with the case of eyes? 144

LEAR   Oho, are you there with me? No eyes in your 145
head, nor no money in your purse? Your eyes are in a
heavy case, your purse in a light, yet you see how this 147
world goes.

GLOUCESTER   I see it feelingly. 149

LEAR   What, art mad? A man may see how this world
goes with no eyes. Look with thine ears. See how
yond justice rails upon yond simple thief. Hark in 152
thine ear: change places and, handy-dandy, which is 153
the justice, which is the thief? Thou hast seen a
farmer's dog bark at a beggar?

GLOUCESTER   Ay, sir.

LEAR   And the creature run from the cur? There thou 157
mightst behold the great image of authority: a dog's 158
obeyed in office. 159
Thou rascal beadle, hold thy bloody hand! 160
Why dost thou lash that whore? Strip thine own back;
Thou hotly lusts to use her in that kind 162
For which thou whipp'st her. The usurer hangs the
cozener. 163

---

86 **Nature's . . . respect** Real life can offer more heart-piercing examples than art.   87 **press money** enlistment bonus.   87–8 **crowkeeper** laborer hired to scare away the crows.   88 **Draw . . . yard** i.e., Draw your bow to the full length of the arrow, a cloth-yard long.   90 **do't** i.e., capture the mouse, an imagined enemy.   **gauntlet** armored glove thrown down as a challenge.   **prove it on** maintain it against 91 **brown bills** soldiers carrying pikes (painted brown), or the pikes themselves.   **well flown, bird** (Lear uses the language of hawking to describe the flight of an arrow.)   **clout** target, bull's-eye   92 **hewgh** (The arrow's noise.)   **word** password.   93 **Sweet marjoram** (A herb used to cure madness.)   97 **like a dog** as a dog fawns   97–8 **told . . . there** i.e., told me I had the white-haired wisdom of old age before I had even attained the manliness of a beard.   98–100 **To . . . divinity** i.e., To agree flatteringly with everything I said was not good theology, since the Bible teaches us to "let your yea be yea and your nay, nay" (James 5:12; see also Matthew 5:37 and 2 Cor. 1:18). 100–3 **When . . . out** i.e., Suffering wet, cold, and storm have taught me about the frailty of the human condition.   103 **Go to** (An expression of impatience.)   105 **ague-proof** immune against illness (literally, fever)   106 **trick** peculiar characteristic   109 **cause** offense.   117 **luxury** lechery   119 **Whose . . . snow** whose frosty countenance seems to suggest frigidity between her legs   120 **minces** affects, mimics   121 **of pleasure's name** the very name of pleasure   122 **The fitchew . . . to't** neither the polecat nor the well-pastured horse indulges in sexual pleasure

124 **centaurs** fabulous creatures with the head, trunk, and arms of a man joined to the body and legs of a horse   126 **But** Only.   **girdle** waist.   **inherit** have possession   130 **civet** musk perfume 134 **piece** (1) fragment (2) masterpiece   134–5 **This . . . naught** Even so will the whole universe come to an apocalyptic end.   137 **squinny** squint   141 **It is** It is taking place, incredibly enough   144 **case** mere sockets   145 **are . . . me?** is that your meaning, the point you are making?   147 **heavy case** sad plight. (With pun on *case* in line 144.)   149 **feelingly** (1) by touch (2) keenly, painfully. 152 **simple** of humble station   153 **handy-dandy** take your choice of hands (as in a well-known child's game)   157 **creature** poor fellow 158–9 **a dog's . . . office** i.e., even currish power commands submission.   160 **beadle** parish officer, responsible for giving whippings 162 **kind** way   163 **The usurer . . . cozener** The moneylender (who can buy out justice) hangs the con man.

Through tattered clothes small vices do appear;   164
Robes and furred gowns hide all. Plate sin with gold,   165
And the strong lance of justice hurtless breaks;   166
Arm it in rags, a pygmy's straw does pierce it.
None does offend, none, I say, none. I'll able 'em.   168
Take that of me, my friend, who have the power   169
To seal th'accuser's lips. Get thee glass eyes,   170
And like a scurvy politician seem   171
To see the things thou dost not. Now, now, now, now!   172
Pull off my boots. Harder, harder! So.

EDGAR [aside]
Oh, matter and impertinency mixed,
Reason in madness!   174

LEAR
If thou wilt weep my fortunes, take my eyes.
I know thee well enough; thy name is Gloucester.
Thou must be patient. We came crying hither.
Thou know'st the first time that we smell the air
We wawl and cry. I will preach to thee. Mark.

GLOUCESTER   Alack, alack the day!

LEAR
When we are born, we cry that we are come
To this great stage of fools.—This' a good block.   183
It were a delicate stratagem to shoe   184
A troop of horse with felt. I'll put 't in proof,   185
And when I have stol'n upon these son-in-laws,
Then, kill, kill, kill, kill, kill, kill!

Enter a Gentleman [with attendants].

GENTLEMAN
Oh, here he is. Lay hand upon him.—Sir,
Your most dear daughter—

LEAR
No rescue? What, a prisoner? I am even
The natural fool of fortune. Use me well;   191
You shall have ransom. Let me have surgeons;
I am cut to th' brains.

GENTLEMAN   You shall have anything.   193

LEAR   No seconds? All myself?   194
Why, this would make a man a man of salt   195
To use his eyes for garden waterpots,
Ay, and laying autumn's dust.
I will die bravely, like a smug bridegroom. What?   198

I will be jovial. Come, come, I am a king,   199
Masters, know you that?   200

GENTLEMAN
You are a royal one, and we obey you.

LEAR   Then there's life in 't. Come, an you get it, you   202
shall get it by running. Sa, sa, sa, sa.   203
                Exit [running, followed by attendants].

GENTLEMAN
A sight most pitiful in the meanest wretch,
Past speaking of in a king! Thou hast one daughter
Who redeems nature from the general curse   206
Which twain have brought her to.   207

EDGAR   Hail, gentle sir.   208

GENTLEMAN   Sir, speed you. What's your will?   209

EDGAR
Do you hear aught, sir, of a battle toward?   210

GENTLEMAN
Most sure and vulgar. Everyone hears that   211
Which can distinguish sound.

EDGAR   But, by your favor,   212
How near's the other army?

GENTLEMAN
Near and on speedy foot. The main descry   214
Stands on the hourly thought.   215

EDGAR   I thank you, sir; that's all.

GENTLEMAN
Though that the Queen on special cause is here,   217
Her army is moved on.

EDGAR   I thank you, sir.
                            Exit [Gentleman].

GLOUCESTER
You ever-gentle gods, take my breath from me;
Let not my worser spirit tempt me again   220
To die before you please!

EDGAR   Well pray you, father.   222

GLOUCESTER   Now, good sir, what are you?   223

EDGAR
A most poor man, made tame to fortune's blows,   224
Who, by the art of known and feeling sorrows,   225
Am pregnant to good pity. Give me your hand.   226
I'll lead you to some biding.   [*He offers his arm.*]

GLOUCESTER   Hearty thanks.   227

164–5 **Through . . . all** i.e., Beggars' small vices are apparent for all to see; rich folk, in expensive clothes, succeed in hiding a great deal. 165 **Plate** Arm in plate armor   166 **hurtless breaks** splinters harmlessly   168 **able** empower, give warrant to   169 **Take . . . me** (1) Learn that from me (2) Take that protection from me   170–2 **Get . . . dost not** If Gloucester were to fit himself out with spectacles (or perhaps with glass eyeballs, though they are not mentioned elsewhere until later in the seventeenth century), he would look wise like a hypocritical politician.   174 **matter and impertinency** sense and nonsense   183 **This'** This is.   **block** mold for a felt hat. (Lear may refer to the weeds strewn in his hair, which he removes as though doffing a hat before preaching a sermon.)   184 **delicate** subtle   185 **felt** i.e., padding to deaden the sound of the footfall.   **in proof** to the test   191 **natural fool** born plaything   193 **cut** wounded   194 **seconds** supporters.   195 **of salt** of salt tears   198 **bravely** (1) courageously (2) splendidly attired.   **smug** trimly dressed. (*Bridegroom* continues the punning sexual suggestion of *die bravely*, "have sex successfully.")

199 **jovial** (1) Jovelike, majestic (2) jolly.   200 **Masters** good sirs   202 **life** i.e., hope still.   **an** if   203 **Sa . . . sa** (A hunting cry.)   206 **general curse** fallen condition of the human race   207 **twain** (1) Goneril and Regan (2) Adam and Eve   208 **gentle** noble   209 **speed you** Godspeed, may God prosper you.   210 **toward** imminent.   211 **vulgar** in everyone's mouth, generally known.   212 **Which** who   214–15 **The main . . . thought** The full view of the main body is expected any hour now.   217 **Though that** Although.   **on special cause** for a special reason, i.e., to minister to Lear   220 **worser spirit** bad angel, or ill thoughts   222 **father** (A term of respect to older men, as also in lines 72, 259, and 290, though with ironic double meaning throughout the scene.)   223 **what** who. (Again, Edgar alters his voice to personate a new stranger assisting Gloucester. See line 48, above, and note.)   224 **tame** submissive   225 **known and feeling** personally experienced and heartfelt   226 **pregnant** prone   227 **biding** abode.

The bounty and the benison of heaven   228
To boot, and boot!

Enter steward [Oswald].

OSWALD   A proclaimed prize! Most happy!   229
                  [He draws his sword.]
That eyeless head of thine was first framed flesh   230
To raise my fortunes. Thou old unhappy traitor,
Briefly thyself remember. The sword is out   232
That must destroy thee.

GLOUCESTER   Now let thy friendly hand   233
Put strength enough to't.   *[Edgar intervenes.]*

OSWALD   Wherefore, bold peasant,
Durst thou support a published traitor? Hence,   235
Lest that th'infection of his fortune take   236
Like hold on thee. Let go his arm.   237

EDGAR   'Chill not let go, zir, without vurther 'cagion. 238

OSWALD   Let go, slave, or thou diest!

EDGAR   Good gentleman, go your gait, and let poor volk 240
pass. An 'chud ha' bin zwaggered out of my life,   241
'twould not ha' bin zo long as 'tis by a vortnight. Nay, 242
come not near th' old man; keep out, 'che vor ye, or 243
Ise try whether your costard or my ballow be the   244
harder. 'Chill be plain with you.

OSWALD   Out, dunghill!

EDGAR   'Chill pick your teeth, zir. Come, no matter vor
your foins.   *[They fight. Edgar fells him with his cudgel.]* 248

OSWALD
Slave, thou hast slain me. Villain, take my purse. 249
If ever thou wilt thrive, bury my body
And give the letters which thou find'st about me   251
To Edmund, Earl of Gloucester. Seek him out
Upon the English party. Oh, untimely death!   253
Death!   *[He dies.]*

EDGAR
I know thee well: a serviceable villain,   255
As duteous to the vices of thy mistress
As badness would desire.

GLOUCESTER   What, is he dead?

EDGAR   Sit you down, father. Rest you. *[Gloucester sits.]*
Let's see these pockets; the letters that he speaks of
May be my friends. He's dead; I am only sorry
He had no other deathsman. Let us see.   262
                  [He finds a letter and opens it.]
Leave, gentle wax, and, manners, blame us not.   263

To know our enemies' minds we rip their hearts;
Their papers is more lawful.   *(Reads the letter.)*
"Let our reciprocal vows be remembered. You have
many opportunities to cut him off; if your will want 267
not, time and place will be fruitfully offered. There is 268
nothing done if he return the conqueror. Then am I 269
the prisoner, and his bed my jail, from the loathed
warmth whereof deliver me and supply the place for 271
your labor.   272
Your—wife, so I would say—affectionate servant,
and for you her own for venture, Goneril."   274
Oh, indistinguished space of woman's will!   275
A plot upon her virtuous husband's life,
And the exchange my brother! Here in the sands
Thee I'll rake up, the post unsanctified   278
Of murderous lechers; and in the mature time   279
With this ungracious paper strike the sight   280
Of the death-practiced Duke. For him 'tis well   281
That of thy death and business I can tell.
                  [Exit with the body.]

GLOUCESTER
The King is mad. How stiff is my vile sense,   283
That I stand up and have ingenious feeling   284
Of my huge sorrows! Better I were distract;   285
So should my thoughts be severed from my griefs,
And woes by wrong imaginations lose   287
The knowledge of themselves.   *Drum afar off.*

[Enter Edgar.]

EDGAR   Give me your hand.
Far off, methinks, I hear the beaten drum.
Come, father, I'll bestow you with a friend.   290
                  Exeunt, [Edgar leading his father].

❖

4.7

*Enter Cordelia, Kent [dressed still in his disguise
costume], and Gentleman.*

CORDELIA
O thou good Kent, how shall I live and work
To match thy goodness? My life will be too short,
And every measure fail me.   3

267 him Albany   **267–8 want not** is not lacking   **268 fruitfully** plentifully and with results   **268–9 There is nothing done** i.e., We will have accomplished nothing   **271 supply** fill   **271–2 for your labor** (1) as recompense for your efforts (2) as a place for your amorous labors.   **274 and for . . . venture** and one ready to venture her own fortunes for your sake   **275 indistinguished . . . will** limitless and incalculable expanse of woman's appetite   **278 rake up** cover up. **post unsanctified** unholy messenger   **279 in . . . time** when the time is ripe   **280 ungracious** wicked. **strike** blast   **281 Of . . . well** of Albany, whose death is plotted. It's a good thing for him   **283 How . . . sense** How obstinate is my deplorable sanity and power of sensation   **284 ingenious** conscious. (Gloucester laments that he remains sane and hence fully conscious of his troubles, unlike Lear.)   **285 distract** distracted, crazy   **287 wrong imaginations** delusions   **290 bestow** lodge. (At the scene's end, Edgar leads off Gloucester; presumably, at line 282 or else here, he must also dispose of Oswald's body in the trapdoor or by lugging it offstage.)
4.7. Location: The French camp.
0.2 *Gentleman* ("*Doctor*" in Q.)   **3 every . . . me** every attempt (to match your goodness) will fall short.

228–9 The bounty . . . and boot! In addition to my thanks, I wish you the bounty and blessings of heaven.   **229 proclaimed prize** one with a price on his head. **happy** fortunate.   **230 framed flesh** born   **232 thyself remember** i.e., say your prayers.   **233 friendly** i.e., welcome, since I desire death   **235 published** proclaimed   **236 Lest that** lest   **237 Like** similar   **238 'Chill** I will. (Literally, a contraction of *Ich will*. Edgar adopts Somerset dialect, a stage convention regularly used for peasants.)   **vurther 'cagion** further occasion.   **240 go your gait** go your own way   **241 An 'chud** If I could.   **zwaggered** swaggered, bullied   **242 'twould . . . vortnight** it (my life) wouldn't have lasted a fortnight.   **243 'che vor ye** I warrant you   **244 Ise** I shall. **costard** head. (Literally, an apple.)   **ballow** cudgel   **248 foins** thrusts.   **249 Villain** Serf   **251 letters** letter. (See 4.5.35 and note.) **about me** upon my person   **253 Upon** on. **party** side.   **255 serviceable** officious   **262 deathsman** executioner.   **263 Leave** By your leave.   **wax** wax seal on the letter

KENT
To be acknowledged, madam, is o'erpaid.
All my reports go with the modest truth,   5
Nor more nor clipped, but so.
CORDELIA   Be better suited.   6
These weeds are memories of those worser hours;   7
I prithee, put them off.
KENT   Pardon, dear madam;
Yet to be known shortens my made intent.   9
My boon I make it that you know me not   10
Till time and I think meet.   11
CORDELIA
Then be't so, my good lord. [*To the Gentleman*] How
   does the King?
GENTLEMAN   Madam, sleeps still.
CORDELIA   O you kind gods,
Cure this great breach in his abusèd nature!
Th'untuned and jarring senses, oh, wind up   16
Of this child-changèd father!   17
GENTLEMAN   So please Your Majesty
That we may wake the King? He hath slept long.
CORDELIA
Be governed by your knowledge, and proceed
I'th' sway of your own will.—Is he arrayed?   21

Enter Lear in a chair carried by servants.

GENTLEMAN
Ay, madam. In the heaviness of sleep
We put fresh garments on him.
Be by, good madam, when we do awake him.
I doubt not of his temperance.
CORDELIA   Very well.   [*Music.*]   25
GENTLEMAN
Please you, draw near.—Louder the music there!
CORDELIA [*kissing him*]
O my dear father! Restoration hang
Thy medicine on my lips, and let this kiss
Repair those violent harms that my two sisters
Have in thy reverence made!
KENT   Kind and dear princess!   30
CORDELIA
Had you not been their father, these white flakes   31
Did challenge pity of them. Was this a face   32
To be opposed against the warring winds?
To stand against the deep dread-bolted thunder   34
In the most terrible and nimble stroke

Of quick cross lightning? To watch—poor perdu!—   36
With this thin helm? Mine enemy's dog,   37
Though he had bit me, should have stood that night
Against my fire; and wast thou fain, poor father,   39
To hovel thee with swine and rogues forlorn   40
In short and musty straw? Alack, alack!   41
'Tis wonder that thy life and wits at once
Had not concluded all.—He wakes! Speak to him.   43
GENTLEMAN   Madam, do you; 'tis fittest.
CORDELIA
How does my royal lord? How fares Your Majesty?
LEAR
You do me wrong to take me out o'th' grave.
Thou art a soul in bliss; but I am bound
Upon a wheel of fire, that mine own tears   48
Do scald like molten lead.
CORDELIA   Sir, do you know me?
LEAR
You are a spirit, I know. Where did you die?
CORDELIA   Still, still, far wide!   51
GENTLEMAN
He's scarce awake. Let him alone awhile.
LEAR
Where have I been? Where am I? Fair daylight?
I am mightily abused. I should ev'n die with pity   54
To see another thus. I know not what to say.   55
I will not swear these are my hands. Let's see;
I feel this pinprick. Would I were assured
Of my condition!
CORDELIA [*kneeling*]   Oh, look upon me, sir,
And hold your hands in benediction o'er me.
                              [*He attempts to kneel.*]
No, sir, you must not kneel.
LEAR   Pray, do not mock me.
I am a very foolish fond old man,   61
Fourscore and upward, not an hour more nor less;
And, to deal plainly,
I fear I am not in my perfect mind.
Methinks I should know you, and know this man,
Yet I am doubtful; for I am mainly ignorant   66
What place this is, and all the skill I have
Remembers not these garments, nor I know not
Where I did lodge last night. Do not laugh at me,
For, as I am a man, I think this lady
To be my child Cordelia.
CORDELIA [*weeping*]   And so I am, I am.
LEAR
Be your tears wet? Yes, faith. I pray, weep not.
If you have poison for me I will drink it.
I know you do not love me, for your sisters
Have, as I do remember, done me wrong.
You have some cause, they have not.

---

5 **All my reports go** All my reports (of my service as Caius to Lear) conform   6 **Nor . . . clipped** i.e., neither more nor less.   **suited** dressed.   7 **weeds** garments.   **memories** remembrances   9 **Yet . . . intent** to reveal my true identity now would alter my carefully made plan.   10 **My . . . it** The favor I seek is.   **know** acknowledge   11 **meet** appropriate.   16 **wind up** tune (as by tightening the slackened string of an instrument)   17 **child-changèd** changed by children's cruelty   21 **I'th' sway** under the direction   25 **temperance** self-control, calm behavior.   30 **reverence** venerable condition   31 **Had you** Even if you had.   **flakes** locks of hair   32 **Did challenge** would have demanded   34 **deep** bass-voiced.   **dread-bolted** furnished with the dreadful thunderbolt

36 **cross** zigzag.   **watch** stay awake (like a sentry on duty).   **perdu** lost one; a sentinel placed in a position of peculiar danger.   37 **helm** helmet, i.e., scanty hair.   39 **Against** before, in front of.   **fain** constrained   40 **rogues forlorn** abandoned vagabonds   41 **short** broken up and hence uncomfortable   43 **concluded all** come to an end altogether.   48 **wheel of fire** (A hellish torment for the eternally damned.)   **that** so that   51 **wide** wide of the mark, wandering.   54 **abused** confused, deluded.   55 **thus** i.e., thus confused, bewildered.   61 **fond** in my dotage   66 **mainly** entirely

CORDELIA   No cause, no cause.
LEAR   Am I in France?
KENT   In your own kingdom, sir.
LEAR   Do not abuse me.   81
GENTLEMAN
    Be comforted, good madam. The great rage,   82
    You see, is killed in him, and yet it is danger
    To make him even o'er the time he has lost.   84
    Desire him to go in. Trouble him no more
    Till further settling.   86
CORDELIA   Will't please Your Highness walk?   87
LEAR   You must bear with me.
    Pray you now, forget and forgive.
    I am old and foolish.
                        Exeunt [all but Kent and Gentleman].
GENTLEMAN   Holds it true, sir, that the Duke of Corn-   91
    wall was so slain?
KENT   Most certain, sir.
GENTLEMAN   Who is conductor of his people?   94
KENT   As 'tis said, the bastard son of Gloucester.
GENTLEMAN   They say Edgar, his banished son, is with
    the Earl of Kent in Germany.
KENT   Report is changeable. 'Tis time to look about; the   98
    powers of the kingdom approach apace.   99
GENTLEMAN   The arbitrament is like to be bloody. Fare   100
    you well, sir.   [*Exit.*]
KENT
    My point and period will be throughly wrought,   102
    Or well or ill, as this day's battle's fought.   *Exit.*   103

❖

5.1

Enter, with drum and colors, Edmund, Regan,
Gentlemen, and soldiers.

EDMUND   [*to a Gentleman*]
    Know of the Duke if his last purpose hold,   1
    Or whether since he is advised by aught   2
    To change the course. He's full of alteration   3
    And self-reproving. Bring his constant pleasure.   4
                                        [*Exit Gentleman.*]
REGAN
    Our sister's man is certainly miscarried.   5

EDMUND
    'Tis to be doubted, madam.
REGAN   Now, sweet lord,   6
    You know the goodness I intend upon you.   7
    Tell me, but truly—but then speak the truth—
    Do you not love my sister?
EDMUND   In honored love.   9
REGAN
    But have you never found my brother's way
    To the forfended place?   11
EDMUND   That thought abuses you.   12
REGAN
    I am doubtful that you have been conjunct   13
    And bosomed with her, as far as we call hers.   14
EDMUND   No, by mine honor, madam.
REGAN
    I never shall endure her. Dear my lord,
    Be not familiar with her.   17
EDMUND
    Fear me not.—She and the Duke her husband!   18

        Enter, with drum and colors, Albany, Goneril,
        [*and*] *soldiers.*

GONERIL   [*aside*]
    I had rather lose the battle than that sister
    Should loosen him and me.
ALBANY   [*to Regan*]
    Our very loving sister, well bemet.   21
    [*To Edmund*] Sir, this I heard: the King is come to his
        daughter,
    With others whom the rigor of our state   23
    Forced to cry out. Where I could not be honest,   24
    I never yet was valiant. For this business,   25
    It touches us as France invades our land,   26
    Not bolds the King, with others whom, I fear,   27
    Most just and heavy causes make oppose.   28
EDMUND   Sir, you speak nobly.
REGAN   Why is this reasoned?   30
GONERIL
    Combine together 'gainst the enemy;
    For these domestic and particular broils   32
    Are not the question here.
ALBANY   Let's then determine
    With th'ancient of war on our proceeding.   34
EDMUND
    I shall attend you presently at your tent.
REGAN   Sister, you'll go with us?
GONERIL   No.

---

81 **abuse** deceive. (Or perhaps Lear feels hurt by the reminder of his having divided the kingdom.)   82 **rage** frenzy   84 **even o'er** fill in, go over in his mind   86 **settling** composing of his mind.   87 **walk** withdraw.   91 **Holds it true** Is it still held to be true   94 **conductor** leader, general   98 **look about** be wary, take stock of the situation   99 **powers of the kingdom** British armies (marching against the French invaders)   100 **arbitrament** decision by arms, decisive encounter   102 **My . . . wrought** i.e., The conclusion of my destiny (literally, the full stop at the end of my life's sentence) will be thoroughly shaped   103 **Or** either.   **as** according as
5.1. Location: The British camp near Dover.
1 **Know** Inquire.   **last purpose hold** most recent intention (to fight) remains firm   2 **since** since then.   **advised by aught** persuaded by any consideration   3 **alteration** vacillation   4 **constant pleasure** settled decision.   5 **man** i.e., Oswald.   **miscarried** lost, perished.

6 **doubted** feared   7 **intend** intend to confer   9 **honored** honorable   11 **forfended** forbidden (by the commandment against adultery)   12 **abuses** degrades, wrongs   13–14 **I . . . hers** I fear that you have been sexually intimate with her to the fullest extent possible.   17 **familiar** intimate   18 **Fear me not** Don't worry about me on that score.   21 **bemet** met.   23 **rigor of our state** harshness of our rule   24 **cry out** rebel.   **Where** In a case where.   **honest** honorable   25 **For** As for   26 **touches us as** concerns us insofar as   27–8 **Not . . . oppose** not because the matter emboldens the King and others who, I fear, are driven into opposition by just and weighty grievances.   30 **Why . . . reasoned?** i.e., Why are we arguing about reasons for fighting, instead of fighting?   32 **particular broils** private quarrels   34 **th'ancient of war** the veteran officers

REGAN
'Tis most convenient. Pray, go with us.   38
GONERIL [aside]
Oho, I know the riddle.—I will go.   39

[As they are going out,] enter Edgar [disguised].

EDGAR [to Albany]
If e'er Your Grace had speech with man so poor,
Hear me one word.
ALBANY [to the others]   I'll overtake you.
                              Exeunt both the armies.
                                        Speak.
EDGAR [giving a letter]
Before you fight the battle, ope this letter.   42
If you have victory, let the trumpet sound   43
For him that brought it. Wretched though I seem,
I can produce a champion that will prove   45
What is avouchèd there. If you miscarry,   46
Your business of the world hath so an end,
And machination ceases. Fortune love you!   48
ALBANY   Stay till I have read the letter.
EDGAR   I was forbid it.
When time shall serve, let but the herald cry
And I'll appear again.   *Exit [Edgar].*
ALBANY
Why, fare thee well. I will o'erlook thy paper.   53

Enter Edmund.

EDMUND
The enemy's in view. Draw up your powers.
                              [He offers Albany a paper.]
Here is the guess of their true strength and forces   55
By diligent discovery; but your haste   56
Is now urged on you.
ALBANY   We will greet the time.   *Exit.* 57
EDMUND
To both these sisters have I sworn my love,
Each jealous of the other as the stung   59
Are of the adder. Which of them shall I take?
Both? One? Or neither? Neither can be enjoyed
If both remain alive. To take the widow
Exasperates, makes mad her sister Goneril,
And hardly shall I carry out my side,   64
Her husband being alive. Now then, we'll use
His countenance for the battle, which being done,   66
Let her who would be rid of him devise
His speedy taking off. As for the mercy   68
Which he intends to Lear and to Cordelia,
The battle done and they within our power,

Shall never see his pardon, for my state   71
Stands on me to defend, not to debate.   72
                                        Exit.

❖

5.2

*Alarum within. Enter, with drum and colors, Lear,
Cordelia, and soldiers, over the stage; and exeunt.*

Enter Edgar and Gloucester.

EDGAR
Here, father, take the shadow of this tree   1
For your good host. Pray that the right may thrive.   2
If ever I return to you again,
I'll bring you comfort.
GLOUCESTER   Grace go with you, sir!   4
                                        Exit [Edgar].

Alarum and retreat within. Enter Edgar.

EDGAR
Away, old man! Give me thy hand. Away!
King Lear hath lost, he and his daughter ta'en.
Give me thy hand. Come on.
GLOUCESTER
No further, sir. A man may rot even here.
EDGAR
What, in ill thoughts again? Men must endure
Their going hence, even as their coming hither;
Ripeness is all. Come on.
GLOUCESTER   And that's true too.   11
                                        Exeunt.

♣

5.3

*Enter, in conquest, with drum and colors, Edmund;
Lear and Cordelia, as prisoners; soldiers, Captain.*

EDMUND
Some officers take them away. Good guard   1
Until their greater pleasures first be known   2
That are to censure them.
CORDELIA [to Lear]   We are not the first   3
Who with best meaning have incurred the worst.   4
For thee, oppressèd King, I am cast down;
Myself could else outfrown false Fortune's frown.
Shall we not see these daughters and these sisters?   7

---

38 convenient proper, fitting.   **39 I know the riddle** i.e., I understand the reason for Regan's enigmatic demand that I accompany her, which is that she wants to keep me away from Edmund.   **42 this letter** i.e., Goneril's letter to Edmund found on Oswald's body.
43 sound sound a summons   **45 prove** i.e., in trial by combat
46 avouchèd affirmed.   **miscarry** lose the battle and die   **48 machination** plotting (against your life)   **53 o'erlook** peruse   **55 guess** estimate   **56 discovery** reconnoitering   **57 We . . . time** We will be ready for whatever happens.   **59 jealous** suspicious   **64 carry . . . side** carry out my end of the bargain in our *reciprocal vows* (4.6.266)
66 countenance backing, authority of his name   **68 taking off** killing.

71 Shall they shall   **71–2 my state . . . debate** my position depends upon maintenance by forceful action, not by talk.
5.2. Location: The battlefield.
0.1 Alarum trumpet call to arms   **1 father** i.e., reverend old man
2 host shelterer.   **4.2 retreat** trumpet signal for withdrawal
11 Ripeness (Humans shouldn't die before their time, just as fruit doesn't fall until it's ripe.)
5.3. Location: The British camp.
1 Good guard Guard them well   **2 their greater pleasures** the wishes of those in command   **3 censure** judge   **4 meaning** intentions
7 Shall . . . sisters? i.e., Aren't we even allowed to speak to Goneril and Regan before they order to prison their own father and sister?

LEAR
    No, no, no, no! Come, let's away to prison.
    We two alone will sing like birds i'th' cage.
    When thou dost ask me blessing, I'll kneel down
    And ask of thee forgiveness. So we'll live,
    And pray, and sing, and tell old tales, and laugh
    At gilded butterflies, and hear poor rogues   13
    Talk of court news; and we'll talk with them too—
    Who loses and who wins; who's in, who's out—
    And take upon 's the mystery of things,   16
    As if we were God's spies; and we'll wear out,   17
    In a walled prison, packs and sects of great ones,   18
    That ebb and flow by th' moon.
EDMUND   Take them away.   19
LEAR
    Upon such sacrifices, my Cordelia,
    The gods themselves throw incense. Have I caught
      thee?   21
    He that parts us shall bring a brand from heaven   22
    And fire us hence like foxes. Wipe thine eyes;   23
    The good years shall devour them, flesh and fell,   24
    Ere they shall make us weep. We'll see 'em starved
      first.   25
    Come.   *Exit [with Cordelia, guarded].*
EDMUND   Come hither, Captain. Hark.
    Take thou this note. [*He gives a paper.*] Go follow them
      to prison.
    One step I have advanced thee; if thou dost
    As this instructs thee, thou dost make thy way
    To noble fortunes. Know thou this: that men
    Are as the time is. To be tender-minded   32
    Does not become a sword. Thy great employment   33
    Will not bear question; either say thou'lt do't   34
    Or thrive by other means.
CAPTAIN   I'll do't, my lord.
EDMUND   About it, and write "happy" when th' hast done.   36
    Mark, I say, instantly, and carry it so   37
    As I have set it down.
CAPTAIN
    I cannot draw a cart, nor eat dried oats;
    If it be man's work, I'll do't.   *Exit Captain.*

    Flourish. Enter Albany, Goneril, Regan, [another
    Captain, and] soldiers.

ALBANY
    Sir, you have showed today your valiant strain,
    And fortune led you well. You have the captives
    Who were the opposites of this day's strife;   43
    I do require them of you, so to use them
    As we shall find their merits and our safety
    May equally determine.
EDMUND   Sir, I thought it fit
    To send the old and miserable King
    To some retention and appointed guard,   49
    Whose age had charms in it, whose title more,   50
    To pluck the common bosom on his side   51
    And turn our impressed lances in our eyes   52
    Which do command them. With him I sent the Queen,   53
    My reason all the same; and they are ready
    Tomorrow, or at further space, t'appear   55
    Where you shall hold your session. At this time
    We sweat and bleed; the friend hath lost his friend,
    And the best quarrels in the heat are cursed   58
    By those that feel their sharpness.   59
    The question of Cordelia and her father
    Requires a fitter place.
ALBANY   Sir, by your patience,   61
    I hold you but a subject of this war,   62
    Not as a brother.
REGAN   That's as we list to grace him.   63
    Methinks our pleasure might have been demanded   64
    Ere you had spoke so far. He led our powers,
    Bore the commission of my place and person,
    The which immediacy may well stand up   67
    And call itself your brother.
GONERIL   Not so hot!
    In his own grace he doth exalt himself
    More than in your addition.
REGAN   In my rights,   70
    By me invested, he compeers the best.   71
GONERIL
    That were the most if he should husband you.   72
REGAN
    Jesters do oft prove prophets.
GONERIL   Holla, holla!   73
    That eye that told you so looked but asquint.   74
REGAN
    Lady, I am not well, else I should answer
    From a full-flowing stomach. [*To Edmund*] General,   76

---

13 gilded butterflies i.e., gaily dressed courtiers and other ephemeral types, or perhaps actual butterflies **16 take upon 's** assume the burden of, or profess to understand **17 God's spies** i.e., detached observers surveying the deeds of humanity from an eternal vantage point. **wear out** outlast **18–19 packs . . . moon** i.e., followers and cliques attached to persons of high station, whose fortunes change erratically and constantly. **21 The gods . . . incense** (The gods make offerings to Cordelia instead of receiving them.) **22–3 He . . . foxes** i.e., Nothing short of a firebrand from heaven will ever part us again. (Firebrands were used to smoke foxes from their lairs; compare also Samson's use of firebrands tied to the tails of foxes in order to punish the Philistines for denying him his wife, in Judges 15:4–5.) **24–5 The good . . . weep** i.e., the years will be good to us and will utterly foil our enemies' attempts to make us sorrowful as long as we are together (?). **32 Are . . . is** i.e., must adapt themselves to stern exigencies. **33 become a sword** i.e., suit a warrior. **34 bear question** admit of discussion **36 write "happy"** call yourself fortunate. **th'** thou **37 carry it** carry it out

43 opposites enemies **49 retention** confinement **50–3 Whose . . . them** whose advanced age had magic in it, and whose title as king had even more, to win the sympathy of the commoners and turn against us the weapons of those very troops whom we impressed into service. (*In our eyes* may suggest retaliation for the blinding of Gloucester.) **55 space** interval of time **58–9 And . . . sharpness** and even the best of causes, at this moment when the passions of battle have not cooled, are viewed with hatred by those who have suffered the painful consequences. (Edmund pretends to worry that Lear and Cordelia would not receive a fair trial.) **61 by your patience** if you please **62 subject of** subordinate in **63 list** please **64 pleasure** wish. **demanded** asked about **67 immediacy** nearness of connection **70 your addition** the titles you confer. **71 compeers** is equal with **72 That . . . most** That investiture would be most complete **73 prove** turn out to be **74 asquint** (Jealousy proverbially makes the eye look *asquint*, "furtively, suspiciously.") **76 full-flowing stomach** full tide of angry rejoinder.

Take thou my soldiers, prisoners, patrimony;   77
Dispose of them, of me; the walls is thine.   78
Witness the world that I create thee here
My lord and master.

GONERIL   Mean you to enjoy him?

ALBANY
The let-alone lies not in your good will.   81

EDMUND
Nor in thine, lord.

ALBANY   Half-blooded fellow, yes.   82

REGAN [to Edmund]
Let the drum strike and prove my title thine.

ALBANY
Stay yet; hear reason. Edmund, I arrest thee
On capital treason; and, in thy attaint   85
This gilded serpent. [Pointing to Goneril] For your
     claim, fair sister,
I bar it in the interest of my wife;
'Tis she is subcontracted to this lord,
And I, her husband, contradict your banns.   89
If you will marry, make your loves to me;   90
My lady is bespoke.

GONERIL   An interlude!   91

ALBANY
Thou art armed, Gloucester. Let the trumpet sound.
If none appear to prove upon thy person
Thy heinous, manifest, and many treasons,
There is my pledge. [He throws down a glove.] I'll make
     it on thy heart,   95
Ere I taste bread, thou art in nothing less   96
Than I have here proclaimed thee.

REGAN   Sick, oh, sick!

GONERIL [aside]   If not, I'll ne'er trust medicine.   99

EDMUND [throwing down a glove]
There's my exchange. What in the world he is   100
That names me traitor, villain-like he lies.
Call by the trumpet. He that dares approach,
On him, on you—who not?—I will maintain
My truth and honor firmly.

ALBANY
A herald, ho!

EDMUND   A herald, ho, a herald!

          Enter a Herald.

ALBANY [to Edmund]
Trust to thy single virtue; for thy soldiers,   106
All levied in my name, have in my name
Took their discharge.

REGAN   My sickness grows upon me.

ALBANY [to Soldiers]
She is not well. Convey her to my tent.
                              [Exit Regan, supported.]
Come hither, herald. Let the trumpet sound,
And read out this.   [He gives a paper.]

CAPTAIN   Sound, trumpet!   A trumpet sounds.

HERALD (reads)   "If any man of quality or degree within   113
the lists of the army will maintain upon Edmund, sup-   114
posed Earl of Gloucester, that he is a manifold traitor,
let him appear by the third sound of the trumpet. He
is bold in his defense."

EDMUND   Sound!   First trumpet.

HERALD   Again!   Second trumpet.

HERALD   Again!   Third trumpet.
                              Trumpet answers within.

          Enter Edgar, armed, [with a trumpeter before
          him].

ALBANY
Ask him his purposes, why he appears
Upon this call o'th' trumpet.

HERALD   What are you?   122
Your name, your quality, and why you answer
This present summons?

EDGAR   Know my name is lost,
By treason's tooth bare-gnawn and canker-bit.   125
Yet am I noble as the adversary
I come to cope.

ALBANY   Which is that adversary?   127

EDGAR
What's he that speaks for Edmund, Earl of
     Gloucester?

EDMUND
Himself. What say'st thou to him?

EDGAR   Draw thy sword,
That, if my speech offend a noble heart,
Thy arm may do thee justice. Here is mine.
                              [He draws his sword.]
Behold, it is the privilege of mine honors,   132
My oath, and my profession. I protest,   133
Maugre thy strength, place, youth, and eminence,   134
Despite thy victor sword and fire-new fortune,   135
Thy valor, and thy heart, thou art a traitor—   136
False to thy gods, thy brother, and thy father,
Conspirant 'gainst this high-illustrious prince,
And from th'extremest upward of thy head   139
To the descent and dust below thy foot   140
A most toad-spotted traitor. Say thou no,   141
This sword, this arm, and my best spirits are bent   142
To prove upon thy heart, whereto I speak,
Thou liest.

---

77 **patrimony** inheritance   **78 the walls is thine** i.e., the citadel of my
heart and body surrenders completely to you.   **81 let-alone** prevent-
ing, denying   **82 Half-blooded** Only partly of noble blood, bastard
85 in thy attaint i.e., as partner in your corruption and as one who
has (unwittingly) provided the *attaint* or impeachment against you
89 banns public announcement of a proposed marriage.   **90 make . . .
me** i.e., sue to me for permission   **91 An interlude!** A play; i.e., you
are being melodramatic, or, what a farce this is!   **95 make** prove
96 in nothing less in no respect less guilty   **99 medicine** i.e., poison.
100 What Whoever   **106 single virtue** unaided prowess

113 **quality or degree** noble birth or rank. (Also in line 123.)
114 lists roster   **122 What** Who   **125 canker-bit** eaten as by the
caterpillar.   **127 cope** encounter.   **132 of mine honors** i.e., of my
knighthood   **133 profession** i.e., knighthood.   **134 Maugre** in spite
of   **135 victor** victorious.   **fire-new** newly minted   **136 heart**
courage   **139 upward** top   **140 descent** lowest extreme   **141 toad-
spotted** venomous, or having spots of infamy.   **Say thou** If you say
142 bent prepared

EDMUND   In wisdom I should ask thy name.   144
But since thy outside looks so fair and warlike,
And that thy tongue some say of breeding breathes,   146
What safe and nicely I might well delay   147
By rule of knighthood, I disdain and spurn.   148
Back do I toss those treasons to thy head,   149
With the hell-hated lie o'erwhelm thy heart,   150
Which—for they yet glance by and scarcely bruise—   151
This sword of mine shall give them instant way,   152
Where they shall rest forever.—Trumpets, speak!   153
                    [He draws.] Alarums. Fight. [Edmund falls.]
ALBANY [to Edgar]
Save him, save him!
GONERIL   This is practice, Gloucester.   154
By th' law of arms thou wast not bound to answer
An unknown opposite. Thou art not vanquished,
But cozened and beguiled.
ALBANY   Shut your mouth, dame,   157
Or with this paper shall I stopple it.—Hold, sir.   158
Thou worse than any name, read thine own evil.
                                 [He shows the letter.]
[To Goneril] No tearing, lady; I perceive you know it.
GONERIL
Say if I do, the laws are mine, not thine.
Who can arraign me for't?
ALBANY   Most monstrous! Oh!
Know'st thou this paper?
GONERIL   Ask me not what I know.
                                                       Exit.
ALBANY
Go after her. She's desperate; govern her.   164
                                   [Exit a soldier.]
EDMUND
What you have charged me with, that have I done,
And more, much more. The time will bring it out.
'Tis past, and so am I. But what art thou
That hast this fortune on me? If thou'rt noble,   168
I do forgive thee.
EDGAR   Let's exchange charity.   169
I am no less in blood than thou art, Edmund;
If more, the more th' hast wronged me.   171
My name is Edgar, and thy father's son.
The gods are just, and of our pleasant vices   173
Make instruments to plague us.
The dark and vicious place where thee he got   175

Cost him his eyes.
EDMUND   Th' hast spoken right. 'Tis true.
The wheel is come full circle; I am here.   177
ALBANY [to Edgar]
Methought thy very gait did prophesy
A royal nobleness. I must embrace thee.
                                   [They embrace.]
Let sorrow split my heart if ever I
Did hate thee or thy father!
EDGAR   Worthy prince, I know't.
ALBANY   Where have you hid yourself?
How have you known the miseries of your father?
EDGAR
By nursing them, my lord. List a brief tale,   185
And when 'tis told, oh, that my heart would burst!
The bloody proclamation to escape   187
That followed me so near—oh, our lives' sweetness,   188
That we the pain of death would hourly die   189
Rather than die at once!—taught me to shift   190
Into a madman's rags, t'assume a semblance
That very dogs disdained; and in this habit   192
Met I my father with his bleeding rings,   193
Their precious stones new lost; became his guide,   194
Led him, begged for him, saved him from despair;
Never—oh, fault!—revealed myself unto him
Until some half hour past, when I was armed.
Not sure, though hoping, of this good success,   198
I asked his blessing, and from first to last
Told him our pilgrimage. But his flawed heart—   200
Alack, too weak the conflict to support—
Twixt two extremes of passion, joy and grief,
Burst smilingly.
EDMUND   This speech of yours hath moved me,
And shall perchance do good. But speak you on;
You look as you had something more to say.
ALBANY
If there be more, more woeful, hold it in,
For I am almost ready to dissolve,   207
Hearing of this.
EDGAR   This would have seemed a period   208
To such as love not sorrow; but another,   209
To amplify too much, would make much more   210
And top extremity. Whilst I   211
Was big in clamor, came there in a man   212
Who, having seen me in my worst estate,
Shunned my abhorred society; but then, finding
Who 'twas that so endured, with his strong arms
He fastened on my neck and bellowed out

144 wisdom prudence   **146 say** smack, taste, indication   **147 safe and nicely** prudently and punctiliously   **148 I . . . spurn** i.e., I disdain to insist on my right to refuse combat with one of lower rank. **149 treasons . . . head** i.e., accusations of treason in your teeth **150 hell-hated** hated as hell is hated   **151 Which . . . bruise** i.e., which charges of treason—since as yet they merely glance off my armor and do no harm   **152 give . . . way** provide them an immediate pathway (to your heart)   **153 Where . . . forever** i.e., my victory in trial by combat will prove forever that the charges of treason apply to you.   **154 Save** Spare. (Albany wishes to spare Edmund's life so that he may confess and be found guilty.)   **practice** trickery, or (said sardonically) astute management   **157 cozened** tricked   **158 stopple** stop up.   **Hold, sir** (Addressed to Edgar or, more probably, Edmund.) **164 govern** restrain   **168 fortune on** victory over   **169 charity** forgiveness (for Edmund's wickedness toward Edgar and Edgar's having slain Edmund).   **171 th' hast** thou hast   **173 pleasant** pleasurable   **175 got** begot

177 The wheel . . . here (Alludes both to the wheel of fortune and to the idea of a completed circle whereby crime meets its appropriate punishment. Edmund sees that everything has at last come around to where it began.)   **185 List** Listen to   **187 The . . . escape** In order to escape the death-threatening proclamation   **188–90 oh . . . at once!** oh, the perversity of our attachment to our lives' sweetness, that we prefer to suffer continually the fear of death rather than die at once and be done with it!   **192 habit** garb   **193 rings** sockets   **194 stones** i.e., eyeballs   **198 success** outcome   **200 flawed** cracked   **207 dissolve** i.e., in tears   **208 a period** the limit   **209–11 but . . . extremity** i.e., but another sorrowful circumstance, adding to what is already too much, would increase it and exceed the limit.   **212 big in clamor** loud in my lamenting

As he'd burst heaven, threw him on my father,   217
Told the most piteous tale of Lear and him
That ever ear received, which in recounting
His grief grew puissant, and the strings of life   220
Began to crack. Twice then the trumpets sounded,
And there I left him tranced.

ALBANY   But who was this?   222

EDGAR
Kent, sir, the banished Kent, who in disguise
Followed his enemy king and did him service   224
Improper for a slave.

    Enter a Gentleman [with a bloody knife].

GENTLEMAN
Help, help, oh, help!

EDGAR   What kind of help?

ALBANY   Speak, man.

EDGAR
What means this bloody knife?

GENTLEMAN   'Tis hot, it smokes.   227
It came even from the heart of—Oh, she's dead!

ALBANY   Who dead? Speak, man.

GENTLEMAN
Your lady, sir, your lady! And her sister
By her is poisoned; she confesses it.

EDMUND
I was contracted to them both. All three
Now marry in an instant.

EDGAR   Here comes Kent.

    Enter Kent.

ALBANY
Produce the bodies, be they alive or dead.
                        [Exit Gentleman.]
This judgment of the heavens, that makes us tremble,
Touches us not with pity.—Oh, is this he?
[To Kent] The time will not allow the compliment   237
Which very manners urges.

KENT   I am come   238
To bid my king and master aye good night.   239
Is he not here?

ALBANY   Great thing of us forgot!
Speak, Edmund, where's the King? And where's
    Cordelia?
    Goneril and Regan's bodies [are] brought out.
See'st thou this object, Kent?   242

KENT   Alack, why thus?

EDMUND   Yet Edmund was beloved.
The one the other poisoned for my sake
And after slew herself.

ALBANY   Even so. Cover their faces.

EDMUND
I pant for life. Some good I mean to do,
Despite of mine own nature. Quickly send—
Be brief in it—to th' castle, for my writ
Is on the life of Lear and on Cordelia.
Nay, send in time.

ALBANY   Run, run, oh, run!

EDGAR
To who, my lord? Who has the office? *[To Edmund]*
    Send   253
Thy token of reprieve.

EDMUND   Well thought on. Take my sword. The captain!
Give it the Captain.

EDGAR   Haste thee, for thy life.
              [Exit one with Edmund's sword.]

EDMUND
He hath commission from thy wife and me
To hang Cordelia in the prison and
To lay the blame upon her own despair,
That she fordid herself.   260

ALBANY
The gods defend her! Bear him hence awhile.
                [Edmund is borne off.]

    Enter Lear, with Cordelia in his arms; [Captain].

LEAR
Howl, howl, howl! Oh, you are men of stones!
Had I your tongues and eyes, I'd use them so
That heaven's vault should crack. She's gone forever.
I know when one is dead and when one lives;
She's dead as earth. Lend me a looking glass;
If that her breath will mist or stain the stone,   267
Why, then she lives.

KENT   Is this the promised end?   268

EDGAR
Or image of that horror?

ALBANY   Fall and cease!   269

LEAR
This feather stirs; she lives! If it be so,
It is a chance which does redeem all sorrows
That ever I have felt.

KENT *[kneeling]*   O my good master!

LEAR
Prithee, away.

EDGAR   'Tis noble Kent, your friend.

LEAR
A plague upon you, murderers, traitors all!
I might have saved her; now she's gone forever!
Cordelia, Cordelia! Stay a little. Ha?
What is't thou say'st? Her voice was ever soft,
Gentle, and low, an excellent thing in woman.
I killed the slave that was a-hanging thee.

CAPTAIN
'Tis true, my lords, he did.

LEAR   Did I not, fellow?

---

217 **As** as if.   **threw . . . father** threw himself on my father's body
220 **His** i.e., Kent's.   **puissant** powerful.   **strings of life** heartstrings
222 **tranced** entranced, senseless.   **224 his enemy king** i.e., the king
who had rejected and banished him   **227 smokes** steams.   **237 compliment** ceremony   **238 Which . . . urges** which common courtesy
requires.   **239 aye good night** farewell forever. (Kent believes he
himself is near death, his heartstrings having begun to crack.)
242 object sight

253 **office** commission.   **260 fordid** destroyed   **267 stone** crystal or
polished stone of which the mirror is made   **268 Is . . . end?** (Kent
may mean "Is this what all our hopes have come to?" Edgar replies
by invoking the Last Judgment.)   **269 image** representation.   **Fall
and cease!** i.e., Let all things cease to be!

I have seen the day, with my good biting falchion   281
I would have made them skip. I am old now,
And these same crosses spoil me.—Who are you?   283
Mine eyes are not o'th' best; I'll tell you straight.   284
KENT
If Fortune brag of two she loved and hated,   285
One of them we behold.   286
LEAR
This is a dull sight. Are you not Kent?
KENT   The same,   287
Your servant Kent. Where is your servant Caius?   288
LEAR
He's a good fellow, I can tell you that;
He'll strike, and quickly too. He's dead and rotten.
KENT
No, my good lord, I am the very man—
LEAR   I'll see that straight.   292
KENT
That from your first of difference and decay   293
Have followed your sad steps—
LEAR   You are welcome hither.
KENT
Nor no man else. All's cheerless, dark, and deadly.   295
Your eldest daughters have fordone themselves,   296
And desperately are dead.
LEAR   Ay, so I think.   297
ALBANY
He knows not what he says, and vain is it
That we present us to him.
EDGAR   Very bootless.   299

Enter a Messenger.

MESSENGER   Edmund is dead, my lord.
ALBANY   That's but a trifle here.
You lords and noble friends, know our intent:
What comfort to this great decay may come   303

Shall be applied. For us, we will resign,   304
During the life of this old majesty,
To him our absolute power; [*to Edgar and Kent*] you, to
your rights,
With boot and such addition as your honors   307
Have more than merited. All friends shall taste
The wages of their virtue, and all foes
The cup of their deservings.—Oh, see, see!
LEAR
And my poor fool is hanged! No, no, no life?   311
Why should a dog, a horse, a rat have life,
And thou no breath at all? Thou'lt come no more,
Never, never, never, never, never!
Pray you, undo this button. Thank you, sir.
Do you see this? Look on her, look, her lips,
Look there, look there!   *He dies.*
EDGAR   He faints.—My lord, my lord!
KENT
Break, heart, I prithee, break!
EDGAR   Look up, my lord.
KENT
Vex not his ghost. Oh, let him pass! He hates him   319
That would upon the rack of this tough world   320
Stretch him out longer.
EDGAR   He is gone indeed.
KENT
The wonder is he hath endured so long.
He but usurped his life.
ALBANY
Bear them from hence. Our present business
Is general woe. [*To Kent and Edgar*] Friends of my soul,
you twain
Rule in this realm, and the gored state sustain.
KENT
I have a journey, sir, shortly to go.   327
My master calls me; I must not say no.
EDGAR
The weight of this sad time we must obey;
Speak what we feel, not what we ought to say.
The oldest hath borne most; we that are young
Shall never see so much nor live so long.   332
Exeunt, with a dead march.

281 **falchion** light sword   283 **crosses spoil me** adversities take away my strength.   284 **I'll . . . straight** I'll recognize you in a moment. 285–6 **If . . . behold** If Fortune were to brag of two persons whom she has subjected to the greatest fall from her favor into her hatred, Lear would have to be one of them.   287 **This . . . sight** i.e., My vision is clouding, or, this is a dismal spectacle.   288 **Caius** (Kent's disguise name.)   292 **see that straight** attend to that in a moment.   293 **from . . . decay** from the beginning of your quarrel (with Cordelia) to your decline of fortune   295 **Nor . . . else** No, not I nor anyone else, or, I am the *very man* (line 291), him and no one else.   296 **fordone** destroyed   297 **desperately** in despair   299 **bootless** in vain. 303 **What . . . come** i.e., whatever means of comforting this ruined king and state of affairs may present themselves

304 **For** As for   307 **With . . . honors** with advantage and such further distinctions or titles as your honorable conduct in this war 311 **poor fool** i.e., Cordelia. (*Fool* is here a term of endearment.) 319 **ghost** departing spirit.   320 **rack** torture rack. (With suggestion, in the Folio and Quarto spelling, "wracke," of shipwreck, disaster.) 327 **journey** i.e., to another world, to death   332.1 *Exeunt* (Presumably the dead bodies are borne out in procession.)

King Lear on Stage

The Elizabethan Era: The Open Stage

Richard Burbage played Lear when he was just under forty years of age and at the height of his powers. Robert Armin, the new comedian in Shakespeare's company, presumably would have played the Fool. In

a passage present only in the Quarto, the Fool calls himself "The one in motley here," suggesting that he may have been wearing the long patchwork coat that was the traditional livery of a fool in an aristocratic home. He must have had a coxcomb, an eared hood, which he could offer to Kent, and probably carried a stick with a carved head to point up his jokes and to mock Lear. In the first scene, a throne would no doubt have been placed on stage to signal the ceremonial nature of the scene, perhaps with banners or other emblems to define the place as that of the English court. Processions coming on stage and assembling in formal groups would have given visual substance to the tragedy's interplay of personal, political, and military forces. The Quarto printed text includes stage directions suggesting a processional entry by Lear's court with one actor bearing a coronet. Similarly when Cordelia and the forces of France, led by the King or Marshall of France, enter in the fourth and fifth acts, the pageantry of the army is plainly indicated in the text. A drum and colors would have signaled Cordelia's arrival. In the Jacobean playhouse, the tiring house façade was an emblem of order and degree; in exposing Lear to the storm outside, the chaos in his family, and the madness within, he was visually expelled from that order to discover himself as "Unaccommodated man" on the forestage.

The Seventeenth Century: Various Stagings and Nahum Tate's Long-lived Adaptation

When the London stage was re-established after the accession of Charles II, *King Lear* became the property of the Duke of York's Company and was performed, occasionally, in a version perhaps not to distant from what Shakespeare wrote. Yet the folk humor of the sort represented by the Fool may well have seemed old-fashioned and indecorous to the more "refined" tastes of Restoration coterie audiences. Nahum Tate's adaptation of *King Lear* (1681) answered to the new times by dispensing with the Fool and making the virtuous Cordelia a larger and more dramatic role, worthy, as Lois Potter puts it, "of a star actress" (in Bevington, A-65). Tate added a love interest between her and Edgar, and provided the happy ending that restored Lear to his throne. He also simplified the role of Edmund, centering that character's evil chiefly upon his predatory sexuality. Tate's Edmund pursued his gratification and died bragging that "rival queens" competed for him. Elizabeth Barry, one of the beautiful Restoration actresses so much admired by Colley Cibber, was the first Cordelia in Tate's adaptation; the banished daughter was represented as a young woman frequently suffering distress, agitation, fear, and dismay. All these emotions would have been visible in facial expressions in the smallish indoor theaters of the era. Tate's adaptation, which ended with Lear, Gloucester, and Kent retiring together to a "cool cell," remained in the repertory for one hundred and fifty years with amendments by George Coleman (1768), David Garrick (1773), and John Philip Kemble (1808). Dr. Samuel Johnson, who could not bear to see Cordelia die, defended Tate on the grounds that Shakespeare's tragic ending might be more true to life

but that "all reasonable beings naturally love justice." By "justice" Dr. Johnson meant tragic justice.

The Eighteenth Century: David Garrick and Others

As the structure of acting companies changed and actor-managers came to dominate theatrical practice, the plays changed as well, often becoming star vehicles rather than scripts for balanced ensembles. Tate's adaptation of *Lear* was performed throughout almost the entire eighteenth century, though in amended form with the Edgar-Cordelia love story backgrounded and Lear's role emphasized. That part became a test of a tragic actor's dimension as well as his emotional versatility. Actors stressed the great moments of Lear's rage, suffering, madness, and finally, pathos. Garrick attempted the role as a newcomer in 1742, then triumphed in it at Drury Lane for thirty years beginning in 1756. With Tate's plot retained, but its emphases shifted and much of Shakespeare's language restored, Lear became one of Garrick's most popular roles. Famed for his nimble, expressive features that delineated passions and probed human psychology in ways that, as Potter puts it, "he praised in Shakespeare and others praised in him," Garrick interpreted the part as an interplay of conflicting emotions. Contemporary observers, including William Hazlitt, noted the power of Garrick's curses. Lear knelt on the forestage close to the audience and delivered the invective in a mounting crescendo that culminated in "thankless child" and a burst of tears. With affecting pathos, Garrick moved his audiences to sympathize deeply with Lear's broken mind, his sufferings of thwarted love at the hands of his cruel daughters, and the fearful consequences of his own foolish relinquishing of power. Garrick attributed his success in these mad scenes to his study of the gestures and expressions of asylum inmates whose nature he claimed to have "copied."

With spoken drama limited to two theaters, Drury Lane and Covent Garden, after the Licensing Act of 1737, and these theaters increasing their audience capacity to as many as three thousand patrons during the late eighteenth century, styles of acting and presentation also changed to suit the new venues. John Philip Kemble and his sister Sarah Siddons, both tall and imposing, were the stars of the era, and Kemble was the quintessential actor-manager. He attempted to forge a unity from details of a production and used more historically accurate sets and costumes than had been previously attempted. Others who followed Garrick adopted similar techniques for building to emotional climaxes like operatic arias. Kemble, beginning in 1788, and Edmund Kean both performed Lear with great physical energy and anguished emotion, although

Kemble, appearing with Siddons as Cordelia, was considered too precise and stiff as compared with other actors who had better portrayed Lear's loss of control in the mad scenes. During this period, Kean attempted to restore the original ending of *King Lear*, in which the King dies over the body of his murdered daughter Cordelia. Audiences did not go along, however.

The Nineteenth Century: Victorian Morality and Domestic Tragedy

In 1838, William Charles Macready at Covent Garden was able to restore the Fool's role to the play, casting an actress in the role, as is sometimes done today. (Emma Thompson was the Fool in England's Renaissance Company production in 1990.) Macready himself was considered one of the few eminent Lears between Garrick and the twentieth century. Striving for both historical "accuracy" and spectacular effects, so that the play might educate and morally improve its audience, Macready created his approximation of the Anglo-Saxon period for sets and costumes. He was the first to introduce suggestions that the pagan context for the tragedy might be a Druid cult.

Both Macready and later Samuel Phelps in 1845 emphasized ensemble playing in their productions, thus diminishing the dominance of a star system that stressed certain "high points" rather than the natural arc of character development. The Duke of Saxe-Meiningen praised Phelps's staging of *Lear* in 1859 for its unity of impact. As a result, Phelps's representation of a coherent dramatic world inspired the formation (see Chapter 5) of the influential Meiningen Players.

Stage interpretations during this period downplayed the authority and stature of the King, emphasizing instead his plight as a rejected and despised father. *King Lear* became a domestic tragedy in which Lear himself was a pathological case study. The notion of presenting Shakespeare for moral improvement continued into Charles Kean's productions, with their massive sets. At the same time, scene changes during this period became so long and cumbersome that Kean had to cut the play heavily, dropping one-third of the text. Henry Irving further developed Macready's visual sense and Kean's historicism, creating for his *Lear* a setting shortly after the departure of the Romans from Britain, with Druid priests and barbaric warriors stalking the ruins. This 1892 staging required extensive cutting and arranging the text to stress Lear's doting fatherhood and his role as outraged patriarch. Irving calibrated the emotional dynamics of the play in order to make the reconciliation of father and daughter Cordelia, played by Ellen Terry, the emotional climax of the performance. She was reduced to tears, it was reported, by Irving's sensitive portrayal of the father

(TOPFOTO)

Artists schooled in the classical forms of India's Kathakali dance drama performed their adaptation of King Lear *at London's Globe Theater in July 1999. Pictured here are the threatening monarch (left) and his Fool.*

begging forgiveness. His Lear was so enfeebled and emotionally distressed that his loving daughter had to support him physically as he left the stage. This Lear was innocent of his own downfall and restored to love and peace by Cordelia. Yet despite all these attempts at moving interpretations, Irving's domesticated and sentimentalized *King Lear* was not a success, and fostered doubts that the tragedy was too difficult to stage.

The Twentieth Century: Redemption, Existentialism, and Archetypes

Reacting to Victorian spectacle, with its expensive and huge verisimilar sets that slowed and fragmented the action, a new generation of stage directors and designers began to stage the play against non-naturalistic backdrops that could be swiftly changed without interrupting the flow of the production. Charles Ricketts's designs for a 1909 Haymarket production drew upon the symbolic effect of large primitive structures, placing the tragedy in a megalithic environment of dark, stony objects. In this context of visual primitivism, *King Lear* was newly canonized by Harley Granville-Barker in his

"Preface" as an actable and relevant work of vibrantly theatrical imagination, filled with universal truths. Edgar became a "Christian gentleman" in a tale of pilgrimage toward redemption. By stressing this mythic, archetypal journey, redemptive readings of the play transcended the harrowing, unjust deaths at the end. Cordelia became a symbol of divine love and Lear a Job figure who achieved the peace that passeth understanding. Laurence Olivier at the Old Vic (in 1946) and John Gielgud (at Stratford-upon-Avon and touring throughout the 1950s) drew upon this tradition in two of the most talked-about interpretations in the immediate aftermath of World War II. The play was now considered the greatest of Shakespeare's tragedies—an assessment that has endured even when darkly pessimistic readings of the play became cultural currency in the 1960s.

As noted earlier, the existential writings of Samuel Beckett and the critical ideas of Jan Kott shaped the famously bleak 1962 production of *King Lear* by director Peter Brook (later, a 1971 film with Paul Scofield). Brook saw the old King of this play as belonging to a harsh world in which nothing is achieved other than through violence. Another dynamic in stagings after the mid-twentieth century has been to characterize the Fool according to contemporary images of clowning and to accord him a close identification with the old King, as in Grigori Kozintsev's film. Adrian Noble cast Antony Sher as a red-nosed, grotesquely lame clown crouching behind the throne, dominating and coaching the king in his responses. In this version Lear (Michael Gambon) accidentally killed the Fool at the end of the mock trial of the evil daughters. Both Lear and this Fool established a close relationship with the audience; thus Noble questioned whether any hierarchical grandeur and dignity was left to post-Imperial Britain.

Gielgud studied the role of Lear under Granville-Barker and played the part in several different productions, beginning in 1950. Reviewers frequently singled out his moving colloquy with Gloucester (4.6) and the recognition scene with Cordelia (4.7). His 1955 appearances in the so-called "Noguchi *Lear*" were problematic; Japanese sculptor Isamu Noguchi, who designed so often for modern dance choreographer Martha Graham, created the starkly beautiful but unwieldy costumes and an incongruous symbolic décor. Neither Gielgud nor anyone else on the artistic or technical staff dared to criticize the costumes or the props. Another noteworthy Lear was Morris Carnovsky, praised for his potent and moving interpretation during 1963 and 1965 seasons at the Shakespeare Festival in Stratford, Connecticut.

King Lear on Film and Video

King Lear has inspired more than twenty film adaptations, two of these silent, and a half-dozen regular productions filmed for television. The first film, starring William V. Ranous in 1909, was one of more than a dozen silent classics by Ranous and director J. Stuart Blackton, including *Othello* and *Macbeth*. Five varying film treatments, Akira Kurosawa's great samurai adaptation *Ran*, and several spin-offs are described here in some detail. They show the remarkable malleability of the play as a fable for our times.

- 1970—Director Grigori Kozintsev, Lenfilm, with Yuri Yarvet (Lear), Karl Sebris (Gloucester), Valentina Shendrikova (Cordelia), Elze Radzinya (Goneril), Galina Volchek (Regan), Reigimantas Adomaitis (Edmund), Oleg Dal (the Fool), Vladimir Yemelyanov (Kent), and Roman Gromadsky (Edgar). (137 min.)

This superbly paced, epic interpretation of the play opens with a long, ceremonial procession of peasants journeying across rocky hills toward Lear's castle; in the background, the Fool's melancholy flute is heard. The Fool is seen as an intimate part of the King himself. First viewed poking his shaved head out from under the folds of Lear's cloak, actor Oleg Dal's Fool suggests the inversion of royal wisdom and clownish folly that will affect not only a family but an entire kingdom. After the love test, Lear (Yuri Yarvet, frail rather than authoritative) tears the map of his kingdom and banishes Cordelia (the exceptionally poised and beautiful Valentina Shendrikova). The howling and braying of animals effectively connote the beast in man. Wolves howl as Edmund tricks his brother into fleeing. When Lear is cast into the storm, he runs across a barren plain where wolves, bears, and boars roam with him. The violence is explicit when Cornwall gouges Gloucester's eye out with a spur. Kozintsev's interpretation has been aptly dubbed an example of Christian Marxism, because love, at last, overrides suffering, and the audience is always aware of the dialectic linking personal, political, and social history. Yarvet's sad face becomes iconic as he crawls among the grasses, picks flowers, gnaws roots, and learns that he is not all in all. The social and political context is always apparent, from the slow ceremonial procession at the outset to the fleeing of refugees from the war, both supported by Shostakovich's swelling orchestral music. Lear meets blind Gloucester before the King is found by Cordelia's soldiers. The Fool plays the flute here, his music helping to heal and restore Lear, while in the background Edmund is sowing chaos as the people run from his advancing troops. Kozintsev eliminates Gloucester's attempted suicide at Dover, substituting instead a touching scene in which Gloucester, staggering on with Poor Tom, suffers a seizure; reaching out, he feels the beggar's face and recognizes Edgar, and then dies, having been restored to his beloved son. Kozintsev intensifies Lear's horrible suffering by showing Cordelia hanging from a hallway arch, then Lear in despair, howling over her body. The Fool is with him, weeping, still playing his flute. The peasants who survive to clear the chaos are emblematic of social continuity and a restored political stability. Edgar simply looks at the camera, then walks away.

- 1971—Director Peter Brook, Filmways/Athena, with Paul Scofield (Lear), Anne-Lise Gabold (Cordelia), Jack MacGowran (the Fool), Alan Webb (Gloucester), Irene Worth (Goneril), Susan Engel (Regan), Cyril Cusack (Albany), Patrick Magee (Cornwall), and Tom Fleming (Kent). (137 min.)

Brook's *King Lear* has a raw, grainy, sometimes brutal look. It is stripped of visual beauty and verbal variety, as if this production were an outcry against poetic eloquence, conventional film spectacle, and redemptive readings of the play. The film begins in silence as the camera pans over a crowd of men outside the castle, then cuts to Lear on his throne in a tomb-like room. The exteriors are just as bleak, with wintry landscapes and frozen ground over which carriages rumble and Lear and his knights ride. No music ameliorates the stark scene. The chill is everywhere; characters again and again huddle near fireplaces. The Edmund and Edgar plot is minimized. To heighten further the nihilism of the ending, Edmund's sudden turn toward good and his attempt to save Lear and Cordelia are eliminated. (In Brook's 1953 television production with Orson Welles, Gloucester's two sons are excised completely.) The dominant images are of cold and cruelty. Kent is set in the stocks, barefoot in the cold. Edgar evades soldiers and disfigures himself to affect his transformation to Poor Tom by rubbing snow on his chest. Lear and the Fool are pummeled by wind and rain.

The blinding of Gloucester and the many murders are unusually savage. Regan bludgeons a servant to death. Edgar kills Edmund with an ax without a hint of the chivalry that usually distinguishes this as a scene from romance. Goneril and Regan's heads are fractured on rocks. Cordelia is seen being hanged. In keeping with this atmosphere, Paul Scofield's Lear is an implacable despot, arrogant and rigid, old and weary. Speaking in a flat monotone, he seems wildly driven from place to place, hounded by pride and shame at his own foolishness. The nonrealistic storm scenes are especially effective as a broken wheel forces Lear to descend unprotected from his carriage into the storm. Lightning flashes and thunderbolts illumine close-ups of the King and his Fool in watery soft-focus as the wind howls and discordant music and sounds screech. Hallucinatory images recur as

Brook superimposes the faces of the Fool upon Lear's, or shows the faces of the wicked daughters as Lear "tries" them in his mock court. The only elements of pathos that remain in Brook's film surround the treatment of Gloucester. Once he is blinded and moaning in a terrible pain that is exacerbated by Regan's cruel revelation that Edmund has betrayed him, a servant cracks an egg open to salve Gloucester's bleeding eye sockets. The pathos becomes almost unbearably tender in the meeting of the blind man and the mad King on the gravel shore at Dover, where their faces—in close-up and brightly lit—seem monumental and serene. A short time afterwards, Lear returns to this beach carrying his dead daughter. Kneeling with her body, he slowly falls backward into death, leaving only a blank, the void. In keeping with Jan Kott's interpretation and Brook's vision of *King Lear*, there is no redemption, no transcendence in this film, which is also cut and edited to create rough, almost violent transitions.

- 1982—Director Jonathan Miller, BBC, with Michael Hordern (Lear), Frank Middlemass (the Fool), John Shrapnel (Kent), Norman Rodway (Gloucester), Gillian Barge (Goneril), Penelope Wilton (Regan), Brenda Blethyn (Cordelia), Julian Curry (Cornwall), Michael Kitchen (Edmund), and Anton Lesser (Edgar). (160 min.)

Miller's production was based upon a widely acclaimed two-hour version of the play for the BBC's Play of the Month series that had been telecast in 1975 shortly before the start of the entire thirty-seven–play BBC series. When Miller then became producer of the series, he urged the BBC to include that 1975 *Lear* as part of the overall plan. Even though the corporation insisted upon a new staging, Miller essentially "remounted his 1975 production and its interpretation, using more of the text but the same leading actors for Lear and the Fool, the same costume and design concepts, even some of the same blocking and characterization" (Susan Willis, 127). Perhaps because they are playing the Fool and Lear for the third time, Middlemass and Hordern give to their scenes together an exceptional intimacy and emotion. Similar in age, these two figures share a long relationship capable of surviving the Fool's bitter provocations of his rash master. The costuming is late Renaissance, as it presumably was in Shakespeare's day. The look is monochromatic, with subtle contrasts between shades of black, gray, and white. As in his televising of *Antony and Cleopatra*, *Othello*, and *King Lear*, Miller explores certain design principles based on Renaissance art and theatrical practice. *Lear*, with a simple nonrepresentational set, shows at its best Miller's exploration of a simple wooden platform as a stage. Here he applies what series chronicler Susan Willis has called a "plank-and-drape approach" to an entire production. Both interior and exterior scenes are shot on or near the platform, with a plain cycloramic curtain and dark fabric spread over the studio floor. This simplicity of decoration leads to some exquisite visual subtleties, including the differences in costume distinguishing Cordelia from her wicked sisters. Cordelia wears a transparent wimple-like cap in the first scene and in the last a coronet that seems a stylized crown of thorns. Miller conceives the play as a spiritual journey—not just for Lear, but also for Gloucester and for the oft-disguised Edgar. Michael Hordern's Lear is a dreadfully self-centered man, unused to being defied as either a father or a king, yet harshly scolded by his sadly wise Fool. From the Fool and from painful experience, Lear learns what it is to become an ordinary man. Edgar, as Poor Tom, dons a crown of thorns and becomes a Christ figure, the very image of suffering humanity. Since little text has been cut for this three-and-a-half hour production, it reveals the full symphonic structure of the tragedy.

■ 1983—Director Michael Elliott with Laurence Olivier, Granada Television, with Colin Blakeley (Kent), Leo McKern (Gloucester), Anna Calder-Marshall (Cordelia), Diana Rigg (Regan), Dorothy Tutin (Goneril), Robert Lindsay (Edmund), David Threlfall (Edgar), and John Hurt (the Fool). (130 min.)

This production is often called the Stonehenge *King Lear*, since its opening and final scenes take place in a ninth-century circle of stones or "henge" like those at the much older Stonehenge. Production designer Roy Stonehouse created the settings for the studio-shot production in such a way as to fulfill director Elliott's wish for a world of "primeval Time, a world of mists and fogs" (Isenberg, 2). Most shots are tight, with a preponderance of close-ups, and much awkward editing and obtrusive cutting. Laurence Olivier, who had first played Lear in 1946 at the age of thirty-nine with a cast that included Alec Guinness as the Fool and Margaret Leighton as Regan, was seventy-five years old when he essayed the role for the last time in this Granada television broadcast. He knew he was terminally ill with cancer (although he would not die until some six years later), and agreed to a demanding three-week taping schedule, paced according to his somewhat weakened condition, at the Manchester RTV Centre. His white-bearded Lear is accordingly a benevolent and frail figure at first; when he rouses himself to vengeful anger at Cordelia for her refusal to flatter him as he wishes, one can see that he is call-

ing on every last ounce of energy at his disposal. Verging on senility, he must struggle to keep his mind from wandering.

Elliott and Olivier have "trimmed" the play to just over two hours, combining Lear's retainers, for instance, into a single knight. Three complete scenes are cut (3.1, 4.3, and 4.4), in order to emphasize Lear's aged irascibility as he attempts to cope with the changes that are coming upon him. Elliott adds wordless visual elements such as the entrance of Edmund and Edgar on horseback, and emphasizes other visual images over verbal ones as well. Most memorably, he shows Olivier's vulnerable Lear asleep on the ground with flowers in his long hair as he slowly awakes and emerges into sanity again. John Hurt makes a mercurial Fool, full of affection for his master. The text is "shaped" to allow Lear to die happily. Thinking he sees Cordelia alive during their final intensely private moments, he lies down to die beside her on the platform that bore his throne in the opening scene.

■ 1998—Director Richard Eyre, National Theatre of Great Britain, with Ian Holm (Lear), David Burke (Kent), Timothy West (Gloucester), Michael Grant (the Fool), Paul Rhys (Edgar), Finbar Lynch (Edmund), Barbara Flynn (Goneril), Amanda Redman (Regan), Victoria Hamilton (Cordelia), and David Lyon (Albany).

This television production, adapted from Richard Eyre's staging of *King Lear* for the National Theatre of Great Britain, was aired on the BBC and in the United States on Mobil Masterpiece Theatre. Influenced scenically by Brook's landmark *A Midsummer Night's Dream*, the staging uses vivid, monochromatic settings—a great red room, a red table and chairs for the opening scenes, for instance, and a plain, brightly lit white one for the mysterious confrontation of the dark knight Edgar and Edmund toward the end. Costumes are simple and timeless. Like Brook, Eyre emphasizes character, contrasting the castle world where Lear has once ruled with outdoor scenes. Those scenes begin (on a cue from Gloucester) with an eclipse of the moon and move on to the intense storms on the heath and at Dover. The simplicity of concept also allows Eyre and his actors to delineate character strongly in many close-ups; very often the focus is upon the listener rather than the speaker, framing subtle reactions. Eyre frequently employs voice-overs, especially for the villain Edmund, whose solo speeches are occasionally transposed to scenes with others; his words play as thoughts while Goneril and Albany, for instance, are speaking of other matters. Holm masterfully moves from volatility through madness towards exhaustion and serenity. He combines the near manic energy of the forgetful Lear with the clear denial of his age and responsibilities. Though on the verge of senility, he roars defiantly at his ungrateful daughters, and later appears angelically composed once the doctor and Cordelia have ministered to him. He humbly recognizes the daughter he has misjudged, and with her tearful help embraces a new state—beyond the reach of the powerful. Lear's Fool is nearly as old as he, and as nimble. When the Fool disappears after the hovel scene, Lear enters wearing the Fool's perky hat. In one of the film's many seemingly spontaneous gestures, Holm's Lear kisses the hat when the King says, "we cry that we are come / To this great stage of fools." Interpretively, Eyre's vision is neither redemptive nor nihilistic. Without sentimentality, Holm creates an empathetic old Lear, truly a man "More sinned against than sinning," a powerful man whose all too human weakness has destroyed him.

Adaptations

■ 1985—*Ran*. Director Akira Kurosawa, with Tatsuya Nakadai (Lord Hidetora Ichimonji), Akira Terao (Taro Takatora Ichimonji), Daisuke Ryu (Saburo Naotora Ichimonji), Mieko Harada (Lady Kaede), Yoshiko Miyazaki (Lady Sué), Peter (Kyoami), Hisashi Igawa (Shuri Kurogane), Masayuki Yui (Tango Hirayama), Mansai Nomura (Tsurumaru), Norio Matsui (Shumenosuke Ogura), Toshiya Ito (Mondo Naganuma), and Kenji Kodama (Samon Shirane). (140 min.)

Shot in breathtaking color, with a stylization often exquisite in its beauty, Akira Kurosawa's epic vision of *King Lear* translates Shakespeare's words into dazzling spectacle set in sixteenth-century Japan. *Ran* unfolds on vivid green mountain slopes and wide volcanic plains where feuding factions ride into battle in color-coded battalions, as rival sons humiliate their Lear-like father Hidetora, while the malignant Lady Kaede moves implacably toward her revenge. Created nearly thirty years after his *Macbeth* film *Throne of Blood*, Kurosawa's *Lear* adaptation restructures several elements of the play to emphasize the theme of violence perpetuating itself across generations, then boomeranging back to destroy both the perpetrator and the prize that Hidetora has so ruthlessly sought. The violent conquests of the house of Ichimonji in the film also stand in for the disastrous imperial ambitions of modern Japan in Manchuria and elsewhere. Not the least of the film's strengths is the facility with which Ran adapts the Lear story to Japanese politics and culture.

Kurosawa makes the most monstrous source of evil in the film a woman, Lady Kaede. She is married to the eldest of Hidetora's three sons, Taro. Kurosawa's Lear, Hidetora, has come into his power as Great Lord through a series of brutal wars in which Lady Kaede's father and brothers, among many others, have been killed. By showing no mercy, Hidetora has gained control of three castles on the plain overlooked by towering mountains. In the opening scenes, Hidetora and his retinue are hunting wild boar, and, as the old Lord rises in his saddle and pulls back on his bow, the image freezes while the movie's title emerges: "Ran" or in English, "Chaos."

Cordelia and the virtuous ideals she represents are split between two characters. The first is Hidetora's blunt, youngest son Saburo (Daisuke Ryu), who questions the father's foolish decision to divide the kingdom by giving one castle to each of his sons, placing fullest authority in the eldest, Taro. Saburo demonstrates the hollowness of sentiment in his father's speech about three arrows being unbreakable if, like the brothers, they act together as one. Saburo breaks the three arrows, thereby forecasting the fraternal discord that will follow. The female Cordelia figure is Sué, the wife of the second son, Jiro. Though she is the daughter of one of Hidetora's former enemies, she has forgiven the past and has cared for her gentle flute-playing brother, Tsurumaru, an amalgam of Gloucester and Edgar. Tsurumaru has been blinded by Hidetora out of fear for the boy's potential to challenge his authority.

Kurosawa transposes other elements from the Gloucester-Edmund-Edgar plot to create a story different from Shakespeare's, yet similar in its exploration of old age and the disintegration of familial and political bonds. Jiro encourages his lieutenant Kurogane to kill Jiro's own brother, Taro. As the tide of savagery washes over the land, Kurosawa creates one harrowing battle after another. Nobles readily betray their lords and mislead Hidetora, as Jiro becomes a puppet manipulated by the snakelike erotic power of Lady Kaede. She exploits her knowledge of Jiro's murder of his brother to blackmail him. She demands that Sué be murdered as well, and that Sué's head be brought to her and Jiro. Kurogane returns instead with the head of an animal statue, a fox, symbolically suggestive of Lady Kaede's sly wickedness. Sué, by contrast, is a paragon of virtue; although her house has also been destroyed by the Ichimonji family, her belief in the Buddha remains unshaken. Of these two starkly contrasting female characters, Marianne McDonald writes as follows: "We never find a woman who is complex (in Kurosawa). In Kurosawa's films, camaraderie is impossible between a woman and a man. Woman is considered to be intellectually as well as morally inferior to the man, reaching the summit only in her capacity for evil. The sainthood of Lady Sué is a sainthood of renunciation" (McDonald, 2).

The devastation at the end is no less than apocalyptic. When Sué visits her blind brother, she finds him living, like Poor Tom, in a hovel like an animal. Hidetora too has seen this specter from his past and has heard the haunting sounds of Tsurumaru's Noh flute—sounds that drive the old lord into madness. Wishing to guide her brother to the safety of the good Saburo's party, Sué must leave him briefly to retrieve the flute he has left behind, giving him an image of the Buddha to protect him. Once she has done so, instead of returning alive, her headless corpse appears clutching the flute in her hand, while her servant lies slain nearby. Gory as these images undoubtedly are, they become beautiful in their own way, and are even more so as battles are fought from horseback with guns and arrows. When Lady Kaede is slaughtered, her blood spurts like a geyser to stain bright red an elegant white shoji screen.

Hidetora miraculously avoids death during these skirmishes only to face an ending even more apocalyptic than Lear's. Wandering out of the burning castle, surrounded by bleeding and dead warriors, he is a figure of ruined majesty whose presence parts the battling soldiers as Moses did the Red Sea. Reunited at last with Saburo, the two of them riding one horse together, Hidetora whispers of his longing to converse with this loving son once they have reached their destination. In that very moment of hope, Saburo is shot and falls forward on the horse, leaving the horrified and bereft Hidetora to die of a broken heart.

The blind Tsurumaru becomes an especially important iconic figure at the film's end. Alone and helpless, he is pictured on the edge of a precipice, silhouetted against the sunset. The vastness of the space around him, and our knowledge that he is unable to see where he is going, create a starkly eloquent image of man alone in an unsympathetic universe. As Kurosawa's camera slowly tracks away, the harsh, stony environment further dwarfs this isolated human figure. He now seems wholly abandoned by the gods, if one can even suppose them to exist. As Kurosawa has told his biographer Aldo Tassone, this ending is meant as a warning to man standing on the edge of the existential void "not to count on the consoling image of a protecting god. If one continues stupidly to look for happiness in strife and in war rather than in harmony or peace, why should heaven intervene to save us from our stupidity?" (283).

Spin-offs

Stage Play

- 1971—*Lear*. Playwright Edward Bond, The Royal Court.

English playwright Edward Bond has rewritten Shakespeare's tragedy in order, as he says, to explore the play "for our time, for our problems." Bond rejects what he calls the "vicious trivialities of the culture of the Absurd," emphasizing instead the violence that shapes our contemporary world in its obsession with destruction. Here, in this epic play influenced by Brecht, all relationships fall apart: Cordelia (who is not Lear's daughter) survives rape and her husband's savage death only to create a new state government as oppressive as Lear's. Because he views Shakespeare as an authoritarian writer, Bond subverts the tragedy by showing that the state itself is the source of cruelty and oppression. Having considered the possibility of dispensing with the King completely and focusing upon the three sisters, Bond has chosen instead to create a despotic Lear who has coerced his enslaved workers into building a wall that he hopes will keep out the enemies of the state. When his daughters Bodice and Fontenelle rebel and wage war against him, Lear is forced to flee, finding safety in the house of a gravedigger's helper. This pastoral interlude is destroyed when soldiers arrive to kill the gravedigger's helper and rape his wife, named Cordelia. She emerges from this brutality determined to lead the opposition against Bodice and Fontenelle. During the inevitable civil war that follows, Cordelia becomes herself a tyrant, comparable in Bond's view to Josef Stalin. Violence spreads to all levels of society. Lear's eyes are removed with more technological efficiency than are Gloucester's in Shakespeare's play.

Like Lear, Bond's King evolves through his madness into some understanding of the nature of the world and of both personal and political relationships. Resolving to take some action in the world as he now apprehends it, Lear commences to tear down the wall with his hands, but is soon shot and killed. The political impact of this retelling of the Lear story is extraordinarily trenchant, even if the writer cancels any possibility of a catharsis or redemptive uplift at the end. Though the wall still stands, Lear finds he must question the validity of his own impulses toward isolation in the name of national security. Many critics have inevitably compared Bond's wall to the Berlin Wall, although events of the twenty-first century have also made clear the play's potency as a larger symbol of division and strife. Pity is the only antidote to madness in Bond's nightmarish world, although even characters of compassion and pity cannot put an end to the play's endless cycle of civil war.

Films

■ 1988—*King Lear: Fear and Loathing*. Director Jean-Luc Godard, Golan/Globus, with Norman Mailer, Woody Allen, Burgess Meredith, Molly Ringwald, Jean-Luc Godard, and Peter Sellars. (92 min.)

In his edgy exploration of themes from Shakespeare's play, the innovative French filmmaker Jean-Luc Godard also charts the demise of his studio-funded project to adapt *King Lear* to a Mafia context. "They're losing confidence in us," Godard says in a voice-over at the beginning of the movie. Nonetheless, he announces, "We are shooting, we are shooting." The first few scenes are multiple takes featuring American novelist Norman Mailer and his real-life daughter. They talk on the telephone, read from a script, and breakfast on the terrace of a posh hotel. They play both themselves in these scenes and also are slated to play the Lear and Cordelia figures in Godard's ill-fated project. Insistent placards on the screen inform us that the film now has a new title: "A Picture Shot in the Back." This is because Godard's studio, The Cannon Group, has decided to withdraw funding from this big-budget film project for financial reasons. Godard has accordingly chosen to feature this betrayal by his studio as a central element of his now-altered film. When, after one day of shooting, the Mailers leave, the remainder of the movie becomes a characteristically disruptive, relentlessly enigmatic film with Burgess Meredith and Molly Ringwald now in the roles of Lear and Cordelia. Also on hand is the *avant-garde* director Peter Sellars, cast in the role of William Shakespeare Jr. V, by way of acknowledging his controversial *auteur* productions of theater and opera classics. Always jotting down notes, Sellars's Shakespeare V steals conversations from the Mafia Lear (Meredith), called Don Learo, and from the Cordelia figure (Ringwald). When Shakespeare V overhears the father talking to his daughter about his dividing his kingdom to unburden himself, Shakespeare V writes the dialogue down to use in his own work, thus raising questions about authorship, originality, ownership of intellectual property, and the authority of the text. Sellars follows the pair into the woods, where the daughter takes dictation on the Las Vegasization of all American art and life, while a man and woman alternately speak philosophical passages from Shakespeare's play in beautifully delivered voice-overs.

Filmmaker Woody Allen appears in a jumble of later scenes involving huge piles of celluloid film and the theme of editing history from such chaos. Intercut images of film and theater icon Orson Welles (who at one time was going to play Godard's Lear) remind viewers of Welles's own appropriation and reworking of Shakespearean material on stage (his Voodoo *Macbeth*) and screen (*Falstaff: Chimes at Midnight*). As he layers more and more allusions in his disrupted story, Godard refers to the history of Shakespeare on film with stills of Orson Welles and shots of a character named for Russian film director Grigori Kozintsev (see above, pp. 760–761). The final scenes, shot in bright white light on a rocky beach, evoke Peter Brook's famous *King Lear* film with Paul Scofield. Cordelia's "body" lies on a rock while Don Learo looks out to sea. In the multiple quick cuts that form a kind of epilogue, we see a horse running, Woody Allen's face, and a placard reading "King Lear: A Study" before the sudden blackout. The film is precisely that, a "study," not a full-scale adaptation. Like many of Godard's films, *King Lear: Fear and Loathing* comments self-reflexively upon itself and upon the difficulty of creating film art in a crassly commercial movie culture.

■ 1998—*The King Is Alive*. Director Kristian Levring, IFC Films, with Jennifer Jason Leigh, David Bradley, Miles Anderson, Janet McTeer, Peter Kubheka, David Calder, and Lia Williams. (98 min.)

In this well-acted, life-imitates-art independent film, a group of stranded desert travelers rehearse and perform many scenes from *King Lear*, while their lives begin to parallel elements of the play's action. A bus driver, trying to navigate with a broken compass, has taken them hundreds of miles away from their destination, and, when they run out of gas at a long-abandoned mining village, their desperation brings out the worst in some of them; the lecherous and self-deceiving Charles (David Calder), for instance, reminds us of Edmund, while an unhappily married wife (Janet McTeer) resembles Regan. To halt their further disintegration, a former actor named Henry (David Bradley) writes out all the roles he can remember from Shakespeare's *King Lear*, assigning each of the characters a part in the tragedy, typecasting as he does so. He senses incompatible marriages and sexual frustration in the women to whom he gives the roles of Goneril and Regan, and a crazy intuitive wisdom in Amanda (Lia Williams) to whom he assigns the Fool's role. In a reversal of expectation, he gives the role of Cordelia to a sexy, devil-may-care young American Gina (Jennifer Jason Leigh), who appears to have been a prostitute or lap dancer. The female French intellectual to whom he first offered the role has refused. As Gina becomes closer to Henry, with his generous artistic spirit, the French woman plots revenge. Bradley takes an effectively restrained approach to his delivery of Lear's speeches, even his most passionate lines.

An Arab storyteller who lives quietly alone on the outpost narrates the tale of this multinational group of travelers, who "ate less every day, but said more words—though not to each other." Among the themes director Levring and co-screenwriter Anders Thomas Jensen explore are the corrosive effects of lust, the place of art as surrogate communication, and the power of theater to heal anxiety, transform hostility, and calm the fear of death. Several stylized scenes are especially memorable. One group of characters seem like timeless pilgrims as they trudge hand-in-hand over a sand dune and then through an immense sand storm to find and bury the body of Jack, the man who earlier set out to find aid for them. The Cordelia figure, Gina, dies, apparently poisoned by her French rival for David's affection. When Charles's arrogance and lechery are exposed, he hangs himself. The other tourists, having come to terms with their fates and with one another, are close to death when they are at last rescued. They have glimpsed both the worst and the best in themselves during their terrifying adventure.

■ 1998—*A Thousand Acres*. Director Jocelyn Moorhouse, Touchstone, with Jason Robards (Larry), Jessica Lange (Ginny), Michelle Pfeiffer (Rose), Jennifer Jason Leigh (Caroline), Colin Firth (Jess Clark), Keith Carradine (Ty Smith), Kevin Anderson (Peter Lewis). (105 min.)

This commercial film is an adaptation of Jane Smiley's novel of the same title, which was itself inspired by the Lear story. A tyrannical Iowa farmer, Larry Cook (played by Robards), decides for tax reasons to transfer his land to his daughters. When the youngest daughter, Caroline, questions the wisdom of this transaction, Larry disowns her. As he sinks into alcoholism and madness, Ginny and Rose quarrel, losing both their husbands and the land. Caroline, having moved away to the city to become an attorney, joins with her father in a suit to reclaim the farm. As the case proceeds, we learn more and more about Larry's incestuous relationships with his two older daughters, with the result that Ginny and Rose become sympathetic broken characters. Unfortunately, in the process of compressing Smiley's epic, Pulitzer Prize–winning novel into a very short span, the film excises nuances of character development and produces instead a plodding soap-opera plot crammed full with adultery, illness, betrayal, and mawkish narration. Yet despite these disappointments (the film was not as well received as the novel), some performances are commendable and even engrossing. Many of the *Lear* parallels in this decidedly downbeat film remain striking.

References and Related Reading

Blau, Herbert. *The Impossible Theater: A Manifesto*. New York, 1964.

Bratton, J. S. *Plays in Performance: "King Lear."* Bristol, 1987.

Buhler, Stephen. *Shakespeare in the Cinema: Ocular Proof*. Albany, N.Y., 2002.

Cavell, Stanley, "The Avoidance of Love: A Reading of *King Lear*." *Shakespeare: "King Lear," a Casebook*. Ed. Frank Kermode. New York, 1992.

Foakes, R. A. The Arden Shakespeare: *King Lear*. Surrey, Eng., 1997.

Howard, Tony. "When Peter Met Orson: The 1953 CBS King Lear." *Shakespeare: The Movie*. Eds. Lynda E. Boose and Richard Burt. London and New York, 1997. 121–134.

Jorgens, Jack. *Shakespeare on Film*. Bloomington, Ind., 1977.

Kott, Jan. *Shakespeare: Our Contemporary*. Trans. Boleslaw Taborski. Preface by Peter Brook. London, 1965.

Kozintsev, Grigori. *Shakespeare: Time and Conscience*. Trans. Joyce Veining. New York, 1966.

Lizard, James P., and June Schuster. *Reading Shakespeare in Performance: "King Lear."* London and Toronto, 1990.

McDonald, Marianne. "The Construction of Literature—Formation of Literary Culture." Unpublished lecture. ICLA, Tokyo, 1991.

Muir, Kenneth, ed. The Arden Shakespeare: *King Lear*. Cambridge, Mass., 1953.

Potter, Lois. "Shakespeare in Performance." *The Complete Works of Shakespeare*. 5th ed. Ed. David Bevington. New York, 2004. A62–73.

Rosenberg, Marvin. *The Masks of Shakespeare*. Berkeley, 1972.

Rothwell, Kenneth S. "In Search of Nothing: Mapping *King Lear*." *Shakespeare: The Movie*. Eds. Lynda E. Boose and Richard Burt. London and New York, 1997. 135–147.

Tassone, Aldo. *Akira Kurosawa*. Paris, 1983/90.

CHAPTER 18

Macbeth

c. 1606

Context and Dating: Spiritual Evil and the Drama of Conscience in the "Scottish" Play

Macbeth, Shakespeare's "most profound and mature vision of evil" (Knight, 140), is the last of his four great tragedies to confront such spiritual darkness. The play is filled with bloody acts; in fact, "blood" is mentioned more times in this relatively short tragedy than in any other play in the canon. In one of the most pessimistic speeches uttered by a major Shakespearean character, the protagonist concludes that life is a mere "tale / Told by an idiot, full of sound and fury, / Signifying nothing" (5.5.26–28). Whereas we can readily appreciate the heroic stature of Shakespeare's other tragic protagonists, we are challenged to summon the same feelings for Macbeth that we invest in Hamlet, Othello, and Lear. Still, the play has always been among Shakespeare's most popular, and its central roles for Macbeth and his wife remain irresistible challenges for actors, though, curiously, few have actually made their reputations with this play. Directors are drawn to its exceptional visual possibilities—the witches, the violent murders, and the thrilling climax in which Macbeth fights to the death with his nemesis, Macduff. Audiences have long enjoyed the play's theatricality and its vivid investigation of horror. *Macbeth* and *Richard III* were the most performed plays in the gold mining camps of California. Ultimately, audiences are drawn to *Macbeth's* portrait of a man who looks evil in the face as few have dared to do. Although he commits heinous deeds, Macbeth does not represent consummate evil; rather he is unforgettable because he is representatively human. His innate sense of right clashes with the intense ambition that drives him to actions he knows to be wrong.

Nonetheless, he succumbs to his desire for kingly power, and thus the story of this "rare monster" with an uncommonly poetic spirit remains as compelling today as it was four hundred years ago.

When Shakespeare wrote *Macbeth*, he had recently completed two of his greatest tragedies, *Othello* and *King Lear*, and would soon thereafter embark upon another, *Antony and Cleopatra*. *Macbeth* is markedly different in style and impact from that of the preceding works, perhaps because it seems to have been influenced by political events in London that appealed to the imaginations of the playwright and his audiences, both private and public.

A Scottish King on the English Throne

Although the first verifiable performance of the play was at the Globe in 1611, *Macbeth* evidently was performed in August 1606 at Hampton Court (a palace built by Henry VIII outside London) where King James I was hosting the Danish king, Christian IV, whose sister James had married in 1589. Three years into his reign, James had largely overcome initial reservations the English may have had about a Scotsman sitting on their throne. Animosities between the English and their northern neighbors were long-standing, and the English had been not only wary of a Scottish king but fearful of civil war. Powerful factions coveted the throne in 1603 since no direct heir stood to inherit the crown in the wake of the childless Elizabeth's death. (James was related to Elizabeth through King Henry VII: he was Henry's great grandson; she, a granddaughter.) Among its many issues, *Macbeth* explores the dangers of regicide and political power struggles, surely two themes that both James I and his Danish guest would have appreciated. James I himself could trace his ancestry to Banquo, a key character in the play. In the opening scene the witches promise Banquo that he will be the progenitor of kings, though never a king himself, and the Stuart family tree clearly showed Banquo as the root of that line.

The Gunpowder Plot

Catholicism had been weakened in England since Henry VIII, Elizabeth's father, abandoned that religion in 1533 in retaliation for the Pope's refusal to grant an annulment of his marriage to his first queen, Catherine of Aragon. Catholics continued to practice their religion, although secretly (as did perhaps Shakespeare's parents in Stratford), and some retained an antipathy to the English monarchy. In early November 1605—a half-year before historians surmise Shakespeare wrote *Macbeth*—English authorities discovered a conspiracy to blow up Parliament with thirty-six barrels of gunpowder. This "Gunpowder Plot" is still celebrated with fireworks and merrymaking on November 5, Guy Fawkes Day, so-named for one of the conspirators. Again we can appreciate the play's concern with regicide and disorder when we realize that English audiences in 1606 had survived this threat to their government and had spent the spring of that year discussing the trial of the Catholic anarchists. Historicist critic Stephen Greenblatt describes *Macbeth* as Shakespeare's "collective ritual of reassurance" to the King and his subjects (337). The play makes specific reference to the Gunpowder Plot in the Porter's speech about "equivocators" in 2.3. The term evokes memories of the trial of Father Henry Garnet, a Jesuit priest indicted in the conspiracy. Garnet, who had published a respected essay on equivocation, defended himself by citing "the privilege of equivocation"—the doctrine that a lie is not a lie if the utterer had in his mind a different meaning in which the utterance was true. Macbeth himself later uses the term (5.5.43) as he reacts to the dreadful news that Birnham Wood is indeed approaching his castle.

Just as *Macbeth* possessed an uncommon topicality for Shakespeare's audiences, subsequent theater and film artists have turned to *Macbeth* as an apt commentary on the political events of their own times. Orson Welles's 1948 film seems to demonstrate the restoration of good in the West after the Allies defeated fascism. By contrast, Roman Polanski's nihilistic 1970 film reflects his angst born of the horrors of World War II and the Cold War; Polanski's native Poland was a battleground for these conflicts, and his reading of *Macbeth* suggests that it is an absurdist drama of the meaninglessness of life. During Tiananmen Spring in 1989, one of this anthology's editors was in China discussing *Macbeth* with graduate students and teachers at precisely the time of the students' pro-democracy movement. The class completed Act 3 before the weekend of the Beijing police's massacre of students in Tiananmen Square

(June 4) and began the discussion of Act 4 the following Tuesday. Macduff's lines—

> Bleed, bleed, poor country!
> Great tyranny, lay thou thy basis sure,
> For goodness dare not check thee . . .
> I think our country sinks beneath the yoke;
> It weeps, it bleeds, and each new day a gash
> Is added to her wounds . . .
>
> (4.3.32–42)

—resonated with remarkable urgency that morning, as still another testimony to the immediacy of Shakespeare's plays in his age—and ours.

At barely two thousand lines, *Macbeth* is among Shakespeare's shortest plays, virtually one-half the length of *Hamlet*. Although the action of the play covers months or even years of actual time (e.g., the expedition to Fife to kill Macduff's family would require considerably more time than is suggested in performance), Shakespeare structures this play without subplots and with only the tiniest bit of comic relief, so that Macbeth's descent into the hell of his misdeeds is swift and irreversible. Most scenes are short (under one hundred lines) by Shakespeare's standards; only one (4.3) is more than two hundred lines, and it is frequently trimmed to minimize the lengthy discourse on tyranny between Malcolm and Macduff. Once he makes his fateful decision to kill Duncan in Act 2, Macbeth's fate is sealed and swift Time metes its justice rapidly. Consequently, this is among Shakespeare's most emotionally intense and cinematic scripts as it "cuts" from one scene to another in rapid succession.

Characters: Moral Character

Although the cast of characters appears lengthy, *Macbeth* is an intimate play, relying largely on a series of two-character scenes. Accordingly, only a few characters are fully developed, and the remainder exist to advance the plot and guide our reactions to the mayhem created by Macbeth and his queen. Most of the characters are based on actual historical personages taken from Holinshed's chronicles (see below): Macbeth and Lady Macbeth, Banquo, King Duncan and his sons, Macduff and his family, and other named lords.

Macbeth and Lady Macbeth are the most fully etched psychological portraits in this tragedy. Both have memorable soliloquies that allow us to penetrate their minds as they plunge further into spiritual darkness. Even in their private moments together (1.5, 1.7, 2.2, and 3.2), the extraordinary candor in their dialogue has the effect of soliloquizing as the innermost thoughts of husband and wife are revealed. Because so much of the play emanates from the minds of its protagonist, *Macbeth* lends itself to expressionistic treatments on stage and in film. Although Expressionism, correctly speaking, is an early twentieth-century artistic style, Shakespeare's probe into the recesses of the human mind—replete with possible hallucinations (i.e., the famous dagger that beckons Macbeth at 2.1.34)—makes the play a forerunner of expressionistic theater and its dramatization of the unconscious.

If *Othello* is about a man who succumbs to a crime of passion, *Macbeth* depicts the fall of a man who coldly rationalizes a despicable act: he kills a lawful king even as the old monarch sleeps in what should be the sanctuary of Macbeth's castle. Macbeth, it must be emphasized, does not kill solely because the Witches or his wife have tempted him with their promises of kingship. They certainly goad him on, but he is not simply the victim of malevolent forces coercing him into a monstrous act he knows full well is wrong. To be sure, the fact that the Weird Sisters predict accurately a future in which Macbeth *will* become king suggests an element of determinism in the matter of his choice. Still, Macbeth exercises his free will, knowing with certainty "the deep damnation" that will befall him if he kills Duncan (see 1.7.19–20). Having killed once, Macbeth further rationalizes more bloodshed (Banquo, Macduff's family): "I am in blood / Stepped in so far that, should I wade no more, / Returning were as tedious as go o'er" (3.4.137–139). Unlike Richard III, who gloats over his crimes and thereby distances audiences from his evil, Macbeth gains a measure of our pity because he has trapped himself in an inescapable hell of his own making. We know him to be a good man and a valiant warrior (see the Captain's speeches in 1.2), yet he succumbs to his human frailty even as he rationalizes his malfeasance in the exquisite language of a poet-philosopher. While audiences do not lament the death of Richard III or the "censure" meted to the "hellish villain," Iago (*Othello*, 5.2.379), they do feel pain at Macbeth's death. "One of the most remarkable aspects of Shakespeare's genius," suggests Barbara Everett, "is the degree to which in the last act he shows the brutish and external Macbeth . . . and yet retains for him a pure human sympathy, so that we can still associate his fate with our own . . . [Macbeth] feels the deepening intensities of the pain of true human failure" (Everett, 105).

Lady Macbeth is perhaps Shakespeare's most fascinating and enigmatic woman in the major tragedies. Certainly great actresses have made their mark playing the "fiendlike queen" (5.8.70) more than in the roles of Gertrude, Ophelia, Desdemona, or Lear's malignant daughters, Regan and Goneril. This theatrical dominance may owe in part to the extraordinary power Lady Macbeth exerts on the play, for it is she who spurs on Macbeth, largely by displaying the ruthlessness that he seems to lack. Unlike her husband, however, she seems to have no misgivings about the heinous crimes that confront them. Only once does she seem pitiably human: she does not participate in the killing of Duncan because the old king reminds her of her own father (2.2.12–13); otherwise, her sangfroid is the equal of any warrior on Scotland's battlefields. Accordingly, Shakespeare invests her

with qualities traditionally associated with masculinity, much like the three Witches—the bearded women—who confront him in Act 1. (In some productions Lady Macbeth actually plays one of the three Witches, a fourth witch, or even a single witch who tempts Macbeth.) Her language is filled with images that reverse her gender ("unsex me here," 1.5.41) to make her as unnatural as the three sisters who "look not like th' inhabitants o'th'earth / And yet are on't" (1.3.41–42). That the role was originally played by an adolescent male invests Lady Macbeth's lines about gender with an exceptional irony.

We do not get nearly as close to the other characters, the most significant of whom are Banquo and Macduff. Banquo is a foil to Macbeth, a good and honest soldier who hears the Witches' prophecy yet remains steadfast. In Holinshed (see below), Banquo is implicated in the murder of Duncan; in absolving him of that crime, Shakespeare is obviously taking pains to establish the lineage of King James's family tree as untainted by crime. Macduff, whose wife and children are slain by Macbeth's henchmen in 4.2, is an ancient archetype—the avenging angel who rights the wrongs of the world. Though such types are found throughout the world's many cultures, the name most often attached to such a character is *nemesis*, after the Greek goddess of fate who punished extravagant pride and ambition.

King Duncan is a much-loved king whose murder at Macbeth's hand is all the more heinous for his goodness; Shakespeare modifies his historical sources, in that the actual Duncan was younger and not as demonstrably saintly. Macbeth's heroic fighting on behalf of Duncan in Act 1—as reported by the "Bloody Captain"—underscores the depths to which Macbeth falls by the final act. Malcolm, the future king, is young and a minor role in the play, although his lengthy discussion with Macduff about tyranny in 4.3 suggests that he has been educated in wariness by the evil he has seen.

Several thanes (feudal lords) such as Seward and Lennox join the roster of characters; of these Ross is the most interesting. He has been used by various directors—notably Polanski—as an agent of apparent loyalty but who, in reality, is as lustful for power as is Macbeth. Casting the play presents us with the problem of the so-called "Third Murderer": two murderers meet with Macbeth in 3.1 to plot the death of Banquo, and yet three participate in the actual murder in 3.3. Directors have tried to account for the third murderer, occasionally by making him one of the named thanes such as Ross (Polanski's film, 1971) or Seward (Houston Shakespeare Festival, 2004). More simply, he may be a third villain whom Macbeth has employed to spy on the other two.

Finally, one of Shakespeare's most famous minor comic roles is the drunken Porter attending the gates at Dunsinane Castle. He appears only briefly—immediately after the murder of King Duncan—and yet he introduces an important thematic element: the Porter imagines himself to be the gatekeeper of hell itself. The play is nothing if not a depiction of a once good man plunging into the depths of a personal hell for his egregious crimes. This brief episode of macabre humor actually heightens the tension with its violent and unexpected lurch to a contrasting mood amidst the bloodletting.

Sources and Inspirations

Holinshed's Chronicles and The Origins of the Scottish People

Shakespeare's primary source for *Macbeth* was Raphael Holinshed's 1587 edition of his popular *Chronicles of England, Scotland, and Ireland*. That Shakespeare borrowed from Holinshed can be ascertained from certain passages in the play that use Holinshed's actual words (e.g., "Weird Sisters"). At the same time, Shakespeare introduces significant changes from his source by collapsing several events and murders for dramatic effect. Shakespeare's glorification of King James may have come from a book that promoted the Stuart myth, *On the Origins of the Scottish People* (1578). Shakespeare himself had contributed to the Tudor myth when he wrote *Richard III* and portrayed the Earl of Richmond—King Henry VII, the progenitor of the Tudor line—as the savior of his country.

James Stuart's Daemonologie

King James was among the most prolific essayists in the history of the English monarchy. He sponsored the widely used version of the Christian Bible that bears his name, and in 1604 he wrote a tract against the use of tobacco, a product brought to Europe from the Americas. As one who was fascinated by the occult, King James wrote *Daemonologie* (1597), a theological and philosophical discussion of witchcraft and evil that Shakespeare may have consulted as he wrote *Macbeth*. Shakespeare was aware of James's essay, if only indirectly, and may have been inspired to include scenes in his plays that illustrated the very ideas the King set forth. More importantly, *Macbeth* represents one of world literature's most astute examinations of the destructive power of evil, a major thematic strain that runs through *Daemonologie*.

Language

Among the play's most intriguing aspects—for readers and actors alike—is the manner in which Shakespeare uses language to chart Macbeth's growing adaptation to his role as ruthless monarch and murderer. Similarly, the playwright traces Lady Macbeth's descent into despair—she who was so self-assured early in the play—by writing passages in which her ability to use

words disintegrates. Her famous sleepwalking speech in 5.1 ("Out, damned spot . . . ") is disjointed and in broken prose in sharp contrast with the rhythmic blank verse speeches she utters in the first two acts. Consider for a moment a passage in 2.2 that illustrates this point. Macbeth has just returned from killing King Duncan:

> MACBETH:
> I have done the deed. Didst thou not hear a noise?
> LADY MACBETH:
> I heard the owl screech and the crickets cry. Did not you speak?
> MACBETH: When?
> LADY MACBETH: Now.
> MACBETH: As I descended?
> LADY MACBETH: Ay.
> MACBETH: Hark! Who lies i'th' second chamber?
> LADY MACBETH: Donalbain.
> MACBETH: [*looking at his hands*]   This is a sorry sight.
> LADY MACBETH:
> A foolish thought, to say a sorry sight.
>
> (2.2.15–25)

This passage skillfully alternates between blank verse and breathless short lines that express the emotional tautness of the moment. Editors sometimes arrange some of the short lines into blank verse ("Did you not speak? / When? / Now. / As I descended?"), but the Folio text gives no clue that this is called for, and in any event the arrangement leaves some speeches still as short lines ("Ay," "Hark?", "This is a sorry sight"), casting doubt on the whole enterprise.

- The passage begins with two blank verse lines in any case. The abnormal stresses in Macbeth's speech show that his mind is troubled by the horrible murder he has just committed: "I have DONE the DEED. DIDST thou NOT HEAR a NOISE?" Note also that the repeated "d" and "t" sounds echo Macbeth's own heartbeat, which surely must be pounding frantically. Lady Macbeth responds with a more regular line: "I HEARD the OWL SCREAM and the CRICKets CRY." It is a five-beat line, just irregular enough to suggest Lady Macbeth's anxiety. Nature is rebelling at the act ("owl scream") and she, too, is a bit unnerved. Vivid sound effects heighten the dialogue. The phrases "owl scream" and "crickets cry" are *onomatopoetic*; that is, they imitate the very sounds they describe to create atmosphere. *Macbeth* is a play about eerie events, and Shakespeare scripts such sound qualities throughout the play. Listen for these while reading or watching the play.

- The following utterances are staccato, as husband and wife respond quickly to one another. Their hurried speeches reflect the way they are jumping at shadows. The dialogue here is as naturalistic and clipped as any modern passage by David Mamet or Quentin

Tarantino. Lady Macbeth's "Ay" and her husband's "Hark!" would seem to denote pauses. Macbeth's inquiry about who is sleeping "i'th' second chamber" elicits from Lady Macbeth a terse reply.

■ Shakespeare then concludes this sequence with two very telling lines. The first, spoken by Macbeth, is short and irregular in its rhythm to reflect his anxiety. The pause implied by the short line suggests that Lady Macbeth takes a moment to compose herself (and to assess Macbeth's panic?). She then responds with a line of perfect iambic pentameter: "a FOOL-ish THOUGHT, to SAY a SORry SIGHT." She is in complete control (or wishes to suggest she is), and her line has a calming effect on Macbeth. The dominance of the "s" (or sibilant) sounds in Lady Macbeth's line is also a stage direction to the actor to "SShhhh" Macbeth.

As the play progresses Lady Macbeth's speech becomes more irregular to reflect her growing madness; by contrast, Macbeth's speech becomes more composed as he adjusts to his status as murderer-king. His final great soliloquy ("Tomorrow, and tomorrow, and tomorrow"), although not written in strict iambic pentameter, is carefully measured, thoroughly controlled—in discernible contrast to his speeches in the first two acts, which are marked by half-thoughts, broken rhythms, and other irregularities. When Macbeth is in a public setting he speaks in remarkably controlled cadences, all part of the mask he wears to project the image of a king in control of himself. The mask slips grotesquely in the banquet scene (3.4): the sight of Banquo's ghost causes Macbeth's language to disintegrate into fractured sentences.

As is his custom, Shakespeare uses recurring verbal images to reinforce the theme of ruin in the play and, as importantly, to create mood. Two images dominate *Macbeth*: blood and pollution. Macbeth's lament in Act 3 is perhaps the most powerful of these: "It will have blood, they say; blood will have blood" (3.4.123). Like *Hamlet*, *Macbeth* also contains numerous references to pollution and decay, an apt symbol for Scotland as it deteriorates under its murderous king's reign. The Witches initiate this imagery in the first scene ("Foul is fair . . . "). The Doctor laments that "Foul whisperings are abroad. Unnatural deeds / Do breed unnatural troubles" (5.1.72–73). Supplementing these speeches are constant reminders that "Hours dreadful and things strange" (2.4.3) are the fate of Scotland under Macbeth's tyranny. Appropriately, paradoxes and oxymorons dominate this text about the subversion of order.

The Witches speak usually in verse and in short lines. As with the fairies in *A Midsummer Night's Dream*, Shakespeare attempts to create an otherworldly aura for the Weird Sisters. Here is their language of incantation from the opening sequence of Act 4:

> Round about the cauldron go;
> In the poisoned entrail throw.
> Toad, that under cold stone
> Days and nights has thirty-one . . .

Other singsong lines, taken from Thomas Middleton's *The Witch* (c. 1612), seem to have been interpolated into the play either by Shakespeare himself or else by those who edited *Macbeth* for the First Folio. Some argue that the mature Shakespeare would not have employed such seeming doggerel, but, given the consistency with which Shakespeare invariably finds precisely the right "voice" for each of his characters, especially in the mature plays, such simple verse is in keeping with his design.

Themes and Issues

The Perils of Pride and Vaulting Ambition

Macbeth has traditionally been considered a warning about the perils of pride and "Vaulting ambition" (1.7.27). Kurosawa's *Throne of Blood* (see below, pp. 812–813) defines these themes in a verse chanted by an invisible chorus of Buddhist monks:

> Men are vain and death is long
> And pride dies within the grave
> For hair and nails are growing still
> When face and fame are gone.

Such themes are self-evident, but others merit consideration.

First, while Macbeth's tragic flaw is often said to be ambition and/or ruthlessness, another quality is often overlooked. Macbeth aspires to be a king, a leader, but he rarely leads. Although Shakespeare makes it clear that Macbeth is ultimately master of his destiny, he is easily—too easily?—prompted by others: the Witches, his wife, even the murderers whose braggadocio incites Macbeth's imagination as they plot the death of Banquo in 3.1. Macbeth is a failed leader in that he follows when he ought to assert his moral certitude. In Shakespeare's age, each person was considered a "little kingdom" unto him/herself; therefore, each "king" or "queen," even a beggar, was obligated to rule one's kingdom wisely. Macbeth fails to rule his personal domain—much less Scotland—nobly.

The greater issue, and the reason why Macbeth is such a fascinating character, is that he knows exactly the moral implications of his choices ("This even-handed justice / Commends th'ingredience of our poisoned chalice / To our own lips," 1.7.10–12), and yet he pursues his "slaughterous thoughts." Macbeth is human in his deliberations, inhumane in his actions. This extraordinary gap between his innate goodness—which knows right from wrong—and his reckless abandonment of his own well-defined principles make him an absorbing figure. Most of us have faced similar dilemmas of conscience, and too we often betray our human nature by ignoring our better instincts in favor of baser ones. Even though most of us are not involved in matters of such import as regicide, we recognize in Macbeth that part of us which succumbs to temptation. If Macbeth possesses tragic greatness—as he surely does, though his tragic stature has been much debated for centuries—he does so by looking evil in the face unflinchingly. Macbeth, as A. C. Bradley has written in *Shakespearean Tragedy* (1904), "challenges fate into the lists. The result is frightful" (299).

Staging Challenges

Even as the play goes about illustrating with uncommon acuteness the inner workings of Macbeth's mind and that of his wife, *Macbeth* is among Shakespeare's most theatrical and visually arresting plays. Thus it presents myriad possibilities to would-be directors; perhaps as much as any of Shakespeare's plays, *Macbeth* invites directors to imagine how a production should "look." Mention Scottish warriors, witches, and ghosts, and people invariably think of kilts and medieval castles, old hags and eerie spirits, and broadswords and pikes. While such images may be endemic to the play, *Macbeth* is rich in many other possibilities as well.

The Setting

Historically, the action of *Macbeth* takes place in north-eastern Scotland, a land once under Viking control. At the time of the play (c. 1040 C.E.), Scotland was a loose collection of tribes, each ruled by a thane—the thane of Cawdor, the thane of Glamis (pronounced *glahmz*)—who answered to the king. The historical Duncan helped unite these independent tribes and was thus especially revered by his people. The land, like the warriors who dwelt upon it, is notoriously rugged, and its rocky hills and inhospitable moors (or "blasted heath[s]," as Shakespeare describes them) are often covered in eerie mists and fogs. Little wonder that this land has spawned folktales about frightful creatures that are "So withered and so wild in their attire" (1.3.40). It is a violent land that begets violent deeds by fearsome and fearless people, and it is still dotted with the places where such deeds took place: Dunsinane Castle, Birnham Wood, and Scone.

At the same time the play takes place in the landscape of Macbeth's mind and that of his wife. Orson Welles's 1948 film of the play created an expressionistic inner world reflecting Macbeth's psychological disintegration. Because *Macbeth* can be read as a parable about political tyranny, it has frequently been staged in lands well beyond Scotland's borders—Haiti, Fascist Italy, Com-

munist Russia, even the criminal underworld (see below, pp. 806 ff.). While we seek to envision the Scotland that Shakespeare's audiences knew, we need to consider also the play's metaphorical nature. Among the most admired productions of the play in the twentieth century was that performed by the Royal Shakespeare Company, under the direction of Trevor Nunn, at Stratford-upon-Avon in 1976. Because The Other Place—an old Quonset hut seating less than two hundred people—did not allow for much scenery, Nunn staged the play on a bare platform, adorned by a supernatural ring of light and an omnipresent golden cloak hung on a mannequin. A dozen actors played all the roles in dark clothing to which symbolic costume pieces were added. The setting could have been medieval Scotland, contemporary Europe—or the inner recesses of Macbeth's mind.

The Witches

If the "Weird Sisters" were played by adolescent males in the early seventeenth century (quite possibly not), Banquo's observation that "Ye should be women / And yet your beards forbid me to interpret / That you are so" (1.2.43–45) would have taken on an odd resonance. How might they have been costumed in London in 1606? We cannot be sure, and yet a woodcut accompanying the text in the first volume of Holinshed's *Chronicles* portrays the Witches dressed in elegant Elizabethan gowns. Might Shakespeare—whose preparatory reading for the play included Holinshed—have suggested such costuming for the actors? Given the play's emphasis on disparities and paradoxes, the sight of elegantly costumed "women" with beards would have established that motif quickly. A contemporary account indicates that Witches were commonly supposed to be "old, lame, bleary-eyed, pale, foul and full of wrinkles"—a description that is in keeping with Banquo's line about one of the witches laying her "chappy finger . . . Upon her skinny lips" (1.3.44–45). The "hag" witch emerged as the most common manifestation on stage until well into the twentieth century, and some modern productions and films (the Welles and Polanski films, Nunn's stage production: see pp. 810–812) have retained this image. To be sure, inventive directors and their designers have offered some intriguing alternatives to the traditional look:

- rocks that came "alive" as the witches rose and retreated rhythmically in and out of the rocks (Madrid, 1980)

- tribal "witchdoctors" (Senegal, Africa, 1969). Welles used a similar approach in his famous 1936 "Voodoo *Macbeth*," set in Haiti (see below, p. 810).

- six witches—three tall males who stood statue-like as three short women screeched the lines (London and New York, 1948–1949)

- satanic demons who remained visible throughout the play, holding out the dagger during Macbeth's famous dagger soliloquy (Odessa, Texas, 1974)

- two naked women and a man, their hands dripping in blood (Cologne, Germany, 1982)

- a single "forest spirit" of Japanese legend who methodically turns a weaver's loom (Kurosawa's *Throne of Blood*, 1957: see below, pp. 812–813).

Some productions have extended the amount of stage time for the Witches, allowing them to remain in view throughout the play as interested observers of the action. Like the audience, they watch with macabre fascination Macbeth's perilous journey from noble warrior to calculated killing machine.

However theatrically exciting they may be, what the Witches wear and how they appear is of less consequence than what they symbolize. Although many people in Shakespeare's era believed that witches walked among them, today we see them as both a concrete symbol of the evil that beckons humans to commit atrocities and as the objectification of psychological states. Concrete or abstract, the power wielded by the Weird Sisters nonetheless is "ultimately demonic" (Curry, 61).

Bloody Deeds

Blood is the play's dominant image, as well as its most frequently used word. After the atmospheric prologue by the Witches, the play begins with a vivid description delivered by a minor character known simply as "the Bloody Captain" (from Duncan's first line, "What bloody man is that?"). The wounded soldier describes Macbeth killing the traitorous Macdonwald by unseaming him "from nave to th' chops" (1.2.22). The play concludes with Macduff carrying Macbeth's severed head aloft, just as Macbeth earlier had carried Macdonwald's head (1.2.23). Such images set the tone for the play and invite directors to invent (indulge in?) gory displays on stage. There is precedent: we know that in Shakespeare's theaters actors often carried animal bladders in their costumes filled with blood obtained from local butcher shops, which, when punctured during fights, spewed gore.

In his 1948 stage version of *Macbeth*, Ingmar Bergman, the renowned Swedish filmmaker, built upon the Captain's vivid description by having the bodies of four men dangling from battlefield's trees as the audience entered the theater; during the banquet scene the human bodies were replaced by the carcasses of slaughtered oxen. In 1994 Greg Boyd staged the tragedy at Houston's Alley Theater, where the killing of Macduff's son was as gruesome as can be imagined. The entire stage floor was covered by an enormous white cloth. After the child was savagely stabbed with a stiletto at downstage right, he slowly crawled diagonally across the stage (some thirty-five feet) oozing blood all over the white cloth.

Questions arise: To what extent should the bloodshed be graphic? Are Shakespeare's words and bloody images sufficient to convey the horror of Macbeth's reign? Can the stage compete with the horrendous dismemberments found in such films as *Saving Private Ryan*? Should it?

The Gory Locks of Banquo's Ghost

The visitation of Banquo's ghost to the banquet celebrating Macbeth's coronation presents an intriguing staging problem. A director has essentially two choices: present the actual figure of Banquo or suggest that the ghost is a hallucination borne of Macbeth's deteriorating mind. Both have been tried with success, although the former is the more common approach. Shakespeare's audiences expected "real" ghosts on stage (Old Hamlet, Caesar, the parade of ghosts that torment Richard III), thus an actor clad as Banquo's ghost no doubt appeared to spectators at the Globe and Blackfriars. Of late, actors of Macbeth have sometimes suggested the presence of a ghost, perhaps influenced by psychological studies and criticism arguing that the ghost is merely a projection of Macbeth's guilt. Only Macbeth sees the ghost, whereas Banquo sees the Witches in the first act. Nunn's 1976 minimalist production for the RSC makes an excellent case for the "ghost-in-Macbeth's-mind" school of thought: Ian McKellen's performance of the encounter with an invisible ghost that seemed to hover over the audience is so chilling that one finds it hard to believe that the ghost did not exist.

"Lay on Macduff"—The Final Fight

Our final impression of the play is predicated upon the fatal confrontation between Macbeth and his nemesis, Macduff. The Folio stage directions are imprecise: the combatants are directed to *"Exeunt, fighting,"* followed by *"Alarums,"* and then *"Enter fighting, and Macbeth slain"* (5.8.34). Macduff, who has entered shortly before this to challenge Macbeth directly, must kill Macbeth in this general melee and then exit with the body, even though he is not specifically named here; he will re-enter at line 53 *"with Macbeth's head."* Throughout the play's stage history, productions invariably have shown Macduff actually kill Macbeth, if only to appease the audience's sense of poetic justice. Nunn's production at Stratford broke tradition: Macbeth merely disappeared eerily in a blackout, which was immediately followed by a light on the royal golden cloak that Macbeth wanted yet never wore.

How Macbeth is killed—if the death is shown at all—has an impact on our perception of the play. Consider the resolution of three films that illustrate this point. Welles's film, made shortly after the end of World War II, depicts the triumph of the Christian West over evil (i.e., Hitler); after Macbeth is slain and his head is raised above Malcolm's soldiers, the warriors jubilantly lift their pikes, many bearing the image the Celtic cross. (To be sure, Welles adds a brief epilogue in which the Three Witches look at the castle through the mists; the tableau serves as a reminder that we must be vigilant because evil, though momentarily defeated, still lurks about us.) Polanski's film, created during the Vietnam War era, depicts the battle between Macbeth and Macduff as an absurd ballet that approaches farce; the tyrant king is killed almost haphazardly by his foe, suggesting that "all events are merely accidents of an indifferent universe" (Pearlman, 255). Polanski's epilogue is even more cynical,

going a step beyond Welles's warning about vigilance. As the thanes head to Scone to crown Malcolm, Polanski inserts a final image: Donalbain, Malcolm's younger brother, furtively enters the cave where the Witches dwell, and thus the cycle of bloodshed is set again in motion. Kurosawa's adaptation, *Throne of Blood*, situates the action in feudal Japan, where the Macbeth character (Washizu), a samurai who has conspired against his lord and master, is killed by the multitude of archers who have pursued him to the castle. The Japanese director interprets the Macbeth legend as an instance of misplaced ambition contributing to the fall of his country's feudal system. By doing so, Kurosawa has fashioned a work that is "the most akin to Shakespeare in the grandeur and spaciousness of its vision" because the characters challenge the prevailing social system (Pearlman, 259). Using essentially the same material as a starting point, the resolution of each film creates a distinctly different impression upon its audience.

Macbeth

[Dramatis Personae

DUNCAN, *King of Scotland*
MALCOLM ⎱ *his sons*
DONALBAIN ⎰

MACBETH, *Thane of Glamis, later of Cawdor, later King of Scotland*
LADY MACBETH

BANQUO, *a thane of Scotland*
FLEANCE, *his son*
MACDUFF, *Thane of Fife*
LADY MACDUFF
SON *of Macduff and Lady Macduff*

LENNOX ⎫
ROSS ⎪
MENTEITH ⎬ *thanes and noblemen of Scotland*
ANGUS ⎪
CAITHNESS ⎭

SIWARD, *Earl of Northumberland*
YOUNG SIWARD, *his son*

SEYTON, *an officer attending Macbeth*
Another LORD
ENGLISH DOCTOR
SCOTTISH DOCTOR
GENTLEWOMAN *attending Lady Macbeth*
CAPTAIN *serving Duncan*
PORTER
OLD MAN
Three MURDERERS *of Banquo*
FIRST MURDERER *at Macduff's castle*
MESSENGER *to Lady Macbeth*
MESSENGER *to Lady Macduff*
SERVANT *to Macbeth*
SERVANT *to Lady Macbeth*
Three WITCHES *or* WEIRD SISTERS
HECATE
Three APPARITIONS

Lords, Gentlemen, Officers, Soldiers, Murderers, and Attendants

SCENE: *Scotland; England*]

1.1

Thunder and lightning. Enter three Witches.

FIRST WITCH
When shall we three meet again?
In thunder, lightning, or in rain?

SECOND WITCH
When the hurlyburly's done,   3
When the battle's lost and won.

THIRD WITCH
That will be ere the set of sun.

FIRST WITCH
Where the place?

SECOND WITCH   Upon the heath.

THIRD WITCH
There to meet with Macbeth.

FIRST WITCH   I come, Grimalkin!   8

SECOND WITCH   Paddock calls.   9

THIRD WITCH   Anon.   10

ALL
Fair is foul, and foul is fair.
Hover through the fog and filthy air.   *Exeunt.*

1.2

*Alarum within. Enter King [Duncan], Malcolm,
Donalbain, Lennox, with attendants, meeting a
bleeding Captain.*

DUNCAN
What bloody man is that? He can report,
As seemeth by his plight, of the revolt
The newest state.

MALCOLM   This is the sergeant   3
Who like a good and hardy soldier fought
'Gainst my captivity.—Hail, brave friend!
Say to the King the knowledge of the broil   6
As thou didst leave it.

CAPTAIN   Doubtful it stood,
As two spent swimmers that do cling together   8
And choke their art. The merciless Macdonwald—   9
Worthy to be a rebel, for to that   10
The multiplying villainies of nature   11
Do swarm upon him—from the Western Isles   12
Of kerns and gallowglasses is supplied;   13

And Fortune, on his damnèd quarrel smiling,   14
Showed like a rebel's whore. But all's too weak;   15
For brave Macbeth—well he deserves that name—   16
Disdaining Fortune, with his brandished steel,
Which smoked with bloody execution,
Like valor's minion carved out his passage   19
Till he faced the slave,   20
Which ne'er shook hands nor bade farewell to him   21
Till he unseamed him from the nave to th' chops,   22
And fixed his head upon our battlements.

DUNCAN
Oh, valiant cousin, worthy gentleman!   24

CAPTAIN
As whence the sun 'gins his reflection   25
Shipwrecking storms and direful thunders break,   26
So from that spring whence comfort seemed to come   27
Discomfort swells. Mark, King of Scotland, mark.   28
No sooner justice had, with valor armed,
Compelled these skipping kerns to trust their heels   30
But the Norweyan lord, surveying vantage,   31
With furbished arms and new supplies of men,
Began a fresh assault.

DUNCAN
Dismayed not this our captains, Macbeth and
    Banquo?

CAPTAIN
Yes, as sparrows eagles, or the hare the lion.   35
If I say sooth, I must report they were   36
As cannons overcharged with double cracks,   37
So they doubly redoubled strokes upon the foe.
Except they meant to bathe in reeking wounds   39
Or memorize another Golgotha,   40
I cannot tell.
But I am faint. My gashes cry for help.

DUNCAN
So well thy words become thee as thy wounds;
They smack of honor both.—Go get him surgeons.
                        [*Exit Captain, attended.*]

Enter Ross and Angus.

Who comes here?

MALCOLM   The worthy Thane of Ross.   45

LENNOX   What a haste looks through his eyes!
So should he look that seems to speak things strange.   47

ROSS   God save the King!

1.1 Location: An open place.
3 hurlyburly tumult   **8 Grimalkin** i.e., gray cat, name of the witch's
familiar—a demon or evil spirit supposed to answer a witch's call
and to allow him or her to perform black magic.   **9 Paddock** toad;
also a familiar   **10 Anon** At once, right away.
1.2. Location: A camp near Forres.
0.1 *Alarum* trumpet call to arms   **3 newest state** latest news.
sergeant i.e., staff officer. (There may be no inconsistency with his
rank of "captain" in the stage direction and speech prefixes in the
Folio.)   **6 broil** battle   **8 spent** tired out   **9 choke their art** render
their skill in swimming useless.   **9–13 The merciless . . . supplied**
The merciless Macdonwald—worthy of the hated name of rebel, for
in the cause of rebellion an ever-increasing number of villainous persons and unnatural qualities swarm about him like vermin—is joined
by light-armed Irish footsoldiers and ax-armed horsemen from the
western islands of Scotland (the Hebrides and perhaps Ireland)

14–15 And Fortune . . . whore i.e., Fortune, proverbially a false strumpet, smiles at first on Macdonwald's damned rebellion but deserts him
in his hour of need.   **16 well . . . name** well he deserves a name that
is synonymous with "brave"   **19 minion** darling. (Macbeth is Valor's
darling, not Fortune's.)   **20 the slave** i.e., Macdonwald   **21 Which . . .
to him** i.e., Macbeth paused for no ceremonious greeting or farewell
to Macdonwald   **22 nave** navel.   **chops** jaws   **24 cousin** kinsman
25–8 As . . . swells Just as terrible storms at sea arise out of the east,
from the place where the sun first shows itself in the seeming comfort
of the dawn, even thus did a new military threat come on the heels of
the seeming good news of Macdonwald's execution.   **30 skipping**
(1) lightly armed, quick at maneuvering (2) skittish   **31 surveying
vantage** seeing an opportunity   **35 Yes . . . eagles** Yes, about as much
as sparrows terrify eagles. (Said ironically.)   **36 say sooth** tell the
truth   **37 cracks** charges of explosive   **39 Except** Unless   **40 memorize** make memorable or famous.   **Golgotha** "place of a skull,"
where Christ was crucified. (Mark 15:22.)   **45 Thane** Scottish title of
honor, roughly equivalent to "Earl"   **47 seems to** seems about to

DUNCAN   Whence cam'st thou, worthy thane?
ROSS   From Fife, great King,
Where the Norweyan banners flout the sky   51
And fan our people cold.   52
Norway himself, with terrible numbers,   53
Assisted by that most disloyal traitor,
The Thane of Cawdor, began a dismal conflict,   55
Till that Bellona's bridegroom, lapped in proof,   56
Confronted him with self-comparisons,   57
Point against point, rebellious arm 'gainst arm,
Curbing his lavish spirit; and to conclude,
The victory fell on us.
DUNCAN   Great happiness!
ROSS   That now
Sweno, the Norways' king, craves composition;   62
Nor would we deign him burial of his men
Till he disbursèd at Saint Colme's Inch   64
Ten thousand dollars to our general use.   65
DUNCAN
No more that Thane of Cawdor shall deceive
Our bosom interest. Go pronounce his present death,   67
And with his former title greet Macbeth.
ROSS   I'll see it done.
DUNCAN
What he hath lost noble Macbeth hath won.
                                        Exeunt.

❧

1.3

Thunder. Enter the three Witches.

FIRST WITCH   Where hast thou been, sister?
SECOND WITCH   Killing swine.
THIRD WITCH   Sister, where thou?
FIRST WITCH
A sailor's wife had chestnuts in her lap,
And munched, and munched, and munched. "Give
    me," quoth I.
"Aroint thee, witch!" the rump-fed runnion cries.   6
Her husband's to Aleppo gone, master o'th' *Tiger*;   7
But in a sieve I'll thither sail,
And like a rat without a tail   9
I'll do, I'll do, and I'll do.   10
SECOND WITCH
I'll give thee a wind.

FIRST WITCH
Thou'rt kind.
THIRD WITCH
And I another.
FIRST WITCH
I myself have all the other,   14
And the very ports they blow,   15
All the quarters that they know   16
I'th' shipman's card.   17
I'll drain him dry as hay.   18
Sleep shall neither night nor day
Hang upon his penthouse lid.   20
He shall live a man forbid.   21
Weary sev'nnights nine times nine   22
Shall he dwindle, peak, and pine.   23
Though his bark cannot be lost,
Yet it shall be tempest-tossed.
Look what I have.
SECOND WITCH   Show me, show me.
FIRST WITCH
Here I have a pilot's thumb,
Wrecked as homeward he did come.   *Drum within.*
THIRD WITCH
A drum, a drum!
Macbeth doth come.
ALL [*dancing in a circle*]
The Weird Sisters, hand in hand,   32
Posters of the sea and land,   33
Thus do go about, about,
Thrice to thine, and thrice to mine,
And thrice again, to make up nine.
Peace! The charm's wound up.

Enter Macbeth and Banquo.

MACBETH
So foul and fair a day I have not seen.
BANQUO
How far is't called to Forres?—What are these,   39
So withered and so wild in their attire,
That look not like th'inhabitants o'th'earth
And yet are on't?—Live you? Or are you aught
That man may question? You seem to understand me
By each at once her choppy finger laying   44
Upon her skinny lips. You should be women,
And yet your beards forbid me to interpret
That you are so.
MACBETH   Speak, if you can. What are you?
FIRST WITCH
All hail, Macbeth! Hail to thee, Thane of Glamis!
SECOND WITCH
All hail, Macbeth! Hail to thee, Thane of Cawdor!
THIRD WITCH
All hail, Macbeth, that shalt be king hereafter!

---

51 flout mock, insult   **52 fan . . . cold** fan cold fear into our troops.
53 Norway The King of Norway.   **terrible numbers** terrifying numbers of troops   **55 dismal** ominous   **56 Till . . . proof** i.e., until Macbeth, clad in well-tested armor. (Bellona was the Roman goddess of war.)   **57 him** i.e., the King of Norway.   **self-comparisons** i.e., matching counterthrusts   **62 Norways'** Norwegians'.   **composition** agreement, treaty of peace   **64 Saint Colme's Inch** Inchcolm, the Isle of St. Columba in the Firth of Forth   **65 dollars** Spanish or Dutch coins   **67 Our** (The royal "we.")   **bosom** close and intimate. **present** immediate
1.3. Location: A heath near Forres.
6 Aroint thee Begone.   **rump-fed runnion** fat-rumped baggage
7 *Tiger* (A ship's name.)   **9–10 like . . . do** (Suggestive of the witches' deformity and sexual insatiability. Witches were thought to seduce men sexually. *Do* means [1] act [2] perform sexually.)

14–17 I . . . card I can summon all other winds, wherever they blow and from whatever *quarter* in the shipman's compass card.   **18 I'll . . . hay** (With a suggestion of sexually draining the seaman's semen.) **20 penthouse lid** i.e., eyelid (which projects out over the eye like a *penthouse* or slope-roofed structure).   **21 forbid** accursed.   **22 sev'n-nights** weeks   **23 peak** grow peaked or thin   **32 Weird Sisters** women connected with fate or destiny; also women having a mysterious or unearthly, uncanny appearance   **33 Posters of** swift travelers over   **39 is't called** is it said to be   **44 choppy** chapped

BANQUO
    Good sir, why do you start and seem to fear
    Things that do sound so fair?—I'th' name of truth,
    Are ye fantastical or that indeed   53
    Which outwardly ye show? My noble partner   54
    You greet with present grace and great prediction   55
    Of noble having and of royal hope,
    That he seems rapt withal. To me you speak not.   57
    If you can look into the seeds of time
    And say which grain will grow and which will not,
    Speak then to me, who neither beg nor fear   60
    Your favors nor your hate.   61
FIRST WITCH   Hail!
SECOND WITCH   Hail!
THIRD WITCH   Hail!
FIRST WITCH
    Lesser than Macbeth, and greater.
SECOND WITCH
    Not so happy, yet much happier.   66
THIRD WITCH
    Thou shalt get kings, though thou be none.   67
    So all hail, Macbeth and Banquo!
FIRST WITCH
    Banquo and Macbeth, all hail!
MACBETH
    Stay, you imperfect speakers, tell me more!   70
    By Sinel's death I know I am Thane of Glamis,   71
    But how of Cawdor? The Thane of Cawdor lives
    A prosperous gentleman; and to be king
    Stands not within the prospect of belief,
    No more than to be Cawdor. Say from whence   75
    You owe this strange intelligence, or why   76
    Upon this blasted heath you stop our way   77
    With such prophetic greeting? Speak, I charge you.
                           Witches vanish.
BANQUO
    The earth hath bubbles, as the water has,
    And these are of them. Whither are they vanished?
MACBETH
    Into the air; and what seemed corporal melted,   81
    As breath into the wind. Would they had stayed!
BANQUO
    Were such things here as we do speak about?
    Or have we eaten on the insane root   84
    That takes the reason prisoner?
MACBETH
    Your children shall be kings.
BANQUO   You shall be king.
MACBETH
    And Thane of Cawdor too. Went it not so?
BANQUO
    To th' selfsame tune and words.—Who's here?

    Enter Ross and Angus.

ROSS
    The King hath happily received, Macbeth,
    The news of thy success; and when he reads   90
    Thy personal venture in the rebels' fight,   91
    His wonders and his praises do contend   92
    Which should be thine or his. Silenced with that, 93
    In viewing o'er the rest o'th' selfsame day
    He finds thee in the stout Norweyan ranks,   95
    Nothing afeard of what thyself didst make,   96
    Strange images of death. As thick as tale   97
    Came post with post, and every one did bear   98
    Thy praises in his kingdom's great defense,
    And poured them down before him.
ANGUS   We are sent
    To give thee from our royal master thanks,
    Only to herald thee into his sight,
    Not pay thee.
ROSS
    And, for an earnest of a greater honor,   104
    He bade me, from him, call thee Thane of Cawdor;
    In which addition, hail, most worthy thane,   106
    For it is thine.
BANQUO   What, can the devil speak true?
MACBETH
    The Thane of Cawdor lives. Why do you dress me
    In borrowed robes?
ANGUS   Who was the thane lives yet,   109
    But under heavy judgment bears that life
    Which he deserves to lose. Whether he was combined 111
    With those of Norway, or did line the rebel   112
    With hidden help and vantage, or that with both
    He labored in his country's wrack, I know not;   114
    But treasons capital, confessed and proved,   115
    Have overthrown him.
MACBETH [*aside*]   Glamis, and Thane of Cawdor!
    The greatest is behind. [*To Ross and Angus*] Thanks for
      your pains.   117
    [*Aside to Banquo*] Do you not hope your children shall
      be kings
    When those that gave the Thane of Cawdor to me
    Promised no less to them?
BANQUO [*to Macbeth*]   That, trusted home,   120
    Might yet enkindle you unto the crown,
    Besides the Thane of Cawdor. But 'tis strange;
    And oftentimes to win us to our harm
    The instruments of darkness tell us truths,
    Win us with honest trifles, to betray 's
    In deepest consequence.—   126
    Cousins, a word, I pray you.   127
               [*He converses apart with Ross and Angus.*]

90–3 **and when . . . his** and when he reads of your extraordinary valor in fighting the rebels, he concludes that your wondrous deeds outdo any praise he could offer. 95 **stout** haughty, determined, valiant   96 **Nothing** not at all   97–8 **As . . . with post** As fast as could be told, i.e., counted, came messenger after messenger. (Unless the text should be amended to "As thick as hail.")   104 **earnest** token payment   106 **addition** title   109 **Who** He who   111 **combined** confederate   112 **line the rebel** reinforce Macdonwald   114 **in . . . wrack** to bring about his country's ruin   115 **capital** deserving death   117 **The greatest is behind** either (1) Two of the three prophecies (and thus the greatest number of them) have already been fulfilled, or (2) The greatest one, the kingship, is still to come.   120 **home** all the way   126 **In deepest consequence** in the profoundly important sequel.   127 **Cousins** i.e., Fellow lords

53 **fantastical** creatures of fantasy or imagination   54 **show** appear. 55 **grace** honor   57 **rapt withal** entranced.   60–1 **beg . . . hate** beg your favors nor fear your hate.   66 **happy** fortunate   67 **get** beget 70 **imperfect** cryptic   71 **Sinel's** (Sinel was Macbeth's father.) 75–6 **Say . . . intelligence** Say from what source you have this disturbing information   77 **blasted** blighted   81 **corporal** corporeal 84 **on** of.   **insane root** root causing insanity; variously identified

MACBETH [*aside*]   Two truths are told,
As happy prologues to the swelling act   129
Of the imperial theme.—I thank you, gentlemen.
[*Aside*] This supernatural soliciting   131
Cannot be ill, cannot be good. If ill,
Why hath it given me earnest of success
Commencing in a truth? I am Thane of Cawdor.
If good, why do I yield to that suggestion
Whose horrid image doth unfix my hair   136
And make my seated heart knock at my ribs,
Against the use of nature? Present fears   138
Are less than horrible imaginings.
My thought, whose murder yet is but fantastical,   140
Shakes so my single state of man   141
That function is smothered in surmise,   142
And nothing is but what is not.   143
BANQUO   Look how our partner's rapt.
MACBETH [*aside*]
If chance will have me king, why, chance may crown
   me
Without my stir.
BANQUO   New honors come upon him,   146
Like our strange garments, cleave not to their mold   147
But with the aid of use.
MACBETH [*aside*]   Come what come may,   148
Time and the hour runs through the roughest day.   149
BANQUO
Worthy Macbeth, we stay upon your leisure.   150
MACBETH
Give me your favor. My dull brain was wrought   151
With things forgotten. Kind gentlemen, your pains
Are registered where every day I turn   153
The leaf to read them. Let us toward the King.
[*Aside to Banquo*]   Think upon what hath chanced,
   and at more time,   155
The interim having weighed it, let us speak   156
Our free hearts each to other.   157
BANQUO [*to Macbeth*]   Very gladly.
MACBETH [*to Banquo*]   Till then, enough.—Come, friends.
                                                            Exeunt.

❖

1.4

*Flourish. Enter King [Duncan], Lennox, Malcolm,
Donalbain, and attendants.*

DUNCAN
Is execution done on Cawdor? Are not
Those in commission yet returned?
MALCOLM   My liege,   2
They are not yet come back. But I have spoke
With one that saw him die, who did report
That very frankly he confessed his treasons,
Implored Your Highness' pardon, and set forth
A deep repentance. Nothing in his life
Became him like the leaving it. He died   8
As one that had been studied in his death   9
To throw away the dearest thing he owed   10
As 'twere a careless trifle.
DUNCAN   There's no art   11
To find the mind's construction in the face.
He was a gentleman on whom I built
An absolute trust.

Enter Macbeth, Banquo, Ross, and Angus.

                             O worthiest cousin!
The sin of my ingratitude even now
Was heavy on me. Thou art so far before   16
That swiftest wing of recompense is slow
To overtake thee. Would thou hadst less deserved,
That the proportion both of thanks and payment   19
Might have been mine! Only I have left to say,   20
More is thy due than more than all can pay.
MACBETH
The service and the loyalty I owe,
In doing it, pays itself. Your Highness' part
Is to receive our duties; and our duties
Are to your throne and state children and servants,   25
Which do but what they should by doing everything
Safe toward your love and honor.
DUNCAN   Welcome hither!   27
I have begun to plant thee, and will labor
To make thee full of growing. Noble Banquo,
That hast no less deserved, nor must be known
No less to have done so, let me infold thee
And hold thee to my heart.
BANQUO   There if I grow,
The harvest is your own.
DUNCAN   My plenteous joys,
Wanton in fullness, seek to hide themselves   34
In drops of sorrow.—Sons, kinsmen, thanes,
And you whose places are the nearest, know
We will establish our estate upon   37
Our eldest, Malcolm, whom we name hereafter
The Prince of Cumberland; which honor must   39
Not unaccompanied invest him only,   40

129 swelling act stately drama   **131 soliciting** tempting   **136 unfix
my hair** make my hair stand on end   **138 use** custom.   **fears** things
feared   **140 whose . . . fantastical** in which the conception of murder
is merely imaginary at this point   **141 single . . . man** weak human
condition   **142 function** normal power of action.   **surmise** speculation, imaginings   **143 And . . . not** and everything seems unreal.
146 stir bestirring (myself).   **come** i.e., which have come   **147–8
cleave . . . use** do not take the shape of the wearer until often worn.
(Macbeth is often connected in the text with clothes that don't really
fit him.)   **149 Time . . . day** time moves relentlessly on, no matter
what else happens.   **150 stay** wait   **151 favor** pardon.   **wrought**
shaped, preoccupied   **153 registered** recorded (in my memory)
155 at more time at a time of greater leisure   **156 weighed it** given
opportunity for reflection on its meaning   **157 Our free hearts** our
hearts freely
1.4. Location: Forres. The palace.

2 in commission having warrant (to see to the execution of Cawdor)
8 Became graced, befitted   **9 been studied** made it his study
10 owed owned   **11 careless** uncared for   **16 before** ahead (in
deserving)   **19–20 That . . . mine** that I might have thanked and
rewarded you in ample proportion to your worth.   **25 Are . . . servants** are like children and servants in relation to your throne and
dignity, existing only to serve you   **27 Safe . . . honor** to safeguard
you whom we love and honor.   **34 Wanton** unrestrained   **37 We**
(The royal "we.")   **establish our estate** fix the succession of our state
39 Prince of Cumberland title of the heir apparent to the Scottish
throne   **40 Not . . . only** not be bestowed on Malcolm alone; other
deserving nobles are to share honors

But signs of nobleness, like stars, shall shine
On all deservers.—From hence to Inverness,   42
And bind us further to you.   43

MACBETH
The rest is labor which is not used for you.   44
I'll be myself the harbinger and make joyful   45
The hearing of my wife with your approach;
So humbly take my leave.

DUNCAN   My worthy Cawdor!

MACBETH [aside]
The Prince of Cumberland! That is a step
On which I must fall down or else o'erleap,
For in my way it lies. Stars, hide your fires;   50
Let not light see my black and deep desires.
The eye wink at the hand; yet let that be   52
Which the eye fears, when it is done, to see.   Exit.   53

DUNCAN
True, worthy Banquo. He is full so valiant,   54
And in his commendations I am fed;   55
It is a banquet to me. Let's after him,
Whose care is gone before to bid us welcome.
It is a peerless kinsman.   Flourish. Exeunt.

❦

1.5

Enter Macbeth's Wife, alone, with a letter.

LADY MACBETH [reads]   "They met me in the day of success; and I have learned by the perfect'st report they   2
have more in them than mortal knowledge. When I
burnt in desire to question them further, they made
themselves air, into which they vanished. Whiles I
stood rapt in the wonder of it came missives from the   6
King, who all-hailed me 'Thane of Cawdor,' by which
title, before, these Weird Sisters saluted me, and referred me to the coming on of time with 'Hail, king
that shalt be!' This have I thought good to deliver thee,   10
my dearest partner of greatness, that thou mightst not
lose the dues of rejoicing by being ignorant of what
greatness is promised thee. Lay it to thy heart, and
farewell."
Glamis thou art, and Cawdor, and shalt be
What thou art promised. Yet do I fear thy nature;   16
It is too full o'th' milk of human kindness
To catch the nearest way. Thou wouldst be great,
Art not without ambition, but without

The illness should attend it. What thou wouldst
   highly,   20
That wouldst thou holily; wouldst not play false,
And yet wouldst wrongly win. Thou'dst have, great
   Glamis,
That which cries "Thus thou must do," if thou have it,   23
And that which rather thou dost fear to do   24
Than wishest should be undone. Hie thee hither,   25
That I may pour my spirits in thine ear
And chastise with the valor of my tongue
All that impedes thee from the golden round   28
Which fate and metaphysical aid doth seem   29
To have thee crowned withal.

Enter [a servant as] Messenger.

                                    What is your tidings?   30

MESSENGER
The King comes here tonight.

LADY MACBETH   Thou'rt mad to say it!
Is not thy master with him, who, were't so,
Would have informed for preparation?   33

MESSENGER
So please you, it is true. Our thane is coming.
One of my fellows had the speed of him,   35
Who, almost dead for breath, had scarcely more
Than would make up his message.

LADY MACBETH   Give him tending;   37
He brings great news.   Exit Messenger.
                        The raven himself is hoarse
That croaks the fatal entrance of Duncan
Under my battlements. Come, you spirits
That tend on mortal thoughts, unsex me here   41
And fill me from the crown to the toe top-full
Of direst cruelty! Make thick my blood;
Stop up th'access and passage to remorse,   44
That no compunctious visitings of nature   45
Shake my fell purpose, nor keep peace between   46
Th'effect and it! Come to my woman's breasts   47
And take my milk for gall, you murd'ring ministers,   48
Wherever in your sightless substances   49
You wait on nature's mischief! Come, thick night,   50
And pall thee in the dunnest smoke of hell,   51
That my keen knife see not the wound it makes,
Nor heaven peep through the blanket of the dark
To cry "Hold, hold!"

Enter Macbeth.

                        Great Glamis! Worthy Cawdor!   54

---

42 **Inverness** the seat or location of Macbeth's castle, Dunsinane
43 **bind . . . you** put me further in your (Macbeth's) obligation by
your hospitality.   44 **The rest . . . you** All activity not devoted to
serving you is mere tediousness and hard work.   45 **harbinger** forerunner, messenger   50 **in my way it lies** (The monarchy was not
hereditary, and Macbeth had a right to believe that he himself might
be chosen as Duncan's successor; he here questions whether he will
interfere with the course of events.)   52–3 **The eye . . . see** Let the eye
shut itself and not see the hand's deed; yet when the deed is done, let
it be fearful to behold.   54 **full so valiant** fully as valiant as you say.
(Apparently, Duncan and Banquo have been conversing privately on
this subject during Macbeth's soliloquy.)   55 **in . . . fed** it nourishes
me to hear him praised
1.5. **Location:** Inverness. Macbeth's castle.
2 **perfect'st** most accurate   6 **missives** messengers   10 **deliver thee**
inform you of   16 **do I fear** I mistrust

20 **illness** evil (that).   **highly** greatly   23 **have** are to have, want to
have   24–5 **And that . . . undone** i.e., and the thing you ambitiously
crave frightens you more in terms of the means needed to achieve it
than in the idea of having it; if you could have it without those means,
you certainly wouldn't wish it undone.   25 **Hie** Hasten   28 **round**
crown   29 **metaphysical** supernatural   30 **withal** with.   33 **informed
for preparation** i.e., sent me word so that I might get things ready.
35 **had . . . of** outstripped   37 **Give him tending** Tend to his needs
41 **tend . . . thoughts** attend on, act as the instruments of, deadly or
murderous thoughts   44 **remorse** pity   45 **nature** natural feelings
46 **fell** fierce, cruel   46–7 **nor . . . and it** nor intervene between my *fell
purpose* and its accomplishment.   48 **for gall** in exchange for gall, or
perhaps *as* gall.   **ministers** agents   49 **sightless** invisible   50 **You . . .
mischief** you aid and abet the wickedness of human nature.   51 **pall**
envelop.   **dunnest** darkest   54 **Hold** Stop

Greater than both by the all-hail hereafter!
Thy letters have transported me beyond   56
This ignorant present, and I feel now
The future in the instant.
MACBETH   My dearest love,
Duncan comes here tonight.
LADY MACBETH   And when goes hence?
MACBETH
Tomorrow, as he purposes.
LADY MACBETH   Oh, never
Shall sun that morrow see!
Your face, my thane, is as a book where men
May read strange matters. To beguile the time,   63
Look like the time; bear welcome in your eye,   64
Your hand, your tongue. Look like th'innocent flower,
But be the serpent under't. He that's coming
Must be provided for; and you shall put
This night's great business into my dispatch,   68
Which shall to all our nights and days to come
Give solely sovereign sway and masterdom.
MACBETH
We will speak further.
LADY MACBETH   Only look up clear.   71
To alter favor ever is to fear.   72
Leave all the rest to me.   *Exeunt.*

❧

1.6

Hautboys and torches. Enter King [Duncan],
Malcolm, Donalbain, Banquo, Lennox, Macduff,
Ross, Angus, and attendants.

DUNCAN
This castle hath a pleasant seat. The air   1
Nimbly and sweetly recommends itself
Unto our gentle senses.
BANQUO   This guest of summer,   3
The temple-haunting martlet, does approve   4
By his loved mansionry that the heaven's breath   5
Smells wooingly here. No jutty, frieze,   6
Buttress, nor coign of vantage but this bird   7
Hath made his pendent bed and procreant cradle.   8
Where they most breed and haunt, I have observed
The air is delicate.

Enter Lady [Macbeth].

DUNCAN   See, see, our honored hostess!

56 letters have i.e., letter has   **63–4 To beguile . . . time** To deceive
everyone, look the way people expect you to look   **68 dispatch** management   **71–2 Only . . . fear** Whatever else you do, keep a cheerful
countenance. To alter one's countenance is to betray a guilty conscience.
1.6. Location: Before Macbeth's castle.
0.1 *Hautboys* oboelike instruments   **1 seat** site.   **3 gentle** (1) noble
(2) refined (by the delicate air)   **4–5 The . . . mansionry** The house
martin, that loves to nest in churches, proves by his devoted nest
building   **6 jutty** projection of wall or building   **7 coign of vantage**
convenient corner, i.e., for nesting   **8 pendent** hanging, suspended.
procreant for breeding

The love that follows us sometime is our trouble,   11
Which still we thank as love. Herein I teach you   12
How you shall bid God 'ild us for your pains,   13
And thank us for your trouble.
LADY MACBETH   All our service
In every point twice done, and then done double,
Were poor and single business to contend   16
Against those honors deep and broad wherewith   17
Your Majesty loads our house. For those of old,   18
And the late dignities heaped up to them,   19
We rest your hermits.
DUNCAN   Where's the Thane of Cawdor?   20
We coursed him at the heels, and had a purpose   21
To be his purveyor; but he rides well,   22
And his great love, sharp as his spur, hath holp him   23
To his home before us. Fair and noble hostess,
We are your guest tonight.
LADY MACBETH   Your servants ever   25
Have theirs, themselves, and what is theirs in compt   26
To make their audit at Your Highness' pleasure,   27
Still to return your own.
DUNCAN   Give me your hand.   28
Conduct me to mine host. We love him highly,
And shall continue our graces towards him.
By your leave, hostess.   *Exeunt.*

❧

1.7

Hautboys. Torches. Enter a sewer, and divers
servants with dishes and service, [and pass] over
the stage. Then enter Macbeth.

MACBETH
If it were done when 'tis done, then 'twere well
It were done quickly. If th'assassination   2
Could trammel up the consequence, and catch   3
With his surcease success—that but this blow   4
Might be the be-all and the end-all!—here,   5

11–12 The love . . . love The love that sometimes forces itself inconve-
niently upon us we still appreciate, since it is meant as love. (Duncan
is graciously suggesting that his visit is a bother, but, he hopes, a welcome one.)   **13 bid . . . pains** ask God to reward me for the trouble
I'm giving you. (This is said in the same gently jocose spirit as lines
11–12.)   **'ild** yield, repay   **16–17 Were . . . Against** would be poor
and small when compared with   **18–20 For . . . hermits** In gratitude
for the dignities heaped upon us in former days and still others more
recently added to them, we are your thankful worshipers who pray
for you like hermits or beadsmen.   **21 coursed** followed (as in a
hunt)   **22 purveyor** an officer sent ahead to provide for entertainment; here, forerunner   **23 holp** helped   **25 We** (the royal "we," also
in lines 13–14 and 29)   **25–8 Your . . . own** Those who serve you hold
their own servants, themselves, and all their possessions in trust from
you, and can render an account whenever you wish, ready always to
render back to you what is yours. (A feudal concept of obligation.)
1.7. Location: Macbeth's castle; an inner courtyard.
0.1 *sewer* chief waiter, butler   **2–4 If . . . success** i.e., If only the assassination of Duncan could proceed without further consequences and
end the matter with the completion of the deed itself. (To *trammel* is to
bind up or entangle in a net; *surcease* means "cessation"; *success*
means "what succeeds or follows.")   **4 that but** so that only   **5 here**
in this world

But here, upon this bank and shoal of time,
We'd jump the life to come. But in these cases   7
We still have judgment here, that we but teach   8
Bloody instructions, which, being taught, return   9
To plague th'inventor. This evenhanded justice   10
Commends th'ingredience of our poisoned chalice   11
To our own lips. He's here in double trust:
First, as I am his kinsman and his subject,
Strong both against the deed; then, as his host,
Who should against his murderer shut the door,
Not bear the knife myself. Besides, this Duncan
Hath borne his faculties so meek, hath been   17
So clear in his great office, that his virtues   18
Will plead like angels, trumpet-tongued, against
The deep damnation of his taking-off;   20
And Pity, like a naked newborn babe
Striding the blast, or heaven's cherubin, horsed   22
Upon the sightless couriers of the air,   23
Shall blow the horrid deed in every eye,
That tears shall drown the wind. I have no spur   25
To prick the sides of my intent, but only
Vaulting ambition, which o'erleaps itself
And falls on th'other—   28

    Enter Lady [Macbeth].

How now, what news?
LADY MACBETH
He has almost supped. Why have you left the
    chamber?
MACBETH
Hath he asked for me?
LADY MACBETH   Know you not he has?
MACBETH
We will proceed no further in this business.
He hath honored me of late, and I have bought   33
Golden opinions from all sorts of people,
Which would be worn now in their newest gloss,   35
Not cast aside so soon.
LADY MACBETH   Was the hope drunk
Wherein you dressed yourself? Hath it slept since?
And wakes it now, to look so green and pale   38
At what it did so freely? From this time
Such I account thy love. Art thou afeard
To be the same in thine own act and valor
As thou art in desire? Wouldst thou have that
Which thou esteem'st the ornament of life,   43
And live a coward in thine own esteem,
Letting "I dare not" wait upon "I would,"   45

Like the poor cat i'th' adage?
MACBETH   Prithee, peace!   46
I dare do all that may become a man;
Who dares do more is none.
LADY MACBETH   What beast was't, then,
That made you break this enterprise to me?   49
When you durst do it, then you were a man;
And, to be more than what you were, you would
Be so much more the man. Nor time nor place   52
Did then adhere, and yet you would make both.   53
They have made themselves, and that their fitness
    now   54
Does unmake you. I have given suck, and know
How tender 'tis to love the babe that milks me;
I would, while it was smiling in my face,
Have plucked my nipple from his boneless gums
And dashed the brains out, had I so sworn as you
Have done to this.
MACBETH   If we should fail?
LADY MACBETH   We fail?
But screw your courage to the sticking place   61
And we'll not fail. When Duncan is asleep—
Whereto the rather shall his day's hard journey
Soundly invite him—his two chamberlains   64
Will I with wine and wassail so convince   65
That memory, the warder of the brain,   66
Shall be a fume, and the receipt of reason   67
A limbeck only. When in swinish sleep   68
Their drenchèd natures lies as in a death,   69
What cannot you and I perform upon
Th'unguarded Duncan? What not put upon
His spongy officers, who shall bear the guilt   72
Of our great quell?
MACBETH   Bring forth men-children only!   73
For thy undaunted mettle should compose   74
Nothing but males. Will it not be received,   75
When we have marked with blood those sleepy two
Of his own chamber and used their very daggers,
That they have done't?
LADY MACBETH   Who dares receive it other,   78
As we shall make our griefs and clamor roar   79
Upon his death?
MACBETH   I am settled, and bend up   80
Each corporal agent to this terrible feat.   81

---

7 jump risk. (But imaging the physical act is characteristic of Macbeth; compare this with line 27.) **8–10 We . . . th'inventor** i.e., we still have punishment for crime in this world, whereby our bloody acts establish guilty precedents and thereby invite the just reciprocity of punishing blood with blood. **11 Commends** presents. **th'ingredience** the contents of a mixture **17 faculties** powers of office **18 clear** free of taint **20 taking-off** murder **22 Striding the blast** bestriding the tempest. (Putti and cherubs are often portrayed this way in Renaissance graphic arts.) **23 sightless couriers** invisible steeds or runners, i.e., the winds **25 tears . . . wind** (Showers of rain were popularly supposed to still the wind.) **28 th'other** the other side. (The image is of a horseman vaulting into his saddle and ignominiously falling on the opposite side.) **33 bought** acquired (by bravery in battle) **35 would** ought to, should **38 green** sickly **43 the ornament of life** i.e., the crown **45 wait upon** accompany, always follow

46 adage (i.e., "The cat would eat fish but she will not wet her feet.") **49 break** broach **52 Nor** Neither **53 adhere** agree, suit. **would** wanted to **54 that their fitness** that very suitability of time and place **61 But** Only. **the sticking place** the notch into which is fitted the string of a crossbow cranked taut for shooting **64 chamberlains** attendants on the bedchamber **65 wassail** carousal, drink. **convince** overpower **66–8 warder . . . only** (The brain was thought to be divided into three ventricles: imagination in front, memory at the back, and between them the seat of reason. The fumes of wine, arising from the stomach, would deaden memory and judgment.) **67 receipt** receptacle, ventricle **68 limbeck** device for distilling liquids **69 drenchèd** drowned (in wine) **72 spongy** soaked, drunken **73 quell** murder. **74 mettle** (the same word as *metal*): substance, temperament **75 received** i.e., as truth **78 other** otherwise **79 As** inasmuch as **80–1 bend up . . . agent** harness and direct every part of me

Away, and mock the time with fairest show.   82
False face must hide what the false heart doth know.
                                                        Exeunt.

❦

2.1

Enter Banquo, and Fleance, with a torch before him.

BANQUO   How goes the night, boy?

FLEANCE
The moon is down. I have not heard the clock.

BANQUO
And she goes down at twelve.

FLEANCE   I take't, 'tis later, sir.

BANQUO
Hold, take my sword. [*He gives him his sword.*] There's
    husbandry in heaven;   4
Their candles are all out. Take thee that too.
                            [*He gives him his belt and dagger.*]
A heavy summons lies like lead upon me,   6
And yet I would not sleep. Merciful powers,   7
Restrain in me the cursèd thoughts that nature
Gives way to in repose!

Enter Macbeth, and a Servant with a torch.

Give me my sword. Who's there? [*He takes his sword.*]

MACBETH   A friend.

BANQUO
What, sir, not yet at rest? The King's abed.
He hath been in unusual pleasure,
And sent forth great largess to your offices.   14
This diamond he greets your wife withal,
By the name of most kind hostess, and shut up   16
In measureless content.   [*He gives a diamond.*]

MACBETH   Being unprepared,   17
Our will became the servant to defect,   18
Which else should free have wrought.   19

BANQUO   All's well.
I dreamt last night of the three Weird Sisters.
To you they have showed some truth.

MACBETH   I think not of them.
Yet, when we can entreat an hour to serve,
We would spend it in some words upon that business,
If you would grant the time.

BANQUO   At your kind'st leisure.

MACBETH
If you shall cleave to my consent when 'tis,   26
It shall make honor for you.

BANQUO   So I lose none   27
In seeking to augment it, but still keep
My bosom franchised and allegiance clear,   29
I shall be counseled.

MACBETH   Good repose the while!   30

BANQUO   Thanks, sir. The like to you.
                            Exit Banquo [with Fleance].

MACBETH [*to Servant*]
Go bid thy mistress, when my drink is ready,   32
She strike upon the bell. Get thee to bed.
                                        Exit [Servant].

Is this a dagger which I see before me,
The handle toward my hand? Come, let me clutch
    thee.
I have thee not, and yet I see thee still.
Art thou not, fatal vision, sensible   37
To feeling as to sight? Or art thou but
A dagger of the mind, a false creation,
Proceeding from the heat-oppressèd brain?   40
I see thee yet, in form as palpable
As this which now I draw.   [*He draws a dagger.*]
Thou marshall'st me the way that I was going,   43
And such an instrument I was to use.
Mine eyes are made the fools o'th'other senses,
Or else worth all the rest. I see thee still,
And on thy blade and dudgeon gouts of blood,   47
Which was not so before. There's no such thing.
It is the bloody business which informs
Thus to mine eyes. Now o'er the one half world
Nature seems dead, and wicked dreams abuse   51
The curtained sleep. Witchcraft celebrates   52
Pale Hecate's offerings, and withered Murder,   53
Alarumed by his sentinel, the wolf,   54
Whose howl's his watch, thus with his stealthy pace,   55
With Tarquin's ravishing strides, towards his design   56
Moves like a ghost. Thou sure and firm-set earth,
Hear not my steps which way they walk, for fear
Thy very stones prate of my whereabout
And take the present horror from the time   60
Which now suits with it. Whiles I threat, he lives;   61

---

82 mock deceive
2.1 Location: Inner courtyard of Macbeth's castle. Time is virtually
continuous from the previous scene.
0.1 *torch* (This may mean "torchbearer," although it does not at line
9.1.)   **4 husbandry** thrift (careful management of resources in the
domestic economy)   **6 summons** i.e., to sleep   **7 would not** am
reluctant to (owing to my uneasy fears).   **powers** order of angels
deputed by God to resist demons   **14 largess** gifts, gratuities.
offices quarters used for the household work.   **16–17 and shut . . .
content** and went to bed professing himself endlessly pleased.
18–19 Our . . . wrought our good will (to entertain the king) was limited by our meager resources (on such short notice), which otherwise
would have poured forth hospitality without restraint.

26 cleave . . . 'tis give me your support, adhere to my view, when the
time comes   **27 So** Provided that   **29 franchised** free (from guilt).
clear unstained   **30 counseled** receptive to suggestion.   **32 drink**
i.e., posset or bedtime drink of hot spiced milk curdled with ale or
wine, as also in 2.2.6   **37 fatal** ominous.   **sensible** perceivable by the
senses   **40 heat-oppressèd** fevered   **43 Thou . . . going** You seem to
guide me toward the destiny I intended, toward Duncan's chambers
47 dudgeon hilt of a dagger.   **gouts** drops   **51 abuse** deceive
52 curtained curtained by night (and by bedcurtains)   **53 Pale
Hecate's offerings** sacrificial offerings to Hecate, the goddess of night
and witchcraft. (She is *pale* because she is identified with the pale
moon.)   **withered** (Murder is pictured as in images of Death,
shrunken and wasted.)   **54 Alarumed** given the signal to action
55 watch watchword or cry   **56 Tarquin's** (Tarquin was a Roman
tyrant who ravished Lucrece.)   **60–1 And take . . . with it** and thus
echo and augment the horror which is so suited to this evil hour, or,
usurp the present horror by breaking the silence.   **61 threat** i.e.,
merely threaten to kill Duncan

Words to the heat of deeds too cold breath gives.   62
                                            A bell rings.

I go, and it is done. The bell invites me.
Hear it not, Duncan, for it is a knell
That summons thee to heaven or to hell.   *Exit.*

❧

2.2

Enter Lady [Macbeth].

LADY MACBETH
That which hath made them drunk hath made me
    bold;
What hath quenched them hath given me fire. Hark!
    Peace!
It was the owl that shrieked, the fatal bellman,   3
Which gives the stern'st good-night. He is about it.   4
The doors are open; and the surfeited grooms   5
Do mock their charge with snores. I have drugged
    their possets,   6
That death and nature do contend about them
Whether they live or die.
MACBETH [*within*]   Who's there? What, ho!
LADY MACBETH
Alack, I am afraid they have awaked,
And 'tis not done. Th'attempt and not the deed
Confounds us. Hark! I laid their daggers ready;   11
He could not miss 'em. Had he not resembled
My father as he slept, I had done't.

Enter Macbeth, [bearing bloody daggers].

My husband!
MACBETH
I have done the deed. Didst thou not hear a noise?
LADY MACBETH
I heard the owl scream and the crickets cry.   16
Did not you speak?
MACBETH   When?
LADY MACBETH   Now.
MACBETH   As I descended?
LADY MACBETH   Ay.
MACBETH   Hark! Who lies i'th' second chamber?
LADY MACBETH   Donalbain.
MACBETH [*looking at his hands*]   This is a sorry sight.
LADY MACBETH
A foolish thought, to say a sorry sight.
MACBETH
There's one did laugh in 's sleep, and one cried
    "Murder!"
That they did wake each other. I stood and heard
    them.

But they did say their prayers, and addressed them   28
Again to sleep.
LADY MACBETH   There are two lodged together.
MACBETH
One cried "God bless us!" and "Amen!" the other,
As they had seen me with these hangman's hands.   31
List'ning their fear, I could not say "Amen"
When they did say "God bless us!"
LADY MACBETH   Consider it not so deeply.
MACBETH
But wherefore could not I pronounce "Amen"?
I had most need of blessing, and "Amen"
Stuck in my throat.
LADY MACBETH   These deeds must not be thought   37
After these ways; so, it will make us mad.   38
MACBETH
Methought I heard a voice cry "Sleep no more!
Macbeth does murder sleep," the innocent sleep,
Sleep that knits up the raveled sleave of care,   41
The death of each day's life, sore labor's bath,   42
Balm of hurt minds, great nature's second course,   43
Chief nourisher in life's feast—
LADY MACBETH   What do you mean?
MACBETH
Still it cried "Sleep no more!" to all the house;
"Glamis hath murdered sleep, and therefore Cawdor
Shall sleep no more; Macbeth shall sleep no more."
LADY MACBETH
Who was it that thus cried? Why, worthy thane,
You do unbend your noble strength to think   49
So brainsickly of things. Go get some water
And wash this filthy witness from your hand.   51
Why did you bring these daggers from the place?
They must lie there. Go, carry them and smear
The sleepy grooms with blood.
MACBETH   I'll go no more.
I am afraid to think what I have done;
Look on't again I dare not.
LADY MACBETH   Infirm of purpose!
Give me the daggers. The sleeping and the dead
Are but as pictures. 'Tis the eye of childhood
That fears a painted devil. If he do bleed,
I'll gild the faces of the grooms withal,   60
For it must seem their guilt.
            [*She takes the daggers, and*] *exit. Knock within.*
MACBETH   Whence is that knocking?
How is't with me, when every noise appalls me?
What hands are here? Ha! They pluck out mine eyes.
Will all great Neptune's ocean wash this blood
Clean from my hand? No, this my hand will rather
The multitudinous seas incarnadine,   66

---

62 **Words . . . gives** Words give only lifeless expression to live deeds,
are no substitute for deeds.
2.2. Location: Scene continues.
3 **bellman** one who rings a bell to announce a death or to mark the
hours of the night   4 **Which . . . good-night** i.e., that announces the
last good-night, death.   5 **grooms** servants   6 **mock their charge**
make a mockery of their guard duty.   **possets** hot bedtime drinks (as
in 2.1.32)   11 **Confounds** ruins   16 **owl, crickets** (The sounds of
both could be ominous and prophetic of death.)

28 **addressed them** settled themselves   31 **As** as if.   **hangman's
hands** bloody hands of the executioner.   37 **thought** thought about
38 **so** if we do so   41 **raveled sleave** tangled skein   42 **bath** i.e., to
relieve the soreness   43 **second course** (Ordinary feasts had two
courses, of which the second was the *chief nourisher;* here, sleep is
seen as following eating in a restorative process.)   49 **unbend** slack-
en (as one would a bow; contrast with "bend up" in 1.7.80)
51 **witness** evidence   60 **gild** smear, coat, as if with a thin layer of
gold. (Gold was ordinarily spoken of as red.)   66 **multitudinous**
numerous and teeming.   **incarnadine** stain red

Making the green one red.   67

Enter Lady [Macbeth].

LADY MACBETH
My hands are of your color, but I shame
To wear a heart so white. (*Knock.*) I hear a knocking
At the south entry. Retire we to our chamber.
A little water clears us of this deed.
How easy is it, then! Your constancy   72
Hath left you unattended. (*Knock.*) Hark! More
   knocking.   73
Get on your nightgown, lest occasion call us   74
And show us to be watchers. Be not lost   75
So poorly in your thoughts.

MACBETH
To know my deed, 'twere best not know myself.   77
                                                        Knock.
Wake Duncan with thy knocking! I would thou
   couldst!   *Exeunt.*

❧

2.3

Knocking within. Enter a Porter.

PORTER   Here's a knocking indeed! If a man were porter
of hell gate, he should have old turning the key.   2
(*Knock.*) Knock, knock, knock! Who's there, i'th'
name of Beelzebub? Here's a farmer that hanged   4
himself on th'expectation of plenty. Come in time!   5
Have napkins enough about you; here you'll sweat for't.   6
(*Knock.*) Knock, knock! Who's there, in th'other
devil's name? Faith, here's an equivocator, that could   8
swear in both the scales against either scale, who
committed treason enough for God's sake, yet could
not equivocate to heaven. Oh, come in, equivocator.
(*Knock.*) Knock, knock, knock! Who's there? Faith,
here's an English tailor come hither for stealing out of   13
a French hose. Come in, tailor. Here you may roast   14
your goose. (*Knock.*) Knock, knock! Never at quiet!   15

What are you? But this place is too cold for hell. I'll
devil-porter it no further. I had thought to have let in
some of all professions that go the primrose way to
th'everlasting bonfire. (*Knock.*) Anon, anon! [*He opens the
gate.*] I pray you, remember the porter.

Enter Macduff and Lennox.

MACDUFF
Was it so late, friend, ere you went to bed,
That you do lie so late?
PORTER   Faith, sir, we were carousing till the second   23
cock; and drink, sir, is a great provoker of three things.   24
MACDUFF   What three things does drink especially
provoke?
PORTER   Marry, sir, nose-painting, sleep, and urine.   27
Lechery, sir, it provokes and unprovokes: it provokes
the desire but it takes away the performance. Therefore much drink may be said to be an equivocator
with lechery: it makes him and it mars him; it sets him
on and it takes him off; it persuades him and dis-
heartens him, makes him stand to and not stand to;   33
in conclusion, equivocates him in a sleep and, giving   34
him the lie, leaves him.   35
MACDUFF   I believe drink gave thee the lie last night.   36
PORTER   That it did, sir, i'the very throat on me. But I   37
requited him for his lie, and, I think, being too strong
for him, though he took up my legs sometimes, yet I   39
made a shift to cast him.   40
MACDUFF   Is thy master stirring?

Enter Macbeth.

Our knocking has awaked him. Here he comes.
                                                  [*Exit Porter.*]
LENNOX
Good morrow, noble sir.
MACBETH   Good morrow, both.
MACDUFF
Is the King stirring, worthy thane?
MACBETH   Not yet.
MACDUFF
He did command me to call timely on him.   45
I have almost slipped the hour.
MACBETH   I'll bring you to him.   46
MACDUFF
I know this is a joyful trouble to you,
But yet 'tis one.

---

67 one red one all-pervading red.   **72–3 Your . . . unattended** Your
preoccupation with yourself has left you inattentive to other matters.
74 nightgown dressing gown   **75 to be watchers** to have been awake
and not abed.   **77 To know . . . myself** To come to terms with what I
have done, I would do best to shut out the horror entirely and deny
who I am.
**2.3. Location: Scene continues. The knocking at the door has
already been heard in 2.2. It is not necessary to assume literally,
however, that Macbeth and Lady Macbeth have been talking near
the** *south entry* **(2.2.70) where the knocking is heard.**
2 old plenty of   **4 Beelzebub** a devil.   **4–5 Here's . . . plenty** i.e., Here's
a farmer who has hoarded in anticipation of a scarcity and will be justly
punished by a crop surplus and low prices.   **5 Come in time!** i.e., You
have come in good time!   **6 napkins** handkerchiefs or towels (to mop
up the sweat)   **8 equivocator** (This is regarded by many editors as an
allusion to the trial of the Jesuit Henry Garnet for treason in the spring of
1606 and to the doctrine of equivocation said to have been presented in
his defense; according to this doctrine, a lie was not a lie if the utterer
had in his mind a different meaning in which the utterance was true.)
13–14 for stealing . . . hose (French fashions, much in demand by style-
conscious courtiers, no doubt provided opportunities for tailors to skimp
in the making of garments while charging customers the full amount.)
14–15 roast your goose heat your tailor's smoothing iron—something
easily done in the flames of hell. (With a pun on the sense, "cook your
goose." A *goose* could also be a long-handled iron, or a prostitute.)

23–4 second cock second crowing of the cock before dawn   **27 Marry**
(Originally, an oath, "by the Virgin Mary.")   **nose-painting** i.e., red-
dening of the nose through drink   **33 makes . . . not stand to** arouses
him sexually but then takes away the ability to perform sexually.
(Repeating the idea of the previous phrases about how it *makes him
and mars him,* etc.)   **34 equivocates . . . sleep** (1) lulls him asleep
(2) gives him an erotic experience in dream only   **34–5 giving him
the lie** (1) deceiving him (2) laying him out flat   **35 leaves him**
(1) dissipates as intoxication (2) is passed off as urine.   **36 gave thee
the lie** (1) called you a liar (2) made you unable to stand and put you
to sleep   **37 i'the . . . me** (1) giving me the deepest insult imaginable
(2) literally, going down my throat. (*On* means "of.")   **39 took . . .
legs** made me unable to stand and threw me to the ground as a
wrestler might do   **40 made a shift** managed.   **cast** (1) throw, as in
wrestling (2) vomit   **45 timely** betimes, early   **46 slipped** let slip

MACBETH
  The labor we delight in physics pain.   49
  This is the door.
MACDUFF   I'll make so bold to call,
  For 'tis my limited service.   *Exit Macduff.*   51
LENNOX   Goes the King hence today?
MACBETH   He does; he did appoint so.
LENNOX
  The night has been unruly. Where we lay,
  Our chimneys were blown down, and, as they say,
  Lamentings heard i'th'air, strange screams of death,
  And prophesying with accents terrible   57
  Of dire combustion and confused events   58
  New hatched to the woeful time. The obscure bird   59
  Clamored the livelong night. Some say the earth
  Was feverous and did shake.
MACBETH   'Twas a rough night.
LENNOX
  My young remembrance cannot parallel
  A fellow to it.

          Enter Macduff.

MACDUFF   Oh, horror, horror, horror!
  Tongue nor heart cannot conceive nor name thee!
MACBETH AND LENNOX   What's the matter?
MACDUFF
  Confusion now hath made his masterpiece!   66
  Most sacrilegious murder hath broke ope
  The Lord's anointed temple and stole thence
  The life o'th' building!
MACBETH   What is't you say? The life?
LENNOX   Mean you His Majesty?
MACDUFF
  Approach the chamber and destroy your sight
  With a new Gorgon. Do not bid me speak;   73
  See, and then speak yourselves.
                    Exeunt Macbeth and Lennox.
                    Awake, awake!
  Ring the alarum bell. Murder and treason!
  Banquo and Donalbain, Malcolm, awake!
  Shake off this downy sleep, death's counterfeit,   77
  And look on death itself! Up, up, and see
  The great doom's image! Malcolm, Banquo,   79
  As from your graves rise up and walk like sprites   80
  To countenance this horror! Ring the bell. *Bell rings.* 81

          Enter Lady [*Macbeth*].

LADY MACBETH   What's the business,
  That such a hideous trumpet calls to parley   83

The sleepers of the house? Speak, speak!
MACDUFF   Oh, gentle lady,
  'Tis not for you to hear what I can speak.
  The repetition in a woman's ear   87
  Would murder as it fell.

          Enter Banquo.

                    Oh, Banquo, Banquo,
  Our royal master's murdered!
LADY MACBETH   Woe, alas!
  What, in our house?
BANQUO   Too cruel anywhere.
  Dear Duff, I prithee, contradict thyself
  And say it is not so.

          Enter Macbeth, Lennox, and Ross.

MACBETH
  Had I but died an hour before this chance   93
  I had lived a blessèd time; for from this instant
  There's nothing serious in mortality.   95
  All is but toys. Renown and grace is dead;   96
  The wine of life is drawn, and the mere lees   97
  Is left this vault to brag of.   98

          Enter Malcolm and Donalbain.

DONALBAIN
  What is amiss?
MACBETH   You are, and do not know't.
  The spring, the head, the fountain of your blood
  Is stopped, the very source of it is stopped.
MACDUFF
  Your royal father's murdered.
MALCOLM   Oh, by whom?
LENNOX
  Those of his chamber, as it seemed, had done't.
  Their hands and faces were all badged with blood;   104
  So were their daggers, which unwiped we found
  Upon their pillows. They stared and were distracted;
  No man's life was to be trusted with them.
MACBETH
  Oh, yet I do repent me of my fury,
  That I did kill them.
MACDUFF   Wherefore did you so?
MACBETH
  Who can be wise, amazed, temp'rate and furious,   110
  Loyal and neutral, in a moment? No man.
  Th'expedition of my violent love   112
  Outran the pauser, reason. Here lay Duncan,
  His silver skin laced with his golden blood,   114
  And his gashed stabs looked like a breach in nature 115
  For ruin's wasteful entrance; there the murderers,   116
  Steeped in the colors of their trade, their daggers

---

49 physics pain i.e., cures that labor of its troublesome aspect.
51 limited appointed   **57 accents terrible** terrifying utterances
58 combustion tumult   **59 New . . . time** newly born to accompany
the woeful nature of the time.   **obscure bird** owl, the bird of darkness
66 Confusion Destruction   **73 Gorgon** one of three monsters with
hideous faces (Medusa was a Gorgon), whose look turned the beholders to stone   **77 downy** feathery, unsubstantial   **79 great doom's
image** simulacrum of the Last Judgment, of Doomsday.   **80 As . . .
rise up** (At the Last Judgment, the dead will rise from their graves to
be judged.)   **sprites** souls, ghosts   **81 countenance** (1) be in keeping
with (2) witness   **83 trumpet** (Another metaphorical suggestion of
the Last Judgment; the *trumpet* here is the shouting and the bell.)

87 repetition recital, report   **93 chance** occurrence   **95 serious in
mortality** worthwhile in mortal life.   **96 toys** trifles.   **97 lees** dregs
98 vault (1) wine-vault (2) earth, with its vaulted sky   **104 badged**
marked, as with a badge or emblem   **110 amazed** bewildered
112 Th'expedition The haste   **114 golden** (See the note for 2.2.60.)
115 breach in nature gap in the defenses of life. (A metaphor of military siege.)   **116 wasteful** destructive

Unmannerly breeched with gore. Who could refrain   118
That had a heart to love, and in that heart
Courage to make 's love known?

LADY MACBETH [*fainting*]   Help me hence, ho!   120

MACDUFF
Look to the lady.

MALCOLM [*aside to Donalbain*]
                        Why do we hold our tongues,
That most may claim this argument for ours?   122

DONALBAIN [*aside to Malcolm*]
What should be spoken here, where our fate,
Hid in an auger hole, may rush and seize us?   124
Let's away. Our tears are not yet brewed.   125

MALCOLM [*aside to Donalbain*]
Nor our strong sorrow upon the foot of motion.   126

BANQUO   Look to the lady.

                    [*Lady Macbeth is helped out.*]
And when we have our naked frailties hid,   128
That suffer in exposure, let us meet
And question this most bloody piece of work   130
To know it further. Fears and scruples shake us.   131
In the great hand of God I stand, and thence   132
Against the undivulged pretense I fight   133
Of treasonous malice.

MACDUFF   And so do I.

ALL   So all.   134

MACBETH
Let's briefly put on manly readiness   135
And meet i'th' hall together.

ALL   Well contented.
                Exeunt [*all but Malcolm and Donalbain*].

MALCOLM
What will you do? Let's not consort with them.   137
To show an unfelt sorrow is an office
Which the false man does easy. I'll to England.   139

DONALBAIN
To Ireland, I. Our separated fortune
Shall keep us both the safer. Where we are,
There's daggers in men's smiles; the nea'er in blood,   142
The nearer bloody.

MALCOLM   This murderous shaft that's shot   143
Hath not yet lighted, and our safest way   144
Is to avoid the aim. Therefore to horse,
And let us not be dainty of leave-taking,   146
But shift away. There's warrant in that theft   147

118 **breeched with gore** covered (as with breeches) to the hilts with
gore.   120 **make 's love known** make manifest his love.   122 **That . . .
ours** we to whom this business matters most.   124 **in an auger hole**
i.e., in some hiding place, in ambush. (An *auger* is a hole-drilling
tool.)   125 **Our . . . brewed** i.e., Our real sorrow has not yet ripened.
126 **upon . . . motion** yet prepared to express itself fully.   128 **our
naked frailties hid** clothed our poor, shivering bodies (which remind
us of our human frailty)   130 **question** discuss   131 **scruples**
doubts, suspicions   132–4 **thence . . . malice** with God's help, I will
fight against the as-yet-unknown purpose that prompted this treason.
133 **pretense** design   134 **malice** enmity.   135 **briefly** quickly.
manly readiness men's clothing and resolute purpose   137 **consort**
keep company, associate   139 **easy** easily.   142–3 **the nea'er . . .
bloody** the closer the relationship, the greater the danger to be feared
of bloody intent.   144 **lighted** alighted, descended   146 **dainty of**
tediously ceremonious in   147 **shift away** disappear by stealth.
warrant justification

Which steals itself when there's no mercy left.
                                Exeunt.

❖

2.4

Enter Ross with an Old Man.

OLD MAN
Threescore and ten I can remember well,
Within the volume of which time I have seen
Hours dreadful and things strange, but this sore night   3
Hath trifled former knowings.

ROSS   Ha, good father,   4
Thou see'st the heavens, as troubled with man's act,   5
Threatens his bloody stage. By th' clock 'tis day,   6
And yet dark night strangles the traveling lamp.   7
Is't night's predominance or the day's shame
That darkness does the face of earth entomb
When living light should kiss it?

OLD MAN   'Tis unnatural,
Even like the deed that's done. On Tuesday last
A falcon, tow'ring in her pride of place,   12
Was by a mousing owl hawked at and killed.   13

ROSS
And Duncan's horses—a thing most strange and
    certain—
Beauteous and swift, the minions of their race,   15
Turned wild in nature, broke their stalls, flung out,
Contending 'gainst obedience, as they would   17
Make war with mankind.

OLD MAN   'Tis said they eat each other.   18

ROSS
They did so, to th'amazement of mine eyes
That looked upon't.

            Enter Macduff.

                    Here comes the good Macduff.—
How goes the world, sir, now?

MACDUFF   Why, see you not?

ROSS
Is't known who did this more than bloody deed?

MACDUFF
Those that Macbeth hath slain.

ROSS   Alas the day,
What good could they pretend?

MACDUFF   They were suborned.   24
Malcolm and Donalbain, the King's two sons,
Are stol'n away and fled, which puts upon them
Suspicion of the deed.

ROSS   'Gainst nature still!

2.4. Location: Outside Macbeth's castle of Inverness.
3 **sore** dreadful, grievous   4 **trifled former knowings** made trivial all
former experiences.   **father** old man   5–6 **the heavens . . . stage** a
solar eclipse threatens disapprovingly our human scene of murder.
(With a theatrical metaphor in *heavens* [the decorated roof over the
stage], *act*, and *stage*.)   7 **traveling lamp** i.e., sun.   12 **tow'ring** cir-
cling higher and higher. (A term in falconry.)   **place** pitch, highest
point in the falcon's flight   13 **mousing** i.e., ordinarily preying on
mice   15 **minions** darlings   17 **as** as if   18 **eat** ate. (Pronounced
"et.")   24 **What . . . pretend?** i.e., what could they hope to gain by it?
suborned bribed, hired.

Thriftless ambition, that will ravin up   28
Thine own life's means! Then 'tis most like   29
The sovereignty will fall upon Macbeth.

MACDUFF
He is already named and gone to Scone   31
To be invested.

ROSS   Where is Duncan's body?

MACDUFF   Carried to Colmekill,   33
The sacred storehouse of his predecessors
And guardian of their bones.

ROSS   Will you to Scone?

MACDUFF
No, cousin, I'll to Fife.

ROSS   Well, I will thither.   36

MACDUFF
Well, may you see things well done there. Adieu,
Lest our old robes sit easier than our new!

ROSS   Farewell, father.

OLD MAN
God's benison go with you, and with those   40
That would make good of bad, and friends of foes!

                              Exeunt omnes.

❖

3.1

Enter Banquo.

BANQUO
Thou hast it now—King, Cawdor, Glamis, all
As the weird women promised, and I fear
Thou played'st most foully for't. Yet it was said
It should not stand in thy posterity,   4
But that myself should be the root and father
Of many kings. If there come truth from them—
As upon thee, Macbeth, their speeches shine—   7
Why, by the verities on thee made good,
May they not be my oracles as well
And set me up in hope? But hush, no more.   10

        Sennet sounded. Enter Macbeth as King, Lady
        [Macbeth], Lennox, Ross, lords, and attendants.

MACBETH
Here's our chief guest.

LADY MACBETH   If he had been forgotten,
It had been as a gap in our great feast
And all-thing unbecoming.   13

MACBETH
Tonight we hold a solemn supper, sir,   14
And I'll request your presence.

BANQUO   Let Your Highness
Command upon me, to the which my duties   16

Are with a most indissoluble tie
Forever knit.

MACBETH   Ride you this afternoon?

BANQUO   Ay, my good lord.

MACBETH
We should have else desired your good advice,
Which still hath been both grave and prosperous,   22
In this day's council; but we'll take tomorrow.
Is't far you ride?

BANQUO
As far, my lord, as will fill up the time
Twixt this and supper. Go not my horse the better,   26
I must become a borrower of the night
For a dark hour or twain.

MACBETH   Fail not our feast.

BANQUO   My lord, I will not.

MACBETH
We hear our bloody cousins are bestowed   31
In England and in Ireland, not confessing
Their cruel parricide, filling their hearers
With strange invention. But of that tomorrow,   34
When therewithal we shall have cause of state   35
Craving us jointly. Hie you to horse. Adieu,   36
Till you return at night. Goes Fleance with you?

BANQUO
Ay, my good lord. Our time does call upon 's.

MACBETH
I wish your horses swift and sure of foot,
And so I do commend you to their backs.   40
Farewell.   *Exit Banquo.*
Let every man be master of his time
Till seven at night. To make society
The sweeter welcome, we will keep ourself   44
Till suppertime alone. While then, God be with you!   45
        Exeunt Lords [and all but Macbeth and a Servant].
Sirrah, a word with you. Attend those men   46
Our pleasure?

SERVANT
They are, my lord, without the palace gate.

MACBETH
Bring them before us.   *Exit Servant.*
                    To be thus is nothing,   49
But to be safely thus.—Our fears in Banquo   50
Stick deep, and in his royalty of nature   51
Reigns that which would be feared. 'Tis much he
  dares;   52
And to that dauntless temper of his mind   53
He hath a wisdom that doth guide his valor
To act in safety. There is none but he
Whose being I do fear; and under him
My genius is rebuked, as it is said   57

---

28 **Thriftless** Spendthrift.   **ravin up** devour ravenously   29 **like** likely   31 **named** chosen. (See the note for 1.4.50.)   **Scone** ancient royal city of Scotland near Perth   33 **Colmekill** Icolmkill, i.e., Cell of St. Columba, the barren islet of Iona in the Western Islands, a sacred spot where the kings were buried; here, called a *storehouse*   36 **Fife** (Of which Macduff is Thane.)   40 **bension** blessing
3.1. Location: Forres. The palace.
4 **stand** stay, remain   7 **shine** beam favorably   10.1 *Sennet* trumpet call   13 **all-thing** in every way   14 **solemn** ceremonious   16 **Command** lay your command

22 **still** always.   **grave and prosperous** weighty and profitable   26 **this** this present moment.   **Go . . . better** Unless my horse makes better time than I expect   31 **bestowed** lodged   34 **invention** falsehood.   35 **therewithal** besides that   35–6 **cause . . . jointly** questions of state occupying our joint attention.   40 **commend** commit, entrust   44 **we . . . ourself** I will keep to myself   45 **While** Till   46 **Sirrah** (A form of address to a social inferior.)   49 **thus** i.e., king   50 **But** unless.   **in** concerning   51 **royalty of nature** natural kingly bearing   52 **would be** deserves to be   53 **to** added to   57 **My genius is rebuked** my guardian spirit is daunted or abashed

Mark Antony's was by Caesar. He chid the sisters   58
When first they put the name of king upon me,
And bade them speak to him. Then, prophetlike,
They hailed him father to a line of kings.
Upon my head they placed a fruitless crown
And put a barren scepter in my grip,
Thence to be wrenched with an unlineal hand,   64
No son of mine succeeding. If't be so,
For Banquo's issue have I filed my mind;   66
For them the gracious Duncan have I murdered,
Put rancors in the vessel of my peace   68
Only for them, and mine eternal jewel   69
Given to the common enemy of man   70
To make them kings, the seeds of Banquo kings.
Rather than so, come fate into the list,   72
And champion me to th'utterance!—Who's there?   73

Enter Servant and two Murderers.

Now go to the door, and stay there till we call.
                                         Exit Servant.
Was it not yesterday we spoke together?
MURDERERS
It was, so please Your Highness.
MACBETH   Well then, now
Have you considered of my speeches? Know
That it was he in the times past which held you
So under fortune, which you thought had been   79
Our innocent self. This I made good to you
In our last conference, passed in probation with you   81
How you were borne in hand, how crossed, the
     instruments,   82
Who wrought with them, and all things else that
     might   83
To half a soul and to a notion crazed   84
Say, "Thus did Banquo."
FIRST MURDERER   You made it known to us.
MACBETH
I did so, and went further, which is now
Our point of second meeting. Do you find
Your patience so predominant in your nature
That you can let this go? Are you so gospeled   89
To pray for this good man and for his issue,
Whose heavy hand hath bowed you to the grave
And beggared yours forever?
FIRST MURDERER   We are men, my liege.   92
MACBETH
Ay, in the catalogue ye go for men,   93
As hounds and greyhounds, mongrels, spaniels, curs,

Shoughs, water-rugs, and demi-wolves are clept   95
All by the name of dogs. The valued file   96
Distinguishes the swift, the slow, the subtle,
The housekeeper, the hunter, every one   98
According to the gift which bounteous nature
Hath in him closed, whereby he does receive   100
Particular addition from the bill   101
That writes them all alike; and so of men.   102
Now, if you have a station in the file,   103
Not i'th' worst rank of manhood, say't,   104
And I will put that business in your bosoms
Whose execution takes your enemy off,   106
Grapples you to the heart and love of us,
Who wear our health but sickly in his life,   108
Which in his death were perfect.
SECOND MURDERER   I am one, my liege,
Whom the vile blows and buffets of the world
Hath so incensed that I am reckless what
I do to spite the world.
FIRST MURDERER   And I another,
So weary with disasters, tugged with fortune,   113
That I would set my life on any chance   114
To mend it or be rid on't.
MACBETH   Both of you
Know Banquo was your enemy.
BOTH MURDERERS   True, my lord.
MACBETH
So is he mine, and in such bloody distance   117
That every minute of his being thrusts   118
Against my near'st of life. And though I could   119
With barefaced power sweep him from my sight   120
And bid my will avouch it, yet I must not,   121
For certain friends that are both his and mine,   122
Whose loves I may not drop, but wail his fall   123
Who I myself struck down. And thence it is   124
That I to your assistance do make love,   125
Masking the business from the common eye
For sundry weighty reasons.
SECOND MURDERER   We shall, my lord,
Perform what you command us.
FIRST MURDERER   Though our lives—
MACBETH
Your spirits shine through you. Within this hour at
     most   129
I will advise you where to plant yourselves,

58 **Caesar** Octavius Caesar.   64 **with** by.   **unlineal** not of lineal descent from me   66 **filed** defiled   68 **rancors** malignant enemies (here visualized as a poison added to a vessel full of wholesome drink)   69 **eternal jewel** i.e., soul   70 **common . . . man** i.e., devil   72 **list** lists, place of combat   73 **champion me** fight with me in single combat.   **to th'utterance** to the last extremity (French, *à l'outrance*).   79 **under fortune** down in your fortunes   81–3 **passed . . . with them** went over the proof with you how you were deceived by false promises, how you were thwarted, who the agents were, who directed their activities   84 **To . . . crazed** even to a half-wit of unsound mind   89 **gospeled** imbued with the gospel spirit   92 **yours** your family   93 **go for** pass for, are entered for

95 **Shoughs . . . clept** shaggy lap-dogs, long-haired water dogs, and dogs that have been crossbred with wolves are called   96 **valued file** list classified according to value   98 **housekeeper** watchdog   100 **in him closed** enclosed in him   101–2 **Particular . . . alike** particular qualification apart from the catalog that lists them all indiscriminately   103–4 **if . . . manhood** if you occupy not the worst of places in the *rank and file* of men   106 **Whose execution** the doing of which   108 **in his life** while he lives   113 **tugged with** pulled about by (as in wrestling)   114 **set** risk, stake   117 **distance** (1) hostility, enmity (2) interval of distance between fencers   118–19 **thrusts . . . life** stabs me to the heart.   120 **With barefaced power** by open use of my supreme royal authority   121 **And . . . avouch it** and use my mere wish as my justification   122 **For** because of, for the sake of   123–4 **wail . . . Who** I must bewail the death of him whom   125 **That . . . love** that I woo your aid   129 **Your . . . you** i.e., Enough; I can see your determination in your faces.

Acquaint you with the perfect spy o'th' time,   131
The moment on't, for't must be done tonight,   132
And something from the palace; always thought   133
That I require a clearness. And with him—   134
To leave no rubs nor botches in the work—   135
Fleance his son, that keeps him company,
Whose absence is no less material to me
Than is his father's, must embrace the fate
Of that dark hour. Resolve yourselves apart;   139
I'll come to you anon.

BOTH MURDERERS   We are resolved, my lord.

MACBETH
I'll call upon you straight. Abide within.
                                     Exeunt [*Murderers*].
It is concluded. Banquo, thy soul's flight,
If it find heaven, must find it out tonight.   [*Exit.*]

❖

3.2

Enter Macbeth's Lady and a Servant.

LADY MACBETH   Is Banquo gone from court?

SERVANT
Ay, madam, but returns again tonight.

LADY MACBETH
Say to the King I would attend his leisure
For a few words.

SERVANT   Madam, I will.   *Exit.*

LADY MACBETH   Naught's had, all's spent,
Where our desire is got without content.   7
'Tis safer to be that which we destroy
Than by destruction dwell in doubtful joy.   9

Enter Macbeth.

How now, my lord? Why do you keep alone,
Of sorriest fancies your companions making,   11
Using those thoughts which should indeed have died 12
With them they think on? Things without all remedy
Should be without regard. What's done is done.   14

MACBETH
We have scorched the snake, not killed it.   15
She'll close and be herself, whilst our poor malice   16
Remains in danger of her former tooth.   17
But let the frame of things disjoint, both the worlds
   suffer,   18
Ere we will eat our meal in fear and sleep
In the affliction of these terrible dreams

That shake us nightly. Better be with the dead,
Whom we, to gain our peace, have sent to peace,   22
Than on the torture of the mind to lie   23
In restless ecstasy. Duncan is in his grave;   24
After life's fitful fever he sleeps well.
Treason has done his worst; nor steel, nor poison,   26
Malice domestic, foreign levy, nothing   27
Can touch him further.

LADY MACBETH   Come on,
Gentle my lord, sleek o'er your rugged looks.   30
Be bright and jovial among your guests tonight.

MACBETH
So shall I, love, and so, I pray, be you.
Let your remembrance apply to Banquo;   33
Present him eminence, both with eye and tongue—   34
Unsafe the while, that we   35
Must lave our honors in these flattering streams   36
And make our faces vizards to our hearts,   37
Disguising what they are.

LADY MACBETH   You must leave this.

MACBETH
Oh, full of scorpions is my mind, dear wife!
Thou know'st that Banquo and his Fleance lives.

LADY MACBETH
But in them nature's copy's not eterne.   41

MACBETH
There's comfort yet; they are assailable.
Then be thou jocund. Ere the bat hath flown
His cloistered flight, ere to black Hecate's summons   44
The shard-borne beetle with his drowsy hums   45
Hath rung night's yawning peal, there shall be done   46
A deed of dreadful note.

LADY MACBETH   What's to be done?

MACBETH
Be innocent of the knowledge, dearest chuck,   48
Till thou applaud the deed. Come, seeling night,   49
Scarf up the tender eye of pitiful day,   50
And with thy bloody and invisible hand
Cancel and tear to pieces that great bond   52
Which keeps me pale! Light thickens,   53
And the crow makes wing to th' rooky wood;   54
Good things of day begin to droop and drowse,

131–2 with . . . on't with full and precise instructions as to when it is to be done. (*Spy* means "espial, observation.")   **133 something from** some distance removed from.   **thought** being borne in mind
134 clearness freedom from suspicion.   **135 rubs** defects, rough spots   **139 Resolve yourselves apart** Make up your minds in private conference
3.2. Location: The palace.
7 content contentedness.   **9 Than . . . joy** than by destroying achieve only an apprehensive joy.   **11 sorriest** most despicable or wretched
12 Using keeping company with, entertaining   **14 without regard** not pondered upon.   **15 scorched** slashed, cut   **16 close** heal, close up again.   **poor malice** feeble hostility   **17 her former tooth** her fang, just as before.   **18 let . . . suffer** let the universe itself fall apart, both heaven and earth perish

22 to gain . . . to peace to gain contentedness through satisfied ambition, have sent to eternal rest   **23 torture** rack   **24 ecstasy** frenzy.
26 nor steel neither steel   **27 Malice domestic** civil war.   **foreign levy** the levying of troops abroad (against Scotland)   **30 Gentle . . . looks** my noble lord, smooth over your rough looks.   **33 Let . . . apply** Remember to pay special attention   **34 eminence** favor
35–6 Unsafe . . . streams we being unsafe at present, we must put on a show of flattering cordiality to make clean our honor. (To *lave* is to wash.)   **37 vizards** masks   **41 nature's . . . eterne** nature's pattern will not continue forever.   **44 cloistered** secluded.   **Hecate** goddess of night and witchcraft, as in 2.1.53   **45 shard-borne** borne on shards, or horny wing cases, or, *shard-born*, bred in cow-droppings (shards)
46 yawning drowsy   **48 chuck** (A term of endearment.)   **49 seeling** eye-closing. (Night is pictured here as a falconer sewing up the eyes of day lest it should struggle against the deed that is to be done.)
50 Scarf up blindfold.   **pitiful** compassionate   **52 that . . . bond** i.e., the bond of natural and moral law (here associated with the full light of day)   **53 pale** sickly, pallid (like moonlight, contrasted with the full light of day); also, pallid from fear.   **Light thickens** Darkness is coming on   **54 crow** rook.   **rooky** full of rooks

Whiles night's black agents to their preys do rouse.   56
Thou marvel'st at my words, but hold thee still.
Things bad begun make strong themselves by ill.
So, prithee, go with me.   *Exeunt.*

❖

3.3

Enter three Murderers.

FIRST MURDERER [*to the Third Murderer*]
    But who did bid thee join with us?
THIRD MURDERER   Macbeth.
SECOND MURDERER [*to the First Murderer*]
    He needs not our mistrust, since he delivers   2
    Our offices and what we have to do   3
    To the direction just.
FIRST MURDERER   Then stand with us.   4
    The west yet glimmers with some streaks of day.
    Now spurs the lated traveler apace   6
    To gain the timely inn, and near approaches   7
    The subject of our watch.
THIRD MURDERER   Hark, I hear horses.
BANQUO (*within*)   Give us a light there, ho!
SECOND MURDERER   Then 'tis he. The rest
    That are within the note of expectation   12
    Already are i'th' court.
FIRST MURDERER   His horses go about.   14
THIRD MURDERER
    Almost a mile; but he does usually—
    So all men do—from hence to th' palace gate
    Make it their walk.

Enter Banquo and Fleance, with a torch.

SECOND MURDERER   A light, a light!
THIRD MURDERER   'Tis he.
FIRST MURDERER   Stand to't.
BANQUO   It will be rain tonight.
FIRST MURDERER   Let it come down!
                    [*They attack Banquo.*]
BANQUO
    Oh, treachery! Fly, good Fleance, fly, fly, fly!
    Thou mayst revenge.—Oh, slave!
                    [*He dies. Fleance escapes.*]
THIRD MURDERER
    Who did strike out the light?
FIRST MURDERER   Was't not the way?   25
THIRD MURDERER
    There's but one down; the son is fled.
SECOND MURDERER
    We have lost best half of our affair.

---

56 to . . . rouse bestir themselves to hunt their prey.
3.3. Location: A park near the palace.
2–4 He . . . just We need not mistrust this man, since the instructions
he brings from Macbeth are so precise.   **6 lated** belated   **7 timely**
arrived at in good time   **12 within . . . expectation** in the list of those
expected   **14 go about** i.e., can be heard as servants take the horses
to the stables (while Banquo and Fleance, provided with a torch, walk
from the palace gate to the castle).   **25 way** i.e., thing to do.

FIRST MURDERER
    Well, let's away and say how much is done.   28
                                        Exeunt.

❖

3.4

Banquet prepared. Enter Macbeth, Lady
[Macbeth], Ross, Lennox, Lords, and attendants.

MACBETH
    You know your own degrees; sit down. At first   1
    And last, the hearty welcome.   [*They sit.*]
LORDS   Thanks to Your Majesty.   2
MACBETH
    Ourself will mingle with society   3
    And play the humble host.
    Our hostess keeps her state, but in best time   5
    We will require her welcome.   6
LADY MACBETH
    Pronounce it for me, sir, to all our friends,
    For my heart speaks they are welcome.

Enter First Murderer [to the door].

MACBETH
    See, they encounter thee with their hearts' thanks. 9
    Both sides are even. Here I'll sit i'th' midst.   10
    Be large in mirth; anon we'll drink a measure   11
    The table round. [*He goes to the Murderer.*] There's
        blood upon thy face.
MURDERER   'Tis Banquo's, then.
MACBETH
    'Tis better thee without than he within.   14
    Is he dispatched?
MURDERER
    My lord, his throat is cut. That I did for him.
MACBETH   Thou art the best o'th' cutthroats.
    Yet he's good that did the like for Fleance;
    If thou didst it, thou art the nonpareil.   19
MURDERER   Most royal sir, Fleance is scaped.
MACBETH
    Then comes my fit again. I had else been perfect,
    Whole as the marble, founded as the rock,   22
    As broad and general as the casing air.   23
    But now I am cabined, cribbed, confined, bound in   24
    To saucy doubts and fears. But Banquo's safe?   25

28.1 Exeunt (Presumably, the murderers drag the body of Banquo offstage as they go.)
3.4. Location: A room of state in the palace.
1 degrees ranks (as a determinant of seating)   **1–2 At . . . last** Once
for all   **3 mingle with society** i.e., leave the chair of state and circu-
late among the guests   **5 keeps her state** remains in her canopied
chair of state.   **in best time** when it is most appropriate   **6 require
her welcome** call upon her to give the welcome.   **9 encounter**
respond to   **10 even** full, with equal numbers on both sides.
11 large liberal, free.   **measure** i.e., cup filled to the brim for a toast
14 'Tis . . . within It is better to have his blood on you than he to
have it within him.   **19 the nonpareil** without equal.   **22 founded**
firmly established   **23 broad and general** unconfined.   **casing**
encasing, enveloping   **24 cribbed** shut in   **25 saucy** sharp, impudent, importunate

MURDERER
Ay, my good lord. Safe in a ditch he bides,
With twenty trenchèd gashes on his head,
The least a death to nature.

MACBETH   Thanks for that.
There the grown serpent lies; the worm that's fled   29
Hath nature that in time will venom breed,
No teeth for th' present. Get thee gone. Tomorrow
We'll hear ourselves again.   *Exit Murderer.*

LADY MACBETH   My royal lord,   32
You do not give the cheer. The feast is sold   33
That is not often vouched, while 'tis a-making,   34
'Tis given with welcome. To feed were best at home;   35
From thence, the sauce to meat is ceremony;   36
Meeting were bare without it.

*Enter the Ghost of Banquo, and sits in Macbeth's
place.*

MACBETH   Sweet remembrancer!   37
Now, good digestion wait on appetite,   38
And health on both!

LENNOX   May't please Your Highness sit?

MACBETH
Here had we now our country's honor roofed   40
Were the graced person of our Banquo present,
Who may I rather challenge for unkindness   42
Than pity for mischance.

ROSS   His absence, sir,
Lays blame upon his promise. Please't Your Highness
To grace us with your royal company?

MACBETH [*seeing his place occupied*]
The table's full.

LENNOX   Here is a place reserved, sir.

MACBETH Where?

LENNOX
Here, my good lord. What is't that moves Your
   Highness?

MACBETH
Which of you have done this?

LORDS   What, my good lord?

MACBETH
Thou canst not say I did it. Never shake
Thy gory locks at me.

ROSS
Gentlemen, rise. His Highness is not well.
                                   [*They start to rise.*]

LADY MACBETH
Sit, worthy friends. My lord is often thus,
And hath been from his youth. Pray you, keep seat.
The fit is momentary; upon a thought   55
He will again be well. If much you note him

You shall offend him and extend his passion.   57
Feed, and regard him not.—[*She confers apart with
   Macbeth.*] Are you a man?

MACBETH
Ay, and a bold one, that dare look on that
Which might appall the devil.

LADY MACBETH   Oh, proper stuff!   60
This is the very painting of your fear.
This is the air-drawn dagger which, you said,   62
Led you to Duncan. Oh, these flaws and starts,   63
Impostors to true fear, would well become   64
A woman's story at a winter's fire,
Authorized by her grandam. Shame itself!   66
Why do you make such faces? When all's done,
You look but on a stool.

MACBETH   Prithee, see there!
Behold, look! Lo, how say you?—
Why, what care I? If thou canst nod, speak too.   70
If charnel houses and our graves must send   71
Those that we bury back, our monuments   72
Shall be the maws of kites.   [*Exit Ghost.*]   73

LADY MACBETH   What, quite unmanned in folly?

MACBETH
If I stand here, I saw him.

LADY MACBETH   Fie, for shame!

MACBETH
Blood hath been shed ere now, i'th'olden time,
Ere humane statute purged the gentle weal;   77
Ay, and since too, murders have been performed
Too terrible for the ear. The time has been
That, when the brains were out, the man would die,
And there an end; but now they rise again
With twenty mortal murders on their crowns,   82
And push us from our stools. This is more strange
Than such a murder is.

LADY MACBETH   My worthy lord,
Your noble friends do lack you.

MACBETH   I do forget.
Do not muse at me, my most worthy friends;
I have a strange infirmity, which is nothing
To those that know me. Come, love and health to all!
Then I'll sit down. Give me some wine. Fill full.
                                   [*He is given wine.*]

Enter Ghost.

I drink to th' general joy o'th' whole table,
And to our dear friend Banquo, whom we miss.
Would he were here! To all, and him, we thirst,   92

---

57 **offend him** make him worse   60 **Oh, proper stuff!** Oh, nonsense!
62 **air-drawn** made of thin air, or floating disembodied in space
63 **flaws** gusts, outbursts   64 **to** compared with.   **become** befit
66 **Authorized by** told on the authority of   70 **thou** Banquo
71 **charnel houses** depositories for bones or bodies   72–3 **our . . .
kites** i.e., we will have to leave the unburied bodies to scavenging
birds of prey.   77 **Ere . . . weal** before the institution of law cleansed
the commonwealth of violence and made it civilized. (*Humane*, inter-
changeable with *human*, means both "appertaining to humankind"
and "benevolent, civilizing.")   82 **mortal murders** deadly wounds.
crowns heads   92 **thirst** desire to drink

29 **worm** small serpent   32 **hear ourselves** personally confer
33 **give the cheer** welcome your guests.   33–5 **The feast . . . welcome**
A feast seems grudgingly and mercenarily given unless it is repeatedly graced with assurances of welcome.   35–7 **To feed . . . without it**
Plain eating is best done in one's own domestic setting; on more
social occasions, the spice to a feast is ceremony; gatherings are too
unadorned without it.   38 **wait on** attend   40 **roofed** under one roof
42 **Who . . . unkindness** whom I hope I may reprove for negligence
55 **upon a thought** in a moment

And all to all.

LORDS   Our duties and the pledge.   93

[*They drink.*]

MACBETH [*seeing the Ghost*]
Avaunt, and quit my sight! Let the earth hide thee!
Thy bones are marrowless, thy blood is cold;
Thou hast no speculation in those eyes   96
Which thou dost glare with!

LADY MACBETH   Think of this, good peers,
But as a thing of custom. 'Tis no other;
Only it spoils the pleasure of the time.

MACBETH   What man dare, I dare.
Approach thou like the rugged Russian bear,
The armed rhinoceros, or th' Hyrcan tiger;   102
Take any shape but that, and my firm nerves   103
Shall never tremble. Or be alive again
And dare me to the desert with thy sword.   105
If trembling I inhabit then, protest me   106
The baby of a girl. Hence, horrible shadow!   107
Unreal mockery, hence!   [*Exit Ghost.*]
                    Why, so; being gone,
I am a man again. Pray you, sit still.

LADY MACBETH
You have displaced the mirth, broke the good meeting
With most admired disorder.

MACBETH   Can such things be,   111
And overcome us like a summer's cloud,   112
Without our special wonder? You make me strange   113
Even to the disposition that I owe,   114
When now I think you can behold such sights
And keep the natural ruby of your cheeks
When mine is blanched with fear.

ROSS   What sights, my lord?

LADY MACBETH
I pray you, speak not. He grows worse and worse;
Question enrages him. At once, good night.   119
Stand not upon the order of your going,   120
But go at once.

LENNOX   Good night, and better health
Attend His Majesty!

LADY MACBETH   A kind good night to all!
                    Exeunt Lords [*and attendants*].

MACBETH
It will have blood, they say; blood will have blood.
Stones have been known to move, and trees to speak;   124
Augurs and understood relations have   125
By maggotpies and choughs and rooks brought forth   126
The secret'st man of blood. What is the night?   127

LADY MACBETH
Almost at odds with morning, which is which.

MACBETH
How say'st thou, that Macduff denies his person   129
At our great bidding?

LADY MACBETH   Did you send to him, sir?

MACBETH
I hear it by the way; but I will send.   131
There's not a one of them but in his house   132
I keep a servant fee'd. I will tomorrow—   133
And betimes I will—to the Weird Sisters.   134
More shall they speak, for now I am bent to know   135
By the worst means the worst. For mine own good
All causes shall give way. I am in blood   137
Stepped in so far that, should I wade no more,   138
Returning were as tedious as go o'er.   139
Strange things I have in head, that will to hand,
Which must be acted ere they may be scanned.   141

LADY MACBETH
You lack the season of all natures, sleep.   142

MACBETH
Come, we'll to sleep. My strange and self-abuse   143
Is the initiate fear that wants hard use.   144
We are yet but young in deed.   *Exeunt.*

❖

3.5

*Thunder. Enter the three Witches, meeting
Hecate.*

FIRST WITCH
Why, how now, Hecate? You look angerly.   1

HECATE
Have I not reason, beldams as you are?   2
Saucy and overbold, how did you dare
To trade and traffic with Macbeth
In riddles and affairs of death,
And I, the mistress of your charms,
The close contriver of all harms,   7
Was never called to bear my part
Or show the glory of our art?
And, which is worse, all you have done
Hath been but for a wayward son,
Spiteful and wrathful, who, as others do,
Loves for his own ends, not for you.
But make amends now. Get you gone,
And at the pit of Acheron   15

93 all to all all good wishes to all, or, let all drink to everyone else.
96 speculation power of sight   **102 armed** armor-plated.   **Hyrcan** of
Hyrcania, in ancient times a region near the Caspian Sea   **103 nerves**
sinews   **105 the desert** some solitary place   **106–7 If . . . girl** If then I
tremble, proclaim me a baby girl, or a girl's doll.   **111 admired disorder**
wondered-at lack of self-control.   **112 overcome** come over   **113–14 You
make . . . owe** You cause me to feel I do not know my own nature (which
I had presumed to be that of a brave man)   **119 At once** To you all; now
120 Stand . . . going Do not take the time to leave in ceremonious order
of rank, as you entered   **124 Stones . . . speak** i.e., Even inanimate
nature speaks in such a way as to reveal the unnatural act of murder
125–7 Augurs . . . blood Prophets versed in the interpretation of occult
mysteries have, by reading the signs of magpies and jackdaws, revealed
secret murderers.   **127 the night** i.e., the time of night.

129 How say'st thou What do you say to the fact   **131 by the way**
indirectly   **132 them** my Scottish nobles   **133 fee'd** i.e., paid to spy.
134 betimes (1) early (2) while there is still time   **135 bent** determined   **137 All causes** all other considerations   **138 should . . . more**
even if I were to wade no farther   **139 were** would be.   **go o'er** to
proceed.   **141 acted . . . scanned** put into performance even before
there is time to scrutinize them.   **142 season** preservative   **143–4 My
. . . use** My strange self-punishing fear is that felt by a novice who
lacks toughening experience.
3.5. Location: A heath. (This scene is probably by another author.)
1 angerly angrily, angry.   **2 beldams** hags   **7 close** secret
15 Acheron the river of sorrows in Hades; here, hell itself

Meet me i'th' morning. Thither he
Will come to know his destiny.
Your vessels and your spells provide,
Your charms and everything beside.
I am for th'air. This night I'll spend
Unto a dismal and a fatal end.   21
Great business must be wrought ere noon.
Upon the corner of the moon
There hangs a vap'rous drop profound;   24
I'll catch it ere it come to ground,
And that, distilled by magic sleights,
Shall raise such artificial sprites   27
As by the strength of their illusion
Shall draw him on to his confusion.   29
He shall spurn fate, scorn death, and bear
His hopes 'bove wisdom, grace, and fear.
And you all know, security   32
Is mortals' chiefest enemy.   *Music and a song.*
Hark! I am called. My little spirit, see,
Sits in a foggy cloud and stays for me.   [*Exit.*]   35
              Sing within, "Come away, come away," *etc.*

FIRST WITCH
Come, let's make haste. She'll soon be back again.
                                                        Exeunt.

❧

3.6

      Enter Lennox and another Lord.

LENNOX
My former speeches have but hit your thoughts,   1
Which can interpret farther. Only I say   2
Things have been strangely borne. The gracious
      Duncan   3
Was pitied of Macbeth; marry, he was dead.   4
And the right valiant Banquo walked too late,
Whom you may say, if't please you, Fleance killed,
For Fleance fled. Men must not walk too late.
Who cannot want the thought how monstrous   8
It was for Malcolm and for Donalbain
To kill their gracious father? Damnèd fact!   10
How it did grieve Macbeth! Did he not straight   11
In pious rage the two delinquents tear
That were the slaves of drink and thralls of sleep?   13
Was not that nobly done? Ay, and wisely too;
For 'twould have angered any heart alive
To hear the men deny't. So that I say

He has borne all things well; and I do think   17
That had he Duncan's sons under his key—
As, an't please heaven, he shall not—they should find 19
What 'twere to kill a father. So should Fleance.
But peace! For from broad words, and 'cause he failed 21
His presence at the tyrant's feast, I hear   22
Macduff lives in disgrace. Sir, can you tell
Where he bestows himself?
LORD   The son of Duncan,   24
From whom this tyrant holds the due of birth,   25
Lives in the English court, and is received
Of the most pious Edward with such grace   27
That the malevolence of fortune nothing
Takes from his high respect. Thither Macduff   29
Is gone to pray the holy king, upon his aid,   30
To wake Northumberland and warlike Siward,   31
That by the help of these—with Him above
To ratify the work—we may again
Give to our tables meat, sleep to our nights,   34
Free from our feasts and banquets bloody knives,   35
Do faithful homage, and receive free honors—   36
All which we pine for now. And this report
Hath so exasperate the King that he   38
Prepares for some attempt of war.
LENNOX   Sent he to Macduff?
LORD
He did; and with an absolute "Sir, not I,"   41
The cloudy messenger turns me his back   42
And hums, as who should say, "You'll rue the time   43
That clogs me with this answer."
LENNOX   And that well might   44
Advise him to a caution, t' hold what distance   45
His wisdom can provide. Some holy angel   46
Fly to the court of England and unfold
His message ere he come, that a swift blessing   48
May soon return to this our suffering country   49
Under a hand accursed!   50
LORD   I'll send my prayers with him.   *Exeunt.*

❧

---

21 **dismal** disastrous, ill-omened   24 **profound** i.e., heavily pendent, ready to drop off   27 **artificial sprites** spirits produced by magical arts   29 **confusion** ruin.   32 **security** overconfidence   35.1 "**Come away**," etc. (The song occurs in Thomas Middleton's *The Witch*.)
3.6. Location: Somewhere in Scotland.
1–2 **My . . . farther** What I've just said has coincided with your own thought. I needn't say more; you can surmise the rest.   3 **borne** carried on.   3–4 **The gracious . . . dead** (Lennox ironically implies that Macbeth's show of sorrow was hypocritical and came only after the murder.)   8 **cannot . . . thought** can help thinking   10 **fact** deed, crime.   11 **straight** straightway, at once   13 **thralls** slaves

17 **borne all things well** managed everything cleverly   19 **an't** if it. **should** would be sure to   21 **from broad words** on account of plain speech   22 **His presence** i.e., to be present   24 **bestows himself** is quartered, has taken refuge. **The son of Duncan** Malcolm
25 **holds . . . birth** withholds the birthright (i.e., the Scottish crown)
27 **Of** by.   **Edward** Edward the Confessor, King of England   29 **his high respect** the high respect paid to him. (Being out of fortune has not lessened the dignity with which Malcolm is received in England.)
30 **upon his aid** in aid of Malcolm   31 **wake Northumberland** rouse the people of Northumberland   34 **meat** food   35 **Free . . . banquets** free our feasts and banquets from   36 **free** freely bestowed, or, pertaining to freemen   38 **exasperate the King** exasperated Macbeth   41 **with . . . I** i.e., when Macduff answered the messenger curtly with a refusal   42 **cloudy** louring, scowling.   **turns me** i.e., turns. (*Me* is used colloquially for emphasis.)   43 **hums . . . say** says "umph!" as if to say   44 **clogs** encumbers, loads   45–6 **Advise . . . provide** warn him (Macduff) to keep what safe distance he can (from Macbeth).
48 **His message** i.e., the request for aid against Scotland that Macduff is going to present to King Edward (see lines 29 ff.)   49–50 **suffering country Under** country suffering under

4.1

[A cauldron.] Thunder. Enter the three Witches.

FIRST WITCH
Thrice the brinded cat hath mewed.   1
SECOND WITCH
Thrice, and once the hedgepig whined.   2
THIRD WITCH
Harpier cries. 'Tis time, 'tis time!   3
FIRST WITCH
Round about the cauldron go;
In the poisoned entrails throw.
Toad, that under cold stone
Days and nights has thirty-one   7
Sweltered venom sleeping got,   8
Boil thou first i'th' charmèd pot.
ALL *[as they dance round the cauldron]*
Double, double, toil and trouble;
Fire burn, and cauldron bubble.
SECOND WITCH
Fillet of a fenny snake,   12
In the cauldron boil and bake;
Eye of newt and toe of frog,
Wool of bat and tongue of dog,
Adder's fork and blindworm's sting,   16
Lizard's leg and owlet's wing,
For a charm of powerful trouble,
Like a hell-broth boil and bubble.
ALL
Double, double, toil and trouble;
Fire burn, and cauldron bubble.
THIRD WITCH
Scale of dragon, tooth of wolf,
Witches' mummy, maw and gulf   23
Of the ravined salt-sea shark,   24
Root of hemlock digged i'th' dark,
Liver of blaspheming Jew,
Gall of goat, and slips of yew   27
Slivered in the moon's eclipse,   28
Nose of Turk and Tartar's lips,
Finger of birth-strangled babe
Ditch-delivered by a drab,   31
Make the gruel thick and slab.   32
Add thereto a tiger's chaudron   33
For th'ingredience of our cauldron.   34

ALL
Double, double, toil and trouble;
Fire burn, and cauldron bubble.
SECOND WITCH
Cool it with a baboon's blood,
Then the charm is firm and good.   38

Enter Hecate to the other three Witches.

HECATE
Oh, well done! I commend your pains,   39
And everyone shall share i'th' gains.
And now about the cauldron sing
Like elves and fairies in a ring,
Enchanting all that you put in.   43
Music and a song: "Black spirits," etc.
[Exit Hecate.]

SECOND WITCH
By the pricking of my thumbs,
Something wicked this way comes.
    Open, locks,
    Whoever knocks!

Enter Macbeth.

MACBETH
How now, you secret, black, and midnight hags?   48
What is't you do?
ALL   A deed without a name.
MACBETH
I conjure you, by that which you profess,
Howe'er you come to know it, answer me.
Though you untie the winds and let them fight
Against the churches, though the yeasty waves   53
Confound and swallow navigation up,   54
Though bladed corn be lodged and trees blown down,   55
Though castles topple on their warders' heads,   56
Though palaces and pyramids do slope   57
Their heads to their foundations, though the treasure
Of nature's germens tumble all together   59
Even till destruction sicken, answer me   60
To what I ask you.
FIRST WITCH   Speak.
SECOND WITCH   Demand.
THIRD WITCH   We'll answer.
FIRST WITCH
Say if thou'dst rather hear it from our mouths
Or from our masters?
MACBETH   Call 'em. Let me see 'em.
FIRST WITCH
Pour in sow's blood, that hath eaten
Her nine farrow; grease that's sweaten   65

4.1. Location: A cavern (see 3.5.15). In the middle, a boiling cauldron (provided presumably by means of the trapdoor; see 4.1.106.
The trapdoor must also be used in this scene for the apparitions.)
1 brinded marked by streaks (as by fire), brindled   **2 hedgepig**
hedgehog   **3 Harpier** (The name of a familiar spirit; probably derived
from *harpy*.)   **cries** i.e., gives the signal to begin   **7–8 Days . . . got** for
thirty-one days and nights has exuded venom, formed during sleep
12 Fillet Slice.   **fenny** inhabiting fens or swamps   **16 fork** forked
tongue.   **blindworm** slowworm, a harmless burrowing lizard
23 mummy mummified flesh made into a magical potion.   **maw and
gulf** gullet and stomach   **24 ravined** ravenous, or glutted with prey (?)
27 Gall gall bladder.   **slips** cuttings for grafting or planting.   **yew**
(A tree often planted in churchyards and associated with mourning.)
28 Slivered broken off (as a branch)   **31 Ditch . . . drab** born in a
ditch of a harlot   **32 slab** viscous.   **33 chaudron** entrails
34 th'ingredience the ingredients

38.1 other (Said because Hecate is a witch, too, not because more
witches enter.)   **39–43 Oh . . . in** (These lines are universally regarded
as non-Shakespearean.)   **43.1 "Black spirits," etc.** (This song is found
in Middleton's *The Witch.*)   **48 black** i.e., dealing in black magic
53 yeasty foamy   **54 Confound** destroy   **55 Though . . . lodged**
though unripe grain be laid flat   **56 warders'** guardsmen's   **57 slope**
bend   **59 nature's germens** seed or elements from which all nature
operates   **60 sicken** be surfeited with its own excess   **65 nine
farrow** litter of nine.   **sweaten** sweated

From the murderer's gibbet throw   66
Into the flame.
ALL   Come high or low,   67
Thyself and office deftly show!   68

Thunder. First Apparition, an armed Head.

MACBETH
Tell me, thou unknown power—
FIRST WITCH   He knows thy thought.
Hear his speech, but say thou naught.
FIRST APPARITION
Macbeth! Macbeth! Macbeth! Beware Macduff,
Beware the Thane of Fife. Dismiss me. Enough.   72
                                    He descends.
MACBETH
Whate'er thou art, for thy good caution, thanks;
Thou hast harped my fear aright. But one word
    more—   74
FIRST WITCH
He will not be commanded. Here's another,
More potent than the first.   76

Thunder. Second Apparition, a bloody Child.

SECOND APPARITION   Macbeth! Macbeth! Macbeth!
MACBETH   Had I three ears, I'd hear thee.
SECOND APPARITION
Be bloody, bold, and resolute; laugh to scorn
The power of man, for none of woman born
Shall harm Macbeth.   *Descends.*
MACBETH
Then live, Macduff; what need I fear of thee?
But yet I'll make assurance double sure,
And take a bond of fate. Thou shalt not live,   84
That I may tell pale-hearted fear it lies,
And sleep in spite of thunder.   86

*Thunder. Third Apparition, a Child crowned, with
a tree in his hand.*

                         What is this
That rises like the issue of a king   87
And wears upon his baby brow the round   88
And top of sovereignty?
ALL   Listen, but speak not to't.   89
THIRD APPARITION
Be lion-mettled, proud, and take no care
Who chafes, who frets, or where conspirers are.
Macbeth shall never vanquished be until

Great Birnam Wood to high Dunsinane Hill
Shall come against him.   *Descends.*
MACBETH   That will never be.
Who can impress the forest, bid the tree   95
Unfix his earthbound root? Sweet bodements, good!   96
Rebellious dead, rise never till the wood   97
Of Birnam rise, and our high-placed Macbeth   98
Shall live the lease of nature, pay his breath   99
To time and mortal custom. Yet my heart   100
Throbs to know one thing. Tell me, if your art
Can tell so much: shall Banquo's issue ever
Reign in this kingdom?
ALL   Seek to know no more.
MACBETH
I will be satisfied. Deny me this,
And an eternal curse fall on you! Let me know.   105
          [The cauldron descends.] Hautboys.
Why sinks that cauldron? And what noise is this?   106
FIRST WITCH   Show!
SECOND WITCH   Show!
THIRD WITCH   Show!
ALL
Show his eyes, and grieve his heart;
Come like shadows, so depart!   111

*A show of eight kings and Banquo last; [the eighth
King] with a glass in his hand.*

MACBETH
Thou art too like the spirit of Banquo. Down!
Thy crown does sear mine eyeballs. And thy hair,
Thou other gold-bound brow, is like the first.   114
A third is like the former. Filthy hags,
Why do you show me this? A fourth? Start, eyes!   116
What, will the line stretch out to th' crack of doom?   117
Another yet? A seventh? I'll see no more.
And yet the eighth appears, who bears a glass
Which shows me many more; and some I see
That twofold balls and treble scepters carry.   121
Horrible sight! Now I see 'tis true,
For the blood-boltered Banquo smiles upon me   123
And points at them for his. *[The apparitions vanish.]*
    What, is this so?   124

---

66 **gibbet** gallows   67 **high or low** of the upper or lower air, from under the earth or in hell; or, one and all   68 **office** function 68.1 *armed Head* (Perhaps symbolizes the head of Macbeth cut off by Macduff and presented by him to Malcolm, or else the head of Macduff, armed in rebellion against Macbeth.)   72.1 *He descends* (i.e., by means of the trapdoor).   74 **harped** hit, touched (as in touching a harp to make it sound)   76.1 *bloody Child* (Symbolizes Macduff untimely ripped from his mother's womb; see 5.8.15–16.)   84 **take a bond of** get a guarantee from (i.e., by killing Macduff, to make doubly sure he can do no harm)   86.1-2 *Child . . . hand* (Symbolizes Malcolm, the royal child; the tree anticipates the cutting of boughs in Birnam Wood, 5.4.)   87 **like** in the likeness of   88–9 **round And top** crown

95 **impress** press into service, like soldiers   96 **bodements** prophecies   97–8 **Rebellious . . . rise** i.e., May the souls of those I have murdered (Banquo, Duncan) never rise again, since trees themself cannot rise. (An image of the Day of Judgment, when bodies are prophesied to rise again; see *Henry V,* 4.1.135–8.)   99–100 **Shall . . . custom** will live out his full life span until it is time for him to expire (*pay his breath*) in the way of all mortals.   105.1 *Hautboys* oboelike instruments.   106 **noise** music   111.1 *eight kings* (Banquo was the supposed ancestor of the Stuart dynasty, leading forward to King James VI of Scotland and James I of England, the *eighth King* here.) 111.2 *glass* (magic) mirror (also in line 119)   114 **other** i.e., second 116 **Start** Bulge from their sockets   117 **th' crack of doom** the thunder-peal of Doomsday at the end of time.   121 **twofold balls** (A probable reference to the double coronation of James at Scone and Westminster, as King of England and Scotland.)   **treble scepters** (Probably refers to James' assumed title as King of Great Britain, France, and Ireland.)   123 **blood-boltered** having his hair matted with blood   124 **for his** as his descendants.

FIRST WITCH

Ay, sir, all this is so. But why   125
Stands Macbeth thus amazedly?   126
Come, sisters, cheer we up his sprites   127
And show the best of our delights.
I'll charm the air to give a sound,
While you perform your antic round,   130
That this great king may kindly say
Our duties did his welcome pay.   132

                            Music. The Witches dance, and vanish.

MACBETH

Where are they? Gone? Let this pernicious hour
Stand aye accursèd in the calendar!
Come in, without there!

                            Enter Lennox.

LENNOX   What's Your Grace's will?

MACBETH

Saw you the Weird Sisters?

LENNOX   No, my lord.

MACBETH

Came they not by you?

LENNOX   No, indeed, my lord.

MACBETH

Infected be the air whereon they ride,
And damned all those that trust them! I did hear
The galloping of horse. Who was't came by?   140

LENNOX

'Tis two or three, my lord, that bring you word
Macduff is fled to England.

MACBETH   Fled to England!

LENNOX

Ay, my good lord.

MACBETH [*aside*]

Time, thou anticipat'st my dread exploits.   144
The flighty purpose never is o'ertook   145
Unless the deed go with it. From this moment   146
The very firstlings of my heart shall be   147
The firstlings of my hand. And even now,   148
To crown my thoughts with acts, be it thought and
        done:
The castle of Macduff I will surprise,   150
Seize upon Fife, give to th'edge o'th' sword
His wife, his babes, and all unfortunate souls
That trace him in his line. No boasting like a fool; 153
This deed I'll do before this purpose cool.
But no more sights!—Where are these gentlemen?
Come, bring me where they are.   *Exeunt.*

                            ❧

125–32 Ay . . . pay (These lines are assumed to have been written by
someone other than Shakespeare.)   **126 amazedly** stunned.
127 sprites spirits   **130 antic round** grotesque dance in a circle
132 pay repay.   **140 horse** horses.   **144 thou anticipat'st** you forestall
145 flighty fleeting   **146 Unless . . . it** unless the execution of the
deed accompanies the conception of it immediately.   **147–8 The
very . . . hand** the firstborn promptings of my heart will become my
first of deeds.   **150 surprise** attack without warning   **153 trace . . .
line** follow him in the line of inheritance.

4.2

                    Enter Macduff's Wife, her Son, and Ross.

LADY MACDUFF

What had he done to make him fly the land?

ROSS

You must have patience, madam.

LADY MACDUFF   He had none.

His flight was madness. When our actions do not,   3
Our fears do make us traitors.

ROSS   You know not   4

Whether it was his wisdom or his fear.

LADY MACDUFF

Wisdom? To leave his wife, to leave his babes,
His mansion, and his titles in a place   7
From whence himself does fly? He loves us not,
He wants the natural touch; for the poor wren,   9
The most diminutive of birds, will fight,
Her young ones in her nest, against the owl.   11
All is the fear and nothing is the love,
As little is the wisdom, where the flight
So runs against all reason.

ROSS   My dearest coz,   14

I pray you, school yourself. But, for your husband, 15
He is noble, wise, judicious, and best knows
The fits o'th' season. I dare not speak much further, 17
But cruel are the times when we are traitors   18
And do not know ourselves, when we hold rumor   19
From what we fear, yet know not what we fear,   20
But float upon a wild and violent sea
Each way and none. I take my leave of you;   22
Shall not be long but I'll be here again.   23
Things at the worst will cease, or else climb upward
To what they were before.—My pretty cousin,
Blessing upon you!

LADY MACDUFF

Fathered he is, and yet he's fatherless.

ROSS

I am so much a fool, should I stay longer
It would be my disgrace and your discomfort.   29
I take my leave at once.   *Exit Ross.*

LADY MACDUFF   Sirrah, your father's dead;   31

And what will you do now? How will you live?

SON

As birds do, mother.

LADY MACDUFF   What, with worms and flies?

SON

With what I get, I mean; and so do they.

4.2. Location: Fife. Macduff's castle.
3–4 When . . . traitors Even when we have committed no treasonous
act, our fearful responses make us look guilty.   **7 titles** possessions to
which he has title   **9 wants . . . touch** lacks the natural instinct to protect his family   **11 Her . . . nest** when her young ones are in the nest
14 coz kinswoman   **15 school** control.   **for** as for   **17 fits o'th' season** violent convulsions of the time.   **18–19 are traitors . . . ourselves**
are alienated from one another by a climate of fear and suspected
treason   **19–20 hold . . . From what we fear** believe every fearful
rumor on the basis of what we fear might be   **22 Each . . . none** this
way and that.   **23 Shall** it shall.   **but** before   **29 It . . . discomfort** I
should disgrace my manhood by weeping and cause you distress.
31 Sirrah (Here, an affectionate form of address to a child.)

LADY MACDUFF   Poor bird! Thou'dst never fear   35
The net nor lime, the pitfall nor the gin.   36

SON
Why should I, mother? Poor birds they are not set for.   37
My father is not dead, for all your saying.

LADY MACDUFF
Yes, he is dead. How wilt thou do for a father?

SON   Nay, how will you do for a husband?

LADY MACDUFF   Why, I can buy me twenty at any
market.

SON   Then you'll buy 'em to sell again.

LADY MACDUFF
Thou speak'st with all thy wit,
And yet, i'faith, with wit enough for thee.

SON   Was my father a traitor, mother?

LADY MACDUFF   Ay, that he was.

SON   What is a traitor?

LADY MACDUFF   Why, one that swears and lies.

SON   And be all traitors that do so?

LADY MACDUFF
Every one that does so is a traitor,
And must be hanged.

SON
And must they all be hanged that swear and lie?

LADY MACDUFF   Every one.

SON   Who must hang them?

LADY MACDUFF   Why, the honest men.

SON   Then the liars and swearers are fools, for there are
liars and swearers enough to beat the honest men and
hang up them.

LADY MACDUFF   Now, God help thee, poor monkey!
But how wilt thou do for a father?

SON   If he were dead, you'd weep for him; if you would
not, it were a good sign that I should quickly have a
new father.

LADY MACDUFF   Poor prattler, how thou talk'st!

Enter a Messenger.

MESSENGER
Bless you, fair dame! I am not to you known,
Though in your state of honor I am perfect.   67
I doubt some danger does approach you nearly.   68
If you will take a homely man's advice,   69
Be not found here. Hence with your little ones!
To fright you thus, methinks, I am too savage;
To do worse to you were fell cruelty,   72
Which is too nigh your person. Heaven preserve you!   73
I dare abide no longer.   *Exit Messenger.*

LADY MACDUFF   Whither should I fly?
I have done no harm. But I remember now
I am in this earthly world, where to do harm
Is often laudable, to do good sometime
Accounted dangerous folly. Why then, alas,

Do I put up that womanly defense
To say I have done no harm?

Enter Murderers.

                              What are these faces?

FIRST MURDERER   Where is your husband?

LADY MACDUFF
I hope in no place so unsanctified
Where such as thou mayst find him.

FIRST MURDERER   He's a traitor.

SON
Thou liest, thou shag-haired villain!

FIRST MURDERER   What, you egg?
                                        [*He stabs him.*]

Young fry of treachery!

SON   He has killed me, mother.   85
Run away, I pray you!   [*He dies.*]
                    Exit [*Lady Macduff*] *crying* "Murder!"
                    [*followed by the Murderers with the Son's body*].

♣

4.3

Enter Malcolm and Macduff.

MALCOLM
Let us seek out some desolate shade, and there
Weep our sad bosoms empty.

MACDUFF   Let us rather
Hold fast the mortal sword, and like good men   3
Bestride our downfall'n birthdom. Each new morn   4
New widows howl, new orphans cry, new sorrows
Strike heaven on the face, that it resounds   6
As if it felt with Scotland and yelled out   7
Like syllable of dolor.

MALCOLM   What I believe, I'll wail;   8
What know, believe; and what I can redress,   9
As I shall find the time to friend, I will.   10
What you have spoke it may be so, perchance.
This tyrant, whose sole name blisters our tongues,   12
Was once thought honest. You have loved him well;
He hath not touched you yet. I am young; but
something   14
You may deserve of him through me, and wisdom   15
To offer up a weak, poor, innocent lamb
T'appease an angry god.

MACDUFF   I am not treacherous.

MALCOLM   But Macbeth is.

---

85 fry spawn, progeny
4.3. Location: England. Before King Edward the Confessor's palace.
3 mortal deadly   **4 Bestride** stand over in defense.   **birthdom** native
land.   **6 that it resounds** so that it echoes   **7–8 As . . . dolor** as if
heaven, feeling itself the blow delivered to Scotland, cried out with a
similar cry of pain.   **8–9 What . . . believe** i.e., What I believe to be
amiss in Scotland I will grieve for, and anything I am certain to be
true I will believe. (But one must be cautious in these duplicitous
times.)   **10 to friend** opportune, congenial   **12 sole** mere   **14 He . . .
yet** i.e., the fact that Macbeth hasn't hurt you yet makes me suspicious of your loyalties.   **young** i.e., inexperienced   **14–15 something
. . . me** i.e., you may win favor with Macbeth by delivering me to him
15 wisdom i.e., it would be worldly-wise

---

35 Thou'dst never fear You are too innocent to be prudently wary of
36 lime birdlime (a sticky substance put on branches to snare birds).
gin snare.   **37 Poor . . . for** i.e., Traps are not set for *poor* birds, as you
call me.   **67 Though . . . perfect** though I am perfectly acquainted
with your honorable state.   **68 doubt** fear   **69 homely** plain
72–3 To . . . person to do actual harm to you would be savage cruelty,
which cruelty is all too near at hand.

A good and virtuous nature may recoil   20
In an imperial charge. But I shall crave your pardon.   21
That which you are my thoughts cannot transpose;   22
Angels are bright still, though the brightest fell.   23
Though all things foul would wear the brows of grace,   24
Yet grace must still look so.
MACDUFF   I have lost my hopes.   25
MALCOLM
Perchance even there where I did find my doubts.   26
Why in that rawness left you wife and child,   27
Those precious motives, those strong knots of love,
Without leave-taking? I pray you,
Let not my jealousies be your dishonors,   30
But mine own safeties. You may be rightly just,   31
Whatever I shall think.
MACDUFF   Bleed, bleed, poor country!
Great tyranny, lay thou thy basis sure,   33
For goodness dare not check thee; wear thou thy
     wrongs,   34
The title is affeered! Fare thee well, lord.   35
I would not be the villain that thou think'st
For the whole space that's in the tyrant's grasp,
And the rich East to boot.
MALCOLM   Be not offended.   38
I speak not as in absolute fear of you.   39
I think our country sinks beneath the yoke;
It weeps, it bleeds, and each new day a gash
Is added to her wounds. I think withal   42
There would be hands uplifted in my right;   43
And here from gracious England have I offer   44
Of goodly thousands. But, for all this,
When I shall tread upon the tyrant's head,
Or wear it on my sword, yet my poor country
Shall have more vices than it had before,
More suffer, and more sundry ways than ever,   49
By him that shall succeed.
MACDUFF   What should he be?   50
MALCOLM
It is myself I mean, in whom I know

All the particulars of vice so grafted   52
That, when they shall be opened, black Macbeth   53
Will seem as pure as snow, and the poor state
Esteem him as a lamb, being compared
With my confineless harms.
MACDUFF   Not in the legions   56
Of horrid hell can come a devil more damned
In evils to top Macbeth.
MALCOLM   I grant him bloody,   58
Luxurious, avaricious, false, deceitful,   59
Sudden, malicious, smacking of every sin   60
That has a name. But there's no bottom, none,
In my voluptuousness. Your wives, your daughters,
Your matrons, and your maids could not fill up
The cistern of my lust, and my desire
All continent impediments would o'erbear   65
That did oppose my will. Better Macbeth   66
Than such an one to reign.
MACDUFF   Boundless intemperance
In nature is a tyranny; it hath been   68
Th'untimely emptying of the happy throne
And fall of many kings. But fear not yet   70
To take upon you what is yours. You may
Convey your pleasures in a spacious plenty,   72
And yet seem cold; the time you may so hoodwink.   73
We have willing dames enough. There cannot be
That vulture in you to devour so many
As will to greatness dedicate themselves,
Finding it so inclined.
MALCOLM   With this there grows
In my most ill-composed affection such   78
A stanchless avarice that, were I king,   79
I should cut off the nobles for their lands,
Desire his jewels and this other's house,   81
And my more-having would be as a sauce
To make me hunger more, that I should forge   83
Quarrels unjust against the good and loyal,
Destroying them for wealth.
MACDUFF   This avarice
Sticks deeper, grows with more pernicious root
Than summer-seeming lust, and it hath been   87
The sword of our slain kings. Yet do not fear;   88
Scotland hath foisons to fill up your will   89
Of your mere own. All these are portable,   90
With other graces weighed.   91
MALCOLM
But I have none. The king-becoming graces,
As justice, verity, temperance, stableness,

20–1 A good . . . charge i.e., Even as good a virtuous nature as you have, Macduff, may give way to the insinuations of a royal command from Macbeth. (With wordplay on the *recoil* of a firearm that is *charged* with power and shot.)   **22 That . . . transpose** My suspicious thoughts cannot change you from what you are, cannot make you evil   **23 the brightest** i.e., Lucifer   **24–5 Though . . . so** Even though evil puts on the appearance of good so often as to cast that appearance into deep suspicion, yet goodness must go on looking and acting like itself.   **25 hopes** i.e., hopes of persuading Malcolm to lead the cause against Macbeth.   **26 Perchance even there** i.e., Perhaps in that same mistrustful frame of mind.   **doubts** i.e., fears such as that Macduff may covertly be on Macbeth's side.   **27 rawness** unprotected condition. (Malcolm suggests that Macduff's leaving his family unprotected could be construed as more evidence of his not having anything to fear from Macbeth.)   **30–1 Let . . . safeties** may it be true that my suspicions of your lack of honor are founded only in my own wariness.   **33 basis** foundation   **34 check** rebuke, call to account.   **wear . . . wrongs** continue to enjoy your wrongfully gained powers   **35 affeered** confirmed, certified.   **38 to boot** in addition.
39 absolute fear complete mistrust   **42 withal** in addition   **43 right cause**   **44 England** the King of England   **49 More . . . ways** suffer more grievously and in more varied ways   **50 What . . . be?** Whom could you possibly mean?

52 grafted (1) engrafted, indissolubly mixed (2) grafted like a plant that will then *open* or unfold   **53 opened** unfolded (like a bud)   **56 confineless** limitless   **58 top** surpass   **59 Luxurious** lecherous   **60 Sudden** violent, impetuous   **65 continent** (1) chaste (2) restraining, containing   **66 will** lust. (Also in line 89.)   **68 nature** human nature   **70 yet** nevertheless   **72 Convey** manage with secrecy   **73 cold** chaste.   **the time . . . hoodwink** you may thus deceive the age.   **78 ill-composed affection** evil disposition   **79 stanchless** insatiable   **81 his** one man's.   **this other's** another's   **83 that** so that   **87 summer-seeming** appropriate to youth (and lessening in later years)   **88 sword** i.e., cause of overthrow   **89 foisons** resources, plenty   **90 Of . . . own** out of your own royal estates alone.   **portable** bearable   **91 weighed** counterbalanced.

Bounty, perseverance, mercy, lowliness,   94
Devotion, patience, courage, fortitude,
I have no relish of them, but abound   96
In the division of each several crime,   97
Acting it many ways. Nay, had I power, I should
Pour the sweet milk of concord into hell,
Uproar the universal peace, confound   100
All unity on earth.
MACDUFF   O Scotland, Scotland!
MALCOLM
If such a one be fit to govern, speak.
I am as I have spoken.
MACDUFF   Fit to govern?
No, not to live. O nation miserable,
With an untitled tyrant bloody-sceptered,   105
When shalt thou see thy wholesome days again,
Since that the truest issue of thy throne
By his own interdiction stands accurst   108
And does blaspheme his breed? Thy royal father   109
Was a most sainted king; the queen that bore thee,
Oft'ner upon her knees than on her feet,
Died every day she lived. Fare thee well.   112
These evils thou repeat'st upon thyself
Hath banished me from Scotland. O my breast,   114
Thy hope ends here!
MALCOLM   Macduff, this noble passion,
Child of integrity, hath from my soul   116
Wiped the black scruples, reconciled my thoughts
To thy good truth and honor. Devilish Macbeth
By many of these trains hath sought to win me   119
Into his power, and modest wisdom plucks me   120
From overcredulous haste. But God above
Deal between thee and me! For even now
I put myself to thy direction and
Unspeak mine own detraction, here abjure   124
The taints and blames I laid upon myself
For strangers to my nature. I am yet   126
Unknown to woman, never was forsworn,   127
Scarcely have coveted what was mine own,
At no time broke my faith, would not betray
The devil to his fellow, and delight
No less in truth than life. My first false speaking
Was this upon myself. What I am truly   132
Is thine and my poor country's to command—
Whither indeed, before thy here-approach,
Old Siward with ten thousand warlike men,
Already at a point, was setting forth.   136

Now we'll together; and the chance of goodness   137
Be like our warranted quarrel!—Why are you silent?   138
MACDUFF
Such welcome and unwelcome things at once
'Tis hard to reconcile.

        Enter a Doctor.

MALCOLM
Well, more anon.—Comes the King forth, I pray you?
DOCTOR
Ay, sir. There are a crew of wretched souls
That stay his cure. Their malady convinces   143
The great essay of art; but at his touch—   144
Such sanctity hath heaven given his hand—
They presently amend.
MALCOLM   I thank you, Doctor.   146
                              Exit [*Doctor*].
MACDUFF
What's the disease he means?
MALCOLM   'Tis called the evil.   147
A most miraculous work in this good king,
Which often, since my here-remain in England,   149
I have seen him do. How he solicits heaven   150
Himself best knows; but strangely-visited people,   151
All swoll'n and ulcerous, pitiful to the eye,
The mere despair of surgery, he cures,   153
Hanging a golden stamp about their necks   154
Put on with holy prayers; and 'tis spoken,   155
To the succeeding royalty he leaves   156
The healing benediction. With this strange virtue   157
He hath a heavenly gift of prophecy,
And sundry blessings hang about his throne
That speak him full of grace.

        Enter Ross.

MACDUFF   See who comes here.
MALCOLM
My countryman, but yet I know him not.   161
MACDUFF
My ever-gentle cousin, welcome hither.   162
MALCOLM
I know him now. Good God betimes remove   163
The means that makes us strangers!
ROSS   Sir, amen.
MACDUFF
Stands Scotland where it did?
ROSS   Alas, poor country,
Almost afraid to know itself. It cannot

---

94 lowliness humility   **96 relish** flavor or trace   **97 division** subdivisions, various possible forms.   **several** separate   **100 Uproar** throw into an uproar   **105 untitled** lacking rightful title, usurping   **108 interdiction** debarring of self   **109 does blaspheme his breed** defames his breeding, i.e., is a disgrace to his royal lineage.   **112 Died . . . lived** lived a life of daily mortification.   **114 breast** heart   **116 Child of integrity** a product of your integrity of spirit; or, you person of perfect integrity   **119 trains** plots, artifices   **120 modest . . . me** wise prudence holds me back   **124 Unspeak . . . detraction** take back all I said in detraction of myself   **126 For** as   **127 Unknown to woman** a virgin   **132 upon** against   **136 at a point** prepared

137–8 the chance . . . quarrel may our chance of success be proportionate to the justice of our cause.   **143 stay** wait for.   **convinces** conquers   **144 essay of art** efforts of medical skill   **146 presently** immediately   **147 evil** i.e., scrofula, supposedly cured by the royal touch; James I claimed this power.   **149 here-remain** stay   **150 solicits** prevails by prayer with   **151 strangely-visited** afflicted by strange diseases   **153 mere** utter   **154 stamp** minted coin   **155–7 and 'tis . . . benediction** it is said that he bequeaths this healing blessedness to his royal progeny.   **157 virtue** healing power   **161 My countryman** (So identified by his dress.)   **know** recognize   **162 gentle** noble   **163 betimes** speedily

Be called our mother, but our grave; where nothing   167
But who knows nothing is once seen to smile;   168
Where sighs and groans and shrieks that rend the air
Are made, not marked; where violent sorrow seems   170
A modern ecstasy. The dead man's knell   171
Is there scarce asked for who, and good men's lives
Expire before the flowers in their caps,   173
Dying or ere they sicken.

MACDUFF   Oh, relation   174
Too nice, and yet too true!

MALCOLM   What's the newest grief?   175

ROSS
That of an hour's age doth hiss the speaker;   176
Each minute teems a new one.

MACDUFF   How does my wife?   177

ROSS
Why, well.

MACDUFF   And all my children?

ROSS   Well too.   178

MACDUFF
The tyrant has not battered at their peace?

ROSS
No, they were well at peace when I did leave 'em.

MACDUFF
Be not a niggard of your speech. How goes't?

ROSS
When I came hither to transport the tidings
Which I have heavily borne, there ran a rumor   183
Of many worthy fellows that were out,   184
Which was to my belief witnessed the rather   185
For that I saw the tyrant's power afoot.   186
Now is the time of help. [*To Malcolm*] Your eye in
    Scotland
Would create soldiers, make our women fight,   188
To doff their dire distresses.

MALCOLM   Be't their comfort   189
We are coming thither. Gracious England hath   190
Lent us good Siward and ten thousand men;
An older and a better soldier none   192
That Christendom gives out.

ROSS   Would I could answer   193
This comfort with the like! But I have words
That would be howled out in the desert air,   195
Where hearing should not latch them.

MACDUFF   What concern they?   196

The general cause? Or is it a fee-grief   197
Due to some single breast?

ROSS   No mind that's honest   198
But in it shares some woe, though the main part
Pertains to you alone.

MACDUFF   If it be mine,
Keep it not from me; quickly let me have it.

ROSS
Let not your ears despise my tongue forever,
Which shall possess them with the heaviest sound   203
That ever yet they heard.

MACDUFF   Hum! I guess at it.

ROSS
Your castle is surprised, your wife and babes
Savagely slaughtered. To relate the manner
Were, on the quarry of these murdered deer,   207
To add the death of you.

MALCOLM   Merciful heaven!
What, man, ne'er pull your hat upon your brows;   209
Give sorrow words. The grief that does not speak
Whispers the o'erfraught heart and bids it break.   211

MACDUFF
My children too?

ROSS   Wife, children, servants, all
That could be found.

MACDUFF   And I must be from thence!   213
My wife killed too?

ROSS   I have said.

MALCOLM   Be comforted.
Let's make us med'cines of our great revenge
To cure this deadly grief.

MACDUFF
He has no children. All my pretty ones?   217
Did you say all? O hell-kite! All?   218
What, all my pretty chickens and their dam
At one fell swoop?   220

MALCOLM   Dispute it like a man.   221

MACDUFF   I shall do so;
But I must also feel it as a man.
I cannot but remember such things were,
That were most precious to me. Did heaven look on
And would not take their part? Sinful Macduff,
They were all struck for thee! Naught that I am,   227
Not for their own demerits, but for mine,
Fell slaughter on their souls. Heaven rest them now!

MALCOLM
Be this the whetstone of your sword. Let grief
Convert to anger; blunt not the heart, enrage it.

167–8 nothing But who nobody except a person who   **168 once** ever
170 marked noticed (because they are so common)   **171 modern
ecstasy** commonplace emotion.   **173 flowers** (Often worn in Elizabethan caps.)   **174 or ere they sicken** before they have had time to
fall ill.   **relation** report   **175 nice** minutely accurate, elaborately
phrased   **176 That . . . speaker** The speaker of news that is scarcely
an hour old is hissed at for reporting stale news   **177 teems** teems
with, yields   **178 well** (Ross quibbles, in his reluctance to tell the bad
news. "The dead are well" means they are at rest.)   **183 heavily**
sadly   **184–6 Of . . . afoot** about many worthy Scots who have been
driven into exile and armed rebellion, which rumor was strengthened
all the more when I saw Macbeth's army on the move (in anticipation
of being attacked).   **188 our women** even our women   **189 doff** put
off, get rid of   **190 Gracious England** i.e., Edward the Confessor
192 none there is none   **193 gives out** tells of, proclaims.   **195 would**
should   **196 latch** catch (the sound of)

---

197 fee-grief a grief with an individual owner, having absolute ownership   **198 Due to** i.e., owned by   **203 possess them with** put them
in possession of   **207 quarry** heap of slaughtered deer at a hunt.
(With a pun on *dear, deer*.)   **209 pull your hat** (A conventional gesture
of grief.)   **211 Whispers** whispers to.   **o'erfraught** overburdened
213 must had to   **217 He has no children** (Referring either to Macbeth, who must not be a father if he can do such a thing, or, to Malcolm, who speaks comfortingly without knowing what such a loss
feels like to a father.)   **218 hell-kite** (The *kite* is a rapacious bird of
prey; a term of disdain and dislike.)   **220 fell** cruel   **221 Dispute**
Strive against, debate   **227 for thee** i.e., as divine punishment for
your sins.   **Naught** Wicked

MACDUFF
Oh, I could play the woman with mine eyes
And braggart with my tongue! But, gentle heavens,
Cut short all intermission. Front to front   234
Bring thou this fiend of Scotland and myself;
Within my sword's length set him. If he scape,   236
Heaven forgive him too!
MALCOLM   This tune goes manly. 237
Come, go we to the King. Our power is ready;   238
Our lack is nothing but our leave. Macbeth   239
Is ripe for shaking, and the powers above
Put on their instruments. Receive what cheer you may.   241
The night is long that never finds the day.   *Exeunt.*

❧

5.1

*Enter a Doctor of Physic and a Waiting-
Gentlewoman.*

DOCTOR   I have two nights watched with you, but can
perceive no truth in your report. When was it she last
walked?
GENTLEWOMAN   Since His Majesty went into the field, I
have seen her rise from her bed, throw her nightgown
upon her, unlock her closet, take forth paper, fold it,   6
write upon't, read it, afterwards seal it, and again
return to bed; yet all this while in a most fast sleep.
DOCTOR   A great perturbation in nature, to receive at
once the benefit of sleep and do the effects of   10
watching! In this slumbery agitation, besides her   11
walking and other actual performances, what, at any
time, have you heard her say?
GENTLEWOMAN   That, sir, which I will not report after her.
DOCTOR   You may to me, and 'tis most meet you should.   16
GENTLEWOMAN   Neither to you nor anyone, having no
witness to confirm my speech.

Enter Lady [Macbeth], with a taper.

Lo you, here she comes! This is her very guise, and,
upon my life, fast asleep. Observe her. Stand close.   20
[*They stand aside.*]
DOCTOR   How came she by that light?
GENTLEWOMAN   Why, it stood by her. She has light by
her continually. 'Tis her command.
DOCTOR   You see her eyes are open.
GENTLEWOMAN   Ay, but their sense are shut.
DOCTOR   What is it she does now? Look how she rubs
her hands.
GENTLEWOMAN   It is an accustomed action with her to
seem thus washing her hands. I have known her
continue in this a quarter of an hour.

LADY MACBETH   Yet here's a spot.
DOCTOR   Hark, she speaks. I will set down what comes
from her, to satisfy my remembrance the more   33
strongly.
LADY MACBETH   Out, damned spot! Out, I say! One—
two—why then, 'tis time to do't. Hell is murky.—
Fie, my lord, fie, a soldier, and afeard? What need we
fear who knows it, when none can call our power to
account? Yet who would have thought the old man to
have had so much blood in him?
DOCTOR   Do you mark that?
LADY MACBETH   The Thane of Fife had a wife. Where is
she now?—What, will these hands ne'er be
clean?—No more o'that, my lord, no more o' that;
you mar all with this starting.   45
DOCTOR   Go to, go to. You have known what you   46
should not.
GENTLEWOMAN   She has spoke what she should not, I
am sure of that. Heaven knows what she has known!
LADY MACBETH   Here's the smell of the blood still. All
the perfumes of Arabia will not sweeten this little
hand. Oh, oh, oh!
DOCTOR   What a sigh is there! The heart is sorely   53
charged.   54
GENTLEWOMAN   I would not have such a heart in my
bosom for the dignity of the whole body.   56
DOCTOR   Well, well, well.
GENTLEWOMAN   Pray God it be, sir.   58
DOCTOR   This disease is beyond my practice. Yet I have
known those which have walked in their sleep who
have died holily in their beds.
LADY MACBETH   Wash your hands, put on your night-
gown; look not so pale! I tell you yet again, Banquo's
buried. He cannot come out on 's grave.   64
DOCTOR   Even so?
LADY MACBETH   To bed, to bed! There's knocking at the
gate. Come, come, come, come, give me your hand.
What's done cannot be undone. To bed, to bed,
to bed!   *Exit Lady.*
DOCTOR   Will she go now to bed?
GENTLEWOMAN   Directly.
DOCTOR
Foul whisperings are abroad. Unnatural deeds
Do breed unnatural troubles. Infected minds
To their deaf pillows will discharge their secrets.
More needs she the divine than the physician.
God, God forgive us all! Look after her;
Remove from her the means of all annoyance,   77
And still keep eyes upon her. So, good night.   78
My mind she has mated, and amazed my sight.   79
I think, but dare not speak.
GENTLEWOMAN   Good night, good Doctor.
Exeunt.

❧

234 intermission delay, interval.   **Front to front** Face to face
236–7 If . . . too! If I let him escape, may he find forgiveness not only
from me but from heaven itself! (This is a condition that Macduff will
not allow to happen.)   **238 power** army   **239 Our . . . leave** we need
only to take our leave (of the English King).   **241 Put . . . instruments**
set us on as their agents, or, arm themselves.
5.1. Location: Dunsinane. Macbeth's castle.
0.1 *Physic* medicine   **6 closet** chest or cabinet   **10–11 do . . . watching** act as though awake.   **16 meet** suitable   **20 close** concealed.

33 satisfy confirm, support   **45 this starting** these startled movements.
46 Go to (An exclamation of reproof, directed at Lady Macbeth.)
53–4 sorely charged heavily burdened.   **56 dignity** worth, value   **58 Pray
. . . sir** Pray God it will turn out well, as you say, sir. (Playing on the
Doctor's *"Well, well,"* i.e., "Dear, dear.")   **64 on 's** of his   **77 annoyance**
i.e., harming herself   **78 still** constantly   **79 mated** bewildered, stupefied

5.2

Drum and colors. Enter Menteith, Caithness,
Angus, Lennox, [and] soldiers.

MENTEITH
The English power is near, led on by Malcolm,
His uncle Siward, and the good Macduff.
Revenges burn in them, for their dear causes   3
Would to the bleeding and the grim alarm   4
Excite the mortified man.
ANGUS   Near Birnam Wood   5
Shall we well meet them; that way are they coming.   6
CAITHNESS
Who knows if Donalbain be with his brother?
LENNOX
For certain, sir, he is not. I have a file   8
Of all the gentry. There is Siward's son,
And many unrough youths that even now   10
Protest their first of manhood.
MENTEITH   What does the tyrant?   11
CAITHNESS
Great Dunsinane he strongly fortifies.
Some say he's mad, others that lesser hate him
Do call it valiant fury; but for certain
He cannot buckle his distempered cause   15
Within the belt of rule.
ANGUS   Now does he feel
His secret murders sticking on his hands;
Now minutely revolts upbraid his faith-breach.   18
Those he commands move only in command,   19
Nothing in love. Now does he feel his title
Hang loose about him, like a giant's robe
Upon a dwarfish thief.
MENTEITH   Who then shall blame
His pestered senses to recoil and start,   23
When all that is within him does condemn
Itself for being there?
CAITHNESS   Well, march we on
To give obedience where 'tis truly owed.
Meet we the med'cine of the sickly weal,   27
And with him pour we in our country's purge   28
Each drop of us.
LENNOX   Or so much as it needs   29
To dew the sovereign flower and drown the weeds.   30
Make we our march towards Birnam.
                        Exeunt, marching.

❖

5.3

Enter Macbeth, Doctor, and attendants.

MACBETH
Bring me no more reports. Let them fly all!   1
Till Birnam Wood remove to Dunsinane,
I cannot taint with fear. What's the boy Malcolm? 3
Was he not born of woman? The spirits that know
All mortal consequences have pronounced me thus: 5
"Fear not, Macbeth. No man that's born of woman
Shall e'er have power upon thee." Then fly, false
     thanes,
And mingle with the English epicures!   8
The mind I sway by and the heart I bear   9
Shall never sag with doubt nor shake with fear.

Enter Servant.

The devil damn thee black, thou cream-faced loon! 11
Where got'st thou that goose look?
SERVANT
There is ten thousand—
MACBETH   Geese, villain?
SERVANT   Soldiers, sir.
MACBETH
Go prick thy face and over-red thy fear,   14
Thou lily-livered boy. What soldiers, patch?   15
Death of thy soul! Those linen cheeks of thine   16
Are counselors to fear. What soldiers, whey-face? 17
SERVANT   The English force, so please you.
MACBETH   Take thy face hence.   [*Exit Servant.*]
                    [*Calling*] Seyton!—I am sick at heart
When I behold—Seyton, I say!—This push   20
Will cheer me ever, or disseat me now.   21
I have lived long enough. My way of life   22
Is fall'n into the sere, the yellow leaf,   23
And that which should accompany old age,
As honor, love, obedience, troops of friends,   25
I must not look to have, but in their stead
Curses, not loud but deep, mouth-honor, breath
Which the poor heart would fain deny and dare not.
Seyton!

Enter Seyton.

SEYTON
What's your gracious pleasure?
MACBETH   What news more?

5.2. Location: The country near Dunsinane.
3–5 their . . . man their grievous wrongs would awaken even the dead to answer the bloody and grim call to battle. **6 well** conveniently **8 file** list, roster **10 unrough** beardless **11 Protest** assert publicly **15 distempered** disease-swollen, dropsical **18 Now . . . faith-breach** every minute now, revolts upbraid him for his violation of all trust and sacred vows. **19 in command** under orders **23 pestered** troubled, tormented **27 Meet we . . . weal** i.e., Let us join forces with Malcolm, the physician of our sick land **28–9 pour . . . of us** i.e., let us shed all our blood as a bloodletting or *purge* of our country. **30 dew** bedew, water. **sovereign** (1) royal (2) medically efficacious

5.3. Location: Dunsinane. Macbeth's castle.
1 Let . . . all! Let all the thanes desert! **3 taint with** become imbued or infected with, weakened by **5 All . . . consequences** all that happens in this mortal life **8 English epicures** luxury-loving Englishmen. **9 sway** rule myself **11 loon** stupid fellow. **14 Go . . . fear** i.e., Go prick or pinch your pale cheeks to bring some color into them. (Current medical theory held that fear caused a retreat of the blood to the abdominal organs, leaving the countenance pale or *lily-livered,* line 15.) **15 patch** domestic fool. **16 Death . . . soul!** May your soul die an eternal death! (An oath.) **linen** i.e., pale, white **17 Are . . . fear** (The fear is contagious to the rest of the body and to other observers.) **20 behold** (Macbeth does not finish this thought.) **push** effort, crisis **21 cheer** (With a suggestion of "chair.") **disseat** dethrone **22 way** course **23 sere** dry and withered **25 As** such as

SEYTON
  All is confirmed, my lord, which was reported.
MACBETH
  I'll fight till from my bones my flesh be hacked.
  Give me my armor.
SEYTON   'Tis not needed yet.
MACBETH   I'll put it on.
  Send out more horses. Skirr the country round.   36
  Hang those that talk of fear. Give me mine armor.
  How does your patient, Doctor?
DOCTOR   Not so sick, my lord,
  As she is troubled with thick-coming fancies
  That keep her from her rest.
MACBETH   Cure her of that.
  Canst thou not minister to a mind diseased,
  Pluck from the memory a rooted sorrow,
  Raze out the written troubles of the brain,   44
  And with some sweet oblivious antidote   45
  Cleanse the stuffed bosom of that perilous stuff
  Which weighs upon the heart?
DOCTOR   Therein the patient
  Must minister to himself.
MACBETH
  Throw physic to the dogs! I'll none of it.   49
  Come, put mine armor on. Give me my staff.   50
                         [Attendants arm him.]
  Seyton, send out. Doctor, the thanes fly from me.—
  Come, sir, dispatch.—If thou couldst, Doctor, cast   52
  The water of my land, find her disease,   53
  And purge it to a sound and pristine health,
  I would applaud thee to the very echo,
  That should applaud again.—Pull't off, I say.—   56
  What rhubarb, senna, or what purgative drug   57
  Would scour these English hence? Hear'st thou of
    them?   58
DOCTOR
  Ay, my good lord. Your royal preparation
  Makes us hear something.
MACBETH   Bring it after me.—   60
  I will not be afraid of death and bane   61
  Till Birnam Forest come to Dunsinane.
                         Exeunt [all but the Doctor].
DOCTOR
  Were I from Dunsinane away and clear,
  Profit again should hardly draw me here.   [Exit.]

                         ✤

5.4

Drum and colors. Enter Malcolm, Siward,
Macduff, Siward's Son, Menteith, Caithness,
Angus, [Lennox, Ross,] and soldiers, marching.

MALCOLM
  Cousins, I hope the days are near at hand   1
  That chambers will be safe.
MENTEITH   We doubt it nothing.   2
SIWARD
  What wood is this before us?
MENTEITH   The wood of Birnam.
MALCOLM
  Let every soldier hew him down a bough
  And bear't before him. Thereby shall we shadow
  The numbers of our host and make discovery   6
  Err in report of us.
SOLDIERS   It shall be done.
SIWARD
  We learn no other but the confident tyrant   8
  Keeps still in Dunsinane and will endure   9
  Our setting down before't.
MALCOLM   'Tis his main hope;   10
  For where there is advantage to be given,   11
  Both more and less have given him the revolt,   12
  And none serve with him but constrainèd things
  Whose hearts are absent too.
MACDUFF   Let our just censures   14
  Attend the true event, and put we on   15
  Industrious soldiership.
SIWARD   The time approaches
  That will with due decision make us know
  What we shall say we have and what we owe.   18
  Thoughts speculative their unsure hopes relate,   19
  But certain issue strokes must arbitrate—   20
  Towards which advance the war.   *Exeunt, marching.* 21

                         ✤

5.5

Enter Macbeth, Seyton, and soldiers, with drum
and colors.

MACBETH
  Hang out our banners on the outward walls.
  The cry is still, "They come!" Our castle's strength
  Will laugh a siege to scorn. Here let them lie
  Till famine and the ague eat them up.   4
  Were they not forced with those that should be ours, 5
  We might have met them dareful, beard to beard,   6

36 **Skirr** Scour   44 **Raze** scrape; erase.   **written troubles of** troubles
recorded in   45 **oblivious** causing forgetfulness   49 **physic** medicine
50 **staff** lance or baton of office.   52 **dispatch** hurry.   52–3 **cast The**
water diagnose disease by the inspection of urine   56 **Pull't off**
(Refers to some part of the armor not properly put on.)   57 **senna** a
purgative drug   58 **scour** purge, cleanse, rid   60 **it** i.e., the armor not
yet put on   61 **bane** ruin
5.4. Location: Country near Birnam Wood.

1 **Cousins** Kinsmen, peers   2 **chambers . . . safe** i.e., we may sleep
safely in our bedchambers.   **nothing** not at all.   6 **discovery** scout-
ing reports   8 **no other but** no other news but that   9 **Keeps**
remains.   **endure** allow, not attempt to prevent   10 **setting down**
before't laying siege to it.   11 **advantage** opportunity (i.e., in military
operations outside Macbeth's castle in which it is possible for would-
be deserters to slip away; in a siege, his forces will be more confined
to the castle and under his watchful eye)   12 **more and less** high and
low   14–15 **Let . . . event** Let us postpone judgment about these
uncertain matters until we've achieved our goal   18 **What . . . owe**
what we only claim to have, as distinguished from what we actually
have. (*Owe* can mean "own.")   19–20 **Thoughts . . . arbitrate** Specu-
lating can only convey our sense of hope; blows must decide the
actual outcome   21 **war** army.
5.5. Location: Dunsinane. Macbeth's castle.
4 **the ague** fever, disease   5 **forced** reinforced   6 **dareful** boldly, in
open battle

And beat them backward home.
A cry within of women.
What is that noise?

SEYTON
It is the cry of women, my good lord.
[He goes to the door.]

MACBETH
I have almost forgot the taste of fears.
The time has been my senses would have cooled   10
To hear a night-shriek, and my fell of hair   11
Would at a dismal treatise rouse and stir   12
As life were in't. I have supped full with horrors; 13
Direness, familiar to my slaughterous thoughts,
Cannot once start me.

[Seyton returns.]

Wherefore was that cry?   15
SEYTON   The Queen, my lord, is dead.
MACBETH   She should have died hereafter;   17
There would have been a time for such a word.
Tomorrow, and tomorrow, and tomorrow   19
Creeps in this petty pace from day to day   20
To the last syllable of recorded time,
And all our yesterdays have lighted fools   22
The way to dusty death. Out, out, brief candle!   23
Life's but a walking shadow, a poor player
That struts and frets his hour upon the stage
And then is heard no more. It is a tale
Told by an idiot, full of sound and fury,
Signifying nothing.   28

Enter a Messenger.

Thou com'st to use thy tongue; thy story quickly.
MESSENGER   Gracious my lord,
I should report that which I say I saw,
But know not how to do't.
MACBETH   Well, say, sir.
MESSENGER
As I did stand my watch upon the hill,
I looked toward Birnam, and anon, methought,
The wood began to move.
MACBETH   Liar and slave!
MESSENGER
Let me endure your wrath if't be not so.
Within this three mile may you see it coming;
I say, a moving grove.
MACBETH   If thou speak'st false,
Upon the next tree shalt thou hang alive
Till famine cling thee. If thy speech be sooth,   40
I care not if thou dost for me as much.

I pull in resolution, and begin   42
To doubt th'equivocation of the fiend
That lies like truth. "Fear not, till Birnam Wood
Do come to Dunsinane," and now a wood
Comes toward Dunsinane. Arm, arm, and out!
If this which he avouches does appear,
There is nor flying hence nor tarrying here.
I 'gin to be aweary of the sun,
And wish th'estate o'th' world were now undone.   50
Ring the alarum bell! Blow wind, come wrack,   51
At least we'll die with harness on our back.   *Exeunt.* 52

❖

5.6

Drum and colors. Enter Malcolm, Siward,
Macduff, and their army, with boughs.

MALCOLM
Now near enough. Your leafy screens throw down,
And show like those you are. You, worthy uncle,   2
Shall with my cousin, your right noble son,
Lead our first battle. Worthy Macduff and we   4
Shall take upon 's what else remains to do,
According to our order.
SIWARD   Fare you well.   6
Do we but find the tyrant's power tonight,   7
Let us be beaten, if we cannot fight.
MACDUFF
Make all our trumpets speak! Give them all breath,
Those clamorous harbingers of blood and death!   10
Exeunt. Alarums continued.

❖

5.7

Enter Macbeth.

MACBETH
They have tied me to a stake. I cannot fly,
But bearlike I must fight the course. What's he   2
That was not born of woman? Such a one
Am I to fear, or none.

Enter young Siward.

YOUNG SIWARD   What is thy name?
MACBETH   Thou'lt be afraid to hear it.
YOUNG SIWARD
No, though thou call'st thyself a hotter name
Than any is in hell.
MACBETH   My name's Macbeth.

---

10 **cooled** felt the chill of terror   11 **my fell of hair** the hair of my
scalp   12 **dismal treatise** sad story   13 **As** as if   15 **start me** make
me start.   17 **She . . . hereafter** She would have died someday, or, she
should have died at some more appropriate time, freed from the
relentless pressures of the moment   19–28 **Tomorrow . . . nothing**
(For biblical echoes in this speech, see Psalms 18:28, 22:15, 90:9; Job
8:9, 14:1–2, 18:6.)   20 **in this** in at this   22 **lighted** (The metaphor is
of a candle used to light one to bed, just as life is a brief transit for
wretched mortals to their deathbeds.)   23 **dusty** (Since life, made out
of dust, returns to dust.)   40 **cling** cause to shrivel.   **sooth** truth

42 **pull in resolution** can no longer give free rein to my self-confident
determination   50 **th'estate** the settled order   51 **wrack** ruin
52 **harness** armor
5.6. Location: Dunsinane. Before Macbeth's castle.
2 **show** appear.   **uncle** i.e., Siward   4 **battle** battalion.   6 **order**
plan of battle.   7 **Do we** If we do.   **power** army   10 **harbingers**
forerunners
5.7. Location: Before Macbeth's castle; the battle action is continuous here.
2 **course** bout or round of bearbaiting, in which the bear was tied to a
stake and dogs were set upon him.

YOUNG SIWARD
  The devil himself could not pronounce a title
  More hateful to mine ear.
MACBETH   No, nor more fearful.
YOUNG SIWARD
  Thou liest, abhorrèd tyrant! With my sword
  I'll prove the lie thou speak'st.
                        Fight, and young Siward slain.
MACBETH   Thou wast born of woman.   12
  But swords I smile at, weapons laugh to scorn,
  Brandished by man that's of a woman born.   *Exit.*

        Alarums. Enter Macduff.

MACDUFF
  That way the noise is. Tyrant, show thy face!
  If thou be'st slain, and with no stroke of mine,
  My wife and children's ghosts will haunt me still.
  I cannot strike at wretched kerns, whose arms   18
  Are hired to bear their staves. Either thou, Macbeth,   19
  Or else my sword with an unbattered edge
  I sheathe again undeeded. There thou shouldst be;   21
  By this great clatter one of greatest note
  Seems bruited. Let me find him, Fortune,   23
  And more I beg not.   *Exit. Alarums.*

        Enter Malcolm and Siward.

SIWARD
  This way, my lord. The castle's gently rendered: 25
  The tyrant's people on both sides do fight,
  The noble thanes do bravely in the war,
  The day almost itself professes yours,   28
  And little is to do.
MALCOLM   We have met with foes
  That strike beside us.
SIWARD   Enter, sir, the castle.   30
                            Exeunt. Alarum.

[5.8]

        Enter Macbeth.

MACBETH
  Why should I play the Roman fool and die   1
  On mine own sword? Whiles I see lives, the gashes   2

  Do better upon them.

        Enter Macduff.

MACDUFF   Turn, hellhound, turn!
MACBETH
  Of all men else I have avoided thee.
  But get thee back! My soul is too much charged
  With blood of thine already.
MACDUFF   I have no words;
  My voice is in my sword, thou bloodier villain
  Than terms can give thee out!   *Fight. Alarum.*
MACBETH   Thou losest labor.   8
  As easy mayst thou the intrenchant air   9
  With thy keen sword impress as make me bleed.   10
  Let fall thy blade on vulnerable crests;
  I bear a charmèd life, which must not yield
  To one of woman born.
MACDUFF   Despair thy charm,   13
  And let the angel whom thou still hast served   14
  Tell thee, Macduff was from his mother's womb
  Untimely ripped.   16
MACBETH
  Accursèd be that tongue that tells me so,
  For it hath cowed my better part of man!   18
  And be these juggling fiends no more believed   19
  That palter with us in a double sense,   20
  That keep the word of promise to our ear   21
  And break it to our hope. I'll not fight with thee. 22
MACDUFF   Then yield thee, coward,
  And live to be the show and gaze o'th' time!   24
  We'll have thee, as our rarer monsters are,
  Painted upon a pole, and underwrit,   26
  "Here may you see the tyrant."
MACBETH   I will not yield
  To kiss the ground before young Malcolm's feet
  And to be baited with the rabble's curse.
  Though Birnam Wood be come to Dunsinane,
  And thou opposed, being of no woman born,
  Yet I will try the last. Before my body   32
  I throw my warlike shield. Lay on, Macduff,
  And damned be him that first cries, "Hold, enough!" 34
                    Exeunt, fighting. Alarums.

        *Enter fighting, and Macbeth slain. [Exit Macduff
        with Macbeth's body.] Retreat, and flourish. Enter,
        with drum and colors, Malcolm, Siward, Ross,
        thanes, and soldiers.*

---

12 s.d. *young Siward slain* (In some unspecified way, young Siward's body must be removed from the stage; his own father enters at line 24.1 and perceives nothing amiss, and in 5.8.38 young Siward is reported *missing* in action. Perhaps Macbeth drags off the body, or perhaps it is removed by soldiers during the alarums.)   **18 kerns** (Properly, Irish foot soldiers; here, applied contemptuously to the rank and file.)   **19 staves** spears.   **Either thou** i.e., Either I find you and sheathe my sword in you   **21 undeeded** having seen no action. **shouldst be** ought to be (judging by the noise)   **23 bruited** announced.   **25 gently rendered** surrendered without fighting **28 professes** declares itself   **30 strike beside us** fight on our side, or miss us deliberately.
5.8. Location: Before Macbeth's castle, as the battle continues; after line 34, within the castle.
1 Roman fool i.e., suicide, like Brutus, Mark Antony, and others
2 Whiles . . . lives i.e., As long as I see any enemy living

8 give thee out name you, describe you.   **9 intrenchant** that cannot be cut, indivisible   **10 impress** make an impression on   **13 Despair** Despair of   **14 angel** evil angel, Macbeth's genius.   **still** always **16 Untimely** prematurely, i.e., by Caesarian delivery   **18 better . . . man** i.e., courage.   **19 juggling** deceiving   **20 palter . . . sense** equivocate with us   **21–2 That . . . hope** that make promises we hear (and think we understand) but then break promise with what we hoped and expected.   **24 gaze o'th' time** spectacle or sideshow of the age. **26 Painted . . . pole** i.e., painted on a board or cloth and suspended on a pole   **32 the last** i.e., my last resort: my own strength and resolution.   **34.3 Retreat** a trumpet call ordering an end to the fighting. **34.3–4 Enter, with drum and colors, etc.** (The remainder of the play is perhaps imagined as taking place in Macbeth's castle and could be marked as a separate scene. In Shakespeare's theater, however, the shift is so nonrepresentational and without scenic alteration that the action is virtually continuous.)

MALCOLM
    I would the friends we miss were safe arrived.
SIWARD
    Some must go off; and yet, by these I see   36
    So great a day as this is cheaply bought.
MALCOLM
    Macduff is missing, and your noble son.
ROSS [to Siward]
    Your son, my lord, has paid a soldier's debt.
    He only lived but till he was a man,
    The which no sooner had his prowess confirmed
    In the unshrinking station where he fought,   42
    But like a man he died.
SIWARD   Then he is dead?
ROSS
    Ay, and brought off the field. Your cause of sorrow
    Must not be measured by his worth, for then
    It hath no end.
SIWARD   Had he his hurts before?
ROSS
    Ay, on the front.
SIWARD   Why then, God's soldier be he!
    Had I as many sons as I have hairs
    I would not wish them to a fairer death.
    And so, his knell is knolled.
MALCOLM   He's worth more sorrow,
    And that I'll spend for him.
SIWARD   He's worth no more.
    They say he parted well and paid his score,   52
    And so, God be with him! Here comes newer comfort.

        Enter Macduff, with Macbeth's head.

36 go off die. **by these** to judge by these (assembled)   **42 unshrinking station** post from which he did not shrink   **52 parted** departed, died.   **score** reckoning

MACDUFF
    Hail, King! For so thou art. Behold where stands   54
    Th'usurper's cursèd head. The time is free.   55
    I see thee compassed with thy kingdom's pearl,   56
    That speak my salutation in their minds,
    Whose voices I desire aloud with mine:
    Hail, King of Scotland!
ALL   Hail, King of Scotland!   *Flourish.*
MALCOLM
    We shall not spend a large expense of time
    Before we reckon with your several loves   62
    And make us even with you. My thanes and kinsmen,   63
    Henceforth be earls, the first that ever Scotland
    In such an honor named. What's more to do
    Which would be planted newly with the time,   66
    As calling home our exiled friends abroad
    That fled the snares of watchful tyranny,
    Producing forth the cruel ministers   69
    Of this dead butcher and his fiendlike queen—
    Who, as 'tis thought, by self and violent hands   71
    Took off her life—this, and what needful else
    That calls upon us, by the grace of Grace
    We will perform in measure, time, and place.
    So, thanks to all at once and to each one,
    Whom we invite to see us crowned at Scone.   76
                       Flourish. Exeunt omnes.

54 stands i.e., on a pole   **55 free** released from tyranny.   **56 compassed . . . pearl** surrounded by the nobles of your kingdom (literally, the pearls encircling a crown)   **62 reckon** come to a reckoning.   **several** individual   **63 make . . . you** repay your worthiness.   **66 would . . . time** should be established at the commencement of this new era   **69 Producing forth** bringing forward to trial.   **ministers** agents   **71 self and violent** her own violent   **76.1** *omnes* all.

Macbeth on Stage

Macbeth has remained among the most performed plays in the canon, partly because of its audience-pleasing sensationalism, mostly because it provides two of the more challenging—and potentially rewarding—roles for Shakespearean actors, despite the superstitions surrounding the play. According to widespread theatrical tradition, actors should avoid saying "Macbeth" except in rehearsals or performance because the name is under a curse. Indeed there are stories supporting this odd belief: actors have been badly injured and even killed while performing the play. Laurence Olivier was almost killed when an iron fly-weight fell upon a chair he had just vacated. Other actors have taken mysteriously ill, and some swear they have seen a fourth witch on stage during performance. Little wonder that actors refer to this only as the "Scottish" play.

The Elizabethan Era: Stagings Outdoors and In

Both theaters that housed productions of *Macbeth* by the King's Men were well-equipped to meet the staging demands of the play. Both presumably had trap doors in the stage floor from whence the witches—and the apparitions in 4.1—might emerge. Possibly an unearthly glow was cast across the stage from a cauldron of ashes placed beneath the stage floor; this would have been especially feasible at the Blackfriars, an indoor theater and the convenient winter quarters of the King's Men after 1608. Among Shakespeare's plays, *Macbeth* is the most nocturnal in that most of its major events happen in the dead of night or in near darkness; as such, it is well suited in a verisimilar way to indoor, nighttime performances at the Blackfriars. The play is so filled with references to night and darkness, mists and fogs, that a receptive audience would have little trouble

Painter George Henry Harlow depicted the actress Sarah Siddons (1755–1831) in the sleepwalking scene (5.1) from her famous interpretation of Lady Macbeth.

The acclaimed Victorian actress Ellen Terry scored one of her many Shakespearean triumphs in the role of Lady Macbeth. She is seen here in an 1888 London production.

imagining the atmosphere, even on London's sunniest afternoons at the Globe, the company's staple theater.

The first documented performance of *Macbeth* was that at the Globe on April 20, 1611, where Simon Forman, an astrologer, fortune-teller, and physician of sorts, saw the play and wrote a somewhat detailed summary of its plot in his diary. Lamentably, Forman says little about the staging, though he mentions that Macbeth and Banquo were "riding through a wood," thus raising the possibility that animals were used on stage. This description, however, may simply echo what we learn from the dialogue.

Both theaters were equipped with machinery to "fly" characters in and out of a scene, though there is no evidence to suggest that the witches literally hovered (see 1.1.12) above the stage at the Globe, suspended by machines housed in the "heavens" that protruded over the stage. Such a spectacle would certainly command the audience's attention, but flying effects may have

been reserved for descents (as in *Cymbeline* and *The Tempest*) that are specified in stage directions. Even if the Witches only appeared through the trap doors in the stage, the effect could be stunning. Later, in 4.1, we find other moments for such audience-pleasing effects, such as *"an armed Head," "a bloody Child,"* and *"a Child crowned, with a tree in his hand,"* followed by a parade of eight kings and the return of Banquo's ghost. The three apparitions evidently were raised from beneath the stage: the stage directions repeatedly specify, "Descends." The play alternates between such scenes of spectacle and more intimate conversations, thus investing events with a cinematic structure that moves from long shot and then zooms in to close-ups of Macbeth and his wife as they plot their foul deeds.

The Restoration and the Eighteenth Century: Improvers and Adapters

Like many of Shakespeare's plays, *Macbeth* was altered by succeeding generations of theater artists in the late seventeenth and eighteenth centuries. In 1663–1664 William Davenant revised the original text to reflect the changing, increasingly neoclassical tastes of Restoration audiences.

Davenant heightened the moral imperatives of the tragedy; in the play's final moment, for instance, Malcolm commanded Macduff to take Macbeth's corpse and

> Hang [it] upon
> A pinnacle in Dunsinane, to show
> To future ages what to those is due
> Who others' right by lawless power pursue.

Elsewhere Davenant added a scene in which Lady Macbeth met Lady Macduff, an invention calculated to provide more opportunities for actresses (who were now a permanent part of the English theater) as much as for any dramatic illustration of contrasts between a good woman and a wicked one. Some of the gory moments (e.g., the slaying of Macduff's children) were deleted so as not to offend audience tastes. Most of all, Davenant transformed this dark tragedy into something akin to opera by adding numerous songs and dances for the Witches. Pepys saw this altered version no less than eight times, and proclaimed it "one of the best plays for the stage, and a variety of dancing and music, that ever I saw." Although David Garrick restored much of Shakespeare's text and intent in 1744, the operatic *Macbeth* retained its popularity until well into the nineteenth cen-

tury; the Mormon Tabernacle Choir sang the musical version in Salt Lake City on New Year's Day, 1865. Garrick also added language to the play, including a death speech—"I sink, Oh! my soul is lost forever!"—for Macbeth, whom the actor-manager played to tremendous acclaim. Garrick and his leading lady, Mrs. Hannah Pritchard, remain among the most admired Macbeth and Lady Macbeth in the play's history. The actors wore eighteenth-century English dress; truly "Scottish" Macbeths are largely a nineteenth-century innovation, though Charles Macklin actually attempted a characteristically Scottish costume as early as 1773. The formal poses presumably reflected contemporary tastes, as a way of portraying life truthfully in an idealized state. In a pamphlet called "An Essay on Acting," Garrick provided an acting lesson for the famous dagger soliloquy:

> [The actor] should not rivet his eyes to an *imaginary* object as if it *really* was there but should show an unsettled motion in his eye . . . . "Come, let me clutch thee" is not to be done by *one* motion only but by several successive catches at it, first with one hand and then with the other, preserving the same motion at the same time with his feet, like a man who, out of his depth and half-drowned in his struggles, catches at the air for substance.

Isuzu Yamada (left) makes a fearsome Lady Macbeth figure in Akira Kurosawa's magnificent 1957 film adaptation of Macbeth *as* Throne of Blood. *In director Roman Polanski's blood-soaked 1971* Macbeth *film, actress Francesca Annis (below, right) employs her porcelain beauty to create a girlish and seductive Lady Macbeth.*

Though grounded in external details, Garrick's advice to actors is historically important because his was the first post-Burbage interpretation to focus on the inner life of the character. Thomas Betterton, who acted the role in Davenant's revised text in the late seventeenth century, was a commendable Macbeth, primarily for his oratorical eloquence rather than any attempt at introspection; at this time actors were expected to possess "an ordered voice . . . and [an]excellence of gesture," the better to portray tragic heroes in an idealized state (Duerr, 178–179). Garrick, however, set the standard for subsequent actors in the role, and is justifiably regarded as among the most admired Macbeths in the play's long stage history, just as Sarah Siddons became a preeminent Lady Macbeth. She performed the role from 1785 until 1815, allowing her to build upon her discoveries. Hers was an extraordinary blend of the termagant (Mrs. Hannah Pritchard's interpretation) and the vulnerable wife. Siddons is believed to be the first actress to play the sleepwalking scene without holding a candle, the better to "wash" her hands during the "Out, damned spot!" sequence. Although Richard Brinsley Sheridan, the famed playwright and manager of the Drury Lane Theatre, was dismayed by Siddons's departure from tradition, William Hazlitt proclaimed that to see Mrs. Siddons's Lady Macbeth was the event of a lifetime.

The Nineteenth Century: Gothic Shakespeare

In the nineteenth century William Charles Macready triumphed in the title role in both England and America. Macready was a meticulous actor-manager who prepared each moment with an obsessive detail. He dressed as a highland chieftain, and his production was noted for its visual splendor as he incorporated several spectacular processions, so typical of Romantic Shakespeare. However, it was in the more intimate scenes with Lady Macbeth that Macready's Macbeth approached brilliance as "a man vacillating between horrified fascination with evil—his Macbeth does not seem to have been moved by ambition—and a highly active moral sense that left him in no doubt as to the dreadful fate to which he was consigning himself" (Williams, 127). Macready's performance as Macbeth precipitated the disastrous Astor Place Riots in New York in May 1849. More than twenty people were killed when the supporters of the English actor Macready clashed with those of Edwin Forrest, America's first native-born superstar actor and an outstanding Macbeth in his own right. During Macready's performance, Forrest's supporters actually threw the carcass of a dead sheep on stage.

The German actor Friedrich Mitterwurzer, noted for his interpretation of Ibsen's realistic dramas, most famously revolutionized the role of Macbeth as he added even more psychological depth to the protago-

Orson Welles makes an imposing Macbeth in his nightmarish 1948 film. Here, during the banquet scene, he rises from the table horrified by the sight of Banquo's ghost.

(JOHN SPRINGER COLLECTION / CORBIS)

nist at the end of the nineteenth century. Mitterwurzer's Macbeth became apoplectic at the sight of Banquo's ghost, first hurling dinnerware and food at the specter, then laughing maniacally as the ghost vanished (Williams, 129). By emphasizing the many inconsistencies in Macbeth's personality, Mitterwurzer anticipated some aspects of German twentieth-century Expressionism.

The Twentieth Century: Freudian Shakespeare and Others

In the twentieth century the play has been approached from many different directions and staged in styles ranging from Method-acting to Artaud's Theater of Cruelty to spiritual ritual. Whatever the style, the general tendency has been to mitigate Macbeth's tragic stature, perhaps in deference to the many critical and scholarly articles questioning the play's tragic impact, as well as the century's experience with such dictators as Hitler and Stalin. Modern and postmodern productions of *Macbeth* have been notable more for their settings and/or attempts to draw parallels with contemporary events than for revelations actors bring to the role. Laurence Olivier played the Scottish king in 1955 in Stratford, as did Ian McKellen (1976), and Antony Sher (1999). Each actor eschewed a heroic approach to the role: Olivier was detached, almost indifferent to the killings, while McKellen made Macbeth a cold, ignoble opportunist, and Sher projected a psychotic poseur who vacillated between hysteria and ennui. Each of these productions featured outstanding Lady Macbeths whose approaches to the role differed vastly, yet effectively: Vivien Leigh, Olivier's wife, was unconventional in that she was a petite woman whose frame belied the monstrous acts she promulgated; Judi Dench, in the Nunn production, was a methodical prompter whose relationship with her husband soured after the killing of Duncan; and Harriet Walter, playing opposite Sher, was a sultry and sophisticated temptress.

An especially memorable twentieth-century *Macbeth* was that staged in Harlem in 1936 by Orson Welles, only twenty years old, for the Negro Theater Unit of the Federal Theater Project. Using a cast of more than one hundred African American performers, Welles relocated the action to Haiti and cut all references to Scotland. Since the Caribbean island is noted for its practice of voodoo, black magic provided the source of the malevolence in Welles's Haiti. Accompanied by the sound of drums and the chanting of an actual *griot*, or bard, voodoo witches were constantly visible on stage, steering the action to its bloody finale. Welles's bold choices, though theatrically fascinating, undercut the tragic dimension of the play and reduced Macbeth (Jack Carter) to a puppet controlled by evil spirits. The opening sequence of Welles's 1948 film suggests some aspects of the 1936 "Voodoo *Macbeth*," though the film itself locates the action in Scotland and uses an exclusively Anglo cast.

Because of its exploration of tyranny and its relatively simple plot, *Macbeth* has been a particular favorite of other cultures and countries. Among several notable African versions of the play, the version called *Umabatha*, "the Zulu *Macbeth*," earned considerable acclaim at the World Theater Season in London in 1972. Like Welles's "Voodoo *Macbeth*," the African production used indigenous music and dance to create its ambience, focusing on the tribe rather than a single character. In 1980 (revived at the Brooklyn Academy of Music in 1990), Yukio Ninagawa fused traditional Japanese theater techniques with those of the West to create an emotionally powerful, stylistically divergent production that enabled audiences to see the play's ritual elements anew. Ninagawa used the haunting music of *Pie Jesu* from Gabriel Faure's *Requiem* as the lights slowly faded on the body of the dead Macbeth.

Macbeth on Film and Video

Given its stage popularity, we might expect to find an unusually large number of films of *Macbeth*. In fact, only two are of note: Welles's 1948 black-and-white version and Polanski's 1971 Technicolor film. Television, on the other hand, has produced at least ten television versions of the tragedy, one as early as 1937. The intimacy of *Macbeth* lends itself to television's penchant for close-ups, as does its brevity.

Macbeth was among the first silent Shakespeare films: in 1905 American Mutoscope made a short film that featured only Macbeth's death. Italian and French filmmakers produced silent versions in 1909 and 1910, respectively, emphasizing the battle scenes and some melodramatic acting. Film history records both American and European *Macbeth*s in the silent era, including one by pioneer film artist D. W. Griffith; lamentably, most of these have been lost. The first "major" film was made in 1947 by David Bradley, an early "indie" filmmaker, for under five thousand dollars. This seventy-three-minute film is most memorable because an aspiring actor, Charlton Heston, played Macbeth—and designed the eighty costumes, most of which were created from material found at rummage sales and secondhand shops. The film was shown, to some acclaim, at the New York Public Library after its premiere in the Chicago area.

Among the most significant and accessible film and television versions of *Macbeth* are:

- 1948—Director Orson Welles, Republic Pictures, with Welles (Macbeth), Jeanette Nolan (Lady Macbeth), Roddy McDowall (Malcolm), and Dan O'Herlihy (Macduff). (89 min., restored 107 min.)

  In 1936 Welles had established his reputation as a director of Shakespeare's plays with his innovative "Voodoo *Macbeth*" (see above). He incorporated elements from that production a dozen years later when he shot *Macbeth* on film in a mere twenty-one days. In the opening sequence the Three Witches are seen creating a doll in a bubbling cauldron; later, when Macduff decapitates the butcher King, the head of that doll is lopped off. The director, who also played Macbeth, built upon the success of his cinematic masterpiece, *Citizen Kane* (1941), by incorporating the *film noir* style he popularized in the story about Kane's fall from prominence. Like *Kane*, *Macbeth* is filmed in black-and-white and uses unexpected camera angles and self-conscious lighting effects to create mood. Macbeth is consistently photographed from low angles to emphasize his powerful status. Welles's boldest and ultimately most successful visual choices are those that reinforce the play's expressionistic possibilities. Much of the film, dark and gloomy throughout, reflects Macbeth's nightmarish view of the world, particularly in Act 5: when Macbeth attempts to intervene and save Lady Macbeth during the sleepwalking scene, she falls to her death amidst bizarrely canted scenery made from *papier-mâché* (since Welles was working with a miniscule budget). The ensuing "Tomorrow, and tomorrow" soliloquy is delivered as an almost out-of-body experience: Welles overlays the speech with shots of ominous, Rorschach-like clouds (coincidentally, a choice Olivier also makes for the "To be or not to be" soliloquy in his film, *Hamlet*, made the same year). Perhaps influenced by his career in radio drama, as well as financial restraints, Welles uses a number of voice-overs throughout the film (e.g., Lady Macbeth's "Unsex me here" speech in 1.5) to heighten his treatment of the play.

Because the film was made only three years after World War II, audiences could not help but draw parallels with Hitler. In a brief prologue to the film (deleted when the film was restored in 1980), Welles announces that the play is an allegory about the battle between "Christian law and order [and] the agents of chaos, priests of hell and magic." To emphasize the religious elements in his interpretation, Welles invents a Holy Man who hovers about the action and even witnesses Macbeth's killing of the grooms attending Duncan. The film thus was seen in 1948 as a battle between the liberators of Europe and a bloody madman (see the discussion of the Macduff-Macbeth fight, p. 773 above). Welles plays Macbeth as a venal, unsympathetic man, spurred by nagging wife. He and his wife are a frustrated, middle-aged couple with little to show for their lives, and hence Welles provides them with a domestic motivation for the crimes they commit.

Although the film has many admirable features, especially in its visuals (e.g., Macbeth and Banquo are trapped in a deluge as they meet the Witches), it is marred by some bombastic acting and artificial Scottish accents. It received mixed reviews from critics and academics. Yet a restored version (including deleted scenes) has resurrected Welles's *Macbeth* so that it is now considered an important film.

■ 1960—Director George Schaefer, Grand Prize Films, with Maurice Evans (Macbeth) and Judith Anderson (Lady Macbeth). (110 min.)

Originally broadcast as a television show by NBC, George Schaefer's *Macbeth*—based on a stage production he had directed in 1954—has also been shown in movie theaters. It is, nonetheless, a made-for-TV show filmed in Scotland with actors wearing tartan plaids. We may think of this as "the anti-Welles" because it was shot in color and in bright light, the antithesis of Welles's gloomy, oppressive film. Macbeth, played by an actor (Maurice Evans) who performed the role for troops in World War II, is decidedly understated, almost as if reciting his lines. By contrast, Dame Judith Anderson, one of the most admired stage Lady Macbeths in the century, could not reduce the size of her acting to the dimensions of film. She emerges as a shrieking witch; one critic even compared her to the Wicked Witch of the West in *The Wizard of Oz*. If Welles's royal couple are frustrated middle-agers, the Evans (fifty-nine) and Anderson (sixty-two) coupling presents an aged couple whom the world has passed by.

■ 1971—Director Roman Polanski, Columbia Pictures, with Jon Finch (Macbeth), Francesca Annis (Lady Macbeth), Terence Bayler (Macduff), and Nicholas Selby (Duncan). (140 min.)

Polanski upended film and television history of *Macbeth* by offering an unusually young and attractive couple in Jon Finch and Francesca Annis, making the central characters ostensibly more sympathetic to a younger audience at whom the film was aimed (it was financed by Hugh Hefner's Playboy enterprises). Similarly, Polanski added to the play an erotic charge that had not been successfully explored in previous films of the play. Polanski's *Macbeth* was very much a product of its time—an age of sexual experimentation, unprecedented violence in film (e.g., Sam Peckinpah's *The Wild Bunch*, Arthur Penn's *Bonnie and Clyde*), and cynicism about people in power (e.g., Lyndon Johnson and Richard Nixon). Furthermore, Polanski's personal life had been shaken by the savage murder of his pregnant wife, actress Sharon Tate, and others at the hands of Charles Manson's infamous "Helter Skelter" family. Not surprisingly, Polanski's was the most graphically violent Shakespeare film of its time.

One need not look further than the opening sequence to understand that Polanski—who had made his reputation for shocking films with *Knife in the Water* and *Rosemary's Baby*—intends to heighten the already bloody nature of the play. The establishing shot, a sunny day (no fog and thunder here) with a placid beach abutting a barren landscape, shows the Witches, two hags and an unattractive young woman, burying grotesque objects—a hangman's noose and a severed hand with a dagger in it—in the sand. Throughout we encounter violent images of men dangling from trees, soldiers brutally dispatching already injured men, and King Duncan being savagely slaughtered. Banquo is also brutally killed in vivid detail, as Polanski, in one of his most arresting inventions, superimposes shots of Macbeth enjoying a bear-baiting at Dunsinane. Most gruesomely, Macbeth's severed head is shown bouncing, not unlike a soccer ball, down the castle steps. Though some have dismissed Polanski's violent images as sensational and gratuitous, they are consistent with the film, which is among the most realistic of Shakespearean movies. Throughout the film Polanski includes myriad realistic touches: Macbeth's castle is filled with laborers pushing carts, chickens and dogs freely running about, and the like. The effect is to depict a normal world into which abnormal, inhumane actions are thrust. Polanski once told a *New York Times* interviewer that he creates horror by setting up a "realistic situation where things don't quite fit in" (Dec. 12, 1971). *Macbeth*, shot mostly in rich colors, embodies Polanski's formula.

The youthful protagonists, although acting in a realistic style that obscures the play's poetry, bring a sexual energy to the text. Kenneth Tynan, who adapted Shakespeare's text for Polanski (and cut about sixty percent of the lines), had recently written the nude musical *Oh! Calcutta!* for Broadway. With Polanski he has created a subtext in which Macbeth is motivated to please his sexually alluring wife. The sleepwalking scene features nudity, and Macbeth encounters several dozen nude witches when he visits the witches' coven in Act 4. The film was among the first to explore the theme of "power as aphrodisiac," soon to become a commonplace in subsequent decades. While such an interpretation may have been provocative, the film—despite its visual brilliance—fails on one major count: Finch's Macbeth is hardly introspective and seems to grow only minimally as he wades deeper and deeper in blood. It is this lack of character growth that makes the film sensational and gratuitous more than its nudity and violence.

Polanski's film is as cynical as it is erotic. The director turns Ross into a self-serving survivor who helps slay Banquo and then participates in the murder and rape of Lady Macbeth. Ross finally emerges as "the keeper of the crown," for it is he who hands the crown to Macbeth and later to Malcolm. Polanski's final shot heightens the cynicism that pervades the film. Macduff's exultant shout that "the time is free" (5.8.55) is cut, and instead the audience sees Donalbain, Malcolm's younger brother, enter the Witches' hovel in a sequence suggesting that the cycle of murders is not yet concluded. Polanski's is a decidedly revisionary ending.

- 1979—Director Trevor Nunn, Thames Television, with Ian McKellen and Judi Dench. (120 min.)

Filmed for television three years after the successful production at the Royal Shakespeare Company's Other Place in Stratford-upon-Avon, this video preserves the feel of the stage version of Nunn's ritualized *Macbeth*, while at the same time it has been thoughtfully directed for television (by Phillip Casson). The RSC's intimate theater encourages the actors to use a conversational delivery without diminishing the power of the language. The style works well for television and its predilection for the close-ups that permit audiences to get very close to Macbeth and his wife.

The style Nunn imposes on the text might best be described as "ritualized theatricality." The video begins with a dozen actors standing in a circle defined by a ring of white light; throughout the production those not involved with the action at center stage watch the tragedy unfold. Rituals abound throughout: Duncan is crowned in a sacred ceremony in the opening; the banquet scene in 3.4 includes a rowdy drinking ritual among the thanes; and a variety of sacred totems are carried by various characters. The dominant image on stage is a shimmering golden cloak on a headless mannequin, suggesting that whoever wears the crown is but a player king "who struts and frets his hour upon the stage / And then is heard no more." The exceptional blend of ritual, theatricality, and naturalistic acting intelligently explores the many layers of *Macbeth*.

- 1983—Director Jack Gold, BBC Shakespeare Plays, with Nicol Williamson (Macbeth) and Jane Lapotaire (Lady Macbeth).

Set in eleventh-century Scotland and featuring an authentic Scot as the murderous king, the BBC *Macbeth* would appear to be a realistic telling of Shakespeare's bloody tale. Yet, the production is stylized, almost static, and—unlike Polanski—rarely capable of showing the graphic elements that have fascinated audiences for centuries: the dagger, the ghost, the parade of kings, and Macbeth's severed head. This *Macbeth* is the tragedy of a single man whose murderous choices unleash havoc on the world about him: thus the emphasis on facial close-ups rather than the externals. The BBC furthers the exploration of the sex-as-aphrodisiac theme hinted at by Polanski. Jane Lapotaire's rendering of the "unsex me here" speech in 1.5 is almost orgasmic. Though perhaps not as visually interesting as in other *Macbeth*s on film and video, the central performances, especially Nicol Williamson's schizophrenic approach (a dignified voice for public encounters, a "possessed" one for private moments) are bold, if sometimes inconsistent in their quality.

Adaptations

Film

- 1957—*Throne of Blood* (also: *Kumonosu-Jo, or The Castle of the Spider's Web*). Director Akira Kurosawa, TOHO Films, with Toshiro Mifune (Macbeth) and Isuzu Yamada (Lady Macbeth). (110 min.)

Technically Kurosawa's film is an adaptation of Shakespeare's play, set by the director in feudal Japan as a samurai fable. It has, nonetheless, entered our consciousness as one of the best interpretations

Toshiro Mifune, the heroic actor who often appears in films by Akira Kurosawa, here plays the dying samurai, Washizu, the Macbeth figure felled by arrows from his own soldiers in Throne of Blood.

(TOHO/THE KOBAL COLLECTION)

for all time of the Macbeth story on stage or screen. Borrowing elements from such diverse sources as the Japanese Kabuki theater (particularly Mifune's *arragoto*—or "manly"—performance), the Noh theater (a chanting chorus, Banquo's ghost, the Spirit of the supernatural Forest), and the American Western movie (e.g., John Ford's black-and-white landscapes), Kurosawa creates a truly mythic work in which Shakespeare's verbal imagery is transformed into poetic visuals. The early scene in which the Macbeth figure (here called Washizu) and the Banquo figure (here named Miki) find themselves trapped in the forest is a masterpiece of cinema: the fog-shrouded forest seems to come alive, its branches and tree limbs ensnaring the samurai warriors until they suddenly find an eerie peace in the presence of an old Forest Spirit weaving upon a loom. By foretelling Washizu's future, this supernatural specter sets in motion his inexorable march to doom. Lady Macbeth (here called Asaji and played by the mesmerizing Isuzu Yamada) is all the more frightening in her seduction of Washizu because she is played in such an extraordinarily understated manner. Her face, so much like an ancient Noh mask, rarely betrays emotion as she keeps her eyes downcast in dutiful obeisance to her lord and master. She nonetheless exerts a powerful influence on him. Washizu's violent death at the hands of his men (see above, p. 774), among the finest moments in modern

cinema, is a just retribution for his violation of the sacred samurai code. "Samurai" means "one who serves"; Washizu's ultimate crime is not his ambitious climb to power, but his failure to protect his master at all costs. Thus, only the samurai brotherhood can kill him. The film is less interested in the psychology of the usurper's guilt—here it is handled in a stylized, rather than realistic, manner—than in telling a Buddhist allegory in which the characters are metaphors for humanity's failings.

Operas and Musicals

The passions engendered by the play have made it a prime candidate for operatic treatments in the modern era. Although not as powerful as *Otello*, Giuseppe Verdi's *Macbeth* (revised in 1865, with libretto by Francesco Maria Piave) has become a staple of opera companies throughout the world, partly because it provides a stunning and passionate role for a baritone. In 2002 Dan Schaaf composed a moderately successful rock-opera titled *The Bloody Deed Is Done*.

Spin-offs

Several commercial films inspired by Shakespeare's tragedy were produced in the silent era. In 1917 an Italian film company made *The Lady from Minsk*, telling the

Close-Up

AKIRA KUROSAWA

Although Akira Kurosawa's *Throne of Blood: The Castle of the Spider's Web* (B&W, 1957) contains not a word of Shakespeare's *Macbeth*, upon which it is based, it is recognized today as one of the greatest film adaptations ever made of a Shakespearean tragedy. In creating political parallels between medieval Japan and medieval Scotland and infusing this world with a sense of samurai adventure and the ceremonial rhythms of Noh drama, Kurosawa has created a work of stark beauty with its own emotional and imagistic integrity. General Washizu, like Macbeth, falls prey to a personal ambition that is fatally abetted by the prophecies of a mysterious spirit (corresponding to Shakespeare's three Weird Sisters) and the urgings of his ambitious wife, Asaji. The film is stunning in its taut compression, its evocation of a terrifying darkness in the natural world, and its equally dark view of human destiny.

Nearly thirty years later, Kurosawa again turned to Shakespeare in *Ran*, a free adaptation of *King Lear*. Here Kurosawa substitutes three sons for Lear's three daughters. He condenses the second plot of *King Lear* about the Duke of Gloucester and his two sons, Edmund and Edgar, so that the villainous Edmund can be transformed into the murderously ambitious daughter-in-law of the film version, the Lady Kaede. The sense of cosmic hopelessness is no less intense than in *Throne of Blood*. Kurosawa considered *Ran* (which means "chaos" or "turmoil") to be his best film, and many critics have been quick to agree. Again, Shakespeare's poetic dialogue has been transformed. Kurosawa's genius is in finding pictorial equivalents and a parallel story from imagined warlord history as a way of recreating the thematic depth and emotional intensity of the Shakespearean original. The mirroring is as indirect as it is indelibly brilliant. Like Giuseppe Verdi in adapting *Macbeth, Othello*, and *The Merry Wives* to the operatic stage, like Orson Welles in transforming *Macbeth, Othello*, and the *Henry IV* plays to the screen, Kurosawa demonstrates how much is to be gained by a bold approach in the hands of a master who confidently understands the divergent strengths of stage and screen.

Kurosawa was born in Tokyo in 1910, the last of seven children of a gentle mother and severe father who had trained to be an army officer. In primary school, Akira Kurosawa was president of his class, and is remembered as fair-minded and friendly though even then, said friends interviewed by critic Donald Ritchie, he was a commanding youngster, showing his spiritual attachment to the old samurai class. As a student, Kurosawa loved language and art, and it was through his years as a painter, from 1927 on, that he came to film. He earned a meager living by painting "for the cooking supplements of ladies' magazines or illustrations for love stories," according to his autobiography. Along with many other dissatisfied young artists, he joined the Proletariat Artists Group, less because he believed in Marxist theory than because he resisted the stagnant state of national affairs, the corruption, and the deadening force of bureaucratic contemporary life. He had a strong interest in such Russian writers as Tolstoy, Turgenev, and Dostoevsky, the last of whom he has often cited as a great influence. Also influential was his older film-loving brother Heigo who, after introducing young Akira to Western movies and literature, unaccountably left for the mountains one day and killed himself, leaving Akira feeling lost and isolated.

In 1936 Kurosawa answered a newspaper ad from a film studio announcing auditions for the position of assistant director. He wrote an essay criticizing and suggesting improvements for Japanese films, and at the audition itself was asked to do a film treatment of a newspaper story. His essay won him an interview with film director Kajiro Yamamoto, who became his teacher. After several years of assisting on in various films within the rigid studio system, Kurosawa made his first film, *Shanshiro Sugata*, in 1943. As a period drama, based on a popular novel about the rivalry between judo and jujitsu, it took up a subject that was considered politically safe enough for him to be entrusted with it, despite his leanings toward the West and particularly toward American culture. The film demonstrated a confidence in tone, image, and style that flourished not long afterwards in *Drunken Angel*, a film of which Kurosawa later said, "I was finally myself." The movie that ultimately brought him to international attention was *Rashomon* (1950), set before a gate in medieval Kyoto, in which three characters mysteriously present four different views of the truth of a crime. The film won first place at the Venice Film Festival and is generally recognized as his first masterpiece.

By his own account, Kurosawa was fascinated by *Macbeth* for some time but held off producing his film version for nearly ten years after Orson Welles had created on film his psychological exploration of the ambitious Scottish nobleman in 1948. *Throne of Blood* followed three years after Kurosawa's *Seven Samurai*, his historical epic depicting the struggle of the human spirit in the face of the chaos that can overwhelm even great personal bravery and courageous action. Kurosawa's adaptation of *Macbeth* takes up a different story, but it perhaps owes something to *Seven Samurai* in the way it moves grimly and forcefully toward Washizu's near-possession by malevolent powers he cannot resist; it melds the sense of movement and adventure in *Seven Samurai* with a countervailing aesthetic, derived from Japanese painting and Noh drama, of ceremonial slowness and meditation. The Lady Macbeth figure, the Lady Asaji, walks with the classic heel-to-toe shuffle of aristocratic women in the Noh drama. Her face suggests a traditional mask. Upon seeing a wall splattered with the blood of the lord against whom she has conspired, she does a formal dance with ritual wringing of her hands that similarly calls to mind the formal gestures of aristocratic traditional drama. Kurosawa's fog-shrouded forest, castles, and forts give tangible and menacing shape to the verbal images in Shakespeare's play of owls, wolves, bats, toads, and beetles. Toward the end of Kurosawa's film, birds from the forest invade the interior of Washizu's castle, presaging the movement from the forest of his enemies and the transfixing of Washizu by scores of arrows from his enemies' bows. Even though he is denied the poetic meditations of Shakespeare's Macbeth, Washizu is nonetheless the protagonist of a terrifying and ironic tragedy of fate.

Ran not only reverses the plot situation of *King Lear* by giving the king three sons instead of three daughters; the film adds to that story the equivalent of Edmund in the Lady Kaede. Her feminized evil is no less terrifying than that of the Lady Asaji in *Throne of Blood*. *Ran*'s visually symbolic tableaux make vivid use of costumes, flags, and other accoutrement of its family members. In both films Kurosawa employs the long shot, giving his films a kind of detachment from which we as spectators are invited to witness personal destruction and cosmic ruin. In neither film does the protagonist achieve tragic illumination; that kind of Shakespearean introspection is subordinated to a grand historical pessimism.

Kurosawa was eighty-eight years old and working on a screenplay when he died in September 1998. Today he is celebrated worldwide as one of the most influential filmmakers of the latter half of the twentieth century. His adaptations from Shakespeare stand as models of intercultural art, for these films have the power to ask Western and Eastern viewers alike to reevaluate the cultural traditions they have inherited. These films amply fulfill Kurosawa's vision of the artist as one who seeks to understand what is compellingly real about human life, and who, having found that truth, "never averts his eyes."

tale from Lady Macbeth's point of view. This concept was expanded in 1961 in the Polish film, *Siberian Lady Macbeth*. Macbeth's nefarious deeds seem a natural for American gangster films. The 1955 film noir *Joe Macbeth* (written by Philip Yordan, directed by Ken Hughes), places the action within a Mafioso context; that idea was echoed in the 1991 film, *Men of Respect* (written and directed by William Reilly). The latter seems more a spin-off of Francis Ford Coppola's *Godfather* trilogy and Martin Scorsese's *Goodfellas*. Both *Joe Macbeth* and *Men of Respect* use fortune-tellers in lieu of the Witches. However inventive these recontextualizations may be, recasting the central character as a ruthless hood reduces these gangster *Macbeth*s to rank melodrama. More recently *Scotland, PA* (2002), a film by Billy Morrissette, situates the action in a small Pennsylvania town where all residents have names beginning with "Mc." Newlyweds Joe and Pat McBeth (sic) work at Duncan's, a burger joint; after failing to get promoted, Joe, egged on by his wife, kills the owner and is ultimately arrested by a cop, Ernie McDuff. The movie, at various times intentionally and at other times unintentionally funny, substitutes three stoned hippies for the Witches. Morrissette's campy film spoofs a series of teen-flick Shakespearean knockoffs.

Curiously, the dark and somber *Macbeth* has inspired several comic playwrights. In 1896 Alfred Jarry, the *enfant terrible* of Parisian theater, wrote *Ubu Roi* (*King Turd*), often cited as the first "absurdist" play. This bitterly comic play is about a stupid, cowardly, and ineffectual Polish king (equal parts Oedipus and

Macbeth) who maintains power by killing and maiming all those who oppose him. To emphasize the depraved king's bloodlust, the playwright scripts the beheading of forty mannequins during the production. Jarry used the play to denounce all that was vulgar and inhumane in a world that was on the verge of the World War I. The Vietnam War produced its variant on this theme: Barbara Garson's *Macbird!* (1967) wryly suggested that Lyndon Johnson was responsible for the death of John F. Kennedy (a.k.a. Ken O'Dunc). Tom Stoppard's *Cahoot's Macbeth* (1977) is a hilarious one-act based on true incidents in Cold War Europe: a small troupe of Czech actors attempt to perform *Macbeth* in a living room but are interrupted by a twisted police magistrate who suspects a subversive message in Shakespeare's play. *Cahoot's Macbeth* is usually coupled with Stoppard's *Dogg's Hamlet* (see *Hamlet*, p. 633) because its comic resolution depends on the reappearance of a character from the Hamlet spoof.

References and Related Reading

Curry, Walter Clyde. *Shakespeare's Philosophical Patterns*. Baton Rouge, La., 1937.

Duerr, Edwin. *The Length and Depth of Acting*. New York, 1962.

Everett, Barbara. "Macbeth Succeeding." *Young Hamlet: Essays on Shakespeare's Tragedies*. Oxford, 1989.

Greenblatt, Stephen. *Will in the World: How Shakespeare Became Shakespeare*. New York and London, 2004.

Kliman, Bernice. *"Macbeth" ("Shakespeare in Performance" Series)*. Manchester and New York, 1992.

Knight, G. Wilson. *The Wheel of Fire*. 1930/65.

Pearlman, E. "*Macbeth* on Film: Politics." *Shakespeare Survey* 39 (1987): 250–260.

Watkins, Ronald, and Jeremey Lemmon. *"Macbeth": In Shakespeare's Playhouse*. Totowa, N.J., 1974.

Williams, Simon. "The Tragic Actor and Shakespeare." *The Cambridge Companion to Shakespeare on Stage*. Ed. Stanley Wells. Cambridge, Eng., 2002. 118–136.

Wills, Garry. *Witches and Jesuits: Shakespeare's* Macbeth. New York and Oxford: 1995.

SHAKESPEARE AND ROMANCE

Lost and Found

As the merrymakers create their mischief in *Twelfth Night*, Fabian says, "If this were played upon the stage, now, I could condemn it as an improbable fiction" (3.4.129–130). Although Fabian's words apply to the near-farcical subplot of that comedy, they are especially appropriate to the quartet of plays Shakespeare wrote between 1608 and 1613: *Pericles*, *Cymbeline*, *The Winter's Tale*, and *The Tempest*. These late plays, collectively known as "the romances," concluded Shakespeare's solo writing career; later, he contributed material to another romance, *The Two Noble Kinsmen*, co-authored with John Fletcher, who became the official playwright of the King's Men after Shakespeare retired in 1613.

Characteristics of the Romance

Romance, as a literary genre, was a term unknown to Shakespeare and his contemporaries; it did not come into common usage until some time after Shakespeare's death. Only during the Victorian Age did the term "romance" become a common feature in the vocabulary of scholars and critics. The Folio of 1623 divides Shakespeare's plays into three categories: "Comedies," "Histories," and "Tragedies." In his catalog of various forms of drama, Polonius cites the "tragical-comical-historical-pastoral" (*Ham.* 2.2.398–399), a joking phrase that nonetheless reflects the romance's synthesis of the potential of tragedy (death is imminent), the resolution of comedy (harmony after chaos), and the epic sweep of history (the plays span many years in the lives of their characters). The action is characteristically situated in green worlds frequented by shepherds, nymphs, and other denizens of the natural landscape—hence the reference to "pastoral." Imagine a play that is equal parts *King Lear* and *As You Like It*, with a smattering of *Henry V*, and one has some sense of the sweep and scope of Shakespeare's romances.

Although love affairs between innocent young women and men are at the heart of these four plays (indeed, love is usually the redeeming force precipitating a joyful resolution), the term has little to do with a love story in the boy-meets-girl tradition. *Romeo and Juliet* is not a romance per se, although it exhibits romantic elements. The term derives from the Latinate "*roman*"; in both the contemporary French and German languages *roman* designates a "novel." Although today a novel specifically refers to a work of prose fiction, it originally applied to literary works in "the new style" popularized by Italian writers such as Guarino Guarini in the early Renaissance. Romances, according to the *Oxford English Dictionary*, are narratives "in which the scenes and incidents are very remote from those of ordinary life." Shakespeare and his literary contemporaries found inspiration in the Italian stories because they transported audiences into the most exotic realms of their imagination.

The romance as it applies to Shakespeare's last plays refers to material that is remote in time and place, plotting that is fantastical, even improbable, and endings that are resoundingly joyful following a period of sorrow. Those storytelling clichés "once upon a time" and "they lived happily ever after" apply to the romance as well as the fairy tale. Shakespeare's opening lines of *Pericles*, spoken by "a Presenter," John Gower, are "To sing a song that old was sung." Royal Shakespeare Company director John Barton included a storyteller who read from an enormous book of fables when he staged *Cymbeline* in the 1970s.

Several distinct features characterize the traditional romance:

- Ingenious plotting of a rapid chain of events typically culminates with a miraculous happening; in one particularly striking example, a statue of a wronged woman assumed to be dead suddenly comes to life in *The Winter's Tale.*

- Stock characters are essentially servants to the plot, although Shakespeare consistently creates brilliant psychological portraits of these time-tested types.

- Extraordinary spectacle is often prompted by exotic locales (ancient Greece, Arthurian England, distant Sicilia and Bavaria, and a mysterious island).

- Comedy freely mixes with serious elements; the humor is as integral to the story as the dramatic sections.

817

- Love contrasts markedly with lust; typically, the goodness of a virginal heroine triumphs over evil to inspire a "brave new world."

- The reunion of separated or estranged family members provides joyous resolutions to the plays; the happy restoration, however, is more than an emotional catharsis as it reinforces the play's cosmic themes.

- Providence and the supernatural are highlighted; although Hamlet may encounter a ghost and Macbeth the witches, in the romance deities can be major figures. For example, Jupiter descends to right human wrongs in *Cymbeline*, while in *The Tempest* three goddesses of fertility and foison bless the impending marriage of Ferdinand and Miranda.

Forgiveness, Reconciliation, and Rejuvenation

Because Shakespeare's romances are essentially mythic tales, they share certain similarities of structure. Typically, a king (Pericles, Cymbeline, Leontes) or duke (Prospero) errs and thus brings about suffering for himself and his children (a daughter is invariably at the center of the play). A positive force (again, invariably a daughter) brings reconciliation and restoration to overpower the malevolent forces created by persons greedy for power. The ruler rejoices and grants forgiveness to his transgressors, and the play ends joyfully with the promise of a new prosperity. In a single play audiences experience both the catharsis of tragedy and comedy's affirmation of life; some critics therefore prefer to call these late plays "tragicomedies."

Consider the following schematic for tragedy, the comedy, and the romance:

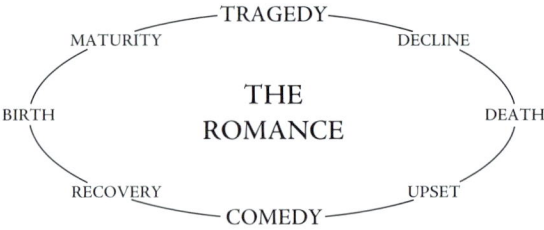

By conflating the parabola for tragedy (which represents "the fall") with that of comedy (whose upward thrust represents recovery from chaos), we arrive at the schematic for the romance: a circle. In his commentary upon Shakespeare's romances, Northrop Frye assesses this fusion of the tragic and comic impulses in the world's great literature:

> The mythical backbone of all literature is the cycle of nature, which rolls from birth to death and back again

to rebirth. The first half of this cycle, the movement from birth to death, spring to winter, dawn to dark, is the basis of the great alliance of nature and reason, the sense of nature and rational order in which all movement is toward the increasingly predictable. . . . drama, tragedy, the history play, and pure irony are centered in this half. . . . Comedy, however, is based on the second half, moving from death to rebirth, decadence to renewal, winter to spring, darkness to dawn (Frye, 119–121, passim).

Shakespeare alludes to this mythic view in *The Winter's Tale* when an earthy shepherd declares: "Thou mett'st with things dying, I with things newborn" (3.3.110–111). Frye and others have noted that this pattern of "birth after death" is reflected in the Bible, as the fall from Eden gives way to Easter's resurrection. This archetypal pattern may also be found in most great myths throughout the world; India's sacred epic, *The Mahabharata*, is a prominent example. Lest we think that the romance is an outmoded remnant from a bygone era, consider that many of the contemporary cinema's most popular works are romances, including *The Lord of the Rings*. The romance remains an integral a part of our contemporary theater experience, just as it was for English audiences in the final years of Shakespeare's writing career.

We may ask the question, Why did Shakespeare suddenly turn to the romance and devote the final portion of his career chiefly to the form? Several probable reasons, both practical and philosophical, help to account for this phase in his evolution as a dramatist. First, romances were becoming increasingly popular. By the end of the first decade of the seventeenth century English audiences clamored for a kind of return to this revitalized form that had long been popular in English culture. Romances were popular in the Middle Ages, serving as secular alternatives to the religious writings of that era. Chaucer included romances in *The Canterbury Tales*, most notably "The Knight's Tale," the inspiration for *The Two Noble Kinsmen*. Robert Greene, Shakespeare's rival, popularized the romance among Elizabethans when, in the late 1580s, he wrote such popular works as *Pandosto*, the source-story for *The Winter's Tale*. By the early seventeenth century Francis Beaumont and John Fletcher were among the most popular playwrights in London, thanks to such romantic dramas as *Philaster, or Love Lies a-Bleeding*. The King's Men needed Shakespeare to produce plays that could compete with those of Beaumont and Fletcher. The English court masque, performed frequently at the court of James I, also encouraged Shakespeare to write dramas reflecting the theatrical appeal of these royal pageants. The fourth act of *The Tempest* contains a sumptuous masque. Advances in theater technology—flying devices, scenic effects, elemental lighting—fueled audiences' thirst for spectacle. Inigo Jones, the scenographer for the court theater, visited Italy in the early seventeenth century and returned with spectacular theatrical visions as yet unseen in England. Just as screenwriters today develop material to showcase computer-generated graphics, so, too, did Jacobean playwrights create stage tales that utilized new scenic practices. The second Blackfriars Theater became the King's Men's winter home in 1608, at just about the time Shakespeare turned his full attention to romance. This indoor theater was especially well equipped for spectacles and "quaint devices" (see the discussion of *The Tempest*, pp. 820ff.).

In addition to these practical reasons why he may have turned to a fascinating new form late in his career, Shakespeare may have had artistic and thematic reasons for shifting predominantly to romance. Having mastered comedy, tragedy, and the history play during the first decade-and-a-half of his writing career, he seemed eager to accept the challenge of a new (to him) form. *Pericles* is almost certainly not by Shakespeare alone; it is an uneven work, though it enjoyed a certain popularity in the early seventeenth century and is not infrequently staged in recent years. *Cymbeline* and *The Winter's Tale* have proved themselves stageworthy, and in *The Tempest* Shakespeare brilliantly manifests his "creative energy in full force" (Spencer, 191).

Although Shakespeare explores the nature of reality vs. illusion throughout his previous works, the theme becomes especially prominent in the romances. The form relies heavily on extraordinary illusions: banquet tables appear and disappear, gods and goddesses manifest themselves, and statues come to life. At the end of his career, Shakespeare, testing the very limits of his art, employs the romance as a vehicle through which to examine both the potency and the shortcomings of the theater. Prospero, in *The Tempest*, is alternately intrigued and disillusioned by his artistry. Some current criticism suggests that Shakespeare turns to the romances to reconcile in himself the very ambiguities about creativity that perplex his sorcerer-duke. Scholar Stephen Greenblatt cautions, however, that while it is "all but irresistible" to "chart [Shakespeare's] psychic and spiritual as well as professional progress" in the last plays, such conjectures about the relationship between his personal and dramatic concerns must be met "with considerable skepticism" (57).

Shakespeare foregrounds the redemptive power of reconciliation in these final plays. The deep interest he has shown in earlier plays about forgiveness and reconciliation, like *All's Well That Ends Well, Measure for Measure,* and *King Lear,* now flourishes in the romances. If, as Theodore Spencer notes in his study of Shakespeare's last plays, tragedies explore the destructive power of evil, in Shakespeare's last plays evil "occupies only a small part of the action and the thought . . . it is the reconciliation that is emphasized and dwelt on, not the violence that precedes it" (Spencer, 202). The final plays offer cautiously optimistic accounts of humanity's faltering but necessary attempts to rise above human failure. As Prospero says, "The rarer action is / In virtue rather than in vengeance" (see 5.1.27–28). Thus the playwright who began his career writing revenge plays (*Titus Andronicus*), who crafted the finest revenge tragedy in Western drama (*Hamlet*), and who dramatized comic vengeance in such comedies as *Much Ado About Nothing* and *Twelfth Night*, culminates his life's work with a series of fanciful tales about humans rising above their most destructive tendencies. In the spirit of reconciliation, they forge a utopia that exists perhaps only in the artistic world of the romance.

References and Related Reading

Bergeron, David M. *Shakespeare's Romances and the Royal Family.* Lawrence, Kan., 1985.

Foakes, R. A. *Shakespeare: From the Dark Comedies to the Last Plays.* Charlottesville, Va., 1871.

Frye, Northrop. *A Natural Perspective: The Development of Shakespearean Comedy and Romance.* New York, 1965.

Greenblatt, Stephen. "General Introduction." *The Norton Shakespeare (Based on the Oxford Edition).* New York, 1997.

Marshall, Cynthia. *Last Things and Last Plays: Shakespearean Eschatology.* Carbondale, Ill., 1991.

Mowatt, Barbara. *The Dramaturgy of Shakespeare's Romances.* Athens, Ga., 1976.

Ryan, Kiernan, ed. *Shakespeare: The Late Plays.* New York, 1999.

Spencer, Theodore. "Shakespeare's Last Plays." *Shakespeare and the Nature of Man.* New York, 1942.

Yates, David. *Shakespeare's Last Plays: A New Approach.* London, 1975.

CHAPTER 19

The Tempest

1611

Context and Dating: "Our Revels Now Are Ended"

Two of Shakespeare's fellow actors, John Heminges and Henry Condell, acting as editors, gave first place to *The Tempest* in the 1623 First Folio edition of his plays. They certainly did not do so because they believed it to be an early work; quite the contrary. Perhaps they thought of it as showing his work at its very best. *The Tempest* does indeed seem to have been his farewell to his art, even if he did, like many persons at the end of a successful career, come briefly out of retirement to collaborate with his successor, John Fletcher, in writing *Henry VIII, Two Noble Kinsmen,* and the lost play *Cardenio* for the King's Men. The idea of *The Tempest* being Shakespeare's farewell to the theater is based upon a reading of Prospero's fine speeches (4.1.148–163; 5.1.33–57; the Epilogue) in which that character undertakes to set aside his magical powers:

> But this rough magic
> I here abjure . . .
>   I'll break my staff,
> Bury it certain fathoms in the earth,
> And deeper than did ever plummet sound
> I'll drown my book.
>
> (5.1.50–57)

This speculative association of Shakespeare with Prospero provides an intriguing view of the play, disputed by some scholars, as the psychological and artistic climax to Shakespeare's roughly twenty-year playwriting career. Yet even if the biographical connection remains uncertain, *The Tempest* can still be appreciated as the capstone to the playwright's career, for here may be found a superb synthesis of his themes, language, and theatricality.

The Tempest is, as far as can be known, one of the few Shakespearean plays for which there is no attributable source for its plot. Bernard Shaw's famous quip that Shakespeare told a good story providing someone told it to him first seems not to apply to *The Tempest*. At the same time, several historical events involving storms at sea and lost ships, as well as a variety of literary sources (discussed later), may have inspired the playwright as he invented this fanciful fiction about revenge, reconciliation, and the redemptive power of art on a mysterious island nominally located in the Mediterranean Sea. As always, the critical point is that Shakespeare has enhanced these accounts to create a superior work. By transforming the island into a place of imagination and magic, Shakespeare takes his characters on a journey into the realm of art where Prospero plays the artist-autocrat, creating situations in which people are tested to learn much of themselves and their values. He practices his benevolent magic to achieve ultimately laudable ends for his daughter Miranda, for Ferdinand, for his servant-sprite Ariel, for the earthy Caliban, for Alonso and the other Italians, and even for his wicked brother Antonio, who long ago usurped Prospero's dukedom in Milan. Forgoing vengeance, Prospero forgives his brother, sees Miranda happily betrothed to Ferdinand, and relinquishes the extraordinary powers he no longer needs before sailing home to Milan where "Every third thought shall be [his] grave" (5.1.315).

The first verifiable performance of *The Tempest* occurred on November 1, 1611, at King James's court theater in Whitehall. Although the point is controversial, some scholars, notably Alvin Kernan, surmise that the script Heminges and Condell included in the Folio was a revision of the 1611 text, amended by Shakespeare to honor a royal wedding in January 1613 when King James's seventeen-year-old daughter Elizabeth married Frederick of Heidelberg, a union that produced the royal Hanoverian line. A week-long celebration at the Banqueting House featured the performance of some twenty plays, including *The Tempest* and "Beatrice and Benedick" (i.e., *Much Ado About Nothing*). The married couple also witnessed several spectacular masques, such as Thomas Campion's *The Lord's Masque*, with set design by England's preeminent scene designer, Inigo Jones. (Kernan provides an especially useful discussion of this possibility and of the politics surrounding *The Tempest* in Chapter Eight of *Shakespeare, the King's Playwright*.) These courtly occasions are an important part of *The Tempest*'s stage history. At the same time, the play must have been performed on many occasions for public audiences at the Globe Theater, to which in fact Prospero seems to refer when he invokes "the gorgeous palaces / The solemn temples, the great globe itself" as an essential part of the "revels" that "now are ended" (4.1.148–153). The Globe Theater and the indoor Blackfriars Theater, where Shakespeare's company performed in wintertime, were *The Tempest*'s first and greatest homes.

Characters: Sprites and Beasts

Shakespeare's earlier plays typically feature multiple plots set in numerous locales across long periods of time. *The Tempest*, on the contrary, exhibits a unique structure by confining itself to a single locale (the island) and a single action (restoring Prospero as the "rightful Duke of Milan"); it spans about two days in actual time (see 1.2.301). A comic subplot—the drunken rebellion of Trinculo, Stephano, and Caliban—is deftly integrated into the major action by demonstrating the ludicrous folly of attempted usurpation. Given its single locale and its unified action within a short passage of time, *The Tempest* is considered Shakespeare's most neoclassical play in its structure, although an early work, *The Comedy of Errors*, also may be described as neoclassical in form. As an adaptation of Plautus's *Menaechmi, or The Twins, The Comedy of Errors* appropriately adheres to the classic "unities" of time, place, and action. *The Tempest* is like Shakespeare's early play in this regard. At the same time, *The Tempest* dramatizes a story about invisible spirits and magical happenings in a way that is thoroughly English rather than neoclassical in its contents.

Indeed, English popular drama in Shakespeare's age was generally more "romantic" than neoclassic; that is, it was not bound by the classical principles fostered by the interpreters of Aristotle and revisited as "the unities" by French and English theorists. Neoclassicism—i.e., the new classicism—looked to ancient Greece and Rome for guidance and inspiration, especially in the arts. Classical influences may be seen in the architecture of Palladio, the sculptures of Michelangelo, the paintings of Raphael (especially *The School of Athens*, a glorification of Greek learning and artistry), and the plays of Ariosto. As the names of these artists suggest, Italy was the center of the new classicism because wealthy nobles established learning academies to preserve the legacy of the Greeks and Romans.

Although Shakespeare does seem consciously to have written a drama with a classical tradition as he created *The Tempest*, his play is nonetheless a bold experiment with form and content. Its unity of time serves the purpose of a story in which impossible and fantastic things happen at every turn. Because Prospero is a man obsessed with accomplishing his mission, time is of the utmost importance, as evidenced by his frequent references to speed, haste, and the passing of the hours. In Act 4 Prospero aborts the wedding masque when he remembers that a plot against him must be dealt with immediately. Such actions seem the province of a man who knows that his time on this island, both that in the Mediterranean and on "the great globe itself," is waning; he has much to accomplish before he can "break his staff."

The Tempest draws upon the traditional characters of the romance; although they are stock characters, Shakespeare individualizes each with varying degrees of psychological complexity. Prospero, the artist-magician, is rooted in the archetype of the scholar-king, a good man who has erred by neglecting his dukedom in favor of his books. He has been sinned against by Antonio, his Machiavellian brother, who had banished him from Milan twelve years earlier. Miranda, Prospero's innocent daughter, is threatened by a creature named Caliban; she is saved by her love for a handsome prince, Ferdinand, the son of King Alonso, whose reign is also threatened by a villainous brother, Sebastian. Gonzalo, a gregarious old man with dreams of a utopian world, plays the role of a faithful counselor.

Prospero lives on the island, accompanied only by his maturing daughter and the two servants who represent his control over the elements above the earth (Ariel) and those of the earth (Caliban). Although his art enables him to master his environment—from the weather to supernatural apparitions such as the goddesses of fertility—this sorcerer focuses his emotional energies on his concern for Miranda's happiness and a still gnawing antipathy toward the conspirators who banished him. In the first scene, Prospero has the opportunity to punish his enemies by drowning them. Yet, like the castaways he tests with his conjuring, he must come to terms with his own nature. He threatens Ariel and Caliban, temporarily enslaves Ferdinand to test his mettle, and plays the overprotective parent to his daughter. At the same time, he seems to have a purpose in these various testings, believing, for example, that Miranda and Ferdinand will better appreciate marital happiness if they can overcome the seeming obstacle of a father's (pretend) hostility. For them, the marriage means romantic happiness; for Prospero, it means a hope of progeny and of political union between Milan and Naples, thus ending the conflict that sent him into exile many years ago. The betrothal of Ferdinand and Miranda, neither of whom requires the moral healing the magical island brings to others, conjoins human nature and the higher law of values achieved through nurture.

The characters Prospero tests represent a hierarchy of human virtues and vices. The thoroughly virtuous, such as Miranda, Ferdinand, and kindly old Gonzalo, possess benevolence that posits a better, if not an ideal, world. The "men of sin," as Ariel terms them (3.3.53), include Antonio, Sebastian, and to a lesser degree Alonso, who repents his transgressions. The poet W. H. Auden, writing during the darkest days of World War II in his essay and poem, *The Sea and the Mirror* (1942), plausibly believes that Antonio will not be reformed despite Prospero's generous act of forgiveness. Trinculo and Stephano, in their perpetually drunken state, may remind audiences exactly how much closer humans are to beasts than to angels. The magical spirit Ariel transcends the limitations of the human world, symbolizing inspiration itself; Ariel invests Prospero's art with extraordinary powers. Caliban, one of the most enigmatic characters in the Shakespeare canon, is on the one hand base and bestial, the product of the devil and a witch (Sycorax). At the same time, he possesses a poetic soul that takes genuine delight in natural beauty. Prospero ultimately accepts this strange duality of the human condition in Caliban—"This thing of darkness I / Acknowledge mine" (5.1.278–279)—and sets him free.

Sources and Inspirations

An extraordinary event in the far-western Atlantic Ocean provided Shakespeare with some material for this captivating romance. In 1609, just two years before the first recorded performance of *The Tempest*, nine English ships set sail for the two-year-old colony at Jamestown, Virginia. On July 24 a powerful storm struck the fleet near the Bermuda Islands, called "the still-vexed Bermudas" (1.2.230) by Shakespeare. Eight ships escaped unscathed and landed safely at Virginia where the mariners reported that their flagship, the *Sea Adventure*, had been lost. Miraculously, however, the crew of the doomed ship survived their ordeal on "the isle of Devils," constructed two small boats, and made the dangerous six-hundred–mile journey to Jamestown, arriving in May 1610. Several accounts of this sensational adventure were quickly published (e.g., crewmember Sylvester Jourdain's *A Discovery of the Bermudas*). The imaginations of the English were fired by such tales from that "brave new world" across the sea. Shakespeare borrowed from Jourdain's account and seems also to have known of William Strachey's 1610 manuscript (not published until 1625), with its striking parallels to *The Tempest*; as in the play, men who were thought to have drowned in a shipwreck eventually returned home in triumph, much changed by their ordeal on a mysterious island.

Aside from these reports of the Bermuda shipwreck and miraculous survivals that provided Shakespeare with plot material, several theatrical developments seem to have inspired elements of *The Tempest*.

The Courtly Masque

Modeled in part on the Italian *intermezzo*, a brief interlude or diversion, the English masque was originally a short allegorical play, or interlude, devised to entertain courtly gatherings. Songs and dances, frequently derived from pastoral plays about shepherds and woodland nymphs (such those found in Act 4), were part of the evening's entertainment. Lavish scenery, costumes, and lighting effects enhanced the performances. Musicians accompanied these spectacles, and such talented poets as Ben Jonson composed eloquent scripts for the occasion. Masques were an integral part of English court life since Henry VIII. He and his masked courtiers "invaded" the banqueting hall at Hampton Court on January 6 (Twelfth Night), 1512, to invite the assembled women to dance. Historian Edward Hall described that lively evening, noting that the "maske . . . after the manner of Italie" was "a thyne not seen afore in England." Despite her reputation for frugality, Queen Elizabeth also enjoyed court spectacles: in 1591 the Gentlemen of Grey's Inn presented her with an extravaganza, *Proteus and the Adamantine Rock*. After 1603, when James I came to the throne, masques became still more numerous and lavish. More than dazzling entertainment, these masques were potent political statements about the glory of the reigning king or queen.

The fourth act of *The Tempest* features a beautiful masque in which Juno, Iris, and Ceres, goddesses of fertility and marriage, bless the impending union between Prospero's daughter Miranda and Ferdinand, son of the King of Naples. The spectacle surely pleased audiences at the Globe or the Blackfriars, as well as those at James's court. A command performance of *The Tempest* during wedding festivities for James's daughter in 1613 would have been all the more poignant as the assembled court heard the goddesses bless marriages, on stage and off:

> Honor, riches, marriage blessing,
> Long continuance, and increasing,
> Hourly joys be still upon you!
>
> (4.1.106–108)

The Tempest also contains an intriguing variant on the anti-masque, a grotesque parody of the stately, dignified masques. In 1609 Ben Jonson inserted an anti-masque featuring monsters and demons into *The Masque of Queens Celebrated*. Prospero's fourth-act masque has its anti-masque in the form of nymphs and "sunburned sicklemen" wearing "rye-straw hats" as they celebrate "holiday" *"in a graceful dance."* Then, too, Ariel's leading a pack of spirits disguised as fierce hounds in pursuit of Caliban, Stephano, and Trinculo is a kind of anti-masque for Shakespeare's own play.

New Technology for the Theater

Throughout the sixteenth century, Italian artists developed extraordinary machinery and scenic techniques to enhance performances at the ducal palaces, such as those of the powerful Medici family in Florence. Inigo Jones, England's foremost scenic artist, visited Italy in 1600 and returned three years later with designs and ingenious machinery for spectacles that mesmerized the English. A discernible shift in English dramaturgy took place as the theater moved from an essentially word-oriented entertainment to one that relied increasingly on spectacle and gimmickry, as evidenced by an intriguing stage direction in 3.3 of *The Tempest*. At Prospero's behest, Ariel sets forth a magnificent banquet to tempt the shipwrecked noblemen; as they prepare to enjoy their feast, it magically disappears. Shakespeare tells us only that it disappears by a *"quaint device."* Just as Shakespeare seemed motivated, in part, to write *The Tempest* to employ new stagecraft, subsequent generations of theater artists have used the play as a medium to celebrate their own quaint devices.

Some Literary Inspirations

Several essays contributed to the play's ideas, if not its plot. Foremost among these were the *Essays* of Michel de Montaigne (published in England in 1603), the most relevant being "Of the Cannibals," a treatise in which the Frenchman contrasted contemporary European culture with the indigenous culture explorers found in the Americas. Caliban's name is an anagram Shakespeare created from "cannibal," itself a corruption of "Caribbean"; originally the term had nothing to do with flesh eating. Just as Montaigne finds many ways in which the society of the decadent Europeans is inferior to that of the natives, Shakespeare, too, exposes to satire the deplorable Machiavellian tactics of Antonio and Sebastian and the coarsely exploitive instincts of Stephano and Trinculo; compared with these characters, Caliban is innocently capable of appreciating the natural beauty of the island, and at times utters the most sensitively poetic language of the play. To be sure, Caliban is also "a savage and deformed slave" who suffers no pangs of conscience for having attempted to rape Miranda. "Oho, oho!" he exults. "Would't had been done!" (1.2.352). The portrait of Caliban is thus a complex reworking of Montaigne. So too with Shakespeare's other literary sources. In Act 2 Gonzalo, counselor to King Alonso, talks longingly about a Utopian world (see 2.1.148-ff.) such as that described by Montaigne and also by Sir Thomas More in his famous treatise of 1516. Utopian literature customarily explores the gulf between humanity's view of an ideal commonwealth and the reality wrought by human error, a central idea in *The Tempest*. That gap is underscored in Act 5 as Miranda emerges from Prospero's cave, where she has been playing chess with Ferdinand. She beholds the assembly of noblemen her father has lured into a mystic circle and joyfully exclaims, "Oh, brave new world / That has such people in't!" (5.1.185-186). Her father, wiser from his encounters with such miscreants as Antonio and Sebastian, replies wryly: " 'Tis new to thee." Shakespeare also draws significantly on Ovid's *Metamorphoses* (7.197-219) for Prospero's eloquent description of the magical power through which he has commanded the elements (5.1.33-57). Thus, although *The Tempest* has no single source for its plot and characters, it is filled with literary borrowings.

Language, Music, and Dance

Shakespeare was at the height of his poetic powers when he wrote *The Tempest*; thus, little more needs to be said here about the play's language and its virtuoso passages. While we might expect Prospero to speak eloquently—he conjures words as well as visions—Shakespeare, as we have seen, assigns some of the play's most poetic speeches to the man-beast Caliban. Ordinarily we expect such a character to speak in prose or perhaps in a patently artificial verse to underscore his other-than-human persona (consider Puck in *A Midsummer Night's Dream*). Caliban, however, speaks some of the most mesmerizing blank verse in the canon, as when he describes the island's music: "The isle is full of noises, / Sounds, and sweet airs, that give delight and hurt not" (see 3.2.137-145). Caliban reviles Prospero for teaching him language—"my profit on't / Is I know how to curse" (1.2.366-367)—but clearly a part of Caliban enables him to respond to the beauty of nature and of language in a way that the best-educated of the Europeans can only approximate. At its most eloquent, Caliban's language invests him with a sympathy that transcends his natural condition.

The Tempest represents Shakespeare's most flexible command of blank verse. We find an inventive use of run-on and shared lines among the speeches, as well as a more pronounced naturalness in the rhetoric than in such early plays as *Romeo and Juliet*. In addition to Caliban's speeches, Shakespeare creates memorable arias for Prospero. His much quoted speech from Act 4 is noted for its shimmering poetry as much as for its philosophical wisdom:

> Our revels now are ended. These our actors,
> As I foretold you, were all spirits and
> Are melted into air, into thin air;
> And, like the baseless fabric of this vision,
> The cloud-capped towers, the gorgeous palaces,
> The solemn temples, the great globe itself,
> Yea, all which it inherit, shall dissolve,
> And, like this insubstantial pageant faded,
> Leave not a rack behind. We are such stuff
> As dreams are made on, and our little life
> Is rounded with a sleep.
>
> (4.1.148–158)

Similarly, the "thousand twangling instruments" (3.2.139) heard by Caliban provide a musical score for *The Tempest*. Shakespeare consistently invests dramatic conventions, such as song and dance, with thematic importance. The play's songs and incidental music, some composed by Robert Johnson, a musician to King James, heighten the mystery of Prospero's isle. For example, Ariel's song "Come unto these yellow sands" (1.2.378–390) is appropriately hypnotic as it lures Ferdinand onto the island. More significantly, the songs underscore the need for harmony among the warring sets of brothers. The dances that are integral to the masque in Act 4 also underscore the play's thematic emphasis on graceful, visual harmony in a world bereft of such qualities when greed usurps them. Peter Greenaway's 1991 film, *Prospero's Books*, employs dances extensively, especially in the depiction of Caliban as played by choreographer-dancer Michael Clark.

Themes and Issues

Virtue and Vengeance

The Tempest and the earlier romances (*Pericles, Cymbeline, The Winter's Tale*) mark a noteworthy change in Shakespeare's thematic concerns. Like the history plays and many of the tragedies, *The Tempest* considers the consequences of usurping the authority that belongs to its lawful occupant—here, the rightful Duke of Milan. Yet in these romances neither vengeance nor violence is offered as a solution to this ancient problem. The *denouement* (the outcome of a complex series of events) offers no counterinsurgency, no death to the usurper, no suicide, not even prison or some similar punishment. Here forgiveness, reconciliation, and redemption triumph over revenge and death. Prospero recognizes that "The rarer action is / In virtue than in vengeance" (see 5.1.27–28). Equanimity replaces the archaic "eye for an eye" mentality that only

provokes further bloodshed. Even more than the marriage of Miranda and Ferdinand, more than the liberation of Ariel and Caliban, reconciliation provides the apparently happy ending of *The Tempest*. The resolution thus evokes—in Northrop Frye's reading of the play—the central myth of Christianity and that of most world religions: humankind loses "a peaceable kingdom, staggers through a long nightmare of tyranny and injustice . . . and eventually regains his original vision [i.e., Paradise]" (133).

Art and Artifice

Shakespeare's plays often use the metaphor of theater to impart their meaning. *The Tempest* is the culminating exemplar of Shakespeare's fascination with the connection between the theater and life beyond the stage. *The Tempest* is the only play in the canon in which the protagonist is an artist, specifically a magician who conjures extraordinary visions. The play opens with a frightful storm—which itself turns out to be an illusion. Thereafter little in the play is what it appears to be. Moreover, Prospero's ability to control human nature is limited to the conditions of his art. When Miranda falls swiftly in love with Ferdinand, she does what her father has wished her to do, and yet the willingness of desire must be her own. When Prospero's slave, Caliban, turns murderous under the influence of the two drunken fools who tempt him with alcohol, Prospero is able to oversee their conspiracy and forestall it, and yet he must ultimately acknowledge the "thing of darkness" that is in Caliban and indeed in Prospero himself. Prospero forgives his brother Antonio, attempting to reform through that most god-like of acts, forgiveness, and yet Prospero must realize that his offer is finally rejected in Antonio's truculent silence (see after 5.1.133). Even his greatest show on earth, the wedding masque, is a mere "vanity" (4.1.41); he must abort his most enthralling but "insubstantial" pageant (4.1.155) to attend to the rebellion of the drunkards. The showman cannot bestow upon an imperfect world the behaviors needed to make it perfect.

Though Prospero may be momentarily disillusioned that art cannot remedy all human problems, neither he nor Shakespeare is cynical at last about the potential of art to move and persuade. The play ends with the actor playing Prospero (probably Richard Burbage in 1611) stepping forward to address the real masters and patrons invoked by the artist: the audience. As Prospero has forgiven Antonio for his crimes, the actor asks of the audience that same forgiveness for his artistic "crimes." As Robert Egan notes in his study of Shakespeare's metatheatrical concerns: "The art of Shakespeare, as well as of Prospero, will prove a vanity unless [the audience] affirms its validity by sharing the moral discovery that informs it, participating in a cognate act of love and forgiveness which are the essence of that discovery" (118). In no other play does Shakespeare so explicitly invest the audience with such powers.

Colonialism

The ensuing stage history of *The Tempest* considers several late twentieth-century productions that examine the value of "civilization" in a postmodern, postcolonial context. History, these productions suggest, has shown colonialism to be capable of unlimited cruelty and greed. Just as Caliban, who often speaks with poetic nuance, questions why he has learned Prospero's language except to learn "how to curse," contemporary critics and directors interrogate the legitimacy of Prospero's authority. The play does raise unsettling questions about exploitation and imperialism, even if Prospero is not a colonialist in the full sense of seeking commercial advantage in an underdeveloped world. Stephano and Trinculo, on the other hand, do participate in a comic version of the colonizer's oppression as they pour wine down Caliban's throat and reduce him to the role of drunken, mindlessly worshipful slave. The villains, Antonio and Sebastian, make it plain that they would not hesitate to exploit the commercial potential of a native islander like Caliban. The history of Caliban on stage illustrates that he can be viewed as the beast of the early explorer's accounts or as the "noble savage" idealized by Jean-Jacques Rousseau in the eighteenth century. At the time Shakespeare wrote *The Tempest*, England was still struggling to control Ireland, an island whose inhabitants most British considered as savage and fierce. From the perspective of the twenty-first century, the play seems to raise questions about the struggle of colonized peoples, whether in Europe or the New World. Such concerns continue to resonate in today's geopolitical climate. Similarly, several recent feminist critics (see Adelman and Stockholder) argue that Prospero's all-controlling magic can be understood as a male's attempt to control a threatening female sexuality, represented by Sycorax, and to replace it with a more tractable generativity, or reproductiveness, that can be regulated in heterosexual marriage.

The ending of the play can be read as not affirming stability. Antonio does not repent. The cycle of revolution on this island (or in Milan) may not necessarily end with Prospero's departure. Critical readings and stage interpretations can render ironic the play's ending because of its ambiguity. Shakespeare addresses political aspects of *The Tempest* in ways that are both limited by their ideologies of his own era and timeless in their representation of the power of art to heal.

Staging Challenges

J. C. Trewin, a British theater critic specializing in Shakespeare-in-performances, divides the *Tempests* he has encountered into two broad categories: "plain" and "spangled" (268). The former relies on the play's poetry to evoke its magic, and there are many critics (e.g., Ann

Barton) and theater artists (Peter Brook) who feel the play is best served by minimal scenic splendor. (Brook, to be sure, also feels free as theater director to cut, rearrange, and rewrite the text.) Others (e.g., Peter Hall) counter that Shakespeare was testing the limits of the theater technology available to him and wrote a play about "illusions"; therefore, they submit, *The Tempest* is best served through grand spectacle. Consider several staging problems—and their thematic implications—that confront those who approach the play, whether on the page or in the theater.

The Tempest and the Shipwreck

Shakespeare knew how to launch a play. From the thrilling swordplay that ignites *Romeo and Juliet* to the ghost and witches that appear in the opening moments of *Hamlet* and *Macbeth*, the playwright immediately engages his audiences. *The Tempest* offers a thrilling opening, both in the initial storm itself and in the ensuing reflections on what the storm has signified. Shakespeare gives us not one, but four descriptions of the tempest and shipwreck (see 1.1, Miranda's opening speech in 1.2, Ariel's speech at 1.2.196ff., and Francisco's at 2.1.115–124) to encourage his audiences to visualize the "The direful spectacle of the wreck." Such vivid details need little scenic embellishment, yet theater designers have for four centuries sought ingenious ways to depict the opening scene: a full scale model of a galleon, a violently fluttering sail representing the whole ship, a swinging lantern creating ghostly images throughout the theater, even total darkness from which the mariners' voices cry helplessly. How the opening scene is depicted on stage—or in film—may establish the tone for the ensuing production. More importantly, the opening scene initiates two central concerns of the play:

- The movement from chaos to harmony: the noise and fury of the opening moments contrasts sharply with the dignified reconciliation in Act 5.
- The nature of illusions: as Ariel makes plain (1.2.218–237), for all its noise the shipwreck is a sorcerer's illusion, a theatrical sleight-of-hand insuring that, ultimately, all will end happily.

The Sprite and the Monster

Ariel and Caliban are more than fanciful stage characters who have entertained audiences for four centuries. The former is a cavorting sprite representing humanity's desire to transcend its mortal bounds, while the latter reminds us of our baser nature. Beyond their symbolic values, Ariel and Caliban remain among Shakespeare's most tantalizingly theatrical characters. As the following stage history (pp. 855ff.) suggests, directors, designers, and actors have portrayed these characters in myriad ways. Ariel is traditionally depicted as a wispy spirit, although a New York production (directed by Julie Taymor in 1991) conceived the sprite as a floating mask on the hand of an actor clad entirely in black, the better to ignite the audience's imagination. Other productions have depicted the sprite as a nearly nude, androgynous figure (the Royal Shakespeare Company, 1978) or as high-wire artiste dressed in a traditional Italian clown outfit (Milan, 1978). Caliban has been embodied in an even greater array of costumes, many reflecting the concerns of a given culture or moment in time. As David Suchet prepared to play the role for the RSC in 1978, he learned that Caliban has been portrayed as a fish, a dog (sometimes with multiple heads), a lizard, an ape, a snake, a Darwinian reptile with fins for arms, and a tortoise (Vaughan and Mason, 192–193). Suchet, under John Barton's direction, opted for "a composite version of Third World peoples." Since the 1960s Caliban especially, and sometimes Ariel as well, have frequently been portrayed as a victims of European colonialism, though that approach has diminished somewhat recently. Directorial and design choices concerning the appearance of these two significantly affects an audience's perception of a play that can be interpreted as, among other things, an enchanting fairy tale, a spiritual ritual, or a political tract.

The Masque

Taking note of the courtly success of masques in the Jacobean England, Shakespeare has created a work of potentially visual splendor, and subsequent generations of theater artists have generally sustained this approach. At the same time, the wedding masque in Act 4 is much more than an extravaganza. It celebrates a fundamental human urge to procreate and thereby continue the species. Historically, the impetus for the masque can be traced to ancient satyr rites of spring celebrating the triumph of life over death, dawn over darkness, spring over winter. Northrop Frye invests the wedding masque with a spiritual importance, noting that in the final analysis it "presents the meeting of earth and heaven under the rainbow" (158). Frye's observation transcends any specific allusion to Judeo-Christian teachings: for Frye, the great myths of the world (e.g., the *Mahabharata* of India) invariably lead to a cosmic vision of hope. Hence, rather than treating this masque as a mere exercise in theatrical razzle-dazzle, we need to imagine, in our mind's eye, a thoughtful stage rendition.

The Magic Circle

Because reconciliation is central to the play's themes, the circle into which Prospero draws the shipwrecked nobles in Act 5 becomes a significant visual symbol of inclusiveness. This perfect circle can, of course, be presented simply: Prospero can merely trace its circumference on the stage floor. It can be elaborate: Peter Greenaway opted for a mystical blue light in his 1991 film. The reconciliation scene in Act 5 is so potent that its staging begs for an extraordinary moment of invention, plain or spangled, for here again meaning and medium are intertwined.

The Tempest

Names of the Actors

ALONSO, *King of Naples*
SEBASTIAN, *his brother*
PROSPERO, *the right Duke of Milan*
ANTONIO, *his brother, the usurping Duke of Milan*
FERDINAND, *son to the King of Naples*
GONZALO, *an honest old counselor*
ADRIAN *and*
FRANCISCO, } *lords*
CALIBAN, *a savage and deformed slave*
TRINCULO, *a jester*
STEPHANO, *a drunken butler*
MASTER *of a ship*

BOATSWAIN
MARINERS

MIRANDA, *daughter to Prospero*

ARIEL, *an airy spirit*
IRIS
CERES,
JUNO,   } *[presented by] spirits*
NYMPHS
REAPERS,

[*Other Spirits attending on Prospero*]

THE SCENE: *An island*

1.1

A tempestuous noise of thunder and lightning heard. Enter a Shipmaster and a Boatswain.

MASTER　Boatswain!

BOATSWAIN　Here, Master. What cheer?

MASTER　Good, speak to th' mariners. Fall to't yarely, or we run ourselves aground. Bestir, bestir!　　*Exit.* 3

Enter Mariners.

BOATSWAIN　Heigh, my hearts! Cheerly, cheerly, my hearts! Yare, yare! Take in the topsail. Tend to th' Master's whistle.—Blow till thou burst thy wind, if room 6 enough! 7 8

Enter Alonso, Sebastian, Antonio, Ferdinand, Gonzalo, and others.

ALONSO　Good Boatswain, have care. Where's the Master? Play the men. 10

BOATSWAIN　I pray now, keep below.

ANTONIO　Where is the Master, Boatswain?

BOATSWAIN　Do you not hear him? You mar our labor. Keep your cabins! You do assist the storm. 14

GONZALO　Nay, good, be patient. 15

BOATSWAIN　When the sea is. Hence! What cares these roarers for the name of king? To cabin! Silence! Trouble us not. 17

GONZALO　Good, yet remember whom thou hast aboard.

BOATSWAIN　None that I more love than myself. You are a councillor; if you can command these elements to silence and work the peace of the present, we will not 23 hand a rope more. Use your authority. If you cannot, 24 give thanks you have lived so long and make yourself ready in your cabin for the mischance of the hour, if it so hap.—Cheerly, good hearts!—Out of our way, 27 I say.　　*Exit.*

GONZALO　I have great comfort from this fellow. Methinks he hath no drowning mark upon him; his complexion is perfect gallows. Stand fast, good Fate, to his 30 31 hanging! Make the rope of his destiny our cable, for our own doth little advantage. If he be not born to be 33

hanged, our case is miserable.　　*Exeunt [courtiers].* 34

Enter Boatswain.

BOATSWAIN　Down with the topmast! Yare! Lower, lower! Bring her to try wi'th' main course. (*A cry* 36 *within.*) A plague upon this howling! They are louder than the weather or our office. 38

Enter Sebastian, Antonio, and Gonzalo.

Yet again? What do you here? Shall we give o'er and 39 drown? Have you a mind to sink?

SEBASTIAN　A pox o'your throat, you bawling, blasphemous, incharitable dog!

BOATSWAIN　Work you, then.

ANTONIO　Hang, cur! Hang, you whoreson, insolent noisemaker! We are less afraid to be drowned than thou art.

GONZALO　I'll warrant him for drowning, though the 47 ship were no stronger than a nutshell and as leaky as an unstanched wench. 49

BOATSWAIN　Lay her ahold, ahold! Set her two courses. 50 Off to sea again! Lay her off!

Enter Mariners, wet.

MARINERS　All lost! To prayers, to prayers! All lost! [*The Mariners run about in confusion, exiting at random.*]

BOATSWAIN　What, must our mouths be cold? 53

GONZALO
The King and Prince at prayers! Let's assist them, For our case is as theirs.

SEBASTIAN　　　　　　　I am out of patience.

ANTONIO
We are merely cheated of our lives by drunkards. 56 This wide-chapped rascal! Would thou mightst lie drowning 57 The washing of ten tides!

GONZALO　　　　　　　He'll be hanged yet, 58 Though every drop of water swear against it And gape at wid'st to glut him. (*A confused noise within:*)　　"Mercy on us!"— 60 "We split, we split!"—"Farewell my wife and children!"— 61 "Farewell, brother!"—"We split, we split, we split!" [*Exit Boatswain.*]

ANTONIO　Let's all sink wi'th' King.

SEBASTIAN　Let's take leave of him.

Exit [with Antonio].

GONZALO　Now would I give a thousand furlongs of sea

Names of the Actors This list appears at the end of the play in the First Folio, in this order, with Miranda's name below that of the men, as was conventional in lists of the period. **PROSPERO,** *the right* the rightful **CALIBAN . . . slave** The Folio reads *"saluage,"* a common alternative spelling of *savage* but perhaps also with a resonance of being salvaged from shipwreck. *Slave* has a range of meanings: wretch, rascal, servile creature, one who is owned by another person, one who is divested of freedom and personal rights.
1.1 Location: On board ship, off the island's coast.
3 Good i.e., It's good you've come, or, my good fellow.　**yarely** nimbly　**6 Tend** Attend　**7 Blow** (Addressed to the wind.)　**7–8 if room enough** as long as we have sea room enough.　**10 Play the men** Act like men, with spirit.　**14 Keep** Remain　**15 good** good fellow　**17 roarers** waves or winds, or both; spoken to as though they were "bullies" or "blusterers"　**23 work . . . present** bring calm to our present circumstances　**24 hand** handle　**27 hap** happen.　**30–1 complexion . . . gallows** appearance shows he was born to be hanged (and therefore, according to the proverb, in no danger of drowning)　**33 our . . . advantage** our own cable is of little benefit.

34 case is miserable circumstances are desperate.　**36 Bring . . . course** Sail her close to the wind by means of the mainsail.　**38 our office** i.e., the noise we make at our work.　**39 give o'er** give up　**47 warrant him for drowning** guarantee that he will never be drowned　**49 unstanched** insatiable, loose, unrestrained. (Suggesting also "incontinent" and "menstrual.")　**50 ahold** ahull, close to the wind.　**courses** sails, i.e., foresail as well as mainsail, set in an attempt to get the ship back out into open water.　**53 must . . . cold?** i.e., must we drown in the cold sea?　**56 merely** utterly　**57 wide-chapped** big-mouthed　**57–8 Would . . . tides!** (Pirates were hanged on the shore and left until three tides had come in.)　**60 at wid'st** wide open.　**glut** swallow　**61 split** break apart.

for an acre of barren ground: long heath, brown furze, 66
anything. The wills above be done! But I would fain 67
die a dry death.   *Exit.*

❧

1.2

Enter Prospero [in his magic cloak] and Miranda.

MIRANDA
If by your art, my dearest father, you have   1
Put the wild waters in this roar, allay them.   2
The sky, it seems, would pour down stinking pitch,
But that the sea, mounting to th' welkin's cheek,   4
Dashes the fire out. Oh, I have suffered
With those that I saw suffer! A brave vessel,   6
Who had, no doubt, some noble creature in her,
Dashed all to pieces. Oh, the cry did knock
Against my very heart! Poor souls, they perished.
Had I been any god of power, I would
Have sunk the sea within the earth or ere   11
It should the good ship so have swallowed and
The freighting souls within her.
PROSPERO   Be collected.   13
No more amazement. Tell your piteous heart   14
There's no harm done.
MIRANDA   Oh, woe the day!
PROSPERO   No harm.
I have done nothing but in care of thee,   16
Of thee, my dear one, thee, my daughter, who
Art ignorant of what thou art, naught knowing
Of whence I am, nor that I am more better   19
Than Prospero, master of a full poor cell,   20
And thy no greater father.
MIRANDA   More to know
Did never meddle with my thoughts.
PROSPERO   'Tis time   22
I should inform thee farther. Lend thy hand
And pluck my magic garment from me. So,
            [laying down his magic cloak and staff]
Lie there, my art.—Wipe thou thine eyes. Have
   comfort.
The direful spectacle of the wreck, which touched   26
The very virtue of compassion in thee,   27
I have with such provision in mine art
So safely ordered that there is no soul—
No, not so much perdition as an hair   30
Betid to any creature in the vessel   31
Which thou heard'st cry, which thou saw'st sink. Sit
   down,   32

For thou must now know farther.
MIRANDA [*sitting*]   You have often
Begun to tell me what I am, but stopped
And left me to a bootless inquisition,
Concluding, "Stay, not yet."   35
PROSPERO   The hour's now come;
The very minute bids thee ope thine ear.
Obey, and be attentive. Canst thou remember
A time before we came unto this cell?
I do not think thou canst, for then thou wast not
Out three years old.
MIRANDA   Certainly, sir, I can.   41
PROSPERO
By what? By any other house or person?
Of anything the image, tell me, that
Hath kept with thy remembrance.
MIRANDA   'Tis far off,
And rather like a dream than an assurance   45
That my remembrance warrants. Had I not   46
Four or five women once that tended me?
PROSPERO
Thou hadst, and more, Miranda. But how is it
That this lives in thy mind? What see'st thou else
In the dark backward and abysm of time?   50
If thou rememb'rest aught ere thou cam'st here,   51
How thou cam'st here thou mayst.
MIRANDA   But that I do not.
PROSPERO
Twelve year since, Miranda, twelve year since,
Thy father was the Duke of Milan and
A prince of power.
MIRANDA   Sir, are not you my father?
PROSPERO
Thy mother was a piece of virtue, and   56
She said thou wast my daughter; and thy father
Was Duke of Milan, and his only heir
And princess no worse issued.
MIRANDA   Oh, the heavens!   59
What foul play had we, that we came from thence?
Or blessèd was't we did?
PROSPERO   Both, both, my girl.
By foul play, as thou say'st, were we heaved thence,
But blessedly holp hither.
MIRANDA   O, my heart bleeds   63
To think o'th' teen that I have turned you to,   64
Which is from my remembrance! Please you, farther.   65
PROSPERO
My brother and thy uncle, called Antonio—
I pray thee mark me—that a brother should
Be so perfidious!—he whom next thyself   68
Of all the world I loved, and to him put
The manage of my state, as at that time   70
Through all the seigniories it was the first,   71

---

66 **heath** heather.   **furze** gorse, a weed growing on wasteland
67 **fain** rather
1.2 **Location:** The island, near Prospero's cell. On the Elizabethan
stage, this cell is implicitly at hand throughout the play, although
in some scenes the convention of flexible distance allows us to
imagine characters in other parts of the island.
1 **art** magic   2 **allay** pacify   4 **welkin's cheek** sky's face   6 **brave**
gallant, splendid   11 **or ere** before   13 **freighting souls** cargo of
souls.   **collected** calm, composed.   14 **amazement** consternation.
piteous pitying   16 **but** except   19 **more better** of higher rank
20 **full** very   22 **meddle** mingle   26 **wreck** shipwreck   27 **virtue**
essence   30 **perdition** loss   31 **Betid** happened   32 **Which** whom

35 **bootless inquisition** profitless inquiry   41 **Out** fully   45–6 **assurance . . . warrants** certainty that my memory guarantees.   50 **backward
. . . time** abyss of the past.   51 **aught** anything   56 **piece** masterpiece,
exemplar   59 **no worse issued** no less nobly born, descended.   63 **holp**
helped   64 **teen . . . to** trouble I've caused you to remember or put you
to   65 **from** out of   68 **next** next to   70 **manage** management, administration   71 **seigniories** i.e., city-states of northern Italy

And Prospero the prime duke, being so reputed   72
In dignity, and for the liberal arts
Without a parallel; those being all my study,
The government I cast upon my brother
And to my state grew stranger, being transported   76
And rapt in secret studies. Thy false uncle—
Dost thou attend me?

MIRANDA   Sir, most heedfully.

PROSPERO
Being once perfected how to grant suits,   79
How to deny them, who t'advance and who
To trash for overtopping, new created   81
The creatures that were mine, I say, or changed 'em,   82
Or else new formed 'em; having both the key   83
Of officer and office, set all hearts i'th' state   84
To what tune pleased his ear, that now he was   85
The ivy which had hid my princely trunk
And sucked my verdure out on't. Thou attend'st not.   87

MIRANDA
Oh, good sir, I do.

PROSPERO   I pray thee, mark me.
I, thus neglecting worldly ends, all dedicated
To closeness and the bettering of my mind   90
With that which, but by being so retired,   91
O'erprized all popular rate, in my false brother   92
Awaked an evil nature; and my trust,
Like a good parent, did beget of him   94
A falsehood in its contrary as great
As my trust was, which had indeed no limit,
A confidence sans bound. He being thus lorded   97
Not only with what my revenue yielded
But what my power might else exact, like one   99
Who, having into truth by telling of it,   100
Made such a sinner of his memory   101
To credit his own lie, he did believe   102
He was indeed the Duke, out o'th' substitution   103
And executing th'outward face of royalty   104
With all prerogative. Hence his ambition growing—   105
Dost thou hear?

MIRANDA   Your tale, sir, would cure deafness.

PROSPERO
To have no screen between this part he played   107
And him he played it for, he needs will be   108
Absolute Milan. Me, poor man, my library   109
Was dukedom large enough. Of temporal royalties   110
He thinks me now incapable; confederates—   111
So dry he was for sway—wi'th' King of Naples   112
To give him annual tribute, do him homage,   113
Subject his coronet to his crown, and bend   114
The dukedom yet unbowed—alas, poor Milan!—   115
To most ignoble stooping.

MIRANDA   O the heavens!

PROSPERO
Mark his condition and th'event, then tell me   117
If this might be a brother.

MIRANDA   I should sin
To think but nobly of my grandmother.   119
Good wombs have borne bad sons.

PROSPERO   Now the condition.
This King of Naples, being an enemy
To me inveterate, hearkens my brother's suit,   122
Which was that he, in lieu o'th' premises   123
Of homage and I know not how much tribute,
Should presently extirpate me and mine   125
Out of the dukedom and confer fair Milan,
With all the honors, on my brother. Whereon,
A treacherous army levied, one midnight
Fated to th' purpose did Antonio open
The gates of Milan, and, i'th' dead of darkness,
The ministers for th' purpose hurried thence   131
Me and thy crying self.

MIRANDA   Alack, for pity!
I, not remembering how I cried out then,
Will cry it o'er again. It is a hint   134
That wrings mine eyes to 't.

PROSPERO   Hear a little further,   135
And then I'll bring thee to the present business
Which now's upon 's, without the which this story
Were most impertinent.

MIRANDA   Wherefore did they not   138
That hour destroy us?

PROSPERO   Well demanded, wench.   139
My tale provokes that question. Dear, they durst
    not,
So dear the love my people bore me, nor set   141
A mark so bloody on the business, but   142

72 prime first in rank and importance   **76 to . . . stranger** i.e., withdrew from my responsibilities as duke.   **transported** carried away   **79 perfected** grown skillful   **81 trash** check a hound by tying a cord or weight to its neck.   **overtopping** running too far ahead of the pack; surmounting, exceeding one's authority   **81–3 new . . . formed 'em** won the loyalty of my officers by appointing them to new posts, or replaced them with others who would be loyal to Antonio, or else redefined the positions and their occupants   **83–5 having . . . ear** having now under his control both the officers and the positions, he set a tone for his rule according to his own inclination. (*Key* is also a metaphor for tuning stringed instruments.)   **87 verdure** vitality.   **on't** of it.   **90 closeness** retirement, seclusion   **91–2 but . . . rate** i.e., were it not that its private nature caused me to neglect my public responsibilities, had a value far beyond what public opinion could appreciate, or, simply because it was done in such seclusion, had a value not appreciated by popular opinion   **94 good parent** (Alludes to the proverb that good parents often bear bad children; see also line 120.)   **of** in   **97 sans** without.   **lorded** raised to lordship, with power and wealth   **99 else** otherwise, additionally   **100–2 Who . . . lie** i.e., who, by repeatedly telling the lie (that he was indeed Duke of Milan), made his memory such a confirmed sinner against truth that he began to believe his own lie.   **103–5 out . . . prerogative** as a result of his making himself my substitute and carrying out all the visible functions of royalty with all its rights and privileges.

107–9 To have . . . Milan In order to eliminate all separation between his role and himself, he insisted on becoming the Duke of Milan in name as well as in fact.   **110 temporal royalties** practical prerogatives and responsibilities of a sovereign   **111 confederates** conspires, allies himself   **112 dry** thirsty.   **sway** power   **113 him** i.e., the King of Naples   **114 his . . . his** Antonio's . . . the King of Naples'.   **bend** make bow down   **115 yet** hitherto   **117 condition** pact.   **th'event** the outcome   **119 but** other than   **122 hearkens** listens to   **123 he** the King of Naples.   **in . . . premises** in return for the stipulation   **125 presently extirpate** at once remove   **131 ministers . . . purpose** agents employed to do this.   **thence** from there   **134 hint** prompting   **135 wrings** (1) constrains (2) wrings tears from   **138 impertinent** irrelevant.   **Wherefore** Why   **139 demanded** asked.   **wench** (Here a term of endearment.)   **141–2 set . . . bloody** i.e., make obvious their murderous intent. (From the practice of marking with the blood of the prey those who have participated in a successful hunt.)

With colors fairer painted their foul ends. 143
In few, they hurried us aboard a bark, 144
Bore us some leagues to sea, where they prepared
A rotten carcass of a butt, not rigged, 146
Nor tackle, sail, nor mast; the very rats 147
Instinctively have quit it. There they hoist us, 148
To cry to th' sea that roared to us, to sigh
To th' winds whose pity, sighing back again,
Did us but loving wrong.

MIRANDA   Alack, what trouble 151
Was I then to you!

PROSPERO   Oh, a cherubin
Thou wast that did preserve me. Thou didst smile,
Infusèd with a fortitude from heaven, 154
When I have decked the sea with drops full salt, 155
Under my burden groaned, which raised in me 156
An undergoing stomach, to bear up 157
Against what should ensue.

MIRANDA   How came we ashore?

PROSPERO   By Providence divine.
Some food we had, and some fresh water, that
A noble Neapolitan, Gonzalo,
Out of his charity, who being then appointed
Master of this design, did give us, with
Rich garments, linens, stuffs, and necessaries, 165
Which since have steaded much. So, of his
    gentleness, 166
Knowing I loved my books, he furnished me
From mine own library with volumes that
I prize above my dukedom.

MIRANDA   Would I might 169
But ever see that man!

PROSPERO   Now I arise. 170
                [He puts on his magic cloak.]
Sit still, and hear the last of our sea sorrow. 171
Here in this island we arrived; and here
Have I, thy schoolmaster, made thee more profit 173
Than other princes can, that have more time 174
For vainer hours and tutors not so careful. 175

MIRANDA
Heavens thank you for't! And now, I pray you, sir—
For still 'tis beating in my mind—your reason
For raising this sea storm?

PROSPERO   Know thus far forth:
By accident most strange, bountiful Fortune,
Now my dear lady, hath mine enemies 180
Brought to this shore; and by my prescience
I find my zenith doth depend upon 182

A most auspicious star, whose influence 183
If now I court not, but omit, my fortunes 184
Will ever after droop. Here cease more questions.
Thou art inclined to sleep. 'Tis a good dullness, 186
And give it way. I know thou canst not choose. 187
                [Miranda sleeps.]
Come away, servant, come! I am ready now. 188
Approach, my Ariel, come.

    Enter Ariel.

ARIEL
All hail, great master, grave sir, hail! I come
To answer thy best pleasure; be't to fly,
To swim, to dive into the fire, to ride
On the curled clouds, to thy strong bidding task 193
Ariel and all his quality.

PROSPERO   Hast thou, spirit, 194
Performed to point the tempest that I bade thee? 195

ARIEL   To every article.
I boarded the King's ship. Now on the beak, 197
Now in the waist, the deck, in every cabin, 198
I flamed amazement. Sometime I'd divide 199
And burn in many places; on the topmast,
The yards, and bowsprit would I flame distinctly, 201
Then meet and join. Jove's lightning, the precursors
O'th' dreadful thunderclaps, more momentary
And sight-outrunning were not. The fire and cracks 204
Of sulfurous roaring the most mighty Neptune 205
Seem to besiege and make his bold waves tremble,
Yea, his dread trident shake.

PROSPERO   My brave spirit! 207
Who was so firm, so constant, that this coil 208
Would not infect his reason?

ARIEL   Not a soul
But felt a fever of the mad and played 210
Some tricks of desperation. All but mariners
Plunged in the foaming brine and quit the vessel,
Then all afire with me. The King's son, Ferdinand,
With hair up-staring—then like reeds, not hair— 214
Was the first man that leapt; cried, "Hell is empty,
And all the devils are here!"

PROSPERO   Why, that's my spirit!
But was not this nigh shore?

ARIEL   Close by, my master.

PROSPERO
But are they, Ariel, safe?

ARIEL   Not a hair perished.
On their sustaining garments not a blemish, 219
But fresher than before; and, as thou bad'st me, 220

---

143 **fairer** apparently more attractive   144 **few** few words.   **bark** ship   146 **butt** cask, tub   147 **Nor tackle** neither rigging   148 **quit** abandoned   151 **Did . . . wrong** i.e., pitied us even as they drove us on.   154 **Infusèd** filled, suffused   155 **decked** covered (with salt tears); adorned   156 **which** i.e., the smile   157 **undergoing stomach** courage to go on   165 **stuffs** supplies   166 **steaded much** been of much use.   **So, of** Similarly, out of   169 **Would** I wish   170 **But ever** i.e., someday   171 **sea sorrow** sorrowful adventure at sea.
173–4 **made . . . can** provided a more valuable education than other royal children (of either sex) can enjoy   175 **vainer** more foolishly spent   180 **my dear lady** (Refers to Fortune, not Miranda.)
182 **zenith** height of fortune. (Astrological term.)

183 **influence** astrological power   184 **but omit** but ignore instead   186 **dullness** drowsiness   187 **give it way** let it happen (i.e., don't fight it).   188 **Come away** Come   193 **task** make demands upon   194 **quality** (1) fellow spirits (2) abilities.   195 **to point** to the smallest detail   197 **beak** prow   198 **waist** midships.   **deck** poop deck at the stern   199 **flamed amazement** struck terror in the guise of fire, i.e., Saint Elmo's fire.   201 **distinctly** in different places   204 **sight-out-running** swifter than sight.   **were not** could not have been.
205 **Neptune** Roman god of the sea   207 **trident** three-pronged weapon   208 **coil** tumult   210 **of the mad** such as madmen feel   214 **up-staring** standing on end   219 **sustaining** protecting   220 **bad'st** ordered

In troops I have dispersed them 'bout the isle.   221
The King's son have I landed by himself,
Whom I left cooling of the air with sighs   223
In an odd angle of the isle, and sitting,   224
His arms in this sad knot.   [*He folds his arms.*]

PROSPERO   Of the King's ship,   225
The mariners, say how thou hast disposed,
And all the rest o'th' fleet.

ARIEL   Safely in harbor
Is the King's ship; in the deep nook, where once   228
Thou called'st me up at midnight to fetch dew   229
From the still-vexed Bermudas, there she's hid;   230
The mariners all under hatches stowed,
Who, with a charm joined to their suffered labor,   232
I have left asleep. And for the rest o'th' fleet,
Which I dispersed, they all have met again
And are upon the Mediterranean float   235
Bound sadly home for Naples,
Supposing that they saw the King's ship wrecked
And his great person perish.

PROSPERO   Ariel, thy charge
Exactly is performed. But there's more work.
What is the time o'th' day?

ARIEL   Past the mid season.   240

PROSPERO
At least two glasses. The time twixt six and now   241
Must by us both be spent most preciously.

ARIEL
Is there more toil? Since thou dost give me pains,   243
Let me remember thee what thou hast promised,   244
Which is not yet performed me.

PROSPERO   How now? Moody?
What is't thou canst demand?

ARIEL   My liberty.

PROSPERO
Before the time be out? No more!

ARIEL   I prithee,
Remember I have done thee worthy service,
Told thee no lies, made thee no mistakings, served
Without or grudge or grumblings. Thou did promise
To bate me a full year.

PROSPERO   Dost thou forget   251
From what a torment I did free thee?

ARIEL   No.

PROSPERO
Thou dost, and think'st it much to tread the ooze
Of the salt deep,
To run upon the sharp wind of the north,
To do me business in the veins o'th' earth   256

When it is baked with frost.

ARIEL   I do not, sir.   257

PROSPERO
Thou liest, malignant thing! Hast thou forgot
The foul witch Sycorax, who with age and envy   259
Was grown into a hoop? Hast thou forgot her?   260

ARIEL   No, sir.

PROSPERO
Thou hast. Where was she born? Speak. Tell me.

ARIEL
Sir, in Argier.

PROSPERO   Oh, was she so? I must   263
Once in a month recount what thou hast been,
Which thou forget'st. This damned witch Sycorax,
For mischiefs manifold and sorceries terrible
To enter human hearing, from Argier,
Thou know'st, was banished. For one thing she did   268
They would not take her life. Is not this true?

ARIEL   Ay, sir.

PROSPERO
This blue-eyed hag was hither brought with child   271
And here was left by th' sailors. Thou, my slave,
As thou report'st thyself, was then her servant;
And, for thou wast a spirit too delicate   274
To act her earthy and abhorred commands,
Refusing her grand hests, she did confine thee,   276
By help of her more potent ministers
And in her most unmitigable rage,
Into a cloven pine, within which rift
Imprisoned thou didst painfully remain
A dozen years; within which space she died
And left thee there, where thou didst vent thy
    groans
As fast as mill wheels strike. Then was this island—   283
Save for the son that she did litter here,   284
A freckled whelp, hag-born—not honored with   285
A human shape.

ARIEL   Yes, Caliban her son.   286

PROSPERO
Dull thing, I say so: he, that Caliban   287
Whom now I keep in service. Thou best know'st
What torment I did find thee in. Thy groans
Did make wolves howl, and penetrate the breasts
Of ever-angry bears. It was a torment
To lay upon the damned, which Sycorax
Could not again undo. It was mine art,
When I arrived and heard thee, that made gape   294
The pine and let thee out.

ARIEL   I thank thee, master.

---

221 troops groups   **223 cooling of** cooling   **224 angle** corner
225 sad knot (Folded arms are indicative of melancholy.)   **228 nook**
bay   **229 dew** (Collected at midnight for magical purposes; compare
with line 324.)   **230 still-vexed Bermudas** ever stormy Bermudas.
(Perhaps refers to the then recent Bermuda shipwreck; see play Introduction. The Folio text reads *"Bermoothes."*)   **232 with . . . labor** by
means of a spell added to all the labor they have undergone
235 float sea   **240 mid season** noon.   **241 glasses** hourglasses.
243 pains labors   **244 remember** remind   **251 bate** remit, deduct
256 do me do for me.   **veins** veins of minerals, or, underground
streams, thought to be analogous to the veins of the human body

257 baked hardened   **259 envy** malice   **260 grown into a hoop** i.e.,
so bent over with age as to resemble a hoop.   **263 Argier** Algiers
268 one . . . did (Perhaps a reference to her pregnancy, for which her
life would be spared.)   **271 blue-eyed** with dark circles under the
eyes or with blue eyelids, implying pregnancy.   **with child** pregnant
274 for because   **276 hests** commands   **283 as mill wheels strike** as
the blades of a mill wheel strike the water.   **284 Save** except.   **litter**
give birth to   **285 whelp** offspring. (Used of animals.)   **hag-born**
born of a female demon   **286 Yes . . . son** (Ariel is probably concur-
ring with Prospero's comment about a "freckled whelp," not contradicting the point about "A human shape.")   **287 Dull . . . so** i.e.,
Exactly, that's what I said, you dullard.   **294 gape** open wide

PROSPERO
If thou more murmur'st, I will rend an oak
And peg thee in his knotty entrails till   297
Thou hast howled away twelve winters.
ARIEL   Pardon, master.
I will be correspondent to command   299
And do my spriting gently.   300
PROSPERO   Do so, and after two days
I will discharge thee.
ARIEL   That's my noble master!
What shall I do? Say what? What shall I do?
PROSPERO
Go make thyself like a nymph o'th' sea. Be subject
To no sight but thine and mine, invisible
To every eyeball else. Go take this shape
And hither come in't. Go, hence with diligence!
                                                        Exit [*Ariel*].
[*To Miranda*] Awake, dear heart, awake! Thou hast
    slept well.
Awake!
MIRANDA   The strangeness of your story put
Heaviness in me.
PROSPERO   Shake it off. Come on,   310
We'll visit Caliban, my slave, who never
Yields us kind answer.
MIRANDA   'Tis a villain, sir,
I do not love to look on.
PROSPERO   But, as 'tis,
We cannot miss him. He does make our fire,   314
Fetch in our wood, and serves in offices   315
That profit us.—What ho! Slave! Caliban!
Thou earth, thou! Speak.
CALIBAN (*within*)   There's wood enough within.
PROSPERO
Come forth, I say! There's other business for thee.
Come, thou tortoise! When?   319

            Enter Ariel like a water nymph.

Fine apparition! My quaint Ariel,   320
Hark in thine ear.   [*He whispers.*]
ARIEL   My lord, it shall be done.   *Exit.*
PROSPERO
Thou poisonous slave, got by the devil himself   322
Upon thy wicked dam, come forth!   323

            Enter Caliban.

CALIBAN
As wicked dew as e'er my mother brushed   324
With raven's feather from unwholesome fen   325
Drop on you both! A southwest blow on ye   326
And blister you all o'er!
PROSPERO
For this, be sure, tonight thou shalt have cramps,

Side-stitches that shall pen thy breath up. Urchins   329
Shall forth at vast of night that they may work   330
All exercise on thee. Thou shalt be pinched
As thick as honeycomb, each pinch more stinging   332
Than bees that made 'em.
CALIBAN   I must eat my dinner.   333
This island's mine, by Sycorax my mother,
Which thou tak'st from me. When thou cam'st first,
Thou strok'st me and made much of me, wouldst give
    me
Water with berries in't, and teach me how
To name the bigger light, and how the less,   338
That burn by day and night. And then I loved thee
And showed thee all the qualities o'th'isle,
The fresh springs, brine pits, barren place and fertile.
Cursed be I that did so! All the charms   342
Of Sycorax, toads, beetles, bats, light on you!
For I am all the subjects that you have,
Which first was mine own king; and here you sty me   345
In this hard rock, whiles you do keep from me
The rest o'th'island.
PROSPERO   Thou most lying slave,
Whom stripes may move, not kindness! I have used
    thee,   348
Filth as thou art, with humane care, and lodged thee   349
In mine own cell, till thou didst seek to violate
The honor of my child.
CALIBAN
Oho, oho! Would't had been done!
Thou didst prevent me; I had peopled else   353
This isle with Calibans.
MIRANDA   Abhorrèd slave,   354
Which any print of goodness wilt not take,   355
Being capable of all ill! I pitied thee,
Took pains to make thee speak, taught thee each hour
One thing or other. When thou didst not, savage,
Know thine own meaning, but wouldst gabble like
A thing most brutish, I endowed thy purposes   360
With words that made them known. But thy vile race,   361
Though thou didst learn, had that in't which good
    natures
Could not abide to be with; therefore wast thou
Deservedly confined into this rock,
Who hadst deserved more than a prison.   365
CALIBAN
You taught me language, and my profit on't
Is I know how to curse. The red plague rid you   367

297 his its   **299 correspondent** responsive, submissive   **300 spriting gently** duties as a spirit willingly.   **310 Heaviness** drowsiness   **314 miss** do without   **315 offices** functions, duties   **319 When** (An exclamation of impatience.)   **320 quaint** ingenious   **322 got** begotten, sired   **323 dam** mother. (Used of animals.)   **324 wicked** mischievous, harmful   **325 fen** marsh, bog   **326 southwest** i.e., wind thought to bring disease

329 Urchins Hedgehogs; here, suggesting goblins in the guise of hedgehogs   **330 vast** lengthy, desolate time. (Malignant spirits were thought to be restricted to the hours of darkness.)   **332 as honeycomb** i.e., as a honeycomb full of bees   **333 'em** i.e., the honeycomb   **338 the bigger . . . less** i.e., the sun and the moon. (See Genesis 1:16: "God then made two great lights: the greater light to rule the day, and the less light to rule the night.")   **342 charms** spells   **345 sty** confine as in a sty   **348 stripes** lashes   **349 humane** (Not distinguished as a word from *human.*)   **353 peopled else** otherwise populated   **354–65 Abhorrèd . . . prison** (Sometimes assigned by editors to Prospero.)   **355 print** imprint, impression   **360 purposes** meanings, desires   **361 race** natural disposition; species, nature   **367 red plague** plague characterized by red sores and evacuation of blood.   **rid** destroy

For learning me your language!
PROSPERO   Hagseed, hence!   368
Fetch us in fuel, and be quick, thou'rt best,   369
To answer other business. Shrugg'st thou, malice?   370
If thou neglect'st or dost unwillingly
What I command, I'll rack thee with old cramps,   372
Fill all thy bones with aches, make thee roar   373
That beasts shall tremble at thy din.
CALIBAN   No, pray thee.
    [Aside]   I must obey. His art is of such power
It would control my dam's god, Setebos,   376
And make a vassal of him.
PROSPERO   So, slave, hence!   377
                                    Exit Caliban.

    Enter Ferdinand; and Ariel, invisible, playing and
    singing. [Ferdinand does not see Prospero and
    Miranda.]

                Ariel's Song.

ARIEL
    Come unto these yellow sands,
        And then take hands;
    Curtsied when you have, and kissed   380
        The wild waves whist;   381
    Foot it featly here and there,   382
        And, sweet sprites, bear   383
    The burden. Hark, hark!   384
        Burden, dispersedly [within].Bow-wow.   385
    The watchdogs bark.
        [*Burden, dispersedly within.*] Bow-wow.
    Hark, hark! I hear
    The strain of strutting chanticleer
    Cry Cock-a-diddle-dow.
FERDINAND
    Where should this music be? I'th'air or th'earth?
    It sounds no more; and sure it waits upon   392
    Some god o'th'island. Sitting on a bank,   393
    Weeping again the King my father's wreck,
    This music crept by me upon the waters,
    Allaying both their fury and my passion   396
    With its sweet air. Thence I have followed it,   397
    Or it hath drawn me rather. But 'tis gone.
    No, it begins again.

                Ariel's Song.

ARIEL
    Full fathom five thy father lies.
    Of his bones are coral made.

    Those are pearls that were his eyes.
        Nothing of him that doth fade
    But doth suffer a sea change
    Into something rich and strange.
    Sea nymphs hourly ring his knell.   406
            Burden [within]. Ding dong.
    Hark, now I hear them, ding dong bell.
FERDINAND
    The ditty does remember my drowned father.   409
    This is no mortal business, nor no sound
    That the earth owes. I hear it now above me.   411
PROSPERO [*to Miranda*]
    The fringèd curtains of thine eye advance   412
    And say what thou see'st yond.
MIRANDA   What is't? A spirit?
    Lord, how it looks about! Believe me, sir,
    It carries a brave form. But 'tis a spirit.   415
PROSPERO
    No, wench, it eats and sleeps and hath such senses
    As we have, such. This gallant which thou see'st
    Was in the wreck; and, but he's something stained 418
    With grief, that's beauty's canker, thou mightst
        call him   419
    A goodly person. He hath lost his fellows
    And strays about to find 'em.
MIRANDA   I might call him
    A thing divine, for nothing natural
    I ever saw so noble.
PROSPERO [*aside*]   It goes on, I see,
    As my soul prompts it.—Spirit, fine spirit, I'll free thee
    Within two days for this.
FERDINAND [*seeing Miranda*]   Most sure, the goddess
    On whom these airs attend!—Vouchsafe my prayer   426
    May know if you remain upon this island,   427
    And that you will some good instruction give
    How I may bear me here. My prime request,   429
    Which I do last pronounce, is—O you wonder!—   430
    If you be maid or no?
MIRANDA   No wonder, sir,   431
    But certainly a maid.
FERDINAND   My language? Heavens!
    I am the best of them that speak this speech,   433
    Were I but where 'tis spoken.
PROSPERO [*coming forward*]   How? The best?
    What wert thou if the King of Naples heard thee?
FERDINAND
    A single thing, as I am now, that wonders   436
    To hear thee speak of Naples. He does hear me,   437

368 learning teaching.   **Hagseed** Offspring of a female demon
369 thou'rt best you'd be well advised   **370 answer other business**
perform other tasks.   **372 old** such as old people suffer, or, plenty of
373 aches (Pronounced "aitches.")   **376 Setebos** (A god of the Patago-
nians, named in Richard Eden's *History of Travel*, 1577.)   **377.2 *Ariel,
invisible*** (Ariel wears a garment that by convention indicates he is invisible to the other characters.)   **380 Curtsied . . . have** when you have curtsied   **380–1 kissed . . . whist** kissed the waves into silence, or, kissed
while the waves are being hushed   **382 Foot it featly** dance nimbly
383 sprites spirits   **384 burden** refrain, undersong.   **385 s.d. *dispers-
edly*** i.e., from all directions, not in unison   **392 waits upon** serves,
attends   **393 bank** sandbank   **396 passion** grief   **397 Thence** i.e.,
From the bank on which I sat

406 knell announcement of a death by the tolling of a bell.
409 remember commemorate   **411 owes** owns.   **412 advance** raise
415 brave excellent   **418 but . . . stained** were it not that his luster is
somewhat darkened   **419 canker** cankerworm (feeding on buds and
leaves)   **426 airs** songs.   **Vouchsafe** Grant   **427 remain** dwell
429 bear me conduct myself.   **prime** chief   **430 wonder** (Miranda's
name means "to be wondered at.")   **431 maid** (1) a human maiden as
opposed to a goddess (2) unmarried (3) a virgin   **433 best** i.e., in
birth   **436 A single . . . now** (1) A single figure who combines into
one person both self and King of Naples (since Ferdinand believes he
has inherited the kingship) (2) A lonely shipwrecked figure
437 Naples the King of Naples.   **He . . . me** I who hear my own
words am the King of Naples

And that he does I weep. Myself am Naples,   438
Who with mine eyes, never since at ebb, beheld   439
The King my father wrecked.
MIRANDA   Alack, for mercy!
FERDINAND
Yes, faith, and all his lords, the Duke of Milan
And his brave son being twain.
PROSPERO [*aside*]   The Duke of Milan   442
And his more braver daughter could control thee,   443
If now 'twere fit to do't. At the first sight
They have changed eyes.—Delicate Ariel,   445
I'll set thee free for this. [*To Ferdinand*] A word, good
    sir.
I fear you have done yourself some wrong. A word!   447
MIRANDA [*aside*]
    Why speaks my father so ungently? This
Is the third man that e'er I saw, the first
That e'er I sighed for. Pity move my father
To be inclined my way!
FERDINAND [*to Miranda*]   Oh, if a virgin,
And your affection not gone forth, I'll make you
The Queen of Naples.
PROSPERO   Soft, sir! One word more.
[*Aside*] They are both in either's powers; but this swift
    business   454
I must uneasy make, lest too light winning   455
Make the prize light. [*To Ferdinand*] One word more: I
    charge thee   456
That thou attend me. Thou dost here usurp   457
The name thou ow'st not, and hast put thyself   458
Upon this island as a spy, to win it
From me, the lord on't.
FERDINAND   No, as I am a man.   460
MIRANDA
There's nothing ill can dwell in such a temple.
If the ill spirit have so fair a house,
Good things will strive to dwell with't.
PROSPERO   Follow me.—   463
Speak not you for him; he's a traitor.—Come,
I'll manacle thy neck and feet together.
Seawater shalt thou drink; thy food shall be
The fresh-brook mussels, withered roots, and husks
Wherein the acorn cradled. Follow.
FERDINAND   No!
I will resist such entertainment till   469
Mine enemy has more pow'r.   470
                He draws, and is charmed from moving.
MIRANDA   O dear father,
Make not too rash a trial of him, for   471

He's gentle, and not fearful.
PROSPERO   What, I say,   472
My foot my tutor?—Put thy sword up, traitor,   473
Who mak'st a show but dar'st not strike, thy
    conscience
Is so possessed with guilt. Come, from thy ward,   475
For I can here disarm thee with this stick
And make thy weapon drop.   [*He brandishes his staff.*]
MIRANDA [*trying to hinder him*]   Beseech you, father!
PROSPERO
Hence! Hang not on my garments.
MIRANDA   Sir, have pity!
I'll be his surety.
PROSPERO   Silence! One word more   479
Shall make me chide thee, if not hate thee. What,
An advocate for an impostor? Hush!
Thou think'st there is no more such shapes as he,
Having seen but him and Caliban. Foolish wench,
To th' most of men this is a Caliban,   484
And they to him are angels.
MIRANDA   My affections
Are then most humble; I have no ambition
To see a goodlier man.
PROSPERO [*to Ferdinand*]   Come on, obey.
Thy nerves are in their infancy again   488
And have no vigor in them.
FERDINAND   So they are.
My spirits, as in a dream, are all bound up.   490
My father's loss, the weakness which I feel,
The wreck of all my friends, nor this man's threats
To whom I am subdued, are but light to me,   493
Might I but through my prison once a day
Behold this maid. All corners else o'th'earth   495
Let liberty make use of; space enough
Have I in such a prison.
PROSPERO [*aside*]   It works. [*To Ferdinand*] Come on.—
Thou hast done well, fine Ariel! [*To Ferdinand*] Follow
    me.
[*To Ariel*] Hark what thou else shalt do me.
MIRANDA [*to Ferdinand*]   Be of comfort. 499
My father's of a better nature, sir,
Than he appears by speech. This is unwonted   501
Which now came from him.
PROSPERO [*to Ariel*]   Thou shalt be as free
As mountain winds; but then exactly do   503
All points of my command.
ARIEL   To th' syllable.
PROSPERO [*to Ferdinand*]
Come, follow. [*To Miranda*] Speak not for him.
                                               Exeunt.

❖

---

438 And . . . weep i.e., and I weep at this reminder that my father is
seemingly dead, leaving me heir.   **439 never . . . ebb** never dry, continually weeping   **442 son** (The only reference in the play to a son of
Antonio.)   **443 more braver** more splendid.   **control** refute
445 changed eyes exchanged amorous glances.   **447 done . . . wrong**
i.e., spoken falsely.   **454 both in either's** each in the other's
455 uneasy difficult   **456 light** cheap. (Playing on *light*, "easy," in
455.)   **457 attend** follow, obey   **458 ow'st** ownest   **460 on't** of it.
463 strive . . . with't i.e., expel the evil and occupy the *temple,* the
body.   **469 entertainment** treatment   **470 s.d. *charmed*** magically
prevented   **471 rash** harsh

472 gentle (1) wellborn (2) easily managed.   **fearful** frightening,
dangerous.   **473 My . . . tutor?** i.e., Do you, as my daughter and thus
bound to me by obedience, dare presume to teach me what to do?
475 ward defensive posture (in fencing)   **479 surety** guarantee.
484 To compared with   **488 nerves** sinews   **490 spirits** vital powers
493 light unimportant   **495 corners else** other corners, regions
499 me for me.   **501 unwonted** unusual   **503 then** if so, then

2.1

Enter Alonso, Sebastian, Antonio, Gonzalo,
Adrian, Francisco, and others.

GONZALO [*to Alonso*]
Beseech you, sir, be merry. You have cause,
So have we all, of joy, for our escape
Is much beyond our loss. Our hint of woe   3
Is common; every day some sailor's wife,
The masters of some merchant, and the merchant,   5
Have just our theme of woe. But for the miracle,   6
I mean our preservation, few in millions
Can speak like us. Then wisely, good sir, weigh   8
Our sorrow with our comfort.
ALONSO   Prithee, peace.   9
SEBASTIAN [*aside to Antonio*]   He receives comfort like
cold porridge.   11
ANTONIO [*aside to Sebastian*]   The visitor will not give   12
him o'er so.   13
SEBASTIAN   Look, he's winding up the watch of his wit;
by and by it will strike.
GONZALO [*to Alonso*]   Sir—
SEBASTIAN [*aside to Antonio*]   One. Tell.   17
GONZALO   When every grief is entertained   18
That's offered, comes to th'entertainer—   19
SEBASTIAN   A dollar.   20
GONZALO   Dolor comes to him, indeed. You have spo-
ken truer than you purposed.
SEBASTIAN   You have taken it wiselier than I meant you
should.
GONZALO [*to Alonso*]   Therefore, my lord—
ANTONIO   Fie, what a spendthrift is he of his tongue!
ALONSO [*to Gonzalo*]   I prithee, spare.   27
GONZALO   Well, I have done. But yet—
SEBASTIAN [*aside to Antonio*]   He will be talking.
ANTONIO [*aside to Sebastian*]   Which, of he or Adrian,   30
for a good wager, first begins to crow?   31
SEBASTIAN   The old cock.   32
ANTONIO   The cockerel.   33
SEBASTIAN   Done. The wager?
ANTONIO   A laughter.   35

SEBASTIAN   A match!   36
ADRIAN   Though this island seem to be desert—   37
ANTONIO   Ha, ha, ha!
SEBASTIAN   So, you're paid.   39
ADRIAN   Uninhabitable and almost inaccessible—
SEBASTIAN   Yet—
ADRIAN   Yet—
ANTONIO   He could not miss't.   43
ADRIAN   It must needs be of subtle, tender, and delicate   44
temperance.   45
ANTONIO   Temperance was a delicate wench.   46
SEBASTIAN   Ay, and a subtle, as he most learnedly   47
delivered.   48
ADRIAN   The air breathes upon us here most sweetly.
SEBASTIAN   As if it had lungs, and rotten ones.
ANTONIO   Or as 'twere perfumed by a fen.   51
GONZALO   Here is everything advantageous to life.
ANTONIO   True, save means to live.   53
SEBASTIAN   Of that there's none, or little.
GONZALO   How lush and lusty the grass looks! How   55
green!
ANTONIO   The ground indeed is tawny.   57
SEBASTIAN   With an eye of green in't.   58
ANTONIO   He misses not much.
SEBASTIAN   No. He doth but mistake the truth totally.   60
GONZALO   But the rarity of it is—which is indeed
almost beyond credit—
SEBASTIAN   As many vouched rarities are.   63
GONZALO   That our garments, being, as they were,
drenched in the sea, hold notwithstanding their fresh-
ness and glosses, being rather new-dyed than stained
with salt water.
ANTONIO   If but one of his pockets could speak, would   68
it not say he lies?   69
SEBASTIAN   Ay, or very falsely pocket up his report.   70
GONZALO   Methinks our garments are now as fresh as
when we put them on first in Afric, at the marriage of
the King's fair daughter Claribel to the King of Tunis.
SEBASTIAN   'Twas a sweet marriage, and we prosper
well in our return.
ADRIAN   Tunis was never graced before with such a
paragon to their queen.   77

2.1. Location: Another part of the island.
3 hint occasion   **5 The masters . . . the merchant** the officers or owners of some merchant vessel and the merchant who owns the cargo
6 for as for   **8–9 weigh . . . comfort** balance our sorrow against our
comfort.   **11 porridge** (Punningly suggested by *peace*, i.e., "peas" or
"pease," a common ingredient of porridge.)   **12 visitor** one bringing
nourishment and comfort to the sick, as Gonzalo is doing   **12–13 give
him o'er** abandon him   **17 Tell** Keep count.   **18–19 When . . . entertainer** When every sorrow that presents itself is accepted without
resistance, there comes to the recipient   **20 dollar** widely circulated
coin, the German thaler and the Spanish piece of eight. (Sebastian
puns on *entertainer* in the sense of paid performer or innkeeper; to
Gonzalo, *dollar* suggests "dolor," grief.)   **27 spare** forbear, cease.
30–1 Which . . . crow? Which of the two, Gonzalo or Adrian, do you
bet will speak (crow) first?   **32 The old cock** Gonzalo.   **33 The cockerel** Adrian.   **35 laughter** (1) burst of laughter (2) sitting of eggs.
(When Adrian, the *cockerel*, begins to speak two lines later, Sebastian
loses the bet. The Folio speech prefixes in lines 38–9 are here reversed
so that Antonio enjoys his laugh as the prize for winning, as in the
proverb "He who laughs last laughs best" or "He laughs that wins."
The Folio assignment can work in the theater, however, if Sebastian
pays for losing with a sardonic laugh of concession.)

36 A match! A bargain; agreed!.   **37 desert** uninhabited   **39 you're
paid** i.e., you've had your laugh.   **43 miss't** (1) avoid saying "Yet"
(2) miss the island.   **44 must needs be** has to be   **45 temperance**
mildness of climate.   **46 Temperance** a girl's name.   **delicate** (Here
it means "given to pleasure, voluptuous"; in line 44, "pleasant."
Antonio is evidently suggesting that *tender, and delicate temperance*
sounds like a Puritan phrase, which Antonio then mocks by applying
the words to a woman rather than an island. He began this bawdy
comparison with a double entendre on *inaccessible*, line 40.)   **47 subtle** (Here it means "tricky, sexually crafty"; in line 44, "delicate.")
48 delivered uttered. (Sebastian joins Antonio in baiting the Puritans
with his use of the pious cant phrase *learnedly delivered*.)   **51 fen** evil-
smelling marshland.   **53 save** except   **55 lusty** healthy   **57 tawny**
dull brown, yellowish.   **58 eye** tinge, or spot. (Sebastian is mocking
Gonzalo's optimism by saying there's precious little green to see anywhere. Antonio echoes him in line 59 with similar sarcasm.)   **60 He
. . . totally** i.e., He's only a tiny 100% wrong. (Sarcastic.)   **63 As . . . are**
(More sarcasm: Just as many alleged strange sights are doubtful,
including this one.)   **68–70 If . . . report** (More wisecracking: Gonzalo's mud-filled pockets would surely give the lie to his talk of clean
fresh garments, thereby *pocketing up* or tabling the *report*.)   **77 to** for

GONZALO   Not since widow Dido's time.   78

ANTONIO [*aside to Sebastian*]   Widow? A pox o' that! How came that "widow" in? Widow Dido!

SEBASTIAN   What if he had said "widower Aeneas" too? Good Lord, how you take it!   82

ADRIAN [*to Gonzalo*]   "Widow Dido" said you? You make me study of that. She was of Carthage, not of Tunis.   84

GONZALO   This Tunis, sir, was Carthage.

ADRIAN   Carthage?

GONZALO   I assure you, Carthage.

ANTONIO   His word is more than the miraculous harp.   88

SEBASTIAN   He hath raised the wall, and houses too.

ANTONIO   What impossible matter will he make easy next?

SEBASTIAN   I think he will carry this island home in his pocket and give it his son for an apple.

ANTONIO   And, sowing the kernels of it in the sea,   94 bring forth more islands.

GONZALO   Ay.   96

ANTONIO   Why, in good time.   97

GONZALO [*to Alonso*]   Sir, we were talking that our garments seem now as fresh as when we were at Tunis at the marriage of your daughter, who is now queen.

ANTONIO   And the rarest that e'er came there.   101

SEBASTIAN   Bate, I beseech you, widow Dido.   102

ANTONIO   Oh, widow Dido? Ay, widow Dido.

GONZALO   Is not, sir, my doublet as fresh as the first   104 day I wore it? I mean, in a sort.   105

ANTONIO   That "sort" was well fished for.   106

GONZALO   When I wore it at your daughter's marriage.

ALONSO
You cram these words into mine ears against
The stomach of my sense. Would I had never   109
Married my daughter there! For, coming thence,   110
My son is lost and, in my rate, she too,   111
Who is so far from Italy removed
I ne'er again shall see her. O thou mine heir
Of Naples and of Milan, what strange fish
Hath made his meal on thee?

FRANCISCO   Sir, he may live.
I saw him beat the surges under him   116
And ride upon their backs. He trod the water,

Whose enmity he flung aside, and breasted
The surge most swoll'n that met him. His bold head
'Bove the contentious waves he kept, and oared   120
Himself with his good arms in lusty stroke   121
To th' shore, that o'er his wave-worn basis bowed,   122
As stooping to relieve him. I not doubt   123
He came alive to land.

ALONSO   No, no, he's gone.

SEBASTIAN [*to Alonso*]
Sir, you may thank yourself for this great loss,
That would not bless our Europe with your daughter,   126
But rather loose her to an African,   127
Where she at least is banished from your eye,   128
Who hath cause to wet the grief on't.

ALONSO   Prithee, peace.   129

SEBASTIAN
You were kneeled to and importuned otherwise   130
By all of us, and the fair soul herself   131
Weighed between loathness and obedience at   132
Which end o'th' beam should bow. We have lost your
son,   133
I fear, forever. Milan and Naples have
More widows in them of this business' making   135
Than we bring men to comfort them.
The fault's your own.

ALONSO   So is the dear'st o'th' loss.   138

GONZALO   My lord Sebastian,
The truth you speak doth lack some gentleness
And time to speak it in. You rub the sore   141
When you should bring the plaster.

SEBASTIAN   Very well.   142

ANTONIO   And most chirurgeonly.   143

GONZALO [*to Alonso*]
It is foul weather in us all, good sir,
When you are cloudy.

SEBASTIAN [*to Antonio*]   Fowl weather?

ANTONIO [*to Sebastian*]   Very foul.   145

GONZALO
Had I plantation of this isle, my lord—   146

ANTONIO [*to Sebastian*]
He'd sow't with nettle seed.

SEBASTIAN   Or docks, or mallows.   147

GONZALO
And were the king on't, what would I do?

---

78 widow Dido Queen of Carthage, deserted by Aeneas. (She was, in fact, a widow when Aeneas, a widower, met her, but Antonio may be amused at Gonzalo's prudish use of the term "widow" to describe a woman deserted by her lover.)   82 take understand, respond to, interpret   84 study of think about   88 miraculous harp (Alludes to Amphion's harp, with which he raised the walls of Thebes; Gonzalo has exceeded that deed by recreating ancient Carthage—*wall and houses*—mistakenly on the site of modern-day Tunis. Some Renaissance commentators believed, like Gonzalo, that the two sites were near each other.)   94 kernels seeds   96 Ay (Gonzalo may be reasserting his point about Carthage, or he may be responding ironically to Antonio, who, in turn, answers sarcastically.)   97 in good time (An expression of ironical acquiescence or amazement, i.e., "sure, right away.")   101 rarest most remarkable, beautiful   102 Bate Abate, except, leave out. (Sebastian says sardonically, surely you should allow widow Dido to be an exception.)   104 doublet close-fitting jacket   105 in a sort in a way.   106 sort (Antonio plays on the idea of drawing lots and on "fishing" for something to say.)   109 The stomach . . . sense my appetite for hearing them.   110 Married given in marriage   111 rate estimation, opinion   116 surges waves

120 oared propelled as by an oar   121 lusty vigorous   122 that . . . bowed that projected out over its (*his*) surf-eroded base, bending down toward the sea   123 As as if   126 That you who   127 But . . . her but would rather turn her loose (or, "lose her")   128–9 Where . . . on't where at least she is not a constant reproach in your eye, which has good reason to weep sorrowfully for this unhappy development.   130 importuned urged, implored   131–3 the fair . . . bow Claribel herself was poised uncertainly, as in a balancing scale, between being unwilling to marry and yet wishing to obey her father.   135 of . . . making on account of this marriage and subsequent shipwreck   138 dear'st heaviest, most costly   141 time appropriate time   142 plaster (A medical application.)   143 chirurgeonly like a skilled surgeon. (Antonio mocks Gonzalo's medical analogy of a *plaster* applied curatively to a wound.)   145 Fowl (With a pun on *foul*, returning to the imagery of lines 30–5.)   146 plantation colonial settlement. (With subsequent wordplay on the literal meaning, "planting.")   147 docks . . . mallows (Weeds; the first was used as an antidote for nettle stings.)

SEBASTIAN   Scape being drunk for want of wine.   149

GONZALO
I'th' commonwealth I would by contraries   150
Execute all things; for no kind of traffic   151
Would I admit; no name of magistrate;
Letters should not be known; riches, poverty,   153
And use of service, none; contract, succession,   154
Bourn, bound of land, tilth, vineyard, none;   155
No use of metal, corn, or wine, or oil;   156
No occupation; all men idle, all,
And women too, but innocent and pure;
No sovereignty—

SEBASTIAN   Yet he would be king on't.

ANTONIO   The latter end of his commonwealth forgets
the beginning.

GONZALO
All things in common nature should produce
Without sweat or endeavor. Treason, felony,
Sword, pike, knife, gun, or need of any engine   164
Would I not have; but nature should bring forth,
Of it own kind, all foison, all abundance,   166
To feed my innocent people.

SEBASTIAN   No marrying 'mong his subjects?

ANTONIO   None, man, all idle—whores and knaves.

GONZALO
I would with such perfection govern, sir,
T'excel the Golden Age.

SEBASTIAN   'Save His Majesty!   171

ANTONIO
Long live Gonzalo!

GONZALO   And—do you mark me, sir?

ALONSO
Prithee, no more. Thou dost talk nothing to me.

GONZALO   I do well believe Your Highness, and did it
to minister occasion to these gentlemen, who are of   175
such sensible and nimble lungs that they always use   176
to laugh at nothing.

ANTONIO   'Twas you we laughed at.

GONZALO   Who in this kind of merry fooling am nothing
to you; so you may continue, and laugh at nothing
still.

ANTONIO   What a blow was there given!

SEBASTIAN   An it had not fallen flat-long.   182

GONZALO   You are gentlemen of brave mettle; you   183
would lift the moon out of her sphere if she would   184

continue in it five weeks without changing.

Enter Ariel [invisible] playing solemn music.

SEBASTIAN   We would so, and then go a-batfowling.   186

ANTONIO   Nay, good my lord, be not angry.

GONZALO   No, I warrant you, I will not adventure my   188
discretion so weakly. Will you laugh me asleep? For I   189
am very heavy.   190

ANTONIO   Go sleep, and hear us.   191
         [All sleep except Alonso, Sebastian, and Antonio.]

ALONSO
What, all so soon asleep? I wish mine eyes
Would, with themselves, shut up my thoughts. I find   193
They are inclined to do so.

SEBASTIAN   Please you, sir,
Do not omit the heavy offer of it.   195
It seldom visits sorrow; when it doth,
It is a comforter.

ANTONIO   We two, my lord,
Will guard your person while you take your rest,
And watch your safety.

ALONSO   Thank you. Wondrous heavy.
                              [Alonso sleeps. Exit Ariel.]

SEBASTIAN
What a strange drowsiness possesses them!

ANTONIO
It is the quality o'th' climate.

SEBASTIAN   Why
Doth it not then our eyelids sink? I find not
Myself disposed to sleep.

ANTONIO   Nor I. My spirits are nimble.
They fell together all, as by consent;   204
They dropped, as by a thunderstroke. What might,
Worthy Sebastian, oh, what might—? No more.
And yet methinks I see it in thy face
What thou shouldst be. Th'occasion speaks thee, and   208
My strong imagination sees a crown
Dropping upon thy head.

SEBASTIAN   What, art thou waking?

ANTONIO
Do you not hear me speak?

SEBASTIAN   I do, and surely
It is a sleepy language, and thou speak'st   212
Out of thy sleep. What is it thou didst say?
This is a strange repose, to be asleep
With eyes wide open—standing, speaking, moving—
And yet so fast asleep.

ANTONIO   Noble Sebastian,
Thou let'st thy fortune sleep—die, rather; wink'st   217

---

149 Scape Escape. **want** lack. (Sebastian jokes sarcastically that this hypothetical ruler would be saved from dissipation only by the barrenness of the island.) **150 by contraries** by what is directly opposite to usual custom **151 traffic** trade **153 Letters** learning **154 use of service** custom of employing servants. **succession** holding of property by right of inheritance **155 Bourn . . . tilth** boundaries, property limits, tillage of soil **156 corn** grain **164 pike** lance. **engine** instrument of warfare **166 it** its. **foison** plenty **171 the Golden Age** an age of prelapsarian abundance and peace; the first of four "ages" of human history, followed by silver, bronze, and lead. **'Save** God save **175 minister occasion** furnish opportunity (for laughter) **176 sensible** sensitive. **use** are accustomed **182 An** If. **flat-long** with the flat of the sword, i.e., ineffectually. **183 mettle** temperament, courage. (The sense of *metal*, indistinguishable as a form from *mettle*, continues the metaphor of the sword. F reads "mettal.") **184 sphere** orbit. (Literally, one of the concentric zones occupied by planets in Ptolemaic astronomy.)

186 a-batfowling hunting birds at night with lantern and *bat*, or "stick"; also, gulling a simpleton. (Gonzalo is the simpleton, or fowl, and Sebastian will use the moon as his lantern.) **188–9 adventure . . . weakly** risk my reputation for discretion for so trivial a cause (by getting angry). **190 heavy** sleepy. **191 Go . . . us** i.e., Get ready for sleep, and we'll do our part by laughing. **193 Would . . . thoughts** would shut off my melancholy brooding when they (my eyes) close themselves in sleep. **195 Do . . . it** do not decline the invitation to drowsiness. **204 They . . . consent** The others all fell asleep simultaneously, as if by common agreement **208 Th' occasion . . . thee** The opportunity of the moment calls upon you **212 sleepy** dreamlike, fantastic **217 wink'st** (you) shut your eyes

Whiles thou art waking.

SEBASTIAN   Thou dost snore distinctly;   218
There's meaning in thy snores.

ANTONIO
I am more serious than my custom. You
Must be so too if heed me, which to do   221
Trebles thee o'er.

SEBASTIAN   Well, I am standing water.   222

ANTONIO
I'll teach you how to flow.

SEBASTIAN   Do so. To ebb   223
Hereditary sloth instructs me.

ANTONIO   Oh,   224
If you but knew how you the purpose cherish   225
Whiles thus you mock it! How, in stripping it,   226
You more invest it! Ebbing men, indeed,   227
Most often do so near the bottom run   228
By their own fear or sloth.

SEBASTIAN   Prithee, say on.
The setting of thine eye and cheek proclaim   230
A matter from thee, and a birth indeed   231
Which throes thee much to yield.

ANTONIO   Thus, sir: 232
Although this lord of weak remembrance, this   233
Who shall be of as little memory   234
When he is earthed, hath here almost persuaded—   236
For he's a spirit of persuasion, only   236
Professes to persuade—the King his son's alive,   237
'Tis as impossible that he's undrowned
As he that sleeps here swims.

SEBASTIAN   I have no hope
That he's undrowned.

ANTONIO   Oh, out of that "no hope"
What great hope have you! No hope that way is   241
Another way so high a hope that even   242
Ambition cannot pierce a wink beyond,   243
But doubt discovery there. Will you grant with me 244
That Ferdinand is drowned?

SEBASTIAN   He's gone.

ANTONIO   Then tell me,
Who's the next heir of Naples?

SEBASTIAN   Claribel.

ANTONIO
She that is Queen of Tunis; she that dwells
Ten leagues beyond man's life; she that from Naples 248
Can have no note, unless the sun were post—   249
The Man i'th' Moon's too slow—till newborn chins
Be rough and razorable; she that from whom   251
We all were sea-swallowed, though some cast again,   252
And by that destiny to perform an act
Whereof what's past is prologue, what to come
In yours and my discharge.   255

SEBASTIAN   What stuff is this? How say you?
'Tis true my brother's daughter's Queen of Tunis,
So is she heir of Naples, twixt which regions
There is some space.

ANTONIO   A space whose ev'ry cubit   259
Seems to cry out, "How shall that Claribel
Measure us back to Naples? Keep in Tunis,   261
And let Sebastian wake." Say this were death   262
That now hath seized them, why, they were no worse
Than now they are. There be that can rule Naples   264
As well as he that sleeps, lords that can prate   265
As amply and unnecessarily
As this Gonzalo. I myself could make   267
A chough of as deep chat. Oh, that you bore   268
The mind that I do! What a sleep were this
For your advancement! Do you understand me?

SEBASTIAN
Methinks I do.

ANTONIO   And how does your content   271
Tender your own good fortune?

SEBASTIAN   I remember   272
You did supplant your brother Prospero.

ANTONIO   True.
And look how well my garments sit upon me,
Much feater than before. My brother's servants   275
Were then my fellows. Now they are my men.

SEBASTIAN   But, for your conscience?   277

ANTONIO
Ay, sir, where lies that? If 'twere a kibe,   278
'Twould put me to my slipper; but I feel not   279
This deity in my bosom. Twenty consciences   280
That stand twixt me and Milan, candied be they   281
And melt ere they molest! Here lies your brother,   282
No better than the earth he lies upon,
If he were that which now he's like—that's dead,
Whom I, with this obedient steel, three inches of it,

---

218 distinctly articulately   **221 if heed** if you heed   **222 Trebles thee o'er** makes you three times as great and rich.   **standing water** water that neither ebbs nor flows, at a standstill.   **223 ebb** recede, decline   **224 Hereditary sloth** i.e., natural laziness and the position of younger brother, one who cannot inherit   **225–6 If . . . mock it!** If you only knew how much you secretly cherish ambition even while your words mock it!   **226–7 How . . . invest it!** How the more you speak flippantly of ambition, the more you, in effect, affirm it, clothing what you have stripped!   **228 the bottom** i.e., on which unadventurous men may go aground and miss the tide of fortune   **230 setting** set expression (of earnestness)   **231 matter** matter of importance   **232 throes** causes pain, as in giving birth.   **yield** give forth, speak about.
233–7 Although . . . alive Although this owner of weak memory, he who will be only weakly remembered when he is dead, has nearly persuaded—since he's a mind or soul devoted solely to persuade—King Alonso that Ferdinand lives   **241 that way** i.e., in regard to Ferdinand's being saved   **242–4 that . . . there** that even ambition for high status cannot see anything higher, and even there it doubts the reality of what it sees (because the place is so supremely high). (What then follows is Antonio's analysis of why they can proceed without fear.)

248 Ten . . . life i.e., further than the journey of a lifetime   **249 note** news, intimation.   **post** messenger   **251 razorable** ready for shaving.   **from** on our voyage from   **252 cast** were disgorged. (With a pun on *casting* of parts for a play.)   **255 discharge** part to play.   **259 cubit** ancient measure of length of about twenty inches   **261 Measure us** retrace our journey.   **Keep** You, Claribel, stay   **262 wake** i.e., to his good fortune.   **264 There be** There are those   **265 prate** speak foolishly   **267–8 I . . . chat** I could teach a jackdaw to talk as wisely, or, be such a garrulous talker myself.   **271–2 And . . . fortune?** And how does your contentment with what I've just said further your good fortune?   **275 feater** more becomingly, fittingly   **277 for** as for   **278 kibe** chilblain, here a sore on the heel   **279 put me to** oblige me to wear   **280–2 Twenty . . . molest!** Even if there were twenty consciences between me and the dukedom of Milan, may they be lumped together or crystallized like candy and then melted down before I'd let them interfere!

Can lay to bed forever; whiles you, doing thus,   286
To the perpetual wink for aye might put   287
This ancient morsel, this Sir Prudence, who
Should not upbraid our course. For all the rest,   289
They'll take suggestion as a cat laps milk;   290
They'll tell the clock to any business that   291
We say befits the hour.

SEBASTIAN   Thy case, dear friend,
Shall be my precedent. As thou got'st Milan,
I'll come by Naples. Draw thy sword. One stroke
Shall free thee from the tribute which thou payest,   295
And I the king shall love thee.

ANTONIO   Draw together;
And when I rear my hand, do you the like
To fall it on Gonzalo.   [*They draw.*]

SEBASTIAN   Oh, but one word.   298
                                                [*They talk apart.*]

        Enter Ariel [invisible], with music and song.

ARIEL [*to Gonzalo*]
My master through his art foresees the danger
That you, his friend, are in, and sends me forth—
For else his project dies—to keep them living.
                                Sings in Gonzalo's ear.
        While you here do snoring lie,
        Open-eyed conspiracy
                His time doth take.   304
        If of life you keep a care,
        Shake off slumber, and beware.
                Awake, awake!

ANTONIO   Then let us both be sudden.

GONZALO [*waking*]   Now, good angels preserve the King!
                                                [*The others wake.*]

ALONSO
Why, how now, ho, awake? Why are you drawn?
Wherefore this ghastly looking?

GONZALO   What's the matter?

SEBASTIAN
Whiles we stood here securing your repose,   312
Even now, we heard a hollow burst of bellowing
Like bulls, or rather lions. Did 't not wake you?
It struck mine ear most terribly.

ALONSO   I heard nothing.

ANTONIO
Oh, 'twas a din to fright a monster's ear,
To make an earthquake! Sure it was the roar
Of a whole herd of lions.

ALONSO   Heard you this, Gonzalo?

GONZALO
Upon mine honor, sir, I heard a humming,
And that a strange one too, which did awake me.
I shaked you, sir, and cried. As mine eyes opened,   322
I saw their weapons drawn. There was a noise,

That's verily. 'Tis best we stand upon our guard,   324
Or that we quit this place. Let's draw our weapons.

ALONSO
Lead off this ground, and let's make further search
For my poor son.

GONZALO   Heavens keep him from these beasts!
For he is, sure, i'th'island.

ALONSO   Lead away.

ARIEL [*aside*]
Prospero my lord shall know what I have done.
So, King, go safely on to seek thy son.
                                Exeunt [separately].

                          ❖

2.2

        *Enter Caliban with a burden of wood. A noise
        of thunder heard.*

CALIBAN
All the infections that the sun sucks up
From bogs, fens, flats, on Prosper fall, and make him   2
By inchmeal a disease! His spirits hear me,   3
And yet I needs must curse. But they'll nor pinch,   4
Fright me with urchin shows, pitch me i'th' mire,   5
Nor lead me, like a firebrand, in the dark   6
Out of my way, unless he bid 'em. But
For every trifle are they set upon me,
Sometimes like apes, that mow and chatter at me   9
And after bite me; then like hedgehogs, which
Lie tumbling in my barefoot way and mount
Their pricks at my footfall. Sometime am I
All wound with adders, who with cloven tongues   13
Do hiss me into madness.

        Enter Trinculo.

                                Lo, now, lo!
Here comes a spirit of his, and to torment me
For bringing wood in slowly. I'll fall flat.
Perchance he will not mind me.   [*He lies down.*]   17

TRINCULO   Here's neither bush nor shrub to bear off   18
any weather at all. And another storm brewing; I hear
it sing i'th' wind. Yond same black cloud, yond huge
one, looks like a foul bombard that would shed his   21
liquor. If it should thunder as it did before, I know not
where to hide my head. Yond same cloud cannot
choose but fall by pailfuls. [*Seeing Caliban*] What have
we here, a man or a fish? Dead or alive? A fish, he
smells like a fish; a very ancient and fishlike smell; a
kind of not-of-the-newest Poor John. A strange fish!   27
Were I in England now, as once I was, and had but
this fish painted, not a holiday fool there but would   29

---

324 verily true.
2.2. Location: Another part of the island.
2 flats swamps   **3 By inchmeal** inch by inch   **4 needs must** have to.
nor neither   **5 urchin shows** elvish apparitions shaped like hedgehogs   **6 like a firebrand** they in the guise of a will-o'-the-wisp
9 mow make faces   **13 wound with** entwined by   **17 mind** notice
18 bear off keep off   **21 foul bombard** dirty leather jug.   **his** its
27 Poor John salted fish, type of poor fare   **29 painted** i.e., painted
on a sign set up outside a booth or tent at a fair

---

286 thus similarly. (The actor makes a stabbing gesture.)   **287 wink**
sleep, closing of eyes.   **aye** ever   **289 Should not** must not be
allowed to   **290 take suggestion** respond to prompting   **291 tell the
clock** i.e., agree, answer appropriately, chime   **295 tribute** (See
1.2.113–24.)   **298 fall it** let it fall   **304 time** opportunity   **312 securing** standing guard over   **322 cried** called out.

give a piece of silver. There would this monster make 30
a man. Any strange beast there makes a man. When 31
they will not give a doit to relieve a lame beggar, they 32
will lay out ten to see a dead Indian. Legged like a
man, and his fins like arms! Warm, o' my troth! I do 34
now let loose my opinion, hold it no longer: this is no 35
fish, but an islander, that hath lately suffered by a
thunderbolt. [*Thunder.*] Alas, the storm is come again!
My best way is to creep under his gaberdine. There is 38
no other shelter hereabout. Misery acquaints a man
with strange bedfellows. I will here shroud till the 40
dregs of the storm be past. 41

         [He creeps under Caliban's garment.]

    Enter Stephano, singing, [a bottle in his hand].

STEPHANO
    "I shall no more to sea, to sea,
      Here shall I die ashore—"
This is a very scurvy tune to sing at a man's funeral.
Well, here's my comfort.   *Drinks.*
(*Sings.*)
    "The master, the swabber, the boatswain, and I, 46
      The gunner and his mate,
    Loved Mall, Meg, and Marian, and Margery,
      But none of us cared for Kate.
    For she had a tongue with a tang, 50
    Would cry to a sailor, 'Go hang!'
    She loved not the savor of tar nor of pitch,
    Yet a tailor might scratch her where'er she did itch. 53
      Then to sea, boys, and let her go hang!"
This is a scurvy tune too. But here's my comfort.
          Drinks.
CALIBAN   Do not torment me! Oh! 56
STEPHANO   What's the matter? Have we devils here? Do 57
you put tricks upon 's with savages and men of Ind, 58
ha? I have not scaped drowning to be afeard now of
your four legs. For it hath been said, "As proper a man 60
as ever went on four legs cannot make him give 61
ground"; and it shall be said so again while Stephano
breathes at' nostrils. 63
CALIBAN   This spirit torments me! Oh!
STEPHANO   This is some monster of the isle with four
legs, who hath got, as I take it, an ague. Where the 66
devil should he learn our language? I will give him 67
some relief, if it be but for that. If I can recover him 68
and keep him tame and get to Naples with him, he's

a present for any emperor that ever trod on neat's 70
leather. 71
CALIBAN   Do not torment me, prithee. I'll bring my
wood home faster.
STEPHANO   He's in his fit now and does not talk after 74
the wisest. He shall taste of my bottle. If he have never 75
drunk wine afore, it will go near to remove his fit. If I 76
can recover him and keep him tame, I will not take too 77
much for him. He shall pay for him that hath him, and 78
that soundly.
CALIBAN   Thou dost me yet but little hurt; thou wilt
anon, I know it by thy trembling. Now Prosper works
upon thee.
STEPHANO   Come on your ways. Open your mouth. Here
is that which will give language to you, cat. Open your 84
mouth. This will shake your shaking, I can tell you, 85
and that soundly. [*Giving Caliban a drink.*] You cannot 86
tell who's your friend. Open your chaps again. 87
TRINCULO   I should know that voice. It should be—but
he is drowned, and these are devils. Oh, defend me!
STEPHANO   Four legs and two voices—a most delicate 90
monster! His forward voice now is to speak well of his
friend; his backward voice is to utter foul speeches and 92
to detract. If all the wine in my bottle will recover him, 93
I will help his ague. Come. [*Giving a drink.*] Amen! I
will pour some in thy other mouth.
TRINCULO   Stephano!
STEPHANO   Doth thy other mouth call me? Mercy,
mercy! This is a devil, and no monster. I will leave
him. I have no long spoon. 99
TRINCULO   Stephano! If thou be'st Stephano, touch me
and speak to me, for I am Trinculo—be not afeard—
thy good friend Trinculo.
STEPHANO   If thou be'st Trinculo, come forth. I'll pull
thee by the lesser legs. If any be Trinculo's legs, these
are they. [*Pulling him out.*] Thou art very Trinculo
indeed! How cam'st thou to be the siege of this 106
mooncalf? Can he vent Trinculos? 107
TRINCULO   I took him to be killed with a thunderstroke.
But art thou not drowned, Stephano? I hope now thou
art not drowned. Is the storm overblown? I hid me 110
under the dead mooncalf's gaberdine for fear of the
storm. And art thou living, Stephano? Oh, Stephano,
two Neapolitans scaped!   *[He capers with Stephano.]*

30–1 make a man (1) make a man's fortune (2) pass for a human being. **32 doit** small coin **34 o' my troth** by my faith. **35 hold it** hold it in **38 gaberdine** cloak, loose upper garment. **40 shroud** take shelter **41 dregs** i.e., last remains (as in a *bombard* or jug, line 21) **46 swabber** crew member whose job is to wash the decks **50 tang** sting **53 tailor . . . itch** (A dig at tailors for their supposed effeminacy and a bawdy suggestion of satisfying a sexual craving.) **56 Do . . . me!** (Caliban assumes that one of Prospero's spirits has come to punish him.) **57 What's the matter?** What's going on here? **58 put tricks upon 's** trick us with conjuring shows. **Ind** India **60 proper** handsome **61 four legs** (The conventional phrase would supply *two legs,* but the creature Stephano thinks he sees has four.) **63 at'** at the **66 ague** fever. (Probably both Caliban and Trinculo are quaking; see lines 56 and 81.) **67 should he learn** could he have learned **68 for that** i.e., for knowing our language. **recover** revive. (Also in line 77.)

70–1 neat's leather cowhide. **74–5 after the wisest** in the wisest fashion. **76 afore** before. **go near to** be in a fair way to **77 recover** restore **77–8 I will . . . much** i.e., no sum can be too much **78 He shall . . . hath him** Anyone who wants him will have to pay dearly for him **84–5 cat . . . mouth** (Allusion to the proverb "Good liquor will make a cat speak.") **85 shake** shake off **86–7 You . . . friend** i.e., You can't tell who's your friend until someone like me provides you with a drink. **87 chaps** jaws **90 delicate** ingenious **92 backward voice** (Trinculo and Caliban are facing in opposite directions. Stephano supposes the monster to have a rear end that can emit *foul speeches* or foul-smelling wind at the monster's *other mouth,* line 95.) **93 If . . . him** Even if it takes all the wine in my bottle to cure him **99 long spoon** (Allusion to the proverb "He that sups with the devil has need of a long spoon.") **106 siege** excrement **107 mooncalf** monstrous or misshapen creature (whose deformity is caused by the malignant influence of the moon). **vent** excrete, defecate **110 overblown** blown over.

STEPHANO Prithee, do not turn me about. My stomach is not constant. 115

CALIBAN
These be fine things, an if they be not spirits. 116
That's a brave god, and bears celestial liquor. 117
I will kneel to him.

STEPHANO How didst thou scape? How cam'st thou hither? Swear by this bottle how thou cam'st hither. I escaped upon a butt of sack which the sailors heaved 121 o'erboard—by this bottle, which I made of the bark of 122 a tree with mine own hands since I was cast ashore.

CALIBAN [kneeling] I'll swear upon that bottle to be thy true subject, for the liquor is not earthly.

STEPHANO Here. Swear then how thou escaped'st.

TRINCULO Swum ashore, man, like a duck. I can swim like a duck, I'll be sworn.

STEPHANO Here, kiss the book. Though thou canst 129 swim like a duck, thou art made like a goose.
[Giving him a drink.]

TRINCULO Oh, Stephano, hast any more of this?

STEPHANO The whole butt, man. My cellar is in a rock by th' seaside, where my wine is hid.—How now, mooncalf? How does thine ague?

CALIBAN Hast thou not dropped from heaven?

STEPHANO Out o'th' moon, I do assure thee. I was the man i'th' moon when time was. 137

CALIBAN
I have seen thee in her, and I do adore thee.
My mistress showed me thee, and thy dog, and thy bush. 139

STEPHANO Come, swear to that. Kiss the book. I will furnish it anon with new contents. Swear.
[Giving him a drink.]

TRINCULO By this good light, this is a very shallow 142 monster! I afeard of him? A very weak monster! The man i'th' moon? A most poor credulous monster! Well drawn, monster, in good sooth! 145

CALIBAN [to Stephano]
I'll show thee every fertile inch o'th'island,
And I will kiss thy foot. I prithee, be my god.

TRINCULO By this light, a most perfidious and drunken monster! When 's god's asleep, he'll rob his bottle. 149

CALIBAN
I'll kiss thy foot. I'll swear myself thy subject.

STEPHANO Come on then. Down, and swear.
[Caliban kneels.]

TRINCULO I shall laugh myself to death at this puppy-headed monster. A most scurvy monster! I could find in my heart to beat him—

STEPHANO Come, kiss.

TRINCULO But that the poor monster's in drink. An 156 abominable monster!

CALIBAN
I'll show thee the best springs. I'll pluck thee berries.
I'll fish for thee and get thee wood enough.
A plague upon the tyrant that I serve!
I'll bear him no more sticks, but follow thee,
Thou wondrous man.

TRINCULO A most ridiculous monster, to make a wonder of a poor drunkard!

CALIBAN
I prithee, let me bring thee where crabs grow, 165
And I with my long nails will dig thee pignuts, 166
Show thee a jay's nest, and instruct thee how
To snare the nimble marmoset. I'll bring thee 168
To clust'ring filberts, and sometimes I'll get thee
Young scamels from the rock. Wilt thou go with me? 170

STEPHANO I prithee now, lead the way without any more talking.—Trinculo, the King and all our com- 172 pany else being drowned, we will inherit here.— 173 Here, bear my bottle.—Fellow Trinculo, we'll fill him by and by again.

CALIBAN (sings drunkenly)
Farewell, master, farewell, farewell!

TRINCULO A howling monster; a drunken monster!

CALIBAN
No more dams I'll make for fish,
Nor fetch in firing 179
At requiring,
Nor scrape trenchering, nor wash dish. 181
'Ban, 'Ban, Ca–Caliban
Has a new master. Get a new man! 183
Freedom, high-day! High-day, freedom! Freedom, 184 high-day, freedom!

STEPHANO O brave monster! Lead the way. Exeunt.

3.1

Enter Ferdinand, bearing a log.

FERDINAND
There be some sports are painful, and their labor 1
Delight in them sets off. Some kinds of baseness 2
Are nobly undergone, and most poor matters 3
Point to rich ends. This my mean task 4
Would be as heavy to me as odious, but 5

---

115 constant steady. **116 an if** if **117 brave** fine, magnificent **121 butt of sack** barrel of Canary wine **122 by this bottle** i.e., I swear by this bottle **129 book** i.e., bottle. (But with ironic reference to the practice of kissing the Bible in swearing an oath; see *I'll be sworn* in line 128.) **137 when time was** once upon a time. **139 dog . . . bush** (The man in the moon was popularly imagined to have with him a dog and a bush of thorn.) **142 By . . . light** By God's light, by this good light from heaven **145 Well . . . sooth!** Well pulled on the bottle, truly! **149 When . . . bottle** i.e., Caliban wouldn't even stop at robbing his god (i.e., Stephano) of his bottle if he could catch him asleep.

156 But that were it not that. **in drink** drunk. **165 crabs** crab apples, or crabs **166 pignuts** earthnuts, edible tuberous roots **168 marmoset** small monkey. **170 scamels** (Possibly *seamews*, mentioned in Strachey's letter, or shellfish, or perhaps from *squamelle*, "furnished with little scales." Contemporary French and Italian travel accounts report that the natives of Patagonia in South America ate small fish described as *fort scameux* and *squame*.) **172–3 all . . . else** all the rest of our shipboard companions **173 inherit** take possession **179 firing** firewood **181 trenchering** trenchers, wooden plates **183 Get a new man** (Addressed to Prospero.) **184 high-day** holiday.
3.1. Location: Before Prospero's cell.
1–2 There . . . sets off Some pastimes are laborious, but the pleasure we get from them compensates for the effort. (Pleasure is *set off* by labor as a jewel is set off by its foil.) **2 baseness** menial activity **3 undergone** undertaken. **most poor** poorest **4 mean** lowly **5 but** were it not that

The mistress which I serve quickens what's dead 6
And makes my labors pleasures. Oh, she is
Ten times more gentle than her father's crabbed,
And he's composed of harshness. I must remove
Some thousands of these logs and pile them up,
Upon a sore injunction. My sweet mistress 11
Weeps when she sees me work and says such baseness
Had never like executor. I forget; 13
But these sweet thoughts do even refresh my labors,
Most busy lest when I do it.

*Enter Miranda; and Prospero [at a distance,
unseen].*

MIRANDA   Alas now, pray you, 15
Work not so hard. I would the lightning had
Burnt up those logs that you are enjoined to pile! 17
Pray, set it down and rest you. When this burns, 18
'Twill weep for having wearied you. My father 19
Is hard at study. Pray now, rest yourself.
He's safe for these three hours.
FERDINAND   O most dear mistress, 21
The sun will set before I shall discharge 22
What I must strive to do.
MIRANDA   If you'll sit down,
I'll bear your logs the while. Pray, give me that.
I'll carry it to the pile.
FERDINAND   No, precious creature,
I had rather crack my sinews, break my back,
Than you should such dishonor undergo
While I sit lazy by.
MIRANDA   It would become me
As well as it does you; and I should do it
With much more ease, for my good will is to it,
And yours it is against.
PROSPERO [*aside*]   Poor worm, thou art infected!
This visitation shows it.
MIRANDA   You look wearily. 32
FERDINAND
No, noble mistress, 'tis fresh morning with me
When you are by at night. I do beseech you— 34
Chiefly that I might set it in my prayers—
What is your name?
MIRANDA   Miranda.—O my father,
I have broke your hest to say so.
FERDINAND   Admired Miranda! 37
Indeed the top of admiration, worth
What's dearest to the world! Full many a lady 39
I have eyed with best regard, and many a time 40
The harmony of their tongues hath into bondage

Brought my too diligent ear. For several virtues 42
Have I liked several women, never any
With so full soul but some defect in her
Did quarrel with the noblest grace she owed 45
And put it to the foil. But you, oh, you, 46
So perfect and so peerless, are created
Of every creature's best!
MIRANDA   I do not know 48
One of my sex; no woman's face remember,
Save, from my glass, mine own. Nor have I seen
More that I may call men than you, good friend,
And my dear father. How features are abroad 52
I am skilless of; but, by my modesty, 53
The jewel in my dower, I would not wish
Any companion in the world but you;
Nor can imagination form a shape,
Besides yourself, to like of. But I prattle 57
Something too wildly, and my father's precepts 58
I therein do forget.
FERDINAND   I am in my condition 59
A prince, Miranda; I do think, a king—
I would, not so!—and would no more endure 61
This wooden slavery than to suffer 62
The flesh-fly blow my mouth. Hear my soul speak: 63
The very instant that I saw you did
My heart fly to your service, there resides
To make me slave to it, and for your sake
Am I this patient log-man.
MIRANDA   Do you love me?
FERDINAND
O heaven, O earth, bear witness to this sound,
And crown what I profess with kind event 69
If I speak true! If hollowly, invert 70
What best is boded me to mischief! I 71
Beyond all limit of what else i'th' world 72
Do love, prize, honor you.
MIRANDA [*weeping*]   I am a fool
To weep at what I am glad of.
PROSPERO [*aside*]   Fair encounter
Of two most rare affections! Heavens rain grace
On that which breeds between 'em!
FERDINAND   Wherefore weep you?
MIRANDA
At mine unworthiness, that dare not offer
What I desire to give, and much less take
What I shall die to want. But this is trifling, 79
And all the more it seeks to hide itself
The bigger bulk it shows. Hence, bashful cunning, 81

6 **quickens** gives life to   11 **sore injunction** severe command. 13 **Had . . . executor** was never before undertaken by so noble a being.   **I forget** i.e., I forget that I'm supposed to be working 15 **Most . . . do it** (Ferdinand seems to say that the busier he is, the less likely he is to forget the sweet thoughts that make his labors pleasant. The line may be in need of emendation.)   17 **enjoined** commanded   18 **this** i.e., the log   19 **weep** i.e., exude resin   21 **these** the next   22 **discharge** complete   32 **visitation** (1) Miranda's visit to Ferdinand (2) visitation of the plague, i.e., infection of love   34 **by** nearby   37 **hest** command.   **Admired Miranda** (Her name means "to be admired or wondered at.")   39 **dearest** most treasured 40 **best regard** thoughtful and approving attention

42 **diligent** attentive.   **several** various. (Also in line 43.)   45 **owed** owned   46 **put . . . foil** (1) overthrew it (as in fencing or wrestling) (2) served as a *foil*, or "contrast," to set it off.   48 **Of** out of   52 **How . . . abroad** What people look like in other places   53 **skilless** ignorant. **modesty** virginity   57 **like of** be pleased with, be fond of.   58 **Something** somewhat   59 **condition** rank   61 **I would** I wish it were 62 **wooden slavery** being compelled to carry wood   62–3 **than . . . mouth** than I would allow flying insects to deposit their eggs in my mouth as if in decaying flesh.   69 **kind event** favorable outcome 70 **hollowly** insincerely, falsely.   **invert** turn   71 **boded** in store for. **mischief** harm.   72 **what** whatever   79 **die** (Probably with an unconscious sexual meaning that underlies all of lines 77–81.)   **to want** through lacking.   81 **bashful cunning** coyness

And prompt me, plain and holy innocence!
I am your wife, if you will marry me;
If not, I'll die your maid. To be your fellow   84
You may deny me, but I'll be your servant
Whether you will or no.

FERDINAND   My mistress, dearest,   86
And I thus humble ever.

MIRANDA   My husband, then?

FERDINAND   Ay, with a heart as willing   89
As bondage e'er of freedom. Here's my hand.

MIRANDA [*clasping his hand*]
And mine, with my heart in't. And now farewell
Till half an hour hence.

FERDINAND   A thousand thousand!   92

Exeunt [*Ferdinand and Miranda, separately*].

PROSPERO
So glad of this as they I cannot be,
Who are surprised with all; but my rejoicing   94
At nothing can be more. I'll to my book,
For yet ere suppertime must I perform
Much business appertaining.   *Exit.*   97

3.2

Enter Caliban, Stephano, and Trinculo.

STEPHANO   Tell not me. When the butt is out, we will   1
drink water, not a drop before. Therefore bear up and   2
board 'em. Servant monster, drink to me.   3

TRINCULO   Servant monster? The folly of this island!   4
They say there's but five upon this isle. We are three
of them; if th'other two be brained like us, the state   6
totters.

STEPHANO   Drink, servant monster, when I bid thee.
Thy eyes are almost set in thy head.   [*Giving a drink.*]   9

TRINCULO   Where should they be set else? He were a   10
brave monster indeed if they were set in his tail.   11

STEPHANO   My man-monster hath drowned his tongue
in sack. For my part, the sea cannot drown me. I   13
swam, ere I could recover the shore, five and thirty   14
leagues off and on. By this light, thou shalt be my   15
lieutenant, monster, or my standard.   16

TRINCULO   Your lieutenant, if you list; he's no standard.   17

STEPHANO   We'll not run, Monsieur Monster.   18

TRINCULO   Nor go neither, but you'll lie like dogs and   19
yet say nothing neither.

STEPHANO   Mooncalf, speak once in thy life, if thou
be'st a good mooncalf.

CALIBAN
How does Thy Honor? Let me lick thy shoe.
I'll not serve him. He is not valiant.

TRINCULO   Thou liest, most ignorant monster, I am in   25
case to jostle a constable. Why, thou deboshed fish,   26
thou, was there ever man a coward that hath drunk so   27
much sack as I today? Wilt thou tell a monstrous lie,
being but half a fish and half a monster?

CALIBAN
Lo, how he mocks me! Wilt thou let him, my lord?

TRINCULO   "Lord," quoth he? That a monster should be
such a natural!   32

CALIBAN
Lo, lo, again! Bite him to death, I prithee.

STEPHANO   Trinculo, keep a good tongue in your head.
If you prove a mutineer—the next tree! The poor mon-   35
ster's my subject, and he shall not suffer indignity.

CALIBAN
I thank my noble lord. Wilt thou be pleased
To hearken once again to the suit I made to thee?

STEPHANO   Marry, will I. Kneel and repeat it. I will   39
stand, and so shall Trinculo.   [*Caliban kneels.*]   40

Enter Ariel, invisible.

CALIBAN
As I told thee before, I am subject to a tyrant,
A sorcerer, that by his cunning hath
Cheated me of the island.

ARIEL [*mimicking Trinculo*]
Thou liest.

CALIBAN   Thou liest, thou jesting monkey, thou!
I would my valiant master would destroy thee.
I do not lie.

STEPHANO   Trinculo, if you trouble him any more in 's
tale, by this hand, I will supplant some of your teeth.   48

TRINCULO   Why, I said nothing.

STEPHANO   Mum, then, and no more.—Proceed.

CALIBAN
I say by sorcery he got this isle;
From me he got it. If Thy Greatness will
Revenge it on him—for I know thou dar'st,
But this thing dare not—   54

STEPHANO   That's most certain.

CALIBAN
Thou shalt be lord of it, and I'll serve thee.

---

84 maid handmaiden, servant. **fellow** mate   **86 will** desire it. **My mistress** i.e., The woman I adore and serve (not an illicit sexual partner)   **89 willing** desirous   **92 A thousand thousand!** A thousand thousand farewells!   **94 with all** by everything that has happened, or, *withal*, "by it"   **97 appertaining** related to this.
3.2 Location: Another part of the island.
1 out empty   **2–3 bear . . . 'em** (Stephano uses the terminology of maneuvering at sea and boarding a vessel under attack as a way of urging an assault on the liquor supply.)   **4 folly of** i.e., stupidity found on   **6 be brained** are endowed with intelligence   **9 set . . . head** fixed in a drunken stare. (But Trinculo answers in a literal sense.)   **10 set** placed   **11 brave** fine, splendid   **13 sack** Spanish white wine. (Also in l. 28.)   **14 recover** gain, reach   **14–15 five . . . on** i.e., a little over a hundred miles, give or take, or, off and on, intermittently. (A drunken hyperbole.)   **15 By this light** (An oath: By the light of the sun.)   **16 standard** standard-bearer, ensign. (But Trinculo answers in the literal sense: Caliban is *no standard,* not able to stand up because he's so drunk.)   **17 list** prefer

18 run run away, retreat (as a standard-bearer should not do) **19 Nor . . . dogs** i.e., You won't even walk, much less run; you'll lie down in the field like the proverbial cowardly dog. (With a play on *lie,* tell falsehoods.)   **25–6 in case** ready, valiant enough **26 deboshed** debauched, drunken   **27 ever . . . coward** ever a coward. (Trinculo appeals to his gargantuan drinking as refutation of the charge that he is *not valiant,* line 24.)   **32 natural** fool, idiot.   **35 the next tree** i.e., you'll hang.   **39 Marry** i.e., Indeed. (Originally an oath, "by the Virgin Mary.")   **40.1 *invisible*** i.e., wearing a garment to connote invisibility, as at 1.2.377.2.   **48 supplant** uproot, displace **54 this thing** i.e., Trinculo

STEPHANO How now shall this be compassed? Canst ⁵⁷
thou bring me to the party?

CALIBAN
Yea, yea, my lord. I'll yield him thee asleep,
Where thou mayst knock a nail into his head.

ARIEL [*mimicking Trinculo*] Thou liest; thou canst not.

CALIBAN
What a pied ninny's this! Thou scurvy patch!— ⁶²
I do beseech Thy Greatness, give him blows
And take his bottle from him. When that's gone
He shall drink naught but brine, for I'll not show him
Where the quick freshes are. ⁶⁶

STEPHANO Trinculo, run into no further danger. Interrupt the monster one word further and, by this hand,
I'll turn my mercy out o' doors and make a stockfish of ⁶⁹
thee.

TRINCULO Why, what did I? I did nothing. I'll go farther
off.

STEPHANO Didst thou not say he lied?

ARIEL [*mimicking Trinculo*] Thou liest.

STEPHANO Do I so? Take thou that. [*He beats Trinculo.*]
As you like this, give me the lie another time. ⁷⁶

TRINCULO I did not give the lie. Out o' your wits and
hearing too? A pox o' your bottle! This can sack and ⁷⁸
drinking do. A murrain on your monster, and the ⁷⁹
devil take your fingers!

CALIBAN Ha, ha, ha!

STEPHANO Now, forward with your tale. [*To Trinculo*]
Prithee, stand further off.

CALIBAN
Beat him enough. After a little time
I'll beat him too.

STEPHANO Stand farther.—Come, proceed.

CALIBAN
Why, as I told thee, 'tis a custom with him
I'th'afternoon to sleep. There thou mayst brain him,
Having first seized his books; or with a log
Batter his skull, or paunch him with a stake, ⁹⁰
Or cut his weasand with thy knife. Remember ⁹¹
First to possess his books, for without them
He's but a sot, as I am, nor hath not ⁹³
One spirit to command. They all do hate him
As rootedly as I. Burn but his books.
He has brave utensils—for so he calls them— ⁹⁶
Which, when he has a house, he'll deck withal. ⁹⁷
And that most deeply to consider is
The beauty of his daughter. He himself
Calls her a nonpareil. I never saw a woman
But only Sycorax my dam and she;
But she as far surpasseth Sycorax
As great'st does least.

STEPHANO Is it so brave a lass? ¹⁰⁴

CALIBAN
Ay, lord. She will become thy bed, I warrant, ¹⁰⁵
And bring thee forth brave brood.

STEPHANO Monster, I will kill this man. His daughter
and I will be king and queen—save Our Graces!—and
Trinculo and thyself shall be viceroys. Dost thou like
the plot, Trinculo?

TRINCULO Excellent.

STEPHANO Give me thy hand. I am sorry I beat thee;
but, while thou liv'st, keep a good tongue in thy head.

CALIBAN
Within this half hour will he be asleep.
Wilt thou destroy him then?

STEPHANO Ay, on mine honor.

ARIEL [*aside*] This will I tell my master.

CALIBAN
Thou mak'st me merry; I am full of pleasure.
Let us be jocund. Will you troll the catch ¹¹⁹
You taught me but whilere? ¹²⁰

STEPHANO At thy request, monster, I will do reason, ¹²¹
any reason.—Come on, Trinculo, let us sing. *Sings.* ¹²²
"Flout 'em and scout 'em ¹²³
And scout 'em and flout 'em!
Thought is free."

CALIBAN That's not the tune. ¹²⁶
Ariel plays the tune on a tabor and pipe.

STEPHANO What is this same?

TRINCULO This is the tune of our catch, played by the
picture of Nobody. ¹²⁹

STEPHANO If thou be'st a man, show thyself in thy
likeness. If thou be'st a devil, take't as thou list. ¹³¹

TRINCULO Oh, forgive me my sins!

STEPHANO He that dies pays all debts. I defy thee. ¹³³
Mercy upon us!

CALIBAN Art thou afeard?

STEPHANO No, monster, not I.

CALIBAN
Be not afeard. The isle is full of noises,
Sounds, and sweet airs, that give delight and hurt not.
Sometimes a thousand twangling instruments
Will hum about mine ears, and sometimes voices
That, if I then had waked after long sleep,
Will make me sleep again; and then, in dreaming,
The clouds methought would open and show riches
Ready to drop upon me, that when I waked
I cried to dream again. ¹⁴⁵

STEPHANO This will prove a brave kingdom to me,
where I shall have my music for nothing.

CALIBAN When Prospero is destroyed.

---

57 compassed achieved. **62 pied ninny** fool in motley. **patch** fool.
66 quick freshes running springs **69 turn . . . o' doors** banish all
merciful feelings. **stockfish** dried cod beaten before cooking
76 give me the lie call me a liar to my face **78 A pox** i.e., A plague.
(A curse.) **79 murrain** plague. (Literally, a cattle disease.) **90 paunch**
stab in the belly **91 weasand** windpipe **93 sot** fool **96 brave utensils** fine furnishings **97 deck withal** furnish it with.

104 brave splendid, attractive **105 become** suit (sexually) **119 jocund**
jovial, merry. **troll the catch** sing the round **120 but whilere** only a
short time ago. **121–2 reason, any reason** anything reasonable.
123 Flout Scoff at. **scout** deride **126.1 tabor** small drum **129 picture of Nobody** (Refers to a familiar figure with head, arms, and legs
but no trunk.) **131 take't . . . list** (A proverbial formula of bravado
and defiance, as in *Romeo and Juliet*, 1.1.40–1.) **133 He . . . debts**
(Another proverbial swagger: Death settles all scores, I'm not afraid
to fight.) **145 to dream** desirous of dreaming

STEPHANO   That shall be by and by. I remember the 149
story.

TRINCULO   The sound is going away. Let's follow it,
and after do our work.

STEPHANO   Lead, monster; we'll follow. I would I could
see this taborer! He lays it on.   154

TRINCULO   Wilt come? I'll follow, Stephano.

Exeunt [following Ariel's music].

❖

3.3

*Enter Alonso, Sebastian, Antonio, Gonzalo,
Adrian, Francisco, etc.*

GONZALO
By'r lakin, I can go no further, sir.   1
My old bones aches. Here's a maze trod indeed
Through forthrights and meanders! By your patience,   3
I needs must rest me.

ALONSO   Old lord, I cannot blame thee,
Who am myself attached with weariness,   5
To th' dulling of my spirits. Sit down and rest.   6
Even here I will put off my hope, and keep it
No longer for my flatterer. He is drowned
Whom thus we stray to find, and the sea mocks
Our frustrate search on land. Well, let him go.   10

[Alonso and Gonzalo sit.]

ANTONIO *[aside to Sebastian]*
I am right glad that he's so out of hope.
Do not, for one repulse, forgo the purpose   12
That you resolved t'effect.

SEBASTIAN *[to Antonio]*   The next advantage
Will we take throughly.

ANTONIO *[to Sebastian]*   Let it be tonight,   14
For, now they are oppressed with travel, they   15
Will not, nor cannot, use such vigilance   16
As when they are fresh.

SEBASTIAN *[to Antonio]*   I say tonight. No more.   17

*Solemn and strange music; and Prospero on
the top, invisible.*

ALONSO
What harmony is this? My good friends, hark!

GONZALO   Marvelous sweet music!

*Enter several strange shapes, bringing in a ban-
quet, and dance about it with gentle actions of
salutations; and, inviting the King, etc., to eat,
they depart.*

ALONSO
Give us kind keepers, heavens! What were these?   20

SEBASTIAN
A living drollery. Now I will believe   21
That there are unicorns; that in Arabia
There is one tree, the phoenix' throne, one phoenix   23
At this hour reigning there.

ANTONIO   I'll believe both;
And what does else want credit, come to me   25
And I'll be sworn 'tis true. Travelers ne'er did lie,
Though fools at home condemn 'em.

GONZALO   If in Naples
I should report this now, would they believe me
If I should say I saw such islanders?
For, certes, these are people of the island,   30
Who, though they are of monstrous shape, yet note,
Their manners are more gentle, kind, than of
Our human generation you shall find
Many, nay, almost any.

PROSPERO *[aside]*   Honest lord,
Thou hast said well, for some of you there present
Are worse than devils.

ALONSO   I cannot too much muse   36
Such shapes, such gesture, and such sound,
expressing—
Although they want the use of tongue—a kind   38
Of excellent dumb discourse.

PROSPERO *[aside]*   Praise in departing.   39

FRANCISCO
They vanished strangely.

SEBASTIAN   No matter, since
They have left their viands behind, for we have
stomachs.   41
Will 't please you taste of what is here?

ALONSO   Not I.

GONZALO
Faith, sir, you need not fear. When we were boys,
Who would believe that there were mountaineers   44
Dewlapped like bulls, whose throats had hanging at
'em   45
Wallets of flesh? Or that there were such men   46
Whose heads stood in their breasts? Which now we
find   47
Each putter-out of five for one will bring us   48
Good warrant of.

ALONSO   I will stand to and feed,   49

---

149 **by and by** very soon.   154 **lays it on** i.e., plays the drum vigorously.
3.3. Location: Another part of the island.
1 **By'r lakin** By our Ladykin, by our Lady   3 **forthrights and meanders** paths straight and crooked.   5 **attached with** seized by   6 **To . . .
spirits** to the point of being dull-spirited.   10 **frustrate** frustrated
12 **for** because of   14 **throughly** thoroughly.   15 **now** now that.
travel (Spelled "trauaile" in the Folio and carrying the sense of labor
as well as traveling.)   16 **use such vigilance** be as vigilant   17.1–2 *on
the top* at some high point of the tiring-house or the theater, on a
third level above the gallery

20 **kind keepers** guardian angels   21 **living drollery** comic entertainment, caricature, or puppet show put on by live actors.   23 **phoenix**
mythical bird consumed to ashes every five hundred to six hundred
years, only to be renewed into another cycle   25 **want credit** lack
credibility   30 **certes** certainly   36 **muse** wonder at   38 **want** lack
39 **Praise in departing** i.e., Save your praise until the end of the performance. (Proverbial.)   41 **viands** provisions.   **stomachs** appetites.
44 **mountaineers** mountain dwellers   45 **Dewlapped** having a
dewlap, or fold of skin hanging from the neck, like cattle   46 **Wallets**
pendent folds of skin, wattles   47 **in their breasts** (I.e., like the
Anthropophagi described in *Othello*, 1.3.146.)   48 **putter-out . . . one**
one who invests money or gambles on the risks of travel on the condition that the traveler who returns safely is to receive five times the
amount deposited; hence, any traveler   49 **Good warrant** assurance.
stand to come forward, fall to. (Also in line 52.)

Although my last—no matter, since I feel   50
The best is past. Brother, my lord the Duke,   51
Stand to, and do as we.   [*They approach the table.*]   52

Thunder and lightning. Enter Ariel, like a harpy,
claps his wings upon the table, and with a quaint
device the banquet vanishes.

ARIEL
You are three men of sin, whom Destiny—   53
That hath to instrument this lower world   54
And what is in't—the never-surfeited sea   55
Hath caused to belch up you, and on this island   56
Where man doth not inhabit, you 'mongst men
Being most unfit to live. I have made you mad;
And even with suchlike valor men hang and drown   59
Their proper selves.   [*Alonso, Sebastian, and Antonio*
                                     draw their swords.]
                          You fools! I and my fellows   60
Are ministers of Fate. The elements
Of whom your swords are tempered may as well   62
Wound the loud winds, or with bemocked-at stabs   63
Kill the still-closing waters, as diminish   64
One dowl that's in my plume. My fellow ministers   65
Are like invulnerable. If you could hurt,   66
Your swords are now too massy for your strengths   67
And will not be uplifted. But remember—
For that's my business to you—that you three
From Milan did supplant good Prospero;
Exposed unto the sea, which hath requit it,   71
Him and his innocent child; for which foul deed
The powers, delaying, not forgetting, have
Incensed the seas and shores, yea, all the creatures,
Against your peace. Thee of thy son, Alonso,
They have bereft; and do pronounce by me
Ling'ring perdition, worse than any death   77
Can be at once, shall step by step attend
You and your ways; whose wraths to guard you
       from—   79
Which here, in this most desolate isle, else falls   80
Upon your heads—is nothing but heart's sorrow   81
And a clear life ensuing.   82

He vanishes in thunder; then, to soft music,
enter the shapes again, and dance, with mocks
and mows, and carrying out the table.

PROSPERO
Bravely the figure of this harpy hast thou   83
Performed, my Ariel; a grace it had devouring.   84
Of my instruction hast thou nothing bated   85
In what thou hadst to say. So, with good life   86
And observation strange, my meaner ministers   87
Their several kinds have done. My high charms work,   88
And these mine enemies are all knit up
In their distractions. They now are in my power;   90
And in these fits I leave them, while I visit
Young Ferdinand, whom they suppose is drowned,
And his and mine loved darling.   [*Exit above.*]
GONZALO
I'th' name of something holy, sir, why stand you   94
In this strange stare?
ALONSO   Oh, it is monstrous, monstrous!   95
Methought the billows spoke and told me of it;   96
The winds did sing it to me, and the thunder,
That deep and dreadful organ pipe, pronounced
The name of Prosper; it did bass my trespass.   99
Therefor my son i'th'ooze is bedded; and
I'll seek him deeper than e'er plummet sounded,   101
And with him there lie mudded.   *Exit.*
SEBASTIAN   But one fiend at a time,   103
I'll fight their legions o'er.
ANTONIO   I'll be thy second.   104
                    Exeunt [*Sebastian and Antonio*].
GONZALO
All three of them are desperate. Their great guilt,   105
Like poison given to work a great time after,   106
Now 'gins to bite the spirits. I do beseech you,   107
That are of suppler joints, follow them swiftly   108
And hinder them from what this ecstasy   109
May now provoke them to.
ADRIAN   Follow, I pray you.
                    Exeunt omnes.

❖

4.1

Enter Prospero, Ferdinand, and Miranda.

PROSPERO
If I have too austerely punished you,
Your compensation makes amends, for I

Have given you here a third of mine own life,   3
Or that for which I live; who once again
I tender to thy hand. All thy vexations   5
Were but my trials of thy love, and thou
Hast strangely stood the test. Here, afore heaven,   7
I ratify this my rich gift. O Ferdinand,
Do not smile at me that I boast her off,   9
For thou shalt find she will outstrip all praise
And make it halt behind her.

FERDINAND   I do believe it   11
Against an oracle.   12

PROSPERO
Then, as my gift and thine own acquisition
Worthily purchased, take my daughter. But
If thou dost break her virgin-knot before
All sanctimonious ceremonies may   16
With full and holy rite be ministered,
No sweet aspersion shall the heavens let fall   18
To make this contract grow; but barren hate,
Sour-eyed disdain, and discord shall bestrew
The union of your bed with weeds so loathly   21
That you shall hate it both. Therefore take heed,
As Hymen's lamps shall light you.

FERDINAND   As I hope   23
For quiet days, fair issue, and long life,   24
With such love as 'tis now, the murkiest den,
The most opportune place, the strong'st suggestion   26
Our worser genius can, shall never melt   27
Mine honor into lust, to take away   28
The edge of that day's celebration   29
When I shall think or Phoebus' steeds are foundered   30
Or Night kept chained below.

PROSPERO   Fairly spoke.
Sit then and talk with her. She is thine own.
              [Ferdinand and Miranda sit and talk together.]
What, Ariel! My industrious servant, Ariel!   33

              Enter Ariel.

ARIEL
What would my potent master? Here I am.

PROSPERO
Thou and thy meaner fellows your last service   35
Did worthily perform, and I must use you
In such another trick. Go bring the rabble,   37

O'er whom I give thee power, here to this place.
Incite them to quick motion, for I must
Bestow upon the eyes of this young couple
Some vanity of mine art. It is my promise,   41
And they expect it from me.

ARIEL   Presently?   42

PROSPERO   Ay, with a twink.   43

ARIEL
          Before you can say "Come" and "Go,"
          And breathe twice, and cry "So, so,"
          Each one, tripping on his toe,
          Will be here with mop and mow.   47
          Do you love me, master? No?

PROSPERO
Dearly, my delicate Ariel. Do not approach
Till thou dost hear me call.

ARIEL   Well; I conceive.   Exit.   50

PROSPERO
Look thou be true; do not give dalliance   51
Too much the rein. The strongest oaths are straw
To th' fire i'th' blood. Be more abstemious,
Or else good night your vow!

FERDINAND   I warrant you, sir,   54
The white cold virgin snow upon my heart   55
Abates the ardor of my liver.

PROSPERO   Well.   56
Now come, my Ariel! Bring a corollary,   57
Rather than want a spirit. Appear, and pertly!—   58
No tongue! All eyes! Be silent.   Soft music.   59

              Enter Iris.

IRIS
Ceres, most bounteous lady, thy rich leas   60
Of wheat, rye, barley, vetches, oats, and peas;   61
Thy turfy mountains, where live nibbling sheep,
And flat meads thatched with stover, them to keep;   63
Thy banks with pionèd and twillèd brims,   64
Which spongy April at thy hest betrims   65
To make cold nymphs chaste crowns; and thy
          broom groves,   66
Whose shadow the dismissèd bachelor loves,   67
Being lass-lorn; thy poll-clipped vineyard;   68
And thy sea marge, sterile and rocky hard,   69
Where thou thyself dost air: the queen o'th' sky,   70

---

3 a third i.e., Miranda, into whose education I have put a third of my life, or (less precisely) who represents a large part of what I have cared about, along with my dukedom and my magical art   **5 tender** offer   **7 strangely** exceptionally   **9 boast her off** i.e., praise her so, or, perhaps an error for "boast of her"; the Folio reads "boast her of"   **11 halt** limp   **12 Against an oracle** even if an oracle should declare otherwise.   **16 sanctimonious** sacred   **18 aspersion** dew, shower   **21 weeds** (In place of the flowers customarily strewn on the marriage bed.)   **23 As . . . you** i.e., as you long for happiness and concord in your marriage. (Hymen was the Greek and Roman god of marriage; his symbolic torches, the wedding torches, were supposed to burn brightly for a happy marriage and smokily for a troubled one.)   **24 issue** offspring   **26–7 the strong'st . . . can** the strongest temptation that the evil spirit within us can propose   **28 to** so as to   **29 edge** keen enjoyment, sexual ardor   **30 or . . . foundered** either that the horses of the sun's chariot have gone lame (thus delaying the night for which I will be so eager)   **33 What** Now then   **35 meaner fellows** subordinates   **37 trick** device.   **rabble** band, i.e., the *meaner fellows* of line 35

41 vanity (1) illusion (2) trifle (3) desire for admiration, conceit   **42 Presently?** Immediately?   **43 with a twink** in the twinkling of an eye.   **47 mop and mow** grimaces.   **50 conceive** understand.   **51 true** true to your promise   **54 good night** i.e., say good-bye to.   **warrant** guarantee   **55 The white . . . heart** i.e., the chaste ideal to which my heart is devoted   **56 liver** (The presumed seat of the passions.)   **57 corollary** surplus, extra supply   **58 want** lack.   **pertly** briskly.   **59 No tongue!** Quiet, everyone!   **59.1 Iris** goddess of the rainbow and Juno's messenger.   **60 Ceres** goddess of the generative power of nature.   **leas** meadows   **61 vetches** plants for forage, fodder   **63 meads** meadows.   **stover** winter fodder for cattle   **64 pionèd and twillèd** undercut by the swift current and protected by roots and branches that tangle to form a barricade   **65 spongy** wet.   **hest** command   **66 broom groves** clumps of broom, gorse, yellow-flowered shrub   **67 dismissèd bachelor** rejected male lover   **68 poll-clipped** pruned, lopped at the top, or *pole-clipped,* "hedged in with poles"   **69 sea marge** shore   **70 thou . . . air** you take the air, go for walks.   **queen o'th' sky** i.e., Juno

Whose wat'ry arch and messenger am I,   71
Bids thee leave these, and with her sovereign grace,   72
              Juno descends [*slowly in her car*].
Here on this grass plot, in this very place,
To come and sport. Her peacocks fly amain.   74
Approach, rich Ceres, her to entertain.   75

      Enter Ceres.

CERES
Hail, many-colored messenger, that ne'er
Dost disobey the wife of Jupiter,
Who with thy saffron wings upon my flowers   78
Diffusest honeydrops, refreshing showers,
And with each end of thy blue bow dost crown   80
My bosky acres and my unshrubbed down,   81
Rich scarf to my proud earth. Why hath thy queen   82
Summoned me hither to this short-grassed green?

IRIS
A contract of true love to celebrate,
And some donation freely to estate   85
On the blest lovers.

CERES   Tell me, heavenly bow,
If Venus or her son, as thou dost know,   87
Do now attend the Queen? Since they did plot   88
The means that dusky Dis my daughter got,   89
Her and her blind boy's scandaled company   90
I have forsworn.

IRIS   Of her society   91
Be not afraid. I met Her Deity   92
Cutting the clouds towards Paphos, and her son   93
Dove-drawn with her. Here thought they to have
   done   94
Some wanton charm upon this man and maid,   95
Whose vows are that no bed-right shall be paid   96
Till Hymen's torch be lighted; but in vain.
Mars's hot minion is returned again;   98
Her waspish-headed son has broke his arrows,   99
Swears he will shoot no more, but play with
   sparrows   100
And be a boy right out.

      [*Juno alights.*]

CERES   Highest Queen of state,   101
Great Juno, comes; I know her by her gait.   102

JUNO
How does my bounteous sister? Go with me   103
To bless this twain, that they may prosperous be,
And honored in their issue.   *They sing:* 105
JUNO
Honor, riches, marriage blessing,
Long continuance, and increasing,
Hourly joys be still upon you!   108
Juno sings her blessings on you.
CERES
Earth's increase, foison plenty,   110
Barns and garners never empty,   111
Vines with clust'ring bunches growing,
Plants with goodly burden bowing;

Spring come to you at the farthest
In the very end of harvest!   115
Scarcity and want shall shun you;
Ceres' blessing so is on you.
FERDINAND
This is a most majestic vision, and
Harmonious charmingly. May I be bold   119
To think these spirits?
PROSPERO   Spirits, which by mine art
I have from their confines called to enact
My present fancies.
FERDINAND   Let me live here ever!
So rare a wondered father and a wife   123
Makes this place Paradise.
      Juno and Ceres whisper, and send
          Iris on employment.
PROSPERO   Sweet now, silence!
Juno and Ceres whisper seriously;
There's something else to do. Hush and be mute,
Or else our spell is marred.
IRIS [*calling offstage*]
You nymphs, called naiads, of the windring brooks,   128
With your sedged crowns and ever-harmless looks,   129
Leave your crisp channels, and on this green land   130
Answer your summons; Juno does command.
Come, temperate nymphs, and help to celebrate   132
A contract of true love. Be not too late.

      Enter certain nymphs.

You sunburned sicklemen, of August weary,   134
Come hither from the furrow and be merry.   135

71 wat'ry arch rainbow   **72.1** *Juno descends* i.e., starts her descent from the "heavens" above the stage   **74 peacocks** birds sacred to Juno and used to pull her chariot.   **amain** with full speed.   **75 entertain** receive.   **78 saffron** yellow   **80 bow** rainbow   **81 bosky** wooded.   **unshrubbed down** open upland   **82 scarf** (The rainbow is like a colored silk band adorning the earth.)   **85 estate** bestow   **87 son** i.e., Cupid.   **as** as far as   **88–91 Since . . . forsworn** Since Venus and her blind son Cupid plotted the means by which Dis (Pluto) carried off my daughter Proserpina to be his bride in Hades, I have forsworn their scandalous company.   **92 Her Deity** i.e., Her Highness   **93 Paphos** place on the island of Cyprus, sacred to Venus   **94 Dove-drawn** (Venus's chariot was drawn by doves.)   **94–5 done . . . charm** inflicted some lustful spell   **96 that . . . paid** that their union will not be sexually consummated   **98 Mars's hot minion** i.e., Venus, the beloved of Mars.   **returned** i.e., returned to Paphos   **99 waspish-headed** hotheaded, peevish   **100 sparrows** (Supposed lustful, and sacred to Venus.)   **101 right out** outright.   **Highest . . . state** Most majestic Queen   **102 gait** i.e., majestic bearing.

103 sister i.e., fellow goddess.   **105 issue** offspring.   **108 still** always   **110 foison plenty** plentiful harvest   **111 garners** granaries   **115 In . . . harvest** i.e., with no winter in between.   **119 charmingly** enchantingly.   **123 wondered** wonder-performing, wondrous.   **wise** (The Folio appears to read "wise" here, but with a tall "s" that resembles an "f," leading to much dispute over this reading. In some copies of the Folio the "s" looks like an "f," perhaps damaged, but evidently as the result of an inkblot, so that the true reading is "s." Even so, an error in transmission would be easy, so that the author's intention is uncertain. The matter bears importantly on whether or not Ferdinand includes Miranda in his vision of paradise.)   **128 naiads** nymphs of springs, rivers, or lakes.   **windring** wandering, winding (?)   **129 sedged** made of reeds.   **ever-harmless** ever innocent   **130 crisp** curled, rippled   **132 temperate** chaste   **134 sicklemen** harvesters, field workers who cut down grain and grass.   **of August weary** i.e., weary of the hard work of the harvest   **135 furrow** i.e., plowed fields

Make holiday; your rye-straw hats put on,
And these fresh nymphs encounter every one   137
In country footing.   138

> *Enter certain reapers, properly habited. They join*
> *with the nymphs in a graceful dance, towards the*
> *end whereof Prospero starts suddenly, and speaks;*
> *after which, to a strange, hollow, and confused*
> *noise, they heavily vanish.*

PROSPERO [*aside*]
I had forgot that foul conspiracy
Of the beast Caliban and his confederates
Against my life. The minute of their plot
Is almost come. [*To the Spirits*] Well done! Avoid; no
    more!   142
FERDINAND [*to Miranda*]
This is strange. Your father's in some passion
That works him strongly.
MIRANDA   Never till this day   144
Saw I him touched with anger so distempered.
PROSPERO
You do look, my son, in a moved sort,   146
As if you were dismayed. Be cheerful, sir.
Our revels now are ended. These our actors,   148
As I foretold you, were all spirits and
Are melted into air, into thin air;
And, like the baseless fabric of this vision,   151
The cloud-capped towers, the gorgeous palaces,
The solemn temples, the great globe itself,   153
Yea, all which it inherit, shall dissolve,   154
And, like this insubstantial pageant faded,
Leave not a rack behind. We are such stuff   156
As dreams are made on, and our little life   157
Is rounded with a sleep. Sir, I am vexed.   158
Bear with my weakness. My old brain is troubled.
Be not disturbed with my infirmity.   160
If you be pleased, retire into my cell   161
And there repose. A turn or two I'll walk
To still my beating mind.
FERDINAND, MIRANDA   We wish your peace.   163
            Exeunt [*Ferdinand and Miranda*].
PROSPERO
Come with a thought! I thank thee, Ariel. Come.   164

            Enter Ariel.

ARIEL
Thy thoughts I cleave to. What's thy pleasure?   165
PROSPERO   Spirit,
We must prepare to meet with Caliban.

ARIEL
Ay, my commander. When I presented Ceres,   167
I thought to have told thee of it, but I feared
Lest I might anger thee.
PROSPERO
Say again, where didst thou leave these varlets?
ARIEL
I told you, sir, they were red-hot with drinking;
So full of valor that they smote the air
For breathing in their faces, beat the ground
For kissing of their feet; yet always bending   174
Towards their project. Then I beat my tabor,
At which, like unbacked colts, they pricked their ears, 176
Advanced their eyelids, lifted up their noses   177
As they smelt music. So I charmed their ears   178
That calflike they my lowing followed through   179
Toothed briers, sharp furzes, pricking gorse, and
    thorns,   180
Which entered their frail shins. At last I left them
I'th' filthy-mantled pool beyond your cell,   182
There dancing up to th' chins, that the foul lake
O'erstunk their feet.
PROSPERO   This was well done, my bird.   184
Thy shape invisible retain thou still.
The trumpery in my house, go bring it hither,   186
For stale to catch these thieves.
ARIEL   I go, I go.   *Exit.* 187
PROSPERO
A devil, a born devil, on whose nature
Nurture can never stick; on whom my pains,
Humanely taken, all, all lost, quite lost!
And as with age his body uglier grows,
So his mind cankers. I will plague them all,   192
Even to roaring.

> *Enter Ariel, loaden with glistering apparel, etc.*

            Come, hang them on this line.   193

> [*Ariel hangs up the showy finery; Prospero and*
> *Ariel remain, invisible.*] *Enter Caliban, Stephano,*
> *and Trinculo, all wet.*

CALIBAN
Pray you, tread softly, that the blind mole may
Not hear a foot fall. We now are near his cell.
STEPHANO   Monster, your fairy, which you say is a
harmless fairy, has done little better than played the
jack with us.   198

---

137 **encounter** join   138 **country footing** country dancing.
138.1 *properly* suitably.   138.5 *heavily* slowly, dejectedly   142 **Avoid**
Withdraw   144 **works** affects, agitates   146 **moved sort** troubled
state, condition   148 **revels** entertainment, pageant   151 **baseless**
fabric unsubstantial theatrical edifice or contrivance   153 **great**
globe (With a glance at the Globe Theatre.)   154 **which it inherit**
who subsequently occupy it   156 **rack** wisp of cloud   157 **on** of
158 **rounded** surrounded (before birth and after death), or crowned,
rounded off   160 **with** by   161 **retire** withdraw, go   163 **beating**
agitated   164 **with a thought** i.e., on the instant, or, summoned by
my thought, no sooner thought of than here.   165 **cleave** cling,
adhere

167 **presented** acted the part of, or, introduced   174 **bending** aiming
176 **unbacked** unbroken, unridden   177 **Advanced** lifted up   178 **As**
as if   179 **lowing** mooing   180 **furzes . . . gorse** prickly shrubs
182 **filthy-mantled** covered with a slimy coating   184 **O'erstunk**
smelled worse than, or, caused to stink terribly   186 **trumpery** cheap
goods, the *glistering apparel* mentioned in the following stage direction   187 **stale** (1) decoy (2) out-of-fashion garments. (With possible
further suggestions of "horse piss," as in line 199, and "steal," pronounced like *stale. For stale* could also mean "fit for a prostitute.")
192 **cankers** festers, grows malignant.   193 **line** lime tree or linden.
193.1–2 *Prospero and Ariel remain* (The staging is uncertain. They
may instead exit here and return with the spirits at line 256.)
198 **jack** (1) knave (2) will-o'-the-wisp

TRINCULO   Monster, I do smell all horse piss, at which
my nose is in great indignation.

STEPHANO   So is mine. Do you hear, monster? If I
should take a displeasure against you, look you—

TRINCULO   Thou wert but a lost monster.

CALIBAN
Good my lord, give me thy favor still.
Be patient, for the prize I'll bring thee to
Shall hoodwink this mischance. Therefore speak
    softly.   206
All's hushed as midnight yet.

TRINCULO   Ay, but to lose our bottles in the pool—

STEPHANO   There is not only disgrace and dishonor in
that, monster, but an infinite loss.

TRINCULO   That's more to me than my wetting. Yet this
is your harmless fairy, monster!

STEPHANO   I will fetch off my bottle, though I be o'er   213
ears for my labor.   214

CALIBAN
Prithee, my king, be quiet. See'st thou here,
This is the mouth o'th' cell. No noise, and enter.
Do that good mischief which may make this island
Thine own forever, and I thy Caliban
For aye thy footlicker.

STEPHANO   Give me thy hand. I do begin to have bloody
thoughts.

TRINCULO [seeing the finery]   O King Stephano! O peer!   222
O worthy Stephano! Look what a wardrobe here is
for thee!

CALIBAN
Let it alone, thou fool, it is but trash.

TRINCULO   Oho, monster! We know what belongs to a
frippery. O King Stephano!   [He puts on a gown.]   227

STEPHANO   Put off that gown, Trinculo. By this hand,
I'll have that gown.

TRINCULO   Thy Grace shall have it.

CALIBAN
The dropsy drown this fool! What do you mean   231
To dote thus on such luggage? Let't alone   232
And do the murder first. If he awake,
From toe to crown he'll fill our skins with pinches,   234
Make us strange stuff.

STEPHANO   Be you quiet, monster.—Mistress line, is   236
not this my jerkin? [He takes it down.] Now is the jerkin   237
under the line. Now, jerkin, you are like to lose your   238
hair and prove a bald jerkin.   239

TRINCULO   Do, do! We steal by line and level, an't like   240
Your Grace.

STEPHANO   I thank thee for that jest. Here's a garment
for't. [He gives a garment.] Wit shall not go unrewarded
while I am king of this country. "Steal by line and
level" is an excellent pass of pate. There's another   245
garment for't.

TRINCULO   Monster, come, put some lime upon your   247
fingers, and away with the rest.

CALIBAN
I will have none on't. We shall lose our time,
And all be turned to barnacles, or to apes   250
With foreheads villainous low.   251

STEPHANO   Monster, lay to your fingers. Help to bear   252
this away where my hogshead of wine is, or I'll turn   253
you out of my kingdom. Go to, carry this.   254

TRINCULO   And this.

STEPHANO   Ay, and this.
        [They load Caliban with more and more garments.]

_A noise of hunters heard. Enter divers spirits, in
shape of dogs and hounds, hunting them about,
Prospero and Ariel setting them on._

PROSPERO   Hey, Mountain, hey!

ARIEL   Silver! There it goes, Silver!

PROSPERO   Fury, Fury! There, Tyrant, there! Hark! Hark!
        [Caliban, Stephano, and Trinculo are driven out.]
Go, charge my goblins that they grind their joints
With dry convulsions, shorten up their sinews   261
With agèd cramps, and more pinch-spotted make
    them   262
Than pard or cat o' mountain.

ARIEL   Hark, they roar!   263

PROSPERO
Let them be hunted soundly. At this hour   264
Lies at my mercy all mine enemies.
Shortly shall all my labors end, and thou
Shalt have the air at freedom. For a little   267
Follow, and do me service.   _Exeunt._

❖

5.1

_Enter Prospero in his magic robes, [with his
staff,] and Ariel._

206 **hoodwink this mischance** cover up (literally, blindfold) this mistake.   **213–14 o'er ears** over my ears in the filthy horse pond (line
182)   **222 King . . . peer** (Alludes to the old ballad beginning, "King
Stephen was a worthy peer.")   **227 frippery** second-hand-clothing
shop. (Trinculo knows that what they have just found is much finer.)
231 The dropsy drown (_Dropsy_ is a disease characterized by
the accumulation of fluid in the connective tissue of the body.)
232 luggage cumbersome trash.   **234 crown** head   **236 Mistress line**
(Addressed to the linden or lime tree upon which, at line 193, Ariel
hung the _glistering apparel._)   **237 jerkin** jacket made of leather
238 under the line under the lime tree. (With punning sense of being
south of the equinoctial line or equator; sailors on long voyages to the
southern regions were popularly supposed to lose their hair from
scurvy or other diseases. Stephano also quibbles bawdily on losing
hair through syphilis, and puns in _Mistress_ and _jerkin_.)   **like** likely
239 bald (1) hairless, napless (2) meager

240 **Do, do!** i.e., Bravo! (Said in response to the jesting or to the taking
of the jerkin, or both.)   **steal . . . level** i.e., steal by means of plumb
line and carpenter's level, methodically. (With pun on _line_, "lime
tree," line 238, and _steal_, pronounced like _stale_, i.e., prostitute, continuing Stephano's bawdy quibble.)   **an't like** if it please   **245 pass of
pate** sally of wit. (The metaphor is from fencing.)   **247 lime** birdlime,
sticky substance (to give Caliban sticky fingers)   **250 barnacles** bar-
nacle geese, formerly supposed to be hatched from barnacles
attached to trees or to rotting timber; here, evidently used, like _apes_,
as types of simpletons   **251 villainous** vilely   **252 lay to** start using
253 this i.e., the _glistering apparel._   **hogshead** large cask   **254 Go to**
(An expression of exhortation or remonstrance.)   **261 dry convulsions** racking cramps   **262 agèd** characteristic of old age   **263 pard**
panther or leopard.   **cat o' mountain** wildcat.   **264 soundly** severely.   **267 little** little while longer
5.1. Location: Before Prospero's cell.

PROSPERO
Now does my project gather to a head.
My charms crack not, my spirits obey, and Time   2
Goes upright with his carriage. How's the day?   3
ARIEL
On the sixth hour, at which time, my lord,   4
You said our work should cease.
PROSPERO   I did say so,
When first I raised the tempest. Say, my spirit,
How fares the King and 's followers?
ARIEL   Confined together
In the same fashion as you gave in charge,
Just as you left them; all prisoners, sir,
In the line grove which weather-fends your cell.   10
They cannot budge till your release. The King,   11
His brother, and yours abide all three distracted,   12
And the remainder mourning over them,
Brim full of sorrow and dismay; but chiefly
Him that you termed, sir, the good old lord,
    Gonzalo.
His tears runs down his beard like winter's drops
From eaves of reeds. Your charm so strongly works
    'em   17
That if you now beheld them your affections   18
Would become tender.
PROSPERO   Dost thou think so, spirit?
ARIEL
Mine would, sir, were I human.
PROSPERO   And mine shall.
Hast thou, which art but air, a touch, a feeling   21
Of their afflictions, and shall not myself,
One of their kind, that relish all as sharply   23
Passion as they, be kindlier moved than thou art?   24
Though with their high wrongs I am struck to th'
    quick,
Yet with my nobler reason 'gainst my fury
Do I take part. The rarer action is   27
In virtue than in vengeance. They being penitent,
The sole drift of my purpose doth extend
Not a frown further. Go release them, Ariel.
My charms I'll break, their senses I'll restore,
And they shall be themselves.
ARIEL   I'll fetch them, sir.
                                              Exit.
    [*Prospero traces a charmed circle with his staff.*]
PROSPERO
Ye elves of hills, brooks, standing lakes, and groves, 33
And ye that on the sands with printless foot
Do chase the ebbing Neptune, and do fly him

When he comes back; you demi-puppets that   36
By moonshine do the green sour ringlets make,   37
Whereof the ewe not bites; and you whose pastime
Is to make midnight mushrooms, that rejoice   39
To hear the solemn curfew; by whose aid,   40
Weak masters though ye be, I have bedimmed   41
The noontide sun, called forth the mutinous winds,
And twixt the green sea and the azured vault   43
Set roaring war; to the dread rattling thunder   44
Have I given fire, and rifted Jove's stout oak   45
With his own bolt; the strong-based promontory   46
Have I made shake, and by the spurs plucked up   47
The pine and cedar; graves at my command
Have waked their sleepers, oped, and let 'em forth
By my so potent art. But this rough magic   50
I here abjure, and when I have required   51
Some heavenly music—which even now I do—
To work mine end upon their senses that   53
This airy charm is for, I'll break my staff,
Bury it certain fathoms in the earth,
And deeper than did ever plummet sound
I'll drown my book.   *Solemn music.*

    Here enters Ariel before; then Alonso, with a
    frantic gesture, attended by Gonzalo; Sebastian and
    Antonio in like manner, attended by Adrian and
    Francisco. They all enter the circle which Prospero
    had made, and there stand charmed; which
    Prospero observing, speaks:

[*To Alonso*] A solemn air, and the best comforter   58
To an unsettled fancy, cure thy brains,   59
Now useless, boiled within thy skull! [*To Sebastian*
    and Antonio] There stand,   60
For you are spell-stopped.—
Holy Gonzalo, honorable man,
Mine eyes, e'en sociable to the show of thine,   63
Fall fellowly drops. [*Aside*] The charm dissolves
    apace,   64
And as the morning steals upon the night,
Melting the darkness, so their rising senses
Begin to chase the ignorant fumes that mantle   67
Their clearer reason.—O good Gonzalo,   68
My true preserver, and a loyal sir
To him thou follow'st! I will pay thy graces   70
Home both in word and deed.—Most cruelly   71
Didst thou, Alonso, use me and my daughter.
Thy brother was a furtherer in the act.—   73

---

2 **crack** collapse, fail. (The metaphor is probably alchemical, as in *project* and *gather to a head*, line 1.) 3 **his carriage** its burden. (Time is no longer heavily burdened and so can go *upright*, "standing straight and unimpeded.") 4 **On** Approaching 10 **line grove** grove of lime trees. **weather-fends** protects from the weather 11 **your release** you release them. 12 **distracted** out of their wits 17 **eaves of reeds** thatched roofs. 18 **affections** disposition, feelings 21 **touch** sense, apprehension 23–4 **that . . . they** I who experience human passions as acutely as they 24 **kindlier** (1) more sympathetically (2) more naturally, humanly 27 **rarer** nobler 33 **Ye . . . groves** This passage, down through line 50, is an embellished paraphrase of Golding's translation of Ovid's *Metamorphoses*, 7.197–219.)

36 **demi-puppets** puppets of half size, i.e., elves and fairies 37 **green sour ringlets** fairy rings, circles in grass (actually produced by mushrooms) 39 **midnight mushrooms** mushrooms appearing overnight 40 **curfew** evening bell, usually rung at nine o'clock, ushering in the time when spirits are abroad 41 **Weak masters** i.e., subordinate spirits, as in 4.1.35 43 **the azured vault** i.e., the sky 44–5 **to . . . fire** I have discharged the dread rattling thunderbolt 45 **rifted** riven, split. **oak** a tree that was sacred to Jove 46 **bolt** thunderbolt 47 **spurs** roots 50 **rough** violent 51 **required** demanded 53 **their senses that** the senses of those whom 58 **air** song. **and** i.e., which is 59 **fancy** imagination 60 **boiled** i.e., extremely agitated 63 **sociable** sympathetic. **show** appearance 64 **Fall** let fall 67 **ignorant fumes** fumes that render them incapable of comprehension. **mantle** envelop 68 **clearer** growing clearer 70 **pay thy graces** requite your favors and virtues 71 **Home** fully 73 **furtherer** accomplice

Thou art pinched for't now, Sebastian. [*To Antonio*]
   Flesh and blood,   74
You, brother mine, that entertained ambition,
Expelled remorse and nature, whom, with Sebastian,   76
Whose inward pinches therefore are most strong,
Would here have killed your king, I do forgive thee,
Unnatural though thou art.—Their understanding
Begins to swell, and the approaching tide
Will shortly fill the reasonable shore   81
That now lies foul and muddy. Not one of them
That yet looks on me, or would know me.—Ariel,
Fetch me the hat and rapier in my cell.
      [*Ariel goes to the cell and returns immediately.*]
I will discase me and myself present   85
As I was sometime Milan. Quickly, spirit!   86
Thou shalt ere long be free.

           Ariel sings and helps to attire him.

ARIEL
   Where the bee sucks, there suck I.
   In a cowslip's bell I lie;
   There I couch when owls do cry.   90
   On the bat's back I do fly
   After summer merrily.   92
  Merrily, merrily shall I live now
  Under the blossom that hangs on the bough.

PROSPERO
   Why, that's my dainty Ariel! I shall miss thee,
But yet thou shalt have freedom. So, so, so.   96
To the King's ship, invisible as thou art!
There shalt thou find the mariners asleep
Under the hatches. The Master and the Boatswain
Being awake, enforce them to this place,
And presently, I prithee.   101

ARIEL
   I drink the air before me, and return
Or ere your pulse twice beat.   *Exit.*   103

GONZALO
   All torment, trouble, wonder, and amazement
Inhabits here. Some heavenly power guide us
Out of this fearful country!

PROSPERO   Behold, sir King,   106
The wrongèd Duke of Milan, Prospero.
For more assurance that a living prince
Does now speak to thee, I embrace thy body;
And to thee and thy company I bid
A hearty welcome.   [*Embracing him.*]

ALONSO   Whe'er thou be'st he or no,
Or some enchanted trifle to abuse me,   112
As late I have been, I not know. Thy pulse   113
Beats as of flesh and blood; and, since I saw thee,
Th' affliction of my mind amends, with which

I fear a madness held me. This must crave—   116
An if this be at all—a most strange story.   117
Thy dukedom I resign, and do entreat   118
Thou pardon me my wrongs. But how should
   Prospero   119
Be living, and be here?

PROSPERO [*to Gonzalo*]   First, noble friend,
Let me embrace thine age, whose honor cannot   121
Be measured or confined.   [*Embracing him.*]

GONZALO   Whether this be
Or be not, I'll not swear.

PROSPERO   You do yet taste
Some subtleties o'th'isle, that will not let you   124
Believe things certain. Welcome, my friends all!
[*Aside to Sebastian and Antonio*] But you, my brace of
   lords, were I so minded,   126
I here could pluck His Highness' frown upon you
And justify you traitors. At this time   128
I will tell no tales.

SEBASTIAN   The devil speaks in him.

PROSPERO   No.
[*To Antonio*] For you, most wicked sir, whom to call
   brother
Would even infect my mouth, I do forgive
Thy rankest fault—all of them; and require
My dukedom of thee, which perforce I know
Thou must restore.

ALONSO   If thou be'st Prospero,
Give us particulars of thy preservation,
How thou hast met us here, whom three hours since   136
Were wrecked upon this shore; where I have lost—
How sharp the point of this remembrance is!—
My dear son Ferdinand.

PROSPERO   I am woe for't, sir.   139

ALONSO
Irreparable is the loss, and Patience
Says it is past her cure.

PROSPERO   I rather think
You have not sought her help, of whose soft grace
For the like loss I have her sovereign aid   143
And rest myself content.

ALONSO   You the like loss?

PROSPERO
As great to me as late, and supportable   145
To make the dear loss, have I means much weaker   146
Than you may call to comfort you; for I   147
Have lost my daughter.

ALONSO   A daughter?
O heavens, that they were living both in Naples,

---

74 **pinched** punished, afflicted   76 **remorse and nature** pity and natural feeling.   **whom** you who   81 **reasonable shore** shores of reason, i.e., minds. (Their reason returns, like the incoming tide.)
85 **discase** disrobe   86 **As . . . Milan** in my former appearance as Duke of Milan.   90 **couch** lie   92 **After summer** following summer as it moves to various parts of the world   96 **So, so, so** (Expresses approval of Ariel's help as valet.)   101 **presently** immediately
103 **Or ere** before   106 **fearful** frightening   112 **trifle** trick of magic. **abuse** deceive   113 **late** lately

116 **crave** require   117 **An . . . all** if this is actually happening.   **story** i.e., explanation.   118 **Thy . . . resign** (Alonso made arrangement with Antonio at the time of Prospero's banishment for Milan to pay tribute to Naples; see 1.2.113–27.)   119 **wrongs** wrongdoings.
121 **thine age** your venerable self   124 **subtleties** illusions, magical powers. (Playing on the idea of "pastries, concoctions.")   126 **brace** pair   128 **justify you** prove you to be   136 **whom** we who   139 **woe** sorry   143 **sovereign** efficacious   145 **late** recent   145–7 **and supportable . . . you** and I have much weaker means to make my loss supportable than you can call upon to comfort you

The king and queen there! That they were, I wish   151
Myself were mudded in that oozy bed   152
Where my son lies. When did you lose your daughter?   153

PROSPERO
In this last tempest. I perceive these lords
At this encounter do so much admire   155
That they devour their reason and scarce think   156
Their eyes do offices of truth, their words   157
Are natural breath. But, howsoever you have   158
Been jostled from your senses, know for certain
That I am Prospero and that very duke
Which was thrust forth of Milan, who most strangely   161
Upon this shore, where you were wrecked, was
    landed
To be the lord on't. No more yet of this,
For 'tis a chronicle of day by day,   164
Not a relation for a breakfast nor
Befitting this first meeting. Welcome, sir.
This cell's my court. Here have I few attendants,
And subjects none abroad. Pray you, look in.   168
My dukedom since you have given me again,
I will requite you with as good a thing,   170
At least bring forth a wonder to content ye
As much as me my dukedom.   172

Here Prospero discovers Ferdinand and Miranda,
playing at chess.

MIRANDA   Sweet lord, you play me false.   173
FERDINAND   No, my dearest love,
I would not for the world.
MIRANDA
Yes, for a score of kingdoms you should wrangle,   176
And I would call it fair play.
ALONSO   If this prove   177
A vision of the island, one dear son   178
Shall I twice lose.
SEBASTIAN   A most high miracle!
FERDINAND [*approaching his father*]
Though the seas threaten, they are merciful;
I have cursed them without cause.   [*He kneels.*]
ALONSO   Now all the blessings
Of a glad father compass thee about!   182
Arise, and say how thou cam'st here.
                                 [*Ferdinand rises.*]
MIRANDA   Oh, wonder!
How many goodly creatures are there here!
How beauteous mankind is! Oh, brave new world   185

That has such people in't!
PROSPERO   'Tis new to thee.
ALONSO
What is this maid with whom thou wast at play?
Your eld'st acquaintance cannot be three hours.   188
Is she the goddess that hath severed us,
And brought us thus together?
FERDINAND   Sir, she is mortal;
But by immortal Providence she's mine.
I chose her when I could not ask my father
For his advice, nor thought I had one. She
Is daughter to this famous Duke of Milan,
Of whom so often I have heard renown,
But never saw before; of whom I have
Received a second life; and second father
This lady makes him to me.
ALONSO   I am hers.
But oh, how oddly will it sound that I
Must ask my child forgiveness!
PROSPERO   There, sir, stop.
Let us not burden our remembrances with
A heaviness that's gone.
GONZALO   I have inly wept,   202
Or should have spoke ere this. Look down, you gods,
And on this couple drop a blessèd crown!
For it is you that have chalked forth the way   205
Which brought us hither.
ALONSO   I say amen, Gonzalo!
GONZALO
Was Milan thrust from Milan, that his issue   207
Should become kings of Naples? Oh, rejoice
Beyond a common joy, and set it down
With gold on lasting pillars: In one voyage
Did Claribel her husband find at Tunis,
And Ferdinand, her brother, found a wife
Where he himself was lost; Prospero his dukedom
In a poor isle; and all of us ourselves   214
When no man was his own.
ALONSO [*to Ferdinand and Miranda*]   Give me your hands. 215
Let grief and sorrow still embrace his heart   216
That doth not wish you joy!
GONZALO   Be it so! Amen!

Enter Ariel, with the Master and Boatswain
amazedly following.

Oh, look, sir, look, sir! Here is more of us.
I prophesied, if a gallows were on land,
This fellow could not drown.—Now, blasphemy,   220
That swear'st grace o'erboard, not an oath on shore?   221
Hast thou no mouth by land? What is the news?
BOATSWAIN
The best news is that we have safely found

151–3 **That . . . lies** I would wish myself buried in that muddy bed
where my son's body lies drowned if that would somehow make
them alive and reigning in Naples.   155 **admire** wonder   156 **devour
their reason** i.e., are openmouthed, dumbfounded   156–8 **and scarce
. . . breath** and scarcely can believe their eyes or their own words.
161 **of** from   164 **of day by day** requiring days to tell, or covering a
long span of time   168 **abroad** anywhere else.   170 **requite** repay
172.1 *discovers* i.e., by opening a curtain, presumably rearstage
173 **play me false** cheat.   176–7 **Yes . . . play** i.e., Yes, even if we were
playing for twenty kingdoms, something less than the whole world,
you would still press your advantage against me, and I would lovingly let you do it as though it were fair play.   178 **vision** illusion
182 **compass** encompass, embrace   185 **brave** splendid, gorgeously
appareled, handsome

188 **eld'st** longest   202 **heaviness** sadness.   **inly** inwardly
205 **chalked . . . way** marked as with a piece of chalk the pathway
207 **Was Milan** Was the Duke of Milan.   **issue** child   214–15 **all . . .
own** all of us have found ourselves and our sanity when we all had
lost our senses.   216 **still** always.   **his** that person's   220 **blasphemy** i.e., blasphemer   221 **That swear'st grace o'erboard** i.e., you who
expel heavenly grace from the ship by your blasphemies.   **not an
oath** aren't you going to swear an oath

Our King and company; the next, our ship—
Which, but three glasses since, we gave out split— 225
Is tight and yare and bravely rigged as when 226
We first put out to sea.

ARIEL [*aside to Prospero*]   Sir, all this service
Have I done since I went.

PROSPERO [*aside to Ariel*]   My tricksy spirit! 228

ALONSO
These are not natural events; they strengthen 229
From strange to stranger. Say, how came you hither?

BOATSWAIN
If I did think, sir, I were well awake,
I'd strive to tell you. We were dead of sleep, 232
And—how we know not—all clapped under hatches,
Where but even now, with strange and several noises 234
Of roaring, shrieking, howling, jingling chains,
And more diversity of sounds, all horrible,
We were awaked; straightway at liberty;
Where we, in all her trim, freshly beheld
Our royal, good, and gallant ship, our Master
Cap'ring to eye her. On a trice, so please you, 240
Even in a dream, were we divided from them 241
And were brought moping hither.

ARIEL [*aside to Prospero*]   Was't well done? 242

PROSPERO [*aside to Ariel*]
Bravely, my diligence. Thou shalt be free.

ALONSO
This is as strange a maze as e'er men trod,
And there is in this business more than nature
Was ever conduct of. Some oracle 246
Must rectify our knowledge.

PROSPERO   Sir, my liege,
Do not infest your mind with beating on 248
The strangeness of this business. At picked leisure, 249
Which shall be shortly, single I'll resolve you, 250
Which to you shall seem probable, of every 251
These happened accidents; till when, be cheerful 252
And think of each thing well. [*Aside to Ariel*] Come
   hither, spirit. 253
Set Caliban and his companions free.
Untie the spell.   [*Exit Ariel.*]
   [*To Alonso*]   How fares my gracious sir?
There are yet missing of your company
Some few odd lads that you remember not. 257

Enter Ariel, driving in Caliban, Stephano, and
Trinculo, in their stolen apparel.

STEPHANO   Every man shift for all the rest, and let no 258
man take care for himself; for all is but fortune. *Corag*- 259

gio, bully monster, *coraggio!* 260

TRINCULO   If these be true spies which I wear in my 261
head, here's a goodly sight.

CALIBAN
O Setebos, these be brave spirits indeed! 263
How fine my master is! I am afraid 264
He will chastise me.

SEBASTIAN   Ha, ha!
What things are these, my lord Antonio?
Will money buy 'em?

ANTONIO   Very like. One of them
Is a plain fish, and no doubt marketable.

PROSPERO
Mark but the badges of these men, my lords, 270
Then say if they be true. This misshapen knave, 271
His mother was a witch, and one so strong
That could control the moon, make flows and ebbs,
And deal in her command without her power. 274
These three have robbed me, and this demidevil—
For he's a bastard one—had plotted with them 276
To take my life. Two of these fellows you
Must know and own. This thing of darkness I 278
Acknowledge mine.

CALIBAN   I shall be pinched to death.

ALONSO
Is not this Stephano, my drunken butler?

SEBASTIAN   He is drunk now. Where had he wine?

ALONSO
And Trinculo is reeling ripe. Where should they 282
Find this grand liquor that hath gilded 'em? 283
[*To Trinculo*] How cam'st thou in this pickle? 284

TRINCULO   I have been in such a pickle since I saw you
last that, I fear me, will never out of my bones. I shall
not fear flyblowing. 287

SEBASTIAN   Why, how now, Stephano?

STEPHANO   Oh, touch me not! I am not Stephano, but a
cramp.

PROSPERO   You'd be king o'the isle, sirrah? 291

STEPHANO   I should have been a sore one, then. 292

ALONSO [*pointing to Caliban*]
This is a strange thing as e'er I looked on.

PROSPERO
He is as disproportioned in his manners
As in his shape.—Go, sirrah, to my cell.
Take with you your companions. As you look
To have my pardon, trim it handsomely. 297

---

225 **glasses** hourglasses.   **gave out split** reported shipwrecked, gave up for lost   226 **yare** ready.   **bravely** splendidly   228 **tricksy** ingenious, sportive   229 **strengthen** increase   232 **dead of sleep** deep in sleep   234 **several** diverse   240 **Cap'ring to eye** dancing for joy to see.   **On a trice** In an instant   241 **them** i.e., the other crew members   242 **moping** in a daze   246 **conduct** director   248 **infest** harass, disturb.   **beating on** worrying about   249 **picked** chosen, convenient   250 **single** privately.   **resolve** satisfy, explain to   251 **probable** plausible   251–2 **of every These** about every one of these   252 **accidents** occurrences   253 **well** favorably.   257 **odd** unaccounted for   258–9 **Every . . . himself** (Stephano drunkenly inverts the saying "Every man for himself.")

259–60 *Coraggio . . . monster* Have courage, gallant monster   261 **true spies** accurate observers (i.e., sharp eyes)   263 **brave** handsome   264 **fine** splendidly attired   270 **badges** emblems worn by servants to indicate whom they serve   271 **say . . . true** say if they are worthy and loyal servants.   274 **And . . . power** and usurp the moon's command (over tides) without her authority. (Sycorax could control the moon and hence the tides.)   276 **bastard** counterfeit   278 **own** acknowledge.   282 **reeling ripe** staggeringly drunk.   283 **gilded 'em** flushed their complexion (from the drink), giving them a ruddy or gilded appearance.   284 **pickle** (1) fix, predicament (2) pickling brine (in this case, horse urine).   287 **flyblowing** i.e., being fouled by fly eggs (from which he is saved by being pickled).   291 **sirrah** (Standard form of address to an inferior, here expressing reprimand.)   292 **sore** (1) tyrannical (2) sorry, inept (3) wracked by pain   297 **trim** prepare, decorate

CALIBAN
    Ay, that I will; and I'll be wise hereafter
    And seek for grace. What a thrice-double ass   299
    Was I to take this drunkard for a god
    And worship this dull fool!
PROSPERO   Go to. Away!
ALONSO
    Hence, and bestow your luggage where you found it.
SEBASTIAN   Or stole it, rather.
               [Exeunt Caliban, Stephano, and Trinculo.]
PROSPERO
    Sir, I invite Your Highness and your train
    To my poor cell, where you shall take your rest
    For this one night; which, part of it, I'll waste   306
    With such discourse as, I not doubt, shall make it
    Go quick away: the story of my life,
    And the particular accidents gone by   309
    Since I came to this isle. And in the morn
    I'll bring you to your ship, and so to Naples,
    Where I have hope to see the nuptial
    Of these our dear-belovèd solemnized;
    And thence retire me to my Milan, where
    Every third thought shall be my grave.
ALONSO   I long
    To hear the story of your life, which must
    Take the ear strangely.
PROSPERO   I'll deliver all;   317
    And promise you calm seas, auspicious gales,
    And sail so expeditious that shall catch   319
    Your royal fleet far off. *[Aside to Ariel]* My Ariel, chick, 320

299 grace pardon, favor.   **306 waste** spend   **309 accidents** occurrences   **317 Take** take effect upon, enchant.   **deliver** declare, relate
319–20 catch . . . far off enable you to catch up with the main part of
your royal fleet, now afar off en route to Naples. (See 1.2.235–6.)

    That is thy charge. Then to the elements
    Be free, and fare thou well!
               [To the others] Please you, draw near. 322
                    Exeunt omnes [except Prospero].

Epilogue   *Spoken by* PROSPERO.

    Now my charms are all o'erthrown,
    And what strength I have 's mine own,
    Which is most faint. Now, 'tis true,
    I must be here confined by you
    Or sent to Naples. Let me not,
    Since I have my dukedom got
    And pardoned the deceiver, dwell
    In this bare island by your spell,
    But release me from my bands   9
    With the help of your good hands.   10
    Gentle breath of yours my sails   11
    Must fill, or else my project fails,
    Which was to please. Now I want   13
    Spirits to enforce, art to enchant,
    And my ending is despair,
    Unless I be relieved by prayer,   16
    Which pierces so that it assaults   17
    Mercy itself, and frees all faults.   18
    As you from crimes would pardoned be,   19
    Let your indulgence set me free.   *Exit.* 20

322 draw near i.e., enter my cell.
Epilogue.
9 bands bonds   **10 hands** i.e., applause (the noise of which could
break a charm).   **11 Gentle breath** Favorable breeze (produced by
hands clapping or favorable comment)   **13 want** lack   **16 prayer** i.e.,
Prospero's petition to the audience   **17 assaults** penetrates the heart
of   **18 frees** obtains forgiveness for   **19 crimes** sins   **20 indulgence**
(1) humoring, lenient approval (2) remission of punishment for sin

The Tempest on Stage

During its long stage history, productions of *The Tempest*—a play about a man who puts on shows—have
ranged from the ultra-spectacular to minimalist. The
former approach has dominated the world's stages, as
producers have created lavish spectacles, sometimes to
the detriment of the text. In 1889 the McVickers Theater in Chicago decorated the play so ornately that it
took eight minutes to change the scenery between the
first two scenes; fifty percent of the text was cut to
allow for other lengthy scene shifts.

The Elizabethan Era: At Whitehall
and the Blackfriars

Thanks to the influence of Inigo Jones's Italianate
scenery, a performance at Whitehall in 1611—and at the
Banqueting Hall two years later—would probably have

been staged more elaborately than at the King's Men's
principal theaters, the Globe and the Blackfriars.
Machinery was typically available in royal performance
spaces that could be used to fly in the trio of goddesses
for the masque, as well as a *"quaint device"* or two for
other of the play's magical moments. Scenic backdrops,
'"wave machines" (painted canvases mounted on
revolving cylinders suggesting the movement of the
sea), and cloud machines may have combined to create
a thrilling storm in the opening minutes. The Globe and
Blackfriars also had devices for lowering and raising
deities (the text of *The Tempest* at 4.1.72 reads, *"Juno
descends,"* and in *Cymbeline*, Jupiter descends from the
heavens), but in many ways the scenic devices at court
were substantially more elaborate than those available
to Shakespeare. He does make effective use of the so-
called "discovery space" backstage when Prospero
draws a curtain and *"discovers Ferdinand and Miranda,
playing at chess"* (5.1, after l.172).

The Seventeenth and Eighteenth Centuries: An Opera and Other Diversions

Like other of Shakespeare's plays, *The Tempest* was altered by the artists who reopened the theaters after the Interregnum of 1642–1660. In 1667 John Dryden and William Davenant substantially revised the play, presenting it as *The Enchanted Isle*. Samuel Pepys, the diarist and avid theatergoer, called their lighthearted revision "the most innocent play I ever saw." To satisfy the neoclassical penchant for symmetry and perhaps to intensify the theme of innocence in a fallen world, Dryden and Davenant invented a sister for Miranda named Dorinda and another for Caliban named Sycorax. Miranda's innocence was paralleled with that of another added character, Hippolito, a young man who has never seen a woman. Hippolito's presence thus conveniently provided Dorinda with someone to marry. Ariel too was given a romantic companion named Milcha. Davenant composed such bawdy language for his innocents that the tone of the play is changed substantially. The murderous plot devised by Antonio and Sebastian was excised, while "eight fat spirits with Corn-o-Copia" were added to the wedding masque. Prospero's role was substantially diminished to that of a "master of cheap ceremonies" (Spencer, 203). The renunciation of his powers, the moving "We are such stuff / As dreams are made on," and other critical speeches by Prospero, were deleted. To satisfy audience tastes, the composers added music generously, including a charming "echo song" between Ariel and Ferdinand.

In 1674 Thomas Shadwell turned the Dryden-Davenant script into even more of an opera and visual extravaganza, inventing such spectacles as a rising sun, a chorus of devils, and a ballet of Winds and Tritons, along with an ensemble of twenty-four musicians. Shadwell's description of the storm suggests the visual appeal late–seventeenth-century audiences demanded: " . . . a thick, Cloudy Sky, a very Rocky Coast, and a Tempestuous Sea in perpetual Agitation. This Tempest (supposed to be raised by Magic) has many dreadful objects in it, as several spirits in horrid shapes flying down among the Sailors . . . and when the ship is sinking, the whole house is darkened, and a shower of fire falls upon them." The Shadwell opera was revived as recently as 1959 at London's Old Vic Theatre, and in 1983 an RSC production included music from the opera in the masque.

Because it was well received, Shadwell's opera became the standard version of *The Tempest* available until the great actor-manager, David Garrick, partly restored Shakespeare's text at the Drury Lane in 1757, a year after attempting his own thirty-two–song operatic version of *The Tempest*. That opera failed, and Garrick returned to the original text (minus about four hundred lines), billing the play as "written by Shakespeare," a novel concept for its time. In 1787 John Philip Kemble created a pastiche opera, using bits from Dryden *et al.*, Shakespeare, and some stage business of his own invention.

The Nineteenth Century: Spectacles and Calibans

In 1838 William Charles Macready, among the nineteenth century's most admired Prosperos, restored much of Shakespeare's text, and his acting edition became the standard text for much of the century. At the same time, most nineteenth-century productions of *The Tempest* continued and substantially expanded the tradition of visually opulent staging begun by Dryden. Two examples can illustrate just how spectacular the productions became throughout Europe and America. The storm sequence at the McVickers Theater (1889), in the tradition of Charles Kean's lavish London production of 1857, included a full-scale sailing vessel, described by a reviewer for the *Chicago Inter-Ocean*: "The swift-passing clouds, penetrated ever and anon by vivid flashes of lightning, the beating waves, ominous in darkness, and the huge ship that comes plunging into view, its decks crowded with people, and is finally driven upon the rocks as a lightning stroke shivers its mast, makes a remarkably realistic picture" (Nilan, 119). In 1904 Sir Herbert Beerbohm Tree, whose Shakespearean spectacles at Her Majesty's Theatre epitomized nineteenth-century scenic excess as that tradition continued on into the early years of the twentieth century, invented a pantomime to bridge Acts 1 and 2 described in his prompt books follows:

> As Ariel exits from Prospero's cell [which contained a library and a couch for Miranda to sleep upon], there is a blackout. The curtain and gauze comes down. "Come Unto These Yellow Sands" is sung by the offstage chorus. As the chorus starts, the curtain goes up in the dark and lights gradually come up to purple, disclosing Nymphs playing in the waters and on the sands. Four Nymphs on wires are behind the first water row. On the last lines of the song, lights actually check down. Nymphs go off slowly behind rocks R[ight] and L[eft] and lights gradually come up amber, revealing the yellow sands.

In the Shadwell opera and throughout the eighteenth century, Caliban was customarily played as a grotesquely comic character in keeping with the lighter tone of the revised play. When, on the other hand, poet Samuel Taylor Coleridge lectured on *The Tempest* in the early nineteenth century, arguing that Caliban had the poetic temperament to elevate him above a mere brute, readers and theater artists took new look at the character, with the result that stage renderings of Caliban became more sympathetic. In Macready's celebrated 1838 revival, George Bennet, an accomplished tragedian, played Caliban as a victim of Prospero's oppression. The actor invented a famous piece of stage business, still often used: Caliban lunged at Prospero during their first encounter, only to be repelled by the sorcerer's magic wand. In 1854 William Evans Burton, a famed American comedian, actually downplayed Caliban's traditional comicality in favor of a "romantic rebel" interpretation. The New York *Times* called Burton's invention "an immense conception," further noting, "Not the great God Pan himself was more the link between the man and beast than this thing."

Charles Darwin's *On the Origin of Species* (1859) provided theater artists with a further elaboration of this approach to Caliban. In 1873 Daniel Wilson published *Caliban: The Missing Link,* drawing connections between Shakespeare's play and Darwin's controversial theories; for Wilson, Caliban was an "intermediate being, between true brute and man." Frank Benson, who staged Shakespeare's plays at Stratford-upon-Avon in the 1890s, actually went to the London zoo to observe apes and monkeys as he prepared his production of *The Tempest,* deciding finally that Caliban ought to enter with a fish in his mouth. An American stage director, Augustin Daly, produced the play in 1897, costuming Caliban as a human covered in brown fur with fish-like scales about his legs. Beerbohm Tree covered Caliban in seaweed and shells to indicate that he was half-man, half-fish. Tree's was among the most sympathetic portraits of Caliban to that time, as the director invented a final tableau in which the character was left forlornly on a rock to watch the departing ship. Darwinian renderings of Caliban persisted well into the mid twentieth century. In 1938 Robert Atkins presented Caliban as a Neanderthal. Such interpretations later gave way to more sociopolitical concerns as Caliban became a symbol of colonial oppression.

The Twentieth Century: Tempests, Plain and Spangled

Peter Brook's 1957 production at the Shakespeare Memorial Theatre in Stratford-upon-Avon marked a turning point in the play's stage history by telling Prospero's tale in simpler—and perhaps more cynical—terms than had previous directors. The opening scene used a single lantern swinging wildly toward the audience to suggest the storm. Only the masque was staged spectacularly to invest it with a glory that contrasted with the spare staging before and after it. John Gielgud, playing Prospero for his third time, fought between his impulse to revenge his wrongs and the desire to reconcile, thus giving the character a greater inner conflict than in his earlier readings. A dozen years later Brook adapted the play for London's Roundhouse Theatre, showing how influenced he had been by his recent experimentation with Artaud's Theater of Cruelty. In this experimental work, more an adaptation of *The Tempest* than an interpretation, Caliban became a primitive rebel who rapes Miranda and sodomizes Prospero after taking over the island.

Among Gielgud's best performances as Prospero was that in 1974 at the National Theatre of Great Britain under Peter Hall's direction. To be sure, the director made far too much of his mistaken belief that Shakespeare wrote *The Tempest* as a response to the shift in Jacobean England to indoor theaters and their scenic possibilities. As a result, the production used self-consciously theatrical gimmicks as the vehicle through which the isle's magic was realized; for instance, Hall recreated a Jacobean court masque as designed by Inigo Jones and employed wing-and-shutter scenery for patently artificial locale shifts. To create the illusion that Ariel exists only in Prospero's mind, the sprite "flew" on an obvious trapeze above his master's head (shades of Brook's *Dream* at the RSC four years earlier?). Still, Gielgud's performance was extraordinary: it was the despairing cry of a disillusioned and world-weary man, who revealed in his epilogue a more melancholic and more introspective vision than had been customary.

In the last third of the twentieth century, directors have seemed less intrigued by the play's visual possibilities than by its politics. Numerous productions have deconstructed *The Tempest* in such a way as to comment on the colonization of the Third World and on racist prejudice directed at nonwhites. To be sure, the idea was not entirely new in the 1960s. As early as 1934 Caliban was portrayed at London's Old Vic as a black man under the control of a white master, even if he was still played by a white (Roger Livesay) who "blacked up" because such key roles were usually not available to minorities. In a 1945 production directed by Margaret Webster, Canada Lee, an African American, broke the color barrier by playing Caliban in a fish-like costume with a grotesque mask. As the American Civil Rights Movement opened opportunities for black actors (James Earl Jones, Earl Hyman), the part of Caliban in *The Tempest* became a vehicle for venting black anger, notably at the Washington, D.C., Shakespeare Festival where Henry Baker played Caliban as "a black militant, angry and recalcitrant" (Vaughan and Vaughan, 191).

Perhaps the best known of the anti-imperialist *Tempest*s was that staged by Jonathan Miller (London, 1970); Caliban and Ariel were portrayed as blacks subjugated by Prospero. Critic Benedict Nightingale described the Caliban of this production as "a tattered field nigger" and the Ariel as a fastidious, well-dressed gentleman's man. Other productions have elaborated upon this concept. One—put on by Tina Packer's Shakespeare & Company, 1980—even added a black Stephano, who, ironically, made a slave of the black Caliban. Director George C. Wolfe's multicultural *Tempest* for the New York Shakespeare Festival in the mid-1980s presented a black Ariel and a black Caliban, competing with each other in their hatred of Prospero. Perhaps no production offered a more venomous Ariel than that staged by Sam Mendes for the Royal Shakespeare Company in 1993: after Prospero set him free ("Be free, and fare thou well!" 5.1.322), Ariel spat in Prospero's face, thereby giving new meaning to the Prospero's next line ("Now my charms all o'erthrown"). Other productions went beyond black-white relations. In 1981 Los Angeles's Globe Playhouse portrayed Caliban as an American Indian; he was the embodiment of both American colonialism and the cannibals in Montaigne's essay. In 1989 the Old Vic portrayed Caliban as a Jamaican Rastafarian. In Peter Brook's most recent production of *The Tempest* (Paris, 1990), roles were dramatically reversed as Caliban was played by a white actor while Prospero and Ariel were played by blacks.

Such "colonialist" *Tempest*s seem to have lost their potency through overexposure. Productions over the past twenty years have, in the main, returned to the Caliban-as-monster motif. Among the more grotesque Calibans of recent years is that at the National Theatre in London (dir., Peter Hall, 1988), a vile being "covered in blood and slime with Frankenstein-like teeth," wrote critic Jill Pearce (Vaughan and Vaughan, 196). Other Calibans have included a monstrosity with three-foot stools strapped to his legs (Trinity Repertory Theater, 1982) and as a punk rocker in sunglasses (New York, 1982). In Mendes's 1993 production for the RSC (see above), the actor playing Caliban wore a one-word sign on his chest: "Monster."

A number of European and Asian productions have invested *The Tempest* with especially inventive magic. In 1978 Giorgio Strehler directed the play for the Piccolo Teatro di Milano and for European and American tours, including a run at the 1984 Olympic Arts Festival in Los Angeles. Strehler used an essentially bare stage dominated by a huge white sail on a fixed mast. After the tempest—which relied solely on flashes of lightning to suggest its chaos—the lights revealed a portion of a ship's deck that doubled as the stage of a makeshift theater. Ariel, costumed as Pierrot and suspended from a wire, flew above the stage and, through a trick of perspective, actually seemed to dance on Prospero's outstretched hand. In Act 5 Prospero freed Ariel simply by detaching the wire from his harness. As Prospero spoke the Epilogue and broke his staff, the entire stage disintegrated to reveal the shabby bricks of the theater and a tattered curtain. In a 1983 production in Madrid, directed by Argentina's Jorge Lavelli, Prospero was played by Spain's leading actress, Nuria Espert, bringing a feminist perspective to the role. The Ariel to this "Prospera" was an entirely imaginary and unseen creature whose recorded lines were played in multitrack stereo. In 1992 in Japan (and later Edinburgh and London) Yukio Ninagawa dramatized Shakespeare's tale as if it were a combination of the ancient Noh theater and the populist Kabuki, two theatrical forms frequently depicting magic and miraculous transformations. Caliban appeared in exotic Kabuki makeup, while the masque was presented as a Noh ritual, an appropriate choice given the fact that *kami* (godplays) are one of the five principal types of Noh drama. Also in 1992, Minoru Fujita, one of Japan's revered puppet masters, created a Bunraku *Tempest* that transformed Shakespeare's drama of reconciliation into a revenge play about feuding war lords in the manner of Japan's esteemed playwright Chikamatsu Monzeon (often referred to as "the Japanese Shakespeare").

Other international productions have similarly used Shakespeare's text as a means to dramatize political conflict. A 1959 Polish production (directed by Krystyna Skuszanka) portrayed Prospero as the symbol of Poland-in-exile under Communist rule. As South Africa struggled to abolish apartheid in 1989, Pretoria audiences witnessed an Afrikaans language version of *The Tempest* that made a strong political statement. Hans Pinaar, writing for Pretoria's *Weekly Mail*, evaluated the production: "All kinds of startling insights into the nature of colonialism emerge. These are wonderfully exposed through the simple move of casting Peter Sephuma in the role of Caliban, wearing no elaborate "monster" costume but his own black-is-beautiful skin" (Rohan Quince, 141). Predictably, Latin American and Caribbean nations have also found political parallels in the play, largely in response to the Cuban poet Roberto Fernandez Retamar's manifesto, "Caliban" (1971). He asks "What is our history, what is our culture, if not the history and culture of Caliban?" Some important derivative plays influenced by Retamar's essay are discussed below as spin-offs.

The Tempest on Film and Television

Curiously, *The Tempest* has a remarkably limited history on film and television, even though those media seem ideally suited to creating special effects to visualize the magic and mystery of Prospero's island. The play has actually enjoyed greater success in the cinema when its story has been transformed to other eras and locales (see "Spin-offs" below, pp. 860–861), and even the two principal films (Derek Jarman's and Peter Greenaway's) are adaptations rather than faithful renderings of Shakespeare's text. Two primary explanations can be offered for the play's paucity of film/video productions:

- Because the text relies on poetic descriptions to establish the isle's magic, the primarily visual media of film and television render Shakespeare's words superfluous.

- The play's ultimate magic rests in a theatrical—as opposed to cinematic—rendering of the text. We know that film and television can create magic through electronic gimmickry, but there is something even more compelling when such feats are created in a space shared with the audience.

Several silent films have attempted to acquaint audiences with Prospero's isle. In 1908 Englishman Percy Snow filmed an eleven-minute "prequel" that illustrated things talked about, but not shown, in the play: Prospero's arrival on the island with books and baby Miranda in hand, the discovery of Caliban, and Ariel's release from the tree. Ariel, played by a young girl, was transformed into a monkey in the film's most inventive shot. Snow concluded his film where Shakespeare begins his play, with Alonso's ship on a storm-tossed sea. Other silent film versions were made in America (1911; no longer extant) and France (1912). The first sound version of the play was actually performed for BBC television in 1939, featuring a young Peggy Ashcroft as Miranda. The BBC made another low-budget version of the play in 1956.

The major film and video versions include:

■ 1960—Director George Schaefer, NBC Television: Hallmark Hall of Fame, with Maurice Evans (Prospero), Lee Remick (Miranda), and Richard Burton (Caliban). (90 min.)

Cut to ninety minutes for television, Schaefer's televised *Tempest* features an exceptional cast, especially Richard Burton as Caliban, deemed "unforgettable" by a number of critics. Given Burton's extraordinary voice and verse-speaking skills, he remains among the most intellectual and anti-primitive interpreters of Caliban in memory. Schaefer treats the play lightly, calling it a "soufflé;" thus some of its darker and more philosophical elements are absent. Other than some photographic tricks that make Ariel appear mere inches high or a towering figure above the villains, Schaefer's rendering of *The Tempest* is mostly a film of a stage version.

■ 1980—Director John Gorrie, BBC Television: The Shakespeare Plays Series, with Michael Hordern (Prospero), Derek Godfrey (Caliban), and Pippa Guard (Miranda). (150 min.)

Although this remains the most accessible film and television version of *The Tempest*, the best that can be said about Gorrie's production is that it is "serviceable"—that is, it is a faithful rendering of Shakespeare's text, thanks largely to Sir Michael Hordern's intelligent reading of Prospero. Like Gielgud, Hordern has played the role a number of times in his career. Despite some attempts to create magic (e.g., the mysterious appearances of Ariel are effected through chroma-key, much as a TV weatherman is superimposed over a map), the BBC *Tempest* is neither particularly theatrical nor cinematic. Although filmed on a 360-degree soundstage to allow for fluidity of action, the production is so conventional that, as a London *Times* review has put it, "there was nothing to stir the blood either to hot flashes of anger or to the electric joy of a new experience. What

we got was some more of the BBC's ghastly middle taste" (Stanley Reynolds, Feb. 28, 1980). The wedding masque, potentially a visual highlight of the play, is marred by some remarkably clumsy dancing.

■ 1980—*The Tempest: by William Shakespeare, as Seen Through the Eyes of Derek Jarman.* Director Derek Jarman, World Northal Films, with Heathcote Williams (Prospero), Jack Birkett (Caliban), and Toyah Wilcox (Miranda). (95 min.)

As its title suggests, Jarman's film does not attempt to recreate Shakespeare's play. Instead, it is a low-budget, *avant-garde* experiment that has outraged many critics. The *New York Times* dismissed it as "nearly unbearable. It's a fingernail scratched on a blackboard, sand in spinach." Jarman's work has captivated other commentators: "Though often bizarre . . . it is genuinely moving and the emotions it arouses are essentially those aroused by Shakespeare's play" (Jackson and Harris). Jarman, a British filmmaker who apprenticed under *enfant terrible* Ken Russell, heavily cuts and restructures the play to create an essentially new work set on "an island of the mind." Some of his inventions are shocking, even to experienced cineastes (those devoted to movies). For example, Sycorax, played as "an obese, naked sorceress, heavily made up and smoking a hookah," breast-feeds a fully grown Caliban, a slobbering voyeuristic monster acted by the blind performance artist Jack Birkett (also known as the Incredible Orlando). The wedding masque, attended by Alonso and his companions, becomes a big band event in which an African American woman (Elisabeth Welch) sings Harold Arlen's classic blues song, "Stormy Weather"—a not necessarily inappropriate choice of music. Other of Jarman's choices seem more campy than thoughtful: Trinculo is portrayed as a drag queen, whistled at adoringly by the male crew of Alonso's ship. Ultimately, Jarman's film emerges as a collage of bizarre images, the antithesis of a play that celebrates harmony. As scholars Lynda Boose and Richard Burt point out in "Totally Clueless" (the introductory essay to their critical anthology *Shakespeare: The Movie*), both Jarman and Peter Greenaway are not only deconstructing "Shakespeare as author, but his radical displacement by the film director; and the interest in any of these films could legitimately be said to lie less in its relation to Shakespeare's play than in its relation to the director's own previous *oeuvre*" (11).

Adaptations

■ 1991—*Prospero's Books.* Director Peter Greenaway, Palace Films, et al., with John Gielgud (Prospero). (129 min.)

Greenaway's mannerist film also has proved controversial, though it has not been denounced in such strident terms as has Jarman's. Much of the film owes its genius to the late John Gielgud, who at eighty-seven years of age had already played Prospero more often than any actor of note in the twentieth century. Gielgud reads Prospero's lines, along with those of all other characters, with unparalleled brilliance. The film exhibits a visual richness focused upon a few recurring images— water, ships, books, the naked human form—to create an imagistic, if not thematic, coherence. Greenaway does not interpret the play, per se; rather, he vividly illustrates the process through which the artist (Shakespeare? Prospero? Gielgud? Greenaway?) conceives a tale such as *The Tempest*. Numerous close-ups of Prospero's hand meticulously inscribing Shakespeare's words in a rich italic script dominate the screen; these shots dissolve into hallucinatory images inspired by the text. Greenaway uses, in his words, "a complex visual cascade" by freely mixing film, high definition video, digital formats, mirrors, and frames-within-frames to "celebrate the text as text, as the master material on which all the magic, illusion, and deception on which the play is based" (Greenaway, 9). He thus creates a phantasmagoria to illustrate both Shakespeare's play and the twenty-four books Prospero has prized above his kingdom. Many images are uncomfortably graphic: we see Ariel urinating on the storm-tossed ship and later we see the Caesarian birth of a child. Most of Greenaway's images are cinematic renderings of Renaissance paintings by Botticelli, Caravaggio, and Messina. Accordingly, the film places a particular emphasis on nudity. Scores of naked men and women of all shapes and ages robotically dance across the director's postmodern landscape to the tune of quasi-Elizabethan electronic music. Greenaway's most intriguing inspiration shows Caliban retrieving Prospero's "final" book after the old sorcerer drowns his library in the finale. That book, *The Tempest*, is placed reverently at the front of the 1623 Folio in the film's concluding shot. In a film with numerous enigmas, Greenaway's most perplexing choice exhibits not one but four Ariels of varying ages. To those familiar with the play and with Renaissance iconography, Greenaway's film often illuminates Shakespeare's text, if disconcertingly so at times; the film's self-consciously artificial images are not at odds with the play's exploration of art's ability to create illusions. To many, however, *The Tempest* according to Greenaway may remain mysterious, even impenetrable. Six years after the film was released, Gielgud, the star of the film and its incessant center of attention, told the *Sunday Times* he felt Greenaway "didn't know the point of the play."

Spin-offs

Several spin-offs are perhaps more successful in capturing the spirit of the original play than most film and video versions of *The Tempest*.

Yellow Sky (1948), directed by William Wellman from a screenplay by LaMar Trotti, relocates *The Tempest* to the American Wild West. A gang of bank robbers, led by the villainous Stretch (Gregory Peck), wander into a ghost town looking for a hideout. An old prospector and his daughter foil the plans of the outlaws, who attempt to rape the daughter but are punished through the old man's mysterious powers. However suspenseful and action-packed the film may be, it offers in its denouement the harsh poetic justice of an O.K. Corral–like gun fight instead of reconciliation and harmony.

The classic derivative of *The Tempest* is the 1954 science fiction film, *Forbidden Planet*, produced by Cyril Hume and directed by Fred McLoud. One London reviewer, characterizing it as "*The Tempest* in space suits," heralded it as "the most rumbustiously enjoyable of all Hollywood planetary melodramas" (Rosenthal, 150). The film's million-dollar budget made it the most expensive and creative sci-fi film to that time. Prospero's island is relocated to the remote planet of Altair-1, where a spaceship, the *Belephron*, has crashed-landed in 2257 C.E. The planet is ruled by Dr. Morbius, a "mad scientist," attended by a robot named Robbie (cf. Ariel). Morbius has discovered a long-lost race of technocrats, the Krel, whom he believes will achieve Utopia. When Morbius's scientific experiments go awry, they unleash an enormous flesh-eating monster in the style of Japanese horror films. The mad doctor ultimately sacrifices himself to save his daughter Altaira, Commander Adams (Ferdinand), and his astronauts. The film, released as the Russians were preparing to launch the first satellite into space, warns of the misuse of science even as it celebrates science as the sorcery of the twentieth century. These topics were calculated to appeal to audiences in the Atomic Age. Despite its somber message, *Forbidden Planet* is a consistently enjoyable, often funny, film that, in sci-fi writer Arthur Clark's estimation, "conveys the wonder and strangeness of space" (Sammons, 145).

Paul Mazursky's *The Tempest* (1982) is a contemporary telling of Shakespeare's tale that is more a witty comedy of manners about "beautiful people" than a classical romance of the 1980s. Phil (Prospero; John Cassavetes), a cynical New York architect, abandons the comforts of his sterile, materialistic world in favor of the Greek islands, where he and his daughter (Molly Ringwald) seek the roots of the classical culture. They are joined by a free-spirited woman, Aretha (Ariel, Susan Sarandon), who tries to seduce Phil. The trio lands on an Aegean island inhabited by a crude goatherd, Kalibanos (Raul Julia), who has learned his language from American television and knows all its clichés. Phil's supernatural powers enable him to draw to the island the yacht of his archenemy, a Mafioso (Vittorio Gassman). Former animosities are eventually forgotten, and the film ends with a melancholy tango before Phil and his daughter sail back to New York. The best dance is that performed by Kalibanos's goats as the Dionysian goatherd plays "New York, New York" on a clarinet. Although such inventive touches attempt to parallel the spirit of *The Tempest*, Mazursky's overlong (2:20) film only "skims the surface of Shakespeare's play, without reaching its soul—leaving *Tempest* as a very pale imitation" (Rosenthal, 154).

The Tempest, a 1998 American Civil War version of Shakespeare's play, involves a Southern gentleman, Gideon Prosper (Peter Fonda), who rejects slavery and fights with his heartless brother for control of the family's plantation. Gideon and his daughter are forced to escape to the bayous, where he is aided by the ghost of a murdered slave (cf. Ariel) and some voodoo magic that Gideon learns from slaves. As the Union Army advances upon the plantation, the warring brothers are reunited during a horrific storm; the siblings are reconciled as the film ends with the freeing of the slaves. Although it is an ingenious and engaging variant on Shakespeare's story, the film replaces metaphysics with sociology and poetry with Southern colloquialisms.

The Tempest has inspired several contemporary playwrights, most notably from the Caribbean and Latin America, whose revised versions challenge our assumptions about Shakespeare's play. A 1969 Creole play called *Une tempte*, by Aimé Césaire, from the island of Martinique, was revived in London in 1998 to mark the one-hundred-fiftieth anniversary of the abolition of slavery in French colonies. In Césaire's drama Caliban accuses Prospero of "lying to me, lying about the world, lying about yourself, and imposing an image of myself . . . and I hate that image!" In 1977 Derek Walcott, the first Caribbean dramatist to win the Nobel Prize for Literature, wrote *Remembrance*, a one-act featuring a play-within-the-play in which Caliban and Ariel discuss liberation as they rehearse Shakespeare's drama. Staged at Havana's Teatro Buendia in 1998, *Otra Tempestad* (*Another Tempest*), by playwrights Raquel Carrio and Flora Lauten, is a fifteen-scene play retaining some of Shakespeare's dialogue in order to contrast it with the colloquial speech of Cuba's poor. Prospero is a Columbus-figure whose expeditions to the New World are financed by Shylock, a Venetian merchant. Caliban is only a muted figure in the play, while Sycorax and the three goddesses of the masque—represented as Afro-Cuban spirits called *orishas*—are central to the action. The play concludes with the death of Miranda, a victim of the island's exploitive patriarchal system.

References and Related Reading

Adelman, Janet. *Suffocating Mothers: Fantasies of Maternal Origins in Shakespeare's Plays, "Hamlet" to "The Tempest."* New York, 1992.

Auden, W. H. *The Sea and the Mirror.* London, 1942.

Boose, Lynda E., and Richard Burt, eds. *Shakespeare: The Movie, Popularizing the Plays on Film, TV, and Video.* New York, 1997.

Egan, Robert. *Drama within Drama: Shakespeare's Sense of His Art.* New York, 1975.

Frye, Northrop. *A Natural Perspective: The Development of Shakespeare's Comedy and Romance.* New York, 1965.

Greenaway, Peter. *Prospero's Books: A Film of Shakespeare's "The Tempest."* London, 1991.

Harris, Diana, and MacDonald Jackson, "Stormy Weather: Derek Jarman's *The Tempest*." *Shakespeare into Film.* Eds. James Welsh, et al. New York, 1998.

Hirst, David. *"The Tempest": Text and Performance.* London, 1984.

Kernan, Alvin. *The King's Playwright: Theater in the Stuart Court, 1603–1613.* New Haven, Conn., 2002.

Mannoni, Ottavio. *Prospero and Caliban: The Psychology of Colonization.* Trans. Pamela Powesland. New York, 1964.

Nightingale, Benedict. "The Tempest." *The New Statesman* 26 June 1970.

Nilan, Mary N. "*The Tempest* at the Turn of the Century: Cross Currents in Production." *Shakespeare Survey* 25 (1972).

Quince, Rohan. *Shakespeare in South Africa: Stage Productions during the Apartheid Era.* New York, 2000.

Retamar Fernandez, Roberto. *Caliban and Other Essays.* Trans. Edward Baker. Minneapolis, 1989.

Reynolds, Stanley. "The BBC's Ghastly Middle." *London Times* 28 Feb. 1980.

Rosenthal, Kenneth. *Shakespeare on Screen.* London, 2000.

Sammons, Eddie. *Shakespeare: A Hundred Years on Film.* Oxford, 2004.

Smith, Cecil. "A Dreadfully Leadfooted *Tempest.*" *Los Angeles Times* 7 May 1980.

Spencer, Hazelton. *Shakespeare Improved: The Restoration Versions in Quarto and On the Stage.* Cambridge, 1927.

Stockholder, Kay. "Sexual Magic and Magical Sex," unpublished paper (1989), quoted in Peter Donaldson, "Shakespeare in the Age of Post-Mechanical Reproduction: Sexual and Electronic Magic in *Prospero's Books.*" *Shakespeare: The Movie.* Eds. Lynda Boose and Richard Burt. New York, 1997. 169–185.

Trewin, J. C. *Going to Shakespeare.* London, 1978.

Vaughan, Alden T., and Virginia Mason Vaughan. *Shakespeare's Caliban: A Cultural History.* Cambridge, Eng., 1991. 192–193. Chapters 7 and 8 provide a comprehensive history of Caliban on stage and in film.

White, R. S., ed. New Casebooks: *The Tempest.* New York, 1999.

CLOSE-UP

JOHN GIELGUD

(1904–2000)

Sir John Gielgud was the last survivor of the triumvirate of British actors who dominated twentieth-century theater in England. Along with Laurence Olivier and Ralph Richardson, he revitalized Shakespeare in performance and inspired what became a golden age of classical theater. Although he was less celebrated toward the end of his life than Olivier (who died in 1989), Gielgud was considered unsurpassed during his era in the intelligence and humanity he brought to the roles of Hamlet, Henry IV, Cassius in *Julius Caesar*, Clarence in *Richard III*, and Prospero in *The Tempest*. As an actor, he was also known for his Romeo, his Angelo in *Measure for Measure,* his Benedick in *Much Ado About Nothing* (which he both performed in and directed for thirty years), as well as for his portrayals of most of the kings in the history plays. Equally at ease with comedy and tragedy, he also demonstrated his mastery of the actor's art in English comedies of the Restoration period (1660–1700), in plays by Oscar Wilde and Anton Chekhov, and in a range of plays by his contemporaries from George Bernard Shaw to Harold Pinter and David Storey.

Although some observers still debate whether his Hamlet—which was never filmed—outshone Olivier's, there is no argument that during his seventy years in the theater, Gielgud spoke Shakespeare's verse with as much insight, beauty, and musicality as the best of his peers. Fellow actor Alec Guinness called that singular voice "a silver trumpet muffled in silk." While Olivier was praised for his versatility and physical daring, and Richardson for his eccentric, comic characterizations, Gielgud's gift was for language, the rhythms and textures of the spoken word. Fortunately many of his Shakespeare performances were recorded on film, television, and radio, and thus can still be seen and heard. The most important of these included his portrayal of a smooth, sleek, increasingly hot-tempered Cassius in the 1953 Joseph Mankiewicz film of *Julius Caesar* (with Marlon Brando as Marc Antony and James Mason as Brutus); his short but potent appearance as Clarence in the *Richard III* film directed by and starring Olivier; his role as the regal, cool, and judgmental father figure, Henry IV, in Orson Welles's *Falstaff:*

Chimes at Midnight; and his magician/playwright Prospero in Peter Greenaway's *Prospero's Books* (1991). Even in his eighties, Gielgud's voice remained, as one *New York Times* reviewer described it in 1988, "supple . . . always oboe-like in its poetic flow and timbre." Beyond his career as an actor, Gielgud's work as a producer and director of an ensemble-based company also left an imprint upon subsequent interpreters of Shakespeare in the theater.

He was born into a theatrical family. Both grandmothers were actors. His father's mother was the Polish star Mme. Aszberger and his mother's mother was Kate Terry, the older sister of the legendary Ellen Terry, whom he saw often and adored, both as an eccentric, loving relative and as a stage artist. Gielgud's passion for theater began when he was seven years old and was given a Victorian toy theater for Christmas. This precious plaything became the center of his fancy for many years. His fascinated play with that toy first revealed how inner-directed and multitalented the boy artist was and would remain. He built sets, created props, and by the age of nine considered himself a producer-director of the little theater, "The New Mars." His older brother Val was the house playwright. Their Slavic father was a natural musician (who became a wealthy stockbroker); young Jack Gielgud also played the piano brilliantly by ear. Yet when he announced that he wished to take his artistic abilities seriously by taking acting lessons instead of going to university, he had to promise his family that if he had not succeeded by the time he reached the age of twenty-five, he would abandon his professional dream and become an architect. Gielgud knew he was dreadful at math; working tirelessly, he instead met his parents' deadline to become an actor.

Gielgud studied at Lady Benson's School where he discovered he could summon emotion on cue and memorize lines, but was shy and ineffective physically. Practicing alone, he transformed his physical stiffness ("a cat with rickets" was how one teacher described him) into the image of a tall, elegant, ever youthful and energetic man. Although he has written that his professional debut as a supernumerary in *Henry V* at the Old Vic was a disaster, he did use his connections to land a position with a cousin's touring production of a melodrama titled *The Wheel*. He next attended the Royal Academy of Dramatic Arts where he studied for a year under the actor Claude Rains. Gielgud performed his first Shakespearean lead as Romeo. Soon thereafter, in 1930, came his first real success after a season of Shakespeare and Shaw at London's Old Vic. His triumph in a piece called *The Good Companions* led him into producing the Old Vic's *The Merchant of Venice* and then a play by Somerset Maugham. In 1933, his production of *Richard of Bordeaux* was a major success. He produced and directed the drama and played the lead. The play's author, Gordon Daviot (a pseudonym for writer Elizabeth Mackintosh), composed the piece shortly after seeing Gielgud in *Richard II*. Her romantic melodrama about Richard included elements of modern comedy. Gielgud suggested many editorial revisions to the playwright, assembled a quality company of actors, and was praised for delivering a moving, coherent production "flowing like music." He was called an actor "at the top of his profession" (Croall, 166). The play ran for a year in London, then toured the country. John Gielgud had made his mark.

Gielgud's production of *Romeo and Juliet* in 1935 became a landmark of the British theater. He and his friend Olivier alternated in the roles of Romeo and Mercutio. Gielgud was most praised as the romantic hero, Romeo, and Olivier as his wittily sardonic friend, Mercutio. Gielgud said that he and Oliver were "complete opposites." He described his friend as a "much more inventive impersonator than I ever was . . . larger than life in a wonderfully dynamic sort of way and I couldn't quite live up to that." The production also transformed the career of actor Peggy Ashcroft, who played Juliet and with whom Gielgud subsequently often appeared. They were most notably paired for many years as Beatrice and Benedick in a long-lived production that "confirmed Gielgud's belief in the value of working with an ensemble of top-class actors" (Croall, 207).

During Gielgud's second trip to the United States in 1937, he appeared as Hamlet, his third undertaking of the role. This Broadway debut brought high praise from critics and audiences. John Mason Brown noted "It will be Mr. Gielgud's voice in the future that we shall hear as the Prince of Denmark . . . such a voice, such diction and such a gift of maintaining the melody of Shakespeare's verse even while keeping it edged from speech to speech with dramatic significance is a new experience." Others described how he broke with tradition by speaking the soliloquies inwardly, rather than roaring with emotion as so many others had done in the part previously. His interpretation's foremost characteristic, wrote critic Laurence Kitchin, "was his speaking of Shakespeare's verse, though he was equally convincing in the prose passages. Then there was a sense of an incurable inward melancholy, offset when called for by flashes of cynical humor. A brooding stage presence and stage gestures natural to a Tudor aristocrat bred on Castiglione's *Courtier* controlled the surface" (Kitchin, 305).

During World War II, Gielgud entertained troops abroad while also performing regularly in London. He took productions of *Hamlet* and Noel Coward's *Blithe Spirit* to Burma and took his stagings of *The Importance of Being Earnest* and William Congreve's satiric Restoration comedy *Love for Love* to New York, where he again scored a major success. He was knighted in 1953.

Just as his great aunt Ellen Terry had devised a recital called *Shakespeare's Heroines*, the newly minted Sir John devised his *Ages of Man,* a one-man show featuring speeches from Shakespeare's characters and lighter recitals from the sonnets, all of this divided into three parts: Youth, Manhood, and Old Age. Gielgud assembled an artful mix of passages from his best-known roles, weaving in commentary and readings from the poems. He toured the show during its first ten years to sixteen countries. In it, he kept gesture and movement to a minimum, saying that "the tendency in doing Shakespeare has too often been to substitute activity and restlessness for the musical and athletic power of the verse, which drives it along if you speak it correctly and are still" (Croall, 401). Many Americans first saw the actor live in this compilation evening, during which he displayed the entire emotional and dynamic range of his incomparable vocal instrument.

When Royal Shakespeare Company founder Peter Hall was casting about for models for the company he wished to form at Stratford-upon-Avon, Peggy Ashcroft and Hall looked to Gielgud's attempts in the 1930s to create a company within the commercial system during seasons at the New Theatre and Queen's Theatre. Gielgud's efforts laid many of the foundations of the postwar Stratford developments that led to the formation of the Royal Shakespeare Company. As a schoolboy, Hall had been impressed by the fine ensemble playing in the Old Vic Company led by Olivier and Ralph Richardson, and by the Gielgud

(continued)

repertory of classics at the Haymarket Theatre (Chambers, 12). It was at the Haymarket that Gielgud allowed Peter Brook to stage rehearsals for his early films; Gielgud was instrumental from that time in advancing Brook's career. Not all of Gielgud's appearances for the RSC were triumphs, to be sure. In 1961, Hall erred by enlisting Gielgud to play Othello in Franco Zeffirelli's "statuesque" production, a throwback to a stylistically different and less race-sensitive era.

Since World War II, the boundary between the classical and the modern actor has blurred somewhat, thanks in part to film. Olivier became known for his Heathcliff in *Wuthering Heights* as well as for his *Henry V* film. Gielgud also crossed that divide on stage and film, though he took up film later and thus came to the attention of a wider American audience somewhat late because his early career was centered principally upon the stage. When he did finally essay film work, he told an interviewer that he was "an overnight success after only forty years' experience." He had often expressed his fear of, and sometimes disdain for, movies and television, noting that he felt he would appear too "hammy," his voice too "plumy" on the screen. Nonetheless, he made his television debut in 1959 on the BBC. He followed that performance with televised productions of Chekhov and some Shakespeare. As movie critic Daniel Rosenthal notes, "The close-up might have been invented for (Gielgud), the man who, as the great drama critic Kenneth Tynan put it, 'was always an actor from the neck up' " (Rosenthal, 196). Later, Gielgud took a leading role in the popular series *Brideshead Revisited*, playing Edward Ryder, the father of Charles (Jeremy Irons), in the popular miniseries eventually broadcast in the United States on public television (PBS). (Olivier played Lord Marchmain.)

Ultimately, Gielgud appeared in sixty-six feature films ranging from the quartet of Shakespearean roles already mentioned to such artistically significant parts as the dying novelist in Alan Resnais's *Providence*, to honored roles such as Lord Irwin in *Gandhi*, and the supercilious, foul-mouthed manservant Hobson in the comedy *Arthur* with Dudley Moore. Among the performances filmed in his last decade, two—one for television, the other for a feature film—have particular significance. Ever the experimenter, Gielgud played Prospero for the fifth time (the first four were on stage) in Greenaway's *Prospero's Books* (1991), an auteur version of *The Tempest* in which Gielgud speaks most of the lines in Shakespeare's play as voice-over. Greenaway, primarily a visual artist, conceived of Prospero as the creator of a play called *The Tempest,* imagining the characters into existence and speaking their words at the center of Greenaway's swirling, water-splashed vision. The concept, Greenaway told Gielgud, was inspired by and modeled upon the actor's voice. Thus, at the age of eighty-six, Gielgud filmed the first scene of the water-saturated film while naked in a pool in an old warehouse in Amsterdam. The startlingly original and dense work (see stage and screen history of *The Tempest*, pp. 855–860) encapsulates his vocal skill and poetic insight as well as his willingness to take artistic risks. His last filmed performance was in modernist Samuel Beckett's short play *Catastrophe,* directed by American playwright David Mamet. British dramatist Harold Pinter also appeared in the production filmed by the Irish television network that aired all of Beckett's plays. The series is now available in the United States on DVD.

Gielgud died in his drawing room on May 2, 2000, having modestly asked only for a simple, private funeral service. Fifty or so friends attended that funeral before his body was cremated at Oxford. "Everybody currently working in the theater will agree that his death brings the end of an era," Trevor Nunn, then director of the Royal National Theatre, told the *New York Times* upon learning of Gielgud's death. Gielgud is widely considered the last in a centuries-long line of theater artists to practice heroic acting; Nunn called him "a seemingly indestructible genius of his age."

References and Related Reading

Chambers, Colin. *Inside the Royal Shakespeare Company.* London and New York, 2004.

Croall, Jonathan. *Gielgud: A Theatrical Life, 1904–2000.* New York, 2001.

Gielgud, John. *An Actor and His Time.* London, 1979.

Gussow, Mel. "Sir John Gielgud, 96, Dies: Beacon of Classical Stage." *New York Times* 23 May 2000: A-1.

Kitchin, Laurence. "John Gielgud." *International Dictionary of Theatre 3: Actors, Directors and Designers.* New York and London, 1996.

Rosenthal, Daniel. *Shakespeare on Screen.* London, 2000.

APPENDIX A

Bibliography

Abbreviations Used

English Literary History	*(ELH)*
Publications of the Modern Language Association of America	*(PMLA)*
Shakespeare Quarterly	*(SQ)*
Shakespeare Studies	*(ShakS)*
Shakespeare Survey	*(ShS)*

Works of Literary Reference

Abbott, E. A. *A Shakespearian Grammar.* New ed. London, 1870.

Allen, Michael J. B., and Kenneth Muir, eds. *Shakespeare's Plays in Quarto.* Berkeley, 1981.

Bentley, G. E. *The Jacobean and Caroline Stage.* 7 vols. Oxford, 1941–1968.

Bergeron, David M. *Shakespeare: A Study and Research Guide.* 1975. 2nd ed. Rev. David Bergeron and Geraldo de Sousa. Lawrence, Kans., 1987.

Bullough, Geoffrey, ed. *Narrative and Dramatic Sources of Shakespeare.* 8 vols. London, 1957–1975.

Chambers, E. K. *The Elizabethan Stage.* 4 vols. Oxford, 1923; rev., 1945.

———. *The Mediaeval Stage.* 2 vols. Oxford, 1903.

———. *William Shakespeare: A Study of Facts and Problems.* 2 vols. Oxford, 1930.

Dent, R. W. *Shakespeare's Proverbial Language: An Index.* Berkeley, 1981.

Garland Shakespeare Bibliographies. Gen. ed. William Godshalk. Published in separate volumes for various plays, at varying dates. Garland: New York.

Greg, W. W. *A Bibliography of the English Printed Drama to the Restoration.* 4 vols. London, 1939–1959.

———, ed. *Shakespeare Quarto Facsimiles.* London, 1939–. (An incomplete set; Greg's work has been supplemented by Charlton Hinman.)

Harbage, Alfred. *Annals of English Drama, 975–1700.* 1964. Ed. Rev. S. Schoenbaum. 3rd ed. Philadelphia, 1989.

Hinman, Charlton, ed. *The Norton Facsimile: The First Folio of Shakespeare.* New York, 1968.

Hosley, Richard, ed. *Shakespeare's Holinshed.* New York, 1968.

Kökeritz, Helge. *Shakespeare's Names.* New Haven, 1959.

———. *Shakespeare's Pronunciation.* New Haven, 1953.

Long, John. *Shakespeare's Use of Music: Comedies.* Gainesville, Fla., 1955. Also see *Final Comedies,* 1961; *Histories and Tragedies,* 1971.

McDonald, Russ. *The Bedford Companion to Shakespeare: An Introduction with Documents.* 1996. 2nd ed. Boston, 2001.

McManaway, James G., and Jeanne Addison Roberts, compilers. *A Selective Bibliography of Shakespeare.* Charlottesville, Va., 1975.

Muir, Kenneth. *Shakespeare's Sources.* 2 vols. London, 1957.

———, and S. Schoenbaum, eds. *A New Companion to Shakespeare Studies.* London and New York, 1971.

Munro, John, ed. *The Shakespeare Allusion Book.* 2 vols. London and New York, 1909; reissued 1932.

Naylor, Edward W. *Shakespeare and Music.* New ed. London, 1931.

Noble, Richmond. *Shakespeare's Biblical Knowledge.* London, 1935.

———. *Shakespeare's Use of Song.* London, 1923.

Onions, C. T. *A Shakespeare Glossary.* Rev. and enlgd. R. D. Eagleson. Oxford, 1986.

Pegasus Shakespeare Bibliographies. Annotated bibliographies of Shakespeare studies in a 12-volume series, gen. ed. Richard L. Nochimson, including *Love's Labor's Lost, A Midsummer Night's Dream,* and *The Merchant of Venice* (Clifford Chalmers Huffman);

Richard II, Henry IV, I and II, and *Henry V* (Joseph Candido); *Hamlet* (Michael E. Mooney); *The Rape of Lucrece, Titus Andronicus, Julius Caesar, Antony and Cleopatra*, and *Coriolanus* (Clifford Chalmers Huffman and John W. Velz); *King Lear* and *Macbeth* (Rebecca W. Bushnell); and *Shakespeare and the Renaissance Stage to 1616* and *Shakespearean Stage History 1616 to 1998* (Hugh Macrae Richmond). Binghamton, N.Y., 1995, and Asheville, N.C., 1996.

Publications of the Modern Language Association of America (PMLA). Annual Bibliography.

Rothwell, Kenneth S., and Annabelle Henkin Melzer. *Shakespeare on Screen: An International Filmography and Videography.* New York and London, 1990.

Schmidt, Alexander. *Shakespeare-Lexicon.* 5th ed. Berlin, 1962.

Seager, H. W. *Natural History in Shakespeare's Time.* London, 1896.

Seng, Peter J. *The Vocal Songs in the Plays of Shakespeare.* Cambridge, Mass., 1967.

Shakespeare Bulletin.

Shakespeare-Jahrbuch.

Shakespeare Newsletter.

Shakespeare Quarterly. Annual Bibliography.

Shakespeare Studies.

Shakespeare Survey.

Spencer, T. J. B., ed. *Shakespeare's Plutarch.* Harmondsworth, Eng., 1964.

Spevack, Marvin. *The Harvard Concordance to Shakespeare.* Cambridge, Mass., 1973.

Sternfeld, Frederick W. *Music in Shakespearean Tragedy.* London, 1963, 1967.

Thomson, J. A. K. *Shakespeare and the Classics.* London, 1952.

Wells, Stanley, ed. *Shakespeare: Select Bibliographical Guides.* London, 1973.

——, ed. *The Cambridge Companion to Shakespeare Studies.* Cambridge, Eng., 1986.

Life in Shakespeare's England

Allen, Don Cameron. *The Star-Crossed Renaissance.* Durham, N.C., 1941.

Baker, Herschel. *The Image of Man: A Study of the Idea of Human Dignity in Classical Antiquity, the Middle Ages, and the Renaissance.* Cambridge, Mass., 1961. (First published in 1947 as *The Dignity of Man.*)

——. *The Wars of Truth: Studies in the Decay of Christian Humanism in the Earlier Seventeenth Century.* Cambridge, Mass., 1952.

Bakhtin, Mikhail M. *Rabelais and His World.* Trans. H. Iswolsky. Cambridge, Mass., 1968.

Barkan, Leonard. *Nature's Work of Art: The Human Body as Image of the World.* New Haven, 1975.

——. *The Gods Made Flesh: Metamorphosis and the Pursuit of Paganism.* New Haven, 1986.

Barroll, J. Leeds. *Politics, Plague, and Shakespeare's Theater: The Stuart Years.* Ithaca, N.Y., 1991.

Bindoff, S. T., et al., eds. *Elizabethan Government and Society.* Essays presented to Sir John Neale. London, 1961.

Bush, Douglas. *The Renaissance and English Humanism.* Toronto, 1939.

Buxton, John. *Elizabethan Taste.* London, 1963.

Byrne, Muriel St. Clare. *Elizabethan Life in Town and Country.* 8th ed. London, 1970.

Camden, Carroll. *The Elizabethan Woman.* Houston, 1952.

Caspari, Fritz. *Humanism and the Social Order in Tudor England.* Chicago, 1954.

Cassirer, Ernst. *The Platonic Renaissance in England.* Trans. J. E. Pettegrove. Austin, Texas, 1953.

De Grazia, Margreta, Maureen Quilligan, and Peter Stallybrass, eds. *Subject and Object in Renaissance Culture.* Cambridge, Eng., 1996.

Einstein, Lewis. *Tudor Ideals.* New York, 1921.

Elizabeth I. *Collected Works.* Eds. Leah S. Marcus, Janel Mueller, and Mary Beth Rose. Chicago, 2000.

Elton, G. R. *The Tudor Revolution in Government.* Cambridge, Eng., 1959.

Fumerton, Patricia, and Simon Hunt, eds. *Renaissance Culture and the Everyday.* Philadelphia, 1999.

Gallagher, Lowell. *Medusa's Gaze: Casuistry and Conscience in the Renaissance.* Stanford, 1991.

Harrison, G. B. *An Elizabethan Journal.* London, 1928; supplements.

——. *A Jacobean Journal . . . 1603–1606.* London, 1941.

——. *A Second Jacobean Journal . . . 1607 to 1610.* Ann Arbor, Mich., 1958.

Haydn, Hiram. *The Counter-Renaissance.* New York, 1950.

Helgerson, Richard. *Forms of Nationhood: The Elizbethan Writing of England.* Chicago, 1992.

Heninger, S. K., Jr. *A Handbook of Renaissance Meteorology.* Durham, N.C., 1960.

Hirst, Derek. *Authority and Conflict: England, 1603–1658.* Cambridge, Mass., 1986.

Huizinga, Johan. *The Waning of the Middle Ages.* London, 1924; Baltimore, 1955.

Hurstfield, Joel. *Elizabeth I and the Unity of England.* London, 1960.

Jones, Ann Rosalind, and Peter Stallybrass. *Renaissance Clothing and the Materials of Memory.* Cambridge, Eng., 2000.

Jordan, Constance. *Renaissance Feminism: Literary Texts and Political Models.* Ithaca, N.Y., 1990.

Judges, A. V., ed. *The Elizabethan Underworld.* 1930. Rpt. London, 1965.

Kewes, Paulina, ed. *Plagiarism in Early Modern England.* Basingstoke, Hampshire, Eng., 2003.

Knights, L. C. *Drama and Society in the Age of Jonson.* London, 1937.

Kocher, Paul. *Science and Religion in Elizabethan England.* San Marino, Calif., 1953.

Lee, Morris. *Great Britain's Solomon: James VI and I in His Three Kingdoms.* Urbana, Ill., 1990.

Lovejoy, A. O. *The Great Chain of Being.* Cambridge, Mass., 1936.

MacCaffrey, Wallace T. *The Shaping of the Elizabethan Regime.* Princeton, 1968.

Marotti, Arthur F., ed. *Catholicism and Anti-Catholicism in Early Modern English Texts.* Basingstoke, Hampshire, Eng., 1999.

Matar, Nabil. *Turks, Moors, and Englishmen in the Age of Discovery.* New York, 1999.

Mattingly, Garrett. *The Armada.* Boston, 1959.

McEachern, Claire, and Debora Shuger, eds. *Religion and Culture in Renaissance England.* Cambridge, Eng., 1997.

McElwee, W. *The Wisest Fool in Christendom.* [About James VI and I.] New York, 1958.

McPeek, James A. S. *The Black Book of Knaves and Unthrifts in Shakespeare and Other Renaissance Authors.* Storrs, Conn., 1969.

Neale, John E. *Elizabeth I and Her Parliaments.* 2 vols. London and New York, 1953–1958.

——. *The Elizabethan House of Commons.* London, 1949.

——. *Queen Elizabeth I.* London, 1934 New York, 1957.

Nichols, John, ed. *The Progresses and Public Processions of Queen Elizabeth.* 3 vols. London, 1823.

Patterson, Annabel M. *Reading Holinshed's "Chronicles."* Chicago, 1994.

Peck, Linda Levy. *Court Patronage and Corruption in Early Stuart England.* Boston, 1990.

Penrose, Boies. *Travel and Discovery in the Renaissance, 1420–1620.* Cambridge, Mass., 1955.

Quinones, Ricardo J. *The Renaissance Discovery of Time.* Cambridge, Mass., 1972.

Rowse, A. L. *The England of Elizabeth: The Structure of Society.* London, 1951.

Stallybrass, Peter, and Allon White. *The Politics and Poetics of Transgression.* Ithaca, N.Y., and London, 1986.

Stone, Lawrence. *The Crisis of the Aristocracy, 1558–1641.* Oxford, 1965.

——. *The Family, Sex and Marriage in England, 1500–1800.* London, 1977.

Stow, John. *Survey of London.* Ed. C. L. Kingsford. Oxford, 1971.

Targoff, Ramie. *Common Prayer: The Language of Public Devotion in Early Modern England.* Chicago, 2001.

Tawney, R. H. *Religion and the Rise of Capitalism.* New York, 1926, 1962.

Tillyard, E. M. W. *The Elizabethan World Picture.* London, 1943, 1967.

Underdown, David. *Revel, Riot, and Rebellion: Popular Politics and Culture in England, 1603–1660.* Oxford, 1985.

Whigham, Frank. *Ambition and Privilege: The Social Tropes of Elizabethan Courtesy Theory.* Berkeley, 1984.

Willson, David Harris. *King James VI & I.* New York, 1956.

Wilson, F. P. *Elizabethan and Jacobean.* Oxford, 1945.

Wilson, J. Dover, ed. *Life in Shakespeare's England.* 1911. 2nd ed. Cambridge, Eng., 1926.

Woodbridge, Linda. *Women and the English Renaissance.* Urbana, Ill., 1984.

Wright, Louis B. *Middle-Class Culture in Elizabethan England.* Chapel Hill, N.C., 1935.

Wrightson, Keith. *English Society, 1580–1680.* New Brunswick, N.J., 1982.

Zeeveld, W. Gordon. *Foundations of Tudor Policy.* Cambridge, Mass., 1948.

Shakespeare's Predecessors and Contemporaries

See also, under "Works of Literary Reference," Bentley, Chambers, Greg, and Harbage; under "London Theaters and Dramatic Companies," McMillin and MacLean; under "Shakespeare Criticism Since 1980," Dollimore, Garber (*Cannibals*), Goldberg, Greenblatt, Jardine, Loomba, Mullaney, Newman, and Skura; under "The Histories," Ribner; and under "The Tragedies," Bushnell.

Altman, Joel B. *The Tudor Play of Mind: Rhetorical Inquiry and the Development of Elizabethan Drama.* Berkeley, 1978.

Bamford, Karen. *Sexual Violence on the Jacobean Stage.* New York, 2000.

Barber, C. L. *Creating Elizabethan Tragedy: The Theater of Kyd and Marlowe.* Chicago, 1988.

Bartels, Emily C. *Spectacles of Strangeness: Imperialism, Alienation, and Marlowe.* Philadelphia, 1993.

Bednarz, James P. *Shakespeare and the Poets' War.* New York, 2001.

Belsey, Catherine. *The Subject of Tragedy: Identity and Difference in Renaissance Drama.* London, 1985.

Berry, Philippa. *Of Chastity and Power: Elizabethan Literature and the Unmarried Queen.* London and New York, 1989.

Bevington, David. *From "Mankind" to Marlowe: Growth of Structure in the Popular Drama of Tudor England.* Cambridge, Mass., 1962.

——. *Tudor Drama and Politics.* Cambridge, Mass., 1968.

——, and Peter Holbrook, eds. *The Politics of the Stuart Court Masque.* Cambridge, Eng., 1991.

Bowers, Fredson T. *Elizabethan Revenge Tragedy, 1587–1642.* Princeton, 1940.

Braden, Gordon. *Renaissance Tragedy and the Senecan Tradition.* New Haven, 1985.

Braunmuller, A. R., and Michael Hattaway, eds. *The Cambridge Companion to English Renaissance Drama.* Cambridge, Eng., 1990.

Bristol, Michael D. *Carnival and Theater: Plebeian Culture and the Structure of Authority in Renaissance England.* London, 1985.

Brooke, C. F. Tucker, ed. *The Shakespeare Apocrypha.* Oxford, 1908.

Brooks, Douglas A. *From Playhouse to Printing House: Drama and Authorship in Early Modern England.* Cambridge, Eng., 2000.

Bruster, Douglas. *Drama and the Market in the Age of Shakespeare.* Cambridge, Eng., 1992.

Burt, Richard. *Licensed by Authority: Ben Jonson and the Discourses of Censorship.* Ithaca, N.Y., 1993.

Bushnell, Rebecca W. *Tragedies of Tyrants: Political Thought and Theater in the English Renaissance.* Ithaca, N.Y., 1990.

Butterworth, Philip. *Theatre of Fire: Special Effects in Early English and Scottish Theatre.* London, 1998.

Caputi, Anthony. *John Marston, Satirist.* Ithaca, N.Y., 1961.

Cohen, Walter. *Drama of a Nation: Public Theater in Renaissance England and Spain.* Ithaca, N.Y., 1985.

Comensoli, Viviana, and Anna Russell, eds. *Enacting Gender on the English Renaissance Stage.* Urbana, Ill., 1999.

Cox, John D., and David Scott Kastan, eds. *A New History of Early English Drama.* New York, 1997.

Craik, T. W. *The Tudor Interlude.* Leicester, 1958, 1962.

Dawson, Anthony B., and Paul Yachnin. *The Culture of Playgoing in Shakespeare's England: A Collaborative Debate.* Cambridge, Eng., 2001.

Deats, Sara Munson. *Sex, Gender, and Desire in the Plays of Christopher Marlowe.* Newark, Del., 1997.

Dessen, Alan C. *Elizabethan Drama and the Viewer's Eye.* Chapel Hill, N.C., 1977.

Diehl, Huston. *Staging Reform, Reforming the Stage: Protestantism and Popular Theater in Early Modern England.* Ithaca, N.Y., 1997.

DiGangi, Mario. *The Homoerotics of Early Modern Drama.* Cambridge, Eng., 1997.

Dillon, Janette. *Theatre, Court and City, 1595–1610: Drama and Social Space in London.* Cambridge, Eng., 2000.

Dolan, Frances E. *Dangerous Familiars: Representations of Domestic Crime in England, 1550–1700.* Ithaca, N.Y., 1994.

Doran, Madeleine. *Endeavors of Art: A Study of Form in Elizabethan Drama.* Madison, Wis., 1954, 1972.

Farley-Hills, David. *Shakespeare and the Rival Playwrights, 1600–1606.* London, 1990.

Findlay, Alison. *A Feminist Perspective on Renaissance Drama.* Oxford, 1999.

———. *Illegitimate Power: Bastards in Renaissance Drama.* Manchester, Eng., 1994.

Finkelpearl, Philip. *John Marston of the Middle Temple.* Cambridge, Mass., 1969.

Freer, Coburn. *The Poetics of Jacobean Drama.* Baltimore, 1981.

Gardiner, H. C. *Mysteries' End.* New Haven, 1946.

Gibbons, Brian. *Jacobean City Comedy.* London, 1968.

Hall, Kim F. *Things of Darkness: Economies of Race and Gender in Early Modern England.* Ithaca, N.Y., 1995.

Hardison, O. B., Jr. *Christian Rite and Christian Drama in the Middle Ages.* Baltimore, 1965.

Hassel, R. Chris. *Renaissance Drama and the English Church Year.* Lincoln, Neb., 1979.

Hattaway, Michael. *Elizabethan Popular Theatre: Plays in Performance.* London, 1982.

Hawkins, Harriett. *Likenesses of Truth in Elizabethan and Restoration Drama.* Oxford, 1972.

Helgerson, Richard. *Adulterous Alliances: Home, State, and History in Early Modern European Drama and Painting.* Chicago, 2000.

Hendricks, Margo, and Patricia Parker, eds. *Women, "Race," and Writing in the Early Modern Period.* London and New York, 1994.

Holbrook, Peter. *Literature and Degree in Renaissance England: Nashe, Bourgeois Tragedy, Shakespeare.* Newark, Del., 1994.

Howard, Jean. *The Stage and Social Struggle in Early Modern England.* London and New York, 1994.

Hunter, G. K. *John Lyly: The Humanist as Courtier.* Cambridge, Mass., 1962.

Kastan, David Scott, and Peter Stallybrass, eds. *Staging the Renaissance: Reinterpretations of Elizabethan and Jacobean Drama.* New York and London, 1991.

Kernan, Alvin. *The Cankered Muse: Satire of the English Renaissance.* New Haven, 1959.

Kiefer, Frederick. *Writing on the Renaissance Stage: Written Words, Printed Pages, Metaphoric Books.* Newark, Del., 1996.

Kirsch, Arthur C. *Jacobean Dramatic Perspectives.* Charlottesville, Va., 1972.

Kolve, V. A. *The Play Called Corpus Christi.* Palo Alto and London, 1966.

Leggatt, Alexander. *Citizen Comedy in the Age of Shakespeare.* Toronto, 1973.

———. *Jacobean Public Theatre.* London, 1992.

Leishman, J. B., ed. *The Three Parnassus Plays (1598–1601).* London, 1949.

Levin, Harry. *The Overreacher: A Study of Christopher Marlowe.* Cambridge, Mass., 1952, 1964.

Levin, Richard. *The Multiple Plot in English Renaissance Drama.* Chicago, 1971.

Margeson, J. M. R. *The Origins of English Tragedy.* Oxford, 1967.

Marrapodi, Michele, ed., with A. J. Hoenselaars. *The Italian World of English Renaissance Drama: Cultural Exchange and Intertextuality.* Newark, Del., 1998.

Maus, Katharine Eisaman. *Inwardness and Theater in the English Renaissance Drama.* Chicago, 1995.

McAlindon, T. *English Renaissance Tragedy.* London, 1986.

McLuskie, Kathleen. *Renaissance Dramatists*. (Feminist Readings.) Atlantic Highlands, N.J., 1989.

——, *The Illusion of Power: Political Theater in the English Renaissance*. Berkeley, 1975.

——. *Impersonations: The Performance of Gender in Shakespeare's England*. Cambridge, Eng., 1996.

——, and Roy Strong. *Inigo Jones: The Theatre of the Stuart Court*. 2 vols. London and Berkeley, 1973.

Ornstein, Robert. *The Moral Vision of Jacobean Tragedy*. Madison, Wis., 1960.

Rabkin, Norman, ed. *Reinterpretations of Elizabethan Drama*. New York, 1969.

Rasmussen, Mark David, ed. *Renaissance Literature and Its Formal Engagements*. Basingstoke, Hampshire, Eng., 2002.

Rose, Mary Beth. *The Expense of Spirit: Love and Sexuality in English Renaissance Drama*. Ithaca, N.Y., 1988.

——. *Gender and Heroism in Early Modern English Literature*. Chicago, 2002.

——, ed. *Renaissance Drama as Cultural History*. Evanston, Ill., 1990.

Sanders, Wilbur. *The Dramatist and the Received Idea: Studies in the Plays of Marlowe and Shakespeare*. Cambridge, Eng., 1968.

Shannon, Laurie. *Sovereign Amity: Figures of Friendship in Shakespearean Contexts*. Chicago, 2002.

Shapiro, James. *Rival Playwrights: Marlowe, Jonson, Shakespeare*. New York, 1991.

Smith, Bruce R. *The Acoustic World of Early Modern England*. Chicago, 1999.

Smith, David L., Richard Strier, and David Bevington, eds. *The Theatrical City: Culture, Theatre and Politics in London, 1567–1649*. Cambridge, Eng., 1995.

Southern, Richard. *The Medieval Theatre in the Round*. London, 1957.

Spivack, Bernard. *Shakespeare and the Allegory of Evil*. New York, 1958.

Traub, Valerie, M. Lindsay Kaplan, and Dympna C. Callaghan, eds. *Feminist Readings of Early Modern Culture: Emerging Subjects*. Cambridge, Eng., 1996.

Vickers, Brian. *"Counterfeiting" Shakespeare: Evidence, Authorship, and John Ford's "Funerall Elegye."* Cambridge, Eng., 2002.

Waith, Eugene M. *The Herculean Hero in Marlowe, Chapman, Shakespeare, and Dryden*. New York, 1962.

Whigham, Frank. *Seizures of the Will in Early Modern English Drama*. Cambridge, Eng., 1996.

White, Paul Whitfield. *Marlowe, History, and Sexuality: New Critical Essays on Christopher Marlowe*. New York, 1998.

——. *Theatre and Reformation: Protestantism, Patronage and Playing in Tudor England*. Cambridge, Eng., 1993.

Wickham, Glynne. *Early English Stages, 1300 to 1660*. 3 vols. London, 1959–1972.

Wilson, F. P. *Marlowe and the Early Shakespeare*. Oxford, 1953.

Woodbridge, Linda. *Women and the English Renaissance: Literature and the Nature of Womankind, 1540–1620*. Urbana, Ill., 1984.

Woolf, Rosemary. *The English Mystery Plays*. Berkeley and Los Angeles, 1972.

Yachnin, Paul. *Stage-Wrights: Shakespeare, Jonson, Middleton, and the Making of Theatrical Value*. Philadelphia, 1997.

Zimmerman, Susan, ed. *Erotic Politics: Desire on the Renaissance Stage*. London and New York, 1992.

London Theaters and Dramatic Companies

See also, under "Works of Reference," Bentley, and Chambers (*Elizabethan Stage*).

Astington, John H., ed. *The Development of Shakespeare's Theater*. New York, 1992.

Beckerman, Bernard. *Shakespeare at the Globe, 1599–1609*. New York, 1962, 1967.

Bentley, Gerald Eades. *The Profession of Dramatist in Shakespeare's Time, 1590–1642*. Princeton, 1971.

——. *The Profession of Player in Shakespeare's Time, 1590–1642*. Princeton, 1984.

Berry, Herbert. *Shakespeare's Playhouses*. New York, 1987.

Bradley, David. *From Text to Performance in the Elizabethan Theatre: Preparing the Play for the Stage*. Cambridge, Eng., 1992.

Clare, Janet. *"Art Made Tongue-Tied by Authority": Elizabethan and Jacobean Dramatic Censorship*. Manchester, Eng., 1990.

Cook, Ann Jennalie. *The Privileged Playgoers of Shakespeare's London, 1576–1642*. Princeton, 1981.

Dutton, Richard. *Mastering the Revels: The Regulation and Censorship of English Renaissance Drama*. Iowa City, 1991.

Feuillerat, Albert, ed. *Documents Relating to the Office of the Revels in the Time of Queen Elizabeth*. Louvain (Louven), Belgium, 1908.

Foakes, R. A., ed. *The Henslowe Papers: The Diary, Theatre Papers, and Bear Garden Papers*. In full and in facsimile. 3 vols. in 2. London, 1976.

——, R. A., and R. T. Rickert, eds. *Henslowe's Diary*. London, 1961.

Gair, W. Reavley. *The Children of Paul's*. Cambridge, Eng., 1982.

Greg, W. W., ed. *Dramatic Documents from the Elizabethan Playhouses: Stage Plots; Actors' Parts; Prompt Books*. 2 vols. Oxford, 1931.

Gurr, Andrew. *Playgoing in Shakespeare's London*. 2nd ed. Cambridge, Eng., 1987, 1996.

——. *The Shakespearian Playing Companies*. Oxford, 1996.

——. *The Shakespearean Stage, 1574–1642*. Cambridge, Eng., 1970; 2nd ed., 1980.

——, and John Orrell. *Rebuilding Shakespeare's Globe*. London and New York, 1989.

Harbage, Alfred. *Shakespeare's Audience*. New York, 1941.

Hodges, C. Walter. *The Globe Restored*. 2nd ed. New York, 1968.

Hosley, Richard. "Was There a Music-room in Shakespeare's Globe?" *ShS* 13 (1960): 113–123.

Ingram, William. *The Business of Playing: The Beginnings of the Adult Professional Theater in Elizabethan London*. Ithaca, N.Y., 1992.

King, T. J. *Casting Shakespeare's Plays: London Actors and Their Roles, 1590–1642*. Cambridge, Eng., 1992.

——. *Shakespearean Staging, 1599–1642*. Cambridge, Mass., 1971.

Knutson, Roslyn Lander. *The Repertory of Shakespeare's Company, 1594–1613*. Fayetteville, Ark., 1991.

——. *Playing Companies and Commerce in Shakespeare's Time*. Cambridge, Eng., 2001.

Linthicum, Marie C. *Costume in the Drama of Shakespeare and His Contemporaries*. Oxford, 1936.

Mann, David. *The Elizabethan Player: Contemporary Stage Representation*. London, 1991.

McMillin, Scott. *The Elizabethan Theatre and "The Book of Sir Thomas More."* Ithaca, N.Y., 1987.

——, and Sally-Beth MacLean. *The Queen's Men and Their Plays*. Cambridge, Eng., 1998.

Nelson, Alan H. *Early Cambridge Theatres: College, University, and Town Stages, 1464–1720*. Cambridge, Eng., 1994.

Nungezer, Edwin. *A Dictionary of Actors*. London and New Haven: Yale UP, 1929.

Shapiro, Michael. *Children of the Revels: The Boys' Companies of Shakespeare's Time and Their Plays*. New York, 1977.

Wickham, Glynne. *Early English Stages, 1300 to 1660*. 3 vols. London, 1959–1972.

Shakespeare's Life and Work

Alexander, Peter. *Shakespeare's Life and Art*. New ed. New York, 1961.

Baldwin, T. W. *William Shakspere's Small Latine and Lesse Greeke*. 2 vols. Urbana, Ill., 1944.

Chambers, E. K. *William Shakespeare: A Study of Facts and Problems*. 2 vols. Oxford, 1930.

Eccles, Mark. *Shakespeare in Warwickshire*. Madison, Wis., 1961.

Greenblatt, Stephen. *Will in the World: How Shakespeare Became Shakespeare*. New York, 2004.

Honan, Park. *Shakespeare: A Life*. Oxford, 1998.

Matus, Irvin Leigh. *Shakespeare, In Fact*. New York, 1994.

Schoenbaum, S. *Shakespeare's Lives*. Oxford and New York, 1970.

——. *William Shakespeare: A Documentary Life*. Oxford, 1975. Also published with fewer illustrations and a slightly revised text as *A Compact Documentary Life*. 1977.

——. *William Shakespeare: Records and Images*. Oxford, 1981.

Wells, Stanley. *Shakespeare: A Life in Drama*. New York and London, 1995.

Wheeler, Richard P. "Deaths in the Family: The Loss of a Son and the Rise of Shakespearean Comedy." *SQ* 51 (2000): 127–153.

Wood, Michael. *Shakespeare*. New York, 2003.

Shakespeare's Language: His Development as Poet and Dramatist

See also, under "Works of Literary Reference," Abbott, Onions, and Schmidt; and under "The Comedies," Elam.

Byrne, Muriel St. Clare. "The Foundations of Elizabethan Language." *ShS* 17 (1964): 223–239.

Cercignani, Fausto. *Shakespeare's Works and Elizabethan Pronunciation*. Oxford, 1981.

Charney, Maurice. *Shakespeare's Roman Plays: The Function of Imagery in the Drama*. Cambridge, Mass., 1961.

——. *Style in "Hamlet."* Princeton, 1969.

Clemen, Wolfgang H. *The Development of Shakespeare's Imagery*. Cambridge, Mass., 1951.

Cruttwell, Patrick. *The Shakespearean Moment and Its Place in the Poetry of the Seventeenth Century*. London, 1954.

Desmet, Christy. *Reading Shakespeare's Characters: Rhetoric, Ethics, and Identity*. Amherst, Mass., 1992.

Dobson, E. J. *English Pronunciation, 1500–1700*. 2 vols. 2nd ed. Oxford, 1968.

Donawerth, Jane. *Shakespeare and the Sixteenth-Century Study of Language*. Urbana, Ill., 1984.

Doran, Madeleine. *Shakespeare's Dramatic Language*. Madison, Wis., 1976.

Empson, William. *The Structure of Complex Words*. 3rd ed. London, 1977.

Hulme, Hilda M. *Explorations in Shakespeare's Language*. London, 1962.

Kermode, Frank. *Shakespeare's Language*. New York, 2000.

Kökeritz, Helge. *Shakespeare's Names*. New Haven, 1959.

——. *Shakespeare's Pronunciation*. New Haven, 1953.

Lanham, Richard A. *The Motives of Eloquence: Literary Rhetoric in the Renaissance*. New Haven, 1976.

Magnussen, Lynne. *Shakespeare and Social Dialogue: Dramatic Language and Elizabethan Letters*. Cambridge, Eng., 1999.

Mahood, M. M. *Shakespeare's Wordplay*. London, 1957.

Miriam Joseph, Sister. *Shakespeare's Use of the Arts of Language*. Rpt. in part as *Rhetoric in Shakespeare's Time*, 1947. New York, 1962.

Nares, Robert. *A Glossary . . . of Shakespeare and His Contemporaries*. New ed. J. O. Halliwell and Thomas Wright. 2 vols. London, 1859, 1905, Rpt. Detroit, 1966.

Partridge, Eric. *Shakespeare's Bawdy*. London, 1947, 1955.

Spurgeon, Caroline. *Shakespeare's Imagery and What it Tells Us*. Cambridge, Eng., 1935.

Thompson, Ann, and John O. Thompson. *Shakespeare: Meaning and Metaphor*. Iowa City, 1987.

Thorne, Alison. *Vision and Rhetoric in Shakespeare: Looking Through Language*. Basingstoke, Eng., and New York, 2000.

Vickers, Brian. *The Artistry of Shakespeare's Prose*. London, 1968.

Willbern, David. *Poetic Will: Shakespeare and the Play of Language*. Philadelphia, 1997.

Willcock, Gladys D. "Shakespeare and Elizabethan English." *ShS* 7 (1954): 12–24.

Wright, George T. *Shakespeare's Metrical Art*. Berkeley, 1988.

Textual Criticism and Bibliography

See also under "*King Lear*," Urkowitz.

Alexander, Peter. *Shakespeare's "Henry VI" and "Richard III."* Cambridge, Eng., 1929.

Blayney, Peter W. M. *The First Folio of Shakespeare*. Washington D.C., 1991.

———. *The Texts of "King Lear" and Their Origins*. Vol. 1. Cambridge, Eng., 1982.

Bowers, Fredson. *Bibliography and Textual Criticism*. Oxford, 1964.

———. *On Editing Shakespeare*. Charlottesville, Va., 1966.

———. *Principles of Bibliographical Description*. Princeton, 1949.

———. *Textual and Literary Criticism*. Cambridge, Eng., 1959.

Chambers, E. K. *William Shakespeare: A Study of Facts and Problems*. 2 vols. Oxford, 1930.

De Grazia, Margreta. *Shakespeare Verbatim: The Reproduction of Authenticity and the 1790 Apparatus*. Oxford, 1991.

Doran, Madeleine. *"Henry VI," Parts II and III: Their Relation to "The Contention" and "The True Tragedy."* Iowa City, 1928.

Duthie, G. I. *Elizabethan Shorthand and the First Quarto of "King Lear."* Oxford, 1949.

Gaskell, Philip. *A New Introduction to Bibliography*. New York and Oxford, 1972.

Greg, W. W. *The Editorial Problem in Shakespeare*. 3rd ed. Oxford, 1954.

———. *Principles of Emendation in Shakespeare*. London, 1928.

———. *The Shakespeare First Folio: Its Bibliographical and Textual History*. Oxford, 1955.

Hart, Alfred. *Stolne and Surreptitious Copies: A Comparative Study of Shakespeare's Bad Quartos*. Melbourne and London, 1942.

Hinman, Charlton. *The Printing and Proof-Reading of the First Folio of Shakespeare*. 2 vols. Oxford, 1963.

Honigmann, E. A. J. *The Stability of Shakespeare's Text*. London and Lincoln, Neb., 1965.

Long, William B. " 'A bed for woodstock': A Warning for the Unwary." *Medieval and Renaissance Drama in England* 2 (1985): 91–118.

Maguire, Laurie E., and Thomas L. Berger, eds. *Textual Formations and Reformations*. Newark, Del., 1998.

Masten, Jeffrey. *Textual Intercourse: Collaboration, Authorship, and Sexualities in Renaissance Drama*. Cambridge, Eng., 1997.

McKerrow, Ronald B. *An Introduction to Bibliography for Literary Students*. Oxford, 1927.

———. *Prolegomena for the Oxford Shakespeare*. Oxford, 1939.

McLeod, Randall, ed. *Crisis in Editing: Texts of the English Renaissance*. New York, 1994.

Mowat, Barbara, and Paul Werstine, eds. *The New Folger Library Shakespeare*. New York, 1992—.

Nosworthy, J. M. *Shakespeare's Occasional Plays: Their Origin and Transmission*. London and New York, 1965.

Pechter, Edward, ed. *Textual and Theatrical Shakespeare: Questions of Evidence*. Iowa City, Iowa, 1996.

Pollard, Alfred W. *Shakespeare Folios and Quartos: A Study in the Bibliography of Shakespeare's Plays, 1594–1685*. London, 1909.

———. *Shakespeare's Fight with the Pirates and the Problems of the Transmission of His Text*. Rev. ed. Cambridge, Eng., 1937.

Sisson, C. J. *New Readings in Shakespeare*. 2 vols. Cambridge, Eng., 1956.

Taylor, Gary, and Michael Warren, eds. *The Division of the Kingdoms: Shakespeare's Two Versions of "King Lear."* Oxford, 1983.

Vickers, Brian. *Shakespeare: Co-Author*. London, 2002.

Walker, Alice. *Textual Problems of the First Folio*. Cambridge, Eng., 1953.

Wells, Stanley, and Gary Taylor. *Modernizing Shakespeare's Spelling*. Oxford, 1979.

Werstine, Paul. " 'Foul Papers' and 'Prompt-books': Printer's Copy for Shakespeare's *Comedy of Errors*." *Studies in Bibliography* 41 (1988): 232–246.

Shakespeare Criticism to the 1930s

Badawi, M. M. *Coleridge: Critic of Shakespeare*. Cambridge, Eng., 1973.

Bradby, Anne, ed. *Shakespeare Criticism, 1919–35*. London, 1936.

Coleridge, S. T. *Coleridge on Shakespeare: The Text of the Lectures of 1811–12*. Ed. R. A. Foakes. Charlottesville, Va., 1971.

———. *Coleridge's Writings on Shakespeare*. Ed. Terence Hawkes. New York, 1959.

Evans, G. Blakemore, ed. *Shakespeare: Aspects of Influence*. Cambridge, Mass., 1976.

Hazlitt, William. *Characters of Shakespear's Plays*. London, 1817.

Johnson, Samuel. *Johnson on Shakespeare*. Ed. Arthur Sherbo. Vol. 7 of *The Yale Edition of the Works of Samuel Johnson*. New Haven, 1968.

Kermode, Frank, ed. *Four Centuries of Shakespearean Criticism*. New York, 1965.

Knight, G. Wilson. *The Shakespearian Tempest*. London, 1932, 1953.

Muir, Kenneth. "Fifty Years of Shakespearian Criticism: 1900–1950." *ShS* 4 (1951): 1–25.

Rabkin, Norman, ed. *Approaches to Shakespeare*. New York, 1964.

Ralli, Augustus. *A History of Shakespearian Criticism*. 2 vols. London, 1932.

Raysor, T. M., ed. *Samuel Taylor Coleridge: Shakespearean Criticism*. 2 vols. 2nd ed. London, 1960.

Schlegel, August Wilhelm. *Lectures on Dramatic Art and Literature*. Trans. John Black, 1846. Rpt. New York, 1965.

Schücking, Levin L. *Character Problems in Shakespeare's Plays*. London, 1917; trans., 1922.

Shaw, G. B. *Shaw on Shakespeare*. Ed. Edwin Wilson. New York, 1961.

Sherbo, Arthur. *Samuel Johnson, Editor of Shakespeare*. Urbana, Ill., 1956.

Smith, David Nichol, ed. *Shakespeare Criticism: A Selection*. World's Classics, Oxford, 1916.

——, ed. *Eighteenth Century Essays on Shakespeare*. 2nd ed. Oxford, 1963.

Stoll, E. E. *Art and Artifice in Shakespeare*. Cambridge, Eng., 1933, 1962.

Vickers, Brian, ed. *Shakespeare: The Critical Heritage*. Several vols. London and Boston, 1974.

Welsford, Enid. *The Fool: His Social and Literary History*. London, 1935; rpt. 1966.

Westfall, A. V. *American Shakespearean Criticism, 1607–1865*. New York, 1939.

Shakespeare Criticism from the 1940s to the 1970s

Armstrong, Edward A. *Shakespeare's Imagination: A Study of the Psychology of Association and Inspiration*. London, 1946.

Bethell, S. L. *Shakespeare and the Popular Dramatic Tradition*. London and Durham, N.C., 1944.

Bevington, David, and Jay L. Halio, eds. *Shakespeare: Pattern of Excelling Nature*. Newark, Del., 1978.

Bloom, Allan, with Harry V. Jaffa. *Shakespeare's Politics*. New York and London, 1964.

Brown, John Russell. *Shakespeare's Plays in Performance*. London, 1966.

Bryant, J. A., Jr. *Hippolyta's View: Some Christian Aspects of Shakespeare's Plays*. Lexington, Ky., 1961.

Burckhardt, Sigurd. *Shakespearean Meanings*. Princeton, 1968.

Burke, Kenneth. *Language as Symbolic Action*. Berkeley, 1966.

Calderwood, James L. *Shakespearean Metadrama*. Minneapolis, 1971.

Coghill, Neville. *Shakespeare's Professional Skills*. Cambridge, Eng., 1964.

Colie, Rosalie L. *Shakespeare's Living Art*. Princeton, 1974.

Council, Norman. *When Honour's at the Stake: Ideas of Honour in Shakespeare's Plays*. London, 1973.

Danby, John F. *Poets on Fortune's Hill: Studies in Sidney, Shakespeare, and Beaumont and Fletcher*. London, 1952.

Dean, Leonard F., ed. *Shakespeare: Modern Essays in Criticism*. New York, 1967.

Driver, Tom F. *The Sense of History in Greek and Shakespearean Drama*. New York, 1960.

Dusinberre, Juliet. *Shakespeare and the Nature of Women*. 1975; 2nd ed. New York, 1996.

Eagleton, Terence. *Shakespeare and Society*. New York and London, 1967.

Edwards, Philip. *Shakespeare and the Confines of Art*. London and New York, 1968.

Empson, William. *The Structure of Complex Words*. London, 1951.

Fiedler, Leslie A. *The Stranger in Shakespeare*. New York, 1972.

Fly, Richard. *Shakespeare's Mediated World*. Amherst, Mass., 1976.

Frye, Roland M. *Shakespeare and Christian Doctrine*. Princeton, 1963.

Garber, Marjorie B. *Dream in Shakespeare: From Metaphor to Metamorphosis*. New Haven and London, 1974.

Goddard, Harold C. *The Meaning of Shakespeare*. Chicago, 1951.

Goldman, Michael. *Shakespeare and the Energies of Drama*. Princeton, 1972.

Granville-Barker, Harley. *Prefaces to Shakespeare*. 2 vols. Princeton, 1946–1947.

Harbage, Alfred. *As They Liked It*. New York, 1947.

——. *Shakespeare and the Rival Traditions*. New York, 1952.

Hawkes, Terence. *Shakespeare's Talking Animals: Language and Drama in Society*. London, 1973.

Hawkins, Harriett. *Poetic Freedom and Poetic Truth: Chaucer, Shakespeare, Marlowe, Milton*. Oxford, 1976.

Holland, Norman. *Psychoanalysis and Shakespeare*. New York, 1966.

——. *The Shakespearean Imagination*. New York, 1964.

Jones, Emrys. *The Origins of Shakespeare*. Oxford, 1977.

Jorgensen, Paul A. *Shakespeare's Military World*. Berkeley and Los Angeles, 1956.

——, ed. *Modern Shakespearean Criticism*. New York, 1970.

Kernan, Alvin B. *The Playwright as Magician: Shakespeare's Image of the Poet in the English Public Theater*. New Haven, 1979.

Kettle, Arnold, ed. *Shakespeare in a Changing World*. London and New York, 1964.

Knights, L. C. *Some Shakespearean Themes*. London, 1959.

Kott, Jan. *Shakespeare Our Contemporary*. New York, 1964.

Leavis, F. R. *The Common Pursuit*. London, 1952.

Levin, Richard. *New Readings vs. Old Plays: Recent Trends in the Reinterpretation of English Renaissance Drama*. Chicago, 1979.

McAlindon, T. *Shakespeare and Decorum*. London and New York, 1973.

Rabkin, Norman. *Shakespeare and the Common Understanding*. New York, 1967.

Righter, Anne. *Shakespeare and the Idea of the Play*. London, 1962.

Rossiter, A. P. *Angel with Horns*. London, 1961.

Sanders, Wilbur. *The Dramatist and the Received Idea: Studies in the Plays of Marlowe and Shakespeare*. Cambridge, Eng., 1968.

Sewell, Arthur. *Character and Society in Shakespeare*. London, 1951.

Soellner, Rolf. *Shakespeare's Patterns of Self-Knowledge*. Columbus, Ohio, 1972.

Spencer, Theodore. *Shakespeare and the Nature of Man*. New York, 1942.

Spivack, Bernard. *Shakespeare and the Allegory of Evil*. New York, 1958.

Stewart, J. I. M. *Character and Motive in Shakespeare*. London, 1949.

Stirling, Brents. *The Populace in Shakespeare*. New York, 1949.

Traversi, Derek. *An Approach to Shakespeare*. 2 vols. Rev. ed. London, 1968.

Van Laan, Thomas F. *Role-Playing in Shakespeare*. Toronto, 1978.

Watson, Curtis Brown. *Shakespeare and the Renaissance Concept of Honor*. Princeton, 1960.

Weimann, Robert. *Shakespeare and the Popular Tradition in the Theater*. Ed. Robert Schwartz. Baltimore, 1978.

Whitaker, Virgil K. *Shakespeare's Use of Learning*. San Marino, Calif., 1953.

Zeeveld, W. Gordon. *The Temper of Shakespeare's Thought*. New Haven and London, 1974.

Shakespeare Criticism Since 1980, Including New Historicism, Gender Studies, and Poststructuralism

See also, under "Shakespeare's Predecessors and Contemporaries," Bednarz, Belsey, Braden, Bristol, Bruster, Cohen, Dolan, Farley-Hills, Findlay (two items), Freer, McLuskie, Orgel, Rasmussen, Rose, Shannon, and Vickers; and under "Shakespeare Criticism from the 1940s to the 1970s," Weimann.

Adelman, Janet. *Suffocating Mothers: Fantasies of Maternal Origin in Shakespeare's Plays, "Hamlet" to "The Tempest."* Chicago, 1992.

Alexander, Catherine M. S., and Stanley Wells, eds. *Shakespeare and Race*. Cambridge, Eng., 2000.

Auden, W. H. *Lectures on Shakespeare*. Ed. Arthur Kirsch. Princeton, 2000.

Bamber, Linda. *Comic Women, Tragic Men: A Study of Gender and Genre in Shakespeare*. Stanford, 1982.

Barber, C. L. *The Whole Journey: Shakespeare's Power of Development*. Berkeley, 1986.

Bate, Jonathan. *The Genius of Shakespeare*. Oxford, 1997.

Belsey, Catherine. *Shakespeare and the Loss of Eden: The Construction of Family Values in Early Modern Culture*. New Brunswick, N.J., 1999.

Berger, Harry, Jr. *Making Trifles of Terrors: Redistributing Complicities in Shakespeare*. Ed. Peter Erickson. Stanford, 1997.

Bergeron, David, ed. *Pageantry in the Shakespearean Theater*. Athens, Ga., 1985.

Bevington, David. *Shakespeare*. Oxford, 2002; 2nd ed., 2005.

Bloom, Harold. *Shakespeare: The Invention of the Human*. New York, 1998.

Boose, Lynda E. "The Father and the Bride in Shakespeare." *PMLA* 97 (1982): 325–347.

Bristol, Michael. *Shakespeare's America, America's Shakespeare*. London and New York, 1990.

Bulman, James C., ed. *Shakespeare, Theory, and Performance*. London and New York, 1996.

Calderwood, James. *Shakespeare and the Denial of Death*. Amherst, Mass., 1987.

Callaghan, Dympna C. *Shakespeare Without Women: Representing Gender and Race on the Renaissance Stage*. London and New York, 2000.

———, ed. *A Feminist Companion to Shakespeare*. Oxford, 2000.

———, Lorraine Helms, and Jyotsna Singh. *The Weyward Sisters: Shakespeare and Feminist Politics*. Cambridge, Eng., 1994.

Carey, John, ed. *English Renaissance Studies*. Oxford, 1980.

Cartelli, Thomas. *Repositioning Shakespeare: National Formations, Postcolonial Appropriations*. London and New York, 1999.

Cavell, Stanley. *Disowning Knowledge in Six Plays of Shakespeare*. Cambridge, Eng., 1987.

Charnes, Linda. *Notorious Identity: Materializing the Subject in Shakespeare*. Cambridge, Mass., 1993.

Cook, Ann Jennalie. *Making a Match: Courtship in Shakespeare and His Society*. Princeton, 1991.

Cox, John D. *Shakespeare and the Dramaturgy of Power*. Princeton, 1989.

Daileder, Celia R. *Eroticism on the Renaissance Stage: Transcendence, Desire, and the Limits of the Visible*. Cambridge, Eng., 1998.

Danson, Lawrence. *Shakespeare's Dramatic Genres.* Oxford, 2000.

Dawson, Anthony B. *Indirections: Shakespeare and the Art of Illusion.* Toronto, 1984.

De Grazia, Margreta, Maureen Quilligan, and Peter Stallybrass, eds. *Subject and Object in Renaissance Culture.* Cambridge, Eng., 1996.

Desmet, Christy. *Reading Shakespeare's Characters: Rhetoric, Ethics, and Identity.* Amherst, Mass., 1992.

———, and Robert Sawyer, eds. *Shakespeare and Appropriation.* London and New York, 1999.

Dobson, Michael. *The Making of the National Poet: Shakespeare, Adaptation, and Authorship, 1660–1769.* Oxford, 1992.

Dolan, Frances E. *Dangerous Familiars: Representations of Domestic Crime in England, 1550–1700.* Ithaca, N.Y., 1994.

Dollimore, Jonathan. *Radical Tragedy: Religion, Ideology and Power in the Drama of Shakespeare and His Contemporaries.* Chicago, 1984; New York, 1989.

———, and Alan Sinfield. *Political Shakespeare: New Essays in Cultural Materialism.* Manchester, Eng., 1985.

Drakakis, John, ed. *Alternative Shakespeares.* London, 1985.

Dubrow, Heather, and Richard Strier, eds. *The Historical Renaissance: New Essays on Tudor and Stuart Literature and Culture.* Chicago, 1988.

Eagleton, Terence. *William Shakespeare.* Oxford, 1986.

Edwards, Philip, et al., eds. *Shakespeare's Styles.* Cambridge, Eng., 1980.

Engle, Lars. *Shakespearean Pragmatism: Market of His Time.* Chicago, 1993.

Erickson, Peter, *Patriarchal Structures in Shakespeare's Drama.* Berkeley, 1985.

———, and Coppélia Kahn, eds. *Shakespeare's Rough Magic: Essays in Honor of C. L. Barber.* Newark, Del., 1985.

French, Marilyn. *Shakespeare's Division of Experience.* New York, 1981.

Frye, Northrop. *Northrop Frye on Shakespeare.* Ed. Robert Sandler. New Haven, 1986.

Fumerton, Patricia, and Simon Hunt, eds. *Renaissance Culture and the Everyday.* Philadelphia, 1999.

Garber, Marjorie. *Coming of Age in Shakespeare.* London, 1981.

———. *Shakespeare's Ghost Writers: Literature as Uncanny Causality.* London and New York, 1987.

———, ed. *Cannibals, Witches, and Divorce: Estranging the Renaissance.* Baltimore, 1987.

———. *Shakespeare After All.* New York, 2004.

Gibbons, Brian. *Shakespeare and Multiplicity.* Cambridge, Eng., 1993.

Gillies, John. *Shakespeare and the Geography of Difference.* Cambridge, Eng., 1994.

Goldberg, Jonathan. *James I and the Politics of Literature: Jonson, Shakespeare, Donne, and Their Contemporaries.* Baltimore, 1983.

———. *Sodometries: Renaissance Texts, Modern Sexualities.* Stanford, 1992.

Grady, Hugh, ed. *Shakespeare and Modernity: Early Modern to Millennium.* London and New York, 2000.

Greenblatt, Stephen. *Learning to Curse: Essays in Early Modern Culture.* London and New York, 1990.

———. *Marvelous Possessions: The Wonder of the New World.* Chicago, 1991.

———. *Renaissance Self-Fashioning: From More to Shakespeare.* Chicago, 1980.

———. *Shakespearean Negotiations: The Circulation of Social Energy in Renaissance England.* Berkeley, 1988.

Habib, Imtiaz. *Shakespeare and Race: Postcolonial Praxis in the Early Modern Period.* Lanham and Oxford, 2000.

Hall, Kim F. *Things of Darkness: Economies of Race and Gender in Early Modern England.* Ithaca, N.Y., 1994.

Hamilton, Donna B. *Shakespeare and the Politics of Protestant England.* Lexington, Ky., 1992.

Hamlin, William M. *The Image of America in Montaigne, Spenser, and Shakespeare: Renaissance Ethnography and Literary Tradition.* New York, 1995.

Hawkes, Terence. *Meaning by Shakespeare.* London and New York, 1992.

———, ed. *Alternative Shakespeares.* Vol. 2. London and New York, 1996.

Holland, Norman, et al., eds. *Shakespeare's Personality.* Berkeley, 1989.

Howard, Jean E. *Shakespeare's Art of Orchestration: Stage Technique and Audience Response.* Urbana, Ill., 1984.

———. *The Stage and Social Struggle in Early Modern England.* London, 1994.

———, and Marion F. O'Connor, eds. *Shakespeare Reproduced: The Text in History and Ideology.* London and New York, 1987.

———, and Scott Cutler Shershow, eds. *Marxist Shakespeares.* London and New York, 2000.

James, Heather. *Shakespeare's Troy: Drama, Politics, and the Translation of Empire.* Cambridge, Eng., 1997.

Jardine, Lisa. *Reading Shakespeare Historically.* London and New York, 1996.

———. *Still Harping on Daughters: Women and Drama in the Age of Shakespeare.* Sussex and Totowa, N.J., 1983; New York, 1989.

Kahn, Coppélia. *Man's Estate: Masculine Identity in Shakespeare.* Berkeley, 1981.

———. *Roman Shakespeare: Warriors, Wounds, and Women.* London and New York, 1997.

Kamps, Ivo, ed. *Materialist Shakespeare: A History.* London, 1995.

———, ed. *Shakespeare Left and Right.* New York and London, 1991.

Kastan, David Scott. *Shakespeare After Theory.* London, 1999.

———. *Shakespeare and the Book.* Cambridge, Eng., 2001.

———. *Shakespeare and the Shapes of Time.* Hanover, N.H., 1982.

———, ed. *A Companion to Shakespeare.* Oxford, 1999.

Kernan, Alvin. *Shakespeare, the King's Playwright: Theater in the Stuart Court, 1603–1613.* New Haven, 1995.

Kerrigan, William. *Shakespeare's Promises.* Baltimore, 1999.

Kirsch, Arthur. *Shakespeare and the Experience of Love.* Cambridge, Eng., 1981.

Knapp, Robert S. *Shakespeare—The Theater and the Book.* Princeton, 1989.

Knowles, Richard, ed. *Shakespeare and Carnival: After Bakhtin.* London and New York, 1998.

Lenz, Carolyn, et al., eds. *The Woman's Part: Feminist Criticism of Shakespeare.* Urbana, Ill., 1980.

Little, Arthur L., Jr. *Shakespeare Jungle Fever: National-Imperial Re-Visions of Race, Rape, and Sacrifice.* Stanford, 2000.

Loomba, Ania. *Gender, Race, Renaissance Drama.* Manchester, Eng., 1989.

———, and Martin Orkin, eds. *Post-colonial Shakespeares.* London and New York, 1998.

Mahon, John W., and Thomas A. Pendleton, eds. *"Fanned and Winnowed Opinion": Shakespearean Essays Presented to Harold Jenkins.* London, 1987.

Mallin, Eric. *Inscribing the Time: Shakespeare and the End of Elizabethan England.* Berkeley, 1995.

Marcus, Leah. *Puzzling Shakespeare: Local Reading and Its Discontents.* Berkeley, 1988.

Mazzio, Carla, and Douglas Trevor, eds. *Historicism, Psychoanalysis, and Early Modern Culture.* London and New York, 2000.

McDonald, Russ, ed. *Shakespeare Reread: The Texts in New Contexts.* Ithaca, N.Y., 1994.

McMullan, Gordon, and Jonathan Hope, eds. *The Politics of Tragicomedy: Shakespeare and After.* London and New York, 1992.

Melchiori, Giorgio. *Shakespeare's Garter Plays: "Edward III" to "Merry Wives of Windsor."* Newark, Del., 1994.

Miola, Robert S. *Shakespeare's Reading.* Oxford and New York, 2000.

———. *Shakespeare's Rome.* Cambridge, Eng., 1983.

Montrose, Louis. *The Purpose of Playing: Shakespeare and Cultural Politics of the Elizabethan Theatre.* Chicago, 1996.

Mullaney, Steven. *The Place of the Stage: License, Play, and Power in Renaissance England.* Chicago, 1988.

Neely, Carol Thomas. *Broken Nuptials in Shakespeare's Plays.* New Haven, 1985.

Newman, Karen. *Fashioning Femininity and the English Renaissance Drama.* Chicago, 1991.

Novy, Marianne. *Love's Argument: Gender Relations in Shakespeare.* Chapel Hill, N.C., 1984.

———, ed. *Women's Re-Visions of Shakespeare.* Urbana, Ill., 1990.

Nuttall, A. D. *A New Mimesis: Shakespeare and the Representation of Reality.* London, 1983.

Orgel, Stephen. *The Authentic Shakespeare and Other Problems of the Early Modern Stage.* London and New York, 2002.

———, and Sean Keilen, eds. *Shakespeare and History; Post-modern Shakespeare; Shakespeare and the Interpretive Tradition; Shakespeare and the Literary Tradition; Shakespeare and Gender; Political Shakespeare.* Separate vols. New York, 1999.

Parker, Patricia. *Shakespeare from the Margins: Language, Culture, Context.* Chicago, 1996.

———, and Geoffrey Hartman, eds. *Shakespeare and the Question of Theory.* London, 1985.

Paster, Gail Kern. *The Body Embarrassed: Drama and the Disciplines of Shame in Early Modern England.* Ithaca, N.Y., 1993.

Patterson, Annabel. *Shakespeare and the Popular Voice.* Oxford, 1989.

Rabkin, Norman. *Shakespeare and the Problem of Meaning.* Chicago, 1981.

Salingar, Leo. *Dramatic Form in Shakespeare and the Jacobeans.* Cambridge, Eng., 1986.

Schwartz, Murray, and Coppélia Kahn, eds. *Representing Shakespeare: New Psychoanalytic Essays.* Baltimore, 1980.

Siemon, James R. *Shakespearean Iconoclasm.* Berkeley, 1985.

Sinfield, Alan. *Faultlines: Cultural Materialism and the Politics of Dissident Reading.* Berkeley, 1992.

Skura, Meredith Anne. *The Literary Use of the Psychoanalytic Process.* New Haven, 1981.

———. *Shakespeare the Actor and the Purposes of Playing.* Chicago, 1993.

Smith, Bruce R. *Homosexual Desire in Shakespeare's England.* Chicago, 1991.

———. *Shakespeare and Masculinity.* Oxford, 2000.

Stockholder, Kay. *Dream Works: Lovers and Families in Shakespeare's Plays.* Toronto, 1987.

Taylor, Gary. *Reinventing Shakespeare: A Cultural History from the Restoration to the Present.* New York, 1989.

Traub, Valerie. *Desire and Anxiety: Circulations of Sexuality in Shakespearean Drama.* London, 1992.

Vickers, Brian. *Appropriating Shakespeare: Contemporary Critical Quarrels.* New Haven, 1993.

Watson, Robert N. *The Rest Is Silence: Death as Annihilation in the English Renaissance.* Berkeley, 1994.

———. *Shakespeare and the Hazards of Ambition.* Cambridge, Mass., 1984.

Wayne, Valerie, ed. *The Matter of Difference: Materialist Feminist Criticism of Shakespeare.* Ithaca, N.Y., 1991.

Weimann, Robert. *Author's Pen and Actor's Voice: Playing and Writing in Shakespeare's Theatre.* Cambridge, Eng., 2000.

Wells, Robin Headlam. *Shakespeare on Masculinity.* Cambridge, Eng., 2000.

———. *Shakespeare, Politics, and the State.* London, 1986.

Wheeler, Richard P. *Shakespeare's Development and the Problem Comedies: Turn and Counter-Turn.* Berkeley, 1981.

White, Paul Whitfield, and Suzanne R. Westfall, eds. *Shakespeare and Theatrical Patronage in Early Modern England*. Cambridge, Eng., 2002.

Williams, Gordon. *Shakespeare, Sex, and the Print Revolution*. London and Atlantic Highlands, N.J., 1996.

Woodbridge, Linda. *The Scythe of Saturn: Shakespeare's Magical Thinking*. Urbana, Ill., 1994.

———, and Edward Berry, eds. *True Rites and Maimed Rites: Ritual and Anti-Ritual in Shakespeare and His Age*. Urbana, Ill., 1992.

Ziegler, Georgianna, ed. *Shakespeare's Unruly Women*. Washington, D.C., 1997.

Shakespeare on Stage; Performance, Dramaturgy

See also, under "Shakespeare Criticism from the 1940s to the 1970s," Goldman and Granville-Barker.

Adler, Steven. *This Rough Magic: Making Theatre at the Royal Shakespeare Company*. Carbondale, Ill., 2001.

Bartholomeusz, Dennis. *Macbeth and the Players*. Cambridge, Eng., 1969.

Barton, John. *Playing Shakespeare*. London, 1984.

Beauman, Sally. *The Royal Shakespeare Company: A History of Ten Decades*. Oxford, 1982.

Bevington, David. *Action is Eloquence: Shakespeare's Language of Gesture*. Cambridge, Mass., 1984.

Brockbank, Philip, ed. *Players of Shakespeare*. Cambridge, Eng., 1985.

Brook, Peter. *The Empty Space*. New York, 1968.

Brown, Ivor. *Shakespeare and the Actors*. London, 1970.

Brown, John Russell. *Shakespeare's Plays in Performance*. London, 1966.

———. *Shakespeare's Dramatic Style*. London, 1970.

Carlisle, Carol Jones. *Shakespeare from the Greenroom: Actors' Criticisms of Four Major Tragedies*. Chapel Hill, N.C., 1969.

Chambers, Colin. *Inside the Royal Shakespeare Company: Creativity and the Institution*. London and New York, 2004.

Cohn, Ruby. *Modern Shakespeare Offshoots*. Princeton, 1976.

Cook, Judith. *Shakespeare's Players*. London, 1983.

Croyden, Margaret. *Lunatics, Lovers and Poets: The Contemporary Experimental Theatre*. New York, 1974.

Dessen, Alan C. *Recovering Shakespeare's Theatrical Vocabulary*. Cambridge, Eng., 1995.

———. *Rescripting Shakespeare: The Text, the Director, and Modern Productions*. Cambridge, Eng., 2002.

———, and Leslie Thomson. *A Dictionary of Stage Directions in English Drama, 1580–1642*. Cambridge, Eng., 1999.

Donohue, Joseph W., Jr. *Dramatic Character in the English Romantic Age*. Princeton, 1970.

Downer, Alan S. *The Eminent Tragedian, William Charles Macready*. Cambridge, Mass., 1966.

Edelman, Charles. *Brawl Ridiculous: Swordfighting in Shakespeare's Plays*. Manchester, Eng., 1992.

Greenwald, Michael L. *Directions by Indirections: John Barton of the Royal Shakespeare Company*. Toronto and London, 1985.

Hodgdon, Barbara. *The Shakespeare Trade: Performances and Appropriations*. Philadelphia, 1998.

Hogan, Charles B. *Shakespeare in the Theatre, 1701–1800*. 2 vols. Oxford, 1952, 1957.

Jackson, Russell, and Robert Smallwood, eds. *Players of Shakespeare 2*. Cambridge, Eng., 1988. Followed by Vols. 3 (1993); and 4, ed. Smallwood (1998).

Jones, Emrys. *Scenic Form in Shakespeare*. Oxford, 1971.

Kozintsev, Grigori. *Shakespeare: Time and Conscience*. Trans. by Joyce Veining. New York, 1966.

Kott, Jan. *Shakespeare Our Contemporary*. Trans. Boleslaw Taborski. Preface by Peter Brook. London, 1965.

Lieter, Samuel L. *Shakespeare Around the Globe: A Guide to Notable Postwar Revivals*. Westport, Conn., 1986.

Lizard, James P., and June Schuster. *Reading Shakespeare in Performance: "King Lear."* London and Toronto, 1990.

Marowitz, Charles. *The Marowitz Shakespeare*. New York, 1978.

Mazur, Cary M. *Shakespeare Refashioned: Elizabethan Plays on Edwardian Stages*. Ann Arbor, Mich.: 1981.

McGuire, Philip C. *Speechless Dialect: Shakespeare's Open Silences*. Berkeley, 1985.

———, and David A. Samuelson. *Shakespeare: The Theatrical Dimension*. New York, 1979.

Odell, George C. D. *Shakespeare from Betterton to Irving*. 2 vols. New York, 1920, 1966.

Olivier, Laurence. *Confessions of An Actor*. London, 1982.

Osbourne, Lisa. *The Trick of Singularity: The Performance Editions*. Iowa City, IA: 1996.

Pearson, Hesketh. *Beerbohm Tree*. New York: 1956.

Poel, William. *Shakespeare in the Theatre*. London, 1913, 1968.

Price, Joseph G., ed. *The Triple Bond: Plays, Mainly Shakespearean, in Performance*. University Park, Pa., 1975.

Quince, Rohan. *Shakespeare in South Africa: Stage Productions during the Apartheid Era*. New York, 2000.

Rosenberg, Marvin. *The Masks of Shakespeare*. Berkeley, 1972.

Rutter, Carol Chillington, ed. *Documents of the Rose Playhouse*. Manchester, Eng., 1999.

———, et al. *Clamorous Voices: Shakespeare's Women Today*. New York, 1989.

Shapiro, Michael. *Gender in Play on the Shakespearean Stage: Boy Heroines and Female Pages*. Ann Arbor, Mich., 1994.

Shattuck, Charles H. *The Shakespeare Promptbooks: A Descriptive Catalogue*. Urbana, Ill., 1965.

———. *Shakespeare on the American Stage from the Hallams to Edwin Booth*. Washington, D.C., 1976; *from Booth and Barrett to Sothern and Marlowe*, Washington, D.C., 1987.

Shaugnessy, Robert. *Representing Shakespeare: England, History and the RSC.* New York, 1994.

Slater, Ann Pasternak. *Shakespeare the Director.* Brighton, Sussex, and Totowa, N.J., 1982.

Speaight, Robert. *William Poel and the Elizabethan Revival.* London, 1954.

Sprague, Arthur Colby. *Shakespeare and the Actors.* Cambridge, Mass., 1944.

———. *Shakespearian Players and Performances.* Cambridge, Mass., 1953.

Styan, J. L. *Shakespeare's Stagecraft.* Cambridge, Eng., 1967.

Todd, Andrew, and Jean-Guy Lecat. *The Open Circle: Peter Brook's Theatrical Environments.* New York, 2003.

Tynan, Kenneth. *The Diaries of Kenneth Tynan.* Ed. John Lahr. New York and London, 2001.

Wells, Stanley. *Royal Shakespeare: Four Major Productions at Stratford-upon-Avon.* Manchester, Eng., 1977.

Shakespeare on Film, Television, and Video

Ball, Robert Hamilton. *Shakespeare on Silent Film.* London, 1968.

Bogdanovich, Peter, and Jonathan Rosenbaum. *This Is Orson Welles.* New York, 1992.

Boose, Lynda E., and Richard Burt, eds. *Shakespeare: The Movie: Popularizing the Plays on Film, TV, and Video.* London and New York, 1997, 1999.

Brady, Leo, and Marshall Cohen, eds. *Film Theory and Criticism.* Oxford, 1974, 1999.

Brode, Douglas, *Shakespeare in the Movies: From the Silent Era to "Shakespeare in Love."* Oxford, 2000.

Buhler, Stephen M. *Shakespeare in the Cinema: Ocular Proof.* Albany, N.Y., 2002.

Bulman, J. C., and H. R. Coursen, eds. *Shakespeare on Television: An Anthology of Essays and Reviews.* Hanover, N.H., 1988.

Burnett, Mark Thomson, and Ramona Wray, eds. *Shakespeare, Film, Fin de Siecle.* Basingstoke, Eng., 2000.

Collick, John. *Shakespeare, Cinema, and Society.* Manchester, Eng., 1990.

Crowl, Samuel. *Shakespeare at the Cineplex.* Athens, Ohio, 2003.

———. *Shakespeare Observed: Studies in Performance on Stage and Screen.* Athens, Ohio, 1992.

Davies, Anthony, and Stanley Wells, eds. *Shakespeare and the Moving Image: The Plays on Film and Television.* Cambridge, Eng., 1994.

Donaldson, Peter. S. *Shakespearean Films/Shakespearean Directors.* Boston, 1990.

Eckert, Charles W., ed. *Focus on Shakespearean Films.* Englewood Cliffs, N.J., 1972.

Holderness, Graham. *Visual Shakespeare: Essays in Film and Television.* Hatfield, Hertfordshire, 2002.

———. and Christopher McCullough, "Shakespeare on the Screen: A Selective Filmography." *Shakespeare and the Moving Image, The Plays on Film and Television.* Eds. Anthony Davies and Stanley Wells. Cambridge, Eng., 1994. 18–49.

Howard, James. *The Complete Films of Orson Welles.* New York, 1991.

Howlett, Kathy M. *Framing Shakespeare on Film.* Athens, Ohio, 2000.

Ivory, James. *Savages, Shakespeare Wallah, Two Films by James Ivory.* New York, 1973.

Jackson, Russell, ed. *The Cambridge Companion to Shakespeare on Film.* Cambridge, Eng., 2000.

Jorgens, Jack L. *Shakespeare on Film.* Bloomington, Ind., 1977.

Kliman, Bernice W. *"Hamlet": Film, Television and Audio Performance.* Cranbury, N.J., 1988.

Lane, Anthony. "Tights, Camera, Action: How Shakespeare Became This Year's Jane Austen." *New Yorker* 25 Nov. 1993: 128:36, 65–77.

Lehman, Courtney, and Lisa S. Starks, *Spectacular Shakespeare: Critical theory and Popular Cinema.* Madison, N.J., and London, 2002.

Manvell, Roger. *Shakespeare and the Film.* London and New York, 1971/77.

McKernan, Luke, and Olwen Terris, eds. *Walking Shadows: Shakespeare in the National Film and Television Archives.* London, 1994.

Morris, Peter. *Shakespeare on Film.* Ottawa, 1972.

Parker, Barry M. *The Folger Shakespeare Filmography.* Washington, D.C., 1977.

Pilkington, Ace. *Screening Shakespeare: From "Richard II" to "Henry V."* Newark and London, 1991.

Rosenthal, Daniel. *Shakespeare on Screen.* London, 2000.

Rothwell, Kenneth S. *A History of Shakespeare on Screen: A Century of Film and Television.* Cambridge, 1999.

———. "In Search of Nothing: Mapping *King Lear.*" *Shakespeare: The Movie.* Eds. Boose and Burt. London and New York, 1997/99. 135–147.

———, and Annabelle Henkin Melzer, eds. *Shakespeare on Screen: An International Filmography and Videography.* London, 1990.

Shaughnessy, Robert, ed. *Shakespeare on Film.* New Casebook series. Basingtoke and London, 1998.

Sinyard, Neil. *Filming Literature: The Art of Adaptation.* London, 1986.

Skovmand, Michael, ed. *Screen Shakespeare.* Aarhus, Denmark, 1994.

Tassone, Aldo. *Akira Kurosawa.* Paris: Flammarion, 1983, 1990.

Uricchio, William, and Roberta E. Pearson. *Reframing Culture: The Case of the Vitagraph Quality Films.* Princeton, 1993.

Welsh, James M., Richard Vela, John C. Tibbetts, et al., *Shakespeare into Film.* New York, 2002.

Willis, Susan. *The BBC Shakespeare Plays: Making the Tele-vised Canon*. Chapel, Hill, N.C., 1991.

Willson, Robert F., Jr. *Shakespeare in Hollywood, 1929–1956*. Madison, N.J., and London, 2000.

Zeffirelli, Franco. *The Autobiography of Franco Zeffirelli*. New York, 1986.

The Comedies

See also, under "Shakespeare Criticism Since 1980," Drakakis (essay by Belsey), Erickson and Kahn (essay by Adelman), and Paster (Chapter 7).

Anderson, Linda. *A Kind of Wild Justice: Revenge in Shakespeare's Comedies*. Newark, Del., 1987.

Barber, C. L. *Shakespeare's Festive Comedy*. Princeton, 1959.

Barton, Anne. *The Names of Comedy*. Toronto, 1990.

Berry, Edward. *Shakespeare's Comic Rites*. Cambridge, Eng., 1984.

Berry, Ralph. *Shakespeare's Comedies: Explorations in Form*. Princeton, 1972.

——. *The Shakespearean Metaphor: Studies in Language and Form*. Totowa, N.J., 1978.

Bloom, Harold, ed. *William Shakespeare: Comedies and Romances*. New York, 1986.

Bradbury, Malcolm, and David Palmer, eds. *Shakespearian Comedy*. London, 1972.

Brown, John Russell. *Shakespeare and His Comedies*. London, 1957, 1968.

——, and Bernard Harris, eds. *Early Shakespeare. Stratford-upon-Avon Studies 3*. London, 1961. (Including an essay by Frank Kermode on "The Mature Comedies.")

Bryant, J. A., Jr. *Shakespeare and the Uses of Comedy*. Lexington, Ky., 1986.

Burke, William Kenneth. *A New Approach to Shakespeare's Early Comedies: Theoretical Foundations*. New York, 1998.

Carroll, William C. *The Metamorphoses of Shakespearean Comedy*. Princeton, 1985.

Champion, Larry S. *The Evolution of Shakespeare's Comedy*. Cambridge, Mass., 1970.

Charlton, H. B. *Shakespearian Comedy*. London, 1938.

Charney, Maurice, ed. *Shakespearean Comedy*. New York, 1980.

Cody, Richard. *The Landscape of the Mind: Pastoralism and Platonic Theory in Tasso's "Aminta" and Shakespeare's Early Comedies*. Oxford, 1969.

Collins, Michael J., ed. *Shakespeare's Sweet Thunder: Essays on the Early Comedies*. Newark, Del., 1997.

Cook, Ann Jennalie. *Making a Match: Courtship in Shakespeare and His Society*. Princeton, 1991.

Cordner, Michael, Peter Holland, and John Kerrigan, eds. *English Comedy*. Cambridge, Eng., 1994.

Dutton, Richard, and Jean E. Howard, eds. *A Companion to Shakespeare's Works: The Comedies*. Malden, Mass., Oxford and Victoria, 2003.

Elam, Keir. *Shakespeare's Universe of Discourse: Language-Games in the Comedies*. Cambridge, Eng., 1984.

Evans, Bertrand. *Shakespeare's Comedies*. Oxford, 1960.

Freedman, Barbara. *Staging the Gaze: Postmodernism, Psychoanalysis, and Shakespearean Comedy*. Ithaca, N. Y., 1991.

Friedman, Michael D. *"The World Must Be Peopled": Shakespeare's Comedies of Forgiveness*. Madison, N. J., and London, 2002.

Frye, Northrop. "The Argument of Comedy." *English Institute Essays 1948*. New York, 1949.

——. *A Natural Perspective: The Development of Shakespearean Comedy and Romance*. New York, 1965.

Hall, Jonathan. *Anxious Pleasures: Shakespearean Comedy and the Nation-State*. Madison, N. J., 1995.

Hamilton, A. C. *The Early Shakespeare*. San Marino, Calif., 1967.

Hassel, R. Chris. *Faith and Folly in Shakespeare's Romantic Comedies*. Athens, Ga., 1980.

Hawkins, Sherman H. "The Two Worlds of Shakespearean Comedy." *ShakS* 3 (1967): 62–80.

Hunter, Robert G. *Shakespeare and the Comedy of Forgiveness*. New York, 1965.

Huston, J. Dennis. *Shakespeare's Comedies of Play*. New York, 1981.

Leggatt, Alexander. *English Stage Comedy, 1490–1990: Five Centuries of a Genre*. London and New York, 1998.

——. *Shakespeare's Comedy of Love*. London and New York, 1974.

——, ed. *Shakespearean Comedy*. Cambridge, Eng., 2002.

Lerner, Laurence, ed. *Shakespeare's Comedies: An Anthology of Modern Criticism*. Baltimore, 1967.

Levin, Richard A. *Love and Society in Shakespearean Comedy: A Study of Dramatic Form and Content*. Newark, Del., 1985.

Miola, Robert S. *Shakespeare and Classical Comedy: The Influence of Plautus and Terence*. Oxford, 1994.

Nevo, Ruth. *Comic Transformations in Shakespeare*. London, 1980.

Newman, Karen. *Shakespeare's Rhetoric of Comic Character*. New York and London, 1985.

Palmer, David J., and Malcolm Bradbury, eds. *Shakespearian Comedy. Statford-upon-Avon Studies 1*. London, 1972.

Palmer, John. *Comic Characters of Shakespeare*. London, 1946.

Pettet, E. C. *Shakespeare and the Romance Tradition*. London, 1949.

Phialas, Peter G. *Shakespeare's Romantic Comedies*. Chapel Hill, N.C., 1966.

Richmond, Hugh M. *Shakespeare's Sexual Comedy*. Indianapolis, 1971.

Salingar, Leo. *Shakespeare and the Traditions of Comedy.* Cambridge, Eng., 1974.

Shaheen, Naseeb. *Biblical References in Shakespeare's Comedies.* Newark, Del., 1993.

Smidt, Kristian. *Unconformities in Shakespeare's Early Comedies.* London, 1986.

Stevenson, David L. *The Love-Game Comedy.* New York, 1946.

Traversi, Derek. *Shakespeare: The Early Comedies.* London, 1960.

Turner, Robert Y. *Shakespeare's Apprenticeship.* Chicago, 1974.

Westlund, Joseph. *Shakespeare's Reparative Comedies: A Psychoanalytic View of the Middle Plays.* Chicago, 1984.

Wheeler, Richard P. "Deaths in the Family: The Loss of a Son and the Rise of Shakespearean Comedy." *SQ* 51 (2000): 127–153.

Williamson, Marilyn. *The Patriarchy of Shakespeare's Comedies.* Detroit, 1986.

THE TAMING OF THE SHREW

See also, under "Shakespeare's Predecessors and Contemporaries," Marrapodi (essay by Bevington); under "Shakespeare Criticism from the 1940s to the 1970s," Garber; under "Shakespeare Criticism Since 1980," Auden, Fumerton and Hunt (essay by Dolan), Kahn, Lenz et al. (essay by Bean), McDonald (essay by Boose), Novy (*Love's Argument*), and Parker and Hartman (essay by Fineman); under "Shakespeare on Stage," Rutter; and under "The Comedies," R. Berry, Charlton, Collins (essays by Dessen and Rutter), Evans, Hawkins, Huston, Leggatt, Nevo, and Stevenson.

Bean, John. "Comic Structure and the Humanizing of Kate in *The Taming of the Shrew.*" *The Woman's Part: Feminist Criticism of Shakespeare.* Eds. Carolyn Ruth Swift Lenz, Gayle Green, and Carol Thomas Neely. Urbana, 1980. 65–78.

Boose, Lynda E. " 'Scolding Brides and Bridling Scolds': Taming the Woman's Unruly Member." *SQ* 42 (1991): 179–213.

Brunvand, Jan Harold. "The Folktale Origin of *The Taming of the Shrew.*" *SQ* 17 (1966): 345–359.

Dolan, Frances E., ed. *"The Taming of the Shrew": Text and Contexts.* New York, 1996.

Freedman, Barbara. *Staging the Gaze: Post-modernism, Psychoanalysis and Shakespearean Comedy.* Ithaca and London, 1991.

Haring-Smith, Tori. *From Farce to Metadrama; A Stage History of "The Taming of the Shrew," 1594–1983.* Westport, Conn., 1985.

Henderson, Diana E. "A Shrew for the Times." *Shakespeare: The Movie.* Eds. Lynda E. Boose and Richard Burt. London and New York, 1997, 1999. 148–168.

Hodgdon, Barbara. "Katerina Bound; or Play (K)ating the Strictures of Everyday Life." *Shakespeare on Film.* Ed. Robert Shaughnessy. New York, 1998. 156–172.

Hosley, Richard. "Was There a 'Dramatic Epilogue' to *The Taming of the Shrew*?" *Studies in English Literature* 1:2 (1961): 17–34.

Hutson, Lorna. *The Usurer's Daughter: Male Friendship and Fictions of Women in Sixteenth-Century England.* London and New York, 1994.

Jayne, Sears. "The Dreaming of *The Shrew.*" *SQ* 17 (1966): 41–56.

Korda, Natasha. "Household Kates: Domesticating Commodities in *The Taming of the Shrew.*" *SQ* 47 (1996): 109–131.

Maguire, Laurie E. "Cultural Control in *The Taming of the Shrew.*" *Renaissance Drama* n.s. 26 (1995): 83–104.

Marcus, Leah. "The Shakespearean Editor as Shrew-Tamer." *English Literary Renaissance* 22 (1922): 177–200.

Newman, Karen. "Renaissance Family Politics and Shakespeare's *The Taming of the Shrew.*" *English Literary Renaissance* 16 (1986): 86–100.

Saccio, Peter. "Shrewd and Kindly Farce." *ShS* 37 (1984): 33–40.

Thompson, Ann, ed. *The Taming of the Shrew.* Cambridge, Eng., 1984.

Thorne, W. B. "Folk Elements in *The Taming of the Shrew.*" *Queen's Quarterly* 75 (1968): 482–496.

A MIDSUMMER NIGHT'S DREAM

See also, under "Life in Shakespeare's England," De Grazia, Quilligan, and Stallybrass (essay by Parker); under "Shakespeare Criticism from the 1940s to the 1970s," Calderwood, Coghill, Garber, Granville-Barker, and Kott; under "Shakespeare Criticism Since 1980," Callaghan (*A Feminist Companion*, essay by Loomba), Mazzio and Trevor (essay by Maus), Montrose, Parker, Paster, and Patterson (Chapter 3); and under "The Comedies," Barber, Bloom (essay by Girard), Brown and Harris (essays by Kermode and Merchant), Carroll, Collins (essay by Halio), Evans, Huston, Leggatt, Lerner, Palmer and Bradbury (essay by Wells), and Smidt.

Bevington, David. " 'But We Are Spirits of Another Sort': The Dark Side of Love and Magic in *A Midsummer Night's Dream.*" *Medieval and Renaissance Studies.* Ed. Siegfried Wenzel. Chapel Hill, N.C., 1978.

Donaldson, E. Talbot. *The Swan at the Well: Shakespeare Reads Chaucer.* New Haven, 1985.

Garner, Shirley Nelson. "*A Midsummer Night's Dream*: 'Jack Shall Have Jill; Nought Shall Go Ill.' " *Women's Studies* 9 (1981): 47–63.

Girard, René. "Myth and Ritual in Shakespeare's *A Midsummer Night's Dream*." *Textual Strategies: Perspectives in Post-Structuralist Criticism*. Ed. Josué V. Harari. Ithaca, N.Y., 1979.

Howard, Skiles. "Hands, Feet, and Bottoms: Decentering the Cosmic Dance in *A Midsummer Night's Dream*." *SQ* 44 (1993): 325–342.

Lamb, Mary Ellen. "*A Midsummer Night's Dream*: The Myth of Theseus and the Minotaur." *Texas Studies in Literature and Language* 21 (1979): 478–491.

———. " 'Taken by the Fairies': Fairy Practices and the Production of Popular Culture in *A Midsummer Night's Dream*." *SQ* 51 (2000): 277–312.

Montrose, Louis Adrian. " 'Shaping Fantasies': Figurations of Gender and Power in Elizabethan Culture." *Representations* 2 (1.2, Spring 1983): 61–94.

Nuttall, A. D. "*A Midsummer Night's Dream*: Comedy as *Apotrope* of Myth." *ShS* 53 (2000): 49–59.

Olson, Paul A. "*A Midsummer Night's Dream* and the Meaning of Court Marriage." *ELH* 24 (1957): 95–119.

Ormerod, David. "*A Midsummer Night's Dream*: The Monster in the Labyrinth." *ShakS* 11 (1978): 39–52.

Pearson, D'Orsay W. " 'Unkinde' Theseus: A Study in Renaissance Mythography." *English Literary Renaissance* 4 (1974): 276–298.

Selbourne, David. *The Making of "A Midsummer Night's Dream."* London, 1982.

Wall, Wendy. "Why Does Puck Sweep?: Fairylore, Merry Wives, and Social Struggle." *SQ* 52 (2001): 67–106.

Warren, Roger. *"A Midsummer Night's Dream": Text and Performance.* London, 1983.

Williams, Gary Jay. *Our Moonlight Revels: "A Midsummer Night's Dream" in the Theatre.* Ames, Iowa, 1997.

Young, David P. *Something of Great Constancy: The Art of "A Midsummer Night's Dream."* New Haven, 1966.

The Merchant of Venice

See also, under "Shakespeare's Predecessors and Contemporaries," Rose (ed. *Renaissance Drama*, essay by Whigham); under "Shakespeare's Language," Donawerth; under "Shakespeare Criticism from the 1940s to the 1970s," Burkhardt, Fiedler, and Granville-Barker; under "Shakespeare Criticism Since 1980," Auden, Callaghan (*A Feminist Companion*, essay by Singh), Dawson, Erickson and Kahn (essays by Kahn and Wheeler), Garber (*Cannibals*, essay by Mullaney), Grady (essays by Drakakis, Freinkel, and Mallin), Howard and O'Connor (essay by Moisan), Mazzio and Trevor (essay by Siemon), Novy (*Love's Argument*, Chapter 4), Rabkin, and Wayne (essay by Leventen); and under "The Comedies," Barber, Bradbury and Palmer (essay by Palmer), Brown and Harris

(essays by J. R. Brown and Kermode), Evans, Leggatt, Levin, Nevo, and Smidt.

Auden, W. H. "Brothers and Others." *"The Dyer's Hand" and Other Essays.* New York, 1948.

Berger, Harry, Jr. "Marriage and Mercifixion in *The Merchant of Venice*: The Casket Scene Revisited." *SQ* 32 (1981): 155–162.

Boose, Lynda E. "The Comic Contract and Portia's Golden Ring." *ShakS* 20 (1988): 241–254.

Bulman, James C. *The Merchant of Venice. Shakespeare in Performance.* Manchester, Eng., 1991.

Cohen, Walter. "*The Merchant of Venice* and the Possibilities of Historical Criticism." *ELH* 49 (1982): 765–789.

Cusack, Sinead. "Portia in *The Merchant of Venice*." *Players of Shakespeare.* Vol. 1. Ed. Philip Brockbank. Cambridge, Eng., 1985. 29–40.

Danson, Lawrence. *The Harmonies of "The Merchant of Venice."* New Haven and London, 1978.

Dessen, Alan C. "The Elizabethan Stage Jew and Christian Example: Gerontus, Barabas, and Shylock." *Modern Language Quarterly* 35 (1974): 231–245.

Edelman, Charles. "Which is the Jew that Shakespeare Knew? Shylock on the Elizabethan Stage." *ShS* 52 (1999): 99–106.

———, ed. *The Merchant of Venice.* Cambridge, 2002. Esp. stage and film history 1–92.

Engle, Lars. " 'Thrift is Blessing': Exchange and Explanation in *The Merchant of Venice*." *SQ* 37 (1986): 20–37.

Fiedler, Leslie. *The Stranger in Shakespeare.* New York, 1972.

Freud, Sigmund. "The Theme of the Three Caskets." *Complete Psychological Works of Sigmund Freud.* Trans. James Strachey et al. London, 1973–4.

Girard, René. " 'To Entrap the Wisest': A Reading of *The Merchant of Venice*." *Literature and Society.* Selected Papers from the English Institute, 1978. Ed. Edward W. Said. Baltimore, 1980.

Hutson, Lorna. *The Usurer's Daughter: Male Friendship and Fictions of Women in Sixteenth-Century England.* London and New York, 1994.

Jardine, Lisa. "Cultural Confusion and Shakespeare's Learned Heroines: 'These Are Old Paradoxes.' " *SQ* 38 (1987): 1–18.

Legatt, Alexander. "*The Merchant of Venice*: A Modern Perspective." The New Folger *Merchant of Venice.* New York, 1992.

Lelyveld, Toby. *Shylock on the Stage.* Cleveland, 1960.

Lever, J. W. "Shylock, Portia, and the Values of Shakespearian Comedy." *SQ* 3 (1952): 383–386.

Lewalski, Barbara K. "Biblical Allusion and Allegory in *The Merchant of Venice*." *SQ* 13 (1962): 327–343.

Mahon, John W., and Ellen MacLeod Mahon, eds. *"The Merchant of Venice": New Critical Essays.* New York and London, 2002.

MacKay, Maxine. "*The Merchant of Venice*: A Reflection of the Early Conflict Between Courts of Law and Courts of Equity." *SQ* 15:4 (1964): 371–375.

Moody, A. D. *Shakespeare: "The Merchant of Venice."* London, 1964.

Newman, Karen. "Portia's Ring: Unruly Women and Structures of Exchange in *The Merchant of Venice.*" *SQ* 38 (1987): 19–33.

Normand, Lawrence. "Reading the Body in *The Merchant of Venice.*" *Textual Practice* 5 (1991): 55–73.

Overton, Bill. *"The Merchant of Venice": Text and Performance.* Atlantic Highlands, N.J., 1987.

Parten, Anne. "Re-establishing Sexual Order: The Ring Episode in *The Merchant of Venice.*" *Women's Studies* 9 (1982): 145–155.

Pettet, E. C. "*The Merchant of Venice* and the Problem of Usury." *English Association Essays and Studies* 31 (1945): 19–33.

Shapiro, James. *Shakespeare and the Jews.* New York, 1996.

Whigham, Frank. "Ideology and Class Conduct in *The Merchant of Venice.*" *Renaissance Drama* 10 (1979): 93–115.

Yaffe, Martin D. *Shylock and the Jewish Question.* Baltimore, 1997.

MUCH ADO ABOUT NOTHING

See also, under "Shakespeare's Predecessors and Contemporaries," Marrapodi (essay by Salingar); under "The Comedies," R. Berry, Brown, Cordner et al. (essay by Everett), Evans, Hunter, Huston, Leggatt, Levin, Nevo, Newman, Salingar, and Stevenson; under "Shakespeare Criticism from the 1940s to the 1970s," Rossiter; and under "Shakespeare Criticism Since 1980," Howard and O'Connor (essay by Howard), Kirsch, Lenz et al. (essay by Hays), and Neely.

Barish, Jonas A. "Pattern and Purpose in the Prose of *Much Ado About Nothing.*" *Rice U. Studies* 60:2 (1974): 19–30.

Berger, Harry, Jr. "Against the Sink-a-Pace: Sexual and Family Politics in *Much Ado About Nothing.*" *SQ* 33 (1982): 302–313.

Cook, Carol. "'The Sign and Semblance of Her Honor': Reading Gender Difference in *Much Ado about Nothing.*" *PMLA* 101 (1986): 186–202.

Cox, John D., ed. *Plays in Performance: "Much Ado About Nothing."* Cambridge, Eng., 1998.

Dawson, Anthony B. "Much Ado about Signifying." *Studies in English Literature* 22 (1982): 211–221.

Dusinberre, Juliet. "Much Ado about Lying." *Shakespeare Readers, Audiences, Players.* Eds. R. S. White, Charles Edelman, and Christopher Wortham. Nedlands, Australia, 1998.

Everett, Barbara. "*Much Ado About Nothing.*" *Critical Quarterly* 3 (1961): 319–335.

Friedman, Michael D. "Male Bonds and Marriage in *All's Well* and *Much Ado.*" *Studies in English Literature* 35 (1995): 231–249.

Jorgensen, Paul A. "*Much Ado About Nothing.*" *SQ* 5 (1954): 287–295. Rpt. in *Redeeming Shakespeare's Words.* Berkeley, 1962.

Lane, Robert. "'Foremost in Report': Social Identity and Masculinity in *Much Ado About Nothing.*" *Upstart Crow* 16 (1996): 31–47.

Lewalski, Barbara K. "Love, Appearance, and Reality: Much Ado About Something." *Studies in English Literature* 8 (1968): 235–251.

Mason, Pamela. *"Much Ado About Nothing": Text and Performance.* Basingstoke, Eng., 1992.

Ormerod, David. "Faith and Fashion in *Much Ado About Nothing.*" *ShS* 25 (1972): 93–105.

Taylor, Michael. "*Much Ado About Nothing*: The Individual in Society." *Essays in Criticism* 23 (1973): 146–153.

TWELFTH NIGHT

See also, under "The Comedies," Barber, E. Berry, Bradbury and Palmer (essay by Anne Barton), Brown, Brown and Harris (essay by Kermode), Hunter, Leggatt, Levin, Nevo, and Salingar; and under "Shakespeare Criticism Since 1980," Callaghan (*A Feminist Companion*, essay by Neely), Erickson and Kahn (essay by Booth), Greenblatt (*Shakespearean Negotiations*, Chapter 3), Hamilton (Chapter 4), Hawkes (essay by Elam), Howard, and Parker and Hartman (essay by Hartman).

Arlidge, Anthony. *Shakespeare and the Prince of Love: The Feast of Misrule in the Middle Temple.* London, 2000.

Auden, W. H. "Music in Shakespeare." *"The Dyer's Hand" and Other Essays.* New York, 1948.

Bloom, Harold, ed. *Modern Critical Interpretations of "Twelfth Night."* New York, 1987.

Booth, Stephen. *Precious Nonsense: The Gettysburg Address, Ben Jonson's Epitaphs on His Children, and "Twelfth Night."* Berkeley, 1998.

Brown, John Russell. "Directions for *Twelfth Night*, or What You Will." *Tulane Drama Review* 5:4 (1961): 77–88.

Downer, Alan S. "Feste's Night." *College English* 13 (1952): 258–265.

Eagleton, Terence. "Language and Reality in *Twelfth Night.*" *Critical Quarterly* 9 (1967): 217–228.

Elam, Keir. "The Fertile Eunuch: *Twelfth Night*, Early Modern Intercourse, and the Fruits of Castration." *SQ* 47 (1996): 1–36.

Hollander, John. "*Twelfth Night* and the Morality of Indulgence." *Sewanee Review* 67 (1959): 220–238.

Hotson, Leslie. *The First Night of* Twelfth Night. New York: 1954.

Hutson, Lorna. "On Not Being Deceived: Rhetoric and the Body in *Twelfth Night.*" *Texas Studies in Literature and Language* 38 (1996): 140–174.

Kerrigan, John. "Secrecy and Gossip in *Twelfth Night.*" *ShS* 50 (1997): 65–80.

Leech, Clifford. *"Twelfth Night" and Shakespearian Comedy.* Toronto, 1965.

Lewalski, Barbara K. "Thematic Patterns in *Twelfth Night.*" *ShakS* 1 (1965): 168–181.

Osbourne, Lisa. *The Trick of Singularity,* The Performance Editions. Iowa City, Iowa, 1996.

Potter, Lois. *"Twelfth Night": Text and Performance.* London, 1985.

Salingar, L. D. "The Design of *Twelfth Night.*" *SQ* 9 (1958): 117–139.

Shannon, Laurie J. "Nature's Bias: Renaissance Homonormativity and Elizabethan Likeness." *Modern Philology* 98 (2000): 183–210.

Wells, Stanley. *Royal Shakespeare.* Manchester, Eng., 1977. (Includes an account of John Barton's production of *Twelfth Night.*)

Welsford, Enid. *The Fool: His Social and Literary History.* London, 1935.

Williams, Porter, Jr. "Mistakes in *Twelfth Night* and Their Resolution." *PMLA* 76 (1961): 193–199.

The Histories

Alexander, Peter. *Shakespeare's "Henry VI" and "Richard III."* Cambridge, Eng., 1929.

Berry, Edward I. *Patterns of Decay: Shakespeare's Early Histories.* Charlottesville, Va., 1975.

Blanpied, John W. *Time and the Artist in Shakespeare's English Histories.* Newark, Del., 1983.

Calderwood, James L. *Metadrama in Shakespeare's Henriad: "Richard II" to "Henry V."* Berkeley, 1979.

Campbell, Lily B. *Shakespeare's "Histories": Mirrors of Elizabethan Policy.* San Marino, Calif., 1947.

Champion, Larry S. *The Noise of Threatening Drum: Dramatic Strategy and Political Ideology in Shakespeare and the English Chronicle Plays.* Newark, Del., 1990.

——. *Perspective in Shakespeare's English Histories.* Athens, Ga., 1980.

Dollimore, Jonathan, and Alan Sinfield, eds. *Political Shakespeare: New Essays in Cultural Materialism.* Manchester, Eng., 1985.

Dorius, R. J. "A Little More Than a Little." *SQ* 11 (1960): 13–26.

Dutton, Richard, and Jean E. Howard, eds. *A Companion to Shakespeare's Works: The Histories.* Malden, Mass., Oxford and Victoria, 2003.

Edwards, Philip. "The Hidden King: Shakespeare's History Plays." *Threshold of a Nation: A Study in English and Irish Drama.* Cambridge, Eng., 1979.

Forker, Charles R. "Shakespeare's Chronicle Plays as Historical-Pastoral." *ShakS* 1 (1965): 85–104.

Hodgdon, Barbara. *The End Crowns All: Closure and Contradiction in Shakespeare's History.* Princeton, 1991.

Holderness, Graham. *Shakespeare's History.* New York, 1985. Largely reprinted in *Shakespeare Recycled: The Making of Historical Drama.* Hempstead, Eng., New York, 1992.

——, ed. *Shakespeare's History Plays: "Richard II" to "Henry V."* London, 1992.

Howard, Jean E., and Phyllis Rackin. *Engendering a Nation: A Feminist Account of Shakespeare's English Histories.* London and New York, 1997.

Jenkins, Harold. "Shakespeare's History Plays: 1900–1951." *ShS* 6 (1953): 1–15.

Jorgensen, Paul A. *Shakespeare's Military World.* Berkeley and Los Angeles, 1956.

Kastan, David Scott. *Shakespeare and the Shapes of Time.* Hanover, N.H., 1982.

Kelly, Henry A. *Divine Providence in the England of Shakespeare's Histories.* Cambridge, Mass., 1970.

Knights, L. C. "Shakespeare's Politics: With Some Reflections on the Nature of Tradition." *Proceedings of the British Academy* 43 (1957): 115–132.

Leggatt, Alexander. *Shakespeare's Political Drama: The History Plays and the Roman Plays.* London, 1988.

Levine, Nina S. *Women's Matters: Politics, Gender, and Nation in Shakespeare's Early History Plays.* Newark, Del., 1998.

Manheim, Michael. "The English History Play on Screen." *Shakespeare and the Moving Image.* Eds. Anthony Davies and Stanley Wells. Cambridge, Eng., 1994. 121–145.

——. *The Weak King Dilemma in the Shakespearean History Play.* Syracuse, N.Y., 1973.

Norwich, John Julius. *Shakespeare's Kings: The Great Plays and the History of England in the Middle Ages: 1337–1485.* London, 1999; New York, 2000.

Ornstein, Robert. *A Kingdom for a Stage.* Cambridge, Mass., 1972.

Palmer, John. *Political Characters of Shakespeare.* London, 1945.

Paris, Bernard J. *Character as a Subversive Force in Shakespeare: The History and Roman Plays.* Rutherford, N.J., and London, 1991.

Patterson, Annabel. *Reading Holinshed's Chronicles.* Chicago, 1994.

Pierce, Robert B. *Shakespeare's History Plays: The Family and the State.* Columbus, Ohio, 1971.

Pilkington, Ace G. *Screening Shakespeare from "Richard II" to "Henry V."* Newark, Del., 1991.

Porter, Joseph. *The Drama of Speech Acts: Shakespeare's Lancastrian Tetralogy*. Berkeley, 1979.

Prior, Moody E. *The Drama of Power: Studies in Shakespeare's History Plays*. Evanston, Ill., 1973.

Pugliatti, Paola. *Shakespeare the Historian*. New York, 1996.

Pye, Christopher. *The Regal Phantasm: Shakespeare and the Politics of Spectacle*. London, 1990.

Rackin, Phyllis. "Anti-Historians: Women's Roles in Shakespeare's Histories." *Theatre Journal* 37 (1985): 329–344.

——. *Stages of History: Shakespeare's English Chronicles*. Ithaca, N.Y., 1990.

Reese, M. M. *The Cease of Majesty*. London and New York, 1961.

Ribner, Irving. *The English History Play in the Age of Shakespeare*. Rev. ed. London, 1965.

Rossiter, A. P. "Ambivalence: The Dialectic of the Histories." *Talking of Shakespeare*. Ed. John Garrett. London, 1954.

Saccio, Peter. *Shakespeare's English Kings: History, Chronicle, and Drama*. New York, 1977, 2000.

Shaheen, Naseeb. *Biblical References in Shakespeare's History Plays*. Newark, Del., 1989.

Siegel, Paul N. *Shakespeare's English and Roman History Plays: A Marxist Approach*. Toronto, 1986.

Sprague, Arthur Colby. *Shakespeare's Histories: Plays for the Stage*. London, 1964.

Sterling, Eric. *The Movement Towards Subversion: The English History Play from Skelton to Shakespeare*. Lanham, Md., 1996.

Tillyard, E. M. W. *Shakespeare's History Plays*. London, 1944, 1961.

Traversi, Derek. *Shakespeare from "Richard II" to "Henry V."* London, 1957.

Velz, John W., ed. *Shakespeare's English Histories: A Quest for Form and Genre*. Binghamton, N.Y., 1996.

RICHARD III

See also, under "The Histories," Alexander, Berry, Campbell, Kelly, Ornstein, Prior, Ribner, and Saccio; under "Shakespeare's Predecessors and Contemporaries," Sanders; under "Shakespeare Criticism from the 1940s to the 1970s," Jones, Rossiter, and Spivack; under "Shakespeare Criticism Since 1980," Dubrow and Strier (essay by Garber), and Lenz et al. (essay by Miner); and under "The Tragedies," Garner and Sprengnether (essay by Rackin), and Hunter.

Anderson, Judith H. "Shakespeare's *Richard III*: The Metamorphosis of Biographical Truth to Fiction." *Biographical Truth: The Representation of Historical Persons in Tudor-Stuart Writing*. New Haven, 1984.

Bevington, David. " 'Why Should Calamity Be Full of Words?' The Efficacy of Cursing in *Richard III*." *Iowa State Journal of Research* 56:1 (1981): 9–21.

Burt, Richard. "The Love that Dare Not Speak Shakespeare's Name: New Shakesqueer Cinema." *Shakespeare: The Movie*. Eds. Lynda E. Boose and Richard Burt. London, 1997, 1999. 240–268.

Cibber, Colley. "*Richard III.*" *Shakespeare Made Fit: Restoration Adaptations of Shakespeare*. Ed. Sandra Clark. London, 1997. 374–459.

Colley, Scott. *Richard's Himself Again: A Stage History of "Richard III."* New York, 1992.

French, A. L. "The World of *Richard III.*" *ShakS* 4 (1968): 25–39.

Hankey, Julie, ed. *Plays in Performance: "Richard III."* 2nd ed. Bristol, 1988.

Hassel, R. Chris, Jr. *Songs of Death: Performance, Interpretation, and the Text of "Richard III."* Lincoln, Neb., 1987.

Hunter, Robert G. *Shakespeare and the Mystery of God's Judgments*. Athens, Ga., 1976.

Kendall, Paul Murray. *Richard the Third*. New York and London, 1956.

Krieger, Murray. "The Dark Generations of *Richard III.*" *Criticism* 1 (1959): 32–48.

Neill, Michael. "Shakespeare's Halle of Mirrors: Play, Politics, and Psychology in *Richard III.*" *ShakS* 8 (1975): 99–129.

Sher, Antony. *Year of the King: An Actor's Diary and Sketchbook*. London, 1985.

Torrey, Michael. " 'The plain devil and dissembling looks': Ambivalent Physiognomy and Shakespeare's *Richard III.*" *English Literary Renaissance* 30 (2000): 123–153.

Wheeler, Richard P. "History, Character, and Conscience in *Richard III.*" *Comparative Drama* 5 (1971–1972): 301–321.

Wood, Alice Ida. *The Stage History of Shakespeare's "King Richard III."* New York, 1909, 1965.

HENRY IV, PART ONE

See also, under "The Histories," Blanpied, Calderwood, Campbell, Dorius, Kelly, Manheim, Ornstein, Palmer, Porter, Prior, Reese, Saccio, Sprague, Tillyard, and Velz (essay by Rumrich); under "Shakespeare Criticism to the 1930s," Johnson and Smith (*Eighteenth Century*, essay by Morgann); under "Shakespeare Criticism from the 1940s to the 1970s," Bevington and Halio (essay by R. G. Hunter), Bryant, Burckhardt, Council, Goldman, Kernan (essay on the "Major History Plays"), Spivack, and Stewart; and under "Shakespeare Criticism Since 1980," Auden, Dollimore and Sinfield (essay by Greenblatt, originally published by *Glyph 8* and in

Shakespearean Negotiations), Nuttall, and Watson; and under "The Comedies," Barber.

Auden, W. H. "The Prince's Dog." *"The Dyer's Hand" and Other Essays*. New York, 1948.

Barber, C. L. "Rule and Misrule in *Henry IV*." *Shakespeare's Festive Comedy*. Princeton, 1959.

Barish, Jonas A. "The Turning Away of Prince Hal." *ShakS* 1 (1965)" 9–17.

Bevington, David, ed. *"Henry IV, Parts One and Two": New Critical Essays*. New York and London, 1986.

Bradley, A. C. "The Rejection of Falstaff." *Oxford Lectures on Poetry*. London, 1909, 1961.

Bryant, J. A., Jr., "Prince Hal and the Ephesians." *Sewanee Review* 67 (1959): 204–219.

Cohen, Derek. "The Rite of Violence in *1 Henry IV*." *ShS* 38 (1985): 77–84.

Dessen, Alan. "Dual Protagonists in *1 Henry IV*." *Shakespeare and the Late Moral Plays*. Lincoln, Neb., 1986.

Doran, Madeleine. "Imagery in *Richard II* and in *Henry IV*." *Modern Language Review* 37 (1942): 113–122.

Dorius, R. J., ed. *Twentieth Century Interpretations of "Henry IV Part I."* Englewood Cliffs, N.J., 1970.

Empson, William. "Falstaff and Mr. Dover Wilson." *Kenyon Review* 15 (1953): 213–262.

Everett, Barbara. "The Fatness of Falstaff: Shakespeare and Character." *Proceedings of the British Academy* 76 (1990): 109–128.

Gottschalk, Paul A. "Hal and the 'Play Extempore' in *1 Henry IV*." *Texas Studies in Literature and Language* 15 (1974): 605–614.

Hawkins, Sherman H. "Virtue and Kingship in Shakespeare's *Henry IV*." *English Literary Renaissance* 5 (1975): 313–343.

Hunter, G. K. "*Henry IV* and the Elizabethan Two-Part Play." *Review of English Studies* n.s. 5 (1954): 236–248.

———. "Shakespeare's Politics and the Rejection of Falstaff." *Critical Quarterly* 1 (1959): 229–236.

Jenkins, Harold. *The Structural Problem in Shakespeare's "Henry the Fourth."* London, 1956.

Kris, Ernst. "Prince Hal's Conflict." *Psychoanalytic Explorations in Art*. New York, 1964.

Levine, Nina. "Extending Credit in the *Henry IV* Plays." *SQ* 51 (2000): 403–431.

McAlindon, Tom. *Shakespeare's Tudor History: A Study of "Henry IV, Parts 1 and 2."* Aldershot, Eng., 2001.

McLuhan, Herbert Marshall. "*Henry IV*, A Mirror for Magistrates." *University of Toronto Quarterly* 17 (1947–1948): 152–160.

McMillin, Scott. *Shakespeare in Performance: "Henry IV, Part One."* Manchester, Eng., 1991.

Palmer, D. J. "Casting Off the Old Man: History and St. Paul in *Henry IV*." *Critical Quarterly* 12 (1970): 267–283.

Poole, Kristen. "Saints Alive! Falstaff, Martin Marprelate, and the Staging of Puritanism." *SQ* 46 (1995): 47–75.

Potter, Lois. "The Second Tetralogy: Performance as Interpretation." *A Companion to Shakespeare's Works, The Histories*. Eds. Richard Dutton and Jean E. Howard. Oxford, 2003.

Toliver, Harold E. "Falstaff, the Prince, and the History Play." *SQ* 16 (1965): 63–80.

Wharton, T. F. *"Henry the Fourth, Parts 1 and 2": Text and Performance*. London, 1983.

Wilson, J. Dover. *The Fortunes of Falstaff*. Cambridge, Eng., 1943.

Womersley, David. "Why Is Falstaff Fat?" *Review of English Studies* n.s. 47 (1996): 1–22.

HENRY V

See also, under "The Histories," Calderwood, Campbell, Jorgensen, Kastan, Ornstein, Porter, Prior, Reese, Ribner, Saccio, and Traversi; under "Shakespeare Criticism to the 1930s," Hazlitt and Schlegel; under "Shakespeare Criticism from the 1940s to the 1970s," Burckhardt, Goddard, Goldman, and Kernan (essay on the "Major History Plays"); under "Shakespeare Criticism Since 1980," Dollimore and Sinfield (essays by Greenblatt and Tennenhouse), Drakakis (essay by Dollimore and Sinfield), Erickson, Mahon and Pendleton (essay by Hammond), Patterson (Chapter 4), and Rabkin (Chapter 2); and under "Shakespeare on Stage," Price (essay by Barton).

Altman, Joel B. " 'Vile Participation': The Amplification of Violence in the Theater of *Henry V*." *SQ* 42 (1991): 1–32.

Beauman, Sally, ed. *"King Henry V": The Royal Shakespeare Company's Production of "Henry V" for the Centenary Season at the Royal Shakespeare Theatre*. Oxford, 1976. (Includes information on Terry Hands's *Henry V*.)

Cubeta, Paul M. "Falstaff and the Art of Dying." *Studies in English Literature* 27 (1987): 197–211.

Eggert, Katherine. "Nostalgia and the Not Yet Late Queen: Refusing Female Rule in *Henry V*." *ELH* 61 (1994): 523–550.

Granville-Barker, Harley. "From *Henry V* to *Hamlet*." *Proceedings of the British Academy* 11 (1925): 283–309.

Gurr, Andrew. "*Henry V* and the Bees' Commonwealth." *ShS* 30 (1977): 61–72.

Hedrick, Donald K. "War Is Mud: Branagh's Dirty Harry V and The Types of Political Ambiguity." *Shakespeare: the Movie*. Eds. Lynda E. Boose and Richard Burt. London and New York, 1997. 45–66.

Levin, Richard. "Hazlitt on *Henry V*, and the Appropriation of Shakespeare." *SQ* 35 (1984), 134–141.

McEachern, Claire. *The Poetics of English Nationhood, 1590–1612*. Cambridge, Eng., 1996.

Neill, Michael. "*Henry V*: A Modern Perspective." The New Folger Shakespeare: *Henry V*. New York, 1995. 253–278.

Smith, Emma, ed. *Shakespeare in Production: "King Henry V."* Cambridge, Eng., 2002.

The Tragedies

See also, under "Shakespeare's Predecessors and Contemporaries," Belsey.

Armstrong, Philip. *Shakespeare's Visual Regime: Tragedy, Psychoanalysis, and the Gaze.* Basingstoke, Eng., and New York, 2000.

Baldo, Jonathan. *The Unmasking of Drama: Contested Representation in Shakespeare's Tragedies.* Detroit, 1996.

Barker, Francis, ed. *The Culture of Violence: Essays on Tragedy and History.* Chicago, 1993.

Barroll, J. Leeds. *Artificial Persons: The Formation of Character in the Tragedies of Shakespeare.* Columbia, S.C., 1974.

Bayley, John. *Shakespeare and Tragedy.* London, 1981.

Bell, Millicent. *Shakespeare's Tragic Skepticism.* New Haven, 2002.

Berry, Philippa. *Shakespeare's Feminine Endings: Disfiguring Death in the Tragedies.* London and New York, 1999.

Berry, Ralph. *Tragic Instance: The Sequence of Shakespeare's Tragedies.* Newark, Del., 1999.

Bradley, A. C. *Shakespearean Tragedy.* London, 1904. (*Hamlet, Othello, King Lear, Macbeth.*)

Brooke, Nicholas. *Shakespeare's Early Tragedies.* London and New York, 1968.

Brown, John Russell, and Bernard Harris, eds. *Early Shakespeare.* London, 1961.

Bulman, James C. *The Heroic Idiom of Shakespearean Tragedy.* Newark, Del., 1985.

Bushnell, Rebecca. *Tragedies of Tyrants: Political Thought and Theater in the English Renaissance.* Ithaca, N.Y., 1990.

Campbell, Lily B. *Shakespeare's Tragic Heroes: Slaves of Passion.* Cambridge, Eng., 1930.

Champion, Larry S. *Shakespeare's Tragic Perspective.* Athens, Ga., 1976.

Charlton, H. B. *Shakespearian Tragedy.* Cambridge, Eng., 1948.

Cunningham, I. V. *Woe or Wonder: The Emotional Effect of Shakespearean Tragedy.* 1951. Rpt. in *Tradition and Poetic Structure.* Denver, 1960.

Danson, Lawrence. *Tragic Alphabet: Shakespeare's Drama of Language.* New Haven and London, 1974.

Dickey, Franklin M. *Not Wisely But Too Well: Shakespeare's Love Tragedies.* San Marino, Calif., 1957.

Dutton, Richard, and Jean E. Howard, eds. *A Companion to Shakespeare's Works: The Tragedies.* Malden, Mass., Oxford and Victoria, 2003.

Eliot, T. S. "Shakespeare and the Stoicism of Seneca." *Selected Essays, 1917–1932.* London, 1932.

Everett, Barbara. *Young Hamlet: Essays on Shakespeare's Tragedies.* Oxford, 1989.

Falco, Raphael. *Charismatic Authority in Early Modern English Tragedy.* Baltimore, 2000.

Farnham, Willard. *Shakespeare's Tragic Frontier.* Berkeley, 1950.

Frye, Northrop. *Fools of Time: Studies in Shakespearean Tragedy.* Toronto, 1967.

Gajowski, Evelyn. *The Art of Loving: Female Subjectivity and Male Discursive Traditions in Shakespeare's Tragedies.* Newark, Del., 1992.

Garner, Shirley Nelson, and Madelon Sprengnether, eds. *Shakespearean Tragedy and Gender.* Bloomington, Ind., 1996.

Goldman, Michael. *Acting and Action in Shakespearean Tragedy.* Princeton, 1985.

Grene, Nicholas. *Shakespeare's Tragic Imagination.* New York, 1992.

Hawkes, Terence. *Shakespeare and the Reason: A Study of the Tragedies and the Problem Plays.* London, 1964.

Held, George F. *The Good That Lives After Them: A Pattern in Shakespeare's Tragedies.* Heidelberg, 1995.

Holloway, John. *The Story of the Night: Studies in Shakespeare's Major Tragedies.* London and Lincoln, Neb., 1961.

Honigmann, E. A. J. *Myriad-Minded Shakespeare: Essays, Chiefly on the Tragedies and Problem Comedies.* New York, 1989.

———. *Shakespeare: Seven Tragedies Revisited: The Dramatist's Manipulation of Response.* 2nd ed. London and New York, 2002.

Hunter, Robert Grams. *Shakespeare and the Mystery of God's Judgments.* Athens, Ga., 1976.

Ide, Richard S. *Possessed with Greatness: The Heroic Tragedies of Chapman and Shakespeare.* Chapel Hill, N.C., 1980.

Kiefer, Frederick. *Fortune and Elizabethan Tragedy.* San Marino, Calif., 1983.

Kirsch, Arthur. *The Passions of Shakespeare's Tragic Heroes.* Charlottesville, Va., 1990.

Knight, G. Wilson. *The Wheel of Fire.* London, 1930, 1965.

Lawlor, John. *The Tragic Sense in Shakespeare.* London, 1960.

Leech, Clifford. *Shakespeare's Tragedies and Other Studies in Seventeenth-Century Drama.* London, 1950.

———, ed. *Shakespeare: The Tragedies.* Chicago, 1965.

Liebler, Naomi Conn. *Shakespeare's Festive Tragedy: The Ritual Foundations of Genre.* London and New York, 1995.

Mack, Maynard. *Everybody's Shakespeare: Reflections Chiefly on the Tragedies.* Lincoln, Neb., 1993.

———. "The Jacobean Shakespeare: Some Observations on the Construction of the Tragedies." *Jacobean Theatre.* Eds. John Russell Brown and Bernard Harris. *Stratford-upon-Avon Studies 1.* London, 1960.

Mack, Maynard, Jr. *Killing the King: Three Studies in Shakespeare's Tragic Structure.* New Haven and London, 1973.

Margolies, David. *Monsters of the Deep: Social Dissolution in Shakespeare's Tragedies.* Manchester, Eng., 1992.

McAlindon, T. *Shakespeare's Tragic Cosmos*. Cambridge, Eng., 1991.

Miola, Robert S. *Shakespeare and Classical Tragedy: The Influence of Seneca*. Oxford, 1992.

Neill, Michael. *Issues of Death: Mortality and Identity in English Renaissance Tragedy*. Oxford, 1997.

Nevo, Ruth. *Tragic Form in Shakespeare*. Princeton, 1972.

Proser, Matthew N. *The Heroic Image in Five Shakespearean Tragedies*. Princeton, 1965.

Rackin, Phyllis. *Shakespeare's Tragedies*. New York, 1978.

Reid, Robert Lanier. *Shakespeare's Tragic Form: Spirit in the Wheel*. Newark, Del., 2000.

Ribner, Irving. *Patterns in Shakespearean Tragedy*. New York, 1960.

Rosen, William. *Shakespeare and the Craft of Tragedy*. Cambridge, Mass., 1960.

Sanders, Wilbur, and Howard Jacobson. *Shakespeare's Magnanimity: Four Tragic Heroes, Their Friends and Families*. Oxford, 1978.

Shaheen, Naseeb. *Biblical References in Shakespeare's Tragedies*. Newark, Del., 1987.

Smith, Molly. *The Darker World Within: Evil in the Tragedies of Shakespeare and His Successors*. Newark, Del., 1991.

Snyder, Susan. *The Comic Matrix of Shakespeare's Tragedies*. Princeton, 1979.

Spivack, Bernard. *Shakespeare and the Allegory of Evil*. New York, 1958.

Whitaker, Virgil. *The Mirror up to Nature*. San Marino, Calif., 1965.

Wilson, Harold S. *On the Design of Shakespearian Tragedy*. Toronto, 1957.

Young, David. *The Action to the Word: Structure and Style in Shakespearean Tragedy*. New Haven, 1990.

ROMEO AND JULIET

See also, under "The Tragedies," Brooke, Brown and Harris (essay by Lawlor), Charlton, Dickey, Nevo, Ribner, and Snyder; under "Shakespeare's Language," Mahood; under "Shakespeare Criticism to the 1930s," Hazlitt; under "Shakespeare Criticism from the 1940s to the 1970s," Calderwood, Granville-Barker, and Rabkin (162–184); under "Shakespeare Criticism Since 1980," Callaghan (*A Feminist Companion*, essay by Berry), Daileader, Edwards et al. (essay by Wells), Erickson and Kahn (essay by Snow), Lenz et al. (essay by Kahn), and Novy (*Love's Argument*); and under "Shakespeare on Stage," Brockbank (essay by Brenda Bruce).

Appelbaum, Robert. " 'Standing to the wall': The Pressures of Masculinity in *Romeo and Juliet*." *SQ* 48 (1997): 251–272.

Auden, W. H. "Commentary on the Poetry and Tragedy of *Romeo and Juliet*." The Laurel Shakespeare. Gen. ed. Francis Fergusson. New York, 1958.

Evans, Bertrand. "The Brevity of Friar Lawrence." *PMLA* 65 (1950): 841–865.

Evans, Robert O. *The Osier Cage: Rhetorical Devices in "Romeo and Juliet."* Lexington, Ky., 1966.

Everett, Barbara. "*Romeo and Juliet*: The Nurse's Story." *Critical Quarterly* 14 (1972): 129–139.

Halio, Jay, ed. *"Romeo and Juliet": Texts, Contexts, and Interpretation*. Newark, Del., 1995.

Hosley, Richard. "The Use of the Upper Stage in *Romeo and Juliet*." *SQ* 5 (1954): 371–379.

Levenson, Jill L. *Shakespeare in Performance: "Romeo and Juliet."* Manchester, Eng., 1987.

Melchiori, Giorgio. "Peter, Balthasar, and Shakespeare's Art of Doubling." *Modern Language Review* 78 (1983): 777–792.

Williams, George W., ed. *The Most Excellent and Lamentable Tragedie of Romeo and Juliet*. Durham, N.C., 1964.

HAMLET

See also, under "Shakespeare's Language," Donawerth; under "The Tragedies," Barker, Bradley, Brooke, Goldman, Holloway, Kirsch, Mack, Mack Jr., Rosen, and Whitaker; under "Shakespeare's Predecessors and Contemporaries," Bowers, and Rabkin (essay by Booth); under "Shakespeare Criticism to the 1930s," Coleridge (*Coleridge's Writings*); under "Shakespeare Criticism from the 1940s to the 1970s," Granville-Barker, Hawkes, and Righter; under "Shakespeare Criticism Since 1980," Cavell (Chapter 5), Drakakis (essay by Rose), Erickson, Garber (*Shakespeare's Ghost Writers*, Chapter 6), Loomba and Orkin (essay by Bertoldi), Mazzio and Trevor (essays by De Grazia and Guillory), McDonald (essay by Parker), Parker and Hartman (essays by Weimann, Ferguson, and Hawkes), Patterson (Chapters 1 and 5), and Schwartz and Kahn (essays by Fineman and Leverenz); and under "Shakespeare on Stage," Bevington.

Alexander, Peter. *Hamlet: Father and Son*. New York, 1955.

Bertram, Paul, and Bernice W. Kliman, eds. *The Three-Text "Hamlet": Parallel Texts of the First and Second Quartos and First Folio*. New York, 1991.

Bowers, Fredson T. "Hamlet as Minister and Scourge." *PMLA* 70 (1955): 740–749.

Branagh, Kenneth. *Hamlet: Screenplay, Introduction and Film Diary*. New York, 1996.

Calderwood, James L. *To Be and Not to Be: Negation and Metadrama in "Hamlet."* New York, 1983.

Charney, Maurice. *Style in "Hamlet."* Princeton, 1969.

Clayton, Thomas, ed. *The "Hamlet" First Published (Q1, 1603): Origin, Form, Intertextualities*. Newark, Del., 1992.

Dawson, Anthony B. *Hamlet. Shakespeare in Performance*. Manchester, Eng., 1995.

Eliot, T. S. "Hamlet and His Problems." *Selected Essays, 1917–1932*. London and New York, 1932.

Erlich, Avi. *Hamlet's Absent Father*. Princeton, 1977.

Ewbank, Inga-Stina. "*Hamlet* and the Power of Words." *ShS* 30 (1977), 85–102.

Fergusson, Francis. *The Idea of a Theater*. Princeton, 1949.

Foakes, R. A. *"Hamlet" versus "Lear": Cultural Politics and Shakespeare's Art*. Cambridge, Eng., 1993.

Frye, Roland Mushat. *The Renaissance "Hamlet": Issues and Responses in 1600*. Princeton, 1984.

Greenblatt, Stephen. *Hamlet in Purgatory*. Princeton, 2001.

Heilbrun, Carolyn G. *Hamlet's Mother and Other Women*. New York, 1990.

James, D. G. *The Dream of Learning*. Oxford, 1951.

Jones, Ernest. *Hamlet and Oedipus*. Rev. ed. New York, 1949, 1954.

Joseph, Bertram. *Conscience and the King*. London, 1953.

Kerrigan, William. *Hamlet's Perfection*. Baltimore, 1994.

Kitto, H. D. F. *Form and Meaning in Drama*. London, 1956.

Knights, L. C. *An Approach to "Hamlet."* London, 1960.

Lacan, Jacques. "Desire and the Interpretation of Desire in *Hamlet*." *Yale French Studies* 55/56 (1977): 11–52.

Lee, John. *Shakespeare's "Hamlet" and the Controversies of Self*. Oxford, 2000.

Levin, Harry. *The Question of Hamlet*. New York and London, 1959.

Lewis, C. S. "Hamlet: The Prince or the Poem?" *Proceedings of the British Academy* 28 (1942): 139–154.

Mack, Maynard. "The World of *Hamlet*." *Yale Review* 41 (1952): 502–523.

McCoy, Richard C. "A Wedding and Four Funerals: Conjunction and Commemoration in *Hamlet*." *ShS* 54 (2001): 122–139.

McGee, Arthur. *The Elizabethan Hamlet*. New Haven, 1987.

Muir, Kenneth, and Stanley Wells, eds. *Aspects of "Hamlet": Articles Reprinted from "Shakespeare Survey."* Cambridge, Eng., 1979. (Esp. essay by Inga-Stina Ewbank.)

Murray, Gilbert. *Hamlet and Orestes*. Annual Shakespeare Lecture for the British Academy, 1914. London, 1919.

Nicoll, Allardyce, ed. *Shakespeare Survey* 9 (1956).

Nietzsche, Friedrich. "The Birth of Tragedy or: Hellenism and Pessimism" (1872). *The Birth of Tragedy and The Case of Wagner*. Trans. Walter Kaufmann. New York, 1967.

Pennington, Michael. *Hamlet: A User's Guide*. New York, 1996.

Righter, Anne. *Shakespeare and the Idea of the Play*. Oxford, 1962.

Rose, Mark. "*Hamlet* and the Shape of Revenge." *English Literary Renaissance* 1 (1971): 132–143.

Rosenberg, Marvin. *The Masks of "Hamlet."* Newark, Del., 1992.

Skulsky, Harold. " 'I Know My Course': Hamlet's Confidence." *PMLA* 89 (1974): 477–486.

States, Bert O. *"Hamlet" and the Concept of Character*. Baltimore, 1992.

Tronch-Pérez, Jesús. *A Synoptic "Hamlet": A Critical-Synoptic Edition of the Second Quarto and First Folio Texts of "Hamlet."* Valencia, Spain, 2002.

Wells, Stanley. *Royal Shakespeare: Four Major Productions at Stratford-upon-Avon*. Manchester, 1977.

Wilson, J. Dover. *What Happens in "Hamlet."* London and New York, 1935, 1951.

Wright, George T. "Hendiadys and *Hamlet*." *PMLA* 96 (1981): 168–193.

Young, David. "Hamlet, Son of Hamlet." *Perspectives on "Hamlet."* Eds. William G. Holzberger and Peter B. Waldock. Lewisburg, Pa., and London, 1975.

OTHELLO

See also, under "The Tragedies," Philippa Berry, Bradley, Dickey, Garner and Sprengnether (essays by Orlin, Hendricks, and Rose), Goldman, Hawkes, Holloway, Knight, Snyder, and Spivack; under "Shakespeare's Language," Doran; under "Shakespeare's Predecessors and Contemporaries," Hendricks and Parker (essays by Boose and Parker); under "Shakespeare Criticism to the 1930s," Coleridge (*Coleridge's Writings*) and Johnson; under "Shakespeare Criticism from the 1940s to the 1970s," Empson, Fiedler, Granville-Barker, and Sewell; and under "Shakespeare Criticism Since 1980," Cavell (Chapter 3), Daileder, Erickson, Erickson and Kahn (essay by Wheeler), Greenblatt (*Renaissance Self-Fashioning*, Chapter 6), Howard and O'Connor (essay by Newman), Kirsch, Lenz et al. (essay by Neely), Loomba and Orkin (essay by Burton), McDonald (essay by Parker), Novy (*Love's Argument*, Chapter 7), and Parker and Hartman (essays by Parker and Showalter).

Adamson, Jane. *"Othello" as Tragedy: Some Problems of Judgment and Feeling*. Cambridge, Eng., 1980.

Altman, Joel B. " 'Preposterous Conclusions': Eros, *Enargeia*, and the Composition of *Othello*." *Representations* 18 (1987): 129–157.

Bartels, Emily C. "Making More of the Moor: Aaron, Othello, and Renaissance Refashionings of Race." *SQ* 41 (1990): 433–454.

Bates, Catherine. "Weaving and Writing in *Othello*." *SQ* 46 (1995): 51–60.

Bayley, John. *The Characters of Love*. London, 1960.

Boose, Lynda E. "Othello's Handkerchief: 'The Recognizance and Pledge of Love.'" *English Literary Renaissance* 5 (1975): 360–374.

Calderwood, James L. *The Properties of "Othello."* Amherst, Mass., 1989.

Dean, Leonard F., ed. *A Casebook on "Othello."* New York, 1961.

Evans, Robert C. "Friendship in Shakespeare's *Othello*." *Ben Jonson Journal* 6 (1999): 109–146.

Everett, Barbara. "Inside *Othello*." *ShS* 53 (2000): 184–195.

——. "Reflections on the Sentimentalist's *Othello*." *Critical Quarterly* 3 (1961): 127–139. (A comment on the Leavis article below.)

Garner, S. N. "Shakespeare's Desdemona." *ShakS* 9 (1976): 233–252.

Hankey, Julie, ed. *Plays in Performance: "Othello."* Bristol, 1987.

Heilman, Robert B. *Magic in the Web: Action and Language in "Othello."* Lexington, Ky., 1956.

Honigmann, E. A. J. *The Texts of "Othello" and Shakespearian Revision*. London, 1996.

Hyman, Stanley Edgar. *Iago: Some Approaches to the Illusion of His Motivation*. New York, 1970.

Jones, Eldred. *Othello's Countrymen: The African in English Renaissance Drama*. London, 1965.

Korda, Natasha. *Shakespeare's Domestic Economies: Gender and Property in Early Modern England*. Philadelphia, 2002. (Chap. 4.)

Leavis, F. R. "Diabolic Intellect and the Noble Hero: Or The Sentimentalist's *Othello*." *The Common Pursuit*. London, 1952.

Muir, Kenneth, ed. *Shakespeare Survey 21* (1968).

Nowottny, Winifred M. T. "Justice and Love in *Othello*." *U. of Toronto Quarterly* 21 (1952): 330–344.

Orkin, Martin. "Othello and the 'plain face' of Racism." *SQ* 38 (1987): 166–188.

Orlin, Lena Cowen. *Private Matters and Public Culture in Post-Reformation England*. Ithaca, N.Y., 1994.

Rosenberg, Marvin. *The Masks of "Othello."* Berkeley, 1961.

Seltzer, Daniel. "Elizabethan Acting in *Othello*." *SQ* 10 (1959): 201–210.

Snyder, Susan, ed. *"Othello": Critical Essays*. New York, 1988.

Stoll, E. E. *"Othello": An Historical and Comparative Study*. Minneapolis, 1915. Rpt. New York, 1964.

Wine, Martin L. *"Othello": Text and Performance*. London, 1984.

KING LEAR

See also, under "Life in Shakespeare's England," De Grazia, Quilligan, and Stallybrass (essay by De Grazia); under "The Tragedies," Bradley, Cunningham, Frye, Goldman, Holloway, Hunter, Kirsch, Knight, and Rosen; Brower; under "Textual Criticism and Bibliography," Blayney, and Taylor and Warren; under "Shakespeare's Language," Doran; under "Shakespeare Criticism to the 1930s," Hazlitt, Johnson, and Stoll; under "Shakespeare Criticism from the 1940s to the 1970s," Bloom (essay by Jaffa), Burckhardt, Empson, Fly, Granville-Barker, Knights, Kott, and Sewell; under "Shakespeare Criticism Since 1980," Auden, Boose, Cavell (Chapter 2, identical with the Cavell entry below), Dollimore, Dollimore and Sinfield (essay by McLuskie), Dubrow and Strier (essay by Strier), Erickson, Erickson and Kahn (essay by Berger), Garber (*Shakespeare's Ghost Writers*, Chapter 5), Greenblatt (*Shakespearean Negotiations*, Chapter 4), Loomba and Orkin (essay by Visser), Novy (*Love's Argument*), Patterson (Chapter 5), and Wayne (essay by Thompson); and under "The Romances," Felperin and Young.

Alpers, Paul J. "*King Lear* and the Theory of the 'Sight Pattern.' " *In Defense of Reading*. Eds. Reuben A. Brower and Richard Poirier. New York, 1962.

Berger, Harry, Jr. "*King Lear*: The Lear Family Romance." *Centennial Review* 23 (1979): 348–376.

Booth, Stephen. *"King Lear," "Macbeth," Indefinition, and Tragedy*. New Haven, 1983.

Bratton, J. S. *Plays in Performance: "King Lear."* Bristol, 1987.

Brownlow, F. W. *Shakespeare, Harsnett, and the Devils of Denham*. Newark, Del., 1993.

Cavell, Stanley. "The Avoidance of Love: A Reading of *King Lear*." *Must We Mean What We Say?* New York, 1969. Rpt. in *Disowning Knowledge in Six Plays of Shakespeare*. Cambridge, Eng., 1987.

Colie, Rosalie L., and F. T. Flahiff, eds. *Some Facets of "King Lear."* Toronto, 1974.

Danby, John F. *Shakespeare's Doctrine of Nature: A Study of "King Lear."* London, 1949.

Delany, Paul. "*King Lear* and the Decline of Feudalism." *PMLA* 92 (1977): 429–440.

Elton, William R. *King Lear and the Gods*. Rpt. Lexington, Ky., 1988.

Everett, Barbara. "The New *King Lear*." *Critical Quarterly* 2 (1960): 325–339.

Foakes, R. A. *"Hamlet" Versus "Lear": Cultural Politics and Shakespeare's Art*. Cambridge, Eng., 1993.

Freud, Sigmund. "The Theme of the Three Caskets." *Complete Psychological Works of Sigmund Freud* 12 (1911–1913). London, 1958. 291–301.

Goldberg, S. L. *An Essay on "King Lear."* Cambridge, Eng., 1974.

Graham, Kenneth J. E. " 'Without the form of justice': Plainness and the Performance of Love in *King Lear*." *SQ* 42 (1991): 438–461.

Hardison, O. B., Jr. "Myth and History in *King Lear*." *SQ* 26 (1975): 227–242.

Heilman, Robert B. *This Great Stage: Image and Structure in "King Lear."* Rpt. Seattle, 1963.

Heinemann, Margot. " 'Demystifying the Mystery of State': *King Lear* and the World Upside Down." *ShS* 44 (1992): 75–83.

James, D. G. *The Dream of Learning.* Oxford, 1951.

Jorgensen, Paul A. *Lear's Self-Discovery.* Berkeley, 1967.

Kahn, Coppélia. "The Absent Mother in *King Lear*." *Rewriting the Renaissance: The Discourses of Sexual Difference in Early Modern Europe.* Eds. Margaret W. Ferguson et al. Chicago, 1986.

Kernan, Alvin. "Formalism and Realism in Elizabethan Drama: The Miracles in *King Lear*." *Renaissance Drama* 9 (1966): 59–66.

Kirsch, Arthur. "The Emotional Landscape of *King Lear*." *SQ* 39 (1988): 154–170.

Kronenfeld, Judy. *King Lear and the Naked Truth: Rethinking the Language of Religion and Resistance.* Durham, N.C., 1998.

Leggatt, Alexander. *King Lear. Shakespeare in Performance.* Manchester, Eng., 1991.

Lothian, J. M. *"King Lear": A Tragic Reading of Life.* Toronto, 1949.

Lusardi, James P., and June Schlueter. *Reading Shakespeare in Performance: "King Lear."* Rutherford, N.J., 1991.

Mack, Maynard. *King Lear in Our Time.* Berkeley, 1965.

Maclean, Norman. "Episode, Scene, Speech, and Word: The Madness of Lear." *Critics and Criticism.* Ed. R. S. Crane. Chicago, 1952.

Michie, Donald M., ed. *A Critical Edition of "The True Chronicle History of King Leir and His Three Daughters, Gonorill, Ragan and Cordella."* New York, 1991.

Murphy, John L. *Darkness and Devils: Exorcism and "King Lear."* Athens, Ohio, 1984.

Reibetanz, John. *The "Lear" World: A Study of "King Lear" in Its Dramatic Context.* Toronto, 1977.

Rosenberg, Marvin. *The Masks of "King Lear."* Berkeley, 1972.

Scott, William O. "Contracts of Love and Affection: Lear, Old Age, and Kingship." *ShS* 55 (2002): 36–42.

Sewall, Richard B. *The Vision of Tragedy.* New Haven, 1959.

Snyder, Susan. "*King Lear* and the Psychology of Dying." *SQ* 33 (1982): 449–460.

Soellner, Rolf. "*King Lear* and the Magic of the Wheel." *SQ* 35 (1984): 274–289.

Tate, Nahum. *The History of King Lear.* 1681. Ed. James Black. Lincoln, Neb. 1975.

Taylor, Gary, and Michael Warren, eds. *The Division of the Kingdoms: Shakespeare's Two Versions of "King Lear."* Oxford, 1983.

Urkowitz, Steven. *Shakespeare's Revision of "King Lear."* Princeton, 1980.

Warren, Michael, preparer. *The Parallel "King Lear," 1608–1623: Parallel Texts of the First Quarto (1608) and the First Folio (1623).* Berkeley, 1989.

Wittreich, Joseph. *"Image of that Horror": History, Prophecy, and Apocalypse in "King Lear."* San Marino, Calif., 1984.

MACBETH

See also, under "The Tragedies," Berry, Bradley, Garner and Sprengnether (essay by Adelman), Goldman, Holloway, Hunter, Kirsch, Mack, Mack Jr., and Rosen; under "Shakespeare Criticism to the 1930s," Smith (essay by De Quincey); under "Shakespeare Criticism from the 1940s to the 1970s," Sanders and Sewell; under "Shakespeare Criticism Since 1980," Garber (*Cannibals*, essay by Adelman), Howard and O'Connor (essay by Goldberg), Mullaney (Chapter 5), Schwartz and Kahn (essay by Gohlke), Watson, and Woodbridge and Berry (essay by Willis); and under "The Histories," Pye.

Bartholomeusz, Dennis. *"Macbeth" and the Players.* Cambridge, Eng., 1969.

Booth, Stephen. *"King Lear," "Macbeth," Indefinition, and Tragedy.* New Haven, 1983.

Brooks, Cleanth. "The Naked Babe and the Cloak of Manliness." *The Well Wrought Urn.* New York, 1947.

Calderwood, James L. *If It Were Done: "Macbeth" and Tragic Action.* Amherst, 1986.

Driver, Tom. *The Sense of History in Greek and Shakespearean Drama.* New York, 1960.

Elliott, G. R. *Dramatic Providence in "Macbeth."* Princeton, 1958.

Fergusson, Francis. "*Macbeth* as the Imitation of an Action." *English Institute Essays 1951* (1952): 31–43.

Freud, Sigmund. "Some Character-Types Met with in Psycho-Analytic Work." *Collected Papers.* Trans. E. Cobern Mayne. Vol. 4. London, 1925.

Gardner, Helen. "Milton's 'Satan' and the Theme of Damnation in Elizabethan Tragedy." *English Association Essays and Studies* n.s. 1 (1948): 46–66.

Jorgensen, Paul A. *Our Naked Frailties: Sensational Art and Meaning in "Macbeth."* Berkeley, 1971.

Kliman, Bernice W. *Macbeth. Shakespeare in Performance.* Manchester, Eng., 1992.

Knights, L. C. "How Many Children Had Lady Macbeth? An Essay in the Theory and Practice of Shakespeare Criticism." *Explorations.* Rpt. Westport, Conn., 1975.

Norbrook, David. "*Macbeth* and the Politics of Historiography." *Politics of Discourse: The Literature and History of Seventeenth-Century England.* Eds. Kevin Sharpe and Steven Zwicker. Berkeley, 1987.

Orgel, Stephen. "Macbeth and the Antic Round." *ShS* 52 (1999): 143–153. Rpt. in Orgel, under "Shakespeare Criticism Since 1980."

Paul, Henry N. *The Royal Play of Macbeth.* New York, 1950.

Purkiss, Diane. *The Witch in History: Early Modern and Twentieth-Century Representations.* London and New York, 1996.

Rosenberg, Marvin. *The Masks of "Macbeth."* Berkeley, 1978.

Sinfield, Alan. "*Macbeth*: History, Ideology and Intellectuals." *Critical Quarterly* 28 (1986): 63–77.

Spender, Stephen. "Time, Violence, and *Macbeth.*" *Penguin New Writing.* Vol. 3. London, 1940–1941.

Williams, Raymond. "Monologue in *Macbeth.*" *Teaching the Text.* Eds. Susanne Kappeler and Norman Bryson. London, 1983.

Wills, Garry. *Witches and Jesuits: Shakespeare's "Macbeth."* Oxford, 1995.

The Romances

See also, under "Shakespeare Criticism Since 1980," McMullan and Hope.

Bergeron, David M. *Shakespeare's Romances and the Royal Family.* Lawrence, Kans., 1985.

Brown, John Russell, and Bernard Harris, eds. *Later Shakespeare.* Stratford-upon-Avon Studies 8. London, 1966.

Danby, John F. *Poets on Fortune's Hill.* London, 1952. Reprinted as *Elizabethan and Jacobean Poets.* London, 1964.

Edwards, Philip. "Shakespeare's Romances: 1900–1957." *ShS* 11 (1958): 1–18. (See also other articles in this issue.)

Fawkner, H. W. *Shakespeare's Miracle Plays: "Pericles," "Cymbeline," and "The Winter's Tale."* Rutherford, N.J., 1992.

Felperin, Howard. *Shakespearean Romance.* Princeton, 1972.

Foakes, R. A. *Shakespeare: From the Dark Comedies to the Last Plays.* London and Charlottesville, Va., 1971.

Frye, Northrop. *Anatomy of Criticism.* Princeton, 1957.

——. *A Natural Perspective: The Development of Shakespearean Comedy and Romance.* New York, 1965.

——. *The Secular Scripture: A Study of the Structure of Romance.* Cambridge, Mass., 1976.

Gesner, Carol. *Shakespeare and the Greek Romance: A Study of Origins.* Lexington, Ky., 1970.

Hartwig, Joan. *Shakespeare's Tragicomic Vision.* Baton Rouge, La., 1972.

Hunter, Robert Grams. *Shakespeare and the Comedy of Forgiveness.* New York, 1965.

James, D. G. "The Failure of the Ballad-Makers," *Scepticism and Poetry.* London, 1937.

Jordan, Constance. *Shakespeare's Monarchies: Ruler and Subject in the Romances.* Ithaca, N.Y., 1997.

Kermode, Frank. *William Shakespeare: The Final Plays.* London, 1963.

Knight, G. Wilson. *The Crown of Life.* London, 1947, 1966.

——. *The Shakespearian Tempest.* London, 1932, 1953.

Leavis, F. R. "A Criticism of Shakespeare's Last Plays." *Scrutiny* 10 (1942): 339–345. Rpt. in *The Common Pursuit.* London, 1952.

Marsh, D. R. C. *The Recurring Miracle: A Study of "Cymbeline" and the Last Plays.* Pietermaritzburg, Natal, 1962, 1964.

Marshall, Cynthia. *Last Things and Last Plays: Shakespearean Eschatology.* Carbondale, Ill., 1991.

Mincoff, Marco. *Things Supernatural and Causeless: Shakespearean Romance.* Newark, Del., 1992.

Mowat, Barbara A. *The Dramaturgy of Shakespeare's Romances.* Athens, Ga., 1976.

Nevo, Ruth. *Shakespeare's Other Language.* New York and London, 1987.

Palfrey, Simon. *Late Shakespeare: A New World of Words.* Oxford, 1997.

Peterson, Douglas L. *Time, Tide, and Tempest: A Study of Shakespeare's Romances.* San Marino, Calif., 1973.

Pettet, E. C. *Shakespeare and the Romance Tradition.* London, 1949.

Platt, Peter G. *Reason Diminished: Shakespeare and the Marvelous.* Lincoln, Neb., 1997.

Richards, Jennifer, and James Knowles, eds. *Shakespeare's Late Plays: New Readings.* Edinburgh, 1999.

Ryan, Kiernan, ed. *Shakespeare: The Late Plays.* New York, 1999.

Smith, Hallett. *Shakespeare's Romances.* San Marino, Calif., 1972.

Strachey, Lytton. "Shakespeare's Final Period." *Books and Characters.* London, 1922.

Traversi, Derek. *Shakespeare: The Last Phase.* New York, 1954.

Yates, Frances A. *Shakespeare's Last Plays: A New Approach.* London, 1975.

Young, David. *The Heart's Forest: A Study of Shakespeare's Pastoral Plays.* New Haven and London, 1972.

THE TEMPEST

See also, under "The Romances," Brown and Harris (essay by Brockbank), Felperin, Frye (*Natural Perspective*), Hartwig, Kermode, Mowat, Peterson, and Young; under "Shakespeare's Predecessors and Contemporaries," Bevington and Holbrook (essay by Bevington); under "Shakespeare Criticism to the 1930s," Coleridge (*Coleridge's Writings*); under "Shakespeare Criticism from the 1940s to the 1970s," Fiedler, Kernan (*Playwright as Magician*, Chapter 6), and Kott; under "Shakespeare Criticism Since 1980,"

Dollimore and Sinfield (essay by Brown), Drakakis (essay by Barker and Hulme), Garber (*Cannibals*, essay by Orgel), Greenblatt (*Shakespearean Negotiations*, Chapter 5), Hamlin, Howard and O'Connor (essay by Cartelli), Lenz et al. (essay by Leininger), Loomba and Orkin (essay by Brotton), McMullan and Hope (essay by Norbrook), and Schwartz and Kahn (essay by Sundelson); and under "The Comedies," Palmer and Bradbury (essay by Wells).

Auden, W. H. "The Sea and the Mirror: A Commentary on Shakespeare's *The Tempest*." *The Collected Poetry*. New York, 1945.

Berger, Harry, Jr. "Miraculous Harp: A Reading of Shakespeare's *Tempest*." *ShakS* 5 (1969): 253–283.

Demaray, John G. *Shakespeare and the Spectacles of Strangeness: "The Tempest" and the Transformation of Renaissance Theatrical Forms*. Pittsburgh, Pa., 1998.

Frey, Charles. "*The Tempest* and the New World." *SQ* 30 (1979): 29–41.

Hamilton, Donna. *Virgil and "The Tempest": The Politics of Imitation*. Columbus, Ohio, 1990.

Hirst, David. *"The Tempest": Text and Performance*. London, 1984.

Hulme, Peter, and William H. Sherman, eds. *"The Tempest" and Its Travels*. Philadelphia, 2000.

James, D. G. *The Dream of Prospero*. Oxford, 1967.

James, Henry. "Introduction to *The Tempest*." Rpt. in *Henry James: Selected Literary Criticism*. Ed. Morris Shapiro. London, 1963.

Mebane, John S. *Renaissance Magic and the Return of the Golden Age: The Occult Tradition and Marlowe, Jonson, and Shakespeare*. Lincoln, Neb., 1989.

Mowat, Barbara A. "Prospero's Book." *SQ* 52 (2001): 1–33.

Orgel, Stephen. "New Uses of Adversity: Tragic Experience in *The Tempest*." *In Defense of Reading*. Ed. Reuben A. Brower and Richard Poirier. New York, 1962.

——. "Prospero's Wife." *Representations* 8 (1984): 1–13. Rpt. in Orgel, under "Shakespeare Criticism Since 1980."

Skura, Meredith Anne. "Discourse and the Individual: The Case of Colonialism in *The Tempest*." *SQ* 40 (1989): 42–69.

Strier, Richard. " 'I am Power': Normal and Magical Politics in *The Tempest*." *Writing and Political Engagement in Seventeenth-Century England*. Ed. Derek Hirst and Richard Strier. Cambridge, Eng., 1999.

Thompson, Ann. " 'Miranda, where's your sister?': Reading Shakespeare's *The Tempest*." *Feminist Criticism: Theory and Practice*. Ed. Susan Sellers. New York, 1991.

Vaughan, Alden T. "Shakespeare's Indian: The Americanization of Caliban." *SQ* 39 (1988): 137–153.

——, and Virginia Mason Vaughan. *Shakespeare's Caliban: A Cultural History*. Cambridge, Eng., 1991.

Vaughan, Virginia Mason, and Alden T. Vaughan, eds. *Critical Essays on Shakespeare's "The Tempest."* New York and London, 1998.

Whit, R. S., ed. New Casebooks: *The Tempest*. New York, 1999.

William, David. "*The Tempest* on the Stage." *Jacobean Theatre*. Eds. John Russell Brown and Bernard Harris. *Stratford-upon-Avon Studies 1*. London, 1960.

APPENDIX B

Videography

The videography is in two parts:

1. Films and videos about Shakespeare, his theater, and the Elizabethan era.
2. Films and videos of the plays contained in this anthology, including subsets:
   a. Film Spin-offs (e.g., *Joe Macbeth; Throne of Blood*)
   b. Operas, Musicals, and Ballets based on the original play (e.g., *Otello; West Side Story*)

The videography does not claim to be complete, especially in its consideration of foreign versions of the plays and less important spin-offs. We have made every attempt to include those films discussed in conjunction with individual plays. For a thorough catalog of film versions of Shakespeare's plays (including numerous international films) and spin-offs, see Eddie Sammons's *Shakespeare: A Hundred Years on Film* (The Scarecrow Press, 2004).

Entries are listed chronologically by title, year of release, principal actor and director (when known), running time, and distributor. A primary distributor for each video is noted; it may be possible that there are other outlets where the video may be obtained. Many can be found on the Internet by entering the title and/or another keyword (e.g., the director). Amazon.com is a reliable source for many of these videos. Other distributors include (with an abbreviation used for this videography):

Facets Performing Arts
  (FPA)   www.facets.org
Films for the Humanities
  (FH)   www.films.com
First Light Media **(FLM)** www.firstlightvideo.com
Insight Media **(IM)** www.insight-media.com
Movies Unlimited **(MU)** www.moviesunlimited.com
Teacher's Video Company
  (TVC)   www.teachersvideo.com

The BBC Shakespeare Series includes thirty-seven plays and may be ordered from Insight Media.

Part One: Shakespeare, His Life, Times, and Theater

SHAKESPEARE: BIOGRAPHY AND TIMES

Shakespeare: Soul of an Age (1962), dir. Howard Sackler, 54 min., NBC News
William Shakespeare: A Life of Drama (1996), 50 min., TVC
Shakespeare Conspiracy (2000), dir. Michael Peer, 60 min., TVC, FPA
The Shakespeare Enigma (2001), 51 min., FH
Shakespeare in London (1999), 50 min., FPA
Shakespeare: Drama's DNA (2000), 60 min., FH
Shakespeare: The Man and His Times (1991), 47 min., IM
William Shakespeare (1995), 46 min., FH
The Maturing Shakespeare (1984), 28 min., FH
"This Earth, This Realm, This England" (2003), w/John Barton, 52 min., FH
Who Wrote Shakespeare's Works? (2001), 90 min., FH

GENRES

Shakespearean Comedy (2000), 30 min., IM
Shakespearean Tragedy (2000), 30 min., IM

SHAKESPEARE AND THE GLOBE THEATER

Shakespeare and His Theater: The Globe, 28 min., FH
Shakespeare's Globe Theater Restored: Much Ado About Something! (1997), 30 min., IM, FPA
Shakespeare's Globe (1998), 2 parts, 20 min. each, IM

PERFORMING SHAKESPEARE

Acting in Shakespearean Comedy (1990), w/Janet Suzman, 60 min., FLM
Classically Shakespeare (2004), 30 min., IM
Muscularity of Language: Motion and Rhythm (2003), w/Cicely Berry, 78 min., IM

Playing Shakespeare (1984), w/John Barton and the Royal Shakespeare Company, 11-part series, FH
    Speaking Shakespearean Verse, 50 min.
    Preparing to Perform Shakespeare, 50 min.
    The Two Traditions, 50 min.
    Using the Verse, 50 min.
    Language and Character, 51 min.
    Set Speeches and Soliloquies, 51 min.
    Irony and Ambiguity, 51 min.
    Passion and Coolness, 52 min.
    Rehearsing the Text (re: *Twelfth Night*), 53 min.
    Exploring a Character (re: *The Merchant of Venice*), 51 min.
    Poetry and Hidden Poetry, 53 min.
Performing Shakespeare (1990), w/Kathleen Conlan, 120 min., IM
Shakespeare's Language (1994), w/Tony Church, 45 min., IM
Shakespeare: Directing for Stage and Film (2001), 20 min., IM
The Shakespeare Sessions (2003), w/John Barton, 60 min., IM
Shared Rhythms and Collective Music, w/Cicely Berry, 90 min., IM
Speech Structures, 88 min., IM
Theater Games: Workshopping Body Language in Shakespeare (w/Cicely Berry), 92 min., FH

Part Two: The Plays, Spin-offs, and Musical Versions

GENERAL: SHAKESPEARE ON STAGE AND FILM

Shakespeare's Women and Claire Bloom (1994), 54 min., FPA
Royal Shakespeare Company: Great Performances (1995), 80 min., FH (Includes interviews with directors and scenes from: *King Lear*, *Twelfth Night*, *A Midsummer Night's Dream*, and *Coriolanus*)
Shakespeare on the Silver Screen (2000), 52 min., FH
Shakespeare Wallah (1965), dir. James Ivory, 125 min., India-set Merchant-Ivory feature with excerpts from *Hamlet*, *Othello*, and *Romeo and Juliet*.
Silent Shakespeare: "Such Stuff as Dreams Are Made On" (2000), 88 min., FPA, Milestone
Reduced Shakespeare Company (2001), dir. Paul Kafno, 90 min., TVC, FPA

HAMLET

Hamlet (1948), dir. Laurence Olivier, 153 min., FPA
Hamlet (1962), Maximilian Schell, dir. Peter Wirth, 130 min., Bavaria Atelier
Hamlet (1964), Richard Burton, dir. John Gielgud, 206 min., FPA
Gamlet (1964), Innokenti Smoktunovsky, dir. Grigori Kozintsev, 140 min., Lenfilm
Hamlet (1969), Nicol Williamson, dir. Tony Richardson, 117 min., Woodfall

Hamlet (1980), Derek Jacobi, dir. Rodney Bennet, 214 min., BBC, IM
Hamlet (1990), Mel Gibson, dir. Franco Zeffirelli, 135 min., TVC, FPA, MU
Hamlet (1990), Kevin Kline, dir. Kirk Browning, 180 min., TVC
Hamlet (1996), Kenneth Branagh, dir. Kenneth Branagh, 242 min., TVC, FPA
Hamlet (2000), Ethan Hawke, dir. Michael Almereyda, 113 min., FPA
Hamlet (2000), Campbell Scott, dir. Campbell Scott, 179 min., FPA, Artisan Home Entertainment
The Tragedy of Hamlet (2001), dir. Peter Brook, 133 min., Arte/BBC
Discovering Hamlet (1990), Kenneth Branagh, dir. Derek Jacobi, 53 min., MU
The Great Hamlets, *Parts One* (55 min.) and *Two* (56 min.), FH
Hamlet: A Critical Guide, 30 min., FH
Hamlet's Soliloquies: Perfecting Perfection, 64 min., FH
A Commedia dell'arte Hamlet (1964), 27 min., FPA
The Marowitz Hamlet (1972), dir. Charles Marowitz, NOS
The Making of a Monologue: Robert Wilson's Hamlet (1995), dir. Robert Wilson, 62 min., FPA

Spin-offs

Hamlet (1920), Asta Nielsen, dir. Sven Gade, 136 min., Art Film
To Be or Not to Be (1942), dir. Ernst Lubitsch, 99 min., Alexander Korda
Strange Illusion (1945), dir. Edgar Ulmer, 85 min., P.R.C., VCI Home Video
The Bad Sleep Well (1960), dir. Akira Kurosawa, 151 min., Home Vision Entertainment
Johnny Hamlet (1972), dir. Enzo Castellari, 115 min., Espana Films
To Be or Not to Be (1983), dirs. Al Johnson and Mel Brooks, 107 min., Brooksfilms
Strange Brew (1983), dirs. Rick Moranis and Dave Thomas, 90 min., MGM
Blue City (1986), dir. Michelle Manning, 95 min., Paramount
Outrageous Fortune (1987), dir. Arthur Hiller, 100 min., Disney
Rosencrantz and Guildenstern Are Dead (1990), dir. Tom Stoppard, 118 min., Brandenberg International
Renaissance Man (1994), dir. Penny Marshall, 124 min., Cinergi-Parkway
In the Bleak Midwinter (a.k.a. *A Midwinter's Tale*) (1995), dir. Kenneth Branagh, 98 min., Midwinter Films
Fuck Hamlet (1996), dir. Cheol-Mean Whang, 90 min., DFFB
Let the Devil Wear Black (1999), dir. Stacy Title, 89 min., Unapix

Henry IV, Part One and Two (Falstaff)

Chimes at Midnight (a.k.a. *Falstaff*, 1966), dir. Orson Welles, 119 min., Now Playing

Henry IV, Part One (1979), Anthony Quayle, dir. David Giles, 165 min., IM

Henry IV, Part One (*Wars of the Roses* series: 1991), dir. Michael Bogdanov, 172 min., FH

Henry IV, Part Two (*Wars of the Roses* series: 1991), dir. Michael Bogdanov, 151 min., FH

Spin-offs

My Own Private Idaho (1991), dir. Gus Van Sant, 102 min., Idaho Productions

Falstaff: Opera

Falstaff—Verdi (1972), Vienna Philharmonic and Vienna State Opera, 136 min., FPA

Falstaff—Verdi (1983), Royal Opera House, 135 min., FPA

The Merry Wives of Windsor—Nicolai (1950), East Germany, 90 min., FPA

Henry V

Henry V (1944), dir. Laurence Olivier, 137 min., FPA

Henry V (1979), David Gwillim, dir. David Giles, 163 min., BBC, IM

Henry V (1989), dir., Kenneth Branagh, 138 min., FPA

King Henry V (*Wars of the Roses* series: 1990) dir. Michael Bogdanov, 175 min., FH

King Lear

King Lear (1971), Paul Scofield, dir. Peter Brook, 132 min., Filmways

Korol Lir (1970), dir. Grigori Kozintsev, 141 min., Lenfilm

King Lear (1974), James Earl Jones, dir. Edwin Sherrin, 180 min., TVC, FPA, Broadway Theater Archive

King Lear (1983), Laurence Olivier, dir. Michael Elliott, MU

King Lear (1982), Michael Hordern, dir. Jonathan Miller, 185 min., BBC, IM

King Lear (1998), Ian Holm, dir. Richard Eyre, 250 min., TVC

King Lear: A Critical Guide, 30 min., FH

King Lear: Text and Performance, 180 min., FH

Spin-offs

House of Strangers (1949), dir. Joseph Mankiewicz, 101 min., Twentieth Century Fox

Broken Lance (1954), dir. Edward Dmytryk, 96 min., Twentieth Century Fox

Harry and Tonto (1974), dir. Paul Mazursky, 115 min.

The Dresser (1983), dir. Peter Yates, 118 min., Columbia

Ran (1985), dir. Akira Kurosawa, 160 min., FPA

King Lear (1987), dir. Jean-Luc Godard, 91 min., Cannon Films

A Thousand Acres (1997), dir. Jocelyn Moorhouse, 105 min., Touchstone Pictures

The King Is Alive (2000), dir. Kristian Levring, 109 min., Zemotropa Entertainments3

The King of Texas (2002), dir. Uli Edel, 180 min., Turner Network Television

Macbeth

Macbeth (1948), dir. Orson Welles, 106 min., Republic

Macbeth (1954), Maurice Evans, 103 min., FPA

Macbeth (1960), Maurice Evans, dir. George Schaefer, 108 min., Grand Prize

Macbeth (1971), Jon Finch, dir. Roman Polanski, 139 min., MU

Macbeth (1978), Ian McKellen, dir. Trevor Nunn, 146 min, FH, TVC, FPA

Macbeth (1983), Nicol Williamson, dir. Jack Gold, 120 min., BBC, IM

Macbeth (1997), Jason Connery, dir. Jeremy Freeston, 129 min., Cromwell

Macbeth (1998), dir. Michael Bogdanov, 87 min., Channel 4 (UK)

Macbeth: A Critical Guide, 30 min., FH

Macbeth: Shakespeare for the Modern Age (2003), Big Adventure Theater Company, 37 min., FH

Ballets

Lady Macbeth of Mtensk—Shostakovich (1992), London Philharmonic, 98 min., FPA

Macbeth (1980), Bolshoi Ballet, 105 min., FPA

Operas

Macbeth—Verdi (1987), dir. Claude D'Anna, 136 min., Daedalus

Spin-offs

Joe Macbeth (1955), dir. Ken Hughes, 90 min., Film Locations

Throne of Blood (*Kumonosu-Jo*, 1957), Toshiro Mifune, dir. Akira Kurosawa, 110 min., Toho

Siberian Lady Macbeth (1961), dir. Andrezej Wajda, 95 min., Facets

Men of Respect (1991), dir. William Reilly, 113 min., Central Film City

Macbeth in Manhattan (1999), dir. Greg Lombardo, 97 min., Cinebard Productions

Macbeth: The Comedy (2001), dir. Allison LiCasi, 91 min., Tristan Films

Scotland, PA (2001), dir. Billy Morrisette, 102 min., Lost 49 Films

Rave Macbeth (2001), dir. Klaus Knosel, 86 min., Framewerk

THE MERCHANT OF VENICE

The Merchant of Venice (1972), Laurence Olivier, dir. Jonathan Miller, 131 min., TVC, MU

The Merchant of Venice (1980), Warren Mitchell, dir. Jack Gold, 157 min., BBC, IM

The Merchant of Venice (2001), Henry Goodman, dir. Trevor Nunn, 135 min., BBC

The Merchant of Venice (2004), Al Pacino, dir./adapter Michael Radford, 131 min., Sony

The Merchant of Venice: A Personal View by Wolf Mankowitz (1998), dirs. David Jones and Sally Kirkwood, 28 min., FH

Shylock (1999), 58 min., FH, National Film Board of Canada

A MIDSUMMER NIGHT'S DREAM

A Midsummer Night's Dream (1935), James Cagney, dir. Max Reinhardt, 135 min., FPA

A Midsummer Night's Dream (1964), Benny Hill, dir. Joan Kemp-Welsh, 111 min., FPA

A Midsummer Night's Dream (1969), Royal Shakespeare Company, dir. Peter Hall, 124 min., Filmways

A Midsummer Night's Dream (1981), Brian Glover, dir. Elijah Moshinsky, 112 min., BBC, IM

A Midsummer Night's Dream (1982), William Hurt, dir. James Lapine, 165 min., ABC

A Midsummer Night's Dream (1984), dir. Celestino Coronado, 77 min., Cabochan Productions (Spain)

A Midsummer Night's Dream (1996), Royal Shakespeare Company, dir. Adrian Noble, 103 min., FPA

A Midsummer Night's Dream (1999), Kevin Kline, dir. Michael Hoffman, 120 min., TVC

A Midsummer Night's Dream: What to Make of Magic, 32 min., FH

The Making of A Midsummer Night's Dream (2000), 50 min., IM

Operas

The Fairy Queen—Purcell (1995), English National Opera, 133 min., FPA

A Midsummer Night's Dream—Britten (1983), Glyndebourne Festival, 194 min., FPA

Oberon—von Weber (1971), dir. Herbert Junkers, 91 min., ZDF

Ballets

A Midsummer Night's Dream—Mendelssohn (1966), chor. George Balanchine, 93 min., PBS/Kultur

The Dream—Mendelssohn (1964), chor. Frederick Ashton, PBS/Kultur

Spin-offs

Sen Noci Svatojanske (Czechoslovakia, 1957), animated puppets, dir. Jiri Trinka, 80 min., Kratky Film Prague

A Midsummer Night's Sex Comedy (1982), dir. Woody Allen, 88 min., Orion

Dead Poets Society (1989), dir. Peter Weir, 129 min., Touchstone Pictures

The Children's Midsummer Night's Dream (2001), dir. Christine Edzard, 115 min., Sands

A Dream in Hanoi (2002), 91 min., IM

MUCH ADO ABOUT NOTHING

Much Ado About Nothing (1973), Sam Waterston, dir. A. J. Antoon, 165 min., FPA

Much Ado About Nothing (1984), Robert Lindsay, dir. Stuart Burge, 138 min., BBC,IM

Much Ado About Nothing (1993), Kenneth Branagh and Emma Thompson, dir. Kenneth Branagh, 111 min., MU

Much Ado About Nothing: A Personal View by Eleanor Bron (1998), dirs. David Jones and Sally Kirkland, 28 min., FH

OTHELLO

The Tragedy of Othello, the Moor of Venice (1951), dir. Orson Welles, 91 min., Films Marceau

Othello (1955), dir. Sergei Youkevich (Russia), 110 min., Mosfilm

Othello (1965), Laurence Olivier, dirs. Stuart Birge and John Dexter, 166 min., British Home Entertainments

Othello (1980), Yaphet Kotto, dir. Liz White, 115 min., Howard University

Othello (1981), Anthony Hopkins, dir. Jonathan Miller, BBC, IM

The Tragedy of Othello, the Moor of Venice (1981), William Marshall, dir. Frank Melton, 195 min., Bard Productions, IM, FPA

Othello (1988), Willard White, Ian McKellen, dir. Trevor Nunn, 210 min., FH

Othello (1988), John Kani, dir. Janet Suzman, 187 min., FH

Othello (1995), Laurence Fishburne, dir. Oliver Parker, 124 min., MU

Othello: A Critical Guide, 30 min., FH

Opera (Verdi)

Otello (1969), Hans Nooker, Berlin Opera, 105 min., FPA
Otello (1958), Mario del Monaco, 134 min., FPA
Otello (1976), Placido Domingo, La Scala, 143 min., FPA
Otello (1987), Jon Vickers, Berlin, 140 min., FPA
Otello (1986), Placido Domingo, dir. Franco Zeffirelli, 123 min., FPA

Spin-offs

Men Are Not Gods (1936), dir. Walter Reisch, 90 min., London Films
A Double Life (1947), dir. George Cukor, 104 min., Universal-International
Jubal (1955), dir. Delmer Daves, 101 min., Columbia
All Night Long (1961), dir. Basil Dearden, 95 min., FPA
Catch My Soul (1973), dir. Patrick McGoohan, 95 min., Metromedia
True Identity (1991), dir. Charles Lane, 93 min., Touchstone Pictures
O (1999), dir. Tim Blake Nelson, 91 min., Lions Gate
Jago (2000), dir. Stephanus Domanig, 55 min., Wiener Film
Othello (2002), dir. Andrew Davies, 100 min., PBS (*Masterpiece Theater*)

ROMEO AND JULIET

Romeo and Juliet (1936), Leslie Howard and Norma Shearer, dir. George Cukor, 130 min., MU
Romeo and Juliet (1964), Laurence Harvey and Susan Shentall, dir. Renato Castellani, 138 min., FPA
Romeo and Juliet (1968), Leonard Whiting and Olivia Hussey, dir. Franco Zeffirelli, 138 min., TVC
Romeo and Juliet (1994), dir. Alan Horrox, 81 min., FPA
William Shakespeare's Romeo+Juliet (1996), Leonardo DiCaprio and Claire Danes, dir. Baz Luhrmann, 120 min., TVC
Romeo and Juliet: A Critical Guide, 30 min., FH

Operas, Ballets, and Musical Theater

Romeo and Juliet—Prokofiev (1968), Nureyev and Paris Opera Ballet, 150 min., FPA
Romeo and Juliet—Prokofiev (1975), Bolshoi Ballet, 108 min., FPA; with Falina Ulanova (1954), Bolshoi, 90 min.
Romeo and Juliet—Prokofiev (1966), Nureyev & Fontaine, Royal Ballet, 126 min., FPA
Romeo and Juliet—Prokofiev (1992), Lyon Opera Ballet, 85 min., FPA
Romeo et Juliette—Gounod (1995), Orchestra and Chorus of the Royal Opera House, 160 min., Pioneer Classics

West Side Story (1961), dir. Robert Wise, 151 min., TVC, FPA

Spin-offs

Aaron Loves Angela (1975), dir. Gordon Parks, Jr., 99 min., Columbia
Fire with Fire (1986), dir. Duncan Gibbins, 104 min., Paramount
China Girl (1987), dir. Abel Ferrera, 90 min., Street Lite
Under the Boardwalk (1989), dir. Fritz Kiersch, 93 min., Star Maker
The Punk and the Princess (1993), dir. Mike Srane, 96 min., Videodrome
Tromeo and Juliet (1996), dir. Lloyd Kaufmann, 104 min., Troma
Shakespeare in Love (1998), dir. John Madden, 127 min., Miramax
Romeo Must Die (2000), dir. Andrzej Bartkowiak, 115 min., Silver Pictures

THE TAMING OF THE SHREW

The Taming of the Shrew (1929), Douglas Fairbanks and Mary Pickford, dir. Sam Taylor, 66 min., United Artists
The Taming of the Shrew (1967), Richard Burton and Elizabeth Taylor, dir. Franco Zeffirelli, 127 min., FPA
The Taming of the Shrew (1976), American Conservatory Theater, dirs. William Ball and Kirk Browning, 120 min., FPA, Broadway Theater Archives
The Taming of the Shrew (1982), dir. Jonathan Miller, 127 min., BBC, IM
The Taming of the Shrew (1982), Stratford (Canada) Festival, dir. Peter Dewes, 163 min., FPA

Musicals

Kiss Me Kate (1953), dir. George Sidney, 110 min., FPA

Spin-offs

10 Things I Hate About You (1999), dir. Gil Junger, 97 min., TVC

THE TEMPEST

The Tempest (1979), dir. Derek Jarman, 95 min., Boyd's Company
Prospero's Books (1991), John Gielgud, dir. Peter Greenaway, 120 min., Allarts
The Tempest (1998), dir. Jack Bender, 88 min., Vidmark, NBC Television
Peter Brook: The Tempest (1968), dir. Peter Brook, 27 min., Saga Films
Julie Taymor: Setting a Scene (1992), 30 min., FPA

Spin-offs

Yellow Sky (1949), dir. William Wellman, 98 min., FMC Library

Forbidden Planet (1956), dir. Fred McLeod Wilcox, 98 min., MGM

Age of Consent (1969), dir. Michael Powell, 104 min., Nautilus Productions

Tempest (1982), dir. Paul Mazursky, 142 min., Columbia

The Tempest (1998), dir. Jack Bender, 120 min., HBO

THE TRAGEDY OF KING RICHARD III

Richard III (1955), dir. Laurence Olivier, 161 min., FPA, MU

Richard III (w/*Henry VI, Parts One–Three*, 1983), Ron Cook, dir. Jane Howell, BBC, IM

Richard III (*Wars of the Roses* series, 1991), dir. Michael Bogdanov, 194 min., FH

Richard III (1995), Ian McKellen, dir. Richard Loncraine, 106 min., United Artists

Spin-offs

Tower of London (1939), dir. Rowland Lee, 92 min., Universal

Tower of London (1962), dir. Richard Corman, 79 min., AIP/Admiral

Looking for Richard (1996), dir. Al Pacino, 112 min., TVC, FPA, MU

The Street King (2002), dir. James Gavin Bedford, 90 min., Universal

TWELFTH NIGHT

Twelfth Night (1980), Felicity Kendal, dir. John Gorrie, 128 min., BBC

Twelfth Night (1986), dir. Neil Armfield, 120 min., Australia Film

Twelfth Night (1991), Frances Barber, dir. Kenneth Branagh, 165 min., FH

Twelfth Night (1996), Imogen Stubbs, dir. Trevor Nunn, 133 min., FPA

Twelfth Night (1998), Helen Hunt, dirs. Nick Hytner and Kirk Browning, 150 min., PBS

Spin-offs

Viola and Sebastian (1972), dir. Ottokar Runza, 93 min., Guertler/Runza

Play On! (2000), dir. Sheldon Epps, 120 min., PBS

APPENDIX C

Family Trees of England's Royal Families: 1399–1625

I. THE LANCASTRIAN KINGS

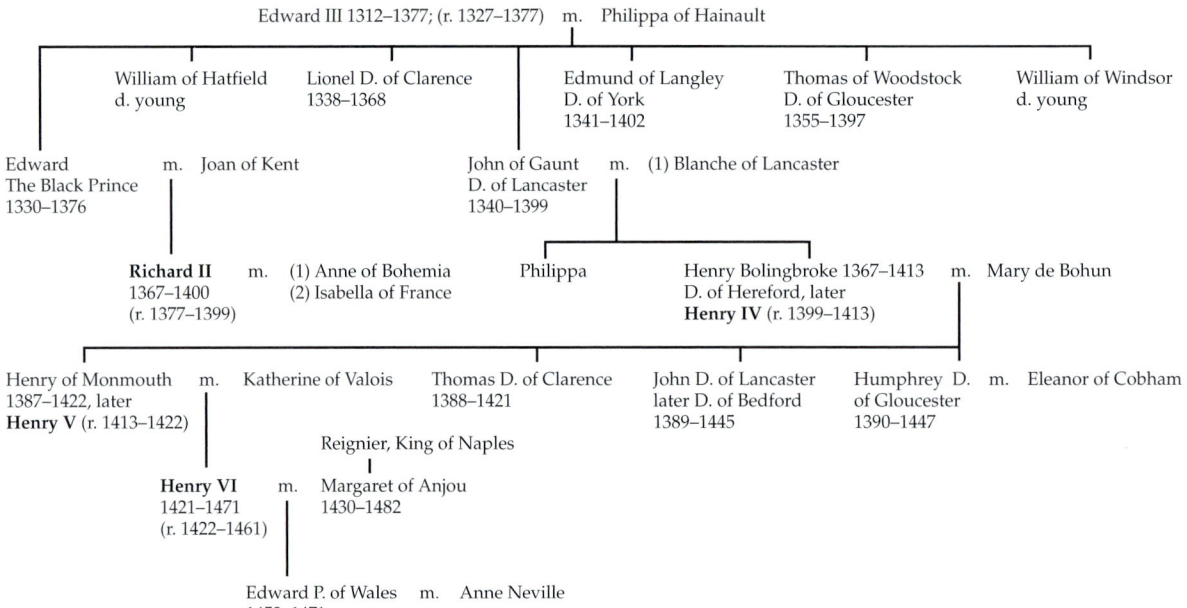

In these diagrams, reigning dates are given in parentheses; other dates indicate life span. Abbreviations: P., Prince, D., Duke, E., Earl; b., born, d., died, m., married. English monarchs are printed in boldface type. The spatial arrangement of names in a family usually but not always indicates order of birth.

In *1 Henry IV*, Shakespeare confuses the Edmund Mortimer who married Glendower's daughter, and died in 1409, with his nephew, the fifth Earl of March,

who asserted a claim to the English throne (see "The Yorkist Kings"). Shakespeare also refers to Henry Percy's (Hotspur's) wife as "Kate," though historically she was named Elizabeth.

Catherine Swynford, third wife of John of Gaunt (see "The Tudor Kings"), bore him children before their eventual marriage. These Beauforts, although later legitimized, were specifically barred from any claim to the English throne.

II. THE YORKIST KINGS

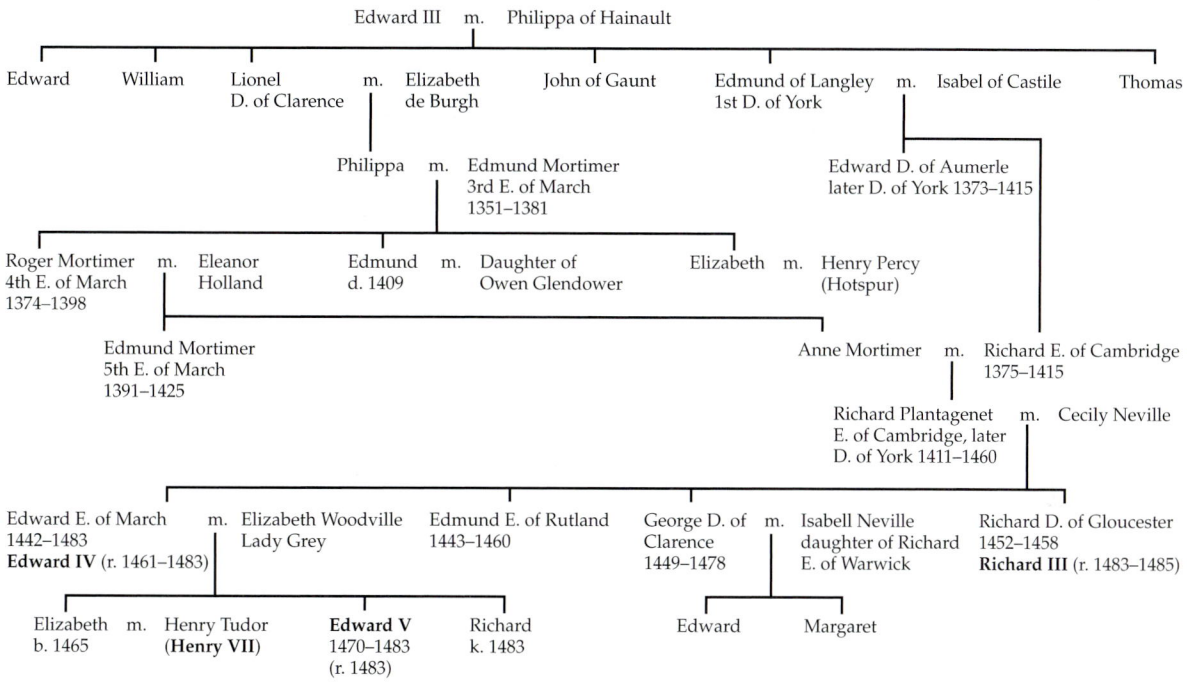

III. THE TUDOR KINGS

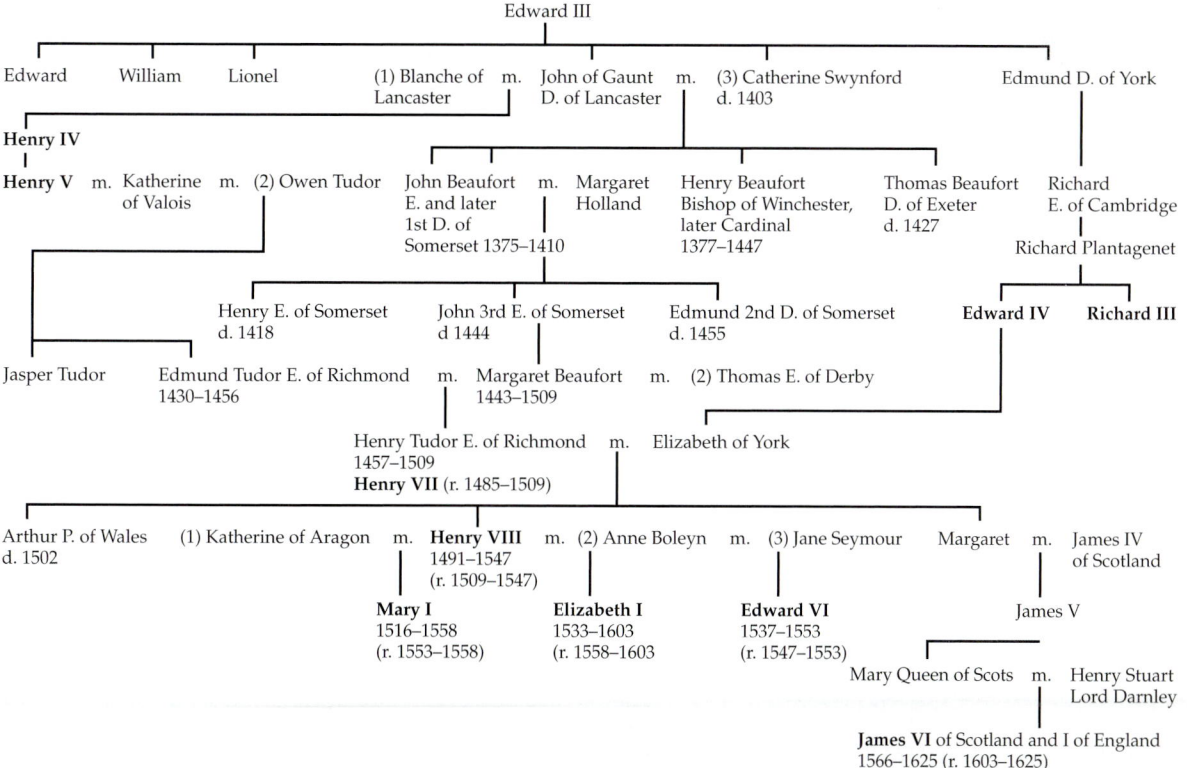

IV. THE ROYAL HOUSES OF ENGLAND AND FRANCE

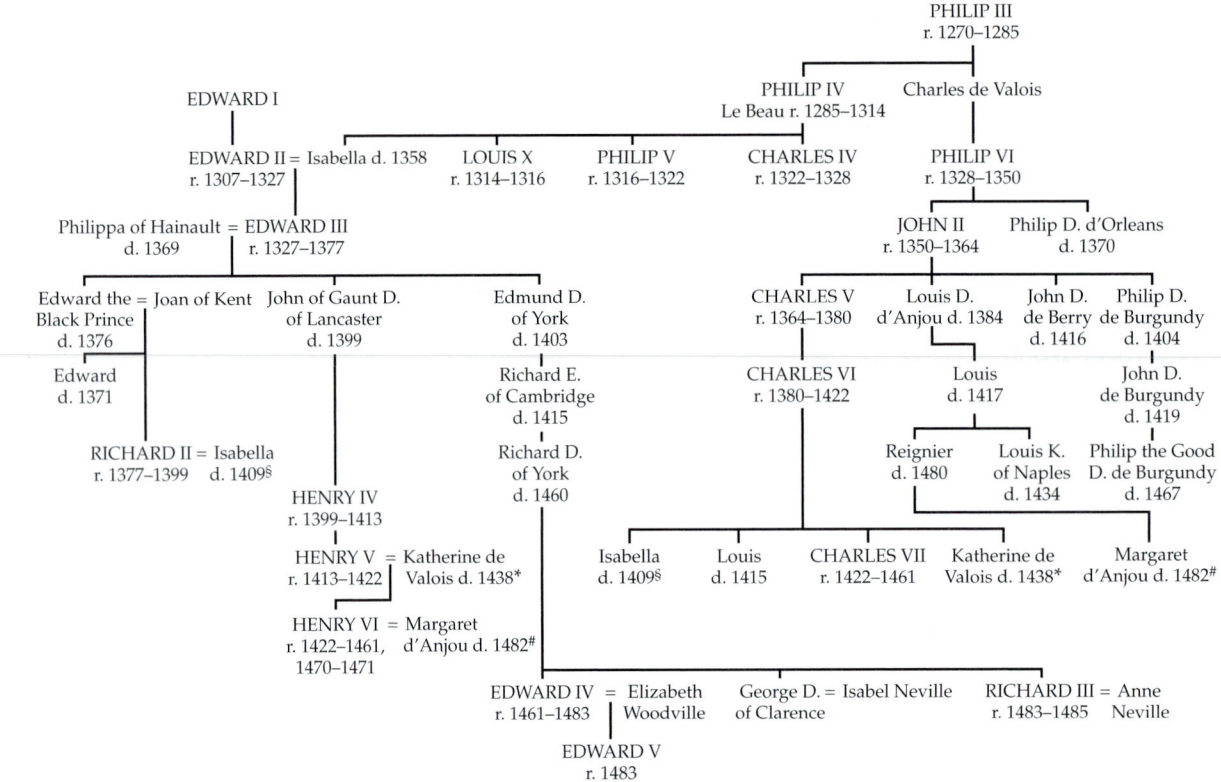

Asterisks, pound signs, and paragraph signs indicate women who appear twice on this diagram owing to marriage

APPENDIX D

Glossary of Terms: Film and Criticism

Cut—This editing term describes a transition between two or more scenes or shots, without traditional optical transitions. Film is merely spliced together, so the frame appears to move quickly.

- **Cross-cut**—The technique of editing together two actions or sequences that are spatially (or even temporally) separate from one another. This technique is primarily used for showing parallel actions occurring between two subjects, such as in a chase scene or a phone conversation.

- **Jump-cut**—This is a type of edit that breaks the fluidity of a subject's motion on the screen. This technique does not follow what is known by cinema theorists as the "thirty-degree-angle rule," a tradition that requires the camera to be placed thirty degrees apart from its previous position when one is filming and editing a subject. Following this rule shows the audience that camera placement and changes of angle are deliberate. Otherwise the image will appear to "jump" on the screen. Formally, a jump-cut is considered a cinematic *faux pas*, unless it is done for purely stylistic purposes.

Diegetic sound—Derived from the term "diegesis," or the narrative world of the film, this type of ambient sound can be easily identified as part of the scene.

Director—The artistic force behind the "look" of the film. The director is in charge of the transformation of the written screenplay into a visual narrative. Ideally, the director should have the most, and usually final, say in all artistic choices from casting to design, shooting, and editing.

Dissolve—An optical effect that gradually merges one series of images with another by briefly superimposing the two series.

Fade—An optical effect that changes the light output on the screen. A "fade-in" refers to a dark screen gradually getting lighter until a picture can be seen clearly. A "fade-out" refers to the picture on the screen gradually becoming darker, until the audience sees black. The term "fade" can also refer to sound gradually growing louder or softer.

Genre film—A term referring to the grouping of films in categories by their similar stylistic or thematic traits, e.g., the Western or *film noir.*

Location—A place in which filming occurs. Location shooting refers to a place outside the studio that has been approved for filming. Malls, schools, or city streets could be considered sites for filming "on location."

Mise-en-scène—The arrangement of and relationship between all of the elements of film in a single shot or frame. In French, literally translated, "the placing of a scene."

Montage—A style of filmmaking that combines images and/or sounds into a coherent narrative. In the United States, montage is traditionally used to show the passing of time. Filmmakers in the Soviet Union pioneered montage as a stylistic movement in the 1920s. In France, montage refers simply to editing.

Narrative—The story creating the momentum of a film. Narratives can be traditionally expressed through dialogue. Visual images can also produce a cinematic narrative such as those in a montage.

Producer—The financial backer of a film, whether a person, group, or corporation. The producer gives the "green light" to a project. The producer selects a director suitable for the project and monitors the progress of the shooting and production.

Screenplay—A film's action, dialogue, camera movements, and effects in a written sequence—usually also visualized on a storyboard—to be shot to produce the final product.

Set—A constructed background, or scene in a film. Normally, most sets are constructed within a production studio.

Shot—The basic unit of film involving both the position and distance of a subject from the camera.

- **Close-up shot**—A camera angle that frames a subject very closely, as in a full view of a subject's face.

- **Framing**—What appears on the screen.
- **Medium shot**—A camera angle that frames the subject from the waist up.
- **Long shot**—A camera angle that is taken at a great distance, usually with a wide-angle lens. The long-shot can be used as an establishing shot, which situates (or establishes) the subject's relative position in the scene.
- **Tracking shot**—A term that describes the motion of a camera. A tracking shot follows (or tracks) the subject(s) with a camera seated on a smooth track, often pulling away from the action or characters at the end of a film.

Voice-over—Typically in the form of narration or internal monologue, a voice-over refers to sound that is "extra-diegetic," which means that it does not come from the narrative world of the scene, rather it is "supplied."

Index

Page ranges in **bold** indicate the page range for the entire play.
Page references followed by *n* indicate a footnote.